The Wordsworth Dictionary of Proverbs

1

The Wordsworth Dictionary of
PROVERBS

ooooooooooooooooooooooooooooooooooooooo

G. L. APPERSON

Revising Editors
STEPHEN J. CURTIS
MARTIN H. MANSER

Wordsworth Reference

In loving memory of
MICHAEL TRAYLER
the founder of Wordsworth Editions

1

Readers who are interested in other titles from
Wordsworth Editions are invited to visit our website at
www.wordsworth-editions.com

For our latest list and a full mail-order service, contact
Bibliophile Books, 5 Thomas Road, London E14 7BN
Tel: +44 (0)20 7515 9222 Fax: +44 (0)20 7538 4115
E-mail: orders@bibliophilebooks.com

This edition published in 1993 by Wordsworth Editions Limited
8B East Street, Ware, Hertfordshire SG12 9HJ
Reset with additions in 2006

ISBN 1 84022 311 1

Typeset in Great Britain by Antony Gray
Printed and bound by Clays Ltd, St Ives plc

Preface

This book is a humble offshoot from the great parent stock of the *Oxford English Dictionary*. Its purpose is to trace, so far as may be possible, the history of English proverbs and proverbial phrases in English use. A very few sayings which have won proverbial rank, such as 'Procrastination is the thief of time' and 'Imitation is the sincerest form of flattery', are of definitely literary origin. These can be accurately dated. But the great mass in most cases cannot be dated with any precision. Many are translated from or based upon Greek or Latin originals; many have been borrowed, undergoing changes in the process, from those of other countries.

In a few score cases, classical originals and parallels, carefully referenced, have been inserted, in square brackets, before the other references; but no attempt has been made to do this exhaustively.

It is obvious that a proverb or proverbial phrase, a crystallised summary of popular wisdom or fancy, is likely, or indeed certain, to have been long current in popular speech before it could make any appearance in literature, or even in collections of such lore. Consequently, the historical method of treatment can only give an approximation to accuracy. But I venture to think that the method adopted in this book is sound, and that the results obtained are worth the eight or nine years' labour that its preparation has involved.

Like the great Oxford work, if one may compare small things with great, this book is based upon the independent collection of material. During the leisure of about seven years I made my collections direct from original sources, as detailed in later paragraphs. Until these collections were as complete as I could make them, I refrained from consulting the *Oxford Dictionary*. When, as the actual writing of my *Dictionary* was in progress, I referred to that monumental work, I found that in a few cases examples which I had collected had already been used therein. These I have not marked, as they were the fruits of my labour, but a small number of other references which I have taken direct from the *Oxford Dictionary* are carefully marked (OED).

The principal early collections of proverbs and proverbial phrases are Taverner's *Proverbes or Adagies out of Erasmus*, 1539; Heywood's *Proverbs*, 1546, and *Epigrams*, 1562; Florio's *First Fruites*, 1578, and *Second Fruites*, 1591; a number in Camden's *Remains*, 1605; Draxe's *Bibliotheca Scholastica Instructissima*, 1633; Clarke's *Paraemiologia Anglo-Latina*, 1639; George Herbert's *Jacula Prudentum*, 1640, and second edition, 1651; Howell's *Proverbs*, 1659; Ray's *Proverbs*, 1670, second edition 1678, third 1737, fourth 1768 and fifth 1813; Walker's *Paraemiologia*, 1672; and Fuller's *Gnomologia*, 1732.

The whole of Ray's collections, except a few offensively dirty or indecent sayings, and a considerable part of the examples in the other books, are included in the present *Dictionary*, but I have excluded a very large number of sententious and moral sentences found in such works as Fuller's *Gnomologia*, which certainly can never have been proverbial, and also sayings which are purely foreign.

Many of the so-called *Proverbs of Alfred, c.*1270, are not proverbs at all, but I have included a few, and also examples from the *Proverbs of Hendyng, c.*1320, which have the genuine ring, and indeed, in some cases, afford early authority for some of our most familiar sayings.

Many English sayings have been found in old dictionaries, such as Horman's *Vulgaria*, 1519; Palgrave's *L'Éclaircissement de la langue Française*, 1530; Withal's *Littel Dictionaire for Children*, 1556, and Lewis's revival of that work, 1586; Huloet's *Abcedarium*, 1552; Baret's *Alvearie*, 1580; Florio's *Worlde of Wordes*, 1598; Cotgrave's *French–English Dictionary*, 1611; Torriano's *Piazza Universale*, 1666; Robertson's *Phraseology Generalis*, 1681; and Berthelson's *English and Danish Dictionary*.

For local sayings all the publications of the English Dialect Society have been searched. I have also examined some thirty other similar works, including such books as Grose's *Provincial Glossary*, second edition 1790; Moor's *Suffolk Words*, 1823; Brockett's *Glossary of North Country Words*, 1825; Carr's *Craven Dialect*, 1828; Forby's *Vocabulary of East Anglia*, 1830; Wilbrahan's *Cheshire Glossary*, 1854; Robinson's *Whitby Glossary*, 1855; *The Dialect of Leeds*, 1862; Brogden's *Provincial Words in Lincolnshire*, 1866; Atkinson's *Cleveland Glossary*, 1868; Parish's *Sussex Dictionary*, 1875; Miss Jackson's *Shropshire Word-Book*, 1879; Mrs Wright's *Rustic Speech and Folk-Lore*, 1913; Dr Bridge's *Cheshire Proverbs*, 1917; and Gepp's *Essex Dialect Dictionary*, 1920. One curious point that emerges from an examination of these books is that not a few proverbial sayings and phrases which were current in literature and general speech in the sixteenth and seventeenth centuries, but which have disappeared from more modern literature and from general colloquial speech, are found still to flourish in the dialectal and provincial vocabulary.

Apart from the special sources indicated above, nearly three thousand works in English literature, dating from the twelfth century (and earlier) to the present day, have been read or examined for the purposes of the present work. Shakespeare and Chaucer have been carefully gone through twice. The books of the Early English Text Society, and other publishing societies, have also been read. This reading has not only provided the illustrative examples and references given, numbering many thousands, of the proverbs brought together in previous collections, but has added a large number of sayings hitherto uncollected.

Wherever possible the illustrative quotations and references have been taken from literature. The various collections are cited only where other references have not been obtained. Reference to the two principal nineteenth-century collections, Bonn's 1855 and Hazlitt's 1869, is made in the few cases only where earlier occurrence in the same form has not been found. Similarly, references to the second, third, fourth and fifth editions of Ray are given only when the saying treated does not appear in an earlier edition In all cases preference has been given to literary illustration. Details as to the system of reference adopted are given in Explanations and Abbreviations on page 9.

I have been more concerned, from the historical point of view, to find the earliest examples I could of the sayings than to illustrate their later use. But, where possible, I have tried to supply, roughly speaking, one quotation or reference for each century, with additional examples to illustrate varying forms of a saying.

The omissions, both of sayings and of illustrations, in a work such as this, undertaken and completed by a single hand, must be many; but as it is really the first attempt at a comprehensive dictionary of the kind, it is hoped that its merits may be found more conspicuous than its deficiencies.

A word must be said as to arrangement. In Ray and other early collections the arrangement is purely fantastic. In more modern books, such as Fuller and Hazlitt, a professional alphabetical order, under the first word of the form of the proverb adopted, is followed. The result of this is whole pages of sayings beginning with A, He, The, We, and other insignificant words, besides the inclusion of the same proverb in several different forms. Proverbs are used and quoted in very varying forms and to find what the searcher wants in collections so arranged is often difficult.

In the present *Dictionary*, an attempt has been made to facilitate reference by adoption of the alphabetical method in a somewhat new way. The arrangement in one alphabet is two-fold.

1 All proverbs relating to the months and seasons of the year, to the days of the week, to saints' days, fasts and festivals, to all animals, birds, insects, etc., are, as a rule, grouped under the month, season, day, etc., to which they refer. Cross-references are supplied to any exceptions. Similarly, sayings related to God, the devil, hell, heaven, the sun, the moon, rain, wind, man, woman, child, and to other subjects which naturally suggest themselves as group-headings, such as fool, time, water, money, life, war, etc., are, as a rule, grouped under their relative headings, with cross-references to exceptions. Sayings relating to places are grouped in like manner.

2 Other proverbs, which do not naturally fall into any of the groups just indicated, take their places in the alphabet under either their first word, if that is significant, or under their first significant word – that by which anyone using the book, who was not certain of the saying's precise form, would naturally look for it. Cross-references have been liberally supplied throughout the work.

By this two-fold arrangement, especially by the grouping system, it is hoped that the book may serve the purposes, not only of a dictionary, but to some extent, at least, of a classified index of English proverbs and proverbial phrases.

G. L. APPERSON

REVISERS' NOTE

In this revised edition we have included over five hundred additional proverbs, such as *The customer is always right*; *There's no such thing as a free lunch*; *If it ain't broke don't fix it*; *Life is too short to stuff a mushroom*; *The family that prays together stays together*; and *Garbage in, garbage out*.

We have also cited earlier dates for many proverbs and given fuller examples of their usage.

S. J. CURTIS
M. H. MANSER

Abbreviations and Explanations

ABBREVIATIONS

B.&F.	Beaumont and Fletcher	P.S.	Parker Society
B.S.	Ballad Society	R.L.S.	Robert Louis Stevenson
E.D.S.	English Dialect Society	Roxb.Cl.	Roxburgh Club
E.E.T.S.	Early English Text Society	S.	Society
F.L.S.	Folk-Lore Society	Ser.	Series
Hunt.Cl.	Hunterian Club	Sh.S.	Shakespeare Society
(N.)	indicates that the quotation so marked is taken from Nare's *Glossary*	Spens.S.	Spenser Society
		s.v.	*sub voce* or *verbo* (under a word or heading, as in a dictionary)
N.&Q.	*Notes and Queries*		
N.Sh.S.	New Shakespeare Society	Tr.	Translation
(OED)	indicates that the quotation so marked is taken from the *Oxford English Dictionary*	T.T.	Tudor Translation
		(W.)	indicates that the quotation so marked is taken from Dr Wright's *Dialect Dictionary*

REFERENCES

The references always precede the quotation, except in the case of the classical quotations within square brackets.

A reference without a quotation indicates that the example occurs either in precisely the same form, or with trifling differences, as in the heading to the article.

References, other than to plays, are to page, or volume and page, unless otherwise indicated. Plays are referred to by act and scene alone.

A date or name in brackets indicates the edition to which reference is made.

1530: Palsgrave	Palsgrave's *L'Eclaircissement de la Langue Française*, Ed. Paris, 1852
1611: Cotgrave	Cotgrave's *French–English Dictionary*, 1611
1633: Draxe	Thomas Draxe's *Bibliotheca Scholastica Instructissima*, 1633
1639: Clarke	John Clarke's *Paraemiologia Anglo–Latina*, 1639
1659: Howell	James Howell's *Proverbs*, 1659
1670, 1678, etc.: Ray	John Ray's *English Proverbs*, 1670 and subsequent editions. Reference is made to the later editions of Ray only when the saying treated does not occur in an earlier edition.
1732: Fuller	Thomas Fuller's *Gnomologia*, 1732
1855: Bohn	H. G. Bohn's *A Hand-Book of Proverbs*, 1855
1869: Hazlitt	W. Carew Hazlitt's *English Proverbs and Proverbial Phrases*, 1869

NOTE   For some of the Latin and Greek quotations I am indebted to Mr H. E. P. Platt's *Alia*, Oxford, 1904.

A

A. 1. A per se = A paragon. 1475: Henryson, *Test. of Cress.*, l. 78, O fair Cresseid! the flour and A-per-se Of Troy and Grece. 1573: Harvey, *Letter-Book*, 104 (Camden S.), A verie A per se A, not her fellowe in Europe. 1631: Brathwait, *Whimzies*, 123 (1859), Such an one is an a per se a for knavery. 1639: Clarke, 104, A per sea.

2. To know not A from the gable-end, or, **from a windmill.** 1401: in T.Wright, *Pol. Poems*, ii. 57 (Rolls Ser., 1861), I know not an a from the wynd-mylne. 1830: Forby, *Vocab. E. Anglia*, 434, He does not know great A from the gable end of a house. Cf. **B** (2).

Aback o' behind like a donkey's tail. 1917: Bridge, *Cheshire Proverbs*, 6.

Abbey to a grange, To bring an. *c.*1480: *Early Miscell.*, 26 (Warton Cl., 1855), And nowe that abbay is torned to a grange. *c.*1540: Bale, *Kynge Johan*, 23 (Camden S.), Our changes are soch that an abbeye turneth to a graunge. 1670: Ray, 161.

Above-board. 1608: J. Hall, *Virtues and Vices*, 15, All his dealings are square, and aboue the boord. 1640: Brome, *Antipodes*, III i, Here's nothing but faire play, and all above boord. 1753: Richardson, *Grandison*, i 185 (1883), All is fair, all is above-board: all is as it was represented. 1891: R.L.S., *Wrecker*, ch ix, 'Oh, everything's open and above board,' he cried. 1924: *The Times*, 25 Jan., p. 11, col. *2*, The public, which likes dealings to be above board.

Absence is a shrew. *c.*1480: in Hazlitt, *Early Pop. Poetry*, ii 13, And therefor it is said in wordes few, how that long absence is a sherew.

Absence makes the heart grow fonder. *c.*1850: T. H. Bayly, *Isle of Beauty*, Absence makes the heart grow fonder. It is often suggested that Bayly was quoting from an anonymous poem in Davison's *Poetical Rhapsody* of 1602. This seems plausible – although the actual source is not easy to find – as the collection contains other poems on the theme of absence such as 'How can the heart forget her?' and 'Absence, Hear Thou my Protestation'. 1848: Anne Brontë, *Tenant of Wildfell Hall*, ' … meantime he exhorts me to the exercise of patience, "that first of woman's virtues", and desires me to remember the saying, "Absence makes the heart grow fonder", and comfort myself with the assurance that the longer

he stays away the better he shall love me when he returns.' The sentiment was certainly current in the 16th century as evidenced by a letter of Sir H. Wotton of 1589: Nothing able to add more to it [affection] than absence. It probably goes back ultimately to a line in Propertius's *Elegies* II: Passion [is] always warmer towards absent lovers.

Absence sharpens love, presence strengthens it. 1732: Fuller, 755.

Absent is always in the wrong, He who is. *See* **Absent party is still faulty.**

Absent party is still faulty, The. *c.*1440: Lydgate, *Fall of Princes*, bk iii. l. 3927, For princis ofte, of furious hastynesse, Wil cachche a quarel, causeles in sentence, Ageyn folk absent, thouh ther be non offence. 1612: Shelton, *Quixote*, Pt I bk iii ch xi, To him that absent is All things succeed amiss. 1710: S. Palmer, *Moral Essays on Proverbs*, 51, The absent party is always to blame. 1732: Fuller, 4390.

Absent without fault. 1633: Draxe, 43, He is neither absent without fault, nor present without excuse.

Abundance depends on sour milk, i.e. thunder-storms aid crops. 1893: Inwards, *Weather Lore*, 119.

Abundance of things ingendereth disdainfulness. 1578: Florio, *First Fruites*, fo. 32, The plenty of things dooth ingender care. 1629: *Book of Meery Riddles*, Prov. 9.

Accidents will happen. 1763: Colman, *Deuce is in Him*, I, Accidents, accidents will happen – No less than seven brought into our infirmary yesterday. 1849: Dickens, *Copperfield*, ch xxviii, 'My dear friend Copperfield,' said Mr Micawber, 'accidents will occur in the best-regulated families.'

Account not that slavery, That brings in penny savoury. 1678: Ray, 221. 1732: Fuller, 6371.

Accounting for tastes, There is no. 1794: A. Radcliffe, *Mysteries of Udolpho* I xi, I have often thought the people he disapproved were much more agreeable than those he admired; – but there is no accounting for tastes. The phrase is based on an old Latin tag *De gustibus non est disputandum* (there is no disputing about tastes), first rendered into English in 1599: J. Minsheu,

Dialogues in Spanish, 6, Against ones liking there is no disputing. 1867: A. Trollope, *Last Chronicle of Barset* I xxxi 263, He had not the slightest objection to recognising in Major Grantly a suitor for his cousin's hand ... There was ... no accounting for tastes. In modern English the form *There is no accounting for taste* is probably more common.

Accusing the times is but excusing our selves. 1732: Fuller, 759.

Ace of trumps. *I will not play my ace of trumps yet.* 1732: Fuller, 2647.

Aces of allowance. *The best must crave their aces of allowance.* 1672: Walker, *Paroem.*, 23.

Aching teeth. *Who hath aking teeth hath ill tenants.* 1670: Ray, 26.

Aching tooth, To have an. Usually to have a longing or desire for – but *See* 1730 quot. 1590: Lodge, *Rosalynde*, 136 (Hunt.Cl.), I have a longing tooth, a longing tooth that makes me crie. 1667: L'Estrange, *Quevedo's Visions*, 201 (1904), 'You have still ... an aching tooth at those poor varlets.' 1730: Bailey, *Dict.*, s.v. 'Ake', To have an aking tooth at one, to be angry at, to have a mind to rebuke or chastise one. 1742: North, *Lives of Norths*, ii 172, He had an aching tooth, as they say, at the mill-stones of a water-mill. 1887: Parish and Shaw, *Dict. of Kent. Dialect*, 1 (E.D.S.), Muster Moppett's man's got a terr'ble aching-tooth for our old sow.

Acorns. *See* **Oak** (5).

Acquaintance of the great will I nought, For first or last dear it will be bought. 15th cent.: in *Reliq. Antiquae*, i 205 (1841), Aqueyntanse of lordschip wyll y noght, For furste or laste dere hit woll be bowght.

Acre to keep a peewit. It would take an. 1917: Bridge, *Cheshire Proverbs*, 86. Said of very poor land.

Action is the proper fruit of knowledge. 1732: Fuller, 760.

Actions speak louder than words. 1628: J. Pym, *Speech*, April 4 ... actions are more precious than words. 1736: *Melancholy State of Province* in A. M. Davis *Colonial Currency* (1911) III 137, Actions speak louder than words, and are more to be regarded. 1856: A. Lincoln *Works* (1953) II 352 'Actions speak louder than words' is the maxim.

Adam. 1. When Adam delved and Eve span, Who was then the gentleman? *c.*1330: R. Rolle in *Religious Pieces*, p. 79 (E.E.T.S. 26), When

Adam dalfe and Eve spane, So spire if thou may spede, Whare was thon the pride of man, That now merres his mede. Before 1500: Hill, *Commonplace-Book*, 131 (E.E.T.S.), Whan Adam delffid and Eve span, who was than a gentilman? 1592: Greene, *Quip*, in *Works*, xi 225 (Grosart), I will not forget the old wiues logick, when Adam delud and Eue spanne, who was then a gentleman? 1630: T. Adams, *Works*, 872. 1732: Fuller, 6421. Ray, 1670, p. 210, adds the couplet, *Upstart a churl and gathered good* [wealth], *And thence did spring our gentle blood.*

2. We are all Adam's children, but silk makes the difference. 1659: Howell, *Proverbs: Span.-Eng.*, 13, We are all Adams sons, silk onely distinguisheth us. 1732: Fuller, 5425. *See also* **Old,** D (2).

Add insult to injury. *See* **Insult.**

Adder. *See* quotations. 1856: *N.&Q.*, 2nd ser, i 401, If the adder could hear and the blindworm could see, No poor man's children could go their way free. 1856: Ibid., 2nd ser, i 331, There is a Kentish proverb ... If I could hear as well as see, No man nor beast should pass by me. 1875: Parish, *Sussex Dict.*, 14, The country people say ... that on the adder's belly will be found the words – 'If I could hear as well as see, No man in life could master me.' 1878: *Folk-Lore Record*, i 15, I have heard of a labourer declaring that the 'queer marks' on the belly of the deaf adder could be made out to be: 'If I could hear as well as see, No mortal man should master me'. *See also* **Deaf** (6); **March** (38); and **Snake** (1).

Adderbury. *See* **Bloxham.**

Addled egg. *As good to be an addled egg as an idle bird.* 1581: Lyly, *Euphues*, 207 (Arber). 1732: Fuller, 681.

Adlant. *See* **Turn,** *verb* (3).

Advantage is a better soldier than rashness. 1855: Bohn, 305.

Adventures are to the adventurous. Meaning that only those who go out in search of excitement or adventure are likely to find it. 1844: Disraeli, *Coningsby*, III l. 244, 'I fear that the age of adventures is past' ... 'Adventures are to the adventurous,' said the stranger. 1914: 'Saki', *Beasts and Superbeasts*, 264, Adventures, according to the proverb, are to the adventurous.

Adversity flattereth no man. 1732: Fuller, 762.

Adversity is easier borne than prosperity forgot. Ibid., No. 763.

Adversity makes a man wise, though not rich.

1633: Draxe, 6, In aduersitie men finde eies. 1678: Ray, 92. 1732: Fuller, 764. *See also* **Prosperity.**

Adversity makes strange bedfellows. The same basic idea has been expressed in a number of different ways. The first word, in particular, often varies. *c.*1611: Shakespeare, *The Tempest* II ii 37, My best way is to creep under his gaberdine: there is no other shelter hereabout. Misery acquaints a man with strange bedfellows. 1837: Dickens, *Pickwick Papers* xli (heading) Illustrative … of the old proverb, that adversity brings a man acquainted with strange bedfellows. 1927: *Times*, 27 Aug., 12 The … alliance of 1923–5 was an illustration of the adage that adversity makes strange bedfellows. The word 'bedfellow' is first recorded in the *Oxford English Dictionary* in 1478.

Advice. 1. Advice comes too late when a thing is done. 1670: Ray, 1. 1748: Richardson, *Clarissa*, iv 119 (1785).

2. Advice to all, security for none. 1855: Bohn, 305.

3. Give neither advice nor salt, until you are asked for it. 1875: A. B. Cheales, *Proverb. Folk-Lore*, 88.

4. In vain he craves advice that will not follow it. 1611: Cotgrave, s.v. 'Croire'. 1670: Ray, 1.

5. We may give advice, but we cannot give conduct. 1736: Franklin, *Way to Wealth*, in *Works*, i 451 (Bigelow).

See also **Woman** (15) and (60).

Affairs, like salt fish, ought to be a good while a soaking. 1855: Bohn, 305.

Afraid of far enough. 1670: Ray, 161. 1917: Bridge, *Cheshire Proverbs*, 8.

Afraid of grass, *c.*1582: G. Harvey, *Marginalia*, 192 (1913), He that is afrayd of euery starting grasse, may not walke in a meddow. 1710: S. Palmer, *Moral Essays on Proverbs*, 195, He that's afraid of every grass must not sleep in a meadow.

Afraid of him that died last year. 1670: Ray, 161. 1732: Fuller, 810, Are you afraid of him that dy'd last year? 1917: Bridge, *Cheshire Proverbs*, 6 … Of that which is never likely to happen.

Afraid of his own shadow. 1567: G. Fenton, *Bandello*, ii 285 (Tudor Tr.), He retorned with more fear of his shadow then true reaporte of that he had in charge. 1580: Baret, *Alvearie*, V 92. And as our English prouerbe is, he is afraid of his owne shadowe. 1672: Walker, *Paroem.*, 53.

Afraid of leaves. 1611: Cotgrave, s.v. 'Peur', Let him thats skared by leaves keep from the wood. 1651: Herbert, *Jac. Prudentum*, 2nd ed., He that is afraid of leaves goes not to the wood.

Afraid of one's friends when none is near. 1699: in *Harl. Miscell.*, ii 38 (1744), No girding satyrist can take up the old proverb against you, and say, That you are afraid of your friends, when there is none near you. 1740: Richardson, *Pamela*, i 222 (1883), You are afraid of your friends, when none are near you.

Afraid of the hatchet, lest the helve stick in his leg. 1917: Bridge, *Cheshire Proverbs*, 7.

Afraid of the wagging of feathers. 1670: Ray, 55, He that's afraid of the wagging of feathers, must keep from among wild fowl.

Afraid of wounds. 1639: Clarke, 310, They that are afraid of wounds, must not come neere a battell. 1670: Ray, 56, He that's afraid of wounds, must not come nigh a battel. 1736: Bailey, *Dict.*, s.v. 'Afraid', He that's afraid of wounds must not go to the wars.

Afraid to ask a price. *See* **He will never.**

After a delay comes a stay. 1732: Fuller, 6177.

After a lank comes a bank. 1678: Ray, 343.

After a storm comes a calm. 1576: C. Holybrand, *French Littleton* E1v, After a storme commeth a calm. 1655: T. Fuller, *The Church-History of Britain* IX viii, After a storm comes a calm. Wearied with a former blustering they began now to repose themselves in a sad silence. Hence the phrase *the calm before the storm*; a time of peace before a period of trouble or disorder.

After death, the doctor. 1611: Cotgrave, s.v. 'Mort', After death drugs. 1681: W. Robertson, *Phraseol. Generalis*, 432. 1732: Fuller, 772. 1826: Brady, *Varieties of Lit.*, 39.

dinner sit awhile; after supper walk a mile. 1588: Cogan, *Haven of Health*, 186 (1612), That old English saying: After dinner sit a while, and after supper walke a mile. 1639: Massinger, *Unnat. Combat*, III i, As the proverb says, for health sake, after dinner, or rather after supper, willingly then I'll walk a mile to hear thee. 1754: Berthelson, *Eng.-Danish Dict.*, s.v. 'Dinner'. 1846: Planché, *Extravag.*, iii 135 (1879), Some tell us after supper walk a mile, But we say, after supper dance a measure.

After drought cometh rain. 15th cent.: in *Reliq. Antiquae*, i 323 (1841), After droght commyth rayne. Before 1529: Skelton, *Magnyfycence*, l. 12, Howe after a drought there fallyth a showre of rayne.

After joy comes sorrow. 15th cent.: in *Reliq.*

Antiquae, i 323 (1841), After plesur commethe payne. 1640: Mabbe, tr. *Exemplary Novels*, i 59 (1900), For as it is in the proverb, after joy comes sorrow.

After meat, mustard. 1605: Camden, *Remains*, 316 (1870). 1694: Motteux, *Rabelais*, bk v ch xxvii 1712: Motteux, *Don Quixote*, Pt I bk iii ch viii, It is just like the proverb, After meat comes mustard. 1822: Scott, *Nigel*, ch iii.

After pear. *See* **Pear** (1).

After wit. 1. After wit comes ower late. 1683: Meriton, *Yorkshire Ale*, 83–7 (1697). 1692: L'Estrange, *Aesop*, 144 (3rd ed.), After-wit comes too late when the mischief is done.

2. After wit is dear bought. 1709: Dykes, *Eng. Proverbs*, 6, After wit is commonly dear bought.

3. After wit is not the best. *c*.1605: in Collier, *Roxb. Ballads*, 88 (1847).

After you is manners. 1738: Swift, *Polite Convers.*, Dial. II, Oh! madam; after you is good manners. 1789: O'Keeffe, *Czar Peter*, III ii, Stop, friend! after me is manners.

After your fling, Watch for the sting. 1917: Bridge, *Cheshire Proverbs*, 7.

Afterthought. *The afterthought is good for nought, except it be to catch blind horses wi'*. S. Devon. 1869: Hazlitt, 355.

Against the grain. 1670: Ray, 178. 1673: Dryden, *Amboyna*, I i, But for this whoreson cutting of throats, it goes a little against the grain, *c*.1730: Swift, *Works*, xiv 250 (Scott), Hither, though much against the grain, The Dean has carried Lady Jane. 1870: Dickens, *Drood*, ch xx, Which again, naturally, rubs against the grain of Mr Bazzard.

Against the hair. *c*.1387: Usk, *Test. of Love* in Skeat's *Chaucer*, vii 58, But ayenst the heer it turneth 1580: Lyly, *Euphues*, 394 (Arber), I will goe against the haire in all things, I may please thee in anye thing. 1609: Shakespeare, *Troilus*, I ii, He is melancholy without cause, and merry against the hair. 1696: *Cornish Comedy*, II, *To have and to hold till us do part, etc.*, goes against the hair. 1754: Berthnelson, *Eng.-Danish Dict.*, s.v. 'Against'.

Against the shins. 1678: Ray, 81, That goes against the shins, i.e. It's to my prejudice.

Against the wool. 1546: Heywood, *Proverbs*, Pt I ch xi, What, should your face thus agayne the woll be shorne For one fall? 1576: R. Peterson, *Galateo*, 25 (1892), For, fromewarde [froward],

signifieth as muche as Shorne against the wooll. 1693: Urquhart, *Rabelais*, bk iii ch xxxvi, Let us turn the clean contrary way, and brush our former words against the wool.

Agamemnon. *See* **Brave** (4).

Age and want. *For age and want save while you may, No morning sun lasts a whole day.* 1736: Franklin, *Way to Wealth*, in *Works*, i 450 (Bigelow).1825: Hone, *Ev. Day Book*, i 1351. 1846: Denham, *Proverbs*, 19 (Percy S.) [with 'summer's' for 'morning'].

Age and wedlock bring a man to his nightcap. 1639: Clarke, 279. 1732: Fuller, 778.

Age and wedlock tame man and beast. 1605: Camden, *Remains*, 317 (1870). 1732: Fuller, 779.

Age and wedlock we all desire and repent of. 1732: Fuller, 780.

Age breeds aches. 1596: Harington, *Metam. of Ajax*, 11 (1814), You have heard the old proverb, 'age breeds aches'.

Age of miracles is past, The. 1599: Shakespeare *Henry V* I i 67, It must be so for miracles are ceas'd. 1602: *All's Well That Ends Well* II iii 1, They say miracles are past; and we have our philosophical persons to make modern and familiar things supernatural and causeless. It has been suggested that the proverb is of earlier origin. 1840: Carlyle *On Heroes and Hero Worship* iv, The Age of Miracles Past? The Age of Miracles is for ever here!

Agree, for the law is costly. 1605: Camden, *Remains*, 316 (1870). 1692: L'Estrange, *Aesop*, 383 (3rd ed.), Agree, agree, says the old saw, the law is costly. 1738: Swift, *Polite Convers.*, Dial. I, Come, agree, agree; the law's costly.

Agree like bells. 1630: T. Adams, *Works*, 192, They tune like bells, and want but hanging. 1683: Meriton, *Yorkshire Ale*, 83–7 (1697), They agree like bells, they want neathing but hanging. 1732: Fuller, 4948, They agree like bells; they want nothing but hanging.

Agreed upon the time. *See* quot. 1855: Bohn, 562, When you are all agreed upon the time, quoth the vicar, I'll make it rain.

Ague in the spring is physic for a king, An. 1659: Howell, 20. 1732: Fuller, 6249. 1846: Denham, *Proverbs*, 34 (Percy S.). 1904: *Co. FolkLore: Northumberland*, 175 (F.L.S.).

Agues come on horseback, but go away on foot. 1678: Ray, 33.

Air of a window. *See* **Draught** (2).

Alciston. *See* **Firle Hill.**

Alder. *See* quot. 1839: G. C. Lewis, *Herefordsh. Words*, 6, When the bud of the aul [alder] is as big as the trout's eye, Then that fish is in season in the River Wye. 1847: Halliwell, *Dict. Prov. Words*, s.v. 'Aul'.

Alderman. *See* **Paced.**

Aldermaston house. *See* quot. 1869: Hazlitt, 457, When clubs are trumps, Aldermaston house shakes.

Aldgate. *See* **Nick and froth;** and **Old,** D (3).

Ale. 1. Ale and history. I have not been able to identify the proverb to which the following quotations refer: Before 1635: Corbet, *Poems*, in Chalmers, v 580, Mine host was full of ale and history. 1654: Gayton, *Pleasant Notes Don Q.*, 195, That truth be in his ale, as history. 1676: Etherege, *Man of Mode*, I, You know the old proverb – ale and history.

2. Ale in, wit out. *See* **Drink,** *subs.* (1).

3. You brew good ale. *c.*1590: Shakespeare, *Two Gent.*, III i, And thereof comes the proverb: 'Blessing of your heart, you brew good ale'. 1826: Scott, *Woodstock*, ch xix, 'I will not say blessing on their hearts,' said he; 'though I must own they drank good ale.'

See also **Fair,** *adv.* (3); **Good ale;** and **Mend** (6).

'Aler. *See* **Hailer.**

Alike every day makes a clout on Sunday. 1732: Fuller, 785. 1846: Denham, *Proverbs*, 5 (Percy S.).

All are good maids, but whence come the bad wives? 1732: Fuller, 499.

All are not abed that have ill rest. 1530: Palsgrave, 422, They be nat all in bedde yet that shall have yvell rest to nyght. 1546: Heywood, *Proverbs*, Pt II ch vii 1670: Ray, 60, All that are in bed must not have quiet rest.

All are not merry. *See* **Merry that dance.**

All are not saints that go to church. 1687: *Poor Robin Alman.*, July.

All are not turners that are dish-throwers. 1678: Ray, 212. 1732: Fuller, 503.

All are presumed good till they are found in a fault. 1640: Herbert, *Jac. Prudentum.*

All asidin as hogs fighten. 1678: Ray, 65.

All blood is alike ancient. 1732: Fuller, 505.

All came from and will go to others. 1611: Cotgrave, s.v. 'Autruy'. 1640: Herbert, *Jac. Prudentum.*

All come to. *You See what we must all come to if we live.* 1678: Ray, 65.

All complain. 1640: Herbert, *Jac. Prudentum.*

All covet all lose. 1297: Robert of Gloucester, 306 (1724) (OED), Wo so coueyteth al, al leseth ywys. 1523–5: Berners, *Froissart*, ch cclix, It is an olde sayenge, He that all coveteth al leseth. 1591: Lodge, *Catharos*, 31 (Hunt.Cl.), The common prouerbe, Hee that coueteth all, oftentimes looseth much. 1664: J. Wilson, *The Cheats*, IV i, This is it, when men must manage their business by themselves. All covet and all lose. 1745: *Agreeable Companion*, 19, All covet, all lose [title of story].

All cry and no wool. *See* **Much cry.**

All cry, fie on the fool. 1659: Howell, *Proverbs: Brit.-Eng.*, 30.

All doors open to courtesy. 1732: Fuller, 512.

All draw water. *See* **Every man wishes water.**

All fear is bondage. 1578: Florio, *First Fruites*, fo. 32, All fearfulnesse is folly. 1629: *Book of Meery Riddles*, Prov. 35.

All feet tread not in one shoe. 1640: Herbert, *Jac. Prudentum.* 1694: D'Urfey, *Quixote*, Pt I Act V sc ii, Let her bequeath it to the devil, or where she pleases: all shoes fit not all feet.

All fellows at football. 1600: *Sir John Oldcastle*, l. 1487 (Malone S.), Al friends at footebal, fellowes all in field. 1641: in *Harl. Miscell.*, iii 228 (1744), If we had stayed but a little while longer, we should have been *All fellows at Football.* 1732: Fuller. No. 498.

All fish are not caught with flies. 1580: Lyly, *Euphues*, 350 (Arber), All fyshe are not caught with flyes. 1598: Meres, *Palladis*, leaf 43. 1732: Fuller, 514.

All flesh is not venison. 1623: Wodroephe, *Spared Houres*, 519. 1670: Ray, 56. 1732: Fuller, 515. 1875: A. B. Cheales, *Proverb. Folk-Lore*, 130.

All fool, or all philosopher. 1732: Fuller, 517.

All Fools' Day. *If it thunders on All Fools' Day, It brings good crops of corn and hay.* 1878: Dyer, *Eng. Folk-Lore*, 255.1882: Mrs Chamberlain. *W. Worcs. Words*, 37 (E.D.S.). 1893: Inwards, *Weather Lore*, 24.

All fruit fails. *See* **Haws** (2).

All go we still, etc. *c.*1430: Lydgate, *Minor Poems*, 150 (Percy S.), An old proverbe groundid on sapience, Alle goo we stille, the cok hath lowe shoon [this line is the refrain – it ends each stanza].

All good things come to an end. 1924: 'D. Vane', *Scar* xxv, All good things come to an end. The feast was over. For the earlier origins of this saying *See* **All things have an end**.

All griefs with bread are less. 1620: Shelton, *Quixote*. Pt II ch lv, Sancho said to him … 'Sorrows great are lessened with meat'. 1640: Herbert, *Jac. Prudentum*.

All-hallon-tide. *Set trees at Allhallontide and command them to grow, Set them after Candlemas and entreat them to grow*. 1678: Ray, 52. *c*.1685: Aubrey, *Nat. Hist. Wilts*, 105 (1847). 1822: Scott, in Lockhart's *Life*, v 184, I hold by the old proverb – plant a tree before Candlemas, and *command* it to grow – plant it after Candlemas, and you must *entreat* it.

All happiness is in the mind. 1855: Bohn, 307.

All have and naught forego. 1562: Heywood, *Epigr.*, No. 278. 1639: Clarke, 40.

All her dishes. *See* **Dish** (1).

All holiday at Peckham. 1825: Hone, *Ev. Day Book*, i 1124. 1848 Forster, *Oliver Goldsmith*, bk i ch vi, 'Oh, that is all a holiday at Peckham,' said an old friend … in a common proverbial phrase.

All in a copse. 1863: Wise, *New Forest*, ch xvi, Forest proverbs … such as … 'All in a copse', that is, indistinct.

All in the day's work. 1738: Swift, *Polite Convers.*, Dial. I, Will you be so kind to tie this string for me, with your fair hands? it will go all in your day's work. 1855: Kingsley, W*est. Ho!*, ch iv, 'It's all in the day's work, as the huntsman said when the lion ate him'. 1908: Lucas, *Over Bemerton's*, ch xv.

All is fair. *See* **Love**, *subs*. (1).

All is fish that comes to net. *c*.1520: in *Ballads from MSS.*, i 95 (B. S.), Alle ys ffysshe that commyth to the nett. 1580: Tusser, *Husbandrie*, 87 (E.D.S.), Alls fish they get that comneth to net. 1664: *Witts Recr.*, Epigr. 644, But Death is sure to kill all he can get, And all is fish with him that comes to net. 1769: Cumberland, *Brothers*, I, Black, brown, fair, or tawny, 'tis all fish that comes in your net. 1852: Dickens, *Bleak House*, ch v.

All is gone, etc. *When all is gone and nothing left, What avails the dagger, with dudgeon haft?* 1583: Melbancke, *Philotinus*, sig. D3, When all is gone and notheinge lefte, farewell dagger with dudgen haft. 1659: Howell, *Letters*, ii 666 (Jacobs) [with 'waits' instead of 'avails']. 1670: Ray, 6. 1732: Fuller, 6393.

All is lost that is put in a riven dish. 1639: Clarke, 169. 1681: W. Robertson, *Phraseol. Generalis*, 1280. 1732: Fuller, 546, All's lost that is pour'd into a crack'd dish. 1880: Spurgeon, *Ploughman's Pictures*, 149 [as in Fuller].

All is not at hand that helps. 1732: Fuller, 526.

All is not lost that is in peril. 1611: Cotgrave, s.v. 'Perdu', All is not lost that in some danger is. 1700: D. Craufurd, *Courtship à-la-Mode*, IV ii, All is not lost that is in hazard, as the saying is. 1880: Platt, *Money*, 32, To realise that 'all is not lost when much is lost.'

All is not won that is put in the purse. 1639: Clarke, 45, 'Tis not all saved that's put i' th' purse. 1732: Fuller, 531. 1758–67: Sterne, *Trist. Shandy*, bk iii ch xxx, All is not gain that is got into the purse. 1875: A. B. Cheales, *Proverb. Folk-Lore*, 100.

All is well. *See* **Man** (78).

All is well save that the worst piece is in the midst. Glos. 1639: in *Berkeley MSS.*, iii 30 (1885).

All is well that ends well. *c Proverbs of hending in Anglia* (1881), IV 182, Wel is him that wel ende mai. 1381: in J. R. Lumby, *Chronicon Henrici Knighton* (1895), II 139, If the ende be wele, than is alle wele. *c*.1426: Audelay, *Poems*, 54 (Percy S.), For al ys good that hath good ende. 1546: Heywood, *Proverbs*, Pt I ch x *c*.1598: Shakespeare, *All's Well that Ends Well* [title]. 1757: Murphy, *Upholsterer*, II i 1850: Smedley, *Frank Fairlegh*, ch xlvii 1901: S. Butler, in *Life*, by H. F. Jones, i 249 (1919).

All is well with him who is beloved of his neighbours. 1611: Cotgrave, s.v. 'Bien', He lives well at home, that is beloved abroad. 1640: Herbert, *Jac. Prudentum*.

All meat is not the same in every man's mouth. 1584: Lodge, *Alarum against Usurers*, 46 (Shakesp. Soc.), Who finding all things meate in the mouth. 1681: W. Robertson, *Phraseol. Generalis*, 597, All meat pleaseth not all mouths. 1732: Fuller, 535.

All meats to be eaten, all maids to be wed. 1546: Heywood, *Proverbs*, Pt II ch ii 1678: Ray, 64.

All men can't be first. 1732: Fuller, 536.

All men can't be masters. 1546: Heywood, *Proverbs*, Pt I ch xii, Every man may not syt in the chayre. 1604: Shakespeare, *Othello*, I i, We cannot all be masters. 1732: Fuller, 537.

All men may say that thou art an ass, then bray, If. 1633: Draxe, 11. 1659: Howell, *Proverbs: Span.-Eng.*, 1, When all tell thee thou art an ass, 'tis time for thee to bray.

All men row galley way. 1813: Ray, 16, i.e. Every one draweth towards himself

All men think all men mortal but themselves. 1924: *Sphere*, 29 March, p. 330, col. 2, That fact is probably explained by the adage, 'All men', etc.

All men's friend. *See* **Friend** (8).

All mouths must be fed. 1710: Ward, *Nuptial Dialogues*, ii 360.

All my eye and Betty Martin. 1785: Grose, *Class. Dict. Vulgar Tongue*, s.v. 'B. M.', That's my eye betty martin, an answer to any one that attempts to impose or humbug. 1828: Carr, *Craven Dialect*, i 128. 1834–7: Southey, *Doctor*, ch cxxv, Who was Betty Martin, and wherefore should she so often mentioned in connexion with my precious eye or yours? 1851: Planché, *Extravag.*, iv 158 (1879), Only your eye and Miss Elizabeth Martin.

All of a dither. *See* quot. 1917: Bridge, *Cheshire Proverbs*, 28, Aw of a dither-a-wack loike a new-baked custhud … = Trembling or shivering.

All of a heap. 1740: Richardson, *Pamela*, ii 119 (1883), Mr Longman, who had struck me of a heap. 1775: Sheridan, *Duenna*, II ii 1817: Scott, *Rob Roy*, ch xxiv 1842: Planché, *Extravag.*, ii 167 (1879).

All of a hommock 1854: Baker, *Northants Gloss.*, s.v. 'Hommock', 'All of a hommock' … is always restricted to a female who, from an excess of ill-made clothing, that sits in heaps or ridges, looks disproportionally stout.

All of a huh. 1886: Elworthy, *West Som. Word-Book*, 357 (E.D.S.), When anything is lopsided, it is said to be 'all of a huh'.

All of a litter, quoth Lambert. 1709: O. Dykes, *Eng. Proverbs*, 43.

All of a spinning = all alike. Staffs. 1889: *Folk-Lore Journal*, vii 294.

All on one side. *See* **Bridgnorth; Chesterfield; Marton; Parkgate; Smoothey's wedding;** and **Takeley Street.**

All one a hundred years hence. 1611: Cotgrave, s.v. 'Fiens', All will be one at the latter day, say we. 1675: in *Bagford Ballads*, ii 722 (B.S.), For 'tis all one a hundred years hence. 1798: Wolcot, *Works*, v 260 (1801). 1895: Pinero, *Benefit of the Doubt*, II.

All one, but their meat goes two ways. 1678: Ray, 78.

All our pomp the earth covers. 1640: Herbert, *Jac. Prudentum.* 1666: Torriano, *Piazza Univ.* 285.

All rivers do what they can for the sea. 1633: Draxe, 180, All rivers run into the sea. 1732: Fuller, 541.

All roads lead to Rome. *See* **Rome** (1).

All Saints Summer. 1924: *Observer*, 28 Sept., p. 7, col. 2, 'All Saints Summer' occasionally gives us a fine spell before or after All Saints' Day on 1 November.

All shall be well. *See* **Jack has his Jill.**

All shearers are honest in the harvest field. 1846: Denham, *Proverbs*, 50 (Percy S.).

All sorts to make a world, It takes. 1620: T. Shelton tr., Cervantes, *Don Quixote* II VI In the world there must surely bee of all sorts. 1767: S. Johnson, *Letter*, Some Lady surely might be found … in whose fidelity you might repose. The World, says Locke, has people of all sorts. 1844: Jerrold, *Story of a Feather*, ch xxviii, 'Well, it takes all sorts to make a world'; and with this worn adage, my new possessor prepared himself to depart. 1901: F. E. Taylor, *Lancs Sayings*, 8, It ta'es o soarts o' folk for t' ma'e a wo'ld.

All that glitters is not gold. [Non teneas aurum totum quod splendet ut aurum, Nec pulchrum pomum quod – libet esse bonum. – Alanus de Insulis (ob. 1294), *Parabolae*, c iii] *c.*1220: *Hali Meidenhad*, 9 (E.E.T.S.), Nis hit nower neh gold al that ter schineth. *c.*1384: Chaucer, *H. Fame*, bk i l. 272, Hit is not al gold, that glareth. *c.*1440: Lydgate, *Fall of Princes*, bk iv 1. 2944 (E.E.T.S.), Al is not gold that shyneth briht. 1583: Greene, *Mamillia*, in *Works*, ii 26 (Grosart), For al is not gold that glysters. 1595: Shakespeare, *Merchant of Venice*, Act II sc vii, All that glisters is not gold. 1703: Ward, *Calves-Head Club*, 5 (1705), We alass see … all is not gold that glisters. 1773: Garrick, Prol. to *Stoops to Conquer*, Thus I begin: 'All is not gold that glitters'. 1859: Sala, *Twice Round the Clock*, 4 p.m. *ad fin.*

All that shakes falls out. 1640: Herbert, *Jac. Prudentum.*

All that shines. *See* **All is not gold.**

All the honesty is in the parting. 1678: Ray, 187.

All the levers you can lay will not do it. Somerset. 1678: Ray, 353. 1732: Fuller, 554, All the levers you can bring will not heave it up.

All the matter's not in my lord judge's hand.
1678: Ray, 76.

All the water in the sea cannot wash out this stain. 1666: Torriano, *Piazza Univ.*, 143, All the water in the sea cannot wash him. 1732: Fuller, No.557.

All the world and Bingham. 1863: *N.&Q.*, 3rd ser, iii 233.

All the world and Little Billing. 1854: Baker, *Northants Gloss.*, s.v. 'L. B.', ... a common mode of expressing that there was a large assemblage people.

All the world and part of Gateshead. 1846–59: *Denham Tracts*, i 80 (F.L.S.). 1892: Heslop, *Northumb. Words*, 2 (E.D.S.), 'Aall the warld an' pairt o' Gyetside' [Gateshead], a common proverb, used jocularly.

All the world goeth by fair speech. Before 1500: Hill, *Commonplace-Book*, 130 (E.E.T.S.).

All things are not to be granted at all times. 1732: Fuller, 562.

All things are possible with God. With reference to Homer's *Odyssey* (with the gods all things can be done) and to Matthew xix 26. 'With men this is impossible; but with God all things are possible'. 1694: P. A. Motteux, tr. *Rabelais' Pantagruel*, V xliii, Drink ... and you shall find its taste and flavor to be exactly that on which you shall have pitched. Then never presume to say that anything is impossible to God. 712: C. mather, *Letter*, 22 Nov. (1971), 17, However, take it again; all things are possible with God. 1826: *Letter*, 1 June, in *Autobiography* (1865), II viii, Sometimes it seems as if persons had too much ... intellect to be converted easily. But all things are possible with God.

All things are soon prepared in a well ordered house. 1611: Cotgrave, s.v. 'Apprestée'. 1670: Ray, 14. 1732: Fuller, 525, All is soon readily in an orderly house.

All things come to those who wait. French proverb *Tout vient à celui qui sait attendre* 'all comes to him who knows how to wait'. 1530 A. Barclay *Eclogues* II 843 Somewhat shall comes who can his time abide. 1863 Longfellow *Poems* (1960) 402 All things come to him who will but wait. 1872 V. Fane *Tout vient à qui sait Attendre* in *From Dawn to Noon* ii 85 Ah! 'All things come to those who wait'. They *come*, but often come *too late*.

All things fit not all men. 1539: Taverner, *Proverbs*, fo. 36, All men can not do all thynges. 1639: Clarke, 82.

All things have a beginning. *c*.1380: Chaucer, *Troylus*, ii 671, For everything, a ginning hath it mede, 1542: Boorde, *Dyetary*, 240 (E.E.T. S.), Yet euery thynge must hauea begynnynge. 1631: Shirley, *Love Tricks*, Prol., Nothing so true As all things have beginning.

All things have an end, with later addition, **and a pudding has two.** *c*.1374: Chaucer, *Troylus*, iii 615, As every thing hath ende. *c*.1490: *Partonope*, l. 11144 (E.E.T.S.), Ye wote wele of all thing moste be an ende. 1530: Palsgrave, 527, Every thynge at the laste draweth to his ende. 1593: Nashe, *Strange Newes*, in *Works*, II 212 (Grosart), Euery thing hath an end, and a pudding hath two. 1613: B.&F., *Burning Pestle*, I ii, All things have end, And that we call a pudding hath his two. 1738: Swift, *Polite Convers.*, Dial. 1, Well, all things have an end, and a pudding has two. 1826: Scott, *Woodstock*, ch x [with the pudding]. 1852: Dickens, *Bleak House*, ch li., 'Well, well!' he cried, shaking it off, 'everything has an end. We shall see!'

All things may be suffered saving wealth. *c*.1390: Gower, *Conf. Amantis*, Prol., l. 787, Bot in proverbe natheles Men sein, ful selden is that welthe Can soffre his oghne astat in helthe. 1611: Cotgrave, s.v. 'Aise', We say, all things may be suffered saving wealth.

All things require skill but an appetite. 1640: Herbert, *Jac. Prudentum.*

All thumbs, or, **Tom All thumbs.** 1598: *Servingmans Comfort*, in *Inedited Tracts*, 107 (Hazlitt, 1868): The clowne, the slouen, and Tom althummes. 1886: Elworthy, *West Som. Word-Book*, 395 (E.D.S.), Leave it alone, all thumbs! why thee art as clumsy as a cow handling a musket. Cf. **Finger** (2).

All tongue. 1828: Carr, *Craven Dialect*, ii 213, 'To be all tongue', to be a great talker.

All truths. *See* **Truth** (23).

All weapons. *See* **Weapon** (1).

All women are good, viz. either good for something, or good for nothing. 1678: Ray, 59. 1738: Swift, *Polite Convers.*, Dial. 1, Which of the goods d'ye mean? good for something, or good for nothing? 1869: Spurgeon, *John Ploughman*, ch xvi.

All work and no play makes Jack a dull boy.

1659: Howell, 12. 1732: Fuller, 6372. 1853: Dickens, in *Letters*, i 313 (1880,) All work and no play may make Peter a dull boy as well as Jack. 1919: J. A. Bridges, *Victorian Recollections*, 160, No doubt, he got sufficient amusement out of his clients to prevent Jack from becoming a dull boy.

All worse and no better, like Tom Norton's wife. 1869: Spurgeon, *John Ploughman*, ch xiii.

All's alike at the latter day; a bag of gold and wisp of hay. 1639: Clarke, 215.

All's lost both labour and cost. 1639: Clarke, 153.

All's out is good for prisoners but naught for the eyes. 1678: Ray, 186.

All's over. *See* **Burying.**

All's well that ends well, as the peacock said when he looked at his tail. 1910: *Devonsh. Assoc. Trans.*, xlii 90.

Allan a Parson. *See* quot. 1846–59: *Denham Tracts*, i 69 (F.L.S.), There never was an Allan a Parson. Spoken of the family of Allan of Blackwell ... and the pedigree of the family fully bears out the saying.

Almond. *See* **Parrot.**

Almost and hard by save many a lie. 1639: Clarke, 106, Almost and wellnigh saves many a lie. 1662: Fuller, *Worthies*, i 82 (1840), I approve the plain country by-word ... 'Almost and very nigh, Have saved many a lie'. 1732: Fuller, 6188.

Almost was never hanged. 1639: Clarke, 3. 1670: Ray, 56.

Alms. 1. Alms never make poor. 1640: Herbert, *Jac. Prudentum*. 1736: Bailey, *Dict.*, s.v. 'Alms', Giving alms never lessens the stock. 1855: Bohn, 309, Alms-giving never made any man poor, nor robbery rich, nor prosperity wise. **2. Alms quencheth sin.** [Water will quench a flaming fire; and almsgiving will make atonement for sin. – *Eccles.* iii 30.] 10th cent.: Aelfric, *Homilies*, ii 106 (Thorpe), thaet seo aelmysse ure synna lig adwaesete. *c.*1175: *Old Eng. Homilies*, 1st ser, 37 (Morris, E.E.T.S.), Al swa thet water acwencheth thet fur swa tha elmesse acwencheth tha sunne. 1303: Robert of Brunne, *Handl. Synne*, l. 7079, Almes fordoth alle wykkednes And quenchyth synne and makyth hyt les.

3. It is an alms-deed to punish him. 1628: Earle, *Microcosm.*, 48 (Arber), No man verifies the prouerbe more, that it is an almes-deed to punish him.

Alone. *See* **Travel** *verb* (3).

Alsager. 1917: Bridge, *Cheshire Proverbs*, 89, Like Auger [Alsager] wenches – all alike.

Altar. *He that serves at the altar, ought to live by the altar.* 1732: Fuller, 2294.

Altringham. 1. *The mayor of Altringham and the mayor of Over, the one is a thatcher, the other a dauber.* 1678: Ray, 301. 1790: Grose, *Prov. Gloss.*, s.v. 'Cheshire'. 1917: Bridge, *Cheshire Proverbs*, 115.

2. *The mayor of Altringham lies in bed while his breeches are mending.* 1678: Ray, 301. 1790: Grose, *Prov. Gloss.*, s.v. 'Cheshire'. 1818: Scott, *Heart of Midl.*, ch xlv, 'But, as we say in Cheshire,' she added, 'I was like the Mayor of Altringham, who lies a bed while his breeches are mending, for the girl did not bring up the right bundle to my room, till she had brought up all the others by mistake.' 1917: Bridge, *Cheshire Proverbs*, 1116.

Always behind. *See* **Miller** (7); and **Mobberley** (1).

Always complains is never pitied, He that. 1732: Fuller, 2038.

Always fears danger always feels it, He that. 1732: Fuller, 2039.

Always in his saddle, never on his way. 1579: Lyly, *Euphues*, Pt II 260 (Bond), Lyke Saint George, who is euer on horse backe yet neuer rideth. 1630: T. Adams, *Works*, 358, He is not like S. Georges statue, euer on horse-backe, and neuer riding. 1788: Franklin, *Autobiog.*, in *Works*, i 286 (Bigelow), He is like St George on the signs, always on horseback and never rides on. 1904: *N. & Q.*, 10th ser, ii 512, I have on several occasions heard the proverb 'Always in his saddle, but never on his way', used with reference to equestrian statues generally, especially where the horse's legs express movement.

Always in the lane (or **field**) **when you should be in the field** (or **lane**). *c.*1791: Pegge, *Derbicisms*, 138 (E.D.S.), To be in the lane, when you should be in the field. 1883: Burne, *Shropsh. Folk-Lore*, 589, He's al'ays i' the lane when he ought to be i' the leasow [meadow]. 1917: Bridge, *Cheshire Proverbs*, 157, Always in the field when you should be in the lane.

Always taking out of the meal-tub, and never putting in, soon comes to the bottom. 1736: Franklin, *Way to wealth*, in *Works*, i 448 (Bigelow). 1880: Spurgeon, *Ploughman's*

Pictures, 11, Always taking out and never putting back soon empties the biggest sack.

Amberley. 1. *See* quot. 1870: Lower, *Hist. of Sussex*, i 8, The local saying, which makes the winter repl*y* to 'Where do you belong?' – 'Amberley, God help us!', and the summer – 'Amberley, where would you live?' [This kind of saying is current about various other places.]

2. *See* quot. 1884: 'Sussex Proverbs', in *N. & Q.*, 6th ser, ix 341, Amberley – God knows. All among the rooks and crows, Where the good potatoes grows.

See *also* **Chichester** (1).

Amen! Parson Penn, more rogues than honest men. 1886: Elworthy, *West Som. Word-Book*, 24 (E.D.S.), A very common saying is: 'Amen', etc.

Amend. 1. *See* quot. 1552 B. Gilpin, *Sermon before Edw. VI*, 41 (1630), It is a proverbe lately sprung up, *No man amendeth himselfe, but every man seeketh to amend other*; and all that while nothing is amended.

2. *See* quot. 1611: Davies (of Hereford), *Sc. of Folly*, 47, in Works, ii (Grosart), Some do amend when they cannot appaire.

Amendment is repentance. 1546: Heywood, *Proverbs*, Pt II ch vi, Let your amendment amende the matter. 1732: Fuller, 789.

Americans. *See* **Good Americans.**

Among friends all things are common. 1477: Rivers, *Dictes and Sayings*, 35 (1877), He … loued aswele to do good to his frendes as to him self, sayng the goodis of frendes ought to be comyn. 1568: W. Fulwood, *Enemie of Idlenesse*, 91 (1593), The benefites of fortune are common amongst friendes. 1694: *Terence made English*, 194, The old proverb says, Among friends all things are common.

Amy Florence. *See* quot. 1854: Baker, *Northants Glossary*, s.v., Any female loosely, untidily and tawdrily dressed. 'She is quite an Amy Florence'.

Ancholme. *See* **Witham.**

Anfield. *See* **Tanfield.**

Anger. 1. Anger and haste hinder good counsel. 1855: Bohn, 313.

2. Anger dieth quickly with a good man. 1670: Ray, 1. 1732: Fuller, 796.

3. Anger edgeth valour. 1639: Clarke, 178.

4. Anger is a short madness. [Ira furor brevis est. – Horace, *Epist.*, I ii 62.] Before 1225: *Ancren*

R., l. 120, Wreththe is a wodschipe. 1477: Rivers, *Dictes and Sayings*, 23 (1877), He that can not refrayne his ire hath no power ouir his witte. *c.*1568: Wager, *Longer thou livest*, sig. C2, Wrath and madnesse they say be all one. *c.*1680: L'Estrange, *Seneca's Morals:* 'Of Anger', ch iv, He was much in the right whoever it was that first call'd Anger, a short madness. 1709: R. Kingston, *Apoph. Curiosa*, 36, Anger is a short fit of madness. 1855: Kingsley, *West. Ho!*, ch xviii, Fear (which, like anger, is a short madness).

5. Anger is a sworn enemy. 1732: Fuller, 793.

6. Anger punishes itself. 1732: Fuller, 799.

Anger a wasp. *See* **Wasp** (4).

Angle, To. 1. To angle all day, and catch a gudgeon at night. 1618: Breton, in *Inedited Tracts*, 190 (Hazlitt, 1868).

2. To angle with a silver (or golden) hook. 1580: Churchyard, *Charge* 28 (Collier), Although you fishe with golden hookes. 1605: Breton, *Honor of Valour*, in *Works*, i (Grosart), To fish for honour with a siluer hooke. 1652: Flecknoe, *Miscellanies*, 126, To exchange ones freedome for a little gain … I ceunt it fishing with a golden hooke. 1725: Bailey, tr. Erasmus' *Colloq.*, 27, For the way of fishing there is according to the proverb, with a golden hook. 1754: Berthelson, *Eng.-Danish Dict.*, s.v. 'Angle', To angle with a golden hook.

Angler. *See* quot. 1658: Franck, *North. Memoirs*, 94 (1821), He's an early angler that angles by moonshine.

Anglesea is the mother of Wales. 1387: Trevisa, tr. Higden, ii 39 (Rolls Ser.), A prouerbe and an olde sawe … Mon moder of Wales, *c.*1440: Anon., tr. Higden, ii 39 (Rolls Ser.), Hit is wonte to be seide prouerbially … Anglesey is the moder of Wales. 1662: Fuller, *Worthies*, iii 508 (1840). 1790: Grose, *Prov. Gloss.*, s.v. 'Anglesey'.

Angry. 1. Angry men make themselves beds of nettles. 1748: Richardson, *Clarissa*, vii 307 (1785).

2. Angry men seldom want woe. 1732: Fuller, 801.

3. He that cannot be angry. *See* quots. 1604: Dekker, *Honest Whore*, Pt II ii, I have heard it often said that he who cannot be angry is no man. *c.*1645: MS. Proverbs in *N. & Q.*, vol 154, p. 27, Hee that cannot be angry is a foole, but hee that will not be angry is more foole.

4. He that is angry is not at ease. 1633: Draxe, 9. 1670: Ray, 1.

5. He that is angry without a cause, must be pleased without amends. *c.*1520: Stanbridge, *Vulgaria*, sig. C2, If ye be angry with me without a cause thou shalt be made at one w'out amendes. 1546: Heywood, *Proverbs*, Pt II ch iv 1642: Fuller, *Holy State:* 'Anger', Be not angry with any without a cause. If thou beest, thou must not only, as the proverb saith, be appeased without amends … 1732: Fuller, 2277.

6. If she be angry, beshrew her angry heart. 1546: Heywood, *Proverbs*, Pt I ch xi

See also **Buckle of belt; Choleric; Hasty man; and Wasp** (1).

Another man's child. *See* quots. 1670: Ray, 52, Put another man's child in your bosom, and he'll creep out at your elbow. *Chesh.* That is, cherish or love him he'll never be naturally affected toward you. 1732: Fuller, 3982 [with 'sleeves' for 'elbow']. 1917: Bridge, *Cheshire Proverbs*, 104.

Another man's dog. *He that keeps another man's dog, shall have nothing left him but the line.* 1639: Clarke, 20. 1670: Ray, 81. 1710: S. Palmer, *Moral Essays on Proverbs*, 275 [with 'string' instead of 'line'].

Another threshed what I reaped. 1732: Fuller, 802.

Another's bread costs dear. 1640: Herbert, *Jac. Prudentum.*

Another's burden, None knows the weight of. 1670: Ray, 1. 1732: Fuller, 3655.

Answer. *See* **Ask** (1);and **Soft answer.**

Ant. 1. If ants their watts do frequent build, Rain will from the clouds be spilled. 1893: Inwards, *Weather Lore*, 146.

2. The ant had wings to do her hurt. 1620: Shelton, *Quixote*, Pt II ch xxxiii 1694: D'Urfey, *Quixote*, Pt I Act IV sc i.

Anthony pig. *See* quots. *c.*1460: *Good Wyfe wold a pylgremage*, l.16, And rene [run] thou not fro hous to house lyke a nantyny gryce [like a St Anthony's pig]. 1593: *Passionate Morrice*, 75 (N.Sh.S.), She followed him at heeles like a tantinie pigge. 1606: Chapman, *Gent. Usher*, IV ii, I have followed you up and down like a Tantalus pig. 1700: Congreve, *Way of the World*, IV xi, Lead on, little Tony – I'll follow thee, my Anthony, my Tantony, sirrah, thou shalt be my Tantony, and I'll be thy pig. 1738: Swift, *Polite*

Convers., Dial. I … like a Tantiny pig. 1762: Bickerstafe, *Love in a Village*, I v, To *See* you Dangling after me everywhere, like a tantony pig. 1836: Wilbraham, *Cheshire Gloss.*, 2nd ed., 112, To follow any one hke a Tantony pig. 1917: Bridge, *Cheshire Proverbs*, 133, To follow one like t' Anthony's pig.

Anticipates. *That which one most anticipates, soonest comes to pass.* [Quid quisque vitet nunquam homini satis Cautum est in horas. – Horace, *Carm.*, II xiii] 1678: Ray, 71, That which one most forehets, soonest comes to pass.

Anvil. 1. An iron anvil should have a hammer of feathers. 1623: Wodroephe, *Spared Houres*, 508, For a hard anveld an hammer of feathers. 1666: Torriano, *Piazza Univ.*, 118, To a hard anvil, a feather hammer. 1710: S. Palmer, *Moral Essays on Proverbs*, 76.

2. The anvil fears no blows. 1666: Torriano, *Piazza Univ.*, 118. 1681: W. Robertson, *Phraseol. Generalis*, 102, The great anvil doth not fear noise or stroaks. 1732: Fuller, 4395. 1869: Spurgeon, *John Ploughman*, ch xxi, The anvil is not afraid of the hammer.

3. When you are an anvil, told you still; when you are a hammer, strike your fill. 1591: Florio, *Second Frutes*, 101. 1696: D'Urfey, *Quixote*, Pt III Act III sc ii 1732: Fuller, 6075.

Any, good Lord, before none. 1886: R. Holland, *Cheshire Gloss.*, 444 (E.D.S.) [supposed exclamation of despairing spinster]. 1917: Bridge, *Cheshire Proverbs*, 8.

Any good. *He that any good would win, at his mouth must first begin.* 1639: Clarke, 136.

Any port in a storm. 1749 J. Cleland *Memoirs of a Woman of Pleasure*, II 133 It was going by the right door and knocking desperately at the wrong one … I told him of it. 'Pooh', says he, 'my dear, any port in a storm'. *c.*1780: J. Cobb, *First Floor*, II ii, in Inchbald's *Farces*, vi 259 (1815), Here is a door open, i' faith – any port in a storm, they say. 1894: R.L.S., *St Ives*, ch xxv, 'Any port in a storm' was the principle on which I was prepared to act.

Any road leads to the end of the world. 1852: FitzGerald, *Polonius*, 86 (1903).

Any stick to beat a dog with. *See* **Stick**, *subs.* (1).

Any tooth, good barber. 1659: Howell, 12. 1678: Ray, 91.

Anything for a quiet life. 1624: T. Heywood, *Captives*, III iii, Anythinge for a quiet lyfe.

1738: Swift, *Polite Convers.*, Dial. I. 1837: Dickens, *Pickwick*, ch xliii., But anythin' for a quiet life, as the man said wen he took the sitivation at the lighthouse. 1841: Planché, *Extravag.*, ii 135 (1879).

Ape, and **Apes. 1. An ape is an ape (or will be an ape), though clad in purple.** 1539: Taverner, *Proverbs*, fo. 21, An ape is an ape, although she weare badges of golde. 1563: Googe, *Eglogs, etc.*, 40 (Arber), An ape wyll euer be an ape, though purple garments hyde. 1683: White Kennett, tr. Erasmus' *Praise of Folly*, 23 (8th ed.), It is a trite proverb, that An ape will be an ape, though clad in purple. 1732: Fuller, 6391, An ape's an ape: a varlet's a varlet, Tho' they be clad in silk or scarlet.

2. An ape is ne'er so like an ape, As when he wears a doctor's cap. 1732: Fuller, 6382. 1869: Spurgeon, *John Ploughman*, ch iii ['popish cape' for 'doctor's cap'. Spurgeon gives the saying a polemical twist].

3. An ape may chance to sit amongst the doctors. 1732: Fuller, 580.

4. An old ape has an old eye. 1605: Camden, *Remains*, 317 (1870). 1653: R. Brome, *Damoiselle*, III ii 1738: Swift, *Polite Convers.*, Dial. I.

5. Ape and whip. *See* quots. 1588: *Mar-Prelate's Epitome*, 7 (1843), Reader cannot chuse but have as great delight therein as a Jack an Apes hath in a whip. 1639: in *Berkeley MSS.*, iii 33 (1885), As proud as an ape of a whip, viz. not proud at all. 1659: Howell, 12, I love it as an ape loves a whipp. 1703: Ward, *Writings*, ii 358, Which every wiseman dreads, as much as an ape does a whip.

6. Apes are never more beasts than when they wear men's clothes. 1732: Fuller, 807.

7. As fine as an ape in purple. 1596: Harington, *Ulysses upon Ajax*, 18 (1814), Howsoever clothed like an ape in purple. 1639: Clarke, 7.

8: As free as an ape is of his tail. 1670: Ray, 205.

9. It is like nuts to an ape. 1732: Fuller, 2970.

10. The ape kills her young with kindness. 1580: Lyly, *Euphues*, 215 (Arber), I should resemble the ape, and kill it by cullyng it. 1586: Whitney, *Emblems*, 188, With kindenes, lo, the ape doth kill her whelpe. 1607: Topsell, *Four-footed Beasts*, 5, She [the ape] killeth that which she loueth, by pressing it to hard. 1732: Fuller, 4396, The ape hugs her darling, till she kills it.

11. The higher the ape goes, the more he shows his tail. *c.*1395: Wyclif, *Bible* (1850), Proverbs iii 35 (*Gloss.*), The filthe of her foli apereth more, as the fylth of the hynd partis of an ape aperith more, whanne he stieth [climbs] on high. *c.*1594: Bacon, *Promus*, No. 924, He doth like the ape that the higher he clymbes the more he shows his ars. 1640: Herbert, *Jac. Prudentum.* 1710: S. Palmer, *Moral Essays on Proverbs*, 218. 1860: Reade, *Cloister and Hearth*, ch lii., Your speech betrays you. 'Tis not till the ape hath mounted the tree that she shows her tail so plain. *See also* **Higher the monkey climbs.**

12. To lead apes in hell. 1575: Gascoigne, *Posies*, in *Works*, i 430 (Cunliffe), I am afrayde my marryage will bee marred, and I may go lead apes in hell. 1599: Shakespeare, *Much Ado*, II i 1658: Cowley, *Cutter of Coleman St*, II viii, I do not intend to die the whining way, like a girl that's afraid to lead apes in hell. 1738: Swift, *Polite Convers.*, Dial. I, Miss, you may say what you please; but faith you'll never lead apes in hell. 1842: Barham, *Ing. Leg.*, 2nd ser, 'Bloudie Jackie', I'm sadly afraid That she died an old maid … So they say she is now leading apes.

13. To say an ape's Paternoster. 1611: Cotgrave, s.v. 'Barboter', To chatter, or didder for cold; to say an apes Paternoster. 1846: Denham, *Proverbs*, 4 (Percy S.), You're saying the ape's Paternoster [said to one whose teeth are chattering with cold].

See also **Bit** (1); and **Wise** (3).

Apothecary. 1. As fit as a thumb with a stone in an apothecary's eye. 1732: Fuller, 679.

2. Apothecaries would not give pills in sugar unless they were bitter. 1670: Ray, 2.

See also **Broken** (1); **Proud**; and **Talk** (9).

Apparel makes the man. 1591: Florio, *Second Frutes*, 115, Though manners makes, yet apparell shapes. 1602: Shakespeare, *Hamlet*, I iii, For the apparel oft proclaims the man. 1617: Greene, *Works*, ix 19 (Grosart), Thy estate may bee great, for the hood makes not the monke, nor the apparrell the man.

Appearances are deceitful. 1666: Torriano, *Piazza Univ.*, 12, Appearance oft deceives. 1750: Smollett, *Gil Blas*, iii 7, Egad, appearances are very deceitful. 1880: Spurgeon, *Ploughman's Pictures*, 27. 1922: A. Bennett, *Prohack*, ch xx iii, I think there is a proverb to the effect that appearances are deceptive.

Appetite comes with eating. This proverb is first recorded in French in 1534: Rabelais's *Gargantua, l'appétit vient en mangeant.* 1653: Urquhart and Motteux, tr. *Rabelais' Gragantua,* I v Appetite comes with eating. 1721: M. Prior, *Dialogues of the Dead* (1907), 227, But as we say in France, the Appetite comes in eating; so in Writing You stil found more to write. 1906: W. Maxwell, *From Yalu to Port Arthur,* i, Appetite comes with eating. Having absorbed Port Arthur and begun on Manchuria, Russia saw no reason why she should not have Korea also.

Apple and **Apples. 1. A rotten apple injures its neighbours.** *See* quots. 1340: *Ayenbite,* 205 (E.E.T.S.), A roted eppel amang the holen maketh rotie the yzounde yef he is longe ther amang. *c.*1386: Chaucer, *Cook's Tale,* l. 42, A proverbe that seith this same word 'Wel bet is roten appel out of hord Than that it rotie al the remenaunt'. 1577: J. Northbrooke, *Treatise against Dicing,* 95 A peny naughtily gotten, sayth Chrysostome, is like a rotten apple layd among sounde apples, which will rot all the rest. 1736: B. Franklin, *Poor Richard's Almanack* (July), The rotten apple spoils his companion. 1855: H. G. Bohn, *Hand-Book of Proverbs,* 514, The rotten apple injures its neighbour.

2. A wink-a-pip [imperfect] **blow Brings apples enow.** 1882: Mrs Chamberlain, *W. Worcs. Words,* 39 (E.D.S.).

3. An apple a day keeps the doctor away. For an alternative version of this proverb, *see* (8). 1913: E. M. Wright, *Rustic Speech, etc.,* 238, Ait a happle avore gwain to bed, An' you'll make the doctor beg his bread (Devon); or as the more popular version runs: An apple a day keeps the doctor away. 1921: F. E. Baily, in *Royal Mag.,* Aug., p. 310.

4. An apple may happen to be better given than eaten. *c.*1300: *Prov. of Hending,* st. 13 (ed. Berlin, 1878), Betere is appel y-yeue then y-ete. 1732: Fuller, 581.

5. Apple and oyster (or **lobster**). *See* quots. 1532: More, *Works,* 724 (1557), No more lyke then an apple to an oyster. 1565: Calfhill, *Answer to Martiall,* 99 (P.S.), Which have learned to make *quidlibet ex quodlibet;* an apple of an oyster. 1594: Shakespeare, *Tam. of Shrew,* IV ii 1667: L'Estrange, *Quevedo's Visions,* 34 (1904), You are no more like … than an apple's like an oyster. 1732: Fuller, 707, As like as an apple is to a lobster.

6. Apples, eggs, and nuts, one may eat after sluts. 1586: L. Evans, *Revised Withals Dict.,* sig. A7, Apples, egges and nuttes, a man may eate thoughe they be dressed by a slute. *c.*1640: in *Roxb. Ballads,* ii 186 (B.S.), My wife is such a beastly slut, Unlesse it be an egge or a nut, I in the house dare nothing eat. 1681: W. Robertson, *Phraseol. Generalis,* 113. 1732: Fuller, 6250, An apple, an egg, and a nut, You may eat after a slut. 1875: A. B. Cheales, *Proverb. Folk-Lore,* 84 [as in Fuller]. 1913: *Folk-Lore,* xxiv 76 [Oxfordsh.], You can eat apples and nuts, after any sluts.

7. Apples, Pears, and nuts spoil the voice. 1659: Howell, *Proverbs: Ital.-Eng.,* 15. 1678: Ray, 41.

8. Eat an apple on going to bed, And you'll keep the doctor from earning his bread. Pembrokeshire and Cornwall. 1866: *N.&Q.,* 3rd ser, ix 153.

9. How we apples swim. 1639: Clarke, 32. 1678: Ray, 253. 1852: FitzGerald, *Polonius,* 51 (1903).

10. If apples bloom in March, etc. 1883: *N.&Q.,* 6th ser, vii 447, In East Sussex the rustics have the following rhyme anent the blooming: If apples bloom in March, In vain for 'um you'll sarch; If apples bloom in April, Why, then they'll be plentiful; if apples bloom in May, You may eat 'um night and day.

11. If good apples you would have, etc. 1883: *N.&Q.,* 6th ser, vii 496, In South Devon the people say: If good apples you would have, The leaves must be in the grave; i.e. the trees should be planted after the fall of the leaf.

12. The apple never falls far from the tree. The proverb is first recorded in German in the 16th century, and is most commonly used to suggest that children take after their parents. 1839: R. W. Emerson, *Letter,* 22 Dec. (1939) II 243, As men say the apple never falls far from the stem, I shall hope that another year will draw your eyes and steps to this old dear odious haunt of the race.

13. To give an apple where there's an orchard; i.e. coals to Newcastle. 1821: Clare, *Rural Life,* 114, Old Fortune, like sly Farmer Dapple, Where there's an orchard, flings an apple. 1854: Baker, *Northants Glossary,* s.v. 'Orchard', Giving an apple where there's an orchard. 1883: Burne, *Shropsh. Folk-Lore,* 590, Those who have an orchard shall have an apple sent them, And those who have a horse shall have another lent them.

14. Won with an apple and lost with a nut; or vice versa. 1546: Heywood, *Proverbs*, Pt I ch x, She is lost with an apple, and woon with a nut. 1573: G. Harvey, *Letter-Book*, 121 (Camden S.), Woone with a napple and loste with a nutt. 1630: *Tinker of Turvey*, 73 (Halliwell), Marian, thinking she had lost her lover with a nut, sent him a present of apples to winne him againe. 1732: Fuller, 2201, He that is won with a nut, may be lost with an apple.

See also **Egg** (8); **Michaelmas** (1); **St Swithin** (2); **Small choice**; and **Two apples**.

Apple-cart, To upset one's. [ὅλην τήν α ἅμαξαν ἐπεσπάσω – Lucian, *Pseudol.*, 32. Plaustrum perculit. – Plautus, *Epid.*, 592.] 1854: E. A. Andrews, *Latin-Eng. Lex.*, s.v. 'Plaustrum', I have upset my apple cart! I am done for! 1880: Courtney, *W. Cornwall Words*, 18 (E.D.S.), In Cornwall 'Down with your dresser', or, 'Over goes your apple-cart'. 1928: Heslop, *Northumb. Words*, 16 (E.D.S.), 'That's upset his apple-cairt for him, sa think', – that has completely stopped his project. 1926: *Church Times*, 8 Jan., p. 46, col. 4, Should he attempt to do anything which in their opinion might upset the ecclesiastical apple-cart.

Appleby. *See* quot. 1690: *New Dict. Canting Crew*, sig. G7, 'Who has any lands in Appleby?' a question askt the man at whose door the glass stands long.

April. 1. A cold April the barn will fill. 1659: Howell, *Proverbs: Span.-Eng.*, 21, A cold April, much bread, and little wine. 1732: Fuller, 6356. 1882: Mrs Chamberlain, *W. Worcs. Words*, 37 (E.D.S.).

2. A dry April Not ike farmer's will: April wet Is what he would get. 1893: Inwards, *Weather Lore*, 22.

3. A flood in April, a flood in May, And a flood to take away the hay. 1917: Bridge, *Cheshire Proverbs*, 162.

4. A raggy [frosty] **April an' a groo** [cold, raw] May, **Gars eydent** [prudent] **farmers ettle out their hay.** 1899: Dickinson, *Cumberland Gloss.*, 112.

5. A sharp April kills the pig. 1893: Inwards, *Weather Lore*, 23.

6. After a wet April a dry June. Ibid., 24.

7. An April cling is good for nothing. Somerset. 1678: Ray, 345. 1846: Denham, *Proverbs*, 43 (Percy S.).

8. An April flood carries away the frog and her brood. 1639: Clarke, 307. 1744: Claridge, in Mills' *Essay on Weather*, 101 (1773). 1893: Inwards, *Weather Lore*, 22.

9. April and May the keys of the year. 1659: Howell, *Proverbs: Span.-Eng.*, 21. 1732: Fuller, 809, April and May are the key of all the year. 1893: Inwards, *Weather Lore*, 23.

10. April cold and wet fills barn and barrel. 1893: Inwards, *Weather Lore*, 23.

11. April comes in with his hack and his bill, And sets a flower on every hill. 1846: Denham, *Proverbs*, 41 (Percy S.). 1879: Henderson, *Folk-Lore of N. Counties*, 95 (F.L.S.).

12. April rains for men [corn]. **May for beasts** [grass], 1893: Inwards, *Weather Lore*, 24.

13. April showers bring May flowers. *c.*1560: in Wright, *Songs, etc., Philip and Mary*, 213 (Roxb.Cl), When Aprell sylver showers so sweet Can make May flowers to sprynge. 1580: Tusser, *Husbandrie*, 103 (E.D.S.), Sweete April showers, Doo spring Maie flowers. 1611: Barry, *Ram-Alley*, V, I'll show you how April showers bring May flowers. 1732: Fuller, 6126. 1921: *Sphere*, 14 May, p. 152, If there was anybody left to believe in the saying that 'April showers bring forth May flowers' ...

14. April snow breeds grass. 1893: Inwards, *Weather Lore*, 23.

15. April wears a white hat. Ibid., 23.

16. April weather, Rain and sunshine, both together. Ibid., 23.

17. Betwixt April and May if there be rain, 'Tis worth-more than oxen and wain. Ibid., 23.

18. He is like an April shower. 1639: in *Berkeley MSS.*, iii 26 (1885), [Of an unconstant man] Hee's like an Aprill shoure, that wets the stone nine times (Glos.).

19. If the first three days, etc. 1861: *N.&Q.*, 2nd ser, xii 303, 'If the first three days in April be foggy, there will be a flood in June', said a Huntingdonshire woman the other day. 1912: R. L. Gales, *Studies in Arcady*, 2nd ser, 105, Fogs in April, floods in June.

20. Moist April, clear June. 1893: Inwards, *Weather Lore*, 24.

21. On the third day of April come in the cuckoo and the nightingale. 1732: Fuller, 6136. 1846: Denham, *Proverbs*, 41 (Percy S.).

22. Snow in April is manure; snow in March devours. 1893: Inwards, *Weather Lore*, 23.

23. The first day of April, you may send a fool whither you will. 1732: Fuller, 6135. 1846: Denham, *Proverbs*, 41 (Percy S.), On the first of April hunt the gowke another mile.

24. Thunderstorm in April is the end of hoar-frost. 1893: Inwards, *Weather Lore*, 24.

25. Till April's dead Change not a thread. Ibid., 23.

26. When April blows his horn [thunder], **It's good for hay and corn.** 1670: Ray, 41. 1744: Claridge, in Mills' *Essay on Weather*, 100 (1773). 1882: *N. & Q.*, 6th ser, v 327.

See also **Cherry** (3); **Cuckoo; Dove's Flood; Frosty winter; January** (14); **March** (6), (13), (21), (24), (27), (34), (39), and (47); and **Potatoes** (2).

Apron-strings. *See* quot. 1678: Ray, 226, To hold by the apron-strings, i.e. in right of his wife.

Apt to promise is apt to forget, A man. 1732: Fuller, 271.

Archer is not known by his arrows, but his aim, A good. Ibid., No. 135.

Architect of one's own fortune. *See* **Every man is the architect.**

Arden, He is the black bear of. 1662: Fuller, *Worthies*, iii 270 (1840). 1790: Grose, *Prov. Gloss.*, s.v. 'Warwickshire', ... Guy Beauchamp, Earl of Warwick, was so called ... This saying was used to express that the person ... so denominated, was really an object of terror.

Argus at home, but a mole abroad. 1732: Fuller, 582. 1813: Ray, 78.

Arm. 1. Don't stretch thy arm farther than thy sleeve will reach. 1541: Coverdale, *Christ. State Matrimony*, sig. I3, Strech out thine arme no farther then thy sleue wyll retche. 1549: Latimer, *Seven Sermons*, 51 (Arber). 1683: Meriton, *Yorkshire Ale*, 83–7 (1697). 1817: Scott, *Rob Roy*, ch xxii, 'Nick,' said he, 'never put out your arm farther than ye can draw it easily back again.' 1901: F. E. Taylor, *Lancs Sayings*, 9, Never put thi arm eawt furr nor thi sleeve'll cover.

2. He's arm i' link wi' him. 1917: Bridge, *Cheshire Proverbs*, 69 ... Very familiar.

Armour is light at table. 1640: Herbert, *Jac. Prudentum*.

Army marches on its stomach, An. 1904: *Windsor Magazine*, Jan. 268 'An army marches on its stomach'. 1911: Hackwood, *Good Cheer*, 313, 'An army marches on its stomach', says the

old proverb. The saying is usually attributed to Napoleon I It encapsulates a report given in Las Cases, *Mémorial de Ste-Hélène* (1823).

Aroint thee, witch, *c.*1605: Shakespeare, *Lear*, III iv 1606: Shakespeare, *Macbeth*, I iii 1670: Ray, *Coll. of Eng. Words*, s.v. 'Rynt ye', By your leave, stand handsomely, as *Rynt you witch*, quoth Besse Locket to her mother. – Proverb – Cheshire. 1816: Scott, *Antiquary*, ch vi, The Antiquary interposed. 'Aroint thee witch! wouldst thou poison my guests with thy infernal decoctions?' 1834: W. Toone, *Glossary*, s.v. 'Aroint'. 1917. Bridge, *Cheshire Proverbs*, 106. [In both Toone and Bridge with the 'Bessie Locket' addition.]

Around, what goes around comes. *See* **Go** (27).

Arrow. 1. He makes arrows of all sorts of wood. 1732: Fuller. No. 1983.

2. The arrow often hits the shooter. Before 1500: Hill, *Commonplace-Book*, 129 (E.E.T.S.), Often times the arow hitteth the shoter. 1709: R. Kingston, *Apoph. Curiosa*, 15, like arrows shot against Heaven, fall upon their own heads.

3. This arrow cometh never out of thine own bow. Before 1500: Hill, *Commonplace-Book*, 129 (E.E.T.S.).

Art. 1. Art hath no enemy but ignorance. 1644: Taylor (Water-poet), 'To John Booker', 5, in *Works*, 2nd coll. (Spens.S., 1873).

2. Art improves nature. 1587: Underdowne, *Heliodorus*, bk iii p. 94 (T.T.), Arte can breake nature. 1732: Fuller, 814, Art helps nature, and experience art. 1827: Hone, *Ev. Day Book*, ii 310, 'Art improves nature', is an old proverb which our forefathers adopted without reflection.

3. Art is long, life short. – Hippocrates, Aph. 1. Inde illa maximi medicorum: exclamatio est, 'vitam brevem esse, longam artem'. – Seneca, *De Brevit. Vit.*, *c* i] *c.*1380: Chaucer, *Parl. of Foules*, l.1, The lyf so short, the craft so long to lerne. 1630: Brathwait, *Eng. Gent.*, *etc.*, 74 (1641), Art is long, life short, Experience deceiving. 1710: S. Palmer, *Moral Essays on Proverbs*, 380. 1850: Dickens, *Chuzzlewit*, ch v 1912: Lucas, *London Lav.*, ch xx, And then there's not time ... Life is short you know, Art can be too long.

4. Art must be deluded by art. 1583: Melbancke, *Philotinus*, sig. G1, It is a chiefe point of art to dissemble art. 1637: Breton, in *Works*, ii *h* 11 (Grosart), I haue heard schollers say, that it is art to conceale art. 1732: Fuller, 815.

Artful fellow. *See* **Devil** (1).

Arthur, King. 1. Arthur could not tame a woman's tongue. 1659: Howell, *Proverbs: Brit.-Eng.*, 23.

2. Arthur was not but whilst he was. 1659: Howell, *Proverbs: Brit.-Eng.*, 35, Arthur himself had but his time. 1662: Fuller, *Worthies*, iii 519 (1840), 'Bu Arthur ond tra fu'. That is, 'Arthur was not, but whilst he was'. 1790: Grose, *Prov. Gloss.*, s.v. 'Cardiganshire', … spoken of a great family reduced to indigence.

3. King Arthur did not violate the refuge of a woman. 1662: Fuller, *Worthies*, iii 519 (1840) … By the woman's refuge, many understand her tongue. 1790: Grose, *Prov. Gloss.*, s.v. 'Cardiganshire'.

Artist lives everywhere, An. 1560: Becon, *Catechism*, 355 (P.S.), According to this common proverb: *Artem quaevis terra alit*; that is to say, 'A man having an occupation shall be able to live wheresoever he become'. 1725: Bailey, tr. Erasmus' *Colloq.*, 238, But you know the old proverb; *a Man of Art will live anywhere*. 1823: D'Israeli, *Cur. of Lit.*, 2nd ser, i 429 (1824), Nero … replied to his censurers by the Greek proverb, 'An artist lives every where'.

Arundel. *See* quot. 1894: A. J. C. Hare, *Sussex*, 221, A proverb says – Since William rose and Harold fell, There have been Earls of Arundel, And Earls old Arundel shall have While rivers flow and forests wave. *See also* **Chichester** (1).

As ever water wet. 1591: Harington, *Orl. Furioso*, bk xvi st. 15, Vnchast and false, as ever water wet. *See also* **Good as ever.**

As far. 1. I have seen as far come as nigh. 1546: Heywood, *Proverbs*, Pt I ch xi *c.*1594: Bacon, *Promus*, No. 638.

2. I've been as far south, as ye've been north. A Wooler saying. 1846–59: *Denham Tracts*, i 26 (F.L.S.).

As good a man. *See* **Honest** (9) and (10).

As good as. *See* **Good.**

As good beat your heels against the ground. 1639: Clarke, 154.

As good do it at first, as at last. 1593: G. Harvey, *Pierces Superer.*, in *Works*, ii 247 (Grosart). 1632: Jonson, *Magnetic Lady*, V vi, Well, you must have it; As good at first as last.

As good do nothing as to no purpose. 1732: Fuller, 684.

As good lost as found. 1605: Camden, *Remains*, 316 (1870).

As good never a whit. *See* **Never a whit.**

As good undone. *See* **Undone** (1).

As good water. *See* **Mill** (1).

As long as I am riche reputed, With solem vyce I am saluted; But wealthe away once woorne, Not one wyll say good morne. 16th cent.: in *Reliq. Antiquae*, i 207 (1841).

As much need on't, as he hath of the pip, or of a cough. 1670: Ray, 187.

As please the painter. *c.*1594: Bacon, *Promus*, Nos. 159 and 1396. 1690: *New Dict. Canting Crew*, sig. I2, *What pleases the painter*, when any representation in the productions of his or any art is unaccountable, and so is to be resolv'd purely into the good pleasure of the artist. 1737: Ray, 61, As it pleases the painter.

As the goodman saith, so say we; But as the goodwife saith, so it must be. 1639: in *Berkeley MSS.*, iii 33 (1885) [with 'so it should be' instead of 'so say we']. 1670: Ray, 51 [with 'good woman' instead of 'goodwife']. 1732: Fuller, 6408. 1875: A. B. Cheales, *Proverb. Folk-Lore*, 7.

Ascension Day. 1. As the weather on Ascension Day, so may be the entire autumn, 1893: Inwards, *Weather Lore*, 41.

2. *See* quot. 1669: *New Help to Discourse*, 284, If it rain upon Ascension Day … it doth betoken scarcity of all kinde of food for cattel, but being fair it signifieth plenty.

Ash. 1. Burn ash-wood green, 'Tis fire for a queen; Burn ash-wood sear, 'Twill make a man swear. 1851: Borrow, *Lavengro*, iii 334, That makes good the old rhyme … 'Ash, when green, is fire for a queen'. 1884: H. Friend, *Flowers and Flower Lore*, 219.

2. If the ash is out before the oak, You may expect a thorough soak; If the oak is out before the ash. You'll hardly get a single splash. *c.*1870: Smith, *Isle of Wight Words*, 62 (E.D.S.) [slightly varied from the foregoing]. 1893: Inwards, *Weather Lore*, 151.

3. Oak, smoke [summer hot]: Ash, squash [summer wet]. 1893: Inwards, *Weather Lore*, 151.

4. When the ash is out before the oak, Then we may expect a choke [drought]; **When the oak is out before the ash. Then we may expect a splash.** Shropshire. Ibid, 151.

It will be noted that 4 is the precise reverse of 2. There are variants of both 2 and 4 which may be found in Inwards.

See also **Oak** (3).

Ashford. *See* quots. 1735: Pegge, *Kentish Proverbs*, in E.D.S., No. 12, p. 67, Naughty Ashford, surly Wye, Poor Kennington hard by. 1899: J. W. Ebsworth, in *Roxb. Ballads*, viii 640 (B.S.), Proud is Ashford, surly is Wye; Lousy Kennington stands hard by.

Ashton. *See* quot. 1869: Hazlitt, 320, Proud Ashton, poor people, ten bells and an old crack't steeple.

Ash Wednesday. 1. As Ash Wednesday, so the fasting time. 1893: Inwards, *Weather Lore*, 40.

2. Wherever the wind lies on Ash Wednesday, it continues during the whole of Lent. 1830: Forby, *Vocab. E. Anglia*, 414. 1893: Inwards, *Weather Lore*, 40.

Ask. 1. Ask a silly question, and you'll get a silly answer. [Proverbs xxvi 5, Answer a fool according to his folly, lest he be wise in his own conceit.] *c.*1300: *South-English Legendary* (E.E.T.S.) 494, Ffor-sothe thou axest as a fol, an swich answere me schul the yive. 1484: Caxton, *Aesop*, V xiii 158, And thus they wente withoute ony sentence For to a folysshe demaunde behoveth a folysshe answere. 1551: R. Robynson, tr. *T. More's Utopia*, I E4, For Salomon the wise sayeth: Answer a foole according to his folishnes, like as I do now. 1721: J. Kelly, *Scottish Proverbs*, 35, A thraward [perverse] Question should have a thrward answer. 1929: R Firbank, *Inclinations*, 'Don't ask silly questions, Daisy, if you don't want foolish answers,' the Countess returned.

2. Ask but enough, and you may lower the price as you list. 1813: Ray, 2.

3. Ask me no questions and I'll tell you no lies. 1773: Goldsmith, *She stoops to Conquer* III 51, Ask me no questions and I'll tell you no fibs. 1818: Scott, *Heart of Midlothian*, I ix, If ye'll ask nae questions, I'll tell ye nae lies. 1900: H. Lawson, *Over Sliprails*, 135, 'Where did you buy the steer, father?' she asked. 'Ask no questions and hear no lies'. 1906: R. Kipling, *Puck of Pook's Hill*, 252, Them that asks no questions isn't told a lie.

4. Ask much to have a little. *c.*1582: G. *Harvey*, *Marginalia*, 191 (1913), Craue and haue. 1640: Herbert, *Jac. Prudentum*

5. Ask my fellow whether I be a thief. 1546: Heywood, *Proverbs*, Pt II ch v 1630: T. Adams, *Works*, 316, This is somewhat to the prouerbe, Aske the sons if the father be a theefe. 1692: L'Estrange, *Aesop*, 355 (3rd ed.), Ask my brother if I'm a thief, 1732: Fuller, 817.

6. Ask the mother if the child be like his father. 1732: Fuller, 818.

7. Ask the seller if his ware be bad. 1666: Torriano, *Piazza Univ.*, 73, Ask mine host whether he have good wine. 1732: Fuller, 819. 1774: C. Dibdin, *The Quaker*, II iii, Ask the vintner if the wine be good.

8. He that asketh a courtesy promiseth a kindness. 1732: Fuller, 2041.

9. He that asketh faintly beggeth a denial. Ibid., No. 2042.

10. He that cannot ask cannot live. 1633: Draxe, 20. 1639: Clarke, 41.

See also **Ax.**

Aspen leaf. 1. To tremble like an aspen leaf. *c.*1374: Chaucer, *Troylus*, iii 1200, Right as an aspes leef she gan to quake. 1449: J. Metham, *Works*, 61 (E.E.T.S.), Than euyn as an espys lef doth schake Ayens the wynd, ryght so than dyd he, Dyd qwake for fere. 1567: Golding, *Ovid*, iii 46, Stoode trembling like an aspen leafe. *c.*1591: Shakespeare, *Titus Andr.*, II iv 1675: C. Cotton, *Burl. upon Burlesque*, 247 (1765), But like an aspen-leaf I shook. 1740: Richardson, *Pamela*, i 228 (1883), She came into bed, but trembled like an aspen-leaf. 1780: Walpole, *Letters*, vii 376 (Cunningham), Lord Mansfield ... quivered on the wool-sack like an aspen. 1828: Scott, *Fair Maid*, ch xxxii 1920: A. A. Milne, *Second*, *plays*, 186 (1921), I was shaking like an aspen leaf.

2. When the aspen leaves are no bigger than your nail, Is the time to look out for truff and peel. 1850: *N. & Q..*, 1st ser ii 511.

Ass and **Asses. 1. A dull ass near home needs no spur.** 1732: Fuller, 83.

2. An ass is but an ass, though laden with gold. 1660: Howell, *Parly of Beasts*, 17, The asse often times carries gold on his back, yet feeds on thistles. 1666: Torriano, *Piazza Univ.*, 15, An asse, though loaded with gold, eats but nettles and thistles. 1732: Fuller, 585.

3. An ass is the gravest beast, the owl the gravest bird. 1732: Fuller, 586. 1886: Swainson, *Folk-Lore of British Birds*, 125 (F.L.S.).

4. An ass laden with gold. *See* quots. 1620: Shelton, *Quixote*, Pt II ch xxxv, The usual proverbs are: 'An ass laden with gold will go lightly uphill' ... 1630: T. Adams, *Works*, 863, Philip was wont to say, that an asse laden with golde would enter the gates of any citie. 1631: Mabbe, *Celestina*, 72 (T.T.), There is not any place so high, where-unto an asse laden with gold will not get up. 1645: Howell, *Letters*, bk i § ii ch ix, There's no fence or fortress against an ass laden with gold. 1732: Fuller, 587, An ass laden with gold overtakes every thing. Ibid., No. 588, An ass loaded with gold climbs to the top of a castle.

5. An ass must be tied where the master will have him. 1732: Fuller, 589.

6. An ass pricked must needs trot. 1629: *Book of Meery Riddles*, Prov. 58.

7. An ass was never cut out for a lap-dog. 1732: Fuller, 592.

8. As proud as an ass of a new pack-saddle. 1823: Scott, *Q. Durward*, ch xxvii.

9. Asses die and wolves bury them. 1732: Fuller, 821.

10. Better ride an ass that carries me, than a horse that throws me. 1633: Draxe, 223. 1732: Fuller, 920. 1880: Spurgeon, *Ploughman's Pictures*, 35. 1929: *Times*, 17 Jan., p. 9, col. 1.

11. Better strive with an ill ass, than carry the wood one's self. 1732: Fuller, 930.

12. Did you ever hear an ass play on a lute? 1556: G. Colvile, tr. Boethius, 18 (1897), Art thou no more apt to vnderstand them then an asse to play on the harpe? 1732: Fuller, 1282. 1781: T. Francklin, *Lucian's Works*, ii 109, What, indeed, as the proverb says, has the ass to do with a lyre?

13. Every ass loves to hear himself bray. 1732: Fuller, 1404.

14. Every ass thinks himself worthy to stand with the king's horses. 1639: Clarke, 254. 1670: Ray, 58. 1732: Fuller, 1405.

15. Hark! I hear the asses bray; We shall have some rain to-day. Rutland. 1893: Inwards, *Weather Lore*, 127.

16. He that makes himself an ass, must not take it ill if men ride him. 1732: Fuller, 2232. 1869: Spurgeon, *John Ploughman*, ch iv, We may make ourselves asses, and then everybody will ride us.

17. It is good to hold the ass by the bridle, and a scoffing foole by his wits end. 1647: *Countrym. New Commonwealth*, 32. 1651: Herbert, *Jac. Prudentum*, 2nd ed. [the first half of the saying only].

18. Jest with an ass, and he will flap you in the face with his tail. 1855: Bohn, 436.

19. Never went out an ass and came home horse. 1732: Fuller, 2668, If an ass goes a travelling, he'll not come home an horse. 1852: FitzGerald, *Polonius*, 48 (1903).

20. Put not an embroidered crupper on an ass. 1732: Fuller, 3984.

21. The ass brays When he pleases. Ibid., No. 4399.

22. The ass that brays most eats least. 1611: Cotgrave, s.v. 'Asne'. 1670: Ray, 3. 1732: Fuller, 822.

23. 'Tis a sorry ass that will not bear his own burden. 1659: Howell, 4.

24. 'Tis time to cock your hay and corn, When the old donkey blows his horn. 1836: *Farmer's Mag.*, vol iv pt I, p. 447. 1893: Inwards, *Weather Lore*, 127.

25. To a rude ass a rude keeper. 1623: Wodroephe, *Spared Houres*, 475.

26. What good can it do an ass to be called a lion? 1732: Fuller, 5490.

27. What, would you have an ass chop logic? Ibid., No. 5527.

28. When an ass climbeth a ladder, you may find wisdom in women. Ibid., No. 5546.

29. Where-ever an ass falleth, there will he never fall again. Ibid., No. 5643.

30. Who drives an ass, and leads a whore, hath pain and sorrow evermore. 1639: Clarke, 259. 1670: Ray, 52. 1687: *Poor Robin Almanac*, July. 1736: Bailey, *Dict.*, s.v. 'Ass'.

31. You will make me believe that an ass's ears are made of horns. 1659: Howell, 8.

See also **All men; Beat,** *verb* (3); **Honey** (8); **Horse** (51) and (75); **Lawyer** (9); and **One mule.**

Ass's head, To wash the. 1578: Florio, *First Fruites*, fo. 34, Who washeth an asses head loseth both labour and sope. 1593: G. Harvey, *Works*, i 276 (Grosart), I ... take small pleasure in washing the asses head. 1660: Howell, *Parly of Beasts*, 28, The old proverb ... He who washeth an asse's head doth lose both time and sope. 1732: Fuller, 5193, To lather an asse's head, is but spoiling of soap.

Assail who will, the valiant attends. 1640: Herbert, *Jac. Prudentum.*

Assfordby Bridge. *He has gone over Assfordby Bridge backwards.* Spoken of one that is past learning. 1678: Ray, 317. 1790: Grose, *Prov.*

Gloss., s.v. 'Leicestershire'. 1881: Evans, *Leics. Words, etc.*, 299 (E.D.S.) … In modern usage [the saying] is applied to one who 'sets the cart before the horse', in word or deed.

Astrology is true, but the astrologers cannot find it. 1640: Herbert, *Jac. Prudentum.*

Atheist is got one point beyond the devil, An. 1732: Fuller, 593. 1875: A. B. Cheales, *Proverb. Folk-Lore*, 124.

Attack is the best form of defence. 1775: W.H. Drayton in R.W. Gibbes *Documentary History of the American Revolution*, (1855) I 174, It is a maxim that it is better to attack than to receive one. 1799: G. Washington, *Writings*, (1940) XXXVII. 250, Make them believe, that offensive operations, often times, is the surest, if not the only … means of defense. The standard American form of this saying is that *The best defense is a good offense.*

Attorney. *See* **Bawds**; and **Lawyer.**

Auger. *See* **Alsager.**

August. 1. As August so the next February. 1893: Inwards, *Weather Lore*, 32.

2. Dry August and warm Doth harvest no harm. 1732: Fuller, 6209. 1893: Inwards, *Weather Lore*, 32.

3. If the first week in August is unusually warm, the winter will be white and long. 1893: Inwards, 33.

4. If the twenty-fourth of August be fair and clear, Then hope for a prosperous autumn that year. 1732: Fuller. No. 6470. 1893: Inwards, 33.

5. None in August should over the land. In December none over the sea. 1893: Inwards, 32.

6. So many August fogs, so many winter mists. Ibid., 32.

See also **Cuckoo** (8), (11), and (12); **March** (15); **Merry be the first; July** (6) and (10); and **Thistle** (2).

Autumn. 1. Clear autumn, windy winter; Warm autumn, long winter. 1893: Inwards, 8.

2. Of fair things the autumn is fair. 1640: Herbert, *Jac. Prudentum.*

See also **Ascension Day** (1); **August** (4); **Blossom; St Bartholomew** (2); and **Spring** (7).

Autumnal agues are long or mortal. 1640: Herbert, *Jac. Prudentum.*

Avarice. *See* **Covetousness.**

Avoidance is the only remedy. *c.*1380: Chaucer, *Minor Poems*, in *Works*, i 340 (Skeat),

Theschewing is only the remedye. Before 1542: Sir T. Wyatt, *Song:* 'From these hie hilles', The first eschue is remedy alone.

Aw makes Dun draw. 1639: Clarke, 93. 1670: Ray, 58. 1881: Evans, *Leics. Words, etc.*, 95 (E.D.S.), Au, au! an exclamation to horses to bid them turn to the left or near side. 'Aw makes Dun draw' is a punning proverb quoted by Ray.

Away the mare. Before 1529: Skelton, *Magnyfycence*, 1. 1342, Nowe then goo we hens, away the mare! *c.*1550: in Hazlitt, *Early Pop. Poetry*, iii 62 (1866), Of no man he had no care, But sung, hey howe, awaye the mare, And made ioye ynough. 1611: Ravenscroft, *Melismata*, No. 6, Heigh ho, away the mare, Let vs set aside all care.

Awls, To pack up one's. 1681: W. Robertson, *Phraseol. Generalis*, 971, To pack up his awls; Colligere vasa. 1694: Motteux, *Rabelais*, Prol. to bk iv, The enemy, who were already packing up their awls … 1762: Bickerstaffe, *Love in a Village*, II iii, So pack up your alls, and be trudging away. 1849: F. T. Dinsdale, *Teesdale Gloss.*, 5, To pack up his awls, is spoken of a person departing in haste. 1881: Evans, *Leics. Words, etc.*, 229 (E.D.S.), Whenever the employer gave a workman his sack, it was an obvious hint to him to pack up his 'alls' and be off.

Ax near, sell dear. 1881: *N.&Q.*, 6th ser, iii 326, [A Lincolnshire J.P.] well versed in rural matters, repeated a short time ago in my hearing this proverb: 'Ax near, sell dear'. That is, if you have corn, cattle, or other matters to sell, you are more likely to get their full market value if you do not ask too much. 1889: Peacock, *Manley, etc., Gloss.*, 366 (E.D.S.).

Axe after the helve. *See* **Throw** (7).

Axe goes to the wood where it borrowed its helve, The. 1732: Fuller, 4401.

Axle-tree. *A pretty fellow to make an axle-tree for an oven.* Cheshire. 1670: Ray, 162. 1732: Fuller, 362. 1917: Bridge, *Cheshire Proverbs*, 5.

Axwell Park. *See* quot. 1846–59: *Denham Tracts*, i 91 (F.L.S.), From Axwell Park to Shotley, A squirrel could leap from tree to tree. [Axwell Park is in the township of Winlaton and parish of Ryton, Durham.]

Ay be as merry as can, For love ne're delights in a sorrowful man. 1678: Ray, 55.

Aylsham treat. 1890: P. H. Emerson, *Wild Life*, 108 *n.*, An Aylsham treat is treat yourself.

B

B. 1. To know not B from a battledore. 1565: J. Hall, *Hist. Expostulation*, 16 (Percy S.), He … knewe not a letter, or a b from a bateldore. 1593: Harvey, *Works*, ii 208 (Grosart), The learnedest of them could not say … B to a battledore. 1630: Taylor (Water-Poet), *Works*, pagin. 2, 59, To the Gentlemen Readers, that vnderstand A. B. from a battledore. 1681: Robertson, *Phraseol. Generalis*, 757, He is as ignorant, he knows not a B from a battle-door.

2. To know not B from a bull's foot. 1401: in Wright, *Pol. Poems*, ii 57 (Rolls Ser., 1861), I know not … a b from a bole foot. 1800: Colman Jr., *Review*, II ii, Fie upon you! – not to know a B from a bull's foot. 1886: Elworthy, *West Som. Word-Book*, 36 (E.D.S.), The common description of a dolt or ignoramus is … he does not know B from a bull's foot. Cf. **A** (2).

Babies in the eyes, To look. 1618: B.&F., *Loyal Subject*, III ii, Can ye look babies, sisters, In the young gallants' eyes? *c.*1685: in *Roxb. Ballads*, vii 445 (B.S.), 'Tis the babes in thine eyes that set my poor heart all on fire. 1709: T. Baker, *Fine Lady's Airs*, I i, Sweeten her again with ogling smiles, look babies in her eyes.

Baby. *See* **Throw** (2).

Bachelor and **Bachelors. 1. A lewd bachelor makes a jealous husband.** 1855: Bohn, 292.

2. Bachelor's fare: bread and cheese and kisses. 1738: Swift, *Polite Convers.*, Dial. I.

3. Bachelors' wives and maids' children be well taught. 1546: Heywood, *Proverbs*, Pt II ch vi 1549: Latimer, *Seven Sermons*, 138 (Arber), The maydes chylde is euer best taughte. 1637: Breton, in *Works*, ii *h*18 (Grosart), For bachelors wiues, and maidens children are pretty things to play withall. 1738: Swift, *Polite Convers.*, Dial. I. 1761: Colman, *Jealous Wife*, IV l, What a pity it is that nobody knows how to manage a wife, but a batchelor. 1920: *Sphere*, 30 March, p. 316, col. 1, But then there is a saying, 'Old maids' children and bachelors' wives are always perfection'.

4. We bachelors grin, but you married men laugh till your hearts ache. 1670: Ray, 48. 1732: Fuller, 5433.

Back. *See* **Scratch**.

Back and edge = entirely, completely. 1639: Clarke, 26, Sticke to him back and edge. 1866: Brogden, *Lincs Words*, 17, He stuck up for me back-and-edge. 1899: Dickinson, *Cumberland Gloss.*, 10. Cf. **Fall**, *verb* (1).

Back door robs the house, The. 1732: Fuller, 4402. 1854: J. W. Warter, *Last of the Old Squires*, 53. *See also* **Fair,** *adj.* (9); and Cf. **Postern door.**

Back is broad enough, His. 1639: Clarke, 86, His back's broad enough to beare jests. 1670: Ray, 163. 1738: Swift, *Polite Convers.*, Dial. I, I suppose you think my back's broad enough to bear everything.

Back may trust but belly won't. 1855: Robinson, *Whitby Gloss.*, 8 … dress may be deferred, but hunger cannot.

Back with that leg. 1678: Ray, 65.

Backare! quoth Mortimer to his sow. 1546: Heywood, *Proverbs*, Pt I ch xi *c.*1550: Udall, *Roister Doister*, I ii 1594: Shakespeare, *Tam. of Shrew*, II i, Let us, that are poor petitioners, speak too: Baccare! you are marvellous forward. 1659: Howell, 20.

Backing. *He's allus backing i' th' breech bent* [breechband]. 1917: Bridge, *Cheshire Proverbs*, 69 … Said of one who is not very 'go-ahead', or energetic.

Bacon. *Where you think there is bacon, there is no chimney.* 1640: Herbert, *Jac. Prudentum. See also* **Save.**

Bad as Jeffreys. 1863: Wise, *New Forest*, ch xvi, 'As bad as Jeffreys' preserves, as throughout the West of England, the memory of one who, instead of being the judge, should have been the hangman.

Bad as Swath Hoome. Staffs. 1889: *Folk-Lore Journal*, vii 294, As bad as Swath Hoome [Hulme], who was two hours getting his shirt on, and then he didna do it right.

Bad bargain. 1685: Meriton, *Yorkshire Ale*, 66, It's an ill made bargain, where beath parties rue. 1732: Fuller, 2839, It is a bad bargain, where both are losers.

Bad broom [slovenly servant] **leaves a dirty room, A.** 1917: Bridge, *Cheshire Proverbs*, 1.

Bad bush. *See* **Bush** (1).

Bad cause that none dare speak in, It is a. 1639: Clarke, 199. 1670: Ray, 4. 1732: Fuller, 2840.

Bad choice where the whole stock is bad, There's but. 1732: Fuller, 4889.

Bad cloth that will take no colour, It is a. 1546: Heywood, *Proverbs*, Pt II ch ix 1592: Lyly, *Gallathea*, IV i 1670: Ray, 71. 1732: Fuller, 2841.

Bad cook. *See* Ill cook.

Bad custom. *A bad custom is like a good cake, better broken than kept.* 1611: Cotgrave, s.v. 'Gasteau'. 1670: Ray, 76. 1732: Fuller, 832, Bad customs are better broke than kept up.

Bad day. 1. A bad day has a good night. 1893: Inwards, *Weather Lore*, 43.

2. It is never a bad day that hath a good night. 1639: in *Berkeley MSS.*, iii 32 (1885), Hee never hath a bad day that hath a good night. 1670: Ray, 6.

Bad excuse (or shift) is better than none, A. *c.*1550: Udall, *Roister Doister*, V ii 1551: T. Wilson, *Rule of Reason*, S6, This is as thei sie in English, better a badde excuse, then none at all. 1579: Gosson, *Sch. of Abuse*, 42 (Arber). 1599: Porter, *Two Angry Women*, in *Old Plays*, vii 360 (Hazlitt), A bad shift is better than none at all. 1692: L'Estrange, *Aesop*, 112 (3rd ed.), And at the worst, a bad shift is better than none. 1732: Fuller, 4.

Bad for a worse, To change a. 1678: Bunyan, *Pilgr. Progress*, Pt I p. 56 (1849), Thou hast done in this according to the proverb, changed a Bad for a Worse.

Bad for the rider. *See* Worse (4).

Bad guides may soon mislead. 1639: Clarke, 1.

Bad is a bad servant, but worse being without him. 1659: Howell, *Proverbs: Brit.-Eng.*, 3.

Bad is the best. 1564: Bullein, *Dialogue*, 77 (E.E.T.S.). 1579: Spenser, *Sheph. Calendar*, Sept., l. 117, Bad is the best (this English is flat). 1606: Day, *Ile of Gulls*, II v, Badd's the best. *c.*1630: B.&F., *Bloody Brother*, IV ii 1753: Richardson, *Grandison*, iii 110 (1883), Bad is my best. 1852: Planché, *Extravag.*, iv 228 (1879), I've no doubt bad enough she'll prove at best. 1905: H. A. Evans, *H. and B. in Oxfordsh. and Cotswolds*, 218, The reader will exclaim that bad is the best.

Bad Jack may have as bad a Jill, A. 1754: Berthelson, *Eng.-Danish Dict.*, s.v. 'Jack', There is not so bad a jack but there is as bad a gill.

Bad lease. *He never hath a bad lease, that hath a good landlord.* Glos. 1639: in *Berkeley MSS.*, iii 32 (1885).

Bad luck often brings good luck. 1732: Fuller, 834.

Bad luck top end. 1917: Bridge, **Cheshire Proverbs**, 29. [Of one not very bright mentally.]

Bad market. *He that cannot abide a bad market, deserves not a good one.* 1678: Ray, 173. 1732: Fuller, 2058.

Bad money drives out good. Generally known as Gresham's law, after Sir Thomas Gresham, (*c.*1519–79), the founder of the Royal Exchange and financial adviser to Elizabeth I, who stated the principle, namely that debased currency will drive good currency out of circulation because people will tend to hoard the good, in a letter to the Queen in 1558. But the principle seems to have been understood by the ancient Greeks, and to have been expounded in the Renaissance by Copernicus. 1858: H.D. Macleod, *Elements of Political Economy* 477, He [Gresham] was the first to perceive that a bad and debased currency is the cause of the disappearance of the good money.

Bad news travels fast. For other earlier and variant forms of this proverb *see* **Ill news flies apace**. 1539: R. Taverner, *Proverbs or Adagies out of Erasmus*, II, Sad and hevy tydynges be easly blowen abroade be they never so vain and false … 1592: Kyd, *Spanish Tragedy* I, Evill newes will flie faster still than good. 1671: Milton, *Samson Agonistes*, l.1538, For evil news rides post, while good news baits. 1694: *Terence's Comedies made English*, 46, Bad News always fly faster than good. 1706: Stevens, *Spanish and English Dictionary*, s.v. Sonarse, Good News is rumour'd but bad News flies. 1935: W. Irwin, *Julius Caesar Murder Case*, xxv, 'Where'd you get it?' 'On the Plains of Philippi'. 'Bad new travels fast,' said Hercules.

Bad padlock invites a picklock, A. 1732: Fuller, 2.

Bad paymaster. *From a bad paymaster get what you can.* 1855: Bohn, 359.

Bad penny. *See* Turn (7).

Bad ploughman beats the boy, A. 1917: Bridge, *Cheshire Proverbs*, 1. Cf. **Ill workman**.

Bad priests bring the devil into the church. 1732: Fuller, 835.

Bad sack. *See* Ill sack.

Bad shearer never had a good sickle, A. 1846: Denham, *Proverbs*, 50 (Percy S.).

Bad stake. *See* Ill stake.

Bad thing never dies, A. 1732: Fuller, 3.

Bad to do evil, but worse to boast of it, It is.

1606: T. Heywood, *If you know not me*, Pt II, in *Dram. Works*, i 275 (1874).

Bad wintering will tame both man and beast. 1846: Denham, *Proverbs*, 6 (Percy S.). Cf. **Wedding.**

Bad words find bad acceptance. 1611: Cotgrave, s.v. 'Meschant'.

Bad words make a woman worse. 1659: Howell, *Proverbs: Brit.-Eng.*, 8.

Bad workman. *See* **Ill workman.**

Badger. *See* **Brock; Greasy; Grizzling;** and **Grey.**

Badger-like, one leg shorter than another. 1659: Howell, 20.

Bag [meal] and pump [water] don't pay like bag and milk. 1877: E. Leigh, *Cheshire Gloss.*, 11. 1886: R. Holland, *Cheshire Gloss.*, 447 (E.D.S.). 1917: Bridge, *Cheshire Proverbs*, 29.

Bag = sack. **1. The bag mouth was open.** 1877: E. Leigh, **Cheshire Gloss.**, 11, 'The bag month was open 'is a Cheshire expression to show that everything that was unknown has become public. 1917: Bridge, *Cheshire Proverbs*, 111.

2. To give the bag = originally, to go off, or abandon a thing or person. Later, to dismiss – *See* 1883 quot. 1576: *Common Conditions*, in Brandl's *Quellen*, 599, This tinkerly trade, wee giue it the bagge. 1592: Greene, *Quip*, in *Works*, xi 263 (Grosart), Lighte witted vpon euery small occasion to geue your maister the bagge. 1607: Dekker and Webster, *Westward Hoe*, IV ii, I fear our oars have given us the bag. 1823: Scott, *Peveril*, ch vii, She gave me the bag to hold, and was smuggling in a corner with a rich old Puritan. 1883: A. Easther, *Almondbury Gloss.*, 7 (E.D.S.), 'To give the bag', which is to dismiss; or 'to get the bag', i.e. to be dismissed.

Bagpipe. *He's like a bag-pipe, he never talks till his belly be fill.* 1623: Wodroephe, *Spared Houres*, 249, Sir, I am like vnto the bagpipes of Bolonia, which can not blow vnlesse they be full of wind. 1678: Ray, 291. 1732: Fuller, 2459.

Bagshot. The sayings in the two following quotations are cearly akin. 1575: R. Laneham, *Letter*, in *Capt. Cox*, 31 (B.S.), Hee ... can talk az much without book, az ony inholder betwixt Brainford [Brentford] and Bagshot. 1670: Ray, 205, As good as any between Bagshot and Baw-waw. There's but the breadth of a street between these two.

Bait hides the hook, The. 1732: Fuller, 4403.

Bake. *As one bakes so one may brew* (or *eat*). Cf. **Brew,** *verb* (1). [Tute hoc intristi; tibi omne est exedendum. – Terence, *Phormio*, II ii 4] 1548: Hall, *Chronicle*, 431 (1809), Such breade as they bake, suche muste they eate. 1577: *Misogonus*, III i, As thou bakst, so shat [shalt] brewe. 1664: Pepys, *Diary*, 15 August, But I will have no more to do with her, let her brew as she has baked. 1775: Garrick, *May-Day*, sc ii, As they bake they shall brew, Old Nick and his crew. 1840: Barham, *Ing. Legends:* 'St Odille'. 1849: C. Brontë, *Shirley*, ch xxi, 'What would Moore have done if nobody had helped him?' asked Shirley. 'Drunk as he'd brewed – eaten as he'd baked'. 1909: De Morgan, *Never can Happen Again*, ch v, 'As they bake, so they will brew', philosophised Mr Challis to himself.

Baker. 1. Be not a baker if your head be of butter. 1640: Herbert, *Jac. Prudentun*. 1732: Fuller, 1321, Don't turn baker, if your head be made of butter.

2. He should be a baker by his bow-legs. 1607: Dekker and Webster, *Westward Hoe*, II ii, Will women's tongues, like bakers' legs, never go straight! 1678: Ray, 91.

3. Quoth the baker to the pillory. *See* quote. 1546: Heywood, Proverbs, Pt II ch ii, We be new kneet, And so late met, that I feare we parte not yeet, Quoth the baker to the pylorie. 1659: Howell, 7, Ile take no leave of you, quoth the baker to the pillory.

Baker's wife. *See* quot. 1598: *Ser9vingman's Comfort*, in *Inedited Tracts*, 166 (Hazlitt), Mee thinkes he myght remember the olde saying: A bakers wyfe may byte of a bunne, a brewers wyfe may drinke of a tunne, and a fysh-mongers wyfe may feede of a cunger, but a seruingmans wyfe may starue for hunger.

Balance distinguisheth not between gold and lead, The. 1640: Herbert, *Jac. Prudentum*. 1670: Ray, 2.

Bald. 1. A bald head is soon shaven. *c.*1450: in *Reliq. Antiquae*, i 75 (1841), A bare berd wyl sone be shave. 1678: Ray, 96. 1732: Fuller, 836.

2. As bald as a bladder of lard. 1886: Elworthy, *West Som. Word-Book*, 41 (E.D.S.). 1894: R.L.S., *St Ives*, ch xv, His head as bald as a bladder of lard. 1901: Raymond, *Idler Out of Doors*, 219.

3. As bald as a coot. *c.*1290: *Treatise of Walter de Biblesworth*, in Wright's *Early Vocab.*, i 165, A balled coote. 1412–20: Lydgate, *Troy-Book*, bk ii l. 4673, He was ballid as a cote. 1566: Adlington, tr. Apuleius, bk v, Older than my father, more bald than a coot. 1604: Breton, in *Works*, ii *k* 13 (Grosart), And left her [head] as bare as a balde coote. *c*.1770: Hall-Stevenson, in *Works*, i 238 (1795), As bare as a coot. 1881: Evans, *Leics. Words, etc.*, 128 (E.D.S.), 'As bald as a coot' is a common simile for baldness.

4. You'll not believe he's bald till you See his brains. 1580: Lyly, *Euphues*, 267 (Arber), As incredulous as those, who thinke none balde, till they *See* his braynes. 1670: Ray, 163. 1732: Fuller, 6032.

Bale. *See* **Boot.**

Balks of good ground, Make not. 1605: Camden, *Remains*, 328 (1870). 1670: Ray, 58. 1732: Fuller, 3316, Make no baulks in good ground. 1846: Denham, *Proverbs*, 6 (Percy S.), Make not a balk of good ground.

Ball. 1. Ball on the bat. 1893: G. L. Gower, *Gloss. of Surrey Words*, 4 (E.D.S.), [Surrey witness *loq.*] 'He'd a mind to make me the ball on the bat between him and the police'.

2. To strike the ball under the line = To fail. 1546: Heywood, *Proverbs*, Pt I ch xi, Thou hast striken the ball vnder the lyne. 1634: S. Rowley, *Noble Soldier*, II ii, She has been strucke under line, master souldier. 1907: Hackwood, *Old English Sports*, 151. Hence [at tennis] came the old proverb, 'Thou hast stricken the ball under the line', meaning one had failed in his purpose.

Baltic. *See* **Drunk as the Baltic.**

Bambroughshire Laird. *See* quot. 1846–59: *Denham Tracts*, i 258 (F.L.S.), He rides like a Bambroughshire Laird. That is, with one spur, and a stick or whip in his opposite hand.

Banbury. 1. As thin as Banbury cheese. 1562: Heywood, *Epigr.*, 6th hundred, No. 24, I neuer saw Banbery cheese thicke enough. 1575: G. Harvey, *Letter-Book*, 91 (Camden S.), More fine then any Banberry cheese. 1600: Shakespeare, *Merry Wives*, I i, *Bardolph*. [*to Slender*.] You Banbury cheese ! 1664: Bp. Griffith Williams, *Sad Condn. of the Clergy in Ossory*, 26, Our lands and glebes are clipped and pared to become as thin as Banbury cheese. 1790: Grose, *Prov. Gloss.*, s.v. 'Oxfordshire', Banbury cheese. 1911: Hackwood, *Good Cheer*, 214, A local saying was of similar significance – 'As thin as a Banbury cheese, nothing but paring'.

2. Banbury ale, a half-yard pot. 1658: *Wit Restor'd*, 159. *c*.1660: in *Roxb. Ballads*, ii 130 (B.S.), Banbury-ale, a two-yard pot.

3. Banbury zeal, cheese and cakes. 1596: Harington, *Anat. of Metam. Ajax*, liiijb, O that I were at Oxenford to eate some Banberie cakes. 1662: Fuller, *Worthies*, iii 5 (1840), Banbury zeal, cheese, and cakes. 1790: Grose, *Prov. Gloss.*, s.v. 'Oxfordshire', Banbury veal [query misprint for 'zeal'], cheese and cakes.

4. Like Banbury tinkers, that in mending one hole make three. 1647: Miles Corbet, *Speech*, in *Harl. Miscell.*, i 274, The malignants do compare this commonwealth to an old kettle with here and there a fault or hole, a crack or flaw in it; and that we (in imitation of our worthy brethren of Banbury) were instructed to mend the said kettle; but, like deceitful and cheating knaves, we have, instead of stopping one hole, made them three or four score. 1790: Grose, *Prov. Gloss.*, s.v. 'Oxfordshire'. Cf. **Tinker** (3).

Banquets every day, never makes a good meal, He that. 1732: Fuller, 2043.

Bapchild. *See* quot. 1735: Pegge, *Kent. Proverbs*, in E.D.S., No. 12, p. 67, If you'd live a little while, Go to Bap-child; If you'd live long, Go to Tenham or Tong.

Bar light law, 'Tis sure to blaw. 1891: R. P. Chope, *Hartland Dialect*, 20 (E.D.S.).

Barber and Barbers. 1. Barbers are correctors of capital crimes. 1659: Howell, 11.

2. Barbers learn to shave by shaving fools. 1611: Cotgrave, s.v. 'Fool', By shaving a foole one learnes to shave. 1654: Whitlock, *Zootomia*, 46, The fools beard teacheth the young barber his trade. 1792: Wolcot, *Works*, ii 446 (1795), Accept a proverb out of Wisdom's schools – 'Barbers first learn to shave by shaving fools!'

3. Common as a barber's chair, or, **Like a barber's chair fit for every one.** 1579: Gosson, *Apol. of Schoole of Abuse*, 66 (Arber), Venus ... that made her self as common as a barbar's chayre. *c*.1598: Shakespeare, *All's Well*, II ii, It is like a barber's chair, that fits all buttocks. 1651: Burton, *Melancholy*, III iv 1, 3, p. 688 (1836), Venus, a notorious strumpet, as common as a barber's chair. 1732: Fuller, 3218, Like a barber's chair, fit for every one. 1825: Hone, *Ev. Day Book*, i 1269, In a newspaper report ... 1825, a person deposing against the prisoner, used the phrase, 'as common as a barber's chair'.

4. No barber shaves so close but another finds work. 1640: Herbert, *Jac. Prudentum*. 1732: Fuller, 3737, One barber shaves not so close but another finds work. 1869: Spurgeon, *John Ploughman*, ch xxii.

Bardney, Lincs. *See* quot. 1905: *N.&Q.*, 10th ser, iii 145, 'I *See* you come from Bardney' is said to a person who has the habit of leaving doors open when he could shut them.

Bardon Hill. *See* quot. 1894: *Leics. N.&Q.*, iii 160, When Bardon Hill has a cap, Hay and grass will suffer for that.

Bare as a bird's tail. *c.*1470: *Mankind*, l. 475, Yt [his purse] ys as clene as a byrdes ars. 1528: Sir T. More, in *Works*, p. 238, col. 1 (1557), And some-tyme as bare as a byrdes arse. 1661: Stevenson, *Twelve Moneths*, 35, Bare as birds britch. 1709: Ward, *Account of Clubs*, 209 (1756). 1889: Peacock, *Manley, etc., Gloss.*, 29 (E.D.S.), Bare as a bo'ds [bird's] tail. Said of a person who has lost everything which he possessed

Bare as a bone. *c.*1460: *Erthe upon Erthe*, 22 (E.E.T.S.), As bare as any bon.

Bare as January. *See* **January** (6).

Bare as Job. Cf. **Poor as Job.** 1530: Palsgrave, 620, I shall make hym as bare as ever was Job. 1542: Udall, tr. Erasmus' *Apoph.*, 236 (1877), Hauing been afore in soch wyse pilled, and left as bare as Job. 1633: Draxe, 137.

Bare as my nail. *See* **Naked as my nail.**

Bare as the back of my hand. 1678: Ray, 281. 1880: Spurgeon, *Ploughman's Pictures*, 21.

Bare as the birch at Yule even. 1822: Scott, *Nigel*, ch xxi, His gentle beggarly kindred ... keep him as bare as a birch at Christmas. 1823: Scott, *Q. Durward*, ch vi, It is ill going to Oliver empty-handed, and I am as bare as the birch in December. 1846: Denham, *Proverbs*, 63 (Percy S.).

Bare as the Bishop of Chester. A sarcastic allusion to the wealth of the bishopric. *c.*1470: in *Reliq. Antiquae*, i 85 (1841), I wolde I were as bare as the beschope of Chester. 1917: Bridge, *Cheshire Proverbs*, 9.

Bare foot is better than none, A. 1611: Cotgrave, s.v. 'Nud'. 1694: D'Urfey, *Quixote*, Pt I Act I sc i, Better a bare foot than no foot at all. 1748: Richardson, *Clarissa*, ii 111 (1785), And hence a third proverb ... Better a bare foot than none at all.

Bare legs, Four. *See* **Marriage** (9).

Bare of a suit. *See* **Lie**, *verb* (1).

Bare walls make giddy housewives. 1605: Camden, *Remains*, 319 (1870). 1670: Ray, 59. 1723: Defoe, *Col. Jack*, ch x, But, as we say, bare walls make giddy hussies. 1732: Fuller, 839, Bare walls make gadding housewives.

Bare words are no good bargain. 1639: Clarke, 85. 1669: *Politeuphuia*, 183, Bare words are no lawful bargain.

Bare words buy no barley. 1732: Fuller, 838.

Barefoot and **Barefooted.** *See* **Thorn.**

Bargain. 1. A bargain is a bargain. 1560: Wilson, *Rhetorique*, 34 (1909), Resting vpon this point, that a bargaine is a bargaine, and must stande without all exception. 1592: Lyly, *Mother Bombie*, III iii 1692: L'Estrange, *Aesop*, 328 (3rd ed.). 1721: C. Cibber. *Refusal*, III. 1860: Reade, *Cloister and Hearth*, ch xxxvi, However ... 'tis ill luck to go back upon a bargain. 1891: Q.-Couch, *Noughts and Crosses*, 77.

2. The bargain is ill made where neither party gains. *c.*1597: A. Douglas, quoted in *N.&Q.*, 10th ser, ii 23, There is a proverb that says, the bargain is ill made where neither of the parties doth gain. 1732: Fuller, 2878, It is a silly bargain, where no body gets.

See also **Bare words;** and **Two to make.**

Bark, *verb.* **1. To bark against the moon.** 1401: in T. Wright, *Political Poems*, ii 53 (Rolls Ser., 1861), But thou, as blynde Bayarde, berkest at the mone. 1530: Palsgrave, 443, This dogge barketh agaynste the moone. 1629: Davenant, *Albovine*, V, Thou bark'st against the moon! 1655: Heywood and Rowley, *Fortune by Land and Sea*, I i, We should in that but bark against the moon. 1736: Bailey, *Dict.*, s.v. 'Bark', To bark at the moon.

2. To bark false. 1639: Clarke, 2, He never barkes false.

Bark, *subs. His* (or *her*) *bark is worse than his* (or *her*) *bite.* [Canis timidus vehementius latrat quam mordet. – Quintus Curtius, *De rebus gestis Alexandri Magni*, vii 14.] 1655: Fuller, *Church History*, bk viii § ii (22), Because politicly presumed to bark the more that he might bite the less, 1860: Reade, *Cloister and Hearth*, ch lxvi, The weakness of her nerves would have balanced the violence of her passions, and her bark been worse than her bite. 1912: Pinero, '*Mind the Paint' Girl*, Act II, p. 89.

Bark and tree. *See* quots. The saying is usually applied as in last quotation. 1546: Heywood,

Proverbs, Pt II ch ii, But it were a foly for mee, To put my hande betweene the barke and the tree. 1580: T*usser,Husbandrie*, 22 (E.D.S.). 1642: D. Rogers, *Naaman*, sig. Cc†, Being so audacious as to go between barke and tree, breeding suspitions … betweene man and wife. 1714: Ozell, *Molière*, iii 185, Cicero says, that between the tree and the finger you must not put the rind. 1820: Scott, *Abbot*, ch iv, Is it for me to stir up strife betwixt them, and put as 'twere my finger betwixt the bark and the tree? 1901: F. E. Taylor, *Lancs Sayings*, 8, It's ill meddlin' between th' bark an' th' tree (It is unwise to interfere between man and wife). Cf. **Oak** (7).

Bark and wood. *Between the bark and the wood.* 1847: Halliwell, *Dict.*, s.v. 'Bark', A well adjusted bargain, where neither party has the advantage. Suffolk. 1866: J. G. Nall, *Great Yarmouth*, etc., 510 [as in Halliwell].

Bark-year. *See* quot. 1863: Wise, *New Forest*, ch xvl, Forest proverbs … such as … 'A good bark-year makes a good wheat-year'.

Barker's knee. *See* **Stiff.**

Barking dog. *See* **Dog** (2).

Barley. 1. Barley makes the heape, but wheat the cheape. Glos. 1639: *Berkeley MSS.*, iii 32 (1885).

2. Sow barley in dree, and wheat in pul [mud]. 1865: Hunt, *Pop. Romances W. of England*, 436 (1896).

See also **Cotswold** (2); **Cuckoo** (3); **Good elm**; **Oak** (8); **October** (1); **St David** (3); **St John** (4); **St Vitus** (2); and **Wheat** (6).

Barley-corn is better than a diamond to a cock, A. 1732: Fuller, 7.

Barley-corn is the heart's key, The. 1659: Howell, *Proverbs: Brit.-Eng.*, 5.

Barley-corn. *See also* **John Barleycorn.**

Barley-straw's good fodder when the cow gives water. 1678: Ray, 51.

Barn. 1. Better a barn fitted than a bed. 1716: Ward, *Female Policy*, 82. 1732: Fuller, 858.

2. When the barn is full, you may thresh before the door. 1647: Howell *Letters*, bk II No. xxiv, When the barn was full any one might thrash in the haggard. 1732: Fuller, 5570. 1846: Denham, *Proverbs*, 5 (Percy S.).

3. You have a barn for all grain. 1732: Fuller, 5910.

Barnaby bright, the longest day and shortest night. 1595: Spenser, *Epithalamion* 266, This day the sunne is in his chiefest hight, With Barnaby the bright. 1659: Howell, 20. 1672: *Westm. Drollery*, Pt II, p. 100 (Eworth), It was in June, and 'twas on Barnaby Bright too, A time when the days are long, and nights are short. 1732: Fuller, 6206. 1901: *N.&Q.*, 9th ser, vii 445, The old saying as preserved in this part of England [Hants] is Barnaby bright, All day and no night.

Barnard Castle. 1. A coward! a coward! O' Barney Castle, Dare na come out to fight a battle! 1846–59: *Denham Tracts*, i 98 (F.L.S.). *c.*1860: Longstaffe, *Richmondshire*, 132. 1913: E. M. Wright, *Rustic Speech, etc.*, 183 [after quoting the saying]. In all probability this refers to the holding of Barnard Castle by Sir George Bowes during the Rising of the North in 1569.

2. Barney Cassel the last place that God made. 1846–59: *Denham Tracts*, i 83 (F.L.S.). *c.*1860: Longstaffe, *Richmondshire*, 132.

3. Come! come! that's Barney Castle! 1846–59: *Denham Tracts*, i 83 (F.L.S.) … an expression often uttered when a person is heard making a bad excuse in a still worse cause.

4. *See* quot. Ibid., i 81, [He] carries his coals round by Richmond to sell at Barnard Castle. This saying is peculiar to the central and mid-southern portions of the county of Durham. It is spoken of a person who is guilty of a circumlocutory act.

See also **Lartington.**

Barnstaple Fair weather = Cold and wet weather. 1893: *Daily Graphic*, 21 April (W.), Throughout all this period – and particularly in September – what Devonians out of their experience call 'Barnstaple fair weather' is to prevail in England.

Barnwell ague, A = Venereal disease. 1678: Ray, 88. 1790: Grose, *Prov. Gloss.*, s.v. 'Cambridgeshire'.

Barometer. 1. First rise after low Foretells stronger blow. 1893: Inwards, *Weather Lore*, 123.

2. When the glass falls low, Prepare for a blow; When it rises high, Let all your kites fly. Nautical. Ibid.

Barrel the better herring, Never a = Not a pin to choose between them. *c.*1540: Bale, *Kynge Johan*, in Manby's *Spec. of Pre-Shaksp. Drama*, i 591 (1903), Lyke lorde, lyke chaplayne; neyther barrell better herynge. 1566: Gascoigne,

Supposes, IV vi 1633: Jonson, *Tale of a Tub*, II, One bad, there's ne'er a good; And not a barrel the better herring among you. 1736: Fielding, *Pasquin*, III, Nor like our misses, about bribing quarrel, When better herring is in neither barrel. 1826: Scott, *Woodstock*, ch xxx, After bestowing a mental curse both on Sectaries and Presbyterians, as being, in his opinion, never a barrel the better herring. 1852: FitzGerald, *Polonius*, 51 (1903).

Barren places. *See* quot. 1610: Holland, tr. Camden's *Britannia*, 692, And haue proved the saying to bee true, That *barrain places giue a good edge to industry*.

Barsen's miller, always behind, Like. 1920: J. H. Bloom, in *N.&Q.*, 12th ser, vii 67. [Said to have been heard in Warwickshire within the last ten years.]

Bartholomew baby, Dressed like a. 1670: Brooks, *Works*, vi 51 (1867) (OED), Men … were dressed up like fantastical antics, and women like Bartholomew-babies. 1790: Grose, *Prov. Gloss.*, s.v. 'London'.

Barton, etc. See quot. 1869:Hazlitt, 80, Barton under Needwood, Dunstall in the Dale, Sitenhill for a pretty girl, and Burton for good ale.

Bashful. 1. As bashful as a Lentel lover. 1846: Denham, *Proverbs*, 32 (Percy S.).

2. His bashful mind hinders his good intent. 1737: Ray, 51.

Bashfulness is an enemy to poverty. 1670: Ray, 2.

Basket, Don't put all your eggs in one, *See* Egg (8).

Basket, You shall have the. Taunton. 1678: Ray, 344.

Basket-Justice will do Justice, right or wrong, A. An ironical saying – *See* 1860 quot. 1678: Ray, 74, A basket Justice; a jyll Justice; a good forenoon Justice. He'll do Justice right or wrong. 1732: Fuller, 8. 1860: Wynter, *Curios. Civiliz.*, 493 (OED), The basket-justices were so called because they allowed themselves to be bought over by presents of game.

Basket of chips. *See* Smile, *verb* (1).

Bastard brood is always proud. 1736: Bailey, *Dict.*, s.v. 'Bastard'.

Bate me an ace, quoth Bolton. 1571: Edwards, *Damon, etc.*, in Hazlitt, *Old Plays*, iv 77. 1578: Whetstone, *Promos and Cassandra*, sig. E3. 1651: Randolph, *Hey for Honesty*, II v 1681: W.

Robertson, *Phraseol. Generalis*, 213. 1732: Fuller, 845.

Bath, The beggars of. 1662: Fuller, *Worthies*, iii 92 (1840). 1790: Grose, *Prov. Gloss.*, s.v. 'Somerset'.

Bathing. *See* May, F. (26).

Bats in the belfry = Of unsound mind. 1926: Phillpotts, *Peacock House*, 219, His father's sister had bats in the belfry and was put away.

Battalions, God *or* **Heaven** *or* **Providence is always on the side of the big.** [*la fortune est toujours, comme disait le pauvre M. de Turenne, pour les gros bataillons* (fortune is always, as poor M. de Turenne used to say, for the big battalions) Mme de Sévigné, *Letter* 22 Dec. 1673] 1822: A. Graydon, *memoirs*, v Heaven was ever found favourable to strong battalions. 1842: A. Allison, *History of Europe*, X lxxviii, Providence was always on the side of dense battalions.

Battersea. *Go to Battersea to be cut for the simples.* 1785: Grose, *Dict. of Vulgar Tongue*, s.v. 'Simples'. 1790: Grose, *Prov. Gloss.*, s.v. 'Surrey'. 1847: Halliwell, *Dict.*, s.v. 'Simples'. 1925: J. G. Taylor, *Our Lady of Batersey*, 93, [Simples, or medicinal herbs, were cultivated at B.] Hence was derived the now forgotten proverb, addressed to one not overburdened with wits, 'You must go to Battersea to get your simples cut!' Cf. **Cut**, *verb* (10).

Battle, Sussex. *See* quot. 1894: A. J. C. Hare, *Sussex*, 103, The capture in 1377 of John de Cariloes, Prior of Lewes, on Rottingdean Hill, by the French, gave rise to the proverb, 'Ware the Abbot of Battel, when the Prior of Lewes is taken prisoner', meaning when one man falls into trouble, his neighbours had better beware.

Bawds and attorneys are like andirons, the one holds the wood, the other their clients till they consume. 1659: Howell, 10.

Bawtry. *The saddler of Bawtry was hanged for leaving his liquor behind him.* 1790: Grose, *Prov. Gloss.*, s.v. 'Yorkshire'. 1878: *Folk-Lore Record*, i 172, There is a Yorkshire saying applied to a man who quits his friends too early at a convivial meeting, that 'He will be hanged for leaving his liquor, like the saddler of Bawtry'. *See also* **Hang**, *verb* (7).

Bayard. 1. As bold as blind Bayard. *c.*1350: *Cleanness*, l.886, *in Allit. Poems*, 64 (E.E.T.S.), Thay blustered as blynde as bayard watz euer. *c.*1386: Chaucer, *Canon's Yeoman's Tale*, l.

860, Ye been as bolde as is Bayard the blinde. 1412–20: Lydgate, *Troy-Book*, bk ii 1. 4731, But ben as bolde as Baiard is, the blynde. *c.*1475: Caxton, *Hist. of Troy*, Prol., And began boldly to run forth as blind Bayard. 1575: *Appius, etc.*, in Hazlitt, *Old Plays*, iv 118, As bold as blind bayard, as wise as a woodcock. 1681: W. Robertson, *Phraseol. Generalis*, 270, Who so bold as blind Bayard? 1825: Scott, *Talisman*, ch xvii, I am no blind Bayard, to take a leap in the dark.

2. Bayard bites on the bridle. *c.*1426: Audelay, *Poems*, 15 (Percy S.).

3. Bayard of ten toes. 1597: *Discouerie of Knights of the Poste*, sig. A3, As I trauelled … upon my well approued hacney (old Bayard of ten toes) [travelled afoot]. 1616: Breton, *Good and Badde*, 35 (OED), The walke of the wofull and his Horse, Bayard of ten-toes. 1866: Brogden, *Lincs Words*, 20, Bayard-of-ten-toes. To walk on foot, a man doing horses' work.

4. To keep Bayard in the stable. *c.*1400: *Beryn*, 1. 3183 (E.E.T.S.), fful trewe is that byword, 'a man to serues-abill, Ledith offt beyard [Bayard] from his owne stabill'. 1546: Heywood, *Proverbs*, Pt I ch xii, To haue kept Bayard in the stable. 1605: Camden, *Remains*, 327 (1870). 1639: Clarke, 278.

Bayton-bargh. See **Brayton-bargh.**

Be as be may is no banning. *c.*1475: *Mankind*, sc ii **st.** 86, Be as be may, I xall do another. 1546: Heywood, *Proverbs*, Pt II ch i 1592: Lyly, *Mother Bombie*, II ii, Well, bee as bee may is no banning. 1670: Ray, 59.

Be as you would seem to be. 1640: Herbert, *Jac. Prudentum*, Be what thou wouldst seem to be. 1732: Fuller, 849.

Be it better, be it worse, do after him that beareth the purse. Before 1500: R. Hill, *Commonplace-Book*, 130 (E.E.T.S.). *c.*1600: T. Deloney, *Thos. of Reading*, ch 8, in *Works*, 244 (Mann), For it is an old prouerbe, Be it better, or be it worse, Please you the man that beares the purse. 1642: D. Rogers, *Matrim. Honour*, 85, And as the proverb saith, Be it better or worse, we must be ruled by him that beares the purse. 1732: Fuller, 6387, Be it better, be it worse. Be ruled by him that bears the purse. 1817: Scott, *Rob Roy*, ch xxvii [as in 1732, with 'has' for 'bears'].

Beacon Hill, near Halifax, Yorks. See quot.

1855: *N. & Q.*, 1st ser, xi 223, You might as well try to bore a hole through Beacon Hill. 1878: *Folk-Lore Record*, i 174.

Beads about the neck and the devil in the heart. 1659: Howell, *Proverbs: Span.-Eng.*, 15, Beads about bis neck, and the devil in his body. 1732: Fuller, 944.

Bean and **Beans. 1. A bean in liberty is better than a comfit in prison.** 1670: Ray, 15. 1732: Fuller, 9.

2. A good year 0f kidney beans, a good year of hops. 1882: Mrs Chamberlain, *W. Worcs. Words*, 38 (E.D.S.).

3. Every bean hath its black. 1639: Clarke, 211. 1709: O. Dykes, *Eng. Proverbs*, 103. 1754: Berthelson, *Eng.-Danish Dict.*, s.v. 'Bean'. 1817: Scott, *Rob Roy*, ch xxxviii, Ye hae had your ain time o't, Mr Syddall; but ilka bean has its black. 1878: *Folk-Lore Record*, i 166, Which is equivalent to every bean hath its black.

4. Like a bean in a monk's hood. 1546: Heywood, *Proverbs*, Pt II ch vi, Like a beane in a moonkis hood. 1611: Cotgrave, s.v. 'Febve'.

5. Plant the bean when the moon is light; Plant potatoes when the moon is dark. 1893: Inwards, *Weather Lore*, 154.

6. Sow beans in the mud and they'll grow like wood. 1639: Clarke, 307. 1647: Fuller, *Good Thoughts in Worse Times*, 112 (1830), His answer was returned me in their country rhyme: Sow beans in the mud, And they'll come up like a wood. 1732: Fuller, 6143. 1893: Inwards, *Weather Lore*, 154.

7. Sow (or **set**) **beans in Candlemas waddle,** i.e. the wane of the moon. Somerset 1678: Ray, 343.

8. The bigger eateth the bean. 1525: *Wydow Edyth: Mery Gestes*, 89 (1864), And yet alway I stand in great doubt, Least that the bigger wyll eate the been. 1546: Heywood, *Proverbs*, Pt II ch v 1611: Davies (of Hereford), *Sc. of Folly*, 45, in *Works*, ii (Grosart), Euer the bigger eateth the beane.

9. The more beans the fewer for a penny. Glos. 1639: *Berkeley MSS.*, iii 31 (1885).

10. To know how many beans make five. 1612: Shelton, *Quixote*, Pt I bk iv ch v, As though I know not how many numbers are five. 1830: Galt, *Lawrie Todd*, II i 42 (1849) (OED), Few men who better knew how many blue beans it takes to make five. 1889: *Daily News*, 4 Nov., p.

6, col. 5, It is as simple as how many blue beans make five.

11. *See* quot. 1905: E. G. Hayden, *Travels round our Village*, 75, 'When parson 'gins the Bible, 'tis time to sow the beans' – thus runs the ancient proverb. [Genesis i is read on Septuagesima Sunday.]

See also **Blue** (6); **Elm-leaves; May**, F. (4); **Pea** (2) and (4); **St David** (1); and **St Valentine** (2).

Bean-belly Leicestershire. *See* **Leicestershire.**

Bear and **Bears,** *subs.* **1. Are you there with your bears?** 1592: Lyly, *Mother Bombie*, II iii 1642: Howell, *Forreine Trauell*, 20 (Arber). 1740: North, *Examen*, 220. 1822: Scott, *Nigel*, ch xxxii 'Ay, man, are you there with your bears?' said the King.

2. As handsomely as a bear picketh muscles. 1546: Heywood, *Proverbs*, Pt II ch v.

3. If it were a bear it would bite him (or **you**). 1633: Draxe, 4. 1690: *New Dict. Canting Crew*, sig. B4, If it had been a bear it would have bit you. 1738: Swift, *Polite Convers.*, Dial. I.

4. Like a bear with a sore head. *See* **Cross,** *adj.* (1).

5. One thing thinketh the bear, but another thinketh his leader. *c.*1374: Chaucer, *Troylus*, bk iv, l. 1453.

6. The bear wants a tail and cannot be a lion. 1662: Fuller, *Worthies*, iii 271 (1840). 1790: Grose, *Prov. Gloss.*, s.v. 'Warwickshire'.

7. To go like a bear to the stake. *c.*1430: Lydgate, *Churl and Bird*, st. 19, To goo at large but as a bere at a stake To passe his boundes but yf he leue take. 1591: Florio, *Second Frutes*, 89, I am as loath to goe to it, as a beare is to goe to the stake. 1642: D. Rogers, *Naaman*, sig. D5, If he goes, yet it is as a beare to the stake. 1722: Defoe, *Moll Flanders*, in *Works*, iii 42 (Bohn), It was easy to see I should go to church like a bear to the stake. 1823: Scott, *Q. Durward*, ch xxi, Pavillion and his lieutenant … faced their fate like bears bound to a stake.

8. To sell the bear's skin. *See* **Sell.**

9. You dare as well take a bear by the tooth. 1601: Dent, *Pathw. Heauen*, 62 (OED), To … take the bear by the tooth. 1639: Clarke, 209. 1690: *New Dict. Canting Crew*, sig. B4, As good take a bear by the tooth, [spoken] of a bold desperate undertaking. 1732: Fuller, 5895.

See also **Cross,** *adj.* (1); **Dancing bear; Guts; Iron nails; King** (8); **Like a young bear;** and **Mastiff** (3).

Bear-garden, To talk. 1678: Ray, 66, He speaks Bear-garden. 1698: Collier, *Short View*, 232, This is brave Bear-Garden language! 1707: Ward, *London Terraefilius*, No. III p. 29, He's as great a master of ill language as ever was bred at a Bear-Garden. 1732: Fuller, 2033, He talks in the Bear-Garden tongue.

Bear-pie. *He that hath eaten a bear-pie, will always smell of the garden*, i.e. the Bear-garden. 1659: Howell, 18. 1670: Ray, 216.

Bear, *verb.* **1. Bear wealth, poverty will bear itself.** 1853: Trench, *Proverbs*, 84 (1905).

2. Bear with evil and expect good. 1640: Herbert, *Jac. Prudentum.* 1670: Ray, 8. 1732: Fuller, 945.

3. Bear with me and I'll bear with thee. 1546: Heywood, *Proverbs*, Pt II ch viii 1639: Clarke, 63.

4. He bears misery best that hides it most. *c.*1590: G. Harvey, *Marginalia*, 95 (1913), He bearith his misery best that hydeth it most. 1732: Fuller, 1810.

5. I bear him on my back. 1639: Clarke, 303, I bore him all the while on my back. 1670: Ray, 164.

6. To bear the bell. *c.*1374: Chaucer, *Troylus*, bk iii l.198, And lat see which of yow shal bere the belle To speke of love a-right! 1468: *Coventry Mysteries*, 161 (SH.S.), Of bewte and of boldnes I bere evermore the belle. Before 1529: Skelton, in *Works*, i 127 (Dyce), Of all prowde knauys thow beryst the belle. 1575: Gascoigne, *Glasse of Govt.*, III vi, So vices brag, but vertue beares the bell. 1633: Herbert, *Temple:* 'Church Porch', st. xxxii, In clothes, cheap handsomenesse doth bear the bell. 1713: Gay, *Wife of Bath*, IV i, Appearance, Sir, bears away the bell, almost in everything. 1812: Combe, *Syntax: Picturesque Tour*, can. xix, That e'en her merchants bore the bell In eating and in drinking well. 1912: Lucas, *London Lav.*, ch iii, But for human features … the capuchin … bears away the bell.

See also **Born.**

Beard. 1. The beard will (or **will not**) **pay for the shaving.** 1830: Forby, *Vocab. E. Anglia*, 431, The beard will pay for the shaving. 1879: G. F. Jackson, *Shropsh. Word-Book*, 28, 'The beard won't pay for the shaving' is a proverbial saying analogous to the French – *Le jeu ne vaut pas la chandelle.* 1883: Burne, *Shropsh. Folk-Lore*, 590 [will not pay]. 1917: Bridge, *Cheshire Proverbs*, 111 [will not pay].

2. 'Tis not the beard that makes the philosopher. 1732: Fuller, 5102.

Beast. 1. Better a beast sold than bought. 1659: Howell, *Proverbs: Brit-Eng.*, 16.

2. The beast that goes always never wants blows. 1640: Herbert, *Jac. Prudentum*.

Beast of many heads. *See* **Many-headed beast.**

Beat. 1. Beat a bush and start a thief. 1622: Drayton, *Polyol.*, xxiii, Where if you beat a bush, 'tis odds you start a thief. 1662: Fuller, *Worthies*, i 194 (1840). 1790: Grose, *Prov. Gloss.*, s.v. 'Bucks'.

2. Better to be beaten than be in bad company. 1670: Ray, 2.

3. He that cannot beat his horse, beats the saddle. 1578: Florio, *First Fruites*, fo. 29, Who cannot beat the horse, let hym beat the saddle. 1629: *Book of Meery Riddles*, Prov. 82. 1732: Fuller, 4174, Since he cannot be reveng'd on the ass, he falls upon the pack-saddle.

4. If you can't beat them, join them. The saying comes from the U.S. where the usual form is *if you can't lick them …* . 1941: Q. Reynolds *The Wounded don't Cry*, i, There is an old political adage which say 'If you can't lick 'em, jine 'em'. 1979: D. Lessing *Shikasta*, 266, I said, Running things, what's the point? He said, If you can't beat 'em, join 'em.

5. To beat (or go) about the bush. 1560: Wilson, *Rhetorique*, 2 (1909), If he … tell it orderly, without going about the bush. 1611: Cotgrave, s.v. 'Aller', To use many circumstances, to goe about the bush. 1696: *Cornish Comedy*, IV ii, He doth not beat about the bush, but falls immediately upon the point. 1884: *Punch*, 29 Nov., p. 256, col. 2, Excuse me … but no good beating about the bush.

6. To beat the bush while others catch the birds. *c.*1390: Gower, *Conf. Amantis*, ii 2355, And takth the bridd to his beyete, Wher othre men the buisshes bete. 1472: *Paston Letters*, iii 44 (Gairdner, 1900), We bette the busschysse and have the losse and the diswor-schuppe and ether men have the byrds. 1580: G. Harvey, in *Works*, i 93 (Grosart), I beate the bushe, the birdes to them doe flye. 1606: *Ret. from Parnassus*, II v, It hath been my luck always to beat the bush, while another killed the hare. 1732: Fuller, 3738, One beateth the bush, and another catcheth the bird. 1828: Scott, letter to Mrs Hughes, in her *Letters*,

etc., *of Scott*, ch xi, Your active benevolence starts the game while others beat the bush.

7. You may beat the devil into your wife, but you'll never bang him out again. 1732: Fuller, 5940.

Beauchamp, As bold as. 1608: Middleton, *Mad World*, V ii, Being every man well hors'd like a bold Beacham. 1612: Drayton, *Polyol.*, xviii 1662: Fuller, *Worthies*, iii 271 (1840). 1790: Grose, *Prov. Gloss.*, s.v. 'Warwickshire'. 1834: W. Toone, *Glossary*, 112, Bold Beauchamp. This person was said to be Thomas Beauchamp, Earl of Warwick, whose prowess [*c.*1400 1350] became proverbial, 'as bold as Beauchamp'.

Beaulieu Fair. *See* **Cuckoo (17).**

Beauty. 1. An enemy to beauty is a foe to nature. 1855: Bohn, 311.

2. Beauty draws more than oxen. 1640: Herbert, *Jac. Prudentum*. 1670: Ray, 2. 1732: Fuller, 948.

3. Beauty draws with a single hair. This proverb has evolved from (2) – *see* quots. 1591 and 1863. 1591: J. Florio, *Second Fruits*, 183, Ten teemes of oxen draw much lesse, Than doth one haire of Helen's tresse. 1693: Dryden, *Persius' Satire* V l. 247, She … Can draw you to her, *with a single hair*. 1712: Pope, *Rape of the Lock*, And beauty draws us with a single hair. 1863: Longfellow, *King Olaf*, xvi, Not ten yoke of oxen Have the power to draw us Like a woman's hair. 1941: 'M. Coles', *They tell no Tales*, xxii, Beauty draws me with a single hair, if it's blonde enough.

4. Beauty is but a blossom. 1633: Draxe, 15. 1670: Ray, 2. 1681: W. Robertson, *Phraseol. Generalis*, 223. 1732: Fuller, 947, Beauty's a blossom.

5. Beauty is but skin-deep. 1606: Davies (of Hereford), *Select Sec. Husb.*, 6, in *Works*, ii (Grosart), Beauty's but skin-deepe. 1730: Lillo, *Silvia*, I ix, She was the handsomest woman in all our parish. But beauty is but skin deep, as the saying is. 1829: Cobbett, *Advice to Young Men*, Lett. III. 1881: Evans, *Leics. Words, etc.*, 101 (E.D.S.), A very common proverb on the lips of the Midland pessimist is: 'Beauty's only skin-deep, but ugly goes to the bone'. 1921: W. H. Hudson, *Traveller in Little Things*, 12.

6. Beauty is in the eye of the beholder. 1742 D. Hume, *Essays Moral and Political*, II 151, Beauty, properly speaking lyes … in the Sentiment or

Taste of the reader. 1769: F. Brooke, *History of Emily Montague*, IV 205, You should remember, my dear, that beauty is in the lover's eye. 1788: R. Cumberland, in *Observer* IV cxviii, Beauty, gentlemen is in the eye. I aver it to be in the eye of the beholder and not in the object itself. 1878: M. W. Hungerford, *Molly Bawn*, I xii, 'I have heard she is beautiful – is she?' 'Beauty is in the eye of the beholder', quotes Marcia. 1893: Lewis Wallace, *Prince of India*, 'Answer, O my Gul-Bahar, more beautiful growing as the days multiply!' 'Thou flatterer! Do I not know beauty is altogether in the eye of the beholder, and that all persons do not see alike?"

7. Beauty is no inheritance. 1633: Draxe, 15, Beauty is no heritage. 1670: Ray, 2. 1732: Fuller, 951.

8. Beauty is only skin-deep. *See* **Beauty is but skin-deep.**

9. Beauty is potent, but money is omnipotent. 1670: Ray, 122. 1732: Fuller, 952, Beauty is potent; but money is more potent.

10. Beauty is soon blasted. 1732: Fuller, 953.

11. Beauty is the subject of a blemish. Ibid., No. 954.

12. Beauty may have fair leaves, yet bitter fruit. Ibid., No. 955.

13. Beauty provoketh thieves sooner than gold. 1599: Shakespeare, *As You Like It*, I iii.

14. Beauty will buy no beef. 1732: Fuller, 956.

15. Beauty without bounty avails nought. 1580: Lyly, *Euphues*, 295 (Arber), Beautie without riches, goeth a begging. 1869: Hazlitt, s.v.

Beccles for a puritan, Bungey for the poor, Halesworth for a drunkard, and Bilborough for a whore. 1670: Ray, 253. 1790: Grose, *Prov. Gloss.*, s.v. 'Suffolk' ['Bilborough' for 'Bli-borough'].

Beck is as good as a Dieu-garde, A. 1546: Heywood, *Proverbs*, Pt I ch x, And thus with a becke as good as a dieu garde, She flang fro me. 1583: Melbancke, *Philotinus*, sig. F4, A becke of yours is as good as a Dieugarde. 1611: Davies (of Hereford), Sc. *of Folly*, 48, in *Works*, ii (Grosart).

Bed. *If the bed would tell all it knows, it would put many to the blush.* 1659: Howell, 4. 1732: Fuller, 2702.

Bed-time for berriers [threshers] **and supper-time for carriers.** Old Cumberland proverb. 1895: T. Ellwood, *Lakeland, etc.*, *Gloss.*, 6 (E.D.S.).

Beddingham. *When Beddingham hills wear a cap, Ripe and Chalvington gets a drop.* 1884: 'Sussex Proverbs', in *N. & Q.*, 6th ser, ix 342.

Bede's chair. *See* quot. 1846–59: *Denham Tracts*, i 67 (F.L.S.), *Has a Chip of Bede's chair in her pouch.* It has been a custom from time immemorial for the ladies, immediately after the conclusion of the marriage ceremony (before Hymen's altar in Jarrow church), to proceed to the vestry and cut a chip off Bede's chair, to ensure their fruitfulness. The saying is generally applied to those females who show signs of fecundity rather early after entering into the happy state of matrimony.

Bedford. 1. Bedford malt-horses. 1622: Drayton, *Polyol.*, xxiii, Of malt-horse, Bedford-shire long since the blazon wan. 1911: Hackwood, *Good Cheer*, 163, As Hampshire men were dubbed 'hogs' in allusion to their pig-breeding, so Bedford folk were nicknamed 'malt-horses' because of the high quality of malt they produced from their barley.

2. The Bailiff of Bedford is coming. 1662; Fuller, *Worthies*, i 167 (1840). 1790: Grose, *Prov. Gloss.*, s.v. 'Bedfordshire'. 1874: Smiles, *Lives of Engineers*, i 15, After a heavy fall of rain, or after a thaw in winter, when the river [Ouse] swelled suddenly, the alarm spread abroad, 'the bailiff of Bedford is coming!' the Ouse passing by that town. 1904: *N. & Q.*, 10th ser, i 391.

Bedfordshire = Bed. 1608: Middleton, *Mad World*, II v, You come rather out of Bedford-shire; we cannot lie quiet in our beds for you. 1670: Cotton, *Scarronides*, bk iv, Each one departs to Bedfordshire; And pillows all securely snort on. 1738: Swift, *Polite Convers.*, Dial. III. 1818: Scott, *Heart of Midl.*, ch xxx, Jeanie heard the highwayman say, to her no small relief, 'She's as fast [asleep] as if she were in Bedfordshire'. 1841: Hood, *Miss Kilmansegg:* 'Her Dream', And there was the bed, so soft, so vast, Quite a field of Bedfordshire clover. 1927: Lucas, in *Punch*, 30 Nov., p. 613, I hear the Dustman drawing near To take you into Bedfordshire; It's time you went to bed. *See also* **Cheshire** (6).

Bedlam broke loose. *c.*1635: Davenant, *News from Plymouth*, IV ii, What's here? Kent Street, Or bedlam broke loose? 1864: 'Cornish Proverbs', in *N. & Q.*, 3rd ser, vi 494, Bedlam broke loose: What a clapper-house!

Bedminster. *See* **Sold.**

Bedpost and **Bedstaff.** *See* **Twinkling.**

Bedworth beggars. 1678: Ray, 317. 1790: Grose, *Prov. Gloss.*, s.v. 'Leicestershire'.

Bee and **Bees. 1. A bee was never caught in a shower.** 1893: Inwards, *Weather Lore*, 146.

2. A dead bee will make no honey. 1578: Florio, *First Fruites*, fo. 25, A dead bee wil make no hony. 1651: Herbert, *Jac. Prudentum*, 2nd ed., A dead bee maketh no honey. 1894: Northall, *Folk Phrases of Four Counties*, 7 (E.D.S.), A still bee gathers no honey. Glos.

3. A swarm of bees in May, etc. *See* quots. 1655: *Reformed Commonwealth of Bees*, 26, It being a proverb, that a swarm of bees in May is worth a cow and a bottle of hay, whereas a swarm in July is not worth a fly. 1676: W. Lawson, *New Orchard and Garden*, 77, A May's swarm is worth a mares foal. 1710: *Tusser Redivivus*, The proverb says, 'A swarm in May is worth a load of hay'. 1744: Claridge. in Mills' Essay *on Weather*, 101 (1773), A swarm of bees in May Is worth a load of hay; But a swarm in July Is not worth a fly. 1850: *N. & Q.*, 1st ser, ii 512, If they swarm in May, They're worth a pound next day; If they swarm in July, They're not worth a fly. Devon. 1883: Burne, *Shropsh. Folk-Lore*, 234, In the retired villages among the Clee Hills the following much more curious version may sometimes be heard: A play o' bees in May's wuth a noble the same day, A play in June's purty soon, A play in July's nod wuth a butterfly. [N.B. – The gold noble, worth 6s. 8d., was first coined 1344.] 1921: *Times*, 7 Oct., p. 8, col. 4, An old rhyme … which says: 'A swarm of bees in May Is worth a load of hay; A swarm of bees in June Is worth a silver spoon: A swarm of bees in July Isn't worth a fly'.

4. As big as a bee's knee. 1797: quoted in *N. & Q.*, 8th ser, x 260, It cannot be as big as a bee's knee. 1894: Northall, *Folk Phrases of Four Counties*, 7 (E.D.S.). 1896: *N. & Q.*, 8th ser, x 199, 'As big as a bee's knee' is a phrase I have frequently heard in South Notts to indicate a very small piece of anything. 1896: Locker-Lampson, *Confidences*, 98 n., It isn't so big as a bee's knee.

5. Bees that have honey in their mouths, have stings in their tails. 1579: Lyly, *Euphues*, 79 (Arber), The bee that hath hunny in hir mouth, hath a sting in hir tayle. 1732: Fuller, 959.

6. Bees will not swarm Before a near storm. 1893: Inwards, *Weather Lore*, 146.

7. Every bee's honey is sweet. 1640: Herbert, *Joe. Prudentum.*

8. He's like the master bee that leads forth the swarm. Glos. 1639: *in Berkeley MSS.*, iii 28 (1885).

9. His head is full of bees = *cares*, fancies, or, he is restless. 1546: Heywood, *Proverbs*, Pt I ch xii, Their hartes full heauy, their heades be full of bees. 1575: Churchyard, *Chippes*, 55 (Collier), About he flees, As though his hed wear full of bees. 1614: Jonson, *Bart. Fair*, I, He will whistle him and all his tunes over at night in his sleep! he has a head full of bees! 1745: Franklin, *Drinker's Dict.*, in *Works*, ii 23 (Bigelow), His head is full of bees [= he is drunk]. 1814: Scott, *Waverley*, ch lxvi, This word had somewhat a sedative effect, but the bailie's head, as he expressed himself, was still 'in the bees'. Cf. No. 13.

10. If bees stay at home, Rain will soon come; If they fly away, Fine will be the day. 1878: Dyer, *Eng. Folk-Lore*, 131. 1893: Inwards, *Weather Lore*, 146.

11. *See* quot. 1863: Wise, *New Forest*, ch xvi, Forest proverbs … such as … 'Like a swarm of bees all in a charm' [or *churm* = noise].

12. To bumble like a bee in a tar-tub. Ibid., ch xvi.

13. To have a bee in one's Bohnet. Cf. No. 9. 1553: *Respublica*, I i, Ye muste perdonne my wyttes, for I tell you plaine, I have a hive of humble bees swarmynge in my braine. 1648: Herrick, *Mad Maid's Song*, Ah! woe is mee, woe, woe is me, Alack and well-a-day! For pitty, Sir, find out that bee, Which bore my love away. I'le seek him in your bonnet brave, I'le seek him in your eyes. 1682: A. Behn, *False Count*, II iii, What means he, sure he has a gad-bee in his brain. 1860: Reade, *Cloister and Hearth*, ch xcvii, He may have a bee in his Bohnet, but he is not a hypocrite. 1922: Weyman, *Ovington's Bank*, ch xxxii, What mare's nest, what bee in the bonnet was this?

14. When bees are old they yield no honey. 1633: Draxe, 146. 1670: Ray, 19. 1732: Fuller, 3706, Old bees yield no honey.

15. When bees to distance wing their flight, Days are warm and skies are bright; But when their flight ends near their home, Stormy weather is sure to come. 1893: Inwards, *Weather Lore*, 146.

16. Where bees are there is honey. 1633: Draxe, 77. 1670: Ray, 60. 1732: Fuller, 5636.

17. Where the bee sucks honey, the spider sucks poison. 1633: Draxe, 123. 1732: Fuller, 5661. 1853: Trench, *Proverbs*, 114 (1905).

See also **Better feed; Brisk; Busy; February** (9); **Honey** (9); **Quick; St Matthew** (2); **Sheep** (4); and **Swine** (2).

Beech in summer and oak in winter. 1884: H. Friend, *Flowers and Fl. Lore*, 220, 'Beech in summer and Oak in winter' [for felling] has now become a common saying.

Beelzebub's Bower. *See* quots. 1362: Langland, *Plowman*, A, ii 100, A bastard i-boren of Belsabubbes kunne. 1546: Heywood, *Proverbs*, Pt II ch iv, But ye be a baby of Belsabubs bowre.

Beer. 1. Beer a bumble, 'twill kill you, afore 'twill make ye tumble. 1869: Hazlitt, 82.

2. What's better than the beer that's made of malt? 1659: Howell, 14.

3. *See* quot. 1913: *Devonshire Assoc. Trans.*, xiv 90, Yu can't 'ave better beer'n wat's putt in the barrow (barrel).

See also **Ale; Cider; Cloth** (2); **July** (3); and **life** (6).

Beetle. *See* **Blind**, *adj.* (12); and **Deaf** (1).

Beg. 1. Beg from beggars and you'll never be rich. 1736: Bailey, *Dict.*, s.v. 'Beg'.

2. To be begged for a fool. 1591: Florio, *Second Frutes*, 187, Euen the vulgar would begge him for a foole that thinks a bungling-stainers dawbing better than the polisht Helen of Zeuxes. 1592: Lyly, *Mother Bombie*, I i, He needs not, sir, Ile beg him for a fool. 1649: in *Somers Tracts*, vii 88 (1811), If there should be a king again, I shall, perhaps, be begg'd for a fool. 1653: Middleton and Rowley, *Spanish Gipsy*, II ii, You are my guardian, best beg me for a fool now. 1707: *Spanish Bawd*, III iii, If he continues so a week longer, his friends will beg him for a fool. 1736: Hervey, *Mem.*, ii 143 (OED), Moyle either deserved to be … begged for a fool, or hanged for a knave.

3. To beg at the wrong door. 1546: Heywood, *Proverbs*, Pt I ch ix, Then of trouth ye beg at a wrong mans dur. 1596: Jonson, *Ev. Man in his Humour*, II vii, He … claps his dish at the wrong man's door. 1659: Howell, 5.

4. To beg like a cripple at a cross. 1812: Brady, *Clavis Cal.*, i 334. We have yet in common usage the old saying of 'He begs like a cripple at a

cross'. 1855: Robinson, *Whitby Gloss.*, 40, 'He begged like a cripple at a cross', very urgently. 1917: Bridge, *Cheshire Proverbs*, 125.

Beggar and **Beggars. 1. A beggar pays a benefit with a louse.** 1678: Ray, 98. 1732: Fuller, 10.

2. A beggar's purse is bottomless. 1539: Taverner, *Proverbs*, fo. 39, A beggers scryppe is neuer fylled. 1639: Clarke, 38. 1670: Ray, 60, A begger can never be bankrupt. 1681: W. Robertson, *Phraseol. Generalis*, 229, A beggers purse is always empty. Cf. **Lady's heart;** and **Proud heart.**

3. A shameless beggar must have a shameful denial. 1639: Clarke, 37. 1732: Fuller, 392 [with 'short' for 'shameful'].

4. Beggars breed and rich men feed. 1639: Clarke, 98. 1670: Ray, 60. 1754: Berthelson, *Eng.-Danish Dict.*, s.v. 'Beggar'.

5. Beggars cannot be choosers. 1546: Heywood, *Proverbs*, Pt I ch x, Beggers should be no choosers. 1616: B.&F., *Scornful Lady*, V iii, Beggars must be no choosers. 1635: Glapthorne, *Hollander*, I, Beggars are no chusers my friend. Before 1726: Vanbrugh, *Journey to London*, III, My lord, says I, beggars must not be choosers. 1819: Scott, *Familiar Letters*, ii 62 (1894), But beggars must not be chusers. 1889: R.L.S., *Ballantrae*, ch iii, For all this we were to pay at a high rate; but beggars cannot be choosers. 1920: Barbellion, *Last Diary*, 13.

6. Beggars make a free company. Before 1658: Cleveland, *Works*, 76 (1742), There was a time when such cattle would hardly have been taken upon suspicion for men in office, unless the old proverb were renewed, That the beggars make a free company, and those their wardens.

7. Better to die a beggar than live a beggar. 1670: Ray, 2. 1732: Fuller, 888.

8. It is better to be a beggar than a fool. 1813: Ray, 81.

9. It would make a beggar beat his bag. 1678: Ray. 228.

10. Much ado to bring beggars to the stocks. 1633: Draxe, 14. 1639: Clarke, 19. 1670: Ray, 60, [with the addition] and when they come there, they'll not pat in their legs.

11. One beggar is enough at a door. 1639: Clarke, 187.

12. One beggar is woe that another by the door should go. 1539: Taverner, *Erasm. Prov.*, 9 (1552) (OED), One begger byddeth wo that another by the dore shuld go. 1608: Armin, *Nest of Ninnies*, 47 (SH.S.). 1681: W. Robertson, *Phraseol. Generalis*, 229, It's one beggers wo to *See* another by the door go. 1736: Bailey, *Dict.*, s.v. 'Beggar' as in 1681].

13. Puling, like a beggar at Hallowmas. *c.*1590: Shakespeare, *Two Gent.*, II i.

14. Set a beggar on horseback and he'll (*a*) **never alight;** (*b*) **ride a gallop;** (*c*) **ride to the devil;** (*d*) **ride to the gallows;** (*e*) **run his horse out of breath;** (*f*) **run his horse to death.** [Asperius nihil est humili, cum surgit in altum. – Claudian, xviii 181.] (*a*) 1576: Pettie, *Petite Pallace*, ii 100 (Gollancz, 1908). 1599: Greene, *Orpharion*, in *Works*, xii 36 (Grosart), Set a begger on horsebacke, and they say he will neuer light. 1620: Rowlands, *Night Raven*, 30 (Hunt.Cl.). (*b*) 1605: Camden, *Remains*, 330 (1870), Set a begger on horseback, and he will gallop. 1651: Burton, *Melancholy*, II iii 2. 1670: Ray, 60. (*c*) 1616: B.&F., *Scornful Lady*, IV ii, Such beggars Once set o' horseback, you have heard, will ride – How far, you had best to look to. 1709: O. Dykes, *Eng. Proverbs*, 98, Set a beggar on horseback, and he'll ride … Whither, but to the devil? 1855: Mrs Gaskell, *North and South*, ch x (*d*) *c.*1626: in *A Pepysian Garland*, 241 (Rollins, 1922), There is an old prouerbe, that oft hath bin try'd, Set a beggar on horseback, to th' gallowes heel ride. (*e*) 1633: Draxe, 163. (*f*) 1594: *Second Part Contention*, 132 (SH.S.), Beggers mounted run their horse to death.

15. Small invitation will serve a beggar. 1855: Bohn, 487.

16. Sue a beggar and catch a louse. 1594: R. Wilson, *Coblers Proph.*, l. 836 (Malone S.), I intreat yee be not ouer nice, What thinke ye as the prouerb goes that beggers haue no lice? 1654: Gayton, *Pleasant Notes Don Q.*, 83, Sue a begger and get a louse. 1681: W. Robertson, *Phraseol. Generalis*, 229. 1721: Bailey, *Eng. Dict.*, s.v. 'Louse'. 1819: Scott, *Bride of L.*, ch ii, I guess it is some law phrase – but sue a beggar, and – your honour knows what follows.

17. The beggar is never out of his way. 1630: T. Adams, *Works*, 120, Vagrant rogues … are neuer out of their way. 1650: Fuller, *Pisgah-Sight*, bk iii ch ii § 7, Fancy is never at a loss, like a beggar never out of his way. 1732: Fuller, 965, Beggars are never out of their way.

18. The beggar may sing before the thief. 1546: Heywood, *Proverbs*, Pt I ch xii, The begger maie syng before the theefe. 1670: Ray, 2. 1732: Fuller, 964. 1829: Scott, in Lockhart's *Life*, vii 173, The last prerogative of beggary, which entitled him to laugh at the risk of robbery.

19. To know one as well as a beggar knows his dish. 1546: Heywood, *Proverbs*, Pt I ch xi, And my selfe knowth him, I dare boldly brag, Euen as well as the begger knowth his bag. 1579: Gossan, *Apol. of Schoole of Abuse*, 74 (Arber), Such as he knew as well as the begger his dishe. 1638: T. Heywood, *Wise W. of Hogsdon*, II i 1779: Mrs Cowley, *Who's the Dupe*, II ii 1822: Scott, *Nigel*, ch xxi.

See also **Merry as beggars; Misery may be;** and **Wish** (1) to (4).

Beggars' Bush. 1564: Bullein, *Dialogue*, 78 (E.E.T.S.), In the ende thei go home … by weepyng cross, by beggers barne, and by knaues acre. 1599: Porter, *Two Angry Women*, in Hazlitt, *Old Plays*, vii 335, They have danc'd a galliard at beggars'-bush for it. 1662: Fuller, *Worthies*, ii 98 (1840), 'This is the way to Beggar's-bush'. It is spoken of such who use dissolute and improvident courses, which tend to poverty; Beggar's-bush being a tree notoriously known, on the left hand of London road from Huntingdon to Caxton. 1790: Grose, *Prov. Gloss.*, s.v. 'Hunts'.

Begin. 1. As you begin the year so you'll end it. 1767: Garrick, Prol. to *Cymon*, There is a good old saying … As you begin the year, you'll surely end it.

2. Good to begin well, better to end well. 1670: Ray, 8.

3. He beginneth to build too soon that hath not money to finish it. 1633: Draxe, 1.

4. He begins to die that quits his desires. 1611: Cotgrave, s.v. 'Abandonner', He truly begins to dye that quits his chiefe desires. 1640: Herbert, *Jac. Prudentum*.

5. Let him that beginneth the song make an end. 1633: Draxe, 12.

6. Life begins at forty. *See* **Life** 2.

Beginning. 1. It is better coming to the beginning of a feast than to the end of a fray. [1546: Heywood, *Proverbs*, Pt II ch vii, It is yll commyng … To thend of a shot [feast], and begynnyng of a fray.] *c.*1590: *Plaine Percevall*,

Dedication, I would it had bin Percevals hap, to haue com to the beginning of a friendly feast, or to the latter ending of so dangerous a fraye. 1597: Shakespeare, 1 *Henry IV*, IV ii 1636: Massinger, *Bashful Lover*, III, Our grandsires ... said, Haste to the beginning of a feast ... but to the end of a fray. 1672: Marvell, *Rehearsal Transpr.*, Pt I, in *Works*, iii 119 (Grosart).

2. It is better coming to the end of a feast than to the beginning of a fray. *c.*1594: Bacon, *Promus*, No. 977. 1670: Ray, 90. 1769: Colman, *Man and Wife*, III ii, I arrived just at the conclusion of the ceremony; but the latter end of a feast is better than the beginning of a fray, they say. 1821: Scott, *Kenilworth*, ch xii 1855: Robinson, *Whitby Gloss.*, 54, 'It is better to come at the far end of a feast than at the fore end of a fray', better late at a feast than early at a fight.

Behappen! [perhaps] says Jack Dallow. 1883: Burne, *Shropsh. Folk-Lore*, 591.

Behind before. *See* **Horse** (25).

Behind the door to mend old breeches, You must go. 1864: 'Cornish Proverbs', in *N. & Q.*, 3rd ser, vi 495.

Believe. 1. Believe not all you hear. 1205: Layamon, *Brut*, 8015, Ful so[t]h seide the seg the theos saye talda: Yif thu ileuest aehcne mon, Selde thu saelt wel don (Very truth said the man who told this saw: If thou believest each man, seldom shalt thou do well). Before 1562: Lord Vaux, *Poems*, 37 (Grosart), Beleve not euery speache. Before 1640: Massinger, *Believe as You List* [title].

2. Believe well and have well. 1546: Heywood, *Proverbs*, Pt II ch ix 1670: Ray, 61. 1732: Fuller, 968.

3. He that believes all, misseth; He that believeth nothing, hits not. 1640: Herbert, *Jac. Prudentum*.

4. We soon believe what, we desire. 1581: tr. Seneca's *Tragedies*, 15 (Spens.S.), What wretches doe most chiefly wishe of all, They soone beleue. 1591: Harington, *Orl. Furioso*, bk i st. 56, It is a proverbe used long ago, We soone beleeve the thing we would have so. 1696: *Cornish Comedy*, Act II, p. 16, What we desire we easily believe. 1709: Manley, *New Atlantis*, ii 77 (1736). 1732: Fuller, 5426, We are apt to believe what we wish for.

Bell and Bells. 1. A crackt bell can never sound well. 1732: Fuller, 6358.

2. Bells call others to church, but go not themselves. 1557: North, *Diall of Princes*, fo. 138 v°, For men y^t reade much, and worke litle, are as belles, the which do sound to cal others, and they themselues neuer enter into the church. 1670: Ray, 3. 1732: Fuller, 969.

3. Bells on one horse. *See* **Hang** (9).

4. He is like a bell that will go for every one that pulls it. 1732: Fuller, 1923.

5. He who cannot bear the clapper, should not pull the bell. 1732: Fuller, 2767, If you love not the noise of the bells, why do you pull the ropes? 1875: A. B. Cheales, *Proverb. Folk-Lore*, 10. 1917: Bridge, *Cheshire Proverbs*, 71.

6. They are like bells; every one in a several note. 1732: Fuller, 4954.

7. To curse with bell, book and candle. Before 1300: *Cursor Mundi*, 1. 17110 (E.E.T.S.), Curced in kirc than sal thai be wid candil, boke, and bell. *c.*1394: in Wright, *Political Poems*, i 341 (Rolls Ser., 1859), Thou shalt be cursed with booke and bell. 1485: Malory, *Morte d'Arthur*, bk xxi ch i, I shall curse you wyth book and belle and candell. 1593: Nashe, *Strange Newes*, in *Works*, ii. 185 (Grosart), The blind vicar would needs ... curse me with bel, book and candle. 1610: Rowlands, *Martin Markall*, 6 (Hunt.Cl.). 1715: Cent-livre, *Gotham Election*, sc vi 1840: Barham, *Ing. Legends:* 'Jackdaw of Rheims'. 1920: Barbellion, *Last Diary*, 138, The *Saturday Review* I cursed with bell, book, and candle.

8. When the bell begins to toll, Lord have mercy on the soul. 1813: Brand, *Pop. Antiq.*, ii 205 (Bohn). 1888: Gilbert, *Yeomen of Guard*, I, The funeral bell begins to toll – May Heaven have mercy on his soul!

See also **Agree like bells.**

Bell the cat. *See* **Cat** (65).

Bellesdon. *In and out like Bellesdon I wot.* 1678: Ray, 317. 1790: Grose, *Prov. Gloss.*, s.v. 'Leicestershire'. 1881: Evans, *Leics. Words, etc.*, 300 (E.D.S.), 'In and out, like Billesdon I wote' ... Billesdon being, or having been, noted for the crookedness of its main thoroughfare.

Bell-grave. *The same again, quoth Mark of Bell-grave.* 1644: J. Taylor (Water-Poet), in *Works*, 2nd coll., 22 (Spens.S.). 1790: Grose, *Prov. Gloss.*, s.v. 'Leicestershire'. 1818: Scott, *Heart of Midl.*, ch xxix.

Belly. 1. A belly full of gluttony will never study willingly. 1678: Ray, 146. 1732: Fuller, 6115.

2. Better belly burst than good drink lost.
1659: Howell, 17. 1738: Swift, *Polite Convers.*,
Dial. II, Come miss; better belly burst than good
liquor be lost. 1917: Bridge, *Cheshire Proverbs*,
30, Better belly burst, than good meat lost.

**3. He whose belly is full believes not him that
is fasting.** 1578: Florio, *First Fruites*, fo. 29, He
that is fed beleeueth not the fasting. 1611:
Cotgrave, s.v. 'Pance', He that hath gorged
himselfe thinkes all mens mawes be full. 1732:
Fuller, 2399.

**4. If it were not for the belly, the back might
wear gold.** 1732: Fuller, 2690. Cf. Nos. 11 and 16.

5. My belly cries cupboard. 1678: Ray, 237, His
belly cries cupboard. 1694: *Terence made
English*, 88, My belly chym'd cupboard above
half an hour ago. 1738: Swift, *Polite Convers.*,
Dial. II. 1826: Scott, *Woodstock*, ch xx, Whose
belly sings cupboard too? 1855: Kingsley, *West.
Ho!*, ch iii, So now away home. My inside cries
cupboard. 1901: F. E. Taylor, *Lancs Sayings*, 24,
Mi bally's cryin' cubbort. Cf. No. 15.

6. My belly thinks my throat cut. 1540:
Palsgrave, *Acolastus*, sig. H2, I am so soore
forhungered, that my bealy weneth my throte is
cutte. 1575: Churchyard, *Chippes*, 127 (Collier),
When hongry mawe thinks throat is cut in deed.
*c.*1630: B.&F., *Love's Pilgrimage*, II ii, Let's walk
apace; hunger will cut their throats else. 1738:
Swift, *Polite Convers.*, Dial. II, You are in great
haste; I believe your belly thinks your throat's
cut. 1901: F. E. Taylor, *Lancs Sayings*, 24, Mi
bally's beginnin' for t'think' at mi throat's cut (I
am hungry).

**7. The belly carries the legs, and not the legs
the belly.** 1620: Shelton, *Quixote*, Pt II ch xxxiv
1694: D'Urfey, *Quixote*, Pt I Act IV sc i 1732:
Fuller, 3194, Let the guts be full, for it's they
that carry the legs.

8. The belly hates a long sermon. 1732: Fuller,
4407.

9. The belly hath no ears. 1539: Taverner,
Proverbs, fo. 47, The bely hath no eares. *c.*1560:
Becon, in *Catechism, etc.*, 601 (P.S.). 1609:
Dekker, *Guls Horne-Booke*, in *Works*, ii 245
(Grosart). 1721: Bailey, *Eng. Dict.*, s.v. 'Belly'.
1853: Trench, *Proverbs*, 29 (1905), We have on
one side the English, Hungry bellies have no
ears.

10. The belly is not fitted with fair words. 1639:
Clarke, 113. 1670: Ray, 61. 1748: *Gent. Mag.*, 21.

1880: Spurgeon, *Ploughman's Pictures*, 18,
Promises don't fill the belly.

11. The belly robs the back. 1619: W. Hornby,
Scourge of Drunkennes, sig. B3, That by his paunch
his backe should fare the worse. 1659: Howell,
Proverbs: Brit.-Eng., 33. Cf. Nos. 4 and 16.

12. The belly teaches all arts. 1855: Bohn, 498.

**13. When the belly is full, the bones would be
at rest.** Before 1500: in Hill, *Commonplace-
Book*, 129 (E.E.T.S.), Whan the beli is fwll, the
bonis wold haue rest. 1553: *Respublica*, III iv
1669: *Politeuphuia*, 182. 1738: Swift, *Polite
Convers.*, Dial. II.

**14. When the belly is full the mind is amongst
the maids.** *c.*1645: MS. Proverbs, in *N. & Q.*, vol
154, p. 27.

15. Your belly chimes, it's time to go to dinner.
1678: Ray, 66. Cf. No. 5.

**16. Your belly will never let your back be
warm.** 1732: Fuller, 6043. Cf. Nos. 4 and 11.

See also **Back may trust; Empty** (1) and (2); **Eye**
(5); **Full; Hard,** *adj.* (8); and **Rule** (3).

Bellyfull is a bellyfull, A. 1666: Torriano, *Piazza
Univ.*, 321. 1694: Motteux, *Rabelais*, bk v ch xxiii
1738: Swift, *Polite Convers.*, Dial. II. 1823: Scott,
St Ronan's, ch x, 'A wamefou is a wamefou', said
the writer, swabbing his greasy chops.

Bellyfull is one of meat, drink, or sorrow, A.
1864: 'Cornish Proverbs', in *N. & Q.*, 3rd ser, vi
495.

Belvoir. *See* **Bever.**

Benacre. *See* **Cowhithe.**

Bench-whistler, He is a. *c.*1430: Lydgate,
Minor Poems, 170 (Percy S.), Al suche benche
whistelers, God late hem never the! [thrive].
1546: Heywood, *Proverbs*, Pt I ch xi That
benchwhistler (quoth I) is a pinchpeny. 1632: T.
Heywood, *Iron Age*, Pt I Act V, A very bench-
whistler.

Bend. 1. Best to bend while 'tis a twig. *c.*1560:
T. Ingdend, *Disobedient Child*, 56 (Percy S.), For
as longe as the twygge is gentell and plyent …
With small force and strength it may be bent.
1590: Lodge, *Rosalynde*, 18 (Hunt. CL), I will
bende the tree while it is a wand. 1667: *Roxb.
Ballads*, vii 696 (B.S.), A twig will bend when it
is young and weak. 1732: Fuller, 971. 1841:
Hood, *Miss Kilmansegg*, As the twig is bent, the
tree's inclined.

2. When you bend the elbow, the mouth opens.
Kentish saying. 1882: *N. & Q.*, 6th ser, v 266.

Benefits please like flowers while they are fresh. 1640: Herbert, *Jac. Prudentum.*

Benfieldside, where the Devil stole the key of the Quakers' Meeting-house. 1846–59: *Denham Tracts*, i 92 (F.L.S.), Benfieldside, in the parish of Lanchester, is celebrated as the site of one of the earliest Quaker meeting-houses in England.

Bent of one's bow, The. 1546: Heywood, *Proverbs*, Pt I ch xi, I, hauyng the bent of your vncles bow. 1579: Lyly, *Euphues*, 75 (Arber), Do you therefore thinke me easely entised to the bent of your bow? 1670: Ray, 164, To have the bent of one's bow.

Berkshire. *See* quot. 1790: Grose, *Prov. Gloss.*, s.v. 'Berkshire', He is a representative of Barkshire [applied to one who coughs]. *See also* **Cheshire** (6).

Berry's wife. *Just the thing, like old Berry's wife.* 1920: J. H. Bloom, in *N. & Q.*, 12th ser, vii 67 [said to have been heard in Warwickshire within the last ten years].

Berwick. 1. From Berwick to Dover; later with addition, *three hundred miles over. c.*1300: R. Brunne, tr. Langtoft's *Chron.*, 305 (Hearne), Alle Inglond fro Berwick vnto Kent. 1560: Wilson, *Rhetorique*, 105 (1909), Whereas oftentimes they [preachers] beginne as much from the matter, as it is betwixt Douer and Berwicke. 1642: D. Rogers, *Naaman*, sig. Hh3, Though you should nrune from Barwicke to Dover. 1662: Fuller, *Worthies*, ii 542 (1840), From Berwick to Dover, three hundred miles over. 1790: Grose, *Prov. Gloss.*, s.v. 'Northumberland' [as in 1662]. 1846–59: *Denham Tracts*, i 283 (F.L.S.) [as in 1662].

2. Once going through Berwick maketh not a man of war. 1846–59: *Denham Tracts*, i 287 (F.L.S.).

Beside the book, To be. 1672: Walker, *Paroem.*, 32, He is quite beside the book; mightily mistaken.

Beside the cushion, To be. 1546: Heywood, *Proverbs*, Pt II ch ix, I may set you besyde the cushyn yit. 1654: Gayton, *Pleasant Notes Don Q.*, 36, He let fly at the Biscaine ... and as we say in our poor English proverb, put him clean beside the cushion. 1681: W. Robertson, *Phraseol. Generalis*, 247, Beside the cushion; Nihil ad rhombum. 1778: H. Brooke, *Female Officer*, I xii, The man did not speak much beside the cushion of common sense.

Besom. *They have need of a besom that sweep the house with a turf.* 1678: Ray, 101. 1683: Meriton, *Yorkshire Ale*, 83–7 (1697).

Best. 1. Best among them. *See* **Fox-cubs.**

2. Best by yourself like Lowd's tup [ram]. 1886: R. Holland, *Cheshire Gloss.*, 447 (E.D.S.), Best by hissel like Lowndes's tup. Said of a disagreeable, quarrelsome fellow. 1917: Bridge, *Cheshire Proverbs*, 29.

3. Best cart. *See* **Cart** (2).

4. Best friends. *See* **Friend** (7).

5. He's one o' th' best eend o' th' worser sort o' folks. 1917: Bridge, *Cheshire Proverbs*, 70.

6. In the deepest water is the best fishing. 1633: Draxe, 66. 1670: Ray, 9. Cf. No. 14.

7. It is best to take half in hand and the rest by and by. 1678: Ray, 354. 1732: Fuller, 2921.

8. Living at the best end of the pig-trough. 1856: E. Hinchliffe, *Barthomley*, 135, The Shropshire farmers, more accustomed to the delicacies of beef and beer, charge ours, in Cheshire, with 'living at the best end of the pig trough'. 1917: Bridge, *Cheshire Proverbs*, 93.

9. Men are best loved furthest off. 1639: Clarke, 71.

10. Sometimes the best gain is to lose. 1640: Herbert, *Jac. Prudentum.*

11. That is the best gown that goes up and down the house. Ibid.

12. The best bred have the best portion. Ibid.

13. The best cloth may have a moth in it. 1732: Fuller, 4411.

14. The best fish swim near the bottom. 1639: Clarke, 212. 1670: Ray, 90. 1732: Fuller, 4412, The best fish swim deep. 1754: Berthelson, *Eng.-Danish Dict.*, s.v. 'Fish'. Cf. No. 6.

15. The best go first, the bad remain to mend. 1855: Bohn, 498.

16. The best ground is the dirtiest. *c.*1393: Langland, *Plowman*, C, xiii 224, On fat londe and ful of donge foulest wedes groweth. 1598: Shakespeare, *2 Henry IV*, IV iv, Most subject is the fattest soil to weeds. 1633: Donne, *Poems*, i 81 (Grierson), There is best land, where there is foulest way. 1676: Cotton, *Walton's Angler*, Pt II ch l., According to the proverb, 'there is good land where there is foul way'. 1846: Denham, *Proverbs*, 3 (Percy S.) [as in 1676]. 1904: *Co. Folk-Lore: Northumberland*, 173 (F.L.S.) [as in 1676]. Cf. **Worse** (4).

17. The best horse needs breaking. 1639:

Clarke, 100. 1670: Ray, 105, The best horse needs breaking, and the aptest child needs teaching. 1732: Fuller, 6441 [as in 1670]. 1868: *Quart. Review*, cxxv 253, The best horse needs breeching, And the aptest child needs teaching.

18. The best is as good as stark naught. 1639: Clarke, 14.

19. The best is best cheap. 1546: Heywood, *Proverbs*, Pt II ch vii 1580: Tusser, *Husbandrie*, 104 (E.D.S.), Count best the best cheape, wheresoeuer ye dwell. 1655: Gurnall, *Christian in Armour*, Verse 11, ch iii, p. 41 (1679), He that sells cheapest shall have most customers, though at last best will be best cheap. 1785–95: Wolcot, *Lousiad*, can. v, 'Best is best cheap' – you very wisely cry.

20. The best is best to speak to. 1683: Meriton, *Yorkshire Ale*, 83–7 (1697).

21. The best is enemy of the good. Meaning that excellence makes what would normally seem acceptable seem poor by comparison. 1861: R. C. Trench, *Commentary on the Epistles to the Seven Churches in Asia*, p. v., 'The best is enemy of the good'; and … many a good book has remained unwritten … because there floated in the mind's eye … the ideal of a better or best. Cf. **Good is the enemy of the best**.

22. The best-laid schemes of mice and men gang aft agley. 1786: Burns, *Poems*, 'To a Mouse', The best-laid schemes o' Mice an' Men, Gang aft agley. 1911: D.H. Lawrence, *Letter*, 21 Sept., I am sorry the bookbinding has gone pop. But there 'The best laid schemes' etc etc. *Gang aft agley* means 'often go awry'. The first line is often misquoted as 'The best-laid plans … '.

23. The best mirror is an old friend. 1611: Cotgrave, s.v. 'Miroir', An old friend an excellent looking-glasse. 1670: Ray, 10. 1732: Fuller, 4905, There is no better looking-glass than an old friend.

24. The best of friends must part. 1385: Chaucer, *Troilus and Criseyde*, V 343, Always frendes may nat been yfeere [may not be together]. 1611: G. Chapman, *MayDay*, iv 70, Friends must part, we came not all together, and we must not goe all together. 1784: J.F.D. Smyth, *Tour in the USA*, I xxxvii, Sooner or later all, even the dearest of friends, must part. 1821: Scott, *Kenilworth*, I xi, 'You are going to leave me then?' … 'The best of friends must part, Flibbertigibbet'.

25. The best of men are but men at the best. 1885: Harley, *Moon Lore*, 191.

26. The best of the sport is to do the deed and say nothing. 1639: Clarke, 326, Sport is sweetest when there be no spectators. 1670: Ray, 25.

27. The best part is still behind. Before 1529: Skelton, *Works*, i 17 (Dyce), Take thys in worth, the best is behynde. 1630: Randolph, in *Works*, i 49 (Hazlitt), For now the proverb true I find, That the best part is still behind. 1659: Howell, 6, The best is behind.

28. The best patch is off the same cloth. 1732: Fuller, 4417.

29. The best remedy against an ill man is much ground between both. 1640: Herbert, *Jac. Prudentum*. 1670: Ray, 14.

30. The best things are worst (or hard) to come by. 1635: Swan, *Spec. Mundi*, 465, Excellent things are hard to come by. 1670: Ray, 61. 1732: Fuller, 4420.

31. The best things in life are free. 1927: B.G. de Silva *et al.* song title, *The Best Things in Life are Free*. The moon belongs to everyone,/The best things in life are free,/The stars belong to everyone,/They gleam there for you and me. 1948: B. Stevenson, *Home-Book of Proverbs*, 887 … Here's a thought for you and me: 'The best things in life are free'..

32. The best things may be abused. 1639: Clarke, 5.

33. To make the best of a bad job (or **bargain**, or **game**, or **market**). 1663: Pepys, *Diary*, 14 Aug., I … therefore am resolved to make the best of a bad market, *c.*1680: L'Estrange, *Seneca's Morals:* 'Happy Life', ch xvi, It is an equal prudence to make the best of a bad game and to manage a good one. 1714: Ozell, *Molière*, ii 142, All the art lies in making the best of a bad market. 1765: Bickerstaff, *Maid of the Mill*, III iv [bad market]. 1823: Scott, *Q. Durward*, ch xxxvi, Her aunt seemed determined to make the best of a bad bargain. 1836: Dickens, *Sketches by Boz:* 'Scenes', ch xiii … a bad bargain. 1923: J. S. Fletcher, *The Diamonds*, ch xxviii, Resolved to … make the best of an undeniably bad job.

34. To put the best (*a*) **foot**, (*b*) **leg, foremost** (or **forward**), (*a*) *c.*1591: Shakespeare, *Titus Andr.*, II iii, Come on, my lords, the better foot before. 1626: Overbury, *Characters:* 'A Footman', His legs are not matches, for he is still setting the best foot forward. 1700: Congreve, *Way of the World*, IV x, You should commence an amour, and put your best foot foremost. 1886: R.L.S., *Kidnapped*, ch xviii, I set my best foot forward. 1901: Raymond, *Idler Out of Doors*, 61, Then he must hurry up best foot afore. (b) c.1500: Medwall, *Nature*, l. 825 (Brandl's *Quellen*, 99), Com behynd and folow me Set out the better leg I warne the. 1633: Jonson, *Tale of a Tub*, II i, Cheer up, the better leg avore. 1742: Fielding, *Andrews*, bk i ch xi, Lovers do not march like horse–guards … they put the best leg foremost. 1838: Dickens, *Twist*, ch v, Now, you must put your best leg foremost, old lady! 1886: Elworthy, *West Som. Word-Book*, 428 (E.D.S.), To put the best leg before is to hasten briskly, not necessarily in walking, but in whatever is in hand.

35. We are usually the best men when in the worst health. 1855: Bohn, 551.

36. You are always best when asleep. Ibid., 575.

Betshanger. *See* quot. 1735: Pegge, *Kent. Proverbs*, in E.D.S., No. 12, p. 75, At Betshanger a gentleman, at Fredvile a Squire, at Bonington a noble knight, at … a lawyer [pron. *lyer*].

Better a blush in the face, than a spot in the heart. 1620: Shelton, *Quixote*, Pt II ch xliv, Better shame in the face than spot in the heart. 1732: Fuller, 859.

Better a clout than a hole out. 1605: Camden, *Remains*, 325 (1870), It is better to see a clout [patch] than a hole out. 1732: Fuller, 6310. 1864: 'Cornish Proverbs', in *N. & Q.*, 3rd ser, v 208.

Better a fair pair of heels than a halter. 1620: Shelton, *Quixote*, Pt II ch lxvii, Better a fair pair of heels than die at the gallows. 1694: D'Urfey, *Quixote*, Pt II Act II sc ii [as in 1620]. 1732: Fuller, 861.

Better a finger off than always aching. Before 1225: *Ancren Riwle*, 360, Betere is finker offe then he eke euer. 1681: W. Robertson, *Phraseol. Generalis*, 252. 1825: Scott, *Fam. Letters*, ii 384 (1894), As to our losing them a few days sooner, one must piece it out with the old proverb, 'Better a finger off than aye wagging'.

Better a good keeper than a good winner. 1611: Cotgrave, s.v. 'Amasseur', A warie keeper is better than a carefull getter. 1623: Wodroephe, *Spared Houres*, 503.

Better a lean jade than an empty halter. 1678: Ray, 166. 1732: Fuller, 863.

Better a lean peace than a fat victory. 1578: Florio, *First Fruites*, fo. 32, Better is a leane agreement then a fat sentence. 1700: in *Thoresby's Correspondence*, i 396 (1832), You will all find the old adage verified, that 'a lean arbitration is better then a fat judgment'. 1732: Fuller, 864. Cf. **lll agreement.**

Better a lean purse than a lere [empty] **stomach.** 1860: Reade, *Cloister and Hearth*, ch xxv.

Better a little fire to warm us, than a great one to burn us. c.1510: A. Barclay, *Eglogves*, 9 (Spens.S.), Then better is small fire one easyly to warme Then is a great fire to do one hurt or harme. 1732: Fuller, 865.

Better a loss at sea than a bad debt at land. 1742: North, *Lives of Norths*, ii 50 (Bohn), The merchants have a proverb, 'Better', etc.

Better a mischief than an inconvenience. The saying was also reversed, see the first two quotations. 1583: Melbancke, *Philotinus*, sig. Zr, Yet must I commit an inconuenience to preuent a mischiefe. 1593: G. Harvey, in *Works*, i 284 (Grosart), So in many priuate cases, better an inconuenience then a mischiefe. 1642: D. Rogers, *Matrim. Honour*, 117, Better admit a mischiefe then an inconvenience. 1681: W. Robertson, *Phraseol. Generalis*, 252, Better once a mischief, then always inconvenience. 1714: *Spectator*, No. 564. 1740: North, *Examen*, 330, Littleton's rule, better a mischief than an inconvenience, sounds oddly, but hath this very meaning.

Better a mouse in the pot than no flesh at all. 1605: Camden, *Remains*, 319 (1870) [has 'louse' for 'mouse']. 1670: Ray, 117 [has 'louse', but adds,] The Scotch proverb saith a mouse, which is better sence, for a mouse is flesh and edible. 1696: D'Urfey, *Quixote*, Pt III Act V sc i ['mouse']. 1732: Fuller, 867 ['mouse']. Cf. **Louse** (1).

Better a new friend than an old foe. 1590: Spenser, *F. Q.*, I ii 243, Better new friend then an old foe is said. 1600: Bodenham, *Belvedere*, 94 (Spens.S.).

Better a portion. *See* **Wife** (6).

Better a quick penny than a dallying shilling. 1894: Northall, *Folk Phrases of Four Counties*, 11 (E.D.S.).

Better a witty fool than a foolish wit. 1601: Shakespeare, *Twelfth Night*, I v.

Better alone than have a false friend for company. 1825: Scott, *Betrothed*, ch xiv Cf. Better be alone, *infra*.

Better an egg in peace than an ox in War. 1611: Cotgrave, s.v. 'Oeuf'.

Better are meals many than one too merry. 1546: Heywood, *Proverbs*, Pt II ch vii *c.*1594: Bacon, *Promus*, No. 494. 1678: Ray, 40.

Better bad than 'bout [without]. 1826: Wilbraham, *Cheshire Gloss.*, s.v. Said by a woman urged to quit a bad husband. 1917: Bridge, *Cheshire Proverbs*, 29.

Better be a fool than a knave. 1616: *Rich Cabinet*, fo. 44, Yet better to bee a foole then a knaue. 1659: Howell, 18. 1875: A. B. Cheales, *Proverb. Folk-Lore*, 164.

Better be alone than in bad company. 1477: Rivers, *Dictes and Sayings*, 8 (1877), It is better a man … to be a lone than to be accompayned with euill people. 1586: B. Young, tr. Guazzo's *Civil Convers.*, fo. 180. 1648: Fuller, *Holy State:* 'Of Company', Better therefore ride alone than have a thief's company. 1732: Fuller, 872. Cf. Better alone, *supra*.

Better be drunk than drowned. 1830: Forby, *Vocab. E. Anglia*, 430.

Better be envied than pitied. 1546: Heywood, *Proverbs*, Pt I ch xi 1584: Lodge, *Alarum against usurers*, 57 (SH.S.). 1670: Ray, 86. 1754: Berthelson, *Eng.-Danish Dict.*, s.v. 'Envyed'.

Better be half blind than have both eyes out. 1639: Clarke, 86. 1670: Ray. 64.

Better be half hanged than ill wed. 1670: Ray, 48.

Better be half hanged than lose estate. 1681: Otway, *Soldier's Fortune*, V iii.

Better be ill spoken of by one before all, than by all before one. 1659: Howell, *Proverbs*, 'To Philologers'. 1670: Ray, 14.

Better be out of the world. *See* Out of the world.

Better be over-manned than over-tooled. 1886: Elworthy, *West Som. Word-Book*, 547 (E.D.S.), A common saying is, – ' 'Tis better to be … ', i.e. that the tool should be rather light than heavy in comparison with the man's strength.

Better be the head of a lizard than the tail of a lion. 1640: Herbert, *Jac. Prudentium*.

Better be the head of a pike (or **dog**) **than the tail of a sturgeon** (or **lion**). 1670: Ray, 101. 1736: Bailey, *Dict.*, s.v. 'Head'. 1823: D'Israeli, *Cur. of Lit.*, ut infra.

Better be the head of an ass than the tail of a horse. 1639: Clarke, 105. 1670: Ray, 101. 1732: Fuller, 928.

Better be the head of the yeomanry than the tail of the gentry. 1639: Clarke, 22. 1670: Ray, 101. 1732: Fuller, 933. 1823: D'Israeli, *Cur. of Lit.*, 2nd ser, i 447 (1824), The ancient … spirit of Englishmen was once expressed by our proverb, 'Better be the head of a dog than the tail of a lion'; i.e. the first of the yeomanry rather than the last of the gentry.

Better be the tail of a horse than the head of an ass. 1639: Clarke, 91.

Better be unmannerly than troublesome. 1659: Howell, 5. 1670: Ray, 153. 1732: Fuller, 880. Cf. **Unmannerliness.**

Better be up to the ankles, than quite to over head and ears. 1732: Fuller, 879.

Better believe it than go where it was done to prove it. 1670: Ray, 164.

Better blue clothes, He's in his, i.e. He thinks himself very fine. 1678: Ray, 66.

Better bow than break, *c.*1374: Chaucer, *Troylus*, i 257, The yerde [twig, branch] is bet that bowen wole and winde Than that that brest [breaks]. 1413: in *Twenty-six Poems*, No. 124, p. 54 (E.E.T.S.), Beter bowe than brest. 1530: Palsgrave, 660, Better plye than breake. 1560: Wilson, *Rhetorique*, 189 (1909). 1611: Davies (of Hereford), *Sc. of Folly*, 44, in *Works*, ii (Grosart). 1732: Fuller, 882.

Better bread than is made of wheat, No. 1546: Heywood, *Proverbs*, Pt II ch vii, Lyke one … That would haue better bread than is made of wheate. 1592: Lyly, *Mother Bombie*, I iii 1611: Cotgrave, s.v. 'Froument', Would you have better bread then's made of wheat. 1712: Motteux, *Quixote*, Pt I bk i ch vii, Rambling up and down like a vagabond, and seeking for better bread than is made of wheat. 1853: Trench, *Proverbs*, 83 (1905), We note very well the folly of one addicted to this, saying: He expects better bread than can be made of wheat.

Better buy man borrow. 1539: Taverner, *Proverbs*, fo. 13, I had leuer bye then begge. 1633: Draxe, 18. 1732: Fuller, 884.

Better children weep than old men. 1541: Coverdale, *Christ. State Matrimony*, sig. 18, Better it is that children wepe then old men. *c.*1594: Bacon, *Promus*, No. 481. 1650: Fuller, *Pisgah Sight*, bk iii ch iv § 1.

Better cut the shoe than pinch the foot. 1732: Fuller, 887.

Better direct well than work hard. Ibid., No. 889.

Better do it than wish it done. 1546: Heywood, *Proverbs*, Pt II ch v, Better it be doone than wishe it had been doone. 1670: Ray, 29 [as in 1546]. 1732: Fuller, 890.

Better dule than dawkin. 1883: A. Easther, *Almondbury Gloss.*, 40 (E.D.S.), The proverb is well known, 'Better have a dule nor a dawkin', i.e. an evil spirit than a fool.

Better early than late. *c.*1225: *Ancren Riwle*, p. 340 (Morton), Better is er then to lete (Better is early, or too soon, than too late). *c.*1520: *Hick-scorner*, in Hazlitt, *Old Plays*, i 193, It is better betime than too late. 1560: *Nice Wanton*, in ibid., ii 168, Better in time than too late. 1817: Scott, *Rob Roy*, ch xviii, Better sune as syne.

Better end of the staff. 1567: Pickering, *Horestes*, l. 168 (Brandl, *Quellen*, 499), By godes ge, iche had not the best end of the staffe. 1667: L'Estrange, *Quevedo's Visions*, 38 (1904), The devil of money has the better end of the staff. 1753: Richardson, *Grandison*, i 360 (1883), Miss Byron, I have had the better end of the staff, I believe. 1924: Shaw, *Saint Joan*, sc v, She does not know everything; but she has got hold of the right end of the stick.

Better eye out than always ache. 1546: Heywood, *Proverbs*, Pt I ch viii 1597: Bacon, *Coulers of good and euill*, 10. 1670: Ray, 86.

Better fed than taught. 1530: Palsgrave, 557, He is better fostred [nourished] than taught. 1548: Hall, *Chron.*, 15 (1809), These monasticall persones ... better fed then taught. 1636: Taylor (Water-Poet), *Travels*, 19, in *Works*, 3rd coll. (Spens.S.). 1820: Scott, *Monastery*, ch i.

Better feed five drones than starve one bee. 1732: Fuller, 935, Better two drones be preserv'd, than one good bee perish. 1875: A. B. Cheales, *Proverb. Folk-Lore*, 126.

Better fill a glutton's belly than his eye. 1590: Greene, in *Works*, ix 167 (Grosart), Now gentlewomen, do I finde the olde prouerbe true: Better fill a mans belly then his eye. 1670: Ray, 96.

Better give a shilling than lend ... 1659: Howell, *Proverbs: Ital.-Eng.*, 14, Better give a penny then lend twenty. 1732: Fuller, 895, Better give a shilling than lend and lose half a crown. 1875: A. B. Cheales, *Proverb. Folk-Lore*, 101, Give a shilling sooner than lend half a crown.

Better give than take. 1493: *Dives and Pauper*, fo. 2 (1536), It is ... more blyssful to giue than to take. 1546: Heywood, *Proverbs*, Pt I ch v 1611: Davies (of Hereford), *Sc. of Folly*, 44, in *Works*, ii (Grosart). 1710: S. Palmer, *Moral Essays on Proverbs*, 351, 'Tis better to give than to receive.

Better go about than fall into the ditch. 1659: Howell, *Proverbs: Span.-Eng.*, 5. 1670: Ray, 1. 1732: Fuller, 897, Better go back than lose your self.

Better go to bed supperless. *See* Supperless.

Better good afar off than evil at hand. 1640: Herbert, *Jac. Prudentum.*

Better have it than hear of it. 1639: Clarke, 256, Better to have than to heare of a good thing. 1670: Ray, 215.

Better have one plough going than two cradles. 1580: Lyly, *Euphues*, 229 (Arber), It is better to haue one plough going, then two cradells. 1716: Ward, *Female Policy*, 82, Therefore it's better to have two ploughs going, than one cradle. 1732: Fuller, 905. 1846: Denham, *Proverbs*, 5 (Percy S.).

Better hazard once than be always in fear. 1732: Fuller, 906.

Better is art than strength. *c.*1205: Layamon, *Brut*, ii 297 (Madden), Hit wes yare i-quethen: that betere is liste thene ufel strenthe (It was said of yore, that better is art than evil strength).

Better is cost upon something worth than expense on nothing worth. 1545: Ascham, *Toxoph.*, 122 (Arber).

Better is the last smile than the first laughter. 1546: Heywood, *Proverbs*, Pt II ch ix *c.*1594: Bacon, *Promus*, No. 501. 1611: Davies (of Hereford), *Sc. of Folly*, 47, in *Works*, ii (Grosart). 1732: Fuller, 929.

Better keep now than seek anon. 1659: Howell, *Proverbs: Brit.-Eng.*, 16.

Better kiss a knave than be troubled with him. 1605: Camden, *Remains*, 326 (1870). 1670: Ray, 110. 1738: Swift, *Polite Convers.*, Dial. I, I had rather give a knave a kiss, for once, than be troubled with him.

Better known than trusted. *c.*1560: in Huth, *Ancient Ballads, etc.*, 228 (1867), They are not so wel trust as knowne. 1592: Chettle, *Kind-Hearts Dream*, 10 (Percy S.), Better knowne than lou'd.

1670: Ray, 183. 1732: Fuller, 909. 1817: Scott, *Rob Roy*, ch xxvi, Rashleigh Osbaldistone is better kend than trusted in Glasgow.

Better late ripe and bear, than early blossom and blast. 1732: Fuller, 910.

Better late than never. [κρεῖττον ἐστὶν ἄρξασθαι ὀψὲ τὰ δέοντα πράττειν ἢ μηδέποτε. – Dionysius of Halicarnassus, ix 9.] *c*.1330: in C. Keller, *Die Mittelenglische Gregoriuslegende* (1941), 146, Better is lat than never blinne [cease] Our soules to maken fre. *c*.1386: Chaucer, *Canon's Yeoman's Tale*, l. 857, For bet than never is late. *c*.1420: Lydgate, *Assembly of Gods*, st. 172, p. 36 (E.E.T.S.), He seyde vyce to forsake ys bettyr late than neuer. 1579: Gosson, *Sch. of Abuse*, 41 (Arber). 1667: Pepys, *Diary*, 17 March, I have been … much ashamed of our not visiting her sooner, but better now than never. 1669: *Politeuphuia*, 183, Better late thrive than never. 1767: Murphy, *Sch. for Guardians*, I iv 1790: M. P. Andrews, [farce] *Better Late than Never* [title]. 1868: Robertson, *Play*, IV.

Better leave than lack. 1546: Heywood, *Proverbs*, Pt I ch v 1681: W. Robertson, *Phraseol. Generalis*, 475, At dinner 'tis better to leave then to lack. 1725: Bailey, tr. Erasmus' *Colloquies*, 71, We had better leave than lack.

Better lose a jest than a friend. 1593: G. Harvey, in *Works*, ii 125 (Grosart), And Papphatchet, it is better to loose a new iest, then an old frend. 1670: Ray, 109. 1732: Fuller, 915.

Better lose cloth than bread. Before 1500: Hill, *Commonplace-Book*, 129 (E.E.T.S.), Better it is, to lese cloth than brede.

Better lost than found. 1584: Robinson, *Handf. Pleas. Delights*, 14 (Arber), For you are better lost than found. 1586: Whitney, *Emblems*, 158, For such a wife is better loste then founde. 1692: L'Estrange, *Aesop*, 121 (3rd ed.). 1821: Scott, *Kenilworth*, ch i, I have one wild slip of a kinsman … but he is better lost than found.

Better luck still, quoth Rowley Burdon. 1846–59: *Denham Tracts*, i 68 (F.L.S.) … An extremely popular toast and saying through nearly the whole of the North of England.

Better my hog dirty home than no hog at all. 1670: Ray, 13. 1712: Motteux, *Quixote*, Pt II ch lxv. 1732: Fuller, 927, Better's a dirty hog than no hog at all.

Better never to begin than never to make an end. 1633: Draxe, 51. 1639: Clarke, 247. 1736:

Bailey, *Dict.*, s.v. 'Better', Better never begun than never ended.

Better one house filled than two spilled. 1670: Ray, 51. 1735: Pegge, *Kenticisms*, in E.D.S., No. 12, p. 48. 1887: Parish and Shaw, *Dict. Kent. Dialect*, 157 (E.D.S.), Spilled. Spoilt. And so the proverb, 'Better one house filled than two spill'd'.

Better one house spoiled (or troubled than) two. 1587: Greene, *Penelope's Web*, in *Works*, v 162 (Grosart), Where the old prouerb is fulfild, better one house troubled then two. 1924: *Folk-Lore*, xxxv 358 [Suffolk], Better one house spoilt than two [said when a witless man marries a foolish woman].

Better one's house. *See* **House** (6).

Better pay the butcher than the doctor. 1875: A. B. Cheales, *Proverb. Folk-Lore*, 82.

Better play a card too much than too little. 1620: Shelton, *Quixote*, Pt II ch xxxvii 1694: D'Urfey, *Quixote*, Pt I Act IV sc i.

Better ride safe, etc. *See* quot. 1821: Scott, *Kenilworth*, ch viii, 'Better ride safe in the dark', says the proverb, 'than in daylight with a cut-throat at your elbow'.

Better riding on a pad than on a horse's bare back. 1792: Wolcot, in *Works*, ii 403 (1795).

Better rule than be ruled by the rout. 1546: Heywood, *Proverbs*, Pt I ch v, And better to rule, than be ruled by the rout. 1605: Camden, *Remains*, 320 (1870). 1670: Ray, 23.

Better say here it is, than here it was. 1683: Meriton, *Yorkshire Ale*, 83–7 (1697). 1732: Fuller, 931.

Better sell than live poorly. 1732: Fuller, 941.

Better shelter under an old hedge, than a young furze-bush. 1639: Clarke, 25, Better to keep under an old hedge than creepe under a new furs-bush. 1732: Fuller, 922.

Better sit still. *See* **Sit** (2).

Better so than worse. 1732: Fuller, 925.

Better sold than bought. 1546: Heywood, *Proverbs*, Pt I ch x, But, for a farthyng, who euer did sell you Myght bost you to be better solde then bought.

Better some of a pudding than none of a pie. 1670: Ray, 135. 1732: Fuller, 924.

Better spare at brim than at bottom. 1523: Fitzherbert, *Husbandry*, 100 (E.D.S.), Thou husbande and huswife, that intend to … kepe measure, you must spare at the brynke, and not at the bottom. 1580: Tusser, *Husbandrie*, 23 (E.D.S.), Some spareth too late, and a number with him, the foole at the bottom, the wise at the brim. 1681: W. Robertson, *Phraseol. Generalis*, 275. 1732: Fuller, 4237. 1869: Spurgeon, *John Ploughman*, ch xvi, He never spares at the brim, but he means, he says, to save at the bottom.

Better spare to have of thine own than ask of other men. 1640: Herbert, *Jac. Prudentum*.

Better spared than ill spent. 1633: Draxe, 196. 1670: Ray, 144.

Better speak to the master, than the man. 1661: Gurnall, *Christian in Armour*, 498 (1679).

Better spent than spared. 1530: Palsgrave, 726, It is better somtyme to spende than to spaare. 1560: Wilson, *Rhetorique*, 189 (1909), It were better sometimes wastefully to spende, then warely to keepe. 1732: Fuller, 926.

Better suffer ill than do ill. 1639: Clarke, 15, Better to suffer wrong than doe wrong. 1640: Herbert, *Jac. Prudentum*. 1875: A. B. Cheales, *Proverb. Folk-Lore*, 164.

Better the day, better the deed. 1607: Middleton, *Mich. Term*, III i 1612: Rowlands, *Knave of Hearts*, 46 (Hunt.Cl.), They say, The better day, the better deede. 1738: Swift, *Polite Convers.*, Dial. I. 1775: Garrick, *May-Day*, sc ii 1870: Dickens, *Drood*, ch x, Ask Mr Landless to dinner on Christmas Eve (the better the day the better the deed).

Better the devil ... *See* **Devil** (11).

Better the feet slip than the tongue. 1586: Pettie, tr. Guazzo's *Civil Convers.*, fo. 55, It is better to slip with the foote, then with the tongue. 1611: Cotgrave, s.v. 'Glisser'. 1670: Ray, 26. 1732: Fuller, 932. 1875: A. B. Cheales, *Proverb. Folk-Lore*, 88. Cf. **Slip of the foot.**

Better the harm I know than that I know not. 1586: D. Rowland, tr. *Lazarillo*, 73 (1924), Remembring the olde proverbe: Better is the evill knowne, than the good which is yet to knowe.

Better to be a-cold than a cuckold. 1678: Ray, 69.

Better to be born lucky than rich. 1639: Clarke, 49, Better to have good fortune then be a rich man's child. 1784: *New Foundl. Hosp. for Wit*, iv 128, Better be fortunate than rich. 1846–59, *Denham Tracts*, i 224 (F.L.S.).

Better to be happy than wise. 1546: Heywood, *Proverbs*, Pt II ch vi 1581: B. Rich, *Farewell*, 7 (SH.S.), There is an old proverbe ... 'It is better to be happie than wise'. 1670: Ray, 99.

Better to be idle than ill occupied. 1560: E. More, *Defence of Women*, Dedication, Better had it bene for hym (as Erasmus sayth) to haue bene ydle then euyll occupyed. 1601: Lyly, *Love's Metam.*, I ii, Yet better idle then ill employed. 1681: W. Robertson, *Phraseol. Generalis*, 252, Better be idle then not well employed. 1725: Bailey, tr. Erasmus' *Colloquies*, 210, Thence comes the proverb, It is better to be idle, than to be doing, but to no purpose.

Better to be safe than sorry. 1837: S. Lover, *Rory O'More* ii xxi, 'Jist countin' them, – is there any harm in that?' said the tinker: 'it's betther be sure than sorry.' 1933: *Radio Times*, 14 Apr., 125, Cheap distempers very soon crack or fade. Better be safe than sorry. Ask for Halls.

Better to be stung by a nettle, than prickt by a rose. That is, better be wronged by a foe than a friend. 1659: Howell, 18.

Better to cry over your goods than after them. 1855: Bohn, 532.

Better to give than to receive. [Acts xx 35, It is more blessed to give than to receive] *c.*1390: Gower, *Confessio Amantis*, v 7725, Betre is to yive than to take. *c.*1527: C. Berthelet, tr. Erasmus' *Sayings of Wise Men*, B2, It is better to gyve than to take, for he that takethe a gyfte of another man is bonde to quyte it, so that his lyberte is gone. 1710: S. Palmer, *Proverbs*, 351, 'Tis better to Give than to Receive, but yet 'tis madness to give so much Charity to others, as to become the Subject of it our Selves.

Better to give the fleece than the sheep. 1578: Florio, *First Fruites*, fo. 32. 1605: Camden, *Remains*, 326 (1870). 1732: Fuller, 896, Better give the wool than the whole sheep.

Better to hang. *See* **Hang** (2).

Better to have loved and lost than never to have loved at all. 1700: Congreve, *The Way of the World*, II i, Say what you will, 'tis better to be left, than never to have lov'd. 1812: Crabbe, *Tales*, xiv, Better to love amiss than nothing to have lov'd. 1850: Tennyson, *In Memoriam*, 'Tis better to have loved and lost Than never to have loved at all.

Better to have than wish. 1546: Heywood, *Proverbs*, Pt II ch iv 1670: Ray, 29.

Better to knit (or knot) than blossom. 1670: Ray, III ['knit']. 1732: Fuller, 2917 ['knot'].

Better to leave than to maintain folly. *c.*1477: Caxton, *Jason*, 116 (E.E.T.S.), For as it is said communly, hit is better to leue folie thenne to mayntene folie.

Better to live in low degree than high disdain. 1589: L. Wright, *Display of Dutie*, 17, It is a true saying, better to liue in lowe degree then high disdaine. 1647: *Countrym. New Commonwealth*, 25, It is better for him to live in low content then in high infamy.

Better to play with the ears than with the tongue. 1611: Davies (of Hereford), *Sc. of Folly*, 46, in *Works*, ii (Grosart). 1633: Draxe, 172.

Better to travel hopefully than to arrive. 1881: R.L. Stevenson, *Virginibus Puerisque*, IV 190, To travel hopefully is a better thing than to arrive, and the true success is to labour.

Better to wear out than to rust out. 1770: G. Whitefield, in Southey, *Wesley*, ii 170 (1858), I had rather wear out than rust out. 1830: Forby, *Vocab. E. Anglia*, 434, It is better to wear up with work, than with rust. 1865: A. K. H. Boyd, *Crit. Essays of Co. Parson*, 40, 'It is better,' said Bishop Cumberland, 'to wear out than to rust out.' 1924: *Folk-Lore*, xxxv 358, It is better to wear up than rust up. Suffolk.

Better tooth out than always ache. 1659: Howell, 7. 1732: Fuller, 869.

Better unborn than untaught. *c.*1270: *Prov. of Alfred*, in *O. E. Miscell.*, 128 (E.E.T.S.), For betere is child vnbore than vnbuhsum [unbuxom = disobedient]. *c.*1460: *How the Goode Wyfe*, l. 203, For a chyld vn-borne wer better Than be vn-taught, thus seys the letter. *c.*1555: in Wright, *Songs, etc.*, *Reign of Philip and Mary*, 6 (Roxb.Cl), Unborne ys better than untought. 1662: Fuller, *Worthies*, i 44 (1840), Our English proverb, 'It is as good to be unborn as unbred'. 1732: Fuller, 937, Better unborn than unbred.

Better unfed than untaught. 1557: Seager, *Sch. of Vertue*, in *Babees Book, etc.*, 348 (E.E.T.S.), The common prouerbe remember ye oughte, 'Better vnfedde then vn-taughte'. 1580: Lyly, *Euphues*, 420 (Arber), I haue beene better taught then fedde.

Better untaught than ill taught. 1678: Ray, 345. 1732: Fuller, 938. 1780: K. O'Hara, *Tom Thumb*, I iii, in Inchbald, *Farces*, vi 174 (1815), Better quite ignorant, than half instructed.

Better wear out shoes than sh E.E.T.S.. 1732: Fuller, 940. 1875: A. B. Cheales, *Proverb. Folk-Lore*, 82.

Better wed over the mixen than over the moor. 1662: Fuller, *Worthies*, i 266 (1840). 1790: Grose, *Prov. Gloss.*, s.v. 'Cheshire'. 1818: Scott, *Heart of Midl.*, ch xxxi 1874: Hardy, *Madding Crowd*, ch xxii 1917: Bridge, *Cheshire Proverbs*, 30.

Better were within, better would come out, If. 1732: Fuller, 2672.

Better workman, the worse husband, The. 1633: Draxe, 62. 1670: Ray, 158. 1754: Berthelson, *Eng.-Danish Dict.*, s.v. 'Workman'. 1901: F. E. Taylor, *Lancs Sayings*, 32, Better workmon – wo'se husbant.

Between promising and performing a man may marry his daughter. 1611: Cotgrave, s.v. 'Donner', *Entre promettre et donner doit on la fille marier*; Betweene promising, and giving the maid ought to be married. 1670: Ray, 22. 1732: Fuller, 974.

Between the anvil (or **beetle**) **and the hammer** (or **block**). 1583: Melbancke, *Philotinus*, sig. Cc2, My spirite was betwixt the anvile and hammer. *c.*1594: Bacon, *Promus*, No. 741, Between the hammer and the anvill. 1613: Hayward, *Norm. Kings*, 274 (OED), Earle William being thus set as it were betweene the beetle and the block – was nothing deiected. 1633: Draxe, 37, Betweene the anuill and the hammer. 1902: in *N.&Q.*, 9th ser, ix 12, The frequency with which the word 'beetle' occurs in proverbial phrases, like … 'Between the beetle and the block' …

Between twelve and two. *See* **Hours.**

Between two stools one falls to the ground. *See* **Two stools.**

Between you and me and the post (or **bed-post, door-post,** etc.). 1838: Dickens, in *Letters*, i 11 (1880), Between you and me and the general post. 1839: Dickens, *Nickleby*, ch x, Between you and me and the post, sir, it will be a very nice portrait. 1843: Planché, *Extravag.*, ii 245 (1879), I fancy between you and me and the post …

Bever. *If Bever have a cap, You churls of the vale look to that.* 1662: Fuller, *Worthies*, ii 226 (1840). 1790: Grose, *Prov. Gloss.*, s.v. 'Leicestershire'. 1881: Evans, *Leics. Words, etc.*, 300 (E.D.S.), I have heard the proverb repeatedly, but always in the form: When Belvoir wears his cap, You churls of the Vale look to that.

Bewails. *He that bewails himself hath the cure in his hands.* 1640: Herbert, *Jac. Prudentum.*

Beware beginnings. 1639: Clarke, 259.

Beware by other men's harms. *See* **Warn** (1).

Beware of breed, i.e. ill breed. Cheshire. 1670: Ray, 65. 1917: Bridge, *Cheshire Proverbs*, 31.

Beware of little expense. 1855: Bohn, 331.

Beware of the forepart of a woman, the hind part of a mule, and all sides of a priest. 1591: Florio, *Second Frutes*, 99, To womens forepartes doo not aspire, From a mules hinder parte retire, And shun all partes of monke or frire. 1623: Wodroephe, *Spared Houres*, 276 [with 'asses' for 'mule']. 1732: Fuller, 978. 1880: Spurgeon, *Ploughman's Pictures*, 118, Beware of a mule's hind foot, a dog's tooth, and a woman's tongue.

Beware the buyer. *See* **Buyer.**

Bewcastler, He's a. 1846–59, *Denham Tracts*, i 72 (F.L.S.), The parallel saying of Cumberland, 'He's a Bewcastler' – i.e. a bad one.

Bibble-babble. *See* Tittle-tattle.

Bible and a stone do well together, The. 1672: Marvell, *Rehearsal Transpr.*, in *Works*, iii 151 (Grosart), The Welch have a proverb, that the Bible and a stone do well together; meaning, perhaps, that if one miss, the other will hit.

Bid me and do it yourself. 1639: Clarke, 232.

Big a liar as Tom Pepper, As. 1862: *Dialect of Leeds*, 405, A noted propagator of untruths is 'as big a liar as Tom Pepper'.

Big as a Dorchester butt. 1838: Holloway, *Provincialisms*, 23, The old saying, you are as big as a Dorchester butt. 1851: *Dorset Gloss.*, 4, As big as a Dorchester butt, i.e. very fat.

Big as a parson's barn. Dorset. 1869: Hazlitt, 58.

Big as bull beef; or, To look as if one had eaten bull beef. 1580: Baret, *Alvearie*, T 270, Such as … looke as though they had eaten bulbeefe. 1681: W. Robertson, *Phraseol. Generalis*, 257, He looks as big as bull beef. 1712: Motteux, *Quixote*, Pt II ch v, You may go, and be a governor, or an islander, and look as big as bull-beef an you will. 1881: Evans, *Leics. Words, etc.*, 112 (E.D.S.), 'As big as bull-beef' is a phrase equivalent to 'as proud as a pump wi' two spouts'. 1901: F. E. Taylor, *Folk-Speech of S. Lancs.*, s.v. 'Bull-beef'.

Big battalions. *See* **Battalions.**

Big in the mouth. 1917: Bridge, *Cheshire Proverbs*, 32, Big i' th' maith [given to boasting].

Bigger they come, the harder they fall, The. Usually attributed to the boxer Robert (Ruby Bob) Fitzsimmons when about to fight a heavier opponent – at least, so reported in the *Brooklyn*

Daily Eagle in August 1900. Earlier fighters such as John L. Sullivan and James J. (Gentleman Jim) Corbett have also been credited with this saying. It is based on an idea that occurs in many forms (*See e.g.* **Tree** 5.) and goes back at least to the fourth-century Latin poet, Claudian (*In Rufinum* I 22) *Tolluntur in altum Ut lapsu graviore ruant*, They are raised on high that they may come down with a heavier fall.

Bilberry. *See* **Blue** (2).

Bilbrough. *See* **Beccles.**

Bill after helve. Apparently equivalent to 'Helve after hatchet'. 1670: Ray, 164.

Billing Hill, between the valleys of Wharfe and Aire. *When Billing Hill puts on its cap, Calverley Mill will get a slap.* 1878: *Folk-Lore Record*, i 169.

Billingsgate. 1. Billingsgate language. 1654: Gayton, *Pleasant Notes Don Q.*, 60, Most bitter Billingsgate rhetorick. 1687: A. Behn, *Lucky Chance*, I ii, She … did so rail at him, that what with her Billinsgate … 1740: North, *Lives of Norths*, i 288 (Bohn), Such Billingsgate language as should not come out of the mouth of any man. 1822: Byron, in *Letters and Journals*, vi 4 (Prothero), I'll work the Laureate before I have done with him, as soon as I can muster Billingsgate therefor. 1918: Muirhead, *Blue Guide to London*, 389, The word 'Billingsgate' as a synonym for coarse language is an aspersion on the fish-porters that is alleged to have passed long since into the domain of pointless slander.

2. You shall have as much favour as at Billingsgate, for a box on the ear. 1659: Howell, 15. 1670: Ray, 215.

Billingshurst. *See* **Rudgwick.**

Billy has found a pin. 1694: Ld. Delamere, *Speech on Arbitrary and Illegal Imprisonments* [quoted in Bridge, below], In our county [Cheshire] when a man makes a great stir about a matter and it ends in nothing that is significant, we say – 'Billy has found a pin!' 1917: Bridge, *Cheshire Proverbs*, 32.

Bind so as you may unbind. 1732: Fuller, 980.

Bingham. *See* **All the world.**

Birch. *See* **Bare as the birch.**

Birchen twigs break no ribs. 1639: Clarke, 75. 1670: Ray, 61. 1732: Fuller, 6380. Cf. **Rod.**

Bird and Birds. 1. A bird in the hand is worth two in the bush. [τὰν παρεοῖσαν ἄμελγε. τί τὸν φεύγοντα διώκεις – Theocritus, xi 75.] *c.*1450: J. Capgrave, *Life of St Katharine*, (E.E.T.S.)

II iii, It is more sekyr [secure] a byrd in your fest, Than to have three in the sky above. Before 1500: in Hill, *Commonplace-Book*, 128 (E.E.T.S.), A birde in hond is better than thre in the wode. *c.*1530: J. Heywood, *Witty and Witless*, 213 (Farmer), Better one bird in hand than ten in the wood. *c.*1550: *Parl. of Byrdes*, l. 196, in Hazlitt, *Early Pop. Poetry*, iii 177, A byrde in hande is worth two in the wood. 1581: Woodes, *Confl. of Conscience*, iv, One bird in the hand is worth two in the bush. *c.*1660: in *Roxb. Ballads*, ii 44 (Hindley). 1696: T. Brown, in *Works*, iv 276 (1696). 1736: Fielding, *Pasquin*, II. 1855: Gaskell, *North and South*, ch xvii.

2. A bird may be caught with a snare that will not be shot. 1732: Fuller, 13.

3. A bird of the air shall carry it; or, A bird told me. [Eccles. x 20, For a bird of the air shall carry the voice, and that which hath wings shall tell the matter.] 1546: Heywood, *Proverbs*, Pt II ch v, I did lately heere … by one byrd that in mine eare was late chauntyng. 1583: Melbancke, *Philotinus*, sig. F3, I had a little bird, that brought me newes of it. 1598: Shakespeare, 2 *Henry IV*, V v 1652: Shirley, *Cardinal*, I i, Take heed; the Cardinal holds Intelligence with every bird i' th' air. 1736: Fielding, *Pasquin*, IV, But I have also heard a sweet bird sing … 1822: Scott, *Nigel*, ch vi 1840: Barham, *Ing. Legends*: 'St Dunstan'. 1919: A. A. Milne, *Camb. Triangle*, in *Sec. Plays*, 149 (1921), How did you know my name? *Dennis*. A little bird told me about you.

4. As the bird is, such is the nest. 1611: Cotgrave, s.v. 'Nid', Such bird, such neast. 1666: Torriano, *Piazza Univ.*, 296.

5. Birds are entangled by their feet, and men by their tongues. 1732: Fuller, 981.

6. Birds in their little nests agree. An admonition to children not to argue amongst themselves. 1715: I Watts, *Divine Songs*, 25, Birds in their little Nests agree; And 'tis a shameful Sight, When children of one Family Fall out, and chide, and fight. 868: L. M. Alcott, *Little Women*, i, 'Birds in their little nests agree,' sang Beth the peacemaker.

7. Birds of a feather flock (or fly) together. [ὡς αἰεὶ τὸν ὁμοῖον ἄγει θεὸς ὡς τὸν ὁμοῖον. – Homer, *Od.*, xvii 218. Pares vetere proverbio cum paribus facillime congregantur. – Cicero, *Sen.*, iii 7.] 1545: W. Turner, *Rescuing of Romish Fox*, B8, Byrdes of on kynde and color flok and flye allwayes together. 1578: Whetstone, *Promos and Cassandra*, sig. C1, Byrds of a fether, best flye together. 1607: Rowlands, *Diog. Lanthorne*, 43 (Hunt.Cl.), Birds of a feather and a kinde, Will still together flocke. 1665: Head and Kirkman, *English Rogue*, i 197. 1729: Fielding, *Author's Farce*, III, Men of a side Like birds of a feather Will flock together. 1850: Dickens, *Chuzzlewit*, ch iii, He has conspired against me, like the rest, and they are but birds of one feather.

8. Each bird loves to hear himself sing. 1659: Howell, *Proverbs: Brit.-Eng.*, 11.

9. He hath brought up a bird to pick out his own eyes. 1639: Clarke, 157. 1672: Walker, *Paroem.*, 53, You bring up a bird to pick out your own eye. 1732: Fuller, 1864.

10. He's in great want of a bird, that will give a groat for an owl. 1678: Ray, 101. 1732: Fuller, 2458.

11. If every bird take back its own feathers, you'll be naked. 1633: Draxe, 18, If euery birde had his owne, he should be as rich as a new shorne sheepe. 1732: Fuller, 2675.

12. Ill fare that bird that picks out the dam's eye. 1639: Clarke, 169.

13. Of all birds give me mutton. 1732: Fuller, 3695.

14. Old birds are not caught with chaff. 1481: Caxton, *Reynard*, 110 (Arber), Wenest thou thus to deceyue me … I am no byrde to be locked ne take by chaf. 1640: R. Brome, *Sparagus Garden*, IV xi, Teach 'hem to licke hony, catch birds with chaffe … 1668: Shadwell, *Sullen Lovers*, V iii, There's no catching old birds with chaff. 1713: Gay, *Wife of Bath*, I. 1852: Dickens, *Bleak House*, ch xlix, He has bought two specimens of poultry, which, if there be any truth in adages, were certainly not caught with chaff.

15. That is the bird that I would catch. 1732: Fuller, 4358.

16. The bird is known by his note, the man by his words. 1659: Howell, *Proverbs: Ital.-Eng.*, 10. 1732: Fuller, 12.

17. The bird that can sing and won't sing, must be made to sing. 1678: Ray, 343. 1681: W. Robertson, *Phraseol. Generalis*, 1133. 1888: Q.-Couch, *Troy Town*, ch i, Remember the proverb about little birds that can sing and won't sing.

18. The birds are flown. 1562: Heywood, *Three Hund. Epigr.*, No. 280.

19. There are no birds of this year in last year's nests. 1620: Shelton, *Quixote*, Pt II ch lxxiv. 1732: Fuller, 4863. 1841: Longfellow, *It is not always May*, There are no birds in last year's nest. 1906: Q.-Couch, *Cornish Window*, 5, He bade his friends look not for this year's birds in last year's nests.

20. To take the bird by its feet. 1678: Ray, 354.

21. We shall catch birds to-morrow. 1546: Heywood, *Proverbs*, Pt II ch viii 1633: Draxe, 2. *See also* **Addled egg; Build** (1); **Child** (3); **Early** (7) and (8); **Every bird; Fine** (12); **Fright a bird; Ill bird; Lion** (10); **Little and little; March** (20), (21), and (23); **Net is spread; Rough net; St Valentine** (1); and **Small birds.**

Birkenhead. *See* **Blacon Point.**

Birmingham. *See* **Sutton.**

Birstal for ringers, Heckmondwike for singers, Dewsbury for peddlers, Cleckheaton for sheddlers [swindlers]. 1878: *Folk-Lore Record*, i 174.

Birth is much but breeding more. 1639: Clarke, 103. 1670: Ray, 63. 1712: Motteux, *Quixote*, Pt II ch lxviii. 1732: Fuller, 983.

Bishop. 1. The bishop hath blessed it. 1528: Tyndale, *Obed. of Chryst. Man*, 166, When a thynge speadeth not well we borowe speach and say 'the byshope hath blessed it', because that nothynge speadeth well that they medyll withall.

2. The bishop has put his foot in it. 1528: Ibid., 166, If the podech be burned to, or the meate over rosted, we say, 'the byshope has put his fote in the potte', or 'the byshope hath played the coke', because the byshopes burn who they lust, and whosoever dis-pleaseth them. 1634: T. Heywood, *Lancs Witches*, II ... till it [burnt milk] stinke worse than the proverbe of the bishops foot. 1790: Grose, *Prov. Gloss.*, s.v. 'Bishop', The bishop has set his foot in it, a saying in the North, used for milk that is burnt-to in boiling. 1825: Brockett, *Gloss. N. Country Words*, 16. 1888: S. O. Addy, *Sheffield Gloss.*, 18 (E.D.S.). 1917: Bridge, *Cheshire Proverbs*, 112.

3. What, a bishop's wife? *eat and drink in your gloves?* This is a cryptic saying. 1678: Ray, 229.

Bishop Auckland i' Bisho' brigg, God help me! 1846–59: *Denham Tracts*, i 93 (F.L.S.).

Bisho' Brigg into Yorkshire, Out o' = Out of the frying pan into the fire. Ibid., i 77.

Bishop-Middleham; where Might rules Right. Ibid., i 93.

Bishop's Nympton. *See* quot. 1889: *N. & Q.*, 7th ser, vii 274, The local saying runs in North Devon ... Bishop's Nympton for length, South Molton for strength, And Chittlehampton for beauty [the reference is to the respective churches].

Bit. 1. A bit and a blow; sometimes with the addition, *as they feed apes.* 1638: D. Turvill, *Vade Mecum*, 81 (3rd ed.), Some againe that doe feed them, but alas! it is as the proverbe saith, with a bit and a knocke. 1672: Walker, *Paraem.*, 10, You feed me like an ape, with a bit and a knock. 1738: Swift, *Polite Convers.*, Dial. I, Why, miss, I find there is nothing but a bit and a blow with you. 1855: Robinson, *Whitby Gloss.*, 14, A bite and a buffet, a maxim, never do a good deed and then upbraid with the obligation. 'Ne'er give a bit And a buffet wi' 't'.

2. A bit in the morning is better than nothing all day; or, **than a thump on the back with a stone.** 1639: in *Berkeley MSS.*, iii 33 (1885), Better a bit then noe bread. 1670: Ray, 33. 1736: Bailey, *Dict.*, s.v. 'Bit'.

Bitch that I mean is not a dog, The. 1732: Fuller, 4426.

Bite, *verb.* **1. He bites the ear, yet seems to cry for fear.** Glos. To bite the ear, was a caress; see *Romeo and Juliet*, II iv 1639: in *Berkeley MSS.*, iii 32 (1885).

2. He that bites on every weed, must needs light on poison. 1639: Clarke, 211. 1669: *Politeuphuia*, 185. 1710: S. Palmer, *Moral Essays on Proverbs*, 24. 1732: Fuller, 2046 [with 'may' for 'must needs'].

3. If you cannot bite, never show your teeth. 1670: Ray, 63. 1736: Bailey, *Dict.*, s.v. 'Bite'.

4. Though I am bitten, I am not all eaten. 1639: Clarke, 32, Though he be bitten, he's not all eaten. 1670: Ray, 164. 1732: Fuller, 6170.

5. To bite the mare by the thumb = ? 1546: Heywood, *Proverbs*, Pt II ch vi, This biteth the mare by the thumbe, as they sey. 1611: Davies (of Hereford), *Sc. of Folly*, 43, in *Works*, ii (Grosart), Thus bitt the mare by the thumbe.

6. To bite upon the bridle. *See* **Bridle** (2).

Bite, *subs. You have taken a bite out of your own arm.* 1732: Fuller, 5925.

Biter is sometimes bit, The. [ὁ νεβρὸς τὸν λέοντα. – Lucian, *Dial. Mort.*, viii.] 1693: D'Urfey, *Richmond Heiress*, Epil., Once in an age the biter should be bit. 1710: Ward, *Nuptial*

Dialogues, ii 179, I think she merits equal praise That has the wit to bite the biter. 1880: Spurgeon, *Ploughman's Pictures*, 16, Biters deserve to be bitten.

Biting and scratching. *See* **Cat** (14).

Bitter. 1. Bitter as gall. *c.*1305: in Wright's *Pol. Songs John to Edw. II*, 193 (Camden S.), Ther hi habbeth dronke bittrere then the galle. 1468: *Cov. Mysteries*, 233 (SH.S.), My mowthe is byttyr as galle. 1581: B. Rich, *Farewell*, 38 (SH.S.), Whose taste I finde more bitter now then gall. 1623: Webster, *Devil's Law-Case*, I ii, *Iol.* Bitter as gall. 1716: Ward, *Female Policy*, 30. 1892: Heslop, *Northumb. Words*, 311, As bitter as gaa [gall].

2. Bitter as soot. *c.*1305: in Wright's *Pol. Songs John to Edw. II*, 195 (Camden S.), Hit falleth the Kyng of Fraunce bittrore then the sote. *c.*1374: Chaucer, *Troylus*, iii 1194, To whom this tale sucre be or soot [i.e. sweet or bitter]. 1758–67: Sterne, *Trist. Shandy*, Vol IV ch xiii (1788), And now thy mouth … is as bitter, I dare say, as soot. 1857–72: Buckland, *Curios. of Nat. Hist.*, iii 29, They are as bitter as soot, if you eats 'em raw.

3. Bitter pills may have wholesome effects, [*c.*1374: Chaucer, *Troylus*, iii 1215, And for to han gladnesse, Men drinken often peyne and greet distresse.] 1732: Fuller, 985.

4. He who hath bitter in his mouth, spits not all sweet. 1640: Herbert, *Jac. Prudentum*. 1670: Ray, 3. 1732: Fuller, 2387 [with 'breast' instead of 'mouth'].

5. That which was bitter to endure, may be sweet to remember. 1732: Fuller, 4385.

Bittern. 1. A bittern makes no good hawk. 1611: Davies (of Hereford), *Sc. of Folly*, 42, in *Works*, ii (Grosart).

2. To roar like a bittern at a seg-root [sedge]. 1883: Burne, *Shropsh. Folk-Lore*, 594.

Blab, *subs. He that is a blab is a scab.* 1639: Clarke, 132. 1670: Ray, 63. 1732: Fuller, 6296, He that is a blab is a meer scab.

Blab, *verb. Blab it wist and out it must.* 15th cent.: *Harl. MS.* 3362 (V. Lean), Labbe hyt whyste, and owt yt must. 1546: Heywood, *Proverbs*, Pt I ch x 1633: Draxe, 16, He cannot hold, but all must out.

Black, *adj.* **1. A black plum is as sweet as a white.** 1633: Draxe, 15, A blacke raisin as good as a white. 1670: Ray, 63. 1732: Fuller, 986, Black plums may eat as sweet as white.

2. A black shoe makes a merry heart. 1659: Howell, 18. 1670: Ray, 216.

3. A black woman hath turpentine in her. 1659: Howell, *Letters*, ii 666 (Jacobs).

4. Although I am black, I am not the devil. 1595: Peele, *Old Wives Tale*, sig. D3.

5. Black as a coal. *c.*1000: *Sax. Leechd.*, ii 332 (OED), And swa sweart swa col. *c.*1260: *King Horn* (Camb.), l. 590 (Hall), Also blak so eny cole. Before 1300: *Cursor M.*, l. 22489. *c.*1386: Chaucer, *Knight's Tale*, l.1834, As blak he lay as any cole. *c.*1450: *Partonope*, l. 3918 (E.E.T.S.), Blak as cole than was his hors. 1599: Breton, in *Works*, ii *c.*14 (Grosart), The other as blacke as a coale. 1640: Tatham, in *Dram. Works*, 20 (1879). 1819: Byron, *Don Juan*, can. iv st. 94, With eyes … black and burning as a coal. 1860: Reade, *Cloister and Hearth*, ch liv., Else our hearts were black as coal.

6. Black as a crow (or **crake**). *c.*1320: *Horn Childe*, l. 1049, in Hall's *King Horn* (1901), Blac as ani crawe. *c.*1386: Chaucer, *Knight's Tale*, l. 1834, Blak he lay as any … crowe. *c.*1540: Bale, *King Johan*, Act I l. 88, I shall cawse the Pope to curse the as blacke as a crowe. 1610: Shakespeare, *Wint. Tale*, IV iv, Cypress black as e'er was crowe. 1716: Ward, *Female Policy*, 86, If brown, think her as black as a crow. 1828: Carr, *Craven Dialect*, i 91, Crake, a crow, as black as a crake. 1876: C. C. Robinson, *Mid-Yorks Gloss.*, 26 (E.D.S.), As black as a crake.

7. Black as a raven. *c.*1300: Robert of Brunne, tr. Langtoft's *Chron.*, 295 (Hearne), His stede was blak as rauen. 1663: Killigrew, *Thomaso*, Pt II Act I sc ii, It keeps him as black as a raven. 1720: Gay, *Trivia*, bk ii l 198, Black as the … glossy raven's back.

8. Black as a sloe. 14th cent.: *Guy of Warwick*, l. 506 (E.E.T.S.), Guy they fonde as blak as sloo. *c.*1386: Chaucer, *Miller's Tale*, l. 60. 15th cent.: *Torrent of Portyngale*, 17 (E.E.T.S.), Ys fytte [his feet] blac ase slon. 1567: Golding, *Ovid*, bk ii l. 315, His wares as blacke as any slo. 1685: *Roxb. Ballads*, viii 418 (B.S.), Hair black as a sloe. 1727: Gay, *Fables*, 1st ser, No. 3, l. 16, The mother's eyes as black as sloes. 1823: Moor, *Suffolk Words*, 363, Her eyes are as black as sloons [sloes]. 1894: R.L.S., *St Ives*, ch xxx.

9. Black as hell. 1506: Guylforde, *Pylgrymage*, 53 (Camden S.), It is comenly derke as hell. 1590: Spenser, *F. Q.*, I viii 355, But all a deepe descent, as dark as hell. 1600: in *Lyrical Poems*, 66 (Percy S.), Aire, made to shine, as blacke as hell shall prove. 1825: Scott, *Talisman*, ch xv, If his treachery be as black as hell.

10. Black as ink. *c.*1510: A. Barclay, *Egloges*, 30 (Spens.S.), At euery tempest they be as blacke as inke. 1590: Spenser, *F. Q.*, I i 201, Deformed monsters, fowle, and blacke as inke. *c.*1685: Aubrey, *Nat. Hist. Wilts*, 21 (1847), Which … became immediately as black as inke. 1721: D'Urfey, *Two Queens of Brentford*, IV, Whose sordid soul, as black as ink … 1893: R.L.S., *Ebb-Tide*, ch i, Clouds … black as ink-stains. 1901: Raymond, *Idler Out of Doors*, 7, The tall elm-top that draws, as black as ink, its tracery of naked limbs.

11. Black as jet. 1412–20: Lydgate, *Troy Book*, bk ii l. 987, It cometh out of Ethiope and Ynde, Blak as is get. 1590: Marlowe, *Tamburlaine*, Pt II Act I sc iii 1682: Evelyn, *Diary*, 19 June, Their nails and teeth as black as jet. 1705: Philips, *Splendid Shilling*, l. 20. 1872: A. Dobson, in *Poet. Works*, 109 (1923), Circling a silky curl as black as jet.

12. Black as Newgate knocker. *See* **Newgate.**

13. Black as soot. 1678: Ray, 281.

14. Black as the devil. *c.*1580: Spelman, *Dialogue*, 42 (Roxb.Cl), His face was as black as a devill in a playe. 1670: Ray, 203. 1754: Berthelson, *Eng.-Danish Dict.*, s.v. 'As'.

15. Black as the devil's nutting-bag. 1866: Gilpin, *Songs* (Cumberland), 393 (W.), Her smock's leyke auld Nick's nuttin' bag. 1879: Henderson, *Folk-Lore N. Counties*, 96, A proverb is current there [Sussex], 'As black as the de'il's nutting-bag'. 1899: *N. & Q.*, 9th ser, iv 478 [saying common in N. Lincs]. 1900: *N. & Q.*, 9th ser, v 38 and 197 [saying common in Berks, Somerset, and Suffolk].

16. Black as thunder. 1839: Planché, *Extravag.*, ii 56 (1879), He looks as black as thunder. 1922: Weyman, *Ovington's Bank*, ch iii, He's in his room and as black as thunder.

17. Black fleet of Norway. *See* **Boston's Bay;** and **England** (11).

18. Black hen. *See* **Hen** (1).

19. Black Jack rides a good horse = Zinc ore gives good promise for copper. 1865: Hunt, *Pop. Romances W. of Eng.*, 194 (1896). 1902: Wright, *Eng. Dial. Dict.*, iii 239.

20. Black lad Monday = Monday in Easter-week. 1846: Denham, *Proverbs*, 32 (Percy S.).

21. Black man. *See* **Red hair.**

22. Black men are pearls in ladies' eyes; or, **A black man is a jewel, etc.** 1599: Chapman, *Hum. Day's Mirth*, sc viii, Oh, sir, black is a pearl in a woman's eye. *c.*1623: B.&F., *Love's Cure*, III iv, The fairest ladies like the blackest men. 1623: Shakespeare, *Two Gent.*, V ii 1670: Ray, 51. 1732: Fuller, 16.

23. No one can say black is my (or **his,** or **your**) **eye** (or **nail**). 1402: Hoccleve, in *Minor Poems*, 76 (E.E.T.S.), That when thow twynnest fro hir companye, another cometh and blered ys thyn ye! 1412: Hoccleve, *Regement*, st. 404, l. 2823 (E.E.T.S.), No man seith onës that blak is his eye. 1583: Stubbes, *Anat. of Abuses*, 88 (N.Sh.S.), And yet maie no man saie blackie is their eye. 1625: Jonson, *Staple of News*, I ii, He … can commit whom he will, and what he will … and no man say black is his eye, but laugh at him. 1711: Steele, *Spectator*, No. 79, The most insolent of all creatures to her friends and domesticks, upon no other pretence in nature but that … no one can say blacke is her eye. 1761: J. Reed, *Reg. Office*, I, in Inchbald's *Farces*, iii 145 (1815), I defy ony body … to say black's my nail. 1771: Smollett, *Clinker*, in *Works*, vi 125 (1817), I challenge you to say black is the white of my eye. 1828: Carr, *Craven Dialect*, i 136, 'Black's my eye', no one can impute blame to me. 1889: Peacock, *Manley, etc.*, *Gloss.*, 52 (E.D.S.), Noäbody niver so much as said black's my naail to me [said anything evil], when I liv'd at Burringham.

24. The black ox treads on one's foot. 1546: Heywood, *Proverbs*, Pt I, ch vii, It was yet but hony moone; The blacke oxe had not trode on his nor hir foote. 1584: Lyly, *Sapho and Phao*, I 199 (1858), Now crowes foote is on her eye, and the black oxe hath trod on her foot. 1633: Jonson, *Tale of a Tub*, IV v, Well, young squire, The black ox never trod yet on your foot. 1738: Swift, *Polite Convers.*, Dial. I, Poor creature! the black ox has set his foot upon her already. 1822: Scott, *Nigel*, ch ii 1883: Burne, *Shropsh. Folk-Lore*, 209, 'The black ox has not trodden on you' – i.e. care has not come near you – is an old Shropshire saying.

25. Those that eat black pudding will dream of the devil. 1738: Swift, *Polite Convers.*, Dial. II.

26. To have the black dog on one's back. 1778: Mrs Thrale, in *Piozzi Letters*, ii 32, I have lost what made my happiness … but the black dog shall not make prey of both my master and myself. 1816: Scott, *Antiquary*, ch vi, Sir Arthur has got the black dog on his back again. 1889: Peacock, *Manley, etc., Gloss.*, 51 (E.D.S.), 'He's gotten th' black dog on his back this mornin'', that is, he is in a bad temper.

See also **Dark.**

Black, *subs.* **1. Above black there is no colour, and above salt no savour.** 1578: Florio, *First Fruites*, fo. 33. 1629: *Booke of Meery Riddles,* Prov. 120. 1659: Howell, *Proverbs: Ital.-Eng.*, 7.
2. Black will take no other hue. 1546: Heywood, *Proverbs*, Pt II ch ix 1593: Peele, *Edward I*, sc viii 1681: W. Robertson, *Phraseol. Generalis*, 262. 1754: Berthelson, *Eng.-Danish Dict.*, s.v. 'Black'.
3. In black and white. *c.*1440: Lydgate, *Fall of Princes*, bk i l. 465, Hauyng no colours but onli whit and blak, To the tragedies which that I shal write. 1596: Jonson, *Ev. Man in his Humour*, IV iii, I have it here in black and white [pulls out the warrant]. 1658: Cowley, *Cutter of Coleman Street*, I v, I saw it from a good hand beyond sea, under black and white. 1678: Bunyan, *Pilgr. Progress*, Author's Apology. 1740: North, *Examen*, 404, A wicked paragraph it is, as ever was put in black and white. 1823: Scott, *St Ronan's*, ch xxiii 1886: Hardy, *Casterbridge*, ch ix. *See also* **Two blacks.**

Blackamoor. To wash (or make) the blackamoor white. [Laterem lavare. – Terence, *Phorm.*, 186.] 1543: Becon, in *Early Works*, 49 (P.S.), Here, therefore, do ye nothing else than, as the common proverb is, go about to make an Ethiop white. 1604: Dekker, *Honest Whore*, Pt II Act I sc i, This is the blackamoor that by washing was turned white. 1673: Wycherley, *Gent. Danc.-Master*, IV i, You wash the blackamoor white, in endeavouring to make a Spaniard of a monsieur. 1748: Richardson, *Clarissa*, ii 160 (1785), I should suspect the whole to be a plot set on foot to wash a blackamoor white. 1853: Planché, *Extravag.*, iv 280 (1879), If any one could wash a blackamoor white It would be Mrs Beecher Stowe.

Blackberries, Plentiful as. 1596: Shakespeare, 1 *Henry IV*, II iv, If reasons were as plentie as blackberries. 1690: *Reason of Mr Bays changing his Religion*, Pt II, p. 35, Were reasons as cheap as blackberries. 1868: *Quart. Review*, cxxv 231,

Parallels are 'as plentiful as blackberries'. 1886: Hardy, *Casterbridge*, ch xvi, Earthworks … were as common as blackberries hereabout. *See also* **Devil** (82).

Blackberry summer. 1846: Denham, *Proverbs*, 57 (Percy S.). 1883: Cope, *Hants Words*, 8 (E.D.S.), Blackberry-summer. Fine weather experienced at the end of September and the beginning of October when blackberries are ripe.

Blacksmith. It is much like a blacksmith with a white silk apron. 1732: Fuller, 2980.

Blackthorn winter. 1789: White, *Selborne*, ii 292 (1813) (OED), The harsh rugged weather obtaining at this season, is called by the country people blackthorn-winter. 1838: Holloway, *Provincialisms*, 13, Blackthorn winter. The cold which is generally experienced at the latter end of April and beginning of May, when the black-thorn is in blossom. 1884: H. Friend, *Flowers and Fl. Lore*, 214.

Blacon Point. *See* quot. 1917: Bridge, *Cheshire Proverbs*, 59, From Blacon Point to Hilbre, A squirrel might leap from tree to tree. [In *N. & Q.*, 4th ser, xi 13 (1873), is the variant, 'From Birkenhead to far Hilbree A squirrel could leap from tree to tree'.]

Blade to haft, True as. 1823: Scott, *Q. Durward*, ch xxiii, I will be true to you as blade to haft, as our cutlers say.

Blake [yellow] **as a paigle** [cowslip or marigold]. [1530: Palsgrave, s.v., Blake, wan of colour.] 1678: Ray, 355. 1683: Meriton, *Yorkshire Ale*, 83 (1697). 1834: Toone, *Glossary*, s.v. 'Paigle'. 1866: Mrs Lynn Linton, *Lizzie Lorton*, ii 217, As blake as marygowds. 1884: H. Friend, *Flowers and Fl. Lore*, 210.

Blake as butter. 1876: C. C. Robinson, *Mid-Yorks Gloss.*, 10 (E.D.S.).

Blames. *He that blames would buy.* 1640: Herbert, *Jac. Prudentum*. 1732: Fuller, 2383, He who findeth fault, meaneth to buy.

Bledlow, Bucks. *See* quot. 1869: Hazlitt, 400, They who live and do abide, Shall see Bledlow church fall into the Lyde.

Bless the king and all his men. A common exclamation when surprised and startled. 1862: *Dialect of Leeds*, 251.

Blessed is the corpse. *See* **Happy.**

Blessing, *subs.* **1. Blessings are not valued till they are gone.** 1732: Fuller, 989.

2. They have need of a blessing that kneel to a thistle. 1639: Clarke, 13. 1670: Ray, 63. 1732: Fuller, 4964.

Blessing of your heart. *See* **Ale** (3).

Blest is the bride. *See* **Happy.**

Blind, *adj.* **1. A blind man cannot (or should not) judge colours.** *c.*1374: Chaucer, *Troylus,* bk ii l. 21, A blind man can nat iuggen wel in hewis. 1412: Hoccleve, *Regement,* 36 (E.E.T.S.), The blynde man of coloures al wrong deemeth. 1530: Palsgrave, 511, A blynde man can nat deme no coulours. 1637: Breton, in *Works,* ii h 44 (Grosart). 1759: Warburton, in *Garrick Corresp.,* i 93 (1831), Proposing an emendation to the generality of those they call scholars, was desiring a blind man to judge of colours.

2. A blind man will not thank you for a looking-glass. 1732: Fuller, 18.

3. A blind man would be glad to see it. 1738: Swift, *Polite Convers.,* Dial. I, A blind man would be glad to see that. 1894: Northall, *Folk Phrases of Four Counties* (E.D.S.), A blind man on a galloping horse would be glad to see it. Cf. Nos. 15 and 18.

4. A man's blind side. 1606: Chapman, *Gent. Usher,* I i, We'll follow the blind side of him. 1681: A. Behn, *Rover,* Pt II I i, The rascals have a blind side as all conceited coxcombs have. 1742: Fielding, *Andrews,* bk iii ch v, If this good man had an enthusiasm, or what the vulgar call a blind side, it was this. 1869: Spurgeon, *John Ploughman,* ch xxi, In the hope of getting on the parson's blind side when the blankets were given away at Christmas.

5. A pebble and a diamond are alike to a blind man. 1732: Fuller, 340.

6. As one blind man said to another, let's behold ourselves. 1612: Shelton, *Quixote,* Pt I bk iv ch xxiii 1694: D'Urfey, *Quixote,* Pt I Act V sc ii 1869: Hazlitt, 258, Let me see, as the blind man said.

7. As the blind man catcheth the hare. 1638: Taylor (Water-Poet), *Bull, Beare,* 10, in *Works,* 3rd coll. (Spens.S.), A blinde man may be taken with a hare [purposely reversed]. 1659: W. Cole, in *Harl. Miscell.,* iv 309 (1745), And so they are as capable to do equity therein, as a blind man to shoot a hare.

8. As the blind man shot the crow. 1546: Heywood, *Proverbs,* Pt II ch ix, As the blind man casts his staffe, or shootes the crow. 1605: Armin, *Foole vpon Foole,* 11 (Grosart), Yet now and then a blinde man may hit a crow. 1732: Fuller, 1393. 1830: Forby, *Vocab. E. Anglia,* 428, Hitty-missy, as the blind man shot the crow.

9. As wary as a blind horse. 1732: Fuller, 745.

10. Better to be blind than to see ill. 1640: Herbert, *Jac. Prudentum.*

11. Blind as a bat. 1639: Clarke, 52, As blind as a bat at noone. *c.*1780: in *Poems on Costume,* 262 (Percy S.), Which makes her as blind as a bat. 1889: J. Nicholson, *Folk Speech E. Yorks,* 16.

12. Blind as a beetle. 1549: Latimer, *Seven Sermons,* 90 (Arber), In this wysdome he is as blynd as a beatel. 1647: in *Polit. Ballads,* 47 (Percy S.), Jack Maynard is a loyall blade, yet blind as any beetle. Before 1704: T. Brown, *Works,* i 236 (1760). 1786: Mrs Cowley, *Sch. for Greybeards,* V ii, Oh, what a beetle, what a blind bat I have been! 1860: Reade, *Cloister and Hearth,* ch l. 1881: Evans, *Leics. Words,* 102 (E.D.S.), 'As blind as a beetle' is a very common simile, the cockchafer being the beetle referred to. 1892: Heslop, *Northumb. Words,* 60 (E.D.S.), Bittle, a beetle, or wooden beater for beating flax or linen clothes. 'As blind as a bittle', a very common expression.

13. Blind as a buzzard. [1377: Langland, *Plowman,* B, x 267, I rede eche a blynde bosarde.] 1577: Kendall, *Flow. of Epigr.,* 143 (Spens.S.), When buzzard blynd thou canst not see what is before thy feete. 1681: Otway, *Soldier's Fortune,* IV iii, I'll … weep till blind as buzzard. 1730: Bailey, *Eng. Dict.,* s.v. 'Buzzard', A stupid senseless fellow; as a blind buzzard. 1823: Moor, *Suffolk Words,* 61, We have the phrase 'as blind as a buzzard'. 1886: Swainson, *Folk-Lore of Brit. Birds,* 133 (F.L.S.), The saying … 'as blind as a buzzard' does not refer to the bird of that name, which is extremely quick-sighted, but rather to the beetle, from the buzzing sound of its flight.

14. Blind as a mole. 1584: B. R., *Euterpe,* 68 (Lang), In the water as blinde as a moale. 1658: Willsford, *Natures Secrets,* 2, When they are as blind as moles. 1785: Wolcot, in *Works,* i 84 (1795). 1823: Scott, *Peveril,* ch xxxii.

15. Blind George. *See* quots. 1633: Jonson, *Tale of a Tub,* II i, That I would fain zee, quoth the blind George of Holloway. 1678: Ray, 268, That would I fain see, said blind George of Hollowee. Cf. Nos. 3 and 18.

16. Blind harpers. *See* **Have among you.**

17. Blind horse. *See* No. 9; *also* **Afterthought;** and **Nod.**

18. Blind Hugh. *See* quots. 1533: J. Heywood, *Pardoner and Friar*, in Hazlitt, *Old Plays*, i 232 (1874), Marry that I would see, quod blind Hew. 1639: in *Berkeley MSS.*, iii 30 (1885), I w'ud I c'ud see't, ka' blind Hugh. 1738: Swift, *Polite Convers.*, Dial. I, Would I could see it, quoth blind Hugh. Cf. Nos. 3 and 15.

19. Blind man's holiday. 1599: Nashe, *Lenten Stuffe*, in *Works*, v 263 (Grosart), What will not blinde Cupid doe in the night which is his blindmans holiday? 1690: *New Dict. Canting Crew*, sig. B6, Blind-man's-holiday, when it is too dark to see to work. 1738: Swift, *Polite Convers.*, Dial. III. 1828: Carr, *Craven Dialect*, i 38. 1891: Q.-Couch, *Noughts and Crosses*, 109, Day was breakin' – a sort of blind man's holiday.

20. Blind whelps. *See* **Hasty bitch.**

21. He's so blind he can't see a hole through a ladder, or, **the holes of a sieve.** 1620: Shelton, *Quixote*, Pt II ch i, How blind is he that sees not light through the bottom of a meal-sieve! 1694: D'Urfey, *Quixote*, Pt I Act I sc i [the holes of a sieve]. 1864: 'Cornish Proverbs', in *N. & Q.*, 3rd ser, vi 494, He's so blind he can't see a hole through a nine-foot ladder.

22. It is a blind man's question to ask, why those things are loved which are beautiful. 1855: Bohn, 426.

23. Men are blind in their own cause. 1546: Heywood, *Proverbs*, Pt II ch v, Folk oft tymes are most blind in their owne cause. 1683: Meriton, *Yorkshire Ale*, 85 (1697), Men are blind in their awn cause.

24. The blind man's wife needs no painting. 1659: Howell, *Proverbs: Span.-Eng.*, 4. 1670: Ray, 3. 1732: Fuller, 992.

25. There's none so blind as those that will not see. 1546: J. Heywood, *Dialogues of Proverbs* II ix, Who is so deafe, or so blynde, as is hee, That wilfully will nother here nor see. 1547: Borde, *Brev. of Helthe*, bk ii fo. vi v°, Who is blynder than he yt wyl nat se. 1670: Ray, 64, Who so blind as he that will not see? 1671: *Westm. Drollery*, 20 (Ebsworth), Ther's none so blind As those that will not see. 1738: Swift, *Polite Convers.*, Dial. III. 1859: Sala, *Twice Round the Clock*, 3 a.m., Homer not unfrequently nods in

Scotland Yard. 'None are so blind as those that won't see', whisper the wicked.

26. What matters it to a blind man, that his father could see? 1855: Bohn, 555.

Blind, *subs.* **1. The blind eat many a fly.** *c.*1430: Lydgate, *Ballade*, in Skeat's *Chaucer*, vii 295, The blind et many a fly. Before 1529: Skelton, in *Works*, i 213 (Dyce), But, as the man sayes, The blynde eteth many a flye. 1609: Rowlands, *Whole Crew of Kind Gossips*, 19 (Hunt.Cl.). 1671: Head and Kirkman, *English Rogue*, ii 88. 1732: Fuller, 4428. 1881: Evans, *Leics. Words*, 300 (E.D.S.), Blind i' th' eye Eats many a fly.

2. When the blind leads the blind, both fall into the ditch. [Luke vi 39.] *c.*897 Alfred *Gregory's Pastoral Care*, (E.E.T.S.) 1, Gif se blinda thone blindan laet, he feallath begen [both] on aenne pytt. *c.*1300: *Body and Soul* (1889), Ac hwanne the blinde lat the blinde, In dike he fallen bothe two. *c.*1450: in *Reliq. Antiquae*, ii 238 (1843), For now the bysom [blind] ledys the blynde. 1583: Melbancke, *Philotimus*, sig. Y1, In the ditch falls the blind that is led by the blind. 1699: Farquhar, *Love and a Bottle*, V i, When the blind leads the blind, no wonder they both fall into – matrimony. 1712: Motteux, *Quixote*, Pt II ch xiii. *See also* **Kingdom** (2).

Blindworm. *See* **Adder.**

Blister on one's tongue, A. 1732: Fuller, 1127, Common fame [= liar] hath a blister on its tongue. 1738: Swift, *Polite Convers.*, Dial. I, I have a blister on my tongue; yet I don't remember I told a lye.

Blood. 1. Blood is thicker than water. [1412–20: Lydgate, *Troy Book*, bk iii l. 2071, For naturelly blod will ay of kynde Draw vn-to blod, wher he may it fynde.] 1857: Hughes, *Tom Brown*, Pt I ch i, With them there is nothing like the Browns, to the third and fourth generation. 'Blood is thicker than water', is one of their pet sayings. 1871: G. Eliot, *Middlemarch*, ch xxxii.

2. Blood without groats is nothing. 1665: J. Wilson, *Projectors*, II, He … compares 'em [great matches] to an ill pudding – all blood and no fat. 1670: Ray, 166, He hath good bloud if he had but groats to him. Cheshire. Good parentage if he had but wealth. 1732: Fuller, 1703, Good blood makes poor pudding without suet. 1825: Brockett, *Gloss. of N. Country Words*, 87, Hence the northern proverb, 'blood without groats is nothing', meaning that family without fortune is of no consequence. 1828: Carr, *Craven Dialect*, i 200. 1917: Bridge, *Cheshire Proverbs*, 68 [as in 1670].

3. Human blood is all of a colour. 1732: Fuller, 2560.

4. The blood of the martyrs is the seed of the church. [Semen est sanguis Christianorum. – Tertullian, *Apologet.*, l.] 1560: J. Pilkington *Aggeus the Prophet*, U4v, Cipriane writes that the bloud of Martirs is the seede of the Church. 1562: J. Wigand, *De Neutralibus et Mediis*, M8v, It is a very goodly and a most true saying: Christian mennes bloud is a sede, and in what felde so ever is sowed, ther spring up Christian men most plenteously thick. 1630: T. Adams, *Works*, 205, So the bloud of martyrs seedes the church. Before 1680: Butler, *Remains*, i 135 (1759), The ancient churches, and the best, By their own martyrs blood increas'd. 1746: *Foundl. Hosp. for Wit*, No. III, p. 41.

5. You can't get blood (or **water**) **out of a stone.** [Nam tu aquam a pumice nunc postulas, Qui ipsus sitiat. – Plautus, *Pers.*, I i 42.] 1599: J. Weever, *Epigrammes*, 17 (1911), For who'le wrest water from a flintie stone? 1666: Torriano, *Piazza Univ.*, 161, There's no getting of bloud out of that wall. 1836: Marryat, *Japhet*, ch iv, I have often heard it said, there's no getting blood out of a turnip. 1865: Dickens, *Mutual Friend*, bk iv ch xv 1917: Bridge, *Cheshire Proverbs*, 158, You cannot whip blood out of a post.

Blossom. *That which doth blossom in the spring, will bring forth fruit in the autumn.* 1633: Draxe, 13. 1670: Ray, 3. 1732: Fuller, 3544, No autumn-fruit without spring-blossoms.

Blot. 1. A blot is no blot till it be hit. A 'blot' in backgammon is an exposed piece which is liable to capture. 1664: J. Wilson, *The Cheats*, V iii, I will join with you in anything, provided always you carry it prudently, for fear of scandal. A blot is no blot till it be hit. 1712: Motteux, *Quixote*, Pt II ch xliii. 1820: Scott, *Fam. Letters*, ii 97 (1894), But then a blot is not a blot till hit.

2. Cleaning a blot with blotted fingers maketh a greater blur. 1732: Fuller, 1112.

Blow, *verb.* **1. Blow devil, the more wind the better boat.** 1724: Defoe, *Tour*, Lett. II, p. 13 [cited as 'a rude sailor's proverb'].

2. Blow first and sip afterwards. 1678: Ray, 103. 1732: Fuller, 995.

3. Blow out the marrow and throw the bone to the dogs. 1678: Ray, 343.

4. Blow, Smith, and you'll get money. 1732: Fuller, 997.

5. Blow the wind high, or blow the wind low. It bloweth good to Hawley's hoe. Plymouth. 1849: Halliwell, *Pop. Rhymes*, 194. 1897: Norway, *H. and B. in Devon, etc.*, 115 [with 'still' for 'good'. and 'hawe' for 'hoe'].

6. Blow thy own pottage and not mine. 1732: Fuller, 998.

7. He can't neither blow nor strike. A blacksmith's description of a useless person. 1926: *Devonsh. Assoc. Trans.*, lvii. 252.

8. He that blows in the dust fills his eyes with it. 1640: Herbert, *Jac. Prudentum*. 1694: D'Urfey, *Quixote*, Pt I Act IV sc i, He that blows in the dust will make himself blind. 1732: Fuller, 2048.

9. To blow at the coal. *c.*1350: Rolle de Hampole, *Prose Treatises*, No. xi, p. 33 (E.E.T.S.), Bot habyde and suffire a while, and go blawe at the fyre, that es, first do thi werkes, and go than allane to thi prayers and thi meditacyons. *c.*1380: *Sir Ferumbras*, 74 (E.E.T.S.), We haue a game in this contray to blowen atte glede [the 'game' is described in the text, ll. 2230–43]. 1485: Caxton, *Charles the Grete*, 119 (E.E.T.S.), By my fayth, syr duc, ye can wel playe and blowe atte cole. *c.*1530: *Detection ... of Dice Play*, 6 (Percy S.), Let them that be acold blow the coals, for I am already on the sure side. 1633: Draxe, 29, Let him that is cold blow at the coale. 1694: *Terence made English*, 11, Were it not much better to try if ye can put that love out of your head, than to indulge your passion thus, stand blowing o' the cole, and to no purpose neither. 1732: Fuller, 3184, Let him that is cold blow the fire. 1837: Mrs Palmer, *Devonsh. Dialect*, 31, To blow a coal, is to make mischief or sow dissension between neighbours.

10. To blow hot and cold. [Simul flare sorbereque baud factu facilest. – Plautus, *Most.*, 791.] 1577: Grange, *Golden Aphroditis*, sig. D2, Out of one mouthe commeth bothe hotte and colde. 1619: H. Hutton, *Follies Anat.*, 12 (Percy S.), Which, Gnato like, doth blowe both hot and cold. 1692: L'Estrange, Aes*op*, 219 (3rd ed.), The old adage of blowing hot and cold; which is taken for the mark and character of a dissembler. 1740: North, *Examen*, 115, So apt are ill men to blow hot and cold. 1853: Dickens, in *Letters*, iii 139 (1882).

11. To blow one's own trumpet. 1799: T. Knight, *Turnpike Gate*, I i, in Inchbald, *Farces*, iii 72 (1815), Or I should not blush so often as I do, by blowing the trumpet of my own praise. 1844: Planché, *Extravag.*, ii 287 (1879), The fellow Blows his own trumpet. 1920: W. H. Hudson, *Dead Man's Plack*, ch ii, The people of her own country, who were great … at blowing their own trumpets.

12. To go blow one's flute. *See* **Pipe in an ivy leaf.**

Blow, *subs. A blow with a reed makes a noise, but hurts not.* 1732: Fuller, 20.

Bloxham for length, Adderbury for strength, but King's Sutton for beauty. Warwickshire church spires. 1878: *N. & Q.*, 5th ser, ix 175.

Bloxwich Bull. *See* quot. 1867: Timbs, *Nooks and Corners*, 261, [The bull to be baited was stolen by a joker, and the expectant crowd were disappointed.] This circumstance gave rise to a local proverb still in use. When great expectations are baffled, the circumstance is instinctively likened to 'the Bloxwich bull'.

Blue, *adj.* **1. Blue as a mazzard.** W. Cornwall, 19th cent. (Mr C. Lee).

2. Blue as a wimberry (bilberry). 1600: Shakespeare, *Merry Wives*, V v, There pinch the maids as blue as bilberry. 1901: F. E. Taylor, *Lancs Sayings*, 1, As blue as a wimberry. 1917: Bridge, *Cheshire Proverbs*, 10.

3. Blue veins in the nose. 1865: Hunt, *Pop. Romances W. of Eng.*, 431 (1896), The old lady of the house had just told her that the child could not live long, because he had a blue vein across his nose. 1889: *N. & Q.*, 7th ser, vii 216, If he has blue veins on the nose, He'll never wear his wedding clothes (Somerset). Born with a blue mark over her nose, She never will live to wear wedding clothes (Worcs.).

4. Once in a blue moon. 1528: Roy and Barlowe, *Rede me, etc.*, 114 (Arber), Yf they saye the mone is belewe, We must beleve that it is true. 1607: Dekker, *Knight's Conjuring*, 25 (Percy S.), She would have trickes (once in a moone) to put the diuell out of his wits. 1880: Braddon, *Barbara*, iii 8, I suppose you would have sent ma a ten-pound note once in a blue moon. 1920: A. G. Bradley, *Book of the Severn*, 18.

5. There may be blue and better blue. 1732: Fuller, 4940.

6. Three blue beans in a blue bladder. 1595: Peele, *Old Wives Tale*, sig. Diii, Three blue beanes in a blue bladder, rattle, bladder, rattle. 1600: Dekker, *Old Fortunatus*, I ii [as in 1595]. 1652: in *Catch that Catch can*, As there be three blew beans in a blew bladder, And thrice three rounds in a long ladder … 1687: Aubrey, *Gentilisme*, 12 (F.L.S.) [as in 1595]. 1715: Prior, *Alma*, can. i l. 29, They say … That, putting all his words together, 'Tis three blue beans in one blue bladder. 1823: Moor, *Suffolk Words*, 23, [as in 1595] – thrice repeated, is as old a frolicsome sort of Suffolk shibboleth as I can recollect; and is still frequently heard.

Blunt wedge will do it, where sometimes a sharp ax will not, A. 1732: Fuller, 19.

Blurt, master constable. 1602: Middleton, *Blurt, Master Constable* [title]. 1659: Howell, 14, Blurt, Mr Constable: spoken in derision. 1855: Kingsley, *West. Ho!*, ch xxx, Blurt for him, sneak-up! say I.

Blush like a black dog, To. 1579: Gosson, *Apol. of Sch. of Abuse*, 75 (Arber), You shall see we will make him to blush like a blacke dogge, when he is graveled. *c.*1590: *Plaine Percevall*, 13 (1860), He is given to blush no more then my black dog. *c.*1591: Shakespeare, *Titus Andr.*,V i 1694: Motteux, *Rabelais*, bk v ch xxviii 1738: Swift, *Polite Convers.*, Dial. I [with 'blue' for 'black'].

Blushing is a sign of grace. 1595: *A Quest of Enquirie*, 4 (Grosart), Margaret blushing (for she hath a little grace yet left her). 1605: R. T., *Sch. of Slovenrie*, 96, When guiltie men beginne to blush, it is a signe of grace. 1670: Ray, 64, Blushing is vertues colour. 1738: Swift, *Polite Convers.*, Dial. I, Well, however, blushing is some sign of grace.

Blustering night, a fair day, A. 1640: Herbert, *Jac. Prudentum.*

Bo to a goose (or **mouse**), **To say.** 1588: *Mar-Prelate's Epistle*, 60 (1843), He is not able to say bo to a goose. 1610; Rowlands, *Martin Markall*, 15 (Hunt.Cl.), He neuer durst say so much as boh to a mouse. 1664: *Wits Recr.*, Epigr. 749, You see, I can cry Bo unto a goose. 1748: Smollett, *Rod. Random*, ch liv. 1885: Pinero, *Magistrate*, I, He is too good-natured to say 'Bo!' to a goose. 1920: Galsworthy, *Tatterdemalion*, 189, We are accustomed to exalt those who can say 'bo' to a goose.

Boar. *See* quot. 1863: Wise, *New Forest*, ch xvi,

'To rattle like a boar in a holme bush', is a thorough proverb of the Forest district, where a 'holme' bush means an old holly. *See also* **Feed** (3).

Boaster and a liar are all one (or **cousins**), **A.** *c.*1374: Chaucer, *Troylus*, bk iii l. 309, Avantour [a boaster] and a lyere, al is on. 1683: Meriton, *Yorkshire Ale*, 83–7 (1697), A vaunter and a lyar is baith yay thing. 1732: Fuller, 21, A boaster and a lyar are cousin-germans. 1869: Spurgeon, *John Ploughman*, ch viii, You will soon find out that a boaster and a liar are first cousins.

Boat. *Ill goes the boat without oars.* 1578: Florio, *First Fruites*, fo. 28. 1629: *Book of Meery Riddles*, Prov. 64. 1659: Howell, *Proverbs: Fr.-Eng.*, 3. *See also* **Oar**; and **Same boat.**

Bocking. *See* **Braintree.**

Bode. *Boad a bagg, and bearn*, i.e. An ill hap falles where it is feared. Glos. 1639: in *Berkeley MSS.*, iii 32 (1885).

Bodkin, To ride. 1638: Ford, *Fancies*, IV i (OED), Where but two lie in a bed, you must be – bodkin, bitch-baby – must ye? 1816: Scott, *Antiquary*, ch xvii, Between the two massive figures … was stuck, by way of bodkin, the slim form of Mary M'Intyre. 1849: Mrs Trollope, *Lottery of Marriage*, ch xiii, Her position as bodkin between her father and mother.

Bodmin. 1. I'll send you to Bodmin = gaol, 1869: Hazlitt, 216.

2. Into Bodmin and out of the world. 1897: A. H. Norway, *H. and B. in Devon, etc.*, 253, The kind of feeling thrown by other Cornishmen into the saying, 'Into Bodmin and out of the world'. Indeed, Bodmin has a very sleepy aspect.

Body. 1. The body is more dressed than the soul. 1633: Draxe, 10, His body is better clothed then his soule. 1640: Herbert, *Jac. Prudentum.*

2. The body is sooner dressed than the soul. 1640: Herbert, *Jac. Prudentum.*

3. The body is the socket of the soul. 1670: Ray, 3.

Body-louse. *Brisk* (with variants) *as a body-louse.* *c.*1570: *Marr. of Wit and Science*, II i, As brag as a body-louse. 1651: Randolph, *Hey for Honesty*, III iii, She is skimming her milk-bowls … as busy as a body louse. 1670: Cotton, *Scarronides*, bk iv, At last she sallies from the house, As fine and brisk as body-louse. 1720: Gay, *Poems*, ii 279 (Underhill), Brisk as a body-louse she trips. 1812: Colman, jr., *Poet. Vagaries*, in *Hum. Works*, 141 (Hotten, 1869), Brisk as a flea.

Boil stones in butter, and you may sip the broth. 1732: Fuller, 1003.

Bolas. *Cold and chilly, like Bolas.* 1883: Burne, *Shropsh. Folk-Lore*, 592.

Bold. 1. Be not too bold with your betters. 1659: Howell, 3. 1855: Bohn, 324, Be bold but not too bold.

2. Bold as a lion. Before 1225: *Ancren R.*, 274, Vor thi beoth euer agean him herdi ase leun ine treowe bileaue. 14th cent.: *Guy of Warwick*, l. 9587 (E.E.T.S.), As stowte as a lyon. *c.*1430: Lydgate, *Minor Poems*, 198 (Percy S.), Force of juventus, hardy as lioun. 1597: Shakespeare, 1 *Henry IV*, III i, Valiant as a lion. 1694: *Terence made English*, 84, I cowhearted? I'm as bold as a lion. 1710: Ward, *Eng. Reform.*, 136 (1716). 1819: Scott, *Bride of L.*, ch xi 1893: R.L.S., *Catriona*, ch xxx.

3. Bold as blind Bayard. *See* **Bayard**

4. Bold as brass. 1789: G. Parker, *Life's Painter*, 162, He died … as bold as brass. 1849: Lytton, *Caxtons*, Pt I ch iv, Master Sisty … as bold as brass. 1922: Weyman, *Ovington's Bank*, ch xvii.

5. Bold as Hector. 1684: *Great Frost*, 20 (Percy S.), Some bold as Hector.

Boldness in business is the first, second and third thing. 1732: Fuller, 1006.

Boldness is blind. Ibid., No. 1005.

Bolney. *Merry Bolney, rick Twineham, Proud Cowfold, and silly Shermanbury.* 1884: 'Sussex Proverbs', in *N. & Q.*, 6th ser, ix 403.

Bolsover. *See* quot. *c.*1791: Pegge, *Derbicisms*, 136 (E.D.S.), Bowser [Bolsover] for bacco-pipes; Tre[e]lton for. trenchers; Laughton for a pretty lass, Whiston for wenches.

Bolt. 1. A bolt from the blue. [Homer, *Od.*, v 102. Horace, *Carm.*, I xxxiv Virgil. *Georg.*, i 487–8.] 1898: H. James, in *Letters*, i 285 (1920), Such an inspiration was your charming note – out of the blue! – of a couple of days ago. 1901: W. James, in *Letters*, ii 142 (1920), In general I don't see how an epigram, being a pure bolt from the blue, with no introduction or cue, ever gets itself writ.

2. A bolt lost is not a bow broken. 1821: Scott, *Kenilworth*, ch xvi.

3. This bolt never came out of your quiver. 1683: Meriton, *Yorkshire Ale*, 83–7 (1697), This bolt com never out of your bag. 1732: Fuller, 4334.

4. To make a bolt or a shaft = To take the risk.

1600: Shakespeare, *Merry wives*, III iv 1608: Middleton, *Trick to Catch, etc.*, II i 1694: *Terence made English*, 12, Since my life's at stake, I'm resolved to make a bolt or a shaft on't. 1732: Fuller, 5201.

See also **Fool** (24).

Bone. 1. A bone to pick (or **bite**) **on.** 1565: Calfhill, *Answ. to Martiall*, 277 (P.S.), Only therefore will I add this, which may be a bone for you to pick on. 1583: Melbancke, *Philotinus*, sig. C1, I cast the[e] a bone to bite on. 1612: Chapman, *Widow's Tears*, II i, [He] has given me a bone to tire on, with a pestilence. 1681: L'Estrange, *Observator*, i, No. 64, But here's a bone for ye to pick. 1795: Cobbett, *A Bone to Gnaw for the Democrats* [title]. 1830: Scott, in Lockhart's *Life*, vii 215, A dish unknown elsewhere, so there is a bone for the gastronomers to pick.

2. Bones bring meat to town. 1639: in *Berkeley MSS.*, iii 31 (1885) … meaninge, Difficult and hard things are not altogether to bee reiected, or things of small consequence. 1642: Fuller, *Profane State:* 'Andronicus', We have an English proverb that *bones bring meat to town*.

3. To have a bone in one's arm, leg, etc. A humorous excuse. 1542: Udall, tr. Erasmus' *Apoph.*, 375 (1877), Demosthenes [having been bribed not to speak] … refused to speake, allegeing that he had a bone in his throte and could not speake. 1666: Torriano, *Piazza Univ.*, 276, The English say, He hath a bone in his arm and cannot work. 1738: Swift, *Polite Convers.*, Dial. III, I can't go, for I have a bone in my leg. 1877: E. Leigh, *Cheshire Gloss.*, 25, When a person has a shooting pain in the arm or leg, it is common to say, 'I've a bone i' th' arm or leg'. 1920: E. F. Benson, *Our Family Affairs*, 15, Panting and bright-eyed she would stop and say, 'Eh, dear, I can't run any more: I ve got a bone in my leg'.

See also **Make** (19).

Bonington. *See* **Betshanger.**

Book by its cover, You can't judge (*or* **tell**). A version, American in origin, of the familiar warning against judging by appearances. 1929: *American Speech*, IV, 465 You can't judge a book by its binding. 1946: Rolfe and Fuller, *Glass Room*, i, 'Forgive me, sir,' he said. 'I had you all wrong. You can never tell a book by its cover.'

Book that is shut is but a block, A. 1732: Fuller, 23.

Boot after bale = Help or relief after woe or distress. Before 1300: *Cursor M.*, l. 21621 (E.E.T.S.), thate with beting was bote of bale For seknes sere to mac paim hale. *c.*1320: in *Reliq. Antiquae*, i 113 (1841), When the bale is hest [highest], Thenne is the bote nest, Quoth Hendyng. *c.*1380: *Gamelyn*, l. 631, in Skeat's *Chaucer*, iv 660, After bale cometh boote thurgh grace of God almight. *c.*1400: *Beryn*, l. 3956 (E.E.T.S.), So 'aftir bale comyth bote'. *c.*1450: *Boke of Nurture*, in *Babees Book*, 119 (E.E.T.S.), 'When bale is hext [highest] than bote is next [nighest]' good sone, lerne welle this. 1567: Golding, *Ovid*, bk xiv l. 557, When that bale is hyghest growne, then boote must next ensew. 1607: *Chester Plays*, 431 (E.E.T.S.), After bale boot thar bringes. 1875: A. B. Cheales, *Proverb. Folk-Lore*, 125, But how often When bale is hext, Boot is next.

Booted. *They that are booted are not always ready.* 1640: Herbert, *Jac. Prudentum.*

Borage. *A leaf of borage might buy all the substance that they can sell.* 1546: Heywood, *Proverbs*, Pt I ch x.

Born. 1. Born in a mill = Deaf. 1578: Whetstone, *Promos and Cassandra*, sig. B3, Were you borne in a myll, curtole? you prate so hye. 1678: Ray, 76.

2. Born on Monday. *See* **Monday** (5).

3. He's born in a good hour who gets a good name. 1732: Fuller, 2455.

4. He that is born to be hanged will never be drowned. 1605: Camden, *Remains*, 324 (1870). 1670: Cotton, *Scarronides*, bk iv, Since as the proverb old 'tis found, *Who's born to hang, will ne'er be drown'd*. 1732: Fielding, *Cov. Garden Tragedy*, I iii, If born to swing, I never shall be drown'd. 1850: Smedley, *Frank Fairlegh*, ch xi.

5. He that's born under a threepenny planet. *See* **Threepenny.**

6. I was not born in a wood to be scared by an owl. 1738: Swift, *Polite Convers.*, Dial. III, Do you think I was born in a wood, to be afraid of an owl? 1830: Forby, *Vocab. E. Anglia*, 429. 1872: J. Glyde, jr., *Norfolk Garland*, 148.

7. She that is born a beauty is half married. 1633: Draxe, 15, Shee that is faire hath halfe her portion. 1732: Fuller, 4141.

8. To be born in a frost = To be blockheaded, dull of apprehension. 1828: Carr, *Craven Dialect*, i 166.

9. We are born crying, live complaining, and die disappointed. 1732: Fuller, 5427.

Borough Hill. *See* quot. 1854: Baker, *Northants Gloss.*, s.v. 'Jackson's pig', 'It's gone over Borough Hill (… near Daventry) after Jackson's pig'. A common phrase in that neighbourhood when anything is lost.

Boroughmen, Bread for. 1639: Clarke, 113, Burrough men merry, more bread than drink. 1678: Ray, 317. 1790: Grose, *Prov. Gloss.*, s.v. 'Leicestershire'.

Borrow. 1. Borrow or flatter. *See* **Contented** (2); and **Rich,** *adj.* (8).

2. He that borrows must pay again with shame or loss. 1639: Clarke, 246, He that will borrow must pay. 1678: Ray, 104.

3. He that goes a-borrowing goes a-sorrowing. 1539: Taverner, *Proverbs*, 46 (OED). 1580: Tusser, *Husbandrie*, 31 (E.D.S.), Who goeth a borrowing, goeth a sorrowing. 1669: *Politeuphuia*, 184. 1714: Ozell, *Molière*, iv 19. 1736: Franklin, *Way to Wealth*, in *Works*, i 448 (Bigelow). 1836: Marryat, *Easy*, ch viii.

4. To borrow on usury brings sudden beggary. 1639: Clarke, 327. 1670: Ray, 153. 1732: Fuller, 6089, To borrow upon usury, bringeth on beggary.

5. Who would borrow when he hath not, let him borrow when he hath. 1855: Bohn, 567.
See also **Swear** (2).

Borrowed. 1. A borrowed loan. *See* **Loan**

2. Borrowed garments never sit well. 1732: Fuller, 1008.

3. Borrowed things will home. 1400: in *Twenty-six Poems*, 2 (E.E.T.S.), And borwed thyng mot home ful nede. *c.*1460: *Prov. of Good Counsel*, in E.E.T.S., Extra Ser., No. 8, p. 68, For borowurd thynge wyll home agayne. *c.*1550: *Parl. of Byrdes*, l. 224, in Hazlitt, *Early Pop. Poetry*, iii 179, Borowed ware wyll home agayne.

4. He that trusts to borrowed ploughs, will have his land lie fallow. 1732: Fuller, 2337.

Borrower nor a lender be, Neither a. [Proverbs xxii 7 the borrower is servant to the lender.] 1600–1: Shakespeare, *Hamlet* I iii, Neither a borrower nor a lender be; For borrowing dulls the edge of husbandry, And loan oft loses both itself and friend.

Boscastle Fair (or Market). *See* quots. 1864: 'Cornish Proverbs', *in N. & Q.*, 3rd ser, v 276, Backwards and forwards like Boscastle Fair. All play and no play, like Boscastle Fair, which begins at twelve o'clock and ends at noon. 1880: Courtney, *W. Cornwall Words*, xiii (E.D.S.), All play, etc. [as in 1864, but with 'Market' for 'Fair'] 1888: Q.-Couch, *Troy Town*, chaps. xiii and xix [as in 1864].

Bosom-friend. *No friend like to a bosom friend, as the man said when he pulled out a louse.* 1732: Fuller, 3571. 1738: Swift, *Polite Convers.*, Dial. I, I'm afraid your bosom friends are become your backbiters.

Boston's Bay. *See* quot. 1869: Hazlitt, 88, Between Boston's Bay and the Pile of Fouldray, shall be seen the black navy of Norway.

Botch and sit, build and flit. 1618: W. Lawson, *New Orchard and Garden*, 9 (1676), Tenants who have taken up this proverb, *Botch and sit, Build and flit.* 1639: in *Berkeley MSS.*, iii 33 (1885).

Both together do best of all. 1639: Clarke, 10.

Bottles. *See* **New wine.**

Bottom of the bag, To bring out the. 1399: in Wright, *Pol. Poems*, i 363 (Rolls Ser., 1859), The grete bagge, that is so mykille, Hit schal be kettord [diminished], and maked litelle; the bothom is ny ougt. 1546: Heywood, *Proverbs*, Pt II ch x, He brought the bottome of the bag cleane out.

Boughs that bear most, hang lowest, The. 1732: Fuller, 4430.

Bought. 1. Bought wit. *See* **Wit** (2) and (12).

2. To be bought and sold. 1639: Clarke, 86, You are bought and sold like sheepe in a market. 1670: Ray, 166, To be bought and sold in a company. 1738: Swift, *Polite Convers.*, Dial. III. 1792: *Looker-on*, No. 11, He was bought and sold by people in power.

Bounce buckram, velvet's dear, Christmas comes but once a year; And when it comes it brings good cheer, But when it's gone it's never the near. 1639: Clarke, 71 [first line only]. 1670: Ray, 211. 1843: Halliwell, *Nursery Rhymes*, 121 [first two lines only]. 1846: Denham, *Proverbs*, 64 (Percy S.) [four lines, but in first 'buckler' for 'buckram', and for last line, 'So farewell Christmas once a year'].

Bound is he that takes gifts. *c.*1460: *How the Good Wife*, l. 70, Bounden he is that gifte takithe.

Bound must obey, The. 1205: Layamon, *Brut*, 1051, Ah heo mot nede beien, the mon the ibunden bith (But he needs must bow, the man that is bounden). *c.*1390: Gower, *Conf. Amantis*,

ii 540, For who is bounden, he mot bowe.
*c.*1410: *Towneley Plays*, 118 (E.E.T.S.), Wo is
hym that is bun, ffor he must abyde. *c.*1520: in
Hazlitt, *Early Pop. Poetry*, iv 92 (1866), The
bounde must euer obaye. 1615: T. Heywood,
Foure Prentises, I, Bound must obey. 1653: R.
Brome, *Mad Couple*, II. 1732: Fuller, 4972,
They that are bound must obey.

Bounty being free itself, thinks all others so.
1855: Bohn, 332.

Bourd. *It is a good bourd to drink of a gourd,*
*c.*1400: *Towneley Plays*, xii p. 115 (E.E.T.S.), It
an is old by-worde, It is a good bowrde, for to
drynk of a gowrde, – It holdys a mett potell.
[Bourd = jest.]

Bourne. *See* **Chichester** (1).

Bout as Barrow was. Cheshire. 1670: Ray, 217.
1691: Ray, *Words not generally Used*, 34
(E.D.S.). 1917: Bridge, *Cheshire Proverbs*, 125
… The meaning is lost. [Bout = without.]

Bout's [Without's] **bare but it's easy.** 1873:
Harland and Wilkinson, *Lancs Leg.*, 202. 1917:
Bridge, *Cheshire Proverbs*, 32 … Common in
Lancashire.

Bow, *subs.* **1. A bow long bent grows weak.**
1541: Coverdale, *Christ. State Matrimony*, sig.
I1, The bowe will breake yf it be to sore bent.
*c.*1577, Northbrooke, *Against Dicing, etc.*, 44
(SH.S.), Euen as too much bending breketh a
bow. 1669: Dudley North, *Obs. and Adv.*
Oeconom., 123, A bow that stands alwayes bent
looseth its strength in the end. 1732: Fuller,
1013, Bows too long bent, grow weake. 1741:
Tom King's: or The Paphian Grove, 10, The bow,
if always bent, will lose It's spring elastic.

2. Draw not thy bow before thy arrow be fixed.
1732: Fuller, 1326.

See also **Robin Hood** (2) and (5).

Bow than break, Better. *See* **Better bow.**

Bow-bell. *To be born within sound of Bow-bell.*
1662: Fuller, *Worthies*, ii 344 (1840). 1753: in
Stukeley Memoirs, i 404 (Surtees S.), Interest is
such a prevailing principle within the sound of
Bow bell. 1793: Grose, *Olio*, 24 (2nd ed.), Born
within the sound of Bow-bell, he rarely ventured
out of it. 1918: Muirhead, *Blue Guide to London*,
351, Any one born within the sound of Bow Bells
is a 'cockney', i.e. a Londoner pure and simple.

Bow-hand. *See* **Wide at the bow-hand.**

Bow-wow. *See* **July** (3).

Bowdon. *Every man cannot be vicar of Bowden.*

1678: Ray, 300. 1790: Grose, *Prov. Gloss.*, s.v.
'Cheshire'. 1917: Bridge, *Cheshire Proverbs*, 54,
Every man was not born to be Vicar of Bowdon.

Bowdon Wakes. *See* quot. 1886: R. Holland,
Cheshire Gloss., 456 (E.D.S.), When Bowdon
Wakes is at Bowdon, winter's at Newbridge
Hollow. 1917: Bridge, *Cheshire Proverbs*, 151.

Bowl of cherries, Life is just a. *See* **Life** (5).

Bowling green. *See* **Three things are thrown**
away.

Bowls. *They that play at bowls must expect* (or
meet with) *rubbers.* 1762: Smollett, *Sir L.*
Greaves, ch x [title], Which sheweth that he who
plays at bowls will sometimes meet with
rubbers. 1824: Scott, *Redgauntlet*, ch xx 1854:
Baker, *Northants Gloss.*, s.v. 'Rubbers'. 1907:
Hackwood, *Old Eng. Sports*, 180, For 'he who
plays at bowls must look out for rubs'. *See also*
Easy to bowl.

Boy and **Boys. 1. Boys to bed, dogs to doors,**
and maidens to clean up the ashes. Cornwall.
1895: J. Thomas, *Randigal Rhymes*, 60.

2. Boys will be boys. 1601: A. Dent *Plain Man's*
Pathway, 64, Youth will be youthfulle, when
you have saide all that you can. 1681: W.
Robertson, *Phraseol. Generalis*, 330, Children
will do like children. 1849: Lytton, *Caxtons*,
Pt XV ch i, 'Well,' said I to myself, 'I will save for
him; boys will be boys.' 1911: G. B. Shaw,
Fanny's First Play, I.

3. Boys will be men. 1611: Cotgrave, s.v.
'Enfant', Or, (as we say) boyes will be men one
day. 1732: Fuller, 1014.

4. The boy has gone by with the cows = has
missed opportunities. Oxfordsh. 1913: *Folk-*
Lore, xxiv 77.

5. To leave boys' play and go to blow point.
1639: Clarke, 197. 1681: W. Robertson, *Phraseol.*
Generalis, 997, To leave boys-play, and fall to
blow point; Relinquere nuces. 1738: Swift,
Polite Convers., Dial. I, Come, let us leave off
children's play, and come to pushpin.

Brabling curs. *See* **Brawling curs.**

Brackley breed, better to hang than feed. 1636:
in *Somers Tracts*, vii 212 (1811), Heer's the full
summe of the reckoning and a pottle over; though
we be Leicestershire fed, yet we be not Brackley
bred, I assure you. 1670: Ray, 246. 1790: Grose,
Prov. Gloss., s.v. 'Northamptonshire'. 1851:
Sternberg, *Dialect, etc., of Northants*, 191.

Bradshaw's windmill, What have I to do with?

i.e. What have I to do with another man's business? 1678: Ray, 317. 1790: Grose, *Prov. Gloss.*, s.v. 'Leicestershire'. 1869: Spurgeon, *John Ploughman*, ch ii.

Brag, *subs.* **1. Brag's a good dog but dares not bite.** 1685: Meriton, *Yorkshire Ale*, 58, Braggs a good dog … But he was hang'd for biting that was ill. 1732: Fuller, 1015.

2. Brag is a good dog but Holdfast is a better. *c.*1598: Deloney, *Gentle Craft*, Pt II ch v, Brag is a good dog (quoth Stutely), but tell vs, hast thou made thy Will? 1599: Shakespeare, *Henry V*, II iii, Men's faiths are wafer-cakes And holdfast is the only dog, my duck. 1709: Dykes, *Eng. Proverbs*, 123. 1748: *Gent. Mag.*, 21. 1861: Dickens, *Great Expect.*, ch xviii 1924: *Devonsh. Assoc. Trans.*, lv. 112.

3. Brag's a good dog but that he hath lost his tail. 1678: Ray, 105.

4. Brag's a good dog if he be well set on. 1670: Ray, 65. 1736: Bailey, *Dict.*, s.v. 'Brag'.

Brag, *verb.* **1. They brag most that can do least.** *c.*1598: Deloney, *Gentle Craft*, Pt II ch vi, It is an old saying, they brag most that can doe least.

2. To brag of many goodmorrows. 1670: Ray, 178.

Brain and **Brains. 1. He carries his brains in his breeches-pocket.** 1883: Borne, *Shropsh. Folk-Lore*, 589.

2. He hath no more brains than a burbolt (bird-bolt). *c.*1550: Udall, *Roister Doister*, III ii, He hath in his head … As much braine as a burbolt. 1672: Walker, *Paroem.*, 11.

3. His brain is not big enough for his skull. 1732: Fuller, 2504.

4. His brains are addle. 1670: Ray, 165.

5. His brains crow. 1678: Ray, 230.

6. His brains will work without barm. Yorks. 1670: Ray, 166. 1732: Fuller, 2505, His brains want no barm to make them work.

7. If the brain sows not corn, it plants thistles. 1640: Herbert, *Jac. Prudentum.* 1659: Howell, 6. 1732: Fuller, 4437.

8. The brains don't lie in the beard. 1732: Fuller, 4431.

Braintree boys, brave boys; Bocking boys, rats; Church Street, puppy dogs; High Garret, cats. 1813: Ray, 246.

Braintree for the pure, and Bocking for the poor, Cogshall for the jeering town, and Kelvedon for the whore. 1670: Ray, 228.

Brandy is Latin for a goose. 1588: *Mar-Prelate's Epitome*, 25 (1843), Can you tell your brother Marprelat with all your learning, howe to decline what is Latine for a goose? 1738: Swift, *Polite Convers.*, Dial. II. 1847: Halliwell. *Dict.*, s.v. 'Pig', *Brandy is Latin for pig and goose*, an apology for drinking a dram after either.

Brass farthing = No value. 1660: *Andromana*, I i, in Hazlitt, *Old Plays*, xiv 197, Some wench, my life to a brass farthing! 1740: North, *Lives of Norths*, i 229 (Bohn), He would not give one brass farthing to buy all the Presbyterians in England. 1801: Colman, jr., *Poor Gent.*, II i, It doesn't signify a brass farthing what they are called. 1911: Shaw, *Fanny's First Play*, Induction, Vaughan is honest, and don't care a brass farthing what he says.

Brass knocker on a barn-door. *See* quot. 1886: Elworthy, *West Som. Word-Book*, 44 (E.D.S.), A very common saying expressive of inconsistency is … may as well put a brass knocker on a barn-door.

Brave, *adj.* **1. A brave retreat is a brave exploit.** 1732: Fuller, 24.

2. Brave actions never want a trumpet. Ibid., No. 1016.

3. Brave man at arms, but weak to Balthasar. 1659: Howell, 5.

4. Brave men lived before Agamemnon. [*Vixere fortes ante Agamemnona Multi* (many brave men lived before Agamemnon) – Horace, *Odes*, iv ix] The saying derives from Horace, and it is very much a poet's saying for the implication is that earlier heroes lived and died in obscurity, unsung by the poetic fraternity. 1616: Jonson, *Forest*, VIII 114, There were brave men before Aiax or Idomen, or all the store That Homer brought to Troy. 1819: Byron, *Don Juan*, I v, Brave men were living before Agamemnon And since, exceeding valorous and sage.

5. Some have been thought brave, because they were afraid to run away. 1732: Fuller, 4214. *See also* **None.**

Brawling curs never want sore ears. 1611: Cotgrave, s.v. 'Hargneux', A brabling curre is never without torne eares. 1694: D'Urfey, *Quixote*, Pt I Act IV sc i, Come, come, sir, babling curs never want sore ears. 1709: R. Kingston, *Apoph. Curiosa*, 9, Barking currs commonly go with bitten ears. 1732: Fuller, 6231. 1865: 'Lancs Proverbs', in *N. & Q.*, 3rd ser, viii 494.

Bray. *The Vicar of Bray will be Vicar of Bray still.*
1662: Fuller, *Worthies*, i 113 (1840). 1707:
Dunton, *Athenian Sport*, 400, The Vicar of Bray;
or, a paradox in praise of the Turncoat Clergy.
1869: Spurgeon, *John Ploughman*, ch xviii, They
admire the Vicar of Bray, whose principle was to
be Vicar of Bray, whether the Church was
Protestant or Popish.

Brayton-bargh. *If Brayton-bargh and
Hambleton hough, and Burton bream, Were all in
thy belly 't would never be team* (full). 1670: Ray,
257. 1683: Meriton, *Yorkshire Ale*, 83–7 (1697).
1790: Grose, *Prov. Gloss.*, s.v. 'Yorkshire'. 1878:
Folk-Lore Record, i 172.

Brazen-nose College, You were bred in. 1732:
Fuller, 6011.

**Bread. 1. Be fair conditioned and eat bread
with your pudding.** 1678: Ray, 79.

**2. Bread and cheese be two targets against
death.** 1655: T. Muffett, *Healths Improvement*,
236. 1666: Torriano, *Piazza Univ.*, 92, Cheese
and bread is physick to such as are in health.

3. Bread is the staff of life, but beer's life itself.
Oxfordsh. 1913. Folk-Lore, xxiv 76.

4. Bread of a day. See **Egg** (3).

**5. Bread with eyes and cheese without eyes,
and wine that leaps to the eyes.** 1666:
Torriano, *Piazza Univ.*, 41. 1670: Ray, 3
[without the 'wine' part]. 1732: Fuller, 1017.

**6. He has got a piece of bread and cheese in
his head** = He is drunk. 1678: Ray, 87.

**7. He that hath store of bread may beg his milk
merrily.** 1659: Howell, *Proverbs: Brit.-Eng.*, 5.

8. His (or **your**) **bread is buttered on both
sides.** 1678: Ray, 232. 1732: Fuller, 6044. 1837:
Lockhart, *Scott*, i 206 n. (1839) (OED),
Wherever Walter goes he is pretty sure to find
his bread buttered on both sides.

**9. It is a good thing to eat your brown bread
first.** 1830: Forby, *Vocab. E. Anglia*, 429. 1872: J.
Glyde, jr., *Norfolk Garland*, 148.

**10. It's no use my leaving off eating bread,
because you were choked with a crust.** 1883:
Burne, *Shropsh. Folk-Lore*, 589.

**11. The bread never falls but on its buttered
side.** 1867: A. D. Richardson, *Beyond Mississippi*,
iii, *His* bread never fell on the buttered side. 1884:
J. Payn, I've never had a piece of toast Particularly
long and wide But fell upon the sanded floor And
always on the buttered side. 1891: J.L. Kipling,
Beast and Man, We express the completeness of

ill-lick by saying 'The bread never falls but on its
buttered side'. This is said to be an old north-
country proverb and is frequently cited as a
variant of Murphy's law – Cf. **If anything can go
wrong** … .

**12. They that have no other meat, bread and
butter, are glad to eat.** 1639: Clarke, 113. 1670:
Ray, 66. 1732: Fuller, 6128.

**13. To know on which side one's bread is
buttered.** 1546: Heywood, *Proverbs*, Pt II ch vii
1564: Bullein, *Dialogue*, 112 (E.E.T.S.), He
knoweth vpon whiche side his breade is buttered
well enough, I warrante you. 1638: Ford, *Lady's
Trial*, II i 1721: C. Cibber, *Refusal*, I, Does his
Grace think I don't know which side my bread's
butter'd on? 1822: Scott, *Nigel*, ch xxiii 1914: H.
A. Vachell, *Quinney's*, bk ii ch xvi (ii.), James is a
bit of a knave, but he knows which side his bread
is buttered.

**14. What bread men break is broke to them
again.** 1630: Taylor (Water-Poet), *Works*, 2nd
pagin., 186, In this the prouerb is approued
plaine, What bread men breake is broke to them
againe.

**15. Who hath no more bread than need, must
not keep a dog.** 1640: Herbert, *Jac. Prudentim.*

**16. You show bread in one hand, and a stone
in the other.** 1732: Fuller, 5994.

See also **Better bread; Better lose; Borough
men; Buying of bread; Eaten; Half a loaf; Loaf;**
and **Wine** (10).

Breage and Germoe. *God keep us from rocks and
shelving sands, And save us from Breage and
Germoe men's hands.* Cornwall. 1887: M. A.
Courtney, in *Folk-Lore Journal*, v 18. 1897:
Norway, *H. and B. in Devon, etc.*, 282, Verse said
to have been current in old days about the two
seaboard parishes just mentioned … God keep
us, etc.

Break, *verb.* **1. A man shall as soon break his
neck as his fast there.** 1546: Heywood, *Proverbs*,
Pt I ch xi 1670: Ray, 165. 1732: Fuller, 3770.

**2. A man that breaks his word, bids others be
false to him.** 1548: Hall, *Chron.*, 184 (1809), But
(as the common prouerbe saieth) he whiche is a
promise breaker, escapeth not alway free. 1732:
Fuller, 311.

**3. Break coals; cut candle; set brand an end,
Neither good housewifery nor good
housewife's friend.** 1666: Torriano, *Piazza
Univ.*, 242. 1732: Fuller, 6424.

4. Break the legs of an evil custom. 1659: Howell, *Proverbs: Span.-Eng.*, 8, Cut off the leg of an ill custome. 1855: Bohn, 333.

5. To break a flint upon a feather-bed. 1659: Gayton, *Art of Longevity*, 20, Just as a feather-bed the flint doth break. 1666: Torriano, *Piazza Univ.*, 123, As the English say, To break, etc.

6. To break a man's back. 1613: Shakespeare, *Henry VIII*, I i, Many Have broke their backs with laying manors on 'em For this great journey. 1632: Rowley, *A New Wonder*, IV, Oh, my poor father! this loss will break his back. 1894: Northall, *Folk Phrases*, 26 (E.D.S.), To break a man's back = To ruin him.

7. To break my head and then give me a plaster. *c.*1430: Lydgate, *Minor Poems*, 56 (Percy S.), To breke myn hede, and yeve me an houffe. 1573: G. Harvey, *Letter-Book*, 52 (Camden S.), To break a mans hed ... and at his laisure, give him a plaster. 1631: Mabbe, *Celestina*, 283 (T.T.), Thou breakest our head, and givest us a plaister. 1738: Swift, *Polite Convers.*, Dial. I. 1818: J. Austen, *Persuasion*, ch xiii, A new sort of way this, for a young fellow to be making love, by breaking his mistress's head! is not it, Miss Elliot? This is breaking a head and giving a plaster truly!

8. To break no squares = To do no harm, to make no difference. 1562: Heywood, *Three Hund. Epigr.*, No. 4, An inch breaketh no square. 1593: Nashe, *Strange Newes*, in *Works*, ii 281 (Grosart), For calling me calfe, it breakes no square. 1675: Crowne, *Country Wit*, I i, Two or three days can break no square. 1707: Cibber, *Comical Lovers*, III, One minute will break no squares, I'll warrant you. 1798: T. Morton, *Speed the Plough*, I ii, I do hope, zur, breaking your head will break noa squares. 1823: Byron, *Don Juan*, can. xiii st. 25, At Blank-Blank Square; – for we will break no squares By naming streets. 1850: Dickens, *Copperfield*, ch xxxix, There are no squares broke between us. I've been into his room already, and we've made it all smooth. 1923: [at a Surrey C.C. Committee meeting, I heard a member (a builder), referring to a small difference between two estimates of cost, say, 'This will break no squares'.

9. To break the ice. 1592: Nashe, *P. Penilesse*, in *Works*, ii 5 (Grosart), He that hath once broke the ice of impudence, neede not care how deepe he wade in discredite. 1631: Shirley, *Love*

Tricks, III i, When I had but broke the ice of my affection, she fell over head and ears in love with me. 1708: tr. Aleman's *Guzman*, i 173, To break the ice in making the first overture. 1848: Dickens, *Dombey*, ch lxi, 'If he would have the goodness to break the – in point of fact, the ice,' said Cousin Feenix.

See also **Broke**; and **Broken**.

Breath. *Keep* (*save*, etc.) *one's breath to cool one's porridge.* *c.*1598: Deloney, *Gentle Craft*, Pt II ch iii, I was about to tell you of a matter, but I see it is to small purpose, and therefore Ile keep my breath to coole my pottage. 1633: Machin, *Dumb Knight*, II, My lord, save your breath for your broth. 1725: Bailey, tr. Erasmus' *Colloq.*, 441, He had as good keep his breath to cool his porridge. 1813: J. Austen, *Pride and Prejudice*, ch vi 1886: R.L.S., *Kidnapped*, ch vii, Instead of asking riddles ... ye would keep your breath to cool your porridge. 1924: Shaw, *Saint Joan*, sc ii.

Bred in the bone will not out of the flesh, What is. [*c.*1290: in Wright's *Pol. Songs John to Edw. II*, 167 (Camden S.), Osse radicatum raro de carne recedit.] 1481: Caxton, *Reynard*, 29 (Arber), That whiche cleuid by the bone myght not out of the flesshe. 1485: Malory, *Morte d' Arthur*, bk ix ch 39, Sir launcelot smyled and said hard hit is to take oute of the flesshe that is bred in the bone. 1546: Heywood, *Proverbs*, Pt II ch viii 1596: Jonson, *Ev. Man in his Humour*, II i 1632: Massinger, *City Madam*, II iii, What's bred in the bone, Admits no hope of cure. 1694: *Terénce made English*, 5. 1713: Gay, *Wife of Bath*, III ii 1842: Barham, *Ing. Legends*, 2nd ser: 'Lay of St Aloysius'.

Bredon Hill. *When Bredon Hill puts on its hat*, *Ye men of the vale, beware of that.* Worcs. 1882: Mrs Chamberlain, *W. Worcs. Words*, 39 (E.D.S.). 1893: Inwards, *Weather Lore*, 101.

Breech makes buttons, His (or **My**) = To be in great fear. *c.*1550: *Jacke Jugeler*, 46 (Grosart, 1873), His arse maketh buttens now. *c.*1618: B.&F., *Bonduca*, II iii 1653: Middleton and Rowley, *Span. Gipsy*, IV iii, O Soto, I make buttons! 1736: Bailey, *Dict.*, s.v. 'Breech'. 1808: Ainsworth, *Lat. Dict.*, i, s.v. 'Button', His tail maketh buttons, *valde trepidat* (OED).

Breeches, To wear the. 15th cent.: *Songs and Carols of 15th Cent.*, 65 (Percy S.), Nova, Nova, sawe you euer such, The most mayster of the hows weryth no brych. 1592: Greene, *Quip*, in

Works, xi 219 (Grosart), I saw a great many of women vsing high wordes to their husbandes: some striuing for the breeches ... 1596: Harington, *Metam. of Ajax*, 63 (1814), I am sure his wife wore the breeches. 1653: R. Brome, *City Wit, or the Woman wears the Breeches*[title]. 1712: Addison, *Spectator*, No. 482, Since you have given us the character of a wife who wears the breeches, pray say something of a husband that wears the petticoat. 1927: *Observer*, 27 March, p. 15, col. 3, Mrs Scally wore the breeches, and her word went in the Scally household.

Breed in the mud are not eels, All that. 1732: Fuller, 549.

Breed is stronger than pasture. 1917: Bridge, *Cheshire Proverbs*, 31.

Breeks off a Highlander, To take the. [Vis nudo vestimenta detrahere? – Plautus, *Asin.*, I i 79.] 1546: Heywood, *Proverbs*, Pt I ch ix, There is nothing more vain ... Than to beg a breeche of a bare arst man. 1580: Baret, *Alvearie*, B, 150, To pull a breeche from a bare arst man. 1630: Taylor (Water-Poet), in *Works*, 2nd pagin., 37, To seek a breech from breechlesse men 'twere vain. 1817: Scott, *Rob Roy*, ch xxvii, It's ill taking the breeks off a Hielandman.

Breeze in one's breech, To have a. Breeze = gadfly. *c.*1630: B.&F., *Monsieur Thomas*, IV vi, What, is the breeze in your breech? 1678: Ray, 232.

Brent Hill. *See* quot. 1893: in *N. & Q.*, 8th ser, iii 209, 'Looking from under Brent Hill' ... used to be very popular [saying] in Devonshire fifty or sixty years ago. It is said of a sullen, frowning person in an ill humour, Brent Hill indicating the eyebrows.

Brentford. *See* quot. 1790: Grose, *Prov. Gloss.*, s.v. 'Middlesex', His face was like the red lion of Brentford. That is, exceeding red.

Brevity is the soul of wit. 1602: Shakespeare, *Hamlet*, II ii 1802: Lamb, *John Woodvil*, III, Brevity is the soul of drinking, as of wit. 1851: Borrow, *Lavengro*, i 311.

Brew, *verb*. **1. As one brews so bake.** *c.*1560: T. Ingelend, *Disob. Child*, in Hazlitt, *Old Plays*, ii 294 (1874), But as he had brewed, that so he should bake. *c.*1626: in *Pepysian Garland*, 241 (Rollins, 1922), For some that are fond, as they brew let them bake. 1670: Cotton, *Scarronides*, bk iv 1766: Garrick and Colman, *Clandest. Marriage*, I i 1847: Planché, *Extravag.*, iii 187

(1879). 1922: Weyman, *Ovington's Bank*, ch xxiii, No, you may go, my lad. As you ha' brewed you may bake!

2. As one brews so drink. *c.*1264: in Ritson, *Songs and Ballads*, 11 (Hazlitt), Let him habbe ase he brew, bale to dryng. Before 1300: *Cursor M.*, l. 2848, Suche as thai brew such haue thai dronkyn. *c.*1390: Gower, *Conf. Amantis*, bk iii l. 1626, And who so wicked alë breweth Ful ofte he mot [must] the wersë drinke. *c.*1425: *Castle of Persev.*, sc viii st. 271, in *Macro Plays*, 171 (E.E.T.S.), As he hath browyn, lete hym drynke. 1596: Jonson, *Ev. Man in his Humour*, II i, Well, as he brews, so shall he drink. 1605: Chapman, etc., *Eastw. Hoe*, IV i 1762: Smollett, *Sir L. Greaves*, ch x 1849: Brontë, *Shirley*, ch xxi 1883: R.L.S., *Treasure I*, ch xxx.

3. To brew in a bottle and bake in a bag. 1542: Boorde, *Dyetary*, 240 (E.E.T.S.), For these men the which do brew in a botyl and bake in a walet, it wyll be long or he can by Iacke a salet. 1678: Ray, 91.

Brewer's horse. *One whom the brewer's horse hath bit = A* drunkard. 1597: Shakespeare, 1 *Henry IV*, III iii, [Falstaff *loq.*] I am a peppercorn, a brewer's horse. 1635: T. Heywood, *Philocothonista*, 45, One whom brewer's horse hath bit. 1847: Halliwell, *Dict.*, s.v. 'Brewer's horse'. 1907: Hackwood, *Inns, Ales, etc.*, 167. 1917: Bridge, *Cheshire Proverbs*, 100.

Briars. 1. It is good to cut the briars in the sere month [August]. *c.*1686: Aubrey, *Gentilisme*, 123 (F.L.S.).

2. In the briars. *See* **Leave,** *verb* (8).

Bribe, *subs*. **1. A bribe I know is a juggling knave.** 1659: Howell, *Proverbs: Brit.-Eng.*, 33.

2. A bribe will enter without knocking. 1619: B. Rich, *Irish Hubbub*, 9 (margin), Honesty stands at the gate and knockes, and bribery enters in. 1633: Draxe, 18, A bribe entreth euery where without knocking. 1670: Ray, 65. 1732: Fuller, 1019.

Bribe, *verb*. *Neither bribe nor lose thy right.* 1640: Herbert, *Jac. Prudentum.*

Bricks without straw, You cannot make. [Exodus v 7, Ye shall no more give the people straw to make brick, as heretofore; let them go and gather straw for themselves.] The meaning of the proverb is that tasks cannot be accomplished without the right materials or tools. 1624: R. Burton, *Anatomy of Melancholy*, I ii, (Hard taske-masters as they are) they take away their straw and compell them to make their number of bricke. 1658: G. Hyde, *Letter* in *Verney Memoirs* (1904), I have made the enclosed. It is an hard task to make bricks without straw, but I have raked together some rubbish. 1909: A. Bennett, *Literary Taste*, iv, You can only acquire really useful general ideas by first acquiring particular ideas ... You cannot make bricks without straw.

Bride. *See* **Happy is the bride** ...

Bridge and **Bridges. 1. Bridges were made for wise men to walk over, and fools to ride over.** 1678: Ray, 106.

2. He is building a bridge over the sea. 1813: Ray, 75.

3. Praise the bridge. *See* **Praise the bridge.**

4. To make a bridge of one's nose. 1678: Ray, 231. 1690: *New Dict. Canting Crew*, sig. H8, You make a bridge of his nose, when you pass your next neighbour in drinking, or one is preferr'd over another's head. 1738: Swift, *Polite Convers.*, Dial. II, Pray, my lord, don't make a bridge of my nose. 1828: Carr, *Craven Dialect*, ii 12, 'To mak a brigg o' yans nose', to pass by him in drinking. 1847: Halliwell, *Dict.*, s.v. 'Nose'.

5. To make (or **build**) **a bridge of gold** (or **silver**) **for a flying enemy.** [1535: Rabelais (*c.*1490–1533), *Gargantua*, liv. i ch 43, Ouurez tousiours a voz ennemys toutes les portes et chemins, et plustost leur faictes ung pont d'argent, affin de les renvoyer.] 1576: Lambarde, *Peramb. of Kent*, 371 (1826), It was well saide of one ... If thine enemie will flie, make him a bridge of golde. 1634: Massinger, *Guardian*, l. i, For a flying foe Discreet and provident conquerors build up A bridge of gold. 1732: Fuller, 3312, Make a silver bridge for your enemy to go over. 1889: R.L.S., *Ballantrae*, ch iv, You may have heard of a military proverb: that it is a good thing to make a bridge of gold to a flying enemy.

Bridgnorth Election, All on one side like. 1841: Hartshorne, *Salopia Ant.*, 336. 1861: in *N. & Q.*, 2nd ser, xi 219, In 1835 I heard a boy say 'all on one side, like Bridgnorth election', in the town of Stone, in Staffordshire. 1883: Burne, *Shropsh. Folk-Lore*, 592 [full explanation of saying]. 1920: A. G. Bradley, *Book of Severn*, 195.

Bridle. 1. A bridle for the tongue is a necessary piece of furniture. 1732: Fuller, 25.

2. To bite upon the bridle. *c.*1390: Gower, *Conf. Amantis*, bk vi l. 929, And as who seith, upon the bridel I chiewe. 1552: Latimer, *Works*, ii 57 (P.S.), Though it goeth hard with us, though we must bite on the bridle. 1605: Chapman, etc., *Eastw. Hoe*, IV ii, They are like to bite o' the bridle [i.e. to fast]. 1642: D. Rogers, *Matrim. Honour*, 300, Be quiet, my soule, bite not upon the bridle. 1750: Smollett. *Gil Blas*, iv 248, The minister was going to retire into his closet, to bite upon the bridle at liberty, *c.*1791: Pegge, *Derbicisms*, 91 (E.D.S.). 'To bite on the bridle', to suffer or fare hard. 1828: Carr, *Craven Dialect*, i 52, To bite on the bridle, to suffer great hardship, to be driven to straits.

Bridport dagger, Stabbed with a = Hanged, hemp being manufactured at Bridport. 1662: Fuller, *Worthies*, i 453 (1840). 1716: Browne Willis, *Notitia Parl.*, quoted in *N. & Q.*, 9th ser, iii 365. 1790: Grose, *Prov. Gloss.*, s.v. 'Dorset'.

Bright. 1. Bright as the sun on a summer's day. *c.*1440: Lydgate, *Lyf of our Lady*, sig. F2 (Caxton), That shone as bright as ony somers day. 1846: Denham, *Proverbs*, 51 (Percy S.).

2. He is only bright that shines by himself. 1640: Herbert, *Jac. Prudentum*.

Brighton. *See* quot. 1884: 'Sussex Proverbs', in *N. & Q.*, 6th ser, ix 342, When the Island's [Wight] seen above the line Brighthelmstone loses weather fine. *See also* **Lewes.**

Brim. *See* **Better spare.**

Brisk as a bee. 1732: Fuller, 666, As brisk as a bee in a tar-pot. 1742: Fielding, *Andrews*, bk iii ch ii, Joseph immediately prevailed with parson Adams, who was as brisk as a bee, to stop. *c.*1770: Hall-Stevenson, *Works*, i 23 (1795), Away skipp'd the urchin, as brisk as a bee. 1901: F. E. Taylor, *Lancs Sayings*, 1.

Brisk as bottled ale. 1720: Gay, *Poems*, ii 278 (Underhill), And merry as a grig is grown, And brisk as bottled ale. 1745: *Agreeable Companion*, 351, Brisk as bottled beer.

Bristol. 1. A Jew cannot live in Bristol. 1790: Grose, *Prov. Gloss.*, s.v. 'Somerset'.

2. Bristol men sleep with one eye open. Ibid., s.v. 'Somerset'. 1868: *Quart. Review*, cxxv. 231, Bristol men, who are currently reported to 'sleep with one eye open'. 1906: Q.-Couch, *Mayor of Troy*, Prol., We slept Bristol fashion, with one eye open.

3. Bristol milk. *See* 1848 quot. 1661: *Antid. against Melanch.*, 156 (Ebsworth), Merrily now let's sing, carouse, and tiple, Here's Bristow milk, come suck this niple. 1668: Pepys, *Diary*, 13 June, Plenty of brave wine, and above all Bristol milk. 1785: Grose, *Class. Dict. of Vulgar Tongue*, s.v. … A Spanish wine called sherry, much drank at that place, particularly in the morning. 1848: Macaulay, *Hist. Eng.*, i 335. The repast was … accompanied by a rich brewage made of the best Spanish wine, and celebrated over the whole kingdom as Bristol milk.

4. The Bristol hogs have built a sty, but cannot find their way into it. 1752: *Journey through England*, 144, quoted in Hazlitt, *Proverbs*, 1869. *See also* **Sold.**

Britain. *See* quot. 1580: Lyly, *Euphues*, 439 (Arber), Whereof there was an olde saying, all countries stande in neede of Britaine, and Britaine of none.

Brittle as glass. 1412–20: Lydgate, *Troy Book*, bk v l. 854, Brotel as glas. *c.*1550: Becon, in *Catechism, etc.*, 437 (P.S.), It is more brittle than glass. 1639: Fuller, *Holy War*, bk ii ch xii, Her fortune being as brittle as her glasses. 1927: J. B. Priestley, *Open House:* 'Midsummer Day's Dream', All this beauty … is as brittle as glass.

Broad. 1. A broad hat does not always cover a venerable head. 1732: Fuller, 26.

2. As broad as narrow like Paddy's plank = 'Much of a muchness'. 1917: Bridge, *Cheshire Proverbs*, 10.

3. It's as broad as it's long. 1678: Ray, 67, As broad as long. Before 1680: Butler, *Remains*, i 110 (1759). 1732: Fuller, 2933. 1821: Byron, *Letters, etc.*, v 379 (Prothero), So that the thing is as broad as it is long. 1907: De Morgan, *Alice-for-Short*, ch xl

Brock = A badger. **1. To stink like a brock.** 1892: Heslop, *Northumb. Words*, 101 (E.D.S.).

2. To sweat like a brock. 1788: in *Reprinted Gloss.*, 23 (E.D.S., No 1), He sweats like a brock [E. Yorks]. 1892: Heslop, *Northumb. Words*, 101 (E.D.S.).

Brockley Hill. *See* quot. 1724: Stukeley, *Itin. Cur.*, 111, They have a proverb here, no heart can think nor tongue can tell, what lys between Brockley Hill and Pennywell. 1849: Halliwell, *Pop. Rhymes and Nursery Tales*, 198 [as in 1724].

Broke his hour that kept his day, He never. 1678: Ray, 122.

Broke, if it ain't … *See* **If.**

Broken, *part. adj.* **1. A broken apothecary, a**

new doctor. 1659: Howell, 13. 1670; Ray, 2.

2. A broken glass can't be hurt. 1732: Fuller, 28.

3. A broken latch (or **what not**) **lasts longer than a good one.** 1883: Burne, *Shropsh. Folk-Lore*, 588.

4. A broken leg is not healed by a silk stocking. 1875: A. B. Cheales, *Proverb. Folk-Lore*, 122.

5. A broken sack will hold no corn. 1629: *Book of Meery Riddles*, Prov. 114, A broken bag can hold no meale. 1633: Draxe, 15. 1670: Ray, 65. 1732: Fuller, No 1022.

6. A broken sleeve holdeth (or **keepeth**) **the arm back.** Before 1500: in Hill, *Commonplace-Book*, 132 (E.E.T.S.), For my brokyn sleve, men me refuce, Pro manica fracta, manus est mea sepe retracta. *c.*1550: *Parl. of Byrdes*, l. 164, in Hazlitt, *Early Pop. Poetry*, iii 175 (1866), It is a terme with John and Jacke, Broken sleue draweth arme a backe. 1625: Jonson, *Staple of News*, I i, And therefore you've another answering proverb, *A broken sleeve keeps the arm back*. 1670: Ray, 66.

7. As broken a ship. *See* **Ship** (1).

8. Trust not to a broken staff. 1580: H. Gifford, *Posie*, 71 (Grosart), To trust her lookes … Is nothing els but trust a broken staffe. 1622: in *Pepysian Garland*, 167 (Rollins, 1922), 'Tis bad to trust a broaken staffe. 1732: Fuller, 5290.

Broken, *part.* **1. He has broken his leg.** 1828: Carr, *Craven Dialect*, i 285, 'He's broke his leg', said of a dissolute person on whom a child has been filiated. 1847: Halliwell, *Dict.*, s.v. 'Leg'.

2. She hath broken her leg at the church-door. Cheshire. *See* 1877 quot. 1670: Ray, 166. 1710: Ward, *Nuptial Dialogues*, i 313, You crown the proverb, *That the nicest maid Becomes the greatest slattern when she's wed*. 1732: Fuller, 4119, She broke her elbow on her wedding-day. 1877: Leigh, *Cheshire Gloss.* (W.) … said of a woman who, as a daughter, was a hard worker and did not spare her elbow grease, but who, after marriage, became lazy and indolent. 1917: Bridge, *Cheshire Proverbs*, 108.

3. She hath broken her leg (or **elbow**) **above the knee** = has had a bastard. 1618: B.&F., *Loyal Subject*, III v, If her foot slip, and down fall she, And break her leg above the knee. Before 1625: B.&F., *Wild-Goose Chase*, IV i 1650: R. Heath, *Epigrams*, 64, And so she broke her elboe 'gainst the bed. 1709: Cibber, *Rival Fools*, V, *Gov* … Your niece! your niece! sir. *Sir*

Ol. What! broke her leg? 1785: Grose, *Class. Dict. of Vulgar Tongue*, s.v. 'Leg'. Cf. **Sprained her ankle.**

Broom. *He bestows his gifts as broom yields honey.* 1586: L. Evans, *Revised Withals Dict.*, sig. D4. 1639: Clarke, 38. 1670: Ray, 177. *See also* **Lads' love; May** (10); and **Under the furze.**

Broom. *To hang out the broom. See* quots. 1773: in *Garrick Corresp.*, i 516 (1831), She [his wife] is gone to fleece my flock at St Mary's ... and I hang out the broom in her absence. *c.*1791: Pegge, *Derbicisms*, 91 (E.D.S.), 'To hang about the broom'. This means, to signify that the wife is from home, and that the goodman's friends may come freely to visit him. 1862: *N.&Q.*, 3rd ser, ii 484 [a proverbial expression in Lancs]. (*See also* **New brooms.**)

Broth. 1. *See* quot. 1913: *Devonsh. Assoc. Trans.*, xlv 286, 'When they'm wit (white), they'm fit; When they'm boil'd, they'm spoil'd'. Meaning that broth should be warmed until a white scum appears on the surface, but should not be boiled or raised to boiling point

2. Many esteem more of the broth, than of the meat sod therein. 1577: Stanihurst, *Descrip. of Ireland*, fo. 4, Setteth hymselfe forth to the gaper, by making more of the broth then y[e] flesh is worth. 1639: in *Berkeley MSS.*, iii 32 (1885).

3. Owd [old] **broth's a jell sooner warmt up tan new made.** 1917: Bridge, *Cheshire Proverbs*, 103. Cf. **Old pottage.**

Brother had rather see the sister rich than make her so, The. 1611: Cotgrave, s.v. 'Frere', The brother would have his sister rich any way, but at his charges. 1678: Ray, 203. 1732: Fuller, 4435.

Brough Hill weather is stormy weather, which often occurs at Fair time. Durham, 1909: *Folk Lore*, xx 75.

Brown as a berry, *c.*1386: Chaucer, *Prol.*, l. 207, His palfrey was as brown as is a berye. 1640: Tatham, *Love Crowns the End*, in *Dram. Works*, 20 (1879), Thy nose is as brown as a berry. 1777: Sheridan, *Sch. for Scandal*, III iii 1843: Dickens, *Letters*, iii 54 (1882). 1874: R.L.S., *Letters*, i 173 (Tusitala ed.), I am back again here, as brown as a berry with sun.

Brown study, To be in a. Originally simply 'in a study', and this form persisted for centuries after the inexplicable 'brown' had been introduced, (*a*) *In a study*, simply, *c.*1300: Robert of Brunne, tr.

Langtoft's *Chron.*, 58 (Hearne), Whan Edward perceyued, his herte was in studie. *c.*1386: Chaucer, *Knight's Tale*, l. 672, Into a studie he fil sodeynly. 1485: Malory, *Morte d'Arthur*, bk i ch 20, The kyng sat in a study. 1576: Pettie, *Petite Pallace* i 72 (1908), This youth stood staring in her face in a great study. 1685: *Mother Bunch's Closet*, 5 (Gomme), I am persuaded you are in a study. 1791: Boswell, *Johnson*, ii 34 (Hill), Dr Johnson, who was still in a profound study. 1875: Parish, *Sussex Dict.*, 116, He seems all in a stud as he walks along, (*b*) *In a brown study. c.*1530: *Dice Play*, 6 (Percy S.), Lack of company will soon lead a man into a brown study. 1591: Greene, in *Works*, x 17 (Grosart), Halfe in a browne study at this strange salutation. 1646: Quarles, *Shep. Oracles*, egl. xi, In a browne studie? ... Speechlesse? 1778: Burney, *Evelina*, Lett. xxxiii, He stood some time quite in a brown study, athinking what he should do. 1841: Dickens, *Barn. Rudge*, ch lxxii, Sitting by the hour together in a brown study. 1908: Lucas, *Over Bemerton's*, ch xxiii, I walked home in a brown study.

Brown wench in face shows that nature gives her grace, A. 1623: Wodroephe, *Spared Houres*, 485.

Brush at his back. *See* **Wear** (2).

Brush, He has bought a = has run away. 1813: Ray, 56.

Buck of the first head, He's like a = brisk, pert, forward. 1678: Ray, 67. 1846–59: *Denham Tracts*, ii 109 (F.L.S.).

Buckets in a well, Like. *c.*1386; Chaucer, *Knight's Tale*, l. 675, Now in the croppë, now doun in the breres, Now up, now doun, as boket in a welle. 1596: Shakespeare, *Rich. II*, IV i *c.*1620: in *Roxb. Ballads*, i 76 (Hindley), In Bath a wanton wife did dwell, She had two buckets to a well. *c.*1705: in *Bagford Ballads*, ii 835 (B.S.), Then be not like buckets, one up, t'other down. 1743: T. Sheridan, in *Garrick Corresp.*, i 15 (1831), I don't know whether the old simile of the two buckets would not do as well. 1893: R.L.S., *Ebb-Tide*, ch viii., The three lives went up and down before him like buckets in a well.

Buckingham. *See* **Old,** A (*b*) (6).

Buckinghamshire bread and beef. 1622: Drayton, *Polyol.*, xxiii, Rich Buckingham doth bear the term of Bread and Beef. 1662: Fuller, *Worthies*. i 194 (1840). 1790: Grose, *Prov. Gloss.*, s.v. 'Buckinghamshire'.

Buckle and thong. 1. *See* quot. 1631: Mabbe, *Celestina*, 71 (T.T.), His mother and I were nayle and flesh, buckle and thong.

2. He'll bring buckle and thong together. 1678: Ray, 232. 1732: Fuller, 2422.

3. To be held to it, buckle and thong. 1658: *Wit Restor'd*, in *Mus. Delicioe, I* 280 (Hotten), When one is held to it hard, buckle and thong. 1678: Ray, 73.

4. To come (or **be brought**) **to bare buckle and thong.** 1546: Heywood, *Proverbs* Pt II ch viii 1600: *Weakest to the Wall*, l. 1053 (Malone S.), My benefice doth bring me in no more But what will hold bare buckle and thong together. Before 1746: *Exmoor Courtship*, sc iii, in *Gent. Mag.*, 297–300 (1746). 1886: Elworthy, *West Som. Word-Book*, 96 (E.D.S.), Poor old blid, her's a'most come to nothin' – can't call her nort but nere bucklen thongs.

Buckle of belt. *If you be angry, turn the buckle of your girdle* (or *belt*) *behind you.* 1599: Shakespeare, *Much Ado*, V i *D. Pedro* … I think he be angry indeed. *Claud.* If he be, he knows how to turn his girdle. 1637: Breton: *Poste with Packet Mad Letters* (N.), If you be angry, turne the buckle of your girdle behind you. *c.*1663: Davenant, *Play-House to be Let*, V 1738: Swift, *Polite Convers.*, Dial. I, If miss will be angry for nothing, take my counsel, and bid her turn the buckle of her girdle behind her. 1817: Scott, *Rob Roy*, ch xxv, If ye're angry, ye ken how to turn the buckle o' your belt behind you. 1917: *Devonsh. Assoc. Trans.*, xlix. 335, 'He may turn his buckle behind his back', meaning, apparently, he may prepare to fight.

Buckley panmug, A face like a. 1917: Bridge, *Cheshire Proverbs*, *2*, Buckley in Flintshire … produces a good deal of coarse red earthenware.

Bucknall, Staffs. *Booked for Bucknall* = Going to be married. 1889: *Folk-Lore Journal*, vii 294.

Build. 1. He builds cages fit for oxen, to keep birds in. 1678: Ray, 352. 1732: Fuller, 1815.

2. He that builds on the people, builds on the dirt. 1633: Draxe, 154. 1641: Jonson, *Timber:* 'Principum Varia', Nor let the common proverb (of he that builds on the people, builds on the dirt) discredit my opinion. 1666: Torriano, *Piazza Univ.*, 212.

3. Who-so that buildeth his house all of sallows, Andpricketh his blind horse over the fallows, And suffereth his wife to seek many hallows, Is worthy to be hanged on the gallows! *c.*1386: Chaucer, *Wife of Bath's Prol.*, ll. 655–8. 1417: in *Reliq. Antiquoe*, i 233 (1841) [with last line, 'God sende hym the blisse of everlasting galos']. 1486: *Boke of St Albans*, sig. f4 [as in 1417]. 1717: Pope, *Wife of Bath*, 347, Oft would he say, who builds his house on sands. Pricks his blind horse across the fallow lands, Or lets his wife abroad with pilgrims roam, Deserves a fool's cap, and long ears at home.

Building and marrying of children are great wasters. 1611: Cotgrave, s.v. 'Abandon', The building of houses and making of feasts, are unlimited wasters of a mans substance. 1640: Herbert, *Jac. Prudentum*. 1670: Ray, 3. 1875: A. B. Cheales, *Proverb. Folk-Lore*, 43.

Building is a sweet impoverishing. 1602–3: Manningham *Diary*, 9 (Camden S.), The proverbe is that building is a theife, because it makes us lay out more money then wee thought on. 1640: Herbert, *Jac. Prudentum*. 1670: Ray, 3.

Bull, *subs.* **1. A mad bull is not to be tied up with a packthread.** 1732: Fuller, 266.

2. As sulky as a bull. 1917: Bridge, *Cheshire Proverbs*, 22.

3. He bellows like a bull, but is as weak as a bulrush. 1639: Clarke, 142.

4. He wears the bull's feather = He is a cuckold. 1533: in *Ballads from MSS.*, i 199 (B.S.), Lyke cokold foles together … we wer an oxes fether, *c.*1680: in *Roxb. Ballads*, iii 418 (B.S.), And to all merry cuckolds who think it no scorn To wear the bull's feather, though made of a horn. 1707: Dunton, *Athen. Sport*, p. 118, col. 2, Pompey, Caesar … were not the less esteem'd for having the bull's feather given 'em by their wives. 1737: Ray, 53.

5. Let him take the bull that stole the calf. 1548: Hall. *Chron.*, 406 (1809). Accordyng to the old prouerbe, let him take, etc. 1569: Grafton, *Chron.*, ii 142 (1809).

6. Like a bull in a china-shop. 1850: Smedley, *Frank Fairlegh*, ch xli., Stigmatising himself as an awkward dog, and comparing himself to a bull in a china-shop. 1899: H. James, in *Letters*, i 349 (1920), Floundering and romping through the arts, both literary and plastic, very much as a bull through a china-shop. 1913: R. E. Francillon, *Mid-Vict. Memories*, 149.

7. No further than you can throw a bull by the tail. 1869: Haxlitt, 293.

8. To take the bull by the horns. 1816: Scott, *Old Mortality*, ch xxv 1849: Lytton, *Caxtons*, Pt II ch i 1869: Spurgeon, *John Ploughman*, ch xi, I have often been told to be bold, and take the bull by the horns.

9. You may play with a bull, till you get his horn in your eye = *Don't* play with edged tools. 1886: R. Holland, *Cheshire Gloss.*, 457 (E.D.S.). 1917: Bridge, *Cheshire Proverbs*, 158.

See also **Lawless; No law;** and **Town bull.**

Bull, *verb. See* 1659 quot. 1612: *Cornucopiae*, 78 (Grosart), Yours is the cow, and you shall keepe the calfe. 1659: Howell, *Proverbs*, 'To Philologers', That [proverb] which began in Henrie the Fourth's time, He that bulls the cow must keep the calf. *c.*1670: in *Roxb. Ballads*, iii 368 (B.S.), Said they 'The calf must with the cow'. 1691: Southerne, *Sir Ant. Love*, IV ii, I had the reputation of it indeed [a bastard]; and should have had the cow with the calf. 1732: Fuller, 5695, Who bulls the cow must keep the calf.

Bullet has its billet, Every. 1575: Gascoigne, *Fruites of Warre*, st. 67, in *Works*, i 154 (Cunliffe), Every bullet hath a lighting place. 1757: Smollett, *Reprisal*, II viii, Every shot has its commission, d'ye see. 1765: Wesley, *Journal*, 6 June, He never received one wound. So true is the odd saying of King William, that 'every bullet has its billet'. 1826–44: Hood, *Comic Poems:* 'Waterloo Ballad', Its billet every bullet has. 1837: Dickens, *Pickwick*, ch xix.

Bungay. *Go to Bungay, to get new-bottomed.* 1830: Forby, *Vocab. E. Anglia*, 434. 1872: J. Glyde, jr., *Norfolk Garland*, 150. *See also* **Beccles.**

Burford bait, A = Drink. 1636: Taylor (Water-Poet), *Cat. of Taverns*, 58, in *Works*, 4th coll. (Spens.S.), Beware of a Burfourd bayt, for it may brew the staggers. 1662: Fuller, *Worthies*, iii 5 (1840), To take a Burford bait. 1790: Grose, *Prov. Gloss.*, s.v. 'Oxfordshire'.

Buried under the gallows. *See* quots. 1678: Ray, 221, He that kills himself with working must be buried under the gallows. 1828: Carr, *Craven Dialect*, i 174 … This is said to be the doom of a man who kills himself with hard working. 1889: Peacock, *Manley, etc., Gloss.*, 227 (E.D.S.), Thaay bury them as kills ther'sens wi' hard wark aneän th' galla's.

Burn, *verb.* **1. Burn not your house to fright away the mice.** 1732: Fuller, 1024.

2. He is burnt to the socket = is dying, is at his last gasp. 1813: Ray, 57.

3. He that burns his house warms himself for once. 1640: Herbert, *Jac. Prudentum.*

4. He that burns most shines most. 1640: Herbert, *Jac. Prudentum.* 1852: FitzGerald, *Polonius*, 92 (1903).

5. He will burn his house to warm his hands. 1481: Caxton, *Reynard*, 78 (Arber), They retche not whos hows brenneth, so that they may warme them by the coles. 1640: Herbert, *Jac. Prudentum.*

6. They that burn you for a witch lose all their coals. 1732: Fuller, 4974. 1846–59: *Denham Tracts*, ii 84 (F.L.S.).

7. To burn daylight. 1587: Churchyard, *Worth. of Wales*, 84 (Spens.S.), Tyme rouleth on, I doe but daylight burne. 1592: Lyly, *Mother Bombie*, II i, Wee burne time. 1692: L'Estrange, *Aesop*, 298 (3rd ed.), Talk does but burn daylight. 1707: Cibber, *Comical Lovers*, II, We burn day-light, lose time, and love. 1828: Carr, *Craven Dialect*, i 58, Burn day-light. To light candles before dark.

8. To burn the house, and run away by the light of it. 1530: Palsgrave, 710, I can set a house a fyre and ronne awaye by the lyght. *c.*1720: J. Smedley, in *Somers Tracts*, xiii 824 (1811), The following English proverbs … Burn the house, and run away by the light of it.

See also **Candle 5.**

Burnt child dreads the fire, A. [Cui dolet, meminit. – Cicero, *Pro Mur.*, 42.] *c.*1300: in *Reliq. Antiquæ*, i 113 (1841), Brend child fur dredeth; Quoth Hendyng. *c.*1400: *Rom. Rose*, l. 1820: Brent child of fyr hath muche drede. 1580: Lyly, *Euphues*, 319 (Arber), A burnt childe dreadeth the fire. 1616: Jonson, *Devil an Ass*, I ii 1725: Bailey, tr. Erasmus' *Colloq.*, 157. *c.*1760: Foote, *Cozeners*, I. 1820: Scott, *Fam. Letters*, ii 73 (1894).

Burroughs end of sheep, Some one = ? 1678: Ray, 68.

Burst at the broadside, To. A drinking phrase. 1670: Ray, 217.

Burthen of one's own choice is not felt, A. 1855: Bohn, 282.

Burton. *See* **Barton.**

Burton-bream. *See* **Brayton-bargh.**

Bury the hatchet, To. *See* **Hatchet.**

Burying a wife. *See* quots. 1847: Halliwell, *Dict.*, s.v. 'Burying-a-wife', A feast given by an apprentice at the expiration of his articles. 1899:

Dickinson, *Cumberland Gloss.*, 23, Berryin' t'ould wife. The treat given by an apprentice on obtaining his freedom.

Burying is gone by, The. *See* quots. *c*.1791: Pegge, *Derbicisms*, 92 (E.D.S.), 'The burying's gone by', i.e. you are too late. 1891: *N.&Q.*, 7th ser, xi 148, 'Th' berrin's gone by, and t'child's called Anthony'. This saying used to be current in Lancashire fifty years ago, when any one appeared just too late for the event he had come to witness.

Bush. 1. A bad (thin, etc.) busk is better than no shelter. *c*.1300: *Prov. of Hendyng*, st. 22 (Berlin, 1878), Under boske shal men weder abide. 1670: Ray, 58, A bad bush is better then the open field. 1732: Fuller, 432, A thin bush is better than no shelter. 1820: Scott, *Monastery*, ch iii, These evil showers make the low bush better than no bield.

2. Bush natural. *See* Hair (3).

3. He thinks every bush a boggard. 1678: Ray, 232.

Bushel. 1. A whole bushel of wheat is made up of single grains. 1732: Fuller, 456.

2. In a bushel of winning is not a handful of cunning. Before 1500: Hill, *Commonplace-Book*, 131 (E.E.T.S.).

3. You should eat a bushel of salt with a man before you trust him. [Aristotle, *Ethics*, viii 4. Multos modios salis simul edisse. – Cicero, *Lael.*, 19.] 1539: Taverner, *Proverbs*, fo. 30, Trust no man onles thou hast fyrst eaten a bushel of salte wyth hym. 1579: Lyly, *Euphues*, 48 (Arber), One should eate a bushel of salt with him whom he meaneth to make his friend. 1637: Shirley, *Hyde Park*, III i, If you allow a bushel of salt to acquaintance ... 1707: Dunton, *Athen. Sport*, 452. 1716: Ward, *Female Policy*, 83. 1875: A.B.Cheales, *Proverb. Folk-Lore*, 95.

Business. 1. Business is business. 1857: Thackeray, *Virginians*, ch i, Business is business, my dear young sir. 1876: Blackmore, *Cripps*, ch iii 1922: Weyman, *Ovington's Bank*, ch xxvi.

2. Business is the salt of life. 1732: Fuller, 1026.

3. Business makes a man as well as tries him. 1855: Bohn, 334.

4. He that thinks his business below him, will always be above his business. 1732: Fuller, 2333.

Busy as a bee. *c*.1386: Chaucer, *Merch. Tale*, Epil., l. 4, For ay as bisy as bees Ben they. 1580: Lyly, *Euphues*, 252 (Arber). 1655: Fuller, *Church Hist.*, bk ix § vii (24). 1709: Cibber. *Rival Fools*, I. 1792: Wolcot, in *Works*, ii 405 (1795). 1834–7: Southey, *Doctor*, ch lxxix. 1901: Raymond, *Idler Out of Doors*, 35, The place is busy as a swarm of bees. Cf. **Busy as bees in a basin.**

Busy as a cat. *See* Cat (9).

Busy as a dog. *See* Dog (17).

Busy as a good wife at oven. 1670: Ray, 203.

Busy as a hen. *See* Hen (2).

Busy as Batty. 1850: *N.&Q.*, 1st ser, i 475, In Devonshire they say 'Busy as Batty', but no one knows who 'Batty' was.

Busy as bees in a basin. 1834: Toone, *Gloss.*, s.v. 'Bees'. There is a proverb in Leicestershire ... 'as busy as bees in a basin'. Cf. Busy as a bee.

Busy folks are always meddling. 1736: Bailey, *Dict.*, s.v. 'Busy'.

Busy will have bands (or bonds). 1633: Draxe, 19. 1670: Ray, 66.

Busy. Who more busy than he that hath least to do? 1633: Draxe, 20. 1670: Ray, 66. 1753: Richardson, *Grandison*, i 294 (1883), I tell the ladies here, that those who have least to do, are generally the most busy people in the world.

Busy-bodies never want a bad day. 1732: Fuller, 1029.

'But,' says Parson Lasky. 1864: 'Cornish Proverbs', in *N.&Q.*, 3rd ser, vi 5. 1888: Q.-Couch, *Troy Town*, ch iv.

But when, quoth Kettle to his mare. Cheshire. 1678: Ray, 276. 1852: in *N.&Q.*, 1st ser, vi 386. 1917: Bridge, *Cheshire Proverbs*, 33.

Butcher. 1. He would have made a good butcher, but for the by-blow. 1639: Clarke, 77.

2. I think this is a butchers horse, he carries a calf so well. 1678: Ray, 232.

3. The butcher looked for his knife and it was in his mouth. 1639: Clarke, 75. *c*.1640: in *Roxb. Ballads*, iii 321 (B.S.), [Kit the butcher] Hee'd with his candell looke his knife, When hee had it in his mouth. 1692: L'Estrange, *Aesop*, 340 (3rd ed.). 1738: Swift, *Polite Convers.*, Dial. I.

4. The butcher looked for the candle, and 'twas in his hat. 1639: Clarke, 75.

Butler's grace = ? 1609: Melton, *Sixfold Politician*, 33, Fidlers, who are regarded but for a baudy song, at a merry meeting, and when they have done, are commonly sent away with butler's grace.

Butter. 1. Butter is gold in the morning, silver at noon, and lead at night. 1588: Cogan, *Haven of Health*, 156 (1612), According to the old English prouerbe: Butter is gold, etc. *c.*1653: in *Somers Tracts*, vii 69 (1811), This butter-print parliament was gold in the morning and lead at night. 1738: Swift: *Polite Convers.*, Dial. I.

2. Butter is good for anything but to stop an oven. 1659: Howell, 6.

3. Butter is in the cow's horn once a year. Ibid., 14. 1670: Ray, 44. 1846: Denham, *Proverbs*, 5 (Percy S.), When the cow is *dried* for calving it is usual to say, 'All the butter is gone into the cow's horn'.

4. Butter is mad twice a year, i.e. when very hard, and very soft. 1625: Jonson, *Staple of News*, II, So butter answer my expectation, and be not mad butter; 'if it be, It shall both July and December see!' 1626: B.&F., *Noble Gent.*, I ii, Mad as May-butter. 1738: Swift, *Polite Convers.*, Dial. I. 1921: in *N.&Q.*, 12th ser, ix 330, A Hertford servant girl, some forty-five years old, when experiencing any difficulty in spreading butter on the bread, used to remark, 'Butter goes mad twice a year, as my grandmother says'.

5. No butter will cleave on my bread. 1546: Heywood, *Proverbs*, Pt II ch vii 1591: Greene, in *Works*, x 22 (Grosart), Well, saith the setter, no butter will cleave on my bread. 1656: Flecknoe, *Diarium*, 38, No butter'd stick upon my bread. 1727: Swift, *Works*, xiv 203 (Scott), But now I fear it will be said, No butter sticks upon his bread. 1824: Scott, *Redgauntlet*, ch xv, The devil a crumb of butter was ever churned that would stick upon my bread.

6. That which will not be butter must be made into cheese. 1678: Ray, 107. 1732: Fuller, 4387.

7. They that have good store of butter may lay it thick on their bread. 1639: Clarke, 49. 1681: W. Robertson, *Phraseol. Generalis*, 1302. 1732: Fuller, 4980.

8. To look as if butter would not melt in one's mouth. 1530: Palsgrave, 620, He maketh as thoughe butter wolde nat melte in his mouthe. 1583: Stubbes, *Anat. of Abuses*, 89 (N.Sh.S.). 1641: Cowley, *Guardian*, III viii 1687: Sedley, *Bellamira*, IV, in *Works*, ii 163 (1778). 1714: Ozell, *Molière*, iv 122. 1850: Dickens,

Chuzzlewit, ch iii 1922: Weyman, *Ovington's Bank*, ch ix.

9. To take butter out of a dog's mouth. 1732: Fuller, 699, As irrecoverable as a lump of butter in a greyhound's mouth. 1886: Elworthy, *West Som. Word-Book*, 202 (E.D.S.), We have an old saying, as easy to get butter out of a dog's mouth, as money out of a lawyer. 1908: T. Ratcliffe, in *N.&Q.*, 10th ser, x 387.

Butter one's bread, To. *See* **Bread** (8) and (12).

Butterbump. *See* **Foot** (3).

Buttermilk wedding, A. A poor affair. 1917: Bridge, *Cheshire Proverbs*, 2.

Button-hole. *See* **Take** (27).

Buy. 1. Buy at a fair but sell at home. 1633: Draxe, 21, A man must buie at the faire, and sell at home. 1670: Ray, 4, Buy at a market, but sell at home. 1732: Fuller, 1034 [as in 1670].

2. He is able to buy an Abbey = He is a spendthrift. 1678: Ray, 352.

3. He that buyeth magistracy, must sell justice. 1642: Fuller, *Holy State:* 'The Good Judge', They that buy justice by wholesale, to make themselves savers must sell it by retail. 1732: Fuller, 2055. Cf. No. 11.

4. He that buys a house. *See* **House** (7).

5. He that buys and lies shall feel it in his purse. 1612: Shelton, *Quixote*, Pt I bk iii ch xi 1712: Motteux, *Quixote*, Pt I bk iii ch xi 1732: Fuller, 2056.

6. He that buys dearly must sell dearly. *c.*1538: Starkey, *England*, II i 175 (OED), He that byth dere may sel dere. 1681: Yarranton, *Eng. Improvement*, Pt II, p. 183, The old saying is, *He that buys dear, must sell dear.*

7. He that buys land buys many stones; He that buys flesh buys many bones; He that buys eggs buys many shells; But he that buys good ale buys nothing else. 1670: Ray, 211. 1732: Fuller, 6422. 1865: in *N.&Q.*, 3rd ser, viii 494. 1901: F. E. Taylor, *Lancs Sayings*, 42, Thoose 'at buy'n beef buy'n booans; Thoose 'at buy'n lond buy'n stooans; Thoose 'at buy'n eggs buy'n shells; Thoose 'at buy'n good ale buy'n nout elze!

8. He that refuseth to buy counsel cheap, shall buy repentance dear. 1647: *Countrym. New Commonwealth*, 39. 1669: *Politeuphuia*, 98. *c.*1670: *Sir Richard Whittington*, 5 (Villon S., 1885).

9. It is good to buy wit with other men's

money. 1672: Walker, *Paroem.*, 30. 1681: W. Robertson. *Phraseol. Generalis*, 297.

10. One may buy gold too dear. 1546: Heywood, *Proverbs*, Pt II ch vii, A man may by gold to deere. 1579: Spenser, *Shep. Cal.*, August, l. 123, So you may buye golde too deare. 1692: L'Estrange, Ae*sop*, 167 (3rd ed.). 1844: Thackeray, *Barry Lyndon*, ch xiii, The fact is, in my opinion, that we often buy money very much too dear.

11. They that buy an office must sell something. 1650: Taylor, *Holy Living*, ch iii § 2, For they that buy the office will sell the act. 1732: Fuller, 4975. Cf. No. 3.

12. To buy and sell and live by the loss. 1633: Draxe, 20. 1660: Fuller, *Mixt Contempl.*, 347 (1830), Merchandising is a ticklish matter, seeing many buy and sell and live by the loss. 1732: Fuller, 1033.

13. To buy dear is not bounty. 1640: Herbert, *Jac. Prudentum.* 1670: Ray, 4.

14. Who always buys and sells, feels not what he spends. 1659: Howell, *Proverbs: Span.-Eng.*, 1. 1732: Fuller, 5693.

15. Who buyeth dear and taketh up on credit, shall ever sell to his loss. 1578: Florio, *First Fruites*, fo. 28, Who buyeth deere, and taketh of credit; consumeth the body and looseth the seede. 1629: *Book of Meery Riddles*, Prov. 70.

Buyer. 1. Let the buyer beware. Often encountered in the Latin form, *Caveat emptor*, a shortening of the legal maxim *Caveat emptor, quia ignorare non debuit quod ius alienum emit* (Let the buyer beware, for he should not be ignorant of the nature of the property that he is buying from another person). 1523: J. Fitzherbert *Husbandry*, 36, And [if] he [a horse] be tame and have ben rydden upon then caveat emptor be ware thou buyer. 1592: Nash, *Pierce Penniless*, I 155, Sed caveat emptor, Let the interpreter beware.1607: E. Sharpham, *Fleire*, II, in Bang, *Materialien*, B. 36, p. 19, Beware the buyer say they, you shall haue enough for your money. 1672: Walker, *Paroem.*, 41, Let the buyer look to himself.

2. The buyer needs a hundred eyes, the seller but one. 1640: Herbert, *Jac. Prudentum.* 1732: Fuller, 1035 [with 'none' for 'but one']. 1869:

Spurgeon, *John Ploughman*, ch xvi, Buyers ought to have a hundred eyes. 1928: *Sporting and Dramatic News*, 7 Jan., p. 27.

Buying and selling is but winning and losing. 1678: Ray, 107. 1732: Fuller, 1036.

Buying of bread undoes us, This. 1678: Ray, 67. 1748: *Gent. Mag.*, 21.

Buzzard. *See* **Blind**, *adj.* (13); **Hawk** (1); **Sparrow-hawk;** and **Too low.**

By and by is easily said. 1855: Bohn, 334.

By chance, as the man killed the devil. 1738: Swift, *Polite Convers.*, Dial. I.

By fits and starts (or girds). 1620: Sanderson, *Serm. ad Pop.*, i 145 (1681) (OED), If thou hast these things only by fits and starts. 1650: Fuller, *Pisgah Sight*, bk i ch ii, That froward people worshipped Him by fits and girds. 1709: Ward, *Acc. of Clubs*, 69 (1756), Yet still, by fits and starts, he'll jadish be. 1732: Fuller, 1039, By fits and girts, as an ague takes a goose. 1748: Richardson, *Clarissa*, iv 318 (1785) … by fits and starts. 1825: Jennings, *Somersetsh. Words*, 42, By fits and gurds. 1840: Dickens, *Curiosity Shop*, ch xxvii *ad fin.* … by fits and starts all night. 1847: Halliwell, *Dict.*, s.v. 'Gurds', Gurds. Fits; starts. *Var. dial.*

By one and one spindles are made. 1578: Florio, *First Fruites, fo.* 25. 1629: *Book of Meery Riddles*, Prov. 62.

By the ears. 1539: Taverner, *Garden of Wysdome*, ch iv, He set a yonge lyon and a very eger dogge togither by the eares. *c.*1580: Spelman, *Dialogue*, 74 (Roxb.Cl) One euyll tonge may sette a nomber of men to gether by the eares. *c.*1630: *Dicke of Devonsh.*, I iii, in Bullen, *Old Plays*, ii 21. 1742: Fielding, *Andrews*, bk ii ch xi 1819: Byron, *Letters, etc.*, iv 295 (Prothero).

By the great. *See* **Work** (4).

Bygones be bygones, Let. – Epictetus, *Disc.*, II xix 34.] 1546: Heywood, *Proverbs*, Pt II ch ix, Let all thinges past pas. 1648: Nethersole, *Parables*, 5 (OED), Let bygans be bygans'. 1710; S. Palmer, *Moral Essays on Proverbs*, 292, Bygones be by-gones, and fair play for time to come. 1857: Borrow, *Rom. Rye*, ch xliv. 1909: De Morgan, *Never can happen Again*, ch xxviii.

C

Ca me, ca thee. *See* **Ka me, ka thee.**

Cackle, *verb*, **I. I would not have your cackling for your eggs.** 1732: Fuller, 2658.

2. She can cackle like a cadowe [jackdaw]. 1579: *Marr. of Wit and Wisdom,* sc iii, p. 26 (SH.S.), Ah, that drabe, she can cacklel like a cadowe. 1886: Swainson, *Folk-Lore of Brit. Birds,* 82 (F.L.S.).

3. You cackle often but never lay an egg. 1732: Fuller, 5867.

Cadbury castle. *See* quot. 1790: Grose, *Prov. Gloss.,* s.v. 'Devonshire', If Cadburye-castle and Dolbury-hill dolven wer, All England might ploughe with a golden sheere.

Caesar's wife must be above suspicion. [Tum Caesar … respondit: Quia suam uxorem etiam suspicione vacare vellet. – Plutarch, *Julius Caesar,* x (4).] 1740: North, *Examen,* 59, A judge should be, like Caesar's wife, neither false nor suspected. 1748: Richardson, *Clarissa,* iii 85 (1785). 1895: Shaw, *Man of Destiny, Lady* [*humbly*] I beg your pardon. Caesar's wife is above suspicion.

Caistor was city when Norwich was none, And Norwich was built of Caistor stone. 1840: *Penny Cyclop.,* xvi 327. 1865: W. White, *Eastern England,* i 64.

Cake. 1. I had rather my cake burn than you should turn it. 1732: Fuller, 2598.

2. One's cake is dough. 1559: Becon, in *Prayers, etc.,* 277 (P.S.), Or else your cake is dough, and all your fat lie in the fire. *c.*1598: Jonson, *Case is Altered,* V iv 1665: Pepys, *Diary,* 27 April, Which puts … me into a great fear, that all my cake will be doe still. 1720: C. Shadwell, *Hasty Wedding,* IV i 1854: Baker, *Northants. Gloss.,* s.v. 'Cake', 'All our cakes are dough'. A proverbial expression, indicating the failure of any undertaking or project. Nares says, obsolete; not so with us. 1886: Hardy, *Casterbridge,* ch xiii, She'll wish her cake dough afore she's done of him.

3. That cake came out of my oven. 1732: Fuller, 4335.

4. There is no cake but there is the like of the same make. 1659: Howell, 5. 1670: Ray, 4. 1762: Smollett, *Sir L. Greaves,* ch x, Crabshaw replied, 'There's no cake but there's another of the same make.'

See also **Eat** (43).

Calais. *See* quot. 1528: Tyndale, *Obed. of Christ. Men,* 239 (P.S.), He shall be cast out of the court, or, as the saying is, conveyed to Calais, and made a captain or an ambassador.

Calder. *See* **Hodder.**

Calenick. *The Mayor of Calenick, who walked two miles to ride one.* 1891: Q.-Couch, *Noughts and Crosses,* 185. 1906: Ibid., *Mayor of Troy,* Prol.

Cales, *See* **Knight.**

Calf and Calves. 1. A calf's head will feed a huntsman and his hounds. 1678: Ray, 108. 1846–59: *Denham Tracts,* ii 108 (F.L.S.).

2. As good luck as the lousy calf, that lived all winter and died in the summer. 1678: Ray, 287.

3. As many calves' skins come to market as of bulls or kine. 1552: Latimer, *Sermons,* 416 (P.S.), It is a common saying, 'There do come, etc'.

4. As wanton as a calf with two dams. 1670: Ray, 208.

5. He who will steal a calf will steal a cow. 1736: Bailey, *Dict.,* s.v. 'Calf'.

6. His calves are gone down to grass. 1678: Ray, 232.

7. That calf never heard church-bell. 1917: Bridge, *Cheshire Proverbs,* 110, A calf born and killed between two Sundays.

8. The largest calves are not the sweetest veal. 1605: Camden, *Remains,* 332 (1870), The greatest calf is not the sweetest veal. 1790: Wolcot, *Works,* ii 111 (1795).

9. To eat the calf in the cow's belly = To reckon one's chickens before they are hatched. 1642: Fuller, *Holy State:* 'Of Expecting Preferment', The law of good husbandry forbids us to eat a kid in the mother's belly, spending our pregnant hopes before they be delivered. 1748: Richardson, *Clarissa,* iii 122 (1785), I ever made shift to avoid anticipations: *I never would eat the calf in the cow's belly,* as Lord M's phrase is. 1792: Wolcot, *Works,* ii 388 (1795). 1875: Smiles, *Thrift,* 264. 1886: Elworthy, *West Som. Word-Book,* 58 (E.D.S.), A very common bucolic saying, precisely expressive of what is called 'discounting' in commercial talk, is eating the calf in the cow's belly.

See also **Bull,** *subs.* (5); **Change,** *subs.* (3); **Cow**

(3), (20), and (31); **Eat** (43); **Essex;** and **Like cow.**

Call. 1. Call one a thief and he will steal. 1838: Carlyle, *Sartor*, bk ii ch i, In a very plain sense the proverb says, Call one a thief, and he will steal.

2. Call over the coals. *See* **Over the coals.**

3. It is too late to call again yesterday. Before 1529: Skelton, *Magnyfycence*, l. 2057, Yesterday wyll not be callyd agayne. 1538: Latimer, *Works*, ii 398 (P.S.). 1639: Davenport, *Too Late to call back Yesterday* [title of dialogue]. 1676: Dryden, *Aureng-Zebe*, V i, To love, once past, I cannot backward move; Call yesterday again, and I may love. 1707: Dunton, *Athen. Sport*, p. 14, col. 2., So can we no more recommend them, than call back yesterday.

4. To call one sir and something else, i.e. sirrah. 1678: Ray, 269.

Calm. 1. Calm after a storm. *See* **Storm** (1) and (2).

2. Calm as a clock. 1831: Hone, *Year-Book*, 622, 'As calm as a clock' has long been a favourite proverb with me.

3. In a calm sea every man is a pilot. [Seneca, Epist. LXXXV. 1639: Clarke, 313 [with 'passenger' for 'man']. 1670: Ray, 4. 1732: Fuller, 2808, In a calm every one can steer.

Calmest husbands. *See* **Husband** (4).

Calverley Mill. *See* **Billing Hill.**

Camberwell. *See* quots. 1588: A. Fraunce, *Lawiers Logike*, fo. 27, All the maydes in Camberwell may daunce in an egge shell. 1861: *N.&Q.*, 2nd ser, xi 449, [as in 1588+] For there are noe maydes in that well. Cf. **Wanswell.**

Cambridge. 1. A Royston horse and a Cambridge Master of Arts are a couple of creatures that will give way to nobody. 1662: Fuller, *Worthies*, i 226 (1840) [with 'boisten' for 'Royston']. 1790: Grose, *Prov. Gloss.*, s.v. 'Cambridgeshire' [as in 1662]. 1885: *Folk-Lore Journal*, iii 85, The proverb, 'A Royston horse and a Cambridge M.A. will give way to no one', refers to the stolid way in which the malt-laden horses of the Hertfordshire town bore their burdens to the London market.

2. Cambridge requires all to be equal. 1662: Fuller, *Worthies*, i 226 (1840). 1790: Grose, *Prov. Gloss.*, s.v. 'Cambridgeshire'.

Cambridgeshire Camels. 1662: Fuller – as before. 1790: Grose – as before. 1874: Smiles,

Lives of Engineers, i 14, The proverb of 'Cambridgeshire Camels' doubtless originated in this old practice of stilt-walking in the Fens.

Cambridgeshire Oaks = Willows. 1785: Grose, *Class. Dict.*, *Vulgar Tongue*, s.v. 1790: Grose – as before.

Can, does … , He who. *See* **Teach** 2.

Candle. 1. A candle lights others and consumes itself. 1855: Bohn, 283.

2. Candle ate the cat. *See* **True** (6).

3. His candle burns within the socket. 1639: Clarke, 279. 1681: W. Robertson, *Phraseol. Generalis*, 307, His candle burns within the socket; Homo depontanus est. 1736: Bailey, *Dict.*, s.v. 'Candle'.

4. Not worth the candle. *See* **Game.**

5. To burn the candle at both ends. 1658: Flecknoe, *Enigm. Characters*, 64, He consuming just like a candle on both ends, betwixt wine and women. 1750: Smollett, *Gil Blas*, iii 116, The butler and steward were in a confederacy, and burnt the candle at both ends. 1842: Barham, *Ing. Legends*, 2nd ser: 'St Cuthbert'. 1889: Peacock, *Manley, etc., Gloss.*, 81 (E.D.S.), Burn candles at both ends. – To be very wasteful.

6. To hold (or set) a candle before the devil. 1461: *Paston Lett.*, ii 73 (Gairdner, 1900), For it is a comon proverbe, 'A man must sumtyme set a candel befor the Devyle'. *c.*1540: *Thersites*, in Hazlitt, *Old Plays*, i 427, It is good to set a candle before the deviL 1672: Wycherley, *Love in a Wood*. I i, You cannot hold a candle to the devil. 1705: Ward, *Hud. Rediv.*, Pt III can. iv, p. 16. 1828: Scott, *Fair Maid*, ch xxix 1871: G. Eliot, *Middle march*, ch xvi, Their impression that the general scheme of things … required you to hold a candle to the devil.

7. To waste a candle and find a flea (or **farthing**). 1623: Wodroephe, *Spared Houres*, 504 … find a flea. 1880: Spurgeon, *Ploughman's Pictures*, 19, They are like Pedley, who burnt a penny candle in looking for a farthing.

See also **Sun** (13).

Candlemas Day. 2 Feb. The Feast of the Purification of the B.V.M. [Before 1529: Skelton, *Garl. of Laurell*, l. 1442, How men were wont for to discerne By candelmas day, what wether shoulde holde.]

a) A FINE CANDLEMAS DAY. *c.*1576: G. Harvey, *Marginalia*, 175 (1913), A faire Candlemas, a fowle Lent. 1584: R. Scot, *Witchcraft*, bk xi ch xv, If Maries purifying-day Be cleare and bright with sunny raie, Then frost and cold shall be much more, After the feast than was before. 1640: *Countrym. Counsellor*, in *Helpe to Discourse*, 224, When on the Purification sun hath shin'd, The greatest part of winter comes behind. 1646: Browne, *Pseudo. Epi.*, bk vi ch iv [cites the old distich: Si Sol splendescat Maria purificante, Major erit glacies post festum quam fuit ante]. 1678: Ray, 51, If Candlemas day be fair and bright Winter will have another flight. 1732: Fuller, 6486 [as in 1678]. 1799: *Gent. Mag.*, Pt I, p. 203, If the sun shines i' th' forenoon [of Candlemas Day], Winter is not half done. 1846: Denham, *Proverbs*, 29 (Percy S.), If Candlemas-day be dry and fair, The half of winter's to come and mair. 1879: Henderson, *Folk-Lore N. Counties*, 76 (F.L.S.), If the sun shines bright on Candlemas Day, The half of the winter's not yet away. 1893: Inwards, *Weather Lore*, 15, If Candlemas Day be fine and clear, Corn and fruits will then be dear [also as in 1640 and 1678]. Ibid., 16, After Candlemas Day the frost will be more keen, If the sun then shines bright, than before it has been. 1904: *Co. Folk-Lore: Northumb.*, 175 (F.L.S.), If Candlemas day is fair and clear, There'll be two winters in the year.

b) A foul Candlemas Day. 1678: Ray, 51, If on Candlemas day it be showre and rain, Winter is gone and will not come again. 1732: Fuller, 6486 [as in 1678]. 1855: *N.&Q.*, 1st ser, xi 421, On Candlemas Day if the thorns hang a-drop, Then you are sure of a good pea-crop. 1893: Inwards, *Weather Lore*, 16 [as in 1678, with slight variation, and as in 1855]. 1917: Bridge, *Cheshire Proverbs*, 164, If Candlemas Day be damp and black, It will carry cold winter away on its back.

c) Candlemas Day and Candles. 1678: Ray, 344, On Candlemas day, throw candle and candlestick away. 1732: Fuller, 6152 [as in 1678]. 1855: *N.&Q.*, 1st ser, xi 239 [as in 1678]. 1893: Inwards, *Weather Lore*, 15 [as in 1678].

d) Candlemas Day and Forage. 1639: in *Berkeley MSS.*, iii 30 (1885), At Candlemas a provident husbandman should have halfe his fodder, and all his corne remaininge. 1732: Fuller, 6487, On Candlemas-day, You must have half your straw, and half your hay. 1855: [a Norfolk correspondent] in *N.&Q.*, 1st ser, xi 239, The farmer should have on Candlemas Day, Half his

stover [winter forage], and half his hay. 1881: C. W. Empson, in *Folk-Lore Record*, iv 127, If it neither rains nor snows on Candlemas Day, You may striddle your horse and go buy hay. Lincs. 1893: Inwards, *Weather Lore*, 15 [as in 1732]. 1916: in *N.&Q.*, 12th ser, ii 118, Rime … known in several North-Midland counties runs: – 'If Candlemas Day comes blithe and gay, You may saddle your horse and buy some hay; But if Candlemas Day comes rugged and rough, You may fodder away – you'll have fodder enough'. Which means that if there be hard weather at the beginning of February it bodes well for the hay and corn crops later on.

e) Candlemas Day and Goose-laying. 1846. Denham, *Proverbs*, 31 (Percy S.), On Candlemas-day a good goose will lay; But on Valentine's day, any goose will lay. 1883: Burne, *Shropsh. Folk-Lore*, 578, At Candlemas Day A good goose should lay; But at St Chad Both good and bad. 1913: E. M. Wright, *Rustic Speech, etc.*, 289, At this date, according to a common proverb: gooid geese all lay; New Candlemas Day, good goose will lay, Old Candlemas Day any goose will lay.

f) Candlemas Day and Sheep. 1732: Fuller, 6485, The shepherd had as live see his wife on the bier, As that Candlemas-day should be pleasant and clear. 1830: Forby, *Vocab. E. Anglia*, 416, On Candlemas Day, if the sun shines clear, The shepherd had rather see his wife on the bier. 1846: Denham, *Proverbs*, 28 (Percy S.) [as in 1732, with 'hind' for 'shepherd']. 1879: Henderson, *Folk-Lore N. Counties*, 76 [as in 1830].

g) Candlemas Day and Snow. 1678: Ray, 43, When Candlemas day is come and gone The snow lies on a hot stone. 1825: Hone, *Ev. Day Book*, i 2 Feb., *ad fin.* [as in 1678]. 1855: *N.&Q.*, 1st ser, xi 239, (1) When Candlemas Day is come and gone, The snow won't lay on a hot stone. [Also] (2) As far as the sun shines in on Candlemas Day, So far will the snow blow in afore old May. 1872: J. Glyde, jr., *Norfolk Garland*, 153 [as in 1855 (1) – 'won't lie']. 1873: *N.&Q.*, 4th ser, xi 275, Snow at Candlemas, Stops to handle us [Rutland].

h) Candlemas Day: Miscellaneous. 1. A Candlemas crack. 1877: F. Ross, etc., *Holderness Gloss.*, 37 (E.D.S.), A Cannlemas-crack [storm] Lays monny a sailor on his back. 2. *As long as the bird* *sings before Candlemas, it will greet after it.* 1846. Denham, *Proverbs*, 27 (Percy S.). 3. *At Candlemas, the cold comes to us.* 1732: Fuller, 6381. 1893: Inwards, *Weather Lore*, 15. 4. *February 2nd, bright and clear, Gives a good flax year.* Ibid., 16. 5. *See* quot. 1910: *Devonsh. Assoc. Trans.*, xlii. 81, 'Green Candlemas, barren Redmas'; proverb used by an old Ashwater man, when a cold May followed a warm early spring ['Redmas' probably = Festival of Invention of Cross, 3 May]. 6. *When the wind's in the east on Candlemas day, There it will stick till the second of May.* 1852: *N.&Q.*, 1st ser, v 462. 1893: Inwards, *Weather Lore*, 16 [as in 1852].

See also **All-hallon-tide;** and **Bean** (7).

Candlemas Eve Wind. 1839: G. C. Lewis, *Herefs. Words*, I22, When the wind blows on Candlemas-eve, it will continue till May-eve. 1858: *N.&Q.*, 2nd ser, v 391, [An old farmer said] it had been observed by him, and by his father before him, that in whatever quarter the wind might be on Candlemas Eve, it 'mainly' remained in that quarter for forty days.

Can't you hit the door? 1639: Clarke, 1.

Canterbury. 1. A Canterbury gallop. 1675: in *Harl. Miscell.*, vii 598 (1746), For his grace at meat, what can I better compare it to, than a Canterbury rack, half-pace, gallop? 1759: Rider, *Dict.*, s.v., In horsemanship, the hard gallop of an ambling horse; probably derived from the monks riding to Canterbury upon ambling horses. 1830: Galt, *Lawrie Todd*, VI vii 280 (1849) (OED), On horse-back, and off at a Canterbury trot.

2. A Canterbury tale. 1549: Latimer. *Seven Sermons*, 49 (Arber), We myghte as well spende that tyme in reading of prophane hystories, of cantorburye tales, or fit of Robyn Hode. 1663: *Roxb. Ballads*, vii 230 (B.S.), A sad relation, a strange Canterbury tale. 1724: Defoe, *Roxana*, in *Works*, xiii 151 (Boston, 1903), That foolish young girl held us all in a Canterbury story; I thought she would never have done with it. 1774: Colman, *Man of Business*, V ii 1785: Grose, *Class. Dict.*, *Vulgar Tongue*, s.v., Canterbury Story, a long roundabout tale.

3. Canterbury is the higher rack, but Winchester is the better manger. 1608: in Harington, *Nugae Antiquae*, ii 87 (1804), A bishop of Winchester [said to have been W. Edington, *ob.* 1366] one day in pleasant talke,

comparing his revenew with the archbishops of Canterburie should say – 'Your Graces will shew better in the racke, but mine will be found more in the maunger'. 1662: Fuller, *Worthies*, ii 5 (1840). 1790: Grose, *Prov. Gloss.*, s.v. 'Hampshire'. 1908: Read, *H. and B. in Hants*, 74, To Edington … is credited the origin of one of Hampshire's proverbs – 'Though Canterbury is the highest rack, Winchester has the deepest manger'.

See also **Deal** (2).

Canting. *See* **Courting.**

Cap, *subs.* **1. If his cap be made of wool** = *A*s sure as his cap is made of wool. 1633: Jonson, *Tale of a Tub*, II ii, Slip, you will answer it, an if your cap be of wool. 1662: Fuller, *Worthies*, ii 68 (1840), Our English garments from head to foot were formerly made thereof [of wool], till the beginning of the reign of King Henry the Eighth, when velvet caps becoming fashionable for persons of prime quality, discomposed the proverb, 'If his cap be made of wool', as formerly comprising all conditions of people how high and haughty soever. 1670: Ray, 167. 1736: Bailey, *Dict.*, s.v. 'Cap'.

2. If the cap fits – wear it. Originally with reference to the fool's or jester's traditional headgear – *see* quots. 1600, 1714. 1600: N. Breton, *Pasquil's Fools-Cap*, A3, Where you find a head fit for this Cappe, either bestowe it upon him for charity, or send him where he may have them for his money. 1714: Ozell, *Molière*, iv 10, If the fool's cap fits any body, let 'em put it on. 1748: Richardson, *Clarissa*, vii 59 (1785), If indeed … the cap fits thy own head … e'en take and clap it on. 1854: Dickens, *Hard Times*, bk ii ch vii.

3. My (or thy) **cap is better at ease than my** (or thy) **head.** 1546: Heywood, *Proverbs*, Pt II ch vii 1659: Howell, 5.

4. She's cap and button too. Said of a lady who 'wears the breeches'. 1887: Croston, *Enoch Crump*, 8 (W.), Th' owd lass were cap and button too i' that house. 1917: Bridge, *Cheshire Proverbs*, 100, Oo's cap and button too.

5. To throw one's cap after a thing. 1607: Shakespeare, *Timon*, III iv, I perceive our masters may throw their caps at their money. 1690: *New Dict. Canting Crew*, sig. C4, He may fling up his cap after it, when a thing or business is past hope.

See also **Considering cap.**

Cap, *verb. See* quot. 1892: Heslop, *Northumb. Words*, 132 (E.D.S.), 'This caps the stack' – is a proverb, meaning something overtopping.

Capel rides a good horse. Cornwall. 1887; M. A. Courtney, *Folk-Lore Journal*, v 187, 'Capel rides a good horse'. Capel is schorl, and indicates the presence of tin.

Capon. 1. Capons were at first but chickens. 1732: Fuller, 1056.

2. If you have not a capon, feed on an onion. 1611: Cotgrave, s.v. 'Chapon'. 1710: S. Palmer, *Moral Essays on Proverbs*, 201.

3. Who gives thee a capon, give him the leg and the wing. 1640: Herbert, *Jac. Prudentum.* 1670: Ray, 11.

See also **Chickens** (1).

Car and Pen, Pol and Tre, Would make the devil run away. Cornwall. 1887: M. A. Courtney, *Folk-Lore Journal*, v 106.

Carcase. *Where the carcase is, the ravens will gather.* 1855: Bohn, 563.

Card of ten. *See* **Outface.**

Cards. 1. Cards are the devil's books. 1676: *Poor Robin Alman. Prognost.*, sig. C4, Cards and dice … the devil's books and the devil's bones. 1745: *Agreeable Companion*, 73, Time out of mind, they [cards] are and have been call'd the devil's books. 1840: Lytton, *Money*, IV ii.

2. Many can pack (or **shuffle**) **the cards, that cannot play well.** 1659: Howell, 10 (8). 1670: Ray, 20. 1694: D'Urfey, *Quixote*, Pt II Act III sc ii, There's many will shuffle the cards that won't play. 1732: Fuller, 3341.

3. When you have told your cards, you'll find you have gained but little. 1546: Heywood, *Proverbs*, Pt I ch xi, Tell thy cardes, and than tell me what thou hast wonne. *c.*1594: Bacon, *Promus*, No. 641 [as in 1546]. 1633: Draxe, 116, Let him count his cardes and see his winnings. 1678: Ray, 68. 1732: Fuller, 5628, When you have counted your cards, you'll find you have little left.

See also **Cooling card; Lucky at cards.**

Care and diligence bring luck. 1732: Fuller, 1057.

Careful. *See* **Good be careful.**

Care is no cure. *c.*1591: Shakespeare, 1 *Henry VI*, III iii 1678: Ray, 108. 1732: Fuller, 1060.

Care killed a cat. 1585–1618: *Shirburn Ballads*, 91 (1907), Let care kill a catte, Wee'le laugh and be fatte. 1599: Shakespeare, *Much Ado*, V i,

What, courage, man! What though care killed a cat. *c.*1630: in *Roxb. Ballads*, ii 103 (Hindley). 1726: Swift, *Poems*, in *Works*, xiv 542 (Scott), Then who says care will kill a cat? 1816: Scott, *Antiquary*, ch xiv 1871: Planché, *Extravag.*, v 287 (1879).

Care never paid a pound of debt, *c.*1640: in *Roxb. Ballads*, i 416 (B.S.).

Care not would have it. 1670: Ray. 67.

Care Sunday, care away, Palm Sunday and Easter-day! 1812: Brady, *Clavis Cal.*, i 242. 1904: *Co. Folk-Lore: Northumb.*, 175 (F.L.S).

Cares not whose child cries, So his laugh, He. 1732: Fuller, 1823.

Careless hussy makes many thieves, A. 1683: Meriton, *Yorkshire Ale*, 83–7 (1697).

Carleton wharlers. *See* 1700 quot. 1622: W. Burton, *Descrip. of Leics.*, 67–8. 1650: Fuller, *Pisgah Sight*, bk ii ch ix, It is observed in a village at Charleton in Leicestershire that the people therein are troubled with wharling in their utterance. 1700: J. Brome, *Travels*, 77, Not far from hence is Carleton, of which we were told, that most persons that are born there … have an ill favoured, un-tunable, and harsh manner of speech, fetching their words with very much ado, deep from out of the throat, with a certain kind of wharling, the letter R being very irksome and troublesome to them to pronounce. 1790: Grose, *Prov. Gloss.*, s.v. 'Leicestershire', Carleton warlers.

Carlisle, a seaport without ships, merchants or trade; and, Nearer God's blessing than Carlisle Fair. Both in 1846–59: *Denham Tracts*, i 180, 181 (F.L.S).

Carpenter is known by his chips, A. 1533: Ld. Berners *History of Arthur* (1582), 162b, I know well my lorde Arthur hath been here … He is a good carpenter, for he hath made here a faire sight of chips. 1611: Coryat, *Crudities*, i 407 (1905), For, according to the old proverbe the best carpenters make the fewest chips. 1653: R. Brome, *Novella*, III i, The best carpenters make fewest chips. 1738: Swift, *Polite Convers.*, Dial. II, They say a carpenter's known by his chips. 1830: Forby, *Vocab. E. Anglia*, 430, You may know a carpenter by his chips. *See also* **Such carpenter.**

Carper can cavil at anything, A. 1732: Fuller, 33.

Carrion kite will never make good hawk, A.

1567: Painter, *Pal. of Pleasure*, iii 68 (Jacobs), It is impossible of a kyte or cormerant to make a good sparhauk. 1605: Camden, *Remains*, 316 (1870). 1669: *Politeuphuia*, 183. 1732: Fuller, 1063. 1820: Scott, *Monastery*, ch xix, For seldom doth a good hawk come out of a kite's egg.

Carry. 1. He carrieth all his wardrobe about him. 1659: Howell, 16.

2. He carries well to whom it weighs not. 1640: Herbert, *Jac. Prudentum.*

3. To carry an M [for 'Master'] **under one's girdle.** *c.*1550: Udall, *Roister Doister*, III iii, Neare [never] an M by your girdle? 1605: Chapman, *Eastw. Hoe*, IV ii, You might carry an M under your girdle to Maister Deputis worship. 1640: Shirley, *Arcadia*, I ii 1738: Swift, *Polite Convers.*, Dial. I. 1816: Scott, *Old Mortality*, ch xxxix, Ye might hae had an M under your belt for *Mistress* Wilson of Milnwood.

4. To carry coals. Before 1529: Skelton, in *Works*, ii 34 (Dyce), Wyll ye bere no coles? 1575: Churchyard, *Chippes*, 37 (Collier), He carryed coales that could abide no geast. 1581: B. Rich, *Farewell*, 112 (SH.S.), He had offended one that would beare no coales. *c.*1602: Chapman, *May-Day*, I, Above all things you must carry no coals. 1631: Mabbe, *Celestina.* 127 (T.T.), He is chollericke, and I can carrie no coles. 1821: Scott, *Kenilworth*, ch xxviii, I am no dog in the manger – but I will not carry coals neither.

5. To carry one's cup even between two parties = To be impartial. 1690: *New Dict. Canting Crew*, sig. D4.

6. To carry one's dish upright. Before 1680: Butler, *Remains*, ii 334 (1759), An affected man carries himself like his dish (as the proverb says) very uprightly. 1725: Defoe, *Everybody's Business*, You must carry your dish very upright, or miss, [the servant] forsooth, gives you warning.

Carshalton. *See* **Sutton.**

Cart. 1. An old cart, well used, may last out a new one abused. 1732: Fuller, 6287.

2. The best cart may overthrow. 1546: Heywood, *Proverbs*, Pt I ch xi 1611: Cotgrave, s.v. 'Chartier'. 1670: Ray, 67. 1732: Fuller, 4410.

3. To keep cart on wheels = To be in a state to carry on business, etc., as usual. 1639: Clarke, 242. 1662: Newcome, *Diary*, 56 (1849) (OED), I must walke closer with God or I cannot keep cart

on wheeles. 1828: Carr, *Craven Dialect*, ii 251 [explained as above].

4. To put the cart before the horse. [ἡ ἅμαξα τὸν βοῦν. – Lucian, *Dial. Mort*, vi 2.] 1528: More, *Works*, p. 154, col. 1 (1557), Muche like as if we woulde go make the carte to drawe the horse. 1542: Udall, tr. Erasmus' *Apoph.*, 359 (1877), The tale ... also setteth the carte before the horses. 1630: Taylor (Water-Poet), *Works*, pagin. 1, 15. 1705: Ward, *Hudibras Rediv.*, Pt II can. iii, p. 27, Excuse me, that the Muses force The cart to stand before the horse. 1893: R.L.S., *Catriona*, ch ix.

Case is altered, The; sometimes with the addition, quoth **Plowden.** (a) With the addition. 1603: *Dekket, Batch. Banq.*, in *Works*, i 235 (Grosart), Then is their long warre come to an end, and the case (as Ployden sayth) cleane altered. *c.*1620: in *Roxb. Ballads*, i 77 (Hindley), Your case is altered in the law quoth Ployden. 1662: Fuller, *Worthies*, iii 54 (1840). 1714: Ozell, *Moliére*, vi 8. 1809: Pegge, *Anonym.*, cent. ii 8. 1841: Hartshorne, *Salopia Antiquae* [said to be still in use in Shropshire]. 1883: Burne, *Shropsh. Folk-Lore*, 591. (b) Without the addition. 1594: Greene, in *Works*, xiv 38 (Grosart), Faith sir, the case is altered; you told me it before in an other manner. *c.*1598: Jonson, *The Case is Altered* [title]. 1634: T. Heywood, *Mayden Head Well Lost*, III. 1714: Ozell, *Moliére*, iii 184. 1824: Scott, *Red-gauntlet*, ch xii, But when you are out of your canonicals the case is altered.

Cask and an ill custom must be broken, A. 1640: Herbert, *Jac. Prudentum.*

Cask savours of the first fill, The. [Quo semel est imbuta recens servabit odorem Testa diu. – Horace, *Epist.*, II ii 69.] *c.*1230: in Wright's *Pol. Songs John to Edw. II*, 31 (Camden S.) [the Horatian line borrowed]. 1509: Barclay, *Ship of Fools*, i 47 (1874), But fyll an erthen pot first with yll lycoure And euer after it shall smell somwhat soure. *c.*1577: Northbrooke, *Against Dicing*, *etc.*, 11 (SH.S.), The vessel will conserve the tast Of lycour very long, With which it was first seasoned. Before 1625: B.&F., *Custom of Country*, I i, With what the maiden vessel Is season'd first – you understand the proverb. 1655: Howell, *Letters*, bk iv, No. 14, The cask savours still of the liquor it first took in. 1820: Colton, *Lacon*, Pt II, No. 203, The new cask takes its odour from the first wine that it receives.

Cast of his office, To give one a. 1577: Grange, *Golden Aphroditis*, sig. N1, Here Boreas with his swelling cheekes shewed a caste of his office. 1666: Torriano, *Piazza Univ.*, 79, The devil gives him a cast of his office. 1690: *New Dict. Canting Crew*, sig. H8, A cast of your office, or a touch of your employment. 1718: W. Taverner, *Artful Wife*, V ii, My chaplain shall give you a cast of his office presently. 1754: Berthelson, *Eng.-Danish Dict.*, s.v. 'Cast'.

Cast, verb. 1. Never cast a clout till May be out. *See* **May** (22).

2. To be cast at cart's arse. 1546: Heywood, *Proverbs*, Pt I ch ix 1611: Davies (of Hereford), *sc of Folly*, 50, in *Works*, ii (Grosart).

3. To cast a sheep's eye. *See* **Sheep** (17).

4. To cast beyond the moon. 1546: Heywood, *Proverbs*, Pt I ch iv, Feare may force a man to cast beyonde the moone. 1579: Lyly, *Euphues*, 78 (Arber), Pardon me, Euphues, if in loue I cast beyond the moone. 1607: T. Heywood, *Woman Killed with Kindness*, IV v, I talk of things impossible, And cast beyond the moon. 1638: Ford, *Lady's Trial*, I ii, He casts Beyond the moon, and will be greater yet, In spight of Don. 1847: Halliwell, *Dict.*, s.v. 'Moon', To cast … , to be very ambitious, to calculate deeply, to make an extravagant conjecture.

5. To cast dust. *See* **Dust.**

6. To cast in one's dish. *See* **Lay a thing.**

7. To cast up accounts = To vomit. 1607: Dekker and Webster, *West. Hoe*, V i, I would not have 'em cast up their accounts here, for more than they mean to be drunk this twelvemonth. 1612: W. Parkes, *Curtain-drawer of the World*, 17 (Grosart). 1745: Franklin, *Drinker's Dict.*, in *Works*, ii 22 (Bigelow), He's casting up his accounts. *c.*1791: Pegge, *Derbicisms*, 93 (E.D.S.).

8. To cast up old scores. 1659: Howell, 2. 1670: Ray, 214. 1732: Fuller, 6145.

9. To cast water into (a) the sea, (b) the Thames, (a) [His qui contentus non est, in mare fundat aquas. – Ovid, *Tr.*, V vi 44.] 1509: Barclay, *Ship of Fools*, i 166 (Jamieson), Or in the se cast water, thynkynge it to augment. 1585: Sir E. Dyer, in *Writings*, 103 (Grosart, 1872), Vnlesse the casters of water into the sea are to be praised for their charitie. 1600: F. Thynne, *Embl. and Epigr.*, 3 (E.E.T.S.), In vaine for mee to … add water to the large sea of your rare lerning. 1654: Gayton, *Pleasant Notes Don Q.*, 127, To doe good to men

unthankfull is to cast water into the sea. (*b*) 1377: Langland, *Plowman*, B, xv 332, And went forth with that water to woke with Themese [to moisten or dilute therewith the Thames]. 1611: Davies (of Hereford), *sc of Folly*, 45, in *Works*, ii (Grosart), To cast water in Thames is superfluous. 1662: Fuller, *Worthies*, ii 347 (1840). 1790: Grose, *Prov. Gloss.*, s.v. 'London'.

Castle and Castles. 1. A castle of comfort. *c.*1560: Becon, *A Castell of Comfort* [title]. 1599: Peele, *Sir Clyomon*, *etc.*, sc xiii, You have a castle of comfort brought in that you have me told. *c.*1630: *Dicke of Devonsh.*, I iii, in Bullen, *Old Plays*, ii 23, I think long till I be at home in our Castle of comfort.

2. A castle that speaketh is near a surrender. 1580: Lyly, *Euphues*, 334 (Arber), Castles that come to parlue, and woemen that delight in courting, are willing to yeelde. 1660: Howell, *Parly of Beasts*, 66, The female and fortress which begins to parly is half-gain'd. 1666: Torriano, *Piazza Univ.*, 93, A fortress that comes to parley, is neer a surrender. Cf. **City.**

3. It is easy to keep a castle that was never assaulted. [1591: Harington, *Orl. Furioso*, bk xliii. st. 25, 'Tis easie to resist where none invade.] 1732: Fuller, 2924. 1883: Burne, *Shropsh. Folk-Lore*, 588, A castle's easy kept as is never stormed.

4. To build castles in Spain. *c.*1400: *Rom. Rose*, l. 2573, Thou shalt make càstels than in Spayne, And dreme of Ioye, al but in vayne. *c.*1477: Caxton, *Jason*, 25 (E.E.T.S.), He began to make castellis in Spaygne as louers doo. 1567: G. Fenton, *Bandello*, ii 249 (T.T.), He began to sighe and build castels in Spaine. 1685–6: Cotton, *Montaigne*, bk iii ch iv, Let me think of building castles in Spain. 1750: Smollett, *Gil Blas*, iii 76, I … fell asleep, in the very act of building castles in Spain. 1853: G. W. Curtis, 'Castles in Spain', in *Putnam's Mag.*, ii 657.

5. To build castles in the air. 1566: Painter, *Pal. of Pleasure*, i 266 (Jacobs), Alerand … was a building of castels in the ayre. 1595: Sidney, *Apol. for Poetrie*, par. 12, As we are wont to say by them that build castles in the air. 1651: Randolph, *Hey for Honesty*, I ii, Castles in the air are very impregnable. 1787: D'Arblay, *Diary*, ii 424 (1876), 'Tis best to build no castles in the air. 1852: Dickens, *Bleak House*, ch xiv, Richard … began, on no other foundation, to build as many castles in the air as would man the great wall of China.

See also **Englishman** (3); **House** (12).

Castleford women. *See* quot. 1868: *Quart. Review*, cxxv. 492, The old rhyme may have been true enough – 'Castleford women must needs be fair, Because they wash both in Calder and Aire'. 1878: *Folk-Lore Record*, i 172 [as in 1868].

Castleton. *See* **Hope, Derbyshire.**

Cat and **Cats. 1. A baited cat may grow as fierce as a lion.** 1620: Shelton, *Quixote*, Pt II ch xiv, If a cat shut into a room, much baited and straitened, turn to be a lion … 1710: S. Palmer, *Moral Essays on Proverbs*, 305.

2. A cat has nine lives. 1546: Heywood, *Proverbs*, Pt II ch iv, A woman hath nyne lyues like a cat. 1592: Shakespeare, *Romeo*, III i, Good king of cats, nothing but one of your nine lives. 1605: Marston, *Dutch Courtezan*, III i, Thou hast nine lives like a cat. 1678: Butler, *Hudibras*, Pt III can. ii l. 1629, With new reversions of nine lives Starts up, and like a cat revives. 1709: Ward, *Acc. of Clubs*, 9 (1756), Assert the same, in spite of her nine lives, to be rank poison to a cat. 1862: Borrow, *Wild Wales*, ch vii, Even a cat, an animal known to have nine lives, cannot live without food.

3. A cat may look at a king. 1546: Heywood, *Proverbs*, Pt II ch v, A cat maie looke on a king, ye know. 1590: Greene, in *Works*, viii 181 (Grosart). 1638: T. Heywood, *Wise Woman*, II. 1714: *A Cat may Look upon a King* [title], in *Somers Tracts*, xiii 509. 1793: Wolcot, in *Works*, ii 475 (1795). 1868: *Quart. Review*, cxxv. 231, 'A cat may look at a king' is but a modern way of putting the Greek adage, 'You're nothing sacred'. 1893: R.L.S., *Catriona*, ch i.

4. A cat's walk: *a little way and back.* Cornwall. 1869: Hazlitt, 5.

5. A muzzled cat was never good mouser. 1605: Camden, *Remains*, 317 (1870). Cf. No. 49.

6. All cats are grey in the dark. 1546: Heywood, *Proverbs*, Pt I ch v, When all candels be out all cats be grey. 1596: Lodge, *Marg. of America*, 56 (Hunt.Cl.). Before 1634: Chapman, *Alphonsus*, III i, By night all cats are grey. 1730: Lillo, *Silvia*, I ix, For, in the night, Sure ev'ry cat is grey. 1880: R.L.S. and Henley, *Deacon Brodie*, I i ix, The grimy cynical night that makes all cats grey.

7. An old cat laps as much milk as a young. 1605: Camden, *Remains*, 318 (1870). 1670: Ray, 68.

8. An old cat sports not with her prey. 1640: Herbert, *Jac. Prudentum.*

9. As busy as a cat in a tripe shop. 1890: J. D. Robertson, *Gloucester Gloss.*, 186 (E.D.S.). 1894: Northall, *Folk Phrases of Four Counties*, 7 (E.D.S.).

10. As nimble as a blind cat in a barn. Glos. 1639: in *Berkeley MSS.*, iii 30 (1885).

11. As the cat licks (or loves) mustard. 1639: Clarke, 235, He loves me as the cat doth mustard. 1659: Howell, 2, As the catt licks mustard. 1754: Berthelson, *Eng.-Danish Dict.*, s.v. 'Love' [as in 1639].

12. As the cat plays with (or watches) a mouse. 1340: *Ayenbite*, 179 (E.E.T.S.), The dyeuel playth ofte … ase deth the cat mid the mous. 1566: J. Studley, tr. Seneca's *Agam.*, in Bang's *Material.*, B. 38, p. 22, With whom (as the cat with the mouse) it liketh her to daly. 1579: Gosson, *Sch. of Abuse*, 25 (SH.S.), To watch their conceates, as the catte for the mouse. 1645: Howell, *Letters*, bk i § iii No. 18, He watch'd her as a cat doth a mouse. 1710: C. Shadwell, *Fair Quaker*, II ii, You play with him as a cat plays with a mouse. 1821: Scott, *Kenilworth*, ch viii, My hang-dog kinsman watching you as close as ever cat watched a mouse. 1886: R.L.S., *Kidnapped*, ch iv. We sat at table like a cat and a mouse, each stealthily observing the other.

13. Before the cat can lick her ear. 1670: Ray, 168. 1732: Fuller, 960.

14. By biting and scratching cats and dogs come together. 1546: Heywood, *Proverbs*, Pt II ch i 1605: Camden, *Remains*, 320 (1870). 1670: Ray, 68. 1732: Fuller, 984, Biting and scratching gets the cat with kitten.

15. Cat will after kind. *c.*1275: *Prov. of Alfred*, A 296, For ofte museth the kat after hire moder. 1546: Heywood, *Proverbs*, Pt I ch xi, Cat after kynde good mouse hunt. 1583: Greene, *Mamillia*, in *Works*, ii 119 (Grosart), Shewing yt the cat wil to kinde. 1601: Shakespeare, *As You Like It*, III ii, If the cat will after kind, So be sure will Rosalind. 1668: Shadwell, *Sullen Lovers*, IV i 1697: Vanbrugh, *Esop*, III. 1716: Ward, *Female Policy*, 93. 1732: Fuller, 1070.

16. Cats eat what hussies spare. 1683: Meriton, *Yorkshire Ale*, 83–7 (1697).

17. Cats hide their claws. 1732: Fuller, 1072.

18. Good liquor will make a cat speak. 1585–

1618: *Shirburn Ballads*, 93 (1907), Who is it but loues good liquor? 'Twill make a catte speake. 1611: Shakespeare, *Tempest*, II ii, Open your mouth; here is that which will give language to you, cat. 1661: *Antid. against Melanch.*, 126 (Ebsworth), Old liquor able to make a cat speak, and a wise man dumb. 1720: *Vade Mecum for Maltworms*, Pt I, p. 35, There … is drink will almost make a cat to speak. 1838: Dickens, *Nickleby*, ch xii, Talk, miss! It's enough to make a Tom cat talk French grammar.

19. He's sure of a cat that hath her skin. 1611: Cotgrave, s.v. 'Chat'.

20. He lives under the sign of the cat's foot = He is henpecked. 1678: Ray, 68. 1880: Spurgeon, *Ploughman's Pictures*, 87.

21. He signifies no more than a blind cat in a barn. 1732: Fuller, 2020.

22. He stands in great need that borrows the cat-dish. 1639: Clarke, 225.

23. He that will play with cats, must expect to be scratched. 1710: S. Palmer, *Moral Essays on Proverbs*, 249.

24. Honest as the cat when the … (*see* quots.). 1732: Fuller, 2524 … meat is upon the hook. 1875: A. B. Cheales, *Proverb. Folk-Lore*, 129 … milk's away. 1880: Spurgeon, *Ploughman's Pictures*, 20 … meat is out of reach.

25. How can the cat help it, if the maid be a fool? 1591: Florio, *Second Frutes*, 41, Is the catt to blame, if maides be fooles with shame? 1623: Wodroephe, *Spared Houres*, 243, What faulte makes the cat when the maidseruant is full of folie and carelessnesse? 1670: Ray, 67. 1732: Fuller, 5595, When the maid leaves open the door blame not the cat.

26. I know a cat from a cowl staff. 1696: T. Dilke, *Lover's Luck*, III i.

27. I will keep no cats that will not catch mice. Somerset. 1678: Ray, 350. 1710: S. Palmer, *Moral Essays on Proverbs*, 358, Keep no more cats than will catch mice. 1732: Fuller, 2638.

28. It would make a cat laugh. 1851: Planché, *Extravag.*, iv 148 (1879), It would have made a cat laugh, or a dog. 1898: Weyman, *Shrewsbury*, ch xxxv, You three all mixed up! It would make a cat laugh, my lad.

29. Kiss the black cat. An' 'twill make ye fat; Kiss the white ane, 'Twill make ye lean. 1878: Dyer, *Eng. Folk-Lore*, 108.

30. Let the cat wink, and let the mouse run.

1522: *World and the Child*, in Hazlitt, *Old Plays*, i 265 (1874), Ah, ah, sirs, let the cat wink. Before 1529: Skelton, *Elynor Runnyng*, l. 306, But drynke, styll drynke, And let the cat wynke. 1546: Heywood, *Proverbs*, Pt II ch iv, Let the cat winke, and leat the mouse ronne. 1659: Howell, 7. 1709: Dykes, *Eng. Proverbs*, 45, And so let the cat be winking.

31. Like a cat he'll still fall upon his legs. 1678: Ray, 282, He's like a cat, fling him which way you will he'll light on's legs. 1732: Fuller, 3220. 1820: Colton, *Lacon*, Pt I No. 348, There are some men who are fortune's favourites, and who, like cats, light for ever upon their legs.

32. Like a cat in a bonfire, don't know which way to turn. Cornwall. 1895: Jos. Thomas, *Randigal Rhymes*, 60.

33. Like a cat in pattens. Oxfordsh. 1913: *Folk-Lore*, xxiv 77, Slipping about like a cat in pattens. 1914: R. L. Gales, *Vanished Country Folk*, 193, 'Like a cat in pattens' was said of an awkward person.

34. Like a cat round hot milk. 1855: Bohn, 442.

35. Little by little as the cat ate the flickle. Before 1500: in Hill, *Commonplace-Book*, 130 (E.E.T.S.), A litill and a litill, the cat etith vp the bacon flicke. 1546: Heywood, *Proverbs*, Pt II ch vii, Yet littell and littell the cat cateth the flickell. 1897: C. Lee, *Widow Woman*, ch vii [with 'candle' for 'flickle'] 1898: E. Peacock, in *N. & Q.*, 9th ser, i 390, 'Do it by degrees, as the cat ate the pestle [pigs foot]', is a proverbial saying in these parts [Kirton-in-Lindsey, Lines].

36. My cat hath no such ears. 1659: Howell, 11.

37. My cat is a good mouse-hunt. Glos. 1639: in *Berkeley MSS.*, iii 27 (1885), My catt is a good moushunt. An vsuall speach when wee husbands commend the diligence of our wives … hee that somtimes flattereth not his wife cannot alwaies please her.

38. Never was cat or dog drowned that could see the shore. *c.*1594: Bacon, *Promus*, No. 590, A catt will never drowne if she sees the shore. 1666: Torriano, *Piazza Univ.*, 36, Neither dog nor cat ever drown, so long as they can discern the shore. 1732: Fuller, 3532.

39. No playing with a straw before an old cat. 1546: Heywood, *Proverbs*, Pt II ch viii 1611: Davies (of Hereford), *sc of Folly*, 47, in *Works*, ii (Grosart). 1792: Wolcot, in *Works*, ii 318 (1795), May stun thee with two proverbs all so pat –

'What, what, Pitt – "play a jig to an old cat?" '
1817: Scott, *Rob Roy*, ch xxvi, They were ower
auld cats to draw that strae afore them.

**40. None but cats and dogs are allowed to
quarrel in my house.** 1732: Fuller, 3643.

41. Send not a cat for lard. 1640: Herbert, *Jac.
Prudentum.*

**42. She paid en like the cat paid the owl –
cross the face.** Newlyn, W. Cornwall, 19th
cent. (Mr C. Lee).

43. That cat is out of kind [nature] **that sweet
milk will not lap.** 1678: Ray, 108.

44. That that comes of a cat will catch mice.
1678: Ray, 109.

**45. The cat and dog may kiss, yet are none the
better friends.** 1855: Bohn, 499.

46. The cat has kittened = Something has
happened. 1883: Burne, *Shropsh. Folk-Lore*,
596.

47. The cat has kittened in your mouth. 1618:
Field, *Amends for Ladies*, II i, *Grace*. Your
mother's cat has kittened in your mouth, sure.

48. The cat hath eaten her count. 1678: Ray,
68.

49. The cat in gloves catches no mice. 1578:
Florio, *First Fruites*, fo. 30, A cat gloued catcheth
no mice. 1623: Wodroephe, *Spared Houres*, 287,
A mufeld cat is not meete to take mice. 1681:
Rycaut, tr. Gracian's *Critick*, 122, The proverb
says, the mousing cat preys not with mittens.
1736: Franklin, *Way to Wealth*, in *Works*, i 444
(Bigelow). 1869: Spurgeon, *John Ploughman*, ch
iii, Do not preach in gloves, for cats in mittens
catch no mice. Cf. No. 5.

50. The cat invites the mouse to a feast. 1732:
Fuller, 4441.

**51. The cat is hungry when a crust contents
her.** 1611: Cotgrave, s.v. 'Chat'. 1670: Ray, 4.

52. The cat is in the cream-pot. 1678: Ray, 233.

53. The cat knows whose lips she licks.
*c.*1210: in Wright's *Essays on Middle Ages*, i 149
(1846), Wel wot hure cat whas berd he licket.
Before 1529: Skelton. *Garl. of Lourell*, l. 1438,
And wele wotith the cat whos berde she likkith.
1670: Ray, 68. 1732: Fuller, 4442.

54. The cat sees not the mouse, ever. 1640:
Herbert, *Jac. Prudentum.* 1670: Ray, 67. 1732:
Fuller, 4443, The cat sees not every mouse.

**55. The cat, the rat, and Lovel the dog, Rule all
England under the hog.** 1542: Fabyan, *Chron.*,
fo. 468, The catte, the ratte, and louel our dogge,

Ruleth all Englande vnder a hogge. The whyche
was mente that Catysby, Ratclyffe, and the lorde
Louell ruled the lande vnder the kynge [Richard
III.], whyche bare the whyte bore for his
conysaunce. 1669: *New Help to Discourse*, 201.
1814: Byron, *Letters, etc.*, iii 29 n. (Prothero).
1816: Scott, *Antiquary*, ch ii, His name, the
young gentleman said, was Lovel. 'What! the
cat, the rat, and Lovel our dog? Was he
descended from King Richard's favourite?'

56. The cat winked when her eye was (or **both
her eyes were**) **out.** 1528: More, in *Works*, p.
241, col. 1 (1557), It was alway that ye cat winked
whan her eye was oute. *c.*1550: *Jacke Jugeler*, 80
(Grosart), The prouerbe olde That the catte
winkid when here eye was out. 1670: Ray, 67 …
both her eyes. 1738: Swift, *Polite Convers.*, Dial.
I, No wonder the cat wink'd, when both her eyes
were out.

**57. The cat would eat fish but would not wet
her feet.** *c.*1250: MS., Trin. Coll., Camb.,
quoted in Farmer's ed. of Heywood's *Proverbs*,
340 (1906), Cat lufat visch, ac he nele his feth
wete. *c.*1384: Chaucer, *H. Fame*, bk iii ll. 693–5.
*c.*1390: Gower, *Conf. Amantis*, iv 1108, And as a
cat wolde ete fisshes Withoute wetinge of his cles
[claws]. 1583: Melbancke, *Philotinus*, sig. O1,
The cat would licke milke, but she will not wette
her feete. 1606: Shakespeare, *Macbeth*, I vii,
Letting 'I dare not' wait upon 'I would', Like the
poor cat i' the adage. 1732: Fuller, 6130, Fain
would the cat fish eat, But she's loth her feet to
wet. 1928: *Sphere*, 7 Jan., p. 36.

58. The liquorish cat gets many a rap. 1611:
Cotgrave, s.v. 'Chat', The lickorous cat hath
many a rap. 1670: Ray, 4. 1732: Fuller, 6228.

**59. The more you rub a cat on the rump, the
higher she sets up her tail.** 1678: Ray, 109.

60. The scalded cat fears cold water. 1611:
Cotgrave, s.v. 'Chat'. 1694: D'Urfey, *Quixote*,
Pt I Act V sc ii 1709: O. Dykes, *Eng. Proverbs*,
147–8.

**61. There are more ways of killing a cat than
choking it with cream.** 1855: Kingsley, *West.
Ho!*, ch xx 1926: *Devonsh. Assoc. Trans.*, lvii.
152, There's more ways o' killin' a cat 'n
chuckin' o' en wi' craim.

**62. They want to know the ins and outs of the
cat's tale.** Said of people who desire full
particulars of anything. 1919: *Devonsh. Assoc.
Trans.*, li. 77.

63. Though the cat winks she is not blind.
1576: *Parad. of Dainty Devices*, in *Brit. Bibliog.*,
iii 59 (1812), I am not blinde although I winke.
1609: Rowlands, *Whole Crew of Kind Gossips*, 20
(Hunt.Cl.), The cat ofte winkes, and yet she is
not blinde.

64. To agree like cat and dog. 1566: Drant,
Horace: Satires, sig. D7, Lyke dogge and catte
these two did then agree. 1579: Gosson, *Sch. of
Abuse*, 27 (Arber), He … shall see them agree like
dogges and cattes. 1629: in *Pepysian Garland*, 301
(Rollins, 1922), Like cat and dog they still agree'd;
Each small offence did anger breed. 1727: Gay,
Fables, 1st ser, No. 12, l. 33, If they like cat and dog
agree … 1878: *Folk-Lore Record*, i 13, You and
your wife will lead a cat-and-dog life.

65. To bell the cat. 1377: Langland, *Plowman*,
B, Prol., ll. 165–81 [the fable of 'belling the cat'
related]. 1388: in Wright, *Pol. Poems*, i 274,
(Rolls Ser., 1859), The cattys nec to bylle [bell].
Before 1529: Skelton, *Col. Clout*, 1.163, They
are … loth to hang the bell Aboute the cattes
necke, For drede to haue a checke. 1623: Taylor
(Water-Poet), in *Works*, pagin. 2, p. 28 (1630),
Not one will aduenture to hang the bell about the
cats necke. 1712: Motteux, *Quixote*, Pt II ch 43,
Who shall hang the bell about the cat's neck?
1830: Scott, *Journal*, 17 July, A fine manly
fellow, who has belled the cat with fortune, and
held her at bay as a man of mould may.

66. To go like a cat on a hot backstone. 1683:
Meriton, *Yorkshire Ale*, 83–7 (1697), As nimble
as a cat on a haite back-stane. 1737: Ray, 222.
1892: S. Hewett, *Peasant Speech of Devon*, 13,
Her 'opp'th like a cat 'pon 'ot bricks.

67. To keep the cat from the tongs = To stay
idly at home. 1598: *Servingmans Comfort*, in
Inedited Tracts, 161 (Hazlitt, 1868), Because his
sonne shalbe sure to keep the catte from the
tonges at home, when other his neighbours
children shall trudge into Fraunce, Flaunders,
and other nations.

68. To let the cat out of the bag. 1760: *Land.
Mag.*, xxix 224 (OED), We could have wished
that the author … had not let the cat out of the
bag. 1849: Brontë, *Shirley*, ch xxxvii, This last
epithet I choose to suppress, because it would let
the cat out of the bag. 1922: *Evening Standard*, 1
July, p. 5, col. 1, The man himself lets the
embarrassed cat out of the bag when the spirit
moves him.

69. To turn cat in pan. Before 1384: Wiclif,
Works, iii 332 (1871), Many men of lawe … bi
here suteltes turnen the cat in the panne. 1543:
Becon, *Against Swearing*, Preface, God saith,
'Cry, cease not'; but they turn cat in the pan, and
say 'Cease, cry not'. 1625: Bacon, *Essays:* 'Of
Cunning', There is a cunning, which we in
England call, The turning of the cat in the pan;
which is, when that which a man sayes to another,
he laies it, as if another had said 't to him. 1688:
Crowne, *City Polit.*, II, You are a villain, have
turn'd cat in pan, and are a Tory. 1740: North,
Examen, 55, Can his lordship's high flying
entrance, huffing speeches, and then turning cat
in the pan, be unknown or ever forgot? 1816:
Scott, *Old Mortality*, ch xxxv, O, this precious
Basil will turn cat in pan with any man!

70. When the cat's away the mice will play.
c.1470: *Harley MS 3362*, in *Retrospective Review*
(1854), May, 309, The mows lordchypythe [has
lordship, rules] there a cat ys nawt. 1578: Florio,
First Fruites, fo. 33, When the cat is abroade the
mise play. 1603: Dekker, *Batch. Banq.*, in *Works*,
i 169 (Grosart). 1732: Fuller, 5572, When the
cat's gone, the mice grow sawcy. 1852: Dickens,
Bleak House, ch liv., So it is, and such is life. The
cat's away, and the mice they play.

**71. When the cat winketh little wots the mouse
what the cat thinketh.** 1678: Ray, 109. 1732:
Fuller, 6453.

**72. Whenever the cat of the house is black,
The lasses of lovers will have no lack.** 1878:
Dyer, *Eng. Folk-Lore*, 108.

73. Which way the cat jumps. 1826: Scott,
Journal, 7 Oct., I would like to be there, were it
but to see how the cat jumps. 1907: De Morgan,
Alice-for-Short, ch xxvii, 'Easy enough to see
which way the cat would jump', or, 'Are you
surprised? I'm not'.

**74. You can have no more of a cat than her
skin.** 1570: in H. G. Wright's *Arthur Hall of
Grantham*, 88 (1919). 1637: Heywood, *Royal
King*, II, Thou canst have no more of the cat but
his skinne. 1738: Swift, *Polite Convers.*, Dial. II.
1894: Northall, *Folk Phrases*, 32 (E.D.S.),
What's a cat but its skin? 1901: F. E. Taylor,
Lancs Sayings, 11, Yo' conno ma'e mooar o' th'
cat nor th' skin.

**75. You shall have what the cat left in the malt-
heap.** 1639: Clarke, 71. c.1660: in Marchant,
Praise of Ale, 138 (1888), The brewer at last

made him to halt; And gave them what the cat left in the malt. 1670: Ray, 168.

See also **Care; Chestnuts; Cry** (1); **February** (18); **Full of sin; Good wife; Kid; Lame; Long and slender; Melancholy; Rat** (4) and (5); **Two cats; Two women.**

Catch, *verb.* **1. Catch that catch can.** *c.*1390: Gower, *Conf. Amantis*, bk vii l. 4422, Bot cacche who that cacche myghte. Before 1529: Skelton, *Magnyfycence*, l. 1773, They catche that catch may, kepe and holde fast. 1614: Jonson, *Bart. Fair*, II, Let him catch this that catch can. 1652: J. Hilton, *Catch that Catch* can [title]. 1761: O'Hara, *Midas*, II viii, There's catch as catch can, hit or miss, luck is all. 1855: Kingsley, *West. Ho!*, ch v, Each shall slay his man, catch who catch can. 1919: A. A. Milne, *Camb. Triangle*, in *Sec. Plays*, 153 (1921), Swords, pistols, fists, catch-as-catch-can – what would you like?

2. First catch your hare. *See* **First.**

3. He that can catch and hold, he is the man of gold. 1654: Gayton, *Pleasant Notes Don Q.*, 243.

4. To catch a Tartar. 1679: A. Behn, *Feign'd Courtezans*, IV ii, Ha – what the devil have I caught – a Tartar? 1708: Cibber, *Lady's Last Stake*, II i, I'm sure catching a husband is catching a Tartar. 1841: Dickens, *Barn. Rudge*, ch lxxx, A poor good-natur'd mean-spirited creetur, as went out fishing for a wife one day, and caught a Tartar.

5. To catch cold by lying in bed barefoot. Said of one who is extremely careful of himself. 1828: Carr, *Craven Dialect*, i 82.

Cater-cousins, They are not. 1519: Horman, *Vulgaria*, fo. 223, They be cater cosyns and almoste neuer a sonder. *c.*1580: Lodge, *Defence of Plays, etc.*, 29 (SHS.), We should find you cater-cosens with a (but hush) you know my meaning. 1670: Ray, 168. 1759: Smollett, in Hill's *Boswell*, i 349, He was humble enough to desire my assistance on this occasion, though he and I were never cater-cousins. 1866: Brogden, *Lincs Words*, 37, We had a chip [tiff], but are now cater-cousins.

Catty put down thy feet. 1917: Bridge, *Cheshire Proverbs*, 35 … used to denote surprise or annoyance at an interruption.

Cavil will enter in at any hole, and if it find none it will make one. 1633: Draxe, 22.

Ceremonious friends are so, as far as a compliment will go. 1732: Fuller, 1078.

Certain as death. *See* **Sure as death.**

Certainty. *He that leaves certainty and sticks to chance, when fools pipe he may dance.* 1546: Heywood, *Proverbs*, Pt II ch xi, Who that leaveth surety and leaneth vnto chance, When fools pipe, by authority he may dance. 1633: Draxe, 22 [as in 1546]. 1670: Ray, 68. 1732: Fuller, 6439.

Chain is only as strong as its weakest link, A. 1856: C. Kingsley, *Letter* 1 Dec. (1877), II 499, The devil is very busy, and no one knows better than he, that 'nothing is stronger than its weakest part'. 1868: L. Stephen, in *Cornhill Magazine* XVII. 295, A chain is no stronger than its weakest link.

Chains of gold are stronger than chains of iron. 1732: Fuller, 1079.

Chairs at home, He has none of his, = He is wrong (*or* weak) in his head. The 1582 passage is a curious anticipation of the Lancashire saying. 1582: R. Robinson, tr. *Assertion of Arthur*, 89 (E.E.T.S.), Whether with like eloquence, grace, and good successe I haue done this, let that by the iudgement of honest and learned persons bee determined. For I knowe very well, *How slender furniture I have at home.* 1864: Ormerod, *Felley fro Rachde*, ch ii (W.), Foke met get it hinto ther yeds us aw'd noane sure cheers owhomme. 1865: 'Lancs Proverbs', in *N. & Q.*, 3rd ser, viii 494.

Chalk and Cheese. 1. I talk of chalk and you of cheese. 1631: Mabbe, *Celestina*, 212 (T.T.), You talke of chalke, and we of cheese. 1681: W. Robertson, *Phraseol. Generalis*, 752. 1721: Bailey, *Eng. Dict.*, s.v. 'Chalk'.

2. To take chalk for cheese; or, **To know one from** (or **compare one with**) **the other.** *c.*1390: Gower, *Conf. Amantis*, ii 2346, And thus fulofte chalk for chese He changeth with ful litel cost. *c.*1550: *John Bon and Mast Person*, in Hazlitt, *Early Pop. Poetry*, iv 15 (1866), For thoughe I have no learning, yet I know chese from chalke. 1586: Pettie, tr. Guazzo's *Civil Convers.*, fo. 144, They know not chaffe from corne, or chalke from cheese, *c.*1615: R. C., *Times Whistle*, 28 (E.E.T.S.), A verier foole Dame Nature never bred, That scarce knowes chalke from cheese, or blew from red. 1849: Brontë, *Shirley*, ch v, 'You think yourself a clever fellow, I know, Scott'. Ay! I'm fairish; I can tell cheese fro' chalk'. 1926: Phillpotts, *Marylebone Miser*, ch vi, Though we're as different as chalk from cheese.

Chalked land makes a rich father but a poor son. 1677: Plot, *Nat. Hist. Oxfordsh.*, 243.

Chalvington. *See* Beddingham.

Chamber of sickness. *See* Sickness.

Chance is a dicer. 1732: Fuller, 1080.

Chance the ducks, To. 1894: Northall, *Folk Phrases*, 12 (E.D.S.), To do a thing and 'chance the ducks' is to do it, come what may. 1917: Bridge, *Cheshire Proverbs*, 149, We mun chance the ducks.

Chancery. *See* Hell (2).

Chances in an hour. *See* Happeth.

Chanctonbury. *See* quot. 1894: A. J. C. Hare, *Sussex*, 161, The proverb 'Old Mother Goring's got her cap on, We shall soon have wet' – refers to Chanctonbury.

Change, *subs.* **1. A change is as good as a rest.** 1890: A. Conan Doyle, in *Lippincott's Monthly Magazine*, Feb. x 198, Well, I gave my mind a thorough rest by plunging into chemical analysis. One of our greatest statesmen has said that a change of work is the best rest. 1895: J. Thomas, *Randigal Rhymes*, 59, Change of work is as good as touchpipe [a short break]. 1967: O. Mills, *Death enters the Lists*, viii, There would be no fish-bits for Whiskers ... but she would buy him some fish-pieces. A change was as good as a rest, she remembered.

2. Change is no robbery. *See* Fair, *adj.* (19).

3. Change of fortune is the lot of life. 1855: Bohn, 336.

4. Change of pasture makes fat calves. 1546: Heywood, Pt II ch iv 1575: Gascoigne, *Glasse of Govt.*, IV iii 1696: D'Urfey, *Quixote*, Pt III Act IV sc i 1732: Fuller, 1081. 1846: Denham, *Proverbs*, 6 (Percy S.).

5. Change of weather is the discourse of fools. 1659: Howell, *Proverbs: Span.-Eng.*, 2. 1670: Ray, 28. 1732: Fuller, 1082. 1846: Denham, *Proverbs*, 3 (Percy S.).

6. Change of women makes bald knaves. 1605: Camden, *Remains*, 320 (1870). 1685: Meriton, *Yorkshire Ale*, 50, But change of women macks lean knaves Ise flaid.

7. Change of work is as good as touch-pipe [short interval of rest], *A.* Cornwall. 1895: Jos. Thomas, *Randigal Rhymes*, 59. See also **Change** (1).

8. Changes never answer the end. 1740: North, *Examen*, 352, Short sentences, commonly called proverbs ... such as, *Honesty is*

the best policy ... Changes never answer the end.

Change, *verb.* **1. Do not change horses in midstream.** *See* Horse (27).

2. I am loath to change my mill. Somerset. 1678: Ray, 349.

3. To change copy. *See* Copy (2).

4. To change the name and not the letter, Is a change for the worse, and not for the better. 1862: Chambers, *Book of Days*, i 723. 1878: Dyer, *Eng. Folk-Lore*, 200. 1901: F. E. Taylor, *Lancs Sayings*, 41, Iv yo' choange yore name beawt choangin' th' letter, youe choange for th' wo'se i'stid o' for th' better.

5. *See* quot. 1853: *N. & Q.*, 1st ser, vii 156, I have frequently in youth heard the proverb, 'You may change *Norman* for a worser (worse) horse'. *See also* Times.

Changeable as a weather-cock. 1548: Hall, *Chron.*, 38 (1809), Which be more variable then the wethercocke. 1615: R. Tofte, tr *Blazon of Iealousy*, 81, Since thou as weather-cocke dost change.

Changeful as the moon. Before 1599: Spenser, *Mutabilitie*, can. ii st. 50, So that as changefull as the moone men use to say.

Changing [exchanging] **of words is the lighting of hearts.** 1855: Bohn, 336.

Chap as married Hannah, The. 1900: *N. & Q.*, 9th ser, vi 346, 'The chap as married Hannah' ... is a very common phrase in South Notts. 'That's the chap as married Hannah' means that is the person or thing I am seeking or that I need. 1900: Ibid., 434, This common here [Worksop], and in many other localities. It is a women's saying, though men occasionally use it. When something has been successfully done, comes out, 'There! That's the chap as married Hannah'.

Char is charred, This (or **That**) = That business (or job) is done. *c.*1400: *Seven Sages*, 88 (Percy S.), 'Sire', scho sayed, 'this char hys heved'. 1593: Peele, *Edward I.*, sc vi, Why, so, this chare is chared. 1670: Ray, 168, That char is char'd (as the good wife said when she had hang'd her husband). 1917: Bridge, *Cheshire Proverbs*, lll, 'That char's charred', as the boy said when he'd killed his father.

Chare-folks are never paid enough. 1678: Ray, 112 [without 'enough']. 1732: Fuller, 1083.

Charing, Smoky. 1735: Pegge, *Kent. Proverbs*, in E.D.S., No. 12, 69.

Charing-Cross. See **Old** (D), (5).

Charitable. 1. He is not charitable that will not be so privately. 1732: Fuller, 1932.

2. The charitable gives out at door, and God puts in at the window. 1678: Ray, 353.

Charity and Pride do both feed the poor. 1669: *Politeuphuia*, 243. 1732: Fuller, 1084, Charity and Pride have different aims, yet both feed the poor.

Charity begins at home. [ἀπωτέρω ἢ γόνυ κνάμα.– Theocritus, xvi 18. Proximus sum egomet mihi. – Terence, *Andr.*, IV i 12.] *c.*1380: Wiclif, in *Eng. Works*, 76 (E.E.T.S.), Whanne charite schuld bigyne at hem-self. 1509: Barclay, *Ship of Fools*, i 277 (1874), For perfyte loue and also charite Begynneth with hym selfe for to be charitable. 1572: T. Wilson, *Disc.*, *upon Usury*, 235 (1925), Charity beginneth first at it selfe. 1641: R. Brome, *Joviall Crew*, II, Good sister Meriel, Charity begins at home. 1763: Murphy, *Citizen*, I ii 1850: Dickens, *Chuzzlewit*, ch xxvii, But charity begins at home, and justice begins next door.

Charterhouse, Sister of the. See quot. 1528: Tyndale, *Obed. of Christ. Man*, 305 (P.S.), Of her that answereth her husband six words for one, we say, 'She is a sister of the Charterhouse': as who should say, 'She thinketh that she is not bound to keep silence; their silence shall be a satisfaction for her'.

Chaste. 1. Although thou be not chaste, yet be chary. 1576: Pettie, *Petite Pallace*, i 32 (Gollancz), Do not some men say that women always live chastely enough, so that they live charily enough? 1612: *Cornucopiae*, 25 (Grosart). 1630: *Tinker of Turvey*, 36 (Halliwell), I learned this old saying in Latin, *Caute, si non caste*. Live charily, if not chastely.

2. She is chaste who was never asked the question. 1695: Congreve, *Love for Love*, III iii.

Chastiseth one, amendeth many, He that. 1633: Draxe, 32. 1670: Ray, 4. 1732: Fuller, 2065.

Chatting to chiding is not worth a chute. 1546: Heywood, *Proverbs*, Pt II ch v.

Chawbent. See **Cheshire** (8).

Cheap. 1. It is as cheap sitting as standing. 1666: Torriano, *Piazza Univ.*, 277, The English say, It is as cheap sitting as standing, my masters. 1738: Swift, *Polite Convers.*, Dial. I. 1776: O'Keeffe, *Tony Lumpkin in Town*, I iii 1854:

Surtees, *Handley Cross*, ch lxiv. 1901: F. E. Taylor, *Lancs Sayings*, 18.

2. It is cheap enough to say, God help you. 1732: Fuller, 2922.

Cheapside, He got it by way of = for less than its value. 1790: Grose, *Prov. Gloss.*, s.v. 'London'.

Cheat, *verb.* **1. Cheat and the cheese will show.** 1917: Bridge, *Cheshire Proverbs*, 35.

2. Cheat me in the price but not in the goods. 1732: Fuller, 1090.

3. He that cheateth in small things is a fool; but in great things is a rogue. Ibid., No. 2066.

4. He that will cheat at play, Will cheat you any way. Ibid., No. 6302.

Cheats never prosper. 1612: J. Harington, *Epigrams* (1618) iv 5, Trason doth never prosper, what's the reason? For if it prosper, none dare call it Treason. 1805: R. Parkinson, *Tour in America*, II xxix, It is a common saying in England, that 'Cheating never thrives': but, in America, with honest trading you cannot succeed. 1903: V.S. Lean, *Collectanea*, II 38, 'Cheating never prospers'. A proverb frequently thrown at each other by young people when playing cards. 1935: R. Crompton, *William – the Detective*, vi, They avenged themselves upon the newcomer … by shouting the time-honoured taunt 'Cheats never prosper'.

Cheek by jowl. *c.*1300: R. Brunne, tr. Langtoft's *Chron.*, i 223 (Hearne), Vmwhile cheke bi cheke. *c.*1534: Berners, *Huon*, ch lv, p. 189 (E.E.T.S.), Rydynge cheke by Cheke by kynge yuoryn. 1599: *Sir Clyomon, etc.*, sig. F2, She went euen cheke by ioule With our head controms wife. 1682: Dryden, Prol. to Southerne's *Loyal Brother*, The devil … Sits cheek by jowl, in black, to chear his heart: Like thief and parson in a Tyburn cart. 1709: Ward, *Clubs*, 252 (1756), Those two sat cheek-by-jole. 1822: Byron, *Vis. of Judg.*, st. 20. 1851: FitzGerald, *Euphranor*, 68 (1855), Victor and vanquisht having to settle down cheek by jowl again. 1922: Weyman, *Ovington's Bank*, ch xxiii.

Cheer up. See **God is where he was.**

Cheerful look makes a dish a feast, A. 1640: Herbert, *Jac. Prudentum*.

Cheese. 1. After cheese comes nothing. 1639: Clarke, 136. 1655: Fuller, *Church Hist.*, bk vi § v (ii. 20), As after cheese, nothing to be expected. 1700: Ward, *London Spy*, 5 (1924). 1732: Fuller, 769.

2. Cheese and money should always sleep together one night. 1917: Bridge, *Cheshire Proverbs*, 35 [said of old when payment was demanded before delivery].

3. Cheese, it is a peevish elf, it digests all things but itself. 1584: Lyly, *Sapho andPhao*, III ii, Cheese … digesteth all things except itselfe. 1630: T. Adams, *Works*, 170, As cheese to digest all the rest, yet it selfe neuer digested. 1678: Ray, 40. 1738: Swift, *Polite Convers.*, Dial. II, They say, cheese digests everything but itself. 1846–59: *Denham Tracts*, ii 215 (F.L.S.), The moral taught was, 'Cheese digests everything but itself'.

4. Cheese of three halfpence a pound won't choke her. 1696: D'Urfey, *Quixote*. Pt III Act III sc i, The jade simpers as if butter would not melt in her mouth; but cheese of three half pence a pound won't choak her, as the old saying is.

5. If you will have a good cheese, and have'n old, You must turn'n seven times before he is cold. Somerset. 1678: Ray, 353. *c.*1685: Aubrey, *Nat. Hist. Wilts*, 105 (1847). 1732: Fuller, 6477.

6. You can't hang soft cheese on a hook. 1852: FitzGerald, *Polomius*, 39 (1903).

See also **Bread** (2), (5), and (6); **Chalk; Cheat** (1); **Eat** (37); **Green** (11); **King** (17); **Suffolk cheese;** and **Toasted cheese.**

Chelsea. *See* **Dead** (6); and **Safe as Chelsea.**

Chepstow born and Chepstow bred, Strong in the arm and weak in the head. Mon. 1905: *Folk-Lore*, xvi 67.

Cherry and Cherries. 1. A cherry year A merry year. 1678: Ray, 52. 1732: Fuller, 6139. 1893: Inwards, *Weather Lore*, 5.

2. Eat not cherries with the great. *c.*1530, *Dialogues of Creatures*, xx, As it is sayde in a commune prouerbe. I counsell not seruauntis to ete churyes with thef bettyrs. Fer they wyl haue the rype and leue them the harde. 1611: Cotgrave, s.v. 'Manger', Mean men are not to eat cherries … with great lords; least the stones of the best flie faster at their eyes then … the worst into their mouthes. 1662: Fuller, *Worthies*, ii 112 (1840), As for the outlandish proverb, 'He that eateth cherries with noblemen, shall have his eyes spurted out with the stones', it fixeth no fault in the fruit. 1732: Fuller, 5026 [as in 1662]. 1854: Doran, *Table Traits*, 209, There is a German proverb which says that 'it is unadvisable to eat cherries with potentates'.

3. If they blow in April, You'll have your fill; But if in May, They'll all go away. 1735: Pegge, *Kent. Proverbs*, in E.D.S., No. 12, p. 75.

4. One cherry-tree sufficeth not two jays. 1576: Lambarde, *Peramb. of Kent*, 269 (1826).

5. What is a tree of cherries worth to four in a company? 1568: in *Loseley MSS.*, 208 (Kempe).

See also **Disgraces; Life** (5); **Pea** (1); **Red; Two bites; Woman** (6).

Cherry's Boose. *See* quots. *c.*1791: Pegge, *Derbicisms*, 90 (E.D.S.), When a man weds a second wife, older and perhaps not so handsome as the first, they say, 'he has put Browney into Cherry's boose' [stall]. 1836: Wilbraham, *Cheshire Gloss.*, 2nd ed., 20, Any person who is got into a comfortable situation is said to be 'put into Cherry's boose'. 1917: Bridge, *Cheshire Proverbs*, 67.

Cheshire. 1. By waif, soc, and theam, You may know Cheshire men. 1917: Bridge, *Cheshire Proverbs*, 33 … Powerful in their legal rights and tenacious of them.

2. Cheshire bred, beef down to th' heels. Said of any very stout person. 1886: R. Holland, *Cheshire Gloss.*, 447 (E.D.S.). 1917: Bridge, *Cheshire Proverbs*, 36.

3. Cheshire born and Cheshire bred, Strong i' th' arm and weak i' th' head; or, **All strong i' th' arm and thick i' th' yed.** 1917: Bridge, *Cheshire Proverbs*, 36.

4. Cheshire chief of men. 1608: in Harington, *Nugae Antiquoe*, ii 276 (1804), He was translated to Chester, the chiefe city of that shire, that some call chiefe of men. 1612: Drayton, *Polyol.*, xi l. 8, For which, our proverb calls her, Cheshire chief of men. 1644: Taylor (Water-Poet), *Crop-eare Curried*, 10, in *Works*, 2nd coll. (Spens.S.), The Cheshire men … tendred themselves as a guard for the person of King Richard the Second, in a time of rebellion, for which they are honoured ever since with the proverb of *Cheshire chiefe of men.* 1790: Grose, *Prov. Gloss.*, s.v. 'Cheshire'. 1917: Bridge, *Cheshire Proverbs*, 36.

5. Cheshire for choice of lads. 1895: C. F. Lawrence, *Hist. Middlewich*, 50, 'Cheshire for choice of lads'. Old Cheshire proverb.

6. Cheshire for men, Berkshire for dogs, Bedfordshire for naked flesh, And Lincolnshire for bogs. *c.*1809, in *N.&Q.*, 9th ser, xi 266. 1917: Bridge, *Cheshire Proverbs*, 37.

7. In Cheshire … (*see* quots.). 1790: Grose, *Prov. Gloss.*, s.v. 'Cheshire', In Cheshire there are Lees as plenty as fleas, and as many Davenports as dogs-tails. 1917: Bridge, *Cheshire Proverbs*, 18, As many Leighs as fleas, Massies as asses, Crewes as crows, and Davenports as dogs' tails.

8. Neither in Cheshire nor Chawbent. = Neither in Kent nor Christendom. Chawbent is a town in Lancashire. 1678: Ray, 301. 1917: Bridge, *Cheshire Proverbs*, 96.

9. To grin like a Cheshire cat. 1792: Wolcot, in *Works*, ii 424 (1795), Yet, if successful, thou wilt be ador'd – Lo, like a Cheshire cat our Court will grin! 1806: A. Ferguson, in Scott's *Fam. Letters*, i 66 (1894), Ever since the Polts have grinned at me like so many Cheshire cats. 1855: Thackeray, *New-comes*, ch xxiv 1917: Bridge, *Cheshire Proverbs*, 135.

Chester. 1. The sweet Rood of Chester. 1575: Gascoigne, *Glasse of Govt.*, They are as much a kynne to the Markgrave as Robyn Fletcher and the Sweet Roode of Chester. 1917: Bridge, *Cheshire Proverbs*, 120.

2. There is more than one yew-bow in Chester. 1662: Fuller, *Worthies*, iii 537 (1840). 1790: Grose, *Prov. Gloss.*, s.v. 'Flintshire'. 1917: Bridge, 118.

3. To kill the Mayor of Chester, on Cevn Cerwyni. 1917: Bridge, 138.

4. Up before the dogs of Chester. 1917: Ibid., 46 [N, Wales saying].

See also **Bare as the Bishop; Easter** (4); and **West Chester.**

Chesterfield steeple, All on one side, like. Derby. 1889: *Folk-Lore Journal*, vii 293.

Chestnuts. *To take the chestnuts out of the fire with the cat's paw.* The story of the ape using the whelp's foot to get chestnuts out of the fire, is told in 1586: G. Whitney, *Emblems*, 58. 1664: J. Wilson, *The Cheats*, V iv, Some few that … make use of us, as the monkey did of the cat's paw, to scrape the nuts out of the fire. 1753: Richardson, *Grandison*, iii 31 (1883), He makes her … become herself the cat's paw to help him to the ready roasted chesnuts. 1855: Kingsley, *West. Ho!*, ch ix, Ready to make a cat's-paw of him or any man, if there be a chestnut in the fire.

Chet. *See* **May** (19).

Chevin. *See* quot. 1678: Ray, 52, Said the chevin to the trout, My head's worth all thy bouk.

Cheviot. *See* quot. 1846–59: *Denham Tracts*, i 317 (F.L.S.), When Cheeyut [Cheviot] ye see put on his cap, Of rain yelle have a wee bit drap. [Variants are given.]

Chew the cud, To. 1382: Wiclif, Hosea, vii 14 (OED), Thei chewiden cud vpon whete, and wyne, and departiden fro me. 1596: Spenser, *F. Q.*, bk v can. vi st. 19, Chawing the cud of griefe and inward paine. *c.*1617: B.&F., *Queen of Corinth*, IV i, Revenge is now the cud That I do chew. 1665: R. Howard, *Surprisal*, I, How he mumbles to himself! sure he does chew the cud of some set speech. 1774: in *Garrick Corresp.*, ii 33 (1832), People are for ever chewing the cud, and ruminating on the unsuccessful passages of their lives. 1827: Southey, *Letter to C. Bowles*, 10 July, Upon this plain statement he is now chewing the cud.

Chichester. 1. A Chichester lobster, a Selsey cockle, an Arundel mullet, a Pulborough eel, an Amberley trout, a Rye herring, a Bourne wheat-ear. 1610: P. Holland, tr. Camden's *Britannia*, 308, Selsey … is most famous for good cockles, and full lobsters. 1653: Walton, *Angler*, Pt I ch viii, Just so doth Sussex boast of four sorts of fish; namely an Arundel mullet, a Chichester lobster, a Shelsey cockle, and an Amerley trout. 1790: Grose, *Prov. Gloss.*, s.v. 'Sussex'.

2. If Chichester church steeple fall, In England there's no king at all. 1861: Lower, in *Sussex Arch. Coll.*, xiii 233.

Chickens. 1. Chickens feed capons. 1678: Ray, 111.

2. The chickens are the country's, but the city eats them. 1640: Herbert, *Jac. Prudentum.* 1670: Ray, 4. 1732: Fuller, 4447.

3. To count (or rechon) one's chickens before they are hatched. [ἀεὶ γεωργὸς εἰς νέωτα πλούσιος. – Philemon, 4 (Mein., 29).] *c.*1570: T. Howell, *New Sonnets*, C2, Counte not thy Chickens that unhatched be. 1577: *Misogonus*, IV i, My chickings are not hatcht; I nil to counte of him as yet. 1579: S. Gosson, *Ephemerides of Philo*, 19, I woulde not have him to counte his Chickens so soone before they be hatcht, nor tryumphe so long before the victorie.1583: Melbancke, *Philotinus*, sig. G2, Why doe we reckon our chickens before they be hatcht. 1664: S. Butler *Hudibras*, II iii, To swallow Gudgeons ere th'are catch'd, And count their Chickens ere th'are hatch'd. 1674: J. Howard, *Eng. Mounsieur*, III iii, Take heed we don't reckon our chicken before they are hatcht. 1725: Bailey, tr. Erasmus' *Colloq.*, 39, You are a little too hasty; you reckon your chickens before they are hatch'd. 1829: Scott, *Journal*, 20 May, But we must not reckon our chickens before they are hatched, though they are chipping the shell now.

See also **Capon** (1); **Children** (1); **Fox** (31); and **July** (7).

Chiddingly. *See* **Hellingly.**

Child. 1. A child may have too much of his mother's blessing. 1639: Clarke, 161 [with 'man' for 'child']. 1659: Howell, 11 (9). 1853: Trench, *Proverbs*, 86 (1905).

2. A child ... (*see* quot.). 1886: Elworthy, *West Som. Word-Book*, 290 (E.D.S.), A very common proverb is: A cheel that can tell [talk] avore he can go [walk], 'll sure t' ha nort but zorrow and wo.

3. A child's birds and a boy's wife are well used. *c.*1430: Lydgate, *Churl and Bird*, st. 52, A childes birde and a knaues wyff Haue ofte sithe grete sorrwe and meschaunce. Before 1529: Skelton, *Garl. of Laurell*, l. 1452, But who may haue a more vngracyous lyfe Than a chyldes birde and a knaues wyfe? 1678: Ray, 351. 1732: Fuller, 37.

4. 'Child my dear,' says Mrs Chapman. 1864: 'Cornish Proverbs', in *N. & Q.*, 3rd ser, vi 6.

5. Child's pig and daddy's bacon. 1678: Ray, 111, Childs pig, but fathers bacon. 1732: Fuller, 1101, Child's pig, but father's hog. 1883: Burne, *Shropsh. Folk-Lore*, 589, Child's pig, and daddy's bacon = nominal ownership.

6. Even a child may beat a man that's bound. 1732: Fuller, 1387.

7. Give a child all he shall crave, And a dog while his tail doth wave; And you'll have a fair dog and foul knave. 1303: Brunne, *Handlyng Synne*, l. 7240, Gyue thy chylde when he wyl kraue, And thy whelpe whyl hyt wyl haue, – than mayst thou make you a stounde A foulë chylde and a feyrë hounde. 1670: Ray, 82. 1732: Fuller, 6456. 1880: Spurgeon, *Ploughman's Pictures*, 70, Yet remember if you give a child his will and a whelp his fill, both will surely turn out ill.

8. He that wipes the child's nose, kisseth the mother's cheek. 1640: Herbert, *Jac. Prudentum*. 1659: Howell, *Proverbs: Span.-Eng.*, 18.

9. Let not a child sleep upon bones, *i.e.* the nurse's lap. Somerset 1678: Ray, 351.

10. The child hath a red tongue like its father. 1678: Ray, 234.

11. The child is father of the man. The character of the adult is formed in childhood. 1671: Milton, *Paradise Regained*, IV 220, The childhood shews the man, As morning shew the day. 1807: Wordsworth, 'The Rainbow', The Child is Father of the Man, And I could wish my days to be Bound each to each by natural piety. 1871: S. Smiles, *Character*, ii, The influences which contribute to form the character of the child ... endure through life ... 'The child is father of the man'.

12. The child says nothing but what it heard by the fire. 1640: Herbert, *Jac. Prudentum*. 1732: Fuller, 4449.

13. The child that's born must be kept. 1605: R. F., *Sch. of Slovenrie*, The Epistle, 'Tis a proverb, The child thats borne must be kept.

14. The child was born ... (*see* quot.). 1605: *London Prodigal*, I i, According to the old proverb, The child was born, and cried, Became a man, after fell sick, and died.

15. To a child all weather is cold. 1640: Herbert, *Jac. Prudentum*. 1670: Ray, 4.

16. When the child is christened you may have godfathers enough. 1639: Clarke, 283, When the child is christ'ned, every man will be god father. 1670: Ray, 69. 1732: Fuller, 5573. *c.*1800: Trusler, *Prov. in Verse*, 29. 1826: Brady, *Varieties of Lit.*, 39.

See also **Another man's child**; **Ask** (6); **Burnt child**; **Cares not**; **Children**; **Good child**; **Happy is the child**; **Innocent**; **Kiss**, *verb* (6); **Nurse** (3) and (4); **Old**, A (1); **One child**; **One pretty**; **Pap**; **Praise the child**; **Quick child**; **Spare the rod**; and **Wise** (7), (31), and (32).

Children. 1. Children and chicken must be always picking. 1573: Tusser, *Huswiferie*, 178 (E.D.S.), Yong children and chickens would euer be eating. 1670: Ray, 33. 1732: Fuller, 6078. 1893: *Co. Folk-Lore: Suffolk*, 156 (F.L.S.), Children and chicken are always a-picking. 1917: Bridge, *Cheshire Proverbs*, 52.

2. Children and fools have merry lives. 1639: Clarke, 298. 1681: W. Robertson, *Phraseol. Generalis*, 330. *c.*1800: Trusler, *Prov. in Verse*, 41.

3. Children and fools speak the truth. 1546: Heywood, *Proverbs*, Pt I ch xi, Children and fooles can not ly. 1591: Lyly, *Endymion*, IV ii,

'Tis an old said saw, 'Children and fools speak true'. *c.*1610: Rowlands, *More Knaues Yet?*, 36 (Hunt.Cl.), Fooles and babes tell true. 1652: Tatham, *Scots Figgaries*, III, I am but a fool, 'tis confest, – but children and fools tell truth sometimes, you know. 1769: Colman, *Man and Wife*, III, Fools and children always speak truth, they say. 1805: Scott, in Lockhart's *Life*, ii 22. 1921: *Evening Standard*, 21 Oct., p. 9, col. 2, *Solicitor* (to a witness in the Bow County Court to-day): – 'Are you telling the truth in this case?' *Witness:* – 'Only children and fools tell the truth'.

4. Children are certain cares, uncertain comforts. *c.*1460: *How the Good Wife*, l. 145, Care he hathe that childryn schalle kepe, 1641: Brathwaite, *Eng. Gent.*, *etc.*, Suppl., p. 27, Children reflect constant cares, but uncertaine comforts. 1707: Dunton, *Athen. Sport*, 389, I shall not be in danger of the certain troubles, but uncertain comforts of children. 1732: Fuller, 1095. 1854: Surtees, *Handley Cross*, ch xxxix.

5. Children are poor men's riches. 1611: Cotgrave, s.v, 'Enfant'. 1670: Ray, 4. 1732: Fuller, 1094. 1875: A. B. Cheales, *Proverb. Folk-Lore*, 47.

6. Children be first a yearm-ache [armache] **and a'terwards a heart-ache.** S.W. Wilts. 1901: *Folk-Lore*, xii 82.

7. Children have wide ears and long tongues. 1732: Fuller, 1097.

8. Children in Holland … (*see* quot.). 1822: Scott, *Nigel*, Introd. Epist., As the nursery proverb goes – 'The children in Holland take pleasure in making What the children in England take pleasure in breaking' [i.e. toys]. 1849: Halliwell, *Pop. Rhymes and Nurs. Tales*, 187.

9. Children pick up words as pigeons pease, And utter them again as God shall please. 1670: Ray, 213.

10. Children should be seen and not heard. Originally applied to girls only – and young women, Cf. **Maid** (9) and (12). 1820: J.Q. Adams, *Memoirs* (1875), My dear mother's constant lesson in childhood, that children in company should be seen and not heard. 1914: Shaw, 'Parents and Children', in *Misalliance*, *etc.*, p. xxi, And impudently proclaim the monstrous principle that little children should be seen and not heard.

11. Children suck the mother when they are young, and the father when they are old. 1678: Ray, 112. 1732: Fuller, 1099 [with 'grown up' for 'old'].

12. Children to bed and the goose to the fire. 1670: Ray, 168. 1675: W. Churchill, *Divi Britannici*, 278, It was high time (as the vulgar proverb hath it) to put the children to bed, and lay the goose to the fire.

13. Children when they are little make parents fools, when great, mad. 1670: Ray, 4. 1748: Richardson, *Clarissa*, iv 120 (1785).

14. He that has no children knows not what is love. 1666: Torriano, *Piazza Univ.*, 89. 1875: A. B. Cheales, *Proverb. Folk-Lore*, 47.

15. He that hath children, all his morsels are not his own. 1640: Herbert, *Jac. Prudentum*. 1666: Torriano, *Piazza Univ.*, 89.

16. He that hath no children feedeth them fat. 1611: Davies (of Hereford), *sc of Folly*, 46, in *Works*, ii (Grosart), Who hath no children feedes them fatt. 1633: Draxe, 58.

17. What children hear at home soon flies abroad. 1611: Cotgrave, s.v. 'Enfant'. 1670: Ray, 4. 1732: Fuller, 5482. 1875: A. B. Cheales, *Proverb. Folk-Lore*, 47.

18. When children stand still, They have done some ill. 1640: Herbert, *Jac. Prudentum* [with 'quiet' for 'still']. 1749: Fielding, *Tom Jones*, bk xv ch ii, I remember a wise old gentleman who used to say, 'When children are doing nothing, they are doing mischief.' 1875: A. B. Cheales, *Proverb. Folk-Lore*, 47.

19. *See* quot. 1913: *Folk-Lore*, xxiv 76, When you've got one, you may run, When you've got two, you may goo, But when you've got three, you must stop where you be. Oxfordsh.

See also **Better children; Boy** (2); **Kindness; Offspring; Old, A** (*b*) (15); and **Woman** (48)

Children's play. *See* **Boy** (5).

Childwall. *See* **Preston.**

Chimney. 1. It is easier to build two chimneys, than to maintain one. 1640: Herbert, *Jac. Prudentum*. 1736: Franklin, *Way to Wealth*, in *Works*, i 450 (Bigelow), It is easier to build two chimneys than to keep one in fuel. 1869: Spurgeon, *John Ploughman*, ch xix.

2. There is not always good cheer where the chimney smokes. 1620: Shelton, *Quixote*, Pt II ch lxv. 1694: D'Urfey, *Quixote*, Pt I Act I sc i 1732: Fuller, 4930.

Chink. *So we have the chink, we will bear with the stink.* 1596: Harington, *Metam. of Ajax*, 68 (1814), So we get the chinks, We will bear with the stinks. 1670: Ray, 4. 1681: W. Robertson, *Phraseol. Generalis*, 332, So we may have the chink, we will away with the stink. 1732: Fuller, 6277, We will bear with the stink, If it bring but in chink. Cf. **Money** (16).

Chip. 1. A chip of the old block. 1633: Rowley, *Match at Midnight*, I, He's a chip o' th' old block. 1644: Quarles, in *Works*, i 166 (Grosart), A true chip of the old block. 1709: Dykes, *Eng. Proverbs*, 30, A chip of the old block, is the vulgar nick-name of a father-like boy. 1762: Colman, *Musical Lady*, II. 1824: Scott, *Redgauntlet*, ch xv, There was my father ... a true chip of the old Presbyterian block. 1850: Dickens, *Chuzzlewit*, ch xviii 1921: Hutchinson, *If Winter Comes*, Pt III ch iii (iii.).

2. Chip in one's eye. *See* **Hews too high.**

3. Like a chip in porridge. 1666: Torriano, *Piazza Univ.*, 182, The English say, like a chip in pottage. 1678: Dryden, *Limberham*, IV i, A note under his hand! that is a chip in porridge; it is just nothing. 1754: Berthelson, *Eng.-Danish Dict.*, s.v. 'Chip', It tastes just like chips in a porridge. 1872: Hardy, *Greenwood Tree*, Pt II ch iv, 'Very well; we'll let en come in', said the tranter feelingly. 'You'll be like chips in porridge, Leaf – neither good nor hurt.'

Chippenham. *See* quot. *c.*1685: Aubrey, *Nat. Hist. Wilts*, 58 (1847), When Chipnam stood in Pewsham's wood, Before it was destroy'd, A cow might have gone for a groat a yeare – But now it is denyed.

Chittlehampton. *See* **Bishop's Nympton.**

Choice of a wife. *See* **Wife** (7).

Choke up – in various phrases. *See* quots. 1605: R. F., *Sch. of Slovenrie*, 6, Say not, God blesse him, but choake vp, or some such matter, rather. 1678: Ray, 343, Choak up, the churchyard's nigh. 1732: Fuller, 1102 [as in 1678]. 1738: Swift, *Polite Convers.*, Dial. I, Choke, chicken; there's more a-hatching. 1871: 'Shropshire Sayings', in *N.&Q.*, 4th ser, vii 9, Choke chicken more hatching. 1883: Burne, *Shropsh. Folk-Lore*, 598, Choke up, Chicken! said to a child choking. 1894: Northall, *Folk Phrases*, 12 (E.D.S.), Choke up, chicken, more a-hatching. Glos. [= There's as good fish in the sea, etc.]

Choleric. 1. From a choleric man, withdraw a little; from him that says nothing, for ever. 1631: Mabbe, *Celestina*, 99 (T.T.), That ancient adage; from an angry man, get the gone but for a while; but from an enemy, for ever. 1640: Herbert, *Jac. Prudentum*.

2. The choleric drinks, the melancholic eats, the phlegmatic sleeps. 1670: Ray, 5.

3. The choleric man never wants woe. 1633: Draxe, 9, The angry man neuer wanted woe. 1659: Howell, 11 (9). Cf. **Hasty man.**

Choose a wife. *See* **Wife** (7).

Choose for yourself and use for yourself. 1639: Clarke, 230.

Choose thy company before thy drink. Ibid., 24.

Chop logic, To. 1528: More, *Workes*, p. 153, col. 2 (1557), She will then waxe copious and chop logicke with her maistres. 1560: Awdeley, *V acabondes*, 15 (E.E.T.S.), Choplogyke is he that when his mayster rebuketh him of hys fault he wyll geue hym xx wordes for one. 1682: A. Behn, *City Heiress*, I i, Send him to chop logick in an University. 1771: Smollett, *Clinker*, in *Works*, vi 21 (1817), A man must not presume to use his reason, unless he has studied the categories, and can chop logic by mode and figure.

Chopt hay, It goes down like. 1678: Ray, 235.

Chrisom child, To die like a. 1599: Shakespeare, *Henry V*, II iii, A' made a finer end and went away an it had been any Christom child, *c.*1620: A. Cooke, in Hunter's *New Ill. of Shakesp.*, ii 60 (1845), He who dieth quietly, without ravings or cursings, much like a chrysom child, as the saying is. 1680: Bunyan, *Badman*, 566 (OED), Mr Badman died ... as they call it, like a chrisom-child, quietly and without fear.

Christ's Cross. *See* quot. 1593: *Tell Trothes N. Yeares Gift*, 33 (N.Sh.S.), Suppose the worst that can happe, imagine shee will neuer be good, building vpon the old sayinge: *Shee that knowes where Christes crosse standes, will neuer forget where great A dwels* ...

Christen. 1. He was christened with pump-water = He has a red face. 1678: Ray, 79.

2. To christen one's own child first. 1659: Howell, 5, Ile christen my own child first. 1694: D'Urfey, *Quixote*, Pt II Act III sc ii, Charity ... begins at home, you know; and ever, while you live, christen your own child first. 1738: Swift, *Polite Convers.*, Dial. I, You know, the parson always christens his own child first. 1864: 'Cornish Proverbs', in *N. & Q.*, 3rd ser, vi 494, They'll christen their own child first. 1893: G. L. Gower, *Gloss. Surrey Words*, 9 (E.D.S.), 'Christen your own child first' [said by a Surrey man].

Christmas. It is noticeable how curiously some of the following sayings contradict one another.

1. A black Christmas makes a fat churchyard. 1846: Denham, *Proverbs*, 62 (Percy S.).

2. A dark Christmas makes a heavy wheatsheaf. 1878: Dyer, *Eng. Folk–Lore*, 54, In Huntingdonshire it is a common saying that 'a dark Christmas sends a fine harvest'. 1878: *N. & Q.*, 5th ser, x 467, [Surrey woman *loq.*] 'They always say a dark Christmas makes a heavy wheatsheaf'.

3. A green Christmas brings a heavy harvest. 1873: *N. & Q.*, 4th ser, xi 212 [Rutland labourer *loq.*].

4. A green Christmas makes a fat churchyard. 1635: Swan, *Spec. Mundi*, 161, They also say, that a hot Christmas makes a fat church-yard. 1642: Fuller, *Holy State*: 'Of Time-Serving', A green Christmas is neither handsome nor healthful. 1710: *British Apollo*, vol iii No. 106, col. 3. 1830: Forby, *Vocab. E. Anglia*, 418. 1879: Henderson, *Folk-Lore of N. Counties*, 75.

5. A kiss at Christmas and an egg at Easter. 1846–59: *Denham Tracts*, II 92 (F.L.S.).

6. A light Christmas makes a full sheaf. 1659: Howell, 12, A light Christmas, a heavy sheaf. 1670: Ray, 4 [as in 1659]. 1881: *N. & Q.*, 6th ser, iv 535. 'A light Christmas makes a full sheaf' … I heard it the other day in Surrey.

7. A windy Christmas and a calm Candlemas are signs of a good year. 1846: Denham, *Proverbs*, 27 (Percy S.). 1893: Inwards, *Weather Lore*, 39.

8. After Christmas comes Lent. 1611: Cotgrave, s.v. 'Banquet', After feasting, fasting. 1678: Ray, 113, After a Christmas comes a Lent. 1732: Fuller, 770. 1846–59: *Denham Tracts*, ii 92 (F.L.S.) [as in 1678].

9. As many mince pies as you taste at Christmas, so many happy months you will have. 1846–59: *Denham Tracts*, ii 91 (F.L.S.).

10. At Christmas great loafs, at Easter clean souls, at Whitsuntide new clothes. 1659: Howell, 11 (9).

11. At Christmas meadows green, at Easter covered with frost. 1893: Inwards, *Weather*

Lore, 38. 1912: R. L. Gales, *Studies in Arcady*, 2nd ser, 108, A green Christmas, a white Easter.

12. At old Christmas the days are longer by a cock's stride. 1830: Forby, *Vocab. E. Anglia*, 418. Cf. No. 17; and **New Year** (2).

13. Better have a new-laid egg at Christmas than a calf at Easter. 1882: Mrs Chamberlain, *W. Worcs. Words*, 38 (E.D.S.).

14. Christmas comes but once a year. 1580: Tosser, *Husb.*, 28 (E.D.S.), At Christmas play and make good cheere, for Christmas comes but once a yeere. 1652: Taylor (Water-Poet), *Christmas In and Out*. 16, in *Works*, 1st coll. (Spens.S.). 1834: Planché, *Extravag.*, i 204(1879). 1892: S. Hewett, *Peasant Speech of Devon*, 68, Cursemas com'th but wance a year.

15. Christmas wet, empty granary and barrel. 1893: Inwards, *Weather Lore*, 38.

16. Coming – like Christmas. 1738: Swift, *Polite Convers.*, Dial. I, Coming! ay, so is Christmas, *c.*1760: Foote, *Maid of Bath*, I, Coming! ay, zo be Christmas. 1839: Planché, *Extravag.*, ii, 60 (1879).

17. From Christmas-tide to New'us-tide, The days do get a cock's stride. 1890: J. D. Robertson, *Gloucester Gloss.* (E.D.S.). Cf. No. 12; and **New Year** (2).

18. He has more business than English ovens at Christmas. *c.*1594: Bacon, *Promus*, No. 912, He hath moe to doe than the ovens in Christmas. 1659: Howell, *Proverbs: Ital.-Eng.*, 1. 1846: Denham, *Proverbs*, 63 (Percy S.), Busy as an oven at Christmas.

19. If Christmas day on a Sunday fall, A troublous winter we shall have all. 15th cent.: Song, in Denham, *Proverbs*, 69, (Percy S. 1846), Yf Crystmas day on the Son day be, A trobolus wynter ye shall see. 1882: *N. & Q.*, 6th ser, v 7.

20. If Christmas day on Monday be, A wintry winter you shall see. 15th cent.: Song, in Denham, *Proverbs*, 70 (Percy S., 1846), Yf Crystemas day on Monday be, A grete wynter that yere have shall ye. 1893: *N. & Q.*, 8th ser, iv 505.

21. If Christmas finds a bridge, he'll break it; if he finds none he'll make one. 1893: Inwards, *Weather Lore*, 38.

22. If the sun shines … *See* quots. 1839: G. C. Lewis, *Herefs. Words*, 122, The following are old sayings current … If the sun shines on Christmas-day, there will be accidents by fire all the year after. 1878: Dyer, *Eng. Folk-Lore*, 249, If the sun shine through the apple-tree on Christmas Day there will be an abundant crop in the following year.

23. Light Christmas; light wheatsheaf: Dark Christmas; heavy wheatsheaf. 1855: *N. & Q.*, 1st ser, xii 490 [current in Kent, and firmly believed]. 1872: *ibid.*, 4th ser, ix 13, I have heard the following saying referred to the neighbourhood of Ledbury, Herefordshire: 'A light Christmas, a light harvest'.

24. The twelve days of Christmas. 1846: Denham, *Proverbs*, 62 (Percy S.).

25. They keep Christmas all the year. 1672: Walker, *Paroem.*, 25. 1681: W. Robertson, *Phraseol. Generalis*, 783.

26. They talk of Christmas so long that it comes. 1611: Cotgrave, s.v. 'Noel', So long is Christmas cryed that at length it comes. 1670: Ray, 26. 1846–59: *Denham Tracts*, ii 92 (F.L.S.).

See also **Bounce buckram; Easter** (1) and (5); **Ice** (1), (2), and (3); **Michaelmas** (1); **Monday** (5); **St Michael** (2); **Simpers; Three things that never;** and **Whitsuntide** (7).

Christmas-Eve. *See* **Ghosts.**

Christmas-pies. *See* **Devil** (71); and **Eat** (17).

Christmas play. *See* **Good as.**

Chuck under the chin, A. *See* quot. 1738: Swift. *Polite Convers.*, Dial. I, Well said, girl! [giving her a chuck]. Take that: they say a chuck under the chin is worth two kisses.

Chue. *See* **Stanton Drew.**

Church have leave to stand in the churchyard, Let the. 1678: Ray, 113. 1732: Fuller, 3192.

Church Street. *See* **Braintree.**

Church Stretton, where they eaten more nor they getten. 1883: Burne, *Shropsh. Folk-Lore*, 583.

Church work goes on slowly. 1639: Fuller, *Holy War*, bk i ch xiii, So that, contrary to the proverb, church work went on the most speedily. 1655: Fuller, *Church Hist.*, bk i § v (iii. 4), Church work is a cripple in going up [building], but rides post in coming down! [destroying a church]. 1732: Fuller, 1106. 1875: A. B. Cheales, *Proverb. Folk-Lore*, 79.

Churchman. *Though you see a Churchman ill, yet continue in the church still.* 1640: Herbert, *Jac. Prudentum.*

Churchyard. *A piece of a churchyard fits everybody.* Ibid.

Churl and **Churls. 1. A churl's churl is often woebegone.**, *c.*1430: Lydgate, *Churl and Bird*, st. 40, For hit was said of folkes yeres agoon A chorles chorle is ofte woo begoon.

2. A churl's feast is better than none at all. 1594: Lodge and Greene, *Looking Glass*, l. 1191, We must feed vpon prouerbes now, as … 'A churles feast is better than none at all'.

3. Give a churl rule. *See* quot. 1485: Malory, *Morte d'Arthur*, bk x ch 61, Hit is an old sawe gyue a chorle rule and there by he wylle not be suffysed.

4. Of churls may no good come. *c.*1489: Caxton, *Blanchardyn, etc.*, 173 (E.E.T.S.), Of churles, bothe man and wyff, can departe noo goode fruyte. Ibid., 173, Men sayen that 'of a kerle may nought come but poyson and fylth, that maketh the place to stynke where he haunted ynne'.

See also **Claw** (1); and **Put** (8).

Churning days, I'll make him know. 1678: Ray, 235.

Cider is treacherous because it smiles in the face, and then cuts the throat. 1653: T. Adams, *Works*, iii 267 (V. Lean) Those bottled windy drinks that laugh in a man's face and then cut his throat. 1738: Swift, *Polite Convers.*, Dial. II, Pray, my lord, how is it [cider] treacherous? *Ld. Sparkish.* Because it smiles in my face, and cuts my throat.

Cider on beer is very good cheer, But beer upon cider's a rider [doesn't mix well]. 1888: Marchant, *Praise of Ale*, 462.

Cipher among numbers, He is a. 1633: Draxe, 29. 1639: Clarke, 70.

Circumstances alter cases. 1678: T. Rymer, *Tragedies of Lost Age* 177, There may be circumstances that alter the case, as when there is sufficient ground of partiality. 1776: W. Heath, *Memoirs* (1798), 92, Our general reflected for a moment, that as circumstances alter cases, Gen. Washington … might wish for some aid. 1870: Dickens, *Drood*, ch ix 1923: J. S. Fletcher, *The Diamonds*, ch ii, Is it not one of your proverbs that circumstances alter cases?

Citizen is at his business before he rise, The. 1640: Herbert, *Jac. Prudentum.*

City which comes to parle is half won, The. 1567: Painter, *Pal. of Pleasure*, iii 48 (Jacobs), For a city is halfe won when they within demaunde for parle. 1651: Herbert, *Jac.*

Prudentum, 2nd ed., A city that parleys is half gotten.

Civil denial is better than a rude grant, A. 1732: Fuller, 38.

Claps his dish at the wrong man's door, He. 1596: Jonson, *Ev. Man in his Humour*, II i 1678: Ray, 239.

Claw, *verb*. **1. Claw a churl by the tail, and he will defile your hand.** 1546: Heywood, *Proverbs*, Pt II ch vii 1568: *Jacob and Esau*, II iii, in Hazlitt, *Old Plays*, ii 216 (1874), This proverb in Esau may be understand: Claw a churl by the tail, and he will file your hand. 1621: Jonson, *Gyps. Metam.* 1670: Ray, 70.

2. Claw me and I'll claw you. 1530: Palsgrave, 486, Clawe my backe, and I wyll clawe thy toe. 1619: H. Hutton, *Follies Anat.*, 31 (Percy S.), Let coxcombs curry favour with a fee, Extoll their braines, with Claw me, I'l claw thee. 1754: Berthelson, *Eng.-Danish Dict.*, s.v. 'Claw'. Cf. **Ka me, ka thee;** and **Scratch me.**

3. He claws it as Clayton claw' the pudding, when he ate bag and all. 1678: Ray, 282. 1732: Fuller, 1826. Cf. **Eat** (38).

Clay and sand. *See* **England** (12).

Clean as a clock. 1669: H. More, *Antid. against Idolatry*, To Reader, Who will be ready to wipe you as clean as a clock, before you come to the castle. 1874: *N.Q Q.*, 5th ser, i 454, 'As clean as a clock'. – A common phrase in Yorkshire, referring to the shining and clean-looking black beetles (always called *clocks* in the North) which are to be found under every piece of cow-dung which has been dropped a few hours.

Clean as a new pin. *See* **New pin.**

Clean as a penny. 1681: W. Robertson, *Phraseol. Generalis*, 338. 1720: Gay, *Poems*, ii 279 (Underhill), Clean as a penny drest. 1828: Carr, *Craven Dialect*, 40, I've lost my knife as clean as a penny. 1854: Baker, *Northants Gloss.*, s.v. 'Penny', 'Clean as a penny' is a common simile for any one that is neatly and cleanly dressed.

Clean as a whistle. 1828: Carr, *Craven Dialect*, ii 256, 'As clean as a whistle', a proverbial simile, signifying completely, entirely. 1851: Planché, *Extravag.*, iv 164 (1879), Or else his head cut off, clean as a whistle. 1925: *Observer*, 14 June, p. 11, col. 3, 'Hay Fever' [a play] is as clean as a whistle – if this matters to anybody.

Clean (or white) as nip. 1838: Holloway, *Provincialisms*, 116, Nepeta cataria, the herb cat-mint, which is covered with a white down; hence the saying 'as white as nep'. 1890: P. H. Emerson, *Wild Life*, 96, Where that have been on the skin that turn as white as nip. 1899: Dickinson, *Cumberland Gloss.*, 378, Clean as a nip. – Smart, very tidy; free from dirt. 1917: Bridge, *Cheshire Proverbs*, 11. Cf. **Nice as nip.**

Clean-fingered huswife, and an idle, folk say, A. 1546: Heywood, *Proverbs*, Pt I ch x.

Clean hands want no washball. 1732: Fuller, 1111

Clean heels, light meals. This 'refers to the superiority of clay land over sand land for yielding milk'. 1886: R. Holland, *Cheshire Gloss.*, 447 (E.D.S.). 1917: Bridge, *Cheshire Proverbs*, 38.

Clean linen only that makes the feast, 'Tis not 1732: Fuller, 5093.

Clean man when dirty-washed, I'm a. 1917: Bridge, *Cheshire Proverbs*, 99, Oi'm a clane mon when dirty-weshed. = Straightforward man even though I may be dirty.

Clean pair of heels. *See* **Show.**

Cleanliness is next to godliness. 1605: Bacon, *Adv. of Learning*, bk ii, Cleanness of body was ever deemed to proceed from a due reverence to God. *c.*1790: quoted in Wesley, *Sermon* 93, 'On Dress', Cleanliness is, indeed, next to godliness. 1861: Dickens, *Great Expect.*, ch iv.

Clear as a bell. 1670: Ray, 203. 1838: Dickens, *Twist*, ch xxiii, Fresh, genuine port wine ... clear as a bell; and no sediment!

Clear as crystal. Before 1300: *Cursor M.*, l. 376, The lift [sky] wit sternes [stars] grete and small wit water clere als cristale. *c.*1350: *Alexander*, l. 2541, It was clerir than cristalle. *c.*1430: Lydgate, *Minor Poems*, 343 (E.E.T.S.), Shewe out in chyldhode as ony crystall clere. 1584: R. Scot, *Witchcraft*, bk xiii ch vi, A stone about the bignesse of a bean, as clear as the crystall. 1605: Sylvester, *Du Bartas*, Week I Day iii l. 141, And, cleer as crystall, in the glasse doth hop. 1700: J. Brome, *Travels*, 36. 1870: Dickens, *Drood*, ch xiv 1884: R.L.S., *Letters*, ii 298 (Tusitala ed.), The weather I have – cloudless, clear as crystal. 1909: Lucas, *Wand, in Paris*, ch i, My duty is clear as crystal.

Clear as the day. 1541: Coverdale, *Christ. State Matrimony*, sig. D8, Euydent it is and as cleare as the daye. 1565: Shacklock. *Hatch, of Heresies*, fo. 76, It is as clear as the daye. 1692: L'Estrange,

Aesop, Life, p. 28 (3rd ed.). 1740: North, *Examen*, 190, The plot was as clear as noon day. 1883: R.L.S., *Treasure* I, ch vi, 'The thing is as clear as noonday,' cried the squire. 1922: A. Bennett, *Prohack*, ch xx (iv.), She *must* be. It's as clear as day-light!

Clear as the sun. *c.*1579: Harvey, *Letter-Book*, 66 (Camden S.), Is it not cleerer then the sonne at noone dayes? 1680: in North, *Lives of Norths*, i 159 (Bohn), Who would make the plot as clear as the sun. 1709: Mandeville, *Virgin Unmask'd*, 133 (1724). 1749: Fielding, *Tom Jones*, bk xii ch vii.

Clear conscience. *See* **Conscience** (1), (2), and (3).

Clear gain that remains by honest gettings, 'Tis. 1659: Howell, 11.

Clear. *See also* **Innocent as a newborn babe.**

Cleave. 1. He cleaves the clouds. 1813: Ray, 75. **2. They cleave together like burs.** 1546: Heywood, *Proverbs*, Pt II ch v 1580: Churchyard, *Charge*, 30 (Collier), Ye cleave together so like burres.

Cleckheaton. *See* **Birstal.**

Clent. *See* quot. 1894: Northall, *Folk Phrases*, 24 (E.D.S.), The people of Clent are all Hills, Waldrons, or devils.

Clerk makes the justice, The. 1660: A. Brome, *Poems:* 'The Leveller', 'Tis we commons make the lords, and the clerk makes the justice. 1691: *Merry Drollery*, 37 (Ebsworth) [as in 1660]. 1729: Defoe, *Compl. Gent.*, Pt I ch vi, p. 239 (1890), So makeing good the old proverb that the clark makes the justice, while the master does just nothing. 1732: Fuller, 3024, It is the Justice's clerk that makes the Justice.

Cleveland in the clay, Bring in two soles and carry one away. 1670: Ray, 257. 1790: Grose, *Prov. Gloss.*, s.v. 'Yorkshire'. 1878: *Folk-lore Record*, i 168.

Cleveland. *See* **Rosebery-Topping.**

Client twist his attorney and counsellor is like a goose twixt two foxes, A. 1659: Howell, 11 (9).

Climb. 1. He that never climbed never fell. 1546: Heywood, *Proverbs*, Pt I ch xii *c.*1594: Bacon, *Promus*, No. 484. 1762: Smollett, *Sir L. Greaves*, ch x, Crabshaw replied ' ... who never climbed, never fell.' **2. Who climbs high his fall is great.** *c.*1430: Lydgate, *Minor Poems*, 120 (Percy S.), Who clymbythe hyest most dredfulle is his falle. *c.*1460: *Wisdom*, sc iii, in *Macro Plays*, 50

(E.E.T.S.), Who clymyt hye, hys fall gret ys. 1513: Bradshaw, *St Werburge*, 40 (E.E.T.S.), Who clymbed to hye often hath a fall. *c.*1580: Spelman, *Dialogue*, 96 (Roxb.Cl), The ould saynge (the higher thou clymeste, and thy foote slyppe, the greater is thy fall). 1631: Mabbe, *Celestina*, 221 (T.T.), It is an ancient proverbe: That the higher a man climbes, the greater is his fall 1884: Gilbert, *Princess Ida*, II, Pray you bear in mind Who highest soar fall farthest.

Cloak. 1. A cloak for the rain = An expedient for every turn of fortune. Before 1529: Skelton, *Magnyfycence*, l. 618, Ye, for your wyt is cloked for the rayne. 1548: Hall, *Chron.*, 701 (1809), Whatsoeuer was saied by the Recorder in his excuse was taken as a cloke for the rain, and a dissimulacion or a mocke. 1601: Munday, etc., *Death of Robert, E. of Hunt.*, III i, Bruce, I tell you plain, Is no sound cloak to keep John from the rain. 1633: Rowley, *Match at Midnight*, III Cf. **Hypocrisy.**

2. Don't have thy cloak to make when it begins to rain. 1639: Clarke, 267, Hee that provides not a cloak before the raine, may chance to be wet to his coste. 1732: Fuller, 1808. 1846: Denham, *Proverbs*, 4 (Percy S.).

3. He hath a cloak for his knavery. 1678: Ray, 235.

4. You may as soon make a cloak for the moon. 1732: Fuller, 6158.

Clock goes as it pleases the clerk, The. 1678: Ray, 114. 1732: Fuller, 4451.

Clocks of London. *See* **London** (6).

Clogs to clogs is only three generations, From; or, There's nobbut three generations between clog and clog. 1871: *N.&Q.*, 4th ser, vii 472 ... A Lancashire proverb, implying that, however rich a poor man may eventually become, his great-grandson will certainly fall back to poverty and clogs. 1875: Smiles, *Thrift*, 292, Hence the Lancashire proverb, 'Twice clogs, once boots'. 1924: *Clogs to Chogs* [title of play produced at Everyman Theatre, London, 10 Nov.].

Close as oak. *See* **Oak** (2).

Close as wax. 1772: Cumberland, *Fash. Lover*, III ii, You mun be as close as wax, d'ye see. 1828: in *Brasenose Ale*, 24 (1878), Sleep seals my eyes as close as wax. 1891: Doyle, *White Company*, ch xx, 'Good lad!' whispered Ford. 'Stick to it close as wax!'

Close is my shirt. *See* **Near.**

Close mouth catches no flies, A. 1605: Camden, *Remains*, 316 (1870). 1670: Ray, 71. 1745: *Agreeable Companion*, 51.

Close mouth makes a wise head, A. 1703: Ward, *Writings*, ii 112.

Close pasture where he can't nibble, It must be a. 1887: *N.&Q.*, 7th ser, iii 514 … This is a common saying in the Midlands, and is probably well known through the country.

Cloth. 1. *See* quot. 1570: Googe, tr. *Popish Kingdom*, 41 (1880), According to the proverbe thus, the cloth must still be shorne, Least it should hap to be consumde with mothes, and all to torne.

2. *See* quot. 1825: Scott, *Betrothed*, ch x, You know the good old saw, – 'Cloth must we wear, Eat beef and drink beer, Though the dead go to bier'.

Clothe thee in war, arm thee in peace. 1640: Herbert, *Jac. Prudentum*.

Clothe thee warm, eat little, drink enough, and thou shalt live. 1578: Florio, *First Fruites*, fo. 34, Cloathe warme, eate little, drink wel, so shalt thou lyue. 1629: *Book of Meery Riddles*, Prov. 129.

Clothes. *He is making clothes for fishes.* 1813: Ray, 75.

Clothmarket, In the = In bed. 1678: Ray, 235. 1738: Swift, *Polite Convers.*, Dial. I.

Cloud and **Clouds. 1. A round-topped cloud, with flattened base, Carries rainfall in its face.** 1893: Inwards, *Weather Lore*, 96.

2. After clouds (or **black clouds**), **clear weather.** *c.*1400: *Beryn*, l. 3955 (E.E.T.S.), ffor 'aftir mysty cloudis there comyth a cler sonne'. 1546: Heywood, *Proverbs*, Pt I ch xi, After cloudes blacke, we shall haue weather cleere. 1685: Meriton, *Yorkshire Ale*, 72, After fowl weather followes a fair day. 1762: Smollett, Sir *L. Greaves*, ch x, Crabshaw replied ' … after clouds comes clear weather'. 1893: Inwards, *Weather Lore*, 88.

3. At sunset with a cloud so black, A westerly wind you shall not lack. Ibid., 86.

4. Clouds that the sun builds up, darken him. 1732: Fuller, 1115. 1893: Inwards, 85.

5. He that pryeth into every cloud, may be struck with a thunderbolt. 1639: Clarke, 31. 1670: Ray, 134. 1732: Fuller, 2255.

6. Hen's scarts [scratchings] **and filly tails**

Make lofty ships carry low sails; also, *If clouds look as if scratched by a hen, Get ready to reef your topsails then.* Nautical. 1893: Inwards, *Weather Lore*, 92.

7. If clouds be bright, 'Twill clear to-night; If clouds be dark, 'Twill rain – do you hark? Ibid., 88.

8. North and south, the sign of drought; East and west, the sign of blast. Ibid., 93.

9. Red clouds in the east, rain the next day. Ibid., 88.

10. The higher the clouds, the finer the weather. Ibid., 85.

11. Trace in the sky the painter's brush, Then winds around you soon will rush. Ibid., 92.

12. When clouds appear like rocks and towers, The earth's refreshed by frequent showers. 1831, Hone, *Year-Book*, 300. 1893: Inwards, 96.

13. When mountains and cliffs in the clouds appear, Some sudden and violent showers are near. 1893: Inwards, 96.

14. When the clouds are upon (or **go up**) **the hills, they'll come down by the mills.** 1678: Ray, 49. 1846: Denham, *Proverbs*, 19 (Percy S.). 1893: Inwards, 99, [as in 1846 *plus*] When it gangs up i' fops [small clouds on hills], It'll fa' down i' drops … North Country. When the clouds go up the hill, They'll send down water to turn a mill. Hants.

15. When the clouds of the morn to the west fly away, You may conclude on a settled, fair day. 1893: Inwards, 86.

See also **Curdly; Flea** (2); **Mackerel; Moon** (16); **Silver** (6); and **Woolly fleeces.**

Cloudy mornings turn to clear evenings. 1546: Heywood, *Proverbs*, Pt II ch ix, Cloudy mornynges turne to cleere after noones. 1681: W. Robertson, *Phraseol. Generalis*, 341. 1732: Fuller, 1116 … may turn … 1846: Denham, *Proverbs*, 6 (Percy S.).

Clout is better than a hole out, A. Corn. 1895: Jos. Thomas, *Randigal Rhymes*, 59.

Clout till may be out, Never cast a. *See* **May** (22).

Clover, To be in. 1813: Ray, 57.

Clown. *See* quots. 1586: Pettie, tr. Guazzo's *Civil Convers.*, fo. 171, You know well the prouerbe – Claw a clown he will thee scratch, Scratch a clown he will thee claw. 1623: Wodroephe, *Spared Houres*, 520, Anoynt a clowne, and hee will grip you, grip a clowne and hee will anoynt you. 1659: Howell, *Proverbs: Fr.-Eng.*, 9, Anoint a clown, and he will prick you.

Clowns are best in their own company, but gentlemen are best everywhere. 1732: Fuller, 1117.

Clowns kill [each] other, and gentles cleave together. 1623: Wodroephe, *Spared Houres*, 520.

Clubs are trumps. Glos. 1639: in *Berkeley MSS.*, iii 29 (1885), Beware, Clubs are trumps; or clubs will prove trumps.

Clude. *To, escape Clude and be drowned in Conway.* Two Welsh rivers. 1662: Fuller, *Worthies*, iii 527 (1840). 1790: Grose, *Prov. Gloss.*, s.v. 'Caernarvonshire'.

Clunton and Clunbury, Clungunford and Clun, are the ... (*see* quots.). 1883: Burne, *Shropsh. Folk-Lore*, 583 ... drunkenest (*or* dirtiest, *or* quietest) places under the sun. 1896: Housman, *Shropsh. Lad*, l. ... quietest places under the sun.

Coaches won't run over him, The = He is in gaol. 1813: Ray, 186.

Coal-pit cale = First come, first served. 1917: Bridge, *Cheshire Proverbs*, 38.

Coals to Newcastle, To send. [In silvam non ligna feras insanius ac si Magnas Graecorum malis implere catervas. – Horace, *Sat.*, I x 34–5.] 1583: Melville, *Autobiog.*, i 163 (Wodrow S.), Salt to Dysart, or colles to Newcastle! 1650: Fuller, *Pisgah Sight*, 128, So far from being needless pains it may bring considerable profit to carry Charcoals to Newcastle. 1682: in *Thoresby Corresp.*, i 16 (1832), To send you our news from England, were to carry coals to Newcastle. 1709: *Labour in Vain; or, Coals to Newcastle* [title of sermon advertised in *Daily Courant*, 6 Oct., 1709]. 1874: R.L.S., *Letters*, i 134 (Tusitala ed.), It seems rather like sending coals to Newcastle to write a lecture to a subsidised professor. 1920: Galsworthy, *Tatterdemalion*, 9, However much she carried coals to Newcastle, or tobacco pouches to those who did not smoke. Cf. **Owl** (9).

Coals. *See* **Over the coals.**

Coarse. *See* **Rough as gorse.**

Coats change with countries. 1659: Howell, 17.

Cob = Mud. *See* quot. 1869: Hazlitt, 142, Give cob a hat and pair of shoes, and he'll last for ever. S. Devon. Provide a stone foundation and a slate coping for a cob [mud] wall. – *Shelly*.

Cobble. *They that cobble and clout shall have work when others go without.* 1670: Ray, 72. 1732: Fuller, 6454.

Cobbler. 1. Cobbler's law, he that takes money must pay the shot. 1678: Ray, 90.

2. Cobbler's Monday. 1825: Brockett, *Gloss. N. Country Words*, 44, Cobbler's-Monday, every Monday throughout the year is a regular holiday among the 'gentle craft'. 1862: *Dialect of Leeds*, 270 ... A day to do nothing in.

3. Cobblers and tinkers are the best ale-drinkers. 1659: Howell, 17. 1670: Ray, 5. 1732: Fuller, 6229. 1886: Bickerdyke, *Curios. of Ale and Beer*, 172, Cobblers and tinkers are your true ale drinkers. 1909: Hackwood, *Inns, Ales, etc.*, 98 [as in 1886].

4. Let not the cobbler go beyond his last. [Denuntiantem ne supra crepidam sutor judicaret. – Pliny, *Nat. Hist.*, xxxv 85.] 1539: Taverner, *Proverbs*, fo. 17, Let not the shoemaker go beyond hys shoe. 1613: Wither, *Abuses Stript, etc.*, To Reader, You will be counted but saucy cobblers to goe beyond your lasts. 1692: L'Estrange, *Aesop*, 205 (3rd ed.). 1754: *World*, No. 55, Extinguished him at once with the famous proverb in use at this day, 'The shoemaker must not go beyond his last'.

5. Let the cobbler stick to his last. For the earlier form of this proverb *see* **Cobbler** (4). 1868: W. Clift, *Tim Bunker Papers*, lix, I understood the use of a plow ... better than the use of a pen ... remembering the old saw 'Let the cobbler stick to his last'.

6. The cobbler deals with all [awl]. A verbal quibble. 1639: Clarke, 32.

7. The richer the cobbler the blacker his thumb. 1710: *Brit. Apollo*, vol iii, No. III, col. 6.

8. Without all [awl] the cobbler's nobody. 1639: Clarke, 71.

Cobwebs. *Where cobwebs are plenty, kisses are scarce.* 1864: 'Cornish Proverbs', in *N. & Q.*, 3rd ser, vi 6. 1906: *Cornish N. & Q.*, 266.

Cock. 1. A cock and bull tale. 1608: Day, *Law Trickes*, IV ii, What a tale of a cock and a bull he tolde my father. *c.*1625: B.&F., *Chances*, II iv, Thou talk'st of cocks and bulls. 1702: T. Brown, in *Works*, ii 94 (1760), Things which some call a cock and a bull, and others the product of a lively imagination. 1762: Hall-Stevenson, *Crazy Tales*, 16, My Cousin's Tale of a Cock and a Bull [title]. 1823: Byron, *Don Juan*, can. vi st. 80. 1858: O. W. Holmes, *Autocrat*, v.

2. A good cock may come out of a bad bag.
1883: Burne, *Shropsh. Folk-Lore*, 590, There'll
come a good cock out of a ragged bag. 1917:
Bridge, *Cheshire Proverbs*, 3.

**3. Better be a cock for a day, than a hen for a
year.** 1659: Howell, 13.

4. Every cock is brave on his own dunghill.
[Gallum in suo sterquilinio plurimum posse. –
Seneca, *Apocol.*, 7.] Before 1225: *Ancren R.*, 140,
Ase me seith 'thet coc is kene on his owune
mixenne'. 1546: Heywood, *Proverbs*, Pt I ch xi
[with 'proude' for 'brave']. 1580: Spenser, *Shep.
Cal.*, Sept., l. 47, As cocke on his dunghill
crowing cranck. 1692: Congreve, *Old Bachelor*,
II ii, For every cock will fight upon his own
dunghill 1869: Spurgeon, *John Ploughman*, ch
xiii, Every cock may crow on his own dunghill
1917: Bridge, *Cheshire Proverbs*, 2, A cock fights
best on his own bouk.

**5. If the cock goes crowing to bed, He's sure
to rise with a watery head.** 1846: Denham,
Proverbs, 18 (Percy S.). 1893: Inwards, *Weather
Lore*, 133. 1920: *N.&Q.*, 12th ser, vii 67, If the
cock crows when he goes to bed, He gets up in
the morn with a wet head [heard in
Warwickshire within the last ten years].

**6. If the cock moult before the hen, We shall
have weather thick and thin:** But if the hen
moult before the cock, We shall have weather
hard as a block. 1670: Ray, 43. *c.*1685: Aubrey,
Nat. Hist. Wilts, 16 (1847), When the hen doth
moult before the cock, The winter will be as hard
as a rock; But if the cock moults before the hen,
The winter will not wett your shoes seame.
1825: Hone, *Ev. Day Book*, i 669. 1893: Inwards,
Weather Lore, 133.

**7. It is a very ill cock that will not crow before
he be old.** 1580: Lyly, *Euphues*, 366 (Arber).

8. The cock crows but the hen goes. 1659:
Howell, 19. 1670: Ray, 5.

**9. The cock does crow, To let us know, If we be
wise, 'Tis time to rise.** 1846: Denham, *Proverbs*,
19 (Percy S.).

10. There is chance in the cock's spur. 1678:
Ray, 111. 1732: Fuller, 4890.

11. To leap like a cock at a blackberry. 1670:
Ray, 209 … Spoken of one that endeavours, but
can do no harm.

Cock's stride. *See* **Christmas** (12); and **New
Year** (2).

Cock on hoop, To set = To be prodigal. Origin

unknown – *see* discussion, s.v., in *Oxford English
Dict.* 1519: Horman, *Vulgaria*, fo. 301, He
setteth al thyngs at cocke in the hope. 1540:
Palsgrave, *Acolastus*, sig. G3, Let us sette the
cocke on the hope, and make good chere. *c.*1568:
Wager, *Longer thou livest*, sig. B2, Make mery,
daunce and sing, Set cocke a whope, and play
care away. 1606: T. Heywood, *If you know not
me*, Pt II, These knaues Sit cock-a-hope, but
Hobson pays for all. 1730: Bailey, *Eng. Dict.*, s.v.,
Cock on hoop [i.e. the cock or spiggot being laid
upon the hoop, and the barrel of ale stunn'd, i.e.
drank out without intermission] at the height of
mirth and jollity.

Cock the little facer, To. Said of one given to
drinking. 1917: Bridge, *Cheshire Proverbs*, 131.

Cockatrice in the shell, Kill the. 1659: Howell,
17 ['Crush' for 'Kill']. 1669: N. Smith, *Quakers
Spirit. Court*, 15, I thought it was best to kill the
cockatrice in the egg. 1732: Fuller, 3124 ['egg'
for 'shell'].

Cocking, Sussex. *See* quot. 1870: Lower,
Hist. Sussex, i 119, When Foxes brewings [mist
among trees] go to Cocking Foxes brewings
come back dropping.

Cockles of the heart. 1685: S. Wesley, *Maggots*,
126, It terrifies the cocales of my heart. 1690:
Reason of Mr Bays changing his Religion, Pt II, p.
33, Now you rejoyce the cockles of my heart.
1792: Scott, in Lockhart's *Life*, i 191, Which
would have delighted the very cockles of your
heart. 1858: Darwin, in *Life, etc.*, ii 112 (1888)
(OED), I have just had the innermost cockles of
my heart rejoiced by a letter from Lyell.

Cockloft is unfurnished, His = Brainless. 1646:
Fuller, *Andronicus*, § vi par. 18, Often the
cockloft is empty in those whom Nature hath
built many stories high. 1678: Ray, 235.

Codnor's Pond. *See* quot. 1884: *Folk-Lore
Journal*, ii 279, When Codnor's Pond runs dry,
The Lords may say good-bye. Derby.

Coggeshall, Essex. 1. *A Coggeshall job.* 1880:
N.&Q., 6th ser, ii 307, This name is generally
shortened into Coxall … . It is the Essex phrase
for any blundering or awkward contrivance.
1913: E. M. Wright, *Rustic Speech, etc.*, 182.
1920: E. Gepp, *Essex Dialect Dict.*, 8, A 'Coxall
job' means a foolish act.

2. Jeering Coxhall. 1662: Fuller, *Worthies*, i 498
(1840). 1790: Grose, *Prov. Gloss.*, s.v. 'Essex',
Jeering Cogshall.

See also **Braintree.**

Coin. *Where coin is not common, commons must be scant.* 1546: Heywood, *Proverbs*, Pt II ch i 1633: Draxe, 1. 1670: Ray, 74.

Colchester, The Weavers' Beef of = Sprats. 1662: Fuller, *Worthies*, i 498 (1840). 1790: Grose, *Prov. Gloss.*, s.v. 'Essex'. 1865: W. White, *Eastern England*, i 145, She had never heard sprats described as 'weavers' beef', as they are (or were) at Colchester. 1866: J. G. Nail, *Great Yarmouth, etc.*, 683.

Cold as a clock. 1579: Lyly, *Euphues*, 106 (Arber), Though Curio bee as hot as a toast, yet Euphues is as colde as [a] clocke. 1583: Melbancke, *Philotimus*, sig. H3. 1592: T. Lodge, *Euphues Shadow*, sig. G2, As coole as a clock.

Cold as a cucumber. *See* **Cool** (2).

Cold as a key. 1501: Douglas, *Pal. Honor*, Pt I st. 61., With quaikand voce and hart cald as a key. 1587: Turbervile, *Trag. Tales, etc.*, 276 (1837), As colde as any kaye. 1702: Farquhar, *Inconstant*, IV iii, Till they be as cold as a key.

Cold as a stone. *c.*1300: Brunne, tr. Langtoft's *Chron.*, 56 (Hearne), He felle dede doun colde as ony stone. 1506: A. Barclay, *Cast, of Labour*, sig. A6, My herte was colde as ony stone. 1697: Dilke, *City Lady*, III iii, In the morning he may find him self as cold as a stone. 1889: R.L.S., *Ballantrae*, ch xi.

Cold as charity. 1640: Shirley, *St Pat. for Ireland*, III i, Would I were a whale in the frozen sea! charity is not cold enough to relieve me. 1675: *Poor Robin Alman.*, Nov., Weather cold as charity. 1909: De Morgan, *Never can happen again*, ch liii.

Cold as clay. 1468: *Coventry Myst.*, 227 (SH.S.), My hert is colde as clay. *c.*1680: in *Roxb. Ballads*, iii 480 (B.S.), Will find the world as cold as clay. 1681: Rycaut, tr. Gracian's *Critick*, 228, His hands were as cold as clay. 1894: W. Raymond, *Love and Quiet Life*, 168, But the old man was as cold as clay.

Cold as ice. 1552: Huloet, *Abced.*, sig. F1, Colde as yse. 1672: Walker, *Paraem.*, 23. 1845: Jerrold, *Mrs Caudle*, v, As cold, too, as any ice. 1889: J. Nicholson, *Folk Speech E. Yorks*, 17, As cawd as ice. 1923: G. Sturt (Bourne), *Wheelwright's Shop*, 13, Feeling my feet cold as ice.

Cold as mutton. Said of weather. Glos. 1911: *Folk-Lore*, xxii 239.

Cold broth hot again, that loved I never; Old love renew'd again, that loved I ever. 1732: Fuller, 6429.

Cold hands, warm heart. Meaning that a reserved exterior may conceal a generous or passionate disposition. 1903: V.S. Lean, *Collectanea*, III 380, A cold hand and a warm heart. 1910: W.G. Collingwood, *Dutch Agnes*, 206, I did take her hand … Cold hand, warm heart.

Cold of complexion good of condition. 1678: Ray, 116. 1732: Fuller, 1119.

Cold pudding settles love. 1685: S. Wesley, *Maggots*, 41, Settle the wit, as pudding settles love. 1709: Ward, *Works*, iv verse 30, Pudding cold, Is said you know in proverb old, To settle love. 1738: Swift, *Polite Convers.*, Dial. II, Cold pudden will settle your love. 1848: Albert Smith, *Chris. Tadpole*, ch lx, The cold plum pudding, too, was a wonder … when Tom Baker said that … there was enough of it to settle everybody's love … they laughed. 1917: Bridge, *Cheshire Proverbs*, 110, Take a little cold pudding to settle your love.

Cold weather and crafty knaves come out of the North. 1659: Howell, 10 (8). 1670: Ray, 19 [omitting 'crafty'.]. Cf. **Three great evils.**

Coldest flint there is hot fire, In. the. 1598: Meres, *Palladis*, fo. 321. 1647: A. Brewer, *Countrie Girle*, sig. C2, The coldest flint has fire, I see. 1670: Ray, 72. 1732: Fuller, 2822.

Cole under candlestick, To play. Nares says, s.v. 'Coal', that Coal-under-candlestick was a Christmas game mentioned in the *Declaration of Popish Impostures* (1603); but the quotations below suggest the sense of – to be secretly deceitful. 1546: Heywood, *Proverbs*, Pt I ch x, Coll vnder canstyk, she can plaie on bothe handis. 1559: Becon, *Display of Popish Mass*, in *Prayers, etc.*, 260 (P.S.), Therefore can ye not play cole under candlestick cleanly. 1659: Howell, 4 [as in 1546, with 'he' for 'she' and 'with' for 'on'].

Coleford. *I've been to Coleford – got both eyes open!* Mon. 1905: *Folk-Lore*, xvi 67.

Cole-prophet, To play. 1546: Heywood. *Proverbs*, Pt I ch ix, Ye plaie coleprophet (quoth I), who takth in hande To knowe his answere before he do his erraunde. 1560: Awdeley, *Vacabondes*, 15 (E.E.T.S.), Cole Prophet is he, that when his maister sendeth him on his errand, he wyl tel his answer therof to his maister or he depart from hym. 1584: R. Scot, *Witchcraft*, bk ix ch iii, To play the cold prophet, is to recount it good or bad luck, when salt or wine falleth on the table, or is shed, etc.

Coleshill. *See* **Sutton.**

Colewort twice sodden = Crambe bis cocta. 1580: Lyly, *Euphues*, 391 (Arber), Who left out nothing that before I put in, which I must omitte, least I set before you, colewortes twice sodden. 1611: Coryat, *Coryats Crambe, or his Colwort twise sodden, etc.* [title]. 1647: Stapylton, *Juvenal*, 126, The same verses i' th' same tune instills, Poore school-masters this twice boil'd lettuce kills.

Collier. 1. As freely as the collier that called my Lord Mayor knave, when he got on Bristow causey [causeway]. 1869: Hazlitt, 63.

2. If you wrestle with a collier, you will get a blotch. 1618: Harington, *Epigrams*, bk ii No. 36, The proverb says, Who fights with durty foes, Must needs be soyl'd, admit they win or lose. 1732: Fuller, 2802.

3. Like a collier's sack; bad without but worse within. Ibid., No. 3221.

Collins' cow, Troubled in mind like. 1906: *Cornish N. & Q.*, 263.

Colly Weston. *See* quots. 1587: Harrison, *Descrip. of Eng.*, Pt I 168 (Furnivall), The Morisco gowns, the Barbarian sleeues, the mandilion worne to Collie weston ward. 1841: Hartshorne, *Salopia Ant.*, 366, Colly Weston ... implies anything awry, or on one side. 1854: Baker, *Northants Gloss.*, s.v., When any thing goes wrong, it is said, 'It is all along o' Colly Weston'. 1917: Bridge, *Cheshire Proverbs*, 82, It's aw along o' Colly Wes(t)on. Cf. **Cotton's neck.**

Coloquintida for Herb-John, You give me. 1732: Fuller, 5905.

Coloquintida spoils all the broth, A little. 1630: T. Adams, *Works*, 711.

Color upon color is false heraldry. 1659: Howell, *Proverbs*, 'To Philologers'. 1738: Swift, *Polite Convers.*, Dial. II, [burlesque version] I have heard that goose upon goose is false heraldry.

Colt. 1. A colt you may break, but an old horse you never can. 1732: Fuller, 45.

2. Cut the colt, he's sure to draw – 'not being so cunning as the "old stagers." ' 1883: Burne, *Shropsh. Folk-Lore*, 589.

3. To have a colt's tooth. *c.*1386: Chaucer, *Reeve's Tale*, l. 34, And yet ik have alwey a coltes tooth. 1588: Greene, *Perimedes*, in *Works*, vii 91 (Grosart), Hee hath beene a wag, but nowe age hath pluckt out all his coltes teeth. *c.*1620: B.&F., *Elder Brother*, II iii, If he should love her now, As he hath a colt's tooth yet ... 1674: Head and Kirkman, *Eng. Rogue*, iii 7, I myself have been good in my time; and still have a colt's tooth in my head. 1770: Colman, *Portrait*, Pt II, in *Dram. Works*, iv 215 (1777), Tho' not in the bloom of my youth, Yet still I have left a colt's tooth. 1841: J. T. Hewlett, *Parish Clerk*, i 81 (OED), They not shedding their colt's teeth yet.

4. When you ride a young colt, see your saddle be well girt. 1659: Howell, 6. 1670: Ray, 5. 1736: Bailey, *Dict.*, s.v. 'Colt'.

See also **Horse** (21); **Ragged as a colt**; and **Ragged colt.**

Comb one's head with a stool, To. 1594: Shakespeare, *Tam. of Shrew*, I i, Doubt not her care should be To comb your noddle with a three-legg'd stool. 1671: *Westm. Drollery*, 38 (Ebsworth), She flew in my face, and call'd me fool, And comb'd my head with a three-legg'd stool. 1785: Grose, *Class. Dict. of vulgar Tongue*, s.v. 'Comb', She combed his head with a joint stool; she threw a stool at him. 1886: Elworthy, *West Som. Word-Book*, 150 (E.D.S.), It is very usual now ... to say of a termagant wife who beats her husband: she will comb out his head with a three-legged stool. 1901: F. E. Taylor, *Lancs Sayings*, 17, Hoo'll comb thi yed wi' a three-leg't stoo'.

Come. 1. As good comes behind as goes before. 1683: Meriton, *Yorkshire Ale*, 83–7 (1697).

2. Come and welcome, go by and no quarrel. 1670: Ray, 169. 1738: Swift, *Polite Convers.*, Dial. II, Faith, colonel, come and welcome; and stay away, and heartily welcome.

3. Come, but come stooping, i.e. well loaded. 1813: Ray, 93.

4. Come day, go day. 1633: Draxe, 98, Come day, goe day, the day is long enough. 1854: Baker, *Northants Gloss.*, s.v. 'Day', 'Come day, go day'. An expression applied to an improvident person ... 'It's come day, go day, with him'. 1876: Robinson, *Whitby Gloss.*, s.v. (E.D.S.). 1893: J. Salisbury, *S.E. Worcs. Gloss.*, 77 (E.D.S.), It is said of a careless person, 'It's all

Come day, go day, God send Sunday with him' (or 'her'). 1921: *N.&Q.*, 12th ser, viii 36, A Leicestershire woman … would often speak of an idle shiftless person as 'a poor come day, go day, God send Sunday creature'.

5. Come dog, come devil. 1600: *Weakest to the Wall*, l. 400 (Malone S.), Come dogge, come diuell, he that scapes best Let him take all.

6. Come every one heave a pound. Somerset. 1678: Ray, 355.

7. Come in if you're fat. 1738: Swift, *Polite Convers.*, Dial. I, Who's there? … come in, if you be fat.

8. Come Sunday, come se'night = Next Sunday but one. 1917: Bridge, *Cheshire Proverbs*, 38.

9. Come what come would. 1546: Heywood, *Proverbs*, Pt I ch xi 1606: Shakespeare, *Macbeth*, I iii, Come what come may, Time and the hour runs through the roughest day. 1639: Clarke, 122, Come what come may.

10. Come wind come weather. *c.*1630: in *Pepysian Garland*, 368 (Rollins, 1922), We needs must drinke come wind come wether.

11. Cometh last to the pot. *See* **Last to the pot.**

12. He that comes after, sees with more eyes than his own. 1732: Fuller, 2067.

13. He that comes every day shall have a cockney and he that comes but now and then shall have a fat hen. 1546: Heywood, *Proverbs*, Pt I ch xi 1633: Draxe, 84.

14. He that cometh last maketh all fast. 1562: Heywood, *Three Hund. Epigr.*, No. 202. 1611: Cotgrave, s.v. 'Porte', The last commer latches the door, maketh all sure. 1670: Ray, 112. 1732: Fuller, 6308. Cf. **Last makes fast.**

15. He who comes uncalled sits un-served. 1597: A. Montgomery, *Poems*, 42 (1821), Quha cum uncallt, unserv'd suld sit. 1732: Fuller, 1123, Come uncall'd; sit unserv'd.

16. 1f they come, they come not; and if they come not, they come. 1662: Fuller, *Worthies*, ii 543 (1840). 1790: Grose, *Prov. Gloss.*, s.v. 'Northumberland'. 1846–59: *Denham Tracts*, i 243 (F.L.S.).

17. If thou wilt come with me, bring with thee. 1578: Florio, *First Fruites*, fo. 33, If thou wilt go with me bryng with thee. 1629: *Book of Meery Riddles*, Prov. 115. 1732: Fuller, 6286, Bring something, lass, along with thee, If thou intend to live with me.

18. It comes by kind, it costs nothing. 1605: Camden, *Remains*, 325 (1870), It cometh by kind [nature], it cost them nothing. 1670: Ray, 182. 1732: Fuller, 5484, What cometh by kind, costeth nothing.

19. To come bluely off. 1678: Ray, 230.

20. To come to fetch fire. *c.*1380: Chaucer, *Troylus*, bk v l. 484, Be we comen hider To fecchë fyr, and rennen hoom ayeyn? 1670: Ray, 175. 1738: Swift, *Polite Convers.*, Dial. I, Where are you going so soon? I hope you did not come to fetch fire.

21. Who cometh late lodgeth ill. 1578: Florio, *First Fruites*, fo. 5. 1732: Fuller, 2381, He who cometh in late, has an ill lodging.

Comfortable as matrimony, As. A two-edged saying. 1736: Bailey, *Dict.*, s.v. 'Comfortable'.

Comforter's head never aches, The. 1640: Herbert, *Jac. Prudentum.* 1670: Ray. 5. 1732: Fuller, 4454.

Coming events cast their shadows before. 1802: Campbell, *Lochiel's Warning* (OED).

Command of custom is great, The. 1640: Herbert, *Jac. Prudentum.*

Command, verb. 1. Command your man, and do it yourself. 1666: Torriano, *Piazza Univ.*, 60 [*plus* 'As the English say']. 1692: L'Estrange, *Aesop*, 53 (3rd ed.), Which is all but according to the old saying. *Command your man and do't yourself.* 1732: Fuller, 1124.

2. Command your wealth, else that will command you. 1732: Fuller, 1125.

3. He commands enough that obeys a wise man. 1640: Herbert, *Jac. Prudentum.* 1670: Ray, 5. 1732: Fuller, 1827.

4. He that commandeth well shall be obeyed well. 1732: Fuller, 2068.

Commend. 1. Commend not your wife, wine, nor house. Ibid., No. 1126.

2. Commend or amend. *c.*1449: R. Pecock, *Repressor*, Pt I ch ix p. 48 (Rolls Ser.), And bi the oolde wijs prouerbe, *A man schulde blame or commende as he fyndeth.* 1868: W. C. Hazlitt, in *N.&Q.*, 4th ser, i 201, Mr Corney ought to bear in mind the old maxim, 'Commend or amend'.

3. Who commends himself. *See* **Neighbour** (2).

Commit. *He that commits a fault thinks every one speaks of it.* 1640: Herbert, *Jac. Prudentum.*

Common, adj. 1. A common servant is no man's servant. 1629: *Book of Meery Riddles*, Prov. 85.

2. Common as a barber's chair. *See* **Barber** (3).

3. Common as a cart-way. 1362: Langland, *Plowman*, *A*, iii 127, [She is] as comuyn as the cart-wei to knaues and to alle. 1493: *Dives and Pauper*, fo. 1 (1536), Other wickednesses ben as common as the carte way. 1566: Drant, *Horace: Sat.*, sig. D6, As common as the carts way. 1678: Ray, 90, As common as the highway.

4. Common as Coleman-hedge. 1639: Clarke, 191. 1670: Ray, 202.

5. Common as Get out. Corn. 1869: Hazlitt, 60.

6. Common as Ratcliff Highway. 1667: L'Estrange, *Quevedo's Visions*, 80 (1904).

7. Common fame is a common liar. 1606: B. Rich, *Faultes*, fo. 46, But Report is a lier. 1710: Ward, *Nuptial Dialogues*, i 214, Since common Fame is but a common lyar. 1821: Scott, *Pirate*, ch xxxix, But common fame, Magnus considered, was a common liar. Cf. **Blister.**

8. Common fame is seldom to blame. 1597: H. Lok, *Poems*, 299 (Grosart), Though prouerbe truely say, by fame's affect, God's iudgement lightly doth a truth detect. 1694: D'Urfey, *Quixote*, Pt II Act I sc i 1732: Fuller, 6120, Common fame Is mostly to blame [another opinion!]. 1853: Trench, *Proverbs*, 13 (1905), *Common fame is seldom to blame* ... is the baser proverb.

9. Keep the common road, and thou'rt safe. 1732: Fuller, 3118.

10. The common people look at the steeple. 1639: Clarke, 148.

11. To be common Jack. 1546: Heywood, *Proverbs*, Pt I ch xi, I haue bene common Iacke to all that hole flocke. 1611: Davies (of Hereford), *Sc. of Folly*, 45, in *Works*, ii (Grosart), Some Iackes are common to all that will play.

Companion. 1. A man knows his companion in a long journey and a little inn. 1732: Fuller, 284.

2. He is an ill companion that has a good memory. 1683: White Kennett, tr. Erasmus' *Praise of Folly*, 167 (8th ed.), It is an old proverb, *I hate a pot-companion with a good memory*. 1710: S. Palmer, *Moral Essays on Proverbs*, 78.

3. It is good to have companions in misery. *c.*1374: Chaucer, *Troylus*, bk i l. 708, Men seyn, 'to wrecche is consolacioun To have another felawe in his peyne'. *c.*1390: Gower, *Conf. Amantis*, bk ii l. 261. 1579: Lyly, *Euphues*, 96 (Arber), In misery Euphues it is great comfort to haue a companion. 1681: W. Robertson, *Phraseol. Generalis*, 348, 'Tis a comfort to have companions in misery. 1709: Centlivre, *Busy Body*, III v, 'Tis some comfort to have a companion in our sufferings. 1850: Planché, *Extravag.*, iv 72 (1879), Well, really, when one's heart is breaking with vexation, To see one's friend in the same distress, is a wond'rous consolation!

Company. 1. Company makes cuckolds. 1639: Clarke, 152. 1678: Ray, 116. 1732: Fuller, 1132.

2. Company's good if you are going to be hanged. 1864: 'Cornish Proverbs', in *N. & Q.*, 3rd ser, vi 495.

3. For company, as Kit went to Canterbury. 1735: Pegge, *Kent. Proverbs*, in E.D.S., No. 12, p. 69.

4. The company makes the feast. 1911: Hackwood, *Good Cheer*, 361, This has been crystallised into the terse English proverb, 'The company makes the feast'.

Comparison. *See* **Nothing** (14).

Comparisons are odious, *c.*1440: Lydgate, in *Pol.*, *Relig.*, *and Love Poems*, 22 (E.E.T.S.), Odyous of olde been comparisonis. 1583: Greene, *Mamillia*, in *Works*, ii 52 (Grosart), I will not make comparisons, because they be odious. 1607: T. Heywood, *Woman Killed with Kindness*, I ii 1742: Fielding, *Andrews*, bk i ch xvi, But comparisons are odious; another man may write as well as he. 1872: H. James, *Letters*, i 32 (1920), Nüremburg is excellent – and comparisons are odious; but I would give a thousand N's for one ray of Verona!

Complains wrongfully on the sea that twice suffers shipwreck, He. 1640: Herbert, *Jac. Prudentum*. 1670: Ray, 23.

Complimenting is lying. 1738: Swift, *Polite Convers.*, Dial. I, I have heard say that complimenting is lying.

Compliments fly when gentlefolk meet. 1894: R.L.S., *St Ives*, ch xxviii 1894: Northall, *Folk Phrases*, 12 (E.D.S.), [ironical version] Compliments pass when beggars meet.

Conceal. *See* **Hide nothing.**

Conceited as a churchwarden. 1917: Bridge, *Cheshire Proverbs*, 11.

Conceited [ingenious] goods are quickly spent. 1678: Ray, 116.

Coney-catching. *See* **Rabbit-hunting.**

Confess and be hanged. 1594: A. Copley, *Wits,*

Fits, etc., 148 (1614), Confesse and be hang'd, and so he was. 1612: Dekker, *If it be not Good, etc.*, in *Dram. Works*, iii 345 (1873), I haue confest, and shal be hangd. 1672: Marvell, *Rehearsal Transpr.*, Pt I, in *Works*, iii 55 (Grosart), After so simple a confession as he hath made, must he now be hang'd too to make good the proverb? 1710: S. Palmer, *Moral Essays on Proverbs*, 199, That unlucky proverb, *Confess and be hang'd*. 1821: Scott, *Pirate*, ch xxxix.

Confess debt and beg days. 1732: Fuller, 1139.

Confessing a fault makes half amends. 1618: Harington, *Epigrams*, bk iii No. 25, A fault confest were half amended. 1670: Ray, 5. 1732: Fuller, 1140.

Confession disarms slander, A generous. 1732: Fuller, 126.

Confession is good for the soul. *c.*1641: in E Beveridge, *D. Ferguson's Scottish Proverbs* (1924), no. 159, Ane open confessione is good for the soul. 1721: J. Kelly, *Scottish Proverbs*, 270, Open Confession is good for the Soul. Spoken ironically to them that boast of their ill Deeds. 1881: J.Payn, *Grape from Thorn*, III xxxix, Confession may be good for the soul, but it is doubtful the avowal of incapacity to the parties desirous of securing our services is quite judicious.

Confession is the first step to repentance. 1654: Gayton, *Pleasant Notes Don Q.*, 66.

Confine your tongue lest it confine you. 1855: Bohn, 338.

Congleton rare. *See* 1862 quot. 1813: Ray, 242, Congleton bears [the clerk of C. is said to have sold the church Bible, to buy a bear for baiting]. 1862: *N.&Q.*, 3rd ser, ii 166, Passing through Congleton some time since, a gentleman heard some tailors, singing, – Congleton rare, Congleton rare, Sold the Bible to pay for a bear. 1917: Bridge, *Cheshire Proverbs*, 39, [*plus* the variant] Like Congleton Bear Town where they sold the Bible to buy a bear. [Similar stories are told of Ecclesfield, and Clifton, a village near Rugby, *N.&Q..*, 3rd ser, ii 236.]

Conies love roast meat. *c.*1685: Aubrey, *Nat. Hist. Wilts*, 59 (1847), 'Tis a saying, that conies doe love rost-meat.

Conquer. *He that will conquer must fight.* 1732: Fuller, 2346.

Conscience. 1. A dear conscience can bear any trouble. Ibid., No. 40.

2. A clear conscience is a sure card. 1581: Lyly, *Euphues*, 207 (Arber). 1659: Howell, *Proverbs: Brit.-Eng.*, 3. 1732: Fuller, 41.

3. A clear conscience laughs at false accusations. 1580: Lyly, *Euphues*, 256 (Arber), A cleere conscience needeth no excuse, nor feareth any accusation. 1669: *Politeuphuia*, 12 [as in 1580]. 1732: Fuller, 42.

4. A conscience as large as a shipman's hose. 1639: Clarke, 66. 1670: Ray, 205.

5. A good conscience is a continual feast. 1633: Draxe, 28. Before 1680: Butler, *Remains*, ii 273 (1759), For a good conscience being a perpetual feast … *c.*1736: Franklin, in *Works*, i 456 (Bigelow), A good conscience is a continual Christmas.

6. A good conscience is the best divinity. 1732: Fuller, 141.

7. A guilty conscience is a self-accuser (or **feels continual fear**). [1580: Sidney, *Arcadia*, bk ii p. 121 (1893), She felt the terrors of her own conscience.] 1598: *Servingmans Comfort*, in *Inedited Tracts*, 99. (Hazlitt), The guyltie conscience thinkes what as is sayd, is alwayes spoken himselfe to vpbrayde. 1604: Drayton, *The Owl*, A guilty conscience feels continual fear. 1679: Crowne, *Ambitious Statesman*, V iii, No hell like a bad conscience. 1732: Fuller, 208, A guilty conscience never thinketh itself safe. *c.*1800: Trusler, *Prov. in Verse*, 112, Conscience is a self-accuser.

8. A quiet conscience causes a quiet sleep. 1732: Fuller, 374, [*plus*, on p. 375] A quiet conscience sleeps in thunder. 1827: Wilson, *Noctes*, in *Blackw. Mag.*, April, 476 (OED), That sweet sound sleep that is the lot o' a gude conscience.

9. An evil conscience breaks many a man's neck. 1678: Ray, 116. 1732: Fuller, 602.

10. Conscience is a cut-throat. 1639: Clarke, 66.

11. Conscience serveth for a thousand witnesses. 1539: Taverner, *Proverbs*, fo. 29, The conscience is a thousande wytnesses. 1629: *Book of Meery Riddles*, Prov. 33. 1633: Draxe, 27 [as in 1539]. 1639: Clarke, 66, Conscience is witness enough.

12. His conscience is made of stretching leather. 1597: *Discouerie of Knights of the Poste*, sig. B4, Their consciences are like chiuerell skins, that will stretch euery way. 1613: Shakespeare, *Henry VIII*, II iii 1737: Ray, 274,

He hath a conscience like a cheverel's skin (That will stretch). A cheverel is a wild goat. Somerset. 1830: Forby, *Vocab. E. Anglia*, 430, Your conscience is made of stretching leather.

13. *See* quot. I do not know to what proverb allusion is made. 1638: Randolph, *Works*, ii 633 (Hazlitt), And since large conscience (as the proverb shows) In the same sense with bad one goes.

14. Whos conscience is combred and stondith nott clene, Of another mans dedis the wursse woll he deme. 15th cent.: in *Reliq. Antiquae*, i 205 (1841).

See also **Friend** (1).

Consideration is half conversion, and Consideration is the parent of wisdom. 1732: Fuller, Nos. 1146 and 1147.

Considering cap, To put on (or off) **one's.** 1605: Armin, *Foole vpon Foole*, 40 (Grosart), The cobler puts off his considering cap. 1618: B.&F., *Loyal Subject*, II i, And now I'll put on my considering cap. 1738: Swift, *Polite Corners.*, Dial. I, Guess who it was that told me; come, put on your considering cap. 1861: Dickens, *Great Expect.*, ch xxxvii, I'll put on my considering cap, and I think all you want to do may be done by degrees.

Constable for your wit, You might be a. 1599: Jonson, *Ev. Man out of Humour*, I, *Sog.* Why, for my wealth I might be a justice of peace. *Car.* Ay, and a constable for your wit. 1678: Ray, 236.

Constant dropping will wear away a stone. [Mr E. Marshall, in *N. & Q.*, 5th ser, viii 513, says: 'The first place in which this proverb, expressing a metaphor which occurs several times in early writers, is found is the fragment of Choerilus, *c* A.c 440 (p. 169, ed. Naëke, Lips., 1817): [πέτρην κοιλαίνει ῥανὶς ὕδατος ἐνδελεχείη'. Gutta cavat lapidem. – Ovid, *Epp. ex Ponto*, IV x 5.] Before 1225, *Ancren R.*, 220 (Morton), Lutle dropen thurleth thene ulint thet ofte ualleth theron. *c.*1387: Usk, *Test, of Love*, in Skeat's *Chaucer*, vii 135, So ofte falleth the lethy water on the harde rocke, til it have thorow persed it. *c.*1477: Caxton, *Jason*, 26 (E.E.T.S.), How well the stone is myned and holowed by contynuell droppyng of water. 1581: Lyly, *Euphues*, 127 (Arber), The lyttle droppes of rayne pearceth hard marble. 1591: Spenser, *Sonnets*, 18. 1631: Mabbe, *Celestina*, 150 (T.T.), Often dropping makes stones hollow. 1736:

Franklin. *Way to Wealth*, in *Works*, i 444 (Bigelow). 1852: Dickens, *Bleak House*, ch l.

Consult your pillow. *See* **Take** (25).

Contemplates. *He that contemplates hath a day without night.* 1640: Herbert, *Jac. Prudentum*. 1670: Ray, 5. 1732: Fuller, 2069 [with 'on his bed' before 'hath'].

Contempt will sooner kill an injury than revenge. 1855: Bohn, 339.

Content, *subs*. **1. Content is all.** 1639: Clarke, 38.

2. Content is happiness. 1666: Torriano, *Piazza Univ.*, 52, Who is contented, enjoys. 1732: Fuller, 1152.

3. Content is more than kingdom. 1639: Clarke, 213, Content is a kingdome. 1732: Fuller, 1153.

4. Content is the philosopher's stone, that turns all it touches into gold. 1732: Fuller, 1154.

5. Content is worth a crown. 1630: Brathwaite, *Eng. Gent.*, 203 (1641).

6. Content lodges oftener in cottages than palaces. 1732: Fuller, 1155.

7. He who wants content, can't find an easy chair. Ibid., No. 2408.

Content, *adj. He who is content in his poverty, is wonderfully rich.* 1623: Wodroephe, *Spared Houres*, 480.

Contented. 1. A contented mind is a continual feast. 1535: Coverdale, *Bible*, Prov. xv 15, A quiet heart is a continual feast. 1592: Warner, *Alb. England*, bk vii ch 37, It is a sweete continuall feast To liue content I see. 1611: Cotgrave, s.v. 'Contenter', We say, a contented minde is a great treasure; or, is worth all. 1681: W. Robertson, *Phraseol. Generalis*, 381. 1725: Bailey, tr. Erasmus' *Colloq.*, 576.

2. He may well be contented who needs neither borrow nor flatter. 1477: Rivers, *Dictes and Sayings*, 69 (1877), Some axed him of howe moche goode[s] a man ought to be content, and he answered to haue so moche as he neded nat to flatre nor borowe of other. 1670: Ray, 5. 1748: Richardson, *Clarissa*, iv 119 (1785), The man was above control who wanted not either to borrow or flatter.

Contentment is the greatest wealth. 1633: Draxe, 31, Contentment is a great riches. 1754: Berthelson, *Eng.-Danisk Dict.*, s.v. 'Wealth'.

Contrary way. *He that goes the contrary way must go over it twice.* 1732: Fuller, 2120.

Controller. *See* quot. 1591: Lodge, *Catharos*, 14 (Hunt.Cl.), It is an olde saying and a true, *A controller is not without contempt.*

Converses. *He that converses not, knows nothing.* 1670: Ray, 5. 1732: Fuller, 2070.

Conway. *See* **Clude.**

Cook. 1. A cook is known by his knife. 1732: Fuller, 50.

2. Cooks are not to be taught in their own kitchen. Ibid., No. 1160. 1911: Hackwood, *Good Cheer*, 234.

3. Every cook praises his own broth. 1663: Gerbier, *Counsel* (1664), Every cook commends his own sauce. 1855: Bohn, 349.

See also **Ill cook**; and **Too many.**

Cook-ruffian, able to scald the devil out of his feathers. 1670: Ray, 169 [with 'in his' for 'out of his']. 1690: *New Dict. Canting Crew*, sig. D1, Cook-ruffian, the devil of a cook, or a very bad one. 1732: Fuller, 1159.

Cool. 1. A cool mouth and warm feet live long. 1611: Cotgrave, s.v. 'Pied', A coole mouth, and a dry foot preserve a man long time alive. 1640: Herbert, *Jac. Prudentum.* 1672: R. Codrington, *Proverbs*, 4.

2. Cool as a cucumber. 1615: Fletcher, *Cupid's Revenge*, I i, Young maids were as cold as cucumbers. 1720: Gay, *Poems*, ii 278 (Underbill), Cool as a cucumber could see The rest of womankind. 1829: Scott, *Journal*, 7 July. I rose as cool as a cucumber. 1909: De Morgan, *Never can happen again*, ch xxxiv.

3. Cool enough to shave a Jew. 1864: 'Cornish Proverbs', in *N. & Q.*, 3rd ser, vi 495.

4. Cool words scald not the tongue. 1733: Fuller, 1161.

Cooling card, A. 1577: *Misogonus*, III ii, Heavy newes for yow, I can tell yow, of a cowlinge carde. 1584: Greene, *Myrr. of Modestie*, in *Works*, iii 24 (Grosart), Hir godly counsel was a cooling carde to their inordinate desires. 1671: Head and Kirkman, *Eng. Rogue*, ii 104, This was a shrewd cooling card to my high hopes.

Cooper's ducks. *See* quot. 1902: *N. & Q..*, 9th ser, ix 127, A short time ago I heard a respectable young master-butcher in London use the following curious saying, viz. 'It would soon have been all Cooper's ducks with me', meaning that death would have resulted had he not quickly recovered from a recent attack of influenza.

Coot. See **Bald** (3).

Copplestone, Crewys and Crocker were home when the Conqueror came. A Devon saying. 1850: *N. & Q.*, 1st ser, ii 511. 1876: *ibid.*, 5th ser, vi 476.

Copy, *subs.* **1. A copy of one's countenance.** *c.*1568: Wager, *Longer thou livest*, sig. C2, It is but a coppie of his countenaunce. 1673: Dryden, *Assignation*, III i, Sure this is but a copy of her countenance; for my heart … whispers to me, she loves me still. Before 1704: T. Brown, in *Works*, iv 232 (1760), All the while he devours you, he cants of moderation, and pretends he does it unwillingly; but this is only a copy of his countenance. 1783: Mrs Brooke, *Rosina*, II, in Inchbald's *Farces*, iii 295 (1815). 1865: Editor, *N. & Q.*, 3rd ser, viii 30, The phrase, 'That is a copy of your countenance', which we have occasionally heard, but which is not of frequent use, *civilly* implies, 'That is not spoken sincerely.

2. To change (or **turn**) **one's copy.** 1523: Berners, *Froissart*, I ccxlix. (OED), Thus the knyghtes and squyers turned theyr copies on both partes. 1553: *Respublica*, II ii, We must now chaunge our coppie. 1584: Lodge, *Alarum against Venus*, 39 (SH.S.), Whereupon, altering his coppie … the king concluded thus … 1606: A. Craig, *Amorose Songes*, 21 (Hunt.Cl.), But being old, hee chaunged copie, and writ as violently against it. 1632: W. Rowley, *New Wonder*, III, Then did my father change his copy, and set up a brewhouse. 1706: *George-a-Greene*, in Thoms, *Early Prose Rom.*, ii 18 (1828), He began to alter his phrases, and changed the copy of his countenance.

Cormorant. *See* **Wet** (2).

Corn. 1. Corn and horn go together. 1678: Ray, 116. 1846: Denham, *Proverbs*, 2 (Percy S.). 1893: Inwards, *Weather Lore*, 5.

2. Corn in good years is hay, in ill years straw is corn. 1640: Herbert, *Jac. Prudentum.* 1670: Ray, 5. 1732: Fuller, 1162.

3. Corn is cleansed with the wind, and the soul with chastening. 1670: Ray, 5.

4. Corn is not to be gathered in the blade but the ear. 1580: Lyly, *Euphues*, 360 (Arber) [with 'budde' for 'blade']. 1732: Fuller, 1163.

5. Much corn lies under the straw that is not seen. 1639: Clarke, 145. 1670: Ray, 73. 1732: Fuller, 3480, Much corn lies in the chaff unseen.

6. The corn hides itself in the snow as an old man in furs. 1640: Herbert, *Jac. Prudentum.*

7. When the corn is in the shock, Then the fish are on the rock. Old Cornish rhyme. 1865: Hunt, *Pop. Romances W. of England*, 428 (1896). *See also* **Candlemas, D; Cuckoo** (3), (7), (16), and (22); **Famine; Fog** (3); **Good seed; July** (1) and (8); **June** (4); **March** (3), (11), and (21); **May**, A (2) and (3), E (1) and (5), and F (12); **Nut** (1); **Old, E** (23); **Up horn; Weeds;** and **Wind, A** (*b*) (1).

Cornish gentlemen are cousins, All. 1602: Carew, *Surv. of Cornwall*, 179 (1811) [cited as 'the proverb']. 1724: Defoe, *Tour*, Lett. III 102. 1880: Courtney, *W. Cornwall Words*, 14 (E.D.S.).

Cornish hug, A. 1638: Nabbes, *Tott. Court*, III iii, You are so taken with your Cornish prentice ... hearing him talke the other day of the hugge ... 1705: in *Harl. Miscell.*, ii 338 (1744). His St Maw's Muse has given the French troops a Cornish hug, and flung them all upon their backs. 1796: Wolcot, *Works*, iv 131 (1796), Give, to black blasphemy, a Cornish hug. 1818: *Gent. Mag.*, i 310, Cornwall is celebrated for athletic exercises, particularly wrestling. A 'Cornish hug' has been long proverbial. 1907: Hackwood, *Old Eng. Sports*, 189, To give a Cornish hug is a proverbial expression.

Corns in the head, To have = To be drunk. 1745: Franklin, in *Works*, ii 23 (Bigelow).

Cornwall. 1. Cornwall will bear a shower every day, and two on Sunday. 1864: 'Cornish Proverbs', in *N. & Q.*, 3rd ser, v 208. 1887: M. A. Courtney, in *Folk-Lore Journal*, v 219.

2. In Cornwall are the best gentlemen. 1851: Borrow, *Lavengro*, ch i *n.* 1864: 'Cornish Proverbs', in *N. & Q.*, 3rd ser, vi 6.

3. There are more saints in Cornwall than in heaven. Ibid., 3rd ser, v 275. 1880: Courtney, *W. Cornwall Words*, xiv (E.D.S.). 1927: J. M. Bulloch, in *Sunday Times*, 15 May, It is a common saying in the West of England that 'there are more saints in Cornwall than in heaven'.

4. *See* quot. 1906: *Cornish N. & Q.*, 293, We all know the old proverb ' 'Tis a bad wind that blows no good to Cornwall'.

5. To send a husband into Cornwall without a boat. *See* 1847 quot. 1567: Painter, *Pal. of Pleasure*, iii 128 (Jacobs), They seemed ... to be iealous ouer their wyues. But ... eyther of them without shipping, sought to send other into Cornouale. 1591: Florio, *Second Frutes*, 143, She spins crooked spindles for her husband, and sends him into Cornwall without ship or boate. 1670: Ray, 223, He doth sail into Cornwall without a bark. 1790: Grose, *Prov. Gloss.*, s.v. 'Cornwall' [as in 1670]. 1847: Halliwell, *Dict.*, s.v., A woman who cuckolds her husband was said to send him into Cornwall without a boat. *See also* **Devil** (87).

Cornwallis Family. *See* **Paston Family.**

Corpus Christi Day clear Gives a good year. 1893: Inwards, *Weather Lore*, 41.

Corrat as Crocker's mare. 1879: *Folk-Lore Record*, 203. 1882: Jago, *Gloss, of Cornish Dialect*, 144, Corrat. Pert, impudent, sharp in rejoinder. 'As corrat as Crocker's mare'. East Cornwall Proverb. 1888: Q.-Couch, *Troy Town*, ch v Cf. **Coy.**

Correction gives understanding. 1552: Latimer, *Sermons*, 501 (P.S.), It is a common saying, *Vexatio dat intellectum*, 'Correction giveth understanding'.

Corruption of best is worst, The. 1642: D. Rogers, *Matrim. Honour*, 34. 1702: Penn, *Fruits of Solitude*, Pt II No. 160, The proverb is verified, The corruption of the best things is the worst and most offensive. 1732: Fuller, 1166.

Corruption of one is the generation of another, The. 1576: Lambarde, *Peramb. of Kent*, 244 (1826), The olde maxime of Philosophie, *Corruptio unius, generatio alterius:* The corruption of one is the generation of another. 1583: Melbancke, *Philotinus*, sig. Y3. *c.*1602: Chapman, *May-Day*, III iii, The corruption of a bawd is the generation of a witch. 1738: Swift, *Polite Convers.*, Dial. II, [a burlesque version] They say that the corruption of pipes is the generation of stoppers.

Cossingland. *See* **Cowhithe.**

Costs little is little esteemed, What. 1612: Shelton, *Quixote*, Pt I bk iv ch vii 1732: Fuller, 5485, What costs little is less esteemed.

Cotherston cheeses will cover a multitude of sins, and **Cotherston, where they christen calves, hopple lops** [fleas], **and kneeband spiders.** Both – 1863: *N. & Q.*, 3rd ser, iii 233.

Cotswold. 1. A Cotswold lion = A sheep, *c.*1440: Satirical rhymes on Siege of Calais, in *Archaeologia*, xxxiii 130, Com rennyng on him fersly as lyons of Cotteswold. 1546: Heywood, *Proverbs*, Pt I ch xi, She is as fierce as a lyon of Cotsolde. 1600: *Sir John Oldcastle*, l. 700

(Malone S.), You old stale ruffin, you lion of Cotswold. 1785: Grose, *Class. Dict. Vulgar Tongue*, s.v., Cotswould Lion, a sheep.

2. It is as long in coming as Cotswold barley. 1662: Fuller, *Worthies*, i 552 (1840). 1790: Grose, *Prov. Gloss.*, s.v. 'Gloucestershire'. 1898: Gibbs, *Cotswold Village*, ch iv, p. 85 (3rd ed.), Two proverbs that are in constant use amongst all classes are … and ' 'Tis as long in coming as Cotswold berle' (barley).

Cottage in possession for a kingdom in hope, I'll not change a. 1639: Clarke, 256. 1670: Ray, 3 [with 'reversion' for 'hope']. 1732: Fuller, 2643 [as in 1670].

Cotton's neck. 1841: Hartshorne, *Salopia Ant.*, 375, 'All awry like Cotton's neck'. A simile applied to any thing that is warped or twisted. 1883: Burne, *Shropsh. Folk-Lore*, 592. Cf. **Colly Weston.**

Cough will stick longer by a horse than a peck (or half a peck) of oats, A. 1678: Ray, 117. 1732: Fuller, 54.

Counsel, *subs.* **1. Counsel breaks not the head.** 1640: Herbert, *Jac. Prudentutn.*

2. Counsel is no command. 1732: Fuller, 1182.

3. Counsel is to be given by the wise, the remedy by the rich. 1855: Bohn, 339.

4. Counsel must be followed, not praised. 1732: Fuller, 1183.

5. Counsel of fools. *See* **Fool** (12).

6. Counsel over cups is crazy. 1670: Ray, 5, Counsels in wine seldom prosper. 1732: Fuller, 1184.

7. Good counsel does no harm: 1633: Draxe, 33. 1639: Clarke, 67.

8. Good counsel is lacking when most needed. *c.*1386: Chaucer, *Tale of Melibeus*, § 13, 'I see wel,' quod this wyse man, 'that the commune proverbe is sooth; that "good conseil wanteth whan it is most nede".'

9. Good counsel never comes amiss. 1732: Fuller, 1708.

10. If the counsel be good, no matter who gave it. Ibid., No. 2704.

11. Ill counsel hurts the counsellor. 1539: Taverner, *Proverbs*, fo. 4, Euyll counsayle is worst to the counseylour. 1639: Clarke, 21.

12. The counsel thou wouldest have another keep, first keep thyself. 1605: Camden, *Remains*, 334 (1870).

Counsel, *verb. He that will not be counselled,*

cannot be helped. 1639: Clarke, 22. 1670: Ray, 6. 1732: Fuller, 2350. 1875: A. B. Cheales, *Proverb. Folk-Lore*, 103.

Counterfeit. *See* quot. *c.*1645: 'MS. Proverbs', in *N. & Q.*, vol cliv, p. 27, Hee is a counterfett who is afraid of the touchstone.

Count every step. *See* **Tell** (5).

Count your chickens … , Don't. *See* **Chicken** (3).

Counting the pothooks. 1917: Bridge, *Cheshire Proverbs*, 44, Said of servants, when in a new place they sit quietly at first and don't quite know what to do or say.

Country. 1. A country man may be as warm in kersey, as a king in velvet. 1732: Fuller, 55. 1869: Spurgeon, *John Ploughman*, ch ii [with 'fustian' for 'kersey'].

2. In the country of the blind, the one-eyed man is king. 1904: H.G. Wells, in *The Strand Magazine*, Apr. 405, short story 'The Country of the Blind', Through his thoughts ran this old proverb … 'In the Country of the Blind, the One-Eyed Man is king'. For the earlier forms of this proverb *see* **Kingdom** (2).

3. The country for a wounded heart. 1906: A. C. Benson, *College Window*, 107, 'The country for a wounded heart', says the old proverb.

4. You must go into the country to hear what news at London. 1678: Ray, 345. 1732: Fuller, 1664 [with 'town' for 'London'].

See also **God made the country; Happy is the country;** and **So many countries.**

County. *See* **Hundred.**

Couple are newly married. *See* quot. 1670: Ray, 53, When a couple are newly married, the first moneth is honeymoon or smick smack; the second is, hither and thither: the third is, thwick thwack: the fourth, the Devil take them that brought thee and I together. 1754: Berthelson, *Eng.-Danish Divt.*, s.v. 'Thwack' [with 'me and thee' for 'thee and I'].

Courage mounteth with occasion. 1855: Bohn, 340.

Courage ought to have eyes as well as arms. 1732: Fuller, 1188.

Courageous foe is better than a cowardly friend, A. Ibid., No. 56.

Course. 1. If that course be fair, again and again quoth Bunny to his bear. 1639: Clarke, 179. 1670: Ray, 163.

2. The course of true love never did run

smooth. 1595: Shakespeare, *Midsummer Night's Dream* i i. 134, For aught that I could ever read, Could ever tell by tale or history, The course of true love never did run smooth. 1857: Reade, *The Course of True Love, etc.* [title]. 1872: Trollope, *Golden Lion*, ch i, He … feels it to be a sort of duty to take care that the course of love shall not run altogether smooth.

Court. 1. At court, every one for himself. 1611: Cotgrave, s.v. 'Court', In court men study only their owne fortunes. 1640: Herbert, *Jac. Prudentum*. 1732: Fuller, 825.

2. Court holy water = Flattery. 1519: Horman, *Vulgaria*, fo. 231,I haue many feyre promessis and haly water of court. 1565: Shacklock, *Hatch, of Heresies*, quoted in *N.&Q.*, 2nd ser, v 411, Therefore were we so wone with courte holy water, that is, fayre and flattring wordes. 1614: B. Rich, *Honestie of This Age*, 52 (Percy S.), Shee may bee rewarded with some *court holy water wordes*. 1692: L'Estrange, *Aesop*, 14 (3rd ed.), A little court holy water washes off all stains. 1740: North, *Examen*, 136, Some words slipt, as it were, from his pen, a drop of mere court holy water. 1785: Grose, *Class. Dict. Vulgar Tongue*, s.v., Court holy water, fair speeches and promises without performance.

3. Courts keep no almanacs. 1640: Herbert, *Jac. Prudentum*, The court hath no almanack. 1670: Ray, 6. 1710: S. Palmer, *Moral Essays on Proverbs*, 318, All Europe has consented to the proverb, that in a Prince's Court there is no almanack. 1732: Fuller, 1192.

4. One of the court, but none of the counsel. 1546: Heywood, *Proverbs*, Pt I ch xi, I was neyther of court nor of counsayle made. 1670: Ray, 170.

Courtesy. 1. A courtesy much entreated is half recompensed. 1732: Fuller, 57.

2. Courtesy on one side only lasts not long. 1640: Herbert, *Jac. Prudentum*. 1670: Ray, 6. 1732: Fuller, 1191.

3. Full of courtesy and full of craft. 1594: Nashe, *Unfort. Trav.*, in *Works*, v 14 (Grosart), Much companie, much knauerie, as true as that olde adage, Much curtesie, much subtiltie. 1639: Clarke, 13. 1670: Ray, 73. 1732: Fuller, 1635.

4. He may freely receive courtesies, that knows how to requite them. 1670: Ray, 22.

Courtier young, beggar old. *c.*1510: A. Barclay, *Egloges*, 20 (Spens.S.), Oft yonge courtiers be beggers in their age. 1579: Lyly, *Euphues*, 185 (Arber), Certes it is an olde saying that who so liueth in the court, shall dye in the strawe. 1613: *Vncasing of Machivils Instr. to his Sonne*, 7, And than do proue the prouerbe often tolde, 'A careless courtier young, a begger olde'. 1732: Fuller, 642, [the converse] An old courtier, a young beggar. Cf. **Live** (15).

Courting and wooing bring dallying and doing. 1605: Camden, *Remains*, 320 (1870). 1670: Ray, 48. 1732: Fuller, 6264 [with 'canting' for 'courting'].

Cousin. 1 Call me cousin, but cozen me not. 1678: Ray, 118. 1732: Fuller, 1046. *c.*1800: J. Trusler, *Prov. in Verse*, 47.

2. Cousin germans quite removed. 1678: Ray, 69. 1732: Fuller, 1193.

3. First cousins may marry, second cousins can't; third cousins will marry, fourth cousins won't. S. Devon. 1869: Hazlitt, 132.

See also **Marry! come up.**

Covent Garden ague, The = Venereal disease. 1678: Ray, 88. 1790: Grose, *Prov. Gloss.*, s.v. 'Westminster'.

Covent Garden is the best garden. 1790: Ibid.

Coventry blue, He is true. 1662: Fuller, *Worthies*, iii 272 (1840). 1790: *Grose, Prov. Gloss.*, s.v. 'Warwickshire'.

Coventry, To send to. 1777: Garrick, in *Garrick Corresp.*, ii 237 (1832), I seemed to be the person marked for displeasure, and was almost literally sent to Coventry. 1787: D'Arblay, *Diary*, ii 427 (1876), This again sent me to Coventry for the rest of the dinner. 1850: Dickens, *Copperfield*, ch v 1874: Smiles, *Lives of Engineers*, ii 239, They thwarted him at every turn, out-voted him, snubbed him, and 'sent him to Coventry'.

Cover your head. *See* **Head** (2).

Cover yourself with your shield, and care not for cries. 1640: Herbert, *Jac. Prudentum*.

Covers me with his wings, and bites me with his bill, He. 1633: Draxe, 97. 1670: Ray, 5. 1732: Fuller, 1829.

Covers thee, discovers thee, He that. 1620: Shelton, *Quixote*, Pt II ch v.

Covet. *He that covets all. See* **All covet**

Covetous, *adj.* **1. A covetous man does nothing well till he dies.** 1539: Taverner, *Proverbs*, fo. 51, A couetous man doth noman good but whan he dyeth. 1572: T. Wilson, *Disc, upon Usury*, 230 (1925). 1732: Fuller, 51.

2. A covetous man is good to none, but worst to himself. 1614: Lodge, tr. Seneca, 443, The couetous man is good to no man, and worst to himselfe. 1669: *Politeuphuia.287.* 1732: Fuller, 53.

3. A covetous man is like a dog in a wheel that roasts meat for others. 1659: Howell, 10 (8). 1670: Ray, 5. 1732: Fuller, 52.

4. A covetous man makes a halfpenny of a farthing, and a liberal man makes sixpence of it. 1855: Bohn, 284.

5. Covetous men live like drudges to die wretches. 1732: Fuller, 1171.

6. The covetous spends more than the liberal. 1640: Herbert, *Jac. Prudentum.*

Covetousness. 1. Covetousness, as well as prodigality, brings a man to a morsel of bread. 1732: Fuller, 1173.

2. Covetousness breaks the sack. *c.*1594: Bacon, *Promus*, No. 616. 1612: Shelton, *Quixote*, Pt I bk iii ch vi 1710: S. Palmer, *Moral Essays on Proverbs*, 34, Covetousness breaks the Jack. Antiquity appears in the face of this proverb; for without doubt 'tis the old black leathern Jack that was in use in the time of our forefathers, that is here designed. [This explanation may well be doubted. Why should 'Jack' have become uniformly 'sack?'] 1712: Motteux, *Quixote*, Pt I bk iii ch vi 1821: Scott, *Kenilworth*, ch iv, Be not over-greedy, Anthony. Covetousness bursts the sack.

3. Covetousness brings nothing home. 1639: Clarke, 37. 1732: Fuller, 1175.

4. Covetousness is always filling a bottomless vessel. 1732: Fuller, 1176.

5. Covetousness is the mother of ruin and mischief. 1387: Trevisa, tr. Higden, iii 475 (Rolls Ser.), Covetise is moder of povert. *c.*1440: Anon., tr. Higden, iii 475 (Rolls Ser.), Covetise is the moder of pouerte. 1533: in *Ballads from MSS.*, i 202 (B.S.), Be ware of covetyse, The rote of all ill vice. 1589: L. Wright, *Display of Dutie*, 10, Couetousnesse is the roote of all euill: the ground of all vice, *c.*1670: *Sir Rich. Whittington*, 26 (Villon S.), It is an old and true saying, Covetousness is the mother of ruine and mischief.

6. Covetousness often starves other vices. 1732: Fuller, 1178.

7. When all sins grow old, covetousness is young. 1560: Becon, *Catechism*, 373 (P.S.),

Covetousness is a vice appropriated as it may seem to old men, according to this old saying: *Cum omnia vitia senescunt, sola avaritia juvenescit:* 'When all vices wax old, covetousness alone waxeth young'. *c.*1570: in Collmann, *Ballads, etc.*, 130 (Roxb.Cl). 1611: Cotgrave, s.v. 'Peché', When all sinnes else be old is avarice young. 1666: Torriano, *Piazza Univ.*, 17.

Cow. 1. A collier's cow and an ale-wife's sow are always well fed. 1678: Ray, 119.

2. A cow will not clem [starve], **if there are three blades of pink grass in the field.** 1877: E. Leigh, *Cheshire Gloss.*, 155 ['an old saying']. 1917: Bridge, *Cheshire Proverbs*, 2.

3. A lowing cow soon forgets her calf. *c.*1330: in Wright's *Pol. Songs*, 332 (Camden S., 6), Hit nis noht al for the calf that kow louweth, Ac hit is for the grene gras that in the medewe grouweth. 1882: Mrs Chamberlain, *W. Worcs. Words*, 39 (E.D.S.). 1894: Northall, *Folk Phrases*, 6 (E.D.S.). 1913: *Folk-Lore*, xxiv 77, A bellowing cow soon forgets her calf. Oxfordsh. 1928: in *London Mercury*, Feb., 439, Common proverb in the West Country is 'A belving cow soon forgets her calf'.

4. A red cow gives good milk. 1917: Bridge, *Cheshire Proverbs*, 5.

5. As comely (or **as nimble**) **as a cow in a cage.** 1399: Langland, *Rich. the Redeless*, iii 262, As becometh a kow to hoppe in a cage! 1546: Heywood, *Proverbs*, Pt II ch i, As comely as is a cowe in a cage. 1577: J. Grange, *Golden Aphroditis*, sig. F1, As seemely as a cowe in a cage. 1678: Ray, 287, As nimble ... 1732: Fuller, 718, As nimble ...

6. As cows come to town, some good some bad. 1639: Clarke, 219.

7. As good luck as had the cow that stuck herself with her own horn. 1678: Ray, 287.

8. As much use as a cow has for side pockets. 1917: Bridge, *Cheshire Proverbs*, 18. Cf. **Toad** (1).

9. Cow's horn. *See* **Butter** (3); and **Milk** (5).

10. Curst cows have short horns. 1509: Barclay, *Ship of Fools*, i 182 (1874), To a wylde cowe god doth short hornys sende. 1588: Greene, *Pandosto*, in *Works*, iv 247 (Grosart), A curst cow hath oftentimes short hornes, and a willing minde but a weake arme. 1599: Shakespeare, *Much Ado*, II i 1721: Centlivre, *Artifice*, III i 1793: Grose, *Olio*, 281 (2nd ed.),

Having thus shown the futility of your criticism, and thereby the truth of that proverb which says, God sends curst cows short horns … 1880: Courtney, *W. Cornwall Words*, xiii (E.D.S.), 'Tis well that wild cows have short horns.

11. He becomes it as well as a cow doth a cart-saddle. [Bovi clitellas imponere: – *ap.* Cicero, *Att.*, V xv 3.] 1530: Palsgrave, 427, As mete to be a great mans keever as a kowe to bear a saddle. 1639: Clarke, 5.

12. He knows no more what to do with it than a cow does with a holiday. Devon. 1882: *Folk-Lore Record*, v 159.

13. His cow has calved. 1596: Jonson, *Ev. Man in his Humour*, IV ii, How now! whose cow has calv'd? 1678: Ray, 70. 1828: Scott, *Fair Maid*, ch xxii, How now – what's the matter? … whose cow has calved?

14. If you buy the cow, take the tail into the bargain. 1732: Fuller, 2743.

15. If you sell the cow, you sell her milk too. Ibid., No. 2786.

16. It is not all butter that comes from the cow. 1546: Heywood, *Proverbs*, Pt II ch ix, It is not all butter that che coow s –. 1666: Torriano, *Piazza Univ.*, 294, All is not butter that the cow makes. 1732: Fuller, 527.

17. Let him that owns the cow take her by the tail. 1611: Cotgrave, s.v. 'Queue' [with 'asse' for 'cow']. 1694: D'Urfey, *Quixote*, Pt II Act III sc ii 1732: Fuller, 3185.

18. Like a crab in a cow's mouth. 1732: Fuller, 2990, It is no more to him than a crab in a cow's mouth. 1913: *Folk-Lore*, xxiv 77, Like a crab in a cow's mouth (Oxfordsh.).

19. Look to the cow and the sow, and the wheat-mow, and [all] will be well enow. Somerset. 1678: Ray, 347. 1846: Denham, *Proverbs*, 19 (Percy S.).

20. Many a good cow hath an evil calf. 1546: Heywood, *Proverbs*, Pt I ch x 1580: Baret, *Alvearie*, H 406. 1605: Chapman, etc., *Eastw. Hoe*, IV ii, Thou art not the first good cow hast had an ill calf. 1681: W. Robertson, *Phraseol. Generalis*, 404, Many a good cow has but a bad calf. 1732: Fuller, 3337. 1846: Denham, *Proverbs*, 3 (Percy S.).

21. Milk the cow that standeth still. *c.*1594: Bacon, *Promus*, No. 553, Milk the standing cowe. Why follow you the flying? 1688: *Gesta Grayorum*, 38 (Malone S.), The proverb is a countrey-proverb, but significative, Milk the cow that standeth still; why follow you her that flieth away?

22. Steal my cow and give away the hide. 1869: Hazlitt, 345.

23. The cow gives good milk, but kicks over the pail. 1599: Porter, *Two Angry Women*, sc xi Be not you like the cowe, that gives a good sope of milke, and casts it downe with her heeles. 1659: Howell, 14, Like a curst cow that gives a paile of milk, and then kicks it down. 1716: Ward, *Female Policy*, 84, A cow that gives good milk, but kicks it to the ground. 1753: Richardson, *Grandison*, iv 148 (1883), You are a pretty cow, my love; you give good store of milk, but you have a very careless heel.

24. The cow knows not what her tail is worth till she has lost it. 1640: Herbert, *Jac. Prudentum.*

25. The cow little giveth, that hardly liveth. 1732: Fuller, 6325.

26. The old brown cow laid an egg. 1917: Bridge, *Cheshire Proverbs*, 117 … used as an answer to importunate questions.

27. The tune the old cow died of. 1732: Fuller, 4360, That is the old tune upon the bag-pipe. 1836:Marryat, *Japhet*, ch lxviii, This tune, 'which the old cow died of', as the saying is, used to be their horror.

28. Till the cows come home. 1625: in *Harl. Miscell.*, iv 125 (1745), Drinking, eating, feasting, and revelling, till the cow come home, as the saying is. 1738: Swift, *Polite Convers.*, Dial. II, I warrant you lay abed till the cows came home. 1836: Marryat, *Easy*, ch vii, Which receipt … was, in point of law, about as valuable as if he had agreed to pay as soon 'as the cows came home'. *c.*1873: John Hay, *Little Breeches*, etc., 22, You may nezoloot till the cows come home. 1924: M. Kennedy, *Constant Nymph*, 320, You can keep on guessing till the cows come home.

29. To grow down like a cow's tail. [Haec colonia retroversus crescit tanquam coda vituli. – Petr., 44.] 1649: in *Somers Tracts*, vii 87 (1811), I would still be growing, though it be downwards. Why should not old lords, as well as old men, be cows-tails? 1653: Urquhart, *Rabelais*, bk ii ch xxvii, Which never grow but like cowes tailes downwards. 1710: Ward, *Nuptial Dialogues*, ii 76, You're growing downwards now, Like tail of heifer or of cow. 1894: Northall, *Folk Phrases*, 19 (E.D.S.), Like a cow's tail, [he *or* she] grows down hill.

30. To have a cow's tongue. 1750: W. Ellis, *Housewife's Companion*, vii, The gossiping sort … have a cow's tongue (as we call it in the country), a smooth side and a rough side.

31. To look on one as a cow on a bastard calf. Somerset. 1678: Ray, 353. 1883: Burne, *Shropsh. Folk-Lore*, 594, To look like a cow at a bastard calf = to look coldly, suspiciously at one.

32. To set a cow to get a hare. 1611: Cotgrave, s.v. 'Vache', A cow may catch a hare. 1683: Meriton, *Yorkshire Ale*, 83–7 (1697), Sett a cow to git a hare. 1883: Burne, *Shropsh. Folk-Lore*, 588, We don't go by size, or a cow would catch a hare.

33. To tip the cow's horn with silver. 1917: Bridge, *Cheshire Proverbs*, 144, When a butcher pays for the cow he has bought, he expects a 'luckpenny' to be returned to him which, in the case of a cow, is usually a shilling, and is technically called 'tipping the cow's horn with silver'.

34. What should a cow do with a nutmeg? 1732: Fuller, 5502.

35. Who will sell the cow must say the word. 1640: Herbert, *Jac. Prudentum*.

36. Who would keep a cow when he may have a quart of milk for a penny? 1659: Howell, *Letters*, ii 666 (Jacobs), In this case it is better to buy a quart of milk by the penny than keep a cow. *c.*1680: in *Roxb. Ballads*, viii 859 (B.S.), What need I keep a cow, or at such charges to be, When I can have a quart of milk for a penny? 1732: Fuller, 5697. 1917: Bridge, *Cheshire Proverbs*, 155 [with 'pottle' for 'quart'].

See also **Calf** (3), (5), and (9); **Horse** (72); **Like cow**; **Lincolnshire where**; **Margery**; **Milk** (5); **Parson's cow**; and **Slender**.

Coward and **Cowards. 1. A coward, a coward.** *See* **Barnard Castle** (1).

2. A coward's fear can make a coward valiant. 1732: Fuller, 58.

3. Cowards are cruel. 1485: Malory, *Morte d'Arthur*, bk xviii ch 24, Euer wylle a coward shewe no mercy. 1591: Harington, *Orl. Furioso*, bk xxxvi, Notes, Cruelty ever proceeds from a vile minde, and often from a cowardly heart. 1639: Clarke, 76, Cruell people are fearefull. 1727: Gay, *Fables*, 1st ser, No. 1, l. 33, Cowards are cruel. 1891: R.L.S., *Wrecker*, ch xxii, For once the proverb was right, cruelty was coupled with cowardice.

4. Cowards die many times before their death. 1599: Shakespeare, *Julius Caesar*, II ii. 32, Cowards die many times before their deaths: The valiant never taste of death but once. 1800: M Edgeworth, *Castle Rackrent*, p. xliv, In Ireland, not only cowards, but the brave, 'die many times before their death'. 1927: *Sphere*, 3 Dec., p. 414, col. I, It is true that cowards die many times before their death.

5. If he be a coward he is a murderer. 1595: *Polimanteia*, sig. N1, Alleadging an olde prouerbe to that ende, *If he be, etc.*

6. Make a coward fight and he will kill the devil. 1669: *New Help to Discourse*, 151. 1732: Fuller, 3980, Put a coward to his mettle, and he'll fight the devil.

7. Many would be cowards, if they had courage enough. 1732: Fuller, 3366.

Cowardly is unlucky. *c.*1386: Chaucer, *Reeve's Tale*, l. 290, 'Unhardy is unsely', thus men sayth.

Cowfold. *See* **Bolney**.

Cowhithe. *See* quot. 1670: Ray, 253, Between Cowhithe and merry Cossingland, The devils – Benacre, look where it stands. 1790: Grose, *Prov. Gloss.*, s.v. 'Suffolk'.

Cowl. *See* **Hood**.

Cowling moon. *See* quot. 1827: Hone, *Table-Book*, 775, In the vulgar vocabulary of Craven a silly fellow is called a 'Cowling moon'.

Cox's pig. *He thought a lie, like Cox's pig.* War. 1920: *N. & Q.*, 12th ser, vii 67.

Coy as a croker's mare. 1546: Heywood, *Proverbs*, Pt II ch i 1670: **Ray**, 202. Cf. **Corrat**.

Crab. *See* **Cow** (18); and **Devil** (122).

Crab of the wood. *See* quot. 1659: Howell, 6, A crabb of the wood is sawce very good for a crabb of the sea, The wood of a crabb is good for a drabb that will not her husband obey. 1670: Ray, 210. 1736: Bailey, *Dict.*, s.v. 'Crab' [very slightly varied].

Crabbed knot must hare a crabbed wedge, A. 1611: Davies (of Hereford), *Sc. of Folly*, 24, in *Works*, ii (Grosart).

Crabs. *The greatest crabs are not always the best meate.* 1546: Heywood, *Proverbs*, Pt I ch xi 1611: Cotgrave, s.v. 'Boeuf'. 1670: Ray, 75.

Crab-tree. *Plant the crab-tree where you will, it will never bear pippins.* 1732: Fuller, 3880.

Crack me that nut. *See* **Nut** (2).

Crack the nut. *See* **Eat** (25).

Crack was a good dog. *See* quot. 1891: S. O. Addy, *Sheffield Gloss. Supp.*, 14 (E.D.S.), There is a proverb which says that 'Crack was a good dog, but he got hung for barking'. It is intended to show that a swaggerer conies to a bad end.

Cradle over thy head, Cast not thy. 1678: Ray, 347.

Cradle straws are scarce out of his breech. 1678: Ray, 346. 1683: Meriton, *Yorkshire Ale*, 83–7 (1697), Credle streays are scarce out of his breech.

Cradle, The hand that rocks the. *See* **Hand** (6).

Craft. 1. All the craft is in the catching. 1631: Mabbe, *Celestina*, 163 (T.T.). Before 1680: Butler, *Remains*, ii 279 (1759), For all the craft is not in the catching (as the proverb says) but the better half at least is being catched.

2. Craft against craft makes no living. 1640: Herbert, *Jac. Prudentum*.

3. Craft bringeth nothing home. 1633: Draxe, 35. 1670: Ray, 6. 1732: Fuller, 1199.

4. Craft is found in clouted shoes. *c.*1600: in *Roxb. Ballads*, ii 574 (B.S.), Craft lies under clowted shoone. 1618: Harington, *Epigrams*, bk i No. 11, I heare some say, and some believe it too, That craft is found ev'n in the clouted shoo.

5. Craft must have clothes, but truth loves to go naked. 1732: Fuller, 1200.

6. He that hath not craft, let him shut up shop. 1640: Herbert, *Jac. Prudentum*.

7. There's craft in daubing. *c.*1454: in *Paston Letters*, i 269 (1900), For her moder … seyth to her that ther is gode crafte in dawbyng. *c.*1520: *Hickscorner*, in Hazlitt, *Old Plays*, i 159, For ye know well, there is craft in daubing: I can look in a man's face and pick his purse. 1670: Ray, 75. 1732: Fuller, 4892. 1901: F. E. Taylor, *Lancs Sayings*, 22, Ther's cunnin' i' dobin' beside layin' it on.

Crafthole. *See* quot. 1602: Carew, *Surv. of Cornwall*, 256–7 (1811), In this parish [Sheviock] standeth Crafthole … a poor village … somewhat infamous, not upon any present desert, but through an inveterate by-word, viz. that it is peopled with twelve dwellings and thirteen cuckolds. Cf. **Strand-on-the-Green**.

Crafty. 1. A crafty fellow never has any peace. 1732: Fuller, 59.

2. A crafty knave needs no broker. 1592: Greene, in *Works*, x 185 (Grosart). 1596: Jonson, *Ev. Man in Humour*, III ii 1639: Breton, in *Works*, ii 11 (Grosart). 1659: Howell, 5 [with 'cunning' for 'crafty'].

3. To a crafty man, a crafty and a half. 1640: Herbert, *Jac. Prudentum*.

Crane's dirt. *See* quots. 1530: Palsgrave, 719, You sayd treuthe, you can well skyll of cranes dyrte, your father was a poulter. 1592: Lyly, *Mother Bombie*, II iii. You are well seene in crane's dirt, your father was a poulter.

Crave in hope, and have in hap, 'oft hast thou heard it'. 1583: Melbancke, *Philotinus*, sig. Ff2.

Crawley, Beds. 1. As crooked as Grawley brook. 1662: Fuller, *Worthies*, i 167 (1840). 1790: Grose, *Prov. Gloss.*, s.v. 'Beds'. 1878: *N.&Q.*, 5th ser, ix 345. As crooked as Crawley.

2. Crawley! God help us. 1878: Ibid., 345.

Crawley, Sussex. *It always rains on Crawley Fair day.* 1884: 'Sussex Proverbs', in *N.&Q.*, 6th ser, ix 342.

Crazy ship. *To a crazy ship all winds are contrary.* 1640: Herbert, *Jac. Prudentum*. 1670: Ray, 6. 1732: Fuller, 5126.

Creaking cart goes long, A. 1900: *N.&Q.*, 9th ser, vi 298, A creaking cart goes long on the wheels [quoted as a common proverb].

Creaking gate (or door) hangs long, A. 1776: T. Cogan, *John Bunch, Junior*, i 239, But they say a creaking gate goes the longest upon its hinges; that's my comfort. 1854: Baker, *Northants Gloss.*, s.v. 'Gate', 'A creaking gate hangs longest on the hinges'. Used figuratively of an invalid, who outlives an apparently healthier person. 1901: F. E. Taylor, *Lancs Sayings*, 7, A creakin' dur 'll hong a good while on it' hinges. 1913: *Folk-Lore*, xxiv 76, Oxfordsh. A creaking door hangs long on its hinges.

Cream of the jest, That's the. 1678: Ray, 69. 1754: Berthelson, *Eng.-Danish Dict.*, s.v. 'Cream'.

Cream-pot love = Cupboard love. 1678: Ray, 69.

Credit 1. Credit keeps the crown of the causeway. 1875: A. B. Cheales, *Proverb. Folk-Lore*, 101.

2. Credit lost is like a Venice glass broke. 1670: Ray, 6. 1732: Fuller, 4021, Reputation crackt, is a Venice-glass broke.

3. Give credit where credit is due. 1777: S. Adams, *Letter*, 29 Oct, in *Collections of the Massachusetts Historical Society* (1917), LXXII 375, May Honor begiven to whom Honor is due. 1834: M. Floy, *Diary*, 17 Jan. (1941), 50, Loudon was be a man of taste … and disposed to give all credit where any credit is due.

4. He that has cracked his credit is half hanged. 1519: Horman, *Vulgaria*, fo. 77, Yf a man haue lost his credence, he is halfe vndon. 1590: Greene, in *Works*, viii 154 (Grosart).

5. He that has lost his credit is dead to the world. 1639: Clarke, 87, To lose a mans credit is the greatest losse. 1640: Herbert, *Jac. Prudentum*. 1670: Ray, 6. 1732: Fuller, 2142.

6. No man ever lost his credit, but he who had it not. 1670: Ray, 6.

Crediton, Devon. **1. As fine as Kerton spinning.** 1790: Grose, *Prov. Gloss.*, s.v. 'Devon'.

2. That's extra. *See* quot. 1901: *Devon N. & Q.*, i 120, Many years ago it was frequently said in Devonshire, ' "That's extra," as the old woman said when she saw "Kirton" ' [Crediton].

3. When Kirton, etc. 1876: *N. & Q.*, 5th ser, vi 364, When Ex'ter was a furzy down, Kirton was a mayor-town. 1892: S. Hewett, *Peasant Speech of Devon*, 145, When Kirton wuz a borough town, Ex'ter wuz a vuzzy-down.

Creditors have better memories than debtors. 1659: Howell, *Proverbs: Span.-Eng.*, 8. 1736: Franklin, *Way to Wealth*, in *Works*, i 450 (Bigelow). *c.*1800: Trusler, *Prov. in Verse*, 53. 1880: Spurgeon, *Ploughman's Pictures*, 18.

Creep before we can go. *See* **First creep.**

Creep up one's sleeve, To. 1821: Clare, *Rural Life*, 161, For there's none apter, I believe, at 'creeping up a mistress' sleeve'. 1854: Baker, *Northants Gloss.*, s.v. 'Creep', Creep up your sleeve. A colloquial phrase for endeavouring to obtain a favour by coaxing or wheedling. 1889: Peacock, *Manley, etc., Gloss.*, 144 (E.D.S.), He's crept up her sleäve till he can do anything wi' her he likes. 1926: Phillpotts, *Yellow Sands*, I, I ain't going to creep up her sleeve because there's money hid there. Cf. **Speak** (20).

Cringing is a gainful accomplishment. 1710: S. Palmer, *Moral Essays on Proverbs*, 266, A man's hat in his hand never did him any harm. 1732: Fuller, 1206.

Cripple. *He that dwells near a cripple will soon learn to halt.* 1579: Lyly, *Euphues*, 131 (Arber), It

is an olde prouerbe that if one dwell the next doore to a creeple he will learne to hault. 1647: *Countrym. New Commonwealth*, 12.

Critics are like brushers of noblemen's clothes. 1651: Herbert, *Jac. Prudentum*, 2nd ed.

Crock as the porridge, She will as soon part with the. Somerset. 1678: Ray, 352.

Crocker. *See* **Copplestone.**

Crooked as a cammock [a bent piece of wood; a cambrel]. Before 1529: Skelton, in *Works*, i 117 (Dyce), Your longe lothy legges, Crokyd as a camoke. 1592: Lyly, *Mother Bombie*, I iii, They study twentie yeares together to make us grow as straight as a wand, and in the end, by bowing us, as crooked as a cammocke.

Crooked as a dog's hind leg. 1886: Elworthy, *West Som. Word-Book*, 170 (E.D.S.), So crooked's a dog's hind-leg … are the superlative absolutes in constant use. 1886: R. Holland, *Cheshire Gloss.*, 445 (E.D.S.), As crookit as a dog's elbow. 1889: Peacock, *Manley, etc., Gloss.*, 146 (E.D.S.). 1926: *Tatler*, 10 Nov., p. 280, He was also as crooked as a dog's hind leg on the turf.

Crooked as a ram's horn. 1658: *Wit Restor'd*, 102, [Ironical] Straight as a rams home is thy nose. 1820: Colton, *Lacon*, Pt II No. 130, The dolphin, which is always painted more crooked than a ram's horn. 1923: *Folk-Lore*, xxxiv 329 [Oxfordsh.].

Crooked as S. 1917: Bridge, *Cheshire Proverbs*, 12.

Crooked logs make straight fires. 1611: Cotgrave, s.v. 'Busche'. 1694: D'Urfey, *Quixote*, Pt I Act I sc ii, Crooked logs make good fires. 1875: A. B. Cheales, *Proverb. Folk-Lore*, 132.

Crooked stick will hare a crooked shadow, A. 1732: Fuller, 61.

Crooked without, crabbed within. 1593: *Passionate Morrice*, 86 (N.Sh.S.).

Crooked. *See also* **Crawley;** and **Wembury.**

Cross, *adj.* **1. As cross as a bear with a sore head.** 1830: Marryat, *King's Own*, ch xxvi, The captain was as savage as a bear with a sore head. 1870: *N. & Q.*, 4th ser, vi 321, Thus we say 'As sulky as a bear with a sore head'. 1922: Weyman, *Ovington's Bank*, ch v, But I assure you, sir, he's like a bear with a sore head.

2. As cross as nine highways. 1855: Bohn, 316.

3. As cross as two sticks. 1831: Scott, *Journal*, 2 Nov., Wind as cross as two sticks. 1854: Baker,

Northants Gloss., s.v. 'Cross' ... A common comparison for an irritable person. 1855: Thackeray, *Newcomes*, ch xxxiii, She scolded her maid and was as cross as two sticks. 1909: Pinero, *Mid-Channel*, III.

Cross and **Crosses**, *subs*. **1. Cross or (and) pile.** [Capita aut navia. – Macrobius, *Sat.*, i 7.] [*c*.1320: in Grose's *Antiq. Repertory*, ii 406 (1808), Item paie a Roi mesmes pour Iewer a Cros et pil ... les Deniers xij.] *c*.1390: Gower, *Conf. Amantis.*, ii 390, Whos tunge neither pyl ne crouche Mai byre. 1552: Huloet, *Abced.*, sig. E2, Cast lottes or crosse and pyle. 1665: J. Wilson, *Projectors*, Prol., That, in effect, 'tis but a cross or pile. In all that's written, whether well or ill. 1673: A. Behn, *Dutch Lover*, I i, Cross or pile who shall go. 1707: Ward, *London Terraefilius*, No. IV, p. 18, He is ready to toss up cross or pile. *c*.1770: Pegge, *Derbicisms*, 15 (E.D.S.), When boys turn up a halfpenny at play, the head side they call cross, and the Britannia pile.

2. Crosses are ladders to heaven. 1633: Draxe, 36, The crosse is the ladder of heauen. 1670: Ray, 6. 1732: Fuller, 1208. 1859: Smiles, *Self-Help*, 341 (1869), 'Crosses', says the old proverb, 'are the ladders that lead to heaven'.

3. He has not a cross [coin] **to bless himself with.** 1540: Palsgrave, *Acolastus*, sig. T4, That hath neuer a crosse left him to blesse him with. 1579: *Marr. of Wit and Wisdom*, sc iii, p. 31 (SH.S.), I have neuer a crose to blesse me. 1632: Rowley, *New Wonder*, III, Your good husband will leave you ne'er a cross i' th' house to bless you with. 1708: tr. Aleman's *Guzman*, i 318, I ... had not a penny left to bless myself with. 1819: Scott, *Bride of L.*, ch iv. The Lord Keeper has got all his estates – he has not a cross to bless himself with.

4. The cross on the breast, and the devil in the heart. 1633: Draxe, 97, The crosse in his breast and the deuill in his actions. 1732: Fuller, 4462.

5. To have neither cross nor coin. 1768: Goldsmith, *Vicar*, ch xxi, You trumpery, to come and take up an honest house without cross or coin to bless yourself with! 1828: Carr, *Craven Dialect*, i 94, 'I've neither cross nor coin', that is, no money at all. 1855: Robinson, *Whitby Gloss.*, 'I'm blest wi' nowther cross nor coin', or as we have otherwise heard it said, 'nowther brass nor benediction'.

6. To make a cross upon anything = Mark with a white stone. 1546: Heywood, *Proverbs*, Pt I ch xi, And now will I make a cross on this gate. **Cross a stile, and a gate hard by, You'll be a widow before you die.** 1864: 'Cornish Proverbs', in *N. & Q.*, 3rd ser, v 208.

Cross the stream where it is ebbest [shallowest]. 1603: Holland, tr. Plutarch's *Morals*, 747, There is still a Lancashire proverb, 'Cross the stream where it is ebbest'.

Cross your bridges till you come to them, Don't. Meaning that there is no purpose in trying to deal with difficulties in advance.1850: Longfellow, *Journal*, 29 Apr. in *Life* (1886), II 165, Remember the proverb, 'Do not cross the bridge till you come to it'. 1895: S.O. Addy, *Household Tales*, xiv, One who anticipates difficulties is told not to cross the bridge till he gets to it. 1927: 'J. Taine' *Quayle's Invention*, xv, Why cross our bridges before we come to them?

Crotchets in the head (or **brain**), **To have.** 1592: G. Harvey, *Works*, i 189 (Grosart), A wilde head ful of mad braine and a thousande crotchets. 1611: Cotgrave, s.v. 'Moucheron', *Avoir des moucherons en teste*. To ... have many ... crotchets in the head. 1660: Howell, *Parly of Beasts*, 49, When a crochet hath got once into his noddle ... 1690: *New Dict. Canting Crew*, sig. D3, Crochets in the crown, whimsies, maggots. 1807: Crabbe, *Par. Reg.*, iii 930 (OED), And gloomy crotchets fill'd his wandering head.

Crouse as a lop [flea] (or **a louse**). 1670: Ray, 203, Crouse as a new washen louse. 1825: Brockett, *Gloss. N. Country Words*, 51 [as in 1670]. 1855: Robinson, *Whitby Gloss.*, 40, 'As crowse as a lop', as brisk as a flea. 1868: Atkinson, *Cleveland Gloss.*, 321, Peert as a lopp, used of a person nimble and active in his movements. 1889: J. Nicholson, *Folk Speech E. Yorks*, 17, As croose (lively) as a loose or lopp.

Crow and **Crows**. **1. As good land as any the crow flies over.** 1684: Bunyan, *Pilgr. Progr.*, Pt II, p. 98 (OED), As fruitful a place, as any the crow flies over. 1690: *New Dict. Canting Crew*, sig. D4.

2. Crows are never the whiter for washing themselves. 1678: Ray, 121. 1732: Fuller, 1210.

3. Crows do not pick out crows' eyes. 1578: Florio, *First Fruites*, fo. 29, One crow wil neuer put out an other crowes eyes. 1629: *Book of Meery Riddles*, Prov. 93. 1732: Fuller, 3744.

1815: Scott, *Mannering*, ch xl, Na, na! hawks shouldna pike out hawks' een.

4. Hoarse as a crow. 1883: R.L.S., *Treasure I*, ch xiv, He was not only red in the face, but spoke as hoarse as a crow. 1911: T. Edwardes, *Neighbourhood*, 116, Tired as a navigator, and hoarse as a crow.

5. It is ill killing a crow with an empty sling. 1678: Ray, 120. 1732: Fuller, 2960.

6. 'Tis long of your eyes, the crows might have helped it when you were young. 1678:Ray, 345.

7. The crow bewails the sheep, and then eats it. 1640: Herbert, *Jac. Prudentum*. 1670: Ray, 6, Carrion crows bewail the dead sheep, and then eat them. 1732: Fuller, 1211.

8. The crow thinks her own birds fairest. 1513: Douglas, *Aeneis*, ix, Prol., 78 (OED), The blak crawe thinkis hir awin byrdis quhite. 1580: H. Gifford, *Posie*, 32 (Grosart), Not vnlike the crow, who alwaies thinkes her owne byrdes fayrest. 1639: Massinger, *Unnat. Combat*, III ii, I … like the foolish crow Believe my black brood swans. 1732: Fuller, 4463. 1855: Gaskell, *North and South*, ch xv, You think you never heard of this wonderful son of mine, Miss Hale. You think I'm an old woman whose … own crow is the whitest ever seen.

9. To have a crow to pluck (or **pull**) **with one.** *c.*1410: *Towneley Plays*, 18 (E.E.T.S.), Na, na, abide, we haue a craw to pull. 1546: Heywood, *Proverbs*, Pt II ch v, We haue a crow to pul. 1592: Lyly, *Mother Bombie*, II i, If I thought thou meanest so … thou shouldst have a crow to pull. 1665: J. Wilson, *Projectors*, V, I've a crow to pluck w' ye. 1754: Berthelson, *Eng.-Danish Dict.*, s.v. 'Crow'. 1841: Dickens, *Barn. Rudge*, ch xiii, Tell him that whenever he comes here I have a crow to pluck with him. 1865: *N.&Q.* 3rd ser, vii 104. 'I've a crow to pluck with you, and a poke to put the feathers in', is I think the usual North country proverb, the poke for the feathers being rather an important part of the threat, judging from the stress the speaker lays upon it.

10. To make the crow a pudding. *c.*1598: Deloney, *Gentle Craft*, Pt II ch iii, Plucke up a good heart woman, let no man … say thou gauest the crow a pudding, because loue would let thee liue no longer. 1599: Shakespeare, *Henry V*, II i, By my troth, he'll yield the crow a pudding one of these days. 1767: Hall Stevenson, *Works*, i 208 (1795), But if he drops him, down he goes, And makes a pudding for the crows. 1889: *Folk-Lore Journal*, vii 292, Derby. He's nowt good-for till he gies crows a pudden [is dead].

11. To say the crow is white. 1528: More, *Works*, p. 207, col. 1 (1557), As he that would say the crowe were white. 1579: *Marr. of Wit and Wisdom*, sc i, p. 10 (SH.S.), Say as she sayeth, although that she Doe say the crowe is white. 1649: in *Somers Tracts*, vi 52 (1811), If they say the crow is white, so must the souldier.

12. To strut like a crow in a gutter. 1579 Fulke *Confut. Sanders*, 675 (OED), He triumpheth like a crow in a gutter. 1690: *New Dict. Canting Crew*, sig. D4, Strut like a crow in a gutter, said in jeer of the stalking of a proud fellow. Before 1729: in *Roxb. Ballads*, viii 812 (B.S.), I used for to vaunt, as if I would fly. And strut like a crow in a gutter. 1880: Spurgeon, *Ploughman's Pictures*, 48, He struts like a crow in a gutter, and thinks himself cock of the walk.

13. When the crow begins to build then sheepe begin to yeald. Glos. 1639: in *Berkeley MSS.*, in. 31 (1885).

See also **Black**, *adj.* (6); **Hungry as June crow; Like crow; March** (20) and (42); **No carrion;** and **Safe as a crow.**

Crowd is not company, A. 1732: Fuller, 62.

Crowland. *See* quots. 1662: Fuller, *Worthies*, ii 268 (1840), All the carts that come to Crowland are shod with silver. 1790: Grose, *Prov. Gloss.*, s.v. 'Lincs' [as in 1662]. 1865: W. White, *Eastern England*, i 281, 'Every cart that comes to Crowland is shod with silver' is a saying that carries us back to days when there was no gravel.

Crown. 1. A crown in pocket doth you more credit than an angel spent. 1732: Fuller, 63.

2. From the crown of the head to the sole of the foot. [Usque ab unguiculo ad capillum summum. – Plautus, *Epid.*, 623.] *c.*1300: *Havelok*, l. 1847 (E.E.T.S.), Fro the croune til the to. 1468: *Coventry Myst.*, 241 (SH.S.), ffro the sool of the ffoot to the hyest asencion. 1547: Borde, *Brev. of Helthe*, fo. vi, Which may be frõ the croune of the heede to the sole of the foote. 1599: Shakespeare, *Much Ado*, III ii 1607: *Chester Plays*, x 439 (E.E.T.S.), From the crowne of the head to the right toe I leave no wholl fell. 1741: Arbuthnot, *Mart. Scriblerus*, bk i ch viii, From the crown of my head to the sole of my foot, I shall ever acknowledge myself your worship's humble servant. 1857: Dickens, *Dorrit*, bk ii ch xxxiii, Mr Merdle was found out from the crown of his head to the sole of his foot the moment he was found out in his pocket.

Crowson's mare. *See* quot. 1841: Hartshorne, *Salopia Ant.*, 381, Here a comes, limping along like owd Crowson's mare. 1883: Burne, *Shropsh. Folk-Lore*, 593 [as in 1841].

Crow-trodden, You look as if you were. 1678: Ray, 237.

Cruelty is a tyrant that's always attended with fear. 1670: Ray, 6. 1732: Fuller, 1213. *c.*1800: Trusler, *Prov. in Verse*, 103.

Cruelty is God's enemy, A man of. 1732: Fuller, 303.

Crumb not your bread before you taste your porridge. 1594: A. Copley, *Wits, Fits, etc.*, 116 (1614), Tast your pottage before you crumb in your bread, *c.*1630: B.&F., *Monsieur Thomas*, IV iv.

Crumbs. *See* **Pick up.**

Crusty. *See* quote. 1592: Lyly, *Mother Bombie*, II iii, You need not bee crustie, you are not so hard backt [baked]. 1678: Ray, 237 [as in 1592]. Ibid., 352, She is as crousty as that is hard bak'd. *Somerset*.

Cry. 1. Cry you mercy killed my cat. 1639: Clarke, 281. 1670: Ray, 68.

2. I cry you mercy I killed your cushion. 1530: Palsgrave, 501, I kry you mercy, I kylled your cussheyn. 1592: Lyly, *Mother Bombie*, IV ii.

3. I cry you mercy, I took you for a joint stool. Ibid., IV ii 1608: Shakespeare, *Lear*, III vi, *Fool.* Cry you mercy, I took you for a joint-stool. 1670: Ray, 186.

4. To cry notch. *See* **Notch.**

5. To cry out before one is hurt. 1548: in *Reliq. Antiquae*, ii 16 (1843), Ye may the better understand that I cry not before I am pricked. 1611: Cotgrave, s.v. 'Anguille', Such as ... crye before their paine approach them. 1818: Byron, *Don Juan*, can. i st. 207, They will not cry out before they're hurt. 1848: Dickens, *Dombey*, ch xxv, My lad ... don't you sing out afore you're hurt.

6. To cry over spilt milk. In the first quotation the proverb is in solution. 1484: Caxton, *Aesope, etc.* ii 270 (Jacobs), The thyrd [doctrine] is that thow take no sorowe of the thynge lost whiche

may not be recouered. 1681: Yarranton, *Englands Improvement*, Pt II, p. 107, Sir, there is no crying for shed milk, that which is past cannot be recall'd. 1741: *True Anti-Pamela*, 131, Well, my dear, said I, it is need less crying after shed milk. *c.*1890: Gilbert, *Foggarty's Fairy*, I, However, it's no use crying over spilt milk. 1923: J. S. Fletcher, *The Diamonds*, ch xxviii, She was one of those women who do not believe in crying over spilled milk.

7. To cry roast meat. *See* **Roast meat** (3).

8. To cry whore. 1676: A. Behn, *Town Fop*, IV iii, She cries whore first, brings him upon his knees for her fault; and a piece of plate, or a new petticoat, makes his peace again. 1738: Swift, *Polite Convers.*, Dial. I, Nay, miss, you cried whore first, when you talked of the knapsack.

9. To cry with one eye and laugh with the other. *c.*1500: quoted in Collier's *Bibliogr. Cat.*, ii 482, Full harde it is to fynde a woman stedfast, For yf one eye wepe, the other dothe contrary. 1667: L'Estrange, *Quevedo's Visions*, 106 (1904), One of them I saw crying with one eye ... and laughing with t'other. 1732: Fuller, 4737, The rich widow cries with one eye and laughs with the other.

Cuckold. 1. A discontented cuckold has not wit. 1612: *Cornucopiae*, 92 (Grosart), Well doth their folly this old saying fit, *A male-contented cuckold hath no wit.*

2. Cuckolds are Christians. 1678: Ray, 69. 1732: Fuller, 1215, Cuckolds are Christians all the world over.

3. Cuckolds are going to heaven. 1659: Howell, 12, In rain and sunshine cuckolds go to heaven. 1670: Ray, 6 [as in 1659]. 1681: Otway, *Soldier's Fortune*, IV i, For all cuckolds go to Heaven, that's most certain. 1699: Farquhar, *Love and a Bottle*, V i 1870: *N.&Q.*, 4th ser, v 366, In the West of England it was in my childhood, and probably is still, a saying, when the sun shines, and it rains at the same time ... that the 'Cuckolds are going to heaven'.

4. Cuckolds are kind. 1620: *Westw. for Smelts*, 40 (Percy S.), Which made her to beleeve that the proverbe is true (cuckolds are kinde men). 1696: Mrs Manley, *Lost Lover*, V i, Vain hopes of having the proverb of your side, *That cuckolds are kind to those who make them so.*

5. If a cuckold come he'll take away the meat. 1678: Ray, 69 ... viz. If there be no salt on the table. 1738: Swift, *Polite Convers.*, Dial. II, Here's no salt; cuckolds will run away with the meat. Cf. No. 9.

6. It is better to be a cuckold and not know it, than be none, and everybody say so. 1659: Howell, *Proverbs: Span.-Eng.*, 14, Better to be a cuckold and none know it, then to be none, and yet to be thought so. 1732: Fuller, 871.

7. Let every cuckold wear his own horns. 1659: Howell, 3. 1670: Ray, 6. 1762: Smollett, *Sir L. Greaves*, ch xiii, Growling within himself, that thenceforward he should let every cuckold wear his own horns.

8. The cuckold is the last that knows of it. 1605: Camden, *Remains*, 332 (1870). 1693: Dryden, *Juvenal*, Sat. x l. 528, For cuckolds hear the last. 1758–67: Sterne, *Trist. Shandy*, ix 4, It is with love as with cuckoldom, the suffering party is generally the last who knows anything about the matter.

9. Think of a cuckold. 1709: *Brit. Apollo*, vol ii No. 59, col. 3, *Q.* When a person is joynting a piece of meat, if he finds it difficult to joynt, he is bid to think of a cuckold. I desire to know whence the proverb? *A.* Thomas Webb, a carver to a Lord Mayor of London in King Charles the First's reign, was as famous for his being a cuckold as for his dexterity in carving; therefore what became a proverb was used first as an invocation, when any took upon him to carve. Cf. No. 5.

10. To be a cuckold and know it not, is no more than to drink with a fly in the cup and see it not. 1580: Lyly, *Euphues*, 284 (Arber), To weare a horne and not knowe it, will do me no more harme then to eate a flye, and not see it. 1593: *Tell-Trothes N. Years Gift*, 20 (N.Sh.S.). 1732: Fuller, 5250 [as in 1580].

11. Who is a cuckold and conceals it, carries coals in his bosom. 1659: Howell, *Proverbs: Span.-Eng.*, 14. 1670: Ray, 6. 1732: Fuller, 2332, He that thinks himself a cuckold, carries live coals in his heart.

See also **Company** (1); and **To-day a man.**

Cuckoo. 1. A cuckoo for one! An expression of contempt or derision. 1633: Rowley, *Match at Midnight*, V, You, a new-fangled fowler, came to show your art i' th' dark; but take this truth, you catched in truth a cuckoo for 't.

2. As scabbed as a cuckoo. 1659: Howell, 5. 1670: Ray, 207. 1797: *Gent. Mag.*, Pt I, p. 456, 'As

scabbed as a cuckoo' is a common saying in the North of England. 1828: Carr, *Craven Dialect*, ii 99. 1866: *Science Gossip*, ii 184, 'As scabbed as a cuckoo' is a common saying in Yorkshire.

3. Bad for the barley, and good for the corn, When the cuckoo comes to an empty thorn. 1883: Burne, *Shropsh. Folk-Lore*, 221. 1893: Inwards, *Weather Lore*, 136.

4. Comes in mid March, Sings in mid April, Stuts in mid May, And in mid June flies away. North country. 1797: *Gent. Mag.*, Pt I, p. 456.

5. Cuckoo oats and woodcock hay, Make a farmer run away. 1864: *N. & Q.*, 3rd ser, v 394. 1891: ibid., 7th ser, xii 486 [with 'Michaelmas' for 'woodcock' – Staffs]. 1893: G. L. Gower, *Gloss. of Surrey Words*, 12 (E.D.S.), Cuckoo oats arc late-sown oats, and are never supposed to yield much. 'There'll be nothing but cuckoo oats this year', said a man in the wet spring of 1889.

6. Hoarse as a cuckoo. 1917: Bridge, *Cheshire Proverbs*, 15.

7. If the cuckoo sings when the hedge is brown, Sell thy horse and buy thy corn. Welsh [You will not be able to afford horse corn]. *If the cuckoo sings when the hedge is green, Keep thy horse and sell thy corn.* Salop [It will be so plentiful that you will have enough and to spare]. 1893: Inwards, *Weather Lore*, 136.

8. In April, come he will; In May, he sings all day; In June he alters his tune; In July, he prepares to fly; In August, go he must; If he stay till September, 'Tis as much as the oldest man can ever remember. Ibid., 24.

9. In April, cuckoo sings her lay; In May, she sings both night and day; In June, she loses her sweet strain; In July, she flies off again. N. Yorks. Ibid., 25.

10. In April the cuckoo can sing her song by rote; In June, out of tune, she cannot sing a note. 1562: Heywood, *Epigr.*, 6th Hund., No. 95.

11. In April the cuckoo shows his bill; In May he sings both night and day; In June he altereth his tune; In July away he'll fly; In August go he must. 1838: Mrs Bray, *Trad. of Devon*, i 326 [slightly varied]. 1846: Denham, *Proverbs*, 42 (Percy S.). 1893: Inwards, *Weather Lore*, 25 [slightly varied].

12. In March The cuckoo starts. In April 'A tune his bill. In May 'A sing all day. In June 'A change his tune. In July Away 'a fly. In August Away's must. In September you'll ollers

remember. In October 'A'll never get over.
East Anglia. 1869: *N. & Q.*, 4th ser, iii 94.

13. March he sits upon his perch; April he soundeth his bell; May he sings both night and day; June he altereth his tune, And July – away to fly. Derby. 1869: *N. & Q.*, 4th ser, iii 94.

14. On the third of April Comes in the cuckoo and nightingale. 1879: J. Hardy, in *Folk–Lore Record*, ii 54, It is a popular saw that …

15. The cuckoo comes in April, Sings a song in May; Then in June another tune, And then she flies away. Glos. 1878: Dyer, *Eng. Folk-Lore*, 56. 1869: Hazlitt, 363, The cuckoo comes in Aperill, and stays the month of May; sings a song at Midsummer, and then goes away. Wilts.

16. The cuckoo comes of mid March, And cucks of mid Aperill; And gauns away of Midsummer month, When the corn begins to fill. 1846: Denham, *Proverbs*, 38 (Percy S.). 1893: Inwards, *Weather Lore*, 20 [with 'Lammas-tide' for 'Midsummer month'].

17. The cuckoo goes to Beaulieu Fair to buy him a petticoat. 1863: Wise, *New Forest*, ch xvi, 'The cuckoo … ', referring to the arrival of the cuckoo about the 15th of April.

18. The cuckoo singeth all the year. 1541: *Sch. House of Women*, l. 321, All beit that few men doo him hear, The cucko singeth all the yeer.

19. The cuckoo sings in April, The cuckoo sings in May, The cuckoo sings at Midsummer, But not upon the day. 1883: Burne, *Shropsh. Folk-Lore*, 222.

20. The first cock of hay Frights the cuckoo away. 1846: Denham, *Proverbs*, 52 (Percy S.). 1879: *Folk-Lore Record*, ii 50. 1924: *Folk-Lore*, xxxv 358.

21. Turn your money when you hear the cuckoo, and you'll never be without it during the year. 1879: *Folk-Lore Record*, ii 90. 1883: Burne, *Shropsh. Folk-Lore*, 219.

22. When the cuckoo comes to the bare thorn, Sell your cow and buy you corn: But when she comes to the full bit, Sell your corn and buy you sheep. 1659: Howell, 16. When the cuckow sitteth on a dry thorn, Sell thy cow, and sow thy corn. 1670: Ray, 43. 1825: Hone, *Ev. Day Book*, i 669. 1893: Inwards, *Weather Lore*, 6.

23. When the cuckoo has pecked up the dirt = Spring. 1830: Forby, *Vocab. E. Anglia*, 430, I will come when the cuckoo, etc. 1893: J. Salisbury, *S.E. Worcs. Gloss.*, 75, In April it is

said that the cuckoo comes and picks up all the dirt. 1904: *Co. Folk-Lore: Northumb.*, 176 (F.L.S.).

24. When the cuckoo … (*see* quot.). 1879: J. Hardy, in *Folk-Lore Record*, ii 58, 'When the cuckoo purls its feathers, the housewife should become chary of her eggs', is a popular saying in many parts of the country.

25. You are like a cuckoo, you have but one song. *c.*1430: Lydgate, *Minor Poems*, 192 (Percy S.), The cokkowe syng can than but oon lay. *c.*1535: *Dialogues of Creatures*, C. (1816), Many folkes … synge allwaye oon songe lyke the cuckowe. 1630: T. Adams, *Works*, 219, He is like the cuckoe, alwaies in one tune. 1681: W. Robertson, *Phraseol. Generalis*, 12, To be still cuckow; or to have always the same song. 1732: Fuller, 5850. 1899: Dickinson, *Cumberland Gloss.*, 144, Ye breed o' the gowk, ye've nae rhyme but ane.

See also **Naked; Nightingale; Ragged; Weirling;** and Welsh ambassador.

Cuckstone. *See* quot. 1735: Pegge, *Kent. Proverbs*, in E.D.S., No. 12, p. 69, If you would goe to a church mis-went, You must go to Cuckstone in Kent. 1849: Halliwell, *Pop. Rhymes, etc.*, 193.

Cucumbers. *See* quot. 1738: Swift, *Polite Convers.*, Dial. II, Madam, I dare not touch it: for they say cucumbers are cold in the third degree. See also **Cool** (2).

Culmstock Fair. *See* quot. 1886: Elworthy, *West Som. Word-Book*, 191 (E.D.S.), Till Culmstock Fair be come and gone, There mid be apples, and mid be none. Cf. **Devil** (43).

Cumberland Jwohny. A satirical appellation for a Cumberland man. 1846–59: *Denham Tracts*, i 166 (F.L.S.).

Cumberland. *See* **Shrewsbury.**

Cunning as a dead pig. 1738: Swift, *Polite Convers.*, Dial. III.

Cunning as Captain Drake. 1678: Ray. 353.

Cunning as Croddock. 1678: Ray, 280. 1846–59: *Denham Tracts*, i 45 (F.L.S.), As cunning as a crafty Cradock. [It is suggested that the saying refers to John Cradock, vicar of Gainford, 1594, who was a high commissioner for Durham, and J.P., etc. He is alleged to have taken bribes and to have been guilty of other underhand practices.]

Cunning as crowder. 1754: *Gent. Mag.*, 211, One saying we have in the Northern parts … *as* *cunning as Crowder* ... and a crowder is a fidler. 1841: Hartshorne, *Salopia Ant.*, 381. 1883: Burne, *Shropsh. Folk-Lore*, 594.

Cunning. *See* **Fox** (4).

Cunning is no burden. 1539: Taverner, *Proverbs*, fo. 22, Cunnynge (they say) is no burthen. 1573: G. Harvey, *Letter-Book*, 121 (Camden S.). 1642: Fuller, *Holy State:* 'The True Gentleman', He knows well that cunning is no burthen to carry. 1732: Fuller, 4182, Skill is no burthen.

Cup. 1. A cup in the pate is a mile in the gait. 1694: Motteux, *Rabelais*, bk iv ch lxv. 1738: Swift, *Polite Convers.*, Dial. II *c*.1791: Pegge, *Derbicisms*, 135 (E.D.S.) [with 'pot' for 'cup'.

2. As merry as cup and can. 1546: Heywood, *Proverbs*, Pt II ch iii, Mery we were as cup and can could holde. 1577: *Misogonus*, II ii, The merye man, with cupp and cann. 1610: Rowlands, *Martin Markall*, 49 (Hunt.Cl.), Where they, as merry as pot and can passe their time in villany and robbery. 1678: Ray, 287.

3. He has got a cup too much. 1678: Ray. 87.

4. There's many a slip between cup and lip. [Saepe audivi inter os atque offam multa intervenire posse. – M. Cato, in Gellius, xiii 17.] 1539: Taverner, *Proverbs*, fo. 15, Many thynges fall betwene the cuppe and the mouth. 1576: Lambarde, *Peramb. of Kent*, 422 (1826), Even as many things happen (according to the proverbe) betweene the cup and the lippe. 1633: Jonson, *Tale of a Tub*, III iv, Many things fall between the cup and lip. 1712: Arbuthnot, *Law a Bott. Pit*, Pt III App. ch iii, Many things happen between the cup and the lip. 1769: Colman, *Man and Wife*, III [as in 1712]. 1840: Barham, *Ing. Legends:* 'Lady Rohesia', There's many a slip 'Twixt the cup and the lip. 1922: Weyman, *Ovington's Bank*, ch vii.

5. To be cup and can = To be 'pals'. 1690: *New Dict. Canting Crew*, sig. C3, As great as cup and can. 1712: Ward, *Poet. Entertainer*, No. *2*, p. 18, Who was as great as cup and kan With the new-marry'd gentleman. 1788: O'Keeffe, *Tantara-rara*, I i, My colonel and he are as great as cup and can.

6. When the cup is fullest, then carry it most carefully. *c*.1320: in *Reliq. Antiquae*, i 112 (1841), 'When the coppe is follest, thenne ber hire feyrest', Quoth Hendyng. 1736: Bailey, *Dict.*, s.v. 'Cup', When the cup's full carry it even.

See also **Such cup.**

Curdly sky will not leave the earth long dry, A; or, will not be twenty-four hours dry. [1736: Bailey, *Dict.*, s.v. 'Curdled', A curdled sky and a painted woman are not of long duration.] 1893: Inwards, *Weather Lore*, 94.

Cure. *See* **Remedy.**

Cured. 1. I have cur'd her from laying [sic] **in the hedge, quoth the goodman when he had wed his daughter.** 1678: Ray, 56. 1732: Fuller, 2604.

2. What can't be cured must be endured. 1377: Langland, *Plowman*, B, x 439, For *qant* OPORTET *vyent en place yl ny ad que* PATI. *c*.1460: *How the Goode Wyfe*, Thynge that may be tyde is for to dowre, my lere childe. 1579: Spenser, *Shep. Cal.*, Sept., ll. 150–4, Better it were, a little to faigne, And clenly couer that cannot be cured, Such ill, as is forced, mought needes be endured. 1639: Massinger, *Unnat. Combat*, II i, What's past help, is Beyond prevention. 1706: Ward, *Hudibras Rediv.*, Pt IX can. xiv, p. 5, 'Tis our prudence to endure With patience what we cannot cure. 1771: Smollett, *Clinker*, in *Works*, iii 191 (1817). 1837: Dickens, *Pickwick*, ch xlviii, What was over couldn't be begun, and what couldn't be cured must be endured. 1851: Borrow, *Lavengro*, ii 54.

Curiosity is endless, restless, and useless, and **Curiosity is ill manners in another's house.** 1732: Fuller, Nos. 1219 and 1220.

Curiosity killed the cat. A comparatively recent warning, from America, against being over inquisitive. 1922: E. O'Neill, *Diff'rent*, ii 252, 'What'd you ask 'em, for instance? ... 'Curiosity killed the cat! Ask me no questions and I'll tell you no lies'. 1939: L.I. Wilder, *By the Shores of Silver Lake*, 'Whatever are you making, Pa? ... Curiosity killed the cat, Pa'.

Curlew. *See* quots. 1866: *N. & Q.*, 3rd ser, x 235, A curlew lean, or a curlew fat, Carries twelve pence upon his back, as they say in North Lincolnshire. [Variant at same reference,] Be it lean, or be it fat, It bears tenpence on its back. 1886: Swainson, *Folk-Lore of Brit. Birds*, 201 (F.L.S.), Be she white or be she black, The curlew has tenpence on her back (Lincolnshire).

Curses come home to roost. *c*.1275: *Prov. of Alfred*, A 84, Eueryches monnes dom to his owere dure churreth (Every man's judgment returns to his own door). *c*.1380: Chaucer, *Parson's Tale*, 41,

And ofte tyme swich cursinge wrongfully retorneth agayn to him that curseth, as a brid that retorneth agayn to his owene nest. 1816: Scott, *Old Mortality*, ch xlii., I have heard a good man say, that a curse was like a stone flung up to the heavens, and maist like to return on the head that sent it. 1894: Northall, *Folk Phrases*, 12 (E.D.S.), Curses, like chickens, come home to roost.

Cursing the weather is bad farming. 1917: Bridge, *Cheshire Proverbs*, 46.

Curst cow. *See* **Cow** (10).

Curst cur must be tied short, A. 1605: Camden, *Remains*, 317 (1870) [with 'dog' for 'cur']. 1670: Ray, 76. 1732: Fuller, 65 [with 'should' for 'must'].

Curtain lectures. [Semper habet lites alternaque jurgia lectus In quo nupta jacet: minimum dormitur in illo. – Juvenal, *Sat.*, vi 267–8.] 1638: *A Curtaine Lecture: as it is read by a Country Farmer's Wife to her Good Man, etc.* [title]. 1649: Quarles, *Virgin Widow*, II, For which I have had already two curtaine-lectures, and a black and blue eye. 1717: Pope, *Wife of Bath*, 165, Or curtain-lectures made a restless night. 1821: Combe, *Syntax in Search of Wife*, can. xxxiv, p. 19, Yes, she may toss her head and hector, But she shall have a curtain lecture. 1846: Jerrold, *Mrs Caudle's Curtain Lectures* [title].

Cushions. *See* quot. I can't identify the proverb to which allusion is made. 1609: Rowlands, *Whole Crew of Kind Gossips*, 12 (Hunt.Cl.), Go to (quoth I) y'are best beat out my braines With cushions now, to make the prouerbe true.

Customer is always right, The. This saying is the motto of Selfridge's Department store in London which opened in 1909; its first occurrence in writing is somewhat later. 1917: B. Pain, *Confessions of Alphonse*, iii, The great success of a restaurant is built up on this principle – *le patron n'a jamais tort* – the customer is always in the right! 1928: C. Sandburg, *Good Morning, America*, 17, Behold the proverbs of a nation … Let one hand wash the other. The customer is always right.

Custom is second nature. *c.*1390: Gower, *Conf. Amantis*, bk vi l 664, For in phisique this I finde, Usage is the seconde kinde. 1422: J. Yonge, *Tr. Of Govt. of Prynces*, 238 (E.E.T.S.), For as ypocras sayth, 'costome is the seconde nature or kynde'. 1558: Bullein, *Govt. of Health*, fo. 98, Custome is like vnto another nature.

1607: Marston, *What You Will*, III. 1712: Addison, *Spectator*, No. 447. 1774: C. Dibdin, *Quaker*, II iii 1817: Scott, *Rob Roy*, ch x, Habit has become a second nature. 1864: Mrs H. Wood, *Trevlyn Hold*, ch xxiv, Habit and use, as we read, are second nature.

Custom makes all things easy. *c.*1598: Deloney, *Gentle Craft*, Pt II ch vi, Labour by custome becommeth easie. *c.*1680: L'Estrange, *Seneca: Epistles*, x, There is nothing so hard, but custom makes it easie to us. 1703: T. Baker, *Tunbridge Walks*, II, Custom … makes every thing familiar. 1732: Fuller, 1225.

Customs, So many countries, so many. *See* **So many countries.**

Custom without reason is but ancient error. 1647: *Countrym. New Commonwealth*, 29, Custome (though never so ancient) without truth, is but an old errour. 1732: Fuller, 1226.

Cut, *verb.* **1. Cut and come again.** 1738: Swift, *Polite Convers.*, Dial. II, I vow, 'tis a noble sirloin, *Neverout.* Ay; here's cut and come again. 1772: Garrick, *Irish Widow*, I i, Give me a slice of a good English surloin; cut and come again. 1848: in Marchant, *Praise of Ale*, 418 (1888), For the boys that can cut and come again Must quaff whole butts of ale.

2. Cut and long tail. *See* **Tag, rag, etc**

3. Cut down an oak. *See* **Oak** (1) and (4).

4. Cut loaf. *See* **Shive**.

5. Cut not the bough. *See* quot. 1528: Tyndale, *Obed. of Christian Men*, 304 (P.S.), 'Cut not the bough that thou standest upon': whose literal sense is, 'Oppress not the commons'.

6. Cut off the head and tail and throw the rest away. 1678: Ray, 346. 1732: Fuller, 1227.

7. Cut or give me the bill. 1732: Fuller, 1228.

8. *See* quot. 1880: Spurgeon. *Ploughman's Pictures*, 36, The old saying is 'Don't cut off your head because it aches'.

9. He has cut his leg = is drunk. 1678: Ray, 87.

10. To be cut for the simples. 1650: in Simpson, *Documents St Paul's*, 148 (Camden S.), The witts of Pauls, or a catalogue of those book-sellers apprentices … which are to be cut of the simples the next spring. 1690: *New Dict. Canting Crew*, sig. L2, He must be cut of the simples, Care must be taken to cure him of his folly. 1738: Swift, *Polite Convers.*, Dial. I, Indeed, Mr Neverout, you should be cut for the simples. 1881: Evans, *Leics. Words*, 239

(E.D.S.), 'A'd ought to be coot for the simples'; a phrase implying that the person spoken of is a fool. Cf. **Battersea**.

11. To cut broad (or large) thongs of another's leather. *c.*1320: in *Reliq. Antiquae*, i 114 (1841), 'Of un-boht hude men kerveth brod thong', Quoth Hendyng. 1484: Caxton, *Aesope*, ii 220 (Jacobs), Ne also it is not honeste to make large thonges of other mennes leder. 1595: *Maroccus Extaticus*, 8 (Percy S.), To cut such large thonges of another mans lether. 1667: L'Estrange, *Quevedo's Visions*, 8 (1904), Those that were in for detraction and calumny, and for cutting large thongs out of other men's leather. 1721: Bailey, *Eng. Dict.*, s.v. 'Thong'. 1853: Trench, *Proverbs*, 100 (1905), On the comparative wastefulness wherewith that which is another's is too often used: *Men cut broad thongs from other men's leather.*

12. To cut large shives of another's loaf. 1630: *Tinker of Turvey*, 31 (Halliwell), By this, the prior perceived that the scull [scullion] had cut a shive [slice] on his loafe. 1670: Ray, 162.

13. To cut off one's nose to spite one's face. [Stultum est vicinum velle ulcisci incendio. – Publ. Syr., 611. Henri iv concut fort bien que détruire Paris, c'étoit, comme on dit, se couper le nez pour faire dépit à son visage. – *c.*1658: Tallemant des Réaux, *Historiettes*, i 17 (1834).] *c.*1560: *Deceit of Women*, I1, He that byteth hys nose of, shameth hys face. 1788: F. Grose, *Dictionary of the Vulgar Tongue* (ed. 2), U3v, He cut off his nose to be revenged of his face, said of one who, to be revenged of his neighbour, has materially injured himself. 1889: R.L.S., *Ballantrae*. ch x, He was in that humour when a man – in the words of the old adage – will cut off his nose to spite his face. 1924: *Times*, 20 Nov., p. 13, col. 1, Continual harassing of the railways, in payment for real or fancied grievances, is much like cutting off one's nose to spite one's face.

14. To cut one's coat according to one's cloth. 1546: Heywood, *Proverbs*, Pt I ch viii, I shall Cut my cote after my cloth when I haue her. 1594: Nashe, *Unfort. Trav.*, in *Works*, v 54 (Grosart), They must shape their cotes good men according to their cloth. 1669: Dryden, *Wild*

Gallant, I ii, I love your wit well, sir; but I must cut my coat according to my cloth. 1720: C. Shadwell, *Sham Prince*, II i, I am a plain dealing man, and am fain to cut my coate according to my cloath. 1869: Spurgeon, *John Ploughman*, ch xii 1926: Inge, *Lay Thoughts*, 187, We must cut our coat according to our cloth and adapt ourselves to changing circumstances.

15. To cut one's comb. 1542: Becon; in *Early Works*, 205 (P.S.), This shall pluck down your comb, as they use to say. 1548: Hall, *Chron.*, 17 (1809), My life stood in ieopardie and my combe was clerely cut. 1584: R. Scot, *Witchcraft*, bk viii ch iii, Since the preaching thereof their combes are cut, and few that are wise regard them. 1642: D. Rogers, *Matrim. Honour*, 45, God cuts their combe, fils their new hopes with new sorrow. 1826: Scott, *Journal*, 13 May, *Malachi* might clap his wings upon this, but, alas! domestic anxiety has cut his comb.

16. To cut one's thong according to one's leather. 1637: R. Whitford, *Werke for Housholders*, sig. F5, Than (after the commune prouerbe) cute your thong after or accordynge vnto your ledder.

17. To cut the grass (or ground) from under the feet. 1567: Fenton, *Bandello*, ii 10 (T.T.), I find a greater fait in my self in suffring an other to cut the earthe frome under my feete. 1576: Pettie, *Petite Pallace*, i 121 (Gollancz), Seeing this young gentleman, as he thought, in great favour ... thought the grass had been cut from under his feet. 1672: Marvell, *Rehearsal Transpr.*, Pt I, in *Works*, iii 195 (Grosart), While you are all this while cutting the grass under his feet, and animating the people against the exercise of his ecclesiastical supremacy. 1760: Murphy, *Way to keep him*, II ii, The grass is cut under my feet if she ever hears a word of it. 1891: Gilbert, *Rosenc. and Guildenstern*, Tabl. II, Thus will you cut the ground from 'neath his feet.

18. To cut the hair. *See* Split hairs.

Cutpurse *A cut-purse is a sure trade, for he hath ready money when his work is done.* 1659: Howell, 8. 1670: Ray, 16.

Cutting out well is better than sewing up well. 1732: Fuller, 1230.

D

Dacre was slain in North Acre, The Lord – at the Battle of Towton, 1461. 1849: Halliwell, *Pop. Rhymes, etc.*, 200. 1868: *Quart. Review*, cxxv. 518, In Saxton churchyard, where is also the tomb of 'The Lord of Dacres Slain in the North Acres', according to the local rhyme.

Daft as a yat [gate] **'at swings beath ways, As.** 1899: Dickinson, *Cumberland Gloss.*, 372.

Daggers drawn, To be at. 1540: Palsgrave, *Acolastus*, sig. F1, We neuer mete togyther, but we be at daggers drawynge. 1618: Harington, *Epigrams*, bk i No. 91, From spightfull words they fell to daggers drawing. 1694: *Terence made English*, 82, The captain and she were almost at daggers drawing when I left 'em. 1736: Bailey, *Dict.*, s.v. 'Dagger', To be at dagger's drawing. 1840: Dickens, *Curiosity Shop*, ch vii, The old man and I will remain at daggers-drawn to the end of our lives. 1867: Mrs H. Wood, *Life's Secret*, Pt I ch ii, I am sure there's no love lost between him and me; we should be at daggers drawn.

Daily cost, and all of it lost, There's a. 1855: Bohn, 524.

Daimport's dog. *See* quots. 1883: Burne, *Shropsh. Folk-Lore*, 595, He talks as Dutch [speaks as unintelligibly] as Daraford's dog. 1917: Bridge, *Cheshire Proverbs*, 144, To talk as Dutch as Daimport's dog.

Dainties. *Who dainties love shall beggars prove.* 1580: Tusser, *Husb.*, 72 (E.D.S.), Who dainties loue, a begger shall proue. 1736: Franklin, *Way to Wealth*, in *Works*, i 447 (Bigelow). 1783: Mrs Cowley, *More Ways than One*, II iv, You know the proverb – those that are dainty ...

Dainty makes dearth. 1590: Spenser, *F.Q.*, I ii 248, So dainty they say maketh derth.

Dainty thing would have a dainty dish, The. 1672: Walker, *Paraem.*, 29 [with 'bit' for 'dish']. 1681: W. Robertson, *Phraseol. Generalis*, 418.

Daisies. *See* Spring (8).

Daisy year. *See* quot. 1901: F. E. Taylor, *Lancs Sayings*, 7, A daisy year's awlus a lazy year (A farmer's saying).

Dally not with money or women. 1640: Herbert, *Jac. Prudentum.* 1669: *New Help to Discourse*, 310.

Dalmanazar, As bright as. 1880: Courtney, *W. Cornwall Words*, xiii (E.D.S.). L

Dalton bell-rope, Like. 1846–59: *Denham Tracts*, i 86 (F.L.S.), Like Dalton bell-rope. That is, a deed half-done. A story is told how, after many vestry meetings holden by the principal inhabitants of this place to take into consideration the propriety of purchasing a new rope for the one bell of their parish church, the churchwardens and ratepayers at last came to the conclusion that the old one should be spliced.

Dam. 1. The dam of that was whisker. Said of a great lie. 1678: Ray, 89.

2. Where the dam leaps over, the kid follows. 1732: Fuller, 5662.

Dame Hockaday's hen, As disconsolate as. Corn. 1869: Hazlitt, 61.

Dance, *verb.* **1. He dances well to whom fortune pipes.** 1578: Florio, *First Fruites*, fo. 25, He daunseth wel, vnto whom fortune pipeth. 1605: Camden, *Remains*, 323 (1870). 1670: Ray, 77. 1732: Fuller, 1832 [with 'merrily' for 'well'].

2. He'll dance to nothing but his own pipe. 1732: Fuller, 2423.

3. If you dance you must pay the fiddler. 1681: in *Roxb. Ballads*, v 67 (B.S.).

4. I'll make him dance without a pipe. = I'll do him an injury, and he shall not know how. 1678: Ray, 71. 1732: Fuller, 2639.

5. They who dance are thought mad by those who hear not the music. Spoken of as an 'old proverb'. 1927: *Times*, 16 Feb., p. 15, col. 4.

6. To dance as another pipes. *c.*1480: *Early Miscellanies*, 25 (Warton Cl., 1855), I wylle dance whylle the world wylle pype. 1546: Heywood, *Proverbs*, Pt II ch xi, Whan fooles pype, by auctoritee he maie daunce. 1593: Giffard, *Dial. on Witches, etc.*, 65 (Percy S.), Ignorant people, which are ready to beleeve all that he telleth, and to dance after his pipe. 1642: D. Rogers, *Matrim. Honour*, 357, If they moove, must not all inferior ones dance after their pipe?

7. To dance attendance on one. Before 1529: Skelton, *Why come ye not*, ll. 625–6, And syr ye must daunce attendaunce And take pacient sufferaunce. 1594: Shakespeare, *Rich. III*, III vii, Welcome, my lord: I dance attendance here. 1645: Howell, *Letters*, bk i § iii No. xiii, Going one morning to speak with the Duke, and having danc'd attendance a long time. 1742: Fielding, *Andrews*, bk ii ch xvi, The man hath danced attendance for about a month. 1923: Lucas, *Advisory Ben*, § vi p. 24, The young men ... were dancing attendance upon creatures more capricious.

8. To dance Barnaby. 1664: Cotton, *Scarronides*, bk i l. 189, Bounce, cries the porthole; out they fly, And make the world dance Barnaby. 1727: in *Roxb. Ballads*, viii 270 (B.S.), Speak, and we'll let your thunder fly, And make the world dance Barnaby.

9. To dance in a net. 1532: More, *Confut. of Tyndale*, cxxvii, I go so bare dawnsyng naked in a net. 1587: Greene, in *Works*, vi 181 (Grosart), At last being Venus scholler, and therefore daring with hir to dance in a net. 1605: Chapman, *All Fools*, II, Think not you dance in nets [think not you are undetected]. 1670: Ray, 6. 1821: Scott, *Kenilworth*, ch iv, Thou canst not dance in a net, and they not see thee.

10. To dance to every man's pipe (or **whistle**). 1670: Ray, 170. 1732: Fuller, 2644, I will not dance to every fool's pipe. 1880: Spurgeon, *Ploughman's Pictures*, 25, If we dance to every fiddle we shall soon be lame in both legs.

11. When you go to dance, take heed whom you take by the hand. 1639: Clarke, 24. 1670: Ray, 77. 1732: Fuller, 5614.

12. You'll dance at the end of a rope without teaching. 1732: Fuller, 6022.

13. You will neither dance nor hold the candle. Ibid., No. 6013.

Dancing bear. *As many tricks* (*antics*, etc.) *as a dancing bear.* 1670: Ray, 163, He hath as many tricks as a dancing bear. 1732: Fuller, 1862 [as in 1670]. 1738: Swift, *Polite Convers.*, Dial. I, I wish you would be quiet, you have more tricks than a dancing bear. 1886: Elworthy, *West Som. Word-Book*, 374 (E.D.S.), He has got more antics than a dancing bear. This is one of the commonest of sayings. 1894: Northall, *Folk Phrases*, 8 (E.D.S.), As full of megrims as a dancing bear.

Dancing days are done, His (or **My**). 1658: Flecknoe, *Enigm. Characters*, 60, His dancing dayes are never done. 1738: Swift, *Polite Convers.*, Dial. I, I doubt her dancing days are over. 1816: Austen, *Emma*, ch xxxviii, My dancing days are over.

Dancing. *They love dancing well that dance among thorns.* 1639: Clarke, 326. 1670: Ray, 77.

1732: Fuller, 4966 [with 'barefoot upon thorns' instead of 'among thorns'].

Danger and **Dangers. 1. A danger foreseen is half avoided.** 1658: R. Franck, *Northern Memoirs*, 95 (1821), Dangers foreseen are the sooner prevented. 1732: Fuller, 67.

2. Better pass a danger once, than be always in fear. 1670: Ray, 9.

3. Danger and delight grow on one stock. 1580: Lyly, *Euphues*, 226 (Arber) [with 'stalke' for 'stock']. 1732: Fuller, 1231.

4. Danger is next neighbour to security. Ibid., No. 1233.

5. Dangers are overcome by dangers. 1651: Herbert, *Jac. Prudentum*, 2nd ed., Danger itself the best remedy for danger. 1732: Fuller, 1232.

6. He that fears danger in time seldom feels it. 1611: Cotgrave, s.v. 'Asseur', He that feares, is assured. 1732: Fuller, 2099.

7. The danger past God is forgotten. 1670: Ray, 6, The danger past and God forgotten. 1732: Fuller, 1234.

Dare not for his (or **my**) **ears, He** (or **I**). 1607: Topsell, *Serpents*, 640 (OED), The yonger not daring for their ears to break into their fathers lands. 1678: Ray, 240 (He). 1754: Berthelson, *Eng.-Danish Dict.*, s.v. 'Ears' (I).

Dark as a wolf's mouth. 1823: Scott, *St Ronan's*, ch xxxvi 1828: Scott, *Fair Maid*, ch xxiv, The moon is quite obscured, and the road as black as a wolf's mouth. 1901: F. E. Taylor, *Lancs Sayings*, 1, As dark as a fox's meawth. 1926: Phillpotts, *Peacock House*, 222, 'Twas blowing and raining that night and dark as a wolf's mouth.

Dark as a Yule (or **Martinmas**) **midnight.** 1814: Scott, *Waverley*, ch xlviii, He may look as black as midnight at Martinmas. 1846: Denham, *Proverbs*, 62 (Percy S.), As dark as a Yule midnight. 1904: *Co. Folk-lore: Northumb.*, 179 (F.L.S.) [as in 1846].

Dark as black hogs. 1869: FitzGerald, *Sea Words and Phrases*, 2.

Dark as Newgate knocker. *See* Newgate.

Dark (or **Black**) **as pitch.** *c.*1300: in *Vernon MS.*, 354 (E.E.T.S.), As blac as eny pich he was. *c.*1380: *Sir Ferumbras*, 81 (E.E.T.S.), Than lai he thar so blac so pych. 1485: Caxton, *Charles the Grete*, 165 (E.E.T.S.), He is as blacke as pytche boylled. 1598: R. Tofte. *Alba*, 39 (Grosart), And darke as pitch shall shew the glistering sunne. 1666: Pepys, *Diary*, 18 Jan., Got home well by coach, though as dark as pitch. 1714: Ozell, *Molière*, iii 217, 'Tis as dark as pitch. 1824: Scott, *Redgauntlet*, ch xvi, All the windows were dark as pitch. 1890: P. H. Emerson, *Wild Life*, 42, The wind roared … It was as dark as pitch.

Dark as the devil's mouth. 1826: Scott, *Woodstock*, ch xii, It is dark as the devil's mouth.

Dark. *See also* **Black.**

Darkest hour is just before the dawn, The. 1650: Fuller, *Pisgah Sight*, bk ii ch xi, It is always darkest just before the day dawneth. 1889: R.L.S., *Letters*, iii 245 (Tusitala ed.), It is always darkest before dawn. 1912: Lucas, *London Lav.*, ch xvi, I'll pull this round safe enough. Things look blackest before the dawn, don't you know.

Darlington. 1. Darnton, where the wind once blew a dog's tongue out. 1846–59: *Denham Tracts*, i 80 (F.L.S.).

2. Dirty Darlington. 1658: R. Franck, *North. Memoirs*, 264 (1821), One course directs us to dirty Darlington. 1846–59: *Denham Tracts*, i 80, Dirty Darnton or Darnton-in-the-dirt.

3. To take Darnton Trod, or May take Darnton Trod. Ibid., i 78.

Darnell for dim sight 1597: Gerarde, *Herbal*, Darnell hurteth the eyes and maketh them dim … and hereupon it seemeth that the old proverbe came, that such as are dim-sighted should be said to eate of darnell. 1917: Bridge, *Cheshire Proverbs*, 49 [spelt 'Darnall' and referred to Cheshire village of Darnhall].

Darnford's dog. *See* **Daimport's dog.**

Darnton. *See* **Darlington.**

Dart, River. *See* quots. 1850: *N. &Q.*, 1st ser, ii 511, River of Dart, oh, river of Dart, Every year thou claim'st a heart. 1897: Norway, *H. and B. in Devon, etc.*, 85 [as in 1850]. 1908: *Folk-Lore*, xix 171, 'The river Dart every year claims its heart' is a South of England saying. Cf. **Don, River.**

Dartford. *See* **Sutton.**

Dasnell dawcock sit among the doctors, The. 1634: Withals, *Dict.*, 558, The dosnell dawcock comes dropping in among the doctors [given as translation of *Graculus inter musas, anser strepit inter olores*]. 1659: Howell, 15 [as in 1634]. 1670: Ray, 217.

Daughter. 1. Daughters and dead fish are no keeping wares. 1732: Fuller, 1235.

2. He that would the daughter win. Must with the mother first begin. 1670: Ray, 49. 1732: Fuller, 6266.

3. When the daughter is stolen, shut Peppergate. 1662: Fuller, *Worthies*, i 291 (1840). 1790: Grose, *Prov. Gloss.*, s.v. 'Cheshire'. 1825: Hone, *Ev. Day Book*, i 430. 1917: Bridge, *Cheshire Proverbs*, 151.

Dava, As ancient as the floods of. 1880: Courtney, *W. Cornwall Words*, xiii (E.D.S.).

Davenham steeple the centre of Cheshire within three barley-corns. 1917: Bridge, *Cheshire Proverbs*, 49.

Davenports. *See* **Cheshire** (7).

Davie Debet = Debt personified, or a bailiff. 1575: Gascoigne, *Posies*, in *Works*, i 65 (Cunliffe), Till Davie Debet in thy parler stand. 1583: Melbancke, *Philotinus*, sig. Q3, Dauie debte stoode watching with a mace at the doore.

Dawes Cross. 1579: *Marr. of Wit and Wisdom*, 28 (SH.S.), Hold heare! thou shalt not lease all; thy purse shall not come home weeping for lose; and as for the, thou shalt be commist to Dawes crosse. 1583: Melbancke, *Philotinus*, sig. Y1, You may sooner be doctors at Dawes crosse. 1596: Nashe, *Haue with you*, in *Works*, iii 16 (Grosart), To grant them their absolute graces, to commence at Dawes Crosse.

Daws. *See* **Norwich.**

Day. 1. A day after Doomsday = Greek kalends. 1540: Palsgrave, *Acolastus*, sig. V1, At the Grekish calendes … or a daye after domesday.

2. A day to come shows longer than a year that's gone. 1732: Fuller, 68.

3. As the day lengthens so the cold strengthens. 1631: E. Pellham, *God's Power*, 27, The New year now begun, as the Days began to lengthen, so the Cold began to strengthen. 1639: in *Berkeley MSS.*, iii 30 (1885), When the daies begin to lengthen the cold begins to strengthen. 1646: Browne, *Pseudo. Epi.*, bk iv ch xiii, We observe the cold to augment, when the daies begin to increase. 1732: Fuller, 6140. 1893: Inwards, *Weather Lore*, 11. *See also* **New Year.**

4. As the days begin to shorten, The heat begins to scorch them. 1893: Inwards, 8.

5. As the days grow longer, The storms grow stronger. 1827: Hone, *Table-Book*, 667. 1893: Inwards, 7.

6. Be the day never so long, at length cometh evensong. *c.*1390: Gower, *Conf. Amantis*, bk vi l.578, Bot hou so that the dai be long, The derke nyht comth ate laste. 1555: Hawes, *Past, of*

Pleasure, 207 (Percy S.), For though the day be never so longe, At last the belles ringeth to evensonge. 1563: Foxe, *Actes, etc.*, vii 346 (1828), His saying was that, although the day was never so long, yet at the last it ringeth to evensong. 1670: Ray, 77. 1732: Fuller, 6132.

7. Day and night; sun and moon; air and light; every one must have, and none can buy. 1732: Fuller, 1237. 1846: Denham, *Proverbs*, 5 (Percy S.).

8. No day passeth without some grief. 1670: Ray, 6.

9. The day is short and the work is long. *c.*1400: *Beryn*, l.3631 (E.E.T.S.).

10. The day that you do a good thing, there will be seven new moons. 1732: Fuller, 4468.

11. 'Tis day still while the sun shines. 1639: Clarke, 294. 1670: Ray, 77.

12. To come a day after the fair. 1546: Heywood, *Proverbs*, Pt I ch viii, A daie after the fayre comth this remors. 1596: Nashe, *Haue with you*, in *Works*, iii 205 (Grosart), A day after the faire when he is hangd Haruey takes him in hand. 1676: Etheredge, *Man of Mode*, III i, I must confess, madam, you came a day after the fair. 1864: Mrs H. Wood, *Trevlyn Hold*, ch xxxiv, They must make good speed, unless they would be 'a day too late for the fair'. 1910: H. James, *Letters*, ii 164 (1920). 1913: E. M. Wright. *Rustic Speech, etc.*, 79, There is an old English proverb: He's a fond chapman that comes the day after the fair.

13. To see day at a little hole. 1546: Heywood, *Proverbs*, Pt I ch x, I see daie at this little hole. *c.*1598: Deloney, *Gentle Craft*, Pt II ch ii, I perceiue you can spie day at a little hole. 1691: J. Wilson, *Belphegor*, IV ii, Men of my station can see day at a little hole – letters make words, and circumstances things! 1714: Ozell, *Molière*, v 153, In love, everything speaks, and in this case daylight is to be spy'd thro' a little hole. 1859: Smiles, *Self-Help*, 391 (1869), As daylight can be seen through very small holes, so little things will illustrate a person's character.

14. What a day may bring, a day may take away. 1732: Fuller, 5475.

Dead, *adj*. **1. A dead wife's the best goods in a man's house.** 1678: Ray, 58. 1738: Swift, *Polite Convers.*, Dial. I, A dead wife under the table is the best goods in a man's house.

2. A dead woman will have four to carry her forth. 1678: Ray, 354.

3. As dead as a door-nail (or **door-tree**). *c.*1350: *Will. Palerne*, 29 (E.E.T.S.), I am ded as dore-nail. 1596: Nashe, *Haue with you*, in *Works*, iii 182 (Grosart), Wee'l strike it as dead as a dore-naile. 1598: Shakespeare, 2 *Henry IV*, V iii 1700: Farquhar, *Constant Couple*, IV ii, I can't tell whether he be dead in law: but he's dead as a door-nail. 1801: Lamb, *Letters*, i 223 (1908), 'The Albion' is dead – dead as nail in door. 1843: Dickens, *Carol*, Stave 1. 1907: De Morgan, *Alice-for-Short*, ch xii, She may be as dead as a door-nail.

4. As dead as a herring. 1600: Shakespeare, *Merry Wives*, II, iii By gar, de herring is no dead so as I vill kill him. 1638: Nabbes, *Tott. Court*, I v, Is shee quite dead? Dead as a herring, sir. 1748: Smollett, *Rod. Random*, ch iv, Ay, ay, I'll warrant him as dead as a herring. 1834: Marryat, *P. Simple*, ch xxix 1880: R.L.S. and Henley, *Deacon Brodie*, IV vii iv, Stabbed to the heart and dead as a herring!

5. As dead as a nit. 1883: Burne. *Shropsh. Folk-Lore*, 594. 1887: Parish and Shaw, *Dict. Kent. Dialect*, 108 (E.D.S.), 'Dead as a nit' is a common expression. 1890: P. H. Emerson, *Wild Life*, 13 *n.*, Dead as nits, a common Norfolk expression. 1923: *Folk-Lore*, xxxiv 329 (Oxfordsh.).

6. As dead as Chelsea. 1823: Egan's Grose's *Class. Dict. of Vulgar Tongue*, s.v. 'Chelsea', To get Chelsea; to obtain the benefit of [Chelsea] hospital. 'Dead Chelsea, by God!' An exclamation uttered by a grenadier at Fontenoy, on having his leg carried away by a cannon ball. [The phrase is not in 1st ed. of Grose, 1785.] 1833: *National Mag.*, quoted in *N. & Q.*, 5th ser, xii 29, Dead as Chelsea.

7. As dead as ditchwater. *See* **Flat as ditchwater.**

8. As dead as mutton. *c.*1770: Bickerstaffe, *Spoiled Child*, II ii, Thus let me seize my tender bit of lamb – (*aside*) there I think I had her as dead as mutton, *c.*1816: in Farmer's *Musa Pedestris*, 80, Your Larry will be dead as mutton, 1860: Reade, *Cl. and Hearth*, ch xxiv 1914: Shaw, 'Parents and Children', in *Misalliance, etc.*, p. vii, The old Bernard Shaw is as dead as mutton.

9. At a dead lift. 1551: R. Robinson, tr. More's *Utopia*, 76 (Arber), Whiche they graunte to be not so good as horses at a sodeyne brunte, and (as we saye) at a deade lifte. 1614: B. Rich, *Honestie of This Age*, 43 (Percy S.), Shee … hath … twenty companions at a becke, that will stick to her at a dead lift. 1640: Shirley, *St Pat. for Ireland*, IV ii, They talk of woman's wit at a dead lift. 1712: Motteux, *Quixote*, Pt I bk iii ch iv 1881: Evans, *Leics. Words, etc.*, 136 (E.D.S.), A dead-lift is a lift or effort that will raise a weight by sheer strength without the intervention of any artificial means.

10. Dead bee. *See* **Bee** (2).

11. Dead dog. *See* **Dog** (25).

12. Dead folks are past fooling. 1732: Fuller, 1238.

13. Dead men bite not (or **do no harm**). 1548: Hall, *Chron.*, 128 (1809), A prouerbe, whiche saith, a dead man doth no harme. 1596: Harington, *Metam. of Ajax*, 64 (1814), I care not, seeing thou art dead, *Mortui non mordent*. 1613: B.&F., *Coxcomb*, II ii, Knock out her brains! And then she'll never bite. 1732: Fuller, 1239, Dead folks can't bite. 1816: Scott, *Old Mortality*, ch xxxiv, Take him [dead man] away now, then, you gaping idiot, and see that he does not bite you, to put an old proverb to shame. 1883: R.L.S., *Treasure I*, ch xi, 'Dead men don't bite,' says he.

14. Dead men tell no tales. 1664: J. Wilson, *Andron. Commenius*, I iv, 'Twere best To knock them i' th' head … The dead can tell no tales. 1681: Dryden, *Span. Friar*, IV i 1795: Mrs Cowley, *The Town*, I ii, The dead do tell no tales! 1860: Reade, *Cl. and Hearth*, ch xxv. 1866 Wilkie Collins, *Armadale* … in five minutes' time the yacht will be scuttled, and the cabin hatch will be nailed down on you. Dead men tell no tales; and the sailing-master's notion is to leave proofs afloat that the vessel has foundered with all on board. 1901: W. James, in *Letters*, ii 154 (1920), We never know what ends may have been kept from realisation, for the dead tell no tales.

15. Dead mice feel no cold. 1678: Ray, 123, A dead mouse feels no cold. 1732: Fuller, 1241.

16. He demands tribute of the dead.

17. He chastises the dead.

18. He paints the dead. All three – 1813: Ray, 75.

19. It's a sad burden to carry a dead man's child. 1655: Fuller, *Church Hist.*, bk ii § v (29), Our women have a proverb, 'It is a sad burden …' 1670: Ray, 53. 1732: Fuller, 2873 [with 'for a woman' after 'burden'].

20. Speak not of a dead man at the table. 1640: Herbert, *Jac. Prudentum*.

21. The dead, and only they, should do nothing. 1732: Fuller, 4469.

22. The dead have few friends. 1303: Brunne, *Handl. Synne*, l. 6302, For the dedë hath few frendys. *c.*1320: in *Reliq. Antiquae*, i 116 (1841), 'Frendles ys the dede,' Quoth Hendyng. 1611: Cotgrave, s.v. 'Ami', The dead have no friends, the sick but faint ones. Before 1701: Sedley, *Ballad*, in *Works*, i 92 (1778), Justice has bid the world adieu, And dead men have no friends.

23. To get a f—t of a dead man. 1546: Heywood, *Proverbs*, Pt I ch xi, I shall … as soone as a farthyng of him. 1605: Chapman, etc., *Eastw. Hoe*, IV ii 1611: Cotgrave, s.v. 'Pet'. 1681: W. Robertson, *Phraseol. Generalis*, 471.

24. To wait for dead men's shoes. 1530: Palsgrave, 644, Thou lookest after deed mens shoes. 1597: Hall, *Satires*, bk ii sat. v, Or if thee list not waite for dead men's shoon. 1631: Mabbe, *Celestina*, 24 (T.T.), He that lookes after dead-mens shooes, may chance to goe barefoote. 1714: Ozell, *Molière*, iii 194. 1757: Murphy, *Upholsterer*, I ii, You have very good pretensions; but then its waiting for dead men's shoes. 1912: Lucas, *London Lav.*, ch iv, 'It's ill waiting for dead men's shoes,' Naomi quoted.

25. To work for a dead horse. 1659: in *Harl. Miscell.*, v 299 (1745), I shall be content to play at any game, but shall be unwilling to play for a dead horse. 1712: Motteux, *Quixote*, Pt II ch lxxi, It shall never be said of me … that I thought it working for a dead horse, because I am paid beforehand. 1785: Grose, *Class. Dict. Vulgar Tongue*, s.v. 'Dead Horse', … to work for wages already paid. 1853: Cooper, *Sussex Provincialisms*, 41, To work out a dead horse is to work out an old debt. 1886: Elworthy, *West Som. Word-Book*, 186 (E.D.S.), Work done in redemption of debt is called working out the dead-horse.

26. When I am dead make me a caudle. 1732: Fuller, 5558.

27. You'll not believe a man is dead, till you see his brains out. 1678: Ray, 67. 1732: Fuller, 6031.

Deadly disease neither physician nor physic can ease, A. 1629: *Book of Meery Riddles*, Prov. 56.

Deaf. 1. As deaf as a beetle. 1867: *N. & Q..*, 3rd ser, xi 34. 1876: Leveson-Gower, *Surrey*

Provincialisms, 86 (E.D.S.), That there horse is as deaf as a beetle. 1887: Parish and Shaw, *Dict. of Kent. Dialect*, 11 (E.D.S.), Beetle. A wooden mallet … The phrase – 'as death [deaf] as a beetle', refers to this mallet, and is equivalent to … 'as deaf as a post'. 1923: *Folk-Lore*, xxxiv 329 (Oxfordsh.).

2. As deaf as a door. 1599: Breton, in *Works*, ii *c* 49 (Grosart), Hee is as deafe as a doore.

3. As deaf as a door-nail. 1572: T. Wilson, *Disc, upon Usury*, 224 (1925), The userer is as deafe as a doore nayle. 1589: L. Wright, *Display of Dutie*, 10. 1633: Draxe, 38. 1837: Mrs Palmer, *Devonsh. Dialect*, 42, As deave [deaf] as a door-nail. 1901: F. E. Taylor, *Lancs Sayings*, 25, He's as deeof as a dur nail.

4. As deaf as a haddock. 1882: Jago, *Gloss. of Cornish Dialect*, 151, There is a term also, 'defe as a haddock', meaning very deaf. 1886: Elworthy, *West Som. Word-Book*, 310 (E.D.S.), We seldom hear … any other than 'so deef's a 'addick'.

5. As deaf as a post. 1575: Churchyard, *Chippes*, 136 (Collier), I thereat seemde dumme and deaffe as post, 1720: Gay, *Poems*, ii 280 (Underhill), Till you grow tender as a chick, I'm dull as any post. 1777: Sheridan, *Sch. for Scandal*, I i, Who you know is as deaf as a post. 1849: Brontë, *Shirley*, ch i.

6. As deaf as an adder. 1605: Chapman, etc., *Eastw. Hoe*, V ii, I will be deafe as an adder. 1618: Minshull, *Essayes, etc.*, 37 (1821). 1702: T. Brown, in *Works*, ii 246 (1760), I would rather chuse to be as deaf as an adder. 1821: Scott, *Pirate*, ch xxviii, As deaf as the adder to the voice of the charmer, 1839: Dickens, *Nickleby*, ch xlvii.

7. Deaf nuts = Nuts without kernels. [1648: Herrick, *Hesp.*, No. 670, As deaf as nuts. 1686: G. Stuart, *Joco-Serious Discourse*, 42, Twou'd vex a man to th' very guts, To sit seaven year cracking deaf nuts.] (*a*) *No deaf nuts. See* quots. 1808: Scott, in Lockhart's *Life*, ii 231, The appointments of our historian are £300 a year – no deaf nuts. 1825: Scott, *Journal*, 5 Dec., I received … a bill for, £750, *no deaf nuts.* 1868: Atkinson, *Cleveland Gloss.*, 138, He does not look as if he lived upon deeaf nuts. 1899: Dickinson, *Cumberland Gloss.*, 95, 'He cracks nea deef-nuts' – said of a well-fed person or animal. 1917: Bridge, *Cheshire Proverbs*, 65, He doesna crack many deaf nuts, (*b*) *To give a*

ha'porth of deaf nuts = A worthless gift. Shropsh. saying. 1917: Bridge, *Cheshire Proverbs*, 65.

8. Deaf men are quick-eyed and distrustful. 1732: Fuller, 1242.

9. Deaf men go away with the blame. 1670: Ray, 6 [with 'injury' for 'blame']. 1732: Fuller, 1243.

10. None so deaf as those that won't hear. 1546: Heywood, *Proverbs*, Pt II ch ix, Who is so deafe or so blynde, as is hee That wilfully will nother here nor see? 1611: Cotgrave, s.v. 'Sourd', No man's worse deafe then he that will not heare. 1714: Ozell, *Molière*, iii 91, 'Tis a true saying, that none are so deaf as those that won't hear. 1869: Spurgeon, *John Ploughman*, ch ii 1905: E. G. Hayden, *Travels round our Village*, 268, 'He! he!' cackled Joane … 'ther be none sa deaf as them who wun't hear!'

11. To be deaf of that ear. 1598: Chamberlain, *Letters*, 12 (Camden S.), I feare we are deafe on that side. 1654: Gayton, *Pleasant Notes Don Q.*, 141, The Don hearing but of one eare. 1754: Berthelson, *Eng.-Danish Dict.*, s.v. 'Deaf', He is deaf of that ear. 1814: Scott, *Waverley*, ch xxxvi, Ye are deaf as adders upon that side of the head.

Deal, Kent. **1. Deal, Dover and Harwich, The devil gave with his daughter in marriage; And by a codicil to his will, He added Helvoet and the Brill.** 1785: Grose, *Class. Dict. Vulgar Tongue*, s.v. 'Devil's Daughter's Portion'

2. Deal savages, Canterbury parrots, Dover sharps, and Sandwich carrots. 1735: Pegge. *Kent. Proverbs*, in E.D.S., No. 12, p. 69.

See also **Dover** (1).

Deals in the world, needs four sieves, He that. 1640: Herbert, *Jac. Prudentum.*

Deansgate, As long as. Manchester. 1869: Hazlitt, 66.

Dear. 1. As dear as cinnamon. Derby. 1889: *Folk-Lore Journal*, vii 291.

2. As dear as saffron. Newlyn, W. Corn., 19th cent. (Mr C. Lee).

3. As dear as two eggs a penny. 1678: Ray, 282.

4. Dear bought. *See* **Far fetched**.

5. Dear child it behoveth to learn. *c*.1320: in *Reliq. Antiquae*, i 110 (1841), 'Luef child lore bynoveth'; Quoth Hendyng. 1377: Langland, *Plowman*, B, v 38, That the leuere childe the more lore bihoueth. *c*.1460: *Good Wyfe wold a*

Pylgremage, l. 11, That lothe chylde lore be-howytt, and leve chyld moche more.

6. It's a dear collop that is cut out of one's own flesh. 1546: Heywood, *Proverbs*, Pt I ch x, For I haue heard saie, it is a deere colup That is cut out of thòwne fleshe. 1639: Clarke, 240, It's a deare collop that's taken out of the flesh.

Dearth always begins. *See* **England** (1).

Dearths foreseen come not. 1640: Herbert, *Jac. Prudentum.*

Death. 1. Death dealeth doubtfully. 1669: *Politeuphuia*, 183.

2. Death devours lambs as well as sheep. 1620: Shelton, *Quixote*, Pt II ch xx 1732: Fuller, 1245.

3. Death is the grand leveller. Ibid., No. 1250.

4. Death keeps no calendar. 1640: Herbert, *Jac. Prudentum.* 1670: Ray, 6. 1732: Fuller, 1251.

5. Death squares all accounts. 1653: Shirley, *Cupid and Death*, in *Works*, vi 357 (Dyce), Death quits all scores. 1685–6: Cotton, *Montaigne*, bk i ch vii, 'Tis a saying, 'That death discharges us of all our obligations'. 1714: Ozell, *Molière*, iii 87, But Death settles all things. 1815: Scott, *Mannering*, ch xxiii, The Laird's dead – aweel, death pays a' scores, 1860: Reade, *Cl. and Hearth*, ch xcii., Death squares all accounts. Cf. **Die** (3).

6. Death when it comes will have no denial. 1611: Cotgrave, s.v. 'Appel', Death admits no appeale. 1681: W. Robertson, *Phraseol. Generalis*, 432.

7. Death's day is Doomsday. 1579: Lyly, *Euphues*, 181 (Arber), Euery ones deathes daye is his doomes daye. 1732: Fuller, 1255.

8. Men fear death as children do to go in the dark. 1659: Howell, 10 (8). 1670: Ray, 7. 1732: Fuller, 3392.

9. Thou hast death in thy house, and dost bewail another's. 1640: Herbert, *Jac. Prudentum.*

Debt. 1. Debt is an evil conscience. 1732: Fuller, 1257.

2. Debt is better than death. 1659: Howell, 6.

3. Debt is the worst poverty. 1732: Fuller, 1258. 1880: Spurgeon, *Ploughman's Pictures*, 19, Too often debt is the worst kind of poverty, because it breeds deceit.

4. Speak not of my debts unless you mean to pay them. 1640: Herbert, *Jac. Prudentum.* 1875: A. B. Cheales, *Proverb. Folk-lore*, 88, Don't talk of my debts unless you mean to pay them.

5. To pay the debt to nature. [1289: in *Lanercost Chron.*, 131 (Maitland Cl.), Quo dicto, debitum naturae statim exsolvit et in Christo quievit.] 1494: Fabyan, *Chron.*, II xli. 28 (OED), Fynally he payde the dette of nature. 1563: Becon, *Reliques of Rome*, fo. 51, When he was an hundred yeare olde, he payed nature her dutye. 1606: Shakespeare, *Macbeth*, V viii, Your son, my Lord, has paid a soldier's debt. 1758–67: Sterne, *Trist. Shandy*, vol v ch iii, *To die*, is the great debt and tribute due unto nature. 1783: Johnson, *Letters*, ii 331 (Hill), Mrs Williams, from mere inanition, has at length paid the great debt to nature. 1845: Planché, *Extravag.*, iii 26 (1879), In peace to pass, with Jason, all her days, Till he or she the debt o' natur' pays. *See also* **Sin**, *subs.* (3).

Debtors are liars. 1640: Herbert, *Jac. Prudentum.* 1869: Spurgeon, *John Ploughman*, ch xii, Debtors can hardly help being liars.

Deceit. 1. Deceit, weeping, spinning, God hath give to women kindly, while they may live. 1809: Hazlitt, 109 … This is a paraphrase of the old leonine verse – Fallere, flere, nere dedit Deus in muliere.

2. There's no deceit in a bag pudding. 1678: Ray, 193.

3. There's no deceit in a brimmer. 1660: A. Brome, *Poems*, in Chalmers, vi 653 (1810), Then quaff it round, No deceit in a brimmer is found. 1738: Swift, *Polite Convers.*, Dial. II. 1750: R. Heath, *Account of Scilly*, 443, Upon the silver mugs in the town of Liskerd it is written, *Qui fallit in poculis, fallit in omnibus*, there is no deceit in a bumper.

Deceive. 1. If a man deceive me once, shame on him; but if he deceive me twice, shame on me. 1736: Bailey, *Dict.*, s.v.

2. To deceive a deceiver is no deceit. *c.*1580: Fulwell *Ars Adulandi.* sig. G3. 1631: Mabbe, *Celestina*, 264 (T.T.), For he that deceives the deceiver, you know what I meane. 1669: *Polieuphuia*, 293. 1732: Fuller, 1261, Deceiving of a deceiver is no knavery.

Deceiver. *See* **Guiler**.

December. 1. *December cold with snow, good for rye*; 2. *December's frost and January's flood Never boded the husbandman's good*; and 3. *Thunder in December presages fine weather* – all in 1893, Inwards, *Weather Lore*, 38. *See also* **August; May, F** (16); and **October** (5).

Deed well done pleaseth the heart, A. *c.*1460: *How the Good Wife*, l. 110, A dede wele done, herte it whemyth [pleaseth].

Deeds are fruits, words are but leaves. 1633: Draxe, 40. 1670: Ray, 7. 1732: Fuller, 1263.

Deeds are males, words are females. 1578: Florio, *First Fruites*, fo. 32. 1581: T. Howell, *Devises*, 31 (1906), Women are wordes, men are deedes. 1645: Howell, *Letters*, bk i § i No. xxxix 1732: Fuller, 5814, Words are for women; actions for men. 1894: Northall, *Folk Phrases*, 12 (E.D.S.), Deeds are Johns, and words Nans. *Warcs.* A local version of the proverb – 'Deeds are males, but words females'.

Deeds not words. 1546: Heywood, *Proverbs*, Pt II ch v, Deede without woords shall driue him to the wall. Before 1681: J. Lacy, *Sawny the Scot*, II.

Deemills. *If thou hadst the rent of Dee mills, thou wouldst spend it.* Cheshire. 1670: Ray, 171. 1790: Grose, *Prov. Gloss.*, s.v. 'Cheshire'. 1917: Bridge, *Cheshire Proverbs*, 77.

Deem [Judge] **not my deeds.** *See* quot. 15th cent.: in *Reliq. Antiquae*, i 205 (1841), Deme noth my dedis, thogh thyne be noght; Say whate thow wilte, knowyst noth my thowght.

Deem the best till the truth be tried out. *c.*1387: Usk, *Test. of Love*, in Skeat's *Chaucer*, vii 26, Thou shalt not juge ne deme toforn thou knowest. 15th cent.: in *Reliq. Antiquae*, i 92 (1841), Deme the best of every doute, Tyl the truthe be tryed out. Before 1500: in Hill, *Commonplace Book*, 131 (E.E.T.S.), Deme no thyng that is in dowt till the trowth be tred owt. 1546: Heywood, *Proverbs*, Pt II ch v, Deeme the best, till time hath tryde the truth out. 1591: Florio, *Second Frutes*, 105, Judge nothing till the end be seene.

Deep as the North. 1869: FitzGerald, *Sea Words and Phrases*, 4, Deep as the North star, said … of a very wide-a-wake babe four months old. 1883: Burne, *Shropsh. Folk-Lore*, 594, As dip [deep = crafty] as the North.

Deeper the sweeter, The. 1596: Jonson, *Ev. Man in Humour*, II iv, My poesy was, 'The deeper, the sweeter.' 1611: Barry, *Ram-Alley*, I. 1661: Davenport, *City Nightcap*, I. 1738: Swift, *Polite Convers.*, Dial. I, Stir it up with the spoon, miss; for the deeper the sweeter.

Deep in the mud. *See* quot. 1914: R. L. Gales, *Vanished Country Folk*, 205, 'One's as deep in the mud as the other in the mire' is a proverb I still sometimes hear.

Deer. *Where the deer is slain, there will some of his blood lie.* 1732: Fuller, 5663.

Defend me and spend me. *c.*1595: Spenser, *State of Ireland*, 624 (Globe ed.), The Irish … saying commonly, 'Spend me and defend me'. 1645: Howell, *Fam. Letters*, bk i § t. No. vii, So that the saying is truly verify'd here, *Defend me, and spend me*. 1737: Ray, 274, Defend me and spend me. (Saith the Irish churl.) 1853: Trench, *Proverbs*, 59 (1905).

Delay. *After a delay comes a let.* 1736: Bailey, *Dict.*, s.v. 'Delay'. *See also* **Wise**, *adj.* (35).

Delays are dangerous. *c.*1300: *Havelok*, l. 1352, Dwelling [delay] haueth ofte scathe [injury] wrouht. *c.*1384: Chaucer, *Troylus*, bk iii l. 853, That peril is with dreeching in y-drawe. 1457: *Paston Lett.*, i 414 (Gairdner, 1900), Taryeng drawyth parell. 1579: Lyly, *Euphues*, 65 (Arber), Delayes breede daungers. 1655: Shirley, *Gent. of Venice*, V i, Shall we go presently? delays are dangerous. 1691: Southerne, *Sir Antony Love*, V iv 1725: Bailey, tr. Erasmus' *Colloq.*, 200, Why not to day rather than to morrow, if delays are dangerous. 1888: R.L.S., *Black Arrow*, bk i ch i, Delay, they say, begetteth peril.

Deliberating is not delaying. 1732: Fuller, 1266.

Demand. *When the demand is a jest, the answer is a scoff.* 1639: Clarke, 86. 1732: Fuller, 5575.

Denshire. *See* **Devonshire**.

Denton. *See* **Heighten**.

Denying a fault doubles it. 1669: *Politeuphuia*, 163, Denials make little faults great. 1732: Fuller, 1267.

Dependence is a poor trade. Ibid., No. 1268.

Depends on another, dines ill and sups worse, He who. 1813: Ray, 164, Who depends upon another man's table often dines late. 1855: Bohn, 399.

Derby ale and London beer. 1614: Cooke, *Greene's Tu Quoque*, in Hazlitt, *Old Plays*, xi 234, I have sent my daughter this morning as far as Pimlico to fetch a draught of Derby ale. 1659: Howell, 14. 1670: Ray, 258. 1703: Ward, *Writings*, ii 122, Two or three gallons of Derby ale had one day set my wits a wooll-gathering.

Derby's bands. 1576: Gascoigne, *Steel Glas*, 71 (Arber), To binde such babes in father Derbies bands. 1592: Greene, *Quip*, in *Works*, xi 244 (Grosart), They tie the poore soule in such

Darbies bands. 1602: Carew, *Surv. of Cornwall*, 49 (1811), For which the poor wretch is bound in Darby's bonds to deliver him two hundred weight of tin at the next coinage.

Derbyshire bom and Derbyshire bred, Strong i' th' arm and weak i' th' head. 1852: *N. & Q.*, 1st sen, v 573. 1884: *Folk-Lore Journal*, ii 279 [with 'thick' instead of 'weak'].

Derbyshire for lead, Devonshire for tin, Wiltshire for hunting plains, And Middlesex for tin. 1669: *New Help to Discourse*, 113, Darbyshire for wooll and lead. *c.*1809: quoted in *N. & Q.*, 9th ser, xi 266.

Desert and reward seldom keep company. 1611: Davies (of Hereford), *Sc. of Folly*, 42, in *Works*, ii (Grosart), Desart and reward be euer farre od. 1670: Ray, 7. 1748: Richardson, *Clarissa*, iv 120 (1785), Desert and reward, I can assure her, seldom keep company together.

Deserve. *See* **First deserve.**

Deserved a cushion, He has. That is, he hath gotten a boy. 1678: Ray, 69.

Deserves no pity that chooseth to do amiss twice, He. 1637: T. Heywood, *Dialogues, etc.*, in Bang's *Materialien*, B. 3, p. 218 [cited as a proverb].

Desire hath no rest. *c.*1582: G. Harvey, *Marginalia*, 201 (1913), Desier sufferith no delay. 1621: Burton, *Melanch.*, I ii 3,11, A true saying it is, desire hath no rest.

Desires are nourished by delays. 1633: Draxe, 41. 1670: Ray, 7.

Desires but little, has no need of much, He that. 1614: Lodge, tr. *Seneca*, 443, He that coueteth little, hath not need of much. 1732: Fuller, 2077.

Despair gives courage to a coward. Ibid., No. 1272.

Desperate diseases must have desperate cures. 1539: Taverner, *Proverbs*, fo. 4, Stronge disease requyreth a stronge medicine. 1600–01: Shakespeare, *Hamlet*, IV iii. Diseases desperate grown By desperate appliance are reliev'd, Or not at all.1670: Shadwell, *Humourists*, IV, Well, a desperate disease must have a desperate cure. 1748: Richardson, *Clarissa*, vii 61 (1785), For desperate diseases must have desperate remedies. 1831: Hone, *Year-Book*, 1416, Desperate cuts must have desperate cures.

Desperate that thinks himself so, He is. 1732: Fuller, 1913.

Devil. 1. An artful fellow is a devil in a doublet. 1732: Fuller, 583.

2. As bad as marrying the devil's daughter, and living with the old folks. 1830: Forby, *Vocab. E. Anglia*, 434.

3. As busy as the devil in a high wind. 1811: *Gent. Mag.*, lxxxi. 505, That adage, so common among the vulgar, 'as busy as the devil in a high gale of wind'. 1821: Scott, *Pirate*, ch viii, They are as busy as the devil in a gale of wind.

4. As great [intimate] as the Devil and the Earl of Kent. 1703: Ward, *Writings*, ii 90, As great as old Nick, and the old Earl of Kent. 1738: Swift, *Polite Convers.*, Dial. III [Scott, in a note to this, says: 'The villainous character given by history to the celebrated Goodwin, Earl of Kent, in the time of Edward the Confessor, occasioned this proverb'].

5. As the devil looks over Lincoln. 1546: Heywood, *Proverbs*, Pt II ch ix 1662: Fuller, *Worthies*, ii 268 (1840), He looks as the devil over Lincoln. 1738: Swift, *Polite Convers.*, Dial. I. 1822: Scott, *Nigel*, ch xxi, When I offer you gold for the winning, you look on me as the devil looks over Lincoln. 1827: Hone, *Ev. Day Book*, ii 1238, The origin of the statue of the devil at Oxford [Lincoln College] is not so certain as that the effigy was popular, and gave rise to the saying of 'the devil looking over Lincoln' [it was taken down in 1731].

6. As the devil loves apple-dumplings. 1858: *Gent. Mag.*, Pt II, p. 401 … This is a not uncommon saying, but to all appearance a very silly one.

7. As the devil loves holy water. *c.*1500: in Hazlitt, *Early Pop. Poetry*, i 227 (1864), They dyd flee fro hym, as the deuyll fro holy water. 1576: Lambarde, *Peramb. of Kent*, 301 (1826), You remember the olde proverbe, how well the divell loveth holy water. 1679: *Roxb. Ballads*, iv 141 (B.S.). 1715: Centlivre, *Wife well Managed*, sc iv, Nothing frights the devil like holy water, – thence comes the proverb, you know. 1828: Carr, *Craven Dialect*, i 232, 'He likes him as the devil likes holy water'; i.e. he mortally hates him. 1913: E. M. Wright, *Rustic Speech, etc.*, 205.

8. As the devil mended his dame's leg. *c.*1542: Brinklow, *Complaynt*, 34 (E.E.T.S.), It is amended, euen as the deuel mendyd his damys legg (as it is in the prouerbe): whan he shuld haue set it right, he bracke it quyte in pecys!

9. Away goes the devil when he finds the door shut against him. 1659: Howell, *Proverbs: Ital. -Eng.*, 4, The devil turns his back at a gate shut up. 1855: Bohn, 323.

10. Better keep the devil at the door, than turn him out of the house. 1732: Fuller, 907.

11. Better the devil you know than the devil you don't know. 1539: R. Taverner, *Proverbs or Adagies out of Erasmus*, 48, *Nota res mala, optima*. An evyl thynge knowen is best. 1576: G. Pettie: *Petit Palace*, 84, You had rather keepe those whom you know, though with some faultes, then take those whom you knowe not, perchance with moe faultes. 1857: A. Trollope, *Barchester Towers*, II vii, 'Better the d— you know than the d— you don't know' is an old saying … but the bishop had not yet realised the truth of it.

12. Between the devil and the deep sea. [Hac urget lupus, hac canis, aiunt. – Horace, *Sat.*, II ii 64.] 1637: quoted in *N.&Q.*, 7th ser, i 453, Betwixt the devill and the deepe sea. 1672: Walker, *Paraem.*, 11, I am in a twittering case; betwixt the devil and the deepe sea. 1762: Smollett, *Sir L. Greaves*, ch last. 1820: Byron, *Letters*, v 4 (Prothero), Between the devil and deep sea, Between the lawyer and trustee – it is difficult to decide. 1902: Sir H. Lucy, *Diary of Journalist*, 170 (1920).

13. Bring you the devil and I'll bring out his dam. 1639: Clarke, 209.

14. Down the lane to the devil. 1546: Heywood, *Proverbs*, Pt II ch vii, The deuel go with the doune the lane. 1619: Chapman, *Two Wise Men*, VII iii, *Her.* By that meanes thou wilt accompanie him to hell. *Sim.* Downe the lane to the divall.

15. Every devil has not a cloven foot. 1726: Defoe, *Hist. of Devil*, Pt II ch vi, p. 242 (4th ed.).

16. Give the devil his due. *1589: Pap with a Hatchet*, 31 (1844), Giue them their due though they were diuels. 1597: Shakespeare, 1 *Henry IV*, I ii 1669: Dryden, *Wild Gallant*, II ii, Let every man speak as he finds, and give the devil his due. 1709: Mandeville, *Virgin Unmask'd*, 28 (1724), Tho' I give the devil his due, I still defy him. 1825: Planché, *Extravag.*, i 25 (1879), You certainly have great merit. I will give the devil his due.

17. He does the devil's work for nothing. 1742: Fielding, *Andrews*, bk ii ch xvi, What a silly fellow must he be who would do the devil's work for nothing! 1830: Forby, *Vocab. E. Anglia*, 433 [said of a common swearer].

18. He is like the devil, always in mischief. 1659: Howell, 13.

19. He that sups with the devil needs a long spoon. *c.*1386: Chaucer, *Squire's Tale*, l. 594, 'Therfor bihoveth him a ful long spoone That shal ete with a feend', thus herde I seye. 16th cent.: in *Reliq. Antiquae*, i 208 (1841), He hath need of a long spoone that eateth with the devill. 1590: Shakespeare, *Comedy of Errors*, iv iii 59, He must have a long spoon that must eat with the devil. 1626: Overbury, *Characters:* 'A Jesuit', A Jesuit is a larger spoon for a traytor to feed with the devil, than any other order. 1840: Barham, *Ing. Legends:* 'St Nicholas'. 1893: R.L.S., *Catriona*, ch xxix.

20. He that (*a*) **takes the devil into his boat,** or (*b*) **that hath shipped the devil must** (*c*) **carry him over the Sound,** or (*d*) **make the best of him.** 1678: Ray, 125 [(*a*) and (*c*), also (*b*) and (*d*)]. 1732: Fuller, 2326 [(*a*) and (*c*)], and No. 2152, He that has purchas'd the devil, must make the most of him. 1853: Trench, *Proverbs*, 143 (1905), He who has shipped the devil, must carry him over the water.

21. He that the devil drives, feels no lead at his heels. 1732: Fuller, 2331.

22. If the devil be a vicar, thou shalt be his clerk. 1670: Ray, 171. 1738: *Gent. Mag.*, 475.

23. If the devil catch a man idle, he'll set him at work. 1732: Fuller, 2705.

24. If you buy the devil you must sell the devil. 1775: Grose, *Antiq. Repertory*, ii 395 (1808), Buying and selling the devil has long been a proverbial expression. 1820: Colton, *Lacon*, Pt II No. 167 *n.*, Booksellers are like horse-dealers in one respect, and if they buy the devil, they must also sell the devil.

25. Ill doth the devil preserve his servant. 1659: Howell, *Proverbs: Brit.-Eng.*, 3.

26. It is a sin to belie the devil. 1548: Hall, *Chron.*, 363 (1809), It wer synne to lye on the deuil. 1607: Dekker, *Knights Coniuring*, 21 (Percy S.), 'Tis sinne to belye the diuell. 1712: Motteux, *Quixote*, Pt I bk iii ch 11. 1732: Fuller, 2884.

27. It is an ill army where the devil carries the colours. 1639: Clarke, 70, 'Tis an ill company where the devil beares the banner. 1670: Ray, 7 [with 'battle' for 'army']. 1732: Fuller, 2896.

28. It is an ill procession where the devil (*a*) **bears the cross,** or (*b*) **holds the candle.** 1633: Draxe, 86 [(*a*)]. 1641: in *Harl. Miscell.*, iii 222

(1744), There is an old saying, *There can be no holy procession where the divel carryes the crosse.* 1694: D'Urfey, *Quixote*, Pt I Act IV sc i [(*b*)]. 1732: Fuller, 2902 [(*b*)].

29. More like the devil than St Lawrence. 1678: Ray, 256.

30. Much about a pitch, Quoth the devil to the witch. 1846–59: *Denham Tracts*, ii 81 (F.L.S.).

31. Never go to the devil with a dish-clout in your hand. 1738: *Gent. Mag.*, 475.

32. One devil is like another. 1612: Shelton, *Quixote*, Pt I bk iv ch iv 1732; Fuller, 3747.

33. One might as well eat the devil as the broth he's boiled in. 1545: Brinklow, *Lamentacyon*, 89 (E.E.T.S.), Yf it be so that God, through the kynge, hath caste out the deuell out of this realme, and yet both he and we soppe of the broth in which the deuell was soden. 1660: T. Hall, *Funebria Florae*, 12, Wee must not so much as tast of the devils broth, lest at last hee bring us to eat of his beef. 1696: D'Urfey, *Quixote*, Pt III Act I, One had as good eat the devil, as the broth he's boiled in. 1738: Swift, *Polite Convers.*, Dial. II. 1834: Taylor, *Philip v Art.*, III i part 2, Hast courage but for half a sin? As good To eat the devil as the broth he's boil'd in. 1865: 'Lancs Proverbs', in *N. & Q.*, 3rd ser, viii 494. 1901: F. E. Taylor, *Lancs Sayings*, 13, Aw'd I as lief eyt the divvle as sup th' broth 'at he's boil't in.

34. Seldom lies the devil dead by the gate (or **in the ditch**), *c.*1400: *Towneley Plays*, xiii, p. 123 (E.E.T.S.), Seldom lys the dewyll dede by the gate. 1670: Ray, 79 [ditch]. 1758–67: Sterne, *Trist. Shandy*, vol viii ch xxviii, Which the devil, who never lies dead in a ditch, had put into her head.

35. She will scold the devil out of a haunted house. 1732: Fuller, 4149.

36. Strike Dawkin! the devil is in the hemp. 1678: Ray, 70. 1889: *Folk-Lore Journal*, vii 293. Derby saying. Strike, Dakeyne! the devil's i' th' hemp.

37. Talk of the devil and he'll appear. [Lupus in fabula. – Terence, *Ad.*, 537. de Varrone loquebamur; lupus in fabula: venit enim ad me. – Cicero, *Att.*, 13, 33, 4.] 1666: Torriano, *Piazza Univ.*, 134, The English say, 'Talk of tiie devil, and he's presently at your elbow'. 1697: Vanbrugh, *Esop*, II i, Talk of the devil, and he's at your elbow'. 1725: Bailey, tr. Erasmus' *Colloq.*, 17 Rather it is according to the old proverb; *talk of the devil and he'll appear*; for we were just now speaking of you. 1799: T. Knight, *Turnpike Gate*, II i, Speak o' th' devil and behold his horns! 1822: Scott, *Nigel*, ch xv, They are the very men we spoke of – talk of the devil, and – humph?

38. The devil always tips at the biggest ruck [heap]. 1886: R. Holland, *Cheshire Gloss.*, 454 (E.D.S.). 1917: Bridge, *Cheshire Proverbs*, 113.

39. The devil and (or) Dick Senhouse. 1826: Brady, *Varieties of Lit.*, 13, A common saying [in Cumberland], 'It will do in spite of the Devil and Dick Senhouse'. 1846–59: *Denham Tracts*, i 167 (F.L.S.), 'I will do it in spite of the Devil and Dick Senhouse'; also 'Either the devil or Dick Senhouse'.

40. The devil and Dr Faustus. 1726: Defoe, *Hist, of Devil*, 326 (4th ed.), It is become a proverb, *as great as the devil and Dr Foster* [Faustus]. 1749: Fielding, *Tom Jones*, bk xviii ch viii, What the devil and Doctor Faustus! shan't I do what I will with my own daughter? 1848: Carleton, *Fardorougha*, 233 (W), You'd beat the divil an' Docthor Fosther.

41. The devil and his dam(e). *c.*1440: *York Plays*, 300 (L. T. Smith), What the deuyll and his dame schall y now doo? 1550: R. Crowley, *Works*, 49 (E.E.T.S.), But they saye that ye purchase the deuill, his dame, and all. *c.*1615: *Times Whistle*, 97 (E.E.T.S.), Me thought as both their heades together came, I saw the devill kissing of his dam. 1657: *Lust's Dominion*, IV v, The devil and his dam, The Moor and my mother. 1830: Scott, *Doom of Devorgoil*, III ii, I have heard of the devil's dam before, But never of his child.

42. The devil and John of Cumber. 1659: Howell, 20.

43. The devil and ninepence go with her. Before 1704: T. Brown, *Works*, iii 245 (1760), The devil and ninepence go with her, that's money and company, according to the laudable adage of the sage mobility! 1738: Swift, *Polite Convers.*, Dial. II, The devil go with him and sixpence; and there's money and company too.

44. The devil and the malster. 1886: Elworthy, *West Som. Word-Book*, 191 (E.D.S.), It is always said that on Culmstock Fair-day, May 21, ' 'tis a fight twixt the devil and the malster' – to decide if there shall be cider to drink, or whether it must be beer. Cf. **Culmstock Fair.**

45. The devil can quote Scripture. This proverb alludes to Matthew iv.6, where the devil quotes Psalm xci:11–12. 1595: Shakespeare, *Merchant of Venice*, I iii, The devil can cite Scripture for his purpose. 1609: Armin, *Maids of More-clacke*, sig. E3, The diuell has scripture for his damned ill. 1821: Scott, *Kenilworth*, ch iv 1850: Dickens, *Chuzzlewit*, ch xi, Does any one doubt the old saw, that the Devil (being a layman) quotes Scripture for his own ends?

46. The devil danceth in a woman's placket. 1659: Howell, 15.

47. The devil dares not peep under a maid's coat. 1675: *Mistaken Husband*, V v, Good Mrs Isbel hide me under your petticoats that the divel may not find me, they say he dares not peep under a maids coat.

48. The devil finds work for idle hands (to do). A similar sentiment is found in the letters of Saint Jerome, Do some work or other that the devil may always find you occupied. 1715: I Watts, *Divine Songs*, 29, In Works of Labour or of Skill I would be busy too: For Satan finds some mischief still for idle Hands to do. 1792: M. Wollstonecraft, *Vindication of the Rights of Woman*, ix, There is a homely proverb that speaks a shrewd truth, that whoever the devil finds idle he will employ. Cf. **Devil** (23); **Idle** (2) and (7).

49. The devil gets up to the belfry by the vicar's skirts. 1659: Howell, *Proverbs: Span.-Eng.*, 20. 1732: Fuller, 4476.

50. The devil goes a nutting on Holy-rood Day. 1689: *Poor Robin Alman.*, Sept., The 14th day [of September], for then, they say, the devil goes a nutting.

51. The devil goes share in gaming. 1855: Bohn, 501.

52. The devil has a chapel wherever God has a church. 1560: Becon, *Catechism*, 361 (P.S.), For commonly, wheresoever God buildeth a church, the devil will build a chapel just by. 1609: Dekker, in *Works*, iv 220 (Grosart), And where God hath a church, the deuill hath a chappell. 1701: Defoe, *True Born Eng.*, Pt I.ll.1–2, Wherever God erects a House of Prayer, The devil always builds a chapel there. 1748: Richardson, *Clarissa*, vii 327 (1785), It is an old proverb … God never had a House of Pray'r, But Satan had a chapel there.

53. The devil has no power over a drunkard.

1635: Glapthorne, *Lady Mother*, III ii, in Bullen, *Old Plays*, ii 160, They say the divell has …

54. The devil hath cast a bone to set strife. 1546: Heywood, *Proverbs*, Pt II ch ii *c*.1594: Bacon, *Promus*, No. 654. 1633: Draxe, 197.

55. The devil is a busy bishop in his own diocese. 1549: Latimer, *Sermon on Ploughers*, 29 (Arber), Who is the most diligent bishoppe and prelate in al England … ? I wyl tel you. It is the deuyl. He is the moste dyligent preacher of al others, he is neuer out of his dioces. 1732: Fuller, 4479. 1910: *N. & Q.*, 11th ser, i 34, The sanctity of the day became violated by the devil, who is 'a busy bishop in his own diocese', the proverb says.

56. The devil is a knave. 1553: *Respublica*, I iii, The devyll ys a knave. 1571: in *Ballads*, 85 (Percy S., No. 1). 1639: Davenport, *New Trick to cheat Devil*, IV i.

57. The devil is an ass. 1616: Jonson, *Devil is an Ass* [title]. 1681: Otway, *Soldier's Fortune*, IV i, The devil's an ass, sir. 1745: *Agreeable Companion*, 304, She found a trick she thought would pass, And prove the devil but an ass.

58. The devil is at home. 1620: Middleton, in *Works*, vii 185 (Bullen), Why, will he have it in's house, when the proverb says, The devil's at home? 1753: Richardson, *Grandison*, i 231 (1883), The devil's at home, is a phrase; and our modern ladies live as if they thought so. 1810: Crabbe, *Borough*, xix 56, A foolish proverb says, 'The devil's at home'.

59. The devil is dead. *c*.1470: *Mankind*, in Manly's *Spec. of Pre-Shakesp. Drama*, i 337, Qwyst, pesse! The deull ys dede! Before 1529: Skelton, *Col. Clout*, l. 36, The deuyll, they say, is dede, The deuell is dede. 1661: Davenport, *City Nightcap*, III, He thinks the devil's dead too. 1671: *Westm. Drollery*, 109 (Ebsworth), The night is our own, for the devil is dead. 1860: Reade, *Cl. and Hearth*, ch lii., Courage, brave wife; the divell is dead.

60. The devil is easier to raise than to lay. 1725: Bailey, tr. Erasmus' *Colloq.*, 202, 'Tis an old saying and a true, 'Tis an easier matter to raise the devil, than 'tis to lay him.

61. The devil is God's ape. 1595: *Polimanteia*, sig. B1, Satan desiring in this to bee Gods ape. 1639: Fuller, *Holy War*, bk iv ch xxi, As the devil is God's ape. 1666: Torriano, *Piazza Univ.*, 67. 1904: J. C. Wall, *Devils*, 22, 'Satan', says

Tertullian, 'is God's ape' – a term which in those days (third century and after) became very general among Christians.

62. The devil is good (or kind) to his own (or to some). 1606: Day, *Isle of Gulls*, II iv, You were not worse then the devil els, for they say hee helps his … seruants. 1660: A. Brome, *Poems*: 'New Montebank', The devil's ever kind to his own. 1738: Swift, *Polite Convers.*, Dial. III, They say, the devil is kind to his own.

63. The devil is good when he is pleased. 1581: Woodes, *Conflict of Conscience*, III iii, The devil is a good fellow, if one can him please. *c.*1600: *Grim the Collier*, II. 1677: *Poor Robin Alman.*, Dec., The devil's good when he is pleased. 1738: Swift, *Polite Convers.*, Dial. II. 1813: Byron, *Letters, etc.*, ii 257 (Prothero), But they say the devil is amusing when pleased.

64. The devil is in the dice. 1678: Ray, 70. 1904: J. C. Wall, *Devils*, 121, Dice are known as the Devil's Bones.

65. The devil is not always at one door. 1611: Cotgrave, s.v. 'Diable'. 1694: D'Urfey, *Quixote*, Pt I, Act IV sc i 1732: Fuller, 4482.

66. The devil is not so black as he is painted. 1596: Lodge, *Marg. of America*. 57 (Hunt. Cl), Wel … diuels are not so blacke as they be painted. 1642: Howell, *Forreine Travell*, 65 (Arber). 1726: Defoe, *Hist. of Devil*, Pt II ch vi, p. 232 (4th ed.), As if the devil was not so black as he was painted. *c.*1770: Foote, *Devil upon Two Sticks*, I. 1860: Reade, *Cl. and Hearth*, ch xxxvii.

67. The devil is seldom outshot in his own bow. 1642: D. Rogers, *Matrim. Honour*, 42.

68. The devil laughs when one thief robs another. 1819: Scott, *Ivanhoe*, ch xxi, The fiend laughs, they say, when one thief robs another.

69. The devil lies brooding in the miser's chest. 1732: Fuller, 4484. 1904: J.C. Wall, *Devils*, 127.

70. The devil loves all colliers. 1583: Melbancke, *Philotinus, sig.* Ll.

71. The devil lurks behind the cross. 1612: Shelton, *Quixote*, Pt I bk i ch vi 1712: Motteux, *Quixote*, Pt II ch xlvii, Your honour ought not to eat any of the things that stand here before you, for they were sent in by some of the convents; and it is a common saying, 'The devil lurks behind the cross'.

72. The devil made askers. 1738: Swift, *Polite Convers.*, Dial. II, Sir John, will you taste my October? … *Sir John*. My lord, I beg your pardon; but they say, the devil made askers. *Ld. Smart* [to the butler]. Here, bring up the great tankard, full of October, for Sir John.

73. The devil makes his Christmas pies of clerks' fingers and lawyers' tongues. 1591: Florio. *Second Frutes*, 179, Of three things the deuill makes his messe, Of lawyers tongues, of scriueners fingers, you the third may gesse. 1630: T. Adams, *Works*, 145, An euill tongue is meate for the deuill, according to the Italian prouerbe: the deuill makes his Christmasse pie of lewd tongues. 1659: Howell, 11 (9).

74. The devil may dance in his pocket – because it contains no *cross* (coin). 1411: Hoccleve, *Reg. of Princes*, 25 (E.E.T.S.), The feende men seyn may hoppen in a pouche Whan that no croys there-inne may a-pere. *c.*1470: *Mankind*, l. 474, The deull may daunce in my purse for ony peny. 1567: Drant, *Horace*, I iii, The deuille may daunce in crosslesse purse. 1623: *New and Merrie Prognos.*, 24 (Halliwell), Some wanting money shall both ban and curse That the devill hath roome to dance in their purse. 1785: Grose, *Class. Dict. Vulgar Tongue*, s.v. 'Devil'. 1826: Scott, *Woodstock*, ch iii, No devil so frightful as that which dances in the pocket where there is no cross to keep him out.

75. The devil on Dun's back. 1639: Clarke, 197. 1677: *Poor Robin's Visions*, 25, In term-time the divel upon Dun rides to and frow.

76. The devil owed a cake and paid a loaf. 1690: *New Dict. Canting Crew*, sig. C3, The devil ow'd her a cake, and has pai'd her a loaf, when instead of a small, a very great disaster, or misfortune has happen'd to a woman. 1732: Fuller, 4477, The devil hath owed me a cake of a long time, and now hath paid me a loaf.

77. The devil owed him a shame. 1542: *Sch. House of Women*, l. 245, The deuil, gossip, ought me a shame. 1679: D'Urfey, *Squire Oldsapp*, V ii, The devil I think ow'd me a shame, and sought to pay it this way. 1753: Richardson, *Grandison*, i 320 (1883), The devil has long, continued he, owed me a shame. 1823: Scott, in Lockhart's *Life*, v 259, I hope the devil does not owe me such a shame.

78. The devil pay the maltman. *c.*1532: R. Copland, *Spyttal Hous*, l. 682, Make we mery as longe as we can, And drynke a pace: the deuill pay the malt man! 1559: Becon, *Prayers, etc.*, 282

(P.S.), To drinke them all out, to set cock on the hoop, let the devil pay the maltman. 1573: Bullein, *Dialogue*, 123 (E.E.T.S.), A dogge hath but a daie. Let the deuill paie the malt manne.

79. The devil rebukes sin. 1666: Torriano, *Piazza Univ.*, 60, The devil corrects sin. 1682: A. Behn, *Roundheads*, V ii, How the devil rebukes sin! 1754: Berthelson, *Eng.-Danish Dict.*, s.v. 'Devil'. 1822: Scott, *Nigel*, ch xxxii, 'I am afraid,' said George Heriot, more hastily than prudently, 'I might have thought of the old proverb of Satan reproving sin.' 1894: R.L.S., *St Ives*, ch x, 'Now, really,' said I, 'is not this Satan reproving sin?'1922: Ramsay Macdonald in Parl., in *Times*, 24 Nov., p. 7, col. 3, That incident is one of the most deplorable examples I have ever known of Satan reproving sin.

80. The devil rides upon a fiddlestick = Much ado about nothing. 1597: Shakespeare, 1 *Henry IV*, II iv, Heigh, heigh! the devil rides upon a fiddlestick: what's the matter? *c.*1620: B.&F., *Hum. Lieut.*, IV iv, The fiend rides on a fiddlestick.

81. The devil run through thee booted and spurred, with a scythe at his back. Called the Sedgeley curse, I know not why. Sedgeley is in Staffordshire. *c.*1620: B.&F., *Woman's Prize*, V ii, A Sedgly curse light on him; which is, Pedro, 'The fiend ride throgh him [as above]'. 1659: Howell, 2. 1726: Defoe, *Hist. of Devil*, Pt II ch ix, p. 297 (4th ed.), And make the devil, as the Scots express it, ride through them booted and spurred. 1790: Grose, *Prov. Gloss.*, s.v. 'Staffs'. 1829: Scott, *Gen. Preface to Waverley*, app. ii, 'May the foul fiend, booted and spurred, ride down his bawling throat, with a scythe at his girdle,' quoth Albert Drawslot.

82. The devil s— upon a great heap. 1659: Howell, 6 [with 'the usurers heaps' for 'a great heap']. 1670: Ray, 80.

83. The devil sometimes speaks the truth. 1635: Glapthorne, *Lady Mother*, I iii, in Bullen, *Old Plays*, ii 123. 1732: Fuller, 5308, Truth may sometimes come out of the devil's mouth.

84. The devil spits on the blackberries, or **puts his foot on them,** or **casts his club over them, on Michaelmas Day.** 1727: Threlkeld, quoted in *Folk-Lore Record*, i 155, After Michaelmas the d—l casts his club over them [blackberries]. 1900: Hudson, *Nature in Downland*, ch xii, In early October the devil flies abroad, as some

believe, to spit on the bramble-bushes, and make its berries uneatable.

85. The devil take the hindmost. [Occupet extremum scabies. – Horace, *A. P.*, 417. *c.*1470: *Mankind*, l. 709, Hens wyth yowur stuff! fast we were gone I be-schrew the last, xall come to hys home!]. *c.*1618: B.&F., *Bonduca*, IV ii 1671: Dryden, *An Evening's Love*, IV iii, If it be come to that once, the devil take the hindmost! 1850: Planché, *Extravag.*, iv 83 (1879).

86. The devil tempts some, but an idle man tempts the devil. 1709: R. Kingston, *Apoph. Curiosa*, 57, An idle person tempts the devil to tempt him. 1820: Colton, *Lacon*, Pt I No. 70, The Turks have a proverb, which says, that *The devil tempts all other men, but that idle men tempt the devil.* 1875: A. B. Cheales, *Proverb. Folk-Lore*, 110.

87. The devil to pay. *c.*1400: in *Reliq. Antiquae*, i 257 (1841), Beit wer be at tome for ay, Than her to serve the devil to pay. 1738: Swift, *Polite Convers.*, Dial. II, I must be with my wife on Tuesday, or there will be the devil and all to pay. 1748: Richardson, *Clarissa*, vi 87 (1785), Here's the devil to pay. 1821: Scott, *Pirate*, ch xxxvi, If they hurt but one hair of Cleveland's head, there will be the devil to pay, and no pitch hot. 1922: Weyman, *Ovington's Bank*, ch xxvi.

88. The devil was sick, the devil a monk would be; The devil was well, the devil a monk was he. [*c.*1450: W. Bower, *Scotichronicon*, ii 292 (Goodall), quoted in *N.&Q.*, 8th ser, xii 331, Lupus languebat monachus tunc esse volebat, Sed cum convaluit lupus ut ante fuit.] 1586: L. Evans, *Withals Dict. Revised*, sig. K8, The diuell was sicke and crasie; Good woulde the monke bee that was lasie. 1692: L'Estrange, *Aesop*, 104 (3rd ed.). 1757: Garrick, *Gamesters*, III *ad fin.* 1875: Smiles, *Thrift*, 314 [with 'saint' for 'monk']. 1875: R.L.S., *Letters*, i 210 (Tusitala ed.), The story shall be called, I think, *When the Devil was well*, in allusion to the old proverb.

89. The devil will not come into Cornwall for fear of being put into a pie. 1790: Grose, *Prov. Gloss.*, s.v. 'Cornwall'. 1891: *N.&Q.*, 7th ser, xii 216.

90. The devil will take his own. 1846: T. Wright, *Essays on Middle Ages*, i 146, We say, 'The devil will take his own'.

91. The devil wipes his tail with the Poor man's pride. 1659: Howell, 12 (10). 1670: Ray, 21.

92. The devil would have been a weaver but for the Temples. 1678: Ray, 91.

93. The devil's behind the glass. 1855: Bohn, 502. 1904: J. C. Wall, *Devils*, 128.

94. The devil's children have the devil's luck. 1678: Ray, 126, The devils child the devils luck. 1776: T. Cogan, *John Buncle, Junior*, i 240, I wish the devil's children devil's luck, that's all. 1865: 'Lancs Proverbs', in *N. & Q.*, 3rd ser, viii 494. 1901: F. E. Taylor, *Lancs Sayings*, 9, The divvle's childer awlus han the divvle's luck.

95. The devil's guts = The surveyor's chain. 1678: Ray, 72.

96. The devil's martyr. 1639: Fuller, *Holy War*, bk ii ch xxix, The unhappy Dutch proverb, 'He that bringeth himself into needless dangers, dieth the devil's martyr'. 1670: Ray, 18 [as in 1748]. 1748: Richardson, *Clarissa*, iv 121 (1785), Then that other fine saying, He who perishes in needless danger, is the Devil's martyr.

97. The devil's meal is half bran. 1611: Cotgrave, s.v. 'Diable', Halfe of the devils meale turns unto branne. 1732: Fuller, 4487, The devil's flour is half bran. 1865: 'Lancs Proverbs', in *N. & Q.*, 3rd ser, viii 494, One half of the devil's meal runs to bran.

98. The devil's mouth is a miser's purse. 1600: Bodenham, *Belvedere*, 128(Spens.S.), The deuils mouth is tearm'd a misers purse. 1669: *Politeuphuia*, 288, A covetous mans purse is called the divels mouth.

99. The devil's run over Jock Wabster – an allusion to one whose affairs are said to be going back in the world. N. of England. 1876: *N. & Q.*, 5th ser, vi 64.

100. There is a devil in every berry of the grape. 1647: Howell, *Letters*, bk ii No. iii, He rails bitterly against Bacchus, and swears there's a devil in every berry of his grape. 1884: H. Friend, *Flowers and Fl. Lore*, 54, Perhaps every one has not heard the proverb, 'There is a devil in every berry of the grape'. This proverb is in use in some parts of England, and is said to have strayed hither from Turkey.

101. To beat the devil round the goose-berry-bush = *To* be wordy, roundabout. 1875: Parish, *Dict. Sussex Dialect*, He did not think the new curate was much of a hand in the pulpit, he did beat the devil round the gooseberry-bush so.

102. To drink the devil dry. 1594: R. Wilson, *Coblers Prophecy*, l. 106 (Malone S.), Ile looke in thy purse by and by: And if thou haue any money in it, Wele drinke the diuell dry, diuell dry.

103. To hug as the devil hugged the witch. 1678: Ray, 286. 1715: *Political Merriment*, Pt III, p. 20, And hug and kiss, and are so great, as the devil and witch of Endor. 1738: Swift, *Polite Convers.*, Dial. I, I've seen her hug you as the devil hugg'd the witch. 1745: *Agreeable Companion*, 251. 1846–59: *Denham Tracts*, ii 84 (F.L.S.), To hug one, as the devil hugs a witch.

104. To lie in the devil's mouth = *To* be wide open. 1609: in *Roxb. Ballads*, vii 437 (B.S.), He could not find a priuy place, for all lay in the diuel's mouth.

105. To patter the devil's Paternoster. *c.*1386: Chaucer, *Parson's Tale*, 506–7, They … grucche and murmure priuely for verray despyt, whiche wordes men clepen the deuelles pater noster. 1552: Latimer, *Sermons*, 350 (P.S.), Go not away with the devil's Paternoster, as some do. Do all things with a good mind. 1567: Golding, *Ovid*, bk ii l. 984, Began to mumble with hir selfe the divels Paternoster. 1641: Jonson, *Sad Shepherd*, II ii, What devil's pater noster mumbles she? 1847: Halliwell, *Dict.*, s.v., To say the devil's pater-noster, to mutter or grumble.

106. To play the devil for God's sake. *c.*1640: in *Harl. Miscell.*, iv 155 (1745), To play the devil for God's sake hath been a common proverb, but was never entered for an article in a sober belief. 1681: L'Estrange, *Dissenters Sayings*, 50 (1685), Which is no more, in short, than playing the devil in God's name. 1820: Scott, *Abbot*, ch xxiv, That would be a serving, as they say, the devil for God's sake.

107. To play the devil in the bulmong. 1670: Ray, 171.

108. To play the devil in the horologe. 1519: Horman, *Vulgaria*, fo. 231, Some for a tryfull play the deuyll in the orlege. *c.*1550: Udall, *Roister Doister*, III ii, *C.C.* What will he? *M.M.* Play the devill in the horologe. 1593: Harvey, in *Works*, i 276 (Grosart), Finding nothing in all those pestilent and virulent sheetes of waste-paper, but meere – meere forgeryes, and the diuell in the horologe. 1659: Howell, 6, The devil's in the orologe.

109. To put out the devil's eye. *See* long story in 1303: Brunne, *Handlyng Synne*, ll. 12165–12252 (Roxb.Cl). 1710: S. Palmer, *Moral Essays on Proverbs*, 81, Come, let's be friends and put out the devil's eye.

110. To set the devil on sale. 1546: Heywood, *Proverbs*, Pt II ch vii, Here is a tale, For honestie, meete to set the diuell on sale.

111. 'Twas surely the devil that taught women to dance, and asses to bray. 1732: Fuller, 5319.

112. What's got over the devil's back is spent under his belly. 1607: Middleton, *Mich. Term*, IV i, What's got over the devil's back (that's by knavery) must be spent under his belly (that's by lechery). 1671: Head and Kirkman, *English Rogue*, ii 97. 1725: Bailey, tr. Erasmus' *Colloq.*, 30. *c.*1800: Trusler, *Prov. in Verse*, 85. 1889: Peacock, *Manley, etc., Gloss.*, 167 (E.D.S.), What's gotten o' th' divil's back goäs oot under his belly. 1917: Bridge, *Cheshire Proverbs*, 150.

113. When it rains and the sun shines at the same time the devil is beating his wife. 1666: Torriano, *Piazza Univ.*, 79 [quoted as 'the French say']. 1703: Ward, *Writings*, ii 299, To go and thrash him round the church-yard, as the devil does his wife in rainy weather when the sun shines. 1738: Swift, *Polite Convers.*, Dial. I, [in mingled rain and sunshine] the devil was beating his wife behind the door with a shoulder of mutton. 1846: T. Wright, *Essays on Middle Ages*, i 130 [saying credited to the Normans]. 1893: Inwards, *Weather Lore*, 110, If it rains while the sun is shining the devil is beating his grandmother. He is laughing and she is crying.

114. When the devil is a hog, you shall eat bacon. 1670: Ray, 217. 1732: Fuller, 5578.

115. When the devil is blind = Never. 1659: Howell, 12. *c.*1670: in *Bagford Ballads*, i 7 (B.S.), They 'l pay me again when the devil is blind. 1709: Ward, *Works*, iv, *Verse* 35, They pay for when the devil's blind. 1815: Scott, *Mannering*, ch xxii, Ay, Tib, that will be when the devil's blind, – and his een's no sair yet. 1847: Halliwell, *Dict.*, s.v., 'Horn'.

116. When the devil is dead … 1678: Ray, 84, When the devil's dead, there's a wife for Humphrey. 1732: Fuller, 5580 [as in 1678, but with 'widow' for 'wife']. 1853: Trench, *Proverbs*, 72 (1905), When the devil is dead, he never wants a chief mourner.

117. When the devil prays, he has a booty in his eye. 1732: Fuller, 5576.

118. When the devil preaches, the world's near an end. 1667: L'Estrange, *Quevedo's Visions*, 21 (1904).

119. When the devil quotes Latin, the priests go to prayers. 1863: *N. & Q.*, 3rd ser, iii 492.

120. Where had the devil the friar, but where he was? 1639: Davenport, *New Trick to cheat Devil*, IV ii 1738: Swift, *Polite Convers.*, Dial. I, Why, where 'twas to be had; where the devil got the friar.

121. Where none else will, the devil must bear the cross. 1579: Lyly, *Euphues*, 53 (Arber). 1732: Fuller, 5652.

122. Why should the devil have all the best tunes? Attributed, by his biographer, to the evangelist and hymn writer Rowland Hill, referring to his predecessor Charles Wesley and his habit of choosing popular secular melodies to set religious words to. 1859: W. Chappell, *Popular Music*, II 748, The Primitive Methodists … acting upon the principle of 'Why should the devil have all the pretty tunes?' collect the airs that are sung at pot and public houses, and set their hymns to them. 1879: J. E. Hopkins, *Work amongst Working Men*, vi, If Wesley could not see why the devil should have all the good tunes, still less should we be able to see why he should have all the good amusements.

123. You can't stand between the oak an' the rain [rind], **where the devil can't go.** Torquay. 1910: *Devonsh. Assoc. Trans.*, xlii. 88. Cf. **Oak** (7).

124. You have daily to do with the devil, and pretend to be frightened at a mouse. 1855: Bohn, 577.

125. You look like a runner, quoth the devil to the crab. 1732: Fuller, 5934.

See also **Bad priests; Beads; Benfield-side; Black**, *adj.* (4), (14), and (15); **Blow**, *verb* (1); **Candle** (6); **Cards** (1); **Dark as the devil's mouth; Deal** (1); **Flatterer** (4); **Friday** (10); **Give** (17); **Go** (8); **God for money; God hath few friends; God sends corn; God sends meat; Happy is the child; Harrow; Idle** (2) and (7); **Innocent as a devil; Leave**, *verb* (5); **Marriage** (2); **Needs must; No sin; Play at small game; Pull devil; Rake hell; Rise** (2); **Saint; Sloth is the devil's cushion;.Sure as the devil; Truth** (3) and (22); **Ugly; Up with it;** and **Woman** (4), (9), and (33).

Devonshire. *See* **Derbyshire**.

Devonshire ground, To. 1607: Norden, *Surv. Dial.*, 228 (OED), They … call it in the west parts, burning of beate, and in the south-east parts, Devonshiring. 1681: Worlidge, *Dict. Rusticum*, s.v., To Denshire, is to cut off the turf of land; and when it is dry, to lay it in heaps and burn it. *c.*1770: Pegge, *Derbicisms*, 16 (E.D.S.), **Denchering**, *sb.* Devonshiring; it being a practice brought from Devonshire. 'Tis when they pare off the sword [sward] and burn it. 1837: Mrs Palmer, *Devonsh. Dialect*, 29, Peat- or sod-burning; an agricultural operation, which appears to have originated in Devonshire, and hence is called Denshiring in many parts.

Devonshire lawyer, To know as much as a. W. Corn., 19th cent. (Mr C. Lee).

Dew. *If nights three dewless there be, 'Twill rain you're sure to see;* and *With dew before midnight, The next day will sure be bright* – both in 1893: Inwards, *Weather Lore*, 103.

Dewsbury. *See* Birstal.

Diamond. 1. A diamond is valuable, tho' it lie on a dunghill. 1732: Fuller, 74.

2. A fine diamond may be ill set. Ibid., No. 97.

3. Diamond cut diamond. 1604: Webster and Marston, *Malcontent*, IV iii, 'Tis found None cuttes a diamond but a diamond. 1693: Congreve, *Double Dealer*, I v, Wit must be foiled by wit; cut a diamond with a diamond. 1738: Swift, *Polite Convers.*, Dial. III, Sharp's the word with her; diamonds cut diamonds. 1844: Thackeray, *Barry Lyndon*, ch x, Among such fellows it was diamond cut diamond. What you call fair play would have been a folly.

Dick's as dapper as a cock-wren. 1732: Fuller, 1281.

Dick's hatband. *See* quots. 1834–7: Southey, *Doctor*, ch cxxv, Who was that other Dick who wore so queer a hat-band that it has ever since served as a standing comparison for all queer things? 1841: Hartshorne, *Salopia Ant.*, 393, As curst as [also 'as fause as', 'as contrary as', 'as cruckit as', 'all across like', 'as queer as', etc.] Dick's hatband, which will come nineteen times round and won't tie at last. 1854: Baker, *Northants Gloss.*, s.v. 'Dick', As queer as Dick's hatband, made of pea-straw, that went nine times round, and would not meet at last. 1917: Bridge, *Cheshire Proverbs*, 25, As queer as Dick's hatband, that went nine times round but was too short to tie. [The saying is used all over the country in differing forms.]

Dick Smith. *See* Dish-clout.

Dickson. *See* quot. 1670: Ray, 171, To get a thing as Dickson did by his distress. That is, over the shoulders, as the vulgar usually say.

Die, *verb.* **1. He dies like a beast who has done no good while he lived.** 1855: Bohn, 370.

2. He that died half a year ago is as dead as Adam. 1732: Fuller, 2079.

3. He that dies pays all debts. 1611: Shakespeare, *Tempest*, III ii Cf. **Death** (5).

4. To die in a fog. 1917: Bridge, *Cheshire Proverbs*, 132 … To give up a task in despair.

5. To die in one's shoes = usually, To be hanged. 1725: *Matchless Rogue*, 87, I have been told by a fortune-teller, that I should die in my shoes. 1725: Gay, *Newgate's Garland*, l. 4, Ye honester poor rogues, who die in your shoes. 1840: Barham, *Ing. Legends*, 1st ser: 'Sucklethumbkin's Story', And there is … all come to see a man 'die in his shoes'! 1917: Bridge, *Cheshire Proverbs*, 68, He'll die in his shoon.

6. When you die of old age, I shall quake for fear. 1738: Swift, *Polite Convers.*, Dial. I, Why, my Lord, when I die for age, she may quake for fear. 1919: *N. & Q.*, 12th ser, v 235 … This was a common saying among peasants and workpeople, when speaking to some one rather older than themselves. Ibid., 325, A common Warwickshire saying round Stratford-on-Avon.

Diet cures more than doctors. 1875: A. B. Cheales, *Proverb. Folk-Lore*, 82.

Dieted bodies. *See* quot. 1655: T. Muffett, *Healths Improvement*, 8, These addle proverbs, 1. Dieted bodies are but bridges to physicians mindes.

Difference. 1. The difference is wide that the sheets will not decide. 1678: Ray, 201. 1732: Fuller, 6155 [with 'very' before 'wide'].

2. There is difference between living long and suffering long. 1732: Fuller, 4893.

3. There is difference between staring and stark blind. 1546: Heywood, *Proverbs*, Pt II ch vii, The difference betwene staryng and starke blynde The wise man at all tymes to folow can fynde. 1593: G. Harvey, in *Works*, ii 235 (Grosart), Hee mought haue spied a difference betweene staring, and starke-blinde.

4. There is difference between staring and stark mad. 1633: Draxe, 44. 1681: W. Robertson, *Phraseol. Generalis*, 471. 1787: Wolcot, *Works*, i 351 (1795), Peter, there's odds 'twixt staring and stark mad …

5. There is difference in servants. 1725: Bailey, tr. Erasmus' *Colloq.*, 507, The old proverb, There is difference in servants.

6. There is no difference of bloods in a bason. 1580: Lyly, *Euphues*, 289 (Arber), You talke of your birth, when I knowe there is no difference of blouds in a basen. 1732: Fuller, 4907.

7. There is some difference between Peter and Peter. 1612: Shelton, *Quixote*, Pt I bk iv ch xx 1631: Mabbe, *Celestina*, 130 (T.T.), Know you not, the proverbe tels us: That there is a great deale of difference betwixt Peter and Peter? 1732: Fuller, 4937.

Different sores must have different salves. 1732: Fuller, 1283.

Different strokes for different folks. An originally and mainly American saying meaning that different people need to be pleased, flattered, or gratified in different ways – or simply that no two people's needs and desires are the same. 1974: *Houston Chronicle Magazine*, 14 Oct., 4, The popular saying around the P[almer] D[rug] A[buse] P[rogram] is 'different strokes for different folks', and that's the basis of the program.

Difficult before they are easy, All things are. Ibid., No. 560.

Difficulty makes desire. Ibid., No. 1284.

Diffidence is the (a) **mother of safety,** (b) **right eye of prudence,** (a) 1754: Berthelson, *Eng.-Danish Dict.*, s.v. 'Mother'. (b) 1732: Fuller, 1286.

Dig one's grave with one's teeth, To. 1630: T. Adams, *Works*, 108, They have digged their graue with their teeth. 1655: Fuller, *Church Hist.*, bk iv § iii (42), Who by intemperance in his diet, in some sort, digged his grave with his own teeth. 1709: Dykes, *Eng. Proverbs*, 173, How many people daily dig their own graves, either with their teeth, their tongues, or their tails. 1880: Smiles, *Duty*, 418, We each day dig our graves with our teeth. 1923: *Observer*, 25 Feb., p. 11, col. 6.

Digs the well at the river, He. 1813: Ray. 75.

Dighton. *When Dighton is pulled down, Hull shall become a great town.* 1670: Ray, 257. 1790: Grose, *Prov. Gloss.*, s.v. 'Yorkshire'. 1878: *Folk-Lore Record*, i 162.

Diligence is the mother of good luck (or **success**). 1612: Shelton, *Quixote*, Pt I bk iv ch xix, It is a common proverb, beautiful lady, that diligence is the mother of good hap. 1712: Motteux, *Quixote*, Pt I bk iv ch xix ['success']. 1736: Franklin, *Way to Wealth*, in *Works*, i 444 (Bigelow) ['good luck']. 1875: Smiles, *Thrift*, 160 ['good luck'].

Diligent scholar, and the master's paid, A. 1640: Herbert, *Jac. Prudentum*.

Diligent spinner has a large shift, The. 1736: Franklin, *Way to Wealth*, in *Works*, i 445 (Bigelow).

Dilly-dally brings night as soon as Hurry-scurry. 1882: Mrs Chamberlain, *W. Worcs. Words*, 39 (E.D.S.).

Dim Sarsnick [Dym Sassenach] **with him, It's =** None so deaf as those who won't hear. 1917: Bridge, *Cheshire Proverbs*, 84.

Dine with Duke Humphrey, To. 1592: G. Harvey, in *Works*, i 206 (Grosart), To seek his dinner in poules with Duke humfrey. 1632: Nabbes, *Covent Garden*, IV iv, Some breake their fasts with Duke Humphrey. 1753: *World*, No. 37, Sometimes I eat as little as those who dine with Duke Humphrey. 1794: *Gent. Mag.*, Pt I, p. 529. 1815: D'Arblay, *Diary*, iv 344 (1876), Or else the whole party … must have made interest to dine with Duke Humphrey. 1850: Dickens, *Chuzzlewit*, ch i, One Diggory Chuzzlewit was in the habit of perpetually dining with Duke Humphrey.

Dines and leaves, lays the cloth twice, He that. 1640: Herbert, *Jac. Prudentum*.

Dinner. *See* quot. 1605: *Fair Maid of Bristow*, sig. C1, For as the old saying is, He that hath a good dinner, knowes better the way To supper.

Dinners cannot be long where dainties want. 1546: Heywood, *Proverbs*, Pt II ch i 1670: Ray, 79.

Dirt. 1. Cast no dirt into the well that hath given you water. 1732: Fuller, 1067.

2. He that flings dirt at another, dirtieth himself most. Ibid., No. 2107.

3. That dirt made this dust. Ibid., No. 4337.

4. Throw dirt enough and some will stick. 1656: *Trepan*, 34, She will say before company, Have you never had the French Pox? speak as in the sight of God; Let them Reply what they will, some dirt will stick. 1660: T. Hall, *Funebria Florae*, 38, Lye lustily, some filth will stick. 1705: Ward, *Hudibras Rediv.*, Pt II. 1769: Colman, *Man and Wife*, Prel., The scandal of others is mere dirt – throw a great deal, and some of it will stick. 1857: Hughes, *Tom Brown*, Pt I ch ix, Only throw dirt enough, and some of it is sure to stick.

Dirt-bird (or **Dirt-owl**) **sings, we shall have rain, The.** 1678: Ray, 80.

Dirty. 1. Dirty grate makes dinner late. Derby. 1884: *Folk-Lore Journal*, ii 279.

2. Dirty hands make clean money. 1869: Hazlitt, 110.

3. Dirty troughs will serve dirty sows. 1732: Fuller, 1292.

4. Dirty water quenches fire. *See* **Foul Water.**

5. Don't throw away dirty water till you have got clean. 1710: S. Palmer, *Moral Essays on Proverbs*, 89. 1738: Swift, *Polite Convers.*, Dial. III, Why, the fellow's rich; and I think she was a fool to throw out her dirty water before she got clean. 1869: Spurgeon, *John Ploughman*, ch viii.

6. To wash one's dirty linen in public. *See* **Wash.**

Discreet. *While the discreet advise, the fool doth his business.* 1640: Herbert, *Jac. Prudentum.*

Discreet women have neither eyes nor ears. 1640: Herbert, *Jac. Prudentum.* 1670: Ray, 7. 1732: Fuller, 1295, Discreet wives have sometimes neither eyes nor ears.

Discretion is the better part of valour. *c.*1477: Caxton, *Jason*, 23 (E.E.T.S.), Than as wyse and discrete he with-drewe him sayng that more is worth a good retrayte than a folisshe abydinge. 1597: Shakespeare, 1 *Henry IV*, V iv, The better part of valour is discretion. 1611: B.&F., *King and No King*, IV iii 1830: Marryat, *King's Own*, ch xxxi 1914: E. V Lucas, *Landmarks*, 37, Mrs Sergison here chose the better part of valour and urged Rudd to go to sleep. *See also* **Valour.**

Disdainful as ditch water. *c.*1386: Chaucer, *Reeve's Tale*, 1. 44, Sche was as deyne as water in a dich As ful of hokir and of bissemare. *c.*1394: *Piers P. Crede*, 1. 375, They ben digne [haughty, disdainful] as dich water that dogges in bayteth.

Disease known is half cured, A. 1725: Bailey, tr. Erasmus' *Colloq.*, 9, When the disease is known, it is half cured. 1732: Fuller, 75.

Disease will have its course. 1655: T. Muffett, *Healths Improvement*, 8, These addle proverbs … 3. Every disease will have its course.

Diseases are the price of ill pleasures. 1670: Ray, 7, Diseases are the interests of pleasures. 1732: Fuller, 1297. *See also* **Sickness.**

Disgraces are like cherries, one draws another. 1640: Herbert, *Jac. Prudentum.*

Dish and **Dishes. 1. All her dishes are chafing dishes.** 1562: Heywood, *Epigr.*, 6th Hund., No. 38, Wyfe, all thy disshes be chaffyng disshes plast; For thou chafest at sight of euery dishe

thou hast. 1639: Clarke, 34, All his meat is in chafing dishes. 1670: Ray, 7.

2. He has got a dish = is drunk. 1678: Ray, 87.

3. Revenge is a dish that is best eaten cold. *See* **Revenge.**

4. The dish wears its own cover. 1680: L'Estrange, *Select Coll. Erasmus*, 135, The dish (as we say) wears its own cover. 1754: Berthelson, *Eng.–Danish Dict.*, s.v. 'Dish'.

Dish-clout 1. I will not make my dish-clout my table-cloth. 1678: Ray, 125. 1732: Fuller, 2646.

2. There's a thing in it quoth the fellow when he drank the dish-clout. 1639: Clarke, 8. 1670: Ray, 196. 1732: Fuller, 4884 … when he drank dish-clout and all. 1883: Burne, *Shropsh. Folk-Lore*, 591, Ahem! as Dick Smith said when he swallowed the dish-clout.

Diss, Norfolk. *See* quot. Before 1852: S. W. Rix, in *Norfolk Arch. Papers*, ii 18 (quoted in *N. &Q.*, 1st ser, vi 303), [Diss] was formerly so little frequented by travellers that it became a proverb at Cambridge to express indifference respecting trivial matters, 'He knows nothing about Diss'.

Dissembled sin is double wickedness. 1633: Draxe, 46, Pretended holiness is double iniquity. 1647: *Countrym. New Commonwealth*, 12 [as in 1633, but with 'Dissembled' for 'Pretended']. 1732: Fuller, 1299.

Distrust *See* quot. 1645: Howell, *Letters*, bk i § v No. xx, It is a rule in friendship, *When distrust enters in at the foregate, love goes out at the postern.*

Ditch. *See* **Hedge** (5).

Ditton. *See* **Hutton.**

Diurnal-maker is the sub-amner to an historian, A. 1659: Howell, 2.

Diversity of humors breedeth tumors. Ibid., 17. 1670: Ray, 7. 1732: Fuller, 6230.

Divide. *See* quot. 1551: T. Wilson, *Rule of Reason*, sig. D8, It is an old saying … he y^t doth well diuide, doth teache well.

Divide and rule. 1588: tr. *M. Hurault's Discourse upon the Present State of France*, 44, It hath been alwaies her [Catherine de Medici's] custome to set in France one against an other, that in the meane while shee might rule in these divisions. 1605: J. Hall, *Meditations*, i 109, For a prince … is a sure axiome, Divide and rule. 1732: Swift, *Poems*, III 805, As Machiavel taught 'em, divide and ye govern. (But Swift was wrong in attributing the source of the principle to Macchiavelli.)

Dizzy (or **Giddy**) **as a goose.** 'Dizzy' was probably used in the old sense of foolish or stupid. 1639: Clarke, 286, As dizzie as a goose. 1670: Ray, 204. 1745: Franklin, *Drinker's Dict.*, in *Works*, ii 24 (Bigelow), He's as dizzy as a gooze. 1774: Burgoyne, *Maid of the Oaks*, IV ii, I am as giddy as a goose, yet I have not touched a drop of liquor to-day. 1788: Colman, jr., *Ways and Means*, III ii, Giddy as a goose.

Do and **Doing. 1. By doing nothing we learn to do ill.** 1567: Fenton, *Bandello*, ii 63 (T.T.), Plato, who affirmeth that in doynge nothyng men lerne to do evill. 1669: *Politeuphuia*, 307. 1732: Fuller, 1038.

2. Do and undo, the day is long enough. 1639: Clarke, 156. 1672: Walker, *Paroem.*, 50. 1736: Bailey, *Dict.*, s.v. 'Do'.

3. Do as I say, not as I do. [Faites ce que nous disons et ne faites pas ce que nous faisons. – Tr. of Boccaccio (3rd day, 7th novel) by A. Sabatier de Castres (1801).] 1546: Heywood, *Proverbs*, Pt II ch v, It is as folke dooe, and not as folke saie. 1631: Mabbe, *Celestina*, 27 (T.T.), Do you that good which I say, but not that ill which I do. 1859: Smiles, *Self-Help*, 360 (1869), The common saying of 'Do as I say, not as I do', is usually reversed in the actual experience of life. 1881: Evans, *Leics. Words, etc.*, 300 (E.D.S.), 'Do as I say an' not as I do' says the paa'son. A *var.* of this which I have heard more than once runs: 'as the paa'son said when they whelt 'im hum in a wheel-barra'.

4. Do as most men do, and men will speak well of you. 1546: Heywood, *Proverbs*, Pt II ch ii, He that dooth as most men doo, shalbe least wondred on. 1670: Ray, 122, Do as the most do, and fewest will speak evil of thee. 1732: Fuller, 1303.

5. Do as you're bidden and you'll never bear blame. 1678: Ray, 101.

6. Do as you would be done by. *c.*1596: A Munday *et al.*, *Sir Thomas More*, 9, A [he] saies trewe: letts do as we may be doon by. 1747: Chesterfield, *Letter* 16 Oct., 'Do as you would be done by' is the surest method that I know of pleasing. 1863: C. Kingsley, *The Water Babies*, v, I shall grow as handsome as my sister … the loveliest fairy in the world … Mrs Doasyou-wouldbedoneby.

7. Do evil and look for the like. 1569: Grafton, *Chron.*, i 482 (1809), So the common prouerbe was verified, as yon have done, so shall you feele.

1633: Draxe, 179, Doe euill and euill will come of it. 1732: Fuller, 1305.

8. Do good and then do it again. 1659: Howell, *Proverbs: Brit.-Eng.*, 12, Do it good, or do it again. 1855: Bohn, 269.

9. Do good: thou dost it for thyself. 1732: Fuller, 1306, Do good, if you expect to receive it. 1864: 'Cornish Proverbs', in *N. & Q.*, 3rd ser, vi 495.

10. Do it by degrees. *See* Cat (35).

11. Do it well that thou may'st not do it twice. 1732: Fuller, 1308.

12. Do-little good, do-little evil, etc. *See* **Come** (4).

13. Do man for thyself, *etc*. *See* quot. 15th cent.: in *Reliq. Antiquae*, i 314 (1841), Do mon for thiselffie, Wyl thou art alyve; For he that dose after thu dethe, God let him never thryve. Quod Tucket.

14. Do not all you can; spend not all you have; believe not all you hear; and tell not all you know. 1855: Bohn, 344.

15. Do nothing hastily but catching of fleas. 1678: Ray, 151, Nothing must be done hastily but killing of fleas. 1732: Fuller, 1309. *c.*1791: Pegge, *Derbicisms*, 136 (E.D.S.), Do nothing rashly, but kill fleas. 1881: Mrs Parker, *Oxfordsh. Words: Suppl.*, 87 (E.D.S.), 'You shouldn do nothun in a 'urry but ketch flaes [fleas]'. A saying.

16. Do the likeliest and hope the best. 1732: Fuller, 1310.

17. Do well and have well. 1362: Langland, *Plowman*, A, viii 97, I con no pardoun fynde, Bote 'dowel, and haue wel and god schal haue thi soule'. *c.*1483: Caxton, *Dialogues*, 47 (E.E.T.S.), I say atte begynnyng, Who doth well shall well haue. 1546: Heywood, *Proverbs*, Pt II ch ix 1611: Cotgrave, s.v. 'Bien', He that does well shall. speed well. 1732: Fuller, 1311.

18. Do what thou oughtest and come what can come. 1659: Howell, 6. 1670: Ray, 7.

19. Doing is better than saying. 1633: Draxe, 41.

20. He does well, but none knows but himself. 1639: Clarke, 145.

21. He doeth much that doeth a thing well. 1732: Fuller, 1839.

22. He may do much ill ere he can do much worse. 1546: Heywood, *Proverbs*, Pt I ch xi 1594: Bacon, *Promus*, No. 956. 1639: Clarke, 150.

23. He that does not love a woman. *See* Hate (1).

24. He that does you an ill turn. *See* Ill turn (2).

25. He that doth amiss may do well. 1629: *Book of Meery Riddles*, Prov. 76.

26. He that doth his own business hurteth not his hand. 1591: Florio, *Second Frutes*, 11 [with 'doth not defile' for 'hurteth']. 1640: Herbert, *Jac. Prudentum* [with 'fouls' for 'hurteth']. 1732: Fuller, 2086.

27. He that doth ill hateth the light. 1629: *Book of Meery Riddles*, Prov. 77.

28. He that doth most at once doth least. 1855: Bohn, 385.

29. He that doth nothing doth ever amiss. 1629: *Book of Meery Riddles*, Prov. 75. 1865: 'Lancs Proverbs', in *N. & Q.*, 3rd ser, viii 494, Those who are doing nothing are doing ill. 1901: F. E. Taylor, *Lancs Sayings*, 10, Thoose 'at are doin' nowt are doin' ill.

30. He that doth well wearieth not himself. 1633: Draxe, 32. 1732: Fuller, 2090.

31. He that doth what he will, doth not what he ought. 1640: Herbert, *Jac. Prudentum*. 1748: Richardson, *Clarissa*, iv 121 (1785), I am sure he has proved the truth of a hundred times, That he who does what he will seldom does what he ought.

32. He that hath done ill once will do it again. 1855: Bohn, 400.

33. He that hath done so much hurt that he can do no more may sit down and rest him. 1633: Draxe, 43. 1639: Clarke, 150.

34. He that would do no ill must do all good, or sit still. 1855: Bohn, 396.

35. I do what I can, quoth the fellow when he thresht in his cloake. 1639: Clarke, 155.

36. If thou thyself canst do it, rely not on another. 1541: Coverdale, *Christ. State Matrimony*, sig. I3, That whych thou cannest do conueniently thy selfe commytte it not to another. 1611: Cotgrave, s.v. 'Faire'. 1670: Ray, 1. 1710: S. Palmer, *Moral Essays on Proverbs*, 152, For what you can do your self don't depend on another. 1831: Hone, *Year-Book*, col. 1612, Never trouble another for what you can do yourself. 1880: Spurgeon, *Ploughman's Pictures*, 33, If you want a thing well done, do it yourself.

37. In doing we learn. 1640: Herbert, *Jac. Prudentum*.

38. That may be done in an hour, which we may repent all our life after. 1658: *Wit Restor'd*, 151.

39. We must do as we may, if we can't do as we would. 1633: Draxe, 32, A man must doe as he can, when hee cannot as he would. 1698: *Terence made English*, 43, They that can't do as they wou'd, must e'en do as they may, as the saying is. 1732: Fuller, 4988.

40. We'll do as they do at … (*see* quots.). 1678: Ray, 80, We'll do as they do at Quern, What we do not do to-day, we must do i' th' morn. 1830: Forby, *Vocab. E. Anglia*, 427, You must do as they do at Hoo, What you can't do in one day, you must do in two. 1919: *Devonsh. Assoc. Trans.*, li. 77, Oh, my dear love! 'e must do same's they doo's in France, the best 'e can.

41. What is done by night appears by day. *c.*1390: Gower, *Conf. Amantis*, bk v 1. 4599, Thing don upon the derke nyht Is after knowe on daies liht. 1666: Torriano, *Piazza Univ.*, 263, That which is done in the dark, appears in the sun shine. 1732: Fuller, 5495.

42. What's done can't be undone. *See* Once done.

43. What we do willingly is easy. 1630: T. Adams, *Works*, 422. 1831: Hone, *Year-Book*, col. 1612, Nothing is troublesome that we do willingly.

44. Who would do ill, ne'er wants occasion. 1640: Herbert, *Jac. Prudentum*.

Dock to a daisy, As like as a. 1639: Clarke, 96, An odious comparison! a dock to a dazie. 1670: Ray, 204, As like as a dock to a daisie. That is very unlike.

Dock. *See* In dock.

Doctor Diet, etc. *See* quots. 1558: Bullein, *Govt. of Health*, fo. 51, The first was called doctor diet, the seconde doctor quiet, the thirde doctor mery-man. 1596: Harington, *Metam. of Ajax*, 99 (1814), Doctor Diet, Doctor Quiet, and Doctor Merryman. 1660: Howell, *Parly of Beasts*, 23, After these two, Doctor Diet and Doctor Quiet, Doctor Merriman is requisit to preserve health. 1738: Swift, *Polite Convers.*, Dial. II, The best doctors in the world are [as in 1596]. 1869: Spurgeon, *John Ploughman*, ch v [as in 1738]. 1920: *Times*, 5 Oct., p. 6, col. 1 [as in 1738].

Doctor Dodipoll. A proverbial name for a simpleton, *c.*1410: *Towneley Plays*, 173 (E.E.T.S.), ffy, dotty-pols, with your bookys! 1550: Latimer, *Sermons*, 245 (P.S.), They, like dodi-poles laughed their godly father to scorn. 1600: *The Wisedome of Dr Dodypoll* [title], in

Bullen, *Old Plays*, vol iii 1639: Clarke, 137, Doctor Dodipoll is more honoured then a good divine. 1881: Evans, *Leics. Words, etc.*, 139 (E.D.S.), Doddipole, a simpleton; noodle. 1889: Peacock, *Manley, etc., Gloss.*, 169 (E.D.S.), Dodipoll – a blockhead.

Doctors differ (or **disagree**). 1677: Wycherley, *Plain Dealer*, I i, Well, doctors differ. 1735: Pope, *Moral Essays*, Epist. iii, Who shall decide when Doctors disagree? 1813: *Gent. Mag.*, Pt I, p. 627, I shall stand protected by the rhyming adage: 'When Doctors disagree, Disciples then are free'. 1830; Colanan, jr., in *Hum. Works*, 429 (Hotten).

Doe in the month of May. *See* quot. *c.*1676: in *Roxb. Ballads*, vii 558 (B.S.), If it be true, as old wives say, 'Take a doe in the month of May, And a forester's courage she soon will allay'.

Doff one's shoes. *See* **Put** (1).

Dog and **Dogs. 1. A bad dog never sees the wolf.** 1611: Cotgrave, s.v. 'Loup', A bad dog hates to looke upon a wolfe. 1640: Herbert, *Jac. Prudentum*.

2. A barking dog never bites (or **bites little**). *c.*1350: *Alexander*, l. 1805, Bot as bremely as he [a 'curre'] baies he bitis never the faster. 1387: Trevisa, tr. Higden, iii 427 (Rolls Ser.), Hit is the manere of the feblest houndes for to berke most. 1581: T. Howell, *Devises*, 30 (1906), Those dogs byte least, that greatest barkings keepe. 1669: *Politeuphuia*, 198, A dog that barketh much will bite but little. 1736: Bailey, *Dict.*, s.v. 'Barking', Barking dogs seldom bite.

3. A dog in a doublet. 1577: J. Grange, *Golden Aphroditis*, sig. F1, As seemely as ... a dogge in a dublet. 1600: Dekker, *Shoem. Hol.*, III i, My maister will be as proud as a dogge in a dublet, al in beaten damaske and velvet. 1639: in *Berkeley MSS.*, iii 33 (1885), As proud as a dog in a doublett, i.e. very proud. 1754: Berthelson, *Eng.-Danish Dict.*, s.v. 'Dog', A meer dog in a doublet. 1894: Northall, *Folk Phrases*, 6 (E.D.S.), A mere dog in a doublet = A mean pitiful creature. Cf. No. 62.

4. A dog in a halter. 1639: Clarke, 274, To take a man up as short as a dog in a halter. 1660: *Roxb. Ballads*, vii 648 (B.S.), For the pence hee's your dog in a halter.

5. A dog is made fat in two meals. 1863: Wise, *New Forest*, ch xvi, 'A dog is made fat in two meals', is applied to upstart or purse-proud people.

6. A dog will not cry if you beat him with a bone. 1659: Howell, *Proverbs: Brit.-Eng.*, 24, The dog will not bite, for being struck with a bone. 1732: Fuller, 79.

7. A dog's life; hunger and ease. 1666: Torriano, *Piazza Univ.*, 276, The English say, Hunger and ease is a dogs life. 1670: Ray, 172.

8. A dog's nose and a maid's knees are always cold. 1639: Clarke, 72, A dog's nose is ever cold. 1659: Howell, 9 (7), A womans knee and a doggs snowt are alwayes cold. 1670: Ray, 51. 1870: 'C. Bede', in *N. &Q.*, 4th ser, vi 495, [Old Hunts cottager *loq.*] Why, that's a very old saying, 'A maid's knee and a dog's nose are the two coldest things in creation'. ['Knee' is sometimes 'elbow'. See a long story of Noah's ark and the leak therein in Lowsley's *Gloss. of Berkshire Words* (1888), quoted in Mrs Wright's *Rustic Speech, etc.*, p. 227 (1913).]

9. A good dog deserves a good bone. 1611: Cotgrave, s.v. 'Bon'. 1633: Jonson, *Tale of a Tub*, II i, A good dog Deserves, sir, a good bone. 1732: Fuller, 144. 1875: A. B. Cheales, *Proverb. Folk-Lore*, 35.

10. A man may provoke his own dog to bite him. 1546: Heywood, *Proverbs*, Pt II ch vii, A man maie handle his dog so That he waie make him byte him, though he would not. 1670: Ray, 7 [with 'cause' for 'provoke']. 1732: Fuller, 298.

11. A still dog bites sore. *c.*1270: *Prov. of Alfred*, in *Old Eng. Miscell.*, 137 (Morris, E.E.T.S.), the bicche bitit ille than he berke still. 1593: *Tell-Trothes N. Yeares Gift*, 15 (N.Sh.S.), A stille dogge bites sore, but the barking cur feares [frightens] more. 1638: D. Tuvill, *Vade Mecum*, 130 (3rd ed.), The slowest barker is the surest biter. 1906: A. C. Doyle, *Sir Nigel*, ch xiv, 'Good!' said he. 'It is the mute hound which bites the hardest.'

12. A toiling dog comes halting home. 1732: Fuller, 441.

13. All the dogs follow the salt bitch. 1639: Clarke, 13. 1670: Ray, 80.

14. An old dog barks not in vain. 1578: Florio, *First Fruites*, fo. 28. 1651: Herbert, *Jac. Prudentum*, 2nd ed. 1732: Fuller, 3711, Old dogs bark not for nothing.

15. An old dog bites sore. 1546: Heywood, *Proverbs*, Pt II ch vi, It is saide of olde: an olde dog byteth sore. 1605: Breton, in *Works*, ii *l* 15 (Grosart). 1716: Ward, *Female Policy*, 46, 'Tis a certain truth that an old dog and ... bite aore.

16. An old dog will learn no new tricks. 1605: Camden, *Remains*, 326 (1870), It is hard to teach an old dog tricks. 1694: D'Urfey, *Quixote*, Pt I Act II sc i 1758–07: Sterne, *Trist. Shandy*, vol iii ch xxxiv, It is a singular blessing, that nature has formed the mind of man with the same happy backwardness and renitency against conviction, which is observed in old dogs, – 'of not learning new tricks'. 1823: Scott, *Peveril*, Introd., par. 2. 1924: I Hay, *The Shallow End*, 5, We are an ancient and dignified people, and you cannot teach an old dog new tricks.

17. As busy as a dog in dough. 1879: G. F. Jackson, *Shropsh. Word-Book*, 128, 'As busy as a dog in duff [dough]' is a proverbial saying heard in some parts of Shropshire. 1894: Northall, *Folk Phrases*, 19 (E.D.S.), Like dogs in dough, i.e. unable to make headway. 1917: Bridge, *Cheshire Proverbs*, 11, As busy (as thrunk) as a dog in dough.

18. As courteous as a dog in a kitchen. Ironical. 1377: Langland, *Plowman*, B, v 261, 'I am holden,' quod he, 'as hende as hounde is in kychyne.'

19. As the old dog barks, so the young one. *c.*1470: G. Ashby, *Poems*, 32 (E.E.T.S.), Aftur the oolde dogge the yonge whelp barkes.

20. As vain as a dog with two tails. 1889: J. Nicholson, *Folk Speech E. Yorks*, 17.

21. At every dog's bark seem not to awake. 1546: Heywood, *Proverbs*, Pt II ch v *c.*1594: Bacon, *Promus*, No. 662, At every dogges bark to awake. 1633: Draxe, 48, Wake not at euery dogges barke.

22. At open doors, dogs come in. 1820: Scott, *Monastery*, ch xxxiii.

23. Better have a dog fawn upon you than bite you. 1639: Clarke, 219. 1678: Ray, 128. 1732: Fuller, 902.

24. Cut off a dog's tail and he will be a dog still. 1578: Florio, *First Fruites*, fo. 33. 1629: *Book of Meery Riddles*, Prov. 122.

25. Dead dogs bark not. 1596: A. Copley, *Fig for Fortune*, 23 (Spens.S.), Dead dogges barke not. 1667: L'Estrange, *Quevedo's Visions*, 252 (1904), A dead dog will never bite.

26. Dog and side pockets. *See* Toad (1).

27. Dog does not eat dog. [… parcit Cognatis maculis similis fera. – Juvenal, *Sat.* xv 160.] 1651: Herbert, *Jac. Prudentum*, 2nd ed., A wolf will never make war against another wolf. 1790: Wolcot, in *Works*, ii 203 (1795), Dog should not prey on dog, the proverb says. 1809: Pegge, *Anonym*, cent. vi 26, It is a common observation that dog will not eat dog. 1869: Spurgeon, *John Ploughman*, ch xiv, Dog won't eat dog, but men will eat each other up like cannibals.

28. Dogs bark as they are bred. 1732: Fuller, 1313. 1875: A. B. Cheales, *Proverb. Folk-Lore*, 140, Dogs bark as they are bred, and fawn as they are fed.

29. Dogs bark before they bite. 1546: Heywood, *Proverbs*, Pt II ch vii, A dog will barke er he bite. 1670: Ray, 81. 1732: Fuller, 1316, Dogs ought to bark before they bite. [Camden (1605, *Remains*, 316 (1870)) reverses the saying – A dog will bite ere he bark.]

30. Dogs bark more from custom than fierceness. 1631: Mabbe, *Celestina*, Epist. Ded., Like dogges that barke by custome. 1647: Wharton, *Merlini Anglici*, Pref., It is a common proverb, 'Dogs bark more for custome than fiercenesse'.

31. Dogs bark not at him. 1546: Heywood, *Proverbs*, Pt II ch v, All dogs barke not at him. 1607: Dekker, *Knight's Conjuring*, 30 (Percy S.), He car'de not what dogges bark'd at him. 1650: Fuller, *Pisgah Sight*, bk iii ch iv § 1, In his peaceable country, where no dog durst bark against him.

32. Dogs begin in jest and end in earnest. 1855: Bonn, 345.

33. Dogs gnaw bones because they cannot swallow them. 1670: Ray, 7.

34. Dogs run away with whole shoulders. 1670: Ray, 172.

35. Dogs that bark at a distance never bite. 1605: Camden, *Remains*, 321 (1870), Dogs barking aloof bite not at hand. 1732: Fuller, 1317.

36. Dogs that put up many hares kill none. 1732: Fuller, 1319. 1846–59: *Denham Tracts*, ii 108 (F.L.S.).

37. Dogs wag their tails not so much in love to you as to your bread. 1611: Cotgrave, s.v. 'Amour', Dogs fawne on a man no longer then he feeds them. 1633: Draxe, 21, The dog waggeth his taile, not for you, but for your bread. 1670: Ray, 7. 1732: Fuller, 1320.

38. Dogs will run away with the meat but not with the work. 1864: 'Cornish Proverbs', in *N.&Q.*, 3rd ser, vi 494.

39. Enough to make a dog laugh. *c*.1603: in Collier, *Roxb. Ballads*, 158 (1847), 'Two'd make a dog laugh. 1664: Pepys, *Diary*, 8 Jan., To hear how W. Symons do commend and look sadly … would make a dogg laugh. 1794: Wolcot, *Works*, ii 528 (1795), Enough to make the sourest cynic smile, Or, as the proverb says, 'make a dog laugh'.

40. Every dog considers himself a lion at home. 1666: Torriano, *Piazza Univ.*, 36, Every dog is a lion at home. 1732: Fuller, 1414, Every dog is stout at his own door. 1865: 'Lancs Proverbs', in *N.&Q.*, 3rd ser, viii 494. 1869: Spurgeon, *John Ploughman*, ch xiii, A dog is a lion when he is at home.

41. Every dog has his day. 1546: Heywood, *Proverbs*, Pt I ch xi, A dog hath a daie. 1573: *New Custom*, II iii, Well, if it chance that a dog hath a day. *c*.1630: in *Roxb. Ballads*, i 184 (Hindley), Let's spend while we may; Each dog hath his day. 1705: Ward, *Hudibras Rediv.*, Pt 2, can. iii, p. 18, I've heard a good old proverb say, That ev'ry dog has got his day. 1860: Reade, *Cl. and Hearth*, ch xxxvi 1864: *N.&Q.*, 3rd ser, v 97, They say in this county [Essex] 'Every dog has his day, and a cat has two Sundays'. 1896: F. M. T. Palgrave, *Hetton-le-Hole Word List*, 3 (E.D.S.), A saying sometimes heard is 'Every dog has its day, and a bitch two afternoons'.

42. For fashion's sake, as dogs go to church. 1732: Fuller, 1590.

43. Give a dog a bad (or an ill) name and hang him. 1706: J. Stevens, *Spanish and English Dictionary*, s.v. Perro, We say, Give a dog an ill Name, and his work is done. 1721: J. Kelly, *Scottish Proverbs*, 124, Give a Dog an ill Name, and he'll soon be hanged. 1760: Colman, *Polly Honeycombe*, sc iv 1815: Scott, *Mannering*, ch xxiii 1922: E. Hutton, in *Sphere*, 8 April, p. 40, 'Give a dog a bad name and hang him' has proved too often to be a true proverb. Cf. Ill name.

44. Hang a dog on a crab-tree and he'll never love verjuice. 1659: Howell, 5, He that is hang'd in a crabb tree will never love verjuyce. 1670: Ray, 81. 1692: L'Estrange, *Aesop*, 59 (3rd ed.). 1753: *World*, No. 32, It is true to a proverb, that if you hang a dog upon a crab-tree, he will never love verjuice.

45. He is a good dog which goes to church. 1826: Scott, *Woodstock*, ch i, Bevis, indeed, fell under the proverb which avers 'He is a good dog which goes to church'.

46. He looks like a dog under a door. 1678: Ray, 70.

47. He that would hang his dog gives out first that he is mad. 1530: Palsgrave, 450, He that wyll kyll his neyghbours dogge beareth folkes in hande he is madde. 1670: Ray, 81. 1732: Fuller, 2362.

48. He went as willingly as a dog to a whip. 1654: Gayton, *Pleasant Notes Don Q.*, 188.

49. He who lies down with dogs will rise with fleas. 1578: Florio, *First Fruites*, fo. 29, Who sleepeth with dogges, shal rise with fleas. 1612: Webster, *White Devil*, V i 1791: Wolcot, *Works*, ii 232 (1795). 1853: Trench, *Proverbs*, 82 (1965).

50. I am not every body's dog that whistles. 1633: Draxe, 18, Hee is ready to runne at euery mans whistle. 1659: Howell, 16, I am not like a dogg that cometh at every ones whisling. 1826: Scott, *Woodstock*, ch ix, You are sure he will come, like a dog at a whistle.

51. I will never keep a dog to bite me. 1732: Fuller, 2640.

52. I'll give you no more quarter than a dog does a wolf. 1725: Bailey, tr. Erasmus' *Colloq.*, 555, So that it is grown into a proverb, *I'll give you, etc.*

53. If the old dog bark, he gives counsel. 1640: Herbert, *Jac. Prudentum*. 1670: Ray, 19. 1732: Fuller, 2709.

54. If you would wish the dog to follow you, *feed him*. 1855: Bonn, 422.

55. Into the mouth of a bad dog, often falls a good bone. 1639: Clarke, 45. 1670: Ray, 82. 1732: Fuller, 2832.

56. It is a good dog that can catch anything. 1678: Ray, 70. 1732: Fuller, 2854.

57. It is a hard winter when dogs eat dogs. 1732: Fuller, 2884.

58. It is a poor dog that does not know 'come out'. 1830: Forby, *Vocab. E. Anglia*, 428.

59. It is a poor dog that is not worth whistling for. 1546: Heywood, *Proverbs*, Pt I ch xi, A poore dogge that is not woorth whystlyng. 1605: Camden, *Remains*, 318 (1870). 1670: Ray, 81 [with 'ill' for 'poor']. 1738: Swift, *Polite Convers.*, Dial. I *c*.1770: Murphy, in *Garrick Corresp.*, ii 335 (1832), If they are determined to think me a dog not worth whistling for. 1881: Evans, *Leics. Words*, 139 (E.D.S.), 'It's a surry doog as een't woo'th a whistle', used by an old man, who, though infirm, would have helped a neighbour in getting in his corn if he had been applied to. The saying is very common.

60. It is hard to make an old dog stoop. 1523: Fitzherbert, *Husbandry*, 45 (E.D.S.), The dogge must lerne it, whan he is a whelpe, or els it wyl not be: for it is harde to make an olde dogge to stoupe. 1611: Davies (of Hereford), *Sc. of Fotty*, 47, in *Works*, ii (Grosart), Its hard to make an olde dogge lye low. 1725: Bailey, tr. Erasmus' *Colloq.*, 75, It is a hard matter to mend the manners of an old sinner. An old dog won't be easily brought to wear a collar.

61. It's an ill dog that deserves not a crust. 1639: Clarke, 91 [with 'bad' for 'ill']. 1670: Ray, 81. 1732: Fuller, 2899.

62. It would make a dog doff his doublet. Cheshire. 1678: Ray, 239. 1917: Bridge, *Cheshire Proverbs*, 86. Cf. No. 3.

63. It would make a dog forget his dinner. *c.*1630: B.&F., *Love's Pilgrimage*, II ii.

64. Let every dog carry his own tail. 1666: Torriano, *Piazza Univ.*, 36, Euery dog values his tail. 1880: Spurgeon, *Ploughman's Pictures*, 47.

65. Let the dog worry the hog. 1659: Howell, 13.

66. Like a dog in a fair. *c.*1520: in Skelton, *Works*, ii 445 (Dyce), Ye come among vs plenty By copies in a peire, As sprites in the haire, Or dogges in the ffayre. 1840: Barham, *Ing. Legends*: 'Jackdaw of Rheims', That little jackdaw kept hopping about; Here and there Like a dog in a fair. 1893: G. L. Gower, *Gloss. Surrey Words*, vii (E.D.S.), They didn't keep nothing reg'lar, it was all over the place like a dog at a fair.

67. Like a dog in a wheel. *c.*1653: in *Somers Tracts*, vii 73 (1811), But I durst undertake to pose him with a riddle, and stand his intelligence in a dog in a wheel. 1748: Richardson, *Clarissa*, iv 120 (1785), [Like] a dog in a wheel, which roasts meat for others. 1827: Scott, *Journal*, 22 March, It … makes me feel like a dog in a wheel, always moving and never advancing.

68. Like a dog in the manger. [καθάπερ τὴν ἐν τῇ φάτνῃ κύνα μήτε αὐτὴν ἐσθίουσαν τῶν κριθῶν μήτε τῷ ἵππῳ πεινῶντι ἐπιτρέπουσαν. – Lucian, *Timon.*] *c.*1390: Gower, *Conf. Amantis*, bk ii l. 84, Thogh it be noght the houndes kinde To ete chaf, yit wol he werne An oxe which comth to the berne, Therof to taken eny fode. 1484: Caxton, *Aesope* [Caxton has the fable of the

Dog, but does not give the proverb or phrase 'dog in a manger' in any form]. 1546: *Supplication of Poore Commons*, 65 (E.E.T.S.), They are lyke to a curre dogge lying in a cocke of haye. For he wyll eate none of the hey hym selfe, nother suffer any other beast that commeth to eate therof. 1580: Tusser, *Husbandrie*, 69 (E.D.S.), To dog in the manger some liken I could. 1663: Pepys, *Diary*, 25 Nov., He wittily replied that there was nothing in the world so hateful as a dog in the manger. 1760: Foote, *Minor*, I, Dead to pleasure themselves, and the blasters of it in others – mere dogs in a manger. 1836: Marryat, *Japhet*, ch lxxii, Why what a dog in the manger you must be – you can't marry them both. 1923: Lucas, *Advisory Ben*, 179, But we mustn't be dogs in the manger: old men like us.

69. Like dogs, if one bark, all bark. 1639: Clarke, 148.

70. Like dogs that snarl about a bone; And play together when they've none. 1732: Fuller, 6431.

71. Many a dog is hanged for his skin, and many a man is killed for his purse. 1639: Clarke, 97.

72. Many a dog's dead since you were a whelp. 1732: Fuller, 3336.

73. The best dog leap the stile first, i.e. let the worthiest person take place. 1678: Ray, 76.

74. The dog that licks ashes trust not with meal. 1640: Herbert, *Jac. Prudentum.* 1670: Ray, 82.

75. The dog that fetches will carry. 1830: Forby, *Vocab. E. Anglia*, 429. 1872: J. Glyde, jr., *Norfolk Garland*, 148.

76. The dog who hunts foulest kits at most faults. 1659: Howell, 1. 1670: Ray, 7. 1732: Fuller, 1318, Dogs that hunt foulest hit off most faults.

77. The foremost dog catcheth the hare. 1670: Ray, 10.

78. The hindmost dog may catch the hare. 1580: Lyly, *Euphues*, 419 (Arber), The last dogge oftentimes catcheth the hare. 1681: W. Robertson, *Phraseol. Generalis*, 728. 1732: Fuller, 4597 [with 'catcheth' for 'may catch'].

79. The mad dog bites his master. 1732: Fuller, 4644.

80. The scalded dog fears cold water. 1561: Hoby, *Courtier*, 191 (T.T.), As dogges, after they have bine once scaulded with hott water, are aferd of the colde. 1611: Cotgrave, s.v. 'Chien', The scaulded dog feares even cold water. 1853: Trench, *Proverbs*, 66 (1905).

81. The worst dog that is will wag his tail. 1578: Florio, *First Fruites*, fo. 33, The worst dog waggeth his tayl. 1666: Torriano, *Piazza Univ.*, 36, The pittyfull'st dog that is will wag his tail.

82: There are more ways of killing a dog than choking it with butter. Cf. **Cat** (61). 1845: W.T. Thompson, *Chronicles of Pineville*, 35, There's more ways to kill a dog besides choking him with butter. 1945: F. Thompson, *Lark Rise*, xvi, A proverb always had to be capped. No one could say, 'There's more ways of killing a dog than hanging it' without being reminded, 'nor of choking it with a pound of fresh butter'.

83. There are more ways to kill a dog than hanging. 1678: Ray, 127. 1725: in Swift, *Works*, vi 478 (Scott), I know that very homely proverb, More ways of killing a dog than hanging him. 1762: Smollett, *Sir L. Greaves*, ch xii [title]. 1836: Marryat, *Easy*, ch v.

84. To beat the dog before the lion. *c.*1386: Chaucer, *Squire's Tale*, l. 491, And for to maken other be war by me, As by the whelp chasted is the leoun. 1602: Chamberlain, *Letters*, 148 (Camden S.), It was so well and cunningly convayed to beate the whelp before the lion, and reade her her lesson in her fellowes booke. 1611: Cotgrave, s.v. 'Batre', *Batre le chien devant le lyon*. To punishe a meane person in the presence, and to the terror, of a great one. 1604: Shakespeare, *Othello*, II iii, As one would beat his offenceless dog to affright an imperious lion. 1892: D. G. Rossetti, *Dante and his Circle*, 314, Since a dog scourged can bid the lion fear.

85. To behave as dogs in a bag. *c.*1380: Wiclif, *Works*, ii 358 (Arnold), Than shulde pees be in the chirche withouten strif of doggis in a poke. *c.*1386: Chaucer, *C. Tales*, A, 4278 (Skeat), They walwe [wallow, roll about, struggle] as doon two piggës in a poke.

86. To give one the dog to hold = To serve one a dog-trick. 1678: Ray, 70.

87. To have a dog in one's sleeve. This seems to mean the same as 'a flea in one's ear'. 1577: J. Grange, *Golden Aphrodities*, sig. L1, Some of the company departed with a dogge in their sleeve.

88. To scorn a thing as a dog scorns tripe. 1670: Ray, 207.

89. To sit where the dog was hanged = 'A

succession of petty mischances'. 1830: Forby, *Vocab. E. Anglia*, 409.

90. To sleep a dog's sleep. 1660: Fuller, *Mixt Contempl.*, 269 (1830). He sleepeth not, but only shutteth his eyes in dogsleep. 1669–96: Aubrey, *Lives*, ii 46 (Clark), He was wont to sleep much in the house [of Commons] (at least dog-sleepe). 1773: in *Garrick Corresp.*, i 571 (1831), Mr Willmot … fell asleep. Dr B— thought it *dog sleep.* 1820: Colton, *Lacon*, Pt II No. 122 *n.*, A Greek quotation … roused our slumbering professor, from a kind of dog sleep, in a snug corner of the vehicle.

91. When a dog is drowning every one offers him water (or **drink**). 1611: Cotgrave, s.v. 'Chien'. 1670: Ray, 7. 1736: Bailey, *Dict.*, s.v. 'Dog'. 1875: A. B. Cheales, *Proverb. Folk-Lore*, 69.

92. When the dog is beaten out of the room, where will they lay their stink? 1732: Fuller, 5581.

93. When the whelp plays the old dog grins. Before 1500: Hill, *Commonplace-Book*, 132 (E.E.T.S.), Whan the whelpe gameth, the old dogge grenneth.

94. While the dog (or **hound**) **gnaweth a bone, he loveth no company.** *c.*1210: in T. Wright, *Essays on Middle Ages*, i 149 (1846), Wil the hund gnagh bon, i-fere neld he non. 1586: L. Evans, *Revised Withals Dict.*, sig. C3, Whiles a dog gnawes a bone, he hateth his fellowe, whom otherwise he loues.

95. *See* quot. 1417: in *Reliq. Antiquae*, i 233 (1841), Who that maketh in Christemas a dogge to his larder, And in Marche a sowe to his gardyner, And in Maye a fole of a wise mannes councell, He shall never have good larder, faire gardeyn, nor wele kepte councell. 1486: *Boke of St Albans*, sig. F4 [as in 1417].

96. Who regards not his dog, will make him a choke-sheep. 1864: 'Cornish Proverbs', in *N. &Q.*, 3rd ser, vi 494.

97. Why keep a dog and bark yourself?. 1583: Melbancke, *Philotinus*, sig. Q2, It is smal reason you should kepe a dog, and barke yourselfe. 1670: Ray, 81. 1738: Swift, *Polite Convers.*, Dial. I, But I won't keep a dog, and bark myself. 1924: Austen Chamberlain, reported in *Times*, 16 Dec., p. 8, col. 3, I said to those with whom I talked: 'We have an English proverb, "Why bark yourself when you keep a dog?" '

98. You can't teach an old dog new tricks. *See* **Dog** (16)

99. You may choke a dog with pudding. 1875: A. B. Cheales, *Proverb. Folk-Lore*, 117.

See also **Another man's dog; Brag; Brawling curs; Butter** (9); **Cat** (14), (38), (40), (45), and (64); **Covetous** (3); **Crack; Curst cur; Eat** (29); **Fight** (2) and (3); **Fit as a pudding; Flesh; Greedy; Greyhound; Hare** (7); **Horse** (66); **Hungry; Lame; Lean dog; Lie,** *verb* (3) and (4); **Living; Look** (19); **Love,** *verb* (10) and (20); **Man** (1); **Many dogs; Mastiff; Musk; One dog; Pleased; Plough,** *verb* (3); **Pudding** (4); **Rise** (5); **Scornful; Silent** (4); **Sleeping dogs; Stick,** *subs.* (1); **Two dogs; Waking; We dogs; Wolf** (18); and **Woman** (8) and (38).

Dog-days. 1. *As the dog days commence, so they end*; 2. *Dog days bright and clear Indicate a happy year; But when accompanied by rain, For better times our hopes are vain*; 3. *If it rains on first dog day, it will rain for forty days after* – all three in 1893: Inwards, *Weather Lore*, 31.

Dogged as does it, It's. 1864: M. B. Chestnut, *Diary*, 6 Aug. (1949) 429, 'It's dogged as does it,' says Isabella. 1867: A. Trollope, *Last Chronicle of Barset*, lxi, There ain't nowt a man can't bear if he'll only be dogged ... . It's dogged as does it. It's nothinking about it. 1916: J. Buchan, *Greenmantle*, i, We've got the measure of the old Boche now, and it's dogged as does it.

Dogmatical tone, a pragmatical pate, A. 1732: Fuller, 77.

Dog-trick, To play or serve one a. *c.*1540: tr. Polydore Vergil's *Eng. Hist.*, 284 (Camden S., No. 36) (OED), I will heere in the way of mirthe, declare a prettie dog tricke or gibe as concerninge this mayden. 1667: Flecknoe, *Tomaso the Wand.*, 11 (1925), By which dog-trick of his ... he made every one an enemy to him. 1690: *New Dict. Canting Crew*, sig. D7, He play'd me a dog-trick, he did basely and dirtily by me.

Dole. *Ye deal this dole out at a wrong door* = Your charity is ill bestowed. 1546: Heywood, *Proverbs*, Pt I ch iii *See also* **Happy man.**

Don, River. *See* quot. 1828: J. Hunter, *South Yorks*, i 2, The shelving shining river Don Each year a daughter or a son, is an old saw often too fatally verified in modern experience. Cf. **Dart, River.**

Doncaster cuts = Horses. Before 1529: Skelton, *Magnyfycence*, l. 296, In fayth, I set not by the worlde two Dauncaster cuttys.

Donkey. *See* **Aback o' behind;** and **Ass.**

Door. 1. Make not the door wider than the house. 1639: Clarke, 11.

2. Who will make a door of gold, must knock a nail every day. 1640: Herbert, *Jac. Prudentum*. *See also* **Opportunity.**

Dorsetshire dorsers. 1662: Fuller, *Worthies*, i 453 (1840). 1790: Grose, *Prov. Gloss.*, s.v. 'Dorset'.

Dotterel. 1. *See* quot. 1878: Dyer, *Eng. Folk-Lore*, 96, The appearance of the dotterel ... is regarded by shepherds as a sign of coming winter, and hence the adage: – 'When dotterel do first appear, it shows that frost is very near; But when the dotterel do go, then you may look for heavy snow'.

2. A dish of dottrells. 1639: Clarke, 220.

Doublet *See* **Put** (1).

Doubt, do nowt, When in. 1874: G.J. Whyte-Melville, *Uncle John*, xx, I should wait. When in doubt what to do, he is a wise man who does nothing. 1884: G. Weatherly, '*Little Folks' Proverb Painting Book*, 64, Err ever on the side that's safe, and when in doubt abstain. 1917: J.C. bridge, *Cheshire Proverbs*, 155, When in doubt, do nowt. This shows the cautious Cheshireman at his best.

Doubts. *He that casteth all doubts shall never be resolved.* 1732: Fuller, 2063.

Dove's flood. *In April* (or *spring*) *Dove's flood Is worth a king's good* [ransom]. 1610: P. Holland, tr. Camden's *Britannia*, 587. 1662: Fuller, *Worthies*, iii 127 (1840). *c.*1791: Pegge, *Derbicisms*, 137 (E.D.S.). 1812: Brady, *Claris Cal.*, i 69. 1852: *N.&Q.*, 1st ser, vi 184.

Dover. 1. A Dover shark and a Deal savage. 1790: Grose, *Prov. Gloss.*, s.v. 'Kent'.

2. A Jack of Dover = A sole. *c.*1386: Chaucer, *Cook's Prol.*, l. 23, For many a pastee hastow laten blood, And many a Iakke of Dover hastow sold. 1604: *Jacke of Dover* [title] (Percy S.). 1790: Grose, *Prov. Gloss.*, s.v. 'Kent'.

3. As sure as there's a dog in Dover. 1735: Pegge, *Kent. Proverbs*, in E.D.S., No. 12, p. 69.

4. Dover, a den of thieves. 1735: Ibid., 70. 1766: Smollett, *Travels*, in *Works*, viii 4 (1872).

5. From Dover to Dunbar; and

6. When it's dark in Dover, *'Tis dark all the world over* – both in 1735: Pegge, *Kent. Proverbs*, in E.D.S., No. 12, p. 70.

See also **Berwick;** and **Deal.**

Dover-court: all speakers and no hearers. Essex. North in 1740 quot. misunderstands the saying. 1662: Fuller, *Worthies*, ii 124 (1840). 1700: T. Brown, in *Works*, iii 66 (1760), The whole room was a perfect resemblance of Dovercourt, where all speak, but no body heard or answer'd. 1740: North, *Examen*, 517, As in the proverbial court at Dover, *all speakers and no hearers.* 1851: *Essex Gloss.*, 6, Dovercourt, a great noise. (Said to have arisen from Dovercourt being famous for its scolds.) 1888: Q.-Couch, *Troy Town*, ch xix, For up ten minutes 'twas Dover to pay, all talkers an' no listeners.

Down, *adv.* **1. Down came Tit, and away tumbled she arsy-varsy.** 1813: Ray, 274.

2. Down the hill goes merrily. 1639: Clarke, 260.

3. Going down the brewe (short, steep declivity] = Failing in health. 1917: Bridge, *Cheshire Proverbs*, 61.

4. He that's down, down with him. 1678: Ray, 129. 1732: Fuller, 2282 [*plus* 'cries the world']. 1875: A. B. Cheales, *Proverb. Folk-Lore*, 154, He that is down, down with him, is an expression of some of the basest feelings of human nature.

5. To go down the wind – To be unfortunate. Cf. **Up the weather.** 1604: Breton, in *Works*, ii *k* 8 (Grosart), My purse grew so bare … two or three yeares brought me so doune the winde … 1663: Pepys, *Diary*, 25 Jan., I perceive he goes down the wind in honour as well as everything else, every day. *c.*1680: L'Estrange, *Seneca's Morals: Happy Life*, ch xviii, When a man goes down the wind, no body comes near him. 1754: Berthelson, *Eng.-Danish Dict.*, s.v. 'Down'. 1827: Scott, *Journal*, 25 April, It is certain the old Tory party is down the wind. 1865: J. Sleigh, *Derbysh. Gloss.*, Down in the wind, bankrupt.

Down, *subs.* **There's no down without eyes, no hedge without ears.** 1864: 'Cornish Proverbs', in *N. & Q.*, 3rd ser, vi 494.

Draff is good enough for swine. *c.*1535: *Gentleness and Nobility*, sig. Cl, Thou sayst trew drafe is good inough for swyne. 1591: Harington, *Orl. Furioso*, bk xx st. 83, Tis fit (quoth he) that swine should feed on draffe. 1683: Meriton, *Yorkshire Ale*, 83–7 (1697). 1732: Fuller, 1324.

Draff was his errand, but drink he would have. 1546: Heywood, *Proverbs*, Pt I ch xi, That draffe is your errand, but drinke ye wolde. 1619: Chapman, *Two Wise Men*, VII i 1670: Ray, 83. 1732: Fuller, 1325.

Draughts. 1. If cold wind reach you through a hole, Say your prayers, and mind your soul. 1846: Denham, *Proverbs*, 16 (Percy S.). 1872: *N. & Q.*, 4th ser, x 83, If draught comes to you through a hole, Go make your will, and mind your soul.

2. The air of a window is as the stroke of a cross-bow. 1678: Ray, 41. 1732: Fuller, 6257.

Draw in one's horns, To. 1577: *Misogonus*, III ii, It will make yow plucke in your hornes, an yow were near [never] so wilde. 1642: D. Rogers, *Naaman*, sig. S1, Let them cause you to be ashamed, or to shrinke in your hornes ever the more. 1672: Walker, *Paroem.*, 15, To pull in his horns; make a retreat. 1776: in *Garrick Corresp.*, ii 140 (1832), Give me your assurance *not*, and I will draw in my horns with great pleasure. 1817: Scott, *Rob Roy*, ch xxvii, He 'drew in his horns', to use the Bailie's phrase, on the instant.

Draw the nail, To. 1917: Bridge, *Cheshire Proverbs*, 132.

Drawn wells are seldom dry. 1639: Clarke, 107. 1670: Ray, 83. 1732: Fuller, 1327. 1853: Trench, *Proverbs*, 104 *n.* (1905), In the sense of the latter half of this proverb we say, *Drawn wells are seldom dry.*

Drawn wells have sweetest water. 1639: Clarke, 107. 1681: W. Robertson, *Phraseol. Generalis*, 1196.

Drayton. See Hodnet.

Dream of a dry summer. See Summer (8).

Dream, To. *See* quots. 1639: Clarke, 236, After a dreame of weddings comes a corse. 1670: Ray, 83 [as in 1639]. 1883: Burne, *Shropsh. Folk-Lore*, 263, We have the sayings, 'To dream of the dead, good news of the living'; 'Dream of a funeral, hear of a wedding'; 'Dream of a death, hear of a birth', and vice versa. Ibid., 264, As they say at Welshampton, To dream of things out of season Is trouble without reason.

Dreams go by contraries. *c.*1400: *Beryn*, Prol., l. 108, ffor comynly of these swevenys [dreams] the contrary men shul fynde. 1566: W. Adlington, tr. Apuleius, bk iv, So the visions of the night do often chance contrary. 1633: Rowley, *Match at Midnight*, IV, O, strange! to see how dreams fall by contraries. 1673: Wycherley, *Gent. Danc.-Master*, IV i, Dreams go by contraries. 1731: Fielding, *Grub-Street Opera*, I xi, Oh! the perjury of men! I find dreams do not always go by contraries. 1851: Planché, *Extravag.*, iv 179 (1879), You know That dreams by their contraries always go. 1922: *Punch*, 7 June, p. 441, col. 2, 'Dreams go by contraries', declares a contemporary. That must be how our Derby-tipster got his information.

Drift is at bad as unthrift. 1659: Howell, 6. 1678: Ray, 71.

Drink, *subs*. 1. Drink in wit out. [In proverbium cessit sapientiam vino obumbrari. – Pliny, XXIII. i 23.] *c.*1390: Gower, *Conf. A mantis*, bk vi l. 555, For wher that wyn doth wit aweie, Wisdom hath lost the rihte weie. 1560: Becon, *Catechism*, 375 (P.S.), For when the wine is in, the wit is out. 1599: Shakespeare, *Much Ado*, III v, *Dogb*. A good old man, sir; he will be talking: as they say, When the age [ale] is in, the wit is out. 1642: D. Rogers, *Naaman*, sig. Ee2, Next day when wine was out, and wit in. 1712: Swift, *Journal to Stella*, Lett, xlii., But after dinner is after dinner – an old saying and a true, 'much drinking, little thinking'. 1854: J. W. Warter, *Last of Old Squires*, 53, When the drink goes in, then the wit goes out.

2. Drink and drought come not always together. 1732: Fuller, 1329.

3. Drink washes off the dawb, and discovers the man. Ibid., No. 1330.

4. Of all the meat in the world, drink goes down the best. 1855: Bohn, 466.

Drink, *verb*. 1. Don't say, I'll never drink of this water, how dirty soever it be. 1710: S. Palmer, *Moral Essays on Proverbs*, 236. 1732: Fuller, 5016.

2. Drink as much after an egg as after an ox. 1608: Harington, *Sch. of Salerne*, sig. A7, Remember … For euexy egge you eate you drink as oft. 1659: Howell, 3. 1670: Ray, 36. 1738: Swift, *Polite Convers.*, Dial. II, And, faith, one should drink as much after an egg as after an ox.

3. Drink in the morning staring, then all the day be sparing. 1659: Howell, 1. 1670: Ray, 39. 1846: Denham, *Proverbs*, 14 (Percy S.).

4. Drink less and go home by daylight. *c.*1320: in *Reliq. Antiquoe*, i 116 (1841), 'Drynk eft lasse, and go by lyhte hom'; Quoth Hendyng.

5. Drink off your drink, and steal no lambs. 1659: Howell, 20. 1670: Ray, 216.

6. Drink only with the duck = Drink water only. 1377: Tangland, *Plowman*, B, v 75, Drynke but myd [with] the doke and dyne but ones.

7. Drink the devil. *See* Devil (102).

8. Drink wine and have the gout; drink no wine and have the gout. 1588: Cogan, *Haven of Health*, Epist. Ded., As I haue heard many gentlemen say ere now: Drinke wine and haue the gowte: drink none and haue the gowt. 1655: T. Muffett, *Health's Improvement*, 5. 1699: in *Harl. Miscell.*, ii 49 (1744) [with 'claret' instead of 'wine']. 1732: Fuller, 1331.

9. He drank till he gave up his half-penny = vomited , 1678: Ray, 87. 1745: Franklin, *Drinker's Dict.*, in *Works*, ii 25 (Bigelow).

10. He drinks like a hen, with head held up. 1675: in *Roxb. Ballads*, iv 45 (B.S.), Though he drinks like a chick, with his eye-balls lift up. 1810: Mary Allen, *Poems for Youth*, The little chickens, as they dip Their beaks into the river, Hold up their heads at every dip, And thank the Giver. 1880: Spurgeon, *Ploughman's Pictures*, 28, There's Solomon Braggs holding up his head like a hen drinking water, but there's nothing in it.

11. He is drinking at the Harrow when he should be at the plough. 1639: Clarke, 47. 1670: Ray, 180. 1732: Fuller, 2456.

12. He that drinketh well sleepeth well, and he that sleepeth well thinketh no harm. 1530: Palsgrave, 721. 1551: T. Wilson, *Rule of Reason*, sig. H8, He that drynkes wel, slepes wel. 1609: Lithgow, *Rare Adventures*, 69 (1906), He that eateth well, drinketh well, he that drinketh well, sleepeth well, he that sleepeth well sinneth not, and he that sinneth not goeth straight through Purgatory to Paradise.

13. If you drink with your porridge, you'll cough in your grave. 1670: Ray, 133. 1738: Swift, *Polite Convers.*, Dial. II.

14. The more one drinks the more one may. 1633: Draxe, 49. 1666: Torriano, *Piazza Univ.*, 25 [with 'would' for 'may'].

15. To drink like a fish. 1646: Shirley, in *Works*, vi.321 (Dyce), I can drink like a fish. 1701: Farquhar, *Sir H. Wildair*, II, Where I may … drink like a fish, and swear like a devil. 1778: H. More, in *Garrick Corresp.*, ii 320 (1832), I shall have nothing to do but to go to Bath and drink like a fish. 1885: A. Dobson, in *Poet. Works*, 297 (1923), Thou drink'st as fishes do. 1894: R.L.S., *St Ives*, ch xiii, He drank like a fish or an Englishman.

16. To drink like a funnel. 1813: Ray, 191.

17. When thou dost drink, beware the toast,

for therein lies the danger most. Glos. 1639: in *Berkeley MSS.*, iii 31 (1885).

18. You drink out of the broad end of the funnel, and hold the little one to me. 1732: Fuller, 5898.

19. You drink vinegar when you have wine at your elbow. Ibid., No. 5899.

Drinking kindness is drunken friendship. Ibid., No. 1333.

Drive, *verb.* **1. Drive the nail that will go.** 1655: Fuller, *Church Hist.*, bk ii § iv (12), Thus he drave that nail … which would go best for the present. 1737: Gay, *Fables*, 2nd ser, No. 9, l. 14, Hence politicians, you suggest, Should drive the nail that goes the best. 1857: Hughes, *Tom Brown*, Pt II ch ii, How often have I told you, Tom, that you must drive a nail where it'll go.

2. Drive the nail to the head. 1639: Clarke, 3.

3. Drive thy business, let not that drive thee. 1736: Franklin, *Way to Wealth*, in *Works*, i 443 (Bigelow).

4. He drives a subtle trade. 1678: Ray, 91.

5. It is ill to drive black hogs in the dark. 1678: Ray, 103. 1732: Fuller, 2963.

6. You can drive out nature with a pitchfork, but she keeps on coming back. A saying, relating to the obstinate reappearance of natural characteristics whatever you do to reform or eradicate them, that originates in a literal translation of Horace's *Epistles* i x 24, *naturam expelles furca, tamen usque recurret.* 1539: R. Taverner, *Proverbs or Adagies out of Erasmus*, 44, Thurst [thrust] out nature with a croche [crook], yet woll she styll runne back agayne. 1831: T.L. Peacock, *Crotchet Castle*, i, Mr Crotchet … seemed … to settle down into an English country gentleman … But as, though you expel nature with a pitchfork, she will always come back. 1867: J.A. Froude, *Short Studies*, II 252, Drive out nature with a fork, she ever comes running back.

Drive a top. *See* **Top.**

Droppings. *See* **Save** (2).

Drought never bred dearth in England. 1533: Heywood, *Play of Weather*, l. 634, And it is sayd syns afore we were borne That drought doth neuer make derth of come. 1640: Herbert, *Jac. Prudentum*, Drought never brought dearth. 1732: Fuller, 1338. 1825: Hone, *Ev. Day Book*, i 669. 1875: Parish, *Sussex Dict.*, 38, Drythe never yet bred dëarth. 1917: Bridge, *Cheshire Proverbs*, 52.

Drown not thyself to save a drowning man. 1732: Fuller, 1340.

Drown the miller, To. 1889: J. Nicholson, *Folk Speech E. Yorks*, 5, If, in making dough, the good wife should put too much water, she has 'dhroonid minler' (drowned the miller). 1899: Dickinson, *Cumb. Gloss.*, 105, One whose liquor has been diluted too much, will say that the miller has been drowned. Cf. **Miller** (14).

Drowning man will catch at a straw, A 1534: Sir T. More, *Dialogue of Comfort* (1553), iii, Lyke a man that in peril of drowning catcheth whatsoever cometh next to hand … be it never so simple a sticke. 1583: J. Prime: *Fruitful and Brief Discourse*, i 30, We do not as men redie to be drowned, catch at every straw. 1614: C. Brooke, *Rich. the Third*, 105 (Grosart), And now like to a man (ready to drowne) Catch at a helplesse thing. *c.*1640: in *Harl. Miscell.*, iv 153 (1745), Sinking she will take hold of reeds. *c.*1680: L'Estrange, *Seneca's Epistles*, xviii, We catch hold of hopes … as drowning men do upon thorns, or straws. 1748: Richardson, *Clarissa*, vi 5 (1785), The dear implacable, like a drowning man, catches at a straw to save herself! 1860: Reade, *Cl. and Hearth*, ch xciii. 1875: R.L.S., *Letters*, i 229 (Tusitala ed.), I cling to you as a drowning man to a straw. 1926: Phillpotts, *Marylebone Miser*, ch ix.

Drum's entertainment = A rough reception. 1583: Melbancke, *Philotinus*, sig. D1, Hee had scarce Jacke Drummes enterteynement. 1592: Greene, *Groatsworth*, in *Works*, xii 129 (Grosart), And so giuing him Jacke Drums entertainment, shut him out of doores. 1634: C. Butler, *Feminine Monarchie*, 64, They gently give them Tom Drums enterteinment. *c.*1685: in *Roxb. Ballads*, viii 869 (B.S.), Thy entertainment shall be like Jack Drums. 1834–7: Southey, *Doctor*, ch cxxv, It is at this day doubtful whether it was Jack Drum or Tom Drum, whose mode of entertainment no one wishes to receive.

Drunk as a beggar. 1622: Massinger, *Virgin Martyr*, III iii, Be drunk as a beggar, he helps you home. 1670: Ray, 204. 1745: Franklin, *Drinker's Dict.*, in *Works*, ii 23 (Bigelow). 1909: Hackwood, *Inns, Ales, etc.*, 169, He may be as … drunk as a beggar or … as a lord.

Drunk as a besom. 1888: S.O. Addy, *Sheffield Gloss.*, 13 (E.D.S.), There is a saying 'as drunk as a beesom'.

Drunk as a boiled owl. 1889: Peacock, *Manley*, *etc.*, *Gloss.*, 182 (E.D.S.).

Drunk as a fiddler. 1884: R.L.S. and Henley, *Adm. Guinea*, II vi, I'm as drunk as a Plymouth fiddler. Pew.

Drunk as a fiddler's bitch. 1362: Langland, *Plowman*, A, v 197, Thenne gon he for to go lyk a gleomonnes bicche, Sum tyme asyde and sum tyme arere. 1830: Forby, *Vocab. E. Anglia*, 27. 1894: Northall, *Folk Phrases*, 8 (E.D.S.). 1901: F. E. Taylor, *Lancs Sayings*, 2.

Drunk as a fish. 1704: Congreve, *Way of World*, IV ix, Thou art both as drunk and as mute as a fish. 1864: T. W. Robertson, *David Garrick*, II, He's drunk as a fish.

Drunk as a lord. 1659: in *Somers Tracts*, vii 184 (1811), Yet the proverb goes, 'As drunk as a lord'. 1670: Cotton, *Scarronides*, bk iv 1731: Coffey, *Devil to Pay*, I ii 1872: Hardy, *Greenwood Tree*, Pt I ch i, Time enough to get as drunk as lords!

Drunk as a mouse. *c.*1307: in *Lyric Poetry*, 111 (Percy S.), When that he is dronke ase a dreynt mous. *c.*1386: Chaucer, *Wife of Bath's Prol.*, l. 246, Thou comest hoom as dronken as a mous. *c.*1470: *Songs and Carols*, 90 (Percy S.). Before 1529: Skelton, *Col. Clout*, l. 803, Dronken as a mouse, At the ale house, *c.*1580: *Tom Tyler*, l. 300, p. 9 (Malone S.). 1889: Peacock, *Manley*, *etc.*, *Gloss.*, 182 (E.D.S.), Drunk as … mice.

Drunk as a piper. 1720: Gay, *Poems*, ii 277 (Underhill), Drunk as a piper all day long. 1772: Graves, *Spirit. Quixote*, bk x ch xxix, He became as drunk as a piper.

Drunk as a rat. 1542: Boorde, *Introduction*, 147 (E.E.T.S.), Although I wyll be dronken other whyles as a rat. 1583: Stubbes, *Anat. of Abuses*, 113 (N.Sh.S.), Till thei were bothe as dronke as rattes. 1691: *Merry Drollery*, 28 (Ebsworth). 1880: Spurgeon, *Ploughman's Pictures*, 41.

Drunk as a swine (or **hog, pig, sow**). *c.*1440: Lydgate, *Fall of Princes*, bk iii l. 2369, Thei lai and slepte lik as dronke swyn. *c.*1500: in Hazlitt, *Early Pop. Poetry*, i 100 (1864), To be as dronke as any swyne. 1681: *Poor Robin Alman.*, June, Well may they say men drunk as hogs I think. 1700: Ward, *London Spy*, 264 (1924), Both were as drunk as swine. 1744: *Foundl. Hosp.*, *for Wit*, No. II, p. 52 (1749), A man for his health to get drunk – as a sow. *c.*1795: Wolcot, *Works*, v 71 (1801), And Dundas gets as drunk as a pig. 1803: Colman, jr., *John Bull*, III ii, There's a hog; – for

he's as drunk as one, I know, by his beastly bawling. 1889: Peacock, *Manley*, *etc.*, *Gloss.*, 182 (E.D.S.), Drunk as a pig.

Drunk as a tinker. 1701: Cibber, *Love Makes a Man*, I, I sent young Louis back again to Marli, as drunk as a tinker. 1909: Hackwood, *Inns, Ales, etc.*, 169, He may be … as drunk as a tinker.

Drunk as a wheelbarrow. 1678: Ray, 87. 1697: T. Dilke, *City Lady*, I i, To have made a German general as drunk as a wheel-barrow. 1745: Franklin, *Drinker's Dict.*, in *Works*, ii 23 (Bigelow).

Drunk as an ape. *c.*1500: in Hazlitt, *Early Pop. Poetry*, i 104 (1864), Such as wilbe as drongen as an ape. 1583: Stubbes, *Anat. of Abuses*, 151 (N.Sh.S.), Swilling and gulling, night and day, till they be as drunke as apes. 1633: Draxe, 49. 1762: Hall-Stevenson, *Crazy Tales*, p. vii, They'll make you drunker than an ape. 1909: Hackwood, *Inns, Ales, etc.*, 169, He may be … as fuddled as an ape.

Drunk as an emperor. 1697: T. Dilke, *City Lady*, III ii, Here's my brother as drunk as an emperor.

Drunk as an owl. 1883: R.L.S., *Treasure* I, ch xxiv, 'Clumsy fellows,' said I; 'they must still be drunk as owls.' 1886: Ehrorthy, *West Som. Word-Book*, 549 (E.D.S.), Com. simile is 'Drunk's a owl'. Why the solemn bird should be taken as the ideal drunkard I know not.

Drunk as Chloe. 1906: Q.-Couch, *Mayor of Troy*, ch ix.

Drunk as David's sow. 1671: Shadwell, *Miser*, IV, I am as drunk … as David's sow, as the saying is. 1711: *Brit. Apollo*, i 572 [gives the story which is said to have originated the saying. It is quoted in *Gent. Mag.*, 1811, Pt I, pp. 634–5]. 1725: Bailey, tr. Erasmus' *Colloq.*, 160, He comes home … as drunk as David's sow. 1834: Marryat, *P. Simple*, ch iii 1901: F. E. Taylor, *Lancs Sayings*, 2, As drunk as David's soo.

Drunk as muck, and **Drunk as soot,** – both in 1889: Peacock, *Manley*, *etc.*, *Gloss.*, 182 (E.D.S.).

Drunk as the Baltic. 1823: Scott, *Peveril*, ch xxvii, Fill him as drunk as the Baltic sea. 1824: Scott, *Red-gauntlet*, ch xiv 1899: *N. & Q.*, 9th ser, iv 336, The phrase is still in use among the seafaring population of the East of Scotland in its homely form of 'as fou's the Baltic'.

Drunk as the devil. *c.*1350: in *Allit. Poems*, 82 (Morris, E.E.T.S.), Now a boster on benche

bibbes ther–of Tyl he be dronkken as the deuel.
1709: Ward, *Account of Clubs*, 272 (1756),
Madam Bibbington, in a chair, as drunk as the
devil. 1864: T. W. Robertson, *David Garrick*, II,
He's as d–d–drunk as the very de–de–devil!

Drunk is as great as a king, He that is. 1672:
Westm. Drollery, Pt II 77 (Ebsworth). 1696:
D'Urfey, *Quixote*, Pt III Act III sc ii.

Drunk. *See also* **Ever drunk.**

Drunkard. *As the drunkard goes, is knowne by his
nose.* 1623: Wodroephe, *Spared Houres*, 491.

Drunkard's purse is a bottle, A. 1640: Herbert,
Jac. Prudentium.

**Drunkards have a fool's tongue and a knave's
heart.** 1732: Fuller, 1342.

Drunken and drowsy. *See* quot. 1596: *Knack to
Know an Honest Man*, l. 657 (Malone S.), The
prouerbe is true that I tell to you, Tis better to be
dronken and drowsie. Than hunger starued and
lousie.

Drunken days have all their tomorrows, as the
old proverb says. 1875: Smiles, *Thrift*, 167.

Drunken general is a bad commander, A – an
old proverb. Before 1704: T. Brown, in *Works*,
iii 256 (1760).

Drunken men never take harm. 1591:
Harington, *Orl. Furioso*, bk xxx st. 13, If fortune
that helps frantike men and drunke Had not him
safe conveyd. 1604: *Meeting of Gallants*, 26
(Percy S.), But there is an oulde prouerbe, and
now confirmed true, a druncken man neuer
takes harme. 1605: Chapman, etc., *Eastw. Hoe*,
III ii 1714: Gay, *Shep. Week*, Sat., l. 127, The
power that guards the drunk, his sleep attends.
1894: R.L.S., *St Ives*, ch xiii, I am well aware
there is a Providence for drunken men.

Drunken night makes a cloudy morning, A.
1601: Cornwallis, *Essayes*, Pt II sig. Dd8 (1610)
[with 'mistie' for 'cloudy']. 1732: Fuller, 81.

**Drunkenness reveals what soberness
conceals.** [Quid non ebrietas designat? Operta
recludit. – Horace, *Epist.*, I v 16.] *c.*1386:
Chaucer, *C. Tales*, B 776 (Skeat), Ther
dronkёnessё regneth in any route, Ther is no
conseil hid, withouten doute. 1539: Taverner,
Proverbs, fo. 30, The thynge that lyeth in a sobre
mans hart is in the tongue of the dronkarde. 1579:
Lyly, *Euphues*, 146 (Arber), It is an old prouerbe,
Whatsoeuer is in the heart of the sober man, is in
the mouth of the drunkarde. 1681: W. Robertson,
Phraseol. Generalis, 508. 1732: Fuller, 6117.

Dry. 1. A dry cough is the trumpeter of death.
1655: Howell, *Letters*, bk iv No. ix 1670: Ray, 5.
1736: Bailey, *Dict.*, s.v. 'Trumpeter'.

2. A dry year never starves itself. *c.*1685:
Aubrey, *Nat. Hist. Wilts*, 33 (1847), 'Tis a saying
in the West, that a dry yeare does never cause a
dearth. 1893: Inwards, *Weather Lore*, 4.

3. As dry as a bone. *c.*1555: in Wright, *Songs,
etc., Philip and Mary*, 14 (Roxb.Cl), Also the
congars, as dry as a bonne. 1678: Ray, 283. 1834:
Marryat, *P. Simple*, ch i, Here, Peter, take mine,
it's as dry as a bone. 1886: Elworthy, *West Som.
Word-Book*, 219 (E.D.S.), Dry as a bone. This is
the almost invariable simile to express the
superlative of dryness.

4. As dry as a chip. 1630: Jonson, *New Inn*, IV i
1725: Bailey, tr. Erasmus' *Colloq.*, 533, By that
time it came to me it was as dry as a chip, and no
more taste in it than a foot of a joint-stool. 1850:
Dickens, *Copperfield*, ch xxxi, 'It's quite dry'.
'So 'tis! … as a chip!' 1877: Ross, *Holderness
Gloss.* (E.D.S.), Ah's as dry as a chip.

5. As dry as a fish. 1862: *Dialect of Leeds*, 405.
1889: Peacock, *Manley, etc., Gloss.*, 182
(E.D.S.), I'm as dry as a fish, do gie us a drink o'
aale.

6. As dry as a kex. 1553: *Republica*, V x
(E.E.T.S.), An ye bydde mee, chill [I will]
squease hym as drie as a kyxe. 1566: Drant,
Horace: Satires, sig. A4, Whose lippes as drye as
any kykkes. 1684: L'Estrange, *Observator*, ii No.
118, The Covenant … squeez'd as dry as a kex.
1725: Bailey, tr. Erasmus' *Colloq.*, 7, You're as
thin a body may see through you, and as dry as a
kecks. 1842: Akerman, *Wilts Gloss.*, 30, As dry as
kecks. 1887: Hardy, *Woodlanders*, ch xlviii, My
throat's as dry as a kex. 1891: Hardy, *Tess*, ch xvii.

7. As dry as dust. 1669: *New Help to Discourse*,
248, Who is by drinking drunk as dry as dust.
1679: D'Urfey, *Squire Oldsapp*, I i, My West-
whaphallan at dinner has made me as dry as
dust.

**8. Be it dry or be it wet, The weather'll always
pay its debt.** 1875: A. B. Cheales, *Proverb. Folk-
Lore*, 18.

**9. Dry bread at home is better than roast meat
abroad.** 1640: Herbert, *Jac. Prudentium.* 1670:
Ray, 13.

10. Dry over head happy. 1659: Howell,
Proverbs: Brit.-Eng., 4, A house dry over head is
happy. 1855: Bohn, 267.

11. It is got into dry cock. A haying simile. 1639: Clarke, 234, You have it in dry cocke. 1672: Walker, *Paraem.*, 13, It is got into dry cock; out of harms way. 1681: W. Robertson, *Phraseol. Generalis*, 678, It is got in a dry cock; Res est jam in vado salutis.

Duck and **Ducks. 1. A duck will not always dabble in the same gutter.** 1732: Fuller, 82.

2. Ducks fare well in the Thames. 1670: Ray, 83. 1735: Pegge, *Kent. Proverbs*, in *E.D.S.*, No. 12, p. 78.

3. Ducks will not lay till they have drunk March water. 1879: *Folk-Lore Record*, ii 202, There is a saying in Luxulyan [Cornwall] that 'ducks will not lay till they have drunk Lide [March] water'.

4. Fine weather for ducks = Wet. [1546: Heywood, *Proverbs*, Pt I ch xiii, Weather meete to sette paddockes (frogs) abroode in.] 1840: Dickens, *Curiosity Shop*, ch ii, From which appearance he augured that another fine week for the ducks was approaching, and that rain would certainly ensue.

5. Like a duck in thunder. 1823: Scott, *Peveril*, ch xi, Till she had … closed her eyes like a dying fowl – turned them up like a duck in a thunderstorm. 1863: Kingsley, *Water Babies*, ch v 1917: Bridge, *Cheshire Proverbs*, 72, He winks and thinks like a duck i' thunner.

6. Like water off a duck's back. 1824: Maginn, *O'Doherty's Maxims*, 128 (1849), The thing passed off like water from a duck's back. 1916: B. Duffy, *The Old Lady*, 12, To let his attentions run off me like water off a duck's back.

7. They follow each other like ducks in a gutter. 1855: Bohn, 525.

8. To make ducks and drakes of money = To squander it. [1585: *Nomenclator*, 299, A stone throwne into the water, and making circles yer it sinke … it is called a ducke and a drake, and a halfe penie cake.] 1605: Chapman, etc., *Eastw. Hoe*, I i, Why, do nothing, be like a gentleman, be idle … make duckes and drakes with shillings. 1653: Shirley, *Cupid and Death*, in *Works*, vi, 349 (Dyce), And play'd at duck and drake with gold, like pebbles. 1765: in *Garrick Corresp.*, i 207 (1831), I had rather make ducks and drakes of my money, than buy his book. 1850: Dickens, *Copperfield*, ch xlvii, He soon made ducks and drakes of what I gave him. 1859: Sala, *Twice Round Clock*, 3 p.m., It is but very rarely indeed that they make ducks and drakes of their customers' money.

9. When ducks are driving through the burn. That night the weather takes a turn. 1893: Inwards, *Weather Lore*, 133.

10. When the ducks eat up the dirt. 1738: Swift, *Polite Convers.*, Dial. II, But, Sir John, when may we hope to see you again in London? *Sir John.* Why, Madam, not till the ducks have eat up the dirt, as the children say. 1910: *N. & Q.*, 11th ser, i 316, Some time in the early sixties I was told in North Lincolnshire that I might go out to play 'when the ducks had picked up [or 'had eaten'] the mud'.

See also **Drink** (6); and **Prate**.

Dudleston. *See* quot. 1883: Burne, *Shropsh. Folk-Lore*, 583, The longer you live the more you see, Dudleston Chapel-bell hung on a tree.

Dudman and Ramhead meet, When. 1602: Carew, *Surv. of Cornwall*, 330 (1811), Amongst sundry proverbs, allotting an impossible time of performance, the Cornishmen have this one, 'When Ram Head and Dudman meet'. 1662: Fuller, *Worthies*, i 307 (1840). 1790: Grose, *Prov. Gloss.*, s.v. 'Cornwall', 1821: Scott, *Kenilworth*, ch iv, Depart – vanish – or we'll have you summoned before the Mayor of Halgaver, and that before Dudman and Ramhead meet. 1865: Hunt, *Pop. Romances W. of Eng.*, 182 (1896), Merlyn is said to have pronounced the following prophecy, standing near St German's Grotto on the shores of Whitsand Bay: – 'When the Rame Head and Dodman meet, Men and women will have cause to greet'.

Dufton. *See* quot. 1846–59: *Denham Tracts*, i 165 (F.L.S.), ' "How's that?" says Dufton.' This saying is very common in Cumberland, and originated with the notorious thief of the name. [He stole corn from farmers' granaries, by boring a hole with an auger through the floor of the granary and holding a sack under it. One farmer had nailed sheet-iron over his boards. When Dufton failed to penetrate this with his auger he said, 'How's that?']

Duke Humphrey. *See* **Dine**.

Dulcarnon, At = At one's wits' end. *c.*1374: Chaucer, *Troylus*, bk iii ll. 930–3, 'I am, til god me bettre minde sende, At dulcarnon, right at my wittes ende.' Quod Pandarus, 'ye, nece, wol ye here? Dulcarnon called is "fleminge of wrecches." ' *c.*1584: Stanihurst, *Descrip. of*

Ireland, 28, These sealie soules were (as all dulcarnanes for the most part are) more to be terrified from infidelitie ... than allured to Christianitie. 1736: Bailey, *Dict.*, s.v., To be at Dulcarnon, to be non-plussed, to be at one's wits end. 1852: *N. & Q.*, 1st ser, v 180, I heard it used the other day by a person who, declaring he was at his wits' end, exclaimed, 'Yes, indeed, I am at Dulcarnon.'

Dule and dawkin. *See* **Better dule.**

Dull as a beetle. 1670: Ray, 204. 1753: *World*, No. 45, 'As dull as a beetle', is a term I have no dislike to.

Dull as a Dutchman. 1639: Clarke, 296. 1681: W. Robertson, *Phraseol. Generalis*, 510.

Dumb as a door. 1362: Langland, *Plowman*, A, xi 94, As doumbe as a dore. *c.*1440: *York Plays*, 322 (L. T. Smith), Bot domme as a dore gon he dwell.

Dumb as a fish. *See* **Mute.**

Dumb man gets no land, The. *c.*1390: Gower, *Conf. Amantis*, bk vi l. 447, For selden get a domb man lond. Tak that proverbe, and understond That wordes ben of vertu grete. 1406: Hoccleve, in *Minor Poems*, 38 (E.E.T.S.), The prouerbe is 'the doumb man no lond getith'. 1670: Ray, 83, Dumb folks get no lands. 1732: Fuller, 84, A dumb man never gets land. 1899: Dickinson, *Cumb. Gloss.*, 106, 'Dumb folk heirs nae Ian" – said when anything is to be or has been obtained by speaking.

Dun as a mouse. 1678: Ray, 283.

Dun cow, To stand like the. 1663: Killigrew, *Parson's Wedding*, II vi, I'll make him jostle like the miller's mare [q.v.] and stand like the dun cow, till thou may'st milk him.

Dun is in the mire. *c.*1386: Chaucer, *Manciple's Prol.*, l. 5, Ther gan our hoste for to iape and pleye, And seyde, 'sirs, what! Dun is in the myre!' 1412: Hoccleve, *Regement*, 86 (E.E.T.S.), Be bis day kept, he rekketh nat a bene, But elles, siker, 'don is in the myre'. Before 1529: Skelton, in *Works*, i 418 (Dyce), Dun is in the myre, dame, reche me my spur. 1592: Shakespeare, *Romeo*, I iv, If thou art Dun, we'll draw thee from the mire. 1694: Motteux, *Rabelais*, bk iv ch lxiii, We were all out of sorts, moping, drooping ... as dull as Dun in the mire. 1905: *N. & Q.*, 10th ser, iii 11, An old proverb 'Dun's in the mire' ... 'Dun' is evidently the name of a horse, and the saying no doubt had its

origin in the dreadful state of the roads in early times.

Dun out of the mire. [To draw Dun out of the mire was an old game, described by Gifford in his edition of Ben Jonson, vii 283.] 1607: Dekker and Webster, *Westw. Hoe*, II iii, I see I'm borne still to draw Dun out oth mire for you: that wise beast will I be. 1663: Butler, *Hudibras*, III iii 110, Who has dragged your dunship out o' th' mire.

Dun's the mouse = Keep still. 1592: Shakespeare, *Romeo*, I iv, Tut, dun's the mouse. 1609: *Ev. Woman in her Humor*, IV i, in Bullen, *Old Plays*, iv 352, I will see and say little; what I say duns the mouse, and welcome my bullies, *c.*1630: in *Roxb. Ballads*, i 69 (Hindley), I'le say no more but duns the mouse.

Dunder [Thunder] **clo gally** [affright] **the beans, The.** Somerset. 1678: Ray, 347.

Dunghill gentleman. *See* **Gentleman** (2).

Dunmow. 1. Dunmow bacon, Doncaster daggers. 1659: Howell, 21. 1670: Ray, 258. 1878: *Folk-Lore Record*, i 172, We hear as a local [Yorks] proverb of 'Dunmow bacon and Doncaster daggers'.

2. They may claim the flitch at Dunmow. 1362: Langland, *Plowman*, A, x 188, Thaugh thei don hem to Donmowe but the deuel helpe To folewen aftur the flucchen fecche thei hit neuere. *c.*1386: Chaucer, *Wife of Bath's Prol.*, l. 217, The bacoun was nat fet for hem, I trowe, That som men han in Essex at Dunmowe. *c.*1580: *Tom Tyler*, l. 760, p. 21 (Malone S.), But you may now go for bacon to Dunmo. 1662: Fuller, *Worthies*, i 498 (1840), He may fetch a flitch of bacon from Dunmow. 1790: Grose, *Prov. Gloss.*, s.v. 'Essex'. 1821: Combe, *Syntax in Search of Wife*, can. xxxiv, p. 57, While I, though I have married been So many years, at least sixteen; Yes, I with honest heart and hand, Can now the *Dunmow Flitch* demand.

3. Who fetcheth a wife from Dunmow, Carrieth home two sides of a sow. 1659: Howell, 21.

Dunstable. *As plain as Dunstable highway*, or *Plain* (or *Downright*) *Dunstable*. 1546: Heywood, *Proverbs*, Pt II ch v, As plaine as dunstable by waie. *c.*1560: in Huth, *Ancient Ballads, etc.*, 1 (1867), As playne ... as Donstable waye. 1599: Breton, in *Works*, ii *c* 48 (Grosart), Alas! to use glosing speeches gives suspicion of little good meaning ... plaine Dunstable is the high way, and yet there are many holes in it. 1658: Dekker,

Witch of Edmonton, I ii, What must it be, Master Frank? or son Frank? I am plain Dunstable. 1718: Dennis, *Works*, ii 344, Look you, my Lord, I am downright, I am dunstable, Gadsbud, and must speak the truth. 1754: Richardson, *Clarissa*, i 217 (1785), That's the plain Dunstable of the matter, Miss! 1790: Grose, *Prov. Gloss.*, s.v. 'Beds', As plain as Dunstable road. Downright Dunstable. 1824: Scott, *Redgauntlet*, ch xviii, If this is not plain speaking, there is no such place as downright Dunstable in being! 1852: M. A. Keltie, *Reminisc. of Thought, etc.*, 101, It was mapped out according to square and rule, and I was not to be substituting any heresies of my own in the room of such good old Dunstable doings.

Dunstall. *See* **Barton.**

Durham. 1. As peppery as Durham mustard. 1846–59: *Denham Tracts*, i 39 (F.L.S.).

2. Durham folks are troubled with afterwit. 1909: *Folk-Lore*, xx 73.

3. He's a Durham man: he's knocker kneed. 1823: Grose, *Class. Dict.*, ed. Egan, s.v. 'Durham man', Durham man. Knocker kneed, he grinds mustard with his knees: Durham is famous for its mustard. 1846–59: *Denham Tracts*, i 48 (F.L.S.).

4. Like a Durham heifer, beef to the heels. 1846–59: Ibid., i 64.

5. *See* quot. 1892: J. Hardy, editor, *Denham Tracts*, i 52, 'There's not much law at Durham for a happeny'. This is spoken of the heavy expenses attending the Probate Court at Durham, and the obtaining of extracts from wills which are deposited there. It is a common saying at Newcastle.

6. Too dear for the Bishop of Durham. 1846–59: *Denham Tracts*, i 39 (F.L.S.), It would appear from the above that the bishops of Durham have been proverbial for their riches from a very early period.

See also **York** (4).

Dursley, You are a man of = one who breaks his word. 1639: *Berkeley MSS.*, iii 26 (1885), Hee'l proove, I thinke, a man of Durseley. 1662: Fuller, *Worthies*, i 551 (1840). 1790: Grose, *Prov. Gloss.*, s.v. 'Gloucest'. 1851: *Gloucestershire Gloss.*, 14.

Dust in a man's eyes, To cast. [Tenebras offudisse indicibus. – Quintil., II xvii 21.] 1581: Pettie, tr. Guazzo's *Civil Convers.*, i 276 (1586) (OED), They doe nothing else but raise a dust to doe out their owne eies. 1633: Draxe, 18. 1690: *New Dict. Canting Crew*, sig. B2. 1718: W. Taverner, *Artful Wife*, I, To throw dust in the eyes of censure is proper. 1928: *Times*, 9 March, p. 14, col. 3, He said that the speech was … designed to throw dust in the eyes of the public.

Dutchman drinketh pure wine in the morning, at noon wine without water, in the evening as it comes from the butt, The. 1659: Howell, 20.

Dutchman drinks his buttons off, the English doublet and all away, The. 1640: Glapthorne, *Ladies Priv.*, III, As is the common proverb, The Dutchman, etc.

Dutchman saith that segging is good cope, The. 1546: Heywood, *Proverbs*, Pt II ch ix.

Dutchman's headache, The = Drunkenness. 1869: Hazlitt, 366.

Dwarf on a giant's shoulder sees farther of the two, A. 1640: Herbert, *Jac. Prudentum.* 1654: Whitlock, *Zootomia*, 218, A proverb … that a child on a giant's shoulder, may see farther than the giant.

Dwarf threatens Hercules, A. *c.*1440: Lydgate, *Fall of Princes*, bk iii l. 531 (E.E.T.S.), But it may falle a dwery [dwarf] in his riht Toutraie a geaunt, for al his grete myht. 1732: Fuller, 85.

Dwells far from neighbours. *see* **Neighbour** (2).

Dying is as natural as living. 1732: Fuller, 1348.

E

Each cross. *See* **Every cross.**

Each man for one. *See* **Every man for himself.**

Eagle and Eagles. 1. Eagles fly alone. 1639: Clarke, 291. 1669: *Politeuphuia*, 185, Eagles flie alone, and they are but sheep that always flock together.

2. The eagle does not catch flies. 1563: *Mirror for Magistrates* (1938), 405, The jolly Egles catche not little flees. 1573: G. Harvey, *Letter-Book*, 50 (Camden S.), Now I se Aquila non capit muscas. 1607: Rowlands, *Guy, E. of Warwick*, 12 (Hunt.Cl.). That proverb in this point might make thee wise, *That princely eagles scorn the catching flies.* 1640: Shirley, *Opportunity*, V ii, Eagles stoop not to flies. 1924: *Sphere*, 27 Sept., p. 386, col. 2, More subtle is the insult in the saying that 'the eagle does not catch flies'.

3. You cannot fly like an eagle with the wings of a wren. 1909: Hudson, *Afoot in England*, ch vi, As the proverb says, 'You cannot', etc.

Eagle-eyed. *He is eagle-eyed in other mens matters, but as blind as a buzzard in his own.* 1633: Draxe, 26.

Ear. *If your ear burns* (or *glows*), *some one is talking about you.* [Quin et absentes [tinnitu] aurium praesentire sermones de se? – Pliny, *Hist. Nat.*, xxviii 2.] *c.*1374: Chaucer, *Troylus*, bk ii l. 1022, And we shal speke of thee som-what, I trowe, Whan thou art goon, to do thyne eres glowe! 1546: Heywood, *Proverbs*, Pt II ch i, I suppose that daie hir eares might well glow, For all the towne talkt of hir, hy and low. 1599: Shakespeare, *Much Ado*, III i, What fire is in my ears? Can this be true? 1687: Aubrey, *Gentilisme*, 110 (F.L.S.), When our cheek burneth, or eare tingleth, we usually say that some body is talking of us. 1755: *Connoisseur*, No. 59, If your right ear or cheek burns, your left friends are talking of you. 1868: Dickens, *Letters*, iii 257 (1882), I dine with Dolby ... and if your ears do not burn from six to nine this evening, then the Atlantic is a non-conductor.

Early. 1. Early ripe. *See* **Soon ripe**.

2. Early riser. *See* **Name** (1).

3. Early sow, early mow. 1639: Clarke, 233. 1670: Ray, 84. 1732: Fuller, 1350.

4. Early to bed and early to rise, makes a man

healthy and wealthy and wise. 1496: *Treatise of Fishing with Angle*, H1, As the olde englysshe proverbe sayth in this wyse. Who soo woll ryse erly shall be holy helthy and zely [fortunate]. 1523: Fitzherbert, *Husbandry*, 101 (E.D.S.), At grammer-scole I lerned a verse, that is this, *Sanat, sanctificat et ditat surgere mane.* That is to say, Erly rysyng maketh a man hole in body, holer in soule, and rycher in goodes. 1577: Rhodes, *Boke of Nurture*, in *Babees Book*, 72 (E.E.T.S.), Ryse you earely in the morning, for it hath propertyes three: Holynesse, health, and happy welth, as my father taught mee. 1670: Ray, 38. 1736: Franklin, *Way to Wealth*, in *Works*, i 443 (Bigelow). 1854: J. W. Warter, *Last of Old Squires*, 60.

5. Early up and never the nearer. 1546: Heywood, *Proverbs*, Pt I ch ii, And I than, their timely weddyng doth clere appere, That they were earely vp, and neuer the nere. 1594: Greene, *Frier Bacon*, sc vi, Your [You are] early up, pray God it be the neere [nearer]. 1633: Jonson, *Tale of a Tub*, Epil., Wherein the poet's fortune is, I fear, Still to be early up, but ne'er lie near. 1732: Fuller, 1351. 1881: Evans, *Leics. Words, etc.*, 200 (E.D.S.), Never-the-near, or Never-the-nigh, *adv.* none the nearer; no forwarder.

6. Early wed, early dead. 1895: *N. & Q.*, 8th ser, viii 516, The old English proverb which says, Early wed, early dead.

7. The early bird catches the worm. 1605: Camden, *Remains*, 333 (1870). 1670: Ray, 84. 1732: Fuller, 5118. 1883: R.L.S., *Treasure I*, ch xxx, And it's the early bird, as the saying goes, that gets the rations.

8. The early bird gets the late one's breakfast. 1882: Mrs Chamberlain, *W. Worcs. Wards*, 39 (E.D.S.).

9. The early sower never borrows of the late. 1659: Howell, 17, The rath sower never horroweth of the late. 1670: Ray, 22 [as in 1659]. 1732: Fuller, 4492.

Earth must to earth. *c.*1480: *Early Miscell.*, 40 (Warton Cl., 1855), How erth schal to erthe he thinkes nothinge. 1593: Peele, *Edward I*, sc xxiv, An old said saw, earth must to earth.

Earth produces all things and receives all again, The. 1732: Fuller, 4493.

Earthen pot must keep clear of the brass kettle, The. Ibid., No. 4494.

Earth's the best shelter. 1659: Howell, *Proverbs: Brit.-Eng.*, 38.

Ease. 1. Ease and success are fellows. *c.*1300: *Havelok the Dane*, l. 1338 (Skeat), Lith and selthe felawes are.

2. **He is at ease who has enough.** *c.*1460: *Wisdom*, sc iv st. 70, Farewell, cousyens! I know not yow; I am at eas, hade I inow. 1493: *Dives and Pauper*, fo. 1 (1536), It is an olde prouerbe, He is wel at ease that hath inough, and can say ho.

3. **He may not have all his ease that shall thrive.** *c.*1460: *How the Good Wife*, l. 130.

4. **He that is at ease seeks dainties.** 1640: Herbert, *Jac. Prudentum*.

Easier said than done. *See* **Said.**

Easier to fall (or **descend**) **than rise** (or **ascend**), **It is.** 1605: Camden, *Remains*, 326 (1870), It is easier to descend than to ascend. 1633: Draxe. 54, A man may sooner fall then rise. 1684: Bunyan, *Pilgr. Progr.*, Pt II, p. 239 (1849), Then said *Mercy*, But the proverb is. *To go down the hill is easy.* 1732: Fuller, 1353, Easier it is fall, than rise.

Easier to pull down than to build up, It is. 1587: J. Bridges, *Defence of Govt. in Church of Eng.*, 518, We may quicklier pull downe with one hande, than wee can easilie builde againe with both. 1732: Fuller, Nos. 2930 and 1354.

Easier to spy two faults than mend one, It is. *c.*1555: Starkey, *Life and Lett.*, I iii 2 (E.E.T.S.), Much easyar hyt ys to spy ii fautes then amend one.

Easily done is soon believed, That which is. 1670: Ray, 8. 1732: Fuller, 4379.

Easily led but dour to drive. Derby. 1889: *Folk-Lore Journal*, vii 292.

Easily won. *See* **Lightly gained.**

East Cheap. *See* quot. *c.*1430: in *Reliq. Antiquae*, i 3 (1841), He that wyll in Eschepe ete a goose so fat, With harpe, pype, and song; He must slepe in Newgate on a mat, Be the nyght never so long.

East Grinstead. *See* quot. 1894: A. J. C. Hare, *Sussex*, 10, A Sussex proverb says [of E. G.] – Large parish, poor people, Large new church, no steeple.

East Looe. *The Mayor of East Looe, who called the King of England 'Brother'.* 1906: Q.-Couch, *Mayor of Troy*, Prol.

East, West, Home's best. 1859: W.K. Kelly, *Proverbs of all Nations*, 'East and west, at home the best' (German).1869: Spurgeon, *John Ploughman*, ch xiii, East and West, Home is best. 1920: Lucas, *Verena in the Midst*, ch xiii, p. 176, None the less I don't envy the traveller. 'East, west, home's best'.

East Wind. *See* **Wind,** B.

Easter. 1. A kiss at Christmas and an egg at Easter. 1846–59: *Denham Tracts*, ii 92 (F.L.S.).

2. **As hard as an egg at Easter.** 1846: Denham, *Proverbs*, 32 (Percy S.).

3. **At Easter let your clothes be new, or else be sure you will it rue.** 1592: Shakespeare, *Romeo*, III i, Didst thou not fall out with a tailor for wearing his new doublet before Easter? 1902: Lean, *Collectanea*, i 378.

4. **At Easter the wind is at Chester.** 1611: in Coryat, *Crudities*, i 93 (1905), And as about the time of Easter,* [*(Note) Prov. At Easter the winde is at Chester. Because it is good for Ireland.] T'enrich the towne and trade of shipping, The winde which evermore is skipping, Is said to come and dwell at Chester …

5. **Easter in snow, Christmas in mud; Christmas in snow, Easter in mud.** 1893: Inwards, *Weather Lore*, 38.

6. **Easter so longed for is gone in a day.** 1659: Howell, 20.

7. **If the sun shines on Easter Day, it shines on Whit Sunday.** 1640: *Countryman's Coms.*, in *Helpe to Discourse*, 224, If the sunne shine on Easter day, it shines on Whit Sonday likewise. 1893: Inwards, *Weather Lore*, 41.

8. **I'll warrant you for an egg at Easter.** 1659: Howell, 2. 1666: Torriano, *Piazza Univ.*, 323, The English tradition was Hai for an egg at Easter. 1738: Swift, *Polite Convers.*, Dial. III, I suppose her ladyship plays sometimes for an egg at Easter.

9. **Late Easter, long, cold spring.** Sussex. 1893: Inwards, *Weather Lore*, 40.

10. **Past Easter frost, Fruit not lost.** Ibid., 41.

11. **Such weather as there is on Easter Day there will be at harvest.** Ibid., 41.

12. **When Easter falls in our Lady's lap, Then let England beware of a rap.** 1648: in Rollins, *Cavalier and Puritan*, 216 (1923), When Easter-day sitteth in Lady-dayes lap, The proverbe bids England beware of a clap. 1659: Howell, 16, When Christ falleth in our Ladies lapp, Then

lett England look for a clapp. 1846: Denham, *Proverbs*, 36 (Percy S.). 1904: *Co. Folk–Lore: Northumb.*, 176 (F.L.S.). 1921: *Sphere*, 2 April, p. 2, Only the very superstitious had their Easter holiday a little dimmed by the ominous falling together of Lady Day and Good Friday [*sic* in 1921], for as the old rhyme runs – When our Lord falls into our Lady's lap, England shall meet with great mishap.

13. When rain falls on Easter Day, We get no grass and little hay. 1851: Sternberg, *Dialect, etc., of Northants*, 189, Rain on Easter-day, Plenty of grass, but little good hay. 1893: Inwards, *Weather Lore*, 41, A good deal of rain upon Easter Day Gives a good crop of grass, but little good hay. Hertfordshire. 1917: Bridge, *Cheshire Proverbs*, 163.

14. You keep Easter, when I keep Lent. 1732: Fuller, 5927.

See also **Christmas** (5), (10), (11); and (13); **Good Friday; Jews; Lady Day;** and **Michaelmas** (5).

Easy as an old shoe. 1894: Northall, *Folk Phrases*, 8 (E.D.S.).

Easy as falling off … 1917: Bridge, *Cheshire Proverbs*, 27, As aisy as fawin off a chair when yo're drunk. 1924: M. Kennedy, *Constant Nymph*, 307, They'd find it as easy as falling off a log, you see!

Easy as kiss my hand. 1670: Cotton, *Scarronides*, bk iv, But you may make 'em, at command, As eas'ly stay as kiss your hand. 1754: Berthelson, *Eng.–Danish Dict.*, s.v. 'Easy'. 1878: Sketchley, *Mrs Brown at Paris Exhib.*, 30, It's as easy as kiss my 'and a-goin' to Paris now-a-days. 1921: *Punch*, 7 Sept., p. 200, I bet if you only liked you could put me on to the winner of the St Leger as easy as kiss me 'and!

Easy as lying. 1602: Shakespeare, *Hamlet*, III ii, It is as easy as lying. 1823: Scott, *St Ronan's*, ch xxvi, Which to me seemed as easy and natural as lying. 1913: L. P. Jacks, *All Men are Ghosts*, 117, Next morning Piecraft bought the book. As no patients came that day he had ample leisure to read it. 'Easy as lying,' he said to himself when he had finished.

Easy as to lick a dish. 1678: Ray, 283.

Easy come, easy go. 1650: A. Bradstreet, *Tenth Muse*, 126, That which easily comes, as freely goes. 1832: *Diary of a Late Physician*, II, xi, 'Easy come, easy go' is … characteristic of rapidly

acquired commercial fortunes. 1960: I Jefferies, *Dignity and Purity*, ii, She's your only daughter, isn't she? … Well, easy come, easy go. *See also* **Light come** … ; **Quickly come** … .

Easy does it. 1863: T. Taylor, *Ticket-of-Leave Man*, iv i, Easy does it, Bob. Hands off and let's take things pleasantly. 1928: J. P. McEvoy, *Showgirl*, 21, No high pressure stuff, sis. Easy does it.

Easy fool is a knave's tool, An. 1732: Fuller, 6189.

Easy that are done willingly, All things are. 1596: Lodge, *Wits Miserie*, 102 (Hunt.Cl.), A good will winneth all things. 1732: Fuller, 561.

Easy to bowl down hill, It is. 1639: Clarke, 151. 1670: Ray, 3. 1732: Fuller, 1352.

Easy to fall into a trap, but hard to get out again, 'Tis. 1732: Fuller, 5072.

Easy to find a stick, etc. *See* **Stick**, *subs.* (1).

Easy to hold the latch, etc. *See* quot. 1917: Bridge, *Cheshire Proverbs*, 81, It's aizy howdin dain th' latch when nobody poos at th' string.

Easy to rob an orchard when no man keeps it, 'Tis. 1639: Clarke, 55. 1670: Ray, 23. 1732: Fuller, 2925.

Easy to wade the stream, etc. *See* quot. 1615: Brathwait, *Strappado*, 222 (1878), (Its easie saies the Prouerb) to wade the streame, Where th' foord's at lowest.

Easy to wed a widow as to catch a dead horse, It's as. 1917: Bridge, *Cheshire Proverbs*, 82, [Shropsh. variant] It's as easy to marry a widow as to put a halter on a dead horse.

Eat. 1. Eat a good dinner. *See* **Good dinner.**

2. Eat and welcome, fast and heartily welcome. 1678: Ray, 84. 1732: Fuller, 1355.

3. Eat at pleasure drink by measure. 1611: Cotgrave, s.v. 'Pain'. 1670: Ray, 38. 1732; Fuller, 6079. 1875: A. B. Cheales, *Proverb. Folk-Lore*, 84, Bread at pleasure Drink by measure is also a maxim much to be commended.

4. Eat enough and it will make you wise. 1592: Lyly, *Mydas*, IV iii [quoted as 'an old proverb'].

5. Eat less and drink less, and buy a knife at Michaelmas. 1659: Howell, 6.

6. Eat peas. *See* **Pea** (1).

7. Eat the devil. *See* **Devil** (32).

8. Eat thy meat and drink thy drink, and stand thy ground, old Harry. Somerset. 1678: Ray, 343.

9. Eat to live not live to eat. [Non vivas ut edas, sed edas ut vivere posses. – Dionysius *in Rom.*, cap. 13.] 1387: J. Trevisa, tr. *Higden's Polychronicon* (1871), III, 281, Socrates seide that meny men wil leve forto ete and drynke, and that they wolde ete and drynke … forto lyve. *c.*1410: tr. of *Secreta Secret.*, 67 (E.E.T.S.), And ypocraas answerde, 'ffair sone, I will ete so that y leue, and noght lyf that y ete'. *c.*1577: Northbrooke, *Dicing, etc.*, 40 (SH.S.), Thou lyuest not to eate, butte eat as thou mayest lyue. 1671: Shadwell, *Miser*, III ii, People should eat to live, not live to eat; as the proverb says. 1733: Fielding, *Miser*, III iii 1911: Pinero, *Preserving Mr Panmure*, II, p. 85.

10. Eat-well is drink-well's brother. 1732: Fuller, 1357.

11. Eat well of the cresses. 1577: J. Grange, *Golden Aphroditis*, sig. F3, Remember the prouerbe, *Eate well of the cresses* [cress was supposed to help the memory].

12. Eat when you're hungry and drink when you're dry. 1917: Bridge, *Cheshire Proverbs*, 52.

13. Eat your own side, speckle-back. 1863: Wise, *New Forest*, ch xvi, 'Eat your own side, speckle-back', is a common Forest expression, and is used in reference to greedy people. It is said to have taken its origin from a girl who shared her breakfast with a snake, and thus reproved her favourite when he took too much.

14. He could eat me without salt (or **with garlic**). 1596: Harington, *Metam. of Ajax*, 3 (1814), The poor sheep still, for an old grudge, would eat him without salt (as they say). 1639: Clarke, 71, You must not think to eat me up without salt. 1670: Ray, 173, He could eat my heart with garlick. That is, he hates me mortally. 1693: D'Urfey, *Richmond Heiress*, V iv, Now could I eat that satyrical devil without salt for my breakfast. 1748: Richardson, *Clarissa*, vii 59 (1785), Yet I can tell thee I could … eat him up without a corn of salt, when I think of his impudence.

15. He eats in plate, but will die in irons. 1732: Fuller, 1842.

16. He has eat up the pot, and asks for the pipkin. Ibid., No. 1868.

17. He has eaten many a Christmas pie. 1639: Clarke, 189.

18. He hath eaten his roast meat first. Glos. 1639: in *Berkeley MSS.*, iii 32, (1885).

19. He is so hungry he could eat a horse behind the saddle. 1678: Ray, 253. 1826: Scott, *Woodstock*, ch xx, I think he could eat a horse, as the Yorkshireman says, behind the saddle.

20. He that eats least eats most. *c.*1645: MS. Proverbs, in *N. & Q.*, vol cliv., p. 27.

21. He that eats most porridge shall have most meat. 1732: Fuller, 2092.

22. He that eats the hard shall eat the ripe. 1640: Herbert, *Jac. Prudentum*.

23. He that eats till he is sick must fast till he is well. 1732: Fuller, 2094.

24. He that eats well and drinks well should do his duty well. 1654: Gayton, *Pleasant Notes Don Q.*, 13, He that eates well does his worke well. 1732: Fuller, 2095.

25. He that will eat the kernel must crack the nut. *c.*1500: in *Antiq. Repertory*, iv 416 (1809), And yf ye wolde the swetnes haue of the kyrnell, Be content to byte vpon the harde shell. 1577: J. Grange, *Golden Aphroditis*, sig. I3, I see the prouerbe is true, *who wil the curnell of the nut must breake the shell*. 1635: Swan, *Spec. Mundi*, 465, For be it so that we desire the sweetnesse of the well relisht kernell, then must we likewise crack the hard shell. 1729: Coffey, *Beggar's Wedding*, II iii, He that wou'd obtain a kernel, must first hazard his teeth in breaking the shell. 1901: F. E. Taylor, *Lancs Sayings*, 9, Theaw mun crack th' nut afore theaw con eyt th' krindle.

26. He'll as soon eat sand as do a good turn. 1732: Fuller, 2421.

27. He'll eat till he sweats, and work till he freezes. Ibid., No. 2424.

28. If she would eat gold he would give it her. 1708: Centlivre, *Busie Body*, III iv, If … eating gold, as the old saying is, can make thee happy, thou shalt be so. 1738: Swift, *Polite Convers.*, Dial. I. 1845: Jerrold, *Mrs Caudle*, xxi, You'd have given me pearls and diamonds to eat, if I could have swallowed 'em.

29. If you eat a pudding at home, the dog shall have the skin. 1605: Camden, *Remains*, 325 (1870). 1732: Fuller, 2751.

30. If you eat till you are cold, you will live to be old, and every one will be tired of you. Oxfordsh. 1923: *Folk-Lore*, xxxiv 328. 1925: *N. & Q.*, cxlviii. 134 [with last eight words omitted].

31. To eat a stake. *See* quots. 1530: Palsgrave, 461, Haste thou eaten a stake, I shall make the[e] bowe. 1667: L'Estrange, *Quevedo's Visions*, 140 (1904), He sat stiff and upright, as if he had swallowed a stake. 1732: Fuller, 1901, He hath swallow'd a stake; he cannot bow.

32. To eat bullbeef. 1583: Melbancke, *Philotinus*, sig. Y2, Thou hast eaten bulbeefe, and braggest highlie.

33. To eat one's heart out. 1539: Taverner, *Proverbs*, fo. 54, Eate not thy harte (that is to saye) consume not thy selfe wyth cares. 1587: Underdowne, *Heliodorus*, bk i, p. 23 (T.T.), And there lived eating (as the proverbe saith) his owne harte out. 1633: Draxe, 123, He eateth his owne heart. 1890: W. A. Wallace. *Only a Sister?*, xviii 155 (OED), Why, there's poor Aikone … eating his heart out and getting no further.

34. To eat one's words. 1577: Stanihurst, *Descrip. of Ireland*, fo. 20, Before I eate these wordes, I will make thee eate a piece of my blade. 1670: Ray, 173. 1710: E. Ward, *Nuptial Dialogues*, i 353, I'll make you eat your words before I've done. 1838: Hood, *Hood's Own*, 1st ser, 486 (1865), The Marine Society must despise me for it … but I cannot eat my words.

35. To eat out of house and home. *c.*1400: *Towneley Plays*, xiii 124 (E.E.T.S.), Bot were I not more gracyus and rychere befar, I were eten outt of howse and of harbar. 1469: *Paston Lett.*, ii 348 (Gairdner), For I eete lyek an horse, of purpose to eete yow owte at the dorys. 1509: Barclay, *Ship of Fools*, ii 93 (1874), They wast and ete theyr mayster out of hous Deuourynge his good, tyll he be pore and bare. 1600: Day, *Blind Beggar*, IV i, Till we have eat him out of house and home in diet. 1668: Shadwell, *Sullen Lovers*, V iii, They would eat me out of house and home, as the saying is. 1734: Fielding, *Intrig. Chambermaid*, II vii, So generously condescend to eat a poor citizen out of house and home. 1909: De Morgan, *Never can happen Again*, i 17, Who was he, that he was to eat his sister out of house and home?

36. To eat sauce. Before 1529: Skelton, *Magnyfycence*, l. 1421, What, wyll ye waste wynde, and prate thus in vayne? Ye haue eten sauce, I trowe, at the Taylers Hall. Before 1529: Skelton, *Bowge of Courte*, l. 72.

37. To eat the cheese in the trap. 1813: Ray, 186.

38. To eat the pudding and the bag. 1659: Howell, 6, You are he that did eat the pudding and the bagg. 1732: Fuller, 1826, He claws it as Clayton claw'd the pudding, when he eat bag and all.

39. We must all eat a peck of dirt before we die. 1639: Clarke, 165, You must eat a peck of ashes ere you die. 1670: Ray, 57, Every man must eat a peck of ashes before he dies. 1709: O. Dykes, *Eng. Proverbs*, 11, So that if we must eat a peck of dirt before we die, it must certainly go down when we are a hungry. 1738: Swift, *Polite Convers.*, Dial. I. 1881: Evans, *Leics. Words*, 209 (E.D.S.), Here, as elsewhere, 'way mut all ate a peck-o'-dut afore way doy' is very commonly current, and almost equally common is the rider, 'but non on us wants it all at woonst'. 1922: *Observer*, 10 Dec., p. 11, col. 7, I suppose a little garbage is necessary in newspapers, just as we must all eat a peck of dirt before we die.

40. Who eats and leaves, has another meal good. 1732: Fuller, 5700.

41. Who eats his cock alone, must saddle his horse alone. 1640: Herbert, *Jac. Prudentum*. 1670: Ray, 8 [with 'dinner' for 'cock']. 1732: Fuller, 5701, Who eats his dinner alone, must saddle his horse.

42. You are what you eat. Well established as a saying in German, but often attributed to Anthelme Brillat-Savarin, the French author of *Physiologie du goût* (1825), who wrote: *Dis-moi ce que tu manges, je te dirai ce que tu es* (Tell me what you eat, and I will tell you what you are). It became very popular in the food-conscious late twentieth century. 1930: J. Gollomb, *Subtle Trail*, ii 55, There flashed through her mind the German saying, 'One is what one eats'. 1940: V.H. Lindlahr, (title) You are what you eat.

43. You cannot eat your cake and have it. 1546: Heywood, *Proverbs*, Pt II ch ix, Wolde ye bothe eate your cake and haue your cake? 1650: R. Heath, *Occasional Poems*, 19, I can't I tro Both eat my cake and have it too. 1738: Swift, *Polite Convers.*, Dial. I, She was handsome in her time; but she cannot eat her cake and have her cake. 1871: Planché, *Extravag.*, v 307 (1879), 'Tis to point to the moral the proverb implies, 'You can't have your cake if you eat it'. 1922: *Punch*, 7 June, p. 441, col. 2, 'You cannot eat your cake and have it', says a physical culture journal. This of course is the distressing experience of many people at sea.

44. You eat above the tongue like a calf. 1678: Ray, 348.

45. You eat and eat but you do not drink to fill you. 1670: Ray, 33.

46. You had as good eat your nails. *c.*1660: in *Roxb. Ballads*, ii 130 (B.S.), Your roaring-boy ... Could never yet make the smith eat his nails. 1738: I Swift, *Polite Convers.*, Dial. I, Say a word more, and you had as good eat your nails. 1784: *New Foundl. Hosp. for Wit*, i 287, Jove would not sooner eat his nails, Than break with us, to humour Juno. 1827: Scott, in Lockhart's *Life*, vii 62, I shall only revenge myself by publishing the whole extracts ... in which he will find enough to make him bite his nails.

47. You must eat another yard of pudding first = grow older. 1830: Forby, *Vocab. E. Anglia*, 428. 1886: Elworthy, *West Som. Word-Book*, 374 (E.D.S.), You must eat some more beef and potatoes first, i.e. wait till you are older – a very common phrase.

Eaten bread it forgotten. 1605: Camden, *Remains*, 321 (1870), Eaten bread is forgot. 1670: Ray, 84. 1732: Fuller, 1358. 1869: Spurgeon, *John Ploughman*, ch xiv, Eaten bread is forgotten, and the hand that gave it is despised. 1913: E. M. Wright, *Rustic Speech, etc.*, 110, Etten cake's sooin forgotten is a proverbial saying [*cake* (Yorks) = bread].

Eating and drinking. *See* quots. 1611: Cotgrave, s.v. 'Mangeant', Eating and drinking will take away any mans stomack. 1738: Swift, *Polite Convers.*, Dial. II, Well; this eating and drinking takes away a body's stomach. 1785: Grose, *Class. Dict. Vulgar Tongue*, s.v. 'Damper', Eating and drinking being, as the proverb wisely observes, apt to take away the appetite.

Eating and scratching. *See* quots. 1732: Fuller, 5158, To eat and to scratch, a man need but begin. 1738: Swift, *Polite Convers.*, Dial. II, They say, eating and scratching wants but a beginning.

Eccles Wakes. *See* **Thrunk.**

Economy. *See* **Frugality.**

Edesn, River. *See* quots. 1659: Howell, 20, Let Uter Pendragon doe what he can, Eden will run the same way she ran. 1766: MS. Tour, quoted in *Denham Tracts*, i 207 (1846–59) (F.L.S.), Let sly Pendragon do all he can, Old Eden will ran where first he ran. 1790: Grose, *Prov. Gloss.*, s.v. 'Westmoreland', Let Uter Pendragon do what he can, The river Eden will run as it ran.

Edged tools, It is ill jesting with. *c.*1568: Wager, *Longer thou Livest*, sig. D1, It is a prouerbe wise and auncient, Beware how you geue any edge toole, Unto madmen that be insipient, Unto a yonge childe, and unto a foole. 1579: Gosson, *Sch. of Abuse*, 57 (Arber), Some say that it is not good iesting with edge toles. 1652: Tatham, *Scots Figgaries*, III, I say again, 'tis dangerous meddling with edge-tools. 1728: Fielding, *Love in several Masques*, IV vii, Sir Apish, jesting with matrimony is playing with edged tools. 1839: Planché', *Extravag.*, ii 58 (1879), To play with edge tools is held unwise.

Education begins a gentleman, conversation completes him. 1732: Fuller, 1359.

Eel and **Eels. 1.** *See* quot. 1879: G. F. Jackson, *Shropsh. Word-Book*, 16, 'Eels are in season when oats are in aw [ear]'. Proverbial saying heard about Aston Botterell.

2. He is as muck out of his element as an eel in a sand-bag. 1732: Fuller, 1912.

3. He that will catch eels must disturb the flood. 1607: *Lingua*, I i.

4. To have an eel by the tail. 1546: Heywood, *Proverbs*, Pt I ch x, Her promise of freendship for any auayle, Is as sure to holde as an ele by the tayle. 1616: B.&F., *Scornful Lady*, II i, I will end with the wise man, and say, 'He that hath a woman has an eel by the tail'. 1640: Shirley, *Arcadia*, V i, But I see a woman and a wet eel have both slippery tails. 1696: T. Dilke, *Lover's Luck*, V i, He that has holt on a young woman has got a slippery eel by the tail. 1754: Berthelson, *Eng.-Danish Dict.*, s.v. 'Eel', There is as much hold of his words as a wet eel by the tail.

5. You cannot hide an eel in a sack. 1640: Herbert, *Jac. Prudentum*. 1670: Ray, 8. 1732: Fuller, 5875.

See also **Breed**; **Mud**; **Nimble**; **Slippery**; and **Wriggle**.

Effect speaks, the tongue needs not, The. 1640: Herbert, *Jac. Prudentum*.

Egg and **Eggs. 1. All your eggs have two yolks apiece, I warrant you.** 1732: Fuller, 573.

2. An egg and to bed. 1639: Clarke, 113. 1670: Ray, 36. 1732: Fuller, 594.

3. An egg of an hour, etc. *See* quots. 1623: Wodroephe, *Spared Houres*, 253–4, An eg of one houre old, bread of one day, a goat of one moneth, wine of six moneths, flesh of a yeare, fish of ten yeares, a wife of twentie yeares, a friend among a hundred, are the best of all number. 1666: Torriano, *Piazza Univ.*, 181, An egg of an hour's laying, bread of a daies, flesh of one year's growth, fish of ten, a woman of fifteen, and a friend of a hundred years standing.

4. An egg will be in three bellies in twenty-four hours. 1678: Ray, 131. 1732: Fuller, 1361, Eggs will be, etc.

5. As full as an egg is of meat. *c*.1565: Still, *Gammer Gurton*, V ii, An egge is not so ful of meate, as she is ful of lyes. 1592: Shakespeare, *Romeo*, III i 1641: Cowley, *Guardian*, I i, The Colonel's as full of waggery as an egge's full of meat. 1696: Vanbrugh, *Relapse*, III. 1758–67: Sterne, *Trist. Shandy*, vol vii ch xxxvii, My remarks through France, which were as full of wit as an egg is full of meat. 1854: Doran, *Table Traits*, 190, An egg is proverbially 'full of meat'.

6. As sure as eggs are eggs. In *N. & Q.*, 3rd ser, vi 203, A. de Morgan suggested that 'as sure as eggs is eggs' = 'corruption of the logician's announcement of identity, "X is X".' 1680: Otway, *Caius Marius*, IV ii, 'Twas to seek for lord Marius, as sure as eggs be eggs. 1720: *Vade Mecum for Malt-worms*, Pt II, p. 48, Certainly, as eggs are eggs. 1772: Graves, *Spirit. Quixote*, bk vii ch xi, If she lives to Lammas-day next she will be but fourteen years old, as sure as eggs is eggs. 1837: Dickens, *Pickwick*, ch xliii., And the Bishop says, 'Sure as eggs is eggs, This here's the bold Turpin!' 1857: Hughes, *Tom Brown*, Pt II ch vi.

7. But one egg and that addled too. 1732: Fuller, 1031.

8. Don't put all your eggs in one basket. 1662: G. Torriano, *Italian Proverbial Phrases*, 125, To put all ones Eggs in a Paniard, viz. to hazard all in one bottom [ship]. 1710: S. Palmer, *Moral Essays on Proverbs*, 344, Don't venture all your eggs in one basket. 1763: Murphy, *Citizen*, I ii, George, too many eggs in one basket.1874: Whyte-Melville, *Uncle John*, ch 27, 'May I carry your basket all my life?' 'If you'll put all your eggs in it, yes', answered Annie boldly. 1894: 'M. Twain', *Pudd'nhead Wilson*, in *Century Magazine*, XLVII. vi 87, The fool saith, 'Put not all thine eggs in one basket' – which is a manner of saying 'Scatter your money and your attention'; but the wise man saith, 'Put all your eggs in one basket and – *watch that basket.*

9. From the eggs to the apples. [Ab ovo Usque ad mala citaret, Io Bacche! – Horace, *Sat.*, I iii 6.] 1639: Clarke, 3, From th' egges to th' apples. 1655: T. Muffett, *Health's Improvement*, 295, The most nourishing meat is first to be eaten

that ancient proverb ratifieth *Ab ovo ad mala*; from the eg to the apples. 1736: Bailey, *Dict.*, s.v. 'End', From the beginning to the end … from the egg to the apples.

10. He has brought his eggs to a fine market. 1883: Burne, *Shropsh. Folk-Lore*, 589, He has brought his eggs to a nice (or fine, or pretty) market; said in irony of a spendthrift or bankrupt trader.

11. He'll dress an egg and give the offal to the poor. 1678: Ray, 90.

12. He'll never be good egg nor bird. 1630: T. Adams, *Works*, 178, Sinne of it selfe is good neither egge nor bird. 1670: Ray, 173, Neither good egg nor bird. 1784: O'Keeffe, *Fontainebleau*, III iv, She was never good, egg, or bird. 1868: Atkinson, *Cleveland Gloss.*, 151, He'll never dow [thrive], egg nor bird.

13. To come in with five (or two) eggs. 1542: Udall, tr. Erasmus' *Apoph.*, 303 (1877), To certain persones comyng in with their fiue egges, how that Sylla had geuen ouer his office of Dictature, as he shuld do … he aunswered that Sylla was not bokishe, nor halfe a good clerke, and therefore gaue vp his Dictature. [In the Appendix to this edition, R. Roberts, editor and publisher, says: 'This was rather a common proverb in the sixteenth century, and has never been explained, but it evidently means a silly rumour, equivalent to "mare's nest." "Will you take eggs for money?" ' (*see* 15 below) belongs to the same family'.] 1551: R. Robinson, tr. More's *Utopia*, 56 (Arber). 1639: Clarke, 19, He comes in with his five egges and foure be rotten. 1683: Meriton, *Yorkshire Ale*, 83–7 (3rd ed., 1697), You come with your five eggs a penny and four of them be rotten. 1711: Swift, *Journal to Stella*, Lett. 34, The Whigs are still crying down our peace, but we will have it, I hope, in spite of them: the Emperor comes now with his two eggs a penny, and promises wonders to continue the war; but it is too late. 1738: Swift, *Polite Convers.*, Dial. I, What! and you must come in with your two eggs a penny, and three of them rotten. 1869: Spurgeon, *John Ploughman*, ch xvi, When there's five eggs a penny, four of them are rotten.

14. To have both the egg and the hen. 1578: Florio, *First Fruites*, fo. 33, There be many that wyl haue both the egge and the hen. 1629: *Book of Meery Riddles*, Prov. 118, In the world there be men That will have the egge and the henne.

15. To have eggs on the spit. 1596: Jonson, *Ev. Man in Humour*, III vi, I have eggs on the spit; I cannot go yet. 1614: Jonson, *Bart. Fair*, I, I have both eggs on the spit, and iron in the fire. 1670: Cotton, *Scarronides*, bk iv, Half-frighted out on's little wit, He now has eggs (i' faith) o' th' spit. 1713: Swift, *Journal to Stella*, 23 April, I write short journals now. I have eggs on the spit. 1827: Scott, *Journal*, 18 Hay, I have other eggs on the spit.

16. To take eggs for money. 1610: Shakespeare, *Wint. Tale*, I ii, *Leon* ... Mine honest friend, Will you take eggs for money? *Mam.* No, my lord, I'll fight. 1666: Pepys, *Diary*, 27 June, By the next fight, if we beat, the Dutch will certainly be content to take eggs for their money (that was his [Sir W. Coventry's] expression). 1720: *New Dict. Canting Crew*, He will be glad to take eggs for his money, i.e. compound the matter with loss. 1847: Halliwell, *Dict.*, s.v., A proverbial expression, used when a person was awed by threats, or had been over-reached into giving money for comparatively worthless things.

17. 1763: Murphy, *Citizen*, I ii, George, too many eggs in one basket.

18. Won with the egg and lost with the shell. 1575: Gascoigne, *Posies*, in *Works*, i 450 (Cunliffe), Nor woman true, but even as stories tell, Wonne with an egge, and lost againe with shell. 1633: Draxe, 75.

See also **Addled egg; Apple** (6); **Better an egg; Christmas** (5) and (13); **Dear** (2); **Drink**, *verb* (2); **Easter** (2) and (8); **Fool** (93); **Half an egg; Hard** (19); **Hen** (1), (8), (10), and (14); **Like as one egg; Omelets; and Reason** (7).

Elbow itches, I must change my bedfellow, My. 1659: Howell, 12.

Elbow-grease gives the best polish. 1672: Marvell, *Rehearsal Transpr.*, i 5 (OED), Two or three brawny fellows in a corner with meer ink and elbow-grease, do more harm than ... 1690: *New Dict. Canting Crew*, sig. E1, It will cost nothing but a little elbow-grease. 1830: Forby, *Vocab. E. Anglia*, 431, Elbow grease gives the best polish. 1872: J. Glyde, jr., *Norfolk Garland*, 149.

Elbow-grease, It smells of. 1639: Clarke, 92. 1670: Ray, 173.

Elden Hole wants filling. Derby. 1670: Ray, 173 [with 'needs' for 'wants']. 1790: Grose, *Prov. Gloss.*, s.v. 'Derbyshire'. 1889: *Folk-Lore*

Journal, vii 292 [Derby sayings], Eldon Hole wants filling up.

Elder. *When elder is white brew and bake a peck*, *When elder is black brew and bake a sack*. 1678: Ray, 352 [Somerset]. 1732: Fuller, 6478. 1904: *Co. Folk-Lore; Northumb.*, 177 (F.L.S.). *See also* **Sheep** (20).

Eldern stake. *See* quot. 1842: Akerman, *Wilts Gloss.*, 19, They have a rhyme in Wiltshire on the formation of a 'stake and ether hedge' – 'An eldern stake and blackthorn ether [hedge] Will make a hedge to last for ever'. 1875: Parish, *Sussex Dict.*

Elephant never forgets, An. Originally modelled on or related to a Greek proverb to the effect that a camel never forgets an injury. Long memory was attributed to elephants by the author Saki (H. H. Munro), who had experience of them, being born in Burma. The saying is now often used without specific reference to ill-treatment or insults. 1910: 'Saki', *Reginald: Reginald on Besetting Sins*, Women and elephants never forget an injury.

Elm. 1928: *Times*, 29 Nov., p. 10, col. 5, 'Every elm has its man' is an old country saying. *See also* **Good elm.**

Elm-leaves. *See* quots. 1856: *N.&Q.*, 2nd ser, i 429, Here is another Worcestershire saying ... When elm leaves are as big as a shilling, Plant kidney-beans, if to plant 'em you're willing. When elm leaves are as big as a penny, You *must* plant kidney-beans, if you mean to have any. 1866: *Field*, 28 April, When the elmen leaf is as big as a mouse's ear, Then to sow barley never fear. When the elmen leaf is as big as an ox's eye, Then says I, 'Hie, boys! hie!' 1881: C. W. Empson, in *Folk-Lore Record*, iv 131 [as in 1856 and 1866]. 1893: Inwards, *Weather Lore*, 152 [as in 1856].

Elm-tree for pears, You ask an. 1732: Fuller, 5862.

Elstow Fair, 3 May, O.S., now 15. *See* quot. 1831: Hone, *Year-Book*, 1595, It is a common saying in many parts of Bedfordshire, when flies first begin to be troublesome on meat, fish, etc., that 'the flies have been to Elstow Fair to buy their bellows'.

Embrace too much. *See* **Grasp.**

Empty, *adj.* **1. An empty belly hears no body.** 1732: Fuller, 596. 1880: Spurgeon, *Ploughman's Pictures*, 52, An empty belly makes no compliments.

2. An empty belly makes a lazy back. 1846–59: *Denham Tracts*, i 42 (F.L.S.), There is much truth contained in the good old northern proverb – A tume [empty] belly makes a lazy back.

3. An empty purse and a new house make a man wise, but too late. 1813: Ray, 20.

4. An empty purse causes a full heart. 1734: Fielding, *Don Quix. in England*, I.vi.

5. An empty purse fills the face with wrinkles. 1633: Draxe, 161. 1670: Ray, 22. 1736: Bailey, *Dict.*, s.v. 'Purse'.

6. An empty purse frights away friends. 1732: Fuller, 597.

7. An empty purse is the devil. 1882: *N. &Q.*, 6th ser, vi 17.

8. Better an empty house than an ill tenant. 1732: Fuller, 870.

9. Empty bags (or sacks) cannot stand upright. 1666: Torriano, *Piazza Univ.*, 245, An empty sack cannot stand upright. 1736: Franklin, *Way to Wealth*, in *Works*, i 449 (Bigelow), It is hard for an empty bag to stand upright. 1849: Lytton, *Caxtons*, Pt VIII ch iii, You have found it more difficult, I fear, than you imagined, to make, the empty sack stand upright. Considering that at least one-third of those born to work cannot find it, why should I? 1880: Platt, *Money*, 199, As empty bags cannot stand upright.

10. Empty barns need no thatch. Suffolk. 1924: *Folk-Lore*, xxxv 358.

11. Empty chambers make foolish maids. 1611: Cotgrave, s.v. 'Chambre', Empty chambers make women play the wantons. 1640: Herbert, *Iac. Prudentum*.

12. Empty hands. *See* **Hawk** (11).

13. Empty vessels make the most sound. 1430: l. Lydgate, *Pilgrimage of Man* (E.E.T.S.), l. 15933, A voyde vessel ... maketh outward a gret soun. Mor than ... what yt was ful. 1547: W. Baldwin, *Treatise of Moral Philosophy*, iv Q4, As emptye vesselles make the lowdest sounde: so they that have least wyt, are the greatest babblers. 1579: Lyly. *Euphues*, 45 (Arber), The emptie vessell giueth a greater sound then the full barrell. 1599–1600: Shakespeare *Henry V*, IV iv, I did never know so full a voice issue from so empty a heart: but the saying is true – The empty vessel makes the greatest sound. 1612: *Cornucopiae*, 90 (Grosart), An emptie vessell giues a mighty sound. 1754: Berthelson, *Eng.-Danish Dict.*, s.v.

'Empty', Empty vessels make the greatest noise. 1913: E. M. Wright, *Rustic Speech, etc.*, 171, Empty barrels make the most noise.

14. That is but an empty purse that is full of other men's money. 1678: Ray, 194. 1732: Fuller, 4352 [with 'folks' for 'men's'].

15. The empty leech sucks sore. 1672: Walker, *Paraem.*, 36. 1681: W. Robertson, *Phrasol. Generalis*, 528.

End, *subs.* **1. In the end things will mend.** 1659: Howell, 9. 1670: Ray, 8. 1736: Bailey, *Dict.*, s.v. 'End'.

2. Next the ende of sorowe, anon entreth joy. *c.*1387: Usk, *Test. of Love*, in Skeat's *Chaucer*, vii 82.

3. The end crowns all (or the work). *c.*1390: Gower, *Conf. Amantis*, bk vi l. 2383, An ende proveth euery thing. 1478: Rivers, tr. C. de Pisa's *Moral Proverbs*, Thende dooth shewe euery werk as hit is. 1578: Florio, *First Fruites*, fo. 29, The end maketh al. 1592: Shakespeare, 2 *Henry VI*, V ii, *O. Clif.* La fin couronne les oeuvres. 1658: R. Brome, *Weeding of Covent Garden*, III i, Was ever good patriot so rudely handled? but the end crowns all. 1820: Scott, *Abbot*, ch xiii, But as the end crowns the work ... 1870: Dickens, *Drood*, ch xviii, Proof must be built up stone by stone ... As I say, the end crowns the work.

4. The end justifies the means. 1583: G. Babington, *Exposition of the Commandments*, 260, The ende good, doeth not by and by make the meanes good. 1718: M. Prior, *Literary Works* (1971), I. 186, The End must justify the Means: He only Sins who Ill intends. 1820: Scott, *The Abbot*, XII, It is in the cause of heaven that I command them to embrace ... the end, sister, sanctifies the means we must use. 1897: C.C. King, *The Story of the British Army*, 341, The districts annexed and righteously governed, had recently ... been 'huge cockpits of slaughter'. The end here unquestionably justified the means.

5. The end makes all equal. 1578: Florio, *First Fruites*, fo. 31, The end maketh al men equal. 1605: Camden, *Remains*, 332 (1870). 1732: Fuller, 4496.

6. The end of our good begins our evil. 1611: Davies (of Hereford), *Sc. of Folly*, 50, in *Works*, ii (Grosart). 1633: Draxe, 117, The end of his good is the beginning of his woe.

7. The end trieth all. 1639: Clarke, 117. 1669: *Politeuphuia*, 183.

Endure, *verb.* **1. He that endures is not overcome.** 1640: Herbert, *Jac. Prudentum.* 1670: Ray, 8.

2. He that can quietly endure over-cometh. *c.*1393: Langland, *Plowman*, C, xvi 138, Quoth Peers the Plouhman '*pacientes uincunt*'. 1629: *Book of Meery Riddles.* Prov. 28.

3. He that will not endure labour in this world, let him not be born. 1578: Florio, *First Fruites*, fo. 28, Who wil not suffer labor in this world, let him not be borne. 1629: *Book of Meery Riddles*, Prov. 7.

Enemy and Enemies. 1. An enemy may chance to give good counsel. 1732: Fuller, 600.

2. An enemy's mouth seldom says well. 1481: Caxton, *Reynard*, I iiii., p. 7 (Arber), Sir Isegrym that is euyl sayd it is a comyn prouerbe An enemyes mouth saith seeld wel.

3. He is no one's enemy but his own. 1600: Cornwallis, *Essayes*, sig. E7 (1610), It smarts not halfe so ill as the phrase, *Euery bodies friend but his owne.* 1664: in *Musarum Delicoe, etc.*, ii 237 (Hotten, 1874), How ere he fail'd in's life, 'tis like Jack Friend, Was no man's foe but's own, and there's an end. 1749: Fielding, *Tom Jones*, bk iv ch v, Tom, though an idle, thoughtless, rattling rascal, was nobody's enemy but his own. 1850: Dickens, *Copperfield*, ch xxv, He is quite a good fellow – nobody's enemy but his own.

4. He that has no enemies has no friends. 1725: Bailey, tr. Erasmus' *Colloq.*, 131, There is this old saying: He that has no enemies has no friends.

5. Take heed of reconciled enemies. *c.*1600: in *Roxb. Ballads*, i 432 (B.S.), Trust not a reconciled friend more than an open foe. 1618: Harington, *Epigrams*, bk i No. 87, Dicke said, beware a reconciled foe. 1656: F. Osborne, *Advice to Son*, 89 (Parry), A reconciled enemy is not safely to be trusted. 1670: Ray, 22, Take heed of enemies reconcil'd, and of meat twice boil'd.

England. 1. A famine in England begins at the horse-manger. 1605: Camden, *Remains*, 329 (1870), No dearth but breeds in the horse-manger. 1662: Fuller, *Worthies*, i 117 (1840). 1790: Grose, *Prov. Gloss.*, s.v. 'England'. 1893: Inwards, *Weather Lore*, 7.

2. England is a little garden full of very sour weeds. 1790: Grose, *Prov. Gloss.*, s.v. 'England', This is said to have been an observation frequently in the mouth of Louis XIV during the victorious Duke of Marlborough's campaigns.

3. England is a ringing island. 1655: Fuller, *Church Hist.*, bk vi § ii (iii.), This, in England, (commonly called the 'ringing-island') was done with tolling a bell. 1790: Grose, *Prov. Gloss.*, s.v. 'England'. 1827: Hone, *Ev. Day Book*, ii 509, England is proverbially called 'the ringing island'.

4. England is the paradise of women, hell of horses, and purgatory of servants – with variant. 1591: Florio, *Second Frutes*, 205, England is the paradise of women, the purgatory of men, and the hell of horses. *c.*1593: Deloney, in *Works*, 377 (Mann, 1912), The wife of euery Englishman is counted blest. 1619: *New Help to Discourse*, 51, England is termed by foreigners the paradise of women, as it is by some accounted the hell of horses, and purgatory of servants. 1642: Howell, *Forreine Travel*, 69 (Arber), Which makes them call England the hell of horses. 1790: Grose, *Prov. Gloss.*, s.v. 'England'.

5. England were but a fling, Save for the crooked stick and the gray-goose wing. 1662: Fuller, *Worthies*, i 116 (1840). 1790: Grose, *Prov. Gloss.*, s.v. 'England'.

6. He that England will win must with Ireland begin. 1567: Diego Ortiz, quoted in Froude, *Hist. of Eng.*, x 480, There is an English proverb in use among them which says – He who would England win, In Ireland must begin. 1592: Warner, *Alb. Eng.*, ch liv. st. 4, It is a saying auncient (not Autenticall, I win) That who-so England will subdew, With Ireland must begin. 1617: Fynes Moryson, *Itin.*, Pt II, p. 3. 1658: Howell, *Lexicon Tetraglotton*, App., p. 2, Get Ireland to-day and England may be thine to-morrow. 1790: Grose, *Prov. Gloss.*, s.v. 'England'. 1868: *N.&Q.*, 4th ser, i 437, A speaker on the Irish Church question lately quoted as an old proverb: – 'He that would England win, Must with Ireland first begin'. Here is a variant – 1918: *N.&Q.*, 12th ser, iv 78, A correspondent, writing to the *Times* under the heading 'Perils of the Coast' on January 3, quoted as an East Anglian proverb of immemorial antiquity: – He who would Old

England win Must at Weybourne Hoop begin.

7. Long beards heartless, painted hoods witless; Gay coats graceless, make England thriftless. 1662: Fuller, *Worthies*, i 119 (1840). 1790: Grose, *Prov. Gloss.*, s.v. 'England', A saying said to have been made by the Scotch in the reign of Edward II, when elated with their victory at Stirling.

8. There is more good victuals in England than in seven other kingdoms. 1639: Clarke, 74.

9. When all England is aloft, etc. *See* quots. 1636: R. James, *Iter Laneast.* (Chetham S.), When all England is aloft, Then happy they whose dwellings in God's Crofte; And where thinke you this crofte of Christ should be, But midst Ribchester's Ribble and the Dee. 1669: *New Help to Discourse*, 114, When as wars is aloft Safe is he that's at Christs croft; And where should this Christs croft be, But betwixt Rible and Mersie.

10. When hemp is spun England is done. 1625: Bacon, *Essays:* 'Prophecies', The triuiall prophecie, which I heard, when I was a childe, and Queene Elizabeth was in the flower of her yeares, was; *When hempe is sponne; England's done.* 1662: Fuller, *Worthies*, i 114 (1840). 1790: Grose, *Prov. Gloss.*, s.v. 'England'. 1812: Brady, *Clavis Cal.*, ii 31.

11. When the black fleet of Norway, etc. *See* quots. These sayings are very obscure. I cannot suggest an interpretation. *c.*1500: in *Thos. of Erceldoune*, App., ii 59 (E.E.T.S.), Then the blake flett of Norwaye is commyn and gone, And drenchid in the flode truly; Mekelle ware hath bene beforne, but after shall none be. [Also] Ibid., 61, Thomas of Asheldon sayeth the egle of the trewe brute shall see all inglond in peas and rest both spirituall and temporall; and euery estate of in thaire degre and the maydens of englonde bylde your howses of lyme and stone. 1625: Bacon, *Essays:* 'Prophecies', There was also another prophecie, before the year of 88, which I doe not well vnderstand. *There shall be seene upon a day, Betweene the Baugh, and the May, The Blacke Fleet of Norway. When that that is come and gone, England build Houses of Lime and Stone For after Warres shall you haue None.* 1662: Fuller, *Worthies*, i 115 (1840), When the black fleet of Norway is come and gone, England build houses of lime and stone, For after wars you

shall have none. 1790: Grose, *Prov. Gloss.*, s.v. 'England' [as in 1662].

12. When the sand feeds the clay [wet summer], **England cries well-a-day; But when the clay feeds the sand** [dry summer] **it is merry with England.** 1662: Fuller, *Worthies*, i 116 (1840). 1790: Grose, *Prov. Gloss.*, s.v. 'England'. 1893: Inwards, *Weather Lore*, 7.

See also **Drought; Hallamshire; Hops; King (14); Lady-day; Mouth (7); Oxford (5); and Sheffield Park.**

English are a nation of shopkeepers, The. Said by Napoleon, according to *Napoleon in Exile* (1822) I 103 by B. E. O'Meara: *L'Angleterre est une nation de boutiquiers.* But similar sentiments had been expressed before then. 1766: J. Tucker, *Four Tracts* (1774), III 132, A shop-keeper will never get the more custom by beating his customers; and what is true of a shop-keeper, is true of a shop-keeping nation. 1776: A. Smith, *The Wealth of Nations*, iv vii (1828), III 41, To found a great empire for the sole purpose of raising a people of customers, may at first sight appear a project fit only for a nation of shopkeepers. 1831: Disraeli, *Young Duke*, I xi, Hast thou brought this, too, about that ladies' hearts should be won … over a counter? … We are indeed a nation of shopkeepers.

English are the Frenchmen's apes, The. 1605: Sylvester, *Du Bartas*, Week I Day ii l. 231, Much like the French (or like our selves, their apes). 1662: Fuller, *Worthies*, i 118 (1840). 1790: Grose, *Prov. Gloss.*, s.v. 'England'. 1826: Brady, *Varieties of Lit.*, 43.

English glutton, The. *c.*1540: in *Reliq. Antiquae*, i 326 (1841), He sayd that Englysshemen ar callyd the grettyste fedours in the worlde. 1662: Fuller, *Worthies*, i 118 (1840). 1790: Grose, *Prov. Antiq.*, s.v. 'England'.

English poke-pudding, The. Ibid., s.v. 'England'.

Englishman. 1. A right Englishman. *See* quots. 1639: Clarke, 78, A right Englishman. 1659: Howell, 10 (8), You are a right Englishman, you cannot tell when you are well. 1670: Ray, 85, A right Englishman knows not when a thing is well.

2. An Englishman Italianate is a devil incarnate. 1586: J. Overton, *Jacobs Troublesome Journey*, 8, As manie of our countrimen haue doone from the other side of the sea ... and are therefore become a by-word vnto the worlde to bee called Deuils incarnate. 1630: T. Adams, *Works*, 12. 1645: Howell, *Letters*, bk i § iii No. ii, There is an ill-favour'd saying, That ... an Englishman Italianate is a devil incarnate. 1823: D'Israeli, *Cur. of Lit.*, 2nd ser, i 468 (1824).

3. An Englishman's house (or home) **is his castle.** 1837: Dickens, *Pickwick Papers*, xxiv, Some people maintains that an Englishman's house is his castle. That's gammon. 1906: G.K. Chesterton, *Charles Dickens*, vii, The man who said that an Englishman's house is his castle said much more than he meant. For earlier versions of this proverb *see* **House** (12).

4. In settling an island. *See* quot. 1790: Grose, *Prov. Gloss.*, s.v. 'England', In settling an island, the first building erected by a Spaniard will be a church; by a Frenchman, a fort; by a Dutchman, a warehouse; and by an Englishman, an alehouse.

5. The Englishman grE.E.T.S.. *See* quot. 1846–59: *Denham Tracts*, i 302 (F.L.S.), The prosperity of our northern neighbours is further celebrated in proverb lore by the following: – the Englishman greets, the Irishman sleeps, but the Scotchman gangs till he gets it.

See also **Scottish mist.**

Enjoy. *If you would enjoy the fruit, pluck not the flower.* 1855: Bohn, 422.

Enough and no more, like Mrs Milton's feast. 1917: Bridge, *Cheshire Proverbs*, 54.

Enough is as good at a feast. [ἐπεὶ τά γ' ἀρκοῦνθ' ἱκανὰ τοῖσι σώφροσιν. – Euripides, *Phoen.*, 554.] *c.*1420: Lydgate, *Assembly of Gods*, 59 (E.E.T.S.), As good ys ynowgh as a gret feste. 1546: Hcywood, *Proverbs*, Pt II ch xi 1590: Greene, *Franc. Fortune*, in *Works*, viii 168 (Grosart), Die not indebted to thy bellie, but enough is a feast. 1605: Chapman, etc., *Eastw. Hoe*, III ii 1696: Vanbrugh, *Relapse*, V, 0, enough's as good as a feast. 1732: Fielding, *Cov. Garden Tragedy*, II vi, A little dish oft furnishes enough: And sure enough is equal to a feast. 1826: Lamb, *Pop. Fallacies*, vi 1855: Kingsley, *West. Ho!*, ch xxv 1922: Weyman, *Ovington's Bank*, ch xix.

Enough is enough. 1546: Heywood, *Proverbs*, Pt II ch xi 1834–7: Southey, *Doctor*, ch xx p.i., As for money, enough is enough; no man can enjoy more. 1924: Shaw, *Saint Joan*, sc vi.

Enough one day. *See* quots. 1639: Clarke, 38, Hee'l have enough one day, when his mouth is full of moulds. 1670: Ray, 173 [as in 1639]. 1732: Fuller, 2428, He'll ne'er have enough, till his mouth is full of mould. 1903: Wright, *Eng. Dial. Dict.*, s.v. 'Mould', Thou'l niver be satisfied til thoo gets thi mooth ful a moud. Yorksh.

Enough who is contented with a little, He hath. 1666: Torriano, *Piazza Univ.*, 52.

Envious heart fretteth itself, An. *c.*1460: *How the Good Wyfe*, l. 109, Enuyos hert hym-selue fretys. 1597: *North. Mothers Blessing*, in *Plasidas*, *etc.*, 167 (Roxb.Cl), For an enuious hert Procures mickle smert.

Envious man is a squint-eyed fool, An. 1732: Fuller, 601.

Envious man shall never want woe, The. 1605: Camden, *Remains*, 333 (1870).

Envious man waxes lean with the fatness of his neighbour, An. 1855. Bohn, 311.

Envy never dies. 1523–5: Berners, *Froissart*, ch 428, There is a comune proverbe, the whiche is true, and that is, howe envy never dyeth.

Envy never enriched any man. 1633: Draxe, 52, A man shall never bee enriched of enuie. 1670: Ray, 8. 1732: Fuller, 1380 [with 'yet' after 'never'].

Envy, Nothing sharpens sight like. Ibid., No. 3674.

Envy shoots at others and wounds herself. *c.*1590: G. Harvey, *Marginalia*, 103 (1913), Enuy shootith at other; but hittith and woundith herself. 1669: *Politeuphuia*, 25. 1732: Fuller, 1381.

Epsom. *See* **Sutton.**

Erith. *See* quot. 1588: A. Fraunce, *Lawiers Logike*, fo. 27, The mayre of Earith is the best mayre next to the mayre of London.

Err is human, to forgive divine, To. 1539: R. Morison, tr. *J.L. Vives' Introduction to Wisdom*, It is naturally gyven to al men to erre, but to no man to persever ... therein. 1578: H. Wotton, tr. *J. Yver's Courtly Controversy*, E3, To offend is humaine, to repent divine, and to persevere divelish. 1711: Pope, *Essay on Criticism*, l. 525, Good-Nature and Good-Sense must ever join; To Err is Humane, to Forgive, Divine.

Error is always in haste. 1732: Fuller, 1382.

Errs and mends. *See* quots. 1620: Shelton, *Quixote*, Pt II ch xxviii, Who errs and mends, to God himself commends. 1732: Fuller, 2037, He that after sinning mends, recommends himself to God.

Escape a scouring, To. 1588: *Mar-Prelate's Epitome*, 31 (1843), His grace shall on [one] day answer me this point or very narrowly escape me a scouringe. 1639: Clarke, 80, He scap'd a scouring. 1753: Richardson, *Grandison*, i 318 (1883), 'Fore God, Sir Hargrave, somebody has escaped a scouring, as the saying is.

Escape the rocks and perish in the sands, To. 1732: Fuller, 5160.

Escape the thunder and fall into the lightning, To. 1651: Herbert, *Jac. Prudentum*, 2nd ed.

Eschewing. *See* **Avoidance**.

Essex calves. 1573: G. Harvey, *Letter-Book*, 135 (Camden S.), Foes mustbe frende, quoth an Essex kalfe. 1599: Buttes, *Dyets Dry Dinner*, sig. I1, Essex calfes the prouerb praiseth. 1605: Chapman, etc., *Eastw. Hoe*, II iv, These women, sir, are like Essex calves. 1677: A. Behn, *Rover*, Pt I II i, Tho' this Essex calf believe them persons of quality. 1704: T. Baker, *An Act at Oxford*, V, Thou art an Essex calf. 1869: Hazlitt, 216, If a man beats a bush in Essex, out jumps a calf.

Essex lions = Calves. 1630: Taylor (Water-Poet), W*it and Mirth*, 79, Essex calves, called lions. 1672: *Poor Robin Alman.*, March, Essex lyons there might live, Which some name of calves do give. 1785: Grose, *Class. Dict. Vulgar Tongue*, s.v., Essex Lion, a calf, Essex being famous for calves.

Essex man. Proverbial for a simpleton. Cf. **Essex calves**, (1573, 1677, and 1704). 1663: Killigrew, *Parson's Wedding*, III v, *Jolly*. Have you no friends in the close committee? *Capt.* Yes, yes, I am an Essex man.

Essex miles. 1662: Fuller, *Worthies*, i 497 (1840).

Essex stiles [ditches], **Kentish miles, Norfolk wiles, many men beguiles** – with variants. 15th cent.: in *Reliq. Antiquae*, i 269 (1841), Suffolk, full of wiles; Norffolk, full of giles. 1580: Tusser, *Husbandrie* 209 (E.D.S.), For Norfolk wiles, so full of giles, Haue caught my toe. 1605: Camden, *Remains*, 321 (1870), Essex stiles, Kentish miles, Norfolk wiles, many men beguiles. 1622: Drayton, *Polyol.*, xxiii, As Essex hath of old been named, Calves and Stiles ... Norfolk many wiles. 1735: Pegge, *Kent. Proverbs*, in E.D.S., No. 12, p. 66 [as in 1605]. 1790: Grose, *Prov. Gloss.*, s.v. 'Essex' [as in 1605].

Estate in two parishes is bread in two wallets. 1640: Herbert, *Jac. Prudentum*.

Este bueth owne brondes = Pleasant is one's own fireside, *c.*1320: in *Reliq. Antiquae*, i 111 (1841).

Even break, Never give a sucker an. *See* **Sucker**.

Even reckoning makes long friends. 1546: Heywood, *Proverbs*, Pt II ch iv, Euen recknyng maketh longe freendis. 1658: *Wit Restor'd*, 151. 1732: Fuller, 1399, Even reckonings keep long friends. 1754: Berthelson, *Eng.-Danish Dict.*, s.v. 'Even'.

Evening. 1. A joyful evening may follow a sorrowful morning. 1732: Fuller, 230.

2. Evening grey and morning red. *See* quots. 1830: Forby, *Vocab. E. Anglia*, 416, Evening gray, and morning red, Send the poor shepherd home wet to his bed. 1846: Denham, *Proverbs*, 9 (Percy S.), But if the evening's grey, and the morning red, Put on your hat or you'll wet your head. 1893: Inwards, *Weather Lore*, 53, An evening grey and a morning red Will send the shepherd wet to bed; [or] Evening grey and morning red Make the shepherd hang his head.

3. Evening oats are good morning fodder. 1639: Clarke, 114 [with 'orts' for 'oats']. 1670: Ray, 86 [as in 1639]. 1732: Fuller, 1401. 1846: Denham, *Proverbs*, 3 (Percy S.).

4. Evening red and morning grey. *See* quots. 1586: L. Evans, *Withals Dict. Revised*, sig.N7, The euening red, the morning gray, Foreshewes a cleare and summers day. 1611: Cotgrave, s.v. 'Matin', The evening red and morning gray presage a faire succeeding day. 1772: Mills, *Essay on Weather*, 34 (1773), The evening red, and the morning grey, is a sign of a fair day. 1830: Forby, *Vocab. E. Anglia*, 416, Evening red and morning gray Are sure signs of a fair day. 1846: Denham, *Proverbs*, 8 (Percy S.), An evening red and morning grey, Will set the traveller on his way. 1893: Inwards, *Weather Lore*, 53 ... Two sure signs of one fine day.

5. Evening words are not like to morning. 1611: Cotgrave, s.v. 'Parole', The evening chat is not like the mornings tattle. 1640: Herbert, *Jac. Prudentum*.

6. The evening crowns the day. 1605: Chapman, *All Fools*, II, Well, th' evening crowns the day. 1633: Ford, 'Tis *Pity, etc.*, II vi *ad fin.*, Welcome sweet night! the evening crowns the day. 1692: L'Estrange, *Aesop*, 264 (3rd ed.). 1754: Berthelson, *Eng.-Danish Dict.*, s.v. 'Evening'.

7. The evening praises the day. 1616: Breton, *Cross, of Proverbs*, 5 (Grosart). 1640: Herbert, *Jac. Prudentum*, [with addition] and the morning a frost.

Evenwood, Co. Durham. *See* quots. 1846–59: *Denham Tracts*, i 84 (F.L.S.), Evenwood, Where never straight tree stood; [or] You've been at Evenwood, where never A straight tree grew; [or] You've been to Evenwood, Where straight tree never stood.

Ever drunk ever dry. 1562: Pilkington, *Works*, 51 (P.S.) (OED), 'A drunken man is always dry', according to the proverb. 1605: Camden, *Remains*, 321 (1870). 1681: W. Robertson, *Phraseol. Generalis*, 508. 1754: Berthelson, *Eng.-Danish Dict.*, s.v. 'Drunk'.

Ever lack evil name. *c.*1460: *How the Good Wife*, l. 45.

Ever out cometh evil spun web. *c.*1320: in *Reliq. Antiquae*, i 115 (1841), 'Ever out cometh evel spoune web'; Quoth Hendyng.

Ever spare and ever bare. 1546: Heywood, *Proverbs*, Pt II ch v 1670: Ray, 144. 1732: Fuller, 6168.

Ever the higher. *See* quot. 15th cent.: in *Reliq. Antiquae*, i 92 (1841), Ever the hiere that thou art, Ever the lower be thy hert.

Every art, In, it is good to have a master. 1640: Herbert, *Jac. Prudentum*.

Every ass. *See* **Ass** (13) and (14).

Every bean. *See* **Bean** (3).

Every beginning is difficult. 1537: R. Whitford, *Werke for Housholders*, sig. A8, Euery begynnynge is harde and of greate diffyculte. 1666: Torriano, *Piazza Univ.*, 219.

Every bird is known by its feathers. 1616: Breton, in *Works*, ii *e* 5 (Grosart). 1732: Fuller, 1407.

Every bird likes its own nest. 1611: Cotgrave, s.v. 'Nid'. 1640: Herbert, *Jac. Prudentum*, The bird loves her nest. 1732: Fuller, 1408, Every bird likes its own nest best. 1846: T. Wright, *Essays on Middle Ages*, i 146, We say 'every bird likes its own nest', a saying which runs thus in the old French: – 'A chescun oysel Son nye li semble bel'.

Every bird must hatch its own eggs. 1616: Breton, in *Works*, ii *e* 6 (Grosart). 1683: Meriton, *Yorkshire Ale*, 83–7 (1697). 1732: Fuller, 1409.

Every body loves his own likeness. 1730: T. Saldkeld, tr. Grecian's *Compl. Gentleman*, 79.

Everybody's business is nobody's business. 1611: Cotgrave, s.v. 'Ouvrage', Every bodies work is no bodies work. 1653: Walton, *Compl. Angler*, Pt I *c* ii, I remember that a wise friend of mine did usually say, 'That which is everybody's business is nobody's business'. 1725: Defoe, *Everybody's Business is Nobody's Business* [title]. 1910: G. B. Shaw, *Misalliance*, p. 10 (ed. 1914).

Everybody's friend. *See* **Friend** (8).

Every commodity hath its discommodity. 1583: Melbancke, *Philotinus*, sig. E1. 1598: Meres, *Palladis*, fo. 159. 1633: Draxe, 24. 1672: Walker, *Paraem.*, 36, No convenience without its inconveniency. 1748: Richardson, *Clarissa*, ii 110 (1785), *There's no inconvenience but has its convenience*, said Betty, giving me proverb for proverb. 1877: L. J. Jennings, *Field Paths*, ch xxi, Sometimes I have thought of taking a missis, but there never was conweniency without an ill conweniency, and so I don't do it.

Every country dogs bite, In. 1640: Herbert, *Jac. Prudentum*. 1666: Torriano, *Piazza Univ.*, 36.

Every country the sun rises in the morning, In. 1640: Herbert, *Jac. Prudentum*. 1670: Ray, 25.

Every couple is not a pair. 1875: A. B. Cheales, *Proverb. Folk-Lore*. 37.

Every cross hath its inscription. 1639: Clarke, 16, Each cross has its inscription. 1670: Ray, 75. *c.*1800: Trusler, *Prov. in Verse*, 62. 1853: Trench, *Proverbs*, 132 (1905), This of ours is Christian both in form and in spirit: *Every cross hath its inscription* – the name, that is, inscribed upon it, of the person for whom it was shaped.

Every day brings a new light. 1732: Fuller, 1413.

Every day brings its bread with it. 1640: Herbert, *Jac. Prudentum*. 1666: Torriano, *Piazza Univ.*, 73, There's no to morrow but brings its bread with it.

Every day cometh night. 1578: Florio, *First Fruites*, fo. 33.

Every day in the week a shower of rain, and on Sunday twain. 1659: Howell, 11 … a proverb in many shires of England. 1670: Ray, 257.

Every day is holiday with sluggards. 1542: Udall, tr. Erasmus' *Apoph.*, 174 (1877), To this matter he wrested the prouerbe, in whiche it is saied: That with the slouthfull and idle lubbers that loue not to do any werke, euery day is holidaye. 1611: Davies (of Hereford), *Sc. of*

Folly, Epigr. 142, in *Works*, ii (Grosart), 'With sluggards eu'ry day is holy day'; And so it is with some that seldome sleepes.

Every day is not Sunday. 1611: Cotgrave, s.v. 'Feste', Feasts last not alwayes … every day is not Sunday (say we). 1666: Torriano, *Piazza Univ.*, 88, Every day is not holy day.

Every day is not yesterday. 1639: Clarke, 124.

Every day's no Yule-day – cast the cat a castock [stump of a cabbage]. 1846: Denham, *Proverbs*, 62 (Percy S.). 1904: *Co. Folk-Lore: Northumb.*, 179 (F.L.S.).

Every dog has his day. *See* Dog (41).

Every door may be shut but death's door. 1666: Torriano, *Piazza Univ.*, 317. 1853: Trench, *Proverbs*, 18 (1905), What were 'All men are mortal', as compared with the proverb: *Every door may be shut but death's door?*

Every evil under the sun, For, there is a remedy, or there is none; if there be one, try and find it, if there be none, never mind it. 1869: **Hazlitt**, 135.

Every extremity is a fault. 1629: *Book of Meery Riddles*, Prov. 30.

Every eye forms its own beauty. 1906: Harper, *Brighton Road*, 249, It is not true that it is the prettiest place, but, of course (as the proverb truly says), 'every eye forms its own beauty'.

Every fault there is folly, In. 1878: J. Platt, *Morality*, 34.

Every fool. *See* Fool (36) and (37).

Every fox. *See* Fox (8).

Every gap hath its bush. 1678: Ray, 354.

Every gracious man is also a grateful man. 1875: A. B. Cheales, *Proverb. Folk-Lore*, 94.

Every grain hath its bran. 1826: Brady, *Varieties of Lit.*, 37.

Every groom. *See* Every man is a king at home.

Every hand fleeceth, Where, the sheep goes naked. 1639: Clarke, 187. 1647: *Countrym. New Commonwealth*, 19. 1670: Ray, 91. 1732: Fuller, No. 5645

Every hill. *See* Hill (6).

Every hog his own apple. 1748: Smollett, *Rod. Random*, ch xli., It was soon spent, because I let them have share and share while it lasted. Howsomever, I should have remembered the old saying, *Every hog his own apple*.

Every horse. *See* Horse (28).

Every ill man hath his ill day. 1640: Herbert, *Jac. Prudentum*. 1710: S. Palmer, *Moral Essays on Proverbs*, 123, Every ill man will have an ill time.

Every Jack. *See* Jack has his Jill.

Every knave has a fool in his sleeve. 1710: S. Palmer, *Moral Essays on Proverbs*, 55.

Every light hath its shadow. 1669: *Politeuphuia*, 262.

Every light is not the sun. 1659: Howell, 13. 1670: Ray, 15.

Every little helps. 1602: P. Gawdy, *Letters I (1906), 118*, The wrenn sayde all helpte when she – in the sea. 1623: W. Camden: *Remains concerning Britain* (ed. 3), 268, Every thing helpes, quoth the Wren when she pist i' the sea. 1787: E. Hazard, in *Collections of the Massachusetts Historical Society* (1877), 5th Ser., II 477, A guinea is a guinea, and every little helps. 1791: O'Keeffe, *Wild Oats*, V iii, Here – it's not much! but every little helps. 1854: *N. & Q.*, 1st ser, ix 409, On the principle that every little helps … I would offer the following suggestions. 1869: Spurgeon, *John Ploughman*, ch xix, Every little helps, as the sow said when she snapped at a gnat.

Every man a knave till found honest. 1720: C. Shadwell, *Irish Hospitality*, I, Besides my maxim is, I think every man a knave, till I find him honest.

Every man a little beyond himself is a fool. 1732: Fuller, 1421.

Every man after the fashion. *See* Every one.

Every man as he loves. 1639: Clarke, 16.

Every man as his business lies. 1678: Ray, 107.

Every man basteth the fat hog. 1546: Heywood, *Proverbs*, Pt I ch xi 1639: Clarke, 10. 1869: Spurgeon, *John Ploughman*, ch xiv, All the cooks baste the fat pig, and the lean one gets burned.

Every man before he dies shall see the devil. *c.*1560: Becon, *Catechism, etc.*, 624 (P.S.), The common people have a saying among them, that 'every man before he dieth shall see the devil'.

Every man born to be rich? Is, 1659: Howell, 9.

Every men can rule (or **tame**) **a shrew.** *See* Shrew (3).

Every man cannot hit the nail on the head. 1605: Camden, *Remains*, 321 (1870). 1659: Howell, 8.

Every man cannot speak with the king. 1611: Cotgrave, s.v. 'Parler', Everie one hath not the kings eare at command. 1681: W. Robertson, *Phraseol. Generalis*, 788, Every man cannot come at the king.

Every man (or one) for himself – (*a*) without addition; (*b*) plus **and the devil for all**; (*c*) *plus and God for ua all*. (a) *c*.1386: Chaucer, *C. Tales*, A 1181 (Skeat), At the kingës court, my brother, Ech man for himself. 1478: *Paston Lett.*, iii 228 (Gairdner, 1900), The wyche ye shall understond more when I come, for ther is eury man for hym selff. 1550: R. Crowley, *Works*, 11 (E.E.T.S.), Where euerye man is for him selfe, And no manne for all. 1615: Brathwait, *Strappado*, 206 (1878), Th' old prouerbe's in request, *each man for one*. 1729: Gay, *Polly*, II iii, Every man for himself, say I. 1869: M. Arnold, *Culture and Anarchy:* 'Sweetness and Light', Our hatred to all limits to the unrestrained swing of the individual's personality, our maxim of 'Every man for himself'. (*b*) 1578: Florio, *First Fruites*, fo. 33, Euery one for him selfe and the diuel for al. (*c*) 1546: Heywood, *Proverbs*, Pt II ch ix, Euery man for him selfe and god for us all. 1641: Cowley, *Guardian*, III vi [as in 1546, but with 'one' for 'man']. 1712: Motteux, *Quixote*, Pt I bk iii ch ii, Every man for himself, and God for us all, say I. 1836: Marryat, *Easy*, ch ix, At certain times, on board ship, it is every man for himself, and God for us all.

Every man gnaw on his own bone, Let. *c*.1430: Lydgate, *Minor Poems*, 160 (Percy S.).

Every man has his faults. 1607: Shakespeare, *Timon*, III i, Every man has his faults, and honesty is his. 1670: Ray, 89. 1732: Fuller, 1427, Every man hath his weak side.

Every man has his humour. 1598: Jonson, *Every Man in his Humour* [title]. 1639: Clarke, 17. 1681: W. Robertson, *Phraseol. Generalis*, 554.

Every man has his price. 1734: W. Wyndham in *Bee*, VIII 97, 'It is an old Maxim, that every Man has his Price', if you can but come up with it. *a*. 1745: R. Walpole, as quoted in W. Coxe, *Memoirs of Sir Robert Walpole* (1798), I lxiv, All those men have their price. 1790: J. Wesley, *Sermons*, 123, That politician … whose favourite saying was, 'Do not tell me of your virtue … : I tell you, every man has his price'.

Every man hath a fool in his sleeve. 1640: Herbert, *Jac. Prudentum* [with 'one' for 'man']. 1732: Fuller, 1424. 1754: Berthelson, *Eng.-Danish Dict.*, s.v. 'Fool'.

Every man hath his proper gift. 1639: Clarke, 89.

Every man in his way. 1677: Yarranton, *Englands Improvement*, 105, Now I see the old saying is true, Every man is a fool when he is out of his own way. 1678: Ray, 84. 1753: Richardson, *Grandison*, iii 72 (1883), I understand you … you need not speak out – every one in their way.

Every man is a king at home. 1611: Davies (of Hereford), *Sc. of Folly*, 42, in *Works*, ii (Grosart), Euery groome is a king at home. 1611: Cotgrave, s.v. 'Roy', Every one is a king in his own house.

Every man is best known to himself. 1633: Draxe, 27. 1670: Ray, 13. 1732: Fuller, 1429.

Every man is not born to be a boatswain. 1817: Scott, in Lockhart's *Life*, iv 76, There is an old saying of the seamen's, 'every man is not born to be a boatswain'.

Every man is the architect of his own fortune – with variants. [Nullum numen abest, si sit Prudentia: nos te, Nos facimus, Fortuna, Deam coeloque locamus. – Juvenal, x 365. Sallust (*De Repub. Ordin.*) attributes the saying to Appius Claudius Caecus, the Censor, 312 B.C.] 1533: N. Udall, *Flowers for Latin Speaking* (1560), 24, A proverbiall spekyng … Every man … is the acuser of his own fortune. 1539: Taverner, *Proverbs*, fo. 37, A mans owne maners do shape hym hys fortune. 1612: Shelton, *Quixote*, Pt I bk i ch iv, And, what is more, every one is son of his works. *c*.1680: L'Estrange, *Seneca's Epistles*, xiii, Every man is the artificer of his own fortune. 1707: Dunton, *Athen. Sport*, 454, It is a highway saying, that we are architects of our own fortune. 1800: Coleridge, *Wallenstein*, Man is made great or little by his own will. 1873: E. Tew, in *N. & Q.*, 4th ser, xii 515, We have not a commoner saying among us than 'Every man is the architect of his own fortune', and we have very few much older.

Every man Jack. 1841: Dickens, *Barn. Rudge*, ch xxxix, 'Every one of 'em,' replied Dennis. 'Every man Jack!' 1883: R.L.S., *Treasure I*, ch ix, I am responsible for the ship's safety and the life of every man Jack aboard of her. Cf. **Every mother's son.**

Every man knows his own business best. 1616: Breton, in *Works*, ii *e 5* (Grosart), Euery man knowes what is best for himselfe. 1742: Fielding, *Andrews*, bk ii ch v, The gentleman stared … and, turning hastily about, said, 'Every man knew his own business'. 1837: J. S. Knowles, *Love-Chase*, V i, But every man, As they say, to his own business.

Every man may not wear a furred hood. 1578: T. Lupton, *All for Money*, sig. C2, By the olde prouerbe euerie man may not weare a fourde hood.

Every man mend one, all shall be mended, If. 1562: Heywood, *Three Hund. Epigr.*, No. 1. 1579: Lyly, *Euphues*, 142 (Arber), Let vs endeaour euery one to amend one, and we shall all soone be amended. 1604: Terilo, *Friar Bakon's Proph.*, 27 (Percy S.), Let every man mend one, And I will not be out. 1740: Richardson, *Pamela*, ii 4 (1883), At least, it will be ... answering the good lesson I learned at school, *Every one mend one*. 1793: D'Arblay, *Diary, etc.*, iii 477 (1876), 'Let every one mend one', as Will Chip says [*Will Chip, or Village Politics*, by Hannah More]; and then states, as well as families, may be safely reformed. 1880: Spurgeon, *Ploughman's Pictures*, 47, Mend your own manners, and if every man does the same all will be ... mended.

Every man must bear his own burden. 1611: Cotgrave, s.v. 'Chasque', Every one must look to his owne charge; or beare his owne burthen. 1855: Kingsley, *Westw. Ho!*, ch xxvi, It was Heaven's will ... and to be borne as such. Every man must bear his own burden.

Every man must row with such oars as he has. 1875: A. B. Cheales, *Proverb. Folk-Lore*, 131.

Every man to his taste. *See* **Every one.**

Every man to his trade (or **craft**, or **business**). 1539: Taverner, *Proverbs*, fo. 33, Let euerye man exercise hym selfe in the facultie that he knoweth. 1597: Shakespeare, 1 *Henry IV*, II ii, *Fal* ... every man to his business. 1682: A. Behn, *False Count*, I ii, Father mine, every man to his business, I say. 1732: Fuller, 1435, Every man to his trade, quoth the boy to the bishop. 1821: Scott, *Kenilworth*, ch xi, Every man to his craft, says the proverb, the parson to the prayer-book, and the groom to his curry-comb. 1895: Shaw, *Man of Destiny*, *Giuseppe* ... Every man to his trade, excellency.

Every man will shoot at the enemy, but few will gather the shafts. 1678: Ray, 202 [with 'go to fetch' for 'gather']. 1732: Fuller, 1436.

Every man wishes water to his own mill. 1578: Florio, *First Fruites*, fo. 14, Euery man draweth

water to hym selfe. 1593: G. Harvey, in *Works*, ii 181 (Grosart), Euery miller is ready to conuey the water to his owne mill. 1670: Ray, 121, Every miller draws water to his own mill. 1740: North, *Lives of Norths*, i 133 (Bohn), The Serjeants ... would have no water go by their mill. 1823: Scott, *Peveril*, ch xxi, I hears on nought, except this Plot, as they call it, that they are pursuing the Papishers about; but it brings water to my mill, as the saying is.

Every man's nose will not make a shoeing-horn. [*c.*1520: Stanbridge, *Vulgaria*, sig. B5, His nose is lyke a shoynge horne.] 1659: Howell, 4, Every one cannot have a nose like a shooing-horn. 1670: Ray, 125. 1732: Fuller, 1434.

Every may be hath a may not be. 1678: Ray, 174. 1932: Fuller, 1437.

Every mile is two in winter. 1640: Herbert, *Jac. Prudentum*.

Every miller. *See* **Every man wishes.**

Every mother's son. [*c.*1310: in Wright's *Pol. Songs*, 312 (Camden S., 6), Sur le sollempnement escomege e maldie Trestuz le fiz de mere ... (Upon it he solemnly excommunicates and curses – every son of a mother ...).] *c.*1350: *Alexander*, l. 2098, For mekely ilka modir sonn. 1485: Malory, *Morte d'Arthur*, bk ii ch 10, And there were slayn mony moders sones. 1560: T. Wilson, *Rhetorique*, 72 (1909), Die we must euery mothers sonne of vs. 1595: Shakespeare, *Mids. N. Dream*, I ii, That would hang us, every mother's son. 1694: *Terence made English*, 260, Ay ev'ry mothers son of 'em. 1710: T. Ward, *Eng. Reform.*, 27 (1716), Convict them every mother's son. 1814: Scott, *Fam. Letters*, i 334 (1894), Fire was maintained at the mouth of the cavern, until every man and mother's son were suffocated. 1883: R.L.S., *Treasure* I, ch xxix, That's about where we are, every mother's son of us. Cf. **Every man Jack.**

Every new thing has a silver tail. 1864: 'Cornish Proverbs', in *N. &Q.*, 3rd ser, vi 495.

Every one after his fashion. 1546: Heywood, *Proverbs*, Pt I ch xi *c.*1594: Bacon, *Promus*, No. 955, Every man after his fashen. 1605: Camden, *Remains*, 321 (1870). 1659: Howell, 8.

Every one can keep house better than her mother till she trieth. 1732: Fuller, 1443. 1875: A. B. Cheales, *Proverb. Folk-Lore*, 49.

Every one fastens where there is gain. 1640: Herbert, *Jac. Prudentum*. 1666: Torriano, *Piazza Univ.*, 109.

Every one gets his own, you'll get the gallows, When. 1732: Fuller, 5550.

Every one is a master and servant. 1640: Herbert, *Jac. Prudentum.*

Every one is kin to the rich man. 1666: Torriano, *Piazza Univ.*, 235.

Every one is (or **should be**) **master in his own house.** 1611: Cotgrave, s.v. 'Maison', ... master within his own doores. Ibid., s.v. 'Maistre', Everyone rules in his own house.

Every one is not born a poet. 1659: Howell, 13.

Every one is weary: the poor in seeking, the rich in keeping, the good in learning. 1640: Herbert, *Jac. Prudentum.* 1666: Torriano, *Piazza Univ.*, 4, Every one will labour, the poor man in seeking what he wants, and the rich man in preserving what he hath.

Every one knows how to find fault. 1732: Fuller, 1447.

Every one puts his fault on the times. 1640: Herbert, *Jac. Prudentum.* 1670: Ray, 26. 1732: Fuller, 1448, Every one lays his faults upon the time.

Every one says. *See* **True** (15).

Every one swale [sell] **his own wuts** [oats]. **Let.** 1917: Bridge, *Cheshire Proverbs*, 89.

Every one takes care of himself, care is taken of all, When. 1855: Bohn, 558.

Every one talks of what he loves. 1732: Fuller, 1450.

Every one that can lick a dish. 1678: Ray, 76.

Every one thinks he knows much. 1732: Fuller, 1451.

Every one thinks his sack heaviest. 1611: Cotgrave, s.v. 'Fardeau', Every one finds his owne burthen heavy enough. 1640: Herbert, *Jac. Prudentum.*

Every one to catch a salmon, 'Tis not for. 1732: Fuller, 5095.

Every one to his taste – (*a*) *plus* **as ... said when he** (or **she**) **kissed the cow;** (*b*) without the cow. (*a*) 1546: Heywood, *Proverbs*, Pt II ch i, Euery man as he loueth Quoth the good man whan that he kyst his coowe. 1630: Davenant, *Just Italian*, III, Th' old amorous deacon that embrac'd his cow Was not so destitute. 1675: Cotton, *Burl. upon Burlesque*, 189 (1765), Why each one as he likes (you know), Quo' th' good man when he kiss'd his cow. 1694: Motteux, *Rabelais*, bk v ch xxix, Every one as they like, as the woman said when she kiss'd her cow. 1738:

Swift, *Polite Convers.*, Dial. I [as in 1694, *plus* 'good' before 'woman']. 1823: Scott, *Peveril*, ch vii, She hath a right to follow her fancy, as the dame said who kissed her cow. 1883: Burne, *Shropsh. Folk-Lore*, 591, Every one to his liking, as the old woman said when she kissed her cow. (*b*) 1611: Cotgrave, s.v. 'Chascun', Every one as hee likes. 1656: Middleton, *Old Law*, II ii, Every one to their liking. 1714: Ozell, *Molière*, ii 110, Every one to his mind. 1759: Sterne, *Trist. Shandy*, bk i ch vii, I never could envy Didius in these kinds of fancies of his: – But every man to his own taste.

Every one's censure is first moulded in his own nature. 1855: Bohn, 351.

Every one's faults are not written in their foreheads. 1678: Ray, 9.

Every path. *See* **Path.**

Every pease hath its veaze – and variant. 1599: Buttes, *Dyets Dry Dinner*, Our common proverb accordeth, speaking somewhat homely: Euery pease wil haue a fease, but euerie beane, fifteene. 1608: Armin, *Nest of Ninnies*, 51 (SH.S.), It was in Lent, when pease pottage bare great sway, and euery pease must have his ease. 1670: Ray, 214, Every pease hath its veaze, and a bean fifteen.

Every peddler thinks well of his pack. 1611: Cotgrave, s.v. 'Panier'. 1631: Mabbe, *Celestina*, 161 (T.T.), Every pedler prayseth his owne needles.

Every penny that is taken is not clear gain. 1732: Fuller, 1454.

Every pleasure hath a pain. 1598: Chapman, *Blind Beggar of Alex*, sc v 1631: Mabbe, *Celestina*, 149 (T.T.), There is no pleasure without sorrow.

Every plummet is not for every sound. 1732: Fuller, 1455.

Every pot has two handles. 1650: Taylor, *Holy Living*, ch ii § 6, There is nothing but hath a double handle, or at least we have two hands to apprehend it. 1827: Hone, *Ev. Day Book*, ii 649, 'Every pot has two handles'. This means 'that one story's good till another story's told', or 'there is no evil without its advantages'.

Every question requireth not an answer. 1578: Florio, *First Fruites*, fo. 32 [with 'woorde' for 'question']. 1629: *Book of Meery Riddles*, Prov. 31. 1875: A. B. Cheales, *Proverb. Folk-Lore*, 118, It is not every question that deserves answer.

Every reed will not make a pipe. 1732: Fuller, 1457.

Every river. *See* **All rivers.**

Every scale hath its counterpoise. 1666: Torriano, *Piazza Univ.*, 53 [with 'balance' for 'scale']. 1732: Fuller, 1458.

Every shoe fits not every foot. 1616: B. Rich, *Ladies Looking Glasse*, 21, As euery shooe is not fit for euery foote. 1670: Ray, 142. 1754: Berthelson, *Eng.-Danish Dict.*, s.v. 'Shoe'.

Every slip is not a fall. 1732: Fuller, 1461.

Every spot is not the leprosy. 1875: A. B. Cheales, *Proverb, Folk-Lore*, 117.

Every thing comes to him who waits. *See* **All things come to those who wait.**

Every thing has an end. *See* **All things have an end.**

Every thing hath a beginning. 1566: Gascoigne, *Supposes*, V v 1661: Middleton, *Mayor of Q.*, IV iii, Everything has beginning.

Every thing hath an ear, and a pitcher has two. 1639: Clarke, 237.

Every thing hath his seed. 1633: Draxe, 12.

Every thing hath its time. 1509: Barclay, *Ship of Fooles*, ii 46 (1874), For euery thynge God hath a tyme puruayde. 1578: *Gorgeous Gallery*, 47 (Rollins), Eche thing must haue a time. 1666: Torriano, *Piazza Univ.*, 283. 1732: Fuller, 1466, Every thing hath its time, and that time must be watch'd. 1875: A. B. Cheales, *Proverb. Folk-Lore*, 12, As another proverb reminds us, Every thing will come into use if you only keep it long enough.

Every thing is as it is taken. 1552: Latimer, *Works*, ii 150 (P.S.), We have a common saying amongst us, 'Every thing is as it is taken'. *c.*1597: in Harington, *Nugae Antiquae*, i 223 (1804), We must say as is oft sayd, 'it was as it was taken'. 1632: Jonson, *Magnetic Lady*, III iii, All counsel's as 'tis taken.

Every thing is good in its season. 1633: Draxe, 184. 1670: Ray, 23. 1732: Fuller, 1467. 1851: Borrow, *Lavengro*, iii 261, He had no objection to tea; but he used to say, 'Every thing in its season'.

Every thing is of use to a housekeeper. 1640: Herbert, *Jac. Prudentum.*

Every thing is the worse for wearing. Before 1529: Skelton, *Magnyfycence*, l. 456, All thynge is worse whan it is worne. 1560: T. Wilson, *Rhetorique*, 151 (1909), Your witte is good enough, if you keepe it still and vse it not, for euery thing, as you knowe, is the worse for the

wearing. 1694: Southerne, *Fatal Marriage*, III ii 1754: Berthelson, *Eng.-Danish Dict.*, s.v. 'Worse'.

Every thing new is fine. 1639: Clarke, 228, Every thing's pretty, when 'tis new. 1666: Torriano, *Piazza Univ.*, 171, A new, every thing is handsome.

Every thing would live. 1670: Ray, 116. 1732: Fuller, 1469.

Every tide will have an ebb. 1583: Melbancke, *Philotinus*, sig. U2, Euerie tide [hath] his eb. 1732: Fuller, 1470.

Every time the sheep bleats. *See* **Sheep** (3).

Every tub must stand on its own bottom. 1564: Bullein, *Dialogue*, 65 (E.E.T.S.), Let euerie fatte [vat] stande vpon his owne bottome. 1678: Bunyan, *Pilgr. Progr.*, Pt I p. 35 (1849), *Sloth* said, *Yet a little more sleep*; and *Presumption* said, *Every tub must stand upon his own bottom.* 1721: C. Cibber, *Refusal*, V 1781: Macklin, *Man of the World*, I. 1857: Borrow, *Rom. Rye*, ch xxix, 'Every vessel must stand on its own bottom,' said I; 'they take pleasure in receiving obligations, I take pleasure in being independent.' 1901: F. E. Taylor, *Lancs Sayings*, 8, Let ev'ry tub stond on it' own bothum.

Every where is no where, He that is. 1586: Pettie, tr. Guazzo's *Civil Convers.*, fo. 63, The prouerbe, That he is not any where, who is euerie where. 1669: *Politeuphuia*, 131, He is no-where that is every-where. 1732: Fuller, 2176.

Every wind bloweth not down the corn. 1546: Heywood, *Proverbs*, Pt II ch ix 1633: Draxe, 234.

Every wind is ill to a broken ship. 1633: Ibid., 171. 1869: Spurgeon, *John Ploughman*, ch vii, Every wind is foul for a crazy ship.

Every woman. *See* quot. 1612: Field, *Woman a Weathercock*, IV ii, They say every woman has a springe to catch a woodcock [gull, or silly fellow].

Evil, *adj.* **1. An evil lesson is soon learned.** 1670: Ray, 8, That which is evil is soon learn't.

2. An evil suspicion has a worse condition. 1886: R. Holland, *Cheshire Gloss.*, 444 (E.D.S.). 1917: Bridge, *Cheshire Proverbs*, 8.

3. Evil beginning hath evil end. *c.*1400: *Mirk's Festial*, 120 (E.E.T.S.), For hyt ys oft sene, all euell bygynnyng hathe a foule endyng. *c.*1440: Lydgate, *Fall of Princes*, bk viii l. 2241, Ther gynnyng cursid hadde a wengable fyn.

4. Evil communications. *See* 11. *Evil words.*

5. Evil crow. *See* **Like crow.**

6. Evil doers. *See* **Ill doers.**

7. Evil guise. *See* **Sluggards guise.**

8. Evil name is evil fame. *c.*1430: in *Babees Book, etc.,* 39 (E.E.T.S.), For he that cacchith to him an yuel name, It is to him a foule fame.

9. Evil news. *See* **Ill news.**

10. Evil will. *See* **Ill will.**

11. Evil words corrupt good manners. *c.*1425: J. Arderne, *Treatises of Fistula* (E.E.T.S.), 5, Shrewed speche corrumpith gode maners. 1530: Palsgrave, 499, Foule wordes corupte good maners. 1533: Sir T. More *Debellation of Salem,* xiv, (As saynt Poule speketh of such heresyes) evyl communication corrupteth good maners.1596: Harington, *Ulysses upon Ajax,* 23 (1814), Evil words corrupt good manners (saith both Paul and Menander). 1 Corinthians xv 33 Be not deceived: evil communications corrupt good manners. 1631: Brathwait, *Eng. Gentlewoman,* 293 (1641), As by good words evill manners are corrected, so by evill words are good ones corrupted. 1749: Fielding, *Tom Jones,* bk xii ch iii, Evil communication corrupts good manners. 1821: Scott, *Pirate,* ch xxx, Gude forgie me for swearing – but evil communication corrupteth good manners.

12. Of evil grain no good seed can come. 1633: Draxe, 13 [without last two words]. 1670: Ray, 8.

13. Of evil life comes evil end. *c.*1300: *King Alisaunder,* l. 753, Soth hit is, in al thyng, Of eovel hi comuth eovel eyndyng. *c.*1440: *La Tour-Landry,* 72 (E.E.T.S.), For gladly euelle lyff hathe euelle ende.

14. The evil wound is cured, but not the evil name. 167: Ray, 18.

Evil, *adv.* Evil gotten, *evil* (or *worse*) *kept* (or *spent*). 1481: Caxton, *Reynard,* 8 (Arber), Therof hym had be better to haue holde his pees for he had stolen it Male quesisti et male perdidisti hit is ryght that it be euil loste that is euil wonne. 1541: Coverdale, *Christ. State Matrimony,* sig. I2, Euyll geten, worse kept. 1579: *Marr. of Wit and Wisdom,* sc iii p. 28 (SH.S.), Euell gotten worse spent. 1670: Ray, 8, Evil gotten evil spent. 1754: Berthelson, *Eng.-Danish Dict.,* s.v. 'Evil', Evil got evil spent.

Evil, *subs.* **1. Evil is soon believed.** 1732: Fuller, 1474.

2. Evil to him that evil thinks (or **seeks**). *c.*1386: Chaucer, *Prioress's Tale,* l. 180, Yvel shal have, that yvel wol deserve. 1484: Caxton, *Aesope,* ii

207 (Jacobs), Now the euyl which men wysshe to other cometh to hym whiche wyssheth hit. 1666: Torriano, *Piazza Univ.,* 200, To who thinks evil, evil befalls him. 1712: Motteux, *Quixote,* Pt I bk iii ch vi, Good betide us all, and evil to him that evil seeks.

3. He that evil does never good weens. *c.*1386: Chaucer, *C. Tales,* A 4320 (Skeat), Him thar nat wenë wel that yvel doth.

4. He that helpeth the evil hurteth the good. *c.*1615: *Time's Whistle,* 45 (E.E.T.S.), For true's the saying … 'He harmes the good that doth the evill spare'. 1669: *Politeuphuia,* 186, He that helpeth an evil man hurteth him that is good. 1732: Fuller, 2163.

5. No evil without its advantages. 1827: Hone, *Ev. Day Book,* ii 649.

6. See no evil, hear no evil, speak no evil. *See* **See (5).**

7. The evil that cometh out of thy mouth, flyeth into thy bosom. 1633: Draxe, 192 [with 'returneth (or falleth)' for 'flyeth']. 1670: Ray, 8. 1732: Fuller, 4505.

8. Whoso will no evil do. *See* quots. 1537: R. Whitford, *Werke for Householders,* sig. D7, The olde prouerbe sayth, who so wyll none euyll do, shulde do nothynge that longeth therto. 1639: Clarke, 202, He that would no evills doe, must shun all things that longs thereto.

Evils. *See* **Misfortunes;** and **Two evils.**

Ewell. *See* **Sutton.**

Example. 1. Example is better than precept. *c.*1400: *Mirk's Festial,* 216 (E.E.T.S.), Then saythe Seynt Austeyn that an ensampull yn doyng ys mor commendabull then ys techyng other prechyng. 1570: Ascham, *Scholemaster,* 61 (Mayor), One example is more valiable … than twenty preceptes written in bookes. 1656: F. Osborne, *Advice to Son,* 34 (Parry), Example prevails more than precept. 1742: Fielding, *Andrews,* bk i ch i, It is a trite but true observation, that examples work more forcibly on the mind than precepts. 1868: W. C. Hazlitt, in *N.&Q.,* 4th ser, i 201, The copy-book says that 'Example is better than Precept'.

2. He is in ill case that gives example to another. 1629: *Book of Meery Riddles,* Prov. 125.

Excellent soldier, he lacks nothing but a heart and a feather, An. 1639: Clarke, 310.

Excellent tale and 'twere told in Greek, An. Ibid., 231.

Exception proves the rule, The. 1664: J. Wilson, *The Cheats*, To Reader, For if I have shown the odd practices of two vain persons pretending to what they were not, I think I have sufficiently justified the brave man even by this reason, that the exception proves the rule. 1771: Smollett, *Clinker*, in *Works*, vi 82 (1817), They serve only as exceptions; which, in the grammarian's phrase, confirm and prove a general canon. 1808: Byron, *Letters and Journals*, i 204 (Prothero), You will recollect that '*exceptions only prove the Rule*'. 1883: Trollope, *Autob.*, ch xii, But the exceptions are not more than enough to prove the rule. 1909: W. H. Helm, *Jane Austen*, 169, The retort … is that they are the exceptions that 'prove' the rule. Cf. **Rule.**

Exception to every rule, There is an. 1579: T.F. *News from the North*, D1v, There is no rule so generall, that it admitteth not exception. 1733: R. Graves, *Spiritual Quixote*, III ix xviii, The rules of Grammar cannot, in any language, be reduced to a strict analogy; but all general rules have some exceptions. 1836: Marryat, *Mr Midshipman Easy*, I xii, I have little reason to speak in its favour … but there must be exceptions to every rule. 1981: *Listener*, 2 May 683, Even they should remember that there is an exception to every rule.

Exchange. *See* **Fair,** *adj.* (19).

Expect. *See* **Pig** (25).

Experience is good, if not bought too dear. 1732: Fuller, 1479.

Experience is sometimes dangerous. 1578: Florio, *First Fruites*, fo. 30, Experience sometymes is perilous. 1629: *Book of Meery Riddles*, Prov. 110.

Experience is the best teacher. 1803: M.L. Weems *Letter* 12 Nov. (1929), 278, Experience, the best of teachers. 1856: F. M. Witcher, *Widow Bedott Papers*, xxix, I … dident know how to do anything as well as I do now … Experience is the best teacher after all. *See also* **Experience is the mistress of fools; Experience is the mother of knowledge;** and **Experience teacheth fools.**

Experience is the father of wisdom, and memory the mother. 1732: Fuller, 1480.

Experience is the mistress of fools. 1579: Lyly, *Euphues*, 123 (Arber), It is commonly said … that experience is the mistresse of fooles. 1618: Breton, in *Inedited Tracts*, 187 (Hazlitt).

1692: L'Estrange, *Aesop*, 185 (3rd ed.), Experience is the mistress of knaves as well as of fools. 1710: S. Palmer, *Moral Essays on Proverbs*, 33, As experience is the school-mistress of fools. *c*.1800: J. Trusler, *Prov. in Verse*, 25.

Experience is the mother of knowledge. 1578: Florio, *First Fruites*, fo. 32, Experience is the mother of al things. 1637: Breton, in *Works*, ii 18 (Grosart), Reading makes a scholler by rule … but experience is the mother of knowledge. 1700: D. Craufurd, *Courtship à-la-Mode*, I ii.

Experience keeps a dear school, but fools will learn in no other. 1736: Franklin, *Way to Wealth*, in *Works*, i 451 (Bigelow). 1875: A. B. Cheales, *Proverb. Folk-Lore*, 115.

Experience teacheth fools. 1732: Fuller, 1484, Experience teacheth fools, and he is a great one that will not learn by it. 1884: *Folk-Lore Journal*, ii 279, Experience makes fools wise. *Derbysh.*

Experience without learning is better than learning without experience. 1855: Bohn, 352.

Extreme right. *See* **Greater the right. Extremes meet.** 1589: *Triumph of Love and Fortune*, IV, in Hazlitt, *Old Plays*, vi 214, A right woman – either love like an angel, Or hate like a devil – in extremes so to dwell. 1780: Walpole, *Letters*, vii 395 (Cunningham), We seem to be plunging into the horrors of France … yet, as extremes meet, there is at this moment amazing insensibility. 1822: Lamb, *Elia:* 'Chimney-Sweepers', That dead time of the dawn, when (as extremes meet) the rake … and the hard-handed artizan … jostle … for the honours of the pavement. 1900: Lucas, *Domesticities*, 24, Oatmeal marks not only the child's breakfast, it is the favourite food of Edinburgh Reviewers. Thus do extremes meet.

Eye and **Eyes. 1. A small hurt in the eye is a great one.** 1732: Fuller, 406.

2. Better eye sore than all blind. *c*.1320: in *Reliq. Antiquae*, i, 110 (1841), 'Betere is eye sor, then al blynd'; Quoth Hendyng. 1846: T. Wright, *Essays on Middle Ages*, i 141, Thus we have the saying 'A sore eye is better than all blind'.

3. He has an eye behind him. *c*.1565: Still, *Gammer Gurton*, II ii, Take hede of Sim Glovers wife, she hath an eie behind her! 1681: W. Robertson, *Phraseol. Generalis*, 1032, He hath an eye behind; a wary man. 1869: P. Fitzgerald, *Comediettas*, 111, Watch every look, every gesture. She has eyes in the back of her head.

4. He shuts his eyes and thinks none sec.
1852: FitzGerald, *Polonius*, 28 (1903).

5. His eye is bigger than his belly. 1640:
Herbert, *Jac. Prudentum* [with 'the' for 'his'].
1738: Swift, *Polite Convers.*, Dial. II, I thought I
could have eaten this wing of a chicken; but my
eye's bigger than my belly. 1828: Carr, *Craven
Dialect*, i 137, 'His eyes are bigger than his belly';
spoken of a glutton. 1889: Peacock, *Manley, etc.*,
Gloss., 193 (E.D.S.), A person is said to have his
'eyes bigger than his belly' who takes more food
upon his plate than he can eat. 1901: F. E. Taylor,
Lancs Sayings, 24, His een are bigger nor his bally.

6. His (or her) eyes draw straws. 1709:
Mandeville, *Virgin Unmask'd*, 98 (1724), My
eyes begin to draw straws … I wish ye a good
repose. 1790: *Gent. Mag.*, Pt II 978, It is a
current expression, in a great part of the
kingdom, to say of a person, when his eyes are
heavy, and he is much inclined to sleep, *that his
eyes draw straws.* 1830: Forby, *Vocab. E. Anglia*,
430. 1883: Burne, *Shropsh. Folk–Lore*, 596, The
eyes are drawing straws = the person is
becoming drowsy.

7. Neither eyes on letters nor hands in coffers.
1578: Florio, *First Fruites*, fo. 33, Neither eyes,
nor handes in other mens writings or purses.
1640: Herbert, *Jac. Prudentum*.

8. Neither my eye nor my elbow. 1894:
Northall, *Folk Phrases*, 20 (E.D.S.), Neither … ,
i.e. neither one thing nor the other. 1907: T.
Ratcliffe, in *N. & Q.*, 10th ser, viii 7, I have never
heard this phrase except from Derbyshire folks.
It is used as a comment on an unsatisfactory
answer, promise, or arrangement, as 'It's neither
my eye nor my elbow' – neither the one thing nor
the other.

**9. One eye of the master's sees more than ten
of the servant's.** 1640: Herbert, *Jac.
Prudentum.* 1670: Ray, 17. 1732: Fuller, 3749.
Cf. Nos. 13 and 17.

10. The eye and religion can bear no jesting.
1630: T. Adams, *Works*, 14, We say … it is no
safe jesting with holy things. 1640: Herbert, *Jac.
Prudentum.* 1710: S. Palmer, *Moral Essays on
Proverbs*, 322, 'Tis ill jesting with your eye and
religion.

11. The eye is a shrew. 1678: Ray, 354.

12. The eye is the pearl of the face. 1580: Lyly,
Euphues, 406 (Arber), As the eye hath euer bene
thought the pearle of the face. 1732: Fuller, 4506.

**13. The eye of a master will do more work than
both his hands.** 1736: Franklin, *Way to Wealth*,
in *Works*, i 445 (Bigelow). 1843: Carlyle, *Past
and Present*, bk ii ch x, But continual vigilance,
rigorous method, what we call 'the eye of the
master', work wonders. Cf. Nos. 9 and 17.

**14. The eye that sees all things else, sees not
itself.** 1732: Fuller, 4507.

15. The eye will have his part. 1640: Herbert,
Jac. Prudentum.

16. The eyes have one language everywhere.
Ibid.

17. The master's eye fats the horse.
[ἐρωτηθεὶς τί μάλιστα ἵππον πιαίνει; Ὁ τοῦ
δεσπότον ὀφθαλμός, ἔφη. – Aristotle, Œcum.,
I vi 4.] 1537: R. Whitford, *Werke for
Housholders*, sig. F5, The eye of the mayster
[maketh] a fatte horse. 1552: Latimer, *Sermons*,
395 (P.S.). 1579: *Lyly, Euphues*, 144 (Arber),
That notable saying of the horse-keeper –
nothing did so fatte the horse as the eye of the
king. 1631: Brathwait, *Whimzies*, 69 (1859),
The proverbe is, The masters eye feedes his
horse. 1709: O. Dykes, *Eng. Proverbs*, 281.
1869: Austen Leigh, *Memoir of Jane Austen*, 35,
Two homely proverbs were held in higher
estimation in my early days than they are now –
'The master's eye makes the horse fat', and …
Cf. Nos. 9 and 13.

**18. To whirl the eyes too much shows a kite's
brain.** 1640: Herbert, *Jac. Prudentum.*

**19. What the eye doesn't see, the heart doesn't
grieve over.** *c.*1477: Caxton, *Jason*, 83
(E.E.T.S.), Men saye communely that ferre ys
from the eye is ferre from the herte. 1546:
Heywood, *Proverbs*, Pt II ch vii 1592: Greene, in
Works, xi 140 (Grosart), What the eie sees not
Phylomela neuer hurteth the heart. *c.*1613:
Rowlands, *Paire of Spy-Knaues*, 7 (Hunt.Cl.),
For what the eye ne're sees, the heart ne're rues.
1653: R. Brome, *City Wit*, III iii 1712: Motteux,
Quixote, Pt II ch 67. 1883: Burne, *Shropsh. Folk–
Lore*, 588, What the eye doesn't see, the heart
doesn't grieve. Cf. **Out of sight out of mind;** and
Seldom seen.

**20. You may put it in the eye and see none the
worse.** 1530: Palsgrave, 478, I maye put my
wynnyng in myn eye. 1545: Ascham, *Toxoph.*,
151 (Arber), So that shoter whiche putteth
no difference, but shooteth in all lyke, in rough
weather and fayre, shall always put his

wynninges in his eyes. 1641: Cowley, *Guardian*, I i, What you get by him you may e'en put i' your eye, and ne'er see the worse for 't. 1738: Swift, *Polite Convers.*, Dial. I.

21. You should never touch your eye but with your elbow, i.e. you should not touch your eye at all. 1640: Herbert, *Jac. Prudentum*, Diseases of the eye are to be cured with the elbow. 1670: Ray, 39. Fuller, 3529, Never rub your eye but with your elbow. 1894: Northall, *Folk Phrases*, 21 (E.D.S.), Rub your sore eye with your elbow, i.e. not at all.

See also **Every eye; Four eyes; Mistress** (3); and **Two eyes.**

Eyelet-holes. *See* quots. 1599: Porter, *Two Angry Women*, in Hazlitt, *Old Plays*, vii 381, 'Twill be a good while, ere you wish your skin full of eyelet-holes. 1678: Ray, 219, It will be long enough ere you wish your skin full of holes. 1738: Swift, *Polite Convers.*, Dial. I, You'll be long enough before you wish your skin full of eyelet holes. 1855: Kingsley, *West. Ho!*, ch iii, I expected to be full of eyelet holes ere I could close with him.

Eye-servant is never good for his master, The. 1659: Howell, 10.

Eye-teeth, To have one's. 1730: Morier, in Atterbury, *Misc. Works*, v 147 (OED), There is no dealing with him without having one's eye teeth. 1778: T. Cogan, *John Buncle, Junior*, ii 148, My ladies have all *their eye teeth about them*, as the saying is. 1870: Emerson, *Works*, ii 7 (Bohn) (OED), Progress that is made by a boy 'when he cuts his eye-teeth'.

F

Face. 1. A face of brass. 1578: Whetstone, *Promos and Cassandra*, Pt II III i, Well, I wyll set a face of brasse on it. 1647: in *Somers Tracts*, v 490 (1811), Had he not had more brass in his face than in his kitchen … 1718: in *Roxb. Ballads*, viii 633 (B.S.), Then, with a face of brass, he ask'd poor Betty more.

2. Face to face the truth comes out. 1732: Fuller, No 1485. 1852: FitzGerald, *Polonius*, 59 (1903), Face to face truth comes out apace.

3. I think his face is made of a fiddle, every one that looks on him loves him. 1678: Ray, 243. 1762: Smollett, *Sir L. Greaves*, ch viii, We may see your honour's face is made of a fiddle; every one that looks on you, loves you. 1816: Scott, *Old Mortality*, ch xxxvii, How could I help it? His face was made of a fiddle, as they say, for a' body that looked on him liked him.

4. The face is index of the heart. 1586: L. Evans, *Withals Dict. Revised*, sig. L7, Your face doth testifie what you be inwardly. *c*.1615: *Times Whistle*, 23 (E.E.T.S.), That olde saying is vntrue, 'the face Is index of the heart'. 1645: Howell, *Letters*, bk i § iii No. xv, The face is oftentimes a true index of the heart. 1713: Ward, *Hist. Grand Rebellion*, i 8, For in the face judicious eyes may find The symptoms of a good or evil mind. 1864: Mrs H. Wood, *Trevlyn Hold*, ch i, You have not to learn that the face is the outward index of the mind within.

Face with a card of ten. *See* **Outface.**

Fact is stranger than fiction. 1853: T.C. Hamiburton, *Sam Slick's Wise Saws*, 5, Facts are stranger than fiction, for things happen sometimes that never entered into the mind of man to imagine or invent. 1881: A. Jessopp, *Arcady for Better or Worse*, iii, I have no desire to convicne the world that … in this … case fact is stranger than fiction. 1929: E.J. Millward, *Copper Bottle*, 64, Facts may be stranger than fiction … but fiction is generally truer than facts. *See also* **truth** (10).

Facts are stubborn things. 1749: Smollett, *Gil Bias*, bk x ch i 1925: E. Lyttelton, *Memories and Hopes*, 228, These are facts; and after all, facts are stubborn things.

Fail at a pinch. *See* **Pinch.**

Fails, He who never, will never grow rich.

1869: Spurgeon, *John Ploughman*, ch xii [cited 'as the proverb is'].

Fain as a fowl. *See* **Fowl.**

Faint at the smell of a wallflower, He will. 1790: Grose, *Prov. Gloss.*, s.v. 'London'.

Faint heart never won fair lady. [*c*.1390: Gower, *Conf. Amantis*, bk v l. 6573, Bot as men sein, wher herte is failed, Ther schal no castell ben assailed.] *c*.1570: in *Black Letter Ballads, etc.*, 16 (Lilly, 1867), Faint harts faire ladies neuer win. 1580: Lyly, *Euphues*, 364 (Arber), Faint heart … neither winneth castell nor lady. 1664: Cotton, *Scarronides*, bk i, Faint heart, you know, ne'er wins fair lady. 1702: Vanbrugh, *False Friend*, III *c*.1750: Foote, *Knights*, II. 1846: Planché, *Extravag.*, iii 130 (1879), And faint heart ne'er fair lady wins, I'll venture – come what may!

Faint praise is disparagement. 1813: Ray, 106.

Fair, *adj.* **1. A fair booty makes many a thief.** 1732: Fuller, 86.

2. A fair day in winter is the mother of a storm. 1639: Clarke, 171, A faire day is mother of a storme. 1651: Herbert, *Jac. Prudentum*, 2nd ed.

3. A fair face cannot have a crabbed heart. 1593: *Passionate Morrice*, 92 (N.Sh.S.), Building vpon the prouerbe, A faire face, etc.

4. A fair face is half a portion. 1633: Draxe, 15, Shee that is faire hath halfe her portion. 1732: Fuller, 89.

5. A fair face may be a foul bargain. 1590: Greene, in *Works*, viii 36 (Grosart), Such as marie but to a faire face, tie themselues oft to a foule bargain. 1732: Fuller, 87, A fair face and a foul bargain. 1875: A. B. Cheales, *Proverb. Folk-Lore*, 35 [as in 1732]. *See also* **Good face.**

6. A fair field and no favour. 1883: E. Pennell-Elmhirst, *Cream Leics.*, 202 (OED), He … asked only for a fair field and a clear course. 1927: *Sphere*, 27 March, p. 492, col. 3, What our small body of genuine talent needs is a fair field and no favour.

7. A fair pawn never shamed his master. 1639: Clarke, 109. 1670: Ray, 130.

8. A fair shop and little gain. 1629: *Book of Meery Riddles*, Prov. 69.

9. A fair wife, a wide house, and a back-door, Will quickly make a rich man poor. *c*.1460: *Prov. of Good Counsel*, in E.E.T.S., Ext. Ser.,

No. 8, p. 69, A nyse wyfe, and a backe dore, Makyth oftyn tymes a ryche man pore. 1647: *Countrym. New Commonwealth*, 43.

10. A fair wife and a frontier castle breed quarrels. 1640: Herbert, *Jac. Prudentum.*

11. A fair wife. *See* **Horse** (34).

12. A fair woman and a slasht gown find always some nail in the way. 1659: Howell, *Proverbs: Ital.-Eng.*, 10. 1670: Ray, 9.

13. A fair woman with foul conditions is like a sumptuous sepulchre full of rotten bones. 1647: *Countrym. New Commonwealth*, 11 [with 'painted' for 'sumptuous']. 1669: *Politeuphuia*, 31.

14. A fair woman without virtue is like patted wine. 1855: Bohn, 285.

15. All's fair in love and war. *See* **Love** (1).

16. As fair as Lady Done. Cheshire. 1670: Ray, 208. 1790: Grose, *Prov. Gloss.*, s.v. 'Cheshire'. 1917: Bridge, *Cheshire Proverbs*, 12, As fair as Lady Done, or, There's Lady Done for you. The wife of Sir John Done (d. 1629) of Utkinton.

17. Expect not fair weather in winter on one night's ice. 1670: Ray, 28.

18. Fair and far off. Wide of the mark. 1690: *New Dict. Canting Crew*, sig. E3.

19. Fair and foolish. *See* quots. 1600: W. Vaughan, *Directions for Health*, Faire and foolish, little and loud, Long and lazie, blacke and proud; Fat and merry, leane and sad, Pale and peevish, red and bad. 1615: R. Tofte, *Blazon of Iealousie*, 34 [as in 1600 but with 'lusty' for 'lazie' and 'pettish' for 'peevish']. Before 1658: Cleveland, *Works*, 268 (1742), Foolish (the proverb says) if fair. 1732: Fuller, 6409: Fair and foolish, black and proud; Long and lazy; little and loud. **Cf. Long and lazy.**

20. Fair exchange is no robbery. 1546: Heywood, *Proverbs*, Pt II ch iv, Chaunge be no robbry. 1628: J. Clavell, *Recantation*, 13, Then chop your horses most familiarly, Exchange you tell them is no roberie. 1771: Smollett, *Clinker*, in *Works*, vi 339 (1817), 'No mistake at all', cried the baronet; 'a fair exchange is no robbery'. 1852: Planché, *Extravag.*, iv 253 (1879), The proverb of 'Exchange no robbery!' 1922: Weyman, *Ovington's Bank*, ch xvii, Exchange is no robbery and I ain't afeard.

21. Fair feathers. *See* **Fine** (12).

22. Fair gainings make fair spendings. 1629: *Book of Meery Riddles*, Prov. 99.

23. Fair in the cradle and foul in the saddle. 1639: Clarke, 83. 1670: Ray, 87. 1709: R. Kingston, *Apoph. Curiosa*, 50, The proverb says, Fair, etc. 1732: Fuller, 6119. Cf. **Foul in the cradle.**

24. Faire is the weather where cup and cover doe hold together, i.e. where husband and wife agree. Glos. 1639: *Berkeley MSS.*, iii 32 (1885).

25. Fair pair of heels. *See* **Show.**

26. Fair play is a jewel. 1824: Scott, *Redgauntlet*, ch xxi, No, no, friend – fair play's a jewel – time about, if you please. 1832: Planché, *Extravag.*, i 104 (1879), Fair play's a jewel, then – let go my hair. 1865: in *N.&Q.*, 3rd ser, viii 317, This saying is or was to be found in Kent, as part of a longer formula – 'Fair play is a jewel! Lucy, let go my hair'. 1898: Weyman, *Shrewsbury*, ch xx, But fair-play is a jewel, my lord … If you would see my face, show me yours!

27. Fair play is good play. 1827: Hone, *Ev. Day Book*, ii 1008, A wooden ball … covered with a plate of silver, which … has commonly a motto – 'Fair play is good play'. 1864: 'Cornish Proverbs', in *N.&Q.*, 3rd ser, vi 495.

28. Fair water makes all clean. 1639: Clarke, 66.

29. Fair without but foul within. 1633: Draxe, 10. 1732: Fuller, 88, A fair face and a foul heart.

30. Fair words and foul deeds cheat wise men as well as fools. 1578: Florio, *First Fruites*, fo. 25, Fayre words and yl deedes deceive both wise and fooles. 1633: Draxe, 46, Faire words and foul deedes deceive many. 1710: S. Palmer, *Moral Essays on Proverbs*, 154.

31. Fair words and foul play cheat both young and old. 1855: Bohn, 353.

32. Fair words break no bones. *c.* 1460: *How the Goode Wyfe*, l. 43, Ne fayre wordis brake neuer bone. 1611: Davies (of Hereford), *Sc. of Folly*, 42, in *Works*, ii (Grosart), Faire wordes breake no bones. 1670: Ray, 158, Soft words break no bones. 1732: Fuller, 6183, Fair words never break a bone, Foul words have broke many a one.

33. Fair words (or **Fine words**) **butter no parsnips.** [ἀλλ᾽ οὐ λόγων λάρ, φασὶν. ἡ ἀγορὴ δεῖται. – Herodas, vii 49.] 1639: Clarke, 12. 1680: L'Estrange, *Select Coll. of Erasmus*, 131, *Co.* Your charity upon earth will be rewarded in heaven. *Pan.* Those words butter no parsnips. 1714: Ozell, *Molière*, iv 222, Meer praise butters no turnips. 1763: Murphy, *Citizen*, I ii, Fine words butter no parsnips. 1826: Scott, *Journal*,

15 April. 1843: Planché, *Extravag.*, ii 205 (1879), Fine words, I grant … But sure, the proverb says, 'No parsnips butter'.

34. Fair words cost nothing. 1712: Gay, *Mohocks*, sc ii, Mr Constable is … a great man, neighbour, and fair words cost nothing.

35. Fair words fill not the belly. 1580: Lyly, *Euphues*, 476 (Arber), Fayre words fatte few. 1732: Fuller, 1491.

36. Fair words foul deeds. 1581: T. Howell, *Devises*, 16 (1906).

37. Fair words hurt not the tongue. 1546: Heywood, *Proverbs*, Pt I ch ix, It hurteth not the tounge to geue fayre wurdis. 1605: Chapman, etc., *Eastw. Hoc*, IV i, O, madam, 'Faire words never hurt the tongue'. 1640: Herbert, *Jac. Prudentum*, Fair language grates not the tongue. 1670: Ray, 158, Soft words hurt not the mouth. 1732: Fuller, 4205 [as in 1670].

38. Fair words make fools fain. *c.*1480: *Early Miscell*, 25 (Warton Cl., 1855), Fayre promese ofte makyth foollis fayne. *c.*1530: *Everyman*, in Hazlitt, *Old Plays*, i 117, Lo, fair words maketh fools fain. *c.*1600: Deloney, *Thos. of Reading*, ch 14, Hold thy peace, faire words make fooles faine. 1732: Fuller, 1492, Fair words please fools. 1820: Scott, *Abbot*, ch xxx, I have on my side put him off with fair words, which make fools fain.

39. Fair words make me look to my purse. 1640: Herbert, *Jac. Prudentum*.

40. Fair words slake wrath. 1421: in *Twenty-six Poems*, 83 (E.E.T.S., No. 124), For fayre speche doth wraththe breke. *c.*1460: *How the Goode Wyfe*, l. 30, Fayre wordes wratthe slakithe. 1597: *North. Mothers Blessing*, in *Plasidas*, 164 (Roxb.Cl), Faire words slaken yre. 1630: Brathwait, *Eng. Gent.*, 236 (1641), As soft words pacifie wrath.

41. Fair words will not make the pot boil. 1736: Bailey, *Dict.*, s.v. 'Fair'.

42. He has a fair forehead to graft on. An allusion no doubt to cuckolding. 1678: Ray, 245. 1732: Fuller, No.1855.

43. He who gives fair words feeds you with an empty spoon. 1855: Bohn, 399.

44. In fair weather prepare for foul. 1732: Fuller, 2818.

45. It's a pity fair weather should do any harm. 1633: Draxe, 45. 1665: R. Howard, *Committee*, I, 'Tis a thousand pities that fair weather should do any hurt. 1738: Swift, *Polite Convers.*, Dial. II,

'Tis a pity that fair weather should ever do any harm. 1846: Denham, *Proverbs*, 6 (Percy S.). 1872: J. Glyde, jr., *Norfolk Garland*, 151 [with 'fine' for 'fair'].

46. Neay, faire words in flighting. 1683: meriton, *Yorkshire Ale*, 83–7 (1697).

47. Some to hide faire faults can make faire weather. 1611: Davies (of Hereford), *Sc. of Folly*, 44, in *Works*, ii (Grosart).

48. To a fair day open the window, but make you ready as to a foul. 1640: Herbert, *Jac. Prudentum*. 1669: *New Help to Discourse*, 310, To a fair day open your window.

49. There was never fair prison nor love with foul face. 1611: Davies (of Hereford), *Sc. of Folly*, 46, in *Works*, ii (Grosart). 1611: Cotgrave, s.v. 'Prison' [omitting 'love with'].

50. Who hath a fair wife needs more than two eyes. 1670: Ray, 9.

Fair, adv. 1. Fair and softly. See **Lawyer** (4); and **Soft and fair**.

2. Fair chieve all where love trucks. 1670: Ray, 47.

3. Fair chieve good ale, it makes many folks speak as they think. 1678: Ray, 93. 1886: Bickerdyke, *Curios. of Ale and Beer*, 404, The old proverb, 'Fair chieve good ale, it makes folk speak what they think'.

4. Fair fall nothing once a year. Glos. 1639: in *Berkeley MSS.*, iii 30 (1885). 1678: Ray, 182. Cf. **Well** (9).

Fair, subs. 1. Fair is fair, work or play. 1710: S. Palmer, *Moral Essays on Proverbs*, 31. 1926: *Humorist*, 20 Nov., p. 409, Fair is fair, when all is said.

2. Fair is not fair, but that which pleaseth. 1640: Herbert, *Jac. Prudentum*. 1670: Ray, 9.

3. Men speak of the fair as things went with them there. 1631: Mabbe, *Celestina*, 84 (T.T.), And as you find your penniworths, so you speake of the faire. 1640: Herbert, *Jac. Prudentum*. 1759: Sterne, *Trist. Shandy*, bk i ch v, For every man will speak of the fair as his own market has gone in it.

4. The fair is done. *c.*1380: *Gamelyn*, l. 270, in Skeat's *Chaucer*, iv 652, For sothe at this tyme this feire is y-doon.

5. The fair lasts all the year. 1541: *Sch. House of Women*, l. 348, in Hazlitt, *Early Pop. Poetry*, iv 118, He need go no farther, the fair is heer; Bye when ye list, it lasteth ouer yeer. 1546:

Heywood, *Proverbs*, Pt II ch ii 1618: Harington, *Epigrams*, bk i No. 72, Her fayre lasts all the yeare. 1633: Draxe, 120.

Fairer the hostess, the fouler the reckoning, The. Before 1635: Corbet, *Poems*, in Chalmers, v 579, A handsome hostesse makes the reckoning deare. 1696: D'Urfey, *Quixote*, Pt III Act IV sc i 1754: Berthelson, *Eng.-Danish Dict.*, s.v. 'Hostess'.

Fairer the paper the fouler the blot, The. 1732: Fuller, 4513.

Fairest looking shoe may pinch the foot, The. Ibid., No. 4514. Cf. **Finest shoe.**

Fairest rose at last is withered, The. 1591: Florio, *Second Frutes*, 105, The fairest and the sweetest rose In time must fade and beauty lose. 1605: Camden, *Remains*, 333 (1870) [with 'in the end' for 'at last']. *c.*1630: *Roxb. Ballads*, i 296 (B.S.), The fairest flower will wither. 1670: Ray, 138. 1732: Fuller, 4515. Cf. **Finest flower.**

Fairest silk is soonest stained, The. 1633: Draxe, 63, The fairest silke will soonest be soiled. 1670: Ray, 88. 1732: Fuller, 4516. Cf. **Finest lawn.**

Fairlight Down. *See* quot. 1884: 'Sussex Proverbs', in *N.&Q.*, 6th ser, ix 403, When Fairlie Down puts on his cap, Romney Marsh will have its sap.

Faith sees by the ears. 1732: Fuller, 1493.

Fall, *verb.* **1. Fall back fall edge** = Whatever may happen. In many English dialects 'back and edge' = thoroughly, entirely – *see* Wright, *Eng. Dial. Dict.*, s.v. 'Back'. 1553: *Respublica*, V v, Fall backe, fall edge, I am ons at a poincte … taduenture a joyncte. 1618: Minshull, *Essayes, etc.*, 68 (1821), Yet fall back, fall edge, thus trauerse wee our ground. *c.*1680: L'Estrange, *Seneca's Morals:* 'Benefits', ch xvii, And, fall back, fall edge, we must be grateful still. 1712: Motteux, *Quixote*, Pt II ch 29, But for all that, fall back fall edge, I must and will discharge my conscience. 1825: Scott, *Journal*, 18 Dec., I will yield to no delusive hopes, and fall back fall edge, my resolutions hold. 1828: Carr, *Craven Dialect*, i 140, 'Fall back', 'fall edge', at all adventures, let what will happen.

2. Fall not out with a friend for a trifle. 1639: Clarke, 25. 1670: Ray, 9.

3. Fall than rise. *See* **Easier.**

4. He falls low that cannot rise again. 1685: Meriton, *Yorkshire Ale*, 72.

5. He that falls into the dirt, the longer he lies the dirtier he is. 1640: Herbert, *Jac. Prudentum.* 1732: Fuller, 2096.

6. He that falls to-day may be up again to-morrow. 1620: Shelton, *Quixote*, Pt II ch lxv. 1732: Fuller, 2097.

7. He that is fallen cannot help him that is down. 1640: Herbert, *Jac. Prudentum.*

8. It falls not under one's cap. 1740: North, *Lives of Norths*, i 62 (Bohn), It fell not under every one's cap to give so good advice.

Falling out of friends is the renewal of love, The. [Amantium irae amoris integratio est. – Terence, *Andr.*, III iii 23.] 1576: *Parad. of Dainty Devices*, No. 42, The fallyng out of faithfull frends is the renuyng of loue. *c.*1610: in *Roxb. Ballads*, i 21 (B.S.), Though falling out of faithfull friends renewing be of loue. 1748: Richardson, *Clarissa*, iv 48 (1785), Old Terence has taken notice of that; and observes upon it, That lovers falling-out occasions lovers falling-in. 1847: Tennyson, *Princess*, i 251, Blessings on the falling out That all the more endears.

Falmouth. *See* quot. 1891: Q.-Couch, *Noughts and Crosses*, 185, The Mayor of Falmouth, who thanked God when the town gaol was enlarged.

False, *adj.* **1. A false abstract comes from a false concrete.** Before 1529: Skelton, *Bowge of Courte*, l. 439.

2. A false knave. *See* **Crafty.**

3. A false report rides post. 1659: Howell, *Proverbs: Brit.-Eng.*, 14.

4. A false tongue will hardly speak truth. 1633: Draxe, 11.

5. As false as a fox. 1886: R. Holland, *Cheshire Gloss.*, 445 (E.D.S.), As fause as a fox.

6. As false as a Scot. 1670: Ray, 204. 1825: Scott, *Talisman*, ch xv, It is enough of folly … to have intrusted your banner to a Scot – said I not they were ever fair and false?

7. As false as fair. 1546: Heywood, *Proverbs*, Pt II ch ix 1825: Scott [as under No. 6].

8. As false as God is true. 1546: Heywood, *Proverbs*, Pt II ch vii, She is, of trouth, as fals as God is trew. 1633: Draxe, 61.

9. As false as hell. 1680: D'Urfey, *Virtuous Wife*, IV iii, Ye are false as hell. 1720: Gay, *Poems*, ii 280 (Underhill), But false as hell, she, like the wind, Changed. 1872: Trollope *Golden Lion*, ch xi, His passion told him every hour … that she was as false as hell.

10. As false as the devil. 1546: Heywood, *Proverbs*, Pt II ch v, The deuill is no falser then is hee. 1639: Clarke, 139.

11. In a false quarrel there is no true valour. 1855: Bohn, 423.

Falsehood in fellowship, There is. *c.*1470: G. Ashby, *Poems*, 26 (E.E.T.S.), Be wele ware of falsehode in felawship. Before 1529: Skelton, *Magnyfycence*, l. 723, Falshode in felowshyp is my sworne brother. 1599: Porter, *Two Angry Women*, in Hazlitt, *Old Plays*, vii 356, I see all is not gold that glitters; there's falsehood in fellowship. 1653: Naunton, *Frag. Regalia*, 204 (1694), That there might be (as the adage hath it) falsity in friendship. 1732: Fuller, 4894.

Falsehood in packing, There is. 1574: R. Scot, *Hoppe Garden*, 49, There is, according to the prouerbe, much falshoode in packing.

Fame is a magnifying glass. 1732: Fuller: No. 1495.

Fame is but the breath of the people. 1611: in Coryat, *Crudities*, i 60 (1905), Fame is but winde. 1732: Fuller, 1497, Fame is but the breath of the people; and that often unwholesome.

Fame is dangerous, All: good, bringeth envy; bad, shame. 1732: Fuller, 513

Fame, like a river, is narrowed at its source and broadest afar off. 1855: Bohn, 353.

Fame to infamy is a beaten road, From. 1732: Fuller, 1628.

Fame (River). *See* **Yoke.**

Familiarity breeds contempt. [Assiduus in oculis hominum, quae res minus verendos magnos homines ipsa satietate facit. – Livy, xxxv 10. Parit enim conversatio contemptum, raritas conciliat ipsis rebus admirationem. – Apuleius, *De Deo Socratis.*] 12th cent.: Alanus de Insulis, in Wright, *Minor Anglo-Latin Satirists*, Record Ser., ii 454. *c.*1386: Chaucer, *Melibeus*, § 55, For right as men seyn, that 'over-greet homlinesse engendreth dispreysinge', so fareth it by to greet humylitee or mekenesse. 1593: G. Harvey, in *Works*, i 293 (Grosart), Truth begetteth hatred; Vertue Enuy, Familiaritie cötempt. 1600: Shakespeare, *Merry Wives*, I i, I hope upon familiarity will grow more contempt. 1689: Shadwell, *Bury Fair*, II i 1769: Smollett, *Adv. of Atom*, 148 (Cooke, 1795), Greater familiarity on his side might have bred contempt. 1852: M. A. Keltie, *Reminisc. of Thought, etc.*, 67, The familiarity which reigns there, and which, according to the old proverb, engenders contempt.

Family that prays together, stays together, The. A professional writer of advertising slogans, Al Scalpone, coined this phrase, and it became the slogan of the U.S. Roman Catholic Family Rosary Crusade, first used in a radio broadcast by Father Patrick Peyton in 1947. It has since been subjected to a number of variations, humorous and otherwise. 1948: *St Joseph Magazine* (Oregon), Apr. 3, 'More things are wrought by prayer than this world dreams of', and 'The family that prays together stays together'. Such religious themes are hardly what one would expect to hear propounded over the air waves of our modern radio. 1949: *Catholic Digest*, June 98, 'The family that prays together stays together'. That is what Father Peyton has made it his business to remind you of every week.

Famine in England. *See* **England** (1).

Famine in the stall [bad hay crop], **After a, comes a famine in the hall** [bad corn crop]. 1678: Ray, 353. 1825: Hone, *Ev. Day Book*, i 1669. 1893: Inwards, *Weather Lore*, 7.

Fan, *verb. He fans with a feather.* 1813: Ray, 75.

Fancy, A little of what you. *See* **Little.**

Fancy is a fool. 1633: Draxe, 6. 1639: Clarke, 28.

Fancy may bolt bran and think it flour. 1546: Heywood, *Proverbs*, Pt II ch iv, Fancy may boult bran and make ye take it floure. 1670: Ray, 88. 1732: Fuller, 1499.

Fancy may kill or cure. 1732: Fuller, 1500.

Fancy surpasses beauty. 1678: Ray, 136, Fancy passes beauty. 1732: Fuller, 1501.

Far-fetched and dear bought is good for ladies. Before 1500: in Hill, *Commonplace-Book*, 132 (E.E.T.S.), A thynge ferre fett is good for ladyes. 1546: Heywood, *Proverbs*, Pt I ch xi, Dere bought and far fet Are deinties for ladies. 1583: Stubbes, *Anat. of Abuses*, 33 (N.Sh.S.), But 'farre fetched and deare boughte' is good for ladyes, they say. 1608: Day, *Law Trickes*, IV i, Fare fech'd and deere bought, is good for you know who. 1696: Vanbrugh, *Relapse*, IV 1738: Swift, *Polite Convers.*, Dial. I. 1886: Elworthy, *West Som. Word-Book*, 799 (E.D.S.), The very common alliterative proverb – far-fetched, dearly bought. 1917: Bridge, *Cheshire Proverbs*, 56.

Far folks fare well. 1633: Draxe, 45, Farre folks fare best. 1678: Ray, 136, Far folks fare well, and fair children die.

Far from Court far from care. 1639: Clarke, 205. 1670: Ray, 73. 1732: Fuller, 1503.

Far from eye. *See* **Eye** (19); **Out of sight**; and **Seldom seen.**

Far from his good is nigh his harm, A man. 1546: Heywood, *Proverbs*, Pt II ch ix 1611: Cotgrave, s.v. 'Plat', We say (more generally) a man thats far from his good is neere his harme. 1670: Ray, 89.

Far from Jupiter, far from thunder. 1692: L'Estrange, *Aesop*, 11 (3rd ed.).

Far from thy kin. *See* quot. 1417: in *Reliq. Antiquae*, i 233 (1841), Far from thy kyn cast the, Wreth not thy neighber next the, In a good corne contrey rest the, And sit downe, Robyn, and rest the.

Far goeth the pilgrim as the post, As. *c.*1594: Bacon, *Promus*, No. 508.

Far shooting never killed bird. 1640: Herbert, *Jac. Prudentum.*

Fare, *verb.* **1. Better fare hard with good men, than feast it with bad.** 1732: Fuller, 893.

2. *See* quot. *c.*1645: MS. Proverbs, in *N.&Q.*, vol 154, p. 27, He feares [fares] like a commissioner for fish and flesh.

3. I never fared worse than when I wished for my supper. 1639: Clarke, 114. 1670: Ray, 157. 1732: Fuller, 2622.

Farewell and be hanged. 1575: G. Harvey, *Letter-Book*, 95 (Camden S.), Farewell and be hanged, goodman cowe. 1634: S. Rowley, *Noble Soldier*, IV ii, Fa? why, farewell and be hang'd. 1668: Davenant, *Rivals*, III. 1707: Dunton, *Athen. Sport*, 108, To say, Farewell, be hang'd, that's twice goodbwy. 1732: Fuller, 1504, Farewel and be hang'd; friends must part.

Farewell fieldfare! This and the three following sayings all seem to have much the same half-contemptuous import as 'Farewell and be hanged'. *c.*1374: Chaucer, *Troylus*, bk iii l. 861, The harm is doon, and fare-wel felde-fare! *c.*1400: *Rom. Rose*, l. 5510, Go, farewel feldefare! 1825: Jennings, *Somersetsh. Words*, 37 … This expression is occasionally heard. It means, I apprehend, that as fieldfares disappear at a particular season, *the season is over; the bird is flown.*

Farewell forty pence! 1583: Melbancke, *Philotinus*, sig. T4, Farewell fortie pence, too deare of [= by] three shillings. 1599: *Sir Clyomon, etc.*, sig. F2, Nay varewell vorty pence, ye are a knaue. 1600: Day, *Blind Beggar*, V, Why,

farewell forty pence! I ha fight fair and caught a frog. 1639: Clarke, 68, Farewell fortie pence, Jack Noble is dead.

Farewell frost! 1564: Bullein, *Dialogue*, 72 (E.E.T.S.), Farewell Frost! [said here sardonically]. 1592: Lyly, *Mother Bombie*, II iii, And so farewell frost, my fortune naught me cost. 1631: *Faire Em*, III. 1637: T. Heywood, *Royal King*, III. 1670: Ray, 174, Farewel frost, nothing got nor nothing lost. 1732: Fuller, 6156 [as in 1670].

Farewell, gentle Geoffrey! 1546: Heywood, *Proverbs*, Pt I ch xi.

Farewell my good days! they will be soon gone. Ibid., Pt II ch ii.

Farmer's care that makes the field bear, 'Tis the. 1732: Fuller, 6350.

Farther from stone. *See* quot. 1865: W. White, *Eastern England*, i 4, We … find the old proverb realised, 'The farther from stone, the better the church'.

Farther. *See also* **Further.**

Farthest way. *See* **Longest way.**

Farthing good silver, To think one's. 1546: Heywood, *Proverbs*, Pt I ch x, She thinkth her farthyng good syluer. *c.*1594: Bacon, *Promus*, No. 636. 1659: Howell, 4, She thinks her farthing as good silver as anothers. Cf. **Halfpenny;** and **Penny** (26).

Farthing is good that makes the penny bud, The. 1623: Wodroephe, *Spared Houres*, 477.

Fashion's sake. *See* **Dog** (42).

Fast and loose is no possession. 1639: Clarke, 159.

Fast and loose. *See also* **Play.**

Fast [asleep] **as a church.** 1708: tr. Aleman's *Guzman*, i 284, I went … to see if he slept still, and found both him and my mistress as fast as a church. 1788: Colman, jr., *Ways and Means*, III iii, All's snug. The baronet's as fast as a church. 1845: Jerrold, *Mrs Caudle*, xxvii, No sooner in bed than you're fast as a church. 1883: Burne, *Shropsh. Folk-Lore*, 594. Cf. **Sleep**, *verb* (6).

Fast as a thief. *See* **Safe as a thief.**

Fast as hops. *See* **Thick as hops.**

Fast bind fast find. 1484: Caxton, Ae*sope*, V iv (Jacobs), For who that wel byndeth well can he vnbynd. *c.*1540: Bale, *Kynge Johan*, in Manly, *Spec. of Pre-Shakesp. Drama*, i 592, As the saynge is, he fyndeth that surely bynde. 1622: B.&F., *Span. Curate*, II ii 1768: Bickerstaffe,

Padlock, I iii, 'Fast bind, safe find', is an excellent proverb. I'll e'en lock her up with the rest. 1824: Scott, *Redgauntlet*, ch xiii.

Fast, *verb*. **1. He fasts enough that has a bad meal.** 1611: Cotgrave, s.v. 'Assez', He that feeds barely fasts sufficiently. 1732: Fuller, 1844.

2. He fasts enough whose wife scolds all dinner-time. Ibid., No. 1845.

3. If I were to fast for my life, I would eat a good breakfast in the morning. 1678: Ray, 67.

4. Is there no mean but fast or feast? 1732: Fuller, 3113.

Fasting belly may never be merry, A. Before 1500: in Hill, *Commonplace-Book*, 131 (E.E.T.S.).

Fat as a fool. 1579: Lyly, *Euphues*, 118 (Arber), That feedeth a louer as fat as a foole. 1630: *Tinker of Turvey*, 59 (Halliwell), To feed him with her faire speeches, till she made him as fat as a foole. 1678: Ray, 283.

Fat as a hen in the forehead. 1611: Cotgrave, s.v. 'Pie', *Maigre comme vne pie*, We say (to the same purpose) as fat as a henne's on the forehead. *c.*1618: B.&F., *Bonduca*, I ii, As fat as hens i' th' foreheads. 1670: Ray, 204. 1738: Swift, *Polite Convers.*, Dial. III, Fat! ay, fat as a hen in the forehead.

Fat as a hog (or **pig**, or **bacon-pig**). 1485: Malory, *Morte d'Arthur*, bk vii ch i, He shall be as fatte ... as a porke hog. 1611: Cotgrave, s.v. 'Cochon', *Gras comme vn cochon*, (Wee say the same) as fat as a pigge. 1653: Walton, *Angler*, Pt I ch x, He will grow not only to be very large, bat as fat as a hog. 1767: Garrick, in *Garrick Corresp.*, i 252 (1831), I am grown as fat as a hog. 1846: Denham, *Proverbs*, 60 (Percy S.), Fat as a bacon-pig at Martlemas.

Fat as a porpoise. 1738: Swift, *Polite Convers.*, Dial. II, I shall grow as fat as a porpoise. 1872: Hardy, *Greenwood Tree*, Pt I ch vii, There's your brother Bob – as fat as a porpoise.

Fat as Big Ben. 1862: *Dialect of Leeds*, 247, 'As fat as Big Ben', is yet a household phrase. A former bellman in great repute upon account of his huge proportions.

Fat as butter. 1678: Ray, 283. 1720: Gay, *Poems*, ii 278 (Underhill), My cheeks as fat as butter grown.

Fat commodity hath no fellow, A. 1659: Howell, 3.

Fat drops fall from fat flesh. 1678: Ray, 137.

Fat, fair, and forty. 1795: O'Keeffe, *Irish Minnie*, II iii, Fat, fair, and forty were all the toast of the young men.

Fat housekeeper (or **kitchen**) **makes lean executors** (or **will**), **A.** 1611: Cotgrave, s.v. 'Testament', A fat kitchin a leane will. Ibid., s.v. 'Cuisine', Great house-keepers leave poor executors. 1670: Ray, 9, A fat housekeeper makes lean executors. 1732: Fuller, 1505 [as in 1670]. 1736: Franklin, *Way to Wealth*, in *Works*, i 446 (Bigelow), A fat kitchin makes a lean will. 1880: Spurgeon, *Ploughman's Pictures*, 11 [as in 1736].

Fat is in the fire, The. *c.*1374: Chaucer, *Troylus*, bk iii st. 95, Or caste al the grewel in the fire. 1559: Becon, in *Prayers, etc.*, 277 (P.S.), Or else your cake is dough, and all your fat lie in the fire. 1603: Dekker, in *Works*, i 174 (Grosart), Then must he trudge to get gossips, such as shee will appoint, or else all the fatte is in the fire. 1633: Jonson, *Love's Welcome*. 1740: North, *Examen*, 506, They might fall in with the King ... and then all the fat was in the fire. 1898: H. James, in *Letters*, i 287 (1920), It is this morning precisely that one feels the fat at last fairly in the fire. 1910: Shaw, *Misalliance*, 15 (1914), I said I was sure I knew nothing about such things, and hadn't we better change the subject. Then the fat was in the fire, I can tell you.

Fat lady. *See* **Opera**.

Fat man knoweth not what the lean thinketh, The. 1640: Herbert, *Jac. Prudentum*.

Fat (or **Fattest**) **land** (or **soil**). *See* **Best** (16).

Fat paunches make lean pates. 1586: B. Young, tr. Guazzo's *Civil Convers.*, fo. 190, The prouerbe is as true as common. That a fat bellie doth not engender a subtill witte. 1592: Shakespeare, *L. L. L.*, I i, Fat paunches have lean pates. 1681: W. Robertson, *Phraseol. Generalis*, 587. 1732: Fuller, 1506.

Fat soil. *See* **Worse for the rider**.

Fat sorrow is better than lean sorrow. 1678: Ray, 137. 1732: Fuller, 1507.

Fat sow. *See* **Sow** (2), (10), and (14).

Fat with the lean, To take the. 1850: Dickens, *Copperfield*, ch li, A man must take the fat with the lean; that's what he must make up his mind to, in this life.

Fate leads the willing but drives the stubborn. 1732: Fuller, 1508.

Father and **Fathers**. **1. Father Derby.** *See* **Derby's bands**.

2. He whose father is judge goes safe to his trial. 1620: Shelton, *Quixote*, Pt II ch xliii, For according to the proverb, 'He that hath the judge to his father, etc.', and I am governor, which is more than judge. 1712: Motteux, *Quixote*, Pt II ch xliii. 1732: Fuller, 2400.

3. His father will never be dead while he is alive. 1672: Walker, *Paroem.*, 50.

4. Like father like son. *See* **Like.**

5. Our fathers who were wondrous wise, Did wash their throats before their eyes. 1613: Wither, *Abuses Stript, etc.*, bk ii Sat. 1, Prethee let me intreat thee now to drinke Before thou wash; Our fathers that were wise, Were wont to say 'twas wholesome for the eyes. 1670: Ray, 212. 1732: Fuller, 6423.

6. The father to the bough, the son to the plough. *See* 1730 quot. 1576: Lambarde, *Peramb. of Kent*, 497 (1826). 1659: W. Cole, in *Harl. Miscell.*, iv 306 (1745), And therefore it is the saying in Kent, The father, etc. 1730: Bailey, *Eng. Dict.*, s.v. 'Gavel-kind', In Gavel-kind, tho' the father be hang'd, the son shall inherit; for their custom is, *the Father to the bough, the son to the plough.* 1790: Grose, *Prov. Gloss.*, s.v. 'Kent'.

7. Thou art thy father's own son. 1672: Walker, *Paroem.*, 30. 1681: W. Robertson, *Phraseol. Generalis*, 587.

Fault and **Faults. 1. A fault is sooner found than mended.** *c.*1580: Fulwell, *Ars Adulandi*, sig. H4.

2. A fault once denied (or **excused**) **is twice committed.** *c.*1590: G. Harvey, *Marginalia*, 100 (1913) [with 'excused']. 1669: *Politeuphuia*, 166 ['excused']. 1732: Fuller, 93 ['denied']. 1875: A. B. Cheales, *Proverb. Folk-Lore*, 165 [as in 1732].

3. Fault confessed. *See* **Confessing.**

4. Faults are thick where love is thin. 1659: Howell, *Proverbs: Brit.-Eng.*, 2. 1670: Ray, 16, Where love fails, we espy all faults. 1732: Fuller, 5676, Where there is no love, all are faults. 1869: Spurgeon, *John Ploughman*, ch x.

5. Faults that are rich are fair. 1855: Bonn, 354.

6. He hath but one fault – he is naught. 1546: Heywood, *Proverbs*, Pt I ch xi 1560: T. Wilson, *Rhetorique*, 153 (1909), Such a man hath no fault but one, and if that were amended, all were well: what is that? (quoth an other). In good faith he is naught. 1633: Draxe, 43 [with 'starke' before 'naught']. 1732: Fuller, 6054, Your main fault is, you are good for nothing.

7. The first faults are theirs that commit them, the second theirs that permit them. 1732: Fuller, 4528.

Faulty stands on his guard, The. 1578: Florio, *First Fruites*, fo. 28, Who is faultie is suspected. 1640: Herbert, *Jac. Prudentum.* 1670: Ray, 9.

Faustus, Dr *See* **Devil** (40).

Favour will as surely perish as life. 1651: Herbert, *Jac. Prudentum*, 2nd ed.

Favour, Without, none will know you, and with it you will not know yourself. 1640: Herbert, *Jac. Prudentum.*

Fawn peckles [Brown freckles] **once made a vow, They never would come on a face that was fou** [foul or ugly]. 1877: E. Leigh, *Cheshire Gloss.*, 152. 1917: Bridge, *Cheshire Proverbs*, 56.

Fear and **Fears,** *subs.* **1. Fear and shame much sin doth tame.** *c.*1550: in Hazlitt, *Early Pop. Poetry*, iii 246.

2. Fear causeth a man to cast beyond the moon. 1546: Heywood, *Proverbs*, Pt I ch iv, Feare may force a man to cast beyonde the moone. 1633: Draxe, 63.

3. Fear gives (or **lends**) **wings.** 1580: Sidney, *Arcadia*, bk ii p. 195 (1893), They all cried, 'O! see how fear gives him wings'. 1590: Spenser, *F. Q.*, III vii 26, Therto fear gave her wings. 1666: Torriano, *Piazza Univ.*, 60, Fear hath wings.

4. Fear hath a quick ear. 1654: Gayton, *Pleasant Notes Don Q.*, 65.

5. Fear is one part of prudence. 1732: Fuller, 1512.

6. Fear is stronger than love. Ibid., No. 1513.

7. Fear keeps the garden better than the gardener. 1640: Herbert, *Jac. Prudentum.*

8. Fear, the beadle of the law. 1651: Ibid., 2nd ed.

9. Fears are divided in the midst. 1640: Ibid.

10. 'Twas fear that first put on arms. 1732: Fuller, 5317.

Fear. *verb.* **1. He that feareth every bush must never go a-birding.** 1580: Lyly, *Euphues*, 354 (Arber). 1732: Fuller, 2098.

2. He that fears death lives not. 1640: Herbert, *Jac. Prudentum.* 1708: tr. Aleman's *Guzman*, i 432, I comforted myself with this saying, *That he that fears death, does not deserve to live.*

3. It is good to fear the worst; the best will save itself. 1633: Draxe, 65. 1639: Clarke, 66, Tis good to fear the worst. 1670: Ray, 89.

4. To fear no colours = To fear no enemy. 1594: *True Trag. Rich. Third*, 15 (SH.S.), I will neuer feare colours. 1601: Yarington, *Two Trag. in One*, I iv, I'le fear no coulours. 1679: Dryden, *Troilus*, II ii, Take a good heart, man ... and fear no colours, and speak your mind. 1704: Swift, *Tale of a Tub*, § xi, He was a person that feared no colours.

Feared men be fearful. 1639: Clarke, 208.

Feast and a bellyful, Little difference between, a. 1659: Howell, 13. 1670: Ray, 215. 1732: Fuller, 3253.

Feast is not made of mushrooms only, A. 1732: Fuller, 96.

Feasting makes no friendship. Ibid., No. 1515.

Feastings are the physicians' harvest, Christmas. 1639: Clarke, 174.

Feather, *subs.* **1. A feather in one's cap.** 1714: Mandeville, *Fable of Bees*, 197, Men ... then put feathers in their caps ... talk of publick-spiritedness. 1754: Berthelson, *Eng.-Danish Dict.*, s.v. 'Feather', That is but feather in his cap. 1803: Colman, jr., *John Bull*, I i, Who ... fancy female ruin a feather in your caps of vanity. 1821: Byron, *Letters and Journals*, v 472 (Prothero). 1922: Weyman, *Ovington's Bank*, ch xvi, It would be a feather in the bank's cap if the money ... were recovered through the bank's exertions.

2. A feather of the same wing. 1639: Clarke, 14.

3. Birds of a feathes. *See* Bird (7)

4. Feather by feather. 1653: Middleton and Rowley, *Span. Gipsy*, II i, Feather by feather birds build nests. 1666: Torriano, *Piazza Univ.*, 174, Quill by quill is a goose pluck'd. 1732: Fuller, 1514, Feather by feather the goose is pluck'd.

5. Let not him that fears feathers come among wild fowl. 1640: Herbert, *Jac. Prudentum*.

6. The feather makes not the bird. 1572: G. Fenton, *Monophylo*, sig. T4, Seing (with the olde prouerbe) as the feather makes not the byrde.

Feather one's nest, To. 1553: *Respublica*, I i, And nowe ys the tyme come ... to make vp my mouth, and to feather my neste. 1590: Greene, in *Works*, viii 138 (Grosart), She sees thou hast fethred thy nest, and hast crowns in thy purse. 1653: Urquhart, *Rabelais*, bk ii ch xvii, If thou didst know what advantage I made, and how well I feathered my nest ... 1709: Ward, *Acc. of Clubs*, 77 (1756), Who, as yet, have not had the lucky opportunity of feathering their nests.

1834–7: Southey, *Doctor*, ch lxiv, He feathered his nest with the spoils of the Loyalists. 1915: Pinero, *Big Drum*, II p. 98.

February. 1. A February spring is not worth a pin. Corn. 1893: Inwards, *Weather Lore*, 13.

2. A Welshman had rather see his dam on her bier than see a fair Februeer. 1678: Ray, 44. 1744: Claridge, in Mills, *Essay on Weather*, 100 (1773). 1846: Denham, *Proverbs*, 31 (Percy S.). 1917: Bridge, *Cheshire Proverbs*, 164.

3. All the months in the year curse a fair Februeer. 1670: Ray, 40. 1732: Fuller, 6151. 1893: Inwards, *Weather Lore*, 13.

4. Double-faced February. Ibid., 13.

5. February fill-dyke. 1557: Tusser, *Hund. Points*, in *British Bibliog.*, iii 20 (1812), And feuerell fill dyke, doth good with his snowe. 1577: Tusser, *Husb.*, ch 34, Feb, fill the dike with what ye like. 1630: Taylor (Water-Poet), *Workes*, 2nd pagin., 257, If foulefac'd February keepe true touch ... By night, by day, by little and by much, It fills the ditch, with either blacke or white. 1799: *Gent. Mag.*, Pt I p. 203, February fill dike Either black or white. 1893: Inwards, *Weather Lore*, 13, February fill the dyke Weather either black or white. Ibid., 14, February fill dyke; March lick it out. February fill dyke, be it black or be it white; But if it be white, it's better to like. 1900: *N. & Q.*, 9th ser, v 384, [Northants] February fills the dykes; March winds blow the organ pipes. 1922: Lucas, *Genevra's Money*, 4, February was filling the dykes to the very margin.

6. February fire lang, March tide to bed gang – a Craven proverb. 1828: Carr, *Craven Dialect*, i 144.

7. February, if ye be fair, The sheep will mend, and nothing mair; *February, if ye be foul* [rainy], *The sheep will die in every pool.* 1846: Denham, *Proverbs*, 29 (Percy S.).

8. February makes a bridge, and March breaks it. 1640: Herbert, *Jac. Prudentum*. 1732: Fuller, 1516. 1846: Denham, *Proverbs*, 27 (Percy S.), February builds a bridge, and March breaks it down.

9. February singing, Never stints stinging. 'If bees get out in February, the next day will be windy and rainy. Surrey'. 1893: Inwards, *Weather Lore*, 13.

10. February's rain, fills the barn. 1611: Cotgrave, s.v. 'Pluye', February rain is the husbandmans gaine. 1666: Torriano, *Piazza Univ.*, 80.

11. Februeer doth cut and shear. 1633: Jonson, *Tale of a Tub*, I i, Old bishop Valentine, You have brought us nipping weather – *Februere doth cut and shear.* Ray, 44. 1893: Inwards, *Weather Lore*, 13 [with 'both' for 'doth'].

12. If February calends be summerly gay, 'Twill be winterly weather in the calends of May. 1882: Mrs Chamberlain, *W. Warcs. Words*, 37 (E.D.S.).

13. If February give much snow, A fine summer it doth foreshow. 1878: Dyer, *Eng. Folk-Lore*, 251.

14. If in February there be no rain, The hay won't goody, nor the grain. 1913: E. M. Wright, *Rustic Speech, etc.*, 317.

15. In February if thou hearest thunder, Thou wilt see a summer's wonder. 1893: Inwards, *Weather Lore*, 14.

16. Reckon right, and February hath one and thirty days. 1640: Herbert, *Jac. Prudentum.* 1670: Ray, 9.

17. When gnats dance in February the husbandman becomes a beggar. 1878: Dyer, *Eng. Folk-Lore*, 251.

18. When the cat lies in the sun in February, she will creep behind the stove in March. 1905: *N. & Q.*, 10th ser, iii 314.

See also **August** (1); **Candlemas**, H (4); **January** (1); **October** (7); **St Matthias**; **St Valentine**; and **Snow** (4).

Feed, *verb*. **1. Feed a cold and starve a fever.** Taken as two separate injunctions combined in one proverb, this saying offers fairly sound medical advice insofar as a healthy diet is helpful for a cold, and fever sufferers are best fed on liquids only. Some writers, however, seem to relate the two parts as cause and effect: by following the first injunction too enthusiastically, one may develop fever. 1852: E. Fitzgerald, *Polonius*, p. ix 'Stuff a cold and starve a fever', has been grievously misconstrued so as to bring on the fever it was meant to prevent. 1867: 'M. Twain', *Celebrated Jumping Frog of Calaveras County*, 69, It was policy 'to feed a cold and starve a fever'. 1939: C. Morley, *Kitty Foyle*, xxxi, I said I better go downstairs and eat a square meal, 'feed a cold and starve a fever' ... 'You misunderstand that,' he says, 'It means if you feed a cold you'll have to starve a fever later.'

2. Feed by measure and defy the physician. 1546: Heywood, *Proverbs*, Pt II ch vii 1670: Ray, 39 [with 'sparingly' for 'by measure'].

3. He that feeds the poor hath treasure. *c.*1460: *How the Good Wife*, l. 15, Tresour he hathe that pouere fedithe.

4. To feed like a boar in a frank. 1598: Shakespeare, *2 Henry IV*, II ii, Where sups he? doth the old boar feed in the old frank? 1631: F. Lenton, *Characters*, sig. C12 (1663), And then feed at ease like a boar in a frank. 1825: Scott, in Lockhart's *Life*, vi 81, From Lowther we reached Abbotsford in one day, and now doth the old *bore* feed in the old frank.

5. To feed like a farmer. 1655: Fuller, *Church Hist.*, bk vi § ii (v. 13), On which the abbot fed as the farmer of his grange. *c.*1680: in *Roxb. Ballads*, vii 278 (B.S.), And if he to a pudding gets, he farmer-like doth feed. 1754: Berthelson, *Eng.-Danish Dict.*, s.v. 'Feed', He feeds like a farmer.

Feeling hath no fellow. 1678: Ray, 138. 1725: *Matchless Rogue*, 56, Tho' seeing is believing, and feeling has no fellow. 1732: Fuller, 1518.

Feet. *See* **Foot**.

Fellow-ruler. *He that hath a fellow-ruler, hath an over-ruler.* 1611: Cotgrave, s.v. 'Avoir'. 1670: Ray, 9.

Female of the species is more deadly than the male, The. 1911: R. Kipling, *Morning Post*, 20 Oct., 7, The she-bear thus accosted rends the peasant tooth and nail, For the female of the species is more deadly than the male.

Fencer hath one trick in his budget more than ever he taught his scholar, A. 1639: Clarke, 127.

Fences. *See* **Good fences**.

Fennel. *See* quot. 1884: Friend, *Flowers and Fl. Lore*, 208, An old proverb says: 'Sowing fennel is sowing sorrow'.

Fern begins to look red, When, then milk is good with brown bread. 1588: Cogan, *Haven of Health*, 152–3 (1612), According to that old saying; when fearne waxeth red, then is milke good with bread. 1659: Howell, 11. 1670: Ray. 35.

Fern is as high as a ladle, When the, You may sleep as long as you are able. 1670: Ray, 35.

Fern is as high as a spoon, When the, You may sleep an hour at noon. Ibid., 34 1732: Fuller, 6186. 1846: Denham, *Proverbs*, 50 (Percy S.). 1904: *Co. Folk-Lore: Northumb.*, 178 (F.L.S.).

Festival. *See* quot. 1660: T. Hall, *Funebria*

Florae, 10, Insomuch that 'tis a common saying, That 'tis *no festival unless there bee some fightings*.

Fetters. *See* **Love**, *verb* (13).

Fever lurden = Laziness. *See* quots. *c.*1500: in Hazlitt, *Early Pop. Poetry*, i 93 (OED), I trow he was infecte certeyn With the faitour, or the fever lordeyn. 1568: W. Fulwood, *Enem. of Idlenesse*, 132 (1593), You have the palsey or eke the feuer lurden. 1606: B. Rich, *Faultes Faults*, sig. F2, One of them growing a little sicke of a feuer lordan. 1678: Ray, 172, He that's sick of a feaver lurden must be cured by the hasel gelding.

Fever of lurk. *See* **Two stomachs.**

Few are fit to be entrusted with themselves. 1732: Fuller, 1523.

Few days pass without some clouds. 1846: Denham, *Proverbs*, 4 (Percy S.).

Few friends. *See* **Friend** (13) and (19).

Few lawyers. *See* **Lawyer** (5).

Few leaves and bad fruit. 1732: Fuller, 1526.

Few men and much meat make a feast. 1639: Clarke, 74.

Few physicians live well. 1605: Camden, *Remains*, 322 (1870).

Few words and many deeds. 1633: Draxe, 40.

Few words are best. *c.*1600: in *Roxb. Ballads*, i 157 (Hindley), It is an old saying, that few words are best. 1660: Tatham, *The Rump*, II, Well, I know what I know; few words are best. 1771: Smollett *Clinker*, in *Works*, vi 70 (1817), I wonder what the devil possessed me – but few words are best. 1828: Scott, *Fair Maid*, ch xxv, Wherefore, few words are best, wench.

Few words the wise suffice. 1546: Heywood, *Proverbs*, Pt II ch vii, Fewe woordis to the wise suffice to be spoken. 1605: Camden, *Remains*, 322 (1870). Before 1680: Butler, *Remains*, i 379 (1759), Few words do best with the wise. 1730: T. Saldkeld, tr. Gracian's *Compl. Gent.*, 60, 'Tis a common saying that few words are sufficient to make a thing intelligible to a man of sense.

Fewer his years, the fewer his tears, The. 1732: Fuller, 6233.

Fewer the better cheer. *See* **More the merrier.**

Fiddle, *subs*. **1. As well try to borrow a fiddle at a wakes.** 1917: Bridge, *Cheshire Proverbs*, 26.

2. He has got the fiddle but not the stick. 1678: Ray, 86. 1732: Fuller, 1871. 1820: Colton, *Lacon*, Pt II No. 231, Those who attempted to imitate them, would find that they had got the fiddle, but not the fiddle-stick.

3. To hang the fiddle at the door. *c.*1791: Pegge, *Derbicisms*, 100 (E.D.S.), 'To hang the fiddle at the door' [said] of a person who is merry and cheerful abroad, but surly and ill-tempered in his family. 1883: Burne, *Shropsh. Folk-Lore*, 597, To hang up the fiddle at the house-door = to be merry abroad and morose at home.

See also **Face** (3); **Fine**; and **Good tune** (3).

Fiddle for shives [slices of bread] **among old wives, Go.** 1639: Clarke, 68 [with 'good' for 'old']. 1670: Ray, 175. 1877: E. Leigh, *Cheshire Gloss.*, 184. 1917: Bridge, *Cheshire Proverbs*, 61.

Fiddler and **Fiddlers. 1. Fiddler's fare.** 1608: *Dumb Knight*, III, in Hazlitt, *Old Plays*, x 169, You have had more than fidler's fare, for you have meat, money, and cloth. 1660: Howell, *Parly of Beasts*, 128, He was dismissed fiddler-like, with meat, drink, and money. 1738: Swift, *Polite Convers.*, Dial. III, Fiddler's fare, meat, drink, and money. 1828: Carr, *Craven Dialect*, i 149 [as in 1738].

2. Fiddlers' dogs and flies come to feasts uncalled. 1683: Meriton, *Yorkshire Ale*, 83–7 (1697).

3. Fiddlers' money = Small change. 1785: Grose, *Class. Dict. Vulgar Tongue*, s.v., Fiddlers' money: all six pences. 1877: *N. &Q.*, 5th ser, vii 138, In Oxfordshire threepenny and fourpenny pieces are called 'fiddler's money'. 1889: Peacock, *Manley*, *etc.*, *Gloss.*, 203 (E.D.S.), Fiddlers' money. Groats, threepenny pieces, pennies. [The expression is common in many parts of the country.]

4. Fiddlers' pay. *See* quots. 1597: 1st part *Return from Parnassus*, I i (OED), He … gave me fidler's wages, and dismiste me. 1690: *New Dict. Canting Crew*, sig. E4, Fiddlers-pay, Thanks and wine.

5. In a fiddler's house. *See* quots. 1640: Herbert, *Jac. Prudentum*, In the house of a fiddler, all fiddle. 1732: Fuller, 2809, In a fidler's house, all are dancers.

6. Like a fiddler's elbow. 1887: T. Darlington, *S. Cheshire Folk Speech*, 187 (E.D.S.). 1917: Bridge, *Cheshire Proverbs*, 79, In and out like a fiddler's elbow. 1926: *Devonsh. Assoc. Trans.*, lvii. 152, 'Too much play, like a fiddler's elbow'. Said of something which had worked loose.

Field, Always in the. *See* **Always in the lane.**

Field requires three things; fair weather, sound seed, and a good husbandman, A. 1846: Denham, *Proverbs*, 3 (Percy S.).

Fields have eyes and woods have ears. 13th cent.: quoted in Wright, *Essays on Middle Ages*, i 168, Wode has erys, felde has sight. *c.*1386: Chaucer, *Knight's Tale*, l. 664, Feeld hath eyen, and the wode hath eres. 1564: Bullein, *Dialogue*, 13 (E.E.T.S.), The fielde haue eyes and the wood haue eares. Therefore we must comen closelie, and beware of blabbes. 1611: Cotgrave, s.v. 'Bois'. 1670: Ray, 95. 1732: Fuller, 1532, Fields have eyes, and hedges ears. 1924: I was told by a Wiltshire woman that a very common saying in that county is, 'Hedges have eyes and walls have ears'.

Fierce as a dig [duck] – a Lancashire and probably a Cheshire proverb. 1877: E. Leigh, *Cheshire Gloss.*, 61.

Fierce as a goose. 1670: Ray, 204.

Fierce as a ratten [rat]. 1862: *Dialect of Leeds*, 406.

Fifth wheel to a coach, A = A hindering superfluity. [1531: C. B. Bouelles, *Proverb. Vulg.*, fo. 36, La cinquiesme roue au chariot, ne faict qu'empescher.] 1631: Dekker, *Match me in London*, I *ad fin.*, Thou tyest but wings to a swift gray hounds heele, And add'st to a running charriot a fift wheele. 1644: Taylor (Water-Poet), *Crop-eare Curried*, 32, in *Works*, 2nd coll. (Spens.S.), As much pertinent as the fift wheele in a coach. 1921: *Observer*, 11 Dec., p. 13, col. 2, Asquithian Liberalism by itself is the fifth wheel to the coach.

Fig for thy friend, and a peach for thine enemy, Provide a. 1629: *Book of Meery Riddles*, Prov. 53. 1678: Ray, 53.

Fight, verb. 1. A man that will fight may find a cudgel in every hedge. 1639: Clarke, 324.

2. Fight dog fight bear. 1583: Stubbes, *Anat. of Abuses*, 178 (N.Sh.S.), Some … will not make anie bones of xx xl *c* pound at once to hazard at a bait [bear-baiting], with 'fight dog, feight beare (say they), the deuill part all!' 1632: R. Brome, *Northern Lasse*, II v, We shall have a foul house on't I fear. But since it is too late, fight dog, fight bear, I'le turn my master loose to her. 1687: A. Behn, *Lucky Chance*, III ii, Why, let 'em fight dog, fight bear; mun, I'll to bed. 1716: E. Ward, *St Paul's Church*, 21, But cry halloo, fight dog, fight bear. 1821: Scott, *Kenilworth*, ch xvii 1831: Scott, *Journal*, 5 March.

3. Fight dog, fight devil. 1656: T. Ady, *Candle in the Dark*, 62. 1873: Spilling, *Molly Miggs*, 5 (W.),

I had had a pratty gude spell o' work morning and night, pull dawg pull devil, as the saying is.

4. He that fights and runs away may live to fight another day. [Post inde aliquanto tempore Philippus apud Chaeroneam proelio magno Athenienses vicit. Tum Demosthenes orator ex eo proelio salutem fuga quaesivit: quumque id ei, quod fugerat, probrose objiceretur; versu illo notissimo elusit, [ἀνὴρ ὁ φεύγων, inquit, καὶ πάλιν μαχήσεται. – Aulus Gellius, *Noct. Att.*, xvii 21.] *c.*1320: in *Reliq. Antiquae*, i. 111. (1841), 'Wel fytht, that wel flyth'; Quoth Hendyng. *c.*1350: *Owl and Nightingale*, l. 174, 'Wel fizt that wel flizt', seith the wise. *c.*1440: *Gesta Rom.*, 374 (E.E.T.S.), It is an olde sawe, he feghtith wele that fleith faste. 1542: Udall, tr. Erasmus' *Apoph.*, 372 (1877), That same man, that renneth awaie, Maie again fight, an other daie. 1663: Butler, *Hudibras*, Pt III can iii, For those that fly may fight again, Which he can never do that's slain. 1761: *Art of Poetry on a New Plan*, ii 147, For he who fights and runs away May live to fight another day. 1849: Planché, *Extravag.*, iii 334 (1879).

5. To fight fire with fire. For the earlier development of this idea, *see* **Fire** (6). 1846: J. F. Cooper, *Redskins*, III, i, If 'Fire will fight fire', 'Indian' ought to be a match for 'Injin' any day. 1869: T. P. Barnum, *Struggles and Triumphs*, xl, I write to ask you what you're intentions are … Do you intend to fight fire with fire?

6. To fight with one's own shadow. 1595: Shakespeare, *M. of Venice*, I ii, He will fence with his own shadow. 1670: Ray, 175. 1736: Bailey, *Dict.*, s.v. 'Shadow'.

Fill the mouth with empty spoons, To. 1639: Clarke, 314. 1670: Ray, 175.

Fill what you will and drink what you fill. 1678: Ray, 88. 1732: Fuller, 6180.

Find, verb. 1. Take heed you find not what you do not seek. 1596: Harington, *Metam. of Ajax*, 122 (1814), Yet he would feel, to seek that he would not find, for fear lest they should find that they did not seek. 1670: Ray, 9. 1732: Fuller, 4309.

2. To find fault. *See* **Blames**.

3. To find things before they are lost. 1546: Heywood, *Proverbs*, Pt I ch xi, If ye seeke to fynde thynges er they be lost. Ye shall fynde one daie you come to your cost. 1633: Draxe, 203, He findeth things before they are lost.

1732: Fuller, 5918, You have found what was never lost

Finders keepers, losers weepers. Meaning that people who find things are entitled to keep them and the original owners must bear the loss – a principle not supported by law! 1825: J.T. Brockett, *Glossary of North Country Words*, 89, No halfers – findee keepee, lossee seekee. 1874: E. Eggleston, *Circuit Rider*, xv, If I could find the right owner of this money, I'd give it to him, but I take it he's buried … 'Finders, keepers', you know.

Findings keepings. 1595: A. Cooke, *Country Errors*, in Harley MS 5247, 108v, That a man finds is his own, and he may keep it. 1863: J. H. Speke, *Discovery of the Source of the Nile*, v, The scoundrels said, 'Findings are keepings by the law of our country; and as we found your cows, so we will keep them'.

Fine, *adj*. **1. A fine new nothing.** 1678: Ray, 342.
2. All is fine that is fit. 1732: Fuller, 523.
3. As fine as a fiddle. 1862: *Dialect of Leeds*, 407.
4. As fine as a horse. 1838: Mrs Bray, *Trad. of Devon*, i 328, This Hobby was very gay and gorgeous, and hence have we, in all probability, the common saying of 'as fine as the horse'. 1883: Burne, *Shropsh. Folk-Lore*, 595, As fine (or proud) as a horse in bells.
5. As fine as a new scraped carrot. 1886: R. Holland, *Cheshire Gloss.*, 445 (E.D.S.). 1917: Bridge, *Cheshire Proverbs*, 13.
6. As fine as Filliloo. 1917: Ibid., 13 … The word [Filliloo] has no particular meaning in Cheshire.
7. As fine as fivepence. 1564: Bullein, *Dialogue*, 62 (E.E.T.S.), Out of the countree … as fine as fippence! *c*.1600: *Grim the Collier*, II, As a man would say, finer than fivepence, or more proud than a peacock. 1685: S. Wesley, *Maggots*, 109, All finer than fippence, they dazzl'd my eye. 1738: Swift, *Polite Convers.*, Dial. III, She was as fine as fi'pence. 1854: Baker, *Northants Gloss.*, s.v. 'Fippence', 'As fine as fippence', is a common proverbial simile. 1901: F. E. Taylor, *Lancs Sayings*, 2, As fine as fippence.
8. As fine as flying pigs. 1883: Burne, *Shropsh. Folk-Lore*, 595.
9. As fine (or proud) as a lord's bastard. 1678: Ray, 284.
10. Fine cloth is never out of fashion. 1732: Fuller, 1537.

11. Fine dressing is a foul house swept before the doors. 1640: Herbert, *Jac. Prudentum*. 1670: Ray, 8 [with 'windows' for 'doors']. 1732: Fuller, 1538.
12. Fine feathers make fine birds. 1592: G. Delamothe, *French Alphabet*, ii 29, The faire feathers, makes a faire foule. 1611: Davies (of Hereford), *Sc. of Folly*, 46, in *Works*, ii (Grosart), The faire feathers still make the faire fowles. 1678: Bunyan, *Pilgr. Progr.*, Pt I p. 35 (1849), Strange! He's another man, upon my word; They be fine feathers, that make a fine bird. *c*.1760: Foote, *Author*, I. 1891: Hardy, *Tess*, ch xxxiv, As everybody knows, fine feathers make fine birds. 1917: Bridge, *Cheshire Proverbs*, 57, Fine feathers make fine birds, but they don't make lady-birds.
13. Fine words. *See* **Fair** (33).
14. To fine folks a little ill finely wrapt. 1640: Herbert, *Jac. Prudentum*.

Finest flower will soonest fade, The. *c*.1570: in Huth, *Ancient Ballads*, *etc.*, 374 (1867). Cf. **Fairest rose**.

Finest lawn soonest stains, The. 1556: Withals, *Dict.*, sig. A2, The finest colours will sonest be staigned. 1600: Bodenham, *Belvedere*, 44 (Spens.S.), The purest lawne is apt for euery staine. 1670: Ray, 90. 1875: A. B. Cheales, *Proverb. Folk-Lore*, 164, The finest silks are soonest stained. Cf. **Fairest silk**.

Finest shoe often hurts the foot, The. 1639: Clarke, 82, The finest shooe fits not every foot. 1670: Ray, 90. Cf. **Fairest looking**.

Finger and Fingers. 1. At one's fingers' ends. 1561: Hoby, *Courtier*, 42 (T.T.), Ye are so good a courtyer that you have at your fingers endes that belongeth thereto. 1596: *Knack to Know Honest Man*, l. 625 (Malone S.), A begger hath flue of the seuen liberall sciences at his fingers ends. *c*.1630: *Dicke of Devonsh.*, III i, Who is more expert in any quality than he that hath it at his fingers ends. 1748: Richardson, *Clarissa*, viii 57 (1785), An hundred more wise adages, which I have always at my fingers end? 1852: M. A. Keltie, *Reminisc. of Thought*, *etc.*, 171, She had the Bible at her fingers' ends. 1906: Lucas, *Listener's Lure*, 156, One has so many thoughts about it all at one's fingers' end.
2. Each finger is a thumb, or All his fingers are thumbs. 1546: Heywood, *Proverbs*, Pt II ch v, Whan he should get ought, eche fynger is a thumbe. *c*.1594: Bacon, *Promus*, No. 660, Ech

finger is thumb. 1642: D. Rogers, *Matrim. Honour*, 141, Though each finger were a thumbe. 1659: Howell, 5, When he should work all his fingers are thumbs. 1732: Fuller, 5556, When he should work every finger is a thumb. 1866:Brogden, *Lincs Words*, 207, His fingers are all thumbs, i.e. he is very awkward. 1920: *Times Lit. Suppl.*, 3 Feb., p.73, col.2, Except on metaphysics (a keyboard upon which his fingers are all thumbs) he has usually disguised sound sense under his purple *panache*.

3. Finger in dish, finger in pouch. 1654: Gayton, *Pleasant Notes Don Q.*, 83.

4. Fingers for fish, prongs for meat. Newlyn, W. Corn. 19th cent. (Mr C. Lee, who says Cf. Boswell, *Tour to Hebrides*, 13 Sept.).

5. Fingers were made before forks. 1567: in *Loseley MSS.*, 212 (Kempe), As God made hands before knives … 1738: Swift, *Polite Convers.*, Dial. II, They say fingers were made before forks, and hands before knives. 1914: Lucas, *Landmarks*, 19, Certain crusted scraps of nursery wisdom were in Sarah's repertory, such as … 'Fingers were made before forks'.

6. His fingers are lime-twigs. 1596: Harington, *Metam. of Ajax*, 65 (1814) (OED), A certain gentleman that had his fingers made of lime-twigs, stole a piece of plate. 1633: Draxe, 203, His fingers are made of lime-twigs. 1672: Walker, *Paraem.*, 14. 1736: Bailey, *Dict.*, s.v. 'Finger'.

7. If I am a fool, put you your finger in my mouth. 1694: D'Urfey, *Quixote*, Pt I Act IV, If you meddle with my mouth, I shall snap at your fingers. 1732: Fuller, 2682.

8. My hand. See quot. 1842: Pulman, *Sketches*, 95 (1871) (W.), My hand's all vingers-an-thums [Devon].

9. The finger next the thumb. 1579: Lyly, *Euphues*, 68 (Arber), I will be the finger next thy thombe. Cf. No. 12.

10. To have a finger in the pie. 1553: *Respublica*, I iii, And first speake for me, bring me in credyte that my hande be in the pye. 1613: Shakespeare, *Henry VIII*, I i, The devil speed him! no man's pie is freed From his ambitious finger. 1694: Southerne, *Fatal Marriage*, I iii, By your good will you would have a finger in every bodies pie. 1798: B. Thompson, *The Stranger*, II iii, The world will be astonished when it comes to light; and not a soul will suppose that Old Solomon had a finger in the pye. 1860: Reade, *Cl. and Hearth*, ch lvi., Their law thrusteth its nose into every platter, and its finger into every pie. 1909: Lucas, *Wand. in Paris*, ch xviii, All the best French Royal Academicians (so to speak) … had a finger in this pie.

11. To put one's finger in the fire. 1546: Heywood, *Proverbs*, Pt II ch ii, To put my finger to far in the fyre. 1633: Draxe, 29, Let him put his finger in the fire that needeth. 1670: Ray, 175. 1732: Fuller, 3986, Put your finger into the fire, and say 'twas your ill fortune.

12. You two are finger and thumb. 1659: Howell, 13. 1670: Ray, 215. 1736: Bailey, *Dict.*, s.v. 'Thumb', They are finger and thumb. Cf. No. 9.

See also **Better a finger**.

Finglesham Church. *See* quot. 1735: Pegge, *Kent. Proverbs*, in E.D.S., No. 12, p. 71, To be married at Finglesham Church. There is no church at Finglesham; but a chalk-pit celebrated for casual amours; of which kind of rencounters the saying is us'd.

Fire. 1. A fire of straw. *See* quots. 1578: Florio, *First Fruites*, fo. 28, Who makes a fire of straw, hath much smoke and nought els. 1629: *Book of Meery Riddles*, Prov. 71, A fire of straw yeelds naught but smoake. 1666: Torriano, *Piazza Univ.*, 97 [as in 1578]. 1732: Fuller, 2236, He that maketh a fire of straw, hath much smoke and but little warmth.

2. As fire kindled by bellows, so is anger by words. 1732: Fuller, 677.

3. Fire and flax (or **tow**). This untoward combination has suggested several sayings. *See* quots. *c*.1386: Chaucer, *C. Tales*, D 89 (Skeat), For peril is bothe fyr and tow t'assemble. *c*.1460: *Good Wyfe wold a Pylgr.*, l. 79 (E.E.T.S.), Feyre and towe i-leyde to-gedore, kyndoll hit woll, be resson. 1530: Palsgrave, 417, Adde fyre to towe and you shal sone have a flame. 1578: Florio, *First Fruites*, fo. 30, Fire and flaxe agree not. 1633: Draxe, 141, There is no quenching of fire with towe. 1637: B.&F., *Elder Brother*, I ii, For he is fire and flax. 1666: Torriano, *Piazza Univ.*, 97 [as in 1578]. 1670: Ray, 175, All fire and tough [tow]. 1717: Pope, *Wife of Bath*, 30, There's danger in assembling fire and tow. 1732: Fuller, 1541, Fire in flax will smoke. 1822: Scott, *Nigel*, ch xxx, 'I know his Majesty's wisdom well,' said Heriot; 'yet there is an old proverb about fire and flax – well, let it pass.'

4. Fire and pride cannot be hid. *c.1375*: Barbour, *Bruce*, bk iv l. 119, For men sais [oft], that fire, na pryd. But discoueryng, may no man hyd.

5. Fire and water are good servants but bad masters. 1562: Bullein, *Bulwarke of Defence*, fo. 12, Water is a very good seruaunt, but it is a cruell maister. 1630: T. Adams, *Works*, 178, We say of water, it is a good seruant, though an ill master. 1659: Howell, 5 [with 'ill' for 'bad']. 1692: L'Estrange, Aes*op*, 38 (3rd ed.), It is with our passions, as it is with fire and water, they are good servants, but bad masters. 1738: Swift, *Polite Convers.*, Dial. II *See also* **Fire** (8).

6. Fire drives out fire. 1592: Shakespeare, *Romeo*, I ii, Tut, man, one fire burns out another's burning. 1608: Shakespeare, *Coriolanus*, iv vii 54, One fire drives out one fire: one nail, one nail. 1629: Quarles, in *Works*, iii 267 (Grosart), Whose desire Was all this while, by fire, to draw out fire; And by a well advised course to smother The fury of one passion with another. 1706: Vanbrugh, *Mistake*, III i, Come! courage, my dear Lopez; fire will fetch out fire. 1732: Fuller, 4523, The fire that burneth, taketh out the heat of a burn.

7. Fire in the one hand and water in the other. 1412–20: Lydgate, *Troy Book*, bk iv l. 4988, On swiche folke, platly, is no trist, that fire and water holden in her fist. 1546: Heywood, *Proverbs*, Pt I ch x 1593: G. Harvey, in *Works*, ii 317 (Grosart), Water in the one hand, fier in the other. 1681: W. Robertson, *Phraseol. Generalis*, 314, He carries fire in one hand, and water in the other. 1732: Fuller, 5886.

8. Fire is a good servant but a bad master. 1615: T. Adams, *Englands Sickness*, 20, The *world*, like fire, may be a good servant, will bee and ill master. 1808: J. Adams, *Works*, (1805–6), VI 533, Like fire, they [aristocrats] are good servants but all-consuming masters. 1841: Dickens, *Barn. Rudge*, ch liii, Fire, the saying goes, is a good servant but a bad master. *See also* **Fire** (5).

9. Fire is as hurtful as healthful. 1669: *Politeuphuia*, 184.

10. Fire is love and water sorrow. 1590: Greene, in *Works*, viii 51 (Grosart), If th' old saw did not borrow, Fier is loue, and water sorrow.

11. Fire of chats. *See* **Love** (35).

12. Fire, quoth the fox, when he p— on the ice. 1639: Clarke, 5. 1670: Ray, 93 1732: Fuller, 1542.

13. If the fire blows. *See* quot. 1839: G. C. Lewis, *Heref. Words*, 122, The following are old sayings current ... If the fire blows (i.e. makes a flaring noise from the escape of gas), wind will soon follow.

14. If you light your fire at both ends, the middle will shift for itself. 1712: Addison, *Spectator*, No. 265 [called 'the old kitchen proverb']. 1732: Fuller, 2765.

15. Make no fire, raise no smoke. 1546: Heywood, *Proverbs*, Pt II ch v.

16. The closer the fire the hotter. *c.1380*: Chaucer, *Leg. of Good Women*, l. 735, Wry [Cover] the gleed [glowing coal], and hotter is the fyr. 1566: L. Wager, *Mary Magdalene*, sig. C2, The more closely that you kepe fyre, no doubt The more feruent it is when it breaketh out. *c.1591*: Shakespeare, *Two Gent.*, I ii, Fire that's closest kept burns most of all.

17. The fire in the flint shows not till it's struck. 1855: Bohn, 504.

18. The fire that does not warm me shall never scorch me. Ibid., 504.

19. The fire which lighteth us at a distance, will burn us when near. Ibid., 504.

20. To get fire out of a pumice-stone. 1658: Willsford, *Natures Secrets*, 21, From whence the old adagie is derived, *To strike fire out of a pumice-stone*, is to expect an impossibility.

21. To go through fire and water. *c.825*: *Vesp. Psalter*, lxv(i.), 12 (OED), We leordun thorh fy and weter. 1530: Palsgrave, 653, He shall passe thorowe fyre and water or he get it. 1600: Shakespeare, *Merry Wives*, III iv, A woman would run through fire and water for such a kind heart. *c.1660*: in *Bagford Ballads*, i 291 (B.S.), Through fire and water I would go I swear. 1708: *Brit. Apollo*, i No. 113, col. 3, That common saying may expound it; I will go thro' fire and water to serve you. 1797: Colman, jr., *Heir at Law*, I ii 1884: R.L.S. and Henley, *Adm. Guinea*, II vi, I'll go through fire and water.

See also **London** (5); and **Smoke** (3) and (5).

Firle Hill. *See* quot. 1884: 'Sussex Proverbs', in *N.&Q.*, 6th ser, ix 341, When Firle Hill and Long Man has a cap, We at A'ston [Alciston] gets a drap.

First and last frosts are the worst, The. 1640: Herbert, *Jac. Prudentum*.

First blow is half the battle, The. Ibid., The first blow is as much as two. 1773: Goldsmith,

She Stoops, II, I fancy, Charles, you're right: the first blow is half the battle. 1790: Burns, *Prol. for Dumfries Theatre*, The first blow is ever half the battle.

First born, first fed. 1633: Draxe, 142. 1659: Howell, *Proverbs: Fr.-Eng.*, 4.

First breath is the beginning of death, The. 1732: Fuller, 4524.

First catch your hare. Supposedly thought to be found either in Mrs Beeton's famous *Book of Household Management* (1851) or in the earlier *Art of Cookery* (1747) by Mrs Glasse, but actually in neither (*see* quote 1896). The idea is essentially that of 'not counting your chickens before they are hatched' (*see* **Chickens** (3)) or not selling the bear's skin (*see* **Sell**). It has a venerable foundation as the first quotation shows. *c*.1300: Bracton, *De legibus Angliae*, iv xxi, *vulgariter dicitur, quod primo oportet cervum capere, et postea cum captus fuerit illum excoriare* (It is a common saying that it is first necessary to catch a deer and, after that, when he has been caught, you skin him). 1801: *Spirit of Farmers' Museum*, 55, How to dress a dolphin, first catch a dolphin. 1855: Thackeray: *The Rose and the Ring*, 'First catch your hare' ... exclaimed his Royal Highness. 1896: *Daily News*, 20 July, 8, The familiar words 'first catch your hare', were never to be found in Mrs Glasse's famous volume. What she really said was, 'Take your hare when it is cased [skinned]'.

First come first served, *c*.1386: Chaucer, *Wife of Bath's Prol.*, l. 389, Who-so that first to mille comth, first grint. *c*.1475: *Paston Lett.*, iii 133 (Gairdner, 1900), For who comyth fyrst to the mylle, fyrst must grynd. 1593: *Pass. Morrice*, 91 (N.Sh.S.), The drift whereof is, that first commers should be first serued. 1614: Jonson, *Bart. Fair*, III, Pardon me, sir, first come first serv'd. *c*.1663: Davenant, *Play-House to be Let*, I. 1720: C. Shadwell, *Irish Hospit.*, II, I was first come, and therefore ought to be first serv'd. 1825: Planché, *Extravag.*, i 24 (1879).

First creep then go. *c*.1350: *Douce MS 52*, no. 16, Fyrst the chylde crepyth and after gooth. *c*.1400: *Towneley Plays*, 103 (E.E.T.S.), ffyrst must vs crepe and sythen go. 1540: Palsgrave, *Acolastus*, sig. b3, They shoulde soner be able perfytely to go, then they coulde afore tymes be able to creepe. 1606: *Wily Beguiled*, in Hazlitt,

Old Plays, ix 266. 1622: Hornby, *Horn-book*, sig. B3, And as the prouerbe old doth teach vs, so We first must creepe, before we well can goe. 1662: Fuller, *Worthies*, iii 210 (1840), We did first creep, then run, then fly into preferment. 1754: Berthelson, *Eng.-Danish Dict.*, s.v. 'Creep', You must learn to creep before you can go. 1823: Scott, *St Ronan's*, ch iii, Folk maun creep before they gang. 1901: F. E. Taylor, *Lancs Sayings*, 11, Yo' mun creep first, an' then goo.

First cut and all the loaf besides, The. 1732: Fuller, 4526.

First deserve and then desire. 1605: Camden, *Remains*, 322 (1870). 1670: Ray. 7 1736: Bailey, *Dict.*, s.v. 'Deserve'.

First dish pleaseth all, The. 1640: Herbert, *Jac. Prudentum*. 1670: Ray, 9. 1732: Fuller, 4527.

First hand buy, At the; At the third let lie. 1732: Fuller, 6337.

First learn then discern. 1568: in *Loseley MSS.*, 207 (Kempe).

First men in the world were a gardener, a ploughman, a grasier, The. 1732: Fuller, 4529.

First of the nine orders of knaves is he that tells his errand before he goes it, The. 1855: Bohn, 504.

First pig, but the last whelp of the litter is the best, The. 1678: Ray, 53. 1732: Fuller, 4530.

First point, The. *Set* Hawk, *verb* (2).

First step is the only difficulty, The. *c*.1596: A. Munday *et al.*, *Sir Thomas More*, 11, Would I were so far on my journey. The first stretch is the worst methinks. 1639: Clarke, 171, The first step is as good as halfe over. 1659: Howell, *Proverbs: Ital.-Eng.*, 7, The hardest step is that over the threshold, viz. the beginning.

First step that is difficult, It is the. *See* **First step is the only difficulty**.

First tale, The. *See* **One tale**.

First things first. 1894: G. Jackson, (title) *First Things First*. 1920: W. Riley, *Yorkshire Suburb*, 36, The dear lady was ... incapable ... of putting first things first.

First time, There is always a (*or* **There's a first time for everything**). 1792: A. Hamilton, *Papers* (1961—) XII 504, But there is always 'a first time'. 1929: W.R. Burnett, *Little Caesar*, iii vii, 'I ain't got nothing to spill ... Did I ever do any spilling?' 'There's a first time for everything'.

First year of wedlock. *See* quot. *c*.1430: Lydgate, *Minor Poems*, 45 (Percy S.), And ever thynk wel on this prouerb trewe ... That the first yere wedlokk is called pleye, The second dreye, and the third yere deye.

Fish, *subs*. **1. Fish and guests (or company) stink in three days.** 1580: Lyly, *Euphues*, 307 (Arber), Fishe and gesse [guests] in three dayes are stale. 1586: L. Evans, *Withals Dict. Revised*, sig. B2, After three dayes fish is vnsauoury, and so is an ill guest. 1678: *Poor Robin Alman.*, As the proverb saies. Guests and fish stink in three days. *c*.1736: Franklin, in *Works*, i 455 (Bigelow), Fish and visitors smell in three days. 1869: *N. & Q.*, 4th ser, iv 272, 'See that you wear not out your welcome'. This is an elegant rendering of the vulgar saying that 'Fish and company stink in three days'.

2. Fish bite the least with wind in the east. 1893: Inwards. *Weather Lore*, 141.

3. Fish bred up in dirty pools will taste of mud. 1563: Googe, *Eglogs, etc.*, 40 (Arber) [with 'stynke' for .'taste']. 1576: Pettie, *Pelite Pall.* ii 100 (Gollancz, 1908).

4. Fish, flesh, etc. *See* **Flesh** nor **fish**, etc.

5. Fish is cast away that is cast in, dry pools. 1546: Heywood, *Proverbs.* Pt I ch xi 1605: Chapman, etc., *Eastw. Hoe*, V ii 1670: Ray, 90, Fishes are cast away, that are cast into dry ponds.

6. Fish make no broth. 1732: Fuller, 1546.

7. Fish marreth water and flesh mendeth it. 1578: Florio, *First Fruites*, fo. 29, Fish marreth the water, and flesh doth dresse it. 1629: *Book of Meery Riddles*, Prov. 104. 1678: Ray, 41, Fish spoils water, but flesh mends it.

8. Fish should swim thrice. 1611: Cotgrave, s.v. 'Poisson', We say, fish must ever swimme twice [water, wine]. 1620: *Westw. for Smelts*, 6 (Percy S.), Fish ... never doth digest well ... except it swimme twice after it comes forth the water: that is, first in butter, so to be eaten: then in wine or beere after it is eaten. 1738: Swift, *Polite Convers.*, Dial. II, They say fish should swim thrice ... first it should swim in the sea ... then it should swim in butter; and at last, sirrah, it should swim in good claret. 1787: O'Keeffe, *Little Hunchback*, II ii, Fish should swim three times; water, sauce, and wine.

9. Fish will not enter the net, but rather turn back. 1623: Wodroephe, *Spared Houres*, 508.

10. Here is fish for catching, etc. *See* quot. 1723: in Bliss, *Reliquiae Hearn.*, ii 154, The people there [Great Marlow] commonly say,

Here is fish for catching, corn for snatching, and wood for fetching.

11. I have other fish to fry. 1660: Evelyn, *Mem.*, iii 132 (1857) (OED), I fear he hath other fish to fry. 1670: Ray, 176. 1710: Swift, *Journal to Stella*, 3 Nov., Which I shall not answer tonight ... No, faith, I have other fish to fry. 1849: Brontë, *Shirley*, ch xx, Your uncle will not return yet, he has other fish to fry. 1910: Lucas, *Mr Ingleside*, ch xv, Most women will continue to be unmoved – they will have other and more primitive fish to fry.

12. It is a silly fish that is caught twice with the same bait. 1732: Fuller, 2879.

13. It is ill catching of fish when the hook is bare. 1583: Greene, in *Works*, ii 63 (Grosart).

14. Like a fish out of water. [Mus in matella. – Petr., 58. Sicut piscis sine aqua caret vita, ita sine monasterio monachus. – Attributed to a Pope Eugenius; but it is adapted from the Greek. It occurs in Sozomen, *Eccl. Hist.*, bk i *c*.13; and still earlier, in a *Life of St Anthony* (*c* 85) attributed to St Athanasius, and not later than A.D. 373. Skeat, *Early Eng. Proverbs*, 89.] *c*.1380: Wiclif, *Gospel Sermons*, cxxxi, in *Works*, ii 15 (Arnold), And how thei weren out of ther cloistre as fishis withouten water. *c*.1386: Chaucer, *Prol.*, l. 180, Ne that a monk whan he is cloysterles Is likned til a fissh that is waterles. 1655: Gurnall, *Christian in Armour*, 117 (1679), You may possibly find a tradesman out of his shop now and then, but he is as a fish out of the water. 1679: Shadwell, *True Widow*, III i 1724: Defoe, *Roxana*, in *Works*, xiii 37 (Boston, 1903), I was like a fish out of water, 1860: Reade, *Cl. and Hearth*, ch xxxi, I have been like a fish out of water in all those great dungeons. 1916: B. Duffy, *The Old Lady*, 17, I feel like a fish out of water here.

15. Like fish that live in salt-water, and yet are fresh. 1732: Fuller, 3228.

16. Sweet is that fish, etc. *See* quot. 1607: E. Topsell, *Four-footed Beasts*, 46, Whence came the prouerbe, *That sweet is that fish, which is not fishe at all* [beaver].

17. That fish will soon be caught that nibbles at every bait. 1732: Fuller, 4342.

18. The fish adores the bait. 1640: Herbert, *Jac. Prudentum*. 1670: Ray, 9, The fish follow the bait. 1754: Berthelson, *Eng.-Danish Dict.*, s.v. 'Bait' [as in 1670].

19. The fish may be caught in a net that will not come to a hook. 1732: Fuller, 4535.

20. There are as good fish in the sea as ever came out of it. [*c*.1380: Chaucer, *Parl. of Foules*, in *Works*, i 356 (Skeat), There been mo sterres, god wot, than a paire!] *c*.1573: G. Harvey, *Letter-Book* (1884), 126, In the mayne sea theres good stoare of fish. 1816: T. L. Peacock: *Headlong Hall*, xiv, There never was a fish taken out of the sea, but left another as good behind. 1822: Scott, *Nigel*, ch xxxv 1881: Gilbert, *Patience*, I, There's fish in the sea, no doubt of it, As good as ever came out of it. 1904: H. James, in *Letters*, ii 10 (1920), I still cling to the belief that there are as good fish in the sea – that is, my sea! …

21. There are lots (or **plenty**) **of good fish in the sea.** For an earlier and alternative version of this, *see* **Fish** (20). 1885: Gilbert *The Mikado*, I, Though there are many who'll wed for a penny, There are lots of good fish in the sea.

22. To find fish on one's fingers. 1587: Greene, in *Works*, iv 140 (Grosart), Who (as the nature of women is, desirous to see and bee seene) thought she should both heare the *parle* and view the person of this young embassadour, and therefore found fish on her fingers, that she might staye still in the chamber of presence. 1590: Lodge, *Rosalynde*, 122 (Hunt.Cl.), Ganimede rose as one that would suffer no fish to hang on his fingers.

23. To make fish of one and flesh of another. 1639: Clarke, 182, I will not make fleshe of one, and fish of the other. 1709: O. Dykes, *Eng. Proverbs*, 137, If the father proves such a partial fool … as to make fish of one [child], and flesh of another. 1738: Swift, *Polite Convers.*, Dial. II. 1828: Carr, *Craven Dialect*, i 151, 'I will not make fish o' yan and fowl of another', an expression by which a person declares that he will shew no partiality.

See also **All fish; All is fish; Best** (14); **Daughter** (1); **Great fish; Little fish; Old, E** (10) and (11); **Sauce; Sea hath fish; Sole; Some fish; Swear** (6); and **Wind, C** (3) and **D** (4).

Fish, *verb*. **1. He has well fished and caught a frog.** 1546: Heywood, *Proverbs*, Pt I ch xi *c*.1548: Latimer, in *Works*, ii 419 (P.S.), As the common saying is, 'Well I have fished and caught a frog.' 1595: Churchyard, *Charitie*, 9 (1816), We angle in the reeds And catch a frog. 1629: in *Pepysian Garland*, 318 (Rollins, 1922), The man that wedds for greedy wealth, he goes a fishing faire, But often times he gets a frog, or very little share. 1732: Fuller, 5903, You fish fair, and catch a frog.

2. It is no sure rule to fish with a cross-bow. 1640: Herbert, *Jac. Prudentum*.

3. Still he fishes that catches one. 1611: Cotgrave, s.v. 'Pescher', And yet he fishes who catcheth one. 1670: Ray, 91. 1732: Fuller, 4262.

4. To fish before the net. *c*.1400: *Towneley Plays*, 104 (E.E.T.S.), Ye fysh before the nett. 1460: Lydgate, *Order of Fools*, l.131 (E.E.T.S., E.S. 8, p. 83), And he ys a fole afore the nette that fysshes. 1596: Harington, *Metam. of Ajax*, 20 (1814), Which either we miss (fishing before the net, as the proverb is) … 1683: Meriton, *Yorkshire Ale*, 83–7 (1697), He that fishes afore the net, lang fish or he fish get.

5. To fish for (or **with**) **a herring and catch a sprat.** 1639: Clarke, 2, I fish't for a herring and catcht a sprat. 1670: Ray, 180 ['for']. 1732: Fuller, 5165 ['with'].

6. To fish in troubled waters. 1569: Grafton, *Chron.*, i 283 (1809), Which alwayes desyre your vnquietnesse, whereby they may the better fishe in the water when it is troubled. 1591: Harington, *Orl. Furioso*, bk xli., Notes, Thinking it (as the prouerb saith) best fishing in troubled waters. 1630: *Pathomachia*, sc i, It is good fishing in troubled waters. 1660: Tatham, *The Rump*, III [as in 1630]. 1756: Murphy, *Apprentice*, I ii, We had better get away from this house; all fishing in troubled waters here.

Fisherman. *See* quot. 1868: *N.&Q.*, 4th ser, ii 94, Never a fisherman need there be, If fishes could hear as well as see (West Kent).

Fisherman's walk, A: three steps and overboard. 1867: Smyth, *Sailor's Word-Book*, s.v.

Fisher's folly. *See* **Kirbie's castle.**

Fishing, *verb. subs.* **1. No fishing like fishing in the sea.** 1575: Churchyard, *Chippes*, 41 (Collier), Some say there is no fishing to the seas. 1605: Camden, *Remains*, 334 (1870), There is no fishing to the sea. 1609: Melton, *Sixfold Politician*, 94 [as in 1605]. 1670: Ray, 90, No fishing to fishing in the sea.

2. The end of fishing is catching. 1580: Lyly, *Euphues*, 396 (Arber). 1732: Fuller, 4497, The end of fishing is not angling, but catching.

Fishing-net. *See* quots. 1528: More, *Works*, 224 (1557), It were as soone done to weue a newe web of clothe as to soue up euery hole in a net. 19th cent.: Newlyn, W. Corn., saying, Like a fishing-net – the more you mend it, the more holes there are in it (Mr C. Lee).

Fit as a fan for a forehorse. 1619: Chapman, *Two Wise Men*, IV iii.

Fit as a fiddle. 1616: Haughton, *Eng. for my Money*, IV i, This is excellent, i' faith; as fit as a fiddle! *c*.1625: B.&F., *Women Pleased*, IV iii 1883: R.L.S., *Treasure I*, ch xxx, Looking fit and taut as a fiddle. 1922: Lucas, *Geneva's Money*, 86, He hasn't been really sober for years and he's as fit as a fiddle.

Fit as a pudding. 1600: Dekker, *Shoem. Hol.*, IV v, Tis a very brave shooe, and as fit as a pudding.

Fit as a pudding for (*a*) **a dog's mouth**; (*b*) **a friar's mouth**, (*a*) 1592: Lyly, *Mother Bombie*, II i, But looke where Prisius' boy comes, as fit as a pudding for a dogges mouth. (*b*) 1578: Whetstone, *Promos and Cassandra*, sig. D3, Your answeare then in sooth, Fyts me as iumpe as a pudding a friars mouth. 1593: Peele, *Edward I*, sc ii 1605: Camden, *Remains*, 318 (1870). 1670: Ray, 204. 1732: Fuller, 678 [with 'fritter' for 'pudding'].

Fit for the chapel. *See* quot. 1579: G. Gates, *Defence of Mil. Profession*, 37, The prouerbe (no lesse wise then it is olde) is also profitable, as it is moste true, He that is fitte for the chappell, is meete for the fielde.

Fitting. *He that is suffered to do more than is fitting, will do more than is lawful*. 1670: Ray, 9.

Five score. *See* **Six score**.

Flanders mare. *See* quots. 1717: in *Six N. Count. Diaries*, 82 (Surtees S.), Uncle told me now we are to see yon damsel of Mr Collingwood's. She's like a Flanders mare. 1732: Fuller, 3229, Like Flanders mares, fairest afar off.

Flanders reckoning, A. 1606: T. Heywood, *If You Know Not Me*, Pt II, in *Dram. Works*, i 271 (1874), God send me but once to finger it, and if I doe not make a Flanders reckoning on't – and that is, as I have heard mad wagges say, receiue it here, and reuell it away in another place …

Flap with a fox-tail, To give one a. 1530: Palsgrave, 563, I flatter hym to begyle hym, or I gyve one a slappe with a foxe tayle. 1565: Calfhill, *Answ. to Martiall*, 292 (P.S.), Break God's [works], and they either look through their fingers, or else give a flap with a fox-tail, for a little money. 1581: B. Rich, *Farewell*, 4 (SH.S.), And when a souldier hath thus served in many a bloudie broile, a flappe with a foxe taile

shall bee his beste reward. 1640: *King and Poore North. Man*, l. 368, in Hazlitt, *Early Pop. Poetry*, iv 307, Where they with brave claret and brave old canary, they with a foxe tale him soundly did pay. 1762: Smollett, *Sir L. Greaves*, ch viii, Your honour has a mortal good hand at giving a flap with a fox's tail, as the saying is. 1808: Scott, in Lockhart's *Life*, ii 218, I owe Jeffrey a flap with a fox-tail on account of his review of Marmion. 1847: Halliwell, *Dict.*, s.v. 'Fox-tail', Fox-tail. Anciently one of the badges of a fool. Hence perhaps the phrase *to give one a flap with a fox-tail*, to deceive or make a fool of him.

Flat as a cake (or **pancake**). 1542: Udall, tr. Erasmus' *Apoph.*, 250 (1877), His nose as flat as a cake, bruised or beaten to his face. 1580: Baret, *Alvearie*, F 649, A nose as flat as a cake. 1631: Mabbe, *Cdestina*, 209 (T.T.), My caske strangely bruised, beaten as flat as a cake. 1758–67, Sterne, *Trist. Shandy*, vol iii ch xxvii, He has crushed his nose … as flat as a pancake to his face. 1786: R. Twining, in *Twining Fam. Papers*, 139 (1887), The Gatinois … is extremely fertile, but as flat as a pancake. 1830: Marryat, *King's Own*, ch xvii, Under which it had lain, jammed as flat as a pancake.

Flat as a dab. 1869: FitzGerald, *Sea Words and Phrases*, 3.

Flat as a flawn, i.e. a custard. 1678: Ray, 355. 1775: Watson, *Hist. of Halifax*, quoted in Hunter's *Hallamsh. Gloss.*, 145, As flat as a flawn (custard), is a proverb. 1887: *Brighouse News*, 23 July (W.), As flat as a flawn.

Flat as a flounder, *c*.1625: B.&F., *Women Pleased*, II iv 1671: E. Howard, *Six Days Adventure*, I, Who lay as flat as flounders. Before 1704: T. Brown, *Works*, i 313, and ii 137 (1760). 1788: O'Keeffe, *Highland Reel*, III i, This instant say in plain, audible English, 'How do you do, Mr McGilpin' – or down you go as flat as a fluke [flounder], *c*.1800: *Irishman in London*, I ii, in Inchbald, *Farces*, ii 95 (1815).

Flat as ditchwater. 1772: in *Garrick Corresp.*, i 465 (1831), 'The Grecian Daughter's' being dead as dish-water after the first act. 1854: Baker, *Northants Gloss.*, s.v. 'Ditchwater', 'As flat', or, 'as dead as ditch-water', said of anything tasteless and insipid. 1862: *Dialect of Leeds*, 406, As dull as ditch-water. 1865: Dickens, *Mutual Friend*, bk iii ch x, He'd be sharper than a serpent's tooth, if he wasn't as dull as ditch water. 1888: Lowsley,

Berks Gloss., 70 (E.D.S.), 'Dead as ditch water' is said of beer that is flat to the taste.

Flatterer. 1. A flatterer's throat is an open sepulchre. 1640: Herbert, *Jac. Prudentum.*

2. Flatterers haunt not cottages. 1732: Fuller, 1550. 1869: Spurgeon, *John Ploughman*, ch xiv.

3. There is no such flatterer as a man's self. 1732: Fuller, 4922.

4. When flatterers meet, the Devil goes to dinner. 1678: Ray, 139. 1799: Wolcot, in *Works*, v 196 (1801), Porteus, there is a proverb thou should'st read, 'When flatt'rers meet, the *Devil goes to dinner*'.

Flattering as a spaniel. 1639: Clarke, 285. 1670: Ray, 204.

Flattery. 1. He that rewards flattery begs it. 1732: Fuller, 2269.

2. Flattery sits in the parlour, when plain dealing is kicked out of doors. Ibid., No. 1552.

3. The coin that is most current among us is flattery. Ibid., No. 4452.

4. There is flattery in friendship. 1600: Shakespeare, *Henry V*, III vii, *Con.* I will cap that proverb with 'There is flattery in friendship'.

Flax. *At leisure, as flax groweth.* 1639: Clarke, 304. *See also* **Candlemas,** H (4); **Fire** (3); and **God will send thee flax.**

Flay a flint (or **stone**). *See* **Skin a flint.**

Flea and **Fleas. 1. A flea in one's ear.** [Comment Panurge auoyt la pulce en l'oreille. – Rabelais, *Pantagruel*, bk iii ch vii, part of title.] *c.*1430: *Pilgr. Lyf. Manhode*, II xxxix 91 (1869) (OED), And manye oothere grete wundres ... whiche ben fleen in myne eres. 1546: Heywood, *Proverbs*, Pt I ch xi, He standth now as he had a flea in his eare. 1602: Middleton, *Blurt, Master Const.*, II ii, I will send him hence with a flea in's ear. 1656: *Musarum Deliciae*, i 65 (Hotten, 1874), Some, telling how they vexed another, say I sent him with a flea in's eare away. 1709: Cibber, *Rival Fools*, III, So, he's gone with this flea in his ear to my uncle, I suppose. 1871: G. Eliot, *Middlemarch*, ch lvi., The best way would be to ... send 'em away with a flea in their ear, when they came spying and measuring. 1922: Weyman, *Ovington's Bank*, ch ix, On which he dismissed her with a flea in her ear.

2. When eager bites the thirsty flea, Clouds and rain you sure shall see. 1639: Clarke, 263, We shall have raine, the fleas bite. 1893: Inwards, *Weather Lore*, 148.

3. When fleas do very many grow, Then 'twill surely rain or snow. 1893: Inwards, *Weather Lore*, 148.

See also **Do** (14); and **Dog** (49).

Flea-bitten horse never tires, A. 1577: Googe, *Heresbach.'s Husb.*, ii 116*b* (1586) (OED), The fleabitten horse prooveth alwaies good in travell. 1696: D'Urfey, *Quixote*, Pt III Act I, Take this proverb with you by way of advice: If you an old flea-bitten ride, you need not fear the dirt; But when you back a young colt, see your saddle be well girt. 1922: *N. & Q.*, 12th ser, xi 169.

Fleece and fell, To have both. 1639: Clarke, 39, Will you have both fleece and fell. 1642: D. Rogers, *Naaman*, sig. Dd2, Thy servant is for thee to use, not tire or teare out: Thou must not take both fleece and flesh too.

Fleet, The. *He may whet his knife on the threshold of the Fleet.* 1662: Fuller, *Worthies*, ii 348 (1840). 1790: Grose, *Prov. Gloss.*, s.v. 'London', Said of persons who are not in debt [and therefore not in danger of arrest].

Flesh never stands so high but a dog will venture his legs. 1678: Ray, 139. 1732: Fuller, 1553.

Flesh nor fish nor good red herring, Neither. 1528: *Rede Me and be not Wrothe*, I iii *b*, Wone that is nether flesshe nor fisshe. 1546: Heywood, *Proverbs*, Pt I ch x, She is nother fyshe, nor fleshe, nor good red hearyng. 1599: Nashe, *Lenten Stuffe*, in *Works*, v 302 (Grosart). 1630: Taylor (Water-Poet), *Workes*, pagin. 1, 34. Before 1704: T. Brown, *Works*, iii 240 (1760), They ... marry their wives, before they know whether they are fish, flesh, or good red herring. 1711: Addison, *Spectator*, No. 165. 1824: Scott, *Red-gauntlet*, ch xii, I never thought twice about it, Mr Fairford; it was neither fish, nor flesh, nor salt herring of mine. 1921: *Times*, 7 Oct., p. 8, col. 4, Its compromise with sentiment and the proprieties leaves it neither fish, flesh, nor good red-herring.

Flesh upon horses and money with women hide a many faults. 1917: Bridge, *Cheshire Proverbs*, 57.

Fletching. *See* quot. 1884: 'Sussex Proverbs', in *N. & Q.*, 6th ser, ix 342, The people of Fletching Live by snapping and ketching.

Flies. See **Fly.**

Flitting of farms makes mailings dear. 1846: Denham, *Proverbs*, 3 (Percy S.).

Float is rotten, What does not. 1813: Ray, 194.

Flow will have an ebb, A. 1412–20: Lydgate, *Troy Book*, bk ii l. 2013, After a flowe, an ebbe folweth ay. 1626: *Scoggins Jests*, 158 (1864), There was never so great a flood, but there may bee as lowe an ebbe. 1670: Ray, 91. 1754: Berthelson, *Eng.-Danish Dict.*, s.v. 'Flow'.

Flower in his garden, It is the finest. 1659: Howell, 15, 'Tis the fairest flower in your garden. 1732: Fuller, 3023.

Flowers in May. *See* **Fresh**; and **Welcome**.

Fly and **Flies, 1. A fly and eke a friar**. *See* quot. *c.*1386: Chaucer, *Wife of Bath's Prol.*, 835, Lo, gode men, a flye and eek a frere Wol falle in every dish and eek matere.

2. A fly hath its spleen. 1580: Lyly, *Euphues*, 316 (Arber), Low trees haue their tops … the flye his splene. 1590: Lodge, *Rosalynde*, 70 (Hunt.Cl.), I tell thee, flies haue their spleene. 1605: Camden, *Remains*, 317 (1870). 1646: Browne, *Pseudo. Epi.*, bk iii ch iii, So is it proverbially said *Formicae sua bilis inest, habet et musca splenem.* 1732: Fuller, 1388, Even a fly hath its spleen. 1924: *Sphere*, 27 Sept., p. 386, col. 2, A Latin tag declares that 'even a fly hath its spleen'.

3. A fly on your nose. *See* quot. 1893: Inwards, *Weather Lore*, 148, A fly on your nose, you slap, and it goes; If it comes back again, it will bring a good rain.

4. Flies come to feasts unasked. 1683: *See* **Fiddler** (2). 1924: *Sphere*, 27 Sept., p. 386, col. 2, Another proverb of unimpeachable veracity proclaims that 'Flies come to feasts unasked'.

5. Flies go to lean horses. 1578: Florio, *First Fruites*, fo. 25, Vnto the leane horses, always resort the flyes. 1631: Mabbe, *Celestina*, 214 (T.T.), Flyes bite none but leane and feeble oxen. 1666: Torriano, *Piazza Univ.*, 43, Flyes do rest upon lean horses.

6. Flies will tickle lions being dead. 1610: Marston, *Histrio-Mastix*, VI.

7. He changes a fly into an elephant. 1736: Bailey, *Dict.*, s.v. 'Elephant', To make of a fly an elephant. 1813: Ray. 75.

8. He takes a spear to kill a fly. Ibid., 75.

9. Into a shut mouth flies fly not. 1640: Herbert, *Jac. Prudentum.* 1869: Spurgeon, *John Ploughman*, ch vi, No flies will go down your throat if you keep your mouth shut.

See also **shut mouth**

10. Like a fly in a tar-box (or **glue-pot**). 1659:

Howell, 19, He capers like a flie in a tar-box. 1670: Ray, 216 [as in 1659]. 1886: Elworthy, *West Som. Word-Book*, 437 (E.D.S.), Like a fly in a glue-pot. Com[mon] expression, to express nervous excitement.

11. More flies are taken with a drop of honey than a tun of vinegar. 1732: Fuller, 3454. 1821: Combe, *Syntax in Search of Wife*, can. xxxiv p. 24, Madam, the ancient proverb says … That one rich drop of honey sweet, As an alluring, luscious treat, Is known to tempt more flies, by far, Than a whole tun of vinegar. 1830: Forby, *Vocab. E. Anglia*, 433, You will catch more flies with a spoonful of honey, than with a gallon of vinegar. 1865: 'Lancs Proverbs', in *N. & Q.*, 3rd ser, viii 494, There's more flies caught with honey than alegar.

12. One cannot catch a fly when he will. 1659: Howell, 11.

13. The fly on the wheel. 1586: Pettie, tr. Guazzo's *Civil Convers.*, fo. 71, The flye, which sitting vppon a cart that was driuen on the waye, sayde he had raysed a very great dust. 1612: Bacon, *Essays:* 'Vainglory', It was pretily deuised of Aesop, *The flie sate vpon the axletree of the chariot wheele, and said, What a dust doe I raise!* 1661: Gurnall, *Christian in Armour*, 299 (1679), Yet these are no more than the flie on the coach. 1732: Fuller, 5476, What a dust have I rais'd! quoth the fly upon the coach. 1814: Byron, in *Letters and Journals*, ii 401 (Prothero), Like the fly in the fable, I seem to have got upon a wheel which makes much dust; but, unlike the said fly, I do not take it all for my own raising. 1922: *Observer*, 5 March, p. 12, col. 5, The fly on the cart-wheel might as well have claimed not only that it was raising all the dust, but that it had built the cart.

14. To a boiling pot flies come not. 1640: Herbert, *Jac. Prudentum.*

15. 'Twould make even a fly laugh. 1732: Fuller, 5340.

16. You must lose a fly to catch a trout. 1640: Herbert, *Jac. Prudentum.*

See also **Eagle** (2); **Elstow; Honey** (3); **Hungry flies**; and **Lion** (5).

Fly, *verb.* **1. Fly, and you will catch the swallow.** 1659: Howell, 13.

2. Fly brass, thy father's a tinker. Ibid., 12.

3. Fly the pleasure that bites tomorrow. 1591: Florio, *Second Frutes*, 99, Flie that present ioye, Which in time will breede annoy. 1623:

Wodroephe. *Spared Houres*, 277, Flee all present pleasure that gives the future payne. 1629: *Book of Meery Riddles*, Prov. 29, Fly that pleasure which paineth afterward. 1640: Herbert, *Jac. Prudentum*. 1710: S. Palmer, *Moral Essays on Proverbs*, 347.

4. He has flown high and let in a cow-clap at last. 1917: Bridge, *Cheshire Proverbs*, 66 … Said of one very particular in choosing a wife, but who has made an ill-assorted marriage after all.

5. He would fain fly, but wanted feathers. 1546: Heywood, *Proverbs*, Pt I ch xi 1681: W. Robertson, *Phraseol. Generalis*, 614, He would flie, but he wants feathers. 1732: Fuller, 2415.

6. To fly at all game. 1670: Ray, 176. 1846–59: *Denham Tracts*, ii 108 (F.L.S.).

Fly-catcher. *See* quot. 1886: Swainson, *Folk-Lore of Brit. Birds*, 49 (F.L.S.), In Somerset these birds are supposed to bring good luck to the homestead they frequent, hence the rhyme:
– 'If you scare the fly-catcher away, No good luck will with you stay'.

Flying enemy. *See* **Bridge** (5).

Flying without wings, No. 1633: Draxe, 124. 1670: Ray, 91. 1732: Fuller, 3569.

Foal. *How can the foal amble, if the horse and mare trot?* 1546: Heywood, *Proverbs*, Pt I ch xi 1614: B. Rich, *Honestie of This Age*, 32 (Percy S.), The olde proverbe is: *If the mother trot how should the daughter amble?* 1670: Ray, 91. 1732: Fuller, 2554. *See also* **Rugged**; and **Trot sire**.

Foe is better than a dissembling friend, A. 1548: Briant, *Dispraise of Life of Courtier*, sig. D3, Alexander sayd assure me my frende Parmeno of those that be dissemblyng frendes, for I wil be ware of them that be my open enemies. 1589: L. Wright, *Display of Dutie*, 19, As good a foe that hurts not, as a friend that helpes not. 1600: Bodenham, *Belvedere*, 176 (Spens.S.). 1647: *Countrym. New Commonwealth*, 13, It is better to have an open foe, then a dissembling friend.

Fog. 1. *See* quot. 1874: W. Pengelly. in *N. & Q.*, 5th ser, ii 184, I often heard the following weather-rhymes in Cornwall in my boyhood: –
… A fog and a small moon Bring an easterly wind soon. 1893: Inwards, *Weather Lore*, 58.

2. A fog cannot be dispelled with a fan. 1846: Denham, *Proverbs*, 1 (Percy S.).

3. A fog from the sea, Brings honey to the bee; A fog from the hills Brings corn to the mills. Pembrokesh. 1889: *N. & Q.*, 7th ser, viii 204.

4. Fog on the hill, water to the mill; Fog in the hollow, fine day to follow. Oxfordsh. 1928: *Spectator*, 3 Nov., p. 640, col. 2.

See also **March** (15), (16), (18), (43). **Folkestone**. *See* quots. 1735: Pegge, *Kent. Proverbs*, in E.D.S., No. 12, p. 71, Folkstone Washer-women. These are the white clouds which commonly bring rain. 1887: Parish and Shaw, *Dict. Kent. Dialect*, 57 (E.D.S.), Folkestone Girls; the name given to heavy rain clouds. Also Folkestone Lasses and Folkestone Washer-women.

Follow, *verb*. **1. Follow love and it will flee; Flee love and it will follow thee.** 1581: T. Howell, *Devises*, 64 (1906), Flee it [love], and it will flee thee, Follow it, and it will follow thee. 1678: Ray, 55. 1732: Fuller, 6258. 1875: A. B. Cheales, *Proverb. Folk-Lore*, 29.

2. Follow the river and you'll get to the sea. 1732: Fuller, 1556.

3. He that follows Nature is never out of his way. Ibid., No. 2108.

4. He that follows truth too closely, etc. *See* quots. 1651: Herbert, *Jac. Prudentum*, 2nd ed., Follow not truth too near the heels, lest it dash out thy teeth. 1681: W. Robertson, *Phraseol. Generalis*, 619, He that follows truth too near the heels, shall have dust thrown in his face. 1820: Colton, *Lacon*, Pt I No. 558, He that follows truth too closely, must take care that she does not strike out his teeth.

5. To follow one's nose. *c*.1350: *Cleanness*, l. 978, in *Allit. Poems*, 67 (Morris, E.E.T.S.), Loth and tho luly-whit his lefly two dezter, Ay folzed here face [followed their face] bifore her bothe yzen. *c*.1520: Stanbridge, *Vulgaria*, sig C2, Ryght forthe on thy nose. Recta via incede. 1637: Heywood, *Royal King*, I, Follow thy nose, and thou wilt be there presently. 1742: Fielding, *Andrews*, bk ii ch ii, The fellow … bade him follow his nose and be d – n'd. 1917: D. Grayson, *Great Possessions*, ch iii, One has only to step out into the open country … and follow his nose.

6. You may follow him long e're a shilling drop from him. 1732: Fuller, 5944.

Folly. 1. Folly grows wtthout watering. 1640: Herbert, *Jac. Prudentum*. 1854: J. W. Warter, *Last of the Old Squires*, ch v p. 53.

2. Folly is never long pleased with it self. 1732: Fuller, 1560.

3. Folly is often sick of itself. Ibid., No. 1559.

4. Folly is wise in her own eyes. 1629: *Book of Meery Riddles*, Prov. 95.

5. Folly may kinder a man of many a good turn. 1694: D'Urfey, *Quixote*, Pt II Act II sc ii.

6. Folly without faults is as reddish [radish] **without salt.** 1608: Armin, *Nest of Ninnies*, 40 (SH.S.).

7. If folly were grief, every house would weep. 1640: Herbert, *Jac. Prudentum.*

8. It is folly to run to the foot when one may run to the head. 1546: Heywood, *Proverbs*, Pt II ch v, Folke show much foly, when things should be sped, To ren to the foote that maie go to the hed. 1633: Draxe, 72.

9. Many for folly themselves fordo. *c.*1460: *How the Good Wife*, l. 140, Many for folye hem self for-doothe.

10. The chief disease that reigns this year is folly. 1640: Herbert, *Jac. Prudentum.*

11. The folly of one man is the fortune of another. 1607: Bacon, *Essays:* 'Fortune'.

12. 'Tis a folly to fret; grief's no comfort. 1813: Ray, 195.

See also **Zeal**.

Fond as a besom. 1855: Robinson, *Whitby Gloss.*, 13, He's as fond as a bezom … very foolish indeed. 1889: Peacock, *Manley, etc., Gloss.*, 44 (E.D.S.), 'He's as fond as a beäsom' signifies that the person spoken of is very foolish. [The phrase is proverbial in other dialects also.]

Fond pride of dress is sure a very curse; Ere fancy you consult, consult your purse. 1736: Franklin, *Way to Wealth*, in *Works*, i 448 (Bigelow).

Fool and **Fools. 1. A fool always comes short of his reckoning.** 1611: Cotgrave, s.v. 'Fol', A foole oft finds himselfe short of his reckonings.

2. A fool and his money are soon parted. 1573: Tusser, *Husb.*, 19 (E.D.S.), A foole and his monie be soone at debate. 1587: J. Bridges, *Defence of the Government in the Church of England*, xv 1294, A foole and his money is soone parted. *c.*1640: in *Roxb. Ballads*, iii 550 (B.S.). 1763: Murphy, *Citizen*, I ii 1894: Shaw, *Arms and the Man*, III.

3. A fool at forty is a fool indeed. 1557: R.Edgeworth, *Sermons*, 301, When he [Reheboam] begonne hys raigne he was one and fortye yeares of age … And he that hath not learned some experience or practice and trade of

the world by that age wil never be wise. *c.*1670: Cotton, *Visions*, No. 1, He who at fifty is a fool, Is far too stubborn grown for school. 1725: Young, *Satires*, No. ii *ad fin.*, Be wise with speed; A fool at forty is a fool indeed. 1820: Colton, *Lacon*, Pt I No. 352 [quotes Young].

4. A fool believes everything. 1625: in *Harl. Miscell.*, iv 130 (1745), Florimundus justified the proverb, A fool believeth every thing.

5. A fool believes the thing he would have so. 1681: W. Robertson, *Phraseol. Generalis*, 620.

6. A fool can dance without a fiddle. 1732: Fuller, 99.

7. A fool is fulsome. 1659: Howell, 10. 1670: Ray, 10. 1686: in *Roxb. Ballads*, viii 604 (B.S.), Prating like a fool is fulsome.

8. A fool knows more in his own house than a wise man in another's. 1620: Shelton, *Quixote*, Pt II ch xliii. 1694: D'Urfey, *Quixote*, Pt II Act V sc i [with 'sees' for 'knows']. 1732: Fuller, 103.

9. A fool looks to the beginning, a wise man regards the end. *c.*1535: *Dialogues of Creatures*, ccvii. (1816), A foole beholdith but onely the begynnynge of his workys, but a wiseman takyth hede to the ende.

10. A fool loseth his estate before he finds his folly. [*c.*1489: Caxton, *Sonnes of Aymon*, 485 (E.E.T.S.), For a fole never byleveth tyll he fele sore.] 1732: Fuller, 104.

11. A fool may make money, but it needs a wise man to spend it. 1869: Spurgeon, *John Ploughman*, ch xix 1875: A. B. Cheales, *Proverb. Folk-Lore*, 100.

12. A fool may sometimes give a wise man counsel – with variants. [πολλάκα γὰρ καὶ μωρὸς ἀνὴρ μάλα καίριον εἶπεν. – Aulus Gellius, ii 6.] 1350: *Ywain and Gawain* (E.E.T.S.) l. 1477, Bot yot a fole that litel kan [knows little], May wele cownsail another man. *c.*1374: Chaucer, *Troylus*, bk i l. 630, A fool may eek a wys man ofte gyde. *c.*1450: *Portonope*, l. 7982, p. 321 (E.E.T.S.), Yet an old proverbe sayd ys all day: Of a foole a wyse man may Take wytt. 1581: Stafford, E*xam. of Complaints*, 11 (N.Sh.S.), Yet fooles (as the prouerbe is) sometimes speake to the purpose. 1678: Ray, 140, A fool may put somewhat in a wise bodies head. 1693: Urquhart, *Rabelais*, bk iii ch 37, I have often heard it said in a vulgar proverb, The wise may be instructed by a fool. 1732: Fuller, 105, A fool may chance to put something into a wise man's head. 1818: Scott, *Heart of Midl.*, ch xlv., And if a fule may gie a wise man a counsel … 1926: Phillpotts, *Marylebone Miser*, ch i, Listen to everybody, for the biggest fool may come out with a bit of sense when you least expect it.

13. A fool may throw a stone into a well, which a hundred wise men cannot pull out. 1640: Herbert, *Jac. Prudentum.* 1854: J. W. Warter, *Last of Old Squires*, 53.

14. A fool on a bridge soundeth like a drum. 1611: Cotgrave, s.v. 'Pont', A foole on a bridge is a drumme in a river. 1623: Wodroephe, *Spared Houres*, 485.

15. A fool or a physician. An association or alternative in various proverbial forms. *See* quots. [Sed gravescente valetudine nihil e libidinibus omittebat, in patientia firmitudinem simulans solitusque eludere medicorum artes atque eos, qui post tricesimum aetatis annus ad internoscenda corpori suo utilia vel noxia alieni consilii indigerunt. – Tacitus, *Annals*, VI xlvi.] 1607: B. Barnes, *Divils Charter*, sig. L3, Eyther mere fooles or good phisitions all. 1634: T. Heywood, *Ma.-Head Well Lost*, III, No matter whether I bee a foole or a phisitian, if I loose, Ile pay. *c.*1645: MS. Proverbs, in *N. & Q.*, vol cliv., p. 27, Every man is either a foole or a physitian. 1678: *The Quacks Academy … A New Art to cross the Old Proverb, and make a Man a Fool and Physician both at a Time* [title], in *Harl. Miscell.*, ii (1744). 1707: Dunton, *Athen. Sport*, p. 13, col. 1, Remember, Every man is a fool, or physician to himself at least. 1732: Fuller, 1428, Every man is a fool, or a physician, at forty. 1777: in *Garrick Corresp.*, ii 219 (1832) [as in 1732]. 1793: O'Keeffe, *World in a Village*, III i [as in 1732].

16. A fool thinketh himself wise. 1557: North, *Diall of Princes*, fo. 91 v°, He may be called a foole that … auaunceth him selfe to be wise. 1601: Shakespeare, *As You Like It*, V i, I do now remember a saying, 'The fool doth think he is wise, but the wise man knows himself to be a fool'.

17. A fool wants [lacks] his cloak on a rainy day. 1732: Fuller, 110.

18. A fool when he hath spoke hath done all, or, **A fool is known by his speech.** 1303: R. Brunne, *Handl. Synne*, l. 2970, By foly wurdys mow men a foyle kenne. 1412–20: Lydgate, *Troy Book*, bk ii l. 7022, For be his tonge a fole is ofte knowe. 1570: Barclay, *Mirrour of Good Manners*, 73 (Spens.S.), A foole is knowen by speche negligent. 1611: Cotgrave, s.v. 'Fol', Fools are wise until they speake. 1732: Fuller, 111, A fool, when he hath spoke, hath done all.

19. A fool will ask more questions than the wisest can answer. 1666: Torriano, *Piazza Univ.*, 69, A fool may ask more than seven wise men can answer. 1670: Ray, 91, A fool may ask more questions in an hour, then a wise man can answer in seven years. 1738: Swift, *Polite Convers.*, Dial. II. 1821: Scott, *Pirate*, ch xviii, He knows a fool may ask more questions than a wise man cares to answer. 1901: F. E. Taylor, *Lancs Sayings*, 7, A foo' con ax mooar questions i' five minits nor a wise mon con answer i' a month.

20. A fool will laugh when he is drowning. 1577: *Misogonus*, I ii, A foole in laughture puttethe all his pleasure. 1616: Breton, in *Works*, ii *e* 6 (Grosart), A foole is euer laughing. 1659: Howell, *Proverbs: Brit.-Eng.*, 2.

21. A fool will not be foiled. 1659: Ibid.,22. 1710: S.Palmer, *Moral Essays on Proverbs*, 127.

22. A fool will not part with his bauble for the Tower of London. Before 1500: in Hill, *Commonplace-Book*, 130 (E.E.T.S.) [with 'geve' for 'part with']. 1509: Barclay, *Ship of Fools*, i 256 (1874), For it is sayd of men both yonge and olde A foole wyll nat gyue his babyll for any golde. 1599: Porter, *Two Angry Women*, in Hazlitt, *Old Plays*, vii 359 [with 'leave' for 'part with']. 1630: T. Adams, *Works*, 774, The foole will not giue his bable for the Kings Exchequer. 1662: Fuller, *Worthies*, ii 342 (1840). 1716: E. Ward, *Female Policy*, 86, Some would not give their babel for the Tower of London. 1790: Grose, *Prov. Gloss.*, s.v. 'London'.

23. A fool's bell is soon rung. *c.*1400: *Rom. Rose*, l. 5266, And fooles can not holde hir tunge; A fooles belle is sone range.

24. A fool's bolt is soon shot. *c.*1270: *Prov. of Alfred*, in *O. E. Miscell.*, 128 (Morris), And sottes bolt is sone i-scohte. *c.*1320: in *Reliq. Antiquae*, i III (1841), 'Sottes bolt is sone shote'; Quoth Hendyng. *c.*1460: *Good Wyfe wold a Pylgr.*, l. 95, A follis bolt ys son i-schot. 1583: Greene, in *Works*, ii 79 (Grosart). 1600: Shakespeare, *Henry V*, III vii 1667: Lord Bristol, *Elvira*, V, How soon a fool's bolt's shot without distinction. 1748: Smollett, *Rod. Random*, ch liii, 'Zounds, I have done,' said he.

'Your bolt is soon shot, according to the old proverb,' said she. 1826: Brady, *Varieties of Lit.*, 21, The implement shot from the cross-bow is called ... by the English a bolt. Hence the saying ... 'the fool's bolt is soonest shot'. 1847: Planché, *Extravag.*, iii 198 (1879).

25. A fool's bolt may sometimes hit the white. 1732: Fuller, 107.

26. A fool's handsel is lucky. 1614: Jonson, *Bart. Fair*, II, Bring him a sixpenny bottle of ale: they say, a fool's handsel is lucky. 1668: Dryden, *Sir Martin Markall*, V iii, A fool's plot may be as lucky as a fool's handsel.

27. A fool's heart is in his tongue. 1566: Drant, *Horace: Satires*, Sat. 2, That sillye foole ... His harte is euer in his toungue. 1622: P. Hannay, *Poet. Works*, 184 (Hunt.Cl.), The wise man's tongue is euer in his heart; The fooles heart's in his tongue. 1641: Quarles, *Enchyridion*, Cent. III cap. lv. 1669: *Politeuphuia*, 37, The heart of a fool is in his mouth. Cf. **Wise**, *adj.* (50).

28. A fool's paper. *See* **White** (11).

29. A fool's paradise. 1462: *Paston Lett.*, ii 109 (Gairdner, 1900), But I wold not be in a folis paradyce. 1549: *Mathew's Bible*, 2 Kings, ch iv, Dyd I desyre a sonne of my Lorde? Dyd I not say that thou shouldest not brynge me in a foles paradyse. 1604: Webster and Marston, *Malcontent*, V iii, Promise of matrimony by a yong gallant, to bring a virgin lady into a fooles paradise! 1632: R. Brome, *Northern Lasse*, V viii, Why I am fubdoodled thus. In I protest and vow a kind of fools Paradise. 1732: Fielding, *Mod. Husband*, I ix, A levee is the paradise of fools. 1894: R.L.S., *St Ives*, ch xxvi, The next moment I had recognised the inanity of that fool's paradise. 1914: Shaw, 'Parents and Children', in *Misalliance*, *etc.*, p. cxiii, A means of pleasing himself and beguiling tedious hours with romances and fairy tales and fools' paradises.

30. A fool's speech is a bubble of air. 1732: Fuller, 109.

31. A fool's tongue is long enough to cut his own throat. Ibid., No. 108.

32. Answer a fool according to his folly. [Answer a fool according to his folly lest he be wise in his own conceit. – *Prov.* xxvi 5.] 1484: Caxton, *Aesope*, ii 175 (Jacobs), To foolish demur [question] behoveth a foolish answer. 1589: Nashe, in *Works*, i 166 (Grosart), It is therefore thought the best way ... to answere the

fooles, according to their foolishness. 1692: L'Estrange, *Aesop*, 10 (3rd ed.), It does not yet become a man of honour ... to answer every fool in his folly. 1740: North, *Lives of Norths*, i 332 (Bohn), And so fools are often answered in their folly.

33. As the fool thinks, so the bell clinks. 1607: *Lingua*, III vii, As the fool thinketh, so the bell clinketh. I protest I hear no more than a post. 1673: Marvell, *Rehearsal Transpr.*, Pt II, in *Works*, iii 387 (Grosart), I understand, sir, what you mean; 'as the fool thinks, so the conscience tinks'. 1738: Swift, *Polite Convers.*, Dial. I, *Miss.* Peace! I think I hear the church-clock. *Neverout.* Why, you know, as the fool thinks ... 1831: Hone, *Year-Book*, 455, As the bell tinks, so the fool thinks; As the fool tinks, so the bell tinks.

34. Bray a fool in a mortar, etc. [Though thou shouldest bray a fool in a mortar among wheat with a pestle, yet will not his foolishness depart from him. – *Prov.* xxvii 22.] *c.*1568: Wager, *Longer thou Livest*, sig. D2, Beate a foole in a morter saith the wise man, and thou shalt not make him leaue his folly. 1694: D'Urfey, *Quixote*, Pt I Act V sc ii, Bray a fool in a mortar, and you'll find all of him but his brains. 1855: Kingsley, *West. Ho!*, ch v.

35. By their words we know fools, and asses by their ears. 1586: L. Evans, *Revised Withals Dict.*, sig. C4.

36. Every fool can find faults that a great many wise men can't remedy. 1732: Fuller, 1416.

37. Every fool is a fiddle to the company. 1616: Sharpham, *Cupid's Whirligig*, IV, They say, euery foole is a fiddle to the companie.

38. Fool's haste is no speed. 1732: Fuller, 1575. 1827: Scott, *Journal*, 12 Jan., I wish it may not prove fool's haste, yet I take as much pains too as is in my nature.

39. Fools and foumarts [polecats]. *See* quot. 1898: *N. & Q.*, 9th ser, ii 88, 'Fools and foumards can't see by day-leet'. I heard this near here [Epworth] the other day.

40. Fools and little dogs are ladies' play-fellows. 1583: Melbancke, *Philotinus*, sig. T3.

41. Fools and madmen speak the truth. 1621: Burton, *Melancholy*, II III viii 429 (1836), For fools and mad men tell commonly truth. 1634: Massinger, *Very Woman*, III i, Wilt thou be my fool? for fools, they say, will tell truth. 1791: Mrs Thrale, in Hayward, *Mrs Piozzi*, i 342 (2nd ed.),

He is quite light-headed, yet madmen, drunkards, and fools tell truth, they say.

42. Fools are all the world over, as he said that shod the goose. 1732: Fuller, 1567. 1880: Spurgeon, *Ploughman's Pictures*, 141.

43. Fools are known by their babbling. 1477: Rivers, *Dictes and Sayings*, 57 (1877), A man may knowe a fole by his moche clatering. 1597: H. Lok, *Ecclesiastes*, 98, Fooles if they once begin, can neuer end. 1641: Jonson, *Timber:* 'Homeri Ulysses', For too much talking is ever the indice of a fool. 1647: *Countrym. New Commonwealth*, 10, Fooles are known by their bablings.

44. Fools are of all sizes. 1901: F. E. Taylor, *Lancs Sayings*, 9, Ther's foo's ov o sizes.

45. Fools are pleased with their own blunders. 1732: Fuller, 1570.

46. Fools are weatherwise. 1887: M. A. Courtney, *Folk-Lore Journal*, v 192, Here [Cornwall] it is well known that 'fools are weatherwise', and that 'those that are weatherwise are rarely otherwise'. 1906: *Cornish N.&Q.*, 271.

47. Fools are wise men in the affairs of women. 1732: Fuller, 1571.

48. Fools build houses and wise men buy them. 1670: Ray, 91. 1732: Fuller, 1573 [with 'enjoy' for 'buy']. *c.*1860: R. S. Hawker, in Byles, *Life, etc.*, 82 (1905) [with 'inhabit' for 'buy']. 1875: A. B. Cheales, *Proverb. Folk-Lore*, 43 [with 'live in' for 'buy'].

49. Fools give, to please all but their own. 1640: Herbert, *Jac. Prudentum.*

50. Fools grow without watering. 1732: Fuller, 1574. 1853: Trench, *Proverbs*, 73 (1905).

51. Fools have fortune. *c.*1568: Wager, *Longer thou Livest*, sig. E2, They say that fooles are fortunable. 1639: Glapthorne, *Wit in a Constable*, III, The old proverbe, of fooles have fortune. 1720: *Vade Mecum for Malt-worms*, Pt II p. 22, Dick ... fulfills the proverb which says, Fools have fortune. *c.*1760: Garrick, *Lying Valet*, 11. Cf. **Fortune favours fools**; and **God sends fortune**.

52. Fools lade the water and wise men catch the fish. 15th cent.: in *Babees Book*, 332 (Furnivall), Folus [Fools] lade polys [pools]; wisemenn ete the fysshe. 1605: Camden, *Remains*, 322 (1870). 1670: Ray, 92. 1732: Fuller, 1581, Fools lade out all the water, and wise men take the fish.

53. Fools laugh at their own sport. 1855: Bohn, 356.

54. Fools live poor to die rich. Ibid., 356.

55. Fools love all that is good. 1738: Swift, *Polite Convers.*, Dial. I, I'm like all fools; I love everything that's good. Cf. **Lord Mayor's fool**.

56. Fools make feasts and wise men eat them. 1578: Florio, *First Fruites*, fo. 30, Fooles make the banquets, and wise men enjoy them. 1683: Meriton, *Yorkshire Ale*, 83–7 (1697). 1736: Franklin, *Way to Wealth*, in *Works*, i 447 (Bigelow). 1823: D'Israeli, *Cur. of Lit.*, 2nd ser, i 449 (1824), A great man in Scotland, who, having given a splendid entertainment, was harshly told that 'Fools make feasts, and wise men eat them ...'

57. Fools may invent fashions that wise men will wear. 1732: Fuller, 1579.

58. Fools never know when they are well. 1519: Horman, *Vulgaria*, fo. 67, He is a foole that can nat holde hym selfe content whan he is well at ease. 1794: Wolcot, in *Works*, ii 528 (1795), Fools never know when they are well. 1822: Scott, *Nigel*, ch xxi, 'Tis always thus – fools and children never know when they are well.

59. Fools no Latin know. 1869: Hazlitt, 134.

60. Fools refuse favours. 1659: Howell, *Proverbs: Brit.-Eng.*, 22.

61. Fools rush in where angels fear to tread. 1711: Pope, *Essay on Criticism*, l. 625, No Place so Sacred from such Fops is barr'd, Nor is Paul's Chruch more safe than Paul's Church-yard: Nay, fly to Altars: there they'll talk you dead; For Fools rush in where Angels fear to tread. 1858: G.J. McRee, *Iredell's Life and Correspondence*, II 277, Rash presumption illustrates the line, 'Fools rush in where angels fear to tread'.

62. Fools set stools for wise men to stumble at. 1605: Camden, *Remains*, 322 (1870). 1613: S. Rowley, *When You See Me*, sig. F3, Yee know what the old prouerbe saies ... When fooles set stocks, and wise men breake their shinnes. 1670: Ray, 91. 1754: Berthelson, *Eng.-Danish Dict.*, s.v. 'Fool'. 1880: Spurgeon, *Ploughman's Pictures*, 141.

63. Fools should not see half done work. I am not sure that this is not a purely Scottish saying. 1818: Scott, in Lockhart's *Life*, iv 216, It is not fit to be shown to 'bairns and fools', who, according to our old canny proverb, should never see half done work.

64. Fools tie knots and wise men loose them. 1639: Clarke, 88. 1670: Ray, 10. 1732: Fuller, 1583.

65. Fools will be fools. 1650: R. Heath, *Satyrs*, 9, Fools will still be fools. 1784: *New Foundl. Hosp. for Wit*, ii 201, Fools will be fools, say what we will.

66. Fools will be meddling. *c.*1380: Chaucer, *Parl. of Foules*, l. 574, But sooth is seyd, 'a fool can noght be stille'. 1670: Ray, 91. 1738: Swift, *Polite Convers.*, Dial. I, Why, madam, fools will be meddling. 1822: Scott, *Nigel*, ch xxiii, Beasts and fools will be meddling, my lord.

67. Fools' paradises are wise men's purgatories. 1763: Colman, *Deuce is in Him*, I i, A fool's paradise is better than a wiseacre's purgatory. 1922: Saintsbury, *Scrap-Book*, 254.

68. Fools' thoughts often fail. *c.*1374: Chaucer, *Troylus*, bk i l. 217, But alday fayleth thing that foolës wenden [imagined], *c.*1387: Usk, *Test. of Love*, ii 8, 122, Thus alday fayleth thinges that fooles wende. *c.*1534: Berners, *Huon*, 502 (E.E.T.S.), It is a comune sayng that many thingis lackethe of folysshe thoughtis.

69. Give a fool a candle to tind [light], He will light it at the ind. 1883: Burne, *Shropsh. Folk-Lore*, 588.

70. He hath great need of a fool that plays the fool himself. 1640: Herbert, *Jac. Prudentum.*

71. He is a fool that deals with fools. *c.*1350: *Parlement of Three Ages*, l. 264 (Gollancz), Fole es that with foles delys.

72. He is a fool that forgets himself. *c.*1270: in *Old Eng. Miscell.*, 59 (Morris, E.E.T.S.). Sot is that is other mannes freond more than his owe. *c.*1374: Chaucer, *Troylus*, bk v l. 98, I have herd seyd, eek tymes twyës twelve, 'He is a fool that wol for-yete himselve'. 1611: Cotgrave, s.v. 'Fol', Hee is a right foole that forgets himselfe. 1683: Meriton, *Yorkshire Ale*, 83–7 (1697).

73. He is a fool that is not melancholy once a day. 1678: Ray, 346. 1683: Meriton, *Yorkshire Ale*, 83–7 (1697), He is a feaul that is not mallancholy yance a day. 1732: Fuller, 2434.

74. He is a fool that makes a wedge of his fist. 1611: Cotgrave, s.v. 'Coing'. 1666: Torriano, *Piazza Univ.*, 221.

75. He is a fool that thinks not that another thinks. 1640: Herbert, *Jac. Prudentum.*

76. He is fool enough himself, who will bray against another ass. 1855: Bohn, 375.

77. He is not the fool that the fool is, but he that with the fool deals. 1683: Meriton, *Yorkshire Ale*, 83–7 (1697).

78. He's a fool that is wiser abroad than at home. 1732: Fuller, 2435.

79. He's a fool. *See* quot. 1846: Denham, *Proverbs*, 65 (Percy S.), He's a fule that marries at Yule; For when the bairn's to bear, The corn's to shear. 1904: *Co. Folk-Lore: Northumb.*, 179 (F.L.S.) [as in 1846].

80. He that sends a fool means to follow him. 1640: Herbert, *Jac. Prudentum.* 1659: Howell, 3, Who sendeth a fool upon an errand, must goe himself after.

81. He who is born a fool is never cured. 1732: Fuller, 2391.

82. If all fools had baubles we should want fuel. 1611: Cotgrave, s.v. 'Marotte', If all that fooles are bables wore, of wood we should have but small store. 1670: Ray, 10, If all fools ware babies fewel would be dear. 1732: Fuller, 2676, If every fool were to wear a bauble, they would grow dear.

83. If all fools wore white caps, we should seem a flock of geese. 1640: Herbert, *Jac. Prudentum.*

84. If fools should not fool it, they shall lose their reason. Ibid.

85. It is the property of fools to be always judging. 1732: Fuller, 3027.

86. Much abides behind what a fool thinks. *c.*1489: Caxton, *Blanchardyn, etc.*, 181 (E.E.T.S.), It ys sayd often in a comyn langage that 'moche abydeth behynde that a fole thynketh'.

87. No one is a fool always, every one sometimes. 1640: Herbert, *Jac. Prudentum.* 1694: D'Urfey, *Quixote*, Pt I Act I sc i, None arc fools always, tho every one sometimes. 1748: Richardson, *Clarissa*, iv 237 (1785). 1854: J. W. Warter, *Last of Old Squires*, 53.

88. One fool in a play is more than enough. Derby. 1889: *Folk-Lore Journal*, vii 293.

89. One fool makes many. 1640: Herbert, *Jac. Prudentum*, One fool makes a hundred. 1654: Gayton, *Pleasant Notes Don Q.*, 140. 1769: Brooke, *Fool of Quality*, iv 228. 1821: Byron, *The Blues*, Ecl. i l. 57. 1860: Reade, *Cl. and Hearth*, ch lxxiv, Loose tongue found credulous ears, and so one fool made many.

90. Only fools and fiddlers sing at meals. 1813: Ray, 9, None but fools and fiddlers sing at their meat. 1889: *Folk-Lore Journal*, vii 293 (Derbyshire).

91. Play with a fool at home, and he will play with you in the market. 1640: Herbert, *Jac. Prudentum*. 1670: Ray, 10. 1732: Fuller, 2763.

92. Send a fool to the market, and a foole he'll return. 1586: G. Whitney, *Emblems*, 178, The foole, that farre is sente some wisedome to attaine; Returnes an ideot, as he wente, and bringes the foole againe. 1604: *Pasquils Jests*, 38 (1864), You may all depart like fooles as you came. 1666: Torriano, *Piazza Univ.*, 147, Who sends a fool expects the same back again. 1732: Fuller, 4096. 1738: Swift, *Polite Convers.*, Dial. I, You may go back again, like a fool as you came.

93. Set a fool to catch a fool. 1654: Gayton, *Pleasant Notes Don Q.*, 178, As they say, set a fool, etc.

94. Set a fool to roast eggs, and a wise man to eat them. 1678: Ray, 241.

95. That which a fool doth at last, a wise man doth at first. 1666: Torriano, *Piazza Univ.*, 197. 1880: Spurgeon, *Ploughman's Pictures*, 20, A wise man does at first what a fool does at last.

96. The first chapter of fools is to esteem themselves wise. 1578: Florio, *First Fruites*, fo. 29 [with 'count' for 'esteem']. 1586: Pettie, tr. Guazzo's *Civil Convers.*, fo. 40. 1659: Howell, 1 [with 'hold' for 'esteem']. 1732: Fuller, 4525.

97. The fool asks much, but he is more fool that grants it. 1633: Draxe, 21. 1670: Ray, 10. 1732: Fuller, 100, A fool demands much; but he's a greater that gives it.

98. The fool is busy in every one's business but his own. 1732: Fuller, 4537.

99. The fool runs away while his house is burning down. Ibid., No. 4538.

100. The fool saith, who would have thought it? 1633: Draxe, 13, It is the part of a foole to say, I had not thought. 1732: Fuller, 4539.

101. The fool wanders, the wise man travels. Ibid., No. 4540.

102. The higher the fool, the greater the fall. 1878: J. Platt, *Morality*, 34.

103. The more riches a fool hath, the greater fool he is. 1732: Fuller, 4666.

104. The praise of fools is censure in disguise. 1855: Bohn, 513.

105. There is no fool like the old fool. 1546: Heywood, *Proverbs*, Pt II ch ii, There is no foole

to the olde foole, folke say. 1592: Lyly, *Mother Bombie*, IV ii 1616: Breton, in *Works*, ii *e*6 (Grosart). 1712: Gay, *Mohocks*, sc ii, Oh Peter, Peter! an old fool of all fools is the worst. 1856: Planché, *Extravag.*, v 157 (1879), In love there's no fool, madam, like an old fool. 1922: Weyman, *Ovington's Bank*, ch viii.

106. To deal fool's dole. 1670: Ray, 171.

107. To the counsel of fools, a wooden bell. 1640: Herbert, *Jac. Prudentum*.

108. We are fools one to another. Ibid.

109. Were there no fools bad ware would not be sold. 1611: Cotgrave, s.v. 'Marché', If fooles went not to markets bad wares would not be sold. 1696: D'Urfey, *Quixote*, Pt III Act I [as in 1611, with 'coxcombs' for 'fooles']. 1732: Fuller, 2677 [as in 1611]. 1869: Spurgeon, *John Ploughman*, ch xvi [as in 1611].

110. When a fool hath bethought himself, the market's over. 1732: Fuller, 5530.

111. When the fool finds a horse-shoe, He thinks always so to do. Ibid., No. 6415.

See also **April** (23); **Certainty; Children** (2) and (3); **Experience; Fortune favours; God sends fortune; Honour** (4); **Many a one; None but fools; None is so wise; Robin Hood** (9); **Wise**, *passim*; **Wit** (4); **Woman** (5); and **World** (7) and (10).

Foolish fear doubleth danger. 1732: Fuller, 1563.

Foolish pity spoils a city. 1556: Heywood, *Spider and Flie*, cap. 70, p. 307 (Farmer), This … Is either not pity, or peevish pity, Which (as th' old saying saith) marreth the city. 1613: Wither, *Abuses Stript, etc.*, bk i sat. 13, A foolish pitty quickly ouerthrowes, In warre an army, and in peace a state. 1670: Ray, 131. 1732: Fuller, 6216 ['ruins' for 'spoils'].

Foolish tongues talk by the dozen. 1640: Herbert, *Jac. Prudentum*.

Foot and **Feet. 1. He thinks his feet be where his head shall never come.** 1546: Heywood, *Proverbs*, Pt I, ch xi 1611: Davies (of Hereford), *Sc. of Folly*, 49, in *Works*, ii (Grosart), Some thinke their feete be where their head shall neuer come.

2. The foot on the cradle, the hand on the distaff. 1659: Howell, *Proverbs: Span.-Eng.*, 2, [*plus*] a sign of a good housewife. 1670: Ray, 14 [as in 1659]. 1732: Fuller, 4541.

3. Thy foot is longer than thy leg. 1917: Bridge,

Cheshire Proverbs, 124, Thou'rt like a butter-bump [bittern], thy foot's longer than thy leg.

4. To have (or know) the length of one's foot. 1580: Lyly, *Euphues*, 290 (Arber), You shal not know the length of my foote, vntill by your cunning you get commendation. 1603: Dekker, in *Works*, i 263 (Grosart), Having now the full length of his foot, then shewes she herselfe what she is. *c.*1663: Davenant, *Play-House to be Let*, V, Well, gossip, I know too the length of your foote. 1720: C. Shadwell, *Irish Hospit.*, II, What I speak is in my own praise, 'tis a very easy matter to get the length of my foot. 1858: Hughes, *White Horse*, ch iii, I have got the length of his foot, and he has asked me to luncheon. 1922: Weyman, *Ovington's Bank*, ch xix, He had taken the length of the Squire's foot.

5. To thrust one's feet under another man's table. 1678: Ray, 272. 1732: Fuller, 5247.

See also **Best** (34); **Leg** (4) and (5); and **One Foot.**

Football. *See* **All fellows**; and **Two to one.**

For ill do well, then fear not hell. 1855: Bohn, 357.

For mad words deaf ears. 1633: Draxe, 69, For foolish talke deafe eares. 1732: Fuller, 1593.

For my part. *See* **Kiln** (1).

Forbearance is no acquittance. 1546: Heywood, *Proverbs*, Pt II ch iv, Sufferaunce is no quittance. 1578: Florio, *First Fruites*, fo. 33, Forbearance is no payment. 1605: T. Heywood, *If You Know Not Me*, in *Works*, i 332 (1874). 1670: Ray, 92. 1732: Fuller, 1587.

Forbidden fruit is the sweetest. [with allusion to Genesis iii 6] *c.*1386: Chaucer, *Parson's Tale*, i 332, The flessh hadde delit in the beautee of the fruyt defended. 1661: *The Wandering Whore*, Pt v ii, The forbidden fruit is sweetest. 1855: Bohn, 357.

Force without fore-cast is of little avail. 1732: Fuller, 1589.

Forced kindness deserres no thanks, A. Ibid., No. 113.

Forced put. *See* quots. 1657: G. Starkey, *Helmont's Vind.*, 328 (OED), To give poysons to purge, in expectation that Nature being forced to play a desperate game, and reduced to a forc't put, may … 1678: Ray, 79, He's at a forc't put. 1754: Berthelson, *Eng.-Danish Dict.*, s.v. 'Put', 'Tis a forced put. 1880: Courtney, *W. Cornwall Words*, 23 (E.D.S.), A fo'ced put is no choice.

Ford. 1. Never praise a ford till you get over. 1633: Draxe, 51, It is not good praysing of a foord, vntill a man be ouer. 1670: Ray, 92 [as in 1633]. 1754: Berthelson,. *Eng.-Danish Dict.*, s.v. 'Ford'.

2. To take the ford as one finds it. 1575: Gascoigne, *Posies*, 6 (Cunliffe), Yet is it true that I must take the foord as I finde it: sometimes not as I woulde, but as I may. 1817: Scott, *Rob Roy*, ch xxvii, Let ilka ane roose the ford as they find it.

Forecast is better than work hard. 1612: Chapman, *Widow's Tears*, II iv [with 'labour' for 'work hard']. 1670: Ray, 92. 1732: Fuller, 1588.

Forehand pay. *See* quots. 1886: Elworthy, *West Som. Word-Book*, 186 (E.D.S.), Hence the old saying 'Vore-hand-pay and never-pay's the wist [worst] of all pay'. 1894: Northall, *Folk Phrases*, 13 (E.D.S.), Forehanded pay is the worst pay as is. Cf. **Pay** (4).

Forehead and the eye, In the, the lecture of the mind doth lie. 1633: Draxe, 60, ['heart is read' for last three words]. 1670: Ray, 92. 1754: Berthelson, *Eng.-Danish Dict.*, s.v. 'Lecture'. Cf. **Face** (4).

Foreheet [Predetermine] **nothing but building churches and louping over them, I'll.** 1678: Ray, 355. 1683: Meriton, *Yorkshire Ale*, 83–7 (1697) [with 'Fore-sheet' for 'Foreheet']. 1691: Ray, *Words not Generally Used*, 43 (E.D.S.).

Fore-horse by the head. *See* quots. 1875: Parish, *Sussex Dict.*, 45, 'He has got the fore-horse by the head' is a Sussex expression for 'he has got matters well in hand'. 1894: Northall, *Folk Phrases*, 28 (E.D.S.), To get the forehorse by the head = To get out of debt: to see one's way clear, etc.

Forelock. *See* **Time** (7).

Forewarned is forearmed, or in some early examples, **half-armed.** [Egon' ut cavere nequeam, cui praedicitur? – Plautus, *Pseudol.*, I v 101.] *c.*1425: J. Arderne, *Treatises of Fistula* (E.E.T.S.), 22, He that is warned afore is noght bygiled. Before 1500: in Hill, *Commonplace-Book*, 132 (E.E.T.S.), He that is warned ys half armed, *c.*1569: in Collmann, *Ballads and Broadsides*, 194 (Roxb.Cl), But they that warned are in tyme, Halfe armed are gainst daungerous crime. 1587: Greene, in *Works*, iv 154 (Grosart), By his fore-warning, thou hadst bene fore-armed. 1620: Shelton, *Quixote*, Pt II ch xvii, He that is warned is half armed. 1673: Wycherley, *Gent. Danc.-Master*, V i 1712: *Spectator*, No. 395.

1834: Marryat, *P. Simple*, ch liv., I now knew the ground which I stood upon; and forewarned was being forearmed. Cf. **Once warned**.

Forget, *verb*. **1. To forget a wrong is the best revenge.** 1639: Clarke, 324. 1670: Ray, 92. *c*.1800: Trusler, *Prov. in Verse*, 101, To forget an injury is the best revenge. Cf. **Forgive** (4).

2. We have all forgot more than we remember. 1732: Fuller, 5442.

Forgetful head makes a weary pair of heels, A. 1869: Hazlitt, 12.

Forgive, *verb*. **1. Forgive and forget.** Before 1225: *Ancren R.*, 124 (OED), Al thet hurt and al thet sore were uorziten and forziuen uor glednesse. 1546: Heywood, *Proverbs*, Pt II ch iii, All our great fraie … Is forgeuen and forgotten betwene vs quight. *c*.1605: Shakespeare, *Lear*, IV vii, Pray you now, forget and forgive. 1696: Southerne, *Oroonoko*, V ii, Endeavour to forget, sir, and forgive. 1792: Holcroft, *Road to Ruin*, V iii, We ought all to forget and forgive. 1823: Scott, *Peveril*, ch xxv, Years had taught Deborah to forget and forgive. 1921: 22 June, King George V, *Speech* at Belfast, opening Ulster Parl., I appeal to all Irishmen to pause, to stretch out the hand of forbearance and conciliation, to forgive and to forget.

2. Forgive any sooner than thyself. 1670: Ray, 10.

3. If we are bound to forgive an enemy, we are not bound to trust him. 1732: Fuller, 2728.

4. Revenge a wrong by forgiving it. 1710: S. Palmer, *Moral Essays on Proverbs*, 81, Forgiveness and a smile is the best revenge. 1831: Hone, *Year-Book*, col. 1417. 1853: Trench, *Proverbs*, 13 (1905), *The noblest vengeance is to forgive:* here is the godlike proverb. Cf. **Forget** (1).

Fork. *I ask you for a fork and you bring me a rake*. 1732: Fuller, 2587. *See also* **Rake**.

Forkle-end. *See* quot. 'Forkle-end' is not in Wright's *Eng. Dialect Dict.* 1869: Hazlitt, 201, He's standing on his forkle-end. S. Devon: i.e. he's well and on his legs, able to get about. – Shelly.

Forms keep fools at a distance. *c*.1750: Foote, *Englishm. returned from Paris*, II, They say forms keep fools at a distance.

Fort *See* **Castle** (2).

Fortunate boor needs but be born, A. 1659: Howell, *Proverbs: Brit.-Eng.*, 26.

Fortunate man may be any where, A. 1732: Fuller, 114.

Fortune and love. *See* quot. Before 1704: T. Brown, in *Works*, iii 167 (1760), The ancient proverb, which says, that fortune and love don't always favour the most deserving.

Fortune can take from us nothing but what she gave us. 1732: Fuller, 1598.

Fortune favour, If. *See* quot. 1670: Ray, 212, If fortune favour I may have her, for I go about her; If fortune fail you may kiss her tail, and go without her.

Fortune favours fools. 1546: J. Heywood, *Dialogue of Proverbs*, ii vi I1v, They saie as ofte, god sendeth fortune to fooles. 1563: Googe, *Eglogs, etc.*, 74 (Arber), But Fortune favours fooles as old men saye. 1599: Jonson, *Ev. Man out of Humour*, I i, *M*. One of those that fortune favours. *C.* The periphrasis of a fool. 1687: Sedley, *Bellamira*, II, Does my patron lose? fortune favours fools. 1737: Gay, *Fables*, 2nd ser, No. 12, l. 119, 'Tis a gross error, held in schools, That Fortune always favours fools. Cf. **Fool** (51); and **God sends fortune**.

Fortune favours the brave (or **bold**). [Fortes fortuna adjuvat. – Terence, *Phorm.*, I iv 26. Audentes fortuna juvat. – Virgil, *Aen.*, x 284. Audentes deus ipse juvat. – Ovid, *Met.*, x 586.] *c*.1385: Chaucer, *Leg. Good Women*, V, Lucretia, l. 94, 'Hap helpeth hardy man alday', quod he. *c*.1390: Gower, *Conf. Amantis*, bk vii l. 4902, And seith 'Fortune unto the bolde Is favorable forto helpe'. 1481: Caxton, *Reynard*, 66 (Arber), Who that is hardy the auenture helpeth him. 1594: Drayton, *Ideas*, lix, Fortune assists the boldest, I reply. 1674: Head and Kirkman, *Eng. Rogue*, iii 142, Fortune helps the bold. 1731: Swift, *Strephon and Chloe*, l. 148, Who had been often told That fortune still assists the bold. 1752: in W. Johnson, *Papers* (1919), IX 86, Make no doubt but that Fortune will favour the brave. 1840: Barham, *Ing. Legends*, 1st ser: 'Grey Dolphin', Fortune … delights to favour the bold. 1885: A. Trollope, *Dr Thorne*, II vii, Fortune, who ever favours the brave, specially favoured Frank Gresham.

Fortune helps him that is willing to help himself. 1611: Cotgrave, s.v. 'Aider'.

Fortune is variant *See* quots. *c*.1420: Lydgate, *Assembly of Gods*, st. 46, p. 10 (E.E.T.S.), Varyaunt she [Fortune] was; ay in short space

Hyr whele was redy to turne without let. *c.*1490: *Partonope*, l. 4389 (E.E.T.S.), Lo, thus ffortune can turne hur dyse Nowe vp, nowe doune; here whele ys vnstabelle. 1509: Barclay, *Ship of Fools*, i 126 (1874), Fortune euer hath an incertayne end. 1692: L'Estrange, *Aesop*, 15 (3rd ed.), The wheel of time, and of fortune is still rolling. 1712: Motteux, *Quixote*, Pt I bk iv ch xx, The old proverb is true again, fortune turns round like a mill-wheel, and he that was yesterday at the top, lies to-day at the bottom. *c.*1824: in Farmer, *Musa Pedestris*, 91, But fortune fickle, ever on the wheel …

Fortune knocks once at least at every man's gate. 1567: Fenton, *Bandello*, ii 148 (T.T.), Fortune once in the course of our life dothe put into our handes the offer of a good torne. 1869: Hazlitt, 136.

Fortune rarely brings good or evil singly. 1732: Fuller, 1605.

Fortune smiles, When, embrace her. 1670: Ray, 10, When fortune smiles on thee, take the advantage. 1732: Fuller, 5553. 1736: Bailey, *Dict.*, s.v. 'Fortune', When fortune knocks be sure to open the door.

Fortune to one is mother, to another is stepmother. 1651: Herbert, *Jac. Prudentum*, 2nd ed.

Forty save one. *See* quots. 1841: Hartshorne, *Salopia Ant.*, 520 [with long explanatory legend, pp. 520–2], Forty sa [save] one like Obitch's [? Holbeach's] cowt. 1883: Burne, *Shropsh. Folk-Lore*, 593, Forty save one, like Rhoden's colt … sometimes 'like Obitch's colt', but not, I think, correctly. 'Obitch's' colt was a spectre.

Foul in the cradle and fair in the saddle. 1605: Camden, *Remains*, 322 (1870), Foul in the cradle proveth fair in the saddle. 1659: Howell, 8. 1754: Berthelson, *Eng.-Danish Dict.*, s.v. 'Foul'. 1889: *Folk-Lore Journal*, vii 292, [Derby sayings] Fou' i' th' cradle, fair i' th' saddle. Cf. **Fair in the cradle.**

Foul water is thrown down the sink. 1683: White Kennett, tr. Erasmus' *Praise of Folly*, 142 (8th ed.), I will take the proverb for a satisfactory reply; namely, *Foul water is thrown down the sink*; which saying, that no person may slight it, may be convenient to advertise that it comes from no meaner an author than that oracle of truth, Aristotle himself.

Foul water will quench fire as well as fair. Sometimes used to suggest that any woman, however ugly etc., can be used to slake a man's sexual appetite. 1546: Heywood, *Proverbs*, Pt I ch v. As this proverbe saieth, for quenchyng hot desire, Foul water as soon as fayre, wyl quenche hot fire. 1592: Lyly, *Mother Bombie*, III iv, Yet I hope foule water will quench hot fire as soone as faire. 1616: *Jack Drum*, I, in Simpson, *Sch. of Shakesp.*, ii 144, Foule water quencheth fire well enough. 1670: Ray, 154, Foul water will quench fire. 1732: Fuller, 1607 [as in 1670].

Four bare legs. *See* **Marriage** (9).

Four eyes see more than two. 1591: A Colynet, *True History of the Civil Wars in France*, 37, Two eyes doo see more than one. 1592: G. Delamothe, *French Alphabet*, II 45, Foure eyes can see more then two.1666: Torriano, *Piazza Univ.*, 175, Four eyes see better than two. 1732: Fuller, 1606.

Four farthings and a thimble, Make a tailor's pocket jingle. 1659: Howell, 15. 1670: Ray, 215. 1732: Fuller, 6328.

Four things drive a man. *See* **Three things drive a man**.

Four things, it is said. *See* quot. 1809: Pegge, *Anonymiana*, cent. ix 45, Four things, it is said, are most to be desired: a good neighbour; a window to every man's heart; that men's tongues and hearts should go together; and an house upon wheels.

Four-pence for that advice, If I had given, I had bought it a groat too dear. 1732: Fuller, 2685.

Four-pence to a groat. *See* **Near as**.

Fowey, The gallants of. Corn. 1602: Carew, *Surv. of Cornwall*, 315 (1811), The merit of which exploit afterwards entitled them Gallants of Foy. 1790: Grose, *Prov. Gloss.*, s.v. 'Cornwall', The gallants of Foy. 1864: 'Cornish Proverbs', in *N. & Q.*, 3rd ser, v 275 … Gallants of Foy. 1904: *Morning Post*, 11 April, quoted in *N. & Q.*, 10th ser, i 505, It was stated that though no charter was in the possession of the parish [Fowey], their rights were traditionally inherited by a grant from the Black Prince, as Duke of Cornwall, in reward for services rendered at sea by 'the Gallants of Fowey', from which the village takes its name.

Fowl of a fair day, As glad as a. 1362: Langland, *Plowman*, A, xi 109, Thenne was I as fayn as foul on feir morwen. *c.*1386: Chaucer, *Canon's Yeoman's Tale*, l. 789, This sotted preest, who was gladder than he? Was never brid gladder agayn the day. *c.*1430: Lydgate, *Minor Poems*, 111 (Percy S.), Sir John was as glad of thys as ever was fowle of daye. 1598: *Servingm. Comfort*, in *Inedited Tracts*, 133 (Hazlitt), Who restes no lesse glad of his place, then the foule of a fayre day. 1639: Clarke, 185.

Fox and Foxes. 1. A fox should not be of the jury at a goose's trial. 1732: Fuller, 116.

2. An old fox need learn no craft. 1639: Clarke, 267. 1670: Ray, 127. 1732: Fuller, 644, An old fox needs not be taught tricks. Cf. Nos. 3 and 19.

3. An old fox understands a trap. 1539: Taverner, *Proverbs*, fo. 27, An olde foxe is not taken in a snare. 1540: Palsgrave, *Acolastus*, sig. Q3 [as in 1539]. 1732: Fuller, 645. 1880: Spurgeon, *Ploughman's Pictures*, 116, An old fox is shy of a trap. Cf. Nos. 2 and 19.

4. As cunning as a klyket [fox]. 1846–59: *Denham Tracts*, ii 107 (F.L.S.).

5. As long as you are in the fox's service, you must hold up his tail. 1738: *Gent. Mag.*, 475.

6. At length the fox is brought to the furrier. 1640: Herbert, *Jac. Prudentum*. 1666: Torriano, *Piazza Univ.*, 199, All foxes are found at the furriers shop. 1880: Spurgeon, *Ploughman's Pictures*, 18, They think it is time that the fox went to the furrier, and they had their share of his skin.

7. At length the fox turns monk. 1611: Cotgrave, s.v. 'Moine'. 1640: Herbert, *Jac. Prudentum*.

8. Every fox must pay his own skin to the flayer. 1639: Clarke, 215. 1670: Ray, 93. 1710: S. Palmer, *Moral Essays on Proverbs*, 123. 1846–59: *Denham Tracts*, ii 107 (F.L.S.).

9. Fie upon heps [query, misprint for 'hen'] **(quoth the fox) because he could not reach them.** 1678: Ray, 142.

10. Foxes dig not their oven holes. 1732: Fuller, 1608. 1846–59: *Denham Tracts*, ii 107 (F.L.S.).

11. Foxes when sleeping have nothing fall into their mouths. 1611: Cotgrave, s.v. 'Emphumé', The sleepy fox hath seldome feathered breakfasts. 1633: Draxe, 98, When the foxe sleepeth, nothing falleth into his mouth. 1670: Ray, 10. 1736: Franklin, *Way to Wealth*, in *Works*, i 443 (Bigelow), The sleeping fox catches no poultry.

12. Foxes are all tail and women all tongue. 1869: Spurgeon, *John Ploughman*, ch vi 1917: Bridge, *Cheshire Proverbs*, 58.

13. Good following the way where the old fox goes. 1639: Clarke, 146.

14. He does not know a fox from a fern-bush. 1587: Bridges, *Def. of Govt. in Church of Eng.*, 99, It seemed (as the saying is) either a foxe or a fearne brake. 1639: in *Berkeley MSS.*, iii 33 (1885), Beware the fox in a fearne bush … Hypocrisy often clokes a knave. 1639: Clarke, 143, He spoke of a fox, but when all came to all, it was but a ferne brake. 1659: Howell, 16 [as in 1639]. 1846–59: *Denham Tracts*, ii 107 (F.L.S.), Does not know a fox from a fern-bush. Cf. **Goose** (20).

15. He has caught a fox = is drunk. *c.*1600: *Fryer Bacon*, in Thorns, *Early Prose Rom.*, i 52 (1848), They kindly thanked Miles for his song, and so sent him home with a foxe at his tayle. 1690: *Neu Dict. Canting Crew*, sig. E7, He has caught a fox, he is very drunk.

16. He that hath a fox for his mate hath need of a net at his girdle. 1640: Herbert, *Jac. Prudentum*.

17. He that will deceive the fox must rise betimes. 1640: Ibid. 1670: Ray, 10. 1732: Fuller, 2357.

18. It is an ill sign to see a fox lick a lamb. 1678: Ray, 142. 1748: *Gent. Mag.*, 21.

19. Old foxes want no tutors. 1732: Fuller, 3712. 1792: Wolcot, in *Works*, ii 318 (1795). Cf. Nos. 2 and 3.

20. The fox had a wound, etc., or **The fox was sick.** 1659: Howell, 12 [wound]. 1678: Ray, 71, The fox was sick, and he knew not where: He clap't his hand on his tail, and swore it was there. 1738: Swift, *Polite Convers.*, Dial. II, Ay; the fox had a wound, and he could not tell where, etc.

21. The fox is taken when he comes to take. *c.*1610: Rowlands, *More Knaues Yet?*, 10 (Hunt.Cl.), And the old ancient prouerbe true did make, Some fox is taken, when he comes to take.

22. The fox is the finder. 1738: Swift, *Polite Convers.*, Dial. I, *Col* … Here's a very bad smell. *Miss.* Perhaps, Colonel, the fox is the finder. 1846–59: *Denham Tracts*, ii 107 (E.D.S.), The fox the finder.

23. The fox kills the lambs, and the hounds the old sheep. 1619: Chapman, *Two Wise Men*, III i [quoted as a proverb].

24. The fox knows much, but more he that catcheth him. 1631: Mabbe, *Celestina*, 264 (T.T.), If the foxe be crafty, more crafty is hee that catches him. 1732: Fuller, 4544. 1846–59: *Denham Tracts*, ii 107 (F.L.S.).

25. The fox may grow grey but never good. 1631: Mabbe, *Celestina*, 207 (T.T.), Though the fox change his haire, yet he never changeth his nature. 1671: E. Howard, *Six Days Adv.*, III p. 41, The fox is gray before he's good. 1732: Fuller, 4545. [1892: Wilde, *lady W.'s Fan*, I, Men become old, but they never become good.]

26. The fox praiseth the meat out of the crow's mouth. 1732: Fuller, 4546.

27. The fox preys furthest from his hole. 1639: Clarke, 127, A crafty fox never preyeth neare his den. 1642: Fuller, *Holy State:* 'Constant Virgin', This they do … to divert suspicion, that they may prey the furthest from their holes. 1670: Ray, 92. 1732: Fuller, 1610 [in the plural]. 1846–59: *Denham Tracts*, ii 107 (F.L.S.), Foxes prey furthest from their earths.

28. The fox that having lost his tail. *See* quots. 1658: Flecknoe, *Enigm. Characters*, 78, Like the fox, who having lost his own taile, would needs perswade all others out of theirs. 1779: Boswell, *Letters*, ii 299 (Tinker), A Scotchman might preach on union to them [the Irish], as a fox who has lost his tail. 1824: Scott, *Redgauntlet*, ch xxiii, 'They that took my land the last time, may take my life this; and that is all I care about it'. The English gentlemen, who were still in possession of their paternal estates … whispered among them of the fox which had lost his tail. 1922: Weyman, *Ovington's Bank*, ch xxxi, Foxes who had lost their tails, they felt themselves marked men until others followed their example.

29. The more the fox is cursed, the better he fares. *c.*1580: Spelman, *Dialogue*, 109 (Roxb.Cl), The fox fareth beste when he is moste careste [cursed]. 1594: Greene, *Friar Bacon, etc.*, sc xi 1660: Tatham, *The Rump*, II, The fox fares best when he is curst. 1712: Motteux, *Quixote*, Pt II ch l., Let them laugh that win; the cursed fox thrives the better. 1853: Trench, *Proverbs*, 79 (1905), For *The fox thrives best when he is most cursed*; the very loudness of the clamour was itself rather an evidence how well they were faring.

30. The tail doth oft catch the fox. 1576: Lambarde, *Peramb. of Kent*, 362 (1826), For as the proverbe is … the taile is ynough to bewray the foxe. 1633: Draxe, 72.

31. Though the fox run, the chicken hath

wings. 1640: Herbert, *Jac. Prudentum*. 1670: Ray, 4. 1732: Fuller, 5008.

32. To be in a fox's sleep. 1672: Walker, *Paroem.*, 25. 1681: W. Robertson, *Phraseol. Generalis*, 639, To be in a foxes sleep; Somnum mentiri. 1796: O'Keeffe. *The Doldrum*, II i, He sleeps … aye like a fox. 1875: *N.&Q.*, 5th ser, iv 286, A few days ago I heard a working-man say, 'I was in a fox's sleep'.

33. To set the fox to keep the geese. 1639: Clarke, 9. 1709: O. Dykes, *Eng. Proverbs*, 45, He sets the fox to keep his geese. 1721: Bailey, *Eng. Dict.*, s.v. 'Fox' [as in 1709].

34. What is the fox but his case? 1637: A. Warwick, *Spare Minutes*, 84 (1829), Methinks the proverbe sutes those sutes [gallants in brave attire], *what is the fox but his case?* Cf. No. 37.

35. When the fox preaches, beware the geese. *c.*1410: *Towneley Plays*, 12 (E.E.T.S.), How! let furth youre geyse, the fox will preche. 1546: Heywood, *Proverbs*, Pt II ch vii 1609: Rowlands, *Whole Crew, etc.*, 14 (Hunt.Cl.), Take in your geese, the fox begins to preach. 1692: L'Estrange, *Aesop*, 319 (3rd ed.). 1754: Berthelson, *Eng.–Danish Dict.*, s.v. 'Fox'.

36. With foxes we must play the fox. 1732: Fuller, 5797.

37. You can have no more of the fox than his skin. 1546: Heywood, *Proverbs*, Pt II ch ix, He can haue no more of the foxe but the skyn. 1659: Howell, 4. Cf. No. 34.

See also False (5); Fire (11); **Flap; Grapes; Lion** (7); **Quietness; Ram; Reynard;** and **Wily.**

Fox-cubs. *See* quot. 1678: Ray, 228, There's ne'er a best among them, as the fellow said by the fox-cubs.

Foxes brewings. *See* **Cocking.**

France. 1. France is a meadow that cuts thrice a year. 1640: Herbert, *Jac. Prudentum.*

2. If that you will France win, Then with Scotland first begin. 1548: Hall, *Chron.*, 55 (1809), The old auncient prouerbe … whiche saieth he that will Fraunce wynne, muste with Scotlande firste beginne. 1599: Shakespeare, *Henry V*, I ii.

Fraud and deceit are always in haste. 1732: Fuller, 1611.

Fredvile. *See* **Betshanger.**

Free as a bird in air. 1635: in *Somers Tracts*, vii 204 (1811), He may trade as free as a bird in ayre.

Free as the wind. 1609: Shakespeare,

Coriolanus, I ix, Were he the butcher of my son, he should Be free as is the wind. *c.*1625: B.&F., *Double Marriage*, IV iii, I am free, free as air. 1822: Peacock, *Maid Marian*, ch xvi, But he roamed where he listed, as free as the wind.

Free lunch, There's no such thing as a. Frequently associated with the American economist Milton Friedman, but not invented by him. 1967: R. A. Heinlein, *The Moon is a Harsh Mistress*, 'Oh, tanstaafl'. Means 'There ain't no such thing as a free lunch'. 1969: *Newsweek*, 29 Dec., 52, I was the taught … the first and only law of economics: 'There is no such thing as a free lunch'.

Free of another man's pottage, You are very. 1732: Fuller, 5861.

Free of her lips free of her hips. 1576: Pettie, *Petite Pall.*, ii 32 (Gollancz), They are as loose of their lips and as free of their flesh as may be. 1678: Ray, 62. 1732: Fuller, 6269.

Free of his gifts as a blind man of his eye, As. 1546: Heywood, *Proverbs*, Pt I ch xi, As free of gyft as a poore man of his eie. 1580: Baret, *Alvearie*, D 994, As we say, he is as true of his promise, as a poore man of his eie. 1633: Draxe, 92, As free of his guift, as a Iewe of his eye. 1670: Ray, 205, As free as a blindman is of his eye.

Freedom. *See* quot. *c.*1430: Lydgate, *Minor Poems*, 183 (Percy S.), I remembre a proverbe said of olde, Who lesethe his fredam, in faith! he loseth all.

Freer than a gift, What is? 1583: Fulke, *Defence*, xv 403 (OED), A gift that is freely giuen … wherof the prouerbe is, what is so free as gift? 1633: Draxe, 80, What is freer than gift? 1670: Ray, 93. 1732: Fuller, 5510.

French leave, To take. 1782: D'Arblay, *Diary*, i 476 (1876), I felt myself extremely awkward about going away, not choosing, as it was my first visit, to take French leave. 1788: Colman, jr., *Ways and Means*, III ii, You'd have taken leave without asking – French leave – if I had not been here. 1824: Scott, *Redgauntlet*, ch xv, I took French leave, and … so I am free of all that business. 1883: R.L.S., *Treasure I*, ch xxii, As I was certain I should not be allowed to leave the enclosure, my only plan was to take French leave, and slip out when nobody was watching.

Frenchmen. *See* quot. 1303: Brunne, *Handl. Synne*, l. 4154, A forbyseyn ys toldë) thys, Seyde on Frenshe men and on Englys, 'That Frenche men synne yn lecherye, And Englys men yn enuye'.

Frenzy, heresy, and jealousy. *See* quots. Before 1529: Skelton, *Replycacion*, l. 406, For be ye wele assured That frensy nor ielousy Nor heresy wyll neuer dye. 1562: Bullein, *Bulw. of Defence*: 'Soreness and Chir.', fo. 75, The old proverb is, that heresy, fransie, and jealousie be so bred by the bone that they will neuer out of the fleshe. 1591: Harington, *Orl. Furioso*, bk xxxi, Notes, Our old English proverb: From heresie, phrenesie, and Iealousie, good Lord deliver me. 1666: Torriano, *Piazza Univ.*, 95, Frensie, jealousy and heresie are never to be cur'd any way.

Fresh as a daisy. 1815: E. S. Barrett, *Heroine*, iii 155 (OED), As fresh as a daisy. 1845: Dickens, *Cricket*, Chirp 2, She presently came bouncing back – the saying is, as fresh as any daisy; *I* say fresher. 1925: I and C. I Gordon, *Two Vagabonds in Languedoc*, 41, Here he comes swinging in from his fifteen kilometres fresh as a daisy.

Fresh as a rose. 1412–20: Lydgate, *Troy Book*, bk v l. 2897, With swetenes freshe as any rose. 1468: *Coventry Mys.*, 154 (SH.S.), Fayr and fresche, as rose on thorn. 1590: Spenser, *F. Q.*, bk ii can. ix st. 36, That was right faire and fresh as morning rose. 1615: in *Roxb. Ballads*, vi 166 (B.S.), Cheeks as fresh as rose in June. 1700: T. Brown, etc., tr. Scarron, ii 182 (1892), The duke … found her as gay and fresh as a rose upon the stalk. 1906: J. M. Rigg, tr. *Decameron*, i 122, A brother, twenty-five years of age, fair and fresh as a rose.

Fresh as an eel. *c.*1410: *Towneley Plays*, 127 (E.E.T.S.), As fresh as an eyll.

Fresh as flowers in May. *c.*1440: Lydgate, *Lyf of our Lady*, sig. G2 (Caxton), Fayrer than floure in maye. 1566: L. Wager, *Mary Magdalene*, sig. B1, Freshe and flourishyng as the floures in May. 1592: Warner, *Alb. England*, ch xxxi st. 4, As peart as bird, as straite as boulte, as freshe as flowers in May. 1631: Heywood, *Fair Maid of West*, Pt II Act I, You shall meete some of them sometimes as fresh as flowers in May. 1714: Gay, *Shep. Week*, Prol., l. 55, But Lansdown fresh as flower of May. 1868: A. Dobson, in *Poet. Works*, 6 (1923), The artless, ageless things you say Are fresh as May's own flowers.

Fresh as paint. 1850: Smedley, *Frank Fairlegh*, ch xli., You are looking as fresh as paint; getting round again, wind and limb, eh? 1859: Sala,

Twice Round Clock, 8 p.m. 1912: Pinero, '*Mind the Paint*' *Girl*, III p. 146, I feel as fresh as paint.

Fresh fish. *See* **Fish** (1).

Fret like gummed taffety, To. 1605: R. F., *Sch. of Slovenrie*, The Epistle, The translator vowes to conclude that either Signior Malevola his sute of gumme is fretted out at elbowes, or … 1732: Fuller, 1846, He frets like gum'd taffety. 1738: Swift, *Polite Convers.*, Dial. II, You have made him fret like gum taffety.

Friar and **Friars. 1. Friar's mouth.** *See* **Fit as a pudding**.

2. Friars observant spare their own and eat other men's. 1578: Florio, *First Fruites*, fo. 30, Obseruant friers spare theyr owne, and eate that which is other mens. 1629: *Book of Meery Riddles*, Prov. 112.

3. Never friar forgot feud. 1820: Scott, *Monastery*, ch x, I might have remembered the proverb, 'Never Friar forgot feud'.

4. The friar preached against stealing and had a goose (or **pudding**) **in his sleeve.** 1526: *Hundred Mery Talys*, No. lxx. p. 120 (Oesterley, 1866) [the story of the stolen pudding falling out of the friar's sleeve]. 1640: Herbert, *Jac. Prudentum* [goose]. 1670: Ray, 95 [pudding]. 1732: Fuller, 4548 [goose]. 1871: Smiles, *Character*, 36, The teaching of the friar was not worth much, who preached the virtue of honesty with a stolen goose in his sleeve.

5. What was good the friar never loved. 1670: Ray, 94.

6. When the friar's beaten, then comes James. 1639: Clarke, 282. 1670: Ray, 94. 1672: Walker, *Paroem.*, 10.

See also **Devil** (118); and **Fly,** *subs.* (1).

Friday. 1. A Friday look (or **face**). 1592: Greene, in *Works*, xii 120 (Grosart), The foxe made a Friday face, counterfeiting sorrow. 1667: L'Estrange, *Quevedo's Visions*, 152 (1904), Look what a Friday-face that fellow makes! 1846: Denham, *Proverbs*, 6 (Percy S.), Has a Friday look (sulky, downcast). 1872: J. Glyde, jr., *Norfolk Garland*, 150, He has a Friday look.

2. A Friday night's dream on the Saturday told, is sure to come true be it never so old. 1626: Overbury, *Characters:* 'Milkmaid', Only a Fridaies dreame is all her superstition: that she conceales for feare of anger. 1831: Hone, *Year-Book*, 252, It is a common saying, and popular belief, that, Friday night's dreams, etc. 1879:

Henderson, *Folk-Lore N. Counties*, 101. 1883: Burne, *Shropsh. Folk-Lore*, 261. 1884: *Folk-Lore Journal*, ii 279 [with 'Sunday' for 'Saturday' – Derby].

3. A Friday's feast. 1639: Davenport, *New Trick, etc.*, III i, I'de make you both make but a Fridayes feast. 1640: in Rollins, *Cavalier and Puritan*, 103 (1923), But now, at last the greedy Scot, Hath a friday's breakefast got, few of such feasts will pull their courage down.

4. A Friday's flit will not long sit. 1868: Atkinson, *Cleveland Gloss.* [with 'never' for 'not long']. 1917: Bridge, *Cheshire Proverbs*, 107 [Lancs]. Cf. **Saturday**.

5. A Friday's sail always fail. 1875: A. B. Cheales, *Proverb. Folk-Lore*, 19. 1924: *Folk-Lore*, xxxv 347, The [Suffolk] fishermen say: 'A Friday's sail Always fail'.

6. As the Friday, so the Sunday. 1853: *N. & Q.*, 1st ser, viii 512, Fine on Friday, fine on Sunday, Wet on Friday, wet on Sunday (Northants). 1875: A. B. Cheales, *Proverb. Folk-Lore*, 19, As the Friday, so the Sunday, As the Sunday so the week. 1886: Elworthy, *West Som. Word-Book*, 271 (E.D.S.), As Friday so Sunday. 1893: Inwards, *Weather Lore*, 43, If on Friday it rain, 'Twill on Sunday again; If Friday be clear, Have for Sunday no fear. Ibid., 42, As the Friday so the Sunday.

7. Friday is the best or the worst day of the week. *c.*1386: Chaucer, *Knight's Tale*, l. 676, Right as the Friday, soothly for to telle, Now it shyneth, now it reyneth faste. 16th cent.: in *Reliq. Antiquae*, ii 10 (1843), Vendredy de la semaine est Le plus beau jour, ou le plus laid. 1830: Forby, *Vocab. E. Anglia*, 415, Friday is either a very fine or a very wet day. 1851: in *N. & Q.*, 1st ser, iii 153, A Shropshire lady tells me that her mother (who was born in 1760) used to say Friday was always the fairest, or the foulest, day of the week. 1893: Inwards, *Weather Lore*, 43. Cf. Nos. 8 and 9.

8. Friday will be either king or underling. Wilts. This seems to be a fanciful version of No. 7. 1875: A. B. Cheales, *Proverb. Folk-Lore*, 19.

9. Friday's a day as'll have his trick The fairest or foulest day O' the wik. Another version of No. 7. 1883: Burne, *Shropsh. Folk-Lore*, 261.

10. Friday's hair and Sunday's horn Go to the Devil on Monday morn. It is considered wrong to cut the hair on Friday or the nails on Sunday.

1678: Ray, 294. 1851: *N. & Q.*, 1st ser, iii 462, The legend that I have heard in Devonshire … ran thus: Friday cut hair, Sunday cut horn, Better that man had never been born. 1878: *N. & Q.*, 9th ser, ii 436.

11. Friday's morn come when it will it comes too soon. [1656: Flecknoe, *Diarium*, 38, Now Friday came, your old wives say, Of all the week's the unluckiest day.] 1825: Brockett, *Gloss. N. Country Words*, 77. 1878: Dyer, *Eng. Folk-Lore*, 243.

12. Friday's noon is Sunday's doom. Corn. 1887: M. A. Courtney, in *Folk-Lore Journal*, v 191.

13. Fridays in the week are never aleek [alike]. *c.*1386: Chaucer, *Knight's Tale*, l. 681, Selde is the Fryday at the wyke i-like. 1850: *N. & Q.*, 1st ser, i 303, The following meteorological proverb is frequently repeated in Devonshire, to denote the variability of the weather on Fridays: – Fridays in the week Are never aleek. 1874: W. Pengelly, in *N. & Q.*, 5th ser, ii 184, [Corn.] Friday and the week Are seldom aleek. 1886: Elworthy, *West Som. Word-Book*, 271 (E.D.S.), On Friday's weather we have … Friday in the week Is seldom alike.

See also **Sing** (4); and **Thursday** (1).

Friend and **Friends. 1. A friend as far as conscience permits.** 1736: Bailey, *Dict.*, s.v. 'Conscience'.

2. A friend in a corner. *c.*1579: Harvey, *Letter-Book*, 80 (Camden S.), Particular contentement of mynde that I have sutch an odd frende in a corner. 1607: Dekker, etc., *Westw. Hoe*, II ii, Had it not been for a friend in a corner [*Takes aqua-vitae*], I had kicked up my heels. *c.*1663: Davenant, *Play-House to be Let*, V, And Caesar, you shall find – a friend in corner. 1681: W. Robertson, *Phraseol. Generalis*, 1056, A friend in a corner for a refuge. 1740: North, *Examen*, 611, For it might … happen that a friend in a corner had been of great service to them.

3. A friend in court is better than a penny in purse. *c.*1400: *Rom. Rose*, ll. 5541–2, For freend in court ay better is Than peny in purs, certis. 1509: Barclay, *Ship of Fools*, i 70 (1874). 1580: Lyly, *Euphues*, 476 (Arber). 1641: Peacham, *Worth of Penny*, in Arber, *Garner*, vi 256 (1883). 1738: *Gent. Mag.*, 475, A friend at court is worth a penny in the purse. 1848: Dickens, *Dombey*, ch xxxviii, I shouldn't wonder – friends at court you know … Cf. **Penny** (6).

4. A friend in need is a friend indeed. *c.*1270: *Prov. of Alfred*, in Kemble, *Salomon and Sat.*, 247 (*Aelfric* S.), A sug fere the his help in mod (A safe fere [companion] is he that helps at need). 1484: Caxton, *Aesope*, ii 251 (Jacobs), The very and trewe frend is fond in the xtreme nede. 1581: T. Howell, *Devises*, 58 (1906), A friend thou art in deede, That helps thy friend in time of nipping neede. 1618: Harington, *Epigrams*, bk ii No. 101, Behold, how much it stands a man in steed, To have a friend answer in time of need. 1772: Graves, *Spirit. Quixote*, bk viii ch xxii [heading].

5. A friend in the market is better than money in the chest. 1732: Fuller, 119.

6. A friend is never known till a man have need. 1303: Brunne, *Handl. Synne*, l. 2251, At nedē shul men proue here frendys. *c.*1470: G. Ashby, *Poems*, 67 (E.E.T.S.), A freende is knowen in necessite. 1546: Heywood, *Proverbs*, Pt I ch xi 1683: Meriton, *Yorkshire Ale*, 83–7 (1697), A friend is not knawn but in need. 1732: Fuller, 118, A friend is never known till needed.

7. A friend is not so soon gotten as lost. 1567: Painter, *Pal. of Pleasure*, ii 177 (Jacobs), As the common prouerbe and wise sayinge reporteth, that the vertue is no lesse to conserue frendship gotten, than the wisedome was great to get and win the same. 1580: Lyly, *Euphues*, 324 (Arber), A friend is long a getting, and soone lost. 1661: Webster and Rowley, *Cure for a Cuckold*, III i, They that study man say of a friend, There's nothing in the world that's harder found, Nor sooner lost. 1732: Fuller, 1612.

8. A friend to all is a friend to none. [ᾧ φίλοι οὐδεὶς φίλος, – Diogenes Laertius, V i Attributed to Aristotle.] 1623: Wodroephe, *Spared Houres*, 475, All men's friend, no man's friend. 1666: Torriano, *Piazza Univ.*, 8, Every bodies friend is nobodies friend. 1732: Fuller, 120. 1779: Johnson, in Boswell's *Life*, 24 April, I believe he is right, Sir … He had friends, but no friend. Cf. **Many friends.**

9. A friend's frown. *See* quots. 1570: A. Barclay, *Mirr. of Good Manners*, 21 (Spens.S.), For much better it is, To bide a frendes anger then a foes kisse. 1659: Howell, *Proverbs: Brit.-Eng.*, 3, A friends frown is better then a fools smiles.

10. A good friend never offends. 1659: Howell, *Proverbs: Brit.-Eng.*, 23.

11. All are not friends that speak us fair. 1639: Clarke, 128. 1670: Ray, 93. 1732: Fuller, 500.

12. Be a friend to thyself, and others will be so too. Ibid., No. 847.

13. Choose thy friends like thy books, few but choice. 1659: Howell, 10 (8).

14. Friends are like fiddle-strings, they must not be screwed too tight. 1855: Bohn, 358.

15. Friends fail flyers. 1548: Hall, *Chron.*, 361 (1809), Frendes fayle fliers. 1605: Camden, *Remains*, 322 (1870). 1639: Clarke, 25.

16. Friends may meet but mountains never. 1530: Palsgrave, 635, Hylles do never mete, but acquayntaunce dothe often. 1653: Wither, *Dark Lantern*, 29, Friends possibly may meet (our proverb sayes) But mountains never. 1754: Berthelson, *Eng.-Danish Dict.*, s.v. 'Friend', Friends may meet but mountains never greet.

17. Friends must part. *c*.1620: in *Roxb. Ballads*, i 253 (B.S.), For friends, you know, must part. 1727: Gay, *Fables*, 1st ser, No. 50, But dearest friends, alas! must part. 1821: Scott, *Kenilworth*, ch xi, The best friends must part.

18. Friends through fortune become enemies through mishap. *c*.1386: Chaucer, *Monk's Tale*, l. 254, For what man that hath freendes thurgh fortune, Mishap wol make hem enemys, I gesse: This proverbe is ful sooth and ful commune.

19. Have but few friends though much acquaintance. 1659: Howell, 5. 1670: Ray, 11. 1732: Fuller, 1807.

20. He is my friend that grindeth at my mill. 1633: Draxe, 74. 1670: Ray, 93. 1732: Fuller, 2464.

21. He is my friend that succoureth me. 1477: Rivers, *Dictes and Sayings*, 57 (1877), He is a good frende that doth the[e] good. *c*.1640: in *Roxb. Ballads*, iii 288 (B.S.), But he is my friend, That helps me i' th' end. 1732: Fuller, 1926, He is my friend that succoureth me, not he that pitieth me.

22. He's a friend that speaks well on's behind our backs. 1678: Ray, 143. 1732: Fuller, 2465.

23. Here's to our friends and hang up the rest of our kindred. 1678: Ray, 347.

24. If you have one true friend, you have more than your share. 1732: Fuller, 2760.

25. It is good to have friends but bad to need them. 1669: *New Help to Discourse*, 15.

26. Make not thy friend too cheap to thee, nor thy self to thy friend. 1659: Howell, 18 [with 'too dear to him' after 'thy self']. 1670: Ray, 10.

27. No man has a worse friend than he brings

with him from home = himself. 1605: Camden, *Remains*, 335 (1870), Where shall a man have a worse friend than he brings from home? 1670: Ray, 94 [as in 1605]. 1738: Swift, *Polite Convers.*, Dial. I, I see there's no worse friend than one brings from home with one. 1831: Hone, *Year-Book*, col. 1417, You may find your worst enemy, or best friend, in yourself. 1853: Trench, *Proverbs*, 139 (1905).

28. One friend watcheth for another. 1611: Cotgrave, s.v. 'Ami', One friend ever watches, or cares for another. 1666: Torriano, *Piazza Univ.*, 8.

29. Save a man from his friends, and leave him to struggle with his enemies. 1869: Hazlitt, 328.

30. The friend that faints is a foe. 1611: Davies (of Hereford), *Sc. of Folly*, 46, in *Works*, ii (Grosart).

31. When a friend asks there is no to-morrow. 1640: Herbert, *Jac. Prudentum.* 1710: S. Palmer, *Moral Essays on Proverbs*, 367.

32. Wherever you see your friend trust yourself. 1639: Clarke, 26.1670: Ray, 94.

33. Who hath too many friends, eats too much salt. 1659: Howell, 10 (8). Cf. **Bushel** (3).

See also **Afraid of one's friends; Among; Best** (23) and (24); **Falling out; God defend me; God hath few; God send me; Good cheer; Kindred; Live** (37); **Lose** (8); **Many humble; Many kinsfolk; Merry when friends; Near friend; New friend; Old, C; Prove; Servant** (7); **True** (10) and (13); **Try** (3); **Two friends;** and **Write** (1).

Friendship. 1. A broken friendship may be soder'd, but will never be sound. 1732: Fuller, 27.

2. Friendship is not to be bought at a fair. Ibid., No. 1619.

3. Friendship that flames goes out in a flash. Ibid., No. 1623. Cf. **Sudden friendship.**

4. While the pot boils friendship blooms. 1875: A. B. Cheales, *Proverb. Folk-Lore*, 95.

Fright a bird is not the way to catch her, To. 1633: Draxe, 2. 1670: Ray, 95. 1732: Fuller, 1627, Frightning of a bird is not the way to catch it. 1875: A. B. Cheales, *Proverb. Folk-Lore*, 127 [as in 1732].

Frog. 1. Frog and feathers. *See* quots. 1823: Lockhart, *Reg. Dalton*, VI i 345 (1842) (OED), Whose coat was as bare of nap as a frog's is of feathers. 1873: *N. & Q.*, 4th ser, xi 63, I well remember a farmer in my parish, saying when describing to me an impoverished house, twenty-five years ago, – 'It was as bare of furniture as a frog is of feathers'. [Another version at the same reference:] 'I'm as bare of brass as a toad is of feathers'.

2. Frog and harrow. See **Toad.**

3. If frogs make a noise in the time of cold rain, warm dry weather will follow. 1846: Denham, *Proverbs*, 3 (Percy S.).

4. Like a frog on a chopping-block. 1678: Ray, 289. 1732: Fuller, 723, As pert as a frog upon a washing-block.

5. The frog cannot out of her bog. 1670: Ray, 95. 1732: Fuller, 6113.

6. When the frog and mouse would take up the quarrel, the kite decided it. 1732: Fuller, 5586. *See also* **April** (8); **Gossips; Thunder** (3); and **Toad.**

Frost. 1. A white frost never lasts more than three days. 1893: Inwards, *Weather Lore*, 114.

2. Bearded frost, forerunner of snow. Ibid., 114.

3. Frost and falsehood have both a dirty gangway. 1846: Denham, *Proverbs*, 5 (Percy S.).

4. Frost and fraud both end in foul. 1605: Camden, *Remains*, 322 (1870), Frost and fraud have always foul ends. 1657: Gurnall, *Christ. in Armour*, Pt II V 14, ch xvii p. 66 (1679), So true is that proverb, that *frost and fraud have dirty ends.* 1709: R. Kingston, *Apoph. Curiosa*, 80 [as in 1657]. 1853: Trench, *Proverbs*, 21 (1905). 1904: *Co. Folk-Lore: Northumb.*, 172 (F.L.S.). 1917: Bridge, *Cheshire Proverbs*, 60.

5. Hoar-frost and gipsies never stay nine days in a place. 1893: Inwards, *Weather Lore*, 114.

6. If hoar-frost come on mornings twain, The third day surely will have rain. Ibid., 114.

7. The frost hurts not weeds. 1732: Fuller, 4550.

8. Three white frosts bring rain. 1881: C. W. Empson, in *Folk-Lore Record*, iv 131. 1893: Inwards, *Weather Lore*, 114, Three white frosts and then a storm. 1917: Bridge, *Cheshire Proverbs*, 163, Three yarry [hoary] frosts are sure to end in rain.

See also **Hail** (1); and **March** (43) and (44).

Frosty nights and hot sunny days Set the corn fields all in a blaze. 1893: Inwards, *Weather Lore*, 43.

Frosty winter, A. See quot. 1846: Denham, *Proverbs*, 68 (Percy S.), A frosty winter, and a dusty March, And a rain about Aperill; And another about the Lammas time, When the corn begins to fill; Is worth a plough of gold, And all her pins theretill. 1893: Inwards, *Weather Lore*, 42.

Frugality is an income. 1542: Udall, tr. Erasmus' *Apoph.*, 44 (1877), Accordyng to the prouerbe: good husbandrie, and sparyng in an hous, is a great penie rent of yerely reuenues. 1681: W. Robertson, *Phraseol. Generalis*, 650, Frugality and good husbandry makes things go far; is great incomes. 1725: Bailey, tr. Erasmus' *Colloq.*, 491, Frugality is a handsome income. 1875: A. B. Cheales, *Proverb. Folk-Lore*, 102, Economy is a good income.

Fruit. 1. Fruit is gold in the morning, etc. *See* quots. 1904: *N. & Q.*, 10th ser, i 251, About fifty years ago a farmer in the county of Durham said in my hearing, 'The late Bishop Barrington used to say, "Fruit is gold in the morning, silver in the afternoon, and lead at night." ' 1922: *Punch*, 20 Sept., p. 279, col. 3, The old adage tells us that 'fruit is gold in the morning, silver at noon and lead at night'.

2. Fruit out of season, sorrow out of reason. 1884: H. Friend, *Flowers and Fl. Lore*, 207, 'Fruit … reason', say the old folk of Sussex; and the same notion is found from Land's End to John o' Groats.

3. He that would have the fruit must climb the tree. 1732: Fuller, 2366.

4. If you would have fruit, you must bring the leaf to the grave, i.e. transplant in autumn. 1678: Ray, 53. 1893: Inwards, *Weather Lore*, 8.

5. No tree bears fruit in autumn that does not blossom in the spring. 1846: Denham, *Proverbs*, 57 (Percy S.).

Fry in one's own grease. *See* **Grease.**

Fry me for a fool and you'll lose your fat in frying. 1864: 'Cornish Proverbs', in *N. & Q.*, 3rd ser, vi 495.

Frying-pan into the fire, Out of the. [Plato, *De Rep.*, viii [ἐς αὐτό, φασί, τὸ πῦρ ἐκ τοῦ καπνοῦ βιαζόμενος. –Lucian, *Necyom.*, 4. Pervenimus igitur de calcaria (quod dici solet) in carbonariam. – Tertullian, *De Carne Christi*, vi.] 1528: More, *Works*, p. 179, col. 2 (1557), Lepe they lyke a flounder out of a frying-panne into the fyre. 1591: Harington, *Orl. Furioso*, bk xiii st. 28, But I was sav'd, as is the flounder, when He leapeth from the dish into the fire. 1621: Burton, *Melancholy*, I iv i 286 (1836), Though, many times, as Aesops fishes, they leap from the frying pan into the fire itself. 1671: Head and Kirkman, *Eng. Rogue*, ii 53. 1772: Garrick, *Irish Widow*, II, Out of the pan into the fire! there's no putting him off. 1842: Barham, *Ing. Legends*, 2nd ser: 'M. of Venice'. 1921: *Times Lit. Suppl.*, 8 Sept., p. 582, col. 2, One is left with an uncomfortable suspicion that Virginia's future may not impossibly exemplify the old saying about the frying-pan into the fire.

See also **Pot** (6).

Fuel to the fire, To add. [οὐ γὰρ χρῆ πῦρ ἐπὶ πῦρ ὀχετεύειν. – Plato, *Legg.*, 666A. Velut materiam igni praebentes. – Livy, xxi 10.] *c.*1380: Chaucer, *Troylus*, bk ii l. 1332, Through morë wode or col, the morë fyr. 1592: Warner, *Alb. England*, ch lix. st. 27, All adding fewel to the fire. 1632: Massinger, *Maid of Honour*, II i, 'Tis far From me, sir, to add fuel to your anger, That … burns Too hot already. 1671: A. Behn, *Amorous Prince*, I iv, Every look adds fuel to my flame. 1712: Motteux, *Quixote*, Pt I bk iv ch vii, Anselmo … so added new fuel to the fire that was to consume his reputation. 1843: Planché, *Extravag.*, ii 248 (1879), Each look is fuel added to my fire.

Full as a jade, quoth the bride. 1678: Ray, 285. 1732: Fuller, 2584.

Full as a piper's bag. 1678: Ray, 284.

Full as a tick. Ibid., 284. 1854: Baker, *Northants Gloss.*, s.v. 'Tick', 'As full as a tick': a state of repletion. 1886: Elworthy, *West Som. Word-Book*, 272 (E.D.S.) … Said of any animal, whether man or beast, which has eaten its fill. 1889: J. Nicholson, *Folk-Speech E. Yorks*, 19 … A tick is a sheep-louse, which has always a full bloated appearance.

Full as a toad of poison. 1678: Ray, 284.

Full as a tun. 1546: Heywood, *Proverbs*, Pt I ch xi, As fulle as a tunne. 1633: Draxe, 79 *bis*, He is fed as full as a tun.

Full as an egg. *See* **Egg** (5).

Full bellies make empty skulls. 1732: Fuller, 1633.

Full belly neither fights nor flies well, A. 1640: Herbert, *Jac. Prudentum*. 1732: Fuller, 1634, Full guts neither run away, nor fight well.

Full bowls make empty brains. 1632: T. Heywood, *Iron Age*, Pt I Act I.

Full cup must be carried steadily, A. *c.*1300: *Prov. of Hending*, st. 16 (ed. Berlin, 1878), When

the coppe is follest, thenne ber hire feyrest. 1732: Fuller, 122.

Full nor fasting. *See* **Never well.**

Full of courtesy. *See* **Courtesy** (3).

Full of himself that he is quite empty, He's so. 1732: Fuller, 2472.

Full of items. 1886: Elworthy, *West Som. Word-Book*, 374 (E.D.S.), One of the commonest of sayings … is 'All full of his items', to describe a restless fidgety person. 1920: *Devonsh. Assoc. Trans.*, lii. 70, 'He's vull o' items', meaning he is very fidgety about things.

Full of sin. *See* quot. 1924: *Devonsh. Assoc. Trans.*, lv. 112, 'Her's zo vull o' sin's a cat is of hairs'.

Full of unbelief. Said of a cow that will not stay in her pasture. 1917: Bridge, *Cheshire Proverbs*, 60.

Full purse makes the mouth to speak, A. 1602: Carew, *Surv. of Cornwall*, 315 (1811), A full purse begetting a stout stomach. 1670: Ray, 22. 1732: Fuller, 123, A full purse makes the mouth run over.

Further East, the shorter West. 1846: Denham, *Proverbs*, 1 (Percy S.). Cf. **Longer East.**

Further off the better looked upon, The. Glos. 1911: *Folk-Lore*, xxii 239.

Further than the wall we cannot go. 1528: More, *Works*, p. 187, col. 1 (1557), I am in this matter euen at the harde walle, and se not how to go further. 1546: Heywood, *Proverbs*, Pt II ch v [with 'he' for 'we']. 1659: Howell, 5.

Further you go, the further behind, The. 1477: Rivers, *Dictes and Sayings*, 144 (1877), He that goth owte of his weye, the more he goth, the ferther he is behinde. 1530: Palsgrave, 852, The farder I go, the more I am behynde. 1670: Ray, 11, The further we go the further behind. 1732: Fuller, 4552, The further you run, the further you are behind.

Furze is out of bloom [= never], **kissing is out of fashion, When the.** 1752: *Poor Robin Alman.*, August, Joan says: 'Furze in bloom is still', and she'll be kiss'd if she's her will. 1855: *N. & Q.*, 1st ser, xi 416, When the gorse is out of blossom, kissing is out of fashion. 1899: Dickinson, *Cumb. Gloss.*, 363, When t' whins is oot o' blossom kissin's oot o' fashion.

Furze. *See also* **Under the furze.**

G

Gabriel blows his horn, When, this question 59: Howell, *Proverbs*, To Philologers.

Gadding gossips shall dine on the pot-lid. 1732: Fuller, 1637.

Gain, *verb.* **1. He gaineth enough whom fortune loseth.** 1611: Cotgrave, s.v. 'Gaigner', Assez gaigne qui malheur perd; He gets enough that misses an ill turn. 1629: *Book of Meery Riddles*, Prov. 60.

2. He that gains time gains all things. 1710: S. Palmer, *Moral Essays on Proverbs*, 380.

3. To gain teacheth how to spend. 1640: Herbert, *Jac. Prudentum*.

Gain, *subs.* **1. No gain without pain.** 1577: J. Grange, *Golden Aphroditis*, sig. M1, Who will the fruyte that haruest yeeldes, must take the payne. 1589: L. Wright, *Display of Dutie*, 4, No gaine without pain. 1670: Ray, 129, Without pains, no gains. 1736: Franklin, *Way to Wealth*, in *Works*, i 443 (Bigelow). 1775: O'Hara, *Two Misers*, II. 1853: Trench, *Proverbs*, 106 (1905), They consequently accept the law of labour, *No pains, no gains.*

2. One man's loss is another man's gain. *See* **Loss.**

3. There's no great loss without some gain. *See* **Loss.**

4. Who heeds not gain, must expect loss. 1864: 'Cornish Proverbs', in *N. & Q.*, 3rd ser, vi 494.

Gainsborough. *See* quot. 1865: W. White, *East. England*, ii 41, Poor Gainsburgh, proud people, Built a new church to an old steeple. 1889: Peacock, *Manley, etc., Gloss.*, 226 (E.D.S.) [without 'Poor'].

Galled horse, Touch a, and he'll kick (or **wince**). Before 1384: Wiclif, *Works*, iii 231 (Arnold), As a horce unrubbed, that haves a sore back, wynses when he is oght touched or rubbed on his rugge. *c.*1483: *Quatuor Sermones*, 27 (Roxb.Cl), A gallyd horse that is touchyd on the sore wynseth and wryeth. 1566: L. Wager, *Mary Magdalene*, Prol., A horse will kick if you touche where he is galled. 1602: Shakespeare, *Hamlet*, III ii, Let the galled jade wince, our withers are unwrung. 1621: Burton, *Melancholy*, Dem. to Reader, 74 (1836), It is not my freeness of speech, but a guilty conscience, a gauled back of

his own, that makes him winch. 1697: Vanbrugh, *Prov. Wife*, V, How the gall'd horse kicks! 1738: Swift, *Polite Convers.*, Dial. I, Touch a gall'd horse, and he'll wince. 1784: *New Foundl. Hosp. for Wit*, ii 32, Like a gall'd jade he winces.

See also **Scabbed horse.**

Gallows groans for you, The. 1577: *Misogonus*, I iv, The gallowes grones for this wage as iust rope ripe. 1585: *Nomenclator*, 525, One for whom ye gallowes grones. 1611: Cotgrave, s.v. 'Pendard', A rake-hell, crack-rope, gallow-clapper, one for whom the gallows longeth. 1738: Swift, *Polite Convers.*, Dial. I. 1754: Berthelson, *Eng.-Danish Dict.*, s.v. 'Gallows', The gallows groans for him.

Gallows will have its own at last, The. 1855: Bohn, 506.

Galtey's cat. *See* quot. 1925: *Devon and Corn. N.&Q.*, xiii 206, His race is jis rin, like Galtey's cat (Mid Cornwall).

Game is not worth the candle, The. 1640: Herbert, *Jac. Prudentum*, It is a poor sport that is not worth the candle. 1668: Cowley, *Essays*, No. 10, Yet when the light of life is so near going out, and ought to be so precious, *Le jeu ne vaut pas la Chandele*, The play is not worth the expence of the candle. 1704: *Gent. Instructed*, 556 (1732), After all, these discoveries are not worth the candle. 1883: Trollope, *Autobiog.*, ch x, To do all this thoroughly was in my heart from first to last; but I do not know that the game has been worth the candle. 1919: J. A. Bridges, *Vict. Recollections*, 163, If he occasionally doubted whether the game was worth the candle, he was generally one of the happiest of men.

Game's end we shall see who gains, At the. 1640: Herbert, *Jac. Prudentum*. 1732: Fuller, 826, At the end of the game you'll see who's the winner.

Gamesters and race-horses never last long. 1640: Herbert, *Jac. Prudentum.*

Gaming, women and wine, while they laugh, they make men pine. Ibid.

Gander. *See* **Goose.**

Gangs up. *See* quot. 1828: Carr, *Craven Dialect*, ii 147, When it gangs up i' sops, It'll fau down i' drops.

Gape, *verb.* **1. He that gapeth till he be fed, Well may he gape until he be dead.** 1546: Heywood, *Proverbs*, Pt I ch ix, He that gapeth till he be fed, Maie fortune to fast and famishe for hounger. 1732: Fuller, 6459. 1869: Spurgeon, *John Ploughman*, ch vii, He that gapes till he be fed, will gape till he be dead.

2. No gaping against an oven. 1577–87, Holinshed, *Chron.*, ii 389 (1807), The legat blushed, and said ... 'A man ought not to chide with a foole, nor gape ouer an ouen'. 1623: Wodroephe, *Spared Houres*, 485, To gape against an ouen. 1670: Ray, 96. 1732: Fuller, 3575.

3. You gape for gudgeons. 1659: Howell, 15.

4. You may gape long enough ere a bird fall in your mouth. 1639: Clarke, 153. 1670: Ray, 96. 1732: Fuller, 5945.

Gape-seed, She is fond of. 1830: Forby, *Vocab. E. Anglia*, 431. 1872: J. Glyde, jr., *Norfolk Garland*, 149.

Gaping is catching. 1736: Bailey, *Dict.*, s.v.

Garbage in, garbage out. A proverbial saying of the computer age, asserting that as a computer is not a miraculous, independently operating machine but relies on its operators, incorrect data put in will cause incorrect data to be put out ('garbage' is computer slang for incorrect data). The phrase is often reduced to an acronym GIGO. 1964: *CIS Glossary of Automated Typesetting and Related Computer Terms* (Composition Information Services, L.A.) 15, The relationship between input and output is sometimes – when input is incorrect – tersely noted by the expression 'garbage in, garbage out'). 1966: E.J. and J.A. McCarthy, *Integrated Data Processing Systems*, v, Many data processing departments put their best operators on verifiers because they wish to avoid the effect of the GIGO principle (Garbage In – Garbage Out).

Gardener, As is the, so is the garden. 1732: Fuller, 701.

Garlands are not for every brow. Ibid., No. 1642.

Garlic. 1. Garlic makes a man wink, drink, and stink. 1594: Nashe, *Unfort. Trav.*, in *Works*, v 71 (Grosart). 1608: Harington, *Sch. of Salerne*, sig A8. [1754: Berthelson, *Eng.-Danish Dict.*, s.v. 'Wink', Onions make a man stink and wink.]

2. *See* quot. 1609: J. Melton, *Sixfold Politician*, 35, (according to the prouerbe): the smel of Garlicke takes away the stink of dunghills. *See also* **Eat** (14); and **White** (17).

Garrick, As deep as. 1880: Courtney, *W. Cornwall Words*, xiii (E.D.S.). 1889: Peacock, *Manley*, *etc.*, *Gloss.*, 162 (E.D.S.). 1907: *N.&Q.*, 10th ser, viii 251, Seventy years ago a common expression in Cornwall and Devon, in description of a specially acute or clever man, was that he was 'as deep as Garrick'. [See an article by A. Smythe Palmer in *Nineteenth Century*, Sept. 1910, pp. 550–2.]

Gaunt as a greyhound. 1678: Ray, 285, As gant as a greyhound. 1848: Thackeray, *Van. Fair*, ch lvii, He was quite well (though as gaunt as a greyhound).

Gauntlet of a hedging-glove, Make not a. 1639: Clarke, 5. 1670: Ray, 96. 1732: Fuller, 3318.

Gay as a goldfinch. 1821: Scott, *Kenilworth*, ch v, Thou art gay as a goldfinch.

Geese. *See* **Goose.**

Gelt. *See* quot. Gelt is the last peak of the Helvellyn Mountains. 1846–59: *Denham Tracts*, i 160 (F.L.S.), When Gelt puts on his night-cap, 'tis sure to rain.

Gentility without ability is worse than plain beggery. 1670: Ray, 96. 1831: Hone, *Year-Book*, 1416 [with 'plain' omitted].

Gentle as a falcon. [1412–20: Lydgate, *Troy Book*, bk ii l. 6605, Ageyn the faukon – gentil of nature ...] Before 1529: Skelton, *Garl. of Laurell*, Gentyll as faucoun. 1579: *Marr.of Wit and Wisdom*, sc ii p. 14 (SH.S.), You shall find him as gentell as a faulcon.

Gentle Craft, The, i.e. shoemaking. 1594: R. Wilson, *Coblers Proph.*, l. 1677 (Malone S.), Ile ... fall to my old trade of the gentle craft the cobler. 1637: L. Price, in *Pepysian Garland*, 447 (1922), The gentle craft doth beare good will to all kind hearted tradesmen still. 1713: Ward, *Hist. Grand Rebellion*, iii 464, When young, of Crispin's gentle craft by trade. 1834–7: Southey, *Doctor*, ch iii, St Crispin is of the Gentle Craft. 1921: *Times Lit. Suppl.*, 29 Dec., p. 868, col. 3, There must have been some reason, in times gone by, for the term of the 'gentle craft', applied only to the shoemaker's occupation.

Gentle heart is tied with an easy thread, A. 1640: Herbert, *Jac. Prudentum.*

Gentle hound should never play the cur, A. Before 1529: Skelton, *Garl. of Laurell*, l. 1436.

Gentle housewife mars the household, A. 1611: Cotgrave, s.v. 'Femme', The over gentle houswife marres her houshold. 1640: Herbert, *Jac. Prudentum.*

Gentle is that gentle does. 1854: J. W. Warter, *Last of Old Squires*, 43, His common saying was 'Gentle is that gentle does'

Gentleman. 1. A gentleman may make a king and a clerk may prove a pope. 1591: Harington, *Orl. Furioso*, bk v, Annot., According to the old proverb, A gentleman, etc.

2. A gentleman of the first head, or, A dunghill gentleman. 1552: Huloet, *Abced.*, sig. N5, Gentlemen of the first head, or *ironice* to be applyed to such as would be estemed a gentleman, hauing no poynt or qualitie of a gentleman, nor gentleman borne. 1583: Stubbes, *Anat. of Abuses*, 122 (N.Sh.S.), Notwithstanding he be a dunghill gentleman, or a gentleman of the first head, as they vse to term them. 1606: *Choice Chance, etc.*, 69 (Grosart), A gull, that for a little wealth was made a gentleman of the first head. 1681: W. Robertson, *Phraseol. Generalis*, 710, A gentleman of the first head; Novus homo.

3. A gentleman ought to travel abroad, but dwell at home. 1732: Fuller, 127.

4. A gentleman should have more in his pocket than on his back. 1732: Ibid., No. 128. 1869: Spurgeon, *John Ploughman*, ch iii.

5. A gentleman will do like a gentleman. 1630: Brathwait, *Eng. Gent.*, 148 (1641) [quoted as 'a common saying amongst us'].

6. A gentleman without an estate is a pudding without suet. 1659: Howell, 12 [with 'money' for 'an estate']. 1732: Fuller, 129.

7. A gentleman's greyhound and a saltbox, seek them at the fire. 1640: Herbert, *Jac. Prudentum.*

8. Gentlemen and rich men are venison in heaven; that is, 'very rare and daintie to haue them come thither'. *c.*1577: Northbrooke, *Against Dicing, etc.*, 22 (SH.S.).

9. He was meant for a gentleman but was spoiled in making. 1738: Swift, *Polite Convers.*, Dial. I, I think she was cut out for a gentlewoman, but she was spoiled in the making. 1830: Forby, *Vocab. E. Anglia*, 434. 1872: J. Clyde, jr., *Norfolk Garland*, 150.

10. It is not the gay coat that makes the gentleman. 1639: Clarke, 124. 1670: Ray, 11.

1732: Fuller, 3002 [with 'fine' for 'gay' and 'fine' before 'gentleman'].

11. Knowledge begins a gentleman, but 'tis conversation that completes him. 1732: Fuller, 3136.

12. What's a gentleman but his pleasure? 1573: G. Harvey, *Letter-Book*, 15 (Camden S.). 1595: *Maroccus Extat.*, 10 (Percy S.), You shall find in an old tracte printed by Winkin de Woorde, this olde sayde sawe: Whats a gentleman but his pleasure? 1670: Ray, 96. 1732: Fuller, 5506.

13. Who would be a gentleman, let him storm a town. 1670: Ray, 11.

See also **Adam.**

Gentry by blood is bodily gentry. 1732: Fuller, 1647.

Gentry sent to market will not buy one bushel of corn. Before 1598: Lord Burghley, in Peck, *Desid. Curiosa*, 47 (1779), For a man can buy nothing in the market with gentility. 1662: Fuller, *Worthies*, iii 441 (1840) [quoted as 'the plain proverb']. 1670: Ray, 96.

Geordy Potter. *See* quot. 1846–59: *Denham Tracts*, i 76 (F.L.S.), Lost in a wood, like Geordy Potter o' Sadberge [there is a rather long explanatory story].

George of Green. *See* **Good as.**

Gerards Bailiff. *See* quot. 1678: Ray, 355, Here is Gerards Bailiff, work or you must die with cold. *Somerset.*

Germain's lips. *See* quots. 1546: Heywood, *Proverbs*, Pt II ch ii, Iust (quoth she), As Iermans lips. 1579: Gosson, *Sch. of Abuse*, 27 (Arber), He … shall see them agree like dogges and cattes, and meete as iump as Germans lippes. 1596: Harington, *Ajax:* 'Apology', 41 (1814), Just as Jermin's lips. 1659: Howell, 3, As just as Jermans lippes; spoken in derision. 1869: *N & Q.*, 4th ser, iii 468, [Referring to the Gosson extract, a correspondent says:] Is not this an allusion to the proverb respecting 'Germain's lips, which came not together by nine mile'? [I have not met with this proverb.]

German's wit is in his fingers, The. 1605: Sylvester, *Du Bartas*, Week II Day ii Pt 3, l. 616, The Northern-man, whose wit in's fingers settles. 1611: Coryat, *Crudities*, ii 81 (1905), In so much that they say, the Germanes have their wit at their fingers ends. 1659: Howell, *Proverbs: Ital.-Eng.*, 17, The Germanes have their wits at their fingers ends, viz. good artificers.

Germoe. *See* Breage.

Get, *verb*. 1. Get up early. *See* Rise.

2. Get what you can, and what you get hold; 'Tis the stone that will turn all your lead into gold. 1736: Franklin, *Way to Wealth*, in *Works*, i 451 (Bigelow).

3. Getting out well is a quarter of the journey. 1732: Fuller, 1648.

4. He gets by that as Dickens did by his distress. 1639: Clarke, 82.

5. He who gets doth much, but he who keeps doth more. 1855: Bohn, 399.

6. To get out of the way of the waggon = To go one's way. Dorset. 1869: Hazlitt, 416.

7. What he gets, he gets out of the fire. 1678: Ray, 246.

Ghosts never appear on Christmas Eve. 1846: Denham, *Proverbs*, 63 (Percy S.).

Giant loves the dwarf, The. 1869: Blackmore, *Lorna Doone*, ch l., And verified the proverb that the giant loves the dwarf.

Giant will starve with what will surfeit a dwarf, A. 1732: Fuller, 209.

Giddy. *See* Dizzy.

Giff-gaff was a good fellow. 1549: Latimer, *Seven Sermons*, 84 (Arber). 1598: *Servingm. Comfort*, in *Inedited Tracts*, 130 (Hazlitt), The giffe gaffe promise he repentes. 1605: Camden, *Remains*, 322 (1870), Give gave is a good fellow. 1670: Ray, 96, Giff gaff was a good man, but he is soon weary. 1824: Scott, *Redgauntlet*, ch xiii, I have pledged my word for your safety, and you must give me yours to be private in the matter – giff-gaff, you know. 1868: Atkinson, *Cleveland Gloss.*, 217, Giff-gaff, *sb*. The interchange of familiar or unstudied conversation on cursory topics. 1913: E. M. Wright, *Rustic Speech, etc.*, 121, Giff-gaff … mutual obligation, reciprocity, used especially in the proverbial saying: giff-gaff makes good friends.

Gift and Gifts, 1. A gift long waited for is sold not given. 1732: Fuller, 130.

2. Don't Look a gift horse in the mouth. [Equi donati dentes non inspiciuntur. – Hier., *Ep. ad Ephes.*, Proem (quoted 'ut vulgare proverbium est').] *c*.1520, Stanbridge, *Vulgaria*, sig. C4, A gyuen hors may not be loked in the tethe. 1539: Taverner, *Proverbs*, fo. 49, A gyuen horse (we saye) maye not be loked in the mouth. 1674: Head and Kirkman, *Eng. Rogue*, iii 158, I am resolved to ride this way [facing the horse's tail], to make good the proverb, that I may not look a

gift horse in the mouth. 1712: Motteux, *Quixote*, Pt II ch lxii. 1826: Lamb, *Pop. Fallacies*, xi. 1871: G. Eliot, *Middlemarch* ch xiv, I thought I was not to look a gift-horse in the mouth, sir.

3. Gifts break a rock. 1640: Mabbe, *Exemplary Novels*, ii 169 (1900), Gifts will break through stone walls. 1732: Fuller, 1649.

4. Gifts enter without knocking. 1633: Draxe, 19. 1640: Herbert, *Jac. Prudentum*, Gifts enter everywhere without a wimble.

5. Gifts from enemies are dangerous. 1732: Fuller, 1650.

6. Gifts make beggars bold. 1669: Politeuphuia, 86. 1732: Fuller, 1651.

7. Gifts on nails. *See* Nails (3).

8. He has a gift. *See* quot. 1828: Carr, *Craven Dialect*, i 182, 'He's a gift at God nivver gave him', i.e. he is a notorious liar.

9. Throw no gift again at the giver's head. 1546: Heywood, *Proverbs*, Pt I ch xi. 1633: Draxe, 80, A man must not throw a gift at the giuers head.

Gilt off the gingerbread, To take the. 1830: Forby, *Vocab. E. Anglia*, 432, It will take the gilding off the gingerbread. 1927: *Observer*, 27 Feb., p. 22, col. 3, It was happy news that our income had increased by £76,000, and that the new year had started with a surplus of £26,000. But Mr Jenkinson quickly removed the gilt from our gingerbread.

Gilt spurs do not make the knight. 1572: J. Bossewell, *Workes of Armorie*, fo. 90, Chaucer sayeth that habite maketh no möcke, ne wearing of gylte spurres maketh no knyghte.

Gimmingham, Trimmingham, Knapton and Trunch, North Repps and South Repps are all of a bunch. 1670: Ray, 245. 1790: Grose, *Prov. Gloss.*, s.v. 'Norfolk'. 1865: W. White, *East. England*, i 188.

Gip. *See* quots. 1659: Howell, 4, Gip quoth Gilbert when his mare f – . 1678: Ray, 85, Gip with an ill rubbing, quoth Badger when his mare kickt. This is a ridiculous expression, used to people that are pertish and froward.

Gipsies. *See* Frost (5).

Girdle will not gird me, That. 1732: Fuller, 4343.

Give. 1. A given bite is soon put out of sight. 1855: Robinson, *Whitby Gloss.*, 71.

2. Give a clown your finger, and he will take your hand. 1640: Herbert, *Jac. Prudentum*. 1670: Ray, 5 [with 'whole' before 'hand'].

3. Give a loaf and beg a shive [slice]. 1678: Ray, 247. 1879: G. F. Jackson, *Shropsh. Word-Book*, 376, 'Er wuz too good-natured; 'er gid the loaf an' 'as to beg the shive.

4. Give advice. *See* **Advice.**

5. Give and be blessed. 1548: Hall, *Chron.*, 16 (1809), Wherof the prouerbe began, geue and be blessed, take awaie and bee accursed.

6. Give her the bells and let her fly. 1603: Dekker, *Pat. Grissil*, I, Ile be hangd if he do not … geue her the belles, let her flye. 1847: Halliwell, *Dict.*, s.v. 'Bells', … an old proverb taken from hawking … applied to the dismissal of any one that the owner has no longer occasion for.

7. Giving is dead and restoring very sick. 1578: Florio, *First Fruites*, fo. 30, Geuyng is dead and restoring is yl at ease. 1670: Ray, 11 [with 'now a days' after 'dead']. 1732: Fuller, 1661 … deadly sick. 1880: Spurgeon, *Ploughman's Pictures*, 154, They used to say that 'Give' is dead, and 'Restore' is buried, but I do not believe it.

8. Giving much to the poor doth enrich a man's store. 1640: Herbert, *Jac. Prudentum.* 1732: Fuller, 6114. 1880: Spurgeon, *Ploughman's Pictures*, 7.

9. Giving to God is no loss. 1875: A. B. Cheales, *Proverb. Folk-Lore*, 126.

10. He can give little to his servant that licks his knife. 1640: Herbert, *Jac. Prudentum.*

11. He gives twice that gives quickly. [Duplex fit bonitas, simul accessit celeritas. – Pub. Syr., 141.] *c.*1385: Chaucer, *Leg. Good Women*, Prol., l. 441, For who-so yeveth a yift, or doth a grace, Do hit by tyme, his thank is wel the more. 1539: Taverner, *Proverbs*, fo. 25, He gyueth twyse yt gyueth quyckely. 1560: T. Wilson, *Rhetorique*, 119 (1909), He giueth twise that giueth sone and cherefully. 1631: F. Lenton, *Characters*, sig. H2 (1663), He that gives timely gives twice. 1712: Motteux, *Quixote*, Pt I bk iv ch vii 1846: Wright, *Essays on Middle Ages*, i 146.

12. He that gives his goods before he be dead. *See* quots. 1640: Herbert, *Jac. Prudentum*, He that gives all before he dies provides to suffer. 1683: Meriton, *Yorkshire Ale*, 83–7 (1697), He that gives all his geir to his bairns may tack a mell and knock out his hares [brains]. 1710: S. Palmer, *Moral Essays on Proverbs*, 27, Give away all before I am dead, And take a beetle and knock me o' th' head. 1735: Inscription on front wall of Hospital at Leominster, founded 1735, He that

gives away all Before he is dead, Let 'em take this hatchet And knock him on ye head.

13. He that gives me small gifts would have me live. *c.*1320: in *Reliq. Anliquae*, i 112 (1841), 'That me lutel geveth, he my lyf ys on'; Quoth Hendyng. 1640: Herbert, *Jac. Prudentum.*

14. He who gives to another bestows on himself. 1681: Rycaut, tr. Gracian's *Critick*, 240. 1732: Fuller, 2114, He that gives to a worthy person, bestows a benefit upon himself.

15. I thought I would give him one, and lend him another, 'i.e. I would be quit with him'. 1670: Ray, 177.

16. They that give are ever welcome. Quoted as 'a sayenge'. *c.*1534: Berners, *Huon*, 235 (E.E.T.S.).

17. To give a thing and take a thing, is to wear the devil's gold ring – with variants. 1611: Cotgrave, s.v. 'Retirer', To weare the devills gold-ring (say we in a triviall proverb). 1663: Killigrew, *Parson's Wedding*, III v, Fie! give a thing and take a thing? 1666: Torriano, *Piazza Univ.*, 79, As the English say, to give a thing, and take it again is the devil's gold ring. 1678: Ray, 146, Give a thing and take again, And you shall ride in hell's wain. 1816: Byron, *Letters and Journals*, iv 11 (Prothero), It is so like these fellows, to do by it as they did by their sovereigns – abandon both; to parody the old rhymes, 'Take a thing and give a thing' – 'Take a king and give a king'. 1894: *N. & Q.*, 8th ser, vi 155, Another saying among boys is – Give a thing and take a thing, To wear the devil's gold ring. 1901: F. E. Taylor, *Lancs Sayings*, 43, Give a thing – tak' a thing; God's gowd ring!

18. To give always, there is never no end. [Largitio fundum non habet. – Cicero, *Off.*, II xv 55.] 1623: Wodroephe, *Spared Houres*, 475.

19. To give and keep there is need of wit. 1620: Shelton, *Quixote*, Pt II ch lviii [as in 1732]. 1670: Ray, 11. 1712: Motteux, *Quixote*, Pt II ch lviii, I guess he stuck to the proverb, To give and keep what is fit, requires a share of wit. 1732: Fuller, 6353, To give and to have, Doth a brain crave.

20. To give one as good as one brings. 1542: Udall, tr. Erasmus' *Apoph.*, i 139 (1877), Plato paied Diogenes home againe well enough, and gaue as good as he brought. 1676: Etherege, *Man of Mode*, I, To him! give him as good as he brings. 1709: O. Dykes, *Eng. Proverbs*, 230, You shall have as good as you bring, at Billingsgate;

not to say, worse. 1843: Carlyle, *Past and Present*, bk ii ch xii, Everywhere we try at least to give the adversary as good as he brings.

21. To give one's head for the washing (or **for nought**). *c.*1500: Medwall, *Nature*, l. 721, A well drawen man ys he and a well taught That wyll not gyue hys hed for nought. 1596: Nashe, *Haue with You*, in *Works*, iii 106 (Grosart), The time was when he would not haue giuen his head for the washing. 1602: Chettle, *Hoffman*, III ii 1615: B.&F., *Cupid's Revenge*, IV iii, And so am I, and forty more good fellows, That will not give their heads for the washing, I take it. 1738: Swift, *Polite Convers.*, Dial. I. 1847: Halliwell, *Dict.*, s.v. 'Head', *To give … washing*, to submit to be imposed upon.

22. To give or to forbear requires judgment. 1736: Bailey, *Dict.*, s.v. 'Give'.

23. To give up the girdle = To submit. *c.*1350: *Alexander*, l. 181, Bot gefe thaim up the girdill. 1655: Howell, *Letters*, bk iv No. xix, The other [French] proverb is, *Il a quitté sa ceinture*, he hath given up his girdle; which intimated as much as if he had become bankrupt, or had all his estate forfeited.

24. What thou sparest from giving for God's sake, the devil will carry another way. 1541: Coverdale, *Christ. State Matrimony*, sig. I4 [cited as 'the common prouerbe'].

25. Who gives to all denies all. 1611: Cotgrave, s.v. 'Donner', He that gives me all denies me all: viz. He that offers me all, meanes to give me nothing. 1640: Herbert, *Jac. Prudentum*.

26. You give me roast and beat me with the spit. 1560: T. Wilson, *Rhetorique*, 131 (1909), Such are not to bee liked that giue a man a shoulder of mutton, and breake his head with the spitte when they haue done. 1658: in *Musarum Deliciae*, i 280 (Hotten). 1716: E. Ward, *Female Policy*, 53, She will give thee roast-meat, but beat thee with the spit. 1855: Robinson, *Whitby Gloss.*, 165, Never invite a friend to a roast and then beat him with the spit. 1913: E. M. Wright, *Rustic Speech, etc.*, 172 [as in 1855].

Glad as a fowl. *See* **Fowl**.

Gladness, A man of, seldom falls into madness. 1659: Howell, 17. 1670: Ray, 11. 1732: Fuller, 6235.

Glass houses. *See* quots. *c.*1385: Chaucer, *Troilus and Criseyde*, ii 867, Who that hath an hed of verre [glass], Fro cast of stones war hym in the

were [wars]! 1640: Herbert, *Jac. Prudentum*, Whose house is of glass, must not throw stones at another. 1720: C. Shadwell, *Sham Prince*, I ii, Ay cousen, no body should throw stones, whose house is made of glass. 1793: Grose, *Olio*, 281 (2nd ed.), One who has a head of glass should never engage in throwing stones. 1842: Barham, *Ing. Legends*, 2nd ser: 'St Medard', If you've any glass windows never throw stones! 1892: Shaw, *Widowers' Houses*, II, People who live in glass houses have no right to throw stones. 1909: De Morgan, *Never can happen Again*, i 159, Why condemn him? No! – Lizarann lived in a glass house, and wouldn't throw stones.

Glass tells you, What your, will not be told by counsel. 1640: Herbert, *Jac. Prudentum*. 1670: Ray, 11.

Glasses and lasses are brittle ware. 1666: Torriano, *Piazza Univ.*, 304, Glass and a maid ever in danger. 1736: Bailey, *Dict.*, s.v. 1875: A. B. Cheales, *Proverb. Folk-Lore*, 4.

Glastonbury. *See* **Old**, D (7); and **Shaftesbury**.

Glean before the cart has carried, To. 1546: Heywood, *Proverbs*, Pt I ch xi, Thou goest a glenyng er the cart haue caried. 1633: Draxe, 175, Hee goeth a gleaning before that the cart haue carried.

Glitters is not gold, All that. *See* **All that glitters …**

Glorious Sixth of May, The. 1917: Bridge, *Cheshire Proverbs*, 114 [6 May, 1807 – see a long story at the reference given].

Gloucester. *See* **Worcester**.

Gloucestershire, As sure as God's in. 1655: Fuller, *Church Hist.*, bk vi § ii (iv 15), Hence the topical wicked proverb … 'As sure as God is in Gloucestershire', as if so many convents had certainly fastened His gracious presence to that place. 1724: Stukeley, *Itin. Cur.*, 64, The old proverb, as sure as God's at Glocester. 1858: P. J. Bailey, *The Age*, 44. 1898: Gibbs, *Cotswold Village*, ch iv. 1920: Ditchfield, *Byways in Berkshire, etc.*, 276.

Gloucestershire kindness, giving away what you don't want yourself. 1894: Northall, *Folk Phrases*, 14 (E.D.S.).

Glowing coals will be sparkling. 1633: Draxe, 84, Glowing coales sparkle often. 1732: Fuller, 6235.

Glow-worm lights her lamp, When the, the air is always damp. 1893: Inwards, *Weather Lore*, 145.

Glue did not hold, The, 'i.e. You were baulked in your wishes: you missed your aim'. 1813: Ray, 196.

Glutton. 1. A glutton is never generous. 1855: Bohn, 287.

2. A glutton young, a beggar old. Cited as 'the old saying'. 1880: Spurgeon, *Ploughman's Pictures*, 11.

3. Non sigheth so sore as the gloton that mai no more. Before 1500: Hill, *Commonplace-Book*, 129 (E.E.T.S.).

4. Who hastens a glutton chokes him. 1640: Herbert, *Jac. Prudentum*.

Gluttony kills more than the sword. *c.*1535: *Dialogues of Creatures*, ccxxviii. (1816), Many moo people be glotonye is slayne, Then in batell or in fight, or with other peyne. 1580: Lyly, *Euphues*, 275 (Arber), More perish by a surfet then the sword. *c.*1625: B.&F., *Women Pleased*, I ii, Surfeits destroy more than the sword. 1669: *Politeuphuia*, 302, By gluttony more die then perish by the sword. 1736: Bailey, *Dict.*, s.v. 'Surfeit', Surfeits slay more than swords. Cf. **More die.**

Go, *verb.* **1. Do not say go, but gaw,** 'viz. go thy self along'. 1659: Howell, 4. 1669: Dudley North, *Obs. and Adv. Oeconom.*, 50, In small families especially in the country, the master may say *Gow* (as we phrase it in East England) or go we, implying that he will accompany them. 1670: Ray, 11. 1823: Moor, *Suffolk Words and Phrases*, A farmer observed, that when his mother called the maids at 'milking time', she never said 'go' but 'gow'.

2. Go forward and fall, go backward and mar all. 1639: Clarke, 102. 1670: Ray, 177. 1738: *Gent. Mag.*, 475, Go back and fall; go forward and mar all.

3. Go here away, go there away, quoth Madge Whitworth, when she rode the mare i' th' tedder. 1678: Ray, 85.

4. Go in God's name, so you ride no witches. 1678: Ray, 247. 1846–59: *Denham Tracts*, ii 83 (F.L.S.).

5. Go it cripples, crutches are cheap. 1869: Hazlitt, 143.

6. Go shake your ears. *See* **Shake your ears.**

7. Go to bed and sleep for wit, and buy land when you have more money. 1886: R. Holland, *Cheshire Gloss.*, 448 (E.D.S.). 1917: Bridge, *Cheshire Proverbs*, 62.

8. Go to the devil and shake yourself, *c.*1816: T. Wilson, *Companion to Ballroom*, 86 [an Irish jig so entitled]. 1846–59: *Denham Tracts*, i 46 (F.L.S.), We have also, in the south of England, 'Go to Bath!' and … the whole of which are pretty much on a par with the still more impious one of 'Go to the devil and shake yourself'. 1862: Borrow, *Wild Wales*, ch xxv, And when I persisted, [he] bade me to go to the Divil and shake myself. Cf. **Shake your ears.**

9. He goes not out of his way that goes to a good inn. 1611: Cotgrave, s.v. 'Fourvoyer'. 1670: Ray, 14. 1732: Fuller, 1851. 1909: Hackwood, *Inns, Ales, etc.*, 189.

10. He goes (or runs) far that never turns. 1546: Heywood, *Proverbs*, Pt II ch ix, He runneth far that never turneth again. 1577: *Misogonus*, I i, He goeth farr that never tournes agayne, as folke say. 1606: T. Heywood, *If You Know Not Me*, Pt II, in *Dram. Works*, i 329 (1874), But he goes far that neuer turns or. 1633: in *Pepysian Garland*, 420 (1922), He runs farre that ne'r returneth, is a prouerbe still in vse. 1732: Fuller, 2012, He runneth far indeed that never returneth.

11. He goes upright that never halts, *c.*1592: *Sir T. More*, 23 (Malone S.).

12. He is going to grass with his teeth upwards = He is going to be buried. 1813: Ray, 196.

13. He that goes and comes maketh a good voyage. 1578: Florio, *First Fruites*, fo. 29 [with 'returneth' for 'comes' 1629: *Book of Meery Riddles*, Prov. 90.

14. He that goes barefoot. *See* **Thorn** (1).

15. He that goes softly, goes safely. 1549: Latimer, *Seven Sermons*, 28 (Arber), For as they say commonly *Qui vadit plane, vadit sane*, that is, He that walketh playnly, walketh safely. 1681: W. Robertson, *Phraseol. Generalis*, 672.

16. He that goes to bed sober. *See* **Often drunk.**

17. He that goes to bed thirsty riseth healthy. 1640: Herbert, *Jac. Prudentum*. 1670: Ray, 36. 1754: Berthelson, *Eng.-Danish Dict.*, s.v. 'Bed'.

18. How does he go through dirt? 1917: Bridge, *Cheshire Proverbs*, 75 … How does he bear suffering or temptation?

19. To go a high lone. 1586: Pettie, tr. Guazzo's *Civil Convers.*, fo. 12, All beastes so soone as they are deliuered from their dam get vpon there feete, and are able to stand a high alone. 1672: Walker, *Paroem.*, 37, To go a high lone; by himself.

20. To go about the bush. *See* **Beat** (4).

21. To go as if dead lice dropped off you. 1672: Walker, *Paroem.*, 20. 1678: Ray, 75. 1893: J. Salisbury, *S.E. Worcs. Gloss.*, 36 (E.D.S.), Look at 'im, 'e creeps along as ef dyud lice wus a drappin' off 'im.

22. To go round land = *To die.* 1888: Q.-Couch, *Troy Town*, ch xi, He went round land at las', and was foun' dead in his bed. 1926: *Devonsh. Assoc. Trans.*, lvii. 152, ' 'E's a gone round land', i.e. died.

23. To go the whole hog. 1836: Marryat, *Japhet*, ch liv., As you are not prepared, as the Americans say, *to go the whole hog*, we will part good friends. 1846: *Bentley Ballads*, 20 (1876), Each a democrat dog, That will go the whole hog.

24. To go to heaven on a feather-bed. 1630: Brathwait, *Eng. Gent.*, 152 (1641), Wee cannot goe to heaven on beds of down. 1681: W. Robertson, *Phraseol. Generalis*, 718, None go to heaven on a feather-bed. 1736: Bailey, *Dict.*, s.v. 'Way'.

25. To go to heaven in a string = To be hanged. Before 1635: Corbet, *Poems*, in Chalmers, v 582, Thou shortly shalt to Heaven in a string … We'll all be glad, Great Tom, to see thee hang'd. 1679: in *Roxb. Ballads*, iv 141 (B.S.), But some are gone to heaven in a string. 1710: T. Ward, *Eng. Reform.*, 178 (1716), And go to heaven in a string. 1778: T. Cogan, *John Buncle, Jr.*, ii 251.

26. To go to pot. *See* **Pot** (7).

27. What goes around comes around. A modern proverb from the U.S.A. usually used to mean that poetic justice operates in the world and that people get what they deserve or it is done unto them as they did unto others. 1974: E. Stone, *Donald writes no More*, XV. No one can say why Donald Goines and Shirley Sailor were murdered. The ghetto philosophy, 'what goes around comes around', is the only answer most people can give. 1987: Tom Wolfe, *The Bonfire of the Vanities*: 'You have to make good on contracts'. 'You have to? Why?' 'Because everybody in the courthouse believes in a saying: "What goes around comes around." That means if you don't take care a me today, I won't take care a you tomorrow'.

28. What goes up must come down. 1929: F.A. Pottle, *Stretchers*, vii, The antiaircraft guns always took a shot for luck. What goes up must come down, and one can be killed quite as neatly by a fragment of his own shrapnel as by the enemy's.1939: L. I. Wilder, *By the Shores of Silver Lake*, 1948: N. Mailer, *The Naked and the Dead*, III vi, In the larger meanings of the curve, gravity would occupy the place of mortality (what goes up must come down) and wind resistance would be the resistance of the medium.

29. Who goes a borrowing. *See* **Borrow** (3).

30. Who goes to bed supperless, all night tumbles and tosses. 1567: Painter, *Pal. of Pleasure*, iii 215 (Jacobs), Accordynge to the prouerbe: He that goeth to bed supperlesse, lyeth in his bed restlesse. 1670: Ray, 37. 1906: J. M. Rigg, tr. *Decameron*, i 201, I have heard you say a thousand times; 'Who fasting goes to bed, uneasy lies his head'.

31. You go as if nine men held you. 1546: Heywood, *Proverbs*, Pt I ch xi, Ye ren to woorke in haste as nine men helde ye. 1672: Walker, *Paroem.*, 20, To go … as if nine men pull'd you and ten men held you. 1678: Ray, 348.

32. You may go farther and fare worse. [Nota mala res optumast. – Plautus, *Trin.*, 63.] 1546: Heywood, *Proverbs*, Pt II ch iv, You … might haue gone further and haue faren wurs. 1632: Shirley, *Love in a Maze*, II ii, I may go farther, and fare worse. 1738: Swift, *Polite Convers.*, Dial. II. 1834–7: Southey, *Doctor*, ch viii p. i., Because if there be no Purgatory, the Dean may have gone farther and fared worse. 1905: E. G. Hayden, *Travels Round our Village*, 95, I reckon them two's a-thinkin' o' gettin' wed … an' he med go furder an' fare wuss, fur she's a swate purty cratur.

Goat and **Goats. 1. An old goat is never the more reverend for his beard.** 1732: Fuller, 646. 1901: *N.&Q.*, 9th ser, viii 510.

2. Contend not about a goat's beard. 1732: Fuller, 1151.

3. Goats are not sold at every fair. Ibid., No. 1667.

4. The goat must browse where she is tied. 1611: Cotgrave, s.v. 'Chevre'. 1640: Herbert, *Jac. Prudentum.* 1714: Ozell, *Molière*, iii 207. 1852: FitzGerald, *Polonius*, 66 (1903).

5. You have no goats, and yet you sell kids. 1732: Fuller, 5922.

God above gets all men's lore, Not. 1639: Clarke, 147. 1670: Ray, 97. 1732: Fuller, 6105.

God Almighty by the toe (or **foot**), **To have.** 1548: Hall, *Chron.*, 462 (1809), The duches thinkyng to haue gotten God by the foote, when she had the deuell by the tayle. 1591: Harington, *Orl. Furioso*, bk xliv, Notes, For if they may match their daughters so as they may say, my lord my sonne, they thinke they haue God almightie by the toe (as the prouerbe saith). 1639: Clarke, 125, He hath got God Almighty by the toe.

God bade ho, One of them to whom. 1546: Heywood, *Proverbs*, Pt I ch xi, She is one of them to whom God bad who; She will all haue, and will right nought forgo. *c.*1594: Bacon, *Promus*, No. 646, He is one of them to whom God bidd how. 1659: Howell, 7.

God comes at last when we think he is furthest off. 1659: Howell, *Proverbs: Ital.-Eng.*, 7. 1670: Ray, 11.

God comes to see without a bell. 1640: Herbert, *Jac. Prudentum*. 1659: Howell, *Proverbs: Span.-Eng.*, 2, God comes to visit us without a bell, viz. without noise.

God comes with leaden feet but strikes with iron hands. 1579: Lyly, *Euphues*, 172 (Arber), Though God haue leaden handes which when they strike pay home, yet hath he leaden feete whiche are as slow to ouertake a sinner. 1630: T. Adams, *Works*, 777, He will strike with yron hands, that came to strike with leaden feet. 1670: Ray, 11. 1853: Trench, *Proverbs*, 140 (1905). Cf. **God stays long.**

God complains not, but does what is fitting. 1640: Herbert, *Jac. Prudentum*.

God defend me from my friends, I'll keep myself from my enemies. 1477: Rivers, *Dictes and Sayings*, 127 (1877), Ther was one that praied god to kepe him from the daunger of his frendis. 1594: A. Copley, *Wits, Fits, etc.*, 50 (1614), A fained friend God shield me from his danger, For well I'le saue my selfe from foe and stranger. 1647: Howell, *Letters*, bk ii No. 75, There is a saying that carrieth with it a great deal of caution; *From him whom I trust, God defend me; for from him I trust not, I will defend myself.* 1710: S. Palmer, *Moral Essays on Proverbs*, 311. 1821: Scott, in Lockhart's *Life*, v 58. 1890: *N.&Q.*, 7th ser, x 428, 'God save me from my friends, I can take care of my enemies

myself' … is generally given as the saying of Maréchal Villars on taking leave of Louis XIV. [It is obviously older.]

God defend me from the still water, and I'll keep myself from the rough. 1666: Torriano, *Piazza Univ.*, 2. 1732: Fuller, 1668.

God deliver me from a man of one book. 1659: Howell, *Proverbs: Ital.-Eng.*, 7, From one that reads but one book … the Lord deliver us. 1855: Bohn, 362.

God deprives him of bread who likes not his drink. 1670: Ray, 11.

God for money, He that serves, will serve the devil for better wages. 1692: L'Estrange, *Aesop*, 100 (3rd ed.) [cited as 'the old saying'].

God grant your early rising do you no harm. 'Spoken jeeringly' 1659: Howell, 11.

God has a church. *See* Devil (50).

God hath done his part. 1556: Heywood, *Spider and Flie*, 4 (1908), God hath done his part: she hath a good face. 1567: Harman, *Caveat*, 48 (E.E.T.S.), But as the prouerbe is 'God hath done his part'. 1605: Chapman, etc., *Eastw. Hoe*, IV ii, (God hath done his part in thee), but thou haste made too much, and beene to proud of that face.

God hath few friends, the devil hath many. *c.*1610: Drayton, *Mooncalf*, in *Works*, ii 483 (1753).

God hath marked, Beware of him whom. 1678: Ray, 347. 1710: S. Palmer, *Moral Essays on Proverbs*, 113, Take heed of him that God has mark'd.

God hath often a great share in a little house. 1611: Cotgrave, s.v. 'Maison' 1670: Ray, 11. 1880: Spurgeon, *Ploughman's Pictures*, 154.

God, He who serves, hath a good master. 1611: Cotgrave, s.v. 'Maistre', The servant of God hath a good master. 1666: Torriano, *Piazza Univ.*, 69. 1853: Trench, *Proverbs*, 138 (1905).

God heals, and the physician hath the thanks. 1640: Herbert, *Jac. Prudentum*. 1660: Howell, *Parly of Beasts*, 77, Though God heals, yet the physitian carries away the fees. *c.*1736: Franklin, in *Works*, i 456 (Bigelow), God heals, the doctor takes the fee. 1861: O. W. Holmes, *Elsie Venner*, ch xxii, 'I dressed his wound and God healed him'. That was an old surgeon's saying.

God help the fool, quoth Pedley. 1678: Ray, 72. 1732: Fuller, 1674.

God help the rich, the poor can beg. 1659: Howell, 16. 1670: Ray, 22. 1732: Fuller, 1675.

God helps them that help themselves. [σὺν
Ἀθηνᾷ καὶ χεῖρα κίνει. – Zenobius, v 93.] 1545:
R. Taverner, *Proverbs or Adagies out of Erasmus*,
57 *Dii facientes adiuvant*. The goddes do helpe
the doers. 1551: T. Wilson, *Rule of Reason*, S1v,
Shipmen cal to God for helpe, and God will
helpe them, but so not withstandying, if they
helpe them selfes. 1580: Baret, *Alvearie*, I 136,
God doth helpe those in their affaires, which are
industrious. 1611: Cotgrave, s.v. 'Ourdi', Begin
to helpe thy selfe, and God will helpe thee. 1736:
Franklin, *Way to Wealth*, in *Works*, i 442
(Bigelow). 1875: Smiles, *Thrift*, 177.

God helps, Where, nought harms. *c.*1300:
Havelok, l. 648, Ther God wile helpen, nouht ne
dereth. *c.*1460: *How the Good Wife*, l. 14, Seldam
is the house pore there God is stywarde. *c.*1534:
Berners, *Huon*, 480 (E.E.T.S.), It is a comune
prouerbe sayde, whome that god wyll ayde no
man can hurte. *c.*1555: in Wright, *Songs, etc.*,
Philip and Mary, 161 (Roxb.Cl), Whom Gode
wolde have holpen he shall never waunte.

**God in thy calling, Serve, it is better than
praying.** 1659: Howell, 9 (7).

God is a good man. 1526: *Hund. Mery Talys*,
No. 85, p. 140 (Oesterley), There came one
which sayde yᵗ god was a good man. 1599:
Shakespeare, *Much Ado*, III v. 1646: Quarles, in
Works, i 79 (Grosart), It is enough for mee to
know, that God is a good man.

**God is at the end when we think he is farthest
off it.** 1640: Herbert, *Jac. Prudentum.*

**God is better pleased with adverbs than with
nouns.** 1570: in *Complete Hist. of England*, ii 502
(1706), That evil was not to be done that good
might come of it: that God was better pleased
with adverbs than with nouns; and more
approved what was done *well* and *lawfully* than
what was otherwise good. 1607: Bp. Hall, *Holy
Observations*, § 14, God loveth adverbs; and cares
not how good, but how well. 1620: Ford, *Line of
Life*, 64 (SH.S.), This man not only liues, but
liues well, remembring alwayes the old adage,
that God is the rewarder of aduerbes, not of
nownes. 1860: Motley, *United Netherlands*, i 2
(1876), Fortunately that member of Parliament
had made the discovery in time … that 'The Lord
was better pleased with adverbs than with nouns'.

God is in the ambry. 1546: Heywood, *Proverbs*,
Pt II ch iv 1633: Draxe, 159. 1659: Howell, 6,
There is God in the almery.

God is no botcher. 1562: Heywood, *Three
Hund. Epigr.*, No. 62. 1659: Howell, 5.

God is where he was. 1530: Palsgrave, 519,
Never dispayre, man, God is there as he was.
1602: Breton, in *Works*, ii g 12 (Grosart), God is
where he was, he hath called me home, follow
me to him. 1678: Ray, 147.

**God kills, That which, is better than that killed
by man.** 1869: Hazlitt, 354.

God knows well which are the best pilgrims.
1611: Cotgrave, s.v. 'Pelerin', God knowes
who's a good pilgrim. 1678: Ray, 147. 1732:
Fuller, 1678.

**God loves, Whom, his house is savoury to
him.** 1620: Shelton, *Quixote*, Pt II ch xliii. 1732:
Fuller, 5724.

**God made the country, and man made the
town.** [*divina natura dedit agros, ars humana
aedificavit urbes* (divine nature gave the fields,
human skill built the towns) – Varro, *De Re
Rustica* iii i] 1667: A. Cowley, in J. Wells *Poems*,
2, My father said … God the first garden made,
and the first city, Cain. 1785: Cowper, *The Task*,
i 40, God made the country, and man made the
town. 1870: H. Tennyson, *Memoir*, 25 Jan.,
(1897) II 96, There is a saying that if God made
the country, and man the town, the devil made
the little country town.

God made, What, he never mars. 1659:
Howell, *Proverbs: Brit.-Eng.*, 24.

**God make you an honester man than your
father.** 1678: Ray, 347.

**God makes and apparel shapes, but it is
money that finishes the man.** 1650: Bulwer,
Anthropomet., 256, I shall a little explain this
proverb; *God makes and the tailor shapes.* 1670:
Ray, 122 [with 'makes' for 'finishes']. 1732:
Fuller, 1680. 1926: *Evening Standard*, 11 Dec.,
p. 5, col. 2.

God never pays his debts with money. Said of
any bad person who falls ill, or meets with
misfortunes. 1893: *Co. Folk-Lore: Suffolk*, 150
(F.L.S.).

God never sends mouths but he sends meat.
1377: Langland, *Plowman*, B, xiv 39, For lente
neuere was lyf but lyflode were shapen. *c.*1560:
Becon, *Catechism, etc.*, 602 (P.S.), There is a
proverb no less true than common: 'God never
made mouth but he made meat'. 1658: R.
Brome, *New Academy*, IV, There comes not a
mouth into the world, but there's meat for't.

1732: Fuller, 1681. 1829: Cobbett, *Advice to Young Men*, Lett. III, 'I do not care how many' [children I have], said the man, 'God never sends mouths without sending meat'.

God only makes heirs. 1669: Dudley North, *Obs. and Adv.* (*Econom.*, 25, Our lawyers have this saying, that God onely makes heirs.

God or a painter, He is either a, for he makes faces. 1592: Shakespeare, *L. L. L.*, V ii 1732: Fuller, 1914.

God, our parents and our master can never be requited. 1670: Ray, 12.

God send me a friend that may tell me of my faults; if not, an enemy, and he will. 1678: Ray, 346 [very slight variation]. 1732: Fuller, 1686 [ending with 'faults'] 1748: Richardson, *Clarissa*, iv 238 (1785).

God send us of our own when rich men go to dinner. 1639: Clarke, 37. 1670: Ray, 129.

God send you joy, for sorrow will come fast enough. 1633: Draxe, 119.

God send you more wit and me more money. 1659: Howell, 15. 1670: Ray, 199. 1732: Fuller, 1689.

God sends cold after clothes. 1546: Heywood, *Proverbs*, Pt I ch iv 1611: Cotgrave, s.v. 'Dieu', God sends men cold according to their cloath; viz. afflictions according to their faith. 1732: Fuller, 1687. 1853: Trench, *Proverbs*, 66 (1905), Many languages have this proverb: *God gives the cold according to the cloth.*

God sends corn end the devil mars the sack. 1633: Draxe, 4 [with 'asketh' for 'sends']. 1670: Ray, 97.

God sends fortune to fools. 1546: Heywood, *Proverbs*, Pt II ch vi *c.*1594: Bacon, *Promus*, No. 493. 1601: Shakespeare, *As You Like It*, II vii, Call me not fool till heaven hath sent me fortune. 1659: Howell, 8. Cf. **Fool** (51); and **Fortune favours fools.**

God sends good luck and God sends bad. 1639: Clarke, 165.

God sends meat and the devil sends cooks. 1542: Boorde, *Dyetary*, 260 (E.E.T.S.), It is a common prouerbe, 'God may sende a man good meate, but the deuyll may sende an euyll coke to dystrue it'. *c.*1600: Deloney, in *Works*, 221 (1912), God sends meate, and the diuell sends cookes. 1674: Head and Kirkman, *Eng. Rogue*, iii 271. 1738: Swift, *Polite Convers.*, Dial. II. 1822: Scott, *Nigel*, ch xxvii 1904: J. C. Wall, *Devils*,

127, 'God sends meat, but the devil sends cooks', is an old adage which Giraldus Cambrensis, in his caustic criticisms on the greed of the monastic Orders, thus revised – 'God sent the abbeys, but the devil sent the kitchens and the cellars'.

'God speed you well,' quo' clerk of Hope. 1889: *Folk-Lore Journal*, vii 292.

God stays long but strikes at last. 1659: Howell, *Proverbs: Brit.-Eng.*, 19. 1878: J. Platt, *Morality*, 34. Cf. **God comes with leaden feet.**

God strikes not with both hands. [1600: Bodenham, *Belvedere*, 1 (Spens.S.), God with his finger strikes, and not his arme.] 1640: Herbert, *Jac. Prudentum*, God strikes not with both hands, for to the sea He made havens, and to rivers fords. 1853: Trench, *Proverbs*, 132 (1905), Nor otherwise with the Spanish: *God never wounds with both hands … for He ever reserves one with which to bind up and to heal.*

God tempers the wind to the shorn lamb. [1594: H. Estienne, *Prémices*, 47, Ces termes, Dieu mesure le froid à la brebis tondue, sont les propres termes du proverbe.] 1640: Herbert, *Jac. Prudentum*, To a close shorn sheep, God gives wind by measure. 1768: Sterne, *Sent. Journey*, 162 (1794), How she had borne it, and how she had got supported, she could not tell – but God tempers the wind, said Maria, to the shorn lamb. 1835: Lytton, *Rienzi*, bk iii ch iii, God help her, and temper the rough wind to the lamb! 1921: *Punch*, 9 Nov., p. 366, col. 2, It was an advertisement of the Only Infallible Hair Producer. Even so is the wind tempered to shorn lambs.

God than gold, Better. 1659: Howell, *Proverbs: Brit.-Eng.*, 16.

God that helps a man, He is a. 1725: Bailey, tr. Erasmus' *Colloq.*, 517, If the proverb be true, *That he is a God that helps a man*, then you are a God to me.

God, The grace of, is worth a fair. *c.*1400: *Mirks Festial*, 86 (E.E.T.S.), Ye haue a comyn sayng among you, and sayn that Godys grace ys worth a new fayre. 1546: Heywood, *Proverbs*, Pt I ch xii *c.*1594: Bacon, *Promus*, No. 37. 1595: Shakespeare, *M. of Venice*, II ii, The old proverb is very well parted between my master Shylock and you, sir: you have the grace of God, sir, and he hath enough. 1659: Howell, 3. 1868: *Quart. Review*, cxxv. 248, Our old and beautiful adage, 'The grace of God is gear enough'.

God white [requite] **you.** 1653: Walton, *Angler*, Pt I ch iv, Marry, God requite you, Sir, and we'll eat it cheerfully. 1917: Bridge, *Cheshire Proverbs*, 61.

God will send thee flax, Get thy spindle and thy distaff ready, and. 1670: Ray, 11.

God will, What, no frost can kill. 1670: Ray, 97. 1732: Fuller, 6106.

God will, When, all winds bring rain. 1633: Draxe, 81, When God will, at all windes it will raine. 1681: W. Robertson, *Phraseol. Generalis*, 674. 1732: Fuller, 5554. 1875: A. B. Cheales, *Proverb. Folk-lore*, 25.

God's blessing, Out of. *See* **Out of.**

God's grace. *See* **Pilling Moss**; and **God, The grace of.**

God's help is better than early rising. 1620: Shelton, *Quixote*, Pt II ch xxxiv 1732: Fuller, 1685.

God's help, Who hopeth in, his help cannot start. 1546: Heywood, *Proverbs*, Pt I ch iv.

God's in his heaven, all's right with the world. A later version of the consolatory maxim **God is where he was** (q.v.). 1841: R. Browning, 'Pippa Passes 'in *Works* (1970), Morning's at seven, The snail's on the thorn, God's in his heaven – All's right with the world. 1928: E. Waugh: *Decline and Fall*, i v, When you've been in the soup as often as I have, it gives you a sort of feeling that everything's for the best, really. You know, God's in his heaven: all's right with the world.

God's mill grinds slow but sure. [ὀψὲ θεῶν ἀλέουσι μύλοι, ἀλέουσι δὲ λεπτά. – *Proverbia e Cod. Coisl.*, No. 396, in Gaisford, *Paroem. Graec.*, 164 (1836).] 1640: Herbert, *Jac. Prudentum.* 1853: Trench, *Proverbs*, 140 (1905), The ancient Greek one: *The null of God grinds late, but grinds to powder. See also* **Mill** (9).

God's name, That never ends ill which begins in. 1639: Clarke, 109. Cf. the reverse, s.v. **In the name of the Lord.**

God. *See also* **Charitable** (2); **Danger** (7); **Devil** (52), (61), and (106); **Gift** (7); **Give** (9) and (24); **Gloucestershire**; **Good spender**; **In time**; **Man** (54), (56), (59), and (77); **Means**; **One God**; **Out of God's blessing**; **Owe** (3); **Pains**; **Please** (7); **Poor** (35); **Sow**, *verb* (9); **Speed the plough**; **Spend** (6); **Sure as God**; and **True** (4).

Godalming. 1. *Godalmin cats;* and 2. *Godalmin rabbits.* 1790: Grose, *Prov. Gloss.*, s.v. 'Surrey'

[Old taunts – the latter based on the story of Mrs Tofts].

3. *See* quot. 1904: Jekyll, *Old West Surrey*, 243, The local saying has it that 'If the sun shines before noon on Godalming fair-day [13 Feb.], the winter isn't half over'.

Godamercy, horse! An almost meaningless proverbial exclamation. 1546: Heywood, *Proverbs*, Pt II ch vii, God haue mercy, hors. 1579: *Marr. of Wit and Wisdom*, sc iii, p. 27 (SH.S.). 1611: *Tarltons Jests*, 24 (SH.S.), But ever after it was a by word thorow London, God a mercy horse, and is to this day. 1647: in *Polit. Ballads*, 51 (Percy S.), Oh, God-a-mercy, parliament. 1664: in *Musarum Deliciae*, ii 232 (Hotten), A taylor is a theef, a sergeant is worse, Who here lyes dead, god-a-mercy horse. 1681: in *Harl. Miscell.*, ii 100 (1744), God-a-mercy horse, this rogue Will was tugging up stream … 1710: *Brit. Apollo*, iii No. 118, p. 3, col. 1, I find I'm whole, *God a mercy horse.* Cf. **Gramercy.**

God-fathers oft give their blessings in a clout. 1611: Davies (of Hereford), sc *of Folly*, 47, in *Works*, ii (Grosart).

Gods love die young, Whom the. [Quem Di diligunt Adolescens moritur. – Plautus, *Bacchides*, IV vi.] 1560: T. Wilson, – *Rhetorique*, 73 (1909), Whom God loueth best, those he taketh sonest. 1651: Herbert, *Jac. Prudentum*, 2nd ed., Those that God loves, do not live long. 1819: Byron, *Don Juan*, can. iv st. 12. 1894: R.L.S., *Letters*, v 125 (Tusitala ed.), I was meant to die young, and the gods do not love me. 1923: Lucas, *Advisory Ben*, § x p. 48, It has never been satisfactorily determined whether the saying about the darlings of the gods dying young means young in years or young in heart.

Going gets tough, the tough get going, When the. A saying popular originally in U.S. political circles. It is usually credited to Senator Joseph P. Kennedy (father of President John F. Kennedy) and was also popular with the aides of the often embattled President Richard M. Nixon. Subsequently used in a pop song and frequently parodied. 1962: J.H. Cutler, 'Honey Fitz', xx, Joe [Kennedy] made his children stay on their toes … He would bear down on them and tell them, 'When the going gets tough, the tough get going'. 1970: *New Yorker*, 3 Oct., 33, Baron Marcel Bich, the millionaire French pen magnate probably spoke for them all last month when he said, 'When the going gets tough, the tough get going!'.

Gold. 1. Gold dust blinds all eyes. 1875: A. B. Cheales, *Proverb. Folk-Lore*, 98.

2. Gold goes in at any gate excePt heaven's. 1630: T. Adams, *Works*, 24, The prouerbe saith, There is no earthly gate, but an asse laden with gold can enter. 1670: Ray, 97. 1736: Bailey, *Dict.*, s.v. 1875: A. B. Cheales, *Proverb. Folk-Lore*, 98.

3. Gold is an orator. 1594: Barnfield, *Affect. Shep.*, 48 (Percy S.), Gold is a deepe-perswading orator. Cf. **Money** (38); and also No. 12 *infra*.

4. Gold is but muck. *c.*1598: Jonson, *Case is Altered*, IV iv [cited as 'the old proverb'].

5. Gold makes a woman penny-white. 1754: Berthelson, *Eng.-Danish Dict.*, s.v. 'Penny' 1894: Northall, *Folk Phrases*, 14 (E.D.S.).

6. Gold maketh an honest man an ill man. 1579: Lyly, *Euphues*, 63 (Arber) [cited as 'a by word amongst vs'].

7. He that has gold may buy land. 1683: Meriton, *Yorkshire Ale*, 83–7 (1697).

8. If gold knew what gold is, gold would get gold, I wis. 1640: Herbert, *Jac. Prudentum*.

9. Pour gold on him, he'll never thrive. 1639: Clarke, 220.

10. That is gold that is worth gold. 1611: Cotgrave, s.v. 'Or'. 1667: Gurnall, *Christian in Armour*, Pt II v 15, ch ix p. 144 (1679), We say, *that is gold which is worth gold*, which we may anywhere exchange for gold. 1853: Trench, *Proverbs*, 87 (1905), Which the brief Italian proverb long ago announced: *Gold's worth is gold*.

11. What words won't do, gold will. 1700: Ward, *London Spy*, 400 (1924) [called an 'old saying'].

12. When gold speaks you may e'en hold your tongue. 1666: Torriano, *Piazza Univ.*, 179, Where gold speaks, every tongue is silent. 1670: Ray, 12, You may speak with your gold and make other tongues dumb. 1732: Fuller, 5555. Cf. No 3, *supra*; and **Money** (38).

13. When we have gold we are in fear, when we have none we are in danger. 1670: Ray, 12. *See also* **All that glitters is not gold; Money;** and **Touchstone.**

Golden. l. A golden dart kills where it pleases. 1732: Fuller, 132.

2. A golden shield is of great defence. Ibid., No. 133.

3. Golden dreams make men awake hungry. 1678: Ray, 129. 1732: Fuller, 1695.

4. Golden hook. *See* **Angle** (2).

5. The golden age never was the present age. 1732: Fuller, 4556.

6. The golden ball never goes up but once. Oxfordsh. 1913: *Folk-Love*, xxiv 77. [No explanation is given.]

7. The golden mean. Before 1225: *Ancren R.,336,*)the middel weie of mesure is euer guldene. 1596: Gosson, *Pleasant Quips*, 14 (Percy S.), The golden meane is free from trips. 1611: Coryat, *Crudities*, ii 150 (1905), To keepe the golden meane in the levell of their thoughts. 1687: Norris of Bemerton, *Poems*, 94 (Grosart). 1754: *World*, No. 95, The golden mean, or middle track of life. 1826: Scott, in Lockhart's *Life*, vi 341, They … are too desirous to make a show, to preserve the golden mean.

8. We must not look for a golden life in an iron age. 1633: Draxe, 242, A man must not … yron world. 1639: Clarke, 124, Expect not a golden life in an iron world. 1670: Ray, 14. 1732: Fuller, 5450.

Good a maid as her mother, A. 1659: Howell, 11.

Good a will as ever I came from school, With as. 1594: Shakespeare, *Tam. of Shrew*, III ii, As willingly as e'er I came from school. 1659: Howell, *Letters*, ii 666 (Jacobs). 1732: Fuller, 5794.

Good action always finds its recompence, A. 1750: Smollett, *Gil Bias*, iv 101 [quoted 'as the proverb says'].

Good against evil, Set. 1640: Herbert, *Jac. Prudentum.*

Good ale is meat, drink, and cloth. 1602: Carew, *Surv. of Cornwall*, 189 (1811), The liquor [ale] itself is the Englishman's ancientest and wholesomest drink, and serveth many for meat and cloth too. *c.*1620: in *Roxb. Ballads*, ii 588 (B.S.), Were't not for this barley broth (Which is meat, drinke, and cloth). 1697: in Marchant, *Praise of Ale*, 403, On the rare virtues of this barley broth! To rich and poor it's meat and drink and cloth. 1738: Swift, *Polite Convers.*, Dial. II. 1815: Scott, *Mannering*, ch xxxix, Sheer ale supports him under everything. It is meat, drink, and cloth, bed, board, and washing.

Good Americans when they die go to Paris. 1858: O. W. Holmes *Autocrat of the Breakfast-Table* To these must certainly be added that other saying of one of the wittiest of men: 'Good

Americans, when they die, go to Paris'. [The man Holmes was referring to was Thomas Gold Appleton (1812–84)]

Good and all, For. 1519: Horman, *Vulgaria*, fo. 208, We begen a newe counte for good and all. 1663: Pepys, *Diary*, 23 June, I do resolve even to let him go away for good and all. 1710: Swift, *Journal to Stella*, 13 Sept., She is broke for good and all, and is gone to the country. 1850: Dickens, *Chuzzlewit*, ch ii, Mr Westlock, sir, going away for good and all, wishes to leave none but friends behind him. 1892: Pinero, *Lady Bountiful*, I p. 45, I've sold my business … and I've cleared out of Baverstoke for good and all.

Good and evil are chiefly in the imagination. 1732: Fuller, 1699.

Good and quickly seldom meet. 1640: Herbert, *Jac. Prudentum*. 1670: Ray, 12. 1736: Bailey, *Dict.*, s.v. 'Soon'.

Good as a Christmas play, As. 1880: Courtney, *W. Cornwall Words*, 24 (E.D.S.) … is said of anything very funny.

Good as a play, As. 1638: Taylor (Water-Poet), *Bull, Beare, etc.*, 43, in *Works*, 3rd coll. (Spens.S.), It was as good as a comedy to him to see the trees fall. 1672: Marvell, *Rehearsal Transpr.*, Pt I in *Works*, iii 41 (Grosart), It was grown almost as good as a play. 1845: Dickens, *Cricket*, Chirp 2, John had such a lively interest in all the parcels, that it was as good as a play. 1915: A. Machen, *Far-off Things*, 130 (1922), The naughty prints and books of Holywell Street were as good as a play.

Good as ever drew sword, As. 1599: Porter, *Two Angry Women*, sc xi, You are as good a man as ever drew sword.

Good as ever flew in the air, As. 1678: Ray, 285.

Good as ever struck, As. *c.*1660: in *Roxb. Ballads*, ii 131 (B.S.), Yet is he as good as ever strooke.

Good as ever the ground went upon, As – with variants. 1599: Porter, *Two Angry Women*, sc xi, You are as good a man … as ere trode on Gods earth. 1678: Ray, 285, As good as ever the ground went upon. *c.*1890: Gilbert, *Foggerty's Fairy*, II, I know you're as good a girl as ever stepped.

Good as ever twanged, As. 1577: *Misogonus*, II ii, I must nedes loue the, i faithe, thart as good as ere twangde. 1667: L'Estrange, *Quevedo's Visions*, 205 (1904), As good a wench as ever twanged. 1678: Ray, 285.

Good as ever water wet, As. 1670: Ray, 205. 1736: Bailey, *Dict.*, s.v. 'Wet'. *See also* **As ever.**

Good as ever went endways, As. 1678: Ray, 285.

Good as George of Green, As. 1670: Ray, 205. 1721: Bailey, *Eng. Dict.*, s.v. 'Greenwich'.

Good as gold, As. 1843: Dickens, *Carol*, Stave 3, 'And how did little Tim behave?' asked Mrs Cratchit … 'As good as gold,' said Bob. 1876: Blackmore, *Cripps*, ch xxxvii, My mother is as good as gold, and much better. 1926: Phillpotts, *Yellow Sands*, II, Him and Emma are both so good as gold.

Good as good for nothing, So. 1639: Clarke, 78.

Good as goose skins that never man had enough of, As. Cheshire. 1670: Ray, 208. 1917: Bridge, *Cheshire Proverbs*, 13 … impossible to explain. The meaning has died out.

Good as one shall see in a summer's day, As. 1599: Porter, *Two Angry Women*, sc xi [with 'upon' for 'in']. 1595: Shakespeare, *Mids. N. Dream*, I ii, A proper man, as one shall see in a summer's day. 1742: Fielding, *Andrews*, bk iv ch xv, As fine a fat thriving child as you shall see in a summer's day.

Good at a distance is better than evil at hand. 1732: Fuller, 1700.

Good bargain is a pick-purse, A. 1611: Cotgrave, s.v. 'Argent', Good cheap commodities are notable pick-purses. 1640: Herbert, *Jac. Prudentum*. 1732: Fuller, 1701, Good bargains are pick-pockets.

Good bargain, On a, think twice. 1640: Herbert, *Jac. Prudentum*. 1710: S. Palmer, *Moral Essays on Proverbs*, 29. Cf. **Great bargain.**

Good be careful, If you can't be. From a Latin phrase (*see* quote 1528). 1303: R. Brunne, *Handlyng Synne* (E.E.T.S.), l. 8316, The apostle seyth thys autoryte, 'Gyf though be nat chaste, be thou pryve [secret]'. 1528: W. Tyndale, *Obedience of a Christian Man*, As oure lawears saye, *si non caste tamen caute*, this is, if ye live not chaste, se ye cary clene, and play the knave secretly. 1903: A.M. Binstead, *Pitcher in Paradise*, viii, Always bear in mind what the country mother said to her daughter who was coming up to town to be apprenticed to the Bond Street millinery, 'For heaven's sake be good; but if you can't be good, be careful'.

Good be good, Though, yet better is better (or better carries it). 1639: Clarke, 105. 1655: Fuller, *Church Hist.*, bk xi § iii, Ded., Good is not good, where better is expected. 1670: Ray, 97.

1736: Bailey, *Dict.*, s.v. 'Good', Good is good, but better is better.

Good be still is worth a groat, A. *c.*1430: Lydgate, *Minor Poems*, 152 (Percy S.), [from a poem in praise of Silence] A good be still is well worth a groote. 1546: Heywood, *Proverbs*, Pt II ch v, A good bestyll is woorth a grote. 1633: Draxe, 190 [in the section on 'Silence'].

Good bearing. *See* quot. *c.*1460: *How the Good Wife*, l. 20, In thi gode berynge begynnythe thy worschipe.

Good beef that costs nothing, It is. 1732: Fuller, 2935.

Good beginning makes a good ending, A. [Non possum togam praetextam sperare, cum exordium pullum videam. – Quint., V x 71.] *c.*1300: *South-English Legendary* (E.E.T.S.), I 216, This was atte verste me thingth [methinks] a god bygynnynge, Ther after was the betere hope to come to god endynge. *c.*1320: in *Reliq. Antiquae*, i 109 (1841), 'God biginning maketh god endyng', Quoth Hendyng. 1477: Rivers, *Dictes and Sayings*, in *Brit. Bibliog.*, iv 239 (1814), And sayd the lokyng vpon the begynnyng of the werke yf it be goode yeueth hope to the endyng. 1546: Heywood, *Proverbs*, Pt I ch x, Of a good begynnyng comth a good end. 1637: Breton, in *Works*, ii *h* 22 (Grosart), A good beginning, with a better proceeding, promiseth a blessed ending. 1710: S. Palmer, *Moral Essays on Proverbs*, 1. 1825: Hone, *Ev. Day Book*, i, 1 Jan. 1854: J. W. Warter, *Last of Old Squires*, 48 [a variant], There was regularly the full service and a good plain sermon, and parson and squire both held to the old saw – Good onset bodes good end! Cf. **Well** (8).

Good blood, You come of, and so does a black pudding. 1855: Bohn, 576.

Good blood. *See* **Blood** (2).

Good bourd [jest] **to drink of a gourd, It is a.** *c.*1410: *Towneley Plays*, 115 (E.E.T.S.), It is an old by-worde, It is a good bowrde for to drynk of a gowrde.

Good broth may be made in an old pot. 1666: Torriano, *Piazza Univ.*, III [with 'sops' for 'broth']. 1880: Spurgeon, *Ploughman's Pictures*, 84, Many a drop of good broth is made in an old pot.

Good building without a good foundation, No. 1732: Fuller, 3578.

Good cake. *See* **Bad custom.**

Good candle-holder proves a good gamester, A. 1659: Howell, 13. 1670: Ray, 4.

Good cards to show for it, He hath. 1678: Ray, 354. 1732: Fuller, 1887.

Good cause makes a stout heart and a strong arm, A. 1732: Fuller, 140.

Good cheap is dear. 1640: Herbert, *Jac. Prudentum*. 1659: Howell, 8, [as in 1640, *plus*] for it tempts one to buy what he needs not. 1732: Fuller, 1704, [as in 1640, *plus*] at long run.

Good cheer. *See* quots. *c.*1477: Caxton. *Book of Curteseye*, 27 (E.E.T.S.), The poete saith hou that a poure borde Men may enriche with cheerful wil and worde. Before 1500: in Hill, *Commonplace-Book*, 131 (E.E.T.S.), In a thyn table, good chere is best sawse. 1639: Clarke, 12, When good cheare is lacking, our friends will be packing. 1670: Ray, 69 [as in 1639]. 1732: Fuller, 6299 [as in 1639]. 1869: Spurgeon, *John Ploughman*, ch xviii [as in 1639, but with 'such' for 'our'].

Good child soon learns, A. *c.*1280: *Prov. of Hendyng*, Sely chyld is sone ylered. *c.*1386: Chaucer, *Prioress's Tale*, l. 60, For sely child wol alday sone lere.

Good cloak, I have a, but 'tis in France. 1732: Fuller, 2602.

Good clothes open all doors. Ibid., No. 1705.

Good company. *See* quots. 1639: Clarke, 291, Good company is a good coach. 1768: Goldsmith, *Vicar*, ch xviii, 'Good company upon the road', says the proverb, 'is the shortest cut'. 1853: Trench, *Proverbs*, 28 (1905), Our own proverb, *Good company on a journey is worth a coach*, has come down to us from the ancient world (Comes facundus in via pro vehiculo est).

Good conscience. *See* **Conscience.**

Good contriver is better than a big eater, A. 1906: *Cornish N. & Q.*, 267 [with 'little' for 'big']. 1909: *Folk-Lore*, xx 73 (Durham).

Good cook. *See* **Ill cook.**

Good corn, He that hath, may be content with some thistles. 1732: Fuller, 2159.

Good cow. *See* **Cow** (20).

Good day will not mend him, nor a bad day impair him, A. 1678: Ray, 71. 1732: Fuller, 143.

Good deed is never lost, A. 1633: Draxe, 40. 1732: Fuller, 1710, Good deeds remain; all things else perish.

Good dinner, He that would eat a, let him eat a good breakfast. 1678: Ray, 124.

Good divine that follows his own instructions, It is a. 1595: Shakespeare, *M. of Venice*, I II

Good eating. *See* quot. 1840: Barham, *Ing. Legends*: 'Bagman's Dog', I've seen an old saw, which is well worth repeating, That says, 'Good Eatynge Deserveth good Drynkynge'.

Good edge is good for nothing, if it has nothing to cut, A. 1732: Fuller, 145.

Good elm, good barley; good oak, good wheat. 1865: W. White, *East. England*, i 38.

Good enough for the parson unless the paint were better, It's. 1678: Ray, 187.

Good enough is never ought. 1678: Ray, 148.

Good estate. *See* quot. 1678: Ray, 78, He has a good estate, but that the right owner keeps it from him.

Good example is the best sermon, A. 1732: Fuller, 146.

Good face is a letter of recommendation, A. 1751: Fielding, *Amelia*, bk ix ch v.

Good face needs no band, A. 1639: Clarke, 131. 1670: Ray, 59. 1709: O. Dykes, *Eng. Proverbs*, 175, In opposition to the fantastical humour of emulating butterflies in the glory of external dress, we commonly say, A good face needs no band. 1738: Swift, *Polite Convers.*, Dial. I.

Good face needs no paint, A. 1581: Lyly, *Euphues*, 204 (Arber), Where the countenaunce is faire, there neede no colours. 1612: T. Heywood, in *Somers Tracts*, iii 575 (1811), A good face needes no painting, and a good cause no abetting. 1732: Fuller, 148.

Good face on a thing, To set a. 1387: Trevisa, tr. Higden, vii 25 (Rolls Ser.), And made good face to the eorle and semblant. 1412–20: Lydgate, *Troy Book*, bk ii l. 4366, And wher thou hast most mater to compleyne, Make ther good face and glad in port the[e] feine. *c.*1540: Bale, *Kynge Johan*, l. 1991, Though it be a foule lye, set upon it a good face. 1580: H. Gifford, *Posie*, 44 (Grosart), But – as the fashione of the worlde is now a dayes – set a good face on a bad matter. 1621: Brathwait, *Natures Embassie*, 107 (1877), Making a good face of an euill matter. 1740: North, *Examen*, 49, His Lordship was not surprised, but ... set a good face upon the matter. 1866: G. Eliot, *Felix Holt*, ch i, Well, madam, put a good face on it.

Good fame is better than a good face, A. 1732: Fuller, 150.

Good fences make good neighbours. 1640: E. Rogers, *Letter in Winthrop Papers* (1944), IV 282, A good fence helpeth to keepe peace between neighbours; but let us take heed that we make not a high stone wall, to keepe us from meeting. 1815: H. H. Brackenridge, *Modern Chivalry*, IV II xiii, I was always with him [Jefferson] in his apprehensions of John Bull ... Good fences restrain fencebreaking beasts, and ... preserve good neighbourhoods. 1914: R. Frost, *North of Boston*, 'Mending Wall', He will not go behind his father's saying And he likes having thought of it so well He says again, 'Good fences make good neighbours'. For a homely British version of this proverb, *see* **Hedge** (1).

Good finds good. 1640: Herbert, *Jac. Prudentum*.

Good fire and clean grate, Just as good as half your meat. Newlyn, W. Corn., 19th cent. (Mr C. Lee).

Good fish if it were caught, It is. 1659: Howell, 12, Good fish, but all the craft is in the catching. 1690: *New Dict. Canting Crew*, sig. E4, Good fish when it is caught. 1732: Fuller, 2936. 1883: Burne, *Shropsh. Folk-Lore*, 589.

Good for something. *See* **All women.**

Good for the back (or head). *See* quots. 1604: James I, *Counterblaste*, 107 (Arber), According to the olde prouerbe, That which is good for the head, is euill for the necke and the shoulders. 1670: Ray, 58, That which is good for the back is bad for the head.

Good Friday. 1. He may eat his part. *See* quots. 1546: Heywood, *Proverbs*, Pt I ch xi, He maie his parte on good fridaie eate, And faste neuer the wurs, for ought he shall geat [get]. 1596: Shakespeare, *King John*, I i, Sir Robert might have eat his part in me Upon Good Friday and ne'er broke his fast.

2. Rain on Good Friday. *See* quots. 1882: Mrs Chamberlain, *W. Worcs. Words*, 37 (E.D.S.), If it rain on Good Friday or Easter Day, 'Twill be a good year of grass, but a sorrowful year of hay. 1890: J. D. Robertson, *Gloucester Gloss.*, 187 (E.D.S.), Rain on Good Friday and Easter Day Brings plenty of grass but little good hay. 1893: Inwards, *Weather Lore*, 40 [to same effect as 1890 quot.]. [Also:] Rain on Good Friday foreshows a fruitful year.

Good friend is my nearest relation, A. 1611:

Cotgrave, s.v. 'Parenté', A sound friend is a second kinsman. 1732: Fuller, 151.

Good garden may have some weeds, A. Ibid., No. 152.

Good goose don't bite. 1592: Shakespeare, *Romeo*, II iv, Nay, good goose bite not. 1599: Porter, *Two Angry Women*, in Hazlitt, *Old Plays*, vii 359, Good goose, bite not. 1678: Ray, 72. 1732: Fuller, 1712.

Good hand good hire. 1639: Clarke, 45. 1788: *Town's Book of Pownall Fee*, quoted in Bridge, *Cheshire Proverbs*, 62, He ... worked sometimes on weekly wages and sometimes good hand good hire, but was never hired for twelve months. 1917: Bridge, *Cheshire Proverbs*, 62 ... Piece-work.

Good harvest, He that hath a, may be content with some thistles. 1639: Clarke, 198. 1670: Ray, 13. 1846: Denham, *Proverbs*, 57 (Percy S.).

Good harvests make men prodigal, bad ones provident. 1611: Cotgrave, s.v. 'Anneé'. 1670: Ray, 13. 1754: Berthelson, *Eng.-Danish Dict.*, s.v. 'Harvest'. 1846: Denham, *Proverbs*, 54 (Percy S.). 1904: *Co. Folk-Lore: Northumb.*, 178 (F.L.S.).

Good health. *See* quot. 1855: Bohn, 400, He who hath good health is young; and he is rich who owes nothing.

Good heed hath good hap. 1681: W. Robertson, *Phraseol. Generalis*, 719. 1736: Bailey, *Dict.*, s.v. 'Heed', Take good heed will surely speed.

Good hope is better than a bad possession, A. 1620: Shelton, *Quixote*, Pt II ch lxv. 1732: Fuller, 154.

Good horse. *See* Horse (3) to (5).

Good house, all things are quickly ready, In a. 1611: Cotgrave, s.v. 'Maison'. 1631: Mabbe, *Celestina*, 152 (T.T.), In a plentifull house a supper is soone provided. 1640: Herbert, *Jac. Prudentum.*

Good housewife. *See* quot. 1678: Ray, 88, She's not a good house-wife that will not wind up her bottom, i.e. take off her drink.

Good husband, Be a = Be thrifty. *See* quot. 1813: Ray, 13, Be a good husband, and you will soon get a penny to spend, a penny to lend, and a penny for a friend.

Good husband makes a good wife, A. 1621: Burton, *Melancholy*, III iii 4, I, p. 648 (1836), For as the old saying is, a good husband makes a good wife. 1702: Farquhar, *Inconstant*, II, i, A good husband makes a good wife at any time. 1753: *World*, No. 21. 1869: Spurgeon, *John Ploughman*, ch xvii Cf. **Good Jack**; and **Good wife.**

Good husbandry is good divinity. 1846: Denham, *Proverbs*, 2 (Percy S.). 1904: *Co. Folk-Lore: Northumb.*, 173 (F.L.S.).

Good husbandry. *See also* **Frugality.**

Good ill that comes alone, 'Tis a. 1620: Shelton, *Quixote*, Pt II ch lv. 1732: Fuller, 5059.

Good Indian is a dead Indian, The only. Associated mainly with the unregenerate days of the old Wild West and with western films; occasionally applied to races and types of people other than Native American Indians. 1868: J.M. Cavanaugh, in *Congressional Globe*, 28 May, 2638, I have never in my life seen a good Indian (and I have seen thousands) excePt when I have seen a dead Indian. 1886: A. Gurney, *Ramble through the United States*, 29, The government ... is at length earnestly endeavouring to do tardy justice to the conquered race; but it was distressing to hear again and again from American lips the remark that 'A *good* Indian is a *dead* Indian'. 1935: L.I. Wilder, *Little House on the Prairie*, xvii, She did not know why the government made treaties with Indians. The only good Indian was a dead Indian.

Good in the mouth and bad in the maw [stomach]. 1669: *Politeuphuia*, 172, What is sweet in the mouth is bitter in the stomach. 1732: Fuller, 5511. 1855: Kingsley, *West. Ho!*, ch xi, Do I not know that it is sweet in the mouth but bitter in the belly? 1925: E. F. Benson, in *London Mercury*, July, 279 [the converse], That crisp little roll which may be bitter to the mouth, but is sweet to the belly.

Good is the enemy of the best, The. Meaning that one may rest satisfied with what is acceptable instead of striving for the truly excellent. 1912: J. Kelman, *Thoughts on Things Eternal*, 108, Every respectable Pharisee proves the truth of the saying that 'the good is the enemy of the best'.

Good is to be sought out, and evil attended [awaited]. 1640: Herbert, *Jac. Prudentum.*

Good Jack makes a good Jill, A. 1605: Camden, *Remains*, 317 (1870). 1670: Ray, 108. 1828: Carr, *Craven Dialect*, i 250. Cf. **Good husband.**

Good Jill may mend the bad Jack, A. 1669: Brathwait, *Hist, of Moderation*, 15, See by experience, what may not a wise woman bring a bad husband to in time? *The good Gill may mend the bad Jack*.

Good judge conceives quickly, judges slowly, A. 1640: Herbert, *Jac. Prudentum*.

Good judgment that relieth not wholly on his own, He hath a. 1710: S. Palmer, *Moral Essays on Proverbs*, 330. 1732: Fuller, 1882.

Good kail is half a meal 1670: Ray, 36. 1732: Fuller, 6252. [In both 'keal' for 'kail'.]

Good kin that none do amiss in, 'Tis a. 1639: Clarke, 160.

Good knife. *See* quots. 1678: Ray, 255, It's a good knife, it will cut butter when 'tis melted. A good knife, it was made five miles beyond Cutwell. 1732: Fuller, 2857, It is a good knife, 'twas made at Dull-edge.

Good land. *See* **Best** (16).

Good language that all understand not, That's not. 1640: Herbert, *Jac. Prudentum*. 1670: Ray, 27.

Good lather is half the shave, A. 1732: Fuller, 5472, Well lather'd is half shaven. 1825: Hone, *Ev. Day Book*, i 1269, He also says, that 'a good lather is half the shave', is a very old remark among the trade [barbers].

Good laws. *See* quots. 1659: Howell, *Proverbs: Fr.-Eng.*, 9, Good laws come from lewd lives. 1855: Bohn, 364, Good laws often proceed from bad manners.

Good life. *See* quots. 1629: *Book of Meery Riddles*, Prov. 27, A good life makes a good death. 1633: Draxe, 113, A good life hath a good death. Ibid., 39, A good life will have a good end. *See also* **Handful**.

Good liquor. *See* **Cat** (18).

Good looks are good cheap. 1639: Clarke, 34.

Good luck comes by cuffing. 1813: Ray, 136.

Good luck for a grey horse. 1862: *Dialect of Leeds*, 316, 'Good luck for a grey horse!' – a common expression of children, accompanied by the act of spitting over their little finger, at the sight of a grey horse. 1922: *N. &Q.*, 12th ser, xi 169.

Good luck in cards bad luck in marriage. 1755: *Connoisseur*, No. 59, She is no less sure of a good one [husband] because she generally has ill luck at cards. 1887: M. A. Courtney, *Folk-Lore Journal*, v 219, Good luck in cards, bad luck in a husband (or wife). (Cornish.)

Good luck lurks under a black deuce. Cornish card saying. 1887: M. A. Courtney, *Folk-Lore Journal*, v 219.

Good luck never comes too late. *c*.1610: Drayton, *Mooncalf*, in *Works*, ii 511 (1753).

Good luck reaches farther than long arms. 1732: Fuller, 1717.

Good luck. *See also* **Calf** (2); and **Cow** (7).

Good maid but for thought, word, and deed, She's a. 1678: Ray, 258.

Good man, A. In a general sense. **1. A good man can no more harm than a sheep.** The first example seems to be a humorous perversion of the saying. 1546: Heywood, *Proverbs*, Pt I ch x, But she can no more harme than can a she ape. 1605: Camden, *Remains*, 316 (1870). 1670: Ray, 98. 1732: Fuller, 160, A good man is no more to be fear'd than a sheep.

2. *See* quot. 1485: Malory, *Morte d' Arthur*, bk xix ch 4, Hit is an old sawe a good man is neuer in daunger but whan he is in the daunger of a coward.

3. He's a good man whom fortune makes better. 1732: Fuller, 2438.

4. If a good man thrive, all thrive with him. 1640: Herbert, *Jac. Prudentum*.

B. = The master of the house. 1. The goodman's the last that knows what's amiss at home. 1670: Ray, 52. 1732: Fuller, 4558. Cf. **Cuckold** (8)

2. When the good man is abroad, the good woman's table is soon spread. 1678: Ray, 61 [with 'from home' for 'abroad', and 'wives' for 'woman's']. 1732: Fuller, 5587. *See also* **As the goodman**.

Good manners, You know, but you use but a few. 1639: Clarke, 2. 1670: Ray, 185. 1732: Fuller, 5919, You have good manners, but never carry them about you.

Good manners. *See* **Lord Mayor** (1).

Good marksman may miss, A. 1732: Fuller, 163.

Good master. *See* quot. *c*.1530: Rhodes, *Boke of Nurture*, 108 (E.E.T.S.), He that hath a good mayster and cannot keepe him, He that hath a good servaunt and not content with hym, He that hath such condicions that no man loueth hym, May well know other, but few men wyll knowe him. 1578: Florio, *First Fruites*, fo. 105.

Good masters make good servants. 1888: Q.-Couch, *Troy Town*, ch xix.

Good maxim is never out of season, A. 1855: Bohn, 288.

Good men are a public good. 1732: Fuller, 1718.

Good men are scarce. 1638: D. Tuvill, *Vade Mecum*, 96 (3rd ed.). 1668: *Poor Robin Alman.*, Sept., Pretending this reason for it, *That good people are scarce.* 1732: Fuller, 3307, Maids, make much of one; good men are scarce. 1738: Swift, *Polite Convers.*, Dial. I, Good folks are scarce.

Good men company, Keep, and you shall be of the number. 1477: Rivers, *Dictes, etc.*, 26 (1877), Acompanye the[e] with good people, and thou shalt be on of them. 1560: T. Wilson, *Rhetorique*, 5 (1909), According to the prouerbe, by companying with the wise, a man shall learne wisedome. 1640: Herbert, *Jac. Prudentum.* 1748: Richardson, *Clarissa*, iv 242 (1785).

Good mind, good find. 1853: Trench, *Proverbs*, 19 (1905).

Good mother says not 'Will you?' but gives, The. 1640: Herbert, *Jac. Prudentum.* 1670: Ray, 18. 1852: FitzGerald, *Polonius*, 74 (1903), The wise mother says not 'Will you?' but gives.

Good name for-winneth, A. *c.*1460: *How the Good Wife*, l. 35.

Good name is better than riches. 1477: Rivers, *Dictes, etc.*, 64 (1877), Good renomme is bettir than richesse. 1506: A. Barclay, *Castell of Labour*, sig. E7, Good name is better than rychesse.

Good name is worth gold, A. *c.*1460: *How the Good Wife*, l. 75, Gode name is golde worthe. 1597: in *Plasidas, etc.*, 166 (Roxb.Cl), For wise men and old Seyne good name is worth gold. 1611: Cotgrave, s.v. 'Assez', A good name is wealth sufficient. 1754: Berthelson, *Eng.-Danish Dict.*, s.v. 'Above', A good name is above the wealth.

Good name keeps its lustre in the dark, A. 1670: Ray, 18.

Good name, Take away my, and take away my life. Ibid., 124. 1732: Fuller, 4306. *c.*1800: Trusler, *Prov. in Verse*, 75.

Good neighbour. *See* Neighbour.

Good news, He that brings, knocks boldly. 1611: Cotgrave, s.v. 'Hardiment'. 1659: Howell, *Proverbs: Span.-Eng.*, 18. 1666: Torriano, *Piazza Univ.*, 213.

Good news may be told at any time, but ill in the morning. 1640: Herbert, *Jac. Prudentum.*

Good night, Nicholas, the moon is in the flock-bed. 1659: Howell, 11.

Good office, He hath a, he must needs thrive. 1678: Ray, 263.

Good often fare the worse for the bad, The. 1712: Motteux, *Quixote*, Pt I bk i ch vii.

Good or ill hap. *See* quot. 1732: Fuller, 6413, The good or ill hap of a good or ill life, Is the good or ill choice of a good or ill wife.

Good orator who convinces himself, He is a. 1855: Bohn, 374.

Good painter can draw a devil as well as an angel, A. 1639: Clarke, 311.

Good palliate a bad action, The. 1855: Bohn, 506.

Good pawn never shames the master, A. 1631: Brathwait, *Whimzies*, 104 (1859). 1639: Glapthorne, *Wit in a Constable*, V 1659: Howell, 11.

Good paymaster is lord of another man's purse, The. 1640: Herbert, *Jac. Prudentum*, A good payer is master of another's purse. 1748: Franklin, in *Works*, ii 119 (Bigelow).

Good paymaster may build Paul's, A. 1732: Fuller, 167.

Good paymaster needs no surety, A. 1620: Shelton, *Quixote*, Pt II ch xiv 1694: D'Urfey, *Quixote*, Pt I Act IV sc i 1732: Fuller, Nos. 1726–7, Good paymasters need no surety. Good paymasters need not bring a pawn.

Good paymaster never wants workmen, A. 1732: Fuller, 168.

Good physician who cures himself, He is a. *c.*1430: Lydgate, *Daunce of Machabree*, l. 424, Good leche is he that can himself recure. 1666: Torriano, *Piazza Univ.*, 148.

Good presence is letters of recommendation, A. 1732: Fuller, 170.

Good reasons. *See* quot. 1623: Wodroephe, *Spared Hours*, 477, Good reasons said, and euill vnderstood, are rozes strawen to hogges, and not so good.

Good recorder sets all in order, A. 1659: Howell, ll 1670: Ray, 22. 1732: Fuller, 6245.

Good reputation is a fair estate, A. 1732: Fuller, 172.

Good riding at two anchors. [ἀγαθαὶ δὲ πέλοντ', ἐν χειμερίᾳ νυκτί θοᾶς ἐκ ναὸς ἀπεσκίμφθαι, δύ' ἄγκυραι. – Pindar, *Olymp.*, Ode VI 170.] 1546: Heywood, *Proverbs*, Pt II ch ix, Good riding at two anchors, men have told, For if the tone fail, the tother may hold. 1579: Lyly, *Euphues*, 116 (Arber), Haue more strings to thy bow then one, it is safe riding at two ankers. 1670: Ray, 151 [as in 1546]. 1716: E. Ward,

Female Policy, 85, It's safe riding with two anchors. 1732: Fuller, 6450 [as in 1546]. Cf. **Two strings**.

Good riding. *See also* **Safe riding**.

Good roller, A, a good rider. 1869: FitzGerald, *Sea Words and Phrases*, 9, 'A good roller a good rider'; that is to say, the breadth of beam and bottom that will make a vessel roll, will also make her ride comfortably at anchor.

Good rye thrives high. 1884: Egerton, *Sussex Folks and Ways*, 82, When I was a growing lad ... a kindly old farmer's wife ... would [say] 'and good rye thrives high'.

Good sailor may mistake in a dark night, A. 1732: Fuller, 173.

Good saver is a good server, A. Somerset. 1678: Ray, 350.

Good scholar is not a good schoolmaster, Every. 1732: Fuller, 1417.

Good seed, Of, proceedeth good corn. *c.*1568: Wager, *Longer thou Livest*, sig. A2.

Good servant must come, A. *See* quots. 1645: Howell, *Letters*, bk i § v No. xiii, He [a footman] will come when you call him, go when you bid him, and shut the door after him. 1738: Swift, *Polite Convers.*, Dial. I, Remember, that a good servant must always come when he's called, do what he's bid, and shut the door after him.

Good servant must have good wages, A. *c.*1555: in Wright, *Songs, etc.*, *Philip and Mary*, 173 (Roxb. CI.), A goode sarvaunte hopes for to be well rewardyde. 1611: Cotgrave, s.v. 'Servir', Good service, of itself, demands reward. 1732: Fuller, 176.

Good service is a great enchantment. 1640: Herbert, *Jac. Prudentum*.

Good shape is in the shears' mouth, A. 1855: Bonn, 289.

Good shift may serve long, but it will not serve ever, A. 1678: Ray, 201. 1732: Fuller, 177.

Good skill in horseflesh. *See* quots. 1670: Ray, 181, He hath good skill in horseflesh to buy a goose to ride on. 1738: Swift, *Polite Convers.*, Dial. I, She had good skill in horse flesh that could choose a goose to ride on.

Good small beer. *See* quot. 1738: Swift, *Polite Convers.*, Dial. II, They say, there is no such thing as good small beer, good brown bread, or a good old woman. Cf. **Good things**.

Good spear, He that hath a, let him try it. 1578: Florio, *First Fruites*, fo. 28 [with 'proue it against

a wal' for 'try it']. 1629: *Book of Meery Riddles*, Prov. 74.

Good spender, To a, God is the treasurer. 1640: Herbert, *Jac. Prudentum*. 1670: Ray, 24. 1732: Fuller, 5127.

Good sport that fills the belly, That is. Ibid., No. 4354.

Good steward abroad when there is a wind frost, There is a. 1830: Forby, *Vocab. E. Anglia*, 431. 1872: J. Glyde, jr., *Norfolk Garland*, 149.

Good stomach is the best sauce, A. Cf. **Hunger**.

Good surgeon. *See* **Surgeon**.

Good swimmers are oftenest drowned. 1611: Cotgrave, s.v. 'Nageur', Good swimmers at the length feed haddocks. 1640: Herbert, *Jac. Prudentum*, Good swimmers at length are drowned. 1732: Fuller, 1729.

Good table, At a, we may go to school. Ibid., No. 823.

Good take-heed doth surely speed. 1639: Clarke, 266. 1670: Ray, 147. 1732: Fuller, 6093.

Good tale ill told is marred in the telling, A. 1546: Heywood, *Proverbs*, Pt II ch vii 1670: Ray, 147. 1732: Fuller, 178, A good tale ill told is a bad one.

Good tale is none the worse for being twice told, A. 1816: Scott, *Old Mortality*, ch vii.

Good that causeth so many good deeds, Needs must it be. *c.*1387: Usk, *Test, of Love*, in Skeat's *Chaucer*, vii 79, Nedes mot it be good that causeth so many good dedes.

Good that does me good, That's my. 1639: Clarke, 109, That's good that doth us good. 1678: Ray, 148. 1732: Fuller, 276, A man has no more goods than he gets good by.

Good that knows not why he is good, He cannot be. 1602: Carew, *Surv. of Cornwall*, 219 (1811), It hath been well said, 'He cannot long be good, that knows not why he is good'. 1732: Fuller, 1819.

Good thing is soon caught up, A. 1670: Ray, 12 [with 'snatch't' for 'caught']. 1732: Fuller, 181.

Good things I do not love. *See* quot. 1678: Ray, 148, Some good things I do not love, a good long mile, good small beer, and a good old woman. Cf. **Good small beer**.

Good, though long stayed for, is good. 1659: Howell, *Proverbs: Brit.-Eng.*, 3.

Good tither a good thriver, A. Somerset. 1678: Ray, 352.

Good to be in the dark, as without light, It's as. 1670: Ray, 77.

Good to be near of kin. *See* quots. 1662: Fuller, *Worthies*, ii 227 (1840), Indeed our English proverb, 'It is good to be near a-kin to land', holdeth in private patrimonies, not titles to crowns. 1748: Richardson, *Clarissa*, i 81 (1785), My sister says, in the words of an old saw, *It is good to be related to an estate.*

Good to fetch a sick man sorrow, or a dead man woe. 1670: Ray, 194 … *Cheshire.* 1738: Swift, *Polite Convers.*, Dial. I, You are fit to be sent for sorrow, you stay so long by the way. 1917: Bridge, *Cheshire Proverbs*, 70.

Good to have some friends both in heaven and hell, It's. 1639: Clarke, 232, It's good having a friend both in heaven and hell. 1670: Ray, 93.

Good to learn at other men's cost, It is. 1546: Heywood, *Proverbs*, Pt I ch xi, It is good to beware by other men's harmes. Before 1651: in Peck, *Desid. Curiosa*, 443 (1779), It is good learning by another's book. 1736: Bailey, *Dict.*, s.v. 'Cost'.

Good to send on a dead man's errand. 1670: Ray, 171 [with 'bodies' for 'man's']. 1738: Swift, *Polite Convers.*, Dial. I, Well, have you been with my Lady Club? You are good to send of a dead man's errand.

Good tongue, Who has not a, ought to have good hands. 1813: Ray, 166.

Good trade. *See* quots. 1659: Howell, *Proverbs: Fr.-Eng.*, 23, He that hath a good trade will have his share. 1732: Fuller, 2386, He who hath a trade, hath a share every where. 1855: Bohn, 566, Who hath a good trade, through all waters may wade.

Good tree brings forth good fruit, A. *c.*1534: Berners, *Huon*, 12 (E.E.T.S.), Alwayes I haue harde say that a good impe [tree] bryngethe forth good freute. 1586: Pettie, tr. Guazzo's *Civil Convers.*, fo. 127, It is seldome seene that a good tree bringeth foorth ill fruites. Cf. **Such tree.**

Good tune played on an old fiddle, There's many a. 1902: S. Butler, *The Way of all Flesh*, lxi, Beyond a haricot vein in one of my legs I'm as young as ever I was. Old indeed! There's many a good tune played on an old fiddle. 1917: Bridge, *Cheshire Proverbs*, 117.

Good turn. *See* **One good turn.**

Good turns, One never loseth by doing. 1670: Ray, 12.

Good voice to beg bacon, He hath a. 1659: Howell, 6.

Good walking with a horse in one's hand, It's. 1591: Lyly, *Endymion*, IV ii, Is it not said, 'It is good walking when one hath his horse in his hand'. 1653: Taylor (Water-Poet), *Short Relation*, 5, in *Works*, 1st coll. (Spens.S.), 'Tis merry walking with a horse in hand. 1685–6: Cotton, *Montaigne*, bk iii ch iii, He may well go a foot, they say, who leads his horse in his hand. 1738: Swift, *Polite Convers.*, Dial. II, I always love to walk with a horse in my hand.

Good ware. *See* quots. 1611: Cotgrave, s.v. 'Marchand', Good chaffer cannot want a chapman. 1616: Breton, in *Works*, ii *e* 5 (Grosart), Good ware makes quick markets. 1659: Howell, *Proverbs: Fr.-Eng.*, 8, Good ware will never want a chapman. 1681: W. Robertson, *Phrasol. Generalis*, 677, Good ware will off. 1754: Berthelson, *Eng.-Danish Did.*, s.v. 'Market' [as in 1616].

Good watch prevents misfortune. 1670: Ray, 28.

Good weight and measure is heaven's treasure. 1732: Fuller, 6161.

Good wheat. *See* **Wheat.**

Good wife and a good cat are best at home, A. 1894: Northall, *Folk Phrases*, 6 (E.D.S.).

Good wife and good name hath no make [mate] in goods nor fame, A. 1623: Wodroephe, *Spared Houres*, 478.

Good wife and health Is a man's best wealth, A. 1732: Fuller, 6313. 1869: Spurgeon, *John Ploughman*, ch xvi.

Good wife makes a good husband, A. 1546: Heywood, *Proverbs*, Pt II ch viii 1659: Howell, 7. 1759: Johnson, in Hill's *Boswell*, i 324, We tell the ladies that good wives make good husbands. Cf. **Good husband;** and **Good Jack.**

Good wife must be bespoke, A; for there's none ready made. 1738: Swift, *Polite Convers.*, Dial. I.

Good wife spares, What the, the cat eats. 1639: Clarke, 242. 1670: Ray, 144. 1732: Fuller, 5520.

Good will, I'll do my, as he said that thresh't in his cloak. 1602–3: Manningham, *Diary*, 131 (Camden S.), 'I will doe myne endeavor', quoth he that thrasht in his cloke. 1670: Ray, 178. 1732: Fuller, 2634.

Good wind. *See* quot. 1592: Lyly, *Mother*

Bombie, II v, I have heard my great grandfather tell how his great grandfather should say, that it was an old proverb, when his great grandfather was a childe, that it was a good wind that blew a man to the wine.

Good wine needs no bush. A bunch of green leaves and twigs (especially ivy the plant of Bacchus), was, and still is in some parts of Europe, the traditional sign of a wine-seller. 1430: J. Lydgate, *The Pilgrimage of Man* (E.E.T.S.), l. 20415, And at tavernys (without wene [doubt]) Thys tooknys [tokens] nor thys bowys grene ... The wyn they mende nat. 1539: Taverner, *Proverbs*, fo. 42, Wyne that is saleable and good nedeth no bushe or garland of yuye to be hanged before. 1575: Gascoigne, *Glasse of Govt.*, I i, The good wyne needeth none iuye garland. 1600: Shakespeare, *As You Like It*, Epilogue, 3, If it be true that good wine needs no bush, 'tis true that a good play needs no epilogue. 1608: Day, *Law Trickes*, IV i 1638: Brathwait, *Barn. Journal*, Pt I *ad fin.*, Good wine no bush it needs, as I suppose. 1711: Addison, *Spectator*, No. 221. 1831: Peacock, *Crotchet Castle*, ch xv.

Good wit, Such a one hath a, if a wise man had the keeping it. 1605: Camden, *Remains*, 331 (1870).

Good wits jump, i.e. agree. 1620: Shelton, *Quixote*, Pt II ch xxxvii, I have heard you say ... 'Good wits will soon meet'. 1664: in *Musarum Deliciae*, ii 85 (Hotten), Like will to like: Good wits will jump (quoth he). 1710: Centlivre, *Man's Bewitch'd*, IV ii, Good wits jump – I resolve to marry too. 1775: in *Garrick Corresp.*, ii 94 (1832), See how good wits jump. *See also* **Great wits.**

Good woman. *See* **Woman** (2), (28).

Good word is as soon said as a bad one, A. *c.*1615: R. C., *Times Whistle*, III (E.E.T.S.). 1736: Bailey, *Dict.*, s.v. 'Word'.

Good words and ill deeds deceive wise and fools. 1611: Davies (of Hereford), sc *of Folly*, 46, in *Works*, ii (Grosart).

Good words anoint us, and ill do unjoint us. 1578: Florio, *First Fruites*, fo. 31, Good woords annoynt a man, the yl woordes kyl a man. 1611: Davies (of Hereford), sc *of Folly*, 43, in *Works*, ii (Grosart).

Good words are worth much and cost little. 1640: Herbert, *Jac. Prudentum*. 1732: Fuller,

1736, Good words cost nothing, but are worth much.

Good words cost no more than bad. 1692: L'Estrange, Ae*sop*, 249 (3rd ed.), A good word, they say, costs no more than a bad. 1732: Fuller, 1735.

Good words cost nought. 1599: Porter, *Two Angry Women*, in Hazlitt, *Old Plays*, vii 356, Good words cost nought: ill words corruPt good manners, Richard. 1670: Ray, 158.

Good words fill not a sack. 1678: Ray, 220. 1732: Fuller, 1737.

Good words make amends for misdeeds. 1604: *Wit of a Woman*, sc i l. 20 (Malone S.) [cited as 'an olde saying'].

Good words quench more than a bucket of water. 1640: Herbert, *Jac. Prudentum.* 1670: Ray, 158, Good words cool more then cold water.

Good words without deeds are rushes and reeds. 1659: Howell, 17. 1670: Ray, 30. 1732: Fuller, 6247. 1875: A. B. Cheales, *Proverb. Folk-Lore*, 86.

Good workman is known by his chips, A. 1869: Hazlitt, 16.

Goodly. *See* **Handsome** (3).

Goodness coming out. *See* quot. 1738: Swift, *Polite Convers.*, Dial. I, *Miss feels a pimple on her face;* Lord! I think my goodness is coming out. [In my boyhood, 1863–73, I heard this expression similarly used. – G. L. A.]

Goodness is not tied to greatness. 1639: Clarke, 226, Greatnesse and goodnesse goe not alwey together. 1655: T. Muffett, *Healths Improvement*, 161, As the Greek proverb saith, Goodness is not tied to greatness, but greatness to goodness.

Goods are theirs who enjoy them. 1578: Florio, *First Fruites*, fo. 31, The ware is not his that gathers it, but his that enjoyes it. 1670: Ray, 12. 1732: Fuller, 1739. Cf. **Wealth** (6).

Goodwin Sands, To set up shop on = To be shipwrecked. 1546: Heywood, *Proverbs*, Pt II ch ix, And so set vp shop vpon Goodwins sands. 1670: Ray, 215, Let him set up shop on Goodwins Sands. 1735: Pegge, *Kent. Proverbs*, in E.D.S., No. 12, p. 72 [as in 1670]. *See also* **Tenterden steeple.**

Goodyer's pig, Like, never well but when he is doing mischief. Cheshire. 1670: Ray, 209. 1852: 'Cheshire Proverbs'. in *N. & Q.*, 1st ser, vi 386. 1917: Bridge, *Cheshire Proverbs*, 89.

Goodyer's pigs. *See* quot. 1678: Ray, 235, They'll come again, as Goodyers pigs did, i.e. never.

Goose and **Geese. 1. A goose cannot graze after him.** *c.*1602: Chapman, *May-Day*, III i, What should he do to him, sir? The pasture is so bare with him that a goose cannot graze upon't. 1639: Clarke, 36. 1670: Ray, 178.

2. A goose go barefoot. *See* **Woman** (3).

3. A goose is a silly bird. *See* quots. 1872: *N.&Q.*, 4th ser, ix 104, That 'a goose is a very silly bird, too much for one but not enough for two', is scarcely a local saying. I have heard it in several widely separated parts of England. 1880: Poole, *Archaic, etc.. Words of Staffs*, 25, The presumed foundation for this proverb is, that a Walsall man, when asked if he and his wife were going to have a goose for their Christmas dinner, replied 'No'; for said he, 'the goose was a silly bird – too much for one to eat, and not enough for two'. 1894: Northall, *Folk Phrases*, 31 (E.D.S.), Too much for one, and not enough for two, like the Walsall man's goose.

4. All his geese are swans. Before 1529: Skelton, *Magnyyfcence*, 1.302, In faythe, els had I gone to longe to scole, But yf I coulde knowe a gose from a swanne. 1615: J. Andrews, *Anat. of Baseness*, 30 (Grosart), That by this art, can make a goose a swanne. 1621: Burton, *Melancholy*, Dem. to Reader, 40 (1836), All their geese are swans. 1725: Bailey, tr. Erasmus's *Colloq.*, 445, For every man's own geese are swans. 1864: Newman, *Apologia*, 68, He was particularly loyal to his friends, and, to use the common phrase, 'all his geese were swans'.

5. As deep drinketh the goose as the gander. 1546: Heywood, *Proverbs*, Pt II ch vii 1580: Lyly, *Euphues*, 275 (Arber). 1659: Howell, *Letters*, ii 666 (Jacobs), The goose will drink as deep as the gander. 1732: Fuller, 671. 1880: Spurgeon, *Ploughman's Pictures*, 136, When the goose drinks as deep as the gander, pots are soon empty, and the cupboard is bare.

6. As great as a goose's egg. *c.*1394: *Piers P. Crede*, l. 225.

7. As is the gander so is the goose. 1732: Fuller, 700.

8. As open as a goose's eye. *c.*1500: Medwall, *Nature*, Pt II l. 130 (Brand), *Quellen*, 120), Nay all ys open that they do there As open as a gose eye.

9. Geese with geese and women with women. 1732: Fuller, 1645.

10. Give the goose more hay. *See* Tittle-tattle.

11. Go flay the geese. 1683: Meriton, *Yorkshire Ale*, 83–7 (1697).

12. Gone is the goose that the great egg did lay. 1732: Fuller, 1696.

13. Goose, gander, and gosling are three sounds, but one thing. 1659: Howell, *Proverbs: Span.-Eng.*, 20. 1670: Ray, 98.

14. Goslins lead the geese to water. 1732: Fuller, 1740.

15. Have a goose and get a goose. 1869: Spurgeon, *John Ploughman*, ch xiv.

16. He hopes to see a goose graze on your head. 1583: Melbancke, *Philotinus*, sig. Ee2, I hope thou shalt eat of the goose that shall tread on her graue. 1670: Ray, 178, He hopes to eat of the goose shall graze on your grave.

17. He that turneth the goose should have the neck. Before 1500: Hill, *Commonplace-Book*, 131 (E.E.T.S.).

18. I have a goose to pluck with you. 1659: Howell, 2. Cf. **Crow** (9).

19. If you eat goose on Michaelmas Day you will never want money all the year round. 1708: *Brit. Apollo*, i No. 74, The custom'd proverb … That who eats goose on Michael's-day, Shan't money lack, his debts to pay. 1825: Hone, *Ev. Day Book*, i 1339 [cited as 'a popular saying']. 1830: Forby, *Vocab. E. Anglia*, 414, If you do not baste the goose on Michaelmas-day, you'll want money all the year. 1904: *Co. Folk-Lore: Northumb.*, 178 (F.L.S.).

20. It is a blind goose that knows not a fox from a fern-bush. 1580: Lyly, *Euphues*, 319 (Arber). 1732: Fuller, 2848.

21. It is a silly goose that comes to a fox's sermon. Ibid., No. 2881.

22. It is a sorry goose that will not baste herself. 1670: Ray, 218. 1732: Fuller, 2886.

23. It is an old goose that will eat no oats. 1591: Lyly, *Endymion*, V ii Cf. No. 36.

24. Shall the goslins teach the goose to swim? 1732: Fuller, 4115.

25. Steal a goose. *See* Steal (6), (7).

26. There's meat in a goose's eye. 1621: Taylor (Water-Poet), *Works*, pagin. I, 105 (1630), For the old prouerbe I must here apply, Good meate men may picke from a gooses eye. 1678: Ray, 148.

27. To as much purpose as the geese slurr [slide] on the ice. Cheshire. 1670: Ray, 190.

1877: E. Leigh, *Cheshire Gloss*,, 191. 1917: Bridge, *Cheshire Proverbs*, 125.

28. To as much purpose as to give a goose hay. Cheshire. 1670: Ray, 190. 1917: Bridge, *Cheshire Proverbs*, 125.

29. To give a goose and charge for the garlic. *c.*1380: Wiclif, in *Eng. Works*, 82 (E.E.T.S.), For thei sillen a faat goos for litel or nought, but the garlek costith many shillyngis.

30. To kill the goose that laid the golden eggs. 1484: Caxton, Ae*sope*, ii 245 (Jacobs) [story told in a fable of Avian]. 1855: Gaskell, *North and South*, ch xvii, And now they come to us, and say we're to take less. And we won't ... They'll have killed the goose that laid 'em the golden eggs, I reckon. 1922: Weyman, *Ovington's Bank*, ch xl, They had cooked their goose with a vengeance – no more golden eggs for them!

31. We desire but one feather out of your goose. 1732: Fuller, 5439.

32. What is sauce for the goose is sauce for the gander. [Idem Accio quod Titio j us esto. – Varro. *ap.* Aul. Gell., *Noct. Att.*, III xvi 13.] 1670: J. Ray, *English Proverbs*, 98, That that's good sawce for a goose, is good for a gander ... This is a woman's proverb. 1671: Head and Kirkman, *Eng. Rogue*, ii 120, I could not justly complain, seeing what was sause for a goose was sause for a gander. 1710: Swift, *Journal to Stella*, 24 Jan. 1785–95: Wolcot, *Lousiad*, can. v 1823: Byron, *Don Juan*, can. xiv st. 83. 1853: Planché', *Extravag.*, iv 364 (1879).

33. You're a man among the geese when the gander's away. 1670: Ray, 177. 1732: Fuller, 5842. 1917: Bridge, *Cheshire Proverbs*, 157.

34. You are a pretty fellow to ride a goose a gallop. 1678: Ray, 248, [*plus*] through a dirty lane. 1732: Fuller, 5843.

35. You find fault with a fat goose. 1678: Ray, 248. 1732: Fuller, 5902.

36. Young is the goose that will eat no oats. 1580: Lyly, *Euphues*, 366 (Arber). 1732: Fuller, 6037. Cf. No. 23.

See also **Bo**; **Candlemas**, E; **Children** (12); **Dizzy**; **Fierce**; **Fool** (82); **Fox** (1), (33), and (35); **Good goose**; **Harborough Field**; **Hare** (16); **Ice** (2); **St Chad**; **St Martin** (1); **St Valentine** (3); **Shoe** (2); **Snow** (6); **Steal** (6) and (7); **Tittle-tattle**; **Wild** (3); **Wise** (2); and **Wolf** (4).

Goose-quill gentleman, A. 1639: Clarke, 226.

Goose-quill is more dangerous than a lion's claw, A. 1732: Fuller, 184. 1868: *Quart. Review*, cxxv. 252, There is ... strong testimony to the superiority of letters to arms, or to the danger of law, in this other, 'A goose quill is more dangerous than a lion's claw'.

Gorse. *See* **Furze**; and **Under the furze.**

Goshawk beats not at a bunting, A. 1639: Clarke, 69. 1670: Ray, 98. 1732: Fuller, 185. 1846–59: *Denham Tracts*, ii 108 (F.L.S.), A goss-hawk strikes not at a bunting.

Gospel, All is (or **is not**), **that one speaks;** or, more recently, **To take for Gospel** = To accept as true; or, **To be Gospel** = to be true. [Credite me vobis folium recitare Sibyllae. – Juvenal, viii 126.] Before 1250: *Owl and Nightingale*, 1268 (OED), Fothi seide Alfred swithe wel And his worde was goddspel. *c.*1374: Chaucer, *Troylus*, bk v l.1265, Every word was gospel that ye seyde! *c.*1400: *Rom. Rose*, l. 7609, Al is not gospel, out of doute, That men seyn in the towne aboute. 1593: Nashe, in *Works*, iv 142 (Grosart), His creditors (thinking all is Gospell he speakes ...). 1691: *Merry Drollery*, 238 (Ebsworth), Now all is Gospel that she saith. 1771: Smollett, *Clinker*, in *Works*, vi 291 (1817), As for Jenkins, she affects to take all her mistress's reveries for gospel. 1883: Trollope, *Autobiog.*, ch v, I merely showed the letter to my wife, declaring my conviction that it must be taken as gospel. 1910: Lucas, *Mr Ingleside*, ch xxii, 'No, no ... I'm too old to be caught like that'. 'It's gospel, I assure you'.

Gossip speaks ill of all, and all of her, A. 1732: Fuller, 186.

Gossiping and lying go together. 1732: Fuller, 1741.

Gossips are frogs – they drink and talk. 1640: Herbert, *Jac. Prudentum*. 1670: Ray, 12.

Gotham – in various sayings. *See* quots. *c.*1400: *Towneley Plays*, 106 (E.E.T.S.), Now god gyf you care foles all sam; Sagh I neuer none so fare bot the foles of Gotham. 1526: *Hund. Mery Talys*, No. xxiv, 'Of the iii wyse men of gotam' [title], p. 45 (Oesterley). 1597: Hall, *Satires*, bk ii sat. v, Saint Fooles of Gotam mought thy parish be. 1639: Taylor (Water-Poet), *Summ. Trav.*, 16, in *Works*, 1st coll. (Spens.S.), I saw the ancient towne of Gotham, famous for the seven sages (or wise men) who are fabulously reported to live there in former ages. 1662: Fuller, *Worthies*, ii 569 (1840), As wise as a man of Gotham. 1703: E.

Ward, *Writings*, ii 316, I happen'd to be a hopeful branch of that ancient and renoun'd family of the wise-men of Gotam. 1754: Berthelson, *Eng.- Danish Dict.*, s.v. 'Wise', A wise man of Gotham. 1842: Halliwell, *Nursery Rhymes*, 19 (Percy S.), Three wise men of Gotham, Went to sea in a bowl: And if the bowl had been stronger, My song would have been longer. [Date of 'song' unknown.] 1863: Kingsley, *Water Babies*, ch viii, On the borders of that island he found Gotham, where the wise men live; the same who dragged the pond because the moon had fallen into it. 1894: A. J. C. Hare, *Sussex*, 74, The proverb, 'As wise as the wise men of Gotham'… is believed to refer to Gotham, a manor partly in the parish of Hailsham, partly in that of Pevensey. [The seat of wisdom is more usually identified with the Nottinghamshire village of Gotham.]

Gout. *See* **Drink,** *verb* (8).

Gown is his that wears it, The, and the world his that enjoys it. 1640: Herbert, *Jac. Prudentum.* 1670: Ray, 28 [with 'hers' for the first 'his']. 1732: Fuller, 4560 [as in 1670].

Grace groweth after governance, 'is an old said saw in each place'. 1566: Becon, in *Early Works*, 395 (P.S.).

Grace of God = Shipwreck. 1659: Howell, 12, O Master Vier, we cannot pay you your rent, for we had no Grace of God this year; No shipwrack upon our coast: a saying of the Cornish.

Grace of God. *See* **God, The grace of.**

Grace will last, beauty will blast. 1639: Clarke, 119 [with 'favour' for 'beauty']. 1670: Ray, 98 [as in 1639]. 1732: Fuller, 6292.

Graft good fruit all, Or graft not at all. Ibid., No. 6335.

Grafting on a good stock, 'Tis good. 1678: Ray, 354. 1732: Fuller, 5082.

Grafts be very good, Let the, or the knife be where it stood. 1855: Bohn, 441.

Grain by grain the hen fills her belly. 1653: Middleton and Rowley, *Span. Gipsy*, II i, Grain pecked up after grain makes pullen fat. 1732: Fuller, 1744.

Grain of prudence is worth a pound of craft, A. Ibid., No. 187.

Graith and grout. *See* quot. 1917: Bridge, *Cheshire Proverbs*, 78, If you've graith [riches] and grout [good breed], You'll never be without.

Gramercy forty pence, Jack Noble's dead. 1659: Howell, 13. 1670: Ray, 215.

Gramercy horse. *c.*1600: in Collier, *Roxb. Ballads*, 29 (1847), The hostler, to maintaine himselfe with money in's purse, Approves the proverbe true, and sayes, gramercy horse. 1631: Brathwait, *Whimzies*, 71 (1859), If he [an ostler] rise to any preferment, he may say, *Gramercy, horse.* 1659: Howell, 14. Cf. **Godamercy horse.**

Grandfather's servants are never good. 1732: Fuller, 1745.

Grant all that is asked, To. *See* quot. 1593: Peele, *Edward I*, sc x, Glocester, an old said saying, – He that grants all is ask'd, Is much harder than Hercules task'd.

Grantham gruel, nine grits and a gallon of water. 1662: Fuller, *Worthies*, ii 269 (1840). Before 1674: in *Roxb. Ballads*, viii 427 (B.S.), Some gruel of Grantham, boyl'd for the nonce. 1790: Grose, *Prov. Gloss.*, s.v. 'Lincs'. 1818: Scott, *Heart of Midl.*, ch xxix, [Newark man *loq.*] Thou wilt get naething at night save Grantham gruel, nine grots and a gallon of water. 1869: Spurgeon, *John Ploughman*, ch xxi.

Grantham steeple stand awry, 'Tis height makes. 1596: Lodge, *Wits Miserie*, 14 (Hunt.Cl.), His beard is cut like the spier of Grantham steeple. 1604: Middleton, *Works*, viii 21 (Bullen), Wresting them quite awry, like Grantham steeple. Before 1659: Cleveland, *Poems*, 63 (1742), Few churchmen can be innocent and high; 'Tis height makes Grantham steeple stand awry. 1732: Fuller, 5086.

Grapes are sour, The. *c.*1580: U. Fulwell, *Ars Adulandi*, sig. E3, I see full well the fox will eate no grapes because he cannot reache them. 1630: T. Adams, *Works*, 69, The foxe dispraiseth the grapes he cannot reach. 1691: *Wit for Money*, 4, And like the fox, to cry the grapes are sowre. 1721: Cibber, *Refusal*, IV, Poor Tom! What are the grapes sour, my dear! 1760: Murphy, *Way to Keep Him*, I, You would be glad to have me: but sour grapes, my dear. 1876: Blackmore, *Cripps*, ch iii, Ah, poor Mary, the grapes are sour.

Grasp all, lose all. *c.*1800: J. Trusler, *Prov. in Verse*, 77. 1880: Spurgeon, *Ploughman's Pictures*, 152.

Grasp no more than thy hand will hold. 1732: Fuller, 1747.

Grasps at too much, He that, holds nothing fast. *c.*1205: Layamon, *Brut*, i 278 (Madden), For the mon is muchel sot The nimeth to him-seoluen Mare thonne he mayen walden (For the man is a great fool who taketh upon himself more than he can manage). *c.*1386: Chaucer, *Melibeus*, § 24, For the proverbe seith: 'he that to muche ebraceth, distreyneth litel'. 1578: Florio, *First Fruites*, fo. 6, Who imbraceth much, litle closeth. 1653: Urquhart, *Rabelais*, bk i ch xlvi., It is too great an undertaking … and (as the proverb is), He that gripes too much, holds fast but little. 1732: Fuller, 2123.

Grass. 1. Grass and hay, we are all mortal. 1631: Brathwait, *Whimzies*, 73 (1859). Which makes him conclude in his owne element; *Grasse and hay, we are all mortall.* 1666: Torriano, *Piazza Univ.*, 277, Good fellows … who say, grass and hay, we are mortal, let's live till we dye.

2. Grass grows not upon the highway, nor **in the market-place.** 1659: Howell, *Proverbs: Brit.-Eng.*, 24, In market growes no grass nor grain. 1678: Ray, 149, Grass grows not upon the highway.

3. Grass never grows when the wind blows. 1846: Denham, *Proverbs*, 7 (Percy S.).

4. No grass grows where the Turk's horse has trod. 1639: Fuller, *Holy War*, bk v ch xxx, According to the old proverbe, Grass springeth not where the grand signior's horse setteth his foot. Before 1658: Cleveland, *Works*, 77 (1742), Of whom you may say, as of the Great Sultan's horse, where he treads the grass grows no more. 1732: Fuller, 5664, Where the great Turk's horse treads, grass never grows.

5. The grass is always greener on the other side of the fence. [*fertilior seges est alienis semper in agris* (the harvest is always richer in another's fields) Ovid, *Ars Amatoria*, I 349] The form of the proverb that is now familiar is not found before the twentieth century, but, as the quotation from Ovid indicates, the sentiment is of very long standing. 1640: G. Herbert, *Jacula Prudentum*, The apples on the other side of the wall are the sweetest. 1959: H and M. Williams, in J.C. Trewin, *Plays of the Year*, XIX 13, (title) The grass is greener.

6. To let the grass grow under one's feet. 1550: Udall, *Roister Doister*, III iii, There hath grown no grass on my heel, since I went hence. 1707: *Spanish Bawd*, IV iii, I have not been idle – I have not let grass grow under my feet. 1864: Mrs H. Wood, *Trevlyn Hold*, ch xlvi., Nora never let the grass grow under her feet, or under any one else's feet, when there was work to do. 1923:

Lucas, *Advisory Ben*, 1, Her disapproval of the pastoral process known as letting the grass grow under your feet was intense.

7. While the grass grows the steed starves. *c.*1440: Capgrave, *Life of St Kath.*, ii 253 (OED), The gray hors, whyl his gras growyth, May sterue for hunger, thus seyth the prouerbe. 1546: Heywood, *Proverbs*, Pt I ch xi. 1593: *Pass. Morrice*, 89 (N.Sh.S.). 1602: Shakespeare, *Hamlet*, III ii, Ay, sir, but 'while the grass grows' – the proverb is something musty. 1621: Burton, *Melancholy*, II iii 3, p. 404 (1836). *c.*1760: Foote, *Commissary*, III, And while the grass grows – you know the proverb … 1869: Spurgeon, *John Ploughman*, ch xv

8. You must look for grass on the top of the oak tree, i.e. 'the grass seldom springs well till the oak comes out'. – Inwards. 1670: Ray, 44. 1893: Inwards, *Weather Lore*, 151. 1917: Bridge, *Cheshire Proverbs*, 159.

See also **Cut** (17).

Grateful man. *See* quots. 1640: Herbert, *Jac. Prudentum*, To a grateful man, give money when he asks. 1732: Fuller, 2113, He that gives to a grateful man, puts out to usury.

Grave as a judge. 1685: S. Wesley, *Maggots*, 2, As grave as judge that's giving charge. 1753: *World*, No. 45, Nor have I any great objection to 'as grave as a judge'. 1836: Marryat, *Easy*, ch xxxii, Mesty sat on the chest between them, looking as grave as a judge. 1907: De Morgan, *Alice-for-Short*, ch viii, 'What a funny little tot it is!' he cried. 'As grave as a judge!'

Grave as an old gate-post. 1678: Ray, 280. 1732: Fuller, 692.

Grave as an owl. 1702: Farquhar, *Inconstant*, III ii, Why, then, look grave as an owl in a barn. 1828: Scott, *Fair Maid*, ch v, What has befallen you, that makes you look as grave as an owl?

Grave, *subs.*, and **Graves. 1. Graves are of all sizes.** 1732: Fuller, 1751.

2. The grave is the general meeting-place. Ibid., No. 4563.

3. The grave's good rest. 1632: Rowley, *Woman never Vexed*, v, But I must go before him; and 'tis said, The grave's good rest when women go first to bed.

4. To the grave with the dead, and them that live to the bread. 1612: Shelton, *Quixote*, Pt I bk iii ch v 1710: S. Palmer, *Moral Essays on Proverbs*, 247. 1732: Fuller, 6347.

Grays Inn for walks, Lincoln's Inn for a wall, The Inner Temple for a garden, and the Middle for a hall. 1659: Howell, 21. 1670: Ray, 258. 1790: Grose, *Prov. Gloss.*, s.v. 'London'.

Graze on the plain, To = To be turned out of doors. 1869: Hazlitt, 418.

Grease, To fry in one's own. [Quasi quom caletur cochleae in occulto latent, Suo sibi suco vivont, ros si non cadit; Item parasiti rebus prolatis latent In occulto, miseri victitant suco suo, Dum ruri rurant homines quos ligurriant. – Plautus, *Capt.*, i 80–4.] *c.*1386: Chaucer, *Wife of Bath's Prol.*, l. 487, But certeinly, I made folk swich chere, That in his owene grece I made him frye For angre. *c.*1400: Lydgate, *Temple of Glas*, 14 (E.E.T.S.), Thus is he fryed in his owene gres, To-rent and torn with his owene rage. 1540: Palsgrave, *Acolastus*, sig. T3, He lyeth and fryeth in his owne grease for anger. Before 1577: Gascoigne, *Works*, i 474 (Hazlitt), The sisters being thus on all sides reiected … began to melt in their owne grease. 1681: in *Roxb. Ballads*, vi 2 (B.S.), And lie like abbey-lubbers stew'd in their own greases. 1898: Weyman, *Shrewsbury*, ch xxiv, If they impeach me, I return to Loo; and they may stew in their own juice!

Grease, *verb.* **1. Grease a fat sow.** *See* **Every man basteth**; and **Sow** (14).

2. He who greases his wheels, helps his oxen. 1732: Fuller, 2384.

3. If you grease a cause well it will stretch. Ibid., No. 2753.

4. It's the squeaking wheel that gets the grease. *See* **Squeaking.**

5. To grease in the fist = To bribe. 1387: Trevisa, tr. Higden, vii 7 (Rolls Ser.), Elsinus … groped here hondes, and gat slyliche a maundmente of the kyng, and was i-put in at Caunterbury. 1569: E. Fenton, *Wonders of Nature*, 135, Annointing their clarkes in the hand with double fee. 1576: Wapull, *Tide tarrieth no Man*, sig. C1, Wherefore he will largely grease me in the hand. 1606: *Ret. from Parnassus*, Pt II ii, Ought his gowty fists then first with gold to be greased? 1681: W. Robertson, *Phraseol. Generalis*, 281, You must grease him in the fist with a new fee, for a bribe. 1789: in Farmer, *Musa Pedestris*, 72, Cease greasing their fist and they'll soon cease their jaw. 1881: Evans, *Leics. Words*, 159 (E.D.S.), A farmer said to me in reference to a douceur

which his landlord's agent appeared to expect, '… but this 'ere giff-gaff grease i' fist sort o' woo'k doon't dew for may'.

6. To grease one's boots = To cajole or flatter. 1813: Ray, 198.

Greasy as a badger. 1917: Bridge, *Cheshire Proverbs*, 14.

Great and good are seldom the same man. 1732: Fuller, 1752.

Great and the little have need of one another, The. Ibid., No. 4564.

Great as the devil and Doctor Faustus. *See* **Devil** (39).

Great bargain, At a, pause. 1736: Franklin, *Way to Wealth*, in *Works*, i 447 (Bigelow), At a great pennyworth pause a while. 1875: A. B. Cheales, *Proverb. Folk-Lore*, 101, At a great pennyworth pause. Cf. **Good bargain.**

Great barkers are no biters. 1605: Camden, *Remains*, 322 (1870). 1659: Howell, 8.

Great birth is a very poor dish at table. 1855: Bonn, 365.

Great boast small roast. *c.*1532: R. Copland, *Spyttel House*, l. 978, Grete boost and small roost. 1591: Harington, *Orl. Furioso*, bk xxv st. 66, As if there were great boast and little rost. *c.*1660: in *Roxb. Ballads*, ii 409 (Hindley). 1732: Fuller, 6297. 1869: Spurgeon, *John Ploughman*, ch xv, Such hopes lead to great boast and small roast.

Great bodies move slowly. 1855: Bohn. 365.

Great book is a great evil, A. The meaning of this saying, originally from ancient Greek, is that the impressive size of a book has no necessary bearing on the impressiveness of its contents. 1628: Burton, *Anatomy of Melancholy* (ed. 3), 7, Often times it falls out … a great Booke is a great mischiefe. 1711: Addison, *Spectator*, 23 July, We do not expect to meet with any thing in a bulky Volume … A great Book is a great Evil. 1909: *British Weekly*, 8 Apr., 13, It may be … said in reference to this unhappy production that a great book is indeed a great evil.

Great braggers little doers. 1539: Taverner, *Proverbs*, fo. 49, Great braggers commonly be least fyghters. 1732: Fuller, 1753. Cf. **Greatest talkers.**

Great businesses turn on a little pin. 1640: Herbert, *Jac. Prudentum.* Cf. **Great engines.**

Great ceremony for a small saint, A. 1732: Fuller, 190.

Great city, A, a great solitude. 1625: Bacon, *Essays:* 'Friendship', The Latine adage meeteth with it a little; *Magna civitas, magna solitudo.* 1732: Fuller, 191.

Great cry. *See* **Much cry.**

Great doings at Gregory's, heat the oven twice for a custard. 1678: Ray, 72. 1732: Fuller, 1755.

Great doings in the North when they bar their doors with tailors, There's. 1678: Ray, 341. 1683: Meriton, *Yorkshire Ale,* 83–7 (1697). 1846–59, *Denham Tracts,* ii 75 (F.L.S.) [with 'steek' for 'bar'].

Great dowry is a bed full of brambles, A. 1640: Herbert, *Jac. Prudentum.* 1670: Ray, 8 [with 'brabbles' for 'brambles']. 1732: Fuller, 193.

Great engines turn on small pivots. 1855: Bohn, 366. Cf. **Great businesses.**

Great fish eateth the little, The. 1575: Churchyard, *Chippes,* 145 (Collier), The whales, you see, eates up the little fishe. 1578: Florio, *First Fruites, fo.* 29. 1633: Draxe, 141.

Great force hidden in a sweet command, There is. 1640: Herbert, *Jac. Pmdentum.*

Great fortune, in the hands of a fool, is a great misfortune, A. 1732: Fuller, 194.

Great fortune is a great slavery, A. Ibid., No. 195.

Great gain makes work easy. Ibid., No. 1756.

Great gifts are for great men. 1639: Clarke, 188. 1670: Ray, 98 [with 'from' for 'for'].

Great Glen. *See* quot. 1678: Ray, 317, At Great Glen there are more great dogs then honest men.

Great harvest. *See* **Harvest** (7).

Great head and little wit. 1562: Heywood, *Epigr.,* 6th Hund., No. 56, Thy head is great … and without wit within. 1633: Draxe, 17. 1670: Ray, 101. 1732: Fuller, 196. 1813: Brand, *Pop. Antiq.,* iii 176 (Bohn).

Great head and small necke is the beginning of a gecke [fool]. 1623: Wodroephe, *Spared Houres,* 518.

Great honours are great burdens. 1670: Flecknoe, *Epigrams,* 53, If that saying be true, Great honours are great burthens.

Great hopes make great men. 1732: Fuller, 1759.

Great journey to the world's end, It is a. 1639: Clarke, 3. 1670: Ray, 158. 1732: Fuller, 2859 [with 'life's' for 'world's'].

Great light a great lanthorn, To a. 1640: Herbert, *Jac. Prudentum.*

Great man, A, and a great river are often ill neighbours. 1732: Fuller, 198. 1813: Ray, 117, A great lord is a bad neighbour.

Great marks are soonest hit. 1732: Fuller, 1760.

Great men have great faults. 1633: Draxe, 127. 1639: Clarke, 160, Great mens faults are never small.

Great men's favours are uncertain. 1736: Bailey, *Dict.,* s.v. 'Favour'.

Great men would have care of little ones, If, both would last long. 1640: Herbert, *Jac. Prudentum.*

Great minds think alike. *See* **Great wits jump.**

Great need of a wife that marries mamma's darling, He has. 1732: Fuller, 1872.

Great oaks. *See* **Oak** (5).

Great ones, There would be no, if there were no little. 1670: Ray, 12. 1732: Fuller, 4868.

Great pain and little gain make a man soon weary. 1633: Draxe, 221. 1670: Ray, 129.

Great pains quickly find ease. 1640: Herbert, *Jac. Prudentum.*

Great pan. *See* quot. 1913: *Devonsh. Assoc. Trans.,* xlv. 90, If yu've a-got a gurt pan an' little to cook, the pan aits the lot, as the zayin' is.

Great promise small performance. 1562: Heywood, *Epigr.,* 5th Hund., No. 10. 1611: Cotgrave, s.v. 'Faiseur', Great promisers, weak performers. 1880: Spurgeon, *Ploughman's Pictures,* 18, Those who are quick to promise are generally slow to perform.

Great put the little on the hook, The. 1640: Herbert, *Jac. Prudentum.*

Great river. *See* quot. Ibid., In a great river great fish are found; but take heed lest you be drowned. 1869: Spurgeon, *John Ploughman,* ch xix.

Great ship asks deep waters, A. 1640: Herbert, *Jac. Prudentum.* 1670: Ray, 24. 1732: Fuller, 203, A great ship must have deep water.

Great shoe fits not a little foot, A. 1633: Draxe, 3. 1639: Clarke, 138.

Great spenders are bad lenders. 1639: Clarke, 262. 1670: Ray, 145. 1732: Fuller, 6169.

Great stirring in the North when old wives ride scout, There's. 1678: Ray, 341. 1846–59: *Denham Tracts,* ii 75 (F.L.S.).

Great strokes make not sweet music. 1640: Herbert, *Jac. Prudentum.* 1670: Ray, 12, The greatest strokes make not the best musick.

Great talkers are great liars. 1736: Bailey, *Dict.*, s.v. 'Talker'.

Great talkers are like leaky pitchers, everything runs out of them. 1855: Bohn, 366.

Great torch may be lighted at a little candle, A. 1583: Melbancke, *Philotinus*, sig. A3.

Great tree hath a great fall, A. *c.*1380: Chaucer, *Troylus*, bk ii ll. 1380–6, Whan that the sturdy ook, On which men hakken oftë, for the nones, Receyvëd hath the happy falling strook, The gretë sweigh doth it come al at ones, As doon these rokkës or these milnë-stones. For swifter cours com'th thing that is of wighte, Whan it descendeth, than don thingës lighte. 1732: Fuller, 204.

Great trees keep under the little ones. Ibid., No. 1769.

Great way to the bottom of the sea, 'Tis a. 1639: Clarke, 4. 1670: Ray, 154. 1732: Fuller, 1850, He goes a great voyage, that goes to the bottom of the sea.

Great wealth and content seldom live together. 1732: Fuller, 1771.

Great weights hang on small wires. 1639: Clarke, 109. 1670: Ray, 154. 1732: Fuller, 1773 [with 'may' before 'hang'].

Great wits have short memories. 1668: Dryden, *Sir M. Markall*, IV i, He has forgot it, sir; good wits, you know, have bad memories. 1720: Swift, in *Works*, ix 191 (Scott, 1883), A common-place book is what a provident punt cannot subsist without, for this proverbial reason, that 'great wits have short memories'. 1763: Murphy, *Citizen*, II, *George* … do you remember what you read, Miss? *Maria.* Not so well as I could wish. Wits have short memories.

Great wits jump. As the later quotations show, this proverb is the original form of *great minds think alike*. The word *jump*, in this old-fashioned sense, means to concur or to coincide. 1618: D. Belchier, *Hans Beer-Pot*, D1, Though he made that verse, Those words were made before … Good wits doe jumpe. 1691. *Wit for Money*, 14, 'Tis much like it, I must confess, hut wits jump. 1758–67: Sterne, *Trist. Shandy*, vol iii ch ix, Great wits jump:—for the moment Dr Slop cast his eyes upon his bag … the very same thought occurred. 1826–44: Hood, *Comic Poems:* 'To Grimaldi', Ah, where thy legs – that witty pair! For 'great wits jump' – and so did they! 1884: *N.&Q.*, 6th ser, x 216, 'Les beaux esprits

rencontrent 'is, of course, the same as our 'Great wits jump together'. 1898: C.G. Robertson, *Voces Academicae*, 24, Curious how great minds think alile. My pupil wrote me the same explanation of his non-appearance … 1922: *Punch*, 27 Dec. p. 601, col. 3, Lord Riddell considers that Mr H. G. Wells is one of the world's greatest minds. Great minds, as the saying is, think alike. Cf. **Good wits.**

Great would have none great, The, and the little all little. 1640: Herbert, *Jac. Prudentum.*

Greater state, the more wisdom, The. Before 1500: in Hill, *Commonplace-Book*, 130 (E.E.T.S.), The grettir state, the more wisedom.

Greater the right, The, the greater the wrong. 1569: Grafton, *Chron.*, ii 228 (1809), According to the adage, the extremitie of iustice is extreme injustice. 1639: Clarke, 182, Extremity of law is extremity of wrong. 1680: L'Estrange, *Tully's Offices*, 18, From whence comes that saying, *Extreme right is extreme wrong.* 1820: Colton, *Lacon*, Pt II No. 139, There is one motto that ought to be put at the head of our penal code, '*Summum jus, summa injuria*'.

Greater the sinner, The, the greater the saint. 1773: R. Graves, *Spiritual Quixote*, II vii xi, It was a maxim with Mr Whitfield, 'The greater the Sinner, the greater the Saint'. 1856: E. Hincliffe, *Barthomley*, 29, How well is the old proverb illustrated … The greater the sinner, the greater the saint. 1913: *Folk-Lore*, xxiv 76 (Oxon).

Greatest barkers bite not sorest, The. 1587: Greene, in *Works*, iv 152 (Grosart), Orlanio … thought the greatest barkers were not always the sorest biters. 1639: Clarke, 153. 1670: Ray, 59. 1732: Fuller, 4567, The greatest barkers arc not the greatest biters.

Greatest boasters are not the boldest men, The. 1509: Barclay, *Ship of Fools*, i 198 (1874), For greattest crakers ar nat ay boldest men. 1570: Barclay, *Mirrour of Good Manners*, 76 (Spens.S.), The greatest crakers are not the boldest men.

Greatest burdens are not the gainfullest, The. 1611: Cotgrave, s.v. 'Acquests'. 1670: Ray, 4.

Greatest calf. *See* **Calf** (8).

Greatest clerks are not the wisest men, The. *c.*1386: Chaucer, *Reeve's Tale*, l. 134, 'The gretteste clerkes been noght the wysest men', As whylom to the wolf thus spak the mare. 1476: *Paston Letters*, iii 153 (Gairdner, 1900), Wherffor, late men deme what they wylle, grettest clerkys are nott alweye wysest men. 1580: Lyly, *Euphues*, 237 (Arber). 1633: Jonson, *Tale of a Tub*, I ii. 1732: Fuller, 4570. 1821: Scott, *Kenilworth*, ch xxxi, He … may be one of those whom Geoffrey Chaucer says wittily, the wisest clerks are not the wisest men.

Greatest hate springs from the greatest love, The. 1732: Fuller, 4573.

Greatest step is that out of doors, The. 1640: Herbert, *Jac. Prudentum.*

Greatest talkers are always the least doers, The. 1594: Shakespeare, *Rich. III*, I iii, Talkers are no good doers. 1607: Marston, *What You Will*, III, Ther's an old fustie proverbe, these great talkers are never good dooers. 1681: W. Robertson, *Phraseol. Generalis*, 1203. 1692: L'Estrange, *Aesop*, 360 (3rd ed.), The boldest talkers are not always the greatest doers. 1754: Berthelson, *Eng.-Danish Dict.*, s.v. 'Talk'. Cf. **Great braggers.**

Greatest vessel hath but its measure, The. 1732: Fuller, 4580.

Greatest wealth is contentment with a little, The. 1659: Howell, 6. 1670: Ray. 28. 1732: Fuller, 4581.

Greedy as a dog. 1639: Clarke, 285. 1670: Ray, 205. 1714: Mandeville, *Fable of Bees*, 187, Dogs, tho' become domestick animals, are ravenous to a proverb.

Greedy is the godless, *c.*1320: in *Reliq. Antiquae*, i 111 (1841), 'Gredy is the godless'; Quoth Hendyng.

Greek Kalends, At the = Never. [In literis cum aliquos nunquam soluturos significare vult Ad Kalendas Graecas soluturos ait. – Suetonius, *Ost.*, 87.] 1540: Palsgrave, *Acolastus*, sig. V1, At the Grekish calendes … or a daye after domesday. 1595: Lodge, *Fig for Momus*, Epist. vii, Yea, when the Grecian Calends come (quoth I). 1653: Urquhart, *Rabelais*, bk i ch xx, The judgment or decree shall be given out and pronounced at the next Greek Calends, that is, never. 1740: North, *Examen*, 477, It must be dated *ad Graecas Calendas.* 1880: *World*, 13 Oct., p. 6, Any prospects of earning a dividend on which must be relegated to the Greek kalends. 1922: *Observer*, 5 March, p. 7, col. 5, The policy … which seemed to postpone to the

Greek Kalends the concessions now freely granted to Egypt.

Greek mE.E.T.S. Greek, then comes the tug of war, When. Often shortened to *When Greek mE.E.T.S. Greek* and meaning that the competition or contest will be particularly fierce when two people of similar calibre encounter one another. 1677: N. Lee, *The Rival Queens*, iv 48, When Greeks joyn'd Greeks, then was the tug of War. 1804: W. irving, *Journals and Notebooks* (1969) I 69, Two upright Postillions … were disputing who was the greatets rogue … 'When Greek meets Greek then comes the tug of war'. 1926: A. Huxley, *Two or Three Graces*, 175, When Greeks meets Greek then comes, in this case, an exchange of anecdotes about the deposed sovereigns of eastern Europe – in a word, the tug of bores.

Greek to one, To be. 1603: Shakespeare, *Caesar*, I ii, But for mine own part, it was Greek to me. 1620: Shelton, *Quixote*, Pt II ch xix, All this to the husbandmen was heathen Greek. 1821: Scott, *Kenilworth*, ch xxix, But this is Greek to you now, honest Lawrence, and in sooth learning is dry work.

Green, *adj.* **1. A green shear is an ill shake.** 1846: Denham, *Proverbs*, 51 (Percy S.).

2. A green wound is soon healed. 1639: Clarke, 283. 1670: Ray, 31. 1732: Fuller, 206.

3. A green Yule. *See* **Christmas** (3) and (4).

4. All green things are gay. 1546: Heywood, *Proverbs*, Pt II ch i, All thing is gay that is greene. 1611: Davies (of Hereford), *Sc. of Folly*, 48, in *Works*, ii (Grosart).

5. As green as a leek. 1585: *Nomenclator*, 180, A colour as greene as a leeke. 1595: Shakespeare, *Mids. N. Dream*, V i, His eyes were green as leeks. 1745: *Agreeable Companion*, 141, If ladies cheek Be green as leek. 1886: Elworthy, *West Som. Word-Book*, 426 (E.D.S.), So green's a leek is the usual simile.

6. As green as grass. 1387: Trevisa, tr. Higden, i 123 (Rolls Ser.), the thridde [third] thre monthes grene as gras. *c.*1420: Lydgate, *Assem. of Gods*, st. 48, p. 11 (E.E.T.S.), Grene as any gresse in the somertyde. 1593: G. Harvey, in *Works*, i 271 (Grosart), As greene as the greenest grasse. *c.*1660: in *Roxb. Ballads*, ii 444 (B.S.), Her gown was of velvet as green as the grass. 1869: Spurgeon, *John Ploughman*, ch iv, Poor soft Tommy, as green as grass, and as ready to bend as a willow.

7. Green wood makes a hot fire. 1477: Rivers, *Dictes, etc.*, 65 (1877), The grene wode is hotter than the other whan it is wel kyndeled. 1586: G. Whitney, *Emblems*, 173, Greenest wood, though kindlinge longe, yet whottest most it burnes. 1670: Ray, 30. 1732: Fuller, 1774.

8. King Green. *See* quot. 1887: Parish and Shaw, *Dict. Kent. Dialect*, 155 (E.D.S.), The use of green meat as a purge gives rise to this old East Kent saying – 'King Grin [i.e. Green], Better than all medcin'.

9. Strew green rushes for the stranger. 1546: Heywood, *Proverbs*, Pt II ch iii, Greene rushes for this straunger. *c.*1594: Bacon, *Promus*, No. 118, Ceremonies and green rushes are for strangers. *c.*1618: B.&F., *Valentinian*, II iv, Where is this stranger? Rushes, ladies, rushes, Rushes as green as summer for this stranger. 1738: Swift, *Polite Convers.*, Dial. I, If we had known of your coming, we would have strewn rushes for you.

10. When there's a green frost = Never. 1883: Burne, *Shropsh. Folk-Lore*, 595.

11. You see no green cheese but your teeth must water. 1546: Heywood, *Proverbs*, Pt II ch ix. 1553: *Respublica*, III iv, Ye can see no grene cheese but your teethe wyll watier. 1670: Ray, 198.

Grenvile family. *See* quot. 1897: Norway, *H. and B. in Devon, etc.*, 183, 'Never a Grenvile wanted loyalty', so say the Cornish still.

Grey and green make the worst medley. 1678: Ray, 149 ['Gray'].

Grey as a badger. 1720: Swift, in *Works*, xiv 134 (Scott), Though she lives till she's grey as a badger all over. 1786: Wolcot, in *Works*, i 140 (1795). 1823: Moor, *Suffolk Words*, 45, We say 'as grey as a badger' of one whose head is 'silvered o'er with age'. 1862: *Dialect of Leeds*, 406. 1880: Courtney, *W. Cornwall Words*, 26 (E.D.S.), 'Grey as a badger' is a Cornish proverb.

Grey as grannum's cat. 1732: Fuller, 693. 1880: Spurgeon, *Ploughman's Pictures*, 48, He will be as grey as grannum's cat before he improves.

Grey before he is good, He's. 1678: Ray, 249.

Grey hairs are death's blossoms. Ibid., 149 ['Gray']. 1853: Trench, *Proverbs*, 70 (1905) ['Gray'].

Grey mare is the better horse, The. 1546: Heywood, *Proverbs*, Pt II ch. iv *c.*1570: *Marr. of Wit and Science*, II i, Break her betimes, and

bring her under by force, Or else the grey mare will be the better horse. 1626: Charles I, in Ellis, *Orig. Letters*, iii 249 (1824), My sister and brother (I place them so, becaus I thinke the gray meare is the best horse). 1723: Steele, *Conscious Lovers*, I i. *c.*1740: Fielding, *Eurydice*. 1849: Macaulay, *Hist. Eng.*, i ch iii *n.*, The vulgar proverb, that the grey mare is the better horse, originated, I suspect, in the preference generally given to the grey mares of Flanders over the finest coach horses of England. 1926: Phillpotts, *Yellow Sands*, II, And when the grey mare's the better hoss, that's no marriage neither.

Greyhound. Proverbial descriptions of the shape of a good grey-hound. 1486: *Boke of St Albans*, sig. Fiiii. v, The propreteis of a goode grehound. A grehounde shulde be heded like a snake, and necked like a drake. Foted like a kat. Tayled like a rat. Syded lyke a terne. Chyned like a berne. 1611: Markham, *Country Contentments*, 39 (1675), An old rime left by your fore fathers, from which you shall understand the true shapes of a perfect grey-hound, and this it is, If you will have a good tike, Of which there are few like, He must be headed like a snake, Neckt like a drake, Backt like a beam, Sided like a bream, Tayled like a rat, And footed like a cat. 1670: Ray, 212, A head like a snake, a neck like a drake, A back like a beam, a belly like a bream, A foot like a cat, a tail like a rat. 1736: Bailey, *Dict.*, s.v. 'Grey-hound' [as in 1670].

Grind or find, I'll either. 1670: Ray, 178.

Grind with every wind, To. 1736: Bailey, *Dict.*, s.v. 'Grind'.

Grist to the mill, To bring. 1583: Golding, *Calvin on Deut.*, 755 (OED), There is no lykelihoode that those thinges will bring gryst to the mill. 1661: Gurnal, *Christian in Armour*, Pt III v 18, ch xxi p. 481 (1679), 'Tis a pick-purse doctrine, contrived to bring grist to the Popes mill. 1720: *Vade Mecum for Malt-worms*, Pt I p. 21, No writs have we, to draw Grist to your mill. 1767: Murphy, *Sch. for Guardians*, I iv, (*A rap at the door*) More grist to the mill. Go and open the door, Peter. 1871: G. Eliot, *Middlemarch*, ch x, Some people make fat, some blood, and some bile – that's my view of the matter; and whatever they take is a sort of grist to the mill.

Grizzling like a badger. Corn. 1895: Jos. Thomas, *Randigal Rhymes*, 60.

Groaning horse and a groaning wife never fail their master, A. 1546: Heywood, *Proverbs*, Pt II ch iv 1611: T. Heywood, *Golden Age*, I, You know the prouerbe: A grunting horse and a groning wife neuer deceiue their maister. 1670: Ray, 51, A grunting horse ... seldom fail their master. 1732: Fuller, 207 [as in 1670, *minus* 'their master'].

Groat is ill saved that shames the master, The. 1605: Camden, *Remains*, 332 (1870). 1670: Ray, 23. 1732: Fuller, 4345. 1853: Trench, *Proverbs*, 103 (1905).

Groats. *See* **Blood** (2).

Groby pool, Leics. **1.** *See* quots. 1678: Ray, 317, For his death there is many a wet eye in Groby pool. 1790: Grose, *Prov. Gloss.*, s.v. 'Leicestershire' [as in 1678]. 1881: Evans, *Leics. Words*, 301 (E.D.S.), This is generally used in the form of a prophecy: 'When a doys, thee'll ba wet oys i' Grewby Pule'.

2. *See* quots. 1678: Ray, 317, Then I'll thatch Groby pool with pancakes. 1790: Grose, *Prov. Gloss.*, s.v. 'Leicestershire' [as in 1678]. 1818: Scott, *Heart of Midl.*, ch xxix, [Newark man *loq.*] Why, when [there's no bad company on the road] ... I'll thatch Groby pool wi' pancakes. 1843: Carlyle, *Past and Present*, bk iii ch i, Think of that. 'Groby Pool *is* thatched with pancakes', – as Jeanie Deans's Innkeeper defied it to be!

Gropes in the dark, He that, finds that he would not. 1659: Howell, 13. 1670: Ray, 12. 1732: Fuller, 2124.

Groundsel, The = Sill or threshold. *See* quots. 1640: Herbert, *Jac. Prudentum*, The groundsel speaks not, save what it heard at the hinges. 1670: Ray, 12 ['grounsel', and 'of' for 'at']. 1732: Fuller, 4583, The groundsel speaketh but what it heard of the hinges.

Ground-sweat cures all disorders, A. *c.*1816: in Farmer, *Musa Pedestris*, 81, We ... sent him to take a ground-sweat [buried him]. 1830: Forby, *Vocab. E. Anglia*, 434. 1872: J. Glyde, jr., *Norfolk Garland*, 150.

Grout [Good breed] **afore brass for me.** 1917: Bridge, *Cheshire Proverbs*, 63.

Grow, *verb.* **1. He grows warm in his harness.** 1623: Wodroephe, *Spared Houres*, 487.

2. *See* quot. 1678: Ray, 72, This grow'd by night. Spoken of a crooked stick or tree, it could not see to grow.

Growing youth. *See* **Wolf** (1).

Grunt. See **Pig** (25).

Grunting horse. *See* **Groaning.**

Guest is never welcome, A constant. 1732: Fuller, 48.

Guildford. 1. Guildford bulls. 1790: Grose, *Prov. Gloss.*, s.v. 'Surrey'. [A Godalming retort in answer to the taunts against the Godalming folk of cats and rabbits. *See* **Godalming.**]

2. Poor Guildford, proud people, three churches, no steeple. 1886: Hissey, *On the Box Seat*, 42.

Guiler is beguiled, The. 1377: Langland, *Plowman*, B, xviii 337, The olde lawe graunteth, That gylours be bigiled. *c.*1386: Chaucer, *Reeve's Tale*, 1. 401, A gylour shal himself bigyled be. *c.*1390: Gower, *Conf. Amantis*, bk vi 1. 1381. 1484: Caxton, *Aesope*, ii 50 (Jacobs), As men saye it is meryte to begyle the begylers ... And therfore he that begyleth other is oftyme begyled hym self. 1598: Bernard, *Terence in English*, 111 (1607), *Frustratur ipse sibi*, he deceiues himselfe, he playeth wilie beguile himselfe. 1606: *Wily Beguiled*, in Hazlitt, *Old Plays*, ix.

Guilt is always jealous. 1732: Fuller, 1779.

Guilty Gilbert. *See* quot. 1608: Armin, *Nest of Ninnies*, 39 (SH.S.), By her cheeks you might find guilty Gilbert, where he had hid the brush.

Gull comes against the rain, The. 1633: Draxe, 189, The gull commeth not, but against a tempest. 1670: Ray, 98.

Gup quean, gup. 'Gup' probably = Go up. 1525: *Wydow Edyth: Mery Gestys*, 36 (1864), Than her lemman cast her vp, Go where she wold: gup quean gup. 1546: Heywood, *Proverbs*, Pt II ch iv, Walke drab, walke! Nay (quoth she), walke knaue walke! 1573: G. Harvey, *Letter-Book*, 118 (Camden S.), Marry gupp, hore, gupp, all the day longe. Cf. **Hop, whore.**

Guts in his brains, He has. 1663: Butler, *Hudibras*, Pt I can. iii 1.1091, Hard matter for a man to do That has but any guts in's brains. 1697: T. Dilke, *City Lady*, III ii, They have no guts in their brains. 1720: Swift, *Right of Precedence*, par. 23, Our vulgar saying, 'that men have guts in their brains', is a vulgar error. 1828: Carr, *Craven Dialect*, i 47, 'You have no guts in your brains'; you are completely ignorant, you are quite destitute of skill or cunning. 1889: *Longman's Mag.*, April, 619 (W.), Maurie has good guts i' her brain.

Guts to a bear, Not fit to carry. 1659: Howell, 17, He is not worthy to carry gutts to a bear. 1670: Ray, 200, Not worthy to carry guts after a bear. 1785–95: Wolcot, in *Works*, i 198 (1795), George thinks us scarcely fit ('tis very clear) To carry guts, my brethren, to a bear. 1826: in Mrs Hughes, *Letters, etc., of Scott*, ch vi, 'So, Sir, I hear you have had the impudence to assert that I am not fit to carry guts to a bear'. 'Oh no! – I defended you: I said you were'.

Gutter Lane, All goeth down. 1631: Brathwait, *Whimzies*, 145 (1859), Whatsoever hee draines from the four corners of the citty, goes in muddy taplash downe Gutter-lane. 1662: Fuller, *Worthies*, ii 348 (1840). 1721: Bailey, *Eng. Dict.*, s.v., All goes down Guttur Lane. 1880: Spurgeon, *Ploughman's Pictures*, 40.

H

Hab or nab. 1542: Udall, tr. Erasmus' *Apoph.*, 209 (1877), To be put to the plounge of making or marring, and of habbe or nhabbe to wynne all, or to lese all. 1595: *Pedlars Prophecy*, 1. 1174 (Malone S.), Sing and be mery, hab or nab; away the mare. 1693: Urquhart, *Rabelais*, bk iii ch xliv., The chance and hazard of a throw of the dice, hab nab, or luck as it will. 1754: Berthelson, *Eng.-Danish Dict.*, s.v., 'Tis meer hab-nab whether it succeeds or not. 1828: Carr, *Craven Dialect*, i 204, To obtain a thing by hab and by nab, i.e. by fair means or foul. 1886: Elworthy, *West Som. Word-Book*, 307 (E.D.S.), Hab or nab = 'get or lose' – 'bit or miss'.

Habit. *See* **Custom.**

Habits. *See* **old** E (12).

Hackney mistress, hackney maid. 1639: Clarke, 217. 1670: Ray, 99. 1732: Fuller, 1780. Cf. **Like mistress like maid.**

Had I fish, is good without mustard. 1639: Clarke, 114. 1670: Ray, 99.

Had I wist, Beware of. *c.*1400: *Beryn*, 1. 2348 (E.E.T.S.), But nowe it is to late to speke of had-I-wist! *c.*1460: *Good Wyfe wold a Pylgr.*, 1. 120, When dede is doun, hit ys to lat; be ware of hady-wyst. Before 1529: Skelton, *Magnyfycence*, 1. 213, Hem, syr, yet beware of Had I wyste! 1587: Greene, in *Works*, iv 110 (Grosart), But alas, had I wist now comes too late. 1651: Taylor (Water-Poet), *Epigr.*, 11, in *Works*, 2nd coll. (Spens.S.), Beware of, had I wist, before thou wed. 1732: Fuller, 976. 1825: Brockett, *Gloss. N. Country Words*, 2, Addiwissen, had I known it. An expression nearly obsolete, though still retained by some old persons. 1868: Atkinson, *Cleveland Gloss.*, 577, Had I wist. Had I known. 1892:

Heslop, *Northumb. Words*, 7 (E.D.S.), Addiwissen … that is, 'Had I but known'.

Had what he hath not. *See* quot. 1546: Heywood, *Proverbs*, Pt II ch ix, Ye, (quoth She), who had that he hath not, woulde Doo that he dooth not, as olde men haue tolde. 1611: Da vies (of Hereford), *Sc. of Folly*, 47, in *Works*, ii (Grosart) [as in 1546].

Had you never miss, What you never *See* **Never had.**

Haddock to paddock, To bring = To lose everything. 1546: Heywood, *Proverbs*, Pt II ch x, And thus had he brought haddocke to paddocke. 1577: Stanihurst, *Descrip. of Ireland*, fo. 10, I had been like to haue brought haddocke to paddocke.

Haddock. *See* **Deaf** (4); and **May,** E (9).

Haft on an old blade, Fresh. *See* quot. 1877: E. Leigh, *Cheshire Gloss.*, 96, 'Dunna waste a fresh haft on an oud blade', Don't throw good money after bad. 1917: Bridge, *Cheshire Proverbs.* 51 [as in 1877].

Hail, *subs.* **1. Hail brings frost in the tail.** 1639: Clarke, 197.1670: Ray, 42. 1825: Hone, *Ev. Day Book*, i 670. 1893: Inwards, *Weather Lore*, 115.

2. He skips like hail on a pack-saddle. 1732: Fuller, 2022.

Hail fellow well met. 1519: Horman, *Vulgaria*, fo. 148, He made so moche of his servaunt that he waxed hayle felowe with hym. *c.*1550: Becon, *Catechism, etc.*, 561 (P.S.), They would be 'hail fellow well-met' with him. *c.*1630: *Dicke of Devonsh.*, IV ii, in Bullen, *Old Plays*, ii 72, The hangman and you had bene 'hayle fellow! well met'. 1748: Richardson, *Clarissa*, v 146 (1785), Who, being no proud woman, is hail fellow, well met, as the saying is, with all her aunt's servants.

1838: Carlyle, *Sartor*, bk i ch x. 1857: Hughes, *Tom Brown*, Pt II ch iii, The ease with which he himself became hail-fellow-well-met with anybody, and blundered into and out of twenty friendships a half year …

Hailer is as bad as the stailer, The = The receiver is as bad as the thief. 1825: Jennings, *Somersetsh. Words*, 43, Hence the very common expression, The heeler is as bad as the stealer. 1879: *Folk-Lore Record*, ii 203, The healer is as bad as the stealer [Corn.]. 1883: Burne, *Shropsh. Folk-Lore*, 588, The heler is as bad as the heaver. 1886: Elworthy, *West Som. Word-Book*, 335 (E.D.S.), Heler … one who covers up or conceals – hence … in the every-day saying: the heler's so bad as the stealer. 1892: S. Hewett, *Peasant Speech of Devon*, 8.

Hailstorm by day denotes a frost at night, A. 1893: Inwards, *Weather Lore*, 115.

Hair. 1. A hair of the dog that bit you. 1546: Heywood, *Proverbs*, Pt I ch xi, I pray the leat me and my felow haue A heare of the dog that bote vs last night – And bitten were we both to the braine aright. 1614: Jonson, *Bart. Fair*, I, 'Twas a hot night with some of us, last night, John: shall we pluck a hair of the same wolf to-day, proctor John? 1674: Head and Kirkman, *Eng. Rogue*, iii 91, If they, in the morning, did fall to drinking again, taking a hair of the old dog … 1717: E. Ward, *Brit. Wonders*, 17, A hair of the same dog next morning, Is best to quench our fev'rish burning. 1817: Scott, *Rob Roy*, ch xii, He poured out a large bumper of brandy, exhorting me to swallow 'a hair of the dog that had bit me'. 1841: Dickens, *Barn. Rudge*, ch lii.

2. His hair grows through his hood = He is on the road to ruin. *c.*1450: in *Reliq. Antiquae*, ii 67 (1843), He that lovyth welle to fare, Ever to spend and never spare, But he have the more good, His here wol grow throw his hood. Before 1529: Skelton, *Bowge of Courte*, l. 350, [of Riot] His here was growen thoroweoute his hat. *c.*1600: Deloney, *Thos. of Reading*, ch v, Out you durty heeles, you will make your husbands haire grow through his hood I doubt. 1694: Motteux, *Rabelais*, bk iv ch Iii., In so much that Snip was condemn'd to make good the stuffs to all his customers; and to this day poor Cabbidge's hair grows through his hood.

3. More hair than wit – often with *Bush natural* prefixed. 1546: Heywood, *Proverbs*, Pt II ch vii,

Thy tales (quoth he) shew long heare, and short wit, wife. 1589: L. Wright, *Display of Dutie*, 38, According to the old prouerbe, bush naturall, more hayre than wit. 1608: Middleton, *Mad World*, II i, There's great hope of his wit, his hair's so long a-coming. 1670: Ray, 166, Bush natural, more hair then wit. 1732: Fuller, 1025 [as in 1670]. 1880: *N. & Q.*, 6th ser, i 403, There was formerly a vague notion that abundance of hair denoted a lack of brains, and from this idea arose a proverb, 'Bush natural, more hair than wit'.

4. Pull hair and hair and you'll make the carle bald. 1639: Clarke, 10. 1670: Ray, 134.

Hake. *See* **Lose** (16).

Haldon, Devon. *See* quots. 1838: Holloway, *Provincialisms*, 147, In Devonshire they say, 'When Haledown has a hat, Let Kenton beware of a skatt [shower of rain]'. 1850: *N. & Q.*, 1st ser, ii 511, When Haldon hath a hat, Kenton may beware a skat. 1893: Inwards, *Weather Lore*, 101 [as in 1838].

Halesworth. *See* **Beccles**.

Half a loaf is better than no bread. 1546: Heywood, *Proverbs*, Pt I ch xi. Throwe no gyft agayne at the givers head, For better is halfe a lofe then no bred. 1605: Camden, *Remains*, 319 (1870). 1642: D. Rogers, *Naaman*, To Reader, He is a foole who counts not halfe a loafe better then no bread. 1681: A. Behn, *Rover*, Pt II II. ii, You know the proverb of the half loaf, Ariadne. *c.*1720: in *Somers Tracts*, xiii 824 (1811). 1793: Grose, *Olio*, 123 (2nd ed.). 1857: Hughes, *Tom Brown*, Pt II ch ii, Yes, he's a whole-hog man, is Tom … Sooner have no bread any day than half the loaf.

Half an acre is good land. 1659: Howell, 4. 1670: Ray, 99. 1732: Fuller, 1782.

Half an egg is better than an empty shell. 1639: Clarke, 86. 1670: Ray, 84. 1732: Fuller, 901. 1855: Robinson, *Whitby Gloss.*, 176, Half an egg is better than a team'd [empty] shell.

Half an eye, To see with. 1531: in State *Papers:* 'Henry VIII', v 266, As with half an eye ye may perceive. 1584: B. R., *Euterpe*, 58 (Lang), Whych any man with halfe an eye may easily discerne. *c.*1660: Jer. Taylor, in *Works*, ix 386 (Edinb. ed.), But half an eye may see the different accounts. 1715: Prior, *Alma*, can. i l. 238. 1876: Blackmore, *Cripps*, ch xl, Anybody with half an eye could see through that conspiracy.

Half an hour is soon lost at dinner. 1738: Swift, *Polite Convers.*, Dial. II.

Half an hour past three quarters, and ready to strike again. 1639: Clarke, 72.

Half an hour's hanging hinders five miles' riding. 1678: Ray, 150.

Half-baked. *See* quot. 1864: 'Cornish Proverbs', in *N. & Q.*, 3rd ser, vi 494, He is only half-baked; he would take a brush more. Cf. **Loaf** (1).

Half-egg, Give him the other, and burst him. 1678: Ray, 241.

Half hanged. *See* **Ill name.**

Half is better than the whole, The. [πλέυν ἥμισυ παντός. – Hesiod, *Works and Days.*] There seems to be an allusion to the saying in the first quotation. 1546: Heywood, *Proverbs*, Pt I ch xiii, Thats iust, if the halfe shall iudge the whole (quoth I). 1550: Latimer, *Sermons*, 277 (P.S.), There is a proverb which I read many years ago, *Dimidium plus toto:* 'The half sometimes more than the whole'. 1726: tr. Gracian's Hero, 4, That seeniingly strange paradox of the wise man of Mitilene, That the half is better than the whole. 1782: T. Twining, in *Twining Fam. Papers*, 104 (1887), The famous saying of old Hesiod, that 'half is more than the whole' ... is to nothing more applicable than to a numerous party.

Half sheweth what the whole meaneth, The. 1546: Heywood, *Proverbs*, Pt II ch vii, This halfe showth what the hole meaneth. 1633: Draxe, 79.

Half the truth is often a whole lie. 1875: A. B. Cheales, *Proverb. Folk-Lore*, 166.

Half the world does not know how the other half lives. 1607: J. Hall, *Holy Observations*, xvii, One half of the world knowes not how the other lives: and therefore the better sort pitty not the distressed ... because they knowe it not. 1640: Herbert, *Jac. Prudentum. c.*1750: *Low Life; or One Half of the World knows not how the Other Half Live* [title]. 1830: Marryat, *King's Own*, ch x. 1925: C. K. S., in *Sphere*, 27 June, p. 392, col. 3, One half the world, we are told, does not know how the other half lives.

Half warned, half armed. 1546: Heywood, *Proverbs*, Pt II ch vi 1605: Camden, *Remains*, 323 (1870). *c.*1625: B.&F., *Women Pleased*, III iii, Since you're so high and hot, sir, you have half arm'd us. 1659: Howell, 8.

Halfpenny good silver, To think one's. 1575: Gascoigne, *Glasse of Govt.*, I v, I thought my halfepeny good siluer within these few yeares past,

and now no man esteemeth me vnlesse it be for counsell. 1586: Pettie, tr. Guazzo's *Civil Convers.*, fo. 115, Shee hath great cause ... to thinke her halfe penie better siluer than other womens. 1633: Draxe, 26, He thinketh his halfpeny good siluer. Cf. **Farthing**; and **Penny** (26).

Halfpenny. *See* **Hand** (8).

Halgaver Court. *See* quots. 1602: Carew, *Surv. of Cornwall*, 296 (1811), Hence is sprung the proverb, when we see one slovenly apparelled, to say 'He shall be presented in Halgaver Court'. 1662: Fuller, *Worthies* (Cornwall), i 307 (1840), He is to be summoned before the Mayor of Halgaver. 1790: Grose, *Prov. Gloss.*, s.v. 'Cornwall' [as in 1662]. 1821: Scott, *Kenilworth*, ch iv, Depart – vanish – or we'll have you summoned before the Mayor of Halgaver. 1880: Courtney, *W. Cornwall Words*, xiii (E.D.S.), To be presented in Halgaver Court.

Halifax. 1. Go to Halifax. 1878: *Folk-Lore Record*, i 165, We have also the expression, 'Go to Halifax'. 1920: L. J. Jennings, *Chestnuts and Small Beer*, 140, I refused to admit that I had made a *faux pas*, and told my critics to go to Halifax.

2. Gooide brade, *etc.* See quot. 1878: *Folk-Lore Record*, i 165, A similarity is also said to exist between the local dialect [Halifax] and that of Friesland and the low countries, whence the following distich: – Gooide brade, botter, and cheese, Is gooid Halifax and gooid Friese.

3. Halifax Law. *See* quots. 1586: Leicester, in Motley, *United Neth.*, i 444 (1860), Under correction, my good Lord, I have had Halifax law – to be condemned first and inquired upon after. 1609: Quoted in *N. & Q.*, 5th ser, iv 154, First executing the prisoner, then enquiring of his demerits, as men say they doe at Halifax. 1708: *Hallifax and its Gibbet-Law placed in a True Light* [title]. 1922: in *N. & Q.*, 12th ser, xi 102, This was the celebrated Halifax Gibbet Law, which gave rise to the well-known proverb: – From Hell, Hull, and Halifax, Good Lord deliver us [q.v. s.v. '**Hell**'].

Hallamshire. *When all the world shall be aloft, Then Hallamshire shall be God's croft.* 1678: Ray, 340. 1790: Grose, *Prov. Gloss.*, s.v. 'Yorkshire'. 1878: *Folk-Lore Record*, i 166.

Halloo before you are out of the wood. *See* **Out of the wood.**

Hallowmas. *See* **Beggar** (13).

Halt before a cripple, Don't. *c.*1374: Chaucer, *Troylus*, bk iv 1. 1457, It is ful hard to halten unespyed Bifore a crepul, for he can the craft. 1592: Lyly, *Gallathea*, IV i, Hee must halt cunningly that will deceive a cripple. 1630: Jonson, *New Inn*, III i, It is ill halting afore cripples. 1653: Urquhart, *Rabelais*, bk i ch xx, Halt not before the lame. 1732: Fuller, 1784, Halt not before a cripple.

Halt before you are lame, You. 1670: Ray, 179. 1754: Berthelson, *Eng.-Danish Dict.*, s.v. 'Halt'.

Halter. 1. A halter and a rope for him that will be Pope, Without all right and reason. 1659: Howell, 11. 1670: Ray, 212.

2. He hath made a halter to hang himself. 1639: Clarke, 200.

3. It is ill talking of a halter in the house of a man that was hanged. 1612: Shelton, *Quixote*, Pt I bk iii ch xi, One should not make mention of a rope in one's house that was hanged. 1710: S. Palmer, *Moral Essays on Proverbs*, 96, Don't talk of a halter in the company of him whose father was hang'd. 1814: Scott, *Waverley*, ch lxxi, 'There were mony good folk at Derby, and it's ill speaking of halters', with a sly cast of his eye toward the Baron.

Halterburn. *See* quot. 1913: E. M. Wright, *Rustic Speech, etc.*, 123, A Northumbrian proverbial saying is: Like the butter of Halterburn, it would neither rug nor rive [be pulled nor torn] nor cut with a knife – it was confounded.

Hambleton-bough. *See* **Bayton.**

Hamilton. *See* **Hood-hill.**

Hampshire ground requires every day of the week a shower of rain, and on Sunday twain. 1790: Grose, *Prov. Gloss.*, s.v. 'Hants'.

Hampshire hog, A = A native of Hampshire. 1622: Drayton, *Polyol.*, xxiii, As Hampshire, long for her, hath had the term of Hogs. 1720: *Vade Mecum for Maltworms*, Pt I 50, Now to the sign of fish let's jog, There to find out a Hampshire Hog, A man whom none can lay a fault on, The pink of courtesie at Alton. 1910: in *N. & Q.*, 11th ser, ii 57, To the circumstance of this county [Hants] having been proverbially famous for its breed of hogs is owing the fact that a native bears the county nickname of 'Hampshire Hog'.

Hand. 1. A hand like a foot. 1732: Fuller, 5921, You have made a hand of it like a foot. 1738: Swift, *Polite Convers.*, Dial. I, Whoe'er writ it, writes a hand like a foot.

2. Don't put or stretch thy hand. *See* **Arm** (1).

3. From hand to mouth. 1605: Sylvester, *Du Bartas*, Week II Day i Pt 4, l. 122, Living from hand to mouth, soon satisfi'd. 1631: Brathwait, *Whimzies*, 143 (1859), All the meanes of his gettings is but from hand to mouth. 1712: Arbuthnot, *John Bull*, Pt II ch iii, He has a numerous family, and lives from hand to mouth. 1790: Cowper, *Letter to Newton*, 5 Feb. 1869: Spurgeon, *John Ploughman*, ch xii, His poor creditors cannot get more than enough to live from hand to mouth.

4. Hand over head. *c.*1440: *Bone Flor.*, 475 (OED), Than they faght hand ovyr hedd. 1530: Palsgrave, 836, Hande over heed, confusedly. 1555: Latimer, *Sermons*, 284 (P.S.), And again sent other servants to bid guests to his bridal, hand-over-head, come who would. 1627: Drayton, *Agincourt*, st. 204, Hand over head pell mell upon them run. 1681: W. Robertson, *Phraseol. Generalis*, 75, Give not your almes hand over head; Do good with discretion. 1769: Bickerstaffe and Foote, *Dr Last in his Chariot*, II, Nor endure to see you run hand over head into all the snares she lays for you. 1823: D'Israeli, *Cur. of Lit.*, 2nd ser, i 462 (1824), Among our own proverbs a remarkable incident has been commemorated; *Hand over head, as men took the Covenant!* [D'Israeli seems to have misunderstood the saying, and taken 'hand over head' as descriptive of a physical attitude. It simply meant, as the other illustrations show – hurriedly, confusedly, unthinkingly.] 1863: Reade, *Hard Cash*, ch i, He laid out all his powers, and went at the leading skiffs hand over head. 1886: Elworthy, *West Som. Word-Book*, 316 (E.D.S.), Hand-over-head. In a reckless thoughtless manner.

5. The hand that gives gathers. 1659: Howell, *Proverbs: Brit.-Eng.*, 34.

6. The hand that rocks the cradle rules the world. 1865: W. R. Wallace, in J.K. Hoyt, *Cyclopaedia of Practical Quotations* (1896), 402, A mightier power and stronger Man from his throne has hurled, For the hand that rocks the cradle Is the hand that rules the world. 1916: 'Saki', *Toys of Peace* (1919), 158, You can't prevent it; it's the nature of the sex. The hands that rocks the cradle rocks the world, in a volcanic sense.

7. Thy hand [is] never [the] worse for doing thy own work. Ibid., 35.

8. To be hand in glove (or **hand and glove**). 1678: Ray, 347, They two are hand and glove. Somerset. 1732: Fuller, 4960, They both put their hands in one glove. 1748: Smollett, *Rod. Random*, ch li., Who was hand and glove with a certain person who ruled the roast. 1824: Scott, *Redgauntlet*, ch xii, Poor Harry Redgauntlet, that suffered at Carlisle, was hand and glove with me. 1883: R.L.S., *Treasure I*, ch xxxiv, I'm on your side now, hand and glove. 1922: Weyman, *Ovington's Bank*, ch xxxvi, He ought to know. Wasn't he hand in glove with them?

9. To have one's hand (or **heart**) **on one's halfpenny** = *To* have an eye to the main chance, or to any particular object. 1546: Heywood, *Proverbs*, Pt I ch vi, So harde is your hande set on your halfpeny, That my reasonyng your reason setteth nought by. 1583: Greene, in *Works*, ii 45 (Grosart), She stood as though her heart had bin on her halfpeny. 1639: Clarke, 231, His heart is on his halfpenny. 1681: W. Robertson, *Phraseol. Generalis*, 885, His mind is on his halfpenny. 1707: in *Thoresby's Correspondence*, ii 62 (1832), I quickly found they had their hand too much upon their halfpenny. 1828: Carr, *Craven Dialect*, i 216, 'To have his hand on his hawpny', a proverbial phrase for being ever attentive to his own interest.

See also **One hand**

Handful of good life is better than a bushel of learning, A. 1640: Herbert, *Jac. Prudentum*. 1748: Richardson, *Clarissa*, iv 120 (1785).

Handful of trade is an handful of gold, An. 1732: Fuller, 603.

Handle thorns, To. *See* **Thorn** (2).

Handle without mittens, To. 1659: Howell, *Proverbs: Fr.-Eng.*, 16, They will not be caught without mittains. 1670: Ray, 216.

Handsaw is a good thing, but not to shave with, A. 1732: Fuller, 210. 1880: Spurgeon, *Ploughman's Pictures*, 31.

Handsel. *See* quot. 1867: Harland, etc., *Lancs Folk-Lore*, 70, Hansell (they [market folk] say) is always lucky when well wet. [First money received is spit upon.]

Handsel Monday. *See* **New Year** (1).

Handsome. 1. A handsome bodied man in the face. 1678: Ray, 73.

2. A handsome woman. *See* quot. 1650:

Bulwer, *Anthropomet.*, 228, The vote of the proverb, for a handsome woman, would have been English to the neck, French to the waste, and Dutch below.

3. Handsome is as handsome does. 1580: Munday, *Sundry Examples*, 78 (SH.S.), But as the auncient adage is, goodly is he that goodly dooth. 1600: Dekker, *Shoem. Hol.*, II i, By my troth, he is a proper man; but he is proper that proper doth. 1659: N.R. *Proverbs*, 49, He is handsome that handsome doth. 1713: Gay, *Wife of Bath*, III i, He is handsome that handsome does. 1768: Goldsmith, *Vicar*, ch i 1826: Lamb, *Pop. Fallacies*, x 1829: Cobbett, *Advice to Young Men*, Lett. III, 'Handsome is that handsome does', used to say to me an old man, who had marked me out for his not over-handsome daughter.

4. He that is not handsome at 20, etc. *See* quots. 1640: Herbert, *Jac. Prudentum*, He that is not handsome at 20, nor strong at 30, nor rich at 40, nor wise at 50, will never be handsome, strong, rich, or wise. 1732: Fuller, 2287 [as in 1640, excePt 'wise' for 'rich at 40', and 'rich' for 'wise at 50']. 1822: Southey, *Letter to Bedford*, 20 Dec., You know the proverb, that he who is not handsome at twenty, wise at forty, and rich at fifty, will never be rich, wise, or handsome.

5. You have a handsome head of hair, pray give me a tester [sixpence]. 1678: Ray, 73.

Handsomest flower is not the sweetest, The. 1855: Bohn, 507.

Hang, *verb.* **1. Better to hang than to hold.** 1639: Clarke, 86. 1685: Meriton, *Yorkshire Ale*, 48, Sike fowkes are fitter to hang than hawd.

2. Hang him that hath no shifts. 1639: Clarke, 42. 1670: Ray, 141. 1732: Fuller, 1785, Hang him that has no shifts; and hang him that has one too many.

3. Hang saving. *See* quots. *c.*1630: *Hang Pinching* [title of ballad], in *Roxb. Ballads*, iii (B.S.). 1666: Torriano, *Piazza Univ.*, 276, As one would say, Hang pinching, let's be mery. 1738: Swift, *Polite Convers.*, Dial. II, Come, hang saving; bring us up a half-p'orth of cheese.

4. Hang yourself for a pastime. 1678: Ray, 73.

5. He may go hang himself in his own garters. 1597: Shakespeare, *1 Henry IV*, II ii, Go hang thyself in thine own heir-apparent garters! 1678: Ray, 246.

6. He was hanged that left his drink behind.

*c.*1640: in *Roxb. Ballads*, i 416 (B.S.), He was hang'd that left his drinke behinde. 1672: *Westm. Drollery*, Pt II 86 (Ebsworth), Yet he was bang'd, nay some say hang'd, That left his drink behind. 1738: Swift, *Polite Convers.*, Dial. II, Stay till this bottle's out; you know, the man was hang'd that left his liquor behind him. 1830: Forby, *Vocab. E. Anglia*, 433, The man was hanged, that left his liquor. *See also* **Bawtry.**

7. I have hanged up my hatchet. *See* **Hatchet.**

8. I'll not hang all my bells on one horse, i.e. give all to one son. 1659: Howell, 14. 1670: Ray, 215. 1732: Fuller, 1786, Hang not all your bells upon one horse. 1913: *Folk-Lore*, xxiv 77, To put all the bells on one horse [Oxfordsh.].

9. If I be hanged, I'll choose my gallows. 1659: Howell, 16. 1670: Ray, 216. 1738: Swift, *Polite Convers.*, Dial. II, If I must be hanged, 1 won't go far to choose my gallows.

10. It hangs together as pebbles in a wyth. 1639: Clarke, 155.

11. Let him hang by the heels. Somerset. Said of a man that dies in debt. 1678: Ray, 353.

12. One might as well be hanged for a sheep as a lamb. *See* **Sheep** (9).

13. To hang in the bell-ropes. *c.*1750: in *N.&Q.*, 3rd ser, xii 91, So what so long has been hanging in the bell-ropes will at last be brought to a happy period. 1867: *N.&Q.*, 3rd ser, xii 139, This is a common phrase in Cumberland at the present day. A couple are said to be 'hingin' i' t' bell reaps' during the period which transpires between the first publication of banns and marriage … In Worcestershire, if marriage does not come off, the deserted one is said to be 'hung in the bell ropes'. [Also common in Leicestershire.] 1884–6: Holland, *Cheshire Words* (E.D.S.), From the time the banns of a couple are completed asking in church, to the time they marry, they are said to 'hing i' th' bell ropes'. 1917: Bridge, *Cheshire Proverbs*, 138.

14. To hang one's ears. 1670: Ray, 179.

Hanged hay never döes [fattens] **cattle,** 1836: Wilbraham, *Cheshire Gloss.*, 33 (2nd ed.). 1917: Bridge, *Cheshire Proverbs*, 64, Hanged hay is hay that has been weighed or hung on the steel-yard [i.e. bought hay].

Hanging. *See* **Marriage** (3).

Hangman, is a good trade, A, he doth his work by daylight. 1678: Ray, 91.

Hangman leads the dance, The. 1615: Stephens, *Essays, etc.*, bk ii No. 28, He [the hangman] hath many dependant followers: for (as the proverb saith) hangman leades the dance.

Hap and a half-penny are world's gear enough. 1639: Clarke, 126, Hap and half-penny goods enough. 1670: Ray, 100, [as in 1639, *plus*] i.e. good luck is enough, though a man have not a penny left him. 1846–59: *Denham Tracts*, i 296 (F.L.S.). 1907: *Introd.* to A. Brewer, *Love-Sick King*, in Bang's *Materialien*, B. 18, p. xii [quoted as 'a very ancient proverb'].

Hap good hap ill. *c.*1489: Caxton, *Sonnes of Aymon*, 332 (E.E.T.S.), 'I care not,' sayd Rychard, 'hap as it hap wyll.' 1530: Palsgrave, 578, Happe what happe shal. 1587: Greene, in *Works*, iv 149 (Grosart), He was so puffed vp with wrath and choller, as hap what hap would, he fell into these tearmes. 1599: Breton, in *Works*, ii *C* 7 (Grosart), Therefore hap good, or hap ill, I will walk on still.

Happeth in one hour, It, that happeth not in seven years. Before 1500: in Hill, *Commonplace-Book*, 128 (E.E.T.S.), Hit fallith in a dai, that fallith not all the iere after. 1546: Heywood, *Proverbs*, Pt L ch xi 1606: T. Heywood, *If You Know Not Me*, Pt II, in *Dram. Works*, i 327 (1874), They say, that may happen in one hour that happens not againe in 7 yeare. 1681: W. Robertson, *Phraseol. Generalis*, 322, It chances in an hour, that happens not in seven years. 1732: Fuller, 2836, It happens in an hour that comes not in an age. 1846: Denham, *Proverbs*, 6 (Percy S.) [as in 1681].

Happy as a king, or, earlier, **Merry as a king.** *c.*1554: *Enterlude of Youth*, in Bang, *Materialien*, B. 12, p. 8, I wyll make as mery as a kynge. 1595: Peele, *Old Wiues Tale*, sig. A3, This Smith leads a life as merrie as a king. 1618: B. Holyday, *Technogamia*, III v, Be as merry as a king. 1661: *Trag. Hist, of Guy, E. of Warwick*, V … have thought ourselves as happy as a king. 1781: D'Arblay, *Diary*, i 359 (1876), Who again stayed dinner, and was as happy as a prince. 1861: Dickens, *Great Expect.*, ch xxxvii, Only tip him a nod every now and then … and he'll be as happy as a king.

Happy as the day is long. 1631: Mabbe, *Celestina*, 54 (T.T.), Even as merry as the day is long. 1772: Graves, *Spirit. Quixote*, bk xi ch viii, They were married in a fortnight's time; and are now as happy as the day is long. 1851: Borrow,

Lavengro, iii 12, I sat there hard at work, happy as the day's long. 1889: Nicholson, *Folk Speech E. Yorks*, 19, As happy as days is long.

Happy as the parson's wife during her husband's life. Query meaning. 1663: Killigrew, *Parson's Wedding*, I i [cited as a proverb].

Happy is he that chastens himself. 1640: Herbert, *Jac. Prudentum*.

Happy is he that is happy in his children. 1732: Fuller, 1787.

Happy is he who knows his follies in his youth. 1659: Howell, 3. 1670: Ray, 12. 1748: Richardson, *Clarissa*, iv 121 (1785) [with 'the man' for 'he'].

Happy is he whose friends were born before him. 1670: Ray, 99. 1732: Fuller, 1790.

Happy is the bride the sun shines on, and happy the corpse the rain rains on. 1607: *The Puritan*, I i, If blessed be the corse the rain rains upon, he had it pouring down. 1632: Randolph, *Jealous Lovers*, V iii, A fair sun Shine on the happy bridegroom. 1827: Hone, *Table-Book*, 667, Blessed is the corpse that the rain falls on. Blessed is the bride that the sun shines on. 1859: E. Peacock, in *N.&Q.*, 2nd ser, viii 319, A superstition prevalent in many parts of Britain … Happy is the wedding that the sun shines on; Blessed is the corpse that the rain rains on. Otherwise thus: – Sad is the burying in the sun shine; But blessed is the corpse that goeth home in rain. 1879: Henderson, *Folk-Lore of N. Counties*, 34, Here, in fact, as all Christendom over – Blest is the bride that the sun shines on! 1922: Lucas, *Genevra's Money*, 4, 'Happy', said some foolish proverbialist, 'are the dead that the rain rains on'.

Happy is the child whose father goes to the devil. 1549: Latimer, *Third Sermon*, 97 (Arber) [cited as 'the old sayinge']. 1590: Greene, in *Works*, vii 235 (Grosart). 1593: Shakespeare, 3 *Henry VI*, II ii, And happy always was it for that son Whose father for his hoarding went to hell. 1655: Howell, *Letters*, bk iv No. ix [cited as 'the City proverb']. 1708: tr. Aleman's *Guzman*, i 405. 1827: Hone, *Table-Book*, 430.

Happy is the country (or land or nation) that has no history. The saying, attributed by Carlyle to the French philosopher Montesquieu, relies on the fact that the history of any country is made up largely of wars and upheavals of various kinds. 1740: B. Franklin, *Poor Richard's Almanack* (Feb.), Happy that Nation – fortunate that age, whose history is not diverting. 1807: T. Jefferson, *Letter*, 29 March, in *Writings* (1904), XI 182, Blest is that nation whose silent course of happiness furnishes nothing for history to say. 1864: Carlyle, *Frederick the Great*, xvi i, Happy the people whose annals are blank in history.

Happy man happy dole. 1546: Heywood, *Proverbs*, Pt I ch iii. 1660: Tatham, *The Rump*, I, A short life and a merry life, I cry. Happy man be his dole. 1671: Crowne, *Juliana*, I i, Here's five thousand crowns bid for his head, Happy man be his dole that catches him. 1796: White, *Falstaff's Letters*, Preface, A man renown'd among his cotemporaries, famous through succeeding centuries, happy be his dole. 1840: Barham, *Ing. Legends*: 'Leech of Folkestone', par. 1, These are genuine and undoubted marks of possession; and if you never experienced any of them, – why, 'happy man be his dole!' 1924: *Punch*, 28 May, p. 573, col. 3, 'The Unemployment Committee are compiling an insular register of persons likely to desire unemployment at the end of the summer season'. *Manx Paper*. Hence the expression, 'Happy Man be his dole!'

Happy than wise, Better be. *c.*1594: Bacon, *Promus*, No. 970. 1605: Camden. *Remains*, 319(1870). 1736: Bailey, *Dict.*, s.v. 'Better'.

Happy that knoweth not himself happy, He is not. 1539: Taverner, *Proverbs*, fo. 51. 1586: Pettie, tr. Guazzo's *Civil Convers.*, fo. 58. 1732: Fuller, 1918, He is happy that knoweth not himself to be otherwise.

Happy the wooing. *See* **Wooing.**

Happy till he dies, Call no man. This is a Greek saying found in Sophocles' *Oedipus Rex* and also cited by Ovid. 1585: R. Taverner, *Proverbs or Adagies out of Erasmus* (ed. 2), 53v, Salon aunsered kynge Cresus, that no man could be named happy, tyl he had happely and prosperouslye passed the course of his lyfe. 1565: Norton and Sackville, *Gorboduc*, iii i, Oh no man happie, till his ende be seen. 1603: Florio, tr. *Montaigne's Essays*, i xviii, We must exspect of man the latest day, Nor e'er he dies, he's happie, can we say. 1891: *Times*, 5 Dec., 9, Call no man happy till he dies is the motto … suggested by the career of Dom Pedro.

Harborne. *See* quot. 1894: Northall, *Folk*

Phrases, 16 (E.D.S.), Hungry Harborne, poor and proud. *Staffs.*

Harborough Field. 1. A goose trill eat all the grass that grows in Harborough Field. 1622: W. Burton, *Descrip. of Leics.*, 128. 1895: Billson, *Co. Folk-Lore: Leics.*, 151 (F.L.S.).

2. I'll throw you into Harborough Field. 1678: Ray, 317. 1790: Grose, *Prov. Gloss.*, s.v. 'Leicestershire'.

Hard, *adj.* **1. A hard beginning hath a good ending.** 1546: Heywood, *Proverbs*, Pt I ch iv, A hard beginnyng makth a good endyng. 1605: Camden, *Remains*, 317 (1870). 1659: Howell, 7.

2. A hard thing it is. *See* quot. 15th cent.: in *Reliq. Antiquae*, i 205 (1841), A harde thynge hit is, y-wys, To deme a thynge that unknowen is.

3. As hard as a flint (or **stone**). *c.*1440: Lydgate, *Fall of Princes*, bk iii 1. 63 (E.E.T.S.), But, hard as ston, Pierides and Meduse. *c.*1489: Caxton, *Sonnes of Aymon*, 347 (E.E.T.S.), A lord that hath no pite in him, hath a hert as harde as a stone. *c.*1510: A. Barclay, *Egloges*, 18 (Spens. S), Thy bread is … harde as a flint. 1587: Churchyard, *Worth, of Wales*, 104 (Spens.S.), A mightie cragge, as hard as flint or steele. 1675: *Poor Robin Alman.*, May, A heart as hard as flint. 1720: Gay, *Poems*, ii 278 (Underhill), Is her heart as flint or stone. 1789: Boswell, *Letters*, ii 364 (Tinker), I should have a heart as hard as a stone were I to remain here. 1823: Scott, *St Ronan's*, ch xxii, A selfish, spiteful heart, that is as hard as a flint. 1908: Hudson, *Land's End*, ch xv, It was not ice but something as hard as stone.

4. As hard as a north toad = tod = fox. 1917: Bridge, *Cheshire Proverbs*, 14.

5. As hard as brazil. 1867: Waugh, *Owd Bl.*, 85, 'Aw'm as hard as brazill', said Tip. 1879: Jackson, *Shropsh. Word-Book*, 48, Brazil [Iron pyrites] is so extremely hard as to have given rise to a common proverbial saying, 'As hard as brazil'. 1917: Bridge, *Cheshire Proverbs*, 15, As hard as brazzil.

6. As hard as horn (or **bone**). *c.*1420: Lydgate, *Assem. of Gods*, st. 89, p. 19 (E.E.T.S.), Hard as any horn. 1545: Ascham, *Toxoph.*, 113 (Arber), This wood is as harde as horn and very fit for shaftes. 1631: Brathwait, *Eng. Gentlewoman*, 196 (1641) … was found to have her elbowes as hard as horne. 1670: Ray, 202. 1824: in Lockhart's *Scott*, v 326, The remainder of the wood was as hard as a bone.

7. As hard as nails. 1838: Dickens, *Twist*, ch ix, 'Hard,' replied the Dodger. 'As nails,' added Charley Bates. 1896: Shaw, *You Never Can Tell*, I, My landlord is as rich as a Jew and as hard as nails. 1922: Weyman, *Ovington's Bank*, ch xxxv, Hard and sharp as nails! I take off my hat to him!

8. Hard cases make bad law. Meaning that difficult and complex cases are not a good basis for establishing clear and readily applicable laws or precedents. 1854: G. Hayes, in W.S. Holdsworth, *History of English Law* (1926). IX 423, A hard case. But hard cases make bad law.

9. Hard fare makes hungry bellies. 1616: Breton, in *Works*, ii *e* 6 (Grosart), Hard fare makes hungry stomackes. 1670: Ray, 100. 1732: Fuller, 1796.

10. Hard winter. *See* **Dog** (57); and **Wolf** (6).

11. Hard with hard never made good wall. 1578: Florio, *First Fruites*, fo. 29. 1655: Fuller, *Church Hist.*, bk ii § ii (69), 'Hard with hard', saith the proverb, 'makes no wall'. 1732: Fuller, 1797, Hard with hard makes not the stone wall.

12. Hard words break no bones. 1697: G. Meriton, *Yorkshire Ale* (ed. 3), 84, Fould words break neay Banes. 1814: G. Morris, *Letter*, 18 Oct. (1889), II xlix, These … are mere words – hard words, if you like, but they break no bones. 1882: Blackmore, *Christowell*, III xvi, 'Scoundrel, after all I have done – '. 'Hard words break no bones, my friend'.

13. It is hard for any man all faults to mend. 1546: Heywood, *Proverbs*, Pt I ch xi. 1611: Davies (of Hereford), *Sc. of Folly*, 49, in *Works*, ii (Grosart).

14. It is hard to be high and humble. 1732: Fuller, 2948.

15. It is hard to be wretched, but worse to be known so. 1640: Herbert, *Jac. Prudentum.*

16. It is hard to carry a full cup without spilling. 1875: A. B. Cheales, *Proverb. Folk-Lore*, 117.

17. It is hard to make a good web of a bottle of hay. 1670: Ray, 154. 1732: Fuller, 2950.

18. It is as hard to please a knave as a knight. 1639: Clarke, 275. 1670: Ray, III. 1732: Fuller, 2907.

19. It is hard to please all. *c.*1430: Lydgate, *Minor Poems*, 60 (Percy S.), To please al folk it is ful hard. 1519: Horman, *Vulgaria*, fo. 93, It is harde to content all menys myndis.

20. It is hard to sail over the sea in an eggshell. 1639: Clarke, 5. 1670: Ray, 139. 1732:

Fuller, 2906. 1880: Spurgeon, *Ploughman's Pictures*, 20.

21. It is hard to shave an egg. 1639: Clarke, 243. 1732: Fuller, 2952. 1869: Spurgeon, *John Ploughman*, ch xii.

22. It is hard to sup and blow with one breath. 1672: Walker, *Paroem.*, 8 [with 'a wind' for 'one breath']. 1681: W. Robertson, *Phraseol. Generalis*, 1190. 1736: Bailey, *Dict.*, s.v. 'Sup', Tis hard to sup and blow at the same time. Cf. **Whistle.**

23. Set hard heart against hard hap. 1639: Clarke, 15. 1670: Ray, 100. 1732: Fuller, 4108.

24. The hard gives no more than he that hath nothing. 1640: Herbert, *Jac. Prudentum* [with omission of 'no']. 1670: Ray, 12.

Hard-fought field where none escapes, It is a. 1546: Heywood, *Proverbs*, Pt I ch xi, A hard foughten feeld where no man skapth vnkyld. 1670: Ray, 59, It's a hard battel where none escapes. 1732: Fuller, 2861.

Hard-hearted as a Scot of Scotland, As. 1678: Ray, 285.

Hardly attained, Things, are long retained. 1639: Clarke, 101. 1670: Ray, 12. 1754: Berthelson, *Eng.-Danish Dict.*, s.v. 'Hardly'.

Hardwick Hall, More window than wall. Derby. 1884: *Folk-Lore Journal*, ii 279.

Hare and Hares. 1. Hare is melancholy meat. 1558: Bullein, *Govt. of Health*, fo. 90, The fleshe of hares be hoote and drye, ingenderers of melancholye. 1666: Torriano, *Piazza Univ.*, 133, A hare being a melancholy meat. 1738: Swift, *Polite Convers.*, Dial. II, They say [hare] 'tis melancholy meat. Cf. No. 3.

2. Hares may pull dead lions by the beard. 1586: Pettie, tr. Guazzo's *Civil Convers.*, fo. 31, Of these this saying rose, That the lion being dead, the verie hares triumph ouer him. 1593: Nashe, in *Works*, ii 198 (Grosart), Strike a man when he is dead? So hares may pull dead lions by the beards. 1596: Shakespeare, *King John*, II i, You are the hare of whom the proverb goes, Whose valour plucks dead lions by the beard. 1639: Clarke, 216.

3. He hath devoured a hare. 1600: W. Vaughan, *Directions for Health*, 17, Hare ... maketh a man to look amiably, according to the prouerb: He hath deuoured a hare. But it is vnwholesome for lazie and melancholick men. Cf. No. 1.

4. He that hunts two hares loses both. 1578:

Florio, *First Fruites*, fo. 28, Who hunteth two hares, loseth the one and leaueth the other. 1630: T. Adams, *Works*, 232, The hound that follows two hares, will catch neither. 1640: Shirley, *Opportunity*, III iii 1732: Fuller, 2782, If you run after two hares, you will catch neither. 1880: Spurgeon, *Ploughman's Pictures*, 24, We shall be like the man who hunted many hares at once and caught none.

5. If a man wants a hare for his breakfast (or **dinner**) **he must hunt overnight.** 1605: Camden, *Remains*, 323 (1870), He that will have a hare to breakfast must hunt overnight. 1670: Ray, 13 [as in 1605]. 1732: Fuller, 2365 [as in 1605]. 1846–59: *Denham Tracts*, ii 107 (F.L.S.) [as in 1605]. 1883: Burne, *Shropsh. Folk-Lore*, 589, If a man wants a hare for his Sunday dinner, he had best catch it over night.

6. It's either a hare or a brake-bush. 1659: T. Pecke, *Parnassi Puerp.*, 143, He can't discern a hare from a brake-bush. 1670: Ray, 179, It's either a hare or a brake-bush. [Πλοῖον ἢ κυνῆ. Aut navis aut galerus. Something if you knew what.

7. Little dogs start the hare but great ones catch it. 1640: Herbert, *Jac. Prudentum.* 1670: Ray, 16. 1732: Fuller, 3254. 1846–59: *Denham Tracts*, ii 108 (F.L.S.).

8. The hare starts when a man least expects it. *c.*1384: Chaucer, *H. Fame*, bk ii l. 173, That been betid, no man wot why, But as a blind man stert an hare. 1712: Motteux, *Quixote*, Pt II ch xxx, But, where we least think, there starts the hare. 1869: Spurgeon, *John Ploughman*, ch x, For hares pop out of the ditch just when you are not looking for them. Cf. No. 9.

9. There goes the hare away. *c.*1500: Medwall, *Nature*, Pt II l. 589 (Brandl, *Quellen*, 134), There went the hare away. Before 1529: Skelton, *Works*, ii 30 (Dyce) [as in 1500]. 1594: Kyd, *Span. Tragedy*, sig. G3 (1618), There goes the hare away. 1670: Ray, 100, Where we least think, there goeth the hare away. 1846–59: *Denham Tracts*, ii 108 (F.L.S.), There goes the hare away. Cf. No. 8.

10. 'Tis as hard to find a hare without a muse, as a woman (or **knave**) **without a 'scuse.** 1576: Pettie, *Petite Pall.*, ii 157 (Gollancz), We ourselves have a common saying amongst us, that women are never without an excuse. 1592: Greene, in *Works*, x 217 (Grosart) ['woman'].

1659: Howell, 12, Take a hare without a muse, and a knave without an excuse, and hang them up. 1732: Fuller, 6081, Find you without excuse, And find an hare without a muse. 1913: E. M. Wright, *Rustic Speech, etc.*, 102, The old English proverbial saying: – [as in 1659].

11. To catch (or hunt) the hare with a taber [drum]. 1399: Langland, *Rich, the Redeless*, i 58, Men myztten as well haue huntyd an hare with a taber. 1546: Heywood, *Proverbs*, Pt I ch ix 1579: Lyly, *Euphues*, 44 (Arber), You shal assoone catch a hare with a tabre. 1611: Cotgrave, s.v. 'Lievre', Hares are not to be caught by drumming. 1642: D. Rogers, *Naaman*, sig. S5 [as in 1579]. 1732: Fuller, 1341, Drumming is not the way to catch an hare. 1901: F. E. Taylor, *Lancs Sayings*, 23, Yo' met as weel try for t' catch a hare wi' thumpin' on a drum. Cf. No. 12.

12. To fright the hare is not the way to catch her. 1846–59: *Denham Tracts*, ii 108 (F.L.S.). Cf. No. 11.

13. To know both hare and hare-gate. 1882: Nodal and Milner, *Lancs Gloss.*, 154 (E.D.S.), 'He knows both th' hare an' th' hare-gate', i.e. he knows both the hare, and the way the hare runs.

14. To run with the hare. *See* Run (18).

15. To seek a hare in a hen's nest. 1599: Porter, *Two Angry Women*, in Hazlitt, *Old Plays*, vii 355, He is gone to seek a hare in a hen's nest, a needle in a bottle of hay.

16. To set the hare's head against the goose giblets. 1546: Heywood, *Proverbs*, Pt II ch iv. 1607: Dekker, etc., *Westw. Hoe*, V 1618: Field, *Amends for Ladies*, I. 1670: Ray, 179. 1732: Fuller, 4109.

See also Blind, *adj.* (7); Cow (32); Dog (36), (77), and (78); First catch … ; Kiss, *verb* (13); Run (18); and We dogs.

Harlow Hill. *See* Heddon.

Harm watch harm catch. 1481: Caxton, *Reynard*, 50 (Arber), Yf he wil seche harm he shal fynde harme. 1614: Jonson, *Bart. Fair*, V iii 1721: Bailey, *Eng. Dict.*, s.v. 1826–44: Hood, *Comic Poems:* 'Hints to Paul Pry', Harm-watching, harm thou still dost catch – That rule should save thee many a sore.

Harms the good, He. *See* Evil, *subs.* (4).

Harp and harrow, To agree like. 1559: Becon, *Prayers, etc.*, 283 (P.S.), Agree together like God and the devil … as the common proverb is, 'Like harp and harrow'. 1589: L. Wright, *Display of*

Dutie, 24, Agreeing like harpe and harrowe. 1659: Howell, 12 (10), They agree like harp and harrow. Before 1704: T. Brown, *Works*, iii 29 (1760), Whether the name and thing be not as disagreeable as harp and harrow?

Harp on a string, To (or on the same string). [Cantilenam eandem canere. – Terence, *Phorm.*, III ii 10. Chorda qui semper oberrat eadem. – Horace, *Ars Poetica*, 356.] *c.*1513: More, *Works*, p. 49, col. 2 (1557), He should harp no more vpon that string. 1594: Shakespeare, *Rich. III*, IV iv, Harp not on that string, madam; that is past. 1644: Quarles, in *Works*, i 176 (Grosart), Doctor, you still harp upon the same string. 1753: Richardson, *Grandison*, i 478 (1883), The poor girl has been harping upon this string ever since you have been gone. 1821: Scott, in Lockhart's *Life*, v 72, All this is extremely like prosing, so I will harp on that string no longer.

Harp on the string that gives no melody, To. 1546: Heywood, *Proverbs*, Pt II ch iv. 1633: Draxe, 222, Hee harpeth on that string that will make no good musicke.

Harrow: the visible church. 1725: Defoe, *Tour*, ii 20, They tell us King Charles II … us'd to say of it [Harrow church] that if there was e'er a visible church upon earth, he believed this was one. 1790: Grose, *Prov. Gloss.*, s.v. 'Middx'. The visible church; i.e. Harrow on the Hill.

Harrow (or Rake) hell and scum the devil. 1670: Ray, 180. 1732: Fuller, 1798, Harrow hell, and rake up the devil.

Harry Sophister. *See* Henry Sophister.

Harry's children of Leigh, never an one like another. Cheshire. 1670: Ray, 217. 1917: Bridge, *Cheshire Proverbs*, 63.

Hartland Light. *See* Padstow Point.

Hartlepool. *Like the Mayor of Hartlepool, you cannot do that.* 1678: Ray, 317. 1790: Grose, *Prov. Gloss.*, s.v. 'Leicestershire'. 1846–59: *Denham Tracts*, i 55 (F.L.S.) … The sense of this saying is, you cannot work impossibilities. A certain mayor of this (at that time) poor but ancient corporation, desirous to show his old companions that he was not too much elated by his high office, told them that, though he was Mayor of Hart-le-pool, *he was still but a man!* there being many things he could not do.

Harvest. 1. A fine harvest a wet hopping. Kent. 1887: Parish and Shaw, *Dict. Kent. Dialect*, 78 (E.D.S.).

2. Harvest comes not every day, tho' it come every year. 1732: Fuller, 1799.

3. Harvest ears, thick of hearing. 1546: Heywood, *Proverbs*, Pt II ch ix, You had on your haruest eares, thicke of hearyng. *c.*1594: Bacon, *Promus*, No. 674, Harvest ears. 1681: W. Robertson, *Phraseol. Generalis*, 715, You hearken not at all; you have on your harvest ears. 1854: Baker, *Northants Gloss.*, s.v., You've got your harvest ears on, I can't make you hear.

4. Harvest will come, and then every farmer's rich. 1732: Fuller, 1800.

5. Short harvests make short addlings [earnings]. 1846: Denham, *Proverbs*, 54 (Percy S.). 1893: Inwards, *Weather Lore*, 8.

6. The harvest moon. 1812: Brady, *Clavis Cal.*, i 55, The Harvest-moon is also used to denote that month in which harvest is usually collected. 1923: *Observer*, 23 Sept., p. 14, col. 1, The feature that distinguishes it from other full moons, and has earned for it the name of harvest moon, is the short interval that separates two successive risings.

7. To make a long harvest of a little corn. 1546: Heywood, *Proverbs*, Pt I ch xii, Ye haue … Made a long haruest for a little corne. 1587: Greene, in *Works*, v 208 (Grosart), I will not make a long haruest for a small crop. 1604: Breton, in *Works*, ii *k* 12 (Grosart), Yee two … haue made a long haruest of a little corne, and haue spent a great deale of money about a little matter. 1681: W. Robertson, *Phraseol. Generalis*, 1207, Not to make a long harvest of so little corn; not to be tedious in a trifle. 1748: Richardson, *Clarissa*, iv 175 (1785), But why … should I make so long a harvest of so little corn? 1893: Inwards, *Weather Lore*, 8, A long harvest, a little corn.

8. When harvest flies hum, Warm weather to come. 1893: Ibid., 148.

See also **Christmas** (2), (3), and (6); **Good harvest**; **Ill sowers**; and **May**, C, and E (2).

Harwich. *See* **Deal.**

Haste, *subs.* **1. Haste and wisdom are things far odd.** 1546: Heywood, *Proverbs*, Pt I ch ii.

2. Haste comes not alone. 1611: Cotgrave, s.v. 'Haste', Haste never comes alone, viz. hath ever some trouble or other t'accompany it. 1640: Herbert, *Jac. Prudentum.*

3. Haste makes waste. *c.*1386: Chaucer, *Tale of Melibee*, l. 1053, The proverbe seith … in wikked haste is no profit. 1546: Heywood, *Proverbs*, Pt I

ch ii. 1583: Greene, in *Works*, ii 28 (Grosart). 1663: Butler, *Hudibras*, Pt I can. iii l. 1254. 1678: Ray, 151, Haste makes waste, and waste makes want, and want makes strife between the good man and his wife. 1864: 'Cornish Proverbs', in *N. & Q.*, 3rd ser, vi 495, Haste makes waste, and waste makes a rich man poor.

4. Haste often rues. *c.*1280: *Prov. of Hendyng*, l. 256, Ofte rap reweth. *c.*1386: Chaucer, *Melibeus*, § 11, The commune proverbe seith thus: 'he that sone demeth, sone shall repente'. 1477: Rivers, *Dictes, etc.*, 62 (1877), Hastynesse engendreth repentaunce. *c.*1580: Spelman, *Dialogue*, 2 (Roxb.Cl), Thinges dunne in haste bringeth spedye repentance.

5. Haste trips up its own heels. 1732: Fuller, 1801. 1869: Spurgeon, *John Ploughman*, ch xix.

6. Make haste slowly. [Latin **festina lente**] *c.*1385: Chaucer, *Troilus and Criseyde*, i 956, He hasteth wel that wisly kan abyde. 1683: Dryden, *Poems* (1958), I 336, Gently make haste … A hundred times consider what you've said. 1744: B. Franklin, *Poor Richard's Almanack* (Apr.), Make haste slowly.

7. Make no more haste when you come down than when you went up. 1604: *Pasquils Jests*, 42 (1864), Take heed that you never get faster downe then you go up. 1678: Ray, 151 … as the man said to him on the tree top. 1692: L'Estrange, *Aesop*, 337 (3rd ed.), You must take care for the future, whenever you climb another tree; that you come no faster down than you went up.

8. More haste less speed. *See* **More haste.**

9. There is no haste to hang true men. *c.*1550: *Jacke Juggeler*, in Hazlitt, *Old Plays*, ii 120, I fear hanging, where-unto no man is hasty. 1599: Porter, *Two Angry Women*, in Ibid., vii 301, There's no haste to hang tnie [honest] men. 1670: Ray, 101. *See also* **No haste.**

Haste, *verb. He hasteth well that wisely can abide. c.*1374: Chaucer, *Troylus*, bk i l.956. *c.*1386: Chaucer, *Melibeus*, § 13. *c.*1430: Lydgate, *Minor Poems*, 121 (Percy S.).

Hastings, He is none of the. *See* quots. 1546: Heywood, *Proverbs*, Pt I ch xi, Ye make such tastingis, As approue you to be none of the hastlingis. 1577: *Misogonus*, I iv, Youil come when yow list, sir … yow are none of y[e] hastlinges. 1658: Flecknoe, *Enig. Characters*, 124, A low spirited man … he is none of the

Hastings'es. 1662: Fuller, *Worthies*, iii 243 (1840), Now men commonly say, They are none of the Hastings, who being slow and slack, go about business with no agility. 1681: W. Robertson, *Phraseol. Generalis*, 1114, You are none of the Hastings; you'll not break your shins for hast. 1790: Grose, *Prov. Gloss.*, s.v. 'Sussex'.

Hasty bitch bringeth forth blind whelps, The. [Festinatio improvida est, et caeca. – Livy, xxii 39.] 1556: R. Robinson, tr. More's *Utopia*, 2nd ed., To Reader, 19 (Arber), But as the latin prouerbe sayeth: The hastye bitche bringeth furth blind whelpes. For when this my worke was finished, the rudenes therof shewed it to be done in poste haste. 1559: Bercher, *Nobil. of Women*, 97 (Roxb.Cl). 1642: D. Rogers, *Matrim. Honour*, 234, They perceive their haste to have brought foorth blind whelpes. 1681: W. Robertson, *Phraseol. Generalis*, 705.

Hasty climbers have sudden falls. *c.*1480: *Digby Plays*, 154 (E.E.T.S.), Who clymyth high, his ffalle grett is. 1592: Greene, in *Works*, xii 158 (Grosart), Hee foreseath not that such as clime hastely fall sodainely. 1616: Breton, in *Works*, ii *e* 9 (Grosart). 1754: Berthelson, *Eng.-Danish Dict.*, s.v. 'Climber'. 1869: Spurgeon, *John Ploughman*, ch xix.

Hasty gamesters oversee themselves. 1678: Ray, 151 [without 'themselves']. 1732: Fuller, 1803.

Hasty glory goes out in a snuff. Ibid., No. 1804.

Hasty love. *See* **Soon hot.**

Hasty (or Angry) man never wants woe, The. *c.*1374: Chaucer, *Troylus*, bk iv l. 1568, For hasty man ne wanteth never care. 1449: Metham, *Works*, 36 (E.E.T.S.), Trwe that prouerbe dan preuyd so, That ouer-hasty man wantyd neuer woo. 1587: Greene, in *Works*, iv 77 (Grosart). 1605: Chapman, etc., *Eastw. Hoe*, V i, 'The hastie person never wants woe', they say. 1712: *Spectator*, No. 438, You are of an impatient spirit, and an impatient spirit is never without woe. 1875: A. B. Cheales, *Proverb. Folk-Lore*, 106. Cf. **Choleric** (3).

Hasty meeting, a hasty parting, A. 1736: Bailey, *Dict.*, s.v. 'Woo'.

Hasty people will never make good midwives. 1659: Howell, 3. 1670: Ray, 101.

Hasty to outbid another, Be not too. 1670: Ray, 3. 1732: Fuller, 853.

Hat is not made for one shower, A. 1640: Herbert, *Jac. Prudentum.*

Hat on the wind's side, Pull down your. 1640: Ibid. 1670: Ray, 29. 1732: Fuller, 3978 [with 'windy' for 'wind's'].

Hatch before the door, It is good to have a = to keep silence. 1546: Heywood, *Proverbs*, Pt I ch xi 1607: Deloney, *Strange Histories*, 70 (Percy S.), A wise man, then, sets hatch before the dore, And, whilst he may, doth square his speech with heed. 1670: Ray, 101. 1732: Fuller, 2941.

Hatchet, To hang up (or bury) the. Before 1327: *Pol. Songs*, 223 (Camden) (OED), Hang up thyn hachet ant thi knyf. *c.*1440: Hoccleve, *Minor Poems*, 136 (E.E.T.S.), Hange vp his hachet and sette him adoun. 1546: Heywood, *Proverbs*, Pt I ch xi, I haue hangd vp my hatchet, God speede him well! 1659: Howell, 6, I have hang'd vp my hatchet and scap'd my self. 1794: Wolcot, *Works*, iv 485 (1796), Gentle Reader, wouldst thou not have imagined that the war hatchet was buried for ever? 1897: W. E. Norris, *Clarissa Furiosa*, ch xliii., She neither affirmed nor denied that she and her husband had buried the hatchet.

Hate, *verb.* **1. He that hates woman sucked a sow.** 1667: L'Estrange, *Quevedo's Visions*, 144 (1904), 'My officious friend,' said I, 'he that does not love a woman sucked a sow.' 1732: Fuller, 2083 [as in 1667]. 1738: Swift, *Polite Convers.*, Dial. I.

2. If you hate a man, eat his bread; and if you love him, do the same. 1732: Fuller, 2756.

Hatfield, Yorks. *See* quot. 1878: *Folk-Lore Record*, i 173, There are no rats at Hatfield, nor sparrows at Lindholme.

Hatherleigh, Devon. *See* quot. 1869: Hazlitt, 382, The people are poor at Hatherleigh moor, and so they have been, for ever and ever.

Hatred is blind as well as love. 1732: Fuller, 1805.

Hatred with friends is succour to foes. 1578: Florio, *First Fruites*, fo. 33, Hatred among friendes is succour vnto strangers. 1633: Draxe, 30.

Have a little. *See* quot. 1917: Bridge, *Cheshire Proverbs*, 64, Have a little, give a little, let neighbour lick the mundle [piece of wood for stirring porridge, cream, etc.] [= Charity begins at home].

Have all, He that will, loseth all. 1481: Caxton, *Reynard*, 95 (Arber), It falleth ofte who that wold haue all leseth alle Ouer couetous was neuer good. 1629: *Book of Meery Riddles*, Prov. 87. Cf. **All covet.**

Have among you blind harpers! 1546: Heywood, *Proverbs*, Pt II ch vii 1593: G. Harvey, *Works*, ii 123 (Grosart), But now there is no remedie, haue amongest you, blind harpers of the printing house. *c*.1663: Davenant, *Ploy-House to be Let*, V, Have w'ee [with you], quoth the blind harper, When he wisht to be as little seen as he saw others. 1785: Grose, *Class. Dict. Vulgar Tongue*, s.v. 'Harp', Have among you, my blind harpers, an expression used in throwing or shooting at random among a crowd.

Have at it, and have it. 1852: FitzGerald, *Polonius*, 123 (1903).

Have in a string, To. 1580: Lyly, *Euphues*, 319 (Arber), Thou hast not loue in a string, affection is not thy slaue. 1631: Shirley, *Love Tricks*, I, They have their conscience in a string, and can stifle it at their pleasure. 1693: Dryden, *Juvenal*, Sat. III l. 72, Since such as they have fortune in a string. 1748: Richardson, *Clarissa*, v 33 (1785), Led us both on – like fools, like tame fools, in a string.

Have one in the wind, To. 1546: Heywood, *Proverbs*, Pt I ch xi, I smelde hir out, and had hir streight in the wynde. 1587: Churchyard, *Worth. of Wales*, 26 (Spens.S.), That hardly we shall haue them in the winde, To smell them forth. 1670: Ray, 199.

Have your cake and eat it, You cannot. *See* **Eat** (43).

Hawk and Hawks. 1. Between hawk and buzzard. 1639: Clarke, 70. 1670: Ray, 164. 1692: L'Estrange, *Aesop*, 318 (3rd ed.), A fantastical levity that holds us off and on, betwixt hawk and buzzard, as we say, to keep us from bringing the matter in question to a final issue. 1745: *Agreeable Companion*, 56, At which, the priest, being driven between hawk and buzzard, told them, he did not know what would please them. 1854: Baker, *Northants Gloss.*, s.v. 'Buzzard', 'Between a hawk and a buzzard'; in a state of perplexity and indecision. 1878: *N.&Q.*, 5th ser, ix. 46, 'Neither hawk nor buzzard' … is used in North and East Derbyshire, and in parts of Notts, and is thus applied: – Persons on being asked how they are will reply, 'Oh! I'm neither hawk nor buzzard', which means a state of being 'rather out of sorts'.

2. By hawk and by hound Small profit is found. 1732: Fuller, 6339.

3. Hawks don't pike [poke] **out hawks' e'en.** 1846–59: *Denham Tracts*, ii 107 (F.L.S.).

4. He's a hawk of the right nest. 1732: Fuller, 2439.

5. High flying hawks are fit for princes. 1639: Clarke, 41. 1670: Ray, 101. 1732: Fuller, 2500. 1846–59: *Denham Tracts*, ii 108 (F.L.S.) [with 'good' for 'fit'].

6. It is easy to reclaim a hawk that has lost its prey. *c*.1300: *Cursor M.*, 3529, For hauk es eth – als i here say – To reclaym pat has tint his pray.

7. She hath one point of a good hawk; she is hardy. 1546: Heywood, *Proverbs*, Pt II ch iv.

8. The gentle hawk half mans herself. 1611: Cotgrave, s.v. 'Debonnaire'. 1670: Ray, 13 [omitting 'half']. 1846–59: *Denham Tracts*, ii 107 F.L.S.) [as in 1670].

9. To know a hawk from a handsaw. 1602: Shakespeare, *Hamlet*, II ii, When the wind is southerly I know a hawk from a handsaw. 1703: Centlivre, *Stolen Heiress*, III iv, He knows not a hawk from a handsaw. 1912: R. L. Gales, *Studies in Arcady*, 2nd ser, 241, I have heard the proverb 'He doesn't know a hawk from a handsaw'. 1920: Barbellion, *Last Diary*, 54, I suspect 'Charlie' … could not tell a hawk front a handsaw, even when the wind was southerly.

10. Unmanned hawks forsake the lure. 1577: J. Grange, *Golden Aphroditis*, sig. G3 [cited as a 'prouerbe'].

11. With empty hands men may no hawks lure. Before 1180: John of Salisbury, *Polycraticus*, lib. v cap. x, Veteri celebratur proverbio: Quia vacuae manus temeraria petitio est. *c*.1386: Chaucer, *Wife of Bath's Prol.*, l.415, With empty hand men may none hawkes lure. *c*.1430: Lydgate, in *Pol.*, *Relig.*, *and Love Poems*, 25 (E.E.T.S.). 1575: Gascoigne, *Posies*, 65 (Cunliffe), For haggard hawkes mislike an emptie hand. 1612: Webster, *White Devil*, III ii, With empty fist no man doth falcons lure. 1717: Pope, *Wife of Bath*, 172, With empty hands no tassels you can lure. 1829: Scott, *Geierstein*, ch xxv, Men lure no hawks with empty hands.

See also **Carrion; Crow** (3)**; Goshawk; Hungry as a hawk; Too low; Wild** (2).

Hawk, *verb.* **1. He has been out a hawking for butterflies.** 1732: Fuller, 1863.

2. The first point of hawking is hold fast.

*c.*1450: in *Reliq. Antiquae*, i 296 (1841), Termes of hawkyng … The first is holde fast when abatith. 1579: Lyly, *Euphues*, 93 (Arber), If thou haddest learned' the first point of hauking, thou wouldst haue learned to haue held fast. 1665: J. Wilson, *Projectors*, II, 'Tis the first part of falconry to hold fast. 1748: *Gent. Mag.*, 21. 1846–59: *Denham Tracts*, ii 108 (F.L.S.).

Hawley's Hoe. *See* **Blow**, *verb* (5).

Haws. 1. Many haws, cold toes. 1855: Robinson, *Whitby Gloss.*, 22, As many haws, So many cold toes. 1879: *N. & Q.*, 5th ser, xii 327, A North Riding saying, 'Many haws, cold toes'. *See also* **Many hips**.

2. When all fruit fails welcome haws. 1732: Fuller, 5544.

Hay. 1. A good hay year a bad fog year. 'Fog' = the aftermath. 1846: Denham, *Proverbs*, 49 (Percy S.). 1893: Inwards, *Weather Lore*, 5.

2. He has hay on his horn. [Foenum habet in cornu. – Horace, *Sat.*, I iv 34.] 1648: Herrick, *Hesp.*, No. 444, He's sharp as thorn And fretful, carries hay in's horn.

3. To make hay while the sun shines. 1509: Barclay, *Ship of Fools*, ii 46 (1874), Who that in July whyle Phebus is shynynge About his hay is not besy labourynge … Shall in the wynter his negligence bewayle. 1546: Heywood, *Proverbs*, Pt I ch iii, Whan the sunne shinth make hay. 1625: Dekker, *Works*, iv 308 (Grosart), He, drawing out one handfull of gold, and another of siluer, cryed … I haue made hay whilst my sunne shined. 1702: T. Brown, *Works*, ii 63 (1760). 1860; Reade, *Cl. and Hearth*, ch lxiii, We must lose no time; we must make our hay while shines the sun. 1915: Pinero, *Big Drum*, I, Some day it'll turn and rend you? Perhaps. Still, if you make hay while the sun shines …

See also **Candlemas, D; Cuckoo** (5) and (20); **Famine; Hanged hay;** and **May, A** (2) and (3), E (1), (5), and (6), and F (2) and (5).

He claws it. *See* **Eat** (38).

He hath but one fault. *See* **Fault** (6).

He is in his own clothes = Let him do as he pleases. 1830: Forby, *Vocab. E. Anglia*, 427.

He that doth what he should not shall feel what he would not. *c.*1386: Chaucer, *C. Tales*, iv 125 (Skeat), And therfore this prouerbe is seyd ful sooth, 'Him thar nat wene wel that yvel dooth' [He must not expect good that does evil]. 1591: Florio, *Second Frutes*, 97, Who dooth what he ought not, Shall finde what he thought not. 1640: Herbert, *Jac. Prudentum*. 1732: Fuller, 2089, He that doth not as he ought, must not look to be done to as he would.

He that has but four and spends five, has no need of a purse. 1623: Wodroephe, *Spared Houres*, 278, Who hath but four and spendeth seauen, Needeth no purse to put his money in. 1732: Fuller, 2134.

He that hath a good neighbour. *See* **Neighbour** (4).

He that hath it, and will not keep it, He that wanteth it and will not seek it, He that drinketh and is not dry, Shall want money as well as I. 1659: Howell, 21. 1670: Ray, 211. 1869: Spurgeon, *John Ploughman*, ch xix.

He that hath plenty of goods shall have more; He that hath but little he shall have less; And he that hath right nought, right nought shall possess. 1546: Heywood, *Proverbs*, Pt I ch xi 1605: Camden, *Remains*, 324 (1870) [first line only]. 1670: Ray, 212.

He that in youth. *See* quot. 15th cent.: in *Reliq. Antiquae*, i 92 (1841), He that in youthe no vertu usit, In age alle honure hym refusit.

He that is in is half way over. 1694: D'Urfey, *Quixote*, Pt I Act IV sc i.

He that is thought to rise betime. *See* **Name** (1).

He that speaks. *See* quot. 1683: Meriton, *Yorkshire Ale*, 83–7 (1697), He that speaks the things he sud not, hears the things he wad not.

He that will no evil do, must do nothing that belongs thereto. 1546: Heywood, *Proverbs*, Pt II ch v 1660: T. Hall, *Funebria Florae*, 12. 1732: Fuller, 6305, He that would no evil do, Must do nought that's like thereto.

He that will not be ruled by his own dame shall be ruled by his stepdame. [14th cent.: *Guy of Warwick*, l. 1593 (E.E.T.S.), For often ichaue herd it say, and y me self it sigge may, 'Who that nil nought leue his fader, He schel leue his steffader'.] 1546: Heywood, *Proverbs*, Pt II ch ix. 1670: Ray, 77.

He that will not when he may, when he will he shall have nay. [Corrigant se, qui tales sunt, dum vivunt, ne postea velint et non possint. – St Augustine, *Opera*, xxxviii 1095 (Migne). Cf. Isaiah lv. 6.] 10th cent.: *A.-S. Homily*, quoted in Skeat, *Early Eng. Proverbs*, vi, the laes, gif he nu nelle tha hwile the he maege, eft thonne he late wille, thaet he ne maege [Lest, if he will not now (do so) while he may, afterwards, when he at last will, he may not]. *c.*1150: John of Salisbury, *Policraticus*, lib. viii *c* xvii, Nam et proverbio dici solet, quia qui non vult cum potest, non utique poterit cum volet. Before 1225: *Ancren R.*, 296, hwo ne deth hwon he mei, he ne schal nout hwon he wolde. 1303: Brunne, *Handl. Synne*, l. 4799, He that wyl nat whan he may, He shal nat when he wyl. 1422: J. Yonge, tr. *Gouernance of Prynces*, 161 (E.E.T.S.), That is to say, 'Who so will not whan he may, he shal not when he wille'. 1546: Heywood, *Proverbs*, Pt I ch iii. *c.*1590: Greene, *Alphonsus*, V iii, No, damsel; he that will not when he may, When he desires, shall surely purchase nay. 1621: Burton, *Melancholy*, III ii vi 5, p. 612 (1836). 1709: O. Dykes, *Eng. Proverbs*, 188. 1880: Mrs Oliphant, *He Who Will Not When He May, When He Wills He Shall Have Nay* [title of novel].

He who hesitates is lost. 1713: Addison, *Cato*, iv i, When love once pleads admission to our hearts … The woman that deliberates is lost. 1865: A. Trollope, *Can You Forgive Her?*, II, x, It has often been said of woman that she who doubts is lost. 1878: H. Beadle, *Western Wilds*, xxi, In Utah it is emphatically true, that he who hesitates is lost – to Mormonism.

He whom God will have kept. *Set* quot. *c.*1489: Caxton, *Blanchardyn*, 155 (E.E.T.S.), Men sayen comynly, that he whome god wyll haue kept, may not be peryshed.

He will never have a thing good cheap that is afraid to ask the price. 1633: Draxe, 4. 1639: Clarke, 41. 1732: Fuller, 2427, He'll ne'er get a pennyworth, that is afraid to ask a price.

He's a fond chapman. *See* **Day** (12).

Head. 1. An head that's white to maids brings no delight. Glos. 1639: in *Berkeley MSS.*, iii 30 (1885).

2. Cover your head by day as much as you will, by night as much as you can. 1678: Ray, 41.

3. He that has no head needs no hat. 1611: Cotgrave, s.v. 'Chaperon', He that hath no head needs no hood. 1670: Ray, 101. 1732: Fuller, 2145, He that has no head, deserves not a laced hat.

4. He that hath a head of wax must not walk in the sun. 1640: Herbert, *Jac. Prudentum*. 1732: Fuller, 2155. 1854: J. W. Warter, *Last of Old Squires*, 53. 1864: 'Cornish Proverbs', in *N. & Q.*, 3rd ser, vi 495, People with wax heads shouldn't walk in the sun.

5. He that will be a head, let him be a bridge. 1790: Grose, *Prov. Gloss.*, s.v. 'Cardiganshire'.

6. Head and feet kePt warm, the rest will take no harm. 1611: Cotgrave, s.v. 'Demeurant', The foot and head kePt warme, no matter for the rest. 1640: Herbert, *Jac. Prudentum*, Dry feet, warm head, bring safe to bed. 1678: Ray, 41, Keep your feet dry and your head hot, and for the rest live like a beast. 1732: Fuller, 6255.

7. Head'full of bees. See **Bee** (9).

8. Heads I win, tails you lose. 1672: Shadwell, *Epsom Wells*, II i, The cheat … worse than *Cross I win, Pile you lose*: but there are some left, that can lose upon the square. 1846: in *Croker Papers*, iii 59 (1884), A game which a sharper once played with a dupe, intituled, 'Heads I win, and tails you lose'. 1909: De Morgan, *Never can happen Again*, ch xxxviii, Women's claims are not allowed in law-courts. It's heads Law wins, tails they lose.

9. Let your head be not higher than your hat. 1580: Lyly, *Euphues*, 284 (Arber), When you match, God send you such a one as you like best: but be sure alwaies, that your head be not higher then your hat. Cf. **Hair** (2).

10. The grief of the head is the grief of griefs. 1659: Howell, 10.

11. The head grey, and no brains yet. 1732: Fuller, 4587.

12. To have a head full of proclamations. 1567: Fenton, *Bandello*, ii 146 (T.T.), At last, beinge past the misterye of his traunce, he repaired to his house with his head full of proclamacions. 1611: Cotgrave, s.v. 'Moucheron', *Avoir des moucherons en teste*. To be humorous, moodie, giddie-headed; or to have many proclamations or crotchets in the head. 1631: Brathwait, *Whimzies*, 97 (1859). 1690: *New Dict. Canting Crew*, sig. 18, His head is full of proclamations, much taken up to little purpose. 1754: Berthelson, *Eng.-Danish Dict.*, s.v. 'Proclamations'.

13. To have a man's head under one's girdle = To have him at one's mercy. 1546: Heywood, *Proverbs*, Pt II ch v, Then haue ye his head fast vnder your gyrdell. 1605: Chapman, etc., *Eastw. Hoe*, IV ii, I list not ha' my head fastened under my child's girdle. 1642: D. Rogers, *Naaman*, sig. Qq3, I will not doe so meane a fellow such honour, as to subdue my spirit, or put my neck under his girdle. 1754: Berthelson, *Eng.-Danish Dict.*, s.v. 'Girdle'. 1829: Scott, *Geierstein*, ch xxv, I am a man little inclined to put my head under my wife's girdle.

14. When the head acheth all the body is the worse. *c.*1230: in Wright, *Pol. Songs John to Edw. II*, 31 (Camden S.), Cui caput infirmum cetera membra dolent. *c.*1399: Gower, *Pr. of Peace*, l. 260, in Skeat's, *Chaucer*, vii 212, Of that the heed is syk, the limmes aken. 1546: Heywood, *Proverbs*, Pt II ch vii. 1620: Shelton, *Quixote*, Pt II ch ii, I mean ... that when the head aches all the body is out of tune. 1670: Ray, 13. 1732: Fuller, 5588 [with 'feels it' for 'is the worse'].

15. You have a head and so has a pin. 1738: Swift, *Polite Convers.*, Dial. I, Thou hast a head, and so has a pin. 1797: Colman, jr., *Heir at Law*, V iii.

16. Your head will never fill your pocket. 1855: Bohn, 582.

17. Your head will never save your legs. 1828: Carr, *Craven Dialect*, i 216, Thy heod'll nivver saav thy legs. 1895: S. O. Jewett, *Life of Nancy*, 253, You'd ought to set her to work, and learnt her head to save her heels.

18. Your head's running upon Jolly Robins = Your wits are wool-gathering. 1917: Bridge, *Cheshire Proverbs*, 159. [Jolly Robin used to figure in old ballads.]

19. Your head's so hot that your brains bubble over. 1732: Fuller, 6050.

See also MacGregor.

Headlam hens lay twice a day. 'A gentle hint in the place of one more discourteous: to wit, that of telling a person he's a liar. Headlam, a small village in the extensive Saxon parish of Gainford'. Durham. 1846–59: *Denham Tracts*, i 89 (F.L.S.). 1909: *Folk-Lore*, xx 73.

Heady is ruled by a fool, He that is. 1732: Fuller, 2178.

Heady man and a fool, may wear the same cap, A. Ibid., No. 212.

Healed as hurt, One is not so soon. 1670: Ray, 13.

Health and money go far. 1640: Herbert, *Jac. Prudentum*.

Health and wealth create beauty. 1855: Bohn, 405.

Health is better than wealth. 1678: Ray, 153. 1736: Bailey, *Dict.*, s.v. 'Health', Health surpasses riches. 1812: Scott, *Fam. Letters*, i 255 (1894), As health is better than wealth, I trust you will hasten the period of your return.

Health it great riches. 1639: Clarke, 314, Health is a jewell. 1672: Walker, *Paroem.*, 45 [as in 1639]. 1732: Fuller, 2477.

Health is not valued till sickness comes. 1666: Torriano, *Piazza Univ.*, 119, In sickness health is known. 1732: Fuller, 2478.

Health without money is half an ague. 1640: Herbert, *Jac. Prudentum*. 1732: Fuller, 2479, Health without wealth is half a sickness.

Healthful man can give counsel to the sick, The. 1651: Herbert, *Jac. Prudentum*, 2nd ed.

Hear, *verb.* **1. He hears not on that side.** 1546: Heywood, *Proverbs*, Pt II ch ix, Than were ye deafe; ye could not here on that syde. 1632: Jonson, *Magnetic Lady*, I, He will not hear of it. *Rut.* Not of that ear. 1681: W. Robertson, *Phraseol. Generalis*, 713, He cannot hear on that ear. 1736: Bailey, *Dict.*, s.v. 'Ear' [as in 1681].

2. He may be heard where he is not seen. 1639: Clarke, 58. 1670: Ray, 180.

3. He that hears much and speaks not at all, shall be welcome both in bower and hall. 1586: G. Whitney, *Emblems*, 191, Heare much; but little speake. 1670: Ray, 102. 1694: D'Urfey, *Quixote*, Pt I Act III sc ii. 1732: Fuller, 6461.

4. He who hears one side only, hears nothing. 1546: Heywood, *Proverbs*, Pt I ch xiii, A man should here all partis, er he judge any. 1750: Smollett, *Gil Bias*, iv 105.

5. Hear all, see all. *See* quots. 1578: Florio, *First Fruites*, fo. 10, Who heares, sees and holds his peace, may alway live in peace. 1623: Wodroephe, *Spared Houres*, 276, Heare all, see all, and hold thee still If peace desirest with thy will. 1925: Yorkshire 'motto' in *N. & Q.*, vol 149, p. 411, Hear all, see all, say now't, tak' all, keep all, gie now't, and if tha ever does ow't for now't do it for thysen'. [There are several variants of this compendium of selfishness.]

6. Hear twice before you speak once. 1855: Bohn, 405.

7. To hear as hogs do in harvest. 1670: G. Firmin, *Real Christian*, II, quoted in *N. & Q.*, 2nd ser, viii 17, The country proverb is Hear as hogs in harvest ... When they are gotten into good shack, when they at home call them or knock at the trough, the hogs will lift up their heads out of the stubble and listen, but fall to their shack again.

Hearers, Were there no, there would be no backbiters. 1640: Herbert, *Jac. Prudentum.*

Hearing. *From hearing comes wisdom; from speaking, repentance.* 1855: Bohn, 359.

Heart 1. Every heart hath its own ache. 1732: Fuller, 1418.

2. He is heart of oak. 1609: *Old Meg of Herefs.* (Nares, s.v. 'Heart'), Here is a doozen of yonkers that have hearts of oake at fourescore yeares. 1672: Walker, *Paroem.*, 24, He was heart of oak; he wore like iron. 1694: *Terence made English*, 125, Marry, I think, you're heart of oak. 1870: Dickens, *Drood*, ch xii, So small a nation of hearts of oak.

3. Heart of the sober man. *See* Drunkenness.

4. Heart on halfpenny. *See* Hand (8).

5. Hearts may agree though heads differ. 1732: Fuller, 2480.

6. His heart is in his hose (or, later, boots). *c.*1410: *Towneley Plays*, 113 (E.E.T.S.), A, thy hart is in thy hose! Before 1529: Skelton, in *Works*, ii 35 (Dyce), Their hertes be in theyr hose. 1616: Breton, *Works*, ii *r* 9 (Grosart), Hanging doune his head as if his heart were in his hose. 1694: Motteux, *Rabelais*, bk v ch xxxvi, If I be not half dead with fear, my heart's sunk down into my hose. 1767: in *Garrick Corresp.*, i 271 (1831), Whose soul and spirit ... are now even in her shoes. 1883: R.L.S., *Treasure I*, ch xiii, My heart sank, as the saying is, into my boots. 1900: Lucas, *Domesticities*, 39, My head was adamant, but, as the saying is, my heart was in my boots.

7. His heart is in his mouth. [Mihi animam in naso esse. – Petr., 62.] 1548: Udall, tr. Erasmus' *Par. Luke*, xxiii 199 (OED), Hauyng their herte at their verai mouth for feare. 1618: B. Holyday, *Technogamia*, V v, My heart's almost at my mouth with feare. 1694: Dryden, *Love Triumphant*, I i, He's come on again; my heart was almost at my mouth. 1740: Richardson, *Pamela*, i 136 (1883), My heart was at my mouth; for I feared ... 1876: Blackmore, *Cripps*, ch ii, She ... glided along with her heart in her mouth. 1883: R.L.S., *Treasure I*, ch iv, A sound that brought my heart into my mouth.

8. Never set at thy heart what others set at their heel. 1546: Heywood, *Proverbs*, Pt I ch xi, Nor suche foly feele, To set at my hert that thou settest at thy heel. *c.*1580: *Tom Tyler*, l. 807, p. 23 (Malone S.), Never set at thy heart, thy wives

churlish part, That she sets at her heel. 1659: Howell, 13, I will not sett at my heart what I should sett at my heel. 1871: *N. & Q.*, 4th ser, viii 506, [A common Lancashire proverb] Never lay sorrow to your heart, when others lay it to their heels.

9. The joy of the heart makes the face merry. 1611: Davies (of Hereford), *Sc. of Folly*, 46, in *Works*, ii (Grosart), The ioy of the heart fairly coulors the face. 1629: *Book of Meery Riddles*, Prov. 54, The heart's mirth doth make the face fayre. 1633: Draxe, 128.

10. The way to a man's heart is through his stomach. *See* **Way**.

11. To take heart of grace. 1530: Palsgrave, 748, They lyved a great whyle lyke cowardes, but at the laste they toke herte a gresse to them. 1560: Becon, *Catechism*, 345 (P.S.), It is now high time to take hart of grease unto them. 1593: *Tell-Trothes New-yeares Gift*, 23 (N.Sh.S.), She ... tooke harte at grasse, and woulde needes trie a newe conclusion. 1630: *Tinker of Turvey*, 53 (Halliwell), Rowland, at this taking heart of grasse, stePt to her. 1687: A. Behn, *Emp. of the Moon*, II ii, Come, come, take heart of grace. 1712: Motteux, *Quixote*, Pt I bk iii ch vi, He took heart of grace, and made shift to carry over one goat, then another. 1826: Scott, *Journal*, 15 Sept., I e'en took heart of grace and finished my task. 1922: Weyman, *Ovington's Bank*, ch v, He took heart of grace.

12. To wear one's heart upon one's sleeve. 1604: Shakespeare, *Othello*, I i, I will wear my heart upon my sleeve For daws to peck at. 1909: Lucas, *Wand, in Paris*, ch xix, Had he too ... carried in his breast or even on his sleeve a great heart ... like Hugo's.

13. What the heart thinks the tongue clinks (or **speaks**). 1477: Rivers, *Dictes, etc.* 26 (1877), The mouth sheweth often what the hert thinketh. 1583: Greene, in *Works*, ii 116 (Grosart), Gonzaga ... thought, what the heart did think, the tongue would clinck. 1670: Ray, 13, What the heart thinketh, the tongue speaketh. 1754: Berthelson, *Eng.-Danish Dict.*, s.v. 'Heart' [as in 1670].

14. Whatever comes from the heart goes to the heart. 1878: J. Platt, *Morality*, 10 [cited as 'an old proverb'].

15. When the heart is a fire, some sparks will fly out of the mouth. 1732: Fuller, 5589.

16. Where hearts are true, Few words will do.
1875: A. B. Cheales, *Proverb. Folk-Lore*, 86.

17. Where the heart is past hope, the face is past shame. 1580: Lyly, *Euphues*, 341 (Arber) [with 'minde' for 'heart']. 1732: Fuller, 5665.

18. With all one's heart and a piece of one's liver. 1598: *Mucedorus*, sig. F4, Weele waite on you with all our hearts. *Clo.* And with a peece of my liuer to [too]. 1738: Swift, *Polite Convers.*, Dial. I, With all my heart, and a piece of my liver.

Heat. *See* **If you can't stand the heat ... .**

Heat nor cold abides always in the sky, Neither. 1678: Ray, 47. 1846: Denham, *Proverbs*, 6 (Percy S.).

Heave and theave, To. Somerset. 1678: Ray, 354.

Heaven upon earth, A. 1618: Breton, *Court and Country*, 5 (Grosart), If there may be a similie of heauen vpon earth ... *See also* **Hell** (6) and (8).

Heavy as lead. *c.*1300: Brunne, *Langtoft's Chron.*, 252 (Hearne), And wex heuy als lede. *c.*1320: in *Reliq. Antiquae*, i 121 (1841), Myn herte is hevy so led. 1414: T. Brampton, *Seven Penit. Psalms*, 13 (Percy S.), My synnes ben hevy as hevy leed. 1592: Shakespeare, *Romeo*, III v, Unwieldy, slow, heavy and pale as lead. 1694: Dryden, *Love Triumphant*, I i, Try his wit, senor, you'll find it as heavy as lead. 1714: Mandeville, *Fable of Bees*, 54, He is heavy as lead; the head is hung down ... 1850: Dickens, *Copperfield*, ch vii, My head is as heavy as so much lead.

Heavy purse makes a light heart, A. *c.*1510: A. Barclay, *Egloges*, 29 (Spens.S.), When purse is heauy oftetime the heart is light. 1595: *Pedlar's Prophecy*, l. 1591 (Malone S.), An heauie purse maketh a mans heart light. 1630: Jonson, *New Inn*, I i. 1670: Ray, 114. 1754: Berthelson, *Eng.-Danish Dict.*, s.v. 'Light'.

Heckmondwike. *See* **Birstal.**

Hector's Cloak, To take = To deceive a friend who confides in one's fidelity. 1662: Fuller, *Worthies*, ii 542 (1840). 1709: Grose, *Prov. Gloss.*, s.v. 'Northumberland'. 1846–59: *Denham Tracts*, i 242 (F.L.S.).

Heddon. *See* quot. 1892: Heslop, *Northumb. Words*, 33 (E.D.S.), East Heddon, West Heddon, Heddon on the Waall, Harlow Hill, an' Horsley, an' Wylam bangs them aall. Old saying.

Hedge and Hedges. 1. A hedge between keeps friendship green. [*See* Prov. xxv 17.] 1710: S. Palmer, *Moral Essays on Proverbs*, 168, A wall between preserves love. 1875: A. B. Cheales, *Proverb. Folk-Lore*, 93. 1917: Bridge, *Cheshire Proverbs*, 3.

2. Hedge abides that fields divides. 1130: *A.-S. Chron.*, in Skeat, *Early Eng. Proverbs*, vi, Man seith to biworde, haege sitteth tha aceres daeleth.

3. Hedges have eyes (or **ears**). 1650: Fuller, *Pisgah Sight*, bk iii ch i § 7, If policy be jealous, that hedges may have ears ... 1738: Swift, *Polite Convers.*, Dial. III, Ay, madam; but they say hedges have eyes, and walls have ears. *c.*1800: J. Trusler, *Prov. in Verse*, 18.

4. If you would a good hedge have, carry the leaves to the grave. 1678: Ray, 350. 1732: Fuller, 6141.

5. Where the hedge is lowest men may soonest over. 1546: Heywood, *Proverbs*, Pt II ch v. 1564: Bullein, *Dialogue*, 65 (E.E.T.S.), Where the hedge is lowest that commonlie is sonest cast to grounde. 1610: Rowlands, *Martin Markall*, 14 (Hunt.Cl.), You will verifie the old saying, where the ditch is lowest, there men goe over thicke and three-fold. 1685: Meriton, *Yorkshire Ale*, 62, Where th' hedge is law, its eath [easy] gitting ore there. 1732: Fuller, 5666 [with 'leap over' for 'may soonest over'].

6. You seek a brack where the hedge is whole. 1639: Clarke, 80, You'd break a gap where the hedge is whole. 1670: Ray, 165.

Hedgehog. *See* quots. 1623: Wodroephe, *Spared Houres*, 487, Decke a hedgehog, and he will seeme a baron. 1659: Howell, *Proverbs: Fr.-Eng.*, 9, Trim up a hedge-hog, and he will look like a lord. 1895: Jos. Thomas, *Randigal Rhymes*, 62, Cornwall. Scrumped up like a hedgehog.

Heeler. *See* **Hailer.**

Heighton, Denton and Tarring All begins with A. 1861: Lower, in *Sussex Arch. Coll.*, xiii 210.

Heler. *See* **Hailer.**

Hell. 1. From Hell, Hull, and Halifax, Good Lord deliver us. 1594: A. Copley, *Wits, Fits, etc.*, 112 (1614), It is prouerbiall in our countrie; From Hull, Hell, and Halifax, Good Lord deliuer vs. 1599: Nashe, in *Works*, v 284 (Grosart), Let them seek him, and neither in Hull, Hell, nor Halifax. 1622: Taylor (Water-Poet), in *Works*, pagin. 2, p. 12 (1630). 1662: Fuller, *Worthies*, iii 398 (1840). 1790: Grose, *Prov. Gloss.*, s.v. 'Yorkshire'. 1875: E. Peacock, in *N. & Q.*, 5th ser, iv 154, From Hull,

Hell, and Halifax, Good Lord, deliver us, is a saying well known in these parts [Lincs]. 1922: in *N.&Q.*, 12th ser, xi 102, This was the celebrated Halifax Gibbet Law [*see* **Halifax**], which gave rise to the well-known proverb: – From Hell, Hull, etc.

2. Hell and Chancery are always open. 1732: Fuller, 2486.

3. Hell hath no fury like a woman scorned. The proverb originally referred to the Furies, the avenging goddesses of Greek mythology, and there are lines in Euripides' play *Medea* that reflect its basic sentiment, though without a mythological reference: when [a woman] has been wronged in a matter of sex, there is no other heart more bloodthirsty. Nowadays, *fury* is often understood in its commoner sense. 1625: Beaumont and Fletcher, *The Knight of Malta*, I i, The wages of scorn'd Love is baneful hate. 1696: C. Cibber, *Love's Last Shift*, IV 71, No Fiend in Hell can match the fury of a disappointed Woman! – Scorned! slighted; dismissed without a parting Pang! 1697: Congreve, *The Mourning Bride*, III 39, Heav'n has no Rage, like Love to Hatred turn'd, Nor Hell a Fury, like a Woman scorn'd.

4. Hell, Hull, and Halifax all begin with a letter; Brag is a good dog, but hold-fast is better. *c.*1791: Pegge, *Derbicisms*, 137 (E.D.S.).

5. Hell is broken loose. 1577: *Misogonus*, II v, I thinke, hell breake louse, when thou gatst ye this porte. 1596: Jonson, *Ev. Man in Humour*, IV i, They should say, and swear, hell were broken loose, ere they went hence. 1667: Milton, *Par. Lost*, iv. 918, Wherefore with thee Came not all Hell broke loose? 1694: D'Urfey, *Quixote*, Pt II Act II sc ii, All hell is broke loose yonder! 1738: Swift, *Polite Convers.*, Dial. I, Hey! what a clattering is here; one would think, hell was broke loose. 1822: Byron, *Vis. of Judg.*, st. 58, And realised the phrase of 'Hell broke loose'.

6. Hell is wherever heaven is not. 1669: *Politeuphuia*, 320. 1732: Fuller, 2489.

7. There is no redemption from hell. 1468: *Coventry Mys.*, 240 (SH.S.), Quia in inferno nulla est redemptio! 1619: Chapman, *Two Wise Men*, I i, It is so deep … that it reacheth to hell, and ther's no redemption. 1662: Fuller, *Worthies*, ii 413 (1840). 1790: Grose, *Prov. Gloss.*, s.v. 'Westminster'. [In the last two examples the saying is applied to a prison at Westminster for the King's debtors.]

8. The road to hell is paved with good intentions. 1574: E. Hellowes, *Guevara's Epistles*, 205, Hell is full of good desires. 1654: Whitlock, *Zootomia*, 203, It is a saying among Divines, that hell is full of good intentions, and meanings. 1775: Johnson, in Boswell, ii 360 (Hill), He said one day, talking to an acquaintance on this subject, 'Sir, Hell is paved with good intentions'. 1825: Scott, in Lockhart's *Life*, vi 82. 1865: Dickens, *Mutual Friend*, bk iv ch x, You recollect what pavement is said to be made of good intentions.

9. They that be in hell ween there is no other heaven. 1546: Heywood, *Proverbs*, Pt I ch xi. 1605: Camden, *Remains*, 334 (1870). 1621: Wither, *Motto*, in *Juvenilia*, iii 681 (Spens.S.), For, those the proverb saith, that liue in hell, Can ne'er conceive what 'tis in heauen to dwell. 1670: Ray, 102, They that be in hell, think there's no better heaven.

See also **Harrow.**

Hellingly, Sussex. *See* quot. 1861: Lower, in *Sussex Arch. Coll.*, xiii 210, Herrin*ly*, Chiddn*ly* and Hoädd*ly*, Three lies and all true.

Hell-kettles, Deep as the. [1577: Harrison, *England*, I xxiv iii 164 (1881) (OED), There are certeine pits, or rather three little pooles, a mile from Darlington … which the people call the kettles of hell, or the diuels kettles. 1727: Defoe, *Tour*, iii 188, As to the Hell Kettles … which are to be seen as we ride from the Tees to Darlington.] 1846–59: *Denham Tracts*, i 79 (F.L.S.), Deep as the hell-kettles … the name of three deep pits at Oxen-le-Hall, in the parish of Darlington.

Help a lame dog. *See* **Lame dog.**

Help at a pinch. *See* **Pinch.**

Help hands! for I have no lands. 1567: Golding, *Ovid*, bk iii l. 745, [An allusion] His handes did serve in steade of landes. 1605: Armin, *Foole vpon Foole*, 36 (Grosart). *c.*1630: in *Roxb. Ballads*, i 305 (B.S.), He passeth some with house and lands; when that decays, he cryes 'Helpe, hands!' 1670: Ray, 99. 1736: Franklin, *Way to Wealth*, in *Works*, i 444 (Bigelow).

Help to salt. *See* **Salt** (1).

Help yourself. *See* quots. *c.*1460: *How the Goode Wife*, in Hazlitt, *Early Pop. Poetry*, i 191, Thi thrifte is thi frendis myrthe, my dere childe. 1738: Swift, *Polite Convers.*, Dial. II, Come, Colonel; help yourself, and your friends will love you the better.

Helps little that helpeth not himself, He. 1629: *Book of Meery Riddles*, Prov. 16.

Helsby (Hill) wears a hood, As lone as, The weather's never very good. 1886: R. Holland, *Cheshire Gloss.*, 445 (E.D.S.). 1917: Bridge, *Cheshire Proverbs*, 161.

Helve after hatchet. *See* **Throw** (7).

Hemp. *See* **England** (10).

Hen. 1. A black hen will lay a white egg. 1633: Draxe, 50, A blacke hen may bring foorth white egges. 1670: Ray, 63. 1738: Swift, *Polite Convers.*, Dial. I, Oh! the wonderful works of nature: That a black hen should have a white egg!

2. Busy as a hen with one chick. 1632: Shirley, *Witty Fair One*, II ii, It has been a proverb, as busy as a hen with one chicken. 1659: Howell, 6 … with ten chickins. 1732: Fuller, 669. 1857: Hughes, *Tom Brown*, Pt II ch ii, In short, as East remarked, cackled after him like a hen with one chick. 1888: Lowsley, *Berks Gloss.*, 30 (E.D.S.), As proud as a hen wi' one chick. 1923: *Folk–Lore*, xxxiv 329 (Oxfordsh.).

3. He has swopped his hen for a hooter [owl] = A bad exchange. 1917: Bridge, *Cheshire Proverbs*, 67.

4. He puts a hat on a hen. 1813: Ray, 75.

5. He that comes of a hen must scrape. 1591: Florio, *Second Frutes*, 179, What is hatcht by a hen, will scrape like a hen. 1611: Cotgrave, s.v. 'Grater', He thats borne of a henne loves to be scraping. 1640: Herbert, *Jac. Prudentum*. 1852: FitzGerald, *Polonius*, 102 (1903). 1880: Spurgeon, *Ploughman's Pictures*, III, That which is born of a hen will be sure to scratch in the dust.

6. If the hen does not prate she will not lay. 1666: Torriano, *Piazza Univ.*, 100, The hen that cakels is she that hath laid. 1732: Fuller, 2799, If you would have a hen lay, you must bear with her cackling. 1830: Forby, *Vocab. E. Anglia*, 427 [Scolding wives make the best housewives]. 1872: J. Glyde, jr., *Norfolk Garland*, 148. Cf. No. 10.

7. It is a sad house where the hen crows louder than the cock. 1578: Florio, *First Fruites*, fo. 33, They are sory houses, where the hennes crowe, and the cock holdes his peace. 1633: Ford, *'Tis Pity*, etc., IV iii, Then I remembered the proverb, that 'where hens crow, and cocks hold their peace, there are sorry houses'. 1678: Ray, 64. 1732: Fuller, 2842 [with 'bad' for 'sad'].

8. It is better to have a hen to-morrow than an egg to-day – but the first reference gives the reverse. 1659: Howell, *Proverbs: Ital.-Eng.*, 1, 'Tis better to have an egg to-day, then a hen to-morrow. 1732: Fuller, 2916.

9. It is no good hen that cackles in your house, and lays in another's. Ibid., No. 2987.

10. It is not the hen that cackles most which lays most eggs. 1865: 'Lancs Proverbs', in *N.&Q.*, 3rd ser, viii 494. 1901: F. E. Taylor, *Lancs Sayings*, 8, It's no' th' hen 'at cackles th' mooest. 'at lays th' mooest eggs. Cf. No. 6.

11. It's a poor hen that can't scratfor one chick. 1882: Mrs Chamberlain, *W. Worcs. Words*, 39 (E.D.S.). 1894: Northall, *Folk Phrases*, 17 (E.D.S.).

12. Never offer your hen for sale on a rainy day. 1768: Goldsmith, *Vicar*, ch xii, I'll warrant we'll never see him sell his hen on a rainy day. 1846: Denham, *Proverbs*, 3 (Percy S.). 1872: J. Glyde, jr., *Norfolk Garland*, 151.

13. The hen discovers her nest by cackling. Before 1225: *Ancren R.*, 66, The hen hwon heo haueth ileid, ne con buten kakelen. And hwat bigit heo therof? Kumeth the coue [chough] anonriht and reueth hire hire eiren. 1694: D'Urfey, *Quixote*, Pt II Act IV sc ii.

14. The hen lays as well upon one egg as many. 1620: Shelton, *Quixote*, Pt II ch vii. 1694: D'Urfey, *Quixote*, Pt I Act IV sc i.

See also **Cock** (3), (6), and (8); **Drink** (10); **Fat as a hen; Grain; January** (10); **Son** (1); and **Woman** (39).

Hengsten Down, well ywrought, Is worth London Town dear ybought. 1602: Carew, *Surv. of Cornwall*, 272 (1811). 1610: Holland, tr. Camden's *Britannia*, 196. 1659: Howell, 21 ['Hinkeson Down']. 1662: Fuller, *Worthies*, i 306 (1840). 1790: Grose, *Prov. Gloss.*, s.v. 'Cornwall'. 1864: 'Cornish Proverbs', in *N.&Q.*, 3rd ser, v 276, Kingston down, well wrought, Is worth London Town, dear bought. 1880: Courtney, *W. Cornwall Words*, xiii (E.D.S.) [as in 1864].

Hen-pen. *See* quot. 1825: Jennings, *Somersetsh. Words*, xiv [as in 1838]. 1838: Holloway, *Provincialisms*, 50, Boys use these words at the game [ducks and drakes] in Somersetshire: – Hen-pen, Duck and mallard, Amen.

Henry Sophister, A, shortened to **Harry-Soph.** Sophista Henricanus. The expression originated in Henry VIII's time. 1662: Fuller,

Worthies, i 227 (1840). 1720: Stukeley, *Memoirs*, i 40 (Surtees S.), I … threw off my ragged Sophs gown … and commenced Harry Soph as its there [Cambridge] styled, and took the habit accordingly. 1790: Grose, *Prov. Gloss.*, s.v. 'Cambs'. 1859: *N. & Q.*, 2nd ser, viii 239, A student at Cambridge, who has declared for Law or Physic, may put on a full-sleeved gown, when those of. the same year, who go out at the regular time, have taken their degree of Bachelor of Arts. He is then styled a *Harry-Soph*, i.e. ἐρισοφός. [This Greek reference is a University joke.]

Herb John. *See* quots. Two contradictory sayings. 1614: T. Adams, *Devil's Banquet*, 307 (OED), Bahne, with the destitution of Gods blessing, doth as much good as a branch of hearb-John in our pottage. 1633: Draxe, 30, He is Iohn herbe in the pottage, that will doe neither good nor hamne. 1659: Howell, 13, Without Herb-John, no good pottage. 1679: *Hist. Jetzer*, 33 (OED), The Bishop of Lausanne, being a flegmatick and heavy piece, moved slowly, and was herb John in the whole proceeding.

Hercules against two. [*See* Plato, *Euthyd.*, 297B; *Phaedo*, 89c.] 1539: Taverner, *Proverbs*, fo. 17, Not Hercules against two, that is to say. 1576: Gascoigne, in *Works*, ii 540 (Cunliffe), But two to one, can be no equall lott For why? the latten proverbe saith you wott … *Ne Hercules enim contra duos*. 1630: T. Adams, *Works*, 372, But *ne Hercules contra duos*, two is odds though against Hercules. 1647: A. Brewer, *Countrie Girle*, sig. G3. 1693: Urquhart, *Rabelais*, bk iii ch xii, And two in fight against Hercules are too strong.

Here a little and there a little. 1633: Draxe, 13.

Here is the door and there is the way. 1546: Heywood, *Proverbs*, Pt I ch xi. 1633: Draxe, 29. 1639: Clarke, 70.

Hereafter comes not yet. 1546: Heywood, *Proverbs*, Pt II ch vii, Though hereafter come not yit. 1577: J. Grange, *Golden Aphroditis*, sig. D4, Here after commeth not yet. 1611: Davies (of Hereford), *Sc. of Folly*, 43, in *Works*, ii (Grosart).

Heresy. *See* **Frenzy**; and **Hops** (1).

Hero to his valet, No man is a. [ὅθεν Ἀντίγονος ὁ γέρων Ἑρμοδότον τίνος ἐν ποιήμασιν αὐτὸν Ἡλίου παῖδα καὶ θεὸν ἀναγορεύοντος οὐ τοιαῦτά μοι. εἶπεν, ὁ λασανοφόρος σύνοιδεν. – Plutarch, *De Iside et Osiride, c* xxiv.] In modern times attributed to a seventeenth-century Frenchwoman Madame Anne Biguet de Cornuel who is credited with remarking that *il n'y a pas de héros pour son valet-de-chambre* (no man is a hero for his valet). But, as the earliest quotations show, the idea was already current in the previous century in the writings of Montaigne. 1603: J. Florio, tr. *Montaigne's Essays*, III ii, Few men have been admired of their familiers. 1685–6: Cotton, *Montaigne*, III ii, Few men have been admired by their own domestics. 1764: Foote, *Patron*, II i, It has been said, and I believe with some shadow of truth, that no man is a hero to his *valet de chambre*. 1899: Wheatley, *Pepysiana*, 240 [as in 1764]. 1924: *Sphere*, 9 Feb., p. 137, col. 2, I referred in these columns to the well-known statement that 'no man was a hero to his valet'.

Herring. 1. Every herring must hang by its own gills. 1609: S. Harward, *MS* (Trinity College, Cambridge) 85, Lett every herring hang by his owne tayle. 1639: Clarke, 20. 1670: Ray, 102. 1694: D'Urfey, *Quixote*, Pt I Act III sc ii. 1817: Scott, *Rob Roy*, ch xxvi, Na, na! let every herring hang by its ain head. 1865: 'Lancs Proverbs', in *N. & Q.*, 3rd ser, viii 494 [with 'should' for 'must']. 1901: F. E. Taylor, *Lancs Sayings*, 7, Every yerrin' should hong bi it' own gills.

2. Gentleman Jack Herring. *See* quot. 1599: Nashe, *Lenten Stuffe*, in *Works*, v 302 (Grosart), He … raised this prouerbe of him, *Gentleman Iacke Herring that puttes his breeches on his head for want of wearing*.

3. Of all the fish in the sea, herring is the king. 1659: Howell, 21.

4. Set a herring to catch a whale. 1869: Hazlitt, 331. Cf. **Sprats**.

5. The herring-man hates the fisherman. [1633: Ames, *Against Cerem.*, Preface, 28 (OED), Its a hard world, when heerring men revile fishermen.] 1869: Hazlitt, 373.

See also **Barrel; Dead** (4); **Fish**, *verb* (5); **Lean; Lose; Red herring; Straight**; and **Wet** (7).

Hertfordshire. 1. Hertfordshire clubs and clouted shorn. 1662: Fuller, *Worthies*, ii 39 (1840). 1790: Grose, *Prov. Gloss.*, s.v. 'Herts', … A gibe at the rusticity of the honest Hertfordshire yeomen and fanners.

2. Hertfordshire hedgehogs. 1662: Fuller, ii 39. 1790: Grose, *Prov. Gloss.*, s.v. 'Herts'.

3. Hertfordshire kindness. 1662: Fuller, ii 40. 1703: Ward, *Writings*, ii 61, For want of a third in our mess, we were fain To use Hertfordshire kindness, *Here's to you again*. 1738: Swift, *Polite Convers.*, Dial. II. 1785: Grose, *Class. Dict. Vulgar Tongue*, s.v., Hertfordshire kindness, drinking twice to the same person.

4. If you wish to go into Hertfordshire, Hitch a little nearer the fire. A rather childish play on the word 'hearth' and the name of the county. 1806: Lysons, *Magna Brit.*, i 117 (Bedford). 1854: Baker, *Northants Gloss.*, s.v. 'Hitch', The distich on the old beam which separated Bedfordshire from an insulated portion of Hertfordshire in the dining-room of the late parsonage house, at Mappershall, near Shefford: *If you wish, etc.*

Hesitates is lost, He who. *See* **He who hesitates … .**

Hesky's library, Like – all outside. 1917: Bridge, *Cheshire Proverbs*, 90.

Hewin or Dick, Be oather = Be either one thing or the other. 1917: Bridge, *Cheshire Proverbs*, 160.

Hews too high may get a chip in his eye, He that. *c.*1300: Brunne, tr. Langtoft's *Chron.*, i 91 (Hearne), Sorow than is his pyne, that he wis ouer his heued, the chip falles in his ine. *c.*1310: in Wright, *Pol. Songs*, 323 (Camden S.), It falles in his eghe, That hackes ovre heghe. *c.*1390: Gower, *Conf. Amantis*, bk i l. 1918: Fulofte he heweth up so hihe, That chippes fallen in his yhe. 1546: Heywood, *Proverbs*, Pt II ch vii, Hewe not to hye lest the chips fall in thine iye. 1589: Peele, in *Works*, ii 270 (Bullen), Thou art too crank, and crowdest all too high; Beware a chip fall not into thine eye. 1659: Howell, 4 [as in 1546]. 1732: Fuller, 2164.

Hexham. Eight sayings. 1846–59: *Denham Tracts*, i 278–81 (F.L.S.), (1) Hexham, the heart of all England. (2) Hexham measure; up heaped, pressed down, and running over. (3) He comes fra' Hexham green, and that's ten miles ayont Hell. (4) Every one for their ain hand, like the pipers O' Hexham. (5) Hexham, where they knee-band lops [fleas], and put spectacles upon blind spiders. (6) Silly – good-natured, like a Hexham goose; bid him sit down, and he will lie down. (7) A Hexham sixpence-worth. (8) Go to Hexham [a Newcastle malediction]. (2) 1892–4: Heslop, *Northumb. Words* (E.D.S.), 'Hexham measure, heaped full an' runnin' over', was a proverb, which … originated in the circumstance that the 'beatment' [quarter-peck measure] at Hexham had twice the capacity of the Newcastle 'beatment'.

Heyden family. *See* **Paston.**

Heytor. *See* quot. 1869: Hazlitt, 458, When Heytor rock wears a hood, Manxton folk may expect no good. *S. Devon.*

Hickup. *See* quot. 1825: Brockett, *N. Country Words*, s.v., Hickup, snick-up, stand up, straight up, One drop, two drops – good for the hiccup. [There are variants.]

Hide can find, They that. *c.*1400: *Seven Sages*, 68 (Percy S.), He may wel fynde that hyde hym selven. 1671: *Westm. Drollery*, 21 (Ebsworth), But now I'm lost, and here am crost, 'Tis they that hide must find. 1740: North, *Examen*, 172, As they say, he that hides can find. 1816: Scott, *Antiquary*, ch xxi, Trust him for that – they that hide ken best where to find. 1855: Bohn, 406, Hiders are good finders. 1917: Bridge, *Cheshire Proverbs*, 71, He that feals [hides slyly] can find.

Hide nothing from thy minister, physician and lawyer. 1578: Florio, *First Fruites*, fo. 27, From the phisition and attorney keepe not the truth hidden. 1596: Harington, *Metam. of Ajax*, 98 (1814), From your confessor, lawyer, and physician, Hide not your case on no condition. 1670: Ray, 103. 1736: Bailey, *Dict.*, s.v. 'Hide', Hide nothing from thy priest, physician. or lawyer; Lest thou wrong thy soul, body, or estate.

Higgledy-piggledy, Malpas shot = All share alike. *See* story of 'Two Rectors', in Leigh's *Ballads and Legends of Cheshire*, 133 (1867). 1869: *N.&Q.*, 4th ser, iii 194. 1913: E. M. Wright, *Rustic Speech, etc.*, 186, The kernel of the story … is the refusal of the then Rector of Malpas [either *temp.* James I. or William III.] to treat the monarch to his share of a dinner at the village inn. In spite of the remonstrances of the Curate, who was also present, the shot was equally divided between the three: higgledy-piggledy all pay alike. Later the monarch caused the same rule to be applied to the benefice, and henceforth the Curate received a moiety of the glebe and tithes. 1917: Bridge, *Cheshire Proverbs*, 73.

High, *adj.* **1. A high building, a low foundation.**
1605: Camden, *Remains*, 316 (1870). 1670: Ray,
103. 1732: Fuller, 2499, High buildings have a
low foundation.

2. As high as three horse loaves. 1546:
Heywood, *Proverbs*, Pt I ch x, As high as twoo
horsen loues hir person is. 1639: Clarke, 73.
1670: Ray, 202.

3. High as a hog. *See* **Hog** (3).

4. High days and holidays. 1653: *The Queen*, I,
in Bang's *Materialien*, B. 13, p. 2, col. 1, Or at a
feast upon high holy dayes. 1857: Hughes, *Tom
Brown*, Pt I ch i, The Pusey horn, which ... the
gallant old squire ... used to bring out on high
days, holidays, and bonfire nights. 1859: Sala,
Twice Round Clock, One p. m., Who consume
an orthodox dinner of meat, vegetables, and
cheese – and on high days and holidays
pudding – at one p.m. 1907: Hackwood, *Old
Eng. Sports*, 2, Popular games and diversions on
all 'high days and holy days'.

5. High places have their precipices. 1616:
Haughton, *Englishm. for my Money*, IV ii, They
say high climbers have the greatest falls. 1732:
Fuller, 2501. Cf. *Higher standing*.

6. High words break no bones. 1584: Greene,
in *Works*, iii 231 (Grosart), Wordes breake no
bones, so we cared the lesse for hir scolding.
1683: Meriton, *Yorkshire Ale*, 83–7 (1697), Foul
words break neay banes. 1734: Fielding, *Don
Quix. in England*, II vi, High words break no
bones. 1774: C. Dibdin, *Quaker*, I viii.

7. To be high in the instep = To be proud.
1542: Boorde, *Introd.*, ch xxvi p. 189
(E.E.T.S.), They be hyghe in the instep, and
stondeth in theyr owne consayte. 1546:
Heywood, *Proverbs*, Pt I, ch xi, He is so hy in
thinstep, and so streight laste [laced]. 1655:
Fuller, *Church Hist.*, bk x § vi (16), Too high in
the instep ... to bow to beg a kindness. 1754:
Berthelson, *Eng.-Danish Dict.*, s.v. 'Instep'.
1854: Baker, *Northants Gloss.*, s.v. 'Instep',
'She's high in the instep', i.e. proud and
haughty.

8. To be on the high ropes. 1690: *New Dict.
Canting Crew*, sig. K5, Upon the high ropes,
Cock-a-hoop. 1771: in *Garrick Corresp.*, i 433
(1831), Who, as I hear, were always upon the
high ropes with her. 1864: Mrs H. Wood,
Trevlyn Hold, ch xxii, Nora was rather on the
high ropes just then, and would not notice him.

**Higham on the Hill, Stoke in the Vale, Wykin
for buttermilk, Hinckley for ale.** 1795–1811:
Nichols, *Hist. of Leics.*, iv 677. 1849: Halliwell,
Pop. Rhymes and Nursery Tales, 197.

Higher standing the lower fall, The. 1633:
Draxe, 7, The higher that I climbe, the greater is
my fall. 1658: Franck, *North. Memories*, 39
(1821), The higher any man rises, the greater is
his fall expected. 1670: Ray, 102. 1709: O.
Dykes, *Eng. Proverbs*, 248, The highest
standing, the lowest fall.

Higher the ape goes. *See* **Ape** (11).

**Higher the monkey climbs, the more he
shows his tail, The.** Originally applied to the
ape (*see* **Ape** (11)). 1873: A. Trollope, *Phineas
Redux*, I xxxiv, He's to be pitchforked up to the
Exchequer ... The higher a monkey climbs –
you know the proverb. 1901: F.E. Taylor, *Lancs
Sayings*, 20, Th' heegher a monkey climbs an'
th'mooar he shows his tail.

Higher the tree. *See* **Plum-tree.**

Highest branch is not the safest roost, The.
1855: Bohn, 507.

Highest flood has the lowest ebb, The. *c.*1555:
in Wright, *Songs, etc.*, *Philip and Mary*, 59
(Roxb.Cl), Thoughe that the flude be great, the
ebe as lowe doth rone. 1598: J. Dickenson,
Greene in Conceipt, 32 (Grosart). 1658: Franck,
North. Memories, 39 (1821), High tides have
their low ebbs. 1709: O. Dykes, *Eng. Proverbs*,
248.

**Highest spoke in Fortune's wheel may soon
turn lowest, The.** 1732: Fuller, 4595.

Highest tree. *See* **Tree** (5).

High Garret. *See* **Braintree.**

**Highgate. 1. I'll make him water his horse at
Highgate.** 1678: Ray, 86. 1790: Grose, *Prov.
Gloss.*, s.v. 'Middx'.

2. To be sworn at Highgate. *See* long accounts in
Hone, *Ev. Day Book*, ii 79–87. *c.*1720: J.
Smedley, in *Somers Tracts*, xiii 825 (1811),
Dined, and was sworn at Highgate. 1769:
Colman, *Man and Wife*, III ii, I have been sworn
at Highgate, Mrs Lettice, and never take the
maid instead of the mistress. 1812: Byron, *Childe
Harold*, can. i st. 70. 1826: G. Daniel, *Sworn at
Highgate* [title]. 1902: Wright, *Dialect Dict.*, s.v.
'Highgate', *He has been sworn in at Highgate*, used
of a man who is very sharp or clever.

Highway is never about, The. 1670: Ray, 13.
1732: Fuller, 4596.

Hill and **Hills. 1. A hill an' a fill an' an o'er-neet.**
1917: Bridge, *Cheshire Proverbs*, 3, Hill = Bed
(covering). Fill = A meal. O'er-neet = A place to
pass the night in. The whole = A night's
lodging.

2. Do on hill as you would do in hall. 1570: A.
Barclay, *Mirrour of Good Manners*, 25, Liue thou
vpon hill as thou would liue in hall. 1732: Fuller,
1307, Do in the hole as thou would'st do in the
hall. 1853: Trench, *Proverbs*, 21 (1905), In the
proverb you will find it [alliteration] of continual
recurrence … Thus … Do on hill as you would
do in hall.

3. Hills are green afar off. 1904: *N. & Q.*, 10th
ser, i 434.

4. The higher the hill the lower the grass. 1732:
Fuller, 4593.

5. There's always a hill against a slack
[hollow]. 1828: Carr, *Craven Dialect*, Ollas a hill
anenst a slack. 1899; Dickinson, *Cumb. Gloss.*,
165, To set hills against slacks is to equalise
matters by giving and taking. Cf. No. 6.

6. There's no hill without his valley. 1583:
Melbancke, *Philotinus*, sig. U2, Euerie hill hath
his dale. 1633: Draxe, 5. Cf. No. 5.

Hinckley. *See* **Higham.**

Hinckley field. *See quots.* 1678: Ray, 317, The
last man that he kill'd keeps hogs in Hinckley
field. Spoken of a coward that never durst fight.
1790: Grose, *Prov. Gloss.*, s.v. 'Leicestershire'.
1881: Evans, *Leics. Words*, 301 (E.D.S.), 'The
last man … Hinckley Field', … is now, and I
imagine always was, applied rather to a boaster
of the 'Ancient Pistol' type.

Hires the horse must ride before, He that.
1639: Clarke, 99. 1670: Ray, 106. 1875: A. B.
Cheales, *Proverb. Folk-Lore*, 99. 1917: Bridge,
Cheshire Proverbs, 71, He who hires the horse
should ride first.

History repeats itself. 1858: 'G. Eliot', *Janet's
Repentance*, in *Scenes from Clerical Life*, II x,
History, we know, is a Pt to repeat itself. 1865: H.
Sedley, *Marian Rooke*, III v i, History, it is said,
repeats itself … Few but are reminded every day
… of something that has gone before.

Hit, *verb*. **1. He that once hits will be ever
shooting.** 1640: Herbert, *Jac. Prudentum*, He
that once hits, is ever bending [his bow]. 1710: S.
Palmer, *Moral Essays on Proverbs*, 378.

2. Hit or miss. 1560: T. Wilson, *Rhetorique*, 87
(1909), Which shot in the open and plaine fieldes

at all aduentures hittie missie. 1656: *Choyce
Drollery*, 21 (Ebsworth), But hit or misse I will
declare The speeches at London and elsewhere.
1678: Ray, 73, Hit or misse for a cow-heel. 1709:
O. Dykes, *Eng. Proverbs*, 272, For we have a
smart saying to this effect, Hit or miss, luck is all.
1823: Byron, *Don Juan*, can. vii st. 33, Renown's
all hit or miss. 1872: J. Glyde, jr., *Norfolk
Garland*, 148, Hitty missy, as the blind man shot
the crow.

3. Hit the nail. See **Nail** (5).

4. To hit over the thumbs = To rebuke. 1540:
Palsgrave, *Acolastus*, sig. B4, Haue men hytte
the[e] vpon the thombes? 1560: T. Wilson.
Rhetorique, 3 (1909), Phanorinus … did hit a
young man ouer the thumbes very handsomely,
for vsing ouer old, and ouer straunge wordes.
1607: Dekker, etc., *Westw. Hoe*, V i, And he,
bristling up his beard to rail at her too, I cut him
over the thumbs thus … 1678: Ray, 349.

5. To hit the bird O' th' eye. 1670: Ray, 181. **Ho**
(or **whooping**), **Out of all** = Out of all bounds.
*c.*1374: Chaucer, *Troylus*, bk ii l. 1034 (1083)
(OED), than gan he telle his wo, But that was
endlees with-outen ho. 1577: *Misogonus*, II iii,
Though you thinke him past whoo, He may yet
reduce him. *c.*1592: *Sir T. More*, 67 (SH.S.),
Would not my lord make a rare player? Oh, he
would vpholde a companie beyond all hoe. 1599:
Shakespeare, *As You Like It*, III ii, O wonderful
… out of all whooping. 1631: Mabbe, *Celestina*,
108 (T.T.), You will hold your peace, will you
not? … What? Is there no ho with you? 1711:
Swift, *Journal to Stella*, Lett. xx. When your
tongue runs there's no ho with you. 1855:
Kingsley, *Westw. Ho!*, ch xxiii, Wonderful, past
all whooping. 1894: Northall, *Folk Phrases*, 20
(E.D.S.), Out of all ho, i.e. immoderately.

**Hoardeth up money, He that, taketh pains for
other men.** 1669: *Politeuphuia*, 130. 1732:
Fuller, 2165.

Hoar-frost. *See* **Frost.**

Hoarse. *See* **Crow** (4); and **Cuckoo** (6).

Hoathly. *See* **Hellingly.**

Hobbledehoy. 1540: Palsgrave, *Acolastus*, sig.
D4, Theyr hobledehoye tyme, the yeares that
one is neyther a man nor a boye. 1670: Ray, 216,
A hoberdehoy, half a man and half a boy. 1738:
Swift, *Polite Convers.*, Dial I. *c.*1791: Pegge,
Derbicisms, 105 (E.D.S.), A hobblety-hoy,
neither man nor boy. 1879: Jackson, *Shropsh.*

Word-Book, 209, Yo' dunna think I'd tak' up ooth a 'obbety-'oy like that fur a sweet'eart! 1894: W. Raymond, *Love and Quiet Life*, 103, No rascally Upton hobbledehoy, half man and half-boy.

Hobson's choice = No choice at all. 1649: in *Somers Tracts*, vii 87 (1811), I had Hobson's choice, either be a Hobson or nothing. 1660: *Bradshaw's Ultimum Vale*, quoted in *N. & Q.*, 6th ser, ii 426, I know no other remedy [for death]; 'tis Hobson's choice. 1712: *Spectator*, No. 509 [the story of Hobson, the Cambridge carrier]. 1718: Cibber, *Non-Juror*, I, Can any woman think herself happy, that's obliged to marry only with Hobson's choice? 1867: Dutton Cook, *Hobson's Choice* [title].

Hockin's duck, Neither mate nor fella, like. Mid-Corn. 1888: Q.-Couch, *Troy Town*, ch xxiv. 1925: *Devon and Corn. N.&Q.*, xiii 206.

Hodder, The. *See* quot. 1869: Hazlitt, 374, The Hodder, the Calder, the Ribble and rain, all meet in a point on Milton's domain.

Hodnet, Shropsh. *See* quot. 1883: Burne, *Shropsh. Folk-Lore*, 579, As sure as Hodnet sends the wind, A rainy day will Drayton find.

Hog. 1. A hog that's bemired endeavours to bemire others. 1732: Fuller, 214.

2. A hog upon trust grunts till he's paid for. Ibid., No. 215.

3. As high as a hog all but the bristles. 1670: Ray, 202.

4. It is hard to break a hog of an ill custom. 1678: Ray, 154. 1732: Fuller, 2949, It is hard to break an old hog off a custom.

5. Like a hog in armour. 1659: Howell, 19, He looketh like a hogg in armour. 1708: Ward, *London Terraefilius*, No. v p. 26. 1740: North, *Examen*, 572, So ridiculous was the figure, as they say, of hogs in armour. 1820: Scott, *Monastery*, ch x. 1847: Halliwell, *Dict.*, s.v., *A hog in armour*, a person finely but very awkwardly dressed. 1867: Larwood and Hotten, *Signboards*, 440, 'Hog in armour' … a favourite epithet applied to rifle volunteers by costermongers, street fishmongers and such like.

6. Lose not a hog. *See* **Sheep** (18).

7. The hog is got into the honey-pot. 1678: Ray, 354, The hogs to the honey pots. 1732: Fuller, 4598.

8. The hog never looks up to him that threshes down the acorns. Ibid., No. 4599.

9. To make a hog or a dog of a thing. 1670: Ray, 217. 1712: Motteux, *Quixote*, Pt II ch xxii, He will go through stitch with it: he will make a hog or a dog of it, I will warrant you.

10. What can you expect of a hog but his bristles? 1813: Ray, 201.

See also **Better my hog; Draff; Drive** (5); **Every hog; Every man basteth; Go** (23); **Hear** (7); **Lincolnshire; October** (2); **One hog; Pig; Swarston Bridge;** and **Swine.**

Hoghton, near Blackburn, Lancs. *See* quot. 1869: Hazlitt, 196, He who would see old Hoghton right, must view it by the pale moonlight.

Hogs Norton. *To be born* (or *brought up*) *at Hogs Norton, where the pigs play on the organs.* It is said that this saying refers to the village of Hock-Norton, Leicestershire, where the organist once upon a time was named Piggs! *c.*1554: *Enterlude of Youth*, in Bang's *Materialien*, B. 12, p. 19, I shall laye the on the eare were thou borne in Trumpington and brought vp at Hogges norton. 1593: Nashe, in *Works*, ii 273 (Grosart), I was brought vp at Hoggenorton, where pigges play on the organs. 1615: Armin, *Val. Welshman*, II iii, This fellow was porne at hogs Norton, where pigges play on the organ. 1670: Ray, 249, You were born at Hogs Norton. 1670: Cotton, *Scarronides*, bk iv, And pillows all securely snort on, Like organists of fam'd Hog's-Norton. 1725: Bailey, tr. Erasmus' *Colloq.*, 317, He being in a violent passion, says to him, out you saucy fellow, where was you drag'd up, *at Hogs Norton?* 1729: Fielding, *Author's Farce*, III, Though his voice be only fit to warble at Hog's Norton, where the pigs would accompany it with organs. 1738: Swift, *Polite Convers.*, Dial. II. 1821: Scott, *Kenilworth*, ch ix, He was born at Hogsnorton, where, according to popular saying, the pigs play upon the organ.

Holbeach, Lincs. *See* quot. 1869: Hazlitt, 206, Holbeach pots, Whaplode pans, Houltan organs, Weston ting-tangs. Higson's *MSS. Coll.*, No. 214, These are four places in South Lincolnshire, and the lines are satirical of the Church bells at each town.

Holborn-hill, He will ride backwards up = He will be hanged. 1790: Grose, *Prov. Gloss.*, s.v. 'London'.

Hold fast when you have it. 1546: Heywood, *Proverbs*, Pt I ch x. 1583: Melbancke, *Philotinus*, sig. F1, As to haue is good happ, so to hould fast is a great vertue. 1605: Camden, *Remains*, 324 (1870). 1659: Howell, 8.

Hold him to it. *See* **Buckle** (3).

Hold one's tongue in an ill time, One may. 1633: Draxe, 5, A man may holde his peace in an ill time. 1670: Ray, 103. 1754: Berthelson, *Eng.-Danish Dict.*, s.v. 'Hold' [as in 1633].

Hold or cut codpiece point. 1678: Ray. 73.

Hold the dish while I shed my pottage. 1670: Ray, 218.

Hold up your dagger-hand. A drinking phrase. 1639: Clarke, 46. 1670: Ray, 216.

Hold up your head: there's money bid for you. 1738: Swift, *Polite Convers.*, Dial. I, Well, methinks here's a silent meeting. Come, miss, hold up your head, girl; there's money bid for you. 1836: Marryat, *Japhet*, ch iv, As the saying is, there's money bid for you.

Hold your tongue, husband, and let me talk that have all the wit. 1678: Ray, 84. 1732: Fuller, 2521.

Hole. 1. He has a hole under his nose, that all his money runs into. 1659: Howell, *Proverbs: Fr.-Eng.*, 10, The hole too ope under the nose, breeds ragged shoes and tattered hose. 1732: Fuller, 1858. 1880: Spurgeon, *Ploughman's Pictures*, 39, He has a hole under his nose, and his money runs into it.

2. The hole calls the thief. 1640: Herbert, *Jac. Prudentum*.

3. To make a hole in the water = To drown oneself. 1813: Ray, 201. 1926: Phillpotts, *Yellow Sands*, I, I'll make a hole in the water – I'll drown to-night sure as death!

4. When you are in a hole, stop digging. 1988: D. Healey, *Observer*, in J. Care (ed.) *Sayings of the Eighties*, It is a good thing to follow the first law of holes; if you are in one, stop digging.

5. You tell how many holes be in a scummer. 1639: Clarke, 146.

Holiday dame, She's an. 1678: Ray, 73.

Hollow as a kex, As. 1678: Ray, 284. 1883: A. Easther, *Almondbury Gloss.*, 73 (E.D.S.), 'He is as hollow as a kex', said of a deceitful man. 1917: Bridge, *Cheshire Proverbs*, 15.

Hollow as a shoe when the foot's out, As. Said of a deceitful person. 1886: R. Holland, *Cheshire Gloss.*, 445 (E.D.S.). 1917: Bridge, *Cheshire Proverbs*, 17.

Holly. *See* quot. 1846: Denham, *Proverbs*, 6

(Percy S.), He never lies but when the hollin's green.

Holmby, It shines like. 1854: Baker, *Northants Gloss.*, s.v. 'Holmby'.

Holme. *See* quot. 1846–59: *Denham Tracts*, i 169 (F.L.S.) … saying, which is prevalent in the north-west part of the county [Cumberland], is valuable as characteristic of the dour and satirical disposition of the natives. When they wish to say a particularly severe thing against any of the gentry, they remark, 'When he dies there will be dry eyes at Holme'. [Holme is pronounced as 'home'.]

Holmsdale, The Vale of, Never won nor never shall. Surrey. 1576: Lambarde, *Peramb. of Kent*, 469 (1826). 1662: Fuller, *Worthies*, iii 204 (1840). 1724: Defoe, *Tour*, Lett. II 104 ['conquered' for 'won']. 1902: G. Thompson, *Picturesque Surrey*, 271. 1906: Harper, *Brighton Road*, § xxix, p. 276, It is … that Vale of Holmesdale Never wonne, ne never shall, as the braggart old couplet lias it, in allusion to the defeat and slaughter of the invading Danes at Ockley, A.D. 851.

Holt, Cheshire. 1. Go to Holt to see Fame Races = *You* are going the wrong way to work. 1917: Bridge, *Cheshire Proverbs*, 62.

2. Holt lions. Ibid., 73 [Bridge has a long discussion of the meaning of the phrase].

Holy, I'll be, I, marry will I. 1639: Clarke, 139.

Holyrood, 14 Sept. *See* quot. 1893: Inwards, *Weather Lore*, 34, If dry be the buck's horn On Holyrood morn, 'Tis worth a kist of gold; But if wet it be seen Ere Holyrood e'en. Bad harvest is foretold. Yorkshire. *See also* **Devil** (48).

Holy Thursday. *See* **Whitsuntide** (2).

Home, He that lives always at, sees nothing but home. 1618: Breton, in *Works*, ii u7 (Grosart) [cited as a 'prouerbe'].

Home is home though never so homely (or poor). *c.*1300: *Prov. of Hending*, st. 14 (Berlin, 1878), Este bueth oune brondes (Pleasant are one's own brands – i.e. one's own fireside). 1546: Heywood, *Proverbs*, Pt I ch iv, Home is homely, though it be poore in syght. 1591: Harington, *Orl. Furioso*, bk xxxix st. 61, For home though homely 'twere, yet is it sweet. 1605: Camden, *Remains*, 324 (1870), Home is homely. Before 1680: Butler, *Remains*, ii 285 (1759), Though *home be homely*, it is more delightful than finer things abroad. 1712: Arbuthnot, *Law a Bott. Pit*, Pt III ch iv, The little I have is free, and I can call it my own! 'Hame's hame, be it never so namely!' 1776: Colman, *Spleen*, I. 1826: Lamb, *Pop. Fallacies*, xii. 1848: Dickens, *Dombey*, ch xxxv, The saying is, that home is home, be it never so homely.

Home is where the heart is. 1870: J.J. McCloskey, in Goldberg and Heffner, *Davy Crockett and Other Plays* (1940), 79, Well, home, they say, is where the heart is. 1950: H.M. Gay, *Pacific Spectator*, IV 91, 'Home is where the heart is', she said, 'if you'll excuse the bromide'.

Home-keeping youths have ever homely wits. *c.*1591: Shakespeare, *Two Gent.*, I i. 1822: Scott, *Fam. Letters*, ii 134 (1894), I hold by the true saying 'untravelled youths have ever homely wits'. 1830: Marryat, *King's Own*, ch xxxvii.

Homer sometimes nods. [Quandoque bonus dormitat Homerus. – Horace, *Ars Poet.*, 359.] 1387: J. Trevisa, tr. *Higden's Polychronicon* (1874), He may take heded that the grete Homerus slepeth sometyme, for in a long work it is laweful to slepe som time.1530: Palsgrave, 897, And ther where they shall se the good Homer have ben aslepe to be wyllyng by good maner to wake him, in correctyng the fautes in the whiche by cause of the same he is fallin. 1648: Herrick, *Hesp.*, No. 95, Homer himself, in a long work, may sleep. 1820: Byron, *Don Juan*, can. v st. 159, Meanwhile, as Homer sometimes sleeps, perhaps You'll pardon to my muse a few short naps.

Home, There's no place like. *See* Place.

Honest, *adj.* **1. An honest good look covereth many faults.** 1732: Fuller, 609.

2. An honest man. *See* Wind, E (2) and F (1).

3. An honest man and a good bowler. 1592: Shakespeare, *L. L. L.*, V ii, An honest man, look you … a marvellous good neighbour, faith, and a very good bowler. 1635: Quarles, *Emblemes*, bk i No. x, The vulgar proverb's crost: He hardly can Be a good bowler and an honest man. 1670: Ray, 181.

4. An honest man's word is as good as his bond. 1670: Ray, 103. 1730: Lillo, *Silvia*, I ix, And every honest man is as good as his word.

5. An honest plain man, without pleats. 1546: Heywood, *Proverbs*, Pt II ch v, Be plaine without pletes. 1659: Howell, 15.

6. An honest shilling is better than a knavish sovereign. Surrey. 1875: A. B. Cheales, *Proverb. Folk-Lore*, 100.

7. An honest woman dwells at the sign of an honest countenance. 1615: in *Harl. Miscell.*, ii 147 (1744) [cited as 'the common saying'].

8. As honest a man as any in the cards when the kings are out. 1639: Clarke, 286. 1678: Ray, 291. 1732: Fuller, 697.

9. As honest a man as ever broke bread. 1599: Porter, *Two Angry Women*, sc xi, You are as good a man … as ere broke bread. 1600: Shakespeare, *Mitch Ado*, III v. 1696: J. Harris, *City Bride*, IV ii. 1793: O'Keeffe, *World in a Village*, I i, As good natur'd a man as ever broke bread.

10. As honest (or good) a man as ever trod on shoe leather. 1599: Porter, *Two Angry Women*, sc xi, You are as good a man as … ere went on neats leather. 1670: Ray, 181. 1754: Berthelson, *Eng.–Danish Dict.*, s.v. 'Shoe'. 1889: J. Nicholson, *Folk Speech E. Yorks*, 19, As good as ivver stepped upo' shoe leather. 1901: F. E. Taylor, *Lancs Sayings*, 33, He were as bonny a lad as ever step't i' shoe-leather.

11. As honest a man as the sun ever shone on. 1789: G. Parker, *Life's Painter*, 26.

12. As honest a woman as ever burnt malt. 1589: *Pap with a Hatchet*, 23 (1844).

13. Honest men do marry but wise men not. 1659: Howell, *Letters*, ii 666 (Jacobs), Honest men use to marry but wise men not. 1696: D'Urfey, *Quixote*, Pt III Act III sc ii, A pure proverb, that says, Honest men marry quickly, but wise men not at all.

14. Nobody so like an honest man as an arrant knave. 1732: Fuller, 2525, Honest men and knaves may possibly wear the same cloth. 1855: Bohn, 463.

15. Of all crafts, to be an honest man is the master craft. 1678: Ray, 13. 1732: Fuller, 3696, Of all crafts to an honest man, downright is the only craft.

16. The honester man the worse luck. 1611: Cotgrave, s.v. 'Mescheoir'. 1670: Ray, 117.

Honesty. 1. A man never surfeits of too much honesty. 1639: Clarke, 213, Too much honesty did never man harm. 1670: Ray, 13.

2. Honesty is a fine jewel, but much out of fashion. 1732: Fuller, 2533.

3. Honesty is ill to thrive by. 1639: Clarke, 30.

4. Honesty is plain, but no good fellow. 1594: *Knack to Know a Knave*, in Hazlitt, *Old Plays*, vi 509.

5. Honesty is the best policy. 1599: Sandys,

Europae Spec., 102 (1632) (OED), Our grosse conceipts, who think honestie the best policie. 1622: P. Hannay, *Poet. Works*, 166 (Hunt.Cl.), Honestie In shew, not deed, is policie. 1638: D. Tuvill, *Vade Mecum*, 27 (3rd ed.), He would ever say that *Honesty is the best policy.* 1671: Head and Kirkman, *Eng. Rogue*, ii 92. 1788: Colman, jr., *Ways and Means*, I ii, My policy was chosen from the proverb. Random; I thought honesty the best. 1850: Dickens, *Copperfield*, ch iv.

6. Honesty may be dear bought, but can never be a dear pennyworth. 1732: Fuller, 2535. 1736: Bailey, *Dict.*, s.v.

7. If honesty cannot knavery should not. 1732: Fuller, 2680.

Honey. 1. A honey tongue, a heart of gall. 1583: Melbancke, *Philotinus*, sig. D3, With honye in her mouth, and a sting in her tayle. *c.*1590: in *Roxb. Ballads*, ii 5 (B.S.). 1670: Ray, 104. 1732: Fuller, 610.

2. Being anointed with honey live sweetly. 1725: Bailey, tr. Erasmus' *Colloq.*, 571 [cited as 'the old saying'].

3. Cover yourself with honey and the flies will eat you. 1620: Shelton, *Quixote*, Pt II ch xlix. 1712: Motteux, *Quixote*, Pt II ch xliii, It is so, daub yourself with honey, and you will never want flies. 1853: Trench, *Proverbs*, 65 (1905), We say: *Daub yourself with honey, and you'll be covered with flies.*

4. He guides the honey ill, that may not lick his fill. 1623: Wodroephe, *Spared Houres*, 503.

5. He that handles honey shall feel it cling to his fingers. 1481: Caxton, *Reynard*, 64 (Arber), How shold ony man handle hony, but yf he lycked his fyngres. 1631: Mabbe, *Celestina*, 158 (T.T.). 1707: *Spanish Bawd*, IV i.

6. He that hath no honey in his pot, let him have it in his mouth. 1633: Draxe, 161, He that hath no honie in his pot, hath none in his mouth. 1640: Herbert, *Jac. Prudentum.* 1659: Howell, *Proverbs: Fr.-Eng.*, 3. 1736: Bailey, *Dict.*, s.v. 'Honey'.

7. Honey is dear bought if licked off thorns, *c.*1175: *Old Eng. Homilies*, i 185 (Morris), Nis nan blisse sothes in an thing thet is utewith, thet ne beo to bitter aboht; thet et huni ther-in, beoth licked of thornes (There is no true bliss in anything external that is not too dearly bought; he that eats honey therein, it is licked off thorns). *c.*1320: in *Reliq. Antiquae*, i 114 (1841), 'Dere is botht the hony that is licked of the thorne';

Quoth Hendyng. 1611: Cotgrave, s.v. 'Acheter', He that licks honey of thornes paies too deare for it. 1732: Fuller, 2215, He that licks honey from a nettle, pays too dear for it. 1827: Hone, *Table-Book*, 686, One who marries an ill-tempered person attempts to lick honey from off a thorn. 1869: Spurgeon, *John Ploughman*, ch xix, Never try dirty dodges to make money. It will never pay you to lick honey off of thorns.

8. Honey is not for the ass's mouth. 1732: Fuller, 2537.

9. Honey is sweet, but the bee stings. 1640: Herbert, *Jac. Prudentum.* 1670: Ray, 13. 1732: Fuller, 2538.

10. Honey is too good for a bear. Ibid., No. 2539.

11. Lick honey with your little finger. 1586: Pettie, tr. Guazzo's *Civil Convers.*, fo. 118, That olde saying, that we must tast honie but with our fingers end. 1670: Ray, 13. 1672: Walker, *Paroem.*, 58.

12. No honey without gall. 1611: Cotgrave, s.v. 'Nul'. 1666: Torriano, *Piazza Univ.*, 313.

13. The best honey. *See* quot. 1924: *Devonsh. Assoc. Trans.*, lv. 111, 'The best honey idd'n got by squeezin' '. Meaning that what is given spontaneously is better than what is gained by pressure.

14. To lick honey through a cleft stick. 1670: Ray, 184. 1732: Fuller, 5197.

See also **Bee; Broom; Fly** (11); **Fog** (3); **Sweet as honey;** and **Wine** (3).**, Honeymoon, It will not always be.** 1639: Clarke, 123.

Honeymoon with them, It is but. 1546: Heywood, *Proverbs*, Pt I ch, vii, It was yet but hony moone. 1633: Draxe, 118. 1659: Howell, 4.

Honour and Honours. 1. Honour and ease are seldom bedfellows. 1640: Herbert, *Jac. Prudentum*, Honour and profit lie not in one sack. 1670: Ray, 13. 1732: Fuller, 2540.

2. Honour bought, temporal simony. 1659: Howell, 9 (7).

3. Honour is but ancient riches. Before 1598: Ld. Burghley, in Peck, *Desid. Curiosa*, 48 (1779), For gentility is nothing else but antient riches. 1618: Breton, *Court and Country*, in *Inedited Tracts*, 190 (Hazlitt), Honour was but ancient riches. 1623: Webster, *Devil's Law-Case*, I i, What tell you me of gentry? 'tis nought else … But ancient riches. 1737: Ray, 52, Nobility is nothing but ancient riches.

4. Honour is unseemly for a fool. 1598: Meres, *Palladis*, fo. 211. 1633: Draxe, 3.

5. Honour will buy no beef. 1668: Shadwell, *Sullen Lovers*, V iii [cited as 'the excellent proverb'].

6. Honour without profit is a ring on the finger. 1611: Cotgrave, s.v. 'Seigneurie', Honour without profit is like a six-penny rent to one that hath nothing else to live on. 1631: Mabbe, *Celestina*, 140 (T.T.). 1659: Howell, *Proverbs: Span.-Eng.*, 19.

7. Honours change manners. [Honores mutant mores. – Polydore Vergil, *Adagia*, Prov. ccii. p. 89 (Basel, 1541).] *c.*1430: Lydgate, in Skeat's *Chaucer*, vii 297, Ther beth four thinges that maketh a man a fool, Honour first putteth him in outrage [extravagant self-importance]. 1552: Latimer, *Sermons*, 437 (P.S.), So they verify that saying *Honores mutant mores*, 'Honours change manners'. 1590: Greene, in *Works*, vii 294 (Grosart), Honours chaungeth manners. 1616: Haughton, *Englishm. for my Money*, IV i [cited as 'an old said saw']. 1711: *Spectator*, No. 259, This good creature is resolved to show the world, that great honour cannot at all change his manners, he is the same civil person he ever was. 1748: Richardson, *Clarissa*, vii 325 (1785). 1820: Scott, *Abbot*, ch xxii, How I have offended the Lord of Lindesay I know not, unless honours have changed manners.

8. Honours nourish arts. *c.*1570: F. Thynn, *Pride and Lowliness*, 22 (SH.S.), Sayeth not the proverbe, honors norishe artes?

9. There is honour among thieves. [Cum igitur tanta vis iustitiae sit, ut ea etiam latronum opes firmet atque augeat. – Cicero, *Off.*, II xi 39.] 1712: Motteux, *Quixote*, Pt II ch lx, The old proverb still holds good, Thieves are never rogues among themselves. 1723: Defoe, *Col. Jack*, ch i, Which is what other thieves make a point of honour of; I mean that of being honest to one another. 1824: Scott, *Red-gauntlet*, ch x. 1840: Dickens, *Curiosity Shop*, ch xlii, 'Honour among – among gentlemen, sir,' returned the other, who seemed to have been very near giving an awkward termination to the sentence.

10. We cannot come to honour under coverlet. 1640: Herbert, *Jac. Prudentum*.

11. Where honour ceaseth, there knowledge decreaseth. 1639: Clarke, 137. 1681: W.

Robertson, *Phraseol. Generalis*, 737. 1736: Bailey, *Dict.*, s.v.

12. Where there is no honour, there is no grief. 1633: Draxe, 91, He that hath no honour hath no soroow. 1640: Herbert, *Jac. Prudentum*.

See also **Prophet**.

Hoo. *See* **Do** (39).

Hoo, Kent. *See* quot. 1735: Pegge, *Kent. Proverbs*, in E.D.S., No. 12, p. 73, He that rideth into the Hundred of Hoo, Besides pilfering seamen, shall find dirt enow.

Hood does not make the monk, The. *c.*1387: Usk, *Test. of Love*, in Skeat's *Chaucer*, vii 91, For habit maketh no monk. *c.*1400: *Rom. Rose*, l. 6192, Habit ne maketh monk ne frere. 1617: Greene, in *Works*, ix 19 (Grosart), The hood makes not the monke, nor the apparrell the man. 1673: Wycherley, *Gent. Dane-Master*, IV i. 1754: *Connoisseur*, No. 10, Mere regimentals no more create a soldier, than the cowl makes a monk. 1820: Scott, *Abbot*, ch xxvi, The cowl makes not the monk, neither the cord the friar.

Hood for this fool, A. *c.*1566: in Collmann, *Ball. and Broadsides*, 93 (Roxb.Cl), A hood, a hood, for such a foole. 1570: in Huth, *Ancient Ballads, etc.*, 128 (1867), And, as the prouerbe doth show very playne, A hood for this foole, to kepe him from the rayne.

Hood-hill [Cleveland, Yorks] **has on his cap, When, Hamilton's sure to come down with a clap.** 1846–59: *Denham Tracts*, ii 14 (F.L.S.). 1878: *Folk-Lore Record*, i 169.

Hook or by crook, By. *c.*1380: Wiclif, in *Eng. Works*, 250 (E.E.T.S.), Comynly thei schulle bie hem with pore mennes goodis with hook or with crook *c.*1390: Gower, *Conf. Amantis*, bk v l. 2872, So what with hepe [hook] and what with crok Thei make here maister ofte winne. 1546: Heywood, *Proverbs*, Pt I ch xi, By hooke or crooke nought could I wyn there. 1583: Stubbes, *Anat. of Abuses*, 75 (N.Sh.S.), Yet will they haue it … eyther by hooke or crooke, by right or wrong, as they say. 1694: Motteux, *Rabelais*, bk v ch xiv, Well, by hook or by crook we must have something out of you. 1761: K. O'Hara, *Midas*, II ii.1860: Reade, *Cl. and Hearth*, ch i. The Church could always maintain her children by hook or by crook in those days.

Hook well lost to catch a salmon, A. 1633: Draxe, 5. 1670: Ray, 104. 1736: Bailey, *Dict.*, s.v.

Hool. *See* **Hutton**.

Hop, *verb.* **1. Hop whore! pipe thief!** 1546: Heywood, *Proverbs*, Pt II ch vii, Where all thy pleasure is, hop hoore, pipe theefe. 1611: Davies (of Hereford), *Sc. of Folly*, 47, in *Works*, ii (Grosart), Hop whoore, pipe theefe, hangman lead the dance.

2. To hop against the hill. *See* quots. 1575: Gascoigne, *Posies*, in *Works*, i 335 (Cunliffe), So strive I now to shewe, my feeble formed will, Although I know my labour lost, to hop against the hill. 1576: Pettie, *Petite Pall*, i 27 (Gollancz), For to hop against the hill and strike [? strive] against the stream, hath ever been counted extreme folly. 1597: Bacon, *Col. of Good and Evil*, 10, Running against the hill: Rowing against the streame, etc.

3. To hop in a person's neck. 1917: Bridge, *Cheshire Proverbs*, 138 … To have one's revenge on him.

Hop o' my thumb = a dwarf. 1530: Palsgrave, p. 232, col. 1 (OED), Hoppe upon my thombe, *fretillon*. 1546: Heywood, *Proverbs*, Pt I ch xi, It is a small hop on my thombe. 1630: *Wine, Beere, Ale, etc.*, 27 (Hanford, 1915), Away hop of my thumbe … I am asham'd of thee. 1888: S. O. Addy, *Sheffield Gloss.*, 112 (E.D.S.), He's a little hop-o-my-thumb, and stands no higher than nine penn'orth of brass.

Hope, Derby. *See* quot. 1889: *Folk–Lore Journal*, vii 293, [Derby sayings] Mony a one lives in Hope as ne'er saw Castleton [one and a half miles away].

Hope, *subs.* **1. He that liveth in hope, danceth without a fiddle.** 1670: Ray, 13 [with 'minstrel' for 'fiddle']. 1732: Fuller, 2224.

2. He that lives on hope will die fasting. 1623: Wodroephe, *Spared Houres*, 302, Hee who liues of hope makes a thinne belly. 1725: Bailey, tr. Erasmus' *Colloq.*, 12, They that feed upon Hope, may be said to hang but not to live. 1736: Franklin, *Way to Wealth*, in *Works*, i 443 (Bigelow). 1869: Spurgeon, *John Ploughman*, ch xv, He who lives on hope has a slim diet.

3. He that wants hope is the poorest man alive. 1732: Fuller, 2342.

4. Hope deferred makes the heart sick. Proverbs xiii 12. *c.*1395: Wyclif, *Bible* (1850), Proverbs, xiii 13, Hope that is deferrid, tormenteth the soule. 1557: R. Edgeworth, *Sermons*, 130v, The hope that is deferred, prolonged, and put of, vexeth the minde. 1631:

Mabbe, *Celestina*, 38 (T.T.), For (as it is in the proverbe) delayed hope afflicteth the heart. 1633: Draxe, 42, Long hope is the fainting of the soule. 1768: Sterne, *Sent. Journey*, 102 (1794), And felt what kind of sickness of the heart it was which arises from hope deferred. 1836: Marryat, *Easy*, ch xxix.

5. Hope is a good breakfast but a bad supper. Before 1626: Bacon, in Aubrey, *Lives*, i 74 (Clark), 'But,' sayd his lordship, 'Hope is a good breakfast, but an ill supper.' 1732: Fuller, 2541. 1817: Mrs Piozzi, in Hayward, *Autobiog., etc., of Mrs P.*, ii 358 (1861), Ah! he was a wise man who said Hope is a good breakfast but a bad dinner. It shall be my supper, however, when all's said and done.

6. Hope is a lover's staff. 1855: Bohn, 408.

7. Hope is as cheap as despair. 1732: Fuller, 2542.

8. Hope is grief's best music. 1855: Bohn, 408.

9. Hope is the poor man's bread. 1640: Herbert, *Jac. Prudentum.*

10. Hope is worth any money. 1732: Fuller, 2543.

11. Hope of long life beguileth many a good wife. *c.*1320, in *Reliq. Antiquae*, i 116 (1841), 'Hope of long lyf Gyleth mony god wyf'; Quoth Hendyng.

12. Hope often blinks at a fool. *c.*1300: *Havelok*, l. 307, Hope maketh fol man ofte blenkes.

13. Hope springs eternal. 1732: Pope, *Essay on Man*, i 95, Hope springs eternal in the human breast. Man never Is, but always To be blest. 1865: Dickens, *Our Mutual Friend*, II iii x, Night after night his disappointment is acute, but hope springs eternal in the scholastic breast.

14. If hope were not heart would break. Before 1225: *Ancren R.*, 80, Ase me seith, gif hope nere, heorte to breke. *c.*1340: Hampole, *Pricke of Con.*, l. 7266 (Morris), And men saye, warn hope ware it [the 'hert'] suld brest. *c.*1440: *Gesta Rom.*, 228 (E.E.T.S.), He made thes wordes to be wreten, 'yf hope wer not, hert shulde breke'. *c.*1590: Harvey, *Marginalia*, 95 (1913), But for hope ye hart woold brust. 1655: A. Brewer, *Love-sick King*, II, in Bang's *Materialien*, B. 18, p. 13, Hope keeps the heart whole. 1748: Richardson, *Clarissa*, vi 200 (1785). 1893: *Co. Folk–Lore: Suffolk*, 150 (F.L.S.), If it warn't for hope, the heart 'ud die.

15. Too much hope deceiveth. 1578: Florio, *First Fruites*, fo. 33. 1629: *Book of Meery Riddles*, Prov. 126.

Hope, *verb.* **1. He that hopes not for good, fears not evil.** 1640: Herbert, *Jac. Prudentum.* 1732: Fuller, 2166, He that hopes no good, fears no ill. 1854: Surtees, *Handley Cross*, ch lxxii, Where no hope is left, is left no fear.

2. I hope better, quoth Benson, when his wife bade him come in cuckold. 1678: Ray, 86. 1732: Fuller, 2608.

3. Hope for the best and prepare for the worst. 1565: Norton and Sackville, *Gorboduc*, I ii, Good is I graunt of all to hope the best, But not to live still dreadles of the worst. 1587: J. Bridges, *Defence of Govt. of Church of Eng.*, 74, I wishe the best, and therefore if I feare the worst I hope I am the easier to bee pardoned. 1590: Spenser, *F. Q.*, IV vi 37, Its best to hope the best, though of the worst affrayd. *c.*1680: L'Estrange, *Seneca's Morals:* 'Happy Life', ch x, I'le hope the best, and provide for the worst. 1706: Ward, *Works*, iii 337 [as in 1680].

4. Hope helpeth. 1568: in *Loseley MSS.*, 209 (Kempe).

5. Hope well and have well. 1583: Melbancke, *Philotinus*, sig. H2. 1647: A. Brewer, *Countrie Girle*, sig. G2. 1712: Motteux, *Quixote*, Pt II ch lxv. 1732: Fuller, 2545, Hope well and have well, quoth Hickwell.

Hopkins. *See* quots. 1678: Ray, 290, As well come as Hopkin, that came to jayl over night, and was hang'd the next morning. 1732: Fuller, 695 [with 'hasty' for 'well come' and 'Hopkins' for 'Hopkin']. 1869: Hazlitt, 113, Don't hurry, Hopkins. This seems to be an Americanism [clearly not].

Hops. 1. Hops and turkeys, carp and beer, Came into England all in one year. As the examples which follow show, there are several versions of this saying. They are brought together here, with cross-references from the various objects named. The year referred to is supposed to be 1520. 1599: Buttes, *Dyets Dry Dinner*, sig. G4, Heresie and beere came hopping into England both in a yeere. 1643: Sir R. Baker, *Chron.*, 298 (1730), About his [Henry VIII's] fifteenth year it happen'd that diverse things were newly brought into England, whereupon this rhime was made: Turkeys, Carps, Hopps, Piccarel, and Beer, Came into England all in one year. *c.*1685: Aubrey, *Nat. Hist. Wilts*, 62 (1847), Greeke, carps, turkey-cocks, and beere, Came into England all in a yeare. 1714: Ward, *Hudib. Brewer*, 21, To the same year's produce, we see, Ascribe both hops and heresy. 1724: Defoe, *Tour*, Lett. II p. 34, Hops, Reformation, bays [baize], and beer, Came, etc. 1809: Pegge, *Anonym.*, Cent. V 88 [as in 1643]. 1826: Brady, *Varieties of Lit.*, 264 [as in 1724]. 1834–7: Southey, *Doctor*, inter-chap. xvi. 1886: Bickerdyke, *Curios. of Ale and Beer*, 67 [as in 1724]. 1909: Hackwood, *Inns, Ales, etc.*, 44.

2. Hops make or break. Referring to the speculative nature of the hop harvest. 1869: Hazlitt, 208.

3. Plenty of lady-birds, plenty of hops. Ibid., 317.

See also **Bean** (2); **St James's Day**; and **Thick as hops.**

Hopton. *See* **Horner.**

Horestone. *See* **Padwell.**

Horn and **Horns. 1. A horn heard soon though hardly seen.** 1659: Howell, *Proverbs: Brit.-Eng.*, 9.

2. He cannot hold a horn in his mouth, but must blow it. *c.*1470: *Songs and Carols*, 23 (Percy S.), I hold hym wyse and wel i-taught, Can bar an horn and blow it naught. 1571: Edwards, *Damon, etc.*, in Hazlitt, *Old Plays*, iv 77, I can wear a horn and blow it not. 1681: W. Robertson, *Phraseol. Generalis*, 733.

3. He had better put his horns in his Pocket than wind them. 1678: Ray, 74. 1732: Fuller, 1852.

4. He that hath horns in his bosom, let him not put them on his head. 1640: Herbert, *Jac. Prudentum.* 1670: Ray, 104. 1732: Fuller, 5704 [with 'forehead' for 'head'].

5. Horns and grey hairs do not come by years. 1678: Ray, 156.

6. Let the horns go with the hide. 1855: Bohn, 441.

7. Your horns hang in your eyes. 1583: Melbancke, *Philotinus*, sig. F2, Her mothers husband … could not see for hornes growing ouer his eyes. 1631: Lenton, *Characters*, No. 32 (N.), A cuckold is a harmelesse horned creature, but they [his horns] hang not in his eies, as your wittals doe. 1709: Ward, *Works*, iv *Verse* 132, To improve your old horns till they hang in your light. 1732: Fuller, 6051. Cf. **Jealous.**

Horn Fair, All is fair at. 1813: Brand, *Pop. Antiq.*, ii 195 (Bohn), So many indecencies were committed upon this occasion on Blackheath ... that it gave rise to the proverb of 'All is fair at Horn fair'. 1862: Chambers, *Book of Days*, i 645 (1869).

Homer, Popham, Wyndham, and Thynne, When the abbot[s] went out, then they came in. 1669–96: Aubrey, *Lives*, i 279 (Clark), Hopton–Horner, Smyth, and Thynne, When abbots went out, they came in. 1790: Grose, *Prov. Gloss.*, s.v. 'Somerset'.

Hornet, He is as mild as a. An ironical Glos. saying. 1639: in *Berkeley MSS.*, iii 30 (1885).

Horse and **Horses. 1. A boisterous horse must have a rough bridle.** 1633: Draxe, 171. 1639: Clarke, 200 [with 'boystrous' for 'rough'].

2. A free horse is soon tired. 1593: *Pass. Morrice*, 93 (N.Sh.S.), How easie is a free horse tired.

3. A good horse cannot be of a bad colour. 1653: Walton, *Angler*, Pt I ch v, It is observed by some that 'there is no good horse of a bad colour'. 1710: S. Palmer, *Moral Essays on Proverbs*, 297, A good horse is never of an ill colour. 1838: Hood, *Hood's Own*, 1st ser, 146 (1865). 1922: *N.&Q.*, 12th ser, xi 169.

4. A good horse oft needs a good spur. 1639: Clarke, 93. 1670: Ray, 105.

5. A good horse should be seldom spurred. 1732: Fuller, 156.

6. A hired horse tired never. 1683: Meriton, *Yorkshire Ale*, 83–7 (1697).

7. A horse foaled of an acorn = the gallows. 1678: Ray, 253, You'll ride on a horse that was foal'd of an acorn. 1762: Smollett, *Sir L. Greaves*, ch viii. 1827: Lytton, *Pelham*, ch lxxxii.

8. A horse is neither better nor worse for his trapping. 1732: Fuller, 217.

9. A horse kiss. 1678: Ray, 74, An horse-kiss. A rude kiss, able to beat one's teeth out. 1732: Fuller, 611 [as in 1678].

10. A horse of another colour. 1840: Barham, *Ing. Legends:* 'Leech of Folkestone', They are manifest asses; but you, good Leech, you are a horse of another colour. 1880: Spurgeon, *Ploughman's Pictures*, 51, Farmer Gripper thinks we can live upon nothing, which is a horse of another colour.

11. A horse stumbles that hath four legs. 1640: Herbert, *Jac. Prudentum*. 1683: Meriton, *Yorkshire Ale*, 83–7 (1697), A horse may stumble on four-feet.

12. A horse that will not carry a saddle must have no oats. 1732: Fuller, 218.

13. A horse that will travel well, a hawk that will fly well, a servant that will wait well and a knife that will cut well. 16th cent.: in *N.&Q.*, 4th ser, iii 10.

14. A horse will not void oats. *See* quot. 1745: Franklin, in *Works*, ii 35–6 (Bigelow), If, as the proverb says, it is unreasonable to expect a horse should void oats, which never eat any.

15. A horse with a wame. *See* quots. 1670: Ray, 44, A nagg with a weamb and a mare with nean. 1828: Carr, *Craven Dialect*, ii 233, 'A horse wi' a waam And a meear in naan'. This Craven distich denotes that a horse should have a large paunch and a mare a small one.

16. A hungry horse makes a clean manger. 1659: Howell, 5. 1670: Ray, 107. 1754: Berthelson, *Eng.-Danish Dict.*, s.v. 'Hungry'.

17. A pair of good spurs to a borrowed horse is better than a peck of haver [oats]. 1683: Meriton, *Yorkshire Ale*, 83–7 (1697).

18. A resty horse must have a sharp spur. 1639: Clarke, 167. 1670: Ray, 105.

19. A spur and a whip for a dull horse. 1639: Clarke, 76.

20. All lay the load on the willing horse. 1546: Heywood, *Proverbs*, Pt I ch xi, Folke call on the horse that will cary alwey. 1611: Cotgrave, s.v. 'Cheval', [as in 1546, *plus*] the willingest are sorest laid unto. 1670: Ray, 116. 1732: Fuller, 532.

21. An inch of a horse is worth a span of a colt. Ibid., No. 636.

22. As holy as a horse. 1530: Palsgrave, 620, He maketh as thoughe he were as holy as a horse.

23. As shortly as a horse will lick his ear. 1546: Heywood, *Proverbs*, Pt II ch ix.

24. As strong as a horse. 1703: Ward, *Writings*, ii 81. 1845: Jerrold, *Mrs Caudle*, xxix, You're not as strong as a horse.

25. *Behind before, before behind, a horse is in danger to be prick't.* 1670: Ray, 44.

26. Choose a horse made and a wife (or man) to make. 1611: Cotgrave, s.v. 'Cheval', A made horse, and a man unarm'd are fittest for use. 1640: Herbert, *Jac. Prudentum* [has two sayings, one 'man', the other 'wife']. 1736: Bailey, *Dict.*, s.v. 'Wife', A horse broken and a wife to break.

27. Do not change horses in midstream. 1864: A. Lincoln, *Collected Works* (1953), VII 384, I am reminded … of a story of an old Dutch farmer, who remarked to a companion once that 'it was best not to swap horses when crossing streams'. 1929: R. Graves, *Goodbye to All That*, xxiii, 'Reverend father we have a proverb in England never to swap horses while crossing a stream.

28. Do not spur a free horse. [Addere calcaria sponte currenti. – Pliny, *Ep.*, I viii 1.] 1477: *Paston Lett.*, iii 200 (Gairdner), It shall never neede to prykk nor threte a free horse. I shall do whatt I can. 1633: Jonson, *Tale of a Tub*, III iv, Spur a free horse, he'll run himself to death. 1712: Motteux, *Quixote*, Pt II ch lxxi, Ride not a free horse to death. 1820: Scott, *Monastery*, ch xxv, Be advised, therefore, by me – Spur not an unbroken horse.

29. Every horse thinks his own pack heaviest. 1732: Fuller, 1420. 1875: A. B. Cheales, *Proverb. Folk-Lore*, 120.

30. Good horses make short miles. 1640: Herbert, *Jac. Prudentum*.

31. Have a horse of your own, and then you can borrow one. 1869: Spurgeon, *John Ploughman*, ch xiv.

32. He hath eaten a horse, and the tail hangs out at his mouth. 1678: Ray, 74.

33. He hath taken my horse and left me the tether. 1672: Walker, *Paroem.*, 17.

34. He is ready to lend a horse who never had one. *c.*1320: in *Reliq. Antiquae*, i 114 (1841), 'He is fre of hors that ner nade non'; Quoth Hendyng.

35. He that hath a white horse and a fair wife is never without trouble. 1586: Pettie, tr. Guazzo's *Civil Convers.*, fo. 124 [with 'woman' for 'wife' – cited as 'an ordinary saying']. 1591: Florio, *Second Frutes*, 191, He that a white horse and a fayre wife keepeth, For feare, for care, for ielousie scarce sleepeth. 1716: Ward, *Female Policy*, 33. 1732: Fuller, 2156.

36. He that hath neither horse nor cart, cannot always load. 1611: Cotgrave, s.v. 'Charger', Hee loads not when he lists that wants both horse and cart. 1623: Wodroephe, *Spared Houres*, 480.

37. He that lets his horse drink at every lake, And his wife go to every wake; Shall never have a good horse, Nor a good wife which is worse. 1640: Herbert, *Jac. Prudentum*, Who lets his wife go to every feast, and his horse drink at

every water, shall neither have good wife nor good horse. 1670: Ray, 28 [as in 1640]. 1696: D'Urfey, *Quixote*, Pt III Act IV sc i, He that lets his wife drink of every cup, ugh, and his horse at every water, shall be sure to have neither of 'em good for any thing. 1732: Fuller, 6187.

38. His horse's head is swollen so big, that he cannot come out of the stable = He owes the ostler so much. 1659: Howell, 6.

39. Horse and man = Completely. 1639: Clarke, 86, He's undone horse and man. 1666: Torriano, *Piazza Univ.*, 134, As much as to say, Undone, horse and man. 1740: Walpole, *Letters*, i 87 (1820) (O), She cheats horse and foot.

40. Horse in hand. *See* **Good walking.**

41. It is a good horse that never stumbles. 1530: Palsgrave, 742, He is a good horse that stumbleth nat sometyme. 1579: G. Harvey, in *Works*, i 23 (Grosart), A good horse that trippeth not once in a iourney. 1616: Breton, in *Works*, ii e 6 (Grosart). 1709: O. Dykes, *Eng. Proverbs*, 19. 1869: Spurgeon, *John Ploughman*, ch x, It is a good horse that never stumbles, And a good wife that never grumbles.

42. It is the bridle and spur that makes a good horse. 1732: Fuller, 3021.

43. It would make a horse break his bridle, or a dog his halter. 1577: Stanihurst, *Descrip. of Ireland*, fo. 6, It would make a horse breake hys halter, to see so dronken a pageant. 1659: Howell, 10, It would make a horse break his halter. 1670: Ray, 165.

44. It's an ill horse can neither whinny nor wag his tail. 1595: *Maroccus Extaticus*, 6 (Percy S.) ['a jade']. 1639: Clarke, 70. 1670: Ray, 105. 1732: Fuller, 2882 ['a silly horse'].

45. Lend thy horse for a long journey, thou mayest have him again with his skin. 1659: Howell, 4. 1670: Ray, 14.

46. Let a horse drink when he will, not what he will. 1678: Ray, 157.

47. Let the best horse leap the hedge first. 1732: Fuller, 3191.

48. Let the quick horse. *See* quot. 1573: Bullein, *Dialogue*, 123 (E.E.T.S.). Mingle the good with the bad, as men saie, lette the quicke horse drawe the deade horse out of the myre.

49. Live, horse! and thou shall have grass. 1738: Swift, *Polite Convers.*, Dial. I. 1901: F. E. Taylor, *Lancs Sayings*, 8, Live, hawse [horse], an' theawst ha' graiss.

50. One white foot. *See* quots. 1659: Howell, *Proverbs: Ital.-Eng.*, 13, A four white-foot horse is a horse for a fool, a three white-foot horse is a horse for a King, and if he hath but one Ile give him to none. 1666: Torriano, *Piazza Univ.*, 59, A horse with one white foot is suppos'd to be best. 1851: FitzGerald, *Euphranor*, 84 (1855), One [white foot], I have heard say, is as good a sign, as all four white are a bad. 1877: *N. & Q.*, 5th ser, vii 64, One white foot, buy a horse; Two white feet, try a horse: Three white feet, look well about him; Four white feet, do without him. 1922: *N. & Q.*, 12th ser, xi 169, One white leg, ride him for your life; Two white legs, give him to your wife; Three white legs, give him to your man; Four white legs, sell him if you can. Ibid., 212, Four white feet and a white nose, Strip off his hide, and give him to the crows. [There is more than one variant of these rhymes.]

51. Put no more on an old horse than he can bear. 1775: Garrick, *May-Day*, sc i [cited as 'an excellent saying'].

52. Ride a horse and a mare on the shoulders, an ass and mule on the buttocks. 1659: Howell, *Proverbs: Ital.-Eng.*, 2 [with 'towards' for each 'on']. 1678: Ray, 53.

53. Steal the horse and carry home the bridle. 1678: Ray, 342. 1732: Fuller, 4173, Sim steals the horse, and carries home the bridle honestly.

54. That horse is troubled with corns = is foundered. 1678: Ray, 74.

55. The biggest horses are not the best travellers. 1732: Fuller, 4425.

56. The blind horse is fittest for the mill. 1692: Southerne, *Maid's Last Prayer*, III i.

57. The common horse is worst shod. 1546: Heywood, *Proverbs*, Pt I ch xi. 1670: Ray, 105.

58. The fault of the horse is put on the saddle. 1620: Shelton, *Quixote*, Pt II ch lxvi, According to the opinion of wise men, the fault of the ass must not be laid upon the pack-saddle. 1640: Herbert, *Jac. Prudentum*. 1732: Fuller, 4519 [as in 1620].

59. The good horse must carry drink. S. Devon. 1869: Hazlitt, 370.

60. The good horse must not cocky to a gally-whacker [start at a scarecrow]. S. Devon. Ibid.

61. The good horse must smell to a pixy [know where the bog is]. S. Devon. Ibid.

62. The horse may starve. *See* Grass (6).

63. The horse next the mill carries all the grist.

1605: Camden, *Remains*, 334 (1870). 1670: Ray, 121. 1694: D'Urfey, *Quixote*, Pt I Act II sc i. 1732: Fuller, 4601.

64. The horse that draws his halter is not quite escaped. 1639: Clarke, 250 1732: Fuller, 4602. 1853: Trench, *Proverbs*, 139 (1905).

65. The horse thinks one thing, and he that saddles him another. 1631: Mabbe, *Celestina*, 264 (T.T.). 1696: D'Urfey, *Quixote*, Pt III Act III sc ii, D'ye hear, friend of mine, the ass thinks one thing, and he that rides him another. 1732: Fuller, 3799, One thing thinketh the horse, and another he that saddles him.

66. The willing horse is always most ridden. 1546: Heywood, *Proverbs*, Pt I ch xi, Folke call on the horse that will cary alwey.

67. They are scarce of horses where two ride on a dog. 1678: Ray, 157, They are scarce of horse-flesh who two and two ride on a dog. 1732: Fuller, 4958.

68. They cannot set their horses together = cannot agree. 1639: Clarke, 94, They cannot set their horses i' th' same stable. 1670: Ray, 181. *c.*1710: Swift, in *Works*, xiv 109 (Scott), And since we're so near, like birds of a feather, Let's e'en, as they say, set our horses together. 1776: in *Garrick Corresp.*, ii 171 (1832), We do not quite set our horses together, though I have done a piece of service lately he knows nothing of, nor ever shall. 1887: Parish and Shaw, *Dict. Kent. Dialect*, 79 (E.D.S.), Muster Nidgett and his old 'ooman can't set their horses together at all.

69. To make a horse's meal, i.e. to eat without drinking. 1793: Grose, *Olio*, 91 (2nd ed.).

70. Trust not a horse's heel nor a dog's tooth. 1678: Ray, 158.

71. When the horse is starved, you bring him oats. 1732: Fuller, 5591.

72. Where the horse lies down, there some hairs will be found. Before 1500: in Hill, *Commonplace-Book*, 129 (E.E.T.S.), Whan the hors waloweth, som hens be loste. 1602: Carew, *Surv. of Cornwall*, 9 (1811), Where the horse walloweth, some haris will still remain. 1662: Fuller, *Worthies*, i 299 (1840). 1732: Fuller, 6331. 1864: 'Cornish Proverbs', in *N. & Q.*, 3rd ser, vi 494.

73. You may take a horse to the water, but you can't make him drink. *c.*1175: *Old Eng. Homilies*, 1st ser, p. 9 (Morris), Hwa is thet mei thet hors wettrien the him-self nule drinken?

(Who is he that may water the horse and not drink himself?). 1546: Heywood, *Proverbs*, Pt I ch xi, A man maie well bring a horse to the water, But he cannot make him drinke without he will. 1616: *Jack Drum*, I, in Simpson, *Sch. of Shakesp.*, ii 143, What! a man may lead a horse to the water, but heele chuse to drinke. 1763: Johnson, in Hill's *Boswell*, i 427, As the proverb says, 'One man may lead a horse to the water, but twenty cannot make him drink'. 1830: Marryat, *King's Own*, ch xxxiv. 1884: J. Platt, *Poverty*, 62.

74. You may beat a horse till he be sad, and a cow till she be mad. 1678: Ray, 98.

75. You may know the horse by his harness. 1670: Ray, 105. 1732: Fuller, 5883, [a contradiction] You can't judge of the horse by the harness.

76. You'll ride a horse that was foaled of an ass. 1855: Bohn, 581.

77. Your horse cast a shoe. 1678: Ray, 349.

See also **Afterthought; Ass** (10) and (14); **Beat** (3); **Better be the tail; Better riding; Blind,** *adj.* (9); **Change,** *verb* (4); **Colt** (1); **Cough; Eat** (19); **Fine** (4); **Flea-bitten; Flesh; Fly** (5); **Foal; Galled; Gift** (8); **Good luck; Grey mare; Groaning; Hang** (9); **Hires; Lazy groom; Like a horse; Like a loader's horse; Mad horse; Man** (1), (55), and (78); **Nod; One saddle; Ox** (7); **Proud horse; Saddle; Scabbed; Scald; Short; Shoulder of mutton; Sick** (4); **Stable-door; Steal** (1) and (5); **Throw** (4); **Two ride; Up the hill; Wife** (12); **Wild** (9); **Willow; Win** (4); and **Young** (9).

Horse-load to a cart-load, To fall away from a. 1678: Ray, 243. 1690: *New Dict. Canting Crew*, sig. G1, Fallen away from a horse-load to a cart-load, spoken ironically of one considerably improved in flesh on a sudden. 1738: Swift, *Polite Convers.*, Dial. I.

Horse-nest. *See* **Mare** (6).

Horsham. *See* **Rudgwick.**

Horsley. *See* **Heddon.**

Horton town. *See* **Wotton hill.**

Hosed and shod, He came in = He was born to a good estate. 1678: Ray, 74.

Host. *See* **Reckon.**

Host's invitation is expensive, An. 1732: Fuller, 612.

Hot as a toast, *c.*1430: *Two Cookery-Books*, 12 (OED), Seene forth alle hote as tostes. *c.*1520: in Skelton, *Works*, ii 415 (Dyce), Chafyng lyke myne hoste, As hott as any toste. *c.*1580: in *Roxb.*

Ballads, i 94 (Hindley), Six pelican chickens as hote as a toast. 1696: D'Urfey, *Quixote*, Pt III Act II sc i, She makes me as hot as a toast. 1714: Ozell, *Molière*, ii 9, You'll have it as hot as a toast, monster! 1860: Reade, *Cl. and Hearth*, ch xxv, They were soon as warm as toast, and fast asleep. 1901: F. E. Taylor, *Lancs Sayings*, 4, As waarm as a toast.

Hot as coals. 1551: T. Wilson, *Rule of Reason*, sig. U4, You shalbe as whote as coles by and by. 1563: Foxe, *Actes, etc.*, v 19 (1846), The bishop and all his doctors were as hot as coals.

Hot as fire. *c.*1350: *Will. Palerne*, 36 (E.E.T.S.), Sum-time it hentis me with hete as hot as ani fure. *c.*1440: *Gesta Rom.*, 46 (E.E.T.S.), For he woll … make me foryete my anger, though I wer as hote as fire. 1579: Spenser, *Shep. Cal.*, March, 1. 48, A stepdame eke as hote as fyre. 1634: Fletcher, *Two Noble Kins.*, V vi, The hot horse, hot as fire. 1786: D'Arblay, *Diary*, ii 212 (1876), I was as hot as fire at this question. 1855: Gaskell, *North and South*, ch xiv, My cheeks were as hot as fire. 1872: Hardy, *Greenwood Tree*, Pt I ch viii., You dance and get hot as fire.

Hot as if he had a bellyful of wasps and salamanders, He is as. 1732: Fuller, 1911.

Hot love hasty vengeance. 1736: Bailey, *Dict.*, s.v. 'Vengeance'.

Hot love is soon cold. 1537: R. Whitford, *Werke for Housholders*, sig. D7, Hote loue is sone colde. 1587: Greene, in *Works*, v 210 (Grosart). 1620: *Two Merry Milkmaids*, II i, The old [adage]. Hot loue's soone cold. 1670: Ray, 46. 1732: Fuller, 2549. 1889: *Folk-Lore Journal*, vii 292 (Derbyshire).

Hot needle. *See* **Put** (11).

Hot porridge (or worts) will soak old crusts. 15th cent.: in *Reliq. Antiquae*, i 82 (1841), This is to saye to your lewde undurstandyng, that hoote wortes erased crusstes makeyn sofft hard wortes. Before 1500: in Hill, *Commonplace-Book*, 132 (E.E.T.S.), Whote wortis make softe crustis. 1917: Bridge, *Cheshire Proverbs*, 75, Hot porridge will soak old crusts.

Hot shot indeed, You are a, 'spoken in a slighting derision'. 1659: Howell, 4. 1678: Ray, 86, He's a hot shot in a mustard pot, when both his heels stand right up. 1732: Fuller, 2440 [as in 1678].

Hot sup, hot swallow. 1639: Clarke, 200. 1670: Ray, 106. 1732: Fuller, 2551.

Hot water. *See* quot. 1654: Gayton, *Pleasant Notes Don Q.*, 79, This same search hath not cost me hot water (as they say).

Hotspurs, You are none of the. 1732: Fuller, 5855, You are none of the hastings, nor hotspurs. 1846–59: *Denham Tracts*, i 228 (F.L.S.), You're none of the hotspurs. Made use of when accusing a noisy braggadocio, be he soldier or civilian, of cowardice.

Houltan. *See* **Holbeach.**

Hound gnaweth bone. *See* **Dog** (94).

Hour in a day between a good housewife and a bad, There's but an. 1678: Ray, 74.

Hour in the morning, before breakfast, is worth two all the rest of the day, An. 1827: Hone, *Ev. Day Book*, ii 477 [cited as 'an old and a true saying']. 1846: Denham, *Proverbs*, 3 (Percy S.).

Hour may destroy what an age was a building, An. 1732: Fuller, 613.

Hour of pain is as long as a day of pleasure, An. Ibid., No. 614.

Hour's cold will suck out seven years' heat, An. 1846: Denham, *Proverbs*, 3 (Percy S.).

Hours Sayings. *See* quots. 1891: R. P. Chope, *Hartland Dialect*, 21 (E.D.S.), 'Twixt twelve an' two You'd zee 'ot the day'll do. 1893: Inwards, *Weather Lore*, 44, Between the hours of ten and two Will show you what the day will do [also as in 1891]. (*See also* **Sleep**)

House. 1. A house built by the wayside is either too high or too low. 1666: Torriano, *Piazza Univ.*, 40, Who buildeth a house in the street, either it is too high or too low. 1670: Ray, 106. 1732: Fuller, 220.

2. A house divided (against itself) cannot stand. [Mark iii 25, And if a house be divided against itself, that house cannot stand.] 1050: Defensor, *Liber Scintillarum* (E.E.T.S.), 133 Drihten segth … aelc ceaster oththe hus todaeled ongean hit sylf, hit na stynt. *c.*1704: in T. Chalkley, *Journal* in *Works* (1751), 42, My mother would often say, *A House divided could not stand.* 1858: A. Lincoln, *Speech*, 16 June, in *Works* (1953) II 461, 'A house divided against itself canot stand'. I believe this government cannot endure permanently half *slave* and half *free.*

3. A house filled with guests is eaten up and ill spoken of. 1855: Bohn, 291.

4. A house ready made and a wife to make. 1611: Cotgrave, s.v. 'Acheter', Buy a house made, and a wife unmar:'d. 1732: Fuller, 222.

5. After the house is finished, leave it. 1640: Herbert, *Jac. Prudentum.*

6. Better one's house too little one day, than too big all the year after. 1670: Ray, 106. 1732: Fuller, 919. 1852: FitzGerald, *Polonius*, 30 (1903). 1868: *Quart. Review*, cxxv. 252 [with last words, 'too large all the year'].

7. Choose not a house near an inn [for noise], **or in a corner** [for filth]. 1640: Herbert, *Jac. Prudentum.*

8. He that buys a house ready wrought hath many a pin and nail for nought. 1605: Camden, *Remains*, 324 (1870). 1670: Ray, 106. 1732: Fuller, 6442.

9. He that hath no house must lie in the yard. 1591: Lyly, *Endymion*, IV ii.

10. His house stands on my lady's ground. 1678: Ray, 75.

11. Much it behoveth him to do that house shall hold. *c.*1460: *How the Good Wife*, l. 120, Mykelle mote hym be-houethe to don that house schall holden.

12. One's house one's castle. 1602–3: Manningham, *Diary*, 21 (Camden S.), His house … is his castle. 1669: Dudley North, *Obs. and Adv. Oeconom.*, 72, Masters of families are much favoured in our law, for their houses are termed their castles. 1767: Murphy, *Sch. for Guardians*, III v, My house is my castle, gentlemen, and nobody must offer violence here. 1848: Dickens, *Dombey*, ch ix, Mrs MacStinger immediately demanded whether an English-woman's house was her castle or not. *See also* **Englishman** (3).

13. Set not your house on fire to be revenged of the moon. 1732: Fuller, 4111. 1880: Spurgeon, *Ploughman's Pictures*, 36 … to spite the moon.

14. The house goes mad when women gad. 1822: Scott, *Nigel*, ch iv.

15. The house shows the owner. 1611: Cotgrave, s.v. 'Maison', The house discovers the owner. 1640: Herbert, *Jac. Prudentum.*

16. To eat out of house and home. *See* **Eat** (35).

17. To throw the house out of the windows. 1562: Bullein, *Bulwarke of Defence*, fo. 28, Haue at all … caste the house out at the window. 1659: in *Pol. Ballads*, 161 (Wright, Percy S.), If we take them there any more, wee'l throw the house out of the window. 1714: Ozell, *Moliére*, i 180, I'll have a virtuous wife, or I'll throw the house out o' th' window. 1836: Dickens, *Sketches by Boz*, 248 (C. D. ed.), The whole family was infected with the mania for Private Theatricals; the house, usually so clean and tidy, was, to use Mr Gattleton's expressive description, 'regularly turned out o' windows'. 1889: Peacock, *Manley, etc.*, *Gloss.*, 563 (E.D.S.), To throw the house out of the windows, To make a great noise, disturbance, or tumult in a house.

18. When house and land are gone and spent. *Then learning is most excellent.* 1753: Foote, *Taste*, I [cited as 'the old saying']. 1773: Garrick, *Prol.* to Goldsmith's *She Stoops*, When ign'rance enters, folly is at hand; Learning is better far than house and land. 1805: Scott, *Fam. Letters*, i 31 (1894), I am at pains with her education, because you know 'learning is better than house or land'. 1859: Planché, *Extravag.*, v 206 (1879) [as in 1805].

19. When my house burns, it is not good playing at chess. 1640: Herbert, *Jac. Prudentum.* 1670: Ray, 106. 1732: Fuller, 5539, When a man's house is on fire, it's time to break off chess.

20. When the house is burned down you bring water. 1732: Fuller, 5592.

21. Who would hold his house very clean, Ought lodge no priest nor pigeon therein. 1611: Cotgrave, s.v. 'Pigeon', He that in a neat house will dwell, must priest and pigeon thence expell. 1666: Torriano, *Piazza Univ.*, 48, Who means to have a clean house, let him not keep pidgeons. 1886: Swainson, *Folk-Lore of Brit. Birds*, 169 (F.L.S.).

See also **Commend** (1); and **Eat** (35).

Housekeeping is a privy thief. 1542: Udall, tr. Erasmus' *Apoph.*, 44 (1877), And (as our Englishe prouerbe saieth) Hous kepyng is a priuie theef. *See also* **Marriage** (5).

Housetop, to be at the = in anger. 1546: Heywood, *Proverbs*, Pt II ch v, He is at three woordis vp in the house roufe. 1626: *Scoggins Jests*, 92 (1864), I defie thee, said Scogins wife (and was up in the house top). 1633: Draxe, 10, At three words he is at the top of the house. 1828: Carr, *Craven Dialect*, i 236, To be at t' house-top, to be in a great rage. 1875: Parish, *Sussex Dialect*, 123, If you says anything to him, he's up-a-top-of-the-house drackly minut.

Housewifery is a great revenue, Good. 1725: Bailey, tr. Erasmus' *Colloq.*, 144. 1869: Spurgeon, *John Ploughman*, ch xvi, A thrifty housewife is better than a great income. Cf. **Frugality.**

How doth your whither go you? = your wife. 1678: Ray, 346.

Howick Hole, No good ever came out of. 1846–59: *Denham Tracts*, ii 364 (F.L.S.).

Hulch and stulch, By = By hook or by crook. 1541: *Schoolhouse of Women*, By huch or by cruch. 1913: E. M. Wright, *Rustic Speech, etc.*, 125. 1917: Bridge, *Cheshire Proverbs*, 33.

Hull cheese, You have eaten some = You are drunk. 1678: Ray, 340. 1790: Grose, *Prov. Gloss.*, s.v. 'Yorkshire'. 1878: *Folk-Lore Record*, i 162.

Hull. *See also* **Dighton**; **Hell** (3); and **Oxford** (1).

Humble-bee in a cow-t—d thinks himself a king, An. 1659: Howell, 1. 1670: Ray, 14.

Humble hearts have humble desires. 1640: Herbert, *Jac. Prudentum.* 1854: J. W. Warter, *Last of Old Squires*, 53.

Humphrey Hambly's ducks, as is said to look larger than they be. 1888: Q.-Couch, *Troy Town*, ch viii.

Hundred and County (or **Shire**). There are two contradictory sayings; or rather, two ways of expressing the same idea, (*a*) *What is won in the hundred is lost in the shire* (or *county*). 1546: Heywood, *Proverbs*, Pt II ch ix, What ye wan in the hundred, ye lost in the sheere. 1605: Camden, *Remains*, 335 (1870), What some win in the hundred, they lose in the shire. 1625: Bacon, *Essays*: 'Of Empire', Taxes and imposts vpon them, doe seldome good to the Kings reuenew, for that he winnes in the Hundred, he leeseth in the Shire. 1682: Bunyan, *Holy War*, ch xv, [Lucifer names two agents] They are Mr Penny-wise-pound-foolish, and Mr Get-i'-the-hundred-and-lose-i'-th'-shire. (*b*) *What is won in the shire* (or *county*) *is lost in the hundred.* 1662: Fuller, *Worthies*, ii 538 (1840), As our English proverb saith, 'What is lost in the hundred will be found in the shire'. 1732: Fuller, 5522, What they lose in the Hundred they gain in the County. 1917: Bridge, *Cheshire Proverbs*, 151, What is got in the County is lost in the Hundred.

Hundred pounds of sorrow pays not one ounce of debt, An. Before 1704: T. Brown, *Works*, iii 247 (1760) [cited as 'the country proverb']. 1869: Spurgeon, *John Ploughman*, ch xii, A hundred years of regret Pay not a farthing of debt.

Hundred tailors, A, a hundred millers, and a hundred weavers make three hundred thieves. 1659: Howell, *Proverbs: Span.-Eng.*, 11. 1672: R. Codrington, *Proverbs*, 4. 1732: Fuller, 615. Cf. **Miller** (10).

Hunger and cold deliver a man up to his enemy. 1813: Ray, 126.

Hunger and ease. *See* Dog (7).

Hunger breaks through stone walls. 1546: Heywood, *Proverbs*, Pt I ch xii, Some saie, and I feele hunger perseth stone wall. *c.*1580: Spelman, *Dialogue*, 121 (Roxb.Cl), As the oulde saynge is, hunger breketh stone walles. 1605: Chapman, etc., *Eastw. Hoe*, V i 1651: Cartwright, *Ordinary*, II i, Hunger may break stone walls, it ne'er hurts men. 1759: Colman, *Rolliad*, can. i, Hunger, they say, thro' stony walls will break. 1821: W. Combe, *Syntax in Search of Wife*, can. xxxiv p. 53, Hunger, by you know whom, 'tis said, Will break through walls to get its bread.

Hunger droppeth out of his nose. Before 1529: Skelton, *Magnyfycence*, l. 2288, I gyue hym Crystys curse, With neuer a peny in his purse … Ye, for *requiem aeternam* groweth forth of his nose. 1546: Heywood, *Proverbs*, Pt I ch xi, Hunger droppeth euen out of bothe their noses. 1611: Cotgrave, s.v. 'Chiche-face', A … wretched fellow; one out of whose nose hunger drops. 1659: Ho well, *Letters*, ii 666 (Jacobs), She will in a short time make hunger to dropp out at your nose.

Hunger fetcheth the wolf out of the woods. 1567: Painter, *Pal. of Pleasure*, iii 216 (Jacobs), I well perceiue that hunger forceth the woulf oute of hir denne. 1611: Cotgrave, s.v. 'Bois', Hunger drives woolves out of the wood. 1750: Smollett, *Gil Blas*, iv 245, Hunger, thou knowest, brings the wolf out of the wood.

Hunger finds no fault with the cookery. 1732: Fuller, 2566. 1869: Spurgeon, *John Ploughman*, ch v with ['cook' for 'cookery'].

Hunger in frost that will not work in heat, They must. 1546: Heywood, *Proverbs*, Pt I ch xi. 1605: Camden, *Remains*, 333 (1870). 1670: Ray, 30. 1754: Berthelson, *Eng.-Danish Dict.*, s.v. 'Hunger'.

Hunger is not dainty. 1732: Fuller, 2567.

Hunger is sharper than thorn. *c.*1560; Becon, *Catechism, etc.*, 601 (P.S.), Ye know the common proverbs …'Hunger is sharper than thorn'. 1884: Cudworth. *Dialect Sketches*, 15 (W.), Hunger, they say, is a sharp thorn, an' begow it's true.

Hunger is the best sauce. [Optimum cibi condimentum fames, sitis potus. – Cicero, *De Finibus*, lib. 2. Cf. Horace, *Sat.*, II ii 38]. *c.*1375: Barbour, *Bruce*, iii 540, That soucht nan othir salso thartill Bot appetyt, that oft men takys (That sought for no other sauce thereto excePt appetite, such as often seizes men). 1542: Udall, tr. Erasmus' *Apoph.*, 2 (1877), Socrates said, the best sauce in the world for meates, is to bee houngrie. 1639: Massinger, *Unnat. Combat*, III i, Nor do you Find fault with the sauce, keen hunger being the best. 1709: O. Dykes, *Eng. Proverbs*, 11, Hunger is sawce for an emperor. 1827: Hone, *Table-Book*, 139, That 'a sharp stomach is the best sauce', is a saying as true as it is common.

Hunger makes dinners, pastime suppers. 1640: Herbert, *Jac. Prudentum*.

Hunger makes hard beans sweet. Before 1500: Hill, *Commonplace-Book*, 133 (E.E.T.S.), Hungre maketh harde bones softe. 1546: Heywood, *Proverbs*, Pt I ch x. 1670: Ray, 107, Hunger makes hard bones sweet beans. 1732: Fuller, 2570, Hunger makes raw beans relish well.

Hungry as a church-mouse. 1670: Ray, 205. 1901: F. E. Taylor, *Lancs Sayings*, 3.

Hungry as a dog. 1862: *Dialect of Leeds*, 405.

Hungry as a hawk. 1652: Taylor (Water-Poet), *Works*, 1st coll., *Christmas In and Out* (Spens.S.), I and my men were as hungry as hawks. 1681: W. Robertson, *Phraseol. Generalis*, 749. 1703: Ward, *Writings*, ii 105, Hungry as hawks, having food to delight 'em. 1883: R.L.S., *Treasure* I, ch vi, I made a hearty supper, for I was as hungry as a hawk.

Hungry as a hunter. 1800: Lamb, *Letters*, i 162 (Lucas), I came home … hungry as a hunter. 1834: Marryat, *P. Simple*, ch ii. 1864: Mrs H. Wood, *Trevlyn Hold*, ch xix, I am as hungry as a hunter. Get me something to eat.

Hungry as a June crow. 1886: C. Swainson, *Folk-Lore of Brit. Birds*, 87 (F.L.S.), About June and July, should there be a drought of long duration, rooks suffer terribly; hence the proverb 'As hungry as a June crow'.

Hungry as a kite. *c*.1555: in Wright, *Songs, etc.*, *Philip and Mary*, 17 (Roxb.Cl), When Lent cummys to the towene as hongré as a glede [kite]. 1855: Robinson, *Whitby Gloss.*, 71, 'As hungry as a glead', ravenous.

Hungry as a wolf. 1540: Palsgrave, *Acolastus*, sig. L1, I am more hungry than any wolfe is. 1611: Cotgrave, s.v. 'Allouvi', As hungry as a woolfe. 1858: Lytton, *What Will He Do?* I iii, I have the hunger of a wolf.

Hungry as the grave. 1880: Courtney, *W. Country Words*, 29 (E.D.S.).

Hungry bellies. *See* **Belly**.

Hungry dogs will eat dirty puddings. [Jejunus raro stomachus vulgaria temnit. – Horace, *Sat.*, II ii 38.] 1546: Heywood, *Proverbs*, Pt I ch v. 1553: *Respublica*, III vi, Suche hongrye doggs will slabbe vp sluttishe puddinges. 1600: Dekker, *Old Fortunatus*, II ii, A hungry dog eats dirty puddings. 1721: Bailey, *Eng. Dict.*, s.v. 'Hungry'. 1830: Colman, jr., in *Hum. Works*, 421 (Hotten). 1893: J. Salisbury, *S.E. Worcs. Gloss.*, 55 (E.D.S.), A 'ongry dog'll yut dirty puddin'. – *Proverb*. 1901: F. E. Taylor, *Lancs Sayings*, 7, A hungry dog's fain o' dirtv puddin'. Cf. **Scornful dogs**.

Hungry flies bite sore. 1546: Heywood, *Proverbs*, Pt II ch ix. 1670: Ray, 107. 1736: Bailey, *Dict.*, s.v.

Hungry, If thou be, I am angry, let us go fight. 1678: Ray, 65.

Hungry man is an angry man, A. *c*.1641: D. Fergusson, *Scottish Proverbs* (S.T.S.), no. 553, Hungry men ar angry. 1659: Howell, 13. 1670: Ray, 14. 1880: Spurgeon, *Ploughman's Pictures*, 52. 1911: Hackwood, *Good Cheer*, 345, A hungry man is an angry man, and an empty stomach has no conscience.

Hungry man smells meat afar off, A. 1732: Fuller, 224.

Hungry men think the cook lazy. Ibid., No. 2574.

Hunt's dog, that will neither go to church nor stay at home, Like. 1678: Ray, 291. 1708: *Brit. Apollo*, i No. 105, col. 3. 1785: Grose, *Class. Dict. Vulgar Tongue*, s.v. [a Shropshire story told]. 1883: Burne, *Shropsh. Folk-Lore*, 593. 1917: Bridge, *Cheshire Proverbs*, 90. 1920: in *N.&Q.*, 12th ser, vii 67 [the correspondent says he had heard the saying in Warwickshire within the last ten years]. Cf. **Wood's dog**.

Hunter's moon, The. 1710; *Brit. Apollo*, iii No. 70, p. 2, col. 1 (OED), The country people call this the Hunters-Moon. 1846: Denham, *Proverbs*, 58 (Percy S.), An October moon is called the 'hunter's moon'. 1855: Kingsley, *West. Ho!*, ch v, The broad, bright hunter's moon. 1873: in *N.&Q.*, 4th ser, xi 45, The Hunter's Moon in October, and the Harvest Moon in September, are not called so simply because hunting begins and harvest is being got in in these months.

Hunters that blow the horn, All are not. 1586: L. Evans, *Wtihals Dict. Revised*, sig. E6, Euery home blower is not a hunter. 1678: Ray, 158. 1869: Spurgeon, *John Ploughman*, ch i, All are not hunters that wear red coats, and all are not working men who call themselves so.

Huntingdon sturgeon, A. *See* quot. 1667: Pepys, *Diary*, 22 May, This day coming from Westminster … we saw at White Hall stairs a fisher-boat, with a sturgeon that he had newly catched in the River; which I saw, but it was but a little one; but big enough to prevent my mistake of that for a colt, if ever I become Mayor of Huntingdon. [Lord Braybrooke's note on this is: 'During a very high flood in the meadows between Huntingdon and Godmanchester, something was seen floating, which the Godmanchester people thought was a black pig, and the Huntingdon folk declared it was a *sturgeon;* when rescued from the waters, it proved to be a *young donkey*. This mistake led to the one party being styled "Godmanchester black pigs," and the other "Huntingdon sturgeons," terms not altogether forgotten at this day. Pepys's *colt* must be taken to be the *colt of an ass'.*] 1790: Grose, *Prov. Gloss.*, s.v. 'Hunts'.

Huntingdonshire. *See* quot. 1865: W. White, *East. England*, ii 95, Huntingdonshire … where, in the words of the proverb, 'they have churches for mile-stones'.

Hurstpierpoint. *See* **Wolstonbury**.

Hurts another hurts himself, He that. 1578; Florio, *First Fruites*, fo. 29. 1629: *Book of Meery Riddles*, Prov. 84.

Husband and **Husbands, 1. A husband must be deaf, and the wife blind, to have quietness**. 1666: Torriano, *Piazza Univ.*, 144. Cf. **Wife** (24).

2. A husband ofttimes makes the best physician. 1840: Barham, *Ing. Legends:* 'Lady Rohesia'.

3. Husbands are in heaven whose wives scold not. 1546: Heywood, *Proverbs*, Pt II ch vii. 1670: Ray, 14 [with 'chide' for 'scold']. 1732: Fuller, 2579 [as in 1670].

4. The calmest husbands make the stormiest wives. 1823: D'Israeli, *Cur. of Lit.*, 2nd ser, i 423 (1824), The husband was reminded of his lordly authority when he only looked into his trencher [*temp.* Elizabeth], one of its learned aphorisms having descended to us, – 'The calmest husbands make the stormyest wives'.

5. When the husband drinks to the wife, all would be well: When the wife drinks to the husband, all is well. 1659: Howell, 9 (7), When the good wife drinketh to the husband all is well in the house. 1670: Ray, 53. 1732: Fuller, 5593.

6. When the husband is fire and the wife tow, the devil easily sets all in a flame. 1732: Fuller, 5594.

See also **Bachelor** (1); **Good husband**; **Hold your tongue**; **Ill husband**; **Maid** (13); **Sorrow for a husband**; and **Wife** (3). (21), and (24).

Husbandman. *See* quot. 1569: Grafton, *Chron.*, ii 5 (1809), The olde auncient adage which sayeth, that the husbandman ought first to taste off the newe growen fruite.

Husk, By the, you may guess at the nut. 1732: Fuller, 1044.

Hustings (or **Hoistings**), **You are all for the.** 1662: Fuller, *Worthies*, ii 349 (1840). 1670: Ray, 244.

Hutton. *See* quot. 1869: Hazlitt, 210, Hutton an' Huyton, Ditton an' Hoo [Hool in Cheshire] are three [? four] of the merriest towns that ever a man rode through. Higson's *MSS. Coll.*, No. 37.

Huyton. *See* **Hutton**; and **Preston**.

Hypocrisy can find out a cloak for every rain. 1573: *New Custom*, II ii *c.*1580: Spelman, *Dialogue*, 56 (Roxb.Cl), [speaking of hypocrites] Such a cloke use they for the rayne.

Hypocrisy is a sort of homage that vice pays to virtue. 1732: Fuller, 2580.

I know what I do when I drink. 1639: Clarke, 85. 1670: Ray, 216.

I made of my friend my foe. *See* quot. 15th cent.: in *Reliq. Antiquae*, i 316 (1841), I made of my frend my foo, I will beware I do no more soo.

I stout. *See* **Stout**.

I was by (quoth Pedley) when my eye was put out. 1678: Ray, 242.

I'll make one (quoth Kirkham) when he danced in his clogs. Cheshire. 1670: Ray, 182. 1917: Bridge, *Cheshire Proverbs*, 78.

I'll tent [prevent] thee, quoth Wood, If I can't rule my daughter, I'll rule my good. Cheshire. 1670: Ray, 52. 1877: E. Leigh, *Cheshire Gloss.*, 208. 1917: Bridge, *Cheshire Proverbs*, 78.

I'm very wheamow [nimble], said the old woman, when she stePt into the milk-bowl. 1670: Ray, 217. 1877: E. Leigh, *Cheshire Gloss.*, 225 [with 'bittlen' for 'milk-bowl']. 1917: Bridge, *Cheshire Proverbs*, 79 [with 'middle of the bittlin' for 'milk-bowl'].

Ice. 1. If at Christmas ice hangs on the willow, clover may be cut at Easter. 1893: Inwards, *Weather Lore*, 39.

2. If the ice will bear a goose before Christmas, it will not bear a duck after. 1846: Denham, *Proverbs*, 62 (Percy S.). 1893: Inwards, *Weather Lore*, 9.

3. If the ice will bear a man before Christmas, it will not bear a goose (or **duck**, or **mouse**) **after.** *c.*1870: Smith, *Isle of Wight Words*, 62 (E.D.S.). 1881: *Folk-Lore Record*, iv 126 ['duck'. Notts]. 1893: Inwards, *Weather Lore*, 39 ['mouse']. 1902: *N. & Q.*, 9th ser, 506 ['goose'].

4. Trust not one night's ice. 1640: Herbert, *Jac. Prudentum*. 1875: A. B. Cheales, *Proverb. Folk-Lore*, 114.

See also **Martinmas** (2); **November** (3); and **St Matthias** (3).

Idle, *adj.* **1. An idle head is a box for the wind.** 1640: Herbert, *Jac. Prudentum*.

2. An idle person is the devil's cushion (or **playfellow**). 1630: T. Adams, *Works*, 197, The idle man is the deuils cushion, whereupon he sits and takes his ease. 1660: Howell, *Parly of Beasts*, 134, To avoid idlenes, which is the devills couch. 1732: Fuller, 620 ['playfellow']. 1859: Smiles, *Self-Help*, 273 (1869), A lazy man [is] the devil's bolster.

3. An idle youth a needy age. 1611: Cotgrave, s.v. 'Jeunesse'. 1651: Herbert, *Jac. Prudentum*, 2nd ed.

4. As idle as Dain's [Dean's] **dog as laid 't deaun t' bark.** 1917: Bridge, *Cheshire Proverbs*, 17. Cf. **Lazy as Ludlam's dog.**

5. Be not idle and you shall not be longing. 1640: Herbert, *Jac. Prudentum.*

6. He is idle that might be better employed. 1732: Fuller, 1919.

7. Idle brains are the devil's workshop. 1602: W. Perkins, *Works* (1603), 906, The idle bodie and the idle braine is the shoppe of the devill. 1678: Ray, 161, An idle brain is the devils shop. 1732: Fuller, 3053 ['workhouses']. 1875: A. B. Cheales, *Proverb. Folk-Lore*, 110. 1901: F. E. Taylor, *Lancs Sayings*, 7, An idle mon's yed's the divvle's smithy.

8. Idle folks have the least leisure. 1869: Spurgeon, *John Ploughman*, ch i.

9. Idle folks lack no excuses. 1639: Clarke, 234. 1670: Ray, 109.

10. Idle folks take tiie most pains. 1678: Ray, 161, Idle folks have the most labour. 1732: Fuller, 3056. 1831: Hone, *Year-Book*, 1416. Cf. **Lazy folks.**

11. Idle men are dead all their life long. 1732: Fuller, 3055.

See also **Devil** (22) and (84).

Idle, *subs. You'll soon learn to shape Idle a coat.* 1602: Carew, *Surv. of Cornwall*, fo. 56 (1769), To reproue one of lazines, they will say, Doest thou make Idle a coate? 1678: Ray, 254.

Idleness is the greatest prodigality in the world. 1650: Taylor, *Holy Living*, ch i § 1. 1732: Fuller, 3060.

Idleness is the key of beggary (or **mother of poverty**). 1616: *Rich Cabinet*, fo. 73, Idlenesse is the mother of pouerty. 1670: Ray, 14, Idleness is the key of beggery. 1754: Berthelson, *Eng.-Danish Dict.*, s.v. [as in 1670]. 1869: Spurgeon, *John Ploughman*, ch i [as in 1670].

Idleness is the parent of all vice. *c.*1440: Lydgate, *Fall of Princes*, bk ii l. 2249 (E.E.T.S.). Mooder off vices, callid idilnesse. *c.*1483: *Quatuor Sermones*, 35 (Roxb.Cl), Fle ydelnesse for it is ... the key of all vyces. *c.*1568: W. Wager, *Longer thou Livest*, sig. C2, Idlenes the parent of all vice. 1630: Brathwait, *Eng. Gent., etc.*, 61 (1641), Idlenesse ... being the mother of all vices. 1851: Borrow, *Lavengro*, i

189, It has been said that idleness is the parent of mischief.

Idleness is the root of all evil. *c.*1390: Chaucer, *Second Nun's Prologue*, l. 158, The ministre and the nprice unto vices, which that men clepe in Englissh ydlenesse. 1422: J. Yonge, in *Secreta Secretorum*, 158, Idylnysse is the rote of vicis. 1538: T. Becon, *Governance of Virtue*, B8v, Idleness ... is the well-spring and root of all vice. 1566: Becon, in *Early Works*, 444 (P.S.), Idleness, which is the well-spring and root of all vice. 1598: *Servingmans Comfort*, in *Inedited Tracts*, 158 (Hazlitt), Idlenesse is the roote of all mischiefe. 1760: Foote, *Minor*, I. 1850: Dickens, *Copperfield*, ch x

Idleness makes the wit rust (or **turns the edge of wit**). 1600: Bodenham, *Belvedere*, 131 (Spens.S.), Idlenes is the canker of the mind. 1650: Taylor, *Holy Living*, I i 14, Idleness is the rust of time. 1670: Ray, 14, Idleness turns the edge of wit. 1732: Fuller, 3061, Idleness makes the wit rust.

Idleness, Of, comes no goodness. 1611: Cotgrave, s.v. 'Gueule'. 1678: Ray, 161. 1732: Fuller, 3698, Of idleness never comes any good.

If a job (*or* **thing**) **is worth doing, it is worth doing well.** *See* Worth (2).

If anything can go wrong it will. Generally assumed to have been coined by George Nichols, project manager for the American aircraft firm of Northrop, on the basis of a remark made by Captain E. Murphy of the Wright Field-Aircraft Laboratory, and hence often known as "Murphy's Law". 1955: *Aviation Mechanics Bulletin*, May–June 11, Murphy's Law: if an aircraft part can be installed incorrectly, someone will install it that way. 1956: *Scientific American*, Apr., 166, Dr Schaefer's observation confirms this department's sad experience that editors as well as laboratory workers are subject to Murphy's Laws, to wit: 1. If something can go wrong it will.

If it ain't broke, don't fix it. An American saying, popularised especially by Bert Lance, President Jimmy Carter's director of the Office of Management and Budget. The traditional British equivalent is *Let well alone* (q.v.). 1977: *Nation's Business*, May 27, Bert Lance believes he can save Uncle Sam billions if he can get the government to adoPt a simple motto: 'If it ain't broke, don't fix it'.

If it be not true here's my elbow. 1659: Howell, 17.

If my aunt had been a man, she'd have been my uncle. 1813: Ray, 202.

If you want clear water, you must go to the head of the well. S. Cornwall, 19th cent. (Mr C. Lee).

If thou won't have me old Shenton will. 1917: Bridge, *Cheshire Proverbs*, 77, [Two men courting a farm-house servant came the same evening] She put one in the brick oven, and being somewhat piqued at the slowness of the other, she said, 'If thou won't have me old Shenton will.' 'Will he?' said Shenton from the oven; and ever since then it has been a saying in that neighbourhood.

If you can't beat them, join them. *See* **Beat** (4).

If you can't be good, be careful. *See* **Good**.

If you can't stand (*or* **don't like) the heat, get out of the kitchen**. A saying associated with President Harry S. Truman, and given by him as a reason for refusing the nomination in 1952, but attributed by him to one of his aides (*see* quot. 1952) and also said to be traditional in Missouri. 1952: *Time*, 28 Apr., 19, President [Truman] gave a ... down-to-earth reason for his retirement. quoting a favorite expression of his military jester, Major General Harry Vaughan: 'If you don't like the heat, get out of the kitchen'.

If you wish a thing done, go; if not, send. 1566: Painter, *Pal. of Pleasure*, i 87 (Jacobs), Always fixe fast in breast, in promPt and ready wise: This prouerbe olde and true, a sentence of the wise: The thing do not expect, by frends for to atchieue: Which thou thyselfe canst doe, thy selfe for to relieue. 1692: L'Estrange, *Aesop*, 53 (3rd ed.), He that would be sure to have his business well done, must either do it himself, or see the doing of it. 1736: Franklin, *Way to Wealth*, in *Works*, i 445 (Bigelow), If you would have your business done, go; if not, send. 1842: Barham, *Ing. Legends*, 2nd ser: 'Ingoldsby Penance'. 1859: Smiles, *Self-Help*, 272 (1869), 'If you want your business done', says the proverb, 'go and do it; if you don't want it done, send some one else'.

Ifs and Ands. *c*.1513: More, *Works*, p. 54, col. 2 (1557), What quod the protectour thou seruest me I wene with iffes and with andes. 1589: Nashe, *Introd.* to Greene's *Menaphon*, 10

(Arber), Sufficeth them to bodge vp a blanke verse with ifs and ands. *c*.1624: Davenport, *King John*, I ii, Well, well, with *ifs* and *ands* Mad men leave rocks and leap into the sands. 1681: W. Robertson, *Phraseol. Generalis*, 90, Without Ifs and Ands; plane, absolute. 1748: Richardson, *Clarissa*, v 237 (1785), Then he came with his If's and And's. 1828: Carr, *Craven Dialect*, i 241, 'Let's hev naan o' yower ifs an' ans', let us have no hesitation, be decisive. 1850: C. Kingsley, *Alton Locke*, I x, 'If a poor man's prayer can bring God's curse down'. ... 'If ifs and ans were pots and pans.' 1889: Peacock, *Manley, etc., Gloss.*, 286 (E.D.S.), If ifs and ands was pots and pans There'd be noä wark for th' tinkers. 1924: Sir R. Horne, in *Times*, 30 May, p. 9, col. 4, If he might vary an old saw he would say, 'If "ifs and ands" could create employment, then there would be little use for the Minister of Labour to tinker at it'.

Ignorance is a voluntary misfortune. 1669: *Politeuphuia*, 63.

Ignorance is bliss, 'tis folly to be wise, Where. 1742: T. Gray, *Ode on a Distant prospect of Eton College*, Thought would destroy their paradise. No more; where ignorance is bliss, 'Tis folly to be wise. 1865: Surtees: *Facey Romford's Hounds*, lxxi, Of course, Facey knew nothing about Lucy, and, upon the principle that where ignorance is bliss 'twere folly to be wise, Soapey was not extra-inquisitive about her.

Ignorance is the mother of devotion. 1559: Bp. Jewell, *Works*, iii Pt ii, 1202 (P.S.), Ignorantia enim, inquit, mater est verae pietatis, quam ille appellavit devotionem. 1573: *New Custom*, I i 1593: G. Harvey, *Works*, ii 138 (Grosart), Ignorance ... was wont to be termed the moother of deuotion. 1621: Burton, *Melancholy*, III iv 1, 2, p. 678 (1836). 1668: Dryden, *Secret Love*, I ii, Your ignorance is the mother of your devotion to me. 1700: T. Brown, *Works*, iii 67–8 (1760).

Ignorance is the mother of impudence. 1666: Torriano, *Piazza Univ.*, 116, Ignorance the mother, of presumption and of errors. Before 1680: Butler, *Remains*, ii 213 (1759), Impudence is the bastard of ignorance. 1732: Fuller, 3067. 1869: Spurgeon, *John Ploughman*, ch ii, His ignorance is the mother of his impudence, and the nurse of his obstinacy.

Ignorance of the law is no excuse. *c*.1412, T. Hoccleve, *De Regimene Principum* (E.E.T.S.),

92, Excuse schal hym naght his ignorance. 1530: St German, *Dialogues in English*, ii xlvi, Ignorance of the law though it be invincible doth not excuse. 1616: T. Draxe, *Adages*, 100, The ignorance of the law excuseth no man. 1654: J. Selden, *Table-Talk* (1689), 30, Ignorance of the Law excuses no man; not that all men know the Law, but because 'tis an excuse every man will plead, and no man can tell how to confute him. **Ignorance**. *See also* **Knowledge**.

Ignorant hath an eagle's wings and an owl's eyes, The. 1640: Herbert, *Jac. Prudentum*.

Ilchester. *See* quots. 1670: Ray, 342, All Ilchester is gaol, say prisoners there. 1790: Grose, *Prov. Gloss.*, s.v. 'Somerset', All Ilchester is gaol.

Ill agreement is better than a good judgment, An. 1640: Herbert, *Jac. Prudentum*. 1666: Torriano, *Piazza Univ.*, 1, A sorry agreement is better than a good sute in law. Cf. **Better a lean peace**.

Ill air where we gain nothing, It is an. 1640: Herbert, *Jac. Prudentum*. 1670: Ray, 1. 1732: Fuller, 2895.

Ill bird lays an ill egg, An. 1586: Pettie, tr. Guazzo's *Civil Convers.*, fo. 127, An ill byrde layeth an ill egge. 1617: *Arraignment of Lewd, etc., Women*, 44. 1716: Ward, *Female Policy*, 93 [cited as 'the old proverb'].

Ill bird that fouls its own nest, It is an. *c.*1250: *Owl and Nightingale*, 99, Dahet habbe that ilkë best That fuleth his owë nest (A curse be upon that beast [creature, bird] that defiles his own nest). 1402: Hoccleve, *Minor Poems*, 80 (E.E.T.S.), An olde proverbe seyde ys in englyssh: men seyn 'that brid or foule ys dyshonest, what that he be and holden ful chirlyssh, that vseth to de-foule his oone neste'. 1509: Barclay, *Ship of Fools*, i 173 (1874), It is a lewde byrde that fyleth his owne nest. 1583: Greene, in *Works*, ii 31 (Grosart), It is a fowle bird defiles the own neast. 1685: *Mother Bunch's Closet, etc.*, 6 (Gomme, 1885), An ill bird befoules its own nest. 1817: Scott, *Rob Roy*, ch xxvi 1851: FitzGerald, *Euphranor*, 13 (1855), You ... must not, like a bad bird, foul your own nest.

Ill boy that goes like a top, no longer than 'tis whipt, He's an. 1732: Fuller, 2449.

Ill cause. *See* quot. 1855: Bohn, 399, He who hath an ill cause, let him sell it cheap.

Ill comes in by ells and goes out by inches. 1640: Herbert, *Jac. Prudentum*. 1666: Torriano, *Piazza Univ.*, 138, Evil cometh by cartloads, and goes away by ounces, cometh on horseback and goes away on foot.

Ill cook that can't lick his own fingers, He's an. *c.*1520: Stanbridge, *Vulgaria*, sig. C4, He is an euyll coke yt can not lycke his owne lyppes. 1592: Shakespeare, *Romeo*, IV. ii 1646: Quarles, *Works*, iii 222 (Grosart), He's but a silly cook that wists not how To lick his fingers. 1738: Swift, *Polite Convers.*, Dial. I. 1822: Scott, *Nigel*, ch vi, They say, a good cook knows how to lick his own fingers.

Ill doers are ill deemers. [Tuo ex ingenio mores alienos probas. – Plautus, *Truc.*, ii 47.] 1738: Swift, *Polite Convers.*, Dial. I, They say ill doers are ill deemers. 1828: Scott, *Fair Maid*, ch xvii.. Put me not to quote the old saw, that evil doers are evil dreaders. 1853: Trench, *Proverbs*, 115 (1905).

Ill done must be done twice, A work. 1659: Howell, *Proverbs: Brit.-Eng.*, 3.

Ill egging makes ill begging. 1605: Camden, *Remains*, 325 (1870). 1670: Ray,84, Illegging makes ill begging. Evil persons by enticing and flattery, draw on others to be as bad as themselves.

Ill fortune, He that hath no, is troubled with good. 1640: Herbert, *Jac. Prudentum*. 1670: Ray, 10 [with 'cloy'd' for 'troubled'].

Ill game that hath not one trump, It is an. 1740: North, *Lives of Norths*, i 357 (Bohn).

Ill gathering of stones where the sea is bottomless, 'Tis. 1659, Howell, 11.

Ill gotten goods (*a*) **thrive not;** (*b*) **thrive not to the third heir,** (*a*) 1519: Horman, *Vulgaria*, fo. 77, Euyll goten ryches wyll neuer proue longe. 1591: Spenser, *Moth. Hubb. Tale*, l. 1149, Ill might it prosper, that ill gotten was. *c.*1630: in *Roxb. Ballads*, i 184 (Hindley), Ill gotten goods never doe thrive. 1732: Fuller, 3070, Ill gotten goods seldom prosper. 1826: Lamb, *Pop. Fallacies*, II. 1842: Barham, *Ing. Legends*, 2nd ser: 'Babes in Wood'. (*b*) 1303: Brunne, *Handl. Synne*, l. 9436, Here mayst thou se, euyl-wunne thyng Wyth eyre shal neuer make gode endyng. Ibid., l. 9479, For thys men se, and sey alday, 'The threde eyre selleth alle away'. *c.*1430: in *Twenty-six Poems*, 149 (E.E.T.S.), Men seyen 'good geten vntrewly, The iijde eyre browke hit ne may'. 1493: *Dives et*

Pauper, It is a common prouerbe … Of euyll gotten goods the thyrde heyre vnneth hath ioy. 1593: Nashe, in *Works*, iv 146 (Grosart), Ill gotten goods neuer touche the third heyre. 1619: *Helpe to Discourse*, 70 (1640), Of piles of wealth, rais'd by unjust extortion, The third heir seldom doth injoy his portion. 1708: tr. Aleman's *Guzman*, i 405, It being next to impossible that ill-got wealth should descend to the third heir. 1875: A. B. Cheales, *Proverb. Folk-Lore*, 101, Ill gotten gear Wilna enrich the third heir.

Ill gotten ill spent. [Male partum male disperit. – Plautus, *Poen.*, IV ii 22.] 1539: Taverner, *Proverbs*, fo. 24, Euyll gotten good go euyll away. 1564: Bullein, *Dialogue*, 72 (E.E.T.S.), For euill gotten goodes are euill spent, saied our curate vpon Sondaie. 1603: Breton, in *Works*, ii i 11 (Grosart). 1680: L'Estrange, *Select Colloq. of Erasmus*, 55, It is but reasonable that what's *Ill got* should be *Worse spent*. 1763: Murphy, *Citizen*, I ii, The moment young master comes to possession, 'Ill got, ill gone', I warrant me.

Ill guest that never drinks to his host, It's an. 1678: Ray, 86.

Ill healing of an old sore, It is. 1546: Heywood, *Proverbs*, Pt II ch viii. 1659: Howell, 4.

Ill husband. 1. He is an ill husband that is not missed. 1633: Draxe, 2.

2. She that has an ill husband shews it in her dress. 1732: Fuller, 4139

Ill language, There were no, if it were not ill taken. 1640: Herbert, *Jac. Prudentum*. 1699: Farquhar, *Love and a Bottle*, IV ii, For as nothing's ill said, but what's ill taken. 1732: Fuller, 4945.

Ill look among lambs, He has an. Ibid., No. 1861.

Ill luck. 1. Ill luck is good for something. 1605: Camden, *Remains*, 326 (1870). 1732: Fuller, 3074.

2. Ill luck is worse than found money. 1670: Ray, 110.

3. What's worse than ill luck? 1639: Clarke, 166. 1641: *Roxb. Ballads*, vii 613 (B.S.), The proverbe sayes, 'What's worse than ill-luck?' 1685: Meriton, *Yorkshire Ale*, 47. 1736: Bailey, *Dict.*, s.v. 'Worse'.

4. When ill luck falls asleep, let nobody wake her. 1659: Howell, *Proverbs: Span.-Eng.*, 1, When ill fortune lies asleep, let none awake her. 1869: Hazlitt, 458.

Ill man lie in thy straw, Let an, and he looks to be thy heir. 1640: Herbert, *Jac. Prudentum*.

Ill marriage is a spring of ill fortune, An. 1633: Draxe, 229.

Ill master makes an ill servant, An. 1666: Torriano, *Piazza Univ.*, 258.

Ill master makes bad scholars, An. 1639: Clarke, 238.

Ill name is half hanged, He that hath an. 1546: Heywood, *Proverbs*, Pt II ch vi. 1560: T. Wilson, *Rhetorique*, 186 (1909). 1613: T. Heywood, *Silver Age*, II, I am halfe hang'd already, for my good name is lost. 1732: Fuller, 2133. 1822: Peacock, *Maid Marian*, ch xviii, Your hero makes laws to get rid of your thief, and gives him an ill name that he may hang him. Cf. **Dog** (43).

Ill natures never want a tutor. 1732: Fuller, 3076.

Ill natures, the more you ask them, the more they stick. 1640: Herbert, *Jac. Prudentum*.

Ill neighbour. *See* **Neighbour** (2) and (3).

Ill news are commonly true. 1611: Davies (of Hereford), *Sc. of Folly*, 42, in *Works*, ii (Grosart). 1633: Draxe, 139.

Ill news flies apace. 1574: E. Hellowes, *Guevara's Epistles*, 91, Euill newes neuer commeth to late. 1629: Massinger, *Picture*, II i, Ill news, madam, Are swallow-wing'd, but what's good walks on crutches. 1694: *Terence made English*, 46, Bad news always fly faster than good. 1792: Holcroft, *Road to Ruin*, II i, Ill news travels fast. 1850: Dickens, *Chuzzlewit*, ch xxxi, There's a true saying that nothing travels so fast as ill news. 1922: Weyman, *Ovington's Bank*, ch xxxviii, Ill news has many feet. Rides apace and needs no spurs.

Ill paymaster never wants excuse, An. 1732: Fuller, 627.

Ill pipe that wants his upper lip, He can. 1546: Heywood, *Proverbs*, Pt II ch ix [with 'lacketh' for 'wants']. 1670: Ray, 131. 1732: Fuller, 6374. 1819: Scott, *Ivanhoe*, ch xxxii, I had mumbled but a lame mass an thou hadst broken my jaw, for the piper plays ill that wants the nether chops.

Ill playing with short daggers, It be. 1546: Heywood, *Proverbs*, Pt I ch xii.

Ill plea should be well pleaded, An. 1855: Bohn, 312.

Ill putting a naked sword in a madman's hand, It is. 1546: Heywood, *Proverbs*, Pt II ch viii. 1670: Ray, 147. 1672: Walker, *Paroem.*, 48.

1736: Bailey, *Dict.*, s.v. 'Sword', Don't put a sword into a madman's hands.

Ill run that cannot go, He may. 1468: *Coventry Mys.*, 97 (SH.S.), He may evyl go that is ner lame; In sothe I com as fast as I may. 1546: Heywood, *Proverbs*, Pt II ch ix. 1670: Ray, 138.

Ill sack that will abide no clouting, It is an. 1546: Heywood, *Proverbs*, Pt II ch iv. 1670: Ray, 23. 1732: Fuller, 2843.

Ill seed ill weed. *c.*1440: Lydgate, *Fall of Princes*, bk v l. 116 (E.E.T.S.), Of froward seed may growe no good corn. 1611: Cotgrave, s.v. 'Moisson'.

Ill servant will never be a good master, An. 1683: Meriton, *Yorkshire Ale*, 83–7 (1697). 1887: *Brighouse News*, 23 July (W.).

Ill shaving against the wool, It's. 1670: Ray, 141.

Ill song who has ne'er a tongue, He makes an. 1855: Bohn, 379.

Ill sowers make ill harvest. 1732: Fuller, 3078.

Ill spun web. *See* quots. *c.*1300: *Prov. of Hending*, st. 35 (Berlin, 1878), Euer out cometh euel sponne web. *c.*1410: *Towneley Plays*, 21 (E.E.T.S.), Ill spon weft ay comes foule out. *c.*1460: *Wyse Man taught hys Sone*, l. 7 (E.E.T.S.), For zrne that is euylle spone Euylle it comes out at the laste. 1670: Ray, 154, An ill-spun weft [web] will out either now or eft … This is a Yorkshire proverb.

Ill stake standeth longest, An. 1659: Howell, 3. 1670: Ray, 14.

Ill stake that can't stand one year in a hedge, It's an. 1546: Heywood, *Proverbs*, Pt II ch iv. 1670: Ray, 145. 1732: Fuller, 2845.

Ill talking between a full man and a fasting, It is. 1823: Scott, *Q. Durward*, ch x 1828: Scott, *Fair Maid*, ch xx 1875: A. B. Cheales, *Proverb. Folk-Lore*, 107.

Ill to himself will be good to nobody, He that's. 1732: Fuller, 2284.

Ill to trust who will trust nobody, He is. 1644: Taylor (Water-Poet), *Cropeare Curried*, 19, in *Works*, 2nd coll. (Spens.S.).

Ill turn. 1. An ill turn is soon done. 1732: Fuller, 631.

2. He that does you a very ill turn, will never forgive you. 1710: S. Palmer, *Moral Essays on Proverbs*, 263 [with 'an injury' for 'a very ill turn']. 1732: Fuller, 2085.

Ill vessels seldom miscarry. 1640: Herbert, *Jac. Prudentutm*.

Ill ware is never cheap. Ibid. 1659: Howell, *Proverbs: Fr.-Eng.*, 8, Bad ware is never too cheap.

Ill weather comes unsent for. 1583: Melbancke, *Philotinus*, sig. F3, Though I come like ill weather, vnsent for. 1846: Denham, *Proverbs*, 3 (Percy S.). Ill weather and sorrow come unsent for. Cf. **Sorrow**.

Ill weather is seen soon enough when it comes. Ibid., 1.

Ill weeds grow apace, *c.*1490: *Harl. MS.*, quoted in Hulme, *Proverb Lore*, 12, Euyl weed ys sone y-growe. 1546: Heywood, *Proverbs*, Pt I ch x, Ill weede growth fast. 1594: Shakespeare, *Rich. III*, II iv, Small herbs have grace, great weeds do grow apace. 1660: Tatham, *The Rump*, I. 1733: Fielding, *Miser*, III v. *c.*1750: Foote, *Knights*, I. 1846: Denham, *Proverbs*, 1 (Percy S.).

Ill will never speaks well. 1566: L. Wager, *Mary Magdalene*, Prol., For euill will neuer said well, they do say. 1599: Shakespeare, *Henry V*, III vii. 1660: Fuller, *Mixt Contempl.*, 300 (1830). 1732: Fuller, 3081.

Ill wind that blows nobody good, It's an. *c.*1540: J. Heywood, *Song against Idleness*. 1580: Tusser, *Husbandrie*, 29 (E.D.S.). *c.*1640: *Capt. Underwit*, II, in Bullen, *Old Plays*, ii 347. 1692: Congreve, *Old Bachelor*, II i. 1769: Smollett, *Adv. of Atom*, 113 (Cooke, 1795). 1837: Dickens, *Pickwick*, ch xxxii. 1917: Bridge, *Cheshire Proverbs*, 81, It's an ill wind that blows no-one any good, but it's well-a-day to them as lost it.

Ill words are bellows to a slackening fire. 1732: Fuller, 3082.

Ill workman quarrels with his tools, An. 1611: Cotgrave, s.v. 'Outil', A bungler cannot find (or fit himselfe with) good tooles. 1696: D'Urfey, *Quixote*, Pt III Act I sc i, 'Tis an ill workman that quarrels with his own tools. 1738: Swift, *Polite Convers.*, Dial. II, They say an ill workman never had good tools. 1818: Byron, *Don Juan*, can. i st. 201, Good workmen never quarrel with their tools. 1859: Smiles, *Self-Help*, 124 (1869), It is proverbial that the bad workman never yet had a good tool.

Ill wound is cured, not an ill name, An. 1640: Herbert, *Jac. Prudentum*.

Ill youth. *See also* **Untoward**.

Image of rye-dough. *See* quot. 1687: Aubrey, *Gentilisme, etc.*, 107 (F.L.S.), We have a saying, She lookes (*or* He stands) like an image of rye-dough. Mdm. In the old time the little images that did adorn the altars were made of rye-dough.

Imitation is the sincerest form of flattery. 1820: Colton, *Lacon*, Pt I No. 217 [omitting 'form']. 1892: B. Pain, *Playthings and Parodies*, § i [title], The Sincerest Form of Flattery.

Impressions soon fade, Slight. *c*.1374: Chaucer, *Troylus*, bk ii l. 1238, For-why men seyth, 'impressiounes lighte Ful lightly been ay redy to the flighte'.

Impudence to show himself a fool, He hath. 1732: Fuller, 1888.

Impudence. *See also* **Ignorance**.

In a quandary. 1577: *Misogonus*, III i, Thou makest me in a greater quandary. 1577: J. Grange, *Golden Aphroditis*, sig. D3, The captaine … standeth in a quandare, not knowing what to doe. 1694: *Terence made English*, 61, I'm in a strange quandary. 1742: Fielding, *Andrews*, bk ii ch iv, 'Poor woman!' says Mrs Slipslop, 'what a terrible quandary she must be in!' 1816: Scott, *Old Mortality*, ch viii. 1894: R.L.S., *St Ives*, ch xxvii, This put me in a quandary. It was a degree of risk I was scarce prepared for.

In dock out nettle, or In nettle dock out = unstable, fickle. *c*.1374: Chaucer, *Troylus*, bk iv l. 461, But canstow pleyen raket, to and fro, Netle in, dokke out, now this, now that, Pandare? 1546: Heywood, *Proverbs*, Pt II ch i, Waueryng as the wynde, in docke out nettle. 1586: L. Evans, *Withals Dict. Revised*, sig. E2, Oute nettle, in docke. 1655: Fuller, *Church Hist.*, bk ii § v (47–8), Thus was it often, 'in dock, out nettle', as they could strengthen their parties. 1732: Fuller, 3831, Out, nettle; in, dock. 1882: Jago, *Gloss, of Cornish Dialect*, 225. 1917: Bridge, *Cheshire Proverbs*, 80.

In for a penny. *See* **Penny** (13).

In the name of the Lord begins all mischief. 1703: Ward, *Writings*, ii 193 [cited as an 'old saying']. Cf. the reverse, s.v. **God's name**.

In the nick; now usually **In the nick of time.** 1577: *Misogonus*, II iv, That came ith nicke. 1577: Stanihurst, *Descrip, of Ireland*, fo. 1, He was so crost in the nycke of thys determination. 1603: Chamberlain, *Letters*, 173 (Camden S.), Mr Gent comming in the nicke. *c*.1620: *Barnavelt*, V iii, in Bullen, *Old Plays*, ii 307, The Prince strikes iust i' th' nick. 1740: North, *Examen*, 255, Why not before or after, but just in

the nick of one judge being absent. 1821: Scott, *Pirate*, ch xi, The fortunate arrival of Mordaunt, in the very nick of time. 1866: G. Eliot, *Felix Holt*, ch vii, Our lucky youngster is come in the nick of time.

In time comes he whom God sends. 1640: Herbert, *Jac. Prudentum*. 1670: Ray, 51 [with 'she' for 'he']. 1732: Fuller, 2831.

Ince, Go to = Go to Jericho. 1917: Bridge, *Cheshire Proverbs*, 63.

Inch. 1. An inch in a miss is as good as an ell. 1605: Camden, *Remains*, 318 (1870). 1670: Ray, 109. 1732: Fuller, 635, An inch in missing is as bad as an ell. Cf. **A miss is as good as a mile**, s.v. **'Miss'** – a less intelligible saying.

2. An inch in a man's nose is much. 1732: Fuller, 634.

3. An inch in an hour is a foot a day. 1678: Ray, 74. 1732: Fuller, 633.

4. Give him an inch and he'll take an ell (or **mile**). 1546: Heywood, *Proverbs*, Pt II ch ix, Whan I gaue you an ynche ye tooke an ell. 1599: Porter, *Two Angry Women*, in Hazlitt, *Old Plays*, vii 357. 1630: Taylor (Water-Poet), *Works*, 2nd pagin., 168, Giue a knaue an inch, hee'l take an ell. 1660: Tatham, *The Rump*. IV 1720: C. Shadwell, *Sham Prince*, Epil., If they encourage him, he thinks if's well, For, give him but an inch, he'll take an ell. 1822: Scott, *Nigel*, ch xxvii. 1865: Dickens, *Mutual Friend*, bk iii ch xiv, Give him an inch, and he'll take an ell. Let him alone this time, and what'll he do with our property next?

5. To see an inch before one's nose. 1683: Meriton, *Yorkshire Ale*, 83–7 (1697), He sees an inch before his nose. 1853: Planché, *Extravag.*, iv 272 (1879), The stupid painters fancied, I suppose, That I might see an inch beyond my nose.

See also **Break** (8).

Inconvenience. *See* **Every commodity**.

Indentures. *See* **Make** (18).

Industry is fortune's right hand and frugality her left. [*c*.1300: *Havelok*, 1. 1338, p. 49 (Skeat), Lith and selthe felawes are (Helpfulness and success companions are).] 1670: Ray, 14. 1732: Fuller, 3092.

Ingleborough. *See* **Pendle**.

Ingratitude drieth up wells, and the time bridges fells. 1623: Wodroephe, *Spared Houres*, 490.

Ingratitude is the daughter of pride. 1620: Shelton, *Quixote*, Pt II ch li. 1732: Fuller, 3094.

Ingratitude is worse than witchcraft. 1846–59: *Denham Tracts*, ii 83 (F.L.S.).

Ink in his pen. *See* quots. 1540: Palsgrave, *Acolastus*, sig. H3, Is there no more of thynge and is there noo more ynke lefte in thy penne, or nothynge yet left the? *Pant*. Nothynge at all. 1678: Ray, 254, He hath no ink in's pen, i.e. no money in his purse, or no wit in his head.

Ink. *See also* **Milk** (3).

Inkle-weavers. *See* **Thick as**.

Inn diversely, but end alike, We. 1639: Clarke, 13.

Inner Temple. *See* **Gray's Inn**.

Innocence is no protection. 1732: Fuller, 3100.

Innocence itself sometimes hath need of a mask. Ibid., No. 3101.

Innocent actions carry their warrant with them. 1578: Florio, *First Fruites*, fo. 31, Innocencie beareth her defence with her. 1732: Fuller, 3102.

Innocent as a devil of two years old, As. 1678: Ray, 286. 1738: Swift, *Polite Convers.*, Dial. I, No, to be sure, my lord! you are as innocent as a devil of two years old.

Innocent as a new-born babe (or as child unborn). 1609: Armin, *Maids of More-clacke*, sig. D3, I … am now as cleare as is the babe new borne. *c*.1679: in *Somers Tracts*, viii 131 (1811), Though they died as innocent as the child unborn. 1745: Swift, *Direct, to Servants*: 'Chambermaid', Offering to take her oath … that she was innocent as the child unborn. 1777: in *Garrick Corresp.*, ii 250 (1832), I am as ignorant of it as the child unborn. 1816: Scott, *Old Mortality*, ch x, If he were as innocent as the new-born infant, they would find some way of making him guilty. 1888: R.L.S., *Black Arrow*, Prol., I am as innocent … as the babe unchristened.

Insult to injury, To add. [Iniuriae qui addideris contumeliam. – Phaedrus, V iii 5.] 1748: E. Moore, *The Foundling*, V ii, This is adding insult to injuries. 1831: Peacock, *Crotchet Castle*, ch ii, To offer me a sandwich, when I am looking for a supper, is to add insult to injury. 1837: Dickens, *Pickwick*, ch xxxv.

Interest will not lie. 1709: R. Kingston, *Apoph. Curiosa*, 80, 'Tis a common proverb, that interest will not lie.

Inward sore puts out the physician's eye, An. 1587: Greene, in *Works*, iii 114 (Grosart).

Ipswich. *See* quot. 1790: Grose, *Prov. Gloss.*, s.v. 'Suffolk', Ipswich, a town without inhabitants, a river without water, streets without names, where asses wear boots.

Iron nails that scratcheth with a bear, He must have. 1678: Ray, 98 [omitting 'with']. 1732: Fuller, 1991. 1801: Wolcot, *Works*, v 124, A man must have, the proverb says, Good iron nails that scratches with a bear.

Iron to swim, He is teaching. 1813: Ray. 75.

Iron windfall, An. *See* quot. 1863: Wise, *New Forest*, ch xvi, Forest proverbs … such as … 'An iron windfall', for anything unfairly taken.

Irons in the fire, To have other (or many). Before 1549: Sir W. Paget, *Lett, to Somerset* (P.R.O. St Pap. Dom. Edw. VI, viii No. 4) (OED), Put no more so many yrons in the fyre at ones. 1576: Lambarde, *Peramb. of Kent*, 336 (1826), To the ende that the King should have at once many yrons (as the saying is) in the fire to attend upon. *c*.1590: G. Harvey, *Marginalia*, 94 (1913), On[e] iron in ye fyer at once. 1612: Chapman, *Widow's Tears*, II i, But you know, brother, I have other irons on th' anvil. 1639: Clarke, 78, He that hath many irons in the fire, some will coole. 1671: Dryden; *An Evening's Love*, IV i, Make haste, then; for I have more irons in the fire. *c*.1750: Foote, *Englishm. in Paris*, I, Leave her to my management, and consider we have more irons in the fire than one. 1849: Lytton, *Caxtons*, Pt VII ch ii, Uncle Jack … had other irons in the fire. 1883: R.L.S., *Letters*, ii 273 (Tusitala ed.), I have many irons in the fire.

Irwell. *See* **Yoke**.

It comes with a fear. 1598: Guilpin, *Skialetheia*, 24 (Grosart), Thou fear'st I am in loue with thee (my deare), I prethy feare not, *It comes with a feare*. 1748: Richardson, *Clarissa*, vi 205 (1785), For they seldom enquire, but when they fear – And the proverb, as my lord has it, says, *It comes with a fear*. That is, I suppose, what they fear generally happens, because there is generally occasion for the fear.

Italians are wise before the deed, the Germans in the deed, the French after the deed, The. 1640: Herbert, *Jac. Prudentum*. 1669: *New Help to Discourse*, 56, The Italian is wise before hand, The German wise in the action, And the French after it is done.

Itch and ease can no man please. 1546: Heywood, *Proverbs*, Pt II ch iv. *c*.1594: Bacon,

Promus, No. 486. 1670: Ray, 14. 1732: Fuller, 6237.

Itch is worse than a smart, An – but the first quotation says the reverse. 1530: Palsgrave, 594, It is better to ytche than to smarte. 1670: Ray, 14. 1732: Fuller, 3114, Itch is more intolerable than smart.

Itch, He that will not bear the, must endure the smart. 1546: Heywood, *Proverbs*, Pt I ch x, And he. Whom in itching no scratchyng will forbere, He must beare the smartyng that shall folow there. 1678: Ray, 162. 1732: Fuller, **2349.**

Iveston (Iceton). *See* **Tanfield.**

Ivinghoe. *See* **Tring.**

J

Jack-a-lent, A. *See* 1827 quot. *c.*1560: in Wright, *Songs, etc., Philip and Mary*, 191 (Roxb. Cl), Then Jacke-a-lent comes justlynge in, With the hedpeece of a herynge. 1575: Churchyard, *Chippes*, 50 (Collier), He was dressed up like Jack a Lent. 1626: Breton, in *Works*, ii *t* 12 (Grosart), It is now Easter, and Jacke of Lent is turned out of doores. 1646: Quarles, *Works*, iii 223 (Grosart), How like a Jack-a-lent He stands, for boys to spend their shrovetide throws. 1742: Fielding, *Andrews*, bk i ch ii, His office was to perform the part the ancients assigned to the god Priapus, which deity the modems call by the name of Jack o' Lent. 1821: Scott, *Pirate*, ch xxxvi. 1827: Hone, *Table-Book*, 135, Jack O' Lent. This was a puppet, formerly thrown at, in our own country, during Lent, like Shrove-cocks.

Jack-a-thrum. *See* **Wise** (5).

Jack-an-apes. 1. Can Jack an apes be merry when his clog is at his heels? 1605: Camden, *Remains*, 321 (1870). 1670: Ray, 71. 1732: Fuller, 1052.

2. There is more ado with one Jack an apes than all the bears. 1633: Draxe, 69. 1694: D'Urfey. *Quixote*, Pt II Act I sc ii. 1732: Fuller, 3464.

Jack and Jill. *See* **Bad Jack,**

Jack at a pinch. *See* quots. 1622: Mabbe, tr. Aleman's *Guzman*, i 130 (OED), When there was neede of my seruice … I was seldome or neuer wanting; I was Iacke at a pinch. 1690: *New Dict. Canting Crew*, sig. G2, Jack at a pinch, a poor hackney parson. 1754: Berthelson, *Eng.-Danish Dict.*, s.v. 'Jack'. 1847: Halliwell, *Dict.*, s.v., *Jack-at-a-pinch*, a sudden unexpected call to do anything. Also, a poor parson.

Jack but there's a Jill, Never a. 1611: Cotgrave, s.v. 'Demander', Like will to like; a Jacke lookes for a Gill. 1735: Pegge, *Kenticisms*, in E.D.S.,

No. 12, p. 51, According to the proverb, 'never a Jack but there's a Gill'. 1738: Swift, *Polite Convers.*, Dial. I. 1912: R. L. Gales, *Studies in Arcady*, 2nd ser, 241, 'For every Jack there's a Jill' was a thoroughly Elizabethan bit of English.

Jack Drum. *See* **Drum's entertainment**.

Jack has his Jill, Every, or **Jack shall have Jill**. Before 1529: Skelton, *Magnyfycence*, l. 290, What auayleth lord-shyp, yourselfe for to kyll With care and with thought howe Jacke shall haue Gyl? 1595: Shakespeare, *Mids. N. Dream*, III ii *ad fin.*, Jack shall have Jill; Nought shaft go ill. 1639: Clarke, 63, All shall be well and Jack shall have Jill. 1725: Defoe, *Everybody's Business*, in *Works*, ii 511(Bohn), For not a Jack among them but must have his Gill. 1823: Scott, *St Ronan's*, ch ii, Every Jack will find a Jill, gang the world as it may. 1886: Bicker-dyke, *Curios. of Ale and Beer*, 168, As every Jack will have his Jill, so … 1911: T. Edwardes, *Neighbourhood*, 10, After much water-spilling and cracking of crowns, Jack has got his Jill, and the wedding-bells are lin-lan-loning.

Jack in a box. 1592: Chettle, *Kind-Hart's Dreame*, 45 (Percy S.), As cunningly … as euer poore cuckoe coulde commend his Iacke in a boxe. *c.*1623: B.&F., *Love's Cure*, III i, My Lord Vitelli's love, and maintenance, Deserves no other Jack i' th' box but he. 1690: *New Dict. Canting Crew*, sig. G2, Jack in a box, a sharper or cheat.

Jack in office. 1670: Ray, 214, To be Jack in an office. 1709: O. Dykes, *Eng. Proverbs*, 117, How uppish and sawcy soever such a Jack-in-an-Office may be … 1732: Fuller, 3050, Jack in an office is a great man. 1785–95: Wolcot, *Lousiad*, can. iv, Some folks are Jacks-in-office, fond of power. 1857: Dickens, *Dorrit*, bk i ch ii, A type of Jack-in-office insolence and absurdity … a beadle.

Jack is as good as his master. As in many of these proverbs, *Jack* here is a generic term for a servant, ordinary sailor, or ordinary man. 1706: J. Stevens, *Spanish and English Dictionary*, s.v. Pedro, Peter is as good as his Master. Like Master, like Man. 1868: Reade and Boucicault, *Foul Play*, II xx, Is it the general opinion of the seamen before the mast? Come, tell us, Jack's as good as his master in these matters.

Jack of all trades. 1618: Minshull, *Essayes, etc.*, 50 (1821), Some broken citizen, who hath plaid Jack-of-all-trades. 1639: Mayne, *City Match*, II v, Why, you mongrel, You John-of-all-trades. 1690: Dryden, *Amphitryon*, I i, Yet I am still in my vocation; for you know I am a jack of all trades. 1732: Fuller, A jack of all trades is of no trade. Hence the contemporary expression *A jack of all trades but master of none*. 1776: Colman, *Spleen*, I, The town Jack of all trades, a mere Jack o' lanthern! half bookseller, half apothecary! 1836: Dickens, *Sketches by Boz:* 'Parish', ch ii, He is a bit of a Jack of all trades, or to use his own words, 'a regular Robinson Crusoe'. 1923: Lucas, *Advisory Ben*, 66, You might have chosen something better to do than to be … a Jack-of-all-trades at the command of anyone with the money to pay your fee.

Jack of both sides. 1557: Grindal, *Lett, to Foxe*, 28 Dec, 233 (P.S.), Nam qui in tota vita praeposterissimus (ut ita dicam) fuit, omnium rerum humanarum et divinarum inversor, consentaneum est ut in scribendo etiam praeposterum sese ostentet, et, ut vulgo dici solet Joannem ad oppositum. 1609: Dekker, in *Works*, iv 158 (Grosart), Who plaid ye iackes on both sides, and were indeede Neuters. 1671: *Westm. Drollery*, 89 (Ebsworth), She'l play Jack a both sides in war, And cares not a pin for her foes. 1729: Defoe, *Compl. Gent.*, Pt I ch i p., 30 (1890), How often have those men of honour … play'd Jack a both sides, to-day for and to-morrow against … as the money could be got or the party was strongest. 1869: Spurgeon, *John Ploughman*, ch xviii, They try to be Jack-o'-both-sides, and deserve to be kicked like a football by both parties.

Jack out of office. 1546: Heywood, *Proverbs*, Pt II ch iii, And Jack out of office she maie bid me walke. *c.*1591: Shakespeare, 1 *Henry VI*, I i. 1598: *Servingmans Comfort*, in *Inedited Tracts*, 166 (Hazlitt), In good credite with his maister at

noone, and Jacke out of office before night. 1735: Pegge, *Kenticisms*, in E.D.S., No. 12, p. 51.

Jack roast beef. 1855: Bohn, 436.

Jack Robinson, Before one can say. 1778: Burney, *Evelina*, Lett, lxxxii, 'Will you?' returned he; 'why, then, 'fore George, I'd do it as soon as say Jack Robinson.' 1812: Miss Edgeworth, *Absentee*, ch ii, I'd get her off before you could say Jack Robinson. 1843: Dickens, *Carol*, Stave 2, Let's have the shutters up … before a man can say Jack Robinson. 1872: Hardy, *Greenwood Tree*, Pt III ch iii, You've got him before you can say … Jack Robinson! 1911: T. Edwardes, *Neighbourhood*, 277, Afore I could s–s–say Jack Robinson.

Jack Sprat could eat no fat. *See* quots. The single appearance – in 1659 – of Jack as an ecclesiastical dignitary is very surprising. 1639: Clarke, 17, Jack will eat no fat, and Jill doth love no leane. Yet betwixt them both, they lick the dishes cleane. 1659: Howell, 20, Archdeacon Pratt would eat no fatt, His wife would eat no lean; Twixt Archdeacon Pratt and Joan his wife, The meat was eat up clean. 1670: Ray, 211, Jack Sprat he loved no fat, and his wife she lov'd no lean: And yet betwixt them both, they lick't the platters clean. 1843: Halliwell, *Nursery Rhymes*, 34, Jack Sprat could eat no fat. His wife could eat no lean; And so, betwixt them both, you see, They lick'd the platter clean.

Jack Sprat would teach his grandame. 1639: Clarke, 4, Jack-Sprat teacheth his grandame. 1670: Ray, 108. 1754: Berthelson, *Eng.-Danish Dict.*, s.v. 'Jack'.

Jack will never make a gentleman. 1681: W. Robertson, *Phraseol. Generalis*, 659. 1721: Bailey, *Eng. Dict.*, s.v. 'Gentleman'.

Jack would be a gentleman. Before 1529: Skelton, *Works*, i 15 (Dyce), Lo, Jack wold be a jentylman! 1546: Heywood, *Proverbs*, Pt I ch xi, Iacke would be a gentleman, if he coulde speake frenche. 1599: Breton, in *Works*, ii C42 (Grosart), And nowe Jacke will bee gentleman, no longer a sheepheard. 1662: Fuller, *Worthies*, i 118 (1840), We ape the French chiefly in two particulars: First, in their language ('which if Jack could speak, he would be a gentleman'). 1732: Fuller, 3052 [as in 1546].

Jack would wipe his nose if he had one. 1659: Howell, 8. 1670: Ray, 108.

Jackasses never can sing well, because they

pitch their notes too high. Said of a foolish person. 1865: 'Lancs Proverbs', in *N. & Q.*, 3rd ser, viii 494. 1901: F. E. Taylor, *Lancs Sayings*, 8.

Jackdaw. *See* quot. 1886: Swainson, *Folk-Lore of Brit. Birds*, 81 (F.L.S.), At Norwich there is an old rhyme – 'When three daws are seen on St Peter's vane together, Then we're sure to have bad weather'. 1893: Inwards, *Weather Lore*, 137 [as in 1886].

Jackson's end. *See* quot. 1889: *Folk-Lore Journal*, vii 294, [Staffs sayings] Fly round by Jackson's end [= to make haste].

Jackson's hens, To fly up with = To become bankrupt. 1577: *Misogonus*, IV ii, Ye may fly vp toth roust with Iacksons hens. 1678: Ray, 86, I'll make him fly up with Jacksons hens; i.e. undo him. 1917: Bridge, *Cheshire Proverbs*, 132.

Jackson's pig. *See* **Borough Hill.**

Jacob Dawson's wife died, We live as. 1777: Nicolson and Burn, *Hist, and Antiq. Of Westmore. and Cumb.*, i 78, On the third pillar in the south ile of the church [of Kendal] is the following inscription: – Here lyes Frances late wife of Jacob Dawson Gent., who departed this life 19th June 1700, in the 25th year of her age: Who by a free and chearful resignation of herself, even *in the midst of this world's affluence*, has left us just grounds to hope she is now happy. – This epitaph we only take notice of, as it hath occasioned a display of the droll humour of the people, who upon any particular occasion of festivity have from hence framed a proverb, 'We live as Jacob Dawson's wife died'. 1918: A Durham correspondent, in *N. & Q.*, 12th ser, iv 214, I have frequently heard this proverb or saying.

Jade eats as much as a good horse, A. 1640: Herbert, *Jac. Prudentum.* 1854: J. W. Waiter, *Last of Old Squires*, 53.

Jailor's conscience and his fetters [are] made both of one metal, A. 1659: Howell, 18.

Jam tomorrow and jam yesterday, never jam today, It's always. 1871: 'L. Carroll, *Through the Looking-Glass*, v, 'The rule is, jam tomorrow and jam yesterday – but never jam to-day'. 'It *must* come sometimes to "jam to-day",' Alice observed. 'No, it can't,' said the Queen.

January. 1. A January haddock, A February bannock, And a March pint of ale [are better than those of any other month]. 1846: Denham, *Proverbs*, 25 (Percy S.).

2. A January spring is worth naething. Ibid., 25. 1913: E. M. Wright, *Rustic Speech, etc.*, 317.

3. A summerish January, a winterish spring. 1893: Inwards, *Weather Lore*, 10.

4. A warm January, a cold May. 1878: Dyer, *Eng. Folk-Lore*, 247. 1893: Inwards, *Weather Lore*, 11. Cf. No. 8.

5. A wet January, a wet spring. 1893: Ibid., 10.

6. As bare as January. 1609: Armin, *Maids of More-clacke*, sig. A1, I will not say as poore as Iob, but as bare as Ianuary.

7. If grain grows in January, there will be a year of great need. 1893: Inwards, *Weather Lore*, 10.

8. If Janiveer's calends be summerly gay, 'Twill be winterly weather till the calends of May. 1732: Fuller, 6483. 1879: Henderson, *Folk-Lore N. Counties*, 75. 1893: Inwards, *Weather Lore*, 10. Cf. No. 4.

9. If January calends fall on Thursday. *See* quot. 1493: *Dives and Pauper*, fo. 66 (1536), The kalendas of Januarie fell on the thursday, whan (as they saye) shulde fall plentie of all good and peace also.

10. If one knew how good it were To eat a hen in Janivere; Had he twenty in the flock, He'd leave but one to go with the cock. 1659: Howell, 21 [with slight variations in third and fourth lines]. 1670: Ray, 213. 1732: Fuller, 6389. 1846: Denham, *Proverbs*, 26 (Percy S.).

11. If the grass grow in Janiveer, It grows the worse for't all the year. 1670: Ray, 40. 1744: Claridge, in Mills, *Essay on Weather*, 100 (1773). 1830: Forby, *Vocab. E. Anglia*, 418, The grass that grows in Janiveer Grows no more all the year. 1893: Inwards, *Weather Lore*, 10 [as in 1744]. 1912: R. L. Gales, *Studies in Arcady*, 2nd ser, 101.

12. If the sun shine the 12th of January, there shall be store of wind that year. 1669: *New Help to Discourse*, 283.

13. If you see grass in January, Lock your grain in your granary. 1893: Inwards, *Weather Lore*, 10.

14. In January if the sun appear, March and April pay full dear. Ibid., 10.

15. Jack Frost in Janiveer, Nips the nose of the nascent year. 1878: Dyer, *Eng. Folk-Lore*, 247. 1893: Inwards, *Weather Lore*, 11.

16. Janiveer freeze the Pot by the fire. 1557: Tusser, *Husbandrie*, in *Brit. Bibliog.*, iii 20

(1812), As Janeuer fryse pot, bidth corne kepe hym lowe. 1670: Ray, 40. 1744: Claridge, in Mills, *Essay on Weather*, 100 (1773). 1879: Jackson, *Shropsh. Word-Book*, 224, Janniwerry-freeze-the-pot-by-the-fire, *sb.* the month of January.

17. January and May. c.1400: Lydgate, *Temple of Glas*, 7 (E.E.T.S.), For it ne sit not vnto fresshe May Forto be coupled to colde Januari. c.1580: Spelman, *Dialogue*, 94 (Roxb.Cl), When I loked apon her husbond with his white hedde and horye berde I judged Janiary and May to be copled together. 1604: *Wit of a Woman*, sc xi (Malone S.), Is not this a prettie world? Ianuary and May make a match? 1656: *Musarum Deliciae*, i 103 (Hotten), Lustfull he was, at forty needs must wed, Old January will have May in bed. 1717: Pope, *January and May* [title]. 1855: Kingsley, *West. Ho!*, ch vii, If they had never allowed that fresh and fair young May to be forced into marrying that old January …

18. January commits the fault and May bears the blame. 1893: Inwards, *Weather Lore*, 11.

19. January never lies dead in a dyke gutter. 1846: Denham, *Proverbs*, 23 (Percy S.).

20. January warm, the Lord have mercy! 1893: Inwards, *Weather Lore*, 10.

21. March in Janiveer, Janiveer in March, I fear. 1678: Ray, 44. 1732: Fuller, 6148. 1893: Inwards, 11. 1912: R. L. Gales, *Studies in Arcady*, 2nd ser, 102.

22. The blackest month in all the year, Is the month of Janiveer. 1846: Denham, *Proverbs*, 26 (Percy S.). 1893: Inwards, 10.

23. The first three days of January rule the coming three months. Ibid., 11.

24. To have January chickens = To have children in old age. 1813: Ray, 202.

25. Who in Janiveer sows oats Gets gold and groats; Who sows in May Gets little that way. 1732: Fuller, 6149. 1893: Inwards, 11.

See also **December**; and **July** (2).

Jape with me. *See* **Play with me.**

Jarrow. 1. Bump against Jarrow. 1825: Brockett, *Gloss, of N. Country Words*, 32 … is a common expression among the keelmen when they run foul of any thing. 1846–59: *Denham Tracts*, i 88 (F.L.S.).

2. It's never dark in Jarrow Church. Ibid., i 89.

Jaws. *See* quot. 1887: T. Darlington, *S. Cheshire Folk Speech*, 280 (E.D.S.), 'Dunna let

yur jaws o'errun your claws' … is a proverbial saying equivalent to 'Do not live beyond your means'. 1917: Bridge, *Cheshire Proverbs*, 50.

Jays. *See* **Cherry** (4).

Jealous head is soon broken, A. 1732: Fuller, 225.

Jealous man's horns hang in his eyes, A. 1666: Torriano, *Piazza Univ.*, 174, A jealouse man hath his horns in his eyes. 1732: Fuller, 226. Cf. **Horn** (7).

Jealousy shuts one door and opens two. 1710: S. Palmer, *Moral Essays on Proverbs*, 370.

Jealousy. *See also* **Frenzy**.

Jemmy Rule's larks, Gone – like. 1888: Q.-Couch, *Troy Town*, ch viii.

Jenny Kemp, who had an occasion for all things, Like. 1864: 'Cornish Proverbs', in *N.&Q.*, 3rd ser, vi 6.

Jericho, Go to. 1648: *Mercurius Aulicus*, 23–30 March, If the Upper House, and the Lower House Were in a ship together, And all the base Committées, they were in another; And both the ships were botomlesse, And sayling on the mayne, Let them all goe to Jericho, And ne'ere be seen againe. 1694: *Terence made English*, 146, Ay, let him be jogging to Jericho for me. 1778: Mrs Thrale, in D'Arblay, *Diary*, i 31 (1876), They wish the poor children at Jericho when they accePt it. 1849: C. Brontë, *Shirley*, ch vii, Her habit was to … come forward hurriedly, yet hesitatingly, wishing herself meantime at Jericho.

Jericho, He. has been to = is drunk. 1745: Franklin, *Drinker's Dict.*, in *Works*, ii 24 (Bigelow).

Jerusalem, He's going to = is drunk. Ibid., ii 24.

Jest breaks no bones, A. 1781: Johnson, in Boswell's *Life*, iv 129 (Hill), It is a certain thing, it is proverbially known, that *a jest breaks no bones*.

Jest, There's many a true word spoken in. *See* **True** (17).

Jesters do oft prove prophets. 1855: Bohn, 436.

Jesting lies bring serious sorrows. Ibid., 436.

Jesting while it pleaseth, Leave, lest it turn to earnest. 1640: Herbert, *Jac. Prudentum*.

Jests are never good till they're broken. 1869: Hazlitt, 250.

Jewel. *See* quot. 1639: Fuller, *Holy War*, bk iii

ch iv, So true it is, none can guess the jewel by the casket.

Jew's eye, Worth a. 1593: G. Harvey, in *Works*, ii 146 (Grosart), As deare as a Iewes eye. 1595: Shakespeare, *M. of Venice*, II v, There will come a Christian by, Will be worth a Jewess' eye. 1842: Barham, *Ing. Legends*, 2nd ser: 'Old Woman in Grey', Hence the late Mr Froude, and the live Dr Pusey, We moderns consider as each worth a Jew's eye. 1886: Elworthy, *West Som. Word-Book*, 382 (E.D.S.), Take care of it, and put it away, it will be worth a Jew's eye some day.

Jews, The, spend at Easter, the Moors at marriages, the Christians in suits. 1640: Herbert, *Jac. Prudentum*. 1670: Ray, 24 [with 'of law' added at end].

Jill. *See* quots. 1678: Ray, 146, There's not so bad a Gill but there's as bad a Will. 1690: *New Dict. Canting Crew*, sig. F2, There's not so ord'nary a Gill, but there's as sorry a Jack. 1732: Fuller, 6112 [as in 1678]. *See also* **Jack**.

Joan Blunt. *See* quot. 1854: Baker, *Northants Gloss.*, s.v., Joan-Blunt. One in the habit of speaking her mind freely, without ceremony.

Joan is a good contriver, My wife; and a good contriver is better than a little eater. 1864: 'Cornish Proverbs', in *N. & Q.*, 3rd ser, vi 6.

Joan is as good as my lady in the dark. 1601: Munday, *Downfall of Earl of Hunt.*, III ii, *Prior* … He is our lady's chaplain, but serves Joan. *Don.* Then, from the friar's fault, perchance, it may be The proverb grew, Joan's taken for my lady. *c.*1640: in *Roxb. Ballads*, i 390 (Hindley). 1720: C. Shadwell, *Irish Hospitality*, I i 1838: Carlyle, *Sartor*, bk i ch x, Much also we shall omit about confusion of Ranks, and Joan and My Lady ['Society in a state of Nakedness'].

Job, Poor as. *See* **Poor** (11).

Job's comforter, A. *Miserable comforters are ye all.* [Job xvi.2] 1630: Brathwait, *Eng. Gent.*, 132 (1641), Iob called his friends miserable comforters. 1724: Defoe, *Roxana*, in *Works*, xii 20 (Boston, 1903), They sat down, like Job's three comforters, and said not one word to me for a great while. 1748: Richardson, *Clarissa*, vii 230 (1785), He called her Small Hopes, and Job's comforter. 1824: Scott, *Redgauntlet*, ch xv, O, this was a new theme for my Job's comforter. 1864: Mrs H. Wood, *Trevlyn Hold*, ch li., 'You are a pretty Job's comforter', gasped Mr Chattaway.

Job's worth doing … If a. *See* **worth** (2).

Jock Wabster. *See* **Devil** (97).

John at night. *See* quot. 1883: Burne, *Shropsh. Folk-Lore*, 596, To be John at night and Jack in the morning = to boast of one's intentions overnight and leave them unfulfilled next day.

John Barley-corn is no body with him, Sir. 1639: Clarke, 306.

John Barley-corn's the strongest knight, Sir. 1670: Ray, 59.

John Dod about him. He has a deal o'. 1917: Bridge, *Cheshire Proverbs*, 68 … Conceited, arrogant. *Dodd* or *Dod* is a well-known Cheshire name.

John Drawlatch. *See* quot. 1546: Heywood, *Proverbs*, Pt II ch viii, Why will ye (quoth he) I shall folow hir will? To make me Iohn drawlache, or such a snekebill.

John Drum. *See* **Drum's entertainment**

John Gray's bird. *See* quote, *c.*1575: Gascoigne, *Fruites of Warre*, cxxxi, The greene knight was amongst the rest Like John Greyes birde that ventured withe the best. 1579: *Quarrell between Hall and Mallerie*, 6, in *Misc. Ant. Angl.* (1816), Maister Robert Audeley … perceiving them to cluster to-gither like John Graves birde, *ut dicitur*, who always loved company.

John Lively. *See* **Kelloe**.

John Long, the carrier. 1546: Heywood, *Proverbs*, Pt I ch xi, I will send it him by Iohn Longe the carier. 1611: Cotgrave, s.v. 'Attendre'. To stay for John Long the Carrier; to tarry long for that which comes but slowly. 1681: W. Robertson, *Phraseol. Generalis*, 839, Whether all things are carried by Tom Long the Carrier; Quo tardissime omnia perferuntur. 1785: Grose, *Class. Dict. Vulgar Tongue*, s.v. 'Tom Long', It is coming by Tom Long the carrier, said of anything that has been long expected, *c.*1791: Pegge; *Derbicisms*, 129 (E.D.S.), Tom Long, carrier, [said] of a person that loiters and is long in coming or returning. 1830: Scott, *Doom of Devorgoil*, II i, A limping sonnet Which he had fashion'd to my cousin's glory, And forwarded by blind Tom Long the carrier. 1883: Burne, *Skropsh. Folk-Lore*, 597, To send by John the long carrier = by a roundabout route.

John of Cumber. *See* **Devil** (41).

John o' Groats. *See* **Land's End,**

John Platt. *See* quot. 1886: R. Holland, *Cheshire Gloss.*, 456 (E.D.S.), Very likely co [quoth] John

Platt. A common saying about Wilmslow. 1917: Bridge, *Cheshire Proverbs*, 148.

John Toy. See quots. 1864: 'Cornish Proverbs', in *N. & Q.*, 3rd ser, vi 6, Like lucky John Toy. 1880: Spurgeon, *Ploughman's Pictures*, 20, The luck that comes to them is like Johnny Toy's, who lost a shilling and found a two-penny loaf. 1883: Burne, *Shropsh. Folk-Lore*, 598, O lucky Tom Hodges! lost five pund an' fund a pig's yok'!

Johnny Middleton's hints, Like. Durham. 1909: *Folk-Lore*, xx 73.

Johnny tuth' Bellas. *See* quot. 1849: Halliwell, *Pop. Rhymes and Nursery Tales*, 200, Johnny tuth' Bellas daft was thy poll, When thou changed Bellas for Henknoll. [Said to date from 1386. Halliwell says we can only account for the saying by supposing that at some former period Bellasyse had been exchanged for lands, but not the manor of Henknoll. He gives an account of the tradition on which the saying is said to be founded.]

Johnson's End. *See* quot. 1860: in *N. & Q.*, 2nd ser, x 249, I have frequently heard it said, in Worcestershire, when a man has become very poor: 'He is gone up Johnson's end'.

Joke never gains over an enemy, but often loseth a friend, A. 1732: Fuller, 228.

Jokes are as bad coin to all but the jocular. 1831: Hone, *Year-Book*, col. 1416.

Jolly as a sandboy. 1863: Kingsley, *Water Babies*, ch viii, She would send them a lot of tops, and balls, and marbles, and ninepins, and make them all as jolly as sandboys. 1894: Northall. *Folk Phrases*, 9 (E.D.S.).

Jone's ale is new. 1594: *Jones Ale is Newe* [title of ballad]. 1630: *Wine, Beere, Ale, etc.*, 30 (Hanford, 1915), 'Tis growne to a prouerbe Iones ale's new.

Journey begins with a single step, The longest. *See* **Longest journey**.

Jove laughs at lovers' lies. [Perjuria ridet amantum Juppiter et ventos irrita ferre jubet. – Tibullus, III vi 49. Cf. Horace, *Carm.*, II viii 13.] 1567: *Lady Lucres*, in *Plasidas, etc.*, 143 (Roxb.Cl), Jupiter rather laughe the then take the angerlye the periurynge of louers. 1592: Shakespeare, *Romeo*, II ii, At lovers' perjuries, They say, Jove laughs. 1627: Massinger, *Great Duke of Florence*, II iii, For the queen of love, As they hold constantly, does never punish, But

smile at lovers' perjuries. 1700: Dryden, *Pal. and Arcite*, ii 149, And Jove but laughs at lovers' perjury! 1829: Cobbett, *Advice to Young Men*, Lett. III, Though I do not approve of the saying, 'At lovers' lies Jove laughs'. 1922: Judge Parry, in *Evening Standard*, 17 Oct., p. 5, col. 1, Perjury in the Divorce Court has been openly permitted to the upper classes for many years, following the maxim, perhaps, which our poets have borrowed from Tibullus, that 'Jove but laughs at lovers' perjury'.

Joy go with you. *See* quot. 1854: Baker, *Northants Gloss.*, s.v., 'Joy go with you, and sixpence; and then you'll want neither love nor money', is a common familiar phrase.

Joy of the heart. *See* **Heart** (9).

Judas kiss, A. *c*.1540: Bale, *Kynge Johan*, l. 2109, A false Judas kysse he hath gyven and is gone. 1570: Barclay, *Mirrour of Good Manners*, 75, Of a flattering foe to haue a Iudas kisse. 1684: in *Roxb. Ballads*, vii 473 (B.S.), They'l giue to you a Judas kisse. 1708: *Brit. Apollo*, i No. 116, col. 5, They once with Judas-kiss With artful smiles ... 1838: Hood, *Hood's Own*, 1st ser, 323 (1865), Her lips were glued on his, in a close 'Judas' kiss'. 1925: *Punch*, 2 Sept., p. 237, col. 1, 'Twas ever thus with misses, They leave the ancient home To plant their Judas kisses Upon some manly dome.

Judge, *subs. He who will have no judge but himself, condemns himself.* 1855: Bohn, 401.

Judge, *verb. He who judges hastily. See* quots. *c*.1450: *Partonope*, l. 9975 (E.E.T.S.), Full yor now hit ys a-goo I haue herd sey, and other moo, That who so yeveth hasty jugegyment Must be the fyrst that shall repent. 1666: Torriano, *Piazza Univ.*, 105, Who suddenly will judge, hastens himself to repentance. 1732: Fuller, 2244, He that passeth a judgment as he runs, overtaketh repentance.

July. 1. A shower in July, when the corn begins to fill, Is worth a plow of oxen, and all belongs there till. 1732: Fuller, 6468. 1893: Inwards, *Weather Lore*, 30.

2. As July so the next January. Ibid., 30.

3. Bow-wow dandy fly, Brew no beer in July. 1846: Denham, *Proverbs*, 54 (Percy S.). 1886: Bickerdyke, *Curios, of Ale and Beer*, 58 [cited as 'the old saying'].

4. If it rains on July 10th, it will rain for seven weeks. 1893: Inwards, *Weather Lore*, 31.

5. If the first of July, it be rainy weather, 'Twill rain, more or less, for four weeks together. 1732: Fuller, 6467. 1893: Inwards, 30.

6. In July, some reap rye, In August, if one will not, the other must. 1831: Hone, *Year-Book*, 1595. 1846: Denham, *Proverbs*, 51 (Percy S.), In July, shear your rye. 1893: Inwards, 30 [both 1831 and 1846 versions].

7. July chickens. *See* quot. 1921: *Observer*, 20 March, p. 5, col. 5, An old saying, which used to be current in my youth, grouped clergymen's sons and doctors' daughters in the same category as July chickens, and declared that, with some exceptions, of course, none of the three ever came to good.

8. No tempest, good July, Lest corn come off bluely. 1732: Fuller, 6208. 1825: Hone, *Ev. Day Book*, i 670 [with 'blue by' [mildew] for 'bluely']. 1893: Inwards, 30 [as in 1825, and also] No tempest, good July, Lest the corn look ruely.

9. To the 12th of July from the 12th of May All is day. 1732: Fuller, 6201, 'Tis said from the twelfth of May To the twelfth of July, all is day. 1893: Inwards, 31.

10. Whatever July and August do not boil, September cannot fry. Ibid., 30.

See also **Bee** (3); **Cuckoo; March** (18); and **Thistle** (2).

June. 1. A cold and wet June spoils the rest of the year. 1893: Inwards, *Weather Lore*, 29.

2. A good leak in June Sets all in tune. 1846: Denham, *Proverbs*, 50 (Percy S.). 1893: Inwards, 29, [as in 1846, with, in addition] A dripping June Brings all things in tune. 1920: *Times*, 21 June, p. 9, col. 2, 'A dripping June puts all things in tune', runs the old adage.

3. A wet June makes a dry September. Corn. 1893: Inwards, 29.

4. Calm weather in June Sets corn in tune. 1732: Fuller, 6207. 1893: Inwards, 28.

5. If it rains on June 27th, it will rain seven weeks. Ibid., 30.

6. If it rain the twenty-fourth day of June, hazel-nuts will not prosper. 1669: *New Help to Discourse*, 284.

7. If on the 8th of June it rain. It foretells a wet harvest, men sain. 1732: Fuller, 6204. Cf. **St Medard.**

8. June damp and warm Does the farmer no harm. 1893: Inwards, 29.

See also **April** (6) and (20); **Bee** (3); **Cuckoo**, *passim;* **March** (14); **May**, B, C, E (2), F (11), (12), (17), and (26); and **Thistle** (2).

Just before you are generous, Be. 1744–6: Mrs Haywood, *Fem. Spectator*, ii 27 (1771), There is, I think, an old saying, that we 'ought to be just before we are generous'. 1777: Sheridan, *Sch. for Scandal*, IV i 1850: Dickens, *Copperfield*, ch xiii.

Just to all, but trust not all, Be. 1855: Bohn, 325.

Justice pleaseth few in their own house. 1640: Herbert, *Jac. Prudentum.*

Justice. *See also* **Basket Justice**.

Ka' me, ka' thee. 1546: Heywood, *Proverbs*, Pt I ch xi, Ka me, ka the, one good tourne askth an other. *c.*1570: in Skelton's *Works*, I lxv. (Dyce), Yea, sayde the hostler, ka me, ka thee; yf she dooe hurte me, I wyll displease her. Before 1627: Middleton, *More Diss. besides Women*, I iv, Ka me, ka thee; if you will ease the melancholy of my mind with singing, I will deliver you from the calamity of boots-haling. 1821: Scott, *Kenilworth*, ch v, Ka me, ka thee – it is a proverb all over the world. 1823: Byron, *Don Juan*, can. xi st. 78. Cf. **Claw** (2); and **Scratch me**.

Kail [Broth] **in a riven dish, He gat his**. 1873: A. C. Gibson, *Folk Speech of Cumb.*, 184,

Kate Mullet. *See* quot. 1888: Q.-Couch, *Troy Town*, ch xi, As knowing as Kate Mullet … they say she was hanged for a fool.

Keep, *verb*. **1. He keepelh a fair castle that keepeth well his mouth,** *c.*1300: in *Vernon MS.*, 340 (E.E.T.S.).

2. He keeps a stir but is no constable. 1639: Clarke, 20.

3. He keeps his road well enough who gets rid of bad company. 1855: Bohn, 378.

4. It is no less praise to keep than to get. 1559: Bercher, *Nobil. of Women*, 97 (Roxb.Cl) [cited as 'theowlde vers'].

5. Keep a thing seven years. *See* quots. 1663: Killigrew, *Parson's Wedding*, II vii, According to the proverb, keep a thing seven years, and then if thou hast no use on't, throw't away. 1816: Scott, *Antiquary*, ch xxi, They say, keep a thing seven year, an' ye'll aye find a use for't. 1826: Scott, *Woodstock*, ch xxviii.

6. Keep bad men company, and you'll soon be of their number. 1640: Herbert, *Jac. Prudentum*, Keep not ill men company, lest you increase the number. 1875: A. B. Cheales, *Proverb. Folk-Lore*, 96.

7. Keep counsel thyself first. 1639: Clarke, 67. 1670: Ray, 5. 1732: Fuller, 3117.

8. Keep some till furthermore come. 1670: Ray, 110. 1736: Bailey, *Dict.*, s.v. 'Keep'.

9. Keep touch in small things. 1732: Fuller, 3120.

10. Keep your feet. *See* **Head** (6).

11. Keep your house and your house will keep you. 1776: Colman, *Spleen*, I [cited as 'the old proverb']. Cf. No. 13.

12. Keep your mouth shut and your eyes open. 1710: S. Palmer, *Moral Essays on Proverbs*, 143.

13. Keep your shop and your shop will keep you. 1605: Chapman, etc., *Eastw. Hoe*, I i, I … garnished my shop … with good wholesome thriftie sentences; as 'Touchstone, keep thy shoppe, and thy shoppe will keepe thee'. 1642: D. Rogers, *Matrim. Honour*, 224. 1712: *Spectator*, No. 509. 1759: Goldsmith, *The Bee*, No. vii 1905: Wells, *Kipps*, bk iii ch iii § 7, 'Shop!' said Kipps. 'That's right. Keep a shop and the shop'll keep you.' Cf. No. 11.

14. Keep your thanks to feed your chickens. 1681: W. Robertson, *Phraseol. Generalis*, 784. 1709: O. Dykes, *Eng. Proverbs*, iii 1732: Bailey, *Dict.*, s.v. 'Thanks'.

15. Keep yourself from the anger of a great man, from the tumult of a mob, from a man of ill fame, from a widow that has been thrice married, from a wind that comes in at a hole, and from a reconciled enemy. 1855: Bohn, 437.

16. To keep band in ike nick = To make things meet. *c.*1791: Pegge, *Derbicisms*, 88 (E.D.S.).

17. To keep it in Pimlico. *See* Pimlico.

18. Why keep a dog and bark yourself? *See* **Dog** (97).

19. You'll keep it no longer than you can a cat in a wheel-barrow. 1732: Fuller, 6025.

Keepers. *See* **Finders Keepers …**

Kelloe. *See* quot. 1849: Halliwell, *Pop. Rhymes and Nursery Tales*, 202, John Lively, Vicar of Kelloe, Had seven daughters and never a fellow.

Kelvedon. *See* **Braintree.**

Kenchester. *See* **Sutton-Well.**

Kendale fox, As craftie as a. 1659: Howell, 20. 1670: Ray, 254.

Kennel of hounds. *See* **Pound of butter.**

Kennington. *See* **Ashford.**

Kenspeckle [Conspicuous] **as a cock on a church broach** [spire], **As**. 1855: Robinson, *Whitby Gloss.*, 95.

Kent. 1. A man of Kent. 1662: Fuller, *Worthies*, ii 122 (1840). *c.*1750: C. Smart, *Fables*, No. ii, Are all to idle discord bent, These Kentish men – those men of Kent. 1887: Parish and Shaw, *Dict. Kent. Dialect*, 98 (E.D.S.), Man of Kent. A title claimed by the inhabitants of the Weald as their peculiar designation; all others they regard as Kentish men.

2. Kent and Christendom. Various proverbial uses. *See* quots. 1579: Spenser, *Shep. Cal.*, Sept., l. 168, Neuer was woolfe seene, many nor some, Nor in all Kent, nor in Christen-dome. 1592: Lyly, *Mother Bombie*, III iv, I care not … I can live in Christendome as well as in Kent. 1599: Nashe, in *Works*, v 221 (Grosart), How William the Conquerour hauing heard the prouerb of Kent and Christendome, thought he had woone a countrey as goode as all Christendome when he was enfeofed of Kent. 1651: Randolph, *Hey for Honesty*, I i, All the cudgels in Christendom, Kent, or New England, shall never make me quiet. 1662: Fuller, *Worthies*, ii 122 (1840), Neither in Kent nor Christendom. 1790: Grose, *Prov. Gloss.*, s.v. 'Kent' [as in 1662].

3. Kent is divided into three parts. *See* quots. 1576: Lambarde, *Peramb. of Kent*, 181 (1826), Very reasonable is their conceite, which doe imagine that Kent hath three steps, or degrees, of which the first (say they) offereth wealth without health: the second, giveth both wealth and health; and the thirde affoordeth health onely, and little or no wealth. 1670: Ray, 234, Some part of Kent hath health and no wealth, viz. East Kent. Some wealth and no health, viz. The weald of Kent. Some both health and wealth, viz. the middle of the countrey and parts near London. 1735: Pegge, *Kent. Proverbs*, in E.D.S., No. 12, p. 76, Health and no wealth; Wealth and no health; Health and Wealth. 1790: Grose, *Prov. Gloss.*, s.v. 'Kent' [abbreviated version of 1670].

4. Kent; red veal and white bacon. 1735: Pegge, *Kent. Proverbs*, in E.D.S., No. 12, p. 61.
See also **Knight of Cales**.

Kentish Jury. *See* **London** (1).

Kentish Long-tails. Versions of the legend or story may be found in 1205: Layamon, *Brut*, ll. 29555–86; also in Polydore Vergil, *Angl. Hist.*, lib. xiii 218 (ed. Basel, 1546). There is a version in Lambarde, *Peramb. of Kent*, 356–62 (1826). *See also* Matthew Paris, 785, 790. 1551: Bale, *Eng. Votaryes*, 30, For castynge of fyshe tayles atthys Augustyne, Dorsett shyre men had tales euer after. But Polydorus applyeth yt vnto Kentysh men at Stroude by Rochester, for

cuttynge of Thomas Beckettes horses tayle. *c.*1600: Deloney, in *Works*, 383 (Mann), The valiant courage and policie of the Kentishmen with long tayles. 1639–61: in *Rump Songs*, Pt II 47 (1662, repr. 1874), I shall not dispute whether Long-tails of Kent, Or papist, this name of disgrace did invent. 1701: T. Brown, *Works*, i 134 (1760), Advice to the Kentish Long-tails, by the Wise Men of Gotham. 1887: Parish and Shaw, *Dict. Kent. Dialect*, 95 (E.D.S.), Long-tails. An old nickname for the natives of Kent.

Kentish miles. *See* **Essex stiles**.

Kentish yeoman. *See* **Knight of Cales**.

Kenton. *See* **Haldon**.

Kentshire, hot as fire. 1735: Pegge, *Kent. Proverbs*, in E.D.S., No. 12, p. 61.

Kent-street distress, A. 1790: Grose, *Prov. Gloss.*, s.v. 'Surrey'.

Kerdon. *See* **Crediton**.

Kernel. *See* **Eat** (25).

Kerton. *See* **Crediton**.

Kettle. *See* **Pot** (6).

Kettle of fish, A pretty! 1742: Fielding, *Andrews*, bk i ch xii, 'Here's a pretty kettle of fish,' cries Mrs Tow-wouse, 'you have brought upon us!' 1767: Brooke, *Fool of Quality*, ii 249, If matters come to this pass, I shall have made a fine kettle of fish on't. 1850: Dickens, *Copperfield*, ch xix, And then it will go in, you know – and then … there'll be a pretty kettle of fish! 1872: Hardy, *Greenwood Tree*, Pt II ch viii, Here's another pretty kettle o' fish for thee.

Kex. *See* **Dry** (6); **Hollow**; and **Light as a kex**.

Key fits not that lock, Your. Before 1529: Skelton, *Works*, i 20 (Dyce), Youre key is mete for euery lok. 1732: Fuller, 6052.

Key under the door, To leave the = To become bankrupt. 1602: Chamberlain, *Letters*, 156 (Camden S.), The mercer of Temple Barre … hath laide the key under the doore and is become banckrupt. 1670: Ray, 182, To lay the key under the threshold. 1677: Yarranton, *Eng. Improvement*, 126, If it hold cheap for three or four years, the tenant lays the key under the door. 1724: Swift, *Drapier Letters*, Lett. I, The shopkeeper … must break, and leave the key under the door.

Keys hang not at one man's girdle, All. Before 1500: Hill, *Commonplace-Book*, 129 (E.E.T.S.). 1546: Heywood, *Proverbs*, Pt I ch xi 1670: Ray, 110. 1732: Fuller, 553.

Keystone. *See* quot. 1863: Wise, *New Forest*, ch xv, The smuggler's local proverb, 'Keystone under the hearth, keystone under the horse's belly'. [The smuggled spirits were concealed either below the fireplace or in the stable.]

Kick, *verb.* **1. To kick against the pricks.** [πρὸς κέντρα μὴ λάκτιζε μὴ πταίσας μογῃς. – Aeschylus, *Agam.*, 1624. Aduorsum stimulum calcas. – Terence, *Phorm.*, I ii 28.] 1382: Wiclif, *Acts*, ix 5 (OED), It is hard to thee, for to kyke aghens the pricke. 1539: Taverner, *Proverbs*, fo. 14, It is harde kyckynge against the gode. 1567: Pickering, *Horestes*, l. 977. *c.*1594: Bacon, *Promus*, No. 962, Folly it is to spurn against the pricke. 1605: Camden, *Remains*, 322 (1870) [as in 1594]. 1638: D. Tuvill, *Vade Mecum*, 46 (3rd ed), It is madnesse in a man to kick against a thorne, to strive against a streame. 1842: Marryat, *P. Keene*, ch iii, It's folly to kick against tenpenny nails.

2. To kick the beam. 1838: Hood, *Hood's Own*, 1st ser, 5 (1865), Despondency … may make you kick the beam and the bucket both at once.

3. To kick the bucket. 1796: Wolcot, *Works*, v 242 (1812), Pitt kicked the bucket. 1828: Carr, *Craven Dialect.* i 55, To kick the bucket, an unfeeling phrase for to die. 1890: G. Allen, *Tents of Shem*, ch x (Farmer), Sir Arthur … will do the right thing in the end before he kicks the bucket.

4. To kick the wind. 1598: Florio, *Worlde of Wordes*, s.v. 'Dar de' calci a Rouaio', To be hang'd, to kicke the wind. 1813: Ray, 203.

Kick, *subs.* **1. I'll give him a kick for a culp** = a Rowland for an Oliver. 1830: Forby, *Vocab. E. Anglia*, 427. 1872: J. Glyde, jr., *Norfolk Garland*, 148.

2. The kick of the dam hurts not the colt. 1732: Fuller, 4611.

Kid. *A piece of a kid is worth two of a cat.* 1546: Heywood, *Proverbs*, Pt II ch vii 1670: Ray, 110. 1732: Fuller, 348.

Kidney, All of a; or Of such and such a kidney. Before 1555: Latimer, *Sermons and Rem.*, 312 (P.S.) (OED), To pronounce all to be thieves to a man, excePt myself, of course, and those men … that are of my own kidney. 1658: R. Franck, *North. Memoirs*, 39 (1821), Such Furiosos, I must confess, are of an odd kidney. 1694: *Terence made English*, 6, If any such has got a tutor of his own kidney, he shall be sure to be ply'd o' the weak side. 1742: Fielding, *Andrews*, bk ii ch viii, I am heartily glad to meet with a man of your kidney. 1854: Baker, *Northants Gloss.*, s.v. 'Kidney', 'All of a kidney'. A common expression when children inherit the bad qualities of their parents; also applied to a number of dissolute associates, 'such young men are all of a kidney'.

Kill, *verb.* **1. He often kills.** *See* quot. *c.*1645: MS. Proverbs, in *N.&Q.*, vol 154, p. 27, Hee often kills that thinks but to hurt that which is worth the restoringe.

2. He that killeth a man when he is drunk shall be hanged when he is sober. 1546: Heywood, *Proverbs*, Pt I ch x 1605: Camden, *Remains*, 324 (1870). 1641: in Marchant, *Praise of Ale*, 154 (1888), Suppose you should kill a man whan you are drunk, you shall never be hanged for it until you are sober. 1732: Fuller, 2204.

3. He that kills himself. *See* Buried.

4. He will kill a man for a mess of mustard. 1562: Heywood, *Three Hund. Epigr.*, No. 207. 1659: Howell, 7.

5. I killed her for good will, said Scot, when he killed his neighbour's mare. 1678: Ray, 85.

6. To kill a man with a cushion. 1639: Clarke, 310. 1670: Ray, 218.

7. To kill one with kindness. 1594: Shakespeare, *Tam, of Shrew*, IV i, This is a way to kill a wife with kindness. 1607: T. Heywood, *A Woman Kilde with Kindnesse* [title]. 1699: Farquhar, *Love and a Bottle*, III i, I bear her an amorous grudge still … I could kill her with kindness. 1761: Colman, *Jealous Wife*, IV i, You absolutely kill him with kindness. 1815: Byron, *Letters and Journals*, iii 205 (Prothero), Don't let them kill you with claret and kindness at the national dinner in your honour. 1876: in *N.&Q.*, 5th ser, vi 246, They say here [Worksop] of a man who … shortened his days by … excess of any kind, that he has 'killed himself with kindness'.

8. To kill two birds with one stone. [Iam ego uno in saltu lepide apros capiam duos. – Plautus, *Cas.*, II viii 40. Una mercede duas res adsequi. – Cicero, *Rosc. Am.*, xxix 80.] 1611: Cotgrave, s.v. 'Coup'. 1671: T. Shadwell, *Miser*, II, And (if you can bring this lady) I should kill two birds with one stone, as that excellent thrifty proverb says. 1734: Fielding, *Univ. Gallant*, V ii, This is better than my hopes! This is killing two birds with one stone. 1850: Dickens, *Chuzzlewit*, ch viii.

9. To kill two flies with one flap. 1678: Ray, 275.

10. We will not kill but whoave [cover]. Cheshire. 1691: Ray, *Words not Generally Used*, 74 (E.D.S.). 1917: Bridge, *Cheshire Proverbs*, 150 … Spoken of a pig or fowl which has been covered by some utensil in readiness to kill.

11. Who was killed by a cannon bullet was curst in his mother's belly. 1659: Howell, 6. 1670: Ray, 110. 1738: Swift, *Polite Convers.*, Dial. I.

See also **Cat** (61); **Dog** (82); **Goost** (30), and **Pace.**

Kiln. 1. For my part burn the kiln boldly. 1639: Clarke, 77.

2. For my peck of malt set the kiln on fire. Ibid., 254. 1666: Torriano, *Piazza Univ.*, 164, The English say, For my peck of malt, set the keel on fire. 1681: W. Robertson, *Phraseol. Generalis*, 982. 1917: Bridge, *Cheshire Proverbs*, 58.

3. Kill's-a-fire. *See* quot. 1851: Sternberg. *Dialect, etc., of Northants*, 58, Kill's-a-fire. A proverbial expression intimating the existence of enmity. 'Kill's-a-fire 'tween they two'.

4. My kiln of malt is on fire. 1605: Camden, *Remains*, 328 (1870).

5. The kiln calls the oven burnt house. 1603: Florio, *Montaigne*, 503 (1634) (OED), Which some say prouerbially, 'Ill may the kill call the ouen "burnt taile"!' 1639: Clarke, 196 (with 'hearth' for 'house']. 1670: Ray, 110. 1853: Trench, *Proverbs*, 63 (1905).

Kim-kam. *See* quots. 1611: Cotgrave, s.v. 'Anguille', To doe a thing cleane kamme, out of order, the wrong way. 1609: Shakespeare, *Coriol.*, III i, *Sic.* This is clean kam. *Bru.* Merely awry. 1637: Clarke, 7, Kim kam arsie versie. 1740: North, *Examen*, 151, The reason of all this chim-cham stuff is … 1879: Jackson, *Shropsh. Word-Book*, 235, Let's 'a none o' yore kim-kam ways.

Kind [Soft] **as a glove.** 1828: Carr, *Craven Dialect*, i 264.

Kind as a kite. 1639: Clarke, 287. 1670: Ray, 202, As kind as a kite, all you cannot eat you'll hide.

Kind as Cockburn. 1600: *Weakest Goeth to the Wall*, II iii, Faith, as kind as Cockburn; I'll break my heart to do them good. [A note on this in Hazlitt's Webster's *Dram. Works*, iv 252, says 'An old proverb'; but I have not met it elsewhere.]

Kind heart loseth nought at last, A. 1639: Clarke, 45.

Kind to-day, cross to-morrow. Ibid., 159.

Kind, *subs. See* **Love;** and **Nature**.

Kinder scout. *See* quot. 1869: Hazlitt, 253, Kinder scout, the cowdest [coldest] place areawt. *Derbyshire*. Higson's *MSS. Coll.*

Kinder than he was wont. *See* **Use** (1).

Kindle not a fire that you cannot extinguish. 1584: B. R., *Euterpe*, 136 (Lang), I will kindle no moe coales then I may well quenche. 1869: Hazlitt, 253.

Kindness is lost that's bestowed on children and old folks. 1639: Clarke, 45.

Kindnesses, like grain, increase by sowing. 1855: Bohn, 437.

Kindred, Wheresoever you see your, make much of your friends. 1659: Howell, 5, For all your kindred make much of your friends. 1670: Ray, 15. 1732: Fuller, 5660.

King and **Kings. 1. A king promises, but observes only what he pleases.** 1855: Bohn, 292.

2. A king without learning is but a crowned ass. *c.*1534: Berners, *Huon*, 730 (E.E.T.S.), For comonly it is said that a kyng without letter or conynge is compared to an asse crowned. *c.*1535: *Dialogues of Creatures*, lv. (1816). 1868: Freeman, *Norman Conquest*, II viii 277 (OED), An unlettered king is a crowned ass.

3. A king's face should give grace. 1831: Croker, Note to *Boswell*, Johnson's letter of 20 June, 1777, The Royal prerogative of mercy, expressed by the old adage, '*The King's face gives grace*'. 1853: Trench, *Proverbs*, 19 (1905).

4. A king's favour is no inheritance. 1678: Ray, 163. 1732: Fuller, 4618.

5. He clips the King's English = *He* is drunk. 1745: Franklin, *Drinker's Dict.*, in *Works*, ii 24 (Bigelow).

6. He shall have the king's horse = He is a liar. 1678: Ray, 89.

7. He that eats the king's goose. *See* quots. 1611: Cotgrave, s.v. 'Oye', He that eats the king's goose doth void fethers an hundred yeares after. 1748: Richardson, *Clarissa*, iv 243 (1785), Often have I thought of that excellent old adage; He that eats the King's goose shall be choaked with his feathers.

8. Kings and bears often worry their keepers. 1738: *Gent. Mag.*, 475.

9. Kings have long arms. 1539: Taverner, *Prov. out of Erasmus*, fo. 4, Kynges haue longe handes. 1581: Lyly, *Euphues*, 76 (Arber). 1669: *Politeuphuia*, 78, Kings have long arms, and rulers large reaches. 1736: Bailey, *Dict.*, s.v. 'King', Kings have long hands.

10. The king and his staff Be a man and a half. 1869: Blackmore, *Lorna Doone*, ch liv. [cited as 'an ancient saying'].

11. The King and Pope. *See* quot. 1659: Howell, 12, The King and Pope, the lion and the wolf: a proverb used in King John's time, in regard of the great exactions.

12. The King can do no wrong. Enshrined in the legal maxim: *rex non potest peccare* (the king cannot do wrong) and used to suggest the sovereign – and sometimes any other ruler – is above the law. (But *see* quot. 1765 for another interpetation). *c.*1538: T. Starkey, *England in the Reign of King Henry VIII* (E.E.T.S.), ɪ iv Wyl you make a kyng to have no more powar then one of hys lordys? Hyt ys commynly sayd … a kyng ys above hys lawys. 1654: J. Selden, *Table-Talk* (1689), 27, The King can do no wrong, that is no Process can be granted against him. 1765: W. Blackstone, *Commentaries on the Laws of England*, ɪ vii, The King can do no wrong … The prerogative of the crown extends not to do any injury: it is created for the benefit of the people, and therefore cannot be exerted to their prejudice. 1888: C.M. Yonge, *Beechcroft at Rockstone*, II xxii, 'So, Aunt Joan, is your Pope.' 'No; she's the King that can do no wrong,' said Gillian, laughing.

13. The king can make a Serjeant, but not a lawyer. 1732: Fuller, No.4613.

14. The king must wait while his beer's drawing. 1869: Hazlitt, 375. 1888: Q.-Couch, *Troy Town*, ch xix, They do say as the Queen must wait while her beer's a-drawin'.

15. The King of England is the king of devils, *c.*1645: Taylor (Water-Poet), *Generall Complaint*, 4, in *Works*, 4th coll. (Spens.S.). 1662: Fuller, *Worthies*, i 118 (1840). 1785–95: Wolcot, *Lousiad*, can. iii, A king of Englis be a king of defils.

16. The king of good fellows is appointed for the queen of beggars. 1605: Camden, *Remains*, 333 (1870). 1732: Fuller, 4616.

17. The king's chaff is better than other people's corn. 1612: Shelton, *Quixote*, Pt I bk iv

ch xii, Men say that a king's crumb is more worth than a lord's loaf. 1738: *Gent. Mag.*, 474. 1825: Scott, *Fam. Letters*, ii 318 (1894), 'King's chaff being better than other folk's corn', his Excellency's lunch served me for my dinner.

18. The king's cheese goes half away in parings. 1659: Howell, 3. 1660: Howell, *Parly of Beasts*, 19, Whence grew the proverb, that the King's cheese goes away three parts in parings? 1709: O. Dykes, *Eng. Proverbs*, 299. 1738: *Gent. Mag.*, 474.

19. The King's English. It will be observed that in 1560, 1600, and 1602, when a queen was on the throne, the phrase used was still 'The King's English'. *c.*1380: Chaucer, *Astrolabe*, Prol., And preye, god save the king, that is lord of this langage. 1560: T. Wilson, *Rhetorique*, 162 (1909), If a man should charge them for counterfeiting the Kings English. 1593: Nashe, *Works*, ii 184 (Grosart), Still he must be … abusing the Queenes English. 1600: *Look About You*, sc ix, in Hazlitt, *Old Plays*, vii 412, Marry, here's a stammerer taken clipping the king's English. 1600: Shakespeare, *Merry Wives*, I iv 1603: Dekker, *Works*, i 136 (Grosart). Before 1681: Lacy, *Sir Hercules Buffoon*, V iv, That is not shorthand, 'tis called clipping the King's English. 1714: *Spectator*, No. 616. 1787: O'Keeffe, *The Farmer*, I jii, My dear ma'am how do you clack away, King George's English hack away. 1864: Alford, *The Queen's English* [title]. 1886: R.L.S., *Kidnapped*, ch x, I have translated it here, not in verse … but at least in the king's English.

20. The king's errand may lie in the cadger's gate. 1826: Scott, *Journal*, 22 Feb.

21. The king's word is more than another man's oath, 1554: Princess Elizabeth, in Ellis, *Orig. Letters*, 2nd ser, ii 255 [cited as 'this olde saynge'].

22. The king's word must stand. 1509: Bp. Fisher, *Eng. Works*, 230 (E.E.T.S.), It is a comyn prouerbe. Verbum regis stet oportet A kynges worde must stande.

See also **Kingdom; Nothing** (36); **Subject;** and **Two Kings**.

King Arthur. *See* **Arthur**.

King Harry. 1. A King Harry's face. 1678: Ray, 73.

2. King Harry loved a man. 1605: Camden, *Remains*, 327 (1870). 1613: S. Rowley, *When You See Me*, sig. D3, King Harry loves a man, I can tell yee. 1653: Naunton, *Frag. Regalia*, 182 (1694), The people hath it to this day in proverb, King Harry loved a man. 1670: Ray, 100, King Harry lov'd a man, i.e. valiant men love such as are so, hate cowards. 1825: Scott, *Talisman*, ch xx, The King of England, who, as it was emphatically said of his successor Henry the Eighth, loved to look upon A MAN …

3. King Harry robbed the Church and died a beggar. 1678: Ray, 354.

4. This was a hill in King Harry's days. Ibid., 73.

King Log, If you despise, you shall fear King Crane. 1732: Fuller, 2749.

King's Sutton. *See* **Bloxham.**

Kingdom. 1. In the kingdom of a cheater, the wallet is carried before. 1640: Herbert, *Jac. Prudentum.*

2. In the kingdom of the blind, the one-eyed is king. Before 1529: Skelton, in *Works*, ii 43 (Dyce), But haue ye nat harde this, How an one eyed man is Well syghted when He is amonge blynde men? 1540: Palsgrave, *Acolastus*, Amongst xx blynde an one-eyed man may be a kynge. 1640: Herbert, *Jac. Prudentum.* 1696: Sir W. Temple, *Miscellanea*, 2nd part, 342 (4th ed.), For among the blind, he that has one eye is a Prince. 1732: Fuller, 2137, He that has but one eye is a prince among those that have none. 1822: Scott, *Fam. Letters*, ii 147 (1894), The *purblind* is a king you know among the blind.

3. Woe to the kingdom whose king is a child, *c.*1513: More, *Works*, p. 63, col. 2 (1557), That the greate wise manne well perceiued, when hee sayde: *Veh regno cujus rex puer est*, Woe is that realme that hathe a chylde to theyr kynge. 1596: Lodge, *Divel Coniured*, 80 (Hunt.Cl.). 1594: Shakespeare, *Rich. III*, II iii, Woe to that land that's govern'd by a child! 1642: Fuller, *Holy State*: 'Gust. Adolphus'.

Kingston Down. *See* **Hengsten Down.**

Kinsman helps kinsman, but woe to him that hath nothing. 1578: Florio, *First Fruites*, fo. 32, Kinsfolkes with kinsfolke, wo to hym that hath nothing. 1629: *Book of Meery Riddles*, Prov. 19.

Kinsman. *See also* **Servant** (7).

Kinsman's ear will hear it, The. 1659: Howell, *Proverbs: Brit.-Eng.*, 4.

Kirbie's castle and Megse's glory, Spinola's pleasure, and Fisher's folly. 1662: Fuller, *Worthies*, ii 343 (1840). 1790: Grose, *Prov. Gloss.*, s.v. 'London'.

Kirby. *See* **Sutton.**

Kiss, *subs.* **1. A kiss of the mouth often touches not the heart.** 1855: Bohn, 292.

2. Kisses are keyes, and Wanton kisses are keyes of sin. 1639: Clarke, 28.

See. also **Christmas** (5).

Kiss, *verb.* **1. Do not make me kiss, and you will not make me sin.** 1855: Bohn, 345.

2. He that doth kiss and do no more, may kiss behind and not before. 1659: Howell, 9 (7).

3. He that kisseth his wife in the market-place, shall have enough to teach him. 1605: Camden, *Remains*, 323 (1870) [with 'many teachers' for 'enough to teach him']. 1670: Ray, 110. 1732: Fuller, 2205.

4. If you can kiss the mistress, never kiss the maid. 1670: Ray, 111. 1742: in Hone, *Ev. Day Book*, ii 377, To kiss with the maid when the mistress is kind, A gentleman ought to be loth, sir.

5. Kiss and be friends, *c.*1300: R. Brunne, tr. Langtoft's *Chron.*, 64 (Hearne), Kisse and be gode frende in luf and in a wille. 1419: in *Twenty-six Poems*, 69 (E.E.T.S.), Make hem kyssen and be frende. 1672: Lacy, *Dumb Lady*, IV, Weep not, Nurse! I am satisfied. Come, kiss and be friends. 1740: Richardson, *Pamela*, ii 73 (1883), Dear aunt, said her kinsman, let's see you buss and be friends. 1775: Franklin, in *Works*, v 450 (Bigelow), 'They should kiss and be friends,' said I. 1847: Tennyson, *Princess*, vi 271.

6. Many kiss the child for the nurse's sake. 13th cent.: MS. quoted in 1846: Wright, *Essays on Middle Ages*, i 150, Osculor hunc ore natum nutricis amore. 1546: Heywood, *Proverbs*, Pt II ch vii 1590: Lodge, *Rosalynde*, 98 (Hunt.Cl.), Aliena … thoght she kist the childe for the nurses sake. 1683: Meriton, *Yorkshire Ale*, 83–7 (1697), For love of the nurse the bairn gets mony a cuss. 1732: Fuller, 3351. 1823: Scott, *Peveril*, ch viii, But among men, dame, many one caresses the infant that he may kiss the child's maid.

7. Many kiss the hand they wish cut off. 1640: Herbert, *Jac. Prudentum.* 1670: Ray, 15. 1754: Berthelson, *Eng.-Danish Dict.*, s.v. 'Kiss', Many do kiss the hands they wish to see cut off.

8. She had rather kiss than spin. 1732: Fuller, 4123.

9. To kiss a man's wife, or wipe his knife, is a thankless office. 1639: Clarke, 45. 1670: Ray, 111.

10. To kiss and tell. 1616: Jonson, *Forest*, V, 'Tis no sin love's fruit to steal, But the sweet theft to reveal. 1675: Cotton, *Burl, upon Burlesque*, 200 (1765), And if he needs must kiss and tell, I'll kick him headlong into Hell. 1695: Congreve, *Love for Love*, II x, Oh fie, Miss, you must not kiss and tell. 1757: Murphy, *Upholsterer*, II, Why must they kiss and tell? 1816: Byron, in *Letters and Journals*, iii 339 (Prothero), The old reproach against their admirers of 'Kiss and tell'. 1910: Shaw, *Misalliance*, 88 (1914). As a gentleman, I do not kiss and tell.

11. To kiss one where he sat on Sunday. 1583: Melbancke, *Philotinus*, sig. Y1, When a mans hose be doune, it is easie to kisse him where he sat on Saterday. *c.*1685: in *Roxb. Ballads*, viii 869 (B.S.), Thou shalt kiss me where I sat on Sunday.

12. To kiss the Counter, *c.*1560: in Huth, *Ancient Ballads, etc.*, 227 (1867), Then some the Counter oft doo kisse, If that the money be not paid.

13. To kiss the hare's foot. *See* quots. 1598: *Servingmans Comfort*, in *Inedited Tracts*, 112 (Hazlitt, 1868), Vpon payne to dyne with Duke Humfrie, or kisse the Hares foote. 1616: Browne, *Brit. Past.*, II ii, 'Tis supper time with all, and we had need Make haste away, unless we mean to speed With those that kiss the hare's foot. 1738: Swift, *Polite Convers.*, Dial. II, Well, I am the worst in the world at making apologies; it was my lord's fault: I doubt you must kiss the hare's foot. 1818: Scott, in Lockhart's *Life*, iv 118, The poor clergyman [got] nothing whatever, or, as we say, *the hare's foot to lick.* 1847: Halliwell, *Dict.*, s.v. 'Kiss', *To kiss the hare's foot, to kiss the post*, to be too late for any thing.

14. To kiss the post. Before 1529: Skelton, *Philip Sparrow*, l. 716, Troylus also hath lost On her moch loue and cost, And now must kys the post. 1595: Churchyard, *Charitie*, 10 (1816), But some that lost their blood in countries right May kisse the post. 1623: *New and Merrie Prognos.*, 19 (Halliwell), That such as come late must kisse the post. 1847: *See* No. 13.

15. You must kiss a parson's wife. 1678: Ray, 86, He that would have good luck in horses, must kiss the parsons wife. 1738: Swift, *Polite Convers.*, Dial. II, *Sir John* ... . I have had devilish bad luck in horse flesh of late. *Ld. Smart.* Why, then, Sir John, you must kiss a parson's wife.

Kissing, *verb. subs.* **1. After kissing comes more kindness.** 1484: Caxton, *La Tour-Landry*, ch xxxiii p. 185 (E.E.T.S.), The kyssynge is nyghe parente and cosyn vnto the fowle faytte or dede. 1639: Clarke, 28. 1661: Davenport, *City Nightcap*, I, She that will kiss, they say, will do worse.

2. Kissing goes by favour. 1605: Camden, *Remains*, 327 (1870). 1649: Quarles, *Virgin Widow*, I. 1725: Bailey, tr. Erasmus' *Colloq.*, 239. 1871: Planché, *Extravag.*, v 300 (1879), And kissing more than ever now is found to go by favour.

See also **Furze**.

Kit after kind = A chip of the old block. 1599: *Life of Sir T. More*, in Wordsworth, *Eccl. Biog.*, ii 112 (1853) (OED), She would now and then show herself to be her mother's daughter, kitt after kinde. 1670: Ray, 183.

Kit to watch your chickens, Never put the. Corn. 1869: Hazlitt, 290.

Kitchen. 1. By a kitchen fat and good makes the poor most neighbourhood. 1623: Wodroephe, *Spared Houres*, 481.

2. If you can't stand the heat, get out of the kitchen. *See* **If.**

3. Kitchen physic is the best physic. 1562: Bullein, *Bulwarke of Defence*, According with kitchen physic, which kitchen, I assure you, is a good potecary's shop. *c.*1670: *Roxb. Ballads*, vii 238 (B.S.), Good kitchen-physick is the best. 1738: Swift, *Polite Convers.*, Dial. II.

4. The smallness of the kitchen makes the house the bigger. 1732: Fuller, 4753.

5. The taste of the kitchen is better than the smell. 1633: Draxe, 41. 1670: Ray, 26. 1732: Fuller, 4784.

Kite sees a dead horse afar off, An hungry. 1732: Fuller, 616.

Kite. *See also* **Carrion; Hungry; Kind; Lark** (1); and **Yellow** (2).

Kitling. 1. Did you ever know a kitling bring a mouse to the old cat? 1917: Bridge, *Cheshire Proverbs*, 50 ... Children are not always ready to support their aged parents.

2. Wanton kitlins may make sober old cats. 1732: Fuller, 5415. Cf. **Untoward girl or boy.**

See also **Kit;** and **Mouse** (10).

Knack me that nut. *See* **Nut** (2).

Knapton. *See* **Gimmingham.**

Knave and **Knaves. 1. A knave discovered is a great fool.** 1732: Fuller, 232.

2. A knave (or **rogue**) **in grain.** 1540: Palsgrave, *Acolastus*, sig. S2, Whan knaues in graine mete. 1593: *Tell-Trothes New-yeares Gift*, 18 (N.Sh.S.), But these of the sixt kinde are knaues in graine. 1640: *The Knave in Grain New VamPt* [title of comedy]. 1728: Swift, in *Works*, xiv 241 (Scott), Among his crew of rogues in grain. 1785: Grose, *Class. Dict. Vulgar Tongue*, s.v., Knave in grain, a knave of the first rate. 1855: Bohn, 299, A rogue in grain is a rogue amain. 1869: Spurgeon, *John Ploughman*, ch xviii, Like corndealers, they are rogues in-grain.

3. As good a knave I know as a knave I know not. 1678: Ray, 74.

4. I'd rather have a knave than a fool. Oxfordsh. 1913: *Folk-Lore*, xxiv 77.

5. If ye would know a knave, give him a staff. 1640: Herbert, *Jac. Prudentum*.

6. Knaves and fools divide the world. 1670: Ray, in. 1690: *New Dict. Canting Crew*, sig. G6, Knaves and fools are the composition of the whole world. 1732: Fuller, 2133.

7. Knaves and whores goby the clock. 1659: Howell, 19.

8. Knaves imagine nothing can be done without knavery. 1732: Fuller, 3135.

9. One of the four, and twenty politics of a knave is to stay long at his errand. 1659: Howell, 2.

10. There I caught a knave in a purse-net. 1639: Clarke, 127. 1670: Ray, 216. 1732: Fuller, 4870.

11. When a knave is in a plum-tree, he hath neither friend nor kin. 1640: Herbert, *Jac. Prudentum*.

Knavery in all trades, There is. 1671: Head and Kirkman, *Eng. Rogue*, ii 115. 1692: L'Estrange, *Aesop*, 161 (3rd ed.), Hence comes the old saying; *There's knavery in all trades, but most in taylors.*

Knavery is in credit, Where, honesty is sure to be a drug. 1754: Berthelson, *Eng.-Danish Dict.*, s.v. 'Drug'.

Knavery may serve a turn, but honesty never fails. 1678: Ray, 164 [with 'is best at long run' for 'never fails']. 1732: Fuller, 3131.

Knavish wit, a knavish will, A. 1736: Bailey, *Dict.*, s.v.

Knife. 1. Carry your knife even, between the paring and the apple. 1732: Fuller, 1065.

2. Every knife. *See* quot. 1877: E. Leigh,

Cheshire Gloss., 96, 'Every knife of his'n has a golden haft', i.e. everything he undertakes turns out well. 1917: Bridge, *Cheshire Proverbs*, 55

Knight of Cales [Cadiz], **A, and a gentleman of Wales, and a laird of the North countree, A yeoman of Kent, with his yearly rent, will buy them out all three.** 1659: Howell, 17. 1662: Fuller, *Worthies*, ii 121 (1840). 1790: Grose, *Prov. Gloss.*, s.v. 'Kent'. 1840: Barham, *Ing. Legends*: 'Leech of Folkestone'. 1887: Parish and Shaw, *Dict. Kent. Dialect*, 193 (E.D.S.).

Knight or a knitter of caps, A. 1580: Lyly, *Euphues*, 285 (Arber), Determining either to be a knight as we saye, or a knitter of cappes.

Knights. *See* quot. 1606: B. Rich, *Faultes*, fo. 28, The prouerbe is olde, and it may be true, that as knights grow poor, ladies grow prowd.

Knipe-scar. *See* quot. 1846–59: *Denham Tracts*, ii 14 (F.L.S.), When Knipe-scar gets a hood, Sackworth may expect a flood. Westmoreland.

Knock at a deaf man's door, To (or **at the wrong door**). 1616: B. Rich, *Ladies Looking Glasse*, 3, Therefore it is but to knocke at a deafe mans doore. 1639: Clarke, 7, You knock at a deafe man's doore, *or* wrong doore.

Knock in the cradle, He got a. 1678: Ray, 255.

Knock under the board, To = To yield. 1678: Ray, 74, Knock under the board. He must do so that will not drink his cup.

Knock Cross, As old as. 1846–59: *Denham Tracts*, i 207 (F.L.S.).

Knot. 1. To find (or **seek**) **a knot in a rush.** 1340: *Ayenbite*, 253, thet zekth tht uel ine the aye other thane knotte ine th resse. 1532: More, *Works*, 778 (1557). 1567: Jewel, *Defence of Apol.*, Pt IV 733 (P.S.), It is a childish labour to seek a knot in a rush, and to imagine doubts where the case is clear. 1579: Gosson, *Sch. of Abuse*, 46 (Arber), They thinke themselues no scholers, if they bee not able to finde out a knotte in euery rushe. 1661: Davenport, *City Nightcap*, III, The trick's come out, And here's the knot i' th' rush. 1740: North, *Lives of Norths*, i 206 (Bohn), To cavil at every step, and raise moot points, like finding knots in bulrushes.

2. To tie a knot with the tongue not to be undone with the teeth. 1580: Lyly, *Euphues*, 468 (Arber), We might knit that knot with our tongues, that we shall neuer vndoe with our teeth. 1617: Greene, *Works*, ix 76 (Grosart), A woman may knit a knot with her tongue, that shee cannot vntie with all her teeth. 1738: Swift, *Polite Convers.*, Dial. I, He has tied a knot with his tongue, that he can never untie with his teeth. 1831: Scott, *Journal*, 6–7 May, I cannot conceive that I should have tied a knot with my tongue which my teeth cannot untie. 1913: E. M. Wright, *Rustic Speech, etc.*, 272, To get married is: to tie a knot wi' the tongue, 'at yan cannot louze wi' van's teeth (Yorkshire and Northamptonshire).

3. Where the knot is loose the string slippeth. 1639: Clarke, 248. 1670: Ray, 111. 1732: Fuller, 5667.

Knott Mill Fair, As throng [busy] as. Manchester. 1869: Hazlitt, 74.

Knotty timber. *See* quots. 1670: Ray, 15, A knotty piece of timber must have smooth wedges. 1855: Bohn, 438, Knotty timber requires sharp wedges.

Know, *verb*. **1. He knows best what good is that has endured evil.** 1855: Bohn, 378.

2. He knows enough that can live and hold his peace. 1586: Pettie, tr. Guazzo's *Civil Convers.*, fo. 55, It is likewise saide, That he knoweth ynough who knoweth nothing if he know how to holde his peace. 1611: Cotgrave, s.v. 'Scavoir', He is cunning enough that can live and hold his peace. 1629: *Book of Meery Riddles*, Prov. 21 [as in 1586].

3. He knows no end of his wealth. 1546: Heywood, *Proverbs*, Pt I ch xi, They know no ende of their good. 1639: Clarke, 97.

4. He knows not whether his shoe goes awry. 1678: Ray, 81.

5. He knows one point more than the devil. Spoken of a cunning fellow. 1620: Shelton, *Quixote*, Pt II ch xxviii, I know that you know an ace more than the devil in all you speak or think. 1659: Howell, *Proverbs: Span.-Eng.*, 2.

6. He knows tin. Corn. 1864: 'Cornish Proverbs', in *N. & Q.*, 3rd ser, vi 495, One who seems to know tin [a cunning fellow]. 1887: M. A. Courtney, *Folk-Lore Journal*, v 187, 'It's a wise man that knows tin 'alludes to the various forms it takes.

7. He that knoweth himself best, esteemeth himself least. 1647: *Countrym. New Commonwealth*, 26.

8. He that knoweth when he hath enough is no fool. 1546: Heywood, *Proverbs*, Pt II ch vii.

9. He that knows little often repeats it. 1732: Fuller, 2209.

10. He that knows not how to hold his tongue, knows not how to talk. 1669: *Politeuphuia*, 157, He that knows not when to hold his peace, knows not when to speak. 1732: Fuller, 2210.

11. He that knows nothing doubts nothing. 1611: Cotgrave, s.v. 'Rien'. 1640: Herbert, *Jac. Prudentum*. 1869: Spurgeon, *John Ploughman*, ch ii, He who knows nothing is confident in everything.

12. He that knows thee will never buy thee. 1667: L'Estrange, *Quevedo's Visions*, 28 (1904) [cited as 'the old proverb'].

13. I know enough to hold my tongue, but not to speak. 1732: Fuller, 2609.

14. I know him as well as if I had gone through him with a lighted link. 1732: Fuller, 2611. 1880: Spurgeon, *Ploughman's Pictures*, 97 [with 'candle' for 'link'].

15. I know him not though I should meet him in my dish. 1672: Walker, *Paroem.*, 13. 1732: Fuller, 2513 [with 'porridge' for 'dish'].

16. I know no more than the man in the moon. 1805: Scott, in Lockhart's *Life*, ii 28, So on I wrote, knowing no more than the man in the moon how I was to end. 1828: Carr, *Craven Dialect*, i 329, 'I kna naa maar nar man ith moon', I am totally ignorant of it. 1878: R.L.S., *Inland Voyage:* 'Down the Oise', I knew no more than the man in the moon about my only occupation.

17. I know no more than the Pope of Rome. 1663: Butler, *Hudibras*, Pt II can. iii l. 894, He knew no more than the Pope of Rome. 1706: *Oxford Jests*, 93, 'Read! truly, my lord,' says he, 'I can read no more than the Pope of Rome.' 1793: *Looker-on*, No. 73, He … assured the gentleman … that he knew no more of Italy than the Pope of Rome. 1863: *N. & Q.*, 3rd ser, iii 470,1 have often heard persons, when professing entire ignorance of any subject, exclaim 'I know no more than the Pope of Rome about it'.

18. In the world who knows not to swim, goes to the bottom. 1640: Herbert, *Jac. Prudentum*.

19. Know thyself. The motto inscribed above the door of the temple at Delphi and rendered into Latin by Juvenal as *nosce teipsum*. 1387: J. Trevisa, tr. *Higden's Polychronicon* (1865), I 241, While the cherle smoot the victor, he schulde ofte seie to hym in this manere … Knowe thyself. 1545: R. Ascham, *Toxophilus*, II 36, Knowe thy selfe: That is to saye, leane to knowe what thou arte able, fitte and aPt unto, and folowe that. 1732: Pope, *Essay on Man*, II 1, Know then thyself, presume not God to scan; The proper study of mankind is Man.

20. Know yourself and your neighbours will not mistake you. 1899: Dickinson, *Cumb. Gloss.*, 184.

21. One may know by his nose what porridge he loves. 1590: Lodge, *Rosalynde*, 91 (Hunt.Cl.), Your nose bewrayes what porredge you loue. 1631: Mabbe, *Celestina*, 104 (T.T.), I know by your nose what porridge you love. 1732: Fuller, 3775.

22. One may know your meaning by your gaping, (*etc.*) 1639: Clarke, 64, I know your meaning by your winking. 1659: Howell, 21, You may know his meaning by his gaping. 1667: L'Estrange, *Quevedo's Visions*, 112 (1904), They might have known their meaning by their mumping. 1670: Ray, 186. 1738: Swift, *Polite Convers.*, Dial. II, I can tell your meaning by your mumping. 1753: Richardson, *Grandison*, iv 226 (1883), You know my meaning by my gaping.

23. They that know one another, salute afar off. 1640: Herbert, *Jac. Prudentum.*

24. To know one from a black sheep. 1670: Ray, 183.

25. To know what's what. *See* **What's what**.

26. To know when one is well. 1553: *Respublica*, IV iv, Thou canst not see, thow wretch, canst thow, whan thow art well? 1576: Wapull, *Tide tarrieth no Man*, Prol., Neyther of them know when they are well. 1692: Southerne, *Wives Excuse*, III ii, You are very happy in the discretion of a good lady, if you know when you're well. 1738: Swift, *Polite Convers.*, Dial. I, I won't quarrel with my bread and butter for all that: I know when I'm well. 1855: Kingsley, *West. Ho!*, ch xix, 'Overboard with you!' quoth Amyas. 'Don't you know when you are well off?'

27. What you don't know can't hurt you. 1576: G. Pettie, *Petit Palace*, 168, Why should I seeke to take him in it? ... So long as I know it not, it hurteth me not. 1908: E. Walter, *Easiest Way*, III 66, What a fellow doesn't know, doesn't hurt him, and he'll love you just the same.

28. With all thy knowledge know thyself. 1659: Howell, 11 (9).

29. You know not where a blessing may light. 1869: Hazlitt, 486.

30. You may know by a handful the whole sack. 1732: Fuller, 5949.

31. You never know what you can do till you try. 1818: Cobbett, *Year's Residence in the USA*, II vi, A man knows not what he can do 'till he tries. 1837: Dickens, *Pickwick*, ch xlix.

Knowledge hath no enemy but ignorance. 1559: W. Cunningham, *Cosmogr. Glasse*, 46 (OED). 1613: Wither, *Abuses Stript, etc.*, bk ii sat. 1, For thus the saying goes, and I hold so; *Ignorance onely is true wisedomes foe.* 1654: Whitlock, *Zootomia*, 160.

Knowledge is a treasure, but practice is the key to it. [c.1460: *Prov. of Good Counsel*, in E.E.T.S., Ext. Ser. No. 8, p. 69, For of all tresure connynge ys flowur.] 1732: Fuller, 3139. Cf. **Knowledge without practice**.

Knowledge is no burden. 1640: Herbert, *Jac. Prudentum.* 1690: *New Diet. Canting Crew*, sig. G7.

Knowledge is power. [Nam et ipsa scientia potestas est. – Bacon, *De Heresibus*. A wise man is strong. – *Prov.* xxiv 5.] 1620: Bacon, *Novum Organum*, 1, Knowledge and human power are synonymous, since the ignorance of the cause frustrates the effect. 1822: Byron, *Letters and Journals*, vi 11 (Prothero), They say that 'Knowledge is Power': I used to think so. 1878: Platt, *Business*, 2, To commercial men knowledge is power. 1923: *Sphere*, 29 Dec., p. 368, col. 1, The old copybook maxim, 'Knowledge is power'.

Knowledge makes one laugh, but wealth makes one dance. 1640: Herbert, *Jac. Prudentum.* 1690: *New Diet. Canting Crew*, sig. G7.

Knowledge without practice makes but half an artist 1732: Fuller, 3141. 1885: *N.&Q.*, 6th ser, xii 450 [cited as 'The English proverb']. Cf. **Knowledge is a treasure**.

Knowledge. *See also* **Gentleman** (11); and **Zeal**. **Kype**. *See* **Scrape**.

L

Labour for one's pains, To have one's. 1589: Nashe: in Greene's *Works*, vi 13 (Grosart), They haue nought but … (to bring it to our English prouerbe) their labour for their trauaile. 1609: Shakespeare, *Troilus*, I i, I have had my labour for my travail. 1675: Cotton, *Burl, upon Burlesque*, 186 (1765), And all that I by that should gain Would be *my labour for my pain*. 1709: Mandeville, *Virgin Unmask'd*, 59 (1724), You'll get nothing but your labour for your pains. 1778: Burney, *Evelina*, Lett. xxxiii, I'm glad the villain got nothing but his trouble for his pains.

Labour in vain is loss of time. 1639: Clarke, 61.

Labour is light where love doth pay. 1594: Drayton, *Ideas*, lix.

Labour to be as you would be thought. *c.*1597: in Harington, *Nugae Antiquae*, i 210 (1804).

Labour. *See also* **Past labour**.

Labourer is worthy of his hire, The. [Luke x.7, *The labourer is worthy of his hire*]. *c.*1390: Chaucer, *Summoner's Tale*, l. 1973, The hye God, that al this world hath wroght, Seith that the werkman worthy is his hyre. 1580: J. Baret, *Alveary*, D697, *Digna canis pabulo* … A Proverbe declaring that the laborer is worthie of his hire. 1824: Scott, *St Ronan's Well*, I x, Your service will not be altogether gratuitous, my old friend – the labourer is worthy of his hire.

Labours and thrives, spins gold, He that. 1640: Herbert, *Jac. Prudentum*. 1670: Ray, 15. 1732: Fuller, 2211.

Lack a tile, lack a sheaf. 1639: Clarke, 10.

Lacketh a stock, Whoso, his gain is not worth a chip. 1546: Heywood, *Proverbs*, Pt II ch ix 1605: Camden, *Remains*, 335 (1870). 1670: Ray, 146. 1732: Fuller, 5731.

Lad to wed a lady. *See* quot. 1513: Bradshaw, *St Werburge*, 43 (E.E.T.S.), By a prouerbe auncyent 'A lad [lout] to wedde a lady is an inconuenyent'.

Ladder to bed, You'll go up the = be hanged. 1678: Ray, 256.

Laden with iron, laden with fear. 1631: Mabbe, *Celestina*, 204 (T.T.), It is not saide in vaine; Laden with iron, laden with feare. 1666: Torriano, *Piazza Univ.*, 88 ['loaded' for 'laden'].

Ladie Lift. *See* quot. Ladie Lift Clump is a clump of trees on the top of a high hill near Bredwardine, Herefordshire. 1881: C. W. Empson, in *Folk-Lore Record*, iv 130, When Ladie Lift Puts on her shift, She feares a downright raine; But when she doffs it, you will finde The rain is o'er and still the winde, And Phoebus shine againe. – *Herefordshire*.

Lads' love's a busk of broom, hot awhile and soon done. Cheshire. 1670: Ray, 46. 1877: E. Leigh, *Cheshire Gloss.*, 34. 1917: Bridge, *Cheshire Proverbs*, 87. Cf. **Love**, *subs.* (31).

Lads' love is lassies' delight, And if lads don't love, lassies will flite. 1828: Carr, *Craven Dialect*, i 273. 1917: Bridge, *Cheshire Proverbs*, 87.

Lady-birds. *See* **Hops** (3).

Lady-day. 1. On Lady-day the latter, The cold comes on the water. 1732: Fuller, 6217.

2. When our Lady. *See* first quot. 1662: Fuller, *Worthies*, i 113 (1840), 'When our Lady falls in our Lord's lap, Then let England beware a sad clap (*or* mishap)'. *Alias* 'Then let the clergyman look to his cap'. I behold this proverbial prophecy, or this prophetical menace, to be not above six score years old, and of Popish extraction since the Reformation. 1790: Grose, *Prov. Gloss.*, s.v. 'England' [as in 1662]. 1812: Brady, *Clavis Cal.*, i 261 [as in 1662]. Cf. **Easter**.

Lady Done. *See* **Fair** (15).

Lady's heart and a beggar's purse, Nothing agreeth worse than a. 1546: Heywood, *Proverbs*, Pt I ch x Cf. **Lord** (1).

Lag puts all in his bag. 1666: Torriano, *Piazza Univ.*, 322, The English say, Lagg puts all in his bagg.

Lamb. 1. A lamb in the house a lion in the field, *c.*1387: Usk, *Test, of Love*, in Skeat's *Chaucer*, vii 24, Lyons in the felde and lambes in chambre. 1589: Puttenham, *Eng. Poesie*, 299 (Arber), We say it is comely for a man to be a lambe in the house, and a lyon in the field. 1593: G. Harvey, *Works*, i 277 (Grosart), A lion in the field, a lamme in the towne.

2. A lamb is as dear to a poor man, as an ox to the rich. [1611: Cotgrave, s.v. 'Povre', An egge's as much to a poor man as an oxe.] 1732: Fuller, 234.

3. Every lamb knows its dam. Ibid., No. 6490.

4. Go to bed with the lamb. *See* **Rise** (12).

5. The first lamb. *See* quot. 1862: R. S. Hawker, in Byles, *Life, etc.*, 357 (1905), Did you ever hear the saying that if the first lamb be a lady the Mistress of the house will govern for that year, and if *versa vice* the first be a gentleman then the Master?

See also **Fox** (18) and (23); **God tempers**; **Mild**; and **Quiet**

Lamb's skin. *See* **Soon goes**.

Lambeth Doctor, A. 1790: Grose, *Prov. Gloss.*, s.v. 'Surrey'.

Lambskin, To lap in a. 1546: Heywood, *Proverbs*, Pt II ch vi, She must obey those lambs, or els a lambs skyn Ye will prouyde for hir, to lap her in. Cf. *The Wyfe lapped in Morels Skyn* (*c.*1570), in Hazlitt, *Early Pop. Poetry*, iv.

Lambtons. *See* quot. 1846–59: *Denham Tracts*, i 106 (F.L.S.), In the northern portion of the bishoprick [of Durham], and southern border of Northumberland, they have an old saw, when speaking of a dashing, flashing, stylish fellow, 'Oh! he's fit to keep company with the Lambtons'.

Lame as a cat, As. 1889: Peacock, *Manley, etc., Gloss.*, 98 (E.D.S.) [a 'proverb'].

Lame as a dog, As. 1886: Elworthy, *West Som. Word-Book*, 202 (E.D.S.), 'Lame as a dog 'is the constantly used expression to denote severe lameness, whether in man or beast.

Lame as a tree, As. 1869: Hazlitt, 65.

Lame dog over a stile, To help a. 1546: Heywood, *Proverbs*, Pt I ch xi, As good a deede As it is to helpe a dogge ouer a style. 1630: Taylor (Water-Poet), *Works*, 2nd pagin., 249, My wit should be so crippled with the gowt, That it must haue assistance to compile, Like a lame dog, that's limping o'r a stile. 1720: C. Shadwell, *Hasty Wedding*, II, You're a clever fellow to lead a lame dog over a stile. 1788: Wolcot, *Works*, i 509 (1795), Let me display a Christian spirit, And try to lift a lame dog o'er a stile. 1901: S. Butler, in H. F. Jones's *Life*, i 344 (1919), When my nightly game of patience goes amiss … I sometimes help a lame dog over a style [*sic*] by a little cheating rather than waste the game.

Lame Giles has played the man. 1639: Clarke, 17.

Lame goes as far as the staggerer, The. 1640: Herbert, *Jac. Prudentum*. 1670: Ray, 15.

Lame hares are ill to help. 1732: Fuller, 3143.

Lame post brings the truest news, The. Ibid., No. 4620.

Lame returns sooner than his servant, The. 1659: Howell, *Proverbs: Brit.-Eng.*, 40.

Lame tongue gets nothing, The. 1605: Camden, *Remains*, 333 (1870). 1732: Fuller, 4619. 1830: Forby, *Vocab. E. Anglia*, 434.

Lame traveller should get out betimes, A. 1732: Fuller, 235.

Lammas, After, corn ripens as much by night as by day. 1678: Ray, 352. 1893: Inwards, *Weather Lore*, 33.

Lammas-tide. *See* **Cuckoo** (16).

Lancashire fair women. 1622: Drayton, *Polyol.*, xxiii, Fair women doth belong to Lancashire again. 1662: Fuller, *Worthies*, ii 191 (1840). 1710: *Brit. Apollo*, iii No. 30, col. 4, Lancashire fair women is past into a proverb. 1790: Grose, *Prov. Gloss.*, s.v. 'Lancs'.

Lancashire law, no stakes, no draw. 1828: Carr, *Craven Dialect*, i 274. 1847: Halliwell, *Dict.*, s.v. … a saying to avoid payment of a bet when verbally made. 1901: F. E. Taylor, *Lancs Sayings*, 41. Cf. **Stopford law**.

Lancashire man. *See* quots. 1599: Buttes, *Dyets Dry Dinner*, sig. A2, Here are neither eg-pies for the Lancashireman, nor … 1622: Drayton, *Polyol.*, xxvii 68, Ye lusty lasses then, in Lancashire that dwell … As ye the egg-pye love, and apple cherry-red. 1655: T. Muffett, *Healths Improvement*, 36, As our Welshmen esteem of cheese, Lancashire men of egg-pies. 1711: Hearne, *Collections*, iii 156 (Oxford Hist. S.), He yt will fish for a Lancashire Lad At any time or tide Must bait his hook with a good egg py or an apple wth a red side. 1911: Hackwood, *Good Cheer*, 163 [as in 1711].

Land and **Lands. 1. He that hath lands, hath quarrels,** 1640: Herbert, *Jac. Prudentum*. 1855: Bohn, 566, Who has land has war.

2. He that hath some land, must have some labour. 1639: Clarke, 59. 1670: Ray, 112. 1732: Fuller, 2161.

3. Land was never lost for want of an heir. 1678: Ray, 165.

See also **House** (17).

Land's End. *See* quots. 1546: Heywood, *Proverbs*, Pt II ch vii, Thou gossepst at home to meete me at landis ende. 1560: T. Wilson, *Rhetorique*, 148 (1909), Some newe fellowes when they thinke one a papist, they will call him streight a catholique, and bee euen with him at the lands end.

Land's End to John o' Groats, From. 1823: Scott, *St Ronan's*, ch x, I can beat Wolverine from the Land's-End to Johnnie Groat's. 1831: Peacock, *Crotchet Castle*, ch iv, Who forages for articles in all quarters, from John o' Groat's House to the Land's End.

Landlords. *See* **Quick landlord**.

Land-mark stones. *See* **Stone** (4).

Lane, In the. *See* **Always in the lane**.

Lansallos treat, A, everybody pay for hisself. 1906: *Cornish N. & Q.*, 265.

Lapped. *See* **Wrapped**.

Lapwing cries most farthest from her nest, The. 1584: Lyly, *Campaspe*, II i, Wherein you resemble the lapwing, who crieth most where her nest is not. *c*.1620: Massinger, *Old Law*, IV ii, He has the lapwing's cunning, I am afraid. That cries most when she's furthest from the nest. 1732: Fuller, 4621.

Lareovers. *See* **Layers**.

Lark and Larks. 1. A leg of a lark is better than the body of a kite. 1546: Heywood, *Proverbs*, Pt I ch iv 1605: Chapman, etc., *Eastw. Hoe*, V i, The legge of a larke is better then the body of a kight. 1732: Fuller, 3765.

2. It were better to hear the lark sing than the mouse cheep. 1855: Bohn, 435.

3. Larks fall there ready roasted. 1659: Howell, *Proverbs: Fr.-Eng.*, 3, He thinks that roasted larks will fall into his mouth; spoken of a sluggard.

See also **Lovers; Rise** (12); and **Sky falls**.

Lartington. *See* quot. 1846–59: *Denham Tracts*, i 81 (F.L.S.), Lartington for frogs, And Barney Castle for butchers' dogs; or, Lartington frogs, And Barney Castle butcher-dogs. 1852: Longstaffe, *Richmondshire*, 133.

Lass in the red petticoat shall pay for all. The. 1664: J. Wilson, *The Cheats*, I ii, That estate Which you believe so fair ... is at present At that low ebb, that if I don't look to't In time, it will be past recovery. Come; the red petticoat must piece up all. 1678: Ray, 80.

Lassies are lads' leavings. Cheshire. 1670: Ray, 217. 1917: Bridge, *Cheshire Proverbs*, 88.

Last benefit is most remembered, The. 1732: Fuller, 4622.

Last but not least. 1580: Lyly, *Euphues*, 343 (Arber), Of these three but one can stand me in steede, the last, but not the least. 1676: Shadwell, *Virtuoso*, IV iv, These are the last, but

not the least. 1782: in *Twining Fam. Papers*, 103 (1887), Upon my word, a goodly party, and the rear well brought up by Mr George T., though 'last, not least'.

Last dog. *See* **Dog** (78).

Last drop makes the cup run over, The. 1655: T. Fuller, *Church History of Britain*, XI ii, When the Cup is brim full before, the last (though least) superadded drop is charged alone to be the cause of all the running over.1855: Bohn, 509.

Last evil smarts most, The. 1732: Fuller, 4623.

Last for his shoe, He has found a. Ibid., No. 1869.

Last has luck: Finds a penny in the muck. Worcs. 1904: Lean, *Collectanea*, iv 27.

Last legs, To be on one's. 1599: Massinger, etc., *Old Law*, V i (OED), *Eugenia*. My husband goes upon his last hour now. *1st Courtier*. On his last legs, I am sure. 1678: Ray, 89, He goes on's last legs. 1753: Richardson, *Grandison*, iv 50 (1883), What would poor, battered rakes and younger brothers do, when on their last legs, were it not for good-natured widows? 1827: Hone, *Ev. Day Book*, ii 1013, The 'regular drama' is on its last legs. 1857: Trollope, *Batch. Towers*, ch i, The bishop was quite on his last legs.

Last makes fast. 1659: Ho well, 6, Last makes fast, viz. Shut the door. 1881: Evans, *Leics. Words*, 302 (E.D.S.), 'Last makes fast' ... is a recognised rule in passing through a gate that has been opened. Cf. **Come** (14).

Last prayers, She is at her. 1678: Ray, 79. 1690: *New Dict. Canting Crew*, sig. L5, Stale maid, at her last prayers. 1698: *Terence made English*, 157 (2nd ed.), S'death! I'm at my last prayers.

Last race-horse brings snow on his tail, The. 1884: 'Sussex Proverbs', in *N. & Q.*, 6th ser, ix 402.

Last straw breaks the camel's back, The. [Quemadmodum clepsydram non extremum stillicidium exhaurit, sed quidquid ante defluxit; sic ultima hora qua esse desinimus, non sola mortem facit, sed sola consummat. – Seneca, *Ep.*, xxiv 19.] 1677: Arch bp. Bramhall, *Works*, iv 59, It is the last feather that breaks the horse's back. 1732: Fuller, 5120 [as in 1677]. 1848: Dickens, *Dombey*, ch ii, As the last straw breaks the laden camel's back ... 1869: P. Fitzgerald, *Comediettas*, It is the Last Straw that breaks the Camel's Back [title of play].

Last suitor wins the maid, The. 1611: Cotgrave, s.v. 'Aimé' [with 'wench' for 'maid']. 1670: Ray, 15. 1732: Fuller, 4624.

Last to the pot is soonest wroth, He that cometh. *c.*1400: *Beryn*, l. 3366, p. 101 (E.E.T.S.), fful soth is that byword, 'to pot, who comyth last! He worst is servid'; and so it farith by me. 1546: Heywood, *Proverbs*, Pt II ch x 1659: Howell, 8.

Last word though he talk bilk for it, He'll have the. 1678: Ray, 228.

Late repentance is seldom true. 1552: Latimer, *Works*, ii 193 (P.S.), It is a common saying, *Paenitentia sera raro vera.* 1639: Clarke, 255. 1732: Fuller, 3145.

Lathom and Knowsley. *See* quot. 1858: *N. & Q.*, 2nd ser, v 211, It is a very common expression [Lancashire] to say of a person having two houses, even if temporarily, that he has 'Lathom and Knowsley' ... Though separate possessions for above 150 years, the expression 'Lathom and Knowsley' still survives.

Latter Lammas = never. 1553: *Res-publica*, III v, Faith youer Marsship will thrive att the latter Lammas. *c.*1566: in Collmann, *Ballads, etc.*, 92 (Roxb.Cl.) 1672: Walker, *Paroem.*, 52, At latter Lammas; at Nevermass. 1709: O. Dykes, *Eng. Proverbs*, xxxvi 1754: *Gent. Mag.*, 416. 1885: W. L. Birkbeck, *Hist. Sketch Distrib. of Land in Eng.*, Pt I ch v, Hence 'Latter Lammas', a later month than Lammas, became proverbial, as an equivalent to the Greek Calends.

Laugh, *verb.* **1. He can laugh and cry both in a wind.** 1670: Ray, 184. 1732: Fuller, 4120 [with 'she' for 'he'].

2. He is not laughed at that laughs at himself first. Ibid., No. 1936.

3. He laughs best that laughs last. *c.*1607: *Christmas Prince* (1923), 109, He laugheth best that laugheth to the end. 1706: Vanbrugh, *Country House*, II v 1823: Scott, *Peveril*, ch xxxviii., Your Grace knows the French proverb, 'He laughs best who laughs last'. But I hear you. 1920: O. Onions, *A Case in Camera*, 147, Very well, young-fellow-me-lad; you watch it! They laugh best that laugh last. It isn't over yet!

4. He laughs ill that laughs himself to death. 1639: Clarke, 201. 1670: Ray, 15. 1732: Fuller, 1962.

5. He who laughs last, laughs longest. A more modern version of **Laugh** (3). 1912: J.

Masefield, *the Widow in Bye Street*, IV 66, In this life he laughs longest who laughs last. 1943: J. Lodwick, *Running to Paradise*, xxx, He who laughs last laughs longest, and in another four days I was able to look at my mug in the mirror without wincing.

6. Laugh and grow fat. 1596: Harington, *Metam. of Ajax*, 68 (1814), Many of the worshipful of the city, that make sweet gains of stinking wares; and will laugh and be fat. *c.*1610: in *Roxb. Ballads*, i 476 (B.S.), Ile laugh and be fatte, for care kils a catte. 1765: Garrick, in *Garrick Corresp.*, i 201 (1831), Laugh and be fat all the world over. 1823: Scott, *Peveril*, ch xxxiii, He seems to have reversed the old proverb of 'laugh and be fat'. 1926: *Humorist*, 9 Oct., p. 237, col. 3, I was told, by my excellent daddy, To laugh and grow fat.

7. Laugh and lie down. Before 1529: Skelton, *Works*, ii 55 (Dyce), Now nothynge but pay, pay, With, laugh and lay downe, Borowgh, cyte, and towne. 1596: A. Copley, *Fig for Fortune*, 24 (Spens.S.), 'Tis faire lie downe and laugh. 1641: R. Brome, *Joviall Crew*, III. 1671: *Westm. Drollery*, 28 (Ebsworth), And when we have done These Innocent sports, we'll laugh and lie down. 1825: Jennings, *Somerset Words*, 52, Laugh-and-lie-down. A common game at cards.

8. Laugh and the world laughs with you; cry and you cry alone. [ut ridentibus arrident, ita flentibus adsunt humani voltus.** (As the faces of men laugh upon those who laugh, so they weep upon those who weep) Horace, *Ars Poetica*, 101] 1883: E.W. Wilcox, *Solitude*, Laugh and the world laughs with you; Weep, and you weep alone. For the sad old earth must borrow its mirth, But has trouble enough of its own.

9. Let them laugh that win. 1546: Heywood, *Proverbs*, Pt I ch v, He laughth that wynth. 1599: Sir *Clyomon, etc.*, sig. F1, Wel let them laugh that win. 1604: Shakespeare, *Othello*, IV i, So, so: they laugh that win. 1674: Head and Kirkman, *Eng. Rogue*, iii 132, If the proverb be true, *Let them laugh that win*. 1767: Garrick, *Epil.* to Colman's *Eng. Merchant*. 1844: Thackeray, *Barry Lyndon*, ch xiii, Let those laugh that win. 1862: Borrow, *Wild Wales*, ch lxiv.

10. Shut your eyes when you laugh, and you'll never see a merry day. W. Corn. (Mr C. Lee).

11. To laugh from the teeth outwards. 1532: More, *Confut. of Tyndale*, cxlviii, He lawgheth but from the lyppes forwarde. 1611: Cotgrave, s.v. 'Rire', *Rire à grosses dents*. From the teeth outwards, say we. 1754: Berthelson, *Eng.-Danish Dict.*, s.v. 'Laugh'.

12. To laugh in one's face and cut one's throat. 1670: Ray, 184. 1716: E. Ward, *Female Policy*, 53, A woman will … laugh in your face, and cut your throat. 1732: Fuller, 5194.

13. To laugh in one's sleeve. [Tu videlicet tecum ipse rides. – Cicero, *De Fin.*, II. xxiii.76] 1546: Heywood, *Proverbs*, Pt II ch v. 1567: Harman, *Caveat*, 46 (E.E.T.S.). Hee laughed in his sleue. 1683: Chalkhill, *Thealma, etc.*, 89 (1820), Now Orandra laugh within her sleeve. 1744–6: Mrs Haywood, *Fem. Spectator*, ii 95 (1771), A certain gentleman … may be laughing in his sleeve at me. 1849: C. Brontë, *Shirley*, ch viii, There was a kind of leer about his lips; he seemed laughing in his sleeve at some person or thing.

14. To laugh like a piskie. 1865: Hunt, *Pop. Romances W. of Eng.*, 82 (1896), They [the fairies] must have been a merry lot, since to 'laugh like a Piskie 'is a popular saying.

15. To laugh on the wrong side of one's mouth. 1666: Torriano, *Piazza Univ.*, 173, Now you can laugh but on one side of your mouth, friend. 1714: Ozell, *Molière*, iv 36, If you provoke me, I'll make you laugh on the wrong side O' your mouth. 1849: C. Brontë, *Shirley*, ch xxx, I see, however, you laugh at the wrong side of your mouth; you have as sour a look at this moment as one need wish to see. 1925: *Times*, 6 March, p. 12, col. 2, You laugh immoderately, and end by laughing on the wrong side of the mouth.

Laughton. *See* **Bolsover.**

Laundress washeth her own smock first, The. 1732: Fuller, 4626.

Lavants, The. *See* quot. 1789: White, *Selborne:* 'Letters to Barrington', xix, The land springs which we call lavants, break out much on the Downs of Sussex, Hampshire, and Wiltshire. The country people say 'When the lavants rise, corn will always be dear'.

Lavishness is not generosity. 1732: Fuller, 3147.

Law and Laws. 1. A suit at law and a urinal bring a man to the hospital. 1670: Ray. 15. 1732: Fuller, 6238.

2. He is a crust of the law; he will never know a crumb of it. 1830: Forby, *Vocab. E. Anglia*, 430.

3. He that goes to law holds a wolf by the ears. 1621: Burton, *Melancholy*, Dem. to Reader, 48 (1836), He that goes to law (as the proverb is) holds a wolf by the ears. Cf. **Wolf** (15).

4. He will go to law for the wagging of a straw. 1615: W. Goddard, *Nest of Wasps*, No. 16, Thou knowst a barlie strawe Will make a parish parson goe to lawe. 1670: Ray, 184. Cf. **Wagging.**

5. In a thousand pounds of law there's not an ounce of love. 1611: Cotgrave, s.v. 'Amour', In a hundred pound of law ther's not a half-peny weight of love. 1670: Ray, 15. 1732: Fuller, 2811, In a thousand pounds worth of law, there is not a shilling's worth of pleasure.

6. Law governs man, and reason the law. 1732: Fuller, 3149.

7. Law, Logic and Switzers may be hired to fight for anybody. 1593: Nashe, *Christs Teares*, in *Works*, iv 148 (Grosart). 1630: Brathwait, *Eng. Gent., etc.*, 7 (1641), It is commonly said that Law, etc … *c.*1640: Davenport, in *Works*, 327 (Bullen), Law, logick, Switzers, fight on any side.

8. Laws catch flies, but let the hornets go free. 1591: Harington, *Orl. Furioso*, bk xxxii, Notes, For the most part lawes are but like spiders webs, taking the small gnats, or perhaps sometime the fat flesh flies, but hornets that have sharpe stings and greater strength, breake through them. 1625: Bacon, *Apoph*, No. 181, One of the Seven was wont to say, 'That laws were like cobwebs: where the small flies were caught, and the great brake thorough'. 1732: Fuller, 3150.

9. The law groweth of sin and doth punish it. 1578: Florio, *First Fruites*, fo. 32. 1629: *Book of Meery Riddles*, Prov. 39 [with 'chastiseth' for 'doth punish'].

10. The law is not the same at morning and at night. 1640: Herbert, *Jac. Prudentum*. 1670: Ray, 15.

11. There's one law for the rich and another for the poor. 1830: Marryat, *King's Own*, I xi, Is there nothing smuggled besides gin? Now if the husbands and fathers of these ladies – those who have themselves enacted the laws – wink at their infringement, why should not other do so? There cannot be on law for the rich and another for the poor. 1913: *Spectator*, 8 Nov., 757, The idea prevails abroad that there is one law for the 'rich' Englishman and another for the 'poor' foreigner.

12. The worst of law is that one suit breeds twenty. 1640: Herbert, *Jac. Prudentum.* 1670: Ray, 15.

See also **Agree; Igorance.**

Lawless as a town-bull, As. 1678: Ray, 286. 1732: Fuller, 706. Cf. **No law.**

Law-makers. *See* **Make** (13).

Lawn. *See* quots. 1546: Heywood, *Proverbs*, Pt I ch viii, He that will sell lawne before he can folde it, He shall repent him before he haue solde it. 1580: Lyly, *Euphues*, 290 (Arber), He that will sell lawne must learne to folde it. *c.*1594: Bacon, *Promus*, No. 474 (as in 1546]. 1670: Ray, 112, He that buyes lawn before, etc … 1732: Fuller, 6443 [as in 1670].

Lawrence. *See* **Lazy Lawrence.**

Lawton-gate a clap, She hath given. 1678: Ray, 300. 1710: *Brit. Apollo*, iii No. 26, col. 7. 1877: E. Leigh, *Cheshire Gloss.*, 43, They say of a girl who from misconduct finds it convenient to leave the county, 'She has given Lawton Gate a clap' – Lawton being the boundary of Cheshire towards Staffordshire. 1917: Bridge, *Cheshire Proverbs*, 109.

Lawyer and **Lawyers. 1. A good lawyer, an evil neighbour.** 1611: Cotgrave, s.v. 'Advocat'. 1670: Ray, 15. 1754: Berthelson, *Eng.-Danish Dict.*, s.v. 'Neighbour', A good lawyer is an ill neighbour. 1831: Hone, *Year-Book*, 125 [quoted as an old French saying].

2. A good lawyer must be a great liar. 1703: E. Ward, *Writings*, ii 319 [cited as 'a common saying'].

3. A wise lawyer never goes to law himself. 1855: Bohn, 303.

4. Fair and softly as lawyers go to Heaven. 1670: Ray, 193. 1694: Motteux, *Rabelais*, bk v ch xxviii, Come, let's now talk with deliberation, fair and softly, as lawyers go to Heaven. 1856: *N. & Q.*, 2nd ser, i 267, The following was related to me the other day by a Salopian: 'An inch every Good Friday, the rate lawyers go to Heaven'. 1894: Northall, *Folk Phrases*, 11 (E.D.S.), By degrees, as lawyers go to Heaven. 1901: F. E. Taylor, *Lancs Sayings*, 15 [as in 1894].

5. Few lawyers die well. 1605: Camden, *Remains*, 321 (1870).

6. He hath as many tricks as a lawyer. 1672: Walker, *Paraem.*, 51.

7. He who is his own lawyer, has a fool for his client. 1809: *Port Folio* (Philadelphia), Aug.,

132, He who is always his own counsellor will often have a fool for his client. 1850: L. Hunt, *Autobiography*, II xi, The proprietor of the *Morning Chronicle* pleaded his own cause, an occasion on which a man is said to have a fool for a client. 1875: A. B. Cheales, *Proverb. Folk-Lore*, 76.

8. Kick an attorney downstairs and he'll stick to you for life. 'A Bar proverb'. 1904: Lean, *Collectanea*, iv 24.

9. Lawyers and asses always die in their shoes. 1867: Harland, etc., *Lancs Folk-Lore*, 20, The proverb that 'lawyers … shoes 'is invariably quoted,

10. Lawyers' gowns are lined with the wilfulness of their clients. 1855: Bohn, 439.

11. Lawyers' houses are built on the heads of fools. 1640: Herbert, *Jac. Prudentum.* 1660: Howell, *Parly of Beasts*, 17, The lawyer replied … this house [his own] is made of asses heads and fools sculls. 1865: 'Lancs Proverbs', in *N. & Q.*, 3rd ser, viii 494 ['Attorneys' for 'Lawyers'].

12. You are one of those lawyers that never heard of Littleton. 1732: Fuller, 5858.

See also **Hide nothing;** and **Part three things.**

Lay a stone at one's door, To = To 'cut' one. 1872: J. Glyde, jr., *Norfolk Garland*, 150, He has laid a stone at my door.

Lay a straw, To = To make a stop, or mark a stopping-place. *c.*1510: A. Barclay, *Egloges*, 47 (Spens.S.), Haue done nowe Faustus, lay here a straw. 1562: Bullein, *Bulwarke of Defence*, fo. 21, But here will I stoppe, and laie a strawe, and fall into my bias againe. 1619: B. Rich, *Irish Hubbub*, 54, But I will here stop and lay a straw.

Lay a thing in one's dish, To = To accuse, or to charge against, one. 1559: Becon, *Prayers, etc.*, 390 (P.S.), Let no man object and lay in my dish old custom. 1560: T. Wilson, *Rhetorique*, Prol. (1909), That it be not yet once again cast in my dish. 1609: in Halliwell, *Books of Characters*, 96 (1857), Your former follies shall be laide in your dish. 1681: W. Robertson, *Phraseol. Generalis*, 806, To lay in ones dish; Aliquid alieni, ut crimen, objicere. 1740: North, *Lives of Norths*, i 191 (Bohn), He found that, when they were pressed, they laid a fresh story in his dish. 1816: Scott, *Old Mortality*, ch x, If I had thought I was to have had him cast in my dish … 1894: Northall, *Folk Phrases*, 31 (E.D.S.), To throw a thing in one's teeth, *or* dish = to reproach.

Lay a water, To = To defer judgment. 1401: in Wright, *Pol. Poems*, ii 43 (Rolls Ser., 1861), But, Jack, thoug thi questions semen to thee wyse, yit lightly a lewid [unlearned] man maye leyen hem a water. 1533: *Ballads from MSS.*, i 228 (B.S.), And care not thoughe the matter were clerely layde a watter. 1546: Heywood, *Proverbs*, Pt I ch iii, The triall therof we will lay a water Till we trie more. 1592: Lyly, *Mydas*, IV iii, I see all his expeditions for warres are laid in water; for now when he should execute, he begins to consult.

Lay it on with a trowel, To. 1601: Shakespeare, *As You Like It*, I ii, Well said: that was laid on with a trowel. 1693: Congreve, *Double Dealer*, III x, Paints, d'ye say? Why, she lays it on with a trowel. 1732: Fuller, 5930, You lay on your butter as with a trowel. 1784: *New Foundl. Hosp. for Wit*, iii 81, They also lay on praise with a trowel, 1860: Reade, *Cl. and Hearth*, ch 1., The old hand laying the court butter on his back with a trowel. 1921: J. C. Squire, in *Observer*, 10 April, p. 4, col. 3, And Disraeli, actor in his own play, who laid the flattery on with a trowel.

Lay on more wood, ashes give money. [1611: Cotgrave, s.v. 'Bois', All wood is worth logs.] 1678: Ray, 65. 1732: Fuller, 3152, Lay on more wood: the ashes will yield money.

Lay things by, they may come to use. Ibid., No. 3154.

Lay thy hand on thy heart and speak the truth. 1659: Howell, 21.

Layers (or **Lay-overs**) **for meddlers.** *See* quots. 1690: *New Dict. Canting Crew*, sig. G7, Lare-over, said when the true name of the thing must (in decency) be concealed. 1785: Grose, *Class. Dict. Vulgar Tongue*, s.v. 'Lareovers', Lareovers for medlers, an answer frequently given to children ... as a rebuke for their impertinent curiosity. 1854: Baker, *Northants Gloss.*, s.v. 'Lay-o'ers', Lay-o'ers-for-meddlers. An expression used to repress childish or impertinent curiosity. A contraction of *lay-overs*, i.e. things laid over, covered up, or protected from meddlers. 1879: Jackson, *Shropsh. Word-Book*, 249, Lay-o'ers-for-meddlers. 1902: *N. & Q.*, 9th ser, x 475, Almost every county has its variation probably of this phrase. The most common form in which it survives, however, is 'Layers for meddlers', and it is generally, though not exclusively so, addressed to over-inquisitive children.

Laziness is not worth a pin unless it is well followed. 1864: 'Cornish Proverbs', in *N. & Q.*, 3rd ser, vi 495.

Laziness travels so slowly that Poverty soon overtakes him. 1736: Franklin, *Way to Wealth*, in *Works*, i 443 (Bigelow).

Lazy as Ludlam's dog, that leant his head against a wall to bark. The quotations show variations in the name of the dog's owner. 1670: Ray, 202. *c.*1791: Pegge, *Derbicisms*, 135 (E.D.S.) ... who laid himself down to bark. 1801: Wolcot, *Works*, v 118 (1801) .... that held his head against the wall to bark. 1850: *N. & Q.*, 1st ser, i 382, As lazy as Ludlum's dog, as laid him down to bark. 1883: Burne, *Shropsh. Folk-Lore*, 595, As lazy as Kittenhallet's dog; 'e laned 'is yed agen a wall to bark. 1886: Elworthy, *West Som. Word-Book*, 420 (E.D.S.), He's like lazy Lawrence's dog, that lied his head agin the wall to bark. 1886: R. Holland, *Cheshire Gloss.*, 445 (E.D.S.), As lazy as Larriman's dog. 1917: Bridge, *Cheshire Proverbs*, 17 [as in 1886, Holland]. Ibid., 91 [as in 1670, with very slight variation]. 1921: Hudson, *Trav. in Little Things*, ch ix 56, Until I knew Dandy I had always supposed that the story of Ludlam's dog was pure invention ... but Dandy made me reconsider the subject; and eventually I came to believe that Ludlam's dog did exist once upon a time, centuries ago perhaps, and that if he had been the laziest dog in the world, Dandy was not far behind him in that respect. Cf. **Idle** (4).

Lazy folk take the most pains. 1734: Franklin, in *Works*, i 416 (Bigelow). 1869: Spurgeon, *John Ploughman*, ch i., It is not much ease that lazy people get by all their scheming, for they always take the most pains in the end.

Lazy groom never loves a grey horse, A. Yorks. 1922: *N. & Q.*, 12th ser, xi 212.

Lazy Lawrence. Several sayings are grouped under this head. In all, Lawrence is the embodiment of laziness. 1784: *Gent. Mag.*, Pt II 349, When a person in hot weather seems lazy, it is a common saying, that Lawrence bids him high wages. [St Lawrence's Day is 10 August.] 1809: Pegge, *Anonymiana*, cent. viii 19, *Laurence bids wages;* a proverbial saying for to be lazy. 1828: Carr, *Craven Dialect*, i 280, When a person is remarkably idle, he is often thus addressed. 'I see lang Lawrence hes gitten hod on thee'. 1830: Forby, *Vocab. E. Anglia* 427, Laurence has got hold of him. 1880: Courtney, *W. Cornwall Words*, 33 (E.D.S.), He's as lazy as Lawrence. One would think that Lawrence had got hold of him. 1882: Jago, *Gloss. of Cornish Dialect*, 205, He is as lazy as Larrence. 1882: *N.&Q.*, 6th ser, v 266, He's got St Lawrence on the shoulder [Kent]. 1886: Elworthy, *West Som. Word-Book*, 420 (E.D.S.), 'So lazy as Lawrence 'is a common saying.

Lazy man. *See* **Idle** (2).

Lazy man's guise, The. 1828: Carr, *Craven Dialect*, i 294, T' lither man's guise, Is nivver to bed And nivver to rise. Cf. **Sluggard's guise.**

Lazy sheep thinks its wool heavy, A. 1732: Fuller, 237. 1869: Spurgeon, *John Ploughman*, ch i, Like lazy sheep, it is too much trouble for them to carry their own wool.

Lead by the nose, To. [τῆς ρινός, φασίν, ἕλκων. – Lucian, *Dial. Deorum*, vi 3.] 1583: Golding, *Calvin on Deut.*, cxxi. 745 (OED), Men ... suffer themselues to bee led by the noses like brute beasts. 1598: Florio, *Worlde of Wordes*, s.v. 'Mener', To leade by the nose. 1625: Bacon, *Essays:* 'Suitors', Let him chuse well his Referendaries, for else he may be led by the nose. 1714: Ozell, *Moliere*, iii 92, Go, go, you must not suffer your self to be led by the nose. 1766: Garrick, *Neck or Nothing*, II i, I heard her say myself that she could lead you by the nose. 1830: Marryat, *King's Own*, ch xxviii, Seven-eighths of the town are led by the nose by this or that periodical work.

Leaden sword. *See* quots. 1562: Heywood, *Three Hund. Epigr.*, No. 71, Thou makst much of thy peynted sheathe. 1568: W. Fulwood, *Enemie of Idlenesse*, 244 (1593), Drawe not (as the prouerbe saith) a leaden sword out of a golden scabbard. 1579: Lyly, *Euphues*, 69 (Arber), Heere you may see ... the paynted sheath with the leaden dagger, the faire wordes that make fooles faine. 1611: Cotgrave, s.v. 'Cousteau', A leaden sword in a golden sheath; a foule heart in a faire body. 1630: Brathwait, *Eng. Gent., etc.*, 47 (1641), The first sort generally, are so miserably enamoured of words, as they care little for substance. These are ever drawing a leaden sword out of a gilded sheath. 1732: Fuller, 238, A leaden sword in an ivory scabbard.

Lean arbitration. *See* **Ill agreement.**

Lean as a rake. *c.*1386: Chaucer, *Prol.*, l. 287, As leene was his hors as is a rake. *c.*1480: *Early Miscell.*, 8 (Warton Cl.), I waxe as leyne as anny rake. 1567: Golding, *Ovid*, bk ii l. 967, Hir bodie leane as any rake. 1653: Urquhart, *Rabelais*, bk ii ch xiv. He was ... as lean as a rake. 1754: Berthelson, *Eng.-Danish Dict.*, s.v. 'Lean'. 1823: Moor, *Suffolk Words*, 305, 'Thin as a rake 'is not an infrequent comparison with us. 1875: Parish, *Sussex Dict.*, 93 ... a common proverb among Sussex people.

Lean as a shotten herring. 1659: Howell, *Proverbs: Fr.-Eng.*, 18. 1754: Berthelson, *Eng.-Danish Dict.*, s.v. 'Shotten', He looks like a shotten herring. 1889: *Folk-Lore Journal*, vii 291 (Derbyshire).

Lean dog for a hard road, A. 1917: Bridge, *Cheshire Proverbs*, 4.

Lean fee is a fit reward for a lazy clerk, A. 1583: Melbancke, *Philotinus*, sig. E3, In deede a leane fee befits a lazye clarke. 1669: *Politeuphuia*, 182.

Lean liberty is better than fat slavery. 1732: Fuller, 3158.

Lean not on a reed. *c.*1586: Deloney, *Garl. of Goodwill*, 13 (Percy S.), But, senseless man, what do I mean Upon a broken reed to lean? 1732: Fuller, 3157.

Lean sorrow is hardest to bear, A. 1895: S. O. Jewett, *Life of Nancy*, 278 [quoted as 'the ancient proverb'].

Leap, *subs. A leap in the dark.* 1697: Vanbrugh, *Prov. Wife*, V v, So, now, I am in for Hobbes's voyage; a great leap in the dark. [Hobbes is said to have used the expression when dying, 1680.] *c.*1716: *The Merry Musician*, i 238, All you that will take a leap in the dark. Think of the fate of Lawson and Clark [both executed]. 1826: Disraeli, *Vivian Grey*, bk ii ch xvi, I saw the feeble fools were wavering, and, to save all, made a leap in the dark.

Leap, *verb.* **1. He is ready to leap over nine hedges.** 1678: Ray, 353.

2. He leaps into a deep river to avoid a shallow brook. 1732: Fuller, 1963.

3. If you leap into a well, Providence is not bound to fetch you out. Ibid., No. 2795.

4. Leap over the stile. *See* **Stile.**

5. Look before you leap. *See* **Look** (11).

6. She Cannot leap an inch from a slut. 1678: Ray, 256 [with 'doth' for 'can' and 'shrew' for 'slut']. 1732: Fuller, 4121.

7. To leap at a crust. 1633: Draxe, 94, Hee will leape at a crust. 1738: Swift, *Polite Convers.*, Dial. I, I believe. Colonel, Mr Neverout can leap at a crust better than you.

8. To leap at a daisy = To be hanged. 1553: *Respublica*, V ii, Some of vs erelong maie happe leape at a daisie. 1592: Greene, *Black Book's Messenger*, To Reader, At last hee leaPt at a daysie … with a halter about his necke. 1604: *Pasquils Jests*, 48 (1864), He sayd: Haue at yon dasie that growes yonder; and so leaped off the gallows.

9. To let leap a whiting = To miss an opportunity. 1546: Heywood, *Proverbs*, Pt II ch vii, There lepte a whityng, (quoth she). 1597: Breton, in *Works*, ii *b* 8 (Grosart), There are many such misfortunes in the world, a man may … leape a whiting, whilst he is looking on a codshead. 1670: Ray, 199. 1754: Berthelson, *Eng.-Danish Dict.*, s.v. 'Whiting', To let go a whiting.

Leap year is never a good sheep year, A. 1846: Denham, *Proverbs*, 17 (Percy S.). 1920: *Sphere*, 3 April, p. 10, Whether it be true to say that – 'A leap year Is never a good sheep year 'remains to be proved so far as this season goes.

Learn not and know not. 1659: Howell, *Proverbs: Brit.-Eng.*, 26.

Learn to lick betimes, you know not whose tail you may go by. 1670: Ray, 117.

Learn to pray, He that will, let him go to sea. 1611: Cotgrave, s.v. 'Mer'. 1640: Herbert, *Jac. Prudentum*. 1732: Fuller, 2368.

Learn to say before you sing. 1639: Clarke, 116. 1670: Ray, 139. 1732: Fuller, 3165.

Learn weeping and thou shalt laugh gaining. 1640: Herbert, *Jac. Prudentum*.

Learning and law, To, there's no greater foe, than they that nothing know. 1592: Greene, *Works*, xii 103–4 (Grosart) [cited as 'an olde said saw'].

Learning in a prince is like a knife in the hand of a madman. 1591: Harington, *Orl. Furioso:* 'Allegory', 413 (1634), The chiefe fault commonly is, in those counsellors that put a sword into a mad-mans hand, by putting such conceits into Princes heads. 1638: D. Tuvill, *Vade Mecum*, 16 (3rd ed.) [with 'dangerous 'before 'knife'].

Learning is the eye of the mind. 1633: Draxe, 111.

Learning makes a good man better and an ill man worse. 1732: Fuller, 3162.

Learning. *See also* **House** (17); **Little learning**.

Learnt young is hard to lose, What is. *c.*1275:

Prov. of Alfred, A, 100–5, The mon the on his youhthe yeorne leorneth Wit and wisdom, and iwriten reden, He may beon on elde wenliche lortheu [good teacher]. *c.*1320: in *Reliq. Antiquae*, i 110 (1841), 'Whose yong Ierneth, olt he ne leseth'; Quoth Hendyng. *c.*1400: *Beryn*, 938, For thing i-take in [youthe, is] hard to put away.

Least boy always carries the biggest fiddle, The. 1670: Ray, 112. 1732: Fuller, 4629 ['always' omitted]. 1880: Spurgeon, *Ploughman's Pictures*, 28, As a rule, the smallest boy carries the biggest fiddle.

Least foolish is wise, The. 1640: Herbert, *Jac. Prudentum*.

Least room. *See* quot. 1913: E. M. Wright, *Rustic Speech, etc.*, 17, A proverbial saying applied to any one who has a great deal to say about the conduct or characters of other people, and is not above suspicion himself, runs: Where there's leeost reawm, there's moast thrutchin' [crowding].

Least said soonest mended. *c.*1460 in W.C. Hazlitt, *Remains of Early Popular Poetry* (1864), III 169, Who sayth lytell he is wyse … And fewe wordes are soone amend. 1555: J. Heywood, *Two Hundred Epigrams*, no. 169, Lyttle sayde, soone amended. 1641: D. Fergusson, *Scottish Proverbs* (S.T.S.) no. 946, Littl said is soon mended. 1776: T. Cogan, *John Buncle, Junior*, i 237–8, But mum's the word; least said is soonest mended. 1818: Scott, *Heart of Midl.*, ch vi 1837: Dickens, *Pickwick*, ch xlviii. 1917: Bridge, *Cheshire Proverbs*, 89, Least said soonest mended, but nout said needs no mending. Cf. **Little meddling**; and **Little said.**

Least talk most work. 1611: Cotgrave, s.v. 'Besongner', The fewer words the more worke. 1666: Torriano. *Piazza Univ.*, 189, Where there is least talk there is most work.

Leather, (There's) nothing like. *See* **Nothing** (24)

Leave, *subs*. 1. He must have leave to speak who cannot hold his tongue. 1683: Meriton, *Yorkshire Ale*, 83–7 (1697). 1732: Fuller, 1992.

2. Leave is light. 1546: Heywood, *Proverbs*, Pt I ch x, Ye might haue knokt er ye came in; leaue is light. *c.*1598: Deloney, *Gentle Craft*, Pt II ch ii, Leaue is light, which being obtained a man may be bold without offence. 1633: Jonson, *Love's Welcome*, Our English proverb, *Leave is light:* 1757: Franklin, in *Works*, ii 518 (Bigelow), I am

sorry, however, that he took it without leave …
Leave, they say, is light. 1827: Hone, *Ev. Day Book*, ii 248.

Leave, verb. 1. He has left off work to go and make bricks. 1864: 'Cornish Proverbs', in *N.&Q.*, 3rd ser, vi. 494.

2. He that leaves the highway, to cut short, commonly goes about. 1732: Fuller, 2213.

3. Leave a jest when it pleases you best. Ibid., No. 6357.

4. Leave boys' play. *See* **Boy** (5).

5. Leave herr on a ley. *See* quots. 1599: Porter, *Two Angry Women*, in Hazlitt, *Old Plays*, vii 355, They should set her on the lee-land, and bid the devil split her. 1659: Howell, 16, Leave her on a ley, and lett the devil flitt her; A Lincolnshire proverb spoken of a scolding wife; viz. tye her to a plow-ridge, and lett the devill remove her to a better pasture. 1847: Halliwell, *Dict.*, s.v. 'Flitten' [as in 1659].

6. Leave off with an appetite. 1558: Bullein, *Govt. of Health*, fo. 37, And so leue with an appetite. 1588: Cogan, *Haven of Health*, 167 (1612), The surest way in feeding is to leaue with an appetite, according to the old saying. 1648: Herrick, *Hesp.*, i 236 (Hazlitt), Go to your banquet then, but use delight, So as to rise still with an appetite. 1693: Penn, *Fruits of Solitude*, No. 64, If thou rise with an appetite, thou art sure never to sit down without one.

7. Leave the Court ere the Court leave thee. 1710: S. Palmer, *Moral Essays on Proverbs*, 61. 1738: *Gent. Mag.*, 475.

8. Leave well (enough) alone. *See* **Let well alone.**

9. To leave in the briers (or **suds**). 1533: Udall, *Flowers out of Terence*, fo. 18, Doest thou not se me brought in the briers through thy devise. 1577: *Misogonus*, III i, Leaue me not now ith breares, yow haue told me thus much of my sonne. *c*.1590: G. Harvey, *Marginalia*, 87 (1913), Lett not any necessary or expedient action lye in the suddes. 1631: Mabbe, *Celestina*, 280 (T.T.), Out alas! … Our solace is in the suds. 1670: Ray, 166, To leave one in the briers (or suds). 1690: *New Dict. Canting Crew*, sig. B8, In the briers, in trouble. 1753: Richardson, *Grandison*, i 86 (1883), How, madam! – Why, we are all in the suds, then! 1784–1815: *Annals of Agric.*, xxxix 83, Very favourable weather must occur, or the fanner is in the suds.

10. To leave in the lurch. 1576: G. Harvey, *Letter-Book*, 163 (Camden S.), Lest he fail in his reckning … and so leave himself in the lurch. 1611: *Tarlton's Jests*, 37 (SH.S.), He leave him in the lurch, and shift for my selfe. Before 1680: Butler, *Remains*, i 255 (1759), And leaves the true ones in the lurch. 1768: Brooke, *Fool of Quality*, iii 240, But here the Master in whom he trusted, happened to leave him in the lurch. 1823: Scott, *Fam. Letters*, ii 182 (1894), It will be an eternal shame if they leave the poor fellow in the lurch after all he has done. 1923: Lucas, *Advisory Ben*, 234, She doesn't like to leave me in the lurch, she says.

11. To leave no stone unturned. [πάντα κινῆσαι πέτρον. – Eur, *Heracl.*, 1002.] *c*.1548: Latimer, in *Works*, ii 427 (P.S.), I will leave no one stone unmoved to have both you and your brother saved. 1560: Becon, *Catechism, etc.*, 313 (P.S.), I would wish that according to the common proverb, every stone should be moved … to win them unto the truth. 1642: D. Rogers, *Matrim. Honour*, 163, Therfore roll each stone to find this grace. 1709: Mandeville, *Virgin Unmask'd*, 144 (1724), I find, Aunt, you leave no stone unturned. 1839: Dickens, *Nickleby*, ch lii, Don't leave a stone unturned. It's always something, to know you've done the most you could. 1925: *Sphere*, 6 June, p. 298, col. 1, No stone should be left unturned in the endeavour to make the piece a success.

12. To leave the meal and take the bran. 1639: Clarke, 5.

13. Who leaveth the old way for the new, will find himself deceived. 1578: Florio, *First Fruites*, fo. 28. 1623: Wodroephe, *Spared Houres*, 278, Who leaues yᵉ old way for to seeke a newe, Is intangled with dangers not a fewe. 1666: Torriano, *Piazza Univ.*, 271. 1862: Borrow, *Wild Wales*, ch xv, 'There is a proverb in the Gerniweg', said I, '… saying, "ne'er leave the old way for the new." '

Leaves, The. 1. He that fears leaves. *See* **Afraid of leaves.**

2. If on the trees the leaves still hold, The coming winter will be cold. 1661: M. Stevenson, *Twelve Moneths*, 48, They say if leaves now [October] hang on the tree, it portends a cold winter, or many caterpillars. 1893: Inwards, *Weather Lore*, 150.

3. Leaves enough but few grapes = Many

words and few deeds. 1659: Howell, *Proverbs: Ital.-Eng.*, 1.

4. When the leaves show their undersides, Be very sure that rain betides. 1893: Inwards, *Weather Lore*, 150.

Lechery and covetousness go together. 1653: *The Queen*, IV, in Bang's *Materialien*, B. 13, p. 30, col. 1 [cited as 'an old proverbe'].

Leek. *See* **Green** (5).

Leeks. *See* **Lovers live.**

Leeks in March. *See* quots. [1558: Bullein, *Govt. of Health*, fo. 64, Leekes purgeth the bloud in march.] *c.*1685: Aubrey, *Nat. Hist. Wilts* 51 (1847), Eate leekes in Lide [March], and ramsins [wild garlic] in May, And all the yeare after physitians may play. 1875: A. B. Cheales, *Proverb. Folk-Lore*, 85, Eat leeks in March, Garlick in May, All the rest of the year The doctors may play. *Sussex.* 1913: E. M. Wright, *Rustic Speech, etc.*, 238 [as in 1685].

Lees. *See* **Cheshire** (7).

Left hand luck. 1540: Palsgrave, *Acolastus*, sig. X2, A lefte hande lucke, this is yll lucke.

Left or right Brings good at night. 1831: Hone, *Year-Book*, 252. 1849: Halliwell, *Pop. Rhymes and Nursery Tales*, 183 [with 'and' for 'or'].

Left shoulder. *See* **Over the shoulder.**

Left side, To rise on one's. 1579: *Marr. of Wit and Wisdom*, sc iii p. 30 (SH.S.), I rose on my lift side [i.e. wrong side] to day. Cf. **Right side.**

Leg and **Legs. 1. Leg of a lark.** *See* **Lark** (1).

2. Stretch your legs according to your coverlet. 1640: Herbert, *Jac. Prudentum*, Every one stretcheth his legs according to his coverlet. 1670: Ray, 25. 1880: Spurgeon, *Ploughman's Pictures*, 136, Stretch your legs according to the length of your blanket, and never spend all you have.

3. To lay one's legs on one's neck (or **to ground**) = To be off. 1611: *Tarlton's Jests*, 41 (SH.S.), The fellow … laid his legges on his neck, and got him gone. 1913; *Devonsh. Assoc. Trans.*, xlv. 290, In phrase 'lay legs to groun', a curious but common idiom, implying speed.

4. To see which leg one is lame of. 1586: D. Rouland, *Lazarillo*, 40 (1924), As for me, when I perceiued upon which foot hee halted, I made hast to eat. 1631: Mabbe, *Celestina*, 212 (T.T.), I now perceive on which foot you halt. 1732: Fuller, 2623,1 now see which leg you are lame of. 1823: Scott, *Q. Durward*, ch xxix, 'Tis a sure sign what foot the patient halts upon.

5. While the leg warmeth the boot harmeth. Before 1500: Hill, *Commonplace-Book*, 128 (E.E.T.S.), While the fote warmith, the sho harmith. 1546: Heywood, *Proverbs*, Pt II ch ii *c.*1594: Bacon, *Promus*, No. 385. 1670: Ray, 113. 1732: Fuller, 6309.

Leg-bail, To give. 1774: Fergusson, *Poems*, 234 (1807) (OED), They took leg-bail and ran awa. 1784: O'Keeffe, *Positive Man*, II ii, I'll give him leg-bail for my honesty (*runs off*). 1819: Scott, *Ivanhoe*, ch xix, Shall we stand fast … or shall we e'en give him leg-bail? 1876: Blackmore, *Cripps*, ch xlii., Two Sundays, when even an attorney may give leg-bail to the Power under whose 'Ca. ad sa'. he lives.

Leicestershire, Bean-belly. 15th cent.: in *Reliq. Antiquoe*, i 269 (1841), Leicesterschir, full of benys. 1622: Drayton, *Polyol.*, xxiii, Bean belly Le'stershire, her attribute doth bear. 1662: Fuller, *Worthies*, ii 225 (1840), Those in the neighbouring counties used to say merrily, 'Shake a Leicestershire yeoman by the collar, and you shall hear the beans rattle in his belly'. 1732: Fuller, 4114 [as in 1662]. 1762: *St James Magazine*, ii 13, Shake a Leicestershire woman by the petticoat, and the beans will rattle in her throat. 1790: Grose, *Prov. Gloss.*, s.v. 'Leicestershire'. 1818: Scott, *Heart of Midl.*, ch xxix, An ye touch her, I'll give ye a shake by the collar shall make the Leicester beans rattle in thy guts.

Leicestershire plover, A = A bag-pudding. 1678: Ray, 317. 1790: Grose, *Prov. Gloss.*, s.v. 'Leicestershire'.

Leighs. *See* **Cheshire** (7).

Leighton Buzzard. *See* **Tring** (2).

Leisure. *He hath no leisure who useth it not.* 1640: Herbert, *Jac. Prudentum.*

Lemster. *See* **Leominster.**

Lend, *verb.* **1. He that doth lend doth lose his money and friend.** 1602: Shakespeare, *Hamlet*, I iii, For loan oft loses both itself and friend. 1666: Torriano, *Piazza Univ.*, 217, Who lends loseth double. 1708: tr. Aleman's *Guzman*, i 240, How much money has been lent and borrowed on the score of friendship, and yet both money and friend have been lost at last. 1869: Spurgeon, *John Ploughman*, ch iv, Very often he that his money lends, loses both his gold and his friends.

2. He that lends, gives. 1640: Herbert, *Jac. Prudentum.*

3. Lend and lose, so play fools. 1737: Ray, 271.

4. Lend never that thing thou needest most. Before 1500: Hill, *Commonplace-Book*, 131 (E.E.T.S.).

5. Lend not horse, nor wife, nor sword. 1574: E. Hellowes, *Guevara's Epistles*, 509, It is an old prouerb that the wife and the sword may bee shewed, but not lent. 1575: Fenton, *Golden Epistles*, 300 (1582), A wife being the dearest of the two things (according to the common saying) which we ought not to lende. 1577: Kendall, *Flow. of Epigr.*, 284 (Spens.S.), Three thinges a man lendeth rife, His horse, his fighting sword, his wife. 1605: Camden, *Remains*, 332 (1870) [as in 1574]. 1647: *Countrym. New Commonwealth*, 43, Thy sword, thy horse, and eke thy wife, Lend not at all, lest it breed strife. 1922: *N.&Q.*, 12th ser, xi 499, The Yorkshire version of this is 'Lend neither your horse nor your wife'. I fear in ancient Yorkshire the horse would come first as being the most valued.

Length of one's foot. *See* **Foot** (4).

Lenson-hill to Pilsen-pen, As much akin as. 1662: Fuller, *Worthies*, i 453 (1840). 1790: Grose, *Prov. Gloss.*, s.v. 'Dorset'.

Lent. 1. Dry Lent, fertile year. 1893: Inwards, *Weather Lore*, 40.

2. He has but a short Lent. *See* quots. 1659: Howell, *Proverbs: Ital.-Eng.*, 11, Who desires a short Lent, let him make a debt to be paid at Easter. 1736: Franklin, *Way to Wealth*, in *Works*, i 450 (Bigelow), Those have a short Lent who owe money to be paid at Easter. 1846: Denham, *Proverbs*, 32 (Percy S.), Lent seems short to him that borrows money to be paid at Easter.

See also **Ash Wednesday; Christmas** (8); and **Shrovetide.**

Leominster bread and Weobley ale. 1610: P. Holland, tr. Camden's *Britannia*, 620, Lemster bread and Weabley Ale … are growne unto a common proverb. 1619: Jonson, *For the Honour of Wales*, 4th song, And what you say to ale of Webley. 1662: Fuller, *Worthies*, ii 70 (1840), Lemster bread, and Weabley ale. 1700: J. Brome, *Travels*, 102, Hence it is grown proverbial among the inhabitants, for Lempster bread and Weobley beer, none can come near. 1725: Defoe, *Tour*, ii 72. 1886: Bickerdyke, *Curios., of Ale and Beer*, 171, 'Lemster bread and Weobley ale 'had passed into a proverb before the seventeenth century. 1905: A. G. Bradley, *March and Borderland of Wales*, 156.

Leominster wool. Before 1530: Barclay, *Egloges*, iv, Cornewall hath tynne and lymsterwoole fine. 1593: Drayton, *Shep. Garland*, Ecl. iv, Her skin as soft as Lemster wool. 1648: Herrick, *Hesp.*, No. 444, And far more Soft than the finest Lemster ore [wool]. 1670: Ray, 258, Monmouth caps and Lemster wooll. 1725: Defoe, *Tour*, ii 72, This town [Leominster], besides the fine wool, is noted for …

Leopard can not change his spots, The. [Jeremiah xiii.23 Can the Ethiopian change his skin, or the leopard his spots?] 1546: J. Bale, *First Exmination of Anne Askew*, 38, Their olde condycyons wyll they change, whan the blackemoreaene change hys skynne, and the catte of the mountayne her spottes. 1596: Shakespeare, *Richard II*, I i 174, Rage mus be withstood … Lions make leopards tame. – Yea, but not change his spots. 1869: A. Henderson, *Latin Proverbs*, 317, *Pardus maculas non deponit*, a leopard does not change his spots.

Leopard, In a, the spots are not observed. 1640: Herbert, *Jac. Prudentum.*

Less is more. 1855: R. Browning, *Andrea del Sarto*, l. 78, Well, less is more, Lucrezia, I am judged. P. Johnson, *Mies van der Rohe*, 49, As in architecture, [Mies] has always been guided by his personal motto, 'less is more'.

Less of your courtesy and more of your purse. 1639: Clarke, 43. 1670: Ray, 74. 1732: Fuller, 3172, Less of your courtship, I pray, and more of your coin.

Less wit a man has, The, the less he knows that he wants it. Ibid., No. 4630.

Let him alone with the saint's bell, and give him rope enough. 1737: Ray, 63.

Let the world pass (or **slide**, or **wag**, etc.). *c.*1400: *Towneley Plays*, 201 (E.E.T.S.), Whoso couthe take hede and lett the warld pas. 1519: *Four Elements*, in Hazlitt, *Old Plays*, i 20, With huffa gallant, sing tirl on the berry, And let the wide world wind! Before 1529: Skelton, *Works*, ii 6 (Dyce), Let the world wag. 1546: Heywood, *Proverbs*, Pt I ch v, To let the world wag, and take mine ease in mine in. 1550: Udall, *Roister Doister*, III iii, Let the world pass. 1594: Shakespeare, *Tam. of Shrew*, Ind. i, Let the world slide. 1678: Dryden, *Limberham*, V i, Let the world pass. 1848: Planché, *Extravag.*, iii 258 (1879), Let the world wag.

Let well alone. [Actum, aiunt, ne agas. – Terence, *Phorm.*, II iii 72.] *c.*1386: Chaucer, *Minor Poems*, in *Works*, i 399 (Skeat), Unwys is he that can no wele endure. *c.*1570: *Scoggin's Jests* (1626), 76, The shomaker thought to make his house greater … They pulled downe foure or five postes of the house … Why said Scoggin, when it was well you could not let it alone. 1740: G. Cheyne, *Essay on Regimens*, p. xxxvi, When a person is tolerably well, and is subject to no painful or dangerous Distemper, I think it is his Duty … to let *Well alone*. 1829: Peacock, *Misfor. of Elphin*, ch ii, It is well: it works well: let well alone. 1863: Kingsley, *Water Babies*, ch i, Let well alone, lad, and ill too at times. 1913: Hankin and Calderon, *Thompson*, III, Why the devil can people never let well alone.

Letter stay for the post, Let your, not the post for the letter. 1666: Torriano, *Piazza Univ.*, 127, Let a letter expect the messenger, not the messenger the letter. 1670: Ray, 15.

Lettuce. *See* **Like lips.**

Lewes, Proud, and poor Brighthelmstone. 1827: Horsfield, *Hist., etc., of Sussex*, ii 34. 1894: A. J. C. Hare, *Sussex*, 99, 'Proud Lewes and poor Brighthelmstone' is a proverb of the days when letters were addressed, 'Brighthelmstone, near Lewes'.

Lewisbam, Long, lazy, lousy. 1790: Grose, *Prov. Gloss.*, s.v. 'Kent'.

Liar and **Liars. 1. A liar is not believed when he speaks truth.** 1477: Rivers, *Dictes, etc.*, 117 (1877), The reward of a lyar is that he be not beleuid of that he reherseth. 1586: Pettie, tr. Guazzo's *Civil Convers.*, fo. 42, The liar neuer is beleeued, although an oath he take. 1645: Howell, *Letters*, bk i § v No. xi, It being one of the punishments … of a lyar, not to be believ'd when he speaks truth. 1681: in *Somers Tracts*, viii 290 (1811), Do not be deceived by an old saying, That when one usually tells lyes, he is not trusted when he speaks truth. 1820: Colton, *Lacon*, Pt I No. 553.

2. A liar is worse than a thief. 1630: Taylor (Water-Poet), *Works*, 2nd pagin., 123, But sure the prouerbe is as true as briefe, A lyer's euer worser then a thiefe. 1639: Clarke, 150.

3. Liar, liar, lick spit. 1602: Chettle, *Hoffman*, V i p. 75 (1852), Liar, liar! – Lick-dish! 1843:

Halliwell. *Nursery Rhymes*, 164, Liar, liar, lick spit, Turn about the candlestick. What's good for liar? Brimstone and fire.

4. Liars should have good memories. [Verumque est illud, quod vulgo dicitur, mendacem memorem esse oportere. – Quintilian, *Instit. Oratoria*, IV ii § 91.] *c.*1531: Latimer, *Works*, ii 312 (P.S.), You may learn how necessary it is for a liar to have a good memory. 1565: Calfhill *Answ. to Martiall*, 88 (P.S.), I see it is true … 'a liar had need have a good remembrance'. 1673: Marvell, in *Works*, iii 367 (Grosart), There is one sort of men, for whose sake there is a common maxime establish'd, that there is an absolute necessity they should have good memories. 1738: Swift, *Polite Convers.*, Dial. I, Here's a pin for that lie; I'm sure liars had need of good memories.

5. Show me a liar and I'll show you a thief. 1607: R. West, *Court of Conscience*, sig. F1, He that will lie will steale. 1630: T. Adams, *Works*, 505. 1725: Bailey, tr. Erasmus' *Colloq.*, 178, It is sometimes for a man's advantage to have pilfering hands; and the old proverb is a witness, that that is a vice that is cousin-german to yours of lying.

Lick honey, To. *See* **Honey** (7), (11), and (14).

Lick one's cauf [calf] **over again, To.** 1917: Bridge, *Cheshire Proverbs*, 140 … To do one's work a second time.

Lick one's self whole again, To. 1670: Ray, 184.

Lick the mundle, To. *See* quots. 1879: Jackson, *Shropsh. Word-Book*, 254, [To] lick the crame-mundle [= to live well]. 1883: Burne, *Shropsh. Folk-Lore*, 597, To lick the crame-mundle = to live well, as in a dairy or farmhouse. [The 'mundle' is a piece of wood used for stirring porridge, cream, etc.] 1917: Bridge, *Cheshire Proverbs*, 64 [as in 1883]. Ibid., 64, That's th' lad as licked the mundle [curried favour].

Lid worthy of the kettle, A. A correspondent of *N.&Q.* (12th ser, ii 7) refers to the story of Crassus laughing at an ass eating thistles, instead of lettuces, finding that they matched his mouth (whence the saying, *Similes habent labra lactiucas – see* **Like lips**), and adds: 'Jerome illustrates the story by another proverb, "*Patellae dignum operculum*," a lid to match the kettle'. 1540: Palsgrave, *Acolastus*, sig. M2, He shall gyue a lydde or couer worthy for … the lyttell panne.

1586: L. Evans, *Withals Dict. Revised*, sig. G7, Like pot, lyke potlid. 1611: Cotgrave, s.v. 'Couvercle', Such pot, such pot-lid, like master like man. 1653: Urquhart, *Rabelais*, Prol. to bk i, If perhaps he had met with as very fools as himself, (and as the proverb saies) a lid worthy of such a kettle. 1732: Fuller, 4276, Such a pot must have such a lid.

Lide [March]. *See* quot. 1639: in *Berkeley MSS.*, iii 30 (1885), Lide pilles the hide: meaninge that March ... pinches the poare man's beast (Glouc).

Lidford. *See* **Lydford.**

Lie, *subs*. **1. A lie begets a lie.** 1732: Fuller, 262, A lye begets a lye, till they come to generations.

2. A lie has no legs. 1666: Torriano, *Piazza Univ.*, 30, A lye hath no feet. 1732: Fuller, 263, A lye has no leg, but a scandal has wings. 1853: Trench, *Proverbs*, 120 (1905).

3. A lie is half way round the world before the truth has got his boots on. The speed with which rumour travels was well-known to the ancients and the roots of this proverb may lie in a line in book four of Virgil's *Aeneid*, *Fama, malum qua non aliud velocius alium* (rumour, than which no other evil thing moves swifter). 1859: C. H. Spurgeon, *Gems from Spurgeon*, 74, It is well said in the old proverb, 'a lie will go round the world while truth is pulling its boots on'.

4. A lie made out of the whole stuff = without foundation. 1830: Forby, *Vocab. E. Anglia*, 427.

5. A lie stands on one leg, and truth on two. 1659: Howell, 10 (8).

6. Ask me no questions and I'll tell you no lies. *See* **Ask** (3).

7. His lies are latticed lies; and you may see through them. 1830: Forby, *Vocab. E. Anglia*, 429.

8. If a lie could have choked him, that would have done it. 1678: Ray, 89.

9. Lies have short wings (or **legs**). 1578: Florio, *First Fruites*, fo. 31, Lyes haue short legges. 1611: Davies (of Hereford), *Sc. of Folly*, 43, in *Works*, ii (Grosart), Lyes haue short wings. 1666: Torriano, *Piazza Univ.*, 30 ... legs.

10. Tell a lie and find out the truth. 1678: Ray, 75. 1732: Fuller, 4324.

11. That's a lie and a loud one. 1678: Ray, 89, That's a loud one. 1819: Scott, *Ivanhoe*, ch xliii., 'That's a lie, and a loud one,' said the Friar.

12. That's a lie with a latchet. 1678: Ray, 89.

1732: Fuller, 6157, [as in 1678, plus] All the dogs in the town cannot match it. 1828: Carr, *Craven Dialect*, i 283, Lee-with-a-latchet. A notorious lie. 1849: Halliwell, *Pop. Rhymes and Nursery Tales*, 182, 'A lee with a latchet', as they say in the North, of a circumstantial self-evident falsehood.

13. That's a lie with a lid on. 1880: Spurgeon, *Ploughman's Pictures*, 99. 1901: F. E. Taylor, *Lancs Sayings*, 28, That's a lie wi' a lid on – an' a brass hondle for t' lift it wi'.

14. Though a lie be well drest, it is ever overcome. 1640: Herbert, *Jac. Prudentum*.

15. To tell a man a lie, and give him a reason for it. 1678: Ray, 257.

Lie, *verb*. To tell a falsehood. **1. He'll not let anybody lie by him** = He is a liar. 1678: Ray, 89.

2. Thou'lt lie all manner of colours but blue, and that is gone to the litting, i.e. dyeing. Ibid., 75.

3. To lie as fast as a dog can lick a dish. 1546: Heywood, *Proverbs*, Pt II ch vii, She will lie as fast as a dogge will licke a dishe. 1670: Ray, 184.

4. To lie as fast as a dog (or **horse**) **will trot.** 1530: Palsgrave, 610, He wyll lye as fast as a dogge wyll trotte. 1589: *Hay any Worke for Cooper*, 65 (1845), Thou canst cog, face and lye, as fast as a dog can trot. 1607: Dekker, etc., *Westw. Hoe*, IV i [dog]. 1694: Motteux, *Rabelais*, bk v ch xxx [dog]. 1737: Ray, 70 [dog]. 1845: J. Petheram, Note to 1589 quotation, p. 83, 'To lie as fast as a dog can trot 'is still in use in Somersetshire. 1869: Spurgeon, *John Ploughman*, ch xii [horse].

5. You licked not your lips since you lied last. 1732: Fuller, 5931.

See also **Swear** (3) and (4).

Lie, *verb*. To be in a recumbent position. **1. He lies bare of a suit** = He has no money. 1830: Forby, *Vocab. E. Anglia*, 434. 1872: J. Glyde, jr., *Norfolk Garland*, 150.

2. He that lies long abed, his estate feels it. 1640: Herbert, *Jac. Prudentum*. 1763: Murphy, *Citizen*, I ii, He that lies in bed, his estate feels it.

3. He that lies on the ground can fall no lower. 1570: A. Barclay, *Mirrour of Good Manners*, 46 (Spens.S.), A man on grounde resting can not much lower fall. 1648: Wither, *Single Si Quis*, 1 (Spens.S.), He that is prostrate on the floor, Lies there, whence he can fall no lower. 1732: Fuller, 2217.

4. He who lies down with dogs will rise with fleas. *See* **Dog** (49).

5. Lie not in the mire and say 'God help me'. *c.*1602: Chapman, *May-Day*, I, Do not lie in a ditch, and say 'God help me!'1710: S. Palmer, *Moral Essays on Proverbs*, 94, Don't lie still and cry God help you. 1869: Spurgeon, *John Ploughman*, ch vii, There's no good in lying down and crying 'God help us!'

6. She lies backward and lets out her fore-rooms. 1639: *Conceits, Clinches, etc.*, No. 278, One asked a gentlewoman in which part of the house she did use to lye. It was answer'd, that she lay backwards and did let out her fore-roomes. 1694: Motteux, *Rabelais*, bk iv ch lxiv. 1785: Grose, *Class. Dict. Vulgar Tongue*, s.v. 'Rooms', She lets out her fore-room and lies backwards, saying of a woman suspected of prostitution.

7. To lie by the wall = *To* be dead. *c.*1430: Lydgate, *Minor Poems*, 230 (Percy S.), To day thawgh thou be stowt and gay, A-morow thou lyyst by the walle. 1823: Moor, *Suffolk Words*, 62, By the walls. An unburied corpse. 'Poor John Smith! he lie by the walls'. 1847: Halliwell, *Dict.*, s.v. 'Laid', Laid. Killed, dead. *Suffolk*. The common phrase is, *laid by the wall.* 1913: *Devonsh. Assoc. Trans.*, xlv. 290, Lied by the wall. The interval between death and burial is always expressed by this phrase. 1920: E. Gepp, *Essex Dialect Dict.*, 21, 'To lay by the wall' is used of a corpse lying in a house awaiting burial.

8. To lie in bed and forecast. 1678: Ray, 75.

9. To lie like a lapwing. 1606: *Sir Giles Goosecappe*, I i.. As fearefull as a haire, and will lye like a lapwing.

10. We shall lie all alike in our graves. 1639: Clarke, 13. 1670: Ray, 56. 1732: Fuller, 5455.

Life. 1. A life of leisure and a life of laziness are two things. 1732: Fuller, 240. 1736: Franklin, *Way to Wealth*, in *Works*, i 445 (Bigelow).

2. Life begins at forty. 1932: W.B. Pitkin, *Life begins at Forty*, i, Life begins at forty. This is the revolutionary outcome of our new era. 1945: *Zionist Review*, 14 Dec., 6, Among Palestine pioneers, life does not 'begin at forty'.

3. Life is a shuttle. 1855: Bohn, 442.

4. Life is half spent before we know what it is. 1600: Cornwallis, *Essayes*, sig. B3 (1610), We begin not to liue before we are ready to die. 1640: Herbert, *Jac. Prudentum.* 1670: Ray, 16. 1732: Fuller, 3208.

5. Life is just a bowl of cherries. 1931: R. Henderson and L. Brown (song title) 'Life is just a bowl of cherries'.

6. Life isn't all beer and skittles. 1855: T.C. Haliburton, *Nature and Human Nature*, I ii, 'This life ain't all beer and skittles'. ... Many a time ... when I am disappointed sadly I say that saw over. 1857: T. Hughes, *Tom Brown's Schooldays*, i ii, Life isn't all beer and skittles. 1888: R. Kipling, *Drums Fore and Aft*, The men ... fell in for their first march, when they began to realise that a soldier's life was not all beer and skittles.

7. Life is sweet. *c.*1350: *Patience*, l. 156, in *Allit. Poems*, 96 (E.E.T.S.), For be monnes lode neuer so luther, the lyf is ay swete. *c.*1390: Gower, *Conf. Amantis*, v 1861, Bot nou our feerfull prelat seith 'The lif is swete'. *c.*1440: *York Plays*, 65 (L. T. Smith), A! dere fadir lyff is full swete. 1576: Pettie, *Petite Pall.*, ii 45 (Gollancz), Life is sweet to every one. 1664: Dryden, *Rival Ladies*, IV iii, Well, life is sweet. 1743: Fielding, *Jon. Wild*, bk iv ch xiii, All this is very true; but life is sweet for all that. 1851: Borrow, *Lavengro*, i 325, Life is sweet, brother.

8. Life is too short to stuff a mushroom. 1975: S. Conran, (epigraph to book) *Superwoman.*

9. Life lies not in living but in liking. 1639: Clarke, 322. 1670: Ray, 113. 1732: Fuller, 3209 [with 'by' for 'but in'.? misprint].

10. Life without a friend is death without a witness. 1640: Herbert, *Jac. Prudentum.* 1670: Ray, 10 [with 'with' for second 'without']. 1732: Fuller, 3211, Life without a friend is death with a vengeance.

11. Life would be too smooth if it had no rubs in it. Ibid., No. 3212.

12. The life of man is a winter way. 1640: Herbert, *Jac. Prudentum.* 1670: Ray, 16, The life of man is a winters day and a winters way. 1694: D'Urfey, *Quixote*, Pt I Act V sc ii [as in 1670]. 1732: Fuller, 6239 [as in 1670].

13. What is life where living is extinct? 1546: Heywood, *Proverbs*, Pt II ch ix 1633: Draxe, 160 [with 'wanting' for 'extinc'].

14. While there's life there's hope. [Modo liceat vivere, est spes. – Terence, *Haut.*, V ii 28. Ut aegroto, dum anima est, spes esse dicitur. – Cicero, *Ad. Att.*, IX x 3.] 1539: Taverner, *Proverbs*, fo. 36, The sycke person whyle he hath lyfe, hath hope. 1671: Crowne, *Juliana*, V,

Madam, he breathes, and whilst there's life There's hope. 1707: C. Cibber, *Double Gallant*, V ii 1761: Murphy, *Old Maid*, II. 1888: R.L.S., *Black Arrow*, bk iv ch ii, But while there is life, Joanna, there is hope!

See also **Variety.**

Lifeless that is faultless, He is. 1546: Heywood, *Proverbs*, Pt I ch xi 1681: W. Robertson, *Phraseol. Generalis*, 825. 1732: Fuller, 1922. 1869: Spurgeon, *John Ploughman*, ch x, The old saying is, 'Lifeless, faultless'.

Light. *See* **Sore eyes.**

Light as a feather. 1548: Hall, *Chron.*, 474 (1809). 1567: Golding, *Ovid*, bk iv l. 765, Now here, now there, as light as any feather. 1629: Shirley, *Wedding*, II iii, Light as a feather, hanging will ne'er kill you. 1778: Johnson, *Letters*, ii 73 (Hill), I hope he will soon shake off the black dog, and come home as light as a feather. 1813: Austen, *Pride and Prejudice*, ch xl 1906: Doyle, *Sir Nigel*, ch ix.

Light as a fly. 1670: Ray, 206.

Light as a kex. 1562: Heywood, *Epigr.*, 1st Hund., No. 47, Ye make my heart light as a kyx.

Light as leaf. *See* **Lind.**

Light as the Queen's groat. 1639: Clarke, 159.

Light beginning, a heavy ending, A. 1593: G. Harvey, *Works*, ii 196 (Grosart).

Light burden far heavy. 1546: Heywood, *Proverbs*, Pt II ch ix, A sir light burdeine far heauy (quoth she). 1594: Drayton, *Ideas*, lix, (Saith he) Light burdens heavy, if far borne. 1670: Ray, 114.

Light cheap lither yield, *c*.1320: in *Reliq. Antiqtuae*, i 114 (1841), 'Lyht chep luthere yeldes'; Quoth Hendyng. *c*.1400: *Towneley Mys.*, xiii 171. 1670: Ray, 114. Cf. **Good cheap.**

Light come. *See* **Lightly.**

Light fare begets light dreams. 1851: Borrow, *Lavengro*, ii 79. Cf. Light suppers.

Light gains make heavy purses. 1546: Heywood, *Proverbs*, Pt I ch xi 1597: Bacon, *Essays:* 'Ceremonies, etc'. 1605: Chapman, etc., *Eastw. Hoe*, I i c.1685: Aubrey, *Nat. Hist. Wilts*, 95 (1847), Perhaps they did not consider the proverb, that 'light gaines with quick returnes make heavy purses'. 1754: Berthelson, *Eng.-Danish Dict.*, s.v. 'Light'.

Light hand makes a heavy wound, A. 1602–3: Manningham, *Diary*, 52 (Camden S.).

Light heart. *See* quots. 1733: C. Coffey,

Boarding-School, sc i, A light heart and thin pair of breeches, Go thro' the world, brave boys. *c*.1742: *Merry Companion*, 175 [as in 1733]. 1748: Smollett, *Rod. Random*, ch v [as in 1733]. 1778: in Doran's *Lady of Last Century*, 243 (1873), He will be in better spirits as a light heart and a thin pair of breeches is a conjunction he has little notion of.

Light heeled mother makes a heavy heeled daughter, A. 1670: Ray, 53. 1732: Fuller, 3214 [in the plural].

Light load. *See* **Light burden.**

Light love will change. 1575: G. Fenton, *Golden Epistles*, 321 (1582), Light loue is an affection great and vehement, and yet lasteth not long. 1576: *Parad. of Dainty Devices*, in *Brit. Bibliog.*, iii 63 (1812), Light love will chaunge.

Light purse is a heavy curse, A. 1732: Fuller, 6493.

Light purse makes a heavy heart, A. 1600: F. Thynne, *Embl. and Epigr.*, 59 (E.E.T.S.). 1716: E. Ward, *Female Policy*, 36, When thy purse is light, then will thy heart be heavy. 1732: Fuller, 241. 1880: Spurgeon, *Ploughman's Pictures*, 12.

Light suppers make clean sheets. 1616: Breton, *Crossing of Proverbs*, 8 (Grosart). 1670: Ray, 36. 1732: Fuller, 3216. Cf. **Light fare.**

Lightening before death, A. 1588: Cogan, *Haven of Health*, 135 (1612), Whereof is growen a Latin prouerbe, *Cygnea cantio*, which among the common people is termed, a lightning before death. 1592: Shakespeare, *Romeo*, V iii 1641: R. Brome, *Joviall Crew*, V 1748: Richardson, *Clarissa*, viii 65 (1785), Her late tranquillity and freedom from pain seemed but a *lightening*, as Mrs Lovick and Mrs Smith call it. 1847: Halliwell, *Dict.*, s.v. ... a proverbial phrase, alluding to the resuscitation of the spirits which frequently occurs before dissolution. 1901: F. E. Taylor, *Lancs Sayings*, 31, He'd a bit of a leetenin' like afore he dee'd.

Lightly come lightly go. *c*.1374: Chaucer, *Troylus*, bk ii l. 1239, For why men seyth, 'impressiounes lighte Ful lightly been ay redy to the flighte'. 1412–20: Lydgate, *Troy Book*, bk ii l 4635, Lightly it cam and lightly went away. 1546: Heywood, *Proverbs*, Pt II ch ix, Light come, light go. *c*.1615: *Times Whistle*, 89 (E.E.T.S.). 1765: Garrick, *Sick Monkey, ad fin.*, What lightly comes, as lightly goes, With all such pretty fellows. 1826: Lamb, *Pop. Fallacies*,

II. 1860: Reade, *Cl. and Hearth*, ch xxxvii 1909: R. Nevill, *Light Come, Light Go* [title].

Lightly gained quickly lost. *c.*1580: Fulwell, *Ars Adulandi*, sig. E2, Experience taught me that easely wonne was lightly loste. 1583: Greene, *Works*, ii 25 (Grosart), He wil iudge that is lightly to bee gained, is as quickly lost. 1898: Besant, *Orange Girl*, II iv (OED), Lightly got, lightly spent.

Lightning. 1. Forked lightning at night, The next day clear and bright. 1893: Inwards, *Weather Lore*, 119.

2. Lightning brings heat. Ibid., 117.

3. Lightning never strikes twice in the same place. 1857: P.H. Myers, *prisoner of Border*, xii, They did not hit me at all … Lightning never strikes twice in the same place, nor cannon balls either, I presume.

4. There's lightning lightly before thunder. 1633: Draxe, 226, Lightly before thunder, lightning. 1670: Ray, 114.

5. When caught by the tempest, wher ever it be, If it lightens and thunders beware of a tree! 1846: Denham, *Proverbs*, 19 (Percy S.).

Like a cat. *See* Cat.

Like a feather on a hill, He's. Glos. Applied to an inconstant man. 1639: in *Berkeley MSS.*, iii 26 (1885).

Like a fiddler's elbow. *See* Fiddler (6).

Like a horse in a mill. *c.*1540: J. Heywood, *Wit and Folly*, 22 (Percy S.), Evyn lyke the myll hors, they be whyppyd amayne. 1607: Dekker, etc., *Northw. Hoe*, I iii, I that like a horse Ran blind-fold in a mill, all in one circle. 1654: Whitlock, *Zootomia*, 432, Carefull men, like horses in a mill, run round in a competency. 1720: Stukeley, *Memoirs*, iii 461 (Surtees S.), The same circle must be observed every day of one's life, like a horse in a mill. 1825: Lamb, *Superann. Man*, par. 11, Like horses in a mill, drudging on in the same eternal round. 1839: Dickens, *Nickleby*, ch lxiv, I am perpetually turning, like a demd old horse in a demnition mill.

Like a house on fire = rapidly. 1857: Dickens, *Dorrit*, bk ii ch xxxiv, I assure you he is making out his case like a house a-fire.

Like a loader's horse, that lives among thieves. Somerset. 1678: Ray, 350. 1732: Fuller, 3223.

Like a ribbon double-dyed, Never worn and never tried. 1864: 'Cornish Proverbs', in *N. & Q.*, 3rd ser, v 209.

Like a silver pin. 1869: Spurgeon, *John Ploughman*, ch xviii, They are like a silver pin, Fair without but foul within.

Like a threeha'penny chick in a wheaten arish [stubble]. Corn. 1895: Jos. Thomas, *Randigal Rhymes*, 60.

Like a young bear with all your sorrows to come. 1870: in *N. & Q.*, 4th ser, vi 321.

Like as one egg to another. [Tam similem quam lacte lacti est. – Plautus, *Mil. Glor.*, II ii 85.] 1542: Becon, *Early Works*, 90 (P.S.), Our houses … are so like one to another, that ye can less discern an egg from an egg … as they say. 1654: Gayton, *Pleasant Notes Don Q.*, 23, Not eggs to eggs are liker. 1738: Swift, *Polite Convers.*, Dial. III *c.*1783: in *Roxb. Ballads*, vii 94 (B.S.).

Like as two peas. [σῦκον εἰκάσαι σύκῳ. – Herodas, vi 60.] 1580: Lyly, *Euphues*, 215 (Arber), Who wer as lyke as one pease is to an other. *c.*1680: in *Roxb. Ballads*, vii 77 (B.S.), And will be as like her as one pea's like another. 1725: Bailey, tr. Erasmus' *Colloq.*, 40. 1846: Planché, *Extravag.*, iii 139 (1879), They are as like each other as two peas! 1884: R.L.S. and Henley, *Adm. Guinea*, II vi 1925: E. Lyttelton, *Memories and Hopes*, 322, He and his twin brother … were as like as two peas.

Like author like book. 1670: Ray, 15.

Like Benjamin's mess. 1628: Earle, *Microcos.*, 124 (1811), His talk at the table is like Benjamin's mess, five times to his part.

Like blood, like goods, and like age, make the happiest marriage. 1639: Clarke, 28. 1681: W. Robertson, *Phraseol. Generalis*, 266. 1732: Fuller, 6184.

Like breeds like. R. Edgeworth, *SermonsI*, 178v, Wyth a frowarde synner, a man shall be naughtye … for lyke maketh like. *c.*1577: *Misogonus*, 2v, The like bredes the like (eche man sayd). 1842: Tennyson, *Poems* (1969) 703, Like men, like manners: Like breeds like they say.

Like carpenter. *See* Such carpenter.

Like carver like cook. 1673: *Vinegar and Mustard*, 23, in Hindley, *Old Book Coll. Miscell.*, iii.

Like cow like calf. 1573: Bullein, *Dialogue*, 21 (E.E.T.S.), Her sonne is like the mother as seemeth by one in the house, like cowe like calfe.

Like crow like egg. 1536: Latimer, *Sermons*, 42 (P.S.), Ye know this is a proverb much used: 'An evil crow an evil egg'. 1611: Cotgrave, s.v. 'Corbeau', Of an ill bird, an ill brood. 1655: T. Muffett, *Healths Improvement*, 135, As the Greek proverb saith, Like crow, like egg.

Like cup. *See* **Such cup.**

Like father like son. *c.*1340: R. Rolle, *Psalter* (1884), 342, Ill sunnys folous ill fadirs. 1377: Langland, *Plowman*, B, ii 28, Qualis pater, talis filius. 1509: Barclay, *Ship of Fools*, i 236 (1874), An olde prouerbe hath longe agone be sayde That oft the sone in maners lyke wyll be Vnto the father. 1605: Camden, *Remains*, 331 (1870), Such a father, such a son. 1721: Bailey, *Eng. Dict.*, s.v. 'Father'. 1860: Reade, *Cl. and Hearth*, ch lxxix. 1907: De Morgan, *Alice-for-Short*, ch xxx, ' "like father, like son" – so people say,' says Alice.

Like fault like punishment. 1542: Becon, *Early Works*, 243 (P.S.) [cited as 'the common proverb'].

Like host like guest. 1540: Palsgrave, *Acolastus*, sig. M2, Such a geste, such an hoste. 1586: L. Evans, *Withals Dict. Revised*, sig. H2, Lyke hoste, lyke guest, *c.*1613: Rowlands, *Poire of Spy-Knaues*, 21 (Hunt. Clo), Such oast, such ghest, the prouerbe sayes. 1654: Gayton, *Pleasant Notes Don Q.*, 9, Like guest like landlord.

Like it or lump it. 1880: Courtney, *W. Cornwall Words*, 36 (E.D.S.), If you don't like it you must lump it. 1901: F. E. Taylor, *Lancs Sayings*, 10, They con like it or lump it, as beggars done pot-bo'.

Like John Gray's bird. *See* **John Gray.**

Like lips like lettuce. [Similem habent labra lactucam (a saying of M. Crassus when he saw an ass eating thistles). – Hieronymus, *Ep.*, vii 5.] 1546: Heywood. *Proverbs*, Pt II ch vii, Suche lips, suche lettice. 1587: Greene, *Works*, iii 60 (Grosart), As you said before, like lips like lettice, as the man is so is his manners. 1634: Massinger, *Guardian*, II iii, There's other lettuce For your coarse lips. 1681: W. Robertson, *Phraseol. Generalis*, 830. 1732: Fuller, 3231. 1853: Trench, *Proverbs*, 21 (1905), In the proverb you will find it [alliteration] of continual recurrence ... Thus ... *Like lips, like lettuce.*

Like lord like chaplain. *c.*1540: Bale, *Kynge Johan*, 73 (Camden S.), Lyke lorde, lyke chaplayne; neyther barrell better herynge.

Like master like man. [Plane qualis dominus talis et servus. – Petr., 58.] *c.*1390: Gower, *Conf.*

Amantis, iii 2421, Such capitein such retenue. 1530: J. Palsgrave, *L'éclaircissement de la Langue Française*, 120v, Suche maystre suche man. 1538: T. Elyot, *Dictionary*, s.v. Similes, A lewde servaunt with an yll master ... Lyke master lyke man. 1568: Fulwell, *Like will to Like*, in Hazlitt, *Old Plays*, iii 330, Like master, like man. 1584: Lyly, *Sapho and Phao*, II iii 1641: Marmion, *Antiquary*, IV 1750: Smollett, *Gil Blas*, iii 189, Scipio, on his side, (for it was like master, like man) kePt table also, in the buttery. 1830: Marryat, *King's Own*, ch xix, She call me d – d nigger, and say like massa like man. 1855: Gaskell, *North and South*, ch xv, What the master is, that will the men be, without overmuch taking thought on his part. *See also* **Trim-tram.**

Like me, God bless the example. 1670: Ray, 184.

Like mistress like maid. 1557: Tusser, *Husbandrie*, in *Brit. Bibliog.*, iii 15 (1812), Such mistres suche mayde. 1620: Rowlands, *Night Raven*, 17 (Hunt.Cl.), Like mistris like maide. 1699: Farquhar, *Love and a Bottle*, II i 1849: Planché, *Extravag.*, iv 19 (1879). Cf. **Hackney mistress.**

Like mother like daughter. 1325: *Cursor Mundi* (E.E.T.S.), l. 18857 O suilk [such] a moder, wel slik [such] a child. 1474: Caxton, *Game of Chess*, II ii, For suche moder suche doughter comunely. 1509: Barclay, *Ship of Fools*, i 236 (1874), An olde prouerbe hath long agone be sayde That oft ... the mayde Or doughter, vnto the mother wyll agre. 1611: *Bible*, Ezek. xvi 44, Every one that useth proverbs shall use this proverb against thee, saying, As is the mother, so is her daughter, 1860: Reade, *Cl. and Hearth*, ch xlvii.

Like priest like people. 1382: Wiclif, *Bible*, Hos. iv 9, As the peple so the prest. 1589: Nashe, *Works*, i 121 (Grosart), *Like people, like priest* begins now to be verified. 1611: *Bible*, Hos. iv 9, Like people, like priest. 1681: Yarranton,. Eng. *Improvement*, Pt II 183, In most places, it is at this day, *like parson, like people*. 1725: Bailey, tr. Erasmus' *Colloq.*, 246, Like people, like priest.

Like punishment and equal pain, both key and key-hole do sustain. 1639: Clarke, 239. 1670: Ray, 135.

Like saint *See* **Such saint.**

Like the boose, To. *See* quot. 1877: E. Leigh, *Cheshire Gloss.*, 170, When men or women marry for fortune they are said … 'To like the boose [stall for cattle] but not the ring-stake', i.e. they like the plenty round but fret at the confinement and chains, with which plenty has been purchased. 1917: Bridge, *Cheshire Proverbs*, 140.

Like the Irishman's pig. *See* quot. 1901: F. E. Taylor, *Lancs Sayings*, 5, He's like th' Oirishmon's pig – he'll noather Ieeod nor droive.

Like the old woman's dish-cloth, looks better dry than wet. Oxfordsh. 1913: *Folk-Lore*, xxiv 76.

Like to one as if spit out of his mouth. *c.*1400: *Beryn*, l. 3232 (E.E.T.S.), Behold thy sone! it semeth crope out of thy mowith. 1602: Breton, in *Works*, ii g 8 (Grosart), The one as like an owle, the other as like an urchin, as if they had beene spitte out of the mouthes of them. 1616: Haughton, *Englishm. for my Money*, IV i, Now look I as like the Dutchman as if I were spit out of his mouth. 1668: Dryden, *Sir Martin Markall*, V i 1703: Centlivre, *Stolen Heiress*, III iv 1738: Swift, *Polite Convers.*, Dial. III. 1828: Carr, *Craven Dialect*, ii 155, 'That barn's as like his fadder, as an he'd been spit out of his mouth', i.e. he very much resembles him. 1887: Parish and Shaw, *Dict. Kent. Dialect*, 158 (E.D.S.). Spit. A double or counterpart. 'He's the very spit of his brother'.

Like water. *See* **Duck** (6).

Like will to like – with varied additions. [Pares autem vetere proverbio cum paribus facillime congregantur. – Cicero, *De Senect.*, 7.) *c.*1375: *Sc. Leg. Saints*, i 543 (Petrus) (OED), Lyk to lyk accordis wele. *c.*1430: Lydgate, *Churl and Bird*, st. 38, Eche thinge draweth to his semblable. *c.*1460: *Prov. of Good Counsel*, in E.E.T.S., Ext. ser, No. 8, p. 70, As for this proverbe dothe specify, 'lyke wyll to lyke in eche company'. 1509: Barclay, *Ship of Fools*, ii 35 (1874), For it is a prouerbe, and an olde sayd sawe That in euery place lyke to lyke wyll drawe. 1546: Heywood, *Proverbs*, Pt I ch iv 1568: Fulwell, *Like will to Like* [title]. 1580: Baret, *Alvearie*, A 589, Lyke will to lyke, quoth the deuill to the colliar. 1614: B. Rich, *Honestie of This Age*, 48 (Percy S.) [as in 1580]. 1664: *Poor Robin Alman. Prognost.*, sig. C5 [as in 1580]. 1670: Ray, 15, Like to like, and Nan for Nicholas. 1679: A. Behn, *Feign'd Curtezans*, V i [as in 1580]. 1732: Fuller, 3239 [as in 1670]; and No. 3240 [as in 1580]. 1823: Scott, *Peveril*, ch xiv, How could I help it? like will to like – the boy would come – the girl would see him. 1922: Weyman, *Ovington's Bank*, ch xxxi, He's learned

this at your d – d counter, sir! That's where it is. It's Like to like.

Like wood like arrows. 1633: Draxe, 113.

Like word like deed. *c.*1386: Chaucer, C. *Tales*, A 741 (Skeat), Eek Plato seith, who-so that can him rede, The wordës mote be cosin to the dede.

Like workman. *See* **Workman** (1).

Likely lies in the mire when Unlikely gets over. 1732: Fuller, 3242.

Likeness causeth liking. 1639: Clarke, 27. 1732: Fuller, 3243, Likeness begets love; yet proud men hate one another.

Likes not his business, Who. *See* quot. 1846: T. Wright, *Essays on Middle Ages*, i 140, We have the saying, 'Who likes not his business, his business likes not him'.

Lilies are whitest in a blackmoor's hand. 1732: Fuller, 3244.

Lill for loll. *See* quot. 1639: in *Berkeley MSS.*, iii 33 (1885), Lill for loll: id est, one for another: as good as hee brought. (Glouc:).

Lily. *See* **White** (2).

Lim hay, To lick it up like. 1670: Ray, 206. 1790: Grose, *Prov. Gloss.*, s.v. 'Cheshire'. 1917: Bridge, *Cheshire Proverbs*, 139. [Lymm is a village on the Mersey where the best hay is got.]

Lime enriches the father and beggars the son. 1846: Denham, *Proverbs*, 6 (Percy S.), Lime makes a rich father and a poor son. 1917: Bridge, *Cheshire Proverbs*, 92.

Lincoln. *See* **Devil** (5).

Lincoln, As loud as Tom of. 1662: Fuller, *Worthies*, ii 267 (1840). 1790: Grose, *Prov. Gloss.*, s.v. 'Lincs'.

Lincoln shall be hanged for London's sake. *c.*1592: Sir *T. More*, 21 (Malone S.), This the olde prouerbe now compleate dooth make, that Lincolne should be hangd for Londons sake.

Lincoln was, London is, and York shall be. 1603: Dekker, *Wond. Yeare*, in *Works*, i 101 (Grosart) [cited as 'that worme-eaten prouerb']. 1662: Fuller, *Worthies*, iii 413 (1840). 1700: J. Brome, *Travels*, 148, Lincoln was, and London is, And York shall be, The fairest city of the three. 1724: Stukeley, *Itin. Cur.*, 85 [as in 1700]. 1725: Defoe, *Tour*, ii 140 [as in 1603]. 1865: W. White, *East. England*, ii 45 [as in 1700].

Lincolnshire. *See* **Cheshire** (6).

Lincolnshire bagpipes. 1590: *Three Lords, etc.*, in Hazlitt, *Old Plays*, vi 393, The sweet ballad of the Lincolnshire bagpipes. 1598: Shakespeare, 1

Henry IV, I ii, I am as melancholy as … the drone of a Lincolnshire bagpipe. 1622: Drayton, *Polyol.*, xxiii, And bells and bagpipes next, belong to Lincolnshire. 1790: Grose, *Prov. Gloss.*, s.v. 'Lincs', Lincolnshire bagpipes.

Lincolnshire where the hogs sh – soap, and the cows fire. 1659: Howell, 21. 1670: Ray, 236. 1790: Grose, *Prov. Gloss.*, s.v. 'Lincs'. 1889: Peacock, *Manley, etc., Gloss.*, 324 (E.D.S.).

Lincoln's Inn. *See* **Gray's Inn.**

Lind [Linden or Lime-tree], **As light as leaf on.** c.1310: in Ritson, *Songs and Ballads*, 56 (Hazlitt), And lef is lyht on lynde. 1377: Langland, *Plowman*, B, i 154, Was neuere leef vpon lynde lighter therafter. c.1386: Chaucer, *Clerk's Tale*, l. 1155. 1457: in *Reliq. Antiquae*, ii 70 (1843), Be ay of chere as lighte as lefe on lynde. 1520: in *Ballads from MSS.*, i 450 (B.S.), As lyght as lefe on lynde.

Lindholme. *See* **Hatfield.**

Line to the wall, Bring your, not the wall to the line. 1732: Fuller, 1021.

Linen in public, To wash one's dirty. *See* **Wash** (5).

Lingering love breeds mislike. 1593: *Pass. Morrice*, 87 (N.Sh.S.).

Lion. **1. A lion among sheep and a sheep among lions.** 1589: Puttenham, *Eng. Poesie*, 299 (Arber), As the prouerbe goeth … a lyon, etc.

2. A lion may be beholden to a mouse. 1639: Fuller, *Holy War*, bk iii ch viii, As the fable telleth us … the mouse [may] befriend the lion. 1732: Fuller, 264, A lyon may come to be beholding to a mouse.

3. A lion's skin is never cheap. 1611: Cotgrave, s.v. 'Lion', A lyons skinne was never bought good cheape. 1670: Ray, 16. 1732: Fuller, 4643.

4. Destroy the lion while he is yet but a whelp. Ibid., No. 1276. 1869: Spurgeon, *John Plough-man*, ch i, You know it is best to kill the lion while it is a cub.

5. Even the lion must defend itself against flies. 1924: *Sphere*, 27 Sept., p. 386, col. 2.

6. He is a lion in a good cause. 1732: Fuller, 1907.

7. (a) **If the lion's skin cannot do it, the fox's shall,** or (b) **To patch a fox's tail to a lion's skin** = to supplement strength by craft. 1605: Camden, *Remains*, 326 (1870) [(a)]. Before 1634: Chapman, *Alphonsus*, I i, And where the lion's hide is thin and scant, I'll firmly patch it with the fox's fell. 1645: Howell, *Letters*, bk i § 1, No. xlii. [(b)]. 1664: J. Wilson, *Andron. Commenius*, IV iv, Craft, where strength doth fail, And piece the lion with the fox's tail! 1670: Ray, 184 [(a)]. 1736: Bailey, *Dict.*, s.v. 'Lion', If the lion's skin cannot the fox's shall. 1745: *Agreeable Companion*, 182, The lion's skin too short, you know … Was lengthen'd by the fox's tail; And art supplies, where strength may fail. 1754: Berthelson, *Eng.-Danish Dict.*, s.v. 'lion' [(b)].

8. If thy hand be in a lion's mouth, get it out as fast as thou canst. 1696: *Cornish Comedy*, V, My hand is in the lion's mouth; I must agree with him. 1732: Fuller, 2724. 1819: Scott, *Ivanhoe*, ch xix, 'Our heads are in the lion's mouth,' said Wamba … 'get them out how we can.'

9. It is a base thing to tear a dead lion's beard off. 1596: Shakespeare, *King John*, II i., You are the hare of whom the proverb goes, Whose valour plucks dead lions by the beard. 1632: Randolph, *Jealous Lovers*, IV iii, Do not, live hare, pull the dead lion's beard. 1656: R. Fletcher, *Ex Otio Negotium*, 95, Be afear'd To pull a deceas'd lyon by the beard. 1732: Fuller, 2846.

10. Little birds may pick a dead lion. Ibid., No. 3250.

11. The lion is not so fierce as he is painted. 1633: Draxe, 64 [with 'furious' for 'fierce']. 1640: Herbert, *Jac. Prudentum.* 1670: Ray, 114 [with 'half' before 'so']. 1732: Fuller, 4642 [as in 1670].

12. To see the lions. Originally the lions in the Tower of London, and, by extension, sights generally. 1590: Greene, *Works*, viii 68 (Grosart), This countrey Francesco was no other but a meere nouice, and that so newly, that to vse the old prouerb, he had scarce seene the lions. 1595: *Maroccus Extaticus*, 8 (Percy S.), Indeed those be the young men that never sawe the lyons. 1765: Mrs Cibber, in *Garrick Corresp.*, i 200 (1831), This is not the right season of the year to show the lions. 1785: Grose, *Class. Dict. Vulgar Tongue*, s.v. 'Lion', To shew the lions and tombs, to point out the particular curiosities of any place. 1843: Dickens, *Letters*, iii 46 (1882), He … has been in London too, and seeing all the lions under my escort.

13. Wake not a sleeping lion. 1580: Sidney, *Arcadia*, bk iv 416 (1893), Dametas, thinking it not good to awake a sleeping lion. 1611: Cotgrave, s.v. 'Esveiller', To awake the sleeping lyon (say we).

1693: Urquhart, *Rabelais*, bk iii ch xiv, As when we say proverbially to incense hornets, to move a stinking puddle, and to awake a sleeping lyon. *See also* **Better be the head**; **Dog** (40) and (83); **Fly** (6); **Hare** (2); **Lamb** (1); **Living dog**; and **Waking dog.**

Lip-honour costs little, yet may bring in much. 1659: Howell, *Proverbs: Ital.-Eng.*, 13, The honor one doth with the mouth avails much and costs little. 1732: Fuller, 3245.

Lip-wisdom that wants experience, All is but. 1580: Sidney, *Arcadia*, bk i 92 (1893). 1647: *Countrym. New Commonwealth*, 22. 1732: Fuller, 522.

Lips hang in your light, Your. Before 1529: Skelton, *Magnyfycence*, l. 1061, Tusshe, thy lyppes hange in thyne eye. 1546: Heywood, *Proverbs*, Pt II ch iv 1611: Davies (of Hereford), *Sc. of Folly*, 49, in *Works*, ii (Grosart), Some lasses lips hang in their light. 1681: W. Robertson, *Phraseol. Generalis*, 621, A born fool; his lips hang in's light.

Lips however rosy must be fed. 1875: A. B. Cheales, *Proverb. Folk-Lore*, 29.

Liquorish. *See* quot. 1668: Davenant, *Man's the Master*, IV, That baggage carries her purse in her bosom; and, according to the Northern proverb, is as liquorish at a penny as at a posset.

Liquorish tongue, A, a lecherous tail. *c.*1386: Chaucer, *Wife of Bath's Prol.*, l. 466, A likerous mouth moste han a likerous tayl. 1560: T. Wilson, *Rhetorique*, 119 (1909), Likerish of tongue, light of taile. 1670: Ray, 16. 1717:Pope, *Wife of Bath*, l. 218, A liquorish mouth must have a lecherous tail. 1732: Fuller, 3205.

Liquorish tongue is the purse's canker, A. 1678: Ray, 169.

Lisping lass is good to kiss, A. 1638: Ford, *Lady's Trial*, IV ii, No, sweet madam, Your lips are destined to a better use, Or else the proverb fails of lisping maids. 1737: Ray, 273. 1917: Bridge, *Cheshire Proverbs*, 4.

Listeners hear no good of themselves. 1647: *Mercurius Elenticus*, 26 Jan–2 Feb., 76, The old Proverb is, hearkners never heare good of them selves. 1678: Ray, 75. 1748: Richardson, *Clarissa*, v 116 (1785), The event ... justified the old observation, that listners seldom hear good of themselves. 1822: Scott, *Nigel*, ch xxxiii, They say that hearkeners hear ill tales of themselves. 1857: Borrow, *Rom. Rye*, ch xi

Lith and selthe. *See* **Ease and success.**

Lithe as lass of Kent. 1579: Spenser, *Shep. Cal.*, Feb., His dewelap as lythe as lasse of Kent. 1735: Pegge, *Kent. Proverbs*, in E.D.S., No. 12, p. 61, Lythe as lass of Kent, i.e. gentle, lithsom, etc.

Lither. *See* **Lazy man's guise**; and **Long as he is lither.**

Lither look. *See* **Wanton look.**

Little and good fills the trencher. 1640: Herbert, *Jac. Prudentum.* 1666: Torriano, *Piazza Univ.*, 211. 1670: Ray, 16 [with 'which is' for 'an'].

Little and little. *See* **Cat** (35).

Little and little, By, the bird makes his nest. 1846: T. Wright, *Essays on Middle Ages*, i 130, We have in England a proverb, 'Little and little make mickle', which appears again under the shape, 'By little and little the bird makes his nest'.

Little and little, By, the poor whore sinks her barn. 1678: Ray, 170.

Little and often fills the purse. 1666: Torriano, *Piazza Univ.*, 211. 1685: L'Estrange, *Observalor*, iii No. 2, But a little and often is a good rule. 1732: Fuller, 3249.

Little barrel can give but a little meal, A. 1732: Fuller, 243.

Little betwixt right and wrong. 1659: Howell, *Proverbs: Brit.-Eng.*, 38.

Little Billing. *See* **All the world.**

Little bird is content with a little nest, A. 1633: Draxe, 115, For a little bird, a little nest. 1732: Fuller, 244.

Little body doth often harbour a great soul, A. 1611: Cotgrave, s.v. 'Lievre', A little bush may hold a great hare; a little body a great heart. 1670: Ray, 16. 1732: Fuller, 3252, Little bodies have commonly great souls. 1875: A. B. Cheales, *Proverb. Folk-Lore*, 9, Little bodies have large souls.

Little, By the, is known the much. 1541: *Sch. House of Women*, l. 846, in Hazlitt, *Early Pop. Poetry*, iv 138.

Little cannot be great unless he devour many, The. 1640: Herbert, *Jac. Prudentum.* 1670: Ray, 16.

Little cattle little care. 1917: Bridge, *Cheshire Proverbs*, 92. Cf. **Little goods.**

Little debt makes a debtor, but a great one an enemy, A. 1732: Fuller, 245.

Little dogs. *See* **Hare** (7).

Little drops. *See* **Constant dropping.**

Little end of the horn. Pictures of the 'horn of suretyship' used to be common – 'I had the horn of suretiship ever before my eyes. You all know the device of the home where the young fellow slippes in at the butts-end and comes squeezed out at the buckall'. – 1605: Jonson, etc., *Eastw. Hoe*, I i *See also* 1624: B.&F., *Wife for a Month*, III iii The horn also represented prison – the wide mouth indicating ease of entrance, the small opening at the other end indicating difficulty of exit. Larwood and Hotten, in *Hist. of Signboards*, 339 (1867), say: 'Among the Roxburghe Ballads (II 138) there is one entitled "The Extravagant Youth, or an Emblem of Prodigality," with a woodcut representing a youth jumping into the mouth of a large horn. On one side stands the father, seemingly in distress; on the other is a mad-house, with the sign of THE FOOL, two of the inmates looking out from behind the bars. The extravagant youth … says:

But now all my glory is clearly decay'd,
And into the horn myself have betray'd
…
All comforts now from us are flown.
My father in Bedlam makes his moan,
And I in the *Counter* a prisoner thrown,
This Horn is a figure by which it is known.

1639–61: in *Rump Songs*, Pt I, 127 (1662, repr. 1874), So that a poor delinquent fleec'd and torn Seems like a man that's creeping through a horn, Finds a smooth entrance, wide, and fit, but when Hee's squeez'd and forc'd up through the smaller end, He looks as gaunt and pin'd, as he that spent A tedious twelve years in an eager Lent. 1887: J. Eliot Hodgkin, in *N. & Q.*, 7th ser, iv 323, 'Coming out of the little end of the horn'. This expression … I first heard it used many years ago by a Warwickshire man.

Little England beyond Wales = Pembrokeshire. 1586: Camden, *Britannia*, 373. 1603: G. Owen, *Descrip. of Pembrokeshire*. 1670: Ray, 258. 1888: E. Laws, *Hist, of Little England beyond Wales* [title]. 1925: *Observer*, 31 May, p. 9, col. 4.

Little fellow, He's a; but every bit of that little is bad. 1732: Fuller, 2441.

Little field. *See* **Little house.**

Little finger. *See* quots. [Cuius pluris erat unguis, quam tu totus es. – Petr., 57.] 1618: B. Holyday, *Technogamia*, I iv, H's more loue in's little finger, then both they in their whole bodyes. 1670: Ray, 175, He hath more in's little finger, then thou in thy whole body. 1738: Swift, *Polite Convers.*, Dial. II, She has more goodness in her little finger, than he has in his whole body.

Little fish are sweet. 1830: Forby, *Vocab. E. Anglia*, 434. 1872: J. Glyde, jr., *Norfolk Garland*, 149.

Little fishes slip through nets, but great fishes are taken. 1598: Meres, *Palladis*, fo. 246.

Little good is soon spent, A. 1605: Camden, *Remains*, 327 (1870). 1670: Ray, 116. 1732: Fuller, 3255, Little goods are soon spent.

Little good to stark naught, To come from. 1639: Clarke, 83. 1670: Ray, 178.

Little goods little care. [*c.*1300: *King Alisaunder*, l. 7365, Beter is, lyte to have in ese Then muche to have[n] in malese.] 1633: Draxe, 161. 1640: Herbert, *Jac. Prudentum*, Little wealth, little care. 1732: Fuller, 3256. 1875: A. B. Cheales, *Proverb. Folk-Lore*, 101, Little wealth, little woe. Cf. **Little cattle.**

Little, He that hath, is the less dirty. 1640: Herbert, *Jac. Prudentum*.

Little helps, Every. *See* **Every Little.**

Little house has a wide mouth, A. 1883: Burne, *Shropsh. Folk-Lore*, 589.

Little house well filled. *See* quots. 16th cent.: in *N. & Q.*, 4th ser, iii 10, A little grounde well tilled, A litel house well filled, A litel wife well willed, Would make him live that weare halfe killed, *c.*1582: G. Harvey, *Marginalia*, 200 (1913), A lyttle house well filled: a lyttle land well tilled. 1670: Ray, 53, [as in 1582, *plus*] and a little wife well will'd. 1738: Swift, *Polite Convers.*, Dial. II [as in 1670]. 1880: Spurgeon, *Ploughman's Pictures*, 156 [as in 1670, but with 'field' for 'land'].

Little in the morning. *See* quots. 16th cent.: in *Reliq. Antiquae*, i 208 (1841), A little in the morning, nothing at noone, And a light supper doth make to live longe. 1619: *Helpe to Discourse*, 125 (1640), A little in the morning is enough, enough at dinner is but a little; a little at night is too much.

Little John. *See* quot. 1605: Camden, *Remains*, 328 (1870), Many a man talks of Little John that never did know him.

Little journeys and good cost bring safe home. 1640: Herbert, *Jac. Prudentum*.

Little kitchen makes a large house, A. Ibid. 1666: Torriano, *Piazza Univ.*, 57.

Little knocks rive great blocks. 1830: Forby, *Vocab. E. Anglia*, 430. 1872: J. Glyde, jr., *Norfolk Garland*, 148.

Little knows the fat sow. *See* Sow (10).

Little labour, much health, A. 1640: Herbert, *Jac. Prudentum*.

Little leak will sink a great ship, A. 1616: T. Adams, *Taming of the Tongue*, 28 in *Sacrifice of Thankfulnesse*, It is a little leake that drowneth a shippe. 1642: Fuller, *Holy State:* 'Good Servant', Many little leaks may sink a ship. 1736: Franklin, *Way to Wealth*, in *Works*, i 447 (Bigelow) [with 'small' for 'little']. 1875: A. B. Cheales, *Proverb. Folk-Lore*, 165 (as in 1736].

Little learning (or **knowledge**) **is a dangerous thing, A.** 1711: Pope, *An Essay on Criticism*, l. 215, A Little Learning is a dang'rous Thing: Drink deep, or taste not the Pierian spring. 1829: P. Egan, *Boxiana*, 2nd Series, II 4, The sensible idea that 'A Little learning is a dangerous thing!'. 1881: T. H. Huxley, *Science and Culture*, iv, If a little knowledge is dangerous, where is the man who has so much as to be out of danger.

Little let [hindrance] **lets an ill workman, A.** 1640: Herbert, *Jac. Prudentum*.

Little London = Penrith. 1846–59: *Denham Tracts*, i 182 (F.L.S.).

Little London beyond Wales = Beaumaris. 1670: Ray, 258.

Little losses amaze, great tame. 1640: Herbert, *Jac. Prudentum*.

Little love and a little money, A. Before 1704: T. Brown, in *Works*, i 293 (1760) [cited as 'a good old proverb'].

Little love, little trust. Before 1500: Hill, *Commonplace-Book*, 47 (E.E.T.S.), An old said sawe … 'Wher is lytill love ther is lytill tryste'.

Little man. *See* quot. 1921: *Times*, 10 Sept., p. 9, col. 4, We are ready to join in the general welcome [to C. Chaplin]. 'A little man may', as the adage truly says, 'cast a great shadow'.

Little mead, little need. Somerset. A mild winter hoped for after a bad summer. 1678: Ray, 352.

Little meddling, Of, cometh great rest (or **ease**), *c.*1386: Chaucer, *Manciple's Tale*, l. 350, That litel jangling causeth muchel rest. 1546: Heywood, *Proverbs*, Pt II ch ii … reste. 1599: Porter, *Two Angry Women*, in Hazlitt, *Old Plays*, vii 337 … rest. 1669: *Politeuphuia*, 166 … much rest. 1694: D'Urfey, *Quixote*, Pt I Act II sc ii …

ease. 1902: in *N. & Q.*, 9th ser, x 475, In chastising a child for undue curiosity, with a view to impress the young mind with the truth of the proverb that 'of little meddling comes great ease'.

Little minds like weak liquors are soonest soured. 1855: Bohn, 444.

Little mischief too much. 1659: Howell, *Proverbs: Brit.-Eng.*, 31.

Little money little law. *c.*1550: *Parl. of Byrdes*, l. 146, in Hazlitt, *Early Pop. Poetry*, iii 174, Than sayde the Comysh daw, Lytle money lytle lawe.

Little neglect may breed great mischief, A. 1736: Franklin, *Way to Wealth*, in *Works*, i 446 (Bigelow).

Little, Of, a, a little. 1611: Cotgrave, s.v. 'Petit', Of a little take a little, of a mickle, mickle. 1631: Mabbe, *Celestina*, 212 (T.T.), That common saying of your little children: Of a little, a little; of much, nothing.

Little of everything is nothing in the main, A. 1732: Fuller, 247.

Little of what you fancy does you good, A. The title of a music hall that became popular enough to acquire proverbial status when taken up by the most famous artiste of the time, Marie Lloyd. *c.*1890: F.W. Leigh and G. Arthurs, (song title) 'A little of what you fancy does you good'.

Little pitchers have big ears. 1546: Heywood, *Proverbs*, Pt II ch v, Auoyd your children: small pitchers haue wide eares. 1594: Shakespeare, *Rich. III*, II iv, Pitchers have ears. 1617: Jonson, *Vis. of Delight* [as in 1594]. Before 1681: J. Lacy, *Sauny the Scot*, IV, I would have it private. Pitchers have ears, and I have many servants. 1721: Bailey, *Eng. Dict.*, s.v. 'Pitchfork'[with 'great' for 'wid']. 1852: Dickens, *Bleak House*, ch xxxvii, Charley verified the adage about little pitchers, I am sure; for she heard of more sayings and doings, in a day, than would have come to my ears in a month. 1914: Lucas, *Landmarks*, ch iv, Certain crusted scraps of nursery wisdom … such as … 'Little Pitchers have long ears'. 1917: Bridge, *Cheshire Proverbs*, 92, Little pigs have long ears.

Little pot is soon hot, A. 1546: Heywood, *Proverbs*, Pt I ch xi 1606: J. Day, *Ile of Gulls*, II iv, Nay, tho I be but a little pot, I shall be as soone hote as another. 1659: Howell, *Letters*, ii 665 (Jacobs). 1732: Fuller, 6173.

Little rain. *See* Rain, *subs.* (3), (22).

Little said soon amended. *c.*1555: in Wright,

Songs, etc., *Philip and Mary*, 31 (Roxb.Cl), Therfor lyttell sayd ys sowne amended. 1577: J. Grange, *Golden Aphroditis*, sig. B1. 1603: Dekker, *Pat. Grissil*, III. 1664: in *Musarum Delicioe, etc.*, ii 162 (Hotten), Little or nothing said, soon mended is. 1748: Richardson, *Clarissa*, V iii (1785), I should be angry if I proceed in my guesses – and little said is soon amended. Cf. **Least said.**

Little saving is no sin, A. 1792: Wolcot, *Works*, ii 313 (1795) [cited as a proverb 'that economic souls rever'].

Little spark. *See* **Spark.**

Little sticks kindle the fire, great ones put it out. 1303: Brunne, *Handlyng Synne*, l. 12438, Thou seest stykkes that are smale, They brenne fyrst feyre. 1640: Herbert, *Jac. Prudentum.* 1670: Ray, 16. 1732: Fuller, 3261.

Little stone may overturn a great wagon, A. *c.*1375: Barbour, *Bruce*, bk xi l.24, A litell stane, as men sayis, May ger weltir ane mekill wane.

Little stream may quench thirst as well as a great river, A. 1732: Fuller, 249.

Little stream will drive a light mill, A. 1639: Clarke, 88, A little stream serveth to drive a light milne. 1670: Ray, 116. 1732: Fuller, 250.

Little string will tie up a little bird, A. Ibid., No. 251.

Little strokes fell great oaks. 1539: Taverner, *Proverbs*, fo. 26, Wyth many strokes is an oke ouerthrowne. 1579: Lyly, *Euphues*, 81 (Arber), Many strokes ouerthrow the tallest oke. 1607: J. Day, *Trav. of Three Eng. Brothers*, 69 (Bullen), By many strokes the tallest okes are shaken. 1736: Franklin, *Way to Wealth*, in *Works*, i 444 (Bigelow). *c.*1800: Truisler, *Prov. in Verse*, 83. 1869; Spurgeon, *John Ploughman*, ch xxii, By little strokes Men fell great oaks.

Little thing, Of a, a little displeaseth. 1640: Herbert, *Jac. Prudentum.*

Little things are good. 1666: Torriano, *Piazza Univ.*, 215, That which is good is ever little.

Little things are great to little men. 1827: Hone, *Table-Book*, 110.

Little things are pretty. 1539: Taverner, *Proverbs*, fo. 50, Vnto lyttle thynges is a certayne grace annexed. 1678: Ray, 169. 1754: *World*, No. 65, Recollecting the proverb, that 'every thing that is little is pretty'.

Little things please little minds. 1576: G. Petie, *Petit Palace*, 39, A litle thyng pleaseth a foole. 1584: Lyly, *Sapho and Phao*, II iv [with 'catch'

for 'please']. 1880: Spurgeon, *Ploughman's Pictures*, 81.

Little tit, all tail. 1546: Heywood, *Proverbs*, Pt I ch x, Little titte all tayle, I haue heard er this. *c.*1570: G. Harvey, *Marginalia*, 139.

Little wealth. *See* **Little goods.**

Little wimble will let in the great auger, The. 1732: Fuller, 4632.

Little wind kindles, much puts out the fire, A. 1586: B. Young, tr. Guazzo's *Civil Convers.*, fo. 193. 1640: Herbert, *Jac. Prudentum.* 1732: Fuller, 253.

Little wit in the head makes much work for the feet. 1855: Bohn, 445. Cf. **Head** (17).

Little wit will serve a fortunate man, A. Ibid., 293.

Little wit, You have a, and it doth you good sometimes. 1670: Ray, 30. 1732: Fuller, 5911.

Little with honesty is better than a great deal with knavery, A. 1659: *London Chanticleers*, sc i, in Hazlitt, *Old Plays*, xii 325 [cited as 'that precise axiom'].

Little with quiet. *See* quots. 1611: Cotgrave, s.v. 'Peu', A little with quietnesse is Gods owne gift. Ibid., s.v., 'Paix', A little with peace is a great blessing. 1640: Herbert, *Jac. Prudentum*, A little with quiet is the only diet.

Little Witham. Used in punning references to lack of wit. 1589: Nashe, in *Works*, i 192 (Grosart), I giue and bequeath … to each of them an aduouson: To the former of small Witam: and to the other of little Brainford. 1595: *Pedlars Prophecy*, l. 481 (Malone S.), At Little Wytham seuen years I went to schoole. 1662: Fuller, *Worthies*, ii 269, He was born at Little Witham. 1790: Grose, *Prov. Gloss.*, s.v. 'Essex' and 'Lines' [as in 1662]. 1818: Scott, *Heart of Midi.*, ch xxxii, 'Has she the capacity of taking care of herself?' 'Why, your Reverence … I cannot just say – I will be sworn she was not born at Wittham'.

Little wood will heat a little oven, A. 1732: Fuller, 254. 1869: Spurgeon, *John Ploughman*, ch v.

Little worm will lie under a great stone, A. 1666: Torriano, *Piaxxa Univ.*, 243, The English say, A little worm, etc.

Live, verb. 1. A man may live upon little, but he cannot live upon nothing. 1855: Bohn, 295.

2. Better to live well than long. Ibid., 330.

3. He lives long that lives till all are weary of him. 1732: Fuller, 1966. 1738: Swift, *Polite*

Convers., Dial. II, I believe I shall live till all my friends are weary of me.

4. He lives long that lives well. 1560: T. Wilson, *Rhetorique*, 83 (1909), For they liued long enough, that haue liued well enough. 1642: Fuller, *Holy State:* 'Good Child', If he chance to die young, yet he lives long that lives well. 1748: Richardson, *Clarissa*, iv 121 (1785), He that lives well, lives long.

5. He lives unsafely that looks too near on things. 1611: Cotgrave, s.v. 'Esplucher' [with 'to matters' for 'on things']. 1640: Herbert, *Jac. Prudentum*.

6. He that lives always at home sees nothing but the same. 1618: Breton, in *Inedited Tracts*, 184 (Hazlitt, 1868) [quoted as a proverb].

7. He that lives ill, fear follows him. 1640: Herbert, *Jac. Prudentum*. 1666: Torriano, *Piazza Univ.*, 286, Who lives ill, fear attends him.

8. He that lives in hope danceth without music. 1591: Florio, *Second Frutes*, 149, He that dooth liue in hope, dooth dance in narrowe scope. 1640: Herbert, *Jac. Prudentum*. 1659: Howell, *Proverbs: Span.-Eng.*, 18.

9. He that lives long suffers much. 1620: Shelton, *Quixote*, Pt II ch xxxii. 1732: Fuller, 2220.

10. He that lives most, dies most. 1640: Herbert, *Jac. Prudentum*.

11. He that lives not well one year, sorrows seven after. 1640: Ibid. 1748: Richardson, *Clarissa*, iv 121 (1785), He that lives ill one year, will sorrow for it seven.

12. He that lives well is learned enough. 1611: Cotgrave, s.v. 'Vivre', He that lives well enough hath skill enough. 1640: Herbert, *Jac. Prudentum*.

13. He that lives well sees afar off. 1640: Ibid. 1748: Richardson, *Clarissa*, iv 121 (1785).

14. He that lives with the muses shall die in the straw. 1732: Fuller, 2223.

15. He that liveth in Court dieth upon straw. 1578: Florio, *First Fruites*, fo. 29. 1579: Lyly, *Euphues*, 185 (Arber). 1629: *Book of Meery Riddles*, Prov. 91. Cf. **Courtier young.**

16. He that liveth overcometh. 1578: Florio, *First Fruites*, fo. 33, Who lyueth vanquisheth. 1629: *Book of Meery Riddles*, Prov. 131.

17. He that liveth wickedly, can hardly die honestly. 1670: Ray, 16.

18. He that will live in peace and rest, Must hear and see and speak the best. *c.*1450: *Prov. of Good Counsel*, l. 52 (E.E.T.S.), Yf thou wylte leve in peas and reste, here, and see, and sey the beste. 1591: Florio, *Second Frutes*, 101, If you wil stil liue at ease, heare and see, and hold your pease. 1605: Camden, *Remains*, 323 (1870) [with 'say' for 'speak']. 1710: S. Palmer, *Moral Essays on Proverbs*, 143, He that means to live at rest, Must hear and see, and say the best. 1732: Fuller, 6182.

19. He who lives by the sword, dies by the sword. *See* **Sword** (2).

20. He would live even in a gravel-pit. 'Spoken of a wary, sparing, niggardly person'. 1678: Ray, 72. 1732: Fuller, 2417.

21. I live, and lords do no more. 1599: Porter, *Two Angry Women*, in Hazlitt, *Old Plays*, vii 307, *Fran.* Well, how doth thy master? *Nich.* Forsooth, live, and the best doth no better. 1732: Fuller, 2616.

22. If you would live for ever. *See* **Wash** (3).

23. If you would live well for a week, etc. *See* 1809 quot. 1666: Torriano, *Piazza Univ.*, 151, Who intends to have a good month, let him to the bath, a good year, let him marry, a good week, let him kill a hog, who will be happy alwaies, let him turn priest. 1809: Pegge, *Anonym.*, cent. ii 19, 'If you would live well for a week, kill a hog; if you would live well for a month, marry; if you would live well all your life, turn priest' [i.e. never marry]. This is an old proverb. 1827: Hone, *Table-Book*, 430 [as in 1809].

24. If you would not live to be old, you must be hanged when you are young. 1670: Ray, 126.

25. Live and learn. *c.*1620: in *Roxb. Ballads*, i 80 (Hindley), A man may live and learne. 1663: Killigrew, *Parson's Wedding*, II iii. 1747: Garrick, *Miss in her Teens*, I ii, I was innocent myself once, but *live and learn* is an old saying, and a true one. 1837: Dickens, *Pickwick*, ch xix. 1885: M. Twain, in *Letters*, 256 (ed. Paine), One lives and learns. I find it takes 7 binderies four months to bind 325,000 books. 1922: Weyman, *Ovington's Bank*, ch xix.

26. Live and let live. 1622: Malynes, *Anc. Law-Merch.*, 229 (OED), According to the Dutch prouerbe … Leuen ende laeten leuen, to liue and to let others liue. 1678: Ray, 170. 1692: L'Estrange, *Aesop*, 127 (3rd ed.), Live and let live is the rule of common justice. 1762: Smollett, *Sir L. Greaves*, ch xvi, You knows, meester, one must live and let live, as the saying is. 1852: Dickens, *Bleak House*, ch xliii. 1909: Lucas, *Wand, in Paris*, ch xiv, Liberty is the very air of the Boulevards. Live and let live.

27. Live well. *See* **Man** (47).

28. Living upon trust is the way to pay double. 1732: Fuller, 3265.

29. Living well is the best revenge. 1640: Herbert, *Jac. Prudentum.*

30. One cannot live by selling ware for words. 1639: Clarke, 156 [with 'I' for 'One']. 1670: Ray, 154. 1732: Fuller, 3741 [with 'goods' for 'wares'].

31. One must live long to learn much. *c.*1568: W, Wager, *The longer thou livest, the more foole thou art* [title]. 1633: Draxe, 58, The longer that one liueth, the more he knoweth. 1666: Torriano, *Piazza Univ.*, 313.

32. She lives by love and lumps in corners. 1678: Ray, 75.

33. They live but ill who always think to live. 1600: Bodenham, *Belvedere*, 228 (Spens.S.). 1732: Fuller, 4971, They seldom live well, who think they shall live long.

34. They live not most at ease that have the world at will. 1577: J. Grange, *Golden Aphroditis*, sig. H2.

35. They that live longest must die at last. 1670: Ray, 116. 1732: Fuller, 4982.

36. They that live longest must go farthest for wood. 1639: Clarke, 190, He that lives longest must fetch his wood furthest. 1670: Ray, 116. 1732: Fuller, 4983.

37. They who live longest will see most. 1620: Shelton, *Quixote*, Pt II ch lii, My mother was used to say that it was needful to live long to see much. 1869: Spurgeon, *John Ploughman*, ch xx, But now they have left they say there's a screw loose, and they who live longest will see most.

38. We can live without our friends, but not without our neighbours. 1732: Fuller, 5435.

39. We must live by the quick and not by the dead. 1578: Florio, *First Fruites*, fo. 34, Quicke with the quicke and dead with the dead. 1605: T. Heywood, *It You Know Not Me*, in *Dram. Works*, i 243 (1874) [quoted as 'the old prouerb']. 1626: Overbury, *Characters:* 'Sexton'. 1694: Southerne, *Fatal Marriage*, IV i, We must live by the living, you know. 1738: Swift, *Polite Convers.*, Dial. II [with 'living' for 'quick'].

40. We shall live till we die. 1600: Dekker, *Shoem. Hol.*, IV iii, Hereof am I sure, I shall live

till I die. 1655: T. Muffett, *Healths Improvement*, 8, We shall live till we dye, in despight of diet. 1889: Jefferies, *Hedgerow*, 65 (W.), The old country proverb, 'Ah, well, we shall live till we die if the pigs don't eat us, and then we shall go acorning'. 1901: F. E. Taylor, *Lancs Sayings*, 10, We shan o live till we dee'n – iv th' dogs dunno wory us. 1917: Bridge, *Cheshire Proverbs*, 149, We … die if the pigs don't eat us. Cf. **Tantera Bobus.**

41. Who lives well dies well. 1506: Pynson. *Kal. of Shepherds*, 169 (1892), He that leuyth well maye not dye amys. 1537: R. Whitford, *Werke for Housholders*, sig. G4, The moste sure way to dye well is well to lyue. 1578: Florio, *First Fruites*, fo. 28. 1639: Clarke, 215, They die well that live well. 1732: Fuller, 1890, He hath liv'd ill that knows not how to die well.

Lively as a cricket. *See* **Merry.**

Lively as a maggot. 1883: Burne, *Shropsh. Folk-Lore*, 595.

Living dog is better than a dead lion, A. 1382: Wiclif, *Bible*, Eccles. ix 4 (O)., Betere is a quyc dogge thanne a leoun dead. 1558: When Queen Mary died, one preacher of a funeral sermon comforted his audience on the virtues of her successor by observing that 'a living dog was better than a dead lion' – *see* Johnson, *Letters*, ii 437 (Hill). 1697: Vanbrugh, *Prov. Wife*, V. 1798: Wolcot, *Works*, v 252 (1801). 1855: Gaskell. *North and South*, ch xlvi, 'I like you twenty times better than Hamlet'. 'On the principle that a living ass is better than a dead lion?' 1909: Lucas, *Wand, in Paris*, ch xii. 1924: Phillpotts, *Human Boy's Diary*, Term 3, 18 April, 'True,' admitted Briggs, 'Better be a live ass than a dead lion.'

Lizard. *See* **Better to be.**

Lizard, The. *See* **Rain**, *subs.* (27).

Loaded. *See* **Laden.**

Loaf and **Loaves. 1. He went in with the loaves and came out with the cakes** = He is 'half-baked'. 1864: 'Cornish Proverbs', in *N. & Q.*, 3rd ser, vi 494, He is only half-baked; put in with the bread and taken out with the cakes. 1896: Northall, *Warwicksh. Word-Book* (E.D.S.), Put in with the bread and pull'd out with the cakes. 1917: Bridge, *Cheshire Proverbs*, 70.

2. Set not your loaf in till the oven's hot. 1732: Fuller, 4110.

3. The loaves and fishes – of office. 1614: Bp. Hall, *Recoll. Treat.*, 954 (OED), If it were not for the loaves and fishes, the traine of Christ would bee lesse. 1789: Wolcot, *Works*, ii 59 (1795), What pity 'tis, in this our goodly land, Amongst the apostolic band, So ill divided are the loaves and fishes! 1816: Scott, *Old Mortality*, ch xxvii, Thou art one of those that follow the Gospel for the loaves and for the fishes. 1880: Spurgeon, *Ploughman's Pictures*, 122, They go to the church for the loaves, and then go over to the Baptist Chapel for the fishes.

See also **Half a loaf.**

Loan should come laughing home, A borrowed. *c.*1300: *Prov. of Hendyng*, st. 25 (Berlin, 1878), Selde cometh lone lahynde hom. 1732: Fuller, 6314.

Lob's pound. Described by A. H. Bullen as 'the thraldom of the henpecked married man': also = a prison. 1595: Peele, *Old Wives Tale*, sig. E1, Lobb be your comfort, and cuckold bee your destenie. 1612: *Cornucopiae*, 64 (Grosart), Thus is the woodcocke fall'n into the gin, And in Lobs-pound in-tangled by a wile. 1623: Massinger, *Duke of Milan*, III ii. 1671: Crowne, *Juliana*, I i, And so there's a heavy bustle, the Cardinal on one side, and the Princess on the t'other, and between 'um both he's got into Lobb's pound. Before 1704: T. Brown, *Works*, iv 323 (1760), Instead of paradise, they have got into lob's pound. 1785: Grose, *Class. Dict. Vulgar Tongue*, s.v. Lob's pound, a prison. 1823: Moor, *Suffolk Words*, 215, Lob's-pound. The bridewell. 1866: J. G. Nall, *Great Yarmouth, etc.*, 595 [as in 1823].

Lobster. *See* **Apple** (5).

Lock and key, To have under. Before 1250: *Owl and Nightingale*, l. 1557 (OED), He hire bi-lukth myd keye and loke. *c.*1390: Gower, *Conf. Amantis*, bk v l. 6621, Which under lock and under keie ... Hath al the Tresor ... *c.*1440: Lydgate, *Fall of Princes*, bk i l. 4886, The brond reseruyng vnder lok and keie. 1584: Robinson, *Handf. Pleas. Delights*, 42 (Arber), Some are as sure as lock and key. 1630: *Wine, Beere, Ale, etc.*, 27 (Hanford, 1915), Art not thou kept vnder locke and key, confinde to some corner of a cellar? 1693: Dryden, *Juvenal*, Sat. vi l. 464, Keep close your women under lock and key. 1740: North, *Examen*, 112, There was a paper found under his lordship's lock and key in his closet. 1894: R.L.S., *St Ives*, ch xii, The great thing is to have me under lock and key. 1925:

Bodieian Quart. Record, iv 192, Books of he smaller sizes, which were kePt under lock and key.

Lock, stock and barrel. 1817: Scott, in Lockhart's *Life*, iv 102, She wants stock, lock, and barrel to put her into repair. 1914: H. A. Vachell, *Quinney's*, bk ii ch xxiii (i.), I'd sooner be ruined, lock, stock, and barrel, than give my daughter to that man!

Lock will hold against the power of gold, No. 1640: Herbert, *Jac. Prudentum*. 1670: Ray, 12. 1732: Fuller, 6236. 1875: A. B. Cheales, *Proverb. Folk-Lore*, 99.

Lockington Wakes, Put up your pipes and go to. 1678: Ray, 317. 1790: Grose, *Prov. Gloss.*, s.v. 'Leicestershire'.

Lombard Street to a china orange, All – with variants for he orange. 1752: Murphy, *Gray's Inn Journal*, No. xi, 30 Dec., I'll lay all Lombard-street to an egg-shell that it is true. 1819: Moore, *Tom Cribb's Mem.*, 38, All Lombard Street to ninepence. 1826: G. Daniel, *Sworn at Highgate*, I iv, I'd bet Lombard Street to a Brummagem sixpence. 1849: Lytton, *Caxtons*, Pt IV ch iii, 'It is Lombard Street to a China orange,' quoth Uncle Jack. 1898: *Sun*, 7 June, Lombard Street to a china orange did not represent the odds against Horsford. 1918: Muirhead, *Blue Guide to London*, 375, Lombard Street, the proverbial wealth of which is indicated in the phrase 'All ... China orange'. 1921: A. Dobson, *Later Essays*, i 11, The eighteenth-century 'All ... China orange'.

London. 1. A London jury; hang half and save half. Said also of Kentish and Middlesex juries – *see* quots. 1608: Middleton, *Trick to Catch Old One*, IV v, Thou that goest upon Middlesex juries, and wilt make haste to give up thy verdict, because thou wilt not lose thy dinner. 1662: Fuller, *Worthies*, ii 340 (1840). 1732: Fuller, 231, A Kentish jury; hang half and save half. 1790: Grose, *Prov. Gloss.*, s.v. 'London'.

2. London Beer. *See* **Derby ale.**

3. London lickpenny. *c.*1440: attrib. to Lydgate, *London Lyckpeny* [title]. 1600: J. Day, *Blind Beggar*, II ii, London lickpenny call ye it, – t'as lick'd me with a witness. 1641: in *Harl. Miscell.*, i 484 (1744), Do as you please, but you will find the old proverb true, *London Lickpenny*. 1710–11: Swift, *Journal to Stella*, 15 Jan., It has cost me three guineas to-day, for a periwig ... Well,

London lickpenny; I find it true. 1790: Grose, *Prov. Gloss.*, s.v. 'London'.

4. She hath been at London to call a strea a straw, and a waw a wall. Cheshire. 1670: Ray, 218. 1790: Grose, *Prov. Gloss.*, s.v. 'Cheshire'. 1913: E. M. Wright, *Rustic Speech, etc.*, 1, There is a very old proverb in Cheshire, applied to any one who goes out of the county for improvement, and returns without having gained much; such a one is said to have 'been at London to learn to call a streea a straw'. 1917: Bridge, *Cheshire Proverbs*, 108.

5. The Fire of London was a punishment for gluttony. 1790: Grose, *Prov. Gloss.*, s.v. 'London'.

6. *They agree like the clocks of London.* 1589: Nashe, in *Works*, i 111 (Grosart), The preachers of England begin to strike and agree like the clocks of England, that neuer meete iumpe on a point together. 1678: Ray, 325. 1823: D'Israeli, *Cur. of Lit.*, 2nd ser, i 469 (1824), It was probably some sarcastic Italian, and perhaps, horologer, who, to describe the disagreement of persons, proverbed our nation – 'They agree like the clocks of London!'

See also **Country** (3); **Lincoln; Lord Mayor; Oxford** (1) and (2); **Ware;** and **Which way**.

London Bridge was built upon wool-packs. *c.*1685: Aubrey, *Nat. Hist. Wilts*, 98 (1847), There is a saying also that London-Bridge … 1708: *Brit. Apollo*, i No. 43, col. 3, Is the receiv'd report of London Bridge's being founded upon wool, true? 1812: Brady, *Clavis Cal.*, i 194, The very common [saying] 'that London Bridge was built upon wool-sacks'. 1913: W. Whitten, *Londoner's London*, 308, The saying that the bridge was 'built upon wool-packs', refers to the impost on wool which helped to defray its cost.

London Bridge was made for wise men to go over and fools to go under. This refers to the danger incurred by boats in 'shooting' the arches of the old bridge. 1639: Clarke, 249. 1670: Ray, 16. 1874: Smiles, *Lives of Engineers*, ii 64. 1913: W. Whitten, *Londoner's London*, 308.

Londoner-like ask as much more as you will take. 1678: Ray, 349.

Lone sheep. *See* **Sheep** (15).

Long = Longdon, Staffs. 1883:Burne, *Shropsh. Folk-Lore*, 583, The stoutest beggar that goes by the way, Can't beg through Long on a midsummer's day.

Long absent soon forgotten. 1611: Cotgrave, s.v. 'Ami', Long absence alters affection. 1670: Ray, 55. 1736: Bailey, *Dict.*, s.v. 'Absent'. Cf. **Out of sight;** and **Seldom seen.**

Long and lazy. 1591: Florio, *Second Frutes*, 189, If long, she is lazy, if little, she is lowde, If fayre, she is slutish, if foule, she is proud. 1648: Herrick, *Hesp.*, No. 357, Long and lazy. That was the proverb. 1732: Fuller, 3267.

Long and slender, like a cat's elbow. Ibid., No. 3268.

Long and the short of it, The. 'The short and the long' was common earlier than the now more usual form, and is still used. *c.*1330: Brunne, tr. Langtoft's *Chron.*, 222 (Hearne), To say longly or schorte, alle [that] armes bare. 1571: Edwards, *Damon, etc.*, in Hazlitt, *Old Plays*, iv 47, Howsover it be, this is the short and long. 1589: Nashe, in *Works*, i 185 (Grosart), This is the short and the long, and the somme of all. 1599: Shakespeare, *Henry V*, III ii … the breff and the long. 1622: Taylor (Water-Poet), in *Works*, 2nd pagin., 3 (1630), Here's the long and short on't. 1676: Shadwell, *Libertine*, II, The short and the long on't is … 1681: W. Robertson, *Phraseol. Generalis*, 837, The long and the short of a business; Summa rei. 1748: Richardson, *Clarissa*, i 289 (1785), The short and the long was … *c.*1760: Foote, *Lame Lover*, II, And that, Mr John, is the long and the short on't. 1838: Dickens, *Twist*, ch xx, 'The short and the long of what you mean,' said Nancy. 1849: C. Brontë, *Shirley*, ch ix, The short and the long of it is … 1850: Dickens, *Chuzzlewit*, ch xxvii, The long and the short of it is … 1886: R.L.S., *Kidnapped*, ch xviii, The short and the long of it is …

Long as he is lither [lazy], **If he were as, he might thatch a house without a ladder.** 1678: Ray, 257. 1828: Carr, *Craven Dialect*, i 294. 1890: P. H. Emerson, *Wild Life*, 72, You are as long as you are lazy. 1917: Bridge, *Cheshire Proverbs*, 76.

Long as I live, I'll spit in my parlour, As. 1732: Fuller, 710.

Long be thy legs, and short be thy life. 1546: Heywood, *Proverbs*, Pt II ch vii.

Long beards heartless, etc. *See* quot. 1589: Puttenham, *Eng. Poesie*, 184 (Arber), The craking Scotts as the Cronicle reportes at a certaine time made this bald rime vpon the Englishman. Long beards hartlesse, Painted hoodes witlesse: Gay coates gracelesse, Make all England thriftlesse. 1602–3: Manningham, *Diary*, 116 (Camden S.). 1605: Camden, *Remains*, 211 (1870), As in the time of King Edward the third ... 'Long beards ...'

Long-Compton. *See* quot. 1719: R. Gale, in *Stukeley Mem.*, iii 155 (Surtees S.), The country tradition joyning them together in a rhyme they all have – If Long Compton thou can'st see, Then King of England thou shalt be. 1743: Stukeley, *Abury*, 83 [as in 1719]. 1849: Halliwell, *Pop. Rhymes and Nursery Tales*, 193 [as in 1719].

Long-Crown. *See* quot. 1847: Halliwell, *Dict.*, s.v., 'That caps Long-Crown, and he capped the Devil', a Lincolnshire saying in reference to a great falsehood.

Long day, Not a, but a good heart rids work. 1611: Cotgrave, s.v. 'Grand', Not long dayes, but strong hearts, dispatch a worke. 1640: Herbert, *Jac. Prudentum.*

Long day that never pay, They take a. 1678: Ray, 188.

Longer east, the shorter west, The. 1546: Heywood, *Proverbs*, Pt I ch xiii. 1605: Camden, *Remains*, 333 (1870). 1670: Ray, 84. 1732: Fuller, 6108, The longer east, the longer [*sic*] west. 1899: Dickinson, *Cumb. Gloss.*, 192, Longer east shorter west. A deficiency in one part is compensated by abundance in another.

Longer forenoon, the shorter afternoon, The. 1546: Heywood, *Proverbs*, Pt I ch xiii.

Longer lives a good fellow than a dear year. 1678: Ray, 170.

Longest day must have an end, The. 1580: Lyly, *Eupkues*, 250 (Arber), The longest summers day hath his euening. 1694: Southerne, *Fatal Marriage*, IV ii [with 'will' for 'must']. 1732: Fuller, 4633.

Longest journey begins with a single step, The. A saying attributed to the Chinese philosopher and founder of Taoism, Lao-Tzu (*c*.604–*c*.531 BC). 1904: L. Giles, tr. *Sayings of Lao Tzu*, 51, A journey of a thousand miles begins with a single step.

Longest way round, nearest way home, The. 1635: Quarles, *Emblemes*, bk iv No. ii, The next way home's the farthest way about. 1681: W. Robertson, *Phraseol. Generalis*, 1300, The farthest way about is the nearest way home. 1734: Fielding, *Intrig. Chambermaid*, I i, The young fellow finds, though he go round about,

It's only to come The nearest way home. 1776: Colman, *Spleen*, II, The longest way about is the shortest way home, you know.

Long foretold Long last. Short notice Soon past. 1875: A. B. Cheales, *Proverb. Folk-Lore*, 26.

Long harvest. *See* **Harvest** (7).

Long home = the grave. 1303: Brunne, *Handlyng Synne*, l. 9195, And thy traueyle shalt thou sone ende, For to thy long home sone shalt thou wende. *c*.1400: *Mirk's Festial*, 295 (E.E.T.S.), Ther is also a meteyorde leyde be hym [the corpse] instede of a staf, in tokenyng that he goth to hys long home. 1598: *Servingmans Comfort*, in *Inedited Tracts*, 128 (Hazlitt), Yet would I, at my owne charges, haue seene him honestly brought foorth to his long home (as the saying is). 1611: *Bible*, Eccles. xii 5. Before 1681: J. Lacy, *Sauny the Scot*, V. 1762: Smollett, *Sir L. Greaves*, ch iv, A fever, which, in a few days, brought Sir Everhard to his long home. 1843: Dickens, *Chuzzlewit*, ch xxv, Playing at berryins down in the shop, and follerin' the order-book to its long home in the iron safe!

Longing than loathing, Better go away. 1732: Fuller, 942.

Long jesting was never good. 1640: Herbert, *Jac. Prudentum.*

Long journey, In a, straw weighs. Ibid.

Long lane and a fair wind, and always thy heels here away, A. 1678: Ray, 75.

Long lane that has no turning, It is a. 1633: *Stationer's Register* (1877), IV 273, Long runns that neere turns. 1670: Ray, 117, It's a long run that never turns. 1748: Richardson, *Clarissa*, iv 237 (1785). 1774: C. Dibdin, *Quaker*, II iii. 1849: Lytton, *Caxtons*, Pt XVII ch i. 1880: A. Dobson, *Old-world Idylls:* 'Dead Letter', II.

Long life hath long misery. 1611: Cotgrave, s.v. 'Vivre', The longer life the greater griefe. 1669: *Politeuphuia*, 203, A long life hath commonly long cares annexed with it. 1732: Fuller, 3270.

Long liveth. *See* **Merry man.**

Long looked for comes at last. *c*.1483: *Quatuor Sermones*, 53 (Roxb.Cl), A thynge that is long desyred at the last it comyth. 1605: Armin, *Foole vpon Foole*, 11 (Grosart), Though long looke for comes at last. 1658: in *Musarum Deliicae, etc.*, i 261 (Hotten). 1740: Richardson, *Pamela*, i 179 (1883), Here's a letter for you: long looked for is come at last.

Long spoon. *See* **Devil** (19).

Long standers. *See* quot. 1600: J. Day *Blind Beggar*, IV iii, 'Tis an old saying in our country [Norfolk], 'Long standers are but short doers'.

Long standing and small offering maketh poor parsons. 1546: Heywood, *Proverbs*, Pt II ch ix 1659: Howell, 4 [with 'poor' for 'small' and 'priests' for 'parsons'].

Long time to know the world's pulse, There needs a. 1640: Herbert, *Jac. Prudentum*. 1670: Ray, 30.

Long tongue is a sign of a short hand, A. 1640: Herbert, *Jac. Prudentum*. 1670: Ray, 26. 1880: Spurgeon, *Ploughman's Pictures*, 28, A long tongue generally goes with a short hand.

Long-tongued wives go long with bairn. 1670: Ray, 49.

Look, *subs. Looks breed love.* 1639: Clarke, 28.

Look, *verb.* **1. A cat may look at a king.** *See* **Cat** (3).

2. A man need not look in your mouth to know how old you are. 1639: Clarke, 280. 1670: Ray, 188.

3. Don't look a gift horse in the mouth. *See* **Gift** (2).

4. He looks as if he had eaten live birds. 1868: *Quart. Review*, cxxv. 231, In modern parlance a person unwontedly animated is told he looks as if 'he had eaten live birds'.

5. He looks as if he had neither won nor lost. 1590: Lodge, *Rosalynde*, 120 (Hunt.Cl.), The shepheard stoode as though hee had neither wonne nor lost. 1594: Greene, *Frier Bacon*, sc xiii. 1678: Ray, 257. 1738: Swift, *Polite Convers.*, Dial. I, What's the matter? You look as if you had neither won nor lost. 1828: Carr, *Craven Dialect*, i 299, He looks as an heed neyther won nor lost.

6. He looks as if he had sold all and took nothing for it. 1659: Howell, 13.

7. He looks like a tooth-drawer, i.e. thin and meagre. 1620: B.&F., *Philaster*, I i, The outlandish prince looks like a toothdrawer. 1678: Ray, 83.

8. He looks not well to himself that looks not ever. 1611: Cotgrave, s.v. 'Garder', He lookes not, that still lookes not, to himselfe. 1640: Herbert, *Jac. Prudentum*.

9. He looks one way and rows another. 1583: Melbancke, *Philotinus*, sig. P1, And so imitate the waterman, which looketh one waye, and roweth another. 1636: Dekker, *Wond. of a Kingdom*, V ii, She has but us'd you As watermen use their fares, for she look'd one way And row'd another. 1694: D'Urfey, *Quixote*, Pt II Act III sc i, Like rowers we look one way – move another. 1740: North, *Examen*, Pref., v, The opposers ... bore a false face, looking one way and rowing another. 1869: Spurgeon, *John Ploughman*, ch xviii.

10. He that looks not before finds himself behind. 1640: Herbert, *Jac. Prudentum*. 1670: Ray, 3. 1736: Bailey, *Dict.*, s.v. Before'.

11. Look before you leap. *c.*1350: *Douce MS*, 52, no. 150, First loke and aftirward lepe. 1528: Tyndale, *Obed. of Chryst. Man*, 304 (P.S.), 'Look ere thou leap'; whose literal sense is, 'Do nothing suddenly, or without advisement'. 1567: Painter, *Pal. of Pleasure*, iii 53 (Jacobs), According to the common saying: He that loketh not before he leapeth, may chaunce to stumble before he sleepeth. 1621: Burton, *Melancholy*, II iii 7, p. 427 (1836). 1705: Steele, *Tender Husband*, III ii, I love to look before I leap. 1849: C. Brontë, *Shirley*, ch ix, When you feel tempted to marry, think of our four sons and two daughters, and look twice before you leap. 1920: Hudson, *Dead Man's Plack*, 41, Let me ... exercise caution and look before I leap.

12. Look behind thee and consider what thou wast. 1659: Howell, 21.

13. Look high and fall low. 1670: Ray, 13, Look high and fall into a cowturd. 1732: Fuller, 3272.

14. Look like a runner. *See* **Devil** (122).

15. Look not too high lest a chip fall in your eye. 1584: Robinson, *Handf. Pleas. Delights*, 39 (Arber). 1696: D'Urfey, *Quixote*, Pt III Act II sc ii. 1732: Fuller, 6316.

16. Look on the wall and it will not bite you. 1678: Ray, 83 ['spoken in jeer to such as are bitten with mustard'. – Ray, 65 (1737)].

17. Look to him, jailor, there's a frog in the stocks. 1678: Ray, 72. 1732: Fuller, 3274.

18. To look as if he had eaten his bedstraw. 1678: Ray, 286.

19. To look as though he had sucked his dam through a hurdle. 1670: Ray, 170. 1732: Fuller, 1971.

20. To look both ways for Sunday. 1828: Carr, *Craven Dialect*, ii 180, 'He was born in the middle of the week, and looked baath ways for Sunday' – a burlesque expression for a person who squints. 1854: Baker, *Northants Gloss.*, s.v.

'Sunday' [as in 1828]. 1920: E. Geppt, *Essex Dialect Dict.*, 35, The phrase 'to look all ways for Sunday' is used of a bewildered person failing to see the obvious. The similar phrase 'to look two ways for Easter' is used in some parts. Cf. No. 24.

21. To look like a dog that hath lost his tail. 1678: Ray, 286.

22. To look like a drowned mouse. *c.*1591: Shakespeare, 1 *Henry VI*, I ii, Or piteous they will look, like drowned mice. 1678: Ray, 286.

23. To look like a Jew. 1611: Coryat, *Crudities*, i 372 (1005), Our English proverbe: To looke like a Jewe (whereby is meant sometimes a weather beaten wasp-faced fellow, sometimes a phrenticke and lunaticke person, sometimes one discontented).

24. To look like a strained hair in a can. 1670: Ray, 206. 1917: Bridge, *Cheshire Proverbs*, 140.

25. To look like the picture of ill luck. 1639: Clarke, 119. 1670: Ray, 206.

26. To look nine ways. 1542: Udall, tr. Erasmus' *Apoph.*, 203 (1877), Squyntyied he was, and looked nyne wayes. Before 1680: Butler, *Remains*, ii 213 (1759), Which commonly is squint-ey'd, and looks nine ways at once. 1688: Crowne, *City Politiques*, I i, He looks ten ways at once. 1696: D'Urfey, *Quixote*, Pt III Act III sc ii, I'll make her look nine ways at once before I have done with her. Cf. No. 18.

27. *To look through the fingers.* 1532: Tyndale, *Expos. St Mathew*, 127 (P.S.), They either look through the fingers, or else give thee a flap with a fox-tail, for a little money. 1535: Coverdale, *Bible*, Lev. xx 4, The people of the londe loke thorowe the fyngers upon that man which hath geuen his sede vnto Moloch. 1583: Stubbes, *Anat. of Abuses*, 100 (N.Sh.S.), The magistrats wincke at it, or els, as looking thorowe their fingers, they see it, and will not see it. 1691: J. Wilson, *Belphegor*, III i, Enough to make a modest woman look through her fingers.

28. To look to one's water. 1546: Heywood, *Proverbs*, Pt I ch xi, By my faith, you come to looke in my water. 1621: B.&F., *Pilgrim*, III iv, Yes still I'll watch his water, he shall pay for it. 1709: Manley, *New Atlantis*, i 132 (1736), He would have watched his waters for him to some purpose. 1894: Northall, *Folk Phrases*, 31 (E.D.S.), To watch one's waters = To keep an eye on a person; to follow his movements.

29. You look for hot water under the ice. 1732: Fuller, 5933.

30. You must look where it is not, as well as where it is. Ibid., No. 5964.

Lookers on see most of the game. [Aiunt homines plus in alieno negotio videre quam in suo. – Seneca, *Ep.*, cix 16.] 1529: J. Palsgrave, in *Arcolastus* (E.E.T.S.), p. xxxviii, It fareth between thee and me as it doth between a player at the chess and a looker on, for he that looketh on seeth many draughts that the player considereth nothing at all. 1597: Bacon, *Essays: 'Followers, etc.'*, To take aduise of friends is euer honorable: *For lookers on many times see more then gamesters.* 1640: R. Brome, *Sparagus Garden*, Epil., For we know lookers on more then the gamsters see. 1706: Vanbrugh, *Mistake*, I i, A stander-by, sir, sees more than a gamester. 1850: Smedley, *Frank Fairlegh*, ch xlvii. 1909: Pinero, *Mid-Channel*, I. p. 43.

Loon in a wash, A, Is as good as a shilling in a poor man's purse. 1886: Swainson, *Folk-Lore of Brit. Birds*, 215 (F.L.S.).

Loose in the haft = unreliable. *c.*1325: in *Pol. Songs*, 339 (Camden) (OED), Unnethe is nu eny man that can eny craft That he nis a party los in the haft. *c.*1555: in Wright, *Songs, etc.*, *Philip and Mary*, 68 (Roxb.Cl), For, alas! she was nat sur in the hafte. 1888–90: Addy, *Sheffield Gloss.* (E.D.S.), He's a bit loose i' t' heft. 1889: Peacock, *Manley, etc.*, *Gloss.*, 329 (E.D.S.), Lohse i' th' heft. That is, loose in the handle. A person of a wild, profligate or wasteful disposition is called 'a lohse i' th' heft'. 1917: Bridge, *Cheshire Proverbs*, 70.

Loose in the hilts = *usually*, unfaithful in marriage, or loose in life. 1623: Webster, *Duchess of Malfi*, II v, She's loose i' th' hilts; grown a notorious strumpet. 1650: Howell, *Epist. Ded.* to Cotgrave's *Dict.*, So in French *cocu* is taken for one whose wife is loose in the hilts. 1712: Motteux, *Quixote*, Pt I bk iii ch vi., The shepherd thought her no better than she should be, a little loose in the hilts, and free of her hips. 1745: Franklin, *Drinker's Dict.*, in *Works*, ii 24 (Bigelow), He's loose in the hilts [drunk]. 1847: Halliwell, *Dict.*, s.v. 'Hilts', She is loose in the hilts, i.e. frail; a common phrase.

Loose stake may stand long, A. 1639: Clarke, 44. Cf. **Low Stake**.

Lopp. *See* Crouse.

Lord. 1. A lord's heart and a beggar's purse agree not. *c.*1430: Lydgate, *Minor Poems*, 160 (Percy S.), A lordis herte, a purs that peiseth lihte [are not commendable], *c.*1510: A. Barclay, *Egloges*, 39 (Spens.S.), A lordes stomake and a beggers pouche Full ill accordeth. 1592: G. Harvey, *Works*, i 207 (Grosart), The two vnmeete companions, a lordes heart, and a beggers purse. 1659: Howell, 5, A lords heart and a beggars purse. Cf. **Lady's heart**.

2. He is a lord for a year and a day, *etc.* 1869: Hazlitt, 164, He is a lord for a year and a day, and she is a lady for ever and aye. This is said of the Lord Mayor of York and his spouse; the latter, it is suggested, never renounces at heart the fugitive dignity conferred on her husband for the year of his mayoralty. Higson's *MSS. Coll.*, No. 24.

Lord Mayor. 1. Good manners to excePt my Lord Mayor. [1655: Fuller, *Church Hist.*, bk iii § vi (14), The richest and proudest (always good manners to excePt Cardinal Wolsey).] 1662: Fuller, *Worthies*, ii 346 (1840), Good manners to excePt my Lord Mayor of London. 1670: Ray, 242. 1790: Grose, *Prov. Gloss.*, s.v. 'London'.

2. I have dined as well as my Lord Mayor of London. 1580: Lyly, *Euphues*, 437 (Arber), Hauing halfe dyned, they say as it were in a prouerbe, yᵃt they are as well satisfied as the Lorde Maior of London whom they think to fare best, though he eate not most. 1633: Rowley, *Match at Midnight*, I. 1659: Gayton, *Art of Longevity*, 12, Shall find a satisfaction in his fare, As great as if h' had din'd with my Lord May'r. 1738: Swift, *Polite Convers.*, Dial. II. 1807: Sir R. Wilson, *Journal*, in *Life*, II viii 253 (1862) (OED), I … would not have exchanged meals with the Lord Mayor of London.

3. Like my Lord Mayor's fool, full of business, and nothing to do. 1738: Swift, *Polite Convers.*, Dial. I.

4. Like my Lord Mayor's fool, I like everything that is good. 1678: Ray, 247, I am a fool, I love everything that is good. 1812: Brady, *Clavis Cal.*, ii 252, 'The Lord Mayor's Fool, who likes everything that is good', is yet a common expression. 1895: J. R. Robinson, *Old Q.*, 123, In drinking as in eating, March was a veritable Lord Mayor's fool; 'the best of everything did for him'.

Lose, *verb.* **1. A man loseth his time that comes early to a bad bargain.** 1732: Fuller, 286.

2. A man may lose his goods for want of demanding them. 1633: Draxe, 17. 1670: Ray, 7.

3. He has lost his leease = *He* has broken down. 1917: Bridge, *Cheshire Proverbs*, 67 … The *leease* is the crossing of the yarn up and down over the warp in regular order. If by chance the warp is divided, the leease is then lost and weaving at a standstill.

4. He has not lost all who has one cast left. 1670: Ray, 16 [with 'throw to cast' for 'cast left']. 1732: Fuller, 1876.

5. He loseth his thanks who promiseth and delayeth. 1633: Draxe, 42. 1681: W. Robertson, *Phraseol. Generalis*, 844. 1732: Fuller, 1977.

6. He loseth many a good bit that striveth with his betters. 1659: Howell, *Proverbs: Brit.-Eng.*, 9.

7. He loseth nothing that loseth not God. 1640: Herbert, *Jac. Prudentum*. 1732: Fuller, 1976, He loseth nothing that keepeth God for his friend.

8. He would rather lose his friend than his jest. Before 1598: Ld. Burghley, in Peck, *Desid. Curiosa*, 49 (1779), They would rather leese their friend then their jest. 1630: Brathwait, *Eng. Gent., etc.*, 137 (1641), These many times … will not sticke to lose their friend rather than their jest. 1709: Cibber, *Rival Fools*, I [with 'dinner' for 'friend']. 1744–6: Mrs Haywood, *Fem. Spectator*, bk 21, iv 135.

9. He'll not lose his jest for his guest, if he be a Jew. 1639: Clarke, 255.

10. I have lost all and found myself. Ibid., 198.

11. Lose a leg rather than life. 1732: Fuller, 3278.

12. Lose a wife. See **Wife** (13).

13. Lose an hour in the morning and you'll be all day hunting for it. 1859: Smiles, *Self-Help*, 275 (1869), It was wittily said by Lord Chesterfield of the old Duke of Newcastle – 'His Grace loses an hour in the morning, and is looking for it all the rest of the day'. 1875: A. B. Cheales, *Proverb. Folk-Lore*, 18.

14. Lose nothing for (want of) asking. 1586: B. Young, tr. Guazzo's *Civil Convers.*, fo. 218, Nothing is lost for asking. 1639: Clarke, 38, Hee'l not lose it for asking. 1665: R. Howard, *Committee*, I, I see thou wouldst not lose any thing for want of asking. 1670: Ray, 58.

15. Lose with a nut. *See* **Apple** (13).

16. What we lose in hake, we shall have in

herring. Corn. 1602: Carew, *Surv. of Cornwall*, 105 (1811). 1639: Clarke, 17. What I lost i' th' salt fish I gained i' th' red herrings. 1750: R. Heath, *Account of Scilly*, 324. 1864: 'Cornish Proverbs', in *N. & Q.*, 3rd ser, vi 494.

17. What you lose on the swings, you gain on the roundabouts. A more modern version of the previous proverb. 1912: P. Chalmers, *Green Days and Blue Days*, 19, What's lost upon the roundabouts, we pulls up on the swings. 1927: *Times*, 24 March, 15, By screwing more money out of taxpayers he diminishes their savings, and the market for trustee securities loses on the swings what it gains on the roundabouts.

18. Who loseth his due getteth no thanks. 1640: Herbert, *Jac. Prudentum*. 1670: Ray, 8. 1732: Fuller, 5709.

19. You cannot lose what you never had. 1593: Marlowe, *Hero and Leander*, I 276, Of that which hath no being do not boast. Things that are not at all are never lost. 1676: Walton, *Compleat Angler* (ed. 5), I v, 'He has broke all; there's half a line and a good hook lost'. 'I [Aye] and a good Trout too'. 'Nay, the trout is not lost, for … no man can lose what he never had. 1788: Wesley, *Works* (1872), VII 41, He only *semeth* to have this … No man can lose what he never had.

Losers leave to speak, Give. 1533: More, in *Works*, 1018 (1557), Hit is an olde curtesye at the cardes perdy, to let the leser haue hys wordes'. 1594: *First Part Content.*, 36 (SH.S.), I can giue the loser leaue to speake. 1630: Taylor (Water-Poet), *Works*, 2nd pagin., 233. 1673: Wycherley, *Gent. Danc.-Master*, V i. 1769: Colman, *Man and Wife*, III, We must give losers leave to talk, you know. 1818: Scott, *Heart of Midl.*, ch xlviii, The Captain … was in the pouting mood not unusual to losers, and which, says the proverb, must be allowed to them.

Losers weepers. *See* **Finders keepers**.

Loss embraceth shame. 1640: Herbert, *Jac. Prudentum*.

Loss is another man's gain, One man's. *c.*1527: T. Berthelet, tr. *Erasmus' Sayings of Wose Men*, D1v, Lyghtly whan one wynneth, an other loseth. 1733: J. Barber, in *Correspondence of Swift* (1965), IV 189, Your loss will be our gain, as the proverb says. 1821: Scott, *The Pirate*, I vi, Doubtless one man's loss is another man's gain.

Loss of one is a gain for two and a chance for

twenty more, The. Corn. 19th cent. (Mr C. Lee).

Loss of the bell more than the loss of the steeple, To fear the. 1678: Ray, 351.

Loss without some gain, There's no great. 1641: D. Fergusson, *Scottish Proverbs* (STS), no. 1408, Thair was never a grit loss without som small vantage. 1868: W. Clift, *Tim Bunker Papers*, 134, However, 'there is no great loss but what there is some small gain', and Jake Frink claims that he has got his money's worth in experience.

Lost, *part. adj.* **1. As good lost as found.** 1639: Clarke, 68. 1670: Ray, 184.

2. Better to have loved and lost than never to have loved at all. *See* **Better**.

3. He who hesitates is lost. *See* **He who hesitates …**

4. It is lost that is unsought. 1546: Heywood, *Proverbs*, Pt I ch xi. 1659: Howell, 14.

5. Lost in the hundred. *See* **Hundred and County.**

6. Lost time is never found again. 1736: Franklin, *Way to Wealth*, in *Works*, i 443 (Bigelow).

'Loth to drink and loth to leave off', they say. 1880: Spurgeon, *Ploughman's Pictures*, 40.

Loud as a horn, As. 1659: Howell, 19. 1670: Ray, 206.

Louse. 1. A louse is better than no meat. 1639: Clarke, 241, Better a louse i' the pot than no flesh at all. 1656: *Musarum Deliciae*, i 31 (Hotten). Cf. **Better a mouse.**

2. As sure as louse in bosom. 1659: Howell, 5. 1670: Ray, 208. 1917: Bridge, *Cheshire Proverbs*, 22.

3. He'd drive a louse a mile for the skin and tallow of 'en. S. Devon. 1869: Hazlitt, 198.

4. He'd skin a louse for the sake of its hide. 1591: Florio, *Second Frutes*, 117, He was such a couetous miser, that he would haue fleade a louse to saue the skin of it. 1623: Wodroephe, *Spared Houres*, 285, He would haue flayed a louse for her skin, he was so couetous. 1916: B. Duffy, *The Coiner*, 7, Thrifty! Man, she'd skin a flea for his hide.

5. If a louse miss its footing on his coat, 'twill be sure to break its neck. 1362: Langland, *Plowman*, A, v 112, But yif a lous couthe lepe I con hit not i-leue Heo scholde wandre on that walk hit was so thred-bare. 1530: Palsgrave, 620,

He hath made my gowne so bare that a lowse can get no holde on it. *c*.1580: Spelman, *Dialogue*, 116 (Roxb.Cl), Truth among clothyers hath lesse harborowe then the lowce upon a thrydbare clothe, *c*.1610: *Ballad*, quoted in Wright, *Essays on Middle Ages*, ii 277 (1846), Thy doublet and breech that were so playne, On which a louse could scarse remayne. 1732: Fuller, 2661.

6. **Louse in Pomfret.** *See* **Pomfret**.

See also **Beggar** (1) and (16); **Crouse**; and **Three skips.**

Love, *subs*. 1. **All's fair in love and war.** *c*.1578: Lyly, *Euphues*, I 236, Anye impietie may lawfully be committed in love, which is lawlesse. 1620: T. Shelton, tr. *Don Quixote*, ii xxi, Love and warre are all one … It is lawfull to use sleights and stratagems to … attaine the wished end. *c*.1630: B.&F., *Lovers' Progress*, V ii, All stratagems In love, and that the sharpest war, are lawful. 1687: A. Behn, *Emp. of the Moon*, I iii, Advantages are lawful in love and war. 1710: Centlivre, *Man's Bewitch'd*, V i, Stratagems ever were allow'd of in love and war. 1850: Smedley, *Frank Fairlegh*, ch l. 1906: Lucas, *Listener's Lure*, 196.

2. **He that hath love in his breast, hath spurs in his sides.** 1640: Herbert, *Jac. Prudentum*. 1732: Fuller, 2160 [with 'at his heels' for 'in his sides'].

3. **In love is no lack.** *c*.1400: *Mirk's Festial*, 165 (E.E.T.S.), For loue hath no lake. 1546: Heywood, *Proverbs*, Pt I ch iv. 1592: Lyly, *Mother Bombie*, I iii. 1641: R. Brome, *Joviall Crew*, III, Where love is, there's no lack. 1670: Ray, 117.

4. **In love's wars he who flyeth is conqueror**, 1732: Fuller, 2819.

5. **Love and a cough cannot be hid.** *c*.1300: *Cursor Mundi*, l. 4276, Luken luue at the end wil kith (Concealed love will show itself at last). 1590: Greene, in *Works*, vii 294 (Grosart), There are foure things cannot be hydden. l. The cough. 2 Loue. 3 Anger. 4 And sorrow. 1640: Herbert, *Jac. Prudentum*. 1709: Mandeville, *Virgin Unmask'd*, 196 (1724). 1732: Fuller, 3298, Love, the itch, and a cough cannot be hid.

6. **Love and business teach eloquence.** 1640: Herbert, *Jac. Prudentum*.

7. **Love and knowledge live not together.** 1611: Cotgrave, s.v. 'Aimer'. 1658: Flecknoe, *Enigm. Characters*, 134, He is bound by the proverb; 'Tis impossible to love and to be wise.

1666: Torriano, *Piazza Univ.*, 7, Knowledge and love, altogether cotten not.

8. **Love and lordship like no fellowship.** [Non bene conveniunt, nec in una sede morantur Maiestas et Amor. – Ovid, *Met.*, ii 846.] *c*.1386: Chaucer, *Knight's Tale*, l. 767, Ful sooth is seyd that love ne lordshipe Wol noght, his thankes, have no felaweshipe. *c*.1440: Lydgate, *Fall of Princes*, bk vi l. 2221, Vnto purpos was saide ful yore agon, How that loue nouther hih lordshippe … Nowther of hem wolde haue no felashipe. 1587: Greene, in *Works*, vi 251 (Grosart), Ambition … not suffring loue or lordship to brooke any fellowship. 1658: R. Brome, *Love-sick Court*, I ii, Love, and ambition (I have heard men say) admit no fellowship. 1681: W. Robertson, *Phraseol. Generalis*, 846. 1736: Bailey, *Dict.*, s.v. 'Love', Love and lordship never like fellowship.

9. **Love and pease porridge will make their way.** 1674: Head and Kirkman, *Eng. Rogue*, iii 176, You know the old proverb, that sad are the effects of love and pease porridge. 1738: Swift, *Polite Convers.*, Dial. I, Ay; they say love and pease porridge are two dangerous things; one breaks the heart; and the other the belly.

10. **Love and pride stock Bedlam.** 1732: Fuller, 3284.

11. **Love asks faith, and faith asks firmness.** 1670: Ray, 16.

12. **Love begets love.** 1648: Herrick, *Hesperides*, 297, Love love begets, then never be Unsoft to him who's smooth to thee. 1812: E. Nares, *I'll consider of It*, iii, 'Love 'says the proverb, 'produces love'. 1909: A. Maclaren, *Epistle to the Ephesians*, Love begets love, and … if a man loves God, then that glowing beam will glow whether it is turned to earth or turned to heaven.

13. **Love cannot be compelled.** *c*.1390: Chaucer, *The Franklin's Tale*, l. 36 Lovve wol nat be constreyned by maistrye. 1534: J. Heywood, *Love*, D1, Wyll wyll not be Forced in love. 1590: Spenser, *Faerie Queene*, III i 25, Ne may love be compeld by maisterye. 1621: R. Burton, *Anatomy of Melancholy* (1651), III ii vi v, 577, You must consider that *Amor cogi non potest*, love cannot be compelled, they must affect as they may.

14. **Love comes in at the window and goes out at the door.** 1605: Camden, *Remains*, 327 (1870).

1670: Ray, 47. 1732: Fuller, 3285 [with 'flies' for 'goes'].

15. Love conquers all. [*Amor vincit omnia*, Virgil, *Eclogues*, x l. 69] Almost better known in the Latin form than in its English equivalent. *c*.1390: Chaucer, *Prologue*, And ther-on heng a broche of gold ful shene, On which ther was first writ a crowned A, And after, *Amor vincit omnia*.

16. Love does much but money does all. 1587: Greene, in *Works*, iii 61 (Grosart). 1611: Cotgrave, s.v. 'Amour'. 1667: L'Estrange, *Quevedo's Visions*, 38 (1904). 1732: Fuller, 3286 [with 'more' for 'all'].

17. Love is a sweet torment. 1633: Draxe, 119.

18. Love is above King or Kaiser, lord or laws. 1583: Greene, in *Works*, ii 122 (Grosart).

19. Love is blind. *c*.1386: Chaucer, *Merch. Tale*, l. 354, For love is blind al day, and may nat see. *c*.1490: *Partonope*, l. 10796, In this case love is blynde. 1566: Painter, *Pal. of Pleasure*, ii 43 (Jacobs). 1621: Burton, *Melancholy*, III ii 4, I, p. 564 (1836), Love is blind, as the saying is. 1733: Gay, *Achilles*, III. 1837: Dickens, *Pickwick*, ch xvii. 1893: Gilbert, *Utopia*, I.

20. Love is full of busy fear. *c*.1374: Chaucer, *Troylus*, bk iv. l. 1645, For I am ever a-gast, for why men rede, That 'love is thing ay ful of bisy drede'. 1506: A. Barclay, *Cast. of Labour*, sig. D2, This prouerbe that I the lere … Loue goth neuer without fere. 1595: Munday, *John a Kent*, 50 (SH.S.), Loove is full of feare. 1654: Flecknoe, *Loves Dominion*, II i, Love's a solicitous thing, and full of fears. 1736: Bailey, *Dict.*, s.v. 'Love', Love is never without jealousy.

21. Love is liberal. 1639: Clarke, 28.

22. Love is not found in the market. 1640: Herbert, *Jac. Prudentum*.

23. Love is the loadstone of love. 1732: Fuller, 3288. 1870: Hawker, *Footprints of Former Men*, 77, No man ever more fully realised the truth of the saying that 'Love makes love'.

24. Love is the true price of love. *c*.1420: in *Twenty-six Poems*, 76 (E.E.T.S.), Loue for loue is euenest boughte. 1569: E. Fenton, *Wonders of Nature*, 66 v°, Al things … be priced at a certaine rate, excePt Loue, which can not be payed but wyth loue. 1631: Mabbe, *Celestina*, 138 (T.T.), Love is never pay'd but with pure love. 1696: Mrs Manley, *Lost Lover*, V iii, What can pay love but love? 1700: Dryden, *Pal. and Arcite*, ii 373, For 'tis their maxim, – Love is love's reward.

1837: J. S. Knowles, *Love-Chase*, I ii, But love's the coin to market with for love. 1852: FitzGerald, *Polonius*, 122 (1903).

25. Love is without law. 1581: B. Rich, *Farewell*, 191 (SH.S.). 1639: Clarke, 27, Love is lawlesse. 1700: Dryden, *Pal. and Arcite*, i 326, Know'st thou not, no law is made for love? Cf. **Lover**.

26. Love lasteth as long as the money endureth. 1474: Caxton, *Chesse*, III iii [cited as 'a comyn proverbe in Englond'].

27. Love laughs at locksmiths. 1803: Colman, jr., *Love Laughs at Locksmiths* [title]. 1898: W. J. Locke, *Idols*, ch vi. 1923: Lucas, *Advisory Ben*, 4, We know how Love treats locksmiths.

28. Love lives in cottages as well as in courts. 1590: Lodge, *Rosalynde*, 95 (Hunt.Cl.), Loue lurkes assoone about a sheepcoate as a pallaice. 1611: Cotgrave, s.v. 'Amourettes' [with 'bides' for 'lives']. 1670: Ray, 16. 1732: Fuller, 3290, Love lives more in cottages than courts.

29. Love locks no cupboards. 1639: Clarke, 26.

30. Love looks for love again. 1570: Barclay, *Mirrour of Good Manners*, 74 (Spens.S.), Shewe thou loue to win loue in worde, heart and dede. 1591: Harington, *Orl. Furioso*, bk xxviii st. 80, And sure love craveth love, like asketh like. 1639: Clarke, 27. 1751: Fielding, *Amelia*, bk v ch ix, But the devil take me, if I think anything but love to be the object of love.

31. Love makes a good eye squint. 1640: Herbert, *Jac. Prudentum*. 1670: Ray, 16.

32. Love makes a wit of the fool. 1774: C. Dibdin, *Quaker*, I viii, According unto the proverb, love maketh a wit of the fool.

33. Love makes men orators. 1583: Greene, in *Works*, ii 57 (Grosart), It hath byn a saying more common then true, that loue makes al men orators. 1630: *Tinker of Turvey*, 63 (Halliwell) [cited as an 'old said saw'].

34. Love makes the world go round. 1865: 'L. Carroll', *Alice's Adventures in Wonderland*, ix, ' "Oh 'tis love, 'tis love, that makes the world go round!" 'Somebody said,' Alice whispered, 'that it's done by everybody minding their own business.' 1902: 'O. Henry', in *Brandur Magazine*, 27. Sept., 4, It's said that love makes the world go round.

35. Love of lads and fire of chats [chips] **is soon in and soon out.** *c*.1460: *Good Wyfe wold a Pylgr.*, l. 83 (E.E.T.S.), A fyre of sponys [wood-shavings], and lowe of gromis, Full soun woll be att a nende. 1670: Ray, 46. Cf. **Lads' love.**

36. Love rules his kingdom without a sword. 1640: Herbert, *Jac. Prudentum*. 1666: Torriano, *Piazza Univ.*, 9. 1853: Trench, *Proverbs*, 130 (1905).

37. Love sees no faults. 1732: Fuller, 3297.

38. Love will creep where it can not (or **may not**) **go.** *c.*1400: *Towneley Plays*, 135 (E.E.T.S.), I trow, kynde will crepe where it may not go. 1481: Caxton, *Reynard*, 70 (Arber), Blood must krepe where it can not goo. *c.*1530: *Everyman*, in Hazlitt, *Old Plays*, i 113 [with 'Kind' for 'Love']. 1569: Grafton, *Chron.*, ii 2 (1809) [with 'Kinne' for 'Love']. 1602: Rowlands, *Merri when Goss. meete*, 20 (Hunt.Cl.), They say loue creepeth where it cannot go. 1658: *Musarum Deliciae*, i 172 (Hotten) ['can not']. 1753 Richardson, *Grandison*, i 403 (1883) ['can not']. 1917: Bridge, *Cheshire Proverbs*, 93 ['can not'].

39. Love will find a way. *c.*1597: Deloney, *Gentle Craft*, ch xv, Thus loue you see, can find a way To make both men and maids obey. *c.*1600: in *Roxb. Ballads*, ii 639 (B.S.) [with 'out 'after 'find']. 1662: Fuller, *Worthies*, ii 227 (1840), But love and money will find or force a passage.

40. Neither for love nor money. 971: *Blickl. Hom.*, 43 (OED), Ne for feo, ne for nanes mannes lufon. *c.*1310: in Wright, *Pol. Songs*, 302 (Camden S.), Pur amy ne pur dener Ray ne dait esparnier (For love nor for pence – A King ought not to spare). 1595: *Pedlars Proph.*, l. 578 (Malone S.), Neither for loue nor mony they will worke. 1669: Shadwell, *Royal Shep.*, Prol., If it were to be had for love or money. 1771: Smollett, *Clinker*, in *Works*, vi 45 (1817), It can't be had for love nor money. 1894: Shaw, *Arms and the Man*, II, You shall never get that out of me, for love or money.

41. The love of a woman, etc. *See* quots. 1578: Florio, *First Fruites*, fo. 25, The loue of a whore and the wine of a bottle at night is good, in the mornyng naught. 1629: *Book of Meery Riddles*, Prov. 57, The love of a harlot, and wine of a flagon, is good in the morning and nought in the evening. 1666: Torriano, *Piazza Univ.*, 9 [as in 1578, with 'woman' for 'whore', 'evening' for 'night', and 'spoyl'd' for 'naught']. 1678: Ray, 55, The love of a woman, and a bottle of wine, Are sweet for a season, but last for a time. 1732: Fuller, 6401 [as in 1678].

42. The love of money and the love of learning rarely meet. 1651: Herbert, *Jac. Prudentum*, 2nd ed.

43. There's love in a budget. 1678: Ray, 258.

44. Though love is blind, yet 'tis not for want of eyes. 1732: Fuller, 5004.

45. When love puts in, friendship is gone. *c.*1630: B.&F., *Lovers' Progress*, I i [quoted – 'as the proverb says'].

46. Where love fails. *See* **Fault** (4).

47. Where love's in the case, the doctor is an ass. 1667: L'Estrange, *Quevedo's Visions*, 111 (1904) [quoted as 'the old rhyme']. 1678: Ray, 50. 1722: Defoe, *Moll Flanders*, in *Works*, iii 35 (Bohn).

See also **Course** (2) **Lucky;** *Old E* (6); **One love.**

Love, *verb.* **1. Better to have loved and lost than never to have loved at all.** *See* **Better.**

2. He loves bacon well that licks the swine-sty door. 1678: Ray, 96. 1732: Fuller, 1978 [with 'sow's breech' for 'swine-sty door'].

3. He that does not love a woman. *See* **Hate** (1).

4. He that loves Glass without G, Take away L and that is he. 1669: *New Help to Discourse*, 265. 1678: Ray, 55. 1732: Fuller, 6260.

5. He that loves the tree loves the branch. 1639: Clarke, 285, If you love the boll, you cannot hate the braunches. 1640: Herbert, *Jac. Prudentum*.

6. I love thee like pudding, if thou wert pie I'd eat thee. 1678: Ray, 349. 1685: S. Wesley, *Maggots*, 24, I love you so that I could eat ye. 1711: *Spectator*, No. 47, Whom the common people of all countries admire, and seem to love so well, that they could eat them, according to the old proverb. 1738: Swift, *Polite Convers.*, Dial. II, I love him like pye, I'd rather the devil had him than I.

7. I love you well but touch not my pocket. 1732: Fuller, 2618.

8. I must love you and leave you. 1917: Bridge, *Cheshire Proverbs*, 79 … Often said on taking leave of a person.

9. If you love not the noise of bells. *See* **Bell** (5).

10. Love me little love me long. 1500: in *Archiv* (1900), CVI. 274, Love me lytyll and longe. 1546: Heywood, *Proverbs*, Pt II ch ii. 1580: Munday, *Sundry Examples*, 73 (SH.S.). 1633: Marlowe, *Jew of Malta*, IV vi. 1711: Steele, *Spectator*, No. 140, My mother says, As he is slow he is sure; He will love me long, if he love me little. 1859: Reade, *Love me Little, Love me Long* [title].

11. Love me love my dog. [Qui me amat, amat et canem meum. – 12th cent.: St Bernard, *Fest. S. Mich.*, Ser. i § 3.] *c.*1480: *Early Miscell.*, 62 (Warton Cl.), He that lovythe me lovythe my hound. 1527: Tyndale, in *Treatises*, 84 (P.S.), We say also, He that loveth not my dog, loveth not me. 1583: Stubbes, *Anat. of Abuses*, 178 (N.Sh.S.). 1664: in *Musarum Deliciae, etc.*, ii 77 (Hotten). 1714: *Spectator*, No. 579. 1826: Lamb, *Pop. Fallacies*, xiii. 1920: W. H. Mallock, *Memoirs*, 42.

12. Love to live and live to love. 1576: Pettie, *Petite Pall.*, i l. 33 (Gollancz), Whatsoever be your common saying, that you must as well love to live as live to love.

13. Love your neighbour yet pull not down your hedge. 1640: Herbert, *Jac. Prudentum.* 1763: Murphy, *Citizen*, I ii. 1875: A. B. Cheales, *Proverb. Folk–Lore*, 93.

14. No man loves his fetters, though they be made of gold. 1546: Heywood, *Proverbs*, Pt I ch viii. *c.*1594: Bacon, *Promus*, No. 475. 1607: Webster, *Sir T. Wyatt*, in *Works*, i 9 (1857), Who would weave fetters though they were all of gold? 1670: Ray, 89. 1732: Fuller, 1522, Fetters of gold are still fetters; and silken cords pinch.

15. One cannot love and be wise. *c.*1527: T. Berthelet, tr. *Erasmus Sayings of Wise Men*, B1v, To have a sadde [serious] mynde and love is nat in one person. 1539: R. Taverner, *Proverbs or Adagies out of Erasmus*, II, A5, To be in love and to be wyse is scase graunted to god. *c.*1601: Shakespeare, *Troilus and Cressida*, III iii … but you are wise; Or else you love not; for to be wise and love Exceeds man's might. That dwells with gods above. 1631: R. Brathwait, *English Gentlewoman*, 32, The lover is ever blinded … with affection … when came that usuall saying One cannot love and be wise. 1872: 'G. Eliot', *Middlemarch*, II III xxvii, If a man could not love and be wise, surely he could flirt and be wise at the same time?

16. She loves the poor well, but cannot abide beggars. Somerset. 1678: Ray, 350.

17. They love like chick. Somerset. Ibid., 347.

18. They love too much that die for love. 1611: Cotgrave, s.v. 'Mourir' [with 'He' for 'They']. 1670: Ray, 16.

19. They who love most are least set by. 1659: Howell, 12. 1670: Ray, 16. 1748: Richardson, *Clarissa*, iv 119 (1785), Those, Mr Belford, who most love, are least set by.

20. To love at the door and leave at the hatch. 1678: Ray, 258. 1732: Fuller, 5200 [omitting each 'at'].

21. To love it as a dog loves a whip. 1678: Ray, 287.

22. Whom we love best, to them we can say least. 1670: Ray, 47. 1732: Fuller, 6259.

23. You love to make much of naught, i.e. yourself. 1678: Ray, 347.

Lover, Who may give law to a? [Quis legem dat amantibus? Maior lex amor est sibi. – 6th cent.: Boethius, *De Consol. Philos.*, bk iii metre xii.] *c.*1386: Chaucer, *Knight's Tale*, l. 306, Wostow nat wel the olde clerkes sawe, That who shal yeve a lovere any lawe? *c.*1450: *Partonope*, l. 8710 (E.E.T.S.), Therfor this ys a full old sawe: Who may gyfe to a louer lawe? 1581: B. Rich, *Farewell*, 131 (SH.S.), What is he, I praie you, that is able to prescribe lawes to love? Cf. **Love,** *subs.* (15), (22).

Lovers live by love as larks live by leeks. Desire for alliteration seems to be the only explanation of the absurd comparison. 1546: Heywood, *Proverbs*, Pt I ch x. 1596: Churchyard, *Pleas. Disc. of Court, etc.*, sig. B4 (Boswell, 1816), All one we liue … By loue as larks do liue by leekes. 1623: Wodroephe, *Spared Homes*, 313, They bee some that do liue of loue, Well yea, as larkes do of leekes. 1670: Ray, 46. 1833: T. Hook, *Parson's Daughter*, vol. i ch xi, One of those sighing swains who, the proverb says – why, nobody has ever exactly ascertained – 'live on love, as larks on leeks'. 1884: H. Friend, *Flowers and Fl. Lore*, Notes, 641.

Loving comes by looking. 1639: Clarke, 28.

Low hedge is easily leaPt over, A. 1605: Camden, *Remains*, 317 (1870). 1670: Ray, 16. 1732: Fuller, 259.

Low stake standeth long, The. 1546: Heywood, *Proverbs*, Pt II ch iv, The lothe stake standeth longe. *c.*1594: Bacon, *Promus*, No. 485. 1732: Fuller, 4637 [in the plural]. Cf. **Loose stake.**

Lower mill-stone grinds as well as the upper, The. 1519: Horman, *Vulgaria*, fo. 153, The lower stone can do no good without the hyar. 1678: Ray, 172. 1732: Fuller, 4638 [with 'much' for 'well'].

Lowly sit, richly warm. 1670: Ray, 117.

Lubberland. *See* quots. Nares (*Glossary*, s.v.) says: 'There was an old proverbial saying about "Lubberland, where the pigs run about ready roasted, and cry Come eat me." ' 1598: Florio, *Worlde of Wordes*, *Cocagna*, as we say Lubberland. 1614: Jonson, *Bart. Fair*, III ii, Will it run off o' the spit into our mouths, think you, as in Lubberland, and cry, *we, we*? 1813: Ray, 64, You'd do well in Lubberland, where they have half a crown a day for sleeping.

Luck. 1. Give a man luck and throw him in the sea. 1576: *Parad. of Dainty Devices*, No. 27, She [Fortune] vseth neuer partiall hands for to offend, or please, Geve me good Fortune all men sayes, and throw me in the seas. 1580: Churchyard, *Charge*, 28 (Collier), Our old proverbe is, given me hap and cast me in the sea. 1632: Rowley, *Woman never Vexed*, I [with 'woman' for 'man']. 1671: Head and Kirkman, *Eng. Rogue*, ii 202. 1709: O. Dykes, *Eng. Proverbs*, 271. 1837: Planché. *Extravag.*, i 268 (1879), Give a man but luck they say, sir, In the sea fling him you may, sir.

2. Luck for the fools and chance for the ugly. 1754: Berthelson, *Eng.-Danish Dict.*, s.v. 'Luck'.

3. Luck is a lord. 1564: Bullein, *Dialogue*, 101 (E.E.T.S.), If good lucke had been our good lord. 1709: O. Dykes, *Eng. Proverbs*, 272, Luck is a lord, we say. 1848: Planché, *Extravag.*, iii 272 (1879).

4. There is luck in leisure. 1855: Bohn, 522.

5. There is luck in odd numbers. 1600: Shakespeare, *Merry Wives*, V i.. This is the third time; I hope good luck lies in odd numbers. 1672: *Dream of the Cabal*, quoted in Wheatley's *Pepys*, vii 229 n., Methought there met the grand Cabal of Seven, (Odd numbers, some men say, do best please Heaven). 1784: *New Foundl. Hosp. for Wit*, ii 118, Odd numbers are lucky. 1883: Burne, *Shropsh. Folk-Lore*, 262, We say now, 'There's luck in odd numbers'.

See also **Good luck; Hit** (2); and **Ill luck.**

Lucky at cards, unlucky in love. 1738: Swift, *Polite Conversation*, III 213, Well, Miss, you'll have a sad Husband, you have such good Luck at Cards. 1866: T. W. Robertson, *Society*, 'I'm always lucky at cards!' ... 'Yes, I know an old proverb about that ... Lucky at play, unlucky in —'. 1925: D. H. Lawrence, *Letter*, Aug., ii 851, Perhaps it's really true, lucky in money, unlucky in love.

Lucky men need no counsel. 1855: Bohn, 447.

Lucky, Third time. *See* **Third time lucky.**

Lucy light, the shortest day and the longest night. [1633: Donne, *Poems*, i 254 (Grierson), Laies thee to sleepe but a Saint Lucies night.] 1659: Howell, *Proverbs: Span.-Eng.*, 13, San Lucy bright, the shortest ... 1678: Ray, 52. 1732: Fuller, 6222. 1881: C. W. Empson, in *Folk-Lore Record*, iv 129, Lucy light! Lucy light! Longest day and shortest night!

Luddington. *See* quot. 1889: Peacock, *Manley, etc., Gloss.*, 333 (E.D.S.), Luddington poor people. With a stoän chech an' a wooden steeple.

Ludgate bird, A. 1639: Clarke, 245.

Ludlam's dog. *See* **Lazy.**

Lunch, There's no such thing as a free. *See* **Free lunch.**

Lundy high, Sign of dry; Lundy plain, Sign of rain. 1891: R. P. Chope, *Hartland Dialect*, 20 (E.D.S.).

Lust. Sec **Pleasure** (4).

Lust is as young as his limbs are old, His. 1659: Howell, 10.

Lydford Law. *See* quots. 1399: Langland, *Richard Redeless*, iii 145, Be the lawe of Lydfford. 1644: Browne, *Lydford Castle*, st. 1, I oft have heard of Lydford Law, How in the morn they hang and draw, And sit in judgment after. 1662: Fuller, *Worthies*, i 399 (1840), First hang and draw, Then hear the cause by Lidford law. 1714: Ozell, *Molière*, iv 215, Hang a man first, and try him afterwards; Lidford law you know! 1838: Mrs Bray, *Trad. of Devon*, iii 12, The old saying of Lydford Law, to express an arbitrary procedure in judgment. 1855: Kingsley, *West. Ho!*, ch xiv, And by Lydfor' law if they will, hang first and try after. 1887: *Cornhill Mag.*, Nov., 523, 'Hang first and try afterwards 'was the fundamental maxim of Lydford Law.

Lying rides on Death's beck. 1736: Franklin, *Way to Wealth*, in *Works*, i 449 (Bigelow). 1875: Smiles, *Thrift*, 242.

Lymm from Warburton, To tear. 1901: F. E. Taylor, *Folk-Speech of S. Lancs*, s.v. 'Limb', Limb-fro'-Warbutton. A term used to denote the division or pulling to pieces of anything. 1917: Bridge, *Cheshire Proverbs*, 144 ... Lymm-cum-Warburton were two medieties of one parish on the Chester side of the Mersey.

Lythe. *See* **Lithe.**

M

M under one's girdle. *See* **Carry** (3).

Macclesfield. *To feed like a freeholder of Macclesfield, who hath neither corn nor hay at Michaelmas.* 1670: Ray, 208. 1790: Grose, *Prov. Gloss.*, s.v. 'Cheshire'. 1917: Bridge, *Cheshire Proverbs*, 65 [with 'Christmas' for 'Michaelmas']. *See also* **Maxfield**; and **Treacle town**.

Macgregor sits is the head of the table, Where. This saying is popularly attributed to Rob Roy (Robert MacGregor of Campbell). The name used sometimes varies, but the sense is that the importance of a person resides with that person and is not conditional on social or other forms of recognition. 1580: Lyly, *Euphues and his England*, II 39, When ... Agesilaus sonne was set at the lower end of the table, and one cast it in his teeth as a shame, he answered: This is the upper end where I sit. 1732: T. Fuller, *Gnomologia*, no. 4362, That is the upper End, where the chief person sits. 1837: Emerson, *American Scholar*, 19, Wherever Macdonald sits, there is the head of the table. 1903: K.D. Wiggin, *Rebecca of Sunnybrook Farm*, If wherever the MacGregor sat was the head of the table, so ... wherever Rebecca stood was the centre of the stage.

Mackerel sky, A. *See* quots. [1669: Worlidge, *Syst. Agric.*, 295 (1681) (OED), In a fair day, if the sky seem to be dapled with white clouds (which they usually term a mackarel-sky) it usually predicts rain.] 1854: Baker, *Northants Gloss.*, s.v. A mackarel sky, Never holds three days dry. *c.*1870: Smith, *Isle of Wight Words*, 62 (E.D.S.), (*a*) Mares' tails and a mackarel sky, Not four and twenty hours dry. (*b*) A mackarel sky and mares' tails Make lofty ships carry low sails. 1886: Elworthy, *West Som. Word-Book*, 453 (E.D.S.), Mackerel-sky! not much wet, not much dry. 1891: Addy, *Sheffield Gloss. Suppl.*, 36 (E.D.S.), In this district it is said that A mackerel sky Is never long dry. 1893: Inwards, *Weather Lore*, 94, [as in 1870 (*b*), plus] (*a*) Mackerel sky, mackerel sky, Never long wet and never long dry. (*b*) Mackerel clouds in sky, Expect more wet than dry. (*c*) Mackerel scales, Furl your sails. (*d*) A mackerel sky, Not twenty-four hours dry.

Mad as a hatter. 1849: Thackeray, *Pendennis*, ch x. 1857: Hughes, *Tom Brown*, Pt II ch iii, He's a

very good fellow, but as mad as a hatter. 1863: F. A. Marshall, *Mad as a Hatter* [title of farce].

Mad as a March hare. *c.*1386: Chaucer, *Friar's Tale*, l. 29, For thogh this Sommour wood [mad] were as an hare. *c.*1450: *Partonope*, l. 7934 (E.E.T.S.), There he rennyth wode [mad] as ony hare. *c.*1500: in Hazlitt, *Early Pop. Poetry*, i 105, And be as braynles as a Marshe hare. 1546: Heywood, *Proverbs*, Pt II ch v, As mad as a marche hare. 1577: Stanihurst, *Descrip. of Ireland*, fo. 14. *c.*1620: Fletcher, *Wild-Goose Chase*, IV iii, They are all, all mad. I came from a world of mad women, Mad as March hares. 1678: Dryden, *Limberham*, V i. 1749: Fielding, *Tom Jones*, bk xii ch vii. 1850: Dickens, *Chuzzlewit*, ch xlvi. 1917: Bridge, *Cheshire Proverbs*, 26, As wyndy [wild] as a March hare.

Mad as a tup. 1883: Burne, *Shropsh. Folk-Lore*, 595, As mad as a tup [ram] in a halter. 1901: in *N.&Q.*, 9th ser, viii 501, In Derbyshire ... there is no commoner saying to express anger shown by any one than to say that he or she was 'as mad as a tup'. 'A tup' is a ram.

Mad as a weaver. 1609: *Ev. Woman in Humor*, I, in Bullen, *Old Plays*, iv 314, If he were as madde as a weaver.

Mad as Ajax. 1592: Shakespeare, *L.L.L.*, IV iii, By the Lord, this love is as mad as Ajax. 1607: Chapman, *Bussy d'Ambois*, III, And run as mad as Ajax. 1732: Fuller, 3287, Love is as mad as Ajax.

Mad, get even, Don't get. *Mad* is used here in the American sense of 'angry'. The saying is associated with President John F. Kennedy (see quot.), though he suggests that it predates him. It was also used by a contemporary of Kennedy's, the Republican minority leader in the Senate, Senator Everett M. Dirksen. 1975: J.F. Kennedy, in C. Bradlee, *Conversations with Kennedy*, 25, Some of the reasons have their roots in that wonderful law of the Boston Irish political jungle: 'Don't get mad, get even'.

Mad horse. *See* quot. 1685: Meriton, *Yorkshire Ale*, 66, A weand [mad] horse I've heard it oft reported And a rotten harrow are seaun parted.

Mad world, my masters, A. 1603: Breton, *A Mad World my Masters* [title], in *Works*, (Grosart), ii. 1608: Middleton, *A Mad World my*

Masters [title]. 1649: Taylor (Water-Poet), *Western Voyage*, l. 1, 'Tis a mad world, my masters.

Mad, You'll never be, you are of so many minds. 1670: Ray, 118. 1738: Swift, *Polite Convers.*, Dial. I.

Madam Parnell, crack the nut and eat the kernel. Howell says that this saying alludes to a woman's labour. It may be noted that 'Pernel' in the seventeenth century and earlier was a name for a woman of loose life. 1659: Howell, l. 1670: Ray, 84.

Madge. *See* **Margery.**

Madman and a fool are no witnesses, A. 1732: Fuller, 267.

Mad parish must have a mad priest, A. Ibid., No. 268.

Maggot bites, When the = When the whim takes one. 1683: L'Estrange, *Observator*, i No. 470, Prethee, where bites the magot to-day, Trimmer? 1709: E. Ward, *Works*, iv, *Verse*, 21, So touchy when the maggot takes him. 1754: Berthelson, *Eng.-Danish Dict.*, s.v. 'Maggot', I shall do it when the maggot bites.

Maggots in the brain, To have = To have whimsies. *c.*1625: B.&F., *Women Pleased*, III iv, Have not you maggots in your brains? 1675: in *Harl. Miscell.* vii 597 (1746), He puts off … the maggots of his own brain for divine inspiration. 1704: D'Urfey, *Tales Trag. and Comical*, 51, The maggots in the brain With novelty possess'd his pate.

Magistracy. *See* quot. 1642: D. Rogers, *Matrim. Honour*, 45, The old speech is, Magistracy makes not the man, but discovers what mettell is in him.

Magnificat, The. 1. To correct Magnificat = To find fault unreasonably, and presumptuously. 1540: Palsgrave, *Acolastus*, sig. B3, Thou … whiche takest vppon the to correct Magnificat. 1583: Melbancke, *Philotinus*, sig. E1, That correcteth Magnificat before he can sing Te Deum. 1589: Nashe, *Works*, i 152 (Grosart), They would correct Magnificat, not knowing *Quid significat.* 1681: W. Robertson, *Phraseol. Generalis*, 388, To correct the Magnificat; Nodum in scirpo quaerere. Ibid., 856 … Lumen soli mutuare. 1694: L'Estrange, *Aesop*, 283 (3rd ed.). 'Tis the same case where subjects take upon them to correct Magnificat, and to prescribe to their superiors. 1736: Bailey, *Dict.*, s.v. 'Correct'.

2. *See* quots. 1588: Bp. Andrewes, *Serm. at Spital*, 24 (1629) (OED), The note is heere all out of place … and so, their note comes in like Magnificat at Matins. 1611: Cotgrave, s.v. 'Magnificat', *Chanter Magnificat à matines*, To doe things disorderly, or use a thing unseasonably. 1653: Urquhart *Rabelais*, bk i ch xi, He … made a mock at the gods, would cause sing Magnificat at Matines.

Magpie. 1. Query the proverb alluded to. 1576: G. Harvey, *Letter-Book*, 163 (Camden S.), Mai perhaps fli at a pie, as ye proverb is, but he is most likeli to catch a dawe.

2. Omens and sayings. 1849: Dinsdale, *Teesdale Gloss.*, 95, One's sorrow, Two's good luck, Three's a wedding, Four's death. 1867: Harland, in *Lancs Folk-Lore*, 144, In Lancashire they say: – 'One for anger, Two for mirth, Three for a wedding, Four for a birth, Five for rich, Six for poor. Seven for a witch, I can tell you no more'. 1878: *Folk-Lore Record*, i 8, In speaking of the magpie they confidently tell you that – 'One is for sorrow, two for mirth, Three for a wedding, Four for a birth'. 1883: Burne, *Shropsh. Folk-Lore*, 224, [as in 1878, *plus*] 'Four for a death', say some; and from Church Stretton we have another variation, 'One for anger, two for luck', etc. 1886: Elworthy, *West Som.Word-Book*, 454 (E.D.S.), One, sign of anger; two, sign o' muth; Dree, sign o' wedding-day; vower, sign o' death; Vive, sign o' zorrow; zix, sign o' joy; Zebm, sign o' maid; an' eight sign o' boy. 1892: S. Hewett, *Peasant Speech of Devon*, 26, Wan is vur zorrow, Tü is vur mirth, Dree is vur a wedding, Vowr is vur death. 1901: F. E. Taylor, *Lancs Sayings*, 41, One for cryin' – two for mirth – Three for a weddin' – four for a d'yeth.

3. Worth one's weight in magpies. Corn. 1869: Hazlitt, 481.

Mahomet and the mountain. 1625: Bacon, *Essays:* 'Boldness', Mahomet cald the hill to come to him, againe, and againe; and when the hill stood still, he was neuer a whit abashed, but said; *If the hill will not come to Mahomet, Mahomet wil go to the hil.* Before 1704: T. Brown, in *Works*, iv 259 (1760), And then 'twas with us in the case of drink, what it was formerly between Mahomet and the mountain. 1874: R.L.S., *Letters*, i 163 (Tusitala ed.).

Maid, Maids, and **Maidens. 1. A maid and a virgin is not all one.** 1639: Clarke, 152.

2. **A maid oft seen, and a gown oft worn, Are disesteem'd, and held in scorn.** 1611: Cotgrave, s.v. 'Fille'. 1670: Ray, 17. 1732: Fuller, 6395.

3. **A maid that giveth yieldeth.** 1611: Cotgrave, s.v. 'Abandonner'. 1670: Ray, 16. 1736: Bailey, *Dict.*, s.v. 'Maid'.

4. **A maid that laughs is half taken.** 1670: Ray, 16. 1732: Fuller, 269.

5. **A maid's knee.** *See* Dog (8).

6. **Every maid is undone.** 1678: Ray, 172.

7. **If the maid be a fool.** *See* Cat (25).

8. **Maidens must be mild and meek; Swift to hear, and slow to speak.** 1732: Fuller, 6410. 1736: Bailey, *Dict.*, s.v.

9. **Maidens should be mim** [silent] **till they're married.** 1917: Bridge, *Cheshire Proverbs*, 93.

10. **Maids' children.** *See* Bachelor (3).

11. **Maids say nay and take.** 1562: Heywood, *Three Hund. Epigr.*, No. 223, Say nay, and take it. 1594: Shakespeare, *Rich. III*, III vii, Play the maid's part, still answer nay, and take it. 1609: W. Rowley, *Search for Money*, 32 (Percy S.). 1694: Motteux, *Rabelais*, bk v ch xxviii. 1738: Swift, *Polite Convers.*, Dial. I.

12. **Maids should be seen and not heard.** *c.*1400: *Mirk's Festial*, 230 (E.E.T.S.), For hyt ys an old Englysch sawe: 'A mayde schuld be seen, but not herd'. 1560: Becon, *Catechism, etc.*, 369 (P.S.) [as in 1400]. Before 1627: Middleton, *More Diss. besides Women*, III i, Virgins should be seen more than they're heard. 1675: Cotton, *Burl. upon Burlesque*, 252 (1765). 1738: Swift, *Polite Convers.*, Dial. I. 1858: G. Eliot, *Clerical Life*: 'Janet's Rep.', ch viii, 'Hush, Lizzie, little gells must be seen and not heard'. 1907: De Morgan, *Alice-for-Short*, ch ix, These [maxims] were the old-fashioned sort, such as – 'Little girls should be seen not heard'. Cf. Children (10).

13. **Maids want nothing but husbands.** 1678: Ray, 347 … *Somerset*. 1732: Fuller, 3309, [as in 1678, *plus*] and then they want every thing.

14. **The worst store [is] a maid unbestowed.** 1659: Howell, *Proverbs: Brit.-Eng.*, 15.

15. **There are never the fewer maids for her.** 1678: Ray, 258.

16. **This maid was born old.** Ibid., 77.

17. **When maidens sue, men live like gods.** 1855: Bohn, 559.

18. **Who knows who's a good maid?** 1678: Ray, 172.

See also **All meats; Good a maid; Meeterly; and Wife** (25).

Main chance, Have an eye to the. 1580: Lyly, *Euphues*, 430 (Arber), Alwayes haue an eye to the mayne, what soeuer thou art chaunced at the buy. *c.*1610: in *Roxb. Ballads*, i 454 (B.S.), She had a care of the main-chance. 1681: W. Robertson, *Phraseol. Generalis*, 322, Have a care of the main chance. 1722: Defoe, *Moll Flanders*, in *Works*, iii 40 (Bohn), A man … getting money, seldom at home, thoughtful of the main chance. 1924: *Sphere*, 29 March, p. 344, col. 1, Ernest Stanton, M.P., has a suave manner and an eye for the main chance.

Main lost, cast the by away, The. 1594: Drayton, *Ideas*, lix. (Proverbs)

Maisemore. *See* quot. 1894: Northall, *Folk Phrases*, 7 (E.D.S.), All together like the men of Maisemore, and they went one at a time.

Make, *verb.* **1. As you make your bed so you must lie on it.** [Tute hoc intristi: tibi omne est exedendum. – Terence, *Phorm.*, 318]. *c.*1590: G. Harvey, *Marginalia*, 88 (1913), Lett them … go to there bedd, as themselves shall make it. 1640: Herbert, *Jac. Prudentum*. He that makes his bed ill, lies there. 1670: Ray, 3 [as in 1640]. 1721: J. Kelly, *Scottish Proverbs*, As you make your bed, so you lie down. According to your Conditions, you have your Bargain. 1732: Fuller, 2233 [as in 1640, but ending 'must be contented to lie ill']. 1842: Barham, *Ing. Legends*, 2nd ser: 'Aunt Fanny', She could not prevent her – 'twas no use in trying it – Oh, no – she had made her own bed, and might lie in it. 1922: Weyman, *Ovington's Bank*, ch xxxi, He has … disgraced our blood … he has done it! He has made his bed and must lie on it!

2. **He that can make a fire well can end a quarrel.** 1640: Herbert, *Jac. Prudentum*.

3. **He that makes his mistress a goldfinch, may perhaps find her a wagtail.** 1647: *Countrym. New Commonwealth*, 8–9.

4. **He that makes the shoe can't tan the leather.** 1580: Lyly, *Euphues*, 224 (Arber), You know that it is not for him that fashioneth the shoe, to make the graine of the leather. 1732: Fuller, 2235.

5. **I'll make you know your driver.** 1678: Ray, 345 … *Somerset*.

6. **I will not make my dish-clout my table-cloth.** 1732: Fuller, 2646. 1737: Ray, 96.

7. Make a-do and have a-do. 1678: Ray, 70.

8. Make haste and leave nothing to waste.
1827: Hone, *Ev. Day Book*, ii 927 [quoted as 'the old proverb'].

9. Make hay. *See* **Hay** (3).

10. Make me a diviner and I will make thee rich. 1578: Florio, *First Fruites*, fo. 30. 1623: Wodroephe, *Spared Houres*, 172, Make me a guesser, and I shall make you rich of it. 1629: *Book of Meery Riddles*, Prov. 111. 1732: Fuller, 3315 [with 'sooth-sayer' for 'diviner'].

11. Make nor meddle. *See* **Meddle**.

12. That which will not make a pot, may make a pot-lid, 1732: Fuller, 4388.

13. They that make laws should not break them. *c.*1386: Chaucer, *Introd. to Man of Law's Prol.*, l. 434, For swich lawe as man yeveth another wight, He sholde him-selven usen it by right. 1598: *Servingmans Comfort*, in *Inedited Tracts*, 154 (Hazlitt), It is a shame for the lawgiuer to break and violate his owne institutions. 1669: *Politeuphuia*, 95, It becometh a law-maker not to be a law-breaker. 1739: *Gent. Mag.*, 427, The old proverb ... that law-makers ought not to be law-breakers. 1830: Marryat, *King's Own*, ch xi [as in 1739].

14. They who make the best use of their time have none to spare. 1855: Bohn, 527.

15. To make a wry mouth = To be hanged. 1611: Cotgrave, s.v. 'Moue', We say of one that's hanged, he makes a wry mouth.

16. To make both ends meet. 1639: Clarke, 242, I cannot make, etc. 1662: Fuller, *Worthies:* 'Cumb'. Worldly wealth he cared not for, desiring onely to make both ends meet. 1748: Richardson, *Clarissa*, iv 137 (1785), Tho' he had a good estate, hardly making both ends meet. 1864: Mrs H. Wood, *Trevlyn Hold*, ch xx, If you have the pleasure of making both ends to meet ... upon the moderate sum of one hundred pounds sterling. 1913: E. M. Wright, *Rustic Speech, etc.*, 14, The sort of life where it is hard to make both ends meet.

17. To make buttons. *See* **Breech**.

18. To make indentures = To walk unsteadily, as when drunk. 1605: R. F., *Sch. of Slovenrie*, 35, Before he with his feete do seeme indentures for to make. 1615: Stephens, *Essays, etc.*, bk ii No. 11, If he bee drunken you must say hee staggers, to avoide aequivocation; for when he is sober hee makes indentures [character of a lawyer's clerk]. 1681: in *Roxb. Ballads*, vi 3 (B.S.), Being so drunk that he cutteth indentures. 1745: Franklin, *Drinker's Dict.*, in *Works*, ii 25 (Bigelow), He makes indentures with his leggs.

19. To make no bones about a thing. 1565: Shacklock, *Hatch. of Heresies*, fo. 14, They haue made no bones at it to say. 1608: Armin, *Nest of Ninnies*, 27 (SH.S.), Which, making no bones of, the sweete youth gaue his doings thus. 1633: T. May, tr. Barclay's *Mirr. of Minds*, 196, Which [dinner] ... they make no bones many times to prolong till supper time. 1740: North, *Examen*, 604, He ... made no bones of telling this passage in all companies. 1894: R.L.S., *St Ives*, ch xxv, 'O, don't make any bones about it!' he interrupted.

20. To make orts of good hay. 1639: in *Berkeley MSS.*, iii 29 (1885), Hee's well served, for bee hath oft made orts of better hay. 1670: Ray, 188. 1732: Fuller, 3317, Make no orts of good hay.

21. To make up one's mouth. This bears more than one meaning. *See* quots. 1546: Heywood, *Proverbs*, Pt I ch xi, His wife to make vp my mouthe, Not onely hir husbandes tauntyng tale auouthe, But therto deuiseth to cast in my teeth, Checks and chokyng oysters. *c.*1570: T. Preston, *Cambysses*, in Hazlitt, *Old Plays*, iv 175, According to the proverb old, My mouth I will up make. 1669: Shadwell, *Royal Shep.*, III i, My mother ... would have made a hard shift to have sat the upper end of my Lord Neander's table, to have had occasion to haye made up a fine mouth, and have said ... Before 1704: T. Brown, in *Works*, iv 202 (1760), All the while she was at church, she made up her mouth as demurely as the best of the congregation. 1888: *N.&Q.*, 7th ser, vi 38, 'A snack of bread and cheese to make up your mouth 'is often the goodwife's suggestion to her fanner lord [Shropsh.].

21. You cannot make an omelette without breaking eggs. *See* **Omelette**.

22. You cannot make bricks without straw. *See* **Bricks without straw.**

23. You can't make a silk purse out of a sow's ear. *See* **Silk purse.**

24. You make the better side the worse. 1678: Ray, 355 ... *Somerset.*

Malachi's child, choke full of sense, Like. 1906: *Cornish N.&Q.*, 266.

Malice hath a sharp sight and strong memory. 1650: Fuller, *Pisgah Sight*, bk ii ch iii, Yet we know malice hath a strong memory. 1732: Fuller, 3328.

Malice hurts itself most. 1639: Clarke, 197. 1732: Fuller, 3327, Malice drinketh up the greatest part of its own poison.

Malice is mindful. 1639: Clarke, 196. 1670: Ray, 118. 1732: Fuller, 3329.

Malice never spoke well. 1574: E. Hellowes, *Guevara's Epistles*, 492, Mallice findes manie faultes. 1605: Camden, *Remains*, 328 (1870).

Malice seldom wants a mark to shoot at. 1855: Bohn, 448.

Malpas ales and Malpas gales [S.W. winds] **Cheer the farmer, fill his pails.** 1917: Bridge, *Cheshire Proverbs*, 164.

Malpas shot. *See* **Higgledy-piggledy.**

Malt is above the water, The = He is drunk. 1678: Ray, 87. 1745: Franklin, *Drinker's Dict.*, in *Works*, ii 26 (Bigelow).

Malt is above wheat with him = He is drunk. 1546: Heywood, *Proverbs*, Pt I ch xi. 1588: Cogan, *Haven of Health*, 217 (1612), Take good heede that malt be not aboue wheate before you parte. *c.*1640: in *Roxb. Ballads*, ii 95 (Hindley), Men will call for it [tobacco] when malt's above wheat. 1824: Scott, *Redgauntlet*, ch xii, 'Come, come, Provost', said the lady, rising, 'if the maut gets abune the meal with you, it is time for me to take myself away'.

Malt to sell, They may sit in the chair that have. 1639: Clarke, 99. 1670: Ray, 68. 1732: Fuller, 4967.

Maltman comes on Monday, The. 1659: Howell, 9.

Malvern Hill. 1. All about Malvern Hill, A man may live as long as he will. 1882: Mrs Chamberlain. *W. Worcs. Words*, 39 (E.D.S.).

2. Go dig at Mavern Hill. Spoken of one whose wife 'wears the breeches'. 1659: Howell, 20. 1790: Grose, *Prov. Gloss.*, s.v. 'Worcestershire'.

Malvern measure, full and running over. 1894: Northall, *Folk Phrases*, 19 (E.D.S.).

Malvern. *See also* **Severn.**

Mamma's milk is scarce out of your nose yet, Your. 1732: Fuller, 6055.

Man and **Men. 1. A man, a horse, and a dog are never weary of each other's company.** 1749: W. Ellis, *Shep. Sure Guide, etc.*, 9 [quoted as a proverb].

2. A man among children will be long a child, a child among men will be soon a man. 1732: Fuller, 270.

3. A man assaulted is half taken. 1629: *Book of Meery Riddles*, Prov. 22.

4. A man at five may be a fool at fifteen. 1736: Bailey, *Dict.*, s.v. 'Five'. 1875: A. B. Cheales, *Proverb. Folk-Lore*, 48.

5. A man at sixteen will prove a child at sixty. 1732: Fuller, 273.

6. A man can do no more than he can. 1530: Palsgrave, 474, No man can do aboue his power. 1626: *Scoggins Jests*, 158 (1864), No man can aske more of a man than hee is able to doe. 1670: Ray, 67. 1814: Scott, in Lockhart's *Life*, iii 152, The islanders retort, that a man can do no more than he can. 1901: F. E. Taylor, *Lancs Sayings*, 11, A body conno' do mooar nor he con, con he?

7. A man cannot live by the air. 1633: Draxe, 180, A man cannot liue by thankes. 1670: Ray, 56. 1748: *Gent. Mag.*, xviii 21.

8. A man every inch of him. 1639: Clarke, 247. 1678: Ray, 76. 1698: *Terence made English*, 64 (2nd ed.), Thou'rt a man every inch of thee. 1870: Carlyle, in Forster's *Dickens*, iii 475, The good, the gentle, high-gifted, ever-friendly noble Dickens – every inch of him an Honest Man.

9. A man has choice to begin love, but not to end it. 1855: Bohn, 294.

10. A man has often more trouble to digest meat than to get it. Ibid., 294.

11. A man hath many enemies when his back is to the wall. 1639: Clarke, 166.

12. A man in distress or despair does as much as ten. 1732: Fuller, 282.

13. A man is a lion in his own cause. 1738: *Gent. Mag.*, 476.

14. A man is a man if he have but a nose on his *face.* 1612: Shelton, *Quixote*, Pt I bk iii ch xi, A man is but a man though he have a nose on his head. 1738: Swift, *Polite Convers.*, Dial. II.

15. A man is a man though he have but a nose on his head. This saying was popular in the 16th and 17th centuries, but its meaning is not clear. It may mean that a man is not to be judged by his apparel, however grotesque that may be. [*c.*1386: Chaucer, *Canon's Yeoman's Tale*, 1.171, Ther I was wont to be right fresh and gay Of clothing and of other good array, Now may I were an hose upon myn heed, And wher my colour was bothe fresh and reed, Now is it wan and of a leden hewe.] 1593: Nashe, in *Works*, ii 249 (Grosart). 1652: Tatham, *Scots Figgaries*, IV. 1664: Cotton, *Scarronides*, bk i. 1709: O. Dykes, *Eng. Proverbs*, 255 (2nd ed.), A man is a man still, if he hath but a hose on his head. 1732: Fuller, 277.

16. A man is as old (or young) as he feels (and a woman is as old as she looks). [Tam miser est quisque, quam credit. – Seneca, *Epist.*, 78.] 1871: V. Lush, *Thames Journal*, 27 Aug. (1975), 114, She is always making me out so much older than I am and that's not fair, for a man is only as old as he *feels*, and a woman is only as old as she *looks*. 1891: W. Morris, *News from Nowhere*, iii, 'How old am I, do you think?' 'Well,' quoth I, 'I have always been told that a woman is as old as she looks.' 1921: R. L. Gales, *Old-World Essays*, 243, 'You are always as young as you feel 'is a saying quoted in this book. I have heard it all my life. 1926: *Times*, 25 March, p. 14, col. 2, A fine figure of a man is Owen Keegan. 'A man is only as old as he feels,' he says.

17. A man is known by the company he keeps. 1541: M. Coverdale, tr. *H. Bullinger's Christian State of Matrimony*, F6, So maye much be spyed also, by the company and pastyme that a body useth. For a man is for the moost parte condicioned even lyke unto them that he kepeth company wythe all. 1591: H. Smith, *Preparative to Marriage*, If a man can be known by nothing els, then he maye bee known by his companions. 1620: Shelton, *Quixote*, Pt II ch lxviii, You may know the man by the conversation he keeps. 1672: Wycherley, *Love in a Wood*, I i, There is a proverb, Mrs Joyner, 'You may know him by his company'. 1748: Richardson, *Clarissa*, vi 362 (1785), Men are known by their companions. 1829: Cobbett, *Advice to Young Men*, Lett. 1, 'Show me a man's companions', says the proverb, 'and I will tell you what the man is'. 1871: Smiles, *Character*, 65, It is a common saying that men are known by the company they keep.

18. A man is not so soon healed as hurt. 1599: Porter, *Two Angry Women*, in Hazlitt, *Old Plays*, vii 357 [with 'whole' for 'healed']. 1670: Ray, 102. 1732: Fuller, 281.

19. A man is weal or woe, As he thinks himself so. [There is a base proverb, thou shalt bee so much esteemed by others, as thou esteemest thy selfe. – 1642: D. Rogers, *Naaman*, sig. E5.] 1732: Fuller, 6312.

20. A man may be an artist tho' he have not his tools about him. Ibid., No. 288.

21. A man may bear till his back break. 1611: Cotgrave, s.v. 'Sommer', *Tant travaille et tracasse l'homme, qu'en fin il se rompt, ou somme;* A man so long doth toile and swink, till under his own charge he sink. 1639: Clarke, 15. 1670: Ray, 59. 1732: Fuller, 3397 [in the plural].

22. A man may come soon enough to an ill bargain. 1633: Draxe, 54. 1639: Clarke, 157.

23. A man may hold his tongue. *See* **Hold one's tongue.**

24. A man may lose. *See* **Lose** (1) and (2).

25. A man may love his house well, though he ride not on the ridge. 1546: Heywood, *Proverbs*, Pt II ch iv 1560: T. Wilson, *Rhetorique*, 189 (1909). 1685: Meriton, *Yorkshire Ale*, 52, He can love the house well that hes [has] Tibb in, And not be alwayes rideing o' th' riggin. 1738: Swift, *Polite Convers.*, Dial. II, A man may love his house very well, without riding on the ridge. 1824: Scott, *Redgauntlet*, ch xiii, Well, now, you see one may love the Kirk, and yet not ride on the rigging of it.

26. A man must go old to the Court, and young to a cloister, that would go from thence to heaven. 1678: Ray, 117.

27. *A man of courage never wants weapons.* 1732: Fuller, 302.

28. *A man of many trades begs his bread on Sundays.* [1642: Fuller, *Holy State:* 'Lady Paula', I know two trades together are too much for one man to thrive upon.] 1732: Fuller, 304.

29. A man of straw is worth a woman of gold. 1591: Florio, *Second Frutes*, 173 [with 'more worth than' for 'worth']. 1647: Howell, *Letters*, bk ii No. iv. 1869: Spurgeon, *John Ploughman*, ch xvii, They say a man of straw is worth a woman of gold, but I cannot swallow it.

30. A man of words and not of deeds, Is like a garden full of weeds. 1659: Howell, 20. 1670: Ray, 211. 1706: Ward, *Hudibras Rediv.*, Pt 5, can. vii p. 9 [in the plural]. 1758: Franklin, in *Works*, iii 36 (Bigelow). 1869: Spurgeon, *John Ploughman*, ch xiv.

31. A man or a mouse. 1541: *Sch. House of Women*, l. 386, Fear not, she saith vnto her spouse, A man or a mouse whether be ye. 1590: *Tarltons Newes out of Purg.*, 54 (SH.S.), What, old acquaintance, a man or a mouse? *c.*1623: B.&F., *Love's Cure*, II ii, I will make a man or a mouse on you. 1681: W. Robertson, *Phraseol. Generalis*, 863. 1709: O. Dykes, *Eng. Proverbs*, 113 (2nd ed.), His … final resolution to make himself either a man or a mouse. 1843: Carlyle, *Past and Present*, bk ii ch vii, To see how Monks elect their Abbot in the Twelfth Century; how the St Edmundsbury mountain manages its midwifery; and what mouse or man the outcome is. 1901: F. E. Taylor, *Lancs Sayings*, 13, Aw'd oather be a mon or a meawse if aw were thee.

32. A man should keep from the blind. *See* quot. 1461: *Paston Lett.*, ii 73 (Gairdner), And also understondyng that he was kynnyes man to my master, and it is a comon proverbe, 'A man shuld kepe fro the blynde and gevyt to is kyn'.

33. A man surprised is half beaten. 1732: Fuller, 310.

34. A man that cannot sit still. *See* quot. 1662: Pepys, *Diary*, 8 Aug., Another rule is a proverb that he hath been taught, which is that a man that cannot sit still in his chamber … and he that cannot say no … is not fit for business.

35. A man that does what no other man does, is wondered at by all. 1387: Trevisa, tr. Higden, viii 19 (Rolls Ser.), that proverbe is ofte had in his mouth … 'Alle men wondreth of hym that doth as noon other doth'. *c.*1440: Anon., tr. Higden, viii 19 (Rolls Ser.), This proverbe: 'A man that doothe a thynge whiche noon other man usethe, causethe alle men to mervayle'.

36. A man that keeps riches and enjoys them not is like an ass that carries gold and eats thistles. 1732: Fuller, 312.

37. A man under no restraint is a bear without a ring. Ibid., No. 313.

38. A man will rather hurt his body than displease his palate. 1659: Howell, 1.

39. A man without money is a bow without an arrow. 1732: Fuller, 316.

40. A man without money is no man at all. Ibid., No. 317.

41. A man without reason is a beast in season. 1659: Howell, 11. 1670: Ray, 22. 1732: Fuller, 6244.

42. A man's best fortune, or his worst, is a wife. 1659: Howell, 5. 1732: Fuller, 306.

43. A man's country is where he does well. 1576: Pettie, *Petite Pall.*, i 40 (Gollancz), I count any place my country where I may live well and wealthily. 1599: Kyd, *Sol. and Perseda*, *IV*, And where a man lives well, there is his country. 1659: T. Pecke, *Parnassi Puerp.*, 94, My countrey is where ever I am well. 1732: Fuller, 5659, Wheresoever we live well, that is our country.

44. A man's praise in his own mouth doth stink. *c.*1615: *Times Whistle*, 37 (E.E.T.S.), Hast thou that aunctient, true saide sawe forgot, That 'a mans praise in his owne mouth doth stink'?

45. A man's wealth is his enemy. 1659: Howell, *Proverbs: Brit.-Eng.*, 3.

46. As a man is friended so the law is ended. 1538: Latimer, in *Works*, ii 399 (P.S.), The assize, where as men be friended, so (they say) things be ended, *c.*1542: Brinklow, *Complaynt*, 25 (E.E.T.S.). 1600: Day, *Blind Beggar*, III ii, Remember this old law 'As men are friended, So either right or wrong their sutes are ended'. 1681: W. Robertson, *Phraseol. Generalis*, 470, As a man is friended, so is his difference, or cause ended. 1738: *Gent. Mag.*, 475.

47. As a man lives, so shall he die; As a tree falls so shall it lie. 1678: Ray, 296.

48. Call no man happy till he dies. *See* **Happy till he dies.**

49. Every man thinks he may live another year. [Nemo enim est tam senex, qui se annum non putet posse vivere. – Cicero, *De Senect.*, vii 24.] *c.*1577: Northbrooke, *Dicing, etc.*, 14 (SH.S.), As Cicero saith, no man is so old and aged, that he perswadeth not him selfe that he may liue a whole yeare. 1669: *Politeuphuia*, 203, No man is so old, but thinketh he may yet live another year. 1784: Johnson, in Boswell's *Ltfe*, iv 270 (Hill), Yet we hope and hope, and fancy that he who has lived to-day may live to-morrow. Cf. **None so old.**

50. Give a man luck. *See* **Luck** (1).

51. He'll be a man among the geese. 1690: *New Dict. Canting Crew*, sig. F3, He'll be a man among the geese when the gander is gone.

52. If a man once fall, all will tread on him. 1530: Palsgrave, 757, Whan a man is thrown under the foote ones. [once], than every man gothe upon hym. 1618: B. Holyday, *Technogamia*, V iv, When a man's once downe, I perceiue he shall be trod vpon. 1681: W. Robertson, *Phraseol. Generalis*, 574. 1754: Berthelson, *Eng.-Danish Dict.*, s.v. 'Fall'.

53. If men become sheep, the wolf will devour them. 1611: Davies (of Hereford), *Sc. of Folly*, 42, in *Works*, ii (Grosart).

54. It is meet that a man be at his own bridal. 1546: Heywood, *Proverbs*, Pt I ch i vi. 1633: Draxe, 230 [with 'euery' for 'a'].

55. Man doth what he can and God what He will. 1633: Draxe, 80 *bis*. 1670: Ray, 97. 1736: Bailey, *Dict.*, s.v. 'Man'.

56. Man hath as many diseases as a horse.
1660: Howell, *Parly of Beasts*, 77.

57. Man is a God to man. 1548: Hall, *Chron.*, 324 (1809), The olde Greke prouerbe to bee very trew, which is that a man to a man shall sometyme be as a God. 1566: L. Wager, *Mary Magd.*, sig. C3. 1630: T. Adams, *Works*, 190. Before 1680: Butler, *Remains*, ii 378 (1759). The philosopher said – Man to man is a God and a wolf.

58. Man is a wolf to man. [Lupus homo homini. – Plautus, *As.*, II iv 88.] *c.*1577: Northbrooke, *Dicing, etc.*, 57 (SH.S.), A man is a wolfe to a man, that is, a devourer one of another. 1585: Sir E. Dyer, in *Writings*, 90 (Grosart), We are (by our owne censures) iudged wolues one to another. 1620: Ford, *Line of Life*, 50 (SH.S.), The old proverbe was … that a man is a beast to a man. 1707: Dunton, *Athen. Sport*, 251, 'Tis enmity makes one man a wolf to another.

59. Man is the head but woman turns it. 1875: A. B. Cheales, *Proverb. Folk-Lore*, 12. 1913: *Folk-Lore*, xxiv 76, [Oxfordsh.] The man's the head, and the woman's the neck, and the neck turns the head. 1917: Bridge, *Cheshire Proverbs*, 93.

60. Man is the measure of all things. A saying originally found in Plato. 1547: W. Baldwin, *Morall Phylosophie*, III, xvi, O6v, Man is the measure of all thynges. 1631: G. Chapman, *Warres of Pompey and Caesar*, ii E2, As of all things man is said the measure, So your full merits measure forth a man.

61. Man proposes, God disposes. [A man's heart deviseth his way; but the Lord directeth his steps. – *Prov.* xvi 9. Sed sicut scriptum esse, Homo cogitat, Deus ordinat. – Ord. Vitalis, *Eccles. Hist.*, bk iii Nam homo proponit, sed Deus disponit. – A'Kempis, *De Imit.*, lib. i cap. xix.] 1377: Langland, *Plowman*, B, xi 36, 'Homo proponit', quod a poete and Plato he hyght, 'And Deus disponit,' quod he. 1509: Bp. Fisher, *Eng. Works*, 222 (E.E.T.S.), It is a comyn prouerbe … Man purposeth and god dysposeth. 1576: Pettie, *Petite Pall.*, ii 44 (Gollancz) [as in 1509], 1640: Herbert, *Jac. Prudentum.* 1700: T. Brown, tr. Scarron, ii 64 (1892). 1854: J. W. Warter, *Last of Old Squires*, 53.

62. Man, remember thy end, And thou shall never be shend. 15th cent.: in *Reliq. Antiquae*, i 316 (1841).

63. Mans best candle [is his] **understanding.** 1659: Howell, *Proverbs: Brit.-Eng.*, 14.

64. Man's extremity. *See* **Need** (6).

65. Man's life is filed by his foe. 1659: Howell, *Proverbs: Brit.-Eng.*, 19.

66. May the man be damned and never grow fat, who wears two faces under one hat. 1855: Bohn, 451.

67. Men are April when they woo, December when they wed. Ibid., 451.

68. Men are never wise but returning from law. 1623: Wodroephe, *Spared Houres*, 501.

69. Men are not to be measured by inches. 1732: Fuller, 3390.

70. Men dream in courtship but in wedlock wake. 1875: A. B. Cheales, *Proverb. Folk-Lore*, 38.

71. Men fear death. *See* **Death** (8).

72. Men may meet but mountains never. *c.*1541: *Mellynge of Dr Barnes and Dr Powell*, It is sene often That men mete now and than, But so do hylles never. 1590: *Three Lords, etc.*, in Hazlitt, *Old Plays*, vi 410, Men may meet, though mountains cannot. 1611: Cotgrave, s.v. 'Montaigne', Men meet often, mountaines never. 1681: W. Robertson, *Phraseol. Generalis*, 760. 1736: Bailey, *Dict.*, s.v. 'Men', Men meet but mountains never greet. 1823: Scott, *Q. Durward*, ch xxxi, Mountains, it is said, may meet, and why not mortal creatures … ?

73. Men muse as they use. 1583: Melbancke, *Philotinus*, sig. G3, Use not, as you muse. 1639: Clarke, 64, You muse as you use. 1670: Ray, 123. 1685: Meriton, *Yorkshire Ale*, 71, You meause wife as ye use. 1710: S. Palmer, *Moral Essays on Proverbs*, 39.

74. Men of principle. See quot. 1820: Colton, *Lacon*, Pref., The old adage may be verified, that 'the men of principle may be the principal men'.

75. Men shut their doors against a setting sun. 1607: Shakespeare, *Timon*, I ii.

76. Men use to worship the rising sun. Before 1634: Chapman, *Alphonsus*, I i, Men rather honour the sun rising than the sun going down. 1639: Clarke, 12. 1670: Ray, 137. 1732: Fuller, 3470, Most men worship the rising sun.

77. Men's vows are women's traitors. 1855: Bohn, 452.

78. Men's years and their faults are always more than they are willing to own. Ibid., 452.

79. No man is a hero to his valet. *See* **Hero**.

80. One man's loss is another man's gain. *See* **Loss**.

81. One man's meat is another man's poison.
See **Meat** (9).

82. The man of God is better by having his bows and arrows about him. 1659: Howell, 4.

83. The man shall have his mare again. 1595: Shakespeare, *Mids. N. Dream*, III ii, The man shall have his mare again, and all shall be well. 1653: R. Brome, *Damoiselle*, IV ii [as in 1595]. 1694: Dryden, *Love Triumphant*, III ii., Then all shall be set right, and the man, etc. 1712: Addison, *Spectator*, No. 481, Honest Sampson ... solves it very judiciously, by the old proverb, that if his first master be still living, *The man must have his mare again.* 1738: Swift, *Polite Convers.*, Dial. I, *Col* ... but her parents forced her to take the old fellow for a good settlement. *Ld. Sparkish.* So the man got his mare again. 1827: Creevey, in *C. Papers*, ii 123 (1904) (OED), No tidings of the Beau yet! but he must have his mare again.

84. Those, or that which, a man knows best, he must use most. [*c.*1384: Chaucer, *H. Fame*, bk i l. 290, Therfor I wol seye a proverbe, That 'he that fully knoweth therbe May saufly leye hit to his yë'.] 1611: Cotgrave, s.v. 'Herbe'.

85. What's a man but his mind? 1639: Clarke, 16.

86. When a man grows angry his reason rides out. 1732: Fuller, No.5533.

87. You'll needs be a man before your time. 1639: Clarke, 267.

See also **Every man; No man; So many; way; Wise man;** and **young.**

Man, *verb.* He that is manned with boys and horsed with colts shall have his meat eaten and his work undone. 1605: Camden, *Remains*, 323 (1870). 1670: Ray, 118. 1732: Fuller, 2286. 1846: Denham, *Proverbs*, 6 (Percy S.).

Manchester bred: long in the arms, and short in the head. 1869: Hazlitt, 273.

Manchester says today, the rest of England says tomorrow, What. A saying that dates from the time in the early nineteenth century when Manchester (and the rest of Lancashire) were at the forefront of opposition to the Corn Laws. It is often applied to other cities and other places. 1898: R. Kipling, *The Day's Work*, 51, What the horses o' Kansas think today, the horses of America will think tomorrow. 1902: V S. Lean, *Collectanea*, I 116, What Lancashire thinks today all England will think tomorrow. This was in the days of the Anti-Corn-Law League. Since then the initiative in political movements proceeds from Birmingham.

Manners and money make a gentleman. 1732: Fuller, 3333.

Manners make often fortunes. 1670: Ray. 17.

Manners make the man *or* **Manners maketh man.** The motto of William of Wykeham (1324–1404), bishop of Winchester, chancellor of England, and the founder of both Winchester College and New College, Oxford. *c.*1350 *Douce Ms 52*, no. 77, Maner makys man. *c.*1450: in *Archiv* (1931), CLIX. 88, Maners and clothyng makes man. *c.*1460: in *Babees Book*, etc., 14 (E.E.T.S.), Nurtur and good maners maketh man. 1513: Bradshaw, *St Werburge*, 131 (E.E.T.S.), Good maners and conynge maken a man. 1602: Rowlands, *Merrie when Goss. meete*, 44 (Hunt.Cl.), The prouerbe sayes 'tis manners that doth make. 1659: Howell, 16, Manners make a man, quoth William of Wickham. 1694: D'Urfey, *Quixote*, Pt II Act I sc i [as in 1659, but with 'the' for 'a']. 1729: Defoe, *Compl. Gent.*, Pt I ch i p. 18 (1890), The manners make the man. 1732: Fuller, 3334 [as in 1659]. 1887: E. J. Hardy, *Manners makyth Man* [title]. 1922: in *Sphere*, 5 Aug., 142, 'Manners', they say, 'make the man'. I maintain also that a climate makes manners.

Manners. *See also* **Unmannerliness.**

Manxton. *See* **Heytor.**

Many. *See also* **So many.**

Many a little makes a mickle. [εἰ γάρ κεν καὶ σμικρὸν ἐπὶ σμικρῷ καταθεῖο, καὶ θαμὰ τοῦτ' ἔρδοις, τάχα κεν μέγα καὶ τὸ γένοιτο. Hesiod, *Works and Days*, 359–60] Before 1225: *Ancren R.*, 54, thus ofte, ase me seith, of lutel wacseth muchel. 1303: Brunne, *Handl. Synne*, l. 2366, For many smale maketh a grete. *c.*1386: Chaucer, *Parson's Tale*, § 21, Manye smale maken a greet. 1546: Heywood, *Proverbs*, Pt I ch xi [as in 1386]. 1593: G. Harvey, *Works*, ii 311 (Grosart), Many a little, by little and little maketh a mickle. 1616: *Jack Drum*, I, in Simpson, *Sch. of Shakesp.*, ii 137, Oh, sir, many a small make a great. 1680: L'Estrange, *Select Colloq. of Erasmus*, 19. 1712: *Spectator*, No. 509. 1758: Franklin, *Poor Rich. Imp.*, in Arber, *Garner*, v 582 (1882). 1869: Spurgeon, *John Ploughman*, ch ix, Many littles make a mickle.

Many a man singeth. *See* quots. *c.*1300: *Prov. of*

Alfred, in *Reliq. Antiquae*, i 178 (1841), Monymon singeth, that wif horn bryngeth; wiste he hwat he brouhte, wepen he myhte. *c.*1320: in Ibid., i 112, 'Moni mon syngeth When he hom bringeth Is yonge wyf; Wyste wot he brohte, Wepen he mohte, Er his lyf syth'; Quoth Hendyng.

Many a mickle makes a muckle. A variant of **Many a little makes a mickle** (q.v.) that is thought of as Scottish. The Scottish origins are dubious and in this form the proverb is, strictly speaking, nonsensical, in that both *mickle* and *muckle* mean "a large amount". 1793: G. Washington, *Writings* (1939), XXXII. 423, A Scotch addage, than which nothing in nature is more true … 'many mickles make a muckle'. 1940: *Huntly Express*, 19 Jan., 3, He said at the close of his address 'As the Scots say, and they should know, mony a mickle mak's a muckle' … As the Scots know, he had quoted the proverb wrongly.

Many a miller. *See* **Miller** (8).

Many a one for land takes a fool by the hand. *c.*1320: in *Reliq. Antiquae*, i 115 (1841), 'Moni mon for londe wyveth to shonde'; Quoth Hendyng. 1639: Clarke, 99, For a little land, take a fool by the hand. 1670: Ray, 116 [as in 1639]. 1678: Ray, 56. 1732: Fuller, 6263.

Many a one says well that thinks ill. 1738: Swift, *Polite Convers.*, Dial. I.

Many a slip between cup and lip, There's. *See* **Cup** (4).

Many are called but few are chosen. [Matthew xxii.14, For many are called but few are chosen.] 1871: J.S.Jones, *Life of J. S. Batkins*, xxviii, The saying that 'many are called, but few are chosen'.

Many a true word spoken in jest, There's. *See* **True** (17).

Many by wit purchase wealth, but none by wealth purchase wit. 1647: *Countrym. New Commonwealth*, 15.

Many can bear adversity, but few contempt. 1732: Fuller, 3340.

Many can brook the weather that love not the wind. 1592: Shakespeare, *L.L.L.*, IV ii.

Many dishes make many diseases. 1655: T. Muffett, *Healths Improvement*, 272 [quoted as a proverb].

Many dogs may easily worry one. 1639: Clarke, 56.

Many drops make a shower. 1616: *Honest*

Lawyer, sig. G2, Many drops; make a floud. 1736: Bailey, *Dict.*, s.v. 'Drop'. 1846: Denham, *Proverbs*, 1 (Percy S.).

Many drops of water will sink a ship. 1732: Fuller, 3345.

Many estates are spent in the getting, Since women for tea forsook spinning and knitting, And men for punch forsook hewing and splitting. 1736: Franklin, *Way to Wealth*, in *Works*, i 446 (Bigelow). 1883: Burne, *Shropsh. Folk-Lore*, 578 [as in 1736, but with 'their beer' for 'punch'. Given as a Chirbury saying].

Many friends no friend. 1875: A. B. Cheales, *Proverb, Folk-Lore*, 96. Cf. **Friend** (8).

Many frosts and many thowes, Make many rotten yowes [ewes]. 1846: Denham, *Proverbs*, 62´ (Percy S.). 1872: J. Glyde, jr., *Norfolk Garland*, 157.

Many hands make light work. *c.*1330: *Sir Beves* (E.E.T.S.), l. 3352, Ascopard be strong and sterk, Mani hondes maketh light werk. 1401: in Wright, *Pol. Poems*, ii 106 (Rolls Ser., 1861), Yit many hondis togider maken ligt werk. *c.*1460: *How the Goode Wife*, in Hazlitt, *Early Pop. Poetry*, i 188, Many handys make light werke, my leue childe. *c.*1550: *Parl. of Byrdes*, l.192, in Ibid., iii 177. 1634: G. Markham, *Art of Archerie*, 20. 1665: Head and Kirkman, *Eng. Rogue*, i 164. 1732: Fuller, 3347. 1923: *Observer*, 11 Feb., p. 9, col. 7, What is the use of saying that 'Many hands make light work 'when the same copybook tells you that 'Too many cooks spoil the broth '?

Many hands will carry off much plunder. 1725: Bailey, tr. Erasmus' *Colloq.*, 342 [cited as 'the old saying'].

Many hare been ruined by buying good penny worths. 1732: Fuller, 3349. 1736: Franklin, *Way to Wealth*, in *Works*, i 447 (Bigelow).

Many haws. *See* **Haws.**

Many-headed beast, The = The multitude. [Bellua multorum es capitum. – Horace, *Epist.*, I i.] 1542: Udall, tr. Erasmus' *Apoph.*, 122 (1877), The multitude of the grosse people, being a beaste of many heades. 1580: Sidney, *Arcadia*, 226 (1893), O weak trust of the many-headed multitude. 1604: Webster, etc., *Malcontent*, III iii, That beast with many heads, The staggering multitude. 1604: J. Wilson, *Andron. Commenius*, III ii., What is this giddy multitude? – this beast Of many heads? 1734: Pope, *Imit. Horace, Epist.* I i l. 121, The people are a many-headed beast. 1773: in *Garrick Corresp.*, i 527 (1831), The public is a many-headed, monster and hard to please. 1810: Scott, *Lady of Lake*, can. v st. 30, Thou many-headed monster-thing. Oh, who would wish to be thy king! 1834–7: Southey, *Doctor*, interch. xxi. I will tell you [the public] what you are; you are a great, ugly, many-headed beast.

Many hips and haws, Many frosts and snaws. 1846: Denham, *Proverbs*, 24 (Percy S.). 1913: E. M. Wright, *Rustic Speech, etc.*, 318, Many hips, many haas, Many frosts, many snaas. Cf. **Haws.**

Many humble servants, but not one true friend. 1732: Fuller, 3350.

Many kinsfolk and few friends. 1546: Heywood, *Proverbs*, Pt I ch xi. 1616: *Rich Cabinet*, fo. 50, A man may haue many kinsfolks, but few friends. 1639: Clarke, 26. 1710: S. Palmer, *Moral Essays on Proverbs*, 252, Many relations, few friends.

Many knacks in his budget, He hath. 1659: Howell, 14.

Many lords many laws. 1633: Draxe, 7.

Many masters. *See* **Toad** (2).

Many men have many minds, But women have but two: Everything would they have, And nothing would they do. Lanes. 1865: *N.&Q.*, 3rd ser, viii 494. 1891: *N.&Q.*, 7th ser, xii 373.

Many nuts (or nits). *See* **Nut** (3).

Many rains, many rowans [mountain-ash berries]; **Many rowans, many yawns.** 1846: Denham, *Proverbs*, 54 (Percy S.).

Many relations. *See* **Many kinsfolk**.

Many sands will sink a ship. 1630: T. Adams, *Works*, 708, Many little sands gather'd to an heape, faile not to swallow a greet vessell. 1639: Clarke, 11. 1670: Ray, 118.

Many seames many beanes. Glos. 1639: in *Berkeley MSS.*, iii 33 (1885).

Many slones [sloes] **many groans.** 1850: *N.&Q.*, 1st ser, ii 511. 1884: H. Friend, *Flowers and Fl. Lore*, 207, In Cornwall they have a proverb … 'Many slones, many groans'.

Many speak much who cannot speak well. 1633: Draxe, 11. 1670: Ray, 17.

Many strike on an anvil, When, they must strike by measure. 1670: Ray, 17. 1732: Fuller, 5561 [with 'observe order' for 'strike by measure'].

Many strokes. *See* **Little strokes**.

Many things are lost for want of asking. 1640: Herbert, *Joe. Prudentum*.

Many things grow in the garden which were never sowed. 1659: Howell, *Proverbs: Span.-Eng.*, 6. 1670: Ray, 12. 1732: Fuller, 3363.

Many things lawful are not expedient. 1855: Bohn, 450.

Many ventures make a full freight. 1633: Draxe, 5. 1670: Ray, 17. 1694: D'Urfey, *Quixote*, Pt II Act IV sc ii.

Many wells, many buckets. 1546: Heywood, *Proverbs*, Pt II ch vii. 1633: Draxe, 237.

Many without punishment, but none without fault. 1633: Draxe, 62. 1670: Ray, 17 [with 'sin' for 'fault'].

Many women. *See* **Woman** (31).

Many words hurt. *See* **Word** (16).

Many words, In. *See* quots. 1548: Hall, *Chron.*, Dedn., I haue redde an olde prouerbe, whiche saithe, that in many woordes, a lye or twayne sone maie scape. 1633: Draxe, 11, Where many words are the truth often goeth by.

Many words will not fill a bucket. 1659: Howell, 9. 1712: Motteux, *Quixote*, Pt I bk iii ch iv [with 'bushel' for 'bucket']. 1732: Fuller, 3365 [as in 1712].

Marazion to learn manners, You must go to. 1864: 'Cornish Proverbs', in *N.&Q.*, 3rd ser, v 275.

Marazion. *See also* **Market-Jew**.

Marbles. *See* quot. 1880: Courtney, *W. Cornwall Words*, xiii (E.D.S.), Those that have marbles may play, but those that have none must look on.

March, *subs.* **1. A bushel of March dust is worth a king's ransom.** 1533: Heywood, *Play of Weather*, 114 (Farmer). 1580: Tusser, *Husbandrie*, 97 (E.D.S.), March dust to be sold, Worth ransome of gold. 1662: Fuller, *Worthies*, i 120 (1840), In England a bushel, etc. 1732: Fuller, 30. 1753: *Gent. Mag.*, 267 [with 'peck' for 'bushel'. Midland Counties). 1812: Brady, *Clavis Cal.*, i 66. 1893: Inwards, *Weather Lore*, 18 [both 'bushel' and 'peck'].

2. A damp rotten March gives pain to farmers. Ibid., 19, March damp and warm Will do farmer much harm.

3. A dry March and a wet May Fill barns and bays with corn and hay. 1886: Holland, *Cheshire Gloss.*, 443 (E.D.S.). 1917: Bridge, *Cheshire Proverbs*, 162.

4. A dry March, an' a windy; A full barn an' a findy. 1876: C. C. Robinson, *Mid-Yorks Gloss.*, 40 (E.D.S.).

5. A dry March never begs its bread. 1846: Denham, *Proverbs*, 31 (Percy S.). 1893: Inwards, *Weather Lore*, 18 [with 'and cold' after 'dry'].

6. A dry March, wet April, and cool May, Fill barn, cellar, and bring much hay. Ibid., 20.

7. A fair March is worth a king's ransom. *c.*1598: Jonson, *Case is Altered*, V iv.

8. A March sun sticks like a lock of wool. 1893: Inwards, *Weather Lore*, 19.

9. A March wind is salt which seasoneth all pulse. *c.*1620: Markham, *Farew. to Husbandry*, 95 (1676) [quoted as 'an old saying among the best' farmers].

10. A March wisher (or whisker) Is never a good fisher. 1732: Fuller, 6127 ['whisker']. 1893: Inwards, *Weather Lore*, 19 ['wisher'].

11. A peck of March dust and a shower in May, Makes the corn green and the fields gay. 1732: Fuller, 6476. 1893: Inwards, 18.

12. A wet March makes a sad harvest. 1878: Dyer, *Eng. Folk-Lore*, 252. 1893: Inwards, 19.

13. A windy March and a rainy April make May beautiful. 1659: Howell, *Proverbs: Span.-Eng.*,21. 1732: Fuller, 468. 1893: Inwards, 20.

14. As it rains in March, so it rains in June. Ibid., 20.

15. As much dew in March, so much fog rises in August. Ibid., 19.

16. As much fog in March, so much rain in summer. Ibid., 19.

17. Dust in March brings grass and foliage. Ibid., 18.

18. Fog in March, thunder in July. Ibid., 19.

19. In beginning or in end, March its gifts will send. Ibid., 18.

20. In March, kill crow, pie and cadow [jackdaw], Rook, buzzard, and raven; Or else go desire them To seek a new haven. 1846: Denham, *Proverbs*, 35 (Percy S.).

21. In March, the birds begin to search; in April, the corn begins to fill; in May, the birds begin to lay. 1869: Hazlitt, 233.

22. In Valentine March lays her line. Ibid., 235.

23. March birds are best. 1678: Ray, 344. 1732: Fuller; No. 3368. 1846: Denham, *Proverbs*, 31 (Percy S.). 1904: *Co. Folk-Lore: Northumb.*, 176 (F.L.S.).

24. March borrows. *See* quots. 1646: Browne, *Pseudo. Epi.*, bk vi ch iv, So is it usual among us … to ascribe unto March certain borrowed days from April. 1670: Ray, 41, April borrows three days of March and they are ill. 1687: Aubrey, *Gentilisme, etc.*, 95 (F.L.S.) [as in 1670]. 1710: *Brit. Apollo*, iii No. 18, col. 4, March borrows of April Three days, and they are ill; April returns them back again Three days, and they are rain. 1732: Fuller, Nos. 6133, 6134, March borrows of April Three days, and they be ill. April borrows of March again Three days of wind and rain. 1893: Inwards, 22, [as in 1732, *plus*] *March* borrowed of April, April borrowed of May, Three days, they say; One rained, and one snew, And the other was the worst day that ever blew. Staffs. March borrowed from April Three days, and they were ill: The first of them is wan and weet, The second it is snaw and sleet, The third of them is peel-a-bane, And freezes the wee bird's neb to the stane. 1921: R. L. Gales, *Old-World Essays*, 250, March borrowed a cloak from his father and pawned it after three days. Cf. **Borrowing days**.

25. March comes in like a lion and goes out like a lamb – very occasionally reversed. 1624: Beaumont & Fletcher, *Wife for a Month*, II i, *Men.* I would choose March, for I would come in like a lion. *Tony.* But you'd go out like a lamb, when you went to hanging. 1670: Ray, 41, March hackham comes in, etc. 1740: North, *Lives of Norths*, i 259 (Bohn), Then came my Lord Shaftesbury, like the month of March, as they say, 'in like a lion, and out like a lamb'. 1849: Brontë, *Shirley*, ch xv, Like March, having come in tike a lion, he purposed to go out tike a lamb. 1893: Inwards, 19, March, black ram Comes in, etc. Ibid., 20, March comes in like a lamb and goes out tike a lion. 1921: *Sphere*, 12 March, p. 254, col. 1, In all proper well-regulated years March comes in like a lion and goes out like a lamb.

26. March comes in with an adder's head, and goes out with a peacock's tail. 1846: Denham, *Proverbs*, 32 (Percy S.). 1921: R. L. Gales, *Old-World Essays*, 250.

27. March dry, good rye; April wet, good wheat. 1893: *Co. Folk-Lore: Suffolk*, 162 (F.L.S.).

28. March dust on an apple-leaf brings all kinds of fruit to grief. 1876: Bull, *Pomona Hereford.*, 50.

29. March flowers make no summer bowers. 1893: Inwards, 18.

30. March grass never did good. 1678: Ray, 44. 1732: Fuller, 6475. 1846: Denham, *Proverbs*, 31 (Percy S.). 1904: *Co. Folk-Lore: Northumb.*, 175 (F.L.S.).

31. March grows never dows [flourishes]. 1855: Robinson, *Whitby Gloss.*, 48, 'March grows Never dows'. March blossom, being premature, is often blighted.

32. March many weathers. 1678: Ray, 44. 1732: Fuller, 6475, March many weathers rain'd and blow'd. 1893: Inwards, *Weather Lore*, 18. 1912: R. L. Gales, *Studies in Arcady*, 2nd ser, 104.

33. March rain spoils more than clothes. 1659: Howell, *Proverbs: Span.-Eng.*, 21, March water is worse than a stain in cloath. 1882: Mrs Chamberlain, *W. Worcs. Words*, 37 (E.D.S.). 1893: Inwards, 19 [as in 1659 and 1882].

34. March, search; April, try; May will prove if you live or die. 1855: *N. & Q.*, 1st ser, xi 416. 1893: Inwards, 20.

35. March sun lets snow stand on a stone. Ibid., 18.

36. March thunder makes all the world wonder. 1895: Rye, *E. Anglian Words*, 228 (E.D.S.).

37. March wind and May sun Makes clothes white and maids dun. 1670: Ray, 41. 1744: Claridge, in Mills, *Essay on Weather*, 100 (1773). 1882: *N. & Q.*, 6th ser, vi 14. 1893: Inwards, 20.

38. March wind kindles the ether [adder] and blooms the whin. 1846: Denham, *Proverbs*, 39 (Percy S.).

39. March winds and April showers Bring forth May flowers. 1886: Elworthy, *West Som. Word-Book*, 461 (E.D.S.). 1893: Inwards, 20.

40. March yeans the lammie And buds the thorn, And blows through the flint Of an ox's horn. Northumb. Ibid., 18.

41. Never come March, never come winter. 1882: Mrs Chamberlain, *W. Worcs. Words*, 37 (E.D.S.).

42. On the first of March, The crows begin to search. 1846: Denham, *Proverbs*,. 39 (Percy S.).

43. So many fogs in March, so many frosts in May. 1669: *New Help to Discourse*, 284, So many mists as there be in March, so many hoar frosts there will be after Easter. 1732: Fuller, 6474, So many mists as in March you see, So many frosts in May will be. 1823: Moor, *Suffolk Words*, 510. 1830: Forby, *Vocab. E. Anglia*, 416. 1879: *N. Q.*, 5th ser, xi 327, 'Fogs in March, frosties in May'

is a common proverb in this part of Surrey [Limpsfield]. 1893: Inwards, 19, [as in 1732, *plus*] As many mistises in March, So many frostises in May. – Wilts. Ibid., 20, Mists in March bring rain, Or in May frosts again.

44. So many frosts in March so many in May. 1659: Howell, 16, If frost in March, there will be some in May. 1737: Ray, 269. 1893: Inwards, 19.

45. The March sun causeth dust, and the wind blows it about. 1670: Ray, 17.

46. *The March sun raises but dissolves not.* 1640: Herbert, *Jac. Prudentam.*

47. Whatever March does not want, April brings along. 1893: Inwards, 23.

48. When it thunders in March, it brings sorrow. Ibid., 19.

See also **April** (22); **Borrowing days; Cuckoo** (4), (12), (13), and (16); **February** (6), (8), and (18); **Frosty winter; January** (1), (14), and (21); **Leeks; Nettles** (3); **September** (2); and **Wheat** (2).

Mare. 1. A mare's shoe and a horse's shoe are both alike. 1732: Fuller, 318.

2. If the mare have a bald [white] **face, the filly will have a blaze.** 1659: Howell, 2. 1696: D'Urfey, *Quixote*, Pt III Act I. 1732: Fuller, 5596. 1828: Carr, *Craven Dialect*, i 21.

3. I'll not go before my mare to the market. 1678: Ray, 259.

4. Mares' tails. *See* **Mackerel sky.**

5. There are more mares in the wood than Grisell. 1678: Ray, 173.

6. To find a mare's nest. 1576: R. Peterson, *Galateo*, 111 (1892), Nor stare in a mans face, as if he had spied a mares nest. 1582: Breton, *Works*, i a 6 (Grosart), To laughe at a horse nest, and whine too like a boy. 1619: B.&F., *Bonduca*, V ii, Why dost thou laugh? What mare's nest hast thou found? 1704: D'Urfey, *Tales Trag. and Comical*, 216 n., An old wife's saw … He has found a mare's nest, and laughs at the eggs. 1864: 'Cornish Proverbs', in *N. & Q.*, 3rd ser, vi 494, They have found a wee's nest [mare's nest], and are laughing over the eggs. 1922: Weyman, *Ovington's Bank*, ch xxxii.

7. Whose mare is dead? = What's the trouble? 1595: *Maroccus Extaticus*, 5 (Percy S.), Whose mare is dead, that you are thus melancoly? *c.*1598: Deloney, *Gentle Craft*, Pt II ch iii. 1598: Shakespeare, 2 *Henry IV*, II i, How now! whose mare's dead? What's the matter? 1738: Swift, *Polite Convers*, Dial, I.

See also **Horse** (52); **Man** (83); **Money** (33): **Ride; Simper as a mare;** and **Tale**(7).

Margaret's flood [Devon] = heavy rain about St Margaret's Day – 20 July. 1850: *N. & Q.*, 1st ser, ii 512.

Margery, good cow. *See* quots. 1546: Heywood, *Proverbs*, Pt II ch vii, Margery good coowe, (quoth he), gaue a good meele, But than she cast it downe again with hir heele. 1639: Clarke, 83 ['gives' for 'gave', and 'kicks' for 'cast']. 1670: Ray, 185, Madge, good cow, gives a good pail of milk, and then kicks it down with her foot.

Mariners' craft it the grossest, yet of handicrafts the subtillest. 1629: *Book of Meery Riddles*, Prov. 101.

Mark after her mother, She hath a. 1678: Ray, 259.

Market. 1. As the market goes wives must sell. 1732: Fuller, 734.

2. Forsake not the market for [because of] **the toll.** 1605: Camden, *Remains*, 322 (1870). 1670: Ray, 119. 1736: Bailey, *Dict.*, s.v. 'Toll'.

3. My market's made. 1590: Lodge, *Rosalynde*, 104 (Hunt.Cl.), Well, sir, if your market may be made no where els, home again. 1649: Quarles, *Virgin Widow*, I, Is it even so? Quack's thread is fairly spun, Quack may go home again, his market's done. 1724: Defoe, *Roxana*, in *Works*, xiii 143 (Boston, 1903), 'In her coach!' said I; 'upon my word, she had made her market then; I suppose she made hay while the sun shone.'

4. No man makes haste to the market where there's nothing to be bought but blows. 1670: Ray, 119. 1732: Fuller, 3651.

5. The market is the best garden. 1640: Herbert, *Joe. Prudentum.* 1670: Ray, 17, [as in 1640, *plus*] At London they are wont to say, Cheapside is the best garden.

6. You may know by the market folks how the market goes. 1546: Heywood, *Proverbs*, Pt I ch xi, Men know … How the market goth by the market men. *c.*1594: Bacon, *Promus*, No. 642. 1600: Day, *Blind Beggar*, IV iii. 1670: Ray, 119. 1716: Ward, *Female Policy*, 94. 1732: Fuller, 5952.

Market-Jew = Marazion, Corn. *In your own light like the Mayor of Market-Jew.* 1859: *N. & Q.*, 2nd ser, viii 451. 1906: Q.-Couch, *Mayor of Troy*, Prol. *See also* **Marazion**.

Mark Lane. *See* quot. 1591: Greene, *Works*, x 99 (Grosart), Perceiued he was bitten [cheated] of all the bite [money] in his bung [purse], and turned to walke penylesse in Marke lane, as the old prouerbe is.

Marls sand, He that. *See* quots. 1753: *Gent. Mag.*, 120, We have an old saying [Lancs]: He that marls sand, may buy land; He that marls moss, suffers no loss; But he that marls clay, throws his money away. 1815: W. Peck, *Topog. Acc. of Isle of Axholme*, 47, If you marle sand, you may buy land; If you marle moss, you shall have no loss; But if you marie clay, you throw all away. 1889: Peacock, *Manley, etc.*, *Goss.*, 341 (E.D.S.) [as in 1815, but with 'there is' for 'you shall have', and 'fling' for 'throw']. 1908: W. Johnson, *Folk Memory*, 220 [as in 1889]. 1917: Bridge, *Cheshire Proverbs*, 72, He who marls sand may buy the land.

Marriage. 1. At marriages and funerals friends are discerned from kinsfolk. 1578: Florio, *First Fruites*, fo. 25, At mariages and burials friends and kinrede is knowen. 1629: *Book of Meery Riddles*, Prov. 55 [as in 1578]. 1732: Fuller, 829.

2. He has a great fancy to marriage that goes to the devil for a wife. Ibid., No. 1856.

3. Marriage and hanging go by destiny. 1519: Horman, *Vulgaria*, fo. 19, It is my destenye to be hanged. 1546: Heywood, *Proverbs*, Pt I ch iii, Wedding is destiny And hanging likewise, saith that proverb. 1595: Shakespeare, *M. of Venice*, II ix, The ancient saying is no heresy. Hanging and wiving goes by destiny. 1624: B.&F., *Wife for a Month*, II i 1664: Butler, *Hudibras*, Pt II can. i l. 839, If matrimony and hanging go By dest'ny, why not whipping too? 1784: *New Foundl. Hosp. for Wit*, v 106.

4. Marriage is a lottery. 1875: Smiles, *Thrift*, 252, The maxim is current, that 'marriage is a lottery'.

5. Marriage is honourable but housekeeping is a shrew. 1616: Breton, *Works*, ii e 8 (Grosart), Marriage is honourable. 1670: Ray, 48. 1780: *Mother Bunch*, 2nd pt, 28 (Gomme, 1885), For although housekeeping is chargeable, yet marriage is honourable.

6. Marriage leapeth up upon the saddle, and repentance upon the crupper. 1669: *Politeuphuia*, 35. 1732: Fuller, 3372.

7. Marriage with peace is this world's Paradise; with strife, this life's Purgatory. 1669: *Politeuphuia*, 227.

8. Marriages are made in heaven. [A prudent wife is from the Lord. – *Prov.* xix. 14.] 1567: Painter, *Pal. of Pleasure*, iii 24 (Jacobs), True it is, that mariages be don in heauen and performed in earth. 1663: Killigrew, *Parson's Wedding*, II vii, Were not those marriages made in heaven? 1738: Swift, *Polite Convers.*, Dial. I. 1850: Smedley, *Frank Fairlegh*, ch xlvii. 1922: Lucas, *Genevra's Money*, ch xi.

9. More belongs to marriage than four bare legs in a bed. 1546: Heywood, *Proverbs*, Pt I ch viii. *c.*1630: in *Roxb. Ballads*, i 166 (Hindley). 1738: Swift, *Polite Convers.*, Dial. I. 1822: Scott, *Nigel*, ch xxxvii, A sort of penny-wedding it will prove, where all men contribute to the young folks' maintenance, that they may not have just four bare legs in a bed thegether.

See also **Age and wedlock; May,** F (14) and (15); **Wedding**; and **Wedlock**.

Married man must turn his staff into a stake, The. 1640: Herbert, *Jac. Prudentium* [with 'turns' for 'must turn']. 1670: Ray, 17.

Marrow to the patch = well suited. 1917: Bridge, *Cheshire Proverbs*, 94.

Marry, *verb.* **1. Before thou marry Make sure of an house wherein to tarry.** 1666: Torriano, *Piazza Univ.*, 144, Before thou marry, get thy habitation ready. 1670: Ray, 17. 1732: Fuller, 6396.

2. He that goes to marry likes to know whether he shall have a chimney to his house. Corn. 1869: Hazlitt, 178.

3. He that marries a slut eats mickle dirt. 1683: Meriton, *Yorkshire Ale*, 83–7 (1697).

4. He that marries late marries ill. 1589: Nashe, *Works*, i 17 (Grosart), Thys common prouerbe, he that marrieth late marrieth euill. 1666: Torriano, *Piazza Univ.*, 143, Who marries late marries amiss.

5. He that marrieth for wealth sells his liberty. 1670: Ray, 17. 1732: Fuller, 2238.

6. He who is about to marry should consider how it is with his neighbours. 1855: Bohn, 400.

7. If you marry in Lent you will live to repent. 1850: *N. & Q.*, 1st ser, ii 259. 1879: Henderson, *Folk-Lore N. Counties*, 34.

8. It is better to marry a quiet fool than a witty scold. 1647: *Countrym. New Commonwealth*, 34. 1669: *Politeuphuia*, 227.

9. It's good to marry late or never. 1670: Ray, 47.

10. Marry and thrive. *See* **Wive and thrive**.

11. Marry first and love will follow. 1714: *Spectator*, No. 605, The old family maxim, that If she marries first, love will come after. 1780: Mrs Cowley, *Belle's Stratagem*, III i.

12. Marry in haste, repent at leisure. 1566: Painter, *Pal. of Pleasure*, i 115 (Jacobs) … leaste in making hastie choise, leasure for repentaunce shuld folow. 1592: Greene, *Works*, xi 86 (Grosart), She was afrayde to match in haste least shee might repent at leysure. 1632: Randolph, *Jealous Lovers*, V ii, Marry too soon, and you'll repent too late. 1692 Congreve, *Old Batchelor*, V viii. 1713: Gay, *Wife of Bath*, I. 1842: Barham, *Ing. Legends*, 2nd ser: 'Aunt Fanny', They 'repent at leisure who marry at random'.

13. Marry your daughters betimes, lest they marry themselves. 1651: Herbert, *Jac. Prudentum*, 2nd ed. 1670: Ray, 47. 1732: Fuller, 3373.

14. Marry your son when you will; your daughter when you can. 1640: Herbert, *Jac. Prudentum.* 1696: D'Urfey, *Quixote*, Pt III Act I. 1736: Bailey, *Dict.*, s.v. 'Daughter'. 1875: A. B. Cheales, *Proverb. Folk-Lore*, 48 [with 'may' for 'can'].

15. To marry the mixen for the sake of the muck = 'to marry an undesirable person for money'. 1737: Ray, 202, You'd marry a midden for muck. 1883: Burne, *Shropsh. Folk-Lore*, 597.

16. Who marries between the sickle and the scythe, Will never thrive. 1678: Ray, 352. 1846: Denham, *Proverbs*, 49 (Percy S.). 1872: J. Glyde, jr., *Norfolk Garland*, 16, They that wive Between sickle and scythe Shall never thrive. Cf. **Sickle** (1).

17. Who marries does well, who marries not does better. 1659: Howell, *Letters*, ii 666 (Jacobs). 1666: Torriano, *Piazza Univ.*, 143.

18. Who marrieth for love without money, hath merry nights and sorry days. 1666: Ibid., 10, He who marries for love, in the night-time hath pleasure, in the day-time sorrow. 1670: Ray, 17. 1732: Fuller, 5710.

See also **May,** F (14) and (15); **Wed; Wife;** and **Widow**.

Marry! come up, my dirty cousin. 1678: Ray, 68. 1700: Ward, *London Spy*, 416 (1924). 1738: Swift, *Polite Convers.*, Dial. II. 1847: Halliwell, *Dict.*, s.v. … a saying addressed to any one who affects excessive delicacy. 1917: Bridge, *Cheshire Proverbs*, 94.

Marsham, Lincs. *See* quots. 1662: Fuller, *Worthies*, ii 269 (1840), They held together as the men of Mar[s]ham when they lost their common. 1790: Grose, *Prov. Gloss.*, s.v. 'Lincs' [as in 1662]. 1818: Scott, *Heart of Midl.*, ch xxix, [Newark man *loq.*] They hold together no better than the men of Marsham when they lost their common.

Marshland, He is arrested by the bailiff of. 1662: Fuller, *Worthies*, ii 447 (1840). 1790: Grose, *Prov. Gloss.*, s.v. 'Norfolk'. 1874: Smiles, *Lives of Engineers*, i 15, When a man was stricken down by the ague, it was said of him, 'he is arrested by the bailiff Pf Marshland',

Martin. *See* **Robin** (5).

Martin Harvey's duck, Weak in paarts, Like. 1906: *Cornish N. & Q.*, 262.

Martin's hammer. *See* quot. 1847: Halliwell, *Dict.*, s.v., 'She has had Martin's-hammer knocking at her wicket', said of a woman who has twins.

Martinmas. 1. Between Martinmas and Yule, Water's worth wine in any Pule. 1846–59: *Denham Tracts*, ii 96 (F.L.S.). 1878: Dyer, *Eng. Folk-Lore*, 261, In the North of England, there is a curious rhyme descriptive of the value of rain in the latter part of the year – ' 'Tween Martinmas and Yule, Water's wine in every pool'.

2. When the ice before Martlemas bears a duck, Then look for a winter o' mire and muck. 1881: Evans, *Leics. Words*, 191 (E.D.S.) [cited as 'a common weather proverb'].

3. Where the wind is on Martinmas Eve, there it will be the rest of the winter. 1893: Inwards, *Weather Lore*, 37 ['an old saying with the people round' – Atherstone].

4. Wind north-west at Martinmas, severe winter to come. Hunts. Ibid., 37.

See also **St Martin**.

Marton Chapel, All on one side like. 1886: Holland, *Cheshire Gloss.*, 444 (E.D.S.). 1917: Bridge, *Cheshire Proverbs*, 9 … The meaning is lost.

Marvel. *See* **Wonder**.

Mass and meat never hindered work. 1817: Scott, *Rob Roy*, ch xxix. 1823: Scott, *St Ronan's*, ch xiv. 1863: *N. & Q.*, 3rd ser, iii 258, Mass and meat never marred work. Ibid,, 439, Mass and meat take up nobody's time. Cf. **Meals and matins; Meat** (5); and **Prayers and provender**.

Master, *subs*. **1. A master of straw eats a servant of steel.** 1640: Herbert, *Jac. Prudentum*.

2. He can ill be master that never was scholar. 1639: Clarke, 149.

3. He that is a master must serve (another). 1640: Herbert, *Jac. Prudentum*.

4. He that is master of himself will soon be master of others. 1732: Fuller, 2182.

5. He that teaches himself has a fool to his master. 1641: Jonson, *Timber*: 'Consilia', For he that was only taught by himself, had a fool to his master. 1692: L'Estrange, *Aesop*, 283 (3rd ed.). 1710: S. Palmer, *Moral Essays on Proverbs*, 32. 1867: F. C. H., in *N. & Q.*, 3rd ser, xi 192, [as to origin of the saying] I believe it has arisen from the following sentence of St Bernard: – 'Qui se sibi magistrum constituit, stulto se discipulum subdit'. Ep. 83 – which may be thus rendered in English: He that will teach himself in school, Becomes a scholar to a fool.

6. If the master say the crow is while, the servant must not say 'tis black. 1672: Walker, *Paroem.*, 10. 1681: W. Robertson, *Phraseol. Generalis*, 871.

7. Masters should be sometimes blind, and sometimes deaf. 1732: Fuller, 3376.

8. The master's eye. *See* Eye (9), (13), and (17).

9. The master's footsteps fatten the soil. 1537: R. Whitford, *Werke for Housholders*, sig. F5, The steppe of the husbande [farmer] maketh a fatte donghyll. 1659: Howell, 10. 1666: Torriano, *Piazza Univ.*, 206 [with 'field' for 'soil'].

See also **Jack; Like;** and **No man**.

Master, *verb. Better master one than engage with ten.* 1732: Fuller, 916.

Master Hogge. *See* quots. 1857: *Archaeologia*, xxxvii 483, 'Master Hogge and his man John, they did cast the first cannon'. [No date given for original.] 1894: A. J. C. Hare, *Sussex*, 125, The Hog House, with a hog and 1581 carved over the door [near Buxted]. It was the residence of the Hogge or Huggett family, of whom Ralf Hogge, in 1543, cast the first iron cannon made in England: – 'Master Huggett and his man John, They did cast the first cannon'.

Mastiff. 1. A mastiff groweth the fiercer for being tied up. 1732: Fuller, 320.

2. The mastiff never loveth the greyhound. 1576: Pettie, *Petite Pall.*, ii 85 (Gollancz) [quoted – 'as the saying is'].

3. Though the mastiff be gentle, yet bite him not by the lip. 1640: Herbert, *Jac. Prudentum*. 1696: D'Urfey, *Quixote*, Pt III Act I sc i, As the proverb says, tho' the bear be gentle, don't bite him by the nose. 1732: Fuller, 5011.

Match, A. *See* quots. 1670: Ray, 216, A match quoth Hatch, when he got his wife by the breech. 1678: Ray, 76, A match quoth Jack, when he kist his dame. 1732: Fuller, 321 [as in 1678, but with 'John' for 'Jack'].

Matter but the mind, 'Tis not Ibid., No. 5105.

Matter lieth a bleeding, His. 1562: Heywood, *Epigr.*, No. 209, Here lieth all and bleedeth. 1633: Draxe, 198 [section on 'Ill success'].

Matty Tasker's jarlers, Like one o' owd. 'Jarler' = anything out of the common. 1917: Bridge, *Cheshire Proverbs*, 91.

Mavern Hill. *See* **Malvern Hill**.

Maxfield measure, heap and thrutch = very good measure. 1670: Ray, 217, Macklesfield measure, heap and thrust. *Cheshire*. 1790: Grose, *Prov. Gloss.*, s.v. 'Cheshire'. 1877: E. Leigh, *Cheshire Gloss.*, 132. 1917: Bridge, *Cheshire Proverbs*, 94, Maxfield measure, hp and thrutch; or, Maxfilt mizzer, upyepped and thrutched [pressed down].

May, *subs*. A. COLD MAY. 1. A cold May and a windy makes a fat barn and findy. 1659: Howell, 21. 1744: Claridge, in Mills, *Essay on Weather*, 101 (1773) [with 'full' for 'fat']. 1825: Hone, *Ev. Day Book*, i 669. 1893: Inwards, *Weather Lore*, 26 [as in 1744].

2. A cold May is good for corn and bad for hay. 1891: C. Wordsworth, *Rutland Words*, 22 (E.D.S.).

3. A cold May is good for corn and hay. 1893: Inwards, *Weather Lore*, 26.

4. A cold May is kind. 1882: Mrs Chamberlain, *W. Worcs. Words*, 17 (E.D.S.), Local proverb ['kind' = favourable].

5. A cold May is kindly, And fills the barn finely. 1893: Inwards, 26.

6. Cold May brings many things. Ibid., 26.

7. Cold May enriches no one. Ibid., 26.

8. For an east wind in May 'tis your duty to pray. Ibid., 26.

B. DRY MAY. 1. A dry May and a dripping June Bring all things into tune. Beds. Ibid., 28.

2. A dry May and a leaking June Make the farmer whistle a merry tune. Ibid., 27.

3. A dry May is followed by a wet June. Ibid., 27.

4. Dry May brings nothing gay. Ibid., 25.

C. MISTY MAY. Mist in May and heat in June, Make the harvest come right soon. 1846: Denham, *Proverbs*, 47 (Percy S.). 1882: Mrs Chamberlain, *W. Warcs. Words*, 37 (E.D.S.). 1893: Inwards, 27, [also] A misty May and a hot June Bring cheap meal and harvest soon.

D. WARM MAY. 1. A hot May makes a fat churchyard. 1659: Howell, 11. 1670: Ray, 42. 1825: Hone, *Ev. Day Book* i.669. 1869: *N.&Q.*, 4th ser, iv 174, A hot May makes a fat church-hay [yard]. Cornwall. 1893: Inwards, 25

2. For a warm May the parsons pray. 1893: Inwards, 25.

E. WET MAY. 1. A dropping May Fills the barns with corn and hay. 1917: Bridge, *Cheshire Proverbs*, 162.

2. A leaky May and a warm June, Bring on the harvest very soon. 1878: Dyer, *Eng. Folk–Lore*, 256.

3. A May flood never did good. 1639: Clarke, 307. 1670: Ray, 41. 1744: Claridge, in Mills, *Essay on Weather*, 101 (1773). 1893: Inwards, 26.

4. A May wet was never kind yet. Ibid., 25.

5. A wet and windy May, Fills the barn with corn and hay. 1917: Bridge, *Cheshire Proverbs*, 162.

6. A wet May brings plenty of hay. 1846: Denham, *Proverbs*, 44 (Percy S.), A weet May Will fill a byre full of hay. 1889: Peacock, *Manley, etc., Gloss.*, 345 (E.D.S.), A weet May Brings plenty o' corn, An' plenty o' haay. 1893: Inwards, 26, [as in 1846, *plus*] A wet May makes a big load of hay. West Shropshire. 1917: Bridge, *Cheshire Proverbs*, 162.

7. May damp and cool fills the barns and wine vats. 1893: Inwards, 25.

8. May rain kills lice. 1846: Denham, *Proverbs*, 43 (Percy S.).

9. The haddocks are good When dipped in May flood. 1862: Chambers, *Book of Days*, i 569 (1869). 1893: Inwards, 25.

10. Water in May is bread all the year. 1666: Torriano, *Piazza Univ.*, 135. 1878: Dyer, *Eng. Folk–Lore*, 256.

F. UNCLASSIFIED, 1. A red gay May. *See* quot. 1623: Wodroephe, *Spared Houres*, 475, A red gay May is best in any yeare; Februare full snow is to ye ground most deare; A whistling March (that makes the ploughman blithe); and moistie April that fits him for the sithe.

2. A snow-storm in May Is worth a waggon-load of hay. 1893: Inwards, 27.

3. As fine as a May-pole on May-day. 1846: Denham, *Proverbs*, 43 (Percy S.).

4. Be it weal or be it woe, Beans blow before May doth go. 1678: Ray, 351. 1732: Fuller, 6202 [with 'should 'before 'blow']. 1893: Inwards, 27 [as in 1678].

5. Be sure of hay Till the end of May. 1732: Fuller, 6197.

6. Blossoms in May Are not good some say. 1893: Inwards, 25.

7. Come it early or come it late, In May comes the cow-quake [tremulous grass]. 1670: Ray, 41, May come she early or come she late, she'll make the cow to quake. 1732: Fuller, 6191, May come early, come late, 'Twill make the cow to quake. 1893: Inwards, 26.

8. He who sows oats in May, Gets little that way. 1846: Denham, *Proverbs*, 47 (Percy S.). 1893: Inwards, 27.

9. If May will be a gardener, he will not fill the granaries. Ibid., 25.

10. If you sweep the house with broom in May, You'll sweep the head of that house away. 1878: *Folk-Lore Record*, i 52. 1879: Henderson, *Folk-Lore N. Counties*, 50 [heard in Sussex]. 1887: Zincke, *His., of Wherstead*, 179, I used to hear the rhymes: – 'Sweep with a broom that is cut in May, And you will sweep the head of the house away'.

11. In May an east-lying field is worth wain and oxen; in June, the oxen and the yoke. 1893: Inwards, 27.

12. Look at your corn in May, and you'll come weeping away: Look at the same in June, and you'll come home in another tune. 1639: Clarke, 307 [a little varied]. 1670: Ray, 41. 1827: Hone, *Table-Book*, 667, He that goes to see his wheat in May Comes weeping away. 1883: Burne, *Shropsh. Folk-Lore*, 579, Of green corn: Go in the May, And come weeping away: Go in the June, And come home another tune. 1893: Inwards, 27 … a proverb alluding to the magical way in which unpromising crops sometimes recover.

13. Many thunderstorms in May, And the farmer sings 'Hey! hey!' Ibid., 27.

14. Married in May will soon decay. 1846: Denham, *Proverbs*, 48 (Percy S.), From the marriages in May All the bairns die and decay. 1872: J. Glyde, jr., *Norfolk Garland*, 16 [as in 1846]. 1917: Bridge, *Cheshire Proverbs*, 93.

15. Marry in May, you'll rue it for aye. 1675: *Poor Robin Alman.*, May, The proverb saies … Of all the moneths 'tis worst to wed in May.

1879: Henderson, *Folk-Lore N. Counties*, 34, The ancient proverb still lives on the lips of the people of Scotland and the Borders – Marry in May Rue for aye. 1913: E. M. Wright, *Rustic Speech, etc.*, 218, Marry in May, you'll rue it for aye, is a Devonshire saying.

16. May and December (or **January**). *c.*1386: Chaucer, *Merch. Tale*, l. 449, That she, this mayden, which that May us highte … should wedded be vnto this Ianuarie. 1606: Dekker, *Works*, ii 71 (Grosart), You doe wrong to Time, enforcing May to embrace December, *c.*1613: Rowlands, *Paire of Spy-Knaues*, 7 (Hunt.Cl.), Yonder goes cold December match'd with May. 1634: Massinger, *Guardian*, I i, I am in the May of my abilities, And you in your December. 1891: R. Buchanan, *Coming Terror*, 267 (OED), When asthmatic January weds buxom May.

17. May and June are twin sisters. 1846: Denham, *Proverbs*, 49 (Percy S.).

18. May-bees don't fly this month. A punning saying. 1738: Swift, *Polite Convers.*, Dial. I, *Miss.* Maybe there is colonel. *Col.* Ay; but May bees don't fly now, miss.

19. May chets bad luck begets. 'Chets' = children in Cornwall, and, hence, kittens also. 1690: Dryden, *Amphitryon*, III, Blear-ey'd, like a Maykitten. 1865: Hunt, *Pop. Romances W. of Eng.*, 430 (1896). 1878: Dyer, *Eng. Folk-Lore*, 176. 1879: Henderson, *Folk-Lore N. Counties*, 115, A certain unluckiness is held all England over to attend a May kitten as well as a May baby. 1882: Jago, *Gloss. of Cornish Dialect*, 131. 1902: *N.&Q.*, 9th ser, x 77, In Huntingdonshire it is a common saying that a 'May kitten makes a dirty cat'. 1913: E. M. Wright, *Rustic Speech, etc.*, 218.

20. May never goes out without a wheatear. 1830: Forby, *Vocab. E. Anglia*, 417. 1893: *Co. Folk-Lore: Suffolk*, 163 (F.L.S.).

21. May-day has come and gone, thou art a gosling and I am none. 1846: Denham, *Proverbs*, 44 (Percy S.). 1904: *Co. Folk-Lore: Northumb.*, 177 (F.L.S.).

22. Never cast a clout till May be out. 1732: Fuller, 6193 [with 'Leave not off' for 'Never cast']. 1886: Elworthy, *West Som. Word-Book*, 467 (E.D.S.), If you would the doctor pay Leave your flannels off in May. 1887: Parish and Shaw, *Dict. Kent. Dialect*, 99 (E.D.S.). 1893: Inwards, *Weather Lore*, 26, Till May be out Leave not off a clout: or, Change not a clout Till May be out.

1906: *N.&Q.*, 10th ser, v 433, Never change a thing Till May comes in. Never cast, etc. Ibid., 474, Button to chin Till May be in; Cast not a clout till May be out.

23. No grass first of May, Fetch another cow to the ley. 1917: Bridge, *Cheshire Proverbs*, 98.

24. The first of May is Robin Hood's day. 1846: Denham, *Proverbs*, 47 (Percy S.).

25. The more thunder in May, the less in August and September. 1893: Inwards, *Weather Lore*, 27.

26. They who bathe in May will soon be laid in clay; They who bathe in June Will sing a merry tune. 1827: Hone, *Table-Book*, 315 [quoted as an 'old saying ... very prevalent in Skipton', Yorks]. 1893: Inwards, 27, [as in 1827, *plus*] They who bathe in July Will dance like a fly.

27. To get up (or **over**) **May hill.** 1825: Hone, *Ev. Day Book*, i 652, The month of May is called a 'trying' month, to persons long ailing with critical complaints. It is common to say 'Ah, he'll never get up May-hill!' or, 'If he can climb over May-hill he'll do'. 1863: Wise, *New Forest*, ch.xvi, 'He won't climb up May Hill', that is, he will not live through the cold spring. 1887: Parish and Shaw, *Dict. Kent. Dialect*, 99 (E.D.S.), I don't think he'll ever get up May hill.

28. To wed in May is to wed poverty. 1878: Dyer, *Eng. Folk-Lore*, 257. 1893: Inwards, *Weather Lore*, 27.

29. Twenty-ninth of May Royal-oak day (or **oaken-apple day**). 1846: Denham, *Proverbs*, 48 (Percy S.).

30. You must not count your yearlings till May-day. 1823: D'Israeli, *Cur. of Lit.*, 2nd ser, i 441 (1824), The state of an agricultural people appears in such proverbs as 'You must not', etc. *See also* **April** (3), (4), (9). (12), (13), and (17); **Bee** (3); **Cuckoo**, *passim;* **Doe; Fresh at flowers; January** (4), (8), (17), and (18); **July** (9); **Leeks; March**, *passim;* **Merry month; Sage; Sheep** (13); and **Thistle** (2).

May, *verb.* **1. That one may not another may.** 1546: Heywood, *Proverbs*, Pt II ch ii.

2. That which may fall out at any time, may fall out today. 1732: Fuller, 4383.

3. What may be done at any time will be done at no time. Ibid., No. 5500.

4. Who that may not as they will, must will as they may. 1546: Heywood, *Proverbs*, Pt II ch v. 1633: Draxe, 1.

5. You may if you list, but do if you dare. 1678: Ray, 350.

Mayors. *See* **Altringham; Calenick; East Looe; Falmouth; Halgaver; Hartlepool; Lord-Mayor; Market-Jew; Northampton; Over; Tregoney;** and **Wigan.**

Mazed. *See* quots. 1895: J. Thomas, *Randigal Rhymes*, 61, Mazed as a curley [Corn.]. 1926: *Devonsh. Assoc. Trans.*, lvii 144, 'Mazed as a brish' [brush] is a common saying about Newton Abbot ... Still commoner, 'mazed as a sheep'. I have also heard 'mazed as a broom-stick'.

Meal make before sail take. Corn. 1869: Hazlitt, 279.

Meals. *See* **Better are meals.**

Meals and matins minish never. 1853: Trench, *Proverbs*, 21 (1905), Meal and matins minish no way. 1863: *N.&Q.*, 3rd ser, iii 209. Cf. **Mass and meat; Meat** (5); and **Prayers and provender.**

Mean as an higgler, As. 1917: Bridge, *Cheshire Proverbs*, 18, Higgler = Huckster or hawker.

Mean as tongs, As. 1899: S. O. Addy, in *N.&Q.*, 9th ser, iv 206 ... I have occasionally heard this phrase in Sheffield.

Means, The end justifies the. *See* **End** (4).

Means, Use the, and God will give the blessing. 1633: Draxe, 109. 1670: Ray, 17. 1732: Fuller, 5413, Use the means, and trust to God for the blessing.

Measure, *subs.* **1. He that loves measure and skill, oft hath his will.** *c.*1460: *How the Good Wife*, l. 55, That mesure louethe, and skille, ofte hathe his wille.

2. Man is the measure of all things. *See* **Man** (60).

3. Measure for measure. 1595: *True Trag. Rich. Duke of York*, 151 (SH.S.), Measure for measure must be answered. 1603: Shakespeare, *Measure for Measure* [title]. 1834–7: Southey, *Doctor*, interch. xxi [title].

4. Measure is a merry mean. *c.*1380: Langland, *Dep. of Rich. II*, 12 (Camden S.), Mesure is a meri mene. *c.*1450: Russell, *Book of Nurture*, in *Babees Book*, 124 (E.E.T.S.). Before 1529: Skelton, *Magnyfycence*, l. 385. 1590: Greene, *Works*, ix. 209 (Grosart). 1670: Ray, 17.

5. Measure is medicine. 1362: Langland, *Plowman*, A, i 33.

6. Measure is treasure. *c.*1225: *Ancren R.*, 336 (Morton), The middel weie of mesure is euer guldene [golden]. *c.*1420: Lydgate, *Minor Poems*, 82 (Percy S.), An olde proverbe – 'mesour is tresoure'. Before 1529: Skelton, *Magnyfycence*, l. 126. 1639: Clarke, 206. 1732: Fuller, 6321.

7. There is measure in all things. [*c.*1450: *Abce of Aristotill*, in E.E.T.S., Ext. Ser., 67 (1869), For a mesurable mene is best for vs alle.] *c.*1385: Chaucer, *Troilus and Criseyde*, II 715, In every thing I woot, there lith mesure [moderation]. 1598–9: Shakespeare, *Much Ado about Nothing*, II i 59, If the prince be too important, tell him there is measure in every thing. 1633: Draxe, 129.

Measure, *verb.* **1. He measures a twig.** 1813: Ray, 75.

2. He that measures not himself is measured. 1640: Herbert, *Jac. Prudentum.*

3. Measure thrice and cut once. 1591: Florio, *Second Frutes*, 97, Alwaies measure manie, Before you cut anie. 1623: Wodroephe, *Spared Howes*, 275, Measure thrice, before thou shapest once. 1670: Ray, 17, Measure thrice what thou buyest, and cut it but once. 1732: Fuller, 3381.

4. To measure another by your own yard. 1589: *Pap with a Hatchet*, To Reader, They measure conscience by their owne yard. 1659: Howell, 12, You measure every one by your own yard. 1883: Burne, *Shropsh. Folk-Lore*, 597, To measure your neighbours cloth by your own yard.

5. To measure another's corn by one's own bushel. 1631: W. Saltonstall, *Picturae Loquentes*, sig. Fi, Her corne stands not long for the sellers sake, and she crosses the proverbe, for shee measures it out by anothers bushell. 1670: Ray, 186, You measure every ones corn by your own bushel. 1713: Gay, *Wife of Bath*, I, Pray do not measure my corn with your bushel, old Drybones! 1828: Carr, *Craven Dialect*, i 58, 'You measure me a peck out of your own bushel'; you judge of my disposition by your own. 1920: L. J. Jennings, *Chestnuts and Small Beer*, 138, No man is inclined to measure his own corn by another man's bushel.

Meat, *subs.* **1. A man is not sure of his meat till it is in his mouth.** 1684: *Great Frost*, 14 (Percy S.) [cited as an old proverb].

2. If 'twasn't for meat and good drink the women might gnaw the sheets 1698: *Terence made English*, 96 (2nd ed.) [quoted as 'the old saying'].

3. Look not on the meat but on the man. 1533: Heywood, *Play of Love*, l. 1230 (Brandl, *Quellen*, 198). 1639: Clarke, 84, Shew me not the meat, but shew me the man. 1678: Ray, 354, To measure the meat by the man.

4. Meat and drink to one, *To be.* 1533: Frith, *Answ. More*, Ej (OED), It ys meate and drinke to this childe to plaie. 1573: G. Harvey, *Letter-Book*, 51 (Camden S.), Whitch were sutch matter … as would be meat and drink to M. Proctor. 1642: Fuller, *Profane State:* 'Hypocrite', Even fasting itself is meat and drink to him, whilst others behold it. 1681: Robertson. *Phraseol. Generalis*, 876, It is meat and drink to me.

5. Meat and mass (or **matins**) **hinder no man's journey** (or **work**). 1639: Clarke, 273, Meat and mattens hinder no mans journey. 1670: Ray, 120 [as in 1639]. 1732: Fuller. No. 3382 [as in 1639, but 'not a' for 'no mans']. 1823: Scott, *Q. Durward*, ch xi, 'Meat and mass' (crossing himself) 'never hindered the work of a good Christian man'. 1893: R.L.S., *Catriona*, ch xix, I beg to remind you of an old musty saw, that meat and mass never hindered man. Cf. **Mass and meat; Meals and matins;** and **Prayers and provender**.

6. Meat is much but manners is more. 1639: Clarke, 93. 1685: Meriton, *Yorkshire Ale*, 54, For meat is mickle but mence [credit] is more. 1732: Fuller, 3383 [with 'malice' for 'manners', but this must surely be a misprint].

7. Meat must be had, but work may stay. 1687: *Poor Robin Alman. Prognost.*, sig. C8 [quoted as 'ancient proverb'].

8. Meat was made for mouths. 1609: Shakespeare, *Coriolanus*, I i.

9. One man's meat is another man's poison. [Tantaque in his rebus distantia, differitasque est, Ut quod aliis cibus est, aliis fuat acre venenum. – Lucretius, iv 638.] 1546: Heywood, *Proverbs*, Pt II ch ii, That one loueth not, an other doth. *c.*1576: T. Whythorne, *Autobiography* (1961), 203, On bodies meat iz an otherz poizon. 1604: *Plato's Cap*, B4, That ould moth-eaten Proverb … One mans meate, is anothermans poyson. 1630: Taylor (Water-Poet), *Works*, 2nd pagin., 254, And one mans meat, anothers poyson is. 1709: O. Dykes, *Eng. Proverbs*, iv (2nd ed.). 1759: Townley, *High Life below Stairs*, I i, Alas, Sir! what is one man's poison is another man's meat. 1883: Trollope,

Autobiog., ch x [with 'food' for 'meat']. 1914: Lucas, *Landmarks*, 197.

10. To be meat for another's mouth. [Non ego sum pollucta pago. – Plautus, *Rud.*, 425.] 1598: Shakespeare, 2 *Henry IV*, II iv, I am meat for your master. 1616: Haughton, *Englishm. for my Money*, II i, I am no meat for his mowing [mouthing], nor yours neither. 1681: Otway, *Soldier's Fortune*, II i, Let my doxy rest in peace, she's meat for thy master. 1738: Swift, *Polite Convers.*, Dial. I, That's meat for your master. 1855: Kingsley, *West. Ho!*, ch viii, And that you can't have, for it's meat for your masters.

11. To bring meat in the mouth. 1580: G. Harvey, *Works*, i 92 (Grosart), Those studies and practises, that carrie as they saye, meate in their mouth. 1639: Clarke, 43, It brings meat i' th' mouth. 1670: Ray, 186.

12. When meat is in anger is out. 1639: Clarke, 178.

Meddle, *verb*. **1. He that will meddle with all things may go shoe the goslings,** *c.*1434: inscrip. in Whalley Church, cited in Farmer's *Heywood's Proverbs*, 377 (1906), Whoso melles of wat men doo, Let hym cum hier and shoo the ghos. 1546: Heywood, *Proverbs*, Pt II ch iii, Who medleth in all thyng maie shooe the goslyng. 1670: Ray, 120. 1732: Fuller, 6445.

2. I will neither meddle nor make, 1593: Nashe, *Works*, iv 151 (Grosart). If in speech you neither meddle nor make with hym. 1609: Shakespeare, *Troilus*, I i, For my part, I'll not meddle nor make no further. 1675: Cotton, *Burl, upon Burlesque*, 259 (1765), I should do very imprudently … Either to meddle or to make. 1730: Lillo, *Silvia*, III v, They are ticklish things, and I don't much care to meddle or make with 'em. 1849: Brontë, *Shirley*, ch xxi, Moore may settle his own matters henceforward for me; I'll neither meddle nor make with them further. 1920: E. Gepp, *Essex Dialect Dict.*, 22, 'I 'on't nuther meddle nor make', I won't interfere.

3. Meddle with your old shoes. 1577: *Misogonus*, II v, What, are you his spoksman? meddle you with your old showes. 1639: Clarke, 18, Meddle with what you have to doe. 1670: Ray, 186. 1681: Robertson, *Phraseol. Generalis*, 877, Meddle with your old shoes; Tua quod nihil refert, ne cures.

Medgelly's cow. *See* quot. 1753: in *Stukeley Memoirs*, iii 179 (Surtees S.), A proverb in this country [Shropsh.], 'Medgelly's cow, for one that gives a deal of milk'.

Medicines be not meat to live by. 1669: *Politeuphuia*, 175.

Medlars are never good till rotten. 1599: J Weever, *Epigr.*, 19 (1911), Medlers are neuer ripe before that they be rotten. 1674: Head and Kirkman, *Eng. Rogue*, iii 259, A medlar, which is never good till rotten. 1678: Ray, 52.

Medlock *See* **Yoke**.

Meet trouble(s) half way, Do not. *See* **Trouble** (2).

Meet with one's match, To. *c.*1305: *Miracle of St James*, 48, in E.E.P., 59 (1862) (OED), the schrewe fond his macche tho. *c.*1400: *Beryn*, 4 (E.E.T.S.), Lo! howe the clowdis worchyn, eche man to mete his mach. 1485: Malory, *Morte d'Arthur*, bk x ch 54, Goo feche sire launcelot or sir Tristram and there shalle ye fynde your matche. 1594: Greene, *Frier Bacon*, sc ix, How now … have you met with your match? 1632: Shirley, *Witty Fair One*, I iii, *Clare*. I am married, sir. *Bra*. Then I hope you have met with your match already. 1700: Congreve, *Way of World*, III-vii, Well, Mr Fainall, you have met with your match. 1874: *N. & Q.*, 5th ser, i 205, Nor insult any one, lest you meet with your match.

Meeterly [Tolerably, Indifferently] **as maids are in fairness**. 1678: Ray, 355. 1683: Meriton, *Yorkshire Ale*, 83–7 (1697).

Meg of Westminster, As long as. 1582: *The Life and Pranks of Long Meg of Westminster* [title]. 1662: Fuller, *Worthies*, ii 413 (1840). 1785: Grose, *Class. Dict. Vulgar Tongue*, s.v. 'Long Meg', A jeering name for a very tall woman, from one famous in story, called Long Meg of Westminster.

Melancholy as a cat, As. 1592: Lyly, *Midas*, V ii 1597: Shakespeare, 1 *Henry IV*, I ii, I am as melancholy as a gib cat. 1599: Chapman, *Hum. Day's Mirth*, sc xi. 1609: in Halliwell, *Books of Characters*, 115 (1857). 1694: D'Urfey, *Quixote*, Pt II Act I sc i, Yonder he lies, and as melancholy as a cat in a church-steeple, expecting my return. 1720: Gay, *Poems*, ii 278, (Underhill), I melancholy as a cat, Am kePt awake to weep. 1785: Grose, *Class. Dict. Vulgar Tongue*, s.v. 'Gib cat', As melancholy as a gib cat; as melancholy as a he-cat who has been catterwauling, whence they always return scratched, hungry, and out of spirits. 1820: Lamb, *South-Sea House*, Melancholy as a gib-cat over his counter all the forenoon.

Melancholy as a collier's horse, As. 1659: Howell, 10.

Melancholy as a sick monkey, As. 1836: Marryat, *Easy*, ch xxi.

Melancholy as a sick parrot, As. 1682: A. Behn, *False Count*, I ii.

Melverley, Shropsh. 1841: Hartshorne, *Salopian Ant.*, 504, Its remoteness, perhaps, and the frequency of inundations to which it is subject, has occasioned the place to pass into a bye word, and its inhabitants to be called Melverly God helps. [Also, after good crops] Melverly where do you think? 1913: E. M. Wright, *Rustic Speech, etc.*, 181, To direct a person to go to a place not to be named to ears polite is to tell him, to go to Melverley, a saying which has arisen from the fact that this village is continually flooded by the irruptions of the Severn, and is therefore a place where ills and misfortunes befall the inhabitants. 1928: *Truth*, 12 Sept., p. 454, col. 2, Melverley God help us! … Melverley, where else?

Memory is the treasure of the mind. 1560: T. Wilson, *Rhetorique*, 209 (1909), The memorie called the threasure of the minde. 1642: Fuller, *Holy State*: 'Memory', Memory … is the treasure-house of the mind.

Memory of happiness makes misery woeful, The. *c.*1440: Lydgate, *Fall of Princes*, bk i l. 650, Nor nothyng more may hertis disauaunce Than off old ioie newe remembraunce. 1669: *Politeuphuia*, 102, The consideration of pleasures past greatly augments the pain present. 1732: Fuller, 4650.

Men. *See* **Man**.

Mend, *verb*. 1. **He may mend but not grow worse**. 1633: Draxe, 43, Some doe mend, when they cannot appaire. 1659: Howell, 7.

2. **If you mend things on your back, you'm sure to lack**, i.e. to want. 1919: *Devonsh. Assoc. Trans*, li 77.

3. **It is never too late to mend**. *See* **Never too late**.

4. **Least said soonest mended**. *See* **Least said**.

5. **Let him mend his manners**, *'twill be his own another day*. 1678: Ray, 76.

6. **Mend one**. *See* **Every man mend one**.

7. **Mend your clothes and you may hold out this year**. 1640: Herbert, *Jac. Prudentum*. 1854: J. W. Warter, *Last of Old Squires*, 53.

8. **To mend as sour ale mends in summer** = To become worse. 1546: Heywood, *Proverbs*, Pt II ch ix, Than wolde ye mend … as sowre ale mendth in summer. 1564: Bullein, *Dialogue*, 77 (E.E.T.S.), The worlde amendes like sower ale in sommer. 1647: Wither, *Amygdala Brit.*, 6 (Spens.S.), And, like sowre ale in summer, mend. 1738: Swift, *Polite Convers.*, Dial. III. 1823: Moor, *Suffolk Words*, 377, ' 'A mend like sour ale in summer' – that is, gets worse and worse.

9. **To mend as the fletcher does his bolt**. 1530: Palsgrave, 634, He mendeth as the fletcher dothe his bolte. 1633: Draxe, 242.

Merchandise. *See* quot. 1593: Nashe, *Works*, iv 139 (Grosart), It is nowe growne a prouerbe *That there is no merchandise but vsury*.

Merchant. 1. A merchant of eel-skins = of refuse, or of nothing. 1545: Ascham, *Toxoph.*, 151 (Arber), He that wyll at all aduenters vse the seas knowinge no more what is to be done in a tempest than in a caulme, shall soone becumme a marchaunt of eele skinnes. 1624: T. Heywood, *Captives*, IV i, Fisher … who knowes but I In tyme may proove a noble marchant? *Clowne*. Yes, of eele skinnes. 1655: A. Brewer, *Love-sick King*, II, in Bang, *Materialien*, B. 18, p.13, Then am I a merchant, not of eels-skins, but lambskins.

2. **A merchant that gains not loses**. 1611: Cotgrave, s.v. 'Gaigner', The marchant loses when he gaines not. 1640: Herbert, *Jac. Prudentum*.

3. **A merchant without either money or ware**. 1546: Heywood, *Proverbs*, Pt II ch v. 1659: Howell, 7.

4. **He is not a merchant bare that hath money-worth or ware**. 1670: Ray, 17. 1732: Fuller, 6240.

5. **He that could know what would be dear, need be a merchant but one year**. 1546: Heywood, *Proverbs*, Pt I ch i. 1611: Cotgrave, s.v. 'Adventure', We say, he that did know what would be deare, might grow full rich within a yeare. 1670: Ray, 78. 1732: Fuller, 6077.

6. **He that loseth is a merchant as well as he that gains**. 1640: Herbert, *Jac. Prudentum*. 1666: Torriano, *Piazza Univ.*, 150.

7. **Merchant May's little summer**. = St Martin's little summer. Corn. 1869: Hazlitt, 280.

8. **To play the merchant** = To rob or cheat. 1593: Nashe, *Works*, iv 240 (Grosart), Is it not a

common prouerbe amongst vs when any man hath cosend or gone beyonde vs, to say, Hee hath playde the merchant with us? 1611: Cotgrave, s.v. 'Larron', Either a merchant or a theefe. 1632: Rowley, *New Wonder*, IV, I doubt, sir, he will play the merchant with us.

Mercury. *See* quot. 1588: Cogan, *Haven of Health*, 45 (1612), It is a common prouerbe among the people, Be thou sicke or whole, put Mercurie in thy koale.

Mere scholar. *See* **Scholar**.

Mere wishes are silly fishes. 1732: Fuller, 6290.

Merrier. *See* **More the merrier**.

Merry and wise. 1546: Heywood, *Proverbs*, Pt I ch ii., Good to be mery and wise, they thinke and feele. 1593: G. Harvey, *Works*, ii 247 (Grosart), It is good, they say, to be merry, and wise. 1668: Davenant, *Man's the Master*, Prol., The proverb says, 'Be merry and be wise'. 1774: Colman, *Man of Business*, I. 1779: Johnson, in *Letters*, ii 114 (Hill), Old Times have bequeathed us a precept, *to be merry and wise*, but who has been able to observe it? 1840: Dickens, *Curiosity Shop*, ch vii.

Merry as a cricket. 1546: Heywood, *Proverbs*, Pt I ch xi. 1597: Shakespeare, 1 *Henry IV*, II iv. 1653: Urquhart, *Rabelais*, bk i ch xxix, And send them home as merry as crickets unto their own houses. 1787: O'Keeffe, *The Farmer*, I ii 1834: Marryat, *Peter Simple*, ch i 1918: Walpole, *Green Mirror*, bk i ch i, Healthy, happy ... lively as crickets – not a happier family in England.

Merry as a Greek, *c*.1551: Udall, *Roister Doister*, I i [one of the characters is Mathew Merygreeke]. 1611: Jonson, in Coryat, *Crudities*, i 17 (1905), Hee is a mad Greeke, no lesse than a merry. 1655: Fuller, *Church Hist.*, bk ii § iii (22), We know the modern proverb of *a merry Greek*. 1670: Cotton, *Scarronides*, bk iv, Merry as Greeks, and drunk as Lords. 1784: *New Foundl. Hosp. for Wit*, iii 176, Make me as merry as a Greek.

Merry as a grig. 1566: Drant, *Horace: Sat.*, I iii, A merry grigge, a iocande frende. 1675: Cotton, *Burl. upon Burlesque*, 195 (1765), A merry grig, and a true toper. Before 1704: T. Brown, in *Works*, ii 188 (1760), They drank till they all were as merry as grigs. 1713: Gay, *Wife of Bath*, V iii, Ah! friend, we were merry grigs in times past. 1775: Jos. Wedgwood, in *Letters* (priv. printed 1903), We have a housefull of children, all as merry as Griggs. 1859: Sala. *Twice Round*

Clock, 3 p..m., They can be as merry as grigs among themselves when they so choose. 1886: Elworthy, *West Som. Word-Book*. 301 (E.D.S.), 'So merry's a grig' and 'So merry's a cricket' are equally common.

Merry as a king. *See* **Happy**.

Merry as a pie. *c*.1386: Chaucer, *Shipm. Tale*, l. 209, And forth she gooth, as iolif as a pye. 1546: Heywood, *Proverbs*. Pt II ch iii. 1590: *Tarltons Newes out of Purg.*, 68 (SH.S.), Home went Lysetta, as merry as a pye. 1600: Dekker, *Shoem. Holiday*, V v, Ile be as merrie as a pie. 1613: S. Rowley, *When You See Me*, sig. C3, Hele lafe and be as merry as a magpie. *c*.1630: B.&F., *Mons. Thomas*, IV ii, At Valentine's house so merry? As a pie, sir.

Merry as beggars. 1659: Howell, 11, As merry as fourty beggars. 1700: Ward, *London Spy*, 264 (1924), Both were ... as merry as beggars. 1724: Swift, *Drapier*, Lett. IV, We should live together as merry and sociable as beggars.

Merry as he that hath nought to lose, Who so? 1672: Walker, *Paroem.*, 39.

Merry as mice in malt. 1639: Clarke, 185. 1659: Howell, 3. 1869: Spurgeon, *John Ploughman*, ch xvi, Some families are as merry as mice in malt on very small wages.

Merry as the maids, *c*.1630: in *Roxb. Ballads*, i 448 (B.S.), For with joviall blades I'm as mery as the maids. 17th cent.: in Marchant, *Praise of Ale*, 249 (1888), We will be as merry as the maides. 1670: Ray, 202.

Merry as three chips. 1546: Heywood, *Proverbs*, Pt I ch vii.

Merry as tinkers. 1659: Howell, 3.

Merry at meat, It is good to be. 1633: Draxe, 66. 1670: Ray, 18.

Merry be the first, and merry be the last, and merry be the first of August. 1869: Hazlitt, 280.

Merry but unlooked-for guest. *See* quot. 1819: Combe, *Syntax Consol. Tour*, can. xxix, And if the proverb says what's true, Which those old saws are aPt to do, The merry, but unlook'd for guest, Full often proves to be the best.

Merry companion, A. *See* quots. 1597: Lyly, *Woman in Moone*, IV, A merry companion is as good as a wagon. 1616: Breton, in *Works*, ii *e* 8 (Grosart), A merry companion is a wagon in the way. 1666: Torriano, *Piazza Univ.*, 49, A merry companion on the way is as good as a nag. 1732: Fuller, 324 ... is musick in a journey.

Merry-go-down = good ale. *c*.1470: in *Songs and Carols*, 92 (Percy S.), I know a drawght off merry-go-downe. 1567: Golding, *Ovid*, bk v l. 556, Out she brought hir by and by a draught of merrie go downe. 1591: Lodge, *Cattaros*, 21 (Hunt.Cl.). *c*.1791: Pegge, *Derbicisms*, 111 (E.D.S.). 1886: Bickerdyke, *Curios, of Ale and Beer*, 120, Used by those ancient worthies in compounding their 'merrie-go-downe'.

Merry in hall when beards wag all, 'Tis. *c*, 1310: *King Alisaunder*, l..1163, Swithe mury hit is in halle, When the burdes wawen alle. 1546: Heywood, *Proverbs*, Pt II ch vii. 1598: Shakespeare, *2 Henry IV*, V iii. 1616: Jonson, *Masque of Christmas*. 1712: Addison, *Spectator*, No. 371. 1846: Wright, *Essays on Middle Ages*, i 43, The object at which they now aimed being to make 'beards wag merry in hall'.

Merry is the company till the reckoning comes. 1678: Ray, 175, Merry is the feast-making till we come to the reckoning. 1732: Fuller, 3409.

Merry man as the sad, As long liveth the. *c*.1300: in *Vernon MS.*, 347 (E.E.T.S.), Lengor liueth a glad mon then a sori. *c*.1550: Udall, *Roister Doister*, I i, As long liveth the merry man (they say), As doth the sorry man, and longer by a day. 1599: Porter, *Two Angry Women*, in Hazlitt, *Old Plays*, vii 308. 1630: *Tinker of Turvey* iv (Halliwell), Lives not a merry-man longer than a sad? 1732: Fuller, 711 ['eart' for 'man']. 1861: Pea, cock, *Gryll Grange*, ch xxxii [as in 1550].

Merry meet merry part. 1678: Ray, 175. 1732: Fuller, 3410.

Merry month of May, The. [1412–20: Lydgate, *Troy Book*, bk i l. 1293, And May was come, the monyth of gladnes.] 1577: J. Grange, *Golden Aphroditis*, sig. K4, It might be the merry moneth of May. 1594: Barn-field, *Affect. Sheph.*, 41 (Percy S.). *c*.1610: in *Roxb. Ballads*, iii 42 (B.S.). *c*.1680: in Ibid., iii 434 (B.S.). 1700: Dryden, *Pal. and Arcite*, ii 44, Observance to the month of merry May. 1889: Gilbert, *Gondoliers*, I, All the year is merry May!

Merry nights make sorry days. Staffs. 1896: *Folk-Lore*, vii 377.

Merry pin, On. *c*.1386: Chaucer, *Merch. Tale*, l. 272, Your herte hangeth on a ioly pin. *c*.1480: *Digby Plays*, 156 (E.E.T.S.), I wyll no more row a-geyn the fflode, I wyll sett my soule on a mery

pynne. 1553: *Respublica*, II iii, Canne Avarice harte bee sett on a merie pynne …? 1639: Davenport, *New Trick to cheat Devil*, I ii, Faith I was never on a merrier pinn, Nor my breast lighter hearted. 1710: Matt. Henry, *Commentary* (Dan. v 4), The cups going round apace, and all upon the merry pin. 1818: *Gent. Mag.*, Pt II 13–17, When a person is much elated, we say he is *in a merry pin*, which no doubt originally meant he had reached that *mark* [in a pegged tankard] which had deprived him of his usual sedateness and sobriety. 1909: Hackwood, *Inns, Ales, etc.*, 146, By which time he was in merry mood, or, as the phrase ran, 'in merry pin'.

Merry that dance, All are not. *c*.1430: Lydgate, *Daunce of Machabree*, l. 392, Al be not merye which that men seen daunce. 1611: Cotgrave, s.v. 'Aise', Every one is not merry that dances. 1640: Herbert, *Jac. Prudentum*, All are not merry that dance lightly.

Merry to keep one's own, It is. *c*.1460: *How the Good Wife*, l. 60, Mery is owne thinge to kepe.

Merry when friends meet, It's. 1639: Clarke, 26.

Merry when gentle-folks meet, 'Tis. 1647: A. Brewer, *Countrie Girl*, sig. H3, And soe – as the proverbe is, tis merry when gentle folkes meete.

Merry when gossips meet, It is. 1616: Breton, in *Works*, ii *e* 6 (Grosart). 1625: Jonson, *Staple of News*, Induction. 1639: Clarke, 184.

Merry when knaves meet, It is. *c*.1520: *Cock Lorells Bote*, 14 (Percy S.), But mery it is whan knaues done mete. 1590: *Three Lords and Three Ladies*, in Hazlitt, *Old Plays*, vi 410. 1639: Clarke, 290.

Merry when maltmen meet, It is. *c*.1630: in *Roxb. Ballads*, i 59 (B.S.), 'Tis merry when kinde maltmen meet. 1631: Brathwait, *Whimzies*, 145 (1859).

Mersey. *See* **Yoke.**

Mettle is dangerous in a blind horse. 1670: Ray, 18, Metal is, etc. 1696: D'Urfey, *Quixote*, Pt III Act I, Too much mettle is, etc. 1732: Fuller, 3411.

Mettle to the back, He is. *c*.1591: Shakespeare, *Titus Andr.*, IV iii, But metal, Marcus, steel to the very back. 1733: Coffey, *Boarding-School*, sc v, The girl is mettle to the back. 1745: *Agreeable Companion*, 105, A notable fellow of his inches, and metal to the back. Cf. **Steel.**

Mice. *See* **Best** (22); **Dead** (15); **Mouse; No larder**; and **Rat** (1) and (6).

Michaelmas. 1. At Michaelmas time, or a little before, half an apple goes to the core; at Christmas time, or a little after, a crab in the hedge, and thanks to the grafter. 1869: Hazlitt, 77.

2. He spent Michaelmas rent in Midsummer moon. 1605: Camden, *Remains*, 323 (1870). 1665: J. Wilson, *Projectors*, II, A good honest man's daughter, that shall bring him no charge … One that shall not spend his Michaelmas rents in Midsummer moon. 1732: Fuller, 2026. 1846: Denham, *Proverbs*, 6 (Percy S.).

3. Michaelmas chickens and parsons' daughters never come to good. 1894: Northall, *Folk Phrases*, 19 (E.D.S.).

4. The Michaelmas moon. *See* **Moon** (17).

5. 'Tis good to have a Michaelmas-groat at Easter. 1710: S. Palmer, *Moral Essays* ON *Proverbs*, 280 … The … proverb is vulgar and peculiar to the watermen, whose business is brisk only in the summer.

See also **Eat** (5); **Goose** (19); **Moon** (13) and (17); **St Michael**; and **Three things that never**.

Mickle ado and little help. 1670: Ray, 120.

Mickle makes a muckle. *See* **Many a mickle**.

Middle Temple. *See* **Gray's Inn**.

Middlesex clowns. 1662: Fuller, *Worthies*, ii 313 (1840) [in the singular]. 1790: Grose, *Prov. Gloss.*, s.v. 'Middlesex'.

Middlesex jury. *See* **London** (1).

Middlesex. *See also* **Derbyshire**.

Midsummer Eve. *See* quot. 1878: Dyer, *Eng. Folk-Lore*, 257, According to an old saying, 'If it rains on Midsummer Eve, the filberts will be spoilt'. 1893: Inwards, *Weather Lore*, 29.

Midsummer moon. *See* quots. 1596: Nashe, *Works*, iii 55 (Grosart), Ere hee bee come to the full Midsommer Moone and raging Calentura of his wretchednes. 1601: Shakespeare, *Twelfth N.*, III iv, Why, this is very midsummer madness. 1670: Ray, 214, 'Tis Midsummer moon with you, i.e. you are mad. 1732: Fuller, 2974 [as in 1670]. 1846: Denham, *Proverbs*, 51 (Percy S.) [as in 1670].

Midsummer rain spoils hay and grain. 1893: Inwards, *Weather Lore*, 7.

Midsummer. *See also* **St John**.

Might is (or overcometh) right. [Plus potest, qui plus valet. – Plautus, *Trucul.*, IV iii 30.] *c.*1311: in Wright, *Pol. Songs John to Edw. II*, 254 (Camden S.), For might is riht. 1546: Heywood, *Proverbs*, Pt II ch v, Might ouercomth right. 1591: Greene,

Works, x 60 (Grosart), Might ouercomes right. 1638: D. Tuvill, *Vade Mecum*, 182 (3rd ed.), It is an old country proverbe, that Might overcomes right. 1742: North, *Lives of Norths*, ii 66 (Bohn) [as in 1591].1836: Marryat, *Easy*, ch vi, This is the age of iron, in which might has become right. 1846: *Bentley Ballads*, 22 (1876), That often Might has vanquished Right, Is now a thrice-told tale.

Might or slight, Either by. 1639: Clarke, 127. 1670: Ray, 186.

Mild as a lamb. 1530: Palsgrave, 626, I can make hym as mylde as a lambe. 1596: Shakespeare, *Rich. II*, II i, In peace was never gentle lamb more mild. 1670: Ray, 206. 1707: tr. Aleman's *Guzman*, ii 62, From a tygress she became as mild as a lamb. 1883: R.L.S., *Treasure I*, ch xiii.

Mile from an ess-midden, He'll never get a. 1886: R. Holland, *Cheshire Gloss.*, 449 (E.D.S.). 1917: Bridge, *Cheshire Proverbs*, 69 … He hasn't the pluck or energy to go far or do much.

Mile of an oak, Within a. 1599: Porter, *Two Angry Women*, sc xi, *Coo.* Where be your tooles? *Nic.* Within a mile of an oake, sir. 1678: A. Behn, *Sir Patient Fancy*, III i, Sir Credulous, where's your mistress? *Sir Cred.* Within a mile of an oak, dear madam, I'll warrant you. 1696: D'Urfey, *Quixote*, Pt III Act V sc i, Your worship can tell within a mile of an oak where he is. 1738: Swift, *Polite Convers.*, Dial. I

Milk, *subs.* **1. His milk boiled over.** 1732: Fuller, 2510.

2. I'll have none of your flat milk. 1659: Howell, 11.

3. Mylke … is white And lieth not in the dike, But all men know it good meate Inke is all blacke And hath an ill smacke No man will it drink nor eat. 1546: Heywood, *Proverbs*, Pt II ch iv.

4. Milk says to wine, 'Welcome friend'. 1640: Herbert, *Jac. Prudentum*.

5. My milk. *See* quot. 1639: in *Berkeley MSS.*, iii 31 (1885), My milke is in the cowes home, now the zunne is 'ryv'd at Capricorne [Glos.].

See also **Nothing** (29).

Mill, *subs.* **1. As good water goes by the mill as drives it.** 1732: Fuller, 691.

2. From mill and market. *See* quots. Before 1225: *Ancren R.*, 88, Vrom mulne and from cheping, from smithe and from ancre huse, me tithinge bringeth. 1611: Cotgrave, s.v. 'Moulin',

An oven and mill are nurseries of news. 1659: Howell, *Proverbs: Fr.-Eng.*, 11, If you will learn news, you must go to the oven or the mill.

3. His mill will go with all winds. 1732: Fuller, 2511.

4. In vain does the mill clack, if the miller his hearing lack. 1631: Mabbe, *Celestina*, 244 (T.T.), To what use serves the clapper in the mil, if the miller be deafe? 1640: Herbert, *Jac. Prudentum*. 1670: Ray, 121. 1732: Fuller, 6388.

5. Mills and wives ever want. 1586: Pettie, tr. Guazzo's *Civil Convers.*, fo. 137, Wherevpon it is said that mils and women euer want something. 1640: Herbert, *Jac. Prudentum*. 1670: Ray, 18.

6. Mills will not grind if you give them not water. 1732: Fuller, 3414.

7. The mill cannot grind with water that's passed. 1633: Draxe, 151, The water that is past cannot make the mill goe. 1640: Herbert, *Jac. Prudentum*. 1712: Motteux, *Quixote*, Pt II ch lxxi, Delay breeds danger. It is best grinding at the mill before the water is past. *c.*1890: S. Doudney, *Lesson of the Watermill*, And a proverb haunts my mind As a spell is cast; 'The mill cannot grind With the water that is passed.

8. The mill gets by going. 1640: Herbert, *Jac. Prudentum*.

9. The mills of God grind slow, but they grind exceeding small. 1870: Longfellow, *Poems* (1960), 331, Though the mills of God grind slowly, yet they grind exceeding small; Though with patience he stands waiting, with exactness grinds he all. 1942: F. Reeding, *Twelve Disguises*, i, That's my business … The mills of God grind slowly, but they grind exceeding small. *See also* God's mill grinds slow.

10. You had rather go to mill than to mass. 1605: Camden, *Remains*, 336 (1870), Ye had as lief go to mill as to mass. 1732: Fuller, 5909.

See also **Born in a mill; Change**, *verb* (1); **First come; Friend** (20); **Grist; Horse** (55) and (62); and **No mill**.

Miller. 1. A miller is never dry = never waits to be thirsty before drinking. 1894: Northall, *Folk Phrases*, 6 (E.D.S.).

2. An honest miller hath a golden thumb – with some variations, *c.*1386: Chaucer, *Prol.*, l. 563, [The Miller] Wel koude he stelen corn and tollen thries, And yet he hadde a thombe of gold, pardee. *c.*1520: *Cock Lorells Bote*, 3 (Percy S.), A myller dusty poll than dyde corne, A Ioly felowe

with a golden thome. 1526: *Hund. Mery Tales*, No. xii p. 22 (Oesterley), I haue hard say that euery trew mylner that tollythe trewlye hath a gyldeyn thombe. 1612: in *Pepysian Garland*, 32 (Rollins), The miller with his golden thumbe … he needs must steale a pecke. 1732: Fuller, 2531, Honest millers have golden thumbs. 1846: Jerrold, *Chron. of Clovernook*, 94, The miller – the prosperous fellow with the golden thumb.

3. As stout as a miller's waistcoat, that takes a thief by the neck every day. 1732: Fuller, 731.

4. It is good to be sure, toll it again, quoth the miller., *c.*1386: Chaucer [*See* the allusion to 'tollen thries 'in the first quotation under No. 2]. 1678: Ray, 91. 1820: Scott, *Monastery*, ch xxxvii, 'It will not be the worse of another bolting', said the Miller; 'it is always best to be sure, as I say when I chance to take multure twice from the same meal-sack'.

5. Like a miller he can set to every wind. 1732: Fuller, 3224.

6. Like a miller's mare = clumsily. 1606: *Choice Chance and Change*, 68 (Grosart), Can seeme as sober as a millers mare. *c.*1620: B.&F., *Little Fr. Lawyer*, IV v, *Nurse* … I can jump yet or tread a measure. *Lam.* like a miller's mare. 1663: Killigrew, *Parson's Wedding*, II vi, I'll make him jostle like the miller's mare, and stand like the dun cow, till thou may'st milk him.

7. Like the miller's filler. *See* quot. 1869: Hazlitt, 199, He's always behind hand, like the miller's filler. *Northampt.*

8. Many a miller many a thief. 1673: *Vinegar and Mustard*, 19, in Hindley, *Old Book-Coll. Miscell.*, iii.

9. No bigger than a miller's thumb. 1675: Cotton, *Burl, upon Burlesque*, 163(1765). 1847: Halliwell, *Dict.*, s.v. 'Miller's thumb', … a common simile.

10. Put a miller, a tailor and a weaver into one bag, and shake them, the first that comes out will be a thief. 1659: Howell, 8. 1670: Ray, 217. Cf. **Hundred tailors**.

11. The miller grinds more men's corn than one. 1596: Nashe, *Works*, iii 25 (Grosart).,

12. The miller sees not all the water that goes by his mill. 1546: Heywood, *Proverbs*, Pt II ch v, Muche water goeth by the myll That the miller knowth not of. 1583: Melbancke, *Philotinus*, sig. Ee3, Muche water passeth besides the mill that the milner seeth not. 1616: *Rich Cabinet*, fo. 31

[as in 1546]. 1670; Ray, 121 [as in 1546]. 1825: Scott, *Betrothed*, ch xxvii, Much water slides past the mill that Hob Miller never wots of.

13. The miller's boy said so = It was a matter of common report. 1872: J. Glyde, jr., *Norfolk Garland*, 149.

14. To Put out the miller's eye. *See* quots. 1678: Ray, 343. 1783: *Gent. Mag.*, 675, The phrase of putting the miller's eye out, when too much liquid is put to any dry or powdery substance. 1854: Baker, *Northants Gloss.*, s.v. 'You've put the miller's eye out'. A general phrase when any liquid is too much diluted with an excess of water. 1887: Parish and Shaw, *Dict. Kent. Dialect.*, 101 (E.D.S.), To put the miller's eye out is when a person, in mixing mortar or dough, pours too much water into the hole made to receive it. 1920: E. Gepp, *Essex Dialect Dict.*, 23 … to overdo the water in a mixture.

15. Ye braide of the millers dogg, Ye lick your mouth or the Poke be open. 1683: Meriton, *Yorkshire Ale*, 83–7 (1607).

See also **Drown the miller**.

Mill-post to a pudding-prick, He hath thwitten [whittled] **a.** 1528: More, in *Works*, p. 236, col. 2 (1557), Thys processe came to a wise purpose, here was a gret post wel thuyted to a pudding pricke. 1611: Cotgrave, s.v. 'Arbre', Wee say of one that hath squandered away great wealth hee hath, etc. 1660: Howell, *Parly of Beasts*, 59, She will bring her poor husband quickly to thwitten a mill-post into a pudding-prick. 1691: Ray, *Words not Generally Used*, 70 (E.D.S.).

Mince-pies. *See* **Christmas** (9).

Mind to me a kingdom is, My. [Mens regnum bona possidet. – Seneca, *Thyestes*, II 380.] 1588: Sir E. Dyer, in Byrd, *Psalmes, etc.*, My minde to me a kingdome is, Such perfect joy therein I finde. *c.*1598: Jonson, *Case is Altered*, I i 1618: Breton, in *Works*, ii *u* 9 (Grosart). 1775: in *Roxb. Ballads*, vii 520 (B.S.), My mind is a kingdom to me, there's danger in being too great. 1871: Smiles, *Character*, 371, ' … ' applies alike to the peasant as to the monarch. 1912: H. James, in *Letters*, ii 253 (1920).

Mind. *See also* **Hand** (8).

Mine ease. *See* **Take** (28).

Miracles is past, The age of. *See* **Age of miracles**.

Mirth and mischief are two things. 1732: Fuller, 3415.

Mirth of the world dureth but a while, The. 1629: *Book of Meery Riddles*, Prov. 11.

Mischief. 1. He that mischief hatcheth, mischief catcheth. 1605: Camden, *Remains*, 324 (1870). 1732: Fuller, 6348.

2. Mischief comes by the pound and goes away by the ounce. 1578: Florio, *First Fruites*, fo. 29, The yll commeth by poundes and goeth away by ounces. 1670: Ray, 121 [in the plural]. 1732: Fuller, 3417.

3. Mischief has swift wings. 1609: J. Melton, *Six-fold Politician*, 13, Mischiefe is well saide to haue swift winges.

4. Mischief is ever too bold. *c.*1604: in *Ballads from MSS.*, ii 47 (B.S.) [quoted as a familiar saying].

5. There is no mischief done. *See* quots. 1577: *Misogonus*, II v, Thers no mischiefe, as they say commenly, but a preist at one end. 1658: *Wit Restor'd*, 150, There is no mischiefe, but a woman is at one end of it. 1670: Ray, 50, There's no mischief in the world done, But a woman is always one. 1732: Fuller, 6405 [as in 1670]. 1875: Cheales, *Proverb. Folk-Lore*, 5, There's no mischief done, But a woman's one.

See also **Better a mischief**.

Miser spares. *See* quot. 1611: Cotgrave, s.v. 'Despendre', That which the wretch [miser] doth spare the waster spends.

Miserly father has a thriftless son, A. 1612: W. Parkes, *Curtaine-Drawer of the World*, 30 (Grosart), Conferme the proverbe, that it currant runne, A miser father finds a thriftlesse sonne.

Misery acquaints a man with strange bed-fellows. 1611: Shakespeare, *Tempest*, II ii 1837: Lockhart, *Life of Scott*, i 411, Literature, like misery, makes men acquainted with strange bed-fellows. Cf. **Poverty**.

Misery enough to have once been happy, It is. 1639: Clarke, 166.

Misery loves company. [Latin: *gaudium est miseris socios habuisse penarum* (it is a joy to the miserable to have companions in their pain). A different version of the same Latin saying is given by Marlowe to the devil Mephistophilis in his *Dr Faustus*.] This saying is now mainly current in America; the preferred modern British form is *A trouble shared is a trouble halved* (*see* **Trouble** (1). 1349: R. Rolle, *Meditation on the Passion*, in C. Horstmann, *Yorkshire Writers*

(1895), I 101, It is a solce to have companie in peyne. 1578: Lyly, *Euphues*, I 238, In miserie Euphues it is a great comfort to have a companion. 1620: T. Shelton, tr. *Cervantes' Don Quixote*, II. xiii, If that which is commonly spoken be true, that to have companions in misery is a lightner of it, you may comfort me. 1851: Thoreau, *Journal*, 1 Spet. (1949), II. 440, If misery loves company, misery has company enough.

Misery may be the mother when one beggar begs of another. 1546: Heywood, *Proverbs*, Pt II ch x 1633: Draxe, 14.

Misfortunes come on wings and depart on foot. 1855: Bohn, 452.

Misfortunes never come singly. *c*.1300: *King Alisaunder*, l. 1281, Men tellen in oldë mone [remembrance], The qued commth nowher alone, *c*.1490: *Partonope*, l. 5542 (E.E.T.S.), For efter won euylle comythe mony mo. 1509: Barclay, *Ship of Fools*, ii 251 (1874), For wyse men sayth ... That one myshap fortuneth neuer alone, *c*.1580: Spelman, *Dialogue*, 3 (Roxb.Cl), A man cannot have one losse, but more will ffolowe. 1602: Shakespeare, *Hamlet*, IV v, When sorrows come, they come not single spies, But in battalions. 1694: *Terence made English*, 30, My misfortunes come one upo' th' neck of another. 1711: Addison, *Spectator*, No. 7. 1743: Fielding, *Jon. Wild*, bk i ch viii, One misfortune never comes alone. 1826: Lamb, *Pop. Fallacies*, xiii, Misfortunes seldom come alone. 1841: Dickens, *Barn. Rudge*, ch xxxii 1914: Lucas, *Landmarks*, 262.

Misfortunes tell us what fortune is. 1732: Fuller, 3420.

Misfortunes, when asleep, are not to be awakened. Ibid., No. 3422.

Misreckoning is no payment 1546: Heywood, *Proverbs*, Pt II ch iv 1670: Ray, 121. 1732: Fuller, No.3423.

Miss is as good as a mile, A. Cf. **Inch in a miss is as good as an ell** – the earlier form of the saying. 1788: *American Museum*, Apr. 382, A miss is as good as a mile.1825: Scott, *Journal*, 3 Dec., He was very near being a poet – but a miss is as good as a mile, and he always fell short of the mark. 1869: Spurgeon, *John Ploughman*, ch vii, A little too late is much too late, and a miss is as good as a mile. 1894: Shaw, *Arms and the Man*, I, A narrow shave; but a miss is as good as a mile.

Miss one's mark, To. 1530: Palsgrave, 638, If I mysse nat my marke, he is a busy felowe. 1639: Clarke, 1, To misse of his marke. 1690: *New Dict. Canting Crew*, sig. B1, He has mist bis aim or end. 1754: Berthelson, *Eng.-Danish Dict.*, s.v. 'Mark'.

Miss the cushion, To. Before 1529: Skelton, *Colin Clout*, l. 998, And whan he weneth to syt, Yet may he mysse the quysshon. 1533: Latimer, in *Works*, ii 366 (P.S.), No doubt he did miss the cushion in many things. 1585: Greene, in *Works*, v 124 (Grosart), Euery one yeelded his verdicte but all mist the cushion. 1639: Clarke, 2, You mist the cushion.

Mist. *See* quots. 1846: Denham, *Proverbs*, 18 (Percy S.), When the mist comes from the hill, Then good weather it doth spill; When the mist comes from the sea, Then good weather it will be. 1891: R. P. Chope, *Hartland Dialect*, 20 (E.D.S.), Mist vrom the say Bring'th vore a dry day; Mist vrom the 'ills, Bring'th watter to the mills. 1893: Inwards, *Weather Lore*, 98 [as in 1846]. Cf. **Fog** (3) and (4).

Mistress. 1. All is well when the mistress smiles. 1659: Howell, 17.

2. The mistress of the mill May say and do what she will. 1864: 'Cornish Proverbs', in *N.&Q.*, 3rd ser, v 208.

3. The mistress's eye feeds the capon. 1616: Breton, in *Works*, ii *e* 8 (Grosart), The mistris eye makes the capon fatt. 1639: Clarke, 163.

4. When the mistress is the master, The parsley grows the faster. Mon. 1905: *Folk-Lore*, xvi 67.

See also **Hackney mistress**; and **Like mistress**.

Misty morning may have a fine day, A. 1732: Fuller, 327.

Misunderstanding brings lies to town. 1639: Clarke, 2. 1670: Ray, 121. 1712: Motteux, *Quixote*, Pt I bk iii ch xi 1732: Fuller, 3424.

Misunderstandings are best prevented by pen and ink. 1831: Hone, *Year-Book*, col. 1416.

Mitcham whisper, A = A shout. 1880: Spurgeon, *Ploughman's Pictures*, 80, They generally speak four or five at a time, and every one in a Mitcham whisper, which is very like a shout. 1881: *N.&Q.*, 6th ser, iii 336, In this town [Leigh, Lancs] an unearthly yell, given at the close of a convivial evening and as a sequel to a popular toast, is called a 'Leigh whisper'.

Mob has many heads but no brains, The. 1732: Fuller, 4653.

Mobberley, Cheshire. **1. Always behind, like Mobberley clock.** 1886: R. Holland, *Cheshire Gloss.*, 444 (E.D.S.). 1917: Bridge, *Cheshire Proverbs*, 7.

2. It rains, it pains. *See* quot. 1917: Ibid., 163, It rains, it pains, it patters i' th' docks, Mobberley wenches are weshin their smocks.

3. The rain always comes out of Mobberley hole. Ibid., 117.

4. Thou'rt like. *See* quot. Ibid., 124, Thou'rt like old Mode o' Mobberley that seed th' new moon i' th' morning.

5. You may know a Mobberley man by his breeches. Ibid., 158.

Mock no panyer-men, your father was a fisher. 1678: Ray, 78. 1732: Fuller, 3425 [with 'if' before 'you'].

Mock not, quoth Mumford, when his wife called him cuckold. 1659: Howell, 9. 1670: Ray, 186. 1732: Fuller, 3426.

Mock the lame you will go so yourself, If you. *c.*1577: Northbrooke, *Dicing, etc.*, 80 (SH.S.), According to the old saying – If thou with him that haltes doest dwell, To learne to halt thou shalt full well. 1732: Fuller, 2774.

Mocking is catching. 1533: Heywood, *Play of Love*, l. 568 (Brandl, *Quellen*, 177), For who so that mocketh shall surely stur This olde prouerbe mockum moccabitur. 1710: S. Palmer, *Moral Essays on Proverbs*, 319. 1738: Swift, *Polite Convers.*, Dial. I. 1880: Spurgeon, *Ploughman's Pictures*, 15, The old saying is, 'Hanging's stretching, and mockmg's catching'.

Moderation in all things. A more modern version of the saying *There is measure in all things* (*See* **Measure** (7)). 1849: H. Melville, *Mardi*, II. lxxvii, I am for being temperate in these things … All things in moderation are good; whence wine is moderation is good. 1879: W.H.G. Kingston, tr. *Swiss Family Robinson*, ii, 'Oh, father, sugar canes … . Do let us take a lot home to mother' … 'Gently, there … Moderation in all things'.

Modest words. *See* quot. *c.*1645: MS. Proverbs, in *N.&Q.*, vol. cliv, p. 27, It is good to find modest words to express immodest things.

Mole – the animal. **1. A mole wants no lanthorn.** 1732: Fuller, 329.

2. He holds a looking-glass to a mole. 1813: Ray. 75.

See also **Blind** (14).

Mole – a growth on the body. **1. A mole on the neck.** *See* quots. 1883: Burne, *Shropsh. Folk-Lore*, 267, A mole on the neck You shall have money by the peck. 1923: *Folk-Lore*, xxxiv 156, Mole on the neck, trouble by the peck (Gloucest.).

2. Five moles in a span, You shall have houses and land. 1883: Burne, *Shropsh. Folk-Lore, 267*.

3. If you've got a mole above your chin You'll never be beholden to any of your kin. Ibid., 267.

Molehill. *See* **Mountain** (3).

Monday. **1. A stranger on Monday means a stranger all the week.** Suffolk. 1924: *Folk-Lore*, xxxv 358.

2. Monday flit, never sit. 1641: Best, *Farming Book*, 135 (Surtees S.), As for Munday, they account it ominous, for they say, Munday flitte, Neaver sitte. Cf. **Saturday** (2).

3. Monday for wealth, etc. *See* quot. 1879: Henderson, *Folk-Lore N. Coun*ties, 33 [Marriage] Monday for wealth, Tuesday for health, Wednesday the best day of all; Thursday for losses, Friday for crosses, And Saturday no luck at all. *Durham*.

4. Monday is Sunday's brother. 1611: *Tarltons Jests*, 41 (SH.S.), One asked Tarlton why Munday was called Sundaies fellow. 1637: in *Pepysian Garland*, 445 (Rollins), Tho Munday Sundayes fellow be, when tuesday comes to worke fall we. 1846: Denham, *Proverbs*, 15 (Percy S.), Monday is Sunday's brother; Tuesday is such another. Wednesday you must go to church and pray; Thursday is half-holiday. On Friday it is too late to begin to spin; The Saturday is half-holiday agen. 1890: J. D. Robertson, *Gloucest. Gloss.*, 187 (E.D.S.), [Cobbler's Creed] Monday is a Saint's day; Tuesday's just another such a day; Wednesday's the middle pin; Thursday's too late to begin; Friday we must fast and pray; Saturday never was but half a day.

5. Monday's child. *See quots.* 1838: Mrs Bray, *Trad. of Devon*, ii 288, Monday's child is fair of face, Tuesday's child is full of grace, Wednesday's child is full of woe, Thursday's child has far to go, Friday's child is loving and giving, Saturday's child works hard for its living; And a child that's born on. Christmas Day Is fair and wise, good and gay. 1877: *N*,

&Q., 5th ser, vii 424, Born on Monday, fair in the face; Born on Tuesday, full of God's grace; Born on Wednesday, sour and sad; Born on Thursday, merry and glad; Bom on Friday, worthily given; Born on Saturday, work hard for your living; Born on Sunday you will never know want [there is a variant at 5th ser, viii 45] 1879: Henderson, *Folk-Lore N. Counties*, 9 [as in 1838, but with 'Sabbath day' for 'Christmas Day', and 'blithe and bonny' for 'fair and wise']. Cf. **Sunday** (4).

Money. 1. All things are obedient to money. [Omnis enim res, virtus, fama, decus, divina humanaque pulchris divitiis parent. – Horace, *Sat.*, II iii 94–6.] 1539: Taverner, *Proverbs*, fo. 14, Vnto money be all thynges obedient. 1542: Becon, *Early Works*, 222 (P.S.). 1611: Cotgrave, s.v. 'Argent', All (earthly) things are commanded, and compassed, by it. 1692: L'Estrange, *Aesop*, 359 (3rd ed.), The old saying, that money does all things, is not much wide of the truth. 1775: Grose, *Antiq. Repertory*, ii 395 (1808), That 'every thing may be had for money', is … no less ancient than true. Cf. No. 31.

2. He that gets money before he gets wit, Will be but a short while master of it. 1732: Fuller, 6432.

3. He that hath money in his purse, cannot want a head for his shoulders. 1659: Howell, 13. 1763: Murphy, *Citizen*, I ii.

4. He that hath no money needeth no purse. 1633: Draxe, 138. 1666: Torriano, *Piazza Univ.*, 63.

5. He that wants money wants all things. 1542: Becon, in *Early Works*, 223 (P.S.), He is a wretch that hath no money. 1611: Cotgrave, s.v. 'Argent'. 1633: Draxe, 24, When wee want mony, we want all. 1772: Cumberland, *Fash. Lover*, II i, In England, he that wants money wants everything.

6. He would get money in a desert. 1813: Ray, 196.

7. He'll find money for mischief, when he can find none for corn. 1732: Fuller, 2425.

8. His money burns in his pocket. *c.*1530: More, in *Works*, 195 (1557), A little wanton money, which … burned out the bottom of his purse. 1601: Cornwallis, *Essayes*, Pt I sig. P4 (1610), Like an vnthrifts money that burnes in his purse. 1637: Shirley, *Hyde Park*, IV iii, My gold has burnt this twelve months in my pocket.

1702: Farquhar, *Inconstant*, V iii, Time lies heavy on my hands, and my money burns in my pocket. 1857: Hughes, *Tom Brown*, Pt I ch vi, Tom's new purse and money burnt in his pocket.

9. His money comes from him like drops of blood. 1678: Ray, 90.

10. If money go before, all ways lie open. 1542: Becon, in *Early Works*, 223 (P.S.), Whosoever hath money may go where he list … at his own pleasure. 1600: Shakespeare, *Merry Wives*, II ii 1666: Torriano, *Piazza Univ.*, 163, Money makes all gates to fly open.

11. If thou wouldest keep money, save money; If thou wouldest reap money, sow money. 1732: Fuller, Nos. 2721 and 2722.

12. If you would know the value of money, try to borrow some. 1640: Herbert, *Jac. Prudentum*, Would you know what money is, go borrow some. 1732: Fuller, 2801 ['a ducat' for 'money', and 'one' for 'some']. 1736: Franklin, *Way to Wealth*, in *Works*, i 448 (Bigelow). 1875: Cheales, *Proverb. Folk-Lore*, 101 [as in 1640].

13. Money answers all things. 1667: L'Estrange, *Quevedo's Visions*, 38 (1904). 1700: Ward, *London Spy*, 400 (1924).

14. Money begets money. 1587: Turbervile, *Trag. Tales, etc.*, 22 (1837), *But where wealth is, there lightlie follows more.* 1625: Bacon, *Essays: 'Usurie'*, They say … that it is against Nature for money to beget money. 1748: Franklin, in *Works*, ii 119 (Bigelow), Money can beget money, and its offspring can beget more. 1865: Dickens, *Mutual Friend*, bk iii ch v, We have got to recollect that money makes money, as well as makes everything else.

15. Money governs the world. 1754: Berthelson, *Eng.-Danish Dict.*, s.v. 'Money'.

16. Money has no smell. 1914: 'E. Bramah', *Max Carrados*, 45, The Romans, Parkinson, had a saying to the effect that gold carries no smell. 1922: A. Bennett, *Prohack*, ch iii (i.), He understood in a flash the deep wisdom of that old proverb … that money has no smell Cf. **Chink**.

17. Money in purse will be always in fashion. 1633: Draxe, 82, Money neuer commeth out of season. 1639: Clarke, 220 [as in 1633]. 1732: Fuller, 3435.

18. Money is a good servant but a bad master. 1855: Bohn, 453.

19. Money is a great traveller in the world. 1616: Breton, in *Works*, ii *e* 5 (Grosart) ['continuall' for 'great']. 1639: Clarke, 98.

20. Money is ace of trumps. 1732: Fuller, 3438.

21. Money is no fool, if a wise man have it in keeping. Glos. 1639: in *Berkeley MSS.*, iii 27 (1885).

22. Money isn't everything. 1927: E. O'Neill, *Marco Millions*, iii, Money isn't everything, not always.

23. Money is oft lost for want of money. 1633: Draxe, 69.

24. Money is round. *See* quots. 1619: *Helpe to Discourse*, 120 (1640), Why is the forme of money round? Because it is to runne from every man. 1666: Torriano, *Piazza Univ.*, 64, Moneys are round, and that makes them rowl away. 1869: Spurgeon, *John Ploughman*, ch xii, Money is round, and rolls away easily.

25. Money is that which art hath turned up trump. 1659: Howell, 18. 1670: Ray, 18.

26. Money is the root of all evil. [A misquotation of 1 Timothy vi.10, The love of money is the root of all evil] *c.*1000: Aelfric, *Homilies* (1843), I 256, Seo gytsung is ealra yfelra thinga wyrtruma (Covetousness is of all evil things the root). *c.*1449: R. Pecock, *Repressor of Blaming of Clergy* (1860), II. 555, Love to money … is worthi to be forborn … as Poul seith, it is 'the roote of al yvel'. 1616: J. Withals, *Dictionary* (rev. ed.) 546, Riches are the root of all evill. 1858: A. Trollope, *Dr Thorne*, I. xii, 'But, doctor, you'll take the money' … 'Quite impossible …' said the doctor … . valiantly rejecting the root of all evil.

27. Money is the sinew of love as well as of war. 1732: Fuller, 3442.

28. Money is welcome though it come in a dirty clout. 1542: Becon, in *Early Works*, 222 (P.S.), The savour of lucre is good, howsoever a man come by it. 1647: Howell, *Letters*, bk ii No. xxv 1670: Ray, 18. 1723: Defoe, *Col. Jack*, ch ii, I have often since heard people say, when they have been talking of money, that they could not get in, I wish I had it in a foul clout.

29. Money is wise, it knows its way. Somerset. 1678: Ray, 352.

30. Money, like dung, does not good till it's spread. 1625: Bacon, *Essays: 'Seditions, etc.'*, Money is like muck, not good excePt it be spread. 1659: Howell, 19, Riches like muck which stinks in a heap, but spread abroad, maketh the earth fruitful. 1670: Ray, 22 [as in 1659]. 1732: Fuller, No.3444.

31. Money makes friends enemies. 1616: Breton, *Crossing of Proverbs*, 6 (Grosart). 1732: Fuller, 3446, Money makes not so many true friends as real enemies.

32. Money makes marriage. Ibid., No. 3445.

33. Money makes mastery. 1602: *Liberality and Prodig.*, I v 1686: *Loyal Garland*, 42 (Percy S.), This masters money, though money masters all things. Cf. No. 1.

34. Money makes the man. [Cf. Pindar, *Isth. Ode*, ii 15.] 1500: in R.L. Greene, *Early English Carols* (1935), 263, Yt ys allwayes sene nowadayes That money makythe the man.1542: Becon, in *Early Works*, 222 (P.S.). 1564: Bullein, *Dialogue*, 102 (E.E.T.S.), That will make readie money, and money maketh a man. *c.*1630: in *Pepysian Garland*, 362 (Rollins), They say tis money makes a man. 1681: Robertson, *Phraseol Generalis*, 892. 1840: Lytton, *Money.* II i 1926: *Evening Standard*, 11 Dec., p. 5, col. 2.

35. Money makes the mare to go. 1578: Florio, *First Fruites*, fo. 30 Money maketh horses runne. 1605 Breton, in *Works*, ii. l7 (Grosart), For money … makes … the olde mare: trot, and the young tit amble. 1691: *Merry Drollery*, 117 (Ebsworth), '*Tis* money makes … the mare to go. *c.*1760: Foote, *Author*, I. 1857: Kingsley, *Two Years Ago*, Introd., I'm making the mare go here … withouth: the money too sometimes.

36. Money makes the merchant. 1468: *Coventry Mys.*, 268 (SH.S.), In old termys I have herd seyde, That mony makyth schapman.

37. Money makes the old wife trot. 1691: *Merry Drollery*, 117 (Ebsworth). 1700: Ward, *London Spy*, 400 (1924). 1732: Fuller, 3433.

38. Money paid and arms broken. 1620: Shelton, *Quixote*, Pt II ch lxxi, It shall never be said of me, 'Money well paid, and the arms broken'. 1631: Mabbe, *Celestina*, 67 (T.T.), How softly she goes! How one leg comes drawling after another! Now she has her money, her armes are broken. 1666: Torriano, *Piazza Univ.*, 257, A servant paid, his arm broke.

39. Money refused loseth its brightness. 1640: Herbert, *Jac. Prudentum.*

40. Money talks. 1586: Pettie, tr. Guazzo's *Civil Convers.*, fo. 88, It is sayd that … the tongue hath no force when golde speaketh. 1666: Torriano, *Piazza Univ.*, 179, Man prates, but gold speaks.

1915: P. G. Wodehouse, *Something Fresh*, ch iii (vi.), The whole story took on a different complexion for Joan. Money talks. 1925: A. Palmer, in *Sphere*, 19 Dec., p. 364, col. 3, 'Money talks', I reminded myself, 'So why not listen to it?'

41. Money will do more than my lord's letter. 1678: Ray, 177. 1732: Fuller, 3447.

42. Money will make the pot boil. 1692: L'Estrange, *Aesop*, 305 (3rd ed.), 'Tis that [Money] which makes the pot boyl (as the proverb says). 1732: Fuller, 3449.

43. Money without love is like salt without pilchers. 1880: Courtney, *W. Cornwall Words*, 42 (E.D.S.).

44. Of money, wit, and virtue, believe one-fourth of what you hear. 1855: Bohn, 466.

45. The abundance of money ruins youth. 1670: Ray, 18.

46. The money you refuse will never do you good. 1855: Bohn, 510.

47. The skilfullest wanting money is scorned. 1670: Ray, 18.

48. They that take money. *See* quot. *c.*1640: in *Roxb. Ballads*, iii 253 (B.S.), The proverb observing – 'They that money take Must pay all the charges'.

49. What will not money do? 1581: T. Howell, *Devises*, 54 (1906), But briefe to bee, what can you craue, That now for golde you may not haue? 1623: Webster, *Devil's Law-Case*, IV i, Lord, lord, To see what money can do! 1681: Robertson, *Phraseol. Generalis*, 892. 1708: tr. Aleman's *Guzman*, i 13, What is not to be done with money?

See also **Beauty** (9); **Fool** (2) and (11); **Little money; Love,** *subs.* (13), (23), (36), and (38); **My son; Pretty things; Ready money;** and **Sinews of war**.

Moneyless man goes fast through the market, A. 1732: Fuller, 330.

Mongst many chapmen there are few that buyes. 1606: Heywood, *If You Know Not Me*, Pt II, in *Works*, i 263 (1874).

Monkey. *See* **Higher the monkey climbs**; and **Melancholy**.

Monkey on the chimney, A = A mortgage or debt on a house. 1877: *N. & Q.*, 5th ser, viii 289, A monkey on the house. 1887: T. Darlington, S. *Cheshire Folk Speech.*, 264 (E.D.S.). 1917: Bridge, *Cheshire Proverbs*, 4.

Monkey's grease, As useless as. 1732: Fuller, 744.

Monkeys. *See* **Pay** (6).

Monmouth caps. *See* **Leominster wool**.

Month of Sundays, A = A prolonged but indefinite period. 1832: Marryat, *N. Forster*, v (OED), It may last a month of Sundays. 1850: Kingsley, *Alton Locke*, ch xxvii, I haven't heard more fluent or passionate English this month of Sundays. 1898: Gibbs, *Cotswold Village*, ch iv 71 (3rd ed.), A joint of mutton is not seen by the peasants more than 'once in a month of Sundays'. 1923: *Punch*, 20 June, p. 582, col. 3, I will engage to talk at that level for a month of Sundays.

Month that comes in good, will go out bad, The. 1893: Inwards, *Weather Lore*, 42.

Month's mind, A = An eager desire. 1575: Gascoigne, *Glasse of Govt.*, II v, She hath a monethes minde vnto Phylosarchus. 1605: *London Prodigal*, I ii, He hath a month's mind here to mistress Frances. 1631: Brathwait, *Eng. Gentlewoman*, 355 (1641), I have a moneth's mind to see the man! 1731: in Peck, *Desid. Curiosa*, 229 (1779), When people earnestly desire a thing, they frequently say, they have a month's mind to it. 1766: Garrick and Colman, *Clandest. Marriage*, *I* i, Persuading a silly girl to do what she has more than a month's mind to do. 1824: Scott, *Redgauntlet*, Lett. III, I have a month's mind … to give thee the history of a little adventure which befell me yesterday. 1877: E. Leigh, *Cheshire Gloss.*, 136, 'To have a month's mind 'is to have a strong inclination to do something. 1913: E. M. Wright, *Rustic Speech, etc.*, 282, To have a month's mind to anything [in general dialectal use]. This alludes to a pre-Reformation practice of repeating one or more masses at the end of a month after death for the repose of a departed soul.

Moon. 1. A dry moon is far north and soon seen. 1893: Inwards, *Weather Lore*, 59

2. A new moon soon seen is long thought of. 1846: Denham, *Proverbs*, 2 (Percy S.). 1904: *Co. Folk-lore: Northumb.*, 171 (F.L.S.).

3. A Saturday's moon. *See* quots. 1732: Fuller, 6491, A Saturday's moon If it comes once in seven years, it comes too soon. 1818: Mrs Piozzi, in Hayward, *Mrs Piozzi*, ii 391 (1861), St David's Day has been a rough one, and your brother Dorset forces me on the reflection that it was a Saturday's moon. 1830: Forby, *Vocab. E. Anglia*, 417, On Saturday new, on Sunday full, Was never good, and never wooll 1846: Denham, *Proverbs*, 9 (Percy S.), A Saturday's moon, Come when it will it comes too soon. Ibid., 18, A Saturday's change brings the boat to the door; But a Sunday's change brings it upon t' mid floor. 1864: 'Cornish Proverbs', in *N. &Q.*, 3rd ser, v 209, A Saturday or a Sunday moon, Comes once in seven years too soon. *c*.1870: Smith, *Isle of Wight Words*, 62 (E.D.S.) [essentially as in 1830]. 1879: Henderson, *Folk-Lore N. Counties*, 114, Throughout Northumberland this couplet is said and believed in: A Saturday's moon and a Sunday's prime Never brought good in any man's time. 1887: M. A. Courtney, *Foik-Lore Journal*, v 191, A Saturday's moon is a sailor's curse. *Cornwall.* 1893: *Co. Folk-Lore: Suffolk*, 161 (F.L.S.) [as in 1830]. 1893: Inwards, *Weather Lore*, 59 [as in 1732,1830, etc.].

4. An old moon in a mist Is worth gold in a kist [chest]; **But a new moon's mist Will never lack thirst.** 1878: Dyer, *Eng. Folk-Lore*, 41. 1893: Inwards, *Weather Lore*, 65. Cf. No. 23.

5. Auld moon mist Ne'er died of thirst. Ibid., 65.

6. Have a care, etc. *See* quot. 1846–59: *Denham Tracts*, ii 57 (F.L.S.), We have, however, an old, very old proverb … to wit; 'Have a care lest the churl fall out o' the moon'.

7. If the full moon rise red expect wind. 1588: A. Fraunce, *Lawiers Logike*, fo. 43, When the moone is red, shee betokeneth wind. 1893: Inwards, 64.

8. If the moon show a silver shield, Be not afraid to reap your field; But if she rises haloed round, Soon we'll tread on deluged ground. 1893: Ibid., 64.

9. In the old of the moon a cloudy morning bodes a fair afternoon. 1639: in *Berkeley MSS.*, iii 31 (1885), A misty morne in th' old o' th' moone doth alwaies bring a faire post-noone. An hilly proverbe about Simondsall (Glouc.). 1678: Ray, 48. 1831: Hone. *Year-Book*, 300, In the waning of the moon, A cloudy morn – fair afternoon. 1893: Inwards, 59, In the decay of the moon A cloudy morning bodes a fair afternoon. Ibid., 64, Near full moon, a misty sunrise Bodes fair weather and cloudless skies.

10. It is a fine moon, God bless he! 1678: Aubrey, in *Antiq. Repertory*, i 73 (1807), Some of

them sitting astride on a gate or stile the first evening the new moon appears, and say, *A fine moon, God bless her!* 1846: Denham, *Proverbs*, 4 (Percy S.).

11. No moon, no man. *See* quot. 1878: Dyer, *Eng. Folk-Lore*, 41, In Cornwall, when a child is born in the interval between an old moon and the first appearance of a new one, it is said that it will never live to reach the age of puberty. Hence the saying, 'No moon, no man'.

12. Pale moon doth rain, red moon doth blow, White moon doth neither rain nor snow. 1639: Clarke, 263.

13. So many days old the moon is on Michaelmas Day, so many floods after. 1661: M. Stevenson, *Twelve Moneths*, 44. 1819: Henderson, *Folk-Lore N. Counties*, 96. 1885: Harley, *Moon Lore.* 185.

14. Sunday's moon. *See* quots. 1851: Steinberg, *Dialect, etc., of Northants*, 110, Thus the proverb, 'Sunday's moon floods 'for 'ts out'. 1893: Inwards, 59, If the moon change on a Sunday, there will be a flood before the month is out. *Worcestershire. See also* No. 3.

15. The full moon brings fine weather. Ibid., 64.

16. The full moon eats clouds. *Nautical.* And, *The moon grows fat on clouds.* Ibid., 64.

17. The Michaelmas moon Rises nine nights alike soon. 1878: Dyer, *Eng. Folk-Lore*, 259.

18. The moon does not heed the barking of dogs. 1813: Ray, 208.

19. The moon is a moon still, whether it shine or not. 1732: Fuller, 4654.

20. The moon is made of green cheese, To believe (or **To tell one) that.** This is one of the most frequently found sayings in 16th- and 17th-century literature. 1529: Frith, *Antith. Works*, p. 105, col. 1 (1573) (OED), They woulde make men beleue … that ye moone is made of grene chese. 1542: Udall, tr. Erasmus' *Apoph.*, 193 (1877), With this pleasaunt mery toye, he … made his frendes beleue the moone to be made of a grene chese. 1584: R. Scot, *Witchcraft*, bk xv ch v 1658: in *Musarum Deliciae, etc.*, i 199 (Hotten), The moon is made of nothing but green cheese. 1696: *Cornish Comedy*, IV i 1754: Berthelson, *Eng.-Danish Dict.*, s.v. 'Believe.'

21. The moon is not seen where the sun shines. 1670: Ray, 122. 1826: Brady, *Varieties of Lit.*, 38.

22. The moon on her back holds water = a sign of rain. 1893: Inwards, *Weather Lore*, 82, The bonnie moon is on her back; Mend your shoes and sort your thack [thatch]. When the new moon lies on her back, She sucks the wet into her lap. Ellesmere. 1895: Rye, *E. Anglia Words*, 143 (E.D.S.).

23. The new moon's mist Is better than gold in a kist [chest]. 1879: Henderson, *Folk-Lore N. Counties*, 115 [quoted as 'A Yorkshire rhyme']. Cf. No. 4.

24. Two full moons in a month bring on a flood. Beds. 1855: *N.&Q.*, 1st ser, xi 416, It will be a wet month when there are two full moons in it. 1893: Inwards, 64.

25. When early seen, 'Tis seldom seen. 1872: J. Glyde, jr., *Norfolk Garland*, 157. 1893: *Co. Folk-Lore: Suffolk*, 163 (F.L.S.).

26. When round the moon there is a burr [halo], **The weather will be cold and rough.** 1631: Brathwait, *Whimzies*, 104 (1859), A burre about the moone is not halfe so certaine a presage of a tempest, as … 1659: Howell, *Proverbs: Span.-Eng.*, 21, The moon with a circle brings water in her beak. 1690: *New Dict. Canting Crew*, sig. C2, *Bur*, a cloud or dark circle about the moon, boding wind and rain. 1830: Forby, *Vocab. E. Anglia*, 417, Near bur, far rain. 1846: Denham, *Proverbs*, 17 (Percy S.). 1887: Parish and Shaw, *Dict. Kent. Dialect*, 23 (E.D.S.), The weatherwise in East Kent will tell you, 'The larger the burr the nearer the rain'. 1893: *Co. Folk-Lore: Suffolk*, 162 (F.L.S.), If it [the halo] is large, the proverb is: – Far burr, near rain; Near burr, far rain. 1893: Inwards, 56 [as in 1659]. 1899: Dickinson, *Cumb. Gloss.*, 48, A far-off burgh tells of a near-hand storm. When t' burrs far t' rains nar.

27. When the moon lies on her back, Then the sou'-west wind will crack; When she rises up and nods, Then northeasters dry the sods. 1867: *Symons' Meteorological Mag.*, Sept., quoted in Inwards, *Weather Lore*, 62.

28. When the moon's in the full, then wit's in the wane. 1846: Denham, *Proverbs*, 4 (Percy S.).

29. You gazed at the moon and fell in the gutter. 1732: Fuller, 5904. 1846: Denham, 5.

See also **Bean** (5); **Changeful;** and **Fog** (1).

Mooney's goose, Like. 1850: *N.&Q.*, 1st ser, ii 153, Full of fun and fooster, like Mooney's goose.

Moonshine in a can. 1639: Clarke, 154, The moone shine i' th' water-pot. 1828: Carr, *Craven Dialect*, i 329, 'To run about moonshine in a can', to be employed in no useful purpose.

Moonshine in the mustard-pot for it, Thou shalt have, i.e. nothing. 1639: Clarke, 68, Moonshine i' th' mustard pot. 1678: Ray, 76.

Moonshine in the water = Nothing. 1468: *Paston Letters*, ii 326 (OED), If Sir Thomas Howys wer … made byleve and put in hope of the moone shone in the water and I wot nat what. 1530: Palsgrave, 865, For moone shyne in the water, *pour une chose de riens*. 1565: Shacklock, *Hatch. of Heresies*, quoted in *N.&Q.*, 2nd ser, v 411. 1592: Shakespeare, *L.L.L.*, V ii 1659: Howell, 15, He waits for moonshine in the water. 1817: Scott, *Rob Roy*, ch xxvi, I care little about that nonsense – it's a' moonshine in water – waste threads and thrums, as we say. 1861: Peacock, *Gryll Grange*, ch iv, He will not break his heart for any moon in the water, if his cooks are as good as his waiting-maids.

Mope-eyed by living so long a maid, You are. 1678: Ray, 346.

More acquaintance the more danger, The. 1732: Fuller, 4656.

More balks. *See* quot. 'Balk' = a strip of unploughed land, also little ridges left in ploughing. 1888: *N.&Q.*, 7th ser, v 194, We have here [Lincs] a proverb, 'More balks, more barley; more seams, more beans'.

More bold than wise (or **welcome).** 1591: Florio, *Second Frutes*, 53, You are not so bold as welcome. 1633: Draxe, 17, He is more bolde than wise. 1738: Swift, *Polite Convers.*, Dial. I, You are more bold than welcome.

More brass than pash = More money than brains. 1877: E. Leigh, *Cheshire Gloss.*, 152. 1917: Bridge, *Cheshire Proverbs*, 160.

More clout than dinner = More show than substance. 1828: Carr, *Craven Dialect*, i 78. Cf. **More poke.**

More cost more worship. 1591: Harington, *Orl. Furioso*, Adv. to Reader, At least (by the old proverbe) the more cost, the more worship. 1615: Markham, *Eng. Housewife*, 163 (1675), According to the old proverb (*Most cost, most worship*). 1670: Ray, 73. 1821: Scott, *Pirate*, ch xi, The mair cost the mair honour.

More cost than worship. 1732: Fuller, 3451. 1738: Swift, *Polite Convers.*, Dial. III, She was as fine as fi'pence; but, truly, I thought there was more cost than worship. 1828: Carr, *Craven Dialect*, i 86, 'More cost than worship', i.e. more expense and trouble than the acquisition is worth. 1877: F. Ross, etc., *Holderness Gloss.*, 45 (E.D.S.), 'It's mair cost-an-worship', it is more trouble than it is worth. 1917: Bridge, *Cheshire Proverbs*, 95, More cost nor worship. Cf. **More trouble**.

More danger, the more honour, The. *c.*1534: Berners, *Huon*, 56 (E.E.T.S.), Where as lyeth grete parelles [perils] there lieth grete honour. *c.*1625: B.&F., *Women Pleased*, III ii, Where the most danger is, there's the most honour. 1671: E. Howard, *Six Days Adventure*, I. 1710: S. Palmer, *Moral Essays on Proverbs*, 85. 1772: Garrick, *Irish Widow*, I iii.

More die by food than famine. 1588: Cogan, *Haven of Health*, 219 (1612), The Greeke poet Theognis most truely hath written, that surfet hath destroied mo than famin. 1732: Fuller, 3453. Cf. **Gluttony**.

More faults than hairs, and more wealth than faults, He has. Ibid., No. 1892.

More folks are wed than keep good houses. 1685: Meriton, *Yorkshire Ale*, 67.

More fool than fiddler. 1678: Ray, 245.

More frightened than hurt – originally, **More afraid** ... 1530: Palsgrave, 558, He was sorer frayed than hurt. 1579: Lyly, *Euphues*, 189 (Arber), Certeinly thou art more afraide then hurte. 1628: J. Clavell, *Recantation*, 12, Thus more afraid than hurt you often are. Before 1704: T. Brown, *Works*, i 74 (1760), Thou art more afraid than hurt. 1768: Sterne, *Sent. Journey*, 34 (1794), All of us ... being ten times more frighten'd than hurt by the very report. 1872: Butler, *Erewhon*, ch xiii, The Erewhonians, therefore, hold that death, like life, is an affair of being more frightened than hurt. 1883: R.L.S., *Treasure* I, ch xxi.

More good victuals. *See* **England** (8).

More guts than brains, He has. 1678: Ray, 249. 1732: Fuller, 1873.

More haste, less speed. *c.*1350: *Douce MS 52*, no 86, The more hast, the worse spede. 1542: Udall, tr. Erasmus' *Apoph.*, 41 (1877), Soche persones, as do make moste hast in the beginning, haue commonly (accordyng to our Englishe prouerbe) worst spede toward the endyng. *c.*1560: *Jacke Jugeler*, in Hazlitt, *Old Plays*, ii 121, When a man hath most haste, he speedeth worst. 1633: Rowley, *Match at Midnight*, *I*. 1705: Ward, *Hudibras Rediv.*, Pt I can. i p. 23, The greater hurry, the worst speed. 1776: Colman, *The Spleen*, I. 1829: Scott, *Journal*, 15 Feb., Unhappily there is such a thing as more haste and less speed. 1919: Weyman, *Great House*, ch xxvii, More haste, less speed, you know.

More have repented speech than silence. 1640: Herbert, *Jac. Prudentum.* 1875: Cheales, *Proverb. Folk-Lore*, 86.

More he hath, The. *See* **Much would have more.**

More hope of a fool than of him that is wise in his own eyes, There is. 1629: *Booh of Meery Riddles*, Prov. 23.

More knave than fool. *c.*1630: in *Roxb. Ballads*, i 72 (Hindley), This man's more knaue than foole. 1634: *Strange Metam. of Man*, sig. G4. 1738: Swift. *Polite Convers.*, Dial II

More knave, the better luck, The. 1550: Latimer, *Sermons*, 280 (P.S.), It is an old proverb, 'the more wicked, the more fortunate'. 1611: Cotgrave, s.v. 'Escheoir', The verier knave the better lucke, say we. 1670: Ray, 111. 1732: Fuller, 6332, He's like Marten; The more knave, the better fortune. 1917: *Devonsh. Assoc. Trans.*, xlix. 68, The greater the rogue, the better the luck.

More knave, the worse company, The. 1546: Heywood, *Proverbs*, Pt I ch xi.

More know Tom Fool than Tom Fool knows. 1723: Defoe, *Col. Jack*, ch xvii [quoted as 'the old English proverb']. 1754: Berthelson, *Eng.-Danish Dict.*, s.v. 'Jack' [with 'jack-pudding' for 'Tom Fool']. 1830: *Forby*, *Vocab. E. Anglia*, 431. 1922: A. B. Walkley, in *Times*, 15 Nov., p.10, col. 2.

More laws, the more offenders, The. 1732 Fuller, 4663.

More light a torch gives, the less while it lasts, The. Ibid., No. 4664.

More maids than Malkin, There are. [*c.*1377: Langland, *Plowman*, B, i 181, Ye ne haue na more meryte in masse ne in houres [church-services] Than Malkyn of hire maydenhode that no man desireth.] 1546: Heywood, *Proverbs*, Pt I ch xi, [If] there was no mo maydes but malkin tho Ye had been lost. *c.*1598: Deloney, *Gentle Craft*, Pt II ch iii 1659: Howell, *Letters*, ii 666

(Jacobs). 1732: Fuller, 4859, There are more maids than Moggy, and more men than Jockey.

More malice than matter. Somerset. 1678: Ray, 352. 1732: Fuller, 3458.

More men threatened than struck, There are. 1640: Herbert, *Jac. Prudentum*. 1670: Ray, 26. 1732: Fuller, 4860.

More mischief, the better sport, The. 1750: Smollett, *Gil Blas*, i 136. 1816: Scott, *Black Dwarf*, ch xii.

More nice than wise. 1581: B. Rich, *Farewell*, 139 (SH.S.), I warrant you, thei can make it more nice than wise. 1599: Buttes, *Dyets Dry Dinner*, Epist. Ded. 1670: Ray, 187. 1754: Berthelson, *Eng.-Danish Dict.*, s.v. 'Nice'.

More noble that deserves than he that confers benefits, He is. 1732: Fuller, 1925.

More noble, the more humble, The. 1633: Draxe, 140. 1670: Ray, 19. 1748: Richardson, *Clarissa*, iv 238 (1785), The more noble any one is, the more humble.

More painful to do nothing than something, It is. 1659: Howell, 6. 1732: Fuller, 2978.

More pigs and less parsons. Derby. 1889: *Folk-Lore Journal*, vii 293.

More places than the parish church, There are. 1579: Gosson, *School of Abuse*, 37 (Arber), There are more houses then parishe churches. 1725: Defoe, *Everybody's Business*. 1760: Colman, *Polly Honeycombe*, sc iv 1864: 'Cornish Proverbs', in *N. &Q.*, 3rd ser, v 276.

More pleasure in loving than in being beloved, There is. 1732: Fuller, 4900.

More poke [bag] **than pudding** = More show than substance. 1828: Carr, *Craven Dialect*, ii 52. 1892: Heslop, *Northumb. Words*, 546 (E.D.S.). Cf. **More clout**.

More riches. *See* **Fool** (102).

More sacks to the mill. 1590: Nashe, *Works*, i 238 (Grosart), To the next, to the next, more sacks to the myll. 1607: Dekker and Webster, *Westw. Hoe*, IV i 1661: in *Harl. Miscell.*, ii 503 (1744), Come, sirs, more sacks unto the mill, More taxes, more free-quarter. 1738: Swift, *Polite Convers.*, Dial. I, [Neverout, as Miss is standing, pulls her suddenly on his lap, and then says] Now, colonel, come sit down on my lap; more sacks upon the mill. 1748: Richardson, *Clarissa*, vii 310 (1785). 1913: E. M. Wright, *Rustic Speech, etc.*, 60, *More sacks to the mill* is a game played in Oxfordshire and Berkshire. It is a

rough-and-tumble boys' game, in which as many boys as possible are heaped together, one above another. As each successive boy is added to the heap – the boys shout: More sacks to the mill!

More said the less done, The. 1760: Colman, *Polly Honeycombe*, sc i, It's an old saying and a true one, The more there's said the less there's done.

More sauce than pig. 1671: *Poor Robin Alman. Prognost.*, sig. C7. 1690: *New Dict. Canting Crew*, sig. K8. 1738: Swift, *Polite Convers.*, Dial. II

More spends the niggard than the liberal. 1557: North, *Diall of Princes*, fo. 199, recto, So sayth the common prouerbe, yt the nigard spendeth asmuche as the liberall. 1639: Clarke, 39. 1666: Torriano, *Piazza Univ.*, 17, A covetous man out-spends a liberal man. Cf. **No feast to a miser's**.

More squeak than wool. 1740: North, *Lives of Norths*, i 220 (Bohn), And for matter of title, he thought there was more squeak than wool. Cf. **Much cry**.

More stars than a pair. *c.*1380: Chaucer, *Parl. of Foules*, l. 595, There been mo sterres, god wot, than a paire!

More store more stink. S.W. Wilts. 1901: *Folk-Lore*, xii 82.

More talk than trouble, There is. 1640: Herbert, *Jac. Prudentum*.

More than enough is too much. 1629: *Book of Meery Riddles*, Prov. 107, More than enough breaks the cover. 1732: Fuller, 3461.

More than nits in *his* **head, There's**. 1917: Bridge, *Cheshire Proverbs*, 118; [also] There's more in his yed nor a smo' tooth comb con fot eawt (Lancashire).

More than we use is more than we want. 1732: Fuller, 3462.

More the merrier, The; the fewer the better fare, (*a*) *The full saying*. 1530: Palsgrave, 885, The mo the meryer; the fewer, the better fare. 1546: Heywood, *Proverbs*, Pt II ch vii 1681: Robertson, *Phraseol. Generalis*, 598 ['cheer' for 'fare']. 1738: Swift, *Polite Convers.*, Dial. II ['cheer']. 1769: Colman, *Man and Wife*, II ['cheer']. 1855: Kingsley, *West. Ho!*, ch v 1863: Kingsley, *Water Babies*, ch vi 1917: Bridge, *Cheshire Proverbs*, 95, More and merrier: less and better fare, like Meg o' Wood's merry meal, (*b*) *The first part only*. *c.*1380: *Pearl* (1953), l. 850, The mo the myryer, so God me blesse. 1553:

Respublica, III v, Come nere, on Goddes halfe, the mo knaves the merier. *c.*1570: *Marr. of Wit and Science*, III ii, The more company the merrier. 1629: Ford, *Lover's Melancholy*, II ii 1696: Vanbrugh, *Relapse*, IV 1727: Vanbrugh and Cibber, *Prov. Husband*, II. 1772: Garrick, *Irish Widow*, I iii, The more the merrier, I say – who's afraid? 1841: Dickens, *Barn. Rudge*, ch lix., Who's afraid? Let 'em come, I say, let 'em come. The more, the merrier. 1918: A. A. Milne, *Make-Believe*, Prol., in *Second Plays*, 6 (1921). (*c*) *The second part only*. 1605: Camden, *Remains*, 332 (1870). 1704: Steele, *Lying Lover*, II ii, The fewer the better cheer.

More thy years, the nearer thy grave, The. 1605: Camden, *Remains*, 333 (1870) ['nigher' for 'nearer']. 1670: Ray, 31. 1732: Fuller, 6248.

More tongue. *See* quot. 1864: 'Cornish Proverbs', in *N.&Q.*, 3rd ser, vi 494, He has more tongue than teeth; better keep a heps [hapse, or hatch] before his mouth. 1880: Courtney, *W. Cornwall Words*. 28 (E.D.S.) ['She' for 'He' and 'her' for 'his'].

More trouble than worship = More trouble than it is worth. 1854: Baker, *Northants Gloss.*, s.v. 'Worship'. Cf. **More cost**.

More ways to kill a cat. *See* **Cat** (61).

More ways to kill a dog. *See* **Dog** (82).

More ways to the wood than one, There are. 1546: Heywood, *Proverbs*, Pt II ch ix. 1579: Gosson, *Sch. of Abuse*, 37 (Arber), There are … more wayes to the woode then one, and more causes in nature then efficients. 1608: Middleton, *Family of Love*, III iv 1664: Falkland, *Marriage Night*, III, Destiny has many ways to the wood. 1732: Fuller, 4861.

More wit the lest courage, The. Ibid., No. 4668.

More witty than wise. 1714: *Spectator*, No. 568, Ay, says he, more witty than wise I am afraid.

More words than one go to a bargain. 1670: Ray, 58. 1732: Fuller, 3465. Cf. **Two words to a bargain**.

More you have (*or* get), the more you want, The. *c.*1340: R. Rolle, *Psalter* (1884), 97, The mare that a man has the brennandere [more ardently] he askis. 1450: *Castle of Perseverance*, l. 3268, The more he hadde, the more he cravyd. 1578: J. Florio, *First Fruits*, 32, The more a man hath, the more he desireth. 1798: W. Manning, *Key of Liberty* (1922), 9, In short he is never easy, but the more he has, the more he wants.

More you heap, the worse you cheap, The. 1670: Ray, 102. 1732: Fuller, 6101.

More you stir, the worse it will stink, The. 1546: Heywood, *Proverbs*, Pt II ch vi 1596: Harington, *Metam. of Ajax*, 105 (1814), As the proverb is, ' 'Tis noted as the nature of a sink, Ever the more it is stirred, the more to stink'. 1632: Jonson, *Magn. Lady*, IV ii 1664: J. Wilson, *Cheats*, V ii, 'Tis a foul business – the more you stir, the worse 'twill be. 1710: S. Palmer, *Moral Essays on Proverbs*, 150, A stink is still worse for the stirring. 1752: Fielding, *Cov. Garden Journal*, No. 7, Pray let Grub Street alone, for the more you stir the more it will stink. 1924: *Folk-Lore*, xxxv 358, The more you stir, the more it stinks (Suffolk).

Morley's ducks, like, born without a notion. 1878: *N.&Q.*, 5th ser, x 10, This was … a Nottinghamshire saying, but a very common one – spoken of some one on the occasion of his committing a stupid action.

Morning. 1. A foul morn may turn to a fair day. [1586: Pettie, tr. Guazzo's *Civil Convers.*, fo. 142, As the prouerbe is, That by the morning it may be gathered how all the day will proue after.] 1732: Fuller, 115.

2. A gaudy morning bodes a wet afternoon. 1893: *Inwards, Weather Lore*, 50.

3. In the morning mountains, in the evening fountains. 1640: Herbert, *Jac. Prudentum*. 1846: Denham, *Proverbs*, 13 (Percy S.), The morn to the mountain, The evening to the fountain.

4. Morning dreams are true. [Post mediam noctem visus quum somnia vera. – Horace, *Sat.*, I x 33.] 1540: Palsgrave, *Acolastus*, sig. 11, After mydnyght men saye, that dreames be true. 1584: R. Scot, *Witchcraft*, bk x ch vii, In the morning … there happen more pleasant and certain dreames. 1611: Jonson, *Love Restored*, last line, And all the morning dreams are true. 1681: Dryden, *Span. Friar*, III iii, At break of day, when dreams, they say, are true. 1713: Gay, *Wife of Bath*, IV ii, Morning dreams, I learned … are most to be relied upon. *c.*1820: Shelley, *Boat on the Serchio*, If morning dreams are true … 1867: Harland, etc., *Lancs Folk-Lore*, 147, Morning dreams are more to be relied on than those of any other time.

See also **Evening**.

Morning sun, or, Morning without clouds. *See* **Sun** (1).

Moroah Downs, Like, hard and never ploughed. 1864: 'Cornish Proverbs', in *N. & Q.*, 3rd ser, v 275.

Morpeth compliment, A. 1834: Service, *Metrical Leg. of Northumb.*, 140, She gav' me nout i' plenty but her tongue, O' that a Morpeth compliment she flung.

Morsel eaten gains no friend, A. 1813: Ray, 140.

Mortar on head. *See* **Rome** (3).

Mortar, To have one's finger in = To dabble in building. 1639: in *Berkeley MSS.*, iii 28 (1885), Dip not thy finger in the morter, nor seeke thy penny in the water. 1662: Gerbier, *Disc. of Building*, 3, Those who say, That a wise-man never ought to put his finger into morter. 1738: Swift, *Polite Convers.*, Dial. II, You are come to a sad, dirty house … but we have had our hands in mortar.

Mort-stone, He may remove. 1662: Fuller, *Worthies*, i 399 (1840). 1790: Grose, *Prov. Gloss.*, s.v. 'Devonshire'.

Morvah Downs – ploughed, not harrowed, Like. Corn. 1895: Jos. Thomas, *Randigal Rhymes*, 61. 1906: *Cornish N. & Q.*, 264, Like Morvah Downs, harved and never ploughed.

Morvah Fair. *See* quot. 1870: Bottrell, *Traditions of W. Cornwall*, 42, The old saying of 'riding three on one horse, like going to Morvah fair'.

Moss and his mare. *See* **Napping**.

Most take all. 1678: Ray, 347.

Most things hare two handles; and a wise man takes hold of the best. 1732: Fuller, 3472.

Most time. *See* **Time**.

Most wild. *See* quot. 1630: T. Adams, *Works*, 498, The prouerbe saith, that the most wilde are in least danger to be starke madde.

Mote is a beam, Every. 1615: R. Tofte, *Blazon of Iealousie*, 29, Hee will then quickly take occasion to be angry with her, and euery mote (as the prouerbe goeth) is a beame in his eye.

Mote may choke a man, A. 1670: Ray, 132.

Mother. 1. It is not as thy mother sayeth, but as thy neighbours say. 1732: Fuller, 2995.

2. Mother's cheek. *See* **Child** (8).

3. Mothers' darlings make but milksop heroes. 1732: Fuller, 3474.

4. The mother's side is the surest. 1548: Hall, *Chron.*, 101 (1809), If the old and trite prouerbe be true that the woman's side is the surer side, and that the childe foloweth the wombe. Before 1627: Middleton, *More Diss. besides Women*, I iii, Only death comes by the mother's side, and that's the surest.

See also **Ask** (6); and **Oven** (1).

Mother-in-law and daughter-in-law are a tempest and hailstorm. 1855: Bohn, 455.

Mother-in-law remembers not that she was a daughter-in-law, The. 1659: Howell, *Proverbs: Brit.-Eng.*, 36. 1732: Fuller, 4675.

Mother-in-law, There is but one good, and she is dead. A New Forest proverb. 1863: Wise, *New Forest*, ch xvi.

Motions are not marriages. 1678: Ray, 56.

Mountain. 1. A mountain and a river are good neighbours. 1640: Herbert, *Jac. Prudentum*.

2. The mountain was in labour and produced a mouse. [Parturiunt montes, nascetur ridiculus mus – Horace, *Ars Poetica*, 139.] *c.*1390: Gower, *Conf. Amantis*, bk vii, ll. 3553–75 [the story of the mountain and mouse]. 1579: Gosson, *Sch. of Abuse*, 21 (Arber), It is a pageant woorth the sight, to beholde how he labors with mountaines to bring foorth mise. 1599: Greene, *Works*, xii 7 (Grosart), Then might you thinke I had sweld with the mountaines, and brought foorth a mouce. 1624: Massinger, *Bondman*, IV iii, *Cleo.* Why do you laugh? *Leost.* To hear the labouring mountain of your praise Deliver'd of a mouse. 1709: O. Dykes, *Eng. Proverbs*, 304 (2nd ed.). 1853: Planché, *Extravag.*, iv 291 (1879), Oft of the mountain in labour you've heard, Which but gave birth to a mouse so absurd.

3. To make a mountain of a molehill. [ἐλέφαντα ἐκ μυίας ποιεῖν. – Lucian, *Musc. Enc.*, *ad fin.*] 1560: Becon, *Catechism*, 338 (P.S.), They make of a fly an elephant, and of a mole-hill a mountain. 1573: G. Harvey, *Letter-Book*, 14 (Camden S.), To make huge mountains of smal low molhils. 1653: R. Brome, *City Wit*, IV i, She takes me for a mountaine, that am but a molehill, *c.*1760: Foote, *Lame Lover*, II, Those people are ever swelling mole hills to mountains. 1834: Marryat, *Peter Simple*, ch xxxvii 1909: De Morgan, *Never can happen Again*, ch xxxviii.

See also **Mahomet; Man** (72); and **Morning** (3).

Mountsorrel Set quot. 1790: Grose, *Prov. Gloss.*, s.v. 'Leicestershire', He leaps like the Bell-giant, or devil of Mountsorrel.

Mouse and Mice. 1. A mouse in time may bite in two a cable. 1546: Heywood, *Proverbs*, Pt II ch vii 1736: Franklin, *Way to Wealth*, in *Works*, i

444 (Bigelow), By diligence and patience the mouse ate in two the cable. 1754: Berthelson, *Eng.-Danish Dict.*, s.v. 'Time'.

2. A mouse must not think to cast a shadow like an elephant. 1732: Fuller, 332.

3. As sure as a mouse tied with a thread. 1546: Heywood, *Proverbs*, Pt II ch vii.

4. As warm as a mouse in a churn. 1678: Ray, 290.

5. Can a mouse fall in love with a cat? 1732: Fuller, 1051.

6. Don't make yourself a mouse, or the cat will eat you. 1875: Cheales, *Proverb. Folk-Lore*, 105.

7. I gave the mouse a hole, and she is become my heir. 1640: Herbert, *Jac. Prudentum.*

8. It must be a bold (or wily) mouse that can breed in the cat's ear. *c.*1430: Lydgate, *Minor Poems*, 167 (Percy S.), An hardy mowse that is bold to breede In cattis eeris. Before 1529: Skelton, *Why Come Ye Not?*, l. 753, Yet it is a wyly mouse That can bylde his dwellinge house Within the cattes eare Withouten drede or feare. 1579: Lyly, *Euphues*, 63 (Arber) ['wily']. 1623: Webster, *Duchess of Malfi*, IV ii, Thou sleepist worse than if a mouse should be fore'd to take up her lodging in a cat's ear. 1732: Fuller, 3040 ['wilely']. 1894: R.L.S., *St Ives*, ch xiv, We ate like mice in a cat's ear.

9. Like a mouse in a cheese. 1658: Flecknoe, *Enigm. Characters*, 16, She is like a mouse in a Holland cheese, her house and diet all the same. 1736: Ainsworth, *Lat. Dict.*, s.v. (OED), He speaketh like a mouse in a cheese.

10. Mice care not to play with kittens. 1732: Fuller, 3412.

11. The escaped mouse ever feels the taste of the bait. 1640: Herbert, *Jac. Prudentum.*

12. The mouse goes abroad where the cat is not lord. Before 1500: in Hill, *Commonplace-Book*, 132 (E.E.T.S.).

13. The mouse that has only one hole is easily taken. *c.*1386: Chaucer, *Wife of Bath's Prol.*, l. 572, I holde a mouses herte not worth a leek, That hath but oon hole for to sterte to. 1586: L. Evans, *Withals Dict. Revised*, sig. C3, That mouse is in an ill case that hath but one hole to lurke in. 1631: Mabbe, *Celestina*, 139 (T.T.), It goes hard (daughter) with that mouse that hath but one hole to trust to. 1717: Pope, *Wife of Bath*, 298, The mouse that always trusts to one poor hole, Can never be a mouse of any soul. 1865:

'Lancs Proverbs', *in N.&Q.*, 3rd ser, viii 494. 1901: F. E. Taylor, *Lancs Sayings*, 7, A meawse 'at's nob-but getten one hole's soon takken.

See also **Best** (22); **Better a mouse; Cat,** *passim;* **Dead** (15); **Dun; Frog** (6); **Lark** (2); **Lion** (2); **Mountain** (2); **No larder; Plough,** *subs.* (3); **Quiet; Rat** (1) and (6); **Safe as a mouse;** and **Water** (4).

Mousehole, where they eat their beef before they sup their broth. Corn., 19th cent. Mr C. Lee says, 'The story is that when the Spaniards raided Mount's Bay, they landed at Mousehole just as the inhabitants were sitting down to their Sunday dinner – broth, duff (dumplings), and beef. Broth and duff had been consumed when the alarm was given, and the diners fled, leaving the Spaniards to eat the beef. Ever since, they have made sure of the beef first. Cf. Scott, *Peveril*, Note P, "Cutlar MacCulloch." '

Mouse-trap smell of cheese, You must not let your. 1659: Howell, 11. 1670: Ray, 18. 1732: Fuller, 3189 [with 'blood' for 'cheese'].

Mouth. 1. A mouth like a Low-country loophole = A wide mouth. 1888: *Yorkshire N.&Q.*, ii 73 (W.).

2. Between the mouth and the morsel. *c.*1594: Bacon, *Promus*, No. 791. Cf. **Cup** (4).

3. He has a mouth for every matter. 1732: Fuller, 1859.

4. He that hath a mouth of his own must not say to another, Blow. 1640: *Jac. Prudentum.* 1732: Fuller, 2130 ['should' for 'must'].

5. Mouth full of mould. *See* **Enough one day**.

6. Mouth in the heart. *See* **Wise** (50).

7. Out of the mouths of babes (and sucklings) [Psalm viii.2, Out of the mouth of babes and sucklings hast thou ordained strength, *and* Matthew 21. 16, Out of the mouth of babes and sucklings thou hast perfected praise] 1899: R. Kipling, *Stalky and Co.* In the present state of education I shouldn't have thought any three boys would be well enough grounded ... But out of the mouths ... 1906: R. Kipling, *Puck of Pook's Hill*, 285, Out of the mouths of babes do we learn.

8. Shut mouth catches no flies. *See* **Shut**.

9. Whoso hath but a mouth Will ne'er in England suffer drought. 1670: Ray, 42. 1893: Inwards, *Weather Lore*, 4. 1904: *Co. Folk-Lore: Northumb.*, 171 (F.L.S.).

10. Your mouth hath beguiled your hands. 1678: Ray, 260. 1732: Fuller, 6057.

Mouthful of moonshine, To give one a. 1813: Ray, 208.

Mow breeze. *See* quot. 1917: Bridge, *Cheshire Proverbs*, 164, It's always dull when there's a Mow breeze [= when wind blows from Mow Cop = east wind].

Much ado about nothing. 1599: Shakespeare, *Much Ado*, etc. [title]. 1692: L'Estrange, *Aesop*, 24 (3rd ed.), [Mountain in labour fable] Moral. Much ado about nothing. 1748: Richardson, *Clarissa*, v 12 (1785), It were better for herself … that she had not made so much ado about nothing. 1863: Kingsley, *Water Babies*, ch vi, I know some people will only laugh at it, and call it much ado about nothing.

Much bran and little meal. 1633: Draxe, 17. 1670: Ray, 65. 1732: Fuller, 3477 ['flour' for 'meal'].

Much bruit little fruit. 1639: Fuller, *Holy War*, bk ii ch xxix. 1670: Ray, 66. 1732: Fuller, 6122.

Much business much pardon. 1750: Franklin, in *Works*, ii 208 (Bigelow), Remember in my favor the old saying, They who have much business must have much pardon.

Much coin much care. [Crescentem sequitur cura pecuniam. – Horace, *Carm.*, III xvi.] 1639: Clarke, 98. 1647: *Countrym. New Commonwealth*, 22. 1732: Fuller, 3478.

Much corn. *See* **Corn** (5).

Much courtesy. *See* **Courtesy** (3).

Much cry and little wool. *c.*1475: Fortescue, *Govern. of England*, ch x 132 (Plummer), And so his hyghnes shal haue theroff, as hadd the man that sherid is hogge, muche crye and litill woll. 1579: Gosson, *Sch. of Abuse*, 28 (Arber), Or as one said at the shearing of hogs, great cry and little wool. 1663: Butler, *Hudibras*, Pt I can. i l. 852, Thou wilt at best but suck a bull, Or shear swine, all cry and no wool. 1711: *Spectator*, No. 251. 1827: Scott, *Journal*, 24 Feb., As to the collection, it was much cry and like woo', as the deil said when he shore the sow. 1871: S. Butler, in H. F. Jones's *Life*, i 143 (1919), So I fought shy of Taine, who, too – for I did read some of him rapidly – seemed to me to be much cry and little wool. 1922: *Punch*, 29 Nov., p. 520, col. 2, Ministers have taken good care that the adage, 'Much cry and little wool', shall not apply to them. Cf. **More squeak**.

Much hath, much behoveth, He that. 1493: *Dives et Pauper*, fo. 4 (1536).

Much heed doth no harm. 1639: Clarke, 66.

Much law but little justice. 1694: *Terence made English*, 139, The old saying's true, You may have much law o' your side, and but little equity. 1732: Fuller, 3482.

Much learning much sorrow. 1639: Clarke, 101 ['science' for 'learning']. 1669: *Politeuphuia*, 183.

Much matter of a wooden platter = Much fuss about nothing in particular. 1639: Clarke, 133. 1670: Ray, 185. 1732: Fuller, 6159.

Much meat much malady. 1639: Clarke, 98. 1670: Ray, 120. 1732: Fuller, 3483. *c.*1800: J. Trusler, *Prov. in Verse*, 22.

Much meddling, Of, comes no sound sleeping. Glos. 1639: in *Berkeley MSS.*, iii 30 (1885).

Much of a muchness. 1727: Vanbrugh and Cibber, *Prov. Husband*, I, *Man*. I hope at least, you and your good woman agree still. *John M.* Ay! ay! much of a muchness. Bridget sticks to me. 1857: Reade, *Never too Late*, ch xviii, Why they are all pretty much of a muchness for that. 1905: E. G. Hayden, *Travels Round our Village*, 24, Folks is folks all the world over – much of a muchness, I reckon, when you gets inside 'um, so to spake.

Much power makes many enemies. 1736: Bailey, *Dict.*, s.v. 'Much'.

Much smoke little fire. Glos. 1639: in *Berkeley MSS.*, iii 32 (1885).

Much spending. *See* quot. 1541: Coverdale, *Christ. State Matrimony*, sig. I3, Mich spendinge and many gyftes make bar[e] celars and empty thystes.

Much wit as three folks, As – two fools and a madman. Cheshire. 1670: Ray, 209. 1732: Fuller, 716. 1828: Lytton, *Pelham*, ch lxxvii, 'No, no, my fine fellow', said Thornton with a coarse chuckle, 'you have as much wit as three folks – two fools and a madman, but you won't *do* me for all that'. 1917: Bridge, *Cheshire Proverbs*, 19.

Much would have more. [Multa petentibus desunt multa. – Horace, *Carm.*, III xvi.] *c.*1350: *Alexander*, l. 4398, Bot ay mekill wald have mare. 1578: Florio, *First Fruites*, fo. 32, The more a man hath, the more he desireth. 1618: W. Lawson, *New Orchard and Garden*, 5 (1676), 'Tis with grounds in this case, as it is with men … Much will have more. 1732: Fuller, 3487, Much would have more; but often meets with less. 1828: Carr, *Craven Dialect*, i 323, Mickle wad hev maar. 1901: F. E. Taylor, *Lancs Sayings*, 9, Mitch would ha' mooar, an' mooar would have o [all].

Muck, *subs.* = manure. **1. Where there's muck there's money** (or **brass**) – with variants. 1678: Ray, 170, Muck and money go together. 1865: W. White, *Eastern England*, i 127, 'The more muck the more money', is an East Anglian proverb. 1866: J. G. Nall, *Gt. Yarmouth, etc.*, 605, Where there's muck, there's money. Norfolk Proverb. 1901: F. E. Taylor, *Lancs Sayings*, 11, Wheer ther's muck – ther's luck. 1917: Bridge, *Cheshire Proverbs*, 95, Muck's the mother of money.

2. You'll have his muck for his meat. 1639: Clarke, 170. 1670: Ray, 186.

Muckhill at his door, He hath a good = He is rich. 1678: Ray, 261.

Muckhill on my trencher, You make a, quoth the bride = You carve me a great heap. 1678: Ray, 77 1732: Fuller, 5936.

Muckle, Many a mickle makes a. *See* **Many a mickle**.

Muck-midden. *See* quot 1846–59: *Denham Tracts*, ii 97 (F.L.S.), There is an old proverb which says 'The muck-midden is the mother of the meal-ark [chest]'.

Muckson up to the buckson = Dirty up to the knuckles. Derby. 1889: *Folk-Lore Journal*, vii 293.

Mud chokes no eels. 1732: Fuller, 3488.

Muddy springs will have muddy streams. Ibid., No. 3489.

Mulberry leaf. *See* quots. 1659: Howell, *Proverbs: New Sayings*, 3, With time and art, the mulberry leafs grow to be sattin. 1852: M. A. Keltie, *Reminiscences of Thought and Feeling*, 36, I would also say, value greatly, and exercise as often as possible, *small* efforts of self-denial. 'By little and little the mulberry leaf becomes satin'.

Mule, As dummel as a. Oxfordsh. 1923: *Folk-Lore*, xxxiv 329.

Mule. *See also* **Beware**; **Horse** (51); and **One mule**.

Mulfra, Cornwall. *See* quot. 1864: 'Cornish Proverbs', in *N. & Q.*, 3rd ser, v 275, All of a motion, like a Mulfra toad oh a hot showl [shovel]. Blown about like a Mulfra toad in a gale of wind.

Mum. *See* **Silence**.

Mumchance. *See* quots. 1690: *New Dict.*

Canting Crew, sig. H5, He looks like Mumchance that was hang'd for saying of nothing. 1694: *Terence made English*, 150, What an unreasonable thing 'tis to make me stand like mum-chance at such a time as this. 1738: Swift, *Polite Convers.*, Dial. I [as in 1690]. 1785: Grose, *Class. Dict. Vulgar Tongue*, s.v. 'Mum', You sit like mumchance who was hanged for saying nothing. 1881: Mrs Parker, *Oxfordsh. Words: Suppl.*, 90 (E.D.S.), Mumchance, to sit quietly thinking. Cf. **Mumphazard**.

Mumphazard. *See* quot. 1670: Ray, 209, He stands like Mumphazard, who was hang'd for saying nothing. *Cheshire*. 1917: Bridge, *Cheshire Proverbs*, 71 [as in 1670]. Cf. **Mumchance**.

Murder will out. Before 1300: *Cursor Mundi*, l. 1084, For-thi men sais into this tyde, Is no man that murthir may hide. *c.*1386: Chaucer, *Prioress's Tale*, l. 124, Mordre wol out, certein it wol not faille, *c.*1400: *Beryn*, l. 2293 (E.E.T.S.), ther may no man hele murdir, that it woll out atte last. *c.*1440: Lydgate, *Fall of Princes*, bk iii l. 2741 (E.E.T.S.). Before 1529: Skelton, *Bowge of Courte*, l. 524, I drede mordre wolde come oute. 1641: Marmion, *Antiquary*, V 1676: Shadwell, *Libertine*, II. 1760: Murphy, *Way to Keep Him*, V 1780: Mrs Cowley, *Belle's Stral.*, I iv, Like murder – Vanity will out. 1840: Barham, *Ing. Legends*, 1st ser: 'Hand of Glory', *ad fin.*

Muse as they use. *See* **Man** (71).

Muses love the morning, The. 1732: Fuller, 4681.

Music as a wheel-barrow, You make as good. Ibid., No. 5938.

Music helps not the toothache. 1640: Herbert, *Jac. Prudentum*. 1670: Ray, 18. 1732: Fuller, 3493.

Musician has forgot his note, When a, he makes as though a crumb stuck in his throat. 1639: Clarke, 108. 1670: Ray, 123. 1732: Fuller, 6471.

Musk in a dog's kennel, Look not for. 1611: Cotgrave, s.v. 'Chien' ['civet' for 'musk']. 1640: Herbert, *Jac. Prudentum*. 1854: J. W. Warter, *Last of Old Squires*, 53. 1894: Northall, *Folk Phrases*, 34 (E.D.S.), You must not expect perfumes in a pigsty.

Must be if we brew, This. 1678: Ray, 87. 1738: Swift, *Polite Convers.*, Dial. III, Well, thus it must be, if we sell ale.

Must be, must be, What. 1519: W. Horman, *Vulgaria*, 20v, That the whiche muste be wyll be. 1616: Beaumont and Fletcher, *The Scornful Lady*, III. i, I must kiss you … What must be, must be.1841: S. Warren, *Ten Thousand a Year*, I. i, It's really very inconvenient … for any of my young man to be absent … but – I suppose – what must be, must be. *See also* **Shall be**; and **Will be**.

Must fly, If you, fly well. 1640: Herbert, *Jac. Prudentum*.

Must is a king's word. *c*.1600: Queen Elizabeth, in Lingard, *Hist, of England*, vi 310, 'Must she?' exclaimed she, 'is must a word to be used to princes?' 1738: Swift, *Polite Convers.*, Dial. I, Must? Why, colonel, must's for the King.

Mustard is very uncivil because it takes one by the nose. 1634: *Strange Metam. of Man*, sig. D8, Hee [mustard] is very snappish, for if you meddle with him, he will strait take you by the nose. 1738: Swift, *Polite Convers.*, Dial. II

Mustard. *See also* **After meat**; **Cat** (11); **Pity**; **Strong**; and **Tewkesbury**.

Muston, Kent. *See* quot. 1576: Lambarde, *Peramb. of Kent*, 224 (1826), The common rythme of the countrie … He that will not live long, Let him dwell at Muston, Tenham, or Tong. 1735: Pegge, *Kent. Proverbs*, in EDS., No. 12, p. 73 [as in 1576].

Mute as a fish. [καὶ πολὺ ἀφωνότερος ἔσομαι τῶν ἰχθύων. – Lucian, *The Dream, or The Cock*.] *c*.1450: Burgh (and Lydgate), *Secrees*, st. 330, p. 73 (E.E.T.S.), Dowmbe as the ffysh. 1620: J. Melton, *Astrologaster*, 38, She shall be as mute as a

fish. 1693: Urquhart, *Rabelais*, bk iii ch xxiv, They are all of them become as dumb as so many fishes. 1704: Congreve, *Way of World*, IV ix, Thou art both as drunk and as mute as a fish. 1788: Wolcot, *Works*, i 477 (1795), The handsome bar-maids stare, as mute as fishes. 1844: Thackeray, *Barry Lyndon*, ch xvi 1915: Galsworthy, *Bit o' Love*, II ii, Round which are gathered five or six sturdy fellows, dumb as fishes.

Mutton is meat for a glutton. 1611: Cotgrave, s.v. 'Mouton', Flesh of a mutton is food for a glutton. 1623: Wodroephe, *Spared Houres*, 514, Flesh of mutton is cheere of glutton. 1666: Torriano, *Piazza Univ.*, 42.

Mutton's going, When the. *See* quot. 1678: Ray, 350, When the shoulder of mutton is going 'tis good to take a slice. 1732: Fuller, 5598 [omitting 'shoulder of'].

Mutton. *See also* **Sheep**.

Muxy. *See* quots. 1633: Draxe, 54, He is gotten out of the myre and is fallen into the riuer. 1849: Halliwell, *Pop. Rhymes, etc.*, 183, He got out of the muxy [dunghill], And fell into the pucksy [quagmire].

My house, my house, though thou art small, thou art to me the Escurial. 1640: Herbert, *Jac. Prudentum*.

My Lord Baldwin's dead. Sussex. 1670: Ray, 163.

My son, put money in thy purse. 1654: Gayton, *Pleasant Notes Don Q.*, 9.

My wife. *See* **Wife** (16).

N

Nab me, I'll nab thee. 1678: Ray, 351.

Nail, *subs*. **1. Another nail in one's coffin**. 1789: Wolcot, *Works*, ii 100 (1795). Care to our coffin adds a nail, no doubt. 1824: Scott, *Redgauntlet*, ch xvi, Every minute he lies here is a nail in his coffin.

2. Drive not a second nail, till the first be clinched. 1732: Fuller, 1334.

3. Nail of wax. *See* quot. 1852: FitzGerald, *Polonius*, 39 (1903), You can't ... drive a nail of wax.

4. Nail that will go. *See* **Drive** (1).

5. To hit the nail on the head. [Acu rem tangere. – Plautus, *Rud.*, V ii 19.] *c*.1520: Stanbridge, *Vulgaria*, sig. B5, Thou hyttest the nayle on the head. *c*.1580: Spelman, *Dialogue*, 115 (Roxb.Cl), How saye you ... to this discourse of this husbondman, I thinke he hath hitte the nayle on the heade. 1656: *Choyce Drollery*, 11 (Ebsworth), 'Tis true what we have sed. In this we hit the naile o' th' head. 1728: Fielding, *Love in Several Masques*, II vi, You have hit the nail on the head, my dear uncle. 1834: Marryat, *P. Simple*, ch xii, He has hit the right nail on the head.

6. Upon the nail. 1596: Nashe, *Works*, iii 59 (Grosart), Speake the word, and I will help you to it vpon the naile. 1637: T. Heywood, *Pleas. Dialogues, etc.*, Dial. 4, in Bang's *Materialien*, B. 3, p. 69, That could not pay One single halfpenny downe vpon the naile. 1692: L'Estrange, *Aesop*, Life, 13 (3rd ed.), Lay down the mony upon the nail, and the business is done. 1729: Gay, *Potty*, I, I'll have her. I'll pay you down upon the nail. 1859: Sala, *Twice Round Clock*, 6 a.m., We would drink brown ale, and pay the reckoning on the nail. 1922: *Punch*, 20 Dec., p. 598, col. 1, I paid for them on the nail – a little over fifteen pounds.

See also **One nail**.

Nails of fingers, etc. 1. Cutting them. 1596: Lodge, *Wits Miserie*, 18 (Hunt.Cl.), He will not ... paire his nailes while Munday, to be fortunat in his loue. 1618: B. Holyday, *Technogamia*, II vi, That you may neuer pare your nailes vpon a Friday. Before 1627: Middleton, *Anything for Quiet Life*, IV ii, What a cursed wretch was I to pare my nails today! a Friday too; I looked for some mischief. 1695: Congreve, *Love for Love*, III ix, As melancholie as if thou hadst ... pared thy nails on a Sunday. 1830: Forby, *Vocab. E. Anglia*, 411, Cut them on Monday, you cut them for health; Cut them on Tuesday, you cut them for wealth; Cut them on Wednesday, you cut them for news; Cut them on Thursday, a new pair of shoes; Cut them on Friday, you cut them for sorrow; Cut them on Saturday, see your true-love tomorrow; Cut them on Sunday, the devil will be with you all the week. 1879: Henderson, *Folk-Lore N. Counties*, 18, [as in 1830, excePt that the last three lines read] Cut them on Saturday, a present tomorrow; But he that on Sunday cuts his horn, Better that he had never been born! Ibid., 17, Better a child had ne'er been born Than cut his nails on a Sunday morn! [Also] Friday hair, Sunday horn. Better that child had ne'er been born! [There are other variants of these sayings – see *N. & Q.*, 9th ser, vi 93, and 12th ser, vii 67.]

2. *See* quot. 1869: Hazlitt, 482, Ye've nails at wad scrat your granny out of her grave. *Leeds*.

3. Specks on nails – commonly called 'gifts'. 1620: J. Melton, *Astrologaster*, 45, That to haue yellow speckles on the nailes of one's hand's a great signe of death. 1646: Browne, *Pseudo. Epi.*, bk v ch xxiii, That temperamental dignotions, and conjecture of prevalent humours, may be collected from spots in our nails, we are not averse to concede ... that white specks presage our felicity, blew ones our misfortunes. 1755: *Connoisseur*, No. 59, A white speck upon the nails made them as sure of a gift, as if they had it already in their pockets. 1854: Baker, *Northants Gloss.*, s.v. 'Gifts', (a) A gift, a friend, a foe, A lover to come, a journey to go. (*b*) A gift on the thumb is sure to come, A gift on the finger is sure to linger. 1879: Jackson, *Shropsh. Wood-Book*, 173 [as in 1854 (*b*)]. 1882: Jago, *Gloss, of Cornish Dialect*, 176 [as in 1854 (*b*)]. 1884–6: Holland, *Chesh. Gloss.* (E.D.S.), The popular belief is that they [white specks on finger-nails] betoken a present, and children say – beginning with the thumb, and ending with the little finger: 'A gift, a friend, a foe, a sweetheart, a journey to go'. The event to happen is indicated by the word which corresponds to the finger on which the white spot is seen. 1886: Elworthy, *West Som. Word-Book*, 284 (E.D.S.) [as in 1854 (*b*), but in plural].

Naked as a cuckoo. 1609: Dekker, *Guls Horne-Booke*, 20 (Hindley), As naked as the cuckoo in Christmas. 1879: J. Hardy, in *Folk-Lore Record*, ii 66, It is from the reported deplumed condition of the cuckoo in winter that the proverb originates, 'As naked as a cuckoo', which I have heard in Northumberland applied to a prodigal.

Naked as a needle, *c*.1350: *Alexander*, l. 4027, And ay is naked a nedill as natour tham schapis. 1377: Langland, *Plowman*, B, xii 162, Bothe naked as a nedle. 1485: Malory, *Morte d'Arthur*, bk xi ch i., She was naked as a nedel. 1858: P. J. Bailey, *The Age*, 75, Nude as a needle.

Naked as a robin. 1883: Burne, *Shropsh. Folk-Lore*, 595.

Naked as a shorn sheep. 1654: Gayton, *Pleasant Notes Don Q.*, 88, As naked and bare as a shorne sheep, as we say in our English proverbe.

Naked as a stone. 14th cent.: in Wright, *Songs and Carols*, 3 (1856), He stod as nakyd as a ston.

Naked as a worm. *c*.1400: *Rom. Rose*, l. 454, For naked as a worm was she.

Naked as my nail. 1533: Heywood, *Play of Wether*, l. 922, Thou myghtest go as naked as my nayle. 1600: Day, *Blind Beggar*, V, Yet would I had her as naked as my nayl. 1629: Massinger, *Renegado*, I i 1681: Robertson, *Phraseol. Generalis*, 905, As naked as ones nail.

Naked as truth. 1647: in *Somers Tracts*, v 491 (1811), Lest it strip him as naked as truth.

Naked sword. See **III putting**.

Name, *subs*. **1. When your name is up you may lie abed.** 1611: Cotgrave, s.v. 'Bruit', Hee that is thought to rise betime, may lie abed till noon. 1659: Howell, 11 (9), He that hath the name to be an early riser may sleep till noon. 1714: *Spectator*, No. 602, So that to use the old proverb, When his name is up he may lye a-bed. *c*.1730: Swift, in *Works*, xiv. 423 (Scott), His name is up, he may in bed lie. 1772: Graves, *Spirit. Quixote*, bk i ch viii, If our name were thus once up … we might lie a-bed.

2. You had not your name for nothing. 1633: Draxe, 135, He hath not his name for naught. 1678: Ray, 261.

Naples. See **See** (4).

Napping, as Moss caught his mare. The allusions to this saying and song in 16th- and 17th-century literature are very numerous. 1569–70: in Arber, *Stat. Registers*, i 193, Recevyd of William Greffeth for his lycense for the pryntinge of a ballett intituled *taken nappynge as Mosse toke his meare*, iiiid. 1597: *Discouerie of Knights of Poste*, sig. C4, Fortune feeding them, as Mosse did his mare, through a hurdle, which made him take her so soone napping. 1641: J. Taylor, *Swarme of Sectaries, etc.* [motto], The cobler preaches and his audience are As wise as Mosse was, when he caught his mare. 1658: *Wit Restored*, 304 (reprint). 1672: *Westminster Drollery*, Pt II 74 (Ebsworth), Her cresses that were wrought Most like the golden snare, My loving heart has caught, As *Mos* did catch the mare. 1785: Grose, *Class. Dict. Vulgar Tongue*, s.v. 'Nap' ['morse' for 'Moss']. 1850: in *N.&Q.*, 1st ser, i 320, There is also a song sung among the farmers of South Devon, of which the last line of each verse is 'As Morse caught the mare'. [There is a version of a song about Moss and his mare in Halliwell's *Nursery Rhymes* (Percy S., No. 17).] 1917: Bridge, *Cheshire Proverbs*, 127.

Natural to him as milk to a calf, As. 1678: Ray, 287.

Nature draws more than ten oxen. 1640: Herbert, *Jac. Prudentum* ['teams' for 'oxen']. 1670: Ray, 18.

Nature gives what no man can take away. Before 1500: in Hill, *Commonplace-Book*, 129 (E.E.T.S.).

Nature it the true law. 1578: Florio, *First Fruites*, fo. 32, Nature is the right law. 1629: *Booh of Meery Riddles*, Prov. 34.

Nature out of the door, Shut. See quot. 1692: L'Estrange, *Aesop*, 61 (3rd ed.), How impossible it is to make are change her biass, and that if we shut her out of the door, she'll come in at the window.

Nature passes nurture. Cf. **Nurture** for a contrary statement. 1647: Stapylton, *Juvenal*, 189, Nature can do more then breeding can. 1732: Fuller, 3505, Nature is beyond all teaching. 1880: Spurgeon, *Ploughman's Pictures*, 70, Nature does sometimes overcome nurture.

Nature requires five. See **Sleep**, *subs*. (1).

Nature, time, and patience are the three great physicians. 1855: Bohn, 457.

Nature will have her course, *c*.1400: *Beryn*, 105 (E.E.T.S.), ffor 'kynde woll have his cours'. 1580: Lyly, *Euphues*, 326 (Arber). *c*.1647: Wither, *Doubtfull Almanack*, 6 (Spens.S.), It is a true saying, Nature will not be hid.

Naught is never in danger. 1639: Clarke, 126. 1678: Ray, 180. 1738: Swift, *Polite Convers.*, Dial. I. 1889: Peacock, *Manley, etc., Gloss.*, 373 (E.D.S.), 'That that's noht's niver e' daanger', a proverb used when a worthless person is prosperous, or a worthless thing escapes destruction. 1889: *Folk-Lore Journal*, vii 293, Nowght's niver i' danger (Derbyshire saying).

Naught is that muse that finds no excuse. 1629: *Book of Meery Riddles*, Prov. 123.

Naught. *See also* **Nothing**; and **Nought**.

Nay, stay, quoth Stringer, when his neck was in the halter. 1678: Ray, 82. 1732: Fuller, 3512.

Near as fourpence to a groat, As. c.1550: *Jacke Jugeler*, 75 (Grosart), And in eueri thing as just as iiii pens to a grot. 1670: Ray, 205 ['like' for 'near']. 1886: Elworthy, *West Som. Word-Book*, 302 (E.D.S.), The usual simile for exactness is ' 'Tis as near's fowerpence is to a groat'. 1894: Northall, *Folk Phrases*, 9 (E.D.S.).

Near burr. *See* **Moon** (26).

Near friend is better than a far-dwelling kinsman, A. 1669: *Politeuphuia*, 184.

Near is my kirtle (or petticoat), but nearer is my smock. (Tunica propior pallio est. – Plautus, *Trin.*, V ii 30.] 1461: *Paston Letters*, i 542 (Gairdner), He answered a geyn in these wordes, 'Nere is my kyrtyl, but nerre [nearer] is my smok'. 1546: Heywood, *Proverbs*, Pt I ch x 1611: Cotgrave, s.v. 'Chair' ['petticoa']. c.1685: in *Roxb. Ballads*, viii 869 (B.S.) ['petticoat']. 1860: Reade, *Cl. and Hearth*, ch xcviii 1894: Northall, *Folk Phrases*, 25 (E.D.S.), The smock is nearer than the petticoat.

Near is my purse, but nearer is my soul. 1860: Reade, *Cl. and Hearth*, ch lxxvi

Near is my shirt, but nearer is my skin. [1539: Taverner, *Proverbs*, fo. 15, My cote is nerer me than my robe or gowne.] c.1570: in *Ballads* (Percy S., No. 1), 99, Neerer is my skin then shirte. 1593: G. Harvey, *Works*, ii 311 (Grosart), That euery man was neerest to himselfe, and the skinne neerer then the shirt. 1685: Meriton, *Yorkshire Ale*, 66 ['sarke' for 'shirt']. 1712: Arbuthnot, *Law a Bott. Pit*, Pt IV ch v, 'My shirt,' quoth he, 'is near me, but my skin is nearer!' 1792: Wolcot, *Works* ii 313 (1795). 1883: A. Easther, *Almondbury Gloss.*, 113 (E.D.S.), A local saying here ... was 'Nar [Near] is mi sark, but narrer's mi skin'. 1890: Caine, *Bondman*, II x (OED).

Near lore by craft maketh the far lore loathed, The. c.1386: Chaucer, *Miller's Tale*, l. 206, Ful sooth is this proverbe, it is no lye, Men seyn right thus, alwey the nye slye Maketh the ferre leve to be looth. c.1390: Gower, *Conf. Amantis*, bk iii 1. 1899, An old sawe is, 'Who that is slyh In place where he mai be nyh, He makth the ferre lieve loth'.

Nearer the bone the sweeter the flesh, The. 1559: in *Ballads* (Percy S., No. 1), 21, The nigher the bone, the flesh is much sweeter. 1614: Cook, *City Gallant, in* Haztitt, *Old Plays*, xi 207. 1661: Davenport, *City Nightcap*, I. 1819: Scott, *Bride of L.*, ch vi, The nearer the bane the sweeter, as your honours weel ken.

Nearer the church the farther from God, The. 1303: Brunne, *Handl. Synne*, l. 9243, The nerë the cherche, the fyrther fro Gode. Before 1500: in Hill, *Commonplace-Book*, 130 (E.E.T.S.). 1579: Spenser, *Shep. Cal.*, July, l. 104, To kirke the narre, to God more farre, has bene an old said saw. 1611: Tourneur, *Atheist's Tragedy*, I. iv. 1662: Fuller, *Worthies*, ii 266 (1840). 1784: *New Foundl. Hosp. for Wit*, iv. 160, The old proverb ... That the nearest the church are the farthest from God. 1824: Scott, *Redgauntlet*, ch xix, For the nearer the church – the proverb is somewhat musty.

Nearer the kin the further in, The. 1591: Harington, *Orl. Furioso*, bk xvi, Moral, The nearer of kin, the sooner in. 1615: R. Tofte, tr. *Blazon of Iealousie*, 28, The nigher kinne the farther in. 1639: Clarke, 26.

Nearest to the well. *See* quot. 1639: in *Berkeley MSS.*, iii 32 (1885), Neerest to the well furthest from the water, Like nearest to the church furthest from God (Gloucst.).

Neat as a new pin. *See* **New pin**.

Neat as ninepence, As. 1659: Howell, 11. 1857: *Blackw. Mag.*, lxxxi 397 (OED), If I didn't see him whip a picture out of its frame, as neat as ninepence. 1911: *Devonsh. Assoc. Trans.*, xliii 94, 'So neat as ninepence' is the common superlative absolute of neatness.

Neat but not gaudy. 1631: Brathwait, *Eng. Gentlewoman*, 399 (1641), Making this her impreze: *Comely, not gaudy*. 1806: Lamb, *Letters*, i 354 (Lucas), A little thin flowery border round, neat not gaudy ... 1838: Ruskin, in *Archit. Mag.*, Nov., 483, That admiration of the 'neat but not gaudy', which is commonly reported to have influenced the devil when he painted his tail pea green.

Necessary. *See* **Sow**, *subs.* (4).

Necessity and opportunity may make a coward valiant. 1732: Fuller, 3514. 1783: Day, *Sandf. and Merton*, 44 (1891), Necessity makes even cowards brave.

Necessity has no law. In the earlier examples it is always **Need** … [Necessitas dat legem, non ipse accipit. – Publ. Syrus. Feriis caret necessitas. – Palladius, I vi 7. Legem non habet necessitas. – St Augustine, *Solil. animae ad Deum, c* 2.] 1377: Langland, *Plowman*, B, xx. 10, Nede ne hath no lawe. *c.*1390: Gower, *Conf. Amantis*, bk iv. l. 1167, For as men sein, nede hath no lawe. *c.*1450: *Partonope*, l. 8268, But this ys a full olde sawe: Nede had no maner of lawe. 1493: *Dives et Pauper*, fo. 123 (1536) [as in.1390]. Before 1529: Skelton, *Colin Clout*, l. 865 [as in 1390]. 1577: Kendall, *Flow. of Epigrams*, 292 (Spens.S.) [as in 1390]. 1608: Rowlands, *Hum. Look. Glasse*, 9 (Hunt.Cl.), Necessitie it hath no law, I must my gelding sell. 1678: Dryden, *Limberham*, III ii, Necessity has no law; I must be patient. 1713: C. Shadwell, *Hum. of the Army*, V ii [as in 1678]. *c.*1800: J. Trusler, *Prov. in Verse*, 79 [as in 1678]. 1864: Mrs H. Wood, *Trevlyn Hold*, ch xxxiv, But necessity has no law, and he was obliged to rise.

Necessity is a hard dart. 1560: Becon, in *Catechism, etc.*, 601 (P.S.) [quoted as 'the common proverb'].

Necessity is coal-black. 1678: Ray, 180.

Necessity is the mother of invention. 1519: Horman, *Vulgaria*, fo. 52, Nede taught hym wytte. 1587: Under-downe, *Heliodorus*, 201 (T.T.), Surely necessitie is the deviser of all manner of shiftes. 1602: Rowlands, *Greenes Ghost*, 32 (Hunt.Cl.), As necessitie is neuer without stratagems. 1672: Wycherley, *Love in a Wood*, III iii, Necessity, mother of invention! 1703: Farquhar, *Twin-Rivals*, I i, If necessity be the mother of invention, she was never more pregnant than with me. 1830: Scott, *Journal*, 11 July. 1860: C. Reade, *Cl. and Hearth*, ch xxxiii.

Necessity knows no law. The form in which the proverb **Necessity has no law** (q.v.) now most commonly appears. 1939: 'D. Yates', *Gale Warning*, vi, 'Don't speak to the man at the wheel 'is a very good rule'. 'So', said I, 'Is "Necessity knows no law." '

Neck and crop. 1816: in Hone, *Ev. Day Book*, i 461, Explain the terms milling – fibbing – cross buttock – neck and crop – bang up – and – prime. 1872: Hardy, *Greenwood Tree*, Pt II ch ii, 'Now 'tis to turn us out of the quire neck and crop', said the tranter. 1894: Caine, *Manxman*, ch xxii.

Neck and heels. 1740: North, *Examen*, 72, The liberty of the subject is brought in neck and heels, as they say, that the Earl might be popular.

Neck as long as my arm, I'll first see thy. 1678: Ray, 261.

Neck of another, One trouble in the. 1533: Udall, *Flowers out of Terence*, fo. 103, One myschiefe on an others necke. 1567: G. Fenton, *Bandello*, i 232 (T.T.), Other straung mischiefes … one in the necke of another, *c.*1640: in *Roxb. Ballads*, i 370 (P.S.), One vice on the neck of another pursues. 1708: tr. Aleman's *Guzman*, i 80, My misfortunes came so upon the neck of one another. 1889: Peacock, *Manley, etc.*, *Gloss.*, 367 (E.D.S.), 'One bad job alus falls on th' neck of anuther', is a common saying when misfortunes follow each other quickly.

Neck or nothing. 1678: Ray, 347. 1708: Cibber, *Lady's Last Stake*, III, But to scamper, neck or nothing, after a mad galloping jade of a hind. 1766: Garrick, *Neck or Nothing* [title]. 1823: Byron, *Don Juan*, can. viii st. 45. 1884: R.L.S. and Henley, *Adm. Guinea*, I ii, By George, it's neck or nothing now. Stand by to back me up.

Need *subs.* **1. Need and night make the lame to trot**. Glos. 1639: in *Berkeley MSS.*, iii 32 (1885).

2. Need makes the naked man run. 1639: Clarke, 225. 1670: Ray, 124. 1754: Berthelson, *Eng.-Danish Dict.*, s.v. 'Need'.

3. Need makes the naked quean spin. 1670: Ray, 124. 1754: Berthelson, s.v. 'Need'.

4. Need makes the old wife trot. *c.*1210: in Wright, *Essays on Middle Ages*, i 149 (1846), Neode makath heald wif eorne. Before 1500: in Hill, *Common place-Book*, 128 (E.E.T.S.), Nede makith the old wiff to trotte. 1573: *New Custom*, III i, For need (they say) maketh the old wife and man both to trudge. 1602: *Liberality and Prod.*, III v 1681: Robertson, *Phraseol. Generalis*, 911. 1712: *Spectator*, No. 509. 1816: Scott, *Old Mortality*, ch viii, Just what gars the auld wives trot – neshessity.

5. Need will have its course. 1678: Ray, 180.

6. When the need is highest, the help is nighest. 1630: T. Adams, *Works*, 619, Mans extremity is Gods opportunitie. 1822: Scott, *Nigel*, ch xxi 1853: Trench, *Proverbs*, 61 (1905), Our own proverb, *Man's extremity*, *God's opportunity*, or as we sometimes have it, *When need is highest, help is nighest*. Cf. **Boot after bale**. *See also* **Necessity**.

Need, *verb*. **1. I may see him need, but I'll not see him bleed.** Spoken by father of erring son. 1639: Clarke, 42. 1670: Ray, 187. 1754: Berthelson, *Eng.-Danish Dict.*, s.v. 'Need'.

2. They need much whom nothing will content. 1639: Clarke, 38. 1670: Ray, 124. 1732: Fuller, 4969.

3. You need not doubt, you are no doctor. 1670: Ray, 172.

Needham. *See* quots. 1580: Tusser, *Husb.*, 188 (E.D.S.), Soone sets thine host at needams shore, to craue the beggers bone. 1662: Fuller, *Worthies*, iii 161 (1840), They are said to be in the highway to Needham who hasten to poverty. 1790: Grose, *Prov. Gloss.*, s.v. 'Suffolk', You are in the highway to Needham. 1869: Spurgeon, *John Ploughman*, ch vii, They will find out their mistake when want finds *them* out … they are already a long way on the road to Needham.

Needingworth, It comes from. 1639: Clarke, 68.

Needk in a bottle of hay, Like a. 1532: More, *Works*, 837 (1557), To seke out one lyne in all hys workes wer to go looke a nedle in a medow. 1592: Greene, *Works*, xi 252 (Grosart), The poore man … gropeth in the darke to find a needle in a bottle of hay. 1608: Day, *Law Trickes*, I ii, My father … is gone to seeke a needle in a bottle of hay. 1691: *Merry Drollery*, 79 (Ebsworth), You'd as soon find a needle in a bottle of hay. 1720: C. Shadwell, *Sham Prince*, II i 1772: Graves, *Spirit. Quixote*, bk iii ch x [with 'bundle' for 'bottle']. 1834: Marryat, *P. Simple*, ch xxii ['bundle']. 1886: R.L.S., *Kidnapped*, ch xx. 1913: R. E. Francillon, *MidVict. Memories*, I discovered what had hitherto been the proverbial needle in the pottle of hay.

Needles and pins, needles and pins, When a man marries his trouble begins. 1843: Halliwell, *Nursery Rhymes*, 122. 1876: Blackmore, *Cripps*, ch lii 1880: *N. & Q.*, 6th ser, ii 205 [with 'girl' for 'man'].

Needs must when the devil drives. *c.*1420: Lydgate, *Assem. of Gods*, st. 3, p. 2 (E.E.T.S.), For hit ys oft seyde by hem that yet lyues He must nedys go that the deuell dryues. 1533:

Heywood, *John, Tyb, etc.*, 77 (Farmer, 1905), He must needs go that the devil driveth. 1594: Kyd, *Span. Trag.*, III xii, Needs must he go that the devils drive. 1633: Jonson, *Tale of a Tub*, III v, Wife, I must go, needs, whom the devil drives. 1672: J. Lacy, *Old Troop*, II *c.*1750: Foote, *Orators*, II. 1822: Scott, *Nigel*, Introd. Epistle. 1840: Barham, *Ing. Legends:* 'St Odille', Needs must when a certain old gentleman drives. 1843: Surtees, *Handley Cross*, III. xi, Needs must when the devil drives … But I'd rather do anything than injure that poor blue-eyed beauty.

Needs must trot afoot, that tires his horse, He. 1607: T. Heywood, *Woman Killed with Kindness*, IV v.

Needy when he is married, shall be rich when he is buried, He that is. 1633: Draxe, 229. 1670: Ray, 48. 1732: Fuller, 2183 [with 'scarce' after 'shall'].

Neighbour and **Neighbours**. **1. Every man's neighbour is his looking-glass.** 1659: Howell, *Proverbs: Brit.-Eng.*, 3.

2. He hath ill neighbours (or dwells far from neighbours) **that is fain to praise himself.** 1548: Hall, *Chron.*, 70 (1809), He that praiseth him self lacketh louyng neighbors. 1599: Porter, *Two Angry Women*, sc xi, You dwell by ill neighbours, Richard; that makes yee praise your selfe. 1631: Brathwait, *Eng. Gentlewoman*, 320 (1641), Beware of self-prayse; it argues you have slow neighbours, or few deserts. 1670: Ray, 125. 1754: Berthelson, *Eng.-Danish Dict.*, s.v. 'Fain'.

3. He's an ill neighbour that is not missed. 1639: Clarke, 75.

4. He that hath a good neighbour hath a good morrow. 15th cent.: in *Reliq. Antiquae*, i 316 (1841), He that hath a good neyghboure hath a good morowe; He that hath a schrewyd wyfe hath much sorowe; He that fast spendyth must nede borowe; But when he schal paye agen, then ys al the sorowe. 1591: Florio, *Second Frutes*, 57, You have a good neighbour then And by consequence a good morrow. 1611: Cotgrave, s.v. 'Matin', … morrow; viz. good words next his heart a mornings. 1633: Draxe, 138. 1670: Ray, 124, A good neighbour, a goodmorrow. 1732: Fuller, 165 [as in 1670].

5. Here's talk of the Turk and the Pope, but it's my next neighbour that does me the harm. 1659: Howell, 4 ['hurt' for 'har']. 1670: Ray, 125. 1732: Fuller, 2497.

6. Hold him not for a good neighbour that's at table and wine at every hour. 1623: Wodroephe, *Spared Houres*, 521.

7. Neighbour's fare. *See* quots. 1678: Ray, 180, Neighbour-quart is good quart, i.e. giffe gaffe [q.v.] is a good fellow. *c.*1680: in *Roxb. Ballads*, iii 419 (B.S.), Since neighbour's fare always is counted the best. 1869: FitzGerald, *Sea Words and Phrases*, 8, I mayn't make a fortune, but I look for neighbour's fare nevertheless. 1901: F. E. Taylor, *Lancs Sayings*, 19, Neighbour's fare's no ill-fare.

8. When thy neighbour's house doth burn, then look to your own. [Nam tua res agitur paries cum proximo ardet. – Horace, *Epist.*, I xviii 84.] 1519: Horman, *Vulgaria*, fo. 126, Whan my neybours house is a fyre, I can nat be out of thought for myn owne. 1548: Hall, *Chron.*, 438 (1809), He remembred the prouerbe that sayth, when thy neighboures house is a fyer, thy staffe standeth nexte the doore. 1593: *Pass. Morrice*, 75 (N.Sh.S.), When our neighbours house is on fier, we haue neede to bestirre vs. 1681: Robertson, *Phraseol. Generalis*, 744. 1732: Fuller, 5599: When the next house is a fire it's high time to look to thy own.

9. Who more ready to call her neighbour scold, than the arrantest scold in all the street? 1639: Clarke, 79 [with 'i' th' parish' for 'in all the street']. 1732: Fuller, 5712.

10. You must ask your neighbour if you shall live in peace. 1639: Clarke, 203. 1670: Ray, 125. 1732: Fuller, 5961. 1855: Bohn, 463, Nobody can live longer in peace than his neighbour pleases.

See also **All is well**; and **Good fences**.

Neither ashore nor afloat. Corn. 1895: Jos. Thomas, *Randigal Rhymes*, 61.

Neither borrow nor flatter. *See* **Rich** (8).

Neither do right nor suffer wrong, He'll. 1678: Ray, 266. 1732:Fuller, 2426 [with 'ne'er' for 'neither'].

Neither end nor side to it, There's. 1917: Bridge, *Cheshire Proverbs*, 119, There's noather eend nor side to 't.

Neither fish nor flesh, etc. *See* **Flesh nor fish**.

Neither give to all nor contend with fools. 1855: Bohn, 458.

Neither great poverty nor great riches will hear reason. 1855: Bohn, 458.

Neither idle nor well occupied. 1567: Harman, *Caveat*, 33 (E.E.T.S.), In the night they be not idle, – nether, as the common saying is, 'well occupied'. *c.*1570: *Marr. of Wit and Science*, IV iv, The proverb is verified, I am neither idle, nor yet well-occupied. 1611: W. Goddard, *A Satirycall Dialogve … Imprinted … for all such gentlewomen as are not altogether idle nor yet well ocvpyed*. 1662: Fuller, *Worthies*, ii 513 (1840), He had an excellent wit, which, the back friends to stage-plays will say, was neither idle nor well employed.

Neither lead nor drive. 1667: L'Estrange, *Quevedo's Visions*, 80 (1904), Another … would neither lead nor drive. 1678: Ray, 75.

Neither maid, wife, nor widow, She is. 1678: Ray, 90, She is neither wife, widow nor maid. 1732: Fuller, 4132.

Neither seeds nor meal. 1892: Heslop, *Northumb. Words*, 471 (E.D.S.), 'Nowther seeds nor meal' – neither one thing nor another – is a common proverb.

Neither sugar nor salt. 1738: Swift, *Polite Convers.*, Dial. I, We were neither sugar nor salt, we were not afraid the rain would melt us. 1880: Banks, *Wooers*, ii 7 (W.), Bless the bairn, shoo's noather sugar nor saut, schoo'l noan melt.

Nene and Welland, The Rivers. *See* quots. 1596: Spenser, *F. Q.*, IV xi 35, And after him the fatal Welland went, That, if old sawes prove true, (which God forbid!) Shall drowne all Holland with his excrement. 1865: W. White, *Eastern England*, i 273, Nene and Welland Shall drown all Holland, recites the ancient saying upon the district … between the two rivers.

Nertown. *See* quot. 1851: in *N. & Q.*, 1st ser, iv. 149, At Taunton, in Somersetshire, there is a similar tradition current: Nertown was a market town When Taunton was a furzy down. This Nertown is a village adjoining Taunton, and lying on the north side of it.

Nests, Birds in their little nests. *See* **Bird** (6).

Net fills though the fisherman sleeps, The. 1683: White-Kennett. tr Erasmus' *Praise of Folly*, 135 (8th ed.), Thus Timotheus, the Athenian commander, in all his expeditions was a mirror of good luck, because he was a little under-witted; from him was occasioned the proverb, *The net fills though the fisherman sleeps*.

Net is spread in sight of the bird, In vain the. [Proverbs i. 17, Surely in vain the net is spread in the sight of any bird] 1581: G. Pettie, tr. *S. Guazzo's Civil Conversation*, i 20v, In vaine (as the Proverb sayth) The net is pitcht in the sight of the birdes. 1888: J.E.T. Rogers, *Economic Interpretation of History*, xxi, The landowners in Pitt's time foresaw this ... They would certainly be caught, and the net was spread in vain in the sight of the bird.

Nettle. 1. Better be stung by a nettle than pricked by a rose. 1670: Ray, 25. 1732: Fuller, 878.

2. He that handles a nettle tenderly is soonest stung. 1579: Lyly, *Euphues*, 65 (Arber), Hee which toucheth the nettle tenderly, is soonest stoung. 1732: Fuller, 2126.

3. Nettles in March. *See* quots. 1846: Denham, *Proverbs*, 38 (Percy S.), If they would drink nettles in March, And eat mugwort in May, So many fine maidens Wouldn't go to the clay. 1882: *N. &Q.*, 6th ser, v 408, If they wad drink nettles in March, And eat muggins in May, Sae mony braw maidens Wad not go to clay. 1913: E. M. Wright, *Rustic Speech, etc.*, 241, As the old rhyme says: [as in 1882].

4. Nip a nettle hard, and it will not sting you. 1830: Forby, *Vocab. E. Anglia*, 430. 1872: J. Glyde, jr., *Norfolk Garland*, 149.

SEE also **In dock**.

Never a fou' face, but there's a fou' fancy, There's. 1917: Bridge, *Cheshire Proverbs*, 119.

Never a whit, As food, as never the better. 1546: Heywood, *Proverbs*, Pt II ch xi 1553: *Respublica*, IV iii 1597: Bacon, *Coulers of Good and Euill*, 10. 1639: Fuller, *Holy War*, bk iv. ch viii 1670: Ray, 125. 1709: R. Kingston, *Apoph. Curiosa*, 72, We say, as good never a whit at all, as never a whit the nearer. 1732: Fuller, 687.

Never be ashamed to eat your meat. 1639: Clarke, 269. 1670: Ray, 57.

Never be weary of well doing. 1633: Draxe, 32, Neuer wearie of that which is good. 1670: Ray, 154.

Never climbed. *See* **Climb** (1).

Never drank was never athirst, He that. 1659: Howell, 13.

Never enough where nothing left, There was. 1639: Clarke, 38. 1670: Ray, 85, Ther's never enough where nought leaves. 1736: Bailey, *Dict.*, s.v. 'Enough'.

Never give a sucher an even treak. *See* **Sucker**.

Never go home. *See* quot. 1888: Lowsley, *Berks Gloss.*, 31 (E.D.S.), Never go whoam Wi'out stick or stwun [stone].

Never good that mind their belly so much. 1678: Ray, 347.

Never had, you never miss, What you've. 1912: 'J. Webster', *Daddy-Long-Legs* (1913), 232, You mustn't get me used to too many luxuries. One doesn't miss what one has never had. 1939: T. Burke, *Living in Bloomsbury*, ii, It has been said that what you've never had you never miss, and from all one can gather, those people were not aware of suffering from lack of holiday.

Never is a long time (*or* day). *c.*1386: Chaucer, *Canon's Yeoman's Tale*, l. 858. Never to thryve were to long a date. 1736: Bailey, *Dict.*, s.v. 'Term', Never is a long term. 1839: Dickens, *Nickleby*, ch last, Never is a long day. 1841: Dickens, *Barn. Rudge*, ch last. 1886: Elworthy, *West Som. Word-Book*, 508 (E.D.S.), Stap cheel! never's a long day. Blackmore: *Springhaven*, I xvii, She never could paye her rent. But 'never is a long time' ... and ... she stood clear of all debt now.

Never less alone than when alone. 1586: Pettie, tr. Guazzo's *Civil Convers.*, fo. 19, Scipio sayd, yt he was neuer lesse alone, then when he was alone. 1596: Lodge, *Divel Coniured*, 9 (Hunt.Cl.), A good man is neuer lesse alone then when alone (as Themistocles said). 1669: *Politeuphuia*, 45, A wise man is never, etc. 1680: L'Estrange, *Tully's Offices*, 141, It was the saying ... of Scipio Affricanus the Elder ... that he was never less idle, or alone, then when he most appeared so to be. 1816: Scott, *Black Dwarf*, ch iv.

Never-mass, At = never. 1639: Clarke, 229.

Never quiet but when she is sleeping, She is. 1631: Brathwait, *Whimzies*, 104 (1859).

Never quit certainty for hope. 1855: Bohn, 459.

Never sigh but send. 1678: Ray, 81, Sigh not but send, he'll come if he be unhang'd. 1738: Swift, *Polite Convers.*, Dial. I, Come, miss, never sigh, but send for him. 1852: FitzGerald, *Polonius*, 78 (1903).

Never tell thy foe that thy foot acheth. *c.*1320: in *Reliq. Antiquae*, i 111 (1841) ... Quoth Hendyng.

Never the nearer. *See* **Early** (5).

Never too late to learn. 1670: Ray, 112 ['old' for 'late'], *c.*1680: L'Estrange, *Seneca's Epistles*, xx, It is never too late to learn what it is always necessary to know. 1726: Southerne, *Money the*

Mistress, V iii 1752: Fielding, *Cov. Garden Journal*, No. 72, An old proverb, which says, It is never too late to grow wise.

Never too late to mend. [ἀκεσταί τοι φρένες ἐσθλῶν. – Homer, *Iliad*, xiii 115.] 1590: Greene, *Neuer too Late* [title]. 1655: Howell, *Letters*, bk iv. No. 38, It is never over-late to mend. 1856: Reade, *It is Never too Late to Mend* [title]. 1891: R.L.S., *Letters*, iv. 54 (Tusitala ed.).

Never too late to repent. 1670: Ray, 112. 1736: Bailey, *Dict.*, s.v. 'Late'.

Never trust a Little. 1846–59: *Denham Tracts*, i 65 (F.L.S.), Never trust a Little. Although this saying is nearly universally used under another name in the bishoprick [Durham], and elsewhere in the North of England, I have reason to believe that the above is the correct form, and the other a mere adaptation. A family of this name (Little) were celebrated rievers, or … thieves.

Never was bad woman fair. 1640: Herbert, *Jac. Prudentum*.

Never well, full nor fasting. 1639: Clarke, 34, Neither pleased full nor fasting. 1659: Howell, 2. 1670: Ray, 170. 1692: L'Estrange, *Aesop*, 265 (3rd ed.). 1738: Swift, *Polite Convers.*, Dial. II, You don't know your own mind; you are neither well, full nor fasting. 1896: *Folk-Lore*, vii 377, He'll neither be satisfied, full nor fasting (Staffs).

New bread. *See* quot. 1888: Lowsley, *Berks Gloss.*, 30 (E.D.S.), New bread, new beer, an' grean 'ood, 'ull bring ruin to any man's house.

Newbridge Hollow. *See* **Bowdon Wakes**.

New brooms sweep clean. 1546: Heywood, *Proverbs*, Pt II ch i, The greene new brome sweepth cleene. 1579: Lyly, *Euphues*, 88 (Arber), Ah well I wot that a new broome sweep-eth cleane. 1659: *Lady Alimony*, II i *c.*1760: Foote, *Cozeners*, I, New acts, like new brooms, make a little bustle at first; but the dirt will return, never fear. 1815: Scott, *Mannering*, ch vi 1905: E. G. Hayden, *Travels Round our Village*, 97, A noo broom swapes clane; but when it's a scrub ther's a job.

Newcastle. 1. Canny Newcastle, 1790: Grose, *Prov. Gloss.*, s.v. 'Northumberland'. 1825: Brockett, *Gloss. N. Country Words*, 37, Canny, a genuine Newcastle word, applied to anything superior or of the best kind … 'Canny Newcassel', *par excellence*, is proverbial. 1846–59: *Denham Tracts*, i 309 (F.L.S.).

2. Coals to Newcastle. *See* **Coals**.
3. He has the Newcastle bur in his throat. 1790: Grose, *Prov. Gloss.*, s.v. 'Northumberland'. 1846–59: *Denham Tracts*, i 292 (F.L.S.).
4. Newcastle grindstone. *See* **Scot** (1).
5. Newcastle hospitality. *See* quot. 1892: Heslop, *Northumb. Words*, 498 (E.D.S.), Newcastle hospitality – that is, roasting a friend to death; or, according to a more popular colloquial phrase, 'killing a person with kindness'.
6. Newcastle Scots are the worst of all Scots. 1846–59: *Denham Tracts*, i 298 (F.L.S.).
7. That is going round by Newcastle to get to Shields. Ibid., ii 364.

New College. *See* quot 1659: Howell, 20, They thrive as New Colledge students, who are golden schollers, silver batchelors and leaden masters.

New friend makes the old forgotten, A. 1611: Cotgrave, s.v. 'Aime'. 1800: Lamb, *Letters*, i 159 (Lucas), But ever the new friend driveth out the old, as the ballad sings. [Mr Lucas notes: 'The ballad I have not found'.]

Newgate. *See* quot. 1662: Fuller, *Worthies*, ii 314 (1840), He that is [at] a low ebb at Newgate, may soon be afloat at Tyburn. 1790: Grose, *Prov. Gloss.*, s.v. 'London' [as in 1662].

Newgate Knocker. *See* quots. 1881: in *N.&Q.*, 6th ser, iii 248, 'As black as Newgate Knocker' – I heard this expressive phrase used the other day by a servant. 1893: G. L. Gower, *Gloss. of Surrey Words*, 12 (E.D.S.), Coming from Croydon on a very dark night the driver remarked 'Ay! it is a dark night, dark as Newgate Knocker'.

New grief awakens the old. 1732: Fuller, 3535.
New honours. *See* **Honour** (7).
New lords, new laws. 1548: Hall, *Chron.*, 233 (1809). *c.*1597: in Harington, *Nugae Antiquae*, i 201 (1804), To such reprovers I answer, *new lords, new laws*. 1605: Sylvester, *Du Bartas*, Week I Day ii l. 97, 1659: R. Brome, *Queen and Concubine*, II v 1712: Motteux, *Quixote*, Pt II ch xliii 1823: Scott, *St Ronan's*, ch xiv, But new lords new laws – naething but fine and imprisonment.

Newmarket heath, A fine morning to catch herrings on. 1639: Clarke, 308.
New meat begets a new appetite. 1633: Draxe, 23, New meats prouoke the appetite. 1670: Ray, 18. 1732: Fuller, 3534, New dishes beget new appetites.
New pin, Clean (or Neat) as a. 1829: Scott, *Journal*, 19 April, It is a great thing to have a

certainty to be clear as a new pin of every penny of debt. R.L.S., *Treasure* I, ch x, Always glad to see me in the galley, which he kept as clean as a new pin. 1886: Elworthy, *West Som. Word-Book*, 504 (E.D.S.), Her was a-dressed off so fine and so nate's a new pin. 1889: Peacock, *Manley, etc., Gloss.*, 366 (E.D.S.), Neat as a new pin. 1923: Alice Brown, *Old Crow*, ch vi, Charlotte told me … he was neat as a new pin.

News. *See* **Country** (3).

New things are fair. [1412–20: Lydgate, *Troy Book*, bk iv. l. 301, It is natural Men to delite in thing that is newe.] 1611: Cotgrave, s.v. 'Nouveau', Every new thing lookes faire. 1651: Herbert, *Jac. Prudentium*, 2nd ed. 1700: T. Brown, *Scarron*, ii 248 (1892), As all new things are aPt to please. 1732: Fuller, 3537, New things are most look'd at.

New wine in old bottles, You can't put. [Matthew ix.17, Neither do men put new wine into old bottles: else the bottles break and the wine runneth out …]1912: L. Strachey, *Landmarks in French Literature*, vi, The new spirits had animated the prose of Chateaubriand and the poetry of Lamartine; but … the *form* of both these writers retained most of the important characteristics of the old tradition. It was new wine in old bottles.

New Year. 1. A good new year and a merry Handsel Monday. 1846: Denham, *Proverbs*, 23 (Percy S.).

2. At New Year's tide The days lengthen a cock's stride. 1710: *Brit. Apollo*, ii No. 90, col. 3, That old saving, that the days lengthen a cock stride. 1759: *Gent. Mag.*, 16, The countryman … has a saying that I believe is very general all over England – At New Year's tide, etc. 1846: Denham, *Proverbs*, 30 (Percy S.), At new-year's day, a cock's stride, At Candlemas, an hour wide. 1904: *Co. Folk-Lore: Northumb.*, 174 (F.L.S.).

3. If New Year's eve. *See* quot. 1846: Denham, *Proverbs*, 23 (Percy S.), If new-year's eve night wind blow South, It betokeneth warmth and growth; If West, much milk, and fish in the sea; If North, much cold, and storms there will be; If East, the trees will bear much fruit – If north-east, flee it man and brute.

4. Pay away money on New Year's day, And all the year through you'll have money to pay. Worcs. and Herefs. 1882: *N. &Q.*, 6th ser, vi 186.

Next to love quietness. 1678: Ray, 194.

Next to no wife. *See* **Wife** (17).

Next way, round about, is at the far door. 1639: Clarke, 8.

Nice as a ha'porth of silver spoons. 1546: Heywood, *Proverbs*, Pt II ch ix, Sodeinly waxen as nyse As it had bene a halporth of syluer spoones. *c.*1550: *Jacke Jugeler*, 40 (Grosart), As denty and nice, as an halpeny worth of silVer spoons.

Nice as a nun's hen. 15th cent.: in *Reliq. Antiquae*, i 248 (1841), Some [women] be nyse as a nanne hene. 1546: Heywood, *Proverbs*, Pt II ch i 1670: Ray, 202. 1847: Halliwell, *Dict.*, s.v. 'Nanny', As nice as a nanny hen, i.e. very affected or delicate. [Halliwell follows the 15th-century example in rendering 'nanne' as 'nanny', but the other references give 'nun's', as also does Wilson in his *Rhetorique*, 1560, p. 219 (1909).]

Nice as nip. 1854: Baker, *Northants Gloss.*, s.v. Nice as nip. Just the thing; to a nicety. A very common colloquial expression. 1901: F. E. Taylor, *Lancs Sayings*, 3. Cf. **Clean as nip**.

Nice wife and a back door Do often make a rich man poor, A. *c.*1450: *Prov. of Good Counsel*, l. 33 (E.E.T.S.), For a nyse wyfe and a backe dore Makyth oftyn tymus a ryche man pore. 1639: Clarke, 218. 1732: Fuller, 6268.

Nichils in nine holes = Nothing at all. Variants of 'holes' are 'pokes', 'nooks', etc. 1584: R. Scot, *Witchcraft*, bk xvi ch vi, And their bodies to the hangman to be trussed on the gallowes, for nichels in a bag. 1662: Fuller, *Worthies*, ch xxv, There is an officer in the Exchequer, called Clericus Nihilorum, or the Clerk of the Nichills, who maketh a Roll of all such sums as are nichill'd by the Sheriff upon their estreats of the Green Wax, when such sums are set on persons, either not found, or not found solvible. 1670: Ray, 188. 1730: Bailey, *Eng. Dict.*, s.v., Nichils (in Common Law) are issues or debts, which the sheriff being opposed, says are worth nothing, by reason that the parties that should pay them are nothing worth. 1852: 'Cheshire Proverbs', in *N. &Q.*, 1st ser, vi 386, Nichils in nine nooks. 1917: Bridge, *Cheshire Proverbs*, 97.

Nicholas Kemp. *See* quot. 1888: Q.-Couch, *Troy Town*, ch xi, Like Nicholas Kemp, he'd occasion for all.

Nick and froth. A proverbial expression for tapsters' tricks. 1600–12: Rowlands, *Four*

Knaves, 48 (Percy S.), With Cannes of beere …
And those they say are fil'd with nick and froth.
1656: R. Fletcher, *Ex Otio Negotium*, 133, From
the nick and froth of a penny pot-house. 1674:
Poor Robin Alman., August, What with nick and
froth, by filling Cans half full for fear of spilling.
1690: *New Dict. Canting Crew*, sig. H7, Nick and
froth built the Pye at Aldgate.

Nick in the post. *See* quot. 1847: Halliwell,
Dict., s.v. 'Nick', The proverbial expression 'to
knock a nick in the post', i.e. to make a record of
any remarkable event.

Niggard. *See* **More spends**.

Niggard never hath enough, The. 1493; *Dives
et Pauper*, fo. 8 (1536).

Night brings is the mother of (or counsel).
1578: Florio, *First Fruites*, fo. 31, The nyght is
the mother of thoughts. 1611: Cotgrave, s.v.
'Conseil', Night gives advice; we say, take
counsell of your pillow. 1640: Herbert, *Jac.
Prudentum*. 1707: Dunton, *Athenian Sport*, 527,
Whence came the saying, *That the night gives
counsels?* 1884: R.L.S. and Henley, *Adm.
Guinea*, III iv, The night brings counsel: to-
morrow shall decide. 1925: Locke, *Great
Pandolfo*, ch ii, The night brings counsel. Cf.
Take (25).

Night brings the crows home. 1901: F. E.
Taylor, *Lancs Sayings*, 9, Neet brings th' crows
whoam.

**Night to run away with another man's wife, A
fine**. 1591: Florio, *Second Frutes*, 165, It were
euen a fine night, etc. *c.*1630: B.&F., *Lovers'
Progress*, III ii, Here were a night to choose to run
away, etc. 1633: Rowley, *Match at Midnight*, IV,
They say a moonshine night is good to run, etc.
1659: Howell, 6, A fit night to steal away a fair
lady, viz. A cleer moonshine. 1738: Swift, *Polite
Convers.*, Dial. I, Oh! 'twas a delicate night to
run, etc.

**Nightingale and cuckoo sing both in one
month, The**. 1639: Clarke, 106. 1696: D'Urfey.
Quixote, Pt III Act V sc i, D'ye hear, sir, as great
as you are, remember this, the nightingale and
cuckoo sing both in a month.

Nightingale cannot sing in a cage, A. 1732:
Fuller, 335.

Nightingale. *See also* **Cuckoo** (14).

Nightingales can sing their own song best.
1732: Fuller, 3542.

Nimble as an eel, As. *c.*1620: B.&F., *Woman's*

Prize, IV i 1675: *The Mistaken Husband*, I iii, As
nimble as an eele riggling in the mud. 1710: T.
Ward, *Eng. Reform.*, 88 (1716), As glib and
nimble As tail of eell 1732: Fuller, 719, As
nimble as an eel in a sand-bag. 1889: Peacock,
Manley, *etc.*, *Gloss.*, 611 (E.D.S.), Wick [Quick]
as an eel.

Nimble as ninepence, As. 1882: Mrs
Chamberlain, *W. Worcs. Words*, 13 (E.D.S.), 'E
gamboled over the yat [gate] as nimble as
ninepence.

**Nimble ninepence is better than a slow
shilling, A**. 1851: *N. & Q.*, 1st ser, iv. 234 [cited
as an 'old proverb']. 1886: Elworthy, *West Som.
Word-Book*, 513 (E.D.S.) [with 'dead' for
'slow']. 1913: E. M. Wright, *Rustic Speech, etc.*,
173.

Nimble penny it worth a slow sixpence, A.
Glos. 1911: *Folk-Lore*, xxii 239.

Nimblest footman is a false tale, The. 1659:
Howell, *Proverbs: Brit.-Eng.*, 3.

Nine crabs high, Ever since I was. Yorks. 1861:
N. & Q., 2nd ser, xii 309 … That is, I suppose,
since I was a mere child.

Nine days wonder, A. [Romania quoque ab
eodem prodigio novendiale sacrum publice
susceptum est, sen voce caelesti ex Albano
monte missa – nam id quoque traditur – seu
aruspicum monitu. – Livy, i 31.] *c.*1374:
Chaucer, *Troylus*, bk iv. l. 588, A wonder last but
nyne night never in toune. 1546: Heywood,
Proverbs, Pt II ch i, This wonder, (as wonders
last,) lasted nine daies. 1600: Kemp, *Nine Days
Wonder* [title]. 1621: Burton, *Melancholy*, II iii 7,
p. 424 (1836), Be content; 'tis but a nine dayes
wonder. 1633: Massinger, *New Way*, *etc.*, IV ii
1767: Murphy, *Sch. for Guardians*, I ii, And
when the nine days wonder is over, I shall pack
off. 1818: Byron, *Don Juan*, can. i st. 188, The
nine days' wonder which was brought to light.
1898: Shaw, *Plays Pleasant, etc.*, I Pref., xii, The
volume … is a curious relic of that nine days
wonder. 1926: Phillpotts, *Peacock House*, 221.

Ninepence to nothing, As like as. 1670: Ray,
206.

Ninepence to nothing, To bring. Before 1729:
in *Roxb. Ballads*, viii 812 (B.S.), A brace of as
delicate jades As ever brought ninepence to
nothing. 1883: Burne, *Shropsh. Folk-Lore*, 596,
To bring one's ninepence to nothing = to lose
property by neglect and waste.

Nine tailors make a man. The meaning of the proverb is disputed. Tailors were popularly supposed to be weak and cowardly, as in the nursery rhyme 'Four and twenty tailors went to catch a snail' or Shakespeare, *2 Henry IV*, III II, where the 'woman's tailor' is named Feeble. Consequently, it was said that it took nine tailors to make up a real man (*See* quots 1771 and 1828), though the earlier examples show an uncertainty about the actual number of tailors required. Later interpretations suggest that a gentleman has to visit nine tailors to make up a good suit of clothes (see quot. 1819). In the twentieth century, it came to be assumed that 'tailor' was a corruption of 'teller' and that the proverb referred to the number of times the bell tolled as a coffin was brought to the church – nine times for a man, six for a woman, three for a child. Before 1603: Q. Elizabeth – *see* 1838 quotation. 1607: Dekker and Webster, *Northw. Hoe*, II, They say three taylors go to the making vp of a man. 1611: *Tarltons Jests*, 20 (SH.S.), Two tailors goe to a man. 1630: Taylor (Water-Poet), *Works*, 3rd pagin., 73, Some foolish knaue (I thinke) at first began The slander that three taylers are one man. 1639–61: *Rump Songs*, Pt I 159 (1662, repr. 1874), like to nine taylors, who if rightly spell'd, Into one man are monosyllabel'd. 1663: Butler, *Hudibras*, Pt I can. ii l. 22, Just like the manhood of nine tailors. 1720: C. Shadwell, *Sham Prince*, II i 1771: Smollett, *Clinker*, in *Works*, vi 236 (1817),Who … made her believe I was a tailor, and that she was going to marry the ninth part of a man. 1819: Scott; *Letter* 26 July (1933), V 427, They say it takes *nine* tailors to make a man – apparently one is sufficient to ruin him. 1908: H.B. Walters, *Church Bells*, v, When the Knell is rung, it is a frequent practice to indicate the … sex of the deceased … The old saying 'nine tailors make a man' is really 'nine tellers', or three times three. 1838: Carlyle, *Sartor*, bk iii ch xi. Does it: not stand on record that the English Queen Elizabeth, receiving a deputation of Eighteen Tailors, addressed them with a 'Good morning, gentlemen both!'

Nineteen bits of a bilberry, He'll make. 1678: Ray, 229.

Nine words at once, To talk. 1611: Cotgrave, s.v. 'Tost', To speak thick, or fast, or (as we say) nine words at once.

Nip the briar in the bud. 1732: Fuller, 3543.

Nippence, no pence, half a groat wanting twopence. 1659: Howell, 12. 1670: Ray, 215, Nipence nopence, etc.

Nits will be lice. 1690: *New Dict. Canting Crew*, sig. H7. 1823: D'Israeli, *Cur. of Lit.*, 2nd ser, i 431 (1824), Oliver Cromwell's coarse, but descriptive proverb … 'Nits will be lice'.

No alchemy to saving. 1640: Herbert, *Jac. Prudentum*. 1710: S. Palmer, *Moral Essays on Proverbs*, 162, No alchymy like to thrift. 1736: Bailey, *Dict.*, s.v. 'Alchymy'. 1928: *Times*, 11 May, p. 17, col. 3.

No better than she should be. 1604: *Pasquils Jests*, 35 (1864), A man whose; wife was no better then she should be. 1666: Torriano, *Piazza Univ.*, 172, A much as to say, she is no saint, she is no better, etc. 1738: Swift, *Polit Convers.*, Dial. I. 1781: Macklin, *Man of the World*, V 1875: Griffiths, *Mem. of Millbank*, 281 (1884), These daughters were not a bit better than they should have been. 1925: *Punch*, 11 Nov., p. 506, col. 3, We're working now on a screen version of the *Iliad* … and Helen no better than she should be.

No bishop no king. 1641: Smectymnuus, *Vind. Answ.*, §16, 208 (OED), King James of blessed memory said, *no Bishop, no King*. 1653: Chetwynd, Dedn. to Harington's *Briefe View of the Church*, Who held that prophetick axiom as a sure truth, and we see it fulfilled, No Bishop, No King. 1709: O. Dykes, *Eng. Proverbs*, 278 (2nd ed). Cf. **No mitre**.

Noble as the race of Shenkin and line of Harry Tudor. An old Shropshire saying. 1871: *N. & Q.*, 4th ser, vii 9.

Noble blood to market, and see what it will bring, Send your. 1732: Fuller, 4099.

Noble housekeeper needs no doors, A. 1640: Herbert, *Jac. Prudentum* [in the plural]. 1670: Ray, 7.

Noble plant suits not with a stubborn ground, A. 1640: Herbert, *Jac. Prudentum*. 1670: Ray, 21, Noble plants suit not a stubborn soil.

Noble to ninepence, To bring a. A proverbial expression for idle dissipation of money. 1568: Fulwell, *Like will to Like*, in Hazlitt, *Old Plays*, iii 344, For why Tom Tosspot, since he went hence. Hath increased a noble just unto ninepence. 1681: Robertson, *Phraseol. Generalis*, 922, A noble quickly brought to ninepence. 1725: Bailey, tr. Erasmus' *Colloq.*, 235, I have brought a noble to nine pence, and of a master of seven arts I am become a workman of but one art. 1854: Baker, *Northants Gloss.*, s.v. 'Noble', It is said of a person who is thoughtless and wasteful in expenditure, 'He'll soon bring his noble to ninepence'. 1886: Elworthy, *West Som. Word-Book*, 516 (E.D.S.), To spend lavishly or to live extravagantly is said to be the way to bring the noble to ninepence. 1914: R. L. Gales, *Vanished Country Folk*, 199, As a child I remember 'Their noble has come to a ninepence' as the commonest of sayings.

Nobody calls himself rogue. 1855: Bohn, 463.

Nobody hath too much prudence or virtue. Ibid., 463.

Nobody is fond of fading flowers. Ibid., 463.

No carrion will kill a crow. 1670: Ray, 76. 1685: Meriton, *Yorkshire Ale*, 49. 1732: Fuller, 3553 ['poison' for 'kill']. 1890: J. D. Robertson, *Gloucester Gloss.*, 186 (E.D.S.).

No chink, no drink. 1659: T. Pecke, *Parnassi Puerp.*, 64.

Nocke anew, nocke anew, i.e. Try again. Glos. 1639: in *Berkeley MSS.*, iii 32 (1885).

No cross, no crown. [1587: Greene, *Works*, iv. 48 (Grosart), He deserueth not to haue the crowne of victorie, which hath not abidde the brunt of the battaile.] 1660: W. Penn, *No Cross No Crown* [title]. 1709: O. Dykes, *Eng. Proverbs*, 278 (2nd ed.). 1853: Trench, *Proverbs*, 21 (1905).

No cut to unkindness. 1659: Howell, 13. 1670: Ray, 27. 1732: Fuller, 3557.

No day so clear but hath dark clouds. 1651: Herbert, *Jac. Prudentum*, 2nd ed.

No deceit in a brimmer. *See* **Deceit** (3).

Nod for a wise man, and a rod for a fool, A. 1732: Fuller, 337.

Nod from a lord is a breakfast for a fool, A. Ibid., No. 338. 1901: F. E. Taylor, *Lancs Sayings*, 7, A nod fro' a lord's a breakfust for a fool'.

Nod is as good as a wink (to a blind horse), A. Often used in the abbreviated form, and usually suggesting that a person understands very well what another person is getting at as any kind of hint or gesture will suffice to communicate it. 1794: W. Godwin, *Caleb Williams*, I viii, Say the word; a nod is as good as a wink to a blind horse. 1802: D. Wordsworth, *Journal* (ed. Knight), i, 129, A wink's as good as a nod with some folks. 1822: Scott, *Nigel*, ch xxv. Let me hear from you tomorrow. Good night, good night, a nod is as good as a wink. 1925: S. O' Casey, *Shadow of a Gunman*, 1. 142, You needn't say no more – a nod's as good as a wink to a blind horse. 1926: Phillpotts, *Peacock House*, 147, So a nod's as good as a wink, Joe.

Nod, Land of = Sleep. 1738: Swift, *Polite Convers.*, Dial. III, I'm going to the land of Nod. 1818: Scott, *Heart of Midl.*, ch xxx.

Nod of an honest man is enough, A. 1732: Fuller, 336.

No fault is, Where, there needs no pardon, *c.*1617: *Machivels Dogge*, fo. 8 ['excuse' for 'pardon']. 1631: Mabbe, *Celestina*, 83 (T.T.), There is no neede of pardon, where there is no fault committed. 1633: Draxe, 28. 1670: Ray, 89. 1732: Fuller, 5651 ['punishment' for 'pardon'].

No feast to a miser's. 1611: Cotgrave, s.v. 'Chiche'. 1670: Ray, 90. 1753: Richardson, *Grandison*, iii 175 (1883), It is an observation that the miser's feast is often the most splendid.

No fee, no law. 1597: G. Harvey, *Works*, iii 26 (Grosart). 1618: B. Holyday, *Technogamia*, II v, A man may as well open an oister without a knife, as a lawyers mouth without a fee.

No fence against a flail. 1670: Ray, 89. 1685: S. Wesley, *Maggots*, 96. 1707: Dunton, *Athenian Sport*, 317, The common old proverb here meant; is that – There's no fence against a flail. 1730: Swift, *Works*, xiv. 256 (Scott). 1830: Forby, *Vocab. E. Anglia*, 428.

No fence against ill fortune. 1605: Camden, *Remains*, 329 (1870) ['for' for 'against']. 1670: Ray, 89. 1732: Fuller, 3566.

No fishing. *See* **Fishing** (1).

No foe to a flatterer. 1576: *Parad, Dainty Devices*, 59 (1810). 1630: T. Adams, *Works*, 194, There is no foe to the flatterer.

No folly to being in love. 1659: Howell, *Proverbs: Brit.-Eng.*, 27, No folly to love. 1678: Ray, 50. 1710: S. Palmer, *Moral Essays on Proverbs*, 137.

No foolery to falling out. 1659: Howell, *Proverbs: Brit.-Eng.*, 27. 1875: Cheales, *Proverb. Folk-Lore*, 106 ['like' for 'to'].

No further. *See* **Bull** (7).

No gain. *See* **Gain** (1).

No garden without its weeds. 1716: E. Ward, *Female Policy*, 89, The finest garden is not free from weeds. 1732: Fuller, 3576.

No going to heaven in a sedan, There is. Ibid., No. 4910.

No gold. *See* No silver.

No good accord where every man would be a lord, There is. 1546: Heywood, *Proverbs*, Pt II ch vi *c.*1594: Bacon, *Promus*, No. 968 ['jack' for 'man']. 1633: Draxe, 8 [omitting 'good'].

No grass grows in the market-place. 1855: Bohn, 461.

No great banquet but none fares ill, There is. 1640: Herbert, *Jac. Prudentum.* 1670: Ray, 2.

No great loss but some small profit. Ibid., 117.

No harm, no force [matter]. 1604: *Pasquils Jests*, 21 (1864), Why then, no harme, no force (quoth the fellow), and so went his wayes.

No haste but good. *c.*1534: Berners, *Huon*, 320 (E.E.T.S.), It is a saynge that an yll haste is not good. 1546: Heywood, *Proverbs*, Pt II ch ix. 1576: Wapull, *Tide tarrieth no Man*, sig. F2, No haste but good, stay yet a while. *c.*1640: in *Roxb. Ballads*, ii 104 (B.S.), No haste but good I hope there be.

No heart *See* quots. 1578: Florio, *First Fruites*, fo. 28, Who hath not a hart let hym haue legges. 1629: *Book of Meery Riddles*, Prov. 78, He that hath no heart, hath legs. 1732: Fuller, 2146, He that has no heart, ought to have heels.

No hell like a troubled conscience. 1590: Lodge, *Rosalynde*, 60 (Hunt.Cl.), There is no stinge to the worme of conscience, no hell to a minde toucht with guilt. 1754: *Connoisseur*, No. 28, A dreadful instance of the truth of that maxim, *There is no hell like a troubled conscience.*

No heralds in the grave. 1732: Fuller, 3581.

No joy without annoy. 1576: *Parad. Dainty Devices*, 64 (1810), No pleasure without some paine. 1587: Greene, *Works*, iii 101 (Grosart), No blisse without bale. 1670: Ray, 109. 1732: Fuller, 6322.

No knaves and fools, If there were, all the world would be alike. Ibid., No. 2715.

No lack to lack a wife. 1546: Heywood, *Proverbs*, Pt II ch xi 1639: Clarke, 329, No lack to a wife.

No land without stones, Or meat without bones. 1875: Cheales, *Proverb. Folk-Lore*, 120.

No larder but hath its mice. 1732: Fuller, 3587.

No law for a town's bull. 1886: R. Holland, *Cheshire Gloss.*, 454 (E.D.S.). 1917: Bridge, *Cheshire Proverbs*, 119. Cf. Lawless.

No law for lying = A man may lie without danger of the law. 1678: Ray, 172.

No living man all things can. [Non omnia possumus omnes. – Virgil.] 1639: Clarke, 147. 1670: Ray, 56.

No longer foster, no longer friend. 'Foster' = food, nourishment. 1412: Hocdeve, *Regement*, st. 238, l. 1661, p. 60 (E.E.T.S.), Styntynge the cause, the effect styntith eek; No lenger forster, no lenger lemman. 1546: Heywood, *Proverbs*, Pt II ch ix, No longer foster, no longer lemman. 1639: Clarke, 12. 1681: Robertson, *Phraseol. Generalis*, 638. 1754: Berthelson, *Eng.-Danish Dict.*, s.v. 'Foster'.

No longer pipe. *See* Pipe.

No love is foul nor prison fair. 1651: Herbert, *Jac. Prudentum*, 2nd ed.

No love to a father's. 1640: Herbert, *Jac. Prudentum.*

No man. *See* quots. 1577: Kendall, *Flow. of Epigrams*, 264 (Spens.S.), No man can doe twoo thyngs at once, the prouerbe old doeth tell. 1611: Cotgrave, s.v. 'Moulin', One cannot be in two places, or follow two businesses at once.

No man can master his own mind. 1764: Garrick, in *Garrick Corresp.*, i 171 (1831) [quoted as 'the old saying'].

No man can please all. Before 1500: in Hill, *Commonplace-Book*, 132 (E.E.T.S.), Ther may no man all men please. 1633: Draxe, 45, One can hardly please all men. 1666: Torriano, *Piazza Univ.*, 204, One cannot please all people.

No man can serve two masters. [Matthew vi.24, No man can serve two masters: for either he will hate the one, and love the other; or else he will hold to the one, and despise the other. Ye cannot serve God and mammon.] *c.*1330: in Wright, *Pol. Songs*, 325 (Camden S.), That no man may wel serve tweie lordes to queme. *c.*1477: Caxton, *Jason*, 57 (E.E.T.S.), For no man may wel serue two maistres for that one corumpeth that other. 1649: T. Forde, *Lusus Fort.*, Epistle, We cannot serve two masters with a single heart. 1924: Shaw, *Saint Joan*, sc *iv.*, Men cannot serve two masters.

No man can stand always upon his guard. 1732: Fuller, 3592.

No man comes to heaven with dry eyes. 1630: T. Adams, *Works*, 180, The prouerbe is too true for many; No man, etc.

No man is born wise. 1620: Shelton, *Quixote*, Pt II ch xxxiii, For no man is born wise, and bishops are made of men and not of stones. 1710: S. Palmer, *Moral Essays on Proverbs*, 285. No man is born a Master of Arts. 1732: Fuller, 3599, No man is born wise or learned.

No man is his craft's master the first day. 1639: Clarke, 35. 1670: Ray, 75. 1754: Berthelson, *Eng.-Danish Dict.*, s.v. 'Crafts-master'.

No man knows what is good excePt he hath endured evil. 1600: Bodenham, *Belvedere*, 6 (Spens.S.), We neuer know what 'tis in heaven to dwell, Till wee haue had some feeling of grim hell. 1633: Draxe, 59. 1670: Ray, 8, No man better knows what good is, then he who hath endured evil. 1736: Bailey, *Dict.*, s.v. 'Endure' [as in 1670].

No man lives so poor as he was born. 1732: Fuller, 3604.

No man liveth without a fault. 1659: Howell, 9.

No man so good. *See* quot. 1662: Fuller, *Worthies*, i 265 (1840), And some will oppose to this narrow county-proverb, an English one of greater latitude, viz. 'No man so good, but another may be as good as he'.

No marvel if water be lue. 1678: Ray, 215.

No mill no meal. 1639: Clarke, 163. 1670: Ray, 120. 1732: Fuller, 3613. 1853: Trench, *Proverbs*, 106 (1905), They courageously accePt the law of labour … *No mill, no meal.*

No mitre no crown. 1639–61: in *Rump Songs*, 121 (1662, repr. 1874), The proverb proves true *No miter no crown.* Cf. **No bishop**.

No money, no Swiss. [1687: Dryden, *Hind and Panther*, iii 177, Those Swisses fight on any side for pay.] Before 1704: T. Brown, *Works*, iii 162 (1760), After long observation, I find it to hold truer *no money, no mistress*, than *no money, no Swiss*. 1737: Gay, *Fables*, 2nd ser, No. 9, l. 61, For these, like Swiss, attend; No longer pay, no longer friend. 1829: Cobbett, *Advice to Young Men*, Lett. V, 'No money, no Swiss', is a proverb throughout the world.

No more mortar no more brick, A cunning knave has a cunning trick. 1678: Ray, 296. 1732: Fuller, 291. 1880: Spurgeon, *Ploughman's Pictures*, 83.

No more purpose, To, than to beat your heels against the ground (or **wind**). 1670: Ray, 190. 1732: Fuller, 5209.

No more sib. *See* **Sieve and riddle**.

No more water than the ship drew, There was. 1546: Heywood,*Proverbs*, Pt II ch viii *c.*1594: Bacon, *Promus*, No. 672. 1659: Howell, 14.

No more wit than a coot. *c.*1540: Bale, *Kynge*

Johan, I l. 176, Thou semyste by thy wordes to have no more wytt than a coote.

No names, no pack-drill. An originally military saying suggesting that if you refuse to name the people who committed a misdemeanour, nobody can be punished or held responsible. Pack-drill was a form of punishment that involved marching up and down for a long time with a full and heavy pack. 1923: O. Onions, *Peace in our Time*, i ii, Men had a way of omitting the names of those of whom they spoke: no names, no pack-drill.

No place like home. *See* **Place**.

None are so wise as those who know nothing. 1875: Cheales, *Proverb. Folk-Lore*, 103.

None but fools lay wagers. 1677: *Poor Robin's Visions*, 16, Your actions verifie a proverb among you; *none but fools lay wagers.* 1711: *Brit. Apollo*, iii No. 146, col. 4, Its an old saying (and I think a true one) That none but knaves or fools lay wagers. 1732: Fuller, 452, A wager is a fool's argument.

None but the brave deserve the fair. 1697: Dryden, 'Alexander's Feast' in *Poems* (1958) III 148, Happy, happy, happy Pair! … None but the Brave deserves the fair. 1829: P. Egan, *Boxiana*, 2nd Series. II 354, The tender sex … feeling the good old notion that 'none but the brave deserve the fair', were sadly out of temper. 1873: A. Trollope, *Phineas Redux*, II xiii, All the proverbs were on his side. 'None but the brave deserve the fair,' said his cousin.

None is born master. 1640: Herbert, *Jac. Prudentum.*

None is offended but by himself. Ibid.

None is so wise but the fool overtakes him. *c.*1205: Layamon, *Brut*, i 32 (Madden), Nis nawer nan so wis mon That me ne mai bi-swiken. *c.*1275: Ibid., ii 211, Thar nis no man so wis That me ne mai bi-swike. 1640: Herbert, *Jac. Prudentum.* 1670: Ray, 29. 1732: Fuller, 3654 [with 'sometimes' after 'fool'].

None knows the weight of another's burden. 1640: Herbert, *Jac. Prudentum.*

None plays the fool well without wit. 1611: Davies (of Hereford), sc *of Folly*, 42, in *Works*, ii (Grosart).

None says his garner is full. 1640: Herbert, *Jac. Prudentum.*

None so blind. *See* **Blind**, *adj.* (25).

None so deaf. *See* **Deaf** (10).

None so good that's good to all. 1639: Clarke, 16.

None so old that he hopes not for a year of life. *c*.1520: *Calisto and Mel.*, in Hazlitt, *Old Plays*, i 78, None so old but may live a year; And there is none so young, but, ye wot well, May die in a day. 1631: Brathwait, *Whimzies*, 45 (1859). Hee seemes to verifie the proverb: *There is none so desperately old, but he hopes to live one yeare longer*. 1732: Fuller, 3653. Cf. **Man** (48).

No news is good news. 1616: James I, in *Loseley MSS.*, 403 (Kempe), No newis is bettir then evill newis. 1632: Lupton, *Lond. and Country:* 'Country', No. 12, The best newes is when we heare no newes. 1776: Colman, *Spleen*, I, No news is good news sometimes, as the proverb goes. 1850: Dickens, *Copperfield*, ch xxxvi 1921: S. Gwynn, in *Observer*, 31 July, p. 5, col. 2, People not unnaturally grow a little impatient under the delays here. But it was never truer that no news is good news.

No one is always wise. 1539: Taverner, *Proverbs*, fo. 37, No man in the worlde is wyse at all houres. 1666: Torriano, *Piazza Univ.*, 249, No body is wise at all times. 1714: Ozell, *Molière*, i 113, If none is wise at all times, yet the shortest errors are the best.

No pain, no gain. *See* **Gain** (1).

No penny, no pardon. 1531: Tyndale, *Expos.* 1 *John*, in *Works*, p. 395, col. 1 (1573) (OED), O Popishe forgiuenesse with whom it goeth after the comon prouerbe, no peny no pardon. 1732: Fuller, 3616.

No penny, no Paternoster. 1528: Tyndale, *Obed. of Christ. Man.* 245 (P.S.), After the common saying, 'No peny, no Paternoster'. 1546: *Suppl. of Poore Commons*, 87 (E.E.T.S.). *c*.1598: Deloney, *Gentle Craft*, Pt II ch vii 1651: Randolph, *Hey for Honesty*, I ii 1709: O. Dykes, *Eng. Proverbs*, 200 (2nd ed.), Whence came this comical saying. *No Peny, no Paternoster*, but from pecuniary Indulgences? 1754: Berthelson, *Eng.–Danish Dict.*, s.v. 'Penny'.

No pipe, no pudding. Glos. 1639: in *Berkeley MSS.*, iii 27 (1885).

No play without a fool in it. 1650: *Newes from New Exchange*, 14, 'Tis an old proverb, there can be no play without a foole in it.

No priest, no mass. 1732: Fuller, 3618.

No raillery is worse than that which is true. 1855: Bohn, 462.

No remedy but patience. 1633: Draxe, 151. 1670: Ray, 190. 1694: Cibber, *Love's Last Shift*, II. 1723: Defoe, *Col. Jack*, ch xviii, I had no remedy but the old insignificant thing, called patience. 1824: Scott, *Red–gauntlet*, ch xv. Cf. **Patience**.

Norfolk capon, A = A red herring. 1785: Grose, *Class. Dict. Vulgar Tongue*, s.v. 1836: in Farmer's *Musa Pedestris*, 121, A Norfolk capon is jolly grub. Cf. **Yarmouth capon**.

Norfolk dumpling, A = A Norfolk man. 1600: Day, *Blind Beggar*, I iii, Make me your cheat, your gull … your Norfolk dumpling. 1608: Armin, *Nest of Ninnies*, 17 (SH.S.), He lookt like a Norfolke dumpling, thicke and short. 1662: Fuller, *Worthies*, ii 446 (1840), Norfolk dumplings … This … relates to the fare they commonly feed on. 1790: Grose, *Prov. Gloss.*, s.v. 'Norfolk'.

Norfolk wiles. *See* **Essex stiles**.

No rogue like to the godly rogue. 1732: Fuller, 3624.

No rose without a thorn. [Nulla est sincera voluptas. – Ovid, *Met.*, vii 453.] *c*.1440: Lydgate, *Fall of Princes*, bk i l. 57, As there is no rose Spryngyng in gardeyns, but ther be sum thorn. 1579: Lyly *Euphues*, 33 (Arber), The sweetest rose hath his prickell. 1681: Robertson, *Phraseol. Generalis*, 1084, No rose without its prickle. 1754: Berthelson, *Eng.–Danish Dict.*, s.v. 'Rose'. 1855: Kingsley, *West. Ho!*, ch viii, True, the rose has its thorn.

North, The. *See* quot. *c*.1670: Aubrey, *Wilts MS. Collect.*, quoted in Halliwell, *Dict.*, s.v. 'North', The North for largeness. The East for health; The South for buildings, The West for wealth.

Northampton. 1. He that must eat a buttered fagot, let him go to Northampton. 1662: Fuller, *Worthies*, ii 501 (1840). 1790: Grose, *Prov. Gloss.*, s.v. 'Northants' ['would' for 'must']. 1851: Sternberg, *Dialect, etc., of Northants*, 191.
2. The mayor of Northampton opens oysters with his dagger. 1662: Fuller, *Worthies*, ii 500 (1840). 1790: Grose, s.v. 'Northants'. 1851: Sternberg, 191. Cf. **Oyster** (1).

Northamptonshire for spires and squires. 1869: Hazlitt, 297.

North country. *See* **Knight of Cales. North–Crawley.** *See* quot. 1854: Baker, *Northants Gloss.*, s.v., How North-Crawley her bonnet stands; i.e. not straight, all on one side.

Northerly wind and blubber Brings home the Greenland lubber. 1846: Denham, *Proverbs*, 20 (Percy S.).

Northern air brings weather fair, A. Ibid., 15.

Northern har [mist] **brings drought from far, A.** 1849: Halliwell, *Pop. Rhymes*, 156.

North Repps. *See* **Gimmingham.**

North wind. *See* **Wind.**

Norwich. *See* **Caistor.**

Norwich, St Peter's. *See* quot. 1869: Hazlitt, 464, When three daws are seen on St Peter's vane together, then we are sure to have bad weather.

Nose. 1. A nose of wax. *See* quots. 1533: in *Ballads from MSS.*, i 206 (B.S.), The text to turne and glose, like a welshe manes hose, or lyk a waxen nose. 1596: Lodge, *Marg. of America*, 40 (Hunt.Cl.), Where-through iustice is made a nose of waxe warmed. 1609: J. Melton, *Six-fold Politician*, 77. They meete with no such noses of waxe as will be so iested withall. 1611: Cotgrave, s.v. 'Tordre', To make a nose of wax of; to wrest, wrie, manage, turne, at pleasure. 1740: North, *Lives of Norths*, i 366 (Bohn), To treat plain words and expressions as a nose of wax to bend one way or other to gratify parties. 1815: Scott, *Mannering*, ch v, Because I let ... the constable draw the warrants, and manage the business his ain gate, as if I had been a nose o' wax. 1847: Halliwell, *Dict.*, s.v. 'Nose', ... a proverbial phrase for anything very pliable.

2. As plain as the nose on a man's face. 1639: Clarke, 188. 1683: White-Kennett, tr. Erasmus' *Praise of Folly*, 25 (8th ed.), I ... can make it (as the proverb goes) *as plain as the nose on your face.* 1773: Graves, *Spirit. Quixote*, bk v ch xviii, The gentleman talks main-well, and has made it as plain as the nose in one's face. 1906: Q.-Couch, *Mayor of Troy*, ch iii.

3. Doth your nose swell (or **eek**, i.e. **itch**) **at that?** 1678: Ray, 77.

4. He can't tell where to turn his nose. *c.*1565: in Huth, *Ancient Ballads, etc.*, 211 (1867) [cited as a 'prouerbe'].

5. He that has a great nose thinks everybody is speaking of it. 1732: Fuller, 2129. 1826: Scott, *Journal*, 24 Jan., I went to the Court for the first time today, and, like the man with the large nose, thought everybody was thinking of me and my mishaps.

6. His nose will abide no jests. 1588: *Mar-Prelate Epit.*, 9 (1843), I am sure their noses can

abide no iest. 1592: Lodge, *Euphues Shadow*, sig. H3, My nose loues no iesting. 1659: Howell, 6. 1678: Ray, 77.

7. If your nose itches, you will shake hands with (or **kiss**) **a fool.** 1738: Swift, *Polite Convers.*, Dial. I, My nose itched, and I knew I should drink wine or kiss a fool. 1755: *Connoisseur*, No. 59.

8. To hold one's nose to the grindstone. 1546: Heywood, *Proverbs*, Pt I ch v, I shall, to reuenge former hurtis, Hold their noses to grinstone. 1653: Middleton and Rowley, *Span. Gipsy*, IV iii, Hold his nose to the grin'stone, my lord. 1732: Fuller, 5187. 1865: Dickens, *Mutual Friend*, bk iii ch xiv.

9. To Put one's nose out of joint. 1581: Rich, *Apolonius and Silla*, 71 (1912), It could be no other than his own man that had thrust his nose so far out of joint. 1607: *The Puritan*, V i, Now all the knights' noses are put out of joint. 1663: Pepys, *Diary*, 22 July, As soon as the King can get a husband for Mrs Stewart, however, my Lady Castlemaine's nose will be out of joynt. 1754: Berthelson, *Eng.-Danish Dict.*, s.v. 'Nose'. 1848: Planché, *Extravag.*, iii 247 (1879), Your lovely eyes Out of joint have put her nose. 1912: Lucas, *London Lav.*, ch xxxvi, Every baby puts some one's nose out of joint.

10. You make his nose warp. 1737: Ray, 204. [Query = the same as 9.]

See also **Cut** (13); **Follow** (5); **Know** (20); and **Lead.**

Nosegay to him as long as he lives, It will be a. 1678: Ray, 262.

No service to the King's. 1484: Caxton, tr. Chartier's *Curial*, 19 (E.E.T.S.), Ne seruyse lyke to the kyng souerayn. *c.*1580: G. Harvey, *Marginalia*, 142 (1913), No fishing to ye sea, nor service to a king. 1618: Breton, *Court and Country*, in *Inedited Tracts*, 190 (Hazlitt). 1659: Howell, 14.

No silver no servant. 1633: Draxe, 179. 1670: Ray, 143. 1732: Fuller, 3629, No silver, no service.

No silver (or **gold**) **without dross.** 1611: Cotgrave, s.v. 'Or', No gold without some drosse. 1633: Draxe, 62, No siluer without his drosse. 1639: Clarke, 80 [as in 1633].

No sin to cheat the devil. 1726: Defoe, *Hist, of Devil*, Pt II ch x, 304 (4th ed.), The old Latin proverb, *Fallere fallentem non est fraus* ... 'tis no sin to cheat the devil.

No song no supper. 1613: B.&F., *Burning Pestle*, II ii, Let thy father go snick–up … let him stay at home, and sing for his supper, boy. 1893: R.L.S., *Ebb–Tide*, ch vii, If you're not there by the time named, there will be no banquet; no song, no supper, Mr Whish!

No sooner up but head in the ambry, and nose in the cup. 1639: Clarke, 136. 1670: Ray, 198. 1736: Bailey, *Dict.*, s.v. 'Aumbry' [ending with 'aumbry'].

No sport, no pie. *c.*1620: B.&F., *Woman's Prize*, I iii, I'll bring it to th' old proverb, 'No sport, no pie'. 1670: Ray, 147.

No sure dungeon but the grave. 1825: Scott, *Talisman*, ch xix, It is an ancient saying, – no sure dungeon but the grave.

No sweat. *See* **Sweat** (3).

Notch (or **Notchel**), **To cry.** 1681: *Dialogue, in Harl. Miscell.*, ii 114, *Will.* The first I think on is the king's majesty (God bless him!), him they cried nochell. *Sam.* What, as Gaffer block of our town cried his wife? *Will.* I do not know what he did; but they voted that nobody should either borrow or lend, nor sell nor buy with him, under pain of their displeasure. 1859: *Blackburn Standard*, quoted in *N.&Q.*, 3rd ser, x 108, On Wednesday there was at Accrington an extraordinary instance of the disgraceful practice of 'notchel crying'. [Bellman sent round first by husband disclaiming responsibility for wife's debts, and then by wife doing the same as regards her husband and also making scandalous charges against him.] 1892: *N.&Q.*, 8th ser, ii, 526, A short time ago, at St Helens County Court, the defendant in an action disclaimed his responsibility on the ground that he had 'cried the notchel', an expression which meant, as explained to the judge, that he had published a notice in the journals that he would not be held responsible for debts contracted by his wife. 1917: Bridge, *Cheshire Proverbs*, 131, To cry notch or nichil (or notchel).

Not free that draws his chain, He is. 1640: Herbert, *Jac, Prudentum.*

No, thank you. *See* quots. 1883: A. Easther, *Almondbury Gloss.*, 20 (E.D.S.), No thank ye has lost mony a gooid butterchauv. 1901: F. E. Taylor, *Lancs Sayings*, 9, 'Nowe, thank yo'' has lost monny a good butter–cake.

Nothing. **1. He has nothing to eat and yet invites guests.** 1732: Fuller, 1877.

2. He that has nothing is frighted at nothing. 1639: Clarke, 41, They that have nothing, need feare to lose nothing. 1732: Fuller, 2150.

3. He that hath nothing is not contented. 1670: Ray, 19.

4. If you put nothing into your purse, you can take nothing out. 1732: Fuller, 2781.

5. It's more painful to do nothing than somethtng. 1670: Ray, 19.

6. Nothing but up and ride? 1639 'Clarke, 116, What? no more but up and ride. 1670: Ray, 198. 1732: Fuller, 5497.

7. Nothing down, nothing up. 1659: Howell, 3. 1670: Ray, 19. Cf. **Nought** (4).

8. Nothing dries sooner than a tear. [Cito arescit lacrima, praesertim in alienis malis. – Cicero, *Part. Or.*, 17.] 1560: T. Wilson, *Rhetorique*, 134 (1909), For as Cicero doth say, nothing drieth soner then teares. 1640: Herbert, *Jac. Prudentum.* 1681: Robertson, *Phraseol. Generalis*, 927, Nothing dries up sooner than tears. 1732: Fuller, 3661 ['woman's tears' after 'a'].

9. Nothing for nothing. Before 1704: T. Brown, in *Works*, i 131 (1760), Thou know'st the proverb, *nothing due for nought.* 1714: Ozell, *Molière*, ii 129, She must refuse all presents offer'd her by men; for now–a–days nothing is given for nothing. 1800: Miss Edge–worth, *Castle Rackrent*, 61 (Everyman), Nothing for nothing, or I'm under a mistake with you, Jason. 1864: Mrs H. Wood, *Trevlyn Hold*, ch xxii, I might have knowed a lawyer wouldn't give nothing for nothing.

10. Nothing hath no savour. 1546: Heywood, *Proverbs*, Pt I ch viii 1559: Becon, in *Prayers, etc.*, 365 (P.S.), Nought hath no savour. 1659: Howell, *Letters*, ii 666 (Jacobs). 1738: Swift, *Polite Convers.*, Dial. I, They say, Something has some savour, but nothing has no flavour.

11. Nothing have, nothing crave. 1670: Ray, 19. 1732: Fuller, 6242.

12. Nothing is a man's truly, that he cometh not by duly. Ibid., No. 6280.

13. Nothing is certain but death and taxes. 1726: Defoe, *History of the Devil*, II vi, Not the Man in the Moon … not the Inspiration of Mother Shipton, or the Miracles of Dr Faustus, Things as certain as Death and taxes, can be more firmly believed. 1789: B. Franklin, *Letter* 13 Nov. in *Writings* (1907) X 69, In this world nothing can be said to be certain, excePt death and taxes.

1939: L. I Wilder, *By the Shores of Silver Lake*, xxv, Everything's more or less a gamble ... Nothing is certain but death and taxes.

14. Nothing is certain but the unforeseen. 1866: J.A. Froude, *Oceana*, vii, There is a proverb that 'nothing is certain but the unforeseen', and in fact few things turn out as we expect them. 1905: A. Maclaren, *Gospel according to St Matthew*, I 322, There is nothing certain to happen, but the unforeseen.

15. Nothing is easy to the unwilling. Ibid., No. 3663.

16. Nothing is good or ill but by comparison. 1676: Shadwell, *Virtuoso*, II, No man is happy but by comparison. 1763: Mrs F. Sheridan, *Discovery*, IV i.

17. Nothing is impossible. *See* quot. 1917: Bridge, *Cheshire Proverbs*, 96, Naught's impossible, as t'auld woman said when they told her cauf had swallowed grindlestone.

18. Nothing is impossible to a willing heart. 1546: Heywood, *Proverbs*, Pt I ch iv. 1555: S. Hawes, *Past. of Pleasure*, 7 (Percy S.), To a willyng harte is nought impossible. 1631: Mabbe, *Celestina*, 183 (T.T.) ['minde' for 'heart']. 1707: *Spanish Bawd*, IV ii [as in 1631].

19. Nothing is lost in a good market. 1827: Hone, *Table-Book*, 8.

20. Nothing is more easily blotted out than a good turn. 1647: *Countrym. New Common-wealth*, 26, Nothing sooner waxeth old then a good turne or benefit. 1732: Fuller, 3669.

21. Nothing is stolen without hands. 1639: Clarke, 149.

22. Nothing is to be bought in the market without a penny. Before 1704: T. Brown, *Works*, i 293 (1760) [quoted as a proverb].

23. Nothing kindles sooner than fire. 1560: T. Wilson, *Rhetorique*, 133 (1909) [cited as 'a common saying'].

24. Nothing like leather. 1692: L'Estrange, *Aesop*, 421 (3rd ed.), Up starts a currier. Gentlemen, says he, when y'ave said all that can be said, there's nothing in the world like leather. 1855: Gaskell, *North and South*, ch x, 'I dare say, my remark came from the professional feeling of there being nothing like leather,' replied Mr Hale.

25. Nothing more proud. *See* quot. 1642: in *Harl. Miscell.*, ii 65 (1744), By his carriage the proverb is verified, *Nothing more proud than basest blood, when it doth rise aloft.*

26. Nothing more smooth than glass, yet nothing more brittle; Nothing more fine than wit, yet nothing more fickle. 1732: Fuller, 6472.

27. Nothing new. *See* quots. 1850: Emerson, *Repr. Men:* 'Montaigne', 'Ah', said my languid gentleman at Oxford, 'there's nothing new or true – and no matter'. 1887: *N. & Q.*, 7th ser, iv. 257, The Cornish version of this proverb has been known to me for many years: 'There's nothing new, and there's nothing true, and it don't sinnify [signify]'.

28. Nothing stake. *See* **Nought** (4).

29. Nothing succeeds like success. 1867: A.D. Richardson, *Beyond Mississippi*, xxxiv, 'Nothing succeeds like success'. There *was* much Southern sympathy on the island; now all our dear friends. 1872: W. Besant, *Ready-Money Mortiboy*, I ix, In Mr Mortiboy's judgement no proverb could be better than ... 'Nothing succeeds like success'. 1882: Sir Stafford Northcote. quoted in *N. & Q.*, 6th ser, v 189. Cf. **Success**.

30. Nothing to be got without pains. 1594: Churchyard, *Mirror of Man*, sig. A4 (Boswell, 1816), Nothing is gotten without toyle and labor. 1611: Cotgrave, s.v. 'Peine', Nor bread, nor ought is gotten without paines. 1732: Fuller, 3677, Nothing to be got without pains, but poverty. 1869: Spurgeon, *John Ploughman*, ch vii [as in 1732, *plus* 'and dirt']. Cf. No. 32.

31. Nothing turns sourer than milk. 1830: Forby, *Vocab. E. Anglia*, 428.

32. Nothing venture, nothing win (or **gain**, or **have**). [Necesse est facere sumptum qui quaerit lucrum. – Plautus, *Asin.*, I iii 65.] *c.*1374: Chaucer, *Troylus*, bk ii 1.807, And seyde, he which that no–thing under-taketh, No-thing ne acheveth, be him looth or dere. *c.*1390: Gower, *Conf. Amantis*, bk iv. 1. 2694, For he which dar nothing beginne, I not what thing he scholde achieve. 1481: Caxton, *Reynard*, 27 (Arber), He that wil wynne he muste laboure and auenture. 1546: Heywood, *Proverbs*, Pt I ch xi, Nought venter, nought haue. 1580: Tusser, *Husb.*, 44 (E.D.S.) [as in 1546]. 1624: T. Heywood, *Captives*, IV i, I see here that nought venters, nothinge gaynes. 1674: Head and Kirkman, *Eng. Rogue*, iii 142. 1709: O. Dykes, *Eng. Proverbs*, 113 (2nd ed.). 1791: Boswell, *Johnson*, iii 189 (Hill). 1840: Lytton, *Money*, III vi 1876: Blackmore, *Cripps*, III iv, We must all have been in France ... if – well, never mind. Nothing venture, nothing win.

33. Nothing will come of nothing. *c.*1374: Chaucer, *Boeth.*, bk v pr. 1, For this sentence is verray and sooth, that 'nothing ne hath his beinge of naught'. 1599: Breton, in *Works*, ii *c* 23 (Grosart), Then of nothing growes nothing, but nothing, *c.*1605: Shakespeare, *Lear*, I i 1652: Flecknoe, *Miscell.*, 73. Of nothing, nothing's made (they say), *c.*1740: Fielding, *Essay on Nothing*, Sect. 1, There is nothing falser than that old proverb which ... is in every one's mouth: '*Ex nihilo nihil fit*'. Thus translated by Shakespeare in Lear's 'Nothing can come of nothing'. 1818: Scott, *Heart of Midl.*, ch i ['can' for 'will']. 1846: Planche, *Extravag.*, iii 117 (1879) [as in 1818].

34. There is nothing done without trouble, only loosingjhe fire out. 1883: Burne, *Shropsh. Folk-Lore*, 588. Cf. No. 28.

35. There is nothing new under the sun. [Ecclesiastes i 9, There is no new thing under the sun.] 1592: G. Delamothe, *French Alphabet*, II 7, Under the large Cope of heaven, we see not a new thing. 1664: A. Bradstreet, *Works* (1867), 53, There is no new thing under the sun. 1801: T. Jefferson, *Writings* (1904) X 229, We can no longer say there is nothing new under the sun. 1850: C. Kingsley, *Alton Locke*, I xviii, There is nothing new under the sun; all that, is stale and trite to a septuagenarian, who has seen where it all ends.

36. There's nothing but is good for something. 1639: Clarke, 72.

37. Where nothing is, a little doth ease. 1546: Heywood, *Proverbs*, Pt I ch x 1639: Clarke, 10. 1694: D'Urfey, *Quixote*, Pt I Act II sc i, Where nothing is, a little goes a great way.

38. Where nothing is, nothing can be had. 1630: Taylor (Water-Poet), *Works*, 2nd pagin., 38, Where nought is, there's nothing to be got. 1675: *Poor Robin Alman.*, Sept., He who hath nothing, nothing can he pay. 1734: Fielding, *Don Quix. in England*, I iii, Where nothing is, nothing can come on't. 1774: Colman, *Man of Business*, Epil., Where nothing's in, there's nothing can come out.

39. Where nothing is, the King must lose his right. 1546: Heywood, *Proverbs*, Pt I ch xii 1594: *True Trag. Rich. Third*, 12–13 (SH.S.), Where nothing is to be had, the King looseth

his right they say. 1664: *Wits Recr.*, in *Mus. Deliciae, etc.*, ii 54 (Hotten). 1709: O. Dykes, *Eng. Proverbs*, 127 (2nd ed.). 1817: Scott, *Rob Roy. ch.* ix.

40. Who nothing save shall nothing have. 1732: Fuller, 6338.

41. Who practiseth nothing shall have nothing. 1580: Tusser, *Husb.*, 48 (E.D.S.).

See also **Naught;** and **Nought.**

No time like the present. 1562: G. Legh, *Accidence of Armoury*, 225v, Mary sir no time better then even now. 1696: Mrs Manley, *Lost Lover* IV i. 1828; Scott, *Fair Maid*, ch ii. 1839: Dickens, *Nickleby*, ch xxxvi 1888: M. Oliphant, *Second Son*, I iv, 'If you were a–passing this way, sir, some time in the morning – ' 'There's no time like the present', answered Roger.

Not Jack out of doors nor yet gentleman. 1639: Clarke, 206.

Not lost that a friend gets, It is. 1642: Taylor, *Answer to Tale of a Tub* (Lean), It is no tint that a friend gets. 1816: Scott, *Old Mortality*, ch xli.

Not lost that comes at last, It is. 1612: Shelton, *Quixote*, Pt I bk iv ch iv 1670: Ray, 117. 1732: Fuller, 2999 ['if it' for 'that']. 1754: Berthelson, *Eng.-Danish Dict.*, s.v. 'Lost'.

Not so good to borrow as be able to lend. 1546: Heywood, *Proverbs*, Pt I ch x

Not so old. 1738: Swift, *Polite Convers* Dial. I, *Col.* Not so old nor yet so cold – You know the rest, miss. [I hope 'Miss' did know the rest – I do not].

Nottingham ale. 1622: Drayton, *Polyol.*, xxiii, Little Rutlandshire is termed raddleman. As Nottingham's, of old (is common) ale and bread. 1708: in *Bagford Ballads*, i 389 (B.S.), With Nottingham ale At every meal. 1763: in Hackwood, *Inns, Ales, etc.*, 99 (1909), I grant that fair Nottingham once bore the bell For our grand sires that tasted the sweets of good ale.

Nottingham, The little smith of, Who doeth the work that no man can. 1634: C. Butler, *Feminine Monarchie*, 17. 1662: Fuller, *Worthies*, ii 570 (1840). 1790: Grose, *Prov. Gloss.*, s.v. 'Notts'.

Not too fast for [fear of] falling. 1580: Baret, *Alvearie*, C 59, As we say, not too fast for breaking your shinnes. 1599: Porter, *Two Angry Women*, in Hazlitt, *Old Plays*, vii 301.

Not too high for the pie, nor too low for the crow. 1546: Heywood, *Proverbs*, Pt II ch vii. 1577: *Misogonus*, II ii. 1670: Ray, 189.

Not worth a (1) **band's end;** (2) **bean; blue point** – *see* No. 29; (3) **button;** (4) **cherry;** (5) **chip;** (6) **cobbler's curse;** (7) **cress;** (8) **curse;** (9) **dodkin;** (10) **farthing;** (11) **fig;** (12) **flea;** (13) **fly;** (14) **gnat;** (15) **gooseberry;** (16) **groat;** (17) **haddock;** (18) **hair;** (19) **haw;** (20) **hen;** (21) **herring;** (22) **leek;** (23) **louse;** (24) **needle;** (25) **nut;** (26) **pea;** (27) **pear:** (28) **pin;** (29) **point** and **blue–point** [a tagged lace or cord]; (30) **potato;** (31) **rush;** (32) **sloe;** (33) **straw;** (34) **tinker's curse;** (35) **an apple;** (36) **egg;** (37) **ivy leaf;** (38) **onion;** (39) **hiring, who talks of tiring;** (40) **shoe–buckles;** (41) **three halfpence.**

(1) 1855: Robinson, *Whitby Gloss.*, 10, 'It is not worth a band's end' – valueless.

(2) 1297: R. Glouc., 497 (OED), Al nas wurth a bene. *c.*1374: Chaucer, *Troylus*, bk iii l. 1167, Swich arguments ne been not worth a bene. *c.*1430: in *Twenty–six Poems*, 131 (E.E.T.S.), I am nat worthe a bene. Before 1529: Skelton, *Bowge of Courte*, l. 95. 1595: *Pedlars Prophecy*, l. 1002 (Malone S.), All is not worthe a beane. 1620: Shelton, *Quixote*, Pt II ch xlvii.. An office that will not afford a man his victuals is not worth two beans. 1823: Scott, *Peveril*, ch xxiii.

(3) 14th cent.: *Guy of Warwick*, l. 2216 (E.E.T.S.), His scheld [shield] nas nought worth a botoun. 1532: More, *Confut. of Tyndale*, Pref., sig. Ee1, All hys welbeloued boke is not worth a boton. 1590: Nashe, *Almond for a Parrot*, 37 (1846). All is not worth a button, if it be too stale. 1609: in Halliwell, *Books of Characters*, 119 (1857). 1776: T. Cogan, *John Bunch, Junior*, I 9. 1857: Hughes, *Tom Brown*, Pt II ch ii, He'll never be worth a button, if you go on keeping him under your skirts.

(4) *c.*1390: *Chevelere Assigne*, l. 329 (E.E.T.S.), I charde not thy croyse [cross] … the valwe of a cherye.

(5) 1672: Walker, *Paroem.*, 15.

(6) 1886: Elworthy, *West Som. Word–Book* 146 (E.D.S.), Cobler's curse. The extreme of valuelessness … Why! he idn a–wo'th a cobbler's cuss. 1897: *N. &Q.*, 8th ser xi 452, Our everyday appraisement is 'not wo'th a cobbler's cuss' [Somerset].

(7) *c.*1350: *Pearl*, l. 343, For anger gaynez the not a cresse [not a mite]. *c.*1387: Usk, *Test, of Love*, in Skeat's *Chaucer*, vii 73, Their might is not worth a cresse. *c.*1390: Gower, *Conf. Amantis*, bk iii l. 588, And so to me nys worth a kerse. *c.*1400:

Beryn, l. 971 (E.E.T.S.). ffor [ne] to body, ne to soule this vaylith nat a karse.

(8) 1820: Byron, in *Letters, etc.*, v 57 (Prothero), The Neapolitans are not worth a curse, and will be beaten.

(9) 1660: B.&F., *Faithful Friends*, IV v, If my trade then prove not worth a dodkin. 1672: Cowell, *Interpreter*, s.v. 'Doitkin' (OED), Hence probably we retain that phrase when we would undervalue a man, to say, *He is not worth a doit or doitkin.* 1881: Duffield, *Don Quix.*, III xxvii 206 (OED), I did not care two dotkins.

(10) 1613: S. Rowley, *When You See Me*, sig. D2, As for the Popes faith (good faith's) not worth a farthing. 1633: *Dux Grammaticus*, quoted in *N. &Q.*, 5th ser, viii 165, All the gaine that thou shalt get by this bargain is not worth a farthing. 1786: Wolcot, *Works*, i 118 (1795). 1824: Scott, *Redgauntlet*, Lett. III. 1876: C. Loftus. *My Youth*, i 87, He was never 'worth a farthing' afterwards; his heart and his spirit were broken.

(11) [Non tressis agaso. – Persius, v 76.] 1528: More, *Works*, 241 (1557). 1596: Harington, *Metam. of Ajax*, 68 (1814), It had not been worth a fig, if they had not … 1667: *Poor Robin Alman.*, July, For what is out of date, is not worth a fig. 1750: Smollett, *Gil Blas*, iii 98, Although it was not worth a fig, it met with great success. 1880: Spurgeon, *Ploughman's Pictures*, 56, Some pretty nothing, not worth a fig.

(12) *c.*1450: Henryson, *Moral Fables*, 195 (OED), For it is said in proverb. But lawté all other vertewis ar nocht worth ane fie. *c.*1640: in *Roxb. Ballads*, i 527 (B.S.), All your warrants are not worth a flee.

(13) 1297: R. Glouc, 428 (1724) (OED), Wat was thy strengthe worth? … ywys not worth a flye. *c.*1352: in Wright, *Pol. Poems*, i 59 (Rolls Ser., 1859), And all thaire fare noght wurth a flye. *c.*1380: *Sir Ferumbras*, l. 4930 (E.E.T.S.). *c.*1386: Chaucer, *Franklin's Tale*, l. 404. 1412: Hoccleve, *Regement*, st. 88, l. 613, By that sette I naght the worth of a flye. 1489: Skelton, in *Works*, i 10 (Dyce), Of whos [life] they counted not a flye. *c.*1550: in Heywood, *Spider and Flie*, 440 (Farmer), *c.*1640: in *Roxb. Ballads*, ii 160 (B.S.), Your speeches are not worth a fly. 1744: Claridge, in Mills, *Essay on Weather*, 101 (1773), But a swarm [of bees] in July Is not worth a fly. 1906: Doyle, *Sir Nigel*, ch xii, Mistress Edith told me that she counted him not a fly.

(14) *c.*1395: *Plowman's Tale*, in Skeat's *Chaucer*, vii 161, Such maters be nat worth a gnat. *c.*1565: Still, *Gammer Gurton*, V ii, Al is not worth a gnat – thou canst sweare till to morow.

(15) 1598: Shakespeare, *2 Henry IV*, I ii, All the other gifts … are not worth a gooseberry.

(16) 1530: Palsgrave, 657, He pyncheth as though he were nat worthe a grote. 1587: Turbervile. *Trag. Tales, etc.*, 309 (1837), He that feares caliuer shot, Can neuer … skirmish woorth a grote. 1694: *Terence made English*, 189, And the woman's not worth a groat. 1709: Ward, *Acc. of Clubs*, 257 (1756), In all its bloom not worth a groat, It does so quickly die. 1784: *New Foundl. Hosp. for Wit*, iv 30, Notions to you not worth a groat.

(17) 1546: Heywood, *Proverbs*, Pt II ch x, Till they both were not woorth a haddocke.

(18) 1613: Wither, *Abuses Stript, etc.*, Epigr. 10, To call you best, or the most faire … Is now not commendations worth a haire. 1639: *Conceits, Clinches, etc.*, No. 18, Give me a man's face: a boyes face is not worth a haire.

(19) *c.*1280: *Castle of Love*, in *Vernon MS.*, 368 (E.E.T.S.), Ne wisdam nis not worth an hawe. *c.*1300: in Ibid., 336, Hit is not worth an hawe. 1412–20: Lydgate, *Troy Book*, bk ii l. 4043. 1468: *Coventry Mys.*, 190 (SH.S.). 1583: Melbancke, *Philotinus*, sig. G1, A whelpe that firste doth misse of his game, doth neuer after proue woorth an haw.

(20) *c.*1386: Chaucer, *Wife of Bath's Tale*, l. 256, Swich arrogance is nat worth an hen. 1508: Dunbar, *Tua Mariit Wemen*, 269 (OED), That hurtis zow nought worth a hen.

(21) *c.*1270: in *Old Eng. Miscell.*, 95 (Morris, E.E.T.S.), Al were sone his prute [pride] agon hit nere on ende wrth on heryng.

(22) *c.*1350: *Alexander*, l. 4229, And your lare of a leke suld nevir the les worth. *c.*1370: Chaucer, *Rom. of Rose*, in *Works*, fo. 130 (1602), Such loue I preise not at a leke. *c.*1400: *Sowdone of Babylone*, 50 (E.E.T.S.), His wittie was not worth a leke. *c.*1480: in Hazlitt, *Early Pop. Poetry*, ii 2. Before 1529: Skelton, *Colin Clout*, l. 183. 1594: Greene, *Works*, xiv. 203 (Grosart). 1612: *Cornucopiae*, 79 (Grosart), This opinion is not worth two leekes.

(23) *c.*1380: *Sir Ferumbras*, l. 439 (E.E.T.S.), Him semede it nas noght worth a lous batayl with him to wage. *c.*1540: in Hazlitt, *Early Pop. Poetry*,

iii 308, Then seke an other house; This is not worth a louse. 1595–6: Gosson, in Ibid., iv. 253, All this new pelfe now sold in shops, In value true not worth a louse. 1639–61: *Rump Songs*, Pt II 168 (1662, repr. 1874). 1698: in *Harl. Miscell.*, ii 276 (1744), But, faith, I'm scarce worth a louse. 1720: *Vade Mecum for Malt-worms*, Pt I 21. 1801: Wolcot, *Works*, v 380 (1801), Life was never worth a louse To the man who ne'er was mellow. 1886: Elworthy, *West Som. Word-Book*, 840 (E.D.S.), An equally common depreciatory saying is, 'He idn a-wo'th a louse'.

(24) Before 1225: *Ancren R.*, 400, And alle theos thinges somed, azean mine bode, ne beoth nout wurth a nelde [needle]. *c.*1395: *Plowman's Tale*, in Skeat's *Chaucer*, vii 172, Such willers wit is nat worth a neld. *c.*1450: *Towneley Plays*, 13 (E.E.T.S.), When all mens corn was fayre in feld Then was myne not worth a neld.

(25) *c.*1300: *Havelok*, l. 1332 (E.E.T.S.), Nouth the worth of one nouthe [nut].

(26) *c.*1393: Langland, *Plowman*, C, x 345, Ich sette by pardon nat a peese. *c.*1430: *Roland and Otuel*, l. 1157 (E.E.T.S.), Your lawes are noghte worthe a pye [pea]. 1561: *Queene Hester*, 21 (Grosart), It is not worth a pease. 1587: Turbervile, *Trag. Tales, etc.*, 393 (1837), With idle words not woorth a parched pease.

(27) 1303: Brunne, *Handl. Synne*, l. 769, For euery gadling nat wurth a pere. *c.*1420: Lydgate, *Assembly of Gods*, 18 (E.E.T.S.), Without myn helpe, be nat worth a peere. 1485: Malory, *Morte d'Arthur*, bk xv ch vi, Vayne glory of the world, the whiche is not worth a pere. *c.*1540: Bale, *Kynge Johan*, 38 (Camden S.), And that is not worth a rottyn wardon [pear].

(28) 1533: Heywood, *Play of Wether*, l. 750, And all our other gere not worth a pyn. 1589: Greene, *Works*, vi 39 (Grosart), Cupide must be … blinde (or all were not worth a pinne). 1685–6: Cotton, *Montaigne*, bk ii ch xvii, I cannot … carve at table worth a pin. 1782: Wolcot, *Works*, i 36 (1795). 1865: Planché, *Extravag.*, v 243 (1879), Your violin Not worth a pin.

(29) 1542: Udall, tr. Erasmus' *Apoph.*, 187 (1877), He was for the respect of his qualitees not to be esteemed worth a blewe point or a good lous. 1547: Borde, *Brev. of Helthe*, fo. xix. v°, All is nat worthe a blewe poynt. 1570: Googe, *Popish Kingdome*, 14 v° (1880), That now he is not worth a poynt, in any kinde of place. 1666:

Torriano, *Piazza Univ.*, 128, A head without tongue is not worth a point. 1672: Walker, *Paroem.*, 59, Not worth a point.

(30) 1823: Byron, *Don Juan*, can. vii st. 4, Who knew this life was not worth a potato.

(31) 1362: Langland, *Plowman*, A, xi 17, Wisdam and wit nou is not worth a russche. *c.*1470: G. Ashby, *Poems*, 39 (E.E.T.S.), Suche maner reule is nat worthe two russhes. 1594: *Willobie's Avisa*, 76 (Grosart), Yet this is all not worth a rush. 1653: Walton, *Angler*, Pt I ch iii, If this chub that you ete of had been kePt till to-morrow, he had not been worth a rush. 1713: Arbuthnot, *John Bull*, Pt V ch vii, His friendship is not worth a rush. 1838: Dickens, *Twist*, ch xxxviii, Don't move a step forward, or your life is not worth a bulrush. 1878: R.L.S., *Letters*, ii 49 (Tusitala ed.), It is a rotten book, and not worth a rush at best.

(32) *c.*1250: *Orison our Lady*, 28, in *Old Eng. Miscell.*, 160 (OED), this liues blisse nis wurth a slo. *c.*1300: *Havelok*, l. 849, Of me ne is me nouth a slo. *c.*1380: *Sir Ferumbras*, l. 4338 (E.E.T.S.), Hit were noght worth a slo. 14th cent.: *Guy of Warwick*, l. 2936 (E.E.T.S.), Scheld no hauberk nas him worth a slo.

(33) *c.*1300: *Havelok*, l. 315, He let his oth al ouer-ga [entirely be disregarded], Therof ne gaf he nouht a stra [Thereof he gave not a straw]. *c.*1386: Chaucer, *Tale of Melibeus*, § 34, And whan that they been accompliced, yet be they nat worth a stree. *c.*1470: G. Ashby, *Poems*, 74 (E.E.T.S.), His wyt is not worth a strawe. Before 1529: Skelton, *Magnyfycence*, l. 1394, Yet lyberte without rule is not worth a strawe. Before 1635: Corbet, *Poems*, 20 (1807), The doctors of the civil law Urg'd ne're a reason worth a straw. 1740: North, *Examen*, 439, Their cogency is not worth a straw. 1863: Reade, *Hard Cash*, ch i, When he has got a headache, Hardie of Exeter is not worth a straw in a boat.

(34) 1894: Northall, *Folk Phrases*, 20 (E.D.S.), Not worth a tinker's curse.

(35) *c.*1489: Caxton, *Sonnes of Aymon*, 544 (E.E.T.S.), The sones of a traytour whiche ben not worthe a roten apple.

(36) *c.*1430: *Roland and Otuel*, l. 222 (E.E.T.S.), That the lawes of Cristyante ne are noghte worthe ane aye [egg], *c.*1500: More, in *Works* (1557), 'Juvenile Poems', And all not worth an egge. 1659: Howell, 14, Tis not worth an egg-shell. 1883: R.L.S., *Letters*, ii 260 (Tusitala ed.), Pouring words upon him by the hour about some truck not worth an egg that had befallen me.

(37) *c.*1390: Gower, *Conf. Amantis*, iv 586, That all nys worth an yvy lef.

(38) 1509: Barclay, *Ship of Fools*, i 63 (1874), A yonge boy that is nat worth an onyon. 1556: Heywood, *Spider and Flie*, cap. 23, p. 103 (Farmer), Your case in law is not worth an inion.

(39) 1883: Burne, *Shropsh. Folk–Lore*, 588, He's not worth hiring, who talks of tiring.

(40) 1670: Ray, 192, Not worth shooe-buckles.

(41) 1672: Walker, *Paroem.*, 26, Not worth three halfpence.

Not worthy to carry books, to loose the latchet of shoes, to wipe one's shoes, etc., etc. *See* quots. *c.*1410: *Towneley Plays*, 196 (E.E.T.S.), I am not worthy for to lawse The leste thwong that longys to his shoyne. 1569: in Huth, *Ancient Ballads, etc.*, 21 (1867), For I with all that I can dooe, Vnworthie … To undoo the lachet of her shooe. 1611: Coryat, *Crudities*, Epist to Reader, i 15 (1905), Travellers of that learning, that I am not worthy to loose their shoe-lachet. 1620: Shelton, *Quixote*, Pt II ch iii, I have seen … of your governors … that are not worthy to wipe my shoes. 1631: Mabbe, *Celestina*, 147 (T.T.), She is not worthy to carry her shooes after her. 1670: Ray, 200, Not worthy to carry his books after him … to be named the same day … to wipe his shoes. 1672: Walker, *Paroem.*, 54, Not worthy to … hold him water to wash his hands. 1709: Mandeville, *Virgin Unmask'd*, 30 (1724), Treats him … as if he was not worthy to wipe her shoes. 1748: Richardson, *Clarissa*, ii 201 (1785) … not worthy to buckle his shoes. 1821: Scott, *Pirate*, ch xiv, Not fit to tie the latchets of John's shoes. 1909: Hudson, *Afoot in England*, ch xxiv, As a poet he was not worthy to unloose the buckles of their shoes. 1926: Phill–potts, *Yellow Sands*, I, You hold your tongue about Arthur. You ain't worthy to black Arthur's boots. *See also* **Guts to a bear.**

Nought. 1. He that hath nought is nought set by. Before 1500: in Hill, *Commonplace-Book*, 132 (E.E.T.S.).

2. He that hath nought shall have nought. *c.*1550: *Part. of Byrdes*, l. 221, in Hazlitt, *Early Pop. Poetry*, iii 179.

3. Nought can restrain consent of twain. [Non caret effectu, quod voluere duo. – Ovid, *Amores*, II iii l6.] 1591: Harington, *Orl. Furioso*, bk xxviii

Nought

Notes, *c*.1596: Marlowe, *Ovid's Elegies*, bk ii el.
3, What two determine never wants effect. 1740:
Richardson, *Pamela*, i 162 (1883), I should have
had a hard task to prevent you, I find; for, as the
saying is. *Nought can restrain consent of twain.*

4. Nought lay down nought take up. *c*.1374:
Chaucer, *Troylus*, bk iv 1 1585, Men seyn …
'who-so wol have leef. he leef mot lete' [He who
will have what he wants must give up what he
likes]. 1546: Heywood, *Proverbs*, Pt I ch vi. 1577:
Misogonus, II iv, Nought stake, nought drawe.
1678: Ray, 206, Nothing stake nothing draw. Cf.
Nothing (7).

**5. Nought won by the one, nought won by the
other.** 1546: Heywood, *Proverbs*, Pt I ch xi.

**6. Where nought is to wed with, wise men flee
the clog.** Ibid., Pt I ch xi. 1605: Camden,
Remains, 335 (1870). 1659: Howell, 10.

See also **Naught**; and **Nothing**.

**November. 1. As November so the following
March.** 1893: Inwards, *Weather Lore*, 36.

2. As November 21 so is the winter. Ibid., 37.

**3. If there's ice in November that will bear a
duck, There'll be nothing after but sludge and
muck.** 1878: Dyer, *Eng. Folk-Lore*, 260. 1891: R.
P. Chope, *Hartland Dialect*, 20 (E.D.S.), Vrost in
November to carr' a duck, The rest o' the winter'll
be a muck. 1893: Inwards, *Weather Lore*, 36.

4. November and flail. *See* **Thresher.**

5. November 10. *See* quot. 1669: *New Help to
Discourse*, 285, If on the 10th of November the
heavens be cloudy, it prognosticates a wet
winter; if clear and dry, a sharp winter.

**6. On the 1st of November, if the weather hold
clear, An end of wheat sowing do make for the
year.** 1580: Tusser, *Husb.*, 181 (E.D.S.), Wife,
some time this weeke, if the wether hold cleere,
an end of wheat sowing we make for this yeere.
1893: Inwards, *Weather Lore*, 36.

7. The third of November. *See* quot. 1659:
Howell, 6, The third of November the Duke of
Vandosm was under water, The fourth of
November the Queen was delivered of a
daughter, The fifth of November we were like to
have a great slaughter, And the sixth of
November was the next day after.

8. Thunder in November a fertile year to come.
1893: Inwards, *Weather Lore*, 36.

No venom to that of the tongue. 1659: Howell,
11.

No vice goes alone. 1732: Fuller, 3637.

No vice like avarice. Ibid., No. 6171.

No weal without woe. 1578: Florio, *First
Fruiies*, fo. 33.

No wheat without its chaff. *c*.1440: Lydgate,
Fall of Princes, bk i l. 6732 (E.E.T.S.), Out off
good corn men may sum darnel weede. 1611:
Cotgrave, s.v. 'Paille', No corne without some
chaffe. 1681: Robertson, *Phraseol. Generalis*,
1312. 1736: Bailey, *Dict.*, s.v. 'Wheat'.

Now I have got. *See* quots. 1732: Fuller, 3691,
Now I have got an ewe and a lamb, every one
cries, Welcome, Peter. 1736: Franklin, *Way to
Wealth*, in *Works*, i 445 (Bigelow), Now I have a
sheep and a cow, everybody bids me good
morrow.

No wisdom to silence. 1659: Howell, *Proverbs:
Brit.-Eng.*, 27.

Now's now. 1631; Mabbe, *Celestina*, 144 (T.T.),
Now is now; and then is then. 1707: *Spanish
Bawd*, III ii [as in 1631]. 1846: Denham, *Proverbs*,
6 (Percy S.), Now's now, but Yule's in winter.

No-where. *See* **Every-where.**

Nowt so queer as folk, There's. 1905: *English
Dialect Dictionary*, IV 304, There's nowt sae
queer as folk, *Old saying*.

Number. *See* **One is no number.**

Numbers the waves, He. 1813: Ray, 75.

Numbers, There's safety in. *See* **Safety.**

**Nurse and Nurses. 1. A nurse spoils a good
huswife.** 1659: Howell, 3.

2. A nurse's tongue is privileged to talk. 1659:
Howell, *Proverbs: Brit.-Eng.*, 4. 1670: Ray, 19.

**3. Nurses put one bit in the child's mouth and
two in their own.** 1639: Clarke, 39.

**4. The nurse is valued till the child is done
sucking.** 1732: Fuller, 4688.

See also **Kiss**, *verb* (6).

Nursed in cotton, To be = To be brought up
very tenderly. 1813: Ray, 209.

Nurture passes nature. [1579: Joubert, *Erreurs
Populaires*, I v 9 (Lean), Nourriture passe
nature.] 1611: Cotgrave, s.v. 'Nourriture',
Nurture surpasseth nature. 1633: Draxe, 50,
Nurture is above nature. 1754: Berthelson,
Eng.-Danish Dict., s.v. 'Nurture', Nurture goes
beyond nature. Cf. **Nature.**

**Nut and Nuts. 1. A good nut year, a good corn
year.** 1846: Denham, *Proverbs*, 55 (Percy S.).
1893: Inwards, *Weather Lore*, 5.

2. Crack me that nut. 1546: Heywood, *Proverbs*,
Pt II ch vii, Knak me that nut. 1564: Bullein,

Dialogue, 62 (E.E.T.S.), Ha, ha, ha, how cracke you this nutte? 1600: Dekker, *Old Fortunatus*, I i, My tongue speaks no language but an almond for a parrot, and crack me this nut. 1670: Ray, 214, Crack me that nut, quoth Bumsted. 1732: Fuller, 1121 [as in 1670]. 1828: Scott, *Fair Maid*, ch xvi, While this prince of revellers exhorted him, – 'Crack me this nut, and do it handsomely'.

3. Many nits [nuts], **many pits** [graves] = If hazel nuts be plentiful, the season will be unhealthy. [1672: Howard, *All Mistaken*, I, A very hopeful generation! sure, This was great nut year!] 1850: in *N. & Q.*, 1st ser, ii 510, Many nits Many pits. A common saying hereabouts [locality not indicated], meaning that if hazel nuts, haws, hips, etc., are plentiful, many deaths will occur. 1884: H. Friend, *Flowers and Fl. Lore*, 207 ... still in use in Devon ... 1891: R. P. Chope, *Hartland Dialect*, 71 (E.D.S.), Many nits, Many pits; Many slones, Many groans.

4. To be nuts to one. 1589: *Hay any Worke for Cooper*, 33 (1845), Like you any of these nuts Iohn Canterbury? [The context shows that 'nuts' is used in this No. 4 sense.] 1674: Head and Kirkman, *Eng. Rogue*, iii 102, It was honey and nuts to him to tell the guests. 1740: North, *Lives of Norths*, i 33 (Bohn), This was nuts to the old lord who thought he had outwitted Frank. 1819: Byron, *Letters, etc.*, iv 294 (Prothero), It will be nuts to all of them: they never had such an opportunity.

See also **Ape** (9); **Apple** (6) and (13); and **Deaf** (7).

Oak and **Oaks. 1. An oak is not felled at one stroke,** *c.*1440: Lydgate, *Fall of Princes*, bk i l. 96, These ookis grete be nat doun ihewe First at a strok. 1477: *Paston Letters*, iii 169 (Gairdner), It is but a sympill oke, That [is] cut down at the first stroke. 1611: Cotgrave, s.v. 'Arbre', Though a little man can fell a great oke, yet fals it not at the first blow. 1732: Fuller, 639 ['chop' for 'stroke']. 1880: Spurgeon, *Ploughman's Pictures*, 127, One stroke fells not an oak.

2. As close as oak = Close as the grain of oak. 1604: Shakespeare, *Othello*, III iii, To seel her father's eyes up close as oak. 1763: Colman, *Deuce is in Him*, II, I am dose as oak, an absolute free-mason for secresy. 1764: Murphy, *The Choice*, I, I never repeat a word; I am as close as oak.

3. Beware of an oak, It draws the stroke; Avoid an ash, It counts the flash; Creep under the thorn, It can save you from harm. 1878: *Folk-Lore Record*, i 43.

4. Cut down an oak and set up a strawberry. 1662: Fuller, *Worthies*, i 396 (1840), I would not wish this county [Devon] the increase of these berries, according to the proverb; 'Cut down', etc. 1670: Ray, 188.

5. Great oaks from tittle acorns grow. Before 1635: Corbet, *Poems*, in Chalmers, v 584, An acorn one day proves an oke. 1732: Fuller, 4576, The greatest oaks have been little acorns. 1852: FitzGerald, *Polonius*, 6 (1903), Every oak must be an acorn. 1923: Mackenzie King, *Speech*, in *Times*, 13 Oct., p. 7, col. 3, Here in England, as nowhere else in the world, 'great oaks from little acorns grow'.

6. Oaks may fall when reeds stand the storm. 1732: Fuller, 3692.

7. To go between the oak and the rind. 1886: Elworthy, *West Som. Word-Book*, 528 (E.D.S.), 'To go 'twixt th' oak and the rind' expresses the making of very fine distinctions – hair splitting; hence the phrase has come to mean the quibbling by which a trimmer agrees with both sides. 1917: *Devonsh. Assoc. Trans.*, xlix. 338, To creep between the oak and the rind. Cf. **Bark and tree**; and **Devil** (120).

8. When the oak puts on his gosling grey, 'Tis time to sow barley, night and day. 1846: Denham, *Proverbs*, 46 (Percy S.). 1893: Inwards, *Weather Lore*, 152. 1904: *Co. Folk-Lore: Northumb.*, 177 (F.L.S.).

See also **Ash; Beech; Good elm; Grass** (7); and **Reed**.

Oar in another's boat, To have (or put) an. 1542: Udall, tr. Erasmus' *Apoph.*, 203 (1877), Whatsoeuer came in his foolyshe brain, Out it should, wer it neuer so vain. In eche mans bote would he haue an ore, But no woorde, to good purpose, lesse or more. 1551: R. Crowley, *Works*, 120 (E.E.T.S.), You had an owre in echmans barge. 1597: G. Harvey, *Works*, iii 33 (Grosart), Those … that will … haue an oare (as we say) in euerie mans boate. 1630: Brathwait, *Eng. Gent.*, *etc.* 6 (1641), Youth … putting his oare in every mans boat. 1712: Motteux, *Quixote*, Pt II ch xxii, He has an oar in every man's boat, and a finger in every pye. 1731: Coffey, *Devil to Pay*, I ii, I will govern my own house without your putting in an oar. 1922: *Weyman. Ovtngton's Bank*, ch xxxv, Then a pretty fool you were to put your oar in !

Oath is better broken than kept, An unlawful. 1670: Ray, 126. 1672: Walker, *Paroem.*, 46.

Oatmeal. *See* quot. 1678: Ray, 352, Where there is store of oatmeal, you may put enough in the crock. *Somerset.*

Oats. *See* **Eel** (1); **Horse** (14); **January** (25); **May, F** (8); **St David** (3); **Water** (21); and **Wild** (7).

Occasion is bald behind. [Fronte capillata, post est occasio calva. – Cato, *Disticha*, ii 26.] 1553: *Respublica*, III vi, The goddesse occasyon … behinde hathe not one heare. 1566: Painter, *Pal. of Pleasure*, i 266 (Jacobs), Occasion … being balde can not easely be gotten againe if she be once let slip. 1629; Quarles, *Arg. and Parth.*, bk i, in *Works*, iii 246 (Grosart). 1634: Massinger, *Guardian*, IV i. 1655: Heywood and Rowley, *Fortune by Land and Sea*, IV i, Occasions head is bald behind. *See also* **Time** (7).

Occasion lost cannot be redeemed, An. 1813: Ray, 144.

October. 1. Dry your barley land in October, Or you'll always be sober. If not, there will be no malt. 1846: Denham, *Proverbs*, 60 (Percy S.). 1893: Inwards, *Weather Lore*, 35.

2. Good October, a good blast, To blow the hog acorn and mast. 1732: Fuller, 6218. 1893: Inwards, 35.

3. In October dung your field, And your land its wealth shall yield. Ibid., 36.

4. Leaves in October. *See* quots. *c.*1630: B.&F., *Bloody Brother*, II ii. And he that will to bed go sober, Falls with the leaf, still in October. 1652: in *Festive Songs*, 60 (Percy S.), Let him drink his small beer and be sober, Whilst we drink sack, and sing as if it were Spring, He shall drop like the leaves in October. 1854: Doran, *Table Traits*,

335, There was an old adage that – He who goes to bed and goes to bed sober, Falls as the leaves do, and dies in October; But he who goes to bed, and goes to bed mellow, Lives as he ought to do, and dies a good fellow. Cf. **Often drunk.**

5. Much rain in October, much wind in December. 1893: Inwards, 35.

6. There are always twenty-one fine days in October. But the number appears to be variable. 1855: Gaskell, *North and South*, ch ii, And when the brilliant fourteen fine days of October came on, her cares were all blown away. 1871: *N.&Q.*, 4th ser, viii 505, It is an old saying that October always gives us twenty-one fine days. 1881: *Folk-Lore Record*, iv 128, October always has twenty-one fine days. 1893: Inwards, *Weather Lore*, 35, There are always nineteen fine days in October. – Kent.

7. Warm October, cold February. Ibid., 35.

Odd numbers. *See* **Luck** (5).

Odds in all things, There are. 1864: 'Cornish Proverbs', in *N.&Q.*, 3rd ser, vi 494.

Odds in evil. 1633: Draxe, 55, In euill there is ods. 1639: Clarke, 197 [as in 1633].

Odds in gossips. 1797: Wolcot, in *Works*, v 44 (1801), '*There's odds in Gossips*', says an old adage.

Odds will beat anybody. 1666: Torriano, *Piazza Univ.*, 320, The English say that odds will beat anybody.

Odious. *See* **Comparisons.**

Offender never pardons, The. 1640: Herbert, *Jac. Prudentum.* Before 1680: Butler, *Remains*, ii 39 (1759), Bad men never use to forgive those whom they have injured, or received any extraordinary obligation from. 1732: Fuller, 2393, He who is the offender, is never the forgiver.

Offer much, To. *See* quots. 1631: Mabbe, *Celestina*, 116 (T.T.), It is a common saying; To offer much to him that asketh but a little, is a kinde of deniall. 1666: Torriano, *Piazza Univ.*, 176, To proffer much is a kind of denyal.

Offices may well be given, but not discretion. 1578: Florio, *First Fruites*, fo. 33 ['are' for 'may well be']. 1629: *Book of Meery Riddles*, Prov. 116.

Offspring of those that are very young or very old, lasts not, The. 1640: Herbert, *Jac. Prudentum.* 1670: Ray, 19. 1748: Richardson, *Clarissa*, iv 121 (1785), The children of very young and very old men … last not long.

Off the hinges. 1611: Cotgrave, s.v. 'Hallebrené', Off the hindges, cleane out of heart. 1645: Howell, *Letters*, bk i § iii No. xxxi, All businesses here are off the hinges. 1661: Webster and Rowley, *Cure for a Cuckold*, V i, Bear with him, sir, he's strangely off o' th' hinges. 1828: Carr, *Craven Dialect*, s.v. 'Hinges', To be off t' hinges, to be out of health. 1894: Northall, *Folk Phrases*, 26 (E.D.S.) … = To be out of temper, or in bad spirits.

Off the hooks – used with various significations. *See* quots. 1621: B.&F., *Pilgrim*, III vi, What fit's this? The pilgrim's off the hooks too! [mad, 'off his head']. 1635: in *Somers Tracts*, vii 188 (1811), If debts … fling not all off the hooks. 1639: Davenport, *New Trick to cheat Devil*, I ii., What, Roger, al amort, me thinkes th'art off o' th' hookes [crestfallen]. 1681: Robertson, *Phraseol. Generalis*, 739, To be off the hooks, or out of humour. 1692: L'Estrange, *Aesop*, life, 8 (3rd ed.), Easily put off the hooks, and monstrous hard to be pleased again. 1740: North, *Lives of Norths*, i 377 (Bohn), He was continued in his office by King James II, but then he was soon off the. hooks. 1824: Scott, *Redgauntlet*, ch i, Then this smart young hopeful is off the hooks with too hard study. 1881: Evans, *Leics. Words*, 205 (E.D.S.), Off-the-hooks, or Off-of-the-hooks … shabby; 'seedy'; worn-out; ailing. 1889: Peacock, *Manley, etc., Gloss.*, 277 (E.D.S.), Maaster seems clear off th' hooks today [ill, or in bad temper].

Off with the old love, before you are on with the new, Be. *See* **Old** E (6).

Oft craving makes soon forgetting. 1869: Hazlitt, 301.

Often and little eating makes a man fat 1670: Ray, 38.

Often drunk, and seldom sober, Falls like the leaves in October. 1732: Fuller, 6219. Cf. **October** (4).

Often happeth evil for a good turne. *c.*1489: Caxton, *Sonnes of Aymon*, 265 (E.E.T.S.) [quoted as a proverb].

Often to the water often to the tatter. Said of linen. 1678: Ray, 347. 1732: Fuller, 6378, Linnen often to water, soon to tatter.

Oil, *subs.* **1. He that measureth oil shall anoint his fingers.** 1611: Cotgrave, s.v. 'Huile' ['besmeares' for 'shall anoint']. 1670: Ray, 126.
2. The oil-bottle. *See* quot. 1827: Hone, *Table-*

Book, 775, 'He's got t' oil bottle in his pocket'. *Craven* = he is double-faced:

3. To bring (or add) oil to fire. [Oleum adde camino. – Horace, *Sat.*, II iii 321.] *c.*1386: Chaucer, *C. Tales*, C. 60 (Skeat), For wyne and youthë doon Venus encrese. As men in fyr wol casten oile or grece. *c.*1560: Ingelend, *Disob. Child*, in Hazlitt, *Old Plays*, ii 280, And, after the proverb, we put oil to the fire. *c.*1605: Shakespeare, *Lear*, II ii, Bring oil to fire, snow to their colder moods. 1647: Cowley, *The Mistress:* 'The Incurable', st. 4, But wine, alas! was oil to th' fire.

4. To cast oil in the fire is not the way to quench it. 1639: Clarke, 167. 1670: Ray, 126. 1732: Fuller, 5142.

5. To hold up oil = To aid and abet, or consent flatteringly. [Narratur belle quidam dixisse, Marulle, Qui te ferre oleum dixit in auriculam. – Martial, *Epigr.*, V lxxviii.] 1387: Trevisa, tr. Higden, iii 447 (Rolls Ser.), Alisaundre gan to boste and make him self more worthy than his fader, and a greet deel of hem [them] that were at the feste hilde up the kynges oyl. *c.*1390: Gower, *Conf. Amantis*, bk vii vol iii 159 (Pauli), For, when he doth extorcion, Men shall not finden one of tho To grueche or speke there agein, But holden up his oile and sain, That all is well that ever he doth.

6. To pour oil on troubled waters. 1855: Kingsley, *West. Ho!*, ch iv, Campion … the sweetest–natured of men, trying to pour oil on the troubled waters.

See also **Truth** (4).

Old, *adj.* Classification: A. **Sayings relating to human life:** (*a*) **General,** (*b*) **Man,** (*c*) **Woman.** B. **Sayings relating to other living creatures.** C. **Sayings relating to books, friends, etc.** D. **Similes.** E. **Unclassified.**

A. Sayings relating to Human Life.

(*a*) **General. 1. An old child sucks hard.** 1602–3: Manningham, *Diary*, 12 (Camden S.) … i.e. children when they growe to age proue chargeable.

2. An old thief desires a new halter. 1639: Clarke, 299. 1670: Ray, 127.

3. Old age is sickness enough of itself. 1672: Walker, *Paroem.*, 33.

4. Old and tough, young and tender. 1678: Ray, 85.

5. Old be or young die. Ibid., 182.

6. Old heads and young hands. Somerset. Ibid., 347.

7. Old heads on young shoulders. 1639: Clarke, 7, You set an old mans head on a yong mans shoulders. *c*.1780: *First Floor*, II i, in Inchbald's *Farces*, vi 243 (1815), Ah, sir, there is no putting an old head on young shoulders. 1850: Dickens, *Chuzzlewit*, ch xi, We should not expect to find old heads upon young shoulders. 1906; Lucas, *Listener's Lure*, 154.

8. Though old and wise, yet still advise. 1640: Herbert, *Jac. Prudentum.* 1670: Ray, 1. 1732: Fuller, 6227. 1875: Cheales, *Proverb. Folk-Lore*, 49.

9. Where old age is evil, youth can learn no good. 1633: Draxe, 145 ['faultie' for 'evil', and 'goodnesse' for 'good']. 1670: Ray, 20. 1736: Bailey, *Dict.*, s.v. 'Youth'.

(b) Man. 1. An old knave is no babe. 1528: More, *Works*, p. 242, col. 1 (1557), They shal for al that well fynde in some of us yt an olde knaue is no chylde. 1546: Heywood, *Proverbs*, Pt II ch ii ['childe' for 'babe']. 1670: Ray, 20.

2. An old man is a bed full of bones. 1678: Ray, 184. 1732: Fuller, 648.

3. An old man never wants a tale to tell. Ibid., No. 649.

4. An old man's end is to keep sheep. 1659: Howell, *Proverbs: Brit.–Eng.*, 2. 1823: D'Israeli, *Cur. of Lit.*, 2nd ser, i 441 (1824), The state of our agricultural people appears in such proverbs as…'An old man's end is to keep sheep'!

5. An old man's staff is the rapper at death's door. 1640: Herbert, *Jac. Prudentum* ['of' for 'at']. 1670: Ray, 19. 1732: Fuller, 4690.

6. An old man who weds a buxom young maiden, biddeth fair to become a freeman of Buckingham. 1790: Grose, *Prov. Gloss.*, s.v. 'Bucks'.

7. An old physician and a young lawyer. 1640: Herbert, *Jac. Prudentum.* 1670: Ray, 36. 1732: Fuller, 652. 1875: Cheales, *Proverb. Folk-Lore*, 75, An old physician and a young lawyer, and confide in both with equal frankness.

8. An old soldier. *See* quot. 1894: R.L.S., *St Ives*, ch xx, I own myself an idiot. Well do they say, *an old soldier, an old innocent*! *See also* **Old E.** (22).

9. An old wise man's shadow is better than a young buzzard's sword. 1640: Herbert, *Jac. Prudentum.*

10. Better be an old man's darling than a young man's warling. 1546: Heywood, *Proverbs*,. Pt II ch vii. 1602: Breton, *Works*, ii *g* 12 (Grosart) ['worldling' for 'warling']. 1611: Barry, *Ram-Alley*. II. 1738: Swift, *Polite Convers.*, Dial. I. 1842: Harr. Ainsworth, *Miser's Daughter*, bk iii ch xv. 1859: Planché, *Extravag.*, v 206 (1879), Better be an old man's darling, Than become a young man's slave.

11. He that would be well old must be old betimes. [Nec enim unquam sum assensus illi veteri laudatoque proverbio, quod monet, mature fieri senem, si diu velis esse senex. – P. Vergil, *Adag. Op.*, 67 (1541).] 1539: Taverner, *Proverbs*, fo. 10, Become an olde man betyme yf thou wylt be an olde man longe. 1583: Melbancke, *Philotinus*, sig. C1, He that will be an old man long, must bee an old man soone. 1640: Herbert, *Jac. Prudentum.* 1670: Ray, 34, (*a*) They who would be young when they are old must be old when they are young. [Also] (*b*) Old young and old long. 1711: Steele, *Spectator*, No. 153, It was prettily said, 'He that would be long an old man must begin early to be one'. 1732: Fuller, 6179 [as in 1670 (*b*)]. Ibid., No. 854, Be old betimes; that thou may'st long be so.

12. He wrongs not an old man that steals his supper from him. 1640: Herbert, *Jac. Prudentum.* 1670: Ray, 19. 1732: Fuller, 2420.

13. Old man, when thou diest give me thy doublet. 1678: Ray, 77.

14. Old men and travellers may lie by authority. 1605: Camden, *Remains*, 330 (1870). 1681: Robertson, *Phraseol. Generalis*, 947. 1732: Fuller, 3715. Cf. **Painters and Poets**; and **Traveller.**

15. Old men are twice children. 1539: Taverner, *Proverbs*, fo. 16, Olde folke are twyse chyldren. 1549: Latimer, *Sec. Sermon*, 56 (Arber). 1588: Cogan, *Haven of Health*, 182 (1612). 1631: W. Saltonstall, *Picturae Loquentes*, sig. B9, Though the proverbe be, once a man and twice a child. 1632: Randolph, *Jealous Lovers*, III vi. 1707: Dunton, *Athenian Sport*, 389, Old men are said to be a second time children. 1825: Hone, *Ev. Day Book*, i, 19 Jan. [as in 1631].

16. Old men go to death; death comes to young men. 1640: Herbert, *Jac. Prudentum.* 1732: Fuller, 3719.

17. Old men. *See* these two quotations. The first is not very intelligible. 1640: Herbert, *Jac. Prudentum*, Old men, when they scorn young, make much of death. 1748: Richardson,

Clarissa, iv 121 (1785), Old men, when they marry young women, are said to make much of death.

18. Old men will die and children soon forget, *c*.1567: in *Black Letter Ballads, etc.*, 53 (Lilly, 1867), Bot as the prouerbe speikis, it plaine appeiris, Auld men will die and barnes will sone forget.

19. When an old man will not drink, look for him in another world. 1666: Torriano, *Piazza Univ.*, 298. 1670: Ray, 20 ['go to see' for 'look for']. 1732: Fuller, 5548, When an old man will not drink, you may safely promise him a visit in the next world.

See also **Young**, *passim*.

(c) **Woman**. **1. An old woman in a wooden ruff** [in an antique dress]. 1678: Ray, 77.

2. He is teaching an old woman to dance. 1813: Ray, 75.

3. Old maids. *See* **Ape** (12).

4. Old maids'children. *See* **Bachelors** (3).

5. Old wife. *See* **Wife** (15).

6. Old wife's fair. Craven. The second day of the fair. 1869: Hazlitt, 303.

7. Old wives' tales. 1387: Trevisa, tr. Higden, iii 265 (Rolls Ser.), And vseth telynges as olde wifes dooth. 1509: Barclay, *Ship of Fools*, i 72 (1874), A fole he is for his moste felycyte Is to byleue the tales of an olde wyfe. 1580: Lyly, *Euphues*, 347 (Arber), thinking euery olde wiues tale to be a truth. 1604: Marlowe, *Faustus*, sc v, Tush; these are trifles, and mere old wives' tales. 1614: Rowlands, *Fooles Bolt*, 12 (Hunt.Cl.). 1672: Marvell, *Works*, iii 39 (Grosart), Who will ... tax up an old–wife's fable to the particularity of history. 1720: C. Shadwell, *Irish Hosp.*, Dram. Pers., *Lady Peevish* ... a mighty observer of cross days, foolish superstitions, and old wives' sayings, 1860: Reade, *Cl. and Hearth*, ch lxxiv., 'These be old wives' fables,' said Jerome contemptuously. 1921: Locke, *Mountebank*, ch iv, Mine differed only in brevity from an old wife's tale.

8. The old wives' Paternoster. Query = the devil's Paternoster – *see* **Devil** (103). 1580: in H. G. Wright, *Arthur Hall of Grantham*, 63 (1919), He plucking his hatte about his eares, mumbling the olde wiues Paternoster, departed.

B. Sayings relating to other Living Creatures.

1. My old mare would have a new crupper. 1546: Heywood, *Proverbs*, Pt II ch i. 1578:

Lupton, *All for Money*, sig. E1, Gylle my olde mare must haue a newe crupper. 1670: Ray, 19, Old mares lust after new cruppers.

2. Old ape. See Ape (4).

3. Old birds and chaff. *See* **Bird** (14).

4. Old cat. *See* **Cat** (7), (8), and (39).

5. Old cattle breed not. 1639: Clarke, 169. 1670: Ray, 127.

6. Old cock. *See* **Young** (17).

7. Old dog. *See* **Dog** (14)–(16), (19), (53), (60), and (93).

8. Old foxes. *See* **Fox** (2), (3), (13). and (19).

C. Sayings relating to Books, Friends, etc.

1. An old friend is a new house. 1640: Herbert, *Jac. Prudentum*.

2. Old friends and old wine are best. 1589: see quot. under No. 3. 1633: Draxe, 75. 1670: Ray, 19. 1736: Bailey, *Dict.*, s.v. 'Old'. 1884: A. Dobson, in *Poet. Works*, 387 (1923), All these I prize, but (*entre nous*) Old friends are best!

3. Old wood to burn. *See* quots. 1589: L. Wright. *Display of Dutie*, 19–20, As olde wood is best to burne; old horse to ride; old bookes to reade; and old wine to drinke; so are old friends alwayes most trusty to vse. 1594: A. Copley, *Wits, Ftis, etc.*, 4 (1614), Olde wood for fewell; an olde horse for easie riding; wine of a yeare olde; olde friendes, and olde bookes. 1773: Goldsmith, *She Stoops*, I i, I love everything that's old! old friends, old times, old manners, old books, old wine. 1816: Scott, *Antiquary*, ch vi, One who professes the maxim of King Alphonso of Castile – old wood to burn – old books to read – old wine to drink – and old friends ... to converse with. Cf. E (11).

D. Similes, 1. An old ewe dressed lamb fashion. 1777: *Gent. Mag.*, xlvii 187, Here antique maids of sixty three Drest out lamb-fashion you might see. 1785: Grose, *Class. Dict. Vulgar Tongue*, s.v. 'Ewe', An old ewe drest lamb fashion, an old woman drest like a young girl. 1909: *N.&Q.*, 10th ser, xii 189.

2. As old as Adam. *c*.1579: G. Harvey, *Letter-Book*, 82 (Camden S.), Yower newe complaynte ... is nye as owlde as Adam and Eve. 1662: in *Roxb. Ballads*, iii 578 (B.S.), If I had as many lives I should be as old as Adam. 1888: Lowsley, *Berks Gloss.*, 38 (E.D.S.), 'As awld as Adam' is the common phrase to denote great age or antiquity.

3. As old as Aldgate. 1725: Defoe, *Tour*, ii 153,

Aldgate was very ancient and decay'd, so that *as old as Aldgate* was a city proverb for many years.

4. As old as Cale-hill. 1639: Clarke, 171.

5. As old as Charing Cross. 1678: Ray, 287.

6. As old as Eggerton. 1709: in *Stukeley Memoirs*, ii 124 (Surtees S.), 'Tis proverbial [Dorset] when they would express what has a long time been, to say, '*tis as old as Eggerton.*

7. As old as Glastonbury tor. Somerset. 1678: Ray, 344.

8. As old as my tongue. *See* quots. 1738: Swift, *Polite Convers.*, Dial. I, I am as old as my tongue, and a little older than my teeth. 1828: Carr, *Craven Dialect*, ii 213, 'As oud as my tongue and ouder ner my teeth', a saucy answer given to the question, 'how oud isto?' 1862: *Dialect of Leeds*, 379 [as in 1828]. 1889: J. Nicholson, *Folk Speech E. Yorks*, 16, As awd as mi tongue, an' a bit awdher then mi teeth.

9. As old as Pandon Gate. 1649: Grey, *Chorographia*, As old as Pandon. 1776: Stukeley, *ltin. Cur.*, cent. ii 65, It is an old proverb in this country [Northumberland], 'As old as Pandon gate'. 1847: Halliwell, *Dict.*, s.v. 'As old as Panton-Gates', a very common proverb. There is a gate called Pandon Gate at Newcastle on Tyne. 1846–59: *Denham Tracts*, i 300 (F.L.S.), As old as Pandon. As old as Pandon Yatts ... The latter is used in the southern portions of the Bishopric [Durham] and the county of York ... Nothing is more general than the above saying, when any one would describe the great antiquity of anything. Pandon Gate is believed to have been of Roman workmanship,

10. As old as Paul's. *See* **Paul's.**

11. As old as the hills. 1820: Scott, *Monastery*, ch ix. 1850: Dickens, *Copperfield*, ch xv. 1924: *Sphere*, 30 Aug., p. 264, col. 1, The capital city, Luxembourg ... old as the hills.

12. As old as the itch. 1732: Fuller, 722.

13. To come the old soldier. 1823: Scott, *St Ronan's*, ch xviii, I should think he was coming the old soldier over me, and keeping up the game.

E. Unclassified. 1. An old band is a captain's honour. 1578: Florio, *First Fruites*, fo. 28, An old ensigne is the honor of a captaine. 1629: *Book of Meery Riddles*, Prov. 65.

2. An old nought will never be ought. 1678: Ray, 184. 1732: Fuller, 6342.

3. An old sack asketh much patching. 1546:

Heywood, *Proverbs*, Pt II ch ii. 1578: Lupton, *All for Money*, sig. E1, When I was a boye it was an olde saying, That an olde sacke would lacke much clouting and patching. 1670: Ray, 127. 1733: Fuller, 3736, Old sacks want much patching.

4. An old thing and a young thing both of an age. 1917: Bridge, *Cheshire Proverbs*, 8 ... Things must be considered old or young by comparison.

5. An old wrinkle never wears out. 1732: Fuller, 654.

6. Be off with the old love before you are on with the new. 1571: R. Edwards, *Damon and Pithias*, in Hazlitt, *Old Plays*, iv 447, 'Tis good to be off wi' the old love Before you are on wi' the new. 1861: Peacock, *Gryll Grange*, ch xxx. 1923: Lucas, *Advisory Ben*, § xxxix. p. 210, That proverb about being off with the old love is a very sound one.

7. Better keep under an old hedge, than creep under a new furze–bush. 1670: Ray, 127. Cf. **Sheltering.**

8. If the old year goes out like a lion, the new year will come in like a lamb. 1893: Inwards, *Weather Lore*, 4.

9. Old enough to lie without doors. 1678: Ray, 77.

10. Old fish and young flesh do feed men best. 1546: Heywood, *Proverbs*, Pt II ch iv. 1588: Cogan, *Haven of Health*, 118 (1612) [quoted as 'that English prouerbe']. 1611: Cotgrave, s.v. 'Chair', Young flesh and old fish (are daintiest). 1666: Torriano, *Piazza Univ.*, 39, Young flesh and old fish. 1717: Pope, *Jan. and May*, 102, There goes a saying, and 'twas shrewdly said, Old fish at table, but young flesh in bed.

11. Old fish, old oil and an old friend are the best. 1678: Ray, 41. Cf. C.

12. Old habits die hard. 1758: B. Franklin, in *London Chronicle*, 26–28 Dec., 632, I hear the reader say, Habits are hard to break, and those ... accustomed to idleness or extravagance do not easily change their manners. 1792: J. Belknap, *Foresters*, ix, Old habits are not easily broken,. 1944: 'H. Talbot', *The Rim of the Pit*, xv, 'Miss Daventry ... started to run. Naturally I ran after her.' Rogan smiled. 'Old habits dies hard.'

13. Old Johnny. 1911: A. S. Cooke, *Off Beaten Track in Sussex*, 285, Ague is also referred to in the phrase, 'Old Johnny has been running his fingers down my back',

14. Old lad. *See* **Devil.**

15. Old muckhills will bloom. 1678: Ray, 77.

16. Old Poacher. *See* **Poacher.**

17. Old porridge is sooner heated than new made. 1670: Ray, 47, Old pottage, etc.1732: Fuller, 3724 ['warmed' for 'heated']. Cf. **Broth** (3).

18. Old praise dies unless you feed it. 1640: Herbert, *Jac. Prudentum.*

19. Old reckonings make new quarrels. 1611: Cotgrave, s.v. 'Dispute', Old accompts breed new differences. 1732: Fuller, 3725.

20. Old sin makes new shame, *c.*1300: *Havelok,* l. 2461. *c.*1390: Gower, *Conf. Amantis,* bk iii l. 2033, Men sein, 'Old senne newe schame'. *c.*1470: Hardyng, *Chron.,* can. 114, st. 18, Thus synnes olde make shames come ful newe. 1578: Florio, *First Fruites,* fo. 32, Old sinne and new penaunce. 1611: Cotgrave, s.v. 'Honte', Old sinne inflicts new shame. 1666: Torriano, *Piazza Univ.,* 197, An old sin, new repentance.

21. Old sins cast long shadows. 1638: Suckling: *Auglara,* v in *Plays* (1971), 110, Our sins, like to our shadowes, When our day is in its glorie scarce appear: Towards our evening how great and monstrous they are. 1924: D. Vane, *Scar,* xxiii, 'You don't look well ... No fresh worry, I hope.' 'No,' wearily. 'Only old sins have long shadows.'

22. Old soldiers never die (they simply fade away). 1920: J. Foley, (song title) *Old soldiers never die.* 1933: F. Richards, *Old Soldiers never Die,* xxviii, We generlly wound up our evenings with the old song, set to the tune of a well-known hymn, 'Old soldiers never die, they simply fade away'. *See also* **Old** A (b) 8.

23. Old sores are hardly cured. 1509: Barclay, *Ship of Fools,* i 164 (1874), In olde sores is grettest ieopardye. 1670: Ray, 19, It's ill healing an old sore. 1732: Fuller, 3727.

24. Old thanks pay not for a new debt. Ibid., No. 3728.

25. Old tree. *See* **Remove.**

26. Old vessels must leak. 1666: Torriano, *Piazza Univ.,* 163. 1732: Fuller, 3729.

27. Out of old fields comes new corn, *c.*1390: Chaucer, *Parl. of Foules,* l. 22, For out of olde feldes, as men seith, Cometh al this newe corn fro yeer to yere.

28. The old withy–tree would have a new gate hung at it. 1732: Fuller, 4691.

29. To bring an old house over one's head = To get into trouble. 1576: Gascoigne, in *Works,* ii 548 (Cunliffe). My boye (qd he) who badd me be so bolde, As for to plucke an olde house on thy hedd? 1607: Dekker and Webster, *Westw. Hoe,* V, Well do so ... and bring an old house ouer your heads if you do. 1687: Sedley, *Bellamira,* II, She may be a person of quality, and you may bring an old house upon your head. 1758–67: Sterne, *Trist. Shandy,* ii ch xvii, If, in our communion, sir, a man was to insult an apostle ... he would have an old house over his head. 1907: De Morgan, *Alice-for-Short,* ch xxxviii, Papa observes in an undertone to Dr Fludyer that he has brought an old house about his ears.

30. To throw an old shoe after one – for luck. 1546: Heywood, *Proverbs,* Pt I ch ix, Nowe for good lucke, cast an olde shoe after mee. 1621: Brathwait, *Natures Embassie,* 204 (1877), One should haue throwne an old shoo after thee. 1665: R. Howard, *Surprisal,* III vii, I shall need nothing now but an old shoe cast after me. 1754: Berthelson, *Eng.-Danish Dict.,* s.v. 'Shoe'. 1842: Tennyson, *Will Waterproof,* And, wheresoe'er thou move, good luck Shall fling her old shoe after.

Older the more covetous, The. 1655: Fuller, *Church Hist.,* bk iv §iii (42). 1659: in *Harl. Miscell.,* iv 311 (1745).

Older the wiser, The. 1639: Clarke, 267. 1683: White-Kennett, tr. Erasmus' *Praise of Folly,* 17 (8th ed.), Contrary to the proverb of *older and wiser,* the more ancient they grow, the more fools they are. 1707: tr. Aleman's *Guzman,* ii 339. If I did not grow wiser as I grew older.

Older the worse, The. 1639: Clarke, 84, The older the worse, like my old shooes. 1732: Fuller, 4693, The older a fool is, the worse he is.

Oldham. *See* quot. 1869: Hazlitt, 233, In Oldham brewis wet and warm, and Rochdale puddings there's no harm. Higson's *MSS. Coll.,* 212.

Olive. *Call me not an olive till thou see me gathered.* 1640: Herbert, *Jac. Prudentum.*

Oliver's Mount. *See* quot. 1878: *Folk-Lore Record,* i 169, When Oliver's Mount puts on his hat, Scarborough town wul pay for that.

Omelette without breaking eggs, you can't make an. Mr A. B. Cheales, in his *Proverbial Folk-Lore,* p. 131 (1875), fathers this saying on

Robespierre. 1859: Gen. P. Thompson, *Audi Alt.* II xc 65 (OED), We are walking upon eggs, and whether we tread East or tread West, the omelet will not be made without the breaking of some. 1894: R.L.S., *St Ives*, ch viii, 'My dear Miss Flora, you cannot make an omelette without breaking eggs,' said I. 1922: Weyman, *Ovington's Bank*, ch xix, But it could not be helped. Without breaking eggs one could not make omelettes.

Once a captain always a captain. 1831: Peacock, *Crotchet Castle*, ch ix. 1838: Mrs Bray, *Trad. of Devon*, iii 239 [cited as 'the old proverb'].

Once a knave and ever a knave. 1659: Howell, 6. 1672: Walker, *Paroem.*, 49, Once a knave and never an honest man.

Once a man twice a child. *See* **Old, A** (*b*) (15).

Once a whore and ever a whore. 1613: H. Parrot, *Laquei Ridiculosi*, bk ii epi. 121. 1659: Howell, 15. 1663: Killigrew, *Thomaso*, Pt I II iv. 1670: Ray, 155. 1703: in *Harl. Miscell.*, v 432 (1745). 1754: *World*, No. 57.

Once a wood. *See* **Pilling Moss.**

Once a year a man may say, On his conscience. 1640: Herbert, *Jac. Prudentum.*

Once an use and ever a custom. 1605: Camden, *Remains*, 330 (1870). 1670: Ray, 153. 1732: Fuller, 3733, Once in use, and ever after a custom.

Once and use it not. 1678: Ray, 263.

Once at a Coronation. Ibid., 263. Once at a wedding. Ibid., 263 and 346, I never see't but once and that was at a wedding.

Once bitten twice shy. [1484: Caxton, *Aesope*, ii 203 (Jacobs), And therfore he that hath ben ones begyled by somme other ought to kepe hym wel fro the same.] 1894: Northall, *Folk Phrases*, 20 (E.D.S.), Once bitten, twice shy. 1920: Conrad, *The Rescue*, Pt III ch ix 168.

Once deceives is ever suspected, He that 1640: Herbert, *Jac. Prudentum.*

Once done is never to be undone, What is. *c.*1450: *King Ponthus* in *Publications of the Modern Language Association of America* (1897), XII, 107, The thynges that be doone may not be undoone. 1546: J. Heywood, *Dialogue of Proverbs*, I x, Things done, can not be undoone. 1601: Yarington, *Two Trag. in One*, I iii, in Bullen, *Old Plays*, iv. 23, Whats done already cannot be undone. 1605–6: Shakespeare, *Macbeth*, III ii,

Things without all remedy should be without regard. What's done is done. *Ibid.* v i, What's done cannot be undone. 1609: *Man in the Moone*, 41 (Percy S.), That which is done cannot be undone. Before 1704: T. Brown, *Works*, i 238 (1760). 1836: Marryat, *Easy*, ch xxxii, I felt much the same; but what's done cannot be undone. Cf. **Thing** (6).

Once in seven years. *See* quot. 1733: Tull, *Horse-hoing Husb.*, Pref., v, Contrary to the proverb that says, That once in seven years, the worst husbands [farmers] have the best corn.

Once in ten years one man hath need of another. 1578: Florio, *First Fruites*, fo. 33. 1666: Torriano, *Piazza Univ.*, 26, Every ten years, one hath need of another. 1732: Fuller, 3732.

Once nought twice somewhat = A first offence counts for nothing. 1889: *Folk-Lore Journal*, vii 295, Once nowt, twice summat.

Once out and always out. 1678: Ray, 77.

Once paid never craved. 1639: Clarke, 182. 1678: Ray, 188.

Once poor. *See* quot. 1618: W. Lawson, *New Orchard and Garden*, 5 (1676), 'Tis with grounds in this case, as it is with men ... Much will have more: and, *Once poor, seldome or never rich.*

Once warned twice armed. 1581: T. Howell, *Devises*, 15 (1906). Cf. **Forewarned.**

One and none is all one. 1670: Ray, 20. Cf. **One is no number.**

One and thirty, He is = He is drunk. 1678: Ray, 87.

One beats the bush. *See* **Beat** (5).

One beggar. *See* **Beggar** (11) and (12).

One body is no body. 1639: Clarke, 44. Cf. **One is no number.**

One bush. *See* quote. 1583: Melbancke, *Philotinus*, sig. L4, One bushe, saith the proverbe, can not harbour two Robin redbreasts. 1586: G. Whitney, *Emblems*, 55, One groane maie not two redbreastes serve. Before 1634: Chapman, *Alphonsus*, I i, Una arbusta non alit duos erithraeos.

One business begets another. 1528: More, *Works*, p. 105, col. 1 (1557), It is an olde said saw, that one busynes begetteth and bryngeth forth another.

One cannot, another can, What. 1630: Davenant, *Cruel Brother*, I

One can't help many, but many can help one. 1917: Bridge, *Cheshire Proverbs*, 99.

One cherry tree. *See* **Cherry** (4).

One child. *See* quot. 1864: 'Cornish Proverbs', in *N.&Q.*, 3rd ser, v 209, With one child you may walk, with two you may ride; When you have three at home you must bide. Cf. **Children** (19).

One cloud is enough to eclipse all the sun. 1732: Fuller, 3743.

One coat, He that has, cannot lend it. Ibid., No. 2135.

One day is sometimes better than a whole year. [*c.*1290: in Wright, *Pol. Songs John to Edw. II*, 176 (Camden S.), Saepe dat una dies quod totus denegat annus.] 1481: Caxton, *Reynard*, 66 (Arber), Oftymes one day is better than somtyme an hole yere. 1631: Mabbe, *Celestina*, 248 (T.T.), Of more worth is one day of a wise man then the whole life of a foole. 1846: Denham, *Proverbs*, 4 (Percy S.).

One day of pleasure is worth two of sorrow. 1732: Fuller, 3746.

One day of respite. *See* quot. *c.*1534: Berners, *Huon*, 128 (E.E.T.S.), It is a commen sayeng, one day of respite is worth c. yere [of endurance].

One devil. *See* **Devil** (32).

One dog, one bull = fair play. 1879: Jackson, *Shropsh. Word-Book*, 309. 1883: Burne, *Shropsh. Folk-Lore*, 447, Only one dog was allowed to be 'loosed' on the bull at a time; hence arose a proverbial saying, 'One dog, one bull', i.e. fair play: now applied in the Collieries to any kind of fight or fray.

One door shuts, another opens, When. 1586: D. Rowland, tr. *Lazarillo*, 32 (1924), This proverbe was fulfild, when one doore is shut the other openeth. 1612: Shelton, *Quixote*, Pt I bk iii ch vii, Where one door is shut another is opened. 1710: S. Palmer, *Moral Essays on Proverbs*, 49. 1869: Spurgeon, *John Ploughman*, ch v, If one door should be shut, God will open another. 1921: R. L. Gales, *Old-World Essays*, 244.

One doth the scathe [harm], and another hath the scorn. 1611: Cotgrave, s.v. 'Faire'. 1670: Ray, 20. 1732: Fuller, 6344, One doth harm, and another bears the blame.

One ear and out at the other, In at. [Nec quae dicentur superfluent aures. – Quintilian, II v 13.] *c.*1374: Chaucer, *Troylus*, bk iv 1. 434, But Troilus ... Tok litel hede of al that ever he mente; Oon ere it herde, at the other out it

wente. *c.*1500: in Hazlitt, *Early Pop. Poetry*, i 229. 1552: Latimer, *Works*, ii 87 (P.S.). *c.*1610: Harington, *Briefe View of Church*, 145 (1653). 1640: *Ar't asleepe Husband?*, Frontispiece, But she might full as well her lecture smother, For ent'ring one eare, it goes out at t'other. 1750: Smollett, *Gil Blas*, iii 182, A world of thanks, which would only have entered at one ear and gone out at the other, had he not assured me ... 1855: Gaskell, *North and South*, ch xxviii 1909: Hudson, *A foot in England*, ch xxii.

One enemy is too much. 1640: Herbert, *Jac. Prudentum*. 1855: Bohn, 468, One enemy is too much for a man in a great post, and a hundred friends are too few.

One extreme produces another. 1748: Richardson, *Clarissa*, vi 213 (1785).

One eye. 1. Better to have one eye than be blind altogether. 1670: Ray, 8. 1736: Bailey, *Dict.*, s.v. 'Better', Better one eye than quite blind.

2. He that has but one eye, had need look well to that. 1611: Cotgrave, s.v. 'Garder', He that hath but one eye had need make much of it, had best looke well to it. 1732: Fuller, 2136.

3. He that hath but one eye, sees the better for it. 1639: Clarke, 44. 1639: *Conceits, Clinches, etc.*, No. 113, Hee that hath but one eye is more like to hit the marke he aimes at then another, because he hath a monstrous sight. [This is a lame explanation of an absurd saying.] 1678: Ray, 134 ... a ridiculous saying.

One eye-witness is better than ten ear-witnesses. [Pluris est oculatus testis unus quam auriti decem. – Plautus, *Truc.*, II vi 8.] 1539: Taverner, *Proverbs*, fo. 43 [with 'of more value' for 'better']. 1582: Robinson, tr. *Assertion of K. Arthur*, 39 (E.E.T.S.), Of more force standes eye witnesse one, Than ten eare witnesses among. 1681: Robertson, *Phraseol. Generalis*, 567. 1732: Fuller, 3750 ['hearsays' for 'ear–witnesses'].

One fair day assureth not a good summer. 1548: Hall, *Chron.*, 42 (1809).

One fair day in winter makes not birds merry. 1640: Herbert, *Jac. Prudentum*.

One false knave accuseth another. 1639: Clarke, 79.

One father is more than a hundred school-masters. 1640: Herbert, *Jac. Prudentum*.

One fault (they say) doth but one pardon need. 1615: Wither, *A Satyre*, l. 720.

One favour qualifies for another. 1732: Fuller, No 3751. Cf. **One kindness.**

One flower makes no garland. 1640: Herbert, *Jac. Prudentum.* 1670: Ray, 10.

One fool. *See* **Fool** (87) and (88).

One foot in the grave. [One foot in Charon's boat. – Lucian, *Apol.*, i.] 1566: Painter, *Pal. of Pleasure*, ii 109 (Jacobs), To visite him, who hath one of his feet alreadie within the graue. 1592: Warner, *Albion's Eng.*, bk ix ch 47, Old doting foole, one foote in graue. *c.*1620: B.&F., *Little Fr. Lawyer*, I i, You that already Have one foot in the grave. 1694: *Terence made English*, 196. 1707: *Spanish Bawd*, III i. 1822: Peacock, *Maid Marian*, ch xiii, What, in the devil's, name, can you want with a young wife, who have one foot in flannels, and the other in the grave?

One foot in the straw, He that hath, hath another in the spittle [hospital]. 1640: Herbert, *Jac. Prudentum.*

One foot is better than two crutches. Ibid.

One for sorrow, two for joy … *See* **Magpie** (2).

One gate. *See* **One Yate.**

One God, no more, but friends good store. 1639: Clarke, 26. 1670: Ray, 94. 1732: Fuller, 6104.

One good forewit is worth two after–wits. 1546: Heywood, *Proverbs*, Pt I ch viii. 1633: Draxe, 169.

One good head is better than an hundred strong hands. 1732: Fuller, 3753.

One good turn deserves (or **asks,** or **requires**) **another.** *c.*1400: in *Bulletin of John Rylands Library* (1930), XIV 92, O [one] good turne asket another. 1546: Heywood, *Proverbs*, Pt I ch xi ['asketh']. *c.*1610: Rowlands, *More Knaues Yet?*, 17 (Hunt.Cl.) ['asketh']. 1638: Randolph, *Amyntas*, V vi ['deserves']. 1670: Cotton, *Scarronides*, bk iv. ['requires']. 1703: Farquhar, *Twin-Rivals*, V iii. 1777: Murphy, *Know your own Mind*, I. 1818: Scott, *Heart of Midl.*, ch xxx. 1894: R.L.S., *St Ives*, ch i [the last four all have 'deserves']. Cf. **One shrewd turn.**

One good wife. *See* quots. 1620: Shelton, *Quixote*, Pt II ch xxii, It was an opinion of I know not what sage man, that there was but one good woman in the world, and his advice was, that every man should think, that was married, that his wife was she. 1707: Dunton, *Athenian Sport*, 333, 'Tis a saying, there is but one good wife in the world, and every man enjoys her. 1738:

Swift, *Polite Convers.*, Dial. I, They say, that every married man should believe there's but one good wife in the world, and that's his own. 1869: Spurgeon, *John Ploughman*, ch xvii.; If there is only one good wife in England, I am the man who put the ring on her finger. Cf. **One shrew;** and **One pretty child.**

One grain fills not a sack, but helps his fellows. 1640: Herbert, *Jac. Prudentum.* 1659: Howell, *Proverbs: Span.Eng.*, 17.

One grief drives out another; and sorrow expelleth sorrow. 1631: Mabbe, *Celestina*, 280 (T.T.).

One had as good be nibbled to death by ducks, or pecked to death by a hen. 1678: Ray, 240.

One hair of a woman draws more than a team of oxen. 1591: Florio, *Second Frutes*, 183, Ten teemes of oxen draw much lesse, Than doth one haire of Helens tresse. 1647: Howell, *Letters*, bk ii No. iv, One hair of a woman can draw more than a hundred pair of oxen. 1712: Pope, *Rape of Lock*, ii 28, And beauty draws us with a single hair. 1732: Fuller, 3757. 1928: *Bystander*, 28 March, p. 624, col. 1, One hair of a woman can draw more than a hundred pair of oxen. Cf. **Beauty** (2).

One hand claweth another. 1567: Jewel. *Defence of Apol.*, Pt IV 692 (P.S.), The proverb is common: 'One hand daweth another'. The Pope was advanced by Pipine; and Pipine was likewise advanced by the Pope.

One hand for yourself and one for the ship. This nautical saying appears in many variant forms, all with the same basic meaning that one should always devote half one's attention to one's own interests or safety. 1799: *Port Folio* (Philadelphia 1812), VII 130, Did I not tell you never to fill both hands at once. Always keep one hand for the owners, and one for yourself. 1902: B. Lubbock, *Round the Horn*, 58, The old rule on a yard is, 'one hand for yourself and one for the ship', which means, hold on with one hand and work with the other.

One hand washeth the other, and both the face. [Manus manum lavat. – Seneca, *Apoc.*, 9, *fin.*] 1578: Florio, *First Fruites*, fo. 34. 1580: Lyly, *Euphues*, 221 (Arber). 1607: Middleton, *Phoenix*, I i, 'Tis through the world, this hand will rub the other. 1640: Herbert, *Jac. Prudentum.* 1732: Fuller, 3759, One hand may wash the other, but both the face.

One hand will not clasp. 1875: A. B. Cheales, *Proverb. Folk-Lore*, 91.

One head for the reckoning. *See* quot. 1573: *New Custom*, III i, I could have tarried longer there [at the tavern] with a good will, But, as the proverb saith, it is good to keep still One head for the reckoning, both sober and wise.

One hog. *See* quot. 1670: Ray, 20, He who hath but one hog, makes him fat, and he who hath but one son makes him a fool. 1732: Fuller, 2138 [as in 1670].

One honest man is worth two rogues. 1855: Kingsley, *West. Ho!*, ch xx.

One honest man scares twenty thieves. *c.*1770: in *Roxb. Ballads*, vii 645 (B.S.) [quoted as a 'saying of old'].

One hour today is worth two tomorrow. 1732: Fuller, 3761.

One hour's sleep. *See* **Sleep**, *subs.* (2).

One ill turn. *See* **One shrewd turn.**

One ill weed mars a whole pot of pottage. 1579: Lyly, *Euphues*, 39 (Arber), One leafe of Colloquintida marreth and spoyleth the whole pot of porredge. 1605: Camden, *Remains*, 329 (1870). 1606: in *Antiq. Repertory*, i 193 (1807), But last of all, to marre all the pottage with one filthy weede, to mar this good prayer with an il conclusion … 1670: Ray, 154.

One ill word asks another. 1546: Heywood, *Proverbs*, Pt I ch ix. 1591: Harington, *Orl. Furioso*, bk xxvi st. 77, Thus one ill word another doth draw on. 1670: Ray, 30. 1685: *Mother Bunch's Closet, etc.*, 15 (Gomme, 1885), One evil word brings in another.

One is a play, and two is a gay [toy]. 1864: 'Cornish Proverbs', in *N.&Q.*, 3rd ser, v 208. 1880: Courtney, *W. Cornwall Words*, 24 (E.D.S.).

One is no number. 1539: Taverner, *Proverbs*, fo. 17, One man no man. 1586: G. Whitney, *Emblems*, 66, The prouerbe saieth, one man is deemed none. 1598: Marlowe, *Hero and L.*, sest. v, For one no number is. 1621: Brathwait, *Natures Embassie*, 268 (1877), Number can ne're consist of lesse then two. 1681: Robertson, *Phraseol. Generalis*, 953, One's as good as none. 1823: Moor, *Suffolk Words*, 236, An old Norfolk and Suffolk saw may be given here – 'One is none – tew is some – three is a sort – four is a mort [Lot]'. 1843: Halliwell, *Nursery Rhymes*, 162, One's none; Two's some, etc. Cf. **One and none;** and **One body.**

One it wise, two an happy, Where. 1710: S. Palmer, *Moral Essays on Proverbs*, 338.

One kindness is the price of another. 1645: Howell, *Letters*, bk i § ii No. ix, Sir, Thanks for one courtesy is a good usher to bring on another. 1732: Fuller, 3764. Cf. **One favour.**

One knock on the iron, and two on the anvil, He gives. Ibid., No. 1849.

One lie makes many. 1533: Udall, *Flowers out of Terence*, fo. 25, One falshode or subtiltie bringeth in an other. 1732: Fuller, 3766, One lie calls for many.

One lordship is worth all his manners. A punning saying – 'manors'. 1670: Ray, 185.

One love expels another. 1666: Torriano, *Piazza Univ.*, 10.

One man is worth a hundred and a hundred is not worth one. 1578: Florio, *First Fruites*, fo. 32. 1629: *Book of Meery Riddles*, Prov. 42.

One man's breath, another's death. 1639: Clarke, 253. 1670: Ray, 128. 1732: Fuller, 6343 [with 'is' after 'breath'].

One man's fault is another man's lesson. 1855: Bonn, 469.

One man's meat. *See* **Meat** (9).

One man's will is another man's wit. 1647: *Countrym. New Commonwealth*, 14.

One mend-fault is worth twenty spy-faults. 1882: Mrs Chamberlain, *W. Worcs. Words*, 39 (E.D.S.). 1901: F. E. Taylor, *Lancs Sayings*, 9, One mend-fawt's wo'th a score o' find-fawts.

One month's cheer is better than a churl's whole life. 1546: Heywood, *Proverbs*, Pt II ch vii. 1633: Draxe, 129.

One mouth doth nothing without another. 1640: Herbert, *Jac. Prudentum.*

One mule scrubs another. [Mutuum muli scabant – Auson., *Idyll.*, xii Praef. monos.] 1638: Randolph, *Muses' Looking-Glass*, III iv. 1666: Torriano, *Piazza Univ.*, 15, Asses scratch one another. 1738: Swift, *Polite Convers.*, Dial. III, It looked like two asses scrubbing one another.

One nail drives out another. Before 1225: *Ancren R.*, 404 (Morton), Vor, al so as on neil driueth ut then otherne … 1387: Trevisa, tr. Higden (Rolls Ser.), vii 25, thanne the kyng drof out on nayle with another. *c.*1570: *Marr. of Wit and Science*, I, Much like the nail, that last came in, and drives the former out. 1607: Tourneur, *Revenger's Trag.*, IV i, Slaves are but nails to drive out one another. 1658: R. Brome, *Love-*

sick Court, V i, Variety of objects Like nails abandon one another. 1725: Bailey, tr. Erasmus' *Colloq.*, 492. 1781: T. Francklin, *Lucian's Works*, ii 136, And thus, according to the old adage, drive out one nail by another. 1852: FitzGerald, *Polonius*, 129 (1903).

One of his hands is unwilling to wash the other for nothing. 1732: Fuller, 3787.

One of these days is none of these days. 1855: Bohn, 470.

One of those gentle ones, that will use the devil himself with courtesy. Ibid., 470.

One pair of ears draws dry a hundred tongues. 1640: Herbert, *Jac. Prudentum*.

One pair of legs is worth two pairs of hands. *c.*1565: Still, *Gammer Gurton*, IV ii, If one pair of legs had not bene worth two paire of hands … 1597: Harvey, *Works*, iii 52 (Grosart). 1600: *Weakest goeth to the Wall*, I ii ['running' before 'legs', and 'working' before 'hands']. 1611: Coryat, *Crudities*, i 35 (1905). 1688: in *Bagford Ballads*, i 375 (B.S.) ['heels' for 'legs']. 1712: Motteux, *Quixote*, Pt II ch lxvii [as in 1688]. 1817: Scott, *Rob Roy*, ch xxv, Take the bent, Mr Rashleigh. Make ae pair o' legs worth twa pair o' hands.

One poison drives out another. 1567: G. Fenton, *Bandello*, ii 218 (T.T.). 1591: Harington, *Orl. Furioso*, bk xxv st. 1, Ev'n as one poyson doth another heale. 1659: Howell, *Proverbs: Brit.-Eng.*, 34, One poyson expels another.

One pretty child. *See* quot. 1917: Bridge, *Cheshire Proverbs*, 119, There's only one pretty child in the world, and every mother has it. Cf. **One good wife**; and **One threw.**

One saddle is enough for one horse. 1732: Fuller, 3791.

One shoe win not fit all feet. 1672: Walker, *Paroem.*, 47, To make one shoe serve for all feet. 1690: *New Dict. Canting Crew*, sig. L2.

One shoulder of mutton drives down another. 1611: Cotgrave, s.v. 'Appetit' ['drawes' for 'drives']. 1738: Swift, *Polite Convers.*, Dial. II. 1811: J. Austen, *Sense and Sens.*, ch xxx. 1840: Barham, *Ing. Legends*, Introd. to 'Look at the Clock'.

One shrew. *See* quots. 1528: More, in *Works*, p. 233, col. 1 (1557), He sayth plainly yt there is but one shrewde wyfe in the worlde; but he sayth in dede that eueri man weneth he hath her. 1588:

Cogan, *Haven of Health*, 252 (1612), Howbeit (as I haue heard say) there is but one shrew in all the world, but euery man thinketh he hath yt one. Cf. **One good wife**; and **One pretty child.**

One shrewd turn asks another. 1509: Barclay, *Ship of Fools*, ii 38 (1874), One yll turne requyreth another be thou sure. 1591: Harington, *Orl. Furioso*, bk viii st. 45, For one ill turne alone is seldome done. 1602: Chamberlain, *Letters*, 126 (Camden S.), One shrewd turne seldome comes alone. 1732: Fuller, 3794. Cf. **One good turn.**

One slumber invites another. 1611: Cotgrave, s.v. 'Attraire' ['drawes on' for 'invites']. 1640: Herbert, *Jac. Prudentum* ['finds' for 'invites']. 1670: Ray, 20.

One sows. *See* **Sow**, *verb* (10).

One step at a time. 1853: C. M. Yonge, *The Heir of Redclyffe*, II 1, One step at a time is all one wants. 1901: R. Kipling, *Kim*, vi, It's beyond me. We can only walk one step at a time in this world. 1919: J. Buchan, *Mr Standfast*, I did not allow myself to think of ultimate escape … One step at a time was enough.

One's too few, three too many. 1678: Ray, 342.

One story. *See* **One tale.**

One stroke. *See* **Oak** (1).

One swallow. *See* **Swallow.**

One sword keeps another in the sheath. 1640: Herbert, *Jac. Prudentum*. 1747: Franklin, in *Works*, ii 57 (Bigelow), It is a wise and true saying, that one sword often keeps another in the scabbard. 1853: Trench, *Proverbs*, 88 (1905) [as in 1747].

One tainted sheep. *See* **Sheep** (10).

One tale is good till another is told. [μηδὲ δίκην δικάσῃς πρὶν ἂν ἀμφοῖν μῦθον ἀκούσῃς. – Cicero, *ad Att.*, vii 18.] 1593: Greene, *Works*, ii 222 (Grosart), Tush syr quoth the Marquesse, one tale is alwayes good vntil another is heard. 1617: Taylor (Water-Poet), *Works*, 3rd pagin., 83. 1662: Fuller, *Worthies*, ii 125 (1840), One story is good till another is heard. 1748: Richardson, *Clarissa*, vii 314 (1785) [as in 1662]. 1827: Hone, *Ev. Day Book*, ii 649, 'Every pot has two handles'. This means 'that one story's good till another story's told'.

One thief robs another. *c.*1510: A. Barclay, *Egloges*, 46 (Spens.S.), It is ill stealing from a thiefe. 1600: *Sir John Oldcastle*, l.1382 (Malone S.), Just the prouerb, one thiefe robs another.

1681: Robertson, *Phraseol. Generalis*, s.v. 'Thief', One thief accuseth another.

One today is worth two tomorrows. 1641: Quarles, *Enchyridion*, Cent. IV, C. xcv. 1736: Franklin, *Way to Wealth*, in *Works*, i 444 (Bigelow). 1875: Cheales, *Proverb. Folk-Lore*, 134, One today is better than ten tomorrows.

One tongue. *See* **Woman** (31).

One tongue and two ears (or **eyes**), *c.*1535: .*Dialogues of Creatures*, cclvi (1816), To euery creature longith but oon tonge and two erys; and so a man shulde suffir more with his tway erys than any man myght speke with oon tonge. 1572: T. Wilson, *Disc, upon Usury*, 211 (1925), You have twoe eares and one tongue, because you shoulde heare more than you speake. 1820: Colton, *Locon*, Pt I No. 112, Men are born with *two* eyes, but with *one* tongue, in order that they should see twice as much as they say.

One trick needs another trick to back it up. 1732: Fuller, 3801, One trick needs a great many more to make it good. 1880: Spurgeon, *Ploughman's Pictures*, 19.

One, two, or three tell you, you are an ass, put on a tail, If. 1732: Fuller, 2697.

One, two, three, four, are just half a score. 1678: Ray, 86.

One vice. *See* quots. 1581: B. Rich, *Farewell*, 197 (SH.S.), Like as we saie, one vice spilles a greate noumber of vertues. 1736: Franklin, *Way to Wealth*, in *Works*, i 446 (Bigelow), What maintains one vice, would bring up two children.

One volunteers. *See* **volunteers.**

One wedding begets another. *c.*1640: in *Roxb. Ballads*, iii 54 (B.S.), 'Tis said that one wedding produceth another. 1713: Gay, *Wife of Bath*, I

One woodcock. *See* **Woodcock.**

One word for me and two for yourself. 1854: Baker, *Northants Gloss.*, s.v. 'Word', … Said to one who is selfish under an appearance of disinterestedness.

One word in time than two afterwards, Better. 1659: Howell, *Proverbs: Brit.-Eng.*, 17. 1736: Bailey, *Dict.*, s.v. 'Better'.

One yate [gate] **for another, good fellow.** 1678: Ray, 263, They father the original of this upon a passage between one of the earls of Rutland and a country fellow. The earl, riding by himself one day, overtook a countryman, who very civilly opened him the first gate they came to, not knowing who the earl was. When they came to the next gate, the earl expecting he should have done the same again, Nay, soft, saith the countryman; one yate for another, good fellow.

One year a nurse and seven years the worse. 1678: Ray, 182. 1732: Fuller, 6377.

One year of joy. *See* quot. 1678: Ray, 63, One year of joy, another of comfort, and all the rest of content. A marriage wish. 1732: Fuller, 3806 [after 'content' – 'make the married life happy']. 1869: Spurgeon, *John Ploughman*, ch xvii [as in 1678].

One year's seed seven years' weed. 1884: H. Friend, *Flowers and Fl. Lore*, 230, If we would keep our gardens free from weeds … let us bear in mind what a Northamptonshire peasant recently told me in the following homely but expressive rhyme, which still passes current as a proverb: – 'One year's seed, Seven years' weed'. Or, as they give it in Oxfordshire: 'One year's seeding makes seven years' weeding'. 1917: Bridge, *Cheshire Proverbs*, 100.

Onion, It may serve with an. An ironical saying. 1659: Howell, 1. 1670: Ray, 214.

Onion's skin very thin, Mild winter coming in; Onion's skin thick and tough, Coming winter cold and rough. A gardener's rhyme. 1893: Inwards, *Weather Lore*, 155.

Onion. *See also* **Capon** (2); **Garlic** (1); and **Spruce.**

On the hip, To have one. *c.*1400: *Beryn*, l. 1781, p. 55 (E.E.T.S.), So within an houre or to, Beryn he had i-caughte Somwhat oppon the hipp, that Beryn had the wers. 1591: Harington, *Orl. Furioso*, bk xlvi st. 117, In fine he doth applie one speciall drift, Which was to get the pagan on the hippe. 1604: Shakespeare, *Othello*, II i, I'll have our Michael Cassio on the hip. 1681: Robertson, *Phraseol. Generalis*, 805, He has him on the hip, at an advantage in Law. 1865: Planché, *Extravag.*, v 262 (1879), Now, infidel, I have thee on the hip.

Open door may tempt a saint, An. 1659: Howell, *Proverbs: Span.-Eng.*, 16, An open gate tempts a saint. 1732: Fuller, 655.

Opens the door with an ax, He. 1813: Ray, 75.

Opera isn't over till the fat lady sings, The. Various suggestions have been advanced to account for this popular modern (and originally American) saying. The obvious explanation is that it relates to what Victor Borge called the 'die arias' of such operatic heroines as Wagner's Isolde and Brunnhilde in *Tristan und Isolde* and *Götterdämmerung* respectively. Alternatively, scholars have suggested that it derives from a particular American diva who sang 'God bless America' before ice hockey matches, from ships' boilers – which were known as 'fat ladies' and 'sang' (i.e. sounded a safety whistle) when they had built up a sufficient head of steam to proceed – or, more prosaically, from a Southern saying 'Church ain't out till the fat lady sings'. 1978: *Washington Post*, 13 June B1, The opera isn't over till the fat lady sings ... One day three years ago, Ralph Carpenter, who was then Texas Tech's sports information director, declared to the press box contingent in Austin, 'The rodeo ain't over till the bull riders ride '. Stirred to top that deep insight, San Antonio sports editor Dan Cook countered with, 'The opera ain't over till the fat lady sings'.

Opinion rules the world. 1615: Markham, *Eng. Housewife*, 70 (1675), Yet it is but opinion, and that must be the worlds master alwayes. 1647: Howell, *Letters*, bk ii No. xxxix, Opinion can do much, and indeed she is that great lady which rules the world. Before 1680: Butler, *Remains*, i 241 (1759), Opinion governs all mankind.

Opinions, So many men, so many. *See* **So many heads.**

Oppenshaw. *The constable of Oppenshaw sets beggars in stocks at Manchester.* 1678: Kay, 301. 1790: Grose, *Prov. Gloss.*, s.v. 'Cheshire'. 1917: Bridge, *Cheshire' Proverbs*, 113.

Opportunity. *See* quot. 1660: Howell, *Parly of Beasts*, 72, Opportunity is the best moment in the whole extension of time. 1869: Hazlitt, 311, Opportunity is the cream of time.

Opportunity is whoredom's bawd. 1605: Camden, *Remains*, 329 (1870).

Opportunity, makes the thief. *c.*1220: *Hali Meidenhad*, 17 (E.E.T.S.), Man seith that eise maketh theof. 1387: Trevisa, tr. Higden, vii 379 (Rolls Ser.), I see wel that ese maketh the to synne. *c.*1440: Anon., tr. Higden, vii 379 (Rolls Ser.), Me thenke that oportunite maketh a thefe. 1591: Florio, *Second Frutes*, 169, Opportunity makes a man committ larcenie. 1611: Cotgrave, s.v. 'Coffre'. 1700: T. Brown, etc., *Scarron*, ii 182 (1892), Yet do I know full well that opportunity makes a thief. 1754: Berthelson, *Eng.-Danish Dict.*, s.v. 'Opportunity'. 1834–7:

Southey, *Doctor*, ch cv, Opportunity, which makes thieves, makes lovers also. 1925: *Sphere*, 14 Nov., p. 197, col. 1.

Opportunity never knocks twice at any man's door. 1567: G. Fenton, *bandello*, 216, Fortune once in the course of our life, dothe put into our handes the offer of a goo torne. 1891: J. J. Ingalls, *Opportunity* in *Truth* (NY) 19 Feb., 17, I [Opportunity] knock unbidden once at every gate! If sleeping, wake: if feasting, rise before I turn away…[for] I return no more. 1941: 'P. Wentworth', *Unlawful Occasions*, xxiv, It was an opportunity with a capital O, and if she threw it away it would never come back again. Opportunity never knocks twice at any man's door. *See also* **Fortune knocks once at least at every man's gate.**

Orchard is his shambles, His. 1639: Clarke, 50.

Orts. *See* **Make** (20).

Ossing comes to bossing = Effort leads to success. 15th cent. MS., Digby, 52, lf. 28, quoted in *N. &Q.*, 10th ser, vii 69, Ossyng comys to bossyng: Vulgus opinatur quod postmodum verificatur. 1691: Ray, *Words not Generally Used*, 58 (E.D.S.) [Cheshire]. 1917: Bridge, *Cheshire Proverbs*, 101.

Other people's fires. *See* quot. 1692: L'Estrange, *Aesop*, Life, 13 (3rd ed.), There's an old saying; *What have we to do to quench other peoples fires?* And I'll e'en keep myself clear of other peoples matters.

Other side of the road always looks cleanest, The. 1852: FitzGerald, *Polonius*, 20 (1903).

Ounce of debt will not pay a pound of care, An. 1599: Porter, *Two Angry Women*, in Hazlitt, *Old Plays*, vii 308.

Ounce of discretion is worth a pound of learning, An. 1630: T. Adams, *Works*, 91. 1670: Ray, 79 ['wit' for 'learning'].

Ounce of fortune is worth a pound of forecast, An. 1611: Cotgrave, s.v. 'Sagesse', An ounce of luck excels a pound of wit. 1732: Fuller, 657.

Ounce of good fortune is worth a pound of discretion, An. 1672: Walker, *Paroem.*, 42.

Ounce of mirth is worth a pound of sorrow, An. 1619: B. Rich, *Irish Hubbub*, 4, A little mirth (they say) is worth a great deale of sorrow. 1734: Carey, *Chronon.*, II iv.

Ounce of mother-wit is worth a pound of clergy [learning], **An.** 1690: *New Dict. Canting Crew*, sig. C7. 1712: Addison, *Spectator*, No.

464, There is a saying among the Scotch, that an ounce of mother is worth a pound of clergy. 1827: Hone, *Table-Book*, 285 ['learning' for 'clergy']. 1880: A. Dobson, in *Poet. Works*, 444 (1923), This was, as Hamlet says, 'a hit'; Clergy was posed by Mother–wit.

Ounce of prudence is worth a pound of gold, An. 1748: Smollett, *Rod. Random*, ch xv.

Ounce of state requires a pound of gold, An. 1629: *Book of Meery Riddles*, Prov. 26.

Ounce of wit that's bought is worth a pound that's taught, An. 1732: Fuller, 6495. Cf. **Wit** (2) and (12).

Out at elbows. 1590: Nashe, *Almond for a Parrot*, 26 (1846), Your witte wilbe welny worn thredbare, and your banquerout inuention cleane out at the elbowes. 1685: S. Wesley, *Maggots*, To the Reader, Who knows but … my stockings happen to be a little out at elbows. 1700: Ward, *London Spy*, 163 (1924), They are one day very richly drest, and perhaps out at elbows the next. 1828: Carr, *Craven Dialect*, i 129, 'Hee's gitten his land out at elbows'; that is, his estate is mortgaged. 1875: Smiles, *Thrift*, 273, He [Steele] died out at elbows on his wife's little property in Wales.

Outface with a card of ten, To. *See* 1847 quot. Before 1529: Skelton, *Bowge of Courte*, l. 315, Fyrste pycke a quarell, and fall oute with hym then, And soo outface hym with a carde of ten. *c.*1542: Brinklow, *Complaynt*, 45 (E.E.T.S.), Eyther he shal haue fauor for his masters sake, or els bragg it out with a carde of x. 1594: Shakespeare, *Tam. of Shrew*, II, Yet I have faced it with a card of ten. 1633: *Dux Grammaticus*, quoted in *N.&Q.*, 5th ser, viii 165, I set very little or nought by him that cannot face out his ware with a card of ten. 1847: Halliwell, *Dict.*, s.v. 'Face', Face. A term at the game of Primero, to stand boldly upon a card … Whence came the phrase *to face it with a card of ten*, to face anything out by sheer impudence.

Out of debt grows rich, He that gets. 1611: Cotgrave, s.v. 'Acquiter'. 1657: Gurnall, *Christian in Armour*, Pt II V 15, ch v p. 129 (1679).

Out of debt out of danger. 1639: Clarke, 82, Out of debt and deadly danger. 1667: Peacham, *Worth of Penny*, in Arber, *Garner*, vi 256 (1883). 1710: S. Palmer, *Moral Essays on Proverbs*, 132. 1869: Spurgeon, *John Ploughman*, ch xii.

Out of debt out of deadly sin. 1605: Camden, *Remains*, 330 (1870).

Out of door out of debt. Somerset. 1678: Ray, 354 … Spoken of one that pays not when once gone.

Out of God's blessing into the warm sun = From better to worse. 1540: Palsgrave, *Acolastus*, sig. H3, To leappe out of the halle into the kytchyn, or out of Chryst's blessynge in to a warme sonne. 1546: Heywood, *Proverbs*, Pt II ch v. 1579: Lyly, *Euphues*, 196 (Arber), Therefore if thou wilt follow my advice … than thou shalt come out of a warme sunne into Gods blessing. 1593: G. Harvey, in *Works*, ii 207 (Grosart), What reason hath Zeale to fly from God's blessing into a warm sunne. *c.*1605: Shakespeare, *Lear*, II ii [The editor of the 'Temple' Shakespeare notes on this passage: 'Prof. Skeat suggests to me that the proverb refers to the haste of the congregation to leave the shelter of the church, immediately after the priest's benediction, running from God's blessing into the warm sun. This explanation seems by far the best that has been suggested'.] 1642: Howell, *Forreine Travell*, 37 (Arber). 1712: Motteux, *Quixote*, Pt I bk iii ch iv. [Motteux takes the saying to mean 'out of the frying pan into the fire' – but the earlier quotations show clearly that this is wrong.] 1846–59: *Denham Tracts*, i 77 (F.L.S.). [This gives the same misinterpretation as in the 1712 reference.]

Out of gunshot. 1551: Robinson, tr. *Utopia*, 26 (Arber), Beyng them selues in the meane season sauffe, and as sayeth the prouerbe, oute of all daunger of gonneshotte. 1672: Walker, *Paroem.*, 25, Out of reach of gunshot. 1678: Ray, 249.

Out of sight out of mind. *c.*1270: *Prov. of Alfred*, in *Old Eng. Miscell.* 134 (Morris, E.E.T.S.), For he that is ute bi-loken [shut out = absent] he is inne sone forgeten. *c.*1320: in *Reliq. Antiquae*, i 114 (1841), 'Fer from eye, fer from herte', Quoth Hendyng. *c.*1386: Chaucer, *Miller's Tale*, l. 206, Ful sooth is this proverbe, it is no lye, Men seyn right thus, 'alwey the nye slye Maketh the ferre leve to be looth'. 1546: Heywood, *Proverbs*, Pt I ch iii. *c.*1570: *Marr. of Wit and Science*, V i. 1697: Vanbrugh, *Esop*, I i. 1711: *Spectator*, No. 77. 1791: Boswell, *Letters*, ii 434 (Tinker). 1863: Kingsley, *Water Babies*, ch i. Cf. **Eye** (19); **Long absent;** and **Seldom seen.**

Out of the North an ill comes forth. 1649: in *Harl. Miscell.*, vii 199 (1746) [quoted as 'the old saying'].

Out of the wood, Don't shout (*or* halloo) till you are. [μήπω μέγ' εἴπῃς πρὶν τελευτήσαντ' ἴδῃς. – Sophocles, in Cicero, *ad Att.*, iv 8 *a* 1.] 1770: B. Franklin, *Papers* (1973), XVIII 356, This is hollowing before you are out of the Wood. 1792: D'Arblay, *Diary*, iii 473 (1876), Mr Windham says we are not yet out of the wood, though we see the path through it. 1840: Barham, *Ing. Legends*, 1st ser: 'Spectre of Tappington', There is a rustic adage, which warns us against self-gratulation before we are quite 'out of the wood'. 1897: W. E. Norris, *Clarissa Furiosa*, ch xliii, I should have told you so before this, only it was better not to shout until we were out of the wood. 1909: De Morgan, *Never can happen Again*, ch xxviii, Marianne is greatly relieved. But we must not halloa before we are out of the wood.

Out of the world, as out of the fashion, As good. 1639: Clarke, 171. 1671: Head and Kirkman, *Eng. Rogue*, 111, in. For out of the fashion, out of the world. 1694: Cibber, *Love's Last Shift*, II. 1752: Fielding, *Cov. Garden Journal*, No. 30. 1903: Ella F. Maitland, *Window in Chelsea*, 31, Better be out of the world than out of the fashion.

Outrun the constable, To. The quotations show the progress from a literal meaning of the phrase to the now current one = to run into debt. 1600: Kemp, *Nine Dates Wonder*, 15, I far'd like one that had … tride the use of his legs to outrun the constable. 1635: in *Somers Tracts*, vii 204 (1811), If the gentleman be predominant, his running nagge will out-run the constable. 1694: *Terence made English*, 241, But we shou'dn't have outrun the constable as the saying is. 1748: Smollett, *Rod. Random*, ch xxiii, 'How far have you over-run the constable?' I told him that the debt amounted to eleven pounds. 1843: Planché, *Extravag.*, ii 197 (1879), *Light* (*whispering*). Outran the constable; lived *fast*, you know.

Outshoot a man in his own bow, To. 1605: Bacon, *Adv. of Learning*, II xxiii 88 *b* (OED), I doubt not but learned men with meane experience, woulde … outshoote them in their owne bowe. 1639: Fuller, *Holy War*, bk iv ch vi Let us see if the Greek church may not outshoot her in her own bow. 1670: Ray, 188. 1732: Fuller, 5212.

Oven. 1. He (or she) **that has been in the oven knows where to look for son, daughter, etc.** This was a very common 16th- and 17th-century saying, and was most frequently said of mother and daughter. 1520: W. de Worde, *Seven Wise Masters*, 40 (Gomme, 1885), But it appereth by a comyn prouerbe, he yᴇ is defectyve or culpable hymself in a synne, he iugeth euery man to be in the same, or elles yʳ fader soughte neuer his sone in yᵉ ouén: but yf he had bin therin hymselfe. 1583: Greene, *Works*, ii 16 (Grosart), They seeke others, where they have been hidde them selues. 1596: Nashe, *Works*, iii 191 (Grosart), That meazild inuention of the good-wife my mothers finding her daughter in the ouen, where she would neuer have sought her, if she had not been there first her selfe: (a hackney prouerb in mens mouths euer since K. Lud was a little boy). 1605: Camden, *Remains*, 329 (1870), No woman seeks another in the oven which hath not before been there. 1678: Dryden, *Limberham*, III ii [an allusion to the saying in a passage too long to quote]. 1740: North, *Lives of Norths*, i 146 (Bohn), For he, as they say, had been in the oven himself, and knew where to look for the pasty. 1785: Grose, *Class. Dict. Vulgar Tongue*, s.v. 'Oven', The old woman would never have looked for her daughter in the oven, had she not been there herself. 1854: Baker, *Northants Gloss.*, s.v. 'Oven', [as in 1785, *plus*] This proverb … is still in common use.

2. It is time to set in when the oven comes to the dough. 1678: Ray, 186. 1714: Ozell, *Molière*, iv 206, Ho, ho! a coming girl! truly – It's time, etc. 1732: Fuller, 3020 ['bread' for 'dough'].

3. Like stopping an oven with butter. 1917: Bridge, *Cheshire Proverbs*, 91.

See also **Christmas** (18).

Over, Cheshire. *See* quot. 1917: Bridge, *Cheshire Proverbs*, 57, For honours great and profits small The Mayor of Over beats them all. *See also* **Altringham.**

Over head and ears. [Ire praecipitem in lutum, per caputque pedesque. – Catullus, xvii 9.] *c.*1565: Still, *Gam. Gurton*, I iii And Gyb, our cat, in the milke pan she spied over head and eares. 1630: *Wine, Beere, Ale, etc.*, 36 (Hanford, 1915), Ouer head and eares in ale. 1679: Crowne, *Ambitious Statesman*, IV ii, Must plunge his soul O'er head and ears betimes in wickedness. 1681: Robertson, *Phraseol. Generalis*, 434, He is in debt over head and ears. 1738: Swift, *Polite Convers.*, Dial. I, Over head and ears in love with some lady. 1831: Peacock, *Crotchet Castle*, ch xvi, The plunge [into love] must have been very sudden, if you are already over head and ears. 1889: Gilbert, *Gondoliers*, II, I am over head and ears in love with somebody else. Cf. **Over shoes.**

Over-niceness may be under-niceness. 1748: Richardson, *Clarissa*, vi 213 (1785).

Oversee workmen, Not to, is to leave them your purse open. 1732: Fuller, 3685. 1736: Franklin, *Way to Wealth*, in *Works*, i 446 (Bigelow).

Over shoes, over boots. 1616: Breton, in *Works*, ii *e*6 (Grosart). 1616: Sharpham, *Cupid's Whirligig*, II, Ouer-shooes, ouer-bootes … now goe deeper euen. 1726: L. Welsted, *Dissemb. Wanton*, IV i, Ho! ho! since she has heard of me, I'll over shoes, over boots. 1740: North, *Examen*, 218, The faction was engaged, over shoes, over boots, and must flounce through. 1824: Scott, *Redgauntlet*, Lett. XIII, Never mind the Court of the Gentiles, man … we will have you into the Sanctuary at once … over shoes, over boots. Cf. **Over head and ears.**

Overtakes at last who tires not, He. 1736: Bailey, *Dict.*, s.v. 'Overtake'.

Over the coals, To fetch (or **haul**) = To rebuke. 1580: *The Bee Hive of the Romish Church … wherein the Catholike Religion is substantially confirmed, and the Heretikes finely fetch'd ouer the coales* [title]. 1639: Fuller, *Holy War*, bk v ch ii, If they should say the Templars were burned wrongfully, they may be fetched over the coals themselves for charging his Holinesse so deeply. 1691: *Merry Drollery*, 228 (Ebsworth). 1818: Byron, *Beppo*, st. iv, They'd haul you o'er the coals. 1825: Brockett, *Gloss. of N. Country Words*, 43, To call over the coals, is to give a severe reprimand. Supposed to refer to the ordeal by fire. 1834: Marryat, *P. Simple*, ch xiii, The captain had been hauling him over the coals for not carrying on the duty according to his satisfaction.

Over the fire-stones. S. Devon, i.e. to prison. 1869: Hazlitt, 312.

Over the shoulder, or **Over the left shoulder.** 1611: Cotgrave, s.v. 'Espaule', Over the shoulder, or the wrong way. 1659: Howell, 17, I have gott it ore the left shoulder. 1670: Ray, 177, To get over the shoulders. 1681: Robertson, *Phraseol. Generalis*, 655, He gains over the left shoulder;

i.e. his gain is mischief. *c.*1750: in Peck, *Desid. Curiosa* 233 (1779), The face of Bacchus, as I have been informed, is very like a certain, *quondam* dean; for whom Verrio [the painter of the Bacchus], they say, had a respect over the left shoulder. 1841: Hartshorne, *Salopia Ant.*, 525, Over the left … a metaphor by which one who speaks by figure is reproved … 'Ah! that's over the left'. 1889: Peacock, *Manley, etc.*, *Gloss.*, 384 (E.D.S.), Over the left. In debt.

Ovington Edge. *See* quot. 1846–59: *Denham Tracts*, i 86 (F.L.S.), Ovington Edge and Cockfield Fell Are the coldest spots 'twixt Heaven and Hell. Ovington is a village near Greta Bridge, in Yorkshire. Cockfield is near Staindrop, in the bishoprick of Durham. They are both lofty and extremely exposed places.

Owe, *verb.* **1. He that ewes nothing, if he makes not mouths at us, is courteous.** 1640: Herbert, *Jac. Prudentum.*

2. He who oweth is in all [? all in] **the wrong.** 1732: Fuller, 2398.

3. I owe God a death. 1597: Shakespeare, 1 *Henry IV*, V i, Why, thou owest God a death. 1655: Heywood and W. Rowley, *Fortune by Land and Sea*, I i, He owed a death, and he hath payed that debt. 1681: Robertson, *Phraseol. Generalis*, 969.

Owl and Owls. 1. An owl is the king of the night. 1633: Draxe, 69. 1639: Clarke, 1.

2. He lives too close to the wood to be frightened by owls. 1864: 'Cornish Proverbs', in *N. & Q.*, 3rd ser, vi 494. 1883: Burne, *Shropsh. Folk-Lore*, 589. 1886: Elworthy, *West Som. Word-Book*, 549 (E.D.S.), Another very common saying now become literary is … I live too near the wood to be frightened by an owl.

3. Like an owl in an ivy bush. 1606: Day, *Ile of Gulls*, V, How say you, my lady? what oule sings out of that ivy bush? 1700: T. Brown, in *Works*, iii 2 (1760), You know that man was made for business, and not to sit amusing himself like an owl in an ivy-bush. 1738: Swift, *Polite Convers.*, Dial. I. *c.*1780: in *Poems on Costume*, 245 (Percy S.), When your hair's finely dress'd, I plainly do see, You look like an owl in an old ivy-tree. 1891: Q.-Couch, *Noughts and Crosses*, 76. 1900: *N. & Q.*, 9th ser, vi 397, 'Like an owl in an ivy bush' is a proverbial saying in North Lincolnshire.

4. The owl flies. *See* quot. 1683: White-Kennett, tr. Erasmus' *Praise of Folly*, 135 (8th ed.), There is also another favourable proverb, *The owl flies, an omen of success.*

5. The owl is not accounted the wiser for living retiredly. 1732: Fuller, 4697. 1886: Swainson, *Folk-Lore of Brit. Birds*, 125 (F.L.S.).

6. The owl thinks all her young ones beauties, *c.*1580: U. Fulwell, *Ars Adulandi*, sig. D3, The oule thought her owne birdes fairest. 1732: Fuller, 4698. 1886: Swainson, *Folk-Lore of Brit. Birds*, 125 (F.L.S.).

7. The owl was a baker's daughter. 1602: Shakespeare, *Hamlet*, IV v, They say the, etc.

8. They have need of a bird, that will give a groat for an owl. *c.*1685: in *Roxb. Ballads*, iv 72 (B.S.).

9. To bring owls to Athens = 'Coals to Newcastle'. [– Aristophanes, *Av.*, 301.] 1583: Melbancke, *Philotinus*, sig. L3, Thy exhortation … is as if thou shouldest bring owles to Athens. 1591: Harington, *Orl. Furioso*, bk xl st. 1, To beare pots (as they say) to Samos Ile … Or owls to Athens, crocodils to Nyle. 1600: F. Thynne, *Embl. and Epigr.*, 3 (E.E.T.S.), Therfore in vaine for mee to bring owles to Athens, or add water to the large sea of your rare lerning. 1693: Hacket, *Life of Williams*, i 217. 1704: *Gent. Instructed*, 545 (1732). 1732: Fuller, 5866.

10. To walk by owl-light = To fear arrest. 1659: Howell, 10. 1670: Ray, 214.

11. When owls whoop much at night, expect a fair morrow. 1886: Swainson, *Folk-Lore of Brit. Birds*, 123 (F.L.S.) [cited as a Sussex saying].

See also **Ass** (3); **Drunk; Grave;** and **Poor** (12).

Own is own. *c.*1320: in *Reliq. Antiquae*, i 114 (1841), 'Owen ys owen, and other mennes edneth', Quoth Hendyng. 1546: Heywood, *Proverbs*, Pt II ch iv, For alwaie owne is owne, at the recknynges eend. 1602: Marston, *Antonios Revenge*, II ii, Loose fortunes rags are lost; my owne's my owne. 1646: Quarles, *Works*, i 72 (Grosart). 1659: Howell, 7.

Owt for nowt. *See* **something for nothing.**

Ox and Oxen. 1. A lazy ox is little better for the goad. 1732: Fuller, 236.

2. A long ox and a short horse. Ibid., No. 257.

3. An old ox makes a straight furrow. 1659: Howell, *Proverbs: Span.-Eng.*, 9, The old ox makes the streightest furrow. 1732: Fuller, 650.

4. An old ox will find a shelter for himself. Ibid., No. 651.

5. An ox is taken by the horns, and a man by

the tongue. 1611: Cotgrave, s.v. 'Homme', An oxe (is bound) by the horne, a man by his word. 1640: Herbert, *Jac. Prudentum.* 1659: Howell, *Proverbs: Span.-Eng.*, 5, Take a bull by the horn, and a man by his word.

6. Seldom dieth the ox that weepeth for the cock. Before 1500: in Hill, *Commonplace-Book*, 133 (E.E.T.S.).

7. Take heed of an ox before, of a horse behind, of a monk on all sides. 1640: Herbert, *Jac. Prudentum.* 1670: Ray, 20 ['asse' for 'horse']. 1736: Bailey, *Dict.*, s.v. 'Ox' [as in 1670]. 1875: Cheales, *Proverb. Folk-Lore. 77.*

8. The ox is never wo till he to the harrow go. 1523: Fitzherbert, *Husb.*, 24 (E.D.S.) [quoted as 'an olde saying'].

9. The ox when weariest treads surest. 1539: Taverner, *Proverbs*, fo. 3, An olde beaten oxe fastenethe hys fote the stronger. 1611: Cotgrave, s.v. 'Boeuf', The weary oxe goes slowly. 1650: Taylor, *Holy Living*, ch ii § 6, The ox, when he is weary, treads surest. 1678: Ray, 186. 1732: Fuller, 4699.

10. To swallow an ox and be choked with the tail. 1659: Howell, 6. 1670: Ray, 194. 1732: Fuller, 5238.

11. Where shall the ox go bid he must labour? 1631: Mabbe, *Celestina*, 78 (T.T.), Which way shall the oxe goe, but he must needs plough? 1670: Ray, 20. 1732: Fuller, 5657.

See also **Black** (24); **Build** (1); **Lamb** (2); **Plough,** *subs.* (5), *verb* (8) and (9); **St Jude;** and **Sow,** *subs.* (5), *verb* (7).

Oxford. 1. Oxford for learning, London for wit, Hull for women, and York for a tit. 1869: Hazlitt, 312.

2. Oxford knives, London wives. 1659: Howell, 21. 1670: Ray, 257. 1790: Grose, *Prov. Gloss.*, s.v. 'Oxfordshire'.

3. Send verdingales [farthingales] to Broadgates, Oxford. 1562: Heywood, *Epigr.*, 5th hund., No. 55, Alas poore verdingales must lie in the streete: To house them, no doore the citee made meete Syns at our narow doores they in can not win, Send them to Oxforde, at Brodegates to get in. 1662: Fuller, *Worthies*, iii 7 (1840). 1790: Grose, *Prov. Gloss.*, s.v. 'Oxfordshire'. 1834: W. Toone, *Gloss.*, s.v. 'Farthingale', They [farthingales, *c.*1600] were so preposterously large, as to give rise to a proverb – 'send fardingales to Broadgates (in Oxford)', for the wearers could not enter an ordinary sized doorway except sideways.

4. Testons are gone to Oxford, to study in Brazennose. 1562: Heywood, *Epigr*, 5th hund., No. 63. 1662: Fuller, *Worthies*, iii 6 (1840) … This proverb began about the end of the reign of King Henry the Eighth, and happily ended about the middle of the reign of Queen Elizabeth. [A teston = a shilling of Henry VIII.] 1790: Grose, *Prov. Gloss.*, s.v. 'Oxfordshire'. 1823: D'Israeli, *Cur. of Lit.*, 2nd ser, i 462 (1824).

5. When Oxford scholars fall to fight. *See* quot. 1662: Fuller, *Worthies*, iii 8 (1840), Mark the chronicles aright, When Oxford scholars fall to fight, Before many months expir'd, England will with war be fir'd. 1790: Grose, *Prov. Gloss.*, s.v. 'Oxfordshire'.

Oyster. 1. He opens an oyster with a dagger. 1732: Fuller, 2001. Cf. **Northampton** (2).

2. Oysters are a cruel meat. *See* quots. 1611: *Tarltons Jests*, 6 (SH.S.), They [oysters] are ungodly, because they are eaten without grace; uncharitable, because they leave nought but shells; and unprofitable, because they must swim in wine. 1738: Swift, *Polite Convers.*, Dial.

II, They say, oysters are a cruel meat, because we eat them alive. Then they are an uncharitable meat, for we leave nothing to the poor; and they are an ungodly meat, because we never say grace.

3. Oysters are not good in the month that has not an R in it. 1599: Buttes, *Dyets Dry Dinner*, sig. N1, The oyster … is vnseasonable and vnholesome in all monethes that haue not the letter R in their name. 1600: W. Vaughan, *Directions for Health*, 22, Oisters … must not bee eaten in those monethes, which in pronouncing wante the letter R. 1655: T. Muffett, *Healths Improvement*, 46, Oisters in all months in whose name an R is found. 1737: Ray, 273, Oysters are not good in a month that hath not an R in it. 1868: *Quart. Review*, cxxv 251, What epicure would act in contravention of the adage that 'Oysters [as in 1737]?'

4. Oysters would be profitable food if the servants could eat the orts [shells]. 1883: Burne, *Shropsh. Folk-Lore*. 590.

5. The oyster is a gentle thing, and will not come unless you sing. 1869: Hazlitt, 381.

See also **Apple** (5); and **St James** (3).

P's and Q's, To mind one's. 1602: Dekker, *Satiromastix*, in *Works*, i 211, (1873), For now thou art in thy Pee and Kue. 1612: Rowlands, *Knave of Hearts*, 20 (Hunt.Cl.), Bring in a quart of Maligo right true: And looke, you rogue, that it be *Pee* and *Kew*. 1779: Mrs Cowley, *Who's the Dupe?*, I ii, You must mind your P's and your Q's with him, I can tell you. 1801: Mrs Piozzi, in Hayward *Autobiog.*, *etc.*, *of Mrs Piozzi*, ii 253 (2nd ed.), I used to tell the borough folks who kept our books, they must *mind their p's and q's*. 1825: Brockett, *Gloss. of N. Country Words*, 167, P's and Q's … perhaps from a French injunction to make proper obeisances, 'Soyez attentifs à vos pies et vos cues'. 1842: Barham, *Ing. Legends*, 2nd ser: 'Lay of St Aloys'. 1885: Pinero, *Magistrate*, I. 1909: De Morgan, *Never can happen Again*, ch xxxii, And then the Rector had to mind his *p's* and *q's*. For he hadn't so much as thought of the text he should preach on.

Pace that kills, It is the. 1850: Thackeray, *Pendennis*, ch 19, You're going too fast, and can't keep up the pace … it will kill you. 1855: S.A. Hammett, *Wonderful Adventures of Captain Priest*, xv, The well-known sporting maxim is that 'It is the pace that kills'. 1901: S. Lane-Poole, *Sir H. Parkes in China*, xx, There is an old proverb about the pace that kills, and … Sir Harry was killing himself by work at high pressure.

Paced like an alderman, He is. 1583: Melbancke, *Philotinus*, sig. I4, Vsing an aldermans pace before he can wel gange. 1611: Cotgrave, s.v. 'Abbé', Alderman's pace, a leasurely walking, slow gate. 1639: Clarke, 32. 1685: S. Wesley, *Maggots*, 1, And struts … as goodly as any alderman. 1754: Berthelson, *Eng.–Danish Dict.*, s.v. 'Alderman', To walk an Aldemans pace.

Pack-drill. *See* **No names.**

Pad in the straw, A. 1530: Palsgrave, 595, There is a padde in the strawe. 1575: Still, *Gam.*

Gurton, V ii, Ye perceive by this lingering there is a pad in the straw. 1616: Haughton, *Englishm. for my Money*, V ii, Yet take heed, wench, there lies a pad in straw. 1650: Fuller, *Pisgah Sight*, bk iii ch iv § 8, *Latet anguis in herba*, 'there is a pad in the straw'. 1737: Ray, 61. 1847: Halliwell, *Dict.*, s.v. *A pad in the straw*, something wrong, a screw loose … . Still in use.

Paddington Fair. *See* quots. 1690: *New Dict. Canting Crew*, sig. 12, Paddington Fair, an execution of malefactors at Tyburn. 1793: Grose, *Olio*, 232 (2nd ed.), Of those advent'rous youths, who make their exit At fair of Paddington. 1898: Weyman, *Shrewsbury*, ch xlii, Send her packing, and see she takes naught of mine, not a pinner or a sleeve, or she goes to Paddington fair for it!

Padstow, The Good Fellowship of. 1602: Carew, *Surv. of Cornwall*, 220 (1811), Some of the idle disposed Cornishmen nick their towns with by-words, as 'The good fellowship of Padstow'. 1864: 'Cornish Proverbs', in *N. &Q.*, 3rd ser, v 275.

Padstow Point. *See* quot. 1870: Hawker, *Footprints of Former Men*, 213, From Padstow Point to Lundy Light, Is a watery grave by day or night. 1897: Norway, *H. and B. in Devon, etc.*, 342 ['Hartland' for 'Lundy'].

Padwell. *See* quot. 1851: Sternberg, *Dialect, etc., of Northants*, 190, If we can Padwell overgoe, and Horestone we can see, Then Lords of England we shall be.

Page of your own age, Make a = Do it yourself. 1633: Draxe, 30, Let him make a page of his age. 1670: Ray,189. 1738: Swift, *Polite Convers.*, Dial. I.

Pain is forgotten where gain follows. 1605: Camden, *Remains*, 330 (1870). 1670: Ray, 129. 1732: Fuller, 3836.

Pain past is pleasure. 1567: G. Fenton, *Bandello*, i 4 (T.T.), The remembrance of the paine that is past is sweete. 1732: Fuller, 3838. 1860: Spurgeon, *John Ploughman*, ch v, Pain past is pleasure, and experience comes by it.

Pains are the wages of ill pleasures. 1732: Fuller, 3839.

Pains be a pleasure to you, If, profit will follow. Ibid., No. 2699.

Pains is the price that God putteth upon all things. 1659: Howell, 19.

Pains to get, care to keep, fear to lose. 1633:

Draxe, 181, There is paine in getting, care in keeping, and griefe in losing riches. 1640: Herbert, *Jac. Prudentum.* 1763: Murphy, *Citizen*, I ii.

Painted pictures are dead speakers. 1616: Breton, in *Works* ii e 5 (Grosart). 1670: Ray, 131.

Painted sheath. *See* **Leaden sword.**

Painters and Poets may lie by authority. 1591: Harington, *Apol. of Poetrie*, par. 3, According to that old verse … Astronomers, painters, and poets may lye by authoritie. 1618: Harington, *Epigrams*, bk ii No. 88, Besides, we poets lie by good authoritie. 1650: R. Heath, *Epigrams*, 35, Poets and painters by authoritie As wel as travellers we say may lie. 1681: Robertson, *Phraseol. Generalis*, 1003. 1736: Bailey, *Dict.*, s.v. 'Poets', Poets and painters lye with license. Cf. **Old, A** (*b*) (14); and **Traveller** (1).

Painting and fighting, On, look aloof. 1640: Herbert, *Jac. Prudentum.* 1670: Ray, 20.

Pair of shears. *See* **Shears.**

Paises its pasture, It = It does credit to its food. Said of a child. 1917: Bridge, *Cheshire Proverbs*, 80.

Pale as ashes. *c.*1385: Chaucer, *Leg. Good Women*, ix. l. 88, Deed wex her hewe, and lyk as ash to sene. *c.*1386: Chaucer, *Knight's Tale*, l. 506, His hewe salow, and pale as asshen colde. *c.*1477: Caxton, *Jason*, 156 (E.E.T.S.), He … after becam pale and dede as asshes. *c.*1490: *Partonope*, l. 10166 (E.E.T.S.). 1567: *Merry Tales, etc.*, No. 48, p. 64 (Hazlitt). 1607: *Conceits of Old Hobson*, 30 (Percy S.), As pale as ashes for feare. 1758–67: Sterne, *Trist. Shandy*, ii ch xix, Seeing her turn as pale as ashes at the very mention of it. 1817: Byron, *Letters, etc.*, iv 51 (Prothero). 1870: Dickens, *Drood*, ch x, He was still as pale as gentlemanly ashes at what had taken place in his rooms.

Pale as clay. *c.*1600: in Collier, *Roxb. Ballads*, 328 (1847), His face was pale as any clay. 1813: Scott, *Rokeby*, V xxvii, He looks pale as clay. 1893: R.L.S., *Letters*, v 11 (Tusitala ed.), He was … as pale as clay, and walked leaning on a stick.

Pale as death. 1567: Painter, *Pal. of Pleasure*, iii 9 (Jacobs), The colour whereof is more pale than death. 1602: Chettle, *Hoffman*, I i, Desert looks pale as death. 1700: T. Brown, etc., *Scarron*, i 214 (1892), He gave a great shriek, turned pale as death … 1751: Fielding, *Amelia*, bk vii ch i. 1815: Scott, *Mannering*, ch xxxv, Lucy …

turned as pale as death. 1886: Hardy, *Casterbridge*, ch xxxix, 'Tis me!' she said, with a face pale as death.

Palm Sunday. *See* quot. 1846: Denham, *Proverbs*, 33 (Percy S.), He that hath not a palm in his hand on Palm Sunday must have his hand cut off. 1904: *Co. Folk-Lore: Northumb.*, 176 (F.L.S.).

Pancake Tuesday. *See* **Shrove-tide.**

Pancridge parson, A. 1612: Field, *Woman a Weathercock*, II, Thou Pancridge parson! 1847: Halliwell, *Dict.*, s.v. … a term of contempt.

Pandon. *See* **Old,** D (9).

Pantofles. *See* **Stand** (7).

Pap before the child be born, Boil not the. 1732: Fuller, 1002.

Pap with a hatchet. 1589: *Pap with a Hatchet* [title of pamphlet]. 1592: Lyly, *Mother Bombie*, I iii, They give us … pap with a hatchet. 1719: D'Urfey, *Pills*, iv 329 (OED), A custard was to him pap with a hatchet. 1847: Halliwell, *Dict.*, s.v. 'To give pap with a hatchet', a proverbial phrase, meaning to do any land action in an unkind manner.

Paradise, He that will enter into, must have a good key. 1640: Herbert, *Jac. Prudentum.* 1670: Ray, 20. 1732: Fuller, 2347 ['come with a right key'].

Pardon all but thyself. 1611: Cotgrave, s.v. 'Pardonner'. 1640: Herbert, *Jac. Prudentum.*

Parings of a pippin are better than a whole crab, The. 1732: Fuller, 4701. 1869: Spurgeon, *John Ploughman*, ch v.

Parings of his nails, He'll not lose the = He is a miser. 1546: Heywood, *Proverbs*, Pt I ch xi, She will not part with the paryng of hir nayles. *c.*1598: Deloney, *Gentle Craft*, Pt II ch i, Such penny fathers and pinch-fistes, that will not part, etc. 1631: Mabbe, *Celestina*, 212 (T.T.), She will not part with anything, no, not so much as the parings of her nailes. 1681: Robertson, *Phraseol. Generalis*, 843. 1894: Northall, *Folk Phrases*, 15 (E.D.S.), He would not give anyone the parings of his nails.

Parkgate, All on one side like. 1886: R. Holland, *Cheshire Gloss.*, 444 (E.D.S.). 1917: Bridge, *Cheshire Proverbs*, 9 … Parkgate consists of a row of houses facing the Dee.

Parrot must have an almond, The. This expression was proverbial in the 16th and 17th centuries, but its meaning is not apparent. Before 1529: Skelton, in *Works*, ii 2 (Dyce), Then Parot must haue an almon or a date. 1590: Nashe, *Almond for a Parrot* [title]. 1609: Shakespeare, *Troilus*, V ii, The parrot will not do more for an almond than he for a commodious drab. 1616: Haughton, *Englishm. for my Money*, IV ii, An almond for parrot! a rope for parrot! 1632: Jonson, *Magnetic Lady*, V v, Almond for parrot. 1635: Taylor (Water-Poet), *A Bawd*, 25, in *Works*, 3rd coll. (Spens.S.), Shee knowes a bribe to a catchpole is as sufficient as an almond for a parrot.

Parrot. *See also* **Melancholy.**

Parsley. 1. Parsley fried will bring a man to his saddle, and a woman to her grave. This seems a meaningless saying. 1678: Ray, 345. 1884: Friend, *Flowers and Fl. Lore*, 209.

2. Parsley must be sown nine times. *See* quots. 1658: R. Barnsley, in *Wit Restored*, 152 (Hotten), Or else the weed, which still before it's born Nine times the devill sees. 1883: Burne, *Shropsh. Folk-Lore*, 248, Parsley must be sown nine times, for the devil takes all but the last. 1885: *N. & Q.*, 6th ser, xi 467, There is a saying in the North Riding of Yorkshire that 'parsley seed (when it has been sown) goes nine times to the devil', a phrase which seems to have originated in the fact that it remains some time in the earth before it begins to germinate.

3. The baby comes out of the parsley-bed. 1640: R. Brome, *Antipodes*, I iv, For I am past a child My selfe to thinke they are found in parsley beds. 1659: *London Chanticleers*, sc ii, My mother indeed used to say that I was born to be a gardener's wife, as soon as ever I was taken out of her parsley bed. *c.*1730: Swift, *Receipt for Stewing Veal*, Some sprigs of that bed Where children are bred. 1883: Burne, *Shropsh. Folk-Lore*, 249, We have the common English saying that the baby, etc. 1886: Elworthy, *West Som. Word-Book*, 557 (E.D.S.), Parsley-bed … the source whence children are told that the little girls come. 1918: *N. & Q.*, 12th ser, iv 256.

See also **Mistress** (4).

Parson gets the children, The. 1663: Killigrew, *Parson's Wedding*, II iii [quoted as a proverb].

Parson of Saddlewick. *See* **Saddle-wick.**

Parson Palmer. *See* 1785 quot. 1682: A. Behn, *Roundheads*, IV iii, Bread, my Lord, no preaching o'er yar liquer. 1709: O. Dykes, *Eng. Proverbs*, 295 (2nd ed.), Dangerous to preach over your liquor. 1738: Swift, *Polite Convers.*,

Dial. II, *Ld. Smart* [*interrupting*]. Pray, Sir John, did you ever hear of parson Palmer? *Sir John.* No, my lord; what of him? *Ld. Smart.* Why, he used to preach over his liquor. 1754: Berthelson, *Eng.-Danish Dict.*, s.v. 'Liquor', To preach over ones liquor. 1785: Grose, *Class. Dict. Vulgar Tongue*, s.v. 'Parson Palmer', Parson Palmer, a jocular name or term of reproach, to one who stops the circulation of the glass by preaching over his liquor, as it is said was done by a parson of that name, whose cellar was under his pulpit.

Parson's cow with a calf at her foot, To come home like the. Cheshire. 1670: Ray, 209. 1917: Bridge, *Cheshire Proverbs*, 131.

Parson's side, To pinch on the. 1579: Lyly, *Euphues*, 87 (Arber), Lucilla perceiuing the drift of the olde foxe hir father … shaped him an aunswere which … pinched Philautus on the persons syde … *c.*1580: Fulwell, *Ars Adulandi*, sig. H1, Pinch on the parsons side, my lorde, the whorsons haue to much. 1630: T. Adams, *Works*, 77, This is a common slander, when the … couetous wretch pincheth on the priest's side. 1690: *New Dict. Canting Crew*, To pinch on the parson's side, or sharp him of his tithes. 1737: Ray, 268.

Parsons are souls' waggoners. 1640: Herbert, *Jac. Prudentum.*

Parsons pay for the clerks. 1812: Combe, *Syntax: Pict. Tour*, can. iv, And there's a proverb, as they say, That for the clerks the parsons pay.

Part of the solution … If you're not. *See* **Solution.**

Part three things, To. *See* quot. 1659: Howell, 17, It is pitie to part three things – the lawyer and his client, the physician and his patient, and a pot of good ale and a toast.

Partridge. 1. If the partridge had the woodcock's thigh, 'Twould be the best bird that ever did fly. 1670: Ray, 44. 1732: Fuller, 6400. 1854: Doran, *Table Traits*, 176, [with the addition] If the woodcock had but the partridge's breast, 'Twould be the best bird that ever was dress'd. 1888: S. O. Addy, *Sheffield Gloss.*, 255 (E.D.S.), If a partridge had but a woodcock's thee [thigh] 'Twere the finest bird that ever did flee.

2. If you had not aimed at the partridge, you had not missed the snipe. 1846–59: *Denham Tracts*, ii 108 (F.L.S.).

See also **Plump.**

Pass the pikes, To = To get out of danger. 1567: G. Fenton, *Bandello*, i 239 (T.T.), Hee wolde graunte him dispence and saffe conduit to passe thorow the pikes of his infortunat dangers. 1581: Pettie, tr. Guazzo's *Civil Convers.*, Pref., Hauing alreadie past the pikes in a daungerous conflict, without wound of honour. 1626: Breton in *Works*, i *e*6 (Grosart), To passe the pikes of Danger's deadly smart. 1682: A. Behn, *Roundheads*, V iv, With much ado … I have pass'd the pikes, my house being surrounded. 1690: *New Dict. Canting Crew*, sig. I5. 1785: Cowper, *Lett, to Lady Hesketh*, 30 Nov. (OED), So far, therefore, have I passed the pikes. The Monthly Critics have not yet noticed me.

Passion entereth at the fore-gate, wisdom goeth out of the postern, When. 1732: Fuller, 5564.

Passion will master you, if you do not master your passion. 1831: Hone, *Year-Book*, col. 1417.

Passionate men. *See* quots. 1692: Sir T. P. Blount, *Essays*, 141, 'Twas the usual saying of a very ingenuous person that passionate men, Like Yorkshire hounds, are apt to overrun the scent. 1732: Fuller, 283: A man in passion rides a horse that runs away with him. 1880: Spurgeon, *Ploughman's Pictures*, 143 [as in 1732].

Past cure past care. 1593: Greene, *Works*, ii 154 (Grosart), Remember the olde prouerbe … past cure, past care, without remedie, without remembrance. 1592: Shakespeare, *L.L.L.*, V ii. *c.*1625: B.&F., *Double Marriage*, I i, But what is past my help is past my care.

Past dying of her first child, She is = She hath had a bastard. 1678: Ray, 240.

Past labour is pleasant. 1539: Taverner, *Proverbs*, fo. 34, Labours ones [once] done be swete. 1732: Fuller, 3845.

Paston Family. 1678: Ray, 327, There never was a Paston poor, a Heyden a coward, nor a Cornwallis a fool. 1790: Grose, *Prov. Gloss.*, s.v. 'Norfolk'.

Pastor Sunday. *See* **Whitsuntide** (3).

Patch and long sit, build and soon fit. 1670: Ray, 21.

Patch by patch. *See* quots. 1639: in *Berkeley MSS.*, iii 33 (1885), Patch by patch is yeomanly; but patch vpon patch is beggerly. 1670: Ray, 129, Patch by patch is good husbandry, but patch upon patch is plain beggery. 1732: Fuller,

6181 [as in 1670, but 'housewifery' for 'husbandry']. 1909: *Folk-Lore*, xx 73, [Durham saying] Patch neighbourly, patch on patch beggarly.

Paternoster. 1. A man may say even his Paternoster out of time. 1732: Fuller, 299.

2. A paternoster while = A little while, a time in which one might say a Paternoster. 1362: Langland, *Plowman*, A, v 192, In a paternoster-while. 1536: Latimer, *Sermons*, 37 (P.S.), Though it be but a Paternoster while. 1584: R. Scot, *Witchcraft*, To Readers, And yet they last not paternoster while the longer. 1888: R.L.S., *Black Arrow*, Prol., And think ever a paternoster-while on Bennet Hatch.

3. He may be in my Paternoster, but never in my Creed. 1546: Heywood, *Proverbs*, Pt II ch ix, He maie be in my Pater noster in deede, But be sure, he shall neuer come in my Creede. *c.*1590: in *Roxb. Ballads*, iii 92 (B.S.). *c.*1594: Bacon, *Promus*, No. 270. 1659: Howell, 5.

4. Paternoster built churches, and Our Father pulls them down. 1630: T. Adams, in *Works*, 16. 1662: Fuller, *Worthies*, i 44 (1840), There is a generation of people who, to prevent the verifying of the old proverb, '*Pater noster* built churches, and *Our Father* plucks them down', endeavour to pluck down both churches and our Father together, neglecting, yea despising the use both of the one and the other. 1670: Ray, 70. 1732: Fuller, 3851.

Path hath a puddle, Every. 1640: Herbert, *Jac. Prudentum*. 1732: Fuller, 1453. 1817: Scott, *Rob Roy*, ch xxxviii, But ilka bean has its black, and ilka path has its puddle. 1852: FitzGerald, *Polonius*, 153 (1903). 1854: Warter, *Last of Old Squires*, 53.

Patience. 1. He preacheth patience that never knew pain. 1855: Bohn, 381.

2. He that hath no patience hath nothing. 1611: Cotgrave, s.v. 'Patience'. 1666: Torriano, *Piazza Univ.*, 194.

3. He that hath patience, hath fat thrushes for a farthing. 1640: Herbert, *Jac. Prudentum*.

4. Let patience grow in your garden. 1546: Heywood, *Proverbs*, Pt I ch xi. 1633: Draxe, 152.

5. Patience carries with it half a release. 1642: D. Rogers, *Matrim. Honour*, 196.

6. Patience conquers, *c.*1374: Chaucer, *Troylus*, bk iv 1. 1584, Men seyn, 'the suffraunt overcometh', pardee. 1611: Davies (of Hereford),

Sc. of Folly, 46, in *Works*, ii (Grosart), Who suffers orecomes. 1639: Clarke, 242, Patient men win the day.

7. Patience is a flower that grows not in every garden. 1645: Howell, *Letters*, bk i § vi No. 58. 1694: D'Urfey, *Quixote*, Pt I Act I sc i. 1732: Fuller, 3854, Patience grows not in every garden. 1869: Spurgeon, *John Ploughman*, ch v, It is not every garden that grows the herbs to make it [patience] with.

8. Patience is a good nag, but she'll bolt. 1875: Cheales, *Proverb. Folk-Lore*, 121.

9. Patience is a plaister for all sores. *c.*1390: Gower, *Conf. Amantis*, bk iii l. 614, And tak into thi remembrance If thou miht gete pacience, Which is the leche of alle offence, As tellen ons these olde wise. *c.*1393: Langland, *Plowman*, C, xx 89, And yet be plastred with pacience. 1560: Wilson, *Rhetorique*, 206 (1909), Pacience is a remedie for euery disease. 1605: Breton, in *Works*, ii *m* 4 (Grosart) ['paine' for 'sores']. 1694: D'Urfey, *Quixote*, Pt II Act I sc i. 1901: F. E. Taylor, *Lancs Sayings*, 9, Payshunce is a plister for o maks o' sores.

10. Patience is a virtue. 1377: Langland, *Plowman*, B, xi 370, Suffraunce is a souereygne vertue. *c.*1386, Chaucer, *C. Tales*, F. 773 (Skeat): Patience is an heigh vertu, certéyn. 1599: Breton, in *Works*, ii *c* 7 (Grosart). 1614: R. Tailor, *Hog hath lost his Pearl*, V 1706: Vanbrugh, *Confederacy*, III ii. 1729: Gay, *Polly*, I. 1798: Morton, *Speed the Plough*, IV iii, There is a point when patience ceases to be virtue. 1821: Byron, *Letters, etc.*, v 287 (Prothero).

11. Patience is the best remedy. 1578: Florio, *First Fruites*, fo. 44, Pacience is the best medicine that is, for a sicke man. 1761: Colman, *Jealous Wife*, IV i. Cf. **No remedy.**

12. Patience, money, and time, bring all things to pass. 1640: Herbert, *Jac. Prudentum*, Patience, time, and money accommodate all things. 1732: Fuller, 3858.

13. Patience perforce. *See* 1847 quot. 1575: Gascoigne, *Patience Perforce* [title of poem]. 1590: Spenser, *F. Q.*, III x 3, But patience perforce; he must abie What future and his fate on him will lay. 1659: Howell, 11 (9), Patience perforce is medicine for a mad horse. 1694: Motteux, *Rabelais*, bk v ch i, Patience per force is a remedy for a mad-dog. 1702: Penn, *Fruits of Solitude*, Pt II No. 188, According to the proverb, *Patience per force*, and *thank you for nothing*. 1837: Southey, *Lett. to Mrs Hughes*, 7 Dec., 'Patience perforce' was what I heard of every day in Portugal. 1847: Halliwell, *Dict.*, s.v. 'Perforce', *Patience perforce*, a phrase when some evil must be endured which cannot by any means be remedied.

14. Patience with poverty is all a poor man's remedy. 1639: Clarke, 15. 1656: Flecknoe, *Diarium*, 6, Patience, vertue of the poor. 1670: Ray, 130. 1732: Fuller, 6361 [omitting 'all'].

See also **Nature; Time;** and **No remedy.**

Patient, and you shall have patient children, Be. 1678: Ray, 346.

Patient is not like to recover who makes the doctor his heir, That. 1659: Howell, *Proverbs: Fr.-Eng.*, 11, He is a fool that makes his physitian his heir. 1732: Fuller, 4368.

Paull, a village on the Humber. *See* quot. 1878: *Folk-Lore Record*, i 167, High Paull, and low Paull, and Paull Holme, There never was a fair maid married at Paull town.

Paul's, Old as. 1662: *in Roxb. Ballads*, iii 577 (B.S.), I can call 'um pritty souls, though they be as old as Pouls. 1667: L'Estrange, *Quevedo's Visions*, 184 (1904), Let her be as old as Paul's. 1738: Swift, *Polite Convers.*, Dial. I. 1752: Fielding, *Cov. Garden Journal*, No. 28, And told me that my secret was not only a lye, but as old as Paul's. 1888: Lowsley, *Berks Gloss.*, 124 (E.D.S.), The expression as 'awld as St Paul's' is used to denote great antiquity.

Paul's steeple, Old as. 1659: Howell, *Proverbs*, Dedn., Some of them may be said to be as old as Pauls steeple. 1670: Ray, 242. 1790: Grose, *Prov. Gloss.*, s.v. 'London'.

Paul's will not always stand. 1593: G. Harvey, in *Works*, i 297 (Grosart), Powles steeple, and a hugyer thing is doune. 1659: Howell, *Proverbs*, Dedn., A very ancient proverb ... viz. Pauls cant alwayes stand. 1670: Ray, 130. 1732: Fuller, 3861.

Paul's. *See also* **Westminster.**

Paves the meadow, He. 1813: Ray, 75.

Pay, *Verb.* **1. He pays him with pen-powder.** 1639: Clarke, 58.

2. He that cannot pay let him pray. 1611: Cotgrave, s.v. 'Argent'. 1670: Ray, 130. 1732: Fuller, 6362.

3. He that payeth another remembereth himself. Ibid., No. 2247.

4. He that payeth beforehand shall have his work ill done. 1591: Florio, *Second Frutes*, 39, He that paieth afore hand, hath neuer his worke well done. 1611: Cotgrave, s.v. 'Bras', ... lames his workeman; or, hath it but lamely done. 1732: Fuller, 2245.

5. He that pays last never pays twice. 1659: Howell, 4, Who payeth last, payeth but once. 1670: Ray, 130. 1732: Fuller, 2246.

6. If you pay peanuts, you get monkeys. The saying is said to be English, although 'peanuts' was originally American slang for a small amount of money – or, in this case, the low wages that will only attract low-grade workers. 1966: L. Coulthard, in *Director*, Aug., 228, Shareholders want the best available businessmen to lead the companies and recognise that you get what you pay for. If you pay in peanuts, you must expect to get monkeys.

7. It is hard to pay and pray too. 1631: F. Lenton, *Characters*, sig. D11 (1663), In his trade, above all others, you must both pray and pay. 1642: D. Rogers, *Matrim. Honour*, 53, And now I adde, pray for it, pay and pray too. 1725: Defoe, *Everybody's Business*, Nor would I be so unchristian to put more upon any one than they can bear; but to pray and pay too is the devil. 1732: Fuller, 2951.

8. Pay what you owe, And what you're worth you'll know. Ibid., No. 6352. 1869: Spurgeon, *John Ploughman*, ch xii. 1875: Smiles, *Thrift*, 89, Who pays what he owes enriches himself.

9. Pay with the same dish you borrow. 1639: Clarke, 14.

10. To pay it with thinking. *See* **Say,** *verb* (9).

11. To Pay one in his own coin. 1589: Greene, *Works*, vii 133 (Grosart), Glad that he had giuen hir a soppe of the same sauce, and paide hir his debt in hir owne coine. 1612: Chapman, *Widow's Tears*, II iii, I did but pay him in's own coin. 1687: A. Behn, *Lucky Chance*, I ii, I would make use of Sir Cautious's cash: pay him in his own coin. 1748: Richardson, *Clarissa*, i 71 (1785), They had best take care he did not pay them in their own coin. 1821: Byron, *Blues*, Ecl. i l. 132, Or he'll pay you back in your own coin. 1851: Borrow, *Lavengro*, iii 353, If you attempt to lay hands on me, I'll try to pay you in your own coin.

12. To pay the debt to Nature. *See* **Debt** (5).

13. To pay the piper. 1638: J. Taylor (Water-Poet), *Taylors Feast*, 98, in *Works*, 3rd coll.

(Spens.S.), Alwayes those that dance must pay the musicke. 1695: Congreve, *Love for Love*, II v, I warrant you, if he danced till doomsday, he thought I was to pay the piper. *c.*1791: Pegge, *Derbicisms*, 115 (E.D.S.), 'To pay the piper', to bear the expense. 1923: *Evening Standard*, 14 Feb., p. 5, col. 1, The old adage of 'He who pays the piper can call the tune' has held good.

14. To pay the shot = To pay the reckoning or bill. 1519: Horman, *Vulgaria*, fo. 165, He loueth well to be at good fare but he wyll pay no scotte. *c.*1534: Berners, *Huon*, 704 (E.E.T.S.), Yf it may please you to let me eat and drynke with you I wyll pay for my scot ['shotte' in 1601 ed.]. 1587: Churchyard, *Worth. of Wales*, 15 (Spens.S.), The shot is great, when each man paies his groate. 1607: Dekker and Webster, *Northw. Hoe*, II i, Did thy father pay the shot? 1611: Cotgrave, s.v. 'Escorter', Every one to pay his shot, or to contribute somewhat towards it. 1842: in Crawhall, *Fishers Garlands*, 109 (1864), Yet still while I have got Enough to pay the shot Of Boniface … 1907: Hackwood, *Old Eng. Sports*, 222, The customers called for their ale … and … expected the losers 'to pay the shot'.

15. You pay more for your schooling than your learning is worth. 1639: Clarke, 59. 1732: Fuller, 5955.

16. You pays your money and you takes your choice. 1846: *Punch* X 16, 'Which is the Prime Minister?' … 'Which ever you please, my little dear. You pays your money and you takes your choice'.

Pea and Pease. 1. Eat peas with the king, and cherries with the beggar. 1732: Fuller, 1356.

2. Sow **peas and beans in the wane of the moon, Who soweth them sooner, he soweth too soon.** 1846: Denham, *Proverbs*, 42 (Percy S.).

3. The smaller the peas. *See* quots. 15th cent.: in *Reliq. Antiquae*, ii 40 (1843), Tho smallere pese tho mo to the pott; Tho fayrere woman tho more gyglott. 1541: *Sch. House of Women*, l. 558, in Hazlitt, *Early Pop. Poetry*, iv 126, The smaller pease, the mo to the pot, The fairer woman the more gillot.

4. To give a pea for a bean = To give a present with an eye to future return. Staffs. 1896: *Folk-Lore*, vii 377.

5. Who hath many peas may put the more in the pot. 1546: Heywood, *Proverbs*, Pt I ch v. 1670: Ray, 21.

See also **Candlemas**, B; **St Benedict;** and **St David** (1).

Peace. 1. If you want peace, prepare for war. [qui desiderat pacem, praeparet bellum. Flavius Vegetius, *Epitoma Rei Militaris* III] 1547: E. Hall, *Chronicle* (1548), Edw. IV, 209, He forgat the olde adage, saynge in tyme of peace provyde for warre. 1593: M. Sutcliffe, *Practice of Arms*, A2v, He that desireth peace, he must prepare for warres. 1624: Burton, *Anatomy of Melancholy*, II iii, The Commonwealth of venice in their Armory have this inscription, Happy is that Citty which in time of peace thinkes of warre, a fit Motto for every mans private house. 1885: C. Lowe, *Prince Bismarck*, II x, Lord Beaconsfield had acted on the maxim 'that if you want peace, you must prepare for war'. *See also* (4).

2. Peace and catch a mouse. 1659: Howell, 11.

3. Peace maketh plenty. 15th cent.: in *Reliq. Antiquae*, i 315 (1841), Pees maketh plenté, Plenté maketh pride, Pride maketh plee, Plee maketh poverté, Povert maketh pees. And therefore, grace growith after governaunce. 1589: Puttenham, *Eng. Poesie*, 217 (Arber), Peace makes plentie, plentie makes pride, Pride breeds quarrell, and quarrell brings warre: Warre brings spoile, and spoile pouertie, Pouertie pacience, and pacience peace: So peace brings warre and warre brings peace. [Puttenham attributes the lines to 'Ihean de Mehune the French Poet'.] 1619: B. Rich, *Irish Hubbub*, 49, An old obseruation, Peace brings plenty, Plenty brings pride, and Pride in the end is it that brings in penury. 1659: Howell, 19, Through peace cometh plenty.

4. 'Tis safest making peace with sword in hand. 1699: Farquhar, *Love and a Bottle*, V iii.

5. Where there is peace, God is. 1640: Herbert, *Jac. Prudentum.*

Peach will have wine, and the fig water, The. 1577: J. Grange, *Golden Aphroditis*, sig. El. 1629: *Book of Meery Riddles*, Prov. 103.

Peacock hath fair feathers but foul feet, The. 1633: Draxe, 10.

Peacock loudly bawls, When the, Soon we'll hare both rain and squalls. 1893: Inwards, *Weather Lore*, 135.

Peacock. *See also* **All's well;** and **Proud.**

Peak, To send a wife to the. 1663: Pepys, *Diary*, 19 Jan., My lord did presently pack his lady into the country in Derbyshire, near the Peake;

which is become a proverb at Court, to send a man's wife to the Devil's arse-á-Peake, when she vexes him.

Pear and Pears. 1. After pear wine, or the priest. 1588: Cogan, *Haven of Health*, 89 (1612), That saying which is commonly used, that peares without wine are poyson. 1608: Harington, *Sch. of Salerne*, sig. B3, Peares wanting wine, are poyson from the tree. 1611: Cotgrave, s.v. 'Poire', After a (cold) peare wine, or the priest. 1666: Torriano, *Piazza Univ.*, 201, A pear must have wine after it, and a fig water.

2. A pear must be eaten to the day, *If you don't eat it then, throw it away.* 1886: *N. & Q.*, 7th ser, ii 506.

3. A pear year, A dear year. 1855: *N. & Q.*, 1st ser, xii 260. 1893: Inwards, *Weather Lore*, 5.

4. Share not pears with your master, either in jest or in earnest. 1611: Cotgrave, s.v. 'Poire', He that eats peares with his lord picks none of the best. 1732: Fuller, 4117.

See also **Apple** (7).

Pearl on your nail, Make a. 1592: Nashe, *Works*, ii 78 (Grosart), After a man hath turnd vp the bottom of the cup, to drop it on hys naile, and make a pearle with that is left. 1678: Ray, 88. 1732: Fuller, 3311. 1909: Hackwood, *Inns, Ales, etc.*, 165, The custom of turning upside down the cup, from which the drinker has quaffed the whole contents, to make a pearl, with the last drop left in the vessel, upon his thumb-nail. Cf. **Supernaculum.**

Pearls before swine, To cast. [Matthew vii 6, Give not that which is holy unto the dogs, neither cast ye your pearls before swine.] 1340: *Ayenbite*, 152 (E.E.T.S.), Huerof zayth ous god ine his spelle. Thet we ne thrauwe nat oure precious stones touore the zuyn. 1401: in Wright, *Pol. Poems*, ii 110 (Rolls Ser., 1861), And the prescious perlis ye strowen to hogges. *c.*1430: Lydgate, *Minor Poems*, 188 (Percy S.), Men shuld not put … perles whight, To-fore rude swyne. 1550: R. Crowley, *Epigr.*, in *Works*, 6 (E.E.T.S.), For before suche swyne no pearles maye be caste. 1606: Day, *Ile of Gulls*, III, To cast eloquence amongst a companie of stincards is all one as if a man should scatter pearls amongst the hoggish animals ecliped swine. 1848: Dickens, *Dombey*, ch xxiii. 1905: Shaw, *How He Lied, etc.*, Introducing a fine woman to you is casting pearls before swine.

Peart. *See* **Pert.**

Pease-field, He is going into the = He is falling asleep. 1678: Ray, 264.

Pease-pottage and tawny Never made good medley. 1659: Howell, 12.

Peckham. *See* **All holiday.**

Peck of dirt. *See* **Eat** (39).

Peck of malt. *See* **Kiln** (2).

Peck of salt. *See* **Bushel** (3).

Peck of troubles, A. *c.*1535: in *Archaeologia*, xxv 97 (OED), The said George … told hym that Mr More was in a pecke of trubles. 1569: Grafton, *Chron.*, i 235 (1809), You bring your selfe into such a pecke of troubles. 1633: Draxe, 37. 1785: O'Keeffe, *Beggar on Horseback*, II iv, I dare say he's in a peck of troubles. 1857: Hughes, *Tom Brown*, Pt I ch viii, A pretty peck of troubles you'll get into.

Pedlar, A small pack becomes a small. 1611: Cotgrave, s.v. 'Mercier', The little pedler a little pack doth serve. 1670: Ray, 143. 1732: Fuller, 409.

Pedlar carry his own burden, Let every. 1659: Howell, 17. 1732: Fuller, 3176.

Pedlar's mare. *See* quot. 1541: Coverdale, *Christ. State Matrimony*, sig. G2, It is no vntrue prouerbe: She that taketh the pedlers mare must be fayne to haue the pedler himself also at the last.

Pedley, Go pipe at, there's a pescod feast. 1678: Ray, 78 ['Padley']. 1790: Grose, *Prov. Gloss.*, s.v. 'Cheshire'. 1917: Bridge, *Cheshire Proverbs*, 62.

Pedley. *See also* **Candle** (7); **God help the fool**; **I was by;** and **Rope** (5).

Peep. I see a knave. 1639: Clarke, 181.

Peeps through a hole may see what will vex him, He who. 1710: Palmer, *Moral Essays on Proverbs*, 135.

Peewit. *See* **Acre.**

Peggy behind Margit, To ride. 1917: Bridge, *Cheshire Proverbs*, 142 … To ride one behind the other.

Peg in, To put the = To give no more credit. 'A peg of wood above the latch inside … effectually locked it'. Ibid., 141.

Pelton. *See* quot. 1846–59: *Denham Tracts*, i 112 (F.L.S.), They'd come back again like the pigs o' Pelton. Ibid., i 113, Thicker and ranker, like pigs o' Pelton.

Pen and ink is wit's plough. 1639: Clarke, 35. 1670: Ray, 130.

Pen and ink never blush. 1577: J. Grange, *Golden Aphroditis*, sig. K2, Better might you haue done it with penne and inke, who (as the prouerbe goeth) neuer blusheth. Cf. **Pens.**

Pen is mightier than the sword, The. 1582: G. Whetstone *Heptameron of Civil Discourses*, iii, The dashe of a Pen, is mor greevous than the counter use of a Launce. 1712: W. King, *The Eagle and the Robin*, in *Poetical Works* (1781), III 49, Poor Bob … A goosequill on for a weapon ty'd. Knowing by use that now and then A sword less hurt does than a pen. 1839: Bulwer–Lytton, *Richelieu*, II ii, Beneath the rule of men entirely great, the pen is mightier than the sword.

Penance. *See* quot. 1593: *Tell–Trothes N. Yeares Gift*, 10 (N.Sh.S.), The old saying is, that he which will no pennance doe, must shonne the cause that belongs thereto.

Pence. *See* **Penny.**

Pendle-Hill, As old as. 1659: Howell, 20. 1670: Ray, 235. 1790: Grose, *Prov. Gloss.*, s.v. 'Lancs'. 1901: F. E. Taylor, *Lancs Sayings*, 3.

Pendle, Ingleborough, and Penigent, Are the three highest hills between Scotland and Trent. 1586: Camden, *Britannia*, 431, Ingleborrow, Pendle and Penigent are, etc. 1622: Drayton, *Polyol.*, xxviii, That Ingleborow hill, Pendle, and Penigent, Should named be the high'st betwixt our Tweed and Trent. 1683: Meriton, *Yorkshire. Ale*, 83–7 (1697). 1790: Grose, *Prov. Gloss.*, s.v. 'Yorks', [as in heading, with variant] Pendle, Penigent, and Ingleborough Are the three highest hills all England thorough. 1878: *Folk-Lore Record*, i 167 [as in 1790].

Penniless bench, On. 1560–1: in W. H. Turner, *Select Rec. Oxf.*, 284 (1880) (OED), Item, to … for mending the peneles benche [*see* note to 1604 quot.]. 1598: Greene, *James IV*, IV iii, Wee will teach him such a lesson as shall cost him a chiefe place on pennilesse-bench for his labour. 1604: Middleton, *Black Book*, in *Works*, viii 27 (Bullen), Pierce should be called no more Pennyless, like the Mayor's bench at Oxford. [Bullen's note: 'At the east end of the old Carfax church at Oxford there was a seat for loungers which was known as Penniless Bench. Hence came the proverb "To sit on Penniless Bench" (= be very poor)'.] 1651: Randolph, *Hey for Honesty*, IV i, I now must pine and starve at Penniless Bench. 1860: Warter, *Sea-board*, ii 43 (OED), Though he have sometimes to sit on the Penniless Bench.

Penny and Pence. 1. A penny at a pinch is worth a pound. 1639: Clarke, 45.

2. A penny earned is better than a shilling given. 1875: Smiles, *Thrift*, 163.

3. A penny for your thought. 1546: Heywood, *Proverbs*, Pt II ch iv, Freend (quoth the good man) a peny for your thought. 1594: Greene, *Frier Bacon, etc.*, sc vi, How cheer you, sir? A penny for your thought! 1602: Marston, *Antonio and Mellida*, II. 1738: Swift, *Polite Convers.*, Dial. I. 1762: Hall Stevenson, *Crazy Tales*, Tale II p. 28, Now, said the Marchioness, and smil'd, I'll give a penny for your thoughts.

4. A penny in purse will bid me drink, when all the friends I have will not. 1670: Ray, 130. 1732: Fuller, 3865 ['make' for 'bid'].

5. A penny in the forehead. *See* quots. This alludes to an old game of making a child believe that a coin pressed on its forehead, and surreptitiously removed, is still there. 1658/9: T. Burton, *Diary*, 9 March, Sir A. Haslerigge turned from the chair, and they called him to speak to the chair. He said, 'I am not bound always to look you in the face like children, to see if you have a penny in your forehead'. 1740: North, *Examen*, 324, We may hope better of their abilities than to be wheedled as children with a penny in the forehead.

6. A penny in the purse is better than a friend at Court. 1875: Smiles, *Thrift*, 126 [quoted as 'a true saying']. Cf. **Friend** (3).

7. A penny more buys the whistle. 1732: Fuller, 341.

8. A penny saved is a penny earned (or **got**). [*c*.1550: *Gentleness and Nobility*, in Heywood, *Spider and Flie*, 447 (Farmer), I tell thee plainly, without any boast, A halfpeny is as well saved as lost.] 1640: Herbert, *Jac. Prudentum*, A penny spared is twice got. *c*.1686: in *Roxb. Ballads*, vi 349 (B.S.), A penny well sav'd is as good as one earn'd. 1711: Steele, *Spectator*, No. 2, He abounds in several frugal maxims … 'A penny saved is a penny got'. 1733: Fielding, *Miser*, III xii. 1852: Dickens, *Bleak House*, ch ix. I saved five pounds out of the brickmaker's affair … It's a very good thing to save one, let me tell you: a penny saved is a penny got! 1923: Wodehouse, *The Inimitable Jeeves*, xi, I can save money this way: and believe me, laddie, nowadays … a penny saved is a penny earned.

9. A penny soul never comes to twopence,

1859: Smiles, *Self-Help*, 297 (1869), Narrow-mindedness ... leads to failure. The penny soul, it is said, never came to twopence.

10. A penny to serve one's need. 1637: in *Pepysian Garland*, 447 (Rollins), The gentle craft doth beare good will, to all kind-hearted tradesmen still, That keepe the prouerbe to fullfill, *a penny to serue their need.*

11. Better penny in silver than any brother. 1659: Howell, *Proverbs: Brit.-Eng.*, 16.

12. Every one hath a penny for the new ale-house. 1678: Ray, 181. 1732: Fuller, 1445.

13. In for a penny in for a pound. 1695: Ravenscroft, *Caut. Guests*, V i (OED), Well than, O'er shooes, o'er boots. And in for a penny, in for a pound. 1815: Scott, *Mannering*, ch xlvi. 1823: Byron, *Letters, etc.*, vi 285 (Prothero). 1877: S. Butler, in *Life* by Jones, i 259 (1919), Feeling, therefore, that if I was in for a penny, I might as well be in for a pound, I wrote about your father's book exactly as I should have done about any one else's.

14. Penny and penny laid up will be many. 1639: Clarke, 35. 1670: Ray, 130. 1732: Fuller, 288.

15. Penny come quick soon makes two Pence. Ibid., No. 3863.

16. Penny in pocket is a good companion. 1659: Howell, 10. 1670: Ray, 130. 1712: Arbuthnot, *John Bull*, Pt II, ch iv, I am sure ... that a penny in the purse is the best friend John can have at last. 1732: Fuller, 3864 ['merry' for 'good'].

17. Penny to bless oneself. *See* **Cross** (3).

18. Penny wise and pound foolish. 1605: Camden, *Remains*, 330 (1870). 1631: Dekker, *Penny-wise, pound-foolish* [title]. 1712: Addison, *Spectator*, No. 295. 1864: Mrs H. Wood, *Trevlyn Hold*, ch xli. 1878: Platt, *Business*, 126.

19. Sometimes a penny well spent is better than a penny ill spared. 1672: Walker, *Paroem.*, 32.

20. Take care of the pence and the pounds will take care of themselves. Before 1724: in *Chesterfield Lett.*, 5. 2. 1750 (OED). 1834–7: Southey, *Doctor*, ch ccxli. 1859: Smiles, *Self-Help*, 305 (1869). 1924: *Observer*, 16 March, p. 2, col. 4. Cf. No. 27.

21. The penny is ill saved that shames the master. 1736: Bailey, *Dict.*, s.v. 'Shame'.

22. The penny is well spent that gets the pound. *c.*1400: *Beryn*, l. 2244, p. 69 (E.E.T.S.), ffor there is a comyn byword, yf ye it herd

havith: 'Wele settip he his peny, pat the pound [therby] savith'. 1536: in *Lisle Papers*, xiv art. 40, The old saying, 'Well is spent', etc.

23. The penny is well spent that saves a groat. 1605: Camden, *Remains*, 332 (1870). 1670: Ray, 130. 1732: Fuller, 4369.

24. There is more honesty in a penny than in five pounds. 1883: Burne, *Shropsh. Folk-Lore*, 588. [Miss Burne says that this is an argument for lending a large sum.]

25. There's no companion like the penny. 1659: Howell, *Proverbs: Span.-Eng.*, 13. 1670: Ray, 21. 1732: Fuller, 4891.

26. To think one's penny good silver. 1580: G. Harvey, *Works*, i 71 (Grosart), Euery one highly in his owne fauour, thinking no man's penny so good siluer as his own. 1637: Breton, in *Works*, ii *h* 20 (Grosart), There are more batchelors then Roger, and my penny is as good siluer as yours. 1732: Fuller, 3112, Is no coin good silver but your penny? Cf. **Farthing**; and **Halfpenny**.

27. Who will not lay up a penny Shall never have many. 1541: Coverdale, *Christ. State Matrimony*, sig. 13, Who so spareth not the penye shall neuer come by the pownde. 1670: Ray, 131 ['keep' for 'lay up']. 1732: Fuller, 6383. Cf. No. 20.

28. You may know by a penny how a shilling spends. 1678: Ray, 78. 1732: Fuller, 5951.
See also **Pennyworth**.

Penny-weight of love is worth a pound of law, A. 1732: Fuller, 343.

Pennyworth, Great. *See* **Great bargain.**

Pennyworth of ease is worth a penny, A. 1605: Camden, *Remains*, 318 (1870). 1678: Ray, 130. 1732: Fuller, 344.

Pennyworth of mirth is worth a pound of sorrow, A. 1678: Ray, 176.

Pennyworth of poker is worth two of coals, A. 1864: 'Cornish Proverbs', in *N. & Q.*, 3rd ser, vi 495.

Penrith, Peerless. 1638: Brathwait, *Barn. Itiner.*, 151 (1774), Thence to Peerless Penrith went I, Which of merchandise hath plenty. 1846–59: *Denham Tracts.*, i 182 (F.L.S.). *See also* **Little London.**

Pensford. *See* **Stanton Drew.**

Pension never enriched a young man. 1640: Herbert, *Jac. Prudentum.*

Pens may blot but they cannot blush. 1596: Harington, *Metam. of Ajax*, vii (1814) [quoted as 'the old saying']. 1639: Clarke, 268. Cf. **Pen and Ink.**

Pentecost. *See* **Whitsuntide.**

Penzance, Not a word of. This refers to the glaring cowardice of the Penzance men when Cornwall was invaded by the Spanish in 1595. 1678: Ray, 350, Not a word of Pensants. 1750: Heath, *Scilly and Cornwall*, 407. 1906: *Cornish N.&Q.*, 264.

People's love is the king's life-guard, The. 1738: *Gent. Mag.*, 475. Cf. **Subject** (1).

Pepper. *See* **Snow** (7).

Pepper-gate. *See* **Daughter.**

Pepper in the nose, To take = To take offence. 1377: Langland, *Plowman*, B, xv 197, And to pore peple han peper in the nose. *c.*1500: Skelton, *Why Come Ye Nat*, l. 381, For drede of the red hat Take peper in the nose [Lest the cardinal take offence]. 1583: Greene, *Works*, ii 52 (Grosart), As old women are soone angry, she tooke pepper in the nose at the sharpe reply. 1607: Marston, *What You Will*, Induction, He's a chollerick gentleman; he will take pepper in the nose instantly. 1682: Bunyan, *Holy War*, ch x. 1714: Ozell, *Molière*, ii 13, I approve of a husband's vigilance in this particular; but I'm afraid you take pepper i' th' nose too soon. 1732: Fuller, 2032. Cf. **Snuff.**

Percys' profit was the Lucys' loss, The. 1846–59: *Denham Tracts*, i 228 (F.L.S.).

Perseverance kills the game. 1813: Ray, 149. 1846–59: *Denham Tracts*, ii 108 (F.L.S.).

Persuasion of the fortunate sways the doubtful, The. 1640: Herbert, *Jac. Prudentum.* 1670: Ray, 10.

PERT and PEART:

(*a*) **Peart as a maggot, As.** Oxfordsh. 1913: *Folk-Lore*, xxiv 77.

Peart as a robin, As. [1592: Warner, *Albion's Eng.*, ch xxxi st. 4, As peart as bird.] 1862: *Dialect of Leeds*, 405. 1901: F. E. Taylor, *Lancs Sayings*, 3, As peeart as a robin.

Peart as a sparrow, As. 1837: Mrs Palmer, *Devonsh. Dialect*, 70 … a common phrase for a lively little chit.

Peart as a spoon, As. 1882: Mrs Chamberlain, *W. Worcs. Words*, 22 (E.D.S.) … means unusually bright and cheerful.

(*b*) **Pert as a pearmonger, As.** 1564: Harding, quoted in Jewel, *Defence of the Apol.*, 822 (P.S.), Here pricketh forth this hasty defender, as pert as

a pearmonger. 1678: Ray, 281, As pert as a pearmongers mare. Before 1732: Gay, *New Song of New Similes*, Pert as a pearmonger I'd be If Molly were but kind. 1738: Swift, *Polite Convers.*, Dial. I. 1855: *N.&Q.*, 1st ser, xi 114, As peart as a pearmonger (Lancs). 1855: Ibid., 232, 'Peart as a pearmonger' does not belong to Lancashire. I have often heard it in Oxon and Bucks.

Pert. *See also* **Crouse.**

Perverseness makes one squint-eyed. 1640: Herbert, *Jac. Prudentum.*

Peter of Wood, Church and mills are all his. Cheshire. 1670: Ray, 217. 1852: *N.&Q.*, 1st ser, vi 386. 1917: Bridge, *Cheshire Proverbs*, 103.

Petworth. 1884: 'Sussex Proverbs', *in. N.&Q.*, 6th ser, x 370, Proud Petworth, poor people, High church, crooked steeple. 1911: A. S. Cooke, *Off Beaten Track in Sussex*, 284, Poor Petworth, proud people, etc.

Physic, *subs.* **1. He takes physic before he is sick.** 1639: Clarke, 283. 1670: Ray, 189.

2. He that liveth fry physicke liveth miserably. 1588: Cogan, *Haven of Health*, Epist. Ded. [quoted as 'a common saying'].

3. If physic do not work, prepare for the kirk. 1678: Ray, 189.

Physician, heal thyself. [Luke iv 23, And he said unto them, Ye will surely say unto me this proverb, Physician, heal thyself: whatsoever we have heard done in Capernaum, do also here in thy country.] *c.*1400: tr. *Honorius of Autun's Elucidarium* (1909), 29, Blynde leches [doctors], heeleth first youre silf! 1511: Colet, *Sermon*, in Dunton's *Phenix*, ii 8 (1708), 'Tis an old proverb, Physician heal thyself. 1543: Becon, in *Early Works*, 385 (P.S.). 1579: Lyly, *Euphues*, 118 (Arber). 1638: D. Tuvill, *Vade Mecum*, 152 (3rd ed.), First therefore physitian, cure thine own ills. 1692: L'Estrange, *Aesop*, 205 (3rd ed.) ['cure' for 'heal']. 1781: Francklin, *Lucian*, ii 134 *n.*, According to the old adage, 'physician, cure thyself'. 1875: Smiles, *Thrift*, 23.

Physicians' faults are covered with earth. 1620: J. Melton, *Astrologaster*, 17, The sunne doth alwayes behold your good successe, and the earth couers all your ignorances. 1637: T. Heywood, *Dialogues, etc.*, in Bang, *Materialien*, B. 3, 197, 'Tis said of all physitians What good comes by their physick, the sun sees: But in their art, if they have bad successe, That the earth covers. 1669: *Politeuphuia*, 175, Physicians are happy men, because the sun makes manifest what good success soever happeneth in their cures, and the earth burieth what fault soever they commit. [As to the Greek original of this saying, by Nicocles, *see N. &Q.*, 8th ser, vi 246.] **Physicians kill more than they cure.** 1703: E. Ward, *Writings*, ii 328 ['an old maxim'].

Physicians. *See also* **Feastings; Feed (1); Few; Fool (15); God heals; Good physician; Hide nothing; Inward sore; Old,** A (*b*)(7); and **Patient.**

Pick a hole in a man's coat, To. 1588: *Mar-Prelate's Epitome*, 3 (1843), There is a deuice to fynde a hole in the coat of some of you puritanes. 1639: Clarke, 80, It's easie to pick a hole in another man's coat, if he be disposed. 1670: Ray, 189. 1745: *Agreeable Companion*, 105, You have great reason to pick holes in your neighbour's coats. 1808: Manning, *Lett. to Lamb*, 110 (1925), God forgive me if I'm censorious, and pick holes in another man's coat.

Pick a quarrel, To. *c.*1449: *Paston Letters*, i 87 (OED), The seyde parsone ... hathe pekyd a qwarell to on Mastyr Recheforthe. 1519: Horman, *Vulgaria*, fo. 128, He begynneth to pyke or fyndeth a quarel of my wordes. *c*1550: *Jacke Jugeler*, 83 (Grosart), Woll sone pike a quarrell, be it wrong or right. 1579: Lyly, *Euphues*, 107 (Arber). 1669: Brathwait, *Hist, of Moderation*, 75, Neighbours ... would be ... ready to pick any quarrel with her. 1894: Caine, *Manxman*, V xiv 325 (OED), Some of the men began to pick quarrels.

Pick and choose and take the worst. 1884: H. Friend, *Flowers and Fl. Lore*, 228, We say more colloquially, 'Pick and choose', etc.

Pick-pockets are sure traders; for they take ready money. 1732: Fuller, 3872.

Pickpockets in a fair, They agree like. 1813: Ray, 178.

Pick up one's crumbs, To = To be convalescent. 1580: Lyly, *Euphues*, 302 (Arber), What with hir merry sporting, and good nourishing, I began to gather vp my crumbes. 1645: Howell, *Letters*, bk i § ii No. 1, I ... am recovering and picking up my crums apace. 1754: Berthelson, *Eng.-Danish Dict.*, s.v. 'Pick'. 1886: Elworthy, *West Som. Word-Book*, 566 (E.D.S.), Our Liz bin ter'ble bad ... but her's pickin' up her crooms again now, like.

Picture is worth a thousand words, One (*or* **A**). A saying particularly associated

with journalism. There is no evidence for the Chinese origin of the saying claimed in the 1927 quot. 1921: *Printer's Ink*, 8 Dec., 96, One look is worth a thousand words. 1927: *Ibid.* 10 March, 114, *Chinese proverb*, One picture is worth ten thousand words. 1979: *Scientific American*, Oct. 118, A picture is worth a thousand words.

Picture tells a story, Every. 1847: C. Brontë, *Jane Eyre*, I i, The letterpress ... I little cared for ... Each picture told a story. 1904: *Daily Mail*, 26 Feb., 18, A London woman and Doan's Backache Kidney Pills ... 'Every picture tells a story'.

Piddinghoe, a Sussex village near Newhaven, in the valley of the Ouse, which has a Gotham-like reputation. *See* quots. 1884: 'Sussex Proverbs', *in N. &Q.*, 6th ser, ix 401, At Piddinghoe they dig for daylight ... moonshine ... [and] smoke. 1911: A. S. Cooke, *Off Beaten Track in Sussex*, 283, More famous Piddinghoe – 'where they shoe their magpies' – with its reputed ague and celebrated chalk-pit – 'where they hang ponds out to dry'. Ibid., 284, Englishmen fight, Frenchmen too: We don't – we live Piddinghoe!

Pie–lid makes people wise. 1678: Ray, 79. 1875: Cheales, *Proverb. Folk-Lore*, 114, One can't tell what a pie is till the lid is off.

Pig and **Pigs. 1. A brinded pig will make a good brawn to breed on** = 'A red headed man will make a good stallion '(Ray, 1737). 1678: Ray, 67.

2. A pig may fly. *See* quots. 1732: Fuller, 4350, That is as likely as to see an hog fly. 1872: De Morgan, *Budget of Paradoxes*, 275, There is a proverb which says, A pig may fly, but it isn't a likely bird.

3. A pig of one's own sow. *c.*1535: *Gentleness and Nobility*, sig. A1, v°, That is euyn a pyg of our own sow. 1579: G. Harvey, *Works*, i 112 (Grosart). A misshapin illfavor'd freshe copy of my precious poems, as it were, a pigg of myne owne sowe. 1608: Day, *Humor out of Breath*, III, 'Tis a pig of your owne sow, madam; and I hope your wit will bestow the nursing of it. 1681: Robertson, *Phraseol. Generalis*, 1110, 'Tis a pig of your own sow, your own self sold it. 1860: Reade, *Cl. and Hearth*, ch xcviii, 'Who more charitable than monks?' 'Go to! They do but give the laity back a pig of their own sow'.

4. A pig of the worse pannier. 1533: Heywood, *John, Tyb, etc.*, 89 (Fanner), And, peradventure, there, he and she Will make me cuckold, even to anger me; And then had I a pig in the worse panyer. 1546: Heywood, *Proverbs*, II ch xi, He hath a pyg of the worse panier sure.

5. A pretty pig makes an ugly old sow. 1732: Fuller, 363.

6. A red pig for an atchern [acorn]. 1886: R. Holland, *Cheshire Gloss.*, 444 (E.D.S.). 1917: Bridge, *Cheshire Proverbs*, 5.

7. As happy as a pig in muck. 1828: Carr, *Craven Dialect*, ii 43. 1889: Peacock, *Manley, etc.*, *Gloss.*, 358 (E.D.S.), 'As happy as pigs e' muck', means having one's fill of sensual pleasure.

8. As Irish as pigs in Shudehill market. Manchester. 1869: Hazlitt, 65.

9. Feed a pig and you'll have a hog. 1732: Fuller, 1517.

10. He has brought his pigs to a fine (or **fair**) **market.** 1600: *Look About You*, sc xiii, My fa-fa-father has brought his ho-ho-hogs to a fa-fa-fair m-m-market. *c*.1613: Rowlands, *Paire of Spy-Knaues*, 9 (Hunt.Cl.), As wise as Iohn of Gotehams calfe: or this fellow brought his hogges to a faire market. 1693: Urquhart, *Rabelais*, bk iii ch xlv, I have fish'd fair now (quoth Panurge) and brought my pigs to a fine market. 1713: C. Shadwell, *Hum. of Army*, V ii, Ah, Gemini, I have brought my hogs to a fair market. 1757: Murphy, *Upholsterer*, I iii, Yes, you've carried your pigs to a fine market. 1806: Lamb, *Mr H –* , II, Your Honour has had some mortification, to be sure … you have brought your pigs to a fine market. 1849: Planché, *Extravag.*, iv 32 (1879), To a fine market you have brought your pigs.

11. He is teaching a pig to play on a flute. 1813: Ray, 75.

12. He knows not a pig from a dog. 1737: Ray, 206.

13. He that loves noise must buy a pig. 1813: Ray, 143.

14. Like a pig, he'll do no good alive. 1589: L. Wright, *Display of Dutie*, 10, A noysome hogg, that is neuer profitable till he dye. 1630: T. Adams, *Works*, 452, Like a two-leg'd hog … neuer doth good, till he is dead. 1732: Fuller, 3226, Like an hog; he does no good till he dies. Ibid., No. 5851, You are like a hog; never good, while living. 1828: Carr, *Craven Dialect*, ii 43, 'He's like a pig, he'll do no good alive', said of a covetous man, regardless of the happiness of others. 1847: Halliwell, *Dict.*, s.v. 'Pig'.

15. Like a pig's tail, going all day, and nothing done at night. 1865: 'Lancs Proverbs', in *N.&Q.*, 3rd ser, viii 494. 1901: F. E. Taylor, *Lancs Sayings*, 5.

16. Pigs can see the wind. 1663: Butler, *Hudibras*, Pt III can. ii l.1105, Had lights when better eyes were blind, as pigs are said to see the wind. 1703: E. Ward, *Writings*, ii 271, 'Tis as natural … as 'tis for a hog to see the wind. 1831: Hone, *Year-Book*, 29 Feb. [quoted as a common saying]. 1890: *N.&Q.*, 7th ser, ix 14, That pigs can see the wind – in particular the east wind – is a notion pretty general in the Midlands. 1916: *N.&Q.*, 12th ser, ii 358, I have often heard it said that wind looks like fire to a pig, and that only a pig can see the wind.

17. Pigs fly in the air with their tails forward. 1639: Clarke, 147. 1670: Ray, 189. 1880: Spurgeon, *Ploughman's Pictures*, 32, They say that if pigs fly they always go with their tails forward.

18. Pigs love that lie together. 1678: Ray, 189. 1707: C. Cibber, *Double Gallant*, V ii, You know the old saying, Sir Solomon, *Lying together makes pigs love.* 1732: Fuller, 3874.

19. Pigs play on the organs. 1639: Clarke, 7, A pig playes, etc. 1670: Ray, 189. 1685: S. Wesley, *Maggots*, 22, Why should not other piggs on organs play, As well as they? 1732: Fuller, 3875. Cf. **Hogs Norton.**

20. The worst pig often gets the best pear. 1855: Bohn, 519.

21. The young pig grunts like the old sow. 1678: Ray, 184.

22. There are more ways. *See* quot. 1883: Burne, *Shropsh. Folk-Lore*, 590, Theer's more ways o' killin' pigs than chokin' 'em 'ooth [with] butter.

23. To buy a pig in a poke [bag]. 1546: Heywood, *Proverbs*, Pt II ch ix, Ye loue not to bye the pyg in the poke. 1583: Greene, *Works*, ii 121 (Grosart), He is a foole, they say, that will buy ye pig in the poke. 1631: F. Lenton, *Characters*, sig. B11 (1663), You may perhaps buy a pigge in a poke. 1694: *Terence made English*, 165, I don't love to buy a pig in a bag. 1705: Steele, *Tender Husband*, III ii, I thought it would be proper to see how I liked you, as not caring to buy a pig in a poke. 1806: Lamb, *Mr H —*, II, No great harm if you had. You'd only have bought a pig in a poke. 1920: Hudson, *Dead*

Man's Plack, ii 20, Athelwold … with a friend's privilege told him not to be so simple as to buy a pig in a poke.

24. To drive pigs to market = To snore. 1738: Swift, *Polite Convers.*, Dial. II, He fell asleep, and snored so hard, that we thought he was driving his hogs to market. 1785: Grose, *Class. Dict. Vulgar Tongue*, s.v. 'Hog', To drive one's hogs, to snore. 1854: Baker, *Northants Gloss.*, s.v. 'Pigs', 'To drive your pigs to market'. To snore. 1901: F. E. Taylor, *Lancs Sayings*, 16, He were droivin' th' pigs to th' market (He was snoring).

25. What can you expect from a pig but a grunt? 1731: *Poor Robin's Almanack*, C6, If we petition a Hog, what can we expect but a grunt. 1827: Scott, *Journal*, 10 April ['sow' for 'pig', and 'grumph' for 'grunt']. 1916: B. Duffy, *Special Pleading*, 7.

26. When pigs carry sticks, The clouds will play tricks; When they lie in the mud, No fears of a flood. 1893: Inwards, *Weather Lore*, 130.

27. When the pig is proffered hold up the poke. *c*.1400: *Douce MS.*, 52, cited in Farmer's *Heywood's Proverbs*, 422 (1906), When me profereth the pigge, open the poghe. 1530: Palsgrave, 594, Whan the pygge is proferd it is good to apen the poke. *c*.1580: Fulwell, *Ars Adulandi*, sig. G1, When pig is proferd, ope the poke. 1670: Ray, 131. 1732: Fuller, 5601.

28. You can never make a good shaft of a pig's tail. 1605: Camden, *Remains*, 328 (1870), Make a pipe of a pig's tail. 1651: Herbert, *Jac. Prudentum*, 2nd ed. 1670: Ray, 104, You can't make a horn of a pigs tail. 1732: Fuller, 5872. 1880: Spurgeon, *Ploughman's Pictures*, 31, There's sense in choosing your tools, for a pig's tail will never make a good arrow.

See also **First Pig; Goodyer's pig; Hog; Like the Irishman's pig; More pigs; Pearls; Pelton; Please** (6); **Sleep,** *verb* (9); **Snug; Sow; Stare; Subtle; Swine;** and **Wilful**.

Pigeon and **Pigeons. 1. Full pigeons find cherries bitter.** 1623: Wodroephe, *Spared Houres*, 509.

2. Pigeons are taken when crows fly at pleasure. 1732: Fuller, 3873.

3. Pigeons never do know woe But when they do a benting go. 1609: T. Ravenscroft, *Deuteromelia*, sig. F3, The pigion is neuer woe, till abenting she goe. 1670: Ray, 44. 1732: Fuller, 6480. *c*.1791: Pegge, *Derbicisms*, 89 (E.D.S.),

Pigeons never know such woe, As when they a-benting go. 1839: G. C. Lewis, *Herefs. Words*, 10. 1842: Akerman, *Wilts Gloss.*, 5.

4. To catch two pigeons with one bean. 1557: North, *Diall of Princes*, fo. 56, For the prouerbe sayeth, that with one beane, a man maye take two pigeons. 1577: J. Grange, *Golden Aphroditis*, sig. E2, In hoping to take two pigeons with one beane you are decyued. 1602: Chamberlain, *Letters*, 124 (Camden S.), You deserve double thanckes, and serve two pigeons with one beane. 1678: Ray, 353.

5. When the pigeons go a benting, Then the farmers lie lamenting. 1830: Forby, *Vocab. E. Anglia*, 417. 1866: Brogden, *Lincs Prov. Words*, s.v. 'Benting', When the dove goes a benting, The farmer is lamenting.

See also **Children** (9); and **House** (20).

Pilchards. 1. Cream upon pilchards, said of a smart dress upon a slatternly woman. S. Corn. 19th cent. (Mr C. Lee).

2. Heat and pilchards. Corn. 1869: Hazlitt, 201.

3. *See* quot. 1875: Cheales, *Proverb. Folk-Lore*, 53, The results of a school of pilchards coming into one of their bays – Meat, money and light, All in one night.

Pilgarlic. Originally a bald head, but became a proverbial name for any unlucky wight, sometimes in self-application. [*c*.1400: *Beryn*, 5 (E.E.T.S.), And yee shull here howe the Tapster made the Pardoner pull Garlik al the longe nyte, til it was nere end day.] Before 1529: Skelton, in *Works*, i 122 (Dyce), Ye loste hyr fauyr quyt; Your pyllyd garleke hed Cowde hocupy there no stede. *c*.1620: B.&F., *Hum. Lieut.*, II ii, There got he a knock, and down goes pilgarlick. 1671: *Westm. Drollery*, 38 (Ebsworth), Then to the cupboard Pilgarlick must hie, To seek for some crusts that have long lain dry. 1676: Shadwell, *Virtuoso*, II, Do you think to make a fool of Pilgarlick? 1709: Centlivre, *Busy Body*, V iii, So, here's everybody happy, I find, but poor Pilgarlick. I wonder what satisfaction I shall have. *c*.1760: Foote, *Lame Lover*, III, So then it seems poor Pill Garlick here is discarded at once. 1813: *Life of Pill Garlick, Rather a Whimsical Sort of Fellow* [title]. 1894: *Punch*, 21 April, 186 (OED), No! 'tis Bull is pilgarlic and martyr.

Pill and **Pills. 1. If the pills were pleasant, they would not want gilding.** 1633: Draxe, 57, If the apothecaries pilles had a good taste, they would neuer gilde them ouer. 1732: Fuller, 2711.

2. To give one a pill to swallow=To tell one something unpleasant. 1567: Painter, *Pal. of Pleasure*, iii 52 (Jacobs), The good lady … swallowed down that pille without chewing. 1889: Peacock, *Manley, etc., Gloss.*, 405 (E.D.S.), It'd be a sore pill for him at his time of life.

Pillar to post, From. Often **From post to pillar.** *c.*1420: Lydgate, *Assembly of Gods*, 34 (E.E.T.S.), Thus fro poost to pylour was he made to daunce. *c.*1532: R. Copland, *Spyttel Hous*, l. 715, And turmoyleth alway fro pyler to post. 1575: *Appius and Virg.*, in Hazlitt, *Old Plays*, iv 151, Thus in hurly burly, from pillar to post, Poor Haphazard daily was toss'd. 1605: Chapman, *All Fools*, III i … from post to pillar. 1609: Dekker, in *Works*, iv 136 (Grosart) … from poste to piller. 1673: Marvell, in *Works*, iii 279 (Grosart) … hunted from post to pillar. 1777: in *Garrick Corresp.*, ii 202 (1832), Your good nature will forgive me, especially when you consider how I am tossed from pillar to post. 1852: Dickens, *Bleak House*, ch xxiv, The man was so badgered, and worried, and tortured, by being knocked about from post to pillar, and from pillar to post … 1903: H. James, *Letters*, i 435 (1902), It all makes me glad I am old, and thereby soon to take leave of a world in which one is driven, unoffending, from pillar to post.

Pilling Moss, Lancs. **1. God's grace and Pilling Moss are endless.** Lancs. 1846–59: *Denham Tracts*, i 180 (F.L.S.).

2. Once a wood, then a sea, now a moss, and e'er will be. 1869: Hazlitt, 305.

Pilsen-pin. *See* **Lenson-hill.**

Pimlico. *See* quots. *c.*1680: Aubrey, *Nat. Hist. Surrey*, v 221, *To walk in Pimblico* became proverbial for a man handsomely drest; as these walks [Pimblico–Path, near the Globe Theatre] were frequented by none else. 1863: *N.&Q.*, 3rd ser, iv 327. There is a Devonshire proverb, 'To keep it in Pimlico', that is, to keep a house in nice order.

Pimpernel. *No heart can think, no tongue can tell, The virtues of the pimpernel.* 1849: Halliwell, *Pop. Rhymes*, 179. 1878: Dyer, *Eng. Folk-Lore*, 26. 1910: *Devonsh. Assoc. Trans.*, xlii 90, No heart can think nor tongue can tell The virtue there is in pimpernel.

Pin and **Pins,** *subs.* **1. A pin a day is a groat a year.** 1712: Addison, *Spectator*, No. 295. 1738: Swift, *Polite Convers.*, Dial. I. 1792: Wolcot, *Works*, ii 313 (1795). 1829: Hunter, *Hallamsh. Gloss.*, 21.

2. He that takes not up a pin, slights his wife. 1640: Herbert, *Jac. Prudentum.* 1670: Ray, 21. 1732: Fuller, 2324.

3. He that will not stoop for a pin, will never be worth a pound. 1667–8: Pepys, *Diary*, 2 Jan., Sir W. Coventry answered: 'I see your Majesty do not remember the old English proverb, "He that will not," etc.' 1732: Fuller, 2355 [with 'point' for 'pound'].

4. He that will steal a pin will steal a better thing. 1537: R. Whitford, *Werke for Housholders*, sig. D7, The chylde yt begineth to pike at a pynne or a poynte wyl after pyke a penny or a pounde. 1639: Clarke, 84, He that begins to steale a pin will be hang'd for a pound one day. 1670: Ray, 145. 1732: Fuller, 6087. 1896: *N.&Q.*, 8th ser, x 320, It is a sin To steal a pin has sometimes helped to keep me straight.

5. Not to care (or pass) a pin. *c.*1410: Towneley Plays, 34 (E.E.T.S.), In fayth thi felowship Set I not at a pyn. *c.*1555: in Wright, *Songs, etc., Philip and Mary*, 89 (Roxb.Cl). Of Goddes ferfull vengance the[y] passyde note a pynne. 1576: Wapull, *Tide tarrieth no Man*, sig. D3, So that for her mother she cares not a pin. 1642: in Marchant, *Praise of Ale*, 234 (1888), Yet I care not a pin, for I see no sin … 1663: in *Amanda, Bagf. Ballads*, 480* (B.S.), Let them laugh that win, I care not a pin. 1779: S. Crisp, in D'Arblay, *Diary*, i 104 (1876), As to your vexation, child, I don't mind it of a pin. 1856: in Marchant, *Praise of Ale*, 415 (1888), For whiskey or gin, I don't care a pin.

6. Pick up pins pick up sorrow. 1883: Burne, *Shropsh. Folk-Lore*, 279, Salopians too say, 'Pick up', etc. 1913: E. M. Wright, *Rustic Speech, etc.*, 220, Pick up pins, pick up sorrow, is a saying which is contradicted by other versions such as [*see* Nos. 7 and 8].

7. See a pin and let it lie, You'll want a pin before you die. 1843: Halliwell, *Nursery Rhymes*, 120, See a pin, and let it lay, Bald luck you'll have all the day! 1872: *N.&Q.*, 4th ser, x 477,1 have frequently heard the following in Cornwall: 'To see a pin and let it lie, You'll want a pin before you die'. 1878: Dyer, *Eng. Folk-*

Lore, 270, *See* a pin … All the day you'll have to cry. 1880: *N.&Q.*, 6th ser, ii 205. 1913: E. M. Wright, *Rustic Speech, etc.*, 220.

8. See a pin and pick it up, All the day you'll have good luck. 1843: Halliwell, *Nursery Rhymes*, 120. 1883: Burne, *Shropsh. Folk-Lore*, 280. 1913: E. M. Wright, *Rustic Speech, etc.*, 220. *See also* **Merry pin.**

Pin, *verb. To pin one's faith on another's sleeve.* 1599: *Life of Sir T. More*, in Wordsworth, *Eccl. Biog.*, ii 149 (1853) (OED), I never intended to pinne my soule to another mans sleeve. 1642: Fuller, *Holy State*: 'Moderation', He never pinned his religion on any man's sleeve. 1656: T. Ady, *Candle in the Dark*, 4, To pin their opinion upon the sleeve of other mens judgements. 1706: E. Ward, *Works*, iii 20, All that pinn'd their faith upon their pastor's sleeve. 1725: *Matchless Rogue*, 17, With your leave, good Mr Poet, we must not pin our faith upon your sleeve. 1809: pegge, *Anonymiana*, cent. iii 63, I find now, that the custom formerly was, for people to wear both badges and presents, such as New-year's gifts, on their sleeves … Hence, I suppose, the expression *to pin one's faith on another's sleeve.*

Pinch, At a. 1489: Caxton, *Faytes of A.*, I xviii 53 (OED), Corageously at a pynche [he] shal renne vpon hem. 1540: Palsgrave, *Acolastus*, sig. Aa3, Do nowe helpe me at a pynche. 1564: Bullein, *Dialogue*, 10 (E.E.T.S.), You are welcome … now helpe at a pinche, or els neuer. 1594: Greene, *Frier Bacon*, sc v, Helpe, Frier, at a pinch. 1614: Jonson, *Bart. Fair*, *I.* 1679: *Counterfeits*, I ii, We women seldom fail at a pinch. 1828: Scott, *Journal*, 4 April, He had not lived so long by the Crown to desert it at a pinch. 1888: R.L.S., *Black Arrow*, bk iv ch i, It … yet might serve him, in a pinch, against Sir Daniel.

Pinch on the parson's side. *See* **Parson's side.**

Pine wishes herself a shrub when the ax is at her root, The. 1732: Fuller, 4705.

Pinnock to pannock. *See* quot. 1552: Huloet, *Abced.*, sig. D3, Brynge somethynge to nothynge, as the vulgare speache is, to brynge pynnock to pannock.

Pint of wine to a vintner is but as a pippin to a coster-monger, A. 1659: Howell, 11.

Pint pot. *See* **Quait.**

Pipe in an ivy leaf, You may go = You may do any silly thing you like. *c.*1370: Wiclif, *Eng. Works*, 372 (E.E.T.S.), The seculer party may

go pipe with an yuy lefe for eny lorde-schipis that the clerkis wille geue hem agen. *c.*1386: Chaucer, *Knight's Tale*, l. 980, That oon of yow, al be him looth or leef, He moot go pypen in an ivy–leef. *c.*1430: Lydgate, *Destr. of Thebes*, Pt II, But let his brother blowe in an horn, Where that him list, or pipe in a reade. *c.*1547: in *Ballads from MSS.*, i 136 (B.S.), They may gowe blowe ther flüett. 1587: Turbervile, *Trag. Tales, etc.*, 309 (1837), Giue him an iuie leafe in stead of pipe to play, That dreads to bourd a gallant dame for feare she say him nay. 1626: *Scoggins Jests*, 109 (1864), Unlesse that hee have some man to speake for him, hec may goe pipe in an ivy leafe.

Pipe, No longer, no longer dance. 1605: Camden, *Remains*, 328 (1870). 1620: Shelton, *Quixote*, Pt II ch vii, It shall be not be said, master, for me, 'No longer pipe, no longer dance'. 1709: O. Dykes, *Eng. Proverbs*, 197 (2nd ed.). 1806: Scott, *Fam. Letters*, i 61 (1894), The vulgar saying of 'No longer pipe, no longer dance', applies to landlord and tenant, chieftain and clan … in short, to all the relations of mankind. 1874: *N.&Q.*, 5th ser, i 205.

Piping hot. *c.*1386: Chaucer, *Miller's Tale*, l. 193, And wafres, pyping hote out of the glede. 1567: Golding, *Ovid*, bk viii l. 850, Whote [Hot] meate came pyping from the fyre. 1595: *Maroccus Extaticus*, iii (Percy S.), A peece of beefe puld piping hot out of the furnace. 1638: H. Shirley, *Martyr'd Souldier*, V, I gave her a messe of porredge piping-hot. 1701: Cibber, *Love Makes a Man*, Prol., A ragou, piping hot from Paris. 1766: Garrick, *Neck or Nothing*, I i. 1821: Byron, *Blues*, ecl. i l. 17, I am just piping hot from a publisher's shop.

Pipkin, She has cracked her. 1681: in *Roxb. Ballads*, v 67 (B.S.), For if you should your pipkin crack, your credit will away. *c.*1685: in *Bagford Ballads*, i 467 (B.S.), Were not my pipkin crackt before, I vow I would be his wife. 1707: *Spanish Bawd*, III ii, If her husband shou'd find out that she has crackt her pipkin, he'll cut your throat. 1732: Fuller, 4124, She has broke her pipkin.

Pirates may make cheap pennyworths of their pillage. 1855: Bohn, 474.

Piss against the wind, To. 1642: Torriano, 19, He who pisseth against the wind wetteth his shirt.

Piss on a nettle, To = To be out of temper.

1546: Heywood, *Proverbs*, Pt II ch x. 1579: *Marr. of Wit and Wisdom*, sc iii p. 30 (SH.S.). 1681: Shadwell, *Lancs Witches*, I. 1714: Ozell, *Molière*, iv 255. 1828: Carr, *Craven Dialect*, ii 8, 'Thou's p. – d of a nettle this mornin'', said of a waspish, ill-tempered person.

Pissed his tallow, He has. *c.*1450: *M. E. Med. Book*, 232 (Heinrich), (OED), Take talow of an hert, suche as he pysseth by twene two seynt mary dayes. 1600: Shakespeare, *Merry Wives*, V v 1694: Motteux, *Rabelais*, bk v ch xxviii, Do but see bow down o' the mouth the curr looks: he's nothing but skin and bones; he has p. – d his tallow. 1737: Ray, 61 … This is spoken of bucks who grow lean after rutting time, and may be applied to men.

Pitch and pay = Pay ready money. 15th cent.: in Hazlitt, *Early Pop. Poetry*, ii 9, Yt ys fule hard bothe to pyche and paye. 1584: in *Roxb. Ballads*, i 6 (B.S.), And there was neither fault nor fray, Nor any disorder any way, But euery man did pitch and pay. 1599: Shakespeare, *Henry V*, II iii, The word is 'Pitch and Pay': Trust none. 1847: Halliwell, *Dict.*, s.v. 'Pitch', Pitch and pay, throw down your money at once, pay ready money.

Pitch. He that touches pitch shall be defiled. [*Ecclesiasticus* xiii 1. Ex quo ostenditur noxium esse vivere cum peccatoribus; qui enim tangit picem, inquinatur ab ea. – St Jerome, *Comment, in Esai.*, vi 5.] 1303: R. Brunne, *Handl. Synne*, l. 6578, Who so handlyth pycche wellyng hote, He shal haue fylthe therof sumdeyl [in some degree], *c.*1380: Wiclif, *Works*, 218 (Matthew, 1880), He that handlith pich schal be foulid thereof. *c.*1440: Lydgate, *Fall of Princes*, bk i l. 4696, Who touchith pich, bassay men may see, It failith nat he shal defouled be. 1579: Lyly, *Euphues*, III (Arber). 1609: Dekker, *Works*, iv 198 (Grosart). 1710: S. Palmer, *Moral Essays on Proverbs*, 249. 1883: R.L.S., *Treasure I*, ch x, 'There,' John would add, 'you can't touch pitch and not be mucked.' 1922: Weyman, *Ovington's Bank*, ch xxxi, You can't touch pitch and keep your hands clean.

Pitcher goes often to the well, but is broken at last, The. 1340: *Ayenbite*, 206 (E.E.T.S.), Zuo longe geth thet pot to the wetere thet hit comth to-broke hom. 1412: Hoccleve, *Regement*, l. 4432, The pot so longe to the watir goth, That hoom it cometh at the laste y-broke. 1481:

Caxton, *Reynard*, 67 (Arber), A pot may goo so longe to water that at the laste it cometh to broken hoom. 1583: Greene, in *Works*, ii 30 (Grosart), So longe the pitcher goeth to the brooke, as in tyme it comes broken home. 1665: Head and Kirkman, *Eng. Rogue*, i 69, I found the proverb verified, The pitcher goes not so often to the well, but that it comes home crackt at last. 1714: Ozell, *Molière*, vi 50. 1748: Smollett, *Rod. Random*, ch lxiv. 1826: Scott, *Journal*, 1 Oct., They talk about the pitcher going to the well; but if it does not go to the well, how shall we get water? 1926: J. S. Fletcher, *Massingham Butterfly*, 275, You know the old proverb about the pitcher going to the well?

Pitchers. *See* **Little pitchers.**

Pitiful surgeon spoileth a sore, A. 1578: Florio, *First Fruites*, fo. 32, A pitifull physition maketh a scabed wound. 1611: Cotgrave, s.v. 'Medecin'.

Pity cureth envy. 1732: Fuller, 3876.

Pity is but one remove from love. 1753: Richardson, *Grandison*, i 34 (1883). [Nowadays the more usual form is, Pity is akin to love.]

Pity's a poor plaster. 1875: Cheales, *Proverb. Folk-Lore*, 122.

Pity without relief Is like mustard without beef. Ibid., 122. 1913: *Devonsh. Assoc. Trans.*, xlv 90, Pity without relief is like pudding without suet [or] like mustard without beef. Cf. **Sympathy.**

Pity, verb. He that pities another remembers himself. 1640: Herbert, *Jac. Prudentum*. 1748: Richardson, *Clarissa*, iv 121 (1785).

Place for everything, and everything in its place, A. 1640: G. Herbert, *Outlandish Proverbs*, no. 379, All things have their place, knew wee how to place them. 1842: Marryat, *Masterman Ready*, II i, In a well-conducted man-of-war … every thing in its place, and there is a place for every thing. 1855: T. C. Haliburton, *Nature and Human Nature*, I vi, There was a place for everything, and everything was in its place. 1875: Smiles, *Thrift*, 66. 1927: *Evening Standard*, 24 Oct., p. 6, col. 1, He appeals to the more rational view that there is a place for everything, but that everything should be in its place.

Place like home, There's no. 1571: T. Tusser, *Husbandry* (rev. ed.) H1v, Though home be but homely, yet huswife is taught, That home hath no fellow to such as have aught. 1823: J. H. Payne, *Clari*, i i, 'Mid pleasures and palaces though we may roam, Be it ever so humble, there's no place like home.

Plain as a pack-saddle. 1553: T. Wilson, *Rhetorique*, 143 (1580) (OED), An honeste true dealyng seruant ... plaine as a packe-saddle. 1613: Wither, *Abuses Stript, etc.*, To the Reader, As plaine (as they say) as a pack-saddle. 1670: Ray, 202. 1736: Bailey, *Dict.*, s.v. 'Plain'.

Plain as a (a) pack-staff; (b) pike-staff. (a) 1532: More, *Works*, 814 (1557). 1542: Becon, *Early Works*, 276 (P.S.), He is as plain as a pack-staff. 1589: Greene, *Works*, vi 68 (Grosart). 1608: Middleton, *Family of Love*, V iii, It shows 'em a flat case as plain as a pack-staff. 1690: Dryden, *Amphitryon*, III i 1881: Evans, *Leics. Words*, 207 (E.D.S.), The common proverbial simile, 'as plain as a pike-staff', is here generally, 'as plain as a pack-staff [the pedlar's staff on which he carries his bundle over his shoulder]. 1886: Elworthy, *West Som. Word-Book*, 552 (E.D.S.), 'So plain's a pack-stave', which literature has corrupted into 'plain as a pike-staff'. (b) 1565: Shackock, *Hatchet of Heresies*, fo. 1, They be as playne as a pyke staff. 1591: Greene, *Works*, x 21 (Grosart), Plain as a pike-staff. 1664: Cotton, *Scarronides*, bk i, Plain as a pike-staff without gilding. *c.*1750: Foote, *Knights*, II. 1859: Dickens, in *C. Dickens as Editor*, 273 (1912), I have read the letter to Evans (which is as plain as a pike staff). 1921: Hutchinson, *If Winter Comes*, Pt I ch i, Can imagine him riling any wife with wrinkling up his nut over some plain as a pikestaff thing.

Plain as the nose. *See* **Nose** (2).

Plain dealing is a jewel. 1583: Melbancke, *Philotinus*, Epist. Ded., Plaine dealing is a iewel (though they that vse it commonly die beggers). 1587: J. Bridges, *Def. of Govt. in Ch. of England*, 124. 1608: Day, *Law Trickes*, II, *Adam* ... thereby grew the prouerbe 'plaine dealing is a jewell'. *Lu.* But he that vseth it shall die a begger. 1630: T. Adams, *Works*, 133 [as in 1608]. 1691: *Merry Drollery*, 81 (Ebsworth) [as in 1608]. 1692: Congreve, *Old Bach.*, IV xxii. 1732: Fuller, 3878 ... ; but they that wear it, are out of fashion. 1775: Garrick, *Bon Ton*, II ii.

Plain dealing is dead. 1616: B. Rich, *Ladies Looking Glasse*, 60, Plaine dealing: honesty is dead. 1732: Fuller: No. 3879, Plain dealing is dead; and dyed without issue. 1880: Spurgeon, *Ploughman's Pictures*, 20 [as in 1732].

Plain dealing is praised more than practised. 1639: Clarke, 138.

Plain fashion it best, The. 1562: Heywood, *Epigr.*, No. 201. 1659: Howell, 7.

Plain of poverty and die a beggar. 1678: Ray, 191.

Planny. *See* **Schemey.**

Plants trees, He that, loves others besides himself. 1732: Fuller, 2248.

Plant thorns. *Set* **Thorn** (1).

Play, women and wine undo men laughing. 1659: Howell, 1. 1670: Ray, 21. 1732: Fuller, 3884. 1880: Spurgeon, *Ploughman's Pictures*, 11, Play, women and wine are enough to make a prince a pauper.

PLAY, *verb:*

Play at chess. *See* **House** (18).

Play at small game before he will sit out, He will. 1605: Camden, *Remains*, 323 (1870). 1631: Brathwait, *Whimzies*, 148 (1859). Before 1680: Butler, *Remains*, i 253 (1759), The devil himself will rather chuse to play At paltry small game, than sit out, they say. 1732: Fuller, 3882 ['stand out' for 'sit out'].

Play Benall, To. Glos. 1639: in *Berkeley MSS.*, iii 27 (1885), I must play Benall with you. A frequent speach when the guest, immediately after meat, without any stay departeth.

Play booty, To = To play a treacherous part. 1540: Palsgrave, *Acolastus*, sig. T4, Shall not I be boty or party felow with the? 1560: Awdeley, *Vacabondes*, 9 (E.E.T.S.), They wil ... consent as though they wil play booty against him. 1692: L'Estrange, *Aesop*, 116 (3rd ed.), We understand what we ought to do; but when we come to deliberate, we play booty against our selves. 1707: Cibber, *Comical Lovers*, II, I believe the Devil plays booty against himself, and tells you of my sins. 1742: Fielding, *Andrews*, bk i ch ii, He had scornfully refused a considerable bribe to play booty on such an occasion. 1817: Scott, *Rob Roy*, ch vii, My uncle is sensible ... that, were he caught playing booty, he would be disarmed. 1838: Dickens, *Twist*, ch ix, Five of 'em strung up in a row, and none left to play booty, or turn white–livered! 1898: Weyman, *Shrewsbury*, ch xii, He had played booty, and played the traitor.

Play fast and loose, To. 1557: *Tottels Miscell.*, 157 (Arber), Of a new maried student that plaied fast or loose. 1580: Lyly, *Euphues*, 326 (Arber),

Thus with the Agyptian thou playest fast or loose. 1601: Yarington, *Two Trag. in One*, III ii, in Bullen, *Old Plays*, iv. 49, Thou ... dastard fast and loose, Thou weathercocke of mutabilitie. 1629: in *Pepysian Garland*, 320 (Rollins), But she that wanton is and fond, that fast and loose will play. 1853: Dickens, *Letters*, iii 139 (1882), The journal itself is blowing hot and cold, and playing fast and loose in a ridiculous way.

Play for nought as work for nought, As good. 1546: Heywood, *Proverbs*, Pt I ch xi 1642: D. Rogers. *Naaman*, sig. Q6, They had as good sit for nought as toyle for nought. 1714: Mandeville, *Fable of Bees*, 218, The fellow ... told him he'd rather play for nothing than work for nothing. 1823: Scott, *Peveril*, ch xxv.

Play in summer starve in winter. 1669: *Poor Robin Alman.*, July.

Play least in sight, To. 1607: R. West, *Court of Conscience*, sig. D1, Now forasmuch as you play least in sight, That Maister Derrick [the hangman] cannot seize vpon you. 1659: Howell, 10. 1678: Ray, 75. 1714: *Spectator*, No. 616, We had with us the attorney, and two or three other bright fellows. The doctor plays least in sight.

Play on both hands, To = To be guilty of double-dealing. 1530: Palsgrave, 433, If he ones apperceyve you howe you play on bothe the handes, he wyll never truste you after. 1633: Draxe, 47, He playeth on both handes.

Play one tune and dance another, They. 1639: Clarke, 18.

Play racket, To. c.1374: Chaucer, *Troylus*, bk iv. 1. 432, Canstow pleyen raket, to and fro, netle in, dokke out? c.1387: Usk, *Test. of Love*, in Skeat's *Chaucer*, vii 13, 'Ye wete wel, lady, eke,' quod I, 'that I have not played raket, "nettil in, docke out," and with the wethercocke waved.'

Plays his money ought not to value it, He that. 1640: Herbert, *Jac. Prudentum.*

Plays more than he sees, forfeits his eyes to the king, He that. 1605: Camden, *Remains*, 324 (1870). 1670: Ray, 132.

Plays well that wins, He. 1562: Heywood, *Three Hund. Epigr.*, No. 230, He pleyth best that wins. 1640: Herbert, *Jac. Prudentum.* 1670: Ray, 132. 1732: Fuller, 2005.

Plays you as fair as if he picked your pocket, He. 1678: Ray, 79.

Play the devil for God's sake. *See* Devil (104).

Play the fool. *See* quots. 1659: Howell,

Proverbs: Brit.-Eng., 7, If thou play the fool, stay for a fellow. 1732: Fuller, 2849, It is a cunning part to play the fool well.

Play the Good Luck, To = To do mischief. 1917: Bridge, *Cheshire Proverbs*, 141.

Play the Jack, To = Query, To play the knave. 1567: Golding, *Ovid*, bk xiii l. 289, Yit durst Thersites bee So bold as rayle vpon the kings, and he was payd by mee For playing so the sawcye Jacke. 1611: Shakespeare, *Tempest*, IV i, Monster, your fairy ... has done little better than played the Jack with us. 1670: Ray, 182.

Play wily beguile, To. 1633: Draxe, 40, He playeth wily beguile you with himselfe. 1732: Fuller, 1895, He hath play'd a wiley trick, and beguil'd himself. 1737: Ray, 66, He hath plaid wily beguiled with himself.

Play with a fool. *See* Fool (91).

Play with boys, you must take boys' play, If you. 1732: Fuller, 2779.

Play with children and let the saints alone. 1659: Howell, *Proverbs: Ital.-Eng.*, 8, Jest with boyes, and leave the saints alone. 1710: S. Palmer, *Moral Essays on Proverbs*, 322.

Play with me and hurt me not, Jest with me and shame me not. 1582: Harvey, *Marginalia*, 188 (1913). 1589: Puttenham, *Eng. Poesie*, 261 (Arber) [quoted as 'this common prouerbe', but with 'Iape' for 'Play', and 'Bourde' for 'Jest']. 1591: Harington, *Orl. Furioso*, bk xii, Moral. 1630: Brathwait, *Eng. Gentleman*, 152 (1641). 1656: F. Osborne, *Advice to Son*, 34 (Parry), Play with me, but hurt me not.

Play with you for shoe-buckles, I'll not. 1639: Clarke, 195, We play not for shoe-buckles. 1678: Ray, 347.

Playden, Sussex. *See* quot. 1894: A. J. C. Hare, *Sussex*, 63, The proverb – 'Sauket church, crooked steeple, Drunken parson, wicked people' refers to Playden, known as Sauket or Saltcot Street, from the salted cod spread on its banks to dry.

Pleasant hours fly fast. 1732: Fuller, 3886.

Please, *verb*. **1. He had need rise betimes that would please everybody.** 1639: Fuller, *Holy War*, bk iv ch xiv, He must rise early, yea, not at all go to bed, who will have everyone's good word. 1670: Ray, 132. 1732: Fuller, 1854. 1875: Cheales, *Proverb. Folk-Lore*, 115, He must rise early that would please everybody.

2. He that all men will please shall never find

ease. 1639: Clarke, 282. 1692: L'Estrange, *Aesop*, 325 (3rd ed.), He that resolves not to go to bed till all the world is pleas'd, shall be troubled with the head-ach. 1880: Spurgeon, *Ploughman's Pictures*, 25.

3. He that would please all and himself too, undertakes what he cannot do. 1659: Howell, 5. 1670: Ray, 132. 1732: Fuller, 6384 … what none could ever do.

4. If you be not pleased, put your hand in your pocket and please yourself. 1678: Ray, 79. 1732: Fuller, 2739 ['content' for 'pleased'].

5. Please the eye and plague the heart. [1611: Cotgrave, s.v. 'Marchandise', Please the eye and picke the purse.] 1655: A. Brewer, *Love-sick King*, III, in Bang, *Materialien*, B. 18, p. 38, She may please your eye a little … but vex your heart. 1754: *World*, No. 80, It is a fatal maxim among women, 'To please the eye, though they torment the heart'. 1829: Cobbett, *Advice to Young Men*, Lett. III, 'Please your eye and plague your heart 'is an adage that want of beauty invented, I dare say, more than a thousand years ago. 1913: *Folk-Lore*, xxiv. 77, (Oxfordsh.) I'll please my eye if I plague my heart.

6. Please the pigs. Before 1704: T. Brown, in *Works*, ii 198 (1760), I'll have one of the wigs to carry into the country with me, and please the pigs. 1755: *Gent. Mag.*, 115. The expression I mean is *An't please the pigs*, in which … *pigs* is most assuredly a corruption of Pyx. [This suggested origin of the phrase is as doubtful as that given in the 1886 quot. *infra*.] 1790: *Gent. Mag.*, 876, 1086–7. 1826–44: Hood, *Comic Poems*: 'Report from Below', 'But please the pigs', – for that's her way of swearing in a passion. 1849: Planché, *Extravag.*, iv. 33 (1879), You'll have no end of money, please the pigs. 1886: Elworthy, *West Som. Word-Book*, 569 (E.D.S.), Pigs. Contraction of pixies, in the common saying, 'Plaze God and the pigs'.

7. When it pleaseth not God, the saint can do little. 1670: Ray, 23.

8. You can't please everyone. 1472: E. Paston, *Letter* 16 May in *Paston Letters* (1971), I 365, I am in serteyn the contrary is true – yt is nomore but that he canot plese all partys. 1616: T. Draxe, *Adages*, 45, One can hardly please all men. 1844: Ruskin, *Journal* 30 Apr. in *Diaries 1835–47* (1956), 274, At Ward's about window – nothing done. Gastineau came up and don't like

mine: can't please everybody. *See also* (1), (2), and (3).

Pleased as a dog with two tails, As. 1889: Peacock, *Manley, etc.*, *Gloss.*, 169 (E.D.S.).

Pleased as if the pot was on, As. Oxfordsh. 1913: *Folk-Lore*, xxiv. 77.

Pleased as Punch, As. 1854: Dickens, *Hard Times*, bk i ch vi, When Sissy got into the school here … her father was as pleased as Punch. 1871: G. Eliot, *Middlemarch*, ch xl., I'm as pleased as Punch, now I've thought of that. 1901: F. E. Taylor, *Lancs Sayings*, 3, As pleeos't as Punch.

Pleasing ware is half sold. 1611: Cotgrave, s.v. 'Chose', Ware that doth please is halfe sold. 1640: Herbert, *Jac. Prudentum*. 1670: Ray, 132. 1732: Fuller, 5617, When ware is lik'd. it is half sold.

Pleasure, *subs*. 1. Consider not pleasures as they come, but as they go. 1855: Bohn, 339.

2. Follow pleasure and pleasure will flee; Flee pleasure and pleasure will follow thee. 1546: Heywood, *Proverbs*, Pt I ch xi 1667: Peacham, *Worth of Penny*, in Arber, *Garner*, vi 261 (1883), ['fly' for first 'flee', and 'be nigh' for 'follow thee']. 1736: Franklin, *Way to Wealth*, in *Works*, i 445 (Bigelow), Fly pleasures, and they will follow you.

3. It is a great pleasure to eat, and have nothing to pay. 1855: Bohn, 427.

4. Let pleasure overcome thee and thou learnest to like it. *c*.1320: in *Reliq. Antiquae*, i 110 (1841), 'Let lust overgon, eft hit shal the lyke', Quoth Hendyng. 1869: Hazlitt, 259.

5. Never pleasure without repentance. 1605: Camden, *Remains*, 329 (1870). 1670: Ray, 21. 1736: Bailey, *Dict.*, s.v. 'Pleasure'.

6. Pleasure has a sting in its tail. 1650: Taylor, *Holy Living*, ch ii § 1, All the instances of pleasure have a sting in the tail. 1692: Congreve, *Old Bach.*, Epil., To think o' th' sting, that's in the tail of pleasure. Before 1704: T. Brown, *Works*, i 313 (1760), You know the old saying, pleasure, etc. 1709: O. Dykes, *Eng. Proverbs*, 172 (2nd ed.), There's a sting in the tail of all unlawful pleasures.

7. The pleasures of the mighty are the tears of the poor. 1633: Draxe, 141. 1670: Ray, 21. 1732: Fuller, 4708, The pleasures of the rich are bought with the tears of the poor.

8. Who will in time present from pleasure refrain, Shall, in time to come, the more

pleasure obtain. 1546: Heywood, *Proverbs*, Pt I ch xi.

See also **Short pleasure.**

Pledge your own health, You must not. 1678: Ray, 152.

Plentiful. *See* **Blackberries**.

Plenty breeds pride. 1639: Clarke, 33.

Plenty is better than a flush, A. 1881: Evans, *Leics. Words*, 202 (E.D.S.), I once quoted the proverb: 'A plenty's better nur a flush', to a farm-labourer, who answered me with: 'Ah, sure! that's what o'd Bendigo Bilson said when the yoong masster gen 'im a chaarge o' rabbit-shot i' the leg'.

Plenty is no dainty. *c.*1449: Pecock, *Repr.*, 184 (OED), Experience wole weel scheme that plente is no deinte. 1546: Heywood, *Proverbs*, Pt II ch iv. 1583: Melbancke, *Philotinus*, sig. Q2, I will not be daintie … suche guests as I be plentie. 1678: Ray, 190.

Plenty know good ale but don't know much after that. N. Corn. 20th cent. (Mr C. Lee).

Plenty makes dainty. 1732: Fuller, 6375, Tis plenty that makes you dainty. 1869: *Spurgeon, John Ploughman*, ch v.

Plenty makes poor. 1590: Spenser, *F. Q.*, I iv. 29, Whose plenty made him poor. 1621: Brathwait, *Natures Embassie*, 269 (1877), She prou'd this true: Much plentie made her poore. 1669: *Politeuphuia*, 130, Plenty begetteth want; for he that hath much needs much.

Plenty never wrings its master by the ear. Glos. 1639: in *Berkeley MSS.*, iii 31 (1885).

Plenty. *See also* **Abundance**; and **Peace** (2).

Plough, *subs.* **1. He that by the plough would thrive, himself must either hold or drive.** 1678: Ray, 191. 1736: Franklin, *Way to Wealth*, in *Works*, i 445 (Bigelow). 1860: A. de Morgan, in *N.&Q.*, 2nd ser, x 390.

2. Keep thy plough jogging, so shalt thou have corn for thy horses. 1659: Howell, 11, If your plow be jogging, you may have meat for your horses. 1732: Fuller, 3119.

3. Never let the plough stand to catch a mouse. 1678: Ray, 265. 1710: S. Palmer, *Moral Essays on Proverbs*, 5. 1869: Spurgeon, *John Ploughman*, ch i. 1917: Bridge, *Cheshire Proverbs*, 50, Don't stop the plough to catch a mouse.

4. The plough goes not well if the ploughman hold it not. 1639: Clarke, 92. 1670: Ray, 132. 1732: Fuller, 4710.

5. The plough goeth before the oxen = The cart before the horse. 1571: *Satir. Poems Reform.*, xxix. 9 (OED), That makis … the plewche befoir the oxin go, the best the man to gyde. 1623: Wodroephe, *Spared Houres*, 501. 1653: Urquhart, *Rabelais*, 1 (Fanner) (OED), He would put the plough before the oxen.

6. There belongs more than whistling to going to plough. 1678: Ray, 191. 1732: Fuller, 4866 ['a plowman' for 'going to plough'].

7. Where the plough shall fail to go, There the weeds will surely grow. 1880: Spurgeon, *Ploughman's Pictures*, 146.

See also **Better have one plough; Borrowed ploughs;** and **Scythe.**

Plough, *verb.* **1. He is ploughing a rock.** 1813: Ray, 75.

2. He ploughs the air. Ibid., 75.

3. I might as well plough with dogs. 1611: Cotgrave, s.v. 'Charruë', The plough that a dog drawes is not worth the driving. 1795: *Gent. Mag.*, Pt I, 299, I have seen a friendly dame, winding a ravelled skain of thread or yarn, exclaim with a curse, 'This is as bad as ploughing with dogs'. 1891: Addy, *Sheffield Gloss. Suppl.*, 44 (E.D.S.), Get on wi' thee; it's as bad as plewin' wi' dogs. 1917: Bridge, *Cheshire Proverbs*, 79.

4. Plough deep while others sleep And you shall have corn to sell and keep. 1659: Howell, *Proverbs: Span.-Eng.*, 8, Plow deep, thou shalt have bread enough. 1736: Franklin, *Way to Wealth*, in *Works*, i 444 (Bigelow) ['sluggards' for 'others']. 1846: Denham, *Proverbs*, 14 (Percy S.). 1872: J. Glyde, jr., *Norfolk Garland*, 158.

5. Plough or plough not, you must pay your rent. 1846: Denham, *Proverbs*, 1 (Percy S.).

6. To plough the headlands before the butts = 'To begin a thing at the wrong end (as by a suitor applying to the father before the daughter!)'. 1883: Burne, *Shropsh. Folk-Lore*, 597.

7. To plough the sands. [Nos tamen hoc agimus tenuique in pulvere sulcos Ducimus et litus sterili versamus aratro. – Juvenal, *Sat.*, vii 48–9.] Before 1529: Skelton, *Speke, Parrot*, l. 342, To sowe corne in the see sande, ther wyll no crope growe. 1576: Pettie, *Petite Pall.*, ii 95 (Gollancz), So that I plough the barren rocks, and set my share into the shore of the sea. 1587: Turbervile, *Trag. Tales, etc.*, 404 (1837), And fruitlesse cleane to sowe the barrain sand. 1647: Stapylton,

Juvenal, 121, Yet still we plow the shoare and sow the sand. 1894: Mr Asquith, *Speech*, 21 Nov., All our time, all our labour, and all our assiduity is as certain to be thrown away as if you were to plough the sands of the seashore the moment that Bill reaches the Upper Chamber. Cf. **Sow**, *verb* (3).

8. To plough with the ass and the ox = To sort things ill. 1813: Ray, 212.

9. You must plough with such oxen as you have. 1678: Ray, 191, A man must, etc. 1732: Fuller, 5968. 1869: Spurgeon, *John Ploughman*, ch i, You know we are obliged to plough with such cattle as we have found for us.

Ploughman. *See* **Bad ploughman;** and **Yeoman.**

Plover. *See* quot. 1655: T. Muffett, *Healths Improvement*, 98, The gray plover is so highly esteemed, that this proverb is raised of a curious and male-contented stomack: *A gray plover cannot please him.*

Plum as a juggle-mear, As = As soft as a quagmire. Devon. 1670: Ray, 218.

Plum year, a dumb year, A. 1678: Ray, 52. 1732: Fuller, 6139. 1856: *N.&Q.*, 2nd ser, i 84 [Norfolk]. 1893: Inwards, *Weather Lore*, 5, A plum year, a dumb year. Kent. In the year when plums flourish all else fails. Devonshire.

Plum. *See also* **Black** (1).

Plumbland Church. 1860: Whellan, *Cumberland, etc.*, 366, The greatest wonder ever was seen Is Plumbland Church on Parsonby Green.

Plump as a partridge, As. 1678: Ray, 281. 1694: *Terence made English*, 62. 1720: Gay, *Poems*, ii 278 (Underhill), Plump as a partridge was I known. 1829: Scott, *Geierstein*, ch xiii 1831: Peacock, *Crotchet Castle*, ch xiv.

Plum-tree. *See* quots. 1639: Clarke, 88. The higher the plum-tree, the sweeter the plumme. 1659: Howell, 17, The higher the tree, the sweeter the plumb; The better the shooe, the blacker the thumb. 1670: Ray, 210, The higher the plum-tree, the riper the plum; The richer the cobler, the blacker his thumb. 1732: Fuller, 6420 [as in 1670].

Plymouth cloak, A = A cudgel. 1625: Massinger, *New Way, etc.*, I i, I must tell you if you but advance Your Plimworth cloke ... 1631: F. Lenton, *Characters*, sig. F7 (1663), A Plimmouth cloake, otherwise call'd a battoone. 1681: A. Behn, *Rover*, Pt II V iii. 1855: Kingsley, *West.*

Ho!, ch vii, 'Thou wilt please to lay down that Plymouth cloak of thine', and he pointed to the cudgel.

Plymouth was a furzy down, When, Plympton was a borough town. 1850: *N.&Q.*, 1st ser, ii 511.

Poacher makes the best gamekeeper, An old. *c.*1390: Chaucer, *Physician's Tale*, l. 83, A theef of venysoun, that hath forlaft His likerousnesse [dishonesty] and al his olde craft, Kan kepe a forest best of any man. 1695: T. Fuller, *Church History of Britain*, ix. iii, Alwayes set a — to catch a —: and the greatest dear-stealers make the best Parke-keepers. 1878: R. Jefferies, *Gamekeeper at Home*, ix, There is an old saying that an old poacher makes the best gamekeeper, on the principle of setting a thief to catch a thief.

Pocket a wrong, etc., To = To accept it without protest. 1595: Munday, *John a Kent*, 28 (SH.S.), I will not pocket this injurious wrong. 1597: Shakespeare, 1 *Henry IV*, III iii, You will not pocket up wrong. 1638: D. Tuvill, *Vade Mecum*, 184 (3rd ed.), To pocket up one wrong, is to allure another. 1772: Graves, *Spirit. Quixote*, bk vi ch xiii, I thought it best to pocket the insult, as well as the money. 1826: Scott, *Woodstock*, ch xxiii, The bravest man sacrifices nothing by pocketing a little wrong which he cannot personally resent.

Poets are born, but orators are made. *c.*1581: Sidney, *Apologie*, 62 (Arber), Therefore is it an old prouerbe, *Orator fit; Poeta nascitur.* 1600: Bodenham, *Belvedere*, 55 (Spens.S.). 1669: *Politeuphuia*, 58.

Poets. *See also* **Painters.**

Poison embitters much sweetness, A little. *c.*1175: *Old Eng. Homilies*, 1st ser, p. 23 (Morris), A lutel ater bitteret muchel swete. 1581: Lyly, *Euphues*, 39 (Arber), One droppe of poyson infecteth the whole tunne of wine.

Poison is poison though it comes in a golden cup. 1630: T. Adams, *Works*, 705. 1633: Draxe, 60, In golden pottes are hidden the most deadly poyson.

Pole-cat, To stink like a. 1639: Clarke, 293, He stinkes like a pole-cat. 1670: Ray, 207. 1700: Ward, *London Spy*, 44 (1924), Which made the crooked vermin out-stink a pole-cat. 1740: North, *Examen*, 172, All which stuff is as rank as a pole-cat. 1889: J. Nicholson, *Folk Speech E. Yorks*, 22, It stinks like a fummat (pole-cat).

Policy goes beyond strength. *c*.1590: G. Harvey, *Marginalia*, 100 (1913), A lytle pollicy praeuaileth when a great deale of strength fayleth. Before 1634: Chapman, *Alphonsus*, II iii, Policy help'd above strength. 1666: Torriano, *Piazza Univ.*, 133. 1754: Berthelson, *Eng.-Danish Dict.*, s.v. 'Policy'.

Polperro. *See* quot. 1906: Q.-Couch, *Mayor of Troy*, ch x, The proverb says that a Polperro jackass is surprised at nothing.

Pomeroy's cat, Hurried in mind, like. 1888: Q.-Couch, *Troy Town*, ch xiii. 1908: *Eng. Ill. Mag.*, Jan., 355.

Pomfret, As sure as a louse in. 1638: Brathwait, *Barn. Journal*, Pt III, A louse in Pomfrait is not surer, Then the poor through sloth securer. 1790: Grose, *Prov. Gloss.*, s.v. 'Yorkshire'. 1878: *Folk-Lore Record*, i 168, As 'sure as a louse in Pomfret', speaks ill for that place.

Pompey is on your back. 1869: Hazlitt, 317, The *black dog Pompey* is said to be on a child's back, when he is fractious. This is a common saying in some parts of the country … In South Devonshire, they say in a similar sense, 'your tail's on your shoulder'.

Pontefract *See* **Pomfret**.

Poole, Dorset. 1790: Grose, *Prov. Gloss.*, s.v. 'Dorset', [three sayings] (1) If Pool was a fishpool, and the men of Pool fish, There'd be a pool for the devil, and fish for his dish. (2) When do you fetch the five pounds? (3) Shoot zaftly, doey now. [(2) refers to a story of a never-claimed bequest of £5 for honesty; (3) refers to a yarn about a man holding a kettle to receive shot discharged from guns.]

Poor, *adj*. **1. A poor beauty finds more lovers than husbands.** 1640: Herbert, *Jac. Prudentum*.
2. A poor man's cow dies, a rich man's child. Ibid.
3. A poor man's debt makes a great noise. 1732: Fuller, 355.
4. A poor man's table is soon spread. 1633: Draxe, 136. 1670: Ray, 132. 1869: Spurgeon, *John Ploughman*, ch v.
5. A poor man's tale. *See* quot. 1639: in *Berkeley MSS.*, iii 31 (1885), A poare mans tale may now be heard: vizt when none speakes the meanest may (Gloucest.).
6. A poor man wants some things, a covetous man all things, *c*.1680: L'Estrange, *Seneca's Epistles*, ii, The poor man wants many things, but the covetous man wants all. 1732: Fuller, 356.
7. A poor spirit is poorer than a poor Purse. Ibid., No. 358.
8. A poor wedding is a prologue to misery. Ibid., No. 359.
9. As poor as a church mouse. [1659: Howell, 13, As hungry as a church-mouse.] 1672: Corye, *Generous Enemies*, I, All that live with him Are as poor as church-rats. 1714: Ozell, *Molière*, iv 38, They're most of them as poor as church mice. 1778: T. Cogan, *John Buncle, Junior*, ii 146. 1803: Colman, jr., *John Bull*, II iii. 1841: Dickens, *Barn. Rudge*, ch lxxviii, I have come back, poorer than a church mouse. 1901: F. E. Taylor, *Lancs Sayings*, 3, As poor as a church-meawse. 1906: Shaw, *Major Barbara*, V.
10. As poor as a rat. 1703: Ward, *Writings*, ii 120, Whilst men of parts, as poor as rats … 1834: Marryat, *P. Simple*, ch xxxi, He's as poor as a rat, and has nothing but his pay. 1866: T. W. Robertson, *Ours*, I, Angus, a distant cousin, poor as a rat. 1907: De Morgan, *Alice-for-Short*, ch xvi.
11. As poor as Job. *c*.1300: Brunne, tr. Langtoft's *Chron.*, 323 (Hearne), Als bare was his toure as Job the pouere man. *c*.1390: Gower, *Conf. Amantis*, bk v l. 2505, To ben for evere til I deie As povere as Job. 1560: T. Wilson, *Rhetorique*, 207 (1909), Thou art as poore as Iob. *c*.1640: in *Roxb. Ballads*, i 503 (B.S.), I am backe return'd, as poore as Job. 1700: Dryden, *Prol. to The Pilgrim*. 1750: Smollett, *Gil Blas*, iii 93. 1822: Scott, *Nigel*, ch viii, Who are all as proud as Lucifer, and as poor as Job. 1850: Dickens, *Copperfield*, ch vi, Old Mrs Mell, his mother, was as poor as Job. 1901: F. E. Taylor, *Lancs Sayings*, 3.
12. As poor as owls. 1862: *Dialect of Leeds*, 405.
13. Every poor man is a fool. 1659: Howell, *Proverbs: Brit.-Eng.*, 3.
14. He is not poor that hath little, but he that desireth much. 1556: G.Colvile, tr. Boethius, 34 (1897), He that fearyth that he shall lacke, and is not contented with that he hath, but soroweth for more … is not ryche, but poore. 1637: A. Warwick, *Spare Minutes*, 4 (1829), Nor her poore that hath but little, but hee that wants more. 1640: Herbert, *Jac. Prudentum*. 1732: Fuller, 1937 ['craves' for 'desireth'].

15. He is poor indeed that can promise nothing. 1039: Clarke, 142, He is poore, can promise nothing. 1670: Ray, 132. 1732: Fuller, 1941.

16. He is so poor that he has not salt to his porridge. Ibid., No. 1945.

17. It's a poor family which hath neither a whore nor a thief in it. 1659: Howell, *Proverbs: Span.-Eng.;* 1, There's no family but there's a whore or a knave of it. 1678: Ray, 9.

18. It's a poor heart that never rejoices. 1834: Marryat, *P. Simple*, ch v, 'Well', continued he, 'it's a poor heart that never rejoiceth'. He then poured out half a tumbler of rum. 1841: Dickens, *Barn. Rudge*, ch iv. 1850: Dickens, *Chuzzlewit*, ch v.

19. Poor and liberal, rich and covetous. 1640: Herbert, *Jac. Prudentum*.

20. Poor and pert. *See* quots. 1887: T. Darlington, *S. Cheshire Folk Speech*, 289 (E.D.S.), He's poor an 'peeart [lively], like th' parson's pig. 1913: E. M. Wright, *Rustic Speech, etc.*, 11 [as in 1887]. 1917: Bridge, *Cheshire Proverbs*, 104 [as in 1887].

21. Poor and proud, fie, fie! 1605: Camden, *Remains*, 330 (1870). 1670: Ray, 132.

22. Poor and proud, still tailor-like. *c.*1620: in *Roxb. Ballads*, ii 580 (B.S.), The saying old hath oft beene told, It plain doth verifie, 'Poore and proud, still taylor-like'. Cf. **Tailor** (4).

23. Poor cook. *See* **Ill cook.**

24. **Poor folk fare the best.** 1639: Clarke, 205.

25. Poor folks are glad of porridge. *c.*1580: Fulwell, *Ars Adulandi*, sig. G1, Poore men are pleasde with potage aye, till better vittailes fall. 1659: Howell, 4, Poor folks must be glad of pottage. 1732: Fuller, 3892.

26. Poor in appetite. *See* quot. 1653: R. Brome, *City Wit*, I ii, It is rightly said, He that is poor in appetite, may quickly be rich in purse.

27. Poor men. *See* **Children** (5).

28. Poor men have no souls. 1562: Heywood, *Three Hund. Epigr.*, No. 167. 1670: Ray, 21.

29. Poor men seek meat for their stomachs; rich men stomachs for their meat. 1594: A. Copley, *Wits, Fits, etc.*, 105 (1614) ['want' for 'seek']. 1678: Ray, 79 ['walketh to get' for 'seek']. 1732: Fuller, 3895. 1820: Scott, in Lockhart's *Life*, v 44, The poor man labours to get a dinner to his appetite, the rich man to get an appetite to his dinner.

30. Poor men's reasons are not heard. 1633: Draxe, 162, A poore mans tale cannot be heard. 1640: Herbert, *Jac. Prudentum*, The reasons of the poor weigh not. 1666: Torriano, *Piazza Univ.*, 214, The poor mans reasons are of no weight. 1732: Fuller, 3897.

31. The poor man's labour is the rich man's wealth. 1846: Denham, *Proverbs*, 6 (Percy S.).

32. The poor man's shilling is but a penny. 1732: Fuller, 4716.

33. The poor man turns his cake, and another comes and eats it. Ibid., No. 4714.

34. The poor must pay for all. 1639: Clarke, 99.

35. They are poor whom God hates. 1633: Draxe, 162. 1659: Howell, 11, Ther's none poor but such as God hates. 1732: Fuller, 2470, He's poor indeed, whom God hates.

36. To be in a poor reed = in poor condition. 1917: Bridge, *Cheshire Proverbs*, 126.

37. To be poor and to look poor, is the devil all over. 1913: *Folk-Lore*, xxiv. 77.

Poorly sit, richly warm. Glos. 1639: in *Berkeley MSS.* iii 30 (1885).

Pope, The. 1. A pope's bull, a dead man's skull, and an old trull, are not all worth a pound of wool. 1616: B. Rich, *Ladies Looking Glasse*, 36. 1647: *Countrym. New Commonwealth*, 42 ['crooked' for 'old', and 'fleece' for 'pound'].

2. If you would be a Pope, you must think of nothing else. 1855: Bohn, 422.

Popham. *See* **Horner.**

Poppies. *See* quot. 1880: *N. & Q.*, 6th ser, ii 164, The other day I heard a Staffordshire man say 'Pluck poppies – make thunder'. This was a proverbial saying that was quite new to me.

Possession is (*a*) **eleven,** (*b*) **nine points of the law.** (*a*) 1630: T. Adams, *Works*, 97, The deuill hath eleuen poynts of the law against you; that is, possession. 1639: Fuller, *Holy War*, bk v ch xxix. 1670: Ray., 132. 1692: L'Estrange, *Aesop*, 291 (3rd ed.). 1709: O. Dykes, *Eng. Proverbs*, 213 (and ed.), Possession is a mighty matter indeed; and we commonly say, 'tis eleven points of the law. 1712: Arbuthnot, *Law a Bott. Pit*, Pt III ch ix, Poor Nic. has only possession; eleven points of the law! 1738: Swift, *Polite Convers.*, Dial. I. 1822: Peacock, *Maid Marian*, ch v, In those days possession was considerably more than eleven points of the law. (*b*) T. Draxe, *Adages*, 163, Possession is nine points of the law. 1659: J.

Ireton, *Oration*, 5 This Rascally-devill ... denys to paya farthing of rent. Tis true, possession is nine points of the law, Yet give Gentlemen, right's right. 1809: Malkin, *Gil Blas*, xxi 20 (OED), She had possession, and that is nine points of the law. 1817: Scott, *Rob Roy*, ch xxxvii, Take all necessary measures to secure that possession, which sages say makes nine points of the law. 1923: J. S. Fletcher, *The Diamonds*, ch iii, He knew that possession is sometimes more than nine points of the law. The following is doubtful, but should probably come under (*a*). 1703: Far–quhar, *Twin-Rivals*, II ii, Upon this you take immediate possession, and so you have the best part of the law on your side.

Post *See* **Pillar**

Postern door makes thief and whore, The. 1605: Camden, *Remains*, 334 (1870). 1670: Ray, 132. 1732: Fuller, 6176. Cf. **Back door**.

Pot, *subs.* **1. A pot that belongs to many is ill stirred and worse boiled.** 1732: Fuller, 360.

2. He's dwindled down from a pot to a pipkin. Ibid., No. 2457.

3. Neither pot broken nor water spilt = No harm done. 1546: Heywood, *Proverbs*, Pt I ch xi. 1619: B. Rich, *Irish Hubbub*, 16. 1659: Howell, 14.

4. Pot and can. *See* **Cup** (2).

5. Pot in the pate. *See* **Cup** (1).

6. The pot calls the kettle black. 1620: Shelton, *Quixote*, Pt II ch lxvii, You are like what is said that the fryingpan said to the kettle, 'Avant, black-brows'. 1639: Clarke, 8, The pot cals the pan burnt-arse. 1679: A. Behn, *Feign'd Courtezans*, V iv, As another old proverb says, do not let the kettle call the pot black-arse! 1685–6: Cotton, *Montaigne*, bk iii ch v *ad fin.*, It is much more easy to accuse one sex than to excuse the other; 'tis according to the saying, 'The pot and the kettle'. 1725: Bailey, tr. Erasmus' *Colloq.*, 365 [as in 1679]. 1732: Fielding, *Cov. Garden Tragedy*, II v, Dares thus the devil to rebuke our sin! Dare thus the kettle say the pot is black! 1834: Marryat, *P. Simple*, ch xxxii, Do you know what the pot called the kettle? 1920: G. Lambert, M.P., in *Times*, 27 March, p. 10, col. 3, I would say to my esteemed leaders that the pot calling the kettle sooty doesn't whiten either of them.

7. To go to pot. 1546: Heywood, *Proverbs*, Pt II ch v, The weaker goeth to the potte, we all daie see. 1591: Harington, *Orl. Furioso*, bk xxxviii st.

60, We may assure our selves if any more We take the field, our side goes to the pot. 1649: in *Somers Tracts*, vii 88 (1811), Many a wiser man than I hath gone to pot. 1694: *Terence made English*, 7, If these brains don't help me out at a dead lift, to pot goes Pilgarlick. 1740: North, *Lives of Norths*, i 151 (Bohn), It was well for us that we were known there, or to pot we had gone. 1828: Carr, *Craven Dialect*, ii 55, 'To go to pot', to be reduced to beggary, to suffer.

8. To make the pot boil. *c.*1663: Davenant, *Play-House to be Let*, V, We'll find out rich husband to make you the pot boil. *c.*1750: C. Smart, *Ballads*, No. xiii, She teaches you economy, Which makes the pot to boil. 1864: Carlyle, *Fredk. Gt.*, XVI ii V 151 (1872) (OED), A feeling that glory is excellent, but will not make the national pot boil.

9. To make the pot with two ears = To put the arms akimbo. 1675: Cotton, *Burl, upon Burlesque*, 236 (1765), *See* what a goodly port she bears, *Making the pot with the two ears!*

10. When the pot boils over, it cooleth itself. 1732: Fuller, 5602.

See also **Ifsand Ands; Lid; Little pot; Pitcher; Quart;** and **Watched pot.**

Potatoes. 1. A dinner of potatoes and point. 1825: J. Neal, *Bro. Jonathan*, i 75 (OED), The potatoes and point of an Irish peasant. 1864: 'Cornish Proverbs', in *N. &Q.*, 3rd ser, vi 495.

2. *See* quot. 1893: Inwards, *Weather Lore*, 23, Plant your 'taturs when you will, They won't come up before April.

See also **Bean** (5).

Pottage. *See* quots. 1678: Ray, 70, With cost one may make pottage of a stool-foot. 1732: Fuller, 5796, With cost, good pottage may be made out of a leg of a joint stool. *See also* **Broth.**

Potterne, Old Ross of. 1659: Howell, 21, He will live as long as old Russe of Pottern, who lived till all the world was weary of him. 1670: Ray, 215 ['Ross' for 'Russe'].

Pound of butter among a kennel of hounds. What is a? 1670: Ray, 66. 1732: Fuller, 5498. 1880: Spurgeon. *Ploughman's Pictures*, 10, His fortune went like a pound of meat in a kennel of hounds.

Pound of care will not pay an ounce of debt, A. 1589: L. Wright, *Display of Dutie*, 29 ['sorrow' for 'care']. 1590: Greene, *Works*, viii 85 (Grosart). 1600: Dekker, *Shoem. Holiday*, III v ['dram' for 'ounce']. 1685: Meriton, *Yorkshire Ale*, 57, A pund of care'l not pay an ounce of debt. 1732: Fuller, 361.

Pour water into a sieve, To. 1639: Clarke, 155, You pour, etc. 1670: Ray, 190. 1732: Fuller, 5979, You pour, etc. 1875: Smiles, *Thrift*, 169, Putting money into her hands is like pouring water through a sieve.

Poverty breeds strife. Somerset. 1678: Ray, 354. 1732: Fuller, 6109, Want makes strife Between the good man and his wife.

Poverty comes in at the door, love flies out of the window, When. 1631: Brathwait, *Eng. Gentlewoman*, 346 (1641), It hath beene an old maxime; that as poverty goes in at one doore, love goes out at the other. 1732: Fuller, 5565 ['creeps' for 'flies']. *c.*1810: C. Dibdin, jr., *My Spouse and I*, Love and poverty they say do not agree; but the love that flies out of the window at the sight of poverty deserves to have the door shut in his face. 1924: Divorce Court evidence in *Evening Standard*, 4 April, p. 9, col. 2, She might then realise that poverty might come in at the door and love fly out of the window.

Poverty destroyeth not, There is no virtue that. 1578: Florio, *First Fruites*, fo. 32, There is no vertue, but pouertie wyl marre it. 1629: *Book of Meery Riddles*, Prov. 8.

Poverty is an enemy to good manners. 1585: Sir E. Dyer, in *Writings*, 97 (Grosart) [quoted as 'a prouerbe amongst vs'].

Poverty is not a crime. 1591: J. Florio, *Second Fruits*, 105, Povertie is no vice. 1640: G. Herbert, *Outlandish Proverbs*, no. 844, Poverty is no sinne. 1785: C. Macklin, *Man of the World*, iv. 56, Her Poverty is not her crime, Sir, but her misfortune. 1839: Dickens, *Nicholas Nickleby*, lv, 'Remember how poor we are.' Mrs Nickleby ... said through her tears that poverty was not a crime.

Poverty is not a shame, but the being ashamed of it is. 1732: Fuller, 3908. 1869: Spurgeon, *John Ploughman*, ch v, Poverty is no shame, but being discontented with it is.

Poverty is no vice but an inconvenience. 1591: Florio, *Second Frutes*, 105. 1616: *Rich Cabinet*, fo. 114, Pouertie is no vice: yet a wofull inconuenience. 1666: Torriano, *Piazza Univ.*, 214. 1781: Macklin, *Man of the World*, IV, Her poverty is not her crime, sir, but her misfortune.

Poverty is still in suspicion, He that is in. 1629: *Book of Meery Riddles*, Prov. 73.

Poverty is the mother of all arts and trades. 1666: Torriano, *Piazza Univ.*, 214.

Poverty is the mother of health. 1377: Langland, *Plowman*, B, xiv 298, Pouerte ... is moder of helthe. 1640: Herbert, *Jac. Prudentum*. 1748: Richardson, *Clarissa*, ii 110 (1785).

Poverty makes strange bed-fellows. 1849: Lytton, *Caxtons*, Pt IV ch iv, I say that life, like poverty, has strange bed-fellows. 1863: Thackeray, *Round. Papers*: 'On Some Carp', par. 2, An illustration of that dismal proverb which tells us how poverty makes us acquainted with strange bed-fellows. Cf. **Misery**.

Poverty parteth fellowship. 1406: Hoccleve, in *Minor Poems*, 29 (E.E.T.S.), Fy! Lak of coyn departith conpaignie. *c.*1470: G. Ashby, *Poems*, 29 (E.E.T.S.), It hathe be, and yet is a comyn sawe, That Poverte departithe felaship. 1546: Heywood, *Proverbs*, Pt I ch xii. *c.*1650: in *Roxb. Ballads*, ii 113 (Hindley). For friendship parts in poverty. 1732: Fuller, 3914, Poverty trieth friends.

Poverty very ill, He bears, who is ashamed of it. Ibid., No. 1811.

Povey't foot. *See* quots. 1841: Hartshorne, *Salopia Ant.*, 535, 'Wos and wos like' [or] 'As large as Povey's foot'. 1883: Burne, *Shropsh. Folk-Lore*, 594, Worse and worse, like Povey's foot.

Powder. *See* **Put** (6).

Power corrupts. 1876: A. Trollope, *Prime Minister*, IV viii, We know that power corrupts, and that we cannot trust kings to have loving hearts. 1887: Lord Acton, *Letter* in *Life and Letters of Mandel Creighton* (1904), I xiii, Power tends to corrupt, and absolute power corrupts absolutely. Great men are almost always bad men, even when they exercise influence and not authority.

Power seldom grows old at Court. 1651: Herbert, *Jac. Prudentum*, 2nd ed.

Power weakeneth the wicked. 1659: Howell, *Proverbs: Brit.-Eng.*, 6.

Powis is the paradise of Wales. 1662: Fuller, *Worthies*, iii 549 (1840). 1790: Grose, *Prov. Gloss.*, s.v. 'Montgomeryshire'.

Practice [originally **Use**] **makes perfect.** 1340: *Ayenbite*, 178 (E.E.T.S.), Uor wone maketh maister. *c.*1530: *Detection ... of Dice Play*, 25 (Percy S.), For use maketh mastery. 1546: Heywood, *Proverbs*, Pt II ch ii, Vse maketh maistry. 1560; T. Wilson, *Rhetorique*, 5 (1909), Eloquence was vsed, and through practise made perfect. 1639: Breton, in *Works*, ii II (Grosart), Use makes perfection in many things. 1766: Anstey, *New Bath Guide*, Lett. V, For practice makes perfect, as often I've read. 1798: Morton, *Speed the Plough*, II ii. 1816: Scott, *Antiquary*, ch xxxv, Use makes perfect. 1829: Scott, *Journal*, 27 Jan., Use makes perfectness. 1870: Dickens, *Drood*, ch xxiii. 1920: P. B. M. Allan, *Book-Hunter at Home*, 96.

Practice toucheth the quick. 1546: Heywood, *Proverbs*, Pt I ch vi.

Practise what you preach. [*c*.1393: Langland, *Plowman*, C, v 118, Tyl that lerede men lyue as thei lere and techen.] *c*.1426: Audelay, *Poems*, 31 (Percy S.), A prechur schuld lyve parfytly, And do as he techys truly. *c*.1680: L'Estrange, *Seneca's Morals*: 'Happy Life', ch ii, We must practise what we preach. 1748: Richardson, *Clarissa*, v 81 (1785), I love … that the clergy should practise what they preach. 1840: Dickens, *Curiosity Shop*, ch xxxvii, Divines do not always practise what they preach.

Praise, *subs.*: **Praise is but the shadow of virtue.** Before 1680: Butler, *Remains*, ii 118 (1759).

Praise makes good men better and bad men worse. 1659: T. Pecke, *Parnassi Puerp.*, 95, Good men are made better; bad, worse by praise. 1732: Fuller, 3918.

Praise of fools. *See* **Fool** (103).

Praise without profit puts little into the pot. 1666: Torriano, *Piazza Univ.*, 131, Praises fill not the belly. 1732: Fuller, 3922.

PRAISE, *verb:*

Praise a hill but keep on the plain. 1591: Florio, *Second Frutes*, 99, Wonder at hills, keepe on the plaine. 1623: Wodroephe, *Spared Houres*, 277, Praise the mountaines, but loue the plaines. 1640: Herbert, *Jac. Prudentum*. Praise a hill, but keep below. 1659: Howell, *Letters*, ii 666 (Jacobs), Commend the hills, but keep thyself on the plains.

Praise at parting, i.e. Praise not too soon, or Praise not till the entertainment is over. *c*.1410: *Towneley Plays*, 108 (E.E.T.S.), Now prays at the partyng. *c*.1440: *Gesta Rom.*, 39 (E.E.T.S.), 'Preyse at the parting', seide knyzt, 'And bihold wele the ende'. *c*.1475: *Rauf Coilyear*, 5 (E.E.T.S.), It is an old saying, praise at the parting. 1611: Shakespeare, *Tempest*, III iii.

Praise day at night – similar in meaning to the preceding saying, *c*.1440: Lydgate, *Fall of Princes*, bk ix. l. 2024, The faire day men do preise at eue. 1605: Camden, *Remains*, 330 (1870), Praise a fair day at night. 1637: Shirley, *Example*, Epil. [as in 1605]. 1681: Robertson, *Phraseol. Generalis*, 324 [as in 1605]. 1732: Fuller, 3919, Praise not the day before night. 1846: T. Wright, *Essays on Middle Ages*, i 148, We say, 'praise the day when it is over'.

Praise no man till he is dead. 1887: R.L.S., *Hanging Judge*, III vi (iii.).

Praise nor dispraise thyself, Neither; thy actions serve the turn. 1640: Herbert, *Jac. Prudentum*. 1670: Ray, 21.

Praise not the ford. *See* **Ford**.

Praise the bridge he goes over, Let every man. 1678: Ray, 106. 1740: North, *Examen*, 368, It is strange men cannot praise the bridge they go over, or be thankful for favours they have had. 1797: Colman, jr., *Heir at Law*, I i, Well, praise the bridge that carried you over. 1817: Scott, in Lockhart's *Life*, iv 59, I am bound to praise the bridge which carried me over. 1875: Cheales, *Proverb. Folk-Lore*, 58, As we have it – Speak well of the bridge that carries you over.

Praise the child and you make love to the mother. 1829: Cobbett, *Advice to Young Men*, Lett. IV [quoted as 'an old saying'].

Praise the sea but keep on land. 1591: Florio, *Second Frutes*, 99, Praise the sea, on shore remaine. 1640: Herbert, *Jac. Prudentum*. 1659: Howell, *Letters*, ii 666 (Jacobs), Commend the sea, but keep thy self ashoar. 1754: Berthelson, *Eng.-Danish Dict.*, s.v. 'Praise'. 1875: Cheales, *Proverb. Folk-Lore*, 83.

Praise the wine before ye taste of the grape, Ye. 1546: Heywood, *Proverbs*, Pt I ch x.

Praiseth himself, spattereth himself, He that. 1640: Herbert, *Jac. Prudentum*.

Praiseth publicly, will slander privately, He that. 1669: *Politeuphuia*, 140, He that praiseth a man openly will not stick to flatter him secretly. 1732: Fuller, 2250.

Prate is prate, but it is the duck that lays the eggs. 1659: Howell, 13. 1670: Ray, 215. 1732: Fuller, 3926. Cf. **Talk is but talk.**

Prate like a parrot, To. 1639: Clarke, 133, He prates like a parrot. 1678: Ray, 265. Cf. **Talk**.

Pray, *verb.* **1. He that would learn to pray, let him go to sea.** 1660: Howell, *Parly of Beasts*, 9, The common saying is, that he who cannot pray, must go to church at sea. 1670: Ray, 133. 1736: Bailey, *Dict.*, s.v. 'Pray'.

2. Pray for yourself, I am not sick. 1546: Heywood, *Proverbs*, Pt II ch vii.

Prayers and provender hinder no journey. 1640: Herbert, *Jac. Prudentum*. 1854: J. W. Warter, *Last of Old Squires*, 53. 1863: *N.&Q.*, 3rd ser, iii 258. 1926: R. A. Knox, *Other Eyes than Ours*, 182, We're letting luncheon get cold, ain't we? I always used to be told that prayer and provender hinder no man. Cf. **Mass and meat; Meals and matins;** and **Meat** (5).

Prayers are done, my lady is ready, When. 1611: Cotgrave, s.v. 'Messe', When prayers were ended, Madame ends her pranking. 1640: Herbert, *Jac. Prudentum*.

Prayers bring down the first blessing, and praises the second. 1659: Howell, 8.

Prayers. *See* quot. 1678: Ray, 191, They shall have no more of our prayers then we of their pies (quoth vicar of Layton).

Prayers. *See also* **Say,** *verb* (4) and (17).

Prays together, stays together, The family that. *See* **Family.**

Preach over liquor. *See* **Parson Palmer.**

Preacher's wages. Before 1635: Corbet, *Poems*, in Chalmers, v 577, Wee all had preacher's wages, thankes and wine.

Preaches war is the devil's chaplain, He that. 1670: Ray, 27. 1732: Fuller, 2251, He that preacheth up war, when it might well be avoided, is the devil's chaplain.

Preaches well that lives well, He. 1620: Shelton, *Quixote*, Pt II ch xx. 1732: Fuller, 2006.

Precepts may lead but examples draw. 1855: Bohn, 475. Cf. **Example.**

Press a stick and it seems a youth. 1640: Herbert, *Jac. Prudentum.*

Preston, Lancs, **1.** *See* quot 1869: Hazlitt, 319, Preston for panmugs, Huyton for pride; Childwall for tolling, and playing beside.

2. Proud Preston. 1727: Defoe, *Tour*, iii 221, The people are gay here, though not perhaps the richer for that; but it has by that obtained the name of Proud Preston. 1835: Walker, *The Original*, No. xi, Preston, then always called Proud Preston, because exclusively inhabited by gentry. 1889: *N.&Q.*, 7th ser, viii 56, Proud Preston, poor people. Built a church and no steeple. 1901: F. E. Taylor, *Lancs Sayings*, 42, Preawd Presson – poor people – Eight bells in a crack't steeple!

Prettiness dies first. 1640: Herbert, *Jac. Prudentum.* 1670: Ray, 21, Prettiness dies quickly. 1732: Fuller, 3930, Prettiness is short-liv'd.

Prettiness makes no pottage. 1678: Ray, 192. 1732: Fuller, 3931.

Pretty as paint, As. 1922: E. V. Lucas, *Geneva's Money*, ch xvi, Now, there's that girl – she's as pretty as paint.

Pretty fellow. *See* **Axle-tree.**

Pretty that have pretty conditions, They are. 1633: Draxe, 15.

Pretty things men make. *See* quots. *c.*1590: *Plaine Percevall*, 19 (1860), He spide a Iacke an apes, in a gaie cote … Good Lord what knacks are made for money, now adaies. 1594: A. Copley, *Wits, Fits, etc.*, 145 (1614), A cockney seeing a squirrell in a shop, greatly admir'd it, and said: Jesu God, what pretty things are made for money. 1604: *Jacke of Dover*, 347 (1864), A jack an apes! quoth she; now, Jesus! what these Fleminges can make for money! – thinking verily it had been a thing made by mens hand. 1732: Fuller, 5503, What pretty things men will make for money, quoth the old woman, when she saw a monkey.

Prevention is better than cure. [Venienti occurrite morbo. – Persius, *Sat.*, iii 64.] *c.*1240: Bracton, *De Legibus*, bk v c.10, § 14 (Rolls Ser, vi 104), Cum melius et utilius sit in tempore occurrere quam post causam vulneratam quaerere remedium. 1630: T. Adams, *Works*, 598, Prevention is so much better then healing. 1685: in *Somers Tracts*, ix. 225 (1811), The wisdom of prevention is better than the wisdom of remedy. 1850: Dickens, *Chuzzlewit*, ch li. 1924: *Sphere*, 4 Oct., p. 2, col. 3, The old copy-book maxim of prevention being better than cure.

Pricketh betimes that will be a good thorn, It. Before 1500: in Hill, *Commonplace-Book*, 128 (E.E.T.S.), Sone hit sharpith, that thorn will be. 1546: Heywood, *Proverbs*, Pt II ch ix. 1568: *Jacob and Esau*, IV iv, It hath been a proverb, before I was born, Young doth it prick, that will be a thorn. 1590: Greene, *Works*, viii 35 (Grosart), Soone prickes the tree that will proue a thorne. 1670: Ray, 84, It early pricks that will be a thorn. 1732: Fuller, 3043.

Pride and grace dwell never in one place. Ibid., No. 6273.

Pride and poverty are ill met, yet often seen together. Ibid., No. 3933.

Pride breakfasted with Plenty, dined with Poverty, and supped with Infamy. 1736: Franklin, *Way to Wealth*, in *Works*, i 449 (Bigelow).

Pride comes before a fall. [Proverbs xvi.18, Pride goeth before destruction, and an haughty spirit before a fall.] 1390: Gower: *Confessio Amantis*, i 3062, Pride ... schal doun falle. 1509: Barclay, *Ship of Fools*, ii 161 (1874), The pryde in them at last sholde haue a fall. Before 1529: Skelton, in *Works*, i 131 (Dyce), I haue red, and rede I xall, Inordynate pride wyll haue a falle. 1593: G. Harvey, *Works*, ii 61 (Grosart), Without more circumlocution, pryde hath a fall. 1654: Gayton, *Pleasant Notes Don Q.*, 8, You see pride will have a fall. 1701: Cibber, *Love Makes a Man*, III ii, So, Pride has got a fall. 1748: Richardson, *Clarissa*, vi 258 (1785). 1848: Dickens, *Dombey*, ch lix., 'Pride shall have a fall, and it always was and will be so!' observes the housemaid. 1856: H. Melville, *Piazza Tales*, 431, The bell's main weakness was where men's blood had flawed in. And so pride went before the fall. 1930: S. Maugham, *Cakes and Ale*, v, I suppose he thinks he's be mayor himself ... Pride goeth before a fall.

Pride costs us more than hunger, thirst, and cold. 1831: Hone, *Year-Book*, col. 1612.

Pride feels no frost 1650: Fuller, *Pisgah Sight*, bk iv. ch vi §7, Some may plead, pride never feels pain. 1670: Ray. 133, Pride feels no cold. 1732: Fuller. No. 3935.

Pride goes before, shame follows after. *c.*1440: *Jacob's Well*, 70 (E.E.T.S.), For pride goth beforn, and schame folwyth after. Before 1500: in Hill, *Commonplace-Book*, 128 (E.E.T.S.). 1509: Barclay, *Ship of Fools*, ii 164 (1874), Pryde goth before, but shame do it ensue. Before 1529: Skelton, in *Works*, i 131 (Dyce). 1605: Chapman, etc., *Eastw. Hoe*, IV i, Nay, nay, eene let pride go afore; shame wil follow after, I warrant you. 1732: Fuller, 3936.

Pride had rather go out of the way, than go behind. Ibid., No. 3937.

Pride in prosperity turns to misery in adversity. Ibid., No. 3940.

Prideis as loud as a beggar as want, and a great deal more saucy. Ibid., No. 3941. 1736: Franklin, *Way to Wealth*, in *Works*, i 448 (Bigelow).

Pride is good even in a wild horse, A little. 1864: 'Cornish Proverbs', in *N. & Q.*, 3rd ser, vi 495.

Pride is in the saddle, shame is on the crupper, When. 1647: *Countrym. New Commonwealth*, 26, Lewis the eleventh, King of France, was wont to say, when pride was in the saddle, mischiefe and shame were on the crupper. 1732: Fuller, 5566.

Pride is the sworn enemy to content. Ibid., No. 3944.

Pride makes naked side, Overdone. *c.*1460: *How the Good Wife*, l.95, Ouere done pride makythe nakid syde.

Pride may lurk under a thread-bare cloak. 1732: Fuller, 3947.

Pride must abide. 1855: Gaskell, *North and South*, ch xxix, I kept myself up with proverbs as long as I could; 'Pride must abide' – and such wholesome pieces of pith! 1901: F. E. Taylor, *Lancs Sayings*, 9, Pride mun abide (Upstart people must bear with rebuffs).

Pride of the rich makes the labours of the poor, The. 1639: Clarke, 18.

Pride rides, shame lacqueys, When. 1732: Fuller, 5567.

Pride scorns the vulgar, yet lies at its mercy. Ibid., No. 3950.

Pride will have a fall. *See* **Pride comes before a fall.**

Pride will spit in pride's face. 1732: Fuller, 3953.

Pride. *See also* **Charity; Fire** (4); and **Love** (10).

Priest and **Priests. 1. Priests love pretty wenches.** 1568: in *Loseley MSS.*, 212 (Kempe).

2. The priest forgets that he was clerk. 1533: Heywood, *John, Tyb, etc.*, 86 (Farmer), But now I see well the old proverb is true; That parish priest forgetteth that ever he was clerk! 1587: Greene, *Works*, iv. 102 (Grosart), Shall the olde prouerbe be verified in thee, that the priest forgets himselfe that euer he was a clerke. 1612: R. Johnson, *Crown Garland*, 48 (Percy S.), The proverb old is come to passe, The priest when he begins the masse, Forgets that ever clarke he was. 1732: Fuller, 4721.

3. To know more than the priest spoke on Sunday. *c.*1540: Bale, *Kynge Johan*, in Manly, *Spec. Pre-Shakesp. Drama*, i 537 (1903), Clargy, marke yt well, I have more to yow to say Than, as the sayeng is, the prest dyd speke a Sonday. 1595: *Pedlars Prophecy*, l. 398 (Malone S.), True maid, fie for shame, why do ye sweare? I know more than the priest spake of a Sunday. 1894:

Northall, *Folk Phrases*, 20 (E.D.S.), More than ever the parson preached about.

4. To the purpose, as priests praise God in the morning. 1623: Wodroephe, *Spared Houres*, 474. *See also* **Bad priests; Beware; Devil** (119); **House** (21); **Such as the priest; Three things are unsatiable;** and **Woman** (59).

Prince that is feared of many must of necessity fear many, The. 1669: *Politeuphuia*, 79.

Princely mind will undo a private family, A. 1732: Fuller, 364.

Princes' privados. *See* quot. 1662: *Fragmenta Aulica*, 108, It is an old adage that princes privados and favourites of Kings were like casting counters, which are used in the exchequer or in play to count by, That sometimes they stand for one, sometimes for ten, sometimes for a hundred.

Priscian's head, To breaks = To speak or write bad Latin, and, by extension, bad English. [The *locus classicus* for the idea that 'speaking false Latin' is equivalent to inflicting violent personal injury on Priscian is Nicodemus Frischlin's comedy *Priscianus Vapulans* (the preface to which is dated 1 January, 1584). – Prof. E. Bensly, in *N. & Q.*, 10th ser, ix 376.] Before 1529: Skelton, *Works*, ii 9 (Dyce), Prisians hed broken now handy dandy. 1589: Puttenham, *Eng. Poesie*, 258 (Arber), As when we speake false English … euery poore scholler knowes the fault, and cals it the breaking of Priscians head, for he was among the Latines a principall grammarian. 1592: Shakespeare, *L.L.L.* V i, Bon, bon, fort bon! Priscian a little scratched: 'twill serve. 1642: Fuller, *Holy State*: 'Hilde-gardis', So that throwing words at random she never brake Priscian's head; as if the Latin had learned to make itself true without the speaker's care. Before 1680: Butler, *Remains*, i 220 (1759), And counted breaking Priscian's head a thing More capital, than to behead a king. 1742: Pope, *Dunciad*, iii 164. 1824: Byron, *Don Juan*, can. xv. st. 24, 'Gainst rhyme I never should have knocked my brows, Nor broken my own head, nor that of Priscian. 1858: O. W. Holmes, *Autocrat*, v, They are bound to speak decent English, unless, indeed, they are rough old campaigners … in which case, a few scars on Priscian's head are pardoned to old fellows that have quite as many on their own.

Probabilities do not make one truth, A thousand. 1855: Bohn, 302.

Problem, If you're not part of the solution, you're part of the. *See* **Solution**.

Proclamations. *See* **Head** (12).

Procrastination is the thief of time. 1742: Young, *Night Thoughts*, i l. 393. 1850: Dickens, *Copperfield*, ch xii.

Prodigal robs his heir, the miser himself, The. 1732: Fuller, 4722.

Proffered service stinks. *c.*1386: Chaucer, *Can. Yeoman's Tale*, l. 513, Ful sooth it is, that swich profred servyse Stinketh, as witnessen these olde wyse. *c.*1480: *Early Miscell.*, 22 (Warton Cl., 1855), I se proferd serves stynkit. 1546: Heywood, *Proverbs*, Pt II ch iv. 1658: R. Brome, *New Academy*, II, She offers up her selfe; now may the proverb Of proffer'd service light upon her. 1710: Swift, *Journal to Stella*, 22 Oct., Is not this vexatious? and is there so much in the proverb of proffered service? 1809: Scott, *Fam. Letters*, i 139 (1894), It is vulgarly said that proffered service is of an evil savour.

Promise and **Promises**, *subs.* **1. All promises are either broken or kept.** 1590: Q. Elizabeth, in Dee, *Diary*, 37 (Camden S.), There was never promisse made, but it was broken or kept. 1641: Taylor (Water-Poet), *Last Voyage*, 8, in *Works*, 2nd coll. (Spens S.). 1692: L'Estrange, *Aesop*, 333 (3rd ed.). 1738: Swift, *Polite Convers.*, Dial. I, Why, madam, you know, promises are either broken or kept.

2. Promise is debt. [*c.*1310: in Wright, *Pol. Songs*, 312 (Camden S.), Promis est dette due, si fay ne seit oublie.] *c.*1386: Chaucer, *Introd.* to *Man of Law's Prol.*, l. 41, Biheste is dette. 1412: Hoccleve, *Regement*, 64 (E.E.T.S.), Of a trewë man, be-heste is dette. *c.*1477: Caxton, *Jason*, 183 (E.E.T.S.), I haue promised hit and promis is dew. *c.*1530: *Everyman*, in Hazlitt, *Old Plays*, i 137, Yet promise is debt; this ys well wot. 1592: G. Harvey, in *Works*, i 174 (Grosart). *c.*1630: in *Roxb. Ballads*, i 201 (B.S.), For promise is a debt. 1664: in *Musarum Deliciae*, ii 177 (Hotten), If it be true that promise is a debt.

3. Promises and pie-crusts are made to be broken. [1599: *Shakespeare, Henry V*, II iii, For oaths are straws, men's faiths are wafer cakes.] 1681: *Heraclitus Ridens*, 16 Aug., He makes no more of breaking Acts of Parliament, than if they were like Promises and Pie-crust made to be broken. 1706: Ward, *Hud. Rediv.*, Pt 5, can. vii p. 9, Fair promises avail but little, Like too rich pye-crust, they're so brittle. 1738: Swift, *Polite Convers.*, Dial. I, Promises and pie-crust are made to be broken. 1773: in *Garrick Corresp.*, i 583 (1831), [as in 1738]. 1828: Carr, *Craven Dialect*, ii 59. 1860: Reade, *Cl. and Hearth*, ch lxxxi, 'Pshaw!' said Catherine, 'promises are pie-crusts.' 1920: Locke, *House of Baltazar*, ch xvi, What about your promise, Mr Baltazar? Pie-crust?

Promise, *verb.* **1. He promises like a merchant but pays like a man of war.** 1639: Clarke, 194. 1670: Ray, 21. 1732: Fuller, 2007.

2. He promises mountains and performs molehills. [Maria et montes polliceri, – Sallust, *C.* xxiii 3.] 1578: Florio, *First Fruites*, fo. 29, He promiseth seas and mountaines. 1629: *Book of Meery Riddles*, Prov. 105. 1880: Spurgeon, *Ploughman's Pictures*, 18, They promise mountains and perform molehills.

3. He that promises too much means nothing. 1633: Draxe, 167, He that promiseth all, deceiueth all. 1732: Fuller, 2253.

4. To promise and give nothing is a comfort for a fool. 1633: Draxe, 167, To promise and giue nought is to comfort a foole. 1670: Ray, 22. 1732: Fuller, 5215.

Promising is the eve of giving. 1578: Florio, *First Fruites*, fo. 29, The eue to geue is to promise. 1640: Herbert, *Jac. Prudentum*. 1666: Torriano, *Piazza Univ.*, 219, Promise is the eve of the gift.

Proof of the pudding is in the eating, The. [Exitus acta probat. – Ovid, *Heroid.*, ii 85.] *c.*1300: *King Alisaunder*, l. 4042, Hit is y-writein, every thyng Himseolf shewith in tastyng. 1623: W. Camden, *remains concerning Britain* (ed. 3) 266, All the proofe of a pudding is in the eating. 1666: G. Torriano, *Italian Proverbs*, 100 (note), As they say at the winding up, or the proof of the pudding is in the eating. 1714: *Spectator*, No. 567. 1828: Scott, *Fair Maid*, ch vi, The thin soft cakes … were done liberal justice to in the mode which is best proof of cake as well as pudding. 1842: Barham, *Ing. Legends*, 2nd ser: 'Black Mousquetaire', can. 2.

Proper that hath proper conditions, He is. 1599: Porter, *Two Angry Women*, sc xi 1670: Ray, 22.

Properer man the worse luck, The. 1633: Jonson, *Tale of a Tub*, III iv. 1670: Ray, 134,

The properer man (and so the honester) the worse luck.

Prophet is not without honour save in his own country, A. [Matthew xiii.57, A prophet is not without honour save in his own country, and his own house.] 1485: Caxton, in Malory *Works* (1967), I p. cxlv, The word of God … sayth that no man is accepte for a prophet in his owne contreye. 1603: J. Florio, tr. *Montaigne's Essays*, III ii, No man hath beene a Prophet … in his owne country, saith the experience of histories. 1771: Smollett, *Humphry Clinker*, III 92, The captain, like the prophets of old, is but little honoured in his own country. 1879: M. Pattison, *Milton*, 153, The homage which was wanting to the prophet in his own country was more liberally tendered by foreigners.

Proposes, God disposes, Man. *See* **Man** (61).

Prospect is often better than possession. 1732: Fuller, 3958.

Prosperity. 1. He who swells in prosperity, will shrink in adversity. 1855: Bohn, 401.

2. In time of prosperity friends will be plenty; In time of adversity not one among twenty, [ἀνδρὸς κακῶς πράσσοντος, ἐκποδὼν φίλοι. – Menander, *Sent.*, 32.] *c.*1500: in *Antiq. Repertory*, iv. 398 (1809), In tyme of prosperite remember adversite. 1659: Howell, 20. 1670: Ray, 11. 1732: Fuller, 6394. 1869: Spurgeon, *John Ploughman*, ch xiv.

3. Prosperity gets followers; but adversity distinguishes them. 1669: *Politeuphuia*, 176, Prosperity getteth friends, but adversity trieth them. 1732: Fuller, 3962.

4. Prosperity lets go the bridle. 1640: Herbert, *Jac. Prudentum.*

Proud as an apothecary. 1639: Clarke, 32. 1678: Ray, 288.

Proud as a peacock. *c.*1290: in Wright, *Pol. Songs John to Edw. II*, 159 (Camden S.), A pruest proud ase a po. *c.*1410: *Towneley Plays*, 117 (E.E.T.S.), Ther shall com a swane as prowde as a po. 1513: Bradshaw, *St Werburga*, 69 (E.E.T.S.), Prowde as a pecocke. 1565: Shacklock, *Hatchet of Heresies*, quoted in *N. & Q.*, 2nd ser, v 411. 1681: Robertson, *Phraseol. Generalis*, 1030. 1753: Richardson, *Grandison*, iv. 152 (1883). 1869: Spurgeon, *John Ploughman*, ch iii.

Proud as Lucifer. *c.*1394: in Wright, *Pol. Poems*, i 315 (Rolls Ser, 1859), They been as proud as

Lucifarre. *c*.1450: *Parlonope*, l. 9740 (E.E.T.S.), Be thow as prowde as Lucifere … 1649: Quarles, *Virgin Widow*, V. *c*.1686: in *Roxb. Ballads*, vii. 21 (B.S.). 1764: Mrs F. Sheridan, *Dupe*, III vii 1822: Scott, *Nigel*, ch viii. 1848: Dickens, *Dombey*, ch xxvi. 1896: Conan Doyle, *Rodney Stone*, ch v.

Proud as old Cole's dog. 1834–7: Southey, *Doctor*, ch cxxv., Who was Old Cole whose dog was so proud that he took the wall of a dung-cart and got squeezed to death by the wheel?

Proud come behind as go before, As. *c*.1565: Still, *Gam. Gurton*, V ii, As proude corns behinde, they say, as any goes before! 1605: Camden, *Remains*, 318 (1870). 1655: Fuller, *Church Hist.*, bk iii § iii (5), Pleasing itself that 'as stout came behind as went before'. 1732: Fuller, 724. 1853: Trench, *Proverbs*, 76 (1905).

Proud eye, A, an open purse, and a light wife, bring mischief to the first, misery to the second, and horns to the third. 1647: *Countrym. New Commonwealth*, 35. 1669: *Politeuphuia*, 281.

Proud folks, for they will not complain, It's good beating. 1639: Clarke, 31. 1670: Ray. 133.

Proud heart and a beggar's purse agree not well together, A. *c*.1430: Lydgate, *Minor Poems*, 56 (Percy S.), A prowde hert in a beggers brest … it accordith nought. *c*.1532: R. Copland, *Spyttel Hous*, l. 977, Lo, here one may see that there is none wors Than is a proude herte and a beggers purs. 1631: Brathwait, *Eng. Gentlewoman*, 272 (1641), Wee say there is no good congruity in a proud heart and a beggers purse. 1670: Ray, 133 ['mind' for 'heart']. 1732: Fuller, 369, A proud mind and a poor purse are ill met. Ibid., No. 6386, There's nothing agrees worse, Than a prince's heart, and a beggar's purse.

Proud horse that will not bear his own provender, A. 1546: Heywood, *Proverbs*, Pt II ch ix. 1597: G. Harvey, *Works*, iii 14 (Grosart), Go too, I say, he is an ill horse that will not carrie his owne prouender. *c*.1660: in *Roxb. Ballads*, ii 159 (Hindley). 1670: Ray, 105 [as in 1597].

Proud look makes foul work in a fine face, A. 1732: Fuller, 367.

Proud looks lose hearts, but courteous words win them. 1647: *Countrym. New Commonwealth*, 18.

Proud man hath many crosses, A. 1732: Fuller, 368.

Prove thy friend ere thou have need. *c*.1400: *Cato's Morals*, in *Cursor Mundi*, p. 1672

(E.E.T.S.), be scarske of thi louing til hit come to prouing of thi gode frende. 1546: Heywood, *Proverbs*, Pt I ch xi. 1670: Ray, 93.

Provender pricks him. 1546: Heywood, *Proverbs*, Pt I ch xi, For whan prouander prickt them a little tyne, They did as thy wife and thou did both dote Eche one on other. 1591: Drayton, *Harmony of Church*, 9 (Percy S.), That now to lust thy prouender doth pricke. 1613: B.&F., *Honest Man's Fortune*, V i, But, by my soul, my provender scarce pricks me. 1716: Ward, *Female Policy*, 84, When provender pricks a woman, then she'll grow knavish.

Proves too much, proves nothing, That which. 1732: Fuller, 4384.

Provide for the worst, the best will save itself. 1546: Heywood, *Proverbs*, Pt I ch v. 1659: Howell, 15. 1680: L'Estrangc, *Citt and Bumpkin*, 6, 'Tis good however to prepare for the worst, and the best (as they say) will help itself.

Providence is always on the side of the big battalions. *See* **Battalions.**

Providence is better than rent. 1640: Herbert, *Jac. Prudentum*. 1670: Ray, 22. 1732: Fuller, 3971.

Providing is preventing. 1883: Burne, *Shropsh. Folk-Lore*, 588.

Prudence. *See* **Ounce**; and **Zeal.**

Prudent pauses forward business. 1732: Fuller, 3976.

Pry'thee lad, shape. 'Shape = set to work – go on – get along'. 1917: Bridge, *Cheshire Proverbs*, 104.

Public. *He that does anything for the public is accounted to do it for nobody.* 1578: Florio, *First Fruites*, fo. 29, Who serueth the commons serueth no body. 1611: Cotgrave, s.v. 'Commun', *Ouvrage de commun ouvrage de nul*; All mens worke is no mans worke; or that which is done for many is acknowledged by none. *Qui sert commun nul ne le paye, et s'il defaut chascun l'abbaye*; The service done to a people no man rewards, the disservices every man railes at. 1732: Fuller, 2082. 1742: North, *Lives of Norths*, ii 120 (Bohn), Which confirms an old lesson, that 'He who serves a community must secure a reward by his own means, or expect it from God'.

Publicity is good publicity, Any *or* **All.** 1933: R. Chandler, in *Black Mask*, Dec. 26, Rhonda Farr said: 'Publicity, darling, Just publicity. Any kind is better than none at all. 1974: P. Cave, *Dirtiest Picture Postcard*, xiv, Haven't you ever heard the old adman's adage … 'any publicity is good publicity'?

Public reproof hardens shame. 1732: Fuller, 3977.

Pudding. 1. A pudding hath two ends. 1598: T. Bastard, *Chrestoleros*, bk iii Ep. 12, A podding merits double praise, a podding hath two ends. 1659: Howell, 11, A pudding hath two ends, but a fool hath none.

2. A pudding in the fire. *See* quot. 1659: Howell, 13, Ther's a pudding in the fire, and my part lies thereinna.

3. If it won't pudding, it will froize = If it won't do for one thing it will for another. 1830: Forby, *Vocab. E. Anglia*, 427. 1872: J. Glyde, jr., *Norfolk Garland*, 148.

4. It would vex a dog to see a pudding creep. *c.*1630: in *Roxb. Ballads*, i 58 (B.S.), Would not a dog for anger swell to see a pudding creepe. 1673: in Halliwell, *Norfolk Anthology*, 17 (1852). 1738: Swift, *Polite Convers.*, Dial. II

5. Pudding before praise. 1847: Barham, *Ing. Legends*, 3rd ser: 'House-Warming', An old proverb says, 'Pudding still before praise!'

6. Pudding for a friar's mouth. *See* **Fit as a pudding.**

7. Pudding is no meat with you. 1639: Clarke, 74.

8. Pudding is poison. *See* quot. 1738: Swift, *Polite Convers.*, Dial. II, O! Madam, they say a pudding is poison when it is too much boil'd.

9. To come in pudding time = To come at the right moment. 1546: Heywood, *Proverbs*, Pt II ch ix, This geare comth euen in puddyng time rightlie. 1568: Fulwell, *Like will to Like*, in Hazlitt, *Old Plays*, iii 319. 1596: Nashe, *Works*, iii 169 (Grosart), In pudding time you have spoken. 1604: Dekker, *Honest Whore*, Pt I V ii, We come in pudding-time, for here's the duke. 1663: Butler, *Hudibras*, Pt I can. ii, l. 865. 1738: Swift, *Polite Convers.*, Dial. II. 1769: Cumberland, *Brothers*, II iv, I want to have a little chat with you, and thought to have dropped in at pudding-time, as they say. 1830: Colman, jr., in *Hum. Works*, 421 (Hotten), The good luck of settling concerns of the greatest consequence, exactly at the critical minute, is expressed by being 'just in pudding time'. 1854: Baker, *Northants Gloss.*, s.v., 'You've hit pudding-time well', is a common salutation to any one who pops in accidentally to dinner.

See also **Cold pudding; Proof;** and **Run** (13).

Puff not against the wind. 1605: Camden, *Remains*, 330 (1870). 1670: Ray, 156. 1846: Denham, *Proverbs*, 7 (Percy S.).

Pulborough. *See* **Chichester.**

Pull devil pull baker. 1759: Colman, *Rolliad*, can. ii, Pull Tom, pull Nick, pull baker, and pull devil. 1831: Planché, *Extravag.*, i 75 (1879), *Orpheus* [*to Pluto*]. But when she went, it was 'pull *you*, pull baker!'1881: in *N. & Q.*, 11th ser, ix. 437, When the Mayor of Birmingham, Alderman Baker, tried to unveil the statue of George Dawson at Birmingham in 1881, the mechanism did not work. The Mayor tugged at the cord in vain. In the strained silence was heard a stage whisper from J. H. Chamberlain, the architect of the canopy, 'Pull devil – pull Baker!' 1922: Ramsay Macdonald in H. of C. *Times*, 14 Dec., p. 8, col. 4, Workmen and employers must see that the old game of 'pull devil, pull baker' was not worth the candle.

Pull down than to build up, It is easier to. *See* **Easier.**

Pullet in the pen is worth an hundred in the fen, A. 1869: Hazlitt, 31.

Pulls with a long rope that waits for another's death, He. 1640: Herbert, *Jac. Prudentum.* 1666: Torriano, *Piazza Univ.*, 159, He pulls at a long rope, who longs for another bodies death.

Punch coal. *See* **Break** (3).

Punctuality is the politeness of princes. Attributed to King Louis XVIII of France (1755–1824). M. Edgeworth, *Helen*, II ix, 'Punctuality is the politeness of princes' … Mr Harley would have ridiculed so antiquated a notion. 1854: Surtees: *Handley Cross*, (ed. 2), xli, Punctuality is the purlitness o' princes, and I doesn't like keepin' people waitin'.

Punctuality is the soul of business. 1869: Hazlitt, 321. 1878: Platt, *Business*, 95, Punctuality … is the very hinge of business.

Punishment is lame, but it comes. 1640: Herbert, *Jac. Prudentum.* 1666: Torriano, *Piazza Univ.*, 199 ['overtakes' for 'comes']. 1853: Trench, *Proverbs*, 140 (1905).

Pure all things are pure, To the. [Titus 115, Unto the pure, all things are pure: but unto them that are defiled and unbelieving is nothing pure.] 1854: Would that our earth were more frequently brightened and purified by such spirits … 'To the pure, all things are pure'. 1895: G. Allen, *The Woman who Did*, vii, Herminia, for her part, never did discover she was talked about. To the pure all things are pure.

Purse. 1. Ask thy purse what thou should'st buy. 1732: Fuller, 820.

2. He hath left his purse in his other hose. 1639: Clarke, 244. 1670: Ray, 22. 1732: Fuller, 1889 ['breeches' for 'hose'].

3. He is purse-sick and lacks a physician. 1546: Heyvrood, *Proverbs*, Pt I, ch xi.

4. He that shows his purse longs to be rid of it. 1639: Clarke, 176. 1670: Ray, 135. 1732: Fuller, 2299, He that sheweth his wealth to a thief, is the cause of his own pillage. Ibid., No. 2301 [as in 1639].

5. His purse and his palate are ill met. Ibid., No. 2513.

6. His purse is made of a toad's skin. 1678: Ray, 90.

7. Keep your purse and your mouth close. 1732: Fuller, 3122.

8. Let your purse be your master. 1639: Clarke, 129. 1670: Ray, 135. 1672: Walker, *Paraem.*, 47.

9. The purse-strings are the most common ties of friendship. 1732: Fuller, 4727.

10. To give ones purse a purgation. 1546: Heywood, *Proverbs*, Pt I ch xi, Ye would by my purs, geue me a purgacion. 1562: Bullein, *Bulw. of Defence*, fo. 27, Can giue his masters purse a purgacion.

See also **Be it better; Devil** (98); **Empty** (3)–(7); **Heavy purse; Less; Light purse; Nothing** (4); **Proud eye; Proud heart; Silk purse; Silver** (2); **Two hands; Wrinkled purses.**

Put, *verb.* **1. He'll not put off his doublet before he goes to bed** = *He'll* not part with his property before death. 1645: Howell, *Letters*, bk i § iii No. xi, This does not suit with the genius of an Englishman, who loves not to pull off his clothes till he goes to bed. 1737: Ray, 186. 1883: Burne, *Shropsh. Folk-Lore*, 597, To doff one's shoon before going to bed = to part with one's property before death.

2. He puts out one of his own eyes, to put out both of his adversary's. 1730: Bailey, *Eng. Dict.*, s.v. 'Solace' [cited as 'the old proverb']

3. Never put off till tomorrow what you can do today. *c.*1386: Chaucer, *Melibeus*, § 71, 'Ther is an old proverbe', quod she, 'seith: that the goodnesse that thou mayst do this day, do it; and abyde nat ne delaye it nat til to-morwe'. 1541: Coverdale, *Christ. State Matrimony*, sig. I3,

What-soeuer thou mayest do to nyght dyferre it not tyll to morowe. 1633: Draxe, 41, Deferre not vntill to morrow, if thou canst do it to day. 1736: Franklin, *Way to Wealth*, in *Works*, i 444 (Bigelow). 1785: *Observer*, No. 96. 1869: Spurgeon, *John Ploughman*, ch vii, These slow coaches ... take for their rule an old proverb turned topsy-turvy – 'Never do to-day what you can put off till to-morrow'.

4. Put in with the bread. *See* **Loaf** (1).

5. Put no more in the pocket than it will hold. 1639: Clarke, 11.

6. Put your trust in God and keep your powder dry. A saying attributed to Oliver Cromwell. 1834: Colonel Blacker, *Oliver's Advice*, in E. Hayes, *Ballads of Ireland* (1856), I 192, Put your trust in God, my boys, and keep your powder dry. 1856: E. Hayes, *Ballads of Ireland* (ed. 2), I 191, Cromwell ... when his troops were about crossing a river ... concluded an adress with these words ... Put your trust in God; but mind to keep your powder dry. 1908: *Times Literary Supplement*, 6 Nov., 383, In thus keeping his powder dry, the bishop acted most wisely, though he himself ascribes the happy result entirely to the observance of the other half of Cromwell's maxim.

7. To be put to one's trumps. *See* **Trumps**.

8. To put a churl upon a gentleman. 1586: L. Evans, *Withals Dict. Revised*, sig. D7, Lay not a churle vpon a gentleman, drinke not beere after wine. 1637: Taylor (Water-Poet), *Drinke and Welcome*, 20, in *Works*, 2nd coll. (Spens.S.), And after to drinke beere, nor will nor can He lay a churle upon a gentleman. 1690: *New Dict. Canting Crew*, sig. C6. 1738: Swift, *Polite Convers.*, Dial. II, *Neverout* [*offered ale*], No, faith, my lord; I like your wine, and won't put a churl upon a gentleman; your honour's claret is good enough for me. 1785: Grose, *Class. Dict. Vulgar Tongue*, s.v. 'Churl'.

9. To put something in the eye. *See* **Eye** (20).

10. To put to bed with a shovel = To bury. 1859: in Farmer, *Musa Pedestris*, 160, With shovels they were put to bed. 1910: *Devonsh. Assoc. Trans.*, xlii 68, She callously replied, 'Oh, he's no güde, 'tis taime he were put to bed wi' a shovel.'

11. To put two and two together. *See* **Two and two.**

12. You put it together with an hot needle and burnt thread. 1678: Ray, 350.

Q

Quake like an oven, To. 1670: Ray, 207.

Quality. *See* quot. 1887: *Folk-Lore Journal*, v 219, To cut an honour for the trump card is unlucky, for 'when quality opens the door there is poverty behind'.

Quarrel, It takes two to make a. *See* **Two to make.**

Quarrel with a knave than with a fool, It is better to. 1820: Colton, *Lacon*, Pt II No. 67, These considerations have given rise to this saying, 'It is better,' etc.

Quarrel with one's bread and butter, To. 1738: Swift, *Polite Convers.*, Dial. I, I won't quarrel with my bread and butter for all that; I know when I'm well. 1748: Richardson, *Clarissa*, v 21 (1785). 1833: Planché, *Extravag.*, i 155 (1879). 1869: Spurgeon, *John Ploughman*, ch xix, He who turns up his nose at his work quarrels with his bread and butter. 1911: T. Edwardes, *Neighbourhood*, 213, Of course I must not quarrel with my bread-and-butter!

Quart into a pint pot, You cannot get a. A quart is a quantity equal to two imperial pints. 1896: *Daily News*, 23 July, 4, They had been too ambitious. They had attempted what he might describe in homely phrase as putting a quart into a pint pot. 1934: C. F. Gregg, *Execution of Diamond Deutsch*, xi, He whistled thoughtfully. 'You can't get a quart into a pint pot – is that it?' asked the South African officer, quick to see the reason.

Quartan ague kills the old and cures the voting, A. 1659: Howell, *Proverbs: Ital.-Eng.*, 15. 1678: Ray, 41. 1732: Fuller, 3991 [in the plural].

Quarter-master where-ever he comes, Hell be. 1678: Ray, 266. 1732: Fuller, 2414, He would be quartermaster at home, if his wife would let him.

Queen Anne's dead. 1722: *Ballad*, in Lady Pennyman, *Miscellanies*, 1740, He's as dead as Queen Anne the day after she dy'd. 1738: Swift, *Polite Convers.*, Dial. I, And pray, what news, Mr Neverout? *Neverout.* Why, madam, Queen Elizabeth's dead. 1797: Colman, jr., *Heir at Law*, I i, Tell 'em Queen Anne's dead, my lady. 1840: Barham, *Ing. Legends*. 1st ser: 'Look at the Clock', Mrs Winifred Pryce was as dead as Queen Anne! 1908: Read, *H. & B. in Hants.*, 353, Portsmouth offers text and reference for the saying 'Queen Anne is dead'.

Queen-apple-tree, To be up the. 1670: Ray, 198.

Queen Dick. 1667: L'Estrange, *Quevedo's Visions*, 50 (1904), This was well enough in the days of Queen Dick, when the poor creatures knew no better.

Queen's English. *See* **King's English.**

Queer as folk, There's nowt so. *See* **Nowt.**

Quern. *See* **Do** (40).

Quest. *See* **Wood-pigeon.**

Question, and you'll get a silly answer, Ask a silly. *See* **Ask** (1).

Question, There are two sides to every. *See* **Two sides.**

Questioneth, He that nothing, nothing learneth. 1732: Fuller, 2241.

Questions and I'll tell you no lies, Ask me no. *See* **Ask** (3).

Quey out of a quey, A, Will breed a byre full of kye. 'Quey' = a heifer. 1846: Denham, *Proverbs*, 14 (Percy S.).

Quick and nimble; more like a bear than a squirrel. 1732: Fuller, 3992.

Quick and nimble 'twill be your own another day. 1678: Ray, 345.

Quick as a bee. 1546: Heywood, *Proverbs*, Pt I ch ix. 1595: Churchyard, *Charitie*, 16 (1816), As quicke as bee, seekes honie euery where. 1633: Draxe, 172.

Quick as lightning. *c.*1440: Lydgate, *Fall of Princes*, bk vi l. 2114, His conquest was swifft as wynd or leuene [lightning], *c.*1623: B.&F., *Love's Cure*, I i, Swift as lightning he came on Upon the other. 1763: Mrs F. Sheridan, *Discovery*, I ii, I am rather petulant, flash, flash, flash, as quick as lightning. 1787: D'Arblay, *Diary*, ii 427 (1876), I turned back, quick as lightning. 1880: R.L.S. and Henley, *Deacon Brodie*, I iii i, I was as quick as lightning.

Quick as thought. Before 1225: *Ancren R.*, 94 (OED), Ase swifte ase is nu monnes thouht. 1412–20: Lydgate, *Troy Book*, bk i l. 1764, By sodeyn chawnge, hasty as a thought. 1468: *Coventry Mys.*, 298 (SH.S.), I am as whyt [quick] as thought. 1594: *Zepheria*, 30 (Spens.S.), But now (old man) flye on, as swift as thought. 1620: Shelton, *Quixote*, Pt II ch xlviii. 1656: R. Fletcher, *Ex Otio Negotium*, 84. 1748:

Richardson, *Clarissa*, vi 13 (1785), Then, as quick as thought … 1894: Northall, *Folk Phrases*, 10 (E.D.S.). 1923: *Punch*, 10 Jan., p. 29, col. 1, As quick as thought I flung myself forward and snatched at the bridle.

Quick at meat, quick at work. 1611: Cotgrave, s.v. 'Bestes'. Ibid., s.v. 'Eschauffer', We say, good at meat, good at worke. 1650: Fuller, *Pisgah Sight*, bk ii ch viii. 1710: E. Ward, *Nuptial Dialogues*, i 307, Speedy at victuals, quick at work's an old proverbial saying. 1738: Swift, *Polite Convers.*, Dial. II. 1829: Cobbett, *Advice to Young Men*, Lett. III, 'Quick at meals, quick at work', is a saying as old as the hills.

Quick baker, A, and a slow brewer. 1732: Fuller, 373.

Quick believers need broad shoulders. 1640: Herbert, *Jac. Prudentum*.

Quick child is soon taught. *c.*1320: in *Reliq. Antiquae*, i 110 (1841), 'Sely chyld is sone y-lered'; Quoth Hendyng. 1869: Hazlitt, 322.

Quick landlord makes a careful tenant, A. 1678: Ray, 165. 1732: Fuller, 3994 [in the plural].

Quick, To the. *See* **Touch** (2).

Quick with the quick. *See* **Live** (38).

Quick. *See also* **Nimble**.

Quickly come, quickly go. 1631: Mabbe, *Celestina*, 29 (T.T.), Quickly be wonne, and quickly be lost.

Quiet as a lamb. 1362: Langland, *Plowman*, A, vi 43, He is as louh [quiet] as a lomb. *c.*1440: Lydgate, *Fall of Princes*, bk i l.6934 (E.E.T.S.), Stille as a lamb, most meek off his visage. 1592: Shakespeare, *Romeo*, II v, I'll warrant him, as gentle as a lamb. 1694: *Terence made English*, 180, I can presently make him as quiet as a lamb. 1787: D'Arblay, *Diary*, ii 337 (1876), I used to … wander about as quiet as a lamb. 1872: Hardy,

Greenwood Tree, Pt V ch i, I walked into the church as quiet as a lamb, I'm sure!

Quiet (or Still) as a mouse. 1656: Flecknoe, *Diarium*, 9, Was wont to be as still as mouse, *c.*1670: in *Roxb. Ballads*, iii 377 (B.S.), I must be silent as a mouse. 1709: Cibber, *Rival Fools*, II, I'm mute as a mouse in a cheese. 1772: Graves, *Spirit. Quixote*, bk ii ch xiv, Tugwell was as still as a mouse during this discourse. 1824: Scott, *Redgauntlet*, ch xvi, A place where you will be as snug and quiet as a mouse in his hole. 1894: R.L.S., *St Ives*, ch xi, Both armies lay as quiet as mice. 1923: *Punch*, 7 March, p. 218, col. 1, If she has her bricks and a pencil and paper she'll be as quiet as a mouse.

Quiet as a 'tatur, As. 1917: Bridge, *Cheshire Proverbs*, 26.

Quiet sleep feels no foul weather. 1732: Fuller, 3997.

Quiet sow, quiet mow. Devon. 1850: *N. & Q.*, 1st ser, ii 512.

Quiet tongue makes a wise head, A. 1562: Heywood, *Epigr.*, 6th hund., No. 83, Hauyng a styll toung he had a besy head. 1776: T. Cogan, *John Buncle, Junior*, i 238, But mum's the word … A quiet tongue makes a wise head, says I

Quietness is best. *See* quots. 1886: R. Holland, *Cheshire Gloss.*, 453 (E.D.S.), Quietness is best, as the fox said, when he bit the cock's head off. 1908: *Eng. Ill. Mag.*, Jan., 357, Quietness is the best noise, as Uncle Johnny said when he knocked down his wife [Cornish]. 1917: Bridge, *Cheshire Proverbs*, 104 [as in 1886].

Quit bridle, quit tit. 1820: Scott, *Abbot*, ch xvii, They are as sharp here north-away as in canny Yorkshire herself, and quit bridle, quit titt, as we say.

Quits his place well that leaves his friend there, He. 1640: Herbert, *Jac. Prudentum*.

Quoth the young cock. *See* **Young** (16).

R

Rabbit for a rat, Who will change a? 1546: Heywood, *Proverbs*, Pt II ch vii.

Rabbit, He's like a, fat and lean in twenty-four hours. 1678: Ray, 288.

Rabbit-hunting. *See* quot. 1732: Fuller, 5170, To go a coney-catching with a dead ferrit.

Race-horse. *See* **Running horse.**

Race is got by running, The. 1732: Fuller, 4728.

Race is not to the swift, nor the battle to the strong, The. [Ecclesiastes ix.11, The race is not to the swift, not the battle to the strong] 1632: Burton, *Anatomy of Melancholy*, II iii, It is not honesty, learning, worth, wisdome, that preferres men. The race is not to the swift, nor the battell to the stronger. 1873: C. M. Yonge, *Pillars of the House*, III xxxii, Poor child! she lay … trying to work out … why the race is not to the swift, nor the battle to the strong.

Race, Slow and steady wins the. *See* **Slow and steady.**

Rack and manger, To lie (or live) at. c.1378: Wiclif, in *Eng. Works*, 435 (Matthew, 1880), It is yuel to kepe a wast hors in stable … but it is worse to have a womman with-ynne or with-oute at racke and at manger. 1590: Greene, *Works*, ix. 178 (Grosart), Mars himselfe hateth to be euer on Venus lappe, he scorneth to lye at rack and manger. 1628: *Robin Goodfellow*, 10 (Percy S.), Leaped and curveted as nimble as if he had beene in stable at rack and manger a full moneth. 1640: Shirley, *Loves Cruelty*, III ii, You think you are at rack and manger, when you divide beans with the horses, and help to foul the stable. 1740: North, *Lives of Norths*, i 335 (Bohn), He took divers of them to rack and manger in his family. 1843: Carlyle, *Past and Present*, bk ii ch i, Tearing out the bowels of St Edmundsbury Convent (its larders namely and cellars) in the most ruinous way, by living at rack and manger there. 1889: Peacock, *Manley*, etc., *Gloss.*, 426 (E.D.S.), To live at rack and manger is to live plentifully; without stint.

Rag on every bush. *See* quot. 1866: in *N.&Q.*, 3rd ser, ix. 474, A Rag upon Every Bush. – This saying, or proverb … is usually applied to young men who are in the habit of showing 'marked attention' to more than one lady at a time. 'Oh, he has a rag on every bush'.

Ragged as a colt, As. 1863: Wise, *New Forest*, ch xvi, The proverb of 'as ragged as a colt Pixey' is everywhere to be heard, and at which Drayton seems to hint in his *Court of Faerie*: 'This Puck seems but a dreaming dolt, Still walking like a ragged colt'. 1894: Northall, *Folk Phrases*, 10 (E.D.S.).

Ragged as a cuckoo, As. Oxfordsh. 1923: *Folk-Lore*, xxxiv. 329.

Ragged as a sheep, As. 1862: *Dialect of Leeds*, 405, If the child of a slatternly woman is seen with tattered garments, it is pronounced at once to be 'as regg'd as a sheep'.

Ragged colt may make a good horse, A. Before 1500: in Hill, *Commonplace-Book*, 128 (E.E.T.S.), Of a rwgged colte cwmeth a good hors. 1546: Heywood, *Proverbs*, Pt I ch xi, For of a ragged colte there comth a good horse. 1605: Chapman, etc., *Eastw. Hoe*, V [with 'prove' for 'make']. 1670: Ray, 72. 1754: Berthelson, *Eng.-Danish Dict.*, s.v. 'Colt'. 1786: Burns, *Dream*, xi (OED), Aft a ragged cowte's been known To mak a noble aiver. 1846: Denham, *Proverbs*, 7 (Percy S.), Of a ragged colt cometh many a good horse.

Ragged colt *See* also **Scald horse.**

Rags o' th' hob, There'll be. 1917: Bridge, *Cheshire Proverbs*, 117 … There will be a quarrel or unpleasantness.

Rain, *subs.* **1. A foot deep of rain Will kill hay and grain; But three feet of snow Will make them come mo'** [more]. 1869: Blackmore, *Lorna Doone*, ch l. [quoted as 'the old sayin']1893: Inwards, *Weather Lore*, 111.

2. After rain comes sunshine (or fair weather). 1484: Caxton, *Fables of Aesope*, II viii (OED), After the rayne cometh the fair weder. 1597: C. Middleton, *Chinon of England*, 26 (E.E.T.S.), After showers at length would come a sunne. 1678: Ray, 194, After rain comes fair weather. 1869: Spurgeon, *John Ploughman*, ch v, After rain comes clear shining. 1893: Inwards, *Weather Lore*, 111, After rain comes sunshine.

3. A little rain stills a great wind. Before 1225: *Ancren R.*, 246, Eft, me seith, and soth hit is, a muchel wind alith mid a lutel rein. c.1430: Lydgate, *Daunce of Machabree*, l. 448, And windes great gon down with litle rein. 1478: Rivers, tr. C. de Pisa's *Morale Prouerbes*, And litle reyne dooth a greet wynd abate, *c.*1534: Berners, *Huon*, 39 (E.E.T.S.), It is sayd that a small rayne abatyth a grete wynd. 1653: Urquhart, *Rabelais*, bk ii ch xi. 1732: Fuller, 410, A small rain may allay a great storm. Cf. No. 11.

4. All the rain avore Midzummer Go'th into the farmer's puss; All the rain afterwards Is zo much the wuss. 1891: R. P. Chope, *Hartland Dialect*, 20 (E.D.S.).

5. A sunshiny shower Won't last half an hour. 1846: Denham, *Proverbs*, 8 (Percy S.). 1872: J. Glyde. jr., *Norfolk Garland*, 155. 1893: Inwards, *Weather Lore*, 111, A sunshiny shower Never lasts half an hour. Bedfordshire. Sunshiny rain Will soon go again. Devon. 1899:*N.&Q.*, 9th ser, iv. 165, There is the rime, Sunshine shower, Rain half an hour, which children used to sing-song if caught in a shower on a summer day coming from school.

6. Between twelve and two You'll see what the day will do. 1872: J. Glyde, jr., *Norfolk Garland*, 155.

7. Bright-backed rain Makes fools fain. 1917: Bridge, *Cheshire Proverbs*, 162 … When a rain cloud is succeeded by a little brightness in the sky, fools rejoice and think it will soon be fair weather.

8. For a morning rain leave not your journey. Before 1500: in Hill, *Commonplace-Book*, 131 (E.E.T.S.), He is no good swayn that lettith his jorney for the rayn. 1640: Herbert, *Jac. Prudentum.*

9. If rain begins at early morning light, 'Twill end ere day at noon is bright. 1893: Inwards, *Weather Lore*, 109.

10. If the rain comes out of the east, 'Twill rain twice twenty-four hours at the least, *c.*1685: Aubrey, *Nat. Hist. Wilts*, 16 (1847). 1830: Forby, *Vocab. E. Anglia*, 417, When it rains with the wind in the east. It rains for twenty-four hours at least. 1893: Inwards, *Weather Lore*, 109, Rain from the east Two days at least.

11. Marry the rain to the wind and you have a calm. Ibid., 110. Cf. No. 3.

12. More rain, more rest. 1864: 'Cornish Proverbs', in *N.&Q.*, 3rd ser, v 208, More rain, more rest; more water will suit the ducks best. 1879: *N.&Q.*, 5th ser, xi 18, Fifty years ago I read in a book of travels, More rain, more rest; Fine weather not the best, as a saying much used by sailors. 1901: F. E. Taylor, *Lancs Sayings*, 41,

Mooar rain – mooar rest: fine weather is no' awlus th' best. Cf. No. 23.

13. No one so surely pays his debt As wet to dry and dry to wet. Wilts. 1893: Inwards, *Weather Lore*, 108.

14. Plenty rain, plenty sunshine, Plenty rain, plenty root. 1899: *N.&Q.*, 9th ser, iv. 165 … old hands know that after an early summer, with nice rains and hot suns alternating, there is sure to be abundance of fruit, corn and root.

15. Rain before seven, Fine before eleven. 1853: *N.&Q.*, 1st ser, viii 512. 1888: Lowsley, *Berks Gloss.*, 30 (E.D.S.), Raain avoor zeven vine avoor 'leven is a very common weather proverb. 1893: Inwards, *Weather Lore*, 44, Rain at seven, fine at eleven; Rain at eight, not fine till eight. 1899: *N.&Q.*, 9th ser, iii 317 … I have always heard this proverb with two additional lines: – If it rains at eleven, 'Twill last till seven.

16. Rain from the south prevents the drought; But rain from the west is always best. 1893: Inwards, *Weather Lore*, 109.

17. Rain has such narrow shoulders it will get in anywhere. 1877: E. Leigh, *Cheshire Gloss.*, 165. 1917: Bridge, *Cheshire Proverbs*, 105.

18. Rain long foretold, long last; Short notice soon past. 1893: Inwards, 109.

19. Rain on the green grass, and rain on the tree, And rain on the house-top, but not upon me. 1846: Denham, *Proverbs*, 8 (Percy S.).

20. Rain, rain, go away, Come again on Saturday. 1687: Aubrey, *Gentilisme, etc.*, 180 (F.L.S.). 1899: in *N.&Q.*, 9th ser, iv 165 [with 'for washing day' for 'on Saturday'].

21. Rain, rain, go to Spain. *See* quots. 1659: Howell, 20, Rain, rain, go to Spain. Fair weather come again. 1837: Mrs Palmer, *Devonsh. Dialect*, 46, Rain, rain, go to Spain; Come again another day: When I brew and when I bake, I'll give you a figgy cake. 1864: 'Cornish Proverbs', in *N.&Q.*, 3rd ser, v 209, [as in 1837, *plus*] and a glass of brandy.

22. Small rain lays a great dust. 1670: Ray, 135. 1732: Fuller, 4193. 1846: Denham, *Proverbs*, 5 (Percy S.) ['will lay' for 'lays'].

23. Some rain some rest. A harvest proverb. 1678: Ray, 80. 1893: Inwards, *Weather Lore*, 108, Some rain, some rest; Fine weather isn't always best. Cf. No. 12.

24. Sunshine and shower, rain again to-morrow. Ibid., 111.

25. The farther the sight the nearer the rain. Ibid., 105.

26. The faster the rain, the quicker the hold up. Norfolk. Ibid., 109.

27. When the Lizard is clear, Rain is near. Corn. Ibid., 105.

28. When the rain raineth and the goose winketh, Little wots the gosling what the goose thinketh. Before 1529: Skelton, in *Works*, i 418 (Dyce). 1667: *Poor Robin Alman.*, Sept.

29. When the rain's before the win', 'Tis time to take the topsails in, But when the wind's before the rain, Let your topsails out again. 1875: A. B. Cheales, *Proverb. Folk-Lore*, 27.

Rain, *verb.* **1. Although it rain, throw not away thy watering-pot.** 1640: Herbert, *Jac. Prudentum.*

2. If it rains before church. *See* quots. [16th cent.: in *Reliq. Antiquae*, ii 10 (1843), Du Dimanche au matin la pluye Bien souvent la semaine ennuye.] 1846: Denham, *Proverbs*, 11 (Percy S.), If it rains on a Sunday before mass, It will rain all the week, more or less. 1881: in *Folk-Lore Record*, iv 130, Rain afore church Rain all the week, little or much. – Norfolk. 1883: Burne, *Shropsh. Folk-Lore*, 261 [as in 1846].

3. If it raineth at tide's flow. *See* quots. *c.*1685: Aubrey, *Nat. Hist. Wilts*, 16 (1847), A proverbial rithme observed as infallible by the inhabitants on the Severne side: – If it raineth when it doth flow, Then yoke your oxe, and goe to plough; But if it raineth when it doth ebb, Then unyoke your oxe, and goe to bed. 1893: Inwards, *Weather Lore*, 107, If it raineth at tide's flow, You may safely go and mow; But if it raineth at the ebb. Then, if you like, go off to bed.

4. If it should rain porridge he would want his dish. [1583: Melbancke, *Philotinus*, sig. Cc3, All the world is otemeale, and my poke left at home.] 1670: Ray, 191. 1692: *Poor Robin Alman.*, May, What is he better for his wish, When it rains porridg to want a dish. 1732: Fuller, 2687. 1895: S. O. Jewett, *Life of Nancy*, 221, 'When it rains porridge hold up your dish,' said Mrs Flagg. 1923: *Devonsh. Assoc. Trans.*, liv. 136, If it shud be rainin' porridge, my dish'd sure to be upside down.

5. It never rains but it pours. 1726: Swift and Pope, *Prose Miscellanies*, [title of paper] It cannot rain but it pours. 1755: Franklin, in *Works*, ii 413 (Bigelow), You will say, It can't rain, but it

pours. 1857: Borrow, *Rom. Rye*, ch xxviii 1860: Reade, *Cl. and Hearth*, ch liii 1904: *Co. Folk-Lore: Northumb.*, 171 (F.L.S.), It does not rain but it pours down.

6. It rains by planets. 1670: Ray, 45. 1809: Pegge, *Anonymiana*, cent. ix. 48, The common people will say in the summer-time, *it rains by planets*. 1828: Carr, *Craven Dialect*, ii 48, 'T' rain faws i' planets', i.e. the rain falls partially. 1887: Parish and Shaw, *Dict. Kent. Dialect*, 117 (E.D.S.), 'It rains by planets', when showers fall in a small compass, in opposition to general rain.

7. It rains cats and dogs. 1653: R. Brome, *City Wit*, IV i, It shall raine ... does and polecats, and so forth. 1738: Swift, *Polite Convers.*, Dial. II, He was sure it would rain cats and dogs. 1829: Scott, *Journal*, 16 April. 1840: Barham, *Ing. Legends*, 1st ser: 'Grey Dolphin.

8. It rains in summer as well as in winter. 1732: Fuller, 3044.

9. To see it rain is better than to be in it. 1639: Clarke, 278. 1670: Ray, 140. 1732: Fuller, 5223, To see a storm is better than to fed it.

Rain, *subs.* and *verb. See also* **After drought; Bee**(10); **Cloud; Devil**(113); **Dew; Dirt-bird; Dog-days; Easter** (13); **Every day in the week; February; Fleas; Friday** (6) and (7); **Frost** (6) and (8); **God will; Good Friday** (2); **July; Mobberley; Peacock; Rainbow; Red at night; St John** (1); **St Mary; St Medard; St Peter; St Swithin; St Vitus; Smoke** (2); **Snail; Spring** (7); **Sun; Whitsuntide;** and **Wind, A** (*a*) (1), (13) and (14); B (2), (5) and (6); D (3) and (5); E (1) and (5); F (5), (8), (9) and (10).

Rainbow. 1. A rainbow in the morning and in the evening. *See* quots. 1555: L. Digges, *Prognostication*, sig. B2, If in the mornyng the raynebow appere, it signifieth moysture ... If in the evening it spend it self, fayre weather ensueth. 1666: Torriano, *Piazza Univ.*, 13, The evening rainbow portends fair weather. 1825: Hone, *Ev. Day Book*, i 670, A rainbow in the morning Is the shepherd's warning; But a rainbow at night Is the shepherd's delight. 1886: R. Holland, *Cheshire Gloss.*, 444 (E.D.S.), A rainbow at morn Is a sign of a storm; A rainbow at night Is a shepherd's delight. 1893: Inwards, *Weather Lore*, 112, [as in 1825, also as follow] The rainbow in the marnin' Gives the shepherd warnin' To car' his gurt cwoat on his back; The rainbow at night is the shepherd's delight, For then no gurt cwoat will he lack. *Wilts.* A dog [small rainbow near the horizon] in the morning, Sailor, take warning; A dog in the night Is the sailor's delight

2. A rainbow in the morn, put your hook in the corn; A rainbow in the eve, put your hook in the sheave. Corn. Ibid., 112.

3. Go to the end of the rainbow and you'll find a crock of gold. 1850: *N. & Q.*, 1st ser, ii 512, Where the rainbow rests is a crock of gold. 1875: Parish, *Sussex Dict.*, 31 [given as a 'Sussex prover'].

4. If the rainbow comes at night, The rain is gone quite. 1830: Forby, *Vocab. E. Anglia*, 417. 1893: *Co. Folk-Lore: Suffolk*, 163 (F.L.S.).

5. If there be a rainbow in the eve, It will rain and leave: But if there be a rainbow in the morrow, It will neither lend nor borrow. 1670: Ray, 43. 1825: Hone, *Ev. Day Book*, i 670. 1893: Inwards, *Weather Lore*, 112.

6. If two rainbows appear at one time, they presage rain to come. 1669: *New Help to Discourse*, 293.

7. Rainbow to windward, foul fall the day; Rainbow to leeward, damp runs away. 1893: Inwards, *Weather Lore*, 112.

Rainy day, To keep something (or **To lay up** or **by**) **for a.** 1582: Breton, in *Works*, i *a* 29 (Grosart), Wise men say Keepe somewhat till a rayny day. 1583: Stubbes, *Anat. of Abuses*, 115 (N.Sh.S.), Is it not good to lay vp something against a stormie day? 1653: R. Brome, *City Wit*, IV i, I hope I had the wit to cozen my husband of somewhat against a rainy day. 1666: Pepys, *Diary*, 31 Oct., I ... do provide for it by laying by something against a rainy day. 1690: Dryden, *Amphitryon*, I ii 1705: Centlivre, *Gamester*, III i. 1744–6: Mrs Haywood, *Fem. Spectator*, i 113 (1771). 1860: Reade, *Cl. and Hearth*, ch lii, So she met current expenses, and laid by for the rainy day she saw coming.

Raise no more spirits than you can conjure down. 1639: Clarke, 247. 1670: Ray, 135. 1732: Fuller, 4000. 1754: Berthelson, *Eng.-Danish Dict.*, s.v. 'Raise' ['lay' for 'conjure'].

Raise one downstairs, To. 1917: Bridge, *Cheshire Proverbs*, 142.

Rake gathers, the fork scatters, What the. 1580: Lyly, *Euphues*, 228 (Arber), Youth ... tedding that with a forke in one yeare, which was not gathered together with a rake, in twentie. *c.*1630: in *Roxb. Ballads*, i 134 (B.S.), Great use

he did take, And for me did rake, Which now with the forke I will scatter. 1775: in *Roxb. Ballads*, vii 520 (B.S.), What the old folks scrap'd together, I spread it abroad with my fork. 1869: Hazlitt, 369, The fork is commonly the rake's heir.

Rake hell and skim the devil, you can't find such another man. 1754: Berthelson, *Eng.-Danish Dict.*, s.v. 'Rake'.

Rake more than the fork, He uses the. 1670: Ray, 190, He is better with a rake then a fork. 1732: Fuller, 2375.

Ram. *See* **Crooked**; and **Sheep** (8).

Ram [fetid] **as a fox, As.** [1601: Shakespeare, *Twelfth Night*, II v, Though it be as rank as a fox. 1693: D'Urfey, *Richmond Heiress*, I, Red and rank as a fox.] 1828: Carr, *Craven Dialect*, ii 69, He's as ram as a fox. 1862: *Dialect of Leeds*, 406. 1889: J. Nicholson, *Folk Speech E. Yorks*, 20, As ram as an awd fox.

Rame Head. *See* **Dudman**.

Ramsey the rich. 1662: Fuller, *Worthies*, ii 98 (1840). 1708: *Brit. Apollo*, i, Suppl. Paper, No. 10, col. 4. 1790: Grose, *Prov. Gloss.*, s.v. 'Hunts'.

Rancor sticks long by the ribs. 1639: Clarke, 178. 1659 = Howell, 16.

Rank courtesy when a man is forced to give thanks for his own, It's a. 1670: Ray, 20. 1732: Fuller, 2871.

Rap. *See* **Haste** (4).

Rap and rend, To=To seize. 1528: Roy, *Rede me*, 74 (Arber), To rappe and rende All that commeth in their fingrynge. 1540: Palsgrave, *Acolastus*, sig. Q2, All that he may gete or laye hande on or rappe and rende. 1817: Scott, *Rob Roy*, ch xxvi, Every ane o' them will maintain as mony ... as he can rap and rend means for. 1866: J. G. Nail, *Gt. Yarmouth, etc.*, 631, ' 'A spend everything 'a can rap and rend', i.e. all he can seize and lay hands on. 1866: Brogden, *Lincs Words*, 163, Rap and rend. – By fair or foul means. 1920: E. Gepp, *Essex Dialect Dict.*, 29, I've giv ye all I could rap and rend.

Rap and run, To. *c.*1386: Chaucer, *Can. Yeoman's Tale*, l.1422, But wasten al that ye may rape and renne. 1607: R. West, *Court of Conscience*, sig. E4, When they haue got what they can rap and run. 1742: North, *Lives of Norths.* ii 280 (Bohn), All that he could (as they say) rap or run went the same way.

Rare thing to do good, It is a. 1659: Howell, 9.

Rashness is not valour. 1732: Fuller, 4002.

Rasp [Put aside] **the scythe: drink some cyder.** S. Devon. 1869: Hazlitt, 323.

Rat and **Rats. 1. He'd starve the rats, and make the mice go upon scritches** [crutches]. S.Devon. 1869: Hazlitt, 198.

2. Rats fly from the falling house. 1625: Bacon, *Essays*: 'Wisdom for Man's Self', It is the wisedome of rats, that will be sure to leaue a house, somewhat before it fall. 1649: T. Forde, *Lusus Fort.*, 32, That ill such friends run from, like mice from a falling house. 1663: Butler, *Hudibras*, Pt I, can. ii l. 939. 1672: Crowne, *Charles VIII*, V, All vermin from a falling palace run. 1724: Defoe, *Tour*, Lett. III, 98, The mice and rats have abandoned many [houses] more, as they say they will, when they are likely to fall. 1748: Richardson, *Clarissa*, vi 324 (1785). 1848: Dickens, *Dombey*, ch lix., It is a great house still … but it is a ruin none the less, and the rats fly from it.

3. Rats leave (or **desert**) **a sinking ship.** A later, and now much more common variant of (2). 1611: Shakespeare, *Tempest*, I ii, A rotten carcass of a boat … the very rats Instinctively have quit it. 1895: J. Payn, *In Market Overt*, ch 26, This is bad news indeed about Barton's pupils … It is a case of rats leaving a sinking ship, I fear.

4. Rats in Ireland. *See* **Rhyme to death.**

5. The rats may safely play when as the cat's away. 1611: Cotgrave, s.v. 'Rat'.

6. Too late repents the rat when caught by the cat. 1591: Florio, *Second Frutes*, 165, Too late repents the ratt, If once her taile be caught by the catt. 1623: Wodroephe, *Spared Houres*, 516.

7. You can't get rats out of mice. Devon. 1882: *Folk-Lore Record*, v 159.

See also **Drunk as a rat; Fierce; Poor; Scot** (1); **Smell** (3); and **Welcome** (7).

Rate thy commodities at home, but sell them abroad. 1611: Cotgrave, s.v. 'Priser'. 1666: Torriano, *Piazza Univ.*, 218, Fix thy rates at home, and in the market sell.

Rather go to bed supperless. *See* **Supperless.**

Raven. Two sayings which = The pot cals the kettle black. 1. **The raven said to the rook, 'Stand away, black-coat'.** 1732: Fuller, 4729. 1886: Swainson, *Folk-Lore Brit. Birds*, 88 (F.L.S.).

2. Thou art a bitter bird, said the raven to the starling. 1678: Ray, 195. 1826: Brady, *Varieties of Lit.*, 38. 1886: Swainson, *ut supra*, 73.

See also **Black**, *adj.* (7); and **Carcase.**

Raw leather will stretch. 1611: Davies (of Hereford), *Sc. of Folly*, 46, in *Works*, ii (Grosart). 1670: Ray, 136. 1732: Fuller, 4004.

Raw pullen, veal and fish make the churchyards fat. 1611: Cotgrave, s.v. 'Poulet', Raw veale, and chickens, make swelling churchyards. 1678: Ray, 41.

Read not before you learn to spell. 1639: Clarke, 4.

Read. *See* quot. 1882: Nodal and Milner, *Lancs Gloss.*, 225 (E.D.S.), A common Lancashire saying among old folks is 'Aw con read [understand] that as ne'er wur printed'.

Read, try, judge, and speak as you find, says old Suffolk. 1813: Ray, 71.

Ready money is a ready medicine. 1611: Cotgrave, s.v. 'Argent'. 1651: Herbert, *Jac. Prudentum*, 2nd ed.

Ready money will away. 1630: Taylor (Water-Poet), *Works*, 1st pagin., 72, For by long proofe, the prouerbe true doth say, *That ready money euer will away*. 1670: Ray, 18.

Ready mouth for a ripe, cherry, You have always a. 1732: Fuller, 5913.

Ready way to lose your friend is to lend him money, A. Ibid., No. 378.

Reason, *subs*, **1. Hearken to reason or she will be heard.** 1640: Herbert, *Jac. Prudentum*. 1736: Franklin, *Way to Wealth*, in *Works*, i 451 (Bigelow), If you will not hear reason, she will surely rap your knuckles.

2. Reason governs the wise man, and cudgels the fool. 1855: Bohn, 479.

3. Reason lies between the spur and the bridle. 1640: Herbert, *Jac. Prudentum*.

4. Reason rules all things. 1633: Draxe, 175, Let reason rule all your actions. 1659: Howell, 9.

5. Reasons are not like garments, the worse for the wearing. 1599: Earl of Essex, quoted in *N.&Q.*, 10th ser, ii 23.

6. The reasons of the poor. *See* **Poor** (30).

7. There's reason in roasting of eggs. 1659: Howell, 12. 1681: Robertson, *Phraseol. Generalis*, 1050. 1762: Bickerstaffe, *Love in a Village*, III i 1855: Planché, *Extravag.*, v 145 (1879), But you'll observe he humbly hopes and begs, Some reason in this roasting of her eggs. *c*.1880: A. Lang, *Poet. Works*, ii 205 (1923), 'There's wit in poaching eggs', the proverb says.

See also **Rhyme.**

Receiver is as bad as the thief, The. 1650: Fuller, *Pisgah Sight*, bk ii ch iv. 1668: Sedley, *Mulberry Garden.*IV 1734: Fielding, *Don Quix. in England*, II xvi. 1830: Marryat, *King's Own*, ch xi.

Receiver, No, no thief. 1546: Heywood, *Proverbs*, Pt I, ch xii, Where be no receiuers, there be no theeues. *c.*1615: R. C., *Times Whistle*, 89 (E.E.T.S.), For every man this olde saide saw beleeves, 'Were no receivers there would be no theeves'. 1670: Ray, 136. 1732: Fuller, 3620. 1884: Jefferies, *Red Deer*, ch v, As there are no receivers … there are no thieves.

(*a*) **Reckon without one's host, To.** Also in the form (*b*) **He that reckons without his host must reckon twice.** *c.*1489: Caxton, *Blanchardyn, etc.*, 202 (E.E.T.S.), It ys sayd in comyn that 'who soeuer rekeneth wythoute his hoste, he rekeneth twys for ones'. 1546: Heywood, *Proverbs*, Pt I ch viii, Reckners without their host must recken twyce. 1579: Lyly, *Euphues*, 84 (Arber), He reckoneth without his hostesse. 1605: Camden, *Remains*, 324 (1870) [as in (*b*)]. 1669: *Politeuphuia*, 183 [as in (*b*)]. 1709: O. Dykes, *Eng. Proverbs*, 262 (2nd ed.) [as in (*b*)]. 1766: Garrick and Colman, *Clandest. Marriage*, III i, Odso! I had quite forgot. We are reckoning without our host here. 1846: Planché, *Extravag.*, iii 140 (1879), Ah, madam, there without your host you reckon! She has deserted us.

Reconciled friend is a double enemy, A. 1732: Fuller, 379.

Recover the horse. *See* **Win** (4).

Red and yellow. *See* quot. 1874: in *N. & Q.*, 5th ser, i 219, An old saying is familiar to me – 'Red and yellow, Tom Fool's colours'. Doubtless the allusion is to the glowing particoloured dress of the Fool or Jester.

Red as a cherry. 1558: Bullein, *Govt. of Health*, fo. 49, Read as chery. 1577: Kendall, *Flow. of Epigrams*, 292 (Spens.S.), Her nipples red as cherries. 1614: *Cobbes Proph.*, sig. D1, (Facs. 1890), When a cup of good sacke … Will make the cheeks red as a cherry. 1720: Gay, *Eclogues*: 'Espousal', l.62, Red as the cherry from the Kentish tree. 1849: Brontë, *Shirley*, ch xi, To-day you see them bouncing, buxom, red as cherries.

Red as a ferret. 1690: *New Dict. Canting Crew*, sig. E4, Eyes as red as a ferret. 1862: *Dialect of Leeds*, 407.

Red as a rose. *c.*1260: *King Horn* (Camb), l. 16 (Hall), Rose red was his colur. Before 1300: *Cursor Mundi*, 571 (E.E.T.S.), As rose reed hit is in spring. *c.*1374: Chaucer, *Troylus*, bk ii l. 1256, 'Nay, nay,' quod she, and wex as reed as rose. *c.*1477: Caxton, *Jason*, 156 (E.E.T.S.), His blood began to chaunge and he woxe rede as a rose. *c.*1565: in Huth, *Ancient Ballads, etc.*, 208 (1867), With bloud, I hard saye, as red as a rose. *c.*1675: in *Roxb. Ballads*, vi 244 (B.S.), She stept to him, as red as any rose. 1798: Coleridge, *Anc. Mariner*, Pt I, st. 9, The bride … Red as a rose is she. 1818: Austen, *North. Abbey*, ch x, My cheeks would have been as red as your roses. 1863: Kingsley, *Water Babies*, ch ii.

Red as a turkey-cock. *c.*1630: B.&F., *Faithful Friends*, III ii, The very sight of his scarlet gown made me blush as red as a turkey-cock. 1733: C. Coffey, *Boarding-School*, sc ii, Your gills look as red as a turkey-cocks. 1880: Spurgeon, *Ploughman's Pictures*, 6, Joe … came from behind the stack, looking as red as a turkey-cock. 1880: Courtney, *W. Cornwall Words*, 36 (E.D.S.), As red as a lubber cock [turkey-cock]. 1894: W. Raymond, *Love and Quiet Life*, 167.

Red as blood. *c.*1205: Lay., 15940 (OED), the oder is milcwhit … the other raed alse blod. 1387: Trevisa, tr. Higden, i 123 (Rolls Ser.), the secounde thre mouthes reed as blood. 1485: Malory, *Mortie d'Arthur*, bk xvii ch iv, Hit was reed as blood. 1594: *First Part Contention*, 22 (SH.S.). 1894: W. Raymond, *Love and Quiet Life*, 246, Wine was dripping into the gutters as red as blood.

Red as fire. *c.*1310: *King Horn* (Oxf.), l. 520 (Hall), Red so any glede. *c.*1489: Caxton, *Sonnes of Aymon*, 27 (E.E.T.S.), He wexed for grete wrathe as redde as ony fyre in his face. 1567: Golding, *Ovid*, bk i l. 954, At this reproch old Phaëton wax as red as any fire. 1681: Robertson, *Phraseol. Generalis*, 267, He blusht as red as fire. 1709: Manley, *New Atlantis*, ii 87 (1736), I blush'd as red as fire. 1722: Defoe, *Moll Flanders*, in *Works*, iii 60 (Bohn).

Red as Martlesham lion=very red. Suffolk. 1892: *E. Anglian Daily Times* (W.).

Red at night and red in the morning. Several sayings to like effect may be conveniently grouped under this heading. Cf. **Evening.** 1551: T. Wilson, *Rule of Reason*, sig. M4, The skie was very red this mornyng. Ergo we are like to have rayne or [ere] nyght. 1584: R. Scot, *Witchcraft*, bk xi ch xv, The skie being red at evening, Foreshewes a faire and clear morning; But if the morning riseth red, Of wind or raine we shall be sped. Before 1627: Middleton, *Anything for Quiet Life*, IV i, You shall find her beauty as malevolent unto you as a red morning, that doth still foretell a foul day to follow. 1661: Webster and Rowley, *Cure for a Cuckold*, III i, like a red morning, friend, that still foretells A stormy day to follow. 1664: in *Musarum Deliciae, etc.*, ii 59 (Hotten), When red the sun goes down, we take to say, It is a signe, we shall have a faire day. 1696: J. Harris, *City Bride*, III i [as in 1661]. 1831: Hone, *Year-Book*, 300, If red the sun begins his race, Expect that rain will fall apace. 1893: Inwards, *Weather Lore*, 50 [as in 1831]. Ibid., 53, Sky red in the morning Is a sailor's sure warning; Sky red at night Is the sailor's delight. 1920: *Punch*, 14 July, p. 36, cols. 2 and 3, 'Red sky at night shepherd's delight,' she quoted … At dawn Titania looked out of the window and gave a wild cry. 'Red sky in the morning shepherd's warning,' she wailed.

Red cap, You shall have the. Said to a marriage-maker. Somerset. 1678: Ray, 353.

Red cow. *See* **Cow** (4).

Red hair. Several sayings are grouped hereunder. 1578: Florio, *First Fruites*, fo. 30, If thou meete a red man, and a bearded woman, greet them three myle of [f]. 1591: Florio, *Second Frutes*, 99, Beware of red men, of women that are bearded, and of such as God hath marked. 1600: W. Vaughan, *Directions for Health*, To a red man reade thy read, With a browne man breake thy bread. 1615: R. Tofte, tr. *Blazon of Iealousie*, 21, The red is wise, the broun trusty, The pale envious, and the blacke lusty. Ibid., 21, [as in 1600, *plus*] At a pale man draw thy knife, From a blacke man keep thy wife. 1619: *Helpe to Discourse*, 153 (1640) [as in the immediately preceding quotation]. 1623: Wodroephe, *Spared Houres*, 276, In all places keepe thee well from redhaired men, from barded women, and from them that are marcked in the face. 1659: Howell, 12, A red beard and a black head, Catch him with a good trick, and take him dead. 1659: Howell, *Letters*, ii 666 (Jacobs), Touching a red-haired man and bearded woman, salute them a hundred paces off. 1670: Ray, 212 [as in first 1659 quot.]. Ibid., 210 [as in second 1615 quot.]. 1732:

Fuller, 1915, He is false by nature that has a black head and a red beard. 1908: W. Johnson, *Folk Memory*, 57, The old saw puts it thus, 'From a black man keep your wife, With the red man beware your knife'.

Red herring. *See* quot. 1678: Ray, 52, Red herring ne'er spake word but een, Broyl my back, but not my weamb [stomach].

Red man. *See* s.v. **Red hair.**

Red petticoat *See* **Lass.**

Red pig. *See* Pig (6).

Red sky at night, shepherd's delight; red sky in the morning, shepherd's warning. *See* **Red at night and red in the morning.**

Reed before the wind lives on, when mighty oaks do fall, A. *c.*1385: Chaucer, *Troilus and Criseyde*, II 1387, And reed that boweth down for every blast, Ful lightly, cesses wynd, it wol aryse. 1621: Burton, *Anatomy of Melancholy*, II iii, Though I live obscure, yet live I cleane and honest, and when as the lofty oake is blowne downe, the silly [frail] reed may fall. 1732: T. Fuller, *Gnomologia*, no. 3692, Oaks may fall, when Reeds stand the Storm. 1954: R. Haydn, *Journal of Edwin Carp*, 20, Remembering that 'a reed before the wind lives on – while mighty oaks do fall, I attempted to remove the pencil marks with my pocket eraser.

Reeds, Where there are, there is water. 1732: Fuller, 5674.

Refuse with the right and take with the left, To. 1639: Clarke, 149. 1732: Fuller, 2009, He refuseth the bribe, but putteth forth his hand.

Regal honours hare regal cares. 1855: Bohn, 479.

Relations. *See* quot. 1858: R. S. Hawker, in Byles, *Life, etc.*, 312 (1905), There is an old English Proverb which hints thus, Love your relations, but live not near them.

Religion is copyhold, and he has not taken it up, His = he has none. 1830: Forby, *Vocab. E. Anglia*, 427. 1872: J. Glyde, jr., *Norfolk Garland*, 148.

Religion is the best armour in the world, but the worst cloak. 1732: Fuller, 4011. 1827: Hone, *Table-Book*, 414.

Religion. *See also* **Eye** (10).

Remedy for all things but death, There is a. *c.*1430: Lydgate, *Daunce of Machabree*, l. 432, Againes Death is worth no medicine. 1620: Shelton, *Quixote*, Pt II ch xliii, There is a remedy for everything but death. 1640: Mabbe, tr. *Exemp. Novels*, i 177 (1900). 1712: Motteux, *Quixote*, Pt II ch xliii.

Remedy for everything, could men find it, There is a. 1651: Herbert, *Jac. Prudentum*, 2nd ed. 1732: Fuller, 4879.

Remedy, If there be no, then welcome Pilvall. 1670: Ray, 189.

Remedy is worse than the disease, The. [Ingratus L. Sulla, qui patriam durioribus remediis, quam pericula erat sanavit. – Seneca, *De Beneficiis*, V xvi 4.] 1607: Bacon, *Essays*: 'Counsel', The doctrine of Italie, and practise of Fraunce hath introduced *Cabanett* Councelles, a remedy worse than the disease. 1624: Massinger, *Bondman*, I i, The cure Is worse than the disease. 1697: Vanbrugh, *Prov. Wife*, V 1762: Hall Stevenson, *Crazy Tales*, 18 [as in 1624]. 1807: Byron, in *Letters, etc.*, i 139 (Prothero), Things will therefore stand as they are; the remedy would be worse than the disease. 1898: Shaw, *Plays Pleasant*, etc., i Pref., xv.

Remove an old tree and it will die. 1570: A. Barclay, *Mirrour of Good Manners*, 67 (Spens.S.), An olde tree transposed shall finde small auauntage. 1605: Camden, *Remains*, 330 (1870). 1670: Ray, 22. 1732: Fuller, 4016, Remove an old tree, and you'll kill it.

Repairs not a part, builds all, He that. 1640: Herbert, *Jac. Prudentum*.

Repentance always comes behind. 1584: Robinson, *Handf. Pleas. Delights*, 38 (Arber).

Repentance comes too late. c.1440: Lydgate, *Fall of Princes*, bk iii l. 915 (E.E.T.S.), Harm doon, to late folweth repentaunce. 1670: Ray, 22, Repentance comes too late, when all is consum'd. 1732: Fuller, 5545, When all is gone repentance comes too late.

Repents is a fool, He that. 1710: S. Palmer, *Moral Essays on Proverbs*, 286, He that repents either was, or is, a fool. 1732: Fuller, 2264, He that repents of his own act, either is, or was a fool by his own confession.

Report *See* **Common** (7).

Reputation is seldom cured, A wounded. 1855: Bohn, 304.

Reputation is the life of the mind, as breath is the life of the body. 1730: T. Saldkeld, tr. Grecian's *Compl. Gent.*, 96.

Reserve the master-blow. 1659: Howell, *Proverbs: Ital.-Eng.*, 13, Reserve thy

masterpiece. 1813: Ray, 20, Reserve the master-blow: i.e. teach not all thy skill, lest the scholar overreach or insult the master.

Resolved mind hath no cares, The. 1640: Herbert, *Jac. Prudentum*.

Respect a man, he will do the more. 1659: Howell, *Proverbs: Brit.-Eng.*, 16.

Respect is younger brother to love. 1691: J. Bancroft, *King Edw. III*, III ii, I have often heard it said, respects the younger brother sure to love.

Respects not is not respected, He that. 1640: Herbert, *Jac. Prudentum*.

Rest a while. *See* **Sit**(6).

Retreat, In a, the lame are foremost. 1640: Herbert, *Jac. Prudentum*.

Revenged every wrong, Had I *See* quots. Before 1500: in Hill, *Commonplace-Book*, 140 (E.E.T.S.), He that will venge euery wreth, the longer he levith, the lesse he hath. 1575: Gascoigne, *Posies*, 147 (Cunliffe), This old sayde sawe, *Had I revenged bene of every harme*, *My coate had never kept me half so warme*. 1639: in *Berkeley MSS.*, iii 32 (1885), Hee that wreakes himselfe at every wronge, Shall never singe the ritch mans songe. 1670: Ray, 136, If I had reveng'd all wrong, I had not worn my skirts so long. 1732: Fuller, 6462 [as in 1670].

Revenge is a dish that is best eaten cold. 1885: C. Lowe, *Prince Bismarck*, He had defended Olmütz, it is true, but ... with a secret resolution to 'eat the dish of his revenge cold instead of hot'. 1895: J. Payn, *In Market Overt*, xvii, Invective can be used at any time; like vengeance, it is a dish that can be eaten cold.

Revenge is sweet. 1566: Painter, *Pal. of Pleasure*, ii 35 (Jacobs), Vengeance is sweete. 1658: *Whole Duty of Man*, Sunday, 16, It is a devilish phrase in the mouth of men, That revenge is sweet. 1691: Southerne, *Sir Antony Love*, IV iii. 1818: Byron, *Don Juan*, can. i st. 124. 1864: Mrs H. Wood, *Trevlyn Hold*, ch lviii, Revenge may be very sweet, but ...

Reverend are ever before, The. 1640: Herbert, *Jac. Prudentum*.

Revess. *See* **Rivaulx**

Revolutions are not made with rose-water. In 1789, two months before the fall of the Bastille, Chamfort, the friend and confidant of Mirabeau, said to Marmontel – 'Je vois que mes espèrances vous attristent: vous ne voulez pas d'une libertè qui coûtera beaucoup d'or et de sang. Voulez-vous qu'on vous fasse des révolutions à l'eau rose?' – Marmontel, *Mèmoires d'un Père*, liv. xiv, in *Oeuvres*, ii 294 (1818–19), 1819: Byron, *Letters, etc.*, iv 358 (Prothero), Revolutions are not to be made with rosewater.

Reynard is still Reynard, tho' he put on a cowl. 1732: Fuller, 4033.

Rhubarb and less diet, More. 1655: T. Muffett, *Healths Improvement*, 8, These addle proverbs … 4. More rubarb and less diet.

Rhyme (and) (nor) (or) reason. [Nec quid nee quare. – Petr., 37. En toy na Ryme ne Raison. – French MS., before 1500, quoted by Skeat, *N. & Q.*, 3rd ser, x 236.] Before 1529: Skelton, *Works*, i 123 (Dyce), Ys ryme yet owte of reson. 1568: *Jacob and Esau*, II iii, Ye shall hear him chafe beyond all reason or rhyme. 1601: Shakespeare, *As You Like It*, III ii, Neither rhyme nor reason can express how much. 1605: Jonson, *Volpone*, Prol., Here is rhyme, not empty of reason. 1714: Ozell, *Molière*, v 134, This gentleman wou'd find neither rhime nor reason in it. 1764: Murphy, *Three Weeks after Marriage*, II, There he owns it … and without rhyme or reason into the bargain. 1849: Lytton, *Caxtons*, Pt IX ch iii, A pretty fellow you are … to leave me all the morning, without rhyme or reason! 1920: P. B. M. Allan, *Book-Hunter at Home*, 87, It does insist most emphatically that there should be a rhyme and a reason for reading any book at any time.

Rhyme, but it accordeth not, It may. Things may be brought together, like riming words, but they will not on that account agree. – Skeat: Note in his *Chaucer*, vii *c*.1387: Usk, *Test. of Love*, in Skeat's *Chaucer*, vii 51, These thinges to-forn-sayd mowe wel, if men liste, ryme; trewly, they acorde nothing, *c*.1430: Lydgate, *Minor Poems*, 56 (Percy S.), It may wele ryme, but it accordith nought. 1562: Heywood, *Three Hund. Epigr.*, No. 265, It may rhyme, but it accordeth not. 1633: Draxe, 45 [as in 1562].

Rhyme to death, as rats in Ireland, To. *c*.1581: Sidney, *Apol.*, 72 (Arber), Nor to be rimed to death, as is sayd to be doone in Ireland. 1601: Shakespeare, *As You Like It*, III ii, I was never so be-rhymed since Pythagoras' time, that I was an Irish rat, which I can hardly remember. 1632: Randolph, *Jealous Lovers*, V ii, My poets Shall … Rhyme 'em to death, as they do rats in

Ireland. Before 1680: Butler, *Remains*, i 377 (1759), Will rather take thee for an Irish rat-catcher, that is said to rhime vermin to death. 1692: Temple, *On Poetry*, in *Works*, iii 418 (1770), The proverb of rhiming rats to death, came I suppose from the same root [Runic incantations].

Ribble, The. *See* **Hodder.**

Ribchester. 1586: Camden, *Brit.*, 431, It is written upon a wall in Rome, Ribchester was as rich as any towne in Christendome. 1662: Fuller, *Worthies*, ii 191 (1840) [as in 1586]. 1790: Grose, *Prov. Gloss.,s.v.* 'Lancs' [as in 1586].

Rich, *adj.* **1. A rich man and a miserable.** 1600: Nashe, *Works*, vi 99 (Grosart), It is a common prouerbe, Diuesque miserque, a rich man, and a miserable.

2. A rich man's money hangs him oftentimes. 1639: Clarke, 98.

3. A rich rogue, two shirts and a rag. 1678: Ray, 80. 1738: Swift, *Polite Convers.*, Dial. I

4. Always you are to be rich next year. 1732: Fuller, 787.

5. As rich as a Jew. 1720: Gay, *Poems*, ii 280 (Underhill), Great as an emp'ror should I be, And richer than a Jew. 1771: Cumberland, *West Indian*, II, She is as rich as a Jew. 1823: Scott, *Peveril*, ch xxvi. 1871: G. Eliot, *Middlemarch*, ch xl. 1896: Shaw, *You Never Can Tell*, I

6. As rich as a new shorn sheep. An ironical saying, [*c*.1440: Lydgate, *Fall of Princes*, bk iii, l. 3262, Bare as a sheep that is but newe shorn.] *c*.1520: *Cock Lorells Bote*, 1 (Percy S.), The nexte that came was a coryar, And a cobeler, his brother, As ryche as a newe shorne shepe. 1595: Churchyard, *Charitie*, 2 (1816). 1637: Breton, in *Works*, ii *h* 11 (Grosart). 1681: Robertson, *Phraseol, Generalis*, 1077. 1732: Fuller, 725.

7. As rich as Croesus. [Superare Crassum divitiis. – Cicero, *Att.*, i *4 fin.*] 1577: Kendall, *Flow, of Epigrams*, 57 (Spens.S.), As riche as Cresus Affric is. 1696: T. Dilke, *Lover's Luck*, II i, And I get a patent for it, I shall be as rich as Croesus. 1724: Defoe, *Roxana*, in *Works*, xiii 73 (Boston, 1903). 1850: Smedley, *Frank Fairlegh*, ch li.

8. He is rich enough that needeth neither to flatter nor borrow. 1669: *Politeuphuia*, 128, He hath riches sufficient that, etc. 1732: Fuller, 1943.

9. He is rich enough that wants nothing, *c*.1387: Usk, *Test. of Love*, in Skeat's *Chaucer*, vii 88, Is he

nat riche that hath suffisaunce? *c.*1577: Northbrooke, *Dicing, etc.*, 48 (SH.S.). Seneca sayeth:
Diues est, non qui magis habet, sed qui minus
cupit. He is riche, not that hath much, but that
coueteth least. 1637: A. Warwick, *Spare Minutes*,
4 (1829), Hee is not rich that hath much, but hee
that hath enough. 1640: Herbert, *Jac. Prudentum.*
1732: Fuller, 1943, He is rich that is satisfied.
1875: Cheales, *Proverb. Folk-Lore*, 101.

**10. He that will be rich before night, may be
hanged before noon.** 1692: L'Estrange, *Aesop*,
337 (3rd ed.), 'Tis a roguy kind of a saying, that
He that will, etc.

**11. In a rich man's house the cloth is soon
laid.** 1712: Motteux, *Quixote*, Pt II ch xliii.

12. Rich men have no faults. 1732: Fuller,
4036.

13. Rich men may have what they will, *c.*1630:
in *Roxb. Ballads*, i 60 (B.S.), Rich people haue
the world at will. 1639: Clarke, 99, Rich men
may doe any thing. 1869: Hazlitt, 325.

14. The richer the cobbler. *See* **Cobbler** (7).

**15. The rich feast, the poor fast, the dogs dine,
the poor pine.** 1630: T. Adams, *Works*, 39.

16. They are rich who have true friends. 1732:
Fuller, 4957.

17. Why should a rich man steal? 1678: Ray,
196. 1732: Fuller, 5736.

**Riches abuse them who know not how to use
them.** Ibid., No. 4040.

Riches are but the baggage of fortune. 1580:
Lyly, *Euphues*, 228 (Arber), To bee rich is the
gift of fortune. 1659: Howell, 8. 1732: Fuller,
4042.

**Riches are gotten with pain, kept with care,
and lost with grief.** 16th cent.: in *Reliq.
Antiquae*, i 208 (1841), Riches are gotten with
labor, holden with feare, and lost with greyfe and
excessive care. 1732: Fuller, 4043.

Riches bring oft harm, and ever fear. 1546:
Heywood, *Proverbs*, Pt I ch xii. 1633: Draxe,
180, Riches bring care and feares.

Riches come to him sleeping. 1754:
Berthelson, *Eng.-Danish Dict.*, s.v. 'Sleep'.

Riches got by craft. *See* quot. 1589: L. Wright,
Display of Dutie, 3, Whereby the prouerbe is
verefied, that riches got with craft is commonly
lost with shame.

Riches have wings. 1855: Bohn, 480.

**Riches, He is not fit for, who is afraid to use
them.** 1732: Fuller, 1934.

Riches increase, the body decreaseth, When.
1670: Ray, 22. 1736: Bailey, *Dict.*, s.v. 'Riches'.

Riches rule the roast 1732: Fuller, 4046.

Riches serve a wise man but command a fool.
Ibid., No. 4047.

Riches. *See also* **Money**; and **Wealth**.

Richmond. *See* **Barnard Castle**.

Ride a free horse. *See* **Horse** (28).

Ride an inch behind the tail, You shall. 1678:
Ray, 266.

Ride as if you went to fetch the midwife, You.
Ibid., 266.

Ride post for a pudding, To. Ibid., 79. 1732:
Fuller, 5219.

Ride softly that you may get home the sooner.
1678: Ray, 204, Ride softly, that we may come
sooner home. 1732: Fuller, 4050.

Rides a tiger is afraid to dismount, He who. A
proverb of Chinese origin, meaning that it is
difficult to with draw from a dangerous
undertaking once it has been embarked upon.
1875: W. Scarborough, *Collection of Chinese
Proverbs*, no. 2082, he who rides a tiger is afraid
to dismount. 1902: A. R. Colquhon, *Mastery of
the Pacific*, xvi, These colonies are … for her
[France] the tiger which she has mounted (to use
the Chinese phrase) and which she can neither
manage nor get rid of.

Rides well that never falls, He. 1485: Malory,
Morte d'Arthur, bk ix ch xxviii, He rydeth wel
that neuer fylle. 1732: Fuller, 2011, He rode sure
indeed, that never caught a fall in his life.

Ride the dun-horse, To = To dun a debtor.
1828: Carr, *Craven Dialect*, i 123.

Ride the fore-horse, To = To be early, or to be
in the front. 1664: Etherege, *Comical Revenge*,
III v, *Palmer [coming late to duel ground.]* I see
you ride the fore-horse, gentlemen. 1754:
World, No. 68, 'You still love to ride the fore-
horse', alluding to his desire of being foremost in
all parties of pleasure. 1823: Scott, *St Ronan's*,
ch i, Determined to ride the fore-horse herself,
Meg would admit no helpmate.

Ride the helps, To. 1864: 'Cornish Proverbs', in
N. & Q., 3rd ser, vi 494, He is put to ride on the
heps. 1880: Courtney, *W. Cornwall Words*, 28
(E.D.S.), When a person has been brought
before his superiors and remanded, he is
figuratively said 'to have been made to ride the
heps [hatch]'.

Ride the high horse, To. 1765: in *Garrick*

Corresp., i 205 (1831), Altogether upon the high horse, and blustering about Imperial Tragedy. 1836: Marryat, *Easy*, ch xii, He was determined to ride the high horse – and that there should be no Equality Jack in future. 1854: Baker, *Northants Gloss.*, s.v. 'Horse', 'To ride the high horse', or 'to be on the high horse', is to assume unbecoming airs, or claim unacknowledged superiority. 1881: Evans, *Leics. Words*, 173 (E.D.S.).

Ride the wild mare, To. 1598: Shakespeare, 2 *Henry IV*, II iv, [He] drinks off candles' ends for flap-dragons, and rides the wild-mare with the boys. 1611: Cotgrave, s.v. 'Asne', *Desferrer l'asne*. To unshooe the asse; we say, to ride the wilde mare.

Ride who will, shod is the mare. 1541: *Sch. House of Women*, l. 572, in Hazlitt, *Early Pop. Poetry*, iv 127.

Ridiculous. *See* subline.

Right as a line. *c.*1430: Lydgate. *Minor Poems*, 373 (E.E.T.S.), Lede us thederward as ryght as a lyne. 1546: Heywood, *Proverbs*. Pt I ch xi *c.* 1602: Chapman, *May-Day*, II

Right as a ram's horn = crooked, *c.*1320: in *Reliq. Antiquae*, ii 19 (1843), As ryt as rams orn. *c.*1400: *Beryn*, 6 (E.E.T.S.), And a red [it] also right as a rammys hornyd. *c.*1430: Lydgate, *Minor Poems*, 171 (Percy S.), Conveyde by lyne ryght as a rammes horne. Before 1529: Skelton, *Colin Clout*, l. 1201, They say many matters be born By the ryght of a rammes horne. 1670: Ray, 207.

Right as a trivet. 1837: Dickens, *Pickwick*, ch xvi. 1847: Barham, *Ing. Legends*, 3rd ser: 'Blasph. Warning'. 1907: De Morgan, *Alice-for-Short*, ch ii, Wait till … she's had time to get sober, and she'll be as right as a trivet.

Right as my glove. 1816: Scott, *Antiquary*, ch xxx, Right, Caxon, right as my glove.

Right as my leg. *c.*1630: in *Roxb. Ballads*, iii 338 (B.S.), That are as right's my leg. 1696: D'Urfey, *Quixote*, Pt III Act III sc ii, And she as right as is my leg. Still gave him leave to touze her. 1701: Farquhar, *Sir H. Wildair*, I, Are they right? No Gray's Inn pieces amongst 'em – all right as my leg. 1737: Ray, 225.

Right as ninepence. 1850: Smedley, *Frank Fairlegh*, ch li, Well, let her say 'no' as if she meant it … and then it will all be as right as ninepence. 1894: R.L.S., *St Ives*, ch xxvii, The members would all be up and 'as right as

ninepence' for the noon-day service. 1901: F. E. Taylor, *Lancs Sayings*, 1, As reet as ninepence.

Right as rain. 1894: W. Raymond, *Love and Quiet Life*, 108, ' 'Tes so right as rain, Zir,' zes I. 1921: Hutchinson, *If Winter Comes*, Pt III ch v (viii), In about a week she'll be as right as rain and writing me letters all day.

Right for the first … miles, You are. 1678: Ray, 343. [Apparently the *lacuna* might be filled at pleasure.]

Right hand from his left, He knows net his. 1681: Robertson, *Phraseol. Generalis*, 1079. 1888: R.L.S., *Black Arrow*, Prol., The poor innocent that cannot tell his right hand from his left

Right, master, right, four nobles a year is a crown a quarter. Cheshire. 1670: Ray, 217. 1917: Bridge, *Cheshire Proverbs*, 105.

Right mixture makes good mortar. 1732: Fuller, 4052.

Right or wrong, put Bagley in the stocks = Give a dog a bad name, etc. 1883: Burne, *Shropsh. Folk-Lore*, 590.

Right reckoning makes long friends. 1537: R. Whitford, *Werke for Householders*, sig. A6, The commune prouerbe is that ofte rekeninge holdeth longe felawshyppe. 1732: Fuller, 4053. 1760: Colman, *Polly Honeycombe*, sc ii *c.*1780: *The First Floor*, I iii, in Inchbald, *Farces*, vi 235 (1815).

Right, Roger. *See* Sow, *subs.* (11).

Right side. *See* quots. 1670: Ray, 195, To take from ones right side, to give to ones left. 1748: Richardson, *Clarissa*, iv. 321 (1785), What the right side gives up, the left, he says, may be better for.

Right side, To rise on the. [It was a good omen for the eagle to appear on Priam's right. – Homer, *Iliad*, xxiv 308–13.] 1540: Palsgrave, *Acolastus*, sig. M3, Howe happily rose I on my ryght syde to-day, *c.*1565: Still, *Gam. Gurton*, II i, Thou rose not on thy ryght syde, or else blest thee not wel. 1607: Marston, *What You Will*, V 1665: J. Wilson, *Projectors*, I, Certain I rise with the right end upward to-day, I have had such good luck! 1670: Ray, 191, He rose on his right side. Cf. **Left side.**

Right wrongs no man. 1853: Trench, *Proverbs*, 8 (1905).

Ring. *Better no ring, than a ring of a rush.* 1732: Fuller, 918.

Ripe. *See* **Beddingham.**

Ripon rowels, As true steel as. 1625: Jonson, *Staple of News*, I iii, There's an angel if my spurs Be not right Ripon. 1662: Fuller, *Worthies*, iii 398 (1840). 1683: Meriton, *Yorkshire Ale*, 83–7 (1697). 1790: Grose, *Prov. Gloss.*, s.v. 'Yorks'. 1807: Hogg, *Gilmanscleuch*, in *Mountain Bard*, The rowels of his silver spurs Were of the Rippon steel. 1878: *Folk-Lore Record*, i 168, To trustworthy persons the expression has been applied – 'As true steel as Rippon rowels'. 1918: *N.&Q.*, 12th ser, iv. 104.

Rip up old sores, To. 1573: G. Harvey, *Letter-Book*, 18 (Camden S.), Sutch ripping up of ould matters. 1652: Walsingham, *Arcana Aulica*, 32 (1694), A hater of those that rip up old offences. 1694: *Terence made English*, 236, What occasion had you to rip up th' old sore? 1712: Arbuthnot, *John Bull*, Pt I ch ix, Such a trial would rip up old sores. 1773: Garrick, in *Garrick Corresp.*, i 518 (1831), I am very much hurt to hear that he has ripped up old sores. 1827: Scott, in *Lockhart's Life*, vii 90, I am not clear that it is a ... healthful indulgence to be ripping up old sores.

Rise, *verb.* **1. As riseth my good so riseth my blood,** *c.*1560: Becon, in *Catechism, etc.*, 599 (P.S.) [quoted as a 'common proverb'].

2. He must rise betimes who will cosen the devil. 1659: Howell, 10 (8).

3. He must rise betimes. *See* **Please,** *verb* (1).

4. He must rise early who can – do this, that, or the other. 1562: Heywood: *Three Hund. Epigr.*, No. 128(9), Who that shall enterprise This measure from thee, for to gleane, Right erly must he rise. 1593: Peele, *Edw. I*, sc x, She riseth early, Joan, that beguileth thee of a Glocester. 1662: Fuller, *Worthies*, i 426 (1840), They must rise early, yea not sleep at all, who over-reach monks in matter of profit. 1681: Robertson, *Phraseol. Generalis*, 1291, They must rise betimes that go beyond him; a very wary man. 1791: R. Jephson, *Two Strings to your Bow*, I i, Let me alone, he must rise early, brother, who makes a fool of Don Pedro. 1838: Dickens, *Twist*, ch xxv, You must get up very early in the morning, to win against the Dodger.

5. He rises betimes that lies in a dog's lair, 1860: Reade, *Cl. and Hearth*, ch xxiv.

6. He that riseth betimes hath something in his head. 1640: Herbert, *Jac. Prudentum.*

7. He that riseth first is first dressed. Ibid.

8. He who does not rise early never does a good day's work. 1633: Draxe, 142, He that riseth not in the morning, loseth his iourney. 1659: Howell, *Proverbs: Span.-Eng.*, 17, Who riseth late must trot all the day. 1736: Franklin, *Way to Wealth*, in *Works*, i 443 (Bigelow), He that riseth late must trot all day, and shall scarce overtake his business at night. 1846: Denham, *Proverbs*, 5 (Percy S.).

9. In vain they rise early that used to rise late. 1611: Davies (of Hereford), *Sc. of Folly*, 46, in *Works*, ii (Grosart). 1639: Clarke, 67, They can't rise early that use to rise late.

10. Rise early and you will see; wake and you will get wealth. 1846: Denham, *Proverbs*, 5 (Percy S.).

11. Rise with an appetite. *See* **Leave** (6).

12. To rise with the lark and go to bed with the lamb. *c.*1555: in Wright, *Songs, etc.*, *Philip and Mary*, 38 (Roxb.Cl), And wythe the larke yche day I ryes. 1580: Lyly, *Euphues*, 229 (Arber), Goe to bed with the lambe, and rise with the larke. 1633: Jonson, *Tale of a Tub*, I iv, Madam, if he had couched with the lamb, He had no doubt been stirring with the lark. 1826: Lamb, *Pop. Fallacies*, xiv, That we should rise with the lark, xv, That we should lie down with the lamb.

Rising of one man is the falling of another, The. 1605: Chapman, etc., *Eastw. Hoe*, I i, As for my rising by other men's fall, God shield me! 1633: Draxe, 7.

Rising tide lifts all boats, A. An American saying that was particularly associated with the Kennedy family. It is generally used to mean that increasing prosperity will benefit all the people in a nation. 1963: J. F. Kennedy, *Address*, 25 June, in *Public Papers of the Presidents of the U.S.* (1964), 519. As they say on my own Cape Cod, a rising tide lifts all the boats. And a partnership be definition, serves both the partners ... . 1988: *Washington Post*, 7 March, A12, The theory used to be that all Americans had a stake in prosperity. The comforting notion was that the rising tide would lift all boats.

Rising, Norfolk. *See* quote. 1815: *N.&Q.*, 1st ser, iii 206, Rising was, Lynn is, and Downham shall be, The greatest seaport of the three. 1865: W. White, *Eastern England*, i 237, Rising was a seaport town When Lynn was but a marsh; Now Lynn it is a seaport town, And Rising fares the worse.

Rivaulx, Yorks. 1754: *Gent. Mag.*, 426, Near Howden, in Yorkshire, when a person cannot easily come at a place, without going a great way about; or … is forced to make use of several synonimous words; or … produces several arguments before he comes to the main point; it is a common saying, that he is going 'Round about Revess' [Abbey of Revess or Rivaulx].

River is deepest. *See* **Still waters.**

River passed and God forgotten, The. 1611: Cotgrave, s.v. 'Sainct', The danger past our vowes are soon forgotten. 1640: Herbert, *Jac. Pruden-tum* ['past']. 1853: Trench, *Proverbs*, 68 (1905), In English we say, [as in 1640].

Rivers need a spring. 1640: Herbert, *Jac. Prudentum.*

River will run as it did, A thousand years hence, the. 1732: Fuller, 436.

Riving Pike do wear a hood, If, Be sure that day will ne'er be good. 1670: Ray, 236. 1790: Grose, *Prov. Gloss.*, s.v. 'Lancs'. 1893: Inwards, *Weather Lore*, 101. 1917: Bridge, *Cheshire Proverbs*, 161.

Roach. *See* **Sound.**

Roads lead to Rome, All. *See* **Rome** (1).

Road to hell is paved with good intentions, The. *See* **Hell** (8).

Roast a stone, To = To waste time and effort. Before 1529: Skelton, in *Works*, ii 30 (Dyce), They may garlycke pyll, Cary sackes to the myll. Or pescoddes they may shyll, Or elles go rost a stone. 1546: Heywood, *Proverbs*, Pt II ch ii, I doo but roste a stone In warnyng hir. 1611: Davies (of Hereford), *Sc. of Folly*, 49, in *Works*, ii (Grosart), He roasts but a stone.

Roast meat. 1. He loves roast meat well that licks the spit. 1670: Ray, 137. 1732: Fuller, 1980. 1880: Spurgeon, *Ploughman's Pictures*, 73, If they are fond of roast beef, they must needs suck the spit.

2. Roast meat dōes cattle. 1877: E. Leigh, *Cheshire Gloss.*, 63, 'Roast meat does cattle', which means that in dry seasons cattle, if they can only get at plenty of water, often milk better than in cold wet seasons, when there is more grass. 1917: Bridge, *Cheshire Proverbs*, 105.

3. To cry roast meat. 1605: Camden, *Remains*, 336 (1870), You cannot fare well but you must cry rost meat. 1616: B.&F., *Scornful Lady*, V iv, Cannot you fare well, but you must cry roast meat? 1681: Robertson, *Phraseol. Generalis*, 1084 [as in 1605]. 1749: Fielding, *Tom Jones*, bk

iv. ch v, They may imagine, that to trumpet forth the praises of such a person, would, in the vulgar phrase, be crying roast-meat, and calling in partakers of what they intend to apply solely to their own use. 1820: Lamb, *Christ's Hospital*. 1822: Scott, *Nigel*, ch xxxvii 1894: Northall, *Folk Phrases*, 27 (E.D.S.), To cry roast meat. (1) to make known one's good luck; (2) to boast of women's favours.

4. You are in your roast meat when others are in their sod. 1639: Clarke, 115. 1670: Ray, 190. 1732: Fuller, 5849.

5. You give me roast meat. *See* **Give** (25).

Rob, *verb.* **1. He that doth not rob makes not a robe or garment.** 1629: *Book of Meery Riddles*, Prov. 83.

2. He that robs a scholar robs twenty men. 1639: Clarke, 243. 1670: Ray, 23. 1732: Fuller, 5716, Who robs a Cambridge-scholar, robs twenty.

3. To rob Peter and pay Paul. [Tanquam si quis crucifigeret Paulum ut redimeret Petrum. – 12th cent.: Herbert of Bosham, 287.] Before 1384: Wiclif, *Works*, iii 174 (Arnold), How schulde God approve that thou robbe Petur, and gif this robbere to Poule in the name of Crist? *c.*1400: Lanfranc, *Cirurgie*, 331 (E.E.T.S.), For sum medicyne is for Peter that is not good for Poul, for the diuersitè of complexioun. *c.*1440: *Jacob's Well*, 138 (E.E.T.S.), the abbot seyde, 'To robbe Petyr, and geue it Powle, it were non almesse but gret synne'. 1546: Heywood, *Proverbs*, Pt I ch xi 1621: Burton, *Melancholy*, Dem. to Reader, 36 (1836). 1637: D. Tuvill, *Vade Mecum*, 36 (3rd ed.). To take from Peter, to give to Paul, is meer oppression. 1661: Heylyn, *Hist. of Reform.*, 121 (1674), The lands of Westminster, so dilapidated by Bishop Thirlby … the rest laid out for reparation to the church of St Paul; pared almost to the very quick in those days of Rapine. From hence first came that significant By-word (as is said by some) of Robbing Peter to pay Paul. [A baseless guess.] 1768: Hall-Stevenson, *Works*, i 27 (1795), I need not steal, like thrifty George, From Paul, in order to pay Peter. 1882: J. Platt, *Economy*, 87, Give credit if they will still have it, and charge for it, but cease to rob Peter to pay for Paul.

4. To rob the spittle [hospital]. 1639: Clarke. 6. 1670: Ray, 191. 1736: Bailey, *Dict.*, s.v. 'Spital'.

Robbers. *See* quot. 1750: Smollett, *Gil Blas*, iv.

12, We got in four days to Oviedo, without meeting with any bad accident on the road, notwithstanding the proverb, which says, that robbers smell the money of travellers afar off.

Robin (redbreast). 1. As blithe as a robin. 1639: in *Berkeley MSS.*, iii 29 (1885), Hee drew it as blith as a Robin reddocke [redbreast].

2. He that hunts robin or wren, Will never prosper boy nor man. 1864: 'Cornish Proverbs', in *N. &Q.*, 3rd ser, v 208.

3. If the robin sings in the bush, Then the weather will be coarse; But if the robin sings on the bam, Then the weather will be warm. 1830: Forby, *Vocab. E. Anglia*, 416. 1893: Inwards, *Weather Lore*, 138.

4. Robin and wren. *See* **Spider** (1).

5. The robin and the wren are God Almighty's cock and hen. *c.*1555: *Harmony of Birds*, 10 (Percy S.), Then sayd the wren, I am called the hen Of our Lady most cumly. 1825: Hone, *Ev. Day Book*, i 647, [as in heading, *plus*] The martin and the swallow Are God Almighty's bow and arrow (Warwickshire). 1830: Forby, *Vocab. E. Anglia*, 409 [as in 1825, except that the last of the four lines=' Are the next two birds that follow']. 1851: Sternberg, *Dialect, etc., of Northants*, 159, The robin and the wren Be God A'-mighty's cock and hen. 1867: Harland, etc., *Lancs Folk-Lore*, 142, A Cock Robin and a Jenny Wren Are God Almighty's cock and hen; A Spink and a Sparrow Are the Devil's bow and arrow. 1879: Henderson, *Folk-Lore of N. Counties*, 123, Those who say – [as in heading, *plus*] Him that harries their nest. Never shall his soul have rest, add – The martin and the swallow Are God Almighty's bow and arrow; or, as it runs in some of our midland counties, – The martin and the swallow Are God Almighty's birds to hollow. 1883: Burne, *Shropsh. Folk-Lore*, 216, [as in heading, *plus*] The martin and the swallow Are God Almighty's scholars. 1913: E. M. Wright, *Rustic Speech, etc.*, 219 … Other versions of this rhyme are: Martins and swallows Are God's teachers and scholars. Robins and wrens Are God's chickens and hens. Those who kill a robin or a wren Will never prosper, boy or man.

See also **Naked; One bush; and Pert.**

Robin Goodfellow. 1. Robin Goodfellow was a strange man. 1639: Clarke, 69.

2. *See* quot. 1567: Harman, *Caveat*, 36 (E.E.T.S.), I verely suppose that when they wer

wel waked with cold, they surely thought that Robin goodfelow (accordinge to the old saying) had bene with them that night.

3. To laugh like Robin Goodfellow. 1830: Forby, *Vocab. E. Anglia*, 431. 1846–59: *Denham Tracts*, ii 85 (F.L.S.).

Robin Hood. 1. A Robin Hood wind. [One correspondent of the *Manchester City News* suggests that the expression belongs originally to the neighbourhood of Rochdale, and refers to the bitter north and east winds that come from the direction of Blackstone Edge, a predominant feature of which hill is Robin Hood's Bed. The thawing winds from the south and west are not referred to as 'Robin Hood winds'. – *N. &Q.*, 12th ser, x 378.] *c.*1855: *Life and Ballads of Robin Hood*, ch ii, Every Yorkshireman is familiar with the observation that Robin Hood could brave all weathers but a thaw wind. 1870: H. Fishwick, in *N. &Q.*, 4th ser, v 58, A Robin Hood Wind. In Lancashire this name is given to a wind that blows during the thawing of the snow. The reason alleged is, that Robin Hood said that he could stand any wind except a thaw wind. 1913: E. M. Wright, *Rustic Speech, etc.*, 189 [to the same effect as 1870 quot.]. 1922: *N. &Q.*, 12th ser, x 411, I have frequently heard in this locality [Clitheroe, Lancs] not only the saying, 'Robin Hood could stand any wind but a thaw wind', but also: 'All sorts of weather could Robin Hood bide, But a cold thaw wind off a high hill side'.

2. As crooked as Robin Hood's bow. Derby. 1889: *Folk-Lore Journal*, vii 291.

3. Come turn about, Robin Hood. 1672: *Westm. Drollery*, Pt II 74 (Ebsworth).

4. Good even, good Robin Hood! Before 1529: Skelton, in *Works*, ii 32 (Dyce).

5. Many talk of Robin Hood that never shot in his bow. *c.*1374: Chaucer, *Troylus*, bk ii l. 861, They speken, but they bente never his bowe. 1401: in Wright, *Political Poems*, ii 59 (Rolls Ser., 1861), Many men speken of Robyn Hood, and shotte nevere in his bowe. 1546: Heywood, *Proverbs*, Pt II ch vi 1631: Brathwait, *Whimzies*, 13 (1859). 1712: E. Ward, *Poet. Entertainer*, No. 2, p. 7, Yet of religion talks, as many do of Robin Hood, whose bow they never drew. 1913: E. M. Wright, *Rustic Speech, etc.*, 189, A Yorkshire proverb runs: Many speak of Robin Hood … i.e. many people talk of doing great things which they can never accomplish.

6. Robin Hood's choice – 'either this or nothing'. 1623: *Vox Graculi*, quoted in J. P. Collier, *Bibliogr. Cat.*, ii 481.

7. Robin Hood's miles = more than ordinary length. 1559: W. Cunningham, *Cosmogr. Glasse*, 57, quoted in *N. & Q.*, 12th ser, x 412.

8. Robin Hood's pennyworths. 1630: T. Adams, *Works*, 207, He makes the world beleeue that he sels Robin-hoods peny-worths. 1662: Fuller, *Worthies*, ii 569 (1840), 'To sell Robin Hood's pennyworths'. It is spoken of things sold under half their value; or, if you will, half sold, half given. 1721: Bailey, *Eng. Dict.*, s.v. ... This proverb is usually apply'd to such as having gotten any thing dishonestly, sell it at a price much below the value. 1889: *Folk-Lore Journal*, vii 293 (Derby.). 1922: *N. & Q.*, 12th ser, x 412.

9. Tales of Robin Hood are good among fools. 1377: Langland, *Plowman*, B, v 402, But I can rymes of Robyn Hood. 1542: Udall, tr. Erasmus's *Apoph.*, Pref., xxv (1877), Old wiues foolishe tales of Robin Hoode. 1546: Heywood, *Proverbs*, Pt II ch ix. 1600: Breton, in *Works*, i g 8 (Grosart), From ... louing idle tales of Robin Hood ... The blessed Lord of heau'n deliuer me. 1681: Robertson, *Phraseol. Generalis*, 1258, Nifles and trifles; vain tales of Robin Hood. 1732: Fuller, 4316 [with 'enough for' instead of 'among'].

10. To go round Robin Hood's barn. Robin Hood's 'barn' must have been the surrounding corn lands. 1878: *N. & Q.*, 5th ser, ix 486, It is used thus. 'Where have you been to-day?' 'All round Robin Hood's barn! I have been all about the country, first here and then there'. 1913: E. M. Wright, *Rustic Speech, etc.*, 189, To go round by Robin Hood's barn (Cambridge and West Midlands) is to go a roundabout way, to go the farthest way. 1922: *N. & Q.*, 12th ser, x 412.

11. To overshoot Robin Hood. 1869: Hazlitt, 425.

See also **May**, F (24).

Rochdale. *See* **Oldham**.

'**Rochester portion, A**, two torn smocks, and what nature gave'. 1690: *New Dict. Canting Crew*, sig. K5. 1735: Pegge, *Kent. Proverbs*, in E.D.S., No. 12, P. 74

Rocks the cradle, is the hand that rules the world, The hand. *See* **Hand** (6).

Rock the cradle empty, If you, Then you shall have babies plenty. Sussex. 1879: Henderson,

Folk-Lore of N. Counties, 19. 1913: E. M. Wright, *Rustic Speech, etc.*, 266, Rock the cradle empty, You'll rock the babies plenty.

Rock the cradle in spectacles, To. 1678: Ray, 69. 1732: Fuller, 5220.

Rod breaks no bones, The. 1633: Draxe, 182. 1639: Clarke, 75. Cf. **Birchen twigs**.

Rod for one's own back, To make a. *c.*1374: Chaucer, *Troylus*, bk i l. 740, For it is seyd, 'man maketh ofte a yerde With which the maker is him-self y-beten In sondry maner'. *c.*1489: Caxton, *Sonnes of Aymon*, 97 (E.E.T.S.), It is often sayd That men make often a rodde for them selfe. Before 1529: Skelton, in *Works*, i 186 (Dyce), For your owne tayle ye made a rod. 1593: *Tell-Trothes N. Yeares Gift*, 35 (N.Sh.S.), To lock vp ones wife ... and to seeke to rule her by correction, when he cannot gouerne himself with discretion, is to gather a rod to beate his owne breeche. 1694: *Terence made English*, 20, But now he makes a rod for his own back. 1738: Swift, *Polite Convers.*, Dial. I, I am not the first man has carried a rod to whip himself.

Rod in pickle, To have a. 1553: *Respublica*, III v, But we have roddes in pysse for them everye chone. 1606: Chapman, *Mons. d'Olive*, I, My little parcel of wits, I have rods in piss for you. 1690: A. Behn, *Widow Ranter*, III i, Here's the young rogue that drew upon us too, we have rods in piss for him, i' faith. 1784: O'Keeffe, *Peeping Tom, ad fin.*, Though you have as poets see, Rods in pickle steeping; Forgive poor Tom of Coventry, And pardon for his peeping. 1854: Baker, *Northants Gloss.*, s.v. 'Rod', 'Rod in pickle (or soak)'. Punishment in store.

Rod in school. *See* **Whip for a fool**.

Rodings, The. *See* quot. 1880: E. Walford, in *N. & Q.*, 6th ser, ii 307, A stupid fellow in Essex is generally said to come from the 'Rodings', or else from the 'sheers' – shires. Cf. **Shires**.

Roger. *See* **Sow**, s*ubs.* (11).

Roger Cary's dinner. 1877: E. Leigh, *Cheshire Gloss.*, 171, Roger Cary's dinner. – A saying when the dinner is scanty, or 'just enoo' and nought to spare. 1917: Bridge, *Cheshire Proverbs*, 87.

Rogue as ever peeped at a speer [chimney-post], **As big a.** Ibid., 10.

Rogue, but he's no fool on the march, He may be a. 1864: 'Cornish Proverbs', in *N. & Q.*, 3rd ser, vi 495.

Rogue in grain. *See* **Knave.**

Rogue's wardrobe is harbour for a louse, A. 1639: Clarke, 71. 1670: Ray, 137. 1732: Fuller, 383.

Roland for an Oliver, A = Tit for tat. 1548: Hall, *Chron.*, 266 (1809), To haue a Rowland for an Olyuer. 1659: Howell, *Letters*, ii 665 (Jacobs), She will alwayes have a Rowland for your Oliver. Before 1704: T. Brown, in *Works*, i 219 (1700), I am resolv'd to give him a Rowland for his Oliver. 1706: Vanbrugh, *Confederacy*, III ii. 1790: Wolcot, *A Rowland for an Oliver* [title]. 1843: Carlyle, *Past and Present*, bk ii ch xii, Look also how my Lord of Clare, coming to claim his undue 'debt' in the Court of Witham, with barons and apparatus, gets a Roland for his Oliver! 1898: Weyman, *Shrewsbury*, ch xvii. 1919: Barbellion, *Journal of Disapp. Man*, 168, It exasperates me to be unable to give a Roland for an Oliver.

Rolling stone gathers no moss, A. 1362: Langland, *Plowman*, A, x 101, Selden moseth the marbelston that men ofte treden. *c.*1406: *Book of Precedence*, 39 (E.E.T.S.), Syldon mossyth the stone That oftyn ys tornnyd and winde. 1546: Heywood, *Proverbs*, Pt I ch xi, The rollyng stone neuer gatherth mosse. 1593: *Passionate Morrice*, 87 (N.Sh.S.). 1606: Marston, *The Fawne*, I ii, Thy head is alwaies working; it roles, and it roles, Dondolo, but it gathers no mosse. *c.*1610: in *Roxb. Ballads*, ii 512 (B.S.). 1720: *Vade Mecum for Malt-worms*, 6 (part 2), The proverb says … That stones, when rolling, gather little moss. 1776: Colman, *The Spleen*, I, Well, well; a rolling stone's always bare of moss, as you say. 1852: Dickens, *Bleak House*, ch xxxiv. 1914: Shaw, 'Parents and Children', in *Misalliance, etc.*, l. xxxiv, We keep repeating the silly proverb that … , as if moss were a desirable parasite. 1917: Bridge, *Cheshire Proverbs*, 5, A rolling stone gathers no moss, but a tethered sheep winna get fat. (In Sussex they add – 'And a sitting hen never grows fat'.)

Rome. 1. All roads lead to Rome, *c.*1380: Chaucer, *Astrolabe*, Prol., Right as diverse pathes leden diverse folk the righte wey to Rome, 1860: Reade, *Cl. and Hearth*, ch xxiv, All roads take to Rome. 1869: Browning, *Ring and Book*, bk v l. 296, Every one soon or late comes round by Rome.

2. Rome was not built in a day. [Non stilla una cavat marmor, neque protinus uno est Condita Roma die. – *c.*1500: Palingenius (ps. for Pietro Angelo Manzolli), *Zodiacus Vitae*, xii 460 (ed. Tauchn.).] 1546: Heywood, *Proverbs*, Pt I ch xi, Rome was not built in one daie. 1593: G. Harvey, *Works*, ii 133 (Grosart). 1658: R. Franck, *North. Memoirs*, 258 (1821). 1660: Tatham, *The Rump*, I. 1763: Murphy, *Citizen*, I ii. 1822: Scott, *Nigel*, ch xxi. 1849: Brontë, *Shirley*, ch vi.

3. To go to Rome. There are several old sayings which all appear to mean – to go on a fool's errand. *See* the quots. *c.*1520: *Hickscorner*, in Hazlitt, *Old Plays*, i 168, For if any of us three be mayor of London … I will ride to Rome on my thumb, *c.*1550: Udall, *Roister Doister*, II ii, It were better to go to Rome on my head than so. 1600: Kemp, *Nine Daies Wonder*, Dedn., Me thinkes I could flye to Rome (at least hop to Rome, as the olde prouerb is) with a morter on my head. 1611: Corbet, *Poems*, in Chalmers, v 562, No more shall man with mortar on his head Set forwards towards Rome. 1653: Middleton and Rowley, *Span. Gipsy*, II ii, A cousin of mine in Rome, I go to him with a mortar.

4. When in Rome, do as the Romans do. [Aristo Punico ingenio inter Poenos usus. – Livy, xxxiv. 61. *See also* St Augustine, Epistle xxxvi, to Casulanus.] Before 1500: in Hill, *Commonplace-Book*, 130 (E.E.T.S.), Whan thou art at Rome, do after the dome; And whan thou art els wher, do as they do ther. 1586: Pettie, tr. Guazzo, *Civil Convers.*, fo. 26, According to the saying, when one is at Rome, to liue as they doe at Rome. 1676: Cotton, Walton's *Angler*, Pt II ch vi, You know the proverb, 'Those who go to Rome must do as they at Rome do'. 1712: Motteux, *Quixote*, Pt II ch liv. *c.*1780: *The First Floor*, II i, in Inchbald, *Farces*, vi 251 (1815). 1842: Barham, *Ing. Legends*, 2nd ser: 'Auto-da-fé'. 1910: Lucas, *Mr Ingleside*, ch xviii.

Romford, The ready way to = ? 1656: *Musarum Deliciae*, i 31 (Hotten), There is a proverb to thy comfort. Known as the ready way to Rumford. That, when the pot ore fire you heat, A lowse is better than no meat.

Romford, To ride to. 1738: Swift, *Polite Convers.*, Dial. II, Well, one may ride to Rumford upon this knife, it is so blunt. 1785: Grose, *Class. Dict. Vulgar Tongue*, s.v. 'Rumford', To ride to Rumford, to have one's backside new bottomed. 1901: *N. & Q.*, 9th ser, viii 306, 'You might ride to

Romford on it'. When a youngster I often heard my old grandmother make this remark *à propos* any blunt carving or other knife which failed to come up to expectations.

Romney Marsh. *See* quot. 1911: A. S. Cooke, *Off Beaten Track in Sussex*, 286, There is an East Sussex saying as to Romney Marsh, which gives the best idea of its area – 'The world is divided into five parts, Europe, Asia, Africa, America – and Romney Marsh!'

Romney Marsh. *See also* **Fairlight Down**.

Roodee, As ronk [rank, rich] **as th'.** 1877: E. Leigh, *Cheshire Gloss.*, 173. 1917: Bridge, *Cheshire Proverbs*, 19. [The Roodee is the Chester racecourse.]

Rook, The. *See* quot. 1872: J. Glyde, jr., *Norfolk Garland*, 154, The weather will fine when the rooks play pitch halfpenny. That is, if flying in flocks some of them stoop down and pick up worms, imitating the action of a boy playing pitch halfpenny. *See also* **Raven**.

Room at the top, There is always. A saying attributed to the American politician Daniel Webster. It is said to have been his reply when he was advised against going into the legal profession because it was already overcrowded. 1900: W. James, *Letter*, 2 Apr. (1920), II 121, Verily there is room at the top. S seems to be the only Britisher worth thinking of. 1914: A. Bennett, *The Price of Love*, vii, The Imperial had set out to be the most gorgeous cinema in the Five Towns; and it simply was. Its advertisements read: 'There is always room at the top'. 1957: J. Braine, *Room at the Top*, xxviii, You're the sort of young man we want. There's always room at the top.

Room than your company, I'd rather have your. 1579: *Marr. of Wit and Wisdom*, sc iii p. 27 (SH.S.), I had rather haue your roome as your componie. 1592: Greene, *Works*, xi 255 (Grosart), Let him depart out of this place, for his roome is better than his company. 1615: Brathwait, *Strappado*, 66 (1878), Whose roome I loue more then his company. 1664: *Witts Recr.*, Epigr. 268. 1798: T. Dibdin, *Jew and Doctor*, II i. 1865: Dickens, *Mutual Friend*, bk i ch vi.

Rootless, must green soon die. *c*.1374: Chaucer, *Troylus*, bk iv. l. 770.

Rope, *subs.* **1. A rope and butter, if one slip the other may hold.** 1678: Ray, 267. 1732: Fuller, 384 ['will' for 'may'].

2. As meet as a rope for a thief. 1540: Palsgrave, *Acolastus*, sig. M2, An host that shalbe as mete for him as a rope is for a thefe. 1579: *Marr. of Wit and Wisdom*, sc ii p. 15 (SH.S.). *c*.1625: B.&F., *Women Pleased*, III iv, As fit for him as a thief for a halter! 1671: *Poor Robin Alman. Prognost.*, sig. C5, A good fire … will be now as seasonable as a rope for a thief is at any time.

3. Give him rope enough and he'll hang himself. 1639: Fuller, *Holy War*, bk v ch vii, They were suffered to have rope enough, till they had haltered themselves in a *praemunire*. 1652: Burroughs, *On Hosea*, iv. 517, As we speak of some, 'Give them line enough, and they will quickly hang themselves'. 1753: Richardson, *Grandison*, i 29 (1883), Give you women but rope enough, you'll do your own business. 1849: Brontë, *Shirley*, ch iii.

4. He puts a rope to the eye of a needle. 1813: Ray, 75.

5. I thought I had given her rope enough, said Pedley, when he hanged his mare. Yorks. 1670: Ray, 191. 1732: Fuller, 2627.

6. Ropes of sand. [τὸ ἐκ τῆς ψάμμου σχοινίον πλέκοντες. – Aristides (ed. Jebb, ii 309).] *c*.1594: Bacon, *Promus*, No. 778, To knytt a rope of sand. 1649: T. Forde, *Lusus Fort.*, 31, One shall sooner knit a rope of sand then unite their affections. 1672: Corye, *Generous Enemies*, II i, 0 woman, woman, thy vows are ropes of sand. Before 1680: Butler, *Remains*, ii 206 (1759), A quibbler … dances on a rope of sand. 1712: in *Somers Tracts*, xiii 144 (1811), I leave to my said children a great chest full of broken promises and cracked oaths; likewise a vast cargo of ropes made with sand. 1845: Carlyle, *Lett. to Emerson*, You have done one very ingenious thing to set Clark upon the Boston booksellers' accounts; Michael Scott setting the devil to twist ropes of sand. [*See* Scott's *Lay of Last Minstrel*, can. ii st. 13 *n*.]

7. Throw the rope in after the bucket. 1732: Fuller, 5042.

Roper's news, That's = no news. 1879: *Folk-Lore Record*, ii 203 (Bodmin). 1880: Courtney, *W. Cornwall Words*, 47 (E.D.S.), That's Roper's news – hang the crier.

Rose proveth a thorn, The. 1546: Heywood, *Proverbs*, Pt I ch x, I toke hir for a rose, but she breedth a burre. 1633: Draxe, 41. 1659: Howell, *Letters*, ii 665 (Jacobs), She may prove a wolf in lambs skin, instead of a rose you will have a burr. 1813: Ray, 155, For the rose the thorn is often plucked.

Rose. *See also* **Fresh; No rose;** and **Red.**

Rosebery Topping wears a cap, When, Let Cleveland then beware a clap. 1610: P. Holland, tr. Camden's *Brit.*, 721. 1700: J. Brome, *Travels*, 164. 1846–59: *Denham Tracts*, i 88 (F.L.S.) ['hat' for 'cap', and 'Morden–Carrs will suffer for that']. 1893: Inwards, *Weather Lore*, 101. 1922: *N. & Q.*, 12th ser, xi 25.

Rosemary. *See* quots. 1884: H. Friend, *Flowers and Fl. Lore*, 217, The old saying respecting another equally popular flower – 'Where Rosemary flourishes the lady rules'. 1911: A. S. Cooke, *Off Beaten Track in Sussex*, 286, Old sayings ... are more often aimed at the weaker sex. 'Except where the missus is master, the rosemary will never blossom', is one such remark.

Rotheras, Every one cannot dwell at. 1659: Howell, 21. 1700: J. Brome, *Travels*, 19 ... Rotheras, it having formerly been a place of too profuse hospitality. 1790: Grose, *Prov. Gloss.*, s.v. 'Herefordshire'. 1868: *Quart. Review*, cxxv. 230, One well known to Herefordshire men, 'Every one can't dwell at Rotheras ' ... a handsome mansion near Hereford, requiring, no doubt, a handsome income to keep it warm.

Rotten apple injures its neighbours, A. *See* **Apple** (1).

Rotten as an asker [newt], **As.** 1917: Bridge, *Cheshire Proverbs*, 19 ... *rotten* because it can drop its tail off.

Rotten case abides no handling, A. 1598: Shakespeare, 2 *Henry IV*, IV i.

Rough as a briar, As. *c.*1410: *Towneley Plays*, 119 (E.E.T.S.), As rugh as a brere.

Rough as gorse, As. 1876: *N. & Q.*, 5th ser, v 94, The English proverb 'As coarse as gorse' ... is common in several parts of England, and about Nottingham I have often heard it 'As coarse as Hickling gorse'. Ibid., 477, 'As coarse as bean-straw' is a common Lincolnshire saying. 1917: Bridge, *Cheshire Proverbs*, 19, As rough as gorse.

Rough as it runs. 1687: T. Brown, in *Dk. Buckingham's Works*, ii 129 (1705) (OED), If you don't like me rough, as I run, fare you well, madam. 1813: Ray, 231, Rough as it runs, as the boy said when his ass kicked him.

Rough as a tinker's budget, As. 1659: Howell, 18. 1670: Ray, 207.

Rough net is not the best catcher of birds,

The. 1546: Heywood, *Proverbs*, Pt I ch ix. 1611: Cotgrave, s.v. 'Douceur'. 1670: Ray, 125.

Rough with the smooth, To take the. *c.*1400: *Beryn*, 37 (E.E.T.S.), Take yeur part as it comyth, of roughe and eke of smooth. 1900: Jerome, *Three Men on Bummel*, 190 (OED), One must take a little rough with one's smooth.

Rouk-town. *See* quot. 1670: Ray, 52, A rouk-town's seldom a good housewife at home. This is a Yorkshire proverb. A rouk-town is a gossiping housewife.

Round about for the next road, To go. 1917: Bridge, *Cheshire Proverbs*, 134.

Roundabouts, What you lose on the swings, you gain on the. *See* **Lose** (17).

Round as a hoop, As. *c.*1555: in Wright, *Songs, etc., Philip and Mary*, 98 (Roxb.Cl), Untyll she ryll as rownd as a hoope. *c.*1660: in *Songs and Ballads*, 132 (Percy S., No. 7), He draws them up as round as a hoop. 1676: Shadwell, *Virtuoso*, I. 1720: Gay, *Poems*, ii 278 (Underhill), Round as a hoop the bumpers flow.

Round table. *See* quots. 1623: Wodroephe, *Spared Houres*, 483, A round table yealds no debate. 1666: Torriano, *Piazza Univ.*, 132, At a round table there's no dispute about the place. 1732: Fuller, 824, At a round table the herald's useless.

Row against the flood. *See* **Strive.**

Rowan tree and red thread Haud the witches a' in dread. 1846–59: *Denham Tracts*, ii 329 (F.L.S.).

Row one way. *See* **Look** (7).

Royston horse. *See* **Cambridge.**

Ruan Vean men. *See* quot. 1895: Jos. Thomas, *Randigal Rhymes*, 61, Like Ruan Vean men – don't knaw and weant be told. [Corn.].

Rub and a good cast. A warning saying, of bowling origin. 1639: Clarke, 213. 1678: Ray, 81, Rub and a good cast. Be not too hasty, and you'll speed the better.

Rub on the gall, To. Before 1529: Skelton, in *Works*, i 365 (Dyce), Yet wrote he none ill, Sauynge he rubbid sum vpon the gall. 1552: Latimer, in *Works*, ii 211 (P.S.), When a thief or a briber heareth this, it rubbeth him on the gall. 1607: *Barley-Breake*, 27 (Grosart), Forbeare to rub me on that sore. 1710: T. Ward, *Eng. Reform.*, 147 (1716), I like not rubbing an old sore.

Rubs in the smoothest road, There will be. 1710: S. Palmer, *Moral Essays on Proverbs*, 364,

No way so smooth but it has some rub. 1821: Scott, *Kenilworth*, ch xvi.

Rudgwick, Sussex. *See quot.* 1884: 'Sussex Proverbs', in *N. &Q.*, 6th ser, ix. 401, Ridgick for riches, Green [Wisborough Green] for poors, Billingshurst for pretty, girls, and Horsham for whores.

Ruffians' Hall, He is only fit for. [Merchant sees his apprentice dressed as a gallant and exclaims: 'Hey day, Ruffians' Hall! Sword, pumps, here's a racket indeed!' – 1605: Chapman, etc., *Eastw. Hoe*, I i.] 1662: Fuller, *Worthies*, ii 347 (1840). 1790: Grose, *Prov. Gloss.*, s.v. 'London'.

Rugged as a foal, As. 1917: **Bridge**, *Cheshire Proverbs*, 19.

Rugged colt. *See* **Ragged.**

Rugged stone grows smooth from hand to hand, A. 1640: Herbert, *Jac. Prudentum.* 1670: Ray, 23.

Rule, verb. **1. He that will not bended by his dame.** *See* **He that win not, etc.**

2. He who will not be ruled by the rudder, must be ruled by the rock. 1666: G. Torrino, *Italian Proverbs*, 286, That ship which will have no *rudder*, must have a rock. 1823: D'Israeli, *Cur. of Lit.*, 2nd ser, i 454 (1824) [cited as 'a Cornish proverb']. 1853: Trench, *Proverbs*, 60 (1905). 1864: 'Cornish Proverbs', in *N. &Q.*, 3rd ser, vi 494.

3. Rule lust, temper tongue, and bridle the belly. 1813: Ray, 20.

4. Rule youth well, for age will rule itself. 1736: Bailey, *Dict.*, s.v. 'Rule'.

5. Rule the roast, *c.*1400: *Carpenter's Tools*, in Halliwell, *Nugae Poeticae*, 17, Whatsoeuer ye brage our boste, My meyster yet shall reule the roste. Before 1529: Skelton, *Colin Clout*, l. 1021, But at the playsure of one That ruleth the roste alone. *c.*1540: Heywood, *Four PP.* in Hazlitt, *Old Plays*, i 361, Nay, if riches might rule the roost, Behold what cause I have to boast! 1593: Greene, *Works*, ii 285 (Grosart), If then it be a woman's wish to haue her owne will, and as the common prouerbe saith, to rule the rost after her owne diet. 1606: Chapman, *Gent. Usher*, V i, I do domineer, and rule the roast. 1637: Nabbes, *Microcosmus*, III, I am my ladies cooke, and king of the kitchin, where I rule the roast. 1696: Vanbrugh, *Relapse*, II. 1736: Fielding, *Pasquin*, II, They bear the name of power, we rule the roast. 1857: Borrow, *Rom. Rye*, ch xxviii, The

son a puppy who … now rules the roast over his father and mother.

Rules are made to be broken. 1942: F. Gruber, *Gift Horse* (1972), v 38, 'That's the rule,' added Happy, unnecessarily. 'Rules are made to be broken,' said Johnny with forced heartiness. 1954: A. C. Clarke, *Expedition to Earth*, 58, It is a fundamental rule of space-flight that … the minimum crew on a long journey shall not consist of less than three men. But rules are made to be broken … .

Rule without an exception, There is no. 1620: Shelton, *Quixote*, Pt II ch xviii 1738: Swift, *Polite Convers.*, Dial. I [with 'general' before 'rule']. 1758–67: Sterne, *Trist. Shandy*, ix. ch xiii Cf. **Exception.**

Run, *verb.* **1. He is run off his legs** = He is bankrupt. 1678: Ray, 89.

2. He runs far. *See* **Go** (10).

3. He runs far back that means to leap a great way. 1681: Robertson, *Phraseol. Generalis*, 480.

4. He that runs fastest gets most ground. 1639: Clarke, 319. 1670: Ray, 138.

5. He that runs fast will not run long. 1855: Bohn, 392.

6. He that runs in the dark may well stumble. 1670: Ray, 19, He that runs in the night stumbles. 1732: Fuller, 2271.

7. He that runs may rally. Ibid., No. 2272.

8. I cannot run and sit still at the same time. Ibid., No. 2590.

9. If you could run as you drink, you might catch a hare. 1640: Herbert, *Jac. Prudentum.*

10. Ill run that cannot go. *See* **Ill run.**

11. It runs in the blood like wooden legs. I heard this saying from the mouth of an Ulsterman, in Surrey, in the sixties of the last century. 1917: Bridge, *Cheshire Proverbs*, 81. 1924: *Devonsh. Assoc. Trans.*, lv. 111. That rins in famlies, like timbern legs.

12. Run tap run tapster. 1678: Ray, 86.

13. To run as swift as a pudding would creep. 1608: Armin, *Nest of Ninnies*, 23 (SH.S.), They puft and they blowede; they ran as swifte as a pudding would creepe.

14. To run at rovers = *To* follow wild or random courses. 1528: More, in *Works*, p. 228, col. 2 (1557), For so shold they nede no such titles at al, nor should nede neither roune at rouers, nor liue in ley mens houses. 1533: Udall, *Flowers out of Terence*, fo. 191, His hart or mynde, whiche now runneth at rouers in ryot and wantonnes. 1567: Painter, *Pal. of Pleasure*, iii 47 (Jacobs), Who I had rather should be somewhat restrayned, than run at rouers to hir dishonour and my shame. 1639: Clarke, 228, You run at random, shoot at rovers. 1847: Halliwell, *Dict.*, s.v. 'Rovers', *Running at rovers*, having too much liberty.

15. To run before one's mare to market. 1709: R. Kingston, *Apoph. Curiosa*, 79, Taking a great deal of pains for nothing, and with the country proverb, is like running before ones mare to the market.

16. To run him through the nose with a cushion. 1672: Walker, *Paraem.*, 57.

17. To run over shoes = To get heavily in debt. 1598: *Servingman's Comfort*, in *Inedited Tracts*, 154 (Hazlitt). He is runne ouershooes. Cf. **Over shoes**.

18. To run with the hare and hunt with the hounds, *c.*1440: *Jacobs Well*, 263 (E.E.T.S.), Thou hast a crokyd tunge heldyng wyth hownd and wyth hare. 1546: Heywood, *Proverbs*, Pt I ch x, To holde with the hare, and run with the hound. 1579: Lyly, *Euphues*, 107 (Arber). 1598: Greene, *James IV*, IV v. 1614: C. Brooke, *Rich. the Third*, 86 (Grosart), And both could runne with hound, and hold with hare. 1705: Ward, *Hud. Rediv.*, Pt 3, can. iv. p. 11. 1893: R.L.S.,

Catriona, ch i, The whole thing … gave me a look of running with the hare and hunting with the hounds. 1897: W. E. Norris, *Clarissa Furiosa*, ch xxxix. 1924: *Times*, Sept. 19, p. 13, col. 4, His policy of running with the hare and hunting with the hounds is becoming a menace to the general safety.

19. You run as if. *See* **Go** (29).

Running horse is an open sepulchre, A. 1578: Florio, *First Fruites*, fo. 28 ['graue' for 'sepulchre']. 1611: Cotgrave, s.v. 'Sepulchre' 1666: Torriano, *Piazza Univ.*, 43. 1732: Fuller, 376 ['race-horse' for 'running horse'].

Rush for him that cares a straw for me, A. 1639: Clarke, 72.

Rushes. *See* **Green** (9).

Russian, Scratch a. *See* **Scratch**.

Rusty sword and empty purse plead performance of covenants, The. 1670: Ray, 23.

Rutland raddleman 'Raddleman' = a dealer in raddle = red ochre. 1622: Drayton, *Polyol.*, xxiii, Little Rutlandshire is termed Raddleman. 1662: Fuller, *Worthies*, iii 38 (1840). 1790: Grose, *Prov. Gloss.*, s.v. 'Rutlandshire'.

Rye (grain). *See* **December; Good rye; July** (6); **March** (27); **St Peter** (2); and **Wheat** (2).

Rye (town). *See* **Chichester;** and **Tenbury**.

Rynt you witch. *See* **Aroint**

S

Sack. 1. A short sack hath a wide mouth. 1583: Melbancke, *Philotinus*, sig.G2.

2. He has given the sack a turn = 'He has turned the tables – reversed the order of things'. 1917: Bridge, *Cheshire Proverbs*, 66.

3. If it isn't in the sack. *See* quot. 1911: *Devonsh. Assoc. Trans.*, xliii 93, 'If 'tisn't in the sack, 'tis in the pig's back'. This means, you will get, one way or the other, your money's value. What you cannot show for it in the meat left in the sack, you will see in what you gain for the fat bacon you have to sell in return for the money spent on the sack's contents.

4. Let every sack stand upon its own bottom. 1659: Howell, 4. Cf. **Every tub.**

5. Many a sack is tied up before it be full. 1607: Rowlands, *Diog. Lanthornme*, 7 (Hunt.Cl.)

[quoted as 'the olde prouerb']. 1612: W. Parkes, *Curtaine-Drawer of the World*, 60 (Grosart) ['knit' for 'tied']. 1671: Head and Kirkman, *Eng. Rogue*, ii 111. When we fell short at meals … he would put us off with an old proverb, that *many a sack is tied up before it be full.*

6. Sacks to the mill. *See* **More sacks.**

7. There comes nought out of the sack, but what was there. 1586: L. Evans, *Withals Dict. Revised*, sig. G1, When the sacke is opened, it is knowne what is therein conteined. 1623: Wodroephe, *Spared Houres*, 489. 1640: Herbert, *Jac. Prudentum:* 1869: Spurgeon, *John Ploughman*, ch ii, Nothing comes out of a sack but what was in it.

See also **Broken** (5); **Empty** (9); **Ill sack; Know** (28); **Old,** E (3); **One grain;** and **Wish** (7).

Sackworth. *See* **Knipe-scar.**

Sad *See* quot. 1550: Udall, *Roister Doister*, III iii, *Merry* ... Why speak ye so faintly, or why are ye so sad? *R.R.* Thou knowest the proverb – because I cannot be had.

Saddle, *subs.* **1. He has a saddle to fit every horse** = a salve for every sore. 1813: Ray, 214.

2. To put the saddle on the right horse. 1607: Dekker and Webster, *Westw. Hoe*, V, How say you wenches, haue I set the sadle on the right horse? 1678: Dryden, *All for Love*, Pref., I suppose he would think it a wiser part to set the saddle on the right horse, and chuse rather to live with the reputation of a plain-spoken honest man, than to die with the infamy of an incestuous villain. 1720: *Vade Mecum for Malt-worms*, Pt I p. 4, Turn Justice to its proper course, And place the saddle on the right horse. 1843: Carlyle, *Past and Present*, bk ii ch x, On all sides he laid about him like a man ... putting consequence on premiss, and everywhere the saddle on the right horse.

3. To set beside the saddle. 1543: Becon, in *Early Works*, 368 (P.S.), Yet by this means have they obtained their purpose, and set the other beggarly fellow besides the saddle. 1630: T. Adams, *Works*, 175, Riot iustles and the wit is turned besides the saddle. 1636: Taylor (Water-Poet), *Travels*, 52, in *Works*, 3rd coll. (Spens.S.), Wines predominant and capitall, To set a horseman quite beside the saddle.

4. Where saddles lack better ride on a pad than on the horse bare-back. 1546: Heywood, *Proverbs*, Pt I ch x 1605: Camden, *Remains*, 335 (1870). 1670: Ray, 139. 1732: Fuller, 6464.

See also **Cow** (11); **Sow**, *subs.* (12); **Win** (4).

Saddle, *verb. You saddle to-day and ride out to-morrow.* 1659: Howell, *Proverbs: Span.-Eng.*, 4, He sadleth to day, and goes to morrow. 1732: Fuller, 5984.

Saddlewick, or ? **Saddleworth.** *See* quots. 1670: Ray, 209, Like the parson of Saddleworth, who could read in no book but his own. Cheshire. 1790: Grose, *Prov. Gloss.*, s.v. 'Cheshire' [as in 1670, but 'Saddlewick']. 1878: *Folk-Lore Record*, i 167, [as in 1790, *plus*] is referable to a Yorkshire town. 1917: Bridge, *Cheshire Proverbs*, 91 [as in 1790].

Sadness and gladness succeed each other. 1639: Clarke, 326. 1670: Ray, 139. 1732: Fuller, 4063.

Safe as a church, As. 1891: Hardy, *Tess*, ch xiv. The plain ones be as safe as churches.

Safe as a crow in a gutter, As. 1639: Clarke, 97 [with 'sowe' for 'crow']. 1670: Ray, 207.

Safe as a mouse in a cheese, As. 1678: Ray, 288.

Safe as a mouse in a malt-heap, As. 1639: Clarke, 47. 1670: Ray, 207.

Safe as a mouse in a mill, As. 1600: *Weakest to the Wall*, l. 345 (Malone S.), And all without feare, safe as mouse in a mill. 1639: Davenport, *New Trick to cheat Devil*, III i, She's safe as mouse in mill.

Safe as a thief in a mill, As. 1623: B.&F., *Maid in Mill*, II i, The thief is as safe as in his mill. 1673: *Vinegar and Must.*, 20, in Hindley, *Old Book-Coll. Miscell.*, iii, You are as safe as so many thieves in a mill. 1738: Swift, *Polite Convers.*, Dial. I. 1847: Halliwell, *Dict.*, s.v. 'Thief', ... very secure. Still in common use. 1889: J. Nicholson, *Folk Speech E. Yorks*, 18, As fast as a thief in a mill. 1901: F. E. Taylor, *Lancs. Sayings*, 2 [as in 1889].

Safe as Chelsea, As. Derby. 1889. *Folk-Lore Journal*, vii 291.

Safe as the bank, As. 1862: Dickens, *Letters*, ii 183 (1880). 1923: J. S. Fletcher, *The Diamonds*, ch xxviii ... safe as the Bank of England.

Safe bind, safe find. *c.*1540: Bale, *Kynge Johan*, l. 1897, As the sayinge is, he fyndeth that surely bynde. 1580: Tusser, *Husbandrie*, 173 (E.D.S.). 1655: Fuller, *Church Hist.*, bk iii § v (6), Sure bind, sure find. 1751: Fielding, *Amelia*, bk xii ch vii 1775: O'Hara, *Two Misers*, I. 1823: Scott, *St.Ronan's*, ch xxxvi 1865: Dickens, *Mutual Friend*, bk iii ch xiv.

Safe from the East Indies, and was drowned in the Thames, He came. 1732: Fuller, 1817.

Safe riding in a good haven, 'Tis. 1659: Howell, 16. 1732: Fuller, 5083, 'Tis good riding in a safe harbour.

Safe than sorry, Better to be. *See* **Better to be safe.**

Safety in numbers, There is. [Proverbs xi.14, In the multitude of counsellors there is safety] 1680: Bunyan: *The Life and Death of Mr Badman*, 133, I verily think (since in the multitude of Counsellors there is safety) that if she had acquainted the Congregation with it ... she had had more peace. 1816: J. Austen, *Emma*, II 1, She determined to cal upon them and seek safety in numbers. 1914: T. Dreiser, *Titan*, xvii, He was beginning to run around with other women. There was safety in numbers.

Saffron. *See* quot. 1904: C. G. Harper, *Newmarket, Bury, etc., Road*, 110, The very least of the benefits it [saffron] conferred was the exhilaration of the spirits, so that the old proverb for a merry fellow was 'He hath slept in a bag of saffron'.

Sage in May. *See* quots. 1588: Cogan, *Haven of Health*, ch, xi p. 32 (1612), In *Schola Salerni* it is demanded, Cur moriatur homo cui saluia crescit in horto? As who should say, such is the vertue of sage, that if it were possible, it would make a man immortall. 1635: Swan, *Spec. Mundi*, 247, Such a desire hath sage to make a man immortall. 1661: M. Stevenson, *Twelve Moneths*, 23, I shall conclude with the old proverb, Set sage in May, and it will grow alway. 1732: Fuller, 6253, He that would live for aye Must eat butter and sage in May. 1846: Denham, *Proverbs*, 44 (Percy S.) [as in 1732, but omitting 'butter and'].

Said than done, Sooner (or **Easier**). [Id dictu quam re, ut pleraque, facilius. – Livy, xxxi 38.] *c.*1534: Berners, *Huon*, 327 (E.E.T.S.), Ye may say your pleasure, but in the doynge is all the mater. 1546: Heywood, *Proverbs*, Pt II ch v, That is … sooner said then doone. 1595: *True Trag. Rich. Duke of York*, 156 (SH.S.), Tis better said then done, my gratious Lord. 1681: Robertson, *Phraseol. Generalis*, 471, 'Tis more difficult then you think for; Sooner said than done. 1766: Garrick, *Neck or Nothing*, I i, That's easier said than done. 1850: Smedley, *Frank Fairlegh*, ch li, Easier said than done, Lawless, unfortunately.

Sail and **Sails**, *subs*. **1. As sails are to a ship, so are the passions to the spirits.** 1736: Bailey, *Dict.*, s.v. 'Spirit'.

2. Make not thy sail too big for the ballast. 1732: Fuller, 3322.

3. To set up a sail to every wind. *c.*1630: B.&F., *Bloody Brother*, IV ii, Then he would sail with any wind. 1670: Ray, 192. 1732: Fuller, 5228. *c.*1733: Swift, *Poems*: 'The Storm', He knows to sail with every wind.

Sail, *verb*. **1. He that will not sail till he have a full fair wind, will lose many a voyage.** 1732: Fuller, 2354.

2. He that will sail without danger must never come upon the main sea. 1639: Clarke, 250.

1670: Ray, 139. 1732: Fuller, 2353, He that will not sail till all dangers are over, must never put to sea.

3. Sail, quoth the king; hold, saith the wind. 1732: Fuller, 4064. 1738: *Gent. Mag.*, 474.

4. To sail with wind and tide. 1580: Sidney, *Arcadia*, bk ii 199 (1893), All men set their sails with the favourable wind, which blew on the fortune of this young prince. 1591: Florio, *Second Frutes*, 97, For wisdom sailes with winde and tide. 1639: Clarke, 15, Sayle with the wind and tide. 1783: Windham, in Boswell's *Johnson*, iv. 201 *n*. (Hill), Set sail, and see where the winds and waves will carry you.

Saint and **Saints. 1. A saint abroad and a devil at home.** 1678: Bunyan, *Pilgr. Progress*, Pt I 81 (1849), Thus, say the common people that know him, *A Saint abroad, and a Devil at home*. 1880: Spurgeon, *Ploughman's Pictures*, 67, They are saints abroad, but ask their maids what they are at home.

2. All saint without, all devil within. 1732: Fuller, 542.

3. They are not all saints that use holy water. 1586: L. Evans, *Withals Dict. Revised*, sig. K6, They be not all saints, of this be you sure, that goe in and out at the churche dore. 1732: Fuller, 4956.

See also **Young** (27).

SAINTS and SAINTS' DAYS:

St Andrew, 30 Nov. 1830: Forby, *Vocab. E. Anglia*, 418, Saint Andrew the King, Three weeks and three days before Christmas comes in.

St Barnabas, 11 June. *On St Barnabas Put a scythe to the grass.* 1659: Howell, *Proverbs: Fr.-Eng.*, 21, At Saint Barnabe the sithe in the medow. 1893: Inwards, *Weather Lore*, 29. *See also* **Barnaby Bright**

St Bartholomew, 24 Aug. **1. All the tears that St Swithin can cry, St Bartlemy's mantle wipes them dry.** 1878: Dyer, *Eng. Folk-Lore*, 258. 1893: Inwards, *Weather Lore*, 32 [with 'dusty' before 'mantle'].

2. As St Bartholomew's Day, so the whole autumn. 1893: Inwards, 33. 1912: R. L. Gales, *Studies in Arcady*, 2nd ser, 107, If St Barthlemy's day be fair and clear, Hope for a prosperous autumn that year.

3. Bathe your eyes on Bartimy Day, You may throw your spectacles away. Mon. 1905: *Folk-Lore*, xvi 67.

4. If the wind change. *See* quot. 1669: *New Help to Discourse*, 284, If the winde change on St Bartholomew's day at night, the following year will not be good.

5. St Bartholomew brings cold dew. 1678: Ray, 52. 1732: Fuller, 6210. 1893: Inwards, *Weather Lore*, 33, At St Bartholomew There comes cold dew.

St Benedict, 21 March. 1678: Ray, 52, S. Benedick sow thy pease or keep them in thy rick. 1893: Inwards, *Weather Lore*, 21 [as in 1678]. 1913: E. M. Wright, *Rustic Speech, etc.*, 290, Then comes Benedick, if you ain't sowed your beans you may keep 'em in the rick.

St Catharine, Isle of Wight. *When St Catharine wears a cap, Then all the Island wears a hat.* *c.*1870: Smith, *Isle of Wight Words*, 61 (E.D.S.). **St Catherine,** 25 Nov. *As at Catherine foul or fair, so will be the next February.* 1893: Inwards, *Weather Lore*, 37.

St Chad, 2 March. *Before S. Chad every goose lays both good and bad.* 1678: Ray, 51. 1732: Fuller, 6163. 1846: Denham, *Proverbs*, 40 (Percy S.), On or before, etc. *See also* **St David;** and **St Valentine** (3).

St David, 1 March. **1. David and Chad sow pease good or bad.** 1659: Howell, 21 [omitting 'pease']. 1670: Ray, 43. 1872: J. Glyde, jr., *Norfolk Garland*, 157, Sow beans and peas on David and Chad, Be the weather good or bad. 1913: E. M. Wright, *Rustic Speech, etc.*, 290, David and Chad sow beans be the weather good or bad.

2. First comes David, next comes Chad, And then comes Winnold [3 March] **as though he was mad.** 1827: Hone, *Ev. Day Book*, ii 284 [quoted as a 'traditional West Norfolk proverbial distich']. 1830: Forby, *Vocab. E. Anglia*, 418. 1893: Inwards, *Weather Lore*, 21 ['Winneral' for 'Winnold'].

3. Upon St David's day, put oats and barley in the clay. 1678: Ray, 346. 1846: Denham, *Proverbs*, 34 (Percy S.). *See also* **St Distaff's day, Neither work nor play.** 1846: Denham, *Proverbs*, 23 (Percy S.).

St George, 23 April. *St George cries 'Goe!' St Mark* [25 April] *cries 'Hoe!'* 1893: Inwards, *Weather Lore*, 25. *See also* **Always in his saddle.**

St Gervatius, 13 May. *Who shears his sheep before St Gervatius' day loves more his wool than his sheep.* Ibid., 28.

St Giles. 1. As lame as St Giles Cripplegate. 1662: Fuller, *Worthies*, ii 349 (1840). 1790: Grose, *Prov. Gloss.*, s.v. 'London'. 1812: Brady, *Clavis Cal.*, ii 134.

2. St Giles's breed; fat, ragged and saucy. 1790: Grose, *Prov. Gloss.*, s.v. 'London'.

3. St Giles's sweat. 1869: Hazlitt, 200, He's in a St Giles's sweat. *Lancashire* … i.e. He lies in bed, while his clothes are being mended.

St Hugh's bones = a shoemaker's took. 1600: Dekker, *Shoem. Holiday*, II iii, Yonder's a brother of the gentle craft; if he bear not Saint Hugh's bones, I'll forfeit my bones. 1637: L. Price, in *Pepysian Garland*, 445 (Rollins), St Hughs bones vp we take in hast, both pinsers, punching alle and last. 1700: Ward, *London Spy*, 139 (1924), So many jolly Crispins in a garret o'er St Hugh's bones. 1825: Hone, *Ev. Day Book*, i 859. 1917: Bridge, *Cheshire Proverbs*, 109.

St Jacob, 20 July. *Clear on St Jacob's Day, plenty of fruit.* 1893: Inwards, *Weather Lore*, 32.

St James, 25 July. **1. If it be fair.** *See* quot. 1669: *New Help to Discourse*, 284, If it be fair three Sundays before St James's day, corn will be good; but wet corn will wither.

2. Till St James's day be come and gone, You may have hops, or you may have none. 1670: Ray, 44. 1732: Fuller, 6469. 1856: *N.&Q.*, 2nd ser., i 226 (Herefs.). 1893: Inwards, *Weather Lore*, 32.

3. Whoever eats oysters on St James's day will never want money. 1846: Denham, *Proverbs*, 51 (Percy S.). 1864: Chambers, *Book of Days*, ii 122.

St John, 24 June. **1. Before St John's Day we pray for rain: after that we get it anyhow.** 1893: Inwards, *Weather Lore*, 29.

2. Cut your thistles before St John, You will have two instead of one. 1830: Forby, *Vocab. E. Anglia*, 418. 1893: Inwards, 30.

3. Never rued the man That laid in his fuel before St John. 1732: Fuller, 6205.

4. Previous to St John's Day we dare not praise barley. 1893: Inwards, 29.

5. Rain on St John's Day, and we may expect a wet harvest. Ibid., 29.

St Joseph, 19 March. *Is't on St Joseph's Day clear, So follows a fertile year.* Ibid., 21.

St Jude, 28 Oct. *On St Jude's Day The oxen may play* = *wet* is expected. Ibid., 36.

St Keverne's bells, No metal will run within the sound of. Corn. 1887: M. A. Courtney, *Folk-Lore Journal*, v 22.

St Lawrence. *See* **Devil** (28); and **Lazy Lawrence**.

St Leonard's saddle [at Bromley, Essex], **A ride upon.** Spoken to a barren woman. 1659: Howell, 20.

St Leran's stone. *See* quot. 1849: Halliwell, *Pop. Rhymes and Nursery Tales*, 193, When with panniers astride A pack-horse can ride Through St Levan's stone, The world will be done.

St Luke, 18 Oct. **1. On St Luke's day. The oxen had leave to play.** 1732: Fuller, 6220.

2. St Luke's Little Summer. 1878: Dyer, *Eng. Folk-Lore*, 260. October the 30th, old St Luke's Day, often brings with it fine sunny weather, and consequently has received the name of 'St Luke's Little Summer'. 1889: Peacock, *Manley, etc.*, *Gloss.*, 455 (E.D.S.), Saint Luke's Summer. A few warm days coming together in October. 1922: Weyman, *Ovington's Bank*, ch xxii.

St Margaret, 13 Aug. *St Margaret's flood.* 1893: Inwards, *Weather Lore*, 33, St Margaret's flood is proverbial, and is considered to be well for the harvest in England.

St Mark. *See* **St George.**

St Martin, 11 Nov. **1. If the geese at Martin's day stand on ice, they will walk in mud at Christmas.** 1893: Inwards, *Weather Lore*, 37.

2. St Martin's summer, *c.*1591: Shakespeare, 1 *Henry VI*, I ii, Expect Saint Martin's summer, halcyon days. 1831: Hone, *Year-Book*, 1343, St Martin's little summer is a term for the fine days which sometimes intervene about the beginning of November. 1869: A. Dobson, in *Poet. Works*, 26 (1923), For these were yet the days of halcyon weather – A 'Martin's summer', when the nation swam ... 1921: Treves, *Riviera*, 42, In age she was just past the meridian. She was, indeed, the embodiment of St Martin's summer.

St Mary, 25 March (Annunciation). *Is't on St Mary's bright and clear, Fertile is said to be the year.* 1893: Inwards, *Weather Lore*, 21.

St Mary, 2 July (Visitation). *If it rains on St Mary's Day, it will rain for four weeks.* Ibid., 30.

St Mary Magdalene, 22 July. *See* quot. 1884: in *Folk-Lore Journal*, ii 279, Alluding to the wet usually prevalent about the middle of July, the saiyng is: – 'St Mary Magdalene is washing her handkerchief to go to her cousin St James's fair' [25 July]. Derbyshire.

St Matthew, 21 Sept. **1. Matthew's Day, bright and clear, Brings good wine in next year.** 1893: Inwards, 35.

2. St Matthee shut up the bee. 1678: Ray, 52. 1732: Fuller, 6211. 1893: Inwards, 34.

3. St Matthew brings on the cold dew. 1732: Fuller, 6212. 1893: Inwards, 34.

4. Saint Matthew get candlestick new, Saint Matthi lay candlestick by. 1830: Forby, *Vocab. E. Anglia*, 418. 1893: Inwards, 35.

St Matthias, 24 Feb. **1. If it freezes on St Matthias' Day, it will freeze for a month together.** 1893: Inwards, 17.

2. Saint Matthias both leaf and grass. 1659: Howell, 21. 1893: Inwards, 17 ['sow' before 'both'].

3. St Matthias breaks the ice; if he finds none he will make it. 1878: Dyer, *English Folk-Lore*, 253 [by a slip 'Matthew' is printed for 'Matthias']. 1893: Inwards, 17.

4. St Matthie all the year goes by. 1678: Ray, 52. 1893: Inwards, 17.

5. St Matthie sends sap into the tree. 1678: Ray, 50. 1893: Inwards, 17.

6. St Mattho take thy hopper [seed-basket] **and sow.** 1678: Ray, 52. 1893: Inwards, 17.

St Medard, 8 June. If on the 8th of June it rain, It foretells a wet harvest, men sain. Ibid., 29.

St Michael, 29 Sept. **1. A Michaelmas rot comes ne'er in the pot.** 1639: in *Berkeley MSS.*, iii 31 (1885). Michaelmas rott comes short of the pott. 1670: Ray, 44. 1732: Fuller, 6215. 1893: Inwards, 35.

2. If St Michael brings many acorns, Christmas will cover the fields with snow. Ibid., 35. *See also* **Michaelmas;** and **Moon** (13) and (17).

St Michael's Mount. *As formal as the Mount.* Newlyn, Corn. Said of an old-fashioned child. 19th cent. (Mr C. Lee).

St Paul's Cathedral. *See* **Paul's.**

St Paul's Day, 25 Jan. *If St Paul's be fine and clear, It doth betide a happy year.* 14th cent.: Robert of Avesbury, *Hist.*, 266 (Hearne), Clara dies Pauli bona tempora denotat anni. Si nix vel pluvia, designat tempora cara. Si fint nebulae, morientur bestia quaeque. Si fiant venti, praeliabunt praelia genti Before 1500: in R. Hill, *Commonplace-Book*, 134 (E.E.T.S.) [as in first two lines of preceding quotation]. 1584: R. Scot, *Witchcraft*, bk xi ch xv, If Paul th' apostles day be clear, It doth foreshew a lucky year. 1658: Willsford, *Natures Secrets*, 145, If Saint Paul's day be fair and clear, It does betide a happy year; But if it chance to snow or rain Then will be clear all kinds of grain: If clouds or mists do dark the skie, Great store of birds and beasts shall die: And if the winds do fly aloft, Then wars shall vex that kingdome oft. 1725: Bourne, *Antiq. Vulgares*, 160 [a shorter version of 1658 quot.]. 1753: *World*, No. 10 [much as in 1658, but omitting the 'clouds or mists' lines]. 1866: *N.&Q.*, 3rd ser, ix. 118, To-day, January 25, has been a lovely day, sunny and mild. A Huntingdonshire cottager said to me: 'We shall have a fine spring, Sir. There is an old proverb that says: "If Paul's day is fine, it will be a fine spring." ' 1893: Inwards, *Weather Lore*, 12 [a slightly varied version of 1658 quot.].

St Peter le Poor, Where's no tavern, alehouse, or sign at the door. 1662: Fuller, *Worthies*, ii 345 (1840), St Peter's in the poor, Where, etc. 1790: Grose, *Prov. Gloss.*, s.v. 'London'.

St Peter's Day, 29 June. 1. If it rains on St Peter's Day, the bakers will have to carry double flour and single water; if dry, they will carry single flour and double water. 1893: Inwards, *Weather Lore*, 30.

2. Peter and Paul will rot the roots of the rye. Ibid., 30.

St Peter's needle, To go through = To have serious misfortune. 1917: Bridge, *Cheshire Proverbs*, 134.

St Pratt's little summer = the fine weather that often occurs at the beginning of autumn. 'St Pratt' = St Protasius, patron saint of Blisland, N. Corn. 1908: Heard by Mr C. Lee.

St Robert gave his cow, As freely as. 1670: Ray, 208.

St Stephen, 26 Dec. 1. Blessed be St Stephen, There's no fast upon his even. 1659: Howell, 21. 1670: Ray, 146. 1846: Denham, *Proverbs*, 66 (Percy S.). 1925: *Church Times*, 24 Dec., 755. col. 1., The old proverb is still remembered: – Blessed be, etc.

2. If you bleed your nag on St Stephen's-day, He'll work your wark far ever and ay! 1528: More, *Works*, p. 194, col. 2 (1557), On saint Stephens day we must let al our horses bloud with a knife, because saynt Stephen was Killed with stones. 1687: Aubrey, *Gentilisme*, 27 (F.L.S.), On St Stephen's day the farrier came

constantly and blouded all the cart-horses, etc. 1744: *Tusser Redivivus*, 148, About Christmas is a very proper time to bleed horses in. 1846: Denham, *Proverbs*, 66 (Percy S.). 1904: *Co. Folk-lore: Northumb.*, 179 (F.L.S.).

St Swithin, 15 July. 1. If it rains on St Swithin's it will rain for forty days. 1599: Jonson, *Ev. Man Out of Humour*, I, O here, St Swithin's ... why it should rain forty days after. 1639: Taylor (Water-Poet), *Part of Summers Travels*, 5, in *Works*, 1st coll. (Spens.S.), Upon Saint Swithin's day, I noted well The wind was calme, nor any rain then fell, Which faire day (as old sawes saith) doth portend, That heav'n to earth, will plenteous harvest send. 1716: Gay, *Trivia*, bk i l. 183, How, if on Swithin's feast the welkin lowers, And ev'ry penthouse streams with hasty showers. Twice twenty days shall clouds their fleeces drain. 1846: Denham, *Proverbs*, 52 (Percy S.), St Swithin's day, if thou dost rain. For forty days it will remain: St Swithin's day, if thou be fair, For forty days 'twill rain na mair.

2. St Swithin is christening the apples. 1813: Brand, *Pop. Antiq.*, i 342 (Ellis, 1895), There is an old saying that when it rains on St Swithin's Day, it is the Saint christening the apples. 1825: Hone, *Ev. Day Book*, i 960. 1893: Inwards, *Weather Lore*, 31. 1912: R. L. Gales, *Studies in Arcady*, 2nd ser, 106.

See also **St Bartholomew.**

St Thomas, 21 Dec. 1. St Thomas gray, St Thomas gray, the longest night, and the shortest day. 1859: *N.&Q.*, 2nd ser, viii, 242.

2. The day of St Thomas, the blessed divine, Is good for brewing, baking, and killing fat swine. 1846: Denham, *Proverbs*, 64 (Percy S.).

St Valentine, 14 Feb. 1. On St Valentine all the birds of the air in couples do join. *c.*1380: Chaucer, *Parl. of Foules*, l. 309, For this was on seynt Valentynes day, Whan every foul cometh ther to chese his make. 1477: *Paston Letters*, iii 169 (Gairdner), And, cosyn, upon Fryday is Sent Volentynes Day, and every brydde chesyth hym a make. 1621: B.&F., *Thierry and Theod.*, III i, When you hear the birds call for their mates, Ask if it be Saint Valentine, their coupling day. *c.*1673: *Roxb. Ballads*, vii 114 (B.S.), There is an old proverb, that 'Birds of a feather Upon St Valentine's Day will meet all together'. 1714: Gay, *Shep. Week*, Thursday, l. 37, Last Valentine, the day when birds of kind

Their paramours with mutual chirpings find. 1828: Scott, *Fair Maid*, ch ii, To-morrow is Saint Valentine's Day, when every bird chooses her mate. 1830: Forby, *Vocab. E. Anglia*, 418.

2. On St Valentine's Day cast beans in clay, But on St Chad sow good and bad. 1639: in *Berkeley MSS.*, iii 33 (1885). 1868: *N. & Q.*, 4th ser, i 361, [Huntingdonshire cottager *loq.*] On Saint Valentine's day, Beans should be in the clay. 1913: E. M. Wright, *Rustic Speech, etc.*, 290, In Rutland there is an old saying: Valentine's Day, sow your beans in the clay.

3. On Valentine's day Will a good goose lay; If she be a good goose, her dame well to pay, She will lay two eggs before Valentine's day. 1678: Ray, 51. 1732: Fuller, 6488. 1882: Mrs Chamberlain, *W. Worcs. Words*, 37 (E.D.S.), By Valentine's day every good goose should lay; But by David and Chad both good and bad.

4. St Valentine set thy hopper [seed-basket] **by mine.** 1678: Ray, 52. 1893: Inwards, *Weather Lore*, 17.

5. To St Valentine the spring is a neighbour. 1659: Howell, *Proverbs: Fr.-Eng.*, 21. 1882: Mrs Chamberlain, *W. Worcs. Words*, 37 (E.D.S.).

See also **Candlemas, E;** and **March** (22).

St Vincent, 22 Jan. *See* quot. 1584: R. Scot, *Witchcraft*, bk xi ch xv, Vincenti festo si sol radiet memor esto. Remember on St Vincent's day. If that the sun his beames display. 1876: *N. & Q.*, 5th ser, v 146, [as in 1584, *plus*]' Tis a token, bright and clear, That you will have a prosperous year.

St Vitus, 15 June. **1. If St Vitus's day be rainy weather, It will rain for thirty days together.** 1846: Denham, *Proverbs*, 49 (Percy S.). 1893: Inwards, *Weather Lore*, 29.

2. Oh! St Vitus, do not rain, so that we may not want barley. Ibid., 29.

Salad. 1. A good salad may be the prologue to a bad supper. 1670: Ray, 139 ['is' for 'may be']. 1732: Fuller, 174.

2. He that sups upon salad goes not to bed fasting. Ibid., No. 2322.

See also Wine (2).

Salisbury Plain is seldom without a thief or twain. 1659: Howell, 17. *c.*1685: Aubrey, *Nat. Hist. Wilts*, 69 (1847) ['never' for 'is seldom']. 1790: Grose, *Prov. Gloss.*, s.v. 'Wilts'. 1908: W. Johnson, *Folk Memory*, 280, Nor, save 'a thief or twain ' … were there any signs of human life [on Salisbury Plain a century ago].

Sally Hatch, Dressed to death, like. 1864: 'Cornish Proverbs', in *N. & Q.*, 3rd ser, vi 6.

Salmon and sermon have both their season in Lent 1659: Howell, *Proverbs: Fr.-Eng.*, 21, Salmons and sermons have their seasons in Lent. 1666: Torriano, *Piazza Univ.*, 246, A sammon and a sermon come much of a season. 1670: Ray, 23. 1917: Bridge, *Cheshire Proverbs*, 106.

Salmon. *See also* **Hook.**

Salt, *adj. Salt cooks bear blame, but fresh bear shame.* 1670: Ray, 73. 1732: Fuller, 6300.

Salt, *subs.* **1. Help me to salt, help me to sorrow.** 1872: J. Glyde, jr., *Norfolk Garland*, 44. 1879: Henderson, *Folk-Lore of N. Counties*, 121. 1883: Burne, *Shropsh. Folk-Lore*, 278. 1910: *N. & Q.*, 11th ser, ii 198.

2. Not worth (or **Worth**) **one's salt.** [Non valet lotium suum. – Petr., 57.] 1830: Marryat, *King's Own*, ch lii, The captain … is not worth his salt. 1883: R.L.S., *Treasure I*, ch xviii, It was plain from every line of his body that our new hand was worth his salt.

3. Of all smells, bread; of all tastes, salt. 1591: Florio, *Second Frutes*, 53, Salt no sauour, God no greater. 1640: Herbert, *Jac. Prudentum.* 1666: Torriano, *Piazza Univ.*, 70, Above salt there's no savour.

4. Salt seasons all things. 1591: Florio, *Second Frutes*, 53, Salt sauoureth, and seasoneth all things. 1659: Howdl. 9.

5. To put salt on a bird's tail. 1580: Lyly, *Euphues and England*, 327 (Arber), It is … a foolish bird that staieth the laying salt on hir taile. 1654: Gayton, *Pleasant Notes Don Q.*, 203, To catch regall birds, by laying salt upon their tailes. 1704: Swift, *Tale of a Tub*, § vii, As boys [catch] sparrows with flinging salt upon their tails. 1806: Lamb, *Mr H –*, II, My name is Finch – Betty Finch … you can't catch me by throwing salt on my tail. 1858: Dickens, *Great Expect.*, ch iv, Plenty of subjects going about, for them that know how to put salt upon their tails.

See also **Black,** *subs.* (1); **Bushel;** and **Neither sugar.**

Salve for every sore, There's a. 1542: *Sch. House of Women*, l. 401, A salue there is for euery sore. 1566: Gascoigne. *Supposes*, II i 1639: Clarke, 15. 1762: Smollett, *Sir L. Greaves*, ch xv, You must have a little patience, Crabshaw – there's a salve for every sore. 1913: *Folk-Lore*, xxiv. 76 (Oxon.).

Salve where you got your sore, Seek your.
1732: Fuller, 4090.

Sam Babb's pig *See* quot. 1925: *Devon and Cornwall N. & Q.*, xiii 206, Like Sam Babb's pig, live 'pon nothing and get fat in a minute: he had water-crease broth all the week and essence o' whip 'pon Sundays (North Cornwall).

Same boat, To be in the. [ταῦτ' ἐμοὶ ζυγὸν τρίβεις. – Herodas, vi 12.] *c*.1594: Bacon, *Promus*, No. 740, You are in the same shippe. 1710: E. Ward, *Nuptial Dialogues*, ii 360, Therefore the sinner, and the saint, Are often in the selfsame boat. 1836: Marryat, *Japhet*, ch lxvi, Well, I will row in the same boat, and I will be a Quaker as well as you both. 1922: Weyman, *Ovington's Bank*, ch xiii, Oh, he's quite right to speak his mind. We are all in the same boat – though we do not all steer.

Same knife cuts bread and fingers, The. 1633: Draxe, 223, The same knife cutteth bread and a mans finger. 1659: Howell, *Proverbs: Span.-Eng.*, 19, The same knife cuts my bread and my finger.

Sammy Dawkin. *See* quot. 1880: Courtney, *W. Cornwall Words*, 48 (E.D.S.), You are a regular Sammy Dawkin, can't scull a boat. A Padstow proverb.

Samson than of Solomon in him, There is more of. 1830: Forby, *Vocab. E. Anglia*, 430.

Samson was a strong man, but he could not pay money before he had it. 1659: Howell, 11 (9), Salomon was a wise man, and Sampson was a strong man, yet neither of them could pay money till they had it. 1732: Fuller, 4066. 1869: Spurgeon, *John Ploughman*, ch xii.

Sand and day. *See* **England** (12).

Sandbach. *See* quot. 1917: Bridge, *Cheshire Proverbs*, 163, A wind from Sandbach in the East, Blows good to neither man nor beast.

Sandwich. *See* **Deal.**

Sandwich Bay (or **Haven**), **Conscience is drowned in**. 1735: Pegge, *Kent. Proverbs*, in E.D.S., No. 12, p. 74 [an explanatory story].

Sap and heart are the best of wood. 1917: Bridge, *Cheshire Proverbs*, 106.

Sarum, Secundum usum. 1589: *Pap with a Hatchet*, 17 (1844), And for the winter nights the tales should be told *secundum Vsum Sarum*. 1655: Fuller, *Church Hist.*, bk iii § i (23), Henceforward the most ignorant parish priest ... understood the meaning of *secundum usum Sarum*, that all service must be ordered 'according to the course and custom of Salisbury church'. *c*.1685: Aubrey, *Nat. Hist. Wilts*, 95 (1847), The consistorie of this church [Salisbury] was as eminent for learning as any in England, and the choire had the best method: hence came the saying *secundum usum Sarum*. 1790: Grose, *Prov. Gloss.*, s.v. 'Wilts', It is done, *secundum usum Sarum*.

Satan. *See* **Devil.**

Saturday. 1. A fine Saturday, a fine Sunday, A fine Sunday, a fine week. 1893: *Co. Folk-lore: Suffolk*, 163 (F.L.S.).

2. Saturday's flit trill never sit. 1851: Sternberg, *Dialect of Northants* 169, Thus the saying – Saturday servants never stay, Sunday servants run away. 1854: Baker, *Northants Gloss.*, s.v. 'Flit', 'Saturday's flit will never sit', is a proverb of prediction with superstitious servants, who reluctantly enter upon a new service on that day. 1917: Bridge, *Cheshire Proverbs*, 107, Saturday's fittings, Light sittings. Cf. **Monday** (2).

3. There is never a Saturday without some sunshine. 1866: *New Suffolk Garland*, 166, There is also a saying that 'the sun is always seen on a Saturday', and this is firmly believed by many of the country people. 1893: Inwards, *Weather Lore*, 43.

4. This is silver Saturday, The morn's the resting day; On Monday up and to't again, And Tuesday push away. 1846: Denham, *Proverbs*, 18 (Percy S.).

See also **Friday** (2); and **Moon** (3).

Sauce before you have caught the fish, Make not your. 1732: Fuller, 3324

Sauce for the goose is sauce for the gander, What is. *See* **Goose** (32).

Save, *verb*. 1. He that saveth his dinner will have the more for supper. 1639: Clarke, 241. 1670 Ray, 79 1732: Fuller, 2288.

2. He would save the droppings of his nose. 1567: Painter, *Pal. of Pleasure*, iii 299 (Jacobs), As vsurers do God knowes, Who cannot spare the dropping of their nose. 1602: J. Cooke, *How a Man may choose Good Wife*, sig. G3, It is such an old snudge, he will not loose the dropping of his nose. 1754: Berthelson, *Eng.-Danish Dict.*, s.v. 'Droppings'. 1828: Carr, *Craven Dialect*, i 119, 'He wad save the vara droppings of his nose', spoken of a penurious person.

3. Save a thief from the gallows, and he'll cut your throat, *c*.1440: Lydgate, *Fall of Princes*, bk vi l. 3253, Who saueth a theef whan the rop is knet Aboute his nekke, as olde clerkis write, With sum fals tourn the bribour wil hym quite. 1484: Caxton, *Aesope*, ii 15 (Jacobs), For as men sayen comynly yf ye kepe a man fro the galhows he shalle neuer loue you after. 1583: Melbancke, *Philotinus*, sig. X4, True is the prouerbe, saue a thief from the gallowes, and he will be the firste shall doe thee a mischiefe. 1622: Massinger, *Virgin Martyr*, II iii, She saved us from the gallows, and, only to keep one proverb from breaking his neck, we'll hang her. Before 1704: T. Brown, in *Works*, ii 290 (1760). 1771: Smollett, *Clinker*, in *Works*, vi 177 (1817). 1820: Scott, *Monastery*, ch x, 'Save a thief from the gallows,' said the Sacristan – 'you know the rest of the proverb.'

4. Save at the spigot and let out at the bung-hole. 1670: Ray, 193 ['Spare' for 'Save']. 1710: S. Palmer, *Moral Essays on Proverbs*, 288. 1754: Berthelson, *Eng.-Danish Dict.*, s.v. 'Spare', To spare at the spigot and let it run out of the bung-hole. 1869: Spurgeon, *John Ploughman*, ch xvi [as in 1754]. 1883: Burne, *Shropsh. Folk-Lore*, 590 ['waste' for 'let out'].

5. Save me from my friends. *See* **God defend me.**

6. Save something for the man that rides on the white horse. 1639: Clarke, 129. 1670: Ray, 139. 1732: Fuller, 4068.

7. Save your breath. *See* **Breath.**

8. To save a snuff he throws away whole candles. 1864: 'Cornish Proverbs', in *N.&Q.*, 3rd ser, iv 495.

9. To save one's bacon. 1682: A. Behn, *City Heiress*, I i, I go [to church] to save my bacon, as they say, once a month. 1729: Fielding, *Author's Farce*, III iii, No tricks shall save your bacon. 1742: North, *Lives of Norths*, ii 193 (Bohn). 1829: in Farmer, *Musa Pedestris*, III, I cuts and runs and saves my bacon.

See also **Penny** (8), (21).

Saving cometh having, Of. 1633: Draxe, 196. 1670: Ray, 139. 1732: Fuller, 6102. 1829: Scott, *Journal*, April 20, It is saving, not getting, that is the mother of riches.

Saving is getting. 1666: Torriano, *Piazza Univ.*, 265, Saving is the first getting. 1732: Fuller, 4069. 1828: Carr, *Craven Dialect*, i 3, Saving's good addlin. 1855: Robinson, *Whitby Gloss*, 2 [as in 1828].

Saving must equal having, *i.e.* you must make both ends meet. 1851: *Gloucester Gloss.*, 14.

Sawtrey, by the way, Now a grange, that was an abbey. 1568: in *Loseley MSS.* 212 (Kempe).

Say, *verb.* **1. Better say nothing than not to the purpose.** 1693: Penn, *Fruits of Solitude*, No. 132. 1732: Fuller, 921.

2. He cannot say his Paternoster. 1552: Latimer, *Sermons*, 389 (P.S.), When we be disposed to despise a man … we say, 'He cannot say his Paternoster'.

3. He grants enough that says nothing. 1611: Cotgrave, s.v. 'Octroyer', He that sayes nothing yields enough. 1623: Wodroephe, *Spared Houres*, 476.

4. He says anything but his prayers, and them he whistles. 1732: Fuller, 2014. 1738: Swift, *Polite Convers.*, Dial. I, Miss will say anything but her prayers, and those she whistles.

5. He who says what he likes shall hear what he does not like. 1539: Taverner, *Proverbs*, fo. 2, He that speaketh what he woll, shall heare what he woll not. 1583: Melbancke, *Philotinus*, sig. Y1, Since they say what they liste, they shall heare what they list not. 1666: Torriano, *Piazza Univ.*, 319, Who says what he lists, hears what is against his will. 1732: Fuller, 6303, He that speaks the thing he should not, Shall hear the thing he would not. 1853: Trench, *Proverbs*, 82 (1905).

6. I will say no more till the day be longer. 1562: Heywood, *Three Hund. Epigr.*, No. 168.

7. I will say nought but mum. 1659: Howell, 7.

8. Say as men say, but think to yourself. 1639: Clarke, 327.

9. Say little but think the more, *c.*1430: Lydgate, *Minor Poems*, 155 (Percy S.), Take no quarelle, thynk mekyl and sey nought, *c.*1490: *Partonope*, 84 (E.E.T.S.), He seyyth butte lytell, butte more thynckyth he. *c.*1535: *Pain of Evil Marriage*, 22 (Percy S.), Therfore thynke moche and saye nought. *c.*1600: Deloney, *Thos. of Reading*, ch 5, Vpon these words away went her husband, and though he said little, hee thought more. *c.*1640: in *Roxb. Ballads*, ii 97 (Hindley), And though he said little, yet he thought the more. 1678: Ray, 82, Though he saith nothing, he pays it with thinking, like the Welchmans jackdaw. 1738: Swift, *Polite Convers.*, Dial. I, Miss says nothing; but I warrant she pays it off with thinking. 1836: Marryat, *Easy*, ch xiv, As for Jack, he said nothing, but he thought the more. 1886: Swainson, *Folk-Lore of Brit. Birds*, 82 (F.L.S.) [as in 1678].

10. Say nay. *See* **Maid** (11).

11. Say no ill of the year till it be past. 1640: Herbert, *Jac. Prudentum.* 1732: Fuller, 4071. 1846: Denham, *Proverbs*, 1 (Percy S.).

12. Say nothing when you are dead, i.e. be silent. 1678: Ray, 82.

13. Say still no, an' ye'll ne'er be married. 1738: Swift, *Polite Convers.*, Dial. I, But if you always say no, you'll never be married. 1869: Hazlitt, 328.

14. Say well is good but do well is better. 1536: in *Brit. Bibliog.*, iv. 283 (1814), Men say wel that do wel. *c.*1550: *Six Ballads*, 6 (Percy S., No. 50). 1639: Clarke, 194, Say well and do well, end with a letter, Say well is good, but do well is better. 1640: Brome, *Sparagus Garden*, IV xi 1732: Fuller, 6447 [as in 1639]. *c.*1791: Pegge, *Derbicisms*, 137 (E.D.S.). 1852: FitzGerald, *Polonius*, 136 (1903) [as in 1639].

15. Say well or be still, *c.*1480: *Early Miscell.*, 63 (Warton Cl., 1855), Ewyre say wylle, or hold the[e] styll. Before 1529: Skelton, in *Works*, i 17 (Dyce), A prouerbe of old, say well or be styll.

16. Say you saw me not. *c.*1520: Stanbridge, *Vulgaria*, sig. C2, Yf ony man aske for me saye thou sawest me not. 1672: Walker, *Paroem.*, 19, Say you saw it not. 1681: Robertson, *Phraseol. Generalis*, 1097.

17. To say his prayers backward. 1678: Ray, 265. 1846–59: *Denham Tracts*, ii 84 (F.L.S.), Ye're like a witch, ye say your prayers backward.

18. You say true, will you swallow my knife? 1678: Ray, 255.

See also **Said**; and **So said**.

Saying and doing are two things. 1546: Heywood, *Proverbs*, Pt II ch v 1572: T. Wilson, *Disc, upon Usury*, 249 (1925), To saye and doe are twoe thynges. 1678: Bunyan, *Pilgr. Progr.*, Pt I 82 (1849), I see that saying and *doing* are two things, and hereafter I shall better observe this distinction. 1712: Motteux, *Quixote*, Pt II ch xxxiv. 1787: O'Keeffe, *The Farmer*, I ii 1869: Spurgeon, *John Ploughman*, ch xx.

Scabbed. *See* **Cuckoo** (2).

Scabbed horse abides no comb, A. *c.*1430: *Pilgr. Lyf. Manhode*, II civ. 114 (1869) (OED), For riht as a scabbed beste hateth hors comb. 1611: Davies (of Hereford), *Sc. of Folly*, 50, in

Works, ii (Grosart). 1732: Fuller, 1639, Gall'd horses can't endure the comb. 1869: Spurgeon, *John Ploughman*, ch iii, If any of you get cross over it, I shall tell you that sore horses cannot bear to be combed.

Scabbed horse is good enough for a scald squire, A. 1540: Palsgrave, *Acolastus*, sig. M2, For suche a scalde squier as he is, a scabbed horse. 1562: Heywood, *Three Hund. Epigr.*, No. 161. 1732: Fuller, 385 ['scabbed knight' for 'scald squire']. 1736: Bailey, *Dict*, s.v. 'Squire' ['shabby' for 'scald']. Cf. **Scald horse.**

Scabbed sheep. *See* **Sheep** (10).

Scabby heads love not the comb. 1623: Wodroephe, *Spared Houres*, 516, A scabbed head doth never loue the combe. 1732: Fuller, 4072. 1801: Wolcot, in *Works*, v 369 (1801), But George disliketh much to hear About his Scottish home; Thus *scabby heads*, the proverb says, For ever hate a *comb*.

Scald head is soon broken, A. Before 1500: in Hill, *Commonplace-Book*, 130 (E.E.T.S.), *A* skalde manis hede is sone brokyn. 1598: Meres, *Palladis*, fo. 302. 1621: Burton, *Melancholy*, III iii 6, 2, p. 589 (1836). 1683: Meriton, *Yorkshire Ale*, 83–7 (1697), A scauld head is seaun broken.

Scald horse is good enough for a scabbed squire, A. 1546: Heywood, *Proverbs*, Pt I ch xi *c.*1580: Fulwell, *Ars Adulandi*, sig. F4, A ragged colte may serue a scabbed squire. 1681: Robertson, *Phraseol. Generalis*, 1098. Cf. **Scabbed horse.**

Scald not your lips in another man's pottage. 1598: *Servingmans Comfort*, in *Inedited Tracts*, 99 (Hazlitt), It is not good to scalde ones lyppes in other mens pottage. 1696: D'Urfey, *Quixote*, Pt III Act II sc ii 1710: S. Palmer, *Moral Essays on Proverbs*, 355. *c.*1800: J. Trusler, *Prov. in Verse*, 58. 1823: Scott, *St Ronan's*, ch viii, I can tell you, Mr Meiklewham … that you are scalding your lips in other folks' kale.

Scandal will rub out like dirt when it is dry. 1732: Fuller, 4076.

Scarborough. *See* **Oliver's Mount.**

Scarborough warning, A = no warning at all. 1546: Heywood, *Proverbs*, Pt I ch xi, Scarbrough warnyng I had (quoth he). *c.*1550–70: in Hindley, *Old Book-Coll. Miscell.*, i 40, This terme, Scarborow warnyng, grew (some say) By hasty hangyng, for rank robbry theare. 1589: Puttenham, *Eng. Poesie*, 199 (Arber). 1593: G.

Harvey, *Works*, ii 225 (Grosart), He meaneth not to come vpon me with a cowardly stratageme of Scarborough warning. 1662: Fuller, *Worthies*, iii 398 (1840). 1790: Grose, *Prov. Gloss.*, s.v. 'Yorkshire'. 1824: Scott, *Redgauntlet*, ch xx, The true man for giving Scarborough warning, first knock you down, then bid you stand. 1913: E. M. Wright, *Rustic Speech*, *etc.*, 189, A Scarborough warning signifies no warning at all. The origin of the saying rests on the statement that in 1557 Thomas Stafford entered and took possession of Scarborough Castle before the townsmen were aware of his approach. [The occurrence of the phrase in 1546, *vide supra*, disproves this theory.]

Scarce of horses. *See* **Horse** (67).

Scarce of news who told that his father was hanged, He was. 1732: Fuller, 2378. 1852: FitzGerald, *Polonius*, 40 (1903), He was scant o' news wha tauld his father was hanged.

Scatter with one hand, gather with two. 1659: Howell, *Proverbs: Brit.-Eng.*, 2.

Sceptre is one thing and a ladle another, A. 1640: Herbert, *Jac. Prudentum*. 1670: Ray, 23. 1732: Fuller, 386.

Schemes of mice and men, The best-laid. *See* **Best** (22).

Schemey must louster, He that can't. 1869: Hazlitt, 482, Yeker that can't scheme must louster. *S. Devon and Cornwall.* 1879: *Folk–Lore Record*, ii 203 (Cornwall). 1913: *Devonsh. Assoc. Trans.*, xlv 291, A common proverb in Devon is, 'He that can't schemey must louster', meaning that he who cannot work with his head must work with his hands. Cf. **Work**, *verb* (3).

Scholar, A mere, a mere ass. 1639: Clarke, 151. 1659: Howell, 3. 1703: Centlivre, *Stolen Heiress*, I, A meer scholar is a meer – you know the old proverb, father. 1732: Fuller, 322, A mere scholar at Court is an ass among apes.

Scholar as my horse Ball, As good a. 1639: Clarke, 145.

Scholar may be gulled thrice, a soldier but once, A. 1659: Howell, *Proverbs: Brit.-Eng.*, 11.

Scholar teacheth his master, The. 1639: Clarke, 4.

Schoolboys. *See* quot. 1678: Ray, 81, School-boys are the reasonablest people in the world, they care not how little they have for their money.

School-butter = a flogging. 1604: *Pasquils Jests*, 24 (1864), An unhappy boy, willing to have one

of his fellowes taste of such schoole-butter as hee had often broke his fast with. 1607: R. West, *Court of Conscience*, sig. D4, [Whipper says] When thou hast tasted some of my schoole-butter, Thy limmes will be so hethy thou wilt leap. 1618: B.&F., *Loyal Subject*, V iv, He was whipt like a top … court school-butter? Is this their diet? 1690: *New Dict. Canting Crew*, sig. K8, School-butter, a whipping.

Scilly, Always a feast or a fast in. 1750: R. Heath, *Acc. of Scilly*, 53, Verifying the proverb, *A feast or a famine in Scilly*. 1864: 'Cornish Proverbs', in *N. & Q.*, 3rd ser, v 275. 1887: M. A. Courtney, *Folk-Lore Journal*, v 38.

Scilly ling is a dish for a king, A. 1864: 'Cornish Proverbs', in *N. & Q.*, 3rd ser, v 208. 1928: *Times*, 25 Sept., p. 10, col. 5.

Scoggin's a doctor, Among the common people. 1639: Clarke, 143. 1670: Ray, 140.

Scold, *subs. Who hath a scold hath sorrow to his sops.* 1659: Howell, 15. 1670: Ray, 23. 1732: Fuller, 5705. Cf. **Sorrow**.

Scold like a cutpurse, To. 1678: Ray, 288.

Scold like a wych-waller [salt-boiler], **To.** 1670; Ray, 208. 1790: Grose, *Prov. Gloss.*, s.v. 'Cheshire'. 1836: Wilbraham, *Cheshire Gloss.*, 91 (2nd ed.) … is a common adage. 1917: Bridge, *Cheshire Proverbs*, 142.

Scold the devil, To. *See* **Devil** (34).

Score twice before you cut once = Look before you leap. 1688: Holme, *Acad. of Armory*, bk iii cap. vi p. 292, The point on the back of the shoemaker's pareing knife is to score or trace out the leather before he venture to cut it, according to the saying score twice before you cut once, else they will cut themselves out of doors. 1917: Bridge, *Cheshire Proverbs*, 107.

Scorn at first makes after-love the more. 1855: Bohn, 482.

Scornful dogs will eat dirty puddings. 1709: Mandeville, *Virgin Unmask'a* 32 (1724), Dirty puddings for dirty dogs. 1738: Swift, *Polite Convers.*, Dial. I. 1816: Scott, *Antiquary*, ch xliii, The messenger (one of those dogs who are not too scornful to eat dirty paddings) … 1824: Scott, *Redgauntlet*, ch xii Cf. **Hungry dogs.**

Scorning it catching, [*c.*1440: Lydgate, *Fall of Princes*, bk iii l. 601 (E.E.T.S.), For it was said sithen go ful yore, He that reioishith to scorne folk in veyn, Whan he wer lothest shal scorned been ageyn.] 1670: Ray, 140. 1732: Fuller, 4081.

1754: Berthelson, *Eng.-Danish Dict.*, s.v. 'Scornfully', After scorning comes catching.

Scot, *subs.* **1. A Scot, a rat, and a Newcastle grindstone, travel all the world over.** 1662: Fuller, *Worthies,* ii 543 (1840), A Scottishman and a Newcastle grindstone, travel all the world over. 1790: Grose, *Prov. Gloss.,* s.v. 'Northumberland'. 1821: in Lockhart, *Life of Scott,* v 99, The old saying, – in every corner of the world you will find a Scot, a rat, and a Newcastle grindstone. 1846–59: *Denham Tracts,* i 301 (F.L.S.).

2. A Scot on Scots bank. 1678: Ray, 81.

3. The Scot will not fight till he see his own blood. 1822: Scott, *Nigel,* ch i.

4. We will not lose a Scot. 1662: Fuller, *Worthies,* ii 542 (1840). 1790: Grose, *Prov. Gloss.,* s.v. 'Northumberland' ['He' for 'We']. 1846–59: *Denham Tracts,* i 248 (F.L.S.), We will not lose a Scot. That is anything, however inconsiderable, which we can possibly save or recover.

See also **Hard-hearted.**

Scotch ordinary, The = The house of office. 1678: Ray, 81.

Scottish mist will wet an Englishman to the skin, A. 1589: *Pap with a Hatchet,* Dedn., We care not for a Scottish mist, though it wet to the skin. 1639: Clarke, 11 ['may' for 'will']. 1641: in *Harl. Miscell.,* iii 228 (1744). 1681: Robertson, *Phraseol. Generalis,* 1100 [as in 1639]. 1732: Fuller, 388 [as in 1639] 1814: Scott, *Waverley,* ch xxv, To beware of Scotch mists, which, she had heard, would wet an Englishman through and through. 1872: J. Glyde, jr., *Norfolk Garland,* 150.

Scottish warming-pan, A = A wench. 1678: Ray, 83. 1685: S. Wesley, *Maggots,* 36, 'Twould better heat a man Than two Bath faggots or Scotch warming-pan. Note. – Scotch warming-pan is the hostesses brown daughter. 1785: Grose, *Class. Dict. Vulgar Tongue,* s.v. 'Warming-pan'. 1826: Brady, *Varieties of Lit.,* 40 … This saying arose from the well-known story of a gentleman travelling in Scotland, who, desiring to have his bed warmed, the servant-maid immediately undressed herself and lay down in it for a while.

Scrambling at a rich man's dole, 'Tis brave. 1639: Clarke, 39. 1670: Ray, 136. 1732: Fuller, 5069.

Scrape and save. *See* quot. 15th cent.: in *Reliq. Antiquae,* i 316 (1841), Kype [Scrape] and save, and thou schalle have; Frest [Lend] and leve, and thou schall crave; Walow and wast, and thou schalle want.

Scratch a beggar before you die, You'll = You will be a beggar. 1639: Clarke, 209, You'l scratch a begger one day. 1670: Ray, 164. 1732: Fuller, 6035.

Scratch a grey head, He will never. 1738: Swift, *Polite Convers.,* Dial. III, I think the countess is very sickly. *Lady Smart.* Yes, madam; she'll never scratch a gray head. 1901: F. E. Taylor, *Lancs Sayings,* 30, He'll never live for t' scrat a grey yed.

Scratch a Russian and you'll find a Tartar. Found more commonly with variant words put in the framework *Scratch a … and you'll find a … (underneath).* This proverb is one of many sayings commonly attributed to Napoleon. The sense is that what a person claims to be may be different from what that person is beneath the surface. 1823: J. Gallatin, *Diary,* 2 Jan (1914), 229, Very true the saying is, 'Scratch the Russian and find the Tartar'. *c.*1863: J. R. Green in *Notes and Queries* (1965) They say if you scratch a Russian you always find the Tartar underneath. 1899: F.A. Ober, *Puerto Rico,* xii, Scratch a Puerto Rican and you find a Spaniard underneath, so the language and home customs of Spain prevail here. 1911: *Spectator,* 2 Dec., 964, Until a short time ago the aphorism, 'Scratch a Russian and you find a Tartar', was the sum of British comprehension of the Russian character.

Scratches his head with one finger, He. 1855: Bonn, 381.

Scratching. *See* **Cat** (14).

Scratch me and I'll scratch thee. [Mutuum muli scabant. – Auson., *Idyll.,* xii, Praef. Monos.] 1611: Cotgrave, s.v. 'Contrelouër', To scratch the back of one who hath already clawed his elbow. 1694: D'Urfey, *Quixote,* Pt II, Act II sc ii, Scratch my back and I'll claw your elbow. 1706: E. Ward, *Works,* iii 145, Scratch me, says one, and I'll scratch thee. Cf. **Claw** (2); and **Ka me.**

Scratch my back and I'll scratch yours, You. The familiar modern form of the previous entry. 1858: 'A. Ward', *Letter,* 27 Jan, in *Maine: Guide 'Down East'* (1937), III 363, You scratch my back and I will scratch your back. 1961: J. Heller, *Catch 22* (1962), iv. 33, A little grease is what makes the world go round. One hand washes the other. Know what I mean? You scratch my back, I'll scratch yours.

Scratch where it does not itch, To. *c.*1510: A. Barclay, *Egloges*, 30 (Spens.S.), I clawe oft where it doth not itche. 1546: Heywood, *Proverbs*, Pt II ch vii, Thou makest me claw where it itcheth not. 1578: Whetstone, *Promos and Cass.* sig. D3, And straight (through feare) where he clawes it doth not ytch. 1639–61: in *Rump Songs*, Pt II 7 (1662, repr. 1874), 'Twould make a man scratch where it does not itch, To see … 1680: Shadwell, *Woman Captain*, I *ad fin.*, 'Twould make one scratch where't does not itch, To see fools live poor to die rich. 1737: Ray, 232 [as in 1680 with very slight variation].

Scythe. *See* quot. 1846: Denham, *Proverbs*, 17 (Percy S.), Where the scythe cuts, and the plough rives, No more fairies and bee-bikes [nests].

Sea complains it wants water, The. 1639: Clarke, 6. 1670: Ray, 192. 1732: Fuller, 4740, The sea complains for want of water.

Sea hath fish for every man, The. 1605: Camden, *Remains*, 334 (1870).

Sea refuses no river, The. 1614: T. Gentleman, *England's Way to win Wealth*, 45 (*marginal note*), The Sailors Proverbe: The Sea and the Gallowes refuse none. 1703: E. Ward, *Writings*, ii 142, The old proverb, The sea and the gallows refuses none. 1732: Fuller, 4741.

Sea, sail, Being on; being on land, settle. 1640: Herbert, *Jac. Prudentum.* 1670: Ray, 23.

Sea. *See also* **Praise the sea.**

Sealed with butter. 1546: Heywood, *Proverbs*, Pt II ch vii, Euery promise that than therin dost vtter Is as sure as it were sealed with butter. 1584: R. Scot, *Witchcraft*, bk ni ch iv, Surely the indentures, containing those covenants, are sealed with butter, *c.*1625: Middleton, *Game of Chess*, I i, I think they have seal'd this with butter. 1634: S. Rowley, *Noble Soldier*, IVii 1670: Ray, 198, A warrant seal'd with butter.

Seaman, A. 1. *See* quot. 1670: Ray, 218, A seaman if he carries a millstone will have a quail out of it. Spoken of the common mariners, if they can come at things that may be eat or drunk

2. A seaman is never broken till his neck be broken. 1671: Head and Kirkman, *Eng. Rogue*, ii 194 [cited as a proverb].

Search not too curiously lest you find trouble. 1659: Howell, 17.

Seasonable. *See* **Snow** (2).

Second blow makes the fray, The. 1597: Bacon, *Colours of Good and Evil*, 10. 1642: D. Rogers, *Matrim. Honour*, 196. 1732: Fuller, 4742. 1875: Cheales, *Proverb. Folk-Lore*, 107.

Second shaft, Shoot the, and perhaps thou mayest find again the first. 1659: Howell, 19.

Second thoughts are best. [αἱ δευτεραί πως φροντίδες σοφωτέραι. – Euripides, *Hippol.*, 438. Posteriores enim cogitationes, ut aiunt, sapientiores solent esse. – Cicero, *Phil.*, xii 5.] 1577: Holinshed, *Chronicles*, 438, Oftentymes it chaunceth, that latter thoughts are better advised than the first. 1581: Pettie, tr. Guazzo's *Civil Convers.*, fo. 23, The second thoughts are euer the best. 1607–12: Bacon, *Essays*: 'Youth and Age', Generally youth is like the first cogitacions, not so wise as the second. 1681: Dryden, *Span. Friar*, 11. ii 1715: Centlivre, *Gotham Election*, sc ii 1787: O'Keeffe, *The Farmer*, I iii, Indeed, Molly, as second thoughts are best, I'll return to my first design, and have you. 1813: Byron, *Letters, etc.*, ii 305 (Prothero), In composition I do not think *second* thoughts are the best, though *second* expressions may improve the first.

Second vice is lying, The, the first being that of owing money. 1732: Fuller, 4743. 1736: Franklin, *Way to Wealth*, in *Works*, i 449 (Bigelow) … the first is running in debt.

Secret, *subs.* **1. If you would know secrets, look for them in grief or pleasure.** 1640: Herbert, *Jac. Prudentum.* 1670: Ray, 23.

2. Wherever there is a secret there must be something wrong. 1837: Lockhart, *Life of Scott*, ii 42 [cited as 'an old saying'].

Secret, *adj.* **1. A secret foe gives a sudden blow.** 1736: Bailey, *Dict.*, s.v. 'Foe'.

2. *See* quot. 1695: Congreve, *Love for Love*, III iii, He only is secret who never was trusted; a satirical proverb upon our sex.

Sedgefield, Durham. Four sayings. *See* quots. 1846–59: *Denham Tracts*, i 85 (F.L.S.), (1) I've been as far travelled as Sedgefield, where the folks call strea—STRAW! (2) Montpellier of the North. To meet with persons here of 80, 90, or even 100 years of age, is no uncommon circumstance. (3) To go at a thing, like a Sedgefield Hunt. Ibid., i 86, (4)' A Sedgefield Chap' = The knave of clubs.

Sedgly curse. *See* **Devil** (79).

See, *verb*. **1. I see much, but I say little, and do less.** 1546: Heywood, *Proverbs*, Pt I ch xi 1576: *Parad. Dainty Devices*, in *Brit. Bibliog.*, iii 86 (1812), The best waie is in all worlds sent, Se all, saie nought, holde thee content.

2. See for your love, buy for your money. 1639: Clarke, 79. 1670: Ray, 184. 1736: Bailey, *Dict.*, s.v. 'Love'.

3. See me and see me not. 1546: Heywood, *Proverbs*, Pt II ch v, If he plaie falsehed in felowship, plaie yee See me, and see me not. 1633: Draxe, 46. 1639: Clarke, 289.

4. See Naples and die. It has been pointed out that, though the origin of the proverb lies in the unique and surpassing beauty of Naples and its setting, the city was a notorious hotbed of diseases and the saying could have a grimmer sense. 1858: O. W. Holmes, *Autocrat of the Breakfast Table* (1892), 126, *See* Naples and die. 1898: Mrs Oliphant, *Kirsteen*, ch 8, This was the Highland girl's devout belief; *vedi Napoli e poi morire* [see Naples and then die]; earth could not have anything to show more fair.

5. See no evil, hear no evil, speak no evil. The saying is often represented by a picture of three monkeys covering their eyes, ears and mouths, respectively, with their paws. It is said to derive from an image of these three wise monkeys over a doorway to the Sacred Stable at Nikko in Japan. 1926: *Army and Navy Stores Catalogue*, 197, The three wise monkeys. 'Speak no evil, see no evil, hear no evil'.

6. To see as far into a millstone as another. 1540: Palsgrave, *Acolastus*, sig. B3, Or wolde seeme to see farther in a myll stone, than excellent auctours haue done before vs. 1575: Gascoigne, *Posies*, in *Works*, i 11 (Cunilffe), They … woulde seeme to see verie farre in a mylstone. 1690: Dryden, *Amphitryon*, V, I am a fool, I must confess; but yet I can see as far into a millstone as the best of you. 1712: Arbuthnot, *Law a Bott. Pit.*, Pt IV ch v, He can see as far into a millstone as another! 1778: Burney, *Evelina*, Lett. xxv 1911: T. Edwardes, *Neighbourhood*, 36, I wur allers th' sort as could see through a brick wall fur as most folk.

7. To see day. *See* **Day** (13).

8. We see not what is in the wallet behind. 1639: Clarke, 52, Wee see not what sits on our shoulder. 1732: Fuller, 5453.

9. What the eye doesn't see, the heart doesn't grieve over. *See* **Eye** (19).

10. What you see is what you get. As the first quotation suggests, the saying – which is of American origin – precedes the computer age. It has become so common in the computer contexts – indicating that what appears on the screen is what will be printed out on paper – that it is frequently shortened to the acronym WYSIWYG. 1971: *New York Times*, 14 Nov., 17, 'What you see is what you get' … is one of those recurring gag lines from the Flip Wilson Show that has quickly drifted into the language, all but become a household expression. 1982: *Economist* May 8, If he wishes to converse with computer buffs, he will have to cope with neologisms such as 'wysiwyg' (what you see is what you get), pronounced 'whizziwig'.

11. Who sees thee by day will not seek thee by night. 1659: Howell, *Proverbs: Ital.-Eng.*, 2.

Seeing is believing. [Pluris est oculatus testis unus, quam auriti decemt. – Plautus, *Truc.*, II vi.] 1639: Clarke, 90. 1706: Farquhar, *Recruiting Officer*, IV iii 1850: Smedley, *Frank Fairlegh*, ch xxxi, 'What an unbelieving Jew it is,' said Archer; 'hand him the list, and let him read it himself. Seeing is believing, they say.' 1879: *N.&Q.*, 5th ser, xi 157, In this part of the country [Boston, Lincs] we say, 'Seeing is believing, but feeling is the truth'. 1901: F. E. Taylor, *Lancs Sayings*, 9, Seein's believin', bu' feelin''s God's truth. 1923: A. Bennett, *Riceyman Steps*, Pt II ch iii.

Seek, *verb*. **1. As good seek nought as seek and find nought.** 1546: Heywood, *Proverbs*, Pt I ch xi.

2. He that seeketh findeth. 1530: in J. Palsgrave, *L'éclaircissement de la Langue Française*, A5, he that wyll seke may fynde And in brefe tyme attayne to his utterest desire. Ibid., Pt I ch x 1578: Florio, *First Fruites*, fo. 34. 1581: B. Rich, *Farewell*, 128 (SH.S.), As the proverbe is (he that sekes shall finde). 1633: Draxe, 185. *See also* **Seek** (5).

3. He that seeks to beguile is overtaken in his will. 1578: Florio, *First Fruites*, fo. 14, Who often seekes others to deceiue, doth rest oppressed and deceyued hym selfe. 1869: Hazlitt, 186.

4. He that seeks trouble never misses. *c.*1460: in *Pol., Rel., and Love Poems*, 69 (E.E.T.S.), Who sechith sorwe, is by [his be] the receyte.

1612: Shelton, *Quixote*, Pt I bk iii ch vi, I heard oft-times the curate … preach that 'He which seeks the danger perisheth therein'. 1640: Herbert, *Jac. Prudentum*. 1732: Fuller, 2291.

5. Seek and ye shall find. [Matthew vii 7, Ask, and it shall be given unto you: seek, and ye shall find.] C. J. Bale, *King Johan* (1931), l. 192, Serche and ye shall fynd in every congrgacyn that long to the pope. *See also* **Seek** (2).

6. Seek till you find and you'll not lose your labour. 1678: Ray, 200. 1732: Fuller, 4089.

7. To seek for a thing one would not find. 1546: Heywood, *Proverbs*, Pt II ch v, But whan she seemed to be fixed in mynde, Rather to seeke for that she was lothe to fynde. 1591: Harington, *Orl. Furioso*, blc. xliii, Notes, It is no wisdome to search for that a man would not find. 1659: Howell, 7, I seek for a thing wife that I would not find.

8. Who seeks what he should not, finds what he would not. 1666: Torriano, *Piazza Univ.*, 44.

Seldom comes a loan laughing home. *c.*1320: in *Reliq. Antiquae*, i 113 (1841), 'Selde cometh lone lahynde home'; Quoth Hendyng.

Seldom comes the better. Before 1272: *MS. Temp. Hen. III*, in Douce, *Ill of Shakesp.*, 334 (1839), Seilde comed se betere. 1519: Horman, *Vulgaria*, fo. 299, It is comynly sayd that selde cometh the better. 1594: Shakespeare, *Rich. III*, II iii 1622: Taylor (Water-Poet), in *Works*, 2nd pagin., 14 (1630). 1740: North, *Examen*, 339, Change, 'tis true, but seldom comes a better. 1820: Scott, *Abbot*, ch vi, And for Roland Graeme, though he may be a good riddance in the main, yet what says the very sooth proverb, 'Seldom comes a better'.

Seldom dieth the ox. *Set* **Ox** (6).

Seldom mosseth the stone. *See* **Rolling stone.**

Seldom seen soon forgotten. 1377: in Wright, *Pol. Poems*, i 216 (Rolls Ser., 1859), Selden seize [seen] and sone forgete [refrain of song]. *c.*1450: in *Reliq. Antiquae*, i 25 (1841), She sayth that she hath seen hit wreten, That seldyn seen is soon for-yeten. 1546: Heywood, *Proverbs*, Pt I ch xi 1620: Middleton, *World Tost at Tennis*, Epil. 1670: Ray, 140. Cf. **Eye** (19); and **Out of sight.**

Seldom thinks is at ease, He that. *c.*1460: *How the Good Wife*, l. 85, At ese he is that seldom thankithe.

Self do, self have. 1546: Heywood, *Proverbs*, Pt I ch viii 1593: *Tell-Trothes N. Yeares Gift*, 7

(N.Sh.S.). 1634: Ford, *Perkin Warbeck*, I ii, Self do, self have – no more words; win and wear her. 1674: Head and Kirkman, *Eng. Rogue*, iii 4. 1748: Richardson, *Clarissa*, i 222 (1785). 1875: Cheales, *Proverb. Folk-Lore*, 137.

Self first, then your next best friend. Oxfordsh. 1913: *Folk-Lore*, xxiv. 76.

Self-love is a mote in every man's eye. 1670: Ray, 141. 1732: Fuller, 4093.

Self-praise is no recommendation. 1612: Shelton, *Quixote*, Pt I bk iii ch ii, Which is such that if I do not praise it, it is because men say that proper praise stinks; but my squire will inform you what I am. 1852: Dickens, *Bleak House*, ch lv. 1865: Dickens, *Mutual Friend*, bk iv. ch ii.

Self-preservation is the first law of nature. Before 1614: Donne, Βιαθάνατος sig. AA (1644) (OED), It is onely upon this reason, that selfe-preservation is of Naturall Law. 1675: Marvell, *Hodge's Vision from Monument*, Self-preservation, nature's first great law. Before 1680: Butler, *Remains*, ii 27 (1759). 1720: C. Shadwell, *Irish Hospitality*, V i, Self-preservation shou'd exert it self, 'tis then indeed the first principle of nature. 1751: Smollett, *P. Pickle*, ch lvii 1838: Dickens, *Twist*, ch x.

Sell as markets go, You must.1584: Greene, in *Works*, iii 224 (Grosart), If thou bee wise … make thy market while the chaffer is set to sale. 1670: Ray, 23, A man must sell his ware after the rates of ye market. 1732: Fuller, 5969.

Sell nothing on trust. *See* **Trust**, *subs.* (2).

Sell the bear's skin before the bear has been caught, To. 1580: Lyly, *Euphues*. 273 (Arber), I trusted so much that I solde the skinne before the beast was taken. 1647: in *Polit. Ballads*, 20 (Percy S., No. 11), Yet they divide the skinne Of the beare among them e're they ha't. 1692: L'Estrange, *Aesop*, 270 (3rd ed.), He bad me have a care for the future, to make sure of the bear, before I sell his skin. 1726: Defoe, *Hist. of Devil*, Pt II ch viii p. 276 (4th ed.), Indeed the devil may be said to sell the bear-skin, whatever he buys. 1819: Scott, *Leg. of Montrose*, ch iii, Somewhat irregular, though, and smells a little too much of selling the bear's skin before he has hunted him.

Selsey. *See* **Chichester.**

Selvage showeth the cloth, The. 1611: Cotgrave, s.v. 'Haistre', We say, the selvidge makes shew of the cloth. 1670: Ray, 141 [as in 1611]. 1732: Fuller, 4744.

Send, *verb.* **1. He sendeth to the Eas Indies for Kentish pippins.** Ibid., No. 2017.

2. Send a fool. *See* **Fool** (91).

3. Send a wise man. *See* **Wise** (33).

4. Send him to the sea and he will not get water. 1683: Meriton, *Yorkshire Ale.* 83–7 (1697).

5. Send not to market for trouble. 1732: Fuller, 4098.

6. To send him for yard-wide packthread = To send on a fool's errand. 1813: Ray, 223.

September. 1. As on the 8th [September], **so for the next four weeks.** 1893: Inwards, *Weather Lore,* 34.

2. As September so the coming March. Ibid., 33.

3. Fair on September 1, **fair for the month.** Ibid., 34.

4. If on September 19 **there is a storm from the south, a mild winter may be expected.** Derby. Ibid., 34.

5. September, blow soft, Till the fruit's in the loft. 1732: Fuller, 6214. 1893: Inwards, 34.

See also **Cuckoo** (8) and (12); **July** (10); and **June** (3).

Serjeant is the spawn of some decayed shop keeper, A. 1626: Overbury, *Characters:* 'A Sargeant'. 1659: Howell, 10.

Serpent by the tail, He holds the. 1813: Ray, 75.

Serpent. *See also* **Snake**.

Serpents engender in still waters. 1732: Fuller, 4100.

Servant and **Servants. 1. A servant and a cock should be kept but a year.** 1732: Fuller, 389.

2. A servant is known in the absence of his master. 1659: Howell, *Proverbs: Ital.-Eng.,* 12. 1732: Fuller, 390.

3. A servant that is diligent. *See* quots. 1590: Greene, *Works,* vii 311 (Grosart), Whereupon an olde Englishe disticke. A servant that is diligent honest and good Must sing at his worke like a bird in the wood. *c.*1597: Deloney, *Gentle Craft,* Pt I ch x, It is an old prouerbe. They proue seruants kind and good, That sing at their businesse like birds in the wood.

4. Don't take a servant off a midden [dung-heap]. 1917: Bridge, *Cheshire Proverbs,* 51.

5. He that would be well served must know when to change his servants. 1855: Bohn, 396.

6. If you pay not a servant his wages, he will pay himself. 1732: Fuller, 2778.

7. If you would have a good servant, take neither a kinsman nor a friend. 1659: Howell, *Proverbs: Span.-Eng.,* 1, Neither take too young a boy, nor kinsman, nor one that is intreated for thy servant. 1855: Bohn, 422.

8. One must be a servant before that he can be a master. 1633: Draxe, 18. Cf. **Serve,** *verb* (2).

9. Servants should put on patience when they put on a livery. 1732: Fuller, 4101.

10. Servants should see all and say nothing. 1771: Smollett, *Clinker,* in *Works,* vi 3 (1817). 1819: Scott, *Ivanhoe,* ch ii, Like good servants, let us hear and see, and say nothing. 1820: Scott, *Abbot,* ch vi [as in 1819].

Serve, *verb.* 1. **He serves the poor with a thump on the back with a stone** = He is a miser. 1678: Ray, 90.

2. He that hath not served knows not how to command. 1539: Taverner, *Proverbs,* fo. 2, No man can be a good ruler, onles he hath bene fyrste ruled. 1578: Florio, *First Fruites,* fo. 28, Who hath not serued can not commaund. 1629: *Book of Meery Riddles,* Prov. 81. Cf. **Servant** (8).

3. He that serves everybody is paid by nobody. 1611: Cotgrave, s.v. 'Abbayer', He that serves a communaltie is controlled by every one, rewarded by none. 1732: Fuller, 2295.

4. He that serves well need not be afraid to ask his wages. 1640: Herbert, *Jac. Prudentum* [omitting 'be afraid to']. 1670: Ray, 23. 1732: Fuller, 2296.

5. Serve God. *See* **God**.

6. To serve two masters. *See* **No man can serve**.

7. To serve two pigeons. *See* **Pigeon** (4).

Service is no inheritance. 1412: Hoccleve, *Regement,* l. 841 (E.E.T.S., Ext. Ser., 72), Seruyse, I wot wel, is non heritage, *c.*1450: *Songs and Carols,* 22 (Warton Cl., 1856), For servyse is non erytage. 1509: Barclay, *Ship of Fools,* i 106 (1874), Thus worldly seruyce is no sure herytage. 1600: T. Heywood, 1 *Edw. IV,* in *Works,* i 51 (1874), Seruice is no heritage. 1640: Herbert, *Jac. Prudentum.* 1712: Centlivre. *Perplex'd Lovers,* I iii 1759: Townley, *High Life below Stairs,* I i 1776: Mrs Cowley, *Runaway,* V i 1830: Marryat, *King's Own,* ch X 1841: Dickens, *Barn. Rudge,* ch lxxx., Though she was but a servant, and knowed that servitudes was no inheritances.

Service without reward is punishment. 1604: Herbert, *Jac. Prudentum.*

Service. *See also* **No service**.

Serving-man. *See* **Young** (8).

Set a good face on it. *See* **Good face**.

Set my house afire only to roast his eggs, He. 1692: L'Estrange, *Aesop*, 375 (3rd ed.), These are the people that set their neighbours houses on fire to roast their own eggs. 1732: Fuller, 2018.

Set up one's rest, To. This is a term taken from the game of Primero. 1576: Lambarde, *Peramb. of Kent*, 430 (1826), She resolved … to set up her last rest, in hope to recover her losses againe. 1590: Lodge, *Rosalynde*, 50 (Hunt.Cl.), Aliena resolued there to set vp her rest. 1592: Shakespeare, *Romeo*, V iii 1653: Middleton and Rowley, *Span. Gipsy*, IV iii, Set up thy rest, her marriest thou or none. *c.*1680: L'Estrange, *Seneca's Epistles*, vii, Teach me … to dispute with Socrates … to set up my rest with Epicurus. 1768: Brooke, *Fool of Quality*, iii 1811. Here I counted to set up my rest for life. 1840: Dickens, *Curiosity Shop*, ch xxi, So we … will set up our rest again among our boyish haunts. 1852: M. A. Keltie, *Reminisc. of Thought and Feeling*, 165, As the estate had then to be sold, it became a question where I was to set up my rest.

Set up one's staff, To. 1573: Harvey, *Letter-Book*, 4 (Camden S.), He hath set down his staf, and made his reckning. 1591: Shakespeare, *Com. of Errors*, III i, Have at you with a proverb: – Shall I set in my staff? 1766: Garrick, *Neck or Nothing*, I i, Then my young master may e'en make a leg to his fortune, and set up his staff somewhere else. 1815: Scott, *Mannering*, ch xix, Here, then, Mannering resolved, for some time at least, to set up the staff of his rest. 1826: Scott, *Journal*, 13 Nov., She has set up the whole staff of her rest in keeping literary society about her. [In these last two passages, Scott has curiously combined this and the preceding proverbial phrase.]

Seven hours' sleep. *See* **Sleep**, *subs.*(1).

Seven may be company but nine are confusion. 1630: Brathwait, *Eng. Gent.*, 178 (1641), Which use was occasion of that adage, *Septem convivium, novem convitium faciunt;* Seven make a banquet, nine a riot. 1681: Robertson, *Phraseol. Generalis*, 598, Seven at a feast, nine at a fray. 1732: Fuller, 4113.

Seven years = any indefinite period. 1362: Langland, *Plowman*, A, v 122, Hit hedde ben vn-sold this seuen yer so me god helpe! *c.*1460:

in Hazlitt, *Early Pop. Poetry*, i 170, For thou may speke a word to-day That vij zer thens may be for thozt. *c.*1475: *Rauf Coilyear*, 25 (E.E.T.S.), Thair suld na man be sa wyse, To gar me cum to Parise, To luke quhair the King lyis, In faith, this seuen yeir! 1519: *Four Elements*, in Hazlitt, *Old Plays*, i 47, That is the best dance without a pipe, That I saw this seven year. 1594: Lodge and Greene, *Looking Glasse*, l. 246, [Thou] shalt not be worth a horse of thine owne this seuen yeare. 1674: J. Howard, *Eng. Mounsieur*, II, I have not seen you these seven years. *Well-bred* … I tell you 'twas not half an hour ago since you saw me. 1778: Burney, *Evelina*, Lett. xxiii, I don't think I shall speak to you again these seven years. 1889: Peacock, *Manley, etc.*, *Gloss.*, 470 (E.D.S.), Seven-year-end. A long but indefinite period. 1913: E.M. Wright, *Rustic Speech, etc.*, 175, A long, indefinite period of time is: from seven year end to seven year end, for years long years and donkey's ears.

Severn, River. **1. Blessed is the eye**. *See* quots. 1659: Howell, 21, Happy is the eye that dwelleth twixt Severn and the Wye. 1662: Fuller, *Worthies*, ii 70 (1840), Blessed is the eye, That is betwixt Severn and Wye. 1790: Grose, *Prov. Gloss.*, s.v. 'Herefordshire' [as in 1662]. 1883: Burne, *Shropsh. Folk-Lore*, 584, Happy is the eye Between Severn and Wye, But thrice happy he Between Severn and Clee.

2. Fix thy pale in Severn [with intent to fence out his water], **Severn will be as before**. 1662: Fuller, *Worthies*, iii 549 (1840). 1790: Grose, *Prov. Gloss.*, s.v. 'Montgomeryshire'.

3. You may as soon sip up the Severn and swallow Mavern [Malvern]. 1659: Howell, 20. 1670: Ray, 258. 1790: Grose, *Prov. Gloss.*, s.v. 'Worcestershire'.

Sexton has snaked his shoo [shovel] **at him, The**. 1917: Bridge, *Cheshire Proverbs*, 120.

Sexton is a fatal musician, The. 1639: Clarke, 215.

Shade your head and go east. 1864: 'Cornish Proverbs', in *N. & Q.*, 3rd ser, vi 495.

Shadow, and lose the substance, Catch not at the. 1855: Bohn, 335.

Shaft or a bolt of it, To make a. 1594: Nashe, *Works*, iii 254 (Grosart), To make a shaft or a bolt of this drumbling subiect of dreames. 1644–55: Howell, *Letters*, I iii 24 (1726), The Prince is preparing for his journey; I shall to it again closely when he is gone, or make a shaft or a bolt of it. 1823: D'Israeli, *Cur. of Lit.* 2nd ser, i 448 (1824), None but true toxophilites could have had such a proverb as 'I will either make a shaft or a bolt of it'! 1907: Hackwood, *Old Eng. Sports*, 103, Hence the old English proverb, 'I will either make a shaft or a bolt of it', signifying the determination that a thing shall not go unused.

Shaftesbury and Glastonbury. 1655: Fuller, *Church Hist.*, bk vi § ii (iv. 14), The country people had a proverb, that 'if the Abbot of Glastonbury might marry the Abbess of Shaftesbury, their heir would have more land than the King of England'. 1894: *Somerset and Dorset N. & Q.*, iii 189, If the Abbot of Glaston could have married the Abbess of Shaston, the King of England would be the poorer man.

Shake a Leicestershire man. *See* **Leicestershire**.

Shake a loose leg, To = To go 'on the loose'. 1869: Hazlitt, 430.

Shake the kettle, and it'll sing. Ibid., 332.

Shake your ears, Go. 1573: G. Harvey, *Letter-Book*, 42 (Camden S.), His Mastership may go shake his eares elswhere. 1601: Shakespeare, *Twelfth Night*, II iii, *Maria*. Go shake your ears. 1647: in *Pol. Ballads*, 69 (Wright, Percy S.), And you may goe and shake your eares, Who had, and could not hold it. 1764: Mrs F. Sheridan, *Dupe*, I iii, March off and leave him to shake his ears.

Shall be, shall be, That which. *c.*1386: Chaucer, *Knight's Tale*, l. 608, As, whan a thing is shapen, it shal be. *c.*1390: Gower, *Conf. Amantis*, bk i l. 1714, Bot nede be mot that nede schal. 1546: Heywood, *Proverbs*, Pt II ch i, That shalbe, shalbe. 1604: Marlowe, *Faustus*, I i, What will be, shall be. 1639: Clarke, 225. *See also* **Must be;** and **Will be.**

Shame, *subs*. **1. He has swallowed shame and drank after it** = *He* has no sense of shame left. 1830: Forby, *Vocab. E. Anglia*, 433.

2. He that has no shame has no conscience. 1732: Fuller, 2148.

3. It's a shame to steal, but a worse to carry home. 1639: Clarke, 190, It's a shame to steale, but a greater shame to bring again. 1670: Ray, 141. 1732: Fuller, 2875.

4. Shame in a kindred cannot be avoyded. 1605: Camden, *Remains*, 330 (1870).

5. Shame is as it is taken. 1534: More, *Works*, 1253 (1557). 1546: Heywood, *Proverbs*, Pt I ch ix.

6. Shame take him that shame thinketh. Ibid., Pt I ch ix. 1596: Spenser, *F. Q.*, IV vi 61, 'Shame be his meede', quoth he, 'that meaneth shame.' 1596: Harington, *Metam. of Ajax*, 104 (1814), Wherefore shame to them that shame think. 1605: Camden, *Remains*, 330 (1870). 1659: Howell, 9.

7. 'Tis no shame to eat one's meat. 1611: Cotgrave, s.v. 'Manger', He thats ashamed to eat is ashamed to live. 1672: Walker, *Paroem.*, 10.

Shameful leaving is worse than shameful eating. 1894: Northall, *Folk Phrases*, 22 (E.D.S.).

Shameless beggar. *See* **Beggar** (3).

Shameless craving must have a shameless nay. 1546: Heywood, *Proverbs*, Pt I ch xi [with 'Shameful' for first word]. 1670: Ray, 141. 1754: Berthelson, *Eng.-Danish Dict.*, s.v. 'Shameless'.

Shameless is graceless, He that is. 1732: Fuller, 2192.

Shankey Hall. *See* quot. 1846–59: *Denham Tracts*, i 69 (F.L.S.), Like Shankey Hall, he takes no hints. A highly popular bishoprick [Durham] proverb.

Share and share alike. 1611: Cotgrave, s.v. 'Escot', Whereat every guest paies his part, or, share and share alike. 1635: in *Somers Tracts*, vii 191, (1811). Not share and share alike, but to every each one the more according to their defects. 1670: Ray, 218, Share and share like, some all, and some never a whit. *Leonina societas.* 1821: Scott, *Pirate*, ch xvii, They say, that a' man share and share equal-equals in the creature's ulzie. 1914: Lucas, *Landmarks*, ch xxxiv, That's the way, Sergison, in married life; share and share alike.

Sharp as a cobbler's elsin [awl]. 1855: Robinson, *Whitby Gloss.*, 52.

Sharp as a needle. Before 1000: *Souls Address*, 120 (OED), zifer hatte se wyrm, the tha eazlas beoth naedle scear-pran. 1552: Huloet, *Abced.*, sig. Ee1, Sharpe lyke a nedle. 1566: Adlington, tr. Apuleius, bk vii, Sharp thorns, as sharp as needles. 1607: T. Heywood, *Fair Maide*, in *Works*, ii 25 (1874). Before 1700: quoted in *N. & Q.*, 3rd ser, xii 341, With a stomach as sharp as a needle. 1725: Bailey, tr. Erasmus' *Colloq.*, 277. 1849: Lytton, *Caxtons*, Pt XVII ch i 1872: Hardy, *Greenwood Tree*, Pt IV ch ii, Lawyer Green – a man as sharp as a needle.

Sharp as a razor. 1519: Horman, *Vulgaria*, fo. 277, My wodknyfe is as sharpe as a rasur. 1577:

Misogonus, IV i, Take my penknif then, ites as sharpe as a racer. 1694: D'Urfey, *Quixote*, Pt I Act I sc ii 1720: Gay, *Poems*, ii 279 (Underhill), Her glance is as the razor keen. 1830: Scott, *Doom of Devorgoil*, III ii, Your razor's polish'd, But, as the proverb goes, 'tis cruel sharp. 1907: De Morgan, *Alice-for-Short*, ch viii.

Sharp as a thorn. 14th cent.: *Early Eng. Met. Rom.*, 15 (Camden. S.), Als scharpe as a thorn, *c.*1480: *Early Miscell.*, 33 (Warton Cl., 1855), And al here eyrns wer scharpe as any thornus. 1648: Herrick, *Hesperides*, No. 444, He's sharp as thorn. 1670: Ray, 207.

Sharp as vinegar. 1631: Mabbe, *Celestina*, 110 (T.T.), And poure forth words as sharpe as vineger. 1693: D'Urfey, *Richmond Heiress*, II i, She's as sharp as vinegar this morning. 1737: Ray, 225. 1821: Scott, *Kenilworth*, ch xxvii, Thou art as sharp as vinegar this afternoon!

Sharper the blast, The shorter 'twill last, The. 1875: Cheales, *Proverb. Folk-Lore*, 19.

Sharply chides is ready to pardon, He that. 1620: Shelton, *Quixote*, Pt II ch lxx. 1732: Fuller, 2298 [with 'the most' before 'ready'].

Sharply too! says Jack Chumley. 1883: Burne, *Shropsh. Folk-Lore*, 591.

Sharp's the word. 1709: Cibber, *Rival Fools*, I, Sharp's the word! we'll have half ours too. 1720: *Vade Mecum for Malt-worms*, Pt II 24, Cry Sharp's the word, and bite that deepest can. 1854: Dickens, *Hard Times*, bk iii ch vii, Thay farewell to your family, and tharp'th the word. 1896: Doyle, *Rodney Stone*, ch i 1922: Weyman, *Ovington's Bank*, ch xvii, Queer old place, and – sharp's the word, here we are.

Sharp stomach makes short devotion, A. 1639: Clarke, 272. 1670: Ray, 142. 1732: Fuller, 4118 [in the plural].

Sheared. *See* quot. 1914: *Devonsh. Assoc. Trans.*, xlvi 92, 'When it is sheared, it likes to be leared'. Used of lambs and then applied as a proverb to persons (Devon).

Shears between them, But a pair of = little or no difference. 1579: Lyly, *Euphues*, 46 (Arber), And as it were but a paire of sheeres to goe betwene their natures. 1603: Shakespeare, *Meas. for Meas.*, I ii 1611: Middleton, *Roaring Girl*, III iii, One pair of shears sure cut out both your coats. 1626: Overbury, *Characters*: 'An Apparator', There went but a paire of sheeres between him and the pursivant

of hell, for they both delight in sinne. 1633: Rowley, *Match at Midnight*, II. *c.*1791: Pegge, *Derbicisms*, 120 (E.D.S.), 'Only shears between them', both alike.

She devils are hard to tame. *c.*1550: in Hazlitt, *Pop. Poetry*, iii 240.

Shed riners with a whaver, To. 1836: Wilbraham, *Cheshire Gloss.*, 68 (2nd ed.), 'To shed riners with a whaver ' ... means to surpass any thing skilful or adroit by something still more so. 1917: Bridge, *Cheshire Proverbs*, 143.

Sheen. *See* **Sion**.

Sheep. [There are two groups of sheep sayings, none of the members of which occurs elsewhere, and it is a little doubtful whether they were ever truly *proverbial*. It will be convenient to enter both groups here. A. 1550–3: *The Decaye of England*, 96 (E.E.T.S.), The more shepe, the dearer is the woll. The more shepe, the dearer is the motton. The more shepe, the dearer is the beffe. The more shepe, the dearer is the corne. The more shepe, the skanter is the whit meate. The more shepe, the fewer egges for a peny. Before 1641: Best, *Farming Book* (Surtees S., No. 33), For as the sayinge is, Sheepe that will live in winter, will live and thrive in summer; and sheepe that growe fleshy with foure teeth, will growe fatte with eight (p. 3) ... The husbandman's sayinge is, that the losse of an ewe's lambe is as greate as the losse of a cowe's calfe (p. 5) ... Hence ariseth the shepheardes phrase, that Whiles the grasse groweth, Ewe dryeth, lambe dyeth (p. 5) ... . The countrey proverbe is, The man that is aboute to clippe his sheepe, Must pray for two faire dayes and one faire weeke (p. 20).]

1. A black sheep is a biting beast, *c.*1550: *Six Ballads*, 4 (Percy S.), The blacke shepe is a perylous beast. 1598: T. Bastard, *Chrestoleros*, bk iv. Ep. 20, Till now I thought the prouerbe did but iest, Which said a blacke sheepe was a biting beast.

2. Every time the sheep bleats, it loses a mouthful. 1623: Wodroephe, *Spared Houres*, 476, The yewe that doth bleate doth loose the most of her meate. 1666: Torriano, *Piazza Univ.*, 23, The sheep that bleats, loseth its pasture. 1732: Fuller, 1471. 1869: Spurgeon, *John Ploughman*, ch v.

3. He loves sheep's flesh well that eats the wool. *c.*1460: *Good Wyfe wold a Pylgremage*, l.

71 (E.E.T.S.), He wyll lowys scheppis flesche, That wettyth his bred in woll. Before 1500: in Hill, *Commonplace-Book*, 131 (E.E.T.S.), He loveth well moton, that weteth his bred in woll. 1546: Heywood, *Proverbs*, Pt II ch v [as in Hill, but with 'sheeps flesh' for 'moton']. 1696: D'Urfey. *Quixote*, Pt III Act I, He loves mutton well that can dine upon the wool. 1732: Fuller, 1979 [as in 1696, but with 'eats' for 'can dine upon']. 1816: Scott, *Antiquary*, ch xliv., They liked mutton weel that licket where the yowe lay.

4. He that hath sheep, etc. *See* quots. 1523: Fitzherbert, *Husbandry*, 74 (E.D.S.), For it is an olde sayinge: he that hath both shepe, swyne, and bees, slepe he, wake he, he maye thryue. 1634: C. Butler, *Feminine Monarchie*, 139, The proverb … Who so keepe wel sheepe and bee'n, Sleepe or wake, their thrift cooms in.

5. He that makes himself a sheep shall be eaten by the wolf. 1583: Melbancke, *Philotinus*, sig. Bb4, He … that will needes be a sheepe, cannot greatly grudge to be bitten with a fox. 1593: Harvey, *Works*, ii 38 (Grosart), It was wont to be said by way of a prouerbe; Hee that will be made a sheepe, shall find wolues inough. 1619: B. Rich, *Irish Hubbub*, 4, He that will make himselfe a sheepe, it is no matter though the wolues doe eat him. 1651: Herbert, *Jac. Prudentum*, 2nd ed. 1710: S. Palmer, *Moral Essays on Proverbs*, 360. 1773: Franklin, *Works*, v 86 (Bigelow), There is much truth in the Italian saying, *Make yourselves sheep, and the wolves will eat you.* 1869: Spurgeon, *John Ploughman*, ch iv, He that makes himself a sheep, will find that the wolves are not all dead.

6. It is a foolish sheep that makes the wolf his confessor. 1670: Ray, 23.

7. It is possible for a sheep to kill a butcher. Ibid., 22 [with 'ram' for 'sheep']. 1732: Fuller, 3010.

8. Let the black sheep keep the white. 1639: Clarke, 69.

9. One might as well be hanged for a sheep as a lamb. 1678: Ray, 350 ['old sheep 'and 'young lamb']. 1732: Fuller, *Gnomologia*, no. 683, As good be hanged for a Sheep as a Lamb. 1748: Richardson, *Clarissa*, i 60 (1785), *So in for the lamb*, as the saying is, *in for the sheep.* 1841: Dickens, *Barn. Rudge*, ch liii, Others … comforted themselves with 4the homely proverb,

that, being hanged at all, they might as well be hanged for a sheep as a lamb. 1920: O. Onions, *Case in Camera*, ii 42, Not worth while going home for lunch now. May as well be hung for a sheep as a lamb. I wonder if they've got a snack of anything here? 1924: Shaw, *Saint Joan*, sc ii.

10. One scabbed sheep infects a whole flock. Before 1500: Hill, *Commonplace-Book*, 129 (E.E.T.S.), One skabbid shepe infectith all the folde. 1586: L. Evans, *Withals Dict. Revised*, sig. C1. 1593: Nashe, *Works*, iv 159 (Grosart). 1630: Taylor (Water-Poet). *Works*, 3rd pagin., 59, One scabbed sheep's enough to spoyle a flocke. 1640: T. Rawlins, *Rebellion*, IV, One tainted sheep mars a whole flock. 1732: Fuller, 3792, One scabby sheep is enough to infect the whole flock. 1796: White, *Falstaff's Letters*, 16, The tainted wether doth infect the whole flock. 1846: Denham, *Proverbs*, 7 (Percy S.) … will mar the whole flock.

11. One sheep follows another. 1816: Scott, *Old Mortality*, ch xxxvi, One sheep will leap the ditch when another goes.first.

12. Shear sheep that has them. 1678: Ray, 201.

13. Shear your sheep in May, And shear them all away. 1670: Ray, 41. 1732: Fuller, 6195. 1893: Inwards, *Weather Lore*, 26.

14. The dust raised by the sheep does not choke the wolf. 1732: Fuller, 4491.

15. The lone sheep's in danger of the wolf. 1639: Clarke, 117. 1670: Ray, 53.

16. There's a scabby sheep in every flock. 1872: J. Glyde, jr., *Norfolk Garland*, 150 [more usually a 'black sheep'].

17. To cast a sheep's eye. 1577: J. Grange, *Golden Aphroditis*, sig. D1, On whom he many a sheepish eye did cast. *c.*1580: *Tom Tyler*, l. 124, p. 4 (Malone S.), If he look but awry; or cast a sheeps eye. *c.*1663: Davenant, *Play-House to be Let*, V, On Cleopatra he has cast a sheep's-eye. 1738: Swift, *Polite Convers.*, Dial. I, I have often seen him cast a sheep's eye out of a calf's head at you. 1855: Kingsley, *West. Ho!*, ch ii, What a plague business had he making sheep's eyes at his daughter?

18. To lose the sheep for a ha'porth of tar. Tar is used to protect sores or wounds in sheep from flies, and the consequent generation of worms. 1600: Day, *Blind Beggar*, V, To him, father; never lose a hog for a halfp'north of tar. 1643: Wither, *Se Defendendo*, 5 (Spens.S.), Much like the saving of a half-peny worth of tarre by the losse of a hogge, jeered in an English proverb. 1749: W. Ellis, *Shepherd's Sure Guide, etc.*, 273, That a sheep may not, according to the proverb, be lost for want of a halfpennyworth of tar. 1846: Denham, *Proverbs*, 7 (Percy S.), Lose not a hog for a halfpenny worth of tar. 1878: Smiles, *Lives of Engineers*, iv 214, He at length came to the conclusion … that it was better 'not to lose a sheep for a ha'porth of tar'. *See also* **sleep** (4).

19. You have no more sheep to shear. 1678: Ray, 344.

20. You may shear your sheep, When the elder blossoms peep. 1893: Inwards, *Weather Lore*, 153.

See also **Better to give; Crow** (7); **Every hand; February** (7); **Lazy sheep; Leap Year; Lion** (1); **Many frosts; Naked; Ragged; St Gervatius; Some good; Soon goes; Stamps; Wolf,** *passim*; **Wool** (5); and **You** (7).

Sheep-skin shoe lasts not long, A. 1732: Fuller, 393.

Sheffield park is ploughed and sown, When, Then little England hold thine own. 1678: Ray, 340. 1790: Grose, *Prov, Gloss.*, s.v. 'Yorkshire'. 1878: *Folk-Lore Record*, i 165.

She hath eaten a snake. 1580: Lyly, *Euphues*, 368 (Arber), Therfore hath it growen to a prouerb in Italy, when one seeth a woman striken in age to looke amiable, he saith she hath eaten a snake.

Shelter against every storm, 'Tis good to have a. 1665: R. Howard. *Committee, I* [called 'a wise saying'].

Sheltering under an old hedge, It is good. 1674: *Learnt to lye Warm; or, An Apology for that Proverb, 'Tis good sheltering under an Old Hedge* [title of tract]. 1732: Fuller, 2939. 1818: Scott, *Heart of Midl.*, ch xlvi, It's better sheltering under an auld hedge than under a new-planted wood. Cf. **old**, E (7).

Shermanbury. *See* **Bolney**.

She that will not. *See* **He that will not.**

Shew. *See* **Show.**

Shields. *See* quots. **1. 1846–59:** Denham Tracts, i 57 (F.L.S.), We'll a' gan' together like the folks o' Shields. 1892: Heslop, *Northumb. Words*, 2 (E.D.S.), Aall togither, like the folks o' Shields.

2. 1846–59: *Denham Tracts*, i 46 (F.L.S.), Go to Shields And fish for eels [a Newcastle phrase].

Shields. *See also* **Newcastle**.

Shilling to ninepence, To bring a. 1546: Heywood. *Proverbs*, Pt II ch v, To bryng a shillyng to ix pens quickely. 1560: T. Wilson, *Rhetorique*, 185 (1909), But yet, sir, your cunning was such that you brought a shilling to nine pence. 1755: *Connoisseur*, No. 91, The old saying was inverted, and we lost eleven-pence out of a shilling.

Shilling. *See also* **Penny** (2).

Shin of beef. *See* quot. 1871: *N. & Q.*, 4th ser, vii 9, Useful as a shin of beef, which has a big bone for the big dog, a little bone for the little dog, and a sinew for the cat [an old Shropshire saying].

Ship and Ships. 1. As broken a ship has come to land. 1732: Fuller, 668. 1800: Colman, jr., *The Review*, I ii, Far more unlikelier ships have com'd into harbour than this. 1823: Scott, *St Ronan's*, ch x, As broken a ship's come to land.

2. A ship and a woman are ever repairing, (or **trimming**). 1602–3: Manningham, *Diary*, 12 (Camden S.), To furnish a shipp requireth much trouble, But to furnishe a woman the charges are double. 1619: *Helpe to Discourse*, 80 (1640), There are two things that cannot bee too much trimmed, and what are they? A ship and a woman. 1640: Herbert, *Jac. Prudentum* … repairing. 1669: *New Help to Discourse*, 310, A ship and a woman always trimming. 1732: Fuller, 394, A ship, a mill, and a woman are always repairing.

3. A ship under sail, a man in complete armour, a woman with a great belly are three of the handsomest sights. 1659: Howell, 2.

4. Don't spoil the ship for a ha'porth of tar. The original form of this proverb enjoined wise people not to *lose the sheep for a ha'porth of tar* (*See* **Sheep** (18)). Its roots are agricultural, not nautical. The change to the present form came about, it is thought, because *ship* is a dialectal form or pronunciation of *sheep*, and also because the same tar that was used to cover wounds and sores on sheep and prevent them from festering was also used to fill the seams in the planking of boats. 1861: C. Reade, *The Cloister and the Hearth*, I i, Never tyne [lose] the ship for want of a bit of tar. 1869: W.C. Hazlitt, *English Proverbs*, 432, To spoil the ship for a halfpennyworth of tar. In Cornwall, I heard a different version, which appeared to me to be more consistent with probability: 'Don't spoil the sheep for a ha'porth of tar'. 1910: *Spectator*, 19 Feb., 289, The ratepayers … are accused of … cheeseparing, of spoiling the ship for a ha'porth of tar.

5. Ships fear fire more than water. 1640: Herbert, *Jac. Prudentum*. 1670: Ray, 24. 1732: Fuller, 4153.

See also **One hand;** and **Woman** (47).

Shipshape and Bristol fashion. 1826: Scott, *Chron. of Canongate*, Introd., Stretching our fair canvas to the breeze, all shipshape and Bristol fashion. 1840: Dana, *Two Years before Mast*, ch xx, Her decks were as white as snow … everything on board 'shipshape and Bristol fashion'. 1914: *N. & Q.*, 11th ser, ix. 446, When a seaman wished to speak well of his vessel, he declared that with her things were 'shipshape and Bristol fashion', although he hailed from another port.

Shipwreck be your sea-mark, Let another's. 1855: Bohn, 440.

Shires, To come out of the. 1735: Pegge, *Kent. Proverbs*, in E.D.S., No. 12, p. 78, To come out of the Shires. This is a proverbial saying relative to any person who comes from a distance. 1875: Parish, *Sussex Dict.*, 103, The true Sussex man divides the world into two parts. Kent and Sussex form one division, and all the rest is 'The Sheeres'. 1882: *N. & Q.*, 6th ser, v 496, The natives [of Kent] speak with contempt of distant compatriots who live 'down in the sheers'. Cf. **Rodings.**

Shirt full of sore bones, I will give you a. 1732: Fuller, 2637.

Shirt knew my design, I'd burn it, If my. 1654: *Clarke Papers*, iii 12 (Camden), (OED), The designe is secrett, knowne to the designer onely, whoe saith if hee thought his shirt knew it hee would burne it. 1732: Fuller, 2695.

Shitten luck is good luck. An unsavoury saying very freely used in the 17th and 18th centuries. 1639–61: in *Rump Songs*, Pt I 137 (1662, repr. 1874). 1691: *Merry Drollery*, 261 (Ebsworth). 1709: Ward, *Acc. of Clubs*, 208 (1756). 1785: Grose, *Class. Dict. Vulgar Tongue*, s.v. 'Luck'. 1894: Northall, *Folk Phrases*, 22 (E.D.S.).

Shive of a cut loaf, It is safe taking a. 'Shive' = slice. 1600: Shakespeare, *Titus Andr.*, II i, And easy it is Of a cut loaf to steal a shive, we know. 1670: Ray, 52. 1732: Fuller, 3012 ['slice' for 'shive']. 1828: Scott, in Lockhart's *Life*, vii 115, 'A shave [? misprint for 'shive'] from a broken

loaf' is thought as little of by the male set of delinquents as by the fair frail. 1901: F. E. Taylor, *Lancs Sayings*, 11, A shoive off a cut loaf's never miss't.

Shive of my own loaf, A. 1670: Ray, 188.

Shoe and Shoes, *subs.* **1. His shoe pinches him** = He is drunk. 1745: Franklin, *Drinker's Dict.*, in *Works*, ii 26 (Bigelow).

2. His shoes are made of running leather. 1575: Churchyard, *Chippes*, 130 (Collier), My minde could never rest at hoem, My shoes wear maed of running leather suer. 1611: Cotgrave, s.v. 'Divague', Straying, ranging … wandring up and downe, whose shooes are made of running leather. 1754: Berthelson, *Eng.-Danish Dict.*, s.v. 'Run'. 1831: Hone, *Year-Book*, col. 1544, This child's shoes are made of running leather.

3. If the shoe fits wear it. A predominantly U.S. version of *If the cap fits … (See* **Cap** (2)). 1773: *New-York Gazette and Weekly Mercury*, 17 May, Why should Mr Vanderbeek apply a general comparison to himself? Let those whom the shoe fits wear it. 1876: W.G. Nash, *Century of Gossip*, 125, If the shoe fits you, you can wear it a little wile [*sic*], Jack.

4. The shoe will hold with the sole. 1546: Heywood, *Proverbs*, Pt II ch v. 1595: *Pedlars Prophecy*, l. 730 (Malone S.), Who should hold with the shoe but the sole? 1605: Camden, *Remains*, 333 (1870). 1670: Ray, 142. 1732: Fuller, 4759, The sole holdeth with the upper leather.

5. Tip at the toe. *See* quot. 1885: J. T. Varden, *E. Anglian Handbook*, 115, A Suffolk rhyme teaches us the significance of the 'wear of shoes': – Tip at the toe, live to see woe; Wear at the side, live to be a bride; Wear at the ball, live to spend all; Wear at the heel, live to save a deal.

6. To know where the shoe pinches, *c.*1386: Chaucer, *Merchant's Tide*, l. 309, I wot best wher wringeth me my sho. 1541: Coverdale, *Christ. State Matrimony*, sig. B5, It maye easely be perceaued where the shoe wryngeth them. 1580: Lyly, *Euphues*, 413 (Arber), I see that others maye gesse where the shooe wringes, besides him that weares it. 1609: Rowlands, *Whole Crew, etc.*, 4 (Hunt. Cl), Ah little do you know where my shoo wrings. 1668: Dryden, *Sir Martin Markall*, IV i, I know where it is that your shoe wrings you. 1693: Urquhart, *Rabelais*, bk iii ch xxviii, That is not … the thing that I fear; nor is it there where my shoe pinches. 1714: Ozell, *Molière*, vi 6, Tho' he has not yet told me any thing, I could lay a wager that there the shoe pinches. 1869: Spurgeon, *John Ploughman*, ch xvi, Those who wear the shoe know best where it pinches. 1922: Weyman, *Ovington's Bank*, ch xxxvii, But there, your honour knows best where the shoe pinches.

See also **Dead** (24).

Shoe, *verb*. **1. To shoe the colt.** 1828: Carr, *Craven Dialect*, i 83, 'To shoe the colt' is also a quaint expression of demanding a contribution from a person on his first introduction to any office or employment. 1886: Elworthy, *West Som. Word-Book*, 664 (E.D.S.), Shoe a colt. To cause to pay colt-ale, or the fine customary on first entering an employment. 1924: *N.&Q.*, cxlvii 126, The old custom of 'shoeing the colt' still obtains in Hampshire.

2. To shoe the goose, *c.*1410: Hoccleve. *Poems*, 13 (1796), Ye medle of al thyng, ye moot shoo the goos. Before 1529: Skelton, *Colin Clout*, l.198, What hath lay men to do The gray gose for to sho? 1583: Stubbes, *Anat. of Abuses*, 117 (N.Sh.S.), But if this [gold in the lawyer's palm] be wanting, than farewel clyent; he may go shooe the goose for any good successe he is like to haue of his matter. 1604: Breton, in *Works*, ii *k* 5 (Grosart), And though I be no great wise man, yet I can doe something else, then shooe the goose for my liuing. 1801: Miss Edgeworth, *Lame Jervas*, ch iii, 'The smith that will meddle with all things may go shoe the goslings', an old proverb which … became ever after a favourite of mine. 1902: *N.&Q.*, 9th ser, x 475 … One of the most curious carvings in the church formerly belonging to the monastery of St John at Beverley, in the East Riding of Yorkshire, represents a blacksmith in the absurd act of hammering a shoe on a goose's foot.

Shoeing-horn to help on his gloves, He calls for a. 1732: Fuller, 1816.

Shoemaker. *See* **Cobbler**; and **Six awls**.

Shoemaker's son is a prince born, A. *c.*1597: Deloney, *Gentle Craft*, ch ix, Then answeared Vrsula, My Royall Father, a shoomakers son is a Prince born. 1637: L. Price, in *Pepysian Garland*, 445 (Rollins), Shoemakers sonnes were princes borne, *c.*1710: *Roxb. Ballads*, vii 35 (B.S.).

Shoemaker's stocks, In the = in shoes too small for the feet. 1678: Ray. 347

Shoemaker's wife, Who is worse shod than the? 1546: Heywood, *Proverbs*, Pt I ch xi .1560: T. Wilson, *Rhetorique*, 119 (1909). 1593: *Pass. Morrice*, 69 (N.Sh.S.). Before 1680: Butler, *Remains*, ii 165 (1759), No man goes worse shod than the shoemaker. 1690: *New Dict. Canting Crew*, sig. L2. 1772: Graves, *Spirit. Quixote*, bk iii ch ii, But, says he, the shoemaker's wife often goes in ragged shoes. 1851: Borrow, *Lavengro*, iii 191, It is said that the household of the shoemaker invariably go worse shod than that of any other craft.

Shoot, *verb*. **1. He hath shot his fry.** 1611: Cotgrave, s.v. 'Pouvoir', He hath shot his frie … done the worst or most he can. 1639: Clarke, 223. 1828: Carr, *Craven Dialect*, i 168, 'To shoot one's fry', to lose the good opinion of others which he had once possessed

2. He shooteth well that hits the mark. 1659: Howell, 20.

3. He shoots like a crow-keeper, *c.*1605: Shakespeare, *Lear*, IV vi, That fellow handles his bow like a crow-keeper, *c.*1770: Barrington, *Hist, of Archery*, quoted in Brady, *Varieties of Lit.*, 22, So that 'to shoot like a crow-keeper' became a proverb.

4. He shoots like a gentleman. 1545: Ascham, *Toxoph.*, 150 (Arber), Tel me somwhat, how I should shoote nere leste that prouerbe myght be sayd iustlye of me some-tyme, He shootes lyke a gentle man fayre and far of.

5. He shoots wide of the mark. 1562: Heywood, *Three Hund. Epigr.*, No. 184, He shooteth wyde. 1659: Howell, 7. 1680: D'Urfey, *Virtuous Wife*, I, You are merry sir, and shoot wide o' th' mark. 1709: Mandeville, *Virgin Unmask'd*, 134 (1724), The King of France has several times shot wide of the mark. 1736: Bailey, *Dict.*, s.v. 'Mark', To shoot wide of the mark.

6. He that shoots always aright forfeits his arrow. 1659: Howell, *Proverbs: Brit.-Eng.*, 34.

7. He that shoots oft shall at last hit the mark. [Quis est enim, qui totum diem jaculans non aliquando collineat? – Cicero, *De Divin.*, ii 59.] 1551: Robinson, tr. More's *Utopia*, 52 (Arber). 1732: Fuller, 2276, He that's always shooting, must sometimes hit.

8. I have shot my bolt. 1826: Brady, *Varieties of Lit.*, 21, The implement shot from the cross-bow is called … by the English a bolt. Hence the saying, 'I have shot my bolt'. Cf. **Fool** (24)

9. To be shot with one's own feathers. 1587:
Underdoune, *Heliodorus*, bk ii 74 (T.T.), That
which greeveth me most, is that (as the proverbe
saith) shee useth mine owne fethers against mee.
1710: S. Palmer, *Moral Essays on Proverbs*, 332,
We are often shot with our own feathers.

10. To shoot at a pigeon and kill a crow. 1639:
Clarke, 2. 1670: Ray, 189. 1787: Colman, jr., *Inkle
and Yarico*, III i, But of all the shots, he's the
worst in the art Who shoots at a pigeon and kills a
crow. 1850: Planché, *Extravag.* iv. 104 (1879).

11. To shoot at rovers. *See* Run (14).

Shorn-bug. *See* quot. 1911: A. S. Cooke.,*Off
Beaten Track in Sussex*, 285, 'To eat shorn-bug
for dinner' is the Sussex way of expressing the
extremity of poverty. 'Shorn-bug' is a beetle.

Short acquaintance brings repentance. 1670:
Ray, 142.

Short and sharp. 1546: Heywood, *Proverbs*, Pt
II ch ii, All thing that is sharpe is short, folke
haue tolde. 1655: Fuller, *Church Hist.*, bk ix. § v
(19), [comment on letter by Lord Burleigh]
Short but sharp. 1926: Phillpotts, *Yellow Sands*,
III, I see a way – short and sharp.

Short and sweet. 1539: Taverner, *Erasm. Prov.*,
68 (1552) (OED), The Englysh prouerbe is thus
pronounced. Short and swete. *c.*1580: Lodge,
Defence of Plays, etc., 28 (SH.S.), Shorte and
sweete if I were judge. 1589: Puttenham, *Eng.
Poesie*, 68 (Arber). 1593: Peele, *Edward I*, sc viii.
1637: Shirley, *Young Admiral*, IV iii 1778: H.
Brooke, *Contending Brothers*, I vii, A few words
in full: multum in parvo, short and sweet! 1883:
R.L.S., *Treasure I*, ch ix. 1901: F. E. Taylor,
Lancs Sayings, 6, Short an' sweet, like a donkey's
gallop.

Short boughs, long vintage. 1640: Herbert,
Jac. Prudentum.

Short counsel is good counsel. 1828: Scott,
Fair Maid, ch vii, 'Short rede, good rede,' said
the Smith. 1846–59: *Denham Tracts*, i 98
(F.L.S.), Short counsel is good counsel; slay ye
the bishop. 1892: Heslop, *Northumb. Words*, 570
(E.D.S.), The proverb is specially associated
with the death of Walcher, the first Bishop of
Durham appointed by William the Conqueror.
At Gateshead the bishop had met the leaders of
the people, and on retiring to the church the cry
was raised, 'Short rede, good rede, slay the
bishop'. The church was thereupon set on fire,
and the bishop was slain. A.D. 1080.

**Short cut of a way without same ill way, There
is no.** 1732: Fuller, 492ı.

Shortest answer is doing, The. 1640: Herbert,
Jac. Prudentum.

Short harvests. *See* Harvest (5).

Short horse is soon curried, A. Before 1500: in
Hill, *Commonplace-Book*, 128 (E.E.T.S.). 1571:
R. Edwards, *Damon and Pithias*, in Hazlitt, *Old
Plays*, iv. 33. 1616: Breton, in *Works*, ii e 6
(Grosart). 1637: Heywood, *Royal King*, II,
Here's a short horse soone curryed. 1732:
Fuller, 395. 1820: Scott, *Abbot*, ch xi, A short
tale is soon told – and a short horse soon curried.
1883: Burne, *Shropsh. Folk-Lore*, 589. 1917:
Bridge, *Cheshire Proverbs*, 4, A little horse is soon
wispt, And a pretty girl is soon kist.

Short life and a merry, A. 1654: Gayton,
Pleasant Notes Don Q., 101, The indicted cry a
merry life and a short. 1660: Tatham, *Rump*, I, A
short life and a merry life, I cry. 1754:
Connoisseur, No. 50, A short life and a merry one
was their favourite maxim. 1855: Kingsley,
West. Ho!, ch xxxii.

Short pleasure long lament. 1468: *Coventry
Mys.*, 32 (SH.S.), Schort lykyng xal be longe
bought. 1556: G. Colvile, tr. Boethius, 66 (1897),
Or as a man woulde saye: for a lytle pleasure,
longe payne. 1611: Cotgrave, s.v. 'Plaisir, 'For a
short pleasure long remembrance. 1681:
Robertson, *Phraseol. Generalis*, 1001. 1732:
Fuller, 4155, Short pleasures, long pains.

Short prayer reaches Heaven, A. *c.*1460: *Good
Wyfe wold a Pylgremage*, 1. 167 (E.E.T.S.), A
schort prayer wynnythe heyvyn. 1493: *Dives et
Pauper*, fo. 74 (1536), It is a common prouerbe,
that a short prayer thirleth [penetrates, or
reaches] heuen. 1666: Torriano, *Piazza Univ.*,
178, A short prayer penetrates. 1732: Fuller, 397,
A short prayer may reach up to the Heaven of
Heavens.

Short reckonings are soon cleared. Ibid., No.
4156. 1869: Spurgeon, *John loughman*, ch xii,
Pay as you go, and keep from small scores. Short
reckonings are soon cleared.

Short reckonings make long friends. 1530: R.
Whitforde, *Work for Householders*, A4, The
commune proverb is that ofte rekenynge holdest
longe felawship. 1641: D. Fergusson, *Scottish
Proverbs* (STS), no. 668 Oft compting makes
good friends.1673: J. Dare, *Counsellot Manners*,
xciii, Short reckonings (we say) make long

friends. 1831: Hone, *Year-Book*, col. 1417. 1918: Orczy, *Man in Grey*: 'Silver-leg', 2.

Short shooting loseth the game. 1546: Heywood, *Proverbs*, Pt II ch ix. [with 'your' for 'the']. *c.*1580: Harvey, *Marginalia*, 147 (1913), Let not short shooting loose yor game. 1670: Ray, 142. 1732: Fuller, 4157.

Short visits make long friends. Oxfordsh. 1923: *Folk-Lore*, xxxiv. 329.

Shotley. *See* **Axwell Park**.

Shoulder of mutton for a sick horse, A. 1541: *Sch. House of Women*, l. 95, As holsome for a man is a woman's corse, As a shoulder of mutton for a sick horse. 1596: Jonson, *Ev. Man in Humour*, II i, Counsel to him is as good as a shoulder, etc. 1639: Clarke, 4, As fit for him as a shoulder, etc. 1678: Ray, 236. 1732: Fuller, 1179.

Shoulder out, To put the=To be annoyed, to take offence. 1917: Bridge, *Cheshire Proverbs*, 142.

Shouter of Gatley, A. Ibid., 6, A shaouter o' Gatley. Said of any loud-spoken boisterous person.

Show a fair (or **clean**) **pair of heels To.** 1546: Heywood, *Proverbs*, Pt II ch vii, Except hir maide shewe a fayre paire of heeles. 1577: J. Grange, *Golden Aphroditis*, sig. D3, The valyaunt souldioure hadde rather truste to the force of hys armes ... than in the fielde a fayre payre of heeles to shew. 1630: T. Adams, *Works*, 55, But for these shackles, debt would often shew credit a light paire of heeles. 1698: *Terence made English*, 241 (2nd ed.), I'd ha' ... shewn him a fair pair of heels for 't. 1737: Ray, 70. 1819: Scott, *Ivanhoe*, ch xl., Or Folly will show a clean pair of heels, and leave Valour to find out his way ... as best he may. 1883: R.L.S., *Treasure I*, ch ii, Black Dog, in spite of his wounds, showed a wonderful clean pair of heels, and disappeared ... in half a minute. 1899: Dickinson, *Cumberland Gloss.*, 66, When a person runs away through fear, he shews a pair of clean heels.

Show me the man. *See* quot. 1819: Scott, *Bride of L.*, ch i, The adage 'show me the man, and I will show you the law', became as prevalent as it was scandalous.

Shows all his wit at once, He. 1633: Draxe, 70. 1670: Ray, 199.

Shrew and **Shrews**, *subs.* **1. A shrew is better than a sheep.** 1580: Tusser, *Husb.*, 157 (E.D.S.), This prouerbe looke in mind ye keepe,

As good a shrew is as a sheepe, For you to take to wiue. *c.*1600: *Grim the Collier*, II, 'Tis better to be a shrew, sir, than a sheep. 1630: Taylor (Water-Poet), *Works*, 3rd pagin., 59. 1659: *Lady Alimony*, V iii, I see one must thank God for a shrew as well as for a sheep. 1732: Fuller, 873, Better be a shrew than a sheep. 1880: Spurgeon, *Ploughman's Pictures*, 89, A shrew is better than a slut. Cf. No. 4.

2. A shrew profitable may serve a man reasonable. 1605: Camden, *Remains*, 317 (1870). 1616: Breton, in *Works*, ii *e* 5 (Grosart) ['is good for' instead of 'may serve']. 1732: Fuller, 398.

3. Every man can rule a shrew but he who has her. 1546: Heywood, *Proverbs*, Pt II ch vi. 1596: Harington, *Metam. of Ajax*, 95 (1814). 1621: Burton, *Melancholy*, II ii 6, 1, p. 364 (1836). 1681: Robertson, *Phraseol. Generalis*, 565. 1732: Fuller, 1444 ['tame' for 'rule']. 1883: Burne, *Shropsh. Folk-Lore*, 588, Every one can manage a bad wife but he who has her.

4. One shrew is worth two sheep. *1575:* Gascoigne, *Glasse of Govt.*, III i [quoted as 'an olde saying']. Cf. No. 1.

5. When all shrews have dined. *See* quots. 1546: Heywood, *Proverbs*, Pt I ch xiii, And when all shrews haue dind, Chaunge from foule weather to faire is oft enclind. 1678: Ray, 243, It will be fair weather when the shrews have dined.

Shrewsbury. *See* quot. 1662: Fuller, *Worthies*, iii 54 (1840), He that fetcheth a wife from Shrewsbury, must cany her into Staffordshire, or else shall live in Cumberland. 1790: Grose, *Prov. Gloss.*, s.v. 'Salop' [as in 1662]. 1846–59: *Denham Tracts*, i 174 (F.L.S.) [as in 1662].

Shrewsbury clock, By. 1597: Shakespeare, 1 *Henry IV*, V iv, We rose both at an instant, and fought a long hour by Shrewsbury clock. 1654: Gayton, *Pleasant Notes Don Q.*, 183, The Knight that fought by th' clock at Shrewsberry. 1681: *Poor Robin Alman.*, March, A great many people shall feed ... three hours together by Shrewsbury Clock. 1783: Mrs Cowley, *More Ways than One*, I i, My master is as strict, and as nice, and exact, as Shrewsperry Clock. 1796: White, *Falstaff's Letters*, 17, Fifteen minutes, as thou say'st, by Shrewsbury clock. 1891: R.L.S., *Letters*, iv 86 (Tusitala ed.), I remember, when I first saw this, laughing for an hour by Shrewsbury clock.

Shrink in the wetting, To. 1540: Palsgrave, *Acolastus*, sig. V4, Where is my golden chain become … it is shrunk in the wetynge. 1596: Lodge, *Divel Coniured*, 4 (Hunt.Cl.), Those conceits are shrunke in the wetting. 1612: Chapman, *Widow's Tears*, II iv, Then had I been here a fool … if for a lady's frown … I should have shrunk in the wetting. 1639: Fuller, *Holy War*, bk v ch xxii, Who washed himself in Jordan, and then shrinking in the wetting returned presently home again. 1825: Scott, *Betrothed*, ch v, They [Flemings] are of an enduring generation, and will not shrink in the washing.

Shropshire is full of trout and Tories. 1883: Burne, *Shropsh. Folk-Lore*, 581.

Shropshire sharp-shins. 15th cent.: in *Reliq. Antiquae*, i 269 (1841), Schropschir, my schinnes ben scharpe. 1622: Drayton, *Polyol.*, xxiii, And Shropshire saith in her, That shins be ever sharp. 1710–12: Leland, *Itin.*, I am of Shropshire, my shinnes be sharpe. 1883: Burne, *Shropsh. Folk-Lore*, 581, 'Sharp-shins' is still applied in Shropshire, 1st to light heels, 2nd to sharp wits. 1913: E. M. Wright, *Rustic Speech.*, *etc.*, 180, Anciently the Salopian was proverbial for sharp shins.

Shrove-tide. 1. Fit as a pancake for Shrove *Tuesday*. 1846: Denham, *Proverbs*, 27 (Percy S.).

2. If it thunder upon Shrove Tuesday it foretelleth winde, store of fruit, and plenty. 1669: *New Help to Discourse*, 283. 1893: Inwards, *Weather Lore*, 40.

3. Rejoice Shrove-tide today; for tomorrow you'll be Ashes. 1732: Fuller, 4009.

4. So much as the sun shineth on Pancake Tuesday, the like will shine every day in Lent. 1669: *New Help to Discourse*, 283. 1893: Inwards, *Weather Lore*, 40.

5. When the sun is shining on Shrovetide Day, it is meant well for rye and peas. Ibid., 40.

Shut mouth catches no flies, A. For an alternative version of this proverb, *see* **Fly** (9). 1599: J. Minsheu, *Spanish Grammar*, 83, In a closed up mouth a flie cannot get in. 1640: G. Herbert, *Outlandish Proverbs*, no. 219, Into a mouth shut, flies flie not. 1659: T. Fuller, *Appeal of Injured Innocence*, I 12, The *Spanish* proverb … is necessary in dangerous … Times, *Where the mouth is shut no Fly doth enter*. 1742: B. Franklin, *Poor Richard's Almanack*, Feb., Speak and speed: the close mouth catches no flies. 1926: T.

Willard, *City of the Sacred Well*, xv, Tell each of them that a shut mouth catches no flies.

Shut not the barn-door. *See* quot. 1860: Reade, *Cl. and Hearth*, ch xxxvi, The law meddles but with men and women, and these cannot utter a story all lies, let them try ever so. Wherefore we shut not the barn-door (as the saying is), against any man's grain. Only having taken it in, we do winnow and sift it.

Shut up shop-windows, He has = He is bankrupt. 1678: Ray, 89.

Sick, adj. 1. As sick as a cat. 1869: Spurgeon, *John Ploughman*, ch xx, These great talkers … make me as sick as a cat.

2. As sick as a cushion. 1678: Ray, 288. 1738: Swift, *Polite Convers.*, Dial. I, Poor miss, she's sick as a cushion, she wants nothing but stuffing.

3. As sick as a dog. 1592: G. Harvey, *Works*, i 161 (Grosart), Now sicke as a dog. 1599: Buttes, *Dyets Dry Dinner*, sig. O4. 1667: L'Estrange, *Quevedo's Visions*, 262 (1904). 1766: *Ganick*, *Neck or Nothing*,I i., I am sick as a dog of being a valet. 1864: Mrs H. Wood, *Trevlyn Hold*, ch xx, Folks have never called him the Squire, though he's as sick as a dog for it.

4. As sick as a horse. 1685: Meriton, *Yorkshire Ale*, 71, It macks me as seeke as a horse. 1758–67: Sterne, *Trist. Shandy*, vol vii ch ii. 1854: Baker, *Northants Gloss.*, s.v. 'Sick as a horse', A common vulgar simile, used when a person is exceedingly sick without vomiting. 1901: F. E. Taylor, *Lancs Sayings*, 4, As sick as a hawse.

5. Ever sick of the slothful guise, Loath to bed and loath to rise. 1639: Clarke, 292. Cf. **Sluggard's guise.**

6. He who was never sick, dies the first fit. 1732: Fuller, 2409.

7. Sick of the fever lurden. *See* **Fever lurden**.

8. Sick o' th' idle crick, and the bellywark i' th' heel. 1678: Ray, 254.

9. Sick of the idles. 1639: Clarke, 144. 1670: Ray, 182.

10. Sick of the Lombard fever. 1659: Howell, 11. 1670: Ray, 215.

11. Sick of the mulligrubs. *c.*1620: B.&F., *Monsieur Thomas*, II iii, Whose dog lies sick o' the mulligrubs? 1634: S. Rowley, *Noble Soldier*, IV ii, The divell lyes sicke of the mulligrubs. 1670: Ray, 218, Sick of the mulligrubs with eating chop't hay. 1738: Swift, *Polite Convers.*, Dial. I [as in 1670].

12. Sick of the silver dropsy. 1633: Draxe, 33, He hath the siluer dropsie. 1639: Clarke, 40.

13. Sick of the simples. 1754: Berthelson, *Eng.-Danish Dict.*, s.v. 'Sick'.

14. Sick of the sullens. 1580: Lyly, *Euphues*, 285 (Arber), She was solitary by walking, with hir frowning cloth, as sick lately of the solens. 1596: Lodge, *Wits Miserie*, 101 (Hunt.Cl.), Rather die sicke of the sullens then tell his griefe. *c.*1620: B.&F., *Woman's Prize*, IV iv, Is fallen sick ... o' th' sullens. 1828: Scott, *Journal*, 9 March, I do not know anything which relieves the mind so much from the sullens as trifling discussion ...

Sickle, *subs*. **1. Between the sickle and the scythe, What is born will never thrive.** Derby. 1884: *Folk-Lore Journal*, ii 279. Cf. **Marry** (16).

2. The sickle and the scythe, that love I not to see, But the good ale-tankard, happy might it be. 1639: Clarke, 47.

3. To put one's sickle into another man's corn. 1387: Trevisa, tr. Higden, viii 183 (Rolls Ser.), And seide to hym, 'Thou hast no leve to sette thyn hook in other men ripe'. *c.*1440: Anon., tr. Higden, in Ibid., viii 183, Hit is not lawefull to the to put a sythe into the corne of other men. 1576: Lambarde, *Peramb. of Kent*, 455 (1826), Least I be blamed for thrusting my sicle into another mans harvest. 1602: Carew, *Surv. of Cornwall*, 211 (1811), I have thrust my sickle overfar into another's harvest. 1681: Robertson, *Phraseol. Generalis*, 291, You have no business to do there; Put not your sickle into your neighbours corn. 1732: Fuller, 5218.

Sickness comes on horseback, but goeth away on foot. 1611: Cotgrave, s.v. 'Maladie', Diseases come on horsebacke and return on foot. 1654: Whitlock, *Zootomia*, 124, Sicknesse posteth to us, but crawleth from us. 1869: Hazlitt, 336.

Sickness is felt, but health not at all. 1732: Fuller, 4160.

Sickness is the chapel of devotion, The chamber of. 1633: Draxe, 190. 1670: Ray, 24. 1732: Fuller, 4444. 1803: *The Moralist's Medley*, 1.

Sickness tells us what we are. 1732: Fuller, 4161.

Side pockets. *See* **Toad**.

Sides to every question. *See* **Two sides**.

Sieve and riddle. *See* quots. 1670: Ray, 207, As

much sib'd [akin] as sieve and ridder, that grew both in a wood together. 1691: Ray, *Words not Generally Used*, 63 (E.D.S.), No more sib'd than, etc. Prov. Cheshire. 1824: Scott, *Redgauntlet*, Lett, xiii, Whilk ye are aware sounds as like being akin to a peatship and a sheriffdom, as a sieve is sib to a riddle. 1917: Bridge, *Cheshire Proverbs*, 98 [as in 1691, but with 'sib' for 'sib'd'].

Sift him grain by grain and he proveth but chaff. 1633: Draxe, 46. 1869: Spurgeon, *John Ploughman*, ch i, Sift a sluggard grain by grain, and you'll find him all chaff.

Sift night and day, and get nothing but bran, You. 1732: Fuller, 5997.

Sigh not. *See* **Never sigh**.

Sight of a man hath the force of a lion, The. 1640: Herbert, *Jac. Prudentum*.

Sign invites you in; but your money must redeem you out, The. 1732: Fuller, 4746.

Silence gives consent. *c.*1387: Usk, *Test, of Love*, in Skeat's *Chaucer*, vii 36, Lo eke an olde proverbe amonges many other: 'He that is stille semeth as he graunted'. 1412: Hoccleve, *Regiment*, st. 442, l. 3093 (E.E.T.S.), And for he naght ne seith, he his assent zeueth therto, by mannës Iugëment. *c.*1490: *Partonope*, 467 (E.E.T.S.), This proverbe was seide fall longe ago: 'Who so holdeth hym still dothe assent'. 1591: Lyly, *Endymion*, V iii, Silence, madam, consents. 1616: Jonson, *Devil an Ass*, I iii, Let me take warrant, lady, from your silence, which ever is interpreted consent. 1638: Randolph, in *Works*, ii 616 (1875), And modest silence gives consent. Before 1754: Fielding, *Fathers*, II ii, At least I shall take your silence for consent. 1768: Goldsmith, *Good-Natured Man*, II. 1821: W. Combe, *Syntax in Search of Wife*, can. xxxv p. 109, But Ma'am said *nought* – though that's *consent*, He thought, if but the adage old Does a decided truth unfold.

Silence is a fine jewel for a woman, but it's little worn. 1732: Fuller, 4166. 1869: Spurgeon, *John Ploughman*, ch vi.

Silence is golden. 1865: W. White, *Eastern England*, ii 129. 1878: Gibbs, *Cotswold Village*, ch iv, 'Silence is golden' is the motto here whilst the viands are being discussed. 1909: A. Dobson, in *Poet. Works*, 403 (1923). Cf. **Speech**.

Silence is the best ornament of a woman. 1539: Taverner, *Proverbs*, fo. 50, Silence garnysheth a woman. 1645: Howell, *Letters*, bk i § iv No. ix. 1670: Ray, 24.

Silence is wisdom (or counsel). *c.*1374: Chaucer, *Troylus*, bk iii l. 294, These wyse clerkes that ben dede Han ever yet proverbed to us yonge, That 'firste vertu is to kepe tonge'. *c.*1470: G. Ashby, *Poems*, 85 (E.E.T.S.), Grete wisdam is, litil to speke. 1540: Palsgrave, *Acolastus*, sig. B2, I dare not … saye mum is counseyle. 1546: Heywood, *Proverbs*, Pt II ch v, I will say nought but mum, and mum is counsell. 1620: *Two Merry Milkmaids*, II ii, Silence lady is the best part of wisdome. 1732: Fuller, 4169, Silence is wisdom, when speaking is folly. 1869: Spurgeon, *John Ploughman*, ch vi.

Silence seldom doth harm. 1630: Brathwait, *Eng. Gent., etc.*, 51 (1641), Silence … may doe good, but can doe little harme. 1670: Ray, 24. 1732: Fuller, 4170, Silence seldom hurts.

Silence. *See also* **No wisdom; Sorrow makes silence;** and **Speech.**

Silent, *adj.* **1. A silent woman [***is***] better than a double-tongued man.** 1659: Howell, 11.

2. As silent as death. 1377: Langland, *Plowman*, B, x 136, As doumbe as deth. 1679: *The Counterfeits*, I i, All the houses silent as Death.

3. As silent as the grave. 1604: Shakespeare, *Othello*, V ii, Ha! no more moving? Still as the grave. 1778: H. Brooke, *Marriage Contract*, I ii, I will be silent as the grave, with respect to your secret. 1829: Scott, *Journal*, 1 July, The house … then became silent as the grave. 1893: R.L.S., *Ebb-Tide*, ch viii.

4. Beware of a silent dog and a still water. 1732: Fuller, 1806. 1875: Cheales, *Proverb. Folk-Lore*, 115.

5. He that is silent gathers stones. 1813: Ray, 159.

Silk and scarlet walks many a harlot, In. 1869: Hazlitt, 234.

Silk purse out of a sow's ear, You can't make a. 1518: A. Barclay, *Eclogues* (E.E.T.S.), v 360, None can make goodly silke of a gotes fleece. 1579: S. Gosson, *Ephemerides of Phialo*, 62v, Seekinge … to make a silke purse of a Sowes eare, that when it shoulde close, will not come togeather. 1611: Cotgrave, s.v. 'Pigeon', A man cannot make a cheverill purse of a sows eare. 1738: Swift, *Polite Convers.*, Dial. II 1748: Richardson, *Clarissa*, iv 119 (1785), Who would expect velvet to be made out of a sow's ear? 1806:

Lamb, *Mr H –* , II. 1877: S. Butler, *Life and Habit*, 201, Every man and every race is capable of education up to a certain point, but not to the extent of being made from a sow's ear into a silk purse. 1921: *Times*, 18 August, p. 7, col. 5, A firm of chemists of Cambridge, Massachusetts, have succeeded in manufacturing a silk purse out of a sow's ear. They admit that it is not yet a commercial proposition, but sufficiently complete and substantial to demonstrate the fallacy of the ancient proverb.

Silks and satins put out the kitchen fire. 1640: Herbert, *Jac. Prudentum*, Silks and satins put out the fire in the chimney. 1736: Franklin, *Way to Wealth*, in *Works*, i 447 (Bigelow) [with 'scarlet and velvets' after 'satins']. 1912: *N. &Q.*, 11th ser, vi 255, In my childhood in Ulster I often heard the proverb, 'Silks', etc.

Silly as a lamb's dad [sheep], **As.** Oxfordsh. 1923: *Folk-Lore*, xxxiv. 329.

Silly fish. *See* **Fish**(12).

Silly goose. *See* **Goose** (3) and (21).

Silly question. *See* **Ask** (1).

Silver, *adj.* and *subs.* **1. A silver key can open an iron lock.** 1732: Fuller, 400.

2. Every cloud has a silver lining. *See* **Silver** (6).

3. He that has no silver in his purse, should have silver on his tongue. [1659: Howell, *Proverbs: Ital.-Eng.*, 5, Who hath not money in his purse, let him have honey in his mouth.] 1732: Fuller, 2149.

4. Silver dropsy. *See* **Sick** (12).

5. Silver hook. *See* **Angle** (2).

6. There is a silver lining to every cloud. 1634: Milton, *Comus*, 221, Was I deceived, or did a sable cloud Turn forth her silver lining on the night? 1852: Dickens, *Bleak House*, ch xviii, I expand, I open, I turn my silver lining outward like Milton's cloud. 1869: P.T. Barnum, *Struggles and Triumphs*, 406, 'Every cloud', says the proverb, 'has a silver lining'. 1885: Gilbert, *Mikado*, II, Don't let's be down-hearted! There's a silver lining to every cloud.

7. To be born with a silver spoon in one's mouth. [Gallinae filius albae. – Juvenal, xiii 141.] 1639: Clarke, 39, He was borne with a penny in's mouth. 1712: Motteux, *Quixote*, Pt II ch lxxiii, Every man was not born with a silver spoon in his mouth. 1850: Dickens, *Chuzzlewit*, ch vi. 1869: Hazlitt, 399, They who are born with silver spoons in their mouths, don't know how to use them. 1922: C. K. Shorter, in *Sphere*, 9 Dec., p. 266, col. 2, Assuredly he was born with a silver spoon in his mouth. He knew none of the struggles and anxieties which some of us have faced.

See also **White** (18).

Sim steals. *See* **Horse** (52).

Simondsall sauce. *See* quot. Simondsall is a Gloucestershire farm on high ground. 1639: in *Berkeley MSS.*, iii 30 (1885), When a man eates little, to say hee wants some of Simondsall sauce.

Simpers as a mare when she eats thistles, She. 1639: Clarke, 120.

Simpers like a bride on her wedding-day, She. 1678: Ray, 288.

Simpers like a furmity kettle, She. 1631: W. Saltonstall, *Picturae Loquentes*, sig. C5, Makes her simper like a pot that's ready to run o're. 1667: L'Estrange, *Quevedo's Visions*, 136 (1904), This sets the widow a-pinking, and simpering like a furmety-kettle. 1738: Swift, *Polite Convers.*, Dial. I. 1846–59: *Denham Tracts*, ii 92 (F.L.S.), She simpers like a frummetty kettle at Christmas.

Simpers like a riven dish, She. 1678: Ray, 288.

Simple as a ha'porth o' soap in a washin mug, As. 1917: Bridge, *Cheshire Proverbs*, 19.

Sin and **Sins,** *subs.* **1. It is a sin to belie the devil.** *See* **Devil** (25).

2. It is a sin to steal a pin. 1875: Cheales, *Proverb. Folk-Lore*, 129 … as we … used to be informed in the nursery. 1914: Lucas, *Land-marks*, ch iv, Certain crusted scraps of nursery wisdom … such as … 'It is a sin to steal a pin'.

3. Our sins and our debts are always greater than we take them to be. 1659: Howell, *Proverbs: Ital.-Eng.*, 1. 1732: Fuller, 4179 ['think' for 'take']. 1774: Franklin, in *Works*, v 291 (Bigelow). 1827: Hone, *Table-Book*, 505 … greater than we think of. 1869: Spurgeon, *John Ploughman*, ch xii [as in 1732].

4. Sins are not known till they be acted. 1640: Herbert, *Jac. Prudentum.*

5. Sin that is hidden is half forgiven. 1567: G. Fenton, *Bandello*, ii 149 (T.T.), Me thinkes a falte don in secrett is halfe perdoned. 1666: Torriano, *Piazza Univ.*, 197, Sin conceal'd, half pardoned.

Sin, *verb. See* quot. *c.*1386: Chaucer, *Melibeus*, § 29, The proverbe seith: that 'for to do sinne is mannish, but certes for to persevere longe in sinne is werk of the devel'.

Sinews of war, The. [Pecuniae belli civilis nervi sunt. – Tacitus, II xxiv. Nervi belli pecunia. – Cicero, *Phil.*, V ii 5.] *c.*1550: *Disc. Common Weal Eng.*, 87 (1893) (OED), These coins and treasures be not with out cause called of wise men … The senowes of warre. 1581: Stafford, *Exam, of Complaints*, 67 (N.Sh.S.). 1594: Peele, *Battle of Alcazar*, I ii, Madam, gold is the glue, sinews, and strength of war. 1623: Massinger, *Duke of Milan*, III i, Money is the sinew of the war. 1653: Urquhart, *Rabelais*, bk i ch xlvi, Coine is the sinews of warre. 1767: Murphy, *Sch. for Guardians*, II iii, You have furnished me with the sinews of war. 1838: Carlyle, *Sartor*, bk ii ch iii, Suppose your sinews of war quite broken; I mean your military chest insolvent.

Sing, *verb.* **1. He may sing before thieves.** [Cantabit vacuus coram latrone viator. – Juvenal, x 22.] *c.*1230: in Wright, *Pol. Songs John to Edw. II*, 35 (Camden S.) [Juvenal's line], *c.*1374: Chaucer, *Boethius*, bk ii Pr. v, A pore man, that berth no richesse on him by the weye, may boldely singe biforn theves, for he hath nat wherof to ben robbed, *c.*1440: Lydgate, *Fall of Princes*, bk iii l. 582 (E.E.T.S.), The poore man affor the theeff doth synge. 1593: Peele, *Edw. I*, sc xii, 'Tis an old said saying … a man's purse-penniless may sing before a thief. 1659: T. Peake, *Parnassi Puerp.*, 21, Clients returning before theefs may sing; For back from London they can't money bring. 1707: Dunton, *Athenian Sport*, p. 155, col. 1, The moneyless traveller can sing before a thief. 1804: Mrs Piozzi, in Hayward, *Mrs Piozzi*, ii 263 (1861), The *poor* traveller always sung safely even in company of thieves.

2. He sings at a deaf man's door. 1633: Draxe, 38.

3. He that sings in disaster [confesses], **Shall weep all his life-time thereafter.** 1612: Shelton, *Quixote*, Pt I bk iii ch viii, 'Here it is quite contrary,' quoth the slave, 'for "He that sings once, weeps all his life after".' 1710: S. Palmer, *Moral Essays on Proverbs*, 197.

4. He that sings on Friday, will weep on Sunday. 1640: Herbert, *Jac. Prudentum.* 1670: Ray, 24.

5. He that sings worst let him begin first, *c.*1410: *Towneley Plays*, 108 (E.E.T.S.), [Here 'worst' is 'best']. Who so can best syng Shall haue the begynnyng. 1725: Bailey, tr. Erasmus'

Colloq., 204, According to the old proverb, He that sings worst let him begin first.

6. Many a one sings that is full sorry. 1561: *Queene Hester*, 19 (Grosart), Yt with their mouth thei sing, Though thei wepe in their hart. 1611: Cotgrave, s.v. 'Chanter'.

7. Sing before breakfast, cry before night. 1530: Palsgrave, 776, You waxe mery this morning. God gyue grace you wepe nat or nyght. 1855: *N. & Q.*, 1st ser, xi 416, If you sing before breakfast, you'll cry before night. 1859: Ibid., 2nd ser, viii 484 [Hants]. 1860: Ibid., 2nd ser, ix. 51 ... very common ... in almost every part of Lincolnshire. 1898: Ibid., 9th ser, ii 436. 1899: Ibid., 9th ser, iii 173 [Northants].

8. Thou singest like a bird called a swine. 1678: Ray, 269. 1732: Fuller, 5230, To sing like, etc.

9. To sing Lachrymae = To be sorry or mournful, *c.*1610: in *Roxb. Ballads*, iii 68 (B.S.), In the prison to stay, Where I sung Lachrima. 1674: *Poor Robin Alman.*, July, The lawyers shall sing Lachrymae over Littletons grave.

10. To sing Placebo = To be flattering or servile. 1340: *Ayenbite*, 60 (OED), the uerthe zenne is thet huanne hi alle zingeth 'Placebo', thet is to zigge: 'mi lhord zayth zuth, mi lhord deth wel'. *c.*1540: Bale, *Kynge Johaon*, 30 (Camden S.), By the mas, me thynke they are syngyng of placebo. 1542: Becon, in *Early Works*, 276 (P.S.), He cannot bear fire in one hand and water in the other. He cannot play *placebo*. 1592: Nashe, *Works*, ii 50 (Grosart), That poets and good fellowes may drinke, and souldiers sing Placebo. 1618: Harington, *Epigrams*, bk ii No. 56, [entitled] Of a Preacher that sings Placebo.

11. To sing the same song (or **one song**). 1580: Baret, *Alvearie*, E 2, They harpe alwaie vpon one string, they are alwaie in one song. 1639: Clarke, 8, To sing the old song. 1670: Ray, 192, To sing the same song. 1681: Robertson, *Phraseol. Generalis*, 1133. 1736: Bailey, *Dict.*, s.v. 'Tune', You are always in the same tune.

12. To sing three thrums = To purr like a cat. 1917: Bridge, *Cheshire Proverbs*, 143.

13. Who can sing so merry a note as he that cannot change a groat. 1546: Heywood, *Proverbs*, Pt I ch xii. 1594: Barnfield, *Affect. Sheph.*, 40 (Percy S.). 1692: L'Estrange, *Aesop*, 390 (3rd ed.) ... the old saying, No man sings a

merrier note Then he that cannot change a groat. 1732: Fuller, 6449 ['the cobler' for 'he'].

14. *See* quot. 1869: Hazlitt, 482, Yeow mussent sing a Sunday, becaze it is a sin; but yeow may sing a Monday, till Sunday cums agin. *Suffolk*.

Singers and ringers are little home bringers. 1893: *Co. Folk-Lore: Suffolk*, 151 (F.L.S.).

Singing man keeps his shop in his throat, The. 1640: Herbert, *Jac. Prudentum*. 1670: Ray, 24. 1732: Fuller, 4747.

Single long, shame at last. 1659: Howell, *Proverbs: Brit.-Eng.*, 21.

Single step, The longest journey begins with a. *See* **Longest**.

Sink in his own sin, He shall. 1546: Heywood, *Proverbs*, Pt I ch x, Thou shalte sure sinke in thine own syn for vs. 1659: Howell, 15.

Sink or swim, To. *c.*1386: Chaucer, *Knight's Tale*, l. 1539, She ... reccheth neuere wher I synke or fleete [float]. *c.*1450: in *Reliq. Antiquae*, i 76 (1841), Whedyr she ever flete, or synke. *c.*1520: in Skelton, *Works*, ii 438 (Dyce), But some shall go astraye, And lerne to swyme or sinke. 1594: Nashe, *Dido*, IV iii, She cares not how we sinke or swimme. *c.*1620: B.&F., *Night-Walker*, III iii. 1667: Pepys, *Diary*, 4 April. 1709: in *Harl.Miscell.*, i 206 (1744). 1748: Richardson, *Clarissa*, vi 211 (1785), She was determined to get out herself as fast as she could, let me sink or swim. 1818: Scott, *Heart of Midl.*, ch xxvi. 1896: Doyle, *Rodney Stone*, ch vii, I sink or swim with my friends! A Whig I started, and a Whig I shall remain.

Sion and Sheen. *See* quots. 1659: Howell, 21, The nun of Sion, with the frier of Shean, Went under water to play the quean. 1790: Grose, *Prov. Gloss.*, s.v. 'Middlesex', The nun of Sion with the friar of Sheen [= birds of a feather].

Sirrah your dogs! 1670: Ray, 192. 1732: Fuller, 6496, Sirrah your dog, but sirrah not me; For I was born before you could see.

Sit, *verb.* **1. Better sit idle than work for nothing.** 1642: D. Rogers, *Matrim. Honour*, 225, Our proverbe saith, better sit for naught, then stir for naught. 1683: Meriton, *Yorkshire Ale*, 83–7 (1697), Better sit idle than work teaum [for nothing].

2. Better sit still than rise up and fall. *c.*1410: *Towneley Plays*, 229 (E.E.T.S.). 1546: Heywood, *Proverbs*, Pt II ch v 1592: Warner, *Albion's England*, bk vii ch 37, And rather sit thou safely still, Then for a fall to rise. 1618: Breton, in *Inedited Tracts*, 190 (Hazlitt), 1732: Fuller, 4181, Sit still, rather than rise and fall down.

3. He sits not sure that sits too high. 1611: Cotgrave, s.v. 'Assuré'.

4. He that sits to work in the marketplace shall have many teachers. 1732: Fuller, 2303.

5. He that sitteth well thinketh ill. 1578: Florio, *First Fruites*, fo. 28, Who sitteth wel thynketh yl. 1629: *Book of Meery Riddles*, Prov. 10.

6. Sit a while and go a mile. 1530: Palsgrave, 436, Rest a whyle and roune a myle. 1639: Clarke, 235.

7. Sit by the good, and by the good arise. 1572: T. Wilson, *Disc, upon Usury*, 359 (1925) [cited as 'an old prouerbe'].

8. Sit in your place and none can make you rise. 1611: Cotgrave, s.v. 'Seoir', He need not fear to be chidden that sits where he is bidden. 1640: Herbert, *Jac. Prudentum*. 1670: Ray, 24. 1732: Fuller, 4180, Sit firm in thy place, and none can hurt thee. 1853: Trench, *Proverbs*, 108 (1905), How excellently this unites genuine modesty and manly self-assertion: *Sit in your place, and no man can make you rise.*

9. To sit on one's skirts. 1546: Heywood, *Proverbs*, Pt I ch v, And also I shall, to reueng former hurtis Hold their noses to grinstone, and syt on theyr skurtis That erst sate on mine. 1598: Bernard, *Terence*, 58, I will be reuenged on thee. I will sit on thy skirts. 1732: Fuller, 2653, I will stick in your skirts for this. 1816: Scott, *Old Mortality*, ch xliii, 'D—n seize me, if I forgive him for it, though!' replied the other; 'and I think I can sit in his skirts now'. 1889: Peacock, *Manley, etc., Gloss.*, 490 (E.D.S.), To sit on a person's skirts is to annoy, baffle, or impede him.

10. To sit still and pill straws. 1672: Walker, *Paroem.*, 21.

11. To sit upon thorns. *See* **Thorn** (8).

Sitenhill. *See* **Barton**.

Six awls make a shoemaker. 1670: Ray, 216.

Sixes and sevens, At. Originally this seems to have been a gambling – dicing – phrase, 'To set at six or seven'. The *Oxford English Dictionary* says – 'probably a fanciful alteration of *to set on cinque and sice*, these being the two highest numbers'. *c.*1340: *Avowyne of Arthur*, st. 65 (Camden S.), Alle in sundur hit brast in six or in seuyn. *c.*1374: Chaucer, *Troylus*, bk iv l.622, Lat

not this wrecched wo thin herte gnawe. But manly set the world on sixe and sevene. *c.*1400: *Towneley Plays*, 169 (E.E.T.S.), Bot be thay past me by by mahowne in heuen, I shall, and that in hy set all on sex and seuen. 1542: Udall, tr. Erasmus' *Apoph.*, 298 (1877), There is a prouerbe, *omnem iacere aliam*, to cast att dice, by whiche is signified, to set al on sixe and seuen, and at al auentures to ieoperd, assaiyng the wild chaunce of fortune, be it good, be it bad. 1596: Shakespeare, *Rich. II*, II ii, All is uneven. And everything is left at six and seven. 1630: Taylor (Water-Poet), *Works*, 2nd pagin., 71, Nor carelessly set all at six and seuen. 1670: Cotton, *Scarronides*, bk iv, But like a dame of wits bereaven, Let all things go at six and seven. 1710: Centlivre, *Man's Bewitch'd*, II iv, Did he make any will? ... No, Sir, he has left all sixes and sevens. 1768: Goldsmith, *Good-natured Man*, I, Haven't I reason to be out of my senses, when I see things going at sixes and sevens? 1829: Cobbett, *Advice to Young Men*, Lett. III, Leaving books and papers all lying about at sixes and sevens. 1920: Locke, *House of Baltazar*, ch xviii, 'We're all at sixes and sevens,' cried Weatherley one day in despair ... 'Unless we're careful, the project will drop to pieces.'

Six feet of earth make all men equal. 1659: Howell, *Proverbs: Ital.-Eng.*, 8. 1666: Torriano, *Piazza Univ.*, 285, Six foot of earth shuts up every one.

Six o'clock with him, It's welly = He is failing in health. 1917: Bridge, *Cheshire Proverbs*, 86.

Six of one and half a dozen of the other. 1852: Dickens, *Bleak House*, ch xxiv, Mostly they come for skill – or idleness. Six of one, and half a dozen of the other. 1859: Sala, *Twice Round Clock*, 3 a.m. 1907: De Morgan. *Alice-for-Short*, ch xvi.

Six score. *See* quots. This is what is known as the 'long hundred'. 1647: in *Somers Tracts* v 488 (1811), For in things without heads six score go to an hundred. 1849: F. T. Dinsdale, *Teesdale Gloss.*, 111, Five score's a hundred of men, money, and pins, Six score's a hundred of all other things. 1881: Evans, *Leics. Words*, 187 (E.D.S.), I have often heard quoted the old rule – [as in 1849]. But the long hundred is now seldom heard of except in piecework in some few trades. 1889: Peacock, *Manley, etc., Gloss.*, 330 (E.D.S.) [as in 1849]. 1917: Bridge, *Cheshire*

Proverbs, 55, Everything is counted six-score except men, money and bricks. Ibid., 96, Naught is counted six score to the hundred but old women and gorse kids [faggots].

Size cinque will not, If. *See* quot. 1678: Ray, 348, If size cinque will not and duce ace cannot, then quatre trey must. The middle sort bear public burthens, taxes, etc., most.

Skeer [Rake out] **your own fire.** This is of the family of 'Sweep before your own door'. 1917: Bridge, *Cheshire Proverbs*, 109.

Skiddaw. 1. If Skiddaw hath a cap, Criffel wots full well of that. In the quotations 1610 to 1709 'Criffel' is given as 'Scruffell'; and in 1790 as 'Scuflel'. 1610: P. Holland, tr. Camden's *Britannia*, 767. 1655: Fuller, *Church Hist.*, bk xi § iii (9). 1709: O. Dykes, *Eng. Proverbs* (at end). 1790: Grose, *Prov. Gloss.*, s.v. 'Cumberland'. 1818: Scott, *Heart of Midl.*, ch xl. 1899: Dickinson, *Cumberland Gloss.*, 54, When Criffel gets a cap, Skiddaw wots well of that.

2. Skiddaw, Lauvellin and Casticand Are the highest hills in all England. 1610: P. Holland, tr.Camden's*Britannia*, 767. 1659: Howell, 21. 1790: Grose, *Prov. Gloss.*, s.v. 'Cumberland'.

Skill and confidence are an unconquered army. 1640: Herbert, *Jac. Prudentum.*

Skimmington, To ride. 1634: C. Butler, *Feminine Monarchie*, 64, Yet when they have it, let them use poore Skimmington as gently as they may; especially in publik, to hide his shame. 1714: E. Ward, *Cavalcade*, 35, That those who knew not the occasion Of such a noisy strange procession, Expected they should find anon The same to be a Skimington. 1825: Jennings, *Somerset. Words*, 68, To ride Skimmerton, is an exhibition ... designed to ridicule some one who, unfortunately, possesses an unfaithful wife. 1886: Hardy, *Casterbridge*, ch xxxix, Have you seen any gang of fellows making a devil of a noise – skimmington riding, or something of the sort?

Skin a flint, To. 1640: Herbert, *Jac. Prudentum*, You cannot flay a stone. 1659: Howell, 11, To skin a stone for a penny, and break a knife of twelvepence. 1670: Ray, 9, No man can flay a stone. 1690: *New Dict. Canting Crew*, sig. E5, He'll flay a flint, of a meer scrab, or miser. 1754: Berthelson, *Eng.-Danish Dict.*, s.v. 'Skin', He would skin a flint. 1841: Hartshorne, *Salopia Ant.*, 567, A covetous person, one who, if it were possible, would 'skin a flint, to save a penny'.

1851: Sternberg, *Dialect, etc., of Northants*, 97, One who, as the proverb says, will 'Skin a flint worth a fardin Spwile [Spoil] a knife worth a grat [groat]'. 1901: *Folk-Lore*, xii 82, [S.W. Wilts] A would skin a vlint vur a varden and spwile a tenpenny nayl in doin' on't. 1910: R. L. Gales, *Studies in Arcady*, 335, The writer ... remembers hearing 'to skin a flint, and spoil a shilling knife in doing it'.

Skin between the brows. *See* quots. 1575: Still, *Gam. Gurton*, V ii, I am as true, I would thou knew, as [the] skin between thy brows. 1599: Shakespeare, *Much Ado*, III v, An old man, sir ... but, in faith, honest as the skin between his brows. 1605: *London Prodigal*, V i, She is ... as true as the skin between any man's brows here. 1696: D'Urfey, *Quixote*, Pt III Act I, I warrant she's as virtuous as the skin between her brows.

Sky falls we shall catch larks, When the. [Quid si? Redeo ad illos qui aiunt: Quid si coelum ruat? – Terence, *Haul.*, IV iii 41.] Before 1500: in Hill, *Commonplace-Book*, 128 (E.E.T.S.), And hewin [heaven] fall, we shall hawe mani larkis. 1546: Heywood, *Proverbs*, Pt I ch iv. ['have' for 'catch']. 1606: Day, *Ile of Gulls*, V ['have' for 'catch']. 1638: Randolph, *Muses' Looking-Glass*, II ii ... Should heaven fall – *Aph.* Why then we should have larks. 1709: R. Kingston, *Apoph. Curiosa*, 17, When the sky shall fall, and blind men catch larks. 1721: Bailey, *Eng. Dict.*, s.v. 'Sky'. 1869: *Spurgeon, John Ploughman*, ch xx. 1914: Shaw, 'Parents and Children', in *Misalliance, etc.*, xxx, Just as I do not admit that if the sky fell we should all catch larks.

Slain that had warning, not he that took it, He was. 1659: Howell, *Proverbs: Brit.-Eng.*, 3.

Slander, but it is no lie, It may be a. 1546: Heywood, *Proverbs*, Pt II ch vii.

Slander flings stones at itself. 1732: Fuller, 4183.

Slander is a shipwreck by a dry tempest. 1640: Herbert, *Jac. Prudentum.*

Slander leaves a scar behind it. 1633: Draxe, 191, Slander leaueth a skarre. 1670: Ray, 24 ['score' for 'scar']. 1681: Robertson, *Phraseol. Generalis*, 1136. 1732: Fuller, 4184 [as in 1670].

Slander one with a matter of truth, To. 1678: Ray, 269.

Slander that is raised is ill to fell, A. *c.*1460: *How the Good Wife*, l. 25, A slaundrer that is reised is euelle to felle.

Slanderer. *The most dangerous of wild beasts is a slanderer; of tame ones a flatterer.* 1855: Bohn, 511.

Slapton, Where fools will happen. 1851: Steinberg, *Dialect, etc., of Northants*, 192.

Slave that cannot command himself, He's a. 1732: Fuller, 2445.

Slavering folks. *See* **Snotty folks.**

Sleep, *subs.* **1. Hours of sleep.** 1666: Torriano, *Piazza Univ.*, 114, Five hours sleepeth a traveller, seven a scholar, eight a merchant, and eleven every knave. 1732: Fuller, 4112, Seven hours' sleep will make a clown forget his design. 1846: Denham, *Proverbs*, 5 (Percy S.) [as in 1732, but with 'the husbandman' for 'a clown']. 1883: Burne, *Shropsh. Folk-Lore*, 578, Nature requireth five, Custom taketh seven, Idleness takes nine, And Wickedness eleven. 1912: *N.&Q.*, 11th ser, v 52, Six hours for a man, seven for a woman, and eight for a fool. The precept seems to be based on the Latin lines: – Sex horis dormire sat est juvenique senique, Septem vix pigro, nulli concedimus octo. – *Collectio Salernitana*, ed. De Renzi, vol v p. 7.

2. One hour's sleep before midnight is worth two after. 1640: Herbert, *Jac. Prudentum* ['three' for 'two']. 1731: in Peck, *Desid. Curiosa*, 226 (1779), As experience it self shews, one hour's rest before twelve of the clock is worth two after. 1829: Cobbett, *Advice to Young Men*, Lett. I ['worth more than two']. 1846: Denham, *Proverbs*, 3 (Percy S.).

Sleep, *verb.* **1. He hath slept well that remembers not he hath slept ill.** 1732: Fuller, 1897.

2. He sleeps with his eyes open. 1586: Pettie, Guazzo's *Civil Convers.*, fo. 140, Which sleepeth (as they say) her eies being open. 1732: Fuller, 1947, He is so wary that he sleeps like a hare, with his eyes open.

3. He that sleeps bites no body. 1567: *Merry Tales, etc.*, No. xxxvi p. 50 (Hazlitt), Here by ye maye se, that many thinges passe by them that slepe, and it is an old sayenge: He that slepeth, byteth no body. 1615: Stephens, *Essays, etc.*, bk i No. 21, Hee that drinkes well, sleepes well, and hee that sleepes well thinkes no harme.

4. I don't sleep to all. 1593: G. Harvey, *Works*, ii 165 (Grosart), Some sleepe not to all: and I watch not to eueryone. 1725: Bailey, tr. Erasmus's *Colloq.*, 487, You know the old proverb, *I don't sleep to all*.

5. Sleep without supping, and wake without owing. 1640: Herbert, *Jac. Prudentum*.

6. To sleep as sound as a church. 1839: Dickens, *Nickleby*, ch xxiii, Asleep she did fall, sound as a church. Cf. **Fast as a church.**

7. To sleep in a field. *See* quot. 1926: *Devonsh. Assoc. Trans.*, lvii 152, 'You've bin sleepin' in a field wi' the gate open'. Said to a man who was fussing about a cold.

8. To sleep in a whole skin. *See* **Whole skin.**

9. To sleep like a pig. 1736: Bailey, *Dict.*, s.v. 'Pig', He sleeps like a pig.

10. To sleep like a top. 1668: Davenant, *Rivals*, III, Or else I shall sleep like a top. 1762: Hall-Stevenson, *Crazy Tales*, 56, Scolded a while, and slept like any top. 1820: Byron, *Letters, etc.*, v 115 (Prothero), I slept like a top. 1855: Gaskell, *North and South*, ch xxiii.

11. To sleep on both ears. [In aurem utramvis otiose ut dormias. – Terence, *Haut.*, II iii 101.] 1540: Palsgrave, *Acolastus*, sig. C4, Than truely lyued I lyke one that sleapeth on bothe his eares. Before 1663: Abp. Bramhall, *Works*, iii 518 (*Ang.-Cath. Lit.*, 1842–4), Let him set his heart at rest; I will remove this scruple out of his mind, that he may sleep securely upon both ears. 1754: Berthelson, *Eng.-Danish Dict.*, s.v. 'Sleep'.

12. To sleep without rocking. 1631: Brathwait, *Whimzies*, 106 (1859), Hee sleepes soundly without rocking. 1738: Swift, *Polite Convers.*, Dial. III, I'm sure I shall sleep without rocking.

Sleeping dogs lie, Let. *c.*1374: Chaucer, *Troylus*, bk iii l. 764, It is nought good a sleping hound to wake. 1546: Heywood, *Proverbs*, Pt I ch x, It is euyll wakyng of a sleepyng dog. 1598: Shakespeare, *2 Henry IV*, I ii, Wake not a sleeping wolf. 1605: Camden, *Remains*, 326 (1870) [as in 1546]. 1850: Dickens, *Copperfield*, ch xxxix, Let sleeping dogs lie – who wants to rouse 'em? 1898: Weyman, *Shrewsbury*, ch xxxii. 1922: *Sphere*, 5 Aug., 132, It is all very well to let sleeping dogs lie, but in this case the dogs are dogs of war.

Sleeping enough in the grave, There will be. 1736: Franklin, *Way to Wealth*, in *Works*, i 443 (Bigelow).

Sleeping lion. *See* **Lion** (13).

Sleepy master makes his servant a lout, A. [*c.*1290: in Wright *Pol. Songs John to Edw. II*, 165 (Camden S.), Mitis praelatus facit ignavos famulatus.] 1640: Herbert, *Jac. Prudentum*.

Sleeveless errand, A. Mr Warwick Bond, in his edition of John Lyly, quotes (iii 503) from Lady Charlotte Guest's translation of the *Mabinogion* ('Dream of Mayen Wledig'): 'Now this was the guise in which the messengers journeyed: one sleeve was on the cap of each of them in front, as a sign that they were messengers, in order that through what hostile land soever they might pass, no harm might be done them'. Mr Bond adds: 'Without the sleeve they might never be able to perform their errand'. This seems to make clear the much disputed origin of the phrase 'A sleeveless errand', i.e. a futile, bootless errand. The use of 'sleeveless' with this signification naturally spread to other things besides errands. One would have expected to find 'sleeveless errand 'at an earlier date than the wider uses; but I have not been able to find examples of the former so early as examples of the latter. There follow illustrations of A, the wider applications of the adjective; and B, the preciser use in 'sleeveless errand'.

A. *c.*1387: Usk, *Test. of Love*, in Skeat's *Chaucer*, vii 76, And mesureth his goodnesse, not by slevelesse wordes … 15th cent.: in *Reliq. Antiquae*, i 83 (1841), Thynke not … y schall telle you a sleveles reson. *c.*1440: *Jacob's Well* 181 (E.E.T.S.), Summe in schryfte schal tarye the preest wyth sleueles talys [idle talk] that nothyng longyth to schryfte. 1593: *Pass. Morrice*, 65 (N.Sh.S.), So vnmannerly to vse him by sleeueles excuses. 1726: in Hone, *Ev. Day Book*, ii 782, Having, under a sleeveless pretence, been deny'd a combat. 1821: Scott, *Fam. Letters*, ii 111 (1894), He … had no honourable mode of avoiding the sleeveless quarrel fixed on him. 1867: Waugh, *Tatlin' Mathy*, 18, Single-step doancin', an' sich like sleeveless wark as that.

B. 1546: Heywood, *Proverbs*, Pt I ch vii, To make … a sleeueles errande. 1604: *Jacke of Dover*, 4 (Percy S.), To whose house I went upon a sleeveles arrand. 1670: Cotton, *Scarronides*, bk iv … 1712: Motteux, *Quixote*, Pt II ch x. 1828: Carr, *Craven Dialect*, ii 290, As I've hed a sleeveless earrant.

Slender in the middle as a cow in the waist, As. 1621: Burton, *Anatomy of Melancholy*, III ii 3, 1, vol iii p. 178 (Shilleto), She stoops, is lame … as slender in the middle as a Cow in the waist. 1670: Ray, 207. 1732: Fuller, 727. 1881: Evans, *Leics. Words*, 242 (E.D.S.), 'As slender', etc. This periphrasis to describe obesity … is still in use.

Slight impressions. *See* **Impressions.**

Slip between cup and lip. *See* **Cup** (4).

Slip of the foot may be soon recovered, A; but that of the tongue perhaps never. 1732: Fuller, 403. Cf. **Better the feet slip.**

Slip one's neck out of the collar, To. 1583: Golding, *Calvin on Deut.*, cxxv. 772 (OED), Albeit we … would slippe our heades out of the coler seeking to shift off ye matter. 1633: Draxe, 189, He draweth his necke out of the coller. 1678: Ray, 350. 1754: Berthelson, *Eng.-Danish Dict.*, s.v. 'Slip'. 1857: Hughes, *Tom Brown*, Pt II ch vii, If we can slip the collar and do so much less without getting caught, that's one to us.

Slippery as an eel. 1412: Hoccleve, *Regement*, l. 1985, p. 72 (E.E.T.S.), Mi wit is also slipir as an eel. *c.*1420: Lydgate, *Assem. of Gods*, 31 (E.E.T.S.), Whyche made the grounde as slepyr as an yele. 1533: Heywood, *Play of Love*, l. 1414 (Brandl, *Quellen*, 204), And coryd [curried (of a horse)] tyll he be slyke as an ele. 1633: S. Marmion, *Fine Companion*, V ii, He is as slippery as an eel, in love. 1690: Shadwell, *Amorous Bigot*, I. 1740: Richardson, *Pamela*, i 207 (1883), You'll find her as slippery as an eel, I'll assure you. 1855: Gaskell, *North and South*, ch xvii.

Sloes. *See* **Black**, *adj.* (8); and **Many slones.**

Sloe-tree's as white as a sheet, When the, Sow your barley whether it be dry or wet. 1678: Ray, 49. 1732: Fuller, 6482. 1825: Hone, *Ev. Day Book*, i 670. 1893: Inwards, *Weather Lore*, 152.

Sloth breeds a scab. 1546: Heywood, *Proverbs*, Pt I ch iii, Sens we see slouth must breede a scab. 1611: Davies (of Hereford), *Sc. of Folly*, 48, in *Works*, ii (Grosart).

Slothful is the servant of the covetous, The. 1640: Herbert, *Jac. Prudentum.*

Slothful man is the beggar's brother, The. 1732: Fuller, 4748. 1917: Bridge, *Cheshire Proverbs*, 6.

Sloth is the devil's cushion or pillow. 1669: *Politeuphuia*, 306.

Sloth is the key to poverty. 1669: *Politeuphuia*, 306 [with 'mother' for 'key']. 1853: Trench, *Proverbs*, 107 (1905), And to many languages another with its striking image, *Sloth, the key of poverty*, belongs.

Sloth, like rust, consumes faster than labour wears. 1736: Franklin, *Way to Wealth*, in *Works*, i 443 (Bigelow).

Sloth makes all things difficult, but industry all things easy. Ibid., i 443.

Sloth turneth the edge of wit. 1579: Lyly, *Euphues*, 126 (Arber). 1670: Ray, 24.

Slow and steady wins the race. Both this and the related saying *Slow and sure* (q.v.) seem to have their origins in one of Aesop's best-known fables, that of the hare and the tortoise. 1762: R. Lloyd, *Poems*, 38, You may deride my awkward pace, But slow and steady wins the race. 1859: S. Smiles, *Self-Help*, xi, Provided the dunce has persistency and application, he will inevitably head the cleverer fellow without these qualities. Slow but sure, wins the race. 1894: G. F. Northall, *Folk-Phrases*, 22, Slow and steady wins the race.

Slow and sure. 1633: Draxe, 111 *bis*, Slownesse is sure. 1639: Fuller, *Holy War*, bk iii ch v, These, though slow, were sure. 1692: L'Estrange, *Aesop*, 337 (3rd ed.), Slow and sure in these cases is good counsel. 1711: Steele, *Spectator*, No. 140, He is rich, and my mother says, As he is slow he is sure. 1768: Goldsmith, *Vicar*, ch xxi, What signifies minding her? … if she be slow she's sure. 1922: Weyman, *Ovington's Bank*, ch v, Slow and sure is a good rule.

Slow help is no help. 1853: Trench, *Proverbs*, 19 (1905).

Slow worm. *See* Adder.

Sluggard makes his night till noon, The. 1732: Fuller, 4749.

Sluggard must be clad in rags, The. 1605: Camden, *Remains*, 333 (1870).

Sluggard's guise. *See* quots. 1639: in *Berkeley MSS.* iii, 32 (1885), Hee is tainted with an evill guise, Loth to bed and lother to rise. 1670: Ray, 143, The sluggards guise, Loath to go to bed and loath to rise. 1732: Fuller, 6368 [as in 1670]. 1825: Jennings, *Somerset. Words*, 70, Sluggardy-guise; Loth, etc. 1842: Akerman, *Wilts Gloss.*, 46, Sluggard's guise Loth to bed And loth to rise.

Sluggard takes an hundred steps because he would not take one in due time, A. 1855: Bohn, 300.

Slut and **Sluts**, *subs.* **1. A slut never wants a clout, Whilst her aipernt** [apron] **holds out.** 1880: Courtney, *W. Cornwall Words*, 1 (E.D.S.).

2. A slud will poison thy gut. 1685: *Mother Bunch's Closet*, 14 (Gomme, 1885) [quoted as 'The old saying'].

3. Of all tame beasts I hate sluts. 1678: Ray, 81. 1732: Fuller, 3697.

4. Sluts are good enough to make a sloven's porridge. 1639: Clarke, 287 [in the singular], *c.*1685: in *Roxb. Ballads*, viii 869 (B.S.) [as in 1639]. 1732: Fuller, 4190.

See also **Apple** (6).

Small birds must have meat. 1600: Shakespeare, *Merry Wives*, I iii, Young ravens must have food. 1639: Clarke, 292. 1670: Ray, 63.

Small cheer and great welcome makes a merry feast. *c.*1600: Shakespeare, *Com. of Errors*, III i.

Small choice in rotten apples, There is. 1594: Shakespeare, *Tam. of Shrew*, I i Before 1681: J. Lacy, *Sauny the Scot*, I. 1875: Cheales, *Proverb. Folk-Lore*, 116.

Smaller the peas. *See* **Pea** (3).

Small family is soon provided for, A. 1732: Fuller, 405.

Small fish than an empty dish, Better are. 1678: Ray, 204. 1732: Fuller, 6369.

Small fish to catch a great one, Venture a. 1639: Clarke, 41. 1670: Ray, 152. 1732: Fuller, 5348. Cf. **Sprat**.

Small heart hath small desires, A. 1640: Herbert, *Jac. Prudentum*.

Small house has a wide throat, A. 1865: 'Lancs Proverbs', in *N. & Q.*, 3rd ser, viii 494. 1901: F. E. Taylor, *Lancs Sayings*, 7, A smo heawse has oft getten a wide throttle.

Small invitation. *See* **Beggar** (15).

Small is beautiful. Not so much a saying, perhaps, as an ecological, economic and technological principle, first enunciated by – and usually associated with E. F. Schumacher (though Schumacher attributed the formulation to his publishers). 1973: E. F. Schumacher, (*book title*) Small is beautiful. 1979: *Journal Royal Society of Arts* July 468/1 It is worth mentioning another and different pressure upon the nature and shape of the hospital: and that is the vague but pervasive notion that 'small is beautiful'.

Small pack. *See* **Pedlar**.

Small pitchers. *See* **Little pitchers**.

Small sore wants not a great plaster, A. 1567: Fenton, *Bandello*, i 222 (T.T.), 'Like as,' sayth he, 'small soares require slender medecins.' 1732: Fuller, 412.

Small spark. *See* **Spark**.

Small stake makes cold play. *c*.1597: in Harington, *Nugae Anttquae*, i 205 (1804), I know the saying … small stake makes colde play.

Small stomachs, light heels. 1855: Bohn, 487.

Small sum will serve to pay a short reckoning, A. 1639: Clarke, 128. 1696: D'Urfey, *Quixote*, Pt III Act V sc i 1732: Fuller, 413. 1753: Foote, *Taste*, I i, A paltry affair, a poor ten-guinea job; however, a small game – you know the proverb.

Smart as a carrot. 1780: in Farmer, *Musa Pedestris*, 56, I still was as smart as a carrot all day. *c*.1791: Pegge, *Derbicisms*, 135 (E.D.S.). 1894: Northall, *Folk Phrases*, 11 (E.D.S.), As smart as a carrot. Said of one gaily dressed. 1923: *Folk-Lore*, xxxiv 329 (Oxfordshire).

Smell, *verb*. **1. He smelleth best that doth of nothing smell** [Quoniam optimus odor in corpore est nullus. Seneca, *Epist.* cviii]. 1598: Meres, *Palladis*, fo. 32, As women do smell well, which smel of nothing. 1607: *Lingua*, IV iii. 1619: *Helpe to Discourse*, 93 (1640), Since as the proverbe is. They smell best that smell of nothing. 1669: *New Helth to Discourse*, 245, They that smell least, smell best.

2. He that smells the first savour, is the fault's first father. Glos. 1639: in *Berkeley MSS.*, iii 32 (1885).

3. To smell a rat. 1533: in *Ballads from MSS.*, i 182 (B.S.), For yf they smell a ratt … *c*.1598: Deloney, *Gentle Craft*, Pt II ch iii, What would you so faine be rid of my company? – If with Gill I smell a rat. 1608: Middleton, *Family of Love*, IV ii, Master Gerardine, disguised and ashore! nay, then I smell a rat. 1669: Dryden, *Wild Gallant*, IV i, Oh, are you thereabouts, sir? then I smell a rat, i' faith. 1714: Ozell, *Molière*, i 102, All these signs betoken no good; I smell a rat. 1872: Butler, *Erewhon*, ch xviii, If they smell a rat about the precincts of a cherished institution, they will always stop their noses to it if they can.

4. To smell of the lamp. [The expression is attributed to Pytheas by Plutarch (*Vit. Demosth.*, c.8).] 1542: Udall, tr. Erasmus' *Apoph.*, 379 (1877), The saiyng of Pytheas is commen and muche spoken of, that the oracions of Demosthenes smelled all of the candle, for that the same did in the night season wryte and recorde soche thinges as he had to saye to the

people in the daye time. 1608: in Harington, *Nugae Antiquae*, ii 190 (1804), A well-labour'd sermon … that smelt of the candle. 1647: Howell, *Letters*, bk ii No. xxi, I thank you heartily for your last letter, in regard I found it smelt of the lamp. 1754: *Connoisseur*, No. 3, Our compositions are so correct that … they may be said to smell of the lamp. 1820: Colton, *Lacon*, Pref., Knowledge … will smell of the lamp.

5. To smell of the oil. 1577: J. Grange, *Golden Aphroditis*, sig. N1, This little volume of mine smelleth of the oyle and candle. 1646: Browne, *Pseudo. Epi.*, To Reader, A work of this nature … should smel of oyl, if duly and deservedly handled. 1883: Trollope, *Autobiog.*, ch x, A man who thinks much of his words as he writes them will generally leave behind him work that smells of oil.

6. Well may he smell fire whose gown burns. 1640: Herbert, *Jac. Prudentum*. 1670: Ray, 9.

Smell of gain is sweet, The. 1621: Brathwait, *Natures Embassie, etc.*, 303 (1877), Smell of gaine makes Labour sweet. 1659: Gayton, *Art of Longevity*, 46.

Smile, *verb*. **1. He smiles like a basket of chips.** Old Shropshire saying. Sometimes with the addition – 'on a frosty morning'. 1871: *N. & Q.*, 4th ser, vii 9.

2. He smiles like a brewer's horse. 1659: Howell, 18.

3. *See* quot. 1702: Centlivre, *Beau's Duel.*, Epil., He surest strikes that smiling gives the blow; Poets, with us, this proverb do defy, We live by smiles, for if you frown we die.

4. You smile and bite. 1732: Fuller, 5999.

Smiling boy seldom proves a good servant, A. 1659: Howell, 8. 1670: Ray, 24. 1852: FitzGerald, *Polonius*, 60 (1903), An old proverb says, 'A smiling boy is a bad servant'.

Smith, *subs.* **1. A right skilful smith.** *See* quot. *c*.1225: *Ancren R.*, 52 (Camden S.), Ofte a ful hawur smith smetheth a ful woc knif (Often does a right skilful smith forge a full weak knife).

2. The smith and his penny are both black. 1640: Herbert, *Jac. Prudentum*. 1657: Gurnall, *Christian in Armour*, Pt II v 15, ch v p. 129 (1679). 1737: Ray, 71. 1875: J. W. Ebsworth, App. to *Merry Drollery*, 373, An old proverb says that the Smith and his penny are both black. So we need not expect that a Sowgelder's song will be cleanly. 1875: Smiles, *Thrift*, 164.

3. The smith hath always a spark in his throat,
i.e. he is always thirsty. 1678: Ray, 90. 1732:
Fuller, 4754. 1880: Spurgeon, *Ploughman's
Pictures*, 39, He is not a blacksmith, but he has a
spark in his throat.

Smithfield bargain, A. 1662: J. Wilson, *Cheats*,
V v, Is not this better than a Smithfield bargain?
1704: T. Baker, *An Act at Oxford*, III ii, Our
marriage is a perfect Smithfield bargain. 1753:
Richardson, *Grandison*, iii 434 (1883), The
hearts of us women … are apt, and are pleaded
with, to rise against the notions of bargain and
sale. *Smithfield bargains*, you Londoners call
them. 1775: Sheridan, *Rivals*, V i.

Smithfield. *See* **Westminster.**

Smithwick *See* quot. 1678: Ray, 291, You been
like Smithwick, either clem'd [starved] or borsten
[replete]. *Cheshire*. 1917: Bridge, *Cheshire
Proverbs*, 157 ['bin' for 'been', and 'bossten' for
'borsten'].

Smocks than shirts. *See* quot. Ray attributes
this saying to Chaucer, but I have failed to find it
in Chaucer. Hazlitt follows Ray, but also gives
no reference. 1678: Ray, 353, He that hath more
smocks then shirts at a bucking [washing], had
need be a man of good forelooking. *Chaucer*.
1732: Fuller, 6427 [as in 1678].

Smoke, *subs.* **1. Smoke follows the fairest.**
1639: in *Berkeley MSS.*, iii 31 (1885), Smoke
will to the smicker. If many gossips sit against a
smokey chimney the smoke will bend to the
fairest. 1646: Browne, *Pseudo. Epi.*, bk v ch
xxiii, That smoak doth follow the fairest, is an
usual saying with us … yet is it the
continuation of a very ancient opinion, as
Petras Victorius and Casaubon have observed,
from a passage in Athenaeus, wherein a
parasite thus describeth himself: – 'To every
table first I come, Whence Porridge I am call'd
by some … Like smoke, unto the fair I fly'.
1687: Aubrey, *Gentilisme, etc.*, 111 (F.L.S.),
That smoak doth follow the fairest is ancient
opinion, as is to be observed in Athenaeus.
1738: Swift, *Polite Convers.*, Dial. I, They say
smoke always pursues the fair. 1851:
Sternberg, *Dialect, etc., of Northants*, 172,
Smoke and dust always follow the fairest.

**2. Smoke, rain, and a very curst wife, Makes a
man weary of house and life.** 1647: *Countrym,
New Commonwealth*, 42. 1683: Meriton,
Yorkshire Ale, 83–7 (1697), A reeking house and

a scawding wife will mack yan weary of his life.
1774: Colman, *Man of Business*, IV ii, She would
ring it in my ears as long as I live – a smoaky
house, and a scolding wife, you know! I need say
no more. – It is a kind of hell to inhabit one, and
the devil himself would scarce live with the
other. Cf. **Three things drive.**

3. There is no smoke without fire. [Flamma
fumo est proxima. – Plautus, *Curculio*, I i 53.]
*c.*1375: Barbour, *Bruce*, bk iv l. 123, And thair
may no man fire sa covir, [Bot] low or reek sall it
discovir. *c.*1440: Hoccleve, *Minor Poems*, 134
(E.E.T.S.), Wher no fyr maad is may no smoke
aryse. 1579: Lyly, *Euphues*, 153 (Arber), Ther can
no great smoke arise, but there must be some fire,
no great reporte without great suspition. 1649:
Quarles, *Virgin Widow*, I, There's no smoake
without some fire. 1679: Shadwell, *True Widow*,
V i, 'Sdeath! there must be some fire under all this
smoke. 1757: Murphy, *Upholsterer*, II i. 1871:
Planché, *Extravag.*, v 302 (1879), Where so much
smoke is, there must be some fire.

**4. The smoke of a man's own house is bttter
than the fire of another.** 1633: Draxe, 93. 1670:
Ray, 20. 1732: Fuller, 4756.

5. To escape the smoke and fall into the fire.
1548: Hall, *Chron.*, 210 (1809). There is an olde
sayd saw, that a man entendyng to auoide the
smoke, falleth into the fyre. 1639: Clarke, 250,
Shunning the smoake he fell into the fire.

**6. When the smoke goes west. Good weather
is past; When the smoke goes east, Good
weather comes neist** [next]. 1846: Denham,
Proverbs, 17 (Percy S.).

**Smoking chimney in a great house is a good
sign, A.** 1732: Fuller, 415.

Smooth as a carpet. 1678: Ray, 289.

Smooth as glass. 1580: Lyly, *Euphues*, 320
(Arber), I see now that there is nothing more
smooth then glasse. 1590: Spenser, *F. Q.*, I i 318,
Could file his tongue as smooth as glas. *c.*1660: in
Roxb. Ballads, ii 445 (B.S.), Her skin was as
smooth as glass. 1720: Gay, *Poems*, ii 279
(Underhill), As smooth as glass, as white as
curds. 1821: Scott, *Pirate*, ch xxii, The bay …
seemed almost as smooth as glass.

Smooth as oil. 1716: E. Ward, *Female Policy*,
51, Her tongue as smooth as oil.

Smooth language grates not the tongue.
1659: Howell, 5.

Smoothy's wedding, All on one side like.

1864: 'Cornish Proverbs', in *N. & Q.*, 3rd ser, vi 6. 1888: Q.-Couch, *Troy Town*, ch viii.

Snail and **Snails,** *subs.* **1. As quick as a snail crawling through tar.** W. Corn. 19th cent. (Mr C. Lee).

2. Snailie, snailie, shoot out your horn. And tell us if it will be a bonnie day the morn. 1893: Inwards, *Weather Lore*, 144.

3. The house is blest Where snail do rest. W. Corn. 19th cent. (Mr C. Lee).

4. The snail slides up the tower at last though the swallow mounteth it sooner. 1580: Lyly, *Euphues*, 419 (Arber), The slow snaile clymeth the tower at last, though the swift swallowe mount it. 1583: Melbancke, *Philotinus*, sig. Ff2, Can the sluggish snayle with creeping pace euer reache the castles tower? 1732: Fuller, 4757.

5. To go a snail's gallop. 1546: Heywood, *Proverbs*, Pt I ch ix, If I shall nedes this viage make ... I will ... thytherward hye me in haste lyke a snayle. 1670: Ray, 193, To drive snails; A snails gallop. 1681: Robertson, *Phraseol. Generalis*, 672, Ye go a snails gallop. 1725: Bailey, tr. Erasmus' *Colloq.*, 32, I see what haste you make, you are never the forwarder, you go a snails gallop. 1803: Colman, jr., *John Bull*, III i, There he comes, in a snail's trot. 1821: Combe, *Syntax in Search of Wife*, can. xxxvi p. 120, He, by degrees, would seldom fail T'adopt the gallop of a snail. 1866: Brogden, *lincs Words*, 188, Sneel-gallop. – A stow pace, compared to the crawl of a snail.

6. When black snails cross your path, Black cloud much moisture hath. 1893: Inwards, *Weather Lore*, 144.

7. When black snails on the road you see, Then on the morrow rain will be. Ibid., 144.

Snake, *subs.* **1. If the snake could hear and the slow-worm could see, Neither man nor beast should e'er go free.** Norfolk. 1856: *N. & Q.*, 2nd ser, i 401. 1871: *N. & Q.*, 4th ser, vii 547. Cf. **Adder**.

2. The head of a snake with garlic is good meat. 1568: in *Loseley MSS.*, 213 (Kempe).

3. There is a snake in the grass. [Latet anguis in herba. – Virgil, *Ecl.*, iii 93.] *c.*1290: in Wright, *Pol. Songs John to Edw. II*, 172 (Camden S.), Cum totum fecisse putas, latet anguis in herba. 1548: Hall, *Chron.*, 236 (1809), But the serpent lurked vnder the grasse, and vnder sugered speache was hide pestiferous poyson. 1593: G.

Harvey, *Works*, ii 294 (Grosart), Take heede of the snake in the grass, or the padd in the straw. 1677: Yarranton, *Eng. Improvement*, 101, Hold, hold, you drive too fast; there is a snake in the bush. 1714: Ozell, *Molière*, iv. 254. 1777: in *Garrick Corresp.*, ii 248 (1832), There are snakes in the grass, and you seem to foster them. 1926: Phillpotts. *Yellow Sands*, I, What cares he for your wishes – young snake in the grass! *See also* **Thunder** (3).

Snapping so short makes you look so lean. 1678: Ray, 345. 1738: Swift, *Polite Convers.*, Dial. I, Snap short makes you look so lean, miss.

Sneck. *See* quot. *c.*1770: Pegge, *Derbicisms*, 65 (E.D.S.), The sneck is the latch itself, and not the string. Hence the proverb: 'to put a sneck before one's snout'.

Sneeze, *subs. See* **quot**. 1732: Fuller, 2436, He's a friend at a sneeze; the most you can get of him is a *God bless you*.

Sneeze, *verb.* **1. He hath sneezed thrice, turn him out of the hospital.** 1659: Howell, 2.

2. Sneeze on a Monday, etc. *See* quots. 1867: Harland, etc., *Lancs Folk-Lore*, 68, Sneeze on a Monday, you sneeze for danger; Sneeze on a Tuesday, you kiss a stranger; Sneeze on a Wednesday, you sneeze for a letter; Sneeze on a Thursday, for something better; Sneeze on a Friday, you sneeze for sorrow; Sneeze on a Saturday, your sweet-heart to-morrow; Sneeze on a Sunday, your safety seek, The Devil will have you the whole of the week. 1878: Dyer, *Eng. Folk-Lore*, 239, In Devonshire, it is said that if you – 'Sneeze on Sunday morning fasting, You'll enjoy your own true love to everlasting'. 1879: Henderson, *Folk-Lore of N. Counties*, 137 [much the same as in 1867, but with the omission of the Sunday couplet]. 1913: E. M. Wright, *Rustic Speech, etc.*, 223 [as in 1867].

Snipe. *See* quots. 1678: Ray, 344, The snite needs not the woodcock betwite [taunt]. *Somerset.* 1732: Fuller, 4939, There is winter enough for the snipe and woodcock too. 1886: Swainson, *Folk-Lore of Brit. Birds*, 192 (F.L.S.) [as in 1732], *See also* **Partridge** (2).

Snotty folks. *See* quot. 1678: Ray, 204, Snotty folks are sweet, but slavering folks are weet. Others have it, Slavering folks kiss sweet, but snotty folks are wise.

Snow, *subs.* **1. A snow year, a rich year.** 1580: J. Frampton, tr. *Monarcles*, ii 162 (T.T.), For this it is said, The yeare of snow, the yeare of fertilise. 1640: Herbert, *Jac. Prudentum*, A snow year, a rich year. 1659: Howell, *Proverbs: Span.-Eng.*, 21, A yeare of snow, a yeare of plenty. 1732: Fuller, 416. 1835: Hone, *Ev. Day Book*, i 670. 1893: Inwards, *Weather Lore*, 5; [also] Snow year, good year.

2. As seasonable as snow in harvest. *c.*1568: Wager, *Longer thou Livest*, sig. F3, As snow in haruest is untimelie. 1595: *Pedlars Prophecy*, l. 237 (Malone S.), As profitable as is snow in harvest. 1605: Camden, *Remains*, 336 (1870) 'summer' for 'harvest']. 1670: Ray, 202 [as in 1605]. 1732: Fuller, 5869, You came as seasonably as snow in summer. 1854: Baker, *Northants Gloss.*, s.v., A provincial sarcasm for want of kindness. 'He looks as cold as snow in harvest'. 1894: Northall, *Folk Phrases*, 34 (E.D.S.), You are come like snow in harvest, i.e. unexpectedly. 1913: *Folk-Lore*, xxiv. 77, As scarce as snow in harvest (Oxfordshire).

3. He roasts snow in a furnace. 1813: Ray, 75.

4. If February give mutch snow, A fine summer it doth foreshow. 1882: Mrs Chamberlain, *W. Worcs. Words*, 37 (E.D.S.), Much February snow A fine summer doth show. 1882: *N.&Q.*, 7th ser, v 297; [also] Snow in February is the crown of the year.

5. If there be neither snow nor rain, Then will be dear all kinds of grain. 1893: Inwards, *Weather Lore*, 4.

6. Snow and geese, *c.*1791: Pegge, *Derbicisms.* 138 (E.D.S.), They are pulling geese in Scotland; so here it snows. 1855: Dickens, *Holly Tree*, Branch 1, I don't know when the snow began to set in; but … I heard the guard remark, 'That the old lady up in the sky was picking her geese pretty hard to-day'. 1917: Bridge, *Cheshire Proverbs*, 121, They're plucking their geese in Wales and sendin' their fithers here [said in a snowstorm]. *See also* Widdecombe.

7. Snow is white And lieth in the dike, And every man lets it lie. Pepper is black, And hath a good smack, And every man doth it buy. Before 1500: in Hill, *Commonplace-Book*, 128 (E.E.T.S.), Thowgh peper be blak, it hath a good smak. *c.*1520: Stanbridge, *Vulgaria*, sig. C1 [as in Hill]. 1546: Heywood, *Proverbs*, Pt II ch iv. 1586: L. Evans, *Withals Dict. Revised*, sig. E4 [the full saying reversed – pepper coming first and snow second]. 1633: Draxe, 16, Pepper is blacke, and snow is white. 1659: Howell, 3. 1681:

Robertson, *Phraseol. Generalis*, 983, Pepper is black, yet it hath a good smack. Ibid., 1142, Snow is white, yet it lyes on the dike.

8. Under water, famine; under snow, bread. 1640: Herbert, *Jac. Prudentum.* 1865: W. White, *Eastern England*, ii 32. 1893: Inwards, *Weather Lore*, 9 ['dearth' for 'famine'].

9. When snow falls in the mud, it remains all winter. Ibid., 116.

10. When now in the ditch the snow doth lie, 'Tis waiting for more by and by. Ibid., 116.

11. When the snow falls dry, it means to lie; But flakes light and soft bring rain oft. Ibid., 116.

12. When the snow is in the orchard, A crab is worth a costard. 1883: Burne, *Shropsh. Folk-Lore*, 579.

13. Whether you boil snow or pound it, you can have but water of it. 1640: Herbert, *Jac. Prudentum.* 1670: Ray, 24. 1732: Fuller, 5687 ['bake' for 'pound'].

See also **April** (14) and (22); **Candlemas**, D and G; **Last racehorse; March** (35); **May**, F (2); **Ram**, *subs.* (1); and **White** (7), (8) and (14).

Snowdon will yield sufficient pasture for all the cattle of Wales put together. 1662: Fuller, *Worthies*, iii 527 (1840). 1790: Grose, *Prov. Gloss.*, s.v. 'Caernarvonshire'.

Snuff in the nose, To take = To take offence. 1610: Rowlands, *Martin Markall*, 34 (Hunt.Cl.), And not by any means to crosse them, least they take snuffe in the nose, and so fall together by the eares. 1661: Pepys, *Diary*, 6 Oct., Who, I expect, should take in snuffe that my wife did not come to his child's christening. 1714: Ozell, *Holière*, i 83, How very hasty you are. You take snuff in a minute. 1821: Scott, *Kenilworth*, ch i, But take no snuff in the nose about it. Cf. **Pepper.**

Snug at a bug in a rug. 1769: *Stratford Jubilee*, II i, I'll have her, as snug as a bug in a rug. 1772: Franklin, in *Works*, iv. 525 (Bigelow), Here Skugg Lies snug As a bug In a rug. 1880: Elworthy, *West Som. Word-Book*, 96 (E.D.S.). 1913: *Folk-Lore*, xxiv 77 (Oxfordshire.)

Snug as a pig in pease-straw. 1639: Davenport, *New Trick, etc.*, III i, He snores and sleepes as snug As any pigge in pease-straw. *c.*1662: in *Bagford Ballads*, i 198 (B.S.), like piggs in the pease-straw, intangld they line.

Soap in a wash tub, They are like a ha'p'orth of. 1855: Bohn, 525.

Sober as a judge. 1694: *Terence made English*, 82, I thought my self as sober as a judge. 1712: Arbuthnot, *John Bull*, Pt III ch vi, Lewis … kept himself sober as a judge. 1896: Doyle, *Rodney Stone*, ch xvi. 1924: *Sphere*, 7 June, p. 259, col. 1, A dignitary proverbially 'sober as a judge'.

Sober man, a soft answer, A. 1659: Howell, *Proverbs: Brit.-Eng.*, 7.

Soberness. *See* **Drunkenness**.

So cunning. *See* **Weather** (3).

Soft and fair goes far. *c.*1400: *Beryn*, 28 (E.E.T.S.), But feir and sofft with ese, homward they hir led. 1542: Udall, tr. *Erasmus' Apoph.*, 286 (1877), The prouerbe, *spede thee faire and softely*, is a lesson of counsaile. 1583: Greene, *Works*, ii 28 (Grosart), Goe as the snaile faire and softly. 1640: Herbert, *Jac. Prudentum*. 1668: Dryden, *Sir Martin Markall*, II ii. 1714: Ozell, *Molière*, ii 13. 1768: Goldsmith, *Good-Natured Man*, IV, Soft and fair, young lady. You that are going to be married think things can never be done too fast. 1818: Scott, *Heart of Midl.*, ch xlv., 'Fair and softly gangs far,' said Meiklehose.

Soft answer turneth away wrath, A. [Proverbs xv. 1, A soft answer turneth away wrath.] *c.*1445: *Peter Idley's Instructions to his Son* (1935), I 84, A softe worde swageth Ire. 1693: C. Mather, *Wonders of the Invisible World*, 60, We would use to one another none but the Soft Answers, which Turn away Wrath. 1826: Southey, *Letter*, 19 July (1912), 414, A soft answer turneth away wrath.

Soft as butter. 1567: Golding, *Ovid*, bk xiii l. 937, More soft than butter newly made. 1620: Shelton, *Quixote*, Pt II ch xii, My lady is as gentle as a lamb and as soft as butter, *c.*1625: Wither, *Schollers Purgat.*, 95 (Spens.S.), I found the words of their mouthes as soft as butter. 1771: Smollett, *Clinker*, in *Works*, vi 8 (1817), She is a poor good-natured simpleton, as soft as butter. 1923: O. Seaman, in *Punch*, 23 May, 482, Soft my words shall be as butter.

Soft as pap. *c.*1590: *Plaine Percevall*, Dedn., The first ladlefull had a smacke as soft as pap. 1720: Gay, *Poems*, ii 279 (Underhill), As soft as pap her kisses are.

Soft as silk. *c.*1307: in *Lyric Poetry*, 36 (Percy S., No. 19), Eythar side soft ase sylk. *c.*1386: Chaucer, *Squire's Tale*, l. 605, And strawe hir cage faire and softe as silk. *c.*1430: Lydgate, *Minor Poems*, 188 (E.E.T.S.), Hir body, softe as selke. *c.*1450: *Partonope*, 66 (E.E.T.S.), Her lees were as softe as sylk. Before 1529: Skelton, *Philip Sparrow*, l. 1119, And handes soft as sylke. 1555: S. Hawes, *Past. of Pleasure*, 63 (Percy S.), By her propre hande, soft as any sylke. 1605: Sylvester, *Du Bartas*, Week II Day iii Pt 1, l. 162. 1782: Wolcot, *Lyric Odes*, Ode viii, in *Works*, i (1795), Sweet is the voice of Praise! – oh, soft as silk. 1892: B. Pain, *Playthings, etc.*, 227, Her cheek was soft as silk.

Soft fire makes sweet malt. Before 1500: in Hill, *Commonplace-Book*, 128 (E.E.T.S.), A softe fire makith swete malte. 1550: Udall, *Roister Doister*, I iii 1617: Greene, *Alcidaa*, in *Works*, ix. 66 (Grosart), The malt is euer sweetest, where the fire is softest. 1694: D'Urfey, *Quixote*, Pt I Act IV ['Slow' for 'Soft']. 1785–95: Wolcot, *Lousiad*, can. ii, Soft fires, the proverb tells us, make sweet malt. 1823: Scott, *Q. Durward*, ch vii ['Slow' for 'Soft'].

Soft pace goes far. 1598: Meres, *Palladis*, fo. 259. 1669: *Politeuphuia*, 182.

Soft wax will take any impression. 1672: Walker, *Param.*, 35.

Soft words and hard arguments. 1670: Ray, 158. 1732: Fuller, 4203 ['are' for 'and'].

Soft words. *See also* **Fair** (31).

Softly as foot can fall. 1530: Palsgrave, 570, I go as softe as foote maye fall. 1587: Turbervile, *Trag. Tales, etc.*, 30 (1837), There stalkte he on, as softe as foote could tread. 1601: Shakespeare, *As You Like It*, III ii 1681: Robertson, *Phraseol. Generalis*, 1145.

Softly, softly catchee monkey. The proverb is said to be African in origin: *catchee* is a typical representation of English as spoken by non-English-speaking colonial peoples. 1907: G. Benham, *Cassell's Book of Quotations*, 849 (Proverbs), 'Softly, softly', caught the monkey – (Negro). 1941: F. Vivian, *Death of Mr Lomus*, iv. 80, 'Managed to dig out a suitable motive for Steadfall?' the Chief Constable asked slyly. 'I haven't done with him yet,' came the slow reply. 'Softly, softly, catchee monkee … '

So got to gone. 1678: Ray, 349.

So great is the ill that doth not hurt me, As is the good that doth not help me. 1578: Florio, *First Fruites*, fo. 32 [slightly varied]. 1629: *Book of Meery Riddles*, Prov. 1.

Sold. *See* quot. Glos. 1639: in *Berkeley MSS.*, iii 29 (1885), He hath sold a beane and bought a peaze. He hath sold a pound and bought a penny. He hath sold Bristoll and bought Bedminster.

Soldiers in peace are like chimneys in summer. 1594: A. Copley, *Wits, Fits,, etc.*, 34 (1614). Before 1598: Lord Burghley, in Peck's *Desid. Curiosa*, 48 (1779). 1611: *Tarltons Jests*, 11 (SH.S.), There was a nobleman that asked Tarlton what hee thought of souldiers in time of peace. Marry, quoth he, they are like chimnies in summer. [Tarlton was a plagiarist.] 1670: Ray, 24. 1732: Fuller, 4207.

Sole is the bread and butter of fish, A. Corn. 1897: *N. & Q.*, 8th ser, xi 448.

Sole. *See* **Shoe**, *subs.* (3).

So like that they are the worse for it, They are. 1678: Ray, 354. 1732: Fuller, 4959 ['both' for the second 'they'].

Solitary man. *See* quots. 1669: *Politeuphuia*, 137, The solitary man is either a God or a beast. 1732: Fuller, 418, A solitary man is either a brute or an angel.

Solomon. *See* **Samson**.

Solomon's wise, loath to go to bed, but ten times loather to rise. 1882: Mrs Chamberlain, *W. Worcs. Words*, 39 (E.D.S.). Cf. **Sluggard's guise.**

So long as you'll crowdy [fiddle] **they'll dance.** E. Corn. 1880: T. Q. Couch, *E. Cornwall Words*, 82 (E.D.S.).

Solution, you're part of the problem, If you're not part of the. 1968: E. Cleaver, *Speech*, in R. Scheer, *Eldridge Cleaver* (1969), 32, What we're saying today is that you're either part of the solution or you're part of the problem.

So many countries, so many customs (or **laws**). 10th cent.: in *A.-Saxon Gnomic Verses*, i 17 (Grein), efen – fela bega, theoda and theawa [an equal number both of countries and customs]. *c.*1320: in *Reliq. Antiquae*, i 109 (1841), 'Ase fele [many] thede [countries], ase fele thewes'; Quoth Hendyng. *c.*1374: Chaucer, *Troylus*, bk ii st. 6, For thus men seyn eche cuntre hath his lawis. Ibid., bk ii l. 28, In sondry londes, sondry ben usages. Before 1634: Chapman, *Alphonsus*, III i, So many lands, so many fashions. 1669: *Politeuphuia*, 224, So many countreys, so many laws. 1670: Ray, 73 ... customs. 1732: Fuller, 4196 ... customs.

So many gipsies, so many smiths. 1846–59: *Denham Tracts*, ii 84 (F.L.S.).

So many heads, so many wits, or **So many men, so many minds** (or **opinions**). [Quot homines, tot sententiae. – Terence, *Phorm.*, II iv. 14.] *c.*1386: Chaucer *Squire's Tale*, l. 195, As many hedes, as many wittes ther been. 1539: Taverner, *Proverbs*, fo. 13, So many men, so many wyttes. 1546: Heywood, *Proverbs*, Pt I ch iii, So many heds so many wits. 1575: Gascoigne, *Glasse of Govt.*, II ii, So many men, so many mindes. 1592: Greene, *Works*, xi 44 (Grosart) [as in 1546]. 1610: Rowlands, *Martin Markall*, 6 (Hunt.Cl.) [as in 1575]. 1692: L'Estrange, *Aesop*: 'Life', 18 [as in 1575]. 1753: Richardson, *Grandison*, iii 477 (1883), So many persons, so many minds. 1859: Sala, *Twice Round Clock*, 3 p.m., The proverb reads aright – as many men, so many minds. 1924: 'A. Carp', *Augustus Carp Esq.*, xii, They were all those things, and they would remember the old saying, so many men, so many opinions.

So many servants, so many foes. 1539: Taverner, *Proverbs*, fo. 34, Loke how many bondmen we haue and so many enemyes we haue. 1586: Pettie, tr. Guazzo's *Civil Convers.* fo. 169, According to the saying, We haue so manie enimies as we haue seruants. 1666: Torriano, *Piazza Univ.*, 257. 1669: Dudley North, *Obs. and Adv. Oeconom.*, 40 ['enemies' for 'foes'].

Some are very busy and yet do nothing. 1732: Fuller, 4211.

Some are wise and some are otherwise. 1659: Howell, 1. 1738: Swift, *Polite Convers.*, Dial. I. 1748: Smollett, *Rod. Random*, ch vi.

Some come, some go; This life is so. 1732: Fuller, 6340.

Some fish, some frogs. *c.*1500: More, *Fortune*, st. 32, in Hill, *Commonplace-Book*, 79 (E.E.T.S.), Lo, in this pond be fishe and froggis bothe. 1579: Lyly, *Euphues*, 196 (Arber), It is in the courte as in all ryuers, some fish some frogges. 1792: Wolcot, *Works*, ii 434 (1795), Whereas it is in Courts, as in a pond, Some fish, some frogs.

Some good, some bad, as sheep come to the fold. 1678: Ray, 247.

Some have hap [luck], **some stick in the gap.** 1639: Clarke, 125. 1659: Howell, 16, Some have the happ and others sticke in the gapp. 1732: Fuller, 6274. 1846–59: *Denham Tracts*, i 296 (F.L.S.).

Some men must lore my lady, and some Joan. 1592: Shakespeare, *L.L.L.*, III last line.

Somerset. *See* quot. 1622: Drayton, *Polyol.*, xxiii, Then Somerset says, Set the bandog on the bull.

Somerton ending, A. Somerset. 1678: Ray, 347. 1790: Grose, *Prov. Gloss.*, s.v. 'Somerset'.

Some save-alls do well in a house. 1678: Ray, 198, Some savers in a house do well 1732: Fuller, 4217.

Something for nothing, You don't get. Often shown or heard in the dialect form *You don't get owt* (or *summat*) *for nowt*. 1845: Disraeli, *Sybil*, I i v, To do nothing and get something formed a boy's ideal of a manly career. 1870: P. T. Barnum, *Struggles and Triumphs*, viii, When people expect to get 'something for nothing' they are sure to be cheated.

Something hath some savour. *c.*1580: Fulwell, *Ars Adulandi*, sig. C2, Somewhat hath some sauor. 1585: Sir E. Dyer, in *Writings*, 87 (Grosart) [as in 1580]. 1611: Davies (of Hereford), *Sc. of Folly*, 43, in *Works*, ii (Grosart). 1656: *Musarum Deliciae*, i 31 (Hotten), Something, you know, will have some savour. 1738: Swift, *Polite Convers.*, Dial. I, They say, something has some savour, but nothing has no flavour. 1754: Berthelson, *Eng.-Danish Dict.*, s.v. 'Savour'.

Somewhat is better than nothing. 1546: Heywood, *Proverbs*, Pt I ch x *c.*1594: Bacon, *Promus*, No. 953. 1620: Shelton, *Quixote*, Pt II ch l., Something is better than nothing. 1659: Howell, 9.

So much is mine. *See* quots. 1578: Florio, *First Fruites*, fo. 32, So much is myne as I enioy, or els geue for Gods sake. 1629: *Book of Meery Riddles*, Prov. 17, So much is mine as I possesse, and give, or lose, for God's sake. 1732: Fuller, 4198, So much is mine as I enjoy, and give away for God's sake.

Son, *subs.* **1. A son of the white hen** = a lucky one. [Qui tu gallinae filius albae, Nos viles pulli nati infelicibus ovis? – Juvenal, xiii 141.] 1630: Jonson, *New Inn*, I i, Yet all, sir, are not sons of the white hen. 1764: *Poor Robin Alman.*, Feb., For money, like a chick of the white hen, has generally luck on its side.

2. He is the son of a bachelor, i.e. a bastard. 1678: Ray, 66. 1732: Fuller, 1949.

3. My son is my son till he have got him a wife;

But my daughter's my daughter all the days of her life. 1670: Ray. 53. 1732: Fuller, 6076. 1851: Planché, in *Extravag.*, iv. 201 (1879), We lose a son who takes a wife, – Our daughter is our daughter all her life.

Song, A, or **An old song** = little value, *c.*1605: Shakespeare, *All's Well*, III ii, I know a man ... hold a goodly manor for a song. 1675: Cotton, *Burl. upon Burlesque*, 266 (1765), And there's an end of an old song. 1694: Crowne, *Regulus*, II i, I bought it for a song. 1704: Swift, *Tale of Tub*, § ix, Hence comes the common saying, and commoner practice, of parting with money for a song. 1714: *Spectator*, No. 597, An hopeful youth ... was forced ... to resign all for an old song. 1849: Lytton, *Caxtons*, Pt XVII ch iv, Jack had ... purchased, on his own account, 'for an old song', some barren land. 1919: J. A. Bridges, *Victorian Recollections*, 187, The inn cost very little to rent; indeed, he might have bought it for a song if he had cared to.

Soon crooketh the tree that good gambrel would be. 'Gambrel' (also 'cambrel' and 'camock)' = a 'bent piece of wood used by butchers to hang carcases on'. *c.*1460: *Good Wyfe wold a Pylgr.*, The tre crokothe son that good cambrel wyll be. 1546: Heywood, *Proverbs*, Pt II ch ix, Timely crooketh the tree that will a good camok bee. 1570: A. Barclay, *Mirrour of Good Manners*, 24 (Spens.S.), Soone crooketh the same tree that good camoke wilbe. 1670: Ray, 75. 1676: W. Lawson, *New Orchard and Garden*, 37, The common homely proverb: Soon crooks the tree That good camrel must be. 1732: Fuller, 6118.

Soon enough. *See* **Well** (19).

Sooner named sooner come. *c.*1550: *Jacke Jugeler*, in Hazlitt, *Old Plays*, ii 116, If I had sooner spoken, he would have sooner been here. 1581: Woodes, *Conflict of Conscience*, III ii, I marvel what doth him from hence so long stay, Sooner named, sooner come, as common proverbs say.

Sooner said. *See* **Said**.

Sooner spared than got. 1541: Coverdale, *Christ. State Matrim.*, sig. I3, A thinge is soner spared then goten.

Soon espied where the thorn pricketh, It is. Before 1529: Skelton, in *Works*, i 418 (Dyce).

Soonest begun soonest over. 1872: Trollope, *Golden Lion*, ch xx.

Soon goes the young sheep as the old to market (or **pot**, etc.), **As**. [*c.*1440: *Gesta Rom.*, 364 (E.E.T.S.), The sone saide, 'alse sone deyeth the yong as the olde ...'] *c.*1520: *Calisto and Meliboea*, in Hazlitt, *Old Plays*, i 78, As soon goeth to market the lamb's fell As the sheep's. 1546: Heywood, *Proverbs*, Pt II ch iv, As soone goth the yonge lamskyn to the market As tholde yewes. 1599: Porter, *Two Angry Women*, in Hazlitt, *Old Plays*, vii 302, Take heed, as soon goes the young sheep to the pot as the old. 1631: Mabbe, *Celestina*, 86 (T.T.), As soone (lady) dies the young lambe as the old sheep. 1712: Motteux, *Quixote*, Pt II ch vii, As soon goes the young lamb to the spit, as the old wether. 1819: Scott, *Bride of L.*, ch iv, As soon comes the lamb's skin to market as the auld tup's.

Soon gotten, soon spent. 1546: Heywood, *Proverbs*, Pt II ch vi 1605: Camden, *Remains*, 331 (1870). 1732: Fuller, 4227. 1849: Brontë, *Shirley*, ch xxvii, 'Unless I heard the whole repeated, I cannot continue it,' she said. 'Yet it was quickly learned.' 'Soon gained, soon gone,' moralized the tutor. 1880: Spurgeon, *Ploughman's Pictures*, 9, This was a case of ... 'soon gotten, soon spent'.

Soon hot soon cold. *c.*1450: Burgh (and Lydgate), *Secrees*, 60 (E.E.T.S.). 1485: Malory, *Morte d'Arthur*, bk xviii ch xxv. 1546: Heywood, *Proverbs*, Pt I ch ii, Than perceiue they well, hotte loue soone colde. 1587: Greene, *Works*, iv 146 (Grosart). 1617: Wither, *Fidelia*, l. 4, Loue that's soon'st hot, is euer soonest cold. 1732: Fuller, 4228.

Soon learnt soon forgotten. *c.*1374: Chaucer, *Troylus*, bk ii l. 1238, Forwhy men seyth, 'impressiones lighte Ful lightly been ay redy to the flighte'. 1869: Hazlitt, 342.

Soon ripe soon rotten. *c.*1393: Langland, *Plowman*, C, xiii 223, And that that rathest rypeth roteth most saunest. 1546: Heywood, *Proverbs*, Pt I ch x 1566: Harman, *Caveat*, cap. xxii 1604: *Jacke of Dover*, 23 (Percy S.) 1683: White-Kennett, tr. Erasmus' *Praise of Folly*, 14 (8th ed.), Therefore for the curbing of too forward parts we have a disparaging proverb. *Soon ripe, soon rotten.* 1756: *Gent. Mag.*, 556. 1889: Peacock, *Manley, etc., Gloss.*, 507 (E.D.S.).

Soon todd [toothed] **soon with God** – an idea which has found expression in several forms. 1659: Howell, 4, Soon todd, soon with God, a Northern proverb, when a child hath teeth too soon. 1670: Ray, 52, Quickly too'd, and quickly go, Quickly will thy mother have moe [more]. Yorksh. Ibid., 26 [as in 1659]. 1879: W. Henderson, *Folk-Lore of N. Counties*, 19, The proverb 'Soon teeth, soon toes', shows another portent of such an event. If baby's teeth come early there will soon be fresh toes, i.e. another baby. 1888: *N. & Q.*, 7th ser, v 285, My mother used always to say, 'soon toothed, soon turfed'.

Sooth bourd. *See* **True** (11).

Sore be healed, Though the, yet a scar may remain. 1732: Fuller, 5013.

Sore eyes. 1. The light is naught for sore eyes. 1580: Lyly, *Euphues*, 394 (Arber), He that hath sore eyes must not behold the candle. 1663: Killigrew, *Parson's Wedding*, II v, *Capt* ... I see you are merry: I'll leave you. I must go a little way to inquire about a business; *Wild.* H' has got a sore eye, I think. 1670: Ray, 114.

2. The sight of you is good for sore eyes. 1738: Swift, *Polite Convers.*, Dial. I. 1893: Raymond, *Gent. Upcott*, ch iv, It's good for sore eyes to see you here.

Sorrow and an evil life maketh soon an old wife. 1639: Clarke, 279. 1670: Ray, 144. 1732: Fuller, 6366.

Sorrow at parting if at meeting there be laughter. *c.*1410: *Towneley Plays*, 292 (E.E.T.S.), Thus sorow is at partyng at metyng if ther be laghter.

Sorrow comes unsent for. 1579: Spenser, *Shep. Cal.*, May, 159, Sorrow, ne neede be hastened on: For he will come without calling anon. 1670: Ray, 144. 1732: Fuller, 4230. 1869: Spurgeon, *John Ploughman*, ch v, Sorrows are visitors that come without invitation.

Sorrow ends not when it seemeth done. 1855: Bohn, 489.

Sorrow for a husband is like a pain in the elbow, sharp and short. 1732: Fuller, 4241.

Sorrow is asleep, wake it not, When. 1659: Howell, 16. 1732: Fuller, 5569. *c.*1850: Song quoted, *N. & Q.*, 8th ser, xi 417, When sorrow sleepeth wake it not.

Sorrow is dry. *c.*1540: Bale, *Kynge Johan*, l. 2459, For heauynesse is drye. *c.*1598: Deloney. *Gentle Craft*, Pt II ch iii, Sorrow they say is dry, and I find it to be true. 1623: Webster, *Devil's Law-Case*, V iv, 'Tis sorrow that is very dry. 1667: Dryden and Davenant, *Tempest*, II i 1714:

Gay, *Shep. Week*, Friday, l. 152, Excessive sorrow is exceeding dry. 1768: Goldsmith, *Vicar*, ch xvii, Deborah, my life, grief, you know, is dry. 1826: Scott, *Woodstock*, ch vii 1901: F. E. Taylor. *Lancs Sayings*, 26, Sorrow will have ale.

Sorrow is good for nothing but sin. 1659: Howell, 4. 1732: Fuller, 4232.

Sorrow makes silence her best orator. 1600: Bodenham, *Belvedere*, 171 (Spens.S.).

Sorrow rode in my cart. 1830: Forby, *Vocab. E. Anglia*, 429.

Sorrow to one's sops, To have. 1546: Heywood, *Proverbs*, Pt II ch viii, I had sorow to my sops ynough, be sure. 1670: Ray, 218. 1788: Grose, *Class. Dict. Vulgar Tongue* (2nd ed.) (OED), Sorrow shall be his sops, he shall repent this.

Sorrow win pay no debt. 1669: *New Help to Discourse*, 310, Sorrow quits no scores. 1670: Ray, 144. 1736: Bailey, *Dict.*, s.v. 'Sorrow'.

Sorrow. *See also* **Lean sorrow; Magpies; Ounce of mirth; Pennyworth of mirth; Sup** (4); and **Weal** (3).

Sorry, Better to be safe than. *See* **Better to be safe**.

Sorry, but I can't cry, I am. 1584: *Three Ladies of London*, in Hazlitt, *Old Plays*, vi 319, Alas! Lucre, I am sorry for thee, but I cannot weep. 1613: B.&F., *Knight of Burning Pestle*, I ii, Beshrew me, sir, I am sorry for your losses, But, as the proverb says, I cannot cry. 1641: *Archy's Dream*, 6, in Hindley, *Old Book-Coll. Miscell.*, iii, Archy said he was very sorry, but could not cry. 1738: Swift, *Polite Convers.*, Dial. I. 1827: Scott, *Journal*, 4 June, We have lost our Coal Gas Bill. Sorry for it, but I can't cry.

So said so done. 1594: Shakespeare, *Tam. of Shrew*, I ii, So said, so done, is well. 1615: T. Heywood, *Foure Prentises*, in *Works*, ii 200 (1874), So said, so done, braue lord.

Soulgrove [February] **is seldom warm.** 1687: Aubrey, *Gentilisme*, 9 (F.L.S.), The shepheards, and vulgar people in South Wilts call Februarie Sowle-grove; and have this proverbe of it: viz. Sowlegrove sil [seldom] lew. February is seldome warme. 1846: Denham, *Proverbs*, 28 (Percy S.), 'Soulegrove sil lew', is an ancient Wiltshire proverb.

Sound as a bell. 1599: Shakespeare, *Much Ado*, III ii, He hath a heart as sound as a bell. 1607: B.Barnes, *Divils Charter*, sig. K1. 1687: Sedley,

Bellamira, III, I am as sound as a bell, fat, plump and juicy. 1720: Gay, *Poems*, ii 278 (Underhill), Hearts sound as any bell. 1862: *Dialect of Leeds*, 406. 1886: Elworthy, *West Som. Word-Book*, 695 (E.D.S.), 'Sound as a bell' is the regular superlative absolute. 1918: Walpole, *Green Mirror*, bk i ch i, Healthy, happy, sound as so many bells.

Sound as an acorn. 1862: *Dialect of Leeds*, 407. 1882: Mrs Chamberlain, *W. Worcs. Words*, 1 (E.D.S.), 'As sound as an ackern' is a local proverb. 1884–6: Holland, *Cheshire Gloss.* (E.D.S.), As sound as a atchern. 1917: Bridge, *Cheshire Proverbs*, 20, As sound as an atchern.

Sound as a roach. 1655: T. Muffett, *Healths Improvement*, 186, According to the old proverb, as sound as a roach. 1668: Shadwell, *Sullen Lovers*, V iii 1697: Vanbrugh, *Prov. Wife*, V 1703: Centlivre, *Love's Contrivance*, I ii *c*.1760: Foote, *Mayor of Garratt*, I i, Tar-water and turpentine will make you as sound as a roach. 1881: Evans, *Leics. Words*, 250 (E.D.S.), Sound as a roach, a common simile.

Sound as a trout. Before 1300: *Cursor Mundi*, l. 11884, Bi that thou com therof oute thou shal be hool as any troute. Before 1529: Skelton, *Magny-fyceence*, l. 1643, I am forthwith as hole as a troute. 1588: Cogan, *Haven of Health*, 142 (1612). 1599: Buttes, *Dyets Dry Dinner*, sig. M1 1678: Ray, 289. 1828: Carr, *Craven Dialect*, ii 219, 'As sound as a troot', applied ... to a person of a sound or good constitution. 1891: P. H. Emerson, *East Coast Yarns*, 43, Now look at 'em with their red skins and dewy noses, healthy as trout.

Sound love is not soon forgotten. 1894: Northall, *Folk Phrases*, 23 (E.D.S.).

Sound travelling far and wide, A stormy day will betide. 1893: Inwards, *Weather Lore*, 106.

Sour ale. *See* **Mend** (6).

Sour apple-tree. *See* quot. 1670: Ray, 193, To be tied to the sowre appletree, i.e. To be married to an ill husband. 1736: Bailey, *Dict.*, s.v. 'Sour' [as in 1670].

Sour as vargis [verjuice]. 1600: Dekker, *Shoom. Holiday*, II i, He lookt upon me as sowre as verjuice. 1709: E. Ward; *Works*, iv, *Verse*, 12, And live on small drink that's as sower as varges. 1854: Baker, *Northants Gloss.*, s.v. 'Vargis', Verjuice, 'As sour as vargis'. 1886: Elworthy, *West Som. Word-Book*, 798 (E.D.S.), Can't drink this yer stuff, 'tis zo zour's varjis. 1917: Bridge, *Cheshire Proverbs*, 20, As sour as vargis (or warjis).

Sour as vinegar. *See* **Sharp**.

Sour as wer [crab-apples]. 1633: Draxe, 194, As soure as a crab. 1691: Ray, *Words not Generally Uused*, 73 (E.D.S.), As sour as wharre. 1877: Leigh, *Cheshire Gloss.*, 225, Sour as wharre. 1917: Bridge, *Cheshire Proverbs*, 21, As sour as wer (or wharre).

Sour as whig [sour whey]. 1854: Baker, *Northants Gloss.*, s.v. 'Whig', ... a common proverbial simile.

South Darne. *See* **Sutton**.

South Molton. *See* **Bishop's Nympton**.

South Repps. *See* **Gimmingham**.

South wind. *See* **Wind**.

Southwold. *See* **Walberswick**.

Sow (female swine), *subs.* **1. A barren sow was never good to pigs.** 1855: Bohn, 281.

2. A fat sow causeth her own bane. 1659: Howell, 7. Cf. **Swine** (1).

3. An alewife's sow is always well fed. 1732: Fuller, 578.

4. As necessary as a sow among young children. 1678: Ray, 287. 1732: Fuller, 717 ['an old sow' for 'a sow'].

5. A sow doth sooner than a cow bring an ox to the plough. Glos. 1639: in *Berkeley MSS.*, iii 31 (1885).

6. A sow to a fiddle. 1639: Clarke, 5. 1670: Ray, 193. 1672: Walker, *Paraem.*, 53.

7. As the sow fills the draff sours. 1639: Clarke, 113. 1685: Meriton, *Yorkshire Ale*, 38, For as the sew [sow] doth fill the draffe doth soure.

8. Every sow to her own trough. 1678: Ray, 204. 1712: Motteux, *Quixote*, Pt II ch xix.

9. It works like soap in a sow's tail – and like expressions. 1592: Lyly, *Mother Bombie*, IV i, This cottons and workes tike wax in a sowes eare. 1659: Howell, 14. 1670: Ray, 193. Ibid., 216, It melts like butter in a sows tail.

10. Little knoweth the fat sow what the lean doth mean. 1546: Heywood, *Proverbs*, Pt I ch x *c.*1560: Becon, in *Catechism, etc.*, 583 (P.S.), Little wot the full sow, that is in the sty, What the hungry sow aileth, that goeth by. 1670: Ray, 89. 1732: Fuller, 3257. 1852: FitzGerald, *Polonius*, xvii (1903), As when we say 'The fat sow knows not what the lean one thinks'.

11. Right, Roger, your sow is good mutton.

1670: Ray, 191. 1732: Fuller, 4054. 1864: 'Cornish Proverbs', in *N.&Q.*, 3rd ser, vi 495, Right, Roger, right; your sow is very good mutton but better pork.

12. Sow and saddle. *See* quots. 1546: Heywood, *Proverbs*, Pt II ch i, As meete as a sow to beare a saddle. 1660: A. Brome, *Poems*: 'New Ballad', But the title of knight, on the back of a knave. Is like a saddle upon a sow. 1671: A. Behn, *Amorous Prince*, IV ii, These clothes become Thee, as a saddle does a sow. 1732: Fuller, 1972, He looks like a sow saddled. 1762: Smollett, *Sir L. Greaves*, ch viii, Lord help his fool's head! it becomes him as a sow doth a cart-saddle. 1917: Bridge, *Cheshire Proverbs*, 80, It becomes him as well as a sow does a cart-saddle

13. To come sailing in a sow's ear. 1670: Ray, 192. 1732: Fuller, 5146.

14. To grease the fat sow. 1546: Heywood, *Proverbs*, Pt I ch xi, What should we (quoth I), grease the fat sow in thars. 1580: Baret, *Alvearie*, S 411, It is as well bestowed vpon him, as to grease a fatte sowe in the arse. 1639: Clarke, 10, To grease a fat sow i' th' taile. 1666: Torriano, *Piazza Univ.*, 243, The more one is rich, the more one may be, usually one greaseth a fat sow in the nose. 1925: *Times*, 8 Dec., p. 8, col. 3, Mr Lansbury said that this was only another instance of 'greasing the fat sow'. Not a single one of these duties would do any good to the working people.

15. To have a good nose to be a poor man's sow. 1530: Palsgrave, 580, He hath a good nose, etc. 1579: *Marr. of Wit and Wisdom*, 27 (SH.S.), I have a good nose, etc. 1670: Ray, 187 [as in 1530, but with 'make' for 'be']. 1738: Swift, *Polite Convers.*, Dial. I, Colonel, I find you would make a very bad poor man's sow.

16. You prick up your ears like an old sow in beans. 1887: Parish and Shaw, *Dict. Kent. Dialect*, 121 (E.D.S.), A proverbial saying is, 'You prick up', etc.

See also **Cow** (1) and (19); **Hog; Pig; Silk purse; Still sow; Swine;** and **Wrong** (4).

Sow, *verb.* 1. As you sow so will you reap. [Galatians vi.7, Whatsoever a man soweth, that shall he also reap.] 8th cent.: Cynewulf, *Christ*, l. 84 (Gollancz), Swa eal manna bearn Sorgum sawath swa eft ripath Cennath to cwealme (All the children of men as they sow in sorrow, so afterwards they reap, they bring forth for death).

*c.*1250: *Owl and Nightingale*, 1037, That man schal erien an sowe Thar he wenth after sum god mowe. *c.*1270: in *Old Eng. Miscell.*, 59 (Morris, E.E.T.S.), Hwenne alle men repen schule, that heo ear seowe. *c.*1420: Lydgate, *Assem. of Gods.* 37 (E.E.T.S.), But suche as ye haue sowe Must ye nedes reepe. *c.*1560: T. Ingelend, *Disob. Child*, in Hazlitt, *Old Plays*, ii 295, But my son ... Shall reap in such wise as he did sow. 1609: Dekker, *Works*, iv. 219 (Grosart), I haue made the olde saying true, who sowes shall reape. 1664: Butler, *Hudibras*, Pt II can. ii l. 504, As you sow, y'are like to reap. 1766: Garrick and Colman, *Clandest. Marriage*, I i 1836: *Marryat, Japhet*, ch xxxi, No, no, Japhet, as I have sown, so must I reap. 1895: Wilde, *Import. of being Earnest*, II, As a man sows so let him reap.

2. Forbear not sowing because of birds. 1640: Herbert, *Jac. Prudentum.*

3. He is sowing on the sand. 1813: Ray, 75. Cf. **Plough**, *verb* (7).

4. He that soweth good seed, shall reap good corn. 1633: Draxe, 12.

5. He that soweth virtue, shall reap fame. 1629: *Book of Meery Riddles*, Prov. 48.

6. He that sows iniquity shall reap sorrow. 1732: Fuller, 2306.

7. He that sows in the highway tires his oxen, and loseth his corn. 1633: Draxe, 222 ['wearieth' for 'tires', and 'labour' for 'corn']. 1732: Fuller, 2305.

8. He that sows thistles shall reap prickles. 1611: Cotgrave, s.v. 'Chardon', ... reaps thornes. 1732: Fuller, 2307.

9. He that sows trusts in God. 1640: Herbert, *Jac. Prudentum.* 1670: Ray, 24, Who sows his corn in the field trusts in God.

10. One sows another reaps. 1709: Dykes, *Eng. Proverbs*, Pref. ii (2nd ed.)

11. Sow dry and set wet. [1580: Tusser, *Husb.*, 101 (E.D.S.), Time faire, to sowe or to gather be bold, but set or remooue when the weather is cold.] 1678: Ray, 49, This rule in gardening, never forget To sow dry, and to set wet. 1846: Denham, *Proverbs*, 11 (Percy S.) ['plant' for 'set']. 1904: *Co. Folk-Lore: Northumb.*, 173 (F.L.S.) [as in 1846].

12. Sow [wheat] **in the slop** (or **sop**), **Heavy at top.** 1823: Moor, *Suffolk Words*, 376. 1830: Forby, *Vocab. E. Anglia*, 417. 1872: J. Glyde, jr., *Norfolk Garland*, 154.

13. Sown corn is not lost. 1875: Cheales, *Proverb. Folk-Lore*, 126.

14. The brain that sows not corn plants thistles. 1670: Ray, 3.

15. To sow the wind and reap the whirlwind. [Hosea viii 7, They have sown the wind, and they shall reap the whirlwind.] 1583: J. Prime, *Fruitful and Brief Discourse*, II, 203, They who sowed a winde, shall reap a whirlewind, but they that sowed in justice shall reape mercie. 1816: Scott, *Black Dwarf*, ch xviii. Indiscriminate profusion ... is sowing the wind to reap the whirlwind. 1895: Purcell, *Life of Manning*, ii 82, He could no longer call an hour in the day his own. He had sown the wind and was reaping the whirlwind.

16. To sow wild oats. *See* **Wild** (7).

17. Who sows little mows the less. Before 1300: *Cursor Mundi*, l. 28831, It was said, 'Qua littil saus, the lesse he mais'. 1611: Cotgrave, s.v. 'Semer', Little sow little mow. 1846: Denham, *Proverbs*, 33 (Percy S.), Sow thin, shear thin.

See also **Quiet sow.**

Sowley hammer. *See* quot. 1863: Wise, *New Forest*, ch vi, Nothing now remains to tell their former importance [iron-works] but a few mounds ... and a country proverb, 'There will be rain when Sowley hammer is heard'.

Space cometh grace, In. 1541: Coverdale, *Christ. State Matrim.*, sig. G8. 1595: *Maroccus Extaticus*, 8 (Percy S.), In space grows grace. 1670: Ray, 144. 1732: Fuller, 6167.

Spade a spade, To call a. [τά σῦκα σῦκα, τὴν σκάφην δὲ σκάφην ὀνομάσων. – Lucian, *Hist. Conscr.*, 41.] 1539: Taverner, *Garden of Wysdome*, sig. C4, Whiche can call ... a spade a spade. 1600: Kemp, *Nine Daies Wonder*, in Arber, *Garner*, vii 34 (1883), That he may, being a plain man, call a spade a spade. 1632: Jonson, *Magn. Lady*, I *ad fin.*, Faith we do call a spade a spade, in Cornwall. 1668: Shadwell, *Sullen Lovers*, IV i 1725: Bailey, tr. Erasmus' *Colloq.*, 181, Who call a fig a fig, and a spade a spade. 1854: Dickens, *Hard Times*, bk i ch vi, There's no imaginative sentimental humbug about me. I call a spade a spade.

Spaniel. *See* **Flattering**; and **Woman** (8).

Spaniels that fawn when beaten, will never forsake their masters. 1732: Fuller, 4236.

Span new. *See* **Spick** and **span.**

Spare at brim. *See* **Better spare.**

Spare not to spend, but spare to go thither.
1659: Howell, 11.

Spare the rod and spoil the child.
[– Menander. Proverbs xiii.24, He that spareth his rod, hateth his son.] *c.*1000: Aelfric, *Hom.*, ii 324 (OED), Se the spareth his yrde, he hatath his cild. 1377: Langland, *Plowman*, B, v 41, Who-so spareth the sprynge spilleth his children. 1422: J. Yonge, tr. *Gouern. of Prynces*, 161 (E.E.T.S.), Salamon sayth, Qui parsit virge odit filium, 'who sparith the yarde he hatyth the chylde'. 1577: *Misogonus*, II iii, He that spareth the rode, hates the childe. 1692: L'Estrange, *Aesop*, 264 (3rd ed.) [as in 1577]. 1732: Fuller, 4238. 1855: Thackeray, *Newcomes*, ch iii, A brother to whom my poor mother spared the rod, and who … has turned out but a spoilt child.

Spare to speak and spare to speed.
*c.*1390: Gower, *Conf. Amantis*, bk i l. 1293, For spechëles may noman spede. *c.*1426: Audelay, *Poems*, 28 (Percy S.), Whosoever sparys fore to speke sparys for to spede. Before 1529: Skelton, *Bowge of Courte*, l. 91, Who spareth to speke, in fayth he spareth to spede. *c.*1597: Deloney, *Gentle Craft*, ch xv 1609: W. Rowley, *Search for Money*, 24 (Percy S.). 1700: Congreve, *Way of World*, IV iv 1730: Lillo, *Silvia*, I ix 1781: Macklin, *Man of the World*, V

Spare well and spend well. 1541: Coverdale, *Christ. State Matrim.*, sig. I3, To spare that thou mayest haue to spend, *c.*1600: in E.E.T.S., Ext. Ser, No. 8, p. 71, Spare in tyme, and spend in tyme. 1869: Hazlitt, 343.

Spare when you are young and spend when you are old. 1541: Coverdale, *Christ. State Matrim.*, sig. I3, Spare for thyne age. 1611: Cotgrave, s.v. 'Souper', Hee that spares when he's young may the better spend when he's old. 1869: Hazlitt, 343.

Spare. *See also* **Spend**.

Sparing is a rich purse. 1541: Coverdale, *Christ. State Matrim.*, sig. I3.

Sparing is the first gaining. 1580: Lyly, *Euphues*, 229 (Arber), Sparing is good getting. 1629: *Book of Meery Riddles*, Prov. 108.

Spark in the throat. *See* **Smith** (3).

Spark makes a great fire, A small. 1412–20: Lydgate, *Troy Book*, bk i l.785, And of sparkys that ben of syghte smale, Is fire engendered that devoureth al. *c.*1470: G. Ashby, *Poems*, 61 (E.E.T.S.), For of a litle sparkle a grete fyre comyth. 1509: Barclay, *Ship of Fools*, i 194 (1874), A small sparcle often tyme doth augment It selfe, and groweth to flames peryllous. 1607: Dekker, etc., *Northw. Hoe*, II, 'Tis a small sparke giues fire to a beautifull womans discredit. 1655: Fuller, *Church Hist.*, bk iii § ii (60), What a great fire doth a small spark kindle! 1748: Richardson, *Clarissa*, vii 306 (1785), How soon a little spark kindles into a flame. 1884: *Folk-Lore Journal*, ii 280, A spark may raise an awful blaze. *Derbysh.*

Sparrow-hawk of a buzzard, You can't make a. *c.*1400: *Rom. Rose*, l. 4033, This have I herd ofte in seying, That man [ne] may, for no daunting, Make a sperhauke of a bosarde.

Sparrow in hand is worth a pheasant that flieth by, A. 1612: Shelton, *Quixote*, Pt I bk iv. ch iv, For 'a sparrow in the fist is worth more than a flying bittour'. 1732: Fuller, 420.

Sparrows fight for corn which is none of their own. Ibid., No. 4242.

Sparrows. *See also* **Pert; Robin;** and **Two sparrows.**

Speak, *verb.* **1. He cannot speak well that cannot hold his tongue.** 1666: Torriano, *Piazza Univ.*, 279, He can hardly speak, who cannot hold his peace. 1732: Fuller, 1820.

2. He never speaks but his mouth opens. 1639: Clarke, 133. 1670: Ray, 193, You never speak, etc. 1690: *New Dict. Canting Crew*, sig. H5.

3. He speaks as if every word would lift a dish. 1732: Fuller, 2024.

4. He speaks one word nonsense, and two that have nothing in them. Ibid., No. 2025.

5. He that speaks ill of his wife, dishonoureth himself. Ibid., No. 2309.

6. He that speaks lavishly shau hear as knavishly. 1670: Ray, 144. 1732: Fuller, 6367.

7. He that speaks me fair and loves me not, I'll speak him fair and trust him not. 1633: Draxe, 67. 1670: Ray, 24.

8. He that speaks, sows, he that hears, reaps. 1670: Ray, 24, He that speaks doth sow, he that holds his peace doth reap. 1694: D'Urfey, *Quixote*, Pt I Act IV sc i [as in 1670, but with 'may' for the second 'doth']. 1732: Fuller, 2310.

9. He that speaks well fights well. *c.*1250: *Owl and Nightingale*, l. 1070, Wel fight that wel speath – seide Alvred.

10. He that speaks without care, shall remember with sorrow. 1732: Fuller, 2311.

11. Never speak ill of the dead. [Latin *de*

mortuis nil nisi bonum (of the dead [say] nothing except good)] 1540: R. Taverner, tr. *Erasmus' Flores Sententiarum*, A6, Rayle not upon him that is deade. 1609: S. Harward, *MS* (Trinity College Cambridge), 81v, Speake not evill of the dead. 1682: W. Penn, *No Cross, No Crown* (ed. 2), xix, Speake well of the dead. 1740: North, *Lives of the Norths*, i 149 (Bohn), It is fit to be silent, because we should not speak ill of the dead. 1945: F Thompson, *Lark Rise*, xiv, 'Never speak ill of the dead' was one of their maxims.

12. Some that speak no ill of any, do no good to any. Ibid., No. 4219.

13. Speak fair and think what you will. 1605: Camden, *Remains*, 331 (1870). 1670: Ray, 144. 1754: Berthelson, *Eng.-Dan. Dict.*, s.v. 'Speak'.

14. Speak fitly or be silent wisely. 1611: Cotgrave, s.v. 'Taire', Better no words then words unfitly placed. 1639: Clarke, 11, Speak to th' purpose or hold your peace. 1640: Herbert, *Jac. Prudentum*.

15. Speak no ill of another, until thou thickest of thy self. 1629: *Book of Meery Riddles*, Prov. 92.

16. Speak of a man as you find him. 1875: Cheales, *Proverb. Folk-lore*, 120.

17. Speak well of the dead. 1670: Ray, 78. *See also* (11).

18. Speak well of your friend, of your enemy say nothing. 1875: Cheales, *Proverb. Folk-Lore*, 88.

19. Speak what you will, an ill man will turn it ill. 1732: Fuller, 6116.

20. Speak when you are spoken to. 1639: Clarke, 20. 1732: Fuller, 4244 [with the addition – 'come when you are called']

21. To speak as though he would creep into one's mouth. 1546: Heywood, *Proverbs*, Pt II ch ix, Ye speake now as ye would creepe into my mouth. 1670: Ray, 170. 1754: Berthelson, *Eng.-Danish Dict.*, s.v. 'Creep', He is ready to creep into his mouth. Cf. **Creep up one's sleeve.**

22. To speak ill of others is the fifth element. 1578: Florio, *First Fruites*, fo. 29. 1654: Whitlock, *Zootomia*, 445.

23. To speak like a mouse in a cheese. [1631: Brathwait, *Whimzies*, 70 (1859), He speakes … like a frog in a well, or a cricket in a wall.] 1659: Howell, 4, He speaks like a mouse in a cheese. 1670: Ray, 186. 1681: Robertson, *Phraseol. Generalis.*, 1157, You speak, etc. 1732: Fuller, 5233.

24. To speak like an oracle, *c.*1676: South, *Serm.*, 341 (1715) (OED), He only now-a-days speaks like an oracle, who speaks tricks and ambiguities. 1738: Swift, *Polite Convers.*, Dial. II, Colonel, you spoke like an oracle.

25. Who so speaketh unwisely. *See* quot. 1493: *Dives lt Pauper*, fo. 75 (1536), It is a common prouerbe, that who so speakethe vnwysely and vaguely, or in an euylle maner, he speketh to moche.

26. Who speaks not, errs not. 1611: Cotgrave, s.v. 'Parler' ['He that' for 'Who']. 1623: Wodroephe, *spared Houres*, 507. 1659: Howell, *Proverbs: Eng.-Fr.*, 11.

27. You speak in clusters, you were begot in nutting. 1678: Ray, 346. 1732: Fuller, 6009.

Spectacles are death's arquebuse. 1640: Herbert, *Jac. Prudentum.*

Speech is silver, silence is golden. Ibid., More have repented speech than silence. 1834: Carlyle, in *Fraser's Magazine*, June, 668, As the Swiss Inscription says: *Sprechen ist silbern, Schweigen is golden* (Speech is silvern, Silence is golden). 1865: A. Richardson, *Secret Service*, ii, A taciturn but edified listener, I pondered upon … 'speech is silver, while silence is golden. 1924: *Punch*, 2 April, p. 363, col. 1, Recollect that maxim old, 'Speech is silver, silence gold'. Cf. Silence.

Speech is the index of the mind. 1630: Brathwait, *Eng. Gent., etc.* 51 (1641). Ibid., 46, Democritus calls speech, the image of life. 1670: Ray, 24, Speech is the picture of the mind. 1870: T. W. Robertson, *Nightingale*, I, Talk! Ha! Speech is the index and mirror of the soul.

Speed is in the spurs, All the. 1732: Fuller, 556.

Speed the plough! originally, **God speed the plough!** 1472: *Paston Letters*, iii 50 (Gairdner), God sped the plowghe. *c.*1500: *God Spede the Plough* [title]. 1542: Boorde, *Introd.*, ch xvii p. 166 (E.E.T.S.), Yf we do not wel, God spede the plow! 1604: Bodley, *Letter*, quoted *Bodl. Quarterly Record*, iii 48, God speede your plough, I am glad your presse is a-foote, and yow so foreward before. 1661: in *Harl. Miscell.*, ii 503 (1744), God speed the plough, plague rooks and crows, And send us years more cheap. 1669: Dryden, *Wild Gallant*, III i, Speed the plough! If I can make no sport, I'll hinder none. 1747: Garrick, *Miss in her Teens*, I i, Well, speed the plough! 1798: Morton, *Speed the Plough* [title of comedy]. 1902: *N.&Q.*, 9th ser, ix 12, The saying implies merely a wish for prosperity, in the same way that 'God speed the plough' applied to the pursuit of agriculture. [In its later uses 'speed the plough' seems to have been little more than an expletive phrase, meaning much the same as 'Good luck to you!']

Spell for spell is fair play = turn for turn. 1855: Robinson, *Whitby Gloss.*, 164.

Spend, *verb.* **1. He that spendeth much.** *See* quot. 15th cent.: in *Relic. Antiquae*, i 316 (1841), He that spendes myche and getythe nowghte, And owith myche and hathe nowghte. And lokys in hys purse and fynde nowghte, He may be sory, thowe he seythe nowghte. *c*: 1530: Rhodes, *Bohe of Nurture*, 107 (E.E.T.S.) [slightly varied by beginning the second and third lines with 'He that']. 1578: Florio, *First Fruites*, fo. 104 [as in 1530].

2. In spending lies the advantage. 1640: Herbert, *Jac. Prudentum.*

3. Know when to spend and when to spare, And yon need not be busy; you'll ne'er be bare. 1732: Fuller, 6437.

4. Never spend your money before you have it. 1831: Hone, *Year-Book*, col. 1612.

5. Spend and be free, but make no waste. 1639: Clarke, 129. 1670: Ray, 24. 1732: Fuller, 4247.

6. Spend and God will send. 1546: Heywood, *Proverbs*, Pt II ch v ['shall' for 'will']. 1575: Gascoigne, *Posies*, 64 (Cunliffe), The common speech is, spend and God will send. 1611: Cotgrave, s.v. 'Manger'. 1710: S. Palmer, *Moral Essays on Proverbs*, 282, There is indeed an unlucky proverb that is often cited on such occasions. Spend, etc. 1869: Spurgeon, *John Ploughman*, ch xvi, He must squander it, always boasting that his motto is, 'Spend', etc.

7. Spend not where you may save; spare not where you must spend. 1678: Ray. 348.

8. What we spent we had; What we gave, we have; What we lent is lost. 1669: *New Help to Discourse*, 250.

9. Who more than he is worth doth spend, He makes a rope his life to end. 1523: Fitzherbert, *Husb.*, 99 (E.D.S.), He that dothe more expende, thanne his goodes wyll extende, meruayle it shall not be, thoughe he be greued with pouertee. 1670: Ray, 24. 1732: Fuller, 6397.

10. Who spends before he thrives, will beg before he thinks, *c.*1460: *Good Wyfe wold a*

Pylgremage, l. 151 (E.E.T.S.), He that spendyth more then he gettythe, a beggarris lyfe he schall lede. 1647: *Countrym. New Commonwealth*, 35. 1732: Fuller, 5720. 1875: Smiles, *Thrift*, 172, He who spends all he gets, is on the way to beggary.

11. Who spends more than he should, shall not have to spend when he would. 1670: Ray, 25. 1732: Fuller, 6074.

See also **Spare**.

Spice, *subs.* **1. If you beat spice, it will smell the sweeter.** 1732: Fuller, 2741.

2. Who hath spice enough may season his meat as he pleaseth. 1640: Herbert, *Jac. Prudentum*, He that hath the spice may season as he list. 1670: Ray, 25. 1732: Fuller, 4140 ['she' for 'he'].

See also **Variety**.

Spick and span new; originally **Span new**, which is now found only in dialectal use. *c.*1300: *Havelok*, l. 968 (E.E.T.S.), And bouthe him clothes, al spannewe. *c.*1374: Chaucer, *Troylus*, bk iii l. 1665, His tale ay was span-newe to biginne Til that the night departed hem a-twinne. 1590: Nashe, *Almond for a Parrot*, 27 (1846). Hee offered her a spicke and spanne new Geneua Bible. 1595: Munday, *John a Kent*, 52 (SH.S.), Heeres a coat, spick and span new. 1614: B. Rich, *Honestie of This Age*, 18 (Percy S.). 1665: Pepys, *Diary*, 15 Nov. 1712: Motteux, *Quixote*, Pt II ch lviii, And all, as they use to say, spick and span new, and shining like beaten gold. 1829: Hunter, *Hallamsh. Gloss.*, 84, Span-new, quite new. 1863: Kingsley, *Water Babies*, ch i, Some spick and span new Gothic or Elizabethan thing. 1886: Elworthy, *West Som. Word-Book*, 696 (E.D.S.), Hav'ee zeed our millerd's span-new cart?

Spick nor crick, There's no. S. Devon. = There is no flaw. 1869: Hazlitt, 396.

Spider, *subs.* **1. But for the robin and the wren A spider would o'ercome a man.** *c.*1870: Smith, *Isle of Wight Words*, 62 (E.D.S.).

2. If you wish to live and thrive, Let a spider run alive. 1863: *N.&Q.*, 3rd ser, iii 262. 1879: Henderson, *Folk-Lore of N. Counties*, 312, He who would wish to thrive, Must let spiders run alive. 1913: E. M. Wright, *Rustic Speech, etc.*, 219.

3. When spiders' web in air do fly, The spell will, soon be very dry. 1893: Inwards, *Weather Lore*, 147.

See also **Bee** (17); **Swallow**, *verb* (1).

Spies are the ears and eyes of princes. 1651: Herbert, *Jac. Prudentum*, 2nd ed.

Spiggot. *See* **Save** (4).

Spin, *verb*. **1. A man cannot spin and reel at the same time.** 1678: Ray, 205. 1732: Fuller, 2591, I cannot spin and weave at the same time.

2. She spins well that breeds her children. 1640: Herbert, *Jac. Prudentum*. 1732: Fuller, 4137, She spins a good thread that brings up her daughter well.

3. Spinning out of time never made good cloth. 1660: Howell, *Parly of Beasts*, 80 [quoted as 'a trite proverb'].

4. That which will not be spun, let it not come between the spindle and the distaff. 1640: Herbert, *Jac. Prudentum*. 1670: Ray, 25. 1732: Fuller, 2726, If 'twill not be spun, bring it not to the distaff.

5. To spin a fair thread. [1412: Hoccleve, *Regement*, l. 1763, p. 64 (E.E.T.S.), Alasse! this likerous dampnable errour. In this londe hath so large a threde I-sponne, That were peple is non vndir the sonne.] 1562: Heywood, *Three Hund. Epigr.*,No. 228, She hath spun a fair thread. 1595: *Locrine*, II iii (Malone S.), O wife I have spunne a faire thredde. *c*.1625: B.&F., *Chances*, III iv, You have spun yourself a fair thread now. 1691.: J. Wilson, *Belphegor*, I iii, And if I lose my place by the bargain, I have spun a fine thread. 1730: Lillo. *Silvia*, III xvii, Ah Lettice, Lettice, what have you been doing? You've spun a fine thread, truly. 1737: Ray, 63.

Spit and a stride, A = A short way. 1621: B.&F., *Pilgrim*. II ii, Wilt thou take a spit and a stride, and see if thou canst outrun us? 1676: Cotton, Walton's *Angler*, Pt II ch ii, You are now … within a spit and a stride of the Peak. 1824: Scott, *Redgauntlet*, ch xvii, I am to carry you to old Father Crackenthorp's, and then you are within a spit and a stride of Scotland, as the saying is. 1828: Carr, *Craven Dialect*, ii 155, Spit and a stride, a very short distance.

Spit, *verb*. **1. Spit in his mouth and make him a mastiff.** It was an old idea that to spit in a dog's mouth gave him pleasure. 1670: Ray, 216.

2. Spit in your hands and take better hold. 1546: Heywood, *Proverbs*, Pt II ch iv, Nay, I will spit in my hands, and take better holde. 1577: J. Grange, *Golden Aphroditis*, sig. H1, Spitte on your handes and take good holde. 1738: Swift,

Polite Convers., Dial. I, I warrant, miss will spit in her hand, and hold fast.

3. To spit in the church. *See* quots. 1591: Florio, *Second Frutes*, 13, Who sometimes make it a matter of conscience to spitt in the church, and at another time will beray the altar. 1640: Herbert, *Jac. Prudentum*, Some make a conscience of spitting in the church, yet rob the altar.

4. Who spits against heaven it falls in his face. 1557: North, *Diall of Princes*, fo. 106, As he whiche spitteth into the element, and the spittel falleth againe into his eies. 1640: Herbert, *Jac. Prudentum*. 1670: Ray, 13. 1732: Fuller, 4252, Spit not against Heaven; 'twill fall back into thy own face.

5. You spit on your own sleeve. 1639: Clarke, 54.

Spiteful as an old maid, As. 1732: Fuller, 730.

Spite of one's teeth, In. 1387: Trevisa, tr. Higden, vii 7 (Rolls Ser.), What I haue longe desired now I haue it maugre thyn teeth. *c*.1489: Caxton, *Sonnes of Aymon*, 109 (E.E.T.S.), Reynawde toke Alarde oute of his enemyes handes, mawgre theyr teeth, *c*.1500: More, *Juvenile Verses*, in *Works* (1557), Maugry thy teeth to lyue cause hym shall I. *c*.1534: Berners; *Huon*, 175 (E.E.T.S.), In the dyspyte of his teth I wyll se my nece. 1567: Painter, *Pal. of Pleasure*, ii 248 (Jacobs), It behoued to obey, and in despite of my teeth to do that which the Romane Emperour commaundeth. 1618: B. Holyday, *Technogamia*, V vi, I will stand here in spight of your teeth. 1678: Otway, *Friendship, in Fashion*, V i, She, like a true wife, may, spite of his teeth, deceive him quite. 1732: B. Mandeville, *Honour and War*, 130, The more I have perceiv'd and felt the truth of it in spight of my teeth. 1768: Walpole, *Lett. to Gray*, 18 Feb., He forced himself upon me at Paris in spite of my teeth and my doors. 1894: R.L.S., *Letters*, v 153 (Tusitala ed.), I read over again … and it is good in spite of your teeth. 1924: Shaw, *Saint Joan*, sc vi.

Spite of the cock and his comb. 1613: Rowlands, *Paire of Spy-Knaues*, 9 (Hunt.Cl.), He will to London spite of cock and's combe.

Split hairs, To. 1678: Ray, 249, To cut the hair, i.e. to divide so exactly as that neither part have advantage. 1732: Fuller, 1122, Come, slit me this hair. Ibid., No. 6457, It's hard to split the hair, That nothing is wanted, and nothing to spare. 1846: Jerrold, *Chron. of Clovernook*, 130,

Whose keen logic would split hairs as a bill-hook would split logs.

Spoil before you spin, You must. 1639: Clarke, 110. 1670: Ray, 145. 1732: Fuller, 5970 [with 'well' after 'spin'].

Spoke in one's wheel, To put a. 1600: *Weakest to the Wall*, l. 848 (Malone S.), Ile set a spoake in your cart. 1682: A. Behn, *Roundheads*, V ii, She speaks as she were Queen, but I shall put a spoke in her rising Wheel of Fortune. 1712: *Spectator*, No. 498, Tho' indeed I thought they had clapt such a spoke in his wheel, as had disabled him. 1848: Dickens, *Dombey*, ch x, Mrs Dombey, eh, ma'am? I think not, ma'am. Not while Joe B. can put a spoke in your wheel, ma'am. 1901: *N. & Q.*, 9th ser, vii 258, The allusion is to the pin or spoke used to lock wheels in machinery; hence, to put an impediment in one's way.

Spoon or spoil a horn, To make a. 1820: Byron, *Letters, etc.*, v 16 (Prothero), I can't cobble: I must 'either make a spoon or spoil a horn'. 1824: Scott, *Redgauntlet*, ch i, His voice faltering, as he replied, 'Ay, ay, I kend Alan was the lad to make a spoon or spoil a horn'. 1910: *N. & Q.*, 11th ser, i 58, A lad showing much promise was commonly referred to [in the Border counties] as one who would 'either make a spoon or spoil a horn'.

Spoon. *See also* **Devil** (19); and **Silver** (6).

Sport is sauce to pains, Some. 1639: Clarke, 191.

Sport is sweetest when no spectators. 1670: Ray, 145.

Sports and journeys men are known, In. 1640: Herbert, *Jac. Prudentum*.

Spot is most seen upon the finest doth, A. 1732: Fuller, 421.

Sprained her ankle, She has. 1785: Grose, *Class. Dict. Vulgar Tongue*, s.v. 'Ankle', A girl who is got with child is said to have sprained her ankle. Cf. **Broken.**

Sprat to catch a macherel (or whale), To throw a – with variants. 1827: Hone, *Ev. Day Book*, ii 1410, It is but 'giving a sprat to catch a herring', as a body may say. 1850: Dickens, *Chuzzlewit*, ch viii, It was their custom, Mr Jonas said … never to throw away sprats, but as bait for whales. 1864: 'Cornish Proverbs', in *N. & Q.*, 3rd ser, vi 495, Give a sprat to catch a mackarel 1869: Hazlitt, 331, Set a herring to catch a whale. 1893: R.L.S., *Letters*, v 87 (Tusitala ed.), Baxter … will let you see a proof of my introduction,

which is only sent out as a sprat to catch whales. Cf. **Small fish.**

Spread nets, To. *See* quot. 1630: Taylor (Water-Poet), *Works*, 2nd pagin., 152, The old prouerb neuer failed yet, Who spreads nets for his friends, snares his own feet.

Spring (the season), *subs.* **1. A late spring Is a great blessing.** 1846: Denham, *Proverbs*, 39 (Percy S). 1893: Inwards, *Weather Lore*, 6.

2. A late spring never deceives. Ibid,, 6.

3. A wet spring, a dry harvest. 1846: Denham, *Proverbs*, 32 (Percy S.), A wet spring is a sign of dry weather for harvest. 1893: Inwards, *Weather Lore*, 6.

4. Better late spring and bear, than early blossom and blast. Ibid., 6.

5. He takes the spring from the year. 1813: Ray, 75.

6. If there's spring in winter, and winter in spring, The year won't be good for anything. 1659: Howell, *Proverbs: Span.-Eng.*, 22, When there is a spring in winter, and a winter in spring, the year is never good. 1893: Inwards, *Weather Lore*, 7.

7. In spring a tub of rain makes a spoonful of mud, In autumn a spoonful of rain makes a tub of mud. Ibid., 6.

8. Spring and the daisies. *See* quots. 1862: Chambers, *Book of Days*, i 312 (1869), Still we can now plant our 'foot upon nine daisies', and not until that can be done do the old-fashioned country people believe that spring is really come, 1878: Dyer, *Eng. Folk-Lore*, 27, 'It ain't spring until you can plant your foot upon twelve daisies', is a proverb still very prevalent. 1881: *Glos. N. & Q.*, i 43 [as in 1878].

9. The spring is not always green. 1846: Denham, *Proverbs*, 31 (Percy S.). 1893: Inwards, *Weather Lore*, 6. 1904: *Co. Folk-Lore: Northumb.*, 175 (F.L.S.).

See also **Blossom; Easter** (9); **January** (2); and **Thunder** (1) and (4).

Spring at his elbow, He hath a. Said of a gamester. 1678: Ray, 351.

Sprotborough, near Doncaster. 1869: Hazlitt, 474, Whoso is hungry, and lists well to eat, let him come to Sprotborough for his meat; and for a night, and for a day, his horse shall have both corn and hay, and no man shall ask him, when he goeth away.

Spruce as an onion, As. 1678: Ray, 289.

Spun. *See* **Spin**.

Spur in the head is worth two in the heel, A.
1670: Ray, 218. 1694: Motteux, *Rabelais*, bk iv.
ch lxv, The horses will perform the better, and
that a spur in the head is worth two in flank; or in
the same horse dialect, That a cup in the pate Is a
mile in the the gate. 1738: Swift, *Polite Convers.*,
Dial. II. 1854: Baker, *Northants Gloss.*, s.v.
'Spur', 'A spur …' A common invitation to a
person on horseback to take a parting glass.

Spur. *See also* **Horse** (4), (5), (17), (18), (19),
(28), and (42).

Spy faults if your eyes were out, You would.
1678: Ray, 271.

Squeaking wheel that gets the grease, It's the.
1937: In J. Bartlett's *Familiar Quotations*, 518,
The wheel that squeaks the loudest is the one
that gets the grease.

Squirrel, *subs.* **1.** *See* quot. 1830: Forby, *Vocab.
E. Anglia*, 420, From the general
discouragement shewn to this sport [squirrel-
hunting on Christmas Day] probably comes the
common saying, 'Hunt squirrels, and make no
noise'.

2. Within a squirrel's jump. Glos. 1911: *Folk-
Lore*, xxii 239.

Stable door after the horse has bolted (or
when the steed is stolen), **To shut the.** [Ne
post tempus praedae praesidium parem. –
Plautus, *Asin.*, 294.] *c.*1390: Gower, *Conf.
Amantis*, bk iv. l. 901, For whan the grete stiede
Is stole, thanne he taketh hiede, And makth the
stable dore fast. 1484: Caxton, *Aesope*, ii 245
(Jacobs), It was not tyme to shette the stable
whan the horses ben loste and gone. 1509:
Barclay, *Skip of Fools*, i 76 (1874), Whan the
stede is stolyn to shyt the stable dore Comys
small pleasure profyte or vauntage. 1579: Lyly,
Euphues, 37 (Arber), It is too late to shutte the
stable doore when the steede is stolne. 1628: J.
Clavell, *Recantation*, 38, This like shutting vp
the stable doore, When as the horse was stolne
out before. 1705: Ward, *Hudibras Rediv.*, Pt 1,
can. i p. 10, And that's but almost like my host,
Who stable shuts when steed is lost. 1725:
Bailey, tr. Erasmus' *Colloq.*, 576. 1886: R.L.S.,
Kidnapped, ch xiv. 1907: De Morgan, *Alice-for-
Short*, ch xxxv, Nothing I have said would
warrant such an absurd mistrust of Providence.
Besides, it would be merely shutting the stable-
door after the steed had broken loose. 1940:

Death of a Peer, x. The horse having apparently
bolted, I shall be glad to assist at the ceremony of
closing the stable door.

Staff, *subs.* **1. If the staff be crooked, the
shadow cannot be straight.** 1640: Herbert,
Jac. Prudentum.

2. To hold at staff's end. *c.*1374: *Anel. and Arc.*,
184 (OED), His new lady holdeth him vp so
narowe Vp by the bridil at the staves ende. 1565:
Shacklock, *Hatchet of Heresies*, fo. 23, They so
helde one an other at the staffes end. 1596:
Lodge, *Wits Miserie*, 83 (Hunt.Cl.), The most
chollericke and troublesome woman living vpon
the earth, shee was alwaies at the staffes end with
my father. 1642: D. Rogers, *Matrim. Honour*,
294–5, Waspish, froward, holding their
husbands at staves end. 1816: Scott, *Antiquary*,
ch xvi 1889: R.L.S., *Ballantrae*, ch ii, Mrs
Henry had a manner of condescension with him
… she held him at the staff's end.

See also **Stick,** *subs.* (1).

Stafford law = the 'law' of the big stick, [*c.*1400:
Towneley Plays, 29 (E.E.T.S.), But thou were
worthi be cled In Stafford blew [= blue from
bruises from beating]; ffor thou art alway adred.]
1589: *Hay any Worke*, 10 (1845), That I
threatned him with blowes, and to deale by
Stafford law. 1624: T. Heywood, *Captives*, III ii,
Mildew. Is this lawe? *Godfrey*. Yes, Stafford's
lawe. 1630: Taylor (Water-Poet), *Works*, 2nd
pagin., 156, If it were lawfull for me to examine
thee at Staffords Law, I would make thee
confesse the receit of ten shillings.

Staffordshire. *See* **Shrewsbury**.

Stale as custom, As. *c.*1592: *Sir Thos. More*, 32
(SH.S.), To vrdge my imperfections in excuse,
Were all as stale as custome.

Stalking-horse, To make a person or thing a.
1601: Shakespeare, *As You Like It*, V iv, He uses
his folly like a stalking-horse. 1604: Webster,
etc., *Malcontent*, IV i, A fellow that makes
religion his stalking-horse. 1642: D. Rogers,
Matrim. Honour, 55, Pretending that their
conscience is the ground, whereas it is but a
staulking-horse. 1714: E. Ward, *Cavalcade*, 3,
And Faith … Was made a stalking-horse to gold.
1740: North, *Examen*, 151, To make a stalking
horse of the exclusion, to shoot him down. 1855:
Kingsley, *West. Ho!*, ch xxix, Mary's death was
as convenient a stalking-horse to him as to the
Pope.

Stamford, As mad as the baiting bull of. 1662: Fuller, *Worthies*, ii 268 (1840). 1732: Fuller, 714 [with 'baited' for 'baiting']. 1790: Grose, *Prov. Gloss.*, s.v. 'Lincs'. 1826: Brady, *Varieties of Lit.*, 15.

Stamps like an ewe upon yeaning, She. Somerset. 1678: Ray, 344.

Stand, *verb.* **1. He stands not surely that never slips.** 1611: Cotgrave, s.v. 'Mescheoir'. 1640: Herbert, *Jac. Prudentum*. Cf. No. 2.

2. He that stands sure. *See* quot. 1412–20: Lydgate, *Troy Book*, bk ii l.1849, The prouerbe that techeth commounly, 'He that stant sure, enhast hym not to meve'. Cf. No. 1.

3. He won't stand keep. 'Said of a person spoilt by prosperity'. 1917: Bridge, *Cheshire Proverbs*, 72.

4. Stand on one side, John Ball, and let my wife see the bar [bear]. 1883: Burne, *Shrops. Folk-Lore*, 590. 1917: Bridge, *Cheshire Proverbs*, 44.

5. To stand buff = To stand firm. 1693: D'Urfey, *Richmond Heiress*, I, I have only hedg'd him into this business to stand buff with his purse upon occasion. 1708: Cibber, *Lady's Last Stake*, III, She ... stands buff at the head of the mode, without the least tincture of virtue to put her out of countenance. 1777: Sheridan, *Sch. for Scandal*, II iii., Ha! ha! that he should have stood buff to old bachelor so long, and sink into a husband at last! 1827: Scott, *Journal*, 4 Sept., There is no reason why he should turn on me, but that if he does, reason or none, it is best to stand buff to him.

6. To stand in one's own light. 1546: Heywood, *Proverbs*, Pt II ch iv, How blindly ye stand in your owne light. 1635: in *Somers Tracts*, vii 188 (1811), If he either stand in his owne light through wilfulnesse ... 1738: Swift, *Polite Convers.*, Dial. I, Mr Neverout, methinks you stand in your own light. 1848: Dickens, *Dombey*, ch xxxix, I ... can't afford to stand in my own light for your good.

7. To stand upon one's pantofles, i.e. on one's dignity. 1573: G. Harvey, *Letter-Book*, 14 (Camden S.), He was altogither set on his merrie pinnes, and walked on his stateli pantocles. 1611: Cotgrave, s.v. 'Bout', To stand upon bis pantofles, or on high tearmes. 1631: Mabbe, *Celestina*, 255 (T.T.), The villaine stands upon his pantofles, and begins to looke big. 1681:

Robertson, *Phraseol. Generalis*, 1031, He is grown very proud; he stands on his pantofles. 1755: Walpole, *Letters*, iii 156 (1846) (OED), I could not possibly today step out of my high historical pantoufles to tell it you.

8. United we stand. *See* united.

Standers by. *See* Lookers on.

Standing pools gather filth. 1639: Clarke, 144. 1670: Ray, 145. 1732: Fuller, 4257.

Stanton Drew. *See* quot. 1776: Stukeley, *Itin. Cur.*, cent. ii. 169, There is an old proverb common in Somersetshire, 'Stanton Drew, a mile from Ponsford, another from Chue'. 1849: Halliwell, *Pop. Rhymes and Nursery Tales*, 198 [as in 1776].

Stare, *verb.* **1.** *See* quot. 1917: Bridge, *Cheshire Proverbs*, 143, To stare like a choked throstle. To stare like a throttled earwig *or* cat.

2. To stare Tike a stuck pig. 1694: Motteux, *Rabelais*, bk v ch ix p. 41 (OED), Panurge star'd at him like a dead pig. 1720: Gay, *Poems*, ii 278 (Underhill), like a stuck pig I gaping stare. 1789: G. Parker, *Life's Painter*, 124, Who gape and stare, just like stuck pigs at each other. 1895: Jos. Thomas, *Randigal Rhymes*, 61.

Starling. *See* Raven.

Stars are not seen by sunshine. 1623: Wodroephe, *Spared Houres*, 503, The starres do not shine at mid-day. 1732: Fuller, 4258. 1846: Denham, *Proverbs*, 5 (Percy S.).

Stars begin to huddle, When the, The earth will soon become a puddle. 1893: Inwards, *Weather Lore*, 65.

Starve 'em. *See* quot. 1785: Grose, *Class. Dict. Vulgar Tongue*, s.v., Starve-'em, Rob'em, and Cheat'em, Stroud, Rochester and Chatham, so called by soldiers and sailors, and not without good reason.

Starve in a cook's shop, To. 1611: Cotgrave, s.v. 'Aimer', He that loves another better than himselfe, starves in a cooks shop. 1630: T. Adams, *Works*, 565, As the by-word is, staruing in a cookes shoppe, wretched in their highest fortunes. 1738: Swift, *Polite Convers.*, Dial. II, No, my lord; I'll never starve in a cook's shop.

Stay, *verb.* **1. He that can stay obtains.** 1611: Cotgrave, s.v. 'Attendre', He that can stay his time, shall compasse any thing. 1640: Herbert, *Jac. Prudentum. c.*1736: Franklin, in *Works*, i 455 (Bigelow), He that can have patience can have what he will.

2. He that stays does the business. 1640: Herbert, *Jac. Prudentum.*

3. She will stay at home, perhaps, if her leg be broke. 1732: Fuller, 4150.

4. Stay a little and news will find you. 1640: Herbert, *Jac. Prudentum.*

5. Stay awhile that we may end the sooner. 1580: Sidney, *Arcadia*, bk i p. 63 (1893), His horse ... taught him that 'discreet stays make speedy journeys'. 1651: Herbert, *Jac. Prudentum*, 2nd ed. 1732: Fuller, 4263, Stop a little, to make an end the sooner. 1823: D'Israeli, *Cur. of Lit.*, 2nd ser, i 431 (1824), Sir Amias Pawlet, when he perceived too much hurry in any business, was accustomed to say, 'Stay awhile, to make an end the sooner'. 1859: Smiles, *Self-Help*, 271 (1869), A wise man used to say, 'Stay a little, that we may make an end the sooner'.

6. Stay till the lame messenger come, if you will know the truth of the thing. 1640: Herbert, *Jac. Prudentum.*

Steady as a buggin [ghost] **in a bush, As.** 1917: Bridge, *Cheshire Proverbs*, 21.

Steal, *verb.* **1. As good steal a horse as stand by and look on.** 1659: Howell, 5.

2. He has stolen a roll out of the brewer's basket. 1678; Ray, 87 ['manchet' for 'roll']. 1732: Fuller, 1900. 1745: Franklin, *Drinker's Dict.*, in *Works*, ii 23 (Bigelow) [as in 1678].

3. He that steals can hide. 1732: Fuller, 2315.

4. He that will steal an egg will steal an ox. 1639: Clarke, 148. 1670: Ray, 145. 1875: Cheales, *Proverb. Folk-Lore*, 129.

5. One may steal a horse while another may not look over the hedge. 1546: Heywood, *Proverbs*, Pt II ch ix, Some man maie steale a hors better Than some other may stande and looke vpone. 1591: Lyly, *Endymion*, III iii, Some man may better steal a horse than another look over the hedge. 1607: Middleton, *Mich. Terme*, I. i., Some may better steal a horse than others look on. 1683: in *Harl. Miscell.*, vi 62 (1745), There is an old proverb, – *That one may better steal a steed, than another peep over the hedge.* 1728: Gay, *Beggar's Opera*, III ii 1772: Garrick, *Irish Widow*, I iii, But an Englishman may look over the hedge, while an Irishman must not stale a horse. 1921: A. Bennett, *Things that have Interested Me*, 315, Strange how one artist may steal a horse while another may not look over a hedge.

6. To steal a goose and give the giblets in alms. 1659: Howell, 1. 1721: Bailey, *Eng. Dict.*, s.v. 'Steal', He steals a goose, and gives, etc. Cf. No. 9.

7. To steal a goose and stick down a feather. 1546: Heywood, *Proverbs*, Pt I ch xi, As dyd the pure penitent that stale a goose And stack downe a fether. 1608: in Harington, *Nugae Antiquae*, ii 200 (1804). 1714: Walker, *Sufferings of Clergy*, Pt II 331, For the managers of those times thought fit, when they stole the goose, to stick down a feather.

8. To steal a pin. *See* **Pin**, *subs.* (4); and **Sin**, *subs.* (2).

9. To steal the hog and give the feet for alms. 1640: Herbert, *Jac. Prudentum.* 1670: Ray, 25. 1732: Fuller, 2028, He steals a hog, etc. Cf. No. 6.

Steed. *See* **Stable door**.

Steel to the back. *c.*1591: Shakespeare, *Titus Andr.*, IV iii, We are ... steele to the very backe. 1633: Draxe, 87. 1678: Ray, 346. Cf. **Mettle**.

Step after step the ladder is ascended. 1611: Cotgrave, s.v. 'Pas', Step after step goes farre. 1640: Herbert, *Jac. Prudentum.* 1670: Ray, 25. 1732: Fuller, 4260.

Step at a time, One. *See* **One step**.

Stern chase is a long chase, A. 1836: Marryat, *Easy*, ch xxix, This will be a long chase; a stern chase always is. 1919: J. A. Bridges, *Victorian Recollections*, 140, English poetry has had a start of some centuries, and a stern chase is proverbially a long one.

Stew in one's own juice. *See* **Grease**.

Stick and Sticks, *subs.* **1. A stick is quickly found to beat a dog with.** 1563: Becon, *Early Works*, Pref., 28 (P.S.), How easy a thing it is to find a staff if a man be minded to beat a dog. 1594: *First Part Contention*, 35 (SH.S.), A staffe is quickly found to beate a dog. 1616: Breton, *Works*, ii *e* 6 (Grosart) ['soone' for 'quickly']. 1664: J.Wilson, *Andr. Commenius*, II i, One need not go far to find A staff to beat a dog, nor circumstance To make him guilty that's before foredoom'd! 1721: *Bailey Eng. Dict.*, s.v. 'Dog', He who has a mind to beat a dog, will easily find a stick. 1842: Planché, *Extravag.*, ii 165 (1879), When you wish to lick A dog, 'tis easy, sir, to find a stick.

2. gave you a stick to break my own head with. 1732: Fuller, 2595.

3. Sticks and stones. *See* quots. 1897: *N. & Q.*, 8th ser, xii 508, I heard this saying in

Warwickshire – 'Sticks and stones will break my bones; but cruel words can never harm me'. 1898: *N. & Q.*, 9th ser, i 177, 'Sticks and stones will break my bones, but scolding will not hurt me', was an old saying in York thirty years ago.

Stick, *verb*. 1. To stick by the ribs. 1670: Ray, 194.

2. To stick like burs. *c.*1510: A. Barclay, *Egloges*, 18 (Spens.S.), Together they cleave more fast then do bums. 1533: Heywood, *Play of Love*, l. 601, I thought her owne tale lyke a bur Stack to her owne back. 1570: Googe, tr. *Popish Kingd.*, 20 (1880), But fast as buries to wooll they sticke. 1654: Flecknoe, *Loves Dominion*, IV ii, Still does this burr stick on me. 1720: Gay, *Poems*, ii 280 (Underhill), Let us like burs together stick. 1821: Scott, *Pirate*, ch xii, He … got rid of his travelling companions, who at first stuck as fast as burs. 1854: Baker, *Northants Gloss.*, s.v. 'Burr', Hence the old adage, 'Sticks like a burr to a beggar's rags'. 1025: *Times Lit. Suppl.*, 21 May, p. 348, col. 2, Phrases that stick like bum in the memory. Cf. **Cleave.**

Stiff as a poker. 1797: Colman, jr., *Heir at Law*, III ii, Stuck up as stiff as a poker. 1828: Carr, *Craven Dialect*, ii 52, 'As stiff as a poker', a proverbial simile generally applied to a haughty coxcomb. 'He's as stiff as an 'ad swallowed a poker'.

Stiff as a stake. *c.*1566: *Albion Knight*, in Malone S.'s *Collns.*, i 236, As styffe as a stake Battayle to make. 1697: T. Dilke, *City Lady*, III iii, In the morning he may find himself as cold as a stone, and as stiff as a stake.

Stiff as Barker's knee. *See* the 1913 quot. 1865: Hunt, *Pop. Rom. W. of England*, 88 (1896). 1882: F. W. P. Jago, *Gloss. of Cornish Dialect*, 112. 1913: E.M. Wright, *Rustic Speech, etc.*, 199, Once upon a time there was a miner called Barker, who was foolhardy enough to say he did not believe there were any Knockers [spirits that haunt Cornish tin-mines]. In revenge for this insult, a crowd of Knockers waylaid him, and pelted him with their tools, causing him a lifelong injury, whence grew up the proverb: As stiff as Barker's knee.

Stile, *subs*. 1. He that will not go over the stile, must be thrust through the gate. 1678: Ray, 206.

2. You would be over the stile before you come at it. 1546: Heywood, *Proverbs*, Pt II ch ix. 1566: Gascoigne, *Supposes*, II i, You would fayne

leape over the stile before you come at the hedge. 1670: Ray, 184, To leap over the stile, before you come at the stile. 1710: S. Palmer, *Moral Essays on Proverbs*, 188, Don't go over, etc. 1712: Motteux, *Quixote*, Pt I bk iii ch iv. [as in 1670]. *See also* Style.

Still as a stone. *c.*1300: *Havelok*, l. 928 (E.E.T.S.), Hauelok sette him dun anon, Also stille als a ston. *c.*1400: *Beryn*, l. 653 (E.E.T.S.), But lay as styll as ony stone. *c.*1490: *Partonope*, l. 1282 (E.E.T.S.), But lyethe as stylle as any stone. *c.*1530: *Thos. of Erceldoune*, l. 233 (Lansdowne, E.E.T.S.), Thomas stode styll as stone. 1768: Brooke, *Fool of Quality*, iii 117. 1820: Scott, *Monastery*, ch xiv. 1922: Weyman, *Ovington's Bank*, ch xxix.

Still dog. *See* **Dog** (11).

Stillest humours are always the worst, The. 1670: Ray, 25. 1732: Fuller, 4768.

Still he fishes. *See* **Fish**, *verb* (3).

Still sow eats up all the draff, The. 1546: Heywood, *Proverbs*, Pt I ch x *c.*1580: *Tom Tyler*, l. 521, p. 15 (Malone S.). 1633: Jonson, *Tale of a Tub*, III v 1641: Cowley, *Guardian*, III viii 1673: Wycherley, *Gent. Danc.-Master*, I ii, The silent sow (madam) does eat most grains. 1714: Ozell, *Molière*, iv. 122 ['drinks' for 'eats']. 1865: *N. & Q.*, 3rd ser, viii 7, We have another pithy proverb [in N. Lancs], which expresses a good deal in little compass: – 'Th' quiet sow eats a' th' draff'. 1920: J. H. Bloom, in *N. & Q.*, 12th ser, vii 507, A few Warwickshire Folk Sayings: – A sly sow eats all the wash.

Still waters run deep. [Altissima quaeque flumina minimo sono labuntur. – *Q.* Curtius, *De Rebus Gestis Alex. Magni*, vii 10.] *c.*1400: *Cato's Morals*, in *Cursor Mundi* (E.E.T.S.), l. 1672, Ther the flode is deppist the water standis stillist. *c.*1430: Lydgate, *Minor Poems*, 186 (Percy S.), Smothe waters ben ofte sithes depe. 1584: Lyly, *Sapho and Phao*, II iv, Water runneth smoothest, where it is deepest. 1618: Field, *Amends for Ladies*, III ii, Deep'st waters stillest go. 1648: Herrick, *Hesperides*, No. 38, Deep waters noiseless are. 1748: Richardson, *Clarissa*, viii 146 (1785), The stillest waters is the deepest. 1781: Macklin, *Man of the World*, I, Smooth water, you know, sir, runs deepest. 1858: D.M. Mulock, *Woman's Thoughts about Women*, xii, In maturer age … the fullest tenderest tide of which the heart is capable may be described by those 'still waters' which 'run deep'.1869; Spurgeon, *John Ploughman*, ch vi, Still waters are the deepest; but the shallowest brooks brawl the most.

Still waters, Take heed of, the quick pass away. 1640: Herbert, *Jac. Prudentum.*

Still waters turn no mills. 1907: F. K. Aglionby, *Life of Bp. E. H. Bickersteth*, 5.

Still. Cf. **Quiet.**

Stink. *See* **Polecat.**

Stinking fish, No man cries. 1664: J. Wilson, *Cheats*, IV ii, Did you ever hear a fishwife cry stinking mackarel? 1708: tr. Aleman's *Guzman*, i 278, He won't cry stinking fish, and tell you he has none that's good. 1801: Wolcot, *Works*, v 302 (1801), Yet people will in answer say, ' 'Tis the world's way – We never hear a man cry "Stinking Fish!" ' 1844: Thackeray, *B. Lyndon*, ch iii, I replied that I was a young gentleman of large fortune (this was not true; but what is the use of crying bad fish?). 1927: *Sphere*, 26 Nov., p. 366, col. 4, I for one should like to cry truce to everlasting criticism … Let us for a while cry no more stinking fish.

Stir with a knife, Stir up strife. 1910: *Devonsh. Assoc. Trans.*, xlii 90. 1917: Bridge, *Cheshire Proverbs*, 77.

Stitch in time saves nine, A. [Principiis obsta. – Ovid, *Rem. Am.*, 91.] 1732: Fuller, 6291, A stitch in time may save nine. 1845: Planché, in *Extravag.* iii 31 (1879), We take a stitch in time that may save nine. 1922: *Times*, 2 June, p. 5, col. 2, With streets, as with clothes, a stitch in time saves nine.

Stitch your seam before you've tacked it, Don't. 1917: Bridge, *Cheshire Proverbs*, 50.

Stoat. *See* quot. 1895: Jos. Thomas, *Randigal Rhymes*, 61, Screech like a whitneck [stoat].

Stocking off a bare leg, It's hard to get a. Spoken of a bankrupt. 1886: R. Holland, *Cheshire Gloss.*, 451 (E.D.S.). 1917: Bridge, *Cheshire Proverbs*, 84.

Stockport. *See* quot. Ibid., 155, When the world was made the rubbish was sent to Stockport.

Stockport chaise, A = Two women riding sideways on one horse. 1828: Carr, *Craven Dialect*, ii 171, Stopport-Chaise, Two women riding together on horseback. Stopport is the Craven pronunciation of Stockport. 1917: Bridge, *Cheshire Proverbs*, 21.

Stoke in the Vale. *See* **Higham.**

Stolen pleasures are sweetest. 1611: *Bible*, Proverbs ix. 17, Stolen waters are sweet. 1632: Massinger, *City Madam*, II i, And, pleasure stolen being sweetest … 1636: Dekker, *Wonder of a Kingdom*, II, Gold barr'd with locks, Is best being stolen. 1671: Head and Kirkman, *Eng. Rogue*, II, Pref. to Reader, Following the proverb, *that stolen meat is sweetest.* 1696: Vanbrugh, *Relapse*, III, Nay, I must confess stolen pleasures are sweet. 1709: Cibber, *Rival Fools*, I, Stolen sweets are best. 1840: Barham, *Ing. Legends*: 'A New Play', Stolen kisses are sweet. 1855: Gaskell, *North and South*, ch xxxi, Some one had told you that stolen fruit tasted sweetest.

Stomach. *See* quot. 1605: Camden, *Remains*, 333 (1870), To have a stomach and lack meat, to have meat and lack a stomach, to lie in bed and cannot rest are great miseries.

Stone and **Stones**, *subs.* **1. A stone in a well is not lost.** 1640: Herbert, *Jac. Prudentum.*

2. It is evil running against a stone wall. 1560: T. Wilson, *Rhetorique*, 189 (1909).

3. The stone that lieth not in your way need not offend you. 1732: Fuller, 4770.

4. Who remove stones bruise their fingers. 1640: Herbert, *Jac. Prudentum.* 1670: Ray, 25. 1732: Fuller, 5715 [with 'landmark' before 'stones'].

See also **Blood** (5); **Stick** (3); and **Still as a stone**.

Stool in the sun. *See* quots. 1659: Howell, 4, Put a stool in the sun, when one knave riseth another comes. 1670: Ray, 146 [as in 1659]. 1732: Fuller, 4105 [as in 1659]. 1780: *Mother Bunch*, Sec. Part, 27 (Gomme, 1885), Remember the old proverb, Set thy stool in the sun, if a knave goes an honest man may come.

Stools one falls to the ground; Between two. *See* **Two stools.**

Stoop so low to take up just nothing at all, I will never. 1732: Fuller, 2641.

Stoop that hath a low door, He must. 1678: Ray, 171. 1732: Fuller, 1995.

Stop, *verb.* **1. He who will stop every man's mouth, must haw a great deal of meal.** 1855: Bohn, 401.

2. Stop stitch. *See* quot. 1828: Carr, *Craven Dialect*, ii 169, 'Stop stitch while I put t'needle in', a proverbial expression … when one wishes … not to be in a hurry about anything.

3. To stop two gaps with one bush. 1546: Heywood, *Proverbs*, Pt II ch ix. *c.*1594: Bacon,

Promus, No. 678. 1639: Fuller, *Holy War*, bk v ch xxii, These Italians stopped two gaps with one bush. 1681: Robertson, *Phraseol. Generalis*, 1174. 1732: Fuller, 5234.

4. To stop two mouths with one morsel. 1639: Clarke, 45. 1670: Ray, 197. 1681: Robertson, *Phraseol. Generalis*, 1174.

5. Ye will as soon stop gaps with rushes. 1546: Heywood, *Proverbs*, Pt II ch ix.

Stopford law, no stake no draw. 1678: Ray, 301. 1790: Grose, *Prov. Gloss.*, s.v. 'Cheshire'. 1917: Bridge, *Cheshire Proverbs*, 110, Stopport law, etc. Cf. **Lancashire law**.

Store is no sore. 1471: Ripley, *Comp. Alch.*, XII viii, in Ashm. 186 (1652), (OED), For wyse men done sey *store ys no sore*. 1553: *Republica*, I i, The worlde waxeth harde, and store (thei saie) is no sore. 1632: Jonson, *Magn. Lady*, II. 1646: Quarles, *Shep. Oracles*, Egl. ii 1720: C. Shadwell, *Sham Prince*, II i 1776: Colman, *Spleen*, I. 1869: Spurgeon, *John Ploughman*, ch xvi, Why not get two or three weeks' supply at once, and so get it cheaper? Store is no sore.

Storm, *subs*. **1. After a storm comes a calm.** 1377: Langland, *Plowman*, B, xviii 409, 'After sharpe shoures,' quod Pees, 'moste shene is the sonne.' 1590: Greene, *Works*, viii 101 (Grosart), Euerie storme hath his calme. 1618: Minshull, *Essayes, etc.*, 18 (1821), After stormes calmes will arise. 1630: Davenant, *Cruel Brother*, I. 1712: Motteux, *Quixote*, Pt II ch xix. 1804: Byron, *Letters, etc.*, i 40 (Prothero). 1893: Inwards, *Weather Lore*, 75.

2. Always a calm before a storm. 1590: Greene, *Works*, viii 57 (Grosart), Little thinking poore soules such a sharp storme shuld follow so quiet a calme. 1597: H. Lok, *Poems*, 208 (Grosart), And stormes insue the calme before that went. 1633: Draxe, 23, After a calme commeth a storme. 1893: Inwards, *Weather Lore*, 75.

3. The sharper the storm, the sooner it's over. Oxfordsh. 1913: *Folk-Lore*, xxiv. 76.

4. The sudden storm lasts not three hours. 1893: Inwards, *Weather Lore*, 74.

5. To raise a storm in a tea-cup. [Fluctus excitare in simpulo. – Cicero, *De Legibus*, iii 16.] 1678: Ormond, in *Hist. MSS. Comm.*, Ormonde MSS., iv. 292 (OED), Our skirmish … compared with the great things now on foot, is but a storm in a cream bowl. 1872: W. Black, *Strange Adv. Phaeton*, ch xix.

Story. *See* **Picture;** and **Tale.**

Story is good till another is told, One. *See* **One tale.**

Stout, I, and thou stout, who shall bear the ashes out? 'Stout' = proud. 1546: Heywood, *Proverbs*, Pt I ch x ['proud' for 'stout']. 1631: J. Donne, *Polydoron*, 44 … carry the dirt out? 1732: Fuller, 6284 [as in 1631].

Straight as a line. 1412–20: Lydgate, *Troy Book*, bk ii l. 6739, The wey hem ladde To the paleis, streight as any lyne. 1587: Churchyard, *Worth. of Wales*, 17 (Spens.S.), Upright as straight as line. 1641: Evelyn, *Diary*, i 28 (Bray, 1883), The river, ten miles in length, straight as a line. 1872: Hardy, *Greenwood Tree*, Pt II ch iii, I say that we all move down-along straight as a line to Pa'son Mayble's'. 1896: Conan Doyle, *Rodney Stone*, ch xv, If I didn't know that he was as straight as a line, I'd ha' thought he was planning a cross and laying against himself. 1901: Raymond, *Idler Out of Doors*, 118, This tidal river, in one part straight as a line …

Straight at a loitch [loach]. 1882: *N. & Q.*, 6th ser, v 28, 'Straight as a loitch' … has been in common use in this part of Yorkshire [Batley] from time immemorial. It is used to express … perfect straightness.

Straight as an arrow. 1592: Warner, *Alb. England*, ch xxxi, st. 4, As peart as bird, as straite as boulte. 1682: A. Behn, *City Heiress*, II i, A back as strait as an arrow. 1713: Ward, *Poet. Entertainer*, No. 5, p. 26, As strait as any arrow. 1817: Scott, *Rob Roy*, ch xxv. 1841: Dickens, *Barn. Rudge*, ch i 1894: R.L.S., *St Ives*, ch xxix. 1924: A. Gissing, *Footpathway in Glouc.*, 114.

Straight as a rush. 1892: Heslop, *Northumb. Words*, 566 (E.D.S.), 'Streit as a rasher' [rush] is a proverbial expression.

Straight as a yard o' pump water, As. 1886: R. Holland, *Cheshire Gloss.*, 446 (E.D.S.) … Often said of a tall, lanky girl.

Straight as my leg. 1720: Gay, *Poems*, ii 279 (Underhill), Straight as my leg her shape appears. 1738: Swift, *Polite Convers.*, Dial. I, Straight! Ay, straight as my leg, and that's crooked at knee.

Straight as the back-bone of a herring. 1678: Ray, 289.

Straight stick is crooked in the water, A. 1732: Fuller, 425.

Straight trees have crooked roots. Ibid., No. 4264.

Strand on the Green, thirteen houses, fourteen cuckolds, and never a house between: – The father and son lay in one house. 1639: Howell, 21. 1790: Grose, *Prov. Gloss.*, s.v. 'Middlesex'. Cf. **Crafthole**.

Strange beast that hath neither head nor tail, It is a. 1633: Draxe, 201. 1639: Clarke, 8.

Stranger's eye sees clearest, A. 1860: Reade, *Cl. and Hearth*, ch lviii [cited as 'a common saying']. Cf. **Lookers on**.

Straw and **Straws**, *subs*. **1. He gives straw to his dog, and bones to his ass.** 1813: Ray, 75.

2. Straws show which way the wind blows. 1654: J. Selden, *Table-Talk* (1689), 31, Take a straw and throw it up into the Air, you shall see by that which way the Wind is … More solid things do not shew the Complexion of the times so well as Ballads and libels. 1799: Cobbett, *Porcupine's Works* (1801), X 161, 'Straws' (to make use of Callender's old hackneyed proverb) … served to show which way the wind blows. 1802: Gouv. Morris, in *Life, etc.*, by Sparks (1832), iii 166 (OED), Straws and feathers … show which way the wind blows. 1860: Reade, *Cl. and Hearth*, ch lvi, Such straws of speech show how blows the wind. 1910: Lucas, *Ingleside*, ch ii 1922: Weyman, *Ovington's Bank*, ch xiii.

3. Who hath skirts of straw needs fear the fire. 1666: Torriano, *Piazza Univ.*, 184, Who hath his tail of straw is afraid of fire. 1670: Ray, 25.

See also **Bricks; Candlemas, D;** and **Drowning.**

Strawberry. *See* **Oak** (4).

Stream can nerer rise above the spring-head, The. 1732: Fuller, No.4771.

Strength. *See* **union.**

Stretcheth his foot beyond the blanket, shall stretch it in the straw, Whoso. *c.*1240: Grosteste, *Book of Husbandry*, quoted Riley, *Memorials of London*, 8, *n.* 4, Whoso streket his fot forthere than the whitel [blanket] will reche, he schal streken in the straw. 1377: Langland, *Plowman*, B, xiv 233, For whan he streyneth hym to streche the strawe in his schetes. *c.*1393: Ibid., C, xvii 76 [as in 1377, but with 'whitel' for 'schetes']. 1736: Bailey, *Dict.*, s.v. 'Arm', Stretch your legs according to your coverlet.

Stretching and yawning leadeth to bed. 1659: Howell, 17. 1670: Ray, 216.

Stretton i' th' street [Rutland], **where shrews meet.** 1678: Ray, 333.

Strife. *See* **Wife** (10).

Strike, *verb*. **1. He strikes with a straw.** 1813: Ray, 75.

2. He that strikes with his tongue, must ward with his head. 1640: Herbert, *Jac. Prudentum.* 1670: Ray, 26. 1732: Fuller, 2319.

3. He that strikes with the sword. *See* **Sword** (1).

4. Strike Dawkin! *See* **Devil** (35).

5. Strike, or give me the bill = Mind what you are about. 1672: Walker, *Paroem.*, 37.

6. To strike while the iron is hot. *c.*1374: Chaucer, *Troylus*, bk ii l.1276, Pandare, which that stood hir faste by, Felte iren hoot, and he bigan to smyte. 1412–20: Lydgate, *Troy Book*, bk ii l. 6110, The iren hoot, tyme is for to smyte. *c.*1489: Caxton, *Sonnes of Aymon*, 136 (E.E.T.S.), Whan the yron is well hoote, hit werketh the better. 1546: Heywood, *Proverbs*, Pt I ch iii, Whan thyron is hot strike. 1603: Dekker, *Works*, i 100 (Grosart), Seeing the dice of Fortune run so sweetly, and resoluing to strike whilst the iron was hote … 1668: Shadwell, *Sullen Lovers*, IV i, Ask no more questions, but to her, and strike while the iron's hot. 1706: Farquhar, *Recruit. Officer*, IV ii *c.*1750: Foote, *Englishm. in Paris*, I. 1841: Dickens, *Barn. Rudge*, ch xliv., Where's the good of putting things off? Strike while the iron's hot; that's what I say. 1922: Weyman, *Ovington's Bank*, ch xli.

Strip it. *See* quot. 1678: Ray, 289, Thou'lt strip it as Slack stript the cat, when he pull'd her out of the churn.

Strive against the stream, To. [Dirigere bracchia contra Torrentem. – Juvenal, iv. 89.] *c.*1270: *Prov. of Alfred*, in Morris, *Old Eng. Miscell.*, 110 (E.E.T.S.), Strong hit is to reowe ayeyn the see that floweth. *c.*1311: in Wright, *Pol. Songs*, 254 (Camden S.), Whoso roweth agein the flod, Off sorwe he shal drinke. *c.*1390: Gower, *Conf. Amantis*, bk iv. l. 1780, Betre is to wayte upon the tyde Than rowe ayein the stremes stronge. *c.*1480: *Digby Plays*, 156 (E.E.T.S.), Ya, I wyll no more row ageyn the fflode. Before 1529: Skelton, in *Works*, i 418 (Dyce), He is not wyse ageyne the streme that stryuith. *c.*1590: Greene, *Alphonsus*, I i, In vain it is to strive against the stream. 1694: *Terence made English*, 207, For what a madness is it to strive against the stream. 1728: Fielding, *Love in* *several Masques*, V xiii 1822: Scott, *Nigel*, Intro. Epistle, No one shall find me rowing against the stream. I care not who knows it – I write for general amusement.

Stroke at every tree without felling any, A. 1855: Bohn, 301.

Strokes are good to give, they are good to receive, If. 1733: Fuller, 2700.

Strokes for different folks, Different. *See* **Different strokes**.

Stroke with one hand, and stab with the other, To. Ibid., No. 5236.

Strong affections give credit to weak arguments. 1639: Clarke, 27.

Strong at a horse. *See* **Horse** (24).

Strong as mustard. 1659: Howell, 18. 1670: Ray, 207. 1720: Gay, *Poems*, ii 277 (Underhill), My passion is as mustard strong.

Stronger house = prison. *See* quot. 1639: Clarke, 209, You'l be sent to a stronger house than ever your father built for you.

Strong man, The. *See* quot. 1871: Smiles, *Character*, 16, 'The strong man and the waterfall', says the proverb, 'channel their own path'.

Stubble in a fallow field, He seeks for. Glos. 1639: in *Berkeley MSS.*, iii 27 (1885).

Studies his content, wants it, He that. 1611: Cotgrave, s.v. 'Aise', Hee that studies his contentment overmuch, ever wants it. 1640: Herbert, *Jac. Prudentum.*

Study, In a. *See* **Brown study**.

Stumble may prevent a fall, A. 1732: Fuller, 424.

Stumble, *verb*. 1. He that stumbles and falls not, mends his pace. 1611: Cotgrave, s.v. 'Choper', He that stumbles without falling, gets the more forward. 1640: Herbert, *Jac. Prudentum.* 1655: Fuller, *Church Hist.*, bk viii § ii (32), He that stumbleth, and doth not fall down, gaineth ground thereby. 1732: Fuller, 2316, He that stumbles and falls not quite, gains a step.

2. He who stumbles twice over the same stone, deserves to break his shins. 1875: Cheales, *Proverb. Folk-Lore*, 114.

3. To stumble at a straw and leap over a block. 1526: *Hund. Mery Tayles*, No. xvi p. 29 (Oesterley), As ye comen prouerb is they stumble at a straw and lepe ouer a blok. 1585: Greene, *Works*, v 90 (Grosart), Tush fond foole, if thou stumble at a straw thou shalt neuer leap ouer a blocke. 1630: T. Adams, *Works*, 327, Doe

they not stumble at our strawes, and leape ouer their owne blockes? 1732: Fuller, 4270.

4. To stumble at the truckle-bed. 1678: Ray, 81.

5. To stumble on plain ground. 1869: Hazlitt, 432.

Sturdy oak. *See* **Great tree**.

Style toward, A, and a wife forward, are uneasy companions. Glos. I do not understand this saying. Perhaps it should be s.v. 'Stile'. 1639: in *Berkeley MSS.*, iii 32 (1885).

Subject, *subs*. 1. The subject's love is the King's life-guard. 1736: Bailey, *Dict.*, s.v. Cf. **People's love**.

2. The subject's riches is the King's power. Ibid.

Subjects. *See* **Wife** (19).

Sublime to the ridiculous is only a step, From the. The saying in its present from derives from a remark made by Napoleon to the Polish ambassador to France, the Abbé de Pradt, concerning his retreat from Moscow. The philosopher Tom Paine, however, had already had a similar thought (*see* quot. 1795). 1795: T. Paine, *Age of Reason*, II 20, The sublime and the ridiculous are often so nearly related, that it is difficult to class them separately. One step above the sublime, makes the ridiculous: and one step above the ridiculous, makes sublime again. 1879: M. Pattison, *Milton*, 16, The Hague tittle-tattle … is set forth in the pomp of Milton's loftiest Latin … The sublime and the ridiculous are here blended without the step between. 1909: *Times Literary Supplement*, 17 Dec., 492, In the case of Louis XVIII, indeed, the ridiculous was, as it is commonly said to be, only a step removed from the sublime.

Subtle as a dead pig, As. 1672: Walker, *Paroem.*, 16. 1681: Robertson, *Phraseol. Generalis*, 1185, He's as subtle as a dead pig; Non plus sapit, quam sus maetata.

Subtlety is better than force. 1736: Bailey, *Dict.*, s.v.

Succeed, try, try, try again. If at first you don't. 1840: T. H. Palmer, *teacher's Manual*, 223, 'Tis a lesson you should heed, Try, try gain. If at first you don't succeed. 1915: E.B. Holt, *Freudian Wish*, iii, The child is frustrated, but not instructed; and it is in the situation where, later on in life, we say to ourselves, 'If at first you don't succeed, Try, try, try again!'

Success is never blamed. 1732: Fuller, 4273. Cf. **Nothing** (27).

Success makes a fool seem wise. 1855: Bohn, 492.

Such a beginning, such an ending. 1546: Heywood, *Proverbs*, Pt II ch ix, Such beginnyng, such ende. 1670: Ray, 3. 1732: Fuller, 4274.

Such a cup, such a cruse. 1549: Latimer, *Seven Sermons*, 143 (Arber).

Such as the priest, such is the clerk. 1666: Torriano, *Piazza Univ.*, 1, Such as the abbot is, such is the monk. 1732: Fuller, 4279.

Such a welcome, such a farewell. 1546: Heywood, *Proverbs*, Pt II ch vii. 1670: Ray, 28. 1732: Fuller, 4278.

Such beef, such broth. 1598: Meres, *Palladis*, fo. 218.

Such carpenter, such chips. 1546: Heywood, *Proverbs*, Pt II ch vii. 1568: Fulwell, *Like to Like*, in Hazlitt, *Old Plays*, iii 330. 1670: Ray, 115, like carpenter like chips.

Such cup, such cover. 1532: More, *Confut. of Tyndale*, Pref., sig. Bb1, A very mete couer for such a cuppe. 1565: Shacklock, *Hatchet of Heresies*, sig. *b*6, As saythe the prouerb, a mete couer for such a cup. 1639: in *Berkeley MSS.* iii, 32 (1885), The cup and cover will hold together. 1642: D. Rogers, *Matrim. Honour*, 277. 1655: Fuller, *Church Hist.*, bk ix. §ii (20), And became great with the Duke de Alva (like cup, like cover!) ...

Such saint, such offering. 1581: T. Howell, *Devises*, 74 (1906), Such saintes, Such seruice. 1651: Herbert, *Jac. Prudentum*, 2nd ed. 1670: Ray, 115, Like saint like offering.

Such tree, such fruit. Before 1300: *Cursor Mundi*, l. 38, O gode pertre coms god peres Were tre, vers fruit it beres. [Of good pear-tree comes good pears Worse tree worse fruit it bears.] *c.*1370: Wiclif, *Eng. Works*, 331 (E.E.T.S.), But who shuld preise this lawe therfore? sith yuel frute witnessith yuel rote. 1402: Hoccleve, *Minor Poems*, 79 (E.E.T.S.), A wikked tre, gode frute may noon forth bryng; for swiche the frute ys as that is the tre. Before 1529: Skelton, *Works*, i 214 (Dyce), For it is an auncyent brute, Suche apple tre, suche, frute. 1584: Greene, *Works*, iii 10 (Grosart). 1611: Cotgrave, s.v. 'Doux', Such as the tree such is the fruit. 1664: J. Wilson, *Andr. Commenius*, III iii, Don't we know the tree By its fruit. 1732: Fuller, 4280 [as in 1611]. Cf. **Tree** (8).

Sucked not this out of my fingers' ends, I. 1546: Heywood, *Proverbs*, Pt I ch xi. 1670: Ray, 25. 1732: Fuller, 2625.

Sucker an even break, Never give a. The saying probably came into being around the 1920s and was certainly popularised – and possibly coined – by the famous film comedian W.C. Fields. It is a rogue's principle, suggesting that however gullible a person looks one should never be tempted to play with him or her. 1925: *Collier's Magazine*, 28 Nov., 26, 'That line of mine that brings the house down always was true, wasn't it?' 'Which line?' I asked. 'Never give a sucker an even break' he [W.C. Fields] answered.

Sudden friendship, sure repentance. Ibid., No. 4281. Cf. **Sudden trust.**

Sudden glory soon goes out. Ibid., No. 4282.

Sudden joy kills sooner than excessive grief. 1620: Shelton, *Quixote*, Pt II ch lii, It is usually said that sudden joy as soon kills as excessive grief. 1732: Fuller, 4283.

Sudden rising hath a sudden fall, A. *c.*1440: Lydgate, *Fall of Princes*, bk ix. l. 1211, Sodeyn clymbyng axeth a sodeyn fall. *c.*1615: R. C., *Times Whistle*, 39 (E.E.T.S.), And 'tis a saying held for true of all, 'A sudden rising hath a sudden fall'.

Sudden trust brings sudden repentance. 1669: *Politeuphuia*, 103. Cf. **Sudden friendship.**

Suds, In the. See Leave, *verb* (8).

Suffer. See **Patience** (6).

Sufferance cometh ease, Of. *c.*1386: Chaucer, *Merch. Tale*, l. 871, Passe over is an ese, I sey namore. *c.*1390: Gower, *Conf. Amantis*, bk iii l. 1672, For suffrance is the welle of Pes [Peace]. 1546: Heywood, *Proverbs*, Pt I ch ix. 1598: Shakespeare, *2 Hen. IV* V iv. 1607: Marston, *What You Will*, Prol., Ile give a proverbe, – Sufferance giveth ease. 1678: Ray, 207. 1736: Bailey, *Dict.*, s.v.

Sufferance. See also **Forbearance.**

Suffer and expect. 1640: Herbert, *Jac. Prudentum.*

Sufferer overcomes. See **Patience** (6).

Suffer the ill and look for the good. 1578: Florio, *First Fruites*, fo. 33, I suffer the bad, hoping for the better. 1629: *Book of Meery Riddles*, Prov.117.

Sufficient unto the day is the evil thereof. [Matthew vi. 34, Sufficient unto the day is the evil thereof] 1766: in L.H. Butterfield et al., *Adams family Correspondence* (1963), I. 56, Sufficient to the Day is the Evil thereof. 1836: J. Carlyle, *Letter*, 1 Apr., in *Letters and Memorials* (1893), I 57, In the meanwhile there were no sense in worrying over schemes for a future, which we may not live to see, 'Sufficient for the day is the evil thereof'.

Suffolk cheese – proverbial for hardness. 1661: Pepys, *Diary*, 4 Oct., I found my wife vexed at her people for grumbling to eat Suffolk cheese. 1662: *Fragm. Aulica*, 60, He could be glad to have had a suffolke cheese and twelfpeny loafe. 1691: Shadwell, *Scourers*, V i, Who snores with fumes from Suffolk cheese and bacon. 1706: Ward, *Works*, iii 114, Curse his thin beer, and rail at Suffolk cheese. 1737: Pope, *Imit. of Horace*, Sat. vi bk ii, Cheese such as men in Suffolk make, But wished it Stilton for his sake. 1865: W. White, *Eastern England*, ii 176, I forebore to ask him if he liked Suffolk cheese, which … is described as hard as grindstones: so hard that even rats and mice refuse it. *See also* Hunger.

Suffolk fair maids. 1622: Drayton, *Polyol.*, xxiii, Fair Suffolk maids and milk. 1662: Fuller, *Worthies*, iii 161 (1840). 1790: Grose, *Prov. Gloss.*, s.v. 'Suffolk'.

Suffolk milk. 1622: Drayton, *Polyol.*, xxiii *ut supra*. 1790: Grose, s.v. 'Suffolk'.

Suffolk stiles = ditches. 1662: Fuller, *Worthies*, iii 161 (1840). Cf. **Essex stiles**.

Suffolk whine, The. 1790: Grose, *Prov. Gloss.*, s.v. 'Suffolk'.

Suit is best that best suits me, That. 1639: Clarke, 16. 1670: Ray, 46 [with 'fits' for 'suits'].

Suits hang half a year in Westminster Hall; at Tyburn half an hour's hanging endeth all. 1869: Hazlitt, 347.

Sulky. *See* **Bull** (2); and **Cross** (1).

Summer, *subs.* **1. A cool summer and a light weight in the bushel.** 1893: Inwards, *Weather Lore*, 8.

2. A dry summer never begs its bread. Somerset. Ibid., 7.

3. A dry summer never made a dear peck. Ibid., 7.

4. A dry summer never made a full Peck. 1882: Mrs Chamberlain, *W. Worcs. Words*, 38 (E.D.S.).

5. An English summer. 1846: Denham, *Proverbs*, 48 (Percy S.) … two fine days and a thunder-

storm. 1854: Doran, *Table Traits*, 27 … three hot days and a thunderstorm. 1893: Inwards, *Weather Lore*, 7 … two hot days and a thunderstorm.

6. Summer in winter, and a summer's flood, Never boded England good. 1846: Denham, Proverbs, 68 (Percy S.). 1893: Inwards, 8 ['an Englishman' for 'England'].

7. There's no summer, but it has a winter. 1846: Denham, 48. 1904: *Co. Folk-Lore: Northumb.*, 178 (F.L.S.).

8. To dream of a dry summer. 1568: W. Fulwood, *Enemie of Idlenesse*, 217 (1593), I thinke you dreame of a drie summer. 1639: Clarke, 64. 1670: Ray, 172.

See also **One fair day; Swallow; and Winter,** *passim.*

Sun, *subs.* **1. A morning sun.** *See* quots. 1640: Herbert, *Jac. Prudentum*, The morning sun never lasts a day. Ibid., A morning sun and a wine-bred child and a Latin-bred woman seldom end well. 1887: *N. & Q.*, 7th ser, iv 447, The old proverb in common use in Yorkshire certainly seventy years ago, which runs thus: 'A morning without clouds, a child that drinks wine, and a woman that talks Latin seldom come to a good end'. 1893: Inwards, *Weather Lore*, 48 [as in 1640, first quot.].

2. A red sun has water in his eye. 1659: Howell, *Proverbs: Span.-Eng.*, 22. 1893: Inwards, 48.

3. He hath the sun on's face, and th' wind on's back. 1639: Clarke, 42.

4. If red the sun begins his race, Expect mat rain will flow apace. 1846: Denham, *Proverbs*, 11 (Percy S.). 1872: J. Glyde, jr., *Norfolk Garland*, 155.

5. If the sun goes pale to bed, 'Twill rain to-morrow, it is said. 1893: Inwards, 52.

6. If the sun in red should set, The next day surely will be wet; If the sun should set in grey, The next will be a rainy day. 1838: Mrs Bray, *Trad. of Devon*, i 6. 1865: Hunt, *Pop. Romances W. of Eng.*, 435 (1896). 1893: Inwards, *Weather Lore*, 51.

7. If the sun sets dear, it is a sign of fair weather. 1754: Berthelson, *Eng.-Danish Dict.*, s.v. 'Clear'.

8. Let not the sun go down upon your wrath. [Ephesians iv. 26, Let not the sun go down upon your wrath] 1642: T. Fuller, *Holy State*, III. viii, S. Paul saith, *let not the Sunne go down on your wrath*; to carry news of the Antipodes in another world of thy revengefull nature. 1709: O. Dykes, *English Proverbs*, 189, We ought not to let the Sun go down upon our Wrath, or our Impenitence.

9. The sun can be seen by nothing but its own light. 1732: Fuller, 4774.

10. The sun is never the worse for shining on a dunghill. 1303: Brunne, *Handlyng Synne*, l. 2299, The sunne hys feyrnes neuer he tynes thoghe hyt on the muk hepe shynes. *c*.1386: Chaucer, *Parsons Tale*, 76, Holy writ may nat been defouled, na-more than the sunne that shyneth on the mixen. 1579: Lyly, *Euphues*, 43 (Arber), The sunne shineth vpon the dounghill, and is not corrupted. 1732: Fuller, 4776. 1846: Denham, *Proverbs*, 5 (Percy S.).

11. The sun shines on both sides of the hedge. Ibid., 49.

12. They that walk in the sun will be tanned at last. 1560: T. Wilson, *Rhetorique*, Prol. (1909), He that goeth in the sunne shall bee sunne burnt, although he thinke not of it. 1638: D. Tuvill, *Vade Mecum*, 56 (3rd ed.), Hee that walketh in the sun shall be tan'd. 1670: Ray, 146. 1732: Fuller, 4986, They that walk in the sun must be content to be tann'd.

13. Though the sun'shine leave not thy cloak at home. 1640: Herbert, *Jac. Prudentum*. 1732: Fuller, 5014, Tho' the sun shines take your cloak. 1846: Denham, *Proverbs*, 1 (Percy S.) ['coat' for 'cloak'].

14. To set forth the sun with a candle. 1551: Robinson, tr. More's *Utopia*, 27 (Arber), They neede not … of me to bee praysed, vnlesse I woulde seeme to shew, and set-furth the brightnes of the sonne with a candell, as the prouerbe saieth. 1586: Whitney, *Emblems*, 107, Bicause it is in vaine, to set a candell in the sonne. *c*.1594: Bacon, *Promus*, No. 688, To help the sunne with lantornes.

15. When the sun is highest he casts the least shadow. 1732: Fuller, 5607.

16. When the sun sets bright and clear, An easterly wind you need not fear. 1846: Denham, *Proverbs*, 20 (Percy S.). 1893: Inwards, *Weather Lore*, 51.

17. When the sun sets in a bank, A westerly wind we shall not want. 1846: Denham, 12. 1893: Inwards, 52 ['lack' for 'want'].

18. When the sun shines, no body minds it; but when he is eclipsed, all consider him. 1732: Fuller, 5608. 1846: Denham, 5.

See also **Candlemas**, A and F; **Christmas** (22); **Cloud** (2)–(4); **Easter** (7); **January** (12) and (14); **March** (18), (35), (37), (45), and (46); **Red at night**; **Saturday** (3); **Shrovetide** (4) and (5); **Sunday** (2); and **Wind**, A (*a*) (18).

Sunday. 1. A wet Sunday, a wet week. 1830: Forby, *Vocab. E. Anglia*, 416.

2. If sunset on Sunday is cloudy, it will rain before Wednesday. 1893: Inwards, *Weather Lore*, 43.

3. Sunday clearing, clear till Wednesday. Ibid., 43.

4. Sunday's child is full of grace, Monday's child is full in the face, Tuesday's child is solemn and sad, Wednesday's child is merry and glad, Thursday's child is inclined to thieving, Friday's child is free in giving, Saturday's child works hard for his living. 1865: Hunt, *Pop. Romances W. of Eng.*, 430 (1896). Cf. **Monday** (5).

5. Sunday shaven, Sunday shorn, Better had'st thou ne'er been born! 1879: Henderson, *Folk-Lore of N. Counties*, 18 (F.L.S.).

6. The first Sunday in the middle of the week = never. 1883: Burne, *Shropsh. Folk-Lore*, 596.

7. When it storms on the first Sunday in the month, it will storm every Sunday. 1893: Inwards, *Weather Lore*, 43.

See also **Alike every day**; **Christmas** (19); **Come** (8); **Friday** (6), (10), and (12); **Monday** (4); **Moon** (3) and (14); and **Saturday** (1).

Sunderland sowies. *See* quot. 1846–59: *Denham Tracts*, i 67 (F.L.S.), This rather coarse and unenviable epithet is, even down to the present day, applied to the fair sex of Sunderland. The meaning of the word sowies, although now nearly forgotten, is evidently the diminutive of sow.

Sunshine but hath some shadow, No. 1658: R. Franck, *North. Memoirs*, 36 (1821), No sun shines without some cloud. 1670: Ray, 146. 1732: Fuller, 3631.

Sunshiny rain. *See* **Rain** (5).

Sup, *verb*. **1. He sups ill who eats up all at dinner.** 1611: Cotgrave, s.v. 'Disner', *Mai soupe qui tout disne:* He sups ill that dines all; after a gluttonous and disordinate youth, followes a needie and hungrie age. 1732: Fuller, 2030.

2. He sups who sleeps. 1860: Reade, *Cl. and Hearth*, ch xxiv, It is ill sitting up wet and fasting, and the byword saith, 'He sups who sleeps'.

3. Sup, Simon. *See* quots. 1607: *The Puritan*, III v, Sup, Simon, now! eat porridge for a month. 1639: Clarke, 46, Sup Simon 'tis best i' th' bottome [or] here's good broth. 1670: Ray, 217, Sup Simon, the best is at the bottom. 1738: Swift, *Polite Convers.*, Dial. II, Sup, Simon; very good broth. 1854: Baker, *Northants Gloss.*, s.v. 'Sup', 'Sup, Simon! its excellent broth'. A common ironical recommendation to any one taking medicine or anything nauseous or disagreeable.

4. To sup sorrow. *c.*1395: *Plowman's Tale*, in Skeat's *Chaucer*, vii 182, Hir servaunts sitte and soupë sorowe! 1738: Swift, *Polite Convers.*, Dial. I, I'll make you one day sup sorrow for this.

5. Who sups well sleeps well. 1666: Torriano, *Piazza Univ.*, 44.

Supernaculum, To drink = to the last drop. *See* 1813 quot. 1592: Nashe, *Works*, ii 78 (Grosart), He is no body that cannot drinke super nagulum. 1617: T. Young, quoted in Brand, *Pop. Antiq.*, ii 331 (Bohn), He is a man of no fashion that cannot drinke supernaculum. 1675: *Mistaken Husband*, IV vi, Pledge the gentleman – supernaculum. 1682: A. Behn, *False Count*, IV i, Your true bred woman of honour drinks all, *Supernaculum*, by Jove. 1709: Ward, *Acc. of Clubs*, 288 (1756), Here's your old health, To the best in Christendom; and off it went to a supernaculum drop. 1813: Brand, *Pop. Antiq.*, ii 342 (Bohn), To drink *supernaculum* was an ancient custom ... of emptying the cup or glass, and then pouring the drop or two that remained at the bottom upon the person's nail that drank it, to show that he was no flincher. 1823: Moor, *Suffolk Words*, 409, Supernaculum. A word well known and occasionally heard in social circles in Suffolk ... something supercurious. [This is a 'supercurious' perversion of the word's meaning.] 1828: Carr, *Craven Dialect*, ii 181, Supernaculum. Good liquor of which there is not even a drop left to wet one's nail. Cf. **Pearl.**

Supperless. *Better to go to bed supperless than to rise in debt.* 1659: Howell, *Proverbs: Span.-Eng.*, 6, 'Tis wholsomer to go to bed without a supper, then rise in debt. 1670: Ray, 7. 1736: Franklin, *Way to Wealth*, in *Works*, i 451 (Bigelow) ['Rather' for 'Better']. 1859: Smiles, *Self-Help*, 305 (1869).

Supple knees feed arrogance. 1855: Bohn, 492.

Sup with the devil. *See* **Devil** (19).

Sure and unsure are not all one. 1639: Clarke, 29.

Sure as a club. 1577: *Misogonus*, III ii, Liturgus bringes him as sure as a clubb. 1584: R. Scot, *Witchcraft*, bk iv ch ix, Her prophesie fell out as sure as a club. 1656: Flecknoe, *Diarium*, 45, Sure as a club 'twill happen t' ye.

Sure as a gun. 1622: B.&F., *Prophetess*, I iii, You are right, master, Right as a gun. 1656: *Musarum Deliciae*, i 94 (Hotten), But when he thought her as sure as a gun, She set up her tail, and away she run. 1693: Congreve, *Double Dealer*, V xx. 1734: Fielding, *Don Quix. in England*, II viii, As sure as a gun – this is he. 1766: Anstey, *New Bath Guide*, Lett. viii. 1846: *Bentley Ballads*, 7(1876). 1886: Elworthy, *West Som. Word-Book*, 729 (E.D.S.), Sure or Safe as a gun. Usual similes.

Sure as a juggler's box. 1650: R. Heath, *Epigrams*, 53, Whom Death hath made sure as his juglers box. 1670: Ray, 207.

Sure as check = Exchequer pay. 1630: Taylor (Water-Poet), *Works*, 1st pagin., 85, But those worthy mariners are dead, and an old prouerbe, As sure as Check with them. 1662: Fuller, *Worthies*, ii 412 (1840), As sure as Exchequer pay. 1670: Ray, 207, As sure as Check, or Exchequer pay. This was a proverb in Queen Elizabeths time. 1732: Fuller, 732 [as in 1662].

Sure as death. *c.*1460: *Wyse Man taught hys Sone*, l. 93 (E.E.T.S.), For deth, my chyld, is, as y trow, The most ryght serteyn [thing] it is. 1484: Caxton, tr. Chartier's *Curial*, 19 (E.E.T.S.), Ne than the deth nothyng more certayn. 1596: Jonson, *Ev. Man in Humour*, II i, Nay as sure as death, That they would say. 1606: Chapman, *Mons. d'Olive*, IV ii, A love-letter from that lady would retrieve him as sure as death. 1726: Defoe, *Hist. of Devil*, Pt II ch vi 232 (4th ed.), Things as certain as death and taxes. 1780: Burgoyne, *Lord of Manor*, I i. 1850: Dickens, *Copperfield*, ch Iii, It is as certain as death. 1926: Phillpotts, *Yellow Sands*, I, I'll drown to-night sure as death!

Sure as God made little apples. 1894: Northall, *Folk Phrases*, 11 (E.D.S.). 1911: *N.&Q.*, 11th ser, iv 289 ... I recently heard this saying twice in the same week in the Manchester district. 1911: Ibid., 377, I have always understood that this was a Devonshire or West Country proverb, and that the full rendering was: 'As sure as God made little apples on big trees'. [Other correspondents at the same reference testify to the use of the saying in the North Midlands, Norwich, and Bristol. The Derbyshire version has 'crab' for 'little'.]

Sure as the coat's on one's back. 1639: Clarke, 209 ['your' for 'one's']. 1670: Ray, 208. 1736: Bailey, *Dict.*, s.v. 'Cap', As sure as the cloths on his back.

Sure as the devil is in London. 1752: Fielding, *Cov. Gard. Journal*, No. 33.

Sure bind. *See* **Safe bind.**

Surety. *See* **Certainty.**

Surety for another. *See* quots. 1539: Taverner, *Proverbs*, 20, Be suretie for an other and harme is at hande. 1633: Draxe, 199, He that is surety for another must pay. 1651: Herbert, *Jac. Prudentum*, 2nd ed., He that will be surety shall pay. 1869: Spurgeon, *John Ploughman*, ch iv, He who is surety is never sure.

Surgeon must have an eagle's eye, a lion's heart, and a lady's hand, A. 1589: L. Wright, *Display of Dutie*, 37, In a good chirurgian, a hawkes eye: a lyons heart: and a ladies hand. 1619: *Helpe to Discourse*, 104–5 (1640) [as in 1589]. 1670: Ray, 36, A good chirurgion must, etc. *c.*1671: in *Roxb. Ballads*, vii 546 (B.S.), This maid with ingenuity had every surgeon's part, A ladle's hand, an eagle's eye, but yet a lyon's heart. 1732: Fuller, 4292. 1868: *Quart. Review*, cxxv 252.

Surgeon. *See also* **Pitiful.**

Surly as a butcher's dog. 1670: Ray, 208. 1869: Spurgeon, *John Ploughman*, ch iv.

Surly as a cow's husband. 1886: R. Holland, *Cheshire Gloss.*, 446 (E.D.S.). 1917: Bridge, *Cheshire Proverbs*, 22.

Suspicion has double eyes. 1597: Shakespeare, 1 *Henry IV*, V ii, Suspicion all our lives shall be stuck full of eyes. *c.*1680: in *Roxb. Ballads*, vi 317 (B.S.), It is a proverb of old, 'Suspicion hath double eyes'.

Sussex weeds = oaks. 1911: A. S. Cooke, *Off Beaten Track in Sussex*, 332, If you are not quite among the 'deep ghylls' at Hartfield, you are certainly among the 'Sussex weed'. The oaks in Buckhurst Park are a sight to gladden the eyes.

Sutton. *See* **York.**

Sutton for mutton. *See* quots. The jingle varies with the county to which the 'Sutton' belongs. The need for 'mutton' to jingle with 'Sutton' in

all is obvious. 1790: Grose, *Prov. Gloss.*, s.v. 'Surrey', Sutton for mutton, Carshalton for beeves, Epsom for whores, and Ewel for thieves. 1878: *N.&Q.*, 5th ser, ix 88 [another Surrey version, as in 1790, but with 'jades' for Epsom]. [A Kent version:] Sutton for mutton, Kirby for beef, South Darne for gingerbread, Dartford for a thief. Ibid., 175, [Warwick] Sutton for mutton, Tamworth for beeves, Brummagem for blackguards, Coleshill for thieves. [Variants for the third line are, 'Walsall for a pretty girl' and 'Walsall for bandy legs'; and for the fourth line, 'Birmingham for a thief'.] 1884: Walford, *Greater London*, ii 207, There is current in the district of West Kent and East Surrey a couplet which runs thus: – 'Sutton for mutton, Kirby for beef, Mitcham for lavender, and Dartford for a thief'.

Sutton-Well and Kenchester are able to buy all London, were it to sell. 1659: Howell, 20. 1790: Grose, *Prov. Gloss.*, s.v. 'Herefordshire'.

Sutton windmill. *See* quot. 1600: Heywood, *Edw. IV*, Pt I, in *Dram. Works*, i 45 (1874), I am just akin to Sutton windmill; I can grind which way soe're the winde blow.

Swallow does not make a summer, One. [μία χελιδών ἔαρ οὐ ποιεῖ. – Aristotle, *Eth. N.*, *I* vii 16.] 1539: Taverner, *Proverbs*, fo. 25, It is not one swalowe that bryngeth in somer. *c.*1597: Deloney, *Iacke of Newberie*, ch i, Nay soft (said the widow) one swallow makes not a summer, nor one meeting a marriage. 1634: C. Butler, *Feminine Monarchie*, 46. 1784: *New Foundl. Hosp. for Wit*, ii 67, One swallow does not make a spring. 1850: Dickens, *Chuzzlewit*, ch xliii. 1854: J. W. Warter, *Last of Old Squires*, 139 [as in 1784]. 1920: *Sphere*, 10 April, p. 27, col. 2, One swallow does not make a summer, but one gazer inevitably makes a crowd.

Swallow. *See also* **Robin** and **Snail** (4).

Swallow, *verb.* **1. He hath swallowed a spider** = He has been bankrupt. 1659: Howell, 6. 1670: Ray, 194. 1754: Berthelson, *Eng.-Danish Dict.*, s.v. 'Swallow'.

2. To swallow a gudgeon = To be gulled. 1579: Lyly, *Euphues*, 68 (Arber), Take heede my Philautus, that thou thy self swallow not a gudgeon. 1584: Lodge, *Alarum against Usurers*, 44 (SH.S.), Those gentlemen who have swallowed the gudgen and have been intangled in the hooke. 1607: Dekker and Webster, *Northw. Hoe*, IV iv, If the gudgeon had been swallowed by one of you it had been vile. 1732: Fuller, 1902, He hath swallow'd a gudgeon. 1847: Halliwell, *Dict.*, s.v. 'Gudgeon', To swallow a gudgeon, i.e. to be caught or deceived, to be made a fool of.

3. To swallow an ox. *See* **Ox** (10).

4. To swallow a stake. *See* **Eat** (31).

5. To swallow a tavern token. *See* **Tavern token.**

Swan sings before death, The. [Olorum morte narratur flebilis cantus, falso ut arbitror aliquot experimentis. – Pliny, *Hist.*, x 23.] 1398: Trevisa, tr. Glanville's *De Propr. Rer.*, XII ii, And whan she [the swan] should dye and that a fether is pyght in the brayn, then she syngethe, as Ambrose sayth. *c.*1430: Lydgate, *Minor Poems*, 157 (Percy S.), The yelwe swan famous and aggreable, Ageyn his dethe melodyously syngyng. 1577: Kendall, *Flow. of Epigrams*, 61 (Spens.S.), The swanne doeth sweetely syng Before his death. 1632: Massinger, *Emp. of East*, V iii, Thus, like a dying swan, to a sad tune I sing my own dirge. 1681: Otway, *Soldier's Fortune*, V v, I'll sing a song like a dying swan. 1712: Pope, *Rape of Lock*, v 66, Thus on Maeander's flowery margin lies The expiring swan, and as he sings he dies. 1819: Byron, *Isles of Greece*, st. 16, There, swan-like, let me sing and die.

Swan. *See also* **Goose.**

Swarm in May is worth a load of hay, A. *See* **Bee** (3).

Swarston Bridge, He's driving his hogs over. Derbysh. 1700: Grose, Prov. Gloss., s.v. 'Derbysh'. 1889: *Folk-Lore Journal*, vii 292, He's driving his hogs o'er Swarson's brig.

Swoar, *verb*. 1. He swears like a gentleman. *c.*1645: MS. Proverbs, in *N. &Q.*, vol 154, p. 27.

2. He swears like a tinker, trooper, etc. 1611: Cotgrave, s.v. 'Chartier', He swears like a carter (we say, like a tinker). 1727: *Devil to pay at St James's*, 7, He swears like a trooper. 1754: Berthelson, *Eng.-Danish Dict.*, s.v. 'Swear', He swears like a tinker.

3. He that sweareth. *See* quots. *c.*1530: Rhodes, *Book of Nurture*, 107 (E.E.T.S.), He that sweareth tyll no man trust him, He that lyeth tyll no man beleeue him; He that boroweth till no man will lende him; Let him go where no man knoweth him. 1578: Florio, *First Fruites*, fo. 104 [as in 1530]. 1880: Spurgeon, *Ploughman's Pictures*, 19 [as in 1530, bat prudishly emended by 'promiseth' for 'sweareth'].

4. He that will swear will lie. 1630: Taylor (Water-Poet), *Works*, 2nd pagin., 189, The prouerbe saies, hee that will sweare will lie. 1650: R. Heath, *Epigrams*, 24. 1692: L'Estrange, *Aesop*, 398 (3rd ed.), Come wife, says he, they that will swear, will lye. .

5. He who sweareth when he is at play, may challenge his damnation by way of purchase. 1659: Howell, 2.

6. If you swear you will catch no fish. 1607: Heywood, *Fair Maid of Exchange*, in *Works*, ii 69 (1874), What are you cursing too? then we catch no fish. *c.*1630: B.&F., *Monsieur Thomas*, I iii, And next, no swearing; Hell catch no fish else. 1790: Wolcot, *Works*, ii 115 (1795), Besides, a proverb, suited to my wish, Declares that swearing never catcheth fish. 1830: Forby, *Vocab. E. Anglia*, 414, If you swear, you will catch no fish. 1872: E. FitzGerald, in *East Anglian*, iv 114, Opinions differ as to swearing. One captain strictly forbade it on board his lugger; but he also, continuing to get no fish, called out, 'Swear away, lads, and see what that'll do'. 1883: Burne, *Shropsh. Folk-Lore*, 588, Dunna swear, or thee'lt ketch no fish.

7. To swear – various extraordinary feats, expressive of rage, perjury, etc. 1658: R. Franck, *North. Memoirs*, 191 (1821), It's thought they would have sworn through a double deal-board, they seem'd so enraged. 1678: Ray, 271, He'll swear dagger out of sheath. Hell swear the devil out of hell. Before 1680: Butler, *Remains*, ii 363 (1759), He will swear his ears through an inch-board. [This seems to suggest the pillory for perjury.] 1731: Swift, *Poems*: 'Judas', Some who can perjure through a two-inch board. 1917: Bridge, *Cheshire Proverbs*, 69, He'll swear through an inch board. Ibid., 100, Oo'd ['Oo' = She] swear the cross off a jackass's back.

**Swearing, *verb. subs. See* quot. 1812: Brady, *Clavis Cal.*, i 339, There was formerly an expression very current, that 'Swearing came in at the head, but is going out at the tail'.

Sweep before your own door. 1650: Fuller, *Pisgah Sight*, bk iii ch i § 5, How soon are those streets made clean, where every one sweeps against his own door. 1684: *Great Frost*, 20 (Percy S.), Each one his sins to God confess; Let every one sweep clean and neat his door. 1732: Fuller, 4296. 1901: F. E. Taylor, *Lancs Sayings*,

22, Thee sweep up thi own dur-step (Look to your own faults).

Sweet, *subs.* **1. All sorts of sweets are not wholesome.** 1732: Fuller, 543.

2. He deserves not sweet that will not taste of sour. [*c*.1387: Usk, *Test. of Love*, in Skeat's *Chaucer*, vii 18, For he is worthy no welthe, that may no wo suffer.] *c*.1535: *Dialogues of Creatures*, xxi (1816), Who that desyryth the swete to assaye, He must taste byttyr, this is no naye. *c*.1575: H. Goldingham. *Garden Plot*, 60 (Roxb.Cl), Indeede he had not deserued thys swete before he had tasted some sowere. 1611: in Coryat, *Crudities*, i 109 (1905), For he no sweet hath merited (they say) That hath not tasted of the sower by th' way. 1670: Ray, 25. 1732: Fuller, 1834.

3. No sweet without sweat. 1576: Pettie, *Petite Pall.*, ii 138 (Gollancz), You … live … by the sweet of other men's sweat. 1639: Clarke, 87. 1681: Robertson, *Phraseol. Generalis*, 1196. 1732: Fuller, 3632 [with 'some' before 'sweat']. 1859: Smiles, *Self-Help*, 305 (1869), No sweat no sweet.

4. Take the sweet with the sour. 1546: Heywood, *Proverbs*, Pt II ch iv. 1560: T. Wilson, *Rhetorique*, 4 (1909), Both can and will ever, mingle sweete among the sower, be he preacher, lawyer, yea, or cooke.

Sweet as a nut. 1599: Buttes, *Dyets Dry Dinner*, sig. O4, As sweete as a nutte. 1654: Gayton, *Pleasant Notes Don Q.*, 34, So have you him uncorrupt … sweet as a nut. 1838: Holloway, *Provincialisms*, 120, We frequently say, 'as sweet as a nut'.

Sweet as honey. 1506: Pynson, *Kal. of Shepherds*, 75 (1892), Swete as hony in oure mouth. *c*.1550: Udall, *Roister Doister, ad fin.*, Custance is as sweete as honey. 1595: Churchyard, *Praise of Poetrie*, 41 (1816), As sweete as honie sure. 1612: Shelton, *Quixote*, Pt I bk iv ch v, All those things are as sweet as honey to me. 1716: E. Ward, *Female Policy*, 51, Her words as sweet as honey. 1844: Planché, *Extravag.* ii 310 (1879), Pay me in smiles and kisses, sweet as honey. 1905: E. G. Hayden, *Trav. Round our Village*, 87, Who'd … hand 'ee over the brass as sweet as honey – never ax 'ee fur a penny, I don't, to put in the bank!

Sweet beauty with sour beggary. 1546: Heywood, *Proverbs*, Pt I ch xiii.

Sweet discourse makes short days and nights. 1670: Ray, 7.

Sweetest wine makes sharpest vinegar. 1567: Painter, *Pal. of Pleasure*, ii 323 (Jacobs), How mutch the sweter is the wyne, the sharper is the egred sawce thereof. 1579: Lyly, *Euphues*, 39 (Arber), The sweetest wine tourneth to the sharpest vineger. 1647: Howell, *Letters*, bk ii No. xvi, This shews, that the sweetest wines may turn to the tartest vinegar. 1681: Robertson, *Phraseol. Generalis*, 1196. 1792: *Looker-on*, No. 2, The sharpest vinegar is made from the sweetest wines. 1852: FitzGerald, *Polonius*, 11 (1903), 'The sweet wine that makes the sharpest vinegar', says an old proverb. 1905: A. S. Palmer, Note in his ed. of Trench's *Proverbs*, 56, The true meaning is that even the best things may be corrupted and turned to evil, as the sweetest wine makes the sourest vinegar.

Sweet heart and bag pudding. 1659: Howell, 6. 1670: Ray, 214.

Sweet heart and honey-bird keeps no house. 1678: Ray, 57. 1732: Fuller, 4297.

Sweet in the mouth. *See* **Good in the mouth.**

Sweet meat will have sour sauce. *c*.1400: *Beryn*, 29. (E.E.T.S.), ffor 'aftir swete, the soure comyth, ful offt, in many a plase'. *c*.1500: *Colyn Blowbols*, l. 131, in Hazlitt, *Early Pop. Poetry*, i 98, Sharpe sawce was ordeigned for swete mete. 1546: Heywood, *Proverbs*, Pt I ch viii. 1620: T. May, *The Heir*, III, Your sweet meat shall have sour sauce. 1670: Cotton, *Scarronides*, IV. 1721: Centlivre, *Artifice*, II ii. 1769: Colman, *Man and Wife*, III ['may' for 'will']. 1771: Johnson, *Letters*, i 180 (Hill).

Swell like a toad, To. 1546: Heywood, *Proverbs*, Pt I ch xi, Streight as she sawe me she swelde lyke a tode. 1672: Walker, *Paroem.*, 26, She swells like a toad. 1754: Berthelson, *Eng.–Danish Dict.*, s.v. 'Toad'.

Swift. *See* **Quick.**

Swift to hear. *See* quot. 15th cent.: in *Reliq. Antiquae*, i 92 (1841), Be swyfte; to here, and slow to speke, Late to wrathe, and lothe to …

Swim, *verb.* **1. He can swim without bladders.** 1649: Howell, *Preem. Parl.*, 17 (OED), My whole life (since I was left to myself to swim, as they say without bladders). 1732: Fuller, 1821.

2. He must needs swim that is held up by the chin. Before 1500: in Hill, *Commonplace-Book*, 129 (E.E.T.S.), He mai lightli swim, that is hold wp by the chin. 1546: Heywood, *Proverbs*, Pt I ch v. *c.*1594: Bacon, *Promus*, No. 473. 1626: *Scoggins Jests*, 119 (1864). 1732: Fuller, 6088.

3. I taught you to swim, and now you'd drown me. Ibid., No. 2626. 1869: Spurgeon, *John Ploughman*, ch xiv. [quoted as 'the old saying'].

4. Who swims on sin, shall sink in sorrow. 1853: Trench, *Proverbs*, 21 (1905).

Swine, *subs.* 1. *A swine over fat is cause of his own bane.* 1546: Heywood, *Proverbs*, Pt II ch vii. 1605: Camden, *Remains*, 318 (1870). 1666: Torriano, *Piazza Univ.*, 213, A hog over fat is the cause of its own death. 1732: Fuller, 428, A swine fatted hath eat its own bane. Cf. **Sow**, *subs.* (2).

2. Swine, women and bees cannot be turned. 1678: Ray, 212. 1732: Fuller, 4299. 1875: Cheales, *Proverb. Folk-Lore*, 6.

3. The swine has run through it. 1879: W. Henderson, *Folk-Lore of N. Counties*, 34, It is unlucky for swine to cross the path in front of a wedding party. Hence the old adage, 'The swine's run through it'.

See also **Hog; Pig; Sheep** (18); and **Sow**, *subs.*

Swings you gain on the roundabouts, What you lose. *See* **Lose** (17).

Sword. 1. He that strikes with the sword shall be stricken with the scabbard. 1546: Heywood,

Proverbs, Pt II ch vii. 1585: Sir E. Dyer, *Nothing*, in *Writings*, 83 (Grosart). 1612: *Cornucopiae*, 48 (Grosart), The prouerbe still doth threate, Who strikes with sword, the scabbard shall him beat. 1670: Ray, 147 [with 'beaten' for 'stricken'].

2. He who lives by the sword, dies by the sword. [Matthew xxvi 52, All they that take the sword shall perish with the sword.] 1652: R. Williams, *Complete Writings* (1963), IV 352, All that take the Sword ... shall perish by it. 1804: G. Morris, *Diary and Letters* (1889), II xlv, To quote the text. 'Those who live by the sword shall perish by the sword'. 916: J. Buchan, *Greenmantle*, vi, I did not seek the war ... It was forced on me ... He that takes the sword will perish by the sword.

3. Sword in madman's hand. *See* Ill putting.

4. The pen is mightier than the sword. *See* **Pen**.

5. Who draws his sword against his Prince, must throw away the scabbard. 1659: Howell, 17. 1670: Ray, 21. 1732: Fuller, 5698.

Sylvester said, As, – fair and softly. 1813: Ray, 232. Cf. **Soft and fair.**

Sympathy without relief Is like mustard without beef. 1914: R. L. Gales, *Vanished Country Folk*, 204. Cf. **Pity.**

T

Table ros more than a thief, The. 1640: Herbert, *Jac. Prudentum.* 1670: Ray, 25. 1732: Fuller, 4782, The table is a great robber.

Tace is Latin for a candle. A humorous hint to be silent. 1676: Shadwell, *Virtuoso*, I, I took him up with my old repartee; Peace, said I, *Tace* is *Latin* for a candle. 1738: Swift, *Polite Convers.*, Dial. II. 1751: Fielding, *Amelia*, bk i ch x .1824: Scott, *Redgauntlet*, ch xii, There are some auld stories that cannot be ripped up again with entire safety to all concerned. *Tace* is Latin for a candle. 1881: *N. & Q.*, 6th ser, iv 157, 'Tace is the Latin for a cat', as I have heard in the north of England when a hint for silence was desirable. Cat, candle, or anything else would do, for *tace* is, of course, the important word.

Tag, rag and bobtail. The quotations show the earlier forms of the phrase. 1553: Bale, *Vocacyon*, in *Harl. Miscell.*, vi 459, All the rable

of the shippe, hag, tag, and rag. 1584: B. R., *Euterpe*, 122 (Lang), To entertayne tagge and ragge all that would come. 1603: Harsnet, *Decl. of Egreg. Popish Impostures*, 50, For all were there tag, and ragge, cut and long-tayle. 1639: Clarke, 236, Tag and rag, cut and long tayle every one that can eat an egge. 1645: *Just Defence John Bastwick*, 16 (OED), That rabble rout tag ragge and bobtaile. 1655: A. Brewer, *Love-sick King*, IV, I think there's some match at foot-bal towards, the colliers against the whole country cut, and long tail. 1660: Pepys, *Diary*, 6 March [as in 1645]. 1694: Motteux, *Rabelais*, bk iv ch xxxiii, It will swallow us all, ships and men, shag, rag, and bobtail, like a dose of pills. *c.*1740: Bramston, *Art of Politics*, l. 10 from end, Tag rag and bobtail. 1762: Smollett, *Sir L. Greaves*, ch xvii [as in 1740]. 1821: Byron, *Blues*, ecl. ii l. 23, By the rag, tag, and bobtail, of those they call

'Blues'. 1907: Hackwood, *Old Eng. Sports*, 276, The usual following of the Rag-Tag-and-Bobtail class.

Tail, *subs*. 1. His tail will catch the chin-cough. Spoken of one that sits on the ground. 1678: Ray, 82.

2. Make not thy tail broader than thy wings. 1659: Howell, 11 (9). 1670: Ray, 147. 1732: Fuller, 3323.

Tailor, *subs*. 1. A tailor's shreds are worth the cutting. 1670: Ray, 147.

2. Like the tailor that sewed for nothing, and found thread himself. 1732: Fuller, 3237.

3. Tailor and needle. See quot. 1917: Bridge, *Cheshire Proverbs*, 160, If you come on to me, you come on your sharps, as tailor said when he showed his needle.

4. Tailor-like. Apparently a proverbial phrase. 1601: Cornwallis, *Essayes*, Pt II, sig. Dd6 (1610), What is his gaine but the marke of an ideot? what his knowledge, but tailor-like and light?

5. Tailors and writers must mind the fashion. 1732: Fuller, 4301.

6. The tailor cuts three sleeves for every woman's gown. 1612: in *Pepysian Garland*, 32 (Rollins), For it is a common prouerbe throughout all the towne, The taylor he must cut three sleeues, for euery womans gowne. 1632: in Ibid., 412, A taylor that will liue in peace, cuts out of one gowne three sleeues.

7. The tailor makes the man. 1625: Jonson, *Staple of News*, I i, And thence, sir, comes your proverb, The tailor makes the man. *c*.1630: B.&F., *Bloody Brother*, III ii, For though he [the tailor] makes the man, The cook yet makes the dishes. 1853: Planché, *Extravag.*, iv 318 (1879), The 'tailor makes the man', we used to say – The tailor makes the manager, to-day.

8. The tailor that makes not a knot, loseth a stitch. 1732: Fuller, 4786.

See also Hundred; **Miller** (10); and **Nine tailors. Tainted sheep.** *See* **Sheep** (10).

Take, *verb*. 1. A man must take such as he finds, or such as he brings. *c*.1386: Chaucer, *C. Tales*, A 4129 (Skeat), I have herd seyd, man sal taa of twa thinges, Slyk as he fyndes, or taa slyk as he bringes. *c*.1590: Greene, *George a Greene*, IV iv, If this like you not, Take that you finde, or that you bring, for me.

2. He has taken his gears in = He is dead. 1917: Bridge, *Cheshire Proverbs*, 67.

3. It takes all mack to make every mack. Ibid., 86 … 'Mack' = sort or kind.

4. I was taken by a morsel, says the fish. 1640: Herbert, *Jac. Prudentum*.

5. Take a doe. *See* **Doe.**

6. Take all and pay the baker. 1678: Ray, 91. 1732: Fuller, 4303.

7. Take all, pay all. 1600: Shakespeare, *Merry Wives*, II ii. 1616: *Jack Drum's Entert.*, I, Rule all, pay all, take all. 1737: Ray, 273, Take all and pay all.

8. Take a thorn. *See* **Thorn** (3).

9. Take away fuel, take away flame. 1639: Clarke, 192. 1670: Ray, 95. 1732: Fuller, 4305, Take away fuel, and you take away fire.

10. Take away the cause and the effect must cease. 1620: Shelton, *Quixote*, Pt II ch lxvii, The cause being removed, the sin will be saved. 1710: Ward, *Nuptial Dialogues*, ii 42, For 'tis a maxim that does seldom miss, Remove the cause and the effect will cease. 1734: in *Walpole Ballads*, 93 (Oxford, 1916).

11. Take care of the pence. *See* **Penny** (20).

12. Take, have, and keep are pleasant words. 1886: Hardy, *Casterbridge*, ch xiv. [quoted as 'the mediaeval saying'].

13. Take heed is a fair thing. 1546: Heywood, *Proverbs*, Pt II ch viii. 1593: Harvey, *Works*, ii 166 (Grosart). 1608: Armin, *Nest of Ninnies*, 29 (SH.S.).

14. Take heed is a good reed [advice]. [*c*.1380: Chaucer, *Troylus*, bk ii l. 343, Avysëment is good before the nede.] 1599: Porter, *Two Angry Women*, in Hazlitt, *Old Plays*, vii 337. 1670: Ray, 102. 1732: Fuller, 6315.

15. Take him in good turn and knock out his brains. 1639: Clarke, 150.

16. Take not counsel in the combat. 1642: D. Rogers, *Matrim. Honour*, 199, As the proverbe saith, take not, etc.

17. Take time by the forelock. *See* **Time** (29).

18. Take your wife's first advice. *See* **Wife** (20).

19. To take a dagger and drown one self. 1678: Ray, 238.

20. To take a leaf out of another's book. 1886: Hardy, *Casterbridge*, ch xvi, You should have taken a leaf out of his book, and have had your sports in a sheltered place like this.

21. To take as falleth in the sheaf. 1546: Heywood, *Proverbs*, Pt II ch iv. 1562: Heywood, *Epigrams*, No. 217, I will take as falleth in the sheaf. 1659: Howell, 7, I will take it [as] faith in the sheaf where ever it fall.

22. To take a thing in snuff. 1592: Shakespeare, *L.L.L.*, V ii, You'll mar the light by taking it in snuff. 1681: Robertson, *Phraseol. Generalis*, 97, He took it in snuff, viz. in anger. Cf. **Snuff.**

23. To take a thorn. *See* **Thorn** (3).

24. To take a venew under the girdle = To be got with child. 1598: Chamberlain, *Letters*, 18 (Camden S.), Some say she hath taken a venew under the girdle and swells upon it.

25. To take counsel of one's pillow. 1573: Harvey, *Letter-Book*, 21 (Camden S.), You counsel me to take counsel of mi pillow. 1611: Cotgrave, s.v. 'Conseil', Night gives advice; We say, take counsell of your pillow. 1676: Cotton, Walton's *Angler*, Pt II ch ii, I will presently wait on you to your chamber, where, take counsel of your pillow; and to-morrow resolve me. 1751: Fielding, *Amelia*, bk ix. ch v, 'I will consult my pillow upon it,' said the doctor. Cf. **Night it the mother.**

26. To take from the right hand and give to the left. 1732: Fuller, 5241.

27. To take one a button-hole (or **peg,** etc.) **lower.** *c.* 1550: Becon, *Catechism, etc.*, 561 (P.S.), This doctrine plucketh them down one staff lower than they were before. 1592: Nashe, *Works*, ii 77 (Grosart), The hard lodging on the boards [will] take their flesh downe a button hole lower. 1592: Shakespeare, *L.L.L.*, V ii, Master, let me take you a button-hole lower. 1633: Shirley, *Triumph of Peace*, in *Works*, vi 28c (Dyce); I'd see the tallest beefeater on you all ... knocking my wife down, and I'll bring him a button-hole lower. 1654: Gayton, *Pleasant Notes Don Q.*, 234, Had not Daplusse taken him a button lower. 1670: Ray, 189, To take one a peg lower. 1764: Mrs F. Sheridan, *Dupe*, IV iv, I must take her down a peg or so. 1829: Peacock, *Misfor. of Elphin*, ch xiii, I have just brought the abbot this pleasant intelligence, and, as I knew it would take him down a cup or two ...

28. To take one's ease in one's inn. 1546: Heywood, *Proverbs*, Pt I ch v, To let the world wag, and take mine ease in mine in. 1597: Shakespeare, 1 *Henry IV*, III iii, *Falstaff* ... Shall I not take mine ease in mine inn but I shall have my pocket picked? 1620: Middleton, *World Tost at Tennis*, in *Works*, vii 185 (Bullen), These great rich men must take their ease i' theirinn.

1821: Byron, *Letters, etc.*, v 481 (Prothero), The traveller can 'take his ease in his inn'.

29. To take one's hands off = To decline a bargain. 1917: Bridge, *Cheshire Proverbs*, 143.

30. To take one up before he is down. 1583: Melbancke, *Philotinus*, sig. L1, Thou louest me well that takest me vp before I fall. 1738: Swift, *Polite Convers.*, Dial. I, You take me up, before I'm down. 1818: Scott, *Heart of Midl.*, ch xviii, 'Sir, under your favour,' replied David ... 'ye take me up before I fall down.' 1880: Courtney, *W. Cornwall Words*, 1 (E.D.S.), He took me up afore I were down.

31. To take out of one pocket to put in the other. 1855: Bohn, 544.

32. To take pet. 1669: *New Help to Discourse*, 252, He thereupon took pet, and so did die. 1706: D'Urfey, *Stories Moral and Comical*, 57, But at his naming of the net, Venus had certainly took pet. 1732: Fuller, 2325, He that takes pet at a feast, loses it all.

Takeley Street. *See* quots. 1880: E. Walford, in *N.&Q.*, 6th ser, ii 307, 'All on one side like Takeley Street' ... the village of Takeley, between Dunmow and Bishop's Stortford, has all the cottages on the one side of the road, and the squire's park on the other. 1896: *N.&Q.*, 8th ser, x 475, A common local saying in Essex is 'All on one side, like Takeley Street'.

Tale, *subs.* **1. A tale never loses in the telling.** 1541: *Schoolhouse of Women*, A4v, What soever commeth to memorye Shall not be loste, for the tellinge. 1581: *Stationer's Register* (1875), II 388, A good tale Cannot to often be Tolde. 1609: S. Harward, *MS* (Trinity College Cambridge), 121, Tales lose nothing by the cariadge. 1633: Draxe, 177, A tale in the carrying is made more. 1710: S. Palmer, *Moral Essays on Proverbs*, 177, A story never loses by carrying. 1869: Spurgeon, *John Ploughman*, ch vi.

2. A tale of a tub. 1538: Bale, *Three Laws*, Act II, Ye saye they folowe your lawe, And varyee not a shawe, Whych is a tale of a tubbe. 1546: Heywood, *Proverbs*, Pt II ch ix, A tale of a tub, your tale no truth auouth. 1576: R. Peterson, tr. *Galateo*, 73 (1892), All thys long babble ... never but a tale of a tubbe. 1633: Jonson, *Tale of a Tub* [title]. 1691: *Merry Drollery*, 225 (Ebsworth), For I think I have told you a Tale of a Tub. 1704: Swift, *Tale of a Tub* [title]. 1710: Centlivre, *Man's Bewitch'd*, I. 1714: Ozell, *Molière*, iv 125,

All is idle talk, trifles, and tales of a tub. 1855: Kingsley, *West. Ho!*, ch vii.

3. A tile twice told is cabbage twice sold. 1732: Fuller, 429. Cf. No. 5.

4. Each tale is ended as it hath favour. *c.*1450: Burgh (and Lydgate), *Secrees*, 51 (E.E.T.S.) [quoted as 'a proverbe'].

5. It ought to be a good tale that is twice told. 1732: Fuller, 3041. Cf. No. 3.

6. One tale good. *See* **One tale.**

7. Tell a tale to a mare. *See* quots. 1567: Pickering, *Horestes*, l. 95 (Brandl, *Quellen*, 496), Tell a mare a tale, and shyell gerd out a fart. 1652: Tatham, *Scots Figgaries*, III [as in 1567]. 1670: Ray, 26 [as in 1567]. 1738: Swift, *Polite Convers.*, Dial. I, Well, miss; tell a mare a tale ... 1869: Hazlitt, 351, Tell a tale to a mare and shell kick thee.

8. The tale runs as it pleases the teller. 1732: Fuller, 4783.

9. To tell tales out of school. 1530: Tyndale, *Pract. of Prelates*, 249 (P.S.), So that what cometh once in may never out, for fear of telling tales out of school. 1546: Heywood, *Proverbs*, Pt I ch x. 1638: Ford, *Fancies*, I ii, Beware of the porter's lodge, for carrying tales out of the school. 1679: Shadwell, *True Widow*, IV i, Fie, miss! fie! tell tales out of school? 1753: Richardson, *Grandison*, iii 110 (1883), Don't tell tales out of school, Emily. 1805: Mary Lamb, in *Letters*, i 315 (Lucas), Write us, my good girl, a long, gossiping letter ... tell me any silly thing you can recollect ... we will never tell tales out of school. 1854: Thackeray, *Newcomes*, ch xii.

See also **Tell**, *verb* (6), (11), (13), and (17).

Tale-bearer is worse than a thief, A. 1736: Bailey, *Dict.*, s.v.

Tale-bearers, Put no faith in. 1855: Bohn, 477.

Talk is but talk. 1620: *Two Mery Milkmaids*, II ii, But talke's but talke, therefore I vse it not. 1639: Chapman and Shirley, *Ball*, V i, You may hear talk; but give me the man that has measured 'em; talk's but talk ... 1678: Ray, 177, Prate is but prate, its money buyes land. 1681: Robertson, *Phraseol. Generalis*, 1203 [as in 1678, but with 'talk' for 'prate']. 1737: Ray, 270 [as in 1681]. Cf. **Prate**; and **Words.** (13).

Talk, *verb*. **1. He that talks much of his happiness, summons grief.** 1640: Herbert, *Jac. Prudentum*.

2. He that talks to himself talks to a fool. 1732: Fuller, 2328.

3. I am talking of hay, and you of horse-beans. Ibid., No. 2586.

4. Many talk like philosophers, and live like fools. Ibid., No. 3358.

5. Talk not too much of state affairs. 1659: Howell, 18.

6. Talk of camps, but stay at home. 1732: Fuller, 4319.

7. Talk of the Devil. *See* **Devil** (37).

8. To talk a bird's (or dog's) **leg off** – and like phrases. 1868: *N.&Q.*, 4th ser, ii 488, In Lancashire a loquacious person, whether man or woman, is said to be able to 'talk a horse's leg off'. Ibid., 591 [also in Norfolk and Midlands]. 1869: Hazlitt, 353, That fellow would talk a horse to death. S. Devon. In the local vernacular: Thilk veller would tell a horse to death. 1893: Gower, *Gloss. of Surrey Words*, lii (E.D.S.), I never see sich a fellow to go on, he would talk his dog's hind leg off any day. 1901: F. E. Taylor, *Lancs Sayings*, 34, He'd talk th' leg off a brass pon [pan].

9. To talk like an apothecary. 1639: Clarke, 133, He prates like a poticary. 1670: Ray, 195. 1708: *Brit. Apollo*, i Suppl. Paper 10, col. 6, Why is a man said, when he speaks at random, to talk like an apothecary? 1769: Smollett, *Adv. of Atom*, 65 (Cooke, 1795), Your grace talks like an apothecary.

Talking comes by nature, Silence by understanding. 1875: Cheales, *Proverb. Folk-Lore*, 86.

Talking pays no toll. 1640: Herbert, *Jac. Prudentum*. 1732: Fuller, 4317. 1869: Spurgeon, *John Ploughman*, ch vi.

Tall, *adj*. **1. As tall as a hop-pole.** 1788: Colman, jr., *Ways and Means*, I ii, Two fine young women ... tall as hop-poles.

2. As tall as a may-pole. 1678: Ray, 289. 1754: Berthelson, *Eng.-Danish Dict.*, s.v. 'May', He is grown so high, that a man dares not come near him by the length of a may-pole.

3. He is a tall man of his hands. 1485: Malory, *Morte d'Arthur*, bk iv, ch xvii, He is a passyng goodman of his handes. 1591: Florio, *Second Frutes*, 117, Is he valiant, and a talle man of his hands? 1678: Ray, 82, A tall man of hands. He will not let a beast rest in's pocket.

4. While the tall maid is stooping, the little one hath swept the house. 1666: Torriano, *Piazza*

Univ., 108, Whilst a tall Meg of Westminster is stooping, a short wench sweeps the house. 1869: Hazlitt, 468.

Tamworth. *See* **Sutton.**

Tanfield fools. *See* quot. 1846–59: *Denham Tracts*, i 68 (F.L.S.), Tanfield fools, and Anfield lubberts, Hungry Iceton with its empty cupboards. Tanfield, Anfield and Iceton (properly Iveston), are villages and hamlets near the source of the river Derwent.

Tangled skein of it to wind off, I have a. 1732: Fuller, 2603.

Tango. *See* **Two to tango.**

Tantera Bobus, who lived till he died, Like. 1864: 'Cornish Proverbs', in *N. & Q.*, 3rd ser, vi 5. 1882: Jago, *Gloss. of Cornish Dialect*, 288, Tantra-bobus, or Tantrum-bobus. Term applied to a noisy, playful child. 'Oh! you tantra-bobus!' 1886: Elworthy, *West Som. Word-Book*, 737 (E.D.S.), Oh! I reckon he lived same's Tantara-bobus – all the days of his life. Cf. **Live** (39).

Tantivy and **Tantony pig.** *See* **Anthony pig.**

Tapster is undone by chalk, The – i.e. by scoring on credit. *c.*1630: in *Roxb. Ballads*, i 71 (Hindley). 1639: Mayne, *City Match*, IV vii, You do offend o' th' score, and sin in chalk.

Tapsters and ostlers are not always the honestest men. 1597: *Discouerie of the Knights of the Poste*, sig. D4.

Tar. *See* **Sheep** (18); and **Ship** (4).

Tarberry Hill, near Hastings. 1894: A. J. C. Hare, *Sussex*, 192, 'Who knows what Tarberry would bear, Must plough it with a golden share', is a proverb.

Tarleton – the Shakespearean jester. 1813: Ray, 71, He answers with monosyllables, as Tarleton did one who out-eat him at an ordinary.

Tarring. *See* **Heighton.**

Tarry-long brings little home. 1732: Fuller, 4320.

Taste, *subs. See* quots. 1633: Draxe, 29, To him that hath lost his taste, sweet is sowre. 1670: Ray, 26 [as in 1633]. 1732: Fuller, 5182, To him that has a bad taste, sweet is bitter.

Taste, *verb. See* quot. 1855: Bohn, 581, You want to taste the broth as soon as the meat is in.

Tastes. *See* **Accounting.**

Taunton. *See* **Nertown.**

Taunton Dean – Where should I be born else? 1662: Fuller, *Worthies*, iii 91 (1840). 1790: Grose, *Prov. Gloss.*, s.v. 'Somerset'.

Tavern bitch, The. *See* quot. 1608: Middleton, *Trick to Catch Old One*, IV v, Faith, the same man still: the tavern bitch has bit him i' th' head [he is drunk].

Tavern haunteth, That. *See* quot. *c.*1460: *How the Good Wife*, l. 50, That tauerne hauntethe his thrifte for-sakithe.

Tavern token, To swallow a = To be drunk. 1596: Jonson, *Ev. Man in Humour*, I iv, Drunk, sir? … Perhaps he swallow'd a tavern token, or some such device. 1604: *Meet. of Gallants*, 17 (Percy S.), Indeed he had swallowed doune many tauerne-tokens, and was infected much with the plague of drunkenness. 1745: Franklin, *Drinker's Dict.*, in *Works*, ii 26 (Bigelow), He's swallowed a tavern token.

Teach, *verb.* **1. He teacheth ill who teacheth all.** 1659: Howell, 4. 1732: Fuller, 2035.

2. He who can, does; he who cannot, teaches. 1903: G.B. Shaw, *Maxims for Revolutionists*, in *Man and Superman*, 230, He who can, does. He who cannot, teaches.

3. Teaching of others teacheth the teacher. Ibid., No. 4323.

4. Teach your father to get children. 1659: Howell, 9 (7). 1754: Berthelson, *Eng.-Danish Dict.*, s.v. 'Father', To teach one's father to get children.

5. Teach your grandmother to suck eggs – and perform other feats. 1542: Udall, tr. Erasmus' *Apoph.*, 380 (1877), A swine to teache Minerua was a prouerbe … for whiche we saie in Englishe, to teache our dame to spinne. 1611: Cotgrave, s.v. 'Apprendre', Wee say to teach his grandame to grope ducks. 1659: Howell, 9 (7), Go teach your granham to grope a goose. 1665: R. Howard, *Committee*, IV, Pish, teach your grannam to spin. 1670: Ray, 178, Teach your grandame to gropen her ducks, to sup sowre milk. 1709: Cibber, *Rival Foots*, II, Go, fools! teach your granums: you are always full of your advice when there's no occasion for 't. 1732: Fuller, 4321 [as in 1665]. 1738: Swift, *Polite Convers.*, Dial. I, You mend it! go, teach your grannam to suck eggs. 1749: Fielding, *Tom Jones*, bk xii ch xiii, A child may sometimes teach his grandmother to suck eggs. 1828: Carr, *Craven Dialect*, i 195, The proverb, 'Gang and teach thy granny to sup sour milk out o' t' ass riddle', is often applied to a confident person, who would attempt to teach another, who has more knowledge than himself.

6. You can't teach an old dog new tricks. *See* **Dog** (16).

Teague – an Irishman. **1. Like Teague's cocks, that fought one another, though all were of the same side.** 1732: Fuller, 3234.

2. You run like Teague, before your errand. Ibid., No. 5983.

Tears are near their eyes, Their. 1864: 'Cornish Proverbs', in *N. & Q.*, 3rd ser, vi 494.

Tears of the tankard. 1678: Ray, 82. 1690: *New Dict. Canting Crew*, sig. M1 … Drops of the good liquor that fall beside.

Tears. *See also* **Nothing** (8).

Tees, Escaped the, and was drowned in the Tyne. 1846–59: *Denham Tracts*, i 313 (F.L.S.).

Teeth. *See* **Tooth.**

Tell. 1. He tells me my way and don't know it himself. 1732: Fuller, 2036.

2. He that can tell. *See* quot. 1921: *Devonsh. Assoc. Trans.*, liii. 162, The old proverbial saying: 'He that can tell [talk] avore 'a can go 'Ull bring he's father ta sorrow an' woe'.

3. He that tells a secret is another's servant. 1640: Herbert, *Jac. Prudentum*. 1736: Bailey, *Dict.*, s.v. 'Tell', Tell your secret to your servant, and you make him your master.

4. He that tells his wife news, is but newly married. 1640: Herbert, *Jac. Prudentum*. 1670: Ray, 49. 1732: Fuller, 2330.

5. If you tell every step, you will make a long journey of it. Ibid., No. 2793.

6. I tell you my tale and my tales man [author]. 1690: *New Dict. Canting Crew*, sig. L8. 1738: Swift, *Polite Convers.*, Dial. I.

7. Tell me it snows. 1639: Clarke, 8, Fiddle, faddle, tell me it snowes. 1681: Robertson, *Phraseol. Generalis*, 1142, Tell me it snows; Piscem natare doces. 1732: Fuller, 4327.

8. Tell me news. 1603: Raleigh, in *Criminal Trials*, i 408 (1832), All this while you tell me news, Mr Attorney. 1639: Clarke, 303, Tell me what I know not. 1670: Ray, 187. 1738: Swift, *Polite Convers.*, Dial. I, I know that already; tell me news.

9. Tell me with whom thou goest. And I'll tell thee what thou doest. 1586: Pettie, tr. Guazzo's *Civil Convers.*, fo. 22, This common prouerbe sheweth, Tell me with whom thou doest goe, and I shall know what thou doest. 1633: Draxe, 25. 1667: L'Estrange, *Quevedo's Visions*, 151 (1904), This minded me of the old saying, 'Tell me thy company, and I'll tell thee thy manners'. 1710: S. Palmer, *Moral Essays on Proverbs*, 36. 1789: G. Parker, *Life's Painter*, 137, 'Tell me your company, and I will describe your manners', is an old saying.

10. Tell money after your own father. 1633: Draxe, 208, A man must tell golde after his owne father. 1639: Clarke, 90. 1656: F. Osborne, *Advice to Son*, 26 (Parry) ['Count' for 'Tell']. 1709: Cibber, *Rival Fools*, V, Always tell money after your father, sir. 1869: Spurgeon, *John Ploughman*, ch viii, Count money after your own kin.

11. Tell-tale-tit, your tongue shall be slit, And all the dogs in the town shall have a little bit. 1843: Halliwell, *Nurs. Rhymes*, 164. 1886: Elworthy, *West Som. Word-Book*, 742 (E.D.S.). 1889: Peacock, *Manley, etc., Gloss.*, 555 (E.D.S.). 1901: F. E. Taylor, *Lancs Sayings*, 43.

12. Tell truth and shame the devil. *See* **Truth** (3).

13. Tell you a tale and find you ears. 1546: Heywood, *Proverbs*, Pt II ch ix, He must both tell, etc. *c.*1594: Bacon, *Promus*, No. 673, A man must tell you tales and find your [*sic*] ears. 1670: Ray, 195. 1738: Swift, *Polite Convers.*, Dial. I, What, miss! must I tell you a story, and find you ears?

14. Tell your cards. *See* **Cards** (3).

15. To be able to tell ten. 1613: B.&F., *Coxcomb*, II i, He cannot be So innocent a coxcomb; he can tell ten, sure!

16. Who tells a lie to save his credit, wipes his nose on his sleeve to save his napkin. 1659: Howell, I.

17. You will tell another tale when you are tried. 1678: Ray, 348.

See also **One Tale; Tale;** and **Time** (32).

Temperance is the best physic. 1855: Bohn, 495.

Temple-brough. *See* **Winkabank.**

Ten. *See* **Hours;** and **Tell,** *verb* (15).

Tenbury. 1882: Mrs Chamberlain, *W. Worcs. Words*, 39 (E.D.S.), Sell wheat and buy rye, Say the bells of Tenbury.

Ten commandments = the ten fingernails. *c.*1560: in Wright, *Songs, etc., Philip and Mary*, 202 (Roxb.Cl), Or els her ten commandments She fastens on hys face. 1594: *First Part Contention*, 16 (S.H.S.), Could I come neare your daintie visage with my nayles, Ide set my ten commandments in your face. 1607: Dekker and Webster, *Westw. Hoe*, V iii, Your harpy that set his ten commandments upon my back. 1814: Scott, *Waverley*, ch xxx. 1830: Marryat, *King's Own*, ch xl, Don't put your tongue into your cheek at me ... or I'll write the ten commandments on your face.

Tender as a chicken. 1678: Ray, 289. 1720: Gay, *Poems*, ii 280 (Underhill), Till you grow tender as a chick.

Tender as a parson's leman. 1546: Heywood, *Proverbs*, Pt I ch x. 1592: Greene, in *Harl. Miscell.*, viii 375 (1746), That had a fayre wench to her daughter, as young and tender as a morrow masse priests lemman. 1611: Cotgrave, s.v. 'Mol'. 1670: Ray, 208.

Tender as Parnell, that broke her finger in a posset-curd. 1678: Ray, 289. 1690: *New Dict. Canting Crew*, sig. M1, Tender-parnel, a very nicely educated creature, apt to catch cold upon the least blast of wind. 1785: Grose, *Class. Dict. Vulgar Tongue*, s.v. 'Tender P'. ['drink' for 'furd']. 1847: Halliwell, dict., s.v. 'Tender' [as in 1785]. 1917: Bridge, *Cheshire Proverbs*, 22.

Ten good turns. I do not understand this dark saying. 1578: Whetstone, *Promos and Cass.*, sig. D2, The prouerbe saies, that tenne good turnes lye dead, And one yll deede, tenne tymes beyonde pretence, By enuious tongues, report abrode doth spread.

Ten pretty. *See* **Twenty** (4).

Tenterden steeple is the cause of Goodwin Sands. 1528: More, *Dialogue*, in *Works*, p. 278, col. 1 (1557) [story of Tenterden steeple being the cause of the choking up by sands of Sandwich harbour]. 1550: Latimer, *Sermons*, 251 (P.S.) [Latimer tells the absurd story]. 1568: in *Loseley MSS.*, 211 (Kempe), Of many people it hath ben said, That Tenterden steeple Sandwich haven hath decayed. 1644: Taylor (Water-Poet), *Crop-Eare*, C. 18, in *Works*, 2nd coll. (Spens.S.), Here is an excellent proofe. Weaker then that of Tenterden Steeple being the cause of Goodwine Sands. 1662: Fuller, *Worthies*, ii 125 (1840). 1790: Grose, *Prov. Gloss.*, s.v. 'Kent'.

Testons. *See* **Oxford.**

Tewkesbury mustard. *See* quots. 1598: Shakespeare, *2 Henry IV*, II iv, His wit's as thick as Tewkesbury mustard. 1634: *Strange Metam. of Man.*, sig. D10, If he [mustard] be of the right

stamp, and a true Tewxbury man. 1662: Fuller, *Worthies*, i 552 (1840), He looks as if he had lived on Tewkesbury mustard. Before 1704: T. Brown, *Works*, iv 236 (1760), When Tewkesbury mustard shall wander abroad. 1790: Grose, *Prov. Gloss.*, s.v. 'Gloucestershire' [as in 1598 and 1662]. 1851: *Gloucestershire Gloss.*, 14 [as in 1662].

Teynham, Kent. *See* **Bapchild**; and **Muston.**

Thakeham, the last place God made. 1884: 'Sussex Proverbs', in *N. & Q.*, 6th ser, ix. 402.

Thames on Fire, To set the. There is no good ground for connecting 'Thames' in this phrase with 'temse', a provincial name for a sieve. *c.*1770: Foote, *Trip to Calais*, III iii, Matt Minnikin ... won't set fire to the Thames, though he lives near the Bridge. 1788: Wolcot, *Works*, i 509 (1795), Whose modest wisdom, therefore, never aims To find the longitude, or burn the Thames. 1818: J. Austen, *Persuasion*, ch v, The Baronet will never set the Thames on fire, but there seems no harm in him. 1863: Kingsley, *Water Babies*, ch viii. 1915: Pinero, *Big Drum*, III.

Thames. *See also* **Cast** (8).

Thank God that your father was born before you, You may. 1855: Bohn, 579.

Thank you for the next, for this I am sure of, I'll. 1678: Ray, 273.

Thatch, *subs. See* **Thick as thack**; and **Wet** (5).

Thatch, *verb,* **1. If a house had to be thatched with muck, there would be more teachers than reachers.** 1762: Smollett, *Sir L. Greaves*, ch xv, Thatch your house with t –, and you'll have more teachers than reachers. 1917: Bridge, *Cheshire Proverbs*, 76.

2. When I have thatched his house, he would throw me down. 1639: Clarke, 170. 1670: Ray, 148. 1732: Fuller, 5559, When I had thatch'd his house, he would have hurl'd me from the roof.

3. Would you thatch your house with Pancakes? Ibid., No. 5829. Cf. **Groby pool.**

That may happen to many, Which doth happen to any. *c.*1590: G. Harvey, *Marginalia*, 101 (1913).

That's for that. 1738: Swift, *Polite Convers.*, Dial. I, So much for that and butter for fish. 1880: Spurgeon, *Ploughman's Pictures*, 34, That's for that, as salt is for herrings ... and Nan for Nicholas.

Th' berrin's. *See* **Burying.**

There or thereabouts, as Parson Smith says. 1678: Ray, 343 ... Proverbial about Dunmow in Essex.

Thetch. *See* **Vetch.**

They say is half a lie. 1666: Torriano, *Piazza Univ.*, 30, To have heard say is half a lye. 1710: S. Palmer, *Moral Essays on Proverbs*, 261. 1869: Spurgeon, *John Ploughman*, ch vi, Hearsay is half lies.

Thick and thin. Through. [Per omne fas ac nefas. – Livy, vi 14.] *c.*1386: Chaucer, *Reeve's Tale*, l. 146, And whan the hors was loos, he ginneth gon Toward the fen, ther wilde mares renne, Forth with wehee, thurgh thikke and thurgh thenne. *c.*1490: *Partonope*, 15 (E.E.T.S.), Alle the day they spare noghte Hym to hvnte thorowe thyke and thynne. 1587: Turbervile, *Trag. Tales, etc.*, 30 (1837), Retchelesse she ran through thick and thin. 1621: B.&F., *Pilgrim*, III ii, He would run through thick and thin to reach me. 1758–67: Sterne, *Trist. Shandy*, vol ii ch ix, Splashing and plunging like a devil thro' thick and thin. 1857: Borrow, *Rom. Rye*, ch xxv. 1895: Pinero, *Benefit of Doubt*, II, He would stand by me through thick and thin.

Thick and threefold. 1552: Huloet, *Abced.*, sig. Ii1, Thicke and thre folde. 1577: Kendall, *Flow. of Epigrams*, 103 (Spens.S.), Thicke and three fold frends will flocke. 1650: Fuller, *Pisgah Sight*, bk ii ch ix, Disaster ... which afterwards fell thick and threefold upon it.

Thick as hail, As. 1205: Layamon, *Brut*, l. 12578, Arwen fluyen ouer wal: al abuten ouer al. swa thicke wes heore uaerae: swulc hit hayel waeren (Arrows flew over the wall all about over all: so thick was their flight, as if it were hail). 1566: Painter, *Pal. of Pleasure*, i 338 (Jacobs), The nomber of shotte, which ... were bestowed so thicke as hayle, vpon euery part of the fort. 1659: *Crown Garland*, 69 (Percy S.), They discharg'd their shafts So thick as hail from sky. 1720: Gay, *Damon and Cupid*, Men fall as thick as hail. 1819: Scott, *Ivanhoe*, ch xxix, This heavy discharge, which continued as thick and sharp as hail. 1907: Hackwood, *Old Eng. Sports*, 111, They fell thick and sharp as hail.

Thick as hops, As. 1599: Porter, *Two Angry Women*, sc xi, Looke, the water drops from you as fast as hops. 1631: Mabbe, *Celestina*, 171 (T.T.), Your presents from all parts ... came

upon me as thicke as hops. 1707: Dunton, *Athenian Sport*, 19, Fly all about as thick as hops. 1733: Swift, *On Poetry*, l. 400, The rest pursue as thick as hops.

Thick as inkle-weavers, As. 'Thick' = close, intimate. 1690: *New Dict. Canting Crew*, sig. C3, As great as two inkle-makers. 1703: Ward, *Writings*, ii. 357 [as in 1690]. 1738: Swift, *Polite Convers.*, Dial. I, Why, she and you were as great as two inkle-weavers. 1788: Cowper, *Letter to Lady Hesketh*, 6 May, When people are intimate, we say they are as great as two inkle-weavers. 1822: Scott, *Nigel*, ch xxiii, We were as loving as inkle-weavers. 1865: *N.&Q.*, 3rd ser, viii 130, 'As thick as inkle-weavers'. – This saying is used in some parts of Cheshire and Lancashire. 1908: *N.&Q.*, 10th ser, x 186, In my early days at Launceston ... and that is now fully seventy-five years ago [when woollen, goods were made at L.], the proverb 'As thick as inkle-makers' was commonly applied to great cronies, because inkle-makers had to work very closely together.

Thick as porridge, etc., As. *c.*1480: *Early Miscellanies*, 87 (Warton Cl., 1855), Thyk as pappe. 1828: Carr, *Craven Dialect*, ii 51, 'As thick as porridge', a proverbial simile frequently applied to beer. 1877: E. Leigh, *Cheshire Gloss.*, 200, As thick as stirrow [hasty pudding]. 1917: Bridge, *Cheshire Proverbs*, 24 [as in 1877].

Thick as thack [thatch]**, As.** 1828: Carr, *Craven Dialect*, ii 198. 1889: Peacock, *Manley, etc.*, *Gloss.*, 558 (E.D.S.).

Thick as thieves, As. Ibid., 558. 1913: L. P. Jacks, *All Men are Ghosts*, 213, But I never would have nothing to do with gypsies; though his Lordship was as thick as thieves with 'em.

Thick as three in a bed, As. 1820: Scott, *Monastery*, Introd. Ep., You twa will be as thick as three in a bed an ance ye forgather. 1828: Can, *Craven Dialect*, ii 201, As thrang as three in a bed. 1889: Peacock, *Manley, etc.*, *Gloss.*, 558 (E.D.S.). Cf. **Thrunk.**

Thickness of a sixpence between good and evil, There is not the. 1732: Fuller, 4933.

Thief and Thieves. 1. All are not thieves that dogs bark at. 1633: Draxe, 48. 1670: Ray, 56. 1694: D'Urfey, *Quixote*, Pt II Act IV sc ii. 1865: 'Lancs Proverbs', in *N.&Q.*, 3rd ser, viii 494. 1901: F. E. Taylor, *Lancs Sayings*, 10, They're not o thieves 'at dogs barken at.

2. A thief knows a thief, as a wolf knows a wolf. 1633: Draxe, 108, One thiefe knoweth another. 1732: Fuller, 430.

3. He that trusts a thief is a fool. *c.*1534: Berners, *Huon*, 706 (E.E.T.S.), It is sayd in a comen prouerbe that a man is taken for a foole that putteth his trust in a thefe.

4. Of all crafts. *See* quot. *c.*1320: in *Reliq. Antiquae*, i 115 (1841), 'Of alle mester men mest me hongeth theves'; Quoth Hendyng. 1869: Hazlitt, 300, 'Of all crafts, the thieving craft is the worst for hanging,' Quoth Hendyng.

5. Set a thief to catch a thief [*c.*1386: Chaucer, *Physic. Tale*, l. 83. A theef of venisoun, that hath forlaft His likerousnesse, and al his olde craft, Can kepe a forest best of any man (= An old poacher makes a good gamekeeper).] 1665: R. Howard, *Committee*. I, According to the old saying, Set a thief to catch a thief. 1702: Brown, *Works*, ii 244 (1760), Always set a knave to catch a knave. 1725: Bailey, tr. Erasmus' *Colloq.*, 457. 1878: Jefferies, *Gamekeeper at Home*, ch ix, There is a saying that an old poacher makes the best gamekeeper, on the principle of setting a thief to catch a thief. 1895: Pinero, *Mrs Ebbsmith*, II

6. The thief is sorry he is to be hanged, but not that he is a thief. 1732: Fuller, 4788.

7. Thieves and rogues have the best luck, if they do but scape hanging. 1670: Ray, 118.

8. Thieves are never rogues among themselves. *See* **Honour**.

9. Thieves' handsell ever unlucky. 1687: Aubrey, *Gentilisme, etc.*, 120 (F.L.S.).

10. When it thunders the thief becomes honest. 1640: Herbert, *Jac. Prudentum*. 1670: Ray, 26. 1732: Fuller, 5691, Whilst it thunders, the thief turns honest.

11. When thieves fall out honest men come by their own. 1546: Heywood, *Proverbs*, Pt II ch ix … true men come to their goode. 1600: Day, *Blind Beggar*, IV i, When false theeves fall out true men come to their own. 1671: *Westm. Drollery*, 51 (Ebsworth), True men might have their own, now knaves fall out. 1710: S. Palmer, *Moral Essays on Proverbs*, 327 ['knaves' for 'thieves']. 1850: Dickens, *Chuzzlewit*, ch xlix, last par., Thanks to this quarrel, which confirms the old saying that when rogues fall out, honest people get what they want.

See also **Ask** (3); **Call** (1); **Careless; Hundred tailors; Miller** (8) and (10); **One thief; Rope** (2);

Thick at thieves; Too many stairs; True (12); Two daughters; and War (6).

Thin as a lath, As. 1744: *Foundl. Hosp. for Wit*, No. ii p. 26 (1749), Our hope grows as thin as a lath. 1799: Dr Burney, in D'Arblay, *Diary*, iv 100 (1876), You used to be as thin as Dr Lind … a mere lath. 1828: Carr, *Craven Dialect*, i 279. 1862: *Dialect of Leeds*, 406, As lean as a lat (lath). 1901: F. E. Taylor, *Lancs Sayings*, 4, As thin as a lat.

Thin as a rasher of wind, As. Oxfordsh. 1923: *Folk-Lore*, xxxiv. 329.

Thin. *See also* **Lean**.

Thin meadow is soon mowed, A. 1659: Howell, 3. 1670: Ray, 26.

Thing and Things. 1. A thing there was, and done it was, and wise was he that did it, Let no man know who knows it not, nor do so no more that did it. 1659: Howell, 3 … Of one who mistook his neighbour's wife for his own.

2. If a thing is worth doing, it's worth doing well. *See* **Worth** (2).

3. If things were to be done twice, all would be wise. 1640: Herbert, *Jac. Prudentum*. 1670: Ray, 27. 1754: Berthelson, *Eng.-Danish Dict.*, s.v. 'Twice'. 1875: Cheales, *Proverb. Folk-Lore*, 115.

4. There's a thing in it. *See* **Dish-clout**.

5. There's many a thing as belongs to everything. 1917: Bridge, *Cheshire Proverbs*, 117.

6. Things done cannot be undone. *c.*1460: *Good Wyfe wold a Pylgremage*, l. 119 (E.E.T.S.), When dede is doun. hit ys to lat. 1539: Taverner, *Proverbs*, fo. 35, The thynge that is done can not be undone. 1546: Heywood, *Proverbs*, Pt I ch x. *c.*1594: Bacon, *Promus*, No. 951. 1649: in Halliwell, *Books of Characters*, 46 (1857), That which is done, cannot be undone. 1718: W. Taverner, *Artful Wife*, III, Your ladiship knows what's done can't be undone. Cf. **Once done.**

7. Things present are judged by things past. 1578: Florio, *First Fruites*, fo. 30. 1629: *Book of Meery Riddles*, Prov. 36.

8. Things well fitted abide. 1640: Herbert, *Jac. Prudentum.*

9. When things come to the worst. *See* **Worst** (9).

Think, *verb*. 1. He that thinks amiss concludes worse. 1651: Herbert, *Jac. Prudentum*, 2nd ed.

2. He that thinks too much of his virtues, bids others think of his vices. 1869: Hazlitt, 188.

3. He thinks himself as great as my Lord Berkeley. Glos. 1639: in *Berkeley MSS.*, iii 26 (1885).

4. He thinks not well that thinks not again.
1611: Cotgrave, s.v. 'Penser', He thinks not well
that thinks of all at once; or thinks not more then
once. 1640: Herbert, *Jac. Prudentum*. 1736:
Bailey, *Dict.*, s.v. 'Think', He thinks ill that
thinks not twice.

5. One may think that dares not speak. 1633:
Draxe, 21. 1670: Ray, 148. 1732: Fuller, 3783.

6. They that think no ill are soonest beguiled.
1546: Heywood, *Proverbs*, Pt II ch v.

**7. They that think they know everything, know
nothing.** 1918: *Devonsh. Assoc. Trans.*, l. 185,
They wat thinks they knows everything, knows
nort.

8. Think and thank God. 1568: in *Loseley M.SS.*,
207 (Kempe).

9. Think first and speak afterwards. 1557: R.
Edgeworth, *Sermons*, B6, Thinke well and thou
shalt speak well. 1623: W. painter, *Chaucer New
Painted*, B1v, Thinke twise, then speak, the olde
Proverbe doth say, Yet Fooles their bolts will
quickely shoot away. 1639: J. Clarke, *Paroemi-
ologia Anglo-Latina*, 133, First thinke and then
speak.

10. Thinking is very far from knowing. 1855:
Bohn, 528.

**11. Think nothing mean that brings in an
honest penny.** 1763: Murphy, *Citizen*, I ii.

12. Think of a cuckold. *See* **Cuckold** (9).

13. Think of ease, but work on. 1640: *Herbert,
Jac. Prudentum.* 1670: Ray, 8.

14. Think on the end before you begin. Before
1300: *Cursor Mundi*, l. 4379, For qua [who] be-
gynne wil any thing euer-mare think on the
endinge. *c.*1400: *Beryn*, 55 (E.E.T.S.), Who take
hede of the begynnyng, what fal shal of the ende,
He leyith a bussh to-fore the gap, ther fortune
wold in ryde. *c.*1470: G. Ashby, *Poems*, 39
(E.E.T.S.), In al your maters, er ye bygynne,
Thenke what ende wol be the conclusion. 1556:
Heywood, *Spider and Flie*, cap. 59, p. 254
(Farmer), This sage saying, the wise have said
and say, – Have an eye to the end, ere thou aught
begin. 1692: L'Estrange, *Aesop*, 81 (3rd ed.). It is
wisdom to consider the end of things before we
embarque, and to forecast consequences. 1704:
Swift, *Tale of a Tub*, § vii, Thus human life is
best understood, by the wise man's rule, of
regarding the end.

15. Think today and speak tomorrow. 1855:
Bohn, 528. *See also* **Think** (9).

16. Think well of all men. 1659: Howell, 10.

**17. To think one's farthing, halfpenny, penny,
good silver.** *See* **Farthing; Halfpenny;** and
Penny (26).

Third heir. *See* **Ill-gotten goods.**

Third time is never like the rest, The. 1875:
Cheales, *Proverb. Folk-Lore*, 133.

Third time lucky. *c.*1840: R. Browning, *Letter*
(1933), 5, 'the luck of the third adventure' is
proverbial. 1882: R.L. Stevenson, *New Arabian
Nights*, II 59, 'The next time we come to blows –
'Will make it the third,' I interrupted ... 'Ay true
... Well the third time's lucky.'

Third time pays for all, The. 1575: Higgins,
Mirr. for Magis.,Pt I: 'Q. Elstride', st. 23, Which
I haue prou'd, therefore the sequel vewe, The
third payes home, this prouerbe is so true. 1599:
Warning for Faire Women, II. 1855: Gaskell,
North and South, ch xvii, 'This is th' third strike
I've seen,' laid she ... 'Well, third time pays for
all.' 1922: *Punch*, 20 Dec., p. 594, col. 3, Mrs
Ellison has already been twice married. The
third time pays for all, so they say.

Thirty days hath September. *See* quots. 1572:
Grafton, *Chron.*, sig. Ff2 v°, Thirty dayes hath
Nouember, Aprill, Iune and September.
February hath xxviij alone, and all the rest have
xxxi. 1577: Holinshed, *Chron.*, 119 [as in 1572,
with addition: 'But in the leape you must adde
one']. 1601: *Ret. from Parnassus*, III i 37 (Arber),
S. *Rad.* How many dayes hath September? *Im.*
Aprill, Iune and Nouember, February hath 28
alone and all the rest hath 30 and one. 1615: A.
Hopton, *Concordancy of Yeares*, 60, Thirtie
dayes hath September, Aprill, Iune, and
November: The rest haue thirtie and one, Saue
February alone Which moneth hath but eight
and twenty meere, Saue when it's bissextile, or
leap-yeare. 1664: *Poor Robin Alman.*, Thirty
days hath September, April, June, and
November, All the rest thirty and one, as I
plainly remember; Onely February hath but
twenty and eight for its store, Except when
tis leap-year, then it hath one more. *c.*1703:
Young Man's Companion, quoted in Denham,
Proverbs, 19 (Percy S.), Thirty days hath
September, April, June, and November;
February eight-and-twenty all alone, And all
the rest have thirty-and-one; Unless that leap-
year doth combine, And give to February
twenty-nine.

This is that must neades be, Quoth the good man, whenn he made his wyfe Pine the bakit. 1579: *Marr. of Wit and Wisdom*, sc iii p. 27 (SH.S.).

Thistle and **Thistles. 1. A thistle is a fat salad for an ass's mouth.** 1732: Fuller, 435.

2. Cut thistles. *See* quots. 1882: Mrs Chamberlain, *W. Worcs. Words*, 38 (E.D.S.), Cut thistles in May They grow in a day. Cut them in June That is too soon. Cut them in July, Then they will die. 1883: Burne, *Shropsh. Folk-Lore*, 579, Cut 'em in June, They'll come again soon. Cut 'em in July, They *may* die. Cut 'em in August, Die they *must*. 1893: Inwards, *Weather Lore*, 156 [as in 1883].

See also **St John.**

Thither as I would go I can go late, Thither as I would not go I know not the gate. 1678: Ray, 296.

Thorn and **Thorns, 1. He that goes barefoot must not plant thorns.** 1611: Cotgrave, s.v. 'Pied'. 1640: Herbert, *Jac. Prudentum*. 1670: Ray, 2, Barefooted men need not tread on thorns. 1732: Fuller, 840, Barefoot must not go among thorns. Ibid., No. 2289, He that scattereth thorns must not go barefoot. 1874: Waugh, in *Manchester Critic*, 14 March, Barfoot folk shouldn't walk upo' prickles. 1901: F. E. Taylor, *Lancs Sayings*, 7 [as in 1874].

2. He that handles thorns shall prick his fingers. 1616: Breton, *Works*, ii e6 (Grosart). 1694: D'Urfey, *Quixote*, Pt I Act III sc ii. 1732: Fuller, 2128, He that handles thorns shall smart for it.

3. I'll not pull the thorn out of your foot and put it into my own. 1659: Howell, *Proverbs: Brit.-Eng.*, 24, I'le never thorn draw from others foot, and having pulld it in mine own put. 1678: Ray, 273. 1753: Richardson, *Grandison*, ii 126 (1883), I should only have taken a thorn out of the foot of another, and put it into my own.

4. Most men have a thorn at their door. 1639: Clarke, 165, Where ever a man dwell he shall be sure to have a thorne-bush neare his doore. 1670: Ray, 149 [as in 1639]. 1732: Fuller, 3469. *c.*1800: J. Trusler, *Proverbs in Verse*, 94, Where'er a man dwells, there's a thorn at his door. 1869: Spurgeon, *John Ploughman*, ch i, Wherever a man lives he is sure to have one thorn-bush near his door, and it is a mercy if there are not two.

5. The thorn comes forth with the point forwards. 1640: Herbert, *Jac.Prudentum*. 1670: Ray, 26.

6. Thorns make the greatest crackling. 1732: Fuller, 5031.

7. Thorns whiten yet do nothing. 1640: Herbert, *Jac. Prudentum*.

8. To sit or stand upon thorns = To be impatient. 1528: More, in *Works*, p. 234, col. 1 (1557), I long by my trouth, quod he, and euen syt on thornes tyll I see that constitucion. 1567: Golding, *Ovid*, bk iv. l. 385, She thought she stoode on thornes untill she went to him. 1633: Massinger, *New Way*, III iii, She ... sitts on thornes till she be private with him. 1636: T. Heywood, *Challenge for Beauty*, III, I stand on thornes till I be in action. 1764: Mrs F. Sheridan, *Dupe*, I ii, The captain will be on thorns till he sees me. 1823: Scott, *Q. Durward*, ch vii, Lord Crawford ... sat as it were on thorns at the royal board. 1886: Elworthy, *W. Som. Word-Book*, 751 (E.D.S.), She has been all upon thorns ever since. 1926: Phillpotts, *Peacock House*, 222, I was on thorns till us met again.

See also **Candlemas, B; No rose;** and **Oak** (3).

Thought, *subs.* **1. The thought hath good legs, and the quill a good tongue.** 1640: Herbert, *Jac. Prudentum*. 1670: Ray, 26. 1732: Fuller, 4790 ['wings' for 'legs'].

2. Thought is free. *c.*1390: Gower, *Conf. Amantis*, bk v l. 4485, I have herd seid that thoght is fre. *c.*1490: *Partonope*, 440 (E.E.T.S.), Therfore this proverbe is seide full truly: Thought to a man is euer ffre. Before 1529: Skelton, *Philip Sparrow*, l. 1201, Thought is franke and fre. 1605: Camden, *Remains*, 332 (1870), Thoughts are free from toll. 1638: Randolph, *Muses' Looking-Glass*, III iv, And yet some think (But thought is free) ... 1860: Reade, *Cl. and Hearth*, ch lii, 'I say not that,' ... 'You do but think it.' 'Thought is free.'

3. Your thoughts close and your countenance loose. 1651: Herbert, *Jac. Prudentum*, 2nd ed.

See also **Second thoughts.**

Thousand pounds and a bottle of hay, is all one at Doomsday, A. 1659: Howell, 4. 1670: Ray, 26. 1732: Fuller, 6398.

Thrash in another man's barn, To. *c.*1400: *Ragm. Roll*, l. 53, in Hazlitt, *Early Pop. Poetry*, i 72, And whoo so lyst may thressyn in your berne.

Thread, *subs.* **1. A thread too fine spun will easily break.** 1732: Fuller, 438.

2. The thread breaks where it is weakest. 1640: Herbert, *Jac. Prudentum.* 1670: Ray, 28. 1732: Fuller, 5647.

3. Thread is spun. 1681: in *Roxb. Ballads*, v 45, Give them what they deserve, their thread is spun. 1819: Scott, *Ivanhoe*, ch xxiv, Fare-thee-well, I say. My thread is spun out – thy task is yet to begin.

Thread-bare coat is armour-proof against highwaymen, A. 1732: Fuller, 437.

Threatened folks live long. *c.*1555: in Collmann, *Ballads, etc.*, 69 (Roxb.Cl), It is a true prouerbe: the threatned man lyues long. 1599: Porter, *Two Angry Women*, in Hazlitt, *Old Plays*, vii 357. 1630: Taylor (Water-Poet), *Works*, 2nd pagin., 152. 1734: Fielding, *Don Quix. in England*, II vi. 1819: Scott, *Leg. of Montrose*, ch *x*. 1870: Dickens, *Drood*, ch xiv, 'The proverb says that threatened men live long,' he tells her lightly.

Threatens many that is injurious to one, He. *c.*1590; G. Harvey, *Marginalia*, 101 (1913), He threatenith many, That hurtith any. 1732: Fuller, 2372.

Threats without power are like powder without ball. 1736: Bailey, *Dict.*, s.v.

Three are too many to keep a secret, and too few to be merry. 1732: Fuller, 5037.

Three bites. *See* **Two bites.**

Three days. *See* **Fish,** *subs.* (1).

Three dear years will raise a baker's daughter to a portion. 1678: Ray, 86. Three flails and cuckoo. 1917: Bridge, *Cheshire Proverbs*, 123, A farmer who at the return of the cuckoo can keep three flails at work cannot … be otherwise than prosperous.

Three great evils come out of the North, a cold wind, a cunning knave, and shrinking cloth. 1614: Jonson, *Bart. Fair*, IV iii, Do my northern cloth zhrink i' the wetting, ha? 1659: Howell, 1, Three ills come from the North, a cold wind, a shrinking cloth, and a dissembling man. 1670: Ray, 19 [as in 1659]. 1683: Meriton, *Yorkshire Ale*, 83–7 (1697). 1846–59: *Denham Tracts*, ii 75 (F.L.S.). Cf. **Cold weather.**

Three-half-pence and twopence = a canter. 1886: Elworthy, *West Som. Word-Book*, 212 (E.D.S.), Dree-half-pence and two-pence … a slow ambling canter. 1896: Graham, *Red Scaur*,

35 (W.), They can hear the … 'three-ha'-pence for tuppence' of a cantering horse.

Three helping one another bear the burden of six. 1640: Herbert, *Jac. Prudentum.*

Three hungry meals. *See* **Two hungry meals.**

Three may keep counsel if two be away. 1546: Heywood, *Proverbs*, Pt II ch v. 1692: L'Estrange, *Aesop*, 399 (3rd ed.) ['when' for 'if']. *c.*1736: Franklin, in *Works*, i 455 (Bigelow), Three may keep a secret, if two of them are dead.

Three merry men. The burden of an old ballad. 1595: Peele, *Old Wives Tale*, sc i, Let us rehearse the old prouerb: 'Three merry men, and three merry men, And three merry men be we; I in the wood, and thou on the ground, And Jack sleeps in the tree'. 1613: B.&F., *Knight of Burning Pestle*, II viii, *Mer.* [*sings*] I am three merry men, and three merry men! *c.*1630: B.&F., *Bloody Brother*, III ii, *Chorus.* Three merry boys, and three merry boys, And three merry boys are we.

Threepence, If you make not much of, you'll never be worth a groat. 1678: Ray, 210. 1732: Fuller, 2771.

Threepenny planet, To be born under a. *See* quots. 1607: Dekker, *Knight's Conjuring*, 32 (Percy S.), All such rich mens darlings are either christened by some left-handed priest, or els born vnder a threepenny planet. 1692: L'Estrange, *Aesop*, 416 (3rd ed.), I'll … make good the old saying to you; *That he that's born under a three-penny planet, shall never be worth a groat.* 1694: Dryden, *Love Triumphant*, I i, And yet his good fortune, and my rascally, threepenny planet, make me suspicious without reason. 1738: Swift, *Polite Convers.*, Dial. I, Egad, I was born under a threepenny planet, never to be worth a groat. 1883: Burne, *Shropsh. Folk-Lore*, 589 [as in 1738]. 1894: Northall, *Folk Phrases*, 15 (E.D.S.), He was born under a threepenny planet, i.e. is avaricious, a curmudgeon. 1901: F. E. Taylor, *Lancs Sayings*, 7 [as in 1692, very slightly varied].

Three removes are as bad as a fire. 1736: Franklin, *Way to Wealth*, in *Works*, i 445 (Bigelow). 1790: Grose, *Prov. Gloss.*, s.v. 'Flit', Two flittings are as bad as one fire. 1881: Evans, *Leics. Words*, 237 (E.D.S.), 'Thray shifts are as bad as a foire', is the Leicestershire form of the common proverb. 1925: *Punch*, 11 Nov., p. 505, col. 3.

Three sisters, The. 1662: Fuller, *Worthies*, iii 548 (1840), 'The three sisters', being a common by-word to express the three rivers of Wye, Severn, Rhiddiall, arising all three in this county [Montgomery].

Three skips of a louse = no value. 1633: Jonson, *Tale of a Tub*, II i, I care not I, sir, not three skips of a louse. Before 1674: in *Roxb. Ballads*, viii 426 (B.S.), And temper it with three leaps of a lowse. 1700: Swift, in *Works*, xiv. 57 (Scott), 'Tis not that I value the money three skips of a louse. 1769: Murphy, in *Garrick Corresp.*, i 340 (1831), I'd cudgel him back, breast and belly for three skips of a louse!

Three slips for a tester – three counterfeit twopenny coins for a sixpence = to give the slip. 1627: F. Grove, *A Quip for a Scornful Lasse, òr, Three Slips for a Tester* [title of ballad]. 1655: *Faithful Post*, 7–14 Sept, He wanted agility of body to give them three slips for a tester. 1678: Ray, 82, Two slips for a tester. *c.*1685: *Roxb. Ballads*, vi 233 (B.S.), *The Forlorn Lover; Declaring how a Lass gave her Love Three Slips for a Tester* [title of ballad], and married another a week before Easter.

Three straws on a staff would make a baby cry and laugh. 1869: Hazlitt, 403.

Three tailors. *See* **Nine tailors**.

Three things a man may be deceived, In. 1736: Bailey, *Dict.*, s.v. 'Three', In three things a man may be easily deceiv'd, viz. In a man, till known, A tree till down, and the day till done.

Three things are not to be credited. 1616: B. Rich, *Ladies Looking Glasse*, 34, There are three things that are not to be credited, a woman when she weeps, a merchant when he sweares, nor a drunkard when he prayes.

Three things are nought worth, fayre face in a whore, Great strength in a porter, fine witt in the poore. 1591: Florio, *Second Frutes*, 191.

Three things are thrown away in a bowling green, namely, time, money and oaths. 1822: Scott, *Nigel*, ch xii, Thus making good the saying, that three, etc.

Three things are to small purpose, if the fourth be away. *c.*1597: Deloney, *Iacke of Newberie*, ch i [cited as 'an old saying'].

Three things are unsatiable, priests, monckes, and the sea. *c.*1560: in Wright, *Songs, etc., Philip and Mary*, 208 (Roxb.Cl).

Three things are untameable, Idiots, women and the salt sea. 1875: Cheales, *Proverb. Folk-Lore*, 8.

Three things cost dear: the caresses of a dog, the love of a mistress, and the invasion of a host. 1855: Bohn, 530.

Three things drive a man out of his house: smoke, rain, and a scolding wife. [Skeat, in a note on *P. Plowman*, C, xx. 297, says: 'Perhaps the original form of this commonly quoted proverb is this: 'tria sunt enim quae non sinunt hominem in domo permanere; fumus, stillicidium, et mala uxor' '(Innocens Papa, *de Contemptu Mundi*, i 18). It is a mere compilation from *Proverbs* x 26, xix. 13, and xxvii 15.] 1377: Langland, *Plowman*, B, xvii 315, Thre thinges there ben that doth a man by strengthe Forto fleen his owne hous as holywryt sheweth. That one is a wikked wyf that wil nought be chasted; Her fiere fleeth fro hyr for fere of her tonge. And if his hous be vnhiled and reyne on his bedde, He seketh and seketh til he slepe drye. And whan smoke and smolder smyt in his syghte, It doth hym worse than his wyf or wete to slepe. *c.*1386: Chaucer, *Melibeus*, § 15, Of whiche wommen, men seyn that 'three thinges dryven a man out of his hous; that is to seyn, smoke, dropping of reyn, and wikked wyves'. *c.*1530: *EvyllMaryage* l.96, in Hazlitt, *EarlyPop. Poetry*, iv 78, And Salamon sayth there be thynges thre, Shrewde wyues, rayne, and smokes blake Make husbandes ofte theyr houses to forsake. 1576: Gascoigne, *Works*, ii 227 (Cunliffe), There are three thinges that suffer not a man to abyde in his owne house. Smooke, rayne, and an evil wyfe. 1590: Greene, *Works*, vii 249, Foure things driues a man from hys house. 1. Too much smoke. 2. A dropping roofe. 3. A fylthie ayre. 4. And a brawling woman. 1597: Shakespeare, 1 *Henry IV*, III i, O, he is as tedious As a tired horse, a railing wife; Worse than a smoky house. 1619: *Helpe to Discourse*, 84 (1640), A smoke, a storme, and a contentious wife, Three ils are found, that tire a husbands life: To which, a fourth is by the proverb sed, When children cry for hunger, wanting bread. 1869: Spurgeon, *John Ploughman*, ch xii, Poverty is hard, but debt is horrible; a man might as well have a smoky house and a scolding wife, which are said to be the two worst evils of our life.

Three things that are not to be lent. *See* **Lend** (5)

Three things that never comes to no good, There be – Christmas pigs, Michaelmas fowls,

and parsons' daughters. Mon. 1882: *N.&Q.*, 6th ser, vi 246.

Three things there be full hard to be known. 1417: in *Reliq. Antiquae*, i 233 (1841), There been thre thinges full harde to be knowen which waye they woll drawe. The first is of a birde sitting upon a bough. The second is of a vessell in the see. And the thirde is the waye of a younge man. 1486: *Boke of St Albans*, sig. f4, Ther be iiii thynges full harde for to know, Wyche way that thay will drawe. The first is the wayes of a yong man. The secunde the cours of a vessayll in the see. The thridde of an edder or a serpent sprent. The iiii of a fowle sittyng on any thyng.

Three things there be which neuer decay whiles the world lasteth, to bake, to brewe, and to powle or sheare, saye the people, or common prouerbe. 1586: L. Evans, *Withals Dict. Revised*, sig. E4.

Three to one. *See* **Two to one.**

Three ways – the universities, the sea, the court, There are. 1612: Shelton, *Quixote*, Pt I bk iv ch xii, There is an old proverb … and it is this, 'The Church, the Sea, or the Court'. 1640: Herbert, *Jac. Prudentum*.

Three women. *See* **Woman** (36).

Three words, At (or In). *See* quots. 1633: Draxe, 10, At three words, he is at the top of the house [i.e. he is greatly excited]. 1659: Howell, 15, In three words she is at the roof of the house.

Thresher take his flail, Let the. *See* quots. 1626: Breton, *Fantasticks*, 10 (Grosart), It is now November, and according to the old prouerbe, Let the thresher take his flayle, And the ship no more sayle. 1661: M. Stevenson, *Twelve Moneths*, 51 [as in 1626]. 1675: *Poor Robin Alman. Prognost.*, sig. C7 [as in 1626]. 1732: Fuller, 6221, November, take flail, Let ships no more sail.

Thrift, subs. 1. Their thrift waxes thin, That spend more than they win. c.1460: *How the Good Wife*, l. 100 ['His' for 'Their']. 1597: *North. Mothers Blessing*, in *Plasidas, etc.*, 167 (Roxb.Cl).

2. Thrift and he are at a fray. 1546: Heywood, *Proverbs*, Pt I ch xi, Whan thrift and you fell fyrst at a fray. You played the man, for ye made thrift ren away. 1670: Ray, 196.

3. Thrift is good revenue. 1659: Howell, *Proverbs: Fr.-Eng.*, 15, Parsimony is the best revenue. 1855: Bohn, 530.

4. Thrift is the philosopher's stone. 1732: Fuller, 5040.

5. Thy thrift is thy friend's mirth. c.1460: *How the Good Wife*, l. 170, Thi thrifte is thi frendis myrthe.

6. When thrift is in the town, he is in the field – or vice versa. 1546: Heywood, *Proverbs*, Pt II ch ix. c.1594: Bacon, *Promus*, No. 675. 1670: Ray, 196.

Thrive, verb. 1. He that thinketh to thrive by hope, may happen to beg in misery. 1647: *Countrym. New Commonwealth*, 23.

2. He that will thrive must ask leave of his wife. c.1470: *Songs and Carols*, 87 (Percy S., No. 73), Fore he that cast hym for to thryve, He must ask off hys wiffe leve. 1523: Fitzherbert, *Husbandry*, 93 (E.D.S.), There is an olde common sayenge, that seldom doth the housbande thryue, withoute the leue of his wyfe. 1669: D. North, *Obs. and Adv. Oeconom.*, 4. 1784: Franklin, *Autobiog.*, in *Works*, i 171 (Biglotw). 1875: Smiles, *Thrift*, 144.

3. He that will thrive must rise at five; He that hath thriven may lie till seven. c.1590: G. Harvey, *Marginalia*, 102 (1913), [as above, *plus*] He that will neuer thryuen may lye till aleuen. 1647: *Countrym. New Commonwealth*, 42 [as in 1590]. 1670: Ray, 148. 1732: Fuller, 6094. 1750: W. Ellis, *Housewife's Companion*, vii, To rise at five is the way to thrive. 1883: Burne, *Shropsh. Folk-Lore*, 578, Them as 'oon thrive Man rise at five, Them as han thruven May lie till seven. 1913: E. M. Wright, *Rustic Speech, etc.*, 173 [as in 1883].

4. He thrives well that God loves. c.1460: *How the Good Wife*, l. 10, Wele thryuethe that God loueth.

Throng [Busy] **as Throp's wife, As**. 1828: Carr, *Craven Dialect*, ii 201, 'As thrang as Throop wife, when she hang'd hersell in her garter', a proverbial simile applied to those who are very busy in trifling things. 1849: F. T. Dinsdale, *Teesdale Gloss.*, 134, There is a phrase, 'As thrang as Throp's wife 'at hanged hersell i' t' dish-clout'. 1892: *N.&Q.*, 8th ser, i 12, I have heard the saying 'I'm as throng as Throp's wife, in Yorkshire, and only a few days ago. 1900: *N.&Q.*, 9th ser, v 414, 'As busy as Throp's wife' – This is a saying current in the dales of North Derbyshire and West Yorkshire. Ibid., 527, In South Notts (where 'throng' =busy is very common) there is a variant, 'As busy as Beck's wife'. Cf. **Thrunk.**

Through stitch, To go = To do a thing thoroughly. 1579: Gosson, *Sch. of Abuse*, 68 (Arber), Philippe of Macedon ... was not able to go thorowe stitche. 1593: Nashe, *Works*, ii 205 (Grosart), What reason haue I ... but to go through stitch with you, as well as him? 1670: Cotton, *Scarronides*, bk iv, Who means to conquer Italy, Must with his work go thorough stitches. 1712: Motteux, *Quixote*, Pt I bk iii ch xi, If you must needs be knocking your noddle, to go through stitch with this ugly job. 1785: Grose, *Class. Dict. Vulgar Tongue*, s.v., To go thorough stitch, to stick at nothing. 1828: Carr, *Craven Dialect*, ii 169, 'To go through stitch', to accomplish a business completely.

Throw, *verb.* **1. Don't throw.** *See* quot. 1883: Burne, *Shropsh. Folk-Lore*, 589, Don't throw your property out through the door with a spade, while your husband is bringing it in through the window with a spoon.

2. Don't throw away dirty water until you have got clean. *See* **Dirty** (5).

3. He that is thrown would ever wrestle. 1640: Herbert, *Jac. Prudentum.* 1732: Fuller, 2196.

4. He who will throw a stone at every dog. *See* quots. *c.*1555: in Collmann. *Ballads, etc.*, 68 (Roxb.Cl), Who flynges a stone at euery dogge, which barketh in the strete, Shall neuer haue a iust reuenge, nor have a pacient sprete. 1575: Gascoigne, *Posies*, in *Works*, i 6 (Cunliffe), He who will throw a stone at everie dogge which barketh, had neede of a great satchell or pocket.

5. Not to have – this or that – **to throw at a dog.** 1546: Heywood, *Proverbs*, Pt II ch vii, To be unable to give a dog a loaf. 1600: Day, *Blind Beggar*, III ii, I have not a horse to cast at a dog, man, not I. 1600: Shakespeare, *Merry Wives*, I iv, He shall not have a stone to throw at his dog. 1607: Heywood, *Fair Maide*, in *Works*, ii 54 (1874), I am not furnish'd of a courting phrase, to throw at a dogge. 1738: Swift, *Polite Convers.*, Dial. I, Here's miss, has not a word to throw at a dog. 1765: Bickerstaff, *Maid of the Mill*, II i, She was struck all of a heap – she had not a word to throw to a dog. 1850: Dickens, *Copperfield*, ch i, It is nothing to say that he hadn't a word to throw at a dog. He couldn't have *thrown* a word at a mad dog. 1884: R.L.S. and Henley, *Beau Austin*, I i, She falls away, has not a word to throw at a dog, and is ridiculously pale.

6. Thrown stone or **spoken word.** *See* quots.

1633: Draxe, 240, A word and a stone let goe, cannot be called backe. 1732: Fuller, 485 [as in 1633]. 1875: Cheales, *Proverb. Folk-Lore*, 88 [as in 1633, but with 'recalled' for 'called backe']. 1924: J. L. Garvin, in *Observer*, 12 Oct., p. 12, col. 3, Never more, says the old proverb, comes back the thrown stone or the spoken word.

7. To throw the baby out with the bathwater. A more modern variant of (9), though known in German from at least the beginning of the sixteenth century. [Cf. J. Kepler *Tertius Interveniens, Das ist Warnung ... das sie ... nicht das Kindt mit dem Badt ausschütten* (This is a warning not to tip out the child with the bathwater)] 1853: T. Carlyle, *Nigger Question* (ed. 2), 29, The Germans say, 'You must empty out the bathing-tub, but not the baby along with it'. ... How to abolish the abuses of slavery, and save the precious thing in it. 1911: G.B. Shaw, *Getting Married* (Preface), 186, We shall in a very literal sense empty the baby out with the bath by abolishing an institution which needs nothing more than a little ... rationalising to make it ... useful. 1957: Ernest Gowers *H. W. Fowler* 14 We can rid ourselves of those grammarians' fetishes which make it more difficult to be intelligible without throwing the baby away with the bath-water.

8. To throw snot about = To weep. 1678: Ray, 82.

9. To throw the helve after the hatchet. 1546: Heywood, *Proverbs*, Pt II ch ix, For here I sende thaxe after the helue awaie. 1587: J. Bridges, *Def. of Govt. in Ch. of England*, 90, If the axe were gone, is this the remedy, to hurle the helve after it? 1685–6: Cotton, *Montaigne*, bk iii ch ix, I abandon myself through despair ... and, as the saying is, 'throw the helve after the hatchet'. 1712: Motteux, *Quixote*, Pt II ch ix. 1829: Scott, *Journal*, 26 April, At night I flung helve after hatchet, and spent the evening in reading the *Doom of Devorgoil* to the girls. 1921: *Observer*, 10 April, p. 10, col. 5, The worst of democracy, as Lord Bryce might admit, is the combination of power and ignorance. Passion is born from the imagination of the thing that is not, and the helve is flung after the hatchet.

10. To throw the house out of the windows. *See* **House** (16).

11. To throw the stone and hide the hand. 1732: Fuller, 5246.

12. To throw water. *See* **Cast** (8).

Thrunk [Crowded] at **Chiddle Wakes, no room areawt, As.** 1917: Bridge, *Cheshire Proverbs*, 24 ['areawt' = out of doors].

Thrunk as Eccles wakes, As. 1901: F. E. Taylor, *Lancs Sayings*, 4.

Thrunk (or Thrang) as three in a bed, As. 1828: Carr, *Craven Dialect*, ii 201, Crowded, 'as thrang as three in a bed'. 1884: *N. & Q.*, 6th ser, x 227, In Yorkshire the expression is 'as thrang as three i' a bed'. 1917: Bridge, *Cheshire Proverbs*, 25. Cf. **Thick as three in a bed**; and **Throng**.

Thrush, avoiding the trap, fell into bird-lime, The. 1732: Fuller, 4792.

Thrushes. *See* **Wish** (3).

Thumb. *See* **Finger** (2), (8), and (11).

Thunder, *subs.* **1. Early thunder, early spring.** 1893: Inwards, *Weather Lore*, 7.

2. If it sinks. *See* quot. 1874: *N. & Q.*, 5th ser, ii 184, If it sinks from the north, It will double its wrath; If it sinks from the south, It will open its mouth; If it sinks from the west, It is never at rest; If it sinks from the east, It will leave us in peace (Kent). 1893: Inwards, 118 [as in 1874].

3. The first thunder of the year awakes All the frogs and all the snakes. Ibid., 117.

4. Thunder in spring Cold will bring. Ibid., 7.

See also **All Fools' Day; April** (24) and (26); **December; Lightning; March** (18), (36), and (48); **May,** F (13) and (25); **November** (8); **Poppies; Shrovetide** (2); **Summer** (5); and **Winter** (7) and (13)–(19).

Thunderbolt hath but its clap, The. 1633: Draxe, 216. 1670: Ray, 148. 1732: Fuller, 4793, The thunder hath but its clap.

Thursday. 1. On Thursday at three Look out, and you'll see What Friday will be. S. Devon. 1893: Inwards, *Weather Lore*, 42.

2. Thursday come, The week's gone. 1640: Herbert, *Jac. Prudentum*, Thursday come, and the week is gone. 1666: Torriano, *Piazza Univ.*, 103, The Thursday come, the week lost. 1878: Dyer, *Eng. Folk-Lore*, 241, Working people are wont to say: – 'Thursday come, The week's gone'.

Thynne. *See* **Horner.**

Tib. A generic name for a girl, as Tom for a boy. *He struck at Tib, but down fell Tom.* 1639: Clarke, 1, [with alternative] but struck downe Tom. 1670: Ray, 196. 1732: Fuller, 2029 [with 'Tim' for 'Tom'].

Tibberton. *See* quot. 1882: Mrs Chamberlain, *W. Worcs. Words*, 39 (E.D.S.), A stone church, a wooden steeple, A drunken parson, a wicked people, is a proverb at Tibberton.

Tib's eve, neither before nor after Christmas. One of the many euphemisms for 'never'. 1785: Grose, *Class. Dict. Vulgar Tongue*, s.v. 'Tib', He will pay you on St Tibbs Eve (Irish). 1854: Baker, *Northants Gloss.*, s.v. 1861: *N. & Q.*, 2nd ser, xi 269, St Tib's Eve is used in Cornwall as equivalent to 'the Greek Kalends'. 1916: B. Duffy, *The Counter-Charm*, 8, If you were boiled in soap from this till Tibb's Eve, you'd be just as sooty.

Tickhill, God help me. 1850: *N. & Q.*, 1st ser, i 247, Can any one tell why a Tickhill man, when asked where he comes from, says, 'Tickhill, God help me'? 1888: S. O. Addy, *Sheffield Gloss.*, 259 (E.D.S.), In speaking to a stranger … a Bawtry man will say of a Tickhill man, 'Oh, he comes from Tickhill-God-help-him', as if nobody need wonder at a Tickhill man's actions.

Tickle my throat with a feather, and make a fool of my stomach. 1678: Ray, 210.

Tid, Mid, Misera. *See* quots. 1788: *Gent. Mag.*, i 188, We have in Northumberland the following couplet, which gives name to every Sunday in Lent, except the first: Tid, and Mid, and Misera, Carting, Palm, and Good-pas-day. 1825: Hone, *Ev. Day Book*, i 379, Tid, Mid, Misera, Calling, Palm, Paste Egg Day.

Tide, *subs.* **1. The tide keeps its course.** 1659: Howell, 10.

2. The tide never goes out so far but it always comes in again. 1864: 'Cornish Proverbs', in *N. & Q.*, 3rd ser, vi. 494.

3. The tide tarries no man. *c.*1440: Lydgate, *Fall of Princes*, bk iii l. 2801 (E.E.T.S.), The tid abit nat for no maner man. 15th cent.: in *Rdiq. Antiquae*, i 268 (1841), Farewele, my frendis, the tide abideth no man. *c.*1530: *Everyman*, in Hazlitt, *Old Plays*, i 105, For, wit thou well, the tide abideth no man. 1546: Heywood, *Proverbs*, Pt I ch iii. 1591: Lyly, *Endymion*, IV ii. 1611: T. Ravenscroft, *Meismata*, sig. B4. Cf. **Time** (15).

4. The tide will fetch away what the ebb brings. 1670: Ray, 26. 1732: Fuller, 4495, The ebb will fetch off what the tide brings in.

See also **Rain,** *verb* (3); and **Rising.**

Tidings make either glad or sad. 1639: Clarke, 229. 1670: Ray, 148.

Tie a knot with the tongue. See **Knot** (2).

Tied by the tooth. 1917: Bridge, *Cheshire*

Proverbs, 124, Sheep and cattle will not break through fences or try to wander if the pasture of the field in which they are grazing is very good. They are 'tied by the tooth'.

Tie it well and let it go. 1640: Herbert, *Jac. Prudentum*.

Tiger. *See* **Rides.**

Tight as a drum, As. 1720: Gay, *Poems*, ii 279 (Underhill), No drum was ever tighter. 1857: Hughes, *Tom Brown*, Pt I ch iv, Tom has eaten … till his little skin is as tight as a drum.

Tight boots, To sin in = To be ill at ease with your host. 1855: Bohn, 543.

Time, *subs.* **1. As good have no time, as make no good use of it.** 1732: Fuller, 686.

2. He that has most time has none to lose. Ibid., No. 2141.

3. He that hath time and looketh for a better time, loseth time. 1578: Florio, *First Fruites*, fo. 28, Who hath tyme and tarieth for time, looseth tyme. 1605: Camden, *Remains*, 323 (1870) [with 'better' omitted]. 1651: Herbert, *Jac. Prudentum*, 2nd ed. … [ending] time comes that he repents himself of time. 1732: Fuller, 2162. 1869: Spurgeon, *John Ploughman*, ch vii [as in 1651].

4. He that hath time hath life. 1578: Florio, *First Fruites*, fo. 28, Who hath tyme hath life. 1596: Nashe, *Works*, iii 70 (Grosart). 1629: *Book of Meery Riddles*, Prov. 14. 1736: Franklin, *Way to Wealth*, in *Works*, i 443 (Bigelow). Then do not squander time, for that is the stuff life is made of.

5. In time of prosperity. *See* **Prosperity.**

6. It is time to yoke when the cart comes to the caples [horses]. Cheshire. 1670: Ray, 48. 1852: *N.&Q.*, 1st ser, vi 386. 1917: Bridge, *Cheshire Proverbs*, 84.

7. Take time (or occasion) by the forelock. Meaning to seize the moment or the opportunity, and based on the ancient image of time as explained in quot. 1539. 1539: R. Taverner, *Proverbs or Adagies out of Erasmus*, C4v, They made her [Time] a goddesse … beynge on the former part of her hed all heavy and on the hynder part balde, so that by the fore parte she may be easily caughte, but by the hynder parte, not so. 1548: Hall, *Chronicle* (1809), 24, It is wisdome to take occasion when the hery side and not the bald side is proferd. 1591: Greene, *Farewell to Folly*, in *Works*, ix. 311, Take time now by the forehead, she is bald

behinde. 1595: Spenser, *Sonnets*, lxx. Tell her the ioyous time wil not be staid, Unlesse she doe him by the forelock take. 1624: T. Heywood, *Captives*, III iii, Loose not this advantadge, But take tyme by the fore-topp. 1767: Brooke, *Fool of Quality*, ii 252, O, then we may take good-man time by the forelock.1824: Scott, *St Ronan's Well*, ch 26, Time was – time is – and if I catch it not by the forelock as it passes, time will be no more. 1882: Blackmore, *Christowell*, ch 47, He had taken time by the forelock now, so far as to seize and hide the cash-box, before the intrusion of the lawyers.

8. Take time when time cometh, for time will away. Before 1529: Skelton, *Works*, i 137 (Dyce), Take tyme when tyme is, for tyme is ay mutable. 1595: A. Montgomery, *Cherrie and Slae*, St 36, Tak time in time, ere time be tint For time will not remain. 1670: Ray, 149 ['is' for 'cometh']. 1732: Fuller, 4313 [as in 1670]. 1846: Denham, *Proverbs*, 5 (Percy S.) [as in 1670].

9. There is a time for everything (or for all things). [Allusion to Ecclesiastes iii.1, To every thing there is a season.]1399: Langland, *Rick, the Redeless*, iii 278, But all thinge hath tyme. 1509: Bp. Fisher, *Eng. Works*, 174 (E.E.T.S.), Euery thynge hath a tyme. 1591: Shakespeare, *Com. of Errors*, II ii. 1605: Chapman, *All Fools*, V ii, For as much, Valerius, as everything has time. 1732: Fuller, 1466, 'Every thing hath its time, and that time must be watch'd. 1818: J. Austen, *Northanger Abbey*, xxx, Your head runs too much upon bath; but there is a time for everything – a time for balls … and a time for work.1861: Peacock, *Gryll Grange*, ch xiii, He held that there was a time for all things. 1926: *Punch*, 28 July, p. 92, col. 2, Nay, nay, there be a time for all things.

10. There is a time to speak, and a time to be silent. [Allusion to Ecclesiastes iii.7, A time to keep silence, and a time to speak.]1485: Caxton, *Charles the Grete*, 56 (E.E.T.S.), Thou knowest the comyn prouerbe that sayth that there is a tyme of spekyng and tyme of beyng stylle. 1523–5: Berners, *Froissart*, ch cccxlviii, John Lyon … sayd, Ther is tyme to be styll and tyme to speke. 1633: Draxe, 190, There is a time to speake and a time to holde ones peace.

11. There is a time to wink, as well as to see. 1732: Fuller, 4885.

12. Time and chance happen to all men. 1709:

O. Dykes, *Eng. Proverbs*, 273 (2nd ed.) [cited as 'a common saw'].

13. Time and chance reveal all secrets. 1709: Manley, *New Atlantis*, ii 230 (1736). Cf. No. 24.

14. Time and patience will wear out stone posts. 1864: 'Cornish Proverbs', in *N. & Q.*, 3rd ser.vi 494 … stonen postes. 1919: *Devonsh. Assoc. Trans.*, li 77, Time and patience wears out most stone paustes.

15. Time and straw make medlars ripe. 1578: Florio, *First Fruites*, fo. 14, With time and with straw, medlers are made ripe. 1611: Cotgrave, s.v. 'Paille', In time and straw are medlers mellowed. 1712: Motteux, *Quixote*, Pt I bk iii ch vi. 1733: Fuller, 5047, Time and straw ripen medlars.

16. Time and tide wait for no man. *c.*1386: Chaucer, *C. Tales*, E118 (Skeat), For thogh we slepe or wake, or rome, or ryde, Ay fleeth the tyme, it nil no man abyde. Before 1529: Skelton, *Works*, i 137 (Dyce), Byde for tyme who wyll, for tyme wyll no man byde. 1596: Nashe, *Works*, iii 78 (Grosart), Yet time and tide (that staies for no man) forbids vs … 1630: Brathwait, *Eng. Gent.*, 189 (1641) Whence we commonly say, Time and tide stayeth for no man. 1736: Bailey, *Dict.*, s.v. 'Time', Time and tide will stay for no man. 1822: Scott, *Nigel*, ch xxvi. 1850: Dickens, *Chuzzlewit*, ch x Cf. **Tide** (3).

17. Time cures all things. 1539: Taverner, *Proverbs*, fo. 38, Tyme taketh away greuaunce. 1698: *Terence made English*, 140 (2nd ed.). 1731: Lillo, *George Barnwell*, V ii, Time and reflection cure all ills. 1736: Bailey, *Dict.*, s.v. 'Time', Time and thought quells the heaviest grief. 1869: Hazlitt, 405, Time and thinking tame the strongest grief.

18. Time fleeth away without delay. 1639: Clarke, 308. 1670: Ray, 149. 1732: Fuller, 6090.

19. Time flies. *c.*1390: Chaucer, *Clerk's Tale*, l. 118, For though we slepe or wake, or rome, or ryde, Ay fleeth the tyme. 1776: W. Fletcher, *Letter*, 21 March, in *Works* (1803), IX 197, Time flies! Years of plenty … disappear before the eternity to which we are all hastening.

20. Time is a file that wears and makes no noise. 1855: Bohn, 531.

21. Time is a great healer. *c.*1385: Chaucer, *Troilus and Criseyde*, v 350, As tyme hem hurt, a tyme doth hem cure. 1591: J. Harington, tr. *Ariosto's Orlando Furioso*, VI ii, *He hurt the wound*

which time perhaps had healed. 1837: Disraeli, *Henrietta Temple*, III VI ix, Time is the great physician. G.B. Shaw, *Translations and Tomfooleries*, 60, Time is the great healer.

22. Time is money. 1607–12: Bacon, *Essays*: 'Despatch', For tyme is the measure of businesse, as money is of wares. 1748: Franklin, in *Works*, ii 118 (Bigelow). 1841: Dickens, *Barn. Rudge*, ch xxiii. 1875: Smiles, *Thrift*, 364. 1903: Gissing, *Henry Ryecroft*: 'Winter', xxiv, Time is money – says the vulgarest saw known to any age or people. Turn it round about, and you get a precious truth – money is time.

23. Time is the father of truth. 1578: Florio, *First Fruites*, fo. 32. 1629: *Book of Meery Riddles*, Prov. 47.

24. Time is the rider that breaks youth. 1640: Herbert, *Jac. Prudentum.* 1670: Ray, 26. 1732: Fuller, 5052 [with 'in' after 'breaks'].

25. Time is tickle. 1546: Heywood, *Proverbs*, Pt I ch iii 1659: Howell, 7.

26. Time lost we cannot win. *c.*1440: Lydgate, *Fall of Princes*, bk iii l. 2811 (E.E.T.S.), Sumtyme departed, ageyn men may nat call. *c.*1535: *Pain of Evil Marriage*, 17 (Percy S.), Tyme passed wyl not agayne retourne. 1605: Camden, *Remains*, 334 (1870). 1659: Howell, 10.

27. Time revealeth all things. 1539: Taverner, *Proverbs*, fo. 37, Tyme discloseth all thynges. 1633: Draxe, 204. 1736: Bailey, *Dict.*, s.v. 'Time', Time brings all things to light. Cf. No. 12.

28. Time stays not the fool's leisure. 1855: Bohn, 531.

29. Time tries truth. 1546: Heywood, *Proverbs*, Pt II ch v, Let time try! Tyme tryeth trouth in euery doubt. 1580: Tusser, *Husbundrie*, 5 (E.D.S.), Time trieth the troth, in euerie thing.

30. Time trieth all things. 1553: *Respublica*, Prol., Yet tyme trieth all. 1599: Porter, *Two Angry Women*, in Hazlitt, *Old Plays*, vii 356, Time and truth tries all. 1607: Marston, *What You Will*, IV. 1633: Draxe, 204.

31. Time undermines us. 1640: Herbert, *Jac. Prudentum.*

32. Time will tell. A later form of *Time revealeth all things* (q.v.). 1771: C. Stuart, *Letter*, 15 Apr., in *Publications of the Mississippi Historical Society* (1925), V 50, Time only will shew how far those Informations have been founded. 1913: E.H. Porter, *Pollyanna*, xxiii, The doctor had looked very grave … and had said that time alone could tell.

33. When time hath turned white sugar to white salt. 1546: Heywood, *Proverbs*, Pt I ch ii. *See also* **Nature; No time;** and **Times.**

Timely blossom, timely fruit. 1639: Clarke, 171 ['beare' for 'fruit'].1670: Ray, 149 ['ripe' for 'fruit']. 1732: Fuller, 5057.

Timely crooketh. *See* **Soon crooketh.**

Times change and we change with them. 1578: Lyly, *Euphues*, I 276, The tymes are chaunged as Ovid sayeth, and wee are chaunged in the times. 1666: G. Torriano, *Italian Proverbs*, 281, Times change, and we with them.

Tinidal. This is a dark saying. I cannot identify 'Tinidal'. 1583: Melbancke, *Philotinus*, sig. Aa2, It is a prouerbe in Englande that the men of Tinidal borderers on ye English midle marches, haue likers, lemmons, and lyerbies.

Tinker and **Tinkers,** *subs.* **1. A tinker and a piper make bad music together.** 1639: Clarke, 5.

2. A tinker's budget is full of necessary tools. Ibid., 72. 1670: Ray, 149.

3. The tinker stops one hole and makes two. 1576: *Common Conditions* in Brandl, *Quellen*, 599, Hoie tiftie toftie tinkers, good followes thei bee, In stoppyng of one hole thei vse to make three. 1630: *Tinker of Turvey*, 10 (Halliwell), Roome for a joviall tinker, He stop one hole, and make three. 1692: L'Estrange, *Aesop*, 189 (3rd ed.), Till it comes at last to the tinker's work of stopping one hole, and making ten. 1738: Swift, *Polite Convers.*, Dial. I. 1872: *N.&Q.*, 4th ser, ix. 375, When I was young it was a proverb in East Cornwall that the tinkers 'repaired one hole and made two'.

4. Tinker's news. 1876: *N.&Q.*, 5th ser, v 168, In Gloucestershire, when any piece of information is mentioned that has been heard or told before, it is called 'tinkers' news'. 1883: Burne, *Shropsh. Folk-Lore*, 599, That's tinker's news; i.e. stale news.

See also **Banbury tinkers; Cobbler** (3); **Merry as tinkers; Not worth** (34); **Rough as a tinker's budget;** and **Swear** (2).

Tint for tant = Tit for tat. Hazlitt suggests derivation from French '*tant* for *tant*'. The *Oxford Dictionary* suggests 'taunt for taunt'. 1620: T. Granger, *Div. Logike*, 124 (OED), like for like, pin driuing out a pin, tint for taunt, etc. 1672: Walker, *Paroem.*, 29, Give him tint for

tant. 1690: *New Dict. Canting Crew*, sig. M2, Tint for tant, hit for hit, and dash for dash. 1828: Carr, *Craven Dialect*, ii 208, 'Tint for tant', a requital similar to *tit for tat*.

Tit for tat. [Par part respondet. – Plautus, *Truc.*, ii 47.] 1546: Heywood, *Proverbs*, Pt II ch iv. 1552: Huloet, *Abced.*, sig. Bb6, Requite as tick for tacke. 1611: Cotgrave, s.v. 'Beau', A tit for a tat … as good every whit as was brought. 1748: Richardson, *Clarissa*, i 153 (1785), They are resolved to break my heart. And they think you are resolved to break theirs: So tit for tat, Miss. 1898: Weyman, *Shrewsbury*, ch xvii. 1922: *Observer*, 10 Dec., p. 13, col. 2, They want their tit for tat with Mr Bonar Law.

Tithe and be rich. 1651: Herbert, *Jac. Prudentum*, 2nd ed.

Tittle, tattle, give the goose more hay. 1659: Howell, 11. 1670: Ray, 214. *c.*1690: Sedley, *Grumbler*, *I* ['Bibble babble' for 'Tittle tattle']. 1732: Fuller, 5058.

Toad, *subs.* **1. The toad and a side-pocket.** *See* quots. Monkey and dog are variants for the toad. 1785: Grose, *Class. Dict. Vulgar Tongue*, s.v. 'Toad', As much need of it as a toad of a side pocket, said of a person who desires anything for which he has no real occasion. 1869: *N.&Q.*, 4th ser, iv 147, The old fellow said: 'I no more wants that than a toad wants side pockets'. 1880: *N.&Q.*, 6th ser, ii 347 ['monkey' for 'toad']. Ibid., 377 ['dog' – Devonsh.]. 1881: *N.&Q.*, 6th ser, iii 76 ['dog' – E. Riding, Yorks]. Ibid. ['toad' – S.W. England and Northants]. 1888: Q. Couch, *Troy Town*, ch x, A bull 's got no more use for religion than a toad for side-pockets. Cf. **Cow** (8).

2. The toad under the harrow. *See* quots. [*c.*1290: in Wright, *Pol. Songs John to Edw. II*, 166 (Camden S.), Dixit bufo crati, 'maledicti tot dominati!'] *c.*1380: Wiclif, *Select Eng. Works*, ii 280, Christene men may seye, as the poete seith in proverbe, the frogge seide to the harwe, cursid be so many lordis. 1720: *Vade Mecum for Maltworms*, Pt I 33, There says, *He lives like toad beneath a harrow*. 1732: Fuller, 3354, Many masters, quoth the toad to the harrow, when every tine turn'd her over. 1817: Scott, *Rob Roy*, ch xxvii, Only muttering between his teeth, 'Ower mony maisters … as the paddock said to the harrow, when every tooth gae her a tig'. 1849: Dinsdale, *Tees dale Gloss.*, 136, 'To live like a toad under a harrow', is an expression denoting extreme personal wretchedness. 1854: Baker, *Northants Gloss.*, s.v. 'Toad under a harrow'. A common simile, applied to any one in a state of mental or bodily disquietude or suffering. 1918: *Devonsh. Assoc. Trans.*, l. 279, The proverbial saying about a man in difficulties, that he is 'like a toad under a harrow'.

See also **Mulfra;** and **Swell.**

Toasted cheese hath no master. 1678: Ray, 82. 1911: Hackwood, *Good Cheer*, 304.

Toast your bread. *See* quot. 1888: Lowsley, *Berks Gloss.*, 30 (E.D.S.), Two-ast yer bread An' rasher yer vlitch, An' as long as 'e lives Thee'ooll never be rich.

Tobacco. *See* quots. 1678: Ray, 296, Tobacco hie, If a man be well it will make him sick. [Also] Will make a man well if he be sick. 1849: Halliwell, *Pop. Rhymes, etc.*, 180, Tobacco hic, Will make you well If you be sick.

Today a man, to-morrow a cuckold. 1669: *New Help to Discourse*, 310.

Today a man, to-morrow a mouse. 1666: Torriano, *Piazza Univ.*, 59. 1732: Fuller, 5152.

Today a man, to-morrow none. Before 1500: in Hill, *Commonplace-Book*, 129 (E.E.T.S.), This dai a man, to morrow non. 1560: T. Wilson, *Rhetorique*, 83 (1909). 1611: Cotgrave, s.v. 'Biere'. 1633: Draxe, 131.

Today at cheer, to-morrow in bier. 1611: Cotgrave, s.v. 'Chere', To day glad, to morrow dead. 1623: Wodroephe, *Spared Houres*, 476. 1880: Spurgeon, *Ploughman's Pictures*, 67, To-day at good cheer, to-morrow on the bier.

Today gold, to-morrow dust. *c.*1500: in *Antiq. Repertory*, iv. 398 (1809), To day a man in golde, to morow closyde in clay. 1869: Hazlitt, 414.

Today is yesterday's pupil. 1732: Fuller, 5153.

Today me, to-morrow thee – or vice versa. Before 1225: *Ancren R.*, 278, And seie … 'Ille hodie, ego cras': Thet is, 'He to dai, ich to morwen'. 1596: Spenser, *F. Q.*, VI i 41, What haps to-day to me to-morrow may to you. 1620: Shelton, *Quixote*, Pt II ch lxv., To-day for thee, and to-morrow for me. 1681: Robertson, *Phraseol. Generalis*, 427. 1732: Fuller, 5154. 1855: Kingsley, *West. Ho!*, ch ix, Today to thee, to-morrow to me. Addio. 1906: Doyle, *Sir Nigel*, ch xv, 'It is the custom of the Narrow Seas,' said they: 'To-day for them; to-morrow for us.'

Today will not, tomorrow may, If. 1732: Fuller, 2725.

Toil of a pleasure, To make a. 1603: Breton, in *Works*, ii j7 (Grosart), I do not low so to make a toyle of a pleasure. Before 1658: Cleveland, in *Works*, 267 (1742), And make a toil of's pleasure.

Toil so for trash, what would you do for treasure, If you? 1639: Clarke, 194.

To it again, no body comes. 1639: Clarke, 303. 1670: Ray, 197. 1672: Walker, *Paroem.*, 53.

Toko for yam. *See* quots. 1823: John Bee, *Slang Dict.*, Toco for yam. – Yams are food for negroes in the West Indies (resembling potatoes), and if, instead of receiving his proper ration of these, blackee gets a whip (*toco*) about his back, why 'he has caught toco' instead of yams. 1855: Planché, *Extravag.*, v 124 (1879) Shan't he get toco For yam as surely As I stand here! 1880: *N.&Q.*, 6th ser, i 455, This is a common expression among sailors in the navy; for instance, 'He'll get toko for yam', i.e 'he'll get paid out', 'hell be punished'.

Toll is mote than the grist, The. 1886: Elworthy, *West Som. Word-Book*, 302 (E.D.S.), Formerly the miller always took his payment in a toll of the corn, and hence one of our most common proverbs … the toll is more than the grist.

Tom All thumbs. *See* **All thumbs.**

Tom, Dick and Harry. 1566: Lindsay, *Dial. between Exper. and a Courtier*, sig. A8 (Purfoot), Wherefore to colliers, carters and cokes To lack and Tom my rime shall be directed. 1604: James I, in Fuller, *Church Hist.*, bk x §i (22). Then Jack, and Tom, and Will, and Dick shall meet and censure me and my Council. 1622: J. Taylor, *Sir Greg. Nonsense*, 16, in Hindley, *Old Book-Coll. Miscell.*, iii, I neither care what Tom, or Jack, or Dick said. 1660: A. Brome, *Poems*: 'Royalist's Answer', Though Dick, Tom, and Jack, Will serve you and your pack. 1885: M. Twain, in *Letters*, 251 (1920), His simple pleasure in the flowers and general ruck sent to him by Tom, Dick and Harry from everywhere. 1921: B. W. Matz, *Inns and Tav. of 'Pickwick'*, 242, He gathered his information from any Tom, Dick or Harry he came in contact with during his wanderings.

Tom Dooley. *See* quot. 1917: Bridge, *Cheshire Proverbs*, 103, Owd Tum Dooley's note, booath barren and dreigh (said of a barren and dry cow).

Tom Drum. *See* **Drum's entertainment.**

Tom Fool. *See* **More know;** and **Red and yellow.**

Tom Hodges. *See* **John Toy.**

Tom Long. *See* **John Long.**

Tom Norton. *See* **All worse.**

Tom of all trades. *See* **Jack of all trades.**

Tomorrow come never. 1678: Ray, 343. 1725: Bailey, tr. Erasmus' *Colloq.*, 34. 1769: *Colman, Man and Wife,* III. 1825: Brockett, *Gloss. N. Country Words,* 150, Nivver, never, 'To-morrow come nivver – when two Sundays meet together'. 1830: Marryat, *King's Own*, ch xxvi. 1917: Bridge, *Cheshire Proverbs*, 141.

Tomorrow is another a new (or day.) Famous in the twentieth century for providing the final line of the film *Gone with the Wind*. *c.*1520: *Calisto and Meliboea,* in Hazlitt, *Old Plays,* i 86, Well, mother, to-morrow is a new day: I shall perform that I have you promised. 1592: Lyly, *Mother Bombie,* V iii. *c.*1620: B.&F., *Night-Walker,* II iii. 1685–6: Cotton, *Montaigne,* bk ii ch iv, To-morrow's a New Day [title of chapter]. 1712: Motteux, *Quixote,* Pt II ch lxviii. 1823: Scott, *St Ronan's,* ch xxxiii. 1956 M. Dickens *Angel in Corner* vi 90 'You can run along now … Those few letters will keep until the morning' … 'But there will be a whole heap of new ones by the morning.' 'I know, dear … If the letters didn't come, that would be the time to start worrying. But tomorrow is another day'.

Tomorrow it untouched. 1846: Denham, *Proverbs*, 1 (Percy S.).

Tomorrow morning I found a horse-shoe. 1620: Shelton, *Quixote,* Pt II ch xliii, That are as much to the purpose as 'To-morrow I found a horse shoe'. 1732: Fuller, 5208. 1926: *Times,* 2 Nov., p. 14, col. 7, The eve of the election finds the Democrats saying, like the man in the proverb, 'To-morrow I found a horse-shoe'.

Tomorrow never comes. A variant and now more common form of *Tomorrow come never* (q.v.). 1523: Lord berners, *Froissart* (1901), II 309, It was sayde every daye among them, we shall fight tomorowe, the whiche day came never. 1602: J. Chamberlain, *Letter,* 8 May (1939) I 142, Tomorrow comes not yet. 1756: B. Franklin, *Poor Richard's Alamanack* (July), To-morrow, every fault is to be amended; but that To-morrow never comes. 1889: Giussing, *Nether World,* III ix, 'It's probably as well for tou that *to-morrow* never comes'.

Tomorrow. *See also* Put (3).

Tom Prodger's job, A. 1854: Baker, *Northants Gloss.,* s.v. 'Prodger', 'A Tom Prodger's job'; a clumsy piece of work is so called.

Tom Tell-truth. 1377: Langland, *Plowman,* B, iv. 17, Tomme Trewe-tonge-telle-me-no-tales. 1542: Udall, tr. Erasmus' *Apoph.,* 202 (1877), (As ye would say in English) Thom trouth, or plain Sarisbuirie. 1550: Latimer, *Sermons,* 289 (P.S.), Master, we know that thou art Tom Truth, and thou tellest the very truth … Thou art plain Tom Truth. 1600: J. Lane, *Tom Tel-Troths Message* [title]. (N.Sh.S.). 1646: Quarles, *Works,* i 93 (Grosart). 1681: Robertson, *Phraseol. Generalis,* 1066, So Tom tell-troth talks and reports. 1709: O. Dykes, *Eng. Proverbs,* p. xxxvi (2nd ed.), Neither do I look upon such scraps, as, Latter Lammas … Tom Tell-Troth … to be fit for my purpose. 1826: Scott, *Journal,* 19 Feb., Yet is he Tom Tell-truth, and totally unable to disguise his real feelings. 1869: Spurgeon, *John Ploughman,* ch xviii, Better be laughed at as Tom Tell-truth than be praised as Crafty Charlie.

Tom Thumb, A tale of. 1659: Howell, 14.

Tong, Kent. *See* **Bapchild;** and **Muston.**

Tongue, *subs.* **1. A good tongue is a good weapon.** 1732: Fuller, 180.

2. At one's tongue's end. 1590: *Tarltons News out of Purg.,* 69 (SH.S.), To blame those wives whose secrets lay at their tongues end. 1652: Walsingham, *Arcana Aulica,* 18 (1694), Upon whose tongues-end lay the disposal of his life. 1751: Fielding, *Amelia,* bk xii ch vii, Having always at her tongue's end that excellent proverb … 1854: Baker, *Northants Gloss.,* s.v. 'I had it at my tongue's end', i.e. I was ready to speak, but on reflection held my tongue.

3. Her tongue runs on pattens. 1546: Heywood, *Proverbs,* Pt II ch vii. *c.*1550: Udall, *Roister Doister,* I iii, Yet your tongue can renne on patins as well as mine. 1611: Davies (of Hereford), *Sc. of Folly,* 46, in *Works,* ii (Grosart).

4. His tongue goes always of errands, but never speeds. 1732: Fuller, 2515.

5. His tongue is as cloven as the devil's foot. Ibid., No. 2516.

6. His tongue is no slander. 1633: Draxe, 121. 1670: Ray, 196. 1736: Bailey, *Dict.,* s.v. 'Tongue'.

7. His tongue is well hung. 1738: Swift, *Polite Convers.*, Dial. I, I warrant this rogue's tongue is well hung. 1754: Berthelson, *Eng.-Danish Dict.*, s.v. 'Hung'.

8. His tongue runs on wheels. *c.*1450: *Partonope*, 420 (E.E.T.S.), They haue no ioy to say the best, Suche mennys tonges gone euer on whelis. 1738: Swift, *Polite Convers.*, Dial. I, Why, wench, I think thy tongue runs upon wheels this morning. 1828: Carr, *Craven Dialect*, ii 213, 'His tongue runs o' wheels'; i.e. he talks fast.

9. Let not thy tongue run away with thy brains. 1732: Fuller, 3190.

10. That tongue doth lye that speakes in hast. 1611: Davies (of Hereford), *Sc. of Folly*, 43, in *Works*, ii (Grosart).

11. The tongue breaks bones, though itself has none. *c.*1270: *Prov. of Alfred*, in *Old Eng. Miscell.* 128 (Morris), For ofte tunge breketh bon theyh heo seolf nabbe non. Before 1384: Wiclif, *Works*, ii 44 (Arnold), Tunge brekith boon, al if the tunge himself have noon. *c.*1470: G. Ashby, *Poems*, 64 (E.E.T.S.), The tonge breketh boon, thaugh he be tendre. 1546: Heywood, *Proverbs*, Pt II ch v, Toung breaketh bone, it selfe hauyng none. 1670: Ray, 26. 1732: Fuller, 4795.

12. The tongue is ever turning to the aching tooth. 1586: G. Pettie, tr. Guazzo's *Civil Convers.*, fo. 221, The tongue rolls there where the teeth aketh. 1659: Howell, *Proverbs: Ital.-Eng.*, 8, Where the tooth pains, the toung is commonly upon it. 1732: Fuller, 4796.

13. The tongue is not steel, yet it cuts. 1546: Heywood, *Proverbs*, Pt I ch x, Her tong is no edge toole, but yet it will cut. 1640: Herbert, *Jac. Prudentum*. 1732: Fuller, 4797 [with 'sorely' after 'cuts']. 1853: Trench, *Proverbs*, 138 (1905).

14. *The tongue is the rudder of our ship.* 1732: Fuller, 4798.

15. The tongue of idle persons is never *idle.* Ibid., No. 4800.

16. The tongue talks at the head's cost. 1640: Herbert, *Jac. Prudentum*. 1670: Ray, 26. 1732: Fuller, 4801.

17. The tongue walks where the teeth steed not. 1640: Herbert, *Jac. Prudentum.*

18. To keep one's tongue between one's teeth. 1672: Walker, *Paroem.*, 18, I shall keep my tongue between my teeth. 1692: L 'Estrange, *Aesop*, 271 (3rd ed.), That have the wit yet to keep their tongues betwixt their teeth. 1709: Cibber, *Rival Fools*, II, If he does not keep his tongue between his teeth, I'll give him a chuck o' the chin, shall chop him in two. 1784: *New Foundl. Hosp. for Wit*, i 287. 1821: Scott, *Kenilworth*, ch vii, Silence, good neighbours! ... keep tongue betwixt teeth.

19. Tongue, whither wilt thou? 1692: L'Estrange, *Aesop*: 'Life', 11 (3rd ed.) [quoted as 'the old proverb'].

20. Your tongue is made of very loose leather. 1732: Fuller, 6062.

21. Your tongue runs before your wit. *c.*1350: *Pearl*, l.294, Thy worde byfore thy wytte con fle. 1540: Heywood, *Proverbs*, Pt II ch iv. *c.*1597: Deloney, *Gentle Craft*, Pt I ch i, Pardon me ... if my tongue doe outslip my wit. *c.*1680: L'Estrange, *Seneca's Epistles*, i, He will no more speak fast, than he will run, for fear his tongue should go before his wit. 1738: Swift, *Polite Convers.*, Dial. I. 1822: Scott, *Nigel*, ch viii, Blisters on my tongue, 'it runs too fast for my wit'.

22. Your tongue runs nineteen to the dozen. 1854: Baker, *Northants Gloss.*, s.v. 'Nineteen', A common expression, when any one talks too fast. 'Your tongue runs nineteen to the dozen, there is no getting in a word with you'. 1901: Raymond, *Idler Out of Doors*, 123, Whilst she talked nineteen to the dozen.

See also **Heart** (12); and **Long tongue.**

Too big a gun. *See* quots. 1732: Fuller, 1824, He carries too big a gun for me. 1912: S. Butler, *Note-Books*, 256, This gentleman had a decided manner and carried quite as many guns as the two barristers ... who sat opposite to us.

Too big for one's fireplace = Beyond one's means. 1893: Gower, *Gloss. of Surrey Words*, 16 (E.D.S.), I'm much obliged to you for letting me look at the farm; but I think that it's too big for my fireplace.

Too busy gets contempt, To be. 1640: Herbert, *Jac. Prudentum.*

Too far East is West. 1853: Trench, *Proverbs*, 93 (1905), This proverb, *Extremes meet*, or its parallel, *Too far East is West*, reaches very far into the heart of things.

Too free to be fat. 1670: Ray, 176. 1681: Robertson, *Phraseol. Generalis*, 641, Too free to be fat; Promus magis quam condus.

Too good is stark naught. 1738: Swift, *Polite Convers.*, Dial. II

Too hasty burnt his lips. 1623: Wodroephe, *Spared Houres*, 519.

Too hasty to be a parish clerk. 1633: Draxe, 10 ['priest' for 'clerk']. 1670: Ray, 180.

Too heavy or too hot. *c.*1386: Chaucer, *Friar's Tale*, l. 138, I spare nat to taken, god it woot, But if it be to hevy or to hoot. 1542: Udall, tr. Erasmus' *Apoph.*, 359 (1877), As being a taker and a bribing feloe, and one for whom nothing was to hotte nor to heauie. 1607: *The Puritan*, I i, Nothing was too hot, nor too dear for me. 1053: Urquhart, *Rabelais*, bk i ch xxvii, They robbed both men and women, and took all they could catch; nothing was either too hot or too heavie for them. 1822: Scott, *Nigel*, ch viii, Such a sight, sweetheart, will make one loth to meddle with matters that are too hot or heavy for their handling. 1890: *N. & Q.*, 7th ser, x 446, 'Nothing but what is too hot and too heavy'. This sentence is a proverbial saying in North Notts, and its application is in respect of those who ... are not particular with regard to the manner in which they procure the means for carrying on their mode of living.

Too high for the stirrup, and not high enough for the saddle. Oxfordsh. 1913: *Folk-Lore*, xxiv 77.

Too hot to hold. 1639: Clarke, 178. 1678: Ray, 346.

Too late to grieve when the chance is past, It is. 1605: Camden, *Remains*, 326 (1870). 1732: Fuller, 5256.

Too late to spars when all is spent. *c.*1555: in Wright, *Songs, etc.*, *Philip and Mary*, 30 (Roxb.Cl), To latte they spare, when all ys goone. 1639: Clarke, 262. 1721: Bailey, *Dict.*, s.v. 'Spare'. 1853: Trench, *Proverbs*, 112 (1905). 1874: *N. & Q.*, 5th ser, i 205.

Too late to spare when the bottom is bare. 1539: Taverner, *Proverbs*, fo. 32, It is to late sparinge at the bottome. *c.*1590: G. Harvey, *Marginalia*, 102 (1913) [as in 1539]. 1670: Ray, 144. 1732: Fuller, 6345.

Too light winning makes the prize light. 1855: Bohn, 545.

Too low for a hawk, too high for a buzzard. 1919: Max Beerbohm, *Seven Men*, 100, I had done for myself, so far as *those* people were concerned. And now that I had sampled *them*, what cared I for others? 'Too low for a hawk, too high for a buzzard'. That homely old saying seemed to sum me up.

Too many cooks spoil the broth. 1575:?J. Hooker, *Life of Carew* (1857), 33, There is the proverb, the more cooks the worse potage. 1662: Gerbier, *Discourse of Building*, 24. 1732: Fuller, 4657, The more cooks the worse broth. 1778: S. Crisp, in D'Arblay, *Diary*, i 84 (1876), In these cases generally the more cooks the worse broth. *c.*1804: J. Austen, *Watsons*, 24 (Walkley, 1923). 1855: Kingsley, *West. Ho!*, ch xv. 1921: *Observer*, 15 May, p. 13, col. 5, Eleven clever gentlemen have made this jolly entertainment, and, contrary to custom, too many cooks have not spoiled the broth.

Too many stairs and back-doors makes thieves and whores. 1662: Gerbier, *Discourse of Building*, 14 [cited as 'the old English proverb'].

Too much bed makes a dull head. Derby. 1884: *Folk-Lore Journal*, ii 279.

Too much breaks the bag. 1666: Torriano, *Piazza Univ.*, 244 ['sack' for 'bag']. 1670: Ray, 26. 1732: Fuller, 5259.

Too much consulting confounds. Ibid., No. 5261.

Too much cordial will destroy. Ibid., No. 5263.

Too much cunning undoes. 1659: Howell, *Proverbs: Brit.-Eng.*, 3.

Too much diligence is hurtful. 1561: Hoby, *Courtier*, 61 (T.T.), It hath bene a proverbe emonge some most excellent peincters of old time, that To muche diligence is hurtfull.

Too much liberty spoils all. 1611: Cotgrave, s.v. 'Bandon', Much liberty brings men to the gallowes. 1681: Robertson, *Phraseol. Generalis*, 822. 1694: *Terence made English*, 123, For too much liberty corrupts an angel.

'Too much money makes men mad, the prouerb plaine doth show'. *c.*1640: in Rollins, *Cavalier and Puritan*, 117 (1923).

Too much of a good thing, You can have. 1601: Shakespeare, *As You Like It*, IV i, Why then, can one desire too much of a good thing? 1611: Cotgrave, s.v. 'Manger', A man may take too much of a good thing. 1809: Syd. Smith, *Works*, i 175 (1867) (OED), This (to use a very colloquial phrase) is surely too much of a good thing.

Too much of nothing but of fools and asses. 1639: Clarke, 73.

Too much of one thing is naught (or good for nothing). *c.*1386: Chaucer, *C. Tales*, iv 645

(Skeat), That that is overdoon, it wol nat preve Aright, as clerkes seyn, it is a vyce. *c.*1450: *Abce of Aristotill*, in E.E.T.S., Ext. Ser., 8, p. 66, For to moche of on thynge was neuer holsome. *c.*1500: in *Antiq. Repertory*, iv. 414 (1809), To muche ys nought of any maner of thynge. *c.*1554: *Interlude of Youth*, in Hazlitt, *Old Plays*, ii 19, Over-much of one thing is nought. 1591: Harington, *Orl. Furioso*: 'Allegory', 408 (1634), Our English prouerbe saith, Too much of one thing is good for nothing. 1634: C. Butler, *Feminine Monarchie*, 170 [as in 1591]. 1681: Robertson, *Phraseol. Generalis*, 877 [as in 1591]. 1725: Bailey, tr. Erasmus' *Colloq.*, 39 [as in 1591]. 1751: Fielding. *Amelia*, bk xi ch iii [as in 1591]. 1871: *N. & Q.*, 4th ser, viii 506, [Lancs] Too much of ought Is good for nought. 1901: F. E. Taylor, *Lancs Sayings*, 10, To' mitch ov owt's good for nowt.

Too much praise is a burthen. 1669: *Politeuphuia*, 140. 1732: Fuller, 5266.

Too much pudding will choke a dog. 1830: Colman, jr., in *Hum. Works*, 421 (Hotten). 1917: Bridge, *Cheshire Proverbs*, 141, Too much pudding would sade [satiate] a dog.

Too much spoileth, too little is nothing. 1659: Howell, *Proverbs: Ital.-Eng.*, 12, Too much spoiles, too little doth not satisfie. 1732: Fuller, 5268.

Too much taking heed is loss. 1640: Herbert, *Jac. Prudentum.*

Too old to learn his accidence, He is now. 1659: Howell, 11 (9).

Too proud as too slow, As well. 1594: Drayton, *Idea*, lix.

Too proud to ask is too good to receive, He that is. 1732: Fuller, 2194.

Too secure is not safe, He that is. Ibid., No. 2195.

Too soon, He's up, That's hanged ere noon, Ibid., No. 6279.

Too soon wise to be long old. 1592: Greene, *Works*, x 238 (Grosart), The neighbours saw, I was too soone wise, to be long olde. 1594: Shakespeare, *Rich. III*, III i, So wise, so young, they say, do never live long. 1738: Swift, *Polite Convers.*, Dial. I, I fear Lady Answerall can't live long, she has so much wit. 1825: Scott, in Lockhart's *Life*, vi 134, I should be sorry the saying were verified in him – 'So wise, so young, they say do ne'er live lag.

Tooth and **Teeth,** *subs.* **1. Tooth and nail** = By all means possible. [Manibus pedibusque. – Terence, *Andr.*, 161.] 1533: Udall, *Flowers out of Terence*, fo. 3, He doeth all thynges … with tothe and nayle, as moche as in him lyeth. 1565: Calfhill, *Answer to Martiall*, 228 (P.S.), Defended with tooth and nail. 1646: Wither, *What Peace to the Wicked?*, 2 (Spens.S.), Some, for themselves, with tooth, and naile. 1710: T. Ward, *Eng. Reform.*, 27 (1716), Then fall with tooth and nail upon 'em. 1766: Garrick, *Neck or Nothing*, II i, She is not to be trusted … tooth and nail against us. 1850: Dickens, *Copperfield*, ch xlii, I've got a motive … and I go at it tooth and nail.

2. Your teeth are longer than your beard. 1855: Bohn, 582.

Too too will in two. Cheshire. 1670: Ray, 149. 1901: F. E. Taylor, *Lancs Sayings*, 10, Too-too will i' two (Friends who are too intimate are sure to quarrel). 1917: Bridge, *Cheshire Proverbs*, 141.

Top. *As soon drive a top over a tiled house.* 1546: Heywood, *Proverbs*, Pt II ch v, I shall as soone trie him or take him this waie, As dryve a top ouer a tyeld house. 1659: Howell, 3, You may drive a toppe over a tylde house as soon. 1678: Ray, 291, As good as ever drave top over til'd house.

Top-heavy, He is = He is drunk. 1678: Ray, 87. 1736: Bailey, *Dict.*, s.v. 1825: Hone, *Ev. Day Book*, ii 859, Being top-heavy with liquor.

Topmost branch is not the safest perch, The. 1875: Cheales, *Proverb. Folk-Lore*, 103.

Totnes, Devon. *See* quot. 1850: *N. & Q.*, 1st ser, ii 511, Here I sit, and here I rest, And this town shall be called Totness. [Said to have been spoken by Brutus of Troy, when he landed there!]

Tottenham, Middlesex, **1. Tottenham is turned French.** 1536: Norfolk, to Cromwell, in *Cal. Lett., etc., Henry VIII*, ii No. 233, It is further written to me that a bruit doth ran that I should be in the Tower of London. When I shall deserve to be there Totynham shall turn French. 1546: Heywood, *Proverbs*, Pt I ch vii. 1631: W. Bedwell, *Briefe Descrip. of … Tottenham*, sig. D3, Three prouerbs, commonly by the neighbours vsed and spoken of Tottenham. The first of those is *Tottenham is turn'd French.* 1662: Fuller, *Worthies*, ii 314 (1840). 1790: Grose, *Prov. Gloss.*, s.v. 'London'.

2. When Tottenham Wood is all on fire, Then Tottenham Street is nought but mire. 1631:

Bedwell, *ut supra*, sig. D4. 1662: Fuller, *Worthies*, ii 314 (1840). 1790: Grose, *Prov. Gloss.*, s.v. 'London'. 1893: Inwards, *Weather Lore*, 51.

3. You shall as easily remove Tottenham-wood. 1631: Bedwell, *ut supra*, sig. D4. 1790: Grose, *Prov. Gloss.*, s.v. 'London'.

Touch, *verb.* **1. I would not touch him with a pair of tongs.** 1639: Clarke, 34, Not to be handled with a pair of tongues. 1658: *Wit Restor'd*, 159, For without a payre of tongs no man will touch her. 1732: Fuller, 2649, I will not touch her with a pair of tongs. 1854: Dickens, *Hard Times*, bk i ch iv, I was so ragged and dirty that you wouldn't have touched me with a pair of tongs. 1876: Blackmore, *Cripps*, ch iii, As if I would touch him with a pair of tongs, sir! 1901: F. E. Taylor, *Lancs Sayings*, 33, Aw wouldno' touch him wi' a pair o' tungs.

2. To touch to the quick. 1546: Heywood, *Proverbs*, Pt I ch vi, Practyse in all, aboue all toucheth the quicke. 1567: Golding, *Ovid*, bk vi l.162, And that did touch Minerva to the quicke. 1602: Shakespeare, *Hamlet*, II ii, I'll tent him to the quick. Before 1658: Cleveland, *Works*, 131 (1742), There I confess I am touched to the quick. 1742: Fielding, *Andrews*, bk i ch xvii, The last appellation stung her to the quick. 1823: Scott, *St Ronan's*, ch xxix, But when you touch me to the quick … you cannot expect me to endure without wincing. 1855: Kingsley, *West. Ho!*, ch i, Her last words had touched him to the quick.

2. Touch and take. 1591: Florio, *Second Frutes*, 197, Touch and take, take and holde. 1620: *Two Merry Milkmaids*, IV ii, I know what the prouerbe saies, touch me and take me. 1662: Davenant, *Law against Lovers*, IV, My grandam left me nothing at her death But a good old proverb, that's Touch and Take. 1819: Scott, *Bride of L.*, ch ix, Touch and try – the gold is good as ever was weighed.

4. Touch pot, touch penny = No credit given. 1654: Gayton, *Pleasant Notes Don Q.*, 83. 1720: Swift, *Elegy on Mr Demar*, He touched the pence when others touched the pot. 1772: Graves, *Spirit. Quixote*, bk iii ch ii, We know the custom at such houses … 'tis touch pot, touch penny – we only want money's worth for our money. 1822: Scott, *Nigel*, ch xvi, Since touch pot touch penny makes every man equal.

5. Touch wood, it's sure to come good. 1906: *N.&Q.*, 10th ser, vi 231.

Touch-stone trieth gold, As the, so gold trieth the hearts of men. 1598: Meres, *Palladia*, fo. 204, As golde is tried by the touchstone, so riches do shew what is in a man. 1669: *Politeuphuia*, 130. 1732: Fuller, 736 [omitting 'the hearts of'].

Tough as leather, As. 1611: Cotgrave, s.v. 'Corias'. 1678: Ray, 290, As tough as whitleather. 1843: Mrs Carlyle, *Lett.*, i 219 (1883) (OED), The 'cold fowl' was … as tough as leather.

Tow. *To have tow on one's distaff* = To have business on hand, to have 'eggs on the spit'. *c.*1386: Chaucer, *Miller's Tale*, l. 588, He hadde more tow on his distaf Than Gerveys knew. 1412: Hoccleve, *Regement*, 45(E.E.T.S.), 'Tow on my distaf haue I for to spynne. More, my fadir, than ye wot of yit.' 1533: Heywood, *Pard. and Friar*, in Hazlitt, *Old Plays*, i 238, I have more tow on my distaff than I can well spin. 1732: Fuller, 4128, She hath other tow on her distaff. 1818: Scott, *Fam. Letters*, ii 4 (1894), I did not much write him *con amore* … above all, I had too much flax on my distaff. 1906: Doyle, *Sir Nigel*, ch xxvi, By my ten finger-bones! … he found more on his distaff that time than he knew how to spin.

Tower of London. *See* **Fool** (22).

Towers build masons. 1639: Clarke, 8.

Town-bull is a bachelor, Then the – i.e. as soon as such an one. 1678: Ray, 66.

Tracies. 1. The Trades have always the wind in their faces. 1662: Fuller, *Worthies*, i 552 (1840). 1790: Grose, *Prov. Gloss.*, s.v. 'Gloucestershire'. 1897: Norway, *H. and B. in Devon, etc.*, 378, Who has not heard of the weird of the Tracys, with ever the wind and the rain in their faces. 1905: *N.&Q.*, 10th ser, iv 335.

2. *See* quot. 1906: Vincent, *H. and B. in Berks*, 121, 'The Tracys, the Lacys, and the Fettiplaces Own all the manors, the parks, and the chases', says the old rhyme.

Trade, *subs.* **1. A handful of trade is worth a handful of gold.** 1736: Bailey, *Dict.*, s.v.

2. A trade is better than service. 1640: Herbert, *Jac. Prudentum*.

3. He that changes his trade. *See* quots. 1611: Cotgrave, s.v. 'Panier', He that meddles with another mans trade, milkes his cow in a pannier [basket]. 1710: S. Palmer, *Moral Essays on Proverbs*, 89, He that changes his trade makes soop in a basket.

4. He that hath a trade. *See* quot. 1611: Cotgrave, s.v. 'Mestier', He that hath a good trade hath a goodly revenue. 1640: Herbert, *Jac. Prudentum*, He that learns a trade, hath a purchase made. 1736: Franklin, *Way to Wealth*, in *Works*, i 444 (Bigelow), He that hath a trade, hath an estate. 1772: Franklin, in *Works*, iv. 538, The proverb says, 'He who has a trade has an office of profit and honour'.

5. Trade is the mother of money. 1633: Draxe, 207. 1670: Ray, 27. 1732: Fuller, 5271.

See also **Good trade; Jack; Knavey; Man** (28); **Tricks;** and **Two of a trade.**

Trail a light harrow, To. 1828: Carr, *Craven Dialect*, i 213, 'To trail a leet [light] harrow'. This expression alludes to the comforts of single blessedness. 1855: Robinson, *Whitby Gloss.*, 79, He trails a light harrow, his hat covers his family.

Traitors. *See* quot. 1678: Ray, 82, Are there traitours at the table that the loaf is turn'd the wrong side upwards? *See also* **Treason.**

Traitors' Bridge [Tower of London], **A loyal heart may be landed under.** 1662: Fuller, *Worthies*, ii 347 (1840). 1790: Grose, *Prov. Gloss.*, s.v. 'London'.

Trap, To understand (or To be up to). 1679: *Counterfeits*, III i, You're deceiv'd in old Gomez, he understands trap. 1699: Farquhar, *Love and a Bottle*, III, We understand trap, sir, you must not catch old birds with chaff. 1700: Ward, *London Spy*, 148 (1924). The rest … look'd as if they had understood trap this twenty years. 1821: Scott, *Pirate*, ch iv, His good lady (who understood trap as well as any woman in the Mearns) … 1828: Carr, *Craven Dialect*, ii 217, 'To be up to trap', to be cunning in business, to be sharp-witted in promoting self-interest. 1854: Baker, *Northants Gloss.*, s.v. 'Trap' [as in 1828]

Trash and trumpery is the highway to beggary. 1678: Ray, 211. 1732: Fuller, 6091.

Travel broadens the mind. 1929: G.K. Chesterton, *Poet and Lunatics*, iii, He may be a trifle cracked … but that's only because his travels have been too much for his intellect. They say travel broadens the mind; but you must have the mind. 1949: N. Streatfield, *Painted Garden*, iii, Foreign travel broadens the mind … and a broadened mind helps all art.

Travel makes a wise man better, but a fool worse. Ibid., No. 5272.

Travel, *verb.* **1. He that travels far knows much.** 1639: Clarke, 276.1670: Ray, 149. 1732: Fuller, 2335 [with 'much' for 'far'].

2. He travelled with Mandeville. Ibid., No. 2374.

3. He travels fastest who travels alone. 1854: Thoreau, *Walden*, The man who goes alone can start today; but he who travels with another must wait till that other is ready. 1888: R. Kipling, *Story of Gadsby* (1889), 94, Down to gehenna, or up to the Throne, He travels fastest who travels alone.

4. He who travelleth not by sea, knows not what the fear of God is. 1623: Wodroephe, *Spared Homes*, 230.

See also **Better.**

Traveller, *subs.* **1. A traveller may lie by authority.** 1509: Barclay, *Ship of Fools*, ii 68 (1874), There thre sortes be Of people lyuynge, whiche may themselfe defende In lesynge [lying], for they haue auctoryte to lye. The first is pylgrymes that hath great wonders sene In strange countres, suche may say what they wyll. *c.*1598: Deloney, *Gentle Craft*, Pt II ch vi, Trauellers … haue liberty to vtter what lies they list. 1630: Brathwait, *Eng. Gent.*, *etc.*, 77 (1641), Whence it is said, that travellers, poets and lyars, are three words al of one signification. 1683: Dryden and Lee, *Duke of Guise*, IV iv, If he has been a traveller, he certainly says true; for he may lie by authority. 1744–6: Mrs Haywood, *Fem. Spectator*, iii 283 (1771), there is a kind of latitude, they say, given to travellers to exceed the truth. 1813: Byron, in *Letters, etc.*, ii 311 (Prothero), I never have, and never should have, alluded to it on my own authority, from respect to the ancient proverb on Travellers. Cf. **Old,** A (*b*) (14); and **Painters.**

2. A traveller must have. *See* quots. The details of equipment vary. 1591: Florio, *Second Frutes*, 93, If you will be a traueller … haue alwayes the eies of a faulcon … the eares of an asse … the face of an ape … the mouth of a hog … the shoulder of a camell … the legges of a stagg … and see that you neuer want two bagges very full, that is one of patience … and another of money. 1594: Nashe, *Works*, v 141 (Grosart), A traueller must haue the backe of an asse to bear all, a tung like the tayle of a dog to flatter all, the mouth of a hog to eate what is set before him, the eare of a merchant to heare all and say nothing. 1611: in Coryat, *Crudities*, i 44 n. (1905), Note reader that a traveller must have the backe of an asse, the mouth of a sow, the eye of a hawke, a merchants eare, etc. 1616: *Rich Cabinet*, fo. 147, Traueller must haue the head of a philosopher ... the heart of a lyon ... the mouth of a swine ... the eyes of a hawke ... the backe of an asse ... the legges of a cammell ... and the vigilancy of a cocke. 1666: Torriano, *Piazza Univ.*, 157 [a slightly varied copy of 1591]. 1678: Ray, 296, To travell safely through the world a must have a falcons eye, an asses eares, an apes face, a merchants words, a camells back, a hogs mouth, and a harts legs.

3. Much spends the traveller more than the abider. 1640: Herbert. *Jac. Prud.*

Treacle Town = Macclesfield. 1917: Bridge, *Cheshire Proverbs*, 146, No good reason has ever been given why it is so called.

Tread on a worm. *See* **Worm** (3).

Tread one's shoe awry, To = To be guilty of a lapse from virtue. *c.*1422: Hoccleve, *Minor Poems*, xxiv 66 (OED), No womman ... But swich oon as hath trode hir shoo amis. 1562: Heywood, *Epigr.*, 6th hund., No. 21, My wife doth euer tread hir shooe a wry. 1590: *Tarltons Newes*, 75 (SH.S.), A faire wife, that ... could not treade right, yet wrincht hir shoe inward ... as secret as she was false. 1616: Sharpham, *Cupid's Whirligig*, *IV*, She hath neuer trode her foot awry. 1639: D'Urfey, *Richmond Heiress*, II ii, A foolish female nice and shy, That never yet trod shooe awry. 1710: Ward, *Nuptial Dialogues*, i 141, But I defy Your servile spies to prove I've trod awry.

Treason, To lore the, but hate the traitor. 1614: C. Brooke, *Rich. Third*, 109 (Grosart), They loue no traytors, that doe traytors vse. 1683: Dryden and Lee, *Duke of Guise*, III i, Hate then the traitor, but yet love the treason. 1692: L'Estrange, *Aesop*, 172 (3rd ed.), We love the treason but we hate the traytor. 1712: Motteux, *Quixote*, Pt I bk iv. ch xii, Who made good to them our Spanish proverb, that the treason pleases, but the traitors are odious.

Treasure is tickle. 1583: Melbancke, *Philotinus*, sig. E3.

Tree and Trees, *subs.* **1. A good tree is a good shelter.** 1732: Fuller, 182.

2. As a tree falls so must it lie. 1549: Latimer, *Seven Sermons*, 118 (Arber), Wheresoeuer the

tree falleth ... there it shall rest. 1556: Heywood, *Spider and Flie*, cap. 88, p. 380 (Farmer), Where the tree falleth there lieth it, – clerks say so. *c.*1630: in *Roxb. Ballads*, i 143 (B.S.), And as he [the tree] falls, so doth he lye. 1820: Scott, *Monastery*, ch viii, There lies the faded tree, and as it fell, so it lies. 1921: Hudson, *Trav. in Little Things*, ch iii.

3. Large trees give more shade than fruit. 1855: Bohn, 439.

4. Set trees poor and they will grow rich, set them rich and they will grow poor. 1678: Ray, 350. 1846: Denham, *Proverbs*, 3 (Percy S.).

5. The highest tree hath the greatest fall. 1605: Camden, *Remains*, 333 (1870). 1670: Ray, 13. 1736: Bailey, *Dict.*, s.v. 'Tree', The higher the tree the greater the fall.

6. There is no tree but bears some fruit. 1616: Breton, in *Works*, ii *e* 8 (Grosart), There is no tree but beareth fruit. 1670: Ray, 149.

7. The tree falls not at the first blow. Before 1500: in Hill, *Commonplace-Book*, 128 (E.E.T.S.), Hit is a febill tre that fallith at the first strok. 1666: Torriano, *Piazza Univ.*, 48. 1736: Bailey, *Dict.*, s.v. 'Tree' ['stroke' for 'blow'].

8. The tree is known by its fruit. [Matthew xii.33, The tree is known by his fruit.] 1528: W. Tyndale, *Obedience of a Christian Man*, 88ᵛ, Judge the tre by his frute, and not by his leves. 1564: Bullein, *Dialogue*, 86 (E.E.T.S.), You shal know that fruicte by the tree. *c.*1630: in *Roxb. Ballads*, i 143 (B.S.). 1670: Ray, 11, A tree is known by the fruit, and not by the leaves. 1719: Prior, in Peck, *Desid. Curiosa*, 222 (1779). 1861: Peacock, *Gryll Grange*, ch v, If you know the tree by its fruit ... Cf. Such tree.

9. The tree that grows slowly keeps itself for another. 1640: Herbert, *Jac. Prudentum*

10. Trees eat but once. Ibid.

11. When the tree is fallen, all go with their hatchet. 1586: Young, tr. Guazzo's *Civil Convers.* fo. 206, The tree is no sooner fallen downe to the grounde, but euerie one is readie to runne vppon it with his hatchette. 1640: Herbert, *Jac. Prudentum.* 1732: Fuller, 4804, The tree is no sooner down, but every one runs for his hatchet. 1875: Cheales, *Proverb. Folk-Lore*, 154, When the tree is down every one runs with his hatchet.

Treelton. *See* **Bolsover.**

Tregeagle, He roars like. 1864: 'Cornish Proverbs', in *N. & Q.*, 3rd ser, vi 6. 1865: Hunt, *Pop. Romances W. of Eng.*, 143 (1896), 'Roaring or howling like Tregeagle', is a common expression amongst the vulgar in Cornwall. 1913: E. M. Wright, *Rustic Speech, etc.*, 196 [Mrs Wright tells the legend at length].

Tregoner. *See* quot. 1906: Q. Couch, *Mayor of Troy*, Prol., The Mayor of Tregoney, who could read print upside-down, but wasn't above being spoken to.

Tre, Pol and Pen, By, You shall know the Cornish men. 1602: Carew, *Survey of Cornwall*, 149 (1811). 1662: Fuller, *Worthies*, i 306 (1840). 1750: R. Heath, *Acc. of Scilly*, 338, By Tre, Pol, and Pen, Ross, Caer, and Lan, You know Cornish men. 1821: Scott, *Kenilworth*, ch i ['may' for 'shall']. 1864: 'Cornish Proverbs', in *N. & Q.*, 3rd ser, v 208 [as in 1750, but with 'shall' before 'know', and 'all' before 'Cornish']. 1928: *Sphere*, 7 Jan., 36, This, of course, is Cornwall … the country of 'Tre, Pol, and Pen'.

Trick, *subs.* **1. A trick to catch an old one.** 1608: Middleton [title of play]. *c.*1624: Davenport, *King John*, IV iii, 'Twas well yet that the trick has catch'd this old one.

2. A trick worth two of that. 1597: Shakespeare, 1 *Henry IV*, II i. 1619: Chapman, *Two Wise Men*, V i. *c.*1620: *Barnavelt*, IV i, in Bullen, *Old Plays*, ii 272, I know a trick worth ten o' that. 1772: Graves, *Spirit. Quixote*, bk iii ch xv. 1879: R.L.S., *Story of a Lie*, ch vi.

3. Trick for trick. 1659: Howell, 4, Trick for trick, and a stone in thy foot besides, quoth one pulling out a stone out of his mares hoof, when she bit him upon the back, and he her upon the buttock. 1670: Ray, 217 [as in 1659]. 1710: Ward, *Nuptial Dialogues*, ii 51, Women … love to shew us trick for trick. 1730: Bailey, *Dict.*, s.v. 'Quid pro quo', Quid pro quo … trick for trick, a Rowland for an Oliver.

Tricks in every trade, There are. For the earlier form of this saying, *see There is knavery in all trades* at **Knavery.** 1857: E. Bennett, *Border Rover*, vi, 'I would be willing to swear you had bewitched this rifle'. … 'Thar's tricks to all trades 'cept ourn'. 1948: F. P. Keyes, *Dinner at Antoine's*, xx, There's tricks to all trades. Running down murderers is one way of making a living, so that makes it a trade.

Trig as a linnet. 1892: Heslop, *Northumb.*

Words, 744 (E.D.S.), 'Trig as a lennard (spruce as a linnet) ' – Newcastle proverb.

Trim as a trencher. *c.*1540: Bale, *Kynge Johan*, 98 (Camden S.), Trymme as a trencher, havynge his shoes of golde. 1542: Udall, tr. Erasmus' *Apoph.*, 276 (1877), Filling vp as trimme as a trencher the space that stoode voide, with his own hand. [In the Appendix, Mr R. Roberts, the editor and publisher of this reprint, says: 'A proverbial saying which may still be heard occasionally, in the country, although trenchers have almost entirely disappeared. A new trencher, neatly turned out of sycamore wood, had a particularly clean and wholesome appearance'.]

Trimmingham. *See* **Gimmingham.**

Trim tram, like master like man – with variants. 1583: Melbancke, *Philotimus*, sig. D3, Trim tram, neither good for God nor man. 1653: Middleton and Rowley, *Span. Gipsy*, IV iii, Trim, tram, hang master, hang man! 1681: Robertson, *Phraseol. Generalis*, 1246. 1714: Ozell, *Molière*, i 159. 1762: Smollett, *Sir L. Greaves*, ch xiii. 1785: Grose, *Class. Dict. Vulgar Tongue*, s.v.

Tring, Wing and Ivinghoe. 1. *See* quots. 1820: *Gent. Mag.*, ii 326, Tring, Wing, and Ivinghoe, did go, For striking the Black Prince a blow. *N. & Q.*, 3rd ser, v 176, The name of Ivanhoe was suggested [to Scott], as the story goes, by an old rhyme recording three names of the manors forfeited by the ancestor of the celebrated Hampden, for striking the Black Prince a blow with his racket, when they quarrelled at tennis … 'Tring, Wing and Ivanhoe, For striking of a blow, Hampden did forego, And glad he could escape so'. [Unluckily for the legend these manors were never in the Hampden family.]

2. Tring, Wing, and Ivinghoe, Three dirty villages all in a row And never without a rogue or two. Would you know the reason why? Leighton Buzzard is hard by. 1852: *N. & Q.*, 1st ser, v 619.

Tripe-broth it better than no porridge. 1732: Fuller, 5274.

Tripe's good meat if it be well wip't. 1678: Ray, 50.

Trojan, Like a. 1846: Planché, *Extravag.*, iii 143 (1879), Upon them! forward! charge like Trojans! – go! 1855: Dickens, *Holly Tree*, Branch 2, He went on a lying like a Trojan about the pony. 1883: R.L.S., *Treasure I*, ch xviii, He had lain like a Trojan behind his mattress in the gallery.

Trot sire, trot dam. *See* quot. 1560: Wilson, *Rhetorique*, 119 (1909), Trot sire, and trot damme, how should the fole amble, that is, when both father and mother were nought, it is not like that the childe will proue good. Cf. **Foal.**

Trouble, *subs.* **1. A trouble shared is a trouble halved.** 1931: D.L. Sayers, *Five Red Herrings*, ix, 'Unbosom yourself,' said Wimsey. 'Trouble shared is trouble halved.' 1966: A. Carter, *Shadow Dance*, viii, He found he wanted to share the experience of the previous night with Edna (a trouble shared is a trouble halved).

2. Do not meet trouble(s) half way. 1598–9: Shakespeare, *Much Ado about Nothing* I i 82, Are you come to meet your trouble? The fashion of the world is to avoid cost, and you encounter it. 1896: J. C. Hutcheson, *Crown and Anchor*, xvi, I can't see the use of anticipating the worst and trying to meet troubles halfway.

3. Let your trouble tarry till its own day comes. 1732: Fuller, 3200. Cf. No. 2.

4. Never trouble trouble till trouble troubles you. Derby. 1884: *Folk-Lore Journal*, ii 280. 1921: R. L. Gales, *Old-World Essays*, 243 [quoted as a West-Country saying]. Cf. No. 1.

5. To have one's trouble for one's pains. *See* **Labour.**

See also **Seek** (4).

Trout. *See* quot. 1893: Inwards, *Weather Lore*, 142, When trout refuse bait or fly, There ever is a storm a-nigh. *See also* **Chevin; and Sound.**

Troy was not took in a day. 1732: Fuller, 5278.

True, *adj.* **1. All be not true that speak fair.** *c*.1460: *How the Good Wife*, l. 65.

2. As true as a corranto. 1632: D. Lupton, *London and Country*: 'Country', No. 12, They [news sheets] have used this trade so long, that now every one can say, its even as true as a currantoe, meaning that its all false.

3. As true as a turtle. *c*.1380: Chaucer, *Parl. of Foules*, l. 355, The wedded turtel with hir herte trewe. *c*.1440: Hoccleve, *Minor Poems*, 141 (E.E.T.S.), As treewe as turtle that lakkith hir feere [mate]. *c*.1470: *Songs and Carols*, 88 (Percy S.), That women be trew as tyrtyll on tre. 1590: Spenser, *F. Q.*, III xi 2, That was as trew in love as turtle to her make. 1670: Ray, 203, As true as a turtle to her mate. 1720: Gay, *Poems*, ii 280 (Underhill), Tho' seeming as the turtle kind, And like the gospel true.

4. As true as God is in heaven. 1737: Ray, 226.

1869: FitzGerald, Sea *Words and Phrases*, 16, As true as God's in heaven, here comes Lord Rochford. 1923: *Folk-Lore*, xxxiv. 329 (Oxfordshire).

5. As true as steel. 1303: Brunne, *Handl. Synne*, l. 2338, And to the ded was as trew as steyl. *c*.1385: Chaucer, *Leg. Good Women*, ix. l. 21, Pitouse, sadde, wyse, and trewe as steel. *c*.1480: *Digby Plays*, 116 (E.E.T.S.), Now, as thou hast byn trew as stylle. 1553: Googe, *Pop. Kingdome*, bk iv l. 537, And sure with no dissembling heart, for true as steele they bee. 1676: Shadwell, *Virtuoso*, III. 1713: Gay, *Wife of Bath*, V iii 1824: Scott, *Redgauntlet*, ch xvi, I am trusty as steel to owners, and always look after cargo. 1849: Brontë, *Shirley*, ch ix. 1923: Lucas, *Advisory Ben*, § xxxix p 208.

6. As true as that the candle ate the cat – with variants. 1666: Torriano, *Piazza Univ.*, 242, The English say, As true as that the candle ate the cat. 1700: Ward, *London Spy*, 230 (1924) [as in 1666, but with 'plain' for 'true']. 1732: Fuller, 4351, That is as true that the cat crew, and the cock rock'd the cradle.

7. As true as the dial to the sun. 1663: Butler, *Hudibras*, III ii 174, True as the dial to the sun Although it be not shined upon. 1742: Fielding, *Andrews*, bk i ch xviii, She was as true to her husband as the dial to the sun.

8. As true as the Gospel. 1540: Palsgrave, *Acolastus*, sig. Q3, That is as trewe as the gospell. 1577: *Misogonus*, III i 1633: Draxe, 210. 1753: Richardson, *Grandison*, i 30 (1883). 1828: Carr, *Craven Dialect*, i 193, 'It's as true as t' gospel', a common asseveration. 1872: Hardy, *Greenwood Tree*, Pt I ch ii, 'That's as true as gospel of this member', said Reuben. 1926: Phillpotts, *Yellow Sands*, III, Is it true what these old men be telling? *Arthur.* True as Gospel!

9. As true as velvet. 1608: *Merry Devil of Edm.*, IV i, Thou speakst as true as velvet. Cf. **Velvet.**

10. A true friend is known in a doubtful matter. 1591: Lodge, *Catharos*, 13 (Hunt.Cl.) [quoted as 'an olde prouerbe'].

11. A true jest is no jest. *c*.1386: Chaucer, *Cook's Prol.*, l. 33, But 'sooth pley, quaad [evil] pley', as the Fleming seith. 1546: Heywood, *Proverbs*, Pt II ch viii, Sooth bourd is no bourd. 1591: Harington, *Apol. of Poetrie*, par. 9 [as in 1546]. 1633: Draxe, 99 [as in 1546]. 1824: Scott, *Redgauntlet*, ch xii, The lady drew up, and the

Provost said, half aside, 'The sooth bourd is nae bourd'. 1825: Hone, *Ev. Day Book*, i 506, To talk now of 'no joke like a true joke' is scarcely passable.

12. A true man and a thief think differently. *c.*1386: Chaucer, *Squire's Tale*, l. 529, But sooth is seyd, gon sithen many a day, 'A trew wight and a theef thenken nat oon'.

13. He is a true friend. *See* quot. Before 1500: in Hill, *Commonplace-Book*, 131 (E.E.T.S.), He ys a trew frend, that loveth me for my love and not for my good [goods, wealth].

14. He that is true. *See* quots. *c.*1300: *King Alisaunder*, l. 7367, Who-so is of dede untreowe Ofte hit schal him sorë reowe. *c.*1390: Gower, *Conf. Amantis*, bk vii l. 1961, The proverbe is, who that is trewe, Him schal his while nevere rewe.

15. It must be true that all men say. 1546: Heywood, *Proverbs*, Pt I ch xi, It must needes be true that euery man sayth. 1570: A. Barclay, *Mirrour of Good Manners*, 52 (Spens.S.), It nedes muste be true which euery man doth say. 1670: Ray, 56, That is true which all men say. 1748: Richardson, *Clarissa*, iv 118 (1785), What every one says must be true. 1829: Scott, *Geierstein*, ch xxii, How should that be false which all men say is true?

16. That's as true as I am his uncle. 1678: Ray, 83.

17. There's many a true word spoken in jest. *c.*1386: Chaucer, *Monk's Prol.*, l. 76, Ful ofte in game a sooth I have herd seye. *c.*1665: in *Roxb. Ballads*, vii 366 (B.S.), Many a true word hath been spoke in jest. 1738: Swift, *Polite Convers.*, Dial. I. 1892: Shaw, *Widowers' Houses*, I. 1920: H. Lucy, *Diary of Journalist*, 21.

18. The truest jests sound worst in guilty ears. 1670: Ray, 14.

19. True blood may not lie. *c.*1489: Caxton, *Sonnes of Aymon*, 248 (E.E.T.S.). But as men sayen 'true blood may not lye'.

20. True blue will never, stain. [*c.*1630: in *Roxb. Ballads*, iii 257 (B.S.), That showes a good fellow true blew.] *c.*1660: in Ibid., iv 495 (B.S.), You know true blew will never stain. 1727: *Harl. MS.*, quoted in *Roxb. Ballads*, iv 495 (B.S.), True blue was the colour which never will stain. 1732: Fuller, 5279. 1875: Cheales, *Proverb. Folk-Lore*, 106.

21. True lovers are sky, when people are by.

c.1760: Foote, *Lame Lover*, II [quoted as 'the old proverb'].

22. True praise roots and spreads. 1640: Herbert, *Jac. Prudentum*. 1670: Ray, 21 ['takes root' for 'roots']. 1736: Bailey, *Dict.* [as in 1670].

Trugs i' th' Hole or by Brokken Cross, Oather by. 1917: Bridge, *Cheshire Proverbs*, 99.

Trumpeter is dead, Your. 1729: Franklin, *Busy-Body*, No. 1, in *Works*, i 329 (Bigelow), I am cautious of praising myself, lest I should be told my trumpeter's dead. 1854: Baker, *Northants Gloss.*, s.v. 'Trumpeter', Trumpeter. An egotist … Sometimes it is said, 'your trumpeter's dead'; i.e. no one sounds your praises, so you are compelled to extol yourself.

Trumps, To be put to one's. 1559: *Mirr. Mag. Jack Cade*, xx (OED), Ere he took me, I put him to his trumps. 1588: *Mar-Prelate's Epitome*, 13 (1843), It would put a man to his trumps, to answer these things soundly. 1615: B.&F., *Cupid's Revenge*, IV i, What is in 't [in a petition] I know not; but it has put him to his trumps. 1730: in *Walpole Ballads*, 35 (Oxford, 1916), And for shifts and excuses Sir William he pumps; Ay, and Bobby the Screen too was put to his trumps. 1825: Scott, in Lockhart's *Life*, vi 7, The great Roman general, Agricola, was strangely put to his trumps at the *Urbs Orrea*.

Trunch. *See* **Gimmingham**.

Truro, Cornwall. **1. Pride of Truro.** 1602: Carew, *Survey of Cornwall*, 220 (1811), Some of the idle disposed Cornishmen nick their towns with bywords, as … 'Pride of Truro'. 1864: 'Cornish Proverbs', in *N.&Q.*, 3rd ser, v 275, The Good Fellowship of Padstow; Pride of Truro; Gallants of Foy.

2. *See* quot. 1662: Fuller, *Worthies*, i 306 (1840), 'Tru-ru, Triveth-en, Ombdina geveth Try-ru'. Which is to say, 'Truru consisteth of three streets; and it shall in time be said, Here Tru-ru stood'.

Trust, *subs.* **1. In trust is treason.** *c.*1460: *Good Wyfe wold a Pylgremage*, l. 76, Syt not with no man a-loune, for oft in trust ys tressoun. *c.*1475: *Mankind*, sc iii st. 107. 1575: Gascoigne, *Posies*, in *Works*, i 404 (Cunliffe). 1628: Rous, *Diary*, 30 (Camden S.), In greatest trust is often greatest treason. 1670: Ray, 149.

2. This day there is no trust, but come to-morrow. 1732: Fuller, 4999. 1855: Bohn, 412, I sell nothing on trust till to-morrow.

3. Trust is dead, ill payment killed it. 1666: Torriano, *Piazza Univ.*, 184. 1911: T. Edwardes, *Neighbourhood*, 109, [Public-house inscription] Poor Trust is dead: bad pay killed him.

4. Trust is the mother of deceit. 1605: Camden, *Remains*, 332 (1870).

Trust, *verb.* **1. Do not trust nor contend, Nor lay wagers, nor lend, And you'll have peace to your life's end.** 1732: Fuller, 6351.

2. He who trusteth not is not deceived. Ibid., No. 2406.

3. He who trusts all things to chance, makes a *lottery of his life.* Ibid., No. 2407.

4. If you trust before you try, you may repent before you die. *c.*1560: in Huth, *Ancient Ballads, etc.*, 221 (1867), Who trusts before he tries may soone his trust repent. 1670: Ray, 149. 1732: Fuller, 6084.

5. I'll trust him no farther than I can fling him. 1618: Harington, *Epigrams*, bk ii No. 74, That he might scant trust him so fane as throw him. 1670: Ray, 197. 1732: Fuller, 5286, Trust him no further than you can throw him. 1901: F. E. Taylor, *Lancs Sayings*, 33, Aw'd trust him no furr nor aw could throw a bull bi t' tail. 1916: B. Duffy, *The Counter-Charm*, 14, I wouldn't trust her as far as I could throw her.

6. I'll trust him no farther than I can see him. 1594: *True Trag. Rich. Third*, 17 (SH.S.), Ile trust neuer ... a Duke in the world, further then I see him. 1611: Cotgrave, s.v. 'Croire', To trust no man further then he sees him. 1694: *Terence made English*, 91, I'll trust ye no farther than I can see ye. 1869: Spurgeon, *John Ploughman*, ch xviii, You may trust some men as far as you can see them, but no further.

7. In whom I trust most. *See* quots. *c.*1450: *Partonope*, 110 (E.E.T.S.), Ther-fore men saith an olde sawe: He to whom a man do trest Euermore may dysceyve hym best. Before 1500: in Hill, *Commonplace-Book*, 130 (E.E.T.S.), In whom I trust most, sounest me deseyvith.

8. I will not trust him though he were my brother. 1546: Heywood, *Proverbs*, Pt I ch xi 1639: Clarke, 140.

9. Trusting often makes fidelity. 1732: Fuller, 5292.

10. Trust me, but look to thyself. Ibid., No. 5288.

11. Trust none better than thyself. *c.*1460: *How*

the Good Wife, l. 125, Leue none better than thi sefie.

12. Trust not a new friend nor an old enemy. 1569: Grafton, *Chron.*, ii 84 (1809), None of vs I beleue is so vn-wise ... to trust a newe friend made of an olde foe. Before 1634: Chapman, *Alphonsus*, I i, Trust not a reconciled friend, for good turns cannot blot out old grudges. 1875: Cheales, *Proverb. Folk-Lore*, 95. Cf. **Reconciled friend.**

13. You may trust him with untold gold. 1633: Draxe, 209, A man may, etc. 1670: Ray, 197. 1711: *Spectator*, No. 202, His master ... could trust him with untold gold. 1870: T. W. Robertson, *Birth*, I, I'd trust him with untold gold.

See also **Put** (6); and **Try** (2).

Truth, *subs.* **1. Fair fatt truth and daylight.** 1678: Ray, 211.

2. In too much dispute truth is lost. 1659: Howell, *Proverbs: Fr.-Eng.*, 1.

3. Tell the truth and shame the devil. 1548: W. Patten, *Expedition into Scotland*, A5, An epigrame ... the whiche I had, or rather (to saie truth and shame the devel, for out it wool) I stale ... from a frende of myne. 1552: Latimer, *Sermons*, 506 (P.S.), There is a common saying amongst us, 'Say the truth and shame the devil'. 1597: Shakespeare, 1 *Henry IV*, III i 1616: Jonson, *Devil is an Ass*, V v, I will tell truth. And shame the fiend. 1670: Cotton, *Scarronides*, bk iv 1710: Centlivre, *Man's Bewitch'd*, III i 1823: Scott, *Peveril*, ch iv, Faith, neighbours, to say truth, and shame the devil, I do not like the sound of it above half. Cf. No. 22.

4. Truth and sweet oil always come to the top. 1620: Shelton, *Quixote*, Pt II ch x, Truth ... tramples on the lie as oil doth upon water. 1640: Herbert, *Jac. Prudentum*, Truth and oil are ever above. 1732: Fuller, 5295 [as in 1640]. 1865: 'Lancs Proverbs', *in N.&Q.*, 3rd ser, viii 494. 1901: F. E. Taylor, *Lancs Sayings*, 10, Truth an' sweet-oil awlus cum'n to th' top.

5. Truth fears no colours, 1732: Fuller, 5296.

6. Truth finds foes where it should find none. 1572: T. Wilson, *Disc., upon Usury*, 188 (1925), It is a common saying, *Vertias odium parit*, Truth purchaseth hatred. 1660: Howell, *Parly of Beasts*, 51, Truth, as the proverb runs, begets hatred often times in the minds of those to whom it is spoken. 1670: Ray, 150, Truth finds foes where it makes none. 1732: Fuller, 5298.

7. Truth has a scratched face. 1875: Cheales, *Proverb. Folk–Lore*, 118.

8. Truth hath a good face but bad clothes. 1600: Bodenham, *Belvedere*, 14 (Spens.S.), Truth most delights, when shee goes meanest clad. 1639: Fuller, *Holy War*, bk iii ch xix, Truth hath always a good face, though often but bad clothes. 1670: Ray, 27. 1694: D'Urfey, *Quixote*, Pt I Act I sc ii, Truth has a good face, tho the quoif be torn. 1732: Fuller, 5929 ['ill' for 'bad'].

9. Truth hath always a sure bottom. 1678: Ray, 211 ['fast' for 'sure']. 1732: Fuller, 5300.

10. Truth is stranger than fiction. 1823: Byron, *Don Juan*, can. xiv. st. 101, For Truth is always strange – Stranger than fiction. *c.*1890: Gilbert, *Foggarty's Fairy*, II

11. Truth is the daughter of Time. 1736: Bailey, *Dict.*, s.v. 'Truth'.

12. Truth is truth to the end of the reckoning. *c.*1581: in *Ballads from M.SS.*, ii 123 (B.S.), Truth wilbe truth, in spite of all defame. 1595: Churchyard, *Charitie*, To Gen. Readers, For truth is truth, when all is saide and done. 1603: Shakespeare, *Meas. for Meas.*, V i.

13. Truth lies at the bottom of a well. [Democritus quasi in puteo quodam sic alta, ut fundus sit nullus, veritatem jacere demersam. – Lactantius, *Inst.*, iii 28.] 1562: J. Wigand, *De Neutralibus*, G6v, The truth lyeth yet syill drowned in the depe. 1578: H. Wotton, tr. *J. Iver's Courtly Controversy*, 90, I shall condust you … unto the Mansion where the truth so long hidden dothe inhabit, the which sage Democritus searched in the bottom of a well.1646: Browne, *Pseudo. Epi.*, bk i ch v, Truth, which wise men say, doth lye in a well. 1758–67: Sterne, *Shandy*, iv, 'Slawkenb. Tale', Whilst the unlearned … were all busied in getting down to the bottom of the well, where TRUTH keeps her little court … 1797: Colman, jr., *Nightg. and Slippers*, 76 (Hotten), And hence the proverb rose, that truth lies in the bottom of a well. 1819: Byron, *Don Juan*, can. ii st. 84, You'd wish yourself where Truth is – in a well. 1852: M. A. Keltie, *Reminisc. of Thought and Feeling*, 3, The thinker … who dives below, and looks for truth in the well wherein she is said to reside.

14. Truth lies on the surface of things. 1824: Maginn, *O'Doherty's Maxims*, 81 (1849), There is not a truer saying in this world, than that truth lies on the surface of things.

15. Truth may be blamed but cannot be shamed. 1468: *Coventry Mys.*, 367 (SH.S.), Trewthe dyd nevyr his maystyr shame. 1542: *Sch. House of Women*, l. 6, Wherby the truthe is often blamed, Yet in no wise truthe may be shamed. 1567: Harman, *Caveat*, 28 (E.E.T.S.). 1655: Fuller, *Church Hist.*, bk iv. § i (56). 1732: Fuller, 5307. 1853: Trench, *Proverbs*, 19 (1905).

16. Truth needs no colours. 1519: Horman, *Vulgaria*, fo. 58, Trewthe nedeth no peynted or colored termes. 1631: Mabbe, *Celestina*, 94 (T.T.), Because truth needeth no colours.

17. Truth needs not many words. *c.*1550: *Part. of Byrdes*, l. 28, Where is many wordes the troueth goeth by. 1732: Fuller, 5309, Truth needs not many words; but a false tale, a large preamble.

18. Truth never grows old. Ibid., No. 5310.

19. Truths and roses have thorns about them. 1855: Bohn, 547.

20. Truth's best ornament is nakedness. 1732: Fuller, 5314.

21. Truth seeks no corners. 1564: Bullein, *Dialogue*, 81 (E.E.T.S.), Well man, well; truth seketh no corners. *c.*1602: Chapman, *May-Day*, IV iii, Why not? Truth seeks no corners. 1732: Fuller, 5311.

22. Truth shameth the devil. 1605: Camden, *Remains*, 334 (1870). 1732: Fuller, 5306, Truth makes the devil blush. Cf. No. 3.

23. Truth should not always be revealed, [*c.*1380: Wiclif, *Eng. Works*, 270 (E.E.T.S.), Sumtyme it harmeth men to seie the sothe out of couenable tyme and euere it harmeth to lie, but sumtyme it profitith to be stille and abide a couenable tyme to speke.] *c.*1387: Usk, *Test. of Love*, in Skeat's *Chaucer*, vii 32, Al sothes be nat to sayne. *c.*1480: *Early Miscell.*, 63 (Warton Cl., 1855), For soothe may not alle day be sayd. *c.*1550: *Parl.*, *of Byrdes*, l. 36, All soothes be not for to saye, It is better some be lefte by reason Than trouth to be spoken out of season. *c.*1680: L'Estrange, *Seneca's Morals*: 'Happy life', ch vii, The thing was true; but all truths are not to be spoken at all times. 1727: Gay, *Fables*, 1st ser, No. 18, l. 24. 1754: Berthelson, *Eng.-Danish Dict.*, s.v. 'Truth' [as in 1680]. 1827: Scott, *Journal*, 16 July, I will erase the passage. Truth should not be spoke at all times. 1846: T. Wright, *Essays on Middle Ages*, i 140, So again, we say 'Every truth is not to be told'.

24. Truths too fine spun are subtle fooleries.
1855: Bohn, 547.

25. Truth trieth. *See* quot. *c.*1475: *Mankind*, sc iii st. 123, The prowerbe seyth 'the trewth tryith the sylfe'. Alas, I have much care.

26. Truth will out. 1439: Lydgate, *Life of St Alban* (1974), 203, Trouthe wil out ... Ryghtwysnesse may nat ben hid. 1596: Shakespeare, *Merchant of Venice*, II ii 73, Truth will come to light; murder cannot be hid long; a man's son may, but in the end truth will out. 1822: M. Edgeworth, *Letter*, 17 Jan. (1971), 324, Whether about a novel or a murder, the truth will out.

27. Truth will prevail. *c.*1400: *Beryn*, 63 (E.E.T.S.), Ffor, aftir comyn seying, 'evir atte ende The trowith wol be previd, how so men evir trend'. *c.*1580: Fulwell, *Ars Adulandi*, sig. E4, Trueth in the ende shall preuayle. 1619: *Helpe to Discourse*, 98 (1640), Truth is the strongest of all, which overcomes all things in the end. 1740: North, *Examen*, 170, According to the proverb, that, *early or late, Truth will out.*

28. Truth will sometimes break out, unlooked for. 1732: Fuller, 5314

See also **Follow** (4).

Try, *verb.* **1. He tries all the keys in the bunch.** 1633: Draxe, 189. 1639: Clarke, 60.

2. Try before you trust, *c.*1460: *Good Wyfe wold a Pylgremage*, l. 118 (E.E.T.S.), A-say [Assay] or euer thow trust. Before 1500: in Hill, *Commonplace-Book*, 47 (E.E.T.S.), Geve trust to them that thow hast preved. 1587: Greene, *Works*, iv. 26 (Grosart), From hence forth trie ere thou trust. 1637: T. Heywood, *Dialogues, etc.*, in Bang, *Materialien*, B. 3, p. 212, Try ere you trust. 1639: Clarke, 31, Try and trust.

3. Try your friend before you have need of him. *c.*1470: *Songs and Carols*, 28 (Percy S.), Man, beware and wyse in dede, Asay thi frend or thou hast nede. 1564: Bullein, *Dialogue*, 67 (E.E.T.S.), It is good trying of friendes before need do require, *c.*1600: in *Roxb. Ballads*, ii 573 (B.S.), First trye thy friend before thou trust. 1659: Howell, 5.

4. Try your skill in gilt first, and then in gold. 1639: Clarke, 60. 1672: Walker, *Paroem.*, 43.

Tub on its own bottom. *See* **Every tub.**

Tub to a whale, To throw a. 1748: Richardson, *Clarissa*, iii 51 (1785), When a man talks to a woman upon such subjects, let her be ever so

much in *Alt*, 'tis strange, if he cannot throw out a tub to the whale; – that is to say, if he cannot divert her from resenting one bold thing, by uttering two or three full as bold; but for which more favourable interpretations will lie. 1763: Mrs Brooke, *Lady J. Mandeville*, 148 (1820), A wise writer ... should throw in now and then an indiscretion in his conduct to play with, as seamen do a tub to the whale. 1912: *Nation*, 29 June, p. 465, col. 2 (OED), He throws a tub to the High Church whale.

Turn Dooley. *See* **Tom Dooley.**

Tune the old cow died of. *See* **Cow** (27).

Turk's hone. *See* **Grass** (4).

Turkeys to market, He is driving, i.e. He cannot walk straight. 1869: Hazlitt, 165.

Turkeys. *See also* **Hops.**

Turn, *verb.* **1. He'll turn rather than burn.** 1639: Clarke, 222, Rather turne than burne. 1678: Ray, 346. 1732: Fuller, 2432. 1855: Kingsley, *West. Ho*, ch vii, None that it [the Inquisition] catches ... but must turn or burn.

2. It is hard to turn tack upon a narrow bridge. 1732: Fuller, 2954.

3. To turn a narrow adlant = To have a narrow escape. [1611: Cotgrave, s.v. 'Charron', A good carter turnes in a narrow corner. 1616: *Honest Lawyer*, sig. E2, He is a cunning coachman that can turne well in a narrow roome.] 1879: Jackson, *Shropsh. Word-Book*, 3, To 'turn on a mighty narrow adlant' is a proverbial saying expressive of a very narrow escape. 1917: Bridge, *Cheshire Proverbs*, 145.

4. To turn one's copy. *See* **Copy** (2).

5. To turn one's tippet = To recant or change one's opinions. 1546: Heywood, *Proverbs*, Pt II ch i, So turned then their tippet by way of exchange. 1576: Pettie, *Petite Pall.*, Pref. Lett., You marvel ... that I should so soon turn my tippet and recant. 1608: *Merry Devil of Edm.*, III ii, The nun will soone at night turne tippit. 1659: Howell, 5, He hath turned his tippet. 1826: Scott, *Woodstock*, ch xxix, A high reward, and pardon for past acts of malignancy, might tempt him once more to turn his tippet.

6. To turn over a new leaf. 1548: Hall, *Chron.*, 180 (1809), When they sawe thenglishmen at the weakest, they turned the leafe and sang another song. 1570: Ascham, *Scholemaster*, 155 (1743), Except such men think themselves wiser than Cicero for teaching of eloquence, they must be content to turn a new leaf. 1593: G. Harvey, *Works*, ii 328 (Grosart), As may schoole him to turne-ouer a new leafe. 1687: Sedley, *Bellamira*, III, When we are marry'd I'll turn over a new leaf. 1750: Smollett, *Gil Blas*, i 228, I ... resolved to turn over a new leaf, and live honestly. 1895: Pinero, *Benefit of Doubt*, I, This ... has been no end of a shocker for me. From to-day I turn over the proverbial new leaf.

7. To turn up like a bad penny. 1824: Scott, *Redgauntlet*, II ii, Bring back Darsie? little doubt of that – the bad shilling is sure enough to come back again. 1884: R.H. Thorpe, *Fenton Family*, iii, Just like as not he'll be coming back one of these days, when he's least wanted. A bad penny is sure to return. 1922: J. Joyce, *Ulysses*, 149, Who's dead, when and what did he die of? Turn up like a bad penny.

8. To turn with the wind (or **tide**). 1591: Harington, *Orl. Furioso*, bk xxv. st. 74, Rogero loves to take the surer side, And turnes his sailes, as fortune tumes her tide. 1670: Ray, 197.

9. Turn about is fair play. 1755: *Life of Captain Dudley Bradstreet*, 338, Hitherto honest Men were kept from shuffling the cards, because they would cast knaves out from the Company of Kings, but we would make them know Turn about was fair Play. 1854: Surtees, *Handley Cross*, xviii, 'Turn about is fair play', as the devil said to the smoke-jack. 1891: R.L.S., *Wrecker*, ch xxiv.

10. Turn-again Lane. *See* 1670 quot. 1531: Tyndale, *Expos. St John*, 140 (P.S.), It is become a turn-again lane with them. 1562: Heywood, *Epigr.*, 5th hund., No. 69, Find means to take a house in Turn-again-lane. 1670: Ray, 243, He must take a house in Turn again Lane. This in old records is called Wind-again Lane, and lieth in the parish of St Sepulchres, going down to Fleet-dike, having no exit at one end. It is spoken of, and to, those who take prodigal or other vicious and destructive courses. 1790: Grose, *Prov. Gloss.*, s.v. 'London' [as in 1670].

11. Turn the buckle. *See* **Buckle of belt**.

Turnips like a dry bed but a wet head. 1917: Bridge, *Cheshire Proverbs*, 147.

Turnips, She has given him = She has jilted him. 1845: Ford, *Handbook Spain*, i 27 *n.* (OED), This gourd forms a favourite metaphor ... she has refused him; it is the 'giving cold turnips' of Suffolk. 1869: Hazlitt, 333, She has given him turnips. *Devonshire.*

Turnspits are dry. 1678: Ray, 83.

Twelfth Day. *See* quots. Ibid., 52, At twelf-day the days are lengthened a cock stride. 1867: *N.&Q.*, 3rd ser, xii 478, On Twelfth Day, the day is lengthened the stride of a fowl (Surrey). 1868: Ibid., 4th ser, i 61, On Twelfth Day the day is a cock-stride longer (East Riding).

Twelve. *See* **Hours**.

Twenty. 1. As good twenty as nineteen. 1670: Ray, 150.

2. I'll go twenty miles on your errand first. Ibid., 177.

3. Twenty sovereigns are worth twenty acres = 'A bird in the hand', etc. 1917: Bridge, *Cheshire Proverbs*, 147.

4. Twenty young. *See* quot. 1591: Florio, *Second Frutes*, 101, And who is not [young] at twentie, And knowes not at thirtie, And hath not at fortie in store. Will not be while he liues, for to know vainely striues, And shall neuer haue anie more. 1882: Mrs Chamberlain, *W. Worcs. Words*, 39 (E.D.S.), Twenty young, Thirty strong, Forty wit, Or never none. I find the following manuscript entry, written in faded ink in an old-fashioned hand, on p. 232 of my copy of Ray's *Proverbs*, 3rd ed., 1737: 'Ten pretty, twenty witty, thirty strong, if ever Forty wise, fifty rich, sixty saint, or never'.

Twice boiled. *See* **Colewort**.

Twig. *See* **Bend** (1).

Twineham. *See* **Bolney**.

Twinkling of a bed-post (originally **bed-staff**), **In the.** 1676: Shadwell, *Virtuoso*, I i, Gad! I'll do it instantly, in the twinkling of a bedstaff. 1685: S. Wesley, *Maggots*, 163, In bedstaff's twinkling I'll be gone. 1700: Ward, *London Spy*, 264 (1924), She could shake 'em off ... in the twinkling of a bed-staff. 1834: Marryat, *P. Simple*, ch xxxvi, Won't I get you out of purgatory in the twinkling of a bed-post? 1847: Planché, *Extravag.*, iii 192 (1879), If any one grumbles I'll scuttle his nob, In the twinkling of a bed post!

Twinkling of an eye, In the. *c.*1300: in *Vernon MS.*, 286 (E.E.T.S.), Ffor in a twynclyng of an eighe ffrom erthe to heuene thou maight styghe. *c.*1400: *Beryn*, 94 (E.E.T.S.), In twynkelyng of an eye To make a short answer. 1549: Latimer, *Seven Sermons*, 117 (Arber), He maye in the twynkejing of an eye, saue a man. 1611: *Bible*, 1 Cor. xv. 52. 1674: Jas. Howard, *Eng. Mounsieur*, IV iii 1704: Defoe, *The Storm*, 195, The rest of his men … in the twinkling of an eye were drown'd. 1884: Gilbert, *Princess Ida*, II, I'll storm your walls. And level your halls, in the twinkling of an eye.

Twist a rope of sand. *See* **Rope**, *subs.* (6).

Twittle, twattle, drink up your posset drink. 1670: Ray, 253 … This proverb had its original in Cambridge, and is scarce known elsewhere. 1790: Grose, *Prov. Gloss.*, s.v. 'Cambridgeshire'.

Two anchors. *See* **Good riding.**

Two and two together, To put. 1855: Thackeray, *Newcomes*, ch xlix., Putting two and two together, as the saying is, it was not difficult for me to guess who the expected Marquis was. 1876: G. Eliot, *Felix Holt*, ch xi, You are men who can put two and two together. 1918: Orczy, *Man in Grey*: 'M. Vaillant', 5 What that purpose was it became my business to learn. It was a case of putting the proverbial two and two together.

Two anons and a by and by is an hour and a half. 1605: Camden, *Remains*, 334 (1870). 1670: Ray, 56. 1732: Fuller, 5321 ['are' for 'is'].

Two apples in my hand and the third in my mouth. 1659: Howell, 10.

Two are company. *See* **Two is company.**

Two bad paymasters, There are. 1773: Foote, *Nabob*, II, There are two bad paymasters; those who pay before, and those who never pay. 1821: Scott, *Pirate*, ch xxxix, There are two bad paymasters – he that pays too soon, and he that does not pay at all.

Two bites of a cherry, To make. 1694: Motteux, *Rabelais*, bk v ch xxviii, Nothing is to be got out of him but monosyllables; by Jingo, I believe he wou'd make three bits of a cherry. 1824: Maginn, *O'Doherty's Maxims*, 69 (1849), The old rule of 'never to make two bites of a cherry' applies with peculiar emphasis to cherry brandy. 1860: Reade, *Cl. and Hearth*, ch xii.

Two blacks will never make a white. 1721: J. Kelly, *Scottish Proverbs*, 321, Two blacks make no white. An Answer to them who, being blam'd, say others have done as ill or worse. 1822: Scott, in Lockhart's *Life*, v 162, To try whether I cannot contradict the old proverb of 'two blacks not making a white'. 1880: Spurgeon, *Ploughm. Pictures*, 92.

Two blows. *See* quot. 1883: Burne, *Shropsh. Folk-Lore*, 589, It takes two blows to make a battle = one swallow does not make a summer (so used and explained).

Two buckets. *See* **Buckets.**

Two candles. *See*. quot. 1883: Burne, *Shropsh. Folk-Lore*, 275, 'Two candles burning And never a wheel turning', is a saying with which, though spinning wheels are no more, careful Staffordshire housewives still reprove 'burning candle to waste'.

Two cats. *See* **Two women.**

Two cats in a gutter, They agree like. 1546: Heywood, *Proverbs*, Pt II ch i 1589: L. Wright, *Display of Dutie*, 24, Agreeing like … two cats in a gutter. 1659: Howell, 3.

Two chimneys. *See* **Chimney** (1).

Two complexions in one face. 1575: G. Fenton, *Golden Epistles*, 292 (1582), A propertie verye familiar with ye moste of them, to haue two colours to one meaning, and (as the saying is) to beare two complexions in one face.

Two cunning knaves need no broker. 1546: Heywood, *Proverbs*, Pt I ch xi ['false' for 'cunning']. 1670: Ray, 111. 1732: Fuller, 5322.

Two daughters and a back door are three arrant thieves. 1670: Ray, 51. 1732: Fuller, 5323.

Two determine. *See* **Nought** (3).

Two dogs fight for a bone, and a third runs away with it. *c.*1386: Chaucer, *Knight's Tale*, l. 1177, We stryve as dide the houndes for the boon … Ther cam akyte that they were so wrothe, And bar awey the boon betwixe hem bothe. 1534: More, *Dialogie of Comfort* (1553), I Aiiiv, Now strive there twain for us, our lord send the grace, that the thyrde dog cary not awaie the bone from them both.1633: Draxe, 30, Two dogs striue for a bone, and the third whiles that they contend, taketh it away. 1692: L'Estrange, *Aesop*, 4 (3rd ed.). 1732: Fuller, 5324. 1880: Spurgeon, *Ploughm. Pictures*, 85.

Two dry sticks will kindle a green one. 1678: Ray, 213. 1732: Fuller, 5325.

Two ears. *See* **One tongue.**

Two eggs a penny. *See* **Egg** (12).

Two evils choose the least, Of. [Nam quod aiunt, minima de malis, id est, ut turpiter potius quam calamitose: an est ullum maius malum turpitudine. – Cicero, *De Officiis*, 3. 29.] *c.*1374: Chaucer, *Troylus*, bk ii l. 470, Of harmes two, the lesse is for to chese. *c.*1440: *Gesta Rom.*, 10 (E.E.T.S.), The knyyt answerid, and seide, 'Sire, hit is wreten, that of too evelis the lasse evill is to be chosyn'. 1546: Heywood, *Proverbs*, Pt I ch v, Of two yls, choose the least, whyle choyse lyth in lot. 1581: Woodes, *Conflict of Conscience*, IV, Howbeit of two evils the least must be choosed. 1694: Cibber, *Love's Last Shift*, III i 1730: Fielding, *Temple Beau*, IV v, Since it is the lesser evil of the two, it is to be preferred. 1913: Galsworthy, *Fugitive*, II, Of two evils, if it be so – choose the least.

Two executors and an overseer make three thieves. 15th cent, in *Reliq. Antiquae*, i 314 (1841).

Two eyes can see more than one. *c.*1594: Bacon, *Promus*, No. 946, Two eyes are better than one. 1605: Camden, *Remains*, 334 (1870). 1681: Robertson, *Phraseol. Generalis*, 567, Two eyes see better than one. 1732: Fuller, 5326 ['may' for 'can'].

Two faces in one hood, To bear = To be double-faced, *c.*1400: *Rom. Rose*, l. 7388, And with so gret devocion They maden her confession, That they had ofte, for the nones, Two hedes in one hood at ones. *c.*1440: Lydgate, *Minor Poems*, 69 (E.E.T.S.), God lovyd neuer two facys in oon hood. Before 1529: Skelton, *Magnyfycence*, l. 720, Two faces in a hode couertly I bere, Water in the one hande, and fyre in the other. 1586: Deloney, *Works*, 462 (1912), With false Iudas you can beare two faces in one hoode. 1668: Shadwell, *Sullen Lovers*, IV i, 'Tis indeed, to be a Pharisee, and carry two faces in a hood, as the saying is. 1754: Berthelson, *Eng.-Danish Dict.*, s.v. 'Face', To carry two faces under a hood. 1841: Dickens, *Barn. Rudge*, ch xl., You are a specious fellow … and carry two faces under your hood, as well as the best. 1893: J. Salisbury, *S. E. Worces. Gloss.*, 45 (E.D.S.), Here's vishing the mon may never get fat, as carries two faces under one hat.

Two feet in one shoe Will never do. 1875: Cheales, *Proverb. Folk-Lore*, 40.

Two folk, To be = To be unfriends. 1631: Mabbe, *Celestina*, 256 (T.T.), I have nothing to say to him; as long as I live, he and I shall be two. 1738: Swift, *Polite Convers.*, Dial. I, Pray, Miss, when did you see your old acquaintance Mrs Cloudy? You and she are two, I hear. 1788: O'Keeffe, *The Toy*, III ii, Mr Metheglin, you and I are now two, so good day to you. 1893: J. Salisbury, *S. E. Worces. Gloss.*, 45 (E.D.S.), Now, Jack, you lazy rascal, uf thee doesn't get on o' thy work, thee un I sh'll be two-folks. 1917: Bridge, *Cheshire Proverbs*, 127.

Two fools in a house are too many. 1580: Lyly, *Euphues*, 283 (Arber), For two fooles in one bed are too many. 1732: Fuller, 5328, Two fools in a house are too many by a couple.

Two fools meet, the bargain goes off, Where. Ibid., No. 5679.

Two forenoons. *See* quot. 1923: *Devonsh. Assoc. Trans.*, liv. 136, 'You can't 'ave two vorenoons in one day'. Meaning you cannot be young more than once.

Two friends have a common purse, one sings and the other weeps, When. 1855: Bonn, 562.

Two friends with one gift, To make. 1681: Robertson, *Phraseol. Generalis*, 797 [with 'favour' for 'gift']. 1732: Fuller, 5205.

Two good days. *See* Wife (5).

Two good men. *See* quot. 1880: Spurgeon, *Ploughm. Pictures*, 154, Another saying, 'There are only two good men, one is dead, and the other is not born'.

Two good things are better than one. 1639: Clarke, 104. 1678: Ray, 212.

Two hands in a dish and one in a puree. 1605: Camden, *Remains*, 333 (1870). 1639: Clarke, 218, One hand in a purse and two in a dish. 1640: Nabbes, *Unfort. Mother*, I iii, Two hands in a dish, The right Court Ordinary. 1738: Swift, *Polite Convert.*, Dial. II

Two heads are better than one. [Σύν τε δύ' ερχομένω. – Homer, *Il.*, x 224.] *c.*1390: Gower, *Confessio Amantis*, I. 1021, Tuo han more wit then on. 1530: Palsgrave, 594, Two wyttes be farre better than one. 1546: Heywood, *Proverbs*, Pt I ch ix. 1558: W. Forrest, *Grisill the Second*, 51 (Roxb.Cl), This olde sayinge, Twoe wytts (or moe) to bee better then one. 1638: Taylor (Water Poet), *Bull, Beare, etc.*, 28, in *Works*, 3rd Coll. (Spens.S.). 1753: Foote, *Taste*, II. 1864: 'Cornish Proverbs', in *N.&Q.*, 3rd ser, vi 494, Two heads are better than one if only sheeps' heads. 1893: S. Butler, in *Memoir*, by Jones, ii 8 (1919), Two are better than one: I heard some one say this and replied: 'Yes, but the man who said that did not know my sisters'. 1894: Northall, *Folk Phrases*, 32 (E.D.S.), Two heads are better than one, even if the one's a sheep's. 1917: Bridge, *Cheshire Proverbs*, 147 [as in 1864.

Two hungry meals make the third a glutton. 1546: Heywood, *Proverbs*, Pt I ch xi 1605: Camden, *Remains*, 331 (1870) ['three' for 'two' and 'fourth' for 'third']. 1655: Fuller, *Church*

Hist., bk vi sect. ii (v. 13). 1732: Fuller, 5329 ['good' for 'hungry', which makes nonsense of the saying].

Two in distress Make trouble less. 1875: Cheales, *Proverb. Folk-Lore*, 32.

Two is company and three is none. 1706: J. Stevens, *Spanish and English Dictionary*, s.v. Compañia, A company consisting of three is worth nothing. 1860: T.C. Haliburton, *Season Ticket*, viii, Three is a very inconvenient limitation, constituting, accoding to the old adage, no company. 1869: 1869: W.C. Hazlitt, *English Proverbs*, 442, Two is company, but three is none. 1871: *N.&Q.*, 4th ser, viii 506 ['are' for 'is']. 1897: E. Lyall, *Wayfaring Men*, ch xxiv, 'Two is company, three is trumpery', as the proverb says. 1907: De Morgan, *Alice-for-Short*, ch viii.

Two kings in one kingdom do not agree well together. 1586: B. Young, *Guazz*, fo. 205.

Two knaves well met. 611: Cotgrave, s.v. 'Chat', *A bon rat bon chat*, Two knaves well met or matched. 1672: Walker, *Paroem.*, 54.

Two losses than one sorrow, Better. 1732: Fuller, 936.

Two masters. *See* No man.

Two may keep counsel if one be away. 1579: Lyly, *Euphues*, 67 (Arber). 1592: Shakespeare, *Romeo*, II iv, Did you ne'er hear say, Two may keep counsel, putting one away? 1630: Brathwait, *Engl. Gent.*, 158 (1641), One may keepe counsell, but two cannot. 1753: Richardson, *Grandison*, ii 8 (1883), The proverb says, Two can keep a secret when one is away.

Two mouths. *See* Stop (4).

Two negatives make an affirmative. 1593: G. Harvey, *Works*, i 293 (Grosart), But euen those two negatiues ... would be conformable enough, to conclude an affirmatiue. 1647: Fuller, *Good Thoughts in Worse Times*, 173 (1830). 1769: Smollett, *Adv. Atom*, 20 (Cooke, 1795), In the English language two negatives amount to an affirmative.

Two of a trade can never agree. [καὶ κεραμεὺς κεραμεῖ κοτέει και τέκτονι τέκτων. –Hesiod, Op. 25.] 1630: Dekker, *Honest Wh.*, Pt 2, IV i, It is a common rule, and 'tis most true. Two of one trade ne'er love. 1752: Murphy, *Gray's Inn Journal*, No. 2, Oct. 8. 1860: Reade, *Cloist. and Hearth*, ch xxxvii.

Two parties to make a quarrel, It takes. 1732:

Fuller, 4942, There must be two at least to a quarrel. 1838: Dickens, *Twist*, ch xv, There must always be two parties to a quarrel, says the old adage. 1925: *Times Lit. Supp.*, Nov. 5, p. 728, col. 2, It takes two to make a quarrel, the proverb says; it takes the world to make a peace.

Two pigeons. *See* Pigeon (4).

Two removes. *See* Three removes.

Two ride on one horse, one must sit behind, When. 1599: Shakespeare, *Much Ado*, III v, An two men ride of a horse, one must ride behind. 1639: in *Berkeley MSS.*, iii 32 (1885). 1883: Burne. *Shropsh. Folk-Lore*, 590, Peggy behind Marget = inferiors last: when two ride one horse, one must ride behind. 1927: *Times*, Feb. 16, p. 10, col. 4.

Two sides to every question, There are. 1802: J. Adams, *Autobiography* (1966), III 269, There were two Sides to a question. 1817: T. Jefferson, *Letter*, 5 May, in L.J. Cappon, *Admas-Jefferson Letters* (1959), II 513, men of energy of character must have enemies; because there are two sides to every question, and ... those who take the other will of course be hostile. 1863: C. Kingsley, *Water Babies*, vi, Let them recollect this, that there are two sides to every question, and a downhill as well as an uphill road.

Two Sir Positives can scarcee meet without a skirmish. 1732: Fuller, 5333.

Two slips *See* Three dips.

Two sorrows of one, Make not.1546: Heywood, *Proverbs*, Pt II ch v *c.*1580: Spelman, *Dialogue*, 4 (Roxb Cl.), As the oulde sainge is; yt is a meere ffollye to make two sorowes of one. 1659: Howell, 5.

Two sparrows on one ear of corn make an iil agreement. 1651: Herbert, *Jac. Prudentum*, 2nd ed. 1732: Fuller, 5334. Two sparrows upon an ear of wheat cannot agree.

Two stomachs to eat and one to work, He has. 1869: Spurgeon *John Ploughman*, ch i, Fellows have two stomachs for eating and drinking, when they have no stomach for work. 1882: *N.&Q.*, 6th ser, v 266 [Kentish saying]. He's got the fever of lurk, Two hearts to eat, and ne'er a one to work. 1880: Peacock, *Manley, etc.*, *Gloss.*, 598 (E.D.S.), He's two bellies fer eätin' an' noan fer wark.

Two stools, Between. *c.*1390: Gower, *Conf. Amantis*, Prol, l.336, Bot it is seid and evere schal, Betwen two stoles lyth the fal. 1546: Heywood, *Proverbs*, Pt I ch iii, While betweene two stooles, my tayle go to grounde. 1593: Giffard, *Dial, on Witches, etc.*, 11 (Percy S.), I perceive your danger is betweene two stooles. 1667–8: Pepys, *Diary*, Jan. 17, And so, between both, as every thing else of the greatest moment do, do fall between two stools. 1791: R. Jephson, *Two Strings to your Bow*, I iii, Well done, Lazarillo; between two stools they say a certain part of a man comes to the ground. 1864: Mrs H. Wood, *Trevlyn Hold*, ch liii, While he keeps me shilly-shallying over this one, I may lose them both. There's an old proverb, you know, about two stools. 1907: De Morgan, *Alice-for-Short*, ch xvi, Charles saw that between the two stools the young couple wouldn't fall to the ground, but would go to the altar.

Two strings to one's bow, To have. [Μηδ' ἐπὶ δυοῖν ἀγκύραιν ὁρμεῖν αὐτοὺς ἐᾶτε. – Demosthenes, *Or.*, 56, 1295 (*fin.*). Nam melius duo defendant retinacula navim. – Prop., ii 22, 41.]. *c.*1477: Caxton, *Jason*, 57 (E.E.T.S.), I wil wel that euery man be amerous and loae but that he haue ij strenges on his bowe. 1578: Florio, *First Fruites*, fo. 6, It is alwayes good for one to haue two stringes to his bowe. 1606: Day, *Ile of Gulls*, II ii, A wise mans bow goes with a two fold string. 1672: Wycherley, *Love in a Wood*, I i *c.*1760: Foote, *Author*, I, I have, I think, at present two strings to my bow; if my comedy succeeds, it buys me a commission; if my mistress, my Laura, proves kind, I am settled for life. 1814: Austen, *Mansfield Park*, ch viii 1859: Planché, *Extravag.*, v 221 (1879). Cf. **Good riding.**

Two Sundays come together, When = never. 1616: Haughton, *Englm. for my Money*, II ii, Art thou so mad as to turn French? *Matt.* Yes, marry, when two Sundays come together. 1681: Robertson, *Phraseol. Generalis*, 1189. 1825: Brockett, *Gloss. N. Country Words*, 150, To-morrow come nivver – when two Sundays meet together. 1854: Baker, *Northants Gloss.*, s.v. 'Sunday', When two Sundays meet. 1881: Evans, *Leicest. Words, etc.*, 276 (E.D.S.), To-morrow come never, when theer's tew Soondays in a wik.

Two tailors. *See* **Nine tailors.**

Two things a man should never be angry at; what he can help, and what he cannot help. 1732: Fuller, 5335.

Two things doth prolong thy life: A quiet heart, and a loving wife. 1607: Deloney, *Strange Histories*, 70 (Percy S.).

Two to one is odds at football. 1567: Pickering, *Horestes*, l. 78, But two is to meyney, the prouerbe douth tell. 1616: Breton, *Works*, i t 24 (Grosart), Two to one is odds. 1654: Gayton, *Pleas. Notes Don Q.*, 220, Three to one is odds. 1658: R. Franck, *North. Memoirs*, 80 (1821), If two to one be odds at football – 1702: Brown in *Works*, ii, 25 (1760). 1742: Fielding, *Andrews*, bk iii ch xii, Who concluded that one at a time was sufficient, that two to one were odds. *c.*1791: Pegge, *Derbicisms*, 138 (E.D.S.).

Two to make a bargain, It takes. For the earlier form of this proverb, *see* **Two words to a bargain.** 1858: Surtees, *Ask Mamma*, ch 75, Unfortunately it requires two parties to these baragins, and Mrs Yammerton would not agree.1943: M. Flavin, *Journey in the Dark*, iv, Takes two to make a bargain, and you both done mighty wrong.

Two to make a quarrel, It takes. 1706: J. Stevens, *Spanish and EÓglish Dictionary*, s.v. Barajar, When one will not, two do not Quarrel. 1732: T. Fuller, *Gnomologia*, no. 4942, There must be two at least to a Quarrel. 1859: H. Kingsley, *Geoffrey Hamlyn*, II xiii, It takes two to make a quarrel, Cecil, and I will not be one.

Two to tango, It takes. The saying comes from the title of a 1952 hit song sung originally by Pearl Bailey. 1952: Haoffmann and Manning, *Takes Two to Tango* (song title), 2, There are lots of things you can do alone! But, takes two to tango. 1965: *Listener*, 24 June, 923, As for negotiation … the President has a firm, and melancholy, conviction: it takes two to tango.

Two trades. *See* **Man** (28).

Two wants of one, To make. 1738: Swift, *Polite Convers.*, i, I don't love to make two wants of one.

Two will. *See* **Nought** (3).

Two women in one house. *See* quots. 1417: in *Retiq. Antiquae*, i 233 (1841), Two wymen in one howse, Two cattes and one mowce, Two dogges and one bone, Maye never accorde in one. 1486: *Boke of St Albans*, sig. F4 ['wyues' for 'women']. 1611: Cotgrave, s.v. 'Accorder', Men say, Two cats and a mouse, two wives in one house, two dogs and a bone, never agree in one. 1670: Ray, 151 [as in 1611]. 1732: Fuller, 6095 [as in 1611]. 1869: Spurgeon, *John Ploughman*, ch xxi [as in 1611, but with last line – 'Will not agree long'.]

Two words to a bargain. 1597: Bacon, *Colours of Good and Evil*, x 68, The seconde worde makes the bargaine. 1598: *Mucedorus*, sig. B2, Tow words to a bargaine. Before 1625: Fletcher, *Wild-Goose Chase*, II iii 1696: Vanbrugh, *Relapse*, III iii 1734: Fielding, *Intrig. Chambermaid*, II iii, There go two words though to that bargain. 1822: Scott, *Nigel*, ch xxxi, There gang twa folk's votes to the unmaking of a bargain, as to the making of ane. 1860: Reade, *Clois, and Hearth*, ch xxiv. Cf. **More words.**

Two wrongs do not make a right. 1783: B. Rush, *Letter*, 2 Aug. (1951), I 308, Three wrongs will not make one right. 1814: J. kerr, *Several Trials of David Barclay*, Two wrongs don't make one right. 1875: Cheales, *Proverb. Folk-Lore*, 120. 1905: S. Weyman, *Starvecrow Farm*, xxiv, He ought to see this! ... After all, two wrongs don't make a right.

Two year old balk. *See* quot. 1841: Hartshorne, *Salopia Ant.*, 314, Hence as it [land which escapes the plough] lies fallow has arisen the proverb that 'a two-year-old balk is as good as a ruck [heap] of muck'.

Twyford, My name is: I know nothing of the matter. 1694: Motteux, *Rabelais*, bk v ch xiii, Hasn't the fellow told you he does not know a word of the business? his name's Twyford. 1732: Fuller, 3502.

Tyburn. *See* **Newgate and Suits hang.**

Tyburn tippet, A = A halter. 1549: 'Latimer, *Seven Sermons*, 63 (Arber), The byshop of Rome sent hym a cardinal's hatte, he should haue had a Tiburne tippet, a halpeny halter. *c.*1570: in Collmann, *Ballads, etc.*, 115 (Roxb.Cl), A Tyborne typett a roope or a halter. 1821: Scott, *Kenilworth*, ch iii. Any one whose neck is beyond the compass of a Tyburn tippet.

Tympany, To have a two-legged = To be with child. 1579: *Marr. of Wit and Wisdom*, 15 (SH.S.), I am afraid it is a timpany with two legges! *c.*1685: in *Roxb. Ballads*, vii 28 (B.S.), The doctor, be sure, is sent for to cure This two-legged tympany. 1732: Fuller, 4127, She hath a tympany with two heels.

Tyne. *See* **Tees.**

Tyrant's breath is another's death, A. 1855: Bohn, 302.

Tyrants seem to kiss, 'Tis time to fear when. Ibid., 534.

U

Ugly as a witch. 1846–59: *Denham Tracts*, ii 84 (F.L.S.).

Ugly at sin. 1821: Scott, *Kenilworth*, ch x, Though I am as ugly as sin. 1891: R.L.S., *Letters*, iv. 75 (Tnsitala ed.), All my other women have been as ugly as sin. 1901: F. E. Taylor, *Lancs. Sayings*, 2, As feaw [ugly] as sin.

Ugly as the devil. 1726: Defoe, *Hist, of Devil*, Pt II ch vii p. 249 (4th ed.) [cited as 'a proverb in his favour'].

Ugly enough to wean a foal. 1917: Bridge, *Cheshire Proverbs*, 147.

Unbidden guest knows not where to sit, An. 1546: Heywood, *Proverbs*, Pt I ch ix. 1612: Webster, *White Devil*, in *Works* (Dyce), 19, An unbidden guest Should travel as Dutch women go to church, Bear their stools with them. 1732: Fuller, 5395. 1736: Bailey, *Dict.*, s.v. 'Unbidden', An unbidden guest must bring his stool with him.

Unbought hide. *See* **Cut** (11).

Uncle Antony. *See* quot. 1909: C. Lee, *Our Little Town*, 17, Idle juniors congenically occupied in 'helping Uncle Antony to kill dead mice', as the phrase goes.

Uncle Jan Knight, never in the right place, Like. Corn. 19th cent. (Mr C. Lee).

Uncover not the church to mend the quire = Rob not Peter to pay Paul. 1570: A. Barclay, *Mirr. of Good Manners*, 30 (Spens.S.), Uncover not the church, therwith to mende the quere.

Under board, To play. 1591: Florio, *Second Frutes*, 134, Thou haste long hands, and vsest them vnderboord. 1642: Fuller. *Holy State* (*Wise Statesman*), The receivers of such [pensions] will play under-board at the councill-table. 1669: Donne, *Poems*, i 102 (Grierson), And often under-boards Spoak dialogues with our feet far from our words. 1669: Dud. North, *Obs. and Adv. Oeconom.*, 71, While the steward fear to be discovered, if he use any underboard play. 1681: Robertson, *Phraseol. Generalis*, 437,

That you should not think I ly at catch, or play under board to deceive you.

Under boake. *See* quot. *c.*1320: in *Reliq. Antiquae*, i 113 (1841), 'Under boske [the greenwood] shal men weder abide,' Quoth Hendyng.

Understanding and reason cannot conclude out of mood and figure. 1639: Howell, 19.

Understands ill, answers ill, Who. 1736: Bailey, *Dict.*, s.v. 'Understand'.

Under the blanket the black one is as good as the white. 1732: Fuller, 5396.

Under the bungo o' th' moon = to be in difficulties. 1917: Bridge, *Cheshire Proverbs*, 148.

Under the furze is hunger and cold, under the broom is silver and gold. 1678: Ray, 348. 1879: *N.&Q.*, 5th ser, xii 447. 1885: *N.&Q.*, 6th ser, xii 309 ['gorse' for 'furze'].

Under the rose. 1546: Dymocke to Vaughan in *State Papers*, Hen. VIII ii 200, The sayde questyons were asked with lysence, and that yt shoulde remayn under the rosse, that is to say, to remayn under the bourde, and no more to be rehersyd. 1639: Chapman and Shirley, *Ball*, II iii, Under the rose, if that will do you a pleasure, The lords do call me cousin, but I am –. 1647: in *Polit. Ballads*, 49 (Percy S.), Any thing may be spoke, if 't be under the rose. 1714: Ozell, *Molière*, vi 7, I must tell you (under the rose) that –.1762: Bickerstaffe, *Love in a Village*, II ii, We all love a pretty girl – under the rose. 1862: Dickens, in *Letters*, ii 178 (1880), I don't know what their pay was, but I have no doubt their principal complements were got under the rose. 1915: Pinero, *Big Drum*, IV, I should *puff* you, under the rose – quietly pull the strings –.

Under the weather. 1891: R.L.S., *Wrecker*, ch iv, You must not fancy I am sick, only over-driven and under the weather. 1926: Phillpotts, *Peacock House*, 222, I've marked you've been a good bit under the weather, and … I should like to help you.

Under water. *See* **Snow** (8).

Undone. 1. **As good undone as do it too soon.** 1546: Heywood, *Proverbs*, Pt II ch v 1659: Howell, 3.

2. **Undone as you would undo an oyster.** 1639: Clarke, 166, He's undone like an oyster. 1672: Walker, *Paroem.*, 34. 1681: Robertson, *Phraseol. Generalis*, Undone as you would undo an oyster; Ne salus quidem ipsa servare potest.

3. **What is done cannot be undone.** *See* **Once done**; and **Thing** (6).

Unexpected always happens, The. 1885: E.J. Hardy, *How to be Happy though Married*, xxv, A woman may have much theoretical knowledge, but this will not prevent unlooked-for obastacles arising … It is the unexpected that constantly happens. 1909: *Times Weekly*, 12 Nov., 732, No place in the world is more familiar than the House of Commons with the 'unforeseen that always happens'. 1938: E. Waugh: *Scoop*, I iii, Have nothing which in a case of emergency you cannot carry in your own hands. But remember that the unexpected always happens.

Unfinished work, Show not fools nor bairns. 1860: Reader, *Cloister and Hearth*, ch lv. [cited as a 'byword'].

Unforeseen, Nothing is certain except the. *See* **Nothing** (14).

Ungirt unblessed. *c.*1477: Caxton, *Book of Curtesye*, 45 (E.E.T.S.), Vngyrte, vnblyssed. seruyng atte table Me semeth hym a seruant nothing able. 1590: Spenser, *F. Q.*, IV v 18. 1646: Browne, *Pseudo. Epi.*, bk v ch xxii, As we usually say, they are unblest until they put on their girdle. 1687: Aubrey, *Gentilisme, etc.*, 43 (F.L.S.), It was accounted before y6 civill warres a very undecent and dissolute thing for a man to goe without his girdle in so much that 'twas aproverbe, 'Ungirt and unbless't'. (*See* Tibullus, *Eleg.*, lib. i ix. 41, and Pers., *Sat.*, iii (31).)

Unhardy is unsely. *See* **Cowardly.**

Union is strength. *c.*1527: T. Berthelet, tr. *Erasmus' Sayings of Wise Men*, A4v, Concorde maketh those thynges that are weake, mighty and stronge. 1654: R. Williams, *Complete Writings* (1963), VI 280, Union strengthens. 1837: in D. Porter, *Early Negro Writing* (1971), 228, In Union is strength. 1848: S. Robinson, *Letter*, 29 Dec., in *Indiana Historical Collections* (1936), XXII 178, 'Union is strength', and that is the only kind that can control the floods of such a 'great father of rivers'.

United we stand, divided we fall. 1768: J. Dickinson, *Liberty Song*, in *Boston Gazette*, 18 July, Then join Hand in Hand brave Americans all, By uniting we stand, by dividing we fall. 1849: G.P. Morris, *Flag of our Union*, in *Poems* (1853), 41, 'United we stand – divided we fall!' It made and preserves a nation!. 1894: J. Jacobs, *Fables of Aesop*, 122, Then the lion attacked them o9ne by one and soon made an end of all four. United we stand, divided we fall.

Unkissed unkind. 1584: Peele, *Arraign. of Paris*, I ii, And I will have a lover's fee; they say, unkiss'd unkind. 1897: Violet Hunt, *Unkist, Unkind* [title].

Unknown, unkissed. *c.*1374: Chaucer, *Troylus*, bk i l. 809, Unknowe, unkist, and lost that is unsought. 1401: in Wright, *Polit. Poems* (Rolls S.), ii 59 (1861), On old Englis it is said, unkissid is unknowen. 1546: Heywood, *Proverbs*, Pt I ch xi, 1579: E. Kirke, *Epist. Ded.*, to Spenser's *Shep. Cal.*, Who for that hee is vncouth (as sayde Chaucer) is vnkist, and vnknowne to most men, is regarded but of a fewe. 1670: Ray, 27. 1732: Fuller, 5403.

Unlikeliest places are often likelier than those that are likeliest, The. 1917: Bridge, *Cheshire Proverbs*, 120.

Unlooked for often comes. 1875: Cheales, *Proverb. Folk-Lore*, 133.

Unlucky in love lucky at play. 1738: Swift, *Polite Convers.*, Dial. III, Well, miss, you'll have a sad husband, you have such good luck at cards. 1868: T. W. Robertson, *Play*, III ii, The old proverb is verified in our case, unlucky in love, lucky at play. *See also* **Lucky at cards.**

Unmannerliness is not so impolite as over-politeness. 1694: D'Urfey, *Quixote*, Pt II I ii, He that has more manners than he ought, is more a fool than he thought. 1732: Fuller, 5404, Unmannerly a little is better than troublesome a great deal. 1736: Bailey, *Dict.*, s.v. 'Unkind', Better unkind than troublesome. 1831: Hone, *Year-Book*, col. 1417. Cf. **Better be unmannerly.**

Unminded, unmoaned. 1546: Heywood, *Proverbs*, Pt I ch ix. 1670: Ray, 27. 1815: Scott, *Mannering*, ch ix, But whon folk's missed, then they are moaned.

Untoward boy, or girl, may make a good man, or woman, An. 1548: Hall, *Chron.*, 12 (1809). Experience teacheth, that ... of a shreude boy, proueth a good man. 1592: Greene, *Works*, x 239 (Grosart), My mother allowed of my vnhappy parts, alluding to this prophane and old prouerbe, an vntoward gyrle makes a good woman. 1633: Draxe, 9, A shrewd boy maketh a good man. 1655: Fuller, *Church. Hist.*, bk x, § iv (52), Verified the proverb, that an untoward boy may make a good man. 1670: Ray, 111, An unhappy lad may make a good man.

Untravelled. *See* **Home-keeping.**

U.P. *See* quots. 1791: *Gent. Mag.*, i 327, 'U.P.K. spells May goslings', is an expression used by boys at play as an insult to the losing party. 1813: Brand, *Pop. Antiq.*, i 219 (Ellis, 1895) [copies the foregoing quotation, with addition –], U.P.K. is 'up pick', that is, up with your pin or peg, the mark of the goal. 1854: Baker, *Northants. Gloss.*, s.v. U.P. spells goslings! Not an uncommon exclamation when any one has completed or attained an object. 1881: Evans, *Leicest. Words, etc.*, 282 (E.D.S.), U.P. spells goslins ... I have heard it not unfrequently, but always as applied to death. 'How's Ted going on?' 'Eh, poor chap, I think it's U.P. spells goslins wi' him', meaning, as I always understood, 'it is all up with him, and the goslings will soon feed on his grave'.

Uphill and against the heart, It goes = It is a hard task. 1883: Burne, *Shropshire Folk-Lore*, 589.

Up horn, Down corn. 1870: *N. & Q.*, 4th ser, vi 259, Another proverb in use about thirty years ago was – 'Up horn, Down con'; meaning that when the price of cattle was 'up', that of corn was 'down'. 1886: *N. & Q.*,7th ser, i 192, The proverb which is common among farmers is generally, 'Up corn, Down horn', meaning when corn is dear beef is cheap.

Up must come down, What goes. *See* **Go** (28).

Uppingham trencher, An. 1678: Ray, 333. 1790: Grose, *Prov. Gloss.*, s.v. 'Rutlandshire', An Uppingham trencher. This town was probably famous for the art of trencher-making. Here, by a statute of Henry VIII, the standard was appointed to be kept for the weights and measures of this county; which might induce turners, and other makers of measures, to settle here.

Up the hill favour me, down the hill beware thee. The horse *loq.* 1639: Clarke, 22. 1670: Ray, 103. 1732: Fuller, 6276, Up-hill spare me; Down-hill forbear me; Plain way, spare me not, Let me not drink when I am hot.

Up the weather, To go = To prosper. Cf. **Down** (5) for the reverse. 1618: Breton, in *Works*, ii *u.* 5 (Grosart), I feare the place you liue in is more costly then profitable; where, for one that goes vp the weather a number goe downe the winde.

Up to one's gossip, To be = To be aware of a person's designs. 1828: Carr, *Craven Dialect*, i 193.

Up to snuff. 1811: Poole, *Hamlet Trav.*, II i (OED), He knows well enough The game we're after: Zooks, he's up to snuff. 1876: *N.&Q.*, 5th ser, v 336, When a man is very acute at a bargain, and 'knows a thing or two', he is said to be 'up to snuff'. 1922: Weyman, *Ovington's Bank*, ch xxxvi, Thank ye, but I am up to snuff. If you ask me I think you're a silly set of fools.

Up to the ears. 1594: Barnfield, *Affect. Sheph.*, 8 (Percy S.), But leave we him in love up to the eares.

Up with it if it be but a devil of two years old. 1639: Clarke, 202.

Usage. *See* **Custom.**

Use is a great matter. 1672: Walker, *Paroem.*, 23.

Use is all. 1639: Clarke, 35.

Use makes perfect. *See* **Practice.**

Use, *verb.* **1. He that useth me better than he is wont, hath betrayed or will betray me.** 1578: Florio, *First Fruites*, fo. 28, Who doth vnto me better then he is woont, he hath betrayed me, or els wil betray me. 1589: Puttenham, *Engl. Poesie*, 295 (Arber), He that speakes me fairer than his woont was too Hath done me harme, or meanes for to doo. 1586: Pettie, *Guazzo*, fo. 36, Hee which maketh more of thee then he was wont, either hath cousened thee alreadie, or else goeth about to cosen thee. 1629: *Book of Meery Riddles*, Prov. 12. 1732: Fuller, 2180, He that is kinder than he was wont, hath a design upon thee.

2. I will use you like a Jew. 1619: W. Hornby, *Scourge of Drunkennes*, sig. A4, Ile vse thee like a dogge, a Iew, a slaue. 1662: Fuller, *Worthies*, ii 346 (1840), I will use you as bad as a Jew. 1670: Ray, 209, To use one like ajew. 1790: Grose, *Prov. Gloss.*, s.v. 'London' [as in 1662].

3. The used key is always bright. 1736: Franklin, *Way to Wealth*, in *Works*, i 443 (Bigelow).

4. Use it or lose it. A modern, originally American proverb. Attributed to Henry Ford, and first used by him in relation to money. Nowadays, it often figures in advice to people on how to retain sexual vigour with advancing age, and was, in the 1990s, adopted by many small post offices in the U.K. (in the form *Use us or lose us*) as a slogan to warn the public that they might be closed if their services were not made use of. 1931: H. Ford: *New York Times*, 11 Aug, Money is like an arm or leg: use it or lose it.

5. Use legs and have legs. *c.*1582: Harvey, *Marginalia*, 188 (1913). Use legges & have legges: use law and have law. Use nether & have nether. 1670: Ray. 153. 1732: Fuller, 5410

6. Use not today what tomorrow may want. 1846: Denham, *Proverbs*, 5 (Percy S.).

7. Use your wit as a buckler, not a sword. 1855: Bohn, 549.

Usual forms of drility oblige no man, The. Ibid., 517.

Usurer is one that tormenteth men for their good conditions, An, viz. The conditions of their bonds. 1659: Howell, 18.

Usurers' purses and women's plackets are never satisfied. Ibid., 7. 1736: Bailey, *Dict.*, s.v. 'Usurer'.

Usury. *See* quot. 1593: Nashe, in *Works*, iv. 139 (Grosart), It is nowe growne a prouerbe That there is no merchandise but vsury.

Uter Pendragon. *See* **Eden.**

V

Vain-glory blossoms but never bears. 1633: Draxe, 212, Vaine glory is a floure that beareth no corne. 1732: Fuller, 5342.

Vain the net is spread in sight of the bird, In. *See* **Net.**

Vale discovereth the hill, The. *c.*1594: Bacon, *Promus*, No. 145 [with 'best' after 'vale']. 1605: Bacon, *Adv. of Learning*, II xxi 71, A proverb more arrogant than sound, 'that the vale discovereth the hill'.

Valiant man's look is more than a coward's sword, A. 1640: Herbert, *Jac. Prudentum*.

Valley, He that stays in the, shall never get over the hill. 1633: Draxe, 42. 1670: Ray, 152. 1732: Fuller, 2314.

Valour can do little without discretion. 1670: Ray, 27. 1732: Fuller, 5343, Valour is brutish without discretion. Cf. **Discretion.**

Valour that parleys is near yielding. 1640: Herbert, *Jac. Prudentum.* 1670: Ray, 27.

Valour would fight, but discretion would run away. 1678: Ray, 214. 1732: Fuller, 5344. Cf. **Discretion.**

Value of money. *See* **Money** (12).

Variety is the spice of life. 1785: Cowper, *The Task*, II 76, Variety's the very speice of life That gives it all its flavour.

Varnishing hides a crack. 1732: Fuller, 5346.

Vavasour family saying. 1659: Howell, 21, A sheriff had he bin, and a Contour, Was no where such a Vavasour. An old said saw of that family.

Veal. 1. In a shoulder of veal there are twenty and two good bits. 1678: Ray, 83 … This is a piece of country wit. They mean by it, There are twenty (others say forty) bits in a shoulder of veal, and but two good ones. 1738: Swift, *Polite Convers.*, Dial. II, They say there are thirty and two good bits in a shoulder of veal.

2. Veal will be cheap: calves fall. 1678: Ray, 83.

Vein across the nose. *See* quot. 1923: *Folk-Lore*, xxxiv. 330, If you have a vein across your nose, You'll never live to wear your wedding clothes (Oxfordsh.).

Velvet true heart, He's a. Cheshire. 1678: Ray, 83. 1852: 'Cheshire Proverbs', in *N.&Q.*, 1st ser, vi 386. 1917: Bridge, *Cheshire Proverbs*, 66, He has a velvet true heart. Cf. **True** (9).

Vengeance, though it comes with leaden feet, strikes with iron hands. 1748: Richardson, *Clarissa*, iv. 120 (1785). Cf. **God comes**.

Venture it, I'll. *See* quots. 1678: Ray, 83, I'll venture it, as Johnson did his wife, and she did well. 1732: Fuller, 1367, E'en venture on, as Johnson did on his wife.

Venture little, hazard little. 1590: Tarlton, *Nerves out of Purg*, To the Readers. Men that venture little, hazard little. Cf. **Nothing** (32).

Venture not all in one bottom. 1639: Clarke, 95. 1672: Walker, *Paroem.*, 53. 1732: Fuller, 5349. 1831: Hone, *Year-Book*, col. 1417, Venture not all you have at once.

Venture out of your depth till you can swim, Never. 1855: Bohn, 459.

Ventures too far, loses all, He that. *c.*1534: Berners, *Huon*, 335 (E.E.T.S.), Some tyme it fortuneth that it is foly to aduenture to moche forward and to late to repent ofter [afterwards]. 1611: Cotgrave, s.v. 'S'adventurer'.

Venus smiles. *See* **Jove laughs.**

Vervain and dill. *See* quots. 1578: Dodoens, *Herbal*, quoted in Aubrey's *Gentilisme* (F.L.S.), Vervaine and dill Hinder witches of their will. 1588: Cogan, *Haven of Health*, ch xxii p. 41 (1612), One olde saying I haue heard of this herbe, That whosoeuer weareth verveine and

dill, May be bold to sleepe on euery hill. 1635: Swan, *Spec. Mundi*, 250 [as in 1588].

Vessel. *See* **Cask;** and **Empty** (13).

Vetch. *See* quot. 1884: H. Friend, *Flowers and Fl. Lore*, 220, Vetches are a most hardy grain, according to the comparison of an old saying – 'A Thetch will go through The bottom of an old shoe'.

Vicar of S. Fools, The. 1562: Heywood, *Epigr.*, 5th Hund., No. 19, Whens come all these? from the vicar of sainct fooles. 1565: Calfhill, *Answ. to Martiall*, 237 (P.S.), Then … a dolt with a dawkin might marry together; and the Vicar of Saint Fools be both minstrel and minister. 1589: Nashe, *Works*, i 13 (Grosart), I must needes sende such idle wits to shrift to the vicar of S. Fooles, who in steade of a worser may be such a Gothamists ghostly father. 1659: Howell, 16, The vicar of fools is his ghostly father. 1670: Ray, 176 [as in 1659].

Vice, *subs.* **1. Vice corrects sin.** 1672: Walker, *Paroem.*, 42. 1693: Penn, *Fruits of Solitude*, No. 45, But the proverb is just, *Vice should not correct Sin*. 1736: Bailey, *Dict.*, s.v. 'Vice'.

2. Vice is often clothed in virtue's habit. Ibid., s.v. 'Vice'.

3. Vice makes virtue shine. 1732: Fuller, 5356.

4. Vice ruleth where gold reigneth. 1669: *Politeuphuia*, 271. 1732: Fuller, 5359.

5. Vices are learned without a master. 1666: Torriano, *Piazza Univ.*, 312. 1732: Fuller, 5361.

6. Where vice is vengeance follows. 1639: Clarke, 325. 1670: Ray, 152. 1681: Robertson, *Phraseol. Generalis*, 1269, Where vice goes before, vengeance follows after. 1732: Fuller, 5681, Where villainy goes before, vengeance follows after.

See also **No vice.**

Vinegar. *See* quots. 1578: Florio, *First Fruites*, fo. 30, Beware of vinegar and sweete wine, and of the anger of a peaceable man. 1640: Herbert, *Jac. Prudentum*, Take heed of the vinegar of sweet wine.

Vine poor, Make the, and it will make you rich, *i.e.* prune it. 1678: Ray, 350.

Vintner. fears false measure, The. 1611: Davies of Hereford, *Sc.of Folly*, 43, in *Works*, ii (Grosart).

Viper in one's bosom, To nourish a. 1670: Ray, 198. 1732: Fuller, 5210.

Virtue. 1. The virtue of a coward is suspicion. 1640: Herbert, *Jac. Prudentum*.

2. To make a virtue of necessity. [*See* Quinct., lib. 1, cap. 8.] Before 1259: *Matt. Paris* (Record Series), i 20, Vitam in tantam sanctitatem commutavit, faciendo de necessitate virtutem. *c*.1374: Chaucer, *Troylus*, bk iv. l.1586, Thus maketh vertue of necessitee By pacience. *c*.1386: Chaucer, *Knight's Tale*, l. 2184. 1412: Hoccleve, *Regement*, 46 (E.E.T.S.), Make of necessite, reed I, vertu. 1584: *Three Ladies of L.*, in Hazlitt, *O. Plays*, vi 332, Thus am I driven to make a virtue of necessity, *c*.1592: Shakespeare, *Two Gent.*, IV i 1618: J. Taylor (Water Poet), *Pennilesse Pilgrim*, I made a vertue of necessity, and went to breakfast in the Sunne. 1748: Smollett, *Rod. Random*, ch xxx, However, making a virtue of necessity, I put a good face on the matter. 1876: Blackmore, *Cripps*, ch xxxiv, He resolved to make a virtue of necessity, as the saying is.

3. Virtue and a trade are the best portion for children. 1640: Herbert, *Jac. Prudentum*.

4. Virtue has all things in (or **below**) **it self.** 1736: Bailey, *Dict.*, s.v. 'Virtue'.

5. Virtue is its own reward. [Ut officii fructus sit ipsum officium. – Cicero, *Fin.*, ii 72] 1509: A. Barclay, *Ship of Fools*, 10v, Vertue hath no rewarde. 1596: Spenser, *Faerie Queene*, III xii, Your vertue selfe her owne reward shall breed, Even immortall praise and glory wyde. 1642: browne, *Religio Medici*, I 87, That vertue is her owne reward, is but a cold principle.1673: Dryden, *Assignation*, III i, Virtue, sir, is its own reward: I expect none from you. 1696: Vanbrugh, *Relapse*, V 1703: Farquhar, *Twin-Rivals*, I ii 1771: Smollett, *Clinker*, in *Works*, vi 158 (1817). 1827: Scott, *Journal*, Sept. 24, This species of exertion is, like virtue, its own reward. 1850: Dickens, *Chuzzlewit*, ch xv. 1919: Weyman, *Great House*, ch xviii, 'Sometimes,' she ventured, 'imprudence is a virtue.' 'And its own reward!' he retorted.

6. Virtue is the only true nobility. 1670: Flecknoe, *Epigrams*, 50, Vertue is onely true nobility. 1732: Fuller, 5382.

7. Virtue never grows old. 1640: Herbert, *Jac. Prudentum.* 1736: Bailey, *Dict.*, s.v. 'Virtue'.

8. Virtue praised increaseth. 1560: Becon, *Catechism*, 351 (P.S.) [quoted as 'the common saying'].

9. Virtues all agree, but vices fight one another. 1732: Fuller, 5392.

10. Virtue which parleys is near a surrender. 1721: Bailey, *Dict.*, s.v. 'Virtue'.

Voice of the people is the voice of God, The. Before 804: Alcuin, *Opp.*, Ep. cxxvii t. 1, p. 191, Ed. Froben, 1777, Nee audiendi sunt ii qui volent dicere, vox populi, vox Dei, cum tumultuositas vulgi semper insaniae proxima est. *c*.1390: Gower, *Conf. Amantis*, Prol., l. 124, And that I take to record Of every lond for his partie The comun vois, which mai noght lie. 1412: Hoccleve, *Regement*, 104 (E.E.T.S.), Thus, my gode lorde, wynneth your peples voice; ffor peples vois is goddes voys, men seyne. 1575: Gascoigne, *Posies*, 143 (Cunliffe), Yet could I never any reason feele, To thinke *Vox populi vox Dei est.* 1646: Browne, *Pseudo. Epi.*, bk i ch iii, Though sometimes they are flattered with that aphorism, will hardly believe, The voice of the people to be the voice of God. 1737: Pope, *Horace: Epistles*, II i 89, The people's voice is odd, It is, and it is not, the voice of God. 1820: Colton, *Lacon*, Pt II No. 266, The voice of the People is the voice of God; this axiom has manifold exceptions. 1914: Shaw, 'Parents and Children', in *Misalliance, etc.*, lxxii, When an experienced demagogue comes along and says, 'Sir: *you* are the dictator: the voice of the people is the voice of God – '

Volunteer is worth two pressed men, One. 1705: T. Hearne, *Journal*, 31 Oct., in *Remarks and Collections* (1885), I 62, 'Tis sd my Ld Seymour presently after Mr Smith was pronounc'd Speaker, rose up, and told them, Gentlemen: you have got a Low Church man; but pray remember that 100 Voluntiers are better than 22 press'd men. 1834: Marryat, *Jacob Faithful*, 'Shall I give you a song?' 'That's right, Tom; a volunteer's worth two pressed men'. 1897: R. Kipling, *Captains Courageous*, x, He presumed Harvey might need a body servant some day or other, and … was sure that one volunteer was worth five hirelings.

Wade's mill. *See* **Ware.**

Wading in an unknown water, No safe. 1630:
T. Adams, *Works*, 748, It is not safe wading
without a bottome. 1670: Ray, 153. 1732: Fuller,
3627. 1831: Hone, *Year-Book*, col. 1417, Wade
not in unknown waters.

Wager. *See* **None but fools.**

Wagging of a straw = a trifle, *c*.1374: Chaucer,
Tr. and Cr., ii 1745 (OED), In titeryng and
pursuyte and delayes The folk deuyne at
waggynge of a stre. 1530: Palsgrave, 468, I can
bring hym out of pacyence with the waggyngof a
strawe. 1577: J. Grange, *Golden Aphroditis*, sig.
I4, The wagging of a strawe ... hindreth the
flight thereof. 1639: Clarke, 34, Angry at the
wagging of a straw. 1678: Ray, 75, He'll laugh at
the wagging of a straw. 1769: Smollett, *Adv.
Atom*, 7 (Cooke, 1795), He will ... at the turning
of a straw take into his bosom the very person
whom he has formerly defamed.

Wait, *verb.* **1. A waiting appetite kindles many
a spite.** 1875: Cheales, *Proverb. Folk-Lore*, 107.

**2. He that waits on another man's trencher,
makes many a late dinner.** 1611: Cotgrave, s.v.
'Escuelle', 'Tis long before he be served that
waits for another mans leavings. 1670: Ray, 27.
1732: Fuller, 2339 ['little' for 'late'].

3. Wait meals, flee chars, *c*.1770: Pegge,
Derbicisms, 11 (E.D.S.), A chare or jobb of work
... see ... the proverb, 'Wait meals, flee chars',
which I take to be the true reading and not *jars.*

Wakefield, Merry. 1662: Fuller, *Worthies*, iii 399
(1840). 1790: Grose, *Prov. Gloss.*, s.v. 'Yorksh'.
1878: *Folk-Lore Record*, i 161, A similar idea is
expressed in the old saying, 'Merry Wakefield'.
[The 'idea' alludes to the sixteenth-century
Yorkshire song, with chorus – 'Yorke, Yorke, for
my monie: Of all the citties that ever I see, For
mery pastime and companie, Except the cittie of
London'. There is probably also a connection
with the famous Pindar of Wakefield.]

Waking dog. *See* quot. 1591: Lyly, *Endymion*,
III i, It is an old saying, madam, that a waking
dog doth afar off bark at a sleeping lion.

Walberswick. *See* quot. 1830: Forby, *Vocab. E.
Anglia*, 430, He is a Walberswick whisperer; you
may hear him over to Southwold.

Wales. *See* **Knight.**

Walk, *verb.* **1. Walk groundly; talk profoundly;
drink roundly; sleep soundly.** 1869: Hazlitt,
446.

2. Walk, knave! walk! 1546: Heywood,
Proverbs, Pt II ch iv, Nay (quoth she) walke
knaue walke. *c*.1630: in *Roxb. Ballads*, i 55
(B.S.), The parrat pralies 'walke, knaues, walke'.
c.1655: in Ibid., vi 211, 'Walk, knaue!' is a
parrot's note. *c*.1685: in Ibid., viii 869, And this
shall be my last reply Go walk up, out knave!
What care I?

3. We must learn to walk before we can run.
For the earlier form of this proverb *see* **First
creep.** 1794: G. Washington, *Letter*, 20 July, in
Writings (1940), XXXIII, We must walk as other
countries have done before we can run. 1851:
Borrow, *Lavengro*, ii 15, Ambition is a very
pretty thing; but, sir, we must walk before we
run. 1878: Platt, *Business*, 124, We must learn
and be strong enough to walk before we can run.
See also **Good walking.**

**Walking-staff hath caught warmth in your
hand, The.** 1546: Heywood, *Proverbs*, Pt I ch x.

Wall, *subs.* **1. Wall between.** *See* **Hedge** (1).

2. Walls have ears. 1575: G. Gascoigne,
Supposes, I i, The tables ... the portals, yes, and
the cupbords them selves have eares. 1591:
Harington, *Orl. Furioso*, bk xxii st. 32, For posts
have eares, and walls have eyes to see. *c*.1600:
Nobody and Somebody, l. 177, There is a way:
but walls have earrs and eyes. 1633: Shirley,
Bird in a Cage, I i, Take heed what you say ...
walls have ears. 1672: Wycherley, *Love in a
Wood*, III iii 1718: Dennis, *Works*, ii 298. 1766:
Garrick, *Neck or Nothing*, II i 1822: Scott, *Nigel*,
ch vi, It is not good to speak of such things ...
stone walls have ears.

Wallington. *See* quots. 1846–59: *Denham Tracts*, i
236 (F.L.S.), To teach one the way to Wallington.
Show me the way to Wallington. 1890: *Monthly
Chron. of N. Country Lore, etc.*, 421–2, Show me
the way to Wallington (title of song).

Walnut-tree: *He who plants a walnut-tree, expects
not to eat of the fruit.* 1732: Fuller, 2401.
See also **Woman** (8).

Walsall. *See* **Sutton.**

Walsall dock, You're too fast, like. 1869:
Hazlitt, 491.

Waltham's calf. *See* **Wise** (6).

Wandsworth, the sink of Surrey. 1790: Grose, *Prov. Gloss.*, s.v. 'Surrey', … This reproach is in a great measure removed. Formerly the town, which lies low, was one continued puddle.

Wanswell. *See* quot. 1639: in *Berkeley M.SS.* iii 29 (1885), All the maids in Wanswell may dance in an egg shell. Glos. Cf. **Camberwell.**

Want, *subs.* **1. For want of a nail, etc.** [*c.*1390: Gower, *Conf. Amantis*, bk v l.4785, For sparinge of a litel cost Ful oftë time a man hath lost The largë cotë for the hod [hood].] 1630: T. Adams, *Works*, 714, The want of a nayle looseth the shooe, the losse of a shoe troubles the horse, the horse indangereth the rider, the rider breaking his ranke molests the company, so far as to hazard the whole army. 1640: Herbert, *Jac. Prudentum*, For want of a nail the shoe is lost, for want of a shoe the horse is lost, for want of a horse the rider is lost. 1736: Franklin, *Way to Wealth,* in *Works*, i 446 (Bigelow) [as in 1640, with 'was' for 'is', *plus*], being overtaken and slain by the enemy; all for want of a little care about a horse-shoe nail. 1875: Cheales, *Proverb. Folk-Lore*, 165 [as in 1736, but ending with 'enemy'].

2. For want of company welcome trumpery. 1678: Ray, 69. 1690: *New Dict. Canting Crew*, sig. M4 [with 'good' before 'company']. 1738: Swift, *Polite Convers.*, Dial. III. 1830: Forby, *Vocab. E. Anglia*, 427.

3. Want goes by such an ones door. Somerset. 1678: Ray, 347.

4. Want is the whetstone of wit. 1611: *Tarlton's Jests*, 36 (SH.S.).

5. Want makes strife. *See* **Poverty breeds**.

6. Want of care admits despair. 1855: Bohn, 551.

7. Want of care does us more damage than want of knowledge. 1736: Franklin, *Way to Wealth*, in *Works*, i 445 (Bigelow).

8. Want of money, want of comfort. 1736: Bailey, *Dict.*, s.v. 'Want'.

Want, *verb.* **1. If you want a thing done well, do it yourself.** *See* **Well** (4).

2. I will not want when I have, and when I haven't too. Somerset. 1678: Ray, 344. 1732: Fuller, 2650.

3. To want a boiled ha'penny: said of weak or silly persons. 1917: Bridge, *Cheshire Proverbs*, 146.

4. What she wants in up and down she hath in round about. 1678: Ray, 346.

5. You want the thing you have. 1629: *Book of Meery Riddles*, Prov. 130.

Wanton look. *See* quots. 13th cent. in *Reliq. Antiquae*, ii 14 (1843), Lither look and twinkling, Titling and tikeling, Opin breast and singing, theise midoutin lesing, Arin toknes of horelinge. 1869: Hazlitt, 447, Wanton look and twinkling, Laughing and tickling, Open breast and singing, these without lying, Are tokens of whoring.

War and Wars, *subs.* **1. He that makes a good war makes a good peace.** 1666: Torriano, *Piazza Univ.* ['who' for 'he' and 'obtaineth' for second 'makes']. 1670: Ray, 28. 1732: Fuller, 2230.

2. He was saying his war prayers, *i.e.* swearing. S. Devon. 1869: Hazlitt, 194.

3. War and physic are governed by the eye. 1640: Herbert, *Jac. Prudentum*.

4. War, hunting and love are as full of troubles as pleasures. 1640: Herbert, *Jac. Prudentum*, In war, hunting, and love, men for one pleasure a thousand griefs prove. 1670: Ray, 28 [with 'law' for 'love']. 1732: Fuller, 5416, War, hunting, and love have a thousand troubles for their pleasure. 1846–59: *Denham Tracts*, ii 109 (F.L.S.) [with 'law' for 'love'].

5. War is death's feast. 1611: Cotgrave, s.v. 'Feste', Warre is the dead mans holy-day. 1640: Herbert, *Jac. Prudentum*. 1732: Fuller, 5417.

6. War makes thieves, and peace hangs them. 1640: Herbert, *Jac. Prudentum*. 1660: *Howell, Party of Beasts*, 117, War makes the thief, and peace brings him to the gallows. 1732: Fuller, 5148

7. War must be waged by waking men. 1639: Clarke, 318. 1670: Ray, 154. 1732: Fuller, 5419, War must not be waged by men asleep.

8. Wars are sweet to those that know them not. 1539: Taverner, *Proverbs*, fo. 49, Batell is a swete thynge to them that neuer assayed it. 1560: E. More, *Def. of Women*, l. 239, As warre is counted pleasaunt to them not tryeng the same. 1575: Gascoigne, *Posies*, 147 (Cunliffe), How sweet warre is to such as knowe it not. Before 1634: Chapman, *Revenge for Honour*, I iii, War is sweet to those That never have experienced it. 1659: Howell, 11. 1816: Scott, *Antiquary*, ch xxviii, It's a rough trade – war's sweet to them that never tried it. 1927: *Sporting and Dramatic*

News, April 30, p. 261, The war correspondent in 'The Desert Song', agrees with the proverb that war is sweet to those who haven't tried it.

9. Wars bring scars. 1670: Ray, 154. 1732: Fuller, 6096. 1826: Scott, *Woodstock*, ch xxvii, Myself am in some sort rheumatic – as war will leave its scars behind, sir.

10. When war begins Hell opens. 1736: Bailey, *Dict.*, s.v. 'War'.

See also **Love** (1).

Wardhall, Cumberland. *See* quot. 1860: Whellan, *Cumbd. and Westm.*, 290 *n.*, Up now ace, and down with the traye, Or Wardhall's gone for ever and aye.

Ware and Wadesmill are worth all London. [1561: *Queene Hester*, 31 (Grosart), Nowe by wades myll, euerye mans wyll Is wonderouslye well.] 1588: A. Fraunce, *Lawiers Logike*, fo. 27, **Ware and Wadesmill bee worth al London.** 1662: Fuller, *Worthies*, ii 39 (1840). 1790: Grose, *Prov. Gloss.*, s.v. 'Herts'.

Wares are gone, shut up the shop-windows, When the. 1612: Webster, *White Devil*, 45 (Dyce), Now the wares are gone we may shut up shop. 1670: Ray. 153. 1732: Fuller, 5609.

Ware skins, quoth Grubber, when he flung the louse into the fire. 1678: Ray, 257. 1732: Fuller, 5420 [with 'shins' for 'skins' and 'Grub' for 'Grubber'].

Warm, *adj.* **1. As warm as toast.** *See* **Hot as a toast.**

2. As warm as wool. 1639: Clarke, 286. 1658: R. Franck, *North. Memoirs*, 163 (1821), Her body was as warm as wool. 1692: L'Estrange, *Aesop*, 411 (3rd ed.), A vengeance on ye, says he, y'are as warm as wool.

3. He that is warm thinks all so. 1640: Herbert, *Jac. Prudentum*. 1875: Cheales, *Proverb. Folk-Lore*, 132.

Warm, *verb.* **1. He warms too near that burns.** 1611: Cotgrave, s.v. 'Brusler', Hee warmes himselfe too neer that burnes himselfe. 1640: Herbert, *Jac. Prudentum*.

2. It is absurd to warm one in his armour. Ibid.

Warn, *verb.* **1. Be warned by others' harms.** [Feliciter sapit qui alieno periculo sapit. – Plautus, *Merc.*, IV iv. 40.] 12th cent, in Wright, *Anglo-Latin Sat. Poets*, i 145, Foelix quem faciunt, aliena pericula cautum. Before 1500: in Hill, *CommonplaceBook*, 132 (E.E.T.S.), He is wysse, that can beware by an other manys harme.

1584: Greene, *Works*, iii 183 (Grosart), It is good indeed … by other mens harmes to learne to beware, *c.*1640: in *Roxb. Ballads*, i 371 (B.S.), For happy is he whom other men's harmes Can make to beware. 1750: W. Ellis, *Housewife's Companion*, iii, Happy is he who by other mens harms learns to beware. 1842: Barham, *Ing. Legends*, 2nd ser, 'Misadv. at Margate'.

2. He that is warned. *See* **Forewarned.**

3. He that will not be warned by his own father, he shall be warned by his stepfather. Before 1500: in Hill, *Commonplace-Book*, 128 (E.E.T.S.). Cf. **He that will not be ruled.**

Wary. *See* **Blind,** *adj.* (9).

Wash, *verb.* **1. For washing his hands none sells his lands.** 1640: Herbert, *Jac. Prudentum*.

2. He washes his sheep with scalding water. 1813: Ray, 75.

3. If you would live for ever you must wash the milk off your liver – a toper's saying. 1611: Cotgrave, s.v. 'Laict', Wash thy milke off thy liver (say we). 1670: Ray, 36. 1732: Fuller, 6073.

4. I will wash my hands and wait upon you. 1678: Ray, 353.

5. To wash one's dirty linen in public. 1809: T. G. Fessenden, *Pills*, 45, The man has always a great itch for scribbling, and has been so fortunate as to procure somebody who pitied his ignorance, to 'wash his dirty linen'. 1867: A. Trollope, *Last Chronicle of Barset*, II xliv, I do not like to trouble you with my private affairs; – there is nothing … so bad as washing one's dirty linen in public. 1886: E.J. Hardy, *How to be Happy though Married*, i, Married epople … should remember the proverb about the home-washing of soiled linen. 1931: *Times*, 3 Aug., 9/ 1, If the Government had made tactful … representations … to the Holy See … the whole matter could have been settled quietly without any washing of dirty linen in public.

6. To wash one's face in an ale-clout. 1546: Heywood, *Proverbs*, Pt I ch x, As sober as she seemth, fewe daies come about But she will onece wasshe hir face in an ale clout.

7. To wash the head. *See* **Wet,** *verb.* (2).

8. To wash the head without soap = To scold. 1581: B. Rich, *Farewell*, 161 (SH.S.), This olde hag, havyng had her head washed thus without sope [having been well scolded] – .

9. Washing days. *See* quots. 1865: Hunt, *Pop. Romances W. of Eng.*, 430 (1896), They that wash

Monday got all the week to dry, They that wash Tuesday are pretty near by, They that wash Wednesday make a good housewife, They that wash Thursday must wash for their life, They that wash Friday must wash in need. They that wash Saturday are sluts in deed. 1888: *N. & Q.*, 7th ser, v 180 ... Monday have all the week to dry ... Tuesday have let a day go by ... Wednesday are not so much to blame ... Thursday wash for very shame ... Friday wash in fearful need ... Saturday are filthy sluts in deed. 1910: *Devonsh. Assoc. Trans.*, xlii 90, Wash Friday, wash for need, Wash Saturday, sluts indeed.

9. Wash your hands often, your feet seldom, and your head never. 1670: Ray, 38. 1926: Inge, *Lay Thoughts*, 226, A hundred and fifty years ago the maxim for ablutions seems to have been, 'Hands often, feet seldom, head never!'

10. You wash out ink with ink. 1639: Clarke, 197.

Washington, To five. *See* quot. 1846–59: *Denham Tracts*, i 92 (F.L.S.), I gave him [or her] Washington. That is, did my work quickly and roughly. But as to whether it alludes to the village of that name in the bishopric [Durham] or the celebrated General Washington I dare not at present decide. The saying is very common in the north of England.

Wasp and Wasps. 1. As angry as a wasp. *c.*1350: *Alexander*, l. 738, As wrath as waspe. Before 1529: Skelton, *Elyn. Rumming*, l. 330, But, Lorde, as she was testy, Angry as a waspy! *c.*1570: in Hazlitt, *E. Pop. Poetry*, iv 194, She is as curste, I dare well swere. And as angry y wis as euer was waspe. 1611: Davies of Hereford, *Sc. of Folly*, 45, in *Works*, ii (Grosart), 'Phryne's as merry as a cricket' sometimes; But angry as a waspe, when she reads my rimes. 1670: Ray, 203.

2. As troublesome as a wasp in one's ear. 1732: Fuller, 740.

3. She is as quiet as a wasp in one's nose. 1659: Howell, 16. 1670: Ray, 215. 1732: Fuller, 4130 ['ear' for 'nose'].

4. To anger a wasp. 1586: Pettie, *Guazzo*, fo. 75, It is a perillous thing to mocke and scoffe at others, and, as the saying is. To anger a waspe. 1659: Howell, *Proverbs: Ital.-Eng.*, 8.

5. Wasps haunt the honey-pot. 1732: Fuller, 5422. 1871: Smiles, *Character*, 228, More wasps are caught by honey than by vinegar.

Waste not want not. 1576: *Par. Dainty Dev.*, in *Brit. Bibliog.*, iii 88 (1812), For want is next to waste. 1732: Fuller, 5423, Waste makes want. 1872: Hardy, *Greenwood Tree*, Pt I ch viii, Taking it across for his own use, on the plea of waste not, want not. 1882: J. Platt, *Economy*, 22, 'Waste not, want not' is a law of nature. 1907: De Morgan, *Alice-for-Short*, ch ix. Cf. **Wilful waste.**

Watched pot never boils, A. 1848: Gaskell, *M. Barton*, ch xxxi, What's the use of watching? A watched pot never boils. 1875: Cheales, *Proverb. Folk-Lore*, 132. 1884: *Folk-Lore Journal*, ii 279, Watch pot never boils. Derbysh. 1906: *Cornish N. & Q.*, 202.

Watch one's water, To. *See* **Look,** *verb* (26).

Water, *subs.* **1. As water in a smith's forge, that serves rather to kindle than quench.** 1579: Lyly, *Euphues*, 61 (Arber), He that casteth water on the fire in the smith's forge, maketh it to flame fiercer. 1639: Clarke, 158.

2. As welcome as water in one's shoes = not welcome at all. 1659: Howell, 11. 1740: North, *Lives of Norths*, i 195 (Bohn), They caressed his lordship very much ... and talked about a time to dine with him; all which, as they say, was 'water in his shoes'. 1880: Spurgeon, *Ploughm. Pictures*, 47. 1901: F. E. Taylor, *Lancs Sayings*, 4, As welcome as wayter i' one's shoon.

3. As welcome as water into a ship, 1580: Lyly, *Euphues*, 381 (Arber), Seeing my counsell is no more welcome vnto thee then water into a ship – 1605: Camden, *Remains*, 317 (1870). 1670: Ray, 203. 1732: Fuller No. 749, As welcome as water in a leaking ship.

4. Don't pour water on a drowned mouse. 1639: Clarke, 9. 1670: Ray, 133. 1710: S. Palmer, *Moral Essays on Proverbs*, 69 ... Don't add affliction to the afflicted, is the plain English of this proverb. 1738: Swift, *Polite Convers.*, Dial. I, Take pity on poor miss; don't throw water on a drownded rat. 1880: Spurgeon, *Ploughm. Pictures*, 20, I would not be hard on a poor fellow, nor pour water on a drowned mouse.

5. He seeks water in the sea. 1813: Ray, 75.

6. He wants all the water to run down his own gutter – said of a covetous person. 1923: *Devonsh. Assoc. Trans.*, liv 136.

7. There's some water. See quots. 1913: E. M. Wright, *Rustic Speech, etc.*, 174, There's aye some water where the stirk [heifer] drowns. 1914: *N. & Q.*, 11th ser, x 29, 'There's some water where the stags drown:' – A friend of mine recently quoted this proverb with the meaning 'There is no smoke without fire'. She has been familiar with it since her early childhood, which was spent under South Yorkshire and Hampshire influences. [It looks as if 'stag 'were a perversion of stirk'. Kelly, *Scottish Proverbs*, 309, gives 'There's aye some water whaur the stirkie (calf) drouns'.]

8. The water that comes from the same spring cannot be fresh and salt both. 1732: Fuller, 4817.

9. To beat water in a mortar. 1576: Lambarde, *Peramb. of Kent*, 423 (1826), The house of Yorke had hitherto but beaten water in a mortar, and lost al their former labour.

10. To carry water in a sieve. 1591: Harington, *Orl. Furioso*, bk xxxii st. 39, Whom your fair speeches might have made beleeve That water could be carrid in a seeve. 1623: *New and Marie Prognos.*, 11 (Halliwell), That none may take up water with a sive. 1681: Robertson, *Phraseol. Generalis*, 1037, It's to no more purpose than to carry water in a riddle. 1716: Ward, *Female Policy*, 23, Giving presents to a woman to secure her love, is as vain as endeavouring to fill a sieve with water. 1736: Bailey, *Dict.*, s.v. 'Wash', To draw water in a sieve.

11. To put water in one's wine. 1567: Painter, *Pal. of Pleasure*, iii 364 (Jacobs), Which if he doe after hee hath well mingled water in his wyne, hee may chaunce to finde cause of repentance. 1599: Chamberlain, *Letters*, 39 (Camden S.), The cheife rebells ... began to put water in theire wine, and to proceed with more temper. *c.*1663: Davenant, *Play-House to be let*, V, Faith, in your wine I perhaps may put water. 1860: Ld. Acton, in Gasquet, *Acton and Circle*, 149 (1906). (OED) I am afraid you will think I have poured a good deal of water into your wine in 'Tyrol' and 'Syria'.

12. Under water. *See* **Snow** (8).

13. Water afar off quencheth not fire. 1586: Young, *Guazzo*, fo. 191, Water a farre of doth [not] quench fier that is nigh. 1640: Herbert, *Jac. Prudentum*. 1666: Torriano, *Piazza Univ.*, 1 ['a neighbouring' before 'fire'].

14. Water, fire and soldiers quickly make room. 1640: Herbert, *Jac. Prudentum*. 1659: Howell, 6 ['war' for 'soldiers']. 1736: Bailey, *Dict.*, s.v. 'Water' [as in 1659].

15. Water into the sea. *See* **Cast** (8).

16. Water into the Thames. *See* **Cast** (8).

17. Water is a good servant. *See* **Fire** (5).

18. Water is as dangerous as commodious. 1669: *Politeuphuia*, 184.

19. Water is a waster. 1672: Walker, *Paroem.*, 27. 1681: Robertson, *Phraseol. Generalis*, 1207.

20. Water past the mill. *See* **Miller** (12).

21. Water trotted is as good as oats. 1640: Herbert, *Jac. Prudentum*.

22. We never know the worth of water till the well is dry. 173: Fuller, 5451. 1832: J. J. Blunt, *Reform, Eng.*, 140 (OED), We know not, says the proverb, what the well is worth till it is dry. 1883: Burne, *Shropsh. Folk-Lore*, 590, We never miss the water till the well runs dry.

23. where the water is shallow no vessel will ride. 1639: Clarke, 245. 1670: Ray, 154. 1732: Fuller, 5682.

Water, *verb*. 1. To water a stake = To waste effort or labour. 1681: Robertson, *Phraseol. Generalis*, 511, Why do I thus water a dull and doltish post? 1732: Fuller, 5897, You do but water a dead stake. 1869: Spurgeon, *John Ploughman*, ch i, I am afraid I have been watering a dead stake.

2. To water one's plants = To weep. 1542: Udall, *Erasm. Apoph.*, 266 (OED), When he read the chronicle of Alexander the greate, he could not forbeare to water his plantes [L. *non tenuit lachrymas*]. 1557: North, *Diall of Princes*, fo. 210 v, They thinke it theyr dutye to water their plantes with teares. 1560: T. Wilson, *Rhetorique*, 80 (1909), So long as my childe liued I fasted, and watered my plants for my yong boye. 1828: Carr, *Craven Dialect*, ii 48.

Wavering as the wind. 1546: Heywood, *Proverbs*, Pt II ch i, But waueryng as the wynde: in docke out nettle. 1672: Walker, *Paroem.*, 14, You are as unconstant as the wind; as wavering as the weathercock.

Wavering man is like a skein of silk, A. 1736: Bailey, *Dict.*, s.v. 'Wavering'.

Waxheads. *See* **Head** (4).

Way of all flesh, The. [1611: *Bible*, Joshua, xxiii 14, And, behold, this day I am going the way of all the earth. Ibid., 1 Kings, ii 2, I go the way of all the earth.] 1611: T. Heywood, Golden Age, III, If I go by land, and miscarry, then I go the way of all flesh. 1631: Heywood, *Fair Maid of West*, Pt II Act IV, She ... by this is gone: the way of all flesh. 1754: Berthelson, *Eng.-Danish Dict.*, s.v. 'Flesh'. 1829: Peacock, *Misf. of Elphin*, ch vii,

Uther Pendragon … went the way of all flesh. 1903: S. Butler, *Way of all Flesh* [title].

Ways of killing a cat than choking it with cream, There are more. *See* **Cat** (61).

Way to a man's heart is through his stomach, The. 1814: J. Adams, *Letter*, 5 April, in *Works1* (*1851*), *VI* 505, *The shortest way to men's hearts is down their throats. 1845: R. Ford*, Hand-Book for Travellers in Spain, I i, The way to many an honest heart lies through the belly. 1857: D.M. Mullock, *John Halifax, gentleman*, xxx, 'Christmas dinners will be much in request'. 'There's a saying that the way to an English-man's heart is through his stomach'.

Way to be gone is not to stay here, The. 1678: Ray, 72.

Way to be safe is never to be secure, The. 1732: Fuller, 4820.

Way to bliss lies not on beds of down, The. 1639: Clarke, 16.

Ways to kill a dog …, There are more. *See* **Dog** (83).

Way to live much is to begin to live well betimes, The. 1732: Fuller, 4821.

Weably. *See* **Leominster.**

Weak, *adj.* **1. As weak as a wassail.** 1828: Carr, *Craven Dialect*, ii 241, 'As wake as a wassail', is a very common phrase to denote excessive weakness.

2. As weak as water, *c.*1320: in *Reliq. Antiquae*, i 122 (1841), Y wake as water in wore. 1545: Ascham *Toxoph.*, 28 (Arber), I found my good bowe clene cast on the one side, and as weake as water. 1611: *Bible*, Ezekiel, vii 17, All hands shall be feeble, and all knees shall be weak as water. 1631: Shirley, *Love Tricks*, I. 1754: Berthelson, *Eng.-Danish Dict.*, s.v. 'Weak', He is as weak as water. 1831: Scott, *Journal*, Oct. 19, I am as weak as water. 1886: R.L.S., *Kidnapped*, ch xx. 1900: Pinero, *Gay Lord Quex*, IV, Yesterday I was as firm as a rock; to-day I'm as weak as water again. **3. The weaker hath the worse.** 1546: Heywood, *Proverbs*, Pt I ch x.

4. The weakest goes to the wall. 1534: in *Two Coventry C. C. Plays*, 47 (E.E.T.S.), You mynde nothynge myne age Bat the weykist gothe eyuer to the walle. 1592: Greene, *Works*, xi 252 (Grosart), Howsoeuer the cause go the weakest is thrust to the wall. 1592: Shakespeare, *Romeo*, I i 1609: Rowlands, *Whole Crew*, 11 (Hunt.Cl.). I know the weakest must vnto the wall. 1689:

Shadwell, *Bury Fair*, III i 1712: Motteux, *Quixote*, Pt I bk iv ch 20. 1834: Marryat, *P. Simple*, ch v 1907: Gairdner, Introd. to *Paston Letters*, IV cc xxxiv, In times of revolution and tumult the weak must go to the wall.

5. The weak may stand the strong in stead. 1577: Kendall, *Flow. of Epigrams*, 249 (Spens.S.), The prouerbe old doth say: The weake may stand the strong in sted.

6. Weak food best fits weak stomachs. *c.*1430: Lydgate, *Minor Poems*, 165 (Percy S.), A proverbe sayde in ful old langage, That tendre browyce made with a marry-boon For fieble stomakes is holsum in potage. 1597: H. Lok, *Poems*, 302 (Grosart), Weake food best fits weake stomacks – as is sayd.

7. Weak men had need be witty. 1639: Clarke, 42. 1670: Ray, 154.

8. Weak things united become strong. 1732: Fuller, 5460.

Weal, *subs.* **1. Weal and woman never Pan**. *See* quots. 1639: Clarke, 118, Weale and women never sam, but sorrow and they can. 1678: Ray, 355, Weal and women cannot pan, *i.e.* close together, But woe and women can. 1828: Carr, *Craven Dialect*, ii 29, We frequently hear it in Craven, 'women and weal can never agree'. 1889: *Folk-Lore Journal*, vii 293 [Derbyshire], Weal and woman never pan But woe and woman can.

2. Weal and worship. 1917: Bridge, *Cheshire Proverbs*, 148, The closing toast of all Congleton festivities, 'May welfare and religion go hand in hand'.

3. Whom weal pricks, sorrow comes after and licks. 1605: Camden, *Remains*, 335 (1870).

Wealth, *subs.* **1. In wealth beware of woe.** *c.*1460: *Proverbs of Good Counsel*, in E.E.T.S., Ext. Ser. 8, p. 69, And ever in welth be ware of woo.

2. Little avails wealth, where there is no health. 1659: Howell, 17.

3. Wealth is best known by want. 1732: Fuller, 5463.

4. Wealth is enemy to health. *c.*1390: Gower, *Conf. Amantis*, Prol. i 30 (1857), But in proverbe netheles Men sain: ful selden is that welthe Can suffre is owne estate in helthe. 1586: Whetstone, *Engl. Myrror*, 14, The rich man's wealth is most enemy unto his health.

5. Wealth is like rheum, it falls on the weakest parts. 1640: Herbert, *Jac. Prudentum*. 1670: Ray, 28.

6. Wealth is not his who hath it, but his who enjoys it. 1659: Howell, *Prov. Ital.-Engl.*, 12. *c.*1736: Franklin, in *Works*, i 455 (Bigelow).

7. Wealth makes wit waver. 1736: Bailey, *Dict.*, s.v., 'Wealth'. 1823: Scott, *Q. Durward*, ch xviii, Where much wealth had, according to the ancient proverb, made wit waver.

8. Wealth makes worship. 1639: Clarke, 99. 1670: Ray, 154. 1732: Fuller, 5464, Wealth wants not for worship.

9. Where wealth, there friends. 1855: Bohn, 564. *See also* **Health; Money;** and **Riches.**

Weapon and Weapons, *subs.* **1. All weapons of war cannot arm fear.** 1578: Florio, *First Fruites*, fo. 32, All the weapons of London wyl not arme feare. 1629: *Book of Meery Riddles*, Prov. 15. 1640: Herbert, *Jac. Prudentum*, All the armes of England will not arme feare.

2. It is ill putting a weapon. *See* **Ill putting.**

3. Weapons bode peace. Before 1500: in Hill, *Commonplace-Book*, 128 (E.E.T.S.), Wepin makith pese divers times. 1869: Hazlitt, 449.

Wear, *verb.* **1. Ever since we wear clothes, we know not one another.** 1640: Herbert, *Jac. Prudentum.*

2. He that wears black must hang a brush at his back. 1639: Clarke, 201 ['They' for 'He']. 1670: Ray, 63. 1732: Fuller, 6298.

3. He wears a whole Lordship on his back. 1639: Clarke, 262.

4. Many who wear rapiers are afraid of goose quills. 1855: Bohn, 450.

5. To wear the breeches. *See* **Breeches.**

6. To wear the willow. 1578: *Gorgeous Gallery*, 84 (Rollins), Which makes men to weare the willow garland. 1612: Field, *Woman a Weathercock*, I, There's Lucida wears the willow garland for you. 1673: Davenant, *Siege*, V, I am content To wear the willow now. 1725: in Farmer, *Musa Pedestris*, 46, Great pity 'twas that one so prim, Should ever wear the willow. 1825: Hone, *Ev. Day Book*, i 1080, The old saying, 'She is in her willows' is here illustrated; it implies the mourning of a female for her lost mate. 1876: J. W. Ebsworth, *Prelude to Bagford Ballads* (B.S.), Lovers who willow wore. 1907: De Morgan, *Alice-for-Short*, ch xii, Having given up wearing the willow on her account, and consoled himself with inferiority.

7. Wear a horn and blow it not. 1639: Clarke, 142. 1670: Ray, 198.

Weasel. *See* quot. 1840: Barham, *Ing Legends*: 'Gengulphus', 'You must, be pretty deep to catch weazels asleep', Says the proverb: that is, 'Take the Fair unawares'.

Weather, *subs.* **1. The weather will fine.** *See* **Rook.**

2. To talk of the weather, it's nothing but folly, For when it rains on the hill, the sun shines in the valley. 1846: Denham, *Proverbs*, 17 (Percy S.).

3. You are so cunning, you know not what weather 'tis, when it rains. 1732: Fuller, 5859.

Weatherwise. *See* quots. 1735: Franklin, *Poor Richard* (1890), 50 (OED), Some are weather wise, some are otherwise. 1875: Cheales, *Proverb. Folk-Lore*, 18, He who is weatherwise is not otherwise. 1893: Inwards, *Weather Lore*, 1, Those that are weather wise are rarely otherwise. Cornwall.

Weaver. *See* **Hundred tailors;** and **Miller (10).**

Webley. *See* **Leominster.**

Wed, *verb.* **He that weds before he's wise shall die before he thrive.** 1546: Heywood, *Proverbs*, Pt I ch viii. 1605: Camden, *Remains*, 335 (1870). 1685: Meriton, *Yorksh. Ale, etc.*, 67, But they that wed before they're wise, it's said Will dee before they thrive. 1710: S. Palmer, *Moral Essays on Proverbs*, 226.

Wedding. *See* **Marriage.**

Wedding. *See* quot. 1888: Q. Couch, *Troy Town*, ch iii, When 'tes over, 'tes over, as Joan said by her weddin'.

Wedding and ill wintering tame both man and beast. *c.*1595: Shakespeare, *Taming of Shrew*, IV i, Thou knowest, winter tames man, woman and beast. 1639: Clarke, 328. 1670: Ray, 47. Cf. **Bad wintering.**

Wedding-ring wears, At your, your cares win wear away. 1678: Ray, 344. 1732: Fuller, 6146, As your wedding ring wears, You'll wear off your cares. 1831: Hone, *Year Book*, 78. 1878: Dyer, *Eng. Folk-Lore*, 192.

Wedge where the beetle drives it, There goes the. 1678: Ray, 216. 1732: Fuller, 4869.

Wedlock is a padlock. 1678: Ray, 56. 1732: Fuller, 6261. 1875: Cheales, *Proverb. Folk-Lore*, 39, Wedlock is a padlock, and therefore is not to be lightly entered upon.

Wednesday. *See* **Sunday** (2), (3), and (4).

We dogs worried the hare. 1678: Ray, 239. 1732: Fuller, 5443, We hounds kill'd the hare, quoth the lap-dog. 1846–59: *Denham Tracts*, ii 108 (F.L.S.).

Weeds overgrow the corn, The. *c.*1450: in *Reliq. Antiquae*, ii 240 (1843), Lest the wede growe over the whete. 1485: Malory, *Morte d'A.*, bk vii ch 8, It is shame that euer ye were made knyghte to see suche a ladde to matche suche a knyghte as the wede ouer grewe the corne. *c.*1554: *Enterlude of Youth*, in Bang, *Materialien*, B. 12, p. 17, Lo Maisters here you may see beforne That the weede ouergroweth the corne. 1638: D. Tuvill, *Vade Mecum*, 95, (3rd Ed.), But alas! the tares have overgrowne the corne. 1721: Kelly, *Sc. Prov.*, 319 (OED), The weeds oergrow the corn, the bad are the most numerous.

Weeds want no sowing. 1732: Fuller, 5466.

Weeds. *See also* **Ill weeds.**

Week of Sundays, A = A considerable, but indefinite, period. 1876: Blackmore, *Cripps*, ch xxxviii, I ain't a been in church now for more nor a week of Sundays. 1894: Raymond, *Love and Quiet Life*, 164.

Weening is not measure. 1640: Herbert, *Jac. Prudentum.*

Weep, *verb.* **1. I wept when I was born, and every day shorn why.** 1654: Whitlock, *Zootomia*, 31, men first brought forth, we cry; Each day brings forth its why. 1670: Ray, 28. 1732: Fuller, 2631.

2. To weep Irish = To feign sorrow. 1589: *Pap with a Hatchet*, 35 (1844), Ile make thee to … weep Irish. 1619: B. Rich. *Irish Hubbub*, 2, Stanhurst, in his History of Ireland [1586], maketh this report of his countreymen; they follow the dead corpse to the ground with howling, and barbarous outcries, pitifull in appearance, whereof (as he supposeth) grew this proverb, 'to weep Irish'. 1650: Fuller, *Pisgah Sight*, II xii 15, Surely the Egyptians did not weep-Irish with feigned and mercenary tears. 1681: Robertson, *Phraseol. Generalis*, 1305.

Weeping Cross = repentance. 1564: Bullein, *Dialogue*, 78 (E.E.T.S.), In the ende thei go home … by weepyng cross. 1610: Rowlands, *Martin Markall*, 29 (Hunt.Cl.), In the end they come home by weeping crosse, and crie *Peccaui*. 1615: Braithwait, *Strappado*, 53 (1878), Goe not along, let my aduise enforce, Least thou returne (my boy) by weeping crosse. 1736: Bailey, *Dict.*, s.v. 'Way', The way to Heaven is by Weeping Cross. 1785. Grose, *Class. Dict. Vulgar Tongue*, s.v., To come home by Weeping Cross, to repent. 1869: Spurgeon, *John Ploughman*, ch v,

We must needs go to glory by the way of Weeping Cross.

Weigh, *verb.* **1. He that weighs the wind must have a steady hand.** 1580: Lyly, *Euphues*, 222 (Arber), Hee that weighes wind, must have a steadie hand to holde the ballaunce. 1732: Fuller, 2345.

2. Weigh justly and sell dearly. 1578: Florio, *First Fruites*, fo. 33, Weigh iust and sel deere. 1640: Herbert, *Jac. Prudentum.* 1732: Fuller, 546. Weigh right, and sell dear.

3. Weigh not what thou givest, but what is given thee. 1659: Howell, 12 (10).

Weight and measure take away strife. 1640: Herbert, *Jac. Prudentum.* 1670: Ray, 28. 1732: Fuller, 5468, Weight, measure, and tale take away strife.

Weirling, The. *See* quot. 1868: *N.&Q.*, 4th ser, i 614 [as in 1886]. 1886: Swainson, *Folk-Lore of British Birds*, 114 (F.L.S.), In Norfolk there is a saying called 'the Wilby warning', frequently quoted by labourers, to this effect: – 'When the weirling shrieks at night, Sow the seed with the morning light, But 'ware when the cuckoo swells its throat, Harvest flies from the moon-call's note.

Welcome, *subs. A hearty welcome is the best cheer.* 1611: Cotgrave, s.v. 'Chere', A hearty welcome is worth halfe a feast. 1725: Bailey, tr. Erasm. *Colloq.*, 429 [cited as 'the old proverb']. 1736: Bailey, *Dict.*, s.v. 'Welcome'. Welcome is the best dish upon the table.

Welcome, *adj.* **1. As welcome as a storm.** 1732: Fuller, 746.

2. As welcome as flowers in May. 1591: Florio, *Second Frutes*, 55, Welcome Maie with his flowres. 1645: Howell, *Letters*, bk i § vi, No. lx., 'Twas as welcome to me as flowers in May. 1793: C. Macklin, *Love à la Mode*, I i, You are as welcome as the flowers in May. 1817: Scott, *Rob Roy*, ch viii. 1893: R.L.S., *Ebb-Tide*, ch vi. 1911: *N.&Q.*, 11th ser iii 367.

3. As welcome as snow in harvest. *See* **Snow** (2).

4. As welcome as the eighteen trumpeters. 1614: R. Heyricke, quoted in *N.&Q.*, 2nd ser, viii 484, You wryte how yow reacayved my lettar … and that … you esteemed yt as wellcome as the 18 trumpytors.

5. As welcome as water in one's shoes, and, as water into a ship. *See* **Water** (2) and (3).

6. He that is welcome fares well. 1736: Bailey, *Dict.*, s.v. 'Welcome'.

7. Welcome death, quoth the rat, when the trap fell. 1659: Howell, 10 … fell down. 1670: Ray, 28 [as in 1659]. 1732: Fuller, 5469.

8. Welcome evil, if thou contest alone. 1640: Herbert, *Jac. Prudentum.* 1732: Fuller, 5471 ['mischief' for 'evil'].

Well, *subs.* **1. If well and them cannot, then ill and them can.** Yorksh. 1670: Ray, 155.

2. Well's a fret. 1853: *N. & Q.*, 1st ser, viii 197, It is a very common practice in Nottingham to say: – 'Well's a fret, He that dies for love will not be hang'd for debt'.

3. When the well is full it will run over. 1736: Bailey. *Dict.*, s.v. 'Well'.

See also **Truth** (13); and **Water** (22).

Well, *adj.* and *adverb.* **1. He's well to live** = He is drunk. 1678: Ray, 87.

2. He that is well sheltered is a fool if he stir out into the rain. 1484: Caxton, *Aesope*, ii 239 (Jacobs), He whiche is in a place wel sure is wel a fole to go fro hit and to putte hym self in grete daunger and perylle. 1589: Puttenham, *Eng. Poesie*, 240 (Arber), It is said by maner of a prouerbiall speach that he who findes himselfe well shuld not wagge. 1732: Fuller, 2199.

3. He that would be well needs not go from his own house. 1640: Herbert, *Jac. Prudentum.*

4. If you want a thing done well, do it yourself. 1541: M. Coverdale, tr. *H. Bullinger's Christian State of Matrimony*, xix, If thou wilt prosper, then loke to every thynge thyne owne self. 1616: T. Draxe, *Adages*, 163, If a man will have his business well done, he must doe it himselfe. 1858: Longfellow, *Poems* (1960), 160, That's what I always say; if you want a thing to be well done, You must do it yourself.

5. If you would be well served, serve yourself. 1869: J. E. Austen-Leigh, *Mem. of Jane Austen*, 35 [quoted as a homely proverb].

6. That is well spoken that is well taken. 1639: Clarke, 111. 1685: Meriton, *Yorkshire Ale, etc.*, 39, It is well spoken that is well tane, I've heard. 1732: Fuller, 4364. 1901: F. E.Taylor, *Lancs. Sayings*, 9, That's weel spokken 'at's weel takken.

7. That which is well done is twice done. 1606: Day, *Ile of Gulls*, V, For, saies my mother, a thinge once wel done is twice done. 1682: A. Behn, *False Count*, III ii [as in 1606]. 1732: Fuller, 4381.

8. They are well off that haven't a house to go to. This seems perilously like nonsense. 1846: Denham, *Proverbs*, 4 (Percy S.).

9. *Well begun is half done.* Dimidium facti qui coepit habet. – Horace, *Epist.*, I ii 40.] *c.*1300: *Prov. of Hendyng*, st. 2 (Berlin, 1878), God beginning maketh god endynge. *c.*1430: in *Babees Book, etc.*, 48 (E.E.T.S.), And whanne a thing is weel bigunne, It makith a good eende at the laste. *c.*1490: *Partonope*, 438 (E.E.T.S.), Thing wele ended is wele be-gonne. 1542: Udall, *Erasm. Apoph.*, 17 (1877), Laertius ascribeth to hym [Socrates] this saiyng also: To haue well begonne, is a thing halfe doen … The saiyng is halfe a verse of the Greke poete Hesiodus: , Begynnyng is halfe of the whole. 1607: *Lingua*, II ii, He that [hath] once begun well, hath half done. 1680: L'Estrange, *Select Coll. of Erasm.*, 208. 1712: Motteux, *Quixote*, Pt II ch xli, A business well begun, you know, is half ended. 1883: Burne, *Shropsh. Folk-Lore*, 273, 'Well begun is half done', is evidently their principle.

10. Well fare nothing once a year. 1639: Clarke, 244. 1659: Howell, 12.

11. Well guessed Kath, here's neither to lack nor to leave. 1639: Clarke, 113.

12. Well horse, winter will come. 1659: Howell, 13.

13. Well is bestowed the meat he eats. *c.*1300: *Havelok*, l. 907, p. 33 (Skeat), Wel is set the mete thu etes.

14. Well is that well does. 1736: Bailey, *Dict.*, s.v. 'Well'.

15. Well paid is well sold. *c.*1630: in *Roxb. Ballads*, i 124 (B.S.).

16. Well rhymed, tutor, brains and stairs. 1639: Clarke, 70 ['traines' for 'brains']. 1670: Ray, 218.

17. Well thriveth that well endureth. *c.*1320: in *Reliq. Antiquae*, i 115 (1841), 'Wei abit that wel may tholye,' Quòth Hendyng.

18. Well to work and make a fire, It doth care and skill require. 1670: Ray, 28. 1732: Fuller, 6246.

19. Well well, is a word of malice. Cheshire. 1670: Ray, 154. 1917: Bridge, *Cheshire Proverbs*, 149.

20. What is well done is done soon enough. 1545: Ascham, *Toxoph.*, 114 (Arber), Thys wyse prouerbe: *Sone ynough, if wel ynough.* 1578: Florio, *First Fruites*, fo. 25, That thing is quickly done, that is done wel. 1598: Meres, *Palladis*, fo. 259 [as in 1545]. 1605: Sylvester, *Du Bartas*, Week i Day i l. 489. 1633: Draxe, 111, *bis*, Soone enough done, if well done. 1666: Torriano, *Piazza Univ.*, 82, That is done soon enough which is well done. 1730: T. Saldkeld, tr. *Gracian Compl. Gent.*, 126, A thing is soon enough done, if well done, was one of the antient sage's maxims.

21. Where men are well used, they'll frequent there. 1659: Howell, 10. 1670: Ray, 27. 1732: Fuller, 5649, Where men are kindly used, they will resort.

See also **All is well.**

Welland, River. *See* **Nene.**

Wellingborough Fair. *See* quot. 1901: *N. & Q.*, 9th ser, viii 421, 'Gone to Wellingborough Fair to blow their bellows'. – This, in addition to several other curious old sayings, I have often during recent years heard from a lady born and bred in Northamptonshire (1830–51).

Wellington round-heads. 1678: Ray, 353. 1790: Grose, *Prov. Gloss.*, s.v. 'Somerset', … A saying, formerly in use, at Taunton, to signify a violent fanatic.

Welsh ambassador, The = The cuckoo. 1608: Middleton, *Trick to Catch*, IV (N.), Thy sound is like the cuckoo, the Welch embassador. *c.*1630: in *Roxb. Ballads*, i 72 (B.S.), Three dozen of Welsh embassadors bakt. 1754: Berthelson, *Eng.-Danish Dict.*, s.v. 'Embassador'. 1878: Dyer, *Eng. Folk–Lore*, 61, In Wales the cuckoo often goes by the name of 'the Welsh Ambassador'. 1917: Bridge, *Cheshire Proverbs*, 121.

Welsh bait, Give your horse a = a rest, without any other refreshment. 1662: Fuller, *Worthies*, iii 489 (1840). 1790: Grose, *Prov. Gloss.*, s.v. 'Wales'.

Welsh blood is up, Her. 1631: Shirley, *Love Tricks*, V iii, *Jen* … Her Welsh plood is up, look you. 1662: Fuller, *Worthies*, iii 488 (1840) ['His' for 'her']. 1790: Grose, *Prov. Gloss.*, s.v. 'Wales'.

Welsh cousin, A. 1790: Grose, *Ibid* … A relation far removed; the Welsh making themselves cousins to most of the people of rank born in the country.

Welshman. 1. The older the Welshman the more madman. 1659: Howell, *Proverbs: Brit.-Engl.*, 31.

2. The Welshman keeps nothing till he has lost it. 1662: Fuller, *Worthies*, iii 520 (1840), 'Ni Cheitw Cymbro oni Gello'. That is, 'The Welchman keeps nothing until he hath lost it'. The historical truth thereof is plain in the British

Chronicles, that when the British recovered the lost castles from the English, they doubled their diligence and valour, keeping them more tenaciously than before. 1790: Grose, *Prov. Gloss.*, s.v. 'Cardiganshire'.

3. The Welshman's jackdaw. *See* **Say** (9).

See also **February** (2).

Welsh pedigree, As long as a. 1662: Fuller, *Worthies*, iii 489 (1840). 1790: Grose, *Prov. Gloss.*, s.v. 'Wales'. 1875: Cheales, *Proverb. Folk–Lore*, 53, As long as a Welsh pedigree … which Walter Scott in one of his couplets … strikingly illustrates.

Wem, Salop. *See* quot. 1883: Burne, *Shropsh. Folk–Lore*, 585, The women of Wem and a few musketeers, Beat Lord Capel and all his cavaliers.

Wembury. *See* quot. 1917: Bridge, *Cheshire Proverbs*, 12, As crooked as Wembury (Wybunbury) steeple.

West Auckland. *See* quot. 1846–59: *Denham Tracts*, i 60 (F.L.S.), By 'grees and 'grees, as the West Auckland lasses get their fortunes.

West Chester, To be sent to. 1851: *N. & Q.*, 1st ser, iii 353, Passing through a village only six miles from London last week, I heard a mother saying to a child, 'If you are not a good girl I will send you to West Chester'. 1851: Ibid., 460, To be sent to *West Chester* [= Chester] (frequently so called in the beginning of the last century) was to be sent into banishment, *i.e.* into Ireland. 1917: Bridge, *Cheshire Proverbs*, 126.

Westgate, Newcastle-on-Tyne. 1655: A. Brewer, *Love-sick King*, II, Here did Thornton enter in With hope, a half penny, and a lambs-skin. 1663: Killigrew, *Parson's Wedding*, II vii, I have heard of Whittington and his cat, and others, that have made fortunes by strange means, but I scarce believe my son would rise from *Hop, a halfpenny and a lamb's-skin.* 1846–59: *Denham Tracts*, i 295 (F.L.S.), At Westgate came Thornton in, With hap [luck], a halfpenny, and a lamb's skin. [Six other slightly varying versions are given at this reference.] Cf. **Hap and a halfpenny.** Thornton was one of the Bailiffs of Newcastle in 1397, later member of Parliament, and the first Mayor. He became very wealthy.

Westminster: *Who goes to Westminster for a wife, to Pail's for a man, or to Smithfield for a horse, may meet with a whore, a knave and a jade.* 1593:

Passionate Morrice, 83 (N.Sh.S.), It is more vncertaine … whether a Smith-feelde horse will proue good or iadish. 1617: Fynes Moryson, *Itinerary*, Pt 3, p. 53, The Londiners pronounce woe to him that buyes a horse in Smythneld, that takes a servant in Pauls Church, that marries a wife out of Westminster [noted for its stews]. 1658: Flecknoe, *Enigm. Characters*, 47, That old saying of choosing a horse in Smithfield, and a serving-man in Pauls. 1790: Grose, *Prov. Gloss.*, s.v. 'London'.

Westminster Hall. *See* **Suits hang.**

Westmoreland Jury. *See* quot. 1846–59: *Denham Tracts*, i 223 (F.L.S.), Wise as the Westmoreland Jury, who found a man guilty of manslaughter who was tried for stealing a grindstone!

Weston. *See* **Holbeach.**

Westridge wood. *See* quot. 1639: in *Berkeley MSS.* iii 29 (1885), When Westridge wood is motley, then it's time to sowe barley. Glos.

Westward for smelts. 1603: *Westward for Smelts, or the Waterman's Fare of Mad, Merry Western Wenches, etc.* [title]. 1607: Dekker, etc., *Westw. Hoe*, II iii, But wenches, with what pullies shall wee slide with some cleanly excuse, out of our husbandes suspition, being gone Westward for smelts all night. 1608: *Great Frost*, in Arber, *Garner*, i 85 (1877), Say, have none gone 'westward for smelts', as our proverbiall phrase is?

Wet, *adj.* **1. After a wet year a cold one.** 1893: Inwards, *Weather Lore*, 4.

2. As wet as a shag (cormorant). 1838: Holloway, *Provincialisms*, 150, 'As wet as a shag', means very wet. 1875: Parish, *Sussex Dict.*, 102 … is a common expression taken from the idea of a cormorant diving frequently under the water.

3. As wet as drip. 1828: Carr, *Craven Dialect*, i 119, 'As wet as drip' is a common phrase, when a person's clothes are so soaked with rain that it falls off in drops.

4. As wet as muck. 1714: Mandeville, *Fable of Bees*, 219, With his cloaths as wet as dung with the rain. 1883: Burne, *Shropsh. Folk-Lore*, 595. 1889: *N.&Q.*, 7th ser, vii 135, A few years ago such a young woman would have said … 'It's as wet as muck'. 1894: Raymond, *Love and Quiet Life*, 215, Made him so wet as a muck.

5. As wet as thatch. 1889: Peacock, *Manley, etc.*, *Gloss.*, 604 (E.D.S.), Weet as thack, *i.e.* wet as thatch. 1917: Bridge, *Cheshire Proverbs*, 26.

6. As wet as wring. Ibid., 26 ['wring' perhaps = coarse, rushy grass].

7. A wet hand will hold a dead herring. 1580: Lyly, *Euphues*, 414 (Arber), A wette hande quoth Flauia will holde a dead hearing. 1732: Fuller, 453.

8. Wet eel. *See* **Eel** (4).

9. With a wet finger = easily, as easily as a wetted finger will turn a page. 1519: Horman, *Vulgaria*, fo. 195, I wyll helpe all this besines with a wete fynger. 1593: G. Harvey, *Works*, ii 32 (Grosart), I hate brawles with my hart: and can turne-ouer a volume of wronges with a wett finger. 1607: Dekker, etc., *Westw. Hoe*, II ii, Ile becken, you shal see ile fetch her with a wet finger. 1721: Cibber, *Refusal*, I, Here's five thousand for you, Mr Granger, with a wet finger. 1824: Scott, *Redgauntlet*, ch xv, He thinks to win them to his turn with a wet finger.

Wet, *verb.* **1. To wet one's whistle.** [τέγγε πνεύμονας – Petr., 34]. *c.*1386: Chaucer, *Reeve's Tale*, l. 235, So was her ioly whistle wel y-wet. *c.*1410: *Towneley Plays*, 119 (E.E.T.S.), Had she oones wett hyr whystyll she couth syng full dere. 1570: Googe, *Popish Kingdome*, 50 (1880), The meate they go, and all with wine their whistles wet. 1685: S. Wesley, *Maggots*, 64, Well may I My whistle wet, for sure the subject's dry. 1886: Hardy, *Casterbridge*, ch xxxvi, Come in and wet your whistle at my expense. 1926: Phillpotts. *Yellow Sands*, iii, He'll want a drop to wet his whistle.

2. To wet the head. *See* quots. 1889: *N.&Q.*, 7th ser, viii 86, Farmer A., who was on his way from the house of Farmer B., where, said he, 'We have been washing the baby's head' [*i.e.* drinking its health]. 1923: *N.&Q.*, 12th ser, xii 63, There is a centuries-old custom connected with the first shoeing of a young horse … known as 'wetting its head'. Ibid., 152, The birth of a child frequently afforded an excuse for a drink, on the plea of 'wetting its head'.

Wettenhall. *See* quot. 1917: Bridge, *Cheshire Proverbs*, 51, Down Wettenhall long lane, the plovers fly backwards. Said in answer to persistent questions. Imparting information which is of no value.

Weybourne Hoop. *See* **England** (6).

Whale. *See* **Herring** (4); **Sprat;** and **Tub to a whale.**

Whaplode. *See* **Holbeach.**

What again? *See* quots. 1639: Clarke, 303, 'What again?' quoth Paul when his wife made him cuckold the second time. 1659: Howell, 11, 'What again?' quoth Palmer.

What d'ye lack? The traditional cry of the London apprentice, which became a proverbial name for a shopkeeper. 1563: Newbery, *Dives Pragmaticus*, sig. A3, What lacke ye, sir what seke you, what wyll you bye? 1630: T. Adams, *Works*, 171, She sits upon the stall, and counts the passengers with a what lacke ye? 1641: *Stage-Players Complaint*, 3, in Hindley, *Old Book Coll. Miscell.*, iii, I'm persuaded that there's never a *What lack you*, *Sir*, in all the City, but is sensible of our calamity. 1685: S. Wesley, *Maggots*, 159, A shop i' th' Change, still damn'd to What d'ye lack!

What greater crime than loss of time? 1732: Fuller, 6324.

What has been, may be. Ibid., No. 5491

What is she, but what has she, Not. 1621: Brathwait, *Natures Embassie*, 233 (1877), 'Tis true what th' prouerbe saith, We aske not what he is, but what he hath. 1732: Fuller, 3687. 1738: Swift, *Polite Convers.*, Dial. I, It is not what is she, but has she now-a-days.

What she wants in up and down. *See* **Want,** *verb* (4).

What's mine's mine own. 1613: H. Parrot, *Laquei ridiculosi*, bk i Epi. 118. 1666: Torriano, *Piazza Univ.*, 278, The English ever say, That which is mine is my own. 1732: Fuller, 5512, What's mine is my own: what's my brother's is his and mine. 1738: Swift, *Polite Convers.*, Dial. II, What's yours is mine, and what's mine is my own. 1830: Forby, *Vocab. E. Anglia*, 430, What's 'hers is mine; what's mine is my own, quoth the husband.

What's what, To know. *c.*1400: *Ywaine and Gawin*, l. 432 (Ritson), For wa I wist noght what was what. *c.*1440: Hoccleve, *Minor Poems*, 138 (E.E.T.S.), And elles woot I neuere what is what. Before 1529: Skelton, *Works*, ii, 60 (Dyce), Yet, whan he toke first his hat, He said he knew what was what. 1542: Udall, tr. *Erasm. Apoph.*, 239 (1877). 1638: Ford, *Lady's Trial*, II i, I know what's what, I know upon which side My bread is butter'd. 1696: Vanbrugh, *Relapse*, III. 1711: Steele, *Spectator*, No. 132, This sly saint ... understands what's what as well as you or I,

widow. 1773: Goldsmith, *She Stoops*, V, I'm an old fellow, and know what's what as well as you that are younger. 1837: Dickens, *Pickwick*, ch xxxvii, That 'ere young lady ... knows wot's wot, she does. 1849: Lytton, *Caxtons*, Pt iv, ch iii.

What the Cheque [Exchequer] **takes not, the Church takes.** 1660: Howell, *Parly of Beasts*, 18.

What they want in meat, let them take out in drink. 1598: Shakespeare, 2 *Hen. IV* V iii, What you want in meat, we'll have in drink. 1631: Heywood, *Fair Maid of West*, Pt I act ii [cited as 'the old proverbe'].

Wheamow. *See* **I.**

Wheat. 1. A good wheat year, a fine plum year. 1887: *N.&Q.*, 7th ser, iv 485 ... This is a prevailing saying in North Notts.

2. Good wheat. *See* quot. 1860: R. S. Hawker, in Byles, *Life, etc.*, 323 (1905), The Farmers have a proverb here [Morwenstow] that good wheat in March should cover a sitting hare.

3. Sow wheat in dirt, and rye in dust. 1732: Fuller, 4235. 1884: H. Friend, *Flowers and Fl. Lore*, 219. 1893: Inwards, *Weather Lore*, 153.

4. Sow your wheat all in a flood, And it will grow up like a wood. 1670: *Poor Robert Alman.*, Sept.

5. Wheat always lies best in wet sheets. 1830: Forby, *Vocab. E. Anglia*, 417.

6. *Wheat is not to be gathered in the blade, but in the ear.* 1732: Fuller, 5528.

7. Wheat or barley. See quot. 1886: Elworthy, **West Som. Word-Book**, 667 (E.D.S.), The old adage about a late season: Wait [wheat] or barley 'll strut [sprout] in June, Nif they baint no higher 'an a spoon.

8. Wheat will not have two praises (summer and winter). 1678: Ray, 348. 1846: Denham, *Proverbs*, 5 (Percy S.).

9. When wheat lies long in bed, it riseth with an heavy head. Gloucest. 1639: in *Berkeley MSS.*, iii 28 (1885).

See also **Bark-year; Barley; Bushel** (1); **Good elm; March** (27); **May** (12); **November** (6); **No wheat;** and **Tenbury.**

Wheel. *See* **Squeaking wheel.**

Wheelbarrow farmer, A. 1917: Bridge, *Cheshire Proverbs*, 27, One who rents only an acre or two of land and is supposed to wheel his manure ... in barrow loads instead of carting it.

Wheels within wheels. [1611: *Bible*, Ezekiel, i 16, Their appearance and their work was as it were a wheel in the middle of a wheel.] 1642: D. Rogers, *Matrim. Honour*, To Reader, This wheele of our conversation ... including many lesser wheeles in, and under it. 1709: Mandeville, *Virgin Unmask'd*, Preface, And as a wheel within a wheel, prefixing it to the Preface. 1740: North, *Lives of Norths*, i 306 (Bohn), Wheels within wheels took place; the ministers turned formalisers, and the court mysterious. 1837: Dickens, *Pickwick*, ch xl, Veels within veels, a prison in a prison. Ain't it, Sir? 1867: Dickens, *Letters*, ii 304 (1880).

Wheelwright's dog is a carpenter's mate, A = A bad wheelwright makes a good carpenter. 1830: Forby, *Vocab. E. Anglia*, 427. 1872: J. Glyde, Jr., *Norfolk Garland*, 148 ['uncle' for 'mate'].

When I did well, I heard it never; When I did ill, I heard it ever. 1732: Fuller, 6414. 1736: Bailey, *Dict.*, s.v. 'When'.

When I lent I was a friend, When I asked I was unkind. 16th cent. in *Reliq. Antiquae*, i 208 (1841).

When thou dost hear a toll or knell, Then think upon thy passing-bell. 1659: Howell, 6. 1670: Ray, 212.

When Tom's pitcher's broken I shall have the shards; *i.e.* Kindness after others have done with it; or refuse. 1678; Ray, 351.

Where a man lives well. *See* **Man** (43).

Where something is found, there look gain. 1732: Fuller, 5658.

Whet is no let, A. Before 1628: J. Preston, *Saint's Daily Exercise*, 32 (1629), (OED), The whetting of the sithe, though there be a stop in the Work for a time, yet, as our common saying is, 'a whet is no let', and the doing of this is no impediment. 1670: Ray, 155. 1709: R. Kingston, *Apoph. Curiosa*, 80, Whetting is no letting. 1732: Fuller, 454, A whet is no let, said the mower.

Whetstone can't itself cut, yet it makes tools cut, A. 1732: Fuller, 455.

Whetstone, To deserve, or, to lie for the. [The tongue compared to a whetstone. – Pindar, *Ol.*, vi 140.] 1364: *Liber Albus*, iv 601 (Rolls), (OED), Juggement de Pillorie par iii heures, ove un ague pier entour soun col, pur mensonges controeves. *c.*1400: *Towneley Plays*, 230 (E.E.T.S.), He lyes for the quetstone. Before 1500 in Hill, *Commonplace-Book*, 110 (E.E.T.S.), I sawe an ege styng a pye; geve me drynke, my mowth ys

drye; Yet ys not long syth I made a lye; I will haue the whetston, and I may. 1580: Lyly, *Euphues*, 238 (Arber), If I meet with one of Creete, I was ready to lye with him for the whetstone. 1625: in *Harl. Miscell.*, iv 87 (1745), Now that this is a lye well worthy of a whetstone, yourself (I hope) will acknowledge. 1732: Fuller, 5991, You shall have the whetstone. 1886: Elworthy, *West Som. Word-Book*, 828 (E.D.S.), Whetstone. The liar's prize – still used thus. 1926: *Star*, Feb. 27, p. 5, col. 1, A country amusement of the day [18th century] was 'lying for the whetstone'.

Which way to London? *See* quots. 1583: Melbancke, *hilotinus*, sig. 63, God geue you good euen, which is the way to Poclinton, a pokeful of plummes. 1633: Draxe, 4, Which way to London? a poke full of plummes. 1639: Clarke, 19 [as in 1633.] 1666: Torriano, *Piazza Univ.*, 100, As they say in English, How many miles to London, answer is made impertinently, a poke fall of plums.

While men go after a leech – = After death the doctor, *c.*1387: Usk, *Test of Love*, in Skeat's *Chaucer*. vii 134, While men gon after a leche the body is buryed.

Whim-wham. *See* quot. 1917: Bridge, *Cheshire Proverbs*, 28, A whim-wham from Yocketon. A whim-wham to wind the sun up. [Answers by old folk to inquisitive young people who interrupt them.]

Whip and whur [whirr] **never made good fur.** 1550: Udall, *R. Doister*, I iii, No haste but good, Madge Mumble-crust; for whip and whur, The old proverb doth say, never made good fur.

Whip for a fool, and a rod for a school, is always in good season, A. 1613: S. Rowley, *When you See Me*, sig. F1, A rod in scoole, a whip for a foole, is alwaies in season. 1670: Ray, 212.

Whip saith the tailor, whit saith the shears, Take a true tailor and cut off his ears. 1659: Howell, 15.

Whip the cat, To = To be drunk. *c.*1600: in *Roxb. Ballads*, ii 382 (B.S.), But mault made hym the cat to whip. 1611: Cotgrave, s.v. 'Bertrand', To bee drunke ... to whip the cat. 1807: *Gent. Mag.*, lxxvii. 1192. 1883: Burne, *Shropsh. Folk-Lore*, 450 [lines formerly on an inn signboard at Albrighton, Salop.], The finest pastime that is under the sun Is whipping the cat at Albrighton.

Whispering. *See* quots. 1678: Ray, 348, Where there is whispering there is lying. 1738: Swift, *Polite Convers.*, Dial. I, There's no whispering, but there's lying. 1753: Richardson, *Grandison*, i 196 (1883), Whisperings in conversations are censurable, to a proverb.

Whist, and catch a mouse. 1639: Clarke, 302. 1670: Ray, 199.

Whistle, *subs. You'll make an end of your whistle though the cart overthrow.* 1678: Ray, 276. 1732: Fuller, 6027 [with 'for it' added].

See also **Wet,** *verb* (1).

Whistle, *verb. You can't whistle and drink at the same time.* 1586: Pettie, *Guazzo*, fo. 137, It is a common saying, that one cannot drinke and whistle altogether. 1659: Howell, *Proverbs: Ital.-Eng.*, 6, One cannot drink and whistle at once. 1869: Hazlitt, 484.

Whistling woman. *See* quots. [1721: Kelly, *Sc. Prov.*, 33, A crooning cow, a crowing hen, and a whistling maid boded never luck to a house.] 1850: *N. & Q.*, 1st ser, ii 164, Hence the old proverb often quoted in this district [Northants.]: A whistling woman and a crowing hen, Is neither fit for God nor men. Ibid., 226, A whistling woman and a crowing hen, Will call the old gentleman out of his den. 1855: T. Q. Couch, in *N. & Q.*, 1st ser, xii 37, An old proverb in use here [Cornwall] says: 'A whistling woman, and a crowing hen, are two of the unluckiest things under the sun'. 1917: Bridge, *Cheshire Proverbs*, 28 … will fear the old lad out of his den.

Whiston. *See* **Bolsover.**

Whist, whist, I smell a bird's nest. 1678: Ray, 276.

White, *adj.* **1. As white as a hound's tooth.** 1923: *Devonsh. Assoc. Trans.*, liv 137, Of a clean floor: 'Er's so white's a hound's tooth.

2. As white as a lily. *c.*1310: *King Horn* (Oxf.), l. 15 (Hall), Whit so any lili flour. 1485: Caxton, *Charles the Grete*, 90 (E.E.T.S.), Hyr chekys rounde, whyt as the flour de lys. *c.*1560: T. Ingelend, *Disobedient Child*, 43 (Percy S.), Your clothes are washte cleane, As whyte as a lylly. 1609: *Ev. Woman in her Humour*, I in Bullen, *O. P.*, iv 319, Thy colour shall be dowlas as white as a lillie. 1682: *A. Behn, City Heiress*, I i, The dearest loveliest hypocrite, white as lillies. 1884: H. Friend, *Flowers and Fl. Lore*, 210, 'As white as a lily' has long since passed into a proverb.

3. As white as a sheet. *c.*1489: Caxton, *Sonnes of Aymon*, 419 (E.E.T.S.), He … becam pale as a white cloth for the grete wrathe that he had. *c.*1611: Shakespeare, *Cymbeline*. II. ii, Fresh lily, And whiter than the sheets! 1751: Fielding, *Amelia*, bk vii ch viii, He entered the room with a face as white as a sheet. 1834: Marryat, *P. Simple*, ch lviii, I turned round to look at the captain; he was as white as a sheet. 1872: Hardy, *Greenwood Tree*, Pt I ch viii, You must be wearied out … you'll be as white as a sheet to-morrow. 1922: Weyman, *Ovington's Bank*, ch xxxvi, He was in the bank, white as a sheet.

4. As white as ivory, (*a*) whale-bone; (*b*) ivory. (*a*) *c.*1307: in *Lyric Poetry*, 34 (Percy S., No. 19), Hire teht [teeth] aren white ase bon of whal. *c.*1380: *Sir Ferumbras*, 80 (E.E.T.S.), That swete thynge as whit as wales bon. 15th cent.: *Torrent of Portyngall*, 29 (E.E.T.S.), Ase whyt ase walles bone. *c.*1450: in *Reliq. Antiquae* i 28 (1841), And sche be whyte as whales bone. 1590: Spenser, *F. Q.*, III i 15, Whose face … through feare, as white as whale's bone. 1592: Shakespeare, *L.L.L.*, V ii. 1609: T. Ravenscroft, *Deuteromelia*, sig. B4, His beard was all on a white a, as white as whale is bone. 1855: Kingsley, *Westw. Ho*, ch vii, The lady herself was of an excellent beauty, like a whale's tooth for whiteness.

(*b*) 1592: Warner, *Alb. England*, bk vii ch 36, Her bodie white as iuorie. 1725: *The Matchless Rogue*, 83, His teeth were as white as ivory. 1781: T. Francklin, *Lucian's Works*, ii 339. 1836: Marryat, *Midsh. Easy*, ch v, He showed a row of teeth white as ivory. 1922: A. Bennett, *Prohack*, ch xxi (iii), The poor lady had gone as pale as ivory.

5. As white as milk. *c.*1300: Brunne, tr. Langtoft *Chron.*, 334 (Hearne), In lynen white as milke. *c.*1380: *Sir Ferumbras*, 124 (E.E.T.S.), As wyt ase melkys fom. *c.*1386: Chaucer, *Prol.* l. 358. *c.*1400: *Rom. Rose*, 1. 1196. *c.*1450: *Partonope*, 66 (E.E.T.S.), And therto whyte as ony mylk. 1555: S. Hawes, *Past. of Pleasure*, 200 (Percy S.), Whyte as the milke, a goodly garment. *c.*1650: in *Poems on Costume*, 119 (Percy S.). 1669–96: Aubrey, *Lives*, i 212 (Clark), A long beard as white as milke. 1748: Smollett, *Rod. Random*, ch viii, A countenance as pale as milk. 1820: Byron, *Don Juan*, can. v st. 77, A slight chemise as white as milk. 1850:

Dickens, *Copperfield*, ch iii, The walls were whitewashed as white as milk. 1883: A. Dobson, in *Poet. Works*, 167 (1923), Her neck is white as milk.

6. As white as nip. *See* **Clean as nip.**

7. As white as driven snow. *c.*1300 in *Vernon MS.*, 418 (E.E.T.S.), Als whit as any dryuen snawe. 1579: Lyly, *Euphues*, 89 (Arber), The fish … is as white as the driuen snow. 1610: Shakespeare, *Wint. Tale*, IV iv, Lawn as white as driven snow. 1622: Drayton, *Polyol.*, xxiv, His head and beard as white as swan or driven snow. 1710: Ward, *Nuptial Dialogues*, i 318, White as the driven snow or thistly down. 1742: Fielding, *Andrews*, bk iv ch vi, His bosom, when a boy, was as white as driven snow. 1823: Byron, *Don Juan*, can. vi st. 25, In sheets white as what bards call 'driven snow'.

8. As white as snow. *c.*1000: *Ags. Gosp.*, Matt. xvii 2 (OED), Hys reaf waeron swa hwite swa snaw. *c.*1280 in *Vernon MS.*, 373 (E.E.T.S.), The castel is whit schinynge So the snowgh. *c.*1360: Mandeville, *Travels*, 139 (E.E.T.S.), And all ben white as snow. *c.*1440: Lydgate, *Lyf of our Lady*, sig. F2 (Caxton), Was whyt in soth as snowe that falleth newe. 1598: Meres, *Palladis*, fo. 195, The hearbe Mary hath a flower as white as snow. 1681: Rycaut, tr. *Graeian's Critick*, 211, Pipes of alablaster as white as snow. 1729: Coffey, *Beggar's Wedding*, I iii, Your head's white as snow. 1883: R.L.S., *Treas. Isl.*, ch i, The next, bright doctor, with his powder as white as snow. 1901: Raymond, *Idler out of Doors*, 5, Orchards, white as snow in early June.

9. As white as whale-bone. *See* No. 4a.

10. A white loaf and a hard cheese never shames the master. 1659: Howell, 11.

11. A white wall is a fool's paper. 1578: Florio, *First Fruites*, fo. 32. 1605: Camden, *Remains*, 319 (1870). 1662: Fuller, *Worthies*, ii 191 (1840), Indeed the Italians have a proverb, 'A wall is the fool's paper', whereon they scribble their fancies. [The Italian proverb is *Muro bianco carta da matti.*] 1732: Fuller, 5692, White walls are fools writing paper. 1868: *Quarterly Review*, cxxv 241, A needful and effectual lesson to wall-scribblers lies in the saw 'Muraille blanche, papier de fou' ('A white wall is the fool's writing-paper').

12. He has made many a white hedge black [? with] *stolen linen.* 1639: Clarke, 191.

13. He is very good at a white-pot = custard or

baked pudding. Gloucest. 1639: in *Berkeley MSS.*, iii 27 (1885).

14. The filth under the white snow, the sun discovers. 1640: Herbert, *Jac. Prudentum.*

15. There's no getting white meal out of a coal-sack. 1865: 'Lancs. Proverbs', in *N. & Q.*, 3rd ser, viii 494. 1869: Spurgeon, *John Ploughman*, ch x, You cannot get white flour out of a coal sack, nor perfection out of human nature. 1901: F. E. Taylor, *Lancs. Sayings*, 10, Ther's no gettin' white meeol eawt of a coal-seek.

16. To mark with a white stone. [O diem laetum, notandumque mihi candidissimo calculo! – Pliny, *Ep.* 6, 11. Creta an carbone notandi? – Horace, *Sat.* II iii 246.] 1540: Palsgrave, *Acolastus*, sig. K1, O festyuall daye … worthye to be marked with a stone as whyte as snowe. 1548: Hall, *Chron.*, 8 (1809), This thing is worthy to be noted with a whitestone. 1632: Massinger, *Emp. of East*, Prol., And, with the whitest stone, To be mark'd in your fair censures. 1693: Dryden, *Persius*, Sat. ii l. 2, Let this auspicious morning be exprest With a white stone. 1748: Smollett, *Rod. Random*, ch lii, He … told me that, in mentioning the white stone, he alluded to the *dies fasti* of the Romans, *albo lapide notati.* 1814: Byron, in *Letters*, etc., iii 57 (Prothero), I shall mark it with the 'white stone' in my calendar. 1888: Marchant, *Praise of Ale*, 581, A day to be marked for ever by Tom with a white stone.

17. White head and green tail. *c.*1386: Chaucer, *Reeve's Tale*, Prol. 1. 24, For in oure mil ther stiketh ever a nayl, To have an hoor heed and a grene tayl, As hath a leek. *c.*1590: Sir J. Davies, in *Poems*, ii 32 (Grosart), Septimus liues, and is like garlick seene, For though his head be white, his blade is greene. 1598: Hall, *Satires*, bk iv s iv, The maidens mocke, and call him withered leeke, That with a greene tayle hath an hoary head. 1651: Cartwright, *Ordinary*, III i, Mine head is white, but, O, mine taile is green. 1693: Urquhart, *Rabelais*, bk iii ch xxviii.

18. White silver draws black lines. 1598: Meres, *Palladis*, fo. 151, Silver although it be white, yet it draweth black lines. 1639: Clarke, 170. 1670: Ray, 142.

Whitneck. *See* **Stoat.**

Whitsuntide. 1. At whitsum. *See* quot. 1659: Howell, 20, At Witson poke Munday, when peeple shear hogs, viz. Never.

2. Fine on Holy Thursday, wet on Whit Monday, Fine on Whit Monday, wet on Holy Thursday. Hunts. 1888: *N. & Q.*, 4th ser, i 551. 1893: Inwards, *Weather Lore*, 41.

3. If it rains on Pastor Sunday [second after Easter] *it will rain every Sunday until Pentecost.* 1893: Inwards, *Weather Lore*, 41.

4. If Whitsunday bring rain, we expect many a plague. Ibid., 41.

5. Rain at Pentecost forebodes evil, Ibid., 41.

6. Whitsunday bright and clear Will bring a fertile year. Ibid., 41.

7. Whitsunday wet, Christmas fat. Ibid., 41.

See also **Christmas** (10) and **Easter** (7).

Whittington's College, He has studied at 1790: Grose, *Prov. Gloss.*, s.v. 'London', He has … That is, he has been confined in Newgate, which was rebuilt A.D. 1423 according to the Will of Sir Richard Whittington, by … his executors.

Whittlesea mere has foaled. 1865: W. White, *Eastern England*, i 255, Among the fenmen the phrase 'Whittlesea Mere has folded '(foaled) signified such a flood as drove fish plentifully from the mere into the dykes and rivers.

Who are you for? I am for him whom I get most by. 1855: Bohn, 565. Who can help sickness, quoth the

drunken wife, when she fell into the gutter? 1732: Fuller, 5696.

Who can hold that they have not in their hand? 1678: Ray, 155.

Who had that he hath not, would do that he doth not. 1546: Heywood, *Proverbs*, Pt II ch ix.

Who hath none to still him, may weep out his eyes. 1640: Herbert, *Jac. Prudentum.* 1670: Ray, 25.

Who may hold that will away? 1546: Heywood, *Proverbs*, Pt II ch vi. 1564: Bullein, *Dialogue*, 121 (E.E.T.S.), Lament no more, good wife, for who can kepe that must needes awaie. 1614: Jonson, *Bart. Fair*, I. 1640: Mabbe, tr. *Exemplary Novels*, 196, i (1900), Keep me not under lock and key, For who can hold what will away?

Who shall keep the keepers? 1567: in *Plasidas*, etc., 132 (Roxb.Cl), In vayne dothe the husbande set kepers ouer her, for who shal kepe those kepers. 1732: Fuller, 5718.

Whole as a fish. Before 1300: *Cursor Mundi*, l. 8175, As any fisshe thou mades me fete [fair]. *c.*1350: *Alexander*, l. 2575, As fast was he fysche-hale. *c.*1400: *Mirk's Festial*, 265

(E.E.T.S.), And anon the lepur [leprosy] fel from hym and he was hole as a fyssche. 1486: *Boke of St Albans*, sig. A4, She shall be hoole as a fysh. *c.*1580: *Tom Tyler*, 19 (1661) (Malone S.), This chafing hath made me as whole as a fish. 1647: A Brewer, *Countrie Girle*, sig. L2, His flesh as whole as a fish. 1707: Dunton, *Athenian Sport*, 304, Fishes exceed all creatures in point of health, even to a proverb. Cf. **Sound as a roach,** and, **as a trout.**

Whole skin, It is good deeping in a. 1543: Becon, in *Early Works*, 354 (P.S.), *c.*1570: *Merie Tales of Skelton*, xii in Skelton's *Works*, i lxv (Dyce), No, sayde the cobler, I am not afearde; it is good to siege in a whole skinne. *c.*1620: Day, *Peregr. Scholastica*, 70 (Bullen), As you think it good sleepeinge in a whole skin. 1664: Etheredge, *Comical Revenge*, IV i, I heard, poor lady, she wept, and charged you to steep in a whole skin. 1749: Fielding, *Tom Jones*, bk xii ch iii, If loving to sleep in a whole skin makes a man a coward – . 1819: Scott, *Bride of L.*, ch.V.

Wholesomest meat it at another man's cost, The. 1659: Howell, 19. 1670: Ray, 1.

Wholesomest way to get a good stomach is to walk on thy own ground, The. 1659: Howell, 18.

Whore in a fine dress is like a clean entry to a dirty house, A. 1736: Bailey, *Dict.*, s.v. *See also* **Once a whore;** and **Young** (10).

Whores affect not you but your money. 1670: Ray, 28. 1732: Fuller, 5726.

Whores and thieves go by the clock. 1678: Ray, 68.

Whoring and bawdry do often end in beggary. 1670: Ray, 28.

Whosoever is king, thou wilt be his man. 1670: Ray, 183. 1732: Fuller, 5734 ['shalt' for 'wilt'].

Whoso in youth. *See* quot. 16th cent, in *Babees Book* 332 (Furnivall), Who so in youthe no vertu vsith In age alle honour him refuseth.

Whoso will no evil do. *See* **Evil** (7).

Why for thy. *See* quot. 1678: Ray, 345, 'Twill not be why for thy. *Somerset.* Of a bad bargain or great loss for little profit.

Why hath its wherefore, Every. 1566: Gascoigne, *Supposes*, I i, I have given you a wherfore for this why many times. *c.*1590: Shakespeare, *Com. of Errors*, II ii, For they say every why hath a wherefore. Before 1704: T. Brown, *Works*, i 40. (1760). 1822: Scott, *Nigel*, ch iii. 1869: Spurgeon, *John Ploughman*, ch xvii.

Wicked, *adj.* **1. A wicked man is his own hell.** 1732: Fuller, 460.

2. A wicked man's gift hath a touch of his master. 1640: Herbert, *Jac. Prudentum.*

3. A wicked woman. *See* Woman (4).

4. It is a wicked thing to make a dearth one's gamer. 1640: Herbert, *Jac. Prudentum.* 1670: Ray, 6. 1732: Fuller, 2890.

5. 'Tis a wicked world, and we make part of it. Ibid., No. 5063.

Wickedness with beauty is the devil's hook baited. Ibid., No. 5739.

Widdecombe folks are picking their geese, Faster, faster, faster. Devon. Said when snow is falling. 1850: *N.&Q.*, 1st ser, ii 512.

Wide at the bow-hand. *i.e.* the left hand = Wide of the mark. 1592: Shakespeare, *L.L.L.*, IV i, Wide o' the bow-hand! i' faith, your hand is out. 1604: Dekker, *Honest Wh.*, Pt I Act. I, Y'are wide o' th' bow-hand still, brother: my longings are not wanton, but wayward. 1654: Webster, *Appius*, III iv, *First serv.*, I take thee to be an honest good fellow. *Clown*, Wide of the bow-hand still: Corbulo is no such man.

Wide ears and a short tongue. 1633: Draxe, 190. 1670: Ray, 8. 1736: Bailey, *Dict.*, s.v. 'Wide'. Wide ears and a short tongue is best.

Wide quoth Bolton when his bolt flew backward. 1591: Florio, *Second Frutes*, To Reader. 1659: Howell, 20. 1678: Ray, 84, Wide quoth Wilson.

Wide will wear but narrow will tear. 1678: Ray, 217. 1732: Fuller, 6097. 1853: Trench, *Proverbs*, 19 (1905), Wide will wear, but tight will tear.

Widow and Widows. 1. A good coming in is all in all with a widow. 1659: Howell, 7.

2. A good occasion for courtship is when the widow returns from the funeral. 1855: Bohn, 288. Cf. No. 9.

3. He that marries a widow and three children, marries four thieves. 1669: *New Help to Discourse*, 310 ['Two' and 'three' for 'three' and 'four']. 1670: Ray, 51. 1696: D'Urfey, *Quixote*, Pt III Act I. 1716: Ward, *Female Policy*, 69. 1732: Fuller, 2237.

4. He that will wed a widow must come day and night. *c.*1597: Deloney, *Iacke of Newb.*, ch xi, He that will wooe a widow, must take time by the forelocke. 1639: Clarke, 27.

5. He who marries a widow will often have a dead man's head thrown in his dish. 1546:

Heywood, *Proverbs*, Pt II ch vii, For I neuer meete the [e] at fleshe nor at fishe, But I haue sure a deade mans head in my dishe. 1605: Marston, *Insat. Countess*, I i, As boldfaced women, when they wed another Banquet their husbands with their dead loves' heads. 1659: Howell, *Letters*, ii 666 (Jacobs), You must also be wary how you marry ... a widdow, for so you will be subject to hav a Deaths head putt often in your Dish. 1736: Bailey, *Dict.*, s.v. 'Widow'.

6. It is as easy to marry a widow as to put a halter on a dead horse. 1883: Burne, *Shropsh. Folk-Lore*, 588.

7. It's dangerous marrying a widow, because she hath cast her rider. 1659: Howell, *Proverbs: Lett. of Advice*, Be wary how you marry one that hath cast her rider ... I mean a widdow. 1678: Ray, 58.

8. Long a widow weds with shame. 1659: Howell, *Proverbs: Brit.-Engl.*, 19.

9. Marry a widow before she leave mourning. 1640: Herbert, *Jac. Prudentum.* Cf. No. 2.

10. Widows are always rich. 1678: Ray, 57. Cf. **Wooers.**

11. Widows' children turn out well. 1897: Mrs Earle, *Pot-Pourri* (Daughters), There is an old saying that widows' children turn out well.

See also **Cross a stile; Woo** (1) and (2); and **Wooers.**

Wife and **Wives,** *subs.* **1. A fair wife without a fortune is a fine house without furniture.** 1732: Fuller, 91.

2. A man's best fortune or his worst is a wife. 1670: Ray, 28.

3. An obedient wife commands her husband. 1732: Fuller, 640.

4. An unchaste wife. *See* quot. 1623: Wodroephe, *Spared Houres*, 484, An unchast wife working mischiefe still, is oft compared to a foule dung hill.

5. A wife brings but two good days, her wedding-day and death day. [πασα γυνὴ χόγος ἐστιν ἔχει δ᾿ ἀγαθὰς δύω ὥρας– Gk. *Anthol.*, xi 381.] *c.*1560: T. Ingelend, *Disob. Child*, 32 (Percy S.) Who sayde with a wyfe are two dayes of pleasure; The first is the joye of the maryage day and nyght, The seconde to be at the wyfes sepulture. 1577: Kendall, *Flow, of Epigrams*, 143 (Spens.S.), Although all women kinde be nought, yet two good dayes hath she: Her marriage day, and day of death, when all she leaues to thee. 1608: Middleton, *Fam. of Love*, I ii. 1745: *Agreeable Companion*, 44, In every marriage two things are allow'd; A wife in wedding-sheets, and in a shroud; How can a marriage-state then be accurst, Since the last day's as happy as the first? 1869: Spurgeon, *John Ploughman*, ch xvii, That very wicked [saying], 'Every man has two good days with his wife – the day he marries her, and the day he buries her'.

6. Better a portion in a wife than with a wife. 1732: Fuller, 868.

7. Choosing a wife: various sayings. *See* quots. 1546: Heywood, *Proverbs*, Pt I ch ii, The best or worst thing to man, for this life, Is good or ill choosing his good or ill wife. 1640: Herbert, *Jac. Prudentum*, In choosing a wife and buying a sword, we ought not to trust another. 1659: Howell, *Proverbs: Span.-Eng.*, 2, Who will have a hansome wife, let him chuse her upon Saturday, and not upon Sunday, viz. when she is in her fine cloaths. 1732: Fuller, 462, A wife is not to be chosen by the eye only. Ibid., No. 1107, Chuse a wife rather by your ear than your eye. 1846: Denham, *Proverbs*, 2 (Percy S.), Chuse a wife on a Saturday rather than a Sunday. 1872: J. Glyde, Jr., *Norfolk Garland*, 150, Choose a wife on Saturday instead of Sunday.

8. He that hath a wife and children must not sit with his fingers in his mouth. 1732: Fuller, 2158.

9. He that hath a wife and children wants not business. 1640: Herbert, *Jac. Prudentum.* 1670: Ray, 29. 1732: Fuller, 2157. 1880: Spurgeon, *Ploughm. Pictures*, 72, Depend on it, he who has a wife and bairns will never be short of care to carry.

10. He that hath a wife hath strife. 1559: Bercher, *Nobility of Women*, 127 (Roxb.Cl), Thear is another common proverbe. Who hathe no controversye hathe no wyffe. 1611: Cotgrave, s.v. 'Noise', He that a wife hath, strife hath.

11. He that hath no wife, beateth her oft. 1629: *Book of Meery Riddles*, Prov. 79.

12. He that lets his wife go to every feast, and his horse drink at every water, shall neither have good wife nor good horse. 1591: Florio, *Second Frutes*, 41, Who lets his wife go to euerie feaste, And lets his horse drinke at euerie puddle, Shall haue of his horse, a starke iadish beast And of his best wife, a twang with a huddle. 1623: Wodroephe, *Spared Houres*, 243 [a variant of 1591]. 1670: Ray, 28.

13. He that loses his wife and sixpence (or a **farthing**) *has lost a tester* (= 6*d.*) (or *a farthing*). 1611: Cotgrave, s.v. 'Femme', He that loses his wife and six pence hath some losse by the money. 1678: Ray, 58, He that loses his wife and a farthing hath a great loss of his farthing. 1694: D'Urfey, *Quixote*, Pt I Act I sc ii [sixpence]. 1699: Farquhar, *Love and a Bottle*, II i, Who throws away a tester and a mistress, loses sixpence. 1738: Swift, *Polite Convers.*, Dial. I [sixpence]. 1869: Spurgeon, *John Ploughman*, ch xvii [as in 1678].

14. He that marries a wife is happy for a month, but he that gets a fat benefice lives merrily all his life. 1725: Bailey, tr. *Erasm. Colloq.*, 27.

15. He that would an old wife wed, Must eat an apple before he goes to bed [Reverse] 1588: Cogan, *Haven of Health*, 88 (1612), Apples … are thought to quench the flame of Venus, according to that old English saying, He that will not a wife wed, must eate a cold apple when he goeth to bed, though some turne it to a contrarie purpose. 1670: Ray, 48.

16. My wife cries five loaves a penny: i.e. she is in travail. 1678: Ray, 71.

17. Next to no wife a good wife is best. 1642: Fuller, *Holy State* 'Marriage', A bachelor was saying, *Next*, etc. 1659: Howell, *Letters*, ii 666 (Jacobs), next to a single life, a married life is best. 1732: Fuller, 3539.

18. Refuse a wife with one fault, and take one with two. 1659: Howell, *Proverbs: Brit.-Eng.*, 13.

19. Subjects and wives. *See* quot. Before 1704: Brown, *Works*, iv 178 (1760), It justifies the old saying, *that subjects and wives, when they revolt from their lawful sovereigns, seldom choose for a better.*

20. Take your wife's first advice. 1666: Torriano, *Piazza Univ.*, 51, Take a woman's first counsel. 1875: Cheales, *Proverb. Folk-Lore*, 159, Take your wife's first advice, and not her second, is a matrimonial maxim that is worth remembering.

21. The cunning wife makes her husband her apron. 1670: Ray, 29.

22. The death of wives and the life of sheep make men rich. 1666: Torriano, *Piazza Univ.*, 164, The English say allusively, If wives fall, and sheep stand, one must grow rich perforce. 1678: Ray, 353.

23. The wife is the key of the house. 1633: Drake, 230. 1670: Ray, 29. 1732: Fuller, 4828.

24. The wife should be blind and the husband deaf. 1539: Taverner, *Garden of Wysdom*, Pt II fo. 4, Wedded persons may thus passe ouer theyr lyues quietly … yf the husbande become deafe, and the wyfe blynde. 1637: T. Heywood, *Dialogues*, etc., in Bang, *Materialien*, B. 3, p. 227, Then marriage may be said to be past in all quietnesse, when the wife is blind, and the husband deafe. 1710: S. Palmer, *Moral Essays on Proverbs*, 338, The husband must not see, and the wife must be blind. Cf. **Husband** (1).

25. The wife that expects to have a good name, Is always at home, as if she were lame: And the maid that is honest, her chiefest delight Is still to be doing from morning to night. 1813: Ray, 49.

26. Wife a mouse, Quiet house; Wife a cat, Dreadful that. 1772: Garrick, *Irish Widow*, I iii [quoted as 'the old saying'].

27. Wife and children are bills of charges. 1659: Howell, 5. 1670: Ray, 29.

28. Wife and children are hostages given to fortune. 1732: Fuller, 5742.

29. Wife and sword. *See* Lend (5).

30. Wives and wind are necessary evils. 1736: Bailey, *Dict.*, s.v. 'Wife'. Cf. **Woman** (45).

31. Wives must be had, be they good or bad. 1639: Clarke, 328. 1670: Ray, 49. 1754: Berthelson, *Eng.-Danish Dict.*, s.v. 'Whether'. 1875: Cheales, *Proverb. Folk-Lore*, 32 [with addition] and so must husbands.

32. Wives must have their will. *See* **Woman** (58).

33. Wives of clouts. 1542: Udall. tr. *Erasm. Apoph.*, 119 (1877), For which we saye in our Englishe prouerbe, wiues of cloutes.

See also **All are good maids; Commend** (1); **Dead** (1); **Fair** (9)–(11) and (49); **Fast**, *verb* (2); **Good or ill hap; Good husband; Good wife; Great need; Horse** (26), (35), and (37); **House** (3); **Husband; Nice wife; No lack; Old A** (*c*) (6)–(8); **One good wife; Proud eye; Quartermaster; Shrewsbury; Smoke** (2); **Speak** (5); **Tell** (4); **This is that must needs be; Westminster;** and **Young** (11).

Wigan, Lancs. *See* quot. 1897: *N. & Q.*, 8th ser, xi 187, Can any one give the origin of a Lancashire saying, when friends touch glasses before drinking, and say, 'Here's to the Mayor of Wigan, that is, our noble selves'?

Wight, The Isle of. 1. An Isle of Wight parson. 1838: Holloway, *Provincialisms*, 150, A shag [cormorant], from its colour and place of resort, is called an 'Isle of Wight parson'.

2. The Isle of Wight hath no monks, lawyers, or foxes. 1607: Webster, etc., *Westw. Ho*, III iii, The Isle of Wight could not of long time neither endure foxes nor lawyers. 1610: P. Holland, tr. Camden's *Britannia*, 274, The inhabitants of this Isle [Wight] were wont merrily to make their boast, that their case was happier than all others, because they had neither hooded monks, nor cavilling lawyers, nor yet crafty foxes. 1662: Fuller, *Worthies*, ii 5 (1840). 1700: J. Brome, *Travels*, 251 [as in 1610]. 1790: Grose, *Prov. Gloss.*, s.v. 'Hants'.

Wild, *adj.* **1. As wild as a buck.** 1639: Clarke, 287. 1670: Ray, 208.

2. As wild as a hawk. 1820: Scott, *Abbot*, ch xviii, Thou lookest wild as a goss-hawk. 1878: Jefferies, *Gamekeeper at Home*, ch vi, Though 'wild as a hawk' is a proverbial phrase, yet hawks are bold enough to enter gardens.

3. A wild-goose chase. [An passim sequeris corvos testaque lutoque. – Persius, iii 61.] 1592: Shakespeare, *Romeo*, II iv, Nay, if thy wits run the wild-goose chase, I have done. 1606: Chapman, *Mons. d'Olive*, I, Let our wits run the wild-goose chase over Court and country. 1621: B.&F., *Pilgrim*, V i, His anger leads him a thousand wild-goose chases. 1772: Graves, *Spirit. Quixote*, bk x ch xvi, Fool enough to … ramble about the country upon such a wild-goose chase. 1868: Dickens, *Uncom. Trav.*, xxii, My mind now began to misgive me that the disappointed coachmaker had sent me on a wild-goose errand. 1891: R.L.S., *Wrecker*, ch vi.

4. A wild goose never lays a tame egg. 1869: Spurgeon, *John Ploughman*, ch i.

5. He looks like a wild cat out of a bush. 1732: Fuller, 1973.

6. The wild duck. *See* quot. 1906: E. Peacock, in *N. & Q.*, 10th ser, v 407, There'll be rain or something waur When the wild duck swims in the pottery car [Doncaster].

7. To sow wild oats. [1542: Becon, in *Early Works*, 204 (P.S.), That they may satisfy the foolish desires of certain light brains and wild oats, which are altogether given to new fangleness.] 1577: *Misogonus*, II iii, He hath not yet sowne all his wilde otes. 1600: Nashe, *Works,* vi 152 (Grosart), Youth ne're aspires to vertues perfect growth, Till his wild oates be sowne. 1687: Sedley, *Bellamira*, III, A certain young captain … ask'd me, if I would never have sown my wild oats. 1748: Richardson, *Clarissa*, iv 240 (1785), You are upon the borders of wedlock, as I may say, and all your wild oats will be sown. 1836: Marryat, *Easy*, ch xiii, He would have turned out a shining character as soon as he had sown his wild oats. 1895: Pinero, *Benefit of Doubt*, I, I'm seven-and-twenty; I'm an old woman; I've sown my wild oats now.

8. Wild and stout never wants a staff. 1659: Howell, *Proverbs: Brit.-Engl.*, 36.

9. Wildest colts make the best horses. 1732: Fuller, 463, A wild colt may become a sober horse. 1829: Cobbett, *Adv. to Young Men*, Lett. 1, These vices of youth are varnished over by the saying, that there must be time for 'sowing the wild oats', and that 'wildest colts make the best horses'.

Wiles often do what force can't. 1736: Bailey, *Dict.*, s.v. 'Wile'.

Wilful as a pig, As. 1678: Ray, 291, As willful as a pig, he'll neither lead nor drive. 1732: Fuller, 750 [as in 1678]. 1880: Spurgeon, *Ploughm. Pictures*, 37.

Wilful man had need be very wise, A. 1732: Fuller, 465. 1736: Bailey, *Dict.*, s.v. 'Wilful'. A wilful man should be very wise.

Wilful man must have his way, A. 1816: Scott, *Antiquary*, ch vi. 1907: De Morgan, *Alice-for-Short*, ch xxxvii.

Wilful man never wants woe, A. 1685: Meriton, *Yorksh. Ale, etc.*, 49, But wilfull fowkes, duz never want weay [woe] its said. 1732: Fuller, 466. Cf. **Hasty man.**

Wilful waste makes woeful want. 1721: J. Kelly, *Scottish Proverbs*, 353, Wilful waste makes woeful want. 1732: Fuller, 5755 ['brings' for 'makes']. 1736: Bailey, *Dict.*, s.v. 'Waste'.

Wilful will to it. 1829: Scott, *Geierstein*, ch xvi, That is as much as to say, wilful will to it. 1875: Cheales, *Proverb. Folk-Lore*, 103, If wilful will to water, wilful must be drowned.

Will, *subs*. 1. He may make a will upon his nail, for anything he has to give. 1732: Fuller, 1986.

2. To take the will for the deed. *c.*1460: *Wisdom*, sc i st. 28, Wyll, for dede oft ys take; Therfor the wyll must, weell be dysposyde. 1593: Nashe, *Christs Teares*, Epist. Ded., Christ accepteth the

will for the deede. 1694: Motteux, *Rabelais*, bk iv ch xlix, We'll take the good-will for the deed, and thank you as much as if we had. 1726: Defoe, *Hist. of Devil*, Pt II ch iv, To take, as we vulgarly express it, the will for the deed. 1804: Byron, *Letters, etc.*, i 47 (Prothero), I dare say he would assist me if he could, so I take the will for the deed. 1852: Dickens, *Bleak House*, ch xv.

3. Where there's a will there's a way. 1640: Herbert, *Jac. Prudentum.*, To him that will, ways are not wanting. 1754: Berthelson, *Eng.-Danish Dict.*, s.v. 'Will' [as in 1640]. 1849: Lytton, *Caxtons*, Pt XVIII ch v, Meanwhile I fall back on my favourite proverb – 'Where there's a will there's a way'. 1911: Shaw, *Fanny's First Play*, Pref., Please do not suppose … that I do not know how difficult it is … But when there's a will there's a way.

4. Where the will is ready, the feet are light. 1640: Herbert, *Jac. Prudentum*, ['your' for 'the']. 1670: Ray, 29. 1754: Berthelson, *Eng.-Danish Dict.*, s.v. 'Will'. Cf. **Willing mind.**

5. Will buyeth and money payeth. 1578: Florio, *First Fruites*, fo. 34, Wyl maketh the market but money maketh payment. 1629: *Book of Meery Riddles*, Prov. 133.

6. Will is the cause of woe. 1639: Clarke, 253. 1670: Ray, 155. 1732: Fuller, 5757.

7. Will will have will though will woe win. 1546: Heywood, *Proverbs*, Pt I ch xi. 1605: Camden, *Remains*, 336 (1870). 1670: Ray, 29. 1732: Fuller, 5758 [with 'its' after 'have'].

8. With will one can do anything. 1859: Smiles, *Self-Help*, 7 (1869), Almost to justify, the proverb that 'with Will one can do anything'. *See also* **Wit** (10) and (19).

Will, *verb*. 1. He that will not be saved, needs no preacher. 1670: Ray, 21. 1732: Fuller, 2351 ['sermon' for 'preacher'].

2. He that will not when he may, when he will he shall have nay. *See* **He that will not** … .

3. He who wills the end, wills the means. 1692: R. South, *Twelve Sermons*, That most true aphorism, that he who wills the end, wills also the means. 1910: *Spectator*, 29 Oct., 677, We won at Trafalgar … because we not only meant to win, but knew how to win – because we understood … the maxim, 'He who wills the end wills the means'.

4. That one will not another will. 1546: Heywood, *Proverbs*, Pt I ch iii, Sens that that one will not on other will – . 1654: Gayton, *Pleasant Notes Don Q.*, 75, If one won't another will. 1709: O. Dykes, *Eng. Proverbs*, 2nd ed., Title-page. If one will not, another will; or, why was the market made? 1771: in *Garrick Corresp.*, i 410 (1831), Well, if one won't, another will, they say.

5. Thy that will not be counselled cannot be helped. 1736: Franklin, *Way to Wealth*, in *Works*, i, 451 (Bigelow).

6. What will be, will be. This proverb exists in several languages, notably in Italian as *che sarà sar*.

7. Will he nill he. *c.*1220: *Hali Meidenhad*, 31 (E.E.T.S.), pat wullen ha nullen ha. Before 1300: *Cursor Mundi*, l. 23729, Nill we, will we, we sal mete. 14th cent., *Guy of Warwick*, l. 7109 (E.E.T.S.), Gon ich mot, wille y so nille. 1485: Malory, *Morte d' A.*, bk i ch viii, Ye shal ouercome hem all whether they wille or nylle. 1595: Munday, *John a Kent*, 18 (SH.S.), Will I, or nill I, all is one to him. 1602: Shakespeare, *Hamlet*, V i, Will he, nill he, he goes. 1607: B.&F., *Woman-Hater*, III iv, Will she, nill she, she shall come running into my house. 1740: North, *Examen*, 67, To which he was peremptorily bound: Will he, nill he, that must be. 1872: Hardy, *Greenwood Tree*, Pt I ch viii, Band played six-eight time; six-eight chaws I, willy-nilly. 1909: De Morgan, *Never can Happen Again*, ch xxxviii, Even my boy is away, and what adds to the cruelty of the position is that, will I nill I, I have to feel glad of his absence.

See also **He that will not.**

Willing horse. *See* **Horse** (20) and (66).

Willing mind makes a light foot, A. 1629: Massinger, *Picture*, V iii, A willing mind makes a hard journey easy. 1732: Fuller, 467. Cf. **Will**, *subs.* (4).

Willingly. *See* **Good a will.**

Willow, *subs.* **1. A willow will buy a horse before an oak will pay for a saddle.** 1846: Denham, *Proverbs*, 33 (Percy S.). 1865: W. White, *Eastern England*, i 280. 1901: Raymond, *Idler out of Doors*, 127, There is a saying that a willow will buy a horse whilst any other tree is paying for the halter.

2. Willows are weak, yet they bind other wood. 1640: Herbert, *Jac. Prudentum*. 1732: Fuller, 5761. 1917: Bridge, *Cheshire Proverbs*, 156.

Wiltshire. *See* **Derbyshire.**

Wiltshire moon-rakers. 1790: Grose, *Prov. Gloss.*, s.v. 'Wilts'. 1863: Wise, *New Forest*, ch xv

n., The expression of 'Hampshire and Wiltshire moon-rakers' had its origin in the Wiltshire peasants fishing up the contraband goods at night.

Wily as a fox, As. 1639: Clarke, 285. 1670: Ray, 208.

Win, *verb.* **1. He's won with a feather and lost with a straw.** 1732: Fuller, 2476.

2. To win and wear. 1576: Pettie, *Pet. Pallace*, i 19 (Gollancz), You would confess, that by force of love I had won you, and were worthy to wear you. 1607: T. Heywood, *Faire Maide*, in *Works*, ii 54 (1874), Court her, win her, weare her, wed her. 1632: S. Marmion, *Holl. Leaguer*, V iv, There she comes! win her, and wear her. 1825: Planché, *Extravag.*, i 31 (1879), You … shall take your chance with the rest. Win me and wear me. 1844: Thackeray, *Barry Lyndon*, ch xi, Now is your time! win her and wear her before the month is over.

3. To win one's spurs. *c.* 1425: Lydgate, *Assembly of Gods*, 980 (OED), These xiiii knyghtes made vyce that day; To wynne theyre spores they seyde they wold asay. 1523–25: Berners, *Froissart*, ch 130, Say to them that they suffre hym this day to wynne his spurres. 1580: Churchyard, *Charge*, 30 (Collier), Perhapps, in winnyng of the spurres, You maie the horse and saddle lose. 1642: D. Rogers, *Naaman*, sig. G3, I doe not accuse you as if ye sought to winne the spurres by your parts. 1859: Smiles, *Self-Help*, 220 (1869), Lord Mansfield … won his spurs by perseverance, knowledge, and ability, diligently cultivated.

4. To win the horse or lose the saddle. 1546: Heywood, *Proverbs*, Pt II ch ix, Recower the hors or leese the saddle too. 1575: Gascoigne, *Posies*, 169 (Cunliffe), It was my full entent, To loose the sadle or the horse to winne. *c.*1620: in *Pepysian Garland*, 383 (Rollins), That either now ile win the horse Or else the saddle lose. 1700: Ward, *London Spy*, 398 (1924), In order to which, he resolves to win the horse, or lose the saddle. 1754: Berthelson, *Eng.-Danish Dict.*, s.v. 'Horse'. 1847: Halliwell, *Dict.*, s.v. 'Mare', To win the mare or lose the halter, to play doable or quits. 1913: *Folk-Lore*, xxiv 77, I'll win the horse or lose the saddle. (Oxfordshire.)

5. Win at first and lose at last. 1678: Ray. 349.

6. Win gold and wear gold. 1583: Melbancke, *Philotinus*, sig. C4, Thou hast woon goulde, now weare gould. 1605: Camden, *Remains*, 336 (1870). 1660: Tatham, *The Rump*, III, He that wins gold, let him wear gold, I cry. 1736: Bailey, *Dict.*, s.v. 'Win'.

7. Win purple and wear purple. 1650: Fuller, *Pisgah Sight*, bk iv. ch vi § 1, Earned with her industry (and good reason – win purple, and wear purple). 1853: Trench, *Proverbs*, 106 (1905).

8. Win whoso may. *See* quot. *c.*1386: Chaucer, *Wife of Bath's Prol.*, l. 414, Winne who-so may for al is for to selle. *à*, and in different forms in English (*See also* **Must be**; and **Shall be**) 1519: W. Horman, *Vulgaria*, 20v, That the whiche muste be wyll be. 1850: Dickens, *David Copperfield*, lvii, 'My love', observed Mr Micawber, ' … I am always willing to defer to your good sense. What will be – will be.'

9. You can't win them all. 1953: R. Chandler, *The Long Good-bye*, xxiv, 122 Wade took him by the shoulder and spun him round. 'Take it easy, Doc. You can't win them all'.

Winchester. *See* **Canterbury** (3).

Winchester goose, The = venereal disease. 1559: Becon, in *Prayers*, etc., 284 (P.S.), Making whole of a Winchester goose. 1611: Cotgrave, s.v. 'Poulain'. A botch in the graine, a Winchester goose. 1730: Bailey, *Eng. Dict.*, s.v. 'Goose'. Winchester goose, a swelling in the thigh.

Wind. Classification. **A. General: (a)** *Literal*, **(b)** *Metaphorical*. **B. East wind. C. North wind. D. South wind. E. West wind. F. Various combinations of directions.**

A. (a) **1. After wind comes rain.** 1548: Hall, *Chron.*, 22 (1809), As the old prouerbe saith, after winde commeth rain. 1569: Grafton, *Chron.*, i 484 (1908).

2. As wroth as the wind. *c.*1350: in *Reliq. Antiquae*, ii 95 (1843), Thanne the kyng wax wrothe as wynde. 1377: Langland, *Plowman*, B. lii 328, Also wroth as the wynde wex Mede [the Lady Meed] in a while, *c.*1400: *Rich, the Redles*, iii 153, Thei woll be wroth as the wynde. 14168: *Coventry Mysteries*, 8 (SH.S.), As wroth as wynde Is kyng Herownde.

3. A veering wind, fair weather, A backing wind, foul weather. 1893: Inwards, *Weather Lore*, 71.

4. Blow the wind never so fast. It will fall at last. 1732: Fuller, 6306. 1869: Spurgeon, *John Ploughman*, ch v ['lower' for 'fall'].

5. *High winds blow on high hills.* [Saepius ventis agitatur ingens Pinus et celsae graviore casu Decidunt turres. – Horace, *Carm.* II x.] Before 1225: *Ancr. Riwle*, 178 (Morton), Vor euer so the hul is more and herre, so the wind is more theron. *c.*1310: in Wright, *Pol. Songs, John to Ed. II*, 207 (Camden S.), Summa petit livor, perflant altissima venti 1484: Caxton. tr. *Chartier's Curial*, 5 (E.E.T.S.), The grete wyndes that blowe in hye courtes. 1578: *Gorgeous Gallery*, 10 (Rollins), As highest seates wee see be subiect to most winde. 1639: Clarke, 23, Huge winds blow on high hills. 1670: Ray, 107 [as in 1639]. 1732: Fuller, 2502.

6. If the wind do blow aloft, then of wars shall we hear oft. 1855: Bohn, 418.

7. If wind follows sun's course, expect fair weather. 1893: Inwards, *Weather Lore*, 71.

8. Look not, like the Dutchman, to leeward for fine weather. Ibid., 69.

9. There's no weather ill when the wind is still. 1605: Camden, *Remains*, 334 (1870). 1670: Ray, 42, No weather's ill If the wind be still. 1732: Fuller, 6493. 1825: Hone, *Ev. Day Book*, i 670. 1893: Inwards, 69.

10. The wind keeps not always in one quarter. 1670: Ray, 1156. 1732: Fuller, 4831.

11. The winds of the daytime wrestle and fight Longer and stronger than those of the night. 1893: Inwards, *Weather Lore*, 69.

12. When the wind backs and the weather glass falls, Then be on your guard against gales and squalls. Ibid., 71.

13. When the wind comes before the rain. You may hoist your topsails up again; But when the rain comes before the winds. *You may reef when it begins.* 1846: Denham, *Proverbs*, 20 (Percy S.).

14. When the wind is still, the shower falls soft. 1814: Scott, *Waverley*, ch xxiv.

15. Where the wind is on Martinmas eve there it will prevail through the winter. 1893: Inwards, *Weather Lore*, 83, If the wind is south-west at Martinmas, It keeps there till after Christmas. 1898: Gibbs, *Cotswold Village*, ch xvii 388 (1909), Last night were Hollandtide [Nov. 11] eve, and where the wind is at Hollandtide there it will stick best part of the winter. 1902: *N. & Q.*, 9th ser, ix. 338, One of our local sayings [Northants.] is … 'Where the wind', etc.

16. Wind and weather do thy worst. 1678: Ray, 277. 1732: Fuller, 5743, Wind and weather do your utmost.

17. Winds at night are always bright; But winds in the morning, sailors take warning. 1893: Inwards, *Weather Lore*, 70.

18. Winds that change against the sun Are always sure to backward run [and] **When the wind veers against the sun, Trust it not, for back 'twill run.** Ibid., 71.

19. You can't catch the wind in a net. 1880: Spurgeon, *Ploughm. Pictures*, 97.

(b) 1. All this wind shakes no corn. 1546: Heywood, *Proverbs*, Pt I ch xi. 1587: Turbervile, *Trag. Tales*, etc., 261 (1837), But al for nought, his winde did shake no corne. 1604: *Wit of a Woman*, sc viii (Malone S.). 1670: Ray, 199.

2. As the wind blows you must set your sail. 1732: Fuller, 738. 1846: Denham, *Proverbs*, 3 (Percy S.).

3. Is the wind at that door? *c.*1490: *Partonope*, 444 (E.E.T.S.), 'What!' seith Gaudyn, 'stonte the wynde in that dore?' 1566: Gascoigne, *Supposes*, III i, Is it even so? is the winde in that doore? *c.*1600: Deloney, *Thos. of Reading*, ch 3, What husband (quoth she) is the winde at that doore? 1641: Tatham, *Distracted State*, I. 1737: Ray, 267, Is the wind in that corner? 1817: Scott, *Rob Roy*, ch viii, 'Whew! sits the wind in that quarter?' inquired the Justice.

4. Let this wind over-blow. 1546: Heywood, *Proverbs*, Pt I ch xi. 1659: Howell, 7.

5. The wind in a man's face makes him wise. 1640: Herbert, *Jac. Prudentum* ['one's' for 'a man's']. 1710: S. Palmer, *Moral Essays on Proverbs*, 190.

6. *To know which way the wind blows, c.*1380: *Tale of Gamelyn*, l. 703, in Skeat's *Chaucer*, iv. 662, To telle him tydinges how the wind was went. 1546: Heywood, *Proverbs*, Pt II ch ix, I know, And knew, which waie the winde blewe; and will blow. 1694: D'Urfey, *Quixote*, Pt I III ii, Why then I know where the wind sits. 1766: Garrick, *Neck or Nothing*, I ii, I always listen to reason, Mr Stockwell. *Stock.* Well, and which way does the wind set now? 1886: R.L.S., *Kidnapped*, ch ix, 'Oho!' says the stranger, 'is that how the wind sets?' And he laid his hand quickly on his pistols. 1906: Doyle, *Sir Nigel*, ch xii, My questions must have shown him whence the wind blew.

7. What wind blew you hither? *c.*1374: Chaucer, *Troylus*, bk ii l.1104, 'Now by your feyth, myn uncle,' quod she, 'dere, What maner windes gydeth yow now here?' *c.*1400: *Beryn*, 51 (E.E.T.S.), Benedicite! what manere wynd hath I brought yewe here? *c.*1489: Caxton, *Sonnes of Aymon*, 106 (E.E.T.S.), Lordes, what ye be, and what wynde dryveth you hyther. 1546: Heywood, *Proverbs*, Pt I ch x. 1657: Sir A. Cokain, *Obstinate Lady*, II iii, What wind brought you hither? 1713: Gay, *Wife of Bath*, I. 1737: Dodsley, *Miller of Mansfield*, I vi 1861: Dickens, *Great Exp.*, ch xliv., 'And what wind,' said Miss Havisham, 'blows you here, Pip?'

B. East Wind. 1. A dry east wind raises the spring. Cornwall. 1893: Inwards, *Weather Lore*, 80.

2. An easterly wind's rain Makes fools fain. Ibid., 80.

3. An east wind is a laxy wind – because it is thin, and will go through you before it will go round you. 1886: R. Holland, *Cheshire Gloss.*, 446 (E.D.S.), 1917: Bridge, *Cheshire Proverbs*, 7. 1922: *N.&Q.*, 12th ser, x 412, I have often heard a cold piercing wind described as a 'lazy wind' – it is too lazy to go round, so it goes through one.

4. A right easterly wind is very unkind. 1855: Bohn, 399.

5. Easterly winds and rain, Bring cockles here from Spain. 1846: Denham. *Proverbs*, 12 (Percy S.).

6. If it rains when the wind is in the east, It will rain for twenty-four hours at least. *c.*1685: Aubrey, *Nat. Hist. Wilts*, 16 (1847), A Wiltshire proverb … If the rain comes out of east, 'Twill rain twice twenty-four houres at the least. 1893: Inwards, *Weather Lore*, 79 [as in 1685, but omitting 'twice']. 1917: Bridge, *Cheshire Proverbs*, 163.

7. If the wind is in the east on Easter day. *See* quot. 1881: Evans, *Leicest. Words*, etc, 169 (E.D.S.), A common Leicestershire saying is: If the wind's i' the East of Easter-dee, Yo'll ha' plenty o' grass, but little good hee [hay].

8. When the wind is in the east, It's good for neither man nor beast. 1600: R. Cawdray, *Treas. of Similies*, 750, The east wind is accounted neither good for man or beast. 1670: Ray, 41. 1732: Fuller, 6224. 1825: Hone, *Ev. Day Book*, i 670. 1893: Inwards, *Weather Lore*,

79. 1913: E. M. Wright, *Rustic Speech, etc.*, 316. *See also* D (1) and F (6) and (9).

C. **North wind. 1. A northern air Brings weather fair** [1611: *Bible*, Job xxxvii 22. Fair weather cometh out of the north.] 1893: Inwards, *WeatherLore*, 77.

2. **A north wind is a broom for the Channel. Cornwall.** 1887: M. A. Courtney, *Folk-Lore Journal*, v 191.

3. **Fishermen in anger froth When the wind is in the north; For fish bite the best When the wind is in the west.** 1893: Inwards, *Weather Lore*, 77.

4. **The north wind doth blow, And we shall have snow.** Ibid., 78.

5. **When the wind is in the north, The skilful fisher goes not forth.** 1846: Denham, *Proverbs*, 17 (Percy S.). 1893: Inwards, 77.

6. **When the wind's in the north, You mustn't go forth.** Ibid., 77.

See also F(6)and(9).

D. **South wind. 1. An out** [southerly] **wind and a fog Bring an east wind home snug.** 1874: W. Pengelly, *in N. & Q.*, 5th ser, ii 184, I often heard the following weather-rhymes in Cornwall in my boyhood: – 'An out, etc. – '

2. **A southerly wind and a cloudy shy, Proclaim a hunting morning.** 1846: Denham, *Proverbs*, 8 (Percy S.). 1893: Inwards, *Weather Lore*, 81.

3. **A southerly wind with showers of rain Will bring the wind from west again.** Ibid., 82.

4. **When the wind is in the south. It blows the bait into the fish's mouth.** 1653: Walton, *Angler*, Pt I ch v, One observes that 'When the wind is south, It blows your bait into a fish's mouth'. 1732: Fuller, 6226. 1825: Hone, *Ev. Day Book*, I. 670. 1893: Inwards, *Weather Lore*, 82.

5. **When the wind is in the south, It's in the rain's mouth.** 1639: Clarke, 263. 1670: Ray, 42. 1732: Fuller, 6225. 1825: Hone, *Ev. Day Book*, I 670. 1893: Inwards, *Weather Lore*, 82, When the wind's in the south, The rain's in its mouth.

See also F (5), (6) and (9).

E. **West wind. 1. A western wind carrieth water in his hand.** 1893: Inwards, 83.

2. **The west wind is a gentleman, and goes to bed** – i.e. *drops in the evening*. 1846: Denham, *Proverbs*, 2 (Percy S.), A west wind and an honest man go to bed together. 1893: Inwards, 83. Cf. F (1).

3. **The wind blows not always west.** 1732: Fuller, 4829.

4. **When the wind is in the west The weather is at the best.** [1606: Chapman, *Gent. Usher*, II i, The wind must blow at west still or she'll be angry.] 1732: Fuller, 6223. 1893: Inwards, 83 ['always' for 'at the']. 1913: E. M. Wright, *Rustic Speech, etc.*, 316, The wind in the west Suits every one best (Lancs.). Cf. F (11).

5. **Wind west Rain's nest.** Devon. 1893: Inwards, 83. Cf. F (8).

See also C (3); D (3); and F (6) and (9).

F. **Various combinations of direction. 1. An honest man and a north-west wind generally go to sleep together.** 1893: Inwards, 79. Cf. E (2).

2. **A north-east wind in May, Makes the shotver-men a prey.** 1735: Pegge, *Kent. Proverbs*, in E.D.S., No. 1270 … Shotver men are the mackarel fishers, and a North-east wind is reckon'd at Dover a good wind for them. [Mackerel fishers' nets are called shot-nets.] 1887: Parish and Shaw, *Dict. Kentish Dialect*, 148 (E.D.S.).

3. **A nor'-wester is not long in debt to a sou wester.** 1893: Inwards, 78.

4. **Do business with men when the wind is in the north-west.** Yorkshire. Ibid., 78.

5. **If the wind is north-east three days without rain, Eight days will pass before south wind again.** Ibid., 78.

6. **North and south the sign o' drouth, East and west the sign of blast.** 1846: Denham, *Proverbs*, 17 (Percy S.) [in reverse order]. 1893: Inwards, 77.

7. **North-west wind brings a short storm; a north-east wind brings a long storm.** Ibid., 79.

8. **The zou'-west Is the rain's nest.** 1891: R. P. Chope, *Hortland Dialect*, 20(E.D.S.). Cf. E (5).

9. **The west wind always brings wet weather, The east wind wet and cold together, The south wind surely brings us rain. The north wind blows it back again.** 1838: Mrs Bray, *Trad. of Devon*, i 5. 1892: S. Hewett, *Peasant Speech of Devon*, 29.

10. **Three south-westers, then one heavy rain.** 1893: Inwards, *Weather Lore*, 83.

11. **When the wind is in the north-west The weather is at its best.** *c.*1685: Aubrey, *Nat. Hist. Wilts*, 16 (1847). 1893: Inwards, 79. Cf. E (4).

Wind. *See also* **Blow**, *verb* (1) and (5); **Candlemas** H (6); **Candlemas Eve; Cloud** (3) and (11); **Every wind; Fire** (12); **Fish,** *subs.* (2); **Fog** (1); **God tampers; God will; Good wind; Ill wind; March** (4), (9), (13) and (37); **Martinmas** (3) and (4); **Moon** (7), (12) and (27); **October** (2) and (5); **Rain,** *subs.* (3), (11) and (29); **Sandbach; Straw** (2); and **Sun** (3). (15) and (16).

Windmill. 1. To have windmills in one's head. 'Windmills' = empty projects, or crotchets. 1612: Shelton, *Quixote*, Pt I bk i ch viii, For they were none other than windmills; nor could any think otherwise, unless he had also windmills in his brains. 1690: *New Dict. Canting Crew*, sig. M7. 1737: Ray, 216. 1869: Spurgeon, *John Ploughman*, ch xv, Poor soul, like a good many others he has windmills in his head.

2. You can't drive a windmill with a pair of bellows. 1640: Herbert, *Jac. Prudentum*, You cannot make a windmill go with a pair of bellows. 1670: Ray, 29. 1732: Fuller, 5880.

3. Your windmill is dwindled into a nut-crack. 1678: Ray, 277. 1732: Fuller, 6064.

Window. 1. A window wench, and a trotter in streete, is neuer good to haue a house to keepe. 1623: Wodroephe, *Spared Houres*, 484.

2. To come in at the window: said of a bastard. 1551: Crowley, *Pleas. and Payne*, 350 (OED), Youe were gladde to take them in, Bycause you knewe that they dyd knowe That youe came in by the wyndowe. 1605: Chapman, *All Fools*, III, Though he came in at the window he sets the gates of your honour open, I can tell you. 1608: Middleton, *Family of Love*, IV iii, Woe worth the time that ever I gave suck to a child that came in at the window. 1664: Cotton, *Scarronides*, bk i, Although he had her not by's wife. But by a fish-wench he was kind to, And so she came in at the window.

Wine, *subs.* **1. He cries wine and sells vinegar.** 1659: Howell, *Proverbs: Span.-Engl.*, 3. 1732: Fuller, 1831.

2. He that drinks not wine after salad is in danger to be sick. 1666: Torriano, *Piazza Univ.*, 308 [slightly varied]. 1670: Ray, 39.

3. Of wine the middle, of oil the top, and of honey the bottom is best. 1659: Howell, *Proverbs: Ital.-Eng.*, 15, Wine in the middle, oyle above, and hony beneath. 1678: Ray, 41.

4. The wine is the master's, the goodness is the drawer's. 1639: Clarke, 204. 1670: Ray, 29. 1732: Fuller, 5747, Wine is the vintner's; but the goodness of it, the drawer's.

5. When the wine is run out, you'd stop the leak. Ibid., No. 5611.

6. When wine sinks, words swim. Ibid., No. 5622. 1736: Bailey, *Dict.*, s.v. 'Wine'.

7. Where wine is not common, commons must be sent. 1605: Camden, *Remains*, 335 (1870). 1659: Howell, 10.

8. Wine and wealth change wise men's manners. 1586: L. Evans, *Revised Withals Dict.*, sig. B7. 1639: Clarke, 33.

9. Wine and wenches empty mens purses. 1586: L. Evans, *Revised Withals Dict.*, sig. O2, Women and wine doe make a man, A doting foole all that they can. 1639: Clarke, 28. 1670: Ray. 52.

10. Wine by the savour. *See* quots. 1578: Florio, *First Fruites*, fo. 29, Wine by the sauour and bread by the heate. 1611: Cotgrave, s.v. 'Vin', Let wine good savour, cloth fresh colour, have. 1629: *Book of Meery Riddles*, Prov. 109, Wine by the savour, bread by the colour. 1666: Torriano, *Piazza Univ.*, 186, Bread by the colour and wine by the taste.

11. Wine counsels seldom prosper. 1640: Herbert, *Jac. Prudentum*.

12. Wine ever pays for his lodging. Ibid.

13. Wine hath drowned more men than the sea. 1669: *Politeuphuia*, 299. 1732: Fuller, 5744.

14. Wine in the bottle quencheth not thirst. 1640: Herbert, *Jac. Prudentum.* 1732: Fuller, 5745 ['hogshead' for 'bottle'].

15. Wine in truth out. 1611: Cotgrave, s.v. 'Mentir', Wine telleth truth and should not be belied. 1659: T. Pecke, *Parnassi Puerp.*, 5, Grant but the adage true, that truths in wine. 1839: Dickens, *Nickleby*, ch xxvii. 1897: Norway, *H. & B. in Devon, etc.*, 52, The old proverb 'In wine there is truth' might with equal propriety be applied to brandy.

16. Wine in, wit out. *See* **Drink,** *subs.* (1).

17. Wine is a turn-coat, first a friend, then an enemy. 1640: Herbert, *Jac. Prudentum.* 1734: Fielding, *Don Q. in England*, I vi, Physic makes you first sick, and then well; wine first makes you well, and then sick.

18. Wine is a whetstone to wit. 1736: Bailey, *Dict.*, s.v. 'Whetstone'.

19. Wine makes all sorts of creatures at table. 1640: Herbert, *Jac. Prudentum.*

20. Wine makes old wives wenches. 1639: Clarke, 192.

21. **Wine neither keeps secrets nor fulfils promises.** 1620: Shelton, *Quixote*, Pt II ch xliii. 1732: Fuller, 5748.

22. **Wine that costs nothing is digested before it be drunk.** 1640: Herbert, *Jac. Prudentum*. 1670: Ray, 29. 1732: Fuller, 5750.

23. **Wine washeth off the daub.** Ibid., No. 5752.

24. **Wine wears no breeches.** 1659: Howell, 7. 1670: Ray, 29. 1736: Bailey, *Dict*, s.v. 'Breeches'. [1781: Cowper, *Convers.*, l.263, When wine has giv'n indecent language birth.]

25. **Wine, wood, women and water.** Herefordshire. 1869: Hazlitt, 476.

26. **Ye praise the wine before ye taste of the grape.** 1546: Heywood, *Proverbs*, Pt I ch x.

27. **You cannot know wine by the barrel.** 1640: Herbert, *Jac. Prudentum*. 1732: Fuller, 5884 ['cask' for 'barrel']. 1869: Spurgeon, *John Ploughman*, ch iii, Though you can not know wine by the barrel, a good appearance is a letter of recommendation even to a ploughman.

See also **Commend** (1); **Drink,** *verb* (8); **Gaming; Good wind; Good wine; Milk** (4); **Old C.; Play, women;** and **Woman** (44), (57) and (66).

Wing. *See* **Tring.**

Wink, *verb.* 1. **All are not blind that wink.** *c.*1570: in Huth, *Ancient Ballads, etc.*, 375 (1867), All winkers are not blind. 1584: Robinson, *Handf. Pleas. Delights*, 45 (Arber), Although I wincke I am not blind. 1615: J. Andrews, *Anat. of Baseness*, 32 (Grosart), Tell me, dost thinke that all are blinde that are content to winke?

2. **He that winketh with the one eye end looketh with the other, I will not trust him though he were my brother.** 1550: Palsgrave, 782. 1546: Heywood, *Proverbs*, Pt I ch xi. 1611: Cotgrave, s.v. 'Borgner', To winke with one eye, and looke with another. 1659: Howell, 8. 1732: Fuller, 6458.

3. **She can wink on the ewe and worry the lamb.** 1546: Heywood, *Proverbs*, Pt I ch x.

4. **Wink at small faults.** 1639: Clarke, 108. 1670: Ray, 156. 1736: Bailey, *Dict.*, s.v. 'Wink'. Wink at small faults, unless you can cast the first stone.

5. **You may wink and choose.** 1639: Clarke, 14, Winke and chuse. 1737: Ray, 216.

Wink *subs. See* **Nod.**

Winkabank and Templebrough, Will buy all England through and through. 1678: Ray, 340. 1790: Grose, *Prov. Gloss.*, s.v. 'Yorkshire'. 1878: *Folk-Lore Record*, i 166.

Winlater, He's a. 1846–59: *Denham Tracts*, i 72 (F.L.S.), He's a Winlater. This saying may be illustrated by using the parallel saying of Cumberland, 'He's a Bewcastler' – *i.e.* a bad one.

Winter, *subs.* 1. **After a rainy winter follows a fruitful spring.** 1893: Inwards, *Weather Lore*, 9.

2. **A good winter brings a good summer.** 1633: Draxe, 12. 1670: Ray, 29.

3. **A green winter makes a fat churchyard.** 1670: Ray, 42. 1732: Fuller, 205. 1825: Hone, *Ev. Day Book*, 1670. 1893: Inwards, *Weather Lore*, 8.

4. **An early winter, a surly winter.** 1846: Denham, *Proverbs*, 61 (Percy S.). 1893: Inwards, 9.

5. **An early winter is surety winter.** Ibid., 9.

6. **A winter fog will freeze a dog.** Ibid., 9.

7. **Four things.** *See* quot. 1636: Breton. in *Works*, ii 7 (Grosart), Foure things ill far the earth: a winter's thunder, a summer's frost, a long drought, and a sudden floud.

8. **He that passeth a winter's day, escapes an enemy.** 1670: Ray, 156.

9. **When winter begins early it ends early.** 1893: Inwards, 9.

10. **Winter finds out what summer lays up.** *c.*1460: *Good Wyfe wold a Pylgremage*, l. 155 (E.E.T.S.), Wynttur ettythe that somer gettyth. *c.*1645; MS. Proverbs *in N. & Q.*, vol 154, p. 27, That which summer getts, winter eats. 1678: Ray, 218, Winter is summers heir. Ibid., 219, Winter finds out what summer lays up. 1732: Fuller, 5753. Winter draws out what summer laid in. 1893: Inwards, 8.

11. **Winter never died in a ditch.** Ibid., 8.

12. **Winter never rots in the sky.** 1639: in *Berkeley MSS.*, iii 33 (1885), Winter never dies in her dams belly. 1655: Gurnall, *Christ, in Armour*, verse 12, ch i p. 61 (1679), May be … no cloud to be seen that portends a storm; but know (as you use to say) Winter does not rot in the clouds, you shall have it at last. 1846: Denham, *Proverbs*, 23 (Percy S.). 1904: *Co. Folk–Lore: N'umberland*, 174 (F.L.S.).

13. **Winter's thunder and summer's flood, Never boded Englishman good.** 1732: Fuller, 6479. 1893: Inwards, *Weather Lore*, 9.

14. **Winter's thunder is a rich man's death and a poor man's wonder.** 1882: Mrs Chamberlain, *W. Worc. Words*, 38 (E.D.S.).

15. **Winter's thunder is summer's wonder.** 1605: Camden, *Remains*, 336 (1870) ['makes' for

'is']. 1611: Cotgrave, s.v. 'Tonner'. 1658: Willsford, *Natures Secrets*, 113, According to the old adigy, Winters thunder is the Sommers wonder. 1731: Coffey, *Devil to Pay*, I v. 1846: Denham, *Proverbs*, 2 (Percy S.). 1926: *Observer*, Jan. 30, p. 17, col. 3, The old Welsh saying [why Welsh?]: – Winter's thunder Brings Summer wonder And a great man's fall.

16. Winter thunder, Poor man's death, rich man's hunger. 1893: Inwards, *Weather Lore*, 9.

17. Winter thunder bodes summer hunger. 1846: Denham, *Proverbs*, 3 (Percy S.).

18. Winter thunder, Rich man's food and poor man's hunger. 1859: *N. &Q.*, 2nd ser, vii 450. 1893: Inwards, 9 … [*i.e.* it is good for fruit and bad for corn.]

19. Winter thunder, To old folks death, to young folks plunder. Ibid., 117.

20. Winter-time for shoeing, Peascod-time for wooing. 1841: Brand, *Pop. Antiq.*, ii 100 (Bohn) [quoted as 'an old proverb in a MS'. Devon Glossary]. 1846: Denham, *Proverbs*, 64 (Percy S.).

21. Winter-weather and women's thoughts change oft. *c.*1450: *Songs and Carols*, 23 (Warton Cl., 1856), Wynteris wether and wommanys thout, And lordis love, schaungit oft. 1590: Greene, in *Works*, vii 293 (Grosart), Wherevnto alludeth our old English prouerbe. Wynters wether, and womens thoght, And gentlemens purposes chaungeth oft. 1670: Ray, 50. Cf. **Woman** (66).

See also **August** (3) and (6); **Autumn** (1); **Candlemas,** A and B.; **Christmas** (19) and (20); **Frosty**; **Leaves** (2); **November** (2) and (5); **September** (4); **Spring** (6); **Summer** (6) and (7); **Wedding**; and **Woodcock**.

Wipe, *verb.* **1 He that wipes the child's nose.** *See* **Child** (8).

2. To wipe a person's nose = To deprive or to cheat. 1577: Holinshed, *Chron.*, ii p. 323, col. 2 (OED), Hee deuised a shifte howe to wype the byshoppes nose of some of his golde. *c.*1597: Deloney, *Gentle Craft*, ch xiv, O John (said Haunce) I have wiped your nose, and Nicks too, you must weare the willow garland. 1639: Chapman and Shirley, *Ball*, III ii, Poor gentleman, how is he beguil'd! *Lam.* your nose is wiped [*aside*]. 1673: Dryden, *Amboyna*, II i, There's … the Dutchman with my mistress; my nose is wiped to-day. 1709: Cibber, *Rival Fools*,

I, I durst lay my life thow wipest this foolish knight's nose of his mistress at last. 1737: Ray, 268, I wip'd his nose on't.

3. To wipe one's nose on one's own sleeve. 1436: *Libell of Engl. Policye*, l. 453, p. 40 (Pauli), And thus, they wolden, if we wil beleve Wipen our nose with our owen sleve. 1546: Heywood, *Proverbs*, Pt II ch ix, I may … make you wype your nose vpon your sleeue. 1577: Stanihurst, *Descr. of Ireland*, fo. 8, For any recompence he is like to haue at mine handes, he may wype his nose in his sleeue. 1659: Howell, *Proverbs: French-Eng.*, 22, He wiped his nose with his own sleeve, viz. he cousened him neatly.

Wire-drawer under his work, To sit like a. Yorkshire. 1670: Ray, 217.

Wisborough Green. *See* **Rudgwick.**

Wisdom. 1. By wisdom peace, by peace plenty. 1605: Camden, *Remains*, 320 (1870). 1670: Ray, 156.

2. He hath wisdom at will that brags not of his skill. 1623: Wodroephe, *Spared Houres*, 514.

3. He hath wisdom at will that with angry heart can hold his tongue still, *c.*1460: *Proverbs of Good Counsel*, in E.E.T.S., Ext. Ser., 8, p. 69, He hathe wysdom at hys wyll that can with angry harte be stylle. 1546: Heywood, *Proverbs*, Pt I ch.xi.

4. 'Tis wisdom sometimes to seem a fool. 1732: Fuller, 5125.

5. Well goes the case when wisdom counsels. 1736: Bailey, *Dict.*, s.v. 'Wisdom'.

6. What is not wisdom, is danger. 1878: J. Platt. *Morality*, 34.

7. Wisdom goes beyond strength. 1736: Bailey, *Dict.*, s.v. 'Wisdom'.

8. Wisdom is a good purchase, though we pay dear for it. 1732: Fuller, 5766

9. Wisdom is wealth to a poor man. 1669: *Politeuphuia*, 45. 1732: Fuller, 5764, Wisdom in a poor man is a diamond set in lead.

10. Wisdom liketh not chance. 1568: in *Loseley MSS.*, 210 (Kempe).

11. Wisdom sometimes walks in clouted shoes. 1732: Fuller, 5771. 1869: Spurgeon, *John Ploughman*, ch xxiv, Wisdom walks often in patched shoes.

Wise, *adj.* and *subs.* **1. As wise as a drake.** 1560: *Impac. Pouerte*, in Bang, *Materialien*, B. 33, p. 27.

2. As wise as a goose (or, **gander**). 1528: More, *Works*, p. 179, col. 2 (1557), And all as wise as wilde geese. 1533: in *Ballads from M.SS.*, i, 230 (B.S.), As wise as a gander, *c.*1580: *Tom Tyler*, l. 840, p. 23 (1661) (Malone S.) [as in 1533]. *c.*1625: R. C. *Times Whistle*, 60 (E.E.T.S.), Till they have made themselves as wise as geese. 1883: Burne, *Shropsh. Folk-Lore*, 595, As wise as a sucking gully [gosling].

3. As wise as an ape. 1530: Palsgrave, 591, She hath so insensed him with folye that he is almoste as wyse as an ape. *c.*1568: Wager, *Longer thou Livest*, sig. C3, To make him shortly as wise as an ape. 17th cent. in Hazlitt, *Ined. Poet. Miscell.* sig. X1 (1870), And sometimes it makes them as wise as an **ape**.

4. As wise as a wisp (or, *woodcock*). 1533. Heywood, *Play of Love*, l. 319 (Brandl, *Quellen*, 170), I shall proue you playne as wyse as a woodcocke. *c.*1560: T. Ingelend, *Disobedient Child*, 31 (Percy S.), As wyse as a wodcocke, without any wytte. 1670: Ray, 203. 1677: *Poor Robin's Visions*, 61, A fool to make woodcocks merry. 1720: Stukeley, *Memoirs*, i 135 (Surtees S.), Lincolnshire proverbs and sayings. As wise as a wisp.

5. As wise as Tom a thrum. Before 1529: Skelton, *Colin Clout*, l. 284.

6. As wise as Waltham's calf. Ibid., l. 811, As wyse as Waltoms calfe. *c.*1570: in *Bl. Lett. Ballads, etc.* (Lilly), 226, (1867), For Walthams calues to Tiburne needes must go To sucke a bull and meete a butchers axe. 1640: J. Taylor (Water Poet), *Diff. Worships*, 26, in *Works*, 1st Coll. (Spens.S.), And each of. them as wise as Walthams calfe. 1667: L'Estrange, *Quevedo*, 256 (1904), A senseless puppy to come back to me with a story of Waltham's calf that went nine miles to suck a bull. 1732: Fuller, 751 [as in 1667].

7. A wise child is father's bliss, *c.*1270: *Prov. of Alfred*, in Kemble, *Salomon and Sat.*, 233 (Aelfric S.).

8. A wise head makes a still tongue. 1732: Fuller, 469, A wise head bath a close mouth to it. 1865: 'Lancs. Proverbs', in *N. &Q.*, 3rd ser, viii. 494.

9. A wise man begins in the end: a fool ends in the beginning. 1732: Fuller, 471.

10. A wise man changes his mind, a fool never will. 1631: Mabbe, *Celestina*, 104 (T.T.), A wise man altreth his purpose, but a foole persevereth in his folly. 1711: Steele, *Spectator*, No. 78.

11. A wise man is a great wonder. 1732: Fuller, 472.

12. A wise man knows his own. 1855: Bohn, 303.

13. A wise man never wants a weapon. 1736: Bailey, *Dict.*, s.v. 'Weapon'.

14. A wise man ought not to be ashamed to change his purpose. 1578. Florio, *First Fruites*, fo. 32. 1629: *Book of Meery Riddles*, Prov. 43 'alter' for 'change']. 1640: Herbert, *Jac. Prudentum*, A wise man needs not blush for changing his purpose.

15. A wise man's thoughts walk within him, but a fool's without him. 1732: Fuller, 478.

16. A wise man turns chance into good fortune. Ibid., No. 475.

17. A wise man will make more opportunities than he finds. Ibid., No. 479.

18. A wise man will make tools of what comes to hand. Ibid., No. 476.

19. A wise woman. *See* Woman (5).

20. He is not a wise man that cannot play the fool. 1586: Pettie, *Guazzo*, fo. 74, To plaie the foole well it behooueth a man first to bee wise. 1687: *Poor Robin Alman.*, July, Sometimes the fool to play, Is wisdom great they say. 1732: Fuller, 1929 [with the addition 'upon occasion'].

21. He is not wise that is not wise for himself. [Qui ipse sibi sapiens prodesse non quit nequiquam sapit. – Enn. ap. Cic., Fam., 7, 6, 2.] 1478: Rivers, tr. C. de Pisa's *Moral Proverbs*, Grete folye is in him, that taketh hede Upon other and not to his owen nede. 1576: Pettie, *Pet. Pallace*, ii 23 (Gollancz), Their wisdom is nothing worth which are not wise for themselves. 1594: Lodge and Greene, *Look. Glass*, l. 723. 1615: Stephens, *Essays, etc.*, bk i, No. 18, Wise enough to keepe his owne. 1681: Robertson, *Phraseol. Generalis*, 291, That wise man is little worth, who is not wise in his own business. 1732: Fuller, 1954, He is wise that hath wit enough for his own affairs. 1781: T. Francklin, *Lucian's Works*, ii 132, After the poet's excellent observation, 'I hate (says he), the wise man, who is not wise tor himself'. 1880: Spurgeon, *Ploughm. Pictures*, 46 [as in 1732].

22. He is wise enough that can keep himself warm. 1546: Heywood, *Proverbs*, Pt II ch ii, Ye are wise inough (quoth he) if ye keepe ye warme. 1579: *Marr. of Wit and Wisdom*, 16 (SH.S.), Thou art a mery fellowe and wise, And if thou

kepe thy selfe warme. 1607: *The Puritan*, III vi,
Which confirms the old beldam's saying. *He's
wisest, that keeps himself warmest.* 1670: Ray, 28.
1820: Scott, *Abbot*, ch xviii, 'The child hath wit
enough to keep himself warm,' said Adam.

23. He is wise that follows the wise. 1852:
FitzGerald, *Polonius*, 132 (1903).

24. He is wise that is honest. 1639: Clarke, 127.
1670: Ray, 13.

25. He is wise that is ware in time. 1303:
Brunne, *Handl. Synne*, l. 8085, Yu a prouerbe
telle men thys 'He wyys ys, that ware ys'. Before
1500: in Hill, *Commonplace Book*, 101, He ys
wyse that ys ware or he harm fele. 1736: Bailey,
Dict., s.v. 'Wary'.

**26. He is wise that knows when he is well
enough.** 1732: Fuller, 2475.

**27. He seemeth wise with whom all things
thrive.** Ibid., No. 2016.

28. He was wise that first gave reward. *c.*1300:
Havelok, l. 1635, He was ful wis that first yaf
mede. *c.*1350: *Sir Tristrem*, l. 626, He was ful wise,
I say, That first yave yift in land. *c.*1390: Gower,
Conf. Amantis, bk v l.4719, For thus men sein, in
every nede, He was wys that ferst made mede.

**29. If the wise erred not, it would go hard with
fools.** 1640: Herbert, *Jac. Prudentum.*

**30. If wise men play the fool, they do it with a
vengeance.** 1855: Bohn, 419. 1875: Cheales,
Proverb. Folk-Lore, 49, When a wise man errs,
he errs with a vengeance.

**31. It is a wise child that knows its own
father.** [Οὐ γάρ πώ τις ἐὸν γόνον αὐτὸς
ἀνέγνω.– Homer, *Od.*, i 216.] 1589: Greene,
Works, vi 92 (Grosart), For wise are the children
in these dayes that know their owne fathers.
1606: Day, *Ile of Gulls*, II i, I am not so wise a
child as you take me for; I neuer knewe my
father. 1633: Rowley, *Match at Midnight*, I,
None but wise children know their own fathers.
1673: Wycherley, *Gent. Danc. Master*, I i, The
children of this age must be wise children indeed
if they know their fathers. 1762: Goldsmith,
Cock Lane Ghost, in *Works*, ii 472 (Gibbs). 1774:
Burgoyne, *Maid of Oaks*, I i 1823: Scott, *Peveril*,
ch xxxiii. 1925: *Sphere*, June 6, p. 294, col. 1.

32. It is a wise father that knows his own child.
1595: Shakespeare, *M. of Venice*, II ii. 1606: B.
Rich, *Faultes*, fo.28. 1640: Shirley, *Opportunity*,
I i.

**33. Send a wise man on an errand, and say
nothing to him.** *c.*1386: Chaucer, *Miller's Tale*,
l.412, Men seyn thus, 'send the wyse, and sey
nothing'. 1640: Herbert, *Jac. Prudentum.* 1670:
Ray, 157.

34. Some are wise. *See* **Some.**

**35. That is a wise delay which makes the road
safe.** 1659: Howell, *Proverbs: Span.-Eng.*, 3,
That delay is good which makes the way the
safer. 1855: Bohn, 495.

36. The wise and the fool have their fellows.
1659: Howell, *Proverbs: Brit.-Eng.*, 4.

**37. The wise hand doth not all that the foolish
mouth speaks.** 1640: Herbert, *Jac. Prudentum.*
1670: Ray, 12.

**38. The wise man, even when he holds his
tongue, says more than the fool when he
speaks.** 1732: Fuller, 4834.

**39. The wise man is deceived but once, the
fool twice.** 1736: Bailey, *Dict.* s.v. 'Wise'.

**40. The wise man must carry the fool upon
his shoulders.** 1623: Wodroephe, *Spared
Houres*, 489.

41. The wise man's tongue. *See* **Fool** (27).

**42. They are wise in other men's matters, and
fools in their own.** 1672: Walker, *Paroem.*, 31.

43. To be wise after the event. [ῥεχθὲν δέ τε
νήπιος ἔγνω. – Homer, *Il.*, 17, 32. Atque illi
modo cauti ac sapientes prompti post eventum
ac magniloque erant. – Tacitus, *Agric.*, xxvii
Eventus, stultorum iste magister est. – Livy,
xxii.39.] 1609: Jonson, *Silent Woman*, II ii,
Away, thou strange justifier of thyself, to be
wiser than thou wert, by the event. 1875: Jowett,
Plato, V 53 (2nd ed.) (OED), There is no merit
… in learning wisdom after the event. 1928:
Sphere, Jan. 21, p. 93, col. 1, Nor is it a case of
being wise after the event.

44. To be wise behind the hand. 1820: Scott, in
Lockhart's *Life*, v 42, The next night, being, like
true Scotsmen, wise behind the hand, the bailies
had a sufficient force … and put down every
attempt to riot. 1892: Heslop, *N'umberland
Words*, 9 (E.D.S.), 'Ahint yor hand', to have
someone to look after your interest in your
absence.

**45. Who is wise, in the day, can be no fool in
the night.** 1659: Howell, *Proverbs: Ital.-Eng.*, 6.

46. Wise fear begets care. 1732: Fuller, 6355.

47. Wise man if thou art. *See* quot. 15th cent, in
Reliq. Antiquae, i 314 (1841), Wyse mon if thou
art, of thi god Take part or thou hense wynde;

For if thou leve thi part in thi secaturs [executor's] ward, Thi part non part at last end. **48. Wise men are caught in wiles,** *c.*1250: Layamon, *Brut.*, 15182, Ac thar nis no man so wis that me ne mai biswike [There is no man so wise that men may not deceive]. 1670: Ray, 156. 1732: Fuller, 5782, Wise men may chance to be caught.

49. Wise men care not for what they cannot have. 1670: Ray, 29. 1732: Fuller, 5775.

50. Wise men have their mouths in their hearts, fools have their hearts in their mouths. 1477: Rivers, *Dictes and Sayings*, 140 (1877), The tonge of a discrete man is in his herte and the herte of a foole is in his tonge. 1574: E. Hellowes, *Guevara's Epis.*, 183, The wise man hath his tong in his hart, and he that is a foole and furious, hath his heart in his tongue. 1630: Brathwait, *Engl. Gent.*, *etc.*, 47 (1641), These are those fooles, which carry their hearts in their mouthes; and farre from those wise men, which carry their mouthes in their hearts. Cf. **Fool** (27).

51. Wise men in the world are like timber-trees in a hedge, here and there one. 1732: Fuller, 5778. 1869: Spurgeon, *John Ploughman*, ch ii.

52. Wise men learn by others' faults, fools by their own. *c.*1380: Chaucer, *Troyluts*, bk iii l.329, For wysë ben by foles harm chastysed. 1591: Florio. *Second Frutes*, 103, A happie man and wise is he, By others harmes can warned be. 1669: *Politeuphuia*, 44, By others faults wise men correct their own offences. 1758: Franklin, *Poor Richard*, in Arber's *Garner*, v 583 (1882), Wise men, as Poor Dick says, learn by others' harms.

53. Wise men make proverbs and fools repeat them. 1710: S. Palmer, *Moral Essays on Proverbs*, Pref. viii. 1823: D'Israeli, *Cur. of Lit.*, 2nd ser, I 449 (1824). *c.*1860: R. S. Hawker, in Byles, *Life*, *etc.*, 82 (1905).

54. Wise men propose and fools determine. 1692: L 'Estrange, *Aesop*, 114 (3rd ed.) [quoted as 'the old saying'].

55. Wise men silent, fools talk. 1639: Clarke, 5.

56. Wise men. *See also* **Fool**, *passim;* and **Gotham**.

57. Wise words and great seldom agree. 1659: Howell, *Proverbs: Brit.-Eng.*, 6.

58. Wise young. *See* **Too soon wise.**

59. You may be a wise man though you can't make a watch. 1670: Ray, 29. 1732: Fuller, 5939 … and yet not know how to make a watch.

Wisely walketh that doth safely go, He. 1600: Bodenham, *Belvedere*, 49 (Spens.S.).

Wish and **Wishes**, *subs.* **1. If wishes were butter-cakes beggars might bite.** 1678: Ray, 219.

2. If wishes were horses beggars would ride. 1584: J. Withals, *Dictionary* (rev. ed.), I 4, Wise sonnes they be in very deede, That knowe their Parentes who did them breed. 1736: Bailey, *Dict.* s.v. 'Wish'. 1628: J. Carmichael, *Proverbs in Scots*, no. 140, And wishes were horses pure [poor] men wald ryde. 1721: J. Kelly, *Scottish Proverbs*, If Wishes were Horses, Beggars would ride.

3. If wishes were thrushes beggars would eat birds. 1605: Camden, *Remains*, 326 (1870). 1670: Ray, 157. 1732: Fuller, 2731.

4. If wishes would bide, beggars would ride. 1670: Ray, 157. 1694: D'Urfey, *Quixote*, Pt I Act V sc ii. 1732: Fuller, 6098.

5. The wish is father to the thought. [Libenter homines id quod volunt credunt. – Caesar, *De Bello G.*, iii 18.] 1598: Shakespeare, 2 *Hen. IV* IV v, Thy wish was father, Harry, to that thought. 1908: W. Johnson, *Folk-Memory*, 229.

6. When a thing is done wishes are too late. 1736: Bailey, *Dict.*, s.v. 'Wish'.

7. Wishes never can fill a sack. 1855: Bohn, 570.

Wishers and wouldert are never good householders. *c.*1520: Stanbridge, *Vulgaria*, sig. C6, Wysshers and wolders ben small house holders. 1590: Greene, *Works*, viii 64 (Grosart). 1616: Breton, in *Works*, ii *e* 8 (Grosart). 1641: in *Harl. Miscell.*, i 483, (1744) Any of those places would suffice you, or myself, but alas! *Wishers and Woulders*, you know how the proverb runs. 1732: Fuller, 6154.

Wishers want will. *c.*1550: *Parl. of Byrdes*, l. 91, in Hazlitt, *Early Pop. Poetry*, iii 171, The hawke sayd, wysshers want wyll, Whether they speake loude or styll.

Wit. 1. Better wit than wealth. 1736: Bailey, *Dict.*, s.v. 'Better'.

2. Bought wit is dear. 1575: Gascoigne, *Posies* in *Works*, i 66 (Cunliffe).

3. He hath no more wit in his head than thou in both thy shoulders. 1670: Ray, 217.

4. He hath some wit but a fool hath the guidance of it. 1602–3: Manningham, *Diary*, 171 (Camden S.), He hath a good witt but it is carried by a foole. 1732: Fuller, 1899.

5. It is wit to pick a lock and steal a horse, but it is wisdom to let them alone. 1659: Howell, 3. 1670: Ray, 30. 1732: Fuller, 3031.

6. The wit of a woman is a great matter. 1599: Breton in *Works*, ii *c* 59 (Grosart) [cited as 'the common proverbe'].

7. The wit of you and the wool of a blue dog, would make a very good medley. 1659: Howell, 11, The wit of you and the wool of an old dogg, will make a piece of linsay-woolsie. 1732: Fuller, 4836.

8. To be at one's wits' end. *c.*1420: Lydgate, *Assem. of Gods*, st. 238, p. 49 (E.E.T.S.), When they were dreuyn to her wyttes ende. *c.*1565: Still, *Gam. Gurton*, IV, ii, And Dame Chat at her wyts ende I have almost set her. 1576: Pettie, *Pet. Pallace*, i 172 (Gollancz), Who … were at their wits' end what medicine to apply. 1694: D'Urfey, *Quixote*, Pt II Act II sc ii, Now is Sancho at his wits-end to know, whether he may believe his eyes and ears or no. 1764: Mrs F. Sheridan, *Dupe*, II iv, I am quite at my wits' end to unriddle it. 1883: R.L.S., *Treas. Isl.*, ch xix, They were at their wits' end what to do. 1923: Lucas, *Adv. Ben*, § xvii p. 95, Can you tell me what to do? I'm at my wits' end.

9. To have wit at will. *c.*1470: *Songs and Carols*, 37 (Percy S., No. 73), If thou have wysdom at thi wyll. *c.*1602: Chapman, *May-Day*, IV iii, Win her and wear her; thou hast wit at will. 1738: Swift, *Polite Convers.*, Dial. I, She's very handsome, and has wit at will. 1772: Graves, *Spirit. Quixote*, bk ix ch vi, My son says, my lady has wit at will, and will hold discourse with any lord or bishop. 1821: Scott, *Pirate*, ch xiv … said Tim, who had wit at will. 1881: A. R. Ellis, *Introd. to Evelina*, i, The living French writer who has the most wit at will.

10. Wit and will strive for the victory. 1736: Bailey, *Dict.*, s.v. 'Wit'.

11. Wit and wisdom are good warison [possession]. *c.*1320: in *Reliq. Antiquae* i 109, (1841), 'Wyt art wysdom is god warysoun,' Quoth Hendyng. 1594: Churchyard, *Mirror of Man*, Wisdome is great wealth.

12. Wit bought is better than taught. 1670: Ray, 157, Wit once bought is worth twice taught. 1875: Cheales, *Proverb. Folk-Lore*, 115. Cf. **Ounce of wit.**

13. Wit goes not all by the hair. *c.*1592: *Sir Thos. More*, 59 (SH.S.), Why, man, he may be without a beard till he come to mariage, for witt goes not all by the hayre.

14. Wit is folly unless a wise man hath the keeping of it. 1813: Ray, 174.

15. Wit is never good till it be bought. *c.*1500: Medwall, *Nature*, Pt II l.1292, Wyt ys nothyng worth tyll yt be dere bought. 1546: Heywood, *Proverbs*, Pt I ch viii. 1579: Lyly, *Euphues*, 34 (Arber), It hath bene an olde sayde sawe … that wit is the better if it be the deerer bought. 1630: Randolph, *Conceited Peddler* in *Works*, i 39 (1875). 1653: R. Brome, *City Wit*, I ii 1678: A. Behn, *Sir P. Fancy*, II i, 'Twas a saying of my grandmother's … that bought wit was best. 1709: T. Baker, *Fine Lady's Airs*, IV ii, My grandmother … says bought wit's best. 1732: Fuller, 1011, Bought wit is best, but may cost too much. 1901: F. E. Taylor, *Lancs. Sayings*, 11, Wit's nowt till its dear bowt. 1917: Bridge, *Cheshire Proverbs*, 156, Wit's n'er owt [aught] Tin dear bowt [Till dear brought].

16. Wits are most wily. *See* quot. 16th cent, in *Reliq. Antiquae*, ii 195, (1843), Wittes are moste wylly where wemen have, wyttes, And curtilly comethe uppon them by ffittes.

17. Wits have short memories. *See* **Great wits**.

18. Wit, whither wilt thou? 1601: Shakespeare, *A. Y. Like It*, IV i, A man that had a wife with such a wit, he might say, 'Wit, whither wilt?' 1659: Howell, 3.

19. Wit will walk where will is bent. 1583: Melbancke, *Philotinus*, sig. Y2.

20. Wit without learning is like a tree without fruit. 1647: *Countrym. New Commenwealth*, 15.

21. Wit without wisdom. *See* quots. *c.*1270: *Prov. of Alfred*, in Kemble, *Salomon and Saturnus*, 229 (Aelfric S.), Wid widutin wisdom is wele ful unwed [wit without wisdom is but little worth]. 1732: Fuller, 5791, Wit without wisdom cuts other men's meat and its own fingers.

22. You have wit enough to drown ships in. 1678: Ray, 277.

23. You may truss up all his wit in an eggshell. Ibid., 84. 1732: Fuller, 5957.

See also **Ounce of wit.**

Witch. *See* **Burn** (6); **Devil** (101); **Go** (4); and **Rowan-tree.**

Witch-wife. *See* quot. 1846–59: *Denham Tracts*, ii 81 (F.L.S.), A witch-wife – an evil, Is three halfpence worse than the deevil.

With a mischief. 1533: Heywood, *John Tib and Sir John*, l. 481, Now go chafe the wax, with a myschyfe. 1541: *Sch. House of Women*, l. 278, And now God giue the shame at last, Commest drunken home with a mischeef. 1623: Massinger, *Duke of Milan*, II i, Pleased, with a mischief! 1681: Robertson, *Phraseol. Generalis*, 760, Be gone with a mischief.

With a vengeance. 1533: Heywood, *John Tib and Sir John*, l. 425, And go with a vengeance. 1593: Peele, *Edw. I*, sc ii, Be gone quickly, or my pikestaff and I will set thee away with a vengeance. 1679: Dryden, *Troilus*, II ii, Nothing, do you call it? This is nothing, with a vengeance. 1701: Cibber, *Love makes a Man*, I, Yes, sir, he has lost with a vengeance. 1778: Burney, *Evelina*, Lett. xxiii, They'd need to be goddesses with a vengeance … for they're mortal dear to look at. 1814: Byron, *Letters, etc.*, iii 124 (Prothero), I got in a passion with an ink-bottle, which I flung out of the window one night with a vengeance. 1922: Weyman, *Ovington's Bank*, ch xl., They had cooked their goose with a vengeance – no more golden eggs for them!

With a wanion – a proverbial expletive phrase, similar to 'With a mischief, vengeance, and witness'. *c.*1568: Wager, *Longer thou Livest*, sig. G2, Get the[e] hence theefe with a wanion. 1606: T. Heywood, *If you know not me*, Pt II, in *Dram. Works*, i 284 (1874), There's your ten pounds; tell it out with a wanion, and take it for your pains, *c.*1627: in *Pepysian Garland* (Rollins), 272, Pray let them both packe with a winion. 1673: *Vinegar and Mustard*, 9, in Hindley, *Old Book Coll. – isc.*, iii, I'll warrant you with a wannion. 1823: Scott, *Peveril*, ch vi, Who calls himself a parson, and whom! hope to fetch down from his perch presently, with a wannion to him!

With a witness. 1703: Ward, *Writings*, ii 273, And the Gown often errs with a witness. 1753: Richardson, *Grandison*, i 225 (1883), *Carried* he should have said; I was carried with a witness!

Witham pike. *See* quots. 1611: Markham, *Country Contentments*, 65 (1675), The ancient proverb is, Ancome eele, and Witham pike, In all England is none sike [such]. 1662: Fuller, *Worthies*, ii 262 (1840), To return to our English pikes, wherein this county [Lincs.] is eminent, especially in that river which runneth by Lincoln, whence grew this proverb, 'Witham

pike England hath none like'. 1874: Smiles, *Lives of Engineers*, i 13 [as in 1662].

Without danger we cannot get beyond danger. 1640: Herbert, *Jac. Prudentum*

Wits. *See* **Good wits and Great wits.**

Wive and thrive both in a year, It's hard to. *c.*1410: *Towneley Plays*, 103 (E.E.T.S.), It is sayde full ryfe, 'a man may not wyfe and also thryfe, And all in a yere'. 1546: Heywood, *Proverbs*, Pt I ch xi. 1580: Tusser, *Husbandrie*, 153 (E.D.S.), It is too much we dailie heare, To wiue and thriue both in a yeare. 1670: Ray, 48. 1738: Swift, *Polite Convers.*, Dial. I, You can't expect to wive and thrive in the same year. 1846: Denham, *Proverbs*, 5 (Percy S.).

Wiving and thriving, a man should take counsel of all the world, In. 1678: Ray. 354.

Wizard Stream, The = The River Dee. 1917: Bridge, *Cheshire Proverbs*, 121.

Woe, *subs.* **1. There is no woe to want.** 1605: Camden, *Remains*, 332 (1870). 1732: Fuller, 4926.

2. *See* quot. 1509: Barclay, *Ship of Fools*, i 284 (1874), For we fynde in an olde sayde sawe Wo is hym that to his maker is vnkynde.

3. Woe to the house where there is no chiding. 1640: Herbert, *Jac. Prudentum*. 1732: Fuller, 5801.

Wogan. *See* quot. 1659: Howell, 21, It shall be done when the king cometh to Wogan, a little village, viz. an impossibility. 1790: Grose, *Prov. Gloss.*, s.v. 'Worcestershire' [as in 659].

Wolf and **Wolves. 1. A growing youth has a wolf in his belly.** 1611: Cotgrave, s.v. 'Ieune', A youth in growing hath a wolfe in his guts. *c.*1625: B.&F., *Women Pleased*, I ii, This ravening fellow has a wolf in's belly. 1754: Berthelson, *Eng.-Danish Dict.*, s.v. 'Dog', To have a dog in ones belly. 1917: Bridge, *Cheshire Proverbs*, 3.

2. A wolf in sheep's clothing. *c.*1460: *Wisdom*, sc iii st. 61, They flatter and lye as they were woode [mad]; Ther ys a wolffe in a lombys skyn. 1509: Barclay, *Ship of Fools*, ii 7 (1874), She is perchaunce A wolfe or gote within a lammys skyn. 1584: Greene, *Works*, iii 11 (Grosart), These two … had … vnder their sheepes skinnes, hidden the bloudie nature of a wolfe. 1657: Gurnall, *Christ. in Armour*, Pt II v 14, ch xvii p. 67 (1679). The hypocrite is the wolf clad in the sheeps skin. 1751: Fielding, *Amelia*, bk ix ch ix, There is the meekness of the clergyman.

There spoke the wolf in sheep's clothing. 1876: Blackmore, *Cripps*, ch xliv., Whose bosom friend is a Jesuit, a fierce wolf in sheep's clothing. 1926: Phillpotts, *Yellow Sands*, III, A wolf in sheep's clothing – that's what she was.

3. By little and little the wolf eateth the sheep. 1633: Draxe, 13.

4. By little and little the wolf eats up the goose. 1611: Cotgrave, s.v. 'Manger'.

5. For the least choice the wolfe tooke the sheepe. 1623: Wodroephe, *Spared Houres*, 500.

6. It is a hard winter when one wolf eats another. 1579. Lyly, *Euphues*, 78 (Arber). 1643: Taylor (Water Poet), *Lett. to London*, 8, in *Works*, 5th Coll. (Spens.S.) ['world' for 'winter']. 1696: D'Urfey, *Quixote*, Pt III Act V sc i 1710: S. Palmer, *Moral Essays on Proverbs*, 327.

7. It is hard to have wolf full and wether whole. 1374: Chaucer, *Troylus*, bk iv l.1373.

8. The death of a young wolf doth never come too soon. 1651: Herbert, *Jac. Prudentum*, 2nd ed.

9. The death of the wolf is the health of the sheep. 1578: Florio, *First Fruites*, fo. 31. 1666: Torriano, *Piazza Univ.*, 132.

10. The wolf eats counted sheep. [Tantum curamus frigora, quantum numerum (ovium) lupus. – Virgil, *Aeneid*, 7, 51]. 1611: Cotgrave, s.v. 'Loup'. The wolfe eats counted (and uncounted) sheepe. 1708: tr. *Aleman's Guzman*, i 435, Your Eminence knows the proverb relating to counted sheep.

11. The wolf eats oft of the sheep that have been warned. 1651: Herbert, *Jac. Prudentum*, 2nd ed.

12. The wolf knows what the ill beast thinks. 1640: Herbert, *Jac. Prudentum*.

13. The wolf must die in his own skin. 1611: Cotgrave, s.v. 'Loup'. 1640: Herbert, *Jac. Prudentum*.

14. To cry wolf = To give a false alarm. 1740: North, *Examen*, 315, They say the false cry of the wolf made the neighbours not regard the cry when the wolf was come in earnest. 1844: Planché, *Extravag.*, ii 288 (1879), Why, you're cried 'Wolf!' till, like the shepherd youth, You're not believed when you do speak the truth.

15. To have a wolf by the ears. [Lupum auribus tenere. – Terence, *Phorm.*, 3, 2, 21.] 1576: Lambarde, *Peramb. of Kent*, 418 (1826), They had but a wolfe by the eares, whom they could

neither well hold, nor might safely let goe. 1642: Quarls, *Works*, i 53 (Grosart), A Prince ... that entertaines Auxiliaries, holds a wolfe by the eares. 1691: J. Wilson, *Belphegor*, II iii, If ever man had a wolf by the ears, I have one now. 1740: North, *Lives of Norths*, i 211 (Bohn), He found ... that it was like a wolf by the ears; he could neither hold it nor let it go.

16. To keep the wolf from the door. 1546: Heywood, *Proverbs*, Pt II ch vii *c.*1597: Deloney, *Gentle Craft*, Pt I ch x, That we may liue out of debt and danger, and driue the woolf from the doore. *c.*1630: in *Roxb. Ballads*, i 167 (Hindley), Though home be but homely, and never so poore, Yet let us keepe, warily, the wolfe from the doore. Before 1704: Brown, *Works*, iii 242 (1760), I shall be very well satisfied if I can keep the wolf from the door, as the saying is. 1860: Reade, *Clois, and Hearth*, ch Iii, And so the brave girl and the brave soldier worked with a will, and kept the wolf from the door. 1921: Sidney Colvin, *Memories, etc.*, 48, Fortunately he had from the first had friends and backers whose appreciation saved him from any serious danger of the wolf at the door.

17. To set the wolf to keep the sheep. [Ovem lupo committere. – Terence, *Eun.*, 5,1,16.] 1639: Clarke, 95, You have given the wolf the weather to keep. 1694: *Terence made English*, 89, Oh you jade, you set the wolf to keep the sheep. 1736: Bailey, *Dict.*, s.v. 'Wolf', To give the wolf the weather to keep.

18. Who hath a wolf for his mate, needs a dog for his man. 1640: Herbert, *Jac. Prudentum*. 1670: Ray, 30.

19. Who keeps company with the wolf will learn to how. 1591: Florio, *Second Frutes*, 57, Who is bread among wolfes, will learne to houle. 1623: Wodroephe, *Spared Houres*, 274, Hee who hantes with wolues doth learne to houle. 1670: Ray, 30. 1748: Richardson, *Clarissa*, iv 119 (1785), Tho' you have kept company with a wolf you have not learnt to howl of him. 1871: Smiles, *Character*, 66, 'Live with wolves', says the Spanish proverb, 'and you will learn to howl'.

20. Who speakes of the wolfe hee seeth his taile. 1623: Wodroephe, *Spared Houres*, 500.

21. Wolves lose their teeth but not their memory. 1633: Draxe, 237. 1670: Ray, 30. 1732: Fuller, 5802, Wolves may lose their teeth, but not their nature.

22. Wolves never prey upon wolves. 1576: Pettie. *Pet. Pallace*, ii 81 (Gollancz). 1651: Herbert, *Jac. Prudentum*, 2nd ed., A wolf will never make war against another wolf.

See also **Dog** (1) and (52); **Hunger fetcheth; Hungry at a wolf; Law** (3); **Man** (53) and (58); and **Sheep** *passim.*

Wolfs mouth. *See* **Dark.**

Wolstonbury, Sussex. *See* quot. 1893: Inwards, *Weather Lore*, 99, When Wolsonbury has a cap, Hurstpierpoint will have a drap.

Woman and **Women. 1. A dishonest woman cannot be kept in, and an honest one will not.** 1732: Fuller, 76.

2. A good woman is worth, if she were sold, the fairest crown that's made of purest gold. 1623: Wodroephe, *Spared Houres*, 484. 1880: Spurgeon, *Ploughm. Pictures*, 88 [omitting 'purest'].

3. As great a pity to see a woman weep as to see a goose go barefoot. 1526: *Hund. Mery Talys*, No. x p. 20 (Oesterley), By thys tale ye may se that the olde prouerbe ys trew that yt is as gret pyte to se a woman wepe as a gose to go barefote. 1621: Burton, *Melanch.*, III II iii 4, 548 (1836), As much pitty is to be taken of a woman weeping, as of a goose going bare-footed. 1716: ward, *Female Policy*, 44. 1850: Sir H. Taylor, *Virgin Widow*, I iii ['gosling' for 'goose'].

4. A wicked woman and an evil is three halfpence worse than the devil. 1639: Clarke, 118. 1670: Ray, 50. 1732: Fuller, 6406. 1875: Cheales, *Proverb. Folk-Lore*, 4, That coarse old saying A wicked woman and an evil Is some nine parts worse than the devil.

5. A wise woman is twice a fool. 1680: L'Estrange, *Select Coll. out of Erasmus*, 220, I have often heard that *One wise woman is two fools.* 1725: Bailey, tr. *Erasm. Coll.*, 256.

6. A woman and a cherry are painted for their own harm. 1659: Howell, *Proverbs: Span.-Eng.*, 18, A woman and a cherry paint themselves for their hurt. 1855: Bohn, 304.

7. A woman and a glass are ever in danger. 1640: Herbert, *Jac. Prudentum.* 1669: *New Help to Discourse*, 310.

8. A woman, a dog, and a walnut-tree, The more you beat them the better they be. 1844: J.O. Halliwell, *Nursery Rhymes of England* (ed. 4), 501, If wishes were horses, Beggars would ride; If turnips were watches, I would wear one by my side. [Nux,asinus, mulier, simili sunt lege ligati: Haec tria nil recta faciunt, si verbera cessent. 16thcent.: Cognatus, *Adagia*, in Grynaeus, *Adagia*, p. 484, col. 1 (1629) (*N. & Q.*, 10th ser, ix 298).] 1586: Pettie, *Guazzo*, fo. 139, A woman, an asse, and a walnut-tree, Bring the more fruite, the more beaten they bee. 1589: L. Wright, *Display of Dutie*, 24, It is sayde that an asse, a walnut-tree, and a woman asketh much beating before they be good. 1596: Nashe, *Works*, iii 110 (Grosart), A nut, a woman, and an asse are like, These three doo nothing right, except you strike. 1608: *Yorksh. Tragedy*, sc i, For you must note, that any woman bears the more when she is beaten. 1612: Webster, *White Devil*, V i, Do you think that she is like a walnut-tree? Must she be cudgelled ere she bear good fruit? 1692: L'Estrange, *Aesop*, 284 (3rd ed.), 'Tis natural for asses, women, and wallnut-trees to mend upon beating. 1732: Fuller, 6404. Walnut trees were beaten not simply, it is said, to bring down the nuts, but in order to break off long twigs and encourage the growth of more fruiting spurs. Thus they figure in the proverb.1878: Dyer, *Engl. Folk-Lore*, 30 ['whip' for 'beat'].

9. A woman can do more than the devil. 1539: Bercher, *Nobility of Women*, 140 (Roxb. C.) [cited as 'a common proverbe'].

10. A woman hath nine lives like a cat. 1546: Heywood, *Proverbs*, Pt II ch iv. 1611: Davies of Hereford, *Sc. of Folly*, 49, in *Works*, ii (Grosart), Some wiues (some say) haue nine liues like a cat. 1738: Swift, *Polite Convers.*, Dial. I, They say, a woman has as many lives as a cat.

11. A woman is an angel at ten, a saint at fifteen, a devil at forty, and a witch at fourscore. 1620: *Swetnam the Woman Hater* (Grosart).

12. A woman is a weather-cock. 1633: Draxe, 238, Women are (oft times) weather-cocks. 1636: W. Sampson, *Vow Breaker*, I iv, in Bang, *Materialien*, B. 42, p. 22, Faith vncle, i' me a woman, and they say, a woman is a wether-cocke.

13. A woman is to be from her house three times; when she is christened, married and buried. 1732: Fuller, 480.

14. A woman need but look upon her apron-string to find an excuse. 1620: *Westward for Smelts*, 17 (Percy S.), Excuses are never further off women than their apron strings. 1672: J. Lacy, *Dumb Lady*, I, They say when a woman means mischief, if she but look upon her apron-strings the devil will help her presently. 1738: Swift, *Polite Convers.*, Dial. III.

15. A woman's counsel. *See* quots. 1620: Shelton, *Quixote*, Pt II ch vii, Woman's advice is but slender, yet he, that refuseth it is a madman. 1639: Clarke, 22, A womans counsell is sometime good. 1659: Howell, 6, A womans advice is best at a dead lift. 1875: Cheales, *Proverb. Folk-Lore*, 5, A woman's advice is a poor thing, but he is a fool who does not take it. Cf. No. 60.

16. A woman's heart and her tongue are not relatives. 1590: Greene, *Works*, viii 90 (Grosart). 1669: *Politeuphuia*, 31.

17. A woman's 'nay'. *See* quots. *c*.1590: Shakespeare, *Pass. Pilgrim*, xix, Have you not heard it said full oft, A woman's nay doth stand for nought? 1611: Davies of Hereford, *Sc. of Folly*, 40, in *Works*, ii (Grosart), A woman's nay's a double yea (they say). 1686: *Loyal Garland*, 31 (Percy S.), A woman's nay is no denial.

18. A woman's place is in the home. 'J. Slick', *High Life*, II 121, A woman's place is her own house, a taking care of the children. 1936: R.A.J. Walling, *Corpse with a Dirty Face*, iv, Mrs Franks, being a dutiful wife, was always on the premises. 'Ah yes – woman's place is in the home,' said Pierce.

19. A woman's reason – because it is so. *c*.1591: Shakespeare, *Two Gent.*, I ii, I have no other but a woman's reason; I think him so, because I think him so. 1601: Lyly, *Love's Metam.*, IV i, Women's reasons; they would not because they would not. 1634: Massinger, *Very Woman*, I i, Shall I lose The privilege of my sex, which is my will, To yield a reason like a man? 1706: Farquhar, *Recruiting Officer*, IV iii *c*.1750: Foote, *Englishm. in Paris*, Prol., To contradict you, I know, is high treason; For the will of a wife is always her reason. 1920: Hudson, *Dead Man's Plack*, Preamble, 9, If any one were to ask me why I dislike him I should probably have to answer like a woman: Because I do.

20. A woman's strength is in her tongue. 1560: Becon, *Catechism*, 345 (P.S.), They shame not to answer: 'A woman hath none other weapon but her tongue ...' 1659: Howell, *Proverbs: Brit.-Engl.*, 29. 1875: Cheales, *Proverbial Folk-Lore*,

8, A woman's tongue is her sword, and she does not let it rust.

21. A woman's tongue is the last thing about her that dies. 1612: Chapman, *Widow's Tears*, IV ii, When a man dies, the last thing that moves is his heart; in a woman her tongue. 1738: Swift, *Polite Convers.*, Dial. III.

22. A woman's work is never done. *c*.1655: in *Roxb. Ballads*, iii 302 (B.S.). 1670: Ray, 50, A womans work is never at an end. 1732: Fuller, 5810 [in the plural]. 1825: Hone, *Ev. Day Book*. I. 1375 [as in 1732]. 1928: *Evening Standard*, Jan. 3, p. 3, col. 2, 'The old adage that woman's work is never done should not be tolerated,' she said.

23. A woman that is wilful. *See* quot. 16th cent. in *Reliq. Antiquae*, ii 195 (1843), A woman thatt ys wylfull ys a plage off the worste, As good live in hell, as withe a wytte that is curste.

24. A woman that loves to be at the window, is like a bunch of grapes on the highway. 1666: *Torriano.Piazza Univ.*, 74, A woman at a window, as grapes on the high way. 1869: Hazlitt, 39.

25. A woman that paints puts up a bill that she is to be let. 1700: Ward, *London Spy*, 420 (1924), For she that paints will doubtless be a whore. 1732: Fuller, 481.

26. A woman that spinnes in vice, hath her smocke full of lice. 1623: Wodroephe, *Spared Houres*, 484.

27. Choose not a woman nor linen by candlelight. 1578: Florio, *First Fruites*, fo. 32, Neither a woman nor lynnen chuse thou by a candle. 1629: *Book of Meery Riddles*, Prov. 18. 1678: Ray, 64, Neither women nor linen by candle-light. 1928: *Bystander*, Oct. 17, p. 138, col. 1. Cf. No. 40.

28. He hath a woman's tongue. 1630: T. Adams, *Works*, 150, The prouerbe came not for nothing, when we say of a brawling man, he ... hath a womans tongue in his head.

29. If a woman were as little as she is good, A peascod would make her a gown and a hood. 1591: Florio, *Second Frutes*, 175 [in the plural]. 1619: *Help to Discourse*, 55 (1640). 1732: Fuller, 6446. 1869: Spurgeon, *John Ploughman*, ch xvii ['peashell' for 'peascod'].

30. Let no woman's fainting Breed thy heart's fainting. 1670: Ray, 20 ['stomachs' for 'hearts']. 1732: Fuller, 6243.

31. Many women many words. *c.*1425: *Castle of Perseverance*, sc vi st. 230, [Where] Ther wymmen arn, are many wordys. 1542: *Skh. House of Women*, l. 482, And where be women, are many woords. *c.*1600: Deloney, *Thos. of Reading*, ch 12, The old prouerbe … Many women many words. 1670: Ray, 214.

32. One tongue is enough for a woman. 1678: Ray, 59. 1738: Swift, *Polite Convers.*, Dial. II.

33. She is a woman and therefore may be wooed, she is a woman and therefore may be won. *c.*1591: Shakespeare, *Titus, Andr.*, II i. 1620: Ford, *Line of Life*, 59 (SH.S.), Women were in theircreation ordained to be wooed, and to be won. 1823: Scott, *Q. Durward*, ch xix, Every woman may be won.

34. Tell a woman she's a beauty, and the devil will tell her so ten times. 1710: S. Palmer, *Moral Essays on Proverbs*, 192, Tell a woman she's handsome but once, And the devil will tell her so fifty times. 1732: Fuller, 4326.

35. The more women look in their glass, the less they look to their house. 1640: Herbert, *Jac. Prudentum*, 1670: Ray, 50 [in the plural]. 1732: Fuller, 4669, The more women look into their glass, the less they look into their hearts.

36. Three women and a goose make a market. 1586: Pettie, *Guazzo*, fo. 115. Doe you not know the prouerbe, that three women make a market? 1607: Rowlands, *Diog. Lanthorne*, 45 (Hunt.Cl.), Three women make a market, for they haue sufficient voyce. 1665: J. Wilson, *Projectors*, 111., If two women and a goose make a market, I see no reason why three may not make a council. 1738: Swift, *Polite Convers.*, Dial. III, Miss, did you never hear, that three women and a goose are enough to make a market? 1865: W. White, *Eastern England*, i 262.

37. Where there are women and geese, there wants no noise. 1659: Howell, *Proverbs: Ital.-Eng.*, 16. 1678: Ray, 64. 1732: Fuller, 5684, Where women are and geese, there wants no gaggling.

38. Woman's instinct is often truer than man's reasoning. 1875: Cheales, *Proverbial Folk-Lore*, 11.

39. Women and dogs set men together by the ears. 1541: *Sch. House of Women*, l. 690, The prouerb olde accordeth right: Women and dogges cause much strife. 1666: Torriano, *Piazza Univ.*, 52, Many women and dogs cause contention.

1670: Ray, 50. 1829: Cobbett, *Adv. to Young Men*, Lett, iv, Soldiers have leisure, too, to play with children, as well as with 'women and dogs', for which the proverb has made them famous.

40. Women and hens by too much gadding are lost. 1611: Cotgrave, s.v. 'Poule', Women and hennes, that gad overmuch, are quickly lost. 1666: Torriano, *Piazza Univ.*, 10.

41. Women and linen look best by candlelight. 1738: Swift, *Polite Convers.*, Dial. III ['shew' for 'look']. 1913: *Folk-Lore*, xxiv 76 (Oxfordshire). Cf. No. 26.

42. Women and music should never be dated. 1773: Goldsmith, *She Stoops*, III.

43. Women and their wills are dangerous ills. 1613: S. Rowley, *When you see me*, sig. L3.

44. Women and wine, game and deceit, Make the wealth small and the wants great. 1591: Florio, *Second Frutes*, 73, Women, wine, and dice, will bring a man to lice. 1732: Fuller, 6416. 1736: Franklin, *Way to Wealth*, in *Works*, i 446 (Bigelow).

45. Women are born in Wiltshire, Brought up in Cumberland, Lead their lives in Bedfordshire, Bring their husbands to Buckingham, And die in Shrewsbury. 1658: *Wit Restor'd*, 99.

46. Women are necessary evils. 1583: Melbancke, *Philotinus*, sig. T2, As all women bee euills, yet necessarie euills. 1591: Florio, *Second Frutes*, 173, Women … are indeed necessarie, but euills. 1639: Clarke, 118. Cf. **Wife** (30).

47. Women are saints in church. *See* quots. 1542: *Sch. House of Women*, l. 658, As holy as saints in church they be, And in street as angels they were, At home, for all their hipocrisie, A deuilish life they lede all the year. 1559: Bercher, *Nobility of Women*, 127 (Roxb.Cl), A woman is a fury and an hurtfull Spyrite in the house, an angell in the churche, an ape in the bead, a mule vnbrideled in the ffelde and a gote in the garden. 1560: E. More, *Defence of Women*, l. 474, At home lyke dyuelles they be, abrode lyke aungelles pure. 1589: Puttenham, *Engl. Poesie*, 299 (Arber), We limit the comely parts of a woman to consist in foure points, that is to be a shrewe in the kitchin, a saint in the church, an angell at the bourd, and an ape in the bed, as the Chronicle reportes by Mistress Shore paramour to king Edward the fourth. 1602: Middleton,

Blurt. Master-Const., III iii, According to that wise saying of you, [women] be saints in the church, angels in the street, devils in the kitchen, and apes in your bed. 1869: Spurgeon, *John Ploughman*, ch xiii, God save us all from wives who are angels in the streets, saints in the church, and devils at home.

48. Women are ships and must be manned, *c.*1630: in *Roxb. Ballads*, i 515. (B.S.).

49. Women be forgetful, children be unkind. *See* quots. *c.*1470: *Songs and Carols*, 34 (Percy S.). Wyves be rekeles, chyldren be onkynd. Execcuturs be covetys and hold that thei fynd. Before 1500: in Hill, *Commonplace-Book*, 138 (E.E.T.S.), Do sum good, man, by thy lyffe, Whiles thow hast thy mynde; Thy children will forgete the sone, Thy wyffe will be unkynd, Thy executours be covytes, And take all that they fynde; Yff thow wilt not, while thow may, They will bryng the behynde. 1603: Stow, *Survey of London*, 116, I wish men to make their owne hands their executors and their eyes their ouerseers, not forgetting the olde prouerbe Women be forgetfull, children be unkinde, Executors be covetous, and take what they finder If anybody aske where the deads goods became, they answer So God mee helpe and holydome Hee dyed a poore man. 1606: T. Heywood, *If you know not me*, Pt II [as in 1603 to 'they finde']. 1632: Rowley, *Woman never vexed*, V [as in 1603, very slightly varied].

50. Women commend a modest man, but like him not. 1732: Fuller, 5805.

51. Women conceal all that they know not. 1640: Herbert, *Jac. Prudentum* and 1670: Ray, 50 [both in the singular number]. 1732: Fuller, 5860.

52. Women have no souls. 1566: L. Wager, *Mary Magdalene*, sig. E4, Women have no soules, this sayng is not newe. *c.*1610: Marston, *Insat. Countess*, V, And lastly, may the opinion of philosophers Prove true, that women have no soules! Before 1680: Butler, *Remains*, i 246 (1759), The souls of women are so small, That some believe th'have none at all. 1708: *Brit. Apollo*, Supp. Paper 12, col. 8, I have often heard say, that the female sex have no soul, I suppose it to be a proverbial saying.

53. Women have two faults. *See* quots. 1606: B. Rich, *Faultes*. fo. 23, Amongst women (some will say) there is but two faults, and those are,

they can neither doe nor say well. 1716: Ward, *Female Policy*, 72, 'Tis said of women, that they have two faults; that is, they can neither say well, nor yet do well 1875: Cheales, *Proverb. Folk-Lore*, 13, Men have many faults, poor women have only two, There's nothing right they say, and nothing right they do!

54. Women in mischief are wiser than men. 1647: *Countrym. New Commonwealth*, 11.

55. Women in state affairs are like monkeys in glass shops. 1659: Howell, 12.

56. *Women laugh when they can and weep when they will.* 1611: Cotgrave, s.v. 'Femme'. A woman laughes, etc. 1640: Herbert, *Jac. Prudentum*. 1670: Ray, 50. 1736: Bailey, *Dict.* s.v. 'Laugh'.

57. Women, money and wine, have their good and their pine. 1611: Cotgrave, s.v. 'Argent', Money, wine, and women, have good and bad things in them. 1623: Wodroephe, *Spared Houres*, 484.

58. Women must have the last word. 1542: *Sch. House of Women*, l. 76, Yet wil the woman haue the last woord. 1655: Fuller, *Church Hist.*, bk i. § iii (7), Whilst women strive for the last word. 1764: Mrs F. Sheridan, *Dupe*, Epil., A prating female will have the last word. 1926: Phillpotts, *Yellow Sands*, III, She was like the rest of your sex, ma'am – she went her own way, and had the last word.

59. Women must have their wills. 1547: Borde, *Brev. Of Helthe*, fo. 96, Let her [the wife] haue her owne wyl for that she wyll haue who so euer say nay. 1602–3: Manningham, Diary, 92 (Camden S.), Women, because they cannot have their wills when they dye, they will have their wills while they live. 1616: Haughton, *Englishm.for my Money*, V iii, Women will have their will 1664: J.Wilson, *Cheats*, V v [as in 1616]. 1733: Gay, Song in *Achilles*, Since woman will have both her word and her way. 1869: Spurgeon, *John Ploughman*, ch xvi, But then the proverb says, a wife ought to have her will during life, because she cannot make one when she dies.

60. Women, priests and poultry never have enough. 1659: Howell, *Proverbs: Ital.-Engl.*, 7. 1670: Ray, 30. 1732: Fuller, 5809.

61. Women's advice is cold advice, *c.*1270: *Prov. of Alfred*, in *Old Eng. Miscell.*, 122 (E.E.T.S.), Cold red Is quene [woman's] red [advice], *c*.1386: Chaucer, *C. Tales*, B. 4446 (Skeat), Wommennes counseils ben full oftë colde. [Skeat says 'colde' = baneful, fatal.] Cf. No. 15.

62. Women's jars breed men's wars. 1642: Fuller, *Holy State* (*Wise Statesman*). 1853: Trench, *Proverbs*. 19 (1905).

63. Women's tongues wag like lambs' tails. *c*.1597: Deloney, *I acke of Newberie*, ch vii, Considering that womens tongues are like lambs tayles, which seldome stand still. 1612: *Cornucopiae*, 7 (Grosart), As womens tongues be like to yong lambs tailes. 1865: 'Lancs. Proverbs', in *N.&Q.*, 3rd ser, viii 494 [in the singular number].

64. Women think Place a sweet fish. 1678: Ray, 59.

65. Women want the best first, and the best always. 1917: Bridge, *Cheshire Proverbs*, 157.

66. Women, wealth and wine have each two qualities, a good and a bad. 1736: Bailey, *Dict.*, s.v. 'Woman'.

67. Women, wind and fortune are given to change. 1639: Clarke, 159, A woman's mind and winter-wind change oft. 1670: Ray, 50 [as in 1639]. 1736: Bailey, *Dict.*, s.v. 'Women'. Ibid., A woman's mind is like the wind in a winter's night.
See also **All women; Bad words; Beware; Black,** *adj.* (3) and (22); **Dally; Dead** (2); **Discreet; Eel** (4); **Every Woman; Fair, adj.** (12) (14); **Flesh upon horses; Fool** (40) **and** (47); **Gaming; Goose** (9); **Handsome** (2); **Hate** (1); **Honest** (7) and (12); **House** (13); **Love** (37); **Luck** (1); **Man** (29) and (59); **Many men; Meat** (2); **Mischief** (5); **Old** A(C), D(I); **One hair; Ship** (2); **Silence; Silent** (1) **Swine** (2); **Two women; Weal** (1) **Whistling; Winter** (21); and **Wit** (6).

Wonder is the daughter of ignorance. 1578: Florio, *First Fruites*, fo. 32, Maruaile is the daughter of ignorance. 1629: *Book of Meery Riddles*, *Prov. 44*, Marvell is, etc. 1677: *Poor Robin's Visions*, 24. 1681: Rycaut, tr. *Gracian's Critick*, 25, Though admiration be the daughter of ignorance. 1732: Fuller, 5811.

Wonders will never cease. 1776: in *Garrick Corresp.* ii 174 (1832). 1844: Jerrold, *Story of a Feather*, ch xx. 1926: Phillpotts, *Marylebone Miser*, ch vii.

Woo. 1. He that woos a maid must come seldom in her sight, But he that woos a widow must woo her day and night. 1639: Clarke, 27,

He that will win a maid must seldom come in her sight. 1670: Ray, 49. 1732: Fuller, 6403.

2. He that would woo a maid. *See* 1669 quot. 1611: Barry, *Ram-Alley*, II, Do, but dally not; that's the widow's phrase. 1618: Field, *Amends for Ladies*, IV i, You have trusted to that fond opinion, This is the way to have a widowhood, By getting to her bed. 1669: N. Smith, *QuakersSpiritual Court*, 13, He told me that I must observe the old proverb … that he that would woe a maid, must fain, lye and flatter, but he that wooes a widow … must down with his britches and at her. 1670: Ray, 49 [as in 1669].

3. To woo is a pleasure in a young man, a fault in an old. Ibid., 30. 1732: Fuller, 5254 ['phrenzy' for 'fault'].
See also **Wooing.**

Wood. 1. To be in a wood = To be puzzled or bewildered. *c*.1616: B. and F., *Mad Lover*, IV, Help the boy; He's in a wood, poor child. 1681: Robertson, *Phraseol. Generalis*, 369, He is confused; he has lost himself in a wood. 1786: D'Arblay, *Diary*, ii 246 (1876), I assured him I was quite in a wood, and begged him to be more explicit. 1854: Baker, *Northants. Gloss.*, s.v. 'Wood', 'All in a wood'. In a state of perplexity and bewilderment.

2. To be unable to see the wood for the trees = To be unable to take a general or comprehensive view. 1546: Heywood, *Proverbs*, Pt II ch iv, Ye can not see the wood for trees. 1581: Woodes, *Confl. of Conscience*, II iii, Why, I was in place long before you came; But you could not see the wood for the trees. 1630: Randolph, *Works*, i 14 (Hazlitt, 1875), We cannot see wood for trees, nor scholars for gowns. 1738: Swift, *Polite Convers.*, Dial. I, Tom, how is it that you can't see the wood for trees? 1910: Hudson, *Shepherd's Life*, ch ii, There are many more which may not be spoken of, since we do not want to lose sight of the wood on account of the trees.

3. Wood half burnt is easily kindled. 1640: Herbert, *Jac. Prudentum*. 1670: Ray, 30. 1732: Fuller, 5812 ['half-coal' for 'half burnt'].

4. Woods have ears. *See* **Fields.** *See also* **Born** (6).

Woodcock does not make a winter, One. 1659: Howell, 11. 1664: J. Wilson, *Cheats*, I ii, One woodcock makes no winter. 1736: Bailey, *Dict.*, s.v. 'Woodcock'. 1846: Denham, *Proverbs*, 31 (Percy S.).

Woodcock. *See* quot. 1921: R. L. Gales, *Old-World Essays*, 251, 'When Daniel's in the lion's den, Then the woodcock comes again'. That is of course some time in October.

Woodcock. *See also* **Partridge** (1); **Snipe**; and **Wise** (4).

Wooden, *adj.* **1. A wooden dagger in a painted sheath.** 1639: Clarke, 6.

2. A wooden leg is better than no leg. 1732: Fuller, 483.

3. I'll not wear the wooden dagger. 1670: Ray, 198.

4. The wooden horse = The gallows. *c.*1550: in Hazlitt, *E. Pop. Poetry*, iii 261, Your happe may be to wagge upon a wodden nagge. 1654: Gayton, *Pleasant Notes Don Q.*, 119, Others ... vaile and couch it, when riding the wooden horse. 1680: D'Urfey, *Virtuous Wife*, II i, I'de ride the wooden horse e're be troubled with her impertinence.

5. To get a wooden suit = To be dead and buried. 1896: *Folk-Lore*, vii 377 (Staffs.).

6. Wooden legs. *See* **Run** (11).

Wood Fidley rain. *See* quot. 1863: Wise, *New Forest*, ch vii, The Forest proverb of 'Wood Fidley rain', that is, rain which lasts all the day.

Woodpecker. *See* quot. *c.*1489: Caxton, *Blanchardyn., etc.*, 173 (E.E.T.S.), Men saye in a comyn langage, that 'never noo wodewoll [woodpecker] dyde brede a sperhawke'.

Wood-pigeon. *See* quot. 1917: Bridge, *Cheshire Proverbs*, 92, Like the Quest [wood-pigeon], always saying 'do, do', but everybody knows it makes the worst nest i' th' wood.

Wood's dog. *See* quots. 1732: Fuller, 3241, Like Wood's dog; he'll neither go to church nor stay at home. 1880: W. D. Parish, in *N. & Q.*, 6th ser, ii 166, 'Why,' said the old man [Selmeston, Sussex], 'it has been a say as long ago as I was a child, Contrairy as Wood's dog, that wouldn't go out nor yet stop at home.' Cf. **Hunt's dog.**

Wooers and widows are never poor. *c.*1550: Udall, *R. Doister*, I ii Cf. **Widow** (10).

Woof or warp of any business, To make. 1639: in *Berkeley MSS.*, iii 30 (1885), Il'e make abb or warp of it (Gloucest.). 1678: Ray. 278.

Wooing. 1. Happy is the wooing that is not long a-doing. 1576: *Parad., of D. Devices*, in *Brit. Bibliog.*, iii 71 (1812), Thrise happie is that woying, That is not long a doyng. 1606: *Sir Giles Goose-cappe*, III ii, ['Blest' for 'Happy']. 1621: Burton, *Melancholy*, III II vi 5, 615 (1836), Blessed is, etc. 1707: Centlivre, *Plat. Lady*, III i, They zay 'tis very unlucky to be long a wooing. 1730: Fielding, *Tom Thumb*, II ix. 1842: Barham, *Ing. Legends*, 2nd ser, 'Sir Rupert'.

2. The wooing was a day after the wedding. 1732: Fuller, 4840.

Wool. 1. He seeks wool on an ass. 1813: Ray, 75.

2. There is no wool so white but a dyer can make it black. 1576: Pettie, *Pet. Pallace*, ii 69 (Gollancz), I see there is no wool so coarse but it will take some colour. 1580: Lyly, *Euphues*, 330 (Arber), There is no wool so white but the diar can make blacke. 1732: Fuller, 4927.

3. To go out for wool and go home shorn. 1599: J. Minsheu, *Dialogues in Spanish*, 61, You will go for wooll, and returne home shorne. 1612: Shelton, *Quixote*, Pt I bk i ch vii, Considering how many there go to seek for wool that return again shorn themselves! 1694: D'Urfey, *Quixote*, Pt I IV i, Several come for wool that return shorn. 1710: Palmer, *Moral Essays on Proverbs*, 148, Many go to seek wool, and come home shorn. 1822: Scott, *Nigel*, ch xxiii, But, lack-a-day! thou art one of those that come out for wool, and art sure to go home shorn.

4. You may keep wool till it's dirt, and flax till it's silk. 1732: Fuller, 5950.

5. You were better give the wool than the sheep. 1670: Ray, 30.

See also **Warm** (2).

Wool-gathering, His wits are. 1560: Wilson, *Rhetorique*, 107 (1909), As though our wittes and our senses were a woll gathering. 1580: Lyly, *Euphues* 415 (Arber), My witts were not at this while a wool-gathering. 1665: Pepys, *Diary*, Oct. 5, My mind is run a' wool gathering and my business neglected. 1748: Richardson, *Clarissa*, viii 220 (1785), That my wits may not be sent a wool-gathering. 1841: Dickens, *Barn. Rudge*, ch liv, He's so dead scared, he's wool-gathering, I think.

Woolly fleeces. *See* quots. 1555: L. Digges, *Prognostication*, sig. B2, If thyck clowdes resemblyng flockes, or rather great heapes of woll, be gathered in many places, they shewe rayne, 1658: Willsford, *Natures Secrets*, 125. When the clouds seem piled upon heaps like fleeces of wool, it presages wet weather, and neer at hand. 1831: Hone, *Year-Book*, 300, If woolly fleeces spread the heavenly way. No rain be sure, disturbs the summer's day [a flat contradiction to 1555 and 1658]. 1846: Denham, *Proverbs*, 50 (Percy S.) [as in 1831].

Wool-seller knows a wool-buyer, A. 1670: Ray, 159. 1732: Fuller, 484.

Worcester. 1. *See* quot. 1882: Mrs Chamberlain, *W. Worc. Words*, 39 (E.D.S.), 'It shines like Worcester against Gloucester' is a very old saying.

2. *Worcester, poor, proud and pretty.* Ibid., 39, It is proverbial that the Worcester ladies are 'Poor, proud, and pretty'. 1894: Northall, *Folk Phrases.* 33(E.D.S.)

Word and **Words. 1. A word and a blow.** *c.*1568: Wager, *Longer thou Livest*, sig. D1, This is manhoode to make thee bolde, Let there be but a worde and a blow. 1592. Shakespeare. *Romeo*, III i, And but one word with one of us? Couple it with something; make it a word and a blow. 1678: Bunyan, *Pilgr. Progr.*, Pt I 71 (1849), So soon as the man overtook me, he was but a word and a blow; for down he knocked me, and laid me for dead. 1720: C. Shadwell, *Irish Hosp.*, I, Come Ned, let's to my sisters, for my uncle is a country wit, a word and a blow. 1768: Franklin, in *Works*, iv 158 (Bigelow), It is said of choleric people, that with them there is but a word and a blow. 1886: R.L.S., *Kidnapped*, ch vii. All, as the saying goes, were 'at a word and a blow' with their best friends.

2. A word and a stone. *See* **Throw** (5).

3. A word before is worth two behind. 1736: Bailey, *Dict.*, s.v. 'Word'.

4. A word spoken is an arrow let fly. 1509: Barclay, *Ship of Fools*, i 108 (1874), A worde ones spokyn reuoked can nat be. 1596: Lodge, *Divel Coniured*, 83 (Hunt.Cl.), Words are like to arrows, which are easily shot out, but hardly got in again. 1639: Clarke, 51, A word spoke is past recalling. 1732: Fuller, 486.

5. A word to the wise is enough. [Dictum sapienti sat est. – Plautus, *Pers.*, 4, 7, 19.] 1513: Dunbar, *Poems* (1979), 206, Few wordis may serve the wyis. 1546: J. Heywood, *Dialogue of Proverbs*, II vii, 14v, Fewe wordis to the wise suffice to be spoken. [2 Thessalonians iii.10, For even when we were with you, this we commanded you, that if any would not work, neither should he eat.] *c.*1535: D. Lindsay, *Satire of the Three Eastates* (E.E.T.S.), 475, *Qui*

non laborat, non manducet … Quha labouris nocht he sall not eit. 1624: Capt. J. Smith, *General History of Virginia*, III x, He that will not worke shall not eate.1577: Rhodes, *Boke of Nurture*, in *Babees Book*, 88 (E.E.T.S.), For few wordes to wyse men is best. *c.*1598: Jonson, *Case is Altered*, I i. Presto. Go to, a word to the wise; away, fly, vanish, 1616: Haughton, *Englishm. for my Money*, III 1., They say, a word to the wise is enough. 1697: Vanbrugh, *Esop*, III. 1711: Addison, *Spectator*, No. 221. 1768: Sterne, *Sent. Journey*, 157 (1794). 1819: Scott, *Bride of L.*, ch vii, But what sayeth the proverb, *verbum sapienti* – a word is more to him that hath wisdom than a sermon to a fool.

6. Deliver your words not by number but by weight. 1855: Bohn, 343.

7. From words to deeds is a great space. 1629: *Book of Meery Riddles*, Prov. 94.

8. He that sells wares for words must live by the loss. 1736: Bailey, *Dict.*, s.v. 'Wares'.

9. His word is his bond. Before 1400: Chaucer, *Book of the Duchesse*, l. 935, Ne lasse flatering in hir worde, That purely, hir simple recorde Was founde as trewe as any bonde. 1630: Brathwait, *Engl. Gent.*, 148 (1641). For his word is his gage. 1631: F. Lenton, *Characters*, sig. G8 (1663), His word is as good as his bond. 1748: Richardson, *Clarissa*, iv 239 (1785), You know that my word has always been looked upon as my bond. 1812: Combe, *Syntax: Pict. Tour*, can. xix. 1886: R.L.S., *Kidnapped*, ch iv, I'm a queer man, and strange wi' strangers; but my word is my bond, and there's the proof of it. 1914: A. Dobson, in *Poet. Works*, 453 (1923), Fixed our word as our bond has been.

10. While the word is in your mouth it is your own; when 'tis once spoken, 'tis another's. 1646: A. Brome, in *Roxb. Ballads*, VIII cix. (B.S.), Our words are our own, if we keep them within. 1736: Bailey, *Dict.*, s.v. 'Word'.

11. Words and feathers are tost by the wind. 1670: Ray, 30.

12. Words are but sands, it's money buys lands. 1659: Howell, 11. 1732: Fuller, 6166.

13. Words are but words, *c.*1620: B. and F., *Little Fr. Lawyer*, I i.

14. Words are wind. Before 1225: *Ancr. Riwle*, 122, hwat is word bute wind? *c.*1390: Gower, *Conf. Amantis*, bk iii l. 2768, For word is wynd. *c.*1450: Lydgate, *Secrees*, 39 (E.E.T.S.), Woord is but wynd leff woord and tak the dede. 1509: Barclay, *Ship of Fools*, i 207 (1874). 1587: Greene, *Works*, iii 102 (Grosart). 1660: Tatham, *Rump*, V 1748: Richardson, *Clarissa*, vi 212 (1785), Words are wind; but deeds are mind. 1823: Scott, *Durward*, ch xix, 'Hard words, or kind ones', said the Zingaro, 'are bat wind.' 1866: G. Eliot, *Felix Holt*, ch *xi*.

15. Words are women. *See* **Deeds.**

16. Words cut more than swords – variously phrased. Before 1225: *Ancr. Riwle*, 74, Mo sleath word thene sweord. 1594: Churchyard, *Mirror of Man*, sig. A4 (1816), Sharp words makes more wounds then surgeons can heale. 1621: Burton, *Melancholy*, I II iv 4, 223 (1836), It is an old saying, a blow with a word strikes deeper than a blow with a sword. 1659: Howell. 13. 1732: Fuller, 575, An acute word cuts deeper than a sharp weapon. 1871: Smiles, *Character*, 170, There are words that strike even harden than blows.

17. Words have long tails; and have no tails. 1678: Ray, 221.

18. Words may pass but blows fall heavy. 1633: Draxe, 103, Words are but winde but blowes are vnkinde. 1678: Ray, 354.

See also **Actions; Pictures Deeds; Fair** (30)– (40); **Few words; Good words; High** (6); **Picture;** and **Soft words.**

Work, *verb.* **1. He that will not work shall not eat.** 1633: Draxe, 109, He that will not labour must not eat. 1639: Clarke, 163.

2. He that works after his own manner, his head aches not at the matter. 1640: Herbert, *Jac. Prudentum.*

3. Those that cannot work. *See* quot. 1864: 'Cornish Proverbs', in *N. & Q.*, 3rd ser, vi 494, Those that cannot work must planny, and those that cannot planny must lowster [hard manual labour]. Cf. **Schemey.**

4. To work by the great = To do piece-work. 1585: *Nomenclator*, 502, He that vndertaketh to doe a peece of worke vpon a prise, and (as they say) by great. 1626: Breton, *Fantasticks*, 13 (Grosart), The labourer by great will be walking toward his worke. 1662: Gertrier, *Disc. of Building*, 26, Let builders put their designs to master-workmen by the great. 1711: *Spectator*, No. 22, Adv. at end., Any person may agree by the great, and be kept in repair by the year. 1742: North, *Lives of Norths*, ii 282 (Bonn), They … keep hirelings in garrets, at hard meat, to write

and correct by the great. 1884: R. Lawson, *Upton-on-Severn Words*, 17 (E.D.S.), Work by the gret, Piece-work. 1917: Bridge, *Cheshire Proverbs*, 146.

5. To work for a dead horse. *See* **Dead** (25).

6. To work for needfire. *See* quot. 1879: Henderson, *Folk-Lore of N. Counties*, 168, The North-country proverb, 'to work as if working for need-fire', shows how prevalent this custom [of producing fire, through the smoke of which cattle were passed, by the friction of two pieces of wood] has been in the border counties as in Scotland.

7. Work to-day, for you know not how much you may be hindered to-morrow. 1846: Denham, *Proverbs*, 3 (Percy S.).

See also **Workman.**

Work, *subs.* **1. All work and no play makes Jack a dull boy.** *See* **All work.**

2. If anything stay let work stay. 1678: Ray, 278. 1732: Fuller, 2671. Cf. **Meat.**

3. It is not work that kills but worry. 1879: D. M. Mullock, *Young Mrs Jardine*, III ix, Working … al day, writing … at night … Roderick had yet … never spent a happier three months … for it is not work that kills, but 'worry'.

4. Work expands to fill the time available. Commonly known as 'Parkinson's Law', after Professor C. Northcote Parkinson, professor of history at the University of Malaya and a wry commentator on people's ability to find unnecessary activities to fill up time. 1955: C.N. Parkinson, in *Economist*, 19 Nov., 635, It is a commonplace observation that work expands so as to fill the time available for its completion.

Workman. 1. As is the workman so is the work. 1611: Cotgrave, s.v. 'Ouvrier', like workman like work. 1732: Fuller, 702.

2. It is working that makes a workman. Ibid., No. 3034.

3. What is a workman without his tools? 1546: Heywood, *Proverbs*, Pt II ch ix. 1559: Becon, in *Prayers, etc.*, 260 (P.S.). 1670: Ray, 30. 1732: Fuller, 5494.

See also **Ill workman.**

World. 1. All the world and his wife. 1738: Swift, *Polite Convers.*, Dial. III, Pray, madam, who were the company? *Lady Smart* Why, there was all the world and his wife. 1766: Anstey, *New Bath Guide*, 130 (1767), How he welcomes at once all the world and his wife. And how civil to folk he ne'er saw in his life! 1816: Byron, *Letters, etc.*, iii 266 (Prothero), In the mean time, I am at war 'with all the world and his wife'. 1848: Dickens, *Dombey*, ch xvii 1920: *Sphere*, April, 10, p. 36, col. 1.

2. A world to see! = wonderful to see. *c.*1475: *Assembly of Ladies*, 1. 539, For yonge and olde, and every maner age, It was a world to loke on her visage. 1519: *Four Elements*, in Hazlitt, *O. Plâys*, i 35, It is a world to see her whirl, Dancing in a round. 1530: Palsgrave, It is a worlde to se him lowte and knele. 1589: Nashe, *Works*, i 149 (Grosart), It is a world to see this world. 1626: Breton, *Works*, i e 8 (Grosart), Oh what a world it is to see what wiles, A silly foole will finde to gather wealth. 1881: Evans, *Leicest. Words, etc.*, 292 (E.D.S.), It's a woo'ld to see that theer little un order the big uns to the roight abaout! A's as marsterful as marsterful!

3. Had you the world on your chessboard, you could not fit all to your mind. 1640: Herbert, *Jac. Prudentum.*

4. The world is a ladder for some to go up and some down. 1659: Howell, *Proverbs: Ital.-Eng.*, 1, The world is like a ladder, one goeth up, the other down. 1732: Fuller, 4841.

5. The world is a tail and happy is he that gets hold on't. 1742: North, *Lives of Norths*, ii 150 (Bohn) [quoted as 'a proverb'].

6. The world is but a day's walk, for the sun goes about it in twenty four hours. 1616: *Rich Cabinet*, fo. 160.

7. The world is full of fools. 1627: in *Harl. Miscell.*, iii 198 (1744). 1642: *Discovery of divers sortes of Asses*, sig. A4 [with addition 'and asses'].

8. The world is his who enjoys it. 1736: Bailey, *Dict.*, s.v. 'World'.

9. The world is his who knows how to wait for it. 1875: Cheales, *Proverbial Folk-Lore*, 48.

10. The world is too narrow for two fools a quarrelling. 1732: Fuller, 4844.

11. The world is well amended with him. 1633: Draxe, 4, The world is somewhat amended for him. 1672: Walker, *Paroem.*, 26.

12. The world runs on wheels. 1546: Heywood, *Proverbs*, Pt II ch vii 1592: Greene, *Works*, x 203, How is it sweete wench, goes the worlde on wheeles, that you tread so daintily on your typtoes? 1614: B. Rich, *Honestie of this Age*, 30 (Percy S.), They were wont to say, the world did runne on wheeles. 1673: *Vinegar and Mustard*, 9,

in Hindley, *Old Book Coll. Misc.*, iii, Now you are come ashore, you think the world runs on wheels, and that all the world is oatmeal.

13. The world was never so dull, but if one will not, another will. 1670: Ray, 158. 1732: Fuller, 6451.

14. This is the world and the other is the country. 1678: Ray, 84.

15. This world is nothing except it tend to another. 1670: Ray, 31.

16. To have the world at will. *c.*1535: *Dialogues of Creatures*, cliv, (1816), He that is prosperows and hath the world at wyl. 1586: Pettie, *Guazzo*, fo. 165, Men hauing the world at will, as he hath, are neuer but merrie. 1629: *Book of Meery Riddles*, Prov. 52, He that hath the world at will, seemes wise. 1680: L'Estrange, *Tully's Offices*, 82, Take a wise man, that has the world at will.

17. To have the world in a string. *See* **Have in a string.**

See also **All sorts; God's in his heaven; Half the world; Hand** (6); **Laugh** (8); **Lie** *subs.* (3); and **Love** *subs.* (34).

Worm and **Worms. 1. Even a worm will turn.** A later and shorter version of (5) *Tread on a worm* (q.v.) 1854: 'M. Langdon' *Ida May*, xi, Even the worm turns when he is trodden upon. 1889: W. James, in *Mind*, XIV 107, Since even the worm will 'turn', the space-theorist can hardly be expected to remain motionless when his editor stirs him up. 1922: Weyman, *Ovington's Bank*, ch ix, The worm will turn … and Thomas did turn.

2. He has a worm in his brain. 1678: Ray, 278. 1754: Berthelson, *Eng.-Danish Dict.*, s.v. 'Worm', He has got a worm in his head.

3. The early bird catches the worm. *See* **Early** (7).

4. To be or to make worms' meat. *c.*1430: Lydgate, *Daunce of Machabree*, 1.640, That wormes food is fine [end] of our liuyng. *c.*1483: *Quatuor Sermones*, 28 (Roxb.Cl), After thyn ende thou shalt be but wormys mete. 1592: Shakespeare, *Romeo*, III i, They have made worms' meat of me. 1611: Cotgrave, s.v. 'Estat', Every creature is wormes meat. 1736: Bailey, *Dict.*, s.v. 'State', Every state is worms meat.

5. Tread on a worm and it will turn. 1546: Heywood, *Proverbs*, Pt II ch iv, Tread a woorme on the tayle, and it must turne agayne. 1592: Greene, in *Works*, xii 143 (Grosart). 1638: Ford,

Fancies, V i, I am, my lord, a worm; pray, my lord, tread on me, I will not turn again. 1710: S. Palmer, *Moral, Essays on Proverbs*, 305. *c*.1800: J. Trusler, *Proverbs in Verse*, 105. 1816: Scott, *Old Mortality*, ch xxvii.

Worse, *adj.* **1. A worse friend.** *See* Friend (27).

2. There is no worse pestilence than a familiar enemy, *c*.1386: Chaucer, *Merchant's Tale*, l.549, For in this world nys worse pestilence Than homly foo, alday in thy presence. 1538: in *Lisle Pipers*, xii Art. 43, It hath been an old proverbe that there is no worse pestilence than a famylar enemy.

3. The worse end of the staff. *See* **Wrong** (3).

4. The worse for the rider, the better for the bider 1639: Clarke, 18, Ill for the rider, good for th'abider. 1659: Howell, 18, A fatt soyl good for the bider, bad for the rider. 1670: Ray, 43. Before 1680: Butler, *Remains*, ii 284 (1759), His discourse is like the road-miles in the North, the filthier and dirtier the longer; and he delights to dwell the longer upon them to make good the old proverb that says – *they are good for the dweller, but ill for the traveller*. 1735: Pegge, *Kent. Proverbs*, in E.D.S., No. 12, p. 75, Bad for the rider, good for th'abider. 1865: W. White, *Eastern England*, ii 35, The latter … still justify in a measure the proverbs – 'Bon pays, mauvais chemin', and 'The worse for the rider, the better for the bider?' Cf. **Best** (16).

5. The worse luck now, the better another time. 1732: Fuller, 4847.

6. The worse the passage, the more welcome the port. Ibid. No. 4848.

7. Worse things have happened at sea. 1869: Spurgeon, *John Ploughman*, ch v.

8. Worse ware. *See* quot. 1762: Smollett, *Sir L. Greaves*, ch xvi, Marry hap, worse ware may have a better chap [market], as the saying goes.

Worship, *s More for worship than for pride*, *c*.1460: *How the good Wife*, l. 90.

Worship, *verb. They that worship God merely for fear, Would worship the devil too, if he appear.* 1732: Fuller, 6419.

Worst, *adj. adv.* and *subs.* **1. He that worst may still holds the candle.** 1546: Heywood, *Proverbs*, Pt II ch ii, Who that woorst maie shall holde the candell. 1576: Pettie, *Pet. Pallace*, ii 54 (Gollancz), How unequally it is provided that those which worst may, are driven to hold the candle! 1639: in *Berkeley MSS.*, iii 32 (1885)

['must hold' for 'still holds']. 1670: Ray, 159. 732: Fuller, 2361.

2. If the worst come to the worst. 1597: *Discouerie of Knights of the Poste*, sig. C3. 1620: Shelton, *Quixote*, Pt II ch lxxiii 1637: Shirley, *Example*, II i 1682: A. Behn, *City Heiress*, III i 1700: Congreve, *Way of World*, III xviii 1719: Defoe, *Crusoe*, 234 (1883), If the worse come to the worst. [This is a more reasonable form of the saying than the usual one.] 1886: R.L.S., *Kidnapped*, ch i 1900: Pinero, *Gay Lord Quex*, III

3. The worst can fall is but a denial. 1546: Heywood, *Proverbs*, Pt *I* ch xi If the woorst fell, we could haue but a naie. 1659: Howell, 14.

4. The worst dog that is. *See* Dog (81).

5. The worst is behind. 1546: Heywood, *Proverbs*, Pt II ch ii 1659: Howell, 6.

6. The worst piece. See All is well.

7. The worst spoke in a cart breaks first. 1678: Ray, 205. 1732: Fuller, 4851.

8. The worst wheel of a cart creaks most. 1586: Pettie, *Guazzo*, fo. 106, The brokenest wheele of the chariot maketh alwaies the greatest noise. 1611: Cotgrave, s.v. 'Crier'. 1666: Torriano, *Piazza Univ.*, 240. 1869: Spurgeon, *John Ploughman*, ch ii.

9. When things are at the worst they will mend. 1600: *Sir John Oldcastle*, l. 1899 (Malone S.), Patience good madame, things at worst will mend. 1691: *Merry Drollery*, 56 (Ebsworth). 1748: Richardson, *Clarissa*, iii 263 (1785). 1824: Scott. *Redgauntlet*, ch xii 1841: Dickens, *Barn. Rudge*, ch xx, When things are at the worst they are sure to mend.

See also **Provide.**

Worth, *adj.* and *subs.* **1. He is worth gold that carries it.** 1732: Fuller, 1956.

2. If a thing (or **job**) **is worth doing, it is worth doing well.** 1746: Chesterfield, *Letter*, 9 Oct. (1932), III 783, Care and application are necessary … In truth, whatever is worth doing at all is worth doing well.1875: Cheales, *Proverb. Folk-Lore*, 138. 1893: R.L.S., *Ebb-Tide*, ch viii 1915: Wells, *Bealby*, ch v § 8, 'If a thing's worth doing at all', said the Professor … 'it's worth doing well.'

3. The worth of a thing is known by its want. 1611: Cotgrave, s.v. 'Cogneu', The worth of things is knowne when they be lost. 1694: D'Urfey, *Quixote*, Pt I V ii 1748: Richardson, *Clarissa*, iv. 238 (1785), Worth is best known by want! I know her's now. *c.*1800: J. Trusler, *Proverbs in Verse*, 24. Cf. **Water** (22).

4. The worth of a thing is what it will bring. 1569: J. Sanforde, tr. *H. C. Agrippa's Vanity of the Arts and Sciences*, xci, The thinge is so muche worthy as it may be solde. 1663: Butler, *Hudibras*, II i 465, For what is worth in any thing, But so much money as 'twill bring. 1847: Halliwell, *Dict.*, s.v. 'Thing'.

5. The worth of water. *See* **Water** (22).

6. To be worth a plum = To be rich. A 'plum' in this sense is usually supposed to be £100,000. 1714: Mandeville, *Fable of Bees*, 83, If a miser, who is almost a plum and spends but fifty pounds a year − . 1754: *Connoisseur*, No. 19, I once saw a grave citizen, worth a plum, order a twopenny mess of broth. 1789: G. Parker, *Life's Painter*, 216, A London merchant worth a plumb.

7. To be worth one's weight in gold. *c.*1500. Medwall, *Nature*, l. 936, Nay ye ar worth thy weyght of gold. 1587: Turbervile, *Trag. Tales, etc.*, 45 (1837), So faire a frend is worth her weight in gold. 1698: *Terence made English*, 224 (2nd ed.), I look upon thee at present to be worth thy weight in gold. 1836: Marryat, *Easy*, ch xxxvi, I have [a servant] … who is worth his weight in gold. 1891: Hardy, *Tess*, ch vi 1926: Phillpotts, *Peacock House*, 40.

See also **Jew's eye**.

Wot, *verb.* = to know. **1. I wot well how the world wags.** 1639: Clarke, 97. 1670: Ray, 158 [as in 1639, *plus* −], he is most lov'd that hath most bags. 1732: Fuller, 6452 [as in 1670]. 1736: Bailey, *Dict.*, s.v. 'Wag' [as in 1670].

2. I wot what I wot, though I few words make. 1546: Heywood, *Proverbs*, Pt II cb. vii 1611: Davies of Hereford, *Sc. of Folly*, 47, in *Works* ii (Grosart), I wott what I wott.

Wotton hill. *See* quot. 1639: in *Berkeley MSS.*, iii 33 (1885). When Wotton hill doth weare a cap, Let Horton towne beware of that.

Wotton under Wever, Where God came never. 1610: P. Holland, tr. Camden's *Britannia*, 587. 1662: Fuller, *Worthies*, iii 127 (1840). 1790: Grose, *Prov. Gloss.* s.v. 'Staffs' ['comes' for 'came'].

Wranglers are never in the wrong. 1633: Draxe, 243, A wrangler neuer wanteth words. 1670: Ray, 31, Wranglers never want words. 1732: Fuller, 5833.

Wrapped in mother's smock, To be = To be born lucky − probably connected with the popular idea of the luck attaching to a caul. 1590: Greene, in *Works*, viii 198; How should I be vsed, but as one that was wrapt in his mothers smock when hee was borne. 1632: Randolph, *Jealous Lovers*, II ii, Did not I tell you, sir, that I was born With a caul upon my face? My mother wrapp'd me In her own smock. 1661: Davenport, *City Nightcap*, II. 1707: Centlivre, *Platonick Lady*, IV ii, My hero! adod thou wert wrapt up in thy mother's − Faith thou wert. 1785: Grose, *Class. Dict. Vulgar Tongue, s.v.* 'Wrapt up', He was wrapt up in the tail of his mother's smock, saying of any one remarkable for his success with the ladies. 1813: Brand, *Pop. Antiq.*, iii 118 (Bohn), The vulgar saying, 'Oh, you are a lucky man; you were wrapped up in a part of your mother's smock'.

Wrath. *See* **Anger** (4); and **Sun** (8).

Wrekin, All friends round the. Shropshire. 1700: Congreve, *Way of World*, III xv, You could intreat to be remember'd then to your friends round the Rekin. 1706: Farquhar, *Recruiting Officer*, Dedn., To all friends round the Wrekin. 1755: *Connoisseur*, No. 119. 1825: Lamb, in *Letters*, ii 680 (Lucas), Love and recollects to all the Wms. Doras, Maries round your Wrekin. 1871: *N.&Q.*, 4th ser, vii 9.

Wren. 1. To bleed a wren according to its veins [which ate very small] = cut your coat according to your cloth, *c.*1430: in *Babees Book, etc.*, 45 (E.E.T.S.), A man must spende as he may that hath but easy good, For aftir the wrenne hath veynes, men must lete hir blood.

2. Wrens may prey where eagles dare not perch. 1855: Bohn, 572.

See also **Eagle** (3); **Robin**; and **Spider** (1).

Wriggle about like a sing [eel] **in a bottle, To.** 1917: Bridge, *Cheshire Proverbs*, 146.

Wrinkled purses make wrinkled faces. 1732: Fuller, 5836. 1880: Spurgeon, *Ploughman Pictures*, 138.

Write. 1. He may even go write to his friends. 1546: Heywood, *Proverbs*, Pt II ch iv, Ye maie wryte to your freendes that ye are in helth. 1670: Ray, 176, He may even go write to his friends. We say it of a man when all his hopes are gone.

2. Write down the advice of him who loves you, though you like it not at present. 1855: Bohn, 572.

3. Write with the learned, but speak with the vulgar. 1732: Fuller, 5837

4. You may write on it. 1901: F. E. Taylor, *Lancs. Sayings*, 23, Yo' may write on't (you may rest assured of it).

Wrong, *adj.* **1. To be in the wrong box.** 1546: Heywood, *Proverbs*, Pt II ch.ix., And therby in the wrong boxe to thryue ye weare. 1590: Greene, in *Works*, viii 88 (Grosart), If ... thou thinkest ... thou arte (sweet seruant) in a wrong box, and sittest far beside the cushion. Before 1658: Cleveland, *Works*, 347 (1742), Faith you were in the wrong box. 1700: Brown in *Works*, iii 41 (1760), Some pert critick will tell me now, that I have lost my way in digressions. Under favour, this critick is in the wrong box, for digressions properly belong to my subject. 1838: Dickens, *Twist*, ch xvii, I very much question ... whether the Clerkinwell Sessions will not find themselves in the wrong box before they have done with me. 1849: Lytton, *Caxtons*, Pt II ch iv.

2. To come on the wrong side of the blanket = To be illegitimate. 1771: Smollett, *Clinker*, in *Works*, vi 381 (1817), My mother was an honest woman. I didn't come on the wrong side of the blanket. 1820: Scott, *Monastery*, ch xxxvii Who, men say, was akin to the Piercie on the wrong side of the blanket. 1901: F. E. Taylor, *Lancs. Sayings*, 38, He were getten o' th' wrank side o' th' blanket.

3. To have the wrong end of the stick. 1534: in *Two Coventry C.C. Plays*, 49 (E.E.T.S.), He schal be sure, asse God me saue, Eyuer the worse yend of the staff to haue. 1573: Harvey, *Letter-Book*, 5 (Camden S.), He was faint to put it up quickly bycause he knew he had the wors end of the staf. 1664: J. Wilson: *Cheats*, I iv, If at any time you find you have the worst end of the staff, leave off your cause and fall upon the person of your adversary. 1740: North, *Lives of Norths*, i 144 (Bohn), He that has the worse end of the staff, is very apt to fling off from the point. 1901: F. E. Taylor, *Lancs. Sayings*, 22, Theaw's getten howd o' th' wrung eend o' th' stick.

4. To have the wrong sow by the ear. 1546: Heywood, *Proverbs*, Pt II ch ix, Ye tooke the wrong way to wood, and the wrong sow by theare. 1596: Jonson, *Ev. Man in his Humour*, II i. When he is got into one o' your city pounds, the counters, he has the wrong sow by the ear, i' faith. 1664: Butler, *Hudibras*, II ii 580, You have a wrong sow by the ear. 1738: Swift, *Polite Convers.*, Dial. I. 1798: T. Dibdin, *Jew and Doctor*, I ii, If you come to apuse Miss Emily, I tell you, you have got de wrong sow in your ear. 1857: Hughes, *Tom Brown*, Pt II ch ii.

5. To rise on the wrong side of the bed. 1653: R. Brome, *Court-Begger*, II [Cit-wit complains that he has been robbed, and continues] – My watch is gone out of my pocket too o' th right side. *Dai* You rose o' the wrong side to-day it seemes. 1676: A. Behn, *Town-Fop*, V i, Sure I rose the wrong way to-day. I have had such damn'd ill luck. 1824: Scott, *Redgauntlet*, ch xx, Thou art angry this morning ... hast risen from thy wrong side, I think. 1828: Carr, *Cravm Dialect*, i 29, Thou's gitten out at wrang side o' th' bed, *i.e.* thou art peevish and ill-tempered. 1921: Hutchinson, *If Winter Comes*, Pt II ch iii (ii), As a matter of fact that's why I came back. I got out of bed the wrong side this morning, didn't I?

6. Ye lean to the wrong shore. 1546: Heywood, *Proverbs*, Pt II ch ii.

Wrong, *subs. All wrong comes to wrack.* 1736: Bailey, *Dict.*, s.v. 'Wrong'.

Wryneck. *See* quot. 1879: Henderson, *Folk-Lore of N. Counties*, 254, Corresponding with the Lancashire saying, 'He caps Wryneck, and Wryneck caps the Dule', i.e. the Devil.

Wybunbury. *See* **Wembury**.

Wye, Kent. *See* **Ashford**.

Wye, River. *See* **Severn**.

Wykin. *See* **Higham**.

Wylam. *See* **Heddon**.

Wyndham. *See* **Horner**.

Wyndy as a w[h]isket [a kind of basket], **As.** Said of a forgetful person. 1917: Bridge, *Cheshire Proverbs*, 27.

Y

Yarmouth capon, A – A herring. 1662: Fuller, *Worthies*, ii 447 (1840). 1785: Grose, *Class. Dict.*, *Vulgar Tongue*, s.v. 1886: J. G. Nall, *Gt. Yarmouth, etc.*, 579, In England a herring is popularly known as a Yarmouth capon. Cf. **Norfolk capon**.

Yarmouth steeple. *See* quot. 1790: Grose, *Prov. Gloss.*, s.v., 'Norfolk', You cannot spell Yarmouth-steeple right.

Year and **Years. 1. A good year will not make him, and an ill year will not break him.** 1736: Bailey, *Dict.*, s.v. 'Year'.

2. As the year is, your pot must seethe. 1640: Herbert, *Jac. Prudentum.*

3. The year doth nothing else but open and shut. Ibid.

4. The year lasts longer than Yule. 1846–59: *Denham Tracts*, ii 92 (F.L.S.).

5. Tis year'd – spoken of a desperate debt. 1678: Ray, 344.

6. Years and years. *See* quot. 1913: E. M. Wright, *Rustic Speech, etc.*, 34, Years ago – years and years and donkey's ears, as the saying is.

7. Years know more than books. 1640: Herbert, *Jac. Prudentum.*

8. Year's mind. *See* Month's mind.

Yellow, *adj.* **1. As yellow as a guinea.** 1852: Planché, *Extravag.*, iv 226 (1879), The Japanese have rich complexions, ninny! Their sovereign is as yellow as a guinea. 1901: Raymond, *Idler Out of Doors*, 3, The white of his eye turns up yellow as a guinea.

2. As yellow as a kite's foot. 1630: Davenant, *Just Italian*, I, Yellow as foot of kite. 1863: Wise, *New Forest*, ch xvi, Forest proverbs … such as 'As yellow as a kite's claw'. 1880: Courtney, *W. Cornwall Words*, 32 (E.D.S.). 20th cent. at Mawgan, W. Cornwall 'Yellow as a kid's foot' (Mr C. Lee).

3. As yellow as a marigold. 1653: Walton, *Angler*, Pt I ch v, The belly of it looked, some part of it, as yellow as a marigold. 1917: Bridge, *Cheshire Proverbs*, 27, As yellow as a meadows-bout [Marsh marigold].

4. As yellow as a paigle [cowslip]. 1735: Pegge, *Kenticisms*, in E.D.S., No. 12, p. 40, As yellow as a pegle. *c.*1791: Pegge, *Derbicisms*, 114 (E.D.S.), Yellow as a peagle. 1854: Baker, *Northants.*

Gloss., s.v. 'Paigle'. Paigle. The cowslip. Now seldom used except in the comparison, as 'yellow as a paigle'. 1887: Parish and Shaw, *Dict. Kent. Dialect*, 115 (E.D.S.) [as in 1735]. Cf. **Blake**.

5. As yellow as gold. 1552: Huloet, *Abced.*, sig. Nn1, Yellow as golde. 1566: L. Wager, *Mary Magdalene*, sig. C3. 1594: *First Part Contention*, 22 (S.H.S.). 1631: Mabbe, *Celestina*, 98 (T.T.), Shall make thy haire as yellow as gold. 1820: Scott, *Monastery*, ch viii, Not her butter, as yellow as gold –

6. As yellow as the golden noble. 1678: Ray, 350.

7. A yellow band and a green wit – an allusion to the fashion for yellow starch. 1619: B. Rich, *Irish Hubbub*, 41 [cited as 'a true proverb'].

8. He wears yellow stockings = He is jealous. 1607: Dekker, etc., *Northw. Hoe*, I, Iealous men are eyther knaues or coxcombes … you weare yellow hose without cause. 1736: Bailey, *Dict.*, s.v. 'Yellow'.

9. Yellow-belly = a fennan. 1790: Grose, *Prov. Gloss.*, s.v. 'lines'. 1866: Brogden, *Lincs. Words*, 227 … said to be derived from the eels with which the fen ditches abound. 1889: Peacock, *Manley, etc., Gloss.*, 620 (E.D.S.), He's a real yalla' belly, you maay tell it by his tung.

Yeoman. *See* quots, 1732: Fuller, 488, A yeoman upon his legs is higher than a prince upon his knees. 1736: Franklin, *Way to Wealth*, in *Works*, i 448 (Bigelow), A ploughman on his legs is higher than a gentleman on his knees.

Yesterday will not be called again. *See* **Call**, *verb.* (3).

Yew. *See* quot. 1908: W. Johnson, *Folk Memory*, 354. The New Forest proverb is almost literally true, 'A post of yew will outlast a post of iron'.

Yoke, Irwell, Medlock, and Fame, when they meet with the Mersey, do lote their name. 1869: Hazlitt, 482 … These are the names of small streams, which flow into the larger one, and so lose their individuality.

York. 1. As much as York excels foul Sutton. 1732: Fuller, 715.

2. I cannot be at York and London at the same time. Ibid., No. 2588.

3. Three P's of York: Pretty, Poor, Proud. 1869: Hazlitt, 403.

4. York has the highest rack, but Durham has the deepest manger. 1846–59: *Denham Tracts*, i 42 (F.L.S.). Cf. **Canterbury.**

5. York, you're wanted. 1816:. T. Morton, *The Slave*, II iv. 1866: *N. &Q.*, 3rd ser, x 355, 'York, you're wanted'. This phrase is commonly used on board a man-of-war when something goes wrong by reason of the absence of 'the right man from the' right place'.

See also **Lincoln** and **Oxford.**

Yorkshire. 1. A Yorkshire tike, or **bite** = A native of Yorkshire, *c*.1600: Deloney, *Thos. of Reading*, ch v, Do you thinke that any can beare the flirts and frumps, which that Northerne tike gaue me the last time he was in towne? 1659: Howell, 21, Yorkshire tikes. 1762: Smollett, *Sir L. Greaves*, ch xxii, I'se a poor Yorkshire tyke … . my name is Tim Crabshaw. 1817: Scott, *Rob Roy*, ch iv, Thou kens I'm an outspoken Yorkshire tyke. 1866: Brogden, *Lincs. Words*, 228, Who respond … by calling the people beyond the Humber 'Yorkshire Bites'. 1893: Crockett, *Stickit Minister*, 268, The dialect of the 'Tykes' of Yorkshire.

2. A Yorkshire way-bit = longer than a mile. 1639–46: in *Rump Sons*, Pt *I* p. 123 (1662), (Repr. 1874), For 'tis (to speak in a familiar style), A Yorkshire wea-bit. longer than a mile. 1640: Rous, *Diary*, 103 (Camden S.), A Yorkshire way-bit, longer then a mile. Before 1658: Cleveland, *Works*. 27 (1742) [as in 1640]. 1790: Grose, *Prov. Gloss.*, s.v. 'Yorkshire'.

3. He's Yorkshire too. Ibid., s.v. 'Yorkshire', Master's Yorkshire too. 1796: Wolcot, *Works*, iv. 102 (1796), But, hang the fellow, 'he was Yorkshire too'. 1803: Kenney, *Raising the Wind*, I i, Aye, and you see I come fra – Yorkshire. 1878: *Folk-Lore Record*, i 174, The saying *He's Yorkshire*, which is equivalent to 'he's a sharp fellow'.

4. To come Yorkshire over one = To overreach or cheat. 1700: *Step to the Bath*, 10 (OED), I ask'd what countrey-man my landlord was? Answer was made full North; and faith 'twas very evident, for he had put the Yorkshire most damnably upon us. 1757: *Lancs. Dialect*, quoted in Sternberg, *Dialect, etc., of Northants.*, 127, Yorshar, to put Yorkshire to a man is to trick or deceive him. 1839: Dickens, *Nickleby*, ch xlii, It's not exactly what we understand by 'coming Yorkshire over us' in London.

See also **Bishop Brigg.**

Yorkshireman. 1. A Yorkshireman's coat of arms: a fly, a flea, a magpie, and a flitch of bacon. 1790: Grose, *Prov. Gloss.*, s.v. 'Yoikshire'. 1846–59: *Denham Tracts*, i 119 (F.L.S.). 1888: *N. &Q.*, 7th ser, vi 368 … a flea, a fly, and a magpie.

2. Give a Yorkshireman a halter, and he'll find a horse. 1869: Hazlitt, 141.

3. Shake a bridle over a Yorkshireman's grave, and he mill arise and steal a horse. 1790: Grose, *Prov. Gloss.*, s.v. 'Yorkshire'. 1922: *N. &Q.*, 12th ser, xi 499.

You. 1. Since you know all and I. 1640: Herbert, *Jac. Prudentum.*

2. You and I draw both in the same yoke. 1732: Fuller, 5840.

3. You are a fine fettow to fetch the devil a priest. Ibid., No. 5841.

4. You are an honest man, and I am your uncle: and that's two lies. Ibid., No. 5845.

5. You are a sweet nut. 1583: Mel bancke, *Philotinus*, sig. X3, You are a swete nut, if you were well crackt you. 1732: Fuller, 5844, You are a sweet nut, if yon were well crackt.

6. You me not one of our paste. 1672: Walker, *Paroem.*, 21.

7. You cannot tell [count], *you are naught to keep sheep.* 1607; Willkins, *Mis. of Enforced Marriage*, in Hazlitt, *O. Plays*, ix 477, And if you cannot tell, beauty, I take the adage for my reply: You are naught to keep sheep, 1666: Torriano, *Piazza Univ.*, 172, If you can't tell you are nought to keep sheep

8. You see your dinner. 1546: Heywood, *Proverbs*, Pt I ch xi, Ye see your fare (sayd she). 1738: Swift, *Polite Convers.*, Dial. II, Lady Answerall, pray eat, you see your dinner.

9. You to the cabbage, and beef. 1732: Fuller, 6007.

Young, *adj.* and *subs.* **1. A man may be young in years, and yet old in hours.** Ibid., No. 296.

2. A young barber and an old physician. 1578: Florio, *First Fruitet*, fo. 32. *c*.1594: Bacon, *Promus*, No. 581. 1666: Torriano, *Piazza Univ.*, 21.

3. A young maid married to an old man is like a new house thatched with old straw. 1659: Howell, 11 (9).

4. A young man, a ruler. *See* quot. 15th cent.: in Reliq. Antiquae, i 316 (1841), A yong man, a rewler, recheles; A olde man a lechowr, loweles; A pore man a waster, haveles; A riche man a thefe, nedeles; A womman a rebawde, shameles. Thes V shalle never thrif blameles

5. A young man married is a young man marred. 1589: G. Puttenham, *Art of English Poesy*, iii xix, 173, The maide that soone married is, soone marred is. 1602: Shakespeare, *All's Well that Ends Well*, ii iii 291, A young man married is a man that's marr'd.

6. A young man negligent, an old man necessitous. 1732: Fuller, 489.

7. A young man old makes the old man young. 1659: Howell, 9 (7).

8. A young prodigal, an old mumper [beggar]. 1732: Fuller, 490.

9. A young serving-man, an old beggar. 1598: *Servingmans Comfort*, in *Inedited Tracts* (Hazlitt, 117.) 1659: R. Brome, *English Moor*, III iii, I am too old to seek out a new master. I will not beg, because Ile crosse the proverb That runs upon old serving creatures. 1706: *George-a-Green*, in Thoms, *Early Prose Rom.*, ii, 9 (1828), An old serving-man made a young beggar. 1732: Fuller, 492.

10. A young trooper should have an old horse. Ibid., No. 493.

11. A young whore an old saint. 1670: Ray, 155. 1754: Berthelson, *Eng.-Danish Dict.*, s.v. 'Young'.

12. A young wife and a harvest goose. *See* quot. *c.*1400: in *Reliquae Antiquae*, ii 113 (1843), A yong wyf and an arvyst gos, Moche gagil with bothe: A man that [hath] ham [= them] yn his clos [possession], Reste schal he wrothe.

13. If the young man would, and the old man could, there would be nothing undone. 1736: Bailey, *Dict.*, s.v. 'Would'.

14. Make the young one squeak, and you'll catch the old one. 1732: Fuller, 3326.

15. Of young men die many, Of old men scape not any. 1666: Torriano, *Piazza Univ.*, 105, Of young people. many dye, of the old none escapes. 1670: Ray, 127: 1732: Fuller, 6379. Cf. No. 23.

16. Quoth the young cock, I'll neither meddle nor make. 1678: Ray, 68. 1710: S. Palmer, *Moral Essays on Proverbs*, 254. 1913: E. M Wright, *Rustic Speech, etc.*, 123 [quoted as 'the old Berkshire proverb'].

17. The young are not always with their bom bent, *i.e.* under rule. 1678: Ray, 353.

18. The young cock crows as he heard the old one. 1509: Barclay, *Ship of Fools*, i 235 (1874), The yonge cok lerneth to crowe hye of the olde. 1589: Pattenham, *Engl. Poesie*, 199 (Arber), As the olde cocke crowes so doeth the chick. 1615: Brathwait, *Strappado*, 176 (1878), Since as the old cocke crowes, the young cock learns. 1710: S. Palmer, *Moral Essays on Proverbs*, 300. 1821: Scott, Pirate. ch xviii [as in 1615. 1910: R. L. Gales, *Studies in Arcady*, 335.

19. Young birds. *See* quot. 1893: Gower, *Gloss, of Surrey Words*, a (E.D.S.), It ain't often that the young birds feed the old uns,

20. Young birds. *See also* **Small birds**.

21. Young cocks love no coops. 1605: Camden, *Remains*, 336 (1870). 1732: Fuller, 6036.

22. Young courtier. *See* **Courtier**.

23. Young doth it prick. *See* **Pricketh betimes**.

24. Young men may die, old men must. 1534: More, *Works*, p. 1139, col. *2* (1557), For as we well wot, that a young man may dye soone; so be we very sure that an olde man cannot liue long. 1605: Camden, *Remains*, 336 (1870). 1670: Ray, 126. 1732: Fuller, 6039. Cf. No. 14.

25. Young men's knocks old men feel. 1670: Ray, 38. 1736: Bailey, *Dict.*, s.v. 'Knock'. 1748: Richardson, *Clarissa*, iv. 121 (1785), Nor is that unworthy of his notice, Young men's frolicks old men feel. My devilish gout, God help me –

26. Young men think old men fools, but old men know the young men are. 1577: J. Grange, *Golden Aphroditis*, sig. O2. 1605: Chapman, *All Fools*, v i 1642: D. Rogers, *Matrim. Honour*, 88, Children will say that old folke dote, and are fooles; but old ones know that children are so. 1738: Swift, *Polite Corners.*, Dial. I, You *think* us old fellows are fools; but we old fellows *know* young fellows are fools. 1901: F. E. Taylor, *Lancs. Sayings*, 11, Young folk think'n 'at owd folk are foo's, but owd folk know'n 'at young uns are.

27. Young prodigal in a coach will be old beggar bare-foot. 1732: Fuller, 6042.

28. Young saint old devil. 1493: *Dives et Pauper*, fo. 34 (1536), It is a common prouerbe yonge saynt olde deuyll. 1552: Latimer, *Sermons*, 431 (P.S.). 1592: Greene, in *Works*, x 239 (Grosart), Fie vpon such as say, young saints, olde devils: it is no doubt a deuillish and damnable saying. 1677: A. Behn, *Rover*, Pt I I ii, There's no sinner like a young saint. 1725: Bailey, tr. *Erasm. Coll.*,

44, There is an old saying, a young saint and an old devil. 1846: T. Wright, *Essays on Middle Ages*, i 146, We say … 'young hypocrite, old devil'.

29. Young wenches make old wrenches. 1639: Clarke, 174. 1670: Ray, 51.

Younger brother. 1. The younger brother hath the more wit. 1616: Sharpham, *Cupid's Whirligig*, III, The reason the younger brothers (according to the old wiues tales) alwayes prooued the wisest men. 1678: Ray, 85.

2. The younger brother the better gentleman. 1642: Fuller. *Holy State*. 'Younger Brother', Some account him the better gentleman of the two, because son to the more ancient gentleman. 1738: Swift, *Polite Convers.*, Dial. I

3. To make a younger brother of one. 1597: *Discouerie of Knights of the Poste*, sig. C2, Drawer (quoth he) thou must not thinke to make a younger brother of me. 1678: Ray, 85, He has made a younger brother of him.

Youth. 1. A lazy youth a lousy age. 1736: Bailey, *Dict*, *s.v.* 'Youth'.

2. If youth knew what age would crave, it would both get and save. 1611: Cotgrave, s.v. 'Ieunesse', If youth knew what to do, and age could do what it knowes, no man would ever be poore. 1670: Ray, 160. 1732: Fuller, 6085.

3. What youth wones [is accustomed to]. *See* quot. 1303: Brunne, *Handl. Synne*, l. 7674, Yu a prouerbe of olde englys Tellë 'men, and sothe hyt ys, 'that yougthe wones, yu agë mones; that thou dedyst ones thou dedyst eftsones'.

4. Youth and age will not agree. 1659: Howell, 19. 1683: Meriton, *Yorksh. Ale*, 83–7 (1697), Youth and Age will never agree.

5. Youth and white paper take any impression. 1579: Lyly, *Euphues*, 37 (Arber), The tender youth of a child is … apt to receive

any forme. 1630: Brathwait, *Engl. Gent.*, *etc.*, 3 (1641), Youth being indeed the philosophers rasa tabula, is apt to receive any good impressure. 1670: Ray, 31. 1732: Fuller, 6066. 1820: Lamb, *South-Sea House*, His mind was in its original state of white paper.

6. Youth riotously led, breedeth a loathsome old age. 1588: Cogan, *Haven of Health*, Epis. Ded., That saying not so common as true: Youth, etc.

7. Youth will be served. 1579: Lyly, *Euphues*, 124 (Arber), We haue an olde (prouerbe), youth wil haue his course. 1633: S. Marmion, *Fine Companion*, *I* vii. Troth, uncle, youth will have his swing. 1851: Borrow, *Lavengro*, iii 291, Youth will be served, every dog has his day, and mine has been a fine one. 1896: Doyle, *Rodney Stone*, ch x 1921: A. Porterfield, '*Youth will be served*' [Story] in *Harper's Mag.*, Nov. 696.

Yule. 1. A Yule feast may be quit at Pasche [Easter]. 1846: Denham. *Proverbs*, 63 (Percy S.).

2. It is easy to cry Yule at other men's cost. 1546: Heywood, *Proverbs*, Pt I ch xi 1736: Bailey, *Dict.*, s.v. 'Yule'. 1846: Denham, *Proverbs*, 62 (Percy S.) ['good' for 'easy'].

3. Yule is come, and Yule is gone, And we have feasted well; So Jack must to his flail again, And Jenny to her wheel. 1846: Denham, *Proverbs*, 67 (Percy S.).

4. Yule is good on Yule even. 1639: Clarke, 307. 1670: Ray, 44. 1846–59: *Denham Tracts*, ii 92 (F.L.S.).

5. Yule, Yule! a pack of new cards and a Christmas fide. 1846: Denham, *Proverbs*, 62 (Percy S.). 1904: *Co. Folk-Lore: N'umberland*, 179 (F.L.S.).

See also **Bare as the birch; Christmas; Dark; Every day's; Fool** (78); **Martinmas** (1); and **Year** (3).

Z

Zeal without knowledge is fire without light 1732: Fuller, 6069.

Zeal without knowledge is the sister of folly. 1611: Davies of Hereford, *Sc. of Folly*, 42 in *Works*, ii (Grosart). 1633: Draxe, 246.

Zeal without prudence is frenzy. 1732: Fuller, 6070.